A SINGLE VENDOR FOR ALL YOUR BRAKE EQUIPMENT NEEDS?

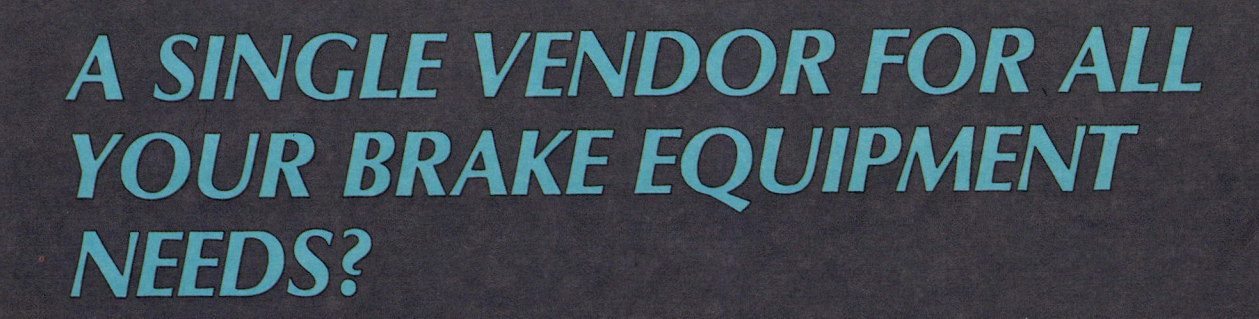

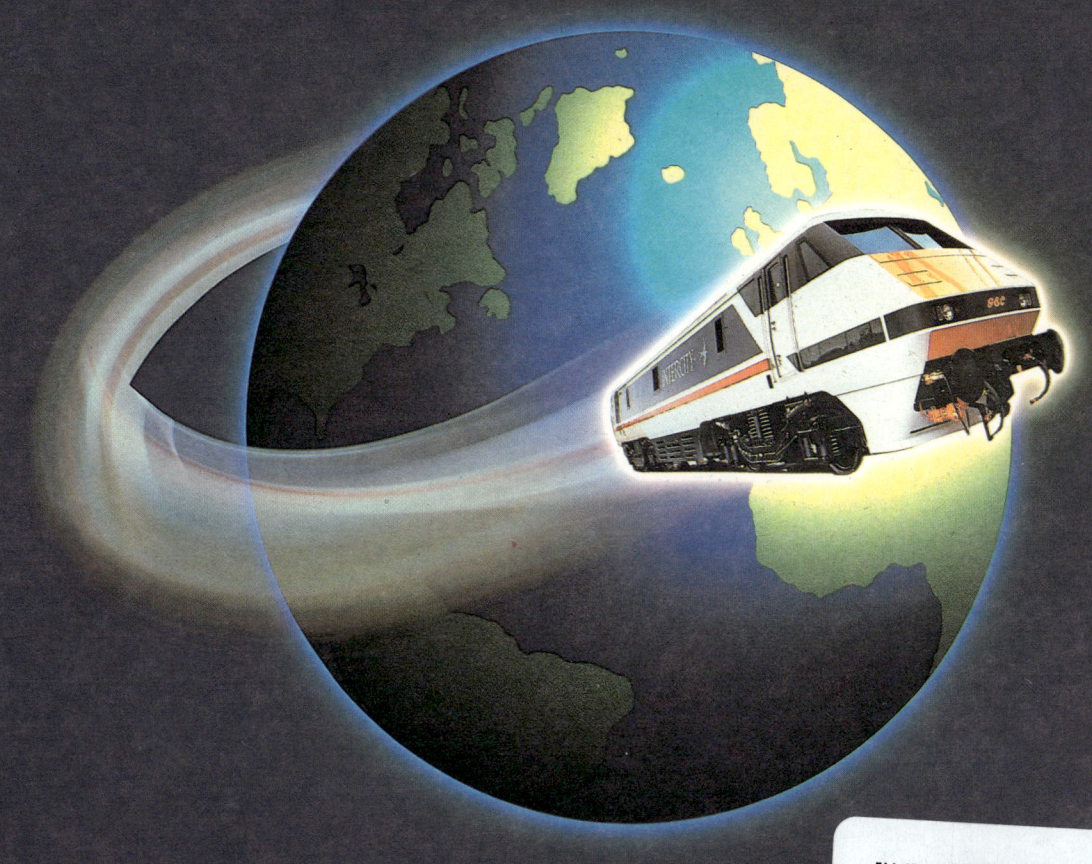

...DAVIES & METCALFE

Davies & Metcalfe p.l.c.
Injector Works Romiley Stockport Cheshire England SK6 3AE
Telephone: 061-430 4272 (five lines) Telex: 668801

THE FUTURE AS A STARTING POINT.

ANSALDO
Trasporti

Ansaldo Trasporti engineers, designs, manufactures, installs, services and maintains railway and urban transit systems, power supply systems for transportation networks and power semiconductors and is the world largest supplier of signalling, automation and control systems for rail-based transportation industries. Ansaldo Trasporti's activities include those of AT Signal System, Union Switch & Signal Inc., Wabco Westinghouse Segnalamento Ferroviario, Wabco Westinghouse Compagnia Italiana Segnali together with participation in CSEE Transport; the company also works in close cooperation with Ercole Marelli Trazione and the other Firema companies. Ansaldo Trasporti, world-class leader in the transportation field, is part of Ansaldo, one of the world's largest manufacturing concerns. With history that dates back 150 years, Ansaldo has more than 16,000 employees in 30 countries around the world. With the strength of its history, coupled to an approach based on the application of advanced technology, on the flexibility of strategies and on the value of ideas and people, today Ansaldo can fully consider the future as a starting point.

ANSALDO

GRUPPO IRI FINMECCANICA

RUSTON RK270
THE SPACESAVER

With unrivalled accessibility the 'space saver' six cylinder, medium speed, RK270 is backed by 50 years of rail traction know how.

The RK270 offers a power range covering 1,700 to 6,000 bhp. For further technical information please contact us today.

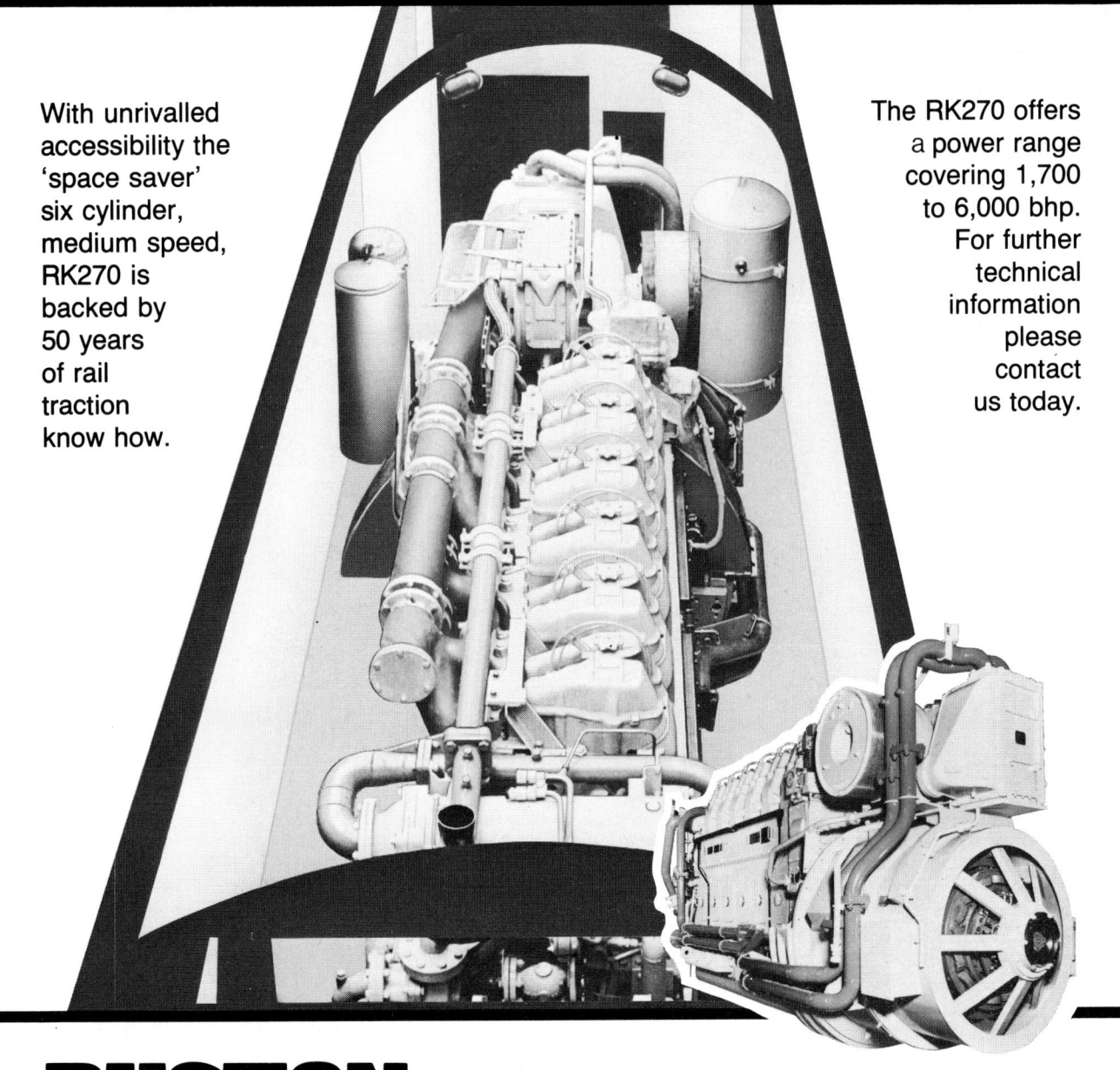

RUSTON DIESELS

Ruston Diesels Limited
Vulcan Works, Newton-le-Willows, WA12 8RU
Merseyside, England.
Tel: 0925 225151.   Telex: 627131   Telefax: 0925 222055

IRI GROUP

FINCANTIERI IS BUILDER OF DIESEL ENGINES

Fincantieri's Diesel Engines Division, based in Trieste, carries out the functions of a typical industrial enterprise for the production and sale of diesel, gas and dual-fuel engines in the marine, industrial and rail traction sectors.
Following the merging of Isotta Fraschini Motori S.p.A., the Division – with the two trademarks GMT and IF – can avail itself of a range of engines covering power outputs from 200 to 33,000 hp per unit.
In addition, Sulzer slow-speed engines are produced for the Italian market and a cross-licencing agreement exists with Sulzer for medium speed engines of the A 320 and ZA 40 S types.

The two production plants of the Division are located at Trieste (530,000 sq.m.) and at Bari (200,000 sq.m.). The production capability results from more than 70 years of skill, experience and advanced technology. The highest standards of excellence are maintained by modern quality control, test facilities and precision machining and fabrication.
Furthermore the Division, with its After Sales Service Department, has in place a world-wide network of service centres integrated by flying-squads capable of being readily deployed wherever necessary, both at land-based plants for energy generation and on board ships even during navigation.

FINCANTIERI
Cantieri Navali Italiani S.p.A.

DIESEL ENGINES DIVISION GMT
Bagnoli della Rosandra 334, Trieste/Italy
Tel. (0) 40 7391 Tlx 460274 FINCGM I
Fax (0) 40 827371

JANE'S WORLD RAILWAYS
1990-91

THIRTY-SECOND EDITION

Edited by
Geoffrey Freeman Allen

JANE'S TRANSPORT DATA

Part of the Jane's Information Group

ISBN 0 7106 0920 5

Copyright © 1990 by Jane's Information Group Limited, Sentinel House, 163 Brighton Road, Coulsdon, Surrey CR5 2NH United Kingdom.

All rights reserved. No part of this publication may be reproduced, stored in a retrieval system, transmitted in any form or by any means electrical, mechanical or photocopied, recorded or otherwise without the prior permission of the publishers. While every care has been taken in the compilation of this publication to ensure its accuracy at the time of going to press the publishers cannot be held responsible for any errors or omissions.

Furthermore, no responsibility for loss occasioned by any person acting or refraining from action as a result from use of any material in this publication can be accepted by the editor and/or authors or publisher.

ADMINISTRATION
Publisher: Ken Harris

Editorial Co-ordinator: Wendy Adamson

Product Group Manager: Ching Lee

EDITORIAL OFFICES
Jane's Information Group Limited, Sentinel House, 163 Brighton Road, Coulsdon, Surrey CR5 2NH, United Kingdom.
Tel: Domestic: 081 763 1030. International +44 81 763 1030.
Fax: Domestic: 081 763 1005. International +44 81 763 1005.
Telex: 916907 JANES G

SALES OFFICES
Send enquiries to: Iain Duncan Smith, Sales Director, Jane's Information Group Limited, UK address as above. Or in the USA to: Joe McHale, Vice-President Sales, Jane's Information Group Inc., 1340 Braddock Place, Suite 300, Alexandria, VA 22314-1651.
Tel: +1 703 683 3700. Fax: + 703 836 0029.

Typesetting and origination by Columns of Reading.
Printed in the United Kingdom by Biddles Limited, Guildford and King's Lynn.

ADVERTISEMENT SALES OFFICES

Group Advertisement Sales Director: Simon Kay.

Australia: Stephen Goddard, Stephen M. K. Goddard Representation, Suite 17, 118 Queen Street, Woolahra, NSW 2025. Tel: +61 2 327 8577. Telex: 177816. Fax: +61 2 327 8357.

Austria: Tony Currow, see United Kingdom.

Benelux: Sandie Palmer, see United Kingdom.

Brazil: L Bilyk, Brazmedia International s/c Ltda, Alameda Gabriel Monteiro da Silva 366, CEP, 01442 São Paulo, Brazil. Tel: +55 11 853 4133. Telex: 32836 BMED BR. Fax: +55 11 852 6485.

Canada: Monika Cornell, see USA.

France: Marie Hélène Causse, Agence MHC, 20-22 rue Valadon, 75007 Paris. Tel: +33 1 45 55 63 43.
Telex: SELEX F 642138 MHC 171. Fax: +33 1 45 55 99 34.

Germany: Tony Currow, see United Kingdom.

Israel: Oreet Ben-Yaacov, Oreet International Media, 39 Hayarkon Street, Bnei-Berak 51204, Israel.
Tel: +972 3 5706335, Fax: +972 3 5791117

Italy and Switzerland: Dott Vittorio Negrone, Ediconsult Internazionale Srl, Piazza Fontane Marose 3, 16123 Genoa.
Tel: +39 10 591955, 583520, 583684. Fax: +39 10 566578.
Telex: 281197 EDINT 1.

Korea: Young-Seoh Chinn, JES Media International, KPO Box 576, Seoul. Tel: +82 2 545 8001, +82 2 549 5561.

Scandinavia: Denise Woodhatch, see United Kingdom.

Singapore, Indonesia, Malaysia, Philippines, Taiwan & Thailand: Hoo Siew Sai, Ad Media Pte, Ltd. 95 South Bridge Road, #09-13 Pidemco Centre, Singapore 0105. Tel: +65 532 4026.
Telex: RS 43370 AMPLS. Telefax: +65 532 4027.

Spain: Jesus Moran Iglesias, VAREX Varenga Exclusiva Internacionales SA. Modesto Lafuente, 4. 28010. Madrid.
Tel: +34 1 448 76 22. Telefax: +34 1 446 01 98.

United States: Monika Cornell, Jane's Information Group Inc, 1340 Braddock Place, Suite 300, Alexandria, VA 22314-1651.
Tel: +1 703 683 3700. Fax: +1 703 836 0029.

United Kingdom/Rest of World: Tony Currow, Denise Woodhatch, Sandie Palmer, Jane's Information Group, Sentinel House, 163 Brighton Road, Coulsdon, Surrey CR5 2NH.
Tel: Domestic: 081 763 1030. International: +44 81 763 1030.
Fax: Domestic: 081 763 1005. International: +44 81 763 1005.
Telex: 916907 JANES G.

KERSHAW

The "INNOVATOR" in track maintenance equipment

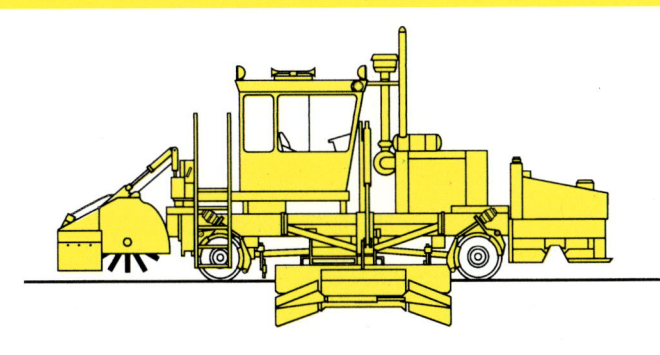

Ballast Regulators
- More than 2500 sold worldwide
- Work speed 0 to 25 km/hr
- Engine 60 to 250 horsepower
- Attachments for snow or sand removal
- Options: Hopper, train formation modification
- Travel speed 80 to 100 km/hr

Sleeper Remover/Inserter
- Wood, concrete, or steel sleepers
- Removes or inserts up to 480 sleepers per hour
- Works from either side of track
- Travel speed 50 to 80 km/hr

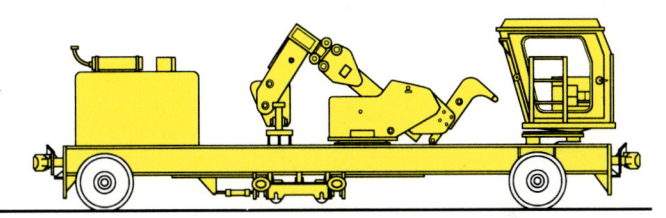

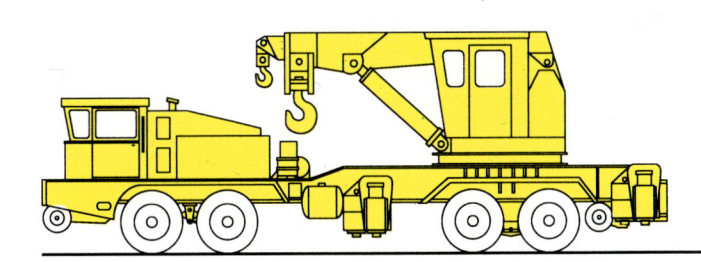

Mobile Wrecking Crane, Series RCH
- Available in 85, 100 or 130 tons capacities
- Two section hydraulic telescopic boom
- Fast set-up without additional rigging
- 360° full revolving upperstructure
- Available with lattice-type boom

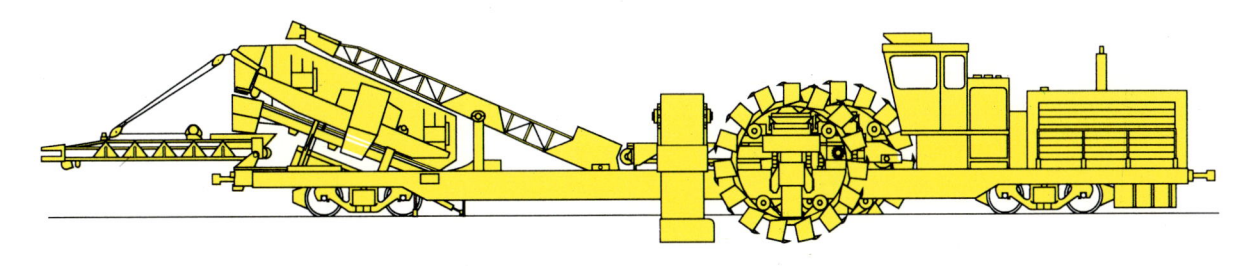

Ballast Cleaning Machines
- Full operation without raising track
- Screen capacity 500 to 650 m^3/hr
- Full section cleaning speed up to 366 m/hr
- Shoulder cleaning speed at least 1500 m/hr
- Spoils discharge 7 meters from track center
- Ready to work within 15 minutes of arrival at site
- Option: "Super System" with 1100 m^3/hr capacity
- Travel speed 80 to 100 km/hr

Also Available:
- Ballast Dressing Machines
- Sleeper Replacement Equipment
- Rail Replacement Equipment
- Rail and Rescue Cranes: up to 136 tons
- Vegetation Control Equipment

KERSHAW

Kershaw Manufacturing Co., Inc.
Post Office Box 17340
Montgomery, AL 36117 USA
Telephone (205) 271-1000
Telex: 593416 Fax: (205) 277-6551

INFORMATION
PUTS YOU IN THE PICTURE ▶▶

Whether you have old Signal Boxes with small TDs

or new ones with the latest colour mimic technology.

They will all be database driven for user friendliness

and will provide essential train data for your other systems.

Network-wide staff information systems

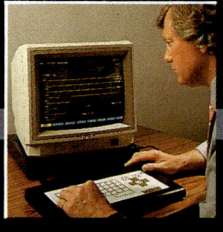

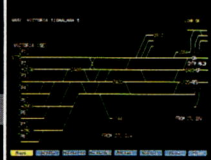

Real time timetable driven systems for many purposes: Passenger Information,

Automatic Train Reporting by Exception, Automatic Code Insertion (Interposing), Automatic Route setting.

Train reporting systems

Public information systems both large and small

All system hardware from the same range of robust industrial equipment.

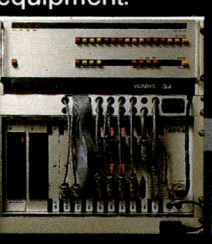

Robust software, well designed well documented using proven MACE Executive

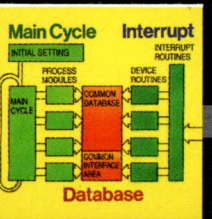

and tested exhaustively before delivery

2P38

VAUGHAN
SYSTEMS
▶▶ **PUTS YOU IN CONTROL**

Vaughan Systems Limited
The Maltings, Hoe Lane, Ware, Hertfordshire SG12 9LR
contact,
Telephone: Ware (0920) 462282
Fax: (0920) 460702   Telex: 81516

Represented in Australasia by **Ventura Projects**
Telephone: +61 2 29 7051   Fax: +61 2 290 3927

Contents

FOREWORD	[51]
MANUFACTURERS	
Locomotives	3
Powered passenger vehicles	77
Diesel engines and transmission systems	151
Electric traction equipment	175
Non-powered passenger vehicles	191
Passenger coach equipment	215
Freight vehicles	231
Brakes and drawgear	265
Bogies and suspensions, wheels and axles	281
Bearings	295
Signalling and telecommunications	301
Passenger information systems	323
Automatic fare systems	329
Fixed electrification equipment	337
Permanent way equipment	347
Freight yard and terminal equipment	387
Workshop, repair and maintenance equipment	401
PRIVATE FREIGHT CAR LEASING COMPANIES	409
INTERNATIONAL RAIL SERVICES IN EUROPE	417
INTERNATIONAL RAILWAY ASSOCIATIONS AND AGENCIES	421
CONSULTANCY SERVICES	429
RAILWAY SYSTEMS	
Afghanistan	464
Albania	464
Algeria	464
Angola	467
Argentina	468
Australia	469
Austria	490
Bangladesh	498
Belgium	499
Benin	505
Bolivia	506
Botswana	507
Brazil	508
Bulgaria	517
Burkina Faso	518
Burma (Myanmar)	518
Cameroon	519
Canada	520
Chile	536
China, People's Republic	539
Colombia	543
Congo	544
Costa Rica	545
Cuba	545
Czechoslovakia	547
Denmark	549
Dominican Republic	554
Ecuador	554
Egypt	555
El Salvador	556
Ethiopia	557
Finland	557
France	561
Gabon	574
Germany, Democratic Republic	575
Germany, Federal Republic	577
Ghana	590
Greece	591
Guatemala	593
Guinea	593
Honduras	594
Hong Kong	594
Hungary	596
India	599
Indonesia	610
Iran	613
Iraq	614
Ireland	616
Israel	618
Italy	620
Ivory Coast	632
Jamaica	632
Japan	633
Jordan	657
Kampuchea	658
Kenya	658
Korea, Democratic People's Republic	660
Korea, Republic	660
Lebanon	662
Liberia	663
Libya	664
Luxembourg	664
Madagascar	665
Malawi	667
Malaysia	667
Mali	669
Mauritania	670
Mexico	670
Mongolia	672
Morocco	672
Mozambique	674
Namibia	674
Nepal	675
Netherlands	675
New Zealand	679
Nicaragua	681
Nigeria	681
Norway	682
Pakistan	685
Panama	688
Paraguay	688
Peru	689
Philippines	690
Poland	691
Portugal	695
Romania	698
Saudi Arabia	699
Senegal	700
South Africa	700
Spain	705
Sri Lanka	713
Sudan	715
Swaziland	716
Sweden	716
Switzerland	722
Syria	740
Taiwan	741
Tanzania	742
Thailand	744
Togo	748
Tunisia	748
Turkey	749
Uganda	752
Union of Soviet Socialist Republics	753
United Kingdom	757
United States of America	765
Uruguay	805
Venezuela	805
Viet-Nam	806
Yugoslavia	806
Zaïre	809
Zambia	810
Zimbabwe	811
RAPID TRANSIT AND UNDERGROUND RAILWAYS	813
INDEX	855

THE TRAM HITS IT OFF AGAIN!

Specifications.

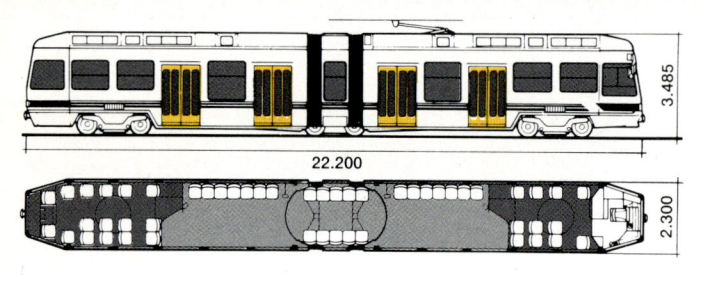

Supply	600 Vcc, overhead line	Continuous power	300 kW
Gauge	1445 mm	Traction motor	150 kW, 540 V, 299 A
Wheel arrangement	B 2 B	(rating)	1630 rpm
Length	22,200 mm	Max speed	> 60 km/h
Width	2,300 mm	Service acceleration	1 m/s^2
Height from rail	3,485 mm	Service deceleration	1.7 m/s^2
Deck height from rail	350 mm	Control system	GTO chopper for each motor with microprocessor control
Mass in running conditions	30,000 kg		
Mass at max load	42,000 kg	Chopper performance	600 V, 500 A max
No. of seats	51	Chopper frequency	600 Hz
Passenger capacity	180	Auxiliary static converter	600/24 Vcc, 7 kW

People are becoming increasingly concerned with improving the quality of life in the places where they live, a concern that also relates to a city's image, the way it's built and its general appearance. This is leading to the rehabilitation of conventional tramlines as a supplement to underground and surface metropolitan transport systems. Fiat Ferroviaria's construction of a tramcar with a low passenger deck is fully in line with this trend. A low-deck car, in fact, is particularly suitable for inner city routes, where infrastructures such as platforms and protected rails would create traffic problems and have a very adverse effect on the appearance of the surroundings.

Moreover, a low deck leads to greater passenger convenience, including ease of access, combined with high efficiency and reliability. All virtues that give this car an excellent performance to costs ratio.

FiatFerroviaria

Alphabetical List of Advertisers

A

AEG Westinghouse Transport System GmbH
15-21 Nonnendammallee, D-1000, 20 Berlin
or
1501 Lebanon Church Road, Pittsburgh,
PA 15236-1491, USA .... *Back Divider*
*Locomotives/Powered Passenger Vehicles/
Engines/Transmissions/Traction Equipment*

Ansaldo Trasporti SpA
Via Nuova delle Brecce 260,
80147 Napoli, Italy .... *Front Endpaper IV*

Ascom Autelca Equipment Division,
Measuring Equipment Division,
Belpstrasse 23, CH-3000 Berne 14,
Switzerland .... [50]

B

BMS
10 Sindalvej, DK-2610 Rodovre,
Denmark .... [38]

Bombardier Inc
1350 Nobel Street, Boucherville,
Quebec J4B 1A1, Canada .... *Inside Front Cover*

Brecknell Willis & Co Ltd
PO Box 10, Chard, Somerset TA20 2DE, UK .... [48]

Breda Costruzioni Ferroviarie SpA
Via Ciliegiole 110-115, 51100 Pistoia, Italy .... [15]

BREL Ltd
St Peter's House, Gower Street, Derby DE1 1AH
UK .... *Front Divider*
Passenger Coaches/Coach Equipment

British Steel Track Products
Moss Bay, Derwent Howe, Workington,
Cumbria CA14 5AE, UK .... [35]

Brown & Root Vickers Ltd
Wessex House, Market Street, Eastleigh, Hampshire SO5 4FD,
UK .... [38]

C

Caterpillar Inc
100 North East Adams Street, Peoria,
USA .... *Front Divider*
Leasing/Associations/Consultancy

Cockerill Mechanical Industries (CMI)
Locomotives and Diesel Engines Department, 1 Avenue Greiner,
B-4100 Seraing, Belgium .... [11]

Cooperativa Bilanciai (Weighing Scales Company)
Via Sergio Ferrai 16, 41011 Campogalliano (Modena),
Italy .... [52]

Craswell Scientific Ltd
Unit 11, Orchard Trading Estate,
Toddington, Gloucestershire GL54 5EB,
UK 321

D

Daewoo Heavy Industries Ltd
PO Box 7955, Daewoo Centre Building, 20th Floor 541,
5-GA Namdaemoon Ro, Jung-gu, Seoul, Republic of
Korea .... *Front Divider*
Rapid Transit & Underground

David Brown Gear Industries Ltd
Park Gear Works, Huddersfield HD4 5DD,
UK .... [44]

Davies & Metcalfe plc
Injector Works, Romiley, Stockport, Cheshire SK6 3AE,
UK .... *Facing Inside Front Cover*

E

EKE-Electronics
1 Westendintie, 02160 ESPOO,
Finland .... *Front Divider*
*Locomotives/Powered Passenger Vehicles/
Engines/Transmissions/Traction Equipment*

F

FIAT Ferroviaria Savigliano SpA
C.50 Ferrucci 112, 10138 Turin, Italy .... [8] & [9]

Fincantieri Cantieri Navali Italiani SpA
Diesel Engines Division, Bagnoli della Rosandra 334,
Trieste, Italy .... [2]

FIREMA Consortium
Corso di Porta Romana 63, 20122 Milan, Italy .... [41]

G

GEC Alsthom Transportation Projects Ltd
PO Box 134, Manchester M60 1AH,
UK .... *Outside Front Cover & Spine*

H

Harmon Industries Inc
1300 Jefferson Court, Missouri 64015, USA ..... *Back Divider*
Signalling/Telecommunications/Fare Systems

Hitachi Ltd
Transportation & Building Systems Dept (XL) 6,
Kanda Surugadai 4-chome, Chiyoda-ku, Tokyo 101,
Japan .... *Back Divider*
Railway Systems

Holec HH Ridderkerk
Ringdijk 390, PO Box 4050,
2980 GB Ridderkerk, The Netherlands .... [23]

I

IPA
Via Provinciale, 24050 Calcinate,
Italy .... [29]

CMI LOCOMOTIVES:
ruggedness, reliability, economy

Cockerill built in 1835 the first steam locomotive running on the continent. Strengthened by the experience acquired, C.M.I. has in the meantime specialized in Diesel-hydraulic and electric traction.

C.M.I. locomotives are fully adapted to the most severe working conditions met in:
– Railway networks
– Urban transportation
– Heavy industry

TECHNICAL CHARACTERISTICS

N° Axles : 2-3-4 and 6
Weight : from 24 to 120 tons
Power : from 200 to 1500 HP
Adaptation to all tracks and gauges.

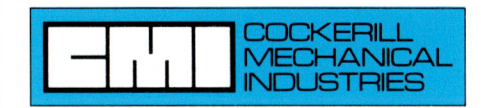

CMI COCKERILL MECHANICAL INDUSTRIES

LOCOMOTIVES AND DIESEL ENGINES DPT

1, Avenue Greiner
B-4100 SERAING/BELGIUM
Tel. + 32.41/30.24.03 - Telex 41.225
Telefax + 32.41/30.23.89

ALPHABETICAL LIST OF ADVERTISERS

J

Jakem Timbers Ltd
The Old Malt House, 125 High Street,
Uckfield, East Sussex TN22 1EG, UK .... [27]

JM Voith GmbH
PO Box 19 40, D-7920 Heidenheim,
West Germany .... [47]

K

Keller Meccanica SpA
Via Francesco Guardione 3, 90139 Palermo, Italy .. [32] & [33]

Kershaw Manufacturing Co Inc
PO Box 17340, Montgomery, AL 36117 USA .... [5]

Knorr-Bremse AG Munchen
PO Box 40 10 60, D-8000, Munchen 40,
Federal Republic of Germany .... [31]

Krauss-Maffei Verkehrstechnik GmbH
Krauss-Maffei-Strasse 2, D-8000 Munich 50,
Federal Republic of Germany .... [19]

KV Limited
43 Burners Lane South, Kiln Farm, Milton Keynes,
Buckinghamshire MK11 3HA, UK .... [40]

L

Lovere Sidermeccanica SpA
Via G. Paglia 45, 24065 Lovere (BG), Italy . *Outside Back Cover*

Luwa GmbH
Railway Air-conditioning Division,
Hanauer Landstrasse 200, D-6000 Frankfurt/Main 1,
Federal Republic of Germany .... *Back Divider
Passenger Coaches/Coach Equipment*

M

Mannesmann Demag Gottwald GmbH
Reisholzer Werftstrasse, PO Box 13 03 29,
D-4000, 13 Dusseldorf,
Federal Republic of Germany .... *Back Index Section*

Marconi Electronic Devices
Power Semiconductor Division
Carholme Road,
Lincoln LN1 1SG, UK .... [38]

Merlin International (Engineers) Ltd
Winery Lane, Walton-le-Dale, Preston PR5 4AZ,
Lancashire, UK .... [35]

Morrison-Knudsen
Railroad Division, PO Box 7808 Boise, Idaho 83729,
USA .... [40]

Motoren-und Turbinen-Union Friedrichshafen GmbH (MTU)
PO Box 2040, D-7990 Friedrichshafen,
Federal Republic of Germany .... [42] & [43]

N

New York Air Brake Company
Starbuck Avenue, Watertown, New York 13601, USA ... [45]

Norprint International Ltd
Boston, Lincolnshire, UK .... [44]

R

Racal Acoustics Limited
Waverley Industrial Park, Hailsham Drive, Harrow,
Middlesex HA1 4TR, UK .... [27]

Rautaruukki Oy
Transtech Division, Kiilakiventie 1, PO Box 217,
SF-90101 Oulu, Finland .... *Back Divider
Freight Vehicles*

RFS Engineering Ltd
PO Box 192, Hexthorpe Road,
Doncaster DN1 1PJ, UK
&
RFS Projects Ltd
2a East Mill,
Bridgefoot, Belper, Derbyshire DE5 1XZ, UK .... [25]

Rolba AG
CH-8620 Wetzikon,
Switzerland .... [39]

Ruston Diesels Ltd
Vulcan Works, Newton-le-Willows, Merseyside WA12 8RU,
UK .... [1]

S

Sécheron Ltd
Traction Components,
CH-1211, Geneva 21, Italy .... [37]

SEMT Pielstick
2 quai de Seine, 93202 Saint-Denis, France .... [44]

Servo Corporation of America
111 New South Road,
Hicksville, New York 11802, USA .... [30]

SIKA Ltd
Watchmead, Welwyn Garden City,
Hertfordshire AL7 1BQ, UK .... *378 & 400*

S.I.L.F.
Via Romagnosi 60, 29100 Piacenza
Italy
&
Via Emilia Pavese 98 SS 10, Sarmato,
Italy .... [48]

Skodaexport Prague
11332, 56 Vaclavske,
Czechoslovakia .... [30]

SOCIMI
Via Varesina 115, 20156 Milano,
Italy .... [13]

Specialist Rail Products Ltd
PO Box 76, Hexthorpe Trading Park,
Doncaster DN4 0EH, UK .... *Back Index Section*

GRUPPO SOCIMI

Socimi means worldwide reliability

Società Costruzioni Industriali Milano S.p.A.

Headquarters and Offices

20156 Milano - Italy
Via Varesina n. 115
Tel. 02/30.09.1
Telex: 323564 Socimi I
Telefax: 02/3085161

Productive Units

20010 Arluno MI
20082 Binasco MI
25020 Brescia
41100 Modena
07100 Sassari
21045 Varese

GRUPPO SOCIMI — SOCIMI — MACCHI — FRANCHI — PADANE

ALPHABETICAL LIST OF ADVERTISERS

Swiss Locomotive & Machine Works (SLM)
CH-8401 Winterthur, Switzerland .... [17]

T

TAKRAF Export/Import
Volkseigener Außenhandelsbetrieb der DDR,
Mohrenstrasse 53-54, DDR-1080 Berlin,
German Democratic Republic .... [49]

Tamper Corporation
PO Box 20, 2401 Edmund Road,
Cayce, West Columbia, South Carolina 29171-0020,
USA .... [21]

Thorn EMI Electronics
Computer Systems Division
Wookey Hole Road, Wells,
Somerset BA5 1AA, UK .... [52]

Transmark
Enterprise House, 169 Westbourn Terrace, London W2 6JY,
UK .... [46]

Transport Design Consortium
5 Heathman's Road, Parsons Green, London SW6 4TJ,
UK .... *Back Index Section*

Twiflex Ltd
The Green, Twickenham TW2 5AQ,
UK .... *Back Index Section*

V

Valdunes
Immeuble Elysees la Defense, 29 Le Parvis, Cedex 35,
92072 Paris-la-Defense, France .... [21]

Vaughan Systems Ltd
The Maltings, Hoe Lane, Ware, Hertfordshire SG12 9LR,
UK .... [6]

W

Westinghouse Brake & Signal Ltd
PO Box 74, Foundry Lane, Chippenham, Wiltshire SN15 1HY,
UK .... *Front Divider*
Brakes/Bogies/Components

Z

Zweiweg-Fahrzeug GmbH & Co Vertriebs-KG
Innlande 18, D-8200 Rosenheim 2, Federal Republic of
Germany .... [36]

BREDA IN THE WORLD.
THE FUTURE TODAY.

Innovation today, to keep abreast of tomorrow, keeping ahead of the times has made Breda's name in Italy and worldwide.

Breda has acquired over one hundred years experience in selecting, designing and supplying the most suitable and complete transportation systems, that respond even to the most demanding needs. Breda is present where innovation counts.

State-of-the-art technology, and solutions today to tomorrow's needs.

Low noise, pollution-free, safe, comfortable and fast vehicles: like the 300 Km/h ETR 500 train, the Dual Bus for Seattle, the Washington subway, the light rail vehicles for Cleveland and the Breda Bus, used all over Italy.

Five rolling stock manufacturing companies belong to the Breda Railway Group: Breda Costruzioni Ferroviarie in Pistoia, Sofer in Naples, Omeca in Reggio Calabria, Ferrosud in Matera, Imesi in Palermo. Five Companies, one Group.

BREDA RAILWAY GROUP

Gruppo EFIM

AVIOFER BREDA

Classified List of Advertisers

The companies advertising in this publication have informed us that they are involved in the fields of manufacture indicated below:

Air brakes
Davies & Metcalfe
Knorr-Bremse
RFS Engineering
Transport Design Consortium
Twiflex
Westinghouse Brake & Signal

Air-conditioning equipment
Bombardier
Daewoo Heavy Industries
Hitachi
Luwa
RFS Engineering
Transport Design Consortium
Westinghouse Brake & Signal

Air filters
Davies & Metcalfe
Transport Design Consortium

Articulated light rail vehicles
Bombardier
Breda Construzioni Ferroviarie
BREL
Daewoo Heavy Industries
Fiat Ferroviaria
FIREMA Consortium
GEC Alsthom Transportation Projects
Hitachi
Rautaruukki
SOCIMI
Transport Design Consortium

Automatic train control systems
Ansaldo Trasporti
GEC Alsthom Transportation Projects
Harmon Industries
Hitachi
Rautaruukki
RFS Engineering

Auxiliary vehicles
AEG Westinghouse Transport Systems
Daewoo Heavy Industries
Keller
Transport Design Consortium

Axleboxes & axlebox fitments
AEG Westinghouse Transport Systems
Brecknell Willis
Daewoo Heavy Industries
JM Voith
S.I.L.F.
SOCIMI
Transport Design Consortium

Axles, railway
Lovere Sidermeccanica
S.I.L.F.
SLM
Transport Design Consortium
Valdunes

Barriers & access control equipment
Thorn EMI Electronics

Baseplates
British Steel Track Products
S.I.L.F.

Battery locomotives
BREL
RFS Engineering
S.I.L.F.
Transport Design Consortium

Bearings
RFS Engineering
S.I.L.F.

Bogies/trucks
Bombardier
Breda Construzioni Ferroviarie
BREL
Daewoo Heavy Industries
Fiat Ferroviaria
Firema Consortium
GEC Alsthom Transportation Projects
Hitachi
Keller
Rautaruukki
RFS Engineering
S.I.L.F.
SOCIMI
Specialist Rail Products
Transport Design Consortium

Breakdown cranes
Daewoo Heavy Industries
RFS Engineering
TAKRAF

Braking systems and equipment
Davies & Metcalfe
Knorr-Bremse
RFS Engineering
New York Air Brake
Transport Design Consortium
Twiflex
Westinghouse Brake & Signal

Brake slack adjusters
Davies & Metcalfe
RFS Engineering
Transport Design Consortium
Westinghouse Brake & Signal

Brake units for disc brakes
Davies & Metcalfe
Knorr-Bremse
RFS Engineering
Transport Design Consortium
Twiflex

Bridge timbers
Jakem Timbers

Buffers
Keller
S.I.L.F.

Car body tilting equipment
Fiat Ferroviaria
Hitachi
SOCIMI
Transport Design Consortium

Cars, passenger
Bombardier
Breda Construzioni Ferroviarie
BREL
Daewoo Heavy Industries
Fiat Ferroviaria
FIREMA Consortium
GEC Alsthom Transportation Projects
Hitachi
Keller
Morrison-Knudsen
RFS Engineering
SOCIMI
Transport Design Consortium

Castings
BREL
Daewoo Heavy Industries
Lovere Sidermeccanica
Transport Design Consortium

Coach heaters
AEG Westinghouse Transport Systems
Daewoo Heavy Industries
Luwa
SOCIMI
Transport Design Consortium

Coal wagons
Breda Construzioni Ferroviarie
Daewoo Heavy Industries
Keller
RFS Engineering
S.I.L.F.
SOCIMI
Transport Design Consortium

Commuter railcars
Ansaldo Trasporti
Bombardier
Breda Construzioni Ferroviarie
BREL
Daewoo Heavy Industries
Fiat Ferroviaria
FIREMA Consortium
GEC Alsthom Transportation Projects
Hitachi
Keller
Morrison-Knudsen
RFS Engineering
SOCIMI
Transport Design Consortium

Consider class

Frankly, there's no such thing as "the SLM locomotive". For each motive power unit is built to fulfill its specific task. One is a hill-climber, another pulls its loads on the flat. Yet another must be both.

Whether your locomotive application calls for a rack or an adhesion system—or both in one—whether you're transporting passengers or goods in a tropical or arctic environment, our engineers have grown up with locomotion and know their craft. And that explains why they never just make "the SLM locomotive". Their capability to make your locomotive puts them in a class of their own. If you're looking for made-to-measure motive power, consider class. Consider SLM.

Swiss Locomotive and Machine Works
CH-8401 Winterthur, Switzerland
Phone 052-85 41 41

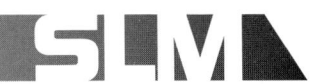

SLM

Locomotion at its best

CLASSIFIED LIST OF ADVERTISERS

Compressed air-conditioning air-dry units
Knorr-Bremse

Compressors
Daewoo Heavy Industries
Davies & Metcalfe
Knorr-Bremse
New York Air Brake
RFS Engineering
SLM
Westinghouse Brake & Signal

Computer-based traffic control systems
AEG Westinghouse Transport Systems
Ansaldo Trasporti
Harmon Industries
Hitachi
Rautaruukki
Vaughan Systems

Computer-controlled marshalling yard systems
Ansaldo Trasporti
GEC Alsthom Transportation Projects

Consultancy services
Ansaldo Trasporti
Bombardier
BREL
Brown & Root Vickers
GEC Alsthom Transportation Projects
Hitachi
SOCIMI
Transport Design Consortium
Transmark

Containers
Rautaruukki
Transport Design Consortium

Control equipment, locomotive
Ansaldo Trasporti
Daewoo Heavy Industries
GEC Alsthom Transportation Projects
Harmon Industries
Hitachi
Knorr-Bremse
Morrison-Knudsen
RFS Engineering
Transport Design Consortium

Control equipment, signal etc
Ansaldo Trasporti
GEC Alsthom Transportation Projects
Harmon Industries
Rautaruukki
RFS Engineering
Vaughan Systems

Couplers
Daewoo Heavy Industries
Davies & Metcalfe
Knorr-Bremse
New York Air Brake
RFS Engineering
Sécheron
SOCIMI
Transport Design Consortium

Crane cars
Brown & Root Vickers
RFS Engineering

Current collectors
AEG Westinghouse Transport Systems
Brecknell Willis
GEC Alsthom Transportation Projects

Dampers
RFS Engineering
Sécheron

Design consultants in product, industrial, engineering, interior, architectural and corporate identity
Transport Design Consortium

Diesel engines
Caterpillar
Cockerill
Fiat Ferroviaria
Fincantieri
RFS Engineering
Ruston Diesels
SEMT Pielstick
Transport Design Consortium

Diesel engines for locomotives
Cockerill
Morrison-Knudsen
RFS Engineering
Ruston Diesels
SEMT Pielstick
Transport Design Consortium

Diesel locomotives
Breda Costruzioni Ferroviarie
BREL
Cockerill
Daewoo Heavy Industries
Fiat Ferroviaria
FIREMA Consortium
Hitachi
Keller
Krauss-Maffei
Morrison-Knudsen
RFS Engineering
S.I.L.F.
SLM
SOCIMI
Transport Design Consortium

Diesel railcars
Breda Costruzioni Ferroviarie
BREL
Daewoo Heavy Industries
Fiat Ferroviarie
GEC Alsthom Transportation Projects
Hitachi
SOCIMI
SLM
Transport Design Consortium

Disc brakes
Davies & Metcalfe
Fiat Ferroviaria
Knorr-Bremse
New York Air Brake
SOCIMI
Transport Design Consortium
Twiflex

Door & window fittings
Breda Costruzioni Ferroviarie
Daewoo Heavy Industries
SOCIMI
Transport Design Consortium
Westinghouse Brake & Signal

Door control equipment
Bombardier
Breda Costruzioni Ferroviarie
Knorr-Bremse
KV Automation Systems
SOCIMI
Transport Design Consortium
Westinghouse Brake & Signal

Door systems for mass transit
Bombardier
Breda Costruzioni Ferroviarie
SOCIMI
Transport Design Consortium
Westinghouse Brake & Signal

Double-decker coaches
Bombardier
Daewoo Heavy Industries
FIREMA Consortium
GEC Alsthom Transportation Projects
Hitachi
Rautaruukki
SOCIMI
Transport Design Consortium

Drawgear
Davies & Metcalfe
New York Air Brake
RFS Engineering
Transport Design Consortium

Drives for diesel traction
JM Voith
MTU
RFS Engineering
Transport Design Consortium
Twiflex

KRAUSS MAFFEI

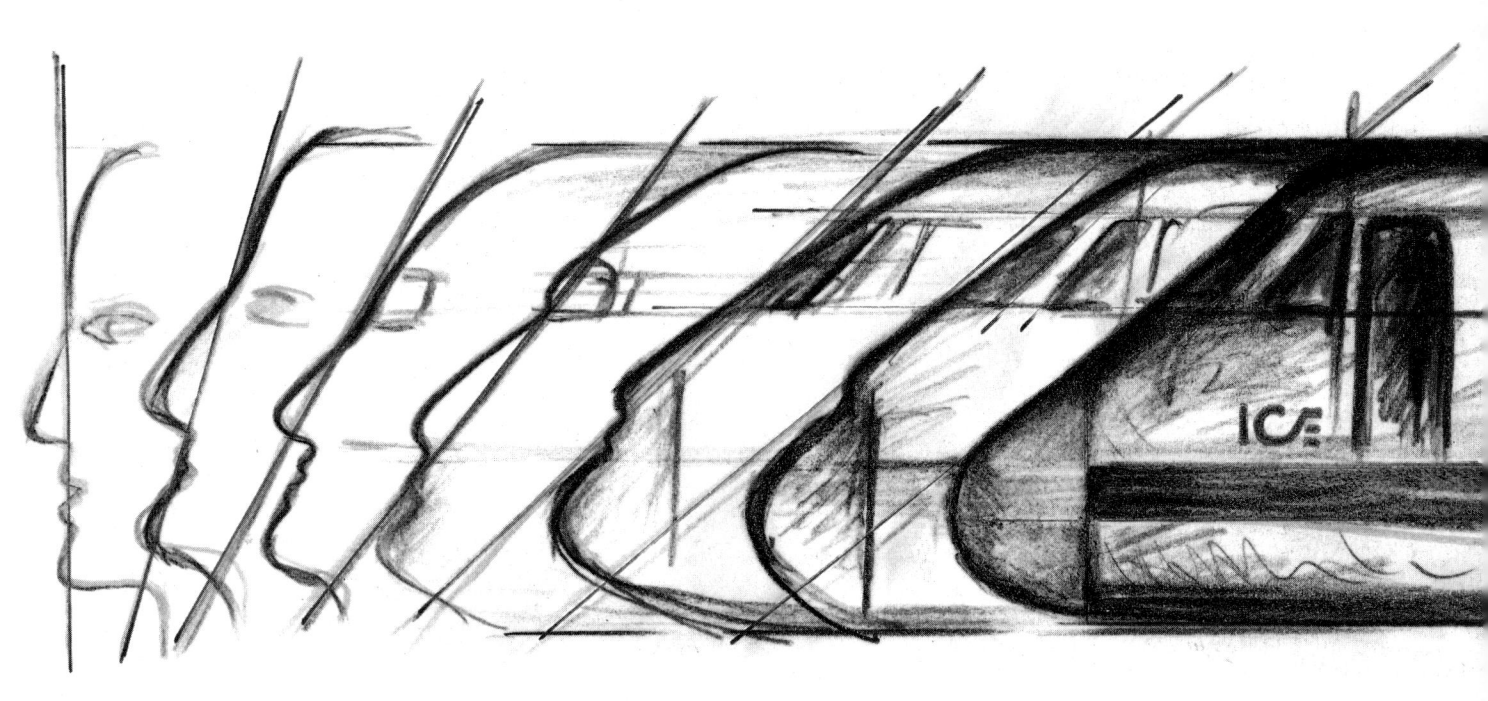

Streamlined Brains for Trains

To flash along the tracks at 406 km.p.h like the superfast ICE (Intercity Express) you need a good head for speed, capable of piloting one of the world's newest and most advanced transport systems.

And you need to have the brains to design, develop and construct a train like the ICE. To give it the right sort of nose, an aerodynamically perfect profile and the smoothest possible skin. And a driver's cab devised for ideal man/machine interaction.

Krauss-Maffei has produced the answer — for the ICE no less than for the TRANSRAPID. The know-how from 150 years of locomotive design and our innovative attitude have given us the right approach.

**Krauss-Maffei
Verkehrstechnik GmbH
Krauss-Maffei-Strasse 2
D-8000 Muenchen 50
Telephone 89/8899 0
Telefax 89/88 99 22 06
Telex 5 23163-91**

CLASSIFIED LIST OF ADVERTISERS

Drives for electric traction
Ansaldo Trasporti
GEC Alsthom Transportation Projects
Hitachi
Transport Design Consortium
Twiflex

Electric battery chargers
Ansaldo Trasporti
Brown & Root Vickers
Harmon Industries
Transport Design Consortium

Electric locomotive equipment
Ansaldo Trasporti
Brecknell Willis
GEC Alsthom Transportation Projects
Ascom Autelca
Hitachi
SOCIMI
Transport Design Consortium

Electric railcars and multiple-units
Ansaldo Trasporti
Breda Construzioni Ferroviarie
BREL
Daewoo Heavy Industries
FIREMA Consortium
GEC Alsthom Transportation Projects
Hitachi
RFS Engineering
Specialist Rail Products

Electric traction equipment
Ansaldo Trasporti
Brecknell Willis
Daewoo Heavy Industries
GEC Alsthom Transportation Projects
Hitachi
Sécheron
SOCIMI
Transport Design Consortium

Electric transmission systems
AEG Westinghouse Transport Systems
Ansaldo Trasporti
GEC Alsthom Transportation Projects
Hitachi
Transport Design Consortium
Vaughan Systems

Electrical cab systems
Ansaldo Trasporti
RFS Engineering
Specialist Rail Products
Westinghouse Brake & Signal

Electro-magnetic brakes
Davies & Metcalfe
SOCIMI
Transport Design Consortium

Electro-pneumatic brakes
Davies & Metcalfe
Transport Design Consortium
Westinghouse Brake & Signal

Electronic control systems for locomotives
AEG Westinghouse Transport Systems
Ansaldo Trasporti
Knorr-Bremse
Krauss-Maffei
GEC Alsthom Transportation Projects
Hitachi
RFS Engineering
Transport Design Consortium

Electronic railcars & multiple-units
AEG Westinghouse Transport Systems
Transport Design Consortium

Electronic seat reservation
Hitachi

End-of-train telemetry systems
Ansaldo Trasporti
GEC Alsthom Transportation Projects

Event recorders
Ansaldo Trasporti
RFS Engineering

Fare collection systems
Thorn EMI Electronics

Filters
Davies & Metcalfe
Transport Design Consortium

Filters for power supply
Sécheron

Fishplates
British Steel Track Products
S.I.L.F.

Flameproof mining locomotives
AEG Westinghouse Transport Systems
Cockerill
Daewoo Heavy Industries
RFS Engineering
Transport Design Consortium

Flexible couplings (rubber)
Davies & Metcalfe
Twiflex

Fluorescent lighting
Transport Design Consortium

Fuel injection test equipment
Merlin

Gears & gearboxes
AEG Westinghouse Transport Systems
Daewoo Heavy Industries
Davies & Metcalfe
Hitachi
JM Voith
New York Air Brake
RFS Engineering
S.I.L.F.
SLM
SOCIMI
Transport Design Consortium

General civil construction of railway lines and yards
Brown & Root Vickers
Transmark

Generators
Daewoo Heavy Industries
Hitachi
SOCIMI
Transport Design Consortium

Grooved rails
S.I.L.F.

Hand brakes
Daewoo Heavy Industries
Transport Design Consortium

High-speed passenger trains
Ansaldo Trasporti
Bombardier
Breda Construzioni Ferroviarie
BREL
Daewoo Heavy Industries
Fiat Ferroviaria
GEC Alsthom Transportation Projects
Hitachi
Keller
RFS Engineering
SOCIMI
Transport Design Consortium

Hydraulic retarders for continuous speed control in marshalling yards
Ansaldo Trasporti
JM Voith

SERVING THE RAILWAY INDUSTRY SINCE 1934

Tamper T

TAMPERS
C.A.R.T. Continuous Action Reciprocating Tamper
"C" Series Production/Switch Tamper
"C" Series Chase/Spot Switch Tamper
Mark III Production/Switch Tampers
Mark I and II Production/Switch Tampers
STM Spot/Switch Tampers

REGULATORS/BROOMS
"C" Series Ballast Regulator
Model BEB-17 Ballast Regulator
"C" Series Double Broom
BEB-17 Style Double Broom

COMPACTORS
"C" Series Crib & Shoulder Consolidators
CSC I Crib & Shoulder Consolidator
CSC II Crib & Shoulder Consolidator

TRACK UNDERCUTTERS
Trac Gopher, Model GO-4
Super Gopher, Model GO-4S

TIE EXCHANGERS
TR-10 High Production
Mini Tie Inserter
Section Gang Machines

TRACK RENEWAL
P-811S Track Renewal System
RCO Rail Change Out
Rail Threaders

TRACK RECORDING
Liteslice Rail Profile Measuring System

TIE PLUGGERS
Skid Mounted Tie Plugger
Tie Gang Plugger (TPG)
Rail Gang Plugger (TPR)

TIE HANDLER
RAIL HEATERS
SNOW REMOVAL/BROOMS
UTILITY VEHICLES
SPIKE DRIVERS/PULLERS
RAIL WELDER - ON TRACK

Tamper T

TAMPER CORP.
2401 Edmund Rd. - Box 20
Cayce-West Columbia, S.C. 29171-0020
(803) 822-9160   Fax (803) 822-8710
USA

RAIL WELDER CRW 500

LIFE EXPECTANCY: 1 500 000 KM

PERFORMANCE:

515,3 km/h*

VALDUNES' WHEELS AND AXLES GIVE BREATH AND WINGS TO THE TGV (HIGH SPEED TRAIN)

Speed Record. Well Done TGV !
Wear Record. Well Done **Valdunes** !
Wheels and axles which give not only
speed, but reliability too.
Today, the daily performance on the Atlantic network,
in addition to the Paris-Lyon network, which has been
in existance for the last 8 years, is befitting that of
a world leader in high performance wheels and wheelsets.

VALDUNES

Exclusive supplier of wheels
and wheelsets for the SNCF TGVs.

Immeuble Elysées la Défense
29, le Parvis - Cedex 35
92072 Paris la Défense 4
Tél. (1) 47 67 91 17

* New world record set on 16 May 1990 by the n° 325 train on the Vendôme St Amand stretch of the Atlantic TGV.

CLASSIFIED LIST OF ADVERTISERS

Information systems
Ansaldo Trasporti
GEC Alsthom Transportation Projects
Harmon Industries
Racal Acoustics
Rautaruukki
Transmark
Westinghouse Brake & Signal
Vaughan Systems

Insulated rail joints
Ansaldo Trasporti
S.I.L.F.

Interlocking signalling equipment
Ansaldo Trasporti
GEC Alsthom Transportation Projects
Harmon Industries

Intermodal equipment and systems
Caterpillar
New York Air Brake
Rautaruukki
Transport Design Consortium

Inverters for power supply
Sécheron

Level crossing equipment
Ansaldo Trasporti
Harmon Industries

Lighting equipment, locomotives
Transport Design Consortium

Lighting equipment, trains
Transport Design Consortium

Light rail slab track
IPA

Light rail vehicles
AEG Westinghouse Transport Systems
Ansaldo Trasporti
Bombardier
Breda Construzioni Ferroviarie
BREL
Daewoo Heavy Industries
Fiat Ferroviaria
FIREMA Consortium
GEC Alsthom Transportation Projects
Hitachi
Keller
RFS Engineering
SOCIMI
Transport Design Consortium

Lightweight track components
S.I.L.F.

Load braking devices
Davies & Metcalfe
Knorr-Bremse
Westinghouse Brake & Signal

Locomotive equipment
Ansaldo Trasporti
AEG Westinghouse Transport Systems
Cockerill
GEC Alsthom Transportation Projects
Hitachi
RFS Engineering
SOCIMI
SLM
Transport Design Consortium

Locomotive fuel management systems
Harmon Industries
Merlin
Transport Design Consortium

Locomotives, diesel
Breda Construzioni Ferroviarie
BREL
Cockerill
Daewoo Heavy Industries
Fiat Ferroviaria
Hitachi
Keller
Krauss-Maffei
Morrison-Knudsen
RFS Engineering
SOCIMI
SLM
Transport Design Consortium

Locomotives, electric
Ansaldo Trasporti
Breda Construzioni Ferroviarie
BREL
Cockerill
Daewoo Heavy Industries
Fiat Ferroviaria
FIREMA Consortium
GEC Alsthom Transportation Projects
Hitachi
Keller
Krauss-Maffei
RFS Engineering
SOCIMI
Skodaexport
SLM
Transport Design Consortium

Locomotives, industrial & mining
Ansaldo Trasporti
Cockerill
Daewoo Heavy Industries
Krauss-Maffei
RFS Engineering
SLM
Transport Design Consortium

Maintenance-of-way machines
Brown & Root Vickers
Caterpillar
Kershaw
Tamper

Maintenance systems packaging
Brown & Root Vickers

Manufacturers-permanent way equipment
Brecknell Willis
Kershaw
Tamper

Manufacturers – yard & terminal
Ansaldo Trasporti
SIKA

Materials handling equipment
TAKRAF

Metro/subway cars
AEG Westinghouse Transport Systems
Ansaldo Trasporti
Bombardier
Breda Construzioni Ferroviarie
BREL
Daewoo Heavy Industries
Fiat Ferroviaria
FIREMA Consortium
GEC Alsthom Transportation Projects
Hitachi
Keller
RFS Engineering
SOCIMI
Transport Design Consortium

Mirrors, platform
Craswell Scientific

Monorail
Bombardier
S.I.L.F.
Transport Design Consortium

Motors, electric
AEG Westinghouse Transport Systems
Ansaldo Trasporti
Daewoo Heavy Industries
GEC Alsthom Transportation Projects
Hitachi
SOCIMI
Transport Design Consortium

Overhead electriciation equipment
Ansaldo Trasporti

CUSTOMISED DRIVE SYSTEMS

modular design with proven components
GTO technology and digital control

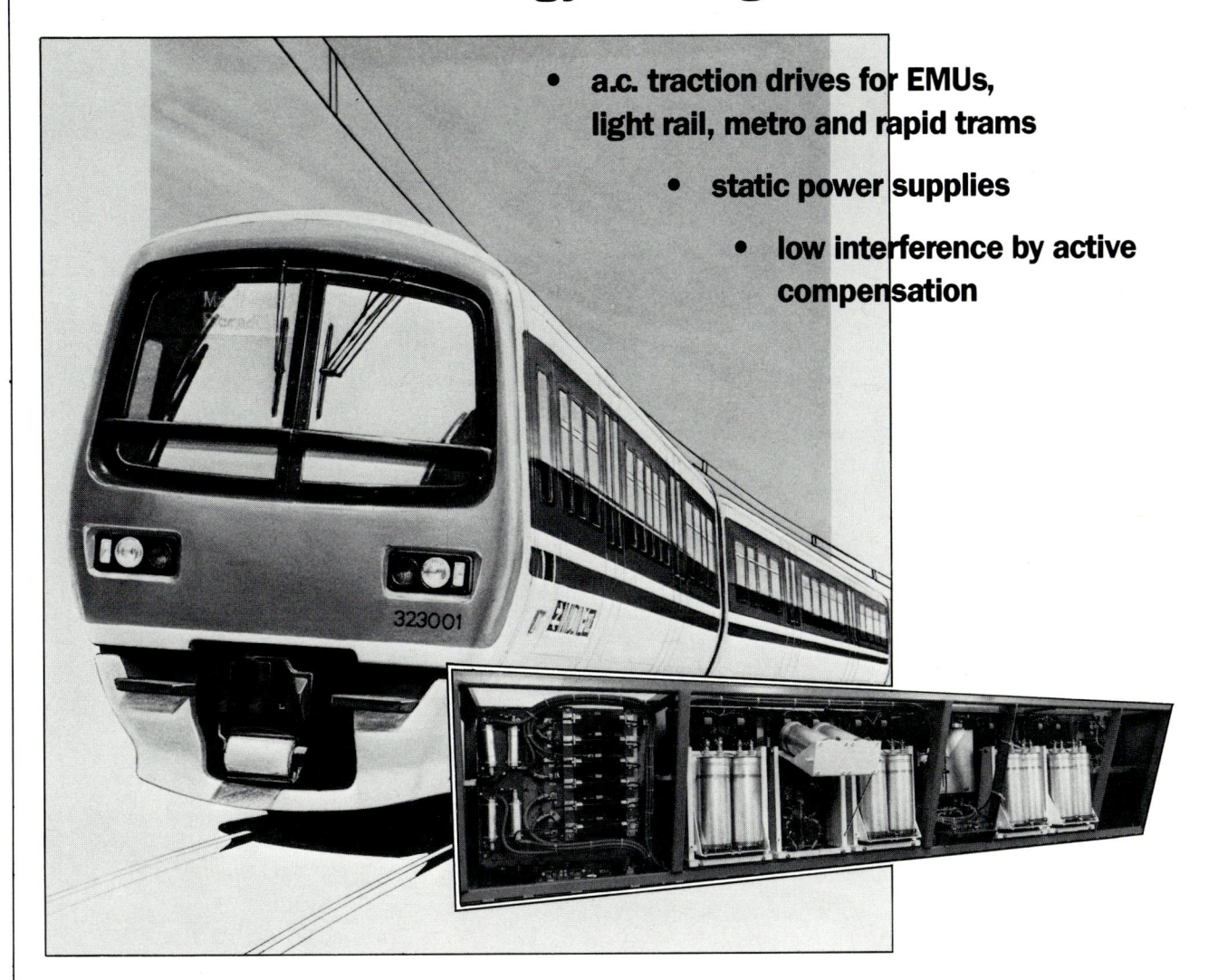

- a.c. traction drives for EMUs, light rail, metro and rapid trams
- static power supplies
- low interference by active compensation

HOLEC ⊢⊣ RIDDERKERK
total commitment to drive technology

Ringdijk 390
P.O. Box 4050
2980 GB Ridderkerk
The Netherlands

Phone: +31.74.465465
Fax: +31.74.465444
Telex: 20377 hslik nl

AQAP-1 certified

CLASSIFIED LIST OF ADVERTISERS

Pantographs
AEG Westinghouse Transport Systems
Ansaldo Trasporti
Brecknell Willis
BREL
SOCIMI
Transport Design Consortium

Parking brake, spring-applied
Davies & Metcalfe
Knorr-Bremse
Transport Design Consortium
Twiflex
Westinghouse Brake & Signal

Passenger brake equipment
Davies & Metcalfe
RFS Engineering
Westinghouse Brake & Signal

Passenger coach brake equipment (energency equipment)
Transport Design Consortium

Passenger coach equipment
Daewoo Heavy Industries
Hitachi
Luwa
Transport Design Consortium

Passenger coaches
Bombardier
BREL
GEC Alsthom Transportation Projects
Keller
RFS Engineering
Transport Design Consortium

Passenger/drive/guard audio communication
Racal Acoustics

Passenger information displays
AEG Westinghouse Transport Systems
Ansaldo Trasporti
Hitachi
Racal Acoustics
Transport Design Consortium
Vaughan Systems
Westinghouse Brake & Signal

Permanent way equipment
TAKRAF

Platforms & crossings
S.I.L.F.

Power rectifiers & inverters
Sécheron

Power supply engineering
Sécheron

Prestressed slabs for turnouts
IPA

Prestressed sleepers for turnouts
IPA

Protection & control relays
Sécheron

Rack railway vehicles and systems
SLM

Radio communications equipment
Ansaldo Trasporti
Harmon Industries

Rail fixing systems
SIKA

Rail grinding equipment
S.I.L.F.
Zweiweg-Fahrzeug

Rail trucks
Breda Construzioni Ferroviarie
RFS Engineering
S.I.L.F.
Transport Design Consortium

Railcar diesel engines
Fiat Ferroviaria
MTU
RFS Engineering
Transport Design Consortium

Railcars, diesel
BREL
Daewoo Heavy Industries
Fiat Ferroviaria
FIREMA Consortium
GEC Alsthom Transportation Projects
Hitachi
Morrison-Knudsen
RFS Engineering
SOCIMI
SLM
Transport Design Consortium

Railcars, electric
AEG Westinghouse Transport Systems
Ansaldo Trasporti
Bombardier
Breda Construzioni Ferroviarie
BREL
Daewoo Heavy Industries
Fiat Ferroviaria
FIREMA Consortium
GEC Alsthom Transportation Projects
Hitachi
Morrison-Knudsen
RFS Engineering
SOCIMI
SLM
Transport Design Consortium

Rails
British Steel Track Products
Servo Corporation of America
S.I.L.F.

Railway cranes
Brown & Root Vickers
Kershaw
Mannesmann Demag
RFS Engineering
S.I.L.F.
Valdunes

Railway equipment
Ansaldo Trasporti
Brecknell Willis
Brown & Root Vickers
RFS Engineering
S.I.L.F.
Transport Design Consortium
Westinghouse Brake & Signal

Rapid transit vehicles
Ansaldo Trasporti
Bombardier
Breda Construzioni Ferroviarie
BREL
Daewoo Heavy Industries
FIREMA Consortium
GEC Alsthom Transportation Projects
Hitachi
RFS Engineering
SOCIMI
SLM
Transport Design Consortium

Rectifiers
AEG Westinghouse Transport Systems
Ansaldo Trasporti
Hitachi
Sécheron

Refrigerated wagons
Breda Construzioni Ferroviarie
Daewoo Heavy Industries
FIREMA Consortium
Transport Design Consortium

The RFS Industries Group -

Stylish Composition

*T*he skills and expertise of three focussed engineering companies together make the RFS Industries Group one of the best and most versatile suppliers of goods and services to the railway industry.

Total quality and service are the keynotes to the RFS philosophy throughout the Group.

RFS Engineering Limited – *rail vehicle construction and lifecare, specialist conversions, equipment and wheelset overhaul.*

Specialist Rail Products Limited – *advanced rail sub-systems.*

RFS Projects Limited – *Industrial design, styling, engineering consultancy and project management.*

With outstanding facilities, strategic locations within the UK rail network, and a highly skilled and motivated workforce, the RFS Industries Group is able to respond to the most exacting engineering requirements.

Conducted with style and professionalism, in tune with the industry's needs.

RFS

RFS Engineering Limited
PO Box 192, Hexthorpe Road,
Doncaster, S Yorkshire DN1 1PJ
Tel: 0302 340700 Fax: 0302 340693
Telex: 547296

Specialist Rail Products Limited
PO Box 76, Hexthorpe Trading Estate,
Hexthorpe Road, Doncaster,
S Yorkshire DN4 0EH
Tel: 0302 328080 Fax: 0302 329911
Telex: 548208

RFS Projects Limited
2a East Mill, Bridgefoot, Belper,
Derbyshire DE5 1XZ
Tel: 0773 821051 Fax: 0773 821045
Telex: 378514

CLASSIFIED LIST OF ADVERTISERS

Remote control equipment
AEG Westinghouse Transport Systems
Ansaldo Trasporti
Caterpillar
Cockerill
Hitachi
Sécheron
Vaughan Systems
Westinghouse Brake & Signal

Retarders
Ansaldo Trasporti

Revenue collection systems & equipment
Transport Design Consortium

Road-rail shunting & track gang vehicles
Caterpillar
Daewoo Heavy Industries
RFS Engineering
Transport Design Consortium
Zweiweg-Fahrzeug

Safety equipment
Ansaldo Trasporti
Brown & Root Vickers
Harmon Industries

Safety equipment & technology
Ansaldo Trasporti
Brown & Root Vickers
Davies & Metcalfe
Harmon Industries
Servo Corporation of America
Specialist Rail Product
Transport Design Consortium
Westinghouse Brake & Signal

Seats, passenger
BREL
Transport Design Consortium

Signalling systems and apparatus
AEG Westinghouse Transport Systems
Ansaldo Trasporti
Harmon Industries
RFS Engineering
Servo Corporation of America
Vaughan Systems

Simulation systems
Ansaldo Trasporti
Ascom Autelca

Slab rack systems
IPA

Sleepers/ties
British Steel Track Products
Harmon Industries
IPA
Jakem Timbers
S.I.L.F.

Solid state interlocking systems
Ansaldo Trasporti
GEC Alsthom Transportation Projects
Harmon Industries

Speed control devices
AEG Westinghouse Transport Systems
Ansaldo Trasporti
Harmon Industries
Hitachi
Krauss-Maffei
New York Air Brake

Station equipment
Ansaldo Trasporti
Transport Design Consortium
Westinghouse Brake & Signal

Suspension components
BREL
Davies & Metcalfe
Knorr-Bremse
Specialist Rail Products
Transport Design Consortium

Switches and switch components
AEG Westinghouse Transport Systems

Switchgears for DC power supply
Sécheron

Tampers, ballast
Brown & Root Vickers
Tamper

Test and measuring units for rail vehicles bogies
Brown & Root Vickers
Transport Design Consortium

Third rail electrification equipment
Ansaldo Trasporti
Brecknell Willis

Thyristors & thyristor equipment
Ansaldo Trasporti
GEC Alsthom Transportation Products
Hitachi

Tickets
Norprint International

Ticket dispensers
Norprint International
Transport Design Consortium

Ties/sleepers
British Steel Track Products
Fiat Ferroviaria
Harmon Industries
IPA
Jakem Timbers
S.I.L.F.

Tower vehicles
Brown & Root Vickers

Track circuit equipment
Ansaldo Trasporti

Track cleaning machines
Kershaw

Track inspection cars
BREL
Brown & Root Vickers
Tamper
Transport Design Consortium

Track machines
Tamper

Track maintenance equipment
Brown & Root Vickers
Caterpillar
Cooperative Bilanciai
Kershaw
Servo Corporation of America
S.I.L.F.
Tamper

Traffic control systems
AEG Westinghouse Transport Systems
Ansaldo Trasporti
Harmon Industries
Hitachi
Vaughan Systems

Way ahead in passenger information systems.

The Racal 'Signboard' product range, using advanced liquid crystal display technology, is a total systems solution to the problems of information display in railway terminals, with the backup and support that can only come from one of the most successful high technology companies.

- Bright, attractive displays with wide viewing angle and choice of colour.
- Choice of character heights and text formats.
- Intelligent interfaces for most standard data transmission protocols.
- On-train information systems.
- All solid state reliability – no moving parts.
- Low life cycle costs, low initial cost.
- Integral lighting control system.
- Versatile mechanical design for front or rear access, and ease of installation.
- Light weight construction.

For further information please contact:

RACAL

Information Display Systems,
Racal Acoustics Limited,
Waverley Industrial Park, Hailsham Drive,
Harrow, Middlesex HA1 4TR.
Tel: 081-427 7727 Fax 081-427 0350

Keep on the right lines with JAKEM

For tough, long-lasting track timbers with expertise to match

Choose from a range of heavy hardwoods for sleepers and crossings; Jarrah, Karri, Kempas, Keruing, Selangan Batu and Ekki.
These timbers have high impact resistance and resilience. They are produced cut-to-size in accordance with established specifications, with all the benefits of Jakem experience. Adzing, end plating, boring and treatment facilities available at source. UK stockholding of standard gauge sleepers and crossings. Technical advice freely given based on a lifetime's experience in the worldwide supply of track timbers.

JAKEM
The Track Timber Specialists

Jakem Timbers Ltd., The Old Malt House, 125 High Street, Uckfield, East Sussex TN22 1EG, England.
Tel: (0825) 768555. Telex: 95670. Fax: (0825) 768483.

Photo by courtesy of British Rail — Crewe remodelling featuring Jarrah/Karri

CLASSIFIED LIST OF ADVERTISERS

Transformers
AEG Westinghouse Transport Systems
Ansaldo Trasporti
Harmon Industries
Hitachi

Transmission systems, traction
Cockerill
David Brown Gear Industries
GEC Alsthom Transportation Products
JM Voith
Twiflex

Trasponders
Ansaldo Trasporti

Two-way vehicles
Ansaldo Trasporti
Brown & Root Vickers
Keller
Transport Design Consortium
Zweiweg-Fahrzeug

Wagons, freight
Brown & Root Vickers
Breda Construzioni Ferroviarie
Daewoo Heavy Industries
Fiat Ferroviaria
FIREMA Consortium
Keller
Rautaruukki
RFS Engineering
Transport Design Consortium

Weighing systems, electronic & mechanical
Brown & Root Vickers
Cooperativa Bilanciai
Westinghouse Brake & Signal

Welding equipment & accessories
Brown & Root Vickers
Daewoo Heavy Industries

Wheel & axle testing equipment
Brown & Root Vickers
RFS Engineering
Transport Design Consortium

Wheels, axles & wheelsets
Lovere Sidermeccanica
Servo Corporation of America
S.I.L.F.
SOCIMI
Tamper
Valdunes

Wheel flange lubricators
Sécheron

Wheelsets
RFS Engineering
S.I.L.F.
Valdunes

Workshop equipment
Ansaldo Trasporti
BMS
Brown & Root Vickers
Merlin
S.I.L.F.
Socimi

Yard and terminal equipment
Kershaw
TAKRAF

ALMOST LIKE FLYING

Hardly a vibration can be felt.
Hardly a sound can be heard. Like flying.
On the basis of this experience, reinforced prestressed cement plates have been produced and put into operation by IPA: a formula which provides for the maximum stability and resilience of railway tracks and the highest level of comfort for the traveller. Even at 300 km/h.
The IPA-Slab Track System shortens the construction time of the line, prevents decay and allows for the transit of emergency road vehicles.
The IPA-Slab Track System was adopted by Italian State Railways for the Udine-Tarvisio line and by Milan metro.
That is, in situations where tomorrow's services are required today.

IPA

INDUSTRIA PREFABBRICATI E AFFINI
PREFABRICATE AND SIMILAR INDUSTRIES
Plants and constructs the development.

IPA - 24050 Calcinate (BG) - Italy
Via Provinciale - Tel. 035/841.291

servo

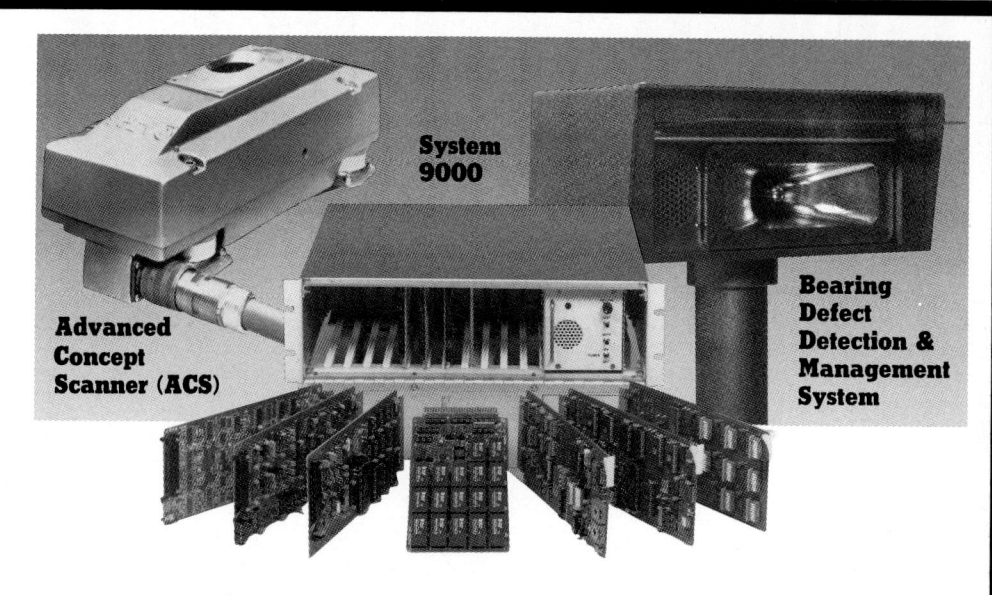

System 9000

Advanced Concept Scanner (ACS)

Bearing Defect Detection & Management System

At the leading edge of derailment prevention technology

SERVO CORPORATION OF AMERICA
111 New South Road
Hicksville, New York 11802
(516) 938-9700 • TWX: 510-221-1872
FAX: (516) 938-9644

Gloucester (Orleans), Ontario, Canada K1C 6K7
(613) 830-5426 • Telefax: 613-837-7482
Chemin du Cap 1-3, 1006 Lausanne, Switzerland
(021) 29-98-73 • Telex: 454-420 SERVO CH
Telefax: 021-29-9874

ŠKODAEXPORT, PRAGUE, CZECHOSLOVAKIA
THE BIGGEST WORLD EXPORTER OF ELECTRIC LOCOMOTIVES

introduces

ŠKODA'S IIIrd Generation:
ELECTRIC LOCOMOTIVE ŠKODA 85E with directly driven axles using asynchronous three-phase motor – 120-140 kmp. Power output control is contactless and continuous . . .

Another ŠKODA's innovations:
DOUBLE SYSTEM ŠKODA 80 E/CSFR-GDR/D/C – 3060 kW, 120 kmp; ŠKODA 93 E – 6 220 kW, 120-150 kmp, six axles.

ŠKODAEXPORT

MADE IN CZECHOSLOVAKIA:
ŠKODA Concern, Plzeň, Tylova 56, 316 00 Plzeň
Czechoslovakia
Telephone (+4219) 215 1111   Telex 154 221-2, 154247
Cables: ŠKODA Plzeň
Telefax: (+4219) 275 589

EXPORTER
ŠKODAEXPORT Prague 11332 Vaclavske n. 56
Czechoslovakia
Telex: 122413 SKEX C   Telephone: (+0422) 236 6407
Cables: ŠKODAEXPORT Prague
Telefax: (+0422) 269563

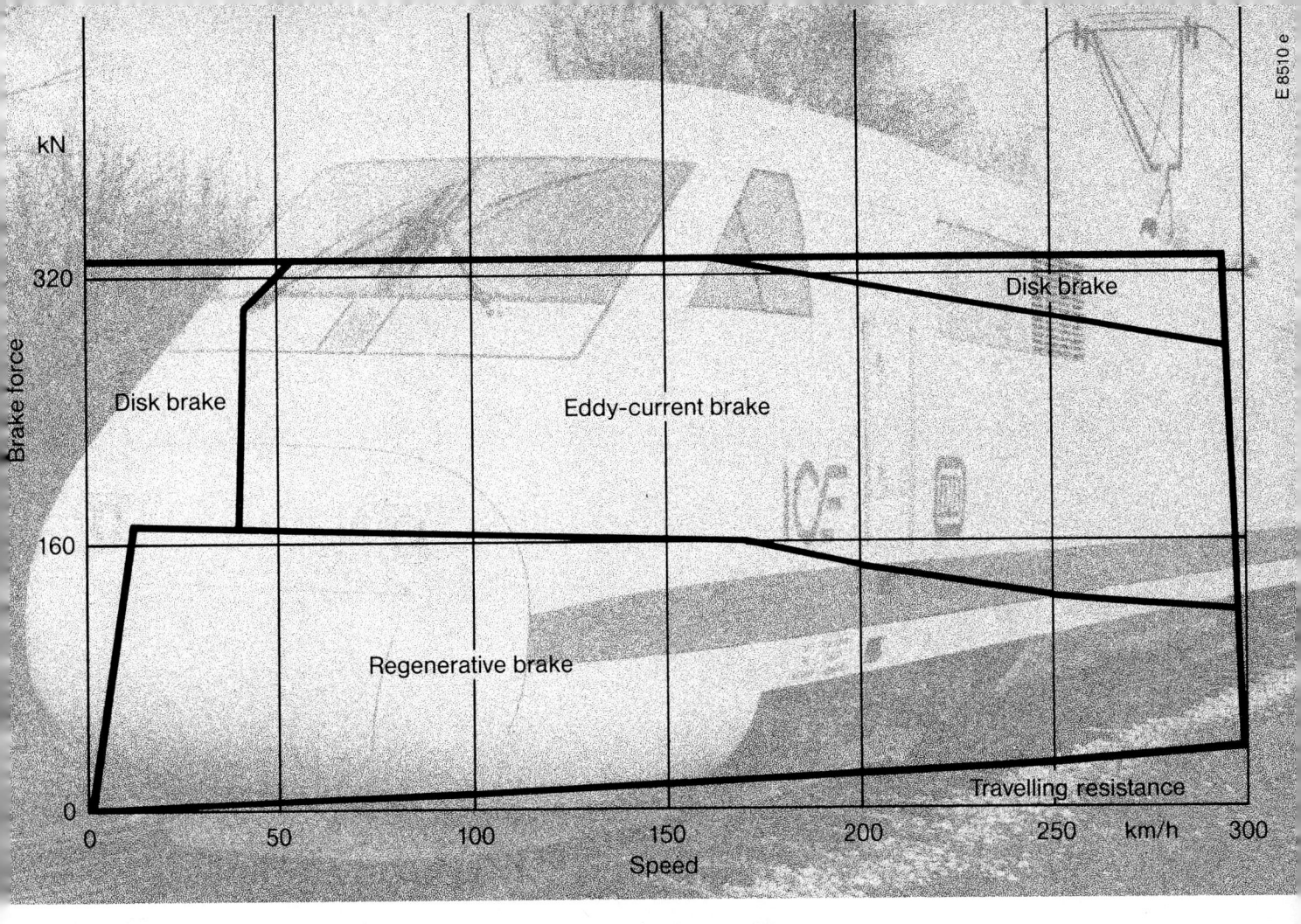

ICE. From 300 to zero.

High-speed trains like the ICE need high-performance brakes to master the enormous kinetic energy unleashed at 300 km/h.

KNORR has taken on this challenge by developing a high-performance braking system capable of handling tomorrow's high-speed trains.

The ICE incorporates an entirely new braking system, a combination of regenerative brakes, KNORR disk brakes and KNORR eddy-current brakes.

The linear eddy-current brake acts straight on the rails through an air gap. There is no friction, so it doesn't wear, and it provides for a high braking effect, even in the very top speed range.

The diagram shows how the three different brakes work together if a full service brake application is performed from a speed of 300 km/h down to zero. The exactly synchronized response of the different brakes is ensured by the electronic microprocessor control system, specifically designed by KNORR for the ICE train, providing for a smooth and gentle braking to increase travelling comfort.

The high control precision permits a very exact stop of the train at a predetermined point. The design of the electronic control system allows modern diagnostic and maintenance procedures which are distinguished by a comprehensive functional monitoring.

This is one more example of KNORR's broad product spectre.

KNORR engineering. Developed for the future. And acknowledged worldwide.

The KNORR-eddy-current brake.

KNORR-BREMSE AG MÜNCHEN

KELLER spa Palermo
KELLER MECCANICA spa
Cagliari

KELLER FREIGHT AND PASSENGER CARS FOR EVERY PURPOSE

TYPE UIC-Z1 INTERNATIONAL AIR CONDITIONED COMPARTMENT PASSENGER CAR

☐ Freight cars of all types ☐ Passenger coaches of all types and classes ☐ Bogies for freight cars and passenger coaches ☐ Special purpose vehicles ☐ Overhead line installation maintenance and inspection cars ☐ Light rail vehicles

HEAD OFFICE: Via Francesco Guardione, 3 - 90139 Palermo (Italy) - TELEPHONE: (091) 586322 - TELEX 911062 KELLDG I - FAX: 091 582784

TYPE K 301 OVERHEAD LINE INSTALLATION INSPECTION AND MAINTENANCE CAR

TYPE VFACCS BOGIE BALLAST WAGON WITH 40 M3 CAPACITY

COVERED BOGIE 80 M3 HOPPER WAGON FOR TRANSPORT OF CEREALS AND OTHER BULK MATERIAL

TRANSPORT

ESSENTIAL INFORMATION SOURCES FOR TRANSPORT PROFESSIONALS

JANE'S URBAN TRANSPORT SYSTEMS 1990

Jane's Urban Transport Systems is the only directory covering the international city passenger transport industry.

It provides comprehensive details on the management, operations, financing and development of over 850 public transport undertakings in over 400 cities worldwide, covering all urban transport modes.

Contact and product information is given for some 700 manufacturers of equipment in over 110 countries. Coverage of consultancy and contracting services worldwide complete this unique information source.

Publication date: May 1990, ISBN 0 7106 0902 7, 680 pp approx, limp bound.

JANE'S WORLD RAILWAYS 1990-91

Jane's World Railways is the long established leading survey of railway systems, new equipment, policies and commercial trends in the rail industry worldwide.

Over 1200 manufacturers of railway equipment are covered, and extensive systems data is provided for over 530 networks in some 110 countries.

As a truly international directory, **Jane's World Railways** also gives full listings of national and international agencies and associations, together with worldwide consultancy services.

Publication date: October 1990, ISBN 0 7106 0920 5, 930 pp approx, laminated covers on boards.

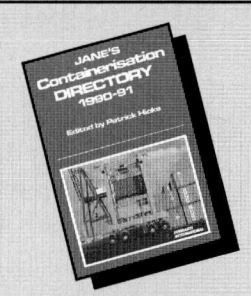

JANE'S CONTAINERISATION DIRECTORY 1990-91

Jane's Containerisation Directory covers all aspects of the international containerisation market. It provides clear and essential information on ports, container operators, container manufacturers, handling equipment suppliers and related services throughout the world. Facilities of some 400 ports and inland terminals in over 100 countries and international operations provided by shipping lines, railways and NVOCs are comprehensively detailed. Container leasing and handling companies, suppliers of products and services are extensively listed, with full contact details and product descriptions.

Publication date: August 1990, ISBN 0 7106 0912 4, 580 pp approx, limp bound

JANE'S HIGH-SPEED MARINE CRAFT 1990

Jane's High-Speed Marine Craft provides full technical descriptions and data for over 600 high-speed craft types capable of more than 20 knots. A complete review is provided of over 350 civil operators of high-speed craft, with contact details, routes operated and fleet inventories.

Manufacturers of principal engineering components, listings of international regulatory authorities, consultants and associations and an extensive bibliography complete this comprehensive directory.

Publication date: June 1990, ISBN 0 7106 0903 5, 720 pp approx, limp bound.

ORDER FORM

Title	Quantity	£	US$
Jane's Urban Transport Systems 1990		110	185
Jane's World Railways 1990-91		115	195
Jane's Containerisation Directory 1990-91		110	185
Jane's High-Speed Marine Craft 1990		105	175
Total Order Value			

Name_____ Job Title_____

Company/Organisation _____

Address _____

_____ Telephone _____

Method of Payment

☐ I enclose a cheque for £/US$ _____ (made payable to Jane's Information Group)

☐ Please invoice my company. Purchase Order number _____

☐ Please charge my credit card Eurocard/Access/Mastercard ☐ American Express ☐ Visa ☐

My card number is ☐☐☐☐☐☐☐☐☐☐☐☐☐☐☐☐   Expiry Date: _____

Signature: _____ (obligatory for credit card orders)

ORDERS FROM THE USA, CANADA & LATIN AMERICA
Jane's Information Group, Dept DSM,
1340 Braddock Place, Suite 300,
Alexandria, VA22314-1651, USA
Telephone: (703) 683-3700

JANE'S · INFORMATION · GROUP

ORDERS FROM EUROPE AND REST OF THE WORLD
Jane's Information Group, Dept DSM,
Sentinel House, 163 Brighton Road
Coulsdon, Surrey CR5 2NH, UK
Telephone: International (+44 81) 763 1030

ONE·STOP SHOPPING

FOR ■ RAILS ■ STEEL SLEEPERS
TRACK LAYING ■ CONTRACTING
SWITCHES & CROSSINGS

British Steel can offer a total package for any rail system. Their engineering expertise and track design capability is renowned throughout the world. For further information on rails, sleepers & track accessories contact British Steel Track Products at Workington – 0900 64321. For switches & crossings and track laying – contact Grant Lyon Eagre at Scunthorpe 0724 862131

S British Steel
Moss Bay, Derwent Howe, Workington, Cumbria CA14 5AE.

MERLIN INJECTION PUMP SERVICE EQUIPMENT

Increase service productivity with the Merlin H1230 Heavy Duty Fuel Pump Test Bench

* Closed Loop Hydrostatic 30 kW (40 hp) Drive or DC Thyristor available.
* Mobile Injector— Calibration Units.
* Capacity up to 18-cylinder In-Line or 'V' configuration pumps or up to 4 single-cylinder pumps.
* Single/Multi-cylinder camboxes.
* Suitable for Engine types: Alco, General Motors, M.A.K. S.E.M.T. Pielstick, etc.

World-wide suppliers to major Railway companies: British, Polish, Indian, Turkish etc
FOR FURTHER INFORMATION CONTACT:

MERLIN INTERNATIONAL (ENGINEERS) LIMITED
Winery Lane, Walton-le-Dale, PRESTON PR5 4AZ, Lancashire, England
Telephone: Preston (0772) 52877/58597
Telegrams: Merlin Preston   Telex: 67376 (Merlin G)   Fax. No. (0772) 203857
Registered UK Defence Contractor to HM Government Reg No: 1W1M01

ADS ASSOCIATION OF DIESEL SPECIALISTS

ZWEIWEG Road Railers

The universal road/rail system for all applications and track gauges. Based on the Mercedes-Benz Unimog.

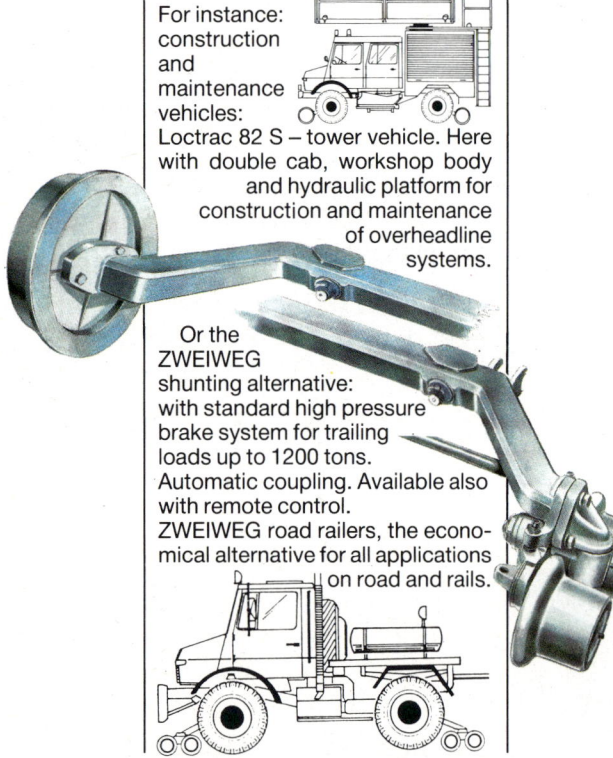

For instance: construction and maintenance vehicles:
Loctrac 82 S – tower vehicle. Here with double cab, workshop body and hydraulic platform for construction and maintenance of overheadline systems.

Or the ZWEIWEG shunting alternative: with standard high pressure brake system for trailing loads up to 1200 tons. Automatic coupling. Available also with remote control.
ZWEIWEG road railers, the economical alternative for all applications on road and rails.

ZWEIWEG-Fahrzeug GmbH & Co. Vertriebs KG
D-8200 Rosenheim · Salinstr. 1 · Tel. 0 80 31/1 50 31,
TTX (17) 803 1 822, Telefax 0 80 31/1 58 99

ZWEIWEG

JANE'S · INFORMATION · GROUP

Leading suppliers of impartial, factual, professional information to the defence, aerospace and transport industries.

The Group's unique capabilities for research and analysis enables it to provide the most comprehensive information from a single source.

Products and Services:
CD-ROM
Subscription Services
Yearbooks and Directories
On-line Services
Journals and Newsletters
Confidential Market Research
Electronic Databases
Symposia

Essential for decision makers in
Sales and Marketing
Procurement
Operations
Research and Development
Training and Recognition
Consultancy

JANE'S INFORMATION GROUP
the unique answer to your intelligence requirements

Jane's Information Group
Sentinel House
163 Brighton Road
Coulsdon
Surrey CR5 2NH
United Kingdom
Tel: (081) 763 1030

Jane's Information Group
1340 Braddock Place
Suite 300
Alexandria VA 22314-1651
United States
Tel: (703) 683 3700

Sécheron

Traction components

Sécheron Ltd draws on more than 100 years of experience in the design, manufacture and marketing of a range of traction components for modern vehicles.

- High-speed DC circuit breakers
- AC vacuum circuit breakers for vehicles
- DC and AC contactors
- Electronic protection devices
- Braking resistors
- Wheel flange lubricators
- Automatic couplings.

Sécheron Ltd

Traction Components
CH-1211 Geneva 21
Phone: +4122/739 41 54
Fax: +4122/739 43 61
Telex: 22130 bbse ch

Marconi
Power Semiconductors for Transport Systems Worldwide

For over 30 years Marconi have been supplying power semiconductors to the railway industry. During that time many new devices have been developed culminating in the GTO thyristor, and even this product has now been refined to reduce the losses even further.

In addition, there are ancillary devices, such as fast recovery diodes, available for use with GTOs besides thyristors and diodes for all traction applications. For your electric traction power semiconductor requirements contact the experts.

Marconi Electronic Devices

Marconi Electronic Devices Ltd.,
Power Semiconductor Division,
Carholme Road,
Lincoln LN1 1SG
Tel: 0522-510500
Telex: 56163
Fax: 0522-510550

Marconi Electronic Devices, S.A.
2 Rue Henri -Bergson,
92600 Asnieres,
France
Tel: (1) 4080 54 00
Telex: 612850
Fax: (1) 4080 55 87

Marconi Elektronik,
Postfach 1929,
Landsberger Strasse 65,
D-8034 Germering,
Federal Republic Of Germany
Tel: (089) 849360 Telex: 5212642
Fax: (089) 8419142

CONTROL THE ACTION IN HIGH POWERED INDUSTRY

Brown & Root Rail Projects

This team can now offer an impartial and professional service for
- Project Management of Turnkey Systems and Modernisation Schemes
- Quality Assurance Services
- Engineering Design Consultancy
- Civil Engineering Design Consultancy
- Q.S. Services

Our clients include
- Caracas Metro
- Hong Kong MTRC
- Kowloon Canton Railway
- London Docklands - (Poplar and Becton Workshops)
- LUL Central and Northern Line
- Istanbul LRT
- Seoul Metro
- Tuen Mun LRT
- Manchester Metrolink
- Adelaide STA
- British Rail Board
- LUL (Quality and Project Management Services)
- Transmanche Link

Try Brown & Root Rail Projects
Contact: Rowland Vye TODAY on :-
Tel: (0703) 625357   Fax: (0703) 619808
United Kingdom

---

30 TONS BOGIE-LIFT

The BMS product range includes hydraulic lifts for bogies and for locomotives, hydraulic pull-off machines for train wheels, arrangements for lifting and dismanteling train bogies and test stand for springs.

BMS
The Danish Building Equipment Pool Ltd.

Sindalvej 10
DK-2610 Rødovre
Denmark
Phone: +45 42 94 90 48
Telefax: +45 42 94 47 30

Summer or winter ... no problem!

Winter or summer, it makes no difference to the railways. Except perhaps for the 5000 to 9000 tonnes of snow which the ROLBA RR-3000 or RR-6000 can clear from the tracks per hour.
And when the weather is fine or perhaps the snow fall not quite so severa, the ROLBA RR-2/200 universal unit takes care of maintenance – all the year round. ROLBA keeps the trains rolling.

rolba

Rolba AG, CH-8620 Wetzikon/Switzerland, Phone 01/933 61 11, Fax 01/933 66 66

Control Systems of the 90's will Open Doors for you...

Modular Pneumatic Control Systems for the Actuation of Automatic Doors

- Designed to your specification
- Compact design
- Labelled port connections
- Many safety features available
- Pre-tested modules
- Minimal pipework
- Low service costs

KV LIMITED
43 Burners Lane South, Kiln Farm, Milton Keynes, Bucks. MK11 3HA England
Tel: (0908) 561515 Telex: 826710 (KAYVEN G) Facsimile: (0908) 561227

KV AUTOMATION SYSTEMS

STEP UP TO THE PLATE.

REMANUFACTURED BY
MORRISON-KNUDSEN
COMPANY, INC.
BOISE, IDAHO

CLASS
MODEL
HORSEPOWER
SERIAL NO.
ORDER NO.

BOISE 1990

THEY DID.

MORRISON KNUDSEN Rail Systems Group

500 plus now in service.
For more information call:
208-386-5950

experience and technology on rail

LRV type T 68
for the GMA Group
Manchester Metrolink
(Prototype Body Shell)

LRV type T 81
for ACOTRAL Rome

FIREMA Consortium
C.so di Porta Romana, 63 - 20122 Milano - Italy
Telex 322255 FIREMA I - Fax (02) 5460133

FIREMA Consortium Engineering

MTU high-performance diesel engines and power systems

Years in the forefront of technology and constant involvement with the specific requirements of our traditional customers have given us the leading edge and the widest experience in the field.

The MTU package

Traction units and peripheral equipment

Diesel Engines

for rail traction and train electricity

Electronics

electronic monitoring and control systems

Systems Engineering

Engineering services for project definition, project handling, field installation and commissioning, as well as locomotive repowering

Product Support

Worldwide product support organization with field engineers, maintenance and repair facilities, parts inventories, operator training and workshop planning service

MTU Motoren- und Turbinen Union
Friedrichshafen GmbH
P. O. Box 2040
D-7990 Friedrichshafen/W.-Germany

Power ratings and railroad applications

Diesel engine series | **Rail Cars**
099   96-152 kW
183   162-580 kW

Diesel engine series | **Main Line Locomotives**
396   1180-1840 kW
956/1163   2460-4100 kW

Diesel engine series | **Shunting and Industrial Locomotives**
183   228- 580 kW
396   785-1840 kW

Diesel engine series | **Mountain Railroad and Narrow-Gauge Railroads**
183   162- 580 kW
396   785-1840 kW

Diesel engine series | **Multi-purpose Locomotives**
183   228- 580 kW
396   785-1840 kW

Diesel engine series | **For continous-duty generator sets, 50 Hz or 60 Hz Train Electricity**
099/183   60- 459 kW
396   (upon request)

mtu
Deutsche Aerospace

THAI RAILWAYS, Locomotive AD 2400 type - 1 S.E.M.T. Pielstick 16 PA4 - V185 engine (1,965 kW)

ASSURANCE OF RELIABILITY

The most extensive range of traction Diesel engines.

- Highest reliability under the most severe operating and climatic conditions.
- Lowest operating costs through availability, easy maintenance and low consumption.
- Compact and light weight design for more horsepower per ton and cubic foot.
- 2,900 Piėlstick traction engines in service throughout the world.

S.E.M.T. PIELSTICK

S.E.M.T. Pielstick
2, quai de Seine - 93202 SAINT-DENIS France
Tél. : 33 (1) 48 09 76 00 - Télex : SEMT 236773 F
Fax : 33 (1) 42 43 81 02

TD PUB

TRANSMISSION CONTROL

When it comes to power transmission, few companies can rival David Brown's 128 year track record. With an impressive design and manufacturing resource, capable of producing a wide range of gears and transmission systems to the highest quality control standards, it's no surprise that many of the world's leading locomotive builders incorporate our products into theirs.
If you would like more information about our comprehensive range of products and services for the railway industry contact:

Clive D. Naylor
Sales and Marketing Manager

DB DAVID BROWN GEAR INDUSTRIES LIMITED

PARK GEAR WORKS, HUDDERSFIELD
WEST YORKSHIRE, ENGLAND HD4 5DD
Telephone: 0484 422180. Fax: 0484 514732

MAGNOR Data SECURITY PRINTING

YOUR SPECIALIST MANUFACTURER.

FEATURING:

ENCODING

MAGNETIC STRIPES

NUMBERING

BAR CODING

SECURITY PRINT

NORPRINT INTERNATIONAL
BOSTON · LINCOLNSHIRE · ENGLAND
TELEPHONE 0205 365161 · TELEX 37578 · FAX 0205 364825

New York Air Brake: on-track worldwide.

ABOVE: NYAB worldwide sales and distribution
RIGHT: New York Air Brake Company general offices and manufacturing facilities at Watertown, New York

New York Air Brake, A Unit of General Signal is long established as a world trader in the international rail transportation community. Our on-going world wide operations include sales and/or distribution in Europe, Asia, Africa, South America, Australia and North America.

This listing underscores NYAB's developing efforts to be on-track worldwide. And we are accomplishing this by competitively meeting our offshore customer's needs with design and manufacturing of brake systems as appropriate to meet AAR or local requirements for locomotives, freight cars, passenger cars and transit vehicles.

In addition, NYAB produces hydraulic and pneumatic brake systems as well as automatic couplers for all types of rail transit applications. Capabilities include: microprocessor based electronic controls, compressors, disc and tread brakes. And behind it all is NYAB's total-capability quality assurance from our systems engineering and testing.

So, write today for our literature. Ask for our SYSTEMS & PRODUCTS books and CAPABILITY book. Or, telephone Jim Pontious, VP Marketing, U.S.A. 315-782-7000.

NYAB

NEW YORK AIR BRAKE
A UNIT OF GENERAL SIGNAL

Starbuck Avenue, Watertown, New York 13601, U.S.A.
Telephone: 315-782-7000
Telex: 93-7303
Telecopier: 315-788-2820

T R A N S M A R K

TRAINING PROGRAMMES

INTERMODAL TRANSPORTATION

A new International Programme for middle level and Senior Managers concerned with Intermodal Systems. It is designed to
- give a state-of-the-art update on the systems available.
- discuss the cost-effective planning, implementation and management of Intermodal Systems.

Synopsis Container Systems
Swap-body Systems
Terminal Equipment
Terminal Layout
Terminal Management
Maintenance Procedures
Inland Clearance Depots, Customs Procedures
Balance between Modes
Costing, Pricing and Marketing

The emphasis is on freight transport and on Road, Rail and Sea modes, but some consideration will be given to interfaces with Air and to the intermodal transfer of passengers.

Location Cheltenham, U.K.

Dates 3 June to 14 June 1991
8 June to 19 June 1992

For further details write to **Training Manager, Transmark, Enterprise House, 169 Westbourne Terrace, London W2 6JY UK. Telex 8953218.**

Transmark is a wholly-owned subsidiary of British Rail.

T R A N S M A R K

TRANSMARK WAS SET UP BY BRITISH RAIL IN 1969 TO OFFER EXPERT PLANNING, SYSTEMS AND TECHNICAL ADVICE TO RAILWAYS AROUND THE WORLD. SINCE THEN WE HAVE GROWN INTO ONE OF THE WORLD'S FOREMOST INDEPENDENT RAILWAY CONSULTANCIES AND ONE OF THE MOST WIDELY EXPERIENCED, ADVISING ON EVERY KIND OF PROJECT IN EVERY CONTINENT OF THE GLOBE.

Transmark has its own specialist Training Unit run by professionals experienced in the design and implementation and evaluation of training programmes at all levels. We run training programmes, lasting from two weeks upwards and based both in Britain and overseas, covering all management and engineering disciplines.

JANE'S INFORMATION GROUP

THE UNIQUE ANSWER TO YOUR

DEFENCE
AEROSPACE
AND TRANSPORT

INTELLIGENCE REQUIREMENTS

Jane's Information Group, Sentinel House, 163 Brighton Road, Coulsdon, Surrey, CR5 2NH
Telephone: 081-763 1030 Fax: 081-763 1005 Telex: 916907

Leading the world!

19,000 rail vehicles in more than **76** countries have Voith drive systems, the best possible proof of Voith quality.

The main features:
- Maximum availability
- Extremely long first life
- Low maintenance costs
- Worldwide servicing

For rail vehicles Voith supplies:
- Turbo transmissions
- Retarders
- Axle drives
- Cooling units
- Cardan shafts

Voith Engineering Ltd.
6 Beddington Farm Road
Croydon, Surrey CR0 4XB
Telephone 081-667 03 33
Telex 946 129
Fax No. 081-667 04 03

VOITH

J.M. Voith GmbH
P.O. Box 19 40, D-7920 Heidenheim
West Germany

at 007.2e

This message is adressed to **KILNS, CEMENT FACTORIES, MINES** and **ANY COMPANY** who whish to improve internal and external transport systems:

we have means to put you on the right track!

S.I.L.F.

Trackworks & Rolling stock

At your complete disposal for your needs about:
rails • fastening equipment • turnouts & switches • wagons • bogies • axles and wheels • supply • design • construction

SALES OFFICES:
Via Romagnosi 60 - 29100 Piacenza - Italy
telex 530122 Rotaia I - Fax +523 385124
phone +523 36377 - +523 27885 - +523 36966

WORKS:
Via Emilia Pavese 98 S.S. 10 - Sarmato (PC) - Italy
phone +523 847543 - +523 847575

FROM LONDON TO SINGAPORE

LEADERS IN TRACTION CURRENT SUPPLY

From the smallest industrial collector to the largest 3rd rail transit electrification system, Brecknell Willis today occupies a premier international position in the design, manufacture and installation of traction current supply equipment. British Rail's new Class 91 locomotives utilise the latest High Speed Pantograph – a design and build area in which Brecknell Willis' pedigree is unmatched.

The third rail systems designed and manufactured for both Singapore MRTC and London Docklands highlight the company's turnkey capability.
Our experience is unparalleled. Contact us now for more information.
- Pantographs ● Short Circuit Equipment
- Line Tensioners ● Depot Overhead Systems
- Third Rail Systems & Components ● Shoe Gear

BRECKNELL WILLIS & CO LTD

PO Box 10, Chard, Somerset, England TA20 2DE. Tel: 0460 64941 (10 lines) Telex: Chard 46518 Fax: 0460 66122

TRADITION
AND
KNOWLEDGE
RELIABILITY
AND
FORMAT

TAKRAF—
railway breakdown cranes are to be found on 4 continents in every imaginable climate as a solution for every demand

TAKRAF—
a world of experience

TAKRAF—
tailored to suit the purpose with simplicity, reliability and economy

TAKRAF—
your guarantee for quality and reliability

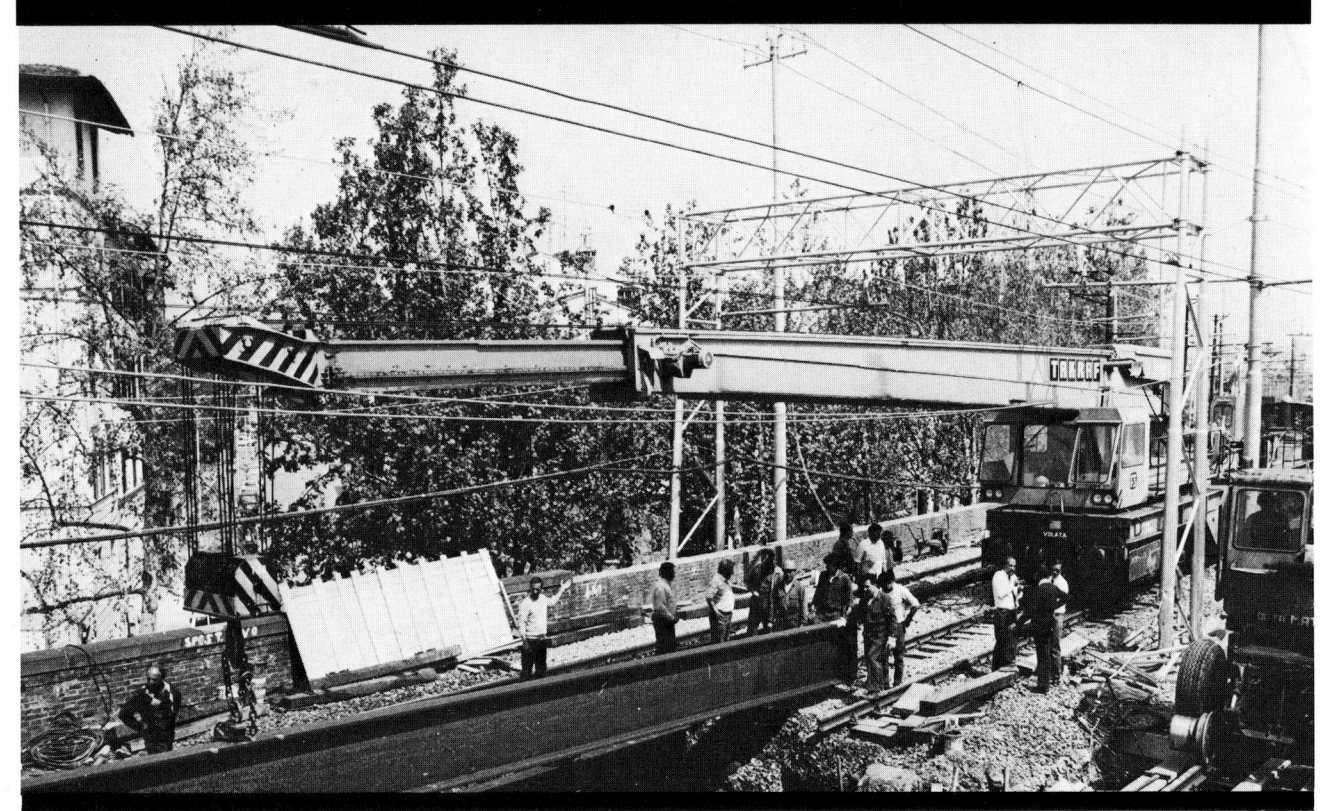

Exporter:
TAKRAF Export/Import
Volkseigener Außenhandelsbetrieb der DDR
DDR - 1080 BERLIN, Mohrenstraße 53/54
Telefon: 48870 und 2240
Telex: 112347, 112348, 115027

To learn more
call or write to us

Hasler TELOC® 2200 – *the key to safe and efficient travel.*

The new Hasler TELOC 2200 data acquisition system from Ascom is extremely compact and economical.
With up to 16 analog and 32 digital signals, it can accurately record residual distance, long-term, event, statistical and operational data. The specially developed user-friendly TELOC UAS software minimizes the time required to search for vitally important data. Special events can be identified more quickly. The clear graphic layout of the data facilitates evaluation. Maintenance of rolling stock becomes more reliable and efficient, not to mention the benefits offered from optimizing timetables.
The TELOC 2200 is small enough to be retrofitted at any time in all types of railcars.

ascom – *we bring savings all round.*

Ascom Autelca Ltd.
Measuring Equipment Division
Belpstrasse 23
CH-3000 Berne 14
Switzerland
Telephone +41 31 63 21 11
Telex 912 674 hasm ch
Telefax +41 31 63 29 19

FOREWORD

The most spectacular rail event of 1990, of course, was French Railways' (SNCF) practical demonstration that the ultimate speed potential of the steel-wheel-on-rail inter-city train is at least 500km/h. Meanwhile, on the TGV-Atlantique the French have already raised par for economical, reliable day-to-day working to 300km/h. Even money is very likely over-generous odds against the current four-year research programme's ability to hoist the norm to 350km/h before TGV network expansion goes much further.

That expansion is set to total 3560 route-km, according to the TGV Network Master Plan published by the French Transport Minister in June 1990 (see France entry in Railway Systems section for details). Some of the projected routes would be partly historic infrastructure upgraded. Even so, the plan is the biggest prospectus of new European rail trunk construction propounded outside the USSR in this century.

How much will get beyond draft, or at best how quickly the plan will be fully implemented, is something else. Of the 14 TGV schemes outlined, the only ones forecast to meet the SNCF's minimum 8.2 per cent return on new TGV route investment are a 49km extension to the TGV-Interconnexion in Paris' southern outskirts, and two trunks: the TGV-Aquitaine from Bordeaux to Tours' and the TGV Provence-Côte d'Azur, a second extension to the TGV-Sud Est, tacking new high-speed tracks to Marseilles and St Raphael on to the TGV Rhône-Alpes bypass of Lyons now in construction. Of the remainder only the TGV Languedoc-Roussillon, a link between Avignon, Narbonne and – perhaps – a future Spanish standard-gauge trunk from Madrid and Barcelona to the French border, scores better than 6 per cent. Propping up the list, economically speaking, is a TGV-Normandie, from the Paris western perimeter to Rouen and Caen. On a prospective return of 0.1 per cent that proposal must be surely a paperwork gesture to the Normans. Unfortunately, too, Provence-Côte d'Azure, the most remunerative scheme and the SNCF's priority, with a completion date of 1997 the target, has come under environmental fire of – for France – unprecedented extent and virulence.

At the time of writing the plan's detail had yet to be taken on board as government policy. But if the French constitution made the country's President absolute ruler, there would be little doubt of that, to judge from the *rail passion* expressed by Francois Mitterand when he inaugurated the Paris-Clermont Ferrand electrification in March 1990.

'I wish', said the President, 'to reaffirm a strong conviction. I believe in the advance of the railway, since it knows how to adapt to evolving demand and competition. I believe in the will and the determination to achieve great infrastructures. I believe in the capacity of the public sector to accomplish them and in so doing to combine economic efficiency with social progress.' France, said the President, had had the sense to sustain a dense railway network even in times of economic weakness. Others had left their railways to founder on aggressive, uncontrolled competition from other modes, or at the mercy of variations in the cost of energy.

Lamenting rail's failure to take a fair share of recent years' strong growth in freight transport demand, President Mitterand said that this decline must be arrested. It was not a matter of favouring one mode over another. The railway must be given a fair competitive deal, so that it could optimise its advantages both for the user and for the community at large, and be sensibly integrated in the global transport system. The latter two objectives, said the President, fully justified state support for intermodal development – and he was speaking with no inkling of a later Gulf crisis and soaraway oil prices that would powerfully reinforce the appeal of electrically-powered rail trunk haulage of merchandise in trailers or demountables.

The quintessential requirement for a national transport system that optimises each mode's practical and economic capabilities is equal treatment of infrastructure provision. France goes part of the way with an annual grant towards French Railways' infrastructure costs. The logical course now adopted in principle, though with administrative and accounting variations, by the Austrians, the Swiss, all the Scandinavians and – prospectively – the Germans, is to make rail infrastructure a public responsibility and charge in the same way as roads. Rental for use of the tracks then approximates to the taxation of road transport. And hopefully the transport ministry will apply consistent economic and social benefit criteria to an integrally planned transport infrastructure development.

At the other extreme is Britain. There, under Margaret Thatcher, railways are treated as an optional add-on to the road system – except, marginally, in provincial areas where withdrawal of all financial support and thus of all trains might put the Parliamentary seats of government supporters at risk. Elsewhere, even in the London-Southeast England commuting network, the quality and development of any rail service is to depend on its ability to sustain fully its infrastructure as well as all operating costs out of affordable tariffs or exploitation of rail-owned property. (But because the biggest BR investments need the support of interest-bearing government loans, Ministers disingenuously preen themselves over BR's capital spending as though this were entirely a dispensation from the state.) The clauses of past Transport Acts that related the Public Service Obligation (PSO) grant – the state's annual financial support – to a BR mandate to sustain all services at levels prevailing in 1968 have never been repealed or even amended. But they have been rubbished by the scale of BR's inescapable cutbacks in the face of remorseless contraction of PSO monies under Mrs Thatcher's rule.

From this it follows naturally that the extra rail infrastructure essential to absorb Channel Tunnel traffic in southeast England is not being built because the government will not put up a penny towards the cost; because the government will not let British Rail borrow on the open market to the extent necessary for a project of such size; and because the return on the exercise, though fully meeting state industry – or French TGV – criteria, will not approach the 18 per cent demand for involvement in construction by Britain's

RAILWAYS WEIGHING SYSTEMS

COOPERATIVA BILANCIAI
WEIGHING SCALES COMPANY

41011 Campogalliano (Modena)
Via Sergio Ferrari, 16 . Telefono 059.526965 r.a.
Telex 511807 BILCOP I . Telefax 059.527079

ELECTRONIC RAILWAYS WEIGHING SYSTEMS WITH PRINTERS.
ELECTRONIC WEIGHING SYSTEMS TO BE INSTALLED ON EXISTING EQUIPMENTS PROVIDED WITH TRACKS SEMIAUTOMATIC DEVICE.
WEIGHBRIDGES FOR ROAD USE.
WEIGHING SYSTEMS FOR SPECIAL APPLICATION.

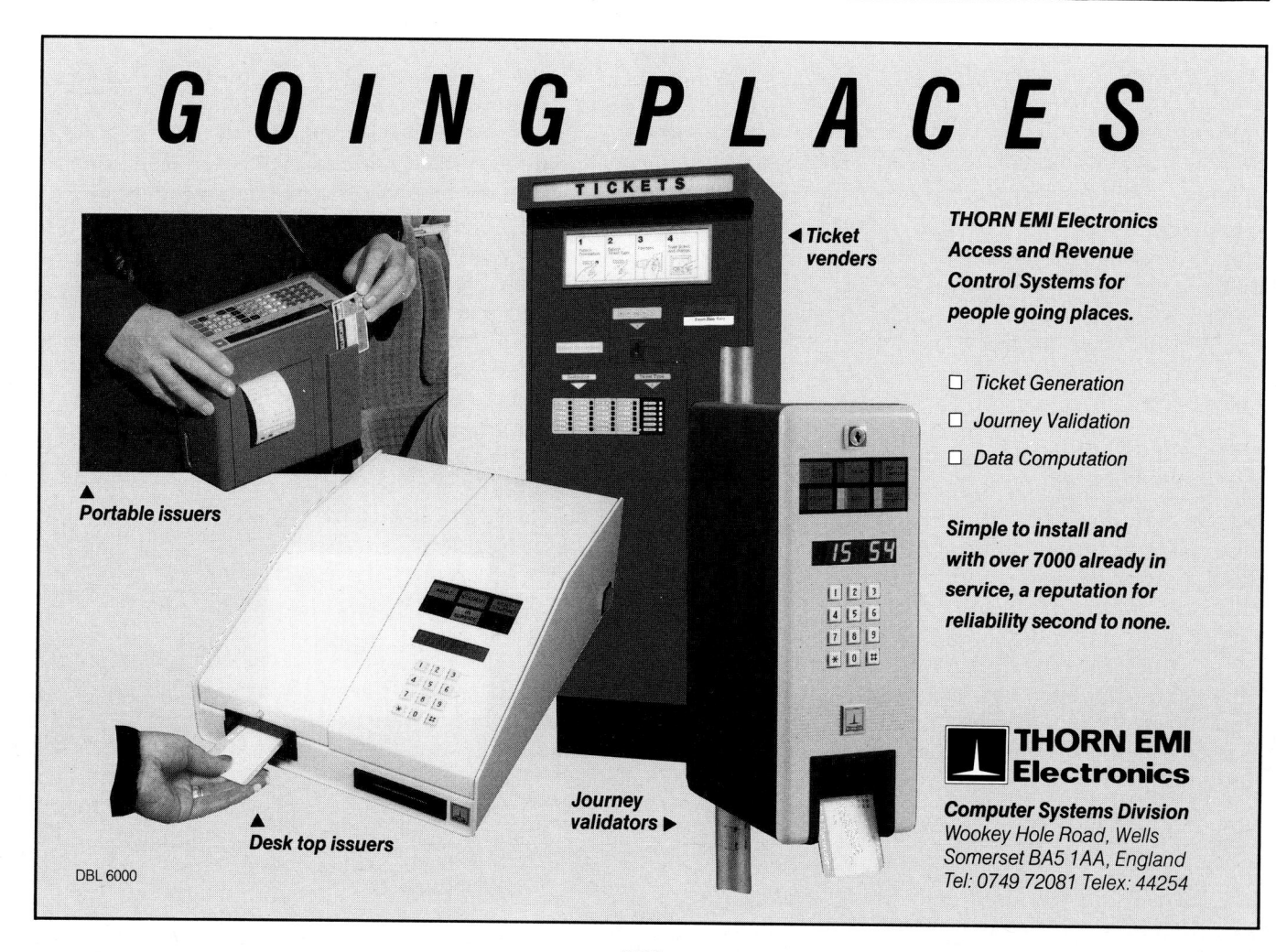

GOING PLACES

◀ Ticket venders

▲ Portable issuers

▲ Desk top issuers

Journey validators ▶

DBL 6000

THORN EMI Electronics Access and Revenue Control Systems for people going places.

☐ Ticket Generation
☐ Journey Validation
☐ Data Computation

Simple to install and with over 7000 already in service, a reputation for reliability second to none.

THORN EMI Electronics

Computer Systems Division
Wookey Hole Road, Wells
Somerset BA5 1AA, England
Tel: 0749 72081 Telex: 44254

endemically short term profit-oriented private industry and institutions. The result, ironically, is less that the London-Paris/Brussels TMST trains will be hampered by the existing network's intensive emu operation, more the converse, because the TMST power cars will be emasculated when they are dieting on a 750V dc third-rail power supply.

It follows, too, that British Rail approaches in disarray the freight opportunities ensuing from the Channel Tunnel's completion and the 1993 European free market. On the mainland railways are gradually getting their act together internationally – for example, by moving for unitary route management; by moves for an integrated approach to intermodal opportunities; by a start in finished auto traffic to efficient pooling of special-purpose wagons so as to minimise empty wagon movement; and by cross-border development, under the EuroCargo logo, of long-distance yard-to-yard direct trains for random wagonloads, intermodal traffic included.

Inevitably defeated by the impossibility of covering infrastructure and marshalling costs within a competitive price, given the limited British scope for lengthy inter-yard unit train hauls, British Rail has been forced to contract sharply its domestic wagonload business for non-bulk freight. That has clearly debilitated BR's campaign to enlist private sector partners, both for terminal development and for penetration of the international total distribution and logistics market. In the late summer of 1990 the precise location of most of BR's proposed European traffic assembly centres was still unknown. An order for 20 dual-voltage electric locomotives will cover only haulage of international trains between London and a Channel Tunnel terminal, not trains direct from the provinces to the mainland. And in late summer 1990 government-approved investment had yet to include modification of clearances between the Tunnel and London to pass common sizes of Continental swap-body on low-floor wagons. Unsurprisingly, a frustrated private sector is not hastening to invest in wagons for potential Channel Tunnel traffic.

Furthermore, whereas Continental freight sent the whole way to a British recipient by road will have free use of Britain's roads, goods railed throughout will pay in their tariffs for use of BR tracks. This is the more anomalous since the European Court of Justice in mid-1990 forced the West Germans to call off their proposed road-use tax on domestic and foreign heavy lorries, which was framed to redress the juggernauts' disproportionate wear of German roads*.

The political attitude to Britain's rail transport that has the depressing consequences outlined, that forces British Rail to charge the highest rail passenger fares in Europe, and which currently has BR sanguinely hunting for bargain-basement means to 250km/h standard speed on its London-Northwest England main line by the mid-1990s, apparently contents BR's new Chairman as a 'good deal for the taxpayer'. That was his concluding response, at a mid-1990 press conference, to his hearers' repeated anxiety at the impact of ever-diminishing state support on the quality, extent and affordability of BR services. President Mitterand's verdict, one feels, would be somewhat different.

Geoffrey Freeman Allen

*The German Federal (DB) entry in the Railway Systems section of this book, forecasting the tax's imposition in July, went to press before the European Court's decision.

Where in the world...

will you find the largest source of impartial defence, aerospace and transport information?

The answer is simple...

Jane's
INFORMATION GROUP

*Jane's Information Group,
Sentinel House, 163 Brighton Road,
Coulsdon, Surrey CR5 2NH, UK.
Telephone: 081-763 1030
Telefax: 081-763 1005*

Manufacturers

Locomotives	3
Powered passenger vehicles	77
Diesel engines and transmission systems	151
Electric traction equipment	175
Non-powered passenger vehicles	191
Passenger coach equipment	215
Freight vehicles	231
Brakes and drawgear	265
Bogies and suspensions, wheels and axles	281
Bearings	295
Signalling and telecommunications systems	301
Passenger information systems	323
Automatic fare systems	329
Fixed electrification equipment	337
Permanent way equipment	347
Freight yard and terminal equipment	387
Workshop, repair and maintenance equipment	401

SOME CREATIONS YOU JUST CAN'T BEAT!

EKE-TRAINNET®
–THE ULTIMATE CONTROL SYSTEM

EKE has developed an efficient network for high-tech trains. This network can be used in any data transmission needed.

Trainnet's specialty is it's unique configuration sequence that makes it possible to use individual coach addresses – for displays, diagnostics, remote control etc.

Sometimes it is hard to handle coach equipment. We have produced at rail engineer's disposal a package deal of electronics to reduce acquisition costs and space needed, to use sophisticated diagnostics and – before all – to get an improved level of coach convenience.

Functions:
- network systems
- remote control device
- heating and ventilation control device
- diagnostics and fault registration
- loudspeaker system and videotape control
- updating destination and information boards
- logical centre for electrical devices (programmable logic for train use!)
- multiple-unit control
- Transfer rate: 275 kbits/s – 1 Mbits/s

EKE-Electronics, Westendintie 1, 02160 ESPOO, Finland. Phone +358 0 420 31, fax +358 0 425 300, telex 12 5492 eke sf

Locomotives/powered passenger vehicles/engines/transmissions/traction equipment

AEG Westinghouse Transportation Systems heading the future

AEG Aktiengesellschaft and Westinghouse Electric Corporation, both world leaders in advanced technologies for electric transportation systems have combined their land-based activities and joined their experience of more than 200 years.

AEG Westinghouse Transportation Systems International offers worldwide innovative solutions for all kinds of long distance traffic inclusive high speed systems and rapid transit and automatic systems including the M-Bahn.

Financial engineering, system planning, overall service and operation know-how combined with modern research, development and manufacturing facilities are the basis for solving any customer requirements related to land bound transportation systems today and in the future.

AEG Westinghouse Transport-Systeme GmbH · Nonnendammallee 15–21 · D-1000 Berlin 20 or AEG Westinghouse Transportation Systems, Inc. · 1501 Lebanon Church Road · Pittsburgh, PA 15236-1491/USA

AEG

Locomotives

ARGENTINA
- AFNE ... 9
- Astarsa ... 9
- Cometarsa ... 20
- General Motors ... 36
- Materfer ... 49

AUSTRALIA
- Clyde ... 18
- Comeng ... 19
- GEC Australia ... 33
- Goninan ... 38
- Moss ... 51

AUSTRIA
- Elin Energieanwendung ... 24
- Jenbacher ... 41
- S-G-P ... 60

BELGIUM
- ACEC Transport ... 8
- BN ... 12
- CMI ... 19
- Jambes-Namur ... 41
- Moës ... 51

BRAZIL
- Emaq ... 24
- General Electric do Brasil ... 33
- Soma ... 66
- Villares ... 73

CANADA
- General Electric of Canada ... 33
- General Motors of Canada ... 36

CHINA, PEOPLE'S REPUBLIC
- Beijing ... 11
- Canton Motive Power ... 15
- Changchow Diesel Locomotive Factory ... 16
- China National Railway Locomotive and Rolling Stock Industry Corp (LORIC) ... 16
- Dalian Locomotive & Rolling Stock Works ... 21
- Datong Locomotive Works ... 21
- Qishuyen Rolling Stock ... 55
- Xiangtan ... 74
- Zhuzou Rolling Stock Works ... 75

CZECHOSLOVAKIA
- ČKD ... 17
- Pragoinvest ... 54
- Škoda ... 62

DENMARK
- ABB Scandia A/S ... 8, 59
- Frichs ... 26

FINLAND
- Saalasti Oy ... 57
- Valmet ... 72

FRANCE
- AFR ... 9
- Batiruhr ... 11
- CFD ... 16
- GEC Alsthom ... 30
- SFL ... 60

GERMANY, DEMOCRATIC REPUBLIC
- LEW ... 46
- Schienenfahrzeuge Export-Import ... 59

GERMANY, FEDERAL REPUBLIC
- ABB ... 4
- Diema ... 21
- Ferrostaal ... 25
- Jung ... 41
- Kaelble-Gmeinder ... 42
- Krauss-Maffei ... 43
- Krupp ... 44
- MaK ... 47
- Newag ... 52
- Ries ... 57
- Ruhrthaler ... 57
- Schöma ... 59
- Siemens ... 60
- Thyssen-Henschel ... 67
- Windhoff ... 74

HUNGARY
- Ganz Electric ... 26
- Ganz-Hunslet ... 26
- Ganz-Mávag ... 27
- Hungarian Railway Carriage ... 39

INDIA
- BHEL ... 12
- CLW ... 17
- DLW ... 22
- PEC ... 53
- SAN ... 58
- Ventra ... 73

IRELAND
- Unilock ... 71

ITALY
- Badoni ... 10
- Breda ... 13
- Casaralta ... 15
- Ferrosud ... 25
- Fiat ... 25
- Firema Consortium ... 25
- Gleismac ... 37
- Imesi ... 41
- Italtrafo ... 41
- OMS ... 52
- Reggiane ... 55
- Socimi ... 66
- SOFER ... 66
- TIBB ... 68
- Zephir ... 75

JAPAN
- Hitachi ... 39
- Kawasaki ... 43
- Kyosan Kogyo ... 46
- Mitsubishi Electric ... 50
- Niigata ... 52
- Nippon Sharyo ... 52
- Toshiba ... 69
- Toyo ... 71

KOREA, REPUBLIC
- Daewoo ... 20
- Hyundai ... 40

NEW ZEALAND
- Price ... 55

POLAND
- Bumar-Fablok ... 14
- Cegielski ... 16
- Kolmex ... 43
- Pafawag ... 52

PORTUGAL
- Sorefame ... 66

ROMANIA
- 23 August ... 10
- Electroputere ... 23
- Mecanoexportimport ... 49

SOUTH AFRICA
- Hudson ... 39
- Hunslet Taylor ... 40
- RSD ... 57
- Union Carriage ... 72

SPAIN
- ATEINSA ... 9
- Babcock & Wilcox Española ... 10
- CAF ... 15
- Inirail ... 41
- Macosa ... 47
- Maquinista, La ... 48

SWEDEN
- ABB Ageve ... 8
- Kalmar ... 42

SWITZERLAND
- Aebi ... 8
- Groupement 50 Hz ... 38
- SLM ... 63

USSR
- Energomachexport ... 24
- Kuibyshev ... 46
- Novocherkassk ... 52
- Voroshilovgrad ... 73

UK
- Barclay ... 11
- BREL ... 13
- Brush ... 14
- GEC Alsthom Traction ... 33
- Hunslet ... 39
- RFS Engineering ... 56

USA
- AEG Westinghouse ... 8
- Anbel ... 9
- Brookville ... 13
- General Electric ... 27
- General Motors ... 34
- Morrison-Knudsen ... 51
- Plymouth ... 53
- Precision National Corporation ... 54
- PSI ... 55
- Republic Locomotive Works ... 56

YUGOSLAVIA
- Duro Daković ... 23

ZIMBABWE
- Zeco ... 75

MANUFACTURERS / Locomotives

ABB
ASEA Brown Boveri

Headquarters: ABB Transportation Management and Systems Development (ABB BTM)
Gottlieb Daimler-Strasse 6, PO Box 100163, 6800 Mannheim 1, Federal Republic of Germany

Telephone: +49 621 468 200
Telex: 462411220 abd
Telefax: +49 621 468 298/9

President: Erich Kocher
Executive Vice President: Åke Nilsson
Vice-President, Marketing: Peter Albexon

Companies of ASEA Brown Boveri, Business Segment Transportation

Africa and Arabian Peninsula Region (AAP)
Regional Traction Manager
AAP c/o ABB Trazione Srl
Via Pietro Coletta 48
20137 Milan
Italy
Telephone: +39 2 55 00 9252
Telex: 310153
Telefax: +39 2 55 00 9261

Australia
ABB Traction Pty Ltd,
PO Box 291, 509 Zillmere Road, Queensland, 4034
Australia
Telephone: +61 7 263 3133
Telex: 40424 aa
Telefax: +61 7 857 0007

Austria
ASEA Brown Boveri Ltd, Division EB
Brown Boveri Strasse 1, 2351 Wr Neudorf, Austria
Telephone: +43 2236 23 661 401
Telex: 131760 obbwa
Telefax: +43 2236 24 417

Brazil
ASEA Brown Boveri Ltd, Transportation & Motors
CP 975, Avenida dos Autonomistas 1496, 06020
Osaco (São Paulo)
Telephone: +55 11 702 2111
Telex: 1171560 abbbr
Telefax: +55 11 704 1991

Denmark
ABB Scandia A/S
Toldbodgade 39, 8900 Randers
Telephone: +45 86 415 300
Telex: 65145 scanes dk
Telefax: +45 86 415 700

Finland
ABB Strömberg Drives Oy
PO Box 184, 00381 Helsinki
Telephone: +358 0 50 69 1
Telex: 124 405 str
Telefax: +358 0 50 69 369

Federal Republic of Germany
ABB Verkehrstechnik GmbH
PO Box 100351
Neustadter Str 62
6800 Mannheim 31
Telephone: +49 621 381 2036
Telex: 462411113 abd
Telefax: +49 621 381 2572

India
ABB Traction AB, Project Office
c/o Asea Brown Boveri Ltd Coordination Office
5 Somm Datt
II Floor
Bhikaiji
Cama Place
New Delhi 110066
Telephone: +91 11 687 27 37
Telex: 031 62561 abb in
Telefax: +91 11 671 405

Italy
ABB Trazione Srl
Via Pietro Coletta 48
CP 1 30 81
20137 Milan
Italy

Electric locomotive for Channel Tunnel equipped with ABB GTO-three-phase propulsion

Class 401 ICE power car for DB

Telephone: +39 2 55 00 91
Telex: 310153
Telefax: +39 2 55 00 92 61

Netherlands
ASEA Brown Boveri BV
Marten Meesweg 3, 3068 AH, Rotterdam
Telephone: +31 10 407 8431
Telex: 21539 abb nl
Telefax: +31 10 456 6927

Norway
EB Strömmens Vaerkstad
Strasjonsveien 1, PO Box 83, Strömmen
Telephone: +47 6 80 97 10
Telex: 71551 svstr
Telefax: +47 6 80 96 01

Portugal
ASEA Brown Boveri Ltd, Traction Division
Apartado 4191
4003 Oporto
Telephone: +351 2 202 2802
Telex: 23599
Telefax: +351 232 5881

Singapore
ASEA Brown Boveri Holdings (SEA) Pte Ltd
Regional Traction Manager South-East Asia
21 Collyer
Qay 15-03
Hong Kong Bank Building
Singapore 0104

Telephone: +65 22 51 000
Telex: 55172
Telefax: +65 22 40 830

Spain
ABB Energia SA Traction (B)
Edificio ABB Calle Ramirez de Arellano 17
28043 Madrid
Telephone: +34 1 581 9393
Telex: 43236 abb m e
Telefax: +34 1 581 9394

Sweden
ABB Traction AB
72173 Västerås
Telephone: +46 21 726 2000
Telex: 40720 abb va-s
Telefax: +46 21 726 2300

Sweden
EB Signal
PO Box 42505
Stockholm
Telephone: +8 46 726 2000
Telefax: +8 46 726 2300

Switzerland
ASEA Brown Boveri Transportation Systems Ltd
Affoltenstrasse 52, PO Box 8242, 8050 Zurich
Telephone: +41 1 315 2216
Telex: 755749/755935 abb
Telefax: +41 1 312 6159

Turkey
Asea Brown Boveri Holdings AS
Regional Traction Manager Middle East
Pakistan, Iran, Iraq, Afghanistan
Kasap Sokak No 2
Oezden Konak
Is Hani Kat 9
80280 Esentepe
Istanbul
Telephone: +90 1 175 28 11
Telex: 27 253
Telefax: +90 1 175 28 21

UK
ASEA Brown Boveri Ltd
48 Leicester Square
London WC2H 7NN
Telephone: +44 71 930 5411
Telefax: +44 71 839 4137

ASEA Brown Boveri Ltd
Derby House, Lawn Central, Telford, Shropshire TF3 4JB
Telephone: +44 952 290 271
Telex: 35284 abbtelg
Telefax: +44 952 291 778

ABB British Wheel Set Manufacturers Ltd
Ashburton Road W, PO Box 14, Manchester M17 1GU
Telephone: +44 61 872 0492
Telex: 668973
Telefax: +44 61 872 2895

BREL Group Ltd
St Peters House
Gower Street
Derby DE1 1AH
Telephone: +44 332 383 850
Telex: 377693
Telefax: +44 332 291 579

USA
ABB Traction Inc
Quaker Bridge Executive Center, 2nd Floor, Grovers Mill Road, Lawrence Township, New Jersey 08648
Telephone: +1 609 275 0111
Telefax: +1 609 275 6852

Products and services: Development, design, engineering, sales, production, installation, maintenance and after-sales service of rolling stock systems and equipment for all railway types, systems and track gauges.

Electric traction vehicles for trunk, feeder, metropolitan, regional, suburban and industrial railway systems and special rolling stock. The group supplies complete rail traction vehicles, a complete range of electrical equipment and sub-systems for all rail traction vehicles, and complete climate equipment for all rail traction vehicles. Also mechanical systems and components, such as bogies and bogie components, wheels and axles, gearboxes and couplings. The group also offers service, minor equipment and spare parts, management of large projects and consultancy.

Recent developments
W Germany
From 1 January 1990, ASEA Brown Boveri Ltd, Mannheim, turned its former VK Division dealing with railway business into an autonomous subsidiary company known as ABB Verkehrstechnik GmbH.

Italy
From 1 January 1990, the traction division of ABB Tecnomasio, Milan, became an autonomous subsidiary known as ABB Trazione Srl.

Switzerland
In 1987 ASEA Brown Boveri AG, Baden, built a new railway equipment manufacturing and vehicle assembly facility named 'TRAMONT' (TRAction Equipment MOuNTing Plant). The vehicle assembly hall, travelling platform, adjoining test track for all usual ac and dc catenary voltages and track gauges were commissioned in the summmer of 1989 and are now fully operational.

TRAMONT assembly capacity is a minimum of 30 complete locomotives and 60 trolleybuses. Electrical equipment volume includes capacity for about 200 rail power and passenger cars, assembled at plants of mechanical partners of ABB.

From 1 January 1990, ASEA Brown Boveri Ltd, Baden, turned its former Transportation Systems Division dealing with railway business into an autonomous subsidiary company known as ABB Transportation Systems Ltd.

Swedish Class X2 high-speed train

Recent contracts
Austria
Austrian Federal Railways (ÖBB) awarded contracts for a number of electric locomotives to the Austrian industry partnership of rolling stock manufacturers; ABB will supply five phase-angle controlled ÖBB Class 1044 electric locomotives out of a further series of 25 units; a second dual-system Bo-Bo 140 km/h ÖBB Class 1822 electric locomotive for operation over the Brenner Pass. ABB is leader for developing the two units with ABB three-phase propulsion and GTO-equipped power converters. Simmering-Graz-Pauker (SGP) produces the mechanical equipment.

Federal Republic of Germany
Krupp-MaK continues to build highly standardised diesel-electric locomotives with ABB three-phase drives for German customers (mostly industrial systems). These are the Classes DE 500 with engine ratings 500-560 kW and DE 102 with 1120-1300 kW. Since the first Class DE 500 locomotive was commissioned in 1981, over 60 units of this class have entered service. The DE 500 units have three axles, a starting tractive effort of 250 kN and a 50 km/h top speed.

The year 1982 saw the first Class DE 1002 locomotive in operation. This locomotive has four axles, all individually driven by three-phase asynchronous squirrel cage motors. The first two series had diesel engines rated at 1120 kW. The third series of eight DE 1002 units have diesel engines rated at 1320 kW, a starting tractive effort of 350 kW and a 70 km/h top speed. These later locomotives started heavy-duty service with the Cologne-Bonn Railways in 1987. They are equipped with ABB MICAS traction control. By 1990 over 80 units of the 'off the shelf' Classes DE 500 and DE 1002 are in service or being built.

Italy
In 1986, FS ordered a prototype series of six Class E 652 5000 kW locomotives with increased power for application in both passenger and freight service. FS has now ordered a series of 30 Class E 652 locomotives with modular traction equipment for their three mono-motor bogies. ABB Tecnomasio is general contractor for the Class E 652 locomotives and manufacturer of the mechanical and electrical equipment.

FS ordered five prototypes of the E 453/454 where Breda and Fiat manufacture the mechanical equipment, and ABB and Ansaldo the electrical equipment. These 80-tonne Bo-Bo 3600 kW units have different gear ratios and top speeds — 120 km/h for the E 453 and 160 km/h for the E 454.

Within a consortium of Italian manufacturers ABB is the contractor for the electrical equipment of the 4200 kW motive power units for the FS Class ETR 500 300 km/h train-sets.

A prototype ETR 500X power car and trailer started trial runs in late 1988. Test runs included reached speeds of up to 350 km/h. Two further prototype Class ETRY 500 trains will be delivered during 1990, each of two power units and ten passenger cars.

Netherlands
Netherlands Railways (NS) ordered a second series of 60 Class DE 6400 diesel-electric locomotives with three-phase transmission from the German partnership of Krupp-MaK in Kiel, and ABB Transportation Technology in Mannheim.

Spain
RENFE (Spanish National Railways) has ordered 75 high-speed electric locomotives from a consortium comprising Siemens (consortium leader), ABB, Krauss-Maffei, Thyssen-Henschel and Macosa of Spain. The original plan was to use these RENFE Class 252 locomotives on the new standard gauge (1435 mm) high-speed network but, due to unforeseen costs, 75 locomotives will now be produced in different versions: 5 standard gauge; 15 standard but adjustable to Spanish gauge; 55 for Spanish gauge but adjustable to standard gauge.

Switzerland
Rhaetian Railways (RhB) ordered a first series of six four-axle Class Ge 4/4 III locomotives, heralding a new generation for its metre-gauge network. The Ge 4/4 III

Zurich S-Bahn regional express train

MANUFACTURERS / Locomotives

will have GTO-equipped power converters and three-phase drives with asynchronous motors. Design will be similar to the BT and SZU locomotives.

Swiss Federal Railways (SBB) ordered a second series of 12 Re 4/4 VI Class 460 high-speed electric locomotives. With a weight of 81 tonnes, 4800 kW continuous and 610 kW short-time power rating, GTO-equipped power converters, three-phase drives and microprocessor control with fault diagnosis, the design is especially tailored with casing and bogies for high line and curve speeds, and for low maintenance requirements.

BLS (Bern-Lötschberg-Simplon), EBT (Emmental-Burgdorf-Thun) and PTT (Swiss Post, Telegraph and Telephone Operations) ordered six Ee 3/3 electric shunters supplied from 15 kV, 16 ⅔ Hz catenary. Four units will go to EBT, one each to BLS and PTT.

USA
New Jersey Transit has ordered another nine units in addition to the six Type ALP-44 electric locomotives recently ordered. ABB Traction Inc of Lawrenceville, NJ, USA with ABB Traction AB, Västerås, Sweden is producing the ALP-44 units. They will power shuttle trains on lines of the Northern New Jersey coast area and on the Newark-Trenton section of the North-East Corridor (Boston– New York–Washington).

UK
In 1989 the British Transmanche Link (TML) group ordered 40 locomotives with the contract going to Brush Electrical Machines (BEM) in Britain and ABB Transportation Systems Ltd, Zürich, Switzerland. The ABB electrical equipment for the 40 Bo-Bo-Bo 130-tonne locomotives with three-phase drives includes: main transformer, input 25 kV, 50 Hz, one-phase; three GTO-equipped power converters, one per bogie; six asynchronous, squirrel cage force-ventilated traction motors rated at 950 kW, working on fully-sprung mechanical power transmissions; control systems; electrodynamic brake for rheostatic and/or regeneration braking; auxiliary service equipment. Deliveries will start in 1991.

Recent deliveries
Australia
Queensland Railways (QR) is receiving 80 locomotives capable of hauling 7000-tonne coal trains with up to 100 cars. The larger part of these ABB-designed units is built in Australia by ABB and its partner Walkers Ltd.

E 652 electric locomotive on assembly line at ABB Tecnomasio's Vado Ligure factory

Federal Republic of Germany
Some 82 units for 41 trainsets of the DB ICE are now in production. ABB Transportation Technology, Mannheim, and other major German railway equipment manufacturers are sharing production of these trains.

DB received three prototype Type DE 1024 diesel-electric locomotives in the spring of 1990. This is a high-powered multipurpose unit developed by a partnership of Krupp-MaK and ABB. DB rents them as Class 240 for extensive in-service trials in the Schleswig-Holstein area.

Italy
Since 1979 ABB has manufactured the prototypes and two series of the chopper-controlled FS Class E 632 and E 633 locomotives. These two classes have the same electrical design but different gear ratios: one for passenger and one for freight operations.

Netherlands
During 1989, the first units of 60 Class DE 6400 diesel-electric locomotives for the Netherlands Railway (NS) with ABB three-phase transmission were delivered. The last unit wil be completed in mid-1991.

Sweden
At the end of 1989, Swedish Railways (SJ) received the first new X2 high-speed trainset. This includes ABB three-phase driven locomotive as motive power unit and a driving trailer at the other end. Further X2 trainsets wil be delivered through 1990 to 1994. They will shorten travel times between Stockholm to Gothenburg, Malmö and Sundsvall, and Gothenburg-Malmö.

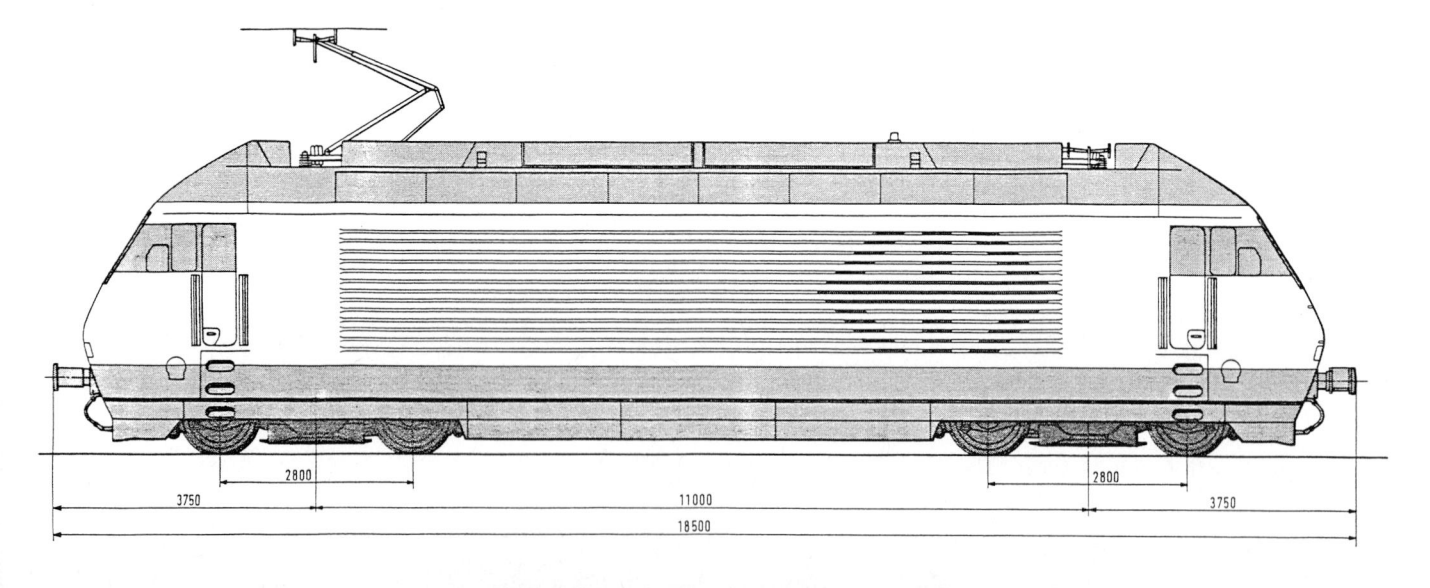

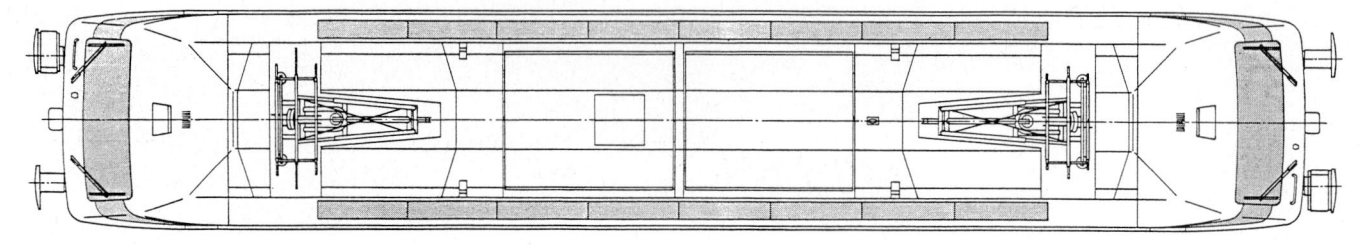

General arrangement of SBB Class 460 'Locomotive 2000'

Locomotives / **MANUFACTURERS**

Switzerland
SBB had received 13 regional express (S-Bahn) Zurich Re 4/4 Class 450 locomotives by the end of 1989.

Mixed adhesion/cog rack Class HGe 4/4 metre-gauge locomotives have been supplied to: Furka Oberalp Railway (FO) (3 units); SBB Brünig (8 units).

The Brig-Visp-Zermatt (BVZ) Railway is due to receive five units.

Turkey
The last units of 35 Class ME 07 diesel-electric locomotives with ABB electrical equipment and three-phase drives will be delivered to the Turkish State Railways by the end of 1990.

South Africa
The first unit of the three two-system 1067 mm (Cape) gauge Bo-Bo Class 14 E locomotives for South African Transport Services (SATS) left Switzerland in late 1989.

USA
ABB is the first to equip 12 locomotives in the USA with three-phase transmission: 10 dual-system (diesel-electric and third rail 650V dc) GM Type FL-9 AC for Metro North, 1 GM Type F-40PH diesel-electric for Amtrak, 1 diesel-electric (MLW type) for CP Rail (No 4744).

In mid-1987 New York Metro North gave ABB a contract for the overhaul and retrofitting of ten FL-9 AC dual-system locomotives. ABB completed this project in the fourth quarter of 1989 with GTO-equipped power converters. Renewed FL-9 AC units include the following ABB equipment:

Three-phase propulsion with two-quadrant input controller; this converts third-rail 650 V or 1400 V dc diesel generator input power for inverters.

Inverters with three-phase outputs for feeding the asynchronous traction motors and auxiliary service equipment.

Microprocessor-based control system.

Inverter for passenger train (hotel) power supply. It is the first time in the US that a locomotive provides this electric power. The inverter is of same design as those for the traction.

Electric locomotive braking system. With third-rail prime power this operates in regenerative mode. Traction motor-generated braking power then returns to the dc supply so long as this system is receptive. With diesel prime mover or when the third-rail dc supply is non-receptive, the electric braking operates in a rheostatic mode. Motor-generated braking power then feeds a resistor.

ABB three-phase propulsion systems, orders to date:

Date built	Number supplied	Designation	Customer
1987/88	60	Electric locomotive E 120	DB
1987–89	60	Diesel locomotive 6400	NS
1988–92	70	Electric locomotive Re 4/4V	SBB
1988–92	120	Emu DT4	Hamburg
1988	1	Power car ETRX 500	FS
1988/89	10	Dual-power (diesel and third-rail dc) Type FL 9	Metro North (New York)
1988/89	26	Electric railcars	SEPTA
1990/91	100	"Arrow III" EMU's (retrofit)	NJ Transit USA
1991	35	Electric light rail cars	Maryland Transit USA
1990/92	24	Electric locomotive Re 4/4V (Railway 2000)	SBB
1988/89	82	Electric locomotive ICE	DB
1989	35	Diesel locomotive ME 07	TCDD
1988/90	3	Electric railcars ABe 4/4	RhB
1989/90	3	Diesel locomotive DE 1024	MaK
1989/92	9	Electric railcars	NSB
1989/94	20	Electric locomotive X 2	SJ
1992/93	6	Electric locomotives Ge 4/4 III	RhB
1990/92	2	Electric locomotives 1822	Ö(u)BB
1991/93	40	Electric locomotives for Euroshuttle auto-ferry trains through channel tunnel	TML
1991/93	60	Diesel-electric locomotives DE 6400	NS
Total*	1105		

* 1) Of this total, 372 are diesel-electric and 10 dual-system (diesel-electric/electric) locomotives, and 15 are diesel-electric rail cars.
2) With ABB Strömberg, Finland, total close to 1200.

ABB thyristor-controlled electric locomotives since 1985

Class	Wheel arrangement	Line voltage	Rated output (kW) IEC 349	Max speed km/h	Weight tonnes	No in service January 1989	Year first built	Builders Mechanical parts	Builders Electrical equipment
South African Railways (SAR) 11E	Co-Co	25 kV/50 Hz	3900	90	168	45	1985	GM-EMD	ABB
Maryland Department of Transportation (MDOT) AEM 7	Bo-Bo	11 kV/25 Hz 12.5–25 kV/60 Hz	4320	201	91	4	1986	GM-EMD	ABB
Queensland Railways (QR) 3500/3600/3900	Bo-Bo-Bo	25 kV/50 Hz	2900	80	108	60	1986	Walkers	Clyde/ABB
Southeastern Pennsylvania Transportation Authority (SEPTA) AEM 7	Bo-Bo	11 kV/25 Hz 12.5–25 kV/60 Hz	4320	201	91	7	1987	GM-EMD	ABB

Electric locomotives equipped by ABB in Federal Republic of Germany since 1983

Class	Wheel arrangement	Line voltage	Rated output continuous	Max speed km/h	Weight tonnes	No in service	Year first built	Builders Mechanical parts	Builders Electrical equipment
NSB EL17	Bo-Bo	15 kV, 16⅔ Hz	3000 kW	150	64	6	1987	TH	ABB
ÖBB 1063	Bo-Bo	15 kV, 16⅔ Hz or 25 kV, 50 Hz	1520 kW	80	84	33	1983	SGP	ABB
DB ICE	Bo-Bo	15 kV, 16⅔ Hz	7600 kW	400	78	82	1985	TH, KM, KI	ABB, Siemens, AEG

Electric locomotives equipped by ABB in Italy 1980–90

Class	Wheel arrangement	Line voltage	Rated output (kW) continuous	Max speed km/h	Weight tonnes	No in service	Year first built	Builders Mechanical parts	Builders Electrical parts
FS E632 (chopper)	B-B-B	3 kV dc	4700	160	102	25	1980	ABB	ABB
FS E652	B-B-B	3 kV dc	6000	160	102	6	1988	ABB	ABB
FNM E620	B-B	3 kV dc	2250	130	72	6	1984	ABB	Ansaldo
FS E652	B-B-B	3 kV dc	5000	160	103	30	1990	ABB	ABB
FS E453/454	2 x Bo-Bo	3 kV dc	13600	120/160	80	5	1989	Sofer/Fiat	ABB/Ansaldo

8 MANUFACTURERS / Locomotives

Diesel locomotives equipped by ABB in Federal Republic of Germany, 1985–90

Class	Wheel arrangement	Transmission	Rated output continuous	Max speed km/h	Weight tonnes	No in service	Year first built	Builders Mechanical parts	Builders Diesel engine	Builders Electrical equipment
RAG DE 1003	Bo	Elec	2 × 500 kW	80	88	4	1989	MaK	MWM	ABB
MaK DE 1024	Co-Co	Elec	2250 kW	180	117	3	1989/90	MaK	MaK	ABB
NL DE 6400	Bo-Bo	Elec	1180 kW	120	80	60	1988	MaK	MTU	ABB
TCDD ME07	Bo-Bo	Elec	785 kW	80	68	35	1985	KM	MTU	ABB
MNCRC, LIRR FL9 (Electro-diesel)	Bo (A-1A)	Elec/650 V dc third rail	2592 or 2350 kW	145	125	10	1989	GM	GM	ABB

ABB Ageve
AB Gävle Vagnverkstad

PO Box 655, 801 27 Gävle, Sweden

Telephone: +46 26 115890
Telex: 47106 ageve s
Telefax: +46 26 187832

Managing Director: Hans Karlstrand
Director, Business Development: Wilhelm Fridell
Marketing Manager: Björn Sylwan

Products: Diesel-hydrostatic shunting locomotives. Recent production has included locomotives which are available in radio remote-controlled versions.

Leading characteristics of RT 36 locomotive
Weight	36 000 kg
Engine: Scania DSI 14A21S	322 kW
Starting tractive effort	7030 kN
Max speed	34 km/h
Fuel tank capacity	400 litres
Electric system	24 V
Storage battery	190 Ah, 2 × 12 V
Wheel diameter	920 mm

Couplings,
 rear: automatic BSI shunting coupling
 front: tow hook

Ageve Type RT 40 diesel hydrostatic shunter

Constitution: In 1989 Ageve was acquired by ASEA Brown Boveri (ABB).

ABB Scandia A/S
See entry on page 56

ACEC Transport
ACEC Transport is a subsidiary of GEC Alsthom

PO Box 4211, B-6000 Charleroi, Belgium

Telephone: +32 71 44 54 11
Telex: 51227 acec b
Telefax: +32 71 43 72 35

Managing Director: Ch Jauquet
Operations Managing Director: R Pellichero
Commercial Director: D Hausman

Products: Electric locomotives: 3 kV dc and 25 kV ac; multi-voltage locomotives: 15 kV, 3 kV dc-15 kV and 25 kV ac; electrical and electronic equipment: choppers, three-phase traction static converters, fault monitoring expert systems.

Latest SNCB electric locomotives equipped by ACEC

SNCB class	Wheel arrangement	Line voltage	Rated output kW continuous one/hour	Max speed km/h	Weight tonnes	Year first built	Builders Mechanical parts	Builders Electrical equipment
27	Bo-Bo	3 kV DC	4180/4380	160	85	1982	BN	ACEC
21	Bo-Bo	3 kV DC	3125/3310	160	85	1983	BN	ACEC
11	Bo-Bo	1.5/3 kV DC 25 kV 50 Hz	3125/3310	160	85	1985	BN	ACEC
21	Bo-Bo	3 kV DC	3125/3310	160	85	1986	BN	ACEC
GECAMINE	Bo-Bo	600 V	480	40	70	1988	GMC	ACEC

Aebi
Robert Aebi AG

Head office: Riedthofstrasse 100, 8105 Regensdorf, Switzerland

Telephone: +41 1 842 5111
Telex: 825 868
Telefax: +41 1 842 5120

Products: Diesel-hydraulic and diesel-mechanical locomotives.

AEG Westinghouse
AEG Westinghouse Transportation Systems Inc

1501 Lebanon Church Road, Pittsburgh, Pennsylvania 15236-1491, USA

Telephone: +1 412 655 5335
Telex: 866267
Telefax: +1 412 655 5860

President: J R Tucker
Vice-President, Commercial Operations: D R Marcucci

Vice-President, Engineering: R T Betler
Vice-President, Manufacturing Operations: T Jost

Products: Electric dc and ac propulsion equipment (cam, chopper, ac inverter, traction motor/gears) for heavy and light rail vehicles, trolleybuses and locomotives; advanced automatic train control and signal-

Locomotives / **MANUFACTURERS**

ling systems for mass rapid transit applications, including car-carried, station, wayside and central control equipment; power supply and distribution systems (sub-stations, switchgear and protection equipment, transmission lines, catenary, third rail distribution, power stations and remote control systems) for railroads, heavy and light rail, commuter rail and automated vehicle systems; train equipment and auxiliary systems (power converters, lighting inverters, couplers, passenger information and ticketing systems) for heavy and light rail vehicles, diesel and trolley buses and railway coaches; a complete range of after-sales products and services including on-site training, traction motor remanufacture, equipment rehabilitation and repair.

AFNE
Astilleros y Fabricas Navales del Estado

Corrientes 672, 1043 Buenos Aires, Argentina

Telephone: +54 1 45 7031/39
Cable: AFNE
Telex: 17924

Products: Diesel-hydraulic locomotives; locotractors manufactured under licence from Cockerill.

AFR
Arbel Fauvet Rail

Head Office: 194 boulevard Faidherbe, 59506 Douai, France
Works: Douai, Arras, Lille

Telephone: +33 27 88 33 11
Cable: Indarbel, Douai
Telex: 130 036 f

President: Conrad Bernstein

Products: Diesel-electric and diesel-hydraulic shunting locomotives of 150 to 1500 bhp at weights of up to 100 tonnes for broad, standard and narrow gauge.

Constitution: The Société Francaise de Locotracteurs, created in 1980, pools the technological experience, research, design and manufacturing of three well-known French and Anglo-French rolling stock companies: Arbel-Fauvet-Rail, GEC Alsthom and De Dietrich.

Anbel
The Anbel Group

2323 South Voss Road, Houston, Texas 77057, USA

Telephone: +1 713 977 9737
Telex: 910 881 1168

President: Kenneth Roy Nichols
Vice-President: Alan R Cripe
Administration Manager: N D Nichols
Field Services: A de la Cruz
Plant Manager: W B Miller

Products: Diesel-hydraulic locomotives (300 to 1500 hp; remanufacture only of diesel-electric locos to 3000 hp).

Astarsa
Astilleros Argentinos Rio de la Plata SA

Head office: Tucumán 1438, 1050 Buenos Aires, Argentina

Telephone: +54 1 40 7014
Cable: Astarsa, Baires
Telex: 21692 astar ar

Works: Calle Solis Y Rio Lujan, 1648 Tigre, Prov Buenos Aires

Telephone: 749 1071 78

Associated company: General Motors Corporation

Products: Diesel-electric locomotives.

Licences: MTE and GEC Alsthom (France & UK)

ATEINSA
Aplicaciones Técnicas Industriales SA

Factoria de Villaverde, Carretera Villaverde, Vallecas 18, Madrid 28041
Telephone: +34 1 796 11 00
Telex: 43521 atfv e
Telefax: +34 1 796 15 08

President: Manuel Costales Gómez-Olea
Managing Director: Eusebio Toral Zuazo
Commercial Director: Pedro Solé Raventos
Export Director: Javier Masoliver y de Marti

Export sales: Inirail, Plaza Marqués de Salamanca 3, 4–5°, Madrid 28006

Products: Locomotives, electric and diesel-electric of up to 1000 hp for shunting, 3600 hp for main-line duty.

Constitution: ATEINSA was set up in 1973 to take over the railway rolling stock production of Astilleros Españoles, SA. In 1988 the company, then owned by Instituto Nacional de Industria (INI), was purchased by Alsthom as part of the arrangements under which Alsthom gained a contract to build high-speed trainsets for Spanish National Railways (RENFE).

Type S-311 three-phase diesel-electric Bo-Bo for RENFE

ATEINSA diesel locomotives in production

Class	Wheel arrangement	Transmission	Rated power (kW)	Max speed km/h	Total weight tonnes	No in service 1988	Year first built	Builders Mechanical parts	Engine & type	Transmission
S-311	Bo-Bo	Electric (three-phase)	750	100	80	1 (+ 60 in manufacture)	1983	ATEINSA BWE	Bazan MTU 396-TC13	MTM-Siemens
DL-300	Bo-Bo	Mechanical	340	50	50	-	1988	ATEINSA CKG	Deutz BA 12M.816 LLKU	CKG-Siemens

ATEINSA electric locomotives in production

Class	Wheel arrangement	Line voltage	Rated output (kW) continuous	Max speed km/h	Weight tonnes	No in service 1988	Year first built	Builders Mechanical parts	Electrical equipment
RENFE S-269	B-B	3000	3100	160	88	131	1982	ATEINSA	WESA/Melco/GEE

10   MANUFACTURERS / Locomotives

23 August
'23 August' Works
Mecanoexportimport supplier

B-dul Muncii 256, Bucharest, Romania

Telephone: +40 0 28 20 10
Telex: 10344

Products: Diesel-hydraulic locomotives of 150–2600 hp and diesel-electric locomotives of 1000–1500 hp for shunting, secondary and main-line duties, under licence from Sulzer, Alco, MTU, MAN, Voith, Clark, Brown Boveri, Gelenkwellen, Oerlikon, Knorr-Bremse and others.

Constitution: The '23 August' Works started production of railcars in 1933 and of diesel locomotives in 1936.

Mecanoexportimport LDE 1100 hp diesel-electric Co-Co built by '23 August' Works

'23 August' diesel locomotives

Class	Wheel arrangement	Transmission	Rated power	Max speed km/h	Total weight tonnes	No in service	Year first built	Builders		
								Mechanical parts	Engine & type	Transmission
L18H (Narrow-gauge)	C (0-6-0)	Hydromechanical	180 hp	28	13.5/16.5	4	1983	"23 August" Works	D2156HMN8 (MAN-licence) Auto-Truck Factory Brasov	C5602 + 4421-701 (Clark-licence) Hidromecanica Brasov
LDH 18	B (0-4-0)	Hydromechanical	180 hp	40	19	20	1982	"23 August" Works	D2156HMN8 (MAN-licence) Auto-Truck Factory Brasov	C5602 + 4421-701 (Clark-licence) Hidromecanica Brasov
LDH 80	B-B	Hydraulic	800 hp	80	50	1	1983	"23 August" Works	8V396 (MTU-licence) "23 August"	TH8 Hidromecanica Brasov
LDE 110	Bo-Bo	Electric	800 kW	80	64	1	1983	"23 August" Works	12V396 (MTU-licence) "23 August"	Ac-dc Electroputere Craiova
LDE 130	Bo-Bo	Electric	950 kW	80	60	7	1982	"23 August" Works	M820SR "23 August"	Ac-dc Electroputere Craiova
LDE 150	Co-Co	Electric	1100 kW	100	105	26	1981	"23 August" Works	6R251FLO (Alco-licence)	Ac-dc Electroputere Craiova

Babcock & Wilcox Española
Sociedad Española de Construcciones Babcock & Wilcox SA

Galindo (Vizcaya)

Telephone: +34 1 495 7011, +34 1 496 6011
Telex: 32235, 32544 bw fbe
Telefax: +34 1 495 6676

Works: Alameda Recalde 27, Bilbao 48009
Lagasca 88, Madrid 28001

Executive President: Manual Fernández Garcia

Products: Main-line diesel-electric and diesel-hydraulic units, shunting locomotives.
  Exports have featured diesel-electric locomotives for Colombia, Guatemala and numerous African railways.
  Current products include a 1600 hp diesel-electric Bo-Bo with the following leading particulars:
Weight: 80 tonnes
Engine: Caterpillar 3516 at 1800 rpm
Max tractive effort, continuous: 14 850 kg at 22 km/h
Alternator: Brush BA 605 B
Continuous ratings: 1.064 kW, 1000 V, 1064 A, 1.800 rpm; 1.064 kW, 665 V, 1600 A, 1.800 rpm
Max speed: 115 km/h

Babcock & Wilcox 1600 hp diesel-electric Bo-Bo

Badoni
Antonio Badoni SpA

Corso Matteotti 7, 22053 Lecco, Italy

Telephone: +39 341 3643 06
Cable: Badoni, Lecco
Telex: 380086 badoni i
Telefax: +39 341 3673 00

Chairman: Gualberto Lesi
Managing Director and General Manager: Giuseppe R Kramer Badoni

Products: Diesel-hydraulic shunting locomotives; radio-controlled shunters; hydrostatic transmission; railway wagons. The company's products include the

Badoni Type VII/D diesel shunter

Badoni diesel locomotives

Class	Wheel arrangement	Transmission	Rated power (kW)	Max speed km/h	Total weight tonnes	No in service 1988	Year first built	Builders Mechanical parts	Builders Engine & type	Builders Transmission
II	0-4-0	Hydrostatic	44	11	6	25	1975	Badoni	FIAT-AIFO	Von Roll/V
V	0-4-0	Hydrostatic	90	18	14	158	1955	Badoni	FIAT-AIFO	Von Roll/V
VI	0-4-0	Hydrostatic	150	18	22	118	1957	Badoni	FIAT-AIFO	Von Roll
VII/D	0-4-0	Hydrostatic	185	24	27	11	1975	Badoni	FIAT-AIFO	Von Roll
VII/C	0-4-0	Hydrostatic	265	25	37	35	1962	Badoni	FIAT-AIFO	Von Roll

Type GR214 130 hp and GR245 500 hp diesel-hydraulic shunters of the Italian State Railways (FS).

The company supplies radio-controlled shunting locomotives whenever high temperature or hazardous conditions advise against control from the driver's cab. The portable battery-fed control equipment is fitted with a dead-man control that stops the shunting locomotive should the driver be suddenly incapacitated. It is also possible to lock the shunting locomotive controls by pushing an emergency button on both sides of the driver's cab.

Barclay
Andrew Barclay, Sons & Co Ltd

Caledonia Works, Kilmarnock, Ayrshire KA1 2QD, Scotland

Telephone: +44 563 23573/4/5/6
Telex: 778497
Telefax: +44 563 41076

Director and General Manager: P E Kewney

Products: Diesel-hydraulic, diesel-electric locomotives (30 to 1000 hp); steam, fireless and crane locomotives; boilers and locomotive components; general engineering and fabrications; iron castings, SG iron castings. The company offers a wide choice of engines in its diesel locomotives, including Rolls Royce, Paxman and Cummins, coupled with Voith or Twin-Disc three-stage torque converters.

600 hp diesel-hydraulic locomotive recently completed for BAOR (British Army of the Rhine)

Batiruhr
A subsidiary of CFD Ateliers de Montmirail

161 rue de Paris, 93000 Bobigny, France

Telephone: +33 844 36 42
Telex: 213966

Products: Diesel-hydraulic, diesel-mechanical, mining and industrial locomotives; electric and diesel personnel coaches for industrial and mining operations.

Beijing
Beijing 'Feb 7th' Locomotive Works

Chang Xindian, Beijing, People's Republic of China

Telephone: +86 1 818408, 818269
Cable: 9927

Member of China National Machinery Import & Export Corporation
Erhtikou, Hsi Chiao, Beijing

Telex: 22328, 22242

Products: Diesel locomotives; diesel engines; hydraulic transmissions; fuel injectors; fuel injection pumps; cardan shafts; bogies.

The BJ series of diesel-hydraulic locomotive is produced in 2700 hp B-B and 5400 hp C-C versions. The B-B has been in series production since 1975. Both types employ the Type 12240 1100 rpm 12-cylinder engine which is also manufactured in the plant. The B-B weighs 92 tonnes, has a starting tractive effort of 23.7 tonnes, a continuous tractive effort of 16.27 tonnes at 24.3 km/h and a maximum speed of 120 km/h.

The works also manufactures the Type Dong Feng 7 diesel-electric Co-Co for heavy shunting. It is fitted with a four-stroke 12-cylinder Vee engine of Type 12240-1, exhaust turbo-charged with intermediate air-cooling, which has a rating of 2200 hp at 1000 rpm. The transmission is ac/dc alternator, employing silicon rectifiers.

Type Dong Feng 7 diesel-electric Co-Co
Weight in working order: 135 tonnes ± 2%
Max axleload: 22.5 tonnes ± 3%
Max designed speed: 80 km/h
Starting tractive effort: 41.14 tonnes
Continuous tractive effort: 30.15 tonnes at 12.7 km/h
Length overall: 18.8 m
Width overall: 3.37 m
Height overall: 4.75 m

Type BJ (Beijing) 2700 hp diesel-hydraulic B-B locomotive

Type Dong Feng 7 2200 hp diesel-electric Co-Co locomotive

MANUFACTURERS / Locomotives

BHEL
Bharat Heavy Electricals Ltd

Bhopal, 462 022 India

Telephone: +91 755 540200
Cable: Bharatelec Bhopal
Telex: 705 264 bhbp in; 705 265 bhbp in
Telefax: +91 755 540 425

General Manager: S K Handa
Additional General Manager, Transportation: B P Jain
Deputy General Manager, Transportation & Oil Field Systems: G P Varshney
Senior Manager, Transportation Systems Engineering: N K Jain

Group companies
Bharat Heavy Electricals Ltd
Jhansi 284 129
(Electric locomotives, diesel-electric shunting locomotives and traction transformers)

Additional General Manager: T S Nanda
Product Manager (Locomotives): Y Pathak

Bharat Heavy Electricals Limited
Transportation Business Department, Lodhi Road, New Delhi 110 003

Telephone: +91 11 616756 (Marketing)
Telefax: +91 11 618837

General Manager: K R Ramachandran

Constitution: BHEL is a multi-product multi-unit company and its corporate office with the Chairman & Board of Directors is located at New Delhi. The electric traction activities are centred at Bhopal which also controls the locomotive manufacturing work at the Jhansi factory.

Products: 350 hp and 700 hp diesel-electric shunting locomotives and 4000 hp 25 kV ac 1676 mm-gauge electric locomotives for Indian Railways. BHEL has also supplied three 80 hp battery-operated narrow-gauge locomotives with chopper control.

4000hp 1676mm-gauge 25 kV ac locomotive

BN
Constructions Ferroviaires et Métalliques
Formerly La Brugeoise et Nivelles SA

avenue Louise 65, 1050 Bruxelles, Belgium

Telephone: +32 2 535 55 11
Cable: Brunag
Telex: 61 736 Brunag
Telefax: +32 2 539 10 17

Managing Director: M Simonart
Executive Director, Transport Division: P Sonveaux
Marketing & Sales Director, Transport Division: J Verraver

Products: Electric and diesel-electric locomotives.
The range of traction equipment supplied to SNCB includes 12 Class 11 dual-voltage electric locomotives (working between Belgium and the Netherlands) and 12 Class 12 dual-voltage electric locomotives (working between Belgium and France).

Constitution: Present style of the BN company dates from July 1977 when La Brugeoise et Nivelles absorbed Constructions Ferroviaires du Centre.
In 1986 Bombardier Inc of Montreal, Canada, became the principal shareholder in BN; it increased its holding to 75 per cent in 1988. Bombardier has had exclusive manufacturing and marketing rights to BN-designed LRVs in North America since 1979.

BN-ACEC main-line electric locomotives supplied to SNCB

Class	27	21	11	12
Year first built	1981	1984	1985	1986
Number	60	30 (30 to be built 1987)	12	12
Tare weight (tonnes)	84	84	84	84
Max speed (km/h)	160	160	160	160
Axle arrangement	Bo-Bo	Bo-Bo	Bo-Bo	Bo-Bo
Gear ratio	1:2.829	1:3.742	1:3.742	1:3.742
Wheel diameter (new) (mm)	1250	1250	1250	1250
Voltage supply	3 kV dc	3 kV dc	3 kV dc 1.5 kV dc	3 kV dc 25 kV ac, 50 Hz
Power (kW) one-hour	4380	3310	3310	3310
continuous	4180	3125	3125	3125
Rated speed (km/h)				
one-hour	88.6	70.4	71.8	70.4
continuous	88.2	71.8	73.5	71.8
Tractive effort (kN)				
one-hour	177.5	165	161.8	165
continuous	166.3	152	149.2	152
Starting effort (kN)	234	234	234	234
Effort at 160 km/h (kN)	78	44	44	44
Max catenary current demand (A)	1700	1300	1300	1300

Class 11 dual-voltage electric locomotive for SNCB

Breda
Breda Costruzioni Ferroviarie SpA

Via Ciliegiole 110/B, 51100 Pistoia, Italy

Telephone: +39 573 3701
Cable: Ferbreda, Pistoia
Telex: 570186 BCF I
Telefax: +39 573 370 292

Chairman: Giuseppe Capuano
General Manager, Breda Railway Group: Corrado Fici
General Manager, Breda Construzioni Ferroviarie: Roberto Cai

Products: Locomotives, light alloy, stainless steel or carbon steel trainsets for long distance, rapid transit and metros.

Current production for the Italian State Railways (FS) includes the related Class E453 and E454 Bo-Bo electric locomotives. These are to a single-cab design, with the E453 intended to work back-to-back in pairs on freight at a maximum of 120 km/h, and the E454 to push-pull medium-distance passenger trains at up to 160 km/h. The design has been studied to secure wide availability for both types over the secondary routes of the FS system and total weight has been contained at 79 tonnes. Innovative features include location of the external access door to the cab well to the latter's rear, so that the cab is completely enclosed and driving comfort enhanced; and rear vestibule connections, so that there is an internal passageway between units working in a back-to-back pair. The bodywork has been styled by Pininfarina.

ETRX 500 high speed power car and trailer

Class E453/4: leading particulars
Wheel arrangement: Bo-Bo
Length of body over buffers: 16 500 mm
Length between bogie centres: 8500 mm
Weight of traction equipment in body: 19.7 tonnes
Weight of bogies with traction motors: 42.2 tonnes
Total weight: 79 tonnes
Continuous rating: 3500 kW
One-hour rating: 3850 kW

The company leads the group involved in producing the 300 km/h Type ETR500 electric train-sets for Italian State Railways (qv).

Type ETR500 electric train-set: leading particulars
Basic consist: 14 vehicles, comprising two motored end-units, 11 passenger coaches and 1 service coach
Seating capacity: approximately 700
Max service speed: 275 km/h
Max tested speed: over 300 km/h
2 Bo-Bo locomotives as motored unit
Total weight of train: 624 tonnes
Weight of one motored unit: 72 tonnes
Weight of one trailer unit: 40 tonnes
Continuous rating at wheel rim: 8500 kW
Inverter-powered triphase asynchronous motors
Motor and trailer bogie wheelbases: 3000 mm
Max acceleration, unbalanced at curve: 1.3 m/s^2

BREL
British Rail Engineering (1988) Ltd

St Peters House, Gower Street, Derby DE1 1AH, England

Telephone: +44 332 383850
Telex: 377693, 377898
Telefax: +44 332 45737

Chairman: Sir David Nicolson
Deputy Chairman: A R Houseman
Managing Director: Peter J Holdstock
Director, New Construction Group: Christopher V Cook
Director, Manufacture Repair Group: Chris P J Sheppard
Finance Director: C R Wood
Marketing Director: P S Coventry
Personnel Director: I M Forrester

Products: Diesel and electric locomotives and multiple-units; passenger coaches; bogies; metro cars; light rail vehicles; railway equipment spares.

In 1988-89 a series of 50 new Class 90 electric locomotives was in course of delivery to British Rail. BREL selected GEC traction and control equipment, which incorporates thyristor control. The Class 90 is a mixed-traffic locomotive with 177 km/h maximum speed.

The 3370 kW Class 90 locomotive is a development of the existing Class 87 first introduced in 1973. The new locomotives benefit from the latest developments in power electronics, microprocessor control and diagnostics, and traction power control. Locomotive weight is 82.5 tonnes. A new streamlined bodyshell has been designed with the cab ends aerodynamically styled, and all power and service connections between locomotive and train concealed behind hinged panels. The design offers improved access for maintenance purposes. Bogies are a derivative of the well-proven BP9 design already fitted to the existing Class 87 locomotives, but improved design features allow longer periods between scheduled overhauls. The brake control system has also been much improved to give smooth transmission and blending between electric and air brakes. Facilities are provided for push-pull operation. Driving cab design features an ergonomic layout of controls, low ambient noise levels and full air-conditioning.

BREL has also co-operated with GEC Transportation Projects and GEC Traction to manufacture the Class 91 high-speed 25 kV electric locomotive fleet for British Rail's newly electrified East Coast Main Line route. An order for 31 of these 225 km/h locomotives is in

Class 91 25 kV ac electric locomotive for British Rail (G Freeman Allen)

Class 90 25 kV ac Bo-Bo electric locomotive for British Rail (John C Baker)

production. BREL is main subcontractor to GEC, responsible for detailed design and manufacture of the mechanical parts. BREL's part of the order is worth £15 million.

Constitution: In January 1989 the British Railways Board approved the purchase of BREL (1988) by a consortium which comprised ASEA Brown Boveri Ltd, Trafalgar House plc and the management and

14 MANUFACTURERS / Locomotives

employees of BREL (1988) Ltd. BREL has two major business groups. The New Construction Group is engaged in the manufacture of locomotives, diesel and electric multiple-units, and locomotive-hauled coaches and bogies. The Manufacture and Repair Group is engaged in the heavy overhaul and repair of locomotives, multiple-units and coaching stock, and the manufacture and repair of a wide range of components for railway rolling stock. The business operates from four works: Derby Carriage, Derby Locomotive, Crewe, and York, and a head office in Derby.

Brookville
Brookville Locomotive Division

20 Pickering Street, Brookville, Pennsylvania 15825, USA

Telephone: +1 814 849 7321
Telex: 866729
Telefax: +1 814 849 5229

President: Dalph S McNeil
Vice President, Production: Larry J Conrad
Export Sales Manager: Steve Koladish
Vice President Marketing: John M Reed

Products: 4 to 35-ton diesel locomotives, personnel carriers for underground coal and hard rock mining and tunneling; 5 to 50-ton yard diesel-hydraulic locomotives; and 65 to 85-ton diesel-hydraulic locomotives for main-, short-, or branch-line railroads.

Brush
Brush Electrical Machines Ltd (Traction Division)
Member of the Hawker Siddeley Group

Falcon Works, Loughborough, Leicestershire LE11 1HJ, England

Telephone: +44 509 611511
Cable: Brush, Loughborough
Telex: 341091
Telefax: +44 509 610440

Chairman: R P Hampson
Managing Director: W M M Petrie
Traction Director: B G Sephton
Manager, Traction Sales and Projects: A L Williams

Products: Main-line diesel-electric and electric locomotives.

Recent contracts have included: 100 Class 60 3100 hp Co-Co diesel-electric freight heavy-haul locomotives for British Railways; and 22 Class 30 3000 kW Bo-Bo-Bo electric locomotives for New Zealand Railways. Orders recently delivered have included: 60 0-4-0 1500 V dc/battery locomotives for Hong Kong Mass Transit System.

Class 60 heavy-haul freight locomotive for BR: leading particulars
Wheel arrangement: Co-Co
Track gauge: 1435 mm
Max service speed: 100 km/h
Total locomotive weight: 126 tonnes
Diesel engine site rating: 3100 hp at 1000 rpm
Diesel engine: Mirrlees Blackstone Type 8 MB 275T
Max available starting tractive effort: 500 kN
Continuous tractive effort: 336 kN
Main alternator: the main alternator is a salient pole machine, fitted with sliprings. The machine is self-ventilated, flange mounted with a single bearing arrangement
Continuous rating: 2055 kVA, 375 V, 3164 A, 1000 rpm.
Auxiliary alternator: The auxiliary alternator is an eight-pole dual-wound machine having a three-phase and six-phase output. The AVR-controlled three-phase winding supplies the auxiliary machines. The six-phase winding provides excitation for the main and auxiliary alternators together with the separately excited traction motors.
Traction motors: the six traction motors are connected in an all parallel arrangement, and are of the four-pole force ventilated, axle-hung type. Continuous rating 300 kW, 462 V, 700 A, 472 rpm.
Bogie arrangement: the bogie is of a low-weight transfer design having all motors mounted facing inboard of the locomotive. Rubber stack secondary suspension is incorporated. Brake actuators are direct acting eliminating the need for brake rigging

Class 89: leading particulars
Wheel arrangement: Co-Co
Track gauge: 1435 mm
Max speed: 200 km/h

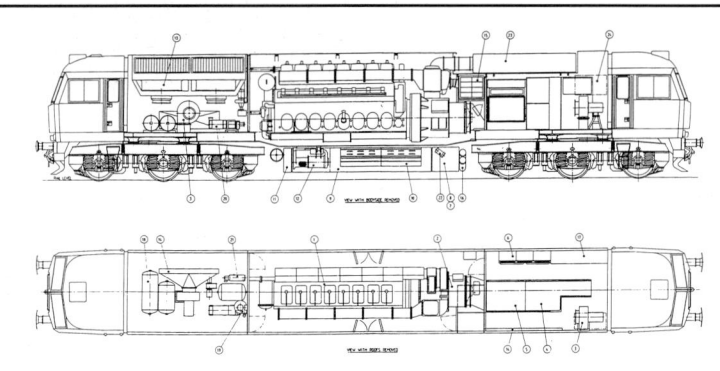

General arrangement of Class 60 locomotive for BR (**1**) engine (8MB 275) (**2**) alternator (**3**) traction motor blower (**4**) control cubicle (**5**) rectifier (**6**) converters/choke cubicle (**7**) battery chargers (**8**) battery charger transformers and chokes (**9**) fuel tank (**10**) battery box (**11**) spillage tank (**12**) compressor (**13**) cooler group (**14**) air filters (**15**) engine secondary filter box (**16**) fire bottles (**17**) brake equipment (**18**) air reservoir (**19**) crankcase extractor fan (**20**) lub oil priming pump (**21**) water heater (**22**) radar unit (**23**) silencer (**24**) space for remote control unit

Class 89 25 kV ac Co-Co electric locomotive for British Rail (*John C Baker*)

Total locomotive weight: 105 tonnes
Total traction motor rating: 4350 kW
Starting tractive effort: 205 kN
Continuous tractive effort: 105 kN at 147 km/h
Power control: Thyristor converter with phase angle control; half-controlled two-stage bridge giving stepless tractive effort control with adjustable speed limit
Traction motors: frame-mounted with hollow shaft drive
Compensated dc motor separately excited: continuous rating 725 kW, 950 V, 808 A, 1450 rpm
Braking system: Primary rheostatic at 200 km/h with blending to air brake at 125 km/h (Rheostatic braking is maintained in case of either short or prolonged loss of supply by using a battery for traction motor excitation)
Auxiliaries: 240 V ac supply from separate winding on main transformer

Shunting and transfer locomotives are also supplied world-wide, the most recent export being of 1100 hp units for the Gabon State Railway.

Constitution: Brush Electrical Engineering Ltd was formed in 1889 with the acquisition of the Falcon Engine and Car Works in Loughborough, and has been involved in electric traction since then. Falcon Works' history of rail traction building began in 1875, with the manufacture of steam locomotives. Originally producing tramcars in large numbers, Brush entered the diesel-electric field in 1948 and has been a major supplier of main-line and shunting locomotives and power equipment, also emu and rapid transit equipment.

Bumar-Fablok
Fabryka Maszyn Budowlanych i Lokomotyw

ul Fabryczna 3 32-500 Chrzanów, Poland

Telephone: +48 22 31-38
Cable: Bumar-Fablok, Chrzanów
Telex: 0312337, 0312338

Export sales: Foreign Trade Company Kolmex, ul Mokotowska 49, 00-950 Warsaw

Products: Diesel-electric locomotives of Type 6Da; brake equipment for diesel locomotives under licence from Oerlikon; Type DRVA brake regulators under licence from SAB; wheel-sets; axles; and gears.

The Type 6Da 800 hp diesel-electric Bo-Bo is intended for heavy shunting yards, and can operate at ambient temperatures ranging from −30° to +40°C, at up to 1200 m above sea level. It is powered with an eight-cylinder V-form, four-stroke, 1000 rpm, water-cooled engine of Type a8Vcc22, without super-charging or air cooling, coupled via a flexible disc with an eight-pole, 512 V, 1090-amp, 558 kW main generator of the LsPa-740 type, fitted with a single bearing and mounted

Locomotives / **MANUFACTURERS** 15

in the underframe by means of rubber-metal elements. A 10 kW auxiliary generator supplying 110 V dc, 291 amps, and running at 450 to 1650 rpm for battery charging and auxiliary circuits, as well as a triple-winding exciter, are mounted on the main generator. Four LSa-430 type series wound traction motors, 445 V 272.2 amps of 105 kW input at 284 rpm, are connected in parallel. Owing to the single-stage field reduction of the traction motors the engine can be operated within a wide output range. For hump shunting a control system has been provided to ensure, at selected constant engine speeds, a tractive effort regulation. The locomotive underframe is fully welded from members of box section, with head-stocks suitable for the application of automatic central couplers, without any further modifications.

Type 6D diesel-electric shunter

CAF
Construcciones y Auxiliar de Ferrocarriles SA

Padilla 17, Madrid 28006, Spain

Telephone: +34 1 435 25 00
Telex: 23197 cafma e
Telefax: +34 1 276 62 63

Export Division: SEMF, Castello 72–1°, 28006 Madrid

Telephone: +34 1 275 64 03
Telex: 27242 semf e
Telefax: +34 1 276 81 08

Works: Beasain, Zaragoza, Irün

President: José I Cangas
Chairman: Pedro Ardaiz
General Manager: Juan José Anza

Products: Electric, diesel-electric and diesel-hydraulic locomotives.
CAF has delivered to RENFE (Spanish National Railways) four Class 269.600 locomotives that have been rebuilt with new bogies and transmissions and with a redesigned front end for 200 km/h operation.

Constitution: The present company, Construcciones y Auxiliar de Ferrocarriles SA, was formed by the merger of Material y Construcciones SA (MMC) into Compañia Auxiliar de Ferrocarriles SA (CAF), retaining

RENFE Class 269.600 Bo-Bo electric locomotive rebuilt for 200 km/h

the initials CAF. It is the largest manufacturer of railway rolling stock in Spain. It was established in 1917 when deliveries started for the Spanish railways.

Canton Motive Power
Canton Motive Power Machinery Works

Canton, Kwangtung, People's Republic of China

Products: Steam locomotives.

Casaralta
Casaralta SpA
A member of the Firema Group

Via Ferrarese 205, 40128 Bologna, Italy

Telephone: +39 51 35 84 54
Cable: Rotabili, Bologna
Telex: 511068 Offcas
Telefax: +39 51 36 38 45

President: Giorgio Regazzoni
Managing Directors: Carlo Filippo Zucchini
Carlo Regazzoni

Products: Electric locomotives and railcars; single- and double-deck passenger coaches; freight wagons.
Recent contracts include the Z1 coach for Italian State Railways (FS) (1989); double-deck coaches, trailers and control trailers for FS (1989); Class E 84 electric train set for ACOTRAL Roma-Italy (1989); double-deck coaches, trailers and control trailers for Nord-Milano Railways, Italy (1989).

Type E656 Bo-Bo-Bo electric locomotive for Italian Railways

16 MANUFACTURERS / Locomotives

Cegielski
Cegielski Locomotive and Wagon Works
Zaklady Przemyslu Metalowego H Cegielski

ul Dzierzynskiego 223/229, 61-485 Poznan, Poland

Telephone: +48 61 212 31
Telex: 0415343

Export sales: Kolmex, 49 Mokotowska, 00-542 Warsaw

Products: Electric locomotives, diesel locomotives of 1700 hp and above.

Constitution: Cegielski is the largest rolling stock works in Poland, building 300 to 400 passenger coaches annually for export alone.

Type EU-07 2000 kW locomotive for Polish State Railways' 3 kV dc electrification

CFD
CFD Industrie

Head office: 9-11 rue Benoît Malon, 92156 Suresnes, France

Telephone: +33 1 45 06 44 00
Telex: 614146
Telefax: +33 1 47 28 48 84

Main works: 51210 Montmirail

After sales office (CFD, Moyse, Batiruhr): 161 rue de Paris, 93000 Bobigny

Telephone: +33 1 48 44 36 42
Telex: 235568
Telefax: +33 1 48 44 60 15

President: F de Coincy
General Manager: P Grau
Sales Manager: M Hallet

Principal subsidiaries
CFD Industrie, CFD Locorem, Desbrugeres, Batiruhr

Products: Diesel locomotives, road-rail vehicles.
Among the company's recent deliveries have been the supply of Type CFB 8000 road-rail vehicles for RENFE (Spain) in 1989; supply of Type BB 800 C' locomotives for Ferrovial (Algeria).

Type GSM 80 137 kW road-rail vehicle

CFD Road Rail Vehicle

Class	Wheel arrangement	Transmission	Rated power (kW)	Max speed	Total weight (T)	Year first built	Builders	
							Mechanical parts	Transmission
CFB 8000	B	on rail: hydrostatic on road: mechanical	180	60 km/h/on rail 90 km/h/on road	19 tons	1985	CFD	RVI/SAUER

Changchow Diesel Locomotive Factory

Changchow, Jiangsu, People's Republic of China

Cable: Equipex, Beijing

Products: Diesel-hydraulic locomotives ranging from 60 to 500 hp, including Type NY380 built for forestry, mine, industrial and shunting operations. Available in all gauges and rated at 380 hp, the NY380 weighs from 24 to 40 tonnes.

China National Railway Locomotive and Rolling Stock Industry Corporation (LORIC)

10 Fu Xing Road, Beijing, People's Republic of China

Telephone: +86 1 45245; +86 1 42685; +86 1 44645
Telex: 222218 loric cn

Products: Diesel-electric and diesel-hydraulic locomotives with various horsepower ratings suiting the needs of passenger, freight and shunting services. Locomotives for 1435 mm and other gauges can be manufactured at the customers' request. LORIC produces a series of diesel locomotives with different continuous horsepower ratings in compliance with UIC standard, for example:
1175 hp Type DFH diesel-hydraulic locomotive;
1800 hp Type DF5 diesel-electric locomotive;
2200 hp Type DF7 diesel-electric locomotive;
2700 hp Types BJ and DFH3 diesel-hydraulic locomotives;
3600 hp Type DF4 diesel-electric locomotive;
4000 hp Type DF4–C diesel-electric locomotive; and
5000 hp Type DF8 diesel-electric locomotive.
Based on IEC standards, LORIC has produced 25 kV ac electric locomotives with the following continuous ratings: Type SS1, 3780 kW; Type SS3, 4350 kW; and Type SS4, 6400 kW.
LORIC also manufactures the steam locomotives: Type QJ for freight service on trunk lines with 2980 hp; Type JS for trunk line, transfer and shunting services with 2270 hp; Type SY-1 for mines, industrial and shunting services with 1300 hp; and metre-gauge Type SY-2 for mines, industrial and shunting services with 1100 hp.
According to the requirements of customers, the factory can manufacture railway steam cranes with lifting capacities of 15 and 60 tons, also diesel railway cranes of 100 tons.
Other products include: rail travelling cranes; various types of medium- and high-speed diesel engines with different ratings (Models 16 240ZB, 12 240Z, 8 240Z, 12 180ZL); a variety of component parts, such as roller bearings, turbochargers, governors, pistons, piston rings, fuel injectors, air compressors, water pumps, springs of all sizes; coupler and draft gear; brake equipments; alternator and traction motor sets; electric

Locomotives / **MANUFACTURERS** 17

control systems; instruments; silicon rectifiers for diesel and electric locomotives; forklift trucks; storage battery cars; refrigerating equipment; and castings and forgings of all sizes.

Constitution: China National Railway Locomotive & Rolling Stock Industry Corporation (LORIC) is a state-owned enterprise under the leadership of the Ministry of Railways. It is authorised to plan production and manage affairs on its own, and is specialised in design, manufacture and overhaul of locomotives and rolling stock as well as parts and components. LORIC manages over 35 factories producing locomotives, rolling stock, machinery and electric motors, as well as four research institutes distributed over 19 provinces, municipalities and autonomous regions throughout China.

ČKD
ČKD Praha
Member of Czechoslovakia's Pragoinvest diesel locomotive exporting group

Head office: U Kolbenky 159, 190 02 Prague 9, Czechoslovakia

Telephone: +42 2 812
Cable: ČKD, Prague
Telex: 121160, 121429

Export sales: Pragoinvest, Ceskomoravská 23, 18 056 Prague 9

Telephone: +42 2 822741–9
Telex: 121 689

Products: Diesel-electric locomotives; diesel engines; electric machinery; truck cranes; tramcars, etc. The works exports through Pragoinvest approximately 400 locomotives a year.

Type LDE 1500 modification of CME 3 Co-Co for Syrian Railways

Class T457.0 600 kW diesel-alternator Bo-Bo prototype for Czechoslovak State Railways

---

CLW
Chittaranjan Locomotive Works

Chittaranjan, Pin-713331, Burdwan District, West Bengal, India

Telephone: Asansol +91 2021/2022
Cable: Engineshala
Telex: 0204 241

General Manager: V K Fondekar
Chief Electrical Engineer: N K Chidambaram
Chief Mechanical Engineer: M H Balakrishnan
Chief Project Manager: S G Bijlani
Financial Adviser/Chief Accounts Officer: S K Sharma
Stores Controller: S N Bhattacharjee
Chief Personnel Officer: A Sharma

Products: Electric locomotives; diesel shunters; narrow-gauge diesel locomotives.

CLW has capacity for an annual production of 100 electric locomotives and 40 diesel locomotives with plans for an increase in production in the near future.

Recent products built for railways in India are:
Class WAG5 25 kV 50 Hz 2830 kW freight locomotive capable of hauling a 4 500-tonne train at a speed of 65 km/h on level. With a maximum speed of 80 km/h, the loco is equipped with rheostatic braking and is suitable for hauling air-braked as well as vacuum-braked stock; it is also designed for working in multiple.

Class WAP1 25 kV 50 Hz 2765 kW passenger locomotive capable of hauling a 1200-tonne 26-coach passenger train at a speed of 120 km/h on the level. With a maximum speed of 130 km/h, the loco is suitable for hauling air-and vacuum-braked stock; it is also designed for working in multiple.

Class ZDM5 narrow-gauge (762 mm) mixed traffic diesel-hydraulic locomotive powered by a 450 hp four-stroke diesel engine capable of running at 50 km/h to haul 185 tonnes on the level with vacuum-braked stock; the loco is also provided with air brakes and is fitted with Voith hydraulic pneumatically-controlled reversible turbo transmission.

Class NDM5 narrow-gauge (610 mm) mixed traffic diesel-hydraulic locomotive powered by a 450 hp four-stroke diesel engine capable of running at 50 km/h to haul 185 tonnes on the level with braked stock. The

Class WAP 3 (WAP 1-FM II) 25 kV 50 Hz ac Co-Co for passenger haulage

Class WAG 5 25 kV 50 Hz ac Co-Co for freight haulage

MANUFACTURERS / Locomotives

loco is also provided with air-brakes and is fitted with Voith hydraulic pneumatically-controlled reversible turbo transmission.

Class WDS4 broad-gauge (1676 mm) 700 hp diesel shunting locomotive with a maximum speed of 65 km/h on the level. It is fitted with Voith reversible hydraulic transmission with jackshaft gearbox. A three-axle coupled-wheel locomotive, it is provided with both air and vacuum brakes for trailing load.

Class YDM2 metre-gauge mixed-traffic diesel locomotive capable of 60 km/h on the level hauling air-or vacuum-braked stock.

CLW is self-sufficient with regard to main sub-assemblies: it builds the Type TAO 659 770 hp traction motor, the HS 15250A 840 hp traction motor and the Mak Type 6M282A(K) diesel engine. CLW has a large steel foundry for casting Co-Co bogies and two furnaces for the manufacture of traction motor components.

Other in-house facilities include the manufacture of underframes, loco body bogies and the manufacture of traction control equipment such as master controllers, reversers, EP and EM contractors, smoothing reactors and inductive shunts. Plans are afoot for the upgrading of electric locos from 3900 hp to 5000 hp, and diesel locos from 700 hp to 1200 hp.

Constitution: This motive power plant, a production unit owned by Indian Railways, was set up to manufacture steam locomotives and went into production in January 1950. Production of electric and diesel locomotives was started in the 1960s and manufacture of steam locomotives tapered down and finally stopped in 1972.

By the end of January 1990, the cumulative production of locos at CLW has totalled 1404 electric locos and 713 diesel locos, as well as some 2531 steam locos.

CLW diesel locomotives

Class and gauge (mm)	Wheel arrangement	Transmission	Rated output (kW)	Max speed km/h	Weight tonnes	Year first built	Builders Mechanical parts	Engine & type	Transmission
WDS4B 1676	C	Hydraulic	525	65	60	1967	CLW	CLW: Type MaK 6M282A (K)	KPC, Pune CLW
ZDM3 762	B-B	Hydraulic	525	50	35	1970	CLW	CLW: Type MaK 6M282A (K)	KPC, Pune CLW
WDS8 1676	Bo-Bo	Electric	525	35	88	1981	CLW	CLW: Type MaK 6M282A (K)	Bharat Heavy Electricals Ltd, Bhopal
ZDM4 762	1B-B1	Hydraulic	525	50	39	1975	CLW	CLW: Type MaK 6M282A (K)	KPC, Pune
ZDM4A 762	1B-B1	Hydraulic	525	50	37.5	1983	CLW	CLW: Type MaK 6M282A (K)	Voith, West Germany
ZDM5 762	B-B	Hydraulic	330	50	22.9	1989	CLW	KCL: Type KTA 1150L	L2r2ZU2 KPC, Pune
NDM5 610	B-B	Hydraulic	330	50	22.0	1987	CLW	KCL: Type KTA 1150L	L2r2U2 KPC, Pune
YDM2 1000	B-B	Hydraulic	525	60	48	1986	CLW	CLW: Type MaK CLW L4r4Zu2 6M282A(K)	KPC, Pune

KPC–Kirloskar Pneumatic Company, Pune
KCL–Kirkloskar Cummins Ltd, Pune

CLW electric locomotives

Class and gauge (mm)	Wheel arrangement	Line voltage	Rated output (kW) continuous	one-hour	Max speed km/h	Weight tonnes	Year first built	Builders Mechanical parts	Electrical equipment
WCM5 1676	Co-Co	1.5 kV dc	2330	2720	120	124	1961	CLW Westinghouse, UK	CLW English Electric, UK
WCG2 1676	Co-Co	1.5 kV dc	3090	–	80	132	1971	CLW, WSF	BHEL
WCAM1 1676	Co-Co	Dual-voltage 25 kV 50 Hz/ 1.5 kV dc	2677 in ac 2155 in dc	–	120	112.8	1975	CLW, WSF	CLW, BHEL GEC Traction, UK
WAG1 1676	B-B	25 kV 50 Hz	2135	2155	80	85.2	1963	CLW, 50 c/s Group	CLW, 50 c/s Group
WAG4 1676	B-B	25 kV 50 Hz	2317	2640	80	87.6	1967	CLW, WSF	CLW, 50 c/s Group BHEL
WAM4 1676	Co-Co	25 kV 50 Hz	2677	–	120	112.8	1971	CLW, WSF	CLW, BHEL, HBB
WAG5 1676	Co-Co	25 kV 50 Hz	2830	–	80	118.8	1978	CLW, WABCO	CLW, BHEL, HBB
WAP1 1676	Co-Co	25 kV 50 Hz	2765	–	130	107	1980	CLW, WABCO	CLW, BHEL, HBB
WAP3 1676	Co-Co	25 kV 50 Hz	2765	–	140	107	1988	CLW, WABCO	CLW, BHEL, HBB

CLW–Chittaranjan Locomotive Works, Chittaranjan
BHEL–Bharat Heavy Electricals Ltd, Bhopal
WSF–Westinghouse Saxby Farmer Ltd, Calcutta
HBB–Hindustan Brown Boveri Ltd, Vadodara
WABCO–Westinghouse Air Brake Company, USA and France

Clyde
Clyde Engineering Motive Power Division

Head office: PO Box 73, Factory Street, Granville, New South Wales 2142, Australia

Telephone: +61 2 637 8288
Telex: 72636
Telefax: +61 2 637 8735

Branches (workshops)
Sydney Road, Bathurst, New South Wales 2795
Somerton Road, Campbellfield, Victoria 3061
Links Avenue, Eagle Farm, Queensland 4007
Somertown Road, Campbellfield, Victoria

Acting General Manager: J M Corbett
National and Export Sales Manager: Kevin C Thomson
Manager, Engineering Design & Development: D E Butters

Products: Diesel-electric and diesel-hydraulic locomotives; electric locomotives; traction motors and associated rolling stock equipment.

In 1988 the company commenced delivery of 12 diesel-electric locomotives to Australian National. The 2240 kW units are of the Clyde/EMD AT 42C Co-Co design and incorporate EMD's latest microprocessor control system and 12-710G3 engine. These latest generation Super 60 Series 118-tonne locomotives are geared for 150 km/h operation.

Constitution: The company delivered steam locomotives to Australian railways over a fifty-year period commencing in 1907. A licensing agreement signed with General Motors Corporation in 1948 prefaced construction and delivery in 1951 of diesel-electric locomotives to GM design and incorporating Electro-Motive Division power equipment. The company is now also engaged in the design of these locomotives to satisfy the specification requirements of the Australian systems and some industrial clients.

Locomotives / **MANUFACTURERS**

Diesel locomotive production since 1985

Class	Wheel arrangement	Transmission	Rated power (kW)	Max speed km/h	Total weight tonnes	No in service 1988	Year first built	Builders		
								Mechanical parts	Engine & type	Transmission
Australian National Railways										
DL (36-47)	Co-Co	Electric	2240	153	118	10	1988	Clyde/EMD	EMD 12-710G3	Clyde/EMD
State Transport Authority of Victoria										
N (450-475)	Co-Co	Electric	1825	115	118	25	1985	Clyde/EMD	EMD 12-645E3B (10) EMD 12-645E3C (15)	Clyde/EMD

Electric locomotive production

Class	Wheel arrangement	Line voltage	Rated output (kW) continuous	Max speed km/h	Weight tonnes	No in service 1988	Year first built	Builders
Queensland Railways								
3X01-3X70	Bo-Bo-Bo	25 kV	2890	80	109.8	50	1986	Clyde/ASEA-Walkers joint venture

CMI
Cockerill Mechanical Industries SA

Head office: avenue Greiner 1, 4100 Seraing, Belgium

Telephone: +32 41 3021 11
Telex: 41225
Telefax: +32 41 3023 89

Works: CMI, Dept Engines and Locomotives, 4100 Seraing

Products: Shunting locomotives of 200 to 2000 hp, on two, three or four axles, for all gauges and types of track. Recent orders have come chiefly from Belgium, Argentina (130 locomotives), Republic of Korea, Zaïre, Peru, France, Angola, Portugal, Algeria, Luxembourg, Gabon, Congo-Brazzaville and Taiwan. In 1982 the company's shunter design was completely reappraised from both technological and ergonomic standpoints. The company has also developed a range of 300 to 800 kW electric locomotives, powered either by a main supply conductor or by batteries affording at least 2 hours' operation without recharging; these locomotives are conceived especially for underground applications where avoidance of pollution is critical. The company is also pursuing high-security remote radio control of shunting locomotives in a system adaptable to all types of locomotive.

Constitution: CMI-Cockerill Mechanical Industries became an independent subsidiary of Cockerill Sambre in December 1982. CMI employs more than 2000 people, and specialises in products for heavy industry including locomotives. It has produced thousands of locomotives of all types and power for both main-line and shunting work and is a leading manufacturer of diesel-hydraulic shunting locomotives.

670 hp 040-040 shunter for Minero Peru

CMI standard three-axle diesel-hydraulic shunter, available with 300–700 bhp ratings and 17-to 25-tonne axleloads (Republic of Korea)

Comeng
A division of the ANI Corporation Limited
Frankston Road, Dandenong, Victoria 3175, Australia
Telephone: +61 3 794 2111
Telex: AA33253
Telefax: +61 3 792 5817

General Manager: A Connor

Products: Electric, diesel-electric locomotives.

Constitution: Comeng is the Rolling Stock Division of The ANI Corporation Limited.

Type 636 2700 kW locomotive rebuilt with full-width air-conditioned cab

Type ELA 101 2900 kW heavy-haul 25 kV 50 Hz ac electric locomotives for Queensland Railways' coal lines

20 MANUFACTURERS / Locomotives

Cometarsa
Cometarsa SAIC

LN Alem 1067, Piso 25, 1001 Buenos Aires, Argentina

Telephone: +54 1 31 6277
Cable: Cometarsa, Baires

Works: Campana, Prov Buenos Aires

Products: Diesel-electric, diesel-hydraulic locomotives.

Daewoo
Daewoo Heavy Industries Ltd

PO Box 7955, Seoul, Republic of Korea

Telephone: Seoul +82 2 752 0211
 Anyang +82 343 52 6171
Cable: Dhiltdincheon
Telex: 23301/25550
Telefax: +82 2 756 2679

Chairman: Woo Choong Kim
President: Kyung Hoon Lee
Executive Vice President: Oh Jun Kwon
Rolling Stock Executive Director: Won Jai Park
Rolling Stock Export Sales Manager: Soo Hwan Kim

Products: Locomotives.

Foreign companies with which Daewoo has technical collaboration arrangements for rail equipment include:
Electric locomotives: 50 c/s Group; ACEC, Belgium; AEG and Siemens, West Germany; GEC Alsthom and MTE, France; BBC, Switzerland
Stainless steel railcars, bogies: Transit America Inc, USA
Electric cars: Hitachi Ltd, Japan
Diesel-hydraulic railcars: Niigata Engineering Co Ltd, Japan
Air-spring bogies, diesel engines: MAN, Federal Republic of Germany
Rubber-spring bogies: Gloucester Railway Carriage & Wagon Co Ltd, England
Barber stabilised bogies: Standard Car Truck Co, USA
Traction motors, motor alternators, design co-operation in electric emu cars: GEC Alsthom Transport Division, England
Alliance couplers: Amsted Industries Inc, USA

Affiliated companies
Daewoo International (America) Corp
100 Daewoo Place, Carlstadt, New Jersey 07072, USA
Tel: +1 201 935 8700
Telex: 133563 daewoo carl

Daewoo International (America) Corp
1005 W Victoria Street, Compton, California 90220, USA
Tel: +1 213 603 9697, 774 1746
Telex: 698368 daewoo cmtn
Telefax: (213) 637 0383

Daewoo International Steel Corp
100 Daewoo Place, Carlstadt, New Jersey 07072, USA
Tel: +1 201 935 8700
Telex: 133563 daewoo carl

Daewoo International Co (Montreal) Ltd
9200 l'Acadie Blvd, Suite 104, Montreal H4N 2TN, Canada
Tel: +1 514 381 4431-3
Telex: 5825826 daewoo

Daewoo International (Panama) SA
Calle Elvira Mandez y Via Espana Edif, Banco de 4TO Piso Aptdo, 6-2240 El Dorado, Panama, Republic of Panama
Tel: +507 23 8144/0394, 64 8537
Telex: 379 2760 daewoo pg

Daewoo Handels GmbH
Hahnstrasse 31-35, 71-Niederrad, Frankfurt/Main, Federal Republic of Germany
Tel: +49 69 664040
Telex: 414957, 16923 daewoo d
Telefax: +49 69 664 0412

Daewoo Industrial Co (UK) Ltd
Templar House, 82 Northolt Road, South Harrow, Middlesex HA2 0YL, England
Tel: +44 81 864 5366
Telex: 887078, 8814285 daewoo g
Cable: Daewootex Harrow
Telefax: +44 81 864 6070

Daewoo France SARL
Centre Seine T41, 23 rue Linois, 75015 Paris, France

Tel: +33 575 1530, 577 9713
Telex: 250837 daewoo f
Telefax: +33 1 577 4934

Daewoo Industrial Co (HK) Ltd
33/F Far East Finance Centre, 16 Harcourt Road, Hong Kong
Tel: +852 5 200826 30
Telex: 75274 dwhkg hx
Cable: Daewoo
Telefax: +852 5 861 0896

Daewoo Malaysia Sdn Bhd
Lot 111, 1st Floor Komplex Antarabangsa, Jalan Sultan Ismail, Kuala Lumpur, Malaysia
Tel: +60 3 526466, +60 3 416556, 416767
Telex: 30067 daewoo ma

Daewoo International (Japan) Corp
Room 404, Toranomon Mitsui Bldg, 8-1, 3-chome, Kasumigaseki, Chiyoda-ku, Tokyo, Japan
Tel: +81 3 502 4301-8

Telex: 222 6754 dwjpn j
Cable: Daewooind Tokyo
Telefax: +81 3 502 4392

International Type Manufacturing & Distribution Co Ltd
PO Box 754, Port Sudan, Sudan
Tel: +249 31 2183-6, +249 31 2188, +249 31 4484-5
Telex: 22187 itmd sd

Daewoo Nigeria Ltd
Plot 1608, Adeola Hopwell Street, Victoria Island, PO Box 8686, Lagos, Nigeria
Tel: +234 1 616953, 616956-7, 616967-8, 617108-9, 6169116
Telex: 22143 daewoo ng
Telefax: +234 1 616953

Société Daewoo Maroc
Tour des Habous, avenue des FAR, Tour 11-8ème Étage, Casablanca, Morocco
Tel: +212 31 0047, 31 0850
Telex: 23056 daewoo ca

740 hp main-line/shunting diesel-electric locomotive for Ghana Railway Corporation

447 kW, 75-tonne diesel-hydraulic B-B, available with fitment for remote control

Locomotives / **MANUFACTURERS**   21

The Sudanese Korean Construction and Contracting Co Ltd
House No 44, Street No 35, PO Box 1873, Khartoum 2, Sudan
Tel: +249 11 76301, 77034, 79984
Telex: 28058 dwskc sd

Constitution: Originating in 1937, the present company was formed to create a major South Korean rolling stock industry in 1973. From manufacture of passenger cars and freight wagons it progressed to construction of electric locomotives and complete multiple-unit trains, including long-haul air-conditioned diesel (Type DEC) and electric (Type EEC) sets for Korean National Railroad. Major export markets for locomotives, passenger vehicles and freight wagons have been created in Bangladesh, Malaysia, Ghana, Tunisia, Sudan, Burma, Singapore, New Zealand, Indonesia and elsewhere. Following technical agreements with MAN of West Germany in 1970 and with several Japanese manufacturers, the company offers a wide range of marine, automotive and industrial diesel engines, and is now expanding into the construction of diesel locomotives and railcars, and electric locomotives.

Daewoo diesel locomotives since 1985

Class	Wheel arrangement	Transmission	Rated power (kW)	Max speed km/h	Total weight tonnes	No in service 1988	Year first built	Engine & type	Transmission
Shunting	0-4-0	Hydraulic	210	25	20	1	1986	Cummins (NT855-L4)	Voith
Shunting	C	Hydraulic	338	30	45	1	1985	Cummins (KT-19L)	Voith
Main line/shunting	B-B	Electric	545	80	56	4	1986	MTU (8V396 TC12)	Toshiba

Daewoo electric locomotives

Daewoo reference	Wheel arrangement	Line voltage	Rated output (kW) continuous	Max speed km/h	Weight tonnes	No in service 1988	Year first built	Electrical equipment	Special features
EL	B-B-B	25 kV ac	3900	85	132	2	1986	Daewoo & 50 c/s Group	Thyristor control

Dalian Locomotive and Rolling Stock Works

Member of China National Machinery Import and Export Corporation

51 Zhong Chang Street, Dalian, Liaoning, People's Republic of China

Telephone: +86 411 403064
Cable: Dallocwks, Dalian
Telex: 86414 daloc cn
Telefax: +86 411 406447

General Manager: Fu Chunli
Deputy General Manager: Shen Yi
Senior Engineer & General Manager, Import & Export: Tan Yukun

Products: Diesel locomotives.
In production is the 2430 kW Type Dong Feng 4C Co-Co diesel locomotive, an improved version of the Dong Feng 4B, which it now supersedes in series production. The Dong Feng 4C has a 23-tonne axleload and is geared for a top speed of 120 km/h as a passenger unit, or 100 km/h in freight service. Powered by a Type 16 V 240ZJC diesel engine with a possible continuous rating of 2650kW at 1000rpm and an idling speed of 430rpm, the engine is fitted with VTC254-13 turbochargers and Type TQFR3000B generator; the Type ZQDR410C traction motor is manufactured by Yongji Motor Plant. The locomotive weighs 138 tonnes and its dimensions are 21.1 m over couplers × 3.309 × 4.725 m. The engine measures 5.02 × 1.79 × 2.99 m.
In 1986 a Type Dong Feng 4, arranged for 120 km/h passenger service, was built and this version was mass-produced in 1988.
In April 1989 the Type Dong Feng 6 high performance 118 km/h diesel-electric locomotive was launched. Its engine has been developed in conjunction with Ricardo Consulting Engineers of Britain, while the transmission system has been developed with the assistance of General Electric Co, USA.
The 16 V 240ZJD diesel engine has a possible continuous rating of 2940kW at 1000rpm with an idling speed of 400rpm and is fitted with a VTC254-13 turbocharger, GE GTA32A1 alternator and GE 752AFC1 traction motor. Axle load is 23 tonnes, service weight 138 tonnes and the locomotive's overall dimensions are 21.1 m over couplers × 3.309m × 4.755 m.
Dalian signed a contract in January 1990 to build two diesel shunters for China Guiyang Gas Co, taking advantage of the loans available through the Overseas Economic Cooperation Fund of Japan.

Type Dong Feng 6 118 km/h diesel-electric locomotive

Datong Locomotive Works

Daqing Road, West Suburbs, Datong, Shanxi, People's Republic of China

Telephone: +86 23845, 23823
Cable: 1001

Products: Diesel locomotives of 2000 hp and 3000 hp gas turbine locomotives. Also on its product list are forged aluminium pistons for 16240 diesels; piston pins; structural metal products; pressure containers; forgings; die forgings; cast steel; common cast iron; nodular cast iron; cast copper and semi-finished products. The works also processes machinery parts.

Datong Locomotive Works offers services to customers world-wide. In addition to those mentioned, it manufactures locomotives for various countries, and also parts, according to customers' specifications or designs and blueprints provided by them.

Diema
Diepholzer Maschinenfabrik Fritz Schoettler GmbH

Diemastrasse 11, PO Box 1170, 2840 Diepholz 1, Federal Republic of Germany

Telephone: +49 5441 3041/43
Cable: Diema, Diepholz
Telex: 941 222
Telefax: +49 5441 3046

Managing Director: Peter Benzien

Products: Standard- and narrow-gauge diesel shunting locomotives, narrow-gauge diesel mine locomotives, narrow-gauge industrial locomotives, hydraulic tippers and motorised work trolleys. Almost 5000 locomotives have been manufactured by the company.
The production range includes:
Diesel locomotives for narrow-gauge: engine output

22 MANUFACTURERS / Locomotives

Diema Type DVD 60 gang trolley

Type DVL 200 diesel shunter

10–300 hp; weight 1–30 tonnes;
Diesel shunting locomotives for standard- and wide-gauge: engine output 15–300 hp, weight 4–30 tonnes;
Diesel locomotives for operation in tunnels and ore mines: engine output 10–300 hp, weight 1–30 tonnes;
Flameproof diesel locomotives for underground service: engine output up to 100 hp, weight 3.5–14 tonnes;
Flameproof battery locomotives for underground mining: up to 44 tonnes weight and 160 kW;
Motorised trolleys for narrow- or standard-gauge as inspection vehicles and heavy-duty work trolleys for track maintenance;
Hydraulic tippers with a load capacity of 2.5 and 5 m^3;
large capacity self-propelled transporter, with 5 or 10 m^3 capacity

DLW
Diesel Locomotive Works

Varanasi 221 004 (UP), India

Telephone: +91 542 64451-55
Cable: Dieseloco
Telex: 0545-230 dlw in

General Manager: R C Sethi
Chief Mechanical Engineer: S Bhattacharya
Controller of Stores: S R Bahadur
Chief Design Engineer: V Anand
Chief Marketing Manager: A S P Sinha

Products: Diesel engines of 1400–2600 hp; diesel generating sets; diesel-electric locomotives of metre-, standard- and broad-gauges; and components for diesel locomotives. The plant was set up in collaboration with Alco and has supplied more than 2450 locomotives so far, mainly to Indian Railways. Recent exports include 15 metre-gauge 1350 hp six-axle locomotives for Viet-Nam National Railways and an equal number to Tanzanian Railways. Standard engine models are: 6-cylinder/1350 hp; 12-cylinder/1950 hp; and 16-cylinder/2600 hp.

Production of a new WDM-6 class of locomotive was begun in 1981 and two were built. This locomotive has a Model 251 D diesel engine and electric transmission. With a 1200 hp rating, it is for hauling medium-load passenger trains on the Indian Railways 1676 mm gauge.

A new locomotive of Type WDS-6 with creep control has been built for the merry-go-round railways in a number of generating stations being set up by the National Thermal Power Corporation of India. The creep control enables the locomotive to operate at a steady 0.4 km/h for loading and unloading of coal. It has provision for automatic wagon door actuation for discharge of its coal trains.

For branch-line services on broad-gauge systems, where less powerful locomotives are required for replacement of steam locomotives, a new 1800 hp Class WDM-7 locomotive has been evolved, incorporating a 12-cylinder Type 251-D engine; 15 units were manufactured in 1987-88.

Some 150 items of spare components for diesel locomotives are manufactured at DLW. These include 16- and 6-cylinder complete diesel power packs,

Class YDM-4 diesel-electric Co-Co

Class WDS-6 diesel-electric Co-Co

DLW diesel locomotives

Class	Wheel arrangement	Transmission	Rated power kW	Max speed km/h	Total weight tonnes	No in service 1989	Year first built	Engine & type	Transmission
WDM-2*	Co-Co	Elec	1790	120	112.8	1671	1964	16V Model 251B	BHEL
YDM-4	Co-Co	Elec	895	100	72	452	1968	6 in-line Model 251D	BHEL
WDS-6*	Co-Co	Elec	895	60	126	318	1975	6 in-line Model 251D	BHEL
WDM-6	Bo-Bo	Elec	895	75	70	2	1981	6 in-line Model 251D	BHEL
WDM-7	Co-Co	Elec	1340	110	96	15	1987	12V Model 251B	BHEL

* Available also with slow-speed creep control

Locomotives / **MANUFACTURERS** 23

Class WDM-7 diesel-electric Co-Co

Class WDM-2 broad-gauge diesel-electric locomotive for Indian Railways

cylinder blocks/heads/liners, connecting rods, camshaft and turbo rotor assemblies etc. Rehabilitation of cylinder blocks is also undertaken.

To meet the growing demand of spares for diesel locomotives, the Ministry of Railways has set up Diesel Component Works at Patiala, where a wide range of components and assemblies are being manufactured. DCW has already started reconditioning traction machines and engine blocks, apart from manufacture of a large number of parts and components. In the second phase, DCW has taken up rehabilitation of power packs and complete locomotives.

Constitution: DLW is a unit of the Indian Railways.

Duro Daković
Duro Daković Industries

PO Box 63, 55001 Slavonski Brod, Yugoslavia

Telephone: +38 55 231 011
Cable: Lokomotive, Slavonski Brod
Telex: 23421/23424

Products: Diesel-electric (610–1840 kW), diesel-hydraulic (150–1176 kW) and diesel-mechanical locomotives.

Constitution: Duro Daković was founded in 1921 as the first Yugoslav locomotive and wagon manufacturer. Diesel locomotives have been produced since 1954.

Electroputere
Electroputere Works, Craiova 1100, Jud Dolj

Calea Bucureşti 144, 1100 Craiova, Romania

Telephone: +40 941 44494/42077
Telex: 41234

Managing Director: Dipl Ing Constantin Udrea

Products: Diesel-electric Co-Co locomotives from 2100 to 4000 hp; electric Co-Co locomotives of 5100 kW.

Since 1960 the works has built 2100 hp diesel-electric locomotives under a Sulzer/Brown Boveri licence. Over 2300 of this type have been built for Romanian Railways and systems in other countries, among them Polish State Railways (422), the Railways Administration in the People's Republic of China (256), and Bulgarian State Railways (130). Powered by a twin-bank 12-cylinder Type 12 LDA 28 diesel engine developing a maximum 2300 hp (under UIC conditions), the locomotive is intended for both passenger and freight service; it has dc/dc transmission and Knorr braking. The first Romanian Railways locomotives of this type have run over 3 million km.

A later unified series of Electroputere locomotives is based on Alco engines with power outputs between 1500 and 4000 hp, manufactured by Reşiţa Works under Alco licence. The 3000 and 4000 hp locomotives so far produced are locally designed. They are intended for mixed traffic and have common features. Engines are four-stroke, pressure-charged with direct injection, at a nominal speed of 1100 rpm, and charge air cooled. The number of cylinders is 12 in the 3000 hp and 16 in the 4000 hp model. Both have self-supporting super-

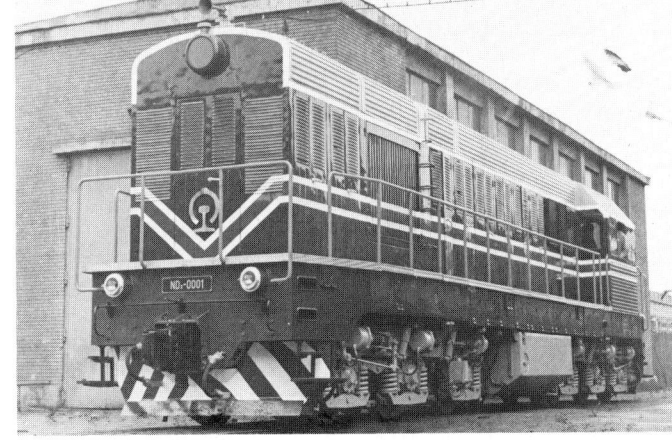

Class ND3 2100 hp diesel-electric shunting Co-Co exported to China

2640 hp diesel-electric Co-Co for Iranian Railways

1200 kW electric heavy-duty shunting Co-Co for Romanian Railways

structures, with cabs at each end, and Flexicoil bogie suspension. All axles are powered with compensated dc, nose-suspended, series excitation traction motors. Transmission is ac/dc in both, and braking equipment is Knorr. Electroputere has already exported 10 4000 hp locomotives to Greece and 10 of 2640 hp to Iran.

The demand for haulage of heavier trains resulted in the development of the most powerful locomotive ever constructed in Romania, a 5100 kW Co-Co electric, which is manufactured under ASEA licence. The first units of this type were delivered to Romanian Railways in 1967 and have since recorded over 2.5 million km in service. To date over 900 electric locomotives have been manufactured and delivered by Electroputere, including 150 exported to Yugoslavia, Bulgaria and China.

Electroputere co-operates with a large number of other factories in Romania supplying auxiliary machines and apparatus, the braking system control and supply equipment, metering equipment lamps etc. Diesel engines are manufactured by ICM Reşiţa and bogies by ICM Caransebeş.

Constitution: A Mecanoexportimport supplier. Electroputere Craiova is the largest manufacturer of industrial electrical equipment in Romania. In 1955–59 the works manufactured for the passenger transport enterprise of Bucharest 161 tramcars, which were the beginning of its rolling stock construction.

Elin Energieanwendung

Penzinger Strasse 76, A-1141 Vienna, Austria

Telephone: +43 1 222 89100-0
Telex: 112763 elin a
Telefax: +43 1 222 8946046

Works: Factory Weiz, Elingasse 3, A-8160 Weiz and Factory Vienna-Floridsdorf, Shuttleworth strasse 4-8, A-1210 Vienna

Chairman: Dipl-Ing Heinrich Trescher
Deputy Chairman: Dkfm Dr Gustav Rose

Director-Railway Division: Prok Dipl-Ing Johann Oismüller

Member companies:
ELIN Deutsche Gesellschaft für Elektrische Industrie

SEA Studiengesellschaft für Energiespeicher und Antriebs-systeme

ELIN Italiana

Elin Wasserwerkstechnik

Voith-Elin Elektronik

Alcatel-Elin Elektronik

Alcatel-Elin Forschungszentrum

Elin Seilbahntechnik

Products: Electric locomotives, traction motors, axle drives, and other components of electric traction units. System engineering for rail and road vehicles, power and auxiliary electronics, vehicle control systems, components, motors, drives (main and auxiliary-ac), transformers and reactors.

Recent contracts include Type 1044, 1063 and 1014 (newly developed) locomotives for ÖBB, together with underground drive systems and tram projects for Vienna municipal services.

Emaq
Emaq-Engenharia e Máquinas SA

Rodovia Estrada Rio-Teresópolis, BR116, Km 121.5
25.900, Magé, Rio de Janeiro, CP 93.609, Brazil

Telephone: +55 21 733 2020
Telex: 21 32200 eloc

Products: Locomotives; rolling stock. The company has licences from MLW, Montreal for diesel-electric locomotive manufacture; from MTE, France for electric locomotives; and from Alco Power Inc of the USA for the EMAQ-251 diesel engine.

Recent contracts include an order from Ferrovia Paulista SA (FEPASA) for 80 electric locomotives, to be delivered 1985–89.

Emaq diesel locomotives

Class	Wheel arrangement	Transmission	Rated power (kW)	Max speed km/h	Total weight tonnes	Year first built	Builders		
							Mechanical parts	Engine & type	Transmission
EM 60	Bo-Bo	Electric	477	28	70	-	Emaq	Saab-Scania DS1-11 6-cyl	BBE
MX 620	Co-Co	Electric	1490	103	96	1980	Emaq	Alco Model EC 251	GE

Emaq electric locomotives for FEPASA

Class	Wheel arrangement	Line voltage	Rated output (kW) continuous	Max speed km/h	Weight tonnes	Builders	
						Mechanical parts	Electrical equipment
EC 362	Bo-Bo	3 kV dc	2540	90	100	Emaq	Various

Energomachexport
V/O Energomachexport

129010 Moscow, Bezbozhny per 25A, USSR

Telephone: +7 095 288 84 56
Cable: Energoexport
Telex: 411965
Telefax: +7 095 288 79 90

Director-General: Vladimir I Filimonov
Deputy Director-General: Grigory I Lapytko
Director, Locomotives: V Dolnakov

Products: Soviet exports of diesel locomotives. Recent deliveries include Type TGM4 and TGM8 750-800 hp diesel-hydraulic units to Egypt and Pakistan, Type M62 diesel-electric 2000 hp units to Poland and Mongolia, and Type TU7 diesel-hydraulic units to Viet-Nam.

Constitution: The company was formed to handle all railway equipment exports from the Soviet Union. Principal partners include the Ludinovo, Kolomna, and Voroshilovgrad locomotive works.

Energomachexport diesel locomotives

Usage	Manufacturer's type reference	Wheel arrangement	Transmission	Rated power (kW)	Max speed km/h	Total weight tonnes	No in service 1988	Year first built	Builders		
									Mechanical parts	Engine & type	Transmission
Shunting and industrial	TGM4, gauge 1435-1676 mm	2-2	Hydraulic	551	55	68	3500	1975	Ludinovo locomotive works	6CN 21/21	Kalyga machine-building plant
Shunting and industrial	TGM8, gauge 1435-1676 mm	2-2	Hydraulic	588	60	80	230	1975	Ludinovo locomotive works	3AE-6D49, Kolomna locomotive works	Kalyga machine-building plant
Shunting	TU7, gauge 750-1676 mm	2-2	Hydraulic	294	50	24	4000	1977	Kambarka locomotive works	1D12 Baznaul machine-building plant	Kalyga machine-building plant
Main-line	M62, gauge 1435 mm	Bo-Bo	Electric	1470	100	116	3500	1965	Voroshilovgrad locomotive works	14D40 Kolomna locomotive works	Kharkov electric plant

Locomotives / **MANUFACTURERS** 25

Ferrostaal
Ferrostaal AG

PO Box 10 12 65, Hohenzollernstrasse 24, 4300 Essen, Federal Republic of Germany

Telephone: +49 201 818 01
Cable: Ferrostaal, Essen
Telex: 0857100

Directors: Dr Hans Singer
Dr F Graf von Ballestran
Helmut Julius
Dr Klaus von Menges
Heinz Staudinger
Gerhard Thulmann

Products: Main-line, shunting and mining locomotives with diesel-hydraulic, diesel-electric and electric traction.

Ferrosud
Ferrosud SpA

PO Box 94, Via Appia Antica Km 13, 75100 Matera, Italy

Telephone: +39 835 2228541
Cable: TF 222841 Ferrosud

Telex: 812525 fersud i
Telefax: +39 835 217137

Chairman: Corrado Fici
Managing Director: Angelo Palmieri
Export Sales: Claudio Marnucci (Breda)

Products: Electric and diesel-electric locomotives.

Constitution: Ferrosud was set up in 1963 for the manufacture and marketing of railway and tramway rolling stock. Production began in 1968. Export sales are handled directly by the company or through Breda Costruzioni Ferroviarie. The company is wholly owned by EFIM through the Gruppo Ferroviario Breda.

Fiat
Fiat Ferroviaria SpA

Piazza Galateri 4, 12038 Savigliano (CN), Italy

Works: 4 Piazza Galateri, 12038 Savigliano (Cuneo)

Telephone: +39 172 2021
Telex: 201234 fiatsv i
Telefax: +39 172 202 426

Chairman: Renato Piccoli
Managing Director and General Manager: Giancarlo Cozza
Deputy General Manager and Project Manager: Pierantonio Losa
Sales Manager: Andrea Parnigoni

Subsidiary Companies
Costruzioni Ferroviarie Colleferro
Elettromeccanica Parizzi

Products: Electric and diesel-electric locomotives.

A recent product is the Type D145 centre-cab diesel-electric locomotive for shunting and light mixed traffic work, of which 38 have been delivered to the Italian State Railways (FS). Developed in conjunction with Elettromeccanica Parizzi, the D145 is also known as the Inloc because of its inverter and three-phase variable voltage frequency ac motor transmission. The Inloc pursues recent Fiat practice in adapting heavy road vehicle diesel engines to rail traction.

The year 1990 saw the first E652 electric full chopper locomotives delivered, representing an important evolution of the well-known E632 with the power increased from 4500 kW to 5000 kW, the speed in one version only gives 160 km/h with unchanged tractive effort.

Constitution: The activity of Fiat in the field of railway rolling stock began in 1917 with the manufacture of passenger and freight cars. In 1931 Fiat put the first diesel railcars into service before beginning production of diesel multiple-units and locomotives, progressing to the tilting body electric 'Pendolino' train.

Class E652 dc 5000 kW 160 km/h electric locomotive for FS

Type D145 inverter locomotive for FS

By the end of 1975 all the activities of Fiat concerning design and manufacture of railway rolling stock were entrusted to Fiat Ferroviaria SpA, the company which now controls Costruzioni Ferroviarie Colleferro SpA, Rome, and Elettromeccanica Parizzi, Milan.

Fiat electric locomotives since 1987

FS class	Wheel arrangement	Line voltage	Rated output (kW) continuous	Max speed km/h	Weight tonnes	Year first built	Builders Mechanical parts	Builders Electrical equipment
E491	Bo-Bo	25 kV ac	3140	140	88	1987	Fiat	Ansaldo
E492	Bo-Bo	25 kV ac	3140	160	88	1987	Fiat	Ansaldo
E652*	Bo-Bo	3 kV dc	5000	160	103	1990	Fiat	Ansaldo ABB

*General layout and project/supply of part of bogies and all the transmissions

Firema Consortium

Head office: Corso di Porta Romana 63, 20122 Milan, Italy

Telephone: +39 2 5465708
Telefax: +39 2 5460133

President: Dr Ing Giorgio Regazzoni

Board Members: Avv Dino Marchiorello
Dr Giorgio Fiore
Procurator: Prof Ing Francesco Perticaroli
Export Manager: Dr Ing Maurizio Fantini

MANUFACTURERS / Locomotives

Member companies

Firema Engineering Srl
Corso di Porta Romana 63, 20122 Milan
Telephone: +39 2 5465708
Telex: 322255
Telefax: +39 2 5460133

Officine di Cittadella SpA
Via Rometta all 'Olmo 5, 35013 Cittadella (Padua)
Telephone: +39 49 597966
Telex: 430854
Telefax: +39 49 9400238

Officina Meccanica della Stanga SpA
Corso Stati Uniti 3, 35100 Padua
Telephone: +39 49 760488
Telex: 430218
Telefax: +39 49 760682

Casaralta SpA
Via Ferrarese 205, 40128 Bologna
Telephone: +39 51 358454
Telex: 511068
Telefax: +39 51 363845

Fiore SpA
General Management: 81020 S Nicola La Strada (Caserta)
Telephone: +39 823 467677
Telex: 720387
Telefax: +39 823 466812
Works: Zona Industriale, 81020 S Nicola La Strada (Caserta)
Via Gabella del Pesce 23, 80056 Ercolano (Naples)

Officine Casertane SpA
81020 S Nicola La Strada (Caserta)
Telephone: +39 823 467499
Telex: 720458
Telefax: +39 823 467691

Metalmeccanica Lucana SpA
85050 Tito Scalo, Potenza
Telephone: +39 971 65088/9
Telex: 812332
Telefax: +39 971 65072

Ercole Marelli Trazione SpA
Viale Edison 110, 20099 Sesto San Giovanni (Milan)
Telephone: +39 2 24941
Telex: 320575
Telefax: +39 2 2488905

Mater SpA
Via Patellani 42, 20091 Bresso (Milan)
Telephone: +39 2 6141751
Telex: 351260
Telefax: +39 2 6141751

Products: Locomotives.
 In September 1988 Officine Casertane received from Italian Railways (FS) an order for 20 3 kV dc locomotives of the new Type E652. These locomotives are similar to the Class E632, but are more powerful.

Frichs
Frichs A/S

PO Box 115, Aarhus C, Denmark

Telephone: +45 6 158555
Telex: 64373

Products: Diesel-electric, diesel-hydraulic and diesel-mechanical locomotives.

Ganz
Ganz Electric Works

Lövöház utca 39, H-1024 Budapest, Hungary
Mail address: PO Box 63, Budapest H-1525, Hungary

Telephone: +36 1 175-3322
Cable: Alterno, Budapest
Telex: 225363 gvm bp
Telefax: +36 1 156-2989

General Manager: Gábor Kara
Director of Traction: Mátyás Rácz

Products: Electric main-line and shunting locomotives.
 Series production of Class V43 2200 kW (3000 hp) locomotives with diode rectifier for Hungarian State Railways (MÁV) started in 1964 and completed in 1983. The next locomotive design was the Type V63 six-axle thyristor-controlled 3600 kW locomotive for mixed traffic. MÁV operates 56 of this type.
 The Type V46 is a thyristor-controlled, four-axle 800kW shunting locomotive; 45 are in service with MÁV.

Constitution: This company developed from the electrical department started by Ganz and Co in 1878.

800 kW 80 km/h 25 kV 50 Hz shunting locomotive for Hungarian State Railways (MÁV)

3600 kW 120 km/h 25kV 50 Hz locomotive for MÁV

Ganz-Hunslet
Ganz-Hunslet Részvénytársaság

Budapest VIII, Vajda Peter u 12, H-1430 Budapest, Hungary

Telephone: +36 1 114 0840, 133-5958
Telex: 22 5575 gmph, 22 5576 gmph
Telefax: +36 1 114 3481, 113 4624

Chief Executive: Harry A Codd
Sales Director: Géza Bereczky
Technical Director: Lászlo Süveges

Ganz-Hunslet is a joint venture company and an associated member of Hunslet (Holdings) PLC of England.

Products: Diesel electric and diesel hydraulic locomotives, a.c. electric locomotives for mainline, shunting and industrial application.

Manufacture of the 662 kW diesel-electric shunter type DVM 12 and of the 820 kW electric shunter type VM 16 is continuing. Under development is a 640 kW diesel electric locomotive type DVM 14 for marshalling and transfer duties fitted with naturally aspirated diesel engine, electro-dynamic brake system and unified bogies with type VM 16.

Ganz-Mávag
Ganz-Mávag Locomotive and Railway Carriage Works

PO Box 28, Könyves Kálmán krt 76, Budapest VIII, Hungary 1967

Telephone: +36 1 335 950, 140 840
Telex: 22 5575/6
Telefax: +36 1 143 481

General Director: József Balogh
Commercial Director: Ferenc Tordai

Products: Diesel-electric and diesel-hydraulic locomotives (250 to 2200 kW).

Diesel-electric shunting locomotives of Type DVM 12 were in manufacture in 1988 following the initial batch of 15 units delivered to Yugoslav Railways (JZ) in 1984-85. Production of Type VM 15 main-line and VM 16 shunting locomotives was continuing in co-operation with Ganz Electric Works.

Type DVM-12 diesel-electric locomotive

GE
General Electric Company
Transportation Systems

2901 East Lake Road, Erie, Pennsylvania 16531, USA

Telephone: +1 814 875 3587
Cable: Geco 14 Eri
Telex: 703531
Telefax: +1 814 875 2976

Export office: International Region, GE Co, 570 Lexington Avenue, New York, New York 10022

General Manager, Locomotive Sales & Marketing Department: M W D Howell
Customer Support: D B Tucker
Manager, Export Sales: S Maier

Products: Diesel-electric and electric locomotives; switching and mining locomotives.

General Electric produces a wide variety of locomotives and locomotive services to meet the worldwide needs for motive power. The product structure includes GE and ALCO locomotive designs powered by ALCO or GE engines as required by specific applications. General Electric Company has strengthened its ability to serve the worldwide locomotive market by combining the advanced technology of its US operation with GE Canada's recently acquired Montreal Locomotive Works (MLW), located in Montreal, Canada.

The company's product range includes the 'Dash 8' locomotive – an advanced microprocessor-controlled locomotive designed for maximum levels of horsepower and tractive effort with optimised system fuel efficiency; the 'Super 7' locomotive which has the advanced performance features of the 'Dash 8', but is simpler in design. The locomotive design can be constructed as a new locomotive, or can be remanufactured from earlier generations of GE locomotives; 'Universal' export locomotives designed to include advanced tractive effort and fuel efficiency within weight and size constraints typical of many of the world's locomotives; and Industrial Switching Locomotives – lower hp units configured to perform typical industrial or railroad shunting tasks, with a simple yet efficient design.

The company's latest domestic product range is the 'Dash 8' series of diesel-electric locomotives. Its features include refinements to the FDL diesel engine, which has accumulated more than 1000 million miles of operating experience in revenue service at the maximum Dash 8 power ratings. A 30 per cent advance in reliability is claimed through the ability of a microcomputer system to work around faults and maintain full power. This system also contributes to reliability by eliminating a multitude of mechanical relays, interlocks used on the power devices, and

'Dash 8' Type 8-40CM Co-Co

Type C30-7 locomotive

GE Type SL 50 switching locomotive

MANUFACTURERS / Locomotives

hundreds of separate wires.

The newly introduced GE-752 AG traction motor is used. The company claims that it significantly reduces operating temperatures and improves moisture resistance. In the Dash 8 it also secures an increased continuous tractive effort ranging from 5 to 11 per cent, depending on the locomotive model. This allows the Dash 8 to take greater advantage of the capabilities of the now computerised Microsentry Adhesion Control System. With Microchec excitation control and the Microsentry system under control of the microcomputer, the Dash 8 is claimed to offer 23 to 26 per cent all-weather adhesion. A traction motor thermal protection system allows full utilisation of motor capacity for faster train acceleration and reduced time on grades. It also allows elimination of Power Match equipment. General Electric's newly improved alternator provides full parallel capability without transition in both four-and six-axle locomotives.

By evaluating and adjusting the locomotive auxiliary system, the microcomputer can increase traction horsepower without increasing the diesel engine brake horsepower. This increase provides higher speed on grades, more rapid acceleration of premium trains, and greater fuel economy. An average 4 per cent fuel saving is achieved with the microcomputer-controlled ac fan and blower drives, a self-contained dynamic braking package, and the new air compressor clutch. Compared to earlier models, fleet average savings are said to reach 10 per cent over 1980 units and 16 per cent over initial 1977 GE New Series locomotives.

The dynamic braking grids are located in a blown self-contained package. This reduces auxiliary load in braking by separating engine speed requirements from grid ventilation. Thus, fuel economy is further improved. When combined with improved performance of the GE-752AG motor, peak braking can be increased by 20 per cent and maximum braking kW by 35 per cent on six-axle units. Similar increases can be achieved on four-axle units.

A clutch allows compressor shutdown when it is unloaded, normally 95 per cent of the time. This extends compressor life, while reducing fuel consumption, compressor maintenance, and lube oil in the air system.

Maintainability and availability are both increased by the Replaceable Unit (RU) concept. All microcomputer control equipment is packaged in replaceable units.

At the centre of a closed-loop, solid-state system are three on-board microcomputers. The three central controllers interface with the control system, continuously adjusting it to operate at maximum efficiency. One computer manages the total locomotive system and control functions; the second is responsible for the main alternator excitation system; and the third computer monitors the auxiliaries. This cluster of computers receives feedback from sensors throughout the locomotive. The computers diagnose how the

'Dash 8' Type 8-40CM Co-Co

Electric locomotives

Model	E60C	E42C	E25B
Rail hp, continuous	5900	3750	2125
Voltage, kV	25/50	25	25
Frequency	50/60	60	60
Number of axles	6	6	4
Minimum weight			
lb	331 000	198 000	240 000
kg	150 000	90 000	109 100
Max speed			
mph	70	68	70
km/h	113	110	113
Continuous tractive effort			
lb	82 000	44 000	55 000
kg	37 200	20 000	25 000
Track gauges			
in	56.5/66	39.4/42	56.5/66
mm	1435/1676	1000/1067	1435/1676
Major equipment			
Traction motors	GE752	GE761	GE752
Line breaker	Vacuum circuit breaker		
Transformer	Sealed design-FOA		
Power converter	Forced air-cooled thyristors		
Ventilating system	Single blower, self-cleaning filters		

'Dash 8' Type B40–8 4000 hp Bo-Bo

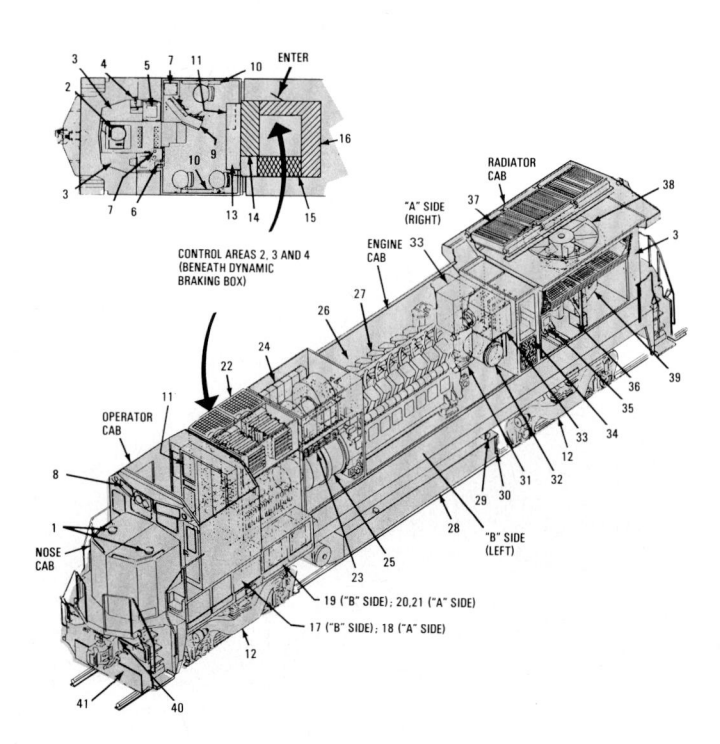

Layout of 'Dash 8' Type B39-8 3900 hp Bo-Bo
(1) sand fill (2) toilet area (3) sand box (4) handbrake (5) refrigerator or cooler (6) emergency brake valve (7) heater and defroster (8) headlight and number light box (9) control area no 5 (control console) (10) heater, side strip (11) engine control panel (12) trucks: 'B', 2 axles per truck; 'C', 3 axles per truck (13) control area no 1 (14) control area no 2 (15) control area no 3 (16) control area no 4 (17) control area no 6 (18) air brake compartment (19) control area no 7 (20) control area no 8 (21) battery box (22) dynamic braking box (23) rectifiers (propulsion) and fuses (24) blower box and air filters (25) alternators (main and auxiliary) (26) engine start station (27) engines: 32B/32C, 12 cylinder FDL-12; 40B/40C, 16 cylinder FDL-16 (28) fuel and retention tanks (29) fuel fill (30) fuel gauge (31) lube oil cooler (32) lube oil filter (33) engine water tank and water control valve (34) engine air filter compartment (35) air compressor (motor driven) (36) control area no 9 (37) radiators (38) radiator fan (39) blower and air filters (no 2 end) (40) anti-climber (optional) (41) pilot plate (snow plough optional)

system is working, make adjustments automatically and work around faults, minimising shutdowns. Performance data is continuously available on the diagnostic display panel in the locomotive cab.

The only running maintenance required within a 92-day period is replenishment of traction motor support bearing oil and gear case lubricant. This results from design improvements in lube oil filters, fuel filters, fuel piping systems and other components. Major overhaul schedules have also been extended by design improvements to engine and traction components, support systems and control equipment.

At the end of 1984 the company completed the delivery of the largest single order in its history, for the supply to Chinese Railways of 220 Type C36-7 4000 hp diesel-electric Co-Cos. A repeat order for 200 C36-7, worth US$230 million, was received in 1985 and delivered from 1986 onward.

In designing the 'Super 7' locomotive, GE merged the features of the company's earlier Dash 7 production line with the advanced Dash 8 design. The result is a locomotive with a tractive effort, fuel efficiency and reliability very similar to that of the Dash 8. The unique feature of the Super 7 design is the facility to update older vintages of GE locomotive to Super 7 standard. Major design features include GE's Microsentry Adhesion Control System, full-time motor parallel connections, motor thermal protection, fuel-efficient 4-cycle GE diesel engine; a separately blown dynamic braking package and radiator fan system with a disengaging eddy current clutch are notable design features.

Licence agreements: General Electric (USA) has locomotive manufacturing agreements with the following:
Australia: A Goninan & Co
Brazil: General Electric do Brasil
Federal Republic of Germany: Krupp
South Africa: Dorbyl

Dash 8' models

Model	B32-8	C32-8	B40-8	C40-8
Wheel arrangement	B-B	C-C	B-B	C-C
Dimensions				
Length	63' 7"	67' 11"	66' 4"	70' 8"
Height	14' 11½"	15' 4½"	14' 11½"	15' 4½"
Width	10' 2¾"	10' 2¾"	10' 2¾"	10' 2¾"
Bolster centres	36' 7"	40' 7"	40' 1½"	43' 4"
Bogie wheelbase	9'	13' 7"	9'	13' 7"
Wheel diameter	40"	40"	40"	40"
Minimum curvature (ft/degree)				
Single	150'/39°	273'/21°	150'/39°	273'/21°
Multiple-unit	195'/29°	273'/21°	195'/29°	273'/21°
Weight (lb)				
*Maximum (nominal ± 2% tolerance)	284 000	390 000	288 000	410 000
Gear ratio				
Standard-maximum speed	83/20-70	83/20-70	83/20-70	83/20-70
Optional-maximum speed	81/22-75	–	81/22-75	–
Maximum continuous tractive effort and speed				
Standard (lb/mph)	71 600/13.8	109 700/8.2	69 200/18.6	108 600/11.0
Optional	63 500/15.6	–	61 400/20.9	–
Supplies				
Fuel (gal)	3250	3900	3250	5000
Water (gal)	350	350	380	380
Lube oil (gal)	365	365	410	410
Sand (ft^3)	48	48	48	48
Control	Microprocessor	Microprocessor	Microprocessor	Microprocessor
Engine data				
Model	FDL-12	FDL-12	FDL-16	FDL-16
Engine type	V-12 4-cycle Turbocharged	V-12 4-cycle Turbocharged	V-16 4-cycle Turbocharged	V-16 4-cycle Turbocharged
Cylinders	12	12	16	16
Traction (hp)	3200	3200	4000	4000
Traction equipment				
Traction alternator and auxiliary alternator	GMG 186	GMG 187	GMG 186	GMG 187
Traction motors	4 752AG	6 752AG	4 752AG	6 752AG

* With heavy options and/or maximum ballast

MANUFACTURERS / Locomotives

Other general purpose models

Model	B23-7	B30-7A	C30-7A	B36-7	C36-7
Wheel arrangement	B-B	B-B	C-C	B-B	C-C
Engine data					
No of engines (all turbocharged) and hp	1 × 2250	1 × 3000	1 × 3000	1 × 3600	1 × 3600
No of cylinders	12	12	12	16	16
Model	GE FDL-12	GE FDL-12	GE FDL-12	GE FDL-16	GE FDL-16
rpm	1050	1050	1050	1050	1000
Dimensions					
Length (m)	18.64	18.64	20.5	18.64	20.5
Height (m)	4.68	4.68	4.68	4.68	4.68
Width (m)	3.1	3.1	3.1	3.1	3.1
Bolster centres (m)	11.18	11.18	12.47	11.18	12.47
Bogie wheelbase (m)	2.74	2.74	4.14	2.74	4.14
Minimum track curvature (radians or degrees)					
for single unit	150' or 39°	150' or 39°	73' or 21°	150' or 39°	273' or 21°
for mu or coupled to train	250' or 23°	250' or 23°	273' or 21°	250' or 23°	273' or 21°
Weight on drivers minimum and max (lb)	253 000/280 000	253 600/280 000	359 000/420 000	259 800/280 000	366 600/420 000
Tractive effort					
Starting at 25% adhesion for minimum and max weight (lb)	63 250/70 000	63 250/70 000	89 750/105 000	64 950/70 000	91 650/105 000
Continuous tractive effort (lb) and speed (mph) on gear ratio indicated	61 000/10.7	64 600/12.0*	96 900/8.8	64 600/12.0*	96 900/11.0
Gear ratio and max speed (mph) (specimen)	3/20-70	83/20-70	83/20-70	83/20-70	83/20-70

* Power match   Note: All units equipped with roller bearing journals.

Switching locomotives

Model	SL80	SL110	SL144
Wheel arrangement	B-B	B-B	B-B
Engine data (all turbocharged)			
No of engines and hp	2 × 300	2 × 300	2 × 550
No of cylinders	6	6	6
Model	Cummins NT-855L4	Cummins NT-855L4	Cummins KTA-1150-L
rpm	2100	2100	2100
Dimensions			
Length (m)	11.58	12.5	13.72
Height (m)	3.92	3.92	4.04
Width (m)	2.9	2.9	2.9
Bolster centres (m)	6.1	6.71	7.62
Bogie wheelbase (m)	2.36	2.36	2.59
Minimum track curvature (radians or degrees)	75' or 77°	75' or 77°	100' or 57°
Weight on drivers minimum and max (lb)	130 000/160 000	170 000/220 000	230 000/288 000
Tractive effort			
Starting at 30% adhesion for minimum and max weight (lb)	39 000/48 000	51 000/66 000	69 000/86 400
Continuous tractive effort (lb) and speed (mph)	31 600/5.4	31 600/5.4	61 560/5.5
Gear ratio and max speed (mph)	20.9/1-21	20.9/1-21	10.52/1-35

Export models

Model	U10B	U11B	U15C	U22C*	U18C	U26C	U30C
Gross hp	1050	1100	1650	2300	1950	2750	3200
Hp for traction	950	1000	1550	2165	1820	2600	3000
Number of axles	4	4	6	6	6	6	6
Track gauge	All gauges from 914 to 1676 mm						
Couplers	To suit railway requirements						
Tractive effort at continuous motor rating (kN)	161	161	241	241	265	265	265
Max speed (km/h)	103	103	103	103	103	103	103
Minimum weight (kg)	49 700	49 700	80 500	88 900	80 500	96 200	96 200
Electrical system	dc/dc	dc/dc	dc/dc	dc/dc	ac/dc	ac/dc	ac/dc
Engine	CAT D379	CAT D398	GE FDL8	GE FDL12	GE FDL8	GE FDL12	GE FDL12
Traction gen/alt	GT 601	GT 601	GT 581	GT 581	GTA11	GTA11	GTA11
Traction motors	GE761	GE761	GE761	GE761	GE761	GE761	GE761

* Streamlined dual cab design available

GEC Alsthom
GEC Alsthom Transport Division

Tour Neptune, 92086 Paris La Défense Cedex 20, France

Telephone: +33 1 47 44 90 00
Telex: 611 207
Telefax: +33 1 47 78 77 55

Other main offices: PO Box 134, Manchester M60 1AH, England

Telephone: +44 61 872 2431
Telex: 667152
Telefax: +44 61 875 2131

Managing Director: Michel Perricaudet
Assistant Managing Director: Brian McCann

Works: Rolling Stock Group
Aytre-la-Rochelle, Belfort, le Creusot, Marly-les-Valenciennes
Managing Director: J M Hoermann (La Defense, Paris)

Traction Group
Ornan, Preston, Tarbes, Trafford Park, Villeurbanne
Managing Director: K Appelbee (Trafford Park, Manchester)

Transportation Projects Group (UK)
Birmingham
Managing Director: B S Ronan (Trafford Park, Manchester)

Transportation Projects Group (France)
Managing Director: A Thinnieres (La Defense, Paris)

Fixed Systems Group (Signalling & Sub-stations)
Borehamwood, Saint Ouen
Managing Director: M Boden (Borehamwood Industrial Park, Rowley Lane, Borehamwood, Herts WD6 5PZ)
Telephone: +44 81 953 9922
Telex: 916129
Telefax: +44 81 207 5905

Products: Diesel and electric locomotives, high-speed electric trains (TGV), suburban emus, metro cars, LRVs and VALs, double-deck motor coaches and trailers, passenger coaches, bogies, electrical propulsion equipment.

Locomotives / **MANUFACTURERS** 31

Overseas Subsidiaries:
ACEC Transport, PO Box 4, 6000 Charleroi, Belgium
Telephone: +32 71 44 57 99
Telex: 51 227 acec b
Telefax: +32 71 43 78 34
Managing Director: C Jauquet

Ateinsa, Factoria de Villaverde, Carretera, Villaverde, Vallecas 18, Madrid 28041, Spain
Telephone: +34 1 796 11 00
Telex: 43521
Telefax: +34 1 796 15 08

Kiepe Elektrik, Thorner Strasse 1, PO Box 13 05 40, D-4000 Düsseldorf 13, W Germany
Telephone: +49 211 74 97 1
Telex: 8581 471
Telefax: +49 211 74 97 300
Traction Dept Manager: W Huober

Macosa, Plaza de la Independencia 8, Madrid, Spain
Telephone: +34 1 522 4787
Telex: 22168

Maquinista, Calle Fernando Junoy 2-64, PO Box 94, 08030 Barcelona, Spain
Telephone: +34 93 345 5700
Telex: 54539
Telefax: +34 93 345 6958

Constitution

In December 1988 a decision was taken to merge the Power Systems Group of the General Electric Company of England with Alsthom of France. The resulting group, with over 85 000 employees and sales of nearly £500 million per annum, is the largest electrical manufacturing company in the EEC.

Each of the partners in this new group had a flourishing rail transport section and their activities now have been combined in the GEC Alsthom Transport Division. The Division employs more than 15 000 people (at 19 factories in six countries) wholly on rail transport and has an annual business of some £1000 million — more than half of which is exported outside the UK and France.

The Division has been involved in the design of railway rolling stock continuously since the very beginning of railways, as one of its constituent companies was Robert Stephenson & Co (set up in 1823 as the first company in the world established specifically to design and manufacture locomotives).

The Division now incorporates the rolling stock and electric traction activities of many well-known companies in Britain including AEI, BT-H, Dick Kerr, English Electric, Metropolitan-Vickers and the Vulcan Foundry. From France have come Brissoneau et Lotz, Franco-Belge, CIMT, CEM Oerlikon, Jeumont Schneider (including Carel Fouché Industries and Alsthom Creusot Rail). Metro-Cammell Ltd of England was acquired in 1989.

In 1988 GEC Alsthom delivered to French Railways the first of 44 units of a new type of electric locomotive, the BB26000 'Sybic' Bo-Bo with self-commutating synchronous ac motors.

The body of the BB26000 is of the self-supporting type, built in semi-stainless steel. At each end, in front of the driving cab, is a protecting shield which absorbs energy in the event of collision. The body interior layout includes two soundproofed driving cabs each equipped with an ergonomic control desk permitting driving to be carried out in either a sitting or standing position; and a central compartment housing the electric and pneumatic equipment blocks.

The power circuits obtain total symmetry between the circuits of the two traction motors. This symmetry is the product of research into an entire equipment functional independence of the two bogies, whether in traction or braking mode.

The central equipment block includes an 'equipment' compartment, and a 'converter' compartment cooled by six motor-ventilator sets. The power semiconductors are housed in freon pollution-free con-

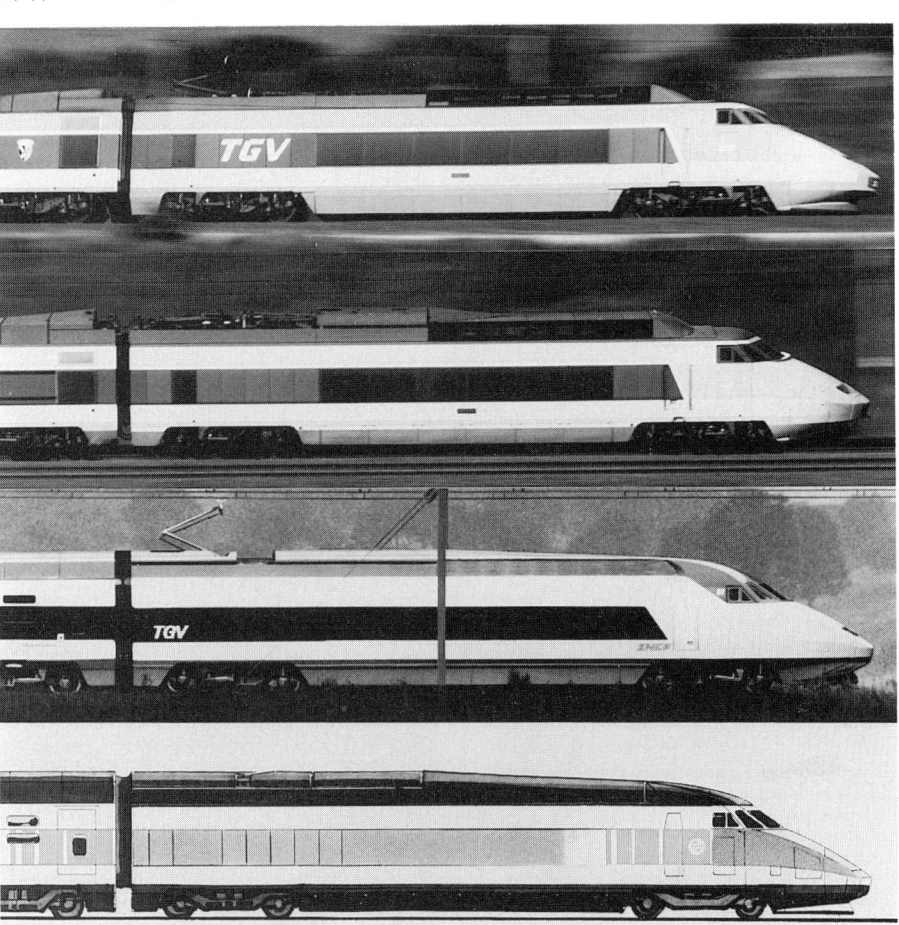

The TGV family

Class BB26000 'Sybic' electric locomotive for SNCF

32 MANUFACTURERS / Locomotives

tainers, and the braking resistances are installed in the upper part of the block. A low voltage cabinet is located on one side.

All auxiliary motors are of the three-phase asynchronous type. Electrical supply to these motors and other consumer items is made through static converters from a regulated 525 V direct current obtained by two step-down choppers drawing energy from the main LC filter.

The braking mode permits automatic blending of the electric and pneumatic brakes irrespective of the type of operation carried out, either by the master controller traction/braking, set speed or by the automatic brake control lever. The electric brake is of the rheostatic type. Holding effort adjustment is obtained by action upon either the traction motor excitation while functioning as an alternator, or the braking rheostat apparent resistance value by the application of the main chopper.

In traction mode the two star-connected inverter units for each motor are mounted in series and supplied under variable current by means of a fixed frequency current chopper which draws its energy from the terminals of a filter. This filter is electrically fed directly from the 1.5 kV catenary, or through the intermediary of a step-down transformer and two rectifier mixed bridges, connected in parallel under 25 kV 50 Hz catenary.

The bogies are of the single motor type. Primary suspension consists of helical springs. The body sits on the bogie central cross member through means of steel-rubber pads called 'sandwich pads'. Hydraulic dampers comprise vertical dampers that ensure dampening of the primary suspension; transversal dampers that control body-bogie displacement; and longitudinal dampers to control hunting movement. Motor torque is transmitted to the gear reduction by means of an elastic coupling.

General characteristics

Length between buffers	17.710 m
Centre distance between bogies	9.684 m
Centre distance between axles	2.797 m
Overall length	3.026 m
Track gauge	1.435 m
Overall height	4.270 m
Total mass in running order	90 tonnes
Three-phase synchronous traction motor:	
Total mass	6400 kg
Power	2800 kW
Maximum speed	1930 rpm
Stator inside diameter	1050 mm
Maximum speed	200 km/h
Developed power over the full 80 to 200 km/h range	5600 kW
Wheelrim effort in traction mode:	
at starting	32 000 daN
at continuous rating (90 km/h)	22 000 daN
at maximum speed (200 km/h)	10 000 daN

The 'wheelrim effort to speed' characteristics permit: haulage of a 750-tonne passenger train (16 Corail coaches) up a 0.25% gradient at 200 km/h; and haulage of a 2050-tonne freight train up a 0.88% gradient (corrected profile) at 80 km/h.

Besides its major role as supplier of TGV train-sets, locomotives, self-powered train-sets and cars to French Railways, and of equipment for the Paris authority, RATP, GEC Alsthom sustains vigorous export business.

In March 1985 the 50 c/s Group, with French industry the chief protagonist, secured from Chinese Railways an order for 150 6400 kW, 184-tonne B-B+B-B electric locomotives valued at FFr2600 million. Delivery of the first locomotive was required within 16 months of signature and completion of the contract within 30 months, demanding an output of 13 locomotives a month. GEC Alsthom is project leader. The contract provided for 10 locomotives of the order to be assembled in China as a preliminary to technology transfer for future construction of complete locomotives to the 50 c/s design in China, but 130 have been assembled in France, mostly by GEC Alsthom at Belfort, where their mechanical parts are chiefly manufactured. Delivery began in 1986.

The 8K locomotive, as the model is classified by Chinese Railways, consists of two Bo-Bo single-cab power units coupled end-to-end creating an articulated eight-axle locomotive with a power of 6400 kW which is particularly apt for hauling heavy trains over sinuous tracks in mountain areas. Each of the units has an automatic 25 kV high voltage roof line coupler which facilitates operations in depots and when uncoupled allows operation of one Bo-Bo as a single unit for hauling light trains. The high adhesion capability of the 8K in heavy freight haulage is due in particular to the bogie structure which allows a good distribution of loads; to the low traction rod connection between the bogie and the body; and to an advanced modern anti-wheelslip device. Taking into account the high power of this locomotive and with the aim of reducing line losses, the 8K locomotive is equipped with a power factor improvement arrangement which improves the all-round efficiency of the line. Each Bo-Bo unit has a pantograph-circuit breaker assembly feeding a roof line common to both units and supplying in each:

A 5126 kVA main transformer, in the tank of which the two smoothing reactors and the eight harmonic filter reactors are incorporated;

A central block housing the rectifier and equipment assemblies; the rectifier assembly comprises 28 thyristors 2200 V, 1700 A and eight diodes 2200 V, 2500 A and the central block is equipped with stabilising resistors for the regenerative braking system;

TAO 649 D 6-pole traction motors with class C insulation.

Nominal voltage	865 V
Nominal current	1200 A
Continuous rating speed	1000 rpm
Max speed	2060 rpm

Front end styling of the TMST

Class 91 4700 kW, 240 km/h 25 kV ac electric Bo-Bo for British Rail

The underframe consists of two main longitudinal beams joined by end and intermediate cross members. The triangulated side walls form with the underframe a beam assembly calculated to resist efforts of 2500 daN. These load-carrying parts are in semi-stainless copper-bearing steel. The driving cab is air-conditioned.

The bogies with two motors have a welded frame structure in 'H' form which allows rapid replacement of the traction motor whilst limiting the bogie wheelbase. The traction motors, nose-suspended on the bogie frame, rest on the axle through the intermediary of a cannon box arrangement. Transmission of the motor torque is by a pinion shrunk on the end of the motor shaft and driving a gear wheel on the axle. To ensure an equal distribution of loads on the rail and good stability a primary suspension system with high flexibility has been adopted.

Class 8K Bo-Bo + Bo-Bo: leading particulars

Length	36 228 mm
Weight in running order	184 000 kg
Length of single-cab power unit	16 746 mm
Width of body	3048 mm
Roof height	3980 mm
Distance between bogie centres of each single-cab power unit	9694 mm
Catenary voltage	25 kV 50 Hz
UIC power at continuous rating	6400 kW
Starting effort	628 kN
Continuous rating effort	471 kN
Max service speed	100 km/h

Locomotives / **MANUFACTURERS** 33

6400 kW 25 kV ac Bo-Bo + Bo-Bo for Chinese Railways; GEC Alsthom was project leader in execution of a 50 c/s Group order for 150 locomotives

Regenerative electric braking
UIC power 5200 kW
Retarding effort at 50 km/h 382.5 kN

Early in 1989 the Moroccan National Railways (ONCF) awarded GEC Alsthom an order for 18 4650 kW electric locomotives closely based on the design of the 7200 and 22200 series locomotives built for the French National Railways (SNCF). The contract is worth FFr345 million. The locomotives will be manufactured jointly with Société Chérifienne de Matériel Industriel et Ferroviaire (SCIF). For this contract GEC Alsthom acquired a stake in the capital of SCIF. This commitment underscored GEC Alsthom's willingness to collaborate with Moroccan industry to meet the requirements of the Moroccan Railways, and to exploit the potential for exports outside Morocco, principally to Algeria and Tunisia.

Significant achievements for GEC Alsthom in 1989 included a world speed record of 482.4 km/h by a TGV Atlantique train set; a world heavy-haul record by Class 9E 50 kV locomotives which helped to haul a train weighing 70 806 tonnes and 7.3 km in length. The Queen's Award for Technological Achievement went to GEC Traction (a member of the Transport Division) for the application of GTOs (Gate Turn Off Thyristors) and microprocessor control to rail traction.

GEC Alsthom Traction
GEC Alsthom Traction Ltd

Head office: PO Box 134, Manchester M60 1AH, England

Telephone: +44 61 872 2431
Telex: 665451, 667152
Telefax: +44 61 875 2131

For further details of personnel and products, see earlier **GEC Alsthom** entry.

GEC Australia
GEC Australia Ltd Heavy Engineering Division

Evans Road, Rocklea, Queensland 4106, Australia

Telephone: +61 7 274 7777
Telex: AA41067
Telefax: +61 7 277 9510

General Manager-Motors & General Engineering Division: T C Fisher

Products: Electric and diesel-electric locomotives; electric and diesel-electric traction power and control equipment.

General Electric Canada
Associate company of General Electric, USA

1505 Dickson Street, Montreal, Quebec H1N 2H7, Canada

Telephone: +1 514 253 7393
Telex: 828841
Telefax: +1 514 253 7334

Managing Director: W D Wrench
Technical Director: R N Guest
General Manager: W Morrell

Products: Diesel-electric locomotives. In February 1989 the company acquired the Rail & Diesel Products Division of Bombardier Inc and the latter's diesel locomotive manufacturing resources.

General Electric do Brasil
General Electric do Brasil SA

Head office: Rua Antonio de Godoy 88, São Paulo, Brazil

Telephone: +55 11 222 1177
Telex: +55 11 24018
Telefax: +55 11 223 6892

Works: Rod SP 101, Campinas, Monte Mór Km 3-8, 13100 Campinas, São Paulo

Telephone: +55 192 401521
Cable: Ingentric Campinas
Telex: (019) 1264
Telefax: +55 192 42 8077, 40 1694

Chairman & CEO GE Brasil: K J Maier
Director & General Manager, Heavy Apparatus Operation: N del Nero
Manager, Locomotive Operations: F E Soares
Manager, Locomotive Sales (Region 1): J C De Almeida
Manager, Locomotive Sales (Region 2): F S Brito

Products: Electric, diesel-electric locomotives, electric traction equipment.

Type U-10-B locomotive recently delivered to Brasil

34 MANUFACTURERS / Locomotives

Recent Deliveries

Customer	Country	Type	QT	HP	Weight Tonnes	Gauge (mm)	Year
Enacar	Chile	DE S/L*	01	470	45	1676	1987
CEB	Angola	DE S/L	06	670	60	1067	1987
Acerias Paz del Rio	Colombia	DE S/L	04	470	41	914	1989
Gécamines	Zaïre	U10B	05	900	70	1067	1989
Recent Orders							
CFM	Mozambique	U20C	05	2200	96	1067	1989
CVRD	Brazil	BB-40-8	06	4100	160	1000	1989
CBA	Brazil	DE S/L	02	470	41	1000	1989
Cutrale	Brazil	C30-7A	07	3235	165	1600	1990
Botswana Railways	Botswana	U15C	10	1650	98	1067	1990

* Shunter/Line

General Motors
Electro-Motive Division

Head office: 9301 West 55th Street, La Grange, Illinois 60525, USA

Telephone: +1 708 387 6543
Cable: Elmodiv, La Grange
Telex: 270041
TWX: 910 691 2186/2187/2188

General Manager: John W Jarrell
General Director, Marketing & Intl Management: Lutz W Elsner

Diesel Division: Box 5160, London, Ontario N6A 4N5, Canada
Telephone: +1 519 452 5000
General Director of Operations: William W Peel

Licensees: General Motors has locomotive manufacturing licence agreements with the following companies:
Clyde Engineering Co Pty Ltd, Granville, NSW, Australia
Duro Dakovic, Slavonski Brod, Yugoslavia
Thyssen-Henschel, Kassel, Federal Republic of Germany
Equipamentos Villares SA, São Paulo, Brazil
Hyundai Rolling Stock Co, Seoul, Republic of Korea

Overseas manufacturing: General Motors has overseas locomotive facilities in the following countries:
General Motors Interamerica Corporation, Buenos Aires, Argentina

Products: Diesel-electric locomotives; remanufacturing and rebuilding services; replacement parts.

The latest 60 Series line of diesel-electric locomotives takes advantage of recent GM-EMD advances in diesel and microprocessor technology and incorporates improvements in many support systems. The locomotives achieve new levels of fuel economy and operating performance but require less maintenance. The 60 Series consists of four main-line models:
The SD60, a 390 000 lb (176 900 kg) six-axle locomotive intended for heavy-duty drag operation or medium-speed freight trains in domestic-type mainline service.
The GP60, a 260 000 lb (117 935 kg) four-axle locomotive for intermediate- and high-speed service.
The GP59, a four-axle, lower-horsepower locomotive for intermediate service.

The models are patterned after the SD50 and GP50 introduced in 1980, but incorporate a number of new and improved components in addition to a new engine and microcomputer controls. They are claimed to be 14 per cent more fuel efficient than the SD50 and GP50 locomotives built in 1980. However, their rating of 3800 traction hp reflects a 300 hp increase.

The 60 Series locomotives are equipped with GM-EMD's new 710G series of two-stroke-cycle 16- and 12-cylinder diesel engines rated conservatively at 4100 and 3200 hp at 900 rpm. They also use three microprocessors to control logic and excitation functions, such as direction and traction motor switching, and diagnostic and display functions. The diagnostic and display system replaces conventional fault annunciators and indicator lights with a four-line display panel and can include many new fault and status indicators as well.

The new D87A traction motor features increased brush face area, improved motor ventilation, and a new polyamide film insulation system; these advances permit higher horsepower without increasing motor size. There have also been a number of improvements in auxiliary systems, which have helped reduce parasitic losses in the 60 Series locomotives to less than 3 per cent of engine ratings. These improvements include:
Increased radiator capacity, combined with other engine efficiency improvements, which reduce demands on the cooling system; this in turn reduces cooling fan horsepower requirements.
Two-speed ac cooling fans that provide five cooling air flows.
Cooling fans cycle that conserve energy.
Improved air ducting to the traction motor blowers which reduces blower horsepower.
Full air flow to motor only when required.
During dynamic braking, the engine runs at the lowest possible speed for motor cooling.

The new 710G series of diesel engines is an evolutionary development of GM-EMD's turbocharged, uniflow scavenged, two-stroke cycle engine, which retains the latter's historical simplicity of design, maintainability and high reliability. The 16-cylinder engine is rated conservatively at 4100 hp at 900 rpm for locomotive applications and has a displacement of 710 in^3 per cylinder.

The design is a logical outgrowth of GM/EMD's previous production series, the 645F. From 1980 to 1983 the fuel efficiency of the 645F was increased by 6 per cent and the compression ratio was increased from 14.5 : 1 to 16 : 1. The 710G is GM/EMD's most fuel-efficient engine. Full load fuel consumption of the model 710G3 engine is down 9 per cent from the 1980 model and 3.4 per cent from the 1983 model.

A major change in the 710G design is greater displacement. The 10 in piston stroke of the predecessor 645FB is increased to 11 in in the 710G engine. This longer stroke at the same bore adds 10 per cent more displacement, from 645 to 710 in^3 per cylinder. The 710G design is 1⅝ in higher and 4⅝ in longer than the 645. The added engine length is the

Type GP60 locomotive

Type SD60M locomotive

Locomotives / **MANUFACTURERS** 35

result of use of a larger and more efficient turbocharger. Entry to the turbine was streamlined to improve gas flow and an improved exhaust diffuser also reduces flow restriction. The turbocharger is deeper to accommodate a larger annulus for a smoother and less restrictive discharge of exhaust gases. It provides a 15 per cent increase in air flow for reduced thermal loading of critical engine components. This higher air flow, in combination with an increased injection rate from the new 9/16in plunger injector, accounts for the increase in fuel economy at rated output with no increase in engine mechanical loading.

Engine specifications compared

Model	16-645FB	16-710G
Bore (in)	9.06	9.06
Stroke (in)	10	11
Displacement (in^3)	645	710
Cylinder spacing (in)	16⅝	16⅝
Bank angle	45°	45°
Compression ratio	16.0 : 1	16.0 : 1
Engine speed (rpm)	950	900
bhp	3800	4100

The GM-EMD microprocessor control system is based on the use of three functionally separate Motorola 6803 microcomputers and associated interface units. The three systems are identified as logic, excitation, and diagnostics and display.

The logic system controls engine speed, locomotive direction, operating mode (power or dynamic brake) and traction motor and generator switching. All the locomotive control devices (throttle, reverser, dynamic brake and so on) provide inputs to the logic computer. The computer responds to these inputs by operating the proper devices (power contactors, switchgear and engine governor speed solenoids) and tells the excitation computer what level of traction power or dynamic braking the locomotive engineer has selected.

The excitation system controls such items as the Super Series wheel creep control, dynamic brake and the latest fuel economy features. This was accomplished in the past with analog and digital integrated circuits on a variety of plug-in modular circuit boards.

The excitation computer receives throttle and brake information from the logic system and establishes power or brake reference limits. Feedback information comes from the main generator, traction motors and dynamic brake system. Comparison of the feedback information and the reference limits determines when and how power is adjusted.

The diagnostic and display system replaces conventional fault annunciators and indicator lights with a four-line display panel. Software allows many new fault and status indications to be added as well.

This system also monitors locomotive operation continuously, detecting abnormal conditions, recording the condition of the locomotive at the time the fault occurred and, in some cases, initiating corrective action. In addition, the archive module will maintain a permanent record of such operational data as mileage, kW-hours and duty cycle.

The menu-driven diagnostic system can analyse fault conditions and provide maintenance workers with detailed information on where the problem is. The display also can be used as a digital voltmeter, displaying up to 12 system parameters simultaneously in real time. In addition, self-test features make it

GM-EMD 60 Series Type SD60 locomotive

Type JT26CW-SS locomotive (British Rail Class 59)

Electric models

Model number		J4FC	GF6C	JF6C	AEM-7
Rated hp		4000	6000	6000	7000
Wheel diameter and gear ratio		40 in 76:19	40 in 70:17	40 in 70:17	51 in 1:3.31
Continuous tractive	lb	67 446	95 180	95 180	NA
	kg	*30 593*	*43 175*	*43 175*	NA
Continuous speed	mph	22	10.3	10.3	NA
	km/h	*35*	*16.52*	*16.52*	NA
Max speed	mph	62	68	68	125
	km/h	*100*	*110*	*110*	*201*
Weight	lb	275 000	330 000	330 000	199 500
	kg	*124 740*	*149 688*	*149 688*	*90 493*
Overall length		62 ft 10 in	68 ft 10 in	70 ft 7 in	51 ft 5¹³⁄₁₆ in
		19.15 m	*20.98 m*	*21.53 m*	*15.7 m*
Overall height		13 ft 7⅞ in	15 ft 4½ in	15 ft 4½ in	14 ft 6 in
		4.16 m	*4.68 m*	*4.68 m*	*4.42 m*
Overall width		9 ft 11½ in	10 ft 7¹³⁄₁₆ in	10 ft 7¹³⁄₁₆ in	10 ft
		3.03 m	*3.24 m*	*3.24 m*	*3.05 m*

Domestic models (diesel-electric)

		Switchers	General purpose B-B locomotives		Special duty C-C locomotives		Passenger locomotives	
Model number		MP15T	GP15T	GP59	GP60	SD60	F40PH-2	F59PH
Engine type		8-645E3C	8-645E3C	12-710G3	16-710G3	16-710G3	16-645E3C	12-710G3
Turbocharged		Yes	Yes	Yes	Yes	Yes	Yes	Yes
Rated hp		1650/1500	1650/1500	3150/3000	3950/3800	3950/3800	3150/3000	3150/3000
Wheel diameter and gear ratio		40 in 62:15	40 in 62:15	40 in 70:17	40 in 70:17	40 in 70:17	40 in 57:20	40 in 66:20
Continuous tractive	lb	46,800	47,000	66,670	66,670	100,000	38,320	51,590
	kg	*21,228*	*21,319*	*30,240*	*30,242*	*45,360*	*17,341*	*23,401*
Continuous speed	mph	9.3	9.16	9.8	9.8	9.8	16.5	18.0
	km/h	*15*	*15*	*16*	*16*	*16*	*27*	*29*
Max speed	mph	70	70	70	70	70	102	87
	km/h	*113*	*113*	*113*	*113*	*113*	*164*	*142*
Weight	lb	248,000	240,000	257,000	260,000	368,000	259,000	260,000
	kg	*112,493*	*108,864*	*116,600*	*117,936*	*166,925*	*117,500*	*117,900*
Overall length		50 ft 2 in	54 ft 11 in	59 ft 9 in	59 ft 9 in	71 ft 2 in	56 ft 2 in	58 ft 2 in
		15.29 m	*16.74 m*	*18.21 m*	*18.21 m*	*21.69 m*	*17.12 m*	*17.73 m*
Overall height		15 ft	15 ft 2⅝ in	15 ft 6 in	15 ft 6 in	15 ft 7⅛ in	15 ft 7¼ in	15 ft 9³⁄₁₆ in
		4.57 m	*4.64 m*	*4.72 m*	*4.72 m*	*4.75 m*	*4.76 m*	*4.80 m*
Overall width		10 ft 4⅞ in	10 ft 3⅛ in	10 ft 3⅜ in	10 ft 3⅛ in	10 ft 3⅛ in	10 ft 7¾ in	10 ft 6 in
		3.17 m	*3.12 m*	*3.13 m*	*3.12 m*	*3.12 m*	*3.24 m*	*3.20 m*

MANUFACTURERS / Locomotives

Export models (diesel-electric)

		B-B locomotives		C-C locomotives			
Model number		G-22CW	G-26CW-2	GT-22CW	GT22LC-2	GT-26CW-2	JT26CW-SS
Engine type		12-645-E	16-645-E	12-645-E3	12-645-E3B	16-645-E3	16-645-E3C
Turbocharged		No	No	Yes	Yes	Yes	Yes
Rated hp		1650/1500	2200/2000	2475/2250	2475/2250	3300/3000	3300/3000
Wheel diameter and gear ratio		40 in 62:15	40 in 62:15	40 in 62:15	36 in 57:16	40 in 62:15	42 in 62:15
Continuous tractive	lb	58 200	57 960	57 840	44 196	67 220	65 080
	kg	26 400	26 290	26 240	20 047	30 490	29 520
Continuous speed	mph	7.2	10.3	12.1	15.8	14.1	14.6
	km/h	11.6	16.6	19.5	25	22.7	23.5
Max speed	mph	65	65	65	68.6	65	70
	km/h	105	105	105	110	105	113
Weight	lb	196 800	209 400	219 750	192 195	255 400	277 000
	kg	89 270	94 980	99 690	87 178	115 850	125 645
Overall length		46 ft 6 in	51 ft 9 in	57 ft	61 ft 10½ in	64 ft	70 ft ½ in
		14.17 m	15.76 m	17.37 m	18.86 m	19.51 m	21.4 m
Overall height		12 ft 7 in	12 ft 7 in	13 ft 3 in	13 ft 4½ in	13 ft 6 in	12 ft 10 in
		3.83 m	3.83 m	4.04 m	4.07 m	4.11 m	3.91 m
Overall width		9 ft 3 in	9 ft 3 in	9 ft 3 in	10 ft 3 in	9 ft 3 in	8 ft 8¼ in
		2.82 m	2.82 m	2.82 m	3.12 m	2.82 m	2.65 m

possible to qualify electrical systems, including radar, contactors and the computer itself.

All chips used in the system are ceramic-based and at or near military grade. They pass reliability tests over the temperature range from −85°F to 257°F. A specially rugged grade of connector is likewise specified. A previous-generation locomotive with typical features has 51 relays and more than 2700 electronic components overall, whereas an equivalent 60 Series locomotive has 15 relays and about 2200 components in total.

The computer also improves reliability by avoiding unnecessary engine shutdowns. Conventional controls automatically shut down the engine when certain types of faults are detected; by contrast, the microcomputer can analyse the fault more precisely and decide whether the problem can be dealt with in some other way. For example, if the cooling water overheats, power is reduced to keep temperatures within acceptable limits. The computer can also reduce repair costs after a failure has occurred by automatically identifying the faulty system or component and by providing helpful (and previously unavailable) information on the status of the locomotive at the time of the failure.

The record of locomotive operation also enables scheduling of routine maintenance and overhauls when they are actually needed. Time-based maintenance schedules customarily reflect average requirements of the locomotive fleet, but since few individual locomotives actually follow the average duty cycle, the majority of the fleet receives maintenance either sooner than necessary or not soon enough. Microprocessor-based controls make it possible to base the maintenance schedule on work performed, as reflected in hp-hours or kW-hours. This maximises the life of components requiring periodic replacement, while safeguarding against continued operation with worn-out equipment.

The EMD-Siemens programme to design and develop F69PH ac traction passenger locomotives has progressed through the design, construction and initial in-plant system testing phases. Both locomotives are currently undergoing extensive testing under all modes of operation at the American Association of Railroads Transportation Test Center at Pueblo, Colorado. Upon completion of this evaluation, the locomotives will enter revenue service on Amtrak.

Plans have been defined to continue the introduction of ac traction in North America through the application of this technology to a heavy haul freight locomotive. EMD and Siemens are proceeding with the development and construction of four SD60MAC six-axle freight locomotives. Based on ac equipment similar to that which has been developed for the F69s, the SD60MAC locomotives will confirm the technical feasibility of ac traction satisfying the performance requirements of freight service, as well as demonstrate under all climatic conditions the reliability and reduced maintenance advantages which are anticipated. A second major feature to be included in this new model freight locomotive will be a three-axle radial steering bogie. Advantages of this new design include improvements in utilisation of adhesion in curves while simultaneously reducing wheel and rail wear. The present schedule calls for demonstration of these locomotives on a major US railroad beginning in late 1991.

General Motors
General Motors Interamerica Corporation-Sucursal Argentina

Sarmiento 1113, Piso 4, Buenos Aires, Argentina

Telephone: +54 1 35 4978/8378/8404/8773
Telex: 21609GMABA AR
Telefax: +54 1 953 4162

Products: Diesel-electric locomotives.

General Motors of Canada
Diesel Division, General Motors of Canada Limited

PO Box 5160, London, Ontario N6A 4N5, Canada

Telephone: +1 519 452 5274
Telex: 064 5850
Telefax: +1 519 452 5380

Locomotive Sales Manager: J K Zerebecki

Products: Diesel-electric locomotives ranging from 1000 to 3800 hp in four- and six-axle configurations for track gauges from 1m to 1680 mm.

The first 3000 hp F59PH locomotives have been delivered to GO Transit. The Canadian version of this new model features a full-width carbody, increased cab size for crew comfort and a desk-type control console. Similar to the SD60 model marketed in Canada and the US, the F59PH incorporates microprocessor controls. The first of these is a logic system which controls engine speed, locomotive direction and traction motor switching. The second receives throttle and brake information from the logic system to control wheel creep, dynamic braking and fuel. The third unit

Locomotive models currently available

Model	Engine	Tractive rating (hp)	Axles	Continuous tractive effort (kg)	Axle weight (kg)	Gauge (mm)
G-18U	8-645E	1000	4	15 240	15 218	1000-1676
G-18W	8-645E	1000	4	17 600	16 307	1435-1676
G-22U	12-645E	1500	4	15 132	18 030	1000-1676
G-22W	12-645E	1500	4	17 600	18 552	1435-1676
G-22CU	12-645E	1500	6	22 969	14 061	1000-1676
G-22CW	12-645E	1500	6	26 399	14 878	1435-1676
GL-22C	12-645E	1500	6	20 194	12 738	1000-1676
G-26CU	16-645E	2000	6	22 861	15 599	1000-1676
G-26CW	16-645E	2000	6	26 290	16 310	1435-1676
GL-26C	16-645E	2000	6	19 976	13 562	1000-1676
GT-22CU	12-645E3	2250	6	22 793	16 677	1000-1676
GT-22CW	12-645E3	2250	6	26 237	18 227	1435-1676
GT-22LC	12-645E3	2250	6	20 047	14 303	1000-1676
GT-26CU	16-645E3	2700	6	24 900	17 585	1000-1676
GT-26CW	16-645E3	3000	6	30 490	19 818	1435-1676
SD40-2	16-645E3C	3000	6	70 200	17 690	1435
SD60F	16-710G3	3800	6	83 600	17 690	1435
F40PH-2	16-645E3C	3000	4	46 800	17 690	1435
F59PH	12-710G3	3000	4	65 000	17 690	1435

Note: *Other gear ratios available.

Locomotives / **MANUFACTURERS** 37

assists railway maintenance personnel with computer diagnostics and plain English displays for the power plant, electrical systems, radar and the other microprocessors.

This new model also includes a separate 500 kW three-phase 575 V ac head-end power system to provide base power for the trailing bi-level commuter cars. The heart of this package is an 8V149TI turbocharged Detroit Diesel engine.

Early indications are showing major fuel economy savings over earlier F40PH locomotives in GO Transit commuter operations.

Type F59PH locomotive for GO Transit, Canada

Type GT22LC-2 2250 hp locomotive for RFC Mali

Type GT18L-2 1500 hp locomotive for Bangladesh Railways

Gleismac
Gleismac Italiana Spa

Viale della Stazione 3, 46030 Bigarello (Mantova), Italy

Telephone: +39 376 45301
Telex: 305 224 gleimn i

Products: Remanufacture of diesel locomotives of 40-2000 hp with electric, hydraulic or mechanical transmission for main-line or shunting duty; manufacture of diesel shunting locomotives of 20–330 hp.

Gleismac diesel locomotives

Class	Wheel arrangement	Transmission	Rated power (kW)	Max speed km/h	Total weight tonnes	Builders		
						Mechanical parts	Engine & type	Transmission
L 80	B	Hydrostatic	74	20	10	Gleismac	Deutz	Sauer
LF 170	B	Hydrokinetic	140	30-50	18	Gleismac	Deutz	Twin-Disc
LF 350	B	Hydrokinetic	294	30-50	40	Gleismac	Deutz	Twin-Disc
CF 120	B	Hydrokinetic	88	60	10	Gleismac	Deutz	Clark
CF 200	B	Hydrokinetic	140	80	18	Gleismac	Deutz	Clark
CF 500	B	Hydrokinetic	235	70	13.5	Gleismac	Deutz	Clark

38 MANUFACTURERS / Locomotives

Goninan
A Goninan & Co Ltd

PO Box 21, Broadmeadow, New South Wales 2292, Australia

Telephone: +61 49 699 299
Cable: Platinum, Newcastle
Telex: AA28061
Telefax: +61 49 69 9250

Chairman: D A W Thomson
Chief Executive & Director: John Fitzgerald
General Manager, Railway Products: Barry Henshaw
Engineering & Sales Manager, Railway Products: Anthony Finnegan

Products: Diesel-electric locomotives.

As licensees of the General Electric Company USA, Goninan has completed contracts of eight CM36-7M and four CM39-8 diesel electric locomotives for Mt Newman Mining Co. Three model CM40-8M modernised diesel electric locomotives have also been delivered to another Australian mining company, which has since placed an order for three more. Contracts are currently held for 15 lightweight CM25-8 units for Westrail and 14 CM30-8 streamlined, high-speed locomotives for Australian National's trans-continental service.

Constitution: A Goninan & Co Ltd is one of Australia's largest heavy engineering companies with manufacturing facilities at Newcastle and Taree (New South Wales) and Perth (Western Australia). In the field of rail transport they hold licence agreements with: General Electric, USA; Pullman Technology Inc, USA; Gloucester Carriage & Wagon Co Ltd, UK; Nippon Sharyo Ltd, Japan.

Type CM25-8 lightweight locomotive for Westrail

Artist's impression of CM30-8 locomotives for Australian National

Groupement 50 Hz
50 c/s Group

PO Box 8524, Baumackerstrasse 46, 8050 Zurich, Switzerland

Telephone: +41 1 312 4680/81
Cable: Coordinat, Zurich
Telex: 823 854 sehz ch
Telefax: +41 1 312 3968

Products: Powered vehicles.

Constitution: The Group comprises ACEC Transport of Belgium, GEC Alsthom of France and UK, AEG Westinghouse and Siemens AG of the Federal Republic of Germany.

Recent contracts

User	No of units	Motive power units	Year introduced	Gauge (mm)	Weight (tonnes)	Continuous rating (kW)	Continuous/max speed (km/h)	Remarks/special features
Portuguese Railways (CP)	15	Three-car units, Class 2100	1982	1665	161.4	1200	64.5/120	Series motors for pulsating dc current, lv tap changer, silicon rectifier, rheostatic braking
	9	Mixed traffic Bo-Bo locos	1987/88	1665	78	2940	160 max	Series motors, dc, silicon rectifiers, bridge connection, tap changer
Turkish Railways (TCDD)	15	Electrical equipments for three-car units	1984	1435	—	1020	64.5/120	Series motors for pulsating dc current, semi-controlled silicon rectifiers, rheostatic braking
	15	ditto	1990					
South African Railways (SAR)	25	Freight locos, Class 7E2	1981	1065	126	2925	35/100	Controlled silicon rectifiers with turn-off circuits, rheostatic braking
	40	Freight locos, Class 7E2	1982	1065	126	2925	35/100	
Ferrocarriles de Costa Rica SA (FECOSA)	12	Dual frequency mixed-traffic locos	1981	1067	64	1270	32/80	Silicon rectifier, lv tap changer, rheostatic braking
National Railways of Zimbabwe (NRZ)	30	Freight locos	1982	1067	114	2466	32/100	Motors for pulsating dc current with mixed excitation, semi-controlled silicon rectifiers with turn-off circuits, rheostatic braking
China National Machinery	150	BB+BB locos	1987/88	1435	184	6400	–/108	—
South African Transport Services (SATS)	3	Dual-voltage Class 14E mixed-traffic electric locos	1989	1065	88	4000	72/160	Asynchronous three-phase ac traction motors, inverter with microprocessor control, rheostatic braking

Locomotives / **MANUFACTURERS** 39

Hitachi
Hitachi Ltd

6 Kanda Suragadai, 4-chome, Chiyoda-ku, Tokyo 101, Japan

Telephone: +81 3 258 1111
Cable: Hitachy, Tokyo
Telex: 22395, 22432, 24491, 26375 hitachy

President: Katsushige Mita
Executive Vice President and Director: Masataka Nishi
Board Director: Toshi Kitamura

Products: Electric locomotives, diesel-electric locomotives, diesel-hydraulic locomotives, propulsion systems, auxiliary power supply, ATP/ATO equipment, computerised total systems for urban transportation, bogie and air-conditioning equipment.

Recent sales have included:
12 Series WAG6 heavy-duty electric locomotives for Indian Railways with rated output of 4560 kW at 25 kV ac. These locomotives have direct digital control using microprocessors, power factor corrective filters and a monitoring system.
12 Series E1250 4290 kW (at 3000 V dc) Co-Co high-speed electric locomotives for ONCF (Morocco), having top speed of 160 km/h.
86 electrical equipments for Class 3100 Bo-Bo coal-haulage locomotives for Queensland Railways (Australia) with rated output of 3000 kW at 25 kV ac. Mechanical parts are built by Comeng (Australia).
98 Class HAU-20 and HBU-20 2000 hp Co-Co diesel-electric locomotives for Pakistan Railways (PR).
Seven HAF-24S 2000 hp Co-Co diesel-electric shunting locomotives for China National Technical Import Corporation.
15 Class 23 2000 hp Co-Co type main-line diesel-electric locomotives and 10 Class 19 650 hp Bo-Bo type branch-line locomotives for Malayan Railway Administration (PKTM).

Class WAG6 4560 kW Co-Co electric locomotive for India

2200 hp Co-Co diesel-electric locomotive for Pakistan

Hitachi diesel locomotives since 1986

Class (Railways own designation)	Manufacturer's type	Wheel arrangement	Transmission	Rated power kW	Max speed km/h	Total weight tonnes	No in service 1987	Year first built	Engine & type	Transmission
HBU-20 (Pakistan)	HFA-22B	Co-Co	ac/dc	1640	125	106.7	60	1986	Alco 12-251C4	Hitachi

Hitachi electric locomotives since 1988

Class (Railway's own designation)	Wheel arrangement	Line voltage	Rated output (kW) continuous	Max speed km/h	Weight tonnes	Overall length mm	No in service 1987	Year first built	Builders Mechanical parts	Builders Electrical equipment
WAG6B (Indian Railways)	Bo-Bo-Bo	25 kV ac	4560	100	123	20 670	6	1988	Hitachi	Hitachi
WAG6C (Indian Railways)	Co-Co	25 kV ac	4560	100	123	20 670	6	1988	Hitachi	Hitachi

Hudson
Robert Hudson South Africa (Pty) Ltd

Van Dyk Road, Benoni, 1500
PO Box 299, Benoni, 1500

Telephone: +27 11 915 2410/13, 915 3410/13
Cable: Raletrux

Telex: +27 11 75 0329
Telefax: +27 11 915 2413

Chairman: W R Hudson
Directors: M E Adams, H A Brooke, P J Hoeben (Sales)

Products: Locomotives from 16 to 65 tonnes with various engine and transmission combinations; surface and underground ore hopper wagons; high-speed rail-mounted self-propelled man transporters for mines.

Hungarian Railway Carriage
Hungarian Railway Carriage & Machine Works

Foreign Trade Department, PO Box 50, 9002 Győr, Hungary

Telephone: +36 96 12 300
Cable: RABA Győr
Telex: 02 4255

Products: Passenger cars and freight wagons.

Hunslet
The Hunslet Engine Company Ltd
Member of Hunslet (Holdings) plc

Hunslet Engine Works, Leeds LS10 1BT, England

Telephone: +44 532 432261
Cable: Hunslt, Leeds
Telex: 55237
Telefax: +44 532 420820

53-tonne 525 hp Hunslet locomotive in Nairobi marshalling yard, Kenya Railways

MANUFACTURERS / Locomotives

603 hp radio-controlled shunter for Canadian Gypsum Terminal

450 hp flashproof locomotive for refinery use in Belgium

Chairman: P J O Alcock
Chief Executive: R J K Beaumont
General Sales Manager: D H Townsley

Products: Diesel-mechanical, diesel-hydraulic, diesel-electric and steam locomotives; fully flameproof surface and underground mine diesel locomotives; electric trolley and battery locomotives; flameproof diesel power packs and standard flameproof components; final drive and reverse gearboxes; diesel exhaust gas conditioners; track maintenance equipment.

Constitution: The Hunslet Engine Company has built locomotives since 1864, introduced diesel shunting locomotives in 1927 and pioneered the first flameproof diesel locomotive for coal mine working in 1939. The Hunslet Engine Company incorporates Kerr Stuart & Co, The Avonside Engine Company, Manning Wardle & Co, Kitson & Co, and The Hunslet Group includes the associate companies Hudswell Clarke & Co Ltd, Greenbat (Engineering) Ltd and Andrew Barclay Sons & Co Ltd.

20-tonne battery/trolley locomotives for Channel Tunnel construction

Hunslet Taylor
Hunslet Taylor Consolidated
An operating unit of Hunslet Handling Equipment (Pty) Ltd

PO Box 4142, Basalt Road, Alrode, 1451 Alberton, South Africa

Telephone: +27 11 864 4707/8
Telex: 4 30366

Directors: P J O Alcock
W J Cotterell

Products: Shunting locomotives for surface operations, from 10 to 80 tonnes; underground locomotives from 2½ to 15 tonnes. As the company is now owned by Hunslet of Leeds, England, it can offer locomotives built and designed by either its own plant or by Hunslet, Leeds.

Hyundai
Hyundai Precision & Ind Co Ltd

Head office: Hyundai Building, 140-2, Gye-Dong, Chongro-ku, Seoul, Republic of Korea
Postal address: KPO Box 1677, Seoul

Telephone: +82 2 719 0649
Telex: 23238, 23720 hdpic k
Telefax: +82 2 719 0741

Works: 621 Deokjeong-Dong, Changwon, Kyungnam
Telephone: +82 551 82 1341/50
Telex: 53744 hdpic k

Chairman: Mong Koo Chung
President: Ki Chyul Yoo
Senior Vice President: Kyung Wook Kim

Products: Electric, diesel-electric and diesel-hydraulic locomotives.
In 1987 the company completed development of a new design of diesel-hydraulic five-car train-set for KNR's prestige Seoul-Pusan 'Saemaul' service. Concentration of the power plant in the leading end of each streamlined power car, one at each end of the unit, enabled intermediate trailer weight to be reduced to 38 tonnes tare. Each end car weighed 68 tonnes tare. Engines are MTU 12V396TC13 and transmission is Voith hydraulic. Maximum design speed is 150 km/h.

Affiliated companies
Hyundai Engineering & Construction Co Ltd
Hyundai Building, 140-2, Kye-Dong, Chongro-ku, Seoul
Telephone: +82 2 741 2111/5
Telex: 23111

Products: Design and construction of high-speed railway and underground systems.

3300 hp diesel-electric locomotives for Iranian Islamic Railways

Streamlined 3700 hp diesel-electric locomotive and train-set for Korean National Railways

Locomotives / MANUFACTURERS

Hyundai Engine Manufacturing Co Ltd
1–5, Chonha-Dong, Ulsan, Kyungnam
Telephone: +82 522 5 4141/9
Telex: 53815, 52191

Products: Engines for industrial use.

Hyundai Electrical Engineering Co Ltd
Hyundai Building, 140-2, Kye-Dong, Chongro-ku, Seoul
Telephone: +82 2 741 4151/60
Telex: 25761

Products: Transformers, generators, motors and circuit breakers.

Constitution: HDPIC, an affiliate of the giant Hyundai Business Group, began rolling stock manufacture in mid-1970 as the Locomotive Division of Hyundai Heavy Industries Company (HHI).

HHI produces diesel-electric locomotives under licence from GM-EMD of the USA.

For desirable concentration on mass transit technology related to all types of railway vehicles, Hyundai Rolling Stock Company (HRS) was incorporated in 1978 and maintained until 1985. Effective from June 1985, HRS was consolidated into HDPIC and is being operated as the Rolling Stock Division of HDPIC.

Imesi
Imesi SpA
(Industrie Metalmeccaniche Siciliane)
A member of the Breda Railway Group

Contada Olivelli Pistone, 90044 Carini, Palermo, Italy

Telephone: +39 91 8668677
Cable: Imesi-SpA, Carini
Telex: 910113 imesi i

Chairman: Giuseppe Capuano
General Manager: Angelo Palmieri

Products: Electric and diesel locomotives.

Inirail

Plaza Marqués de Salamanca 3-4, Madrid 28006, Spain

Telephone: +34 1 435 57 08, 435 00 16, 275 15 43
Telex: 49681 dbe e
Telefax: +34 1 577 16 80

Chairman: Eusebio Toral Zuazo
Managing Director: Javier Masolivier y de Marti

Products: Electric, diesel-electric and diesel-hydraulic main-line locomotives; diesel-electric and diesel-hydraulic industrial and shunting locomotives; electric multiple-units; diesel-electric and diesel-hydraulic railcars and multiple-units for underground and suburban service; passenger vehicles, single- and double-deck, baggage, restaurant, etc; wagons with two axles and with bogies, closed platform, low-sided, high-sided, etc; special-purpose wagons, hopper, tank, transport of heavy loads, etc.

Constitution: Inirail was founded in 1982 to promote and co-ordinate the export sales of its two member companies: Ateinsa and Maquinista.

Italtrafo
Italtrafo SpA
Via Nuova delle Brecce 260, Naples, Italy

Telephone: +39 81 266022/7520633
Telex: 71131

Products: Electric and diesel-electric locomotives.

Constitution: Member of Finmeccanica Group.

Jambes-Namur
Ateliers de Construction de Jambes-Namur SA

Rue du le Gare Fleurie 16, 5100 Jambes, Belgium

Telephone: +32 30 18 51
Cable: Jamur Jambes
Telex: 59127

Managing Director: Etienne Offergeld
Chief of Sales: Paul De Groote

Products: Locopulseur Pulso shunting machine, a single-wheel vehicle capable of moving freight cars weighing 160 to 200 tons on straight level track. It can also move cars in curves, split a line of cars and handle a car on a turntable.

Jenbacher
Jenbacher Werke AG

6200 Jenbach, Austria

Telephone: +43 5244 2291-0
Cable: Motor Jenbach
Telex: 053756-7

Managing Director: F Franer
Technical Director: Dr Ebner
Production Manager: Ing Truppe

Products: Diesel-mechanical and diesel-hydraulic rail tractors and locomotives; diesel engines; diesel compressors; diesel generator and pumping sets.

The company's range of locomotives starts with JW-engined diesel-mechanical tractors covering outputs of 6, 7.5, 11 and 15 kW and gauges of 430 to 1435 mm; it includes models with adjustable gauge and others for underground duty.

In locomotives of up to 880 kW a fluid-drive reversing gearbox simplifies application of remote radio control; locomotives of more than 440 kW are also fitted with electronic anti-slip protection.

Constitution: The company was started in 1946 for the manufacture of diesel engines and combined units.

Diesel-hydraulic shunter standard range

	DH200B26	DH400B40	DH700C60	DH1000 B-B80
Power output (kW)	164	300	530	735
No of axles	2	2	3	4
Gauge (mm)	1435	1435	1435	1435
Weight (tonnes)	26	32/42	54	80
Starting traction (kN)	84.4	103.8/129.8	195	260
Speed (km/h)	30	35	60	40
Minimum turning radius (m)	35	35	70	50
Engine	Perkins TV8.540	Mercedes-Benz OM 204	Jenbach C240S	Jenbach C320S
Gearbox model	Clark 32 000	Clark 8000	Clark 16 000 or Voith	Voith

---

Jung
Arn Jung Lokomotivfabrik GmbH

Postfach 20, 5242 Jungenthal bei Kirchen a/d Sieg, Federal Republic of Germany

Telephone: +49 2741 6831
Cable: Lokomotivfabrik, Kirchen-Sieg
Telex: 08 753 19

Products: Electric and diesel locomotives.

Typical of recent production is the RC 43 C diesel-hydraulic locomotive designed for shunting and branch-line duties. Designed as a three-axle rigid-frame locomotive, it is driven by an MTU four-stroke diesel engine and equipped with Voith hydrodynamic forward/reverse transmission. The axles are driven via cardan shafts and axle gear boxes. Axles have rubber springs and are equipped with hydraulic shock absorbers. Controls are electro-pneumatic. In service with Deutsche Bundesbahn the locomotive is frequently equipped with radio control equipment.

MANUFACTURERS / Locomotives

Kaelble-Gmeinder
Kaelble-Gmeinder GmbH

Postfach 1355, 6950 Mosbach, Baden, Federal Republic of Germany

Telephone: +49 6261 80617
Cable: Gmeinder, Mosbachbaden
Telex: 04 66111
Telefax: +49 6261 80660

Managing Director: Olof N E Enmark
Head of Rail Traction Division: Gerhard Wuschick

Products: Diesel locomotives with electric, hydrodynamic or hydrostatic power transmission systems and engine output up to 1100 kW, suitable for narrow-, standard- or broad-gauge; locomotives with dual power systems, diesel-electric/electric, battery/electric for operations in tunnels; flameproof diesel locomotives for chemical industries and flameproof battery locomotives for underground mining operations; propulsion bogie systems for application to any kind of special railway vehicles, such as snow ploughs, rail grinding and track maintenance vehicles.

Kaelble-Gmeinder Type D75 B-B

Kaelble-Gmeinder Type D60C

Kaelble-Gmeinder Type D construction locomotive for Singapore MRT

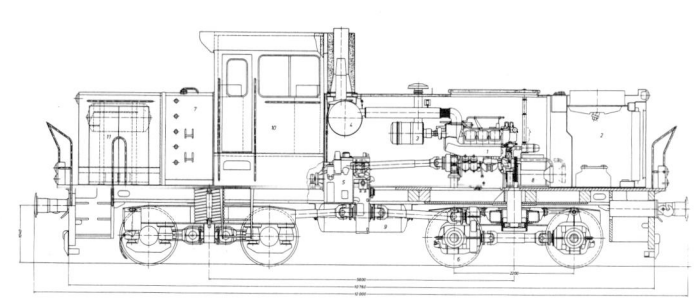

Kaelble-Gmeinder Type D100 B-B

General arrangement of Type D100 B-B

Kalmar
Kalmar Verkstads AB

PO Box 943, S-39129 Kalmar, Sweden

Telephone: +46 480 15070
Cable: Kvab, Kalmar
Telex: 43029
Telefax: +46 480 18979

Chairman: Sven Arnerius
Managing Director: K Harry Eriksson

Products: Diesel-electric locomotives, diesel-hydraulic shunting locomotives.
Important recent sales have been: 33 diesel-electric locomotives, for Swedish State Railways (SJ). In collaboration with ABB the company is involved in the design and delivery to SJ of 20 Type X-2 tilt-body 200 km/h train-sets.

SJ Type T44 1650 hp diesel-electric locomotive for heavy shunting and freight haulage geared for 105–140 km/h max speeds

Locomotives / **MANUFACTURERS** 43

Development in progress includes diesel shunting locomotives.

Constitution: Kalmar Verkstad was founded in 1902 and is Swedish State Railways' (SJ) major supplier of diesel locomotives, railcars and passenger cars. In 1989 Kalmar Verkstad was acquired by ASEA Brown Boveri (ABB).

Co-operation agreements: Kalmar Verkstad is associated with General Motors Electromotive Division, USA.

Kawasaki
Kawasaki Heavy Industries Ltd, Rolling Stock Group

Head office: World Trade Centre Building, 4-1 Hamamatsu-cho 2-chome, Minato-ku, Tokyo, Japan

Telephone: +81 3 2867 3 0022
Cable: Kawasaki Heavy, Tokyo
Telex: 22672, 26888, (domestic) 242-4371

Works: 1/18 Wadayama-Dori 2-chome, Hyogo-ku, Kobe
Telephone: +81 78 671 5021

2857-2, Naka Okamoto, Kawachi-cho, Kawachi-Gun, Tochigi Pref
Telephone: +81 3 435 2589

Chairman: Zenji Umeda
President: Kenko Hasegawa
Executive Vice Presidents: Renzo Nihei
　　　　　　　　　　　　　Yutaki Onishi
Director (Rolling Stock): Masahiko Ishizawa

Products: Electric, diesel-electric, diesel-hydraulic locomotives.

Kawasaki has been a member of Japanese consortia supplying 80 electric locomotives to Chinese National Railways and 26 diesel-electric locomotives to the Malayan Railway Administration.

Constitution: Kawasaki Heavy Industries Ltd was formed in 1969 by the merger of Kawasaki Rolling Stock Manufacturing Co, Kawasaki Aircraft Co and Kawasaki Dockyard Co Ltd. In 1972 Kisha Seizo Kaisha Ltd was taken over and merged into Kawasaki Heavy Industries Ltd.

Kolmex
Foreign Trade Enterprise Co Ltd

Mokotowska 49, 00-542 Warsaw, Poland

Telephone: +48 22 28 22 91
Cable: Kolmex, Warsaw
Telex: 813270; 813714
Telefax: +48 22 295879

Managing Director: Aleksander Gudzowaty

Sales Directors: Aleksander Kociszewski
　　　　　　　　　Wieslaw Husraski
　　　　　　　　　Elzbieta Zaleska

Products: Electric and diesel locomotives.
The Type 302 D main-line diesel locomotive is an example of the family being manufactured by Cegielski Works. This locomotive is powered by a 3000 hp engine, has electric transmission, and incorporates an internal combustion engine to drive its electric heating generator. Maximum speed is 140 km/h. Its power unit is an air-cooled, supercharged Type 2116 SSF 16-cylinder engine, built under Fiat licence, and a synchronous 150 c/sec frequency ac main generator. All basic recommendations of the international UIC requirements have been taken into account in the design and construction.

Constitution: Kolmex acts as sole exporter of railway motive power, passenger and freight stock manufactured in Poland, and as purchaser of imported equipment. Between 1947 and 1989 Kolmex export production has totalled 2536 locomotives, 9250 passenger coaches, 201,374 freight wagons and 33,377 containers. Kolmex has exported rolling stock units and containers to 44 countries.

Type 201E 3040 kW 3 kV dc Co-Co electric in Polish State Railways (PKP) service as Class ET22

Type 302 D 2200 kW diesel-electric locomotive

Krauss-Maffei
Krauss-Maffei Aktiengesellschaft

Krauss-Maffei Strasse 2, 8000 Munich 50, Federal Republic of Germany

Telephone: +49 89 88991
Cable: Kraussmaffei, Münchenallach
Telex: 05 23 163-91
Telefax: +49 89 8899 2206

Board of Directors: Dipl Ing Werner Görlitz
　　　　　　　　　　Wolfgang Harttrumpf
Sales Director: Walter Tichy

Products: Electric, diesel-electric and diesel-hydraulic locomotives; electronic slip and speed control systems, automatic drive and brake control systems; test stands and simulators for testing of railway vehicles and components; tracked high-speed transport systems based on contact-free magnetic levitation and guidance (Transrapid) system.

For 150 years Krauss-Maffei has been associated with important innovations in rail-wheel transport. Krauss-Maffei's current programme comprises electric and diesel locomotives for all duties, gauges, speeds and for both main-line and industrial services. In 1988 the company was supplying Class 120 electric locomotive series with three-phase motors and the power units of the high-speed Intercity Express train-sets to the German Federal Railway (DB). The Transrapid

Standard three-axle Type MH 05 700 hp diesel-hydraulic shunter

Standard 1000 hp multi-purpose diesel locomotive, offered with ac/ac or ac/dc transmission, as supplied to Turkish State Railways

44 MANUFACTURERS / Locomotives

Class 120 5600 kW locomotive with three-phase propulsion for DB

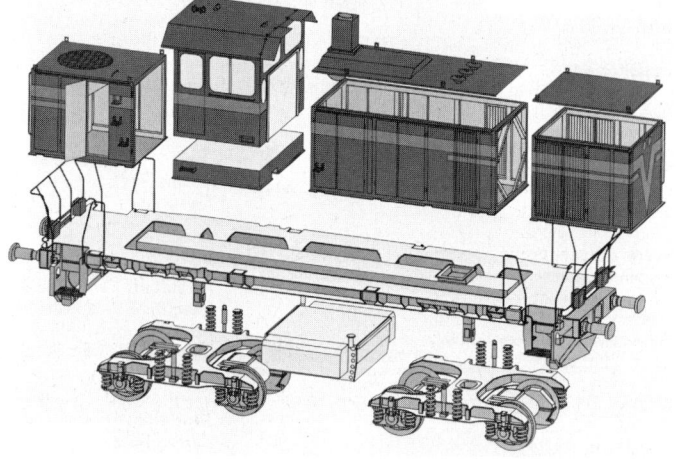

Modular design of K-M standard 1000 hp Type ME 07/DE 1000 diesel-electric locomotive

magnetically-levitated high-speed train with a capacity of 200 passengers reached 412 km/h in early 1988.

In addition Krauss-Maffei offers a comprehensive programme of peripheral systems for wheel-rail transport. Activities range from the development and supply of electronic control and diagnosis systems to the design and supply of highly sophisticated test stands and simulators.

Constitution: The present firm of Krauss-Maffei was created by the merger in 1931 of two locomotive builders, J A Maffei AG, founded in 1837, and Krauss & Co KG, founded in 1866. In 1935–37 a factory, replacing the former two plants, was erected at Allach, a suburb of Munich.

Prototype ICE high-speed train-set with three-phase propulsion for DB

Krauss-Maffei recent electric locomotives

Class (Railway's own designation)	Wheel arrangement	Line voltage	Rated output (kW) continuous/ one-hour	Max speed km/h	Weight tonnes	Overall length mm	No in service 1988 (on order)	Year first built	Builders — Mechanical parts	Builders — Electrical equipment	Remarks
Class 120 (DB)	Bo-Bo	15 kV 16⅔ Hz	5600	200	84	19 200	5 27 (+33)	1980 1987 1988	Krauss-Maffei,† Krupp, Thyssen-Henschel	AEG, BBC, Siemens	Three-phase propulsion system
Class 401 ICE power unit (DB)	Bo-Bo	15 kV 16⅔ Hz	4800	300	76	20 810	2 (80§)	1985 1989	Krauss-Maffei,‡ Krupp, Thyssen-Henschel	AEG, BBC, Siemens	Three-phase propulsion system

† Jointly designed, developed and supplied by Krauss-Maffei, Krupp and Thyssen-Henschel under leadership of Krauss-Maffei
‡ Jointly designed, developed and supplied by Krauss-Maffei, Krupp and Thyssen-Henschel under leadership of Krupp
§ One prototype and 80 series units to be supplied 1989-91

Krauss-Maffei recent diesel locomotives

Class (Railway's own designation)	Manufacturer's type	Wheel arrangement	Transmission	Rated power (kW)	Max speed km/h	Total weight tonnes	No in service 1988	Year first built	Builders — Mechanical parts	Builders — Engine & type	Builders — Transmission
*	MH 05	C	Hydraulic	500	40	60/66	5	1984	Krauss-Maffei	MTU 6 V 396TC12 6 V 396TC13	Voith L 3r4U2
TCDD Class 11000 (Turkey)	ME 07/ DE 1000	Bo-Bo	Electric	735	90	68	50	1985	Krauss-Maffei	MTU 8 V 396TC13	BBC ac/dc GEC ac/ac
RENFE Class 354 (Spain)	M 4000 B-B	B-B	Hydraulic	3070	180	80	8	1982	Krauss-Maffei	2× MTU 16 V 396TC13	Voith L 520rzU2

* Various industrial and private railway companies
† Components for 30 locomotives produced under license by TÜLOMSAS/Eskisehir

---

Krupp
Krupp Maschinentechnik GmbH

Helenenstrasse 149, 4300 Essen 1, Federal Republic of Germany

Telephone: +49 201 363-0
Cable: Krupp, Essen
Telex: 8 57 767-0 kmd
Telefax: +49 201 324449

Chairman: Dr Ing Gerd Weber
Vice-Chairman, Mechanical Engineering: Dipl Ing Günter Kaes
General Manager, Railway Engineering: Dipl Ing Heinrich Gerdsmeier
Marketing Manager: Dipl Vw Horst Boege

Products: Electric, diesel-electric and diesel-hydraulic locomotives; power supply systems for LRV, emus, railcars and coaches.

Recent contracts have covered:
1986/88: Burma Railways Corporation: 19 diesel-hydraulic locomotives Type M 1200, 920 kW.
1987: ONATRA, Zaire: five diesel-electric locomotives Type U15C, 1265 kW.
1987/89: German Federal Railway: 20 three-phase locomotives Class E 120, 5600 kW.
1989/91: German Federal Railway: 28 Class 401 power units, 4800 kW for ICE high-speed train-sets.

The Krupp standard diesel locomotive range includes locomotives with both hydraulic and electric transmissions. The diesel-electric locomotives are equipped with engines and electric equipment made by the General Electric Company, USA. The engine is of the

Locomotives / **MANUFACTURERS** 45

FDL series in 8-or 12-cylinder versions with exhaust-driven turbocharger and charge-air inter-cooler.

For the lower power range transmission is by dc generator, in the medium power range either by dc generator or alternator with subsequent full-wave rectifying system, and in the upper power range by alternator. Both dc generator and alternator are diesel engine-mounted.

Control devices are grouped in dust- and moisture-resistant steel compartments. Reverser and line contactors are electro-pneumatically operated. Other contactors are magnetically-operated. The locomotives can be built either with only one driver's cab (with one or two control desks) or with a driver's cab at each end.

Bogies are of the high-adhesion, lateral-motion, swivel type, and can be supplied in cast-steel or fabricated in all gauges from 1000 to 1676 mm. There is a choice of Bo-Bo, A1A-A1A or Co-Co arrangements. Braking options include rheostatic.

Type M1200 diesel-hydraulic B-B for Burma Railways Corporation

Class ET 401 power car of IC-Express high-speed production train-sets for German Federal Railway

Type U30C 2394 kW diesel-electric locomotive for Tazara Railway

Type BB 304 1269 kW diesel-hydraulic B-B for Indonesian State Railways (PJKA)

Class E120 5600 kW electric locomotive for DB

46 MANUFACTURERS / Locomotives

Krupp electric locomotives recently delivered

Railway's own designation	Wheel arrangement	Line voltage	Rated output (kW) continuous	Max speed km/h	Weight tonnes	Overall length mm	No delivered (on order)	Years built	Builders		
									Mechanical parts	Electrical equipment	Remarks special features
DB E120.1	Bo-Bo	15 kV 16⅔ Hz	5600	200	84	19200	20 (60)	1987/88	Krupp (Henschel Krauss-Maffei)	AEG, BBC, Siemens	Universal locomotive three-phase transmission
DB ET410	Bo-Bo	15 kV 16⅔ Hz	3640	350	78	20810	1 (2)	1985	Krupp (Henschel, Krauss Maffei)	AEG, BBC, Siemens	Power unit of ICE (prototype three-phase transmission
DB ET401	Bo-Bo	15 kV 16⅔ Hz	4800	250	80	20560	28 (82)	1989/91	Krupp (Henschel, Krauss Maffei)	AEG, BBC, Siemens	Power unit of ICE three-phase transmission

Krupp diesel locomotives recently delivered

Railway	Manufacturer's type	Wheel arrangement	Transmission	Rated power (kW)	Max speed km/h	Total weight tonnes	No delivered	Years built	Builders		
									Mechanical parts	Engine & type	Transmission
Burma DD 1200	M1200	B-B	Hydraulic	920	90	48.8	19	1986/88	Krupp	MTU 12V396TC12	Voith
Indonesia BB 304	M1500	B-B	Hydraulic	1140	120	52	25	1976/83	Krupp	MTU 12V652TB11	Voith
Zaire/ONATRA	U15C	Co-Co	Electric	1265	103	99	13	1982/87	Krupp	GE 8FDL7	GE
Zambia	U20C	Co-Co	Electric	1537	103	99	10	1981	Krupp	Ge 12FDL7	GE
Botswana BD	UM22C	Co-Co	Electric	1552	114	96	12	1982	Krupp	GE 12FDL7	GE
Thailand	AD2400	Co-Co	Electric	1655	100	82.5	15	1981	Krupp	Pielstick 16PA4-185VG	Alsthom
Tanzania/ Zambia (TAZARA)	U30C	Co-Co	Electric	2394	103	120	14	1983/84	Krupp	GE 12FDL7	GE

Kuibyshev
Kuibyshev Diesel Locomotive Works

Kolomensk, USSR

Products: Diesel locomotives. Current production for the Soviet Railways comprises Classes TEP60, 2TEP60 and TEP70 (for details see under USSR in Railway Systems section).

Kyosan Kogyo
Kyosan Kogyo Co Ltd

8-36 Mikawa-minami-machi, Fukushima 960, Japan

Telephone: +81 245 34 4191

Products: Diesel-hydraulic locomotives.

LEW
VEB Lokomotivbau-Elektrotechnische Werke "Hans Beimler"

Head office: 1422 Hennigsdorf, German Democratic Republic

Export sales: AHB Schienenfahrzeuge Export-Import

Telephone: +37 50
Cable: Elektrolok
Telex: 01 158 531

Type EL 20 electric locomotive in service in the USSR

Type BR 243 main-line electric locomotive

Locomotives / **MANUFACTURERS** 47

LEW electric locomotives

Class	Wheel arrangement	Line voltage	Rated ouput (kW) continuous	Max speed km/h	Weight tonnes	No in service	Year first built	Builders Mechanical parts	Electrical equipment
BR 212/243	Bo-Bo	15 kV 16⅔ Hz	3720	140/120	82.5	102	1982	LEW	LEW
EL 20 + 2 motor dump wagons	Bo-Bo + Bo-Bo + Bo-Bo	10 kV 50 Hz	3 × 1840	50	3 × 122	4	1983	LEW	LEW
EL 21	Bo-Bo-Bo	1.5 kV	2100	65	160	135	1981	LEW	LEW
EL 16/03	B	112 V*	17	6	12	8	1982	LEW	LEW

* Battery voltage

Products: Electric, diesel-hydraulic and diesel-electric locomotives; special electric locomotives.

Recent products include the Type 243 B-B 15 kV 16⅔ Hz electric locomotive for Deutsche Reichsbahn (DR). The thyristor-controlled Type 243 is a 3720 kW machine weighing 82.5 tonnes, with a length of 16.64 m and a starting tractive effort of 248 kN. By early 1988 310 had been built for the DR.

The high-voltage power control embodies a 31-step multiple-contact switch and a thyristor regulator with opto-electronic transmission elements. The controlling and regulating circuits, a complex information electronics unit, have been designed on the basis of highly integrated circuits.

A new offer for industrial users is the Type EL 20, an assembly of three motorised Bo-Bo vehicles of which only one is a control cab unit; the other two are dumper wagons each with a load capacity of 55 tonnes. The EL 20 is essentially an electric vehicle, which can be arranged for either overhead or conductor-rail current pick-up, but for work in excavation areas without traction current supply it can operate as a diesel-electric powered by an 810 kW diesel engine. All power equipment is concentrated in the control unit. Each of the three motorised Bo-Bo units has a 1840 kW rating on electric power, so that the set can cope with a trailing load of up to 1800 tonnes on gradients as steep as 1 in 25 (with diesel-electric power the limiting grade on such tonnage is 1 in 100). The EL 20 is designed for work in temperatures ranging from –50 to +40°C.

The range of industrial locomotives made by Kombinat VEB LEW Hennigsdorf includes the electric EL 21, which has been developed for open-cast mine duty; 135 of the type, which was introduced in 1981, are in service in the USSR. The EL21 is an articulated Bo-Bo-Bo suited to operate at ambient temperatures as low as –50°C and for employment on gradients as steep as 4 per cent. Its force-ventilated, series-wound, nose-suspended motors can be arranged either in series, with two motors each in three parallel groups, or all in parallel to achieve a maximum economy in operation. Control of tractive force, electric brake power and speed is by a contactor control system and with force-ventilated starting and braking resistors.

Macosa
Material y Construcciones, SA

Head office: Plaza de la Independencia 8, Madrid 28001, Spain

Telephone: +34 1 522 4787
Cable: Material, Madrid
Telex: 22168

Works: Herreros 2, Barcelona
Telephone: +34 3 307 05 00; Telex: 52286
San Vicente 273, Valencia
Telephone: +34 6 377 39 00; Telex: 62452

Marqués de Mudela 10, Alcazar de San Juan
Telephone: +34 26 54 1124   Telex: 23692

President: Eduardo Santos
Vice President: Pedro Nueno
Managing Director: Emilio Daroca
Financial Director: José Miguel Olabarria
Rolling Stock Director: Andrés Soler
Export Director: José Sanz

Products: Electric, diesel-electric and diesel-hydraulic locomotives.

The company builds General Motors-type diesel-electric locomotives under licence and on this basis has recently supplied Type GT26CU-2 units to CVRD, Brazil; Type J26CW/AC locomotives to Iraq; and Type G22 locomotives to Yugoslavia.

Recent work for Spanish National Railways (RENFE) has included reconstruction of 20 Class 319 diesel-electric locomotives as heavy freight hauliers.

Constitution: This company was formed in 1947 by the merger of Material para Ferrocarriles y Construcciones SA of Barcelona and Construcciones Devis SA of Valencia.

MaK
Krupp MaK Maschinenbau GmbH

PO Box 9009, 2300 Kiel 17, Federal Republic of Germany

Telephone: +49 431 3811
Cable: MaK, Kiel
Telex: 02 99877/78

Directors: Dr-Ing M Link
H-O Brockmeier
Dr-Ing U Schaller
Dr rer-pol Hollunder

MaK Type DE 1002 1350 kW three-phase diesel-electric locomotives for Netherlands Railways

MaK Type G 763 diesel-hydraulic shunting locomotives for Genoa port authority, Italy

MaK Type DE 502 with three-phase electric transmission

MANUFACTURERS / Locomotives

Products: Diesel-hydraulic locomotives from 315 kW up to 2650 kW; diesel-electric three-phase locomotives from 500 kW to 2650 kW; axle drives for diesel-electric and diesel-hydraulic locomotives; bogies; electronic control equipment.

In conjunction with ABB, the company has received an order from Netherlands Railways for 120 diesel-electric locomotives with three-phase transmission based on the MaK standard Type DE1002 design. The locomotives are being built at MaK's Kiel works and delivery began in January 1988.

Constitution: A member of the Krupp group, Krupp MaK has designed and produced diesel locomotives since 1925.

Prototype Type DE 1024 2600 kW diesel-electric locomotive for trial service on DB

MaK three-phase standard locomotive designs for narrow-gauge

Service	Heavy shunting and light line	Line	Heavy line
Axle arrangement	Co-Co	Co-Co	Co-Co
Service weight*	90 tonnes	90 tonnes	105 tonnes
Max speed*	80 km/h	100 km/h	100 km/h
Starting tractive effort*	31 tonnes	31 tonnes	36 tonnes
Diesel engine MaK	6 M 282	8 M 282	12 M 282
Type	Water-cooled, four-stroke, exhaust turbocharged with charge-air cooling		
Cylinder arrangement	6 in line	8 in line	12 vee
Engine rating	1200 kW (1600 hp)	1600 kW (2200 hp)	2650 kW (3600 hp)
Engine speed		1000 rpm	
Power transmission BBC	Three-phase asynchronous traction motors controlled by static converters		

* Alternative lay-out possible

MaK three-phase locomotive designs for standard-/broad-gauge

Service	Heavy shunting and light line	Line	Heavy line
Axle arrangement	Bo-Bo	Bo-Bo	Co-Co
Service weight*	80 tonnes	80 tonnes	120 tonnes
Max speed*	80 km/h	120 km/h	120 km/h
Starting tractive effort*	27 tonnes	27 tonnes	41 tonnes
Diesel engine MaK	6 M 282	8 M 282	12 M 282
Type	Water-cooled, four-stroke, exhaust turbocharged with charge-air cooling		
Cylinder arrangement	6 in line	8 in line	12 vee
Engine rating	1200 kW (1600 hp)	1600 kW (2200 hp)	2650 kW (3600 hp)
Engine speed		1000 rpm	
Power transmission BBC	Three-phase asynchronous traction motors controlled by static converters		

* Alternative lay-out possible

MaK diesel locomotives in production

Class	Wheel arrangement	Transmission	Rated power (kW)	Max speed km/h*	Total weight tonnes*	Year first built	Engine & type	Transmission
G 321	B	Hydr	315	22; 35	32–40	1981	KHD BF 10L 413F	Voith L2r4
G 760	C	Hydr	560	32; 40	60–68	1977	MTU 6V 396 TC 13	Voith L3r4
DE 502	Co	Elec (3-phase)	560	45	60–66	1980	MTU 6V 396 TC 13	ABB
DE 1002	Bo-Bo	Elec (3-phase)	1180	90	80–100	1982	MTU 12V 396 TC 13	ABB
			1350	90	80–100	1986	MWM TBD 604 DV12	
G1203	B-B	Hydr	750	35–70	70–100	1980	MTU 8V 296 TC 13	Voith L4r4
G1204	B-B	Hydr	1120	42–80	80–100	1978	MTU 12V 396 TC 13	Voith L5r4
DE 6400	Bo-Bo	Elec (3-phase)	1170	120	80	1988	MTU 12V 396 TC 13	ABB
DE 1024	Co-Co	Elec (3-phase)	2650	160	120	1989	MaK 12 M 282	ABB

* available alternatives

Maquinista, La
La Maquinista Terrestre y Maritima SA

General offices, technical bureaus and works: Calle Fernando Junoy 2-64, PO Box 94, 08030 Barcelona, Spain

Telephone: +34 93 345 5700
Cable: Maquinista, Barcelona
Telex: 54539 maqui e
Telefax: +34 93 345 6958

President: D Miguel Sa enz de Viguera y Aizpurua
Commercial Director: Pere Solé Raventós
Export Director: D Javier Masoliver y de Marti

Locomotives / **MANUFACTURERS** 49

Products: Electric and diesel locomotives (200–6000 hp); bogies and freight wagons; diesel engines for locomotives and railcars; traction motors; generators; converters and miscellaneous electrical equipment.

In 1988 the company was manufacturing for RENFE 60 Type S-311 diesel-electric shunting locomotives.

Constitution: Since 1855 La Maquinista has specialised in production of railway equipment. Largest shareholder is the Instituto Nacional de Industria (INI).

Type DH-700 720 hp diesel-hydraulic shunter for RENFE

Type S-311 750 kW diesel-electric shunting locomotive with three-phase asynchronous motors for RENFE, the first all-Spanish industry locomotive design

Electric locomotives by La Maquinista

Class	Wheel arrangement	Line voltage	Rated output (kW) continuous/one-hour	Max speed km/h	Weight tonnes	No in service 1988	Year first built	Builders	
								Mechanical parts	Electrical equipment
250 (RENFE)	Co-Co	3000 dc	4600/4940	160	120	36	1982	MTM	BBC

Diesel locomotives by La Maquinista

Class	Wheel arrangement	Transmission	Rated power (kW)	Max speed km/h	Total weight tonnes	No in service 1988	Year first built	Builders		
								Mechanical parts	Engine & type	Transmission
1600 (FEVE)	B+B	Elec (three-phase)	1102	80	60	10	1985	MTM	SACM 175V16BZSHR	
DH-700 (RENFE)	C	Hyd	530	50	54	20	1985	MTM	Bazán MTU 6V396TC13	Voith
DH-200	B	Hyd	132	24	26	6	1978	MTM	Pegaso 9105	Voith
DH-300	B	Hyd	228	40	40	8	1980	MTM	Pegaso 9156	Voith
DH-600	C	Hyd	456	50	60	1	1982	MTM	Guascor E-318 TO	Voith
S-311	Bo-Bo	Elec (three-phase)	750	100	80	1 (+ 60 in manufacture)	1985	Ateinsa BWE	Bazán MTU 8V396TC13	MTM-Siemens

Materfer
Materfer SA

Suipacha 1109, Pisos 2° and 5°, 1008 Buenos Aires, Argentina

Telephone: +54 1 313 0870/1296
+54 1 313 0927/0900
Telex: 25175 catmg ar
Telefax: +54 1 331 5491

Works: Fábrica Materfer SA
Ruta 9, Km 694, 5123 Ferreyra, Córdoba, Argentina
Telephone: +54-51 97 2730/32/34
Telefax: +54-51 97 2489
Telex: 51300 MAT SA

President: Lic Eduardo Jorge Nava
Vice-President: Dr Edgardo Héctor Iriarte
General Manager: Ing Enzo Nicolás Filipelli
Commercial Director: Antonio Maltana

Group companies: Centro de Actividades Termomécanicas SA (CAT), Grandes Motores Diésel SA (GMD) and Industrias de Generación de Energia Electromecánica SA (INGEAS).

Products: Diesel-electric locomotives, rotating electrical equipment.

Materfer has manufactured 42 1000–2000 kW dc locomotives and rebuilt 42 1200 kW ones.

GMD has a contract for the systematisation of 28 different locomotive types such as: 15 GE 18C locomotives using A230 12 series engines; 12 GAIA locomotives using AL 230 8 series engines; 1 GAIA locomotive using the ALCO 255B engine.

INGESA is a regular supplier of rotating electrical equipment and spares, recently having rebuilt over 1500 traction motors and manufactured more than 500 new ones.

GMD-CAT, together with Materfer and INGESA, have a contract for sequential revision at 200,000 km of ALCO RSD 16 locomotives.

The group of companies is also rebuilding 40 ALCO RSD 16 locomotives, manufacturing 40 new ALCO 251C 2050 hp engines, and repairing 40 WABCO compressors.

Mecanoexportimport

10 Mihail Eminescu Street, Bucharest, Romania

Telephone: +40 0 1198 55
Cable: Mecanex, Bucharest
Telex: 10 269
Telefax: 22 107

Products: Electric, diesel-electric and diesel-hydraulic locomotives, multi-function rail/road vehicles, rotary snowploughs.

Mecanoexportimport is the export sales company for the Romanian railway supply industry. (For the

Type DE626 BL2 diesel-electric locomotive

50 MANUFACTURERS / Locomotives

majority of the locomotive designs available see the entries for Electroputere and '23 August' Works.) Recent exported products include:

Type DE626 BL2 diesel-electric locomotive
Wheel arrangement: Co-Co
Power: 2640 hp
Gauge: 1435 mm
Type of diesel engine: Alco 12R251ELO
Max speed: 100 km/h
Total weight: 120 tonnes
Length over couplers: 19 200 mm
Continuous tractive effort: 240 kN
Max tractive effort: 314 kN

LEM 25 kV ac electric locomotive
Gauge: 1435 mm
Wheel arrangement: Co-Co
Power: 1200 kW
Max speed: 100 km/h
Total weight: 126 tonnes
Length over couplers: 18 000 mm
Continuous tractive effort: 270 kN
Max tractive effort: 390 kN

LEM 1200 kW 25 kV ac electric locomotive

Recent electric locomotives

Type	Wheel arrangement	Line voltage	Rated output (kW) continuous/one-hour	Max speed km/h	Weight tonnes	Overall length mm	Year first built	Builders Mechanical parts	Electrical equipment
46.000	Co-Co	25 kV ac	5100/5400	130	126	19 800	1986	Electroputere ICM Caransebes	Electroputere
LEM	Co-Co	25 kV ac	1200/1270	80	111/126	18 000	1984	Electroputere ICM Caransebes	Electroputere
LEMC	Bo	3 × 380 V ac	170	17	28/34	7520	1986	Electroputere ICM Caransebes	Electroputere
LEML	Bo	3 × 660 V ac	84	15	126	16 190	1988	Electroputere	Electroputere

Recent diesel locomotives

Type	Wheel arrangement	Transmission	Rated power (kW)	Max speed km/h	Total weight tonnes	Year first built	Builders Mechanical parts	Engine & type	Transmission
ND3	Co-Co	dc/dc	1540/1200	100	126	1984	Electroputere ICM Coransebes	ICM Reşita Sulzer 12 LDA28	Electroputere
61	Co-Co	ac/dc	1940/1450	100	114	1984	Electroputere ICM Coransebes	ICM Reşita Alco 12R 251	Electroputere
60-351÷360	Co-Co	ac/dc	1940/1450	100	120	1986	Electroputere ICM Coransebes	ICM Reşita Alco 12R 251	Electroputere
DE626BL2	Co-Co	ac/dc	1940/1380	100	120	1989	Electroputere ICM Caransebes	ICM Reşita Alco 12R251	Electroputere

Mitsubishi Electric
Mitsubishi Electric Corporation

Mitsubishi Denki Building, 2-3 Marunouchi, 2-chome, Chiyoda-ku, Tokyo 100, Japan

Telephone: +81 3 218 2111
Cable: Melco, Tokyo
Telex: 24532

President: Moriya Shiki
Vice-President, International Operations Group: Shinichi Yufu
General Manager, Overseas Marketing Division, Heavy Machinery: Kenji Kimura

Products: Complete electric locomotives, diesel-electric locomotives.

Recent sales have included: 30 Series 251 B-B-B chopper-controlled locomotives with rated output of 4650 kW at 3 kV dc; 169 Series 269, 279, 289 B-B locomotives; and four Series 269 B-B chopper-controlled locomotives for Spanish National Railways (RENFE) with rated output of 3100 kW at 3 kV dc, maximum speed 160 km/h, weight 88 tonnes. Traction and auxiliary electrical equipment for 56

Class 251 B-B-B with chopper control for Spanish National Railways (RENFE)

Class 6K 25 kV 4800 kW Bo-Bo-Bo for China: mechanical parts by Kawasaki Heavy Industry, electrical equipment by Mitsubishi

Locomotives / **MANUFACTURERS** 51

Electric locomotives equipped by Mitsubishi Electric since 1985

Class	Railway	Wheel arrangement	Line voltage	Rated output (kW) continuous	Max speed km/h	Weight tonnes	No in service	Year first built	Builders Mechanical parts	Electrical equipment
Ac electric locomotives										
ED (for Burma)	–	Bo-Bo	25 kV	440	48	48	4	1986	Kawasaki Heavy Industry	Mitsubishi Electric
6K (for China)	–	Bo-Bo-Bo	25 kV	4800	100	138	80†	1987	Kawasaki Heavy Industry	Mitsubishi Electric

† To be built

diesel-electric locomotives and 64 electric locomotives for NSW SRA of Australia.
110 electric locomotives for JNR (since 1970).
In 1988 delivery continued of Chinese Railways order for 80 ac electric locomotives with advanced features such as large-capacity thyristor technology and microcomputer-digital control.

Constitution: A member of the Mitsubishi Group.

Moës
Moteurs Moës, SA

62 rue de Huy, 4370 Waremme, Belgium

Telephone: +32 19 32 23 52, 32 64 53
Cable: Motormoës
Telex: 41568
Fax: +32 19 323448

Chairman: M Fraidbise
Managing Director: M Thirion
Sales Director: J Antoine

Products: Narrow-gauge diesel-hydraulic, diesel-mechanical, diesel-mining locomotives of 3–30 tonnes, 15–254 hp.

Morrison Knudsen
Morrison Knudsen Corporation

Mailing Address: PO Box 73, Boise, Idaho 83707, USA

Telephone: +1 208 386 5950
Cable: Emkayan
Telex: 368439 emkayan bse e
Telefax: +1 208 386 6171

Chairman & Chief Executive Officer: W M Agee
President: F M Adams
Rail Systems Group President: J G Fearon
Director, Marketing and Sales: M Monteferrante

Principal subsidiary companies
MK-Ferguson Company
MK-Environmental Services Division
MKE Transportation and Water Resources Division

Products: Locomotive remanufacturing.
Morrison Knudsen Corporation, or MK, maintains three major facilities for remanufacture: in Boise, Idaho; in Hornell, New York; and in Mountaintop, PA. Locomotive services include: complete engine rebuild, complete rewiring, electrical cabinet update and modification, bogie rebuilding, cab and hood fabrication, fuel tank fabrication, repainting, load testing, wheel trueing, air brake rebuild and frame fabrication.

GP40M-2 locomotive

SD40M-2 locomotive

Moss
George Moss Ltd

PO Box 136, Mount Hawthorn 6016, 461 Scarborough Beach Road, Osborne Park 6017, Western Australia, Australia

Telephone: +61 9 4468844
Cable: Gemco, Perth
Telex: 92645
Telefax: +61 9 446 3404

Products: Industrial locomotives and mineral wagons.

MANUFACTURERS / Locomotives

Newag
Newag GmbH & Co KG

Blumenstrasse 56, PO Box 101201, 4100 Duisburg 1, Federal Republic of Germany

Telephone: +49 203 334061
Telex: 8 55526 newag d

Products: Remanufacture of diesel-electric and diesel-hydraulic locomotives of 30–3000 hp. Remanufacturing capability covers all gauges and remanufactured products are covered by an extensive warranty.

Constitution: The company is closely associated with Gleismac Italiana SpA (qv).

Niigata
Niigata Engineering Co Ltd

4-1 Kasumigaseki 1-chome, Chiyoda-ku, Tokyo 100, Japan

Telephone: +81 3 504 2111
Cable: Nite, Tokyo
Telex: 222 7111

Chairman: Hideo Washio
Managing Director: Mitsuaki Ishiyama
Chief Sales Director: Toshio Nakamura

Products: Electric and diesel railcars; diesel-hydraulic locomotives; passenger cars; rotary snow plough; transit system work cars.

Recent products include rail grinding units for the Toronto Transit Commission. These consist of a diesel locomotive, a rail grinding car and a flat/crane car. The rail grinding car is equipped with stones both for initial grinding of running rails and for subsequent refinishing.

Constitution: Niigata has been engaged in the manufacture of rolling stock for more than 80 years. It began production in 1896, just one year after its foundation, when the company launched its first passenger, freight and mail cars.

Nippon Sharyo
Nippon Sharyo Ltd

Head office: 1-1 Sanbonmatsu-cho, Atsuta-ku, Nagoya, Japan

Telephone: +81 52 882 3315
Cable: Nishiya, Nagoya
Telex: 447 3411
Telefax: +81 52 887 3337

Works: Toyokawa

President: Osamu Shinohara
Managing Director and Chief of Export Division: Kenji Nishimura

Products: Electric locomotives.

Novocherkassk
The Novocherkassk Electric Locomotive Works

V/O Sovelektzo, 1/4 Deguninskaya ul, 127486 Moscow, USSR

Telephone: 487 31 87
Telex: 411926, 411965

Products: Electric locomotives.

9400 kW VL 85 locomotive

6160 kW VL 80R locomotive

Recent Novocherkaask electric locomotives

Class	Wheel arrangement	Line voltage	Rated output (kW) continuous/one hour	Max speed km/h	Weight tonnes	Year first built	Builders	
							Mechanical parts	Electrical equipment
VL 15	2(Bo-Bo-Bo)	3000 V dc	8400/9000	100	300	1985	Novocherkassk Works	Tbilisi Works
VL 86F	2(Bo-Bo-Bo)	25 kV 50 Hz	10 800	110	288	1985	Novocherkassk Works	Novocherkassk Works

---

OMS
Officina Meccanica della Stanga
Member of Firema Consortium

Corso Stati Uniti 3, 35100 Padua, Italy

Telephone: +39 49 8700866
Telex: 430218 omspd i
Telefax: +39 49 76 06 82

Chairman: Dr Dino Marchiorello
Vice Chairman: Ing Aldo Iaia
Managing Director: Dr-Ing Ugo Soloni

Products: Diesel-electric locomotives.

Pafawag
FW Pafawag

Fabryka Wagonow Pafawag, ul Pstrowskiego 12, 53-609 Wroclaw, Poland

Telephone: +48 71 56 21 11
Telex: 0712432

Export sales: Kolmex, 49 Mokotowska, 00-542 Warsaw

Engineering Manager: R Geppert
Commercial Director: K Krzyczmonik

Products: Electric locomotives.

Pafawag Type 104E passenger electric locomotive for Polish State Railways

Locomotives / **MANUFACTURERS** 53

Pafawag electric locomotives

Class	Wheel arrangement	Line voltage	Rated output (kW) continuous	Max speed km/h	Weight tonnes	No in service	Year first built	Builders Mechanical parts	Builders Electrical equipment
Passenger 104E	Bo-Bo	3000	2920	160	83.5	Prototype	1986	Pafawag	Elta Lódz, Dolmel-Wroclaw
Freight 206E	Bo-Bo-Bo	3000	3000	100	120	Prototype	1990	Pafawag	Elta Lódz{a}, Dolmel-Wroclaw

Electric railcars or multiple-units

Class	Cars per unit	Line voltage	Motor cars per unit	Motored axles per motor car	Rated output (kW) per motor	Max speed km/h	Weight tonnes per unit (M motor, T trailer)	Total seating capacity	Length per unit mm (M motor, T trailer)	No in service	Rate of acceleration m/s^2	Year first built	Builders Mechanical parts	Builders Electrical equipment
Suburban traffic 6WE	3	3000	1	4	206	100	M53 T40/36	154	M6400 T4000	Prototype	0.6	1989	Pafawag	Elta-Lódz{a}, Dolmel-Wroclaw

PEC
The Projects & Equipment Corporation of India Ltd
A Government of India Enterprise

Hansalaya, 15 Barakhamba Road, New Delhi 110 001, India

Telephone: +91 11 3313542, 3314419, 3313356
Cable: PECOIND
Telex: 031 65199, 031 65256
Telefax: +91 11 331 5279

Chairman: S N Malik
Executive Director: R Khosla
Chief Marketing Manager (Railway Equipment Division): M Chatterji

Products: Diesel-electric, diesel-hydraulic, electric, industrial and mining locomotives; spares for locomotives, for export.
Diesel-electric locomotives have been exported to Tanzania and to Viet-Nam; a Vietnamese contract for spares has recently been completed.

Constitution: PEC was formed in 1971 as a corporation under the Indian Ministry of Commerce to handle and boost the export of railway equipment and engineering goods.
Locomotives are manufactured in Indian Railway units such as Diesel Locomotive Works, Varanasi, Chittaranjan Locomotive Works, Asansol and in the private sector by Venkateswara Transmission, Hyderabad, and SAN Engineering and Locomotives Ltd, Bangalore, for the smaller hp ranges.

Plymouth
Plymouth Locomotive International Inc

PO Box 105, 607 Bell Street, Plymouth, Ohio 44865, USA

Telephone: +1 419 687 4881
Telex: 241551
Telefax: +1 419 687 8112

Chairman: John Frecka
President: Art Evans
Export Sales: Miles Fate Christian

Products: Diesel-hydraulic locomotives for industrial, rapid transit, and mining/tunnelling customers in standard form, or custom-manufactured to detailed specifications.
Industrial locomotives are available in sizes from small (5 US tons) to large (120 US tons), in a wide variety of track gauges. The customer can choose from Caterpillar, Cummins, Detroit Diesel or Deutz engines to power the locomotive.
Rapid Transit models are available for maintenance purposes as well as for towing a disabled transit train. The locomotives can be equipped with snow ploughs on the bumpers, and an auxilliary diesel-powered snow blower can be coupled with the locomotive for heavy snow removal.

Plymouth Model MDT 45-ton diesel-hydraulic locomotive

Plymouth Model CR-8T 50-ton diesel-hydraulic locomotive in rapid transit system service

Plymouth diesel locomotives

Industrial

	H	D	J/JW	M/W	CR-8	CR-8XT
Weight (tonnes)	4-8	10-15	15-25	30-45	45-65	70-120
Power (hp)	60-100	125-200	150-250	300-450	600-1000	600-1200
Haulage capacity (tonnes)	200	375	625	1125	1625	3000
Wheel arrangement	0-4-0	0-4-0	0-4-0 (J) 0-6-0 (JW)	0-4-0 (M) 0-6-0 (W)	Bo-Bo	Bo-Bo

Engines: Caterpillar, Cummins, Detroit Diesel or Deutz

Mining

	TMDR	HMD	DMD	JMD	MMD
Weight (tonnes)	4-6	4-8	10-16	15-25	25-45
Power (hp)	50-90	60-100	125-225	150-250	300-400
Haulage capacity (tonnes)	150	200	375	625	1125
Wheel arrangement	0-4-0	0-4-0	0-4-0	0-4-0	0-4-0

Engines: Caterpillar and Deutz with MSHA Schedule 24 and 31 approved

54 MANUFACTURERS / Locomotives

Pragoinvest
Czechoslovak locomotive export group

Českomoravská 23, 19000 Prague 9, Czechoslovakia

Telephone: +42 2 822741, 820840
Telex: 122 379, 122 601

Works: ČKD, Prague

General Director: Miloslav Kočárek
Sales Manager: Josef Žák

Products: Diesel-electric shunting locomotives. Export sales agency for Czechoslovak locomotive industry.

The T669.1 was specifically designed to Soviet Railways (SZD) requirements as a heavy shunter and over 5000 have been acquired by SZD, but it is also used in Czechoslovakia, Poland, Albania, India and Iraq; more batches were exported to Albania, Poland and the SZD in 1989. The SZD classifies it as the Type CME3. The T448.0 has been redeveloped as the Type 446.2, with increased top speed of 90 km/h and lower axleload of 16 tonnes for Czechoslovak State Railways (ČSD), which operates over 200. Recent additions to the range are the T457.0 for light shunting and mainline mixed traffic; the T419.0 for industrial plant shunting; and the metre-gauge Type D12E for Viet-Nam Railways, to which more units were exported in 1989-90.

Type CME3 diesel for Soviet Railways (SZD)

Type T466.2 diesel for Czechoslovak Railways (ČSD)

Type T419.0 industrial shunter

Metre-gauge Type D12E Bo-Bo for Viet-Nam Railways

Type T457.0 light shunter

Pragoinvest diesel-electric locomotives

Type	CME3 (SZD)	T419.0	T448.0 (ČSD)	T457.0	T466.2 (ČSD)	T478.4 (ČSD)	D12E
Wheel arrangement	Co-Co	Bo-Bo	Bo-Bo	Bo-Bo	Bo-Bo	Bo-Bo	Bo-Bo
Gauge	1520 mm	1435 mm	1435 mm	1435 mm	1435 mm	1435 mm	1000 mm
Length over buffers/coupler	17.22 m	15.18 m	13.58 m	14 m	13.58 m	16.54 m	13.48 m
Body width	3.08 m	3.08 m	3.06 m	3.084 m	3.06 m	3.07 m	2.754 m
Total wheelbase	12.6 m	10.2 m	9.1 m	9.6 m	9.1 m	11.4 m	9.1 m
Bogie wheelbase	4 m	2.6 m	2.4 m	2.4 m	2.4 m	2.4 m	2.4 m
Wheel diameter	1.05 m	1.05 m	1 m	1 m	1 m	1 m	1 m
Minimum curve radius	80 m	70 m	80 m	80 m	80 m	100 m	80 m
Weight in working order	123 tonnes	84 tonnes	72 tonnes	69.5 tonnes	64 tonnes	73 tonnes	55 tonnes
Max service speed	95 km/h	80 km/h	70 km/h	80 km/h	90 km/h	100 km/h	80 km/h
Continuous tractive effort	226 kN/11.4 km/h	128.6 kN/12.8 km/h	131 kN/18 km/h	102 kN/15 km/h	121 kN/19 km/h	120 kN/30 km/h	118 kN/15.9 km/h
Engine	CKD K6S 310DR	CKD K6S 230DR	CKD K6S 230DR	CKD K6S 230DR	CKD K6S 230DR	CKD K12V 230DR	CKD K6S 230DR
Rating	990 kW/750 rpm	600 kW/1150 rpm	883 kW/1250 rpm	600 kW/1150 rpm	883 kW/1250 rpm	1460 kW/1100 rpm	846 kW/1150 rpm

Precision National Corporation

908 Shawnee Street, Mt Vernon, Illinois 62864, USA

Telephone: +1 618 244 0405
Telefax: +1 618 244 0405

President: Dean Manes
Vice-President, Operations: Bill Fesler
Purchasing Manager: Ken Bradley
Customer Service/Sales: Carol Rudofski

Products: Locomotive remanufacture, locomotive sales and hire, parts, mobile service and repairs.

Price
A & G Price Ltd

Private Bag, Thames, New Zealand

Telephone: +64 9 399526
Cable: Priceco, Thames
Telefax: +64 9 392 819

Chief Executive Officer: A D Gatland
Resident Manager: T W Just
Production Manager: B J O'Sullivan

Products: Diesel-hydraulic, diesel-mechanical and battery locomotives.

Constitution: This company stems from a foundry and workshop set up at Onehunga near Auckland in 1868 by two brothers, Alfred and George Price.

PSI
Peaker Services Inc

8080 Kensington Court, Brighton, Michigan 48116, USA

Telephone: +1 313 437 04174
    1 800 622 4224 (USA only)
Telefax: +1 313 437 8280

President: Richard R Steele
Vice President, Marketing and Sales: Ray B Sykes
Director, Locomotive Sales: Thomas Psillas
Sales Promotion: Sam Breck

Products: Locomotive remanufacturing; diesel engine rebuilding, maintenance; exchange service for diesel engine components; personnel training.

Peaker Services Inc (PSI) is an independently-owned company specialising in large diesel engines and locomotives manufactured by the Electro-Motive Division of General Motors Corporation. Work is performed at its plant in Green Oak Township, Michigan, approximately 40 km north-west of Detroit, or on-site anywhere in the world. Services include complete locomotive remanufacturing, engine conversions and upgrading, unit exchange components, engine overhaul, field repairs, service contracts, application studies, crankcase lineboring and repairs, locomotive inspections and evaluations, and personnel training in locomotive maintenance and repair.

PSI also has developed expertise in redesigning the electrical systems of EMD locomotives for greater efficiency, prolonged service life of the unit, and convenient access and repair.

Re-manufactured EMD switching locomotive with remote control feature

---

Qishuyen
Qishuyen Locomotive and Rolling Stock Works

Changzhou, Jiangsu, People's Republic of China

Telephone: +86 71711 4472
Cable: 2058

Products: Diesel-electric locomotive manufacture and repair; component manufacture for locomotives and rolling stock; rolling stock maintenance and repair.

In addition to meeting domestic needs, the works' products are exported to more than 30 countries in Europe, America, Asia, and Africa. A major product is the 3310 kW Dong Feng 8 freight diesel locomotive with ac-dc electric transmission, first built in October 1984. It is powered by a single V-type, 4-stroke diesel engine (Type 16V 280 ZJ) of 16 cylinders, each of 280 mm bore diameter and 285 mm piston stroke. The separately excited ac traction generator has a rated capacity of 3330 kVA at 1000 rpm. The 480 kW traction motors are series-excited dc. The cooling system comprises a plate-fin water radiator and static hydraulic-driven cooling fan. The two three-axle bogies, which are interchangeable, are pedestal-less, with no centre plate or balance beam. At the end of 1987 24 units were in service.

Type Dong Feng 8 4500 hp diesel-electric Co-Co

Main technical specifications:
Track gauge: 1435 mm
Wheel arrangement: Co-Co
Designed speed: 100 km/h
Continuous speed: 30.2 km/h
Axleload: 23 tonnes ± 3%
Starting tractive effort: 45 500 kg
Tractive effort per wheel cycle: 32 400 kg

Minimum curvature radius: 145 m
Driving wheel diameter: 1050 mm
Max height (rail surface to top end): 4736 mm
Max width: 3288 mm
Length (coupler to coupler): 22 000 mm
Distance between bogie centres: 12 324 mm
Coupler height: 880 mm ± 10 mm

Reggiane
Officine Meccaniche Italiano SpA

PO Box 431, 27 Via Vasco Agosti, 42100 Reggio Emilia, Italy

Telephone: +39 522 5881
Telex: 530665 regom
Telefax: +39 522 588243

Chairman: Dr Giuseppe Ivan Bonora
General Manager: Vincenzo Giuliano

Products: Electric, diesel-electric, diesel-hydraulic and diesel-mechanical locomotives.

Reggiane participates in development and production of Italian State Railways' new Class E402 electric locomotive

56 MANUFACTURERS / Locomotives

Reggiane has been engaged in railway locomotives and rolling stock since 1905. The company also manufactures mechanical sub-assemblies for other companies, such as bogies for locomotives complete with quill drive or toothed gearing.

Constitution: Founded in 1904 to build rolling stock and, a few years later, steam locomotives. After being largely destroyed during 1943 the works were rebuilt and re-equipped. Reggiane OMI is a subsidiary of Efimpianti, a member of the EFIM group.

Republic
Republic Locomotive Works Inc

1861 West Washington Road, Greenville, South Carolina 29601, USA

Telephone: +1 803 271 4000
Telefax: +1 803 233 2103
President & CEO: Hugh B Hamilton Jr
Vice President, Locomotive Sales: William J Leonard
Vice-President, Finance-Administration: Robert W Rhoton
Vice-President, Manufacturing: David G Tennent
Vice-President, Communications: Susan R Franklin

Principal subsidiaries:
Republic Locomotive Works Inc, Republic Group Inc, Republic Raileasing Inc

Products: New and remanufactured locomotives, custom designed and built to any gauge, weight and power; export capabilities; locomotive lessors; contract switching; contract maintenance; supplier of new and remanufactured parts and components; full service locomotive repair including major wreck damage; extensive parts and field service.

The RL2000
The RL2000 locomotive is a modern 2000 hp railroad freight locomotive designed for use in both mainline and branchline service. The RL2000 has superior fuel economy and shutdown/restarting capability, and with its microprocessor control systems, provides greater tractive effort than previously available.

The RL1000/1500
Republic's goal in designing the RL1000/1500 series of Caterpillar powered locomotives was to apply modern technology to the application of heavy industrial switchers. The result of this programme has been a switcher with very high fuel efficiency, greatly improved adhesion, substantially lower maintenance requirements, excellent cold weather starting and operating characteristics, and a much longer life expectancy. More specifically, fuel savings in a switching application have been in the range of 30 to 50%.

RL2000 2000 hp freight locomotive

The RL400
The design of an all-new locomotive, the RL400, in concept is very similar to Republic's RL1000/1500s, but offers specification options for a myriad of uses. This unit can be manufactured to accommodate narrow to broad gauge, 400 to 1000 hp, and can weigh from 40 to 100 tonnes.

Recent contracts include the remanufacture of 10 FL9 dual-mode ac commuter units for the Metro-North Commuter Railroad Company of New York City, due for completion in 1990.

New York City Transit Authority awarded a contract to Republic in 1988 to build seven new RL400 locomotives which will be 50-tonne, 400 hp switching units to pull worktrains throughout the New York City subway system. Completion of the contract is scheduled for 1990.

A contract for two RL2000 locomotives for industrial use in bauxite mining operations for Jamalco in Jamaica has been executed and delivered.

Republic has been awarded a contract from Cogentrix for one RL1000 locomotive, the fourth unit built specifically to Cogentrix's specifications. This new unit will be utilised for switching application at the new cogenerating station at Rocky Mount, N Carolina. Delivery is scheduled for 1990.

One RL1500 locomotive is scheduled for delivery on lease to the Nebraska Machinery Company in 1990 for shortline railroad switching. Similarly, one RL1500 has been ordered by the Amoco Chemical Company for switching.

RFS Engineering Ltd

PO Box 192, Hexthorpe Road, Doncaster DN1 1PJ, England

Telephone: +44 302 340700
Telex: 547296
Telefax: +44 302 340693

Works: Kilnhurst Works, Rotherham, Yorks S62 5TD

Managing Director: P Page
Director: E Harrison

Products: Locomotive manufacture and repair.

Following acquisition by RFS Engineering Ltd of Thomas Hill (Rotherham) Ltd in mid-1989, the Company has developed and consolidated its market position as a major supplier of new and remanufactured locomotives, and of the Trackmaster range of dual-mode road/rail shunters.

New Vanguard locomotives generally comprise the 'Steelman' shaft-drive disc-braked model, lately improved by cardan shaft drive to final drive gear boxes and installation of hydraulic shock absorbers between axleboxes and frame. The 'Steelman' range starts with 25 tonnes gross, 200 hp, two-axle units and rises to 75-tonne, 750 bhp three-axle versions. Both diesel-hydraulic and diesel-electric transmissions are incorporated, powered from alternative diesel engines including Cummins, Caterpillar and Perkins, and the units can be equipped for remote radio control.

Older locomotives may be fully remanufactured and repowered at the extensively equipped Kilnhurst

The 'Steelman' locomotive

Locomotives / **MANUFACTURERS** 57

workshops which have long specialised in retrofits and have over 10 years' experience in radio (remote) control of shunting locomotives, petrol-chemical standard flameproofing requirements etc.

With the transfer of the Class 08 GR contract to Kilnhurst and the development of its field service and spares support activity, RFS Engineering has evolved a comprehensive locomotive capability with industrial and mining locomotives centred at Kilnhurst and main line locomotive conversions and erection facilities at Doncaster.

Recent contracts include Orient Express coach overhaul (November 1989); TML 150 hp shunting locomotive (mid-1989).

Ries
Adolf Ries Maschinenenbau GmbH

Schnabel-Henning Strasse 30, PO Box 2240, 7520 Bruchsal 1, Federal Republic of Germany

Telephone: +49 7251 15031
Telex: 07 822204 ries d

Products: Road/rail tractors.

RSD
A Division of Dorbyl Ltd

PO Box 229, Boksburg 1460, South Africa

Telephone: +27 11 52 8276
Cable: Dorlonsa, Johannesburg
Telex: 4-29576
Telefax: +27 11 52 5714

Chairman: M J Smithyman
Marketing Manager: D L Cope

Products: Diesel-electric locomotives, electric (25 kV 50 Hz ac) locomotives, industrial locomotives, mining locomotives.

Funkey range of diesel locomotives
C H Funkey is now a wholly-owned subsidiary of Dorbyl Railway Products. For closer connection with the latter's Boksburg plant, C H Funkey has moved to new premises in Boksburg.

Products: Mining battery locomotives, mining diesel locomotives, underground pantograph locomotives, inspection trolleys; 22-man gang trolleys and industrial shunting locomotives from 10 to 65 tonnes.

In the electronic field Dorbyl Railway Products has supplied SATS with a Train Dynamics Analyser. The TDA is a computerised simulated locomotive control panel and guides a simulated train across a video screen, showing engineers more efficient ways to use their traction and solving problems for the technical staff.

Dorbyl Railway Products started supplying locomotives from their Boksburg works in 1960, building to General Electric drawings and specifications. Over 850 locomotives have been supplied. These include diesel-hydraulics and the new SATS Class 7E1 electric locomotives, of which a contract for 110 has been delivered.

Constitution: The company is a subsidiary of Dorbyl Ltd, which was established in South Africa as Wade & Dorman Ltd, Structural Engineers in 1909. The manufacture of rolling stock was begun in 1944.

Ruhrthaler
Ruhrthaler Maschinenfabrik, Schwarz & Dyckerhoff KG

Postfach 10 16 54, Scheffelstrasse 14-28, 4330 Mülheim/Ruhr, Federal Republic of Germany

Telephone: +49 208 44131
Cable: Ruhrtaloko, Mülheimruhr
Telex: 856710
Telefax: +49 208 479041

Export Manager: Karl-Heinz Krull

Products: Diesel-hydraulic narrow gauge mining locomotives; suspended monorail diesel locomotives for underground transportation of personnel and material.

Saalasti Oy

Arinatie 4, 00370 Helsinki 37, Finland

Telephone: +358 0 557 775
Telex: 124694 insa sf
Telefax: +358 0 550 780

Chairman: Eng Tapio Saalasti
Locomotive Sales: Teijo Saalasti

Products: Diesel shunting locomotives; road/rail shunting tractor; permanent way train crane tractors; shunting couplings; snow ploughs.

Two new models of OTSO locomotive were launched in 1989: OTSO 8 and 10 are both part of a new generation of ergonomically-designed locomotives. In the patented control of OTSO locomotives, start-up, speed control, change of direction and braking are operated from a single control wheel. When the driver's grip releases the handwheel or the drive lever of the radio control apparatus, the brakes are applied, the locomotive stops and the engine idles. Previous OTSO locomotives have had hydrodynamic transmission, while the OTSO 8 and 10 are equipped

Rolling snowplough mounted on Finnish State Railways railroad tractor

NALLE road/rail tractor, as supplied to Finnish State Railways (VR)

Work train crane tractor by Saalasti Oy

58 MANUFACTURERS / Locomotives

Type OTSO 4 diesel shunter

OTSO 8/10 diesel locomotive-general arrangement

with Voith turbohydraulic transmission and Caterpillar engines. The locomotives can be equipped with antislip device and radio control, shunting couplers and snow plough. Some OTSO locomotive models can be supplied for metre-gauge operation.

Saalasti Oy delivered new rolling snow ploughs to Finnish State Railways in 1989.

Saalasti Oy shunting locomotives

	NALLE[1]	OTSO 2	OTSO 4	OTSO 5	OTSO 8	OTSO 10
Weight (tonnes)	14	20–25	40–44	56	80	84
Power (hp (kW))	120 (88)	200 (150)	400 (295)	560 (410)	750 (560)	1000 (750)
Engine	Scania	Scania	Caterpillar	Caterpillar	Caterpillar	Caterpillar
Drawbar pull (kN)	45	70	130	168	240	250
Speed (km/h)	20	20	25	20	35	35
Overall length (mm)	5200	6000	7600	8080	11580	11580
Overall height (mm)	4000	3750	3850	3900	4300	4300
Max width (mm)	3300	3100	3100	3200	3200	3200
Wheelbase (mm)	2000	2500	3100	3800/1400[3]	2400/5800[4]	
Wheel diameter (mm)	800	800	960	960	1050	1050
Transmission	BW & S[5]	Voith	BW & S	BW & S	Voith & KG[6]	Voith & KG
Axle arrangement	B	B	B	C	B'B'	B'B'
Rail gauge (mm)				1435/1524		

[1] Bi-modal rail/road tractor
[2] Also available 1500 hp
[3] Outmost axles/front axles
[4] Bogie wheel base/pivot centers
[5] Torque converter Borg Warner, Gearbox Saalasti Oy
[6] Turbo transmission Voith, Axle drives Kaelble-Gmeinder

Accessories available: OTSO coupling, OTSO R coupling, VAPITI coupling, brush, pointed and side ploughs, radio control, equipment for paired running

---

SAN
SAN Engineering & Locomotive Co Ltd

PO Box 4802, Whitefield Road, Bangalore 560048, India

Telephone: +91 812 842271-6
Cable: Sunaya 560 048
Telex: 0845 2006 fuya in

Managing Director: Lenin K Thakkar

Western Region Manager, Bombay: D V Jhalam
232 Arun Chambers, Tardeo Road, Bombay 400 034

Telephone: +91 22 4941157/4941884
Telex: 011 75253 san in

Branch Manager, Calcutta: S K Bhuchar
7/1 Monica, 9-B Lord Sinha Road, Calcutta 700 071

Telephone: +91 33 431023/432209
Telex: 021 4256 san in

Branch Manager, New Delhi: A S Thakur
19 Osian (5th Floor), 12 Nehru Place, New Delhi 110 019

Telephone: +91 11 6410874
Telex: 031 61704 san in

Principal subsidiary:
San Transmissions Division, Plots 1 & 10, Hebbal Industrial Area, Belawadi Post, Mysore 571 106

Products: Diesel-hydraulic and diesel-electric locomotives, transmissions for locomotives and industrial applications, gears and gear boxes. Locomotives manufactured are used by industries such as cement plants, oil refineries, petrochemical complexes, steel plants, fertiliser plants, thermal plants, construction sites etc. Locomotives are tailored to customer needs.

The company also manufactures flameproof locomotives for underground coal mines. Locomotives for refineries and petrochemical complexes are built to oil companies materials association specification MEC-1 standard; and for coal mines application, locomotives are certified by the Directorate General of Mines Safety, Dhanbad.

Recent contracts obtained include the supply of five 350 hp and four 650 hp diesel-hydraulic locomotives for Maharahtra State Electricity Board; two 800 hp diesel-hydraulic locomotives for Gujarath Electricity Board; two 60-tonne diesel-electric rail cranes to Steel Plants.

SAN diesel locomotives

Recent contracts fulfilled include two 650 hp diesel-hydraulic locomotivers for Calcutta Port Trust; one 650 hp diesel-hydraulic flameproof locomotive for Bharat Petroleum Corporation.

Constitution: This plant was set up in 1969 at Bombay and moved to Bangalore as a public limited company in 1972. Since then the company has produced 416 locomotives in the 30–900 hp range to varying gauges and axleloads.

The company has collaboration agreements with Voith GmbH for the manufacture of turbo reversing transmissions L2 r2 ZU2 and L3 r4 U2; Brush Electrical Machines Limited (Hawker Siddeley Group) for the manufacture of Brush propulsion equipment for diesel-electric locomotives; and Takraf Export/ Import Volkseigener Aussenhandelsbetrieb (GDR) for the manufacture of rail cranes.

Locomotives / **MANUFACTURERS** 59

Recent SAN diesel locomotives

Gauge	Manufacturer's type	Wheel arrangement	Transmission	Rated power (kW)	Max speed km/h	Total weight tonnes	No in service 1987	Year first built	Builders Mechanical parts	Engine & Type	Transmission
Broad	DL-900	B-B	Hydrodynamic	672	12–50	90	1	1986	SAN	DDA 12V71X2	Twin Disc
Broad	DL-800	B-B	Hydrodynamic	597	32	90	3	1985	SAN	KCL, VTA-1710-L	Voith L3 r4 U2
Broad	DL-650	C	Hydrodynamic	507/597	35	67.5	27	1983	SAN	KCL, VTA-1710-L	Voith L3 r4 U2; L4 r2 U2
Metre	DL-600	B-B	Hydrodynamic	447	35	60	1	1987	SAN	KCL, KTA-1150-L	Voith L3 r4 U2
Broad	DL-450	C	Hydrodynamic	335	24–35	54	9	1984	SAN	KCL, V-1710-L	Voith L3 r4 U2; L4 r2 U2
Broad	DL-400	B	Hydrodynamic	298	17	45	3	1986	SAN	KCL, NTA-855-L	Voith-SAN L2 r2 ZU2
Metre	DL-400	C	Hydrodynamic	298	17	45	1	1987	SAN	KCL, NTA-855-L MWM TD 232 V12	Voith-SAN L2 r2 ZU2
Special	DL-90	B	Hydrodynamic	70	15	12–14	6	1983	SAN	KOEL, RB-66	KPC-TC + SAN-GB
Broad	DEL-300	B	Electric dc/dc	250	35	45	5	1986	SAN	KCL, NT-855-L4	Brush
BG/MG	DL-200	B	Hydrodynamic	153	15	30	85	1974	SAN	KCL, N-743-L	KPC TC/SAN GB
BG/MG	DL-125	B	Hydrodynamic	93	15	13–16	29	1976	SAN	KCL, N-495-L	KPC TC/SAN GB
BG/MG	DL-70	B	Hydrodynamic	52	15	8–10	12	1975	SAN	Simpsons P6 Ruston YD4	KPC TC/SAN GB
BG/MG	DL-300	B	Hydrodynamic	250	17	36–45	51	1976	SAN	KCL NT-855L	Voith SAN L2 r2 U2
BG/MG	DL-300	B	Hydrodynamic	250	17	36–45	75	1974	SAN	KCL NT-855L	KPC TC & SAN
BG/MG	DL-150	B	Hydrodynamic	112	20	25	10	1975	SAN TATA	OM312	Voith RS14Y
NG/MG	DL-45	B	Hydrodynamic	34	15	6	75	1971	SAN	Simpsons-P4	KPC & SAN
NG/MG	DL-30	B	Mechanical	22	12	4	13	1974	SAN	Simpsons-P3	David Brown & SAN GB

Scandia Randers
ABB Scandia A/S

Toldbodgade 39, 8900 Randers, Denmark

Telephone: +45 86 425300
Cable: ABB Scandia, Randers
Telex: 65145 scanas dk
Telefax: +45 86 415700

President: Henning Balle Kristensen
Vice President: Ragnar Sjöström
Export Manager: Kjeld Hvid

Products: Light weight diesel and electrical multiple units constructed according to the modular principle, light rail vehicles, service, and systems of interior styling.

Schienenfahrzeuge Export-Import
Volkseigener Aussenhandelsbetrieb der DDR
Export agency of VEB Kombinat Schienenfahrzeugbau and member of Vereinigter Schienenfahrzeugbau der DDR e V

Ötztaler Strasse 5, Berlin GDR-1100, German Democratic Republic

Telephone: +37 2 48040
Telex: 114372
Telefax: +37 2 472 8132

Products: Locomotives, emus and wagons

Constitution: Sole exporter of all rail vehicles and rail vehicle equipment built in the German Democratic Republic.

Schöma
Christoph Schöttler Maschinenfabrik GmbH

PO Box 1509, 2840 Diepholz 1, Federal Republic of Germany

Telephone: +49 5441 2047
Cable: Schöma, Diepholz
Telex: 41217
Telefax: +49 5441 7702

Manager: Ing Fritz Schöttler
Sales Manager: Ing L Niermeyer

Products: Shunting, narrow-gauge and mining locomotives with hydrodynamic, hydrostatic or mechanical transmission; gang trolleys.
The company has extended its product range to locomotives of 55 tonnes weight and 450 kW output.
Specimen particulars:

CFL-500 DCL-3 (NCZ Kafue, Zambia)
Gauge: 1067 mm
Weight: 45 tons
Wheel arrangement: 0-6-0
Max speed: 65 km/h
Engine: Caterpillar 3412 DITT
Output: 486 kW at 2100 rpm
4-speed powershift transmission with torque converter

CFL-200 B-B (CODELCO, Chile)
Gauge: 1435 mm
Weight: 32 tons
Wheel arrangement: 0-4-0 + 0-4-0
Max speed: 45 km/h
Engine: Deutz BF12L 413 FW
Output: 230 kW at 2150 rpm
3-speed powershift transmission with torque converter
Electro-magnetic rail brakes

Recent sales have included: 20 narrow-gauge locomotives, Model CFL-200 DCL-3, for Société des Sucreries, Egypt; and 26 trolleys, Model CS 300, for Tanzania-Zambia Railways.

Model CS 300 trolleys for Tanzania-Zambia Railways

Model CFL-500 DCL-3 three-axle shunting locomotive

SFL
Société Française de Locotracteurs

40 boulevard Henri-Selher, 92156 Suresnes Cedex, France

Telephone: +33 1 42 04 01 39
Telex: 614720
Telefax: +33 1 47 28 71 39

Managing Director: Henri Caijo
Commercial Director: Gerhard Schulze
Plant Manager: Christian Thuilliez

Products: Diesel-electric, diesel-hydraulic and electric shunting locomotives of 150 to 1500 bhp at weights up to about 100 tonnes for standard-, broad- and narrow-gauge.

The group's latest products include a heavy-duty unit of 1000 hp conceived primarily for steel industry use, designed for adaptability to a variety of engines and transmissions, and for equipment as desired with dynamic braking, creep control and for remote operation. Three diesel-hydraulic units of 1000 hp and 105 tonnes service weight have been delivered to a French steel plant. These units are provided with double end cabs, remote control, creep control, dynamic brake, wheel-slip device and a microprocessor to control all logical functions. A dominant item in the group's recent production has been the construction for French Railways (SNCF) of 330 Type Y8000 diesel-hydraulic shunters; these are two-axle machines with a 300 hp Poyaud engine, Voith L2r4sU2 transmission, cardan shaft drive and a weight of 36 tonnes. Further batches totalling 135 units are being supplied over the period 1989–92; of these 90 would be equipped for remote radio control.

Other shunter orders have been processed for Algeria, Cameroon, Congo, Egypt, Ethiopia, Madagascar, Senegal, Zimbabwe, Tunisia and Morocco. By early 1990 over 700 locomotives had been exported to 48 countries. The group's output is characterised by modular design for standardisation of parts and sub-assemblies and similarly by use of printed circuit electronic modules to minimise electro-mechanical switchgear. Extras such as constant speed or creep control and automatic wheel-slip safeguards are available throughout the group's range. The group also supplies electric control equipment.

The company's latest development concerns the improvement of maintenance and adaptability through use of microprocessors to control logic, excitation, and diagnostic and display functions. A first unit has been delivered to a steel plant in Northern France for on-site testing. One of the features of the new system is its memorisation of all important operational data, so that overhaul is ordered only when needed and not at average numbers of service hours. It also permits easy detection of faults and therefore helps to cut down repair costs.

Constitution: The Société Française de Locotracteurs, created in 1980, pools the technological experience, research, design and manufacturing of five well-known French rolling stock companies: Arbel-Fauvet-Rail, GEC Alsthom, and De Dietrich, Carel Fouché.

Type Y8000 300 bhp diesel-hydraulic shunting locomotive for French Railways (SNCF)

1000 hp diesel-hydraulic shunter

1000 bhp diesel-electric shunting locomotive

S-G-P
Verkehrstechnik Gesellschaft mbH

Head office: PO Box 103, Brehmstrasse 16, 1110 Vienna, Austria

Telephone: +43 1 22 74 69
Telex: 131891, 132574
Telefax: +43 1 22 74 51 48

General Manager: Dr Herbert Ziegler
Sales Director: Dipl Ing Heinz Butz

Technical Director: Dipl Ing Roland Himmelbauer

Products: Electric locomotives, diesel locomotives, rack locomotives, shunting locomotives, fireless steam locomotives.

Class (Railways own designation)	Wheel arrangement	Line voltage	Rated output (kW) continous/ one-hour	Max speed km/h	Weight tonnes	Overall length mm	No in service 1989	Year first built	Builders Mechanical parts	Builders Electrical equipment
1044 (OBB)	Bo-Bo	15 kV 16⅔ Hz	5000/5200	160	84	16060	134	1974	SGP	BES*
1063 (OBB)	Bo-Bo	15 kV 16⅔ Hz und 25 kV 50 Hz	1700/1700	100	82	15700	37	1983	SGP	BES*
1064 (OBB)	Co-Co	15 kV 16⅔ Hz	1520/1520	100	111	18540	8	1985	SGP	BES*
EL 1	Co-Co	25 kV 50 Hz	2400 34 km/h	100	114	19040	30	1983	ZECO/SGP	50 c/s Group

* BES is an Austrian consortium of ABB, Elin and Siemens

Siemens
Siemens AG

Head Office, Transportation Systems Group
Werner-von-Siemens-Strasse 50, Postfach 32 40, D-8520 Erlangen, Federal Republic of Germany

Telephone: +49 9131 72 4157
Cable: Siemens, Erlangen
Telex: 62021 508 si d
Telefax: +49 9131 726840

Transportation Systems Group President:
W O Martinsen
Main Line Rolling Stock Division: R Stubenrauch

Mass Transit & Rolling Stock Division: G Scholtis

Products: Electric and diesel-electric vehicles and associated electrical equipment for main-line, inter-urban, urban rapid transit, underground, narrow-gauge, industrial and mine railways, and also for trolleybus systems (see Siemens entry in Electrification section for power supply and control systems detail).

Locomotives / **MANUFACTURERS**   61

In late 1988 RENFE, the Spanish national railway, awarded a German-Spanish consortium under the leadership of Siemens an order for 75 high-performance locomotives of three-phase ac design. The consortium includes Krauss-Maffei, Thyssen-Henschel and Macosa for the mechanical part; and ABB Switzerland and Siemens for the electrical equipment. The order is worth some DM 600 million. The order is connected with the reorganisation of the Spanish Railway industry, and so members of the consortium will have a financial interest in the Spanish companies which will build 80% of these 'universal' locomotives.

The locomotives will represent the latest state of the art of three-phase ac drive technology. The drives, which use GTO thyristor converters to feed induction traction motors, are also in service with the German Federal Railway in their locomotives and high-speed trains. Control duties are performed by the Sibas 16 microcomputer system, a Siemens development. The locomotives are designed for a continuous rating of 5600 kW and are suitable both for goods trains and for high-speed passenger trains operating at speeds up to 220 km/h.

Other contracts lately in hand or completed include traction equipment for: Class 252 'universal' electric main-line locomotives of Spanish National Railways (RENFE); Class 14E dual-system main-line locomotives for SA Transport Services; Class F 69 PH-AC diesel-electric passenger locomotives with three-phase drive for Amtrak, USA; Class 1822 dual-system main-line locomotives for the Austrian Federal Railway (ÖBB); Class 1063/1064 electric shunting locomotives for the Austrian Federal Railway (ÖBB); and Class DE500 diesel-electric locomotives for industrial railways.

Recent technological developments include three-phase ac drives for locomotives, and Type SIBAS 16 static logic control units which use microprocessor techniques for computing all functions of propulsion systems including dynamic and regenerative braking and for fault detection and diagnostics. More than 3500 units of the latter design are in revenue service or will shortly be commissioned.

Amtrak Class F69 PH-AC diesel-electric with three-phase drive

Artist's impression of Class 252 locomotive for RENFE

Dual-voltage Type 14E locomotive for Spoornet (South Africa)

Recent electric locomotives with electrical equipment by Siemens

Class	Wheel arrangement	Line voltage	Rated output (kW) one-hour	Max speed km/h	Weight tonnes	Year first built	Remarks
South Africa 8E	Bo-Bo	3000 V dc	686	75	82	1983	Chopper-controlled
Germany E120	Bo-Bo	15 kV 16⅔ Hz	5600	200 (250)	84	1987	Three-phase drive
Denmark EA3000	Bo-Bo	25 kV 50 Hz	4000	160 (175)	80	1984	Three-phase drive
South Africa 14 E	Bo-Bo	25 kV 50 Hz 3 kV dc	4000	140 (160)	92	1989	Three-phase drive
Austria 1822	Bo-Bo	15 kV 16⅔ Hz 3 kV dc	4400	140	82	1990	Three-phase drive
Austria 1044	Bo-Bo	15 kV 16⅔ Hz	5000	160	83.2	1976	Three-phase drive
Austria 1063	Bo-Bo	15 kV 16⅔ Hz 25 kV 50 Hz	1520	80	75.5	1981	Three-phase drive
Austria 1064	Co-Co	15 kV 16⅔ Hz	1520	80	112.2	1981	Three-phase drive
Austria 1012	Bo-Bo	15 kV 16⅔ Hz	6000	200	80	1992	Three-phase drive
China 8K	Bo-Bo+Bo-Bo	19-29 kV 50 Hz	6400	100	184	1986-87	Three-phase drive
Spain 252	Bo-Bo	25 kV 50 Hz	5600	220	86	1992	Three-phase drive (GTO Thyr)

62 MANUFACTURERS / Locomotives

Recent diesel locomotives with electrical equipment by Siemens

Class	Wheel arrangement	Transmission	Rated power (kW)	Max speed km/h	Total weight tonnes	Year first built	Builders Mechanical parts	Engine & type
Spain Mabi I	Bo-Bo	Elec	785	90	80	1986	MTM	MTU
USA F69 PH-AC	Bo-Bo	Elec	2260	177	120	1989	GM	GM

Škoda
Škoda Group Plzeň

Námesti Ceskych Bratri 8, 31600 Plzeň, Czechoslovakia

Telephone: +42 19 215
Cable: Škoda, Plzeň
Telex: 154221

Export sales: Škodaexport, Václavské 56, 113 32 Prague 1

Telephone: +42 2 240851
Telegrams: Škodaexport, Prague
Telex: 122413

Managing Director: M Mikeš

Products: Electric locomotives.
The Škoda works in Plzeň has built more than 5000 locomotives, many of them for the railways of the Soviet Union, Bulgaria and Poland as well as those of Czechoslovakia. The plant has been completing a manufacturing changeover to its second-generation range of electric locomotives, features of which include:
New suspension systems employing steel coil springs in both stages, with liquid shock absorbers fitted in parallel to secure a good ride at up to 200 km/h;
New body design with a weight-saving main frame;
Controlled auxiliary drives including a static accumulator battery charger;
In high-power locomotives, 1000 kW tractive power per axle;
Electrodynamic braking with a short-time rating of up to 1250 kW per axle;
Control electronics for commutator-type traction motors;
Automatic speed control and diagnostic equipment;
Air conditioning of a redesigned cab with standardised driving desk;
Electronic anti-skid and anti-slip protection;
Power economy improvements in both traction and auxiliary circuits;
Measures for reduction of maintenance costs.
Locomotives of the second-generation family for Czechoslovak State Railways (ČSD) with these features are the dual-voltage Class 363 (Škoda Type 69E), the 25 kV ac Class 263 (Škoda Type 70E) and the 3 kV dc Class 163 (Škoda Type 71E). All were in series production in 1988. Types embodying the same concepts and principles have been built for the

Type 82E 6160 kW, 160 km/h, 3 kV dc Bo-Bo+Bo-Bo for Soviet Railways

Type 69E 3060 kW 3 kV dc/25 kV 50 Hz ac dual-system locomotive for ČSD

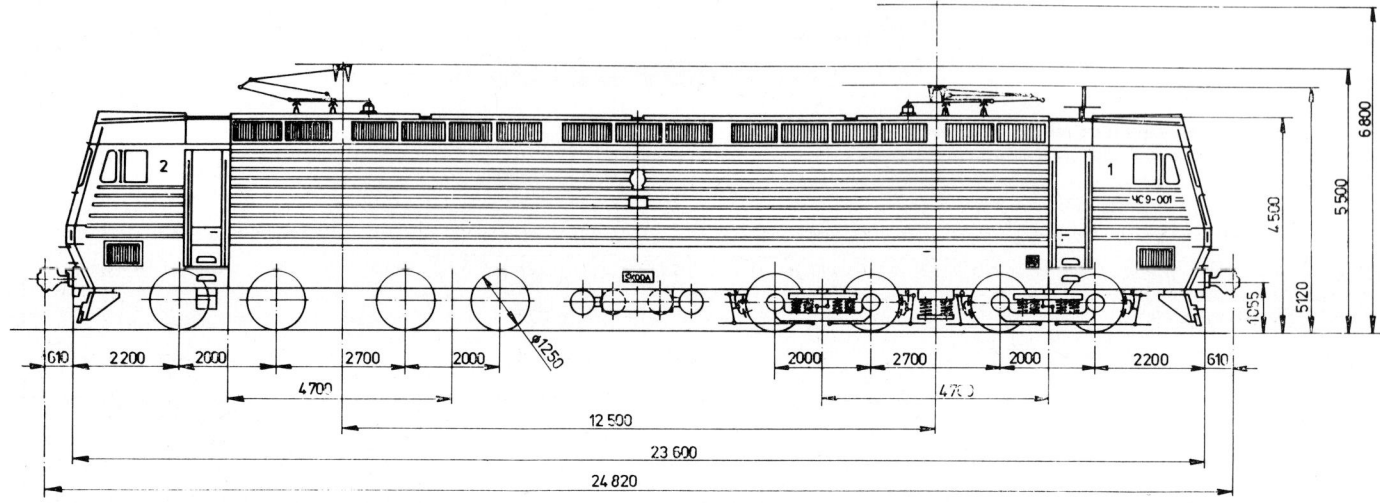

General arrangement of Type 86EO due for prototype production in 1996

Locomotives / MANUFACTURERS

Class 85E third-generation 3 kV dc Bo-Bo with asynchronous motors

Bulgarian and Soviet railways. In the mechanical part all three locomotives have mutually interchangeable bogies, a uniform concept of locomotive body and of driver's position. In the electrical part they employ contactless control of the traction output, and feature an electrodynamic brake, automatic speed control and controlled auxiliary drives with the use of diagnostics.

Development is in progress on a third-generation range of locomotives employing commutatorless induction motors in high- and low-speed variants, and with new electronic control systems. The objective is to extend periods between maintenance to 500 000 km for the mechanical parts and to 1 million km for the electronic equipment. On-board diagnostics, either acoustic or optical, will include a memory feature to simplify operation and maintenance. A Class 85E Bo-Bo prototype with Škoda asynchronous motors for 3 kV dc has been produced.

Class 85E: leading particulars
Current system: 3 kV dc
Axle arrangement: Bo-Bo
Diameter of wheels: 1250 mm
Top speed: 120/160 km/h
Weight of locomotive: 84 tonnes
Continuous-duty output of traction motors: 2600 kW and 3200 kW
Three-phase traction motor rating: 4 × 650 kW, 1200 V, 227 A; 4 × 800 kW, 1200 V, 252 A
Electrodynamic brake rating: 2800 kW, 3200 kW

Recent production has also included a series of dual-voltage Type 80E for ČSD and the German State Railway (DR), the first locomotives built by Škoda for DR, which designates them Class 230. Their ČSD classification is 372.

Type 80E dual-voltage locomotive for ČSD and DR

Type 71E 3060 kW, 120 km/h, 3 kV dc, mixed-traffic Bo-Bo for ČSD

A twin-unit version of this type is under development for prototype production by 1996. It is provisionally classified Type 86EO.

Škoda electric locomotives in production

Class (Railway's* own designation)	Manufacturer's type	Wheel arrangement	Line voltage	Rated output (kW) continuous	Max speed km/h	Weight tonnes	Overall length mm	No in service 1988	Year first built	Electrical equipment	Remarks– special features
SZD CS-200	66E	Bo-Bo+Bo-Bo	3 kV dc	8000	200	156	33 080	12	1975	Škoda	
SHD	27E	Bo+Bo+Bo	1.5 kV dc	2190	65	155/165	21 560	40	1984	Škoda	
ČSD 210	51E	Bo-Bo	25 kV 50 Hz	880	80	72	14 400	74	1973	Škoda + ČKD	
ČSD 111	78E	Bo-Bo	3 kV dc	760	80	72	14 478	36	1977	Škoda + ČKD	
SZD CS-8	81E	Bo-Bo+Bo-Bo	25 kV 50 Hz	7200	160	170	32 780	32	1983	Škoda + ČKD	
SZD CS-7	82E	Bo-Bo+Bo-Bo	3 kV dc	6160	160	172	34 040	210	1983	Škoda	
ČSD 363	69E	Bo-Bo	3 kV dc/25 kV 50 Hz	3060	120	87	16 740	147	1981	Škoda + ČKD	
ČSD 263	70E	Bo-Bo	25 kV 50 Hz	3060	120	85	16 800	12	1984	Škoda	
ČSD 163	71E	Bo-Bo	3 kV dc	3060	120	84	16 740	60	1984	Škoda + ČKD	
–	85E	Bo-Bo	3 kV dc	2600/3200	110	88	18 000	1	1987	Škoda	Prototype with asynchronous motors

* ČSD: Czechoslovak State Railways
SZD: Soviet Railways
BDŽ: Bulgaria State Railways
SHD: North Bohemian Coal District

SLM
Schweizerische Lokomotiv-und Maschinenfabrik
Swiss Locomotive and Machine Works

8401 Winterthur, Switzerland

Telephone: +41 52 85 41 41
Cable: Locomotive, Winterthur
Telex: 896 131 slm ch
Telefax: +41 52 2387 65

President, Board of Management: H Hegi
General Manager: K Vogel

Assistant Vice President, Technical Department: R Kummrow
Commercial Department, Deputy Vice President: Dr M Knüsli
Works Department, Assistant Vice President: O Heiniger
Sales Department, Assistant Vice President: W Grütter

Products: General contractor for complete locomotives; supplier of the mechanical parts (complete bogies and superstructure) for main-line and shunting locomotives, gearing specialist for rail motive power or special vehicles; service enterprise for engineering (including wheel-rail dynamics, measuring and control system technology), gear cutting, machining and sheetmetal working.

The company's recent output has included eight high-performance electric locomotives for Swiss private railways, six for the Bodensee-Toggenburg Railway and two for the Sihltal-Zurich-Uetliberg Railway. The lightweight mechanical equipment designed and built by SLM features main components grouped in assemblies, and a functional layout for ease of operation, maintenance and upkeep. The three-phase asynchronous motors have SLM's patented shifting

64 MANUFACTURERS / Locomotives

axle-drive, which allows lateral as well as radial adjustment of lightweight wheel-sets in conjunction with Flexicoil spring axlebox links. Flexicoil springs are also interposed between bogies and self-supporting body. Tractive effort is transmitted through low-level traction rods that are centrally arranged.

BT and SZU electric locomotives: leading particulars
Gauge: 1435 mm
Wheel arrangement: Bo-Bo
Wheel diameter, new: 1100 mm
Locomotive mass: 72 tonnes
Mass of mechanical part: 31.5 tonnes
Starting tractive effort: 240 kN
Continuous (UIC) rating at motor shaft: 3000 kW
Max rating (traction and electric braking): 3200 kW at wheel rim
Max braking force: 140 kN
Max speed: 130 km/h
Overhead line voltage: 15 kV 16⅔ Hz

SLM is building the Swiss Federal (SBB) Class 450 locomotives for the Swiss Federal Railway's forthcoming Zurich S-Bahn service with bi-level passenger cars. This will be a push-pull operation with units each comprising a locomotive, two intermediate trailers and a control (Bt) trailer. The Class 450 is a single-cab locomotive with an air-conditioned cab; it accommodates a luggage compartment.

Lightweight construction of both body, which has corrugated sheet metal walls for strength, and bogies is a feature. These units also have SLM's shifting axle drive. Wear of track and wheel-sets will be minimised by lightweight wheel-sets with low unsprung mass, employing monobloc wheels on a bonded shrink-fit and hollow-forged axle; by use of Flexicoil spring axlebox links; by transverse decoupling of wheel-sets in relation to bogie and traction motors; and by trapezoidally-arranged links between traction motor and a bogie's centre girder, which afford radial adjustment of the wheel-sets even when tractive effort is being exerted.

Hy Class 450 locomotive: leading particulars
Gauge: 1435 mm
Wheel arrangement: Bo-Bo
Wheel diameter, new: 1100 mm
Locomotive mass, tare: 74 tonnes
Additional load (luggage): 4 tonnes
Mass of mechanical part: 37 tonnes
Continuous rating (UIC) at motor shaft: 3000 kW
Max rating (traction and electrical braking) at wheel: 3200 kW
Starting tractive effort at V = 0–48 km/h: 240 kN
Max braking effort: 140 kN
Max speed: 130 km/h
Overhead line voltage: 15 kV 16⅔ Hz

SLM is constructing the first 24 SBB Class 460 electric locomotives, the new type associated with the SBB's 'Rail 2000' concept. Entry into service is scheduled for 1991. These four-axle high-performance locomotives are designed to be equally as suitable for duty on the existing SBB network with its numerous curves as for high-speed passenger traffic on SBB's new lines. Consequently for the first time optimal high-speed and curve negotiation capabilities have been combined in the same motive power unit. A completely new basic design has been applied to the body and especially to the bogies. Noteworthy features include: elastic mounting of the traction motor and gear transmission unit on the bogie and body (this mounting concept is optimised in relation to springing and damping properties and guarantees stable running at speeds ranging up to 230 km/h); minimal wear and stressing of wheel and rail in curves thanks to wheelsets with radial self-steering capability at any tractive effort; high secondary springs that allow high

Type Re 4/4 Bo-Bo locomotive with three-phase drive for Sihltal-Zurich-Uetliberg Railway (SZU)

SBB Class 450 power car for Zurich S-Bahn

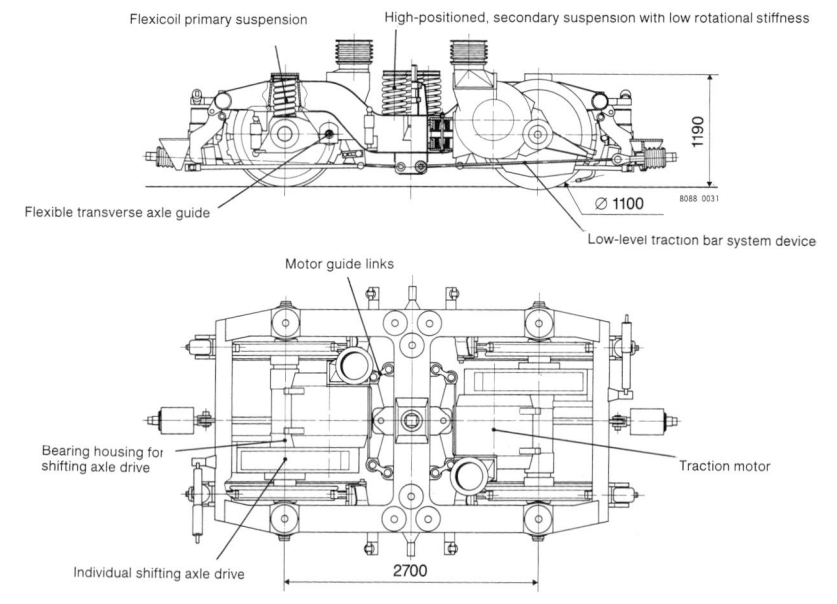

General arrangement of SLM shifting axle drive bogie

SLM diesel locomotives

Class	Wheel arrangement	Transmission	Output diesel UIC kW	Max speed km/h	Total weight tonnes	No in service 1988	Year first built	Builders Mechanical parts	Builders Engine & type	Builders Transmission
V1–4S15–1180 Bolivia	Bo-Bo	diesel-electric	1180	65	60	2	1985	SLM	MTU 12 V 396 TC 13	BBC
BB 20401–20410 Indonesia	Bo-2-Bo	diesel-electric	1050	Adh 60 Rack 20	55	10	1982	SLM	MTU 12 V 396 TC 12	BBC
Tm IV	B	diesel-hydraulic	280	60	30	90	1970	SLM	MTU	–

Locomotives / MANUFACTURERS

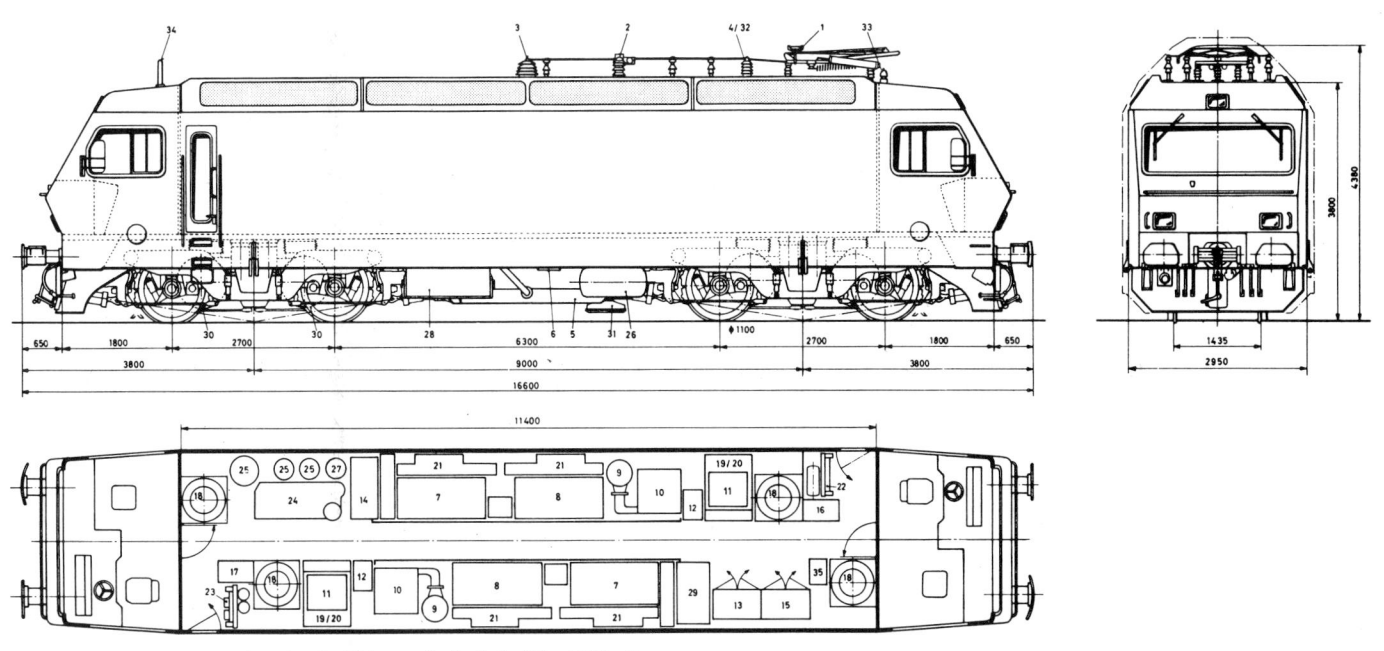

General arrangement of three-phase Type Re 4/4 locomotive for Swiss BT and SZU railways

speeds in curves with minimum rolling motion of the body; and hollow cardan shaft drive allowing large relative movements between wheelset and gear transmission unit.

The regenerative brake acts as service brake. As a mechanical back-up, the locomotive is equipped with brake units with sintered metal shoes and a permanent magnet rail brake.

Structural design of the lightweight body has been computer-optimised with the overall configuration developed in wind tunnel tests. The air-conditioned and pressure-tight driver's cabs will be of fibre-reinforced sandwich construction.

The electrical equipment supplied by ABB Switzerland will embody frequency converter technology with three-phase traction motors and the latest GTO (gate turn-off) power thyristors.

SBB Class 460: leading particulars

Axle arrangement: Bo-Bo
Gauge: 1435 mm
Wheel diameter new/worn: 1100 mm/1030 mm
Locomotive weight: 81 000 kg
Weight of mechanical part including gear transmission: 41 000 kg
Continuous output (UIC) at motor shaft: 5200 kW
Maximum output at wheel between 80 and 200 km/h (traction and braking): 6100 kW
Starting tractive effort and braking force at wheel, freely programmable, between 0 and 80 km/h: 275 kN
Maximum speed: 230 km/h
Overhead line voltage/frequency: 15 kV/16⅔ Hz

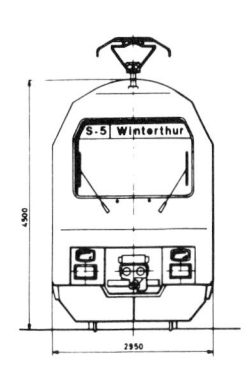

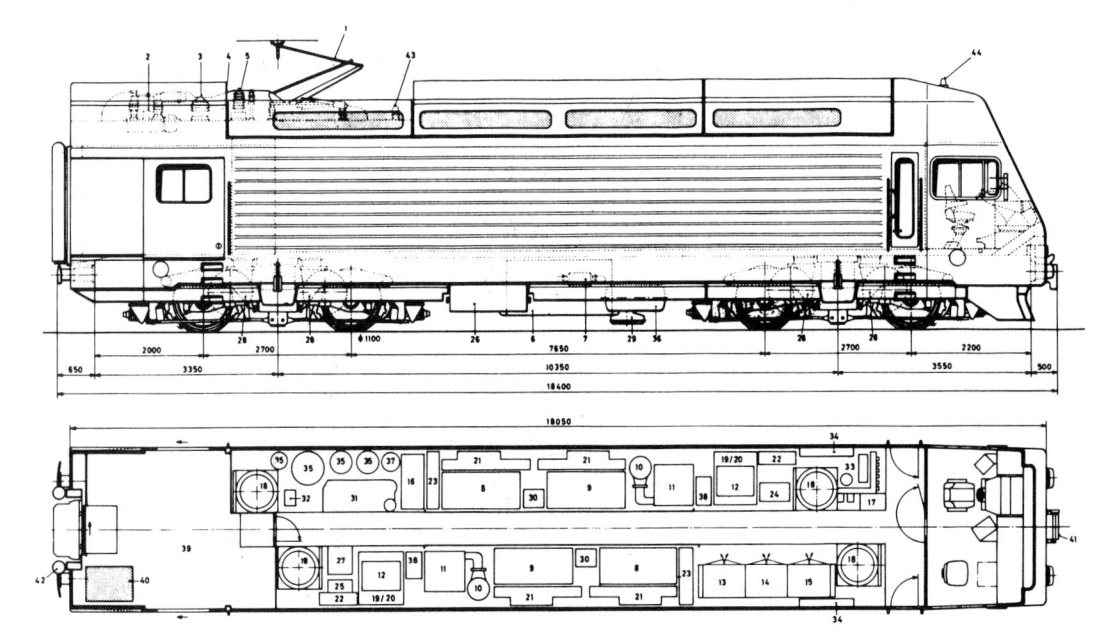

Steerable-axle drive bogie of SBB Class 450

General arrangement of three-phase Class 450 locomotive for Zurich S-Bahn service

66 MANUFACTURERS / Locomotives

SLM electric locomotives

Class	Wheel arrangement	Gauge mm	Line voltage	Rated output (kW) continuous/ one-hour	Tractive effort continuous/ at starting (kN)	at speed (km/h)	Max speed km/h	Weight tonnes	No in service 1989	Year first built	Electrical equipment
SBB Re 4/4 IV	Bo-Bo	1435	15 kV	4872/5072	200/300	86	160	80	4	1982	ABB
SBB Ee 6/6 II	Co-Co	1435	15 kV	730/860	353/360	10	85	106	10	1980	ABB
SBB Re 6/6	Bo-Bo-Bo	1435	15 kV	7434/8028	235/394	111	140	120	89	1972	ABB
SBB Re 4/4 II	Bo-Bo	1435	15 kV	4447/4780	149/255	105	140	80	303	1964	ABB
GDe 4/4	Bo-Bo	1000	840 V dc	1016/1068	81/172	45	100	50	6	1983	ABB
Furka-Oberalp Ge 4/4 III	Bo-Bo	1000	11 kV	1520/1700	102/179	53	90	50	2	1980	ABB
RhB Ge 4/4 II	Bo-Bo	1000	11 kV	1520/1700	102/179	53	90	50	23	1973	ABB
PTT Ee 3/3	Co	1435	15 kV	580/624	80/130	28	60	48	4	1985	ABB
HGe 4/4 II*	Bo-Bo	1000	15 kV	1660/1750	–	–	100	62.3	2	1985	ABB
HGe 4/4 II	Bo-Bo	1000	11 kV	1660/1750	–	–	90	64	3	1985	ABB
Re 4/4†	Bo-Bo	1435	15 kV	3000	240	–	130	69	6	1987	ABB
SBB Class 450	Bo-Bo	1435	15 kV	3000	240	–	130	74	19	1989	ABB
SBB Class 460	Bo-Bo	1435	15 kV	5200	275	–	230	81	–	1990	ABB

* Rack and adhesion locomotive
† Converter

Socimi
Società Costruzioni Industriali Milano SpA

Head office: Via Varesina 115, 20156 Milan, Italy

Telephone: +39 2 30091
Telex: 323564
Telefax: +39 2 3085161

Main works
Via Enrico Fermi n 25, 20082 Binasco (Milan)
Telephone: +39 2 9055605/6/7/8

Via Donatori del Sangue n 100, 20010 Arluno (Milan)
Telephone: +39 2 9017666, 9017803

Viale Porto Torres, Reg Zentu Figghi, 07100 Sassari
Telephone: +39 79 260206

Type 214 130 hp diesel-hydraulic shunter for Italian State Railways (FS)

Via I Maggio, 21045 Gazzada Schianno (Varese)
Telephone: +39 332 461313

Chairman: Dr Eng Alessandro Marzocco
Managing Director: Dr Eng Pierino Sacchi

Assistant to Chairman: Dr Eng Corrado Landolina

Products: Diesel-electric and diesel-hydraulic locomotives, diesel-mechanical locomotives, electric locomotives, tractors.

SOFER
SOFER–Officine Ferroviarie, SpA

Via Miliscola 33, Pozzuoli (Naples), Italy

Telephone: +39 81 526 2522
Cable: SOFER, Pozzuoli
Telex: 710048
Telefax: +39 81 526 2288

Chairman: Dr Ing Corrado Fici
General Manager: Dr Ing Giovanni Alfano

Products: Electric, diesel-electric and diesel-hydraulic locomotives; shunting locomotives.

Soma
Soma Equipamentos Industrias SA

Head office: Parque Industrial Mariano Ferraz, Avenida Soma 700, Sumaré, São Paulo, Brazil

Telephone: +55 11 192 73 1000
Telex: 019 1923
Telefax: +55 11 192 73 2472

São Paulo office: Avenida Brigadeiro Faria Lima, 1709, 7° Andar, Conjumto 7A, São Paulo

Telephone: +55 11 212 5311
Cable: Somafer
Telex: (011) 23692

President: Victorio Walter dos Reis Ferraz
Executive Vice President: Victorio Mariano Ferraz
Commercial Vice President: Carlos Marcondes Ferraz

Products: Battery locomotives. Recent products include a 14-tonne, flameproofed mining locomotive, manufactured under licence from Arn Jung Lokomotivfabrik of Kirchen, Federal Republic of Germany, with an output of 49.2 kW.

Constitution: The company was founded in 1929 and was the first company in South America to manufacture freight cars. It has specialised in the development of refrigerator cars and tank cars which are leased to various transport concerns.

Sorefame
Sociedades Reunidas de Fabricaçoẽs Metálicas, SA

Head office: Rua Vice-Almirante Azevedo Coutinho, PO Box 5, 2701 Amadora Codex, Portugal

Telephone: +351 1 976051
Cable: Sorefame, Amadora
Telex: 12 608 sorfam p
Telefax: +351 1 977210

Works: Amadora

Chairman: Rui Vilares Cordeiro
Rolling Stock Division Manager: M Andrade Gomes
Marketing Director: Luiz Veloso

Products: Diesel and electric locomotives.
The company's recent products includes the follow-

Class CC-3000 diesel-electric Co-Co for CP

Locomotives / **MANUFACTURERS** 67

Recent Sorefame electric locomotives

Class	Wheel arrangement	Line voltage	Rated output (kW)	Max speed km/h	Weight tonnes	No in service 1988	Year first built	Builders	
								Mechanical parts	Electrical equipment
BB-2880	B-B	25 kV	2880	160	78	9	1986	Sorefame/Alsthom	50 Hz Group (Alsthom, MTE, ABB, Siemens)

Recent Sorefame diesel locomotives

Class	Wheel arrangement	Transmission	Rated power kW	Max speed km/h	Total weight tonnes	No in service 1988	Year first built	Builders		
								Mechanical parts	Engine & type	Transmission
CC-3000	Co-Co	Elec	2425	120	120	30	1980–81	Sorefame Alsthom	SACM AGO V12 DSHR	Alsthom

ing order for the Portuguese Railways (CP): nine 2880 kW 25 kV ac 50 Hz electric locomotives built by Sorefame in association with 50 c/s Group, with the mechanical parts manufactured by Sorefame under Alsthom licence.

Constitution: The company was established in 1943, and has supplied rolling stock for Portugal, Africa, North America and Brazil as well as hydro-mechanical equipment for dams, electro-mechanical equipment for hydro-electric and thermal power stations (classical and nuclear).

Class 2500 electric Bo-Bo for CP

Thyssen Henschel
Thyssen Industrie AG, Henschel

Henschelplatz 1, 3500 Kassel 2, Federal Republic of Germany

Telephone: +49 561 8011
Cable: Henschel, Kassel
Telex: 099793 thksl d
Telefax: +49 561 8016338

President: Klaus Bax
Senior Vice President, Traffic Systems: Hans-Richard Hippenstiel

Vice President, Locomotives: Manfred Kunis
Director of Engineering: Prof Siegfried Kademann

Products: Locomotives for main-line and shunting service covering a wide power range and designed for all gauges and axle loads; diesel locomotives with hydraulic and electric (ac/dc and ac/ac) transmission; electric locomotives for all current systems; dual-power locomotives; Henschel electronic control systems; Henschel Flexi-Float bogies; axle drives for locomotives; rapid transit vehicles; spring-suspended gear wheels for railbound vehicles; research and development of new rail transport technologies such as Maglev vehicles; complete after-sales facilities;

rehabilitation and modernisation of existing locomotives, including retrofitting of electronic control equipment.

The Thyssen Group is heavily involved in rail transport, both as supplier and user of railroad equipment. The Group also has one of Europe's largest industrial railway systems, operated by Eisenbahn und Häfen, and many Thyssen plants have a railway department operating their own locomotives.

From October 1984, Waggon Union GmbH and the Herne and Kassel plants of Thyssen Getriebe-und Kupplungswerke were incorporated into the Thyssen-Henschel business sector. Thyssen-Henschel intend to offer complete railway systems from one source.

Class DHG 700 diesel-hydraulic 0–6–0 for Thailand

Class EA 3000 4000 kW 25 kV ac three-phase electric locomotive for Danish State Railways

68 MANUFACTURERS / Locomotives

The various sections of the Thyssen-Henschel Group comprise component research, development, design and manufacture, and are located as follows: locomotives in Kassel; vehicles at Siegen and in Berlin; and new transportation technologies, including magnetic levitation (Maglev), in Munich and Kassel. Besides the production of standardised locomotives and those built to specifications to European and overseas railways systems, which since 1848 have totalled almost 33 000 units, Henschel has always been actively engaged in high-speed transportation. First trials in this field took place already in the early years of this century.

In recent years Henschel has played an active part in the wheel/rail research programme sponsored by the Federal German Ministry of Research and Technology. Within this programme Henschel developed from their standard Flexi-Float bogie design, which is characterised by draw-and-push-rods between axle boxes and bogie as well as between bogie and chassis, the UmAn bogie concept. In the latter, unsprung masses can be transferred hydromechanically from the bogie frame to the main frame during high-speed running on tangent track, thereby reducing lateral and horizontal forces on wheels and rails and also avoiding critical speeds. During high-speed tests carried out with the Henschel-BBC diesel-electric three-phase motor DE2500 UmAn research locomotive, speeds of 250 km/h on rails and 300 km/h on a roller-rig test-bed were attained without any difficulties.

As a result of these tests the design of the bogies for the power cars of the ICE high-speed research train-set was evolved from the Henschel UmAn bogie. For the ICE the design was modified and simplified by replacing the mechanical and controlled coupling of unsprung masses such as the traction motor, gears and wheelsets (active coupling) with hydraulic shock absorbers having special characteristics (passive coupling) for safe speeds of up to 400 km/h.

Class 120 5600 kW universal Bo-Bo electric locomotive for German Federal Railway

In recent years diesel-electric main-line locomotives employing GM power and transmission equipment have been supplied amongst others to Egypt (Class 3000, 2500 hp, a repeat order) and Pakistan (Class HGMU-30, 3300 hp). Three-axle diesel-hydraulic locomotives of 700 hp have been supplied to Thailand.

In the field of electric locomotives the Norwegian State Railways (NSB) took delivery of further Class EL 17 3000/3300 kW units and the German Federal Railway (DB) of Class 120 (5600 kW with BBC three-phase power transmission). All bogie locomotives are equipped with Henschel Flexi-Float bogies.

In 1974 Thyssen-Henschel began research and development work in the field of long-stator magnetic levitation technology to create an alternative concept to the line of development being pursued at the time. By adopting a development strategy aimed at the practical application of the magnetic levitation system, Thyssen-Henschel succeeded in establishing this concept as an independent line of development and advancing it to a state of operational readiness through large-scale projects, such as the IVA 79 demonstration facilities and the Transrapid test facilities in Emsland (TVE).

In parallel with these applications there was further development of long-stator magnetic levitation technology within the framework of a comprehensive technology programme subsidised by the Federal Ministry for Research and Technology to promote the realisation of operational, highly reliable components and subsystems, such as the failsafe 'magnetic wheel'. After 10 years of successful development and project activity, Thyssen-Henschel assumed the lead in magnetic levitation systems development. The findings of the application studies based on the system data generated by Thyssen-Henschel show the medium's competitiveness with other transport systems. In addition, Thyssen-Henschel has succeeded in using this acquired know-how outside the field of magnetic levitation development for the improvement and the development of new products.

Thyssen-Henschel diesel locomotives delivered or in production

Class	Wheel arrangement	Transmission	Rated power kW	Max speed km/h	Total weight tonnes	No in service	Year first built	Builders		
								Mechanical parts	Engine & type	Transmission
DE 3300	Co-Co	DE ac/dc	2460	125	120	30	1985	Henschel	EMD GM 16–645 E3C	EMDGMARIO-D18
DE 1650	Co-Co	DE dc/dc	1230	90	84	5	1985	Henschel	GM 12–645	EMD GM D25
DHG 700	C	DH	495	58	47	10	1985	Henschel	MTU 6 V 396 TC 12	L 3r 4U2
DHG 1000	B-B	DH	743	90	44	57	1972	Henschel	MTU 12 V 396 TC 12	
DE 3000	Co-Co	ac/dc	1845	120	122	247	1976	Henschel	EMD GM 12–645E3	EMD GM ARIO/D14

Thyssen-Henschel electric locomotives delivered or in production

Class	Wheel arrangement	Line voltage	Rated output (kW) continuous	Max speed km/h	Weight tonnes	No in service	Year first built	Builders	
								Mechanical parts	Electrical equipment
ICE (DB)	Bo-Bo	15 kV/16⅔ Hz	4200	300 (350)	78	1	1984	Henschel	BBC
EL 17 (NSB)	Bo-Bo	15 kV/16⅔ Hz	3000	140	64	12	1981	Henschel	BBC
EA 3000 (DSB)	Bo-Bo	25 kV/50 Hz	4000	175	80	10	1984	Henschel	BBC
E 120 (DB)	Bo-Bo	15 kV 16⅔ Hz	5600	200	84	60	1986	Henschel Krauss-Maffei Krupp	AEG BBC Siemens

TIBB
Tecnomasio Italiano Brown Boveri SpA
Transport Division
(A member of the ABB Group)

Casella postale 10225, 20100 Milan, Italy

Telephone: +39 2 57971
Cable: Tecnomasio, Milan
Telex: 310153
Telefax: +39 2 57972740
　　　　　57972756

Products: Electric and diesel-electric locomotives.
The company developed the full chopper control for the experimental Italian State Railways (FS) electric locomotive No E444.005 of 1976, which embodied the first application of solid-state technology to high-power

Class D145 diesel-electric locomotive for Italian State Railways

Locomotives / **MANUFACTURERS** 69

electronic drives for 3 kV dc systems. Since 1979, TIBB has manufactured the prototypes and two series of the chopper-control locomotives Classes E632 and E633. In 1986 FS ordered a pre-series of six units of Class E652 with increased power and only one gear ratio to cover both passenger and freight services. The E652 has a continuous rating of 5000 kW, a 36/64 gear ratio, a max speed of 160 km/h and tractive efforts of 278 kN starting and 180 kN continuous.

The 102-tonne E652 locomotive has a single, fully-suspended motor on each bogie, but is not articulated like earlier FS B-B-B types; the body, with a welded steel frame, is one-piece, with freedom of movement in the centre bogie. Electro-mechanical shoe- or disc-braking is combined with an automatic skid device, supplemented by rheostatic braking. The electrical equipment comprises: modular traction equipment on three motors, each fed by its own two-column chopper; choppers operating at fixed frequency steps with automatic checking of their precision; protection against over-voltage and excess current with electronic primer; provision for automatic attainment of the speed required with control of acceleration and absorbed current; motors' separate excitation with static feeder, regulated to obtain a series-indirect effect and automatic drop-out of the fields (the latter are interconnected in series, to ensure stability of the motor operation and prevent slipping); rheostatic braking; static converter for three-phase ac feed of the auxiliary services.

Since 1979 TIBB has manufactured 20 mixed-traffic Class D145 diesel-electric locomotives for FS. The main feature of this centre-cab design is its employment of three-phase traction technology. Each two-axle bogie is fitted with two three-phase asynchronous, nose-suspended and force-ventilated motors and the power transmission is by a synchronous, six-pole generator with three-phase exciter. The main exciting current is rectified by means of rotating diodes without sliprings. One side of each motor shaft is connected to the pinion of the reduction gear, which has a 15/79 ratio. There is an electronic control and regulation system for voltage and frequency, and rheostatic braking is fitted. The 12-cylinder, four-stroke engine has BBC turbochargers.

The FS ordered a further batch of 42 Class D145 from TIBB in 1985.

The ETR500 train-set is the Italian State Railways' high-speed project for the 1990s. The basic composition of each train is two locomotives enclosing up to 14 trailers.

The main technical features are:
Two Bo-Bo locomotives, total power: 8400 kW
Max speed: 300 km/h
Traction motors: Three-phase asynchronous
Drive: inverters
Tare weight of full train: 680 tonnes
Seats: 700

Technical fulfilment of the project is by a consortium of the main Italian manufacturers in which TIBB is responsible for the development and the production of the electrical traction equipment (chopper, inverters, traction motors, controls).

Constitution: TIBB has been in existence since 1903. In 1919 the Vado Ligure factory was taken over by Tecnomasio Italiano Brown Boveri. Mechanical components and electrical equipment for rolling stock are still manufactured at Vado Ligure while electronic equipment is produced at the Vittuone factory. Over 700 electric locomotives have been built for Italian State Railways (FS).

Electric locomotives or power cars

Class	Wheel arrangement	Line voltage	Rated output (kW) continuous	Max speed km/h	Weight tonnes	No	Year first built	Builders Mechanical parts	Builders Electrical equipment
FS E652	B-B-B	3 kV dc	5000	160	102	6	1988	TIBB	TIBB
FS ETR 500	B-B	3 kV ac	4000	300	72	3	1988	Breda/Fiat	TIBB/Ansaldo

Diesel locomotives

Class	Wheel arrangement	Transmission	Rated power kW	Max speed km/h	Total weight tonnes	No in service or on order to 6/86	Year first built	Builders Mechanical parts	Builders Engine & type	Builders Transmission
FS D145.2000 (FS)	Bo-Bo	Elec ac/dc/ac	840	100	70	62	1983	TIBB	1 × IF-ID369912V	TIBB

Toshiba
Toshiba Corporation
Railway Projects Department

Toshiba Building, 1-1, Shibaura 1-chome, Minato-ku, Tokyo 105, Japan

Telephone: +81 3 457 4924
Cable: Toshiba Tokyo
Telex: 22587 toshiba
Telefax: +81 3 457 8385

Products: Electric, diesel-electric and diesel-hydraulic locomotives; electric traction equipment; auxiliary power supply units.

A major item of recent production has been design of ac electric locomotives for Turkish State Railways. The locomotive is of the monocoque body type with a driving cab at each end, and with six axle-hung nose-suspended traction motors developing 3180 kW and mounted on a three-bogie (Bo-Bo-Bo) configuration. It is designed to operate at a nominal line voltage of 25 kV but can operate at any voltage within the range of 19 kV to 27.5 kV. Two locomotives can operate in multiple-unit.

Leading particulars
Wheel arrangement: Bo-Bo-Bo
Track gauge: 1435 mm
Max operating speed: 90 km/h
Total weight: 120 tonnes
Rated capacity: 3180 kW
Continuous rated tractive effort: 280 kN at 40 km/h
Powering control: Notchless voltage control by main converter with phase angle control
Braking control: Dynamic brake with field excitation control and air brake
Primary power supply is drawn from the 25 kV 50 Hz single-phase ac overhead catenary via the pantograph. The earth return path is through earthing brushes furnished in the traction motor suspension tubes making contact with the axles. From secondary windings of the main transformer, the controlled traction power is conducted to the dc traction motors via a main converter and smoothing reactors.

A phase-converter powered from tertiary winding of main transformer provides 380 V 50 Hz three-phase power for auxiliary rotating machines. An auxiliary alternator accommodated with the common yoke to the phase converter supplies the power for charging the nickel cadmium batteries. Power for miscellaneous service equipment is provided from a tertiary winding of the main transformer.

An electro-pneumatically controlled, automatic compressed air brake and spring-type parking brake are provided. An electrical dynamic brake system is also provided; the last two locomotives will have both dynamic and regenerative braking.

Microprocessor control covers: armature converter

1900 kW Bo-Bo electric locomotive for Japan Freight Railway Company

control for both groups; field converter control for each motor; speed calculation; wheel diameter compensation; automatic compensation of locomotive weight transfer; wheel slip/slide control; and various protection items.

The main transformer is of a shell type and has eight windings, such as a primary, four secondary for armature converter, a tertiary for auxiliary power converter, a fourth for train heating and a fifth for field converter. Oil-immersed with forced air, forced oil cooling, it has a continuous rating of 5398 kVA-4572 kVA-140 kVA-600 kVA-86 kVA.

A main converter has functions both of armature and field current control, and for their control too a microprocessor is used. Four thyristor-diode mixed bridge units are divided into two groups, and connected in cascade-connection respectively. Six thyristor bridge

MANUFACTURERS / Locomotives

units for field control are connected to fifth winding of main transformer in parallel, and each unit controls field current relating to the armature current drawn on same traction motor individually. Continuous rating: 4374 kW-2 × 900 V-2430 A for armature converter; 51 kW-6 × 25 V-338 A for field converter.

Each traction motor is of the four-pole pulsating current, separately excited and axle-hung type. The six motors are connected in two groups of three. All parallel-connected motors are controlled individually via a main converter. Continuous rating: 530 kW-900 V-635 A-1050 rpm.

Among advanced technology equipment under trial manufacture is a pulse width modulation converter for the traction power supply of the next generation of train-sets for JNR's Shinkansen. The input for this converter is 50/60 Hz 20 to 25 kV and GTO thyristors of high capacity are adopted.

Toshiba electric locomotives

Class	Wheel arrangement	Line voltage	Rated output kW	Max speed km/h	Weight tonnes	Gauge mm	Notes	Builders Mechanical parts	Builders Electrical equipment
ED-45	B-B	20 000 ac (50 Hz)	1300		60	1067		Toshiba	Toshiba
ED-71	B-B	20 000 ac (50 Hz)	2040		64	1067		Toshiba	Toshiba
ED-72	B-2-B	20 000 ac (60 Hz)	2050	100	82	1067		Toshiba	Toshiba
ED-72	B-2-B	20 000 ac (60 Hz)	1900		87	1067		Toshiba	Toshiba
ED-73	B-B	20 000 ac (60 Hz)	1900		67	1067		Toshiba	Toshiba
ED-75	B-B	20 000 ac (50 Hz)	1900		67.2	1067		Toshiba	Toshiba
ED-76	B-2-B	20 000 ac (60 Hz)	1900		87	1067		Toshiba	Toshiba
ED-76	B-2-B	20 000 ac (50 Hz)	1900		90.5	1067		Toshiba	Toshiba
ED-77	B-2-B	20 000 ac (50 Hz)	1900	100	75	1067		Toshiba	Toshiba
EF-30	B+B+B	20 000 ac (60 Hz) 1500 dc	1800		96	1067	Ac-dc dual use	Toshiba	Toshiba
EF-71	B-B-B	20 000 ac (50 Hz) 1500 dc	2700	100	96	1067	Ac-dc dual use	Toshiba	Toshiba
EF-80	B-B-B	20 000 ac (50 Hz) 1500 dc	1950		96	1067	Ac-dc dual use	Toshiba	Toshiba
WAG-2	B-B	25 000 ac (50 Hz)	2400 (2×1200)	80	86.5	1676	Box type, silicon rectifier, HT tap changer, mono-motor system	Toshiba	Toshiba
E43000 (TCDD)	B-B	380 ac (50 Hz)	180 (4×45)		145	1524	Centre cab, thyristor phase control with radio remote control device	Toshiba	Toshiba
	B-B-B	25 000 ac (50 Hz)	3180	90	120	1435	Thyristor converter and microprocessor control with dynamic or dynamic/regenerative braking	Toshiba Tulomsas	Toshiba
DEROI	1C+C1	3000 dc	1920 (6×320)		135	1435	Centre cab, non-automatic multiple operation with rheostatic brake	Toshiba	Toshiba
	B-B	1200 dc	955 (4×239)		85	1435	Centre cab, non-automatic multiple operation with rheostatic brake	Toshiba	Toshiba
Ea	B-B	1500 dc	960 (4×240)	72	54	1067	Box type, single cab, multiple operation, non-automatic rheostatic brake for speed suppression for steep gradient operation	Toshiba	Toshiba
10E	C-C	3000 dc	3090 (6×515)		126	1067	Box type, multiple operation, chopper control with regenerative/rheostatic brake	UCW	Toshiba
	B-B	1200 dc	850 (4×212.5)		73	1435	Centre cab, non-automatic multiple operation with rheostatic brake	Toshiba	Toshiba
	B-B	1200 dc	955 (4×239)		80	1435	Centre cab, non-automatic multiple operation with rheostatic brake	Toshiba	Toshiba
	B-B	1200 dc	955 (4×239)		85	1435	Centre cab, non-automatic multiple operation with rheostatic brake	Toshiba	Toshiba
	B-B	1500 dc	955 (4×239)		85	1435		Toshiba	Toshiba
LOCO-EBB-30	B-B	500 dc	400 (4×100)		30	1067	Centre cab, non-automatic indirect control with rheostatic brake, with pole type current collector	Toshiba	Toshiba
EB-10	B-B	1500 dc	135		23	1067		Toshiba	Toshiba
ED-16	1B+B1	1500 dc	900		77	1067		Toshiba	Toshiba
ED-17	B+B	1500 dc	915		60	1067		Toshiba	Toshiba
ED-31	B-B	1200 dc	456		41	1067		Toshiba	Toshiba
ED-33	B-B	1200 dc	588		52	1067		Toshiba	Toshiba
ED-35	B-B	1500 dc	340		35	1067		Toshiba	Toshiba
ED-38	B-B	1500 dc	588		50	1067		Toshiba	Toshiba
ED-42	B+B	600 dc	525		63	1067	Rack adhesion type	Toshiba	Toshiba
ED-42	B+B	1500 dc	440		63	1067	Rack adhesion type	Toshiba	Toshiba
ED-42	B-B	1500 dc	510		63	1067	Rack adhesion type	Toshiba	Toshiba
ED-61	B-B	1500 dc	1560		60	1067		Toshiba	Toshiba
EF-10	1C+C1	1500 dc	1380		98	1067		Toshiba	Toshiba
EF-11	1C+C1	1500 dc	1380		98	1067		Toshiba	Toshiba
EF-12	1C+C1	1500 dc	1650		100	1067		Toshiba	Toshiba
EF-13	1C+C1	1500 dc	1650		100	1067		Toshiba	Toshiba
EF-15	1C+C1	1500 dc	1950		101	1067		Toshiba	Toshiba
EF-16	1C+C1	1500 dc	1900		106	1067		Toshiba	Toshiba
EF-18	2C+C2	1500 dc	1900		110	1067		Toshiba	Toshiba
EF-52	2C+C2	1500 dc	1350		108	1067		Toshiba	Toshiba
EF-53	2C+C2	1500 dc	1350		100	1067		Toshiba	Toshiba
EF-58	2C+C2	1500 dc	1650		98	1067		Toshiba	Toshiba
EF-58	2C+C2	1500 dc	1950		115	1067		Toshiba	Toshiba
EF-60	B-B-B	1500 dc	2550		96	1067		Toshiba	Toshiba
EF-62	C-C	1500 dc	2550		96	1067		Toshiba	Toshiba
EF-63	B-B-B	1500 dc	2550		108	1067		Toshiba	Toshiba
EF-64	B-B-B	1500 dc	2550		96	1067		Toshiba	Toshiba
EF-65	B-B-B	1500 dc	2550		96	1067		Toshiba	Toshiba
EH-10	(B-B)+(B-B)	1500 dc	2530		120	1067		Toshiba	Toshiba
ED-79	B-B	20000 ac	1900		67.2	1067	Toshiba	Toshiba	

Locomotives / **MANUFACTURERS**

Toshiba diesel locomotives

Class	Wheel arrangement	Rated power hp/rpm	Total weight tonnes	Gauge mm	Notes	Builders		
						Mechanical parts	Engine & type	Transmission
	B-B	500/1800	52	1000	Hood type, non-automatic shunter, 4×52kW	Toshiba	Caterpillar D348TA	Toshiba
	B-B	1050/1300	64	1600	Hood type, non-automatic, shunter, 4×117kW	Toshiba	Caterpillar D398TA Series B	Toshiba
	C-C	2400/1500	90	1000	Box type, main line	Toshiba Kawasaki	SEMT-Pielstick 16PA4-V-200VG	Toshiba
DSJ	B-B	475/1800	52	1067	Semi-centre cab, shunter, non-automatic, 4×55kW	Toshiba	Cummins KTA-1150-L	Toshiba
DSG	B-B	2×475/1800	56	1067	Centre cab, twin-engine, non-automatic, with constant speed control device, 4×110 kW	Toshiba	Cummins 2×KTA-1150-L	Toshiba
	B-B	500/1500	52	1067	Hood type, multiple operation, non-automatic, 4×52 kW	Toshiba	Maybach Mercedes-Benz MB-836Bb	Toshiba
	B-B	1050/1300	105	1435	Hood type, shunter, non-automatic, 4×141 kW	Toshiba	Caterpillar D398-TA	Toshiba
	A1A-A1A	750/600	106	1435		Toshiba		Toshiba
	B-B	1050/1300	58	1067	Hood type, non-automatic, with wheel slip/slide detection device, 4×140 kW	Toshiba	Caterpillar D398TA Series B	Toshiba
DD-10	A1A-A1A	600/900	69	1067		Toshiba		Toshiba
DD-41	B-B	660/1000	60	1067		Toshiba	Cooper-Bessemer FWL-6T	Toshiba
DF-50	B-B-B	1400/1000	82	1067		Toshiba	MAN V6V 22/30mA	Toshiba
	B-B	600/1500	50	1067		Toshiba	Niigata DMF31SB1	Toshiba
	0-B-0	153/1800	20	1067		Toshiba	Hino DA59C	
	B-B	500/1500	60	1435		Toshiba	Niigata DMF31BS	Toshiba
	0-B-0	153/1800	20	1067		Toshiba	Hino DA59C	Toshiba
	0-B-0	180/1500	25	1067		Toshiba	Niigata DMH17C	Toshiba
	0-B-0	110/1800	10	1067		Toshiba	Hino DS50	Toshiba

Toyo
Toyo Denki Seizo KK
Toyo Electric Manufacturing Co Ltd

Yaesu Mitsui Building, No 7-2 Yaesu, 2-chome, Chuo-ku, Tokyo 104, Japan

Telephone: +81 3 271 6374
Cable: Yohden, Tokyo
Telex: 222 4666

President: Atsushi Doi

Products: Electric locomotives; diesel-electric locomotives.

Constitution: Established in 1918, this company produces traction motors and control equipment for home and export. It was responsible for the axle drive with cardan shaft and steel blade coupling which is used as standard equipment by the Japanese National Railways and by many of the private railways in Japan.

Unilok
Unilokomotive Ltd
A subsidiary of Killeen Investments (Irl) Ltd

Mervue Industrial Estate, Galway, Republic of Ireland

Telephone: +353 91 57034
Telex: 50113 ulok ei
Telefax: +353 91 51373

Sales Director: Michael Lalor

Products: Unilok shunting/switching locomotives manufactured in three basic configurations: C Series, for rail only duty; D Series, for rail/off rail duty on smooth terrain; and E Series, for rail/off rail duty on rough terrain.

Models are classified according to maximum possible drawbar pull. All Unilok machines except the E-552 use the principle of weight transfer whereby weight is borrowed from the adjacent wagon, thereby increasing significantly the traction weight of the Unilok itself. Using this principle, the E-125 is capable of achieving a drawbar pull of 12 500 kg and of hauling loads up to 1700 tonnes. At the other end of the scale, the E-55 develops 5500 kg drawbar pull and is suitable for smaller loads up to 7000 tonnes.

Depending on the model, auxiliary drives and specification engine sizes vary from 70 to 150 hp. Typical towing speed at maximum load is 5–10 km/h with a maximum speed on rail of 20 km/h and 30 km/h on road.

All machines are available with infinitely variable hydrostatic drive transmission and a wide range of optional equipment including wagon air/vacuum brakes, deadmans vigilance system, steel, polyurethane or rubber rail tyres, explosion proofing, radio remote control. Additionally the machines may be fitted with auxiliary equipment such as snow-plough (road and rail), sweeper, fork lift, hydraulic crane etc.

Uniloks are in service worldwide and are available in all gauges and coupler systems.

Recent exports include deliveries to Pakistan, UK, Germany, Iran, Syria and Holland.

Unikok E–55 operating under remote radio control at Hamburg   Unilok Series E-125 at Cementas Tolteca, Mexico

72 MANUFACTURERS / Locomotives

Constitution: Manufactured and sold from West Germany 1966 to 1976 by Hugo Aeckerle Co of Hamburg. All production and sales moved to the Republic of Ireland in 1976.

Unilok Series D-105 locomotive at WAPDA, Pakistan

Union Carriage
Union Carriage & Wagon Co (Pty) Ltd

PO Box 335, Marievale Road, Vorsterkroon, Nigel 1490, Transvaal, South Africa

Telephone: +27 11 739 2411
Cable: Unicarwag
Telex: 750524 unicar
Telefax: +27 11 739 5156

Chairman: G S E Courcourakis
Managing Director: R Bingham
Commercial Manager: A A M Lyle
Technical Manager: J J R Wetten
Manufacturing Manager: T D Floyd

Products: Electric and diesel locomotives.

Since 1959 the company has manufactured over 11 000 locomotives and passenger coaches for South African Transport Services (SATS), for export and for industrial organisations.

The company manufactures diesel locomotives with hydraulic and electric transmissions for shunting and branch-line operations in a standard range of mass and power configurations of up to 80 tonnes and 1100 kW. Designs incorporate multiple-unit control, slow speed/ high speed control, deadman or vigilance system, anti-slip slagtipping devices, dual train brakes etc.

Constitution: General Mining and Union Corp, Anglo-American Corp and Matsak Ltd are the principal shareholders of this company. Less than 25 per cent in value of all the contracts received is spent overseas, mostly on electric traction equipment which is not obtainable from South African sources. Formed in 1957 to supply South African Railways with passenger coaches, Union Carriage has expanded its business to supply the export market and to become a major manufacturer of main-line and shunting electric locomotives.

Thyristor-chopper-controlled Class 8E shunting locomotive for SATS (main contractor, ABB-Siemens consortium)

Class 10E locomotive for South African Transport Services (SATS)

Valmet
Valmet Corporation, Railway Division

PO Box 387, 33101 Tampere, Finland

Telephone: +358 31 658111
Telex: 22112
Telefax: +358 31 657044

General Manager: Esko Määttänen
Marketing Manager: Matti Kurkela
Export Manager: Olavi Kivimäki

Products: Diesel-hydraulic and diesel-electric locomotives.

Valmet is building 19 of the M-series Type Dr 16 diesel-electric locomotive for Finnish State Railways, delivery of which will take place during 1990–92. The Dr 16 is a multi-purpose locomotive which can be used in main line service and for heavy shunting duties.

The first unit of Valmet's new diesel-electric N-series locomotive was delivered in 1990. It is suited for main line operation as well as shunting and marshalling work. Low operating costs are achieved by ac-drive for

Scale model of the new Valmet N-locomotive

for high efficiency, and modular construction for ease of maintenance.

The new Valmet bogie used on the N-locomotive is a significant development: it has wheel sets with radial steering and divided axles which give the advantages of extra-durable flanges, quiet running in curves and low transverse forces against the rail.

Type Dr 16 diesel-electric locomotive for VR

Valmet diesel locomotives

Class	Wheel arrangement	Transmission	Rated power kW	Max speed km/h	Total weight tonnes	No in service	Year first built	Builders		
								Mechanical parts	Engine & type	Transmission
Tve4/Move 250	B	Hyd & Mech	283	75	34	45	1978	Valmet	Scania DS 14	Clark C8612 + Clark 8420
Move 66	C	Hyd	400	60	60	21	1967	Valmet	General Motors 16V-71N	Twin Disc CF 13800
Move 500	C	Hyd	520	50	57	1	1983	Valmet	Caterpillar 3412 PCTA	Voith L3r4U2
Dv 12	B-B	Hyd	1030	130	66	128	1964	Valmet	Tampella MGO V16 BSHR	Voith L216rs
Dr 16	Bo-Bo	Elec	1677	140	84	6	1985	Valmet	Pielstick 12PA4V200VG	Strömberg
Dr 16	Bo-Bo	Elec	1500	140	84	2	1987	Valmet	Wärtsilä 8V22	Strömberg
N	Bo-Bo	Elec	730	120	64	1	1990	Valmet	Caterpillar 3508	Strömberg

Ventra
Ventra Locomotives Ltd

10-5-3/A/1 (First Floor) Masab Tank, Hyderabad 500028, India

Telephone: +91 222081
Telex: 425 6928 vntr in

Director: Arvind N Vakil
General Manager: T O Verghese

Products: Diesel locomotives of up to 1200 hp; battery locomotives up to 100 hp; self-propelled wagons, Granby cars and OHE cars.

Diesel shunter by Ventra

Villares
Equipamentos Villares SA

Av Senador Vergueiro No 2000, São Bernardo do Campo 09700, SP, Brazil

Telephone: +55 11 443 5500
Telex: +55 11 44068

Managing Director: J Carlos do Couto Viana
Manufacturing Director: J Cassio Daltrini
Sales Manager: Renato Franco

Products: Diesel locomotives under EMD licence; electric locomotives under GEC licence; diesel shunting locomotives.

Type JT26CW 2684 kW diesel-electric locomotive for ENAFER, Peru

Recent Villares diesel locomotives

Type	Wheel arrangement	Transmission	Rated power kW	Max speed km/h	Total weight tonnes	No in service 1988	Year first built	Engine & type	Transmission
SD40-2	Co-Co	Elec	2684	105	180	19 (on order)	1985	EMD 16-645E3C	Villares
GT-22 CUM-2	Co-Co	Elec	1846	105	120	10	1986	EMD 12-645E3B	Villares
JT-26 CW	Co-Co	Elec	2684	100	120	6	1986	EMD 16-645E3C	Villares
GT-26 CW-2B	Co-Co	Elec	2684	85	120	30	1988	EMD 16-645E3C	Villares

Voroshilovgrad
Voroshilovgrad Diesel Locomotive Works

Voroshilovgrad, USSR

Products: Diesel locomotives.

Constitution: Member of Energomachexport.

74 MANUFACTURERS / Locomotives

Windhoff
Rheiner Maschinenfabrik Windhoff AG

Head office: Hovstrasse 10, Postfach 1160, 4440 Rheine, Federal Republic of Germany

Telephone: +49 5971 58-0
Telex: 09 81643 wir d

Works: Rheine (rolling stock)
Rheine-Neuenkirchen (heat exchangers)

President: Dr Bernd Windhoff
Managers: Heinz Lörfing
Günter Knieper
Franz-Josef Cramer
Christoph Wessels
Herbert Bucksch
Export Manager: Helmut Pühs

Products: Standard types of shunting vehicle; Windhoff Tele-Trac with tractive forces up to 40 000 daN, diesel or electro-hydraulically driven, control of shunting and coupling operations by radio or by interlinking with the loading programme; shunting equipment for railway connections and sidings; turntables and traversers of all kinds for track vehicles; axle and bogie lifts for vehicle maintenance; multipurpose track maintenance machines with extensive attachments; rail crane trucks; crib ballast removers; light trailers for track motor cars; overhead line inspection cars.

The Windhoff FU 80 is equipped with a hydraulic working platform, a workshop for all operational requirements, a spacious crew room and a driver's stand in each travelling direction. The vehicle is driven by a 10-cylinder air-cooled diesel engine and has a maximum speed of 80 km/h. Shift transmission is normal, but for stop-and-go operations on site a hydrostatic drive is provided. The tractive power permits the coupling of additional loads that may be required on site, while at the same time the pneumatic braking system is designed for coping with any such loads.

Overhead line inspection car

Xiangtan
Xiangtan Electric Manufacturing Works, Import & Export Corp

Xiashesi, Xiangtan, Hunan, People's Republic of China

Telephone: +86 732 23300 21922-243
Telex: 998002 XEMW CN

Cable: 3000
Telefax: +86 732 23300/24236

Standing Deputy Director: Fan Shi Ang

Products: Electric locomotives. The plant produced China's first electric Co-Co locomotive in 1958, a 3900 hp unit based on the Soviet-designed N-60s.

Type ZG100-1500-S Bo+Bo+Bo+Bo for industrial use

Two-car unit manufactured by Xiangtan Works

Zeco
Zimbabwe Engineering Ltd

PO Box 1874, Bulawayo, Zimbabwe

Telephone: +263 9 78931
Cable: Tensile Belmont
Telex: 33171 ZW
Telefax: +263 9 72259

Works: 38 London Road, Belmont, Bulawayo, Zimbabwe

Chairman: J R T Moxon
Managing Director: E L Venables
Divisional Managers, Rolling Stock: J J Cann
Traction: K A Meth
Marketing: M I Macdonald

Products: Construction of diesel-electric, diesel-hydraulic and electric locomotives and rolling stock; overhaul and rebuilding of steam, diesel-electric, diesel-hydraulic and electric locomotives and rolling stock. Supply of complete bogies, bogie components and all spares for freight wagons.

Contracts completed and obtained during 1989 include the rebuilding of 30 steam locomotives for National Railways of Zimbabwe; supply of 590 freight wagons to Botswana Railways; supply of 50 phosphate, 25 tanker and 75 low-sided wagons to Tanzania Railways Corporation; and supply of 275 high-sided and 50 covered wagons for Tazara.

Zephir
Zephir SpA

Via S Allende 85, 41100 Modena, Italy

Telephone: +39 59 252554
Telex: 510247 BENFRA I Attn ZEPHIR
Telefax: +39 59 253759

Chairman: Dalla Rovere
Managing Director: Vittorio Cereghini

Products: Road-rail shunting tractors, diesel-powered with powershift transmission and four rubber drive wheels for rail gauges from 1000 to 1900 mm, engines 80 to 300 hp, weight 9 to 26 tonnes, drawbar pull from 4.5 to 15 tonnes. Optional fitments include automatic hook and brake system for railcars, tow hooks for industrial trailers; snow blades; rail-sweepers; pneumatic sandsprayer; anti-pollution system; anti-explosion system; opening front window of cab; remote control; portable two-way radio, puncture-proof and CSE tyres.

Zephir manufactures two models of diesel-engined ro-ro tractors (4 × 4) with 169 to 210 hp. These machines have powershift or automatic gearbox, two forward and two reverse speeds (or three forward and three reverse speeds). They can lift more than 25 tonnes on the fifth wheel and are suitable for 75 000 kg. A 180° slewing seat can be supplied on ro-ro models.

Due to increased sales, Zephir opened a new assembly plant in October 1989 – ZEPHIR 2 – with a production line capable of an annual output of over 200 tractors. Larger orders for tractors are dealt with here, with a manufacturing capacity of up to 20 units per month.

Sales and deliveries at the beginning of December 1989 totalled 14 ro-ro 171P25 tractors to Tanzania Harbours Authority and a further 10 to an unspecified southern Italian port authority. Zephir has been awarded a contract to supply 12 drawbar tractors to the Port of Casablanca, making a total order to date from Morocco of some 84 tractors.

Locomotives / **MANUFACTURERS**

Zephir shunting tractor

Zhuzou Rolling Stock Works

Zhuzou, Hunan, People's Republic of China

Products: Electric locomotives, traction motors and other electrical apparatus.

A typical product is the Type 'Shaoshan-1' 25 kV, 50 Hz ac Co-Co electric locomotive, weight 138 tonnes, with a continuous rating of 3780 kW and a maximum speed of 90 km/h. The 'Shaoshan-3' is a 138-tonne locomotive with a top speed of 100 km/h and a 4800 kW rating.

Constitution: Built in 1936, the works was rebuilt and extended in 1949 and began to produce and overhaul steam locomotives, passenger coaches and goods wagons. In 1959, it produced its first main-line mixed traffic electric locomotive of Type 'Shaoshan-1'. In 1964 it began to manufacture traction motors for both electric and diesel-electric locomotives. Overhaul of steam locomotives, passenger coaches and goods wagons ceased in 1980 and since then the works has engaged in mass production of high-power semi-conductor electric locomotives, traction motors for both electric and diesel-electric locomotives, traction transformers and many kinds of electrical apparatus. It has become the first electric locomotive works of China National Railway Technical Equipment Corporation.

'Shaoshan-3' 4800 kW 25 kV ac 50 Hz Co-Co

Powered passenger vehicles

ARGENTINA
Materfer 122

AUSTRALIA
Comeng 93
Goninan 110
Walkers 149

AUSTRIA
BRW 89
Jenbacher 114
S-G-P 137

BELGIUM
ACEC Transport 79
BN 85
TAU 143

BRAZIL
Cobrasma 93
Engesa–FNV 100
Mafersa 120
Santa Matilde 134
Villares 148

CANADA
Bombardier 86
UTDC 147

CHINA
Changchun Railway Works 93
China National Railway Corporation 93

CZECHOSLOVAKIA
Czechoslovak Wagon Works 95
Strojexport 142

DENMARK
ABB Scandia A/S 79, 134
Frichs 103

EGYPT
SEMAF 136

FINLAND
Valmet 148

FRANCE
ANF-Industrie 82
CFD 92
De Dietrich 97
GEC Alsthom 106
Matra 124
Soulé 141

GERMANY, DEMOCRATIC REPUBLIC
LEW 118

GERMANY, FEDERAL REPUBLIC
ABB 78
Duewag 98
Ferrostaal 100
Linke-Hofmann-Busch 119
MAN GHH 121
MBB 125
Newag 129
Schöma 136
Siemens 137
Talbot 143
Transrapid International 145
Waggon Union 148

HUNGARY
Ganz Electric 104
Ganz-Hunslet 105
Ganz-Mávag 105

INDIA
ICF 113
Jessop 114
PEC 132

ITALY
Ansaldo Trasporti 83
Breda 87
Casaralta 92
Ferrosud 100
Fiat 100
Firema 102
Gleismac 109
Imesi 114
OMECA 131
OMS 131
Reggiane 132
Socimi 139
SOFER 140

JAPAN
Alna Koki 80
Fuji 103
Fuji Car 104
Hitachi 111
Kawasaki 115
Kinki Sharyo 115
Mitsubishi Electric 127
Niigata 129
Nippon Sharyo 130
Tokyu 143
Toshiba 144

KOREA
Daewoo 96
Hyundai 112
Korea Shipbuilding & Engineering 118

MEXICO
Concarril 95

NORWAY
Strømens (NEBB) 142

POLAND
Cegielski 92
Kolmex 117
Konstal 117

PORTUGAL
Sorefame 140

ROMANIA
23 August 84
Mecanoexportimport 125

South Africa
RSD 133
Union Carriage 147

SPAIN
ATEINSA 84
Babcock & Wilcox 84
CAF 90
Macosa 119
La Maquinista 121

SWEDEN
ABB Traction AB 79
Kalmar 114

SWITZERLAND
Alusuisse 80
Groupement 110
Schindler 134
Schindler Waggon Altenrhein 135
SLM 138
VeVey 148

USSR
Energomachexport 100
Mytischy 129
Riga 132

UK
Alexander 80
BREL 88
Hunslet TPL 112
Metro-Cammell 125
RFS 132
Wickham 149

USA
AEG Westinghouse 80
Morrison-Knudsen 129

YUGOSLAVIA
Duro Daković 100
GOŠA 110

ZIMBABWE
More Wear 129

78 MANUFACTURERS / Powered passenger vehicles

ABB
ASEA Brown Boveri
Transportation Management and Systems GmbH
(ABB BTM)

Corporate Headquarters: PO Box 100163, 1 Gottlieb-Daimler Strasse 6, 6800 Mannheim 1, Federal Republic of Germany

Telephone: +49 621 468 200
Telex: 462411220
Telefax: +49 621 468 298/9

President: Eric Kocher
Executive Vice-President: Åke Nilsson
Vice President, Marketing: Peter Albexon

For full list of ABB companies, see ABB entry in Locomotives section.

Products: Development, design, engineering, sales, production, installation, maintenance and after-sales service of rolling stock systems and equipment for all railway types, systems and track gauges of the following:
Electric multiple- or single-unit traction vehicles for trunk, feeder, metropolitan, regional, suburban and industrial railway systems, and special rolling stock as complete rail traction vehicles; also complete range of electrical equipment and sub-systems for all rail traction vehicles; and complete climate equipment for all rail traction vehicles.

The group also offers:
Mechanical systems and components: bogies and bogie components; wheels and axles; gearboxes and couplings.
Service, minor equipment and spare parts.
Large projects management and consultancy.

Recent contracts:
Federal Republic of Germany
Linke-Hofmann-Busch (LHB) and ABB have obtained an order from an LHB company, the Taunus Railway. This is a feeder to Frankfurt/Main and bought 11 two-car Class VT/VS 2E units. With similar types of these double-unit cars with ABB equipment already operating in Austria, Norway and Spain since the early 1980s, the total number now exceeds 100.

Norway
Since 1985 Norwegian State Railways (NSB) has operated 15 ABB-designed diesel-electric train sets with three-phase propulsion. These comprise the Class BM 92 rail power cars with BS 92 driving trailers. Producers were BBC (now ABB Transportation Technology, Mannheim, Germany) and EB Strömmens Verksted. The NSB order to ABB in 1989 for nine four-car IC 70 train sets for intercity services is in production. They will operate over shorter distances between Oslo and other cities in the southern part of Norway. The train compositions include an electric rail power car, a maximum of three intermediate passenger cars and a driving trailer. The rail power cars with ABB three-phase propulsion for the IC 70 train sets will feature the most advanced GTO-equipped design of traction and auxiliary power converters. Many components will be the same as applied for the Swiss Federal Railways (SBB) Class 460 locomotive (Locomotive 2000). Producers are ABB Transportation Systems, Zürich, Switzerland, and EB Strömmens Verksted. Expected delivery is late 1992. Once the latest IC 70 train sets are delivered the NSB will have 103 train sets produced by companies of the ABB Group.

Sweden
ABB Traction AB, Västerås has received an order for 20 train sets, each comprising electric rail power car and driving trailer. Deliveries will start in 1991 and extend to 1993. These sets will be serving in various regions of Sweden and are a further development of earlier phase-angle controlled sets in operation in and around Stockholm, Gothenburg and Malmö. Once the trains now on order are commissioned, almost 100 sets will be operating all over Sweden.

Switzerland
Over the last 10 years regional railway systems in Switzerland have been modernising or expanding their motive power fleets: Bern-Solothurn (RBS), Wynental-Suhrental (WSB) and Bremgarten-Dietikon (BD) (three private regional railway systems) have placed a joint

Austrian Federal Railways 760 mm gauge diesel-electric power car for the Zell-Krimml line of the Salzburg area.

Diesel-electric double-unit Class VT/VS 2 E in service with various German regional railway companies.

Rhaetian Railway Bernina line, Class ABe III with freight train.

contract for 22 low-floor, light rail power cars. These cars – all with same mechanical and electrical equipment – are being built by Schindler Waggon Ltd, Altenrhein and ABB Transportation Systems Ltd, Zürich. The low-floor concept requires mounting of electrical equipment on the roof. Delivery of the light rail power cars in three-week intervals will be starting in September 1991.

In 1990, the Swiss "Ferrovie Autolinee Regionali Ticinese" (FART) and the Italian "Società Subalpina di Imprese Ferroviarie" (SSIF) ordered 10 low-floor, articulated light rail Type ABe 4/6 power cars with three-phase drives. Eight units will go to FART, two go to SSIF. The latter has an option for two additional units. For regional operation, these cars are the first units to be realised in "VeVey" low-floor design. Constructions mécaniques de VeVey SA (ACMV) will produce the car bodies and the trailer bogies; Swiss Industry Company (SIG), manufactures the motor bogies; ABB Transportation Systems, Zürich will make all the electrical equipment. Deliveries start in early 1992, one car per month.

Jungfrau Railway (JB) ordered four double-unit Class BDhe 4/8 dc electric power cars. This cog/rack railway has a three-phase supply. Regenerative braking energy is fed back into the three-phase power supply. The power conversion from the three-phase supply to the DC traction motors is by a fully controlled three-phase bridge circuit. Delivery of the first unit will be in summer 1992, and the last will be supplied at the end of 1992.

SEZ, GBS and BN Railways are part of the BLS (Bern-Loetschberg-Simplon) Railway Operation Group. This Group ordered four additional Class RBDe 4/4 units and four driving trailers Bt.

GFM (Gruyère-Fribourg-Morât) Railways of the Fribourg Railway Group ordered two additional Class RABDe 4/4 units and driving trailers.

RVT (Chemin de fer Régional du Val-de-Travers) Railway ordered one additional Class RBDe 4/4 unit and driving trailer.

SBB ordered a third series of shuttle trains with 20 RBDe 4/4 power cars (rated 1760 kW, 140 km/h maximum speed) and 20 driving trailers Bt. With new intermediate passenger cars the three series ordered since 1984 were called 'New Shuttle Train' (NPZ = Neuer Pendel-Zug). They are now known as Colibri trains, on account of their lively colors. Including the third series, the SBB has now bought 86 Colibri train sets.

PBr (Chemins de fer Pont Brassus) Railway is another regional system which ordered two shuttle trains (Class RBDe 4/4 electric rail car and driving trailer Bt) of the same design as the second series of the SBB trains.

Austria
Montafon Railway of the Vorarlberg country bordering on Switzerland ordered a shuttle train comprising an electric power car with ABB thyristor-based phase-angle control and a Bt driving trailer. These vehicles are of the same type as the latest series of the Swiss SBB Class RBDe 4/4 power cars and Bt driving trailer.

Austrian Federal Railways ordered a second series of two diesel-electric Class 5090 rail power cars from ABB. These will operate on the 760 mm gauge line in Salzburg country, from Zell am See to Krimml. The 5090 unit power rating is 235 kW and its maximum speed 70 km/h.

Australia
Western Australia Railways – Westrail, Perth – has ordered another series of 22 two-car trains, in addition to the first 21-unit series now in production. The second series differs from the first in as much as the first car will have four and the second two traction motors. All motors are rated 195 kW. Maximum train speed will be 110 km/h. The 22 units will operate on a new line, the North corridor Perth – Joondalup. These trains will be produced by ABB Traction, ABB Västerås in Sweden and ABB Traction Pty Ltd in Australia. The last of the 45 two-car trains now on order will be delivered by the end of 1992

United Kingdom
London Underground Ltd (LUL) ordered 680 rail power cars for tube trains from BREL in Derby, with electrical equipment by ABB Transportation Systems Ltd, Zürich, Switzerland. This contract is the largest single award ever issued for rolling stock in the UK. The new cars will have individual axle drives, GTO-equipped chopper controls and regenerative braking. These features will provide good adhesion and quick acceleration. The electrodynamic braking will substantially save supply energy. The 680 cars will be combined into 85 trains with 8 units each. LUL has an option for an additional 80 cars. The new series will replace older rolling stock on the Central Line of the London Underground System.

USA
MTA (Mass Transit Administration) Baltimore (Maryland), placed in early 1989 a contract for 35 light rail power cars, with ABB Traction Inc., Lawrenceville (NJ) and ABB Traction AB, Västerås (Sweden). These vehicles will be operating on the 27-mile Central Light Rail Line being built. The cars will feature GTO-based three-phase ac propulsion and inverter for three-phase auxiliary on-board power. Deliveries will start in 1990.

New Jersey Transit (NJT) placed a contract with ABB Traction Inc., Lawrenceville (NJ) in early June 1989, for the overhaul and propulsion upgrade of 100 Arrow II emus. There is an option for the same work on an additional 130 emus. Supported by ABB Traction AB, Västerås (Sweden), ABB Traction Inc., Lawrenceville, will retrofit these units. Installed will be three-phase ac propulsion including ac single phase 25 and 60 Hz catenary input equipment, GTO-based converters, asynchronous traction motors, and on-board power inverter for ac supply to auxiliary loads. An ABB micro-processor system type TRACS will control traction and auxiliary power and the braking system will be refurbished. Deliveries start during 1990.

Southeastern Pennsylvania Transportation Authority (SEPTA) – for their Philadelphia-Norristown line – placed a contract for 26 four-axle regional light rail power cars with ABB Traction Inc., Lawrenceville (NJ), and ABB Traction AB, Västerås (Sweden). These are the first units in the USA with three-phase ac propulsion. The ABB electrical equipment for the 600 V dc third rail-supplied vehicles includes two inverters, four 150 kW asynchronous motors and an onboard supply power converter for auxiliary services and the air conditioning system.

The production and order books of all companies now in the ABB Business Segment Transportation include:

Electric rail power cars or multiple units – A total of over 800 cars or multiple units, or the complete electrical equipment for them, over 100 with three-phase propulsion. On the order books are close to 900 units, many with three-phase propulsion, including cars to be retrofitted.

Diesel-electric rail power cars or multiple units – A total of over 120 cars or multiple units, or the complete electrical equipment for them, some with three-phase propulsion. On the order books are 13 units.

New Jersey Transit Arrow II emu before retrofit.

ABB Scandia A/S
See entry on page 134.

ABB Traction AB
ABB Railcar AB

891 83 Örnsköldsvik, Sweden

Telephone: +46 660 800 00
Telex: 6051 haeggs
Telefax: +46 660 181 81

Chairman: Lars Olof Nilsson
President: Anders Dalborg

Products: Car bodies for electric locomotives, Type X10 emus with ABB electrical equipment for Swedish State Railways (SJ), rapid transit surface and underground cars, street (tram) cars. Main contractor for suburban trains for Sweden's Roslagsbanan.

Constitution: Hägglunds was founded in 1899 and is the largest engineering company in northern Sweden. In 1972 it became a subsidiary company of ASEA of Västerås. In 1973 Hägglunds acquired the railcar and locomotive division of ASJ of Linköping and production was transferred to Örnsköldsvik. In January 1988, the company became one of six wholly-owned subsidiaries of the Hägglund Group. ABB Traction acquired Hägglunds Traction Division in December 1989.

ACEC Transport
ACEC is a subsidiary of GEC Alsthom

PO Box 4211, B-6000 Charleroi, Belgium

Telephone: +32 0 71 44 54 11
Telex: 51227 acec b
Telefax: +32 0 71 43 72 35

Managing Director: Ch Jauquet
Operations Managing director: R Pellichero
Commercial Director: D Hausman

Products: Electric multiple-units from 3 kV and 1.5 kV dc to 25 kV ac; GTO choppers and inverters, switchgear and circuit breakers, static converter fault monitoring system.

ACEC Transport has built and operated a 3 kV emu equipped with ac motors on SNCB lines since 1988. The four 200 kW motors are controlled by a current inverter providing a 0.55 m/s^2 acceleration. At braking, a high regeneration rate is achieved by avoiding the use of limitation resistors. The equipment complies with the minimum impedance and maximum harmonic current prescriptions imposed by the SNCB to ensure compatibility with signalling equipment.

Latest electric multiple-units equipped by ACEC

Class	Cars per unit	Line voltage	Motor cars per unit	Motored axles per motor car	Rated output (kW) per motor	Max speed km/h	Weight tonnes per set	Total seating capacity	Length per set mm	Rate of acceleration m/s^2	Year first built	Builders Mechanical parts	Builders Electrical equipment
AM80 (for SNCB)	2	1kVDC	1	4	310	160	126	171	25 075	0.75	1981	BN	ACEC
ONCFM	3	3kVDC	1	4	351	160	170	271	25 075	0.53	1983	BN	ACEC
AM86 (for SNCB)	2	3kVDC	1	4	171.5	120	126	175	26 400	0.55	1988	BN	ACEC
SCNB	2	3kVDC	1	4	200	130	123	165	26 400	0.55	1987	BN	ACEC

80 MANUFACTURERS / Powered passenger vehicles

AEG Westinghouse
AEG Westinghouse Transportation Systems Inc

1501 Lebanon Church Road, Pittsburgh, Pennsylvania 15236-1491, USA

Telephone: +1 412 655 5335
Telex: 866267
Telefax: +1 412 655 5860

President: J R Tucker
Vice Presidents: Commercial Operations:
    D R Marcucci
    Engineering: R T Betler
    Manufacturing Operations: T Jost

Products: In November 1989, AEG Westinghouse Transportation Systems Inc was selected by the Port Authority of New York and New Jersey to provide construction, operation and maintenance for a fully-automated people mover system at John F Kennedy International Airport.
In September 1989 the Company was selected to supply vehicles and system components for extensions to the Metromover, an automated people mover in metropolitan Dade County, Miami, Florida.

Miami Metromover, Florida

AL
Alusuisse-Lonza Services Ltd

Head office: Buckhauserstrasse 11, CH-8048 Zurich, Switzerland

Telephone: +41 1 497 44 22
Telex: 817 555 32
Cable: Alusuisse
Telefax: +41 1 497 45 85

Main works: Alusuisse Swiss Aluminium Ltd, CH-3960 Sierre, Switzerland
Alusingen GmbH, D-7700 Singen/Hohentwiel, Federal Republic of Germany
Alusuisse France SA, F-89600 St Florentin, France

Director: Jürg Zehnder
Marketing Manager: Jochen Warner

Products: Design of aluminium body shells, manufacture of prototypes as well as static and fatigue testing of bodies for all types of passenger rolling stock and components; production of large aluminium extrusions up to 800 mm width.
In 1990, Alusuisse-Lonza Services held co-operation agreements with more than 20 car manufacturers worldwide. Projects with which the company has recently been concerned include: ETR 500 for FS, IC-70 for NSB and Type 465 dmu (BR Class 158) for British Rail.

Class 158 Super Sprinter for British Rail

Alexander
Walter Alexander & Co (Coachbuilders) Ltd

91 Glasgow Road, Falkirk, Stirlingshire FK1 4JB, Scotland

Telephone: +44 324 21672
Telex: 777650
Telefax: +44 324 32469

Products: Diesel railbuses employing the company's standard road bus body shell of riveted aluminium alloy construction.

Alna Koki
Alna Koki Company Ltd

Head office and works: No 4-5, Higashinaniwa-cho, 1-chome, Amagasaki 660, Japan

Telephone: +81 6 401 7283
Telex: 5242782 alnosk
Telefax: +81 6 401 6168

President: Jitokuro Sakai
Managing Director, Production: Yoshinobu Sugimoto
Chief Engineer and Director: Kiyoyuki Yamagami
Managing Director, Sales and Marketing: Masahiro Higuchi

Products: Aluminium and steel electric railcars and passenger coaches; LRVs.

Major sales in 1987–90 included:
185 aluminium electric railcars for Hankyu Corporation;

Alna Koki electric railcars or multiple-units

Class	Cars per unit	Line voltage (dc)	Motor cars per unit	Motored axles per motor car	Rated output (kW) per motor	Max speed km/h	Weight tonnes per car (M-motor T-trailer)	Total seating capacity per car	Length per car mm	No in service 1989	Rate of acceleration m/s^2	Year first built	Builders Mechanical parts	Builders Electrical equipment
Hankyu 8300	8	1500	4	4	170	120	35.5 (Mi) 23.5 (Ti)	End car 48 Others 54	18 900	16	0.72	1989	Alna Koki	Toyo
Okayama 7900	1	600	1	2	45	40	16.5 (Mi)	32	12 200	1		1989	Alna Koki	Toyo

18 aluminium, 14 steel and 194 stainless steel electric railcars for Tobu Railways;
18 aluminium electric railcars and 4 aluminium linear motor cars for Osaka MTB;
27 aluminium electric railcars for Kitaosaka Kyuko Railway;
67 LRV and 53 refurbished railcars for Japanese private railway companies.
3 special purpose railcars and 296 remodelled railcars for Japanese private railways.

Constitution: Established in 1947 by Hankyu Corporation under the name of Naniwa Koki Company Ltd; became Alna Koki Co Ltd in 1970. Capacity is just over 20 passenger cars and 50 freight wagons a month.

Series 8300 aluminium-bodied VVVF emu for Hankyu Corporation

Series 7900 LRV for Okayama Electric Railways

Series 20 000 chopper-controlled emu for Tobu Railway

Series 8800 VVVF emu LRV for Kumatomo MTB

82 MANUFACTURERS / Powered passenger vehicles

ANF-Industrie
Société ANF-Industrie

Tour Aurore, Cedex 5, 92080 Paris Défense, France

Telephone: +33 1 47 78 62 62
Telex: 610 817 anf courb
Telefax: +33 1 47 78 62 66

Chairman: Michel de Lambert de Boisjean
Sales Manager: Jean-Claude Viche

Products: Electric multiple-units, metro cars, diesel multiple-units, turbotrains. From December 1989, ANF-Industrie became a subsidiary of Bombardier.

Turbine powered train-sets, called 'Turbotrains' in France, have been designed and manufactured to run at higher speeds than conventional trains on non-electrified and non-dedicated lines. Up to the end of 1986 74 such trains operating in France, the USA, Egypt and Iran, had run some 200 million km.

Three turbotrains began revenue service in Egypt between Cairo and Alexandria in 1983. More recently, the American operator, Amtrak, has launched a programme of upgrading its turbotrain fleet with the new Turmo XII turbine which is more powerful and fuel-efficient.

Turbotrains are reversible and train make-up consists of two driving power cars at train ends, and several intermediate trailer cars, the number dependent on the passenger load expected, and also on the performance to be attained. The Turmo XII traction turbines from Turbomeca are rated at 1200 kW each. The transmission is a Voith hydrodynamic gearbox, fully automatic. A combination of shoe brake, disc brake, electromagnetic emergency brake and hydrodynamic brake enables a turbotrain to stop from 160 km/h within 900 m. Special attention has been paid to comfort. The turbotrains feature air-conditioning, good riding quality, a grill bar, and reclining and rotating seats. Based on the same engineering principles, a new generation of turbotrains will be capable of a maximum speed of 240 km/h.

ANF-Industrie has been French Railways' (SNCF) only diesel train-set manufacturer since 1960. In that period there has been continuous improvement: the original 330 kW engine has been changed for a 440 kW engine, and the design modified several times for better comfort and performance. Recent orders of SNCF for new railcars and light alloy trailer cars raise the total supplied to 1300 vehicles. A new design of diesel railcar has been produced for metre-gauge lines.

The Class Z2N suburban electric double-deck emus for the SNCF enclose two or three trailer cars between two power cars, which are supplied in single and dual-voltage versions. In each power car two dc motors are controlled by choppers for an output of 2800 kW per train-set. Braking is regenerative and air-operated disc and shoe.

SNCF has so far taken delivery of, or has on order, a total of 265 double-deck dual-voltage and dc power cars. The first 1.5 kV dc train-sets were introduced into

Turbotrain for Egyptian Railways

Type X2200 diesel railcar and trailer for SNCF

'Club'-type car of TGV-Atlantique train-set, French Railways

Type Z2N emu power car for French Railways

Powered passenger vehicles / **MANUFACTURERS**   83

ANF-Industrie diesel railcars or multiple-units and turbotrains

Class	Cars per unit	Motor cars per unit	Motored axles per motor car	Trans-mission	Rated power (kW) per motor	Max speed km/h	Weight tonnes per car (M-motor T-trailer)	Total seating capacity	Length per car m (M-motor T-trailer)	No in service	Year first built	Engine & type	Transmission
SNCF X 2100 X 2200	1	1	2	Hydro-kinetic	440	140	42	57	22.4	53 (+60 on order)	1980	Saurer	Voith
SNCF ETG (Turbo)	4	2	2	Hydro-kinetic	Turmo III: 860 Diesel: 330	160	M & T 163	188	87.2	14	1970	Turbomeca; Saurer	Voith
SNCF RTG (Turbo)	5	2	2	Hydro-kinetic	Turmo XII: 1200 Turmo III: 850	200	M & T 225	280	M & T 129	39	1973	Turbomeca	Voith
Turbotrain (Iran)	5	2	2	Hydro-kinetic	Turmo III: 850	160	M & T 225	280	M & T 129	4	1973/1974	Turbomeca	Voith
Turbotrain (USA)	5	2	2	Hydro-kinetic	Turmo XII: 1200	160	M & T 281	276	M & T 129	7 (+6 Type SNCF)	1973/1974	Turbomeca	Voith
Turbotrain (Egypt)	10	2	2	Hydro-kinetic	Turmo XII: 1200	160	M & T 465	600	M & T 260	(1983) 3 units	1982	Turbomeca	Voith

ANF-Industrie electric railcars or multiple-units

Class	Cars per unit	Line voltage	Motor cars per unit	Motored axles per motor car	Rated output (kW) per motor	Max speed km/h	Weight tonnes per car (M-motor T-trailer)	Total seating capacity	Length per car mm (M-motor T-trailer)	No of sets in service	Rate of acceleration m/s^2	Year first built	Builders Mechanical parts	Builders Electrical equipment
SNCF Z2N	4 or 5	1.5 kV or 25 kV	2	4	350	140	M 66-70 T 42	166/220	M 25 100 T 24 280	10	0.9	1982	ANF + CIMT	TCO; Jeumont-Schneider

commercial operation in November 1983. The SNCF aims to operate more than 50 per cent of its suburban lines with similar double-deck vehicles in the near future. Maximum standing and seated capacity in a five-car train-set exceeds 1700 passengers, but comfort is superior to that of preceding single-level cars.

Electronics have been standardised in traction and braking choppers, auxiliaries supply converter and rectifier bridge (dual-current version). Power and control equipment is grouped on the power cars in homogeneous units so as to limit the number and length of the pneumatic and electric connections, to provide a high reliability and to simplify maintenance and overhaul.

Metro cars have been supplied to Paris, Marseilles, Mexico, Santiago and Caracas. Among recent activities in this field, the company has acted as consortium leader in the manufacture of 225 metro Type R68 motor cars for the New York City Transit Authority. Despite a comparatively light tare weight of carriage structure, these 225 cars are designed to sustain harsh vertical compressive, tensile and torsion constraints. A second order for 200 Type R68 motor cars was placed in mid-1986. The total of 425 cars was completed in August 1988.

In December 1988 the RATP awarded ANF-Industrie a contract for the design and manufacture of nine MF 88 type train-sets. The RATP also entrusted the company with the management of the contract and the integration of the main components.

This equipment, which foreshadows the Paris Metro steel-wheel cars of the year 2000, will benefit from the latest developments in computer technology. The on-board system of the vehicles will ensure the monitoring of main equipment and interpret the received commands from the train-set driver. This represents the first stage of integration which will lead to a fully automated driving mode. The system comprises on-board computers and broadly uses a standardised data transmission network; it will mean greater trouble-shooting facilities and availability of printed circuits and will simplify wiring. In addition, this equipment will allow assistance for automated maintenance.

After receiving an order from the RATP at the beginning of 1988 to equip BOA cars with running gear comprising steerable axles and independent wheels, and with asynchronous traction, ANF-Industrie was awarded a contract for the integration of this equipment on the BOA2 train-sets. The steerable axles with independent wheels using activated or de-activated differential constitutes a world first in the application of such a system.

117 Z2N double-deck power cars recently have been ordered by SNCF.

Ansaldo Trasporti

Ansaldo Trasporti SpA
Head Office: 425 Via Argine, 80147 Naples, Italy
Works: 260 Via Nuova delle Brecce 80147, Naples, Italy

Telephone: +39 81 7810111
Telex: 710131 ans na i
Telefax: +39 81 7810698-699

Other offices:
336 Viale Sarca, 20126 Milan, Italy
Telephone: +39 2 64451
Telex: 331279
Telefax: +39 2 6438032

25 Corso Perrone, 16161 Genoa, Italy
Telephone: +39 10 65511
Telex: 271274
Telefax: +39 10 495044

Chairman: Giovanni Nobile
Vice President and Managing Director: Emilio Maraini
General Director: Francesco Granito
General Co-Director: Alberto G Rosania
Technical Director: Salvatore Bianconi
R & D and Commercial Director: Carlo Rizzi

Products: Electric propulsion equipment, either rheostatic or electric, for railway, urban and suburban vehicles with ac and dc motors; electronic converters and controls; auxiliary apparatus; planning designing and management methodologies for public transport: sale, assembly, start-up and servicing.

Recently electrical equipment has been provided for 35 chopper-controlled Class Ale 582 and 30 Class Ale 642 electric railcars of Italian Railways (FS). Chopper-controlled traction units together with driving trailers have been supplied to Ferrovie Nord Milano (FNM); 33 chopper-controlled multiple-units have been supplied to the Circumvesuviana Railway and six multiple-units to SEPSA.

FS Class Ale 582 electric railcar

84 MANUFACTURERS / Powered passenger vehicles

ATEINSA
Aplicaciones Técnicas Industriales SA

Factoria de Villaverde, Carretera Villaverde, Vallecas 18, Madrid 28041 Spain

Telephone: +34 1 796 11 00
Telex: 43521 atfve
Telefax: +34 1 796 15 08

President: Manuel Costales Gómez-Olea
Managing Director: Eusebio Toral Zuazo

Commercial Director: Pedro Solé Raventos
Export Director: Javier Masoliver y de Martí

Products: Electric train-sets for main-line, suburban and underground systems; diesel railcars; Ferrostaal-type railbuses.

Electric railcars or multiple–units in production

Cars per unit	Line voltage	Motor cars per unit	Motored axles per motor car	Rated output (kW) per motor	Max speed km/h	Weight tonnes per car	Total seating capacity	Length per car mm	Rate of acceleration m/s^2	Year first built	Builders Mechanical parts	Electrical equipment
RENFE Type S-444												
3	3000 V	1	4	290	140	151	212	79.864	0.5	1985	ATEINSA	GEE/Melco

Diesel railcars or multiple–units in production

Cars per unit	Motor cars per unit	Motored axles per motor car	Trans-mission	Rated power (kW) per motor	Max speed km/h	Weight tonnes per car	Total seating capacity	Length per car mm	No in service 1988	Year first built	Builders Mechanical parts	Engine & type	Trans-mission
RENFE Type S-592													
3	2	2	Hydraulic	169	120	131	228	70.214	132	1980	ATEINSA	MAN D3256 BTXUE	Voith

23 August
"23 August" Works
Mecanoexportimport supplier

B–dul Muncii 256, Bucharest, Romania

Telephone: +40 0 28 20 10
Telex: 10344

Products: Diesel railcars.

Constitution: The "23 August" Works started production of railcars in 1933 and of diesel locomotives in 1936.

23 August diesel railcars or multiple-units

Class	Cars per unit	Motor cars per unit	Motored axles per motor car	Trans-mission	Rated power per motor	Max speed km/h	Weight tonnes per car (M-motor T-trailer)	Total seating capacity	Length per car mm (M-motor T-trailer)	No in service	Year first built	Builders Mechanical parts	Engine & type	Trans-mission
AD 20	3 (M+2T)	1	1	Hydro-mechanical	192 hp	80	M 21 T 16	52+ 2×60 =172	16 000 (M=T)	1	1983	"23 August" Auto-Truck Factory Brasov	D2156HM81U/85 (MAN-licence)	16HRS 5302-703 (Clark-licence) Hidromecanica Brasov
A20 DP	3 (M+2T)	1	2	Hydro-mechanical	141	60	M = 24 T=18	39 + 2×45 =129	15920 (M=T)	30 units + 40T	1983	"23 August" Bucharest	D2156HM6U (MAN-licence) RABA – Hungary	16HRS 5302-704 (Clark-licence) Hidromecanica Brasov
AD 20	6 ((2M+ +4T)	2	1	Hydro-mechanical	141+ 141= 282	80	M=26 T=20	2×63+ 4×84= 462	16 000 (M=T)	1 unit	1985	"23 August" Bucharest	D2156HM6U (MAN-licence) RABE – Hungary	16LHRS 5302-700 (Clark-licence) Hidromecanica Brasov
AD 2×19	6 (2M+ 4T)	2	2	Hydro-mechanical	2×141+ 2×141= 564	80	M=27 T=18	2×43+ 4×56 310	15240 (M=T)	2 units +22T	1989	"23 August" Bucharest	D2156HM6U (MAN-licence) RABA – Hungary	16LHRS 5302-701 (Clark-licence) Hidromecanica Brasov

Babcock & Wilcox Española
Sociedad Española de Construcciones Babcock & Wilcox SA

Galindo (Vizcaya) 9, Spain

Telephone: +34 4 4966011, +34 4 4957011
Telex: 32235, 32544 bw fbe

Works: Alameda Recalde 27, 48009 Bilbao
Lagasca 88, 28001 Madrid

Executive President: Manual Fornándoz Garcia

Products: Electric train units and metro train-sets.

Electric train-set for FEVE

Powered passenger vehicles / **MANUFACTURERS** 85

BN
Constructions Ferroviaires et Métalliques
Formerly La Brugeoise et Nivelles SA

Avenue Louise 65, 1050 Bruxelles, Belgium

Telephone: +32 2 535 55 11
Cable: Brunag
Telex: 61 736 Brunag
Telefax: +32 2 539 10 17

Managing Director: M Simonart
Executive Director, Transport Division: P Sonveaux
Marketing & Sales Director, Transport Division: Jean Verraver

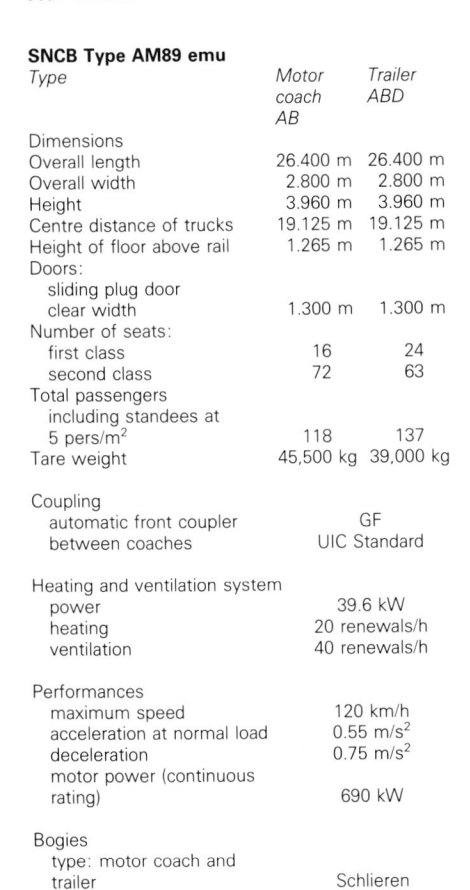

SNCB Type AM89 emu

Type	Motor coach AB	Trailer ABD
Dimensions		
Overall length	26.400 m	26.400 m
Overall width	2.800 m	2.800 m
Height	3.960 m	3.960 m
Centre distance of trucks	19.125 m	19.125 m
Height of floor above rail	1.265 m	1.265 m
Doors:		
sliding plug door		
clear width	1.300 m	1.300 m
Number of seats:		
first class	16	24
second class	72	63
Total passengers		
including standees at		
5 pers/m^2	118	137
Tare weight	45,500 kg	39,000 kg
Coupling		
automatic front coupler	GF	
between coaches	UIC Standard	
Heating and ventilation system		
power	39.6 kW	
heating	20 renewals/h	
ventilation	40 renewals/h	
Performances		
maximum speed	120 km/h	
acceleration at normal load	0.55 m/s^2	
deceleration	0.75 m/s^2	
motor power (continuous rating)	690 kW	
Bogies		
type: motor coach and trailer	Schlieren	
secondary suspension	col spring	
track gauge	1435 mm	
two motor bogies and		
two trailer bogies		
wheelbase	2670 mm	2500 mm
wheel diameter	1010 mm	1010 mm

Type AM86 emu for SNCB

Delivery of 45 8-axle 'Stadstrams' for Amsterdam began in March 1990

Brake system
type: Oerlikon ESt3
electro-pneumatic friction
brake system with two disc
brakes per axle
disc braking only
disc diameter:
  motor coach   Ø 820 mm
  trailer   Ø 700 mm
electronic anti-skid system
according to latest UIC
specifications
air-operated emergency
brake
parking brake: on one trunk
per coach

Constitution: Present style of the BN company dates from July 1977 when La Brugeoise et Nivelles absorbed Constructions Ferroviaires du Centre.
In 1986 Bombardier Inc of Montreal, Canada, became the principal shareholder in BN, increasing its holding to 90 per cent in 1988. Bombardier has had exclusive manufacturing and marketing rights to BN-designed LRVs in North America since 1979.

Products: LRV, Guided Light Transit (GLT), and metro stock; emus.
At the end of 1989 BN obtained an order from Moroccan Railways for six 3-car emus. Belgian Railways (SNCB) ordered 68 intermediate cars for existing emu sets and 17 2-car stoptrain emus identical to the AM 86 series previously delivered. In association with HOLEC (Netherlands), BN received an order from PT INKA (Indonesian Railways) for seven suburban 4-car trains which will be operated in Jakarta. London's Docklands Light Railway ordered 44 fully automated 6-axle LRVs, with delivery starting at the end of 1990. This contract is being undertaken in conjunction with Hawker-Siddeley. The Brussels Public Transport Authority (MIVB-STIB) ordered 32 motor coaches which will be used as intermediate cars in the existing

Recent BN electric railcars or multiple-units

Class	Cars per unit	Line voltage	Motor cars per unit	Motored axles per motor car	Rated output (kW) per motor	Max speed km/h	Weight tonnes set	Total seating capacity	Length per car mm	Rate of acceleration m/s^2	Year first built	Electrical equipment
SNCB Class AM 80	2	3 kV	1	4	1240	160	105	171	25 075	0.75	1982	ACEC
Moroccan Railways	3	3 kV	1	4	1416	160	145	271	25 075	0.53	1983	ACEC
SNCB Class AM 86	2	3 kV	1	4	690	120	106	175	26 400	0.55	1987	ACEC
Class AM 89		3 kV	1	4	690	120	106	175	26 400	0.55	1990	ACEC

86 MANUFACTURERS / Powered passenger vehicles

dual metro car units. The delivery of 45 Amsterdam 8-axle 'Stadstram' LRVs began in October 1989. These LRVs feature a low central floor section for ease of access. After trials on BN's test track, the first of 13 6-axle 'Sneltram' LRVs was supplied to GVBA (City of Amsterdam) in March 1990.

BN has also developed a new generation of full-length, low-floor trams. This development is based on an innovative articulated bogie design without rigid axles which confers excellent cornering abililty. Because of this new technology, the vehicle floor has a constant level of 350 mm from end to end.

BN is the builder of the GLT-Guided Light Transit. The GLT is a bimodal, rubber-tyred vehicle which can run either in manually steered or guided mode. First operated during the 1988 tourist season, the GLT is at present operating between Rochefort and Jemelle in southern Belgium.

Bombardier
Bombardier Inc

Mass Transit Division

1350 Nobel Street, Boucherville, Quebec J4B 1A1

Works: CP 580, La Pocatière, Quebec G0R 1Z0

Telephone: +1 514 655 3830
Telex: 055 61576
Telefax: +1 514 655 4257

President: Gilles Bacon
Vice President, Marketing & Sales: Thomas C Owen
Director, Marketing & Sales (International): Salem Wahby

Principal subsidiaries: TGI (Transportation Group Inc), Orlando, Florida; BN (formerly Brugeoise et Nivelles), Brussels, Belgium; ANF-Industrie, France.

Products: Bombardier offers a complete range of rail transit vehicles for urban, commuter and intercity transit: rubber-tyred and steel-wheeled metro cars, articulated light rail vehicles, self-propelled gallery commuter cars, commuter train cars, bi-level transcontinental train coaches, the PeopleMover and Monorail systems, and finally the LRC high-speed train which is the only high-speed train of North American design.

In 1974 Bombardier began to diversify, breaking in to the mass transit field with a contract to supply the Montreal Urban Community with subway cars. To fill the order, the Company converted its La Pocatière plant and acquired the technology for rubber-tyred subway equipment through a licensing agreement with the French firms CIMT and AT-BL, which later became part of the GEC Alsthom group.

Bombardier then proceeded to master technologies related to a wide range of rail transit vehicles. This was accomplished by signing manufacturing and marketing licence agreements for various types of vehicles including the PeopleMover and Monorail systems originally designed by the Walt Disney organisation (1984). The Company also acquired all Pullman and Budd vehicle designs (1987).

In keeping with a strategy aimed at expanding its activities in the field of mass transit, Bombardier created a US subsidiary in 1985, The Transportation Group Inc (TGI). Based in Orlando, Florida, this subsidiary offers integrated transportation systems to the North American market.

Bombardier operates two plants in North America: one in La Pocatière, Quebec, and another in Barre, Vermont. Since 1974, the Company has obtained orders totalling over $2.5 billion in value, the most significant of which was a Canadian $1 billion contract to supply 825 subway cars to New York City between 1982 and 1987. Bombardier has delivered urban transit equipment to Montreal, New York City, Mexico City, and Portland, Oregon. Its commuter cars are operated in Connecticut, New Jersey, Massachusets and Pennsylvania, as well as in Quebec. Amtrak, the national rail carrier of the USA, has ordered intercity train cars, and VIA Rail in Canada operates the high-speed LRC train between the major cities of Quebec and Ontario.

The transportation Group Inc, a US subsidiary located in Orlando, Florida, is responsible for marketing monorail cars that meet urban transit operating

Commuter car for the USA National Railroad Passenger Corporation (AMTRAK)

Bombardier monorail at Disneyworld, Florida

Car for Massachusetts Bay Transportation Authority

Powered passenger vehicles / **MANUFACTURERS** 87

requirements and therefore can be offered to public transit authorities.

The Company's Austrian Division in Vienna, Bombardier-Rotax, manufactures tramways for the Austrian market.

Through two transactions made in February 1986 and February 1988 respectively, Bombardier acquired a 90.6 per cent interest in the capital stock of the Belgian company BN Constructions Ferroviaires et Mètalliques SA, thus becoming the majority shareholder of one of Europe's leading manufacturers of rolling stock.

Another major move was made in December 1989 through the acquisition of ANF-Industrie, the second largest manufacturer of the French railway industry. This transaction has enabled Bombardier to consolidate its position in the European rolling stock industry.

Recent production has included 104 Intercity Passenger Cars for Amtrak (USA National Railroad Passenger Corporation) as well as a total of 62 commuter cars for Boston and New Jersey Transit. In December 1989, Bombardier was asked to play a key role in the new Technology Test Train programme of the New York City Transit Authority when it was awarded a contract to develop, build and test nine prototype subway cars in connection with the Authority's plan to renew its fleet by the year 2000.

Bombardier, BN and ANF-Industrie are members of the Euroshuttle consortium which was chosen to build shuttle trains for the transportation of cars and buses in the English Channel tunnel. Their joint contribution to this project is the design and manufacture of the train carriages.

Through BN and ANF-Industrie, Bombardier is involved in various TGV high-speed train projects in Europe (TGV-Atlantique, TGV-Europe, TGV-Transmanche). In addition, under an industrial and commercial co-operation agreement with the French-British group GEC Alsthom, Bombardier is responsible for marketing the TGV in North America and will act as manufacturing leader for any TGV project on this continent.

The New York R-110 prototype test train

SEPTA car maintenance centre

Breda

Breda Costruzioni Ferroviarie SpA

Via Ciliegiole 110/B, 51100 Pistoia, Italy

Telephone: +39 573 3701
Cable: Ferbreda, Pistoia
Telex: 570186 BCF I
Telefax: +39 573 370 292

Chairman: Giuseppe Capuano
General Manager, Breda Railway Group: Corrado Fici
General Manager, Breda Costruzioni Ferroviarie: Roberto Cai

Products: Light alloy or steel electric train-sets for long distances, for rapid transit of commuters and for underground lines. The company also manufactures passenger coaches, LRVs, locomotives, trucks and freight wagons.

Recent contracts include 30 stainless steel rapid transit cars for SCRTD of Los Angeles, USA; 32 light alloy rapid transit cars for Lima Metro, Peru; 68 light alloy rapid transit cars for WMATA (Washington DC, USA; 33 bi-articulated light rail vehicles for SFSM (Naples); 261 freight wagons and nine amenity coaches for TML (Channel Tunnel Project); electric trains (ETR 500 high-speed train) for Italian State Railways (FS).

The rapid transit cars for SCRTD are bi-directional and comprise two powered cars (A & B) which are structurally identical although they have different equipment. The cars can operate in trains of up to three married pairs. The cars are made of stainless steel and the propulsion system is regulated by chopper with two motors for each truck. The vehicle is controlled by an ATC system which controls speed, braking, stopping etc. The truck has trade brakes and it is powered by third rail.

The rapid transit cars for Lima Metro, Peru, are bi-directional and comprise two powered cars (A & B) which are structurally identical although they have different equipment and the possibility of adding a trailer car. The different parts of the carbody represent a unique self-bearing shell structure keeping the empty weight low. Mono-motor trucks of the bolster beam type are mounted on Torpress air springs with rolling journal boxes and primary suspension composed of stainless steel helical springs. The motor cars are equipped with a static, full-chopper traction and braking equipment with microprocessor regulation.

The Ale 582 power car, with electrical equipment by Ansaldo Trasporti, is of a new emu design for Italian Railways' cross-country intercity service. Bodies are of aluminium alloy with polyester reinforced fibreglass cab ends.

The ETR 500 high speed train for Italian State Railways is composed of two motor coaches and 1st/2nd class trailer coaches. The design has been arrived at through the use of 1:5 scale models tested in wind tunnels. The train's aerodynamic shape reduces turbulence, thereby improving passenger comfort.

The motor coach has been designed to carry powerful and complex electric traction equipment and auxiliaries, to support mechanically the gear units sprung to the frame and to provide suitable interfaces to the trucks. The primary structure is made from high resistance steel and the internal linings from large aluminium extrusions. The aerodynamic head, which includes the operator's cab, has been the cause of a number of engineering difficulties. Kevlar, a polyamide compound impregnated with epoxy resins, has been used for part of the vehicle's structure.

88 MANUFACTURERS / Powered passenger vehicles

The ETR X 500 propulsion equipment is composed of two completely independent modules, each of them supplying a truck and functioning as a seperate activation. double power conversion through the thyristor converters affects the power supply deriving from the contact line. The four 1000 kW traction motors, supplied by an inverter, are of the asynchronous type. The traction motors and gear units of the bimotor truck are directly sprung to the carbody so as to reduce to a minimum the weight resting on the rail, offering a uniform weight distribution.

Passenger compatments are equipped with a closed type luggage area located over the windows along both sides. The seats are arranged in the running direction and opposite so the passengers can choose the most comfortable position. The vehicle has four doors provided with inflatable seals to ensure a tight fit. The watertight vestibule forms an integral part of the gangway (900 mm) which is made of a thick rubber acoustically insulated membrane.

The air-conditioned passenger area is located between the truck pivot and a sliding door separates it from the vestibules. Double-glazed windows provide sound and heat insulation. To further minimise discomfort caused by vibration, the passenger seats are mounted on elastic supports.

Class Ale 582 power car

Type ETR electric train-set: leading particulars
Basic consist: 14 vehicles, comprising two motored end-units, 11 passenger coaches and 1 service coach
Seating capacity: approximately 700
Max service speed: 275 km/h
Max tested speed: over 300 km/h
2 Bo-Bo locomotives as motored unit

Total weight of train: 624 tonnes
Weight of one motored unit: 72 tonnes
Weight of one trailer unit: 40 tonnes
Continuous rating at wheel rim: 8000 kW
Inverter-powered triphasic asynchronous motors
Motor and trailer bogie wheelbases: 3000 mm
Max acceleration, unbalanced at curve: 1.2 m/s^2

BREL
BREL (1988) Ltd

St Peters House, Gower Street, Derby DE1 1AH, England

Telephone: +44 332 383850
Telex: 377693
Telefax: +44 332 45737

Chairman: Sir David Nicolson
Deputy Chairman: A R Houseman
Managing Director: Peter J Holdstock
Director, New Construction Group: Christopher V Cook
Director, Manufacture Repair Group: Chris P J Sheppard
Finance Director: C R Wood
Marketing Director: P S Coventry
Personnel Director: I M Forrester

Products: Diesel and electric multiple-units; metro cars; light rail vehicles; railway equipment spares.

BREL continues its major involvement in the manufacture of Sprinter diesel multiple-units for British Rail. Orders now total over 500 vehicles. These trains utilise a bodyshell design derived from recent classes of suburban electric multiple-units, themselves based on the BR Mark III InterCity coach. They incorporate comfortable high-backed seating in a 3 + 2 layout, double-glazed windows, power-operated sliding doors with passenger controls, and heating system using waste heat from the engine. Public address system and fluorescent lighting are fitted. The trains are powered by Cummins NT-855-R5 engines rated at 285 hp (213 kW) at 2100 rpm, driving Voith 211 hydraulic transmission via cardan shafts, with Gmeinder final drive assemblies. Bogies are of the successful Series 3 family. Secondary suspension is by airbags, and incorporates a levelling valve for maintaining standard floor height. Air-operated tread brakes using composition blocks are fitted. The system incorporates SAB cylinders and slack adjusters. Fully automatic BSI couplers including pneumatic and electrical systems are fitted at the outer ends of the driving vehicles. Within each set the cars are linked by semi-permanent bar-couplers.

The latest contracts are for a fleet of 229 diesel multiple-unit cars for use on BR's longer-distance provincial express routes. Based on the earlier fleets of Sprinter trains, the new units, designated Class 158, incorporate welded aluminium bodyshell construction, high-quality interior accommodation including air-conditioning, public telephone, power-operated sliding plug doors and Series 4 bogies with air-bag secondary suspension. The new trains are capable of 145 km/h maximum speed.

A series of 60 four-car dual-voltage emus has been built at BREL's York works. These Class 319 trains operate British Rail's Thameslink cross-London services, utilising both 25 kV ac overhead and 750 V dc third-rail current supply. They have been followed by a further fleet of 46 similar single voltage (25 kV ac only) four-car trains (Class 321) to operate London outer suburban services.

Class 321 emu for BR (John C Baker)

Class 442 Waterloo-Bournemouth-Weymouth emu for BR (John C Baker)

BREL (1988) Limited subsequently secured a £28 million order for a total of 66 emu cars for British Rail's provincial sector. The 22 three-car, 160 km/h electric trains will update local services radiating from Glasgow. Known as Class 320, they are being financed by the Strathclyde Passenger Transport Executive with support from the Scottish office.

BREL have also won two major orders for electric multiple-units from British Rail's Network SouthEast. The larger order, worth £21 million, is for 24 two-car Class 456 emus to operate on the Southern Region's 750 V dc third-rail supply; they will be compatible with the fleet of Class 455 vehicles which have been in service over some years. The second order, worth £7 million, is for five four-car Class 322 emus to run the new Liverpool Street to Stansted Airport shuttle service. Based on the bodyshell of BREL's Class 321 emu, the Class 322 units will have an internal configuraion more suited to an airport shuttle service, with 2 + 2 rather than 3 + 2 seating and increased luggage storage. Both the Class 456 and Class 322 units are being built at BREL's York Works, with bogies manufactured by the company's dedicated bogie production plant at Derby Locomotive Works.

A contract worth over £7 million has been secured from the Battersea Leisure Group for three four-car electric multiple-units. They are the first trains to be built by BREL for a private company to run on BR lines.

Powered passenger vehicles / **MANUFACTURERS** 89

Mock-up of Class 158 emu for BR

Class 319 dual-voltage emu for BR Thameslink service (*John C Baker*)

Called the 'Battersea Bullet' the trains are to provide a private rail service across the Thames, linking London Victoria station with the Battersea Palace of Entertainment which is being created on the site of Battersea Power Station by Battersea Leisure, part of the Alton Group, owners of Europe's greatest leisure park, Alton Towers.

BREL has recently completed delivery of 24 five-car Class 442 long-distance emus for the London-Bournemouth-Weymouth route. The trains are capable of a maximum speed of 160 km/h, and include buffet accommodation, standard-class seating saloons and first-class side-corridor compartment accommodation.

Constitution: The British Railways Board announced in January 1989 that it has selected as the preferred purchaser of its engineering subsidiary BREL (1988) Limited, a consortium which comprises the management and employees of BREL, Trafalgar House plc, and ASEA Brown Boveri Ltd.

BRW
Bombardier-Rotax-Wien Produktions-und VertriebsgesmbH

Donaufelder Strasse 73-79, A-1210 Vienna, Austria

Telephone: +43 222 25 56 45 0
Telex: (47) 114791
Telefax: +43 222 25 91 383, +43 222 25 56 45 200

Managing Director: Dr R Kremlicka
General Manager, Rail Vehicles & Metal construction: A Schiruk
General Manager, Administration/Control: Dipl J W Borghans

Products: Light rail vehicles, diesel and bi-currency commuter cars, funicular cars, special-purpose maintenance rail vehicles, body shells, bogies and other rolling stock components.

Recent work has included 65 trailers (Type c5) and 15 six-axle articulated single-end tramcars (Type E2) as well as 23 Stadtbahn coaches (Type E6) and trailers (Type c6) for the Vienna Transport Authority; maintenance-tower vehicle and narrow-gauge diesel-electric commuter cars for the Federal Austrian Railways and for the Styria Local Railways; dual-voltage commuter cars (15kV 16⅔ Hz/800 V dc) for the private railway enterprise Stern & Hafferl; and various special-purpose maintenance vehicles (eg tower vehicles, maintenance vehicles etc and overhaul contracts).

Designs have been produced for six-, eight-, and ten-axle articulated high-capacity light rail vehicles with body shell constructed in lightweight steel and a reinforced fibreglass body insulation achieving up to 40 per cent weight reduction and therefore substantial energy savings. Research has lead to improved designs of special articulation safety linings for new and existing cars, and devices have been developed which

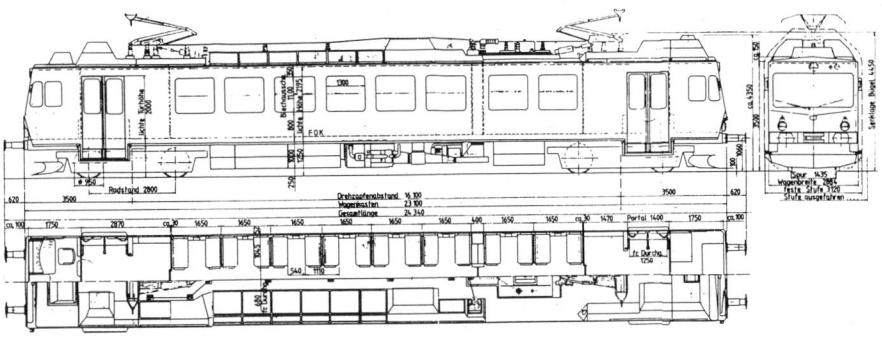

BRW double-ended commuter car

MANUFACTURERS / Powered passenger vehicles

reduce noise levels by up to 75 per cent. To meet the trend towards low-floor tramcars, BRW has such a vehicle under development.

The company has specialised in the development of track-bed cleaning machines for subway lines that provide an economic and reliable solution to the safety problems arising from dust and wear on tunnels (causing failures in the electric and electronic systems) by using a wet cleaning vacuum sytem; this eliminates the danger of dust explosions.

Due to the increasing requirement of maintenance vehicles for tunnel walls, stations and track-beds, BRW has developed a 'wet vacuum cleaning system' in a compact modular system that reduces risks of fire and operational breakdowns, and improves the attractiveness of the transport system. This modular system is easy to adapt to special profiles, conditions and requirements.

BRW low-floor metro car

BRW track-bed and tunnel cleaning machine

CAF
Construcciones y Auxiliar de Ferrocarriles, SA

Head office
Padilla, 17, 28006 Madrid, Spain

Telephone: +34 1 435 25 00
Telex: 23197 cafma e
Telefax: +34 1 276 62 63

Export division
SEMF, Castelló 72 1°, 28006 Madrid, Spain

Telephone: +34 1 275 64 03
Telex: 27242 semf e
Telefax: +34 1 276 81 08

Works: At Beasain, Zaragoza and Irún

President: José I Cangas
Chairman: Pedro Ardaiz
General Manager: Juan J Anza

Products: Diesel and diesel-electric multiple-units, metro units, light rail vehicles, all types of motor and

Class 444.500 intercity emu for RENFE

Powered passenger vehicles / **MANUFACTURERS**

trailer bogies and other rolling stock components.

RENFE (Spanish National Railways) has followed an initial purchase of six Series 444.500 emus with an order for a further 25 units. Air-conditioned and of M-T-Tc configuration like the first six, the second series has improved exterior styling and interior comfort. By January 1989 CAF had delivered 11 units. The units' maximum speed is 160 km/h and power rating in continuous service for a line voltage of 3000 V dc is 1160 kW. They can be operated as trains of up to 12 cars (using either M-T-Tc or M-Tc sets). Carbody width is 2.95 m and maximum height 4.2 m. Primary suspension is coil spring with oil damping, secondary, pneumatic. The motor car has dynamic brake, the trailers air brake. Motor car, trailer and trailer with driving cab car have a total seating capacity of 212 passengers.

RENFE has also ordered 100 three-car air-conditioned units for suburban services with M-T-M configuration. Power rating is 1920 kW, maximum speed 100 km/h, total passenger capacity 152 seated and 607 standing. Suspension is pneumatic.

GTO chopper, air-conditioned cars for Barcelona Metro

Series 2000 train-set for Madrid Metro

CAF electric railcars or multiple-units

Railway	Type	Cars per unit	Line voltage	Motor cars per unit	Motored axles per motor car	Rated output (kW) per motor	Max speed km/h	Weight tonnes per car (M-motor T-trailer)	Total seating capacity per car (M-motor T-trailer)	Length per car mm (M-motor T-trailer)	No in service 1988 (on order)	Rate of acceleration m/s²	Year, first built	Electrical equipment
RENFE	444	3	3000 V	1	4	290	140	M 64 T 39 Tc 48	M 72 T 88 Tc 52	M 26400 T 26670 Tc 26800	14	0.45	1980	WESA GEE MELCO
RENFE	444.500	3	3000 V	1	4	290	160	M 64 T 39 Tc 48	M 72 T 88 Tc 52	M 26400 T 26670 Tc 26800	6 (25)	0.45	1987 MELCO	CENEMESA CONELEC
RENFE	445	3	3000 V	2	4	240	100	M 56		M 26400	1 (50)	0.79	1984	GEE MTM WESA
RENFE	440	3	3000 V	1	4	290	140	M 61 Tc 39 T 48	M 68 Tc 92 T 100	M 26200 Tc 26200 T26160	255	0.39	1974	CENEMESA CONELEC MELCO
RENFE	443 Electrotren Basculante	4	3000 V	4	2	220	180	MA 31 MB 20 MC 64 MD 52	MA 27000 MB 24900 MC 24900 MD 27000		1		1976	
Madrid Metro	5000	2	600 V	2	4	235	70	32.5	40	17400	130	1.05	1974	AEG GEE
Madrid Metro	2000	2	600 V	2	4	148.5	70	MA 27.8 MB 28.3	24	14000	6	1.2	1984	AEG GEE
Madrid Metro	2000	2	600 V	1	4	148.5	70	M 27.3 T 20.5	M 24 T 24	M 14000 T 14000	70 (25)	1.2	1985	AEG GEE
Barcelona	3000	5	1500 V 1200 V	4	4	150	90	M 34.2 T 23.4	M 32 T 40	M 16500 T 16500	9	1	1986	MELCO CENEMESA
FGV	Tren Articulated	2	1500 V	2	2	220	80	23.44	51	14500	8	1	1987	BBC
ET/FV		3	1500 V	2	4	240	80	M 32.5 T 27	M 62 T 68	M 17235 T 17180	20			CENEMESA
FEVE		3	1500 V	1	4	120		M 29 T 19.7 Tc 23.8	M 32 T 38 Tc 30	M 15240 T 15240 Tc 15240	37	0.8	1977	AEG GEE

MANUFACTURERS / Powered passenger vehicles

CAF diesel railcars or multiple-units

Railway	Type	Cars per unit	Motor cars per unit	Motored axles per motor car	Trans-mission	Rated power (kW) per motor	Max speed km/h	Weight tonnes per car (M-motor T-trailer)	Total seating capacity per car (M-motor T-trailer)	Length per car mm (M-motor T-trailer)	No in service 1988	Year first built	Builders Engine	Transmission
RENFE	593	3	2	2	Mech	206	120	M 48 T 40	M 72 T 84	M 23580 T 22440	62	1982	FIAT	FIAT

Madrid Metro (CMM) continues acquisition of Series 2000 for rolling stock renewal on its small-profile lines. By January 1989 CAF had delivered 91 units. Each unit consist of motor car and trailer and up to three units can operate in multiple. Each motor car is provided with two double motors (2 × 120 kW). Total length of unit is 29440 mm; gauge 1445 mm; line voltage 600 V dc and seating capacity per car, 48.

Barcelona Metro (MB) which at first ordered 30 trains (18 small-profile; 12 large-profile), each one consisting of motor car-trailer-three motors cars (M-T-MMM), has increased its orders to 12 new trains. Each motor car has a continuous rating of 600 kW for a line voltage of 1200 v dc. Electric equipment employs four-quadrant GTO thyristors. Length of each car is 16 500 mm. Seating capacity is motor car 32, and trailer 40. Maximum speed is 90 km/h.

Constitution: The present company, Construcciones y Auxiliar de Ferrocarriles, SA, was formed by the merger of Material y Construcciones, SA (MMC) into Compañía Auxiliar de Ferrocarriles, SA (CAF) retaining the initials CAF. It is the largest manufacturer of railway rolling stock in Spain. It was established in 1917 when deliveries started for the Spanish Railways.

Interior of Class 444.500 emu first-class saloon: note roof-mounted video screens

Casaralta
Casaralta SpA
A member of the Firema Group

Via Ferrarese 205, 40128 Bologna, Italy

Telephone: +39 51 35 84 54
Cable: Rotabili, Bologna
Telex: 511068
Telefax: +39 51 36 38 45

President: Giorgio Regazzoni
Managing Directors: Carlo Filippo Zucchini
Carlo Regazzoni

Products: Electric railcars.

Electric railcars for Italian local railway

Cegielski
Cegielski Locomotive and Wagon Works
Zaklady Przemyslu Metalowego H Cegielski

ul Dzierzynskiego 223/229, 61-485 Poznan, Poland

Telephone: +48 61 212 31
Telex: 0415343

Export sales: Kolmex, 49 Mokotowska, 00-542 Warsaw

Products: Diesel railcars.

Constitution: Cegielski is the largest rolling stock works in Poland, building 300 to 400 passenger coaches annually for export alone.

CFD
CFD Industrie
Head office: 9.11 rue Benoît Malon, 92150 Suresnes, France

Telephone: +33 1 4506 44 00
Telex: 614 146

Main works: 51210 Montmirail
After sales office (CFD, Moyse, Batiruhr): 161 rue de Paris, 93000 Bobigny

Telephone: +33 1 844 36 42
Telex: 213966

President: F de Coincy
General Manager: P Grau
Sales Manager: A Lapiczak

Products: Diesel-hydraulic railcars for all track gauges.

CFD diesel railcars or multiple-units

Class	No of motored axles per motor car	Transmission	Rated power (kW) per motor	Max speed km/h	Weight tonnes per car	Total seating capacity	Year first built	Builders Mechanical parts	Transmission
X 2200	2	Mechanical	2 × 160	80	18	50/60	72	CFD	CFD
X 2300	2	Mechanical	2 × 160	110	21	50/60	76	CFD	CFD
X 5000	4	Power shift	2 × 225	110	30	50/60	80	CFD	CFD
X 240	2	Hydraulic	300	100	30	50/60	82	CFD	Voith

Powered passenger vehicles / **MANUFACTURERS**

Changchun Railway Passenger Car Works

5 Qingyin Road, Changchun, Jilin, People's Republic of China

Telephone: +86 73981
Telex: 83031 cpcf cn

Products: Metro railcars.
  The plant has also developed a new design of 750 V dc third-rail rapid transit cars designated DK6 with chopper voltage regulation and DK8 with varistor control. All cars are motored (4 × 76 kW) and designed to work in multiples of two, four or six. Car bodies are of integral loaded construction and mounted on air-suspension bogies. Passenger capacity per car, standing and seated, is 180 and tare weight 34 tonnes. Acceleration rate is 0.9 m/s^2 up to a maximum speed of 80 km/h; deceleration rate is 1.0 m/s^2.

Type DK6/DK8 rapid transit emu

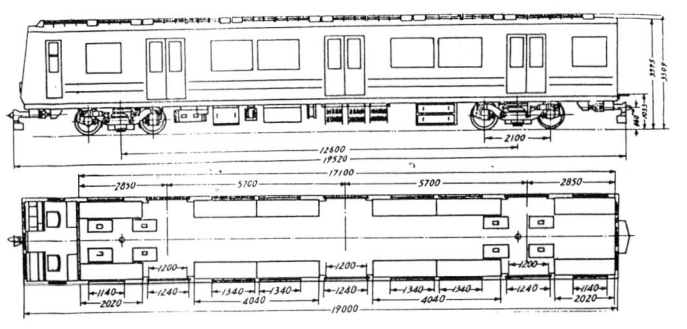

Layout of rapid transit emu car

Interior of rapid transit emu car

China National Railway Locomotive and Rolling Stock Industry Corporation

10 Fu Xing Road, Beijing, People's Republic of China

Telephone: +86 45245; +86 42685; +86 44645
Telex: 222218 loric cn

Products: Electric subway cars and electric multiple-units for speeds of up to 160 km/h.

Cobrasma SA

Head office: Rua da Estacão 523, Osasco, São Paulo, Brazil

Telephone: +55 11 704 6122
Telex: 71545, 71589

Works: Km 104 Via Anhanguera, Sitio São João, Distrito de Hortolândia, Sumaré, São Paulo

President: Luis Eulálio de Bueno Vidigal
Vice-Presidents: Marcos V Xavier da Silveira
  Luis Eulálio de Bueno Vidigal Filho
Marketing Director: Alberto Martinez
Export Director: Eduardo Hubert Kirmaier Monteiro

Products: Metro cars; LRVs.
  The company has lately delivered 100 emus to Ferrovia Paulista SA (FEPASA) for the São Paulo suburban system and a further 60 to Brazilian Federal Railways (RFFSA) for the Rio de Janeiro suburban network, together with 26 of the 68 light rail vehicles ordered by Companhia do Metropolitano do Rio de Janeiro. The company has also supplied 25 emus for the Demetro rapid transit system of Belo Horizonte and 25 stainless steel-bodied, chopper-controlled emu cars for the São Paulo Metro.

Constitution: Founded in 1944, the company has the capacity to produce 3000 freight wagons and 300 passenger coaches, emus, and metro cars and LRVs annually, as well as intercity buses and trolley buses.

Electric multiple-units by Cobrasma

Class	Cars per unit	Line voltage	Motor cars per unit	Motored axles per motor car	Rated output (kW) per motor	Max speed km/h	Weight tonnes per car (M-motor T-trailer)	Total seating capacity	Length per car mm (M-motor T-trailer)	Rate of acceleration m/s^2	Year first built	Builders Mechanical parts	Builders Electrical equipment
Demetro Belo Horizonte	4	3000	2	4	282	80	M 60 T 42	1030	M 22 400 T 22 000	8	1985	Cobrasma	MTE/JS (France)

Comeng

A Division of the ANI Corporation Limited

Frankston Road, Dandenong, Victoria 3175, Australia

Telephone: +61 3 794 2111
Telex: AA33253
Telefax: +61 3 792 5817

General Manager: A Connor
Commercial Manager: G Daniels

Products: Diesel railcars, electric multiple-units, light rail vehicles, passenger cars.

  Recent contracts have included: diesel-electric suburban railcars for Adelaide, delivered June 1988; light rail vehicles for Hong Kong, delivered July 1988; articulated light rail vehicles for Melbourne; and Intercity double-deck cars for SRA of NSW which were delivered in 1989.

94 MANUFACTURERS / Powered passenger vehicles

Electric railcars or multiple-units

Class	Type	Cars per unit	Line voltage	Motor cars per unit	Motored axles per motor car	Rated output (kW) per motor	Max speed km/h	Weight tonnes per car (M-motor T-trailer)	Total seating capacity per car (M-motor T-trailer)	Length per car mm (M-motor T-trailer)	No in service 1989	Rate of acceleration m/s²	Year first built	Builders Mechanical parts	Builders Electrical equipment
NSW Intercity	EMU 104	4	1500 dc	2	4	156	130	60M 45T	96M 112T	23968M 23828T	306	0.65	1968	Comeng	Mitsubishi
Melbourne Suburban	EMU 102	3	1500 dc	2	4	121	115	50M 34T	94M 102T	24025M 23210T	575	0.8	1981	Comeng	GEC
KCRC Tuen Mun LRV	Tuen Mun T5000	1	750 dc	1	4	242	80	27	60	20192	70	1.3	1987	Comeng	AEG
MTA C4000	MTA T4000	1	600 dc	1	4	195	80	32.5	76	24640	30	1.4	1988	Comeng	AEG

Twin-unit articulated light rail vehicle for Melbourne: these double-cab cars are used in street service and on tracks previously used by suburban trains

Stainless steel, fully air-conditioned suburban diesel-electric railcar with three-phase traction motors for the STA of SA, for commuter service in Adelaide

Rack drive passenger cars for the Skitube railway in New South Wales; at 3.7m these are the widest cars of this type in the world. Power supply is at 1500 V dc

Stainless steel air-conditioned express diesel-hydraulic railcar with fully blended hydrodynamic brakes; these narrow gauge cars operate at a maximum speed of 120 km/h on the Westrail system of Australia

Stainless-steel, air-conditioned, double-deck interurban cars for the SRA of NSW; these cars operate at a maximum speed of 130 km/h in four- and eight-car sets

Powered passenger vehicles / **MANUFACTURERS** 95

Stainless steel single-unit light rail vehicle for the new system based at Tuen Mun in the New Territories of Hong Kong

Diesel railcars or multiple-units

Class	Type	Cars per unit	Motor cars per unit	Motored axles per motor car	Trans-mission	Rated power (kW) per motor	Max speed km/h	Weight tonnes per car (M-motor T-trailer)	Total seating capacity per car (M-motor T-trailer)	Length per car mm	No in service 1988	Year first built	Builders Mechanical parts	Engine & type	Trans-mission
ADP ADQ	DMU 106	4	4	2	Mechanical	350	120	46	40 DM 60 NDM	21160	5	1987	Comeng	Cummins KTA-19-R75	Voith
3000	DMU 105	1	1	2	Electric	354	90	46.5	113	25774	20	1987	Comeng	Mercedes OM 444	Stromberg 3ph motors

Concarril
Constructora Nacional de Carros de Ferrocarril SA

San Lorenzo No 925, 5 Piso, Col del Valle 03100, Mexico, DF

Telephone: +52 5 688 5233
Telex: 1771738
Telefax: +52 5 688 8482

Works: Ciudad Sahagun, HGO

General Director: Lic Jorge Tamayo
Commercial Director: Lic Ignacio Riva Palacio
Industrial Director: Ing Juan Ollivier Fierro

Products: Electric multiple-units, metro cars, light rail vehicles, rail cars, rebuilding of locomotives.
Concarril currently has orders for light rail vehicles for Mexico City and Monterrey; light rail vehicles have just been delivered to Guadalajara City.
The company is currently working on designs for medium-sized cities; access to Duewag technology acquired to LRV bogies.

Czechoslovak Wagon Works
Československé Vagónky
(Member of Strojexport, Foreign Trade Co Ltd, Prague)

Nám Dukelskych hrdinů 95, 058 01 Poprad, Czechoslovakia

Telephone: +42 25242
Telex: 078 348

Works: Vagónka Studénka, 742 13 Studénka
Vagónka Poprad, 058 80 Poprad
Vagónka Česka Lipa, 470 79 Česka Lipa

Chairman: Stefan Tužinsky
Managing Director: Jan Hlavačik
Sales Director: Karol Kosik

Products: Type M152 light steel diesel railcars and trailers.

Type M153 catenary inspection car derivative of railbus

MANUFACTURERS / Powered passenger vehicles

Diesel railcars

Class	Cars per unit	Motor cars per unit	Motored axles per motor car	Trans-mission	Rated power (kW) per motor	Max speed km/h	Weight tonnes per car (M-motor T-trailer)	Total seating capacity (M-motor T-trailer)	Length per car mm (M-motor T-trailer)	Year first built	Engine
M: Bzmot 002 T: Bzx	M+2T	1	1	Hydro-mechanical	141.2	70	M 19 T 15	M 55 T 67	M 13 970 T 13 970	1983	Skoda ML-634
M 153.0	1	1	1	Hydro-mechanical	141.2	80	23.5	5+1 inspection car	13 970	1983	Skoda ML-634

Type Bzmot 141 kW railbus

Daewoo
Daewoo Heavy Industries Ltd

PO Box 7955, Seoul, Republic of Korea

Telephone: Seoul +82 2 752 0211. Anyang +82 343 52 6171
Cable: Dhiltdincheon
Telex: 23301/25550
Telefax: +82 2 756 2679

Chairman: Woo Choong Kim
President: Kyung Hoon Lee
Executive Vice President: Oh Jun Kwon
Rolling Stock Executive Director: Won Jai Park
Rolling Stock Export Sales Manager: Soo Hwan Kim

(For list of affiliated companies, see Daewoo entry in Locomotives section.)

Products: Railcars, electric multiple-unit and car components, including traction motors.

Recent production has included two new types of train-set for the Korean National Railroad. One is a diesel-hydraulic train-set for the 'Saemaul' Seoul-Pusan passenger traffic, basically of five cars but with provision for expansion to seven or eight. The five-car format comprises two end power cars, and three trailers, one incorporating a restaurant and bar. The stainless steel car bodies are air-conditioned and equipped with sliding-plug entrance doors. All seats are reclining and rotating, and interior appointments include automatic power-operated vestibule doors and public address. Bogies have coil-spring primary and air secondary suspension. Each motor car is fitted with an MTU 1145 kW engine driving a body-mounted Voith L520rU2 transmission, the latter featuring a hydro-dynamic brake to complement axle disc braking, and a 440 V ac 250 kVA engine-generator set for auxiliary supply. Maximum speed is 150 km/h. Each trailer seats 64, each power car 24, and there are 20 non-dining seats in the restaurant-bar trailer.

For suburban service Daewoo has produced a dual-voltage 25 kV ac, 1.5 kV dc emu featuring a GTO static inverter in its auxiliary power unit. The carbody has two end frames including the body bolster of high-strength carbon steel, a roof panel of anticorrosion steel plate (SPA), the remaining structures of mild steel, and with hinged-type top and fixed-type bottom aluminium frame windows of laminated and tinted glass. Seats are longitudinal and covered with moquette. Three large air-conditioners are installed in the ceiling.

The control system is a multi-notch, motor-operated camshaft. The system can also be used for dynamic

Emu for Seoul Subway Lines 3 and 4

Diesel-hydraulic 'Saemaul' inter-city train-set for KNR

Powered passenger vehicles / **MANUFACTURERS**

braking. In the ac power section, 25 kV ac power is stepped down and rectified to 1.5 kV dc by transformer and rectifier for supply of the traction motors and the auxiliary power supply system of the 110 kVA GTO inverter. Each power motor car has four 120 kW motors. The bogie incorporates a rigid fabricated box section 'H' frame, primary suspension, swing bolster, spring arrangement, wheel sets and brake rigging.

Foreign companies with which Daewoo has technical collaboration arrangements for rail equipment include:
Electric locomotives: 50 c/s Group; ACEC, Belgium; AEG and Siemens, West Germany; GEC Alsthom and MTE, France; ABB, Switzerland
Stainless steel railcars, bogies: Transit America Inc, USA
Electric cars: Hitachi Ltd, Japan
Diesel-hydraulic railcars: Niigata Engineering Co Ltd, Japan
Air-spring bogies, diesel engines: MAN, Federal Republic of Germany
Rubber-spring bogies: Gloucester Railway Carriage & Wagon Co Ltd, England
Barber stabilised bogies: Standard Car Truck Co, USA
Traction motors, motor alternators, design co-operation in electric emu cars: GEC Traction International Ltd, England
Alliance couplers: Amsted Industries Inc, USA

Emu for Seoul subway Line 2

Daewoo diesel inter-city multiple-units

Daewoo reference	Cars per unit	Motor cars per unit	Motored axles per motor car	Transmission	Rated power (kW) per motor	Max speed km/h	Weight tonnes per car (M-motor T-trailer)	Total seating capacity	Length per car m (M-motor T-trailer)	No in service 1987	Year first built	Engine & type	Transmission
DEC	5 or 2	2	4	Electric	84	110	PM: 58.5 M: 42.8 T: 38.5	192	21	12	1979	Cummins KTA-1150L	Daewoo
DHC	2	2	2	Hydraulic	160	120	PM1: 47 PM2: 47	172	21	12	1984	Cummins VTA-28L2	NICO (Japan)
DHC	3	2	2	Hydraulic	160	120	PM1: 47 PM2: 47 Tc: 41	251	21	16	1984	Cummins VTA-28L2	NICO (Japan)
Saemaul	5	2	2	Hydraulic	445	150	NA	196	M 23.8 T 23.5	2	1987	MTU 12V 369TC13	Voith L520rU2

Daewoo electric railcars or multiple-units

Class	Cars per unit	Line voltage	Motor cars per unit	Motored axles per motor car	Rated output (kW) per motor	Max speed km/h	Weight tonnes per car (M-motor T-trailer)	Total seating capacity (M-motor T-trailer)	Length per car m	No of cars in service 1987	Rate of acceleration km/h/s	Year first built	Electrical equipment
Subway Commuter	4, 6, 8 or 10	25 kV ac or 1500 V dc	2, 4 or 6	4	120	110	Tc: 34.5 M: 43.5 M': 46.5	T: 48 M: 54 M': 54	20	261	2.5	1976	Daewoo & Hitachi (Japan)
Subway Commuter	4, 6, 8 or 10	1500 V dc	4 or 6	4	150	100	MC: 41.5 M1: 40.5 M2: 40.5	MC: 48 M1: 54 M2: 54	20	32	3.0	1980	Hitachi
Subway Commuter	4, 6, 8 or 10	1500 V dc	2, 4 or 6	4	150	100	Tc: 33.0 M1: 42.2 M2: 41.8 T: 31.7	Tc: 48 M1: 54 M2: 54 T: 54	20	402	3.0	1983	GEC Traction
Inter-city	10	25 kV ac	6	4	120	100	Tc: 43.5 M: 51.5 M': 51.0 Tb: 40.0 Ts: 37.5	561	20	20	2.0	1979	Daewoo & Hitachi

De Dietrich
De Dietrich & Cie

Reichshoffen, 67110 Niederbronn-les-Bains, France

Telephone: +33 88 80 25 00
Cable: Dietriwagons
Telex: 870 850
Telefax: +33 88 80 25 12

Sales organisation: De Dietrich & Cie
Railway and Mechanical Division

President: Gilbert de Dietrich
Director, Rolling Stock Division: Maurice Canioni

Products: Light rail vehicles (LRV), Electric multiple units (emu). In July 1988 De Dietrich signed a contract with Luxembourg Railways for 22 Z2 train sets, delivery of which commenced in the summer of 1990 at a rate of one set per month. Completion is due in late summer 1992.

98 MANUFACTURERS / Powered passenger vehicles

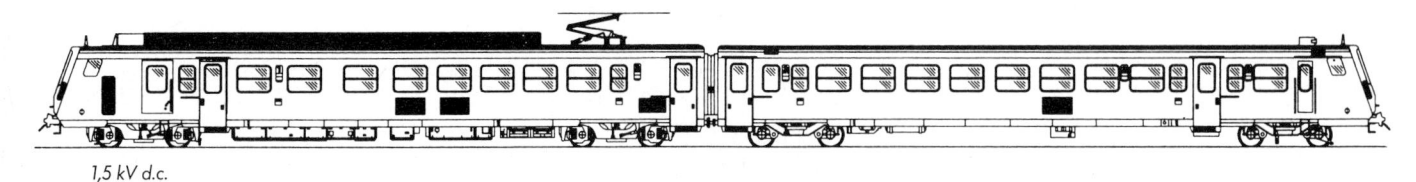

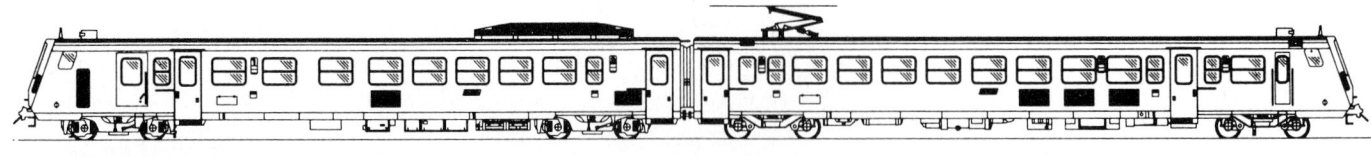

1,5 kV d.c.

25 kV 50 Hz

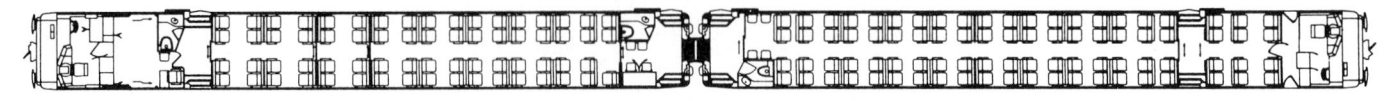

SNCF local services

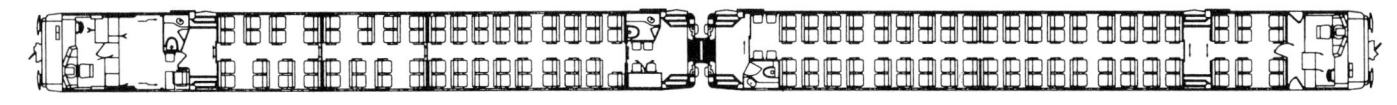

SNCF express

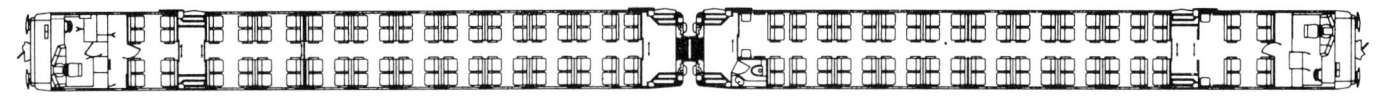

Luxembourg National Railways (C.F.L.)

De Dietrich Z2 emu-general arrangement

Duewag Aktiengesellschaft
Werk Düsseldorf

Königsberger Strasse 100, 4000 Düsseldorf, Federal
Republic of Germany

Telephone: +49 211 73431
Telex: 8582 722
Telefax: +49 211 7343 205

Main Works
Duisburger Strasse 145, 4510 Krefeld-Uerdingen

Type DT8 Stuttgart LRV

Plug-door entrance of Type DT8

Powered passenger vehicles / MANUFACTURERS

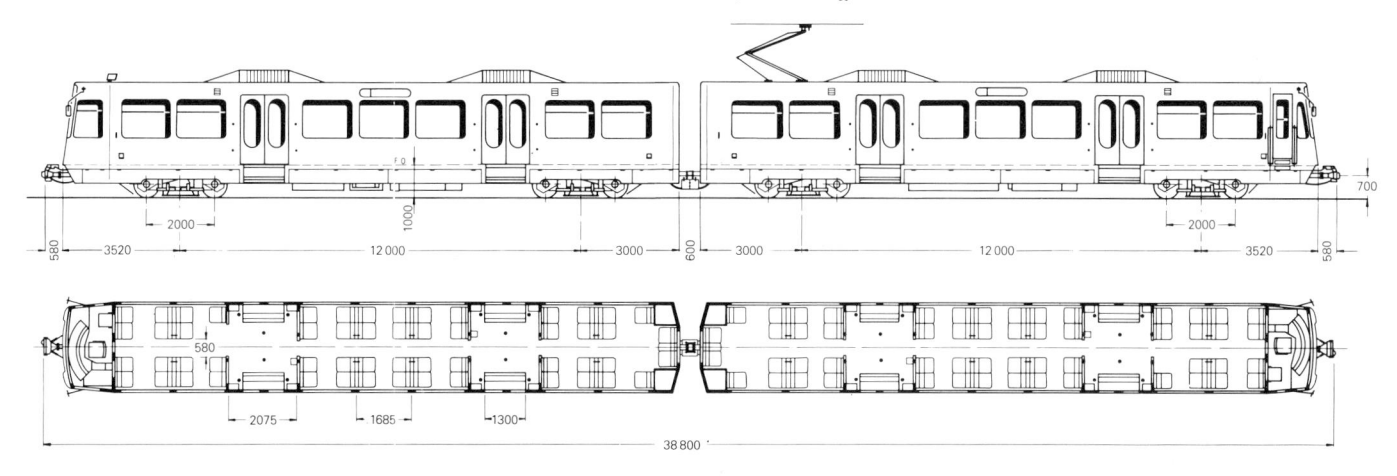

General arrangement of Type DT8

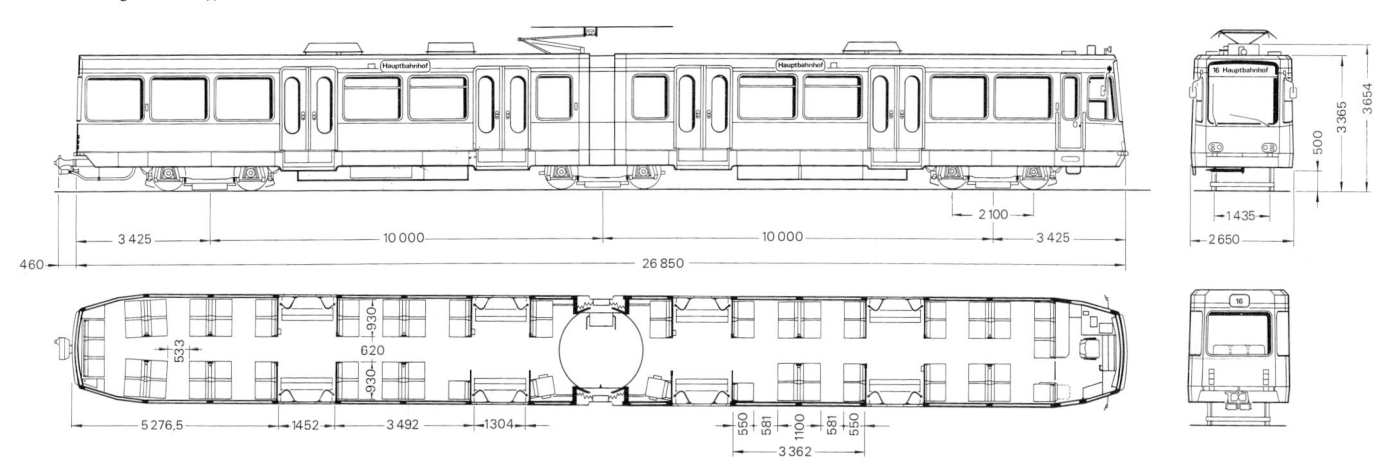

General arrangement of Type B80D

Executive Board: K Capellmann
H Atzorn
P Koch
Dr T Wichterich
E Volckmar
Vice President: W Brand
Sales Director: W Grawenhoff

Overseas associate: Deuwag Corporation, Sacramento, USA

Type B80D Cologne LRV

Interior of Type B80D

Products: Cars for full metro and pre-metro systems; vehicles for light rail and conventional tramway systems; bogies for these cars; reinforced glass-fibre components; advanced transport systems.

Cities which have placed vehicle orders with Deuwag include Cologne, Bonn, Frankfurt, Düsseldorf, Duisburg, Dortmund, Essen, Kassel, Freiburg, Edmonton, Calgary, Pittsburgh, Sacramento, San Diego and Rotterdam. Recent contracts are LRVs for Stuttgart, Cologne, Bochum, Düsseldorf, Kassel, Essen, Freiburg and Karlsruhe.

Deuwag has also supplied bogies for the Hong Kong Mass Transit Corporation and Kowloon Canton Railway vehicles, built by Metro-Cammell; and is supplying bogies for the 396 cars under construction by Kawasaki for Singapore mass transit system. Further bogie contracts are in production and delivery for Mexico City, Guadalajara and Monterrey.

MANUFACTURERS / Powered passenger vehicles

Duro Daković
Duro Daković Industries

PO Box 63, 55001 Slavonski Brod, Yugoslavia

Telephone: +38 55 231-011
Cable: Lokomotive, Slavonski Brod
Telex: 23421/23424

Products: Light rail vehicles and trams; diesel railcars and train-sets.

Constitution: Duro Daković was founded in 1921 as the first Yugoslav locomotive and wagon manufacturer. Diesel locomotives have been produced since 1954.

Energomachexport
V/O Energomachexport

Pr Kalinina, 12109 Moscow, USSR

Telephone: +7 095 203 15 71
Cable: Energoexport
Telex: 411965, 411003

Director General: Vladimir I Filiminov
Deputy Director-General: Grigory I Lapytko
Director, Transmach: Georgy B Stepnov

Products: Electric train-sets; metro cars.
Recent exports have included 15 four-car suburban emus of Type ER-31 to Yugoslavia.

Constitution: The company was formed to handle all railway equipment exports from the Soviet Union. Principal partners include the Ludinovo, Novocherkassk, and Voroshilovgrad locomotive works.

Engesa-FNV
FNV Veiculos e Equipamentos S/A
An Engesa Company

Avenida Tucunaré 125/211, 06400 Barueri, São Paulo, Brazil

Telephone: +55 11 421 4711
Telex: 11 71302 enes br
Telefax: +55 11 421 4445

President: José Luiz Whitaker Ribeiro
Vice-President: José Guilherme Whitaker Ribeiro
Directors: Sérgio Antonio Bardella

Armando Ulbricht Junior
Marco Aurelio de Barros Montenegro
Vail Eduardo Gomes
José Carlos Pereira de Carvalho
Marcos Puglisi de Assumpão

Products: Electric train-sets.

Ferrostaal
Ferrostaal AG

PO Box 10 12 65, Hohenzollernstrasse 24, 4300 Essen, Federal Republic of Germany

Telephone: +49 201 818 01
Cable: Ferrostaal, Essen
Telex: 0857100

Directors: Dr Hans Singer
Dr F Graf von Ballestrem
Helmut Julius
Dr Klaus von Menges
Heinz Staudinger
Gerhard Thulmann

Recife, Brazil, emu featuring body-shells, bogies, pa system and other electrical and mechanical components by Ferrostaal

Products: Electric or diesel-electric railcars, rail buses, light rail vehicles and other multiple-units for urban public transport; motor and trailer bogies; components of rolling stock such as wheels, axles, assembled wheelsets, bearings, suspensions, couplers, electrical equipment; track materials.

Ferrosud
Ferrosud SpA

PO Box 94, Via Appia Antica Km 13, 75100 Matera, Italy

Telephone: +39 835 222841
Telex: 812525 fersud i
Telefax: +39 835 217137

Chairman: Corrado Fici
Managing Director: Angelo Palmieri
Export sales: Claudio Mannucci (Breda)

Products: Railcars and trailers for electric and diesel trains; all types of bogies. Recent contracts have included an order from Italian Railways (FS) for 120 motor and 120 trailer bogies, plus a further order of 82 emu trailer bogies.

Fiat
Fiat Ferroviaria SpA

Piazza Galateri 4, 12038 Savigliano (CN) Italy

Telephone: +39 172 2021
Telex: 210234 fiatsv i
Telefax: +39 172 202 426

Works: 4 Piazza Galateri, 12038 Savigliano (Cuneo)

Chairman: Renato Piccoli
Managing Director and General Manager: Giancarlo Cozza
Deputy General Manager and Project Manager: Pierantonio Losa
Sales Manager: Andrea Parnigoni

Principal subsidiaries: Costruzioni Ferroviarie Colleferro; Elettromeccanica Parizzi

Type ETR 450 tilt-body 250 km/h train-set

Powered passenger vehicles / **MANUFACTURERS**

Fiat diesel railcars or multiple-units since 1980

FS Class	Cars per unit	Motor cars per unit	Motored axles per motor car	Transmission	Rated power(kW) per motor	Max speed km/h	Weight tonnes per car	Total seating capacity	Length per car mm	No in service/ on order 1987	Year first built	Builders		
												Mechanical parts	Engine & type	Trans- mission
Italian State Railways (FS)														
ALn668 (3200)	1	1	2	Mech	169	131	38	69	23 540	105	1980	Fiat	Fiat	Fiat
ALn668	1	1	2	Mech	169	110/130	38	73	23 540	83	1981	Fiat	Fiat	Fiat
ALn668	1	1	2	Mech	168	124	38	69	23 540	5	1982	Fiat	Fiat	Fiat
ALn668	1	1	2	Mech	169	110/130	40	63	23 540	120	1982	Fiat	Fiat	Fiat
ALn663	1	1	2	Mech	240	114	38	85	23 540	10	1982	Fiat	Fiat	Fiat
ALn663	1	1	2	Mech	250	100	40	85	23 540	9	1984	Fiat	Fiat	Fiat
ALn663	1	1	2	Mech	230	137	40	76	23 540	6	1985	Fiat	Fiat	Fiat
ALn668 330 CV	1	1	1	Mech	243	130	40	68	23 540	2	1986	Fiat	Fiat	Fiat
ALn663	1	1	2	Mech	176	95	39	68	23 540	2	1986	Fiat	Fiat	Fiat
ALn668	1	1	2	Mech	240	110	38	68	23 540	3		Fiat	Fiat	Fiat
Swedish State Railways (SJ)														
Y1	1	1	2	Hyd	147	133	42	68	24 400	100	1979	Fiat	Fiat	Fiat
Narrow- gauge	1	1	4	Mech	184	100	30	52	18 170	6	1986	Fiat	Fiat	Fiat
ALn776	1	1	2	Mech	187	130	40	76	23 540	2	1987	Fiat	Fiat	Fiat
ALn776	1	1	2	Mech	250	137	40	76	23 540	3	1987	Fiat	Fiat	Fiat
ALn776	1	1	2	Mech	250	137	40	76	23 540	5	1988	Fiat	Fiat	Fiat

Fiat electric railcars or multiple-units since 1980 continued

Class	Cars per unit	Line voltage	Motor cars per unit	Motored axles per motor car	Rated output(kW) per motor	Max speed km/h	Weight tonnes per car (M-motor T-trailer)	Total seating capacity	Length per car mm (M-motor T-trailer)	No in service 1987 or on order (M-motor T-trailer)	Year first built	Builders	
												Mechanical parts	Electrical equipment
LRV	1	600 V dc	1	B + 2 + B	210	75	43	290	29 494	51	1982	Fiat	AEG/Ansaldo
Milan Metro Line 2	3	1500 V dc	2	B + B	270	90	M 30 T 19	32 40	M 17 540 T 17 540	M28 M 14	1985	Fiat	Ansaldo/Marelli
Milan Metro Line 2 AD inverter	3	1500 V dc	2	B + B	270	90	M 32 R 19	32 40	M 17 540 R 17 540	M 8 T 4	1986	Fiat	Ansaldo/Parizzi
Low-floor streetcar	1	600 V dc	1	B + 2 + B	150	60	28	173	22 280	54	1987	Fiat	Ansaldo
ETR450	14	3 kV dc	10	1A + A1	350	250	44	460	M 27 350 M* 25 600	14	1987	Fiat	Fiat/Marelli Ansaldo
ETR500 Prototype†	2	3000 V dc	1	Bo-Bo	1000	275	M 72 T 40	– –	M 20 000 T 26 000	M1 T 1	1987	Fiat/Breda	Ansaldo/TIBB
Rome Metro (Lido)	6	1500 V dc	4	B + B	220	100	M32 M* 31 T 19	133	17 640	6	1987	Fiat	Ansaldo/Marelli
Milan Metro Line 3 Inverter	3	1500 V dc	2	B + B	270	90	M 32 T 40		M 17 540 T 17 540	M26 T 13	1987	Fiat	Ansaldo/Parizzi/TIBB Marelli/Hitachi/Socimi
ETR500(*)		3000 V dc		Bo-Bo	1000	300	M 72 T 40	714	M 20 000 T 26 000	1990	1989	Fiat/Breda	Ansaldo/ABB
Milan Metro Line 2		1500 V dc		Bo-Bo	270 T40	90 8	M 32 T 26 000	16 1991	M 17550		1991	Fiat	Ansaldo-ABB-Marelli

(*)Pre-production trains, each one composed of two locomotives and 10 coaches.

* Intermediate motor car   † Bogies and transmission

Products: Electric and diesel railcars; tilting-body trains; multiple-units; metro cars; LRVs; tramcars; bogies and components.

Fiat is now supplying low-floor tramcars for Turin, metro cars for Milan and bogies for Rome Line B metro cars. The ETR 450 trains, well-known as 'Pendolino' are now running on the Italian FS network connecting the main towns like Rome, Milan, Naples, Turin, Venice and Florence. Journey time has been reduced from 5 hours to 4 hours between Rome and Milan.

Based on this succesful performance other important European countries have disclosed their interest for this solution. Amongst others, DB ordered components for 10 VT 610 diesel-electric trains to be made in cooperation with local manufacturers.

Fiat is also actively working within an Italian consortium consisting of Breda, Ansaldo, ABB and Fiat for a new high-speed Type ETR 500 train. This has already been tested at over 300 km/h using smooth-running Fiat bogies and transmissions.

Fiat recently delivered the first new units for Milan Metro Line 3.

Costruzioni Ferroviarie Colleferro obtained an order from Interfrigo for 770 refrigerated wagons and is also producing a mid-range passenger coach for FS.

Fiat is currently engaged in the supply of 24 vehicle bodies for Milan Metro's Line 2. Ten diesel railcars also have been ordered by private Italian railways.

Constitution: The activity of Fiat in the field of railway rolling stock began in 1917 with the manufacture of passenger and freight cars. In 1931 Fiat put the first diesel railcars into service before beginning production of diesel multiple-units and locomotives, progressing to the tilting body electric 'Pendolino' train.

Type ALn776 diesel railcars for Central Umbria Railway

102 MANUFACTURERS / Powered passenger vehicles

By the end of 1975 all the activities of Fiat concerning design and manufacture of railway rolling stock were entrusted to Fiat Ferroviaria SpA, the company which now controls Costruzioni Ferroviarie Colleferro Spa, Rome.

Inverter-control train-set for Rome Metro (Lido)

Firema Consortium

Head office: Corso di Porta Romana 63, 20122 Milan, Italy

Telephone: +39 2 5465708
Telefax: +39 2 5460133

President: Dr Ing Giorgio Regazzoni
Board Members: Avv Dino Marchiorello
Dr Giorgio Fiore
Procurator: Prof Ing Francesco Perticaroli
Export Manager: Dr Ing Maurizio Fantini

(For full list of member companies see Firema entry, Locomotives section.)

Products: Multiple-units, railcars, underground rolling stock and light rail vehicles.

The Firema Class E126 emu for 3 kV dc standard-gauge local railways with maximum axleload of 16–17 tonnes has been developed from single-unit 3 kV dc railcars supplied to the Benevento-Naples and Modena-Sassuolo Railways. Each train-set can have two or three cars formed from a power car, control trailer and intermediate trailer.

Principal characteristics of Class E126 emu

Formation	M+Tc	M+T+Tc
Gauge	1435 mm	
Power supply	3 kV dc	
Total length	46 040 mm	69 060 mm
Width	2900 mm	
Height above rail level	3600 mm	
Wheel diameter	910 mm	
Tare weight	77.8 tonnes	107.2 tonnes
Hourly rating	720 kW	
Max speed	120 km/h	
Seats	176	272
Standard capacity	224	340
Total capacity	400	612

Independently wheeled articulating bogie of prototype low-floor tram

Prototype low-floor Milan articulated tram

Class E126 electric train-set for Modena-Sassuolo railway

Artist's impression of Type E82 emu for SEPSA, Naples

Within the Firema group the body-shells are built by Officine di Cittadella, then fitted out by Casaralta, while the bogies are produced by Officina Meccanica della Stanga and the electrical equipments and traction motors by Metalmeccanica Lucana.

In December 1984 Officina Meccanica della Stanga and Officine di Cittadella, both of the Firema Consortium, presented the new prototype of an articulated low-floor tramway for ATM of Milan. The project was financed by the Italian National Research Council within the Finalised Transportation Project, the object of which has been, since 1980, the acquisition of advanced technologies in the tramway field.

The vehicle was entirely designed by OMS, which also built the prototype independently-wheeled articulating bogie. Cittadella carried out all the modifications of the two 1928-type tramway bodies (ATM series 1500) which were used to construct the prototype. The new vehicle has retained the old cars' driving bogies (modified in their primary suspension to increase comfort, and to which electromagnetic skid brakes have been added) and the front and rear parts of the bodies above the driving bogies.

The central part of the vehicle has been rebuilt with a floor height of 364 mm from the rails, but this height is reduced to 346 mm around the four access doors by inclination of the floor. The entire central part of the

Powered passenger vehicles / **MANUFACTURERS**

Firema electric railcars or multiple-units

Class	Cars per unit	Line voltage	Motor cars per unit	Motored axles per motor car	Rated output (kW) per motor	Max speed km/h	Weight tonnes per car (M-motor T-trailer)	Total seating capacity (M-motor T-trailer)	Length per car mm (M-motor T-trailer)	No in service	Year ordered	Builders Mechanical parts	Builders Electrical equipment
Italian State Railways													
ALe 582	*	3 kV dc	(M)	4	1100	140	56.7	58	25 995	34	1983	Fiore	Metalmeccanica Lucana
ALe 582	*	3 kV dc	(M)	4	1100	140	56.7	58	25 995	11	1983	Fiore	Ansaldo
Le 562	*	3 kV dc	(Tc)	–	–	140	34.6	56	25 995	45	1983	OMS	OMS
Le 562	*	3 kV dc	(Tc)	–	–	140	34.6	56	25 995	23	1983	Fiore	Fiore
Le 763	*	3 kV dc	(T)	–	–	140	33	76	25 540	22	1983	Fiore	Fiore
Benevento-Napoli Railway													
E126	3	3 kV dc	1	4	600	120	M 48 / T 29.4 / Tc 29.8	272	M 23 020 / T 23 020 / Tc 23 020	2	1983	Firema Consortium	Firema Consortium
Modena-Sassuolo Railway													
E126	2	3 kV dc	1	4	600	120	M 48 / Tc 29.8	176	M 23 020 / Tc 23 020	2	1983	Firema Consortium	Firema Consortium
CTL Rome G Line													
LRV	3	1.5 kV dc	†	8	720	80	59.7	66	32 400	6	1983	Firema Consortium	Ansaldo-TIBB
ACOTRAL Rome													
E84	2	3 kV dc	1	4	1000	90	M 44.2 / Tc 32	128	M 21 530 / Tc 21 530	6	1983	Firema Consortium	Firema Consortium
SEPSA Naples													
E81	2	3 kV dc	2	2	275	100	M + M 80.5	M + M 72	M + M 50 660	6	1987	Firema Consortium	Ansaldo

* M + Tc or M + T + Tc † Three-car articulated train-set

vehicle has the same floor level; the two ends of the vehicle are at 834 mm from the rails and are connected to the central part by two steps.

The vital item of the project is the independently wheeled bogie under the articulation, which has been designed with an eye to applications in vehicles of entirely new construction. Each wheel is mounted on a short axle with the interposition of spherical roller bearings. The axle is connected to the bogie frame with an articulation and through a pneumatic primary suspension with telescopic damper. Each wheel is also provided with a pneumatic brake acting on the wheel rim with a single shoe. Both the primary suspension and the brake are housed within a vertical structure disposed above and between the wheels. This leaves the entire central part of the bogie free so that the transversal central beam, carrying the structure of the articulation, can be lowered almost to rail level.

From this prototype, now in regular service after many months of trials, a new series of low-floor LRVs has been developed for Italian cities (Firema Types T61 and T62).

In May 1987 OMS recieved an order from Milan Transport Authority (ATM) for the design of coach bodies for ATM's Line 3 vehicles. These three-car train-sets (motor + trailer + motor coaches M+T+M) have light alloy welded bodies and inverter traction equipment. OMS is building 14 train-sets: the other 26, based on OMS design, are being built by three other Italian builders.

In June 1987 Fiore received an order from SEPSA, Naples (Cumana and Circumflegrea Railways), for six Type E81 two-car 3 kV dc emus. The design of the coach bodies and of the bogies is by Firema Engineering; the bodies are being built by Fiore at Caserta works and the bogies by OMS at Padua. These emus, rated at 1100 kW, with top speed of 100 km/h and passenger capacity of 522, have light alloy welded bodies. The inner bogies of each car are motored, with chopper traction equipment by Ansaldo Trasporti.

In 1988 Italian Railways (FS) ordered 30 electric railcars of the new series ALe 642 and 30 matching trailers of Type Le 764 from Fiore of Caserta; in the same period OMS of Padua received an order for 10 Le 764 trailers and for 20 control trailers of Type Le 682. These vehicles with light alloy bodies, are similar to the emus of Class ALE 582/Le 562 already delivered to FS.

Artist's impression of Type E82 emu interior

Frichs
Frichs A/S

PO Box 115, Åarhus C, Denmark

Telephone: +45 6 158555
Telex: 64373

Products: Diesel and electric railcars; diesel and electric multiple-units.

Fuji Car
Fuji Car Manufacturing Co Ltd

28 Hachiman-cho, Minami-ku, Osaka 542, Japan

Telephone: +81 6 213 2711
Telex: 5225279 fujosk j

President: Tetsuhiro Nishi

Vice President: Junichi Takano
Export Sales: Kazuo Okazaki

Products: People mover systems (FAST).

Fuji
Fuji Heavy Industries Ltd
Transport Equipment Division

7-2, 1-chome Nishishinjuku 1-chome, Shinjuku-ku, Tokyo 160, Japan

Telephone: +81 3 347 2436
Telex: 232 2268 fuji j
Telefax: +81 3 347 2117

MANUFACTURERS / Powered passenger vehicles

Model Mooka 63 railbus for a Japanese private railway

Main works
Utsunomiya Rolling Stock Plant
1-11, 1-chome, Yonan, Utsunomiya-shi
Tochigi Prefecture 320, Japan

President: Toshihiro Tajima
Senior Managing Director: Sadasuke Nakazato
General Manager, Transport Equipment Division: Noboru Yuzawa
General Manager, Overseas Business Dept: Kinji Hitomi

Products: Diesel train-sets and railcars.

Constitution: Fuji Heavy Industries stems from the Nakajima Aircraft Company. The Nakajima Company was dissolved in 1945, but in 1953 it was reorganised as Fuji Heavy Industries, specialising in building SUBARU automobiles, buses, rolling stock and aircraft.

Model K1HA 183 Kei diesel railcar for JR-Hokkaido

GANZ
GANZ Electric Works

Lövöház utca 39, Budapest H-1024, Hungary
Mail address: PO Box 63, Budapest H-1525, Hungary

Telephone: +36 1 175-3322
Cable: Alterno, Budapest
Telex: 225363 gvm bp
Telefax: +36 1 156-2989

General Manager: Gábor Kara
Director of Traction Division: Mátyás Rácz

Products: Main-line and suburban railcars and train-sets; LRVs, trams and metro cars.
Between 1976–84, Ganz produced as a standard product the three-unit, 25 kV 50 c/s 1200 kW commuter emu. Two versions of this thyristor-controlled unit are running, one in Yugoslavia and one (metre-gauge) in Tunisia. The commuter train has one power car, which carries most of the electrical equipment under its floor.
A new Ganz electric train-set began trials in 1987. This 25 kV 50 Hz (4-car unit) asynchronous traction motor with current-inverters, a total with 356 passenger seats, features 1460 kW output and regenerative braking. The motor car and one of the three trailers are cabbed.

Budapest Metro car

A six-coach underground train-set has run 100 000 km on the Budapest Metro since it was put into operation at the end of 1986. Chopper control, dynamic braking and automatic regeneration depending on the voltage level of the third rail are characteristics of the design. The three, all-axle driven, coach types enable variation of train-set length to suit traffic density.
Recent contracts obtained include: 18 four-car electric trainsets with asynchronous traction motors and current inverters, 1460 kW output and regenerative braking, for Hungarian State Railways; and three articulated tramcars with chopper control for Hungarian cities.

Constitution: This enterprise developed from the electrical department started by Ganz and Co in 1878.

GANZ electric multiple-units

Railway	Cars per unit	Line voltage	Motor cars per unit	Motored axles per motor car	Rated output (kW) per set	Max speed km/h	Weight per set tonnes	Total seating capacity	Length per set m	No in service 1989	Rate of acceleration m/s²	Year first built	Builders Mechanical parts	Builders Electrical equipment
JZ*	3	25 kV 50 Hz	1	4	1200	120	143.5	236	72.41	50	0.5	1976	Ganz-Mávag	Ganz Electric
SNCFT	3	25 kV 50 Hz	2	2	1200	120	142	200	72.41	6	0.7	1984	Ganz-Mávag	Ganz Electric
Budapest Metro	6	750 V dc	6	4	3360	80	201	276 + 840 standing	116	1	1.2	1986	Ganz-Mávag	Ganz Electric
MÁV	4	25 kV 50 Hz	1	4	1460	120	183	356	103.8	6	0.6	1987	Ganz-Mávag	Ganz Electric

* 1435 mm gauge
† 1000 mm gauge

Ganz-Hunslet
Ganz-Hunslet Részvénytársaság
Budapest VIII, Vajda Péter u.12, H-1430 Budapest
PO Box 29, Hungary

Telephone: +36 1 114 0840, 113 5950
Telex: 22 5575/6 gmbp
Telefax: +36 1 114 3481, 113 4624

Chief Executive: Harry A Codd
Sales Director: Géza Bereczky
Technical Director: László Süveges

An Anglo-Hungarian joint venture company, associated member to the Hunslet (Holdings) PLC of Leeds. Bearer of goodwill and tradition of the 1844 established Ganz and later Ganz-Mávag companies.

Products: Diesel and electric railcars, multiple unit sets and rapid transit vehicles.
10 Ganz Ikarus railbus sets of recent delivery are in service with the Malayan Railway Administration (KTM), five sets are three-car type and five sets five car respectively with two and three motored units.
The total number of the four car mainline commuter sets in service with MAV with static inverter fed three phase asynchronous traction motors have been increased to 20.
An inter-regional version of the emu set with re-shaped cab and with VIC Z-type intermediate trailers is under development for 1991 delivery.

Powered passenger vehicles / **MANUFACTURERS**

Diesel railcars and multiple-units

Class	Cars per unit	Motor cars per unit	Motored axles per motor car	Trans-mission	Rated power (kW) per motor	Max speed km/h	Weight tonnes per car (M-motor T-trailer)	Length per car mm (M-motor T-trailer)	No in service	Year first built	Builders
OSE A 6460	3	1	4	Hyd	840	100	M 49	M 19 480	11	1985	Ganz
KTM RBC	3	2	1–1	Hyd	240	100	Mc 44 M 35 T 35	Mc 12 200 M 10 200 T 10 200	5	1988	Ganz
KTM RBC	5	3	1–1	Hyd	240	100	Mc 44 M 35 T 35	Mc 12 200 M 10 200 T 10 200	5	1988	Ganz
Cummins Twin Disc							NTA 855R	Tac 22			
Cummins Twin Disc							NTA 855R	Tac 22			
Ganz Pielstick Voith							8PA4-185VG	L520rU2			

Electric railcars and multiple-units
MAV BDV mot. No. in service: 20

Ganz-Mávag
Ganz-Mávag Locomotive and Railway Carriage Works

PO Box 28, Könyves Kálmán krt 76, Budapest VIII, Hungary 1967

Telephone: +36 1 335 950, 140 840
Telex: 22 5575/6
Telefax: +36 1 143 481

General Director: József Balogh
Commercial Director: Ferenc Tordai

Products: Diesel railcars, multiple-units, and rapid transit vehicles.

The Ganz-Ikarus demonstrator railbus has completed a successful 180 000 km trial on Malaysian Railways. The vehicle is designed for powering with a Cummins engine. Individual vehicle length is 25 m, weight is 26 tonnes and the vehicle is designed with a maximum speed of 100 km/h. The prototype has 86 seats, but this arrangement can be modified. The Ganz Locomotive and Railway Carriage Works is to develop several versions of the railbus. Following the trial, Malaysian Railways ordered 10 railbus-sets for 1988 delivery; five sets are three-car type and five sets five-car, respectively with two and three motored units.

Projects developed in co-operation with Ganz Electric Works are a six-unit chopper-control metro set for the Budapest Transit Authority on evaluation test and two prototype four-car main-line commuter sets for MÁV. The power cars of the latter are driven by static inverter-fed three-phase asynchronous traction motors. The prototype sets will be followed by manufacture of 18 sets.

Power car of prototype commuter emu for MÁV

Electric railcars or multiple-units

Railway and type	Cars per unit	Line voltage	Motor cars per unit	Motored axles per motor car	Rated output (kW) per motor	Max speed km/h	Weight tonnes per car (M-motor T-trailer)	Total seating capacity	Length per car mm (M-motor T-trailer)	No in service	Rate of acceleration m/s²	Year first built	Builders Mechanical parts	Electrical equipment
NZR EM/ET	2	1.5 kV dc	1	4	100	100	M 37.6 T 34.5	148	M 21 530 T 21 530	44	(0-80 km/h) 0.4	1981	Ganz-Mávag	GEC Traction
SNCFT YZ-E	3	25 kV ac	1	4	305	120	Tc 45.3 M 52 Tc 44.6	200	Tc 24 500 M 23 410	6	(0-50 km/h) 0.65	1984	Ganz-Mávag	Ganz Electric
MÁV BDV mot	4	25 kV ac	1	4	760	120	M 66 Tc 39	344 + 12	M 24 600 T, Tc 26 400	2	(0-60 km/h) 0.6	1987	Ganz-Mávag	Ganz Electric

Diesel railcars or multiple-units

Class	Cars per unit	Motor cars per unit	Motored axles per motor car	Trans-mission	Rated power (kW) per motor	Max speed km/h	Weight tonnes per car (M-motor T-trailer)	Total seating capacity	Length per car mm (M-motor T-trailer)	No in service	Year first built	Builders Mechanical parts	Engine & type	Transmission
SNCFT ZB411	3	1	2	Hyd	883	130	M 60 T 51 Tc 38.5	170	M 22 990 T 25 660 Tc 25 890	15	1979	Ganz-Mávag	Ganz-Pielstick 8PA4-185VG	Ganz H-122-10
SNCFT YZB671	3	1	2	Hyd	883	130	M 60 T 42 Tc 34	148	M 22 290 T 22 660 Tc 22 590	5	1979	Ganz-Mávag	Ganz-Pielstick 8PA4-185VG	Ganz H-122-10
Railbus	2	1	1-1	Hyd	254	100	289	86	25 200		1983	Ganz-Mávag Ikarus	Cummins NTA855R	Twin-Disc TAC-22
OSE A 6460	3	1	4	Hyd	840	100	M 49 T 32 Tc 28	128	M 19 480 T 19 160 Tc 19 480	11	1985	Ganz-Mávag	Ganz-Pielstick 8PA4-185VG	Voith L520rU2

MANUFACTURERS / Powered passenger vehicles

GEC Alsthom
GEC Alsthom Transport Division

Tour Neptune, 92086 Paris La Défense Cedex 20, France

Telephone: +33 1 47 44 9000
Telex: 611 207 alstr f
Telefax: +33 1 47 78 77 55

Managing Director: Michel Perricaudet
Assistant Managing Director: Brian McCann

Works: See GEC Alsthom entry in Locomotives section

Products: Metros, light rail vehicles, automated light vehicles, diesel and electric multiple-units, railcars, electric and electronic traction equipment. Railway engineering: turnkey transport systems.

Other main offices:
PO Box 134, Manchester M60 1AH, England

Telephone: +44 61 872 2431
Telex: 667152
Telefax: +44 61 875 2131

Early in 1986 French Railways placed an initial order for 73 TGV-Atlantique train-sets (with an option on a further 22) with GEC Alsthom as leader of a group formed with Francorail. Since then a further 32 TGV-Atlantique sets have been ordered plus 80 TGV-R (Reaseau or Regional) trainsets. These latter are intended to link the PSE and Atlantique routes with the new Nord route to Lille and Brussels. The Atlantique and PSE sets are dual voltage (25 kV and 1500 V dc) whilst the Regional train-sets are designed in addition for operation on the 3000 V dc network of Belgium.

Each TGV-Atlantique train-set comprises 12 vehicles composed of two power cars framing an articulated 10-trailer consist. The units will be dual-voltage, able to work off 25 kV 50 Hz ac and 1.5 kV dc.

Each bogie of a power car is equipped with two synchronous star-connected traction motors. Power conversion is by means of thyristor diode single-phase mixed bridges and by direct current chopper.

Each synchronous traction motor is associated with a thyristor current inverter. The power equipment semi-conductors are cooled in a two-phase R 113 Flugene atmosphere (liquid and gas). The equipment also includes a power factor improvement device. Power equipment is controlled by a microprocessor ensuring the operating and control functions of the two motors of a bogie and permitting execution of numerous tests in addition to fault memorisation in the case of power transmission chain element failure.

The auxiliaries supply system of a train-set comprises two step-down choppers delivering a 500 V direct voltage. This network feeds two 330 kVA inverters for all 10 trailers' requirements and five 50 kVA inverters for the auxiliaries of each power car. All inverters are of the GTO type (gate turn-off thyristors), and all motors driving auxiliaries, including the variable speed auxiliaries, are of the variable-frequency, three-phase asynchronous type.

In addition to the conventional safety equipment for travelling over conventional infrastructures (automatic vigilance, repetition of pre-indicated signals), a power car also includes: cab signal equipment; on-board microprocessor central unit centralising all train-set information, controlling a certain number of power car and trailer car functions and carrying out tests and controls; data transmission radio enabling exchange with the ground (stations, maintenance workshops) of known or on-board, central unit-controlled information; multiplexing system for traction control and signalling functions between power cars and between train-sets; and public address and train-set personnel communication system.

The articulated consist comprises three first-class and six second-class trailers plus a catering service car, all equipped with pneumatic suspension. Two of the first-class trailers are of new layout, with four-seat compartments. Other novel features include areas arranged for families and groups, and for children. Interior decoration and arrangement have been revised by comparison with the TGV-PSE units and employ new colours, comfortable seating in first-class cars, and cloth-covered seats and curtains in second-class cars.

New passenger amenities include: public telephone booth; nursery; WC for physically-handicapped passengers; and a redesigned and more spacious bar car. Two cars are equipped with galleys for tray lunch catering to seated passengers.

All cars are air-conditioned, the system being operable under two different ventilating rate conditions, depending upon external climatic conditions. Particular care has been given to the soundproofing of the intercommunication platforms and annular articulations; this increases comfort while moving through the train since the intercommunication doors between trailer cars have been suppressed.

Each car has a passenger information system comprising a liquid crystal screen which displays the following: train name; passenger car reservation number; destinations or stations served; and information on services at the passenger's disposal.

Each of the 10 trailers is locally controlled by microprocessor-operated equipment which safeguards door opening and closing, anti-slip-slide control, air conditioning, passenger information system, data management of public address system and telephone booths. All trailer microprocessor-operated equipment is linked to the leading driving cab central unit by a high-output transmission network which enables dialogue between all equipment of the train-set.

In December 1989 30 TGV train-sets were ordered for express services between London and Paris/

TGV-Atlantique train-set

TGV-A train-set: first-class saloon area for conferences

LRV for Grenoble, note low entrance for ease of access by handicapped passengers

Brussels through the Channel Tunnel. These trains are known as the Trans Manche Super Trains (TMST) and are derived from the domestic French TGV but with significant mechanical differences to accommodate the smaller British loading gauge. There are electrical differences also, for example, for operation on 750 V dc third rail on the Southern Region of BR in the UK, and also to work safely with the signalling systems of all three countries. To date, no fewer than 350 TGV train-sets have been ordered of which half have been delivered already.

Leading particulars of the TGV-Atlantique train-sets

Train-set consist: M+10T+M
Motor axle layout (UIC): 2 Bo-Bo power cars
Electrical supply: 25 kV 50 Hz, 1.5 kV dc
Power conversion: Thyristors (single-phase mixed bridges, direct current chopper)
Number of powered axles: 8
New wheel diameter: 920 mm
Total tare weight of train-set in running order: 450 tonnes
Total train-set adhesion weight under normal load: 136 tonnes
Motor or carrying axle load: 17 tonnes
Dimensions
    overall length M+10T+M: 237 600 mm
    overall width: 2904 mm
    bogie rigid wheelbase: 3000 mm
Traction motor
    type: three-phase synchronous
    number per train-set: 8
    location: underfloor
    type of transmission: gear reduction, spline shaft transmission and final drive gear box
Maximum speed in commercial service
    on new high-speed line: 300 km/h
    on conventional line: 220 km/h
Passenger capacity
    first-class: 116
    second-class: 369
Maximum wheel rim power: 8700 kW

In 1988 GEC Alsthom was to deliver to French Railways the first of 44 units of a new type of electric locomotive, the BB26000 'Sybic' Bo-Bo with synchronous ac motors.

Besides its major role as supplier of TGV train-sets, locomotives, self-powered train-sets and cars to French Railways, and of equipment for the Paris authority, RATP, GEC Alsthom sustains vigorous export business in traction units and cars.

In late 1988 GEC Alsthom gained the contract to supply 24 25 kV ac high-speed train-sets (*Tren de Alta Velocidad*), or TAV for Spain's new Madrid–Seville line. As the latter is now to be built to 1435 mm gauge, the TAV can be very closely based on the design of the second-generation TVG-Atlantique train-sets, with the same traction equipment, braking and electronic systems. The interior arrangement (materials and colours) will be adapted to Spanish needs and taste. It will be possible to operate two coupled sets multiple-unit.

Each TAV will consist of two power cars and eight trailer coaches with an expected 361-seat capacity in addition to 25 tip-up seats in the access areas. There will be 81 first-class and 280 second-class seats. Of the two first-class trailers, one will have 45 lounge-type seats with a meeting room for management groups located at one of the coach ends, and the other 36 compartment-type seats. Meals will be served at seats.

There will be a snack-bar coach for second-class, including an area for a shop and a public telephone.

The five second-class coaches will be of the 56-seat lounge type with areas arranged for families and children. Both first-class and second-class coaches will be equipped with video systems.

In 1988 GEC Alsthom was completing delivery of the second-generation bi-level emus for the SNCF's Paris suburban system. These latest Type Z2N units are characterised by employment of asynchronous motor traction, improved passenger comfort through a better space arrangement (seats, accesses), and seating capacity increased by 25 per cent in the trailers (or 12 per cent in a two power-coach + two-trailer train-set), compared to the first generation. These important gains were attained without increasing tare weight, though length is increased by 8 per cent and the number of transported passengers was increased.

TGV-A train-set: first-class 'club' semi-compartment seating

TGV-A driving cab

Artist's impression of snack-bar car for Spanish TAV

108 MANUFACTURERS / Powered passenger vehicles

TGV-A motor bogie

TGV-A trailer bogie

Type Z2N asynchronous motor bi-level emu for SNCF

Nantes LRV based on standard tram design

Furthermore, a review of maintenance costs led to the standardisation of a great number of interior elements.

Type Z2N emu: leading particulars
Dual current power supply: 1500 V dc/25 kV–50 Hz
Traction-braking system with chopper/inverter
Regenerative electric braking
80 kVA static converter group (1 per motorcoach) delivering voltages of:
  220 V single phase-50 Hz for the auxiliary motors
  380 V three phase-50 Hz for the motorcompressor
  72 V direct current for the battery charge and low voltage circuits
The heating plant and static converter are supplied under 1500 V dc
72 V-180 Ah capacity lead battery supplying the train functioning safety circuits and emergency lighting
Compressed air production by compressor delivering 1500 l/minute under 9 bars pressure
Device for brake adjusting in function of load

Train-set characteristics

Train-set consist	Length of train-set	No seated passengers	Passenger capacity under normal load conditions	Total weight under normal load conditions
Two motorcoaches + one 2nd class trailercoach + one 1st and 2nd class trailercoach	103 M	600	1,064	298.7 T
Two motorcoaches + two 2nd class trailercoaches + one 1st and 2nd class trailercoach	129.4 M	804	1,413	366.2 T

Electric transmission:
4 fully suspended forced ventilated asynchronous motors, per motorcoach.
1 current inverter per motor.
Continuous rating per motor   375 kW
Current at continuous rating per motor   440 A
Maximum current per motor   700 A

Performances and operation
Maximum speed: 140 km/h.
Service acceleration at starting with two motorcoaches and two trailers: 0.9 m/s^2 in normal load condition.
Normal track gauge: 1.435 m.
Suburban service.

Bogies:
Motor bogies
2 twin motor per motor coach.
New wheel diameter: 1020 mm.
Transmission: fully suspended motor and gear reduction hollow shaft type coupling and cardan.
Body/bogie drive: central pivot and precompressed sandwich blocks.

Two stage suspension:
  primary: springs and link rods,
  secondary: high clearance pneumatic springs.
Mechanical braking: one brake block per wheel.
Carrying bogies
2 carrying bogies per trailercoach.
New wheel diameter: 840 mm.
Body/bogie drive: by intermediate cross-member and driving roads.
Two stage suspension:
  primary: springs and axle guide rods,
  secondary: pneumatic springs.
Mechanical braking: 2 discs per axle,
             1 brake block per wheel.

Driving cab:
Access to cab by way of the equipment compartment;
double-deck motorcoaches are designed to be driven by one driver;
all driving function and train service controls in addition to the monitoring instruments are positioned on the driving desk within the seated driver's reach;
interphone: between two driving cabs
       between driver and passengers
       between driver and central control post.

Interior arrangement:
In general, the compartments and passenger accesses are arranged for suburban service conditions;
the individualised 'anti-vandalism' material-covered seats are arranged face-to-face in five place rows in second class and four place rows in first class;
vehicle access doors of the two-leafed dual pneumatic plug-in operating type with automatic closing and assisted opening, providing a 1300 mm free passage on the motorcoach and a 1800 mm passage on the trailercoach;
half-opening type windows;
distribution of air blown through ducts located under the seats.

Options:
Air-conditioning;
stainless steel structures;
adaptation to network loading gauges;
adaptation of fittings to other types of service.

RATP, the Paris public-transport authority, has ordered a first batch of nine three-vehicle Type MF 88 train-sets with driving cab and intercommunication (one prototype and eight series train-sets). ANF Industrie is the project leader in charge of the body and running gear; GEC Alsthom is in charge of the traction/body elements. Commercial service foreseen in May 1991. The MF 88 will employ the BOA technology of independent-wheeled steering axles and intercommunication between vehicles providing a throughway extending the whole length of the train, that has been evolved by RATP. Asynchronous motor propulsion will be supplied by GEC Alsthom.

In 1985 the company delivered to Nantes the first examples of the French Standard Tram, an articulated twin-unit LRV which has also been supplied to the

Powered passenger vehicles / **MANUFACTURERS**

Low-floor loading benefit of Grenoble LRV

Grenoble authorities. The initial examples have been built for 1435 mm gauge, but the design is adaptable to metre-gauge and also to a three-body configuration. The articulating bogie is non-powered. Each end bogie is monomotor-powered by a self-ventilated, chopper-controlled 275 kW motor working off 750 V dc. Transmission is by cardan shaft and reduction gear and resilient wheels are fitted. Primary suspension is by two elastometer pads for each axlebox, secondary suspension by two pairs of chevron-type springs. Regenerative braking down to speeds of approximately 5 km/h is complemented by electro-mechanically-operated disc brakes, emergency electro-magnetic track brakes, anti-skid and anti-slip devices on powered bogies and anti-skid on the centre bogie. The body structure is of light alloy, the hinged skirting of aluminium alloy and the front-end fairings of moulded glass-polyester.

French Standard Tram

Length over couplers	28 500 mm
Body width	2300 mm
Height of body	3250 mm
Interior height	2080 mm
Floor height, new wheels	850 mm
worn wheels	825 mm
Normal load, seated	60
standing (4 passengers/m^2)	108
Total	168
Crush load, seated	60
standing (6.6 passengers/m^2)	178
Total	238
Weights, unloaded	35 500 kg
normal load	47 260 kg
crush load	52 160 kg

	Empty	Normal load
Max speed	80 km/h	80 km/h
Max acceleration on starting	1.60 m/s^2	1.10 m/s^2
Normal braking	1.70 m/s^2	1.50 m/s^2
Emergency braking	3.50 m/s^2	3.00 m/s^2
Adhesion on starting	22%	18%
Ratio, adhesion weight/ total weight	0.70	

The authorities of the Saint Etienne city tramway (7.2 km with 24 stations) in France have decided to renew their rolling stock fleet. As a first stage of this programme, they have ordered from GEC Alsthom 12 double articulated elements with an option of one to three supplementary elements. This new vehicle is being developed in co-operation with the Swiss company Ateliers Mecaniques de Vevey, which is designing and will supply the vehicle body, carrying bogie, articulation, the Duewag motor bogies and the Hanning & Kahl brakes. All these elements are identical to or derivatives of those in the Berne three-unit tramset of Switzerland. The global sharing of this order (development costs and vehicles) amounts to 65 per cent for GEC Alsthom and 35 per cent for Vevey. This new narrow body, low-floor, metre-gauge material is notably lighter in weight and less expensive than that of the Grenoble tramway and the Nantes light metro. Service commissioning of the first element is foreseen for April 1991 and that of the final element in February 1992.

The city of Taipei in Taiwan has awarded the Matra/Transport company the contract for a VAL-type automatic light metro line. The rolling stock will be built by Alsthom and represents approximately half the contract. The vehicles of the VAL 256 type will be similar to those which will equip the US schemes in Chicago and Jacksonville. The Taipei order concerns 102 vehicles (or married pairs). Entry into revenue service is foreseen for January 1992.

The GMA Group, of which GEC Alsthom is part, has been chosen to design, build and operate Phase 1 of the Manchester Metrolink in England. GEC Alsthom is responsible for all electrical and mechanical aspects of the project, including the vehicles. The Group has international railway construction experience, including the Docklands Light Railway in London, as well as experience of operating public transport services.

Interior of Type Z2N bi-level emu

Constitution
See GEC Alsthom entry in Locomotives section

Gleismac
Gleismac Italiana SpA

Viale della Stazione 3, 46030 Bigarello (Mantova), Italy

Telephone: +39 376 45301
Telex: 305 224 gleimn i

Products: Remanufacture of diesel and electric rail-cars and multiple-units, passenger cars and freight wagons; manufacture of inspection and construction trolleys for track maintenance, construction and electrification.

110 MANUFACTURERS / Powered passenger vehicles

Goninan
A Goninan & Co Ltd

PO Box 21, Broadmeadow, New South Wales 2294, Australia

Telephone: +61 49 69 9250
Cable: Platinum, Newcastle
Telex: A28061
Telefax: +61 49 69 9250

Chairman: D A W Thomson
Chief Executive & Director: John Fitzgerald
General Manager, Railway Products: Barry Henshaw
Engineering & Sales Manager, Railway Products: Anthony Finnegan

Products: Diesel-hydraulic and electric passenger railcars, and fabricated rail bogies.

Goninan are now the major supplier of stainless steel, double-deck emus for the Sydney Suburban Network. Following previous orders for over 400 cars, Goninan received a contract from the SRA of New South Wales for 450 'Tangara' commuter cars of striking appearance valued at A$530 million.

The 'Tangara' units feature smooth stainless steel exteriors with large glass areas extending through both decks, and full glass bi-parting doors. Bogies manufactured to Nippon Sharyo designs are enclosed by metal skirts to reduce noise. Electrical traction systems incorporating 1500 V dc chopper control are supplied by Mitsubishi.

Constitution: A Goninan & Co Ltd is one of Australia's largest heavy engineering companies with manufacturing facilities at Newcastle and Taree (New South Wales) and Perth (Western Australia). In the field of rail transport they hold licence agreements with: General Electric USA; Pullman Technology Inc USA; Gloucester Carriage & Wagon Co Ltd UK; Nippon Sharyo Ltd Japan.

'Tangara' double-deck cars

GOŠA
SOUR Industrija GOŠA
Rolling Stock Manufacturing Division

Head office: Industrijska 70, 11 420 Smederevska Palanka, Yugoslavia
Sales office: Goša Commerce, Sitnička 39, 11 000 Belgrade

Telephone: +38 26 32 022
Cable: Goša Smederevska Palanka
Telex: 11 684
Telex (sales): 12605

Chairman: Momir Pavlićević
Managing Director: Miodrag Bajčić
Export Sales: Slavko Djorić

Products: Diesel and electric train-sets.

Diesel railcars or multiple-units

Class	Cars per unit	Motor cars per unit	Motored axles per motor car	Transmission	Rated power (kW) per motor	Max speed km/h	Weight tonnes per car (M-motor T-trailer)	Total seating capacity	Length per car mm	No in service	Year first built	Builders Mechanical parts	Engine & type	Transmission
2	2	1	1	Electro-mechanical	150	90	M 20 T 14	122	13 000	200	1953	Goša	Famos	GZF

Electric railcars or multiple-units

Cars per unit	Line voltage	Motor cars per unit	Motored axles per motor car	Rated output (kW) per motor	Max speed km/h	Weight tonnes per car (M-motor T-trailer)	Total seating capacity	Length per car mm	No in service	Rate of acceleration m/s^2	Year first built	Builders Mechanical parts	Electrical equipment
3	25 kV 50 Hz	1	4	300	120	M 54 T 35	228	24 300	2	0.64	1969	Goša	50 c/s Group

Groupement 50 Hz
50 c/s Group

PO Box 8524, Baumackerstrasse 46, 8050 Zurich, Switzerland

Telephone: +41 1 312 46 80/81
Cable: Coordinat, Zurich
Telex: 823 854 sehz ch
Telefax: +41 1 312 3968

Products: Electric train-set equipment.

Constitution: The Group comprises ACEC Transport of Belgium, GEC Alsthom of France and UK, AEG Westinghouse and Siemens AG of the Federal Republic of Germany.

Recent contracts

User	No of units	Motive power units	Year introduced	Gauge (mm)	Weight (tonnes)	Continuous rating (kW)	Continuous/max speed (km/h)	
Portuguese Railways (CP)	15	Three-car units, Class 2100	1982	1665	161.4	1200	64.5/120	Series motors for pulsating dc current, lv tap changer, silicon rectifier, rheostatic braking
Turkish Railways (TCDD)	22	Electrical equipments for three-car units	1984	1435	—	1020	64.5/120	Series motors for pulsating dc current, semi-controlled silicon rectifiers, rheostatic braking
	15	Electrical equipments for three-car units	1990					

Hitachi
Hitachi Ltd

6 Kanda Suragadai, 4-chome, Chiyoda-ku, Tokyo 101, Japan

Telephone: +81 3 258 1111
Cable: Hitachy, Tokyo
Telex: 22395, 22432, 24491, 26375 hitachy

President: Katsushige Mita
Executive Vice President and Director: Masataka Nishi
Board Director: Toshi Kitamura

Products: Electric railcars, diesel railcars, monorail cars, propulsion systems, auxiliary power supply, ATP/ATO equipment, computerised total systems for urban transportation, bogie and air-conditioning equipment.

Recent sales have included:
120 cars all stainless steel transit vehicles with chopper control for Metropolitan Atlanta Rapid Transit Authority (MARTA), USA;

Series 100 Shinkansen car for Central Japan Railway Company

Hitachi electric railcars or multiple-units

Class	Cars per unit	Line voltage	Motor cars per unit	Motored axles per motor car	Rated output (kW) per motor	Max speed km/h	Weight tonnes per car (M-motor T-trailer)	Total seating capacity per car (M-motor T-trailer)	Length per car mm (M-motor T-trailer)	No in service 1988	Rate of acceleration m/s^2	Year first built	Builders Mechanical parts	Builders Electrical equipment
3000 (Nagoya Subway)	4	1500 V dc	4	4	135	100	M36.4-39.1	48-54	20 000	34	0.85	1989	Hitachi	Hitachi and others
200 (East Japan Railway Co)	12	25 kV ac	12	4	230	230	M57-62	45-95	25 000–25 100	128	–	1980	Hitachi	Hitachi and others
1000 (Kita-Kyushu Rapid Railroad Co)	4	1500 V dc	4	4	75	80	27	34-40	13 900–14 800	36	1.0	1981	Hitachi	Hitachi
5000 (Nagoya Subway)	6	600 V dc	4	4	95	65	M24.2 T22	M44 T38	M14 800 T13 450	36	0.9	1982	Hitachi	Hitachi and others
100 (Trensurb, Brazil)	4	3000 V dc	2	4	315	90	M58.3 T43.5	M54 T60	M22 760 T22 760	32	0.8	1985	Hitachi	Hitachi and others
200 (Marta, USA)	8	750 V dc	8	4	136	112	36.7	68	22 860	120	1.3	1985	Hitachi	Garrett and others
100 (Central Japan Railway Co)	16	25 kV dc	12	4	230	240	54-64	60-100	25 800 24 500	76	–	1985	Hitachi	Hitachi and others
1000 (Fukuoka Subway)	6	1500 V dc	4	4	150	90	M40-41 T34	M54 T45	20 000 24 500	6	0.92	1986	Hitachi	Hitachi and others
10-000 (Tokyo Subway)	8	1500 V dc	6	4	165	120	M34.5-38 T28	M58 T50	20 000	38	0.92	1986	Hitachi	Hitachi and others
10 (Kyoto Subway)	6	1500 V dc	4	4	130	105	M34.8-36.8 T28.5-29	50-58	20 000	30	0.92	1987	Hitachi	Hitachi and others
205 (East Japan Railway Co)	10	1500 V dc	6	4	120	100	M34.9-36.2 T24.5-26.5	M54 T48-54	20 000	150	–	1985	Hitachi	Hitachi and others
211 (East Japan Railway Co)	15	1500 V dc	6	4	120	110	M33.6-35.3 T24.1-26.4	M58-68 T55-68	20 000	28	–	1986	Hitachi	Hitachi and others
783 (Kyushu Railway Co)	7	20 kV ac	4	4	150	130	M40.1-40.6 T29.3-30	M60-64 T29-44	20 000	13	–	1988	Hitachi	Hitachi and others
7000 (Sagami Railway Co)	10	1500 V dc	4	4	180	110	M35.8 T24.9-29.8	M54 T48-54	20 000	40	0.7	1988	Hitachi	Hitachi

32 Series 100 all stainless steel cars for Trensurb (Brazil);
21 25 kV ac electric cars for Argentine Railways (FA);
12 1500 V dc electric cars for Indonesian State Railways (PJKA);
12 Series 100 Shinkansen cars and 62 Series 200 Shinkansen cars for Japan Railways Group;
80 Series 205 commuter service electric cars for East Japan Railway Company;
30 Series 10 subway cars for Kyoto Municipal Transportation Bureau, six Series 1000 for Fukuoka Municipal Transportation Bureau, 36 Series 5000 for Nagoya Municipal Transportation Bureau, 24 Series 20 for Osaka Municipal Transportation Bureau;
36 urban monorail cars for Kitakyushu Monorail, four cars for Osaka Monorail and 10 cars for Tokyo Monorail;
15 310 hp stainless steel diesel railcars with air-conditioning for TRA (Taiwan);
Eight 180 hp diesel railcars for PJKA (Indonesia);
17 212 hp stainless steel diesel railcars for RSR (Thailand).

Recent developments:
Hitachi has developed lightweight stainless steel carbodies to reduce maintenance costs and extend service life. These new carbodies are as light as their aluminium equivalents. This was made possible by

112 MANUFACTURERS / Powered passenger vehicles

using thin component members which employ high-tensile strength low-carbon stainless steel developed for electric cars, and a new, stronger joint structure, as well as the simple structure realised through the use of projection bead panels. The ability of the carbody to be formed into any sectional shape and the flexibility of the door and window layouts, make it applicable to a wide range of vehicle designs.

Hitachi recently completed a prototype tram set of an advanced urban monorail car (four-coach) for delivery to the Osaka Rapid Transit Railways. The car is now in trial operation on a 6.7 km stretch prior to revenue service in 1990. A specially designed roof-mounted thin-type inverter air-conditioner in the lowest package is used to enhance the roominess of the passenger compartment. A hollow, extruded aluminium alloy has been liberally utilised for the structural members to minimise weight. A field chopper is used in the control system in order to reduce energy consumption. Pre-assembled units and block layout design are used for the underfloor equipment and construction. This facilitates manufacture and maintenance and also helps to muffle the noise from the bogie portion.

Series 7000 aluminium alloy emu for Sagami Railway Company, Japan

Constitution: Fabrication and assembly of railcars takes place at the Kasado works while locomotives are assembled at Mito.

Series 783 stainless steel emu for Kyushu Railway, Japan

Hunslet TPL
Hunslet Transportation Projects Limited
Member of Telfos Holdings Plc

Dogpool Mills, Stirchley, Birmingham, B30 2XJ, England

Telephone: +44 21 471 1047
Telex: 334269 HTPL-G
Telefax: +44 21 414 1369

Chairman: J Mallins
Managing Director: T M Jefferies
Sales Director: P C Johnson

Associate companies
Hunslet (Holdings) Plc
Hunslet Engine Works, Leeds, LS10 1BT, England

Telephone: +44 532 432261
Telex: 55237
Telefax: +44 532 420820

Hunslet-Barclay Limited
Caledonia Works, Kilmarnock, Ayrshire, KA1 2QD, Scotland

Telephone: +44 563 23573
Telex: 778497
Telefax: +44 563 41076

Products: Emu/railcars, dmu/railcars, metro cars, trams, LRVs and coaches.

Constitution: In the early part of 1989, Hunslet–TPL was formed as a project oriented company to co-ordinate the interest of the Hunslet Group in the design, manufacture and supply of emu, dmu, metro, tram and LRV vehicles and passenger coaches.

Hyundai
Hyundai Precision & Ind Co Ltd

Head office: Hyundai Building, 140-2, Gye-Dong, Chongro-ku, Seoul, Republic of Korea
Postal address: KPO Box 1677, Seoul

Telephone: +82 2 719 0649
Telex: 23238, 23720 hdpic k
Telefax: +82 2 719 0741

Works: 621 Deokjeong-Dong, Changwon, Kyungnam
Telephone: +82 551 82-1341/50
Telex: 53744 hdpic k

Chairman: Mong Koo Chung
President: Ki Chyul Yoo
Senior Vice President: Kyung Wook Kim

Products: Emu railcars, dmu railcars, railbuses, metro cars, trams/LRVs.

Affiliated companies
Hyundai Engineering & Construction Co, Ltd
Hyundai Building, 140-2, Gye-Dong, Chongro-ku, Seoul
Telephone: +82 2 741 2111/5
Telex: 23111

Products: Design and construction of high-speed railway and underground systems.

Hyundai Engine Manufacturing Co, Ltd
1-5, Chonha-Dong, Ulsan, Kyongnam
Telephone: +82 1522 5 4141/9
Telex: 53815, 52191

Products: Engines for industrial use.

Hyundai Electrical Engineering Co, Ltd
Hyundai Building, 140-2, Gye-Dong, Chongro-ku, Seoul
Telephone: +82 2 741 4151/60
Telex: 25761

Powered passenger vehicles / **MANUFACTURERS** 113

Streamlined 3700 hp diesel-electric locomotive and train-set for Korean National Railways

Stainless steel-bodied emu for Pusan metro

Products: Transformers, generators, motors and circuit breakers.

In 1987 the company completed development of a new design of a diesel-hydraulic five-car train-set for KNR's prestige Seoul-Pusan 'Saemaul' service. Concentration of the power plant in the leading end of each streamlined power car, one at each end of the unit, enabled intermediate trailer weight to be reduced to 38 tonnes tare. Each end car weighed 68 tonnes tare. Engines are MTU 12V396TC13 and transmission is Voith hydraulic. Maximum design speed is 150 km/h.

In 1987 the company delivered an additional six streamlined locomotives for KNR, 56 stainless steel-bodied emus for Pusan Metro, to be followed by 36 diesel railcars for KNR in 1988. HDPIC also supplied 68 emus to Seoul Metro to increase operating capacity for the period of the 24th Olympic Games held in Seoul in September 1988.

Constitution: HDPIC, an affiliate of the giant Hyundai Business Group, began rolling stock manufacture in mid-1970 as the Locomotive Division of Hyundai Heavy Industries Company (HHI).

For desirable concentration on mass transit technology related to all types of railway vehicles, Hyundai Rolling Stock Company (HRS) was incorporated in 1978 and maintained until 1985. Effective from June 1985, HRS was consolidated into HDPIC and is being operated as the Rolling Stock Division of HDPIC.

Hyundai electric multiple-units

Operator	Manufacturer's type	Cars per unit	Line voltage	Motor cars per unit	Motored axles per motor car	Rated output (kW) per motor	Max speed km/h	Weight tonnes (M-motor T-trailer)	Total seating capacity (M-motor T-trailer)	Length per car mm (M-motor T-trailer)	No in service 1988	Rate of acceleration	Year first built	Builders Mechanical parts	Builders Electrical equipment
KNR	Subway Line 1	6	1500 V dc 25 kV ac	4	4	120	110	TC 34.2 M 43 M 47.6 T 33	TC 48 M 54 M 54 T 54	TC 20 000 M 20 000 M 20 000	92	2.5 km/h/s (0.7 m/s^2)	1981	HDPIC	MELCO
SMSC	Subway Line 2	4	1500 V dc	4	4	150	100	MC 41.5 M 41.5 T 32	MC 48 M 50	MC 20 000 M 20 000	190	3.0km/h/s (0.83 m/s^2)	1980	HDPIC	MELCO
PCG	Subway Line 1	6	1500 V dc	4	4	165	80	TC 27.6 M1 37.8 M2 36.7 T 25.7	TC 48 M1 56 M2 56	TC 18 000 M 18 000	186	1.0m/s^2	1983	HDPIC	MELCO
KNR	Subway Line 1	10	1500 V dc 25 V dc	4	4	120	110	M 43 T 33	M 54 T 54	19 500	11	2.5	1988	Hyundai	Hyundai

Hyundai diesel train-sets

Operator	Cars per unit	Motor cars per unit	Motored axles per motor car	Transmission	Rated power (kW) per motor	Max speed km/h	Weight tonnes (M-motor T-trailer)	Total seating capacity per car (M-motor T-trailer)	Length per car mm (M-motor T-trailer)	No in service 1988	Year first built	Builders Mechanical parts	Builders Engine & type	Builders Transmission
KNR	6	2	2	Hydraulic	1123	150	M 68 T 38	M 24 T 64	M 23 500 T 23 030	12	1987	HDPIC	MTU 12V396TC/3	Voith
KNR Push-pull	6	2	2	Voith	1100	150	67	A 68 B 64 TR 20	23 565	1	1987	Hyundai	MTU 12V396	TC13 Voith L520RU2
KNR Type DHC	8	2	2	Voith	1450	150	70	A 68 B 64 SP 60	23 565	1	1988	Hyundai	MTU 16V396	TC13 Voith L520RUZU2

ICF
The Integral Coach Factory

Perambur, Madras 600 038, India
Telephone: +91 44 618920, 618091

Cable: Raildib, Madras
Telex: 7390

Diesel railcars

Class	Cars per unit	Powered cars per unit	Powered axles per motor car	Transmission	Rated power (kW) per motor	Max speed km/h	Weight tonnes per car	Total seating capacity	Length per car mm	No in service	Year first built	Engine & type	Transmission
I & II	2	2	2	Hyd	212	100	30.4	78	19 500	6	Prototype 1964, remainder 1970-71	Leyland, UK Type REO-680 Kirloskar Cummins NHHR TØ-6B1	BUT, UK Kirloskar Cummins

MANUFACTURERS / Powered passenger vehicles

ICF electric multiple-units

Class	Cars per unit	Line voltage	Motor cars per unit	Motored axles per motor car	Rated output (kW) per motor	Max speed km/h	Weight tonnes per car (M-motor T-trailer)	Total seating capacity	Length per car mm	No in service (M-motor T-trailer)	Rate of acceleration m/s²	Year first built	Builders Mechanical parts	Builders Electrical equipment
BG I & II	4	25 kV ac	1	4	167 Cont 187 1 hr	105	M 59.5 DT 32.0 T (A type) 30.0 T (C type) 32.0	408	20 726	M 400 DT 338 T (A type) 318 T (C type) 347	0.55	1962-63	Coach builders: ICF Brake equipments: Westinghouse/ Escorts	Hitachi AEI BHEL/India
BG I & II	3	1.5 kV dc	1	4	149 Cont 164 1 hr	105	M 52.6 T 34.53 DT 35.13	296	20 726	M 131 DT 122 T 126	0.54	1969-70	Coach builders: ICF Brake equipments: Westinghouse/ Escorts	BHEL/India GEC
MG I & II	4	25 kV ac	1	4	128 Cont 145 1 hr	90	M 44.5 T 22.3 DT 23.4	298	19 500	MC 45 DT 49 T 96	0.45	1965	Coach builders: ICF Brake equipments: Westinghouse/ Escorts	Fuji/Toyo Denki

General Manager: Kuldip Narain

Products: Electric multiple-units for ac and dc traction; diesel railcars; metro cars.

Constitution: This is a production unit under the Indian Ministry of Railways, set up during the first Five Year Plan in collaboration with Swiss Car Elevator Manufacturing Corporation, Zurich. The collaboration agreement ended in 1961 and since then all new type of coaches have been designed and engineered entirely by ICF. Up to the end of December 1986 output had totalled 19 240 coaches of over 100 different types.

Imesi
Imesi SpA

(Industrie Metalmeccaniche Siciliane)
A member of the Breda Railway Group

Contada Olivelli Pistone, 90044 Carini, Palermo, Italy

Telephone: +39 91 8668677
Cable: Imesi-SpA, Carini
Telex: +39 910113 imisi i

Chairman: Giuseppe Capuano
General Manager: Angelo Palmieri

Products: Electric multiple-units; railcars; trailer passenger coaches.

Inirail
(See Locomotives Section)

Jenbacher
Jenbacher Werke AG

6200 Jenbach, Austria

Telephone: +43 5244 2291-0
Cable: Motor Jenbach
Telex: +43 53756-7

Managing Director: F Franer
Technical Director: Dr Ebner
Production Manager: Ing Truppe

Products: Diesel railcars. Recent products include the new Type 5047 419kW diesel-hydraulic railcar for Austrian Federal Railways (ÖBB).

Constitution: The company was started in 1946 for the manufacture of diesel engines and combined units.

Jessop
Jessop & Co Ltd, Calcutta

63 Netaji Subhas Road, Calcutta 700 001, India

Telephone: +91 33 25 3420/5041
Cable: Jessops, Calcutta
Telex: 021-5054; 021-5298

Works: Jessore Road, Dum Dum, Calcutta

Telephone: +91 33 57 2321

Chairman: S R Choudhury
Managing Direcror: S N Sinha
Director (Engineering & Commercial): R N Bhowal
Director (Production): D Sen

Products: All types of rolling stock including electric multiple-unit coaches and LRVs.

Constitution: Jessop and Co was founded in 1788, one of the oldest engineering firms in India. The works at Dum Dum, which cover 80 acres, comprise six separate units: wagon, coach, structural, road roller, mechanical and paper works. The works at Durgapur, built on 116 acres, manufacture heavy-duty iron castings.

Kalmar
Kalmar Verkstads AB

PO Box 943, S-39129 Kalmar, Sweden

Telephone: +46 480 62600
Cable: Kvab, Kalmar
Telex: 43029
Telecopier: +46 480 18975

Chairman: Sven Arnerius
Managing Director: K Harry Eriksson

Products: Diesel-hydraulic railcars.
Important recent sales have been 30 railcars (in collaboration with Fiat Ferroviaria Savigliano SpA) for Swedish State Railways (SJ). In collaboration with ABB the company is involved in the design and delivery to SJ of 20 Type X-2 tilt-body 200 km/h train-sets.

Constitution: Kalmar Verkstad was founded in 1902 and is Swedish State Railways' (SJ) major supplier of diesel locomotives, railcars and passenger cars. Kalmar Verkstad is a subsidiary of the Kalmar Industries Group.

Co-operation agreements: Kalmar Verkstad is associated with General Motors Electromotive Division, USA.

Kalmar diesel railcars

Class	Transmission	Rated power (kW) per motor	Max speed km/h	Weight tonnes per car	Total seating capacity	Length per car mm	No in service	Year first built	Builders Mechanical parts	Builders Engine & type	Builders Transmission
Y1	Hyd	295	130	45	68	24 400	30	1980	Kalmar Verkstad/Fiat	Fiat 8217 12	Fiat SRM

Powered passenger vehicles / **MANUFACTURERS** 115

Kawasaki
Kawasaki Heavy Industries Ltd, Rolling Stock Group

Head office: World Trade Centre Building, 4-1 Hamamatsu-cho 2-chome, Minato-ku, Tokyo, Japan

Telephone: +81 3 2867 3 0022
Cable: Kawasaki Heavy, Tokyo
Telex: 22672, 26888, (domestic) 242-4371

Works: 1/18-adayama-Dori 2-chome, Hyogo-ku, Kobe
Telephone: +81 78 671 5021

2857-2, Naka Okamoto, Kawachi-cho, Kawachi-Gun, Tochigi Pref
Telephone: +81 3 435-2589

Chairman: Zenji Umeda
President: Kenko Hasegawa
Executive Vice Presidents: Renzo Nihei
 Yutaki Onishi
Director (Rolling Stock): Masahiko Ishizawa

Keihan Electric Railways Series 6000 emu

Car type	Motor cars per unit	Motored axles per motor car	Rated output (kW) per motor	Max speed km/h	Weight tonnes per car (M-motor T-trailer)
MC1	1	4	130 (at 600 V)	120	M 32.5
MC2	1	4	155 (at 1.5 kV)		M 32.5
M1	1	4			M 32
M2	1	4			M 32
T1					T 22
T2					T 22
T					T 24

SEPTA light rail vehicle

Series 203 emu for Japan Rail

Products: Electric and diesel railcars.

The company was one of five manufacturers entrusted with construction of 432 cars forming the Series 200 train-sets for the 25 kV 50 Hz Tohoku and Joetsu Shinkansen of Japanese National Railways (JNR).

Other recent sales to JNR have included the 1.5 kV dc chopper-controlled Series 203 emu. It is fabricated in unpainted light alloy from large hollow-formed sections. Based on the JNR Series 201, the 203 was designed for the opening of through service between the JNR Johban and Tokyo Corporation Chiyoda Lines. The route is severely graded in many places, so high acceleration and deceleration rates were specified. The weight of the car was also lowered substantially in order to reduce the thermal load of the main circuit equipments such as the main motor. All four axles in a motor car are powered with 150 kW motors and motor car weights are either 34.9 or 35.4 tonnes, with 54 seats. Maximum speed is 100 km/h. Each car is 20 metres long and trailers weigh 24 to 26.5 tonnes, with 48 or 54 seats.

In 1987 150 KHI-built cars were running on the Singapore MRTC lines. A fleet of 246 cars was added in 1988. All are equipped with state-of-the-art electronic control systems. KHI's contract with MRTC, amounting to US 285 million, was signed in April 1984. It involved delivery of 66 train systems comprising 396 cars.

KHI recently won a US$ 200 million contract from MTA (Metropolitan Transportation Authority) to supply 200 subway cars to the New York City Transit Authority (NYCTA). This is NYCTA's second contract placed with KHI. Under the first contract, KHI completed delivery of 325 air-conditioned, graffiti-proof, stainless steel subway cars in July 1985. They are now running on NYCTA's Lexington Line connecting the Bronx district with Manhattan.

Under Chinese National Railway's (CNR) electrification plan, five KHI-built cars are running between Zhengzhou and Baoji.

In the US, KHI's Yonkers plant, New York, became operational in March 1987 and is producing and renovating cars for US rapid transit systems. 95 new cars were produced and delivered in November 1987 to the Port Authority of Trans Hudson Corporation (PATH), a division of the Port Authority of New York and New Jersey. In addition, 248 cars have been overhauled for PATH at the facility, with mid-1988 set as the deadline.

In April 1988, the plant was assembling new subway cars for the New York City Transit Authority (NYCTA).

Constitution: Kawasaki Heavy Industries Ltd was formed in 1969 by the merger of Kawasaki Rolling Stock Manufacturing Co, Kawasaki Aircraft Co and Kawasaki Dockyard Co Ltd. In 1972 Kisha Seizo Kaisha Ltd was taken over and merged into Kawasaki Heavy Industries Ltd.

Kinki Sharyo
The Kinki Sharyo Co Ltd
Kinki Rolling Stock Manufacturing Co Ltd

Head office and Tokuan factory: 3-9-60, Inada-Shinmachi, Higashi Osaka City, Osaka 577, Japan

Telephone: +81 6 746 5240
Cable: Kinsha Fuse
Telex: 5278911
Telefax: +81 6 745 5135 (GIII)

Tokyo office: 527 Nippon Bldg, Ohtemachi, Chiyoda-ku, Tokyo 100

Telephone: +81 3 270 3431
Telex: 222 3105
Telefax: +81 3 245 0238 (GIII)

President: Seihei Katayama
Executive Vice President, Admin: Akira Kitamori
Senior Managing Director, Rolling Stock: Hisatsugu Sugano
Senior Managing Director, Accounts: Yoshio Yoshii
Managing Director, Tokyo Branch/Sales Management: Yasuji Yukawa
Director, Domestic & Export Sales: Takumi Ono
Director, Manufacturing: Teijiro Itoh

Series 2600 'Sakura Liner' for Kinki Nippon Railway

MANUFACTURERS / Powered passenger vehicles

Principal subsidiary companies:
The Kinki Kogyo Co Ltd
Kinki Aluminium Co Ltd
Kinki Golf Centre Co Ltd
Kinsha Service Co Ltd
Techno Design Co Ltd
Kinki Metal Industrial Co Ltd

Products: Electric and diesel railcars.

In 1981, the company entered into a licensing agreement with SIG, Switzerland, which allows Kinki to produce articulated light railway vehicles to SIG's proven design.

Major purchasers of Kinki products include such domestic clients as Japan Railways Group, Kinki Nippon Railway Co, Ltd, Teito Rapid Transit Authority, Tokyo Metropolitan Government Transport Authority, Osaka, Fukuoka and Kyoto Municipal Transportation Bureaus, as well as customers in such countries as the Republic of Korea, Taiwan, Hong Kong, Philippines, Thailand, Myanmar, Bangladesh, Indonesia, Singapore, Australia, New Zealand, Egypt, East Africa, Nigeria, Zambia, USSR, USA, Mexico, Peru, Brazil and Argentina.

Representative products include Shinkansen electric cars for JR Group, double-deck express electric cars for Kinki Nippon Railway Co, Ltd, and the chopper-control cars for Teito Rapid Transit Authority, Fukuoka and Kyoto Municipal Transportation Bureaus. The company manufactures aluminium and stainless steel as well as steel cars.

Typical of recent commuter emu products are the all-stainless steel sets for the JR Group, the aluminium alloy sets for the Kyoto Municipal Transportation Bureau and the 02 and 03 series of aluminium alloy sets for the Teito Rapid Transit Authority.

More than 900 LRVs have been supplied to authorities in Egypt, including 480 tramcars for the Cairo Transport Authority, 305 for the Heliopolis Co for Housing and Development, and 138 for the Alexandria Passenger Transport Authority. Kinki Sharyo also won a contract from the Massachusetts Bay Transportation Authority, USA, for 100 articulated LRVs, which were delivered in 1986–88.

In 1988 the Japanese Ministry of Trade and Industry awarded Kinki Sharyo its annual prize for good design for the company's Series 211 Limited Express electric cars for West Japan Railway and its Series 21000 'Urban Liner' Limited Express and Series 5200 Express electric cars for the Kinki Nippon Railway. In 1986 the company gained this award for its six-car 'Super Electric Commuter' emus for the Kinki Nippon Railway's Higashi Osaka line.

Interior of Kinki Nippon Railway 'Sakura Liner'.

Series 211 Limited Express emu for West Japan Railway

Induction motor-powered bogie of Kinki Nippon Railway 'Super Commuter Car'

Motor bogie of LRV for MBTA

Advanced technology features of the 'Super Electric Commuter' unit include induction motors and GTO thyristor VVVF (variable voltage variable frequency) inverter units for control equipment. Two VVVF inverter units are mounted on each motor car and controlled by a bogie drive unit to localise failures and reduce the wheel diameter maintenance control between bogies. Regenerative braking is supplemented by and blended with air brake equipment.

The line on which the emus operate has long tunnels and inclines and the third rail system was adopted; diagnostic display equipment is therefore installed in the cab to enable quick response to failures. A microcomputer control unit is installed for the ATC equipment, automatic announcing system and cooling system.

Bodies are all steel and all cars have four doors on a side. Doors are a double sliding type, 1300 mm wide, operated by a motor installed on the door header. The gangway between cars features sliding doors and new interlock-type vestibule diaphragms with stainless steel frames.

Auxiliary equipment such as a brushless motor generator and air compressor on trailer cars, and the main circuit equipment such as the inverter, gate control box, line breaker box and filter reactors on the motor cars, are underfloor-mounted. The layout of the equipment and cross beams on the latter is specially designed to reduce the number of equipment suspension points and thickness of steel plates. Aluminium wire ducts and small cross-section WL wires (cross-linked polyethylene insulated wire) are also used to reduce weight.

The bogie is a standard air-sprung, direct connection, and side bearer-support type. To improve passenger comfort and ease maintenance, the axle box suspension device and frame are of new design. The laminated cylindrical rubber units arranged in a wing-type structure are combined with the axle spring. Both ends of the side beams are cast steel and are welded with steel plates to form a one-piece bogie. Cylindrical roller bearing package units are used. The brake equipment, of single tread type, is installed at each wheel. Trailer bogies at the front and end of a train have wheel tread cleaning equipment. On some bogies the current collector from the third rail is installed on the axlebox.

Powered passenger vehicles / **MANUFACTURERS**   117

'Urban Liner': principal features

Gauge	1435 mm
Line current	1500 V dc
Tare weight	45 tons (2 cars), 44 tons (3 cars), 43 tons (1 car)
Seating capacity	56 (regular car), 42 (deluxe car)
Traction motors	4 × 125 kW/car
Control system	Rheostatic cam shaft control with dynamic brake and speed balancing brake
Brake system	Electromagnetic straight air brake Dynamic brake
Auxiliary power supply system	dc/dc converter type 70 kW
Max operating speed	120 km/h
Max acceleration	2.5 km/h/s
Max deceleration	4.0 km/h/s

Series 21000 'Urban Liner' electric train-set for Kinki Nippon Railway

Recent contracts

Customer	No of cars	Type of vehicle
JR East	16	Series 415 Suburban
	10	Series 251 Limited express, sight-seeing
	21	Series 253 Limited express, airport access
JR Tokai	16	Series 311 Suburban
	16	Shinkansen 'Bullet Train'
JR West	16	Shinkansen 'Bullet Train'
	42	Series 221 Suburban
JR Shikoku	12	Series 7000 Commuter
JR Kyushu	2	Series 783 Limited express
Teito Rapid Transit Authority, Tokyo	32	Subway car
Osaka Municipal Transportation Bureau	2	Subway car
Kinki Nippon Railway	4	Express
	4	Express, party-trip
	21	Commuter

The Series 2100 'Urban Liner' electric railcars were produced for the Kinki Nippon Railway to improve passenger services between Osaka and Nagoya. Composed of three two-car units, the Urban Liner connects Osaka and Nagoya (185 km) in about two hours non-stop. The train's maximum speed is 120 km/h, the fastest provided by conventional private railways in Japan. All axles are motored, so that output has been increased by 40 per cent compared to the Kinki Nippon Railway's conventional limited-express electric railcars.

The Series 2600 Limited express luxury train, known as the 'Sakura Liner' and built for Kinki Nippon Railway Co Ltd (KINTETSU), entered revenue service in March 1990. Its purpose is to improve the sightseeing service of cherry blossom (Sakura) in Yoshino, Nara, the most famous location for cherry blossom in Japan.

The Series 251 Limited express luxury train, known as the 'Odoriko', was completed for East Japan Railway in April 1990.

Kinki Sharyo LRVs

	MBTA	Cairo	Alexandria
Gauge (mm)	1 435	1 000	1 435
Line current (V dc)	600	600	600
Tare weight (tonnes)	38.5	21.5	18.7
Passenger capacity			
Total	201	163	137
Seated	50	44	36
Length overall (mm)	21 945.6	15 800	12 900
Width overall (mm)	2 641.6	2500	2300
Height to top of roof (mm)	3 352.8	3340	3220
Bogie centre distance (mm)	7 010.4	8400	6500
Wheelbase (mm)	1905	1905	1850
Wheel diameter (mm)	660.4	660	660
1 h rating output (kW) per motor	103	52	52
Motored axles per motor car	4	4	4
Max speed (km/h)	88.4	64	50

Kinki Sharyo commuter emus

	Fukuoka		Kyoto		Teito		Kinki Nippon 'Super Commuter'	
	(Power car)	(Trailer car)	(Power car)	(Trailer car)	(Power car)	(Trailer car)	(Power car)	(Trailer car)
Gauge (mm)	1067		1435		1067		1435	
Line current (V dc)	1500		1500		1500		750	
Tare weight (tonnes)	34	40	36	26.3	35.7	37 (TC)	28–34 (M&T)	
Passenger capacity								
Total	136	144	150	170	136	144	125	135
Seated	48	54	50	58	48	54		
Car length overall (mm)		20 000		20 000		20 000	18 200	18 000
Width overall (mm)		2840		2780		2830	2900	
Height to top of roof (mm)		4090		4040		3920	3745	
Bogie centre distance (mm)		14 000		14 100		13 800	12 400	
Wheelbase (mm)		2100		2100		2200	2100	
Wheel diameter (mm)		860		860		860	860	
1 h rating output (kW) per motor		150		130		160	140	
Motored axles per motor car		4		4		4	4	
Max speed (km/h)		90		75		100	70	

Kolmex
Foreign Trade Enterprise Co Ltd

Mokotowska 49, 00-542 Warsaw, Poland

Telephone: +48 22 28 22 91
Cable: Kolmex, Warsaw
Telex: 813270; 813714
Telefax: +48 22 295879

Managing Director: Aleksander Gudzowaty
Sales Directors: Aleksander Kociszewski
 Wieslaw Husarski
 Tomasz Suprowicz
 Elzbieta Zaleska

Products: Electric train-sets.

Konstal
Steel Construction Works Konstal

ul Metalowcow 7, 41-501 Chorzów, Poland

Export sales: Kolmex, 49 Mokotowska, 00-542 Warsaw

Telephone: +48 22 411051-58
Cable: Konstal, Chorzów
Telex: 0312451

Products: Trams and LRVs.

118 MANUFACTURERS / Powered passenger vehicles

Konstal Type 105r light rail vehicle

Stainless steel electric railcars for Pusan City Government

Konstal LRV

Class	Wheel arrangement	Line voltage	Rated output kW	Max speed km/h	Weight tonnes	No in service	Year first built	Builders	
								Mechanical parts	Electrical equipment
105 N	Bo-Bo	600 dc	166	70	17	1500	1974	Konstal-Chorzów	Elta-Lódź

Korea Shipbuilding & Engineering
Korea Shipbuilding & Engineering Corporation

Head office: 1, 1-Ka Jongro, Jongro-ku, Seoul, Republic of Korea
CPO Box 1520, Seoul

Telephone: +82 2 739 5577
Telex: 23669; 23415 ksecs
Telefax: +82 2 733 8113

Pusan factory: 370-6 Tadae-dong, Saha-ku, Pusan
PO Box 74, Busan

Telephone: +82 51 204 0541
Telex: 53613 ksecs
Telefax: +82 51 204 0626

Chairman: Ryun Namkoong
President: Ho Namkoong
Executive Director: Jong-Chul Mun
Sales Director: Jun Kil Suh

Products: Diesel railcars, electric railcars.

In recent years, KSEC has delivered over 5000 units of various kinds of rolling stock to Korean National Railways and to Malaysia, Saudi Arabia, Indonesia, Sudan, Thailand, Argentina, New Zealand and elsewhere.

Latest deliveries have included 12 sets of electric railcars for Pusan City Government with carbodies of stainless steel.

Electric multiple-units for Pusan City Government

Cars per unit	Line voltage	Motor cars per unit	Motored axles per motor car	Rated output (kW) per motor	Max speed km/h	Weight tonnes per car (M-motor T-trailer)	Total seating capacity (M-motor T-trailer)	Length per car m	No of cars in service	Rate of acceleration km/h/s	Year first built	Builders	
												Mechanical parts	Electrical equipment
6	1500 V dc	4	4	165	80	TC 26.3 M1 36 M2 35	TC 48 M1 56 M2 56	17.5	6	Normal: 1 Max: 1.26	1985	KSEC	KSEC & Marubeni (Japan)

LEW
VEB Lokomotivbau-Elektrotechnische Werke "Hans Beimler"

Head office: 1422 Hennigsdorf, German Democratic Republic

Export sales: AHB Schienenfahrzeuge Export-Import

Telephone: +37 50
Cable: Elektrolok
Telex: 01 158 531

Products: Multiple-unit trains.

LEW has constructed the short-distance emu of Type BR 270 for the city railway of Berlin. Chopper control and combined regenerative/rheostatic brake are features. Information electronics for control, regulation and protection increases operational security. Lightweight construction used for non-bearing car body structures and bogie sub-assemblies help to reduce energy consumption. Each two-car unit offers 102 seats and room for 404 standing.

Within a joint agreement between the GDR rail vehicle industry and AEG, LEW supplied the first of 12 diesel-electric Intercity emu trains to Greek Railways (OSE) in 1989. The Series DE-IC 2000 N-OSE vehicles will be taken into service on the Athens–Thessaloniki line. A characteristic of the car bodies is lightweight steel construction. Sheet steel with a coat of copper alloy has been used for exterior sheet metal lagging.

Type BR 270 emu for Berlin

A computerised control system of the drive unit guarantees optimal fuel consumption by adapting the diesel-generator set to actual traction conditions. Comfort is ensured by electro-dynamic and pneumatic brakes, thermal and noise insulation and air-conditioning. Each emu consists of two motor coaches with luggage compartment, driver's compartment, two machine compartments and passenger compartments; and two intermediate trailers either entirely saloon or sub-divided into two compartments and one bar/kitchen compartment. Total capacity amounts to 36 first-class and 144 second-class seats.

Powered passenger vehicles / **MANUFACTURERS** 119

LEW electric multiple-units

Class	Cars per unit	Line voltage	Motor cars per unit	Motored axles per motor car	Rated output (kW) per motor	Max speed km/h	Weight tonnes per car (M-motor T-trailer)	Total seating capacity	Length per car mm (M-motor T-trailer)	No in service	Rate of acceleration m/s²	Year first built	Builders Mechanical parts	Builders Electrical equipment
BR 270	4	750 V dc	2	4	150	90	M 33.5 T 23.5	208	M 18 150 T 18 050	2	0.7	1980	LEW	LEW
GIII	4	750 V dc	4	4	120	70	M 22.5 T 21.1	126	M1 14 650 M2 14 650	25	0.8	1984	LEW	LEW

Linke-Hofmann-Busch
Linke-Hofmann-Busch Waggon-Fahrzeug-Maschinen GmbH

Postfach 411160, 3320 Salzgitter 41, Federal Republic of Germany

Telephone: +49 5341 21 1
Cable: Linkebusch, Salzgitter 41
Telex: 954452
Telefax: +49 5341 214156

Technical & Commercial Director: Wolfgang von Waldstätten
Production Director: Hilmar Kobriger
Chief Sales Director: Dr Alfred Henning
Manager Export Sales: Reiner Schmidt

Products: Passenger and freight cars; electric and diesel railcars and train-sets; long-haul, suburban and underground passenger cars; tramcars and light rail vehicles.

Constitution: Established in 1839 at Breslau under the name of Carbuilding Workshops of Gottfried Linke, the company amalgamated with Gebruder Hofmann & Co in 1912 to form Linke-Hofmann Werke AG, Breslau. In 1928 the Waggon & Maschinenfabrik AG was formed. Busch joined the company to form Linke-Hofmann-Busch. After the Second World War the company's works at Breslau had to be abandoned, but in 1949 LHB resumed its activities at Salzgitter-Watenstedt, near Brunswick.

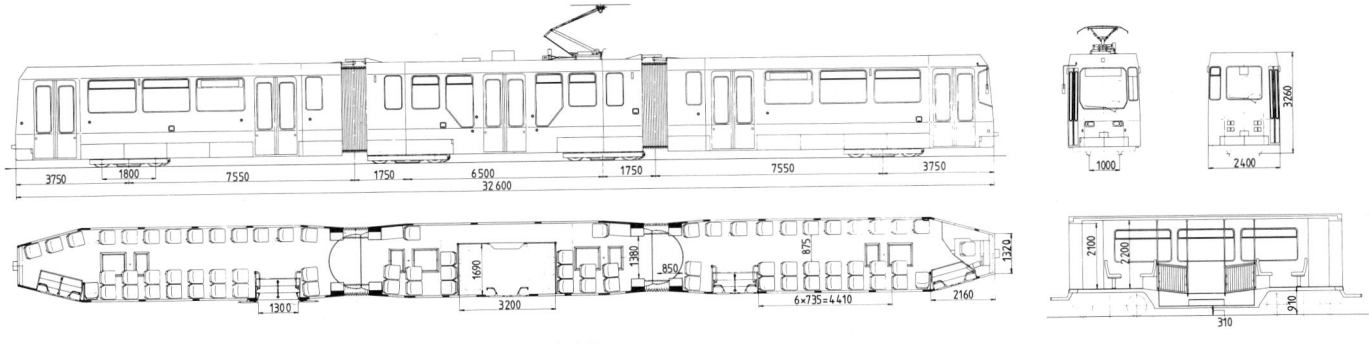

Type DT4 four-car underground train-set for Hamburg (HHA)

Layout of new-generation Type GTW8/8 LRV for Würzburger Strassenbahn GmbH

Macosa
Material y Construcciones, SA

Head office: Plaza de la Independencia 8, Madrid 28001, Spain

Telephone: +34 1 522 4787
Cable: Material, Madrid
Telex: 22168

Macosa diesel railcars or multiple-units

Class	Cars per unit	Motor cars per unit	Motored axles per motor car	Transmission	Rated power (kW) per motor	Max speed km/h	Weight tonnes per car (M-motor T-trailer)	Total seating capacity	Length per car mm (M-motor T-trailer)	No in service	Year first built	Builders Mechanical parts	Builders Engine & type	Builders Transmission
RENFE 592	3	2	2	Hydr	169	120	M 46 T 39	228	M 22 620 T 23 000	70	1981	Macosa	MAN	Voith
712 ZTO	3	1	2	Hydr	214	120	M 29.5 T 21.5	145	M 17 200 T 17 200	20	1975	Macosa	MAN	Voith
712/714 ZTP	2	1	2	Hydr	214	120	M 28 T 29.5	144	M 21 566 T 21 566	35	1981	Macosa MAN Duro Dakovic	MAN	Voith
ENAFER	1	1	2	Hydr	228	80	M 34.5	120	M 18 250 T 18 200	6	1984	Macosa	MAN	Voith
FEVE	1	1	2	Elec	360	120	M 25	208	16 200	30	1985	Macosa MTM	MAN	MTM BBC

MANUFACTURERS / Powered passenger vehicles

Works: Herreros 2, Barcelona
Telephone: +34 3 307 05 00; Telex: 52286
San Vicente 273, Valencia
Telephone: +34 6 377 39 00; Telex: 62452
Marqués de Mudela 10, Alcazar de San Juan
Telephone: +34 54 1124; Telex: 23692

President: Eduardo Santos

Vice President: Pedro Nueno
Managing Director: Emilio Daroca
Financial Director: José Miguel Olabarria
Rolling Stock Director: Andrés Soler
Export Director: José Sanz

Products: Diesel railcars and dmus; emus and electric railcars; subway cars.

Constitution: This company was formed in 1947 by the merger of Materialpara Ferrocarriles y Construcciones, SA of Barcelona and Construcciones Devis, SA of Valencia.

Macosa electric railcars or multiple-units

Class	Cars per unit	Line voltage	Motor cars per unit	Motored axles per motor car	Rated output (kW) per motor	Max speed km/h	Weight tonnes per car (M-motor T-trailer)	Total seating capacity	Length per car mm (M-motor T-trailer)	No in service (on order)	Rate of acceleration m/s²	Year first built	Builders Mechanical parts	Builders Electrical equipment
RENFE 445 CDTI	2	3 kV dc	2	4	240	100	M 56	152	24 600	1	0.79	1984	Macosa CAF MTM	GEE MTM Westinghouse SA
RENFE 440	3	3 kV dc	1	4	290	140	M 61 T 37 T 42	260	M 26 205 T 26 177 T 26 205	172 (20)	–	1972	Macosa	Westinghouse SA GEE MELCO
RENFE 444	3	3 kV dc	1	4	290	140	M 64 T 39 T 48	212	M 26 400 T 26 200 T 26 295	14	–	1980	Macosa	Westinghouse SA MELCO GEE
FGC111/181	3	1.2 kV dc	2	4	276	90	M 32 T 21	176	M 20 225 T 19 800	20	1.2	1983	Macosa	MTM AA
FGC211/281	3	1.5 kV dc	2	4	276	90	M 30 T 20	148	M 18 125 T 17 700	5	1.2	1984	Macosa	MTM AA

Mafersa
Sociedade Anônima

Av Raimundo Pereira de Magalha es 230, CEP 05092, São Paulo, SP, Brazil

Telephone: +55 11 261 8911
Cable: Mafersa
Telex: +55 11 83862
Telefax: +55 11 832 1607

Chairman: Marcos Ferraz Miranda
Commercial Director: Carlos Roberto Doll
Industrial Director: Seijió Ogusku

Commercial Managers: Tamas Ivan Fodor, Sergio Mendes Chieco, José Manoel C M David

Products: Stainless steel passenger cars for metro and suburban traffic and long-distance services; passenger cars of carbon steel for suburban traffic and long-distance services; light rail vehicles; all-purpose freight cars; underframes for railway cars and steel welded trucks; forging wheels for railway and crane bridges; forged railway axles; ingots and casting steel.

São Paulo Metro east-west line train-set

Constitution: Mafersa, an authentic Brazilian company, is one of the largest industrial railway equipment complexes in Latin America with three factories in Brazil (two in the state of São Paulo and one in the state of Minas Gerais). Annual production capacity is 300 stainless steel railway passenger cars; 1200 freight cars; 120 LRVs; 140 000 forging wheels; 12 000 forged railway axles; 600 steel welded bogies; and 600 underframes for railway cars.

Recent contracts include 132 passenger cars for the São Paulo subway system (1988); 28 push-pull stainless steel passenger cars for Northern Virginia Transit Commission, USA (contract signed 1990); and 40 carbody shells for the Mitsui Corporation of Japan (contract signed 1990).

Mafersa electric multiple-units

Type	Cars per unit	Line voltage	Motor cars per unit	Motored axles per motor car	Rated output (hp) per motor	Max speed km/h	Weight tonnes per car (M-motor T-trailer)	Total seating capacity per train-set	Length per train-set mm	Rate of acceleration m/s²	Year first built	Builders Mechanical parts	Builders Electrical equipment
São Paulo Metro	6	750 V dc	6	4	170	100	34	2000	21 120	1.12	1972	Budd Mafersa Wabco Fresinbra	Welco Villares
Rio de Janeiro Metro	6	750 V dc	6	4	190	100	40.5	2000	21 500	1.12	1977	Budd Mafersa Wabco Fresinbra	Welco Villares
Suburban (RFFSA) T A2	4	3 kV dc	2	4	388	90	M 58	1300	22 100	0.8	1981	Mafersa Tokyu Car	Hitachi Toshiba
São Paulo Metro L/O	6	750 V dc	6	4	190	100	36	2000	21 235	1.12	1982	Mafersa Fresinbra Villares	Welco Villares

Powered passenger vehicles / **MANUFACTURERS** 121

MAN GHH
MAN Gutehoffnungshuette AG

Head office: PO Box 11 02 40, Bahnhofstrasse 66, 4200 Oberhausen 11, Federal Republic of Germany

Telephone: +49 208 692.1
Telex: 856691 oghhd
Telefax: +49 208 692 2887

Main works: MAN GHH Rolling Stock Division, PO Box 44 01 00, Frankenstrasse 150, 8500 Nuremberg 44

Telephone: +49 208 18 2632
Telex: 622 291 mnd
Telefax: +49 208 18 2375

Vice President, Railway Rolling Stock Division: Heinz Hennig
Senior Sales Manager: Wolfgang Knörk
Senior Design Manager: Gerhold Sames

Products: Diesel and electric railcars and multiple-unit diesel stock; metro railway stock; light rail vehicles, especially low-floor designs; suspended monorails.

Car bodies are fabricated in steel, light metal or stainless steel (Nirosta). In 1988 manufacture of twin-car metro units for Munich was completed. Manufacture of carbody shells for the short-distance system under construction in Medellin, Colombia, was resumed.

In 1989 prototype diesel train-sets for the Greek State Railway (OSE) were under construction: a single-car version for standard-gauge and for short distances up to 150 km; a twin-car version for metre-gauge and poor permanent way with severe gradients; and a triple-car version, also for metre-gauge, but with comfort of European inter-city stock standard.

The German Federal Railway ordered further triple-car train-sets of DB Class 420 for suburban traffic in the region of Munich. It also authorised MAN GHH to develop, together with partners in a consortium, a new diesel train-set of Class 610 employing the Fiat automatic tilt-body apparatus. A series of 10 train-sets is envisaged.

Constitution: MAN GHH in Oberhausen ranks among the leading engineering and contracting companies worldwide and has been active for more than 200 years. Its activities in the railway rolling stock sector are based on its Nuremberg plant. Since 1841 more than 160 000 rail vehicles have been shipped from this plant.

Class 420 emus of German Federal Railway

Munich metro two-car train-set

Maquinista, La
La Maquinista Terrestre y Maritima SA

General offices, technical bureaus and works: Calle Fernando Junoy 2–64, PO Box 94, 08030 Barcelona, Spain

Telephone: +34 93 345 5700
Cable: Maquinista, Barcelona
Telex: 54539 maqui e
Telefax: +34 93 345 6958

President: D Miguel Säenz de Viguera y Aizpurua
Commercial Manager: Pere Solé Raventós
Export Director: Javier Masoliver y de Marti

Type S446 emu for FGV Valencia

MANUFACTURERS / Powered passenger vehicles

Products: Electric and diesel train-sets and railcars; train-sets for underground networks; bogies; traction motors; generators; converters and miscellaneous electrical equipment.

In 1988 the company was working to contracts with RENFE for 50 ST-446 emus for suburban services; and five bi-level train-sets. For Ferrocarril Metropolitano de Barcelona the company was manufacturing seven Type S-4000 five-car train-sets.

Constitution: Since 1855 La Maquinista has specialised in production of railway equipment. Largest shareholder is the Instituto Nacional de Industria (INI).

Five-car train-set for Barcelona Metro

Series 3000 emu for FC Metropolitano di Barcelona

Diesel railcars or multiple-units by La Maquinista

User	Cars per unit	Motor cars per unit	Motored axles per motor car	Transmission	Rated power (kW) per motor	Max speed km/h	Weight tonnes per car (M-motor T-trailer)	Total seating capacity	Length per car mm (M-motor T-trailer)	No in service 1987	Year first built	Builders Mechanical parts	Builders Engine & type	Builders Transmission
FEVE (Spain)	3	2	2	Elec	228	100	M 33.8 T 22.1	101	M 16 500 T 16 500	14	1983	MTM	MAN D3256 BTYUE	BBC-MTM
RCFS (Senegal)	4	1	2	Elec	700	100	M 58 T 25	248	M 23 992 T 19 050	4	1986	MTM	SACM MGO V 12 A SHR	AA-MTM
FEVE	2	2	2	Elec	228	100	33.8	70	16 500	30	1985	MTM	MAN D3256 BTYUE	BBC-MTM
FEVE (FEMA type)	2	2	2	Elec	254	80	32.5	84	17 170	18	1987	MTM	MTM Pegaso 96 RUAZ	NA

Electric railcars or multiple-units by La Maquinista

User	Cars per unit	Line voltage	Motor cars per unit	Motored axles per motor car	Rated output (kW) per motor	Max speed km/h	Weight tonnes per car (M-motor T-trailer)	Total seating capacity	Length per car mm (M-motor T-trailer)	No in service 1988	Rate of acceleration m/s^2	Year first built	Builders Mechanical parts	Builders Electrical equipment
UT Generalitat	3	1500 1200	2	4	276	90	M 39 T 28	176	M 20 330 T 19 810	17	1	1983	MTM	AA-MTM
FFCC Grandes Pendientes	2	1500	2	2	180	37/19	24	112	13 330	3	1	1985	MTM-SLM	BBC-MTM
Metro Barcelona	5	1500 1200	4	4	120	80	M 34 T 23	168	16 500	24	1	1986	MTM	MTM-Melco
FGV Valencia	2*	1500	2	4	188	80	46.88†	80	29 800	18	1	1986	CAF, Macosa, MTM	BBC-MTM
FGV Valencia S.446	3	3000	2	4	240	100	M 58.9 T 41.2	M 66 T 72	M 25057 T 24 685	NA	1	1985	MTM, Macosa, CAF	Cenemesa, Conelec, Melco

* Articulated B-2-B
† Total weight of unit

Materfer
Materfer SA

Suipacha 1109, Pisos 2° and 5°, 1008 Buenos Aires, Argentina

Telephone: +54 1 313 0870/1296/0900/0927
Telex: 25175 cat mg ar
Telefax: +54 1 331 5491

Works: Fábrica Materfer SA
Ruta 9, Km 694, (5123) Ferreyra, Córdoba, Argentina
Telephone: +54 51 97 2730/32/34
Telefax: +54 51 97 2489
Telex: 51300 MAT SA

President: Lic Eduardo Jorge Nava

Vice-President: Dr Edgardo Héctor Iriarte
General Manager: Enzo Filipelli
Commercial Manager: Antonio Maltana

Group companies: Centro de Actividades Termomecánicas SA (CAT), Grandes Motores Diésel SA (GMD), Ingesa SA, and AGRITEC Tractores Fiat.

Powered passenger vehicles / **MANUFACTURERS**   123

Products: Electric and diesel railcars; metro cars; light rail cars; pre-metro cars; LRVs.

Recent products include 27 two-car emus for the Buenos Aires metro with full chopper control and regenerative braking. The sets are in service on lines A, C, D, and E of the railway and are compatible with existing rolling stock. All axles are powered. Each car has a driver's cab at one end. The passenger compartment has 15 single and 13 double seats with room for 129 standing passengers (6 per square metre). Each coach has four electro-pneumatic sliding doors on each side which are controlled automatically, although they can be controlled manually in an emergency. The driver's cab has its own mechanical sliding plug-in door, but may also be entered through a sliding door from the car. Standard Scharfenberg automatic couplings facilitate operation of up to three loaded sets in multiple, more when units are empty. The air-suspension bogies have joints with spherical bearings for easy negotiation of sharp curves. Longitudinal mounting of the 750 V dc, 185 kW motors, one per bogie with drives at both ends of the shaft to gearboxes and universal joints, enables simultaneous driving of both bogie axles and enhances adhesion. Electrical equipment is by Siemens.

The company's latest product is the prototype CML light diesel railcar, adaptable to metre-, 1435 mm and 1676 mm gauges. It can be supplied with engine power up to 400 kW and with hydraulic or mechanical transmission, and in powered and trailer variants; the power car can be equipped with a cab at one or both ends, the trailer with or without a single cab. Seating capacity with cab is 56, without cab 60, and there is standing room for 56–60. Overall length is 15 834 mm, maximum width 2700 mm and tare weight 20 tonnes. Optional equipment includes design of seats; baggage racks; for cold-climate service, liquid heating in power cars, electrical in trailers; Bourrelets-type intercommunication in cars of train-sets; one or two toilet areas per car (each toilet area replaces four seats); air-conditioning (available only in power cars); and access doors at both ends of a car. CML railcars in twin-unit sets have been sold to the Argentine Railways for the latter's Mitre suburban line.

As part of another consortium, with electrical equipment by Siemens, Materfer has built 25 four-axle articulated 'Pre-metro' LRVs, designed to allow mu operation of two units, as an extension of a contract for the Buenos Aires light rail Line E2, which runs underground and on the surface in mixed street traffic. Materfer manufactured the bogies under agreement with BN Constructions Ferroviaries et Metalliques (Belgium). Leading particulars of these vehicles are: Glass-fibre reinforced plastic (GFRP) front end; length 15 560 mm; width 2500 mm; height 3225 mm (from upper rail level); resilient wheels; gauge 1435 mm; full load of passengers, 200; total full load weight, 15 000 kg; operating voltage, 750 dc; top speed (with new wheels), 70 km/h; maximum acceleration (with normal load), 1.0 m/s^2 ± 10 per cent; deceleration (with normal load), 1.3 m/s^2 ± 10 per cent; number of motors per vehicle, 2; power rating of motor, 185 kW; contractor-resistance driving and braking control; main braking system, electro-dynamic; secondary braking, electro-hydraulic with shoes on discs; emergency brake, electro-magnetic on rail; bogies, Manila type, BN single-motor design.

Since 1960, Materfer has produced 2660 rail units of various types and models for Argentine Railways and has entered into agreements to reconstruct over 950 passenger cars. Materfer has exported 463 units to Chile, Uruguay, Bolivia and Cuba.

Constitution: Fiat-Materfer began production of railway rolling stock in 1960. In 1983 it became Materfer SA. Materfer is a licensee of Bombardier (Canada) and the MTE-Jeumont/Schneider Group of France.

'Pre-metro' car for Buenos Aires Line F2

Interior of Buenos Aires 'pre-metro' car

Materfer Buenos Aires metro and Pre-metro train-sets

Type	Cars per unit	Line voltage	Motor cars per unit	Motored axles per motor car	Rated output(kW) per motor	Max speed km/h	Weight tonnes per car	Total seating capacity	Length per car mm	No in service 1988	Rate of acceleration m/s^2	Year first built	Electrical equipment
Metro	2	1.5 kV dc	2	4	185	80	32.07 31.69	41	17 770	40	0.8	1980	Siemens AEG
Pre-metro LRV	1–2	750 V dc	1–2	4	185	70	25	24	15 560	5	1 m/s^2 ± 10%	1988	Siemens AEG

MANUFACTURERS / Powered passenger vehicles

Materfer diesel railcars

Manufacturer's type	Cars per unit	Motor cars per unit	Motored axles per motor car	Rated power (kW) per motor	Max speed km/h	Weight tonnes per car (M-motor T-trailer)	Total seating capacity per car	Length per car mm	No in service 1987	Year first built	Engine & type	Transmission
CML Railcar	1–4	1–2	2	166–250	100	M 24.5 T 19.0	112-120	15 834	16	1987	Diesel	Detroit Diesel Allison Transmissions (USA)

Materfer emus for Argentine Railways urban service

Cars per unit	Line voltage	Motor cars per unit	Motored axles per motor car	Rated output (kW) per motor	Max speed km/h	Weight tonnes per car (M-motor T-trailer)	Total passenger capacity (M-motor T-trailer)	Length per car mm	No in service	Rate of acceleration m/s^2	Year first built	Builders Mechanical parts	Builders Electrical equipment
3	25 kV ac single phase 50 Hz	2	4	220	120	M 52 T 50 T 38	M 64 T 68 T 68	25 000	104 52	0.8	1983/ 85	Materfer (Arg) Dccion Gral de Fabricaciones Militares (Arg) Nippon Sharyo (Jap) Sumitomo (Jap) Kinki Sharyo (Jap)	SIAM (Arg) Toshiba (Jap) Hitachi (Jap)

CML light railcar set for Argentine Railways' Mitre line

Matra

Matra Transport
Subsidiary of Matra SA

2 rue Auguste Comte, 92170 Vanves, France

Telephone: +33 1 45 29 29 29
Telex: 205079
Telefax: +33 1 45 29 29 08

Chairman: Bernard Felix
Vice Chairman and President: Alain Nicolaidis
Senior Vice President, Technical: Daniel Ferbeck
Senior Vice President, Export: Norbert Charbit
Senior Vice President, France: Jean-Pierre Weiss

Main works: Vanves, Lille, Le Bourget

Subsidiaries: Matra Transit (USA), Comeli (O & M Lille, France), IMCA (Mexico)

Products: The automated, unmanned VAL rapid transit system, first installed in Lille, France (see Rapid Transit section). Matra has since been awarded contracts to build VAL systems in Toulouse, Strasbourg and Bordeaux, Orly Airport, France, and in Chicago Airport and Jacksonville, USA; also a second line in Lille.

The SACEM control, operations and maintenance assistance system for regional transit lines (RER, suburban) in Paris, France.

MAGGALY, a full automation system for existing urban network (metro), in process of installation in Lyons, France.

Automatic train control and automatic train operation (ATC/ATO), installed in the urban networks of Paris, Mexico, Santiago, Caracas and Budapest.

The SCADA supervisory control and data acquisition system, installed in urban and industrial networks, and equipping the second VAL line in Lille.

The ARAMIS small fully automatic transit system.

The VAL fully automatic AGT system uses either: lightweight two-car sets 6 ft 9 in wide (VAL 206) with capacity for 124 passengers (68 seated with 24 folding seats down and 56 standing with 4 passengers on 11 ft^2), equipped with six doors sets in down-town AGT application; or a lightweight 8 ft 5 in wide single car (VAL 256) with capacity for 112 passengers (12 seated and 100 standing), equipped with four large doors in down-town AGT application. Both run on a metallic or precast concrete guideway (depending on the prevailing weather conditions of the site).

Primary suspension is by rubber tyres, with further pairs of horizontal tyres bearing on H-type guidebars to provide lateral guidance. All axles are powered by 120 kW motors, with current collected at 750 V dc from the guidebars.

VAL is a fixed-block system in which trains are detected by an ultrasonic sensor. As the train proceeds through the section, signals are emitted inductively from the train to a continuous cable laid in the track. The signalling logic detects the train's signal until it is proved to have left the section by the ultrasonic detector. Two further inductive cables are used to control train speed. These have transpositions arranged so as to induce running at normal speed, or to initiate braking. In the event of out-of-course running, a computer at the operations centre will automatically speed up or slow down trains to restore normal timetable running.

Lille VAL 206 units

Interior of Lille VAL 206 unit

Powered passenger vehicles / **MANUFACTURERS**   125

Traffic regulation is achieved by a series of aluminium blades located in the track in such a way that a train in normal operation passes over one blade every two seconds. All trains receive a clock pulse from the control centre at two-second intervals, and by comparing the number of pulses with the number of blades, train speed can be adjusted to maintain the correct schedule.

City VAL 206 has been in service in Lille, France, since 1983; a second line is under construction, selected for the cities of Toulouse, Strasbourg and Bordeaux.

Airport VAL 206 is selected for the connection between RER and Paris Metro network and Orly Airport south and west terminals (ORLY-VAL).

City VAL 256 is in construction at Jacksonville (USA) and Airport VAL 256 is in construction at Chicago O'Hare airport.

MBB
Messerschmitt-Bölkow-Blohm GmbH
Transportation Technology Division

PO Box 1353, 8850 Donauwörth, Federal Republic of Germany

Telephone: +49 906 71-1
Telex: 51843 mbb d
Telefax: +49 906 71 898

General Manager: Dieter v Hummel
Director, Engineering and Programmes: Dr Christian Günther

Products: Rail vehicles in lightweight construction for underground and rapid transit commuter services, diesel and electrically powered train-sets.

Recent orders have included 25 two-car VT 628/VS 928 diesel train-sets and 12 Type ET 420/421 rapid transit emus for the German Federal Railway.

Aluminium-bodied dmu for Yugoslav Railways (JZ)

MBB diesel multiple-units

Class	Cars per unit	Motor cars per unit	Motored axles per motor car	Transmission	Rated power (kW) per motor	Max speed km/h	Weight tonnes per car (M-motor T-trailer)	Total seating capacity	Length per car mm (M-motor T-trailer)	No in service 1988	Year first built	Builders Mechanical parts	Engine & type	Transmission
JZ 713/715	2	1	2	Hydr	367	120	M 31.2 T 25	128	M23 580 T 23 580	27	1983	MBB	Daimler-Benz OM 424A	Voith
DB VT 628/ VS 928	2	1	1	Hydr	410	120	M 39 T 28	143	22 700	12	1988	MBB	Daimler-Benz OM 444A	Voith

MBB electric railcars or multiple-units

Class	Cars per unit	Line voltage	Motor cars per unit	Motored axles per motor car	Rated output (kW) per motor	Max speed km/h	Weight tonnes per unit	Total seating capacity	Length per unit mm	Rate of acceleration m/s^2	Year first built	Builders Mechanical parts	Electrical equipment
DB ET 420/1	3	15 kV	3	4	200	120	130	194	67 400	1.0	1989	MBB	ABB, AEG, Siemens

Mecanoexportimport

10 Mihail Eminescu Street, Bucharest, Romania

Telephone: 40 1198 55
Cable: Mecanex, Bucharest
Telex: 10 269
Telefax: 40 22 107

Products: Electric, diesel-electric, diesel-hydraulic locomotives and railcars; passenger coaches; freight wagons.

Mecanoexportimport is the export sales company for the Romanian railway supply industry. (For the majority of the locomotive designs available see the entries for Electroputere and "23 August" Works).

Type AD19 railbus for Romanian State Railways (CFR)

Metro-Cammell
Metro-Cammell Ltd

PO Box 248, Leigh Road, Washwood Heath, Birmingham B8 2YJ, England

Telephone: +44 21 328 5455
Cable: Metro, Birmingham
Telex: 337601
Telefax: +44 21 327 6430

Chairman: A H Sansome
Managing Director: B S Ronan
Sales Manager: Ken Willis

Products: Rapid transit cars for surface, sub-surface and underground routes; design and supply of cars for pre-metro and full metro and suburban rapid transit systems; electric and diesel multiple-units; main contractors for railway mechanical and electrical engineering systems.

Completion of Metro-Cammell's orders for 576 railcars for the Hong Kong Mass Transit Railway Corporation in 1984 led to provision of 53 eight-car trains for operation on the Tsuen Wan Line and 25 six-car trains for the Kwun Tong and Island Lines. Both chopper-and camshaft-controlled motor cars were involved.

The company subsequently gained a £50 million order from the Hong Kong MTRC for 53 emu cars, plus a further 33 cars following approval by the Hong Kong

126 **MANUFACTURERS** / Powered passenger vehicles

government of plans for the new Hong Kong cross-harbour tunnel.

In 1985 the company won a £30 million contract to supply 75 more railcars to the Kowloon-Canton Railway. The new vehicles included additional design features to meet KCR's need for greater passenger capacity. Traction control equipment was updated by incorporating thyristors in place of tap-changer equipment. (This equipment was based on the proven design for British Rail's Class 317 stock.) Increased passenger crush capacity was provided by reducing the number of seats to give more standing space; thus the seating is 2 + 2 across the cars instead of 3 + 2. In 1988 the company secured a further contract worth £50 million for up to 16 new six-car emus for KCR.

The company has supplied to London Underground two prototype new-generation Tube train-sets. One set has BBC Brown Boveri, the other GEC-TPL electrical equipment. Metro-Cammell is also the main contractor for the supply to London Underground of 16 six-car train-sets and three spare cars to the 1983 Tube

Interior of Type C prototype London Tube train

Prototype Type C London Underground Tube train

Class 156 dmu for British Rail

1983 tube stock for London Transport

Kowloon-Canton Railway emu

Metro-Cammell diesel multiple-units

Class (Railway's own designation)	Cars per unit	Motor cars per unit	Motored axles per motor car	Transmission	Rated power (kW) per motor	Max speed km/h	Weight tonnes per car (M-motor T-trailer)	Total seating capacity per car	Length per car mm (M-motor T-trailer)	Year first built	Engine & type	Transmission
BR 151	3	3	2	Hydro-mechanic	212	120	DM 31.9 NDM 31.3 DML 32.7	80 84 68	DM 19 975 DM 19 600 DM 19 975	1983	Cummins NT855-R4	Twin Disc
BR 156	2	2	2	Automatic Hydrodynamic	285	121	DMSL 35.2 DMSB 35.2	79 84	DM 23 000 DM 23 000	1987	Cummins NT855-R5	Voith T 2118

Powered passenger vehicles / **MANUFACTURERS**

stock design to supplement the existing fleet of such vehicles on London's Jubilee Line.

Following delivery to British Rail of Metro-Cammell's two prototype Class 151 three-car dmus the company received a British Rail order for 114 two-car dmus; built to a 23 m body length, they are designated Class 156.

A major order from British Rail appoints Metro-Cammell as main contractor for the supply of 31 nine-car trains to a new BR Mk 4 car design, plus four spare cars to make the total 283 vehicles, for BR's East Coast Main Line electrification now in progress. All train-sets are for push-pull working, so that each includes a driving trailer (DVT); one DVT is also among the four spares. For the rest, two train-sets will feature three Pullmans, one tourist open, one tourist open with disabled person's toilet, two service vehicles and one tourist end car; the remainder will comprise two Pullmans, three tourist open, one tourist open with disabled person's toilet, one service vehicle and one tourist end car. The remaining spare cars will consist of a tourist open, a service vehicle and a tourist end car.

There is an option for the supply of a further 31 tourist open cars.

Constitution: In the latter part of 1966 Metropolitan-Cammell absorbed the railway rolling stock business of Cravens of Sheffield. In 1969 Vickers Ltd relinquished their 50 per cent shareholding and a new company was formed for railway matters under the style of Metro-Cammell Ltd. In May 1989 the company was acquired by GEC-Alsthom.

Diesel multiple-units

Class	Cars per unit	Motor cars per unit	Motored axles per motor car	Transmission	Rated power (kW) per motor	Max speed km/h	Weight tonnes per car (M-motor T-trailer)	Total seating capacity	Length per car mm (M-motor T-trailer)	Year first built	Builders Mechanical parts	Builders Engine & type	Builders Transmission
BR 151	3	3	2	Hydro-mech	212	120	DM 31.9 NDM 31.3 DML 32.7	80 84 68	DM 19 975 DM 19 600 DM 19 975	1983	Metro-Cammell	Cummins NT 855-R4	Twin Disc

Metro-Cammell electric multiple-units

Type*	Cars per unit	Line voltage	Motor cars per unit	Motored axles per motor car	Continuous rated output (kW) per motor	Max speed km/h	Weight tonnes per car (M-motor T-trailer)	Total seating capacity	Length per car mm (M-motor T-trailer)	No in service	Rate of acceleration m/s^2	Year first built	Builders Mechanical parts	Builders Electrical equipment
MTRC A B C D	6 or 8	1.5 kV dc	6	4	91	90	M 38.4 M 37.4 M 38.8 T 28	48 each car	M 22 850 M 22 000 M 22 000 T 22 000	156 79 235 106	1.3	1978 1980 1978 1982	Metro-Cammell	GEC
KCR 6B 5 6 4	3	25 kV ac	1	4	245	120	T 34 M 51.5 T 32.2 T 32.9	84 88 84 54	T 23 770 M 23 530 T 23 770 T 23 770	45 45 16 29	0.6	1981	Metro-Cammell	GEC
D78 single-ended unit	6	600 V dc	4	4	50	72	DM 27.7 NDM 26.7 TC 18.3	280 136	DM 18 372 NDM 18 119 TC 18 119	390 60	1.0	1978	Metro-Cammell	GEC
double-ended unit	3		2	4										
D83 motor car trailer car	3	600 V dc	2	2	44	72	144 per 3-car unit		M 17 726 T 17 676	90	1.1	1983	Metro-Cammell	GEC and Brush
T&W twin-body articulated unit	1	1.5 kV dc	1	4	180	80	39.4	84	27 800	88	1.0	1978	Metro-Cammell	GEC

* MTRC: Mass Transit Railway Corporation, Hong Kong
  KCR: Kowloon-Canton Railway
  D78: London Transport
  D83: London Transport
  T&W: Tyne and Wear PTE

Mitsubishi Electric
Mitsubishi Electric Corporation

Mitsubishi Denki Bldg, 2-3 Marunouchi, 2-chome, Chiyoda-ku, Tokyo 100, Japan

Telephone: +81 03 218 2111
Cable: Melco, Tokyo
Telex: 24532

President: Moriya Shiki
Vice-President, International Operations Group: Shinichi Yufu
General Manager, Overseas Marketing Division, Heavy Machinery: Kenji Kimura

Products: Power propulsion equipment (traction motors, main drive gears, traction control gears, main transformers, rectifiers, main alternators, VVVF inverters); auxiliary electrical equipment (converters, inverters, motor-alternators); automatic train control equipment; air brake equipment for multiple-unit trains, light rail vehicles, rubber-tyred vehicles on segregated tracks; monorails and electric buses.

Recent sales have included:
30 Series 251 B-B-B chopper-controlled locomotives with rated output of 4650 kW at 3 kV dc; 169 Series 269, 279, 289 B-B locomotives; and four Series 269 B-B chopper-controlled locomotives for Spanish National Railways (RENFE) with rated output of 3100 kW at 3 kV dc, maximum speed 160 km/h, weight 88 tonnes; Traction and auxiliary electrical equipment for 216 suburban double-deck emus, 48 inter-urban double-deck emus, 56 diesel-electric locomotives and 64 electric locomotives for NSW SRA of Australia;
64 emus for Argentine Railways;
1521 chopper-controlled emu cars for Mexico Metro;
175 four-quadrant chopper-controlled emu cars for Barcelona Metro, Spain;
396 four-quadrant chopper-controlled emu cars for Singapore Metro;
126 sets of 65 kVA, 1.5 kV dc/415 V ac brushless motor alternators for Victorian Railways of Australia;
5984 traction motors, 850 main transformers, 300 silicon rectifiers, 404 tap-changers and 150 ATC equipments for Shinkansen train-sets of Japanese National Railways (JNR);
110 electric locomotives for JNR (since 1970);
200 chopper-controllers for Teito Rapid Transit Authority (TRTA), Tokyo, and other Japanese municipal transportation authorities.

Latest products include:
750 V dc third-rail eight-car emu with eight 128 kW traction motors, regenerative braking, and two-phase chopper control, with natural cooling by boiling and condensing heat transfer (freon cooling), chopping frequency 400 Hz, maximum speed 80 km/h, for Osaka Municipal Transportation Bureau (similar electrical equipment has been produced for Mexico City emus);
1.5 kV dc emu featuring 130 kW traction motor, two-phase chopper control provided with freon cooling, and micro-computerised monitoring system, for Kyoto MTB;
1.5 kV dc emu featuring two-phase chopper control with freon cooling, reversible blending control between regenerative brake and rheostatic brake, for Hong Kong MRTC;
1.5 kV dc 10-car emu, including six power cars, 1067 mm gauge, with 150 kW one-hour rating traction motors incorporating WN gear coupling, two-phase AVF chopper control, regenerative braking, freon cooling, chopping frequency 660 Hz, microcomputerised dynamic testing system, maximum speed 100 km/h, for TRTA Hanzomon line;
A 600-volt ac, 60 Hz three-phase, rubber-tyred guideway bus system, in which the vehicles feature four 90 kW dc motors per set of two motor cars and one trailer with thyristor control, regenerative braking and computerised fully automatic operation, for Kobe port lines;

MANUFACTURERS / Powered passenger vehicles

Recent electric railcars or multiple-unit cars with Mitsubishi chopper control and VVVF inverter control

Class	Cars per unit	Line voltage	Motor cars per unit	Motored axles per motor car	Rated output (kW) per motor	Max speed km/h	Weight tonnes per car (M-motor T-trailer)	Total rated seating capacity	Length per car m (M-motor T-trailer)	No in service 1988	Rate of acceleration m/s^2	Year first built	Builders
Hong Kong Metro	8	1500	6	4	109	90	M 40 T 30	–	22	20	0.8	1983	Metro-Cammell
Yokohama	6	750	4	4	120	90	M 36 T 28	880	M 18 T 18	18	0.888	1983	Tokyu Car Corporation
Shin-Keisei (8000)	6	1500	4	–	110	100	M 35	150*	M 18	18	–	1981	–
Namkai (8200)	6	1500	4	4	160	115	M 39 T 27	–	–	24	–	1982	Tokyu Car Corporation
Hanshin (3100)	3	1500	2	–	110	110	M 36.5 T 30.5	–	–	18	–	1983	–
Kumamoto (8200)	1	600	1	2 VVVF	120 ac motor	40	19.0	70	12.8	2	0.833	1982	Nippon Sharyo
Hiroshima LRV (800)	1	600	1	2	60	40	20.5	91	13.5	2	0.833	1984	Alna Koki Co
Sapporo LRV (8500)	1	600	1	2 VVVF/GTO	60 ac motor	40	19.5	100	13.0	2	0.833	1985	Kawasaki Heavy Industry
Sapporo (6000)	6	1500	3	8	75	72	M 25 T 23	736	18.0	66	0.972	1976	Kawasaki Heavy Industry
Mexico City Trolleybus	1	600	1	1	105	65	10.0	101	11.5	2	0.833	1984	MASA (Mexico)
Sendai (1000)	4	1500	2	4	165	85	M 37 T 27	648	20.0	44	0.833	1985	Kawasaki Heavy Industry
Pusan City Subway	6	1500	4	4	165	80	M 35 T 24.5	327	18.0	186	1.0	1984	Hyundai (Korea)
TRTA (01)	6	600	3	4 4QCH/GTO	120	65	M 28.5 T 26	608	16.0	44	0.833	1984	Kawasaki Heavy Industry
Kinki Nippon (1250)	2	1500	1	4 VVVF/GTO	165 ac motor	110	M 39 T 35.5	340	20.0	1	0.700	1984	Kinki Sharyo
Higashi Osaka Ikoma	6	750	3	4 VVVF/GTO	140 ac motor	70	M 35 T 30	810	18.7	1	0.833	1984	
Osaka Metro (20)	6	750	3	4 VVVF/GTO	140 ac motor	70	M 35 T 31	810	18.7	1	0.700	1984	Kawasaki Kinki Sharyo
Shin-Keisei	8	1500	4	4 VVVF/GTO	135	100	M 34 T 28	–	18.0	8	0.77	1985	Nippon Sharyo
Odakyu	6	1500	4	4 VVVF/GTO	175	110	M 36.7	324	20.0	2	0.75	1985	Kawasaki Heavy Industry
Tokyo Municipal	2	1500	1	4 VVVF/GTO	120	70	M 26.5	–	16.5	2	0.833	1985	Tokyu Car Corporation
SRA, NSW, Australia (Suburban)	4	1500	2	4 4QCH/GTO	155	130	M 48.5 T 40	–	–	56	0.75	1985	Goninan
(Interurban)	4	1500	2	4 4QCH/GTO	140	130	M 59.8 T 45.0	–	–	62	0.65	1985	Comeng
Barcelona, Spain (Line 1)	5	1500	4	4 4QCH/GTO	150	90	M 36.1 T 24.5	–	–	85	1.0	1985	Macosa
(Line 3)	5	1200	4	4 4QCH/GTO	150	90	M 35.1 T 23.4	–	–	90	1.0	1985	CAF, MTM
Singapore MRT	6	750	4	4 4 QCH/GTO	145	80	M 37 T 27	62	22.8	396	1.0	1986	Kawasaki
NSW SRA (Tangara)	4	1500	2	4 4 QCH/GTO	170	130	M 50.1 T 42.2	M 120 T 112	–	450	0.8	1987	Goninan
Tianjin Metro	3	750	2	4	130	80	M 37 T 28	M 58 T 50	19	2	0.917	1987	Tokyu Car Corporation, Mitsubishi, Changchun Car Factory
Spain RENFE Class 446	3	3000	2	4	200	100	M 62 T 40	M 53 T 56	25	50	0.75	1988	CAF, Mitsubishi, Cenemesa, Conelec

* Per car

Teito RTA Ginza Line emu with four-quadrant chopper control

VVVF inverter-controlled emu for Kinki Nippon Railway

1.5 kV dc four-car emu, including two power cars, with eight 160 kW traction motors, separate excitation by two-phase field chopper control, regenerative/rheostatic braking, freon cooling, chopping frequency 482 Hz, maximum speed 110 km/h, for Kinki Nippon Railways;

750-volt dc emu with two 140 kW three-phase traction motors driven by VVVF inverter with freon cooling and microprocessor control for Osaka Municipal Transportation Bureau and Higashi-Osaka Ikoma Railway;

1.5 kV dc emu equipped with 165 kW three-phase traction motors driven by a VVVF inverter, with gate turn-off (GTO) thyristors (4500 V, 2000 A), freon cooling and microprocessor control, for Kinki Nippon Railways;

the VVVF ac motor control has been designed for practical use with the voltage capacity GTO thyristor; 600-volt dc LRVs with two 60 kW three-phase traction motors driven by VVVF inverter with freon cooling and microprocessor control, for Sapporo Municipal Transportation Bureau;

750-volt dc emus with two 140 kW three-phase

traction motors driven by VVVF inverters with GTO thyristors (2500 V, 2000 A), freon cooling and microprocessor control for Osaka Municipal Transportation Bureau and for Kinki Nippon Railways (Higashi-Osaka line);
Two series of 1.5 kV dc emus with 165 kW three-phase traction motors driven by VVVF inverter with GTO thyristors (4500 V, 2000 A), freon cooling and microprocessor control, for Kinki Nippon Railways;
1.5 kV dc emus with 120 kW three-phase traction motors driven by VVVF inverter and GTO thyristors (4500 V, 2000 A), freon cooling and microprocessor control for Transportation Bureau of Tokyo Metropolitan Government;
1.5 kV dc emus with 130 kW three-phase traction motors driven by VVVF inverter with GTO thyristors (4500 V, 2000 A), freon cooling and microprocessor control for Shinkeisei Railway;
1.5 kV dc emus with 175 kW three-phase traction motors driven by VVVF inverter with GTO thyristors (4500 V, 2000 A), freon cooling and microprocessor control for Odakyu Railway.

Delivery has proceeded of two important overseas contracts. Chinese Railways have ordered 80 ac electric locomotives with advanced features such as large-capacity thyristor technology and microcomputer-digital control; New South Wales State Railway Authority have ordered 450 emu power units with GTO thyristor four quadrant chopper control for their Tangara train-sets.

Constitution: A member of the Mitsubishi Group.

More Wear
More Wear Industrial Holdings Ltd

PO Box 2199, Harare, Zimbabwe

Telephone: +263 4 67802
Telex: 24110 MORWER ZW
Telefax: +263 4 67807

Works: 53 Plymouth Road, Southerton, Harare, Zimbabwe

Group General Manager: Ronald Murahwa
Group Co-ordinator/Exports Executive: Isaiah C Mlambo
Group Financial Manager: Maurice B Buhera
Group Marketing Manager: Phillip Madziva
Group Purchasing Manager: Domingos M Dos Santos

Principal subsidiary companies
More Wear Industries (Private) Ltd
More Wear Industries Bulawayo (Private) Ltd
More Wear Consolidated Industries (Private) Ltd
Lysaght & Co (Private) Ltd

Products: Passenger cars.

Morrison Knudsen
Morrison Knudsen Corporation
Rail Systems Group

Mailing Address: PO Box 73, Boise, Idaho 83707, USA

Telephone: +1 208 386 5950
Cable: Emkayan
Telex: 368439 emkayan bse e
Telefax: +1 208 386 6171

Chairman & Chief Executive Officer: W M Agee
Executive Vice President: F M Adams
Rail Systems Group President: J G Fearon
Director of Marketing & Sales: M Monteferrante

Principal subsidiary companies
MK-Ferguson Company
MK-Environmental Services Division
MKE Transportation & Water Resources Division

Products: Transit, commuter and passenger car remanufacturing; electrical rotating and component remanufacturing; diesel generator sets.

Morrison Knudsen Corporation, or MK, maintains three major facilities to remanufacture transit, commuter, passenger cars and generator sets: a shop in Boise, Idaho; Hornell, New York; and Rocky Mt, North Carolina.

Transit services include: carbody fabrication, repair and modification, electrical component and electrical rotating equipment rebuilding, bogie rebuilding and interior refurbishing. Generator set services include: design, building, installation and service of power supply systems. An authorised distributor of EMD diesel engine power products servicing 17 East Coast states and the Caribbean.

Remanufactured Type R-42 transit car for New York City Transit Authority

Mytischy
Mytischy Railway Car Works

Mytischy, USSR

Products: Passenger coaches; subway cars.

Constitution: Member of Energomachexport.

Newag
Newag GmbH & Co KG

Blumenstrasse 56, PO Box 101201, 4100 Duisburg 1, Federal Republic of Germany

Telephone: +49 203 334061
Telex: 8 55526 newag d

Products: Remanufacture of passenger cars. Remanufacturing capability covers all gauges and remanufactured products are covered by an extensive warranty.

Constitution: The company is closely associated with Gleismac Italiana SpA (qv).

Niigata
Niigata Engineering Co Ltd

4-1 Kasumigaseki 1-chome, Chiyoda-ku, Tokyo 100, Japan

Telephone: +81 3 504 2111

Cable: Nite, Tokyo
Telex: 222 7111

Chairman: Hideo Washio
Managing Director: Mitsuaki Ishiyama
Chief Sales Director: Toshio Nakamura

Products: Passenger cars; rotary snow plough; transit system work cars.

Constitution: Niigata has been engaged in the manufacture of rolling stock for more than 80 years. It began production in 1896, just one year after its foundation, when the company launched its first passenger, freight and mail cars.

Niigata electric railcars

Class	Cars per unit	Line voltage	Motor cars per unit	Motored axles per motor car	Rated output (kW) per car	Max speed km/h	Weight tonnes per car	Total seating capacity	Length per car m	No in service	Year first built	Builders Mechanical parts	Builders Electrical equipment
1000 1200 1300	3	1.5 kV dc	8	4	400	90	37	66	20	3	1976	Niigata	Toyo Electric
6000	2	1.5 kV dc	8	4	400	90	37	58	20	2	1981	Niigata	Toyo Electric
250	1	1.5 kV dc	4	4	400	90	36	52	20	2	1981	Niigata	Toyo Electric

MANUFACTURERS / Powered passenger vehicles

Niigata diesel railcars

Class	Cars per unit	Motor cars per unit	Motored axles per motor car	Transmission	Rated power (kW) per motor	Max speed km/h	Weight tonnes per car	Total seating capacity	Length per car m	No in service	Year first built	Builders Mechanical parts	Engine & type	Transmission
KIHA 40	1	1	1	Hyd torque converter	164	95	36.4	66	21.3	219	1977	Niigata	Niigata DMF15HSA	Niigata Converter DW 10
KIHA 183 limited express	7 or 10	7 or 10	1	Hyd torque converter	164	100	46.0	40	21.3	14	1979	Niigata	Niigata DMF15HSA	Niigata Converter DW 10
KIHA 184 limited express	7 or 10	7 or 10	1	Hyd torque converter	164	100	44.2	52	21.3	6	1979	Niigata	Niigata DMF15HSA	Niigata Converter DW 9A
KIHA 182 limited express	7 or 10	7 or 10	1	Hyd torque converter	328	100	42.7	68	21.3	32	1979	Niigata	Niigata DMF30HSI	Niigata Converter DW 9A
KIRO 182 limited express		1		Hyd torque converter	328	100	44.7	32	21.3	6	1979	Niigata	Niigata DMF30HSI	Niigata Converter DW 9A
KIHA 37	1	1	1	Hyd torque converter	157	95	30.8	66	20	2	1981	Niigata	Niigata DMF13S	Niigata Converter DF115A

Nippon Sharyo
Nippon Sharyo Ltd

Head office: 1-1 Sanbonmatsu-cho, Astuta-ku, Nagoya, Japan

Telephone: +81 52 882 3315
Cable: Nishiya, Nagoya
Telex: 447 3411
Telefax: +81 52 882 3337

Tokyo office: Telephone: +81 3 668 3330
Telex: 252 2095
Telefax: +81 3 669 0238

Works: Toyokawa

President: Osamu Shinohara
Managing Director and Senior Vice-President: Eiichi Okumura
Chief of Export Division: Kenji Nishimura (Tokyo office)
General Manager, Rolling Stock Division: Kazuhiko Iwadare

Products: Electrical and diesel railcars.

Odakyu Electric Railway Series 10000 for commuter service

Car interior of Odakyu 10000 series

Driver's cab of Odakyu 10000 series

Linear motor car for Osaka Municipal Transportation Bureau subway

Nagoya Railroad 1000 series electric train-set

Powered passenger vehicles / **MANUFACTURERS** 131

Recent Nippon Sharyo electric railcars or multiple-units

Railway	Cars per unit	Line voltage	Motor cars per unit	Motored axles per motor car	Rated output (kW) per motor	Max speed km/h	Weight tonnes per car (M-motor T-trailer)	Total seating capacity per car	Length per car mm (M-motor T-trailer)	No in service 1988	Rate of acceleration m/s²	Year first built	Builders Mechanical parts	Builders Electrical equipment
Odakyu Electric Railway 10 000 Series	11	1.5 kV dc	9		140	110	Mc 32.9 M 25 T 22.5	432	Mc 16350 M 12500 T 12500	22	0.57 (2)	1987	Nippon Sharyo Kawasaki	
Nagoya Railroad 1000 Series	4	1.5 kV dc	2	4	150	110	Tc 37.0 M 40	212	Tc 20380 M 19730	36	0.56 (2)	1988	Nippon Sharyo,	Toshiba
Osaka Municipal Transportation Bureau LIM	2	1.5 kV dc	2	2	65*	70	M 16	49	12600	2	0.83 (3)	1987	Nippon Sharyo	Hitachi
JR (Japanese Railway Group) Shinkansen TEC 100	16	25 kV ac	12	4	230	230	56.5	1229	25000		0.44	1984 Tokyu	Nippon Sharyo, Hitachi, Kawasaki, Toyo, Shinko	Hitachi, Toshiba, Mitsubishi, Fuji Electric,
JR Group, 211 Series	10	1.5 kV dc	4	4	120	110	M 34.1 T 23.9	654	M 20000 T 20000			1985	Nippon Shryo, Toshiba, Tokyu, Hitachi, Kinki, Kawasaki	Hitachi, Mitsubishi, Fuji Electric, Toyo

* Linear motor

Recent Nippon Sharyo diesel railcars or multiple-units

Railway	Cars per unit	Motor cars per unit	Motored axles per motor car	Transmission	Rated power (hp) per motor	Max speed km/h	Weight tonnes per car	Total seating capacity per car	Length per car mm	No in service 1989	Year first built	Builders Mechanical parts	Builders Engine & type	Builders Transmission
JR Group 85 Series for suburban service	4	4	2	C-DW14A	2 × 350	120	41.5	244	21300	8	1989	Nippon Sharyo, Fuji, Niigata	Cummins NTA885-R1	Niigata Converter

JR Group Series 85 emu for suburban service

OMECA
OMECA SpA

Works: Reggio Calabria, Italy

Products: Railcars.

Constitution: The OMECA plant is jointly owned by Fiat Ferroviaria Savigliano and Aviofer Breda (EFIM).

OMS
Officina Meccanica della Stanga
Member of Firema Consortium

Corso Stati Uniti 3, 35100 Padua, Italy

Telephone: +39 49 76 04 88
Cable: OMS, Padova
Telex: 430218 omspd i
Telefax: +39 49 76 06 82

Chairman: Dr Dino Marchiorello
Vice-Chairman: Ing Aldo Iaia
Managing Director: Dr-Ing Ugo Soloni

Products: Electric and diesel railcars and multiple-unit train-sets.

Recent contracts have included: 20 motor and 10 trailer cars for ATM Milan Metro Line 1; and 24 low-floor Light Rail Vehicles for ATM Turin in co-operation with FIAT Ferroviaria.

Development projects in hand include: bogies, powered and non-powered, with independently-mounted wheels for low-floor vehicles; and a low-floor LRV for urban transit.

132 MANUFACTURERS / Powered passenger vehicles

PEC
The Projects & Equipment Corporation of India Ltd
A Government of India Enterprise

Hansalaya, 15 Barakhamba Road, New Delhi 110 001, India

Telephone: +91 331 3542, 331 419, 331 3356
Cable: Pecoind
Telex: 31 65199, 31-65256
Telefax: +91 11 331 5279

Chairman: S N Malik
Chief Marketing Manager (Railway Equipment Division): M Chatterji
Executive Director: R Khosla

Products: Electric multiple-units.

Constitution: PEC was formed in 1971 as a corporation under the Indian Ministry of Commerce to handle and boost the export of railway equipment and engineering goods.

The Indian coach building industry comprises the Integral Coach Factory, Madras (an Indian Railway unit), BEML, Bangalore (a unit under the Ministry of Defence) and Jessop & Co Ltd with a combined annual capacity of approximately 1700 units. These companies also regularly supply Indian Railways.

Reggiane
Officine Meccaniche Italiano SpA

PO Box 431, 27 Via Vasco Agosti, 42100 Reggio Emilia, Italy

Telephone: +39 522 5881
Telex: 530665
Telefax: +39 522 588243

Chairman: Dr Giuseppe Ivan Bonora
General Manager: Vincenzo Giuliano

Products: Railcars; rolling stock components.

Reggiane has been engaged in railway locomotives and rolling stock since 1905.

RFS Engineering Ltd

PO Box 192, Hexthorpe Road, Doncaster DN1 1PJ, England

Telephone: +44 302 340700
Telex: 547296
Telefax: +44 302 340693

Managing Director: P Page
Technical Director: D W Theyers
Finance Director: B J Pierce
Director: E Harrison
Commercial Manager: M Rowe

Products: Conversion, overhaul and repair of powered passenger vehicles and equipment.

Constitution: The vehicle division is equipped to handle all types of railway rolling stock and provides a complete service of constructing, converting and overhauling of all types of railway vehicles. Operating alongside the vehicle division, the specialist wheelset division provides an overhaul and assembly service for all types of wheelsets and the components division concentrates on the overhaul and repair of H.V. equipment, other types of rail-vehicle components including hydraulic dampers, brake equipment, electrical machines and many more.

Recent contracts include the Class 142 Pacer gearbox conversion (1989) for BR.

Class 142 Pacer gearbox conversion for BR

Riga
Riga Carriage Building Works-RVR

201 Lenin Street, Riga, Latvia, USSR

Telephone: +7 365 363
Cable: Riga Wagonzavod
Telex: 161124 rail

Technical Director: Dr Robert Reingardt
Manager: Victor Zhivs
Sales Manager: Arkadi Solovyov
Export Manager: Maina Tshertock

Products: Diesel and electric (ac and dc) multiple-units.

Recent products have included a Type ER-2R emu for suburban traffic and a Type ER-31 25 kV ac emu for Yugoslav Railways (JZ).

The Series 412/416 25 kV 50 Hz ac electric train is for suburban services on 1435 mm-gauge railways. The basic consist is two end motor cars and two trailers. Two or three such sets can be multipled. The cars have passenger exits on to both low and high platforms, the motor cars two and the trailer cars three at each side. The saloons are fitted with semi-upholstered seats having head and arm rests, and also with luggage shelves, forced ventilation, air heaters,

Riga-built Series 412/416 suburban emu for Yugoslav Railways (JZ)

Interior of Series 412/416 emu

and stoves. The passenger saloons have a PA system. Each car has a lavatory, and the end cars also have luggage compartments. Laminated paper plastics of various colours and aluminium sections are used for finishing the interiors. The cars have balloon-type transition vestibules. The bogies have axleboxes without pedestal liners and central suspension without cradles. The train is fitted with rheostatic brakes and with Oerlikon and MZT-Skopje brake and pneumatic equipment and automatic stopping device and Scharfenberg automatic couplers.

Series 412/416 emu
Traction motors per set: 8 × 210 kW
Tare weight, motor car: 60.1 tonnes
 trailer car: 48.5 tonnes
Max axleload: 18 tonnes
Max speed: 120 km/h
Average acceleration to 60 km/h: 0.7 m/s^2
Passenger capacity, four-car set
 seated: 294
 total: 598
Length of set: 102 m
Width of car over corrugations: 2.81 m
Heating: air heaters and stoves
Door control: electro-pneumatic from driver's cab

The Type DR-1A six-car diesel train is for suburban passenger service. It consists of two end driving motor and four trailer cars. The design provides for passenger exit on to low or high platforms. The passenger saloons have semi-upholstered seats facing both ways, broad windows and luggage shelves. The walls of the cars are finished with laminate plastics. Air heaters use the heat of the train power plant cooling water. The control system automatically maintains the temperature of the air in the passenger saloons within 15 ± 3°C at an ambient temperature as low as –40°C. In warm weather, fresh air is delivered. The power plant in each end car is an M756B four-stroke turbocharged engine rated at 736 kW, driving through a hydraulic transmission with two torque convertors. These and the air compressor are mounted on a common frame and fastened to the carbody's frame via shock absorbers. Disc brakes are fitted.

Type AP-1A diesel-hydraulic train-set
Gauge: 1520 mm
Engine rating: 2 × 736 kW
Tare weight, motor car: 60 tonnes
 trailer car: 36.5 tonnes
Max speed: 120 km/h
Seating capacity, six-car train: 648
 motor car: 68
 trailer car: 128
Length over couplers, motor car: 26 012 mm
 trailer car: 25 582 mm
Car wheelbase: 18 000 mm
Bogies: without cradle, with two-stage spring suspension and underslung frame

Constitution: Member of Energomachexport.

Type DR-1A diesel-hydraulic suburban train-set by Riga

Interior of Type DR-1A diesel train-set

Riga electric multiple-units

Type	Cars per unit	Line voltage	Motor cars per unit	Motored axles per motor car	Rated output (kW) per motor	Max speed km/h	Weight tonnes per car (M-motor T-trailer)	Total seating capacity per car (M-motor T-trailer)	Length per car mm	No of cars in service 1988	Rate of acceleration m/s^2	Year first built	Builders Mechanical parts	Builders Electrical equipment
ER-2T	12	3 kV	6	4	235	130	M 57.2 $T_2$1 39.8 $T_2$2 41.6	M 98 $T_2$1 98 $T_2$2 74	19600	538	0.72	1987	RVR	REZ
ER9T	10	25 kV 50 hZ	5	4	190	130	M 61 $T_2$1 37 $T_2$2 39	M 107 $T_2$1 98 $T_2$2 74	19600	140	0.72	1988	RVR	REZ, TEZ

RSD
A Division of Dorbyl Ltd

PO Box 229, Boksburg 1460, South Africa

Telephone: +27 11 52 8276
Cable: Dorlonsa, Johannesburg
Telex: 4-29576
Telefax: +27 11 52 5714

Chairman: M J Smithyman
Executive Director: C J O Rehder

Products: The 24-module (96 coaches in total) Class 8M Stainless Steel New Generation train-set is an electrically controlled system which significantly reduces power consumption and improves the riding quality of the coaches. It has regenerative braking, automatic wheelslip prevention and is manufactured using predominantly high strength 301L stainless steel to reduce tare and minimise maintenance.

Stainless steel Class 8M new generation trainset

134 MANUFACTURERS / Powered passenger vehicles

Santa Matilde
Cia Industrial Santa Matilde

Export sales and head office: Av Koeler 260, Petrópolis 25.685, Rio de Janeiro, Brazil

Telephone: +55 242 43 8656
Telex: 021 36694/5/6 cism br

Products: Emus; passenger coaches

The company operates an industrial unit in Três Rios (RJ), with a covered area of 90 000 m² and a total area of 309 650 m². The company is equipped to produce annually 60 four-car electric train units, 300 passenger cars, 10 000 hand brake units, 10 000 brake triangles, 7200 fibreglass hatch covers for cars and a number of fibreglass items for passenger cars and electric train units, such as seats, panels, etc.

Constitution: Companhia Industrial Santa Matilde, founded in 1916 was initially engaged in mining manganese ore. In 1926 it began repairing railway passenger and freight cars. Manufacture of rolling stock and electric train units began in 1946.

Scandia
ABB Scandia A/S

Toldbodgade 39, 8900 Randers, Denmark

Telephone: +45 86 425300
Telex: 65145 scanas dk
Telefax: +45 86 415700

Danish Railways IC3 train-set

President: Henning Balle Kristensen
Vice President: Ragnar Sjöström
Export Manager: Kjeld Hvid

Products: Light weight diesel and electrical multiple units, constructed according to the modular principle, light rail vehicles, service, and systems of interior styling.

The new IC3 intercity train set for the DSB consists of two power cars with diesel-mechanical traction and one intermediate trailer. The train sets can be coupled to a maximum of five sets (15 cars). Each power car will have two 294 kW engines which enable the train to accelerate from 0 to 140 km/h in less than 120 sec. The maximum speed of the train is 180 km/h. The total weight of a three-car set is 92 tonnes. This low weight is obtained by use of Jacob's bogies, aluminium for the car body and sandwich materials for the interior.

The basic idea of the IC3 is a train which guarantees increased passenger revenue and reduced operation and maintenance costs. Accordingly top priority has been given to passenger comfort. High-quality interior design, catering, passenger information services, five-channel stereo, telephone, and telefax. The train is modular built and standard components have been employed wherever possible.

The first train sets were delivered in 1989.

Constitution: ABB Scandia A/S is jointly owned by ASEA Brown Boveri A/S, Den Danske Bank, and Employees' Capital Pension Fund a.o.

Interior of IC3 train-set (*G Freeman Allen*)

Schindler
Schindler Carriage & Wagon Co Ltd

4133 Pratteln, near Basle, Switzerland

Telephone: +41 61 825 91 11
Telex: 968010
Telefax: +41 61 825 9205

Managing Director: P Piffaretti
Technical Director and Director of Works: H Knecht
Sales Manager: R Meury

Products: Electric railcars and multiple-units for all track gauges.

Entrance to low-floor central section of Basle Be 4/8 LRV

Basle LRV converted to Type Be 4/8 with new central low-floor section

Powered passenger vehicles / **MANUFACTURERS**

The company has delivered to Swiss Federal Railways (SBB) two series of Type NPZ (*Neue Pendelzüge*) two-car electric units consisting of a power car and driving trailer (RBDe 4/4 and Bt), intended primarily for the SBB's Regional services but capable also of commuter operation. The welded-steel bodies are similar to those of the standard emu lately produced for nine private railways, including the Bern-Lötschberg-Simplon (BLS) and Bodensee-Toggenburg (BT). The doors, 1.4 m wide, are opened by passenger use of a push-button. They close automatically behind the passenger as he breaks a light beam and passes over a sensor-plate on the footstep. The power equipment features thyristor control and regenerative braking.

In 1988 the SBB ordered a further 20 Type RBDe 4/4 power cars and Type Bt trailers.

Leading particulars of RBDe 4/4 + Bt
Gauge: 1435 mm
Length over couplers: 50 000 mm
Car body width: 2650 mm
Distance between bogie centres: 2 × 21 300 mm
Bogie wheelbase: 2500 mm
Seating capacity (power car): 56
 (trailer): 71 + 1 compartment for disabled
Standees (power car): 28
 (trailer): 40
Tare weight (power car): 69.5 tonnes
 (trailer): 37.5 tonnes
Max speed: 140 km/h
One hour rating at wheel: 1650 kW

For Baselland Transport Company (BLB) the company has converted 18 six-axle articulated LRVs into eight-axle vehicles with a low-floor central section. For this purpose, the car is separated into two halves at the articulation. A new central section of 6.2 m length, an additional trailer bogie and an articulation are needed to form the new eight-axle, double articulated vehicle. A low-floor entry without step, an increased carrying capacity, sufficient space for prams, bicycles etc are some of the advantages gained. In 1988 Basle Transport Authority ordered 28 Be 4/6 articulated vehicles from the company.

Schindler electric railcars or multiple-units

Class	Cars per unit	Line voltage	Motor cars per unit	Motored axles per motor car	Rated output (kW) per motor (one-hour)	Max speed km/h	Weight tonnes per car (M-motor T-trailer)	Total seating capacity	Length per car mm (M-motor T-trailer)	No in service	Rate of acceleration m/s^2	Year first built	Builders† Mechanical parts	Builders† Electrical equipment
RABDe 4/12*	2 or 3	15 000 16⅔ Hz	1	4	425	125	M 69.7 T 35.0	206	M 25 000 T 25 500	32 (31 under construction)	1.2‡	1982	SWP/SWS	ABB
RBDe 4/8	2	15 000 16⅔ Hz	1	4	425	140	M 69.5 T 37.5	127	25 000	4	1.4‡	1984	SWP/SWA	ABB
Tram 2000 (VBZ, Zurich)	2 (articulated)	600	1	4 (mono-motor bogie)	138	65	26.5	50	21 400	113 (23 ordered)	1.2††	1976	SWP	ABB
Tram 2000 (VBZ, Zurich)	1 4-axle	600	1	2 (mono-motor bogie)	138	65	18.5	36	15 400	20(15 ordered)	1.2††	1985	SWP	ABB
Tram Be 4/4 (Basle)	1	600	1	4 (mono-motor bogie)	150	65	19.5	30	13 970	26	1.2††	1986	SWP/SIG	Siemens ABB
BDe 4/4 +Bt (Waldenburg)	2	1500	1	4	223	75	M 24 T 16.5	81	M 18 200 T 18 200	4	1.2**	1985	SWP/SIG	ABB
Be 4/8 (Bern-Solothurn)	1	600	1	4	138	65	M 36	74	M 31 200	9	1.2**	1987	SWP/SIG	ABB

*Customers: BLS, BN, GBS, SEZ, EBT, SMB, VHB, RVT, GFM (all Switzerland)
†SWP = Schindler Carriage & Wagon Co Ltd
 SWA = Schindler Carriage & Wagon Co Ltd, Altenrhein Works
 SIG = Swiss Industrial Company
 ABB = ASEA Brown Boveri
‡ at full load excluding standing passengers
††at full load including standing passengers
**with medium passenger load

Recent contracts include first and second class Mk IV passenger cars for Swiss Federal Railways (1989); Bt driving trailers for Swiss Federal Railways (1989); double-deck passenger cars and driving trailers for Zurich S-Bahn (Swiss Federal Railways) (1989). Main orders received in 1990 include 90 double-deck cars for Zurich S-Bahn; 31 motor coaches, driving trailers and passenger cars for different Swiss private railways; 23 Type Be 4/6 motor coaches and 15 Type Be 2/4 driving trailers for Zurich Transport Authority; 9 Mk IV passenger cars for Swiss private railways.

Interior of the double-deck 2nd class passenger coach

Schindler Waggon Altenrhein
Schindler Waggon Altenrhein AG

9423 Altenrhein, Switzerland

Telephone: +41 71 43 43 43
Telex: 881530 swa ch
Telefax: +41 71 43 44 45

Chairman: Dr Luciano Caroni
President: Hans Kubat
Sales Director: Robert Séquin

Products: Powered passenger cars of lightweight steel and aluminium alloy design for all gauges; bogies for all types of car; streetcars; tram bogies. Special

Swiss Federal Railways' NPZ 'Colibri' shuttle train

MANUFACTURERS / Powered passenger vehicles

constructions for all purposes; designs; understructure; modification; and individual components and sub-assemblies.

As the main contractor within the SWA/SWP/SIG/ABB group, the company has been involved in manufacture of 30 shuttle trains for Swiss Federal Railways (SBB). The company is manufacturing 30 motor coaches.

Constitution: The company was founded in 1925 as Flug- und Fahrzeugwerke AG Altenrhein (FFA). During 1931–35 the first funiculars and suspension cars were built, and the rail carriage department began in 1945–47. At the start of 1987 FFA was taken over by the Schindler company and in the following June its railway vehicle building and general engineering were separated from its aircraft manufacture, the former activities taking the new title of Schindler Waggon Altenrhein AG. The company supplies rolling stock for the SBB (Swiss Federal Railways) as well as for a large number of private and municipal railway undertakings.

Schöma
Christoph Schöttler Maschinenfabrik GmbH

PO Box 1509, 2840 Diepholz 1, Federal Republic of Germany

Telephone: +49 5441 2047
Cable: Schöma, Diepholz
Telex: 41217
Telefax: +49 5441 7702

Manager: Ing Fritz Schöttler
Sales Manager: Ing L Niermeyer

Products: Diesel railcars and trailers.

Schöma diesel railcars

Class	Cars per unit	Motor cars per unit	Motored axles per motor car	Transmission	Rated power (kW) per motor	Max speed km/h	Weight tonnes per car (M-motor T-trailer)	Total seating capacity	Length per car mm (M-motor T-trailer)	No in service 1988	Year first built	Engine & type	Transmission
CS 300/ CS 299*	1-3	1	2	6-speed	157	80	M 12 T 5 (unloaded)	7	M 8240 T 7500	M 46 T 22	1983	Deutz F8L 413F	Clark HR 28620
Klv 53/ Kla 03*	1-3	1	2	6-speed	82	70	M 8 T 4	7	M 6000 T 5900	M 160 T 420	1967	Deutz F6L 912	Clark 28620

* Matching trailer

SEMAF
Société Générale Egyptienne de Matériel des Chemins de Fer

Ein Helwan, Cairo, Egypt

Telephone: +202 782358; 782177; 782716; 782306; 630097; 782625; 782625
Cable: SEMAF, Ein Helwan
Telex: 23342 semaf un
Telefax: +202 788413

Chairman: Eng T El-Maghraby
Technical Manager: Eng A Rahik
Commercial/Financial Manager: A Farid
Works Manager, Coach & Metro: Dr Eng L Melek
Works Manager, Wagon & Bogie: Eng El-Sherbini

Products: Power cars, passenger cars; first, second and third class air-conditioned or normally ventilated cars with two package units or seven roof units; railcar/trailers, trams and metro cars.

Recent output has included sleeping coaches for Egyptian National Railways, 1991; power and trailer cars for Sudan Railways, 1990; emu cars for Cairo Regional Metro, 1989; Metro cars for Heliopolis, 1989.

Interior of Cairo emu car

Electric railcars by SEMAF

Class	Cars per unit	Line voltage	Motor cars per unit	Motored axles per motor car	Rated output (kW) per motor	Max speed km/h	Weight tonnes per car	Total seating capacity	Length per car mm (M-motor MC-motor composite class)	Rate of acceleration m/s^2	Year first built	Builders Mechanical parts	Builders Electrical equipment
5753-5800B	3	1500	2	4	260	100	33.6	48	19600	0.9	1988	SEMAF	Alsthom
2	3	600	3	4	52	67	21.6	144	16320 M 15800 MC	0.8	1989	SEMAF	Toshiba

Emu car for Cairo Regional Metro

Powered passenger vehicles / **MANUFACTURERS** 137

S-G-P
SGP Verkehrstechnik Gesellschaft mbH

Head office: PO Box 103, Brehmstrasse 16, A-1110 Vienna, Austria

Telephone: +43 222 7469
Telex: 131891, 132574
Telefax: +43 222 745148

Simmering works: Leberstrasse 34, 1110 Vienna, Austria
Graz works: Eggenbergerstrasse 31, 8021 Graz, Austria

General Manager: Dr Herbert Ziegler
Sales Director: Dipl Ing Heinz Butz
Technical Director: Dipl Ing Roland Himmelbauer

Products: Electric railcars, diesel railcars, rack railcars; tramways, underground railway stock and suburban trains.

Type GTW6 articulated six-axle LRV for Salzburg Local Railways (SVB); up to four units can be operated in mu formation (*John C Baker*)

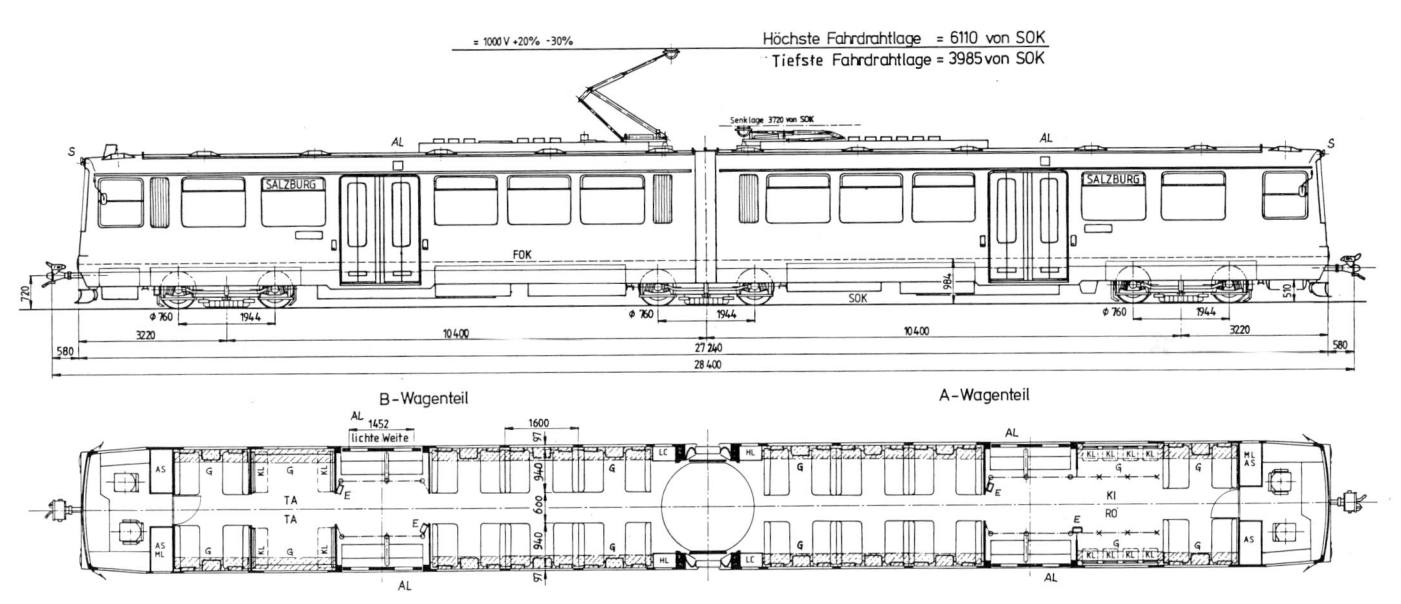

Layout of GTW6 LRV. Note space for prams with associated tip-up seats (KI and KL); also baggage space (TA)

Siemens
Siemens AG

Transportation Systems Group
Werner-von-Siemens-Strasse 50, Postfach 32 40, D-8520 Erlangen, Federal Republic of Germany

Telephone: +49 9131 725176
Cable: Siemens, Erlangen
Telex: 62921 508 si d
Telefax: +49 9131 727748

Transportation Systems Group President: W O Martinsen
Main Line Rolling Stock Division: R Stubenrauch
Mass Transit Rolling Stock Division: G Scholtis

Products: Electric and diesel-electric vehicles and associated electrical equipment for main-line, inter-urban, urban rapid transit, underground, narrow-gauge, industrial and mine railways, and also for trolleybus systems (see Siemens entry in Fixed Electrification Equipment section for power supply and control systems detail).

Contracts recently completed or in hand include Class 420 electric multiple-units for the German Federal Railway; Class 610 diesel-electric multiple-units with automatic body-tilting for German Federal Railway; Medellin Metro and Shanghai Metro emus; a new generation of Type B80-AC three-phase LRVs for Cologne and Bochum-Gelsenkirchen; LRVs for Province of Alberta, Canada (three-phase ac), San Diego (USA), Sacramento (USA), Monterrey (Mexico), Stuttgart, Mexico City, Mulheim-Ruhr, St Louis (USA), and Tunis; low-floor LRVs for Munich, Würzburg, Bochum-Gelsenkirchen, Kassel and VÖV-project; Class 480 emus for Berlin (West) S-Bahn; three-phase ac metro cars for Munich, Vienna, Lisbon and Madrid; rack-motor cars for Bavaria's Zugspitzbahn, Rochers de Naye (Switzerland) and Wendelsteinbahn; and trolleybuses for Lucerne (Switzerland); motor cars for Uetliberg (Zürich); and trolleybuses for the Swiss cities of Luzern, La Chaux-de-Fonds and Geneva.

Recent technological developments include GTO-

Class 401 Intercity Express (ICE) power car for DB

138 MANUFACTURERS / Powered passenger vehicles

based three-phase ac drives for heavy and light rail vehicles and Type SIBAS 16 static logic control units which use microprocessor techniques for computing all functions of propulsion systems including dynamic and regenerative braking and for fault detection and diagnostics. More than 3000 units of the latter design are in revenue service or will shortly be commissioned. The company also participates in automated suspended DPM system called H-Bahn.

A significant example is the low-maintenance, fully suspended integral transverse drive with an enclosed, three-phase induction motor, two-stage spur gearing and disc brakes. It guarantees passengers optimum ride quality and vehicle performance at low noise level, high efficiency and extended maintenance free operation.

Furthermore, Siemens completed the development of low floor LRT vehicles with floor heights of approximately 350 mm above the rails. The vehicles are equipped with three-phase ac drive technology and microcomputer controls. Orders are in hand for Bochum (20), Kassel (15, but dc-chopper), Munich (3), and VÖV (3). Fifteen low-floor LRTs with dc chopper are on order for Kassel.

Services
Engineering, development, manufacture and supply of equipment or complete vehicles, with worldwide turnkey project capability comprising planning, design and construction for power supply, rolling stock, control and safety systems, civil works, project management, installation and commissioning, training of maintenance and operating staff; after-sales service and financing.

Emu for the Medellin Metro, Columbia

Recent diesel multiple-units and rail cars with electrical equipment by Siemens

Class	Wheel arrangement	Transmission	Rated power (kW)	Max speed km/h	Total weight tonnes	Year first built	Builders Mechanical parts	Engine & type
Germany Class 610	1A-A1 + 1A-A1	Elec	2 × 485	160	104	1990	MAN MBB Duewag	MTU
Austria Class 2068	B-B	Hyd	785	100	74	1989	Jenbacher Werke	SGP JW

Recent electric railcars or multiple-units with electrical equipment by Siemens

Class	Cars per unit	Line voltage	Motor cars per unit	Motored axles per motor car	Rated output kW	Max speed km/h	Weight tonnes per power car	Year first built
South Africa 7M	4	3000 V dc	2	4	290	100	43	1984
Germany ICE	5	15 kV 16⅔ Hz	2	4	700	350	78	1985
Germany 420	3	15 kV, 16⅔ Hz	3	4	200	120	72	1989

SLM
Schweizerische Lokomotiv-und Maschinenfabrik
Swiss Locomotive and Machine Works

8401 Winterthur, Switzerland

Telephone: +41 52 85 41 41
Cable: Locomotive, Winterthur
Telex: 896 131 slm ch
Telefax: +41 52 2387 65

President, Board of Management: H Otmar
General Manager: K Vogel
Assistant Vice President, Technical Department: R Kummrow
Commercial Department, Deputy Vice President: Dr M Knüsli
Works Department, Assistant Vice President: O Heiniger
Sales Department, Assistant Vice President: W Grütter

Products: General contractor for complete railcars; supplier of the mechanical parts (complete bogies and superstructure) for railcars and pilot cars for adhesion, rack and combined rack-and-adhesion operation; gearing specialist for rail motive power or special vehicles; service enterprise for engineering (including wheel-rail

Type BDhe 4/8 twin-unit for Wengernalp Railway, Switzerland

Powered passenger vehicles / **MANUFACTURERS**

Leading particulars

	WAB BDhe 4/8	Bayerische Zugspitzbahn	Wendelsteinbahn
Total output at motor shafts			
continuous rating	804 kW	864 kW	1012 kW
Total tractive effort at wheel rims			
(rack)			
continuous rating	168 kN	160 kN	160 kN
starting	216 kN	300 kN	300 kN
Max speeds			
uphill	28 km/h	25%: 18 km/h	23.7%: 25 km/h
downhill on 12%	21.5 km/h		
on 18%	17 km/h		
on 25%	14 km/h	25%: 15 km/h	23.7%: 15 km/h
adhesion		70 km/h	30 km/h
Weight per double railcar in			
running order			
tare	43.1 tonnes	54 tonnes	54 tonnes
gross	58.1 tonnes	69.3 tonnes	69.3 tonnes
Total passenger accommodation	200	204	204
seated	64	114	130
folding seats	16		
standing (6 per m^2)	120	90	74
Transmission ratio			
rack drive	1:15.65	1:11.889	1:10.803
adhesion drive		1: 6.019	1:12.906
Line data			
overhead line voltage	1500 V dc	1650 V=/cc/dc	1500 V
maximum gradients			
rack section	19%	25%	23.7%
adhesion section	25%	4%	3.7%
gauge	800 mm	1000 mm	1000 mm
rack system	Riggenbach	Riggenbach	Strub
Electrical equipment	ABB	Siemens	Siemens

dynamics, measuring and control system technology), gear cutting, machining and sheetmetal working.

The company's recent output has included four double railcars and a pilot car of Type BDhe 4/8 for the 19 km mountain rack system of Switzerland's Wengernalpbahn, part of the BOB group.

Automatic couplings, multiple control capability and electrical braking control enable sets from two to five railcars to be operated by one driver.

The interior design features a large entrance space in the middle of each car with ski racks and fold-away seats, modern-styled passenger compartments including attractive seating with upholstery for the summer season, practical holding grips and luggage racks. Slide-down windows and glass partitions inside offer good viewing.

The four nearly identical bogies, optimised with regard to high security against derailment, each have a nose-suspended drive block acting on the downhill axle with transverse-mounted traction motor and two independent, efficient, electropneumatically controlled stopping brakes.

For the Zugspitz mountain railway in Bavaria SLM supplied two Type Beh 4/8 double railcars capable of mixed adhesion and rack service which make it unnecessary to change trains from the 7.5 km adhesion line to the 11.2 km rack section. Each half of the close-coupled railcars has two single-motor bogies. Features included adjustable pulse control of the brakes and modern dc chopper technique for the drive.

Two almost identical sets were ordered in the summer of 1988 by the Wendelstein Railway for its mixed rack and adhesion line 7.66 km long.

SLM electric railcars or multiple-units

Class	Type and operator	Gauge mm	Max gradient	Cars per unit	Line voltage	Motor cars per unit	Motored axles per motor car	Rated output (kW) per motor	Max speed km/h (r=rack a=adhesion)	Total weight tonnes	Total seating capacity	Length per unit mm	No in service 1988	Year first built	Builders Mechanical parts	Builders Electrical equipment
BDhe 4/8	Rack car (WAB)	800	25%	2	1.5 kV dc	1	4	201	r=28	42.4	64	31 160	4	1988	SLM	ABB
Beh 4/8	Rack and adhesion car (FRG)	1000	25%	2	1650 V dc	2	2	216	r=21 a=70	54	114	29 300	2	1987	SLM	Siemens
ABeh 4/4	Rack and adhesion car (BOB)	1000	15%	1	1.5 kV dc	1	4	314	r=21.5 a=70	44.7	36	17 584	3	1986	SLM	ABB
Beh 4/8	Rack and adhesion car (Spain)	1000	15%	2	1.5 kV dc	2	2	181	r=19 a=35	50	112	28 080	3	1986	SLM (MTM)	ABB
Bhe 4/4 + Bt	Rack (ARB/VRB)	1435	25%	2	1.5 kV dc	1	4	206	r=30	42	139	33 352	2	1982	SLM	ABB
Beh 4/8	Rack and adhesion (FRG)	1000	23.7%	2	1.5 kV dc	1	4	253	r=25 a=30	54	130	29 300	–	1990	SLM	Siemens

Socimi
Società Costruzioni Industriali Milano SpA

Head office: Via Varesina 115, 20156 Milan, Italy

Telephone: +39 2 30091
Telex: 323564
Telefax: +39 2 3085161

Main works
Via Enrico Fermi n 25, 20082 Binasco (Milan)
Telephone: +39 2 9055605/6/7/8

Via Donatori del Sangue n 100, 20010 Arluno (Milan)
Telephone: +39 2 9017666, 9017803

Taiwan Railways emus supplied by Socimi

140 MANUFACTURERS / Powered passenger vehicles

Viale Porto Torres, Reg Zentu Figghi, 07100 Sassari
Telephone: +39 79 260206

Via I Maggio, 21045 Gazzada Schianno (Varese)
Telephone: +39 332 461313

Chairman: Dr Eng Alessandro Marzocco
Managing Director: Dr Eng Pierino Sacchi
Assistant to Chairman: Dr Eng Corrado Landolina

Products: Diesel-electric and diesel-hydraulic train-sets and railcars; diesel-mechanical railcars and rail-buses; double-deck electric and diesel railcars; automatic tilt-body systems, railcars, subway cars and trailer cars; monorail cars; tramcars and LRVs.

The Socimi Tilting System (STS) is independent and self-contained on each vehicle. It comprises these by subsystems:
Electronic processor: receives transductor signals and controls the hydraulic system.
Electronic-hydraulic system: performs carbody tilt and adjustment according to the commands sent by the electronic processor.
Socimi FAST-RIDE 14KR-AB-TB bogie: on which the hydraulic tilt cylinders and transductors are installed.

A lateral pneumatic suspension between bogie and twist beam consists of four double-acting pneumatic cylinders piloted by two pressure regulating valves. This suspension supplies a progressive flexibility characteristic and has a self-centering effect to guarantee maximum comfort of ride in rectilinear and high speed curves. The twist beam ends are fitted to the hydraulic tilt cylinders.

On each bogie there are the transductors (gyroscope, accelerometer, resolvers and speedometer) to generate the electronic-processor signals. These transductors are housed in sealed containers fixed with suitable counter-vibration materials.

STS detects curve entries and exits, determines the optimal car-body tilt degree value depending on speed, curve, radius and superelevation, and realises the requested trim variation as the railcar reaches the constant radius of the curve.

Experimental railcar with Socimi STS body-tilt system in 220 Km/h trials, hauled by FS E444 locomotive, on Rome–Florence Direttissima

SOFER
SOFER – Officine Ferroviarie, SpA

Via Miliscola 33, Pozzuoli (Naples), Italy

Telephone: +39 81 5262522 Cable: SOFER, Pozzuoli
Telex: 710048
Telefax: +39 81 5262288

Chairman: Dr Ing Corrado Fici
General Manager: Dr Ing Giovanni Alfano

Products: Electric and diesel multiple-unit train-sets; motor and carrying bogies for articulated electric train-sets.

Recent contracts include Breda-built metro cars for the Washington and Los Angeles metros.

Motor bogie for Washington metro car, USA

Sorefame
Sociedades Reunidas de Fabricações Metálicas, SA

Board of Directors: Av Antonio Augusto de Aguiar, 163, 3° Dto, 1000 Lisbon, Portugal

Telephone: +351 1 524059
Telex: 64882 sorfam p

Head office: Rua Vice-Almirante Azevedo Coutinho, PO Box 5, 2701 Amadora Codex, Portugal

Telephone: +351 1 976051
Cable: Sorefame, Amadora
Telex: 12 608 sorfam p
Telefax: +351 1 977210

Works: Amadora

Chairman: Rui Vilares Cordeiro
Rolling Stock Division Manager: M Andrade Gomes

Products: Diesel and electric multiple-unit train-sets, diesel and electric railcars.

Sorefame supplies carbody shells according to its own or the client's design. The self-supporting shells are in stainless steel. All sheets and profiles, visible or not, used in the structure of the shell are in stainless steel except the end underframes which are built in low alloy, high tensile steels. Stainless steel profiles are obtained in draw-bench machines from strip coils.

Three-car emu for São Paulo suburban service, Brazil

Powered passenger vehicles / **MANUFACTURERS**   141

Recent Sorefame diesel railcars or multiple-units

Class	Cars per unit	Motor cars per unit	Motored axles per motor car	Trans-mission	Rated power (kW) per motor	Max speed km/h	Weight tonnes per car (M-motor)	Total seating capacity	Length per car mm	No in service 1989	Year first built	Builders Mechanical parts	Engine & type	Transmission
600	2	2	2	Hydro	386	120	M 55 M 54	194	25 880	26	1986	Sorefame	Jeumont Rail Saurer SDHR 1	EMG Voith Type T420

The company's recent products have included, for the Portuguese Railways (CP), six diesel-hydraulic two-car units, with propulsion system supplied by EMG and MTE, an extension of an order for identical units built in 1978.

Constitution: The company was established in 1943, and has supplied rolling stock for Portugal, Africa, North America and Brazil as well as hydro-mechanical equipment for dams, electro-mechanical equipment for hydro-electric and thermal power stations (classical and nuclear).

Two-car dmu for Portuguese Railways (CP)

Recent Sorefame electric railcars or multiple-units

Class	Cars per unit	Line voltage	Motor cars per unit	Motored axles per motor car	Rated output (kW) per motor	Max speed km/h	Weight tonnes per car (M-motor T-trailer)	Total seating capacity	Length per car mm	No in service 1988	Rate of acceleration m/s²	Year first built	Builders Mechanical parts	Electrical equipment
2151	3	25 kV	1	4	260	120	M 61 T 33	60 96	22 620 22 820	18	0.64	1976	Sorefame	50 Hz Group
2201	3	25 kV	1	4	260	120	M 61 T 33	60 96	22 620 22 820	15	0.64	1983	Sorefame	50 Hz Group
M 215 C₁ 215 C₂ 215 Cl 215	4	1.5 kV dc	1	4	96	90	M 49 T₂1 28 T₂1 28 T₂3 27	64 63 63 68	19 000 19 000 19 000 19 000	8	0.35–0.5	1977	Sorefame	GEC
M 199 C₂1 119 C₂2 119	3	1.5 kV dc	1	4	96	90	M 49 T 28	64 63	19 000 19 000	6	0.35 0.5	1977	Sorefame	GEC
9500	3	3 kV dc	1	4	259	90	M 46 T 32 T 27	180	M 19 550 T 19 200	50	1.1	1979	Consortium (Sorefame, Mafersa, ACEC, Villares)	ACEC/Villares
ML 79 (Lisbon)	2	750 V dc	2	4	217	72	31	80	16 000	28	1.1	1983	Sorefame Alsthom (MTE for bogies)	Siemens/Alsthom

Soulé
Soulé SA

PO Box 1, 65200 Bagnères-de-Bigorre, France

Telephone: +33 62 95 07 31
Cable: Soulé, Bagnères de Bigorre
Telex: 530 179
Telefax: +33 62 95 55 65

Chairman: Arnaud de Boysson
Vice-President: Guy Thomas

Products: Diesel railcars and trailers.

The company has developed a range of diesel-electric railcars, in a design adaptable to 1000, 1067 or 1435 mm gauge, which is specially conceived to suit operation in equatorial and tropical territory.

A diesel-hydraulic train set (2 x 175 kW) for Corsican Railways, delivered in 1989, comprises of a railcar with two motors and bogies, and a pilot trailer with bogies. With a seating capacity of 105, the railcar has a total length of 36.6 m and a width of 2.5 m; there is one

Two-axle railcar for Brittany region of French Railways

MANUFACTURERS / Powered passenger vehicles

driving cab in each vehicle and one toilet.

A two-axle railcar, the A2E will be delivered to the Region Bretagne of SNCF during 1990. With a rated power of 210 kW and hydraulic transmission (one carrying axle, one driving axle), the A2E has a seating capacity of 50; a length of 15.6 m and width of 3 m; two driving cabs and one toilet.

2 x 175 kW diesel hydraulic trainset for Corsican Railways

Soulé single diesel railcars

Motored axles per car	Transmission	Rated power (kW) per motor	Max speed km/h	Weight tonnes	Total seating capacity	Length per car m	No in service	Year first built	Builders Mechanical parts	Engine & type	Transmission
2	Elec	400	90	43	30-50	22.5	30	1965	Alsthom	SACM	Alsthom
2	Elec	400	90	39	30-50	17.5	5	1967	Alsthom	Poyaud	Alsthom
4	Elec	620	110	52	30-50	22.5	8	1969	CEM	Poyaud	CEM
2	Elec	700	110	52	30-50	22.5	2	1973	Alsthom	SACM	Alsthom
2	Elec	700	110	54	30-50	23.5	7	1976	Alsthom	SACM	Alsthom
4	Elec	700	110	56	30-50	23.5	2	1977	CEM	SACM	CEM
2	Elec	700	110	52	30-50	18	2	1982	Alsthom	SACM	Alsthom
2	Hydro	370	110	35	60	18.7	1	1984	Voith	SACM	Voith
4	Hydro	175x2	100	35	50	18.3	3	1989	Voith	SACM	Voith
1	Hydro	210	100	25	50	15.6	3	1990	ZF	Cummins	Voith

Strojexport Company Ltd
(Czechoslovak foreign trade corporation for the export and import of machines and machinery equipment)

Václavské n 56, 11326 Prague 1, Czechoslovakia

Telephone: +422 2131
Cable: Strojexport, Prague
Telex: 121671, 122604
Telefax: +422 2323084, 2323092

General Director: Ing Josef Regner
Deputy General Director: Ing Stanislav Vrabec

Commercial Director: Ing František Forgács

Products: Strojexport handles all transactions for the export of passenger and freight rolling stock built by Czechoslovak wagon works. In 1988-90 Strojexport was delivering to the USSR diesel multiple-units for main-line traffic.

Strojexport diesel railcars or multiple-units

Class	Type	Cars per unit	Motor cars per unit	Motored axles per motor car	Transmission	Rated power (kW) per motor	Max speed km/h	Weight tonnes per car (M-motor T-trailer)	Total seating capacity per car (M-motor T-trailer)	Length per car mm (M-motor T-trailer)	No in service 1989	Year first built	Builders Mechanical parts	Engine & type	Transmission
AČ-2	AČ-2	3	1	2	hydr	746	120	M 59 T 37	M 70 T 123	M 25 000 T 25 000	46	1988	ČSSR	USSR	USSR

Strømens
EB Strömens Verksted

PO Box 83, 2011 Strømen, Norway

Telephone: +47 6 809600
Cable: Verkstedet, Strømen
Telex: 71 551
Telefax: +47 6 809601

Managing Director: P Hauan
Technical Director: J Jacobsen

Products: Electric train-sets; diesel railcars; tramcars and subway cars.

Constitution: The company was established in 1873 for the manufacture of railway rolling stock and is now the only car builder in Norway. Since 1988, EB Strömens Verksted is a subsidiary of EB, a member of the ABB Group.

An order from Norwegian State Railways for nine intercity electric train-sets, will be delivered in 1990.

Norwegian State Railways electric multiple-units manufactured by Strømens Verksted and ABB

Class	Cars per unit	Line voltage	Motor cars per unit	Motored axles per motor car	Rated output (kW) per motor	Max speed km/h	Weight tonnes per car (M-motor T-trailer)	Total seating capacity	Length per car mm (M-motor T-trailer)	No in service	Rate of acceleration m/s^2	Year first built	Builders Mechanical parts	Electrical equipment
NSB 69ABC	2	15 kV 16⅔ Hz	1	4	297	130	M 53 T 30	191	24 000	49	1.0	1970	Strømens Vaerksted	NEBB
69D	3	15 kV 16⅔ Hz	1	4	297	130	M 60 T 34	300	24 000	25	1.0	1983	Strømens Vaerksted	NEBB
IC70	4	15 kV 16⅔	1	4	400	160	M 69 T 52	270	M 24750 T 26400	–	0.7	1990	Strømens	Vaerksted

Powered passenger vehicles / **MANUFACTURERS** 143

Talbot
Waggonfabrik Talbot

Postfach 1410, Jülicherstrasse 213-237, 5100 Aachen, Federal Republic of Germany

Telephone: +49 241 18210
Cable: Talbot, Aachen
Telex: 08 32 845
Telefax: +49 241 1821214

Products: Electric and diesel railcars.

TAU
Transport Automatisé Urbain

ACEC SA Transport Department, PO Box 4, 6000 Charleroi, Belgium

Telephone: +32 71 44 21 11
Telex: 51227 acec b
Telefax: +32 71 43 78 34

Products: Automated steel-wheel/steel-rail light metro, TAU (Transport Automatisé Urbain).

TAU has been developed by a Belgian consortium headed by ACEC and including BN, Constructions Ferroviaires et Métalliques, CRTH and RDW. The aim was to achieve cost reductions over heavy metro whilst retaining steel-wheel/steel-rail technology. Savings of up to 50 per cent on civil engineering costs are claimed. A test track has been built at Jumet near Charleroi, and in 1985 it was announced that Liège was to be the first city to be served by the system. A 16 km route is planned for opening in three phases (see Liège entry, Rapid Transit section), with the first 6 km scheduled to open 1990-95.

In the TAU system, lightweight small-profile cars run on conventional metre-gauge track. Cars are bogie-mounted, each bogie comprising a pair of independently-driven wheels and a pair of smaller wheels providing guidance only. All four wheels are independently mounted and the bogie frame is hinged, allowing sufficient flexibility for the cars to run through 10 m radius curves. Traction power is collected at 950 V three-phase by under-running pick-ups from totally-enclosed conductor rails. Braking is regenerative. Full automatic control is provided by three computers at the operations centre which transmit commands to processors on-board via an inductive link to a cable laid between the running rails. Transpositions in the cable every 35 m allow the cars to calculate their location, which is continuously reported to the control centre. Should any one of the three computers fail, operation would continue with two computers. In normal operation TAU is unmanned, but cars have a control panel for emergency manual operation.

An important feature of TAU is the modular system adopted for rapid cut-and-cover construction. The narrow-gauge and small profile of the cars makes for a considerable reduction in the scale of civil engineering works, and prefabricated modular sections have been developed for tunnels and stations. Tunnel sections typically 2.25 m long by 5.2 m wide and 3.70 m high internally, are lowered into a trench dug in the road and can be covered in immediately.

Tokyu
Tokyu Car Corporation

Head office: 1 Kamariya-cho, Kanazawa-ku, Yokohama, Japan
Sales and Export Department: 2-7-2, Yaesu, Chuo-ku, Tokyo

Telephone: +81 45 272 8091/3
Cable: Tokyucarcorp Tok
Telex: 0222 2020
Telefax: +81 45 272 3656

Chairman: Ihaho Takahashi
President: Kiyoshi Yasuzumi
Executive Vice-Presidents: Hikaru Honda
    Takatoshi Tozawa

Products: Electric and diesel railcars.

Recent production has included the Series 1000 commuter emu for the Odakyu Railway. The carbody is of high-strength stainless steel with a very lightweight structure and VVVF inverter control propulsion is employed. The latter and resultant increase of adhesion enables limitation of motored cars to one per two vehicles. A static inverter capable of 140 kVA is applied for auxiliary power supply. The brake system is electrically controlled with regenerative brake predominant and air brake supplementary.

The Series 211 for Shikoku Japan Railway and Series 213 for West Japan Railway, both commuter emus with stainless steel bodies, employ a newly-designed field chopper control using rehabilitated existing controller and propulsion equipment to reduce the initial manufacturing costs. Regenerative braking system is another feature.

The Series 1500 commuter emu for Keihin Express Railways has a carbody of painted aluminium alloy with all cars motored. A static inverter is provided for auxiliary power supply. Other equipment includes ATS and regenerative braking.

For the New Haven line of the Metro North Commuter Railroad, New York, the company has provided the Series M4 for commuter and express use; 54 cars were delivered in 1987. The carbody is of lightweight high-tensile stainless steel structure with a GRFP front-end. The cars are dual-voltage ac/dc. A static inverter serves auxiliary electric supply. A fabricated bogie with air suspension is used for the first time in New York's M Series emu cars.

For the forthcoming small-bore Line 12 of the Tokyo metro the company has produced two prototype Type 12-000 (Mc + Tc) units. In these stainless steel body cars the floor height is 850 mm above the rail, about 300 mm lower than existing cars, to secure maximum possible passenger compartment height. New technologies applied to achieve light weight and improved maintenance and energy saving include ac propulsion, VVVF inverter control with regenerative brake, a large-capacity static inverter as auxiliary power supply and bolsterless air-spring bogies.

In the VVVF (variable voltage variable frequency) inverter control system, power running/regenerative brake and forward/reverse changeovers are achieved

2000 Series commuter car for Nankai Electric Railroad

4000 Series commuter car for Seibu Railway

by the inverter. Use of 4500 V 2000 A GTO thyristors greatly simplifies the power circuitry and reduces size and weight. Microcomputer control secures improved accuracy and reliability. Use of a freon cooler to cool the thyristors eliminates a blower and makes for improved maintenance and low noise level.

The three-phase squirrel cage induction motor is particularly suitable for small diameter wheels and low-floor cars. The drive gear is parallel cardan-type comprising a fully-enclosed, one stage reduction gear unit and a gear-type coupling.

The TB-12 brake system is electrically controlled with regenerative brake predominant and air brake supplementary. On receipt of a digital command, the processor directly analog-controls the electro-pneumatic change valves of Mc cars and Tc cars; brake cylinder pressure is thus continuously controlled. Optical fibre is used for the brake command line from the on-board centralised control equipment to the transfer unit.

Under the supervision of ATC, ATO automatically controls power, train braking and coasting operations such as constant speed running and stopping at stations.

In addition, this equipment provides automatic public address and connection to the line's operation control system through data transfer, allowing automated train operation.

The on-board centralised control equipment is a hierarchical computer system which controls and monitors all major items. The system consists of microprocessor terminals and a central unit processor

MANUFACTURERS / Powered passenger vehicles

interlinked by an optical-fibre network. The equipment controls propulsion and braking equipment, also the auxiliary equipment for compartment lighting, cooling, heating and blowing etc. Light transfer terminals are used for major equipment control and optical-fibre contactless relays for auxiliary equipment. In the event of an abnormality, the equipment notifies the operator on a VDU and also provides guidance on counter-measures. The emergency report unit digitalises control signals as well as voice signals and transfers them through PCM light transmission. Commands to the liquid crystal destination and operation display device are transferred through the light transfer passages of the on-board centralised control system.

Leading particulars:
Gauge: 1435 mm
Electrical system: 1500 V dc overhead
Formation: Tc + Mc (4M4T at 8 car formation)
Weight: Mc 27 tons, Tc 24 tons
Passenger capacity: 88 (36 seating)
Carbody dimensions: 16 500 × 2500 × 3045 mm (Mc)
 16 250 × 2499 × 3045 mm (Tc)
Height of floor level: 850 mm
Traction motor: 3 phase induction motor 120 kW × 4
Control system: VVVF inverter control system with regenerative brake
Brake system: Electrically controlled regenerative brake and supplementary airbrake

Max operating speed: 70 km/h
Max acceleration: 3 km/h/s
Max deceleration: 3.5 km/h/s
 (emergency): 4.5 km/h/s

Constitution: This company was formed in 1948, its predecessors being the Yokohama Plant of the Tokyo Electric Express Railway Co. It built the first stainless steel train-set in Japan following technical agreement with the Budd Company of USA in 1960. Merging Teikoku Car & Manufacturing Co of Osaka into its organisation in 1968, the company is now the largest Japanese supplier of rolling stock to home and overseas railways.

Tokyu electric railcars or multiple-units

Class (Railway's own designation)	Cars per unit	Line voltage	Motor cars per unit	Motored axles per motor car	Rated output (kW) per motor	Max speed km/h	Weight tonnes per car (M-motor T-trailer)	Total seating capacity per car (M-motor T-trailer)	Length per car mm	No in service	Rate of acceleration m/s^2	Year first built	Builders Mechanical parts	Builders Electrical equipment
Japanese National Railways New Shinkansen 100	16	25 kV 60 Hz	12	4	230	258	927 per unit	1st 132 Economy 1153 per unit	25 000	80	0.28	1985	Tokyu, Kawasaki, Nippon, Kinki, Hitachi	
Japanese National Railways 207	10	1500 V dc	6	4	150	100	301.4 per unit	528 (1424) per unit	20 000	10	0.92	1986	Tokyu Kawasaki	
Tokyu Corporation 9000	8	1500 V dc	4	4	170	120	M 33.8 Tc 26.4 T 24.3	M 56 Tc 49 T 56	20 000	8	0.86	1986	Tokyu	Hitachi
Nankai Electric Railroad 1000	2	1500 V dc	1	4	145	110	M 39.0 T 33.0	64	20 825	8	0.70	1986	Tokyu	Mitsubishi
Izu Express 2100	6	1500 V dc	3	4	120	100	M 37.0 Tc 35.5 T 30.0	M 50 Tc 52 T 48	20 000	14	0.56	1986	Tokyu	Toshiba
Tokyo Metropolitan Transportation Authority 12000	2	1500 V dc	1	4	120	70	M 26.5 T 24.5	36	16 500	—	0.83	1986	Tokyu	Mitsubishi
Odakyu Electric Railroad 1000	4	1500 V dc	2	4	175	110	M 38.1 Tc 29.8	M 58 Tc 50	20 000	32	0.92	1987	Tokyu, Kawasaki, Nippon	Mitsubishi
Keihin Kyuko Electric Railroad 1500	6 or 4	1500 V dc	6 or 4	4	100	130	—	Mc 48 M 52	18 000	16	0.97	1987	Tokyu, Kawasaki	Tokyo Mitsubishi
JR Nishi Nihon Railroad 213	3	1500 V dc	1	4	120	110	Mc 38 T 24.5 Tc 27	Mc 60 T 64 Tc 58	20 000	24	0.31	1987	Tokyu, Kawasaki, Nippon, Kinki, Hitachi	
JR Shikoku Railroad 211	2	1500 V dc	1	4	110	100	Mc 42 Tc 27	62	20 000	38	0.52	1987	Tokyu, Kawasaki, Kinki, Hitachi	
Metro North Railroad Co, USA M4	3	13.2 kV ac 60 Hz 700 V dc	3	4	220/115	160	186 per unit	356 per unit	25 900	54	0.83	1987	Tokyu	General Electric

Toshiba
Toshiba Corporation
Railway Projects Department

Toshiba Building, 1-1, Shibaura 1-chome, Minato-ku, Tokyo 105, Japan

Telephone: +81 3 457 4924
Cable: Toshiba Tokyo
Telex: 22587 toshiba
Telefax: +81 3 457 8385

JNR's first VVVF inverter-driven emu, Series 207, with 1330 kVA VVVF inverters

Powered passenger vehicles / **MANUFACTURERS** 145

Products: Electric and diesel railcars; trolleybuses; monorails; electric traction equipment; auxiliary power supply units; coach air-conditioner; industrial rolling stock.

Series 8000 4M + 4T emu with VVVF inverter drive systems of Kita-Osaka Kyuko Railway Corp, Osaka

Toshiba electric railcars or multiple-units for export

Train formation	Line voltage	Gauge (mm)	Rated output (kW) per motor	Max speed km/h	Control system	Builders Mechanical parts	Builders Electrical equipment
M-T	1500 dc	1676	132 × 4	96	Multiple-unit up to 8 coaches, rheostatic, unit switch control	Nippon Sharyo	Toshiba
T-M-T	3000 dc	1000	170 × 4	90	Multiple-unit up to 12 coaches, rheostatic, cam control	Kawasaki Heavy Ind	Toshiba
M	800 dc	1676	190 × 2	135	Multiple-unit up to 12 coaches, rheostatic, cam control with rheostatic brake	Kawasaki Heavy Ind	Toshiba
M	800 dc	1676	190 × 2	135	Multiple-unit up to 12 coaches, rheostatic, cam control with rheostatic brake	Nippon Sharyo	Toshiba
all M	600 dc	1000	52 × 4	70	Multiple-unit, rheostatic, cam control with emergency rheostatic brake	Kinki Sharyo	Toshiba
MM TM	600 dc	1000	52 × 4	60	Multiple-unit, rheostatic, cam control with emergency rheostatic brake	Kinki Sharyo	Toshiba
M	600 dc	1000	(52 × 4)	–	Multiple-unit, rheostatic, cam control with emergency rheostatic brake	Kinki Sharyo	Toshiba
MT	1500 dc	1435	150 × 4	115	Multiple-unit, rheostatic, cam control with emergency rheostatic brake	Comeng	Toshiba
MTTM	3000 dc	1676	280 × 4	130	Multiple-unit, rheostatic, cam control with rheostatic brake	Kawasaki Heavy Ind	Toshiba
MTTM	3000 dc	1676	280 × 4	160	Multiple-unit, rheostatic, cam control with rheostatic brake	Kawasaki Heavy Ind	Toshiba
M	600 dc	1435	142 × 2	100	Multiple-unit up to 8 coaches, rheostatic, cam control	Kinki Sharyo	Toshiba
M	600 dc	1435	142 × 2	100	Multiple-unit up to 8 coaches, rheostatic, cam control	Kinki Sharyo	Toshiba
MTM	600 dc	1000	52 × 4	60	Multiple-unit, rheostatic, cam control with emergency rheostatic brake	Kinki Sharyo	Toshiba
MM	600 dc	1000	52 × 4	65	Multiple-unit, rheostatic, cam control with emergency rheostatic brake	Kinki Sharyo	Toshiba
MMM	600 dc	1435	52 × 4	60	Multiple-unit, rheostatic, cam control with emergency rheostatic brake	SEMAF	Toshiba
MM	600 dc	1435	52 × 4	50	Multiple-unit, rheostatic, cam control with emergency rheostatic brake	SEMAF	Toshiba
MTTM	3000 dc	1600	315 × 4	90	Multiple-unit, rheostatic, cam control with rheostatic brake	Hitachi	Toshiba
MTTM	3000 dc	1600	315 × 4	90	Multiple-unit, rheostatic, cam control with rheostatic brake	Mafersa	Toshiba
TMT	3000 dc	1600	315 × 4	90	Multiple-unit, rheostatic, cam control	Mafersa	Toshiba
MMT	25 kV ac 60 Hz/ 1500 V dc (dual)	1435	120 × 4	110	Multiple-unit, rheostatic, cam control	Hitachi, Daewoo	Toshiba
MTM	25 kV ac 50 Hz	1676	220 × 4	120	Multiple-unit up to 9 coaches, thyristor phase control with rheostatic brake	Nippon Sharyo	Toshiba

Toshiba diesel railcars or multiple-units

Cars per unit	Motor cars per unit	Gauge & wheel arrangement	Transmission	Rated power hp/rpm	Max speed km/h	Weight tonnes per car (M-motor T-trailer)	Total seating capacity (M-motor T-trailer)	Length per car mm (M-motor T-trailer)	Notes	Builders Mechanical parts	Builders Engine & type	Builders Transmission
2	2	1067 mm A1A-2+2-B	Electric	1010/ 1300	112	M1 66 M2 48	M1 36 M2 60	M1 22 860 M2 22 860	Limited express RM1-RM2	Kawasaki Heavy Industries Ltd	Caterpillar D398TA	Toshiba
5	4	1435 mm 2-B+B-B+ 2-2+B-B+B-2	Electric	970/ 1900	110	PMc 64.4 M 50 T 45.3	PMc 28 M 56 Tr 24	PMc 21 000 M 21 000 Tr 21 000	Super express PMc-M-Tr-M-PMc	Daewoo Heavy Industries Ltd	Cummins KTA-2300-L × 2 sets	Toshiba

Transrapid International
Gesellschaft für Magnetbahn-Systeme

PO Box 80 18 44, Anzinger Strasse 1/V, 8000 Munich 80, Federal Republic of Germany

Telephone: +49 89 40 67 67
Telex: 5 29 032 attn. TRI
Telefax: +49 89 49 39 59

Directors: Rolf Kretzschmar
Wolfgang Harttrumpf
Hans-Georg Raschbichler

Products: Transrapid magnetically-levitated (Maglev) transportation system.

The consortium is a joint venture formed in 1982 by Krauss-Maffei AG, Messerschmitt-Bölkow-Blohm GmbH (MBB) and Thyssen Industrie AG Henschel to further development of the Transrapid system and foster its introduction world-wide. Its purpose is to bring to the attention of the general public, potential operators, legislators, government executives, the media and other opinion leaders, the claimed benefits of the Transrapid system so as to foster the system's acceptance, to make application and other studies, and to optimise the existing system.

Under financial sponsorship of the Federal German Ministry for Research and Technology, a full-scale, entirely elevated test track has been erected in

MANUFACTURERS / Powered passenger vehicles

Interior of Transrapid 06

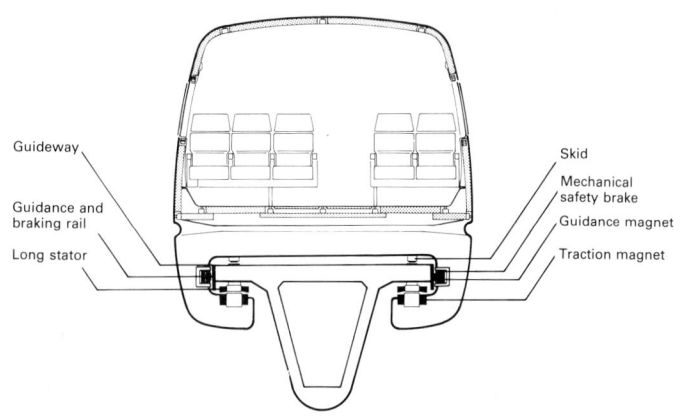

Main components of Transrapid guidance and traction system

Emsland, north Germany, to permit vehicle tests at up to 450 km/h. The test track is now managed by MVP, a company in which the German Federal Railway, Lufthansa and IABG are equal partners.

The guideway of the Emsland test facility is designed so that the vehicle can achieve the following top speeds: a constant 400 km/h over 5.5 km; a maximum of 450 km/h. One loop has a radius of only 1000 metres, and is banked at 12 degrees, and to prove the system's adaptability to changing contours without loss of speed, the test track features gradients of up to 3.5 per cent. The 2.8 metre-wide guideway, mounted on A-shaped concrete supports, is formed partly of prestressed concrete and partly of steel beams. The equipment for levitation, guidance and propulsion is fitted to the concrete guideway after the beams are positioned, but where the beams are steel the guidance components are partly incorporated in the supporting structure. Support height is generally 5 metres, the most common span 25 metres. The flexible switches consist of a continuous steel beam which is elastically bent over its entire length; they allow speeds of up to 200 km/h over the diverging track. The southern loop of the test track was to be completed and commissioned in February 1988.

The full-size Transrapid 07 prototype vehicle, with which the R&D programme on the test track is now conducted, is manufactured from an aluminium framework, to which are cemented riveted panels that sandwich a phenolplast-soaked aramid- paper-honeycomb core between aluminium sheeting. Weighing 80 tonnes, the vehicle is in two 25.5 m- long, 3.8 m-wide sections, which together can seat up to 200.

Transrapid 07 is designed for a cruising speed of 400 km/h and is able to attain a top speed of 500 km/h. It is streamlined for minimum air resistance and minimum susceptibility to cross winds. At top speed, its aerodynamic drag is only about 52 kN. Via pneumatic springs, the two body sections rest on the eight bogies with the levitation and guidance system. The self-levelling suspension guarantees a constant static load distribution in all operating modes.

The train is fitted with electromagnets, while the track features ferromagnetic armature rails. The levitation magnets pull the train up to the track and the guidance magnets keep it centred. The electromagnetic levitation and guidance system incorporates individually hinged magnets and a decentralised control concept (magnetic wheel) in modular construction.

In each train section, the electromagnetic levitation and guidance forces are generated by 15 levitation and 12 guidance magnets, each of which is 3 metres long. While the levitation magnets are of the longitudinal flux type, the guidance magnets carry a magnetic flux perpendicular to the track. Via a primary spring, each magnet is connected with the levitation bogie. Each section features four bogies which keep the magnets in the proper parallel position and convey the forces generated by the levitation and guidance systems. The bogies also incorporate anti-friction sledge elements and the contactless, eddy current brake system which operates independently of the drive system. The anti-friction sledge elements are individually suspended and keep the train properly on the track when it comes to a stop.

The eddy current brake system consists of four independent brake circuits. If, in the event of a defect, the electrical brake of the linear drive system fails to operate properly, the eddy current brake system can take over the braking function without problems.

The levitation and guidance system is supplied with power from an on-board set of batteries fed by linear generators. To ensure that the system will always function properly even in the event of a defect, the power supply is decentralised: each magnet has two independent supplies through dc power modulators. On average 110 kW are required to suspend and guide each section along the track.

To stabilise the air gap of 8 mm between the train and the track and the magnetic forces generated by the individual levitation and guidance magnets, the dc power modulator of each magnet is controlled by an independent control system. This system utilises certain parameters, such as the width of the air gap between the train and the track, the rate of acceleration and the magnetic flux through the individual magnets.

A synchronised electric long stator linear motor has been specially developed to drive Transrapid 07. The ferromagnetic stator with the three-phase track windings is fastened to the guideway, while the exciter is constituted by the levitation magnets incorporated in the train.

The long stators located on both sides of the guideway beams are fed with three-phase current of varying frequency directly from the track. In this way they generate a travelling field which propels the train in the desired direction. To achieve best efficiency and to use the voltage optimally, the entire track circuit is subdivided into several power feed and switch sections, which are then activated according to the momentary position of the train. The energy drawn from the national 110 kV grid is fed into the long stator sections via transformers and frequency converters, the frequency being used to control the speed of the train.

Serving as the standard brake system, the linear motor decelerates the train electrically without any frictional contact between the train and the track. By varying the voltage, frequency and polarisation, a converter controls the driving force of the linear motor to provide the requisite propulsion or braking force.

A contactless eddy current brake is also incorporated as an additional brake system available in emergencies.

The Transrapid vehicles are the first full-sized trains built with contact-free energy transmission. The nucleus of this system is constituted by the linear generator. As the train moves along the track, the long stator built into the track generates magnetic field variations in the pole pieces of the levitation magnets. These field variations, in turn, induce a speed-related voltage in a generator winding within the pole pieces, as a result of which electrical power is fed into the on-board grid.

The linear generator is designed to provide the power required for the levitation and guidance system at speeds above approximately 75 km/h. As soon as the train reaches a speed of more than 125 km/h, the additional power provided by the generator reloads the buffer batteries.

Top speed so far achieved by Transrapid TR06 is 435 km/h, in December 1989.

A public revenue-earning Transrapid system within the Federal Republic is now considered essential to realise overseas sales of the technology. Routes under evaluation in 1988 were Hannover-Hamburg, Augsburg-Munich II Airport, and Hannover-Braunschweig-Wolfsburg. Foreign interest concerns particularly the following corridors: Seoul-Pusan, South Korea; Shanghai-Nanjing, China; Tampa-Orlando and Las Vegas-South Carolina, USA.

Transrapid 07 prototype at Hamburg IVA exhibition, 1988

Union Carriage
Union Carriage & Wagon Co (Pty) Ltd

PO Box 335, Marievale Road, Vorsterkroon, Nigel 1490, Transvaal, South Africa

Telephone: +27 11 739 2411
Cable: Unicarwag
Telex: 750524
Telefax: +27 11 739 5156

Chairman: G S E Coucourakis
Managing Director: R Bingham
Commercial Manager: A A M Lyle
Technical Manager: J J R Watten

Products: Electric multiple-unit cars and locomotive-hauled passenger coaches.

Since 1959 the company has manufactured over 11 000 locomotives and passenger coaches for South African Transport Services (SATS), for export and for industrial organisations.

During 1986 the company began manufacture of 33 coaches making up 11 three-car electrical multiple-units for the Taiwan Railway Administration, to operate on the 25 kV single-phase ac 60 Hz system at maximum speeds of 120 km/h. Electric traction equipment for these vehicles is by GEC Traction Projects, UK.

Constitution: General Mining and Union Corp, Anglo-American Corp and Malbak Ltd are the principal shareholders of this company. Less than 25 per cent in value of all the contracts received is spent overseas, mostly on electric traction equipment which is not obtainable from South African sources. Formed in 1957 to supply South African Railways with passenger coaches, Union Carriage has expanded its business to supply the export market and to become a major manufacturer of main-line and shunting electric locomotives.

Emu car for Taiwan

Union Carriage & Wagon electric multiple-units

Class	Cars per unit	Line voltage	Motor cars per unit	Motored axles per motor car	Motor output (kW) one-hour	Max speed km/h	Weight tonnes per car (M-motor T-trailer)	Total seating capacity	Length per car mm	No in service	Rate of acceleration m/s²	Year first built	Builders Mechanical parts	Builders Electrical equipment
SATS suburban	8	3 kV	2	4	225	96	M 63 T 31	472 (2150 including standing capacity)	18 500	Up to 550 8-car sets	0.455	1961	Union Carriage & Wagon (Pty) Ltd	GEC
Taiwan Railway Administration	3	25 kV 60 Hz	2	4	140	120	M 47.5 T 38	144	19 300	–	–	1986	Union Carriage & Wagon (Pty) Ltd	GEC

UTDC
UTDC Inc

PO Box 70, Station 'A', Kingston, Ontario, Canada K7M 6P9

Telephone: +1 613 384 3100
Telex: 066 3357
Fax: +1 613 389 6382
Cable: URBANTRANS KGTN

President & CEO: David Pattenden
Senior Vice President, Marketing: Herb Goldman
Vice President, Sales & Proposals: Richard Giles

Main works: Thunder Bay and Kingston, Ontario

Products: The UTDC group of companies designs, delivers and commissions complete urban transportation systems. Products and services include: single and articulated light rail vehicles and systems; automated transit systems; people-mover systems; heavy rail transit vehicles and systems; intercity and suburban rail coaches (bi-level and single-level); frame-braced and steerable axle bogies; freight and material handling systems; and complete transportation system implementation and operation services (operations and maintenance planning, manual production, training, testing, commissioning and on-going operations and maintenance management).

Three of UTDC's advanced light rapid transit (ALRT) systems are in revenue service. Toronto's Scarborough line opened in March 1985 and Vancouver's 22.5 km system, one of the longest automated transit systems in the world, opened in January 1986. These automated systems use linear induction motors, steerable-axle bogies, system health monitoring, compact and lightweight aluminium carbodies and moving-block automatic train operation. The Detroit People Mover, a 4.7 km single-track elevated loop serving the downtown core, commenced operation in 1987.

Other recent orders include 60 bi-level (double-decked) commuter cars for GO (Government of Ontario) Transit's regional commuter service; and 16 automated vehicles for the Vancouver SkyTrain. UTDC also operates and maintains a new 108 km commuter line servicing the surrounding counties of Miami, Florida.

Articulated light rail vehicle
(Santa Clara County Transit District (California) specifications)

Description: A double-ended, articulated, six-axle light rail vehicle capable of operating singly or in trains of up to four units.

Construction
Frame: low-alloy, high-tensile (LAHT) steel
Exterior walls: LAHT steel
Interior finish: trim panels
Insulation: fibreglass and Aquaplas
Floor: corrugated steel with steel sheeted plywood overlay

Performance
Max speed: 104 km/h
Max grade: 1.33 m/s²
Service acceleration (initial): 1.34 m/s²
Service deceleration: 1.57 m/s²
Emergency deceleration: 2.68 m/s² (max)
Minimum horizontal curve radius: 25 m
Minimum vertical curve radius: 505 m
Seating capacity: 75
Total capacity (design load): AW2 (4/m²) 166
 (crush load): AW4 (8/m²) 257
Empty weight: 44 898 kg

Articulation unit: Carbodies are attached to the bogie bolster through two double-ring bearings. Body torsion transfer link forms part of the roof structure. The centre frame hinges on the bolster and is connected to the carbodies by weathertight bellows. Interior passageway incorporates two fixed side panels in combination with four curved panels which close all gaps between carbodies and articulation section. Vehicle is designed to handle a wide range of horizontal and vertical curves.

Extensive research into the limitations of standard rail freight bogies led UTDC to develop a frame-braced bogie for freight cars. Simple bracing and cushioning modifications to a standard three-piece bogie improve performance considerably while lowering operating and also maintenance costs, by significantly reducing both wheel and track wear. Tested and used successfully by several North American railroads, the frame-braced bogie's increased stability allows bulk and intermodal cars to operate at higher train speeds, even with very heavy loads.

Articulated LRV for Santa Clara County, California, USA

Constitution: UTDC is a leading supplier of ground transportation systems, equipment and services. The Canadian company has developed and applied innovative technologies in a variety of transit, industrial, airport and railroad applications.

In addition to advanced research and development, the UTDC offers complete life-cycle support. Offering traditional turnkey services – planning, designing, building, and maintaining its systems – the company also assembles original financing packages for clients that sometimes includes equity participation by the company.

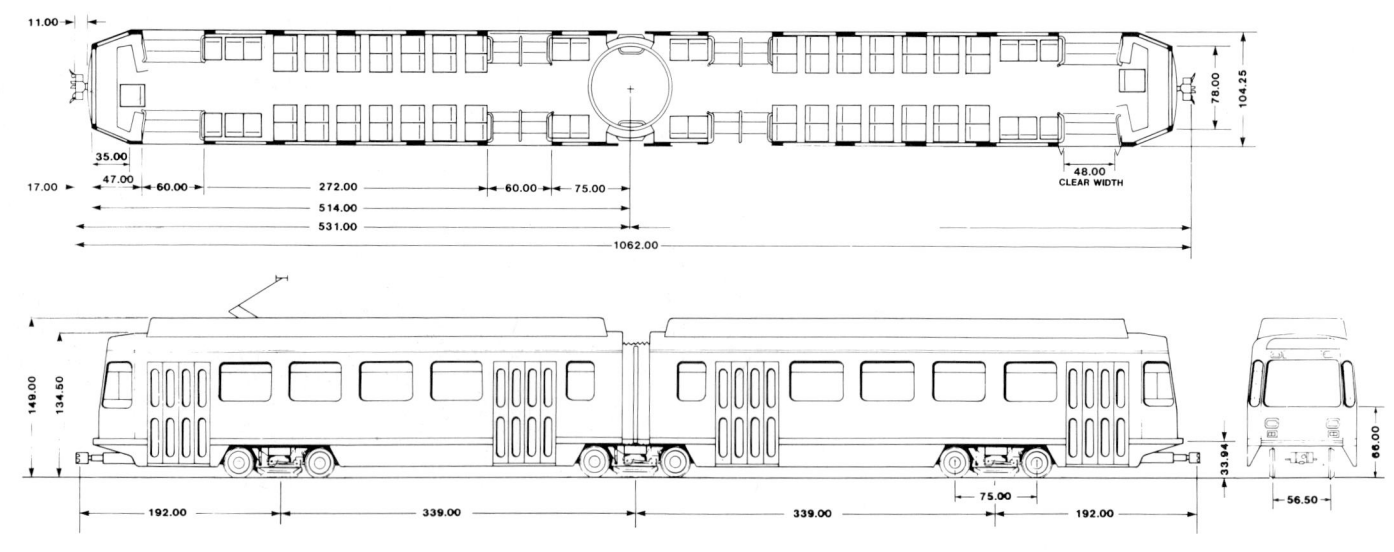

148 MANUFACTURERS / Powered passenger vehicles

General arrangement of Santa Clara CTD articulated LRV

Valmet
Valmet Corporation, Railway Division

PO Box 387, 33101 Tampere, Finland

Telephone: +358 31 658111
Telex: 22112
Telefax: +358 31 657044

General Manager: Esko Määttänen
Marketing Manager: Olavi Kivimäki

Products: Electric multiple-unit trains; rapid transit trains; articulated tramcars.

Metro train for the City of Helsinki by Valmet

Valmet electric railcars or multiple-units

Class	Cars per unit	Line voltage	Motor cars per unit	Motored axles per motor car	Rated output (kW) per motor	Max speed km/h	Weight tonnes per car	Total seating capacity	Length per car mm	No in service	Rate of acceleration m/s^2	Year first built	Builders Mechanical parts	Builders Electrical equipment
Electric train Sm2	2	25 kV	1	4	155	120	47+29	200/204	53 250	50	1.0	1975	Valmet	Strömberg
Metro train	2	750 V	2	4	125	90	30	134	44 200	42	1.2	1979	Valmet	Strömberg

VeVey
VeVey Engineering Works Ltd

Railway Division: 1844 Villeneuve, Switzerland

Marketing Manager: Fritz Hess

Products: Electric train-sets, light rail vehicles and tramcars, low-floor railcars for urban and suburban passenger service; powered and unpowered bogies.

Telephone: +41 21 960 42 51
Telex: 453 105 vey ch
Telefax: +41 21 960 42 56

Villares
Equipamentos Villares SA

Av Senador Vergueiro No 2000, São Bernardo do Campo 09700, SP, Brazil

Telephone: +55 11 443 5500
Telex: +55 11 44068

Managing Director: J Carlos do Couto Viana

Manufacturing Director: J Cassio Daltrini
Sales Manager: Renato Franco

Products: Multiple-unit train-sets.

Von Roll Habegger
Von Roll Habegger SA

Industriestrasse 2, CH–3601 Thun, Switzerland

Telephone: +41 33 21 99 88
Telex: 921 201 roha
Telefax: +41 33 23 20 43

Von Roll Habegger of America Inc

753 West Main Street, Watertown, NY 13601

Telephone: +1 315 788 12 80
Telex: 494 61 81 vrh awtr
Telefax: +1 315 788 13 21

Products: Monorail systems.

Von Roll Habegger of Australia Pty Ltd

2nd Level, 31 Miller Street, North Sydney, NSW 2060

Telephone: +61 2 959 31 99
Telefax: +61 2 959 32 02

Products: Monorail systems for local and urban transportation. The company has 20 installations operational in countries worldwide.

Waggon Union
Waggon Union GmbH

PO Box 2240, 5902 Netphen 2, Federal Republic of Germany

Telephone: +49 271 702 1
Cable: Waggonunion, Siegen
Telex: 08 72843

General Manager: Dipl-Ing Hans-Richard Hippenstiel

Products: Electric and diesel-powered railcars, railbuses, and multiple-unit train-sets; tramways, underground trains; double-deck buses and fabricated bogies for passenger coaches.

Walkers
Walkers Ltd
A member of the Evans Deakin Industries Group

Bowen Street, Maryborough, Queensland 4650, Australia

Telephone: +61 71 21 8100
Telex: AA 49718 itolzak
Telefax: +61 71 224400

General Manager: R Hardy
Secretary: A Warren

Products: Eighty 25 kV electric locomotives have been delivered to Queensland Railways; 50 Class 35/600 are employed on coal haulage while 30 Class 3900 are dedicated to main line passenger and freight services. These units were manufactured in a joint venture by Clyde/Asea Walkers in the period 1985–89.

Two hundred and sixty four 25 kV suburban emu electric railcars were delivered to Queensland Railways by the joint venture company Walkers-Asea Pty Ltd in the period 1979–87. This contract was followed by a contract for 20 25 kV emu railcars for operation on the 120 km/h 'Spirit of Capricorn' service operating between Brisbane and Rockhampton. The cars were also produced by Walkers-Asea Pty Ltd and delivered in 1988-89.

Currently, Walkers-Asea Pty Ltd is engaged in a contract with the Western Australian Government Railways Commission (Westrail) to manufacture 43 two-car sets of 25 kV emu railcars for the electrification of the Perth suburban rail system. The first of these units will be delivered during mid-1990.

25 kV emu railcar for operation on the 600 km route from Brisbane to Rockhampton

Constitution: Walkers was founded at Ballarat Victoria in 1864 and the works at Maryborough were opened on the present site in 1868.

Wickham
D Wickham & Co Ltd

Crane Mead, Ware, Hertfordshire SG12 9QA, England

Telephone: +44 920 462491/7
Cable: Wickham, Ware
Telex: 81340 wickhm g
Telefax: +44 920 460733

Joint Managing Directors: D S Holden and T H Bailie
Sales Director: G P Redfern
Technical Director, Product Sales-Home & Export: A P Mott

Products: Diesel railcars and railbuses.

Constitution: D Wickham & Co, which was incorporated as a private limited company in 1912, has been building railway vehicles since 1922. The company pioneered the use of roller bearing axleboxes, welded steel frames, underslung springs and all steel bodies, using solid drawn square steel tubing to eliminate the conventional underframe and produce cars with a high power/weight ratio for operating under arduous mountain conditions. The company specialises in track maintenance and inspection vehicles and offers a wide range of equipment for this purpose.

Diesel engines and transmission systems

ARGENTINA
Fiat Concord 157
GMD 160

AUSTRIA
JW 162

BELGIUM
ABC 152
ACEC 152
CMI 154
Möes 164

CHINA
Beijing 153
Dalian 155

FRANCE
GEC Alsthom Traction 159
Paulstra Hutchinson 166
SEMT Pielstick 168
Turbomeca 170
UNI Diesel Sarl 171

GERMANY, DEMOCRATIC REPUBLIC
Gotha 161
Strömungsmaschinen 170

GERMANY, FEDERAL REPUBLIC
ABB 152
BSI 153
Deutz MWM 156
EMG 157
Hurth 161
Kaelble-Gmeinder 162
KHD Deutz 162
MaK 163
MTU 164
Siemens 170
Thyssen-Henschel 170
Voith 173

HUNGARY
Ganz 157

ITALY
Fiat 157
GMT 161
Isotta Fraschini Motori 162
MPM 164

JAPAN
Fuji Electric 157
Hitachi 161
NICO 165
Niigata 165
Shinko 169

ROMANIA
August 23 Works 153
Hidromecanica 161
UCMR Resita 171

SWEDEN
Scania 166
SRM 170

USSR
Kolomna 163
VO Energomachexport 172

UK
Brush 153
David Brown 156
Gardner 158
GEC Diesels 159
Hunslet 161
Mirrlees 163
Perkins Engines 166
SCG 167
Twiflex 171

USA
Alco Power 152
Caterpillar 153
Cummins 155
Detroit Diesel 156
GE 158
General Motors Corporation 160
Kim Hotstart 162
L&M Radiator 163
Twin Disc 171

MANUFACTURERS / Diesel engines and transmission systems

ABB
ASEA Brown Boveri Transportation Management and System Development

Headquarters: PO Box 100163, Gottlieb-Daimler-Strasse 6, 6800 Mannheim 1, Federal Republic of Germany

Telephone: +49 621 468 200
Telex: 4624 11220 abd memo: btm gmbh
Telefax: +49 621 468 298/9

For full list of ABB group companies, see ABB entry in Locomotives section.

Products: Development, design, engineering, sales, production, installation, maintenance and after-sales-service of electrical and mechanical power transmission systems and equipment for all railway types, systems and track gauges.

Electrical power transmissions for traction vehicles for trunk, feeder, metropolitan, regional, suburban and industrial railway systems, and special rolling stock; complete range of electrical equipment and subsystems for all rail traction vehicles.

Mechanical power transmission systems and components: bogies and bogie components; axle drives; wheels and axles; gearboxes and couplings.

Service, minor equipment and spare parts; large projects management and consultancy.

ABB has delivered a large number of electrical and mechanical power transmission systems over many years and offers such systems within its engineering and supply of complete traction vehicles; or of complete electrical equipment for traction vehicles; or as sub-supplier with sub-systems and/or components.

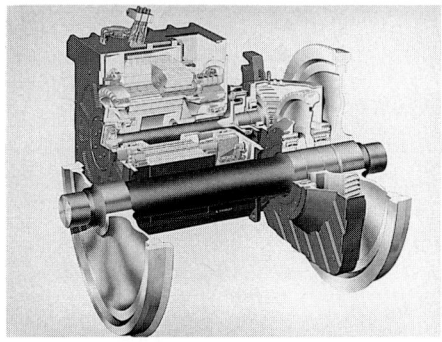

Transmission unit for heavy duty with suspended traction motor, gearbox and coupling

ABC
Anglo Belgian Corporation NV
43 Wiedauwkaai, 9000 Ghent, Belgium

Telephone: +32 91 23 45 41
Telex: 11298 abc gt b

Products: Diesel engines.

Formed in 1912, to take over the SA des Anciens Ateliers Onghena which had been building gas engines since 1904, the company manufactures four-stroke diesel engines for marine, industrial and rail traction services.

DXS and DXC Series
Type: 6- and 8-cylinder vertical in-line, 4-cycle turbocharged and charge air cooled (DXC), water cooled.
Cylinders: Bore 242 mm. Stroke 320 mm. Swept volume 14–72 litres per cylinder. Compression ratio 12.05:1. Cast iron wet type cylinder liners with three rubber seal rings. Cast iron cylinder heads secured by studs.
Fuel injection: Direct injection with one pump per cylinder.
Supercharger: Exhaust gas turbo-blower.
Cooling system: Panel radiator with one centrifugal pump.
Starting: Electric or compressed air.

DZC Series
Type: 6- and 8-cylinder vertical in-line, 4-stroke turbocharged and charge air cooled, water cooled.
Cylinders: Bore 256 mm. Stroke 310 mm. Swept volume 15.956 litres per cylinder. Compression ratio 12.1:1. Cast iron wet type cylinder liners with three rubber seal rings. Cast iron cylinder heads secured by studs.
Fuel injection: Individual Bryce Mk II pumps per cylinder. Direct injection.
Supercharger: Exhaust gas turbo-blower.
Cooling system: Water cooled. Panel radiator with one centrifugal pump.
Starting: Electric or compressed air.

Model		DXS	DXC		6DZC	8DZC
Turbo-charged		Yes	Yes	Yes	Yes	Yes
No of cylinders		6	6	8	6	8
Continuous rating	hp	650	9090	1200	1803	2404
	(kW)	(478)	(662)	(883)	(1326)	(1768)
Max engine speed	rpm	750	750	750	1000	1000
Mbep continuous	lb/in²	125	174	174	236	236
	(bar)	(8.8)	(12.22)	(12.22)	(16.6)	(16.6)
Bmep max 10% overload	lb/in²	138	191	191	260	260
	(bar)	(9.68)	(13.44)	(13.44)	(18.26)	(18.26)
Weight	lb	16 984	17 336	23 003	20 460	28 600
(dry without flywheel)	(kg)	(7720)	(7880)	(10 456)	(9300)	(13 000)
Length	in	129	129	158	158	194
	(mm)	(3270)	(3270)	(4025)	(4025)	(4925)
Width	in	55	55	55	57	59
	(mm)	(1400)	(1400)	(1400)	(1450)	(1495)
Height	in	64	64	64	72	73
	(mm)	(1620)	(1620)	(1620)	(1830)	(1850)
Consumption fuel	lb/hp/h	0.354	0.347	0.347	0.349	0.349
	(g/kW/h)	(218.5)	(214)	(214)	(215)	(215)
Lube oil			0.5% fuel consumption		0.6% fuel consumption	Vol + 3% LCV = 42 000 kJ/kg

Rated output: ISO 3046/1

ACEC Transport
ACEC Transport is a subsidiary of GEC Alsthom

PO Box 4211, B-6000 Charleroi, Belgium

Telephone: +32 0 71 44 54 11
Telex: 51227 acec b
Telefax: +32 0 71 43 72 35

Managing Director: Ch Jauquet

Operations Managing Director: R Pellichero
Commercial Director: D Hausman

Products: Electrical transmissions for diesel-electric locomotives

Alco Power Inc
A subsidiary of Bombardier Inc, Montreal

100 Orchard Street, Auburn, New York 13021, USA

Products: Alco continues to manufacture diesel engines for both stationary and marine applications. The Montreal plant handles sales for locomotives, and through licenses in various parts of the world including Argentina, Australia, India and Romania. It also continues to supply renewal parts and rebuilding components on a world-wide basis.

Alco was the first manufacturer in the USA to introduce turbo-supercharging for a diesel engine. The 12- and 16-cylinder V-type 244 model was introduced in the 1940s. First rated at 1580 hp at 1000 rpm, it was developed to give 1760 hp at the same speed. The V16 model gave 2360 hp. The 251 series with the same bore and stroke supersedes these. The engine design is approved by international regulating bodies ABS, Lloyds, GL, CnV, Bv for stationary and marine service.

251 Series
Type: 6-cylinder in-line, 8-, 12-, 16- and 18-cylinder Vee, 4-cycle high pressure turbo-charged with charge air cooling.

251 Series specifications

No of cylinders		6 in-line	8V	12V	16V	18V
Turbo-charged		Yes	Yes	Yes	Yes	Yes
Continuous rating	bhp	1500	1700	3000	3900	4500
Engine speed	rpm	1100	1000	1100	1100	1100
Bmep max	lb/in²	269	252	269	263	270
	(kg/cm²)	(18.9)	(17.7)	(18.9)	(18.5)	(19)
Engine weight (dry)	lb	24 700	26 400	32 300	42 500	49 000
	(kg)	(11 200)	(12 000)	(14 700)	(19 300)	(22 200)

251 Series Locomotive ratings

		6F	8V-F	12V-F	16V-F	18V-G
Turbo-charger		Single	Single	Single	Single	Single
Continuous rating	GHP	1500	1700	3000	3900	4500
Max rated speed	rpm	1100	1000	1100	1100	1100
Bmep	lb/in²	269	252	269	263	270
	(kg/cm²)	18.9	17.7	18.9	18.5	19
Engine weight	lb	22 500	25 700	33 000	42 000	49 200
	(kg)	10 206	11 658	14 969	19 051	22 317
Length	ft in	12 10	11 7	15	17 9	20 7
	(mm)	3912	3531	4572	5410	6274
Width	ft in	4 8	5 1	5 1	5 1	5 1
	(mm)	1422	1549	1549	1549	1549
Height	ft in	7 5	8 5	9 1	9 1	9 5
	(mm)	2261	2565	2769	2769	2870

Base ratings @ 90°F; 28.25" Hg 1500'–19 620 BTU/# D2 fuel (Ref DEMA)

Cylinders: Bore 9 in (228 mm). Stroke 10½ in (267 mm). Swept volume 668 in^3 per cylinder. Compression ratio 11.5:1. Cast iron cooled heat treated cylinder liners, chrome plated on inner surface. Cast iron-nickel alloy cylinder heads.
Fuel injection: Design for flat fuel-consumption curves. System is high-pressure with fuel supplied to cylinders by individual single-acting plunger pumps.
Turbo-charger: High pressure ratio exhaust gas driven turbo-charger. Alco-designed and built with replaceable blades on the turbine wheel. Water cooled charge air cooler.
Fuel: ASTM specification 2-D. Other fuels can be used (heavy oils, natural gas, crudes, etc) with suitable standard modifications to fuel injection equipment and governing apparatus.
Cooling system: Varies with type, locomotive or other installation. One Alco pump, gear driven from engine.
Starting: Motored main generator, or air.
Mounting: 4-point.

August 23 Works
Mecanoexportimport Supplier

Bd Muncii 256, Bucharest, Romania

Telephone: +40 0 27 73 10, +40 0 28 20 10
Telex: 10344

Products: The 23 August Works, under the trading name of FAUR, builds diesel engines to its own design or under licence.

The diesel engines for rail traction range from 220 to 1050 kW and are used for a wide variety of traction installations in both diesel-electric and diesel-hydraulic locomotives.

The Types 6, 8, and 12 V 396 four-stroke turbo-charged engines are built under licence from MTU of Germany and feature charge air cooling with direct injection; bore is 165 mm and stroke 185 mm. The Type 491 four-stroke turbo-charged engine also features charge air cooling and direct injection; bore is 175 mm and stroke 205 mm.

Types 6, 8 and 12 V 396 engines

Type designation	Speed rpm	Rated output kW/hp	Weight kg	Dimensions mm		
				Length	Width	Height
6V396TC12	1800	525/715	1900	1501	1424	1345
8V396TC12	1800	700/950	2400	1721	1442	1345
12V396TC12	1800	1050/1430	3350	2251	1522	1405

Type 491 engines

Type designation	Speed rpm	Rated output kW/hp	Weight kg	Dimensions mm		
				Length	Width	Height
6L491	1500	515/700	3200	2360	970	1600
12V491	1500	1030/1400	4200	2375	1310	1515

Beijing
Beijing "Feb 7th" Locomotive Works
Member of China National Machinery Import and Export Corporation

Erhlikou, Hsichiao, Beijing, China

Telex: +86 1 22328; +86 1 22242

Products: The main diesel engine produced at China's "Feb 7th" works is the type 12240, having passed GB 1105-74 testing for diesel locomotives: 100-hour typing test (rated power at 1100 rpm, 2700 hp; hourly overload 3000 hp); 500-hour endurance and reliability test (rated power 2700 hp; hourly overload 3000 hp); and 100-hour intensification test (rated power 3000 hp; hourly overload 3300 hp).

Type 12240 diesel engine
Type: 12 cylinder, 4-stroke, single acting, Vee 45 degree.
Cylinders: Bore 240 mm. Stroke, main cylinder 260 mm, auxiliary cylinder 273-51 mm. Compression ratio 12.5:1.

Type 12240 engine

	Diesel engine standard design		Intensified design		
hp	2700	3000	2700	3000	3000
rpm	1100	1100	1100	1100	1100
Fuel consumption (g/hp/h)	153.4	156.9	149.5	152	153
Max combustion pressure (kgf/cm^2)	120	124	113.2	119.6	130.25
Temp at turbine entrance (°C)	540	563	545	575	605
Exhaust gas index (Bosch)	1	1.6	0.95	0.95	1.45
Pressure of intake gas (kgf/cm^2)	2.25	2.46	2.265	2.44	2.712
Temp of intake gas (°C)	62	66	58	60	66.5
Mean effective pressure (kgf/cm^2)	15.65	17.4	15.65	19.4	19.13
Co-efficient of mechanical load (m^2/min^2)	75.5	75.5	75.5	75.5	75.5
Co-efficient of thermal load (hp/cm^2)	0.477	0.53	0.477	0.58	0.58
Co-efficient of intensification (kg/cm^2.m/s)	149.1	166	149.1	166	183

Fuel injection: Solid direct.
Weight, dry: 14 600 kg.

Brush
Brush Electrical Machines Ltd
(Traction Division)
A Hawker Siddeley company

PO Box 18, Loughborough, Leicestershire LE11 1HJ, England

Telephone: +44 509 611511
Telex: 341091

Products: Electric transmission systems of up to 6000 hp.

BSI
Bergische Stahl-Industrie
A member of Thyssen Guss AG

Papenberger Strasse 38, PO Box 100165, 5630 Remscheid 1, Federal Republic of Germany

Telephone: +49 2191 3641
Telex: 8513858
Telefax: +49 2191 30765

Mülheim works: Oberhausener Strasse 1, 4330 Mülheim/Ruhr

Telephone: +49 208 771
Telex: 856589
Telefax: +49 208 777355

General Manager: W Wiebelhaus
Senior Sales Manager: O Berghaus

Products: Axle drives for urban, underground and rapid transit railway vehicles; more than 28 500 in use world-wide. For details see BSI entry in Electric Traction Equipment section.

Caterpillar
Caterpillar Inc
Engine Division, PO Box 610, Mossville, Illinois 61552, USA

Telephone: +1 309 578 6193
Telex: 190423 catswmsvl
Telefax: +1 309 578 6466

Caterpillar Overseas SA
J E Bachelin, Manager OEM Sales
Caterpillar Overseas SA
PO Box 456, 1211 Geneva 6, Switzerland

MANUFACTURERS / Diesel engines and transmission systems

Model		3616	3612	3608	3606	3516	3512	3508	3412	3408	3406	3306	3304
Bore & stroke	in	11 × 11.8	11 × 11.8	11 × 11.8	11 × 11.8	6.6 × 7.5	6.7 × 7.5	6.7 × 7.5	5.4 × 6	5.4 × 6	5.4 × 6	4.75 × 6	4.75 × 6
	(mm)	(280 × 300)	(280 × 300)	(280 × 300)	(280 × 300)	(170 × 190)	(170 × 190)	(170 × 190)	(137 × 152)	(137 × 152)	(137 × 165)	(121 × 152)	(121 × 152)
No of cylinders		V16	V12	I8	I6	V16	V12	V8	V12	V8	I6	I6	I4
Turbo-charged		Yes	Yes	Yes	Yes	Yes	Yes	Yes	Yes	Yes	Yes	Yes	Yes
Aftercooled		Yes	Yes	Yes	Yes	Yes	Yes	Yes	Yes	Yes	Yes	Yes	Yes
Locomotive rating	bhp*	6000	4500	3000	2250	2075	1480	975	750	503	402	300	165
	rpm	1000	1000	1000	1000	1800	1800	1800	2100	2100	2100	2200	2200
Weight (dry)	lb	64 500	52 900	45 000	36 900	17 100	12 600	10 500	4720	3365	2960	2160	1655
	(kg)	(29 500)	(23 990)	(20 410)	(16 735)	(7763)	(5715)	(4763)	(2141)	(1526)	(1340)	(980)	(750)
Length	in	225.47	189.25	198.03	165.74	132.5	106.2	85	78.5	62.6	65.4	62	50.3
	(mm)	(5727)	(4807)	(5030)	(4210)	(3366)	(2699)	(2159)	(1995)	(1590)	(1660)	(1575)	(1280)
Width	in	66.93	66.93	66.93	66.93	73.9	67	67	60.4	48.5	35.5	30.8	32.3
	(mm)	(1700)	(1700)	(1700)	(1700)	(1878)	(1703)	(1703)	(1535)	(1230)	(902)	(785)	(820)
Height	in	103.38	103.38	102.83	102.83	67.1	67.7	67.7	68.2	54.2	52.6	46.1	39.4
	(mm)	(2626)	(2626)	(2612)	(2612)	(1703)	(1720)	(1720)	(1730)	(1376)	(1335)	(1170)	(1110)

* Ratings dependent on service.

Products: Caterpillar has been a supplier of diesel engine power to the railroad industry since 1931 and currently builds a range of diesel engines from 165 to 6000 hp. Caterpillar has been developing new engines to meet the demands of improving both fuel consumption and performance, and the 3500 and 3600 Series engines are well suited in size, power, and performance for locomotive applications. Caterpillar diesel traction engines have been installed by more than 30 locomotive manufacturers and are currently in service with railroads world-wide, as well as in numerous maintenance of way equipment and industrial and mining applications. Also offered are certified flameproof engines of 85 to 240 hp for use in gassy mines and other hazardous environment applications.

In addition to a non-load control, electro-pneumatic, eight-notch controller, Caterpillar also offers its own microprocessor-based digital electronic locomotive control system. The Locomotive Programmable Electronic Engine Control (PEEC) provides engine governing and generator load control to minimise fuel consumption; offers fully adjustable acceleration and deceleration ramp rates, with two programmes for yard and main-line operation; and performs wheelslip control and modulated generator unload as well as voltage and current limiting. PEEC eliminates the power dips or surges that normally occur with conventional electronic locomotive controls when fast response power changes are required.

PEEC consists of a control module, a rack actuator, a rack position feedback transducer, an engine speed sensor, and a wiring harness to connect the sensors, actuator, and control module to the locomotive's wiring system. The wiring system provides the proper notch code signals, a wheelslip signal, a generator load signal, and signals proportional to generator output voltage and current to the Locomotive PEEC.

The control module monitors engine speed, engine rack position (fuel delivery), generator voltage and current, wheelslip and generator load signals to determine the proper outputs to the rack actuator and generator exciter coil. Engine speed is controlled independently of generator load. Generator output is controlled as a function of engine speed, rack position, generator voltage, generator current, wheel-slip and generator load signals.

Minimum fuel consumption is obtained by operating the engine at its minimum fuel consumption point for each operating load. Since the engine operates at discrete power outputs for each notch, locomotive PEEC can be programmed to run the engine at minimum fuel consumption for the power specified in each notch. When shifting from a lower to a higher notch, the generator power output follows the minimum fuel consumption path. Decreasing power output follows the same path in reverse order. The programmable operating curve allows the engine operation to be tailored to prevent undesirable operating modes from a fuel consumption/smoke/noise/cylinder pressure/turbo-charger/etc viewpoint.

Locomotive PEEC uses linear speed and load control ramps. Engine speed is ramped at a constant rate between notches. The linear speed ramp provides a smooth and continuous rate of power change when transitioning between notches since the power output is determined as a function of engine speed rather than notch position. Two different sets of engine speed ramp rates can be programmed into the control. One set of engine speed ramp rates (increasing and decreasing engine speed) can be selected for switch yard application and a second set specified for main-line operation. A switch input is provided for selecting one of the two operating modes.

Locomotive PEEC ramps power down when a wheelslip condition occurs. A wheelslip detection system on the locomotive sends a signal to the governor to indicate the wheels are slipping. The control then ramps power output down until the wheelslip condition clears, then power is ramped back up to the desired level as specified by the notch setting.

Locomotive PEEC performs internal diagnostics or a self-health test to insure that the control is functioning properly and the sensors are sending valid signals to the control. When faulty sensor signals are detected the control either substitutes a calculated value for the reading or switches to another mode of operation for which the control has valid signals.

Locomotive PEEC units have accumulated approximately 18 000 development and field test hours with minimal development failures. All failures have been corrected with proven design solutions. Locomotive PEEC is now available in a production version for the 3500, 3400 and 3600 Series Caterpillar engines.

Specifications for all engine models:
Cylinders: Removable wet type cylinder liners of hardened cast iron. Alloy cast iron cylinder heads with water directors and removable injectors/prechambers. The 3500 and 3600 Series utilise individual cylinder heads for serviceability.
Fuel injection: Caterpillar-designed unit injectors and pumps on all models of the direct injection type. Caterpillar also offers the 3300 and 3400 families with indirect injection fuel systems for use in mining and other environment-sensitive applications. Standard arrangements utilise replaceable full flow fuel filters.
Aspiration: All models utilise turbo-charging and aftercooling (intercoolers). The 3300s are also offered in naturally aspirated versions.
Fuel: No 2 diesel fuel oil (ASTM specification D396-48T). Premium diesel fuel oil can be used, but is not recommended. The 3600 Series is also capable of heavy fuel operation.
Lubrication: Full pressure systems including gear-type pumps, replaceable full flow filters and water cooled oil coolers.
Cooling systems: Centrifugal-type circulating pumps with thermostatically-controlled bypass. All systems are capable of pressurisation and designed to use antifreeze solutions.
Starting: Air or electric.

CMI
Cockerill Mechanical Industries SA
Engines & Locomotives Department

Avenue Greiner 1, 4100 Seraing, Belgium

Telephone: +32 41 30 21 11
Telex: 41225 cklsam b
Telefax: +32 41 30 23 89

Products: Launched in 1965, the present 240CO series is now in its third generation. Developing 1170 to 3120 kW (1590–4240 hp) at 1000 rpm, it is being used worldwide for rail traction, marine propulsion and power generation.

A recent contract provided for delivery of 18 8TR240CO engines to power 84-tonne diesel-electric Co-Co locomotives of a new design for Viet-Nam.

Series 240CO
Type: 6 and 8 cylinders in-line, 12 and 16 cylinders in Vee, 4-cycle water cooled.
Cylinders: Bore 9½ in (24.31 mm). Stroke 12 in (304.8 mm). Swept volume 13.92 litres per cylinder. Cast iron wet cylinder liners, separate cast iron cylinder heads, direct injection combustion chambers.
Fuel injection: Mechanical pumps and nozzles.
Lubrication: One pressure pump.
Cooling system: One centrifugal water pump.

		240CO Series			
		6TR	8TR	V12TR	V16TR
No of cylinders		6	8	12	16
Turbo-charged		Yes	Yes	Yes	Yes
Charge air cooled		Yes	Yes	Yes	Yes
Weight (dry)	lb	18 722	24 230	34 500	45 815
	(kg)	(8500)	(11 000)	(15 700)	(20 800)
Length	in	129.92	156.93	171.77	232.28
	(mm)	(3300)	(3986)	(4363)	(5900)
Width	in	47.64	48.03	86.62	84.25
	(mm)	(1210)	(1220)	(2200)	(2140)
Height	in	104.73	104.73	93.11	105.08
	(mm)	(2660)	(2660)	(2365)	(2669)
Speed			1000 rpm		
Continuous power*	hp	1590	2120	3180	4240
	(kW)	(1170)	(1560)	(2340)	(3120)
Bmep	lb/in²	243	243	243	243
	(kg/cm²)	(17.2)	(17.2)	(17.2)	(17.2)
Piston speed	ft/min	1999	1999	1999	1999
	(m/s)	(10.16)	(10.16)	(10.16)	(10.16)
Fuel consumption	lb/hp/h	0.336	0.338	0.332	0.332
	(g/hp/h)	(150.5)	(151.5)	(148.5)	(144)

* To UIC 623-1

Constitution: CMI-Cockerill Mechanical Industries became an independent subsidiary of Cockerill Sambre in December 1982. CMI employs more than 2000 people, and specialises in products for heavy industry including diesel engines.

The first CMI diesel engine was built in 1913 with assistance from its inventor Rudolf Diesel.

Diesel engines and transmission systems / **MANUFACTURERS**

Cummins
Cummins Engine Co, Inc
Box 3005, Columbus, Indiana 47202-3005, USA

Telephone: +1 812 377 3355
Telex: 217 410
Telefax: +1 812 377 3082

Vice President, Industrial Markets: M A Levett
Manager, Rail Marketing: M L Clancy

Products: Cummins Engine Co manufactures a range of diesel engines from 76 to 2000 hp for a wide variety of rail-associated applications. Experience in maintenance of way, railcar, head-end power and locomotive traction installations, covers more than 40 years. Over 5900 sales and service outlets are located throughout the world.

Aftercooler: Large-capacity aftercooler results in cooler, denser intake air for more efficient combustion and reduced internal stresses for longer life. Aftercooler is located in engine coolant system eliminating need for special plumbing.
Cooling system: Gear-driven centrifugal water pump. Large volume water passages provide even flow of coolant around cylinder liners, valves, and injectors. Four modulating by-pass thermostats regulate coolant temperature. Spin-on corrosion resistors check rust and corrosion, control acidity, and remove impurities.
Cylinder block: Alloy cast iron with removable wet liners. Cross-bolt support to main bearing cap provides extra strength and stability.
Cylinder heads: Alloy cast iron. Each head serves one cylinder. Valve seats are replaceable corrosion-resistant inserts. Valve guides and crosshead guides are replaceable inserts.
Cylinder liners: Replaceable wet liners dissipate heat faster than dry liners and are easily replaced without reboring the block.
Fuel system: Cummins exclusive low pressure PT system with wear compensating pump and integral dual flyball governor. Camshaft-actuated fuel injectors give accurate metering and timing. Spin-on fuel filters.
Lubrication: Large capacity gear pump provides pressure lubrication to all bearings and oil supply for piston cooling. All pressure lines are internal drilled passages in block and heads. Oil cooler, full-flow filters, and by-pass filters maintain oil condition and maximise oil and engine life.
Turbo-charger: Two AiResearch exhaust gas-driven turbo-chargers mounted at top of engine. Turbocharging provides more power, improved fuel economy, altitude compensation, and lower smoke and noise levels.

Engine	Maximum rating hp	rpm	Continuous traction rating hp	rpm	Displacement in³ (litres)	Bore and stroke in (mm)	Number of cylinders	Aspiration	Net weight lb (kg)
Industrial engines									
4B 3.9	76	2500	64	2200	239 (3.9)	4.02 × 4.72 (102 × 120)	4	N	715 (324)
4BT 3.9	100	2500			239 (3.9)	4.02 × 4.72 (102 × 120)	4	T	740 (336)
4BTA 3.9	116	2500	91	2200	239 (3.9)	4.02 × 4.72 (102 × 120)	4	T/A	767 (348)
6B 5.9	115	2500			359 (5.8)	4.02 × 4.72 (102 × 120)	6	N	908 (412)
6BT 5.9	152	2500	122	2200	359 (5.8)	4.02 × 4.72 (102 × 120)	6	T	933 (423)
6BTA 5.9	177	2500	141	2200	359 (5.8)	4.02 × 4.72 (102 × 120)	6	T/A	967 (439)
6C 8.3	150	2200	134	2200	505 (8.3)	4.49 × 5.32 (114 × 135)	6	N	1320 (599)
6CT 8.3	210	2200	173	2200	505 (8.3)	4.99 × 5.32 (114 × 135)	6	T	1359 (616)
6CTA 8.3	234	2200	199	2200	505 (8.3)	4.49 × 5.32 (114 × 135)	6	T/A	1402 (636)
Locomotive engines									
N-855-L3	235	2100	210	2100	855 (14)	5.5 × 6 (140 × 152)	6	N	2590 (1175)
NTA-855-L4	335	2100	285	2100	855 (14)	5.5 × 6 (140 × 152)	6	T/A	2625 (1191)
NTA-855-L3	400	2100	340	2100	855 (14)	5.5 × 6 (140 × 152)	6	T/A	2750 (1247)
KT-19-L	450	2100	380	2100	1150 (19)	625 × 6.25 (159 × 159)	6	T	3450 (1565)
KTA-19-L	600	2100	510	2100	1150 (19)	6.25 × 6.25 (159 × 159)	6	T/A	3500 (1588)
KTTA-19-L	650	2100	550	2100	1150 (19)	6.25 × 6.25 (159 × 159)	6	T/A	3600 (1633)
VTA-28-L3	725	2100	615	2100	1710 (28)	5.5 × 6 (140 × 152)	12	T/A	5780 (2621)
VTA-28-L2	800	2100	680	2100	1710 (28)	5.5 × 6 (140 × 152)	12	T/A	5780 (2621)
KT-38-L	900	2100	765	2100	2300 (38)	6.25 × 6.25 (159 × 159)	12	T	7300 (3315)
KTA-38-L	1200	2100	1020	2100	2300 (38)	6.25 × 6.25 (159 × 159)	12	T/A	9250 (4200)
KTA-50-L	1600	2100	1360	2100	3067 (50)	6.25 × 6.25 (159 × 159)	16	T/A	12 000 (5455)
KTTA-50-L	1800	2100	1530	2100	3067 (50)	6.25 × 6.25 (159 × 159)	16	T/A	12 100 (5500)
Railcar engines									
N-855-R2	235	2100	210	2100	855 (14)	5.5 × 6 (140 × 152)	6	N	2600 (1185)
NT-855-R5	335	2100	285	2100	855 (14)	5.5 × 6 (140 × 152)	6	T	2700 (1200)
NTA-855-R	400	2100	340	2100	855 (14)	5.5 × 6 (140 × 152)	6	T/A	2800 (1255)
KTA-19-R	600	2100	510	2100	1150 (19)	6.25 × 6.25 (159 × 159)	6	T/A	3900 (1770)

Dalian
Dalian Locomotive and Rolling Stock Works
Member of China National Machinery Import and Export Corporation

Dalian, Liaoning, People's Republic of China

Telephone: +86 411 403064
Telex: 86414 daloc cn
Telefax: +86 411 406447

Products: Diesel-generator sets for 'Dong Feng' type diesel locomotives. Main specifications of the Model 16V 240ZJB engine produced for the 'Dong Feng 4' are:
Bore: 240 mm
Stroke: 275 mm
Total displacement: 199 litres
Compression ratio: 12.5:1
Rated speed: 1000 rpm
Lowest idle speed: 430 rpm
Continuous power rating: 2650 kW
Mean effective pressure: 1.598 mPa
Max firing pressure: 12.258 mPa
Specific fuel consumption: 210 + 7 g/kW/h
Specific oil consumption: <2.9 g/kW/h
Exhaust gas temperature: <620°C
   Main specifications of the Model 8240 ZJ engine built for the 'Dong Feng 5' are:
Bore: 240 mm
Stroke: 275 mm
Compression ratio: 12.5:1
Rated speed: 1000 rpm
Lowest idle speed: 400 rpm
Continuous power rating: 1320 kW
Mean effective pressure: 1.598 mPa
Specific fuel consumption: 210 + 7 g/kW/h
Specific oil consumption: <2 g/kW/h

Model 16V 240ZJB diesel engine for Dong Feng 4 locomotive

156 **MANUFACTURERS** / Diesel engines and transmission systems

David Brown
David Brown Corporation plc
David Brown Vehicle Transmissions Limited

Park Gear Works, Lockwood, Huddersfield HD4 5DD, England

Telephone: +44 484 422180
Telex: 9312110238 db g
Telefax: +44 484 435292

Managing Director: J A Vigor
Director & General Manager: R S Tadman
Marketing Manager: S Ambler
Sales Manager: P Dalton

Products: David Brown Vehicle Transmissions offer a comprehensive engineering and manufacturing service to the rail industry, including new transmissions such as the right-angled main axle drives used on the British Rail Class 91 high-speed electric locomotive; and redesign and reconditioning of rail gear units as carried out on the Tyne and Wear Passenger Transport Executive's light rail transit system.

The company's design and engineering services are available to assist with performance studies, analysis and prediction of service failures, as well as being used to design optimum units for new applications or the redesigning and upgrading of existing transmissions.

The company has the capability to design, manufacture and heat-treat all gear, shaft and case components required in the production of new and reconditioned rail gear units for the widest range of applications.

Right-angled main axle drive gear unit of BR Class 91 electric locomotive (four per locomotive)

Detroit Diesel
Detroit Diesel Corporation

13400 Outer Drive West, Detroit, Michigan 48239-4001, USA

Telephone: +1 313 592 5000
Telex: 4320091
Telefax: +1 313 592 7580

Chief Executive Officer and Chairman: Roger S Penske
President & Chief Operating Officer: Ludvik F Koci
Vice-President International: Paul A Moreton
Vice-President, Construction & Industrial Sales: James T Marcoux

Products: Diesel engines, generator sets, horsepower ranges of 200 to 2200 bhp.

Deutz MWM
Motoren-Werke Mannheim AG

PO Box 102263 Carl-Benz Strasse 5, 6800 Mannheim 1, Federal Republic of Germany

Telephone: +49 621 3840
Telex: 462341
Telefax: +49 621 384328

Sales Director: Guenter Schau
Overseas Sales: Wolfgang Libbach
European Sales: Friedrich Mette

Products: The Deutz MWM engine programme now ranges from 100 to 1940 kW (134 to 2600 hp). Within this programme the 234, 816 and 604B series are the most important for railway application.

The 234 series comprises V-type engines with 6, 8, 12 and 16 cylinders which cover a power spectrum from 100 to 900 kW at speeds between 1500 and 2300 rpm. The engines are supplied with turbo-charger and charge air cooling. The 6-, 8- and 12-cylinder versions are also available as naturally aspirated engines. These engines, introduced on the market in 1981, achieve good specific values: the fuel consumption of the 16-cylinder engine is as low as 194 g/kWh at 2100 rpm. The engines have an optimal weight per unit power of 2.1 kg/kW.

The 816 series, with its 6- and 8-cylinder in-line engines and 12- and 16-cylinder V-engines, spans a power range from 85 to 1230 kW at speeds between 1000 and 2000 rpm. Turbo-charger and charge air cooling are standard equipment. The in-line engines can be supplied as naturally aspirated engines.

The 604B series presented in 1985 has been developed from the 603/604 family. Its development significantly increased power to weight and power to volume ratios. With a brake mean effective pressure of about 18 bar the maximum power per cylinder is 120 kW at a speed of 1800 rpm. A 6-cylinder in-line engine and 90° V-engines with 8, 12 and 16 cylinders

Locomotive of the Köln-Bonn Railway powered by Deutz MWM Type TBD 604B V12 diesel engine with UTC output of 1320 kW at 1800 rpm

Rolba rotary snowploughs of Yugoslav Railways (JZ) equipped with 12-cylinder engines of Deutz MWM 234 series. With an output of 770 kW, this 34 tonne unit can clear up to 10 000 tonnes/hour

Model		TBD 234 V6	TBD 234 V8	TBD 234 V12	TBD 234 V16	BA6M 816	BA8M 816	BA12M 816	BA16M 816	TBD 604B L6	TBD 604B V8	TBD 604B V12	TBD 604B V16
No of cylinders		V6	V8	V12	V16	6 in-line	8 in-line	V12	V16	6 in-line	V8	V12	V16
Turbo-charged		Yes	Yes	Yes	Yes	Yes	Yes	Yes	Yes	Yes	Yes	Yes	Yes
Charge air cooled		Yes	Yes	Yes	Yes	Yes	Yes	Yes	Yes	Yes	Yes	Yes	Yes
Output (cont)	kW	300	400	600	800	383	511	766	1022	670	892	1340	1784
UIC Code 623VE	(hp)	(408)	(544)	(816)	(1088)	(521)	(695)	(1042)	(1390)	(911)	(1213)	(1822)	(2426)
Engine speed	rpm	2100	2100	2100	2100	1800	1800	1800	1800	1800	1800	1800	1800
Length	mm	1390	1565	1835	2525	1796	2175	2120	2600	2194	1913	2629	3129
Width	mm	865	910	910	1220	1112	947	1510	1565	1143	1389	1389	1389
Height	mm	1135	1130	1125	1245	1459	1473	1402	1425	1582	1667	1810	1810
Weight	kg	940	1100	1500	2250	1605	2085	2980	3730	2155	3000	4075	5495

and a maximum power up to 1940 kW are available.

The individual cylinder heads of these engines have been provided with two inlet ports, one designed as a swirl port and the other matched to optimal air supply. A throttle plate controls the air supply to the port and is designed for optimal air supply. With decreasing load the throttle plate closes the air supply port and more air is forced through the swirl port. In view of the increased specific swirl at low load it is possible, together with a respective adaption of the injected fuel quantity, to realise a significant torque increase without inadmissible smoke content in the exhaust emission.

EMG
Elektro-Mechanik GmbH Wendenerhütte

5963 Wenden 2, Federal Republic of Germany

Telephone: +49 2762 612-0
Telex: 876 416
Telefax: +49 2762 612237

Products: Cardan shaft axle drives, electrical equipment for diesel railcars.

EMG cardan shaft axle drive for diesel railcars

Fiat
Fiat Ferroviaria SpA

Piazza Galateri 4, 12038 Savigliano (CN), Italy

Telephone: +39 172 2021
Telex: 210234 fiatsv i
Telefax: +39 172 202 426

Chairman: Renato Piccoli
Managing Director & General Manager: Giancarlo Cozza
Deputy General Manager: Pierantonio Losa
Sales Manager: Andrea Parnigoni

Principal subsidiaries: Costruzioni Ferroviarie Colleferro; Elettromeccanica Parrizi

Products: Electric and diesel locomotives, electric and diesel railcars, tilting body trains; multiple units; metro cars; tramcars; bogies and components.

Diesel engines for rail applications derived directly from Iveco large volume powerplants for road trucks. This results in low initial investment and spares costs, plus the inherent advantages derived from extensive large scale operating experience. This particularly applies to Type 8217.

Design and manufacture of components and transmission for rail vehicles, in particular diesel railcar transmissions, output ratings 200 to 280 hp (147 to 205 kW), both hydro-mechanical (hydraulic coupling and five-speed gearbox) and hydraulic (torque converter); recently, the mechanical version has been improved by introducing a microprocessor device for automatic control of transmission. Also drives for locomotives, metro car tractive units and tramcars in monomotor and twin-motor versions with traction motors mounted longitudinally or transversally. Drives for high speed (up to 300 km/h) motor bogies are currently under development.

Fiat engines for rail traction

Model	8217	8280	8297
No of cylinders	6	8	12
Output (UIC) standard	260 kW (280 hp)	316 kW (430 hp)	515 kW (700 hp)
No of strokes	4	4	4
Cylinder arrangement	Horizontal	90° Vee	90° Vee
Bore	5¼ in (147 mm)	5¾ in (145 mm)	5¾ in (145 mm)
Stroke	6 in (156 mm)	5 in (130 mm)	5 in (130 mm)
Capacity	842 in^3 (13 797.7 cm^3)	1048 in^3 (17 173 cm^3)	1572 in^3 (25 761 cm^3)
Engine speed (UIC)	2000 rpm	2200 rpm	2100 rpm
Firing order	1-5-3-6-2-4	1R-3R-7L-2R-6L-5L-4R-8L	1R-12L-5R-8L-3R-10L 6R-7L-2R-11L-4R-9L
Turbo-charger	Single	Twin + Intercooler	Twin + Intercooler
Engine dimensions			
Height	25¾ in (653 mm)	49¼ in (1250 mm)	49¼ in (1262 mm)
Length	92 in (2341 mm)	55½ in (1410 mm)	75½ in (1918.5 mm)
Width	47¼ in (1200 mm)	47¼ in (1200 mm)	57¾ in (1470 mm)
Weight (dry)	3138 lb (1420 kg)	3536 lb (1600 kg)	4530 lb (2050 kg)

Fiat Concord
Fiat Concord SAIC
Cerrito 740, 1309 Buenos Aires, Argentina

Telephone: +54 1 35 3044
Telex: 012 11141

Products: Diesel engines.

Fuji Electric
Fuji Electric Co Ltd

New Yurakucho Building, 12-1 Yurakucho 1-chome, Chiyoda-ku, Tokyo 100, Japan

Telephone: +81 3 211 7111
Telex: 22331
Telefax: +81 3 347 2117

Chairman: Fukushige Shishido

President: Hideo Abe
Executive Vice President: Teruhisa Shimizu
Senior Executive Managing Director: Takeshi Nakao
Products: Complete electric transmissions for locomotives and multiple-units.

Ganz
Ganz Machinery Works

Kóbányai út 21, 1087 Budapest, Hungary

Telephone: +36 1 753322

Products: Hydraulic transmissions with input power of 250 to 1800 kW. Transmission types include a hydraulic transmission family of two-converter type, comprising:

Type	Traction power kW	Nominal input speed rpm	Output speed rpm	Weight without oil kg
H182-20	1820	1500	2570	4200
H182-10	1420	1500	2020	4200
H122	820	1500	2270	3300
H92	660	1500	2250	2400
H52	330	1500	2100	1300

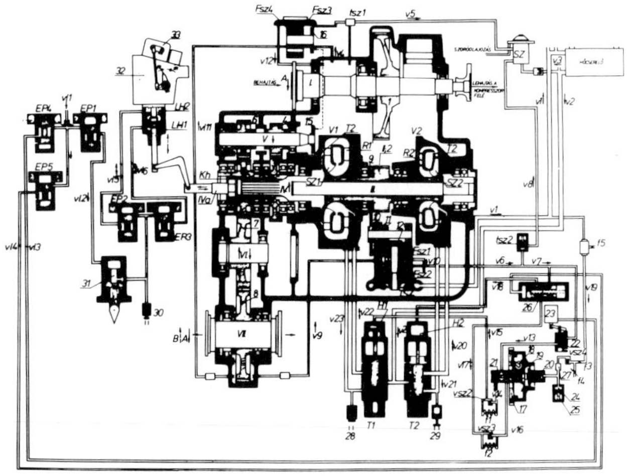

Ganz Type H122 transmission

158 **MANUFACTURERS** / Diesel engines and transmission systems

Also offered are hydraulic couplings of Types K 4-10, K 5-10 and K 6-10 for cooling fans of locomotives and railcars. The hydraulic coupling is built into the hub of the runner and it is fastened to the stator of the fan.

The company also manufactures other kinds of hydraulic transmissions for railcars and locomotives, such as hydraulic-reverse type; hydraulic torque converters for oil drilling aggregates; and hydraulic couplings for ventilators, fans, pumps and belt conveyor drives.

Ganz Machinery build various diesel engines, mainly for their own makes of locomotive and railcar. Two typical products are:

SEMT-Pielstick 12PA4V-185 VG made under licence
Type: 12 cylinders in Vee, 4-stroke with variable geometry combustion chamber, turbo-charged and intercooled.
Cylinders: Bore 185 mm, stroke 210 mm, swept volume 5.65 litres per cylinder. Individual cylinder heads and separate cast-iron water jackets with wet liners. Nodular graphite iron pistons with internal oil cooling.
Fuel injection: Conventional type injection pump and pintle type injectors.
Output: Nominal power rating 1472 kW/200 hp at 1500 rpm.
Dry weight: About 6700 kg complete with all accessories.
PA4 engine range also comprises 6-, 8-, 16- and 18-cylinder models.

Type 12 VFE 17/24
Type: 12 cylinders in Vee, 4-stroke with pre-chamber, turbo-charged and intercooled.
Cylinders: Bore 170 mm, stroke 240 mm, swept volume 5.45 litres per cylinder. Individual cylinder heads, wet liners and light metal of cooled pistons.
Fuel injection: Jendrassik type spring injection pump and semi-open injectors.
Output: Nominal power rating 736 kW/1000 hp at 1250 rpm.
Dry weight: About 5000 kg complete with accessories.
17/24 range also comprises 8- and 16-cylinder models.

Ganz Type H122 transmission as fitted to Type DHM12 diesel-hydraulic locomotive for Bangladesh

Gardner
L Gardner & Sons Ltd
Specialised engines division of Perkins Engines

Barton Hall Engine Works, Patricroft, Eccles, Manchester M30 7WA, England

Telephone: +44 61 789 2201
Telex: 668 023
Telefax: +44 61 787 7549

General Manager: Brian Willmott
Sales & Marketing Manager: Allan Littlemore
OE Sales Manager: Bill McArdle

Model		6LXB	6HLXB	6LXCT	6HLXCT	6LXDT	6LYT
No of cylinders		6	6	6	6	6	6
Max bhp		180	180	230	230	290	350
Engine speed	rpm	1850	1850	1900	1900	1900	1800
Weight approx	lb	1560	1707	1892	1892	1890	2407
	(kg)	(707.6)	(774.3)	(858)	(858)	(858)	(1091)
Length	in	55	55	60½	61½	62	63
	(mm)	(1397)	(1397)	(1536)	(1566)	(1569)	(1585)
Width	in	244¼	55	24	67	28	30
	(mm)	(667)	(1397)	(608)	(1706)	(706)	(754)
Height	in	45¼	26	37¼	27	45	51
	(mm)	(1149)	(660)	(948)	(687)	(1140)	(1283)

Now owned by Perkins Engines Group, Gardner will make full use of its parent's comprehensive technical resources. All Gardner engines are now being developed at Perkins' Peterborough headquarters, which has what is claimed to be the world's largest diesel research facilities. These include noise cells and more than 100 test beds linked to computer programmes to simulate every conceivable operating condition. Perkins also has some of the most sophisticated combustion research equipment available, which should ensure that Gardner engines retain their reputation for fuel economy.

Gardner will continue to use the latest production machinery to make precision components, which are then hand-built by one man from the crankcase up before being performance tested.

Products: Horizontal and vertical engines from 180–350 bhp featuring high torque, low weight and exceptionally low fuel consumption. The engines are proven in rail applications as well as truck, bus, coach and marine operation throughout the world.

GE
General Electric Co
Transportation Systems Business Operations

2910 East Lake Road, Erie, Pennsylvania 16531, USA

Products: Diesel engines and complete electric transmissions.

Series FDL (8-, 12- and 16-cylinder 45° Vee) engines
Type: 4-cycle turbo-charged with water cooled charge air cooler.
Cylinders: Bore 9 in (229 mm). Stroke 10½ in (267 mm). Swept volume 668 in^3 per cylinder. Individual unitised cast cylinder with renewable liner and head. Compression ratio 12.7:1.
Fuel injection: Individual injectors and fuel pumps.
Turbo-charger: One, exhaust driven (no gear drive to crankshaft).
Lubrication: Forced full flow filtered oil to all bearings and pistons, gear type engine driven pump.
Cooling system: Forced circulation water cooling of cylinders, turbo-charger, and intercoolers. The water passages are external of the crankcase and main frame.

Current engine specifications

Model	7FDL8	7FDL12	7FDL16
No of cylinders	8	12	16
Output (UIC) standard	1970	3233	3940
Stroke cycle	4	4	4
Cylinder arrangement	45° Vee	45° Vee	45° Vee
Bore	9 in (228.6 mm)	9 in (228.6 mm)	9 in (228.6 mm)
Stroke	10½ in (266.7 mm)	10½ in (266.7 mm)	10½ in (266.7 mm)
Compression ratio	12:7:1	12:7:1	12:7:1
Idle speed	385 rpm	385 rpm	385 rpm
Full-rated speed	1050 rpm	1050 rpm	1050 rpm
Firing order	1R-1L-2R-2L-4R-4L-3R-3L	1R-1L-5R-5L-3R-3L-6R 6L-2R-2L-4R-4L	1R-1L-3R-3L-7R-7L-4R-4L 8R-8L-6R-6L-2R-2L-5R-5L
Turbo-charger	Single	Single	Single
Engine dimensions			
Height (excluding stack)	86¼ in (2191 mm)	90⅛ in (2289 mm)*	90⅛ in (2289 mm)
Length (overall)	128½ in (3264mm)	159½ in (4051 mm)	193 in (4902 mm)
Width (overall)	68¼ in (1734 mm)	68⅜ in (1740 mm)	68⅜ in (1740 mm)
Weight (dry)	27 000 lb (12 200 kg)	35 000 lb (15 900 kg)	43 500 lb (19 700 kg)

* Note: Domestic (USA) type engines only. The export model has a lower water header (86¼ in, 2191 mm)

Diesel engines and transmission systems / MANUFACTURERS

GEC Alsthom Traction

GEC Alsthom Transport Division

Tour Neptune, 92086 Paris La Défense Cedex 20, France

Telephone: +33 1 47 44 00 00
Telex: 611207 alstr f
Telefax: +33 1 47 78 77 55
PO Box 134, Manchester M60 1AH, England

Telephone: +44 61 872 2431
Telex: 667152
Telefax: +44 61 875 2131

For full list of companies in the group, see GEC Alsthom entry in Locomotives section.

Products: Full range of electric transmissions.

GEC Diesels

Vulcan Works, Newton-le-Willows, Merseyside WA12 8RU, England

Products: Diesel engines.

GEC Diesels is the parent company of Ruston Diesels Ltd and Paxman Diesels Ltd.

Ruston Diesels Ltd

Vulcan Works, Newton-le-Willows, Merseyside WA12 8RU

Telephone: +44 925 225151
Telex: 627131
Telefax: +44 925 222055

Managing Director: J M MacKinnon
Engineering Director: M Whattam
Traction Manager: R R Smith

Products: The company offers rail traction engines within a power range of 1600 to 6000 bhp.

Ruston RK series

The RKC engine provides a maximum output of 313 hp (233 kW) per cylinder at 1000 rpm. The engine is manufactured in 6-cylinder in-line and Vee 8-, 12- and 16-cylinder forms (Vee angle 45°). The engine covers a power band up to 5000 hp (3730 kW) at 1000 rpm under ISO standard reference conditions. The RKC medium-speed engine with cylinder dimensions of 254 mm (10 in) bore and 305 mm (12 in) stroke throughout the range offers long periods between overhauls with a high degree of interchangeability of components.

Type: 4-stroke water cooled, turbo-charged/charge air cooled.
Fuel injection: Individual pumps and injectors for each cylinder.
Turbo-charger: Normally Napier turbo-chargers are specified but other makes can be supplied.

Lubrication: Jacket cooling system thermostatically-controlled using an engine-driven water pump.
Starting: Electric starting from the locomotive battery, either by starting windings in the driven machine or by starter motors mounted on the engine.

The supply and commissioning of 50 Ruston 12RKC 3300 bhp engines for British Rail Class 58 locomotives has now been completed. Two Ruston 6RK270 engines have successfully undergone four years service evaluation in BR Class 37 locomotives, having previously obtained type approval test certificates.

The first locomotives to incorporate the RK270 engines have now successfully completed four years service handling heavy mineral traffic. Further rehabilitation was undertaken during 1989 in Tanzania and other African railway locomotives are programmed for similar updating during 1990.

RK215 series

The RK215 is a range of compact, high power/weight ratio 4-stroke medium speed diesel engines producing

Engine type	Speed rpm	No of cylinders	Standard power brakepower		Length		Approx dimensions Width		Height		Approx weight of engine with flywheel	
			hp	kW	mm	in	mm	in	mm	in	kg	lb
6RKC	850	6	1660	1240	4648	183	1397	55	2235	88	12 109	26 670
	900	6	1730	1290	4648	183	1397	55	2235	88	12 109	26 670
	1000	6	1775	1325	4648	183	1397	55	2235	88	12 109	26 670
8RKC	850	8	2220	1655	4343	171	1702	67	2337	92	14 213	31 340
	900	8	2325	1735	4343	171	1702	67	2337	92	14 213	31 340
	1000	8	2375	1770	4343	171	1702	67	2337	92	14 213	31 340
12RKC	850	12	3325	2480	5207	205	1829	72	2235	88	19 293	42 540
	900	12	3460	2580	5207	205	1829	72	2235	88	19 293	42 540
	1000	12	3550	2650	5207	205	1829	72	2235	88	19 293	42 540
16RKC	850	16	4440	3310	6325	249	1803	71	2311	91	23 864	52 620
	900	16	4650	3470	6325	249	1803	71	2311	91	23 864	52 620
	1000	16	4750	3540	6325	249	1803	71	2311	91	23 864	52 620

Engine type	Speed rpm	No of Cyls	Brake Power		Approx dimensions Length		Width		Height		Approx dry weight	
			kW	hp	mm	in	mm	in	mm	in	kg	lb
6RK215T	850	6	920	1230	2597	102	1480	58	2145	84	6500	14300
	900	6	970	1300	2597	102	1480	58	2145	84	6500	14300
	950	6	1030	1375	2597	102	1480	58	2145	84	6500	14300
	1000	6	1080	1450	2597	102	1480	58	2145	84	6500	14300
8RK215T	850	8	1220	1640	2422	95	1707	67	2600	102*	8000	17600
	900	8	1300	1740	2422	95	1707	67	2600	102	8000	17600
	950	8	1370	1830	2422	95	1707	67	2600	102	8000	17600
	1000	8	1440	1930	2422	95	1707	67	2600	102	8000	17600

Powers for traction duty in accordance with UIC test conditions, weights include oil filter, oil cooler and damper but exclude flywheel.
* height of 8RK215T can be reduced to 2200mm by using alternative turbocharger position.

Engine type	Speed rpm	No of cylinders	Brakepower		Length		Approx dimensions Width		Height		Approx weight of engine	
			hp	kW	mm	in	mm	in	mm	in	kg	lb
6RK270T	850	6	2100	1585	3455	136	1480	58	2330	93	13 300	29 300
	900	6	2170	1620	3455	136	1480	58	2330	92	13 300	29 300
	950	6	2240	1670	3455	136	1480	58	2330	92	13 300	29 300
	1000	6	2305	1720	3455	136	1480	58	2330	92	13 300	29 300
8RK270T	850	8	2800	2090	2870	113	1740	69	2345	92	16 650	36 700
	900	8	3895	2160	2870	113	1740	69	2345	92	16 670	36 700
	950	8	2980	2225	2870	113	1740	69	2345	92	16 650	36 700
	1000	8	3080	2300	2870	113	1740	69	2345	92	16 650	36 700
12RK270T	850	12	4200	3130	3660	144	1830	72	2255	89	21 230	46 800
	900	12	4340	3240	3660	144	1830	72	2255	89	21 230	46 800
	950	12	4480	3340	3660	144	1830	72	2255	89	21 230	46 800
	1000	12	4610	3440	3660	144	1830	72	2255	89	21 230	46 800
16RK270T	850	16	5600	4180	4850	191	1830	72	2255	89	27 300	62 400
	900	16	5790	4320	4850	191	1830	72	2255	89	28 300	62 400
	950	16	5960	4450	4850	191	1830	72	2255	89	28 300	62 400
	1000	16	6160	4600	4850	191	1830	72	2255	89	28 300	62 400

The powers shown are available for traction duty in accordance with UIC Test Conditions: 27°C; charge air cooler water temperature not exceeding 50°C; altitude 110 m a maximum power output of 180 kW/cylinder at 1000 rpm. The versions currently available are six in-line and eight vee.

They feature rugged cast iron crankcases with underslung crankshafts running in unplated aluminium-based bearings. Also featured are individual cylinder heads housing combined unit injectors, integral charge coolers and dual turbochargers.

The firing pressure limit of 172 bar results in an engine with low fuel consumption.

Bore & stroke: 215 x 175 mm
BMEP at max power: 21.7 bar
Max continuous speed: 1000 rpm

RK270 series

The RK270 engine represents the latest stage in the evolutionary development of the well-known RK series of engines and, with a bore of 270 mm (10.63 in) and a stroke of 305 mm (12.00 in), offers higher horsepowers, improved access for maintenance and lower operating costs.

Paxman Diesels Ltd

Paxman Works, Hythe Hill, Colchester, Essex CO1 2HW, England

Telephone: +44 206 575151
Telex: 98151
Telefax: +44 206 577869

First introduced into railway traction in 1930, the Paxman engines in the present range are of compact design while providing maximum accessibility for maintenance. They combine high power-to-weight ratio with the rugged construction necessary for reliable traction service. British Rail's fleet of High Speed Trains (HSTs) is powered by Paxman. Each train-set has two Valenta 12CL engines, over 200 of which have now been supplied and to date the fleet has recorded nearly 12 million running hours. Similar units have been supplied for the XPT train-sets of the State Rail Authority, New South Wales.

Engine type	*Turbo-charged or turbo-charged/ inter-cooled*	*No of cylinders*	*Cont traction rating kW brake (bhp)*	*Engine speed rpm*	*Bmep bar (lbf/in^2)*	*Piston speed m/s (ft/min)*	*Full load fuel con-sumption g/bhp/h (lb/bhp/h)*	*Bore mm (in)*	*Stroke mm (in)*	*Displace-ment litres (in^2)*	*Com-pression ratio*	*Approx dimensions mm (in)* Length	Width	Height	Crank-case centre line height	*Approx dry weight kg (lb)*
Ventura (6CL)	TC/I	6	840 *(1125)*	1500	17.07 *(248)*	10.8 *(2125)*	170 *(0.376)*	197 *(7.75)*	210 *(8.5)*	39.4 *(2405)*	13.0:1	2780 *(63)*	1200 *(56)*	1850 *(70)*	635 *(21)*	4700 *(10 364)*
Ventura 8CL	TC/I	8	1120 *(1000)*	1500	17.07 *(165)*	10.8 *(2125)*	165 *(0.363)*	197 *(7.75)*	210 *(8.5)*	52.6 *(3207)*	13.0:1	2010 *(67)*	1580 *(52.5)*	1850 *(83)*	585 *(23)*	3855 *(8500)*
Ventura 12CL	TC/I	12	1119 *(1500)*	1500	11.4 *(165)*	10.8 *(2125)*	165 *(0.363)*	197 *(7.75)*	210 *(8.5)*	78.9 *(4811)*	13.0:1	2060 *(81)*	1335 *(52.5)*	2010 *(79)*	585 *(23)*	5111 *(11 270)*
Ventura 16CL	TC/I	16	1492 *(2000)*	1500	11.4 *(165)*	10.8 *(2125)*	166 *(0.365)*	197 *(7.75)*	210 *(8.5)*	105.1 *(6415)*	13.0:1	2670 *(105)*	1335 *(52.5)*	2060 *(81)*	585 *(23)*	6789 *(14 970)*
Valenta 6CL	TC/I	6	839 *(1125)*	1500	17 *(247)*	10.8 *(2125)*	170 *(0.376)*	197 *(7.75)*	210 *(8.5)*	39.4 *(2405)*	13.0:1	2673 *(105.25)*	1073 *(42.25)*	1804 *(71)*	635 *(25)*	4730 *(10 430)*
Valenta 8CL	TC/I	8	1119 *(1500)*	1500	17 *(247)*	10.8 *(2125)*	170 *(0.376)*	197 *(7.75)*	210 *(8.5)*	52.6 *(3207)*	13.0:1	1936 *(76.25)*	1460 *(57.5)*	2350 *(92.5)*	740 *(29)*	5057 *(11 150)*
Valenta 12CL	TC/I	12	1679 *(2250)*	1500	17 *(247)*	10.8 *(2125)*	165 *(0.363)*	197 *(7.75)*	210 *(8.5)*	78.9 *(4811)*	13.0:1	2458 *(96.75)*	1460 *(57.5)*	2305 *(90.75)*	740 *(29)*	6735 *(14 850)*
Valenta 16CL	TC/I	16	2238 *(3000)*	1500	17 *(247)*	10.8 *(2125)*	173 *(0.382)*	197 *(7.75)*	210 *(8.5)*	105.1 *(6415)*	13.0:1	2980 *(117.5)*	1460 *(57.5)*	2350 *(92.5)*	740 *(29)*	9010 *(19 870)*
Valenta 18CL	TC/I	18	2522 *(3380)*	1500	17 *(247)*	10.8 *(2125)*	166 *(0.366)*	197 *(7.75)*	210 *(8.5)*	118.3 *(7217)*	13.0:1	3207 *(126)25)*	1460 *(57.5)*	2260 *(89)*	740 *(29)*	9873 *(21 770)*
6SETCAL	TC/I	6	538 *(721)*	1500	18.75 *(272)*	9.5 *(1870)*	158 *(0.348)*	160 *(7)*	190 *(7.5)*	–	13.8:1	1915 *(75.4)*	1120 *(44.1)*	1521 *(59.9)*	543 *(21.4)*	2150 *(4741)*
12SETCAL	TC/I	12	1075 *(1441)*	1500	18.75 *(272)*	9.5 *(1870)*	164 *(0.362)*	160 *(7)*	190 *(7.5)*	–	13.8:1	2638 *(103.9)*	1410 *(55.5)*	1770 *(69.7)*	646 *(25.4)*	4207 *(9276)*
16SETCAL	TC/I	16	1432 *(1920)*	1500	18.75 *(272)*	9.5 *(1870)*	164 *(0.362)*	160 *(7)*	190 *(7.5)*	–	13.8:1	3245 *(127.8)*	1410 *(55.5)*	1770 *(69.7)*	646 *(25.4)*	4930 *(10 871)*

Engine ratings: Continuous traction rating corrected for altitude of 150 m (500 ft), air temperature of 30°C (85°F) and water temperature to intercooler 45°C (113°F).
Dimensions: These are for engines with standard equipment.
Engine weights: These include fuel and lubricating oil filters, oil cooler damper and sump, but exclude flywheel, air filters and mounting. Those for 8, 12 and 16 Ventura include fabricated housing. SE weights do include the flywheel and mounting but not the air filters.

General Motors Corporation

Electro-Motive Division

La Grange, Illinois 60625, USA

The Electro-Motive Division of General Motors first developed the Model 567 diesel engine in 1938 when it began locomotive manfuacture at La Grange, Illinois, USA.

To provide increased horsepower and greater efficiency, the Model 645 engine was introduced in mid-1965. The major change in the Model 645 over the 567 was the increase in cylinder liner bore from 216 mm (8½ in) to 230 mm (9⅙ in), the stroke remaining at 254 mm (10 in).

The turbo-charged 645E3B engine introduced in 1979 and the turbo-charged 645F3 engine introduced in 1981 were a result of the search for increased product reliability, performance, and fuel economy. With increased horsepower and fuel economy these engines could haul more tonnage at the same speed or the same tonnage at a higher speed than their predecessors.

The new 710G series of engines unveiled in 1984 offers increased reliability, better fuel efficiency, and the potential for significantly higher horsepower in the future. The design is an evolutionary development of GM/EMD's turbo-charged, uniflow-scavenged, two-stroke cycle engine. The 16-cylinder 710G is rated conservatively at 3950 hp at 900 rpm for locomotive applications and has a displacement of 710 in^3 per cylinder.

The design of the 710G follows logically from GM/EMD's current production series, the 645F engines. The most recent version of this series, the 645FB, is the result of a succession of improvements to the engine. From 1980 to 1983, for example, the fuel efficiency of the 645F was increased by 6 per cent and the compression ratio from 14.5:1 to 16:1. Greater displacement and an advanced turbo-charger give the 710G the capacity for significant increases in horsepower. It is the product of four years of development at GM/EMD. Total development cost was $60 million; tooling cost alone was $78 million.

Full load fuel consumption of the model 710G3 engine is down 9 per cent from the 1980 model and 3.4 per cent from the 1983 model in the 645 range. Among the ways fuel efficiency has been increased is by reducing parasitic losses. Fuel consumption is further reduced by use of a low 200 rpm idle speed for railroad service.

A major change in the 710G design is greater displacement. The 10 in piston stroke of the predecessor 645FB is increased to 11 in, and this longer stroke at the same bore adds 10 per cent more displacement, from 645 to 710 in^3 per cylinder. This added displacement is a key factor in the 710G's promise of greater horsepower in future models.

The longer stroke and added displacement led to these structural improvements in the engine: Model G crankcase; larger diameter plunger injectors; larger diameter crankshaft; new camshaft; longer cylinder liner; and longer piston and rod assembly. The 710G design also increased the overall dimensions: the new engine is 1⅝ in higher and 4⅝ in longer.

The increase in length is the result of a larger, more efficient turbo-charger. Entry to the turbine was streamlined to improve gas flow. An improved exhaust diffuser also reduces flow restriction. The turbo-charger is deeper to accommodate a larger annulus for a smoother and less restrictive discharge of exhaust gases. This new state-of-the-art G turbo-charger provides a 15 per cent increase in air flow for reduced thermal loading of critical engine components. This higher air flow, in combination with an increased injection rate from the new ⁹⁄₁₆ in plunger injector, accounts for the increase in fuel economy at rated output with no increase in engine mechanical loading.

A key concern in the development of a large displacement engine has been reliability. Throughout the development of the 710G, GM/EMD used advanced laboratory techniques to analyse stress and predict performance. Finite element analysis and comprehensive strain-gauge testing were used extensively.

Model		*16-645FB*	*16-710G*
Bore	in	9.06	9.06
Stroke	in	10	11
Displacement	in^3	645	710
Cylinder spacing	in	16⅝	16⅝
Bank angle		45	45
Compression ratio		16.0:1	16.0:1
Engine speed	rpm	950	900
bhp		3800	4100

GMD

Grandes Motores Diesel SA
Suipacha 1109, 2° and 5° floors, 1008 Buenos Aires, Argentina

Telephone: +541 313 0870/1296/0927/0900
Telex: 25175 cat mg ar
Telefax: +541 331 5491

Works: Grandes Motores Diesel S.A. Industrial Plant, Ruta 9, Km. 695 (5123) Ferreyra–Córdoba

Telephone: +5451 97 2425/2501/2214/2237
Telex: 51592 gmd ar
Telefax: +5451 97 2212

President: Dr Edgardo Héctor Iriarte
Vice-President: Sr Marcos Garfunkel
General Manager: Sr Hugo Norberto Castagnasso
Commercial Director: Ing Enrique Walter Beles

Group Companies: Materfer
CAT Centro de Actividades Termomecánicas-
INGESA Industrias de Generación de Energía Electromecánica-
AGRITEC Tractores Fiat

Products: GMD manufactures the ALCO 251 engine under General Electric Inc license. GMD's plant is equipped with the latest technology in horizontal machining centres, computer-controlled lathes, digital-controlled copying milling machines. A complete heat-treatment facility includes induction hardening, carburising, gas and salt bath nitriding, furnace hardening/annealing and shot blast. Control equipment includes a specially-designed metrology room, destructive lab with X-ray, gear profile control machine, and the most advanced CMM, besides computerised engine test-beds.

Together with CAT, the company manufactures spares for Fiat GMT engines, and in 1989/90 had contracts for: 30 ALCO 251C (rebuilding from 251B); 36 ALCO 251C (mounted in ALCO RS16); 24 ALCO 251D (mounted in ALCO RS35); 40 ALCO 251C (mounted in ALCO RS16).

GMT
Grandi Motori Division
Fincantieri-Cantieri Navali Italiani SpA

PO Box 497, 34100 Trieste, Italy

Telephone: +39 40 8991
Telex: 462074/5 fincgm i

Products: Grandi Motori Division of Fincantieri builds diesel engines for railway traction, marine and industrial applications. For rail traction its locomotive engine range includes series A210 and BL230 from 620 to 4400 kW.

Series A210
Type: 4-stroke, turbo-charged, with charge air cooling.
Cylinders: Bore 210 mm. Stroke 230 mm.

The company has completed supply of 95 12-cylinder engines of Type A210 for the Italian State Railways Class D445 locomotives.

Series BL230
Type: 4-stroke, turbo-charged, with charge air cooling.
Cylinders: Bore 230 mm. Stroke 310 mm.

Other main characteristics, common to the two types of engine, are as follows:
Turbo-charging: Achieved by means of exhaust gas turbo-blowers operating with pulse systems. The air is then cooled in suitable coolers.
Fuel injection pumps: Of plunger type with a spiral groove. The fuel injection is controlled by rotating the plunger by means of a transversal rack.
Fuel: Gas oil.

A210 engine

Version	Cylinder	Output kW (UIC)	Weight kg	Length mm	Width mm	Height mm
A 210.4	4 V	620	4400	1700	1770	1570
A 210.6	6 V	930	5500	2000	1770	1570
A 210.8	8 V	1240	7000	2250	1820	1930
A 210.12	12 V	1860	9800	2835	1820	2020
A 210.16	16 V	2480	12 00	3415	1820	1980
A 210.20	20 V	3100	14 800	4050	1820	2020

Length: at crankshaft *Width:* overall *Height:* from underside of feet

Engine speed: 1500 rpm
Fuel consumption: 215 g/kW/h

BL230 engine

Version	Cylinder	Output kW (UIC) at 1050 rpm	Output kW (UIC) at 1200 rpm	Weight kg	Length mm	Width mm	Height mm
BL 230.4	4 L	810	880	5900	2710	1200	1960
BL 230.6	6 L	1215	1320	8000	3335	1200	1960
BL 230.8	8 V	1620	1760	10 500	3160	1740	2170
BL 230.12	12 V	2430	2640	14 700	4204	1740	2200
BL 230.16	16 V	3240	3520	18 700	4536	1740	2250
BL 230.20	20 V	4050	4400	24 500	5536	1740	2380

Lubrication: Force fed by directly-driven gear pump.
Cooling: Fresh water fed by two centrifugal pumps, one for the engine, one for the oil and air cooling system.

Gotha
Getriebewerk Gotha

Karl-Liebknecht-Strasse 26, 5800 Gotha, German Democratic Republic

Products: Axle gearings for diesel- and electrically-powered vehicles.

Hidromecanica
Mecanoexportimport supplier

Hidromecanica Works, 78 Boulevard Lenin, 2200 Brasov, Romania

Telephone: +40 21 34082
Telex: 61279

Products: Hydraulic transmissions.

Hitachi
Hitachi Ltd

6 Kanda Suragadai, 4-chome, Chiyoda-ku, Tokyo 101, Japan

Telephone: +81 3 258 2111
Telex: 22395; 22432; 24491; 26385 hitachi

Products: Complete control equipment, electric transmissions and hydraulic transmissions.

Hunslet
Hunslet Precision Engineering Ltd

Hunslet Engine works, Leeds LS10 1BT, England

Telephone: +44 532 432261
Telex: 55237

Products: Main transmission gears, forward and reverse and final drives; axle drive units for diesel-mechanical; mechanical change-speed, hydraulic and hydro-mechanical transmissions of up to 1000 hp; gearing for electrical transmissions; gears and gearboxes.

Hurth
Carl Hurth Maschinen-und Zahnradfabrik

Holzstrasse 19, 8000 Munich 5, Federal Republic of Germany

Telephone: +49 89 23 70 21
Telex: 5216021

Products: Jackshaft gears; hollow shaft and bevel gear axle drive units; cardanic axle couplings; mechanical change-speed gears; alternate-speed and reverse-reduction gears of up to 500–600 hp.

MANUFACTURERS / Diesel engines and transmission systems

Isotta Fraschini Motori SpA
Via Milano 7, Saronno 21047, Italy

Telephone: +39 2 960 3251/2/3
Telex: 332403

Products: Hydraulic and mechanical transmissions for locomotives and railcars. Axle drives for electric and diesel-powered vehicles. Diesel engines for rail and road traction, marine and industrial applications. For rail traction the locomotive engine range includes: series ID 38 from 200 to 400 hp and series ID 36 from 300 to 2700 hp.

ID 38 series
Type: 6 cylinders, 90° Vee, 4-stroke, direct injection, water cooled.
Cylinders: Bore 128 mm. Stroke 126 mm. Swept volume 1.62 litres per cylinder. The output is based on UIC specifications.

ID 36 series
Type: 6, 8, 12 and 16 cylinders, 90° Vee, 4-stroke, direct injection, water cooled.
Cylinders: Bore 170 mm. Stroke 1700 mm. Swept volume 3.858 litres per cylinder.
The output is based on UIC specifications. Engine speed maximum 1900 rpm. Engine type ID 36/38 V can be supplied with cylinders opposed for railcar applications.

		ID 38 series		ID 36 series							
Model		N6V	SS6V	N6V	SS6V	N8V	SS8V	N12V	SS12V	N16V	SS16V
No of cylinders		6	6	6	6	8	8	12	12	16	16
Turbo-charged		–	Yes	–	Yes	–	Yes	–	Yes	–	Yes
Charge air cooled		–	Yes	–	Yes	–	Yes	–	Yes	–	Yes
bhp (UIC)		200	400	300	640	400	850	600	1285	800	2700
Engine speed	rpm	2800	2800	1650	1650	1650	1650	1650	1650	1650	1900
Weight (dry)	lb	1655	1766	3780	4000	5115	5335	7115	7445	–	9277
	(kg)	(750)	(800)	(1700)	(1800)	(2300)	(2400)	(3200)	(3350)		(4200)
Length max	in	39.37	42.91	–	53.15	–	63	–	88.55	–	118.11
	(mm)	(1000)	(1090)		(1350)		(1600)		(2250)		(3000)
Width max	in	35.43	35.43	–	47.24	–	47.24	–	47.24	–	51.18
	(mm)	(900)	(900)		(1200)		(1200)		(1200)		(1300)
Height max	in	37	37	–	51.57	–	49.60	–	58.26	–	70.86
	(mm)	(940)	(940)		(1310)		(1260)		(1480)		(1800)
Fuel consumption		Normally aspirated and turbo-charged = 170 g/hp/h									
All models		Turbo-charged and intercooled = 165 g/hp/h									

N = Naturally aspirated, SS = Turbo-charged and intercooled.

JW
Jenbacher Werke AG
6200 Jenbach, Austria

Telephone: +43 5244 2291 0
Telex: 953756 7

Products: Formed in 1946, this company builds diesel locomotives and diesel engines for industrial and marine purposes up to 3000 hp.

LM Series
Type: 6-, 8- and 12-cylinder 90° Vee, 2-stroke, water cooled, direct injection.
Cylinders: Bore 240 mm. Stroke 250 mm. Swept volume 11.3 litres per cylinder. Cast iron with centrifugally cast wet cylinder liners. Individual cylinder heads.
Fuel injector: Gear-driven from flywheel end of crankshaft.
Scavenge blower: Centrifugal type driven from flywheel end of crankshaft.
Lubrication: Gear pump.
Starting: Electric or compressed air.

Model		LM750	LM1000	LM1500
No of cylinders		6	8	12
Output	kW	768	1025	1538
Speed	rpm	1000	1000	1000
Weight (dry)	kg	7400	8900	11 800
Length	mm	2502	2862	3672
Width	mm	1715	1715	1715
Height	mm	2150	2150	2150
Fuel consumption	g/kWh	215	215	215

Kaelble-Gmeinder
Kaelble-Gmeinder GmbH

PO Box 1260, 6950 Mosbach/Baden, Federal Republic of Germany

Telephone: +49 6261 806-0
Telex: 04 66111
Telefax: +49 6261 806-60

Products: Axle drives; gears; alternate-speed and reduction gears for transmissions with jackshaft or cardan shaft drives for motive power transmission applications in locomotives, rapid transit, urban and underground railway vehicles, tramways and special railway vehicles.

KHD Deutz
KHD Antriebs-und Luftfahrttechnik GmbH

PO Box 80 05 09, 5000 Cologne 80, Federal Republic of Germany

Under the tradename KHD Deutz, air-cooled diesel engines are offered in the power range from 2.3 kW (3.1 hp) to 441 kW (600 hp). Some 2 million of these engines are operating successfully all over the world.

As a result of comprehensive development of the FL 413 engines a new engine series has been produced in the upper power range with the type designation FL 513. It covers finely stepped power requirements from 86 kW (117 hp) to 441 kW (600 hp).

Model		F6L513[3]	F8L513	F10L513	F12L513[3]	BF6L513R	BF6L513RC	BF8L513	BF8L513C	BF8L513CP	BF10L513	BF12L513	BF12L513C	BF12L513CP
No of cylinders		6V	8V	10V	12V	6 in-line	6 in-line	8V	8V	8V	10V	12V	12V	12V
Turbo-charged		–	–	–	Yes	Yes	Yes	Yes	Yes	Yes	Yes	Yes	Yes	Yes
Charge air cooled		–	–	–	–	–	Yes	–	Yes	Yes	–	–	Yes	Yes
Output	kW	141	188	235	282	177	210	235	265	294	294	353	386	441
	(hp)	(192)	(256)	(320)	(383)	(241)	(286)	(320)	(360)	(400)	(400)	(480)	(525)	(600)
Engine speed	rpm	2300	2300	2300	2300	2300	2300	2300	2300	2300	2300	2300	2300	2300
Length[1]	mm	885	1050	1216	1380	1390	1390	1047	[3]	[3]	1215	1380	1380	[3]
Width	mm	1038	1038	1038	1038	790	830	1138	[3]	[3]	1138	1192	1192	[3]
Height	mm	860	860	999	1007	1034	1036	1042	[3]	[3]	1055	1087	1112	[3]
Weight[2]	kg	665	835	995	1130	865	895	920	[3]	[3]	1140	1250	1300	[3]

[1] to reference surface
[2] including cooling system
[3] for queries, consult head-office

Kim Hotstart
Kim Hotstart Manufacturing Inc

PO Box 42, East 5724 Broadway, Spokane, Washington 99210, USA

Telephone: +1 509 534 6171
Telefax: +1 509 534 4216

Vice-President and General Manager: Rick Robinson
Director, Sales and Marketing: John R Schratz

Manager, Industrial Products: Bill Harnish

Products: Layover protection systems for diesel engines, coolant only; coolant and lube oil; and lube oil, coolant and diesel fuel.

Diesel engines and transmission systems / **MANUFACTURERS** 163

Kolomna
Kolomensky Plant Manufacturing Association

Partisan Street, Kolomna 140408, USSR

Telephone: +7 3-81-85
Telex: 846517/8 vympel

General Manager: M E Kiselshtein
Engineer-in-Chief: V A Berezhkov
Commercial Manager: N S Churashkin

Products: D49 series of diesel locomotive engines. Type: 4-stroke, turbocharged; 8, 12, 16, 20 cylinders in V-versions.
The D49 engine is built on a modular concept basis providing high manufacturing, operation and maintenance efficiency.
The main modules are:
Cast-welded cylinder block: the crankcase portion of the cylinder block is formed by a series of components common to all units depending on the number of cylinders;
Cylinder set (including cylinder head with an underslung cylinder liner with piston and connecting rod attached);
Tray (housing) with a camshaft and drive unit for valves of both cylinder rows;
Drive units of valve timing and attached devices formed by a box-like double-walled housing with built-in gear mechanisms mounted on cylinder block ends;
Turbocharger.

Engine type	Output kW	Output hp	Length	Width	Height	Diesel engine Weight, kg	Power unit Weight, kg	Type of locomotive to which fitted in USSR
8 VD49	590–1620	800–2200	3370	1665	2330	10070	—	TGM 6V, TGM 8
12 VD49	1100–2650	1500–3600	5425	1920	3030	14392	22135*	2TE 116, TEM 7A
16 VD49	1840–3520	2500–4800	6740	2020	3030	17766	27240*	2TE 116, 2TE 121, TEP 70
20 VD49	3700–4750	5000–6500	8461	2125	3275	20879	34425*	2TE 136, TEP 80

Output, specific fuel consumption and weight values are for ISO standard reference conditions (3040/I).
* Weight values are for power units including diesel engine, generator, devices attached to the engine and base frame.

D49 diesel locomotive engines
Specification:
Bore, mm 260
Stroke, mm 260
Speed, $\min^{-1}$ 750–1000
Mean effective pressure, MPa 1.1–1.96
Mean piston speed, m/s 6.8–8.6
Specific fuel consumption, g/kW.h 190

L & M Radiator, Inc
1414 East 37th Street, Hibbing, Minnesota 55746, USA

Telephone: +1 218 263 8993
Telex: 29-4448

President: Alex Chisholm
Vice President: Richard Braun

Principal subsidiaries
L & M Radiator, Inc, Texas
L & M Radiator, Ltd, Winnipeg, Manitoba, Canada
L y M de Mexico
L & M Radiator Pty Ltd, Australia; and South Africa

Products: Radiators and radiator cores.

MaK
Krupp MaK Maschinenbau GmbH Kiel
PO Box 9009, 2300 Kiel 17, Federal Republic of Germany

Telephone: +49 431 3811
Telex: 02 99877 mak d
Telefax: +49 431 381 2193

Directors:
Dr-Ing M Link
H O Brockmeier
Dr-Ing U Schaller
Dr rer pol J Hollunder

Products: Axle drives for locomotives. Four-stroke diesel engines. For rail traction the company offers the Series M 282 engine in 6, 8 and 12 cylinder form, in a power range from 1000 to 2650 kW.

Series M 282
The M 282 rail traction engine is the result of a continuous search for product improvement. It is a medium-speed engine with high performance and extended overhaul periods. This engine has been in operation with Indian Railways since 1968 and is being produced under licence in Indian's Chittaranjan locomotive Works. The engine is also in service with many private railways in Germany, Luxembourg and Italy, as well as with the German Federal Railway (DB) since 1968. In 1986 it successfully completed the Diesel Engine Type Approval Test of British Railways.

Constructional features: Closed engine housing with hanging bearings and underhung sump. Main and big-end bearings of the bronze-lined steel shell type, with lead-tin bearing surface. The bearings can be exchanged without removing the crankshaft.
Fuel injection: Bosch injectors with individual Bosch pumps.
Supercharger: Exhaust gas turbo-blower, ASEA Brown Boveri.
Starting: Compressed air.
Mounting: Elastic suspension by metal bonded rubber elements.

Model		6 M 282	8 M 282	12 M 282
No of cylinders		6 in line	8 in line	12 in V
Turbo-charger		Yes	Yes	Yes
Cooling system		single circuit	single circuit	single or double circuit
Continuous power (UIC)	kW	1200	1600	2650
Speed	rpm	1000	1000	1000
Max bmep	bar	18.96	18.96	20.93
Max piston speed	m/s	9.33	9.33	9.33
Bore	mm	240	240	240
Stroke	mm	280	280	280
Weight, dry	tonnes	7.8	9.4	12
Fuel consumption	g/kW/h	197	195	195
Lube oil consumption	g/kW/h	1.4–2	1.4–2	1.4–2

Mirrlees
Mirrlees Blackstone (Stamford) Ltd
(a Hawker Siddeley Company)

Ryhall Road, Stamford, Lincolnshire PE9 1UH, England

Telephone: +44 780 64641
Telex: 32234
Telefax: +44 780 65850

The MB 190 is a high-reliability engine designed for heavy-duty operation with long periods between overhauls. An efficient thermodynamic cycle ensures low fuel consumptions. Built in 6 and 8 cylinders in-line with 12 and 16 cylinders Vee-form, all engines in the range are turbo-charged and intercooled.
A cost effective design, the ESL Mk 2 sets new standards of accessibility for maintenance, reliability in service and economy of operation. A 45° Vee angle results in a very compact engine with clean lines.

MB190 Bore 190 mm × stroke 210 mm, bmep 20.0 bar

Engine type	Brake power kW 1200 rpm	hp 1200 rpm	Brake power kW 1500 rpm	hp 1500 rpm	Weight kg
6MB190	716	960	895	1200	8230
8MB190	955	1280	1194	1600	10 290
12MB190	1432	1920	1790	2400	11 900
16MB190	1910	2560	2387	3200	14 880

ESL Mk 2 Bore 222 mm × stroke 292 mm, mbep 19.7 bar

Engine type	Brake power kW 900 rpm	hp 900 rpm	Brake power kW 1000 rpm	hp 1000 rpm	Weight kg
ESL12 Mk 2	2060	2700	2235	3000	16 000
ESL16 Mk 2	2685	3600	2985	4000	19 740

Mirrlees Blackstone (Stockport) Ltd
(a Hawker Siddeley Company)

Hazel Grove, Stockport SK7 5AH, England

Telephone: +44 61 483 1000
Telex: 667314
Telefax: +44 61 487 1465

164 MANUFACTURERS / Diesel engines and transmission systems

Modern techniques have been used in design and production to produce an engine which maintains high specific outputs in concert with acceptable operating limits. High cylinder pressures ensure an efficient thermodynamic cycle with attendant low fuel consumptions. All engines are turbo-charged and intercooled.

MB272 Bore 275 mm {h5} × {h7} stroke 305 mm, mbep 19.1 bar

Engine type	Brake power kW	900 rpm hp	Brake power kW	1000 rpm hp	Weight kg
6MB275	1575	2112	1750	2345	20 500
8MB272	2070	2775	2300	3085	24 500

Möes
Moteurs Möes SA
62 rue de Huy, 4370 Waremme, Belgium

Products: Diesel-electric generator sets up to 1000 kVA.

MPM
MPM-Meccanica Padana Monteverde SpA

Via Penghe, Caselle di Selvazzano, 35030 Padua, Italy

Telephone: +39 49 8975599
Telex: 430320 mpm pd i
Telefax: +39 49 8975598

Directors: Ing Vittorio Rasera
Marino Battini
Ing Salvatori Basile

Product Manager: Gianni Cappellato

Parent company: ZF Friedrichshafen

Products: Traction gears, special gearboxes, special axle drive units. MPM is staffed and equipped to design and manufacture complete transmissions for rail vehicles with case-hardened ground gears and profile correction for long life and smooth running.

The company has developed computer programmes for calculation and projecting custom-engineered gears and gear drives. Transmissions can also be tested under operating conditions on a simulator using a method in which torque and speed can be varied independently while the transmission is running.

Recent contracts for Italian State Railways include: double reduction Type MPM PFA 18 DR axle drives for the Class DE 245 locomotives; bevel gears for ETR 450 high-speed trains; traction gears for ETR-Y-500 high-speed power cars; and gears for Class E633, E652 and E656 locomotives.

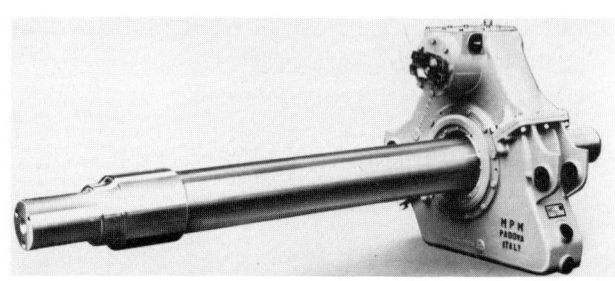

MPM axle drive unit

MPM double-reduction drive unit

MTU
Motoren-und Turbinen-Union Friedrichshafen GmbH
PO Box 2040, Olgastrasse 75, Friedrichshafen 1, Federal Republic of Germany

Telephone: +49 7541 29 1
Telex: 0734 280-0 mtd
Telefax: +49 7541 292247

MTU produces diesel engines for marine propulsion, railroad locomotives, electric power generation and heavy vehicular applications. To date, more than 53 000 MTU diesels have come off the assembly line, of which over 8500 units rated at some 12 million kW (16 million hp) have been applied to railroad shunting and main line service with hydraulic or electric power transmissions. By virtue of their compactness and favourable power/volume ratios, MTU engines also qualify for electric power generation to provide train heating and air conditioning, as well as for locomotive repowering.

MTU diesels are liquid-cooled, direct injection, four-stroke engines with turbo-charging and charge air cooling. Salient engine characteristics are: low weight; operating economy, low fuel consumption; compact design; and integrated, easily accessible accessory equipment for convenience in maintenance.

MTU Series 183 129-580 kW diesel engine

Rail traction applications

Engine	Speed rpm	Output (UIC) kW	Output (UIC) hp	Weight kg	Length mm	Width mm	Height mm
6R 099* AZ11	2400	96	131	440	1015	630	920
6R 099* TA11	2400	126	171	450	1015	730	920
6R 099* TE11	2400	152	207	495	1015	730	915
6R 183* AA12H**	1800	162	220	820	1315	1110	670
6R 183* TA12H**	1800	204	277	840	1315	1300	635

Diesel engines and transmission systems / **MANUFACTURERS**   165

Rail traction applications continued

Engine	Speed rpm	Output (UIC) kW	Output (UIC) hp	Weight kg	Length mm	Width mm	Height mm
8V 183* TA11	1800	228	310	880	1250	1090	1045
8V 183* TA12	1800	267	363	930	1250	1090	1045
8V 183* TE12	1800	327	445	950	1330	1070	1145
12V 183* TA12	1800	400	544	1 300	1430	1215	1065
12V 183* TE12	1800	485	660	1 380	1440	1215	1175
12V 183* TD12	1800	580	789	1 380	1440	1215	1175
8V 396 TC14	1800	785	1065	2 840	2140	1530	1530
12V 396 TC14	1800	1180	1600	3 850	2600	1530	1700
16V 393 TC14	1800	1570	2135	4 950	3060	1530	1750
8V 396 TE14	1800	920	1250	3 010	2140	1530	1530
12V 396 TE14	1800	1380	1875	4 020	2600	1530	1700
16V 396 TE14	1800	1840	2500	5 000	3060	1530	1750
12V 956 TB12	1500	2460	3350	10 900	3310	1600	2290
16V 956 TB12	1500	3280	4460	13 710	4000	1600	2315
20V 956 TB12	1500	4100	5580	16 280	4690	1600	2335
12V 1163 TB12	1200	2460	3350	11 400	3310	1660	2340
16V 1163 TB12	1200	3280	4460	14 350	4000	1660	2365
20V 1163 TB12	1200	4100	5580	17 050	4690	1660	2385

* MTU Series 099 and 183, based on Mercedes-Benz Series 300 and 400
** In-line engine, horizontal

Train electric power supply applications

Engine	Speed rpm	Output (UIC) kW	Output (UIC) hp	Weight kg	Length mm	Width mm	Height mm
6R 099* AZ11	1500	60	82	440	1015	630	920
	1800	72	98				
6R 099* TA11	1500	84	114	450	1015	730	920
	1800	100	136				
6R 099* TE11	1500	94	128	495	1015	730	915
	1800	113	154				
6R 183* AA12	1500	129	175	815	1325	820	1165
	1800	152	207				
6R 183* TA12	1500	180	245	835	1325	820	1165
	1800	195	265				
8V 183* TA11	1500	206	280	880	1250	1090	1045
	1800	229	311				
8V 183* TA12	1500	240	326	930	1250	1090	1045
	1800	255	347				
8V 183* TE12	1500	255	347	950	1330	1070	1145
	1800	295	401				
12V 183* TA12	1500	360	490	1300	1430	1215	1065
	1800	382	520				
12V 183* TE12	1500	407	554	1380	1440	1215	1175

NICO
Niigata Converter Co Ltd

Asano Sinjuku Building, 27-9, Sendagaya 5-chome, Shibuya-ku, Tokyo 151, Japan

Telephone: +81 3 354 7111
Telex: 232 3105 nicotoj
Telefax: +81 3 341 5365

Main works
Kamo plant: Gejo 405, Kamo, Niigata 159-13
Omiya plant: 405-3, Yoshinocho 1-chome, Omiya, Saitama 330

President: R Sakauchi
Managing Director: T Iwata
Directors, Domestic Sales: S Kobayashi
  Y Kasuga
Director, Sales Engineering: K Kobayashi
Director, International Operations: T Honda

Principal subsidiary company:
NICO Transmission (Singapore) Pte Ltd
301 Jurong Town Hall Road, Singapore 2260

Telephone: +65 562 1100
Telex: 25983 rs
Telefax: +65 563 6941

Products: Single-stage torque converters, three-stage torque converters, power-shift transmissions, hydraulic couplings for engines rated from 50 to 1400 hp.
 Recent products include:
Model TACN-22-1600 two-speed forward, two-speed reverse power-shift transmission with Type 8 single-stage torque converter for 330 hp diesel railcars;
Model DW 14 two-speed forward, two-speed reverse power-shift transmission with three-stage torque converter for 330 hp express diesel railcars.

Niigata
Niigata Engineering Co Ltd

4-1 Kasumigaseki 1, Chiyoda-ku, Tokyo, Japan

Founded in 1895, one of Japan's leading engineering manufacturers, Niigata builds diesel engines for marine and industrial use up to 29 700 hp and for rail traction up to 2000 hp.

DMPP81Z
Type: 16-cylinder Vee, water cooled, 4-stroke turbo-charged and charge air cooled.
Cylinders: Bore 180 mm. Stroke 200 mm. Swept volume 5.09 litres per cylinder.

DMF31ZN
Type: 6-cylinder vertical in-line, water cooled, 4-stroke turbo-charged and charge air cooled.

Cylinders: Bore 180 mm. Stroke 200 mm. Swept volume 5.09 litres per cylinder.

General specifications for both models
Cylinders: Monobloc cast iron cylinder block and crankcase, removable cast iron liners with integral water jacket. Cast iron cylinder heads secured by studs.
Fuel injection: Bosch type injectors and Bosch type pump.
Turbo-charger: Niigata-Napier type turbo-blower. Two for DMP81Z, one for DMF31SDI.
Lubrication: Forced feed.
Starting: Electric starter.

Model		DMP81Z	DMF31SDI
Turbo-charged		Yes	Yes
Charge air cooled		Yes	Yes
No of cylinders		16V	6
Power rating (max)	hp	2000	650
Engine speed	rpm	1500	1500
Bmep (max)	lb/in^2	209	181
	(kg/cm^2)	(14.73)	(12.178)
Piston speed	ft/min	1970	1970
	(m/s)	(10)	(10)
Weight (dry)	lb	19 600	6940
	(kg)	(8900)	(3150)
Length	in	170	109.3
	(mm)	(4322)	(2775)
Width	in	74	54.2
	(mm)	(1880)	(1376)
Height	in	78	69.4
	(mm)	(1978)	(1762)
Fuel consumption	lb/hp/h	0.370	0.352
	(g/hp/h)	(168)	(160)

MANUFACTURERS / Diesel engines and transmission systems

Paulstra Hutchinson
Paulstra Hutchinson
Railway Department

61 rue Marius Aufan, 92305 Levallois-Perret, France

Telephone: +33 1 47 57 31 13
Telex: 613990 antiv f
Telefax: +33 1 47 57 44 20

Products: Tetraflex coupling of 4000 mN torque capacity, part of a new family of power transmission couplings developed by Paulstra. Used between electric motors and gearboxes, they are characterised by a reduced axial thickness and a radial misalignment capacity of several mm. The torque range available is between 2000 and 8000 mN with a maximum speed of 3500 to 3000 rpm.

Perkins Engines
Perkins Group Ltd

Eastfield, Peterborough, Cambridgeshire PE1 5NA, England

Telephone: +44 733 67474
Telex: 32501 perken g
Telefax: +44 733 582240

Perkins Engines was founded in 1932 and manufactures high-performance diesel engines for all applications from 30 to 1200 bhp. It has made major advances in diesel engine design, and has established a high reputation for the quality and reliability of its engines. Since 1932, more than 10 million units have been built and half of them remain in current service.

Perkins has been passing through its most intensive period of new product launches since it was founded. New ranges include the 2-litre 500 Series, and the four- and six-cylinder 1000 Series incorporating the revolutionary Quadram combustion system. Latest ranges from Perkins Engines (Shrewsbury), where the company builds its larger engines, are the 2000 Series of six-cylinder engines and the eight- and twelve-cylinder Vee-configuration 3000 Series. Included in the 2000 Series range is the 2006-TWH, a horizontal engine capable of powering 145 km/h railcars. This engine, developing between 186 kW (250 bhp) at 1900 rpm and 260 kW (350 bhp) at 2100 rpm, has been designed for high-speed intercity and urban operations by cars carrying around 80 passengers. The 2006-TWH has passed the toughest test for diesel traction in the world, British Rail's new Type Test. It has been selected by British Rail to power the second generation Class 158 railcars and the new Class 165 railcars.

Engine	Turbo-charged	No of cylinders	Bore in (mm)	Stroke in (mm)	Swept volume in³ (litres)	Continuous rating to BS 5514:1982 bhp (kW)	eng speed rpm	Max intermittent rating to BS AU 141a:1971 bhp (kW)	eng speed rpm	Max gross torque lb/ft (Nm)	Engine speed rpm	Typical bare engine dimensions Length in (mm)	Width in (mm)	Height in (mm)	Bare engine dry weight lb (kg)
D3.152	No	3	3.6 (91.4)	5.0 (127.0)	152.7 (2.5)	34.0 (25.5)	1800	47.0 (35.0)	2250	128.0 (173.0)	1250	24.3 (616.7)	20.0 (508.9)	31.4 (798.1)	463 (210)
3.1524	No	3	3.6 (91.4)	5.0 (127.0)	152.7 (2.5)	39.0 (29.1)	1800	52.0 (39.0)	2500	128.0 (173.0)	1600	24.3 (616.7)	20.0 (508.9)	31.4 (798.1)	463 (210)
T3.1524	Yes	3	3.6 (91.4)	5.0 (127.0)	152.7 (2.5)	–	–	55.0 (41.0)	2250	140.0 (190.0)	1500	24.6 (625.4)	22.8 (579.4)	30.9 (783.8)	478 (217)
4.2032	No	4	3.6 (91.4)	5.0 (127.0)	203.6 (3.3)	–	–	60.0 (44.5)	2600	156.0 (212.0)	1500	28.2 (717.2)	19.5 (494.9)	29.4 (746.4)	520 (236)
4.236	No	4	3.9 (98.4)	5.0 (127.0)	235.9 (3.9)	57.0 (42.7)	1800	81.0 (60.5)	2600	197.0 (267.0)	1300	27.0 (685.2)	21.9 (556.3)	31.3 (797.4)	565 (257)
T4.236	Yes	4	3.9 (98.4)	5.0 (127.0)	235.9 (3.9)	86.0 (64.0)	1800	102.0 (76.0)	2600	251.0 (340.0)	1600	27.5 (698.9)	29.0 (735.0)	30.7 (779.0)	607 (276)
6.3544	No	6	3.9 (98.4)	5.0 (127.0)	354 (5.8)	77.5 (57.8)	1800	122.0 (91.0)	2600	283.0 (384.0)	1400	36.2 (919.7)	23.0 (584.0)	33.0 (837.8)	960 (435)
T6.3544	Yes	6	3.9 (98.4)	5.0 (127.0)	354 (5.8)	122.0 (91.0)	1800	145.0 (108.0)	2600	346.0 (469.0)	1600	35.5 (901.0)	29.3 (743.9)	31.1 (788.2)	981 (445)
T6.3544cc (water/air intercooled)	Yes	6	3.9 (98.4)	5.0 (127.0)	354 (5.8)	–	–	158.0 (118.0)	2400	391.0 (530.0)	1600	37.2 (944.0)	24.3 (743.1)	31.5 (801)	1001 (445)
TV8.540	Yes	8	4.3 (108.0)	4.8 (120.7)	539 (8.8)	168.0 (125.0)	1800	240.0 (179.0)	2600	570.0 (774.0)	1800	42.6 (1081.5)	32.6 (827.6)	32.6 (827.6)	1525 (692)
1004-4	No	4	3.94 (100)	5.0 (127)	243 (4.0)	–	–	90 (67)	2600	215 (291)	1500	28.0 (711)	24.0 (610)	30.2 (767)	600 (273)
1004-4T	Yes	4	3.94 (100)	5.0 (127)	243 (4.0)	–	–	113 (84)	2600	264 (358)	1600	28.0 (711)	24.0 (610)	30.2 (767)	614 (279)
1006-6	No	6	3.94 (100)	5.0 (127)	365 (6.0)	–	–	133 (99)	2600	324 (440)	1400	37.2 (944)	24.0 (610)	30.7 (780)	902 (410)
1006-6T	Yes	6	3.94 (100)	5.0 (127)	365 (6.0)	119 (89)	1500	165 (123)	2600	402 (545)	1600	37.2 (944)	26.7 (677)	30.7 (780)	922 (419)
1006-6TW (water/air intercooled)	Yes	6	3.94 (100)	5.0 (127)	365 (6.0)	–	–	125 (131.5)	2600	418 (567)	1600	37.2 (944)	26.7 (677)	30.7 (780)	946 (430)
2006-12T1	Yes	6	5.125 (130.2)	6 (152.4)	742.6 (12.17)	236 (176)	1800	270 (201)	2100	872.0 (1190.0)	1000	61.5 (1563)	27.1 (715)	42.5 (1123)	2300 (1050)
2006-12T2	Yes	6	5.125 (130.2)	6 (152.4)	742.6 (12.17)	284 (212)	1800	320 (239)	2100	1090.0 (1480.0)	1100	61.5 (1563)	27.1 (715)	42.5 (1123)	2300 (1050)
2006-12TW	Yes	6	5.125 (130.2)	6 (152.4)	742.6 (12.17)	315 (235)	1800	354 (264)	2100	1180.0 (1600.0)	1100	61.5 (1563)	29.3 (775)	41.3 (1091)	2350 (1070)
2006-TA	Yes	6	5.125 (130.2)	6 (152.4)	742.6 (12.17)	350 (261)	1800	400 (298)	2100	1400.0 (1600.0)	1000	61.5 (1563)	27.1 (715)	42.5 (1123)	2300 (1050)
3008-17T	Yes	8	5.31 (135)	5.98 (152)	1062 (17.4)	393 (293)	1800	450 (336)	2100	1295.0 (1756.0)	1300	44.9 (1141)	42.3 (1075)	48.4 (1230)	2950 (1340)
3008-17TW (intercooled)	Yes	8	5.31 (135)	5.98 (152)	1062 (17.4)	518 (387)	1800	550 (410)	2100	1530.0 (2074.0)	1300	44.9 (1141)	45.7 (1160)	50.0 (1272)	3050 (1390)
3008-17TA (intercooled)	Yes	8	5.31 (135)	5.98 (152)	1062 (17.4)	566 (422)	1800	600 (448)	2100	1785.0 (2420.0)	1300	44.9 (1141)	45.7 (1160)	48.1 (1340)	2950 (1340)
3012-26TW1 (intercooled)	Yes	12	5.31 (135)	5.98 (152)	1593 (26.1)	660 (492)	1800	700 (522)	2100	1960.0 (2657.0)	1500	59.5 (1511)	50.4 (1280)	53.9 (1369)	4250 (1930)
3012-26TW (intercooled)	Yes	12	5.31 (135)	5.98 (152)	1593 (26.1)	754 (567)	1800	800 (597)	2100	2240.0 (3037.0)	1500	59.5 (1511)	50.4 (1280)	53.9 (1369)	4250 (1930)
3012-26TA (intercooled)	Yes	12	5.31 (135)	5.98 (152)	1593 (26.1)	848 (633)	1800	900 (671)	2100	2520.0 (3417.0)	1500	59.5 (1511)	50.4 (1280)	51.2 (1300)	4186 (1900)
Horizontal Engine															
2006-TWH	Yes	6	5.125 (130.2)	6 (152.4)	742.6 (12.17)	–	–	350.0 (261.0)	2100	1150.0 (1560.0)	1100	75.5 (1918)	68.3 (1735)	24.2 (615)	2730 (1240)

Scania
Saab-Scania AB, Scania Division

151 87 Södertälje, Sweden

Telephone: +46 755 81000
Telex: 10200 Scania S
Telefax: +46 755 83180

The company, which produced its first internal combustion engine in 1897 and its first diesel engine in 1936, specialises in high-speed engines.

New developments and improvements were introduced to the Scania series in 1981. By modifying the engines and introducing a completely new series of injection equipment, higher outputs were attained, as well as a reduction in fuel consumption and a considerable decrease in smoke emission. In addition, the introduction of charge air cooling widened the output range.

Scania's industrial engine programme now comprises engines with outputs ranging from 59 to 361 kW. The programme is in part a preparedness for future demands for reduced emission levels in industrial engines. Here charge air cooling is a distinct advantage in optimising the engines to meet more stringent regulations without loss of fuel economy.

Diesel engines and transmission systems / **MANUFACTURERS** 167

The new engines are especially adapted for operation with high average output utilisation, and the fact that the user does not always have the opportunity to run-in the engine has been taken into consideration. To reduce the danger of piston ringstick in extremely heavy operation, a Keystone-ring is fitted as upper compression ring on the piston. Increased top land clearance provides for low lubrication oil consumption, down to 0.4 g/kWh.

Generating set engines have been specially adapted for the generator speeds of 1500 and 1800 rpm. The new injection pump and single-speed Bosch RQ governor provides faster and more precise governing of engine speed. With this governor the requirements for Class A1 (high requirements of governing accuracy) in ISO 3046 are fulfilled and governing is made possible down to a lower speed droop. The new governor is also particularly well suited for governing in parallel operation of multi-engine installations.

Locomotives and railway equipment form part of the extensive product programme manufactured by Valmet Oy in Finland. The 250 B is a shunting locomotive built by Valmet and powered by a Scania DS14 with a rated output in this configuration of 283 kW (385 bhp) at 2100 rpm. A Clark power-shift transmission is used to optimise traction (a full 13.2 tonnes coupling traction) and obtain a top speed of 75 km/h. A combination of the long 4.5-metre axle distance and pivoted, full suspension axles with ballast between the axles gives a smooth and comfortable ride. The low noise emission level of the DS14 engine, with a silenced engine compartment, ensures that the sound level in the driver's cab is as low as 66 dBA. Two 250 Bs are already operational in Sweden.

Other makes of equipment employing Scania engines include the OTSO locomotives manufactured by Saalasti Engineering in Finland. The OTSO 2R is powered by a Scania DS11 with an output of 217 kW (295 hp); its operating weight is 30 tonnes and tractive effort 90 kN. The locomotive is radio-controlled. The bigger OTSO 3 HSJ has a Scania DS14 rated at 243 kW (330 hp); its operating weight is 38 tonnes and tractive effort 107 kN. Maximum speed of both models is 25 km/h.

The Type LH shunting locomotive by Moteurs Möes SA, Belgium is equipped with a Scania DN8 engine rated at 99 kW (135 hp) and has a tractive effort of 40 kN and a maximum speed of 15 km/h.

Plasser & Theurer of Linz, Austria has used Scania engines in its track maintenance equipment for many years and recently received an order from the Brazilian Federal Railways (RFFSA) for 64 units each powered by a Scania DS11 engine.

Types D11, DS11
6-cylinder in-line, 4-stroke, water cooled.
Cylinders: Bore and stroke 127 × 145 mm (5 × 5.71 in). Wet type centrifugal cast iron cylinder liners, the outer surfaces directly flushed by cooling water. Alloy cast iron cylinder heads, each covering three cylinders.

Types DN9, DS9
Cylinders: The cylinder block is integral with the upper half of the crankcase and is one piece of alloy cast-iron. Exchangeable wet-type cylinder liners in direct contact with the coolant. Sealing between the coolant jacket and the crankcase is provided by rings of oil- and heat-resistant rubber. Alloy cast iron cylinder heads each cover one cylinder.
Lubrication: By gear pump located in the front of the sump.
Fuel system: By injection pump with multi-orifice nozzles.

Cooling: Coolant is pumped horizontally through oil cooler and into cylinder block which communicates with cooling jackets of cylinder head. From cylinder heads coolant passes through two-way thermostat back to radiator.
Turbo-charger: Single-stage radial turbine and single-stage centrifugal compressor. DN9 is naturally aspirated.

Type DS14
8-cylinder Vee, 4-stroke, water cooled.
Cylinders: Bore and stroke 127 × 140 mm (5 × 5.51 in). Alloyed cast iron cylinder heads, one for each cylinder.
Fuel injection: Multi-hole type injectors with special cold starting device. Helical gear driven injection pump.
Turbo-charger: Exhaust gas turbo-charger.
Fuel: Diesel fuel.
Lubrication: Forced feed to all bearings and gear trains with intermittent oil supply to the valve rocker mechanism. One gear-type pump.
Cooling: One centrifugal type water pump driven from the crankshaft through Vee-belts (DS14 through gear chain). Thermostatic control for low temperature operation.
Starter: Electric.

Generator drive engines for power generation

Model	Nominal engine gross	Prime duty*		Stand-by duty†	
		50 Hz	60 Hz	50 Hz	60 Hz
DN9(174)	kW(hp)	84(114)	100(136)	– (–)	– (–)
DS9(227)	kW(hp)	139(189)	155(211)	164(223)	184(250)
DS9(254)	kW(hp)	156(212)	177(241)	180(245)	203(276)
DS11(306)	kW(hp)	194(264)	217(295)	– (–)	– (–)
DS11(331)	kW(hp)	204(277)	228(310)	231(314)	259(352)
DSI11(438)	kW(hp)	248(337)	278(378)	287(390)	322(438)
DSC11(469)	kW(hp)	270(367)	300(408)	310(421)	345(469)
DS14(427)	kW(hp)	259(352)	292(397)	307(417)	344(468)
DSI14(555)	kW(hp)	317(431)	351(477)	366(498)	408(555)
DSC14(571)	kW(hp)	339(461)	374(508)	381(518)	420(571)

Speed variations as per ISO 3046/IV, class A1
Standards: ISO 3046, DIN 6271, SAE J 1349, B.S. 5514

* Prime power: For continuous operation under varying load factors with a 10% overload capability for 1 hour in every 12 hours.
† Stand-by power: The engine is allowed to work continuously, under normal varying load factors for the duration of a power outage. Stand-by ratings should, however, not be used in applications designed to repeatedly require more than 300 service hours per year, and are intended for electrical networks, which under normal conditions are well established.

Industrial engines

Model	DN9(174)	DS9(227)	DS9(254)	DN11(215)	DS11(331)	DSI11(367)	DSC11(358)	DS14(427)	DSI14(458)	DSC14(477)
No of cylinders	6 in-line	6 in-line	6 in-line	6 in-line	6 in-line	6 in-line	6 in-line	V8	V8	V8
Cylinder volume, cm³	8480	8480	8480	11020	11020	11020	11020	14190	14190	14190
Intermittent output* kW(hp)rpm	126(174)2200	167(227)2200	187(244)2200	158(215)2200	243(331)2100	270(367)2100	283(385)2100	314(427)2100	337(458)2100	351(477)2100
Max torque intermittent Nm(rpm)	605(1200)	884(1400)	1001(1350)	777(1350)	1365(1300)	1488(1300)	1584(1300)	1726(1400)	1821(1400)	1946(1350)
Specific fuel consumption g/kWh(g/hph) at 1500 rpm	226(166)	201(148)	201(148)	227(167)	204(150)	200(147)	195(143)	205(151)	206(152)	200(147)
Weight (dry) kg	810	825	825	905	930	950	1020**	1160	1180	1256**

* Full power 1h in 6h. No limitation on running hours. Standards: ISO 3046, DIN 6271. SAE J 1349 and B.S. 5514
** Weight incl. radiator and expansion tank.

SCG
Self-Changing Gears Ltd

Lythalls Lane, Coventry, West Midlands CV6 6FY, England

Telephone: +44 203 688881
Telex: 31644
Telefax: +44 203 666660

Managing Director: D J Webster
Rail Sales Manager: D B Smith

Products: A range of automatic transmission systems for passenger trains and heavy transmission systems for shunting locomotive applications.

The latest generation of lightweight diesel railcars for British Rail, the Class 142, 143 and Class 144, employ SCG transmission systems. These vehicles are fitted with R500 series transmissions and RF420i final drives developed by SCG. The R500 series design recognises the experience gained on the Class 141 railcars which entered service with British Rail early 1984. In Class 141 vehicles a fluid coupling was mounted on the engine and drove an RRE5 bi-directional gearbox via a propshaft. A further propshaft took the drive from the transmission output on the RF420i final drive unit, which is axle-mounted.

Under a recent refurbishment programme Class 141 railcars have been updated with the latest specification R500 transmission, as currently fitted to Class 142, 143 and 144 vehicles.

The R500 includes a sophisticated microprocessor-based controlled which provides simplicity in use with versatility in operation and an advanced diagnostics capability.

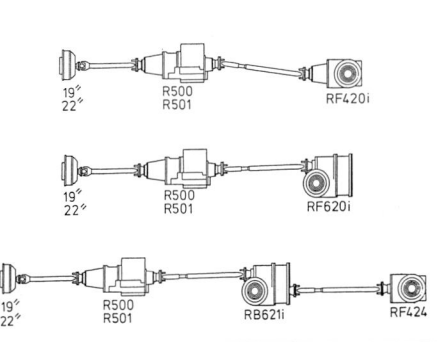

A OIL FILLER
B BEVEL WHEEL
C BEVEL PINION
D INPUT COUPLING
E OIL PUMP
F AXLE SHAFT

RF420i axle

Driveline configuration

168 MANUFACTURERS / Diesel engines and transmission systems

The combination of epicyclic gearing, brake band operation, advanced electronic controls and pressurised lubrication sets the highest standards for mechanical efficiency in railcar transmissions.

RF420i final drives feature an efficient bevel and pinion arrangement incorporating a self-contained, pressurised lubrication system. An isolating device that allows the drive to be disconnected is available as an option.

The company also offers heavy-duty reverse and reduction final drive units applicable to diesel shunting locomotives in the 100-650 hp range. These are based on the RF11, which is offered in Thomas Hill locomotives and as an option on Andrew Barclay locomotives in the UK. RF11 is also offered in equipment of overseas manufacturers.

A two-speed planetary gearset can be included as an option to provide suitable ratios for trip-shunting applications.

In addition to the company's standard range, SCG operates as a design and development house to devise solutions to customers' transmission requirements. SCG transmissions are built under licence in seven countries throughout the world.

Thomas Hill 'Steelman' locomotive incorporating SCG final drive

S.E.M.T-Pielstick
2 Quai de Seine, BP 75, 93202 Saint-Denis Cedex 1, France

Telephone: +33 1 48 09 76 00
Telex: 236773 semt f
Telefax: +33 1 42 43 81 02

PA4-185 Series
Type: 6-cylinder in-line horizontal; 6-cylinder in-line vertical; 6, 8, 12 and 16 Vee (90°), 4-cycle, water cooled.
Cylinders: Bore 185 mm. Stroke 210 mm. Swept volume 5.65 litres per cylinder. Wet liners, individual cast iron cylinder heads. Central pre-combustion chamber fitted with pintle-type injectors.
Fuel injection: Pintle-type injectors fitted to pre-combustion chambers. Monobloc injection pump located inside Vee, controlled by hydraulic governor.
Superchargers: Exhaust gas turbo-chargers, one for 6-and 8-cylinder engines, one for 12 cylinders and two for 16 and 18 cylinders, between cylinder banks. Air coolers arranged on timing gear side.
Cooling: Water pumps fitted on timing gear end of frame.
Starting: Either electrically or by compressed air.

PA4-200 Series
Type: 8, 12 and 16 Vee (90°), 4 cycles, water cooled. 2 models:
VG: Variable geometry pre-combustion chamber
VGA: High ratio turbo-charging
Cylinders: Bore 200 mm. Stroke 210 mm. Swept volume 6.6 litres per cylinder. Wet liners, individual cast iron cylinder heads.
Pistons: Cast iron pistons cooled by pressure lubricating oil fed through connecting rod and piston pin into an annular chamber level with top compression ring.
Fuel injection: Monobloc injection pump inside the Vee, controlled by hydraulic governor.
Superchargers: Exhaust gas turbo-chargers, one for 8-cylinder engine, two for 12 and 16 cylinders, between cylinder banks. Air coolers arranged on timing gear side.
Cooling: Water pumps fitted on timing gear end of frame.
Starting: Either electrically or by compressed air.

PA5-255 Series
Type: 6 and 8 cylinders in line, 12 and 16 cylinders Vee, supercharged, water cooled.
Cylinders: Bore 255 mm. Stroke 270 mm. Swept volume 13.79 litres per cylinder. Wet liners directly mounted in the crankcase, without cooling jackets. Individual cast iron cylinder heads. Single combustion chamber. Direct injection.
Fuel injection: Direct injection by means of injectors of the multi-hole type. Individual injecting pump housed in the crankcase, directly controlled by the camshafts. Injection controlled by hydraulic speed governor.
Turbo-chargers: Two per engine, driven by a turbine on the exhaust gas, and housed in the centre line of the engine above each end of the crankcase. Air cooler at supercharger outlets, housed above the middle of the crankcase, and crossed by a special water line.

The PA5 engine has successfully run 100 hours UIC tests (12 PA5 V) and BR type tests (6 PA5 L).

PA6-280 Series
Type: 6, 7 and 8 cylinders in line, 12 and 16 cylinders Vee, supercharged, water cooled.
Cylinders: Bore 280 mm. Stroke 290 mm. Swept volume 17.85 litres per cylinder. Wet liners directly mounted in the crankcase, without cooling jackets. Individual cast iron cylinder heads. Single combustion chamber. Direct injection.
Fuel injection: Direct injection by means of injectors of the multi-hole type. Individual injecting pump housed

PA4-185 VG						
No of cylinders	6(H)	6(L)	6(V)	8(V)	12(V)	16(V)
Turbo-charged	Yes	Yes	Yes	Yes	Yes	Yes
Charge air cooled	Yes	Yes	Yes	Yes	Yes	Yes
Power rating (hp)	1000	1000	1000	1335	2000	2670
Engine speed (rpm)	1500	1500	1500	1500	1500	1500
Piston speed (m/s)	10.5	10.5	10.5	10.5	10.5	10.5
Bmep (bar)	17.3	17.3	17.3	17.3	17.3	17.3
Weight (dry) (kg)	3280	3400	3140	3870	5620	7120
Length (mm)	3115	3120	1640	1940	2540	3140
Width (mm)	1710	910	1450	1450	1450	1450
Height (mm)	860	1700	1865	1865	1865	1865

	PA4-200 VG			PA4-200 VGA		
No of cylinders	8(V)	12(V)	16(V)	8(V)	12(V)	16(V)
Turbo-charged	Yes	Yes	Yes	Yes	Yes	Yes
Charge air cooled	Yes	Yes	Yes	Yes	Yes	Yes
Power rating (hp)	1600	2400	3200	1880	2820	3760
Engine speed (rpm)	1500	1500	1500	1500	1500	1500
Piston speed (m/s)	10.5	10.5	10.5	10.5	10.5	10.5
Bmep (bar)	17.8	17.8	17.8	23	23	23
Weight (dry) (kg)	4400	6000	7720	4450	6800	8400
Length (mm)	1925	2525	3125	1925	2625	3125
Width (mm)	1575	1450	1700	1575	1450	1700
Height (mm)	1865	1865	1865	1865	1865	1865

PA5-255				
No of cylinders	6(L)	8(L)	12(V)	16(V)
Turbo-charged	Yes	Yes	Yes	Yes
Charge air cooled	Yes	Yes	Yes	Yes
Power rating (UIC) (hp)	1955	12 610	3915	5220
Engine speed (rpm)	1000	1000	1000	1000
Piston speed (m/s)	9	9	9	9
Bmep (bar)	19	19	19	19
Weight (dry) (kg)	10 500	13 500	17 000	21 000
Length (mm)	3650	4440	4135	5175
Width (mm)	1260	1280	1980	2230
Height (mm)	2310	2400	2610	2705

PA6-280					
No of cylinders	6(L)	7(L)	8(L)	12(V)	16(V)
Supercharged	Yes	Yes	Yes	Yes	Yes
Charge air cooled	Yes	Yes	Yes	Yes	Yes
Power rating (UIC) (hp)	2400	2800	3200	4800	6400
Engine speed (rpm)	1050	1050	1050	1050	1050
Piston speed (m/s)	10.15	10.15	10.15	10.15	10.15
Piston speed (ft/min)	18.8	18.8	18.8	18.8	18.8
Weight (dry) (kg)	11 200	13 100	14 400	18 800	24 100
Length (mm)	3865	4285	4705	3675	4595
Width (mm)	1405	1405	1405	1780	1780
Height (mm)	2690	2690	2690	2480	2480

in the crankcase, directly controlled by the camshafts. Injection controlled by hydraulic speed governor.
Turbo-chargers: Two per engine, driven by a turbine on the exhaust gas, and housed in the centre line of the engine above each end of the crankcase.
Air cooler at supercharger outlets, housed above the middle of the crankcase, and crossed by a special water line.
Cooling: Two water pumps of the centrifugal type, driven by the timing train, one for jacket and cylinder head line, the other for air-cooler and lube-oil line.
Starting: Compressed air.

360-hour UIC test
The 18-cylinder 18PA6V-280 engine has officially run its 360-hour UIC locomotive test in accordance with ORE regulations.

In Turkey, under a World Bank loan, SEMT Pielstick received in 1989 an order from TCDD for 29 16 PA4V185 VG engines to repower Alsthom MTE 24000 type locomotives. These engines would be partially manufactured and assembled under SEMT Pielstick supervision by Tülomsas, subsidiary of TCDD.

In Finland, after three years of severe tests, Finnish Railways chose the 12 PA4V200 VG type SEMT Pielstick engine to power its Valmet DR16 locomotives which are of advanced technology (ac/ac with GTO thyristors). The contract relates to 10 engines, plus an option for 23 engines.

Shinko
Shinko Engineering Co Ltd

1682 Motoima-cho, Ogaki 503, Japan

Telephone: +81 584 89 3121
Telex: 4793 624
Telefax: +81 584 89 2139

Products: This is a subsidiary of Kobe Steel Ltd. Manufacture of high-speed diesel engines for rail traction began in 1950 and the present range is from 140 to 200 hp. It also builds hydraulic torque converters capable of up to 1600 hp and cardan shaft drive hydro-mechanical transmissions for outputs of up to 1600 hp.

Vertical in-line water cooled 4-cycle

DMF 13C	6-cylinder normally aspirated
DMH 17C	8-cylinder normally aspirated
DMH 17S	8-cylinder turbo-charged
DMH 17SB	8-cylinder turbo-charged
DMF 18ZB	8-cylinder turbo-charged and charge air cooled
DMF 31SB	6-cylinder turbo-charged
DMF 31SI	6-cylinder turbo-charged and charge air cooled
DMF 31ZB	6-cylinder turbo-charged and charge air cooled
DMH 41S	8-cylinder turbo-charged
DMH 41Z	8-cylinder turbo-charged and charge air cooled
DMH 41ZB	8-cylinder turbo-charged and charge air cooled

Horizontal in-line water cooled 4-cycle

DMH 17H	8-cylinder normally aspirated
DMH 17HS	8-cylinder turbo-charged
DMF 15HS	8-cylinder turbo-charged
DML 30HS	12-cylinder turbo-charged opposed cylinder

Vee-type water cooled 4-cycle

DML 61S	12-cylinder turbo-charged
DMH 61Z	12-cylinder turbo-charged and charge air cooled
DML 61ZA	12-cylinder turbo-charged and charge air cooled
DML 61ZB	12-cylinder turbo-charged and charge air cooled
DMP 81Z	16-cylinder turbo-charged and charge air cooled

Vertical in-line

		DMF 13C	DMH 17C	DMF 18ZB	DMF 31SB	DMF 31Z	DMF 31S1	DMF 31ZB	DMH 41S	DMH 41Z	DMH 41ZB
Bore	in	5.12	5.12	5.91	7.09	7.09	7.09	7.09	7.09	7.09	7.09
	(mm)	(130)	(130)	(150)	(180)	(180)	(180)	(180)	(180)	(180)	(180)
Stroke	in	6.3	6.3	6.69	7.87	7.87	7.87	7.87	7.87	7.87	7.87
	(mm)	(160)	(160)	(170)	(200)	(200)	(200)	(200)	(200)	(200)	(200)
No of cylinders		6	8	6	6	6	6	6	8	8	8
Displacement	in³	777	1036	1100	1864	1864	1864	1864	2483	2483	2483
	(litres)	(12.74)	(16.98)	(18.02)	(30.55)	(30.55)	(30.55)	(30.55)	(40.7)	(40.7)	(40.7)
Turbo-charged		–	–	Yes	Yes	Yes	Yes	Yes	Yes	Yes	Yes
Charge air cooled		–	–	Yes	–	Yes	Yes	Yes	–	Yes	Yes
Power rating continuous	hp	140	180	550	500	550	600	750	700	800	1000
Engine speed	rpm	1500	1500	2000	1500	1500	1500	1500	1500	1500	1500
Mbep	lb/in²	93.7	90.5	195.3	139.8	153.6	167.8	209	146.5	167.8	209
	(kg/cm²)	(6.59)	(6.36)	(13.7)	(9.83)	(10.8)	(11.8)	(14.7)	(10.3)	(11.8)	(14.7)
Piston speed	ft/min	1576	1576	2233	1970	1970	1970	1970	1970	1970	1970
	(m/s)	(8)	(8)	(11.3)	(10)	(10)	(10)	(10)	(10)	(10)	(10)
Weight (dry)	lb	2430	3090	5290	6830	7055	7276	7716	9921	9987	10 031
	(kg)	(1100)	(1400)	(2400)	(3100)	(3200)	(3300)	(3500)	(4500)	(4500)	(4550)
Length	in	65.4	79.2	69.5	105.2	105.4	109.1	105	126.6	126.6	126.6
	(mm)	(1661)	(2011)	(1766)	(2672)	(2677)	(2772.6)	(2667)	(3210)	(3217)	(3216)
Width	in	44.5	44.5	38.5	37.8	49.9	51.2	49.9	42	41.9	41.9
	(mm)	(1131)	(1131)	(977)	(961)	(1269)	(1300)	(1268)	(1066.5)	(1066)	(1066)
Height	in	38.9	38.9	59.5	78.6	66.7	66.7	66.7	71	70.9	70.9
	(mm)	(987)	(987)	(1511)	(1995)	(1695)	(1695)	(1695)	(1803.5)	(1803)	(1803)
Fuel consumption	lb/hp/h	0.419	0.419	0.360	0.397	0.397	0.386	0.386	0.397	0.397	0.386
	(g/hp/h)	(1990)	(190)	(163)	(180)	(180)	(175)	(175)	(180)	(180)	(175)

Horizontal / Vee-type

Model		DMH 17H	DMH 17HS	DMF 15HS	DML 30HS	DML 61S	DML 61Z	DML 61ZA	DML 61ZB	DMP 81Z
Bore	in	5.12	5.12	5.5	5.5	7.09	7.09	7.09	7.09	7.09
	(mm)	(130)	(130)	(140)	(140)	(180)	(180)	(180)	(180)	(180)
Stroke	in	6.3	6.3	6.3	6.3	7.87	7.87	7.87	7.87	7.87
	(mm)	(160)	(160)	(160)	(160)	(200)	(200)	(200)	(200)	(200)
No of cylinders		8	8	8	12	12	12	12	12	16
Displacement	in³	1036	1036	901	1803	3728	3728	3728	3728	4970
	(litres)	(16.98)	(16.98)	(14.78)	(29.56)	(61.1)	(61.1)	(61.1)	(61.1)	(81.5)
Turbo-charged		–	Yes	Yes	Yes	Yes	Yes	Yes	Yes	Yes
Charge air cooled		–	–	–	–	–	Yes	Yes	Yes	Yes
Power rating continuous	hp	180	250	250	500	1000	1100	1250	1500	2000
Engine speed	rpm	1500	1500	1600	1600	1500	1500	1500	1550	1500
Bmep	lb/in²	90.5	125.6	135.1	135.1	139.8	153.6	174.9	203.3	209
	(kg/cm²)	(6.36)	(8.83)	(9.5)	(9.5)	(9.83)	(10.8)	(12.3)	(14.3)	(14.7)
Piston speed	ft/min	1576	1576	1674.5	1674.5	1970	1970	1970	2035	1970
	(m/s)	(8)	(8)	(8.5)	(8.5)	(10)	(10)	(10)	(10.33)	(10)
Weight (dry)	lb	2420	2420	3968	7495	12 130	12 240	12 346	14 330	19 842
	(kg)	(1550)	(1550)	(1800)	(3400)	(5500)	(5550)	(5600)	(6500)	(9000)
Length	in	93.2	105.9	64.8	97.5	108.1	108.1	108.9	108.9	141
	(mm)	(2392)	(2691)	(2149.5)	(2477)	(2746)	(2746)	(2768)	(2768)	(3582)
Width	in	53.7	48.2	61.4	76.5	65	72.4	72.4	74	74
	(mm)	(1363)	(1225)	(1561)	(1944)	(1652)	(1840)	(1840)	(1880)	(1880)
Height	in	29.6	29.5	28.2	37.6	36.9	36.9	72.2	72.2	72.6
	(mm)	(753)	(750)	(716)	(955)	(936)	(936)	(1833)	(1833)	(1844)
Fuel consumption	lb/hp/h	0.419	0.408	0.397	0.386	0.397	0.397	0.386	0.395	0.395
	(g/hp/h)	(190)	(185)	(180)	(180)	(180)	(180)	(175)	(170)	(170)

MANUFACTURERS / Diesel engines and transmission systems

Siemens
Siemens AG Transportation Systems Group

Werner-von-Siemens-Strasse 50, Postfach 3240, D-8520 Erlangen, Federal Republic of Germany

Telephone: +49 9131 724157
Telex: 6291508 si d
Telefax: +49 9131 726840

Group President: W O Martinsen

Mainline Rolling Stock Division: R Stubenrauch
Mass Transit Rolling Stock Division: G Scholtis

Products: Electrical equipment for all types of rolling stock (see also Siemens entry in Locomotives section).

SRM
SRM Hydromekanik AB

Sorterargatan 2, 2r, S-162 11 Vällingby, Sweden

Telephone: +46 8 38 02 30
Telefax: (09) 38 54 24

Managing Director: Ewald Vetter
Chief Engineer: Per-Olof Bergström

Products: SRM hydraulic transmission of 30 to 2000 hp.

Licensees: Fiat SpA (Italy), Zahnraderfabrik Renk AG (Federal Republic of Germany), ČKD Praha (Czechoslovakia) and OTO Melara SpA (Italy).

Strömungsmaschinen
VEB Strömungsmaschinen

Postfach 64, 8300 Pirna Sonnenstein, German Democratic Republic

Telephone: +37 820
Telex: 028322

Works: Otto-Buchwitz-Strasse 96, 8060 Dresden

Products: Hydraulic couplings, hydraulic and hydrodynamic transmissions, flow converters.

Over 8000 hydraulic transmissions made by VEB Strömungsmaschinen have been installed in diesel locomotives. A recent development in response to demand for more powerful diesel shunting locomotives has been a hydraulic reversing gear. The GS 20-20/5.5 hydraulic transmission is a four-stage converter gear with two hydraulic converters for each direction of travel which features: hydrodynamic wear-free braking with subsequent reversal; 20-fold extension of the operating time to brake base renewal; stepless adaptation to all operating conditions; vibration damping and shock-reducing design; low maintenance cost; and enhanced drawbar power.

Specifications of GS 20-20/5.5
Rated input power, max: 880 kW
Rated primary capacity, max: 880 kW
Input speed: 1000–1500 rpm
Nominal output speed, low gear: ≥ 750 rpm
  high gear: ≥ 1750 rpm
Lowest output speed on CD: 0.17 n2nenn
Starting torque, low gear: ≤ 65 700 Nm
  high gear: ≤ 28 224 Nm
Auxiliary power take-off 1, speed: 3100 rpm
  take-off 2, speed: 1800 rpm
Gear efficiency at vortex: 0.80
Weight of gear unit, empty: 5000 kg
Weight of oil filling: 350 kg

GS 20/4-2 hydraulic transmission

The GS 20/4-2 hydraulic transmission with two torque converters of different transmission ratios ensures optimal operation of shunting locomotives, overhead contact wire inspection locomotives and railcar trains. Its range of applications is extended by the incorporation of a reverse gear for cardan drives. Among its features are: vibration-damping and shock-absorbing; stepless torque/speed adjustment; fully automatic operation; and low maintenance cost.

Thyssen-Henschel
TGW Thyssen Getriebe-und Kupplungswerke GmbH

Südstrasse 111, 4690 Herne 1, Federal Republic of Germany

Telephone: +49 2323 497-1
Telex: 8229868

Products: Monomotor traction gears; axle drives with rubber pad couplings or hollow shaft type rubber pad couplings (inside positioned); FWH-Duewag axle drive; Simotrac twin-axle longitudinal drive-unit.

Turbomeca

64320 Bordes, France

Telephone: +33 59 32 84 37
Telex: 560 928
Telefax: +33 59 53 15 12

Subsidiary company:
Turbomeca Engine Corporation
2709 Forum Drive, Grand Prairie
Texas 75051, USA

Telephone: +1 21 46 41 66 45
Telex: 247 575

Products: Small gas turbines in the 100 to 2000 kW range.

Since 1970, Turbomeca has actively participated in the developments of efficient and economic high speed trains. 73 turbotrains have been built to date and are operated in France, USA, Egypt and Iran, involving the Turmo III and Turmo XII gas turbines (1 or 2 units, per train) for traction through hydrokinetic transmission, and the Astazou gas turbine for on-board electric power generation. The favourable weight/power ratio of these engines is 0.4 kg/kW. Turbomeca traction gas turbines are of the two-shaft type (gas generator + power turbine), with annular combustion chamber and fuel injection through centrifugal wheel ensuring homogeneous temperature and high life potential. Engine efficiency is up to 28%.

Rail traction applications

Engine	Type	Output Speed rpm	Output kW	Output hp	Weight kg	Length mm	Width mm
Turmo III	2-shaft	6500	820	1115	355	2130	760
Turmo XII	2-shaft	6500	1200	1630	488	2100	715
Makila	2-shaft	6500	1200	1830	410	1850	700

Train electric power supply

Engine	Type	Output Speed rpm	Output kW	Output hp	Weight kg	Length mm	Width mm
Astazou IV	1-shaft	1500	330	450	300	1500	700

Diesel engines and transmission systems / **MANUFACTURERS**

Twiflex
Twiflex Ltd

The Green, Twickenham, Middlesex TW2 5AQ, England

Telephone: +44 81 894 1161
Telex: 261704
Telefax: +44 81 894 6056

Sales Director: Alan Hughes

Products: Layrub and Laylink flexible shafts and couplings; industrial and marine disc brakes and Flexi-clutch couplings.

Both the Layrub and the Laylink type couplings incorporate compressed cylindrical rubber blocks. The Laylink type coupling carries these blocks in links, while the Layrub coupling carries them in a carrying plate. The use of these couplings and flexible shafts allows large amounts of angular and axial misalignment to be accommodated; it also absorbs shock, controls vibrations and simplifies close coupling in confined spaces. The units need no servicing or lubrication and can cater for very high operating speeds and transmission of high powers without loss.

The range of Twiflex disc brakes covers all applications from the lightest tensioning duties to the heaviest emergency stopping applications. Braking forces up to 430 kN per caliper are available. Unlimited disc diameter means that available braking torque is limitless. The range includes actuation calipers with pneumatic, hydraulic, mechanical and electrical actuation; and throughout the range, spring applied versions are available. All calipers can be provided with control systems and brake discs, and pad wear and operation monitoring is available.

The Flexi-clutch range comprises four different sizes of clutch coupling which have very soft torsional stiffness characteristics; thus a single unit combines the functions of a clutch and flexible coupling. Engaging speeds are pre-set according to particular requirements and momentary overload protection is facilitated. The units are totally automatic in operation and allow motors and engines to be started under no load condition with a smooth take-up of power.

Orders executed in 1988 included supply of: Layrub couplings to Sweden for locomotive and power car traction drives operating in Sweden, Australia and India; Layrub traction drives and Layrub for British Rail Class 90 locomotive, railbus and Sprinter alternator transmissions; and Layrub and Laylink. Traction quill shafts and couplings for BR HST train-sets.

Twin Disc
Twin Disc Incorporated

1328 Racine Street, Racine, Wisconsin 53403, USA

Telephone: +1 414 634 1981
Telex: 264432
Telefax: +1 414 634 1989

Vice President, International Marketing (Racine): J McIndoe
Director of Marketing (Belgium): K Sethi
Managing Director (Twinfel): J Thomas
Managing Director (Twinpac): C Rawlings
Managing Director (Twinvaal): B Nagl
General Manager, UK: R Lewis
Niigata Converter: S Igeta

Principal Subsidiary Companies
Twin Disc International SA, Chaussee de Namur 54, 1400 Nivelles, Belgium

Telephone: +32 67 21 4941
Telex: 57414
Telefax: +32 67 21 9577

Twin Disc International SA, UK Branch, 11 High Street, Strood, Rochester, Kent, ME2 4AB, England

Telephone: +44 634 719440
Telex: 96182
Telefax: +44 634 719443

Twin Disc (Pacific) Pty Ltd, Post Office Box 442, Zillmere, Queensland 4034, Australia

Telephone: +61 7 265 1200
Telex: 42051

Telefax: +61 7 865 1371

Twin Disc (South Africa) Pty Ltd, PO Box 40542, Cleveland 2022, Republic of South Africa

Telephone: +27 11 613 5717
Telex: 4-26341 sa
Telefax: +27 11 613 5710

Twin Disc (Far East) Ltd, PO Box 155, Jurong Town Post Office, Singapore 9161

Telephone: +65 2618909
Telex: 24284
Telefax: +65 2642080

Products: Universal joints; hydraulic torque converters, power-shift transmissions and controls suitable for locomotives and railcars.

UCMR
UCMR Resita

Mecanoexportimport supplier

1 Golului Street, 1700, Resita, Romania

Telephone: +40 17 111
Telex: 74 215; 74 269

General Manager: Vasile Uscat

Products: Diesel engines manufactured under ALCO and Sulzer licence.

ALCO R 251 series engines

No of cylinders	6	8	12	16	18
Rpm range	400-1100	400-1100	400-1100	400-1100	400-1100
Compression ratio	(12.5) 11.5:1	(12.5) 11.5:1	:12.5) 11.5:1	(12.5) 11.5:1	(12.5) 11.5:1
Bore × stroke (mm)	228 × 267	228 × 267	228 × 267	228 × 267	228 × 267
Displacement (dm^3)	65.7	87.6	131.4	175.2	197.1
Turbo-charged	Yes	Yes	Yes	Yes	Yes
Aftercooled	Yes	Yes	Yes	Yes	Yes
Fuel system type	Mech	Mech	Mech	Mech	Mech
Heat diss rate					
oil (k cal/hp min)	1.2	1.2	1.2	1.2	1.2
water (k cal/hp min)	5.5	5.5	5.5	5.5	5.5
Starting system	Air motor	Air motor	Air motor	Air motor	Air motor
m^3/start average	7	7	7	7	7
Pressure range (bar)	6-10	6-10	6-10	6-10	6-10
Weight					
dry (tons)	10.2 10.6	11.7 11.8	15.0 15.4	19.1 19.6	22.3 23.2
wet (tons)	1.8 11.7	12.0 12.5	15.4 16.2	19.6 20.6	23.0 24.8

Note: Dual-Fuel/blending intermediate fuel operation available. Electric starting motor on special request.

UNI Diesel Sarl
Sales and Marketing Company of the SACM diesel group

157 avenue Charles de Gaulle, BP 138, 92203 Neuilly sur Seine Cedex, France

Telephone: +33 1 47 47 51 00
Telex: 620207 unidl
Telefax: +33 1 47 45 28 67

Main works
SACM Mulhouse (Société Alsacienne de Constructions Mécaniques de Mulhouse)
1 rue de la Fonderie, BP 1210, 68054 Mulhouse Cedex, France

Telephone: +33 89 46 01 08
Telex: 881699 sacmm
Telefax: +33 89 46 01 08

SSCM (Société Surgerienne de Constructions Mécaniques)
BP 13, 17700 Surgères, France

Telephone: +33 46 07 62 10
Telex: 790831 poyaud
Telefax: +33 46 07 62 10 ext 446

UNI Diesel engines

| Model | Low speed range | | | High speed range | | | Engine dimensions | | | Dry |
	rpm	kW	hp	rpm	kW	hp	mm	mm	mm	kg
UD 18 H6 R3	2200	217	295	2500	243	330	1750	1235	750	1100
UD 18 L6 R3	2200	217	295	2500	243	330	1600	810	1190	1100
UD 18 V8 R3	2200	287	390	2500	323	440	1540	1285	1210	1500
UD 18 V12 R3	2200	433	590	2500	485	660	1990	1285	1240	1900
UD 25 H6 R4	1500	367	500	1800	367	500	2780	1880	840	2600
UD 25 L6 R3	1500	294	400	1800	294	400	1950	1230	1780	2400
UD 25 L6 R4	1500	367	500	1800	367	500	1950	1230	1780	2500
UD 25 V12 R3	1500	588	800	1800	588	800	2760	1585	1970	4600
UD 25 V12 R4	1500	736	1000	1800	736	1000	2760	1585	1970	4750

MANUFACTURERS / Diesel engines and transmission systems

UNI Diesel engines continued

Model	Low speed range rpm	kW	hp	High speed range rpm	kW	hp	Engine dimensions mm	mm	mm	Dry kg
UD 30 H6 R6	1200	410	560	1650	570	770	2595	2250	920	3800
UD 30 L6 R6	1200	410	560	1650	570	770	2400	1310	1950	3800
UD 30 V8 R6	1200	560	760	1650	770	1040	2200	1550	1785	4100
UD 30 V12 R6	1200	825	1120	1650	1130	1540	2660	1520	1890	5550
UD 30 V16 R6	1200	1060	1440	1650	1455	1980	3150	1540	1890	6900
UD 33 V12 R6	1200	1280	1740	1650	1760	2395	3500	1720	2080	6500
UD 33 V16 R6	1200	1680	2285	1650	2310	3140	4200	1720	2220	8800
UD 33 V20 R6	1200	2080	2820	1650	2860	3890	4700	1720	2220	10 500
UD 45 L6 R6	1000	975	1330	1350	1225	1665	3600	1840	2800	9000
UD 45 L8 R6	1000	1300	1770	1350	1630	2220	4100	1590	2450	12 000
UD 45 V12 R6	1000	1990	2710	1350	2500	3400	3460	1960	2410	14 000
UD 45 V16 R6	1000	2670	3630	1350	3355	4650	4560	2000	2500	19 000
UD 45 V20 R6	1000	3340	4540	1350	4190	5700	6100	2200	2700	25 000

Ratings at engine PTO according to UIC 623-1 OR specification
H6 engines are horizontal versions.

The new name UNI Diesel now covers former SACM and SSCM engines, of which 4000 are in use on all types of locomotives, shunters and railcars on about 50 railway systems world-wide.

Low fuel consumption, easy maintenance, a high availability rate and proven reliability under the most adverse climatic conditions are some of the features claimed for the engines. Their sizes and weights are compatible with the engining and re-engining of all types of locomotives and other rail vehicles. Horizontal engine versions up to 700 hp UIC are available and single engines of up to 6000 hp UIC for locomotives.

VO Energomachexport
25A Bezbozhny per, 129010 Moscow, USSR

Telephone: +7 095 288 84 56
Telex: 411965
Telefax: +7 095 288 79 90

Director-General: Vladimir I Filimonov
Sales Directors: A Zigalov
V Doluakov

Products: Diesel engines.

Series		D100				D40	D45
Type		2-stroke, opposed piston				2-stroke Vee	2-stroke Vee
Bore in			8.15			9.06	9.06
(mm)			(207)			(230)	(230)
Stroke in			10			11.8/11.98	11.8/11.98
(mm)			(254)			(300/304.3)	(300/304.3)
Model		6D100	2D100	10D100	9D100-F	1D40	11D45
No of cylinders		8	10	10	12	12	16
Output hp		2000	2000	3000	4000	2000	3000
Engine speed rpm		850	850	850	900	750	750
Piston speed ft/min		1417	1417	1417	1496	1476	1476
(m/s)		(7.2)	(7.2)	(7.2)	(7.6)	(7.5)	(7.5)
Bmep lb/in²		111	88	132	108	115	129
(kg/cm²)		(7.8)	(6.2)	(9.3)	(7.6)	(8.1)	(9.1)
Weight lb		43 200	42 750	46 300	50 700	23 100	30 400
(kg)		(15 500)	(19 400)	(21 000)	(23 000)	(10 500)	(13 800)
Length in		238.3	240.7	243.3	260.6	145.7	158.3
(mm)		(6052)	(6115)	(6180)	(6620)	(3700)	(4020)
Width in		66.5	56.7	68.1	59.1	6.97	66.9
(mm)		(1690)	(1440)	(1730)	(1500)	(1770)	(1700)
Height in		118.6	127.6	126.4	124.0	95.3	97.2
(mm)		(3013)	(3240)	(3210)	(3150)	(2421)	(2470)

Principal specifications of diesel locomotive engines

Engine model	2-5D49	1A-5D49	3-5D49R2	14D40	2-6D49	0E-1L	3A-6D49	211D-2T	1D12-400	U1D6-250TKC4	JA3-L204A
No of strokes	4	4	4	2	4	4	4	4	4	4	2
Rated power (hp)	4000	3000	2800 (2600)	2000 (1690)	1450	1200 (1030)	1200	750	400	250	120
Cylinder arrangement	Vee-type	Vee-type	Vee-type	Vee-type	Vee-type	In-line	Vee-type	In-line	Vee-type	In-line	In-line
No of cylinders	16	16	16	12	8	6	8	6	12	6	4
Diameter of cylinder (mm)	260	260	260	230	260	318	260	210	150	150	108
Piston stroke (mm)	260	260	260	300/304.3	260	330	260	210	180	180	127
Rated speed (rpm)	1000	1000	1000	750	1000	750	1000	1400	1600	1500	2000
Specific fuel consumption, g/bhp/h	157 + 5%	151 + 5%	158 + 5%	160 + 5%	150 + 5%	165 + 5% (174 + 5%)	150 + 5%	155 + 5%	170	160 + 5%	190
Locomotives on which engine is used	TZ129	TZ109	RZ114	L62	RZL6Q	RZL2	RDL6A RDL8	RDL4A RDL4	RDL23B RW72	RDJ2	RW6A

Series		D49				D50			D70			M		1D
Type		4-stroke Vee				4-stroke in-line			4-stroke Vee			4-stroke Vee		4-stroke Vee
Bore in		10.24				12.5			9.45			7.09		5.9
(mm)		(260)				(318)			(240)			(180)		(150)
Stroke in		10.24				13			10.63			7.88/8.26		7.09/7.35
(mm)		(260)				(330)			(270)			(200/208.8)		(180/186.7)
Model		4D49	12D49	D49-V16	D49-F	D50	D50M	11D1M	8D70	12D70	D70	D70F	M753	M756	1D12
No of cylinders		6	12	16	16	6	6	6	8	12	16	16	12	12	12
Output hp		1200	2000	3000	4000	1000	1000	1200	1200	2000	3000	4000	750	1000	400
Engine speed rpm		1000	1000	1000	1000	740	740	750	1000	1000	1000	1000	1400	1500	1600
Piston speed ft/min		1713	1713	1713	1713	1604	1604	1624	1772	1772	1772	1772	1837/1929	2087/2205	1890
(m/s)		(8.7)	(8.7)	(8.7)	(8.7)	(8.15)	(8.15)	(8.25)	(9)	(9)	(9)	(9)	(9.3/9.8)	(10.6/11.2)	(9.6)
Bmep lb/in²		188	156	174	232	110	110	131	196	175	196	262	105	131	82.5
(kg/cm²)		(13.2)	(11)	(12.2)	(16.3)	(7.7)	(7.7)	(9.2)	(13.8)	(12.3)	(13.8)	(18.4)	(7.4)	(9.2)	(5.8)
Weight lb		14 300	24 200	30 900	30 900	39 700		24 700	31 300	37 500	37 500	35 300	39 700	41 900
(kg)		(6500)	(11 000)	(14 000)	(14 000)	(18 000)		(11 200)	(14 200)	(17 000)	(17 000)	(16 000)	(18 000)	(19 000)
Length in		96	142	170	170	205		157	181	217	220	89.4	95.3	61.4
(mm)		(2400)	(3600)	(4300)	(4300)	(5200)		(4000)	(4600)	(5500)	(5600)	(2270)	(2420)	(1560)
Width in		55	63	63	63	59		63	63	63	63	42.7	44.1	33.7
(mm)		(1400)	(1600)	(1600)	(1600)	(1500)		(1600)	(1600)	(1600)	(1600)	(1085)	(1120)	(856)
Height in		90	102	110	110	98		110	114	118	118	47.3	58.3	42.3
(mm)		(2300)	(2600)	(2800)	(2800)	(2500)		(2800)	(2900)	(3000)	(3000)	(1200)	(1480)	(1075)

Voith
J M Voith GmbH
Power Transmission Engineering

PO Box 1940, 7920 Heidenheim/Brenz, Federal Republic of Germany

Telephone: +49 7321 37 0
Telex: 71479980 vh d
Telefax: +49 7321 373104
Voith Managing Director: Dr M Rogowski
Railway Division Manager: Dr H Bruns
Sales & Application Engineering Manager:
K O Dahler

UK subsidiary: Voith Engineering Ltd, 6 Beddington Farm Road, Croydon, Surrey CR0 4XB, UK
Telephone: +44 81 667 0333
Telex: 946129
Telefax: +44 81 667 0403

Products: Voith hydrodynamic transmissions and brakes, torque converters and automatic hydro-mechanical transmissions; axle-drive gearboxes, cardan shafts cooling units and torsional couplings.

Voith automatic hydrodynamic transmissions are specifically developed for installation in rail vehicles. The basis components are hydraulic torque converters and hydraulic couplings which work on the Föttinger principle. In combination they provide tractive effort over a wide speed range at an efficiency which fully satisfies the demands of railway service. The characteristic feature of the Voith turbo transmission is its ability to engage and disengage the hydraulic circuits by automatic filling or emptying. Thus the changeover from one circuit to another takes place without any wear, which is of great importance, especially with transmissions of high power. With Voith turbo-reversing transmissions for shunting locos, this principle is extended to reversing, which is also carried out without wear and without interruption. Voith turbo transmissions for mainline locomotives can be fitted with wear-free hydrodynamic retarders.

In 1989-90 production is concentrated on transmissions for diesel railcars such as the T 211rz for Class 158 and 165 railcars of British Railways, and T 320rT 311r for German Federal Railways.
Further large orders have been obtained from Far Eastern countries.

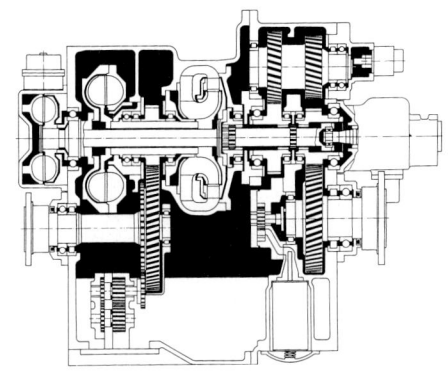

T 211rz transmission for railcars up to 400 hp engine output, embodying torque converter for acceleration and fluid coupling for operating at medium and high speeds: optionally with retarder

Electric traction equipment

ARGENTINA
Dearmedelec 183

AUSTRALIA
Clyde 183
SMC 188

BELGIUM
ACEC 175

BRAZIL
SIGLA 188

FRANCE
Alsthom 179
CGE 183
Faiveley 184
Ferraz 184

FINLAND
Strömberg 188

GERMANY, FEDERAL REPUBLIC
ABB 176
AEG Westinghouse 177
BSI 182
Kiepe Elektrik 186
Siemens 188
Stemmann 189

HUNGARY
Ganz 185

INDIA
BHEL 181

ITALY
Ansaldo Trasporti 180
CGE 183
ML 187
Parizzi 187
Socimi 188
TIBB 189

JAPAN
Fuji Electric 184
Hitachi 185
Toshiba 189
Toyo Denki 189

NETHERLANDS
Holec 185

POLAND
Pafawag 187

SPAIN
CENEMESA 183

SWITZERLAND
ABB 175
BBC-Sécheron 181
Groupement 185
Sécheron 189

UK
Brecknell, Willis 183
Bristol 183
Brush 183
GEC 185
Marconi 187
Siemens Plessey 188

USA
AEG Westinghouse 178
EFE North America Inc 184
National 187
Siemens 188

MANUFACTURERS / Electric traction equipment

ABB
Asea Brown Boveri Transportation

(For full details of ABB companies, see ABB entry in Locomotives section)

Products: Development, design, engineering, sales, production, installation, maintenance and after-sales service of equipment for all railway types, systems and track gauges; retrofitting of traction vehicles; electrical systems and components; transformers and chokes; main breakers; electro-mechanical control systems; electronic control and diagnosis systems; solid state dc and ac power converters; ac and dc traction motors; service, minor equipment and spare parts; and large projects management and consultancy.

Recent contracts have included:
Hong Kong
Both Kowloon-Canton Railway Corporation car operating in one of its 85 suburban trains, and Mass Transit Railway Corporation, rail cars are to test an ABB on-board power Type BUR converter for train power bus supply.
Italy
Metro Naples will equip 45 railcars with ABB on-board power converters for train power bus supply.
Switzerland
The SBB (Swiss Federal Railways) has ordered a retrofit of 80 Class RBe 4/4 electric railcars, originally built between 1959 and 1966. Their electric traction equipment still includes main transformer tap-changer control with electro-mechanical load switches in parallel. As replacement for these maintenance-intensive components ABB now provides Type NU 28 thyristor load switches. Updating of the 80 units also includes selective door controls, improved train safety devices and train radio. They will serve in the SBB regional express network (S-Bahn) starting in 1990.

Other European railway administrations have also shown interest in the NU 28 for their older electric motive power units still equipped with transformer tap-changer control.

SBB has also ordered a retrofit of 10 four-system electric shunters of Class Ee3/3 IV. These SLM/Sécheron-built units commissioned in 1962 were originally equipped with mercury-arc rectifiers. They serve in Swiss border stations with France and Italy.

ABB, having taken over the Sécheron traction equipment facilities, is replacing the mercury-arc rectifiers with solid-state traction power converters and also providing new electronic on-board power converters for the auxiliary services. Deliveries were to start in August 1989 with one set of equipment per month.

To the EBT/VHB/SMB railway group the partnership of Swiss Wagon Schlieren, Sécheron and Brown Boveri supplied eight electric railcars of Class RBDe 4/4 in 1974. Since then SWS has been taken over by Schindler Wagon Pratteln (SWP); Brown Boveri is now ASEA Brown Boveri and also includes the traction equipment facilities of Sécheron. The eight units were originally equipped with contactor control and oil-cooled diode rectifiers, the latter chosen in 1974 as the signalling cables of this railway group could not cope with the harmonics generated by thyristor-controlled motive power. ABB is now supplying new electric traction equipment with phase-angle control and thyristor rectifiers. Equipment deliveries will be completed by end 1989. The retrofitted RBDe 4/4 units will then have the same traction equipment as newer railcars of the same class supplied over the past few years.

On-board modular Series BUR power converter with three modules for battery charging, intermediate circuit dc voltage, and variable three-phase voltage. Dust-and splash-proof modules with the finned coolers outside are here turned down for inspection

---

ACEC
ACEC Transport

BP 4, 6000 Charleroi, Belgium

Telephone: +32 71 44 57 99
Telex: 51 227 acec b
Telefax: +32 71 43 78 34

General Manager: Ch Jauquet
Commercial Director: D Hausman

Products: Electrical equipment for locomotives and electric multiple-units (750 V, 1500 V and 3 kV dc; 25 kV ac; diesel-electric), LRV and metro coaches, streetcars and trolleybuses; ac and dc traction motors; GTO choppers and inverters; switchgears and circuit-breakers; static converters for auxiliary loads; microprocessor-based control electronics including slip/slide detection, speed control, fault monitoring, expert systems, etc.

ACEC has built and operated a 3 kV emu equipped with ac motors on SNCB lines since 1957. The four 200 kW motors are controlled by a current inverter, providing a 0.55 m/s^2 acceleration. At braking, a high regeneration rate is achieved by avoiding the use of limitation resistors. The equipment complies with the minimum impedance and maximum harmonic current prescriptions imposed by the SNCB to ensure compatibility with the signalling equipment.

In 1989 ACEC was delivering to British Rail a batch of 317 three-phase 33 kVA static converters. The PWM inverter is directly fed by the catenary giving minimum weight and volume and high reliability. ACEC was also commissioning 15 chopper equipments for GECAMINE (Zaïre) locomotives. Another recent order concerns the rehabilitation of propulsion equipment of Antwerp streetcars using GTO choppers.

SNCB Class 27 3 kV dc Bo-Bo

Latest SNCB electric locomotives equipped by ACEC

SNCB class	Wheel arrangement	Line voltage	Rated output (kW) continuous/one-hour	Max speed km/h	Weight tonnes	Year first built	Builders Mechanical parts	Builders Electrical equipment
27	Bo-Bo	3 kV dc	4180/4380	160	85	1982	BN	ACEC
21	Bo-Bo	3 kV dc	3125/3310	160	85	1983	BN	ACEC
11	Bo-Bo	1.5/3 kV dc	3125/3310	160	85	1985	BN	ACEC
12	Bo-Bo	3 kV dc/ 25 kV 50 Hz	3125/3310	160	85	1986	BN	ACEC
21	Bo-Bo	3 kV dc	3125/3310	160	85	1986	BN	ACEC
Gecomine	Bo-Bo	600 V	480	40	70	1988	GMC	ACEC

Electric traction equipment / **MANUFACTURERS** 177

Latest electric multiple-units equipped by ACEC

Class	Cars per unit	Line voltage	Motor cars per unit	Motored axles per motor car	Rated output(kW) per motor	Max speed km/h	Weight tonnes per set	Total seating capacity	Length per set mm	Rate of acceleration m/s^2	Year first built	Builders Mechanical parts	Electrical equipment
AM.80 (for SNCB)	2	3 kV dc	1	4	310	160	126	171	25 075	0.75	1981	BN	ACEC
ONCFM	3	3 kV dc	1	4	351	160	170	271	25 075	0.53	1983	BN	ACEC
AM.86 (for SNCB)	2	3 kV dc	1	4	171.5	120	126	175	26 400	0.55	1988	BN	ACEC
SNCB	2	3 kV dc	1	4	200	130	123	165	26 400	0.55	1987	BN	ACEC

Constitution: Founded 1904. In 1984 ACEC partitioned its former Transport Division into Rolling Stock and Signalling & Transportation Systems Divisions. In January 1989 the railway business of ACEC was taken over by the Alsthom group through a new subsidiary company, ACEC Transport.

Chopper equipment for SNCB Class 27

AEG Westinghouse
AEG Westinghouse Transport-Systeme GmbH

Nonnendammallee 15-21, D-1000 Berlin 20, Federal Republic of Germany

Telephone: +49 30 3305-0
Telefax: +49 30 3305 2169

Director General: Prof Dipl-Ing Dr K Milz
Production Director: Dr-Ing H-P Gold
Director Research and Design: Dipl-Ing J Körber
Commercial Director: R Stark

Principal subsidiary company
FABEG GmbH, Carl-Benz-Strasse 2, 7518 Bretten

Berlin S-Bahn train-set: AEG Westinghouse participated in development and delivery commenced in mid-1990

Berlin S-Bahn train-set bogie with three-phase ac motors

ICE train of German Federal Railways (DB)

Products: Electrical equipment for ac/dc/undulatory-current and three-phase locomotives, railcars, multiple-units (including diesel-electric) for main-line and branch-line services, mining and industrial locomotives, transit stock for suburban and underground railways, trams and trolleybuses.

Recent traction vehicle work has included participation with the 50 c/s Group in the equipment of many locomotives in Europe and overseas. Several orders for equipment totalling more than 300 tramcars and underground railcars were in hand in 1990.

In West Germany, AEG Westinghouse Transport-Systeme intensified activities in the field of three-phase traction. Besides supplies for the German Federal (DB) Class 120 locomotives, the company has been successfully engaged in development and design for the high-speed Intercity Express (ICE) trains and the prototype Intercity Experimental unit, which has successfully proven its ability with a world record of 406 km/h for rail vehicles. German Federal Railway has ordered a series of 41 ICE train-sets for completion in 1991-92. AEG Westinghouse Transport-Systeme is an important partner in the realisation of these trains.

Contributions of the company to the ICE include

178 MANUFACTURERS / Electric traction equipment

asynchronous traction motors of most modern design as well as energy-saving auxiliary supplies with static converters and GTO application. Through-train buses enable 1000 V connection of energy demand in the intermediate cars using new high-voltage couplings. The train control system includes microcomputers and fibreglass optics which likewise serve to control the brake system comprising electric regenerative braking, eddy-current brakes and disc brakes. It also has ample capacity for data transmission for passengers' information, etc.

Current activities in the field of suburban traffic systems are equipment for light rapid transit vehicles for Melbourne, Oslo, Hong Kong, Frankfurt, Kassel and Stuttgart, metros in Buenos Aires, Calcutta, Madrid, Oslo, and Vienna: also a complete automation system for the Amsterdam Metro. With Daimler-Benz, AEG Westinghouse Transport-Systeme has developed a Dual Power Bus (DUO-Bus) for passenger transport in Essen and Esslingen. In the suburbs the normal output of the diesel engine is used. On urban routes, the power supply is received via overhead line and the vehicle driven by an electric motor. Both drives are operated by the same pedals and levers to avoid extra work for the driver; system change-over takes approximately 30 seconds.

Delivery of 41 double-unit Series 480 trainsets for Berlin (West) S-Bahn with three-phase ac drives started in mid-1990.

A fully automated maglev railway, the M-Bahn, is under construction in West Berlin.

Constitution: Manufacture of traction equipment started in 1889. AEG has been concerned with the development of generation, distribution and consumption of electric power for all purposes.

AEG Westinghouse
AEG Westinghouse Transportation Systems Inc
Transportation Systems and Support Division

1501 Lebanon Church Road, Pittsburgh, Pennsylvania 15236-1491, USA

Telephone: +1 412 655 5335
Telex: 866267
Telefax: +1 412 655 5860

President: J R Tucker
Vice Presidents: Commercial Operations:
  D R Marcucci
Engineering: R T Betler
Manufacture: T Josk

Products: Electric ac and dc propulsion equipment (cam, chopper, ac inverter, traction motors/gears) for heavy and light rail vehicles, locomotives and trolley buses.

AEG Westinghouse Transportation Systems Inc propulsion equipment has been or is being installed on the following transit systems:
Cam equipment: New York City Transit Authority (heavy rail); Washington Metropolitan Area Transit Authority (heavy rail); Massachusetts Bay Transportation Authority (heavy rail); Port Authority Trans Hudson (heavy rail).
Chopper equipment: Bay Area Rapid Transit (heavy rail); São Paulo Metro Transit (heavy rail); Rio de Janeiro Metro Transit (heavy rail); Southeastern Pennsylvania Transit Authority (light rail); Washington Metropolitan Area Transit Authority (heavy rail); Vancouver Regional Transit System (trolleybus); Baltimore Mass Transportation Administration (heavy rail); Metro-Dade Transportation Administration (heavy rail); Niagara Frontier Transportation Authority (light rail); Massachusetts Bay Transportation Authority (light rail).
AC propulsion: Municipality of Metropolitan Seattle (trolleybus).

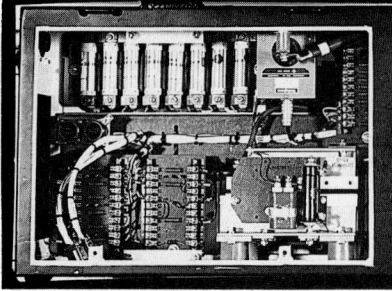

AEG Westinghouse thyristor chopper control

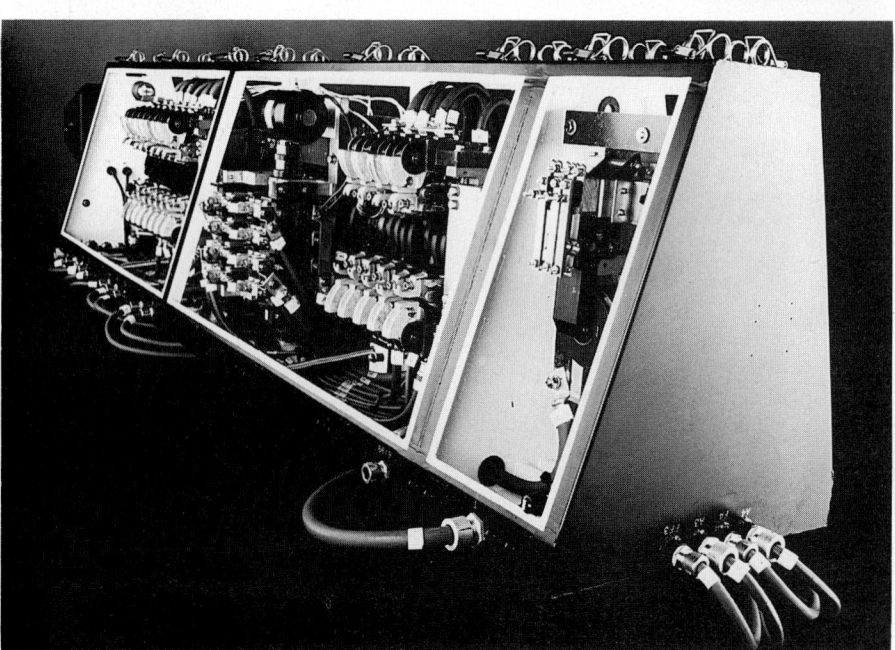

AEG Westinghouse ac inverter

AEG Westinghouse electric cam control

Electric traction equipment / **MANUFACTURERS** 179

Alsthom
GEC Alsthom
Transportation Division

Tour Neptune, 92086 Paris La Défense Cedex 20, France

Telephone: +33 1 47 44 9000
Telex: 611 207 alstr f
Telefax: +33 1 47 78 77 55

General Manager: Michel Perricaudet
Assistant General Manager: Michel Olivier

Plants: Belfort, Tarbes, Aytre-La Rochelle, Raismes, Ornans, Villeurbanne, Saint-Ouen, Marly-Les-Valenciennes, Aubevoye, Le Creusot

Subsidiaries and affiliates:
For full list see Alsthom entry in Locomotives section.

Products: All electrical and mechanical equipment; conventional and electronic switchgear, choppers, rectifiers, traction motors, bogies, signalling and automation. Control equipment for locomotives and railcars for urban, suburban and main line transportation, equipped with dc motors or with ac synchronous or induction motors; with dc power supply via JH electromechanical controllers; or with ac or dc power supply via electronic choppers (dc drive systems) or via chopper-inverters (synchronous and induction drive systems).

Static converters for power supply of motor vehicle auxiliaries; step-type control equipment; starting or braking rheostats, with or without forced ventilation; electronic auxiliary regulation systems and control logic; controllers and reversing equipment; driver's cabs and control desks; high-speed single-pole circuit breakers 1000 amps at 750 volts dc or 3000 amps at 1500 volts and 3000 volts dc, for traction equipment.

An order for four-car bi-level Type Z2N emus placed with Alsthom and ANF Industrie by French Railways early in 1986 specified equipment with asynchronous motors. The units are for the Paris RER Line C and delivery began in 1988. An option on a further 29 four-car sets covered their equipment with asynchronous motors also.

The electrical equipment is similar to the prototype applied in April 1985 to bi-level Z2N unit No Z8895. This unit can work in multiple with other dual-current emus and is itself able to operate under 1.5 kV dc and 25 kV ac catenary. Its equipment for each powered bogie comprises two asynchronous motors, and a fixed-frequency chopper series feeding two I-inverters, each inverter driving one motor. This equipment enables regenerative braking under both dc and ac overhead. Switchover from driving to braking mode is achieved through static components: reversal is simply obtained by modifying the thyristor-firing sequence of motor phases.

The main current feeding the inverters is regulated by the chopper. A microprocessor controls the inverter, the frequency of which is precalculated from the motor speed measurement. At low frequencies, the motor wave current is sub-chopped to reduce torque pulsations. The semi-conductors composing the chopper and the inverters are plunged in 113 freon inside air-tight tanks, the gills of which are forced-air cooled.

The Type 4 FLA 3258 traction motor is a squirrel-cage induction motor, mechanically interchangeable with the dc motors standardised on earlier Z2N units, but weighing 430 kg less. This motor is C class-insulated, self-ventilated and has four poles. Its main characteristics are as follows:
Frequency: 50 Hz
Output at shaft: 397.5 kW
Voltage: 580 V
Current: 470 A
Torque at shaft: 2580 Nm
Speed of rotation: 1470 rpm
Slip value: 0.02
Cos phi: 0.912
Weight: 1380 kg

Its maximum speed is 3036 rpm corresponding, with wheels at their mid-life, to 140 km/h for the train-set.

Alsthom has also developed prototype asynchronous motor systems for RATP, the Paris metro operator. The first equipment set, installed on the MF 67-type motorcoach M 10024, is of the impulse width-modulation voltage inverter-type. The two power coach monomotor bogies are equipped with self-ventilated asynchronous motors, each motor being supplied by a thyristor-type voltage inverter.

The second equipment set, installed on the MF 77-type motorcoach M 30029, includes one self-ventilated asynchronous motor, a current inverter and one chopper per bogie.

For the two traction chains, the use of flugene 113 (freon) as a heat transfer fluid permitted the realisation of natural convection equipment, while retaining motorcoach weights practically identical to those equipped with conventional traction chains.

Commercial operation of the two train-sets has validated the technical and technological options of the two projects. Subsequent progress achieved in the field of semi-conductors, and more particularly in the field of gate turn-off thyristors (GTO), enables a further considerable reduction in the number of power components, thus improving reliability. For the voltage

Synchronous traction motor for French Railways 'Sybic' Class BB 26000 locomotive

Asynchronous motor of French Railways bi-level suburban emu

Traction chopper for Lille VAL Line 1 Bis train-set

180 MANUFACTURERS / Electric traction equipment

inverter this permits the removal of the auxiliary turn-off circuits. For current inverter equipment the chopper is simplified due to the removal of the forced turn-off circuits.

Joint Alsthom-GEC Company: In December 1988 Alsthom's Board approved an agreement to combine the activities of Alsthom and the Power Systems Group of General Electric Company plc (GEC) of the UK under a jointly-owned company, titled GEC–Alsthom, in which Alsthom and GEC participate as to 50 per cent each. The scope of the joint company's activities include the development, production and marketing of equipment for rail transport. The supervisory board of the joint company is composed equally of representatives of CGE (Alsthom's French parent) and GEC. The Chairman of the Management Board is Jean-Pierre Desgeorges and the Vice-Chairman, Robert J Davidson. The company's principal operating office is in Paris.

Synchronous traction motor for French Railways TGV-Atlantique power car

Alsthom standard Type R-460 monomotor bogie for urban train-sets

Dc traction motor for Type Z2N bi-level motor car of French Railways

Ansaldo Trasporti
Ansaldo Trasporti SpA
A member of the Ansaldo Group

Head Office: 425 Via Argine, 80147 Naples, Italy
Works: 260 Via Nuova delle Brecce 80147, Naples, Italy

Telephone: +39 81 7810111
Telex: 710131 ans na i
Telefax: +39 81 7810698-699

Other offices:
336 Viale Sarca, 20126 Milan, Italy

Telephone: +39 2 64451
Telex: 331279
Telefax: +39 2 6438032

25 Corso Perrone, 16161 Genoa, Italy

Telephone: +39 10 65511
Telex: 271274
Telefax: +39 10 495044

Light traction motor by Ansaldo Trasporti

Electric traction equipment / **MANUFACTURERS** 181

Chairman: Giovanni Nobile
Vice President and Managing Director: Emilio Maraini
General Director: Francesco Granito
General Co-Director: Alberto G Rosania
Technical Director: Salvatore Bianconi
R & D and Commercial Director: Carlo Rizzi

Products: Electric propulsion equipments, either rheostatic or electric, for railway, urban and suburban vehicles with ac and dc traction motors; electronic converters and controls; auxiliary apparatus; planning, design and management methodologies for public transport; sales, assembly, start-up servicing.

Power cabinet of Italian Railways' Class E402 electric locomotive's electronic drive

Heavy traction motor for Italian Railways Type E491/2 ac electric locomotive under test

Assembly of static converters for locomotive auxiliaries

BBC-Sécheron
BBC-Sécheron Ltd
Transportation Systems
Company of the ASEA Brown Boveri Group

14 avenue de Sécheron, 1211 Geneva 21, Switzerland

Telephone: +41 22 394111
Telex: 22130
Telefax: +41 22 342194

Products: Components for electric locomotives, electric and diesel-electric traction vehicles of all kinds including dc high-speed circuit breakers, dc and ac contactors, braking resistors, commutators, reversers, relays, isolating switches, manipulators and current collectors. Electronic control systems for electric and diesel-electric traction vehicles.

The Type CER electronic control system is specially designed to modernise electric vehicles with motors controlled electromechanically. The CER is microprocessor-driven. Modernisation is confined generally to the control equipment; power circuits remained unchanged. The CER system narrows the technological gap between vehicles of modern conception and those of the previous generation. The service life of such vehicles is lengthened at a small fraction of the cost of new vehicles.

Recourse to electronics brings about not only technological progress but provides also for monitoring functions, yielding the important benefits of system protection and optimal performance and utilisation of the vehicle, thanks to reduced stressing of the power equipment.

BBC-Sécheron has now supplied more than 2400 electronic control systems for locomotives, train-sets, tramways, underground railways, LRVs and trolleybuses.

Constitution: Member of the ASEA Brown Boveri Group. The company was founded as A de Meuron & Cuénod in 1879 for the manufacture of electrical equipment.

BHEL
Bharat Heavy Electricals Ltd

Bhopal, 462 022 India

Telephone: +91 755 540200
Cable: Bharatelec Bhopal
Telex: 705 264 bhbp in; 705 265 bhp in
Telefax: +91 755 540425

General Manager: S K Handa
General Manager, Transportation: B P Jain
Deputy General Manager, Transportation & Oil Field Systems: G P Varshney
Deputy General Manager, Transportation Systems Engineering: N K Jain

Group companies
Bharat Heavy Electricals Ltd
Jhansi 284 129
(Electric locomotives, diesel-electric shunting locomotives and traction transformers)
Additional General Manager: T S Nanda
Product Manager, Locomotives: Y Pathak

MANUFACTURERS / Electric traction equipment

Bharat Heavy Electricals Limited
Transportation Business Department, Lodhi Road, New Delhi 110 003

Telephone: +91 11 616756
Telefax: +91 11 618837 (Marketing)
General Manager: K R Ramachandran

Constitution: BHEL is a multi-product multi-unit company and its corporate office with the Chairman and Board of Directors is located at New Delhi. The electric traction activities are centred at Bhopal which also controls the locomotive manufacturing work at the Jhansi plant.

Products: Electrical propulsion equipment for electric, diesel-electric and battery vehicles (locomotives, electric multiple-units and tram cars), equipment for traction sub-stations. BHEL is the major supplier of electrical equipment to the locomotive and coach building works of Indian Railways and have supplied about 3000 sets of electrics, including more than 20 000 traction motors and generators with matching control gear, locomotive transformers etc. The 76 coaches operating commercial services on India's maiden underground railway at Calcutta are all equipped with BHEL electrics. Metre-gauge diesel electric locomotives incorporating BHEL electrics have been exported to Tanzania and Vietnam.

Metre-gauge emus incorporating thyristor control equipment from BHEL (in collaboration with GEC Alsthom) have recently completed performance, signalling and telecommunications compatibility tests on Southern Railways and now have been cleared for commercial services.

BSI
Bergische Stahl-Industrie Verkehrstechnik

PO Box 1001 65, D 5630 Remscheid 1, Federal Republic of Germany

Telephone: +49 21 91 150
Telex: 8513858
Telefax: +49 21 91 152215

Main works:
Papenberger Strasse 38, D 5630 Remscheid 1
Oberhausener Strasse 1, D 4330 Mülheim/Ruhr

Member of Board: Dr Ing H Zeuner
General Manager: W Wiebelhaus
Senior Sales Manager: O Berghaus

Products: Axle drives for urban, underground and rapid transit railway vehicles; more than 35 000 in use world-wide.

Two bevel gear systems are offered. In System 1, the weight of the power package is supported by the axle. There is no contact to the bogie frame. The jointing elements between the axle drive and the axle are flexible coupling discs or rubber pad couplings.

In System 2 the power package is coupled to the bogie frame. Two tandem-joined rubber-pad couplings, which are tightly connected to the hollow shaft of the gearbox on one side and on the other to the axle shaft, maintain a centering effect on a second hollow shaft that passes through the gearbox between the axle shaft and the hollow shaft of the gearbox. For each system axle drives adaptable to all types of city street cars, rapid transit and metro cars, are available.

As to design and construction, the two-piece casing is made of sphereolitic cast iron or, particularly for underground and rapid transit cars, of light alloy. Both housing halves are centred and connected by high-tensile necked-down bolts. A hollow shaft, enclosing the axle with clearance, is bearing-supported within the casing. The sealing between the housing and the hollow shaft is achieved by contract-free and maintenance-free labyrinth packings, having three oversize square chambers. This design ensures absolute oil-tightness.

The bevel gear drive with axle offset is designed according to the Klingelnberg cyclo-palloid toothing system. The gears are case-hardened and HPG cutted. In order to determine optimal toothing properties, dimensioning criteria for every case of application, such as axleload, cruising programme and operating conditions, are considered. The pinion shaft and crown wheel are made of high-tensile drop-forged case-hardened steel. The crown-wheel is frictionally connected to the hollow shaft by bolts and fitting screws. The connection between the pinion shaft and the armature shaft of the motor is secured as a rule by a two-hinged tooth coupling which is greased by transmission oil.

The company's bogie-suspended motor drive for rapid transit, underground or heavy rail systems is claimed to have these advantages: low unsprung weight by virtue of bogie suspension and a light alloy casing; resilient and silent running through use of double helical toothing and torsion bar drive, compact design that saves mounting space, and easy mounting through the shrink-disc fit of the ring gear.

Single-axle drives with parallel shaft motor are chiefly used in three-phase current systems, all the more so as BSI Verkehrstechnik has introduced various refinements:

Heat and noise generation is reduced owing to the high efficiency of the single-helical or double-helical spur gear unit with optimal helix angle.

The input diaphragm coupling with cardan action and provided with a torsion shaft allows motor suspension in the bogie, which reduces unsprung masses. This feature is enhanced by the lightweight gear unit with its axle-mounted greater wheel and a torque-restraining arm connected with the bogie.

A further development is a high-speed three-phase current motor and a spur gear unit, for instance as a two-stage variant.

The motor and the gear unit are connected by a torsionally stiff, flexurally elastic Rigiflex shaft coupling. So the pinion bearing serves as the second support point of the overhung motor shaft.

The entire mechanical and electrical drive is fixed in the bogie.

The gear unit and the axle are connected by means of a hollow-shaft wedge rubber pad coupling, which is a tried and tested BSI development.

Double helical toothing ensures smooth running thanks to its high helix angle and a long service life as axial thrust on the bearing is avoided.

Additionally, single-helical or spur toothing is available, the bearing system having to be adapted to requirements in each case.

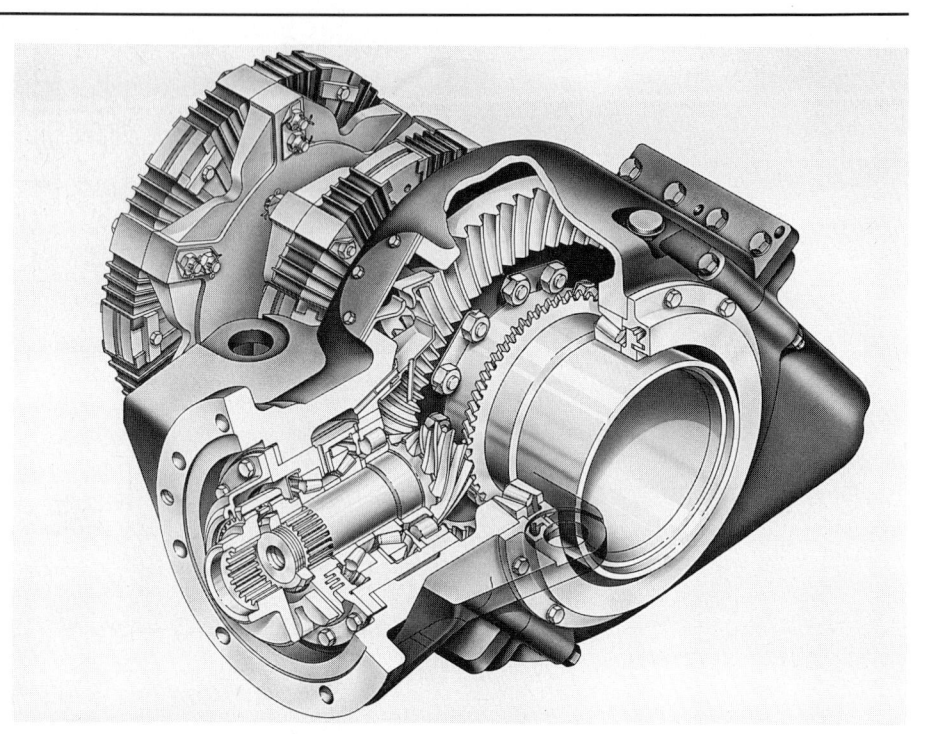

BSI bogie-mounted bevel gear

BSI compact-design drive with two-stage spur gear unit, disc brake and actuator, single-side hollow-shaft rubber-pad coupling and integrated three-phase current motor (bogie drive)

Electric traction equipment / **MANUFACTURERS** 183

Brecknell, Willis
Brecknell, Willis & Co Ltd
Member of the Fandsten Electric Group

Chard, Somerset TA20 2DE, England

Telephone: +44 460 64941
Telex: 46518
Telefax: +44 935 79140

Chairman: Lord Tanlaw
Managing Director: Tony Hobbs
Marketing & Projects Manager: Tony White

Products: A complete range of current collection and power distribution equipment for all applications in the transportation sector. These include a range of pantographs for railways, tramways, metros and light rail systems.

Also complete third rail systems for railway and metro applications covering design, manufacture, supply and installation of third rail electrification systems.

Automatic gas tensioning equipment. Brecknell Willis supplies gas tensioning equipment for better tensioning control in catenary and contact wire systems. A range of spring boxes is also available.

One of the most recent projects has been the completion of 7.3 km of the South Hampshire Electrification Scheme for Network SouthEast using aluminium/stainless steel conductor rail.

Brecknell Willis' involvement in the Docklands Light Railway City Extension is due to be completed at the end of 1990.

The Company has manufactured pantographs for BREL for the Class 90 and 91 locomotives, as well as Classes 319, 320 and 321 emus.

Third rail shoegear – including vehicles – for the Beckton Extension, and an order from BN of Belgium for third rail collectors and auxiliary equipment complete the list of recent contracts.

Bristol
Bristol Pneumatic Ltd

Chequers Bridge, Gloucester GL1 4LL, England

Telephone: +44 452 28431
Telex: 43233 wiljay g
Telefax: +44 452 507394

Products: Pantograph air compressor: a compact air-cooled compressor direct-coupled to dc motor (0.7 kW). Constructed in heavy duty cast iron this compressor offers maximum scope for choice of mounting position on locomotive. Charging rate: 126 litres/min over pressure range 0 to 75 psi (0 to 5 bar). Maximum operating pressure: 100 psi (7 bar). Dimensions: 46 cm × 26 cm × 27 cm; weight with motor, 43 kg.

Brush
Brush Electrical Machines Ltd (Traction Division)

PO Box 18, Falcon Works, Loughborough, Leicestershire LE11 1HJ, England

Telephone: +44 509 611511
Telex: 341091
Telefax: +44 509 610440

Chairman: R P Hampson
Managing Director: W M M Petrie

Traction Director: B G Sephton
Sales & Projects Manager: A L Williams

Products: Electrical transmission equipment including main and auxiliary alternators, traction motors and control equipment. 100 sets of electrical transmission equipment for Class 60 diesel locomotives for British Rail.

Electrical propulsion equipment including control equipment, traction motors, transformers and electrical auxiliary equipment for electric locomotives, suburban and intercity trains, metro cars and light rail vehicles.

Recent contracts include: 76 sets of electrical propulsion equipment for BR Class 321 emus; five sets of electrical propulsion equipment for BR Class 322 emus; 22 sets of electrical propulsion equipment for BR Class 320 emus; eight sets of electrical propulsion equipment for Taiwan Railway emus; 33 sets of propulsion equipment for London Underground metro cars; and 52 sets of electrical propulsion equipment for Toronto ALRVs (Canada).

CENEMESA
Constructora Nacional de Maquinaria Electrica SA

Victor Hugo 4, Madrid 28004, Spain

Telephone: +34 1 2317200
Cable: Cnmesa
Telex: 22430
Telefax: +34 1 2323118

General Manager: José Maria Aldeanueva Abaunza
Director, Traction Group: Angel de Nicolás y Diaz de Garayo

Works: Reinosa: motors, motor-generators sets, motor-compressors and reactors
Erandio: control equipments, static inverters and electric switch-gear for substations
Madrid: main resistors, services

Products: Traction motors, motor-generator sets, motor compressors, reactors, static inverters, main resistors, cam-shaft and chopper-controlled equipment for electric locomotives, electric motor units, rectifier sub-stations both mobile or static, after-sale service, maintenance and repair works.

CENEMESA has lately built electric equipment for the following: 20 emus for suburban service between Bilbao and Plencia, 960 kW 1500 V dc chopper-controlled; 35 M-T-MMM train-sets for Barcelona Metro 2400/1900 kW, 1500/1200 V dc chopper-controlled; 31 Series 444-500 emus for RENFE, 1160 kW 3000 V dc cam-shaft controlled; and 50 Series 446 emus for RENFE, 2300 kW 3000 V dc chopper-controlled (freon-cooled GTO thyristors).

Constitution: Member of the CENEMESA group of companies.

CGE
Compagnie Générale d'Electricité

54 rue de la Boétie, 75382 Paris Cedex 08, France

Telephone: +33 1 4 563 14 14
Cable: Electricté, Paris 8
Telex: 280953

The companies within the CGE Group covering electrical contracting are: CGEE Alsthom; Comsip Entreprise; and Controle Bailey

Products: Electrical and electronic equipment and construction.

The Group has been concerned with numerous metro constructions in France and abroad, including those of Lyons, Marseilles, Montreal, Santiago, São Paulo, Mexico City, Rio de Janeiro, Caracas, Lisbon and Cairo.

CGE
Compagnia Generale di Electricta SpA

Via dei Missaglia 97, Milan, Italy

Telephone: +39 2 82 29 1
Telex: 333851

Products: Electric transmissions.

CLYDE
Clyde Engineering Co Pty Ltd

Motive Power Division

Factory Street, Granville, PO Box 73, New South Wales 2142, Australia

Telephone: +61 2 637 8288
Telex: 21647
Telefax: +61 2 637 8735

Products: Traction motors.

Dearmedelec
Dearmedelec SAIC

Juramento 4182/86, 1430 Buenos Aires, Argentina

Telephone: +54 1 526766/3409/7036

Products: Static exciting systems, traction motor transition systems, battery charge regulator.

184 MANUFACTURERS / Electric traction equipment

EFE North America Inc
OB Transit Products

380 North Main St, Mansfield, Ohio 44903-1319, USA

Telephone: +1 419 522 7111
Telex: 987414
Telefax: +1 419 522 7069

Main Works address: PO Box 7758, Huntington, WV 25778, USA

President: John Russell
Product Manager: Joe Reed

Products: Catenary and trolley subsystem equipment and components; transit car electrical and electromechanical equipment, coupling and collection.

Recent contracts include the supply of traction power substations for a light rail system in Monterrey, Mexico. The design is similar to units supplied at an earlier date for a light rail system in San Diego, California.

Faiveley
Faiveley SA
Transportation Department

93 rue du Docteur Bauer, 93407 Saint Ouen Cedex, France

Telephone: +33 1 4264 12 60
Telex: 290653
Telefax: +33 1 4606 0001

Products: Pantographs and collector shoes. The company's range of single-arm pantographs includes: the LV unit, for installation on dc or ac locomotives and power cars; and the LVT unit, for tramways and light rail vehicles. A Faiveley double-stage pantograph was mounted on the TGV unit with which French Railways secured a new world rail speed record of 380 km/h in February 1981.

(For further details of company see Faiveley entry in Passenger Coach Equipment section).

Faiveley double-stage pantograph on French Railways TGV train-set

Faiveley Type LV2600 pantograph with electric control

Ferraz SA

28 rue Saint Philippe, 69003 Lyon, France

Telephone: +33 72 22 66 11
Telex: 300534
Telefax: +33 72 22 67 13

Works:
28 rue Saint Philippe, 69003 Lyon, France
BP No 3025 69391 Lyon CEDEX 3

70 Avenue de la Gare, BP No 18-38290 La Verpilliere, France

Rue Vaucanson-69720 St Bonnet de Mure, France

Marketing Manager: M Renart
Export Sales Manager: H Behr

Principal subsidiary companies: Fouilleret, Ferraz Corporation (USA), Nihon Ferraz (Japan), worldwide representation in more than 40 countries

Products: Earth return current units; brush-holders for electric traction motors; current-collecting device on live rail; fuses with very high breaking capacity for protection; automatic earthing device with large short-circuit capability; resistors.

Recent contracts include the supply of traction brush-holders for ETR 450 and 500 trains (Italian Railways); disconnectors for TGV-A (SNCF); Protistor fuses for Loc 1044 (Austrian Federal Railways).

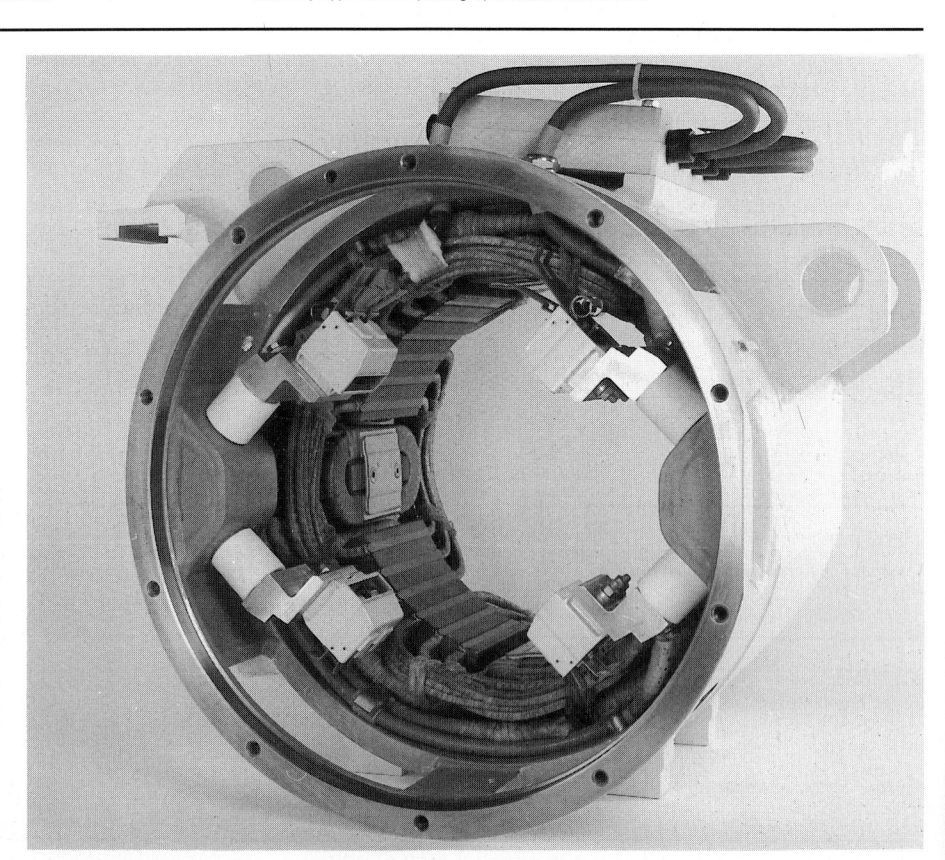

A brush-holder assembly on a GEC Alsthom traction motor

Fuji Electric
Fuji Electric Co Ltd

New Yurakucho Building 12-1, Yurakucho 1-chome, Chiyoda-ku, Tokyo 100, Japan

Telephone: +81 3 211 7111
Telex: 22331, 26374
Telefax: +81 3 214 2744

Products: Traction motor with chopper control, static converter, brushless motor generating set, pantograph for Shinkansen (250 km/h); power supply equipment; remote supervisory control equipment with computer, freon cooling silicon rectifier. SF6 gas circuit breakers and mini high-speed circuit breakers; moulded transformer; total control system including electric power management, station office apparatus control, data management and disaster prevention management.

Electric traction equipment / **MANUFACTURERS** 185

GANZ
GANZ Electric Works

PO Box 63, Budapest H-1525, Hungary
Lövöház u39, Budapest H-1024, Hungary

Telephone: +36 1 175 3322
Telex: 225363 gvm bp
Telefax: +36 1 156 2989

General Manager: Gábor Kara

Products: Traction motors, auxiliary machinery, traction transformers, reactors; traction rectifiers, inverters and controls; traction apparatus – pantographs, resistors, control gears, jumps etc.

GEC Transmission and Distribution Projects
GEC Transmission and Distribution Projects Ltd

PO Box 27, Stafford ST17 4LN, England

Telephone: +44 785 57111
Telex: 36203
Telefax: +44 785 52540

Managing Director: K J Ralls
Sales Director: E G Nolan

Products: Variable voltage, variable frequency, pulse width modulated inverter systems for ac drives incorporating transistor or GTO thyristor techniques; levitation and drive control systems for magnetic levitation schemes.

Recent contracts include: 1983 to 1986: transistorised power conversion units installed on light rail vehicles for Intermediate Capacity Transit Systems at Scarborough in Ontario, Vancouver in British Columbia and Detroit in the USA; 1984: battery chargers, propulsion and levitation controls for Maglev vehicles at Birmingham Airport, UK; and 1989: GTO power conversion units for vehicles in light rail system Milan, Italy.

Groupement 50 Hz
50 c/s Group

Baumackerstrasse 46, PO Box 8524, 8050 Zurich, Switzerland

Telephone: +41 1 312 46 80/312 46 81
Cable: Coordinat, Zurich
Telex: 823 854 sehz ch
Telefax: +41 1 312 3968

Products: Traction rolling stock and stationary equipment for all aspects of railway electrification including planning, design, technical co-ordination and installation.
Electrifications completely furnished by the Group have included: the Lisbon-Oporto line of Portuguese Railways (CP); Jung Ang, Tae Baeg and Yeong Don lines of Korean National Railroad (KNR); and the Linea Bananera of Ferrocarriles de Costa Rica (FECOSA).

Constitution: The Group comprises ACEC Transport of Belgium, GEC Alsthom of France and UK, AEG Westinghouse and Siemens AG of the Federal Republic of Germany.

Hitachi
Hitachi Ltd

6 Kanda Suragadai, 4-chome, Chiyoda-ku, Tokyo 101, Japan

Telephone: +81 3 258 1111
Cable: Hitachi, Tokyo
Telex: 22395, 22432, 24491, 26385 hitachy

President: Katsushige Mita
Executive Vice President and Director: Masataka Nishi
Board Director: Toshi Kitamura

Products: Propulsion systems, auxiliary power supply, ATP/ATO equipment, computerised total systems for urban transportation, bogie and air-conditioning equipment.
Recent sales have included:
63 VVVF inverter control equipments for Tokyu Corporation, Kinki Nippon Railway, controller for linear motor driven electric cars.
546 chopper controllers for private railways and subways (since 1970).
Computerised total system and automatic train operation system based on fuzzy control for Sendai Municipal Transportation Bureau.
Recent developments:
In view of developing use of ac induction motor propulsion systems, Hitachi has been busy in bringing out VVVF inverters for train-sets of 1500 V dc railways.
The small size of Hitachi VVVF inverters has been achieved by use of 4500 V high-voltage GTO thyristors. Direct digital control with monitoring system by 16-bit microprocessors provides excellent accuracy in constant speed control, slip-skid correction control and start control on up gradients. The signalling system is protected from noise and electromagnetic interference by extensive shielding and optimised wiring layout.
Hitachi Cable has developed fibre-optic cables for use in monitoring and control systems in electric train cars. They are being used in the latest versions of Japanese National Railways' Tokaido and Sanyo Shinkansen line cars.

Holec Ridderkerk
Holec Machines and Apparaten BV

Head office: PO Box 4050, 2980 GB Ridderkerk, Netherlands

Telephone: +31 74 465000/465465
Telex: 20377 hslik hl
Telefax: +31 74 465444

Works: Ringdijk 390, Ridderkerk

Managing Director: Ir H Smidt
Product Group Manager, Traction: Ir A Hoogerwaard

Modular Holec chopper installation in tramway car of The Hague

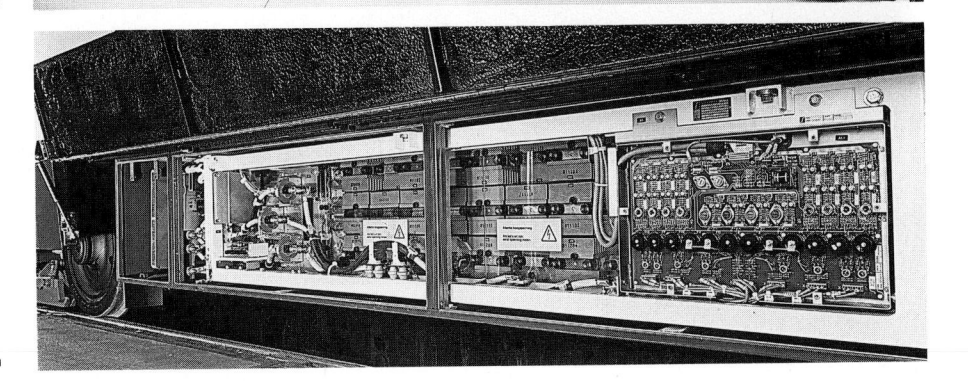

Microprocessor-controlled three-phase ac inverter using totally enclosed cage induction motors in traction system

MANUFACTURERS / Electric traction equipment

Products: Manufacturers of electrical equipment for rolling stock, offering design, manufacture and commissioning of complete traction systems following conventional designs or designs based on power electronics for vehicles to operate on main-line, interurban, urban rapid transit, underground, tramway or trolleybus systems.

Thyristor inverter with air cooling for Rotterdam tramcar

Kiepe Elektrik
Kiepe Elektrik GmbH

Thorner Strasse 1, 400 Düsseldorf 13, Federal Republic of Germany

Telephone: +49 211 74 97-1
Telex: 8581471
Telefax: +49 211 7497 300

General Manager: M Martin
Commercial Sales Director: G Rubach
Traction Department Manager: W Huober

Parent company: Alsthom SA

Products: Propulsion control equipment for 600 and 750 V dc supply, including three-phase ac and dc chopper power electronics for LRVs with regenerative braking, and rotating camshaft controller or contactor bank controller (switched resistor) for underground or LRVs with control electronics in microprocessor technology; dc contactors, reversers, switches; master controllers; braking resistors; power electronics; door and step controls; weight, speed and displacement transducers; time delay-, light- and blinker-relays; and static converters.

LRV master controller by Kiepe

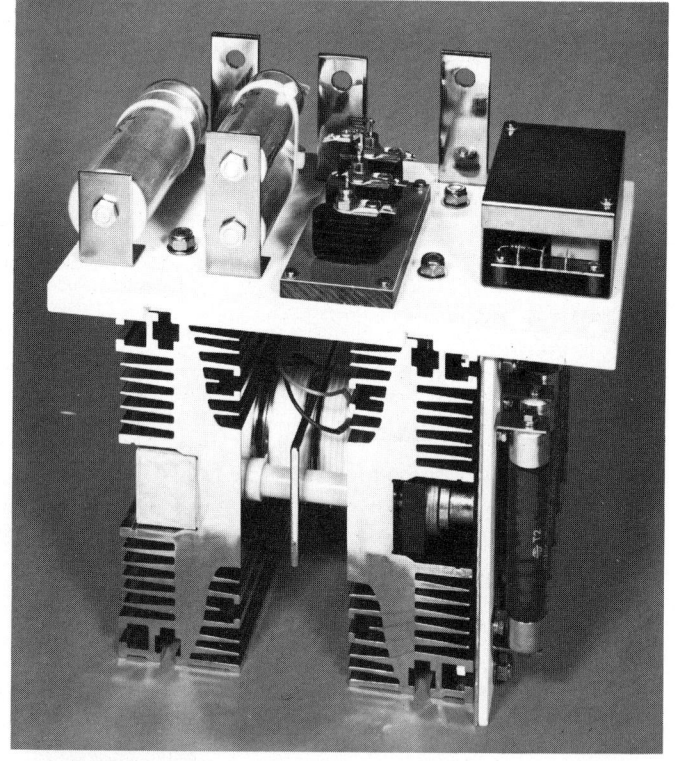

Thyristor power module for three-phase ac equipment by Kiepe

Electronically-controlled camshaft controller for Alexandria, Egypt, LRV by Kiepe

Major contracts currently held cover: Tube stock vehicles; battery/line locomotives for various metro and LRV operators; three-phase ac equipment for low-floor trams. Kiepe supplies components and sub-assemblies for most LRV and underground projects in the Federal German Republic. The company is also expert in installing and wiring the electrical equipment of vehicles at a carbuilder's factory.

Constitution: In 1988 Alsthom acquired full ownership of Kiepe Elektrik, which was formerly a subsidiary of ACEC in Belgium. The transaction also included the subsidiary Kiepe Electric in Vienna, Austria.

This purchase allows Alsthom's Rail Transport Division to reinforce its range of electrical equipment with highly specialised products.

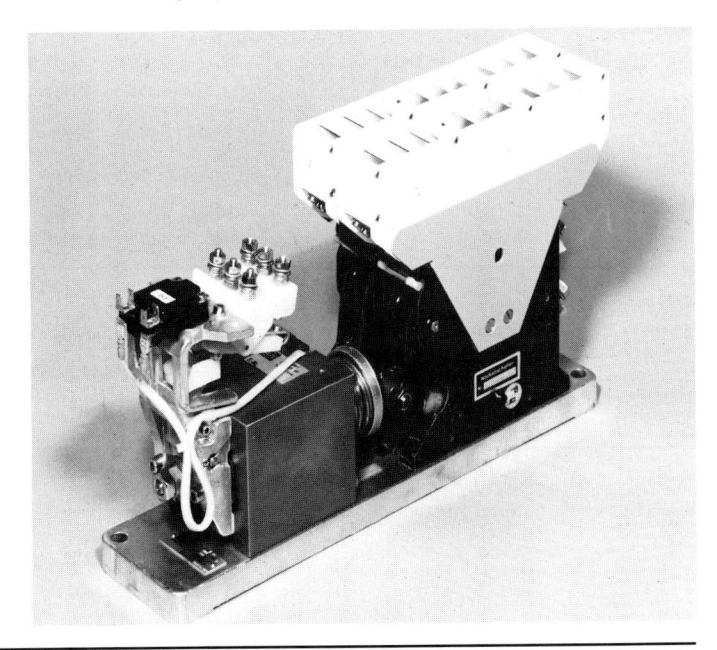

Dc contactor, two-pole, 750 V dc, 400 A by Kiepe

Marconi
Marconi Electronic Devices Limited

Lincoln Industrial Park, Doddington Road, Lincoln LN6 3LF, England

Telephone: +44 522 500500
Telex: 56380
Telefax: +44 522 500550

Main works address: Power Semiconductor Division, Carholme Road, Lincoln, LN1 1SG, UK

Telephone: +44 522 510500
Telex: 56163
Telefax: +44 522 510550

Managing Director: A J Sadler
Sales Director: W W Reid
Director, Power Semiconductor Division: R J Francey
Sales/Marketing Manager, Power Semiconductor Division: N G Hobdey
Export Manager, Power Semiconductor Division: S F Coley

Products: Power semiconductor devices: thyristors, diodes, transistors, gate turn-off thyristors (GTOs) and air, oil, water and phase change cooling assemblies. These products may be used for on-board or track-side equipment.

Contracts executed and obtained have covered: SNCF BB 7200 (1979 to 1983); SNCF/RATP Interconnections M179 (1979 to 1983); SNCF Z2N and Z2N-2U (1981 to 1983); BRB Class 317 emu (1984); Seoul Metro Lines C and D (1984); RATP MI84 Metro (1985); SNCF TGV Sud-Est (1979 to 1983); Switzerland, various projects (1980 onwards); BRB Class 319 in service 1988; BRB Class 90 and 91; SNCF TGV Atlantique.

ML
Metalmeccanica Lucana

85050 Tito Scalo (Potenza), Italy

Telephone: +39 971 65088
Telex: 812332
Telefax: +39 971 65072

Products: Electric traction equipment, comprising both rotating machines and traditional and electronic equipment, for railways and urban transit systems; traction motors and auxiliary dc motors; chopper equipments for 3 kV dc electric motor coaches for commuter and intercity services; electric equipments for heavy-duty six-axle 3 kV dc locomotives; electric equipments for 3 kV dc train-sets for local railways; static dc/ac and dc/dc converters for locomotives and motor coaches.

National
National Electrical Carbon Corporation

PO Box 1056, Greenville, South Carolina 29602, USA

Telephone: +1 803 458 7777
Telex: 205 248
Telefax: +1 803 281 0180

President: R P Kimlin
Vice President, Marketing: M Cox
Marketing Manager: R F Zegar
International Sales Manager: K Osman

Principal subsidiaries
National Electrical Carbon BV, Hoorn, Holland
National Electrical Carbon Canada, Mississauga, Ontario
National Electrical Carbon Limited, Sheffield, England

Products: Carbon brushes for all traction, commutator, motor generator and auxiliary equipment, carbon brush holders and wheel flange lubricators.

Pafawag
Fabryka Wagonow Pafawag

ul Pstrowskiego 12, 53-609 Wroclaw, Poland

Telephone: +48 71 56 21 11
Telex: 0712432

Management Engineer: R Geppert
Commercial Director: K Krzyczmonik

Products: Single-arm current collector for supply of standard-gauge traction vehicles from overhead trolley wire with the voltage of 3000 V, maximum speed 160 km/h and rated current 1000 A. Weight of collector, 258 kg; sliding height when folded, 386 mm; lifting time, 15 sec; folding time (adjustable) 5–20 sec.

Parizzi
Elettromeccanica Parizzi SpA

Via C Romani 8/10, 20091 Bresso (Milan), Italy

Telephone: +39 2 6106301
Telex: 332831 elepar i
Telefax: +39 2 6140408

Spanish subsidiary
Systemas Electronicos de Potencia, SA
Albatros, 7 y 9, pinto (Madrid)

Telephone: +341 6915311 61
Telex: 22253 sept e
Telefax: +341 2227697

Products: Energy converters: mono and poli-current static converters fed by the primary power line to supply power for on-board auxiliary systems in three-phase 50 Hz ac (input voltages: 3000 V dc, 1500 V dc, 1500 V ac, 50 Hz, 1000 V ac 16⅔ Hz. Powers: 40 to 85 kVA); mono and poli-current static battery chargers fed by the primary power line (input voltages: as above, 600, 750 and 1500 V dc. Powers: 1, 5 to 14 kW); inverters and converters; UPS.

Traction equipment: variable frequency and voltage inverters for the supply and control of asynchronous traction motors for diesel-electric locomotives and metro multiple-units; ac traction motors.

Components: electrical and electro-pneumatic components for rail cars and locomotives; automatic starters; controllers and reverse switches; electrical connectors for multiple traction; various transducers.

Electro-mechanical devices: battery chargers operated from the axle of the bogie of railway vehicles.

Electronic systems: microprocessor-based control and diagnostic systems; centralised tachometric/tachographic and event-recording systems; electronic anti-slide devices to adapt the braking force to the instantaneous adhesion condition of railway vehicles; electronic anti-slip devices for locomotives; bivalent anti-slide/anti-slip devices.

MANUFACTURERS / Electric traction equipment

Siemens
Siemens AG Transportation Systems Group

Werner-von-Siemens-Strasse 50, Postfach 32 40, D-8520 Erlangen, Federal Republic of Germany

Telephone: +49 9131 724157
Cable: Siemens, Erlangen
Telex: 6291508 si d
Telefax: +49 9131 726840

Transportation Systems Group President: W O Martinsen
Mass Transit Rolling Stock Division: Gerhard Scholtis
Mainline Rolling Stock Division: R Stubenrauch

Products: Electrical traction equipment for ac and dc vehicles such as dc motors and three-phase asynchronous motors, static converters/inverters (GTO); SIBAS 16 a universal microcomputer systems for any control application in traction vehicles; dc contactors and choppers, transformers, pantographs; electrical equipment for trolley buses, complete traction vehicles. (See Siemens entry in Locomotives and Powered Passenger Vehicles section for fuller detail.)

Siemens
Siemens Energy & Automation Inc
Transportation Industry

150 Hembree Park Drive CS 100150, Roswell, Georgia 30077-7150, USA

Telephone: +1 404 751 3180
Telex: 543281
Telefax: +1 404 664 0672

Products: Electric traction equipment.

The company was associated with Duewag in the supply of LRVs for the Port Authority of Allegheny County, Pittsburgh, Pennsylvania, San Diego MTDB and Sacramento Regional Transit.

Siemens Plessey
Siemens Plessey Controls Limited

Sopers Lane, Poole, Dorset BH17 7ER, England

Telephone: +44 202 782000
Telex: 41272
Telefax: +44 202 782331

General Manager: D G Hornby
Marketing Manager: A J Rose
Product Manager: B J Watkins
Sales Manager: M T Deem

Products: Control and monitoring systems to allow locomotives to be connected in tandem or operate in push-pull mode. A high-speed multiplexed data system transmits control and indications through a minimum of two wires along the length of the train. The systems are designed to meet the severe traction environment and are in regular service on a number of main line electric and diesel locomotives.

SIGLA
Sigla Equipamentos Elétricos SA

Av Brigadeiro Faria Lima 2003, 14 andar 01451 São Paulo SP, Brazil

Main works: Avenida da Saudade, s/No 13170 Sumaré/SP, Brazil

Telephone: +55 11 210 3299
Telex: 11 83171
Telefax: +55 11 813 09 43
Marketing Director: D M Elie Huet
Director, Branch Transportation: M A Giavina-Bianchi

Products: Chopper control systems for traction, high and low voltage switchboards, self inductive coils, resistors and static convertors, traction rectifiers, control boards, auxiliary switchboards and low voltage rectifiers. Axle counters, way circuits, energy and signalling synoptic panels, data transmission boards, relay racks and impedance bonds.
Recent contracts include rolling stock modifications for the Metro de São Paulo's East/West subway and installation of electrification system on the Paulista Subway (substation and auxiliary supplies).

SMC
SMC Pneumatics (Australia) Pty Ltd
Transport Division

161 Showground Road, Castle Hill, New South Wales 2154, Australia

Telephone: +61 2 680 3222
Telex: 7123152
Telefax: +61 2 634 7764

Manager: Robert Jolly

Products: Current collections pantographs and carbon wear strips for ac and dc power supply.
Recent contracts have included supply of pneumatic door-operating equipment and current collection pantographs for the Hong Kong KCRC LRV project, SRA of NSW suburban, inter-urban and XPT passenger cars, 25 kV pantographs for Queensland Rail heavy-haulage locomotives, high-speed locomotive pantographs for the Indian Railways and pneumatics for passenger doors and current collection pantographs for the Perth (Australia) electrification project.

SMC-Schunk WB-85 air-bag pantograph

Socimi
Società Costruzioni Industriali Milano SpA

Head office: Via Varesina 115, 20156 Milan, Italy

Telephone: +39 2 30091
Telex: 323564

Main works
Via Enrico Fermi 25, 20082 Binasco (Milan)
Telephone: +39 2 9055605/6/7/8

Via Donatori del Sangue 100, 20010 Arluno (Milan)
Telephone: +39 2 9017666, 9017803

Viale Porto Torres, Reg Zentu Figghi, 07100 Sassari
Telephone: +39 79 260206

Chairman: Alessandro Marzocco
Managing Director: Pierino Sacchi
Assistant to Chairman: Corrado Landolina

Products: Pantographs, electrically or air-operated.

Strömberg
A member of the ASEA Brown Boveri Group

PO Box 184, 00381 Helsinki, Finland

Telephone: +358 0 5641
Cable: Dynamo, Helsinki
Telex: 124405
Telefax: +358 0 554 620

President: Matti Ilmari

Profit Centre Manager, Traction Drives: Börje Stjernberg
Marketing Manager, Traction Drives: Keijo Kärhä
Engineering Manager, Traction Drives: Juhani Helosvuori

Products: Electric drives, especially traction drives for trains, undergrounds, locomotives, trams and trolleybuses.
Twenty ac propulsion drives will be delivered for diesel-electric railcars built by Comeng. The cars will be operated by the State Rail Authority of South Australia in Adelaide.
Finnish State Railways has ordered 23 diesel-electric locomotives equipped with Strömberg's ac induction motor drive.
The company has been selected to participate in a demonstration programme of advanced metro car drives together with Garrett Corporation, with which Strömberg has co-operation in USA. This co-operation has also resulted in an order for 150 static auxiliary inverters for the metro cars of San Francisco.

Electric traction equipment / **MANUFACTURERS**

Stemmann
Stemmann-Technik GmbH

PO Box 1460, D 4443 Schültorf, Federal Republic of Germany

Telephone: +49 5923 81 0
Telex: 9 8813
Telefax: +49 5923 81 100

Products: Standard pantographs for light rail vehicles, underground tramways and suburban transit systems per German DIN specification 43 187, and modified versions to suit customer requirements; heavy-duty pantographs for trunk railroads for all catenary voltages (up to 25 kV) in conventional (diamond) and contemporary single-arm style; pantographs for industrial locomotives, custom designed to suit any catenary arrangement.

TIBB
Tecnomasio Italiano Brown Boveri SpA
(Company of the ASEA Brown Boveri Group)

CP 10225, 20137 Milan, Italy

Telephone: +39 2 5797 1
Cable: Tecnomasio, Milan
Telex: 310153

Products: Static and rotary converters for auxiliary services; dc and ac generators; single-arm pantographs and electromagnetic rail brakes; substations for dc traction.

Toshiba
Toshiba Corporation
Railway Projects Department

Toshiba Building, 1-1, Shibaura 1-chome, Minato-ku, Tokyo 105, Japan

Telephone: +81 3 457 4924
Cable: Toshiba Tokyo
Telex: 22587 toshiba
Telefax: +81 3 457 0843

Overseas Offices: New York, San Francisco, Houston, Vancouver; Mexico, Caracas, Bogota, Rio de Janeiro, Buenos Aires; London, Berlin, Vienna, Athens; Cairo, Tehran, Baghdad, Dubai, Jeddah; Beijing, Guangzhou, Shanghai, Taipei, Hong Kong, Manila, Bangkok, Jakarta, New Delhi; Sydney.

Toshiba International Corporation: San Francisco, Houston, Tulsa, Vancouver

Toshiba International Corporation Pty Ltd: Sydney

Toshiba International (Europe) Ltd: London

Products: Electric traction equipment; auxiliary power supply units; coach air-conditioner; industrial rolling stock.

One of the systems of advanced technology that has been under development, in this case in conjunction with Japanese National Railways, is the propulsion system for the next generation of Shinkansen Super-Hikari train-sets, which consists of a 3000 kW pulse width modulation converter with 4500 V-2000 A GTO, 1760 kVA VVVF inverter also with 4500 V-2000 A GTO, and eight 320 kW induction motors.

Toyo Denki
Toyo Denki Seizo KK
Toyo Electric Manufacturing Co Ltd

Yaesu Mitsui Building, No 7-2 Yaesu, 2-chome, Chuo-ku, Tokyo 104, Japan

Telephone: +81 3 271 6374
Cable: Yohden, Tokyo
Telex: 222 4666

President: Atsushi Doi

Products: Traction motors and electric machinery and apparatus for railway vehicles; ac induction and dc traction motors; bogie-mounted and nose-suspended traction motors for emus, electric and diesel-electric locomotives; ac generators for diesel-electric locomotives; chopper control systems; automatic field exciting chopper control systems; camshaft control systems; VVVF control systems; thyristor inverter, brushless motor-generator set; pantograph; door motors; speedometers; and traction equipment of New Transportation system.

Constitution: Established in 1918, this company produces traction motors and control equipment for home and export. It was responsible for the axle drive with cardan shaft and steel blade coupling which is used as standard equipment by the Japanese National Railways and by many of the private railways in Japan.

Addendum

Sécheron
Sécheron Ltd

Avenue de Sécheron 14, 1211 Genève 21, Switzerland

Telephone: +41 22 739 41 11
Telex: 22130 bbse
Telefax: +41 22 738 73 05

General Manager: Claude Chabanel

Products: Vacuum circuit breakers for ac traction vehicles. Type BVAC 15·08 is for 15 kV 16⅔ Hz overhead electrification and has 25kA rated short-circuit breaking current. Type BVAC 25·06 is for 25 kV 50-60 Hz electrification and has 16 kA rated short-circuit breaking current. Both are suitable for current up to 1000 A.

Both breakers are interchangeable with the BBC type DBTF device, and can be fitted with external contacts for a bipolar earthing switch type BTE.

Prototypes have been in service for over two years and series are being supplied for the RENFE type 252 locomotives, the SBB 2000 RE 4/4-VI locomotives and Stadtbahn Karlsruhe in the Federal Republic of Germany.

Non-powered passenger vehicles

ARGENTINA
Materfer 205

AUSTRALIA
Comeng 197
Goninan 201

AUSTRIA
Jenbacher 203
S-G-P 210

BELGIUM
BN 195

BRAZIL
CCC 197
Cobrasma 197
Engesa-FNV 199

CANADA
Alcan 192
Bombardier 195
UTDC 212

CHINA
Changchun Railway Works 197
China National Railway Corporation 197
Pu Zhen 207

CZECHOSLOVAKIA
Czechoslovak Wagon Works 198
Strojexport 210

DENMARK
ABB Scandia A/S 192, 207

EGYPT
SEMAF 209

FINLAND
Valmet 213

FRANCE
ANF-Industrie 193
De Dietrich 198
GEC Alsthom 201
Soulé 210

GERMANY, DEMOCRATIC REPUBLIC
Ammendorf 192
Bautzen 194
Görlitz 201
Schienenfahrzeuge Export-Import 207

GERMANY, FEDERAL REPUBLIC
Bremer 196
Ferrostaal 199
MAN-GHH 205
MBB 206
Siemens 210
Talbot 211
Waggon Union 213

HUNGARY
Ganz-Hunslet 200
Hungarian Railway Carriage 202

INDIA
BEML 195
ICF 203
Jessop 203
PEC 207

ITALY
Breda 196
Casaralta 197
CFC 197
Costamasnaga 197
Ferrosud 199
Fiat 199
Firema 200
Gallinari 200
Imesi 203
OFV 206
OMECA 206
OMS 206
Reggiane 207
SGI 209
Socimi 210
Sofer 210

JAPAN
Alna Koki 192
Fuji Car 200
Fuji Heavy Industries 200
Kawasaki 204
Kinki Sharyo 204
Nippon Sharyo 206
Tokyu 212

KOREA
Daewoo 198
Hyundai 202
Korea Shipbuilding & Engineering 204

MOROCCO
SCIF 209

NORWAY
Strømens 210

PAKISTAN
Pakistan Railways Carriage 207

POLAND
Cegielski 197
Kolmex 204
Pafawag 207

PORTUGAL
Sorefame 210

ROMANIA
Arad 193
Mecanoexportimport 206
Turnu-Severin 212

SOUTH AFRICA
Union Carriage 212

SPAIN
ATEINSA 193
Babcock & Wilcox 194
CAF 196
Dimetal 199
La Maquinista 204
Macosa 204
Tafesa 211
Talgo 211

SWEDEN
Kalmar 203

SWITZERLAND
Alusuisse-Lonza 192
Schindler 208
Schindler Waggon Altenrhein 208

UK
BREL 196
GEC Alsthom 201
Hunslet 202
RFS 207

USA
Miner Railcar Services 204
RPS 207

YUGOSLAVIA
Duro Daković 199
GOŠA 202

MANUFACTURERS / Non-powered passenger vehicles

New aluminium rolling stock for Stockholm's Roslagsbanan bodywork by AL

ABB Scandia A/S
See entry on page 207

AL
Alusuisse-Lonza Services Ltd

Head office: Buckhauserstrasse 11, CH-8048 Zurich, Switzerland

Telephone: +41 1 497 44 22
Telex: 817 555 32
Cable: Alusuisse
Telefax: +41 1 497 45 85

Main works: Alusuisse Swiss Aluminium Ltd, CH-3960 Sierre, Switzerland
Alusingen GmbH, D-7700 Singen/Hohentwiel, Federal Republic of Germany
Alusuisse France SA, F-89600 St Florentin, France

Director: Jürg Zehnder
Marketing Manager: Jochen Warner

Products: Design and manufacture of prototypes and fatigue testing of body shells for all types of passenger rolling stock and components; supply of aluminium semis and composite materials; large aluminium extrusions up to 800 mm width.
Design of self-supporting welded aluminium bodies using large extrusion technology for replacing ageing rolling stock of motor cars, trailers and intermediate cars for Stockholm's SLJ Roslagsbanan. First and second orders comprise 35 and 66 vehicles respectively. Material supply to AB Railcar AB (formerly Hägglunds Traction AB) for all cars.

Alcan
Alcan Canada Products Ltd

Box 269, Toronto-Dominion Centre, Toronto, Ontario M5K 1K1, Canada

Telephone: +1 416 366 7211
Cable: Alcan, Toronto
Telex: 06-22641

Products: More than 30 years of experience designing lightweight aluminium rolling stock for passenger service. Supplies aluminium sheet, plate, and extrusions for rail transport applications of all kinds.
All-aluminium LRC locomotive and cars in service with VIA Rail Canada are designed jointly by Alcan, Bombardier-MLW, and Dofasco.

Alna Koki
Alna Koki Company Ltd

4-5, Higashinaniwa-cho, 1-chome, Amagasaki 660, Japan

Telephone: +81 6 401 7283
Telex: 5242782 alnosk
Telefax: +81 6 401 6168

President: Jitokiro Sakai
Managing Director, Production: Yoshinobu Sugimoto
Chief Engineer & Director: Kiyoyuki Yamagami
Managing Director, Sales & Marketing: Masahiro Higuchi

Products: Various types of aluminium and steel passenger coaches.

Ammendorf
VEB Waggonbau Ammendorf
Member of VEB Kombinat Schienenfahrzeugbau and of Vereinigter Schienenfahrzeugbau der DDR e V

Merseburger Strasse 89, 4011 Halle, German Democratic Republic

Telephone: +37 4650
Telex: 04216

Exports: Schienenfahrzeuge Export-Import Volkseigener Aussenhandelsbetrieb der DDR, Oltztaler Strasse 5, 1100 Berlin, German Democratic Republic

Products: Long-distance passenger and restaurant cars; bogies. With government agreement a new generation of long-distance passenger cars is projected, including first- and second-class air-conditioned couchette cars, second-class couchette cars with forced ventilation, air-conditioned couchette cars with buffet compartment, and air-conditioned dining cars.
A prototype of the air-conditioned second-class Type WPX/K car was built and tested in the USSR in 1986. The carbody is of all-welded, self-supporting construction employing high-strength steel of grade HS 52-3. The car is equipped with Type KWS-ZNII-M bogies, Type SA3 centre buffer-couplers, a 135 V, 32 kW three-phase generator driven by a centre axle gear box and a 300 Ah nickel-iron battery. A three-phase inverter feeds the motors of the air-conditioning plant and a single-phase inverter supplies other equipment such as drinking-water cooler, refrigerator, reading lamps, sockets for shavers, cleaning devices and the samovar. Water tanks with a capacity of 1200 litres are made of nirosta-steel. The heating boiler, which combines use

Interior of WPX-Club coach by Ammendorf

Non-powered passenger vehicles / MANUFACTURERS

of solid fuels and electricity, is fed by 300 V dc or ac from the main bus bar. Air temperature is controlled electronically by a microcomputer. The central switch cabinet in the attendant's compartment includes a diagnostic device and a fire extinguishing plant; the fire alarm is connected to monitor devices in all compartments and rooms of the car.

In 1987-88 the company delivered an order received in 1985 from MBTA Boston for 34 commuter cars, which was extended in 1986 to a total of 67 cars. The order covered both control trailer and pure trailer cars. Except for the underframes the carbodies will be fabricated of aluminium extrusions. Length over buffers will be 26 010 mm and seating capacity 96 in the trailers, 94 in the control trailers.

Among other recent deliveries to Soviet Railways (SZD) have been a series of 240 Type SK K restaurant cars Model 356. Features of this air-conditioned car are: a 48-seat dining saloon; hot-water heating system that can be operated either electrically or with solid fuel; a 32 kW three-phase generator driven by a centre axle gear box; and an oil-burned kitchen range.

Constitution: Originating as a carriage works in 1823, the plant took up tramcar, bus and narrow-gauge passenger car construction in 1945, but from the early 1950s it developed as a specialised coach-builder for SZD, to which it had delivered over 23 000 vehicles by the end of the 1980s.

ANF-Industrie
Société ANF-Industrie

Tour Aurore, 92080 Paris La Défense Cedex 5, France

Telephone: +33 1 47 78 62 62
Telex: 610 817 anf courb
Telefax: +33 1 47 78 62 66

Chairman: Michel de Lambert de Boisjean
Sales Manager: Jean-Claude Viche

Products: Passenger coaches and trailer cars of all types.
Recent orders received include 126 double-deck tourist wagons for Eurotunnel; 160 TGV-R first class passenger cars and an additional 20 TGV-A 'Club' cars for SNCF.

Arad
Arad Car and Passenger Coach Building Enterprise

Intreprinderia de Vagoane Arad, Cal Aurel Vlaicu 41-45, 2900 Arad, Romania

Telephone: +40 66 37020
Cable: Vagoane Arad
Telex: 76256

Products: Sleeping and dining cars; first-, second- and third-class coaches; saloon coaches; train-heating cars; brake and luggage vans; power-generating cars; mail vans; observation and conference saloons; lounge coaches; four- and multi-axled freight cars, covered high-board open, flat with or without side and front walls and stanchions, tipping of 40 or 25 m³, gondola, grain transport, pellet, etc; four- and six-axle dumpers; flat cars on four, six, 10, 12 or 20 axles for heavy transport; ore transport cars; sliding-roof or side-wall cars, etc, for any gauge from 900 to 1676 mm.

Constitution: Mecanoexportimport supplier.

ATEINSA
Aplicaciones Técnicas Industriales SA

Head office: Zurbano 70, Madrid 28010, Spain

Telephone: +34 1 419 95 50
Cable: Ateinsa, Madrid
Telex: 22055
Telefax: +34 1 410 09 45

Works: Factoria de Villaverde, Carretera Villaverde, Vallecas 18, Madrid 28041

President: Manuel Costales Gómez-Olea

Passenger cars for Iraqi Railways by ANF-Industrie

Type B6 Dux driving trailer for French Railways by ANF-Industrie

Second-class inter-city passenger car for RENFE (ATEINSA)

Restored restaurant car of 'Al Andalus' cruise train (ATEINSA)

194 MANUFACTURERS / Non-powered passenger vehicles

Products: Passenger cars, including restaurant and cafeteria cars.

In 1985 Ateinsa was commissioned by Spanish National Railways to rebuild historic cars and build new vehicles to create the 'Al Andalus' luxury landcruise trains. The work comprised the complete rehabilitation and conversion of four 1920s-vintage restaurant cars, reconstruction of two luggage vans as shower cars and construction of new cars to establish a train-set of two power vans, four cars serving as restaurant, recreation or discotheque cars, four sleeping cars, one couchette car for train staff and generator car. The 1920s cars were painstakingly restored to the full splendour of their original period panelling, furnishing and general decor. The train-set is the first in Spain to feature retention toilet systems.

Of the day vehicles, the recreation car includes a bar, a video room and a gaming area. The discotheque car also has a bar. Each of the two shower cars has 10 modules individually divided into shower and washbasin compartments. Each shower car also has a waiting area with lounge seating and an electronic panel indicating the occupancy of each module and the temperature of its water supply.

Export Sales: Inirail, Plaza Marqués de Salamanca 3, 4–5°, Madrid 28006

Constitution: ATEINSA was set up in 1973 to take over the railway rolling stock production of Astilleros Españoles, SA. Owned by Instituto Nacional de Industria (INI).

Babcock & Wilcox Española
Sociedad Española de Construcciones Babcock & Wilcox SA

Galindo (Vizcaya), Spain

Telephone: +34 4966011, 4957011
Telex: 32235, 32544 bw fbe
Telefax: +34 4956676

Works: Alameda de Recalde, 48009 Bilbao 9, Spain
Lagasca 88, Madrid 28001

Executive President: Manual Fernández Garcia

Telephone: +34 4018300, +34 4018754
Telex: 27657

Products: Passenger cars. Recent contracts have included 22 couchette cars for Spanish National Railways (RENFE).

Power output: 2 × 225 kW generating sets
Length between buffers: 26 620 mm
Weight: 52 tonnes
Max load: 8 tonnes
Max speed: 160 km/h

Constitution: Owned by Instituto Nacional de Industria (INI).

Inter-city car for RENFE (Babcock & Wilcox)

Type X restaurant car interior (Bautzen)

Bautzen
VEB Waggonbau Bautzen
A member of VEB Kombinat Schienenfahrzeugbau and Vereinigter Schienenfahrzeugbau der DDR e V

Neuesche Promenade 920, 8600 Bautzen, German Democratic Republic

Telephone: +37 5350
Telex: 0287225

Exports: Schienfahrzeuge Export-Import Volkseigener Aussenhandelsbetrieb der DDR, Otztaler Strasse 5, 1100 Berlin

Products: Passenger, couchette, restaurant and baggage cars.

Recent production has included 100 Type X 11-compartment second-class cars with central power supply for the Czechoslovak State Railways (CSD). Features of these cars include lower weight due to extensive use of lightweight components and of high-strength steels for parts subjected to high static and dynamic loads. The cars are fitted with disc-braked Type GP 200 bogies.

The automatically-controlled, combined heating and ventilating system has air inlets in the side walls; filter, fan and heat exchanger are arranged under the coach floor and the air ducts are an integral part of the floor. Passengers can adjust the temperatures individually while air rates are kept at a constant level.

The broad sliding plug doors are power-operated and have a central interlocking device. Compartment walls are made of composite wood board faced with decorative plastic laminate on both sides.

Each compartment has eight seats which are adjustable in reclining angle by 105 mm. Interior cleaning is made easy by considerably reduced floor area, a floor covering that is rounded to the corridor walls and by elimination of heater panels.

The central power supply plant is fed by direct or alternating 3000 V current or from the train bus-bar and supplies 24 V current for the electrical equipment and for charging the NC battery, which has a capacity of 375 Ah.

Current output features second-class passenger coaches for Czechoslovak State Railways with luggage compartment and a compartment for disabled persons with a special lifting device for the wheelchair and a special lavatory; and couchette cars for Chinese State Railways.

In 1989 the factory was to produce Type X dining cars for Polish State Railways. Dining cars of this type have already been delivered to the Hungarian, Bulgarian and German State Railways. Further production will comprise 50 open-saloon and 250 couchette cars for the People's Republic of China and passenger coaches for high-speed trains for the Greek State Railway.

Recent production has included passenger coaches for the Ghana Railway Corporation (GRC). This contract comprised first-and second-class cars, second-class cars with luggage compartment, tourist cars, buffet cars and sleeping cars. The cars are of lightweight steel construction, mounted on modified 'Gorlitz V' bogies and fitted with vacuum braking. Interiors are ventilated by electrically-powered fans.

Constitution: Opened as an iron foundry and machinery plant in 1846, the works took up tram manufacture in 1897. After 1945 it developed from passenger and freight vehicle repair into construction of a wide variety of vehicles from long-haul passenger cars to railbuses and freight wagons, but has since 1970 specialised in RIC passenger cars.

Second-class car for Czechoslovak State Railways (ČSD) (Bautzen)

Non-powered passenger vehicles / **MANUFACTURERS**

Interior of new DR inter-city first-class saloon (Bautzen)

Second-class saloon interior of new DR inter-city vehicles (Bautzen)

New design of inter-city first saloon with 200 km/h operating capability for German State Railway (DR) (Bautzen)

First-class car for Ghana Railways Corporation (GRC) (Bautzen)

BEML
Bharat Earth Movers Ltd
Railcoach Division

Unity Buildings, J C Road, Bangalore 560 002, India

Telephone: +91 812 560 075
Cable: Bemrail
Telex: 398 bg

Chairman and Managing Director: M B Ajwani
General Manager: Col A R Sharma
Senior Manager (R & D): K S Jagannatha

Products: Integral passenger coaches in steel; welded lightweight stock such as second-class coaches, brake and luggage vans, sleeping coaches; heavy-duty road trailers and earth-moving equipment.

Constitution: The Railcoach Division of Bharat Earth Movers Ltd was the first factory in India to take up manufacture, in 1947, of all-metal broad-gauge coaches, steel, welded, lightweight passenger coaches, postal vans, parcel vans, brake and luggage vans, day-cum-sleeper coaches, motor cum-parcel coaches. The Division has since supplied over 8400 coaches of different types for Indian Railways. Coaches have also been exported to Bangladesh and Sri Lanka.

BN
Constructions Ferroviaires et Métalliques
Formerly La Brugeoise et Nivelles SA

Avenue Louise 65, 1050 Bruxelles, Belgium

Telephone: +32 2 535 55 11
Telex: 61 736 brunag
Telefax: +32 2 539 10 17

Managing Director: M M Simonart

Executive Director, Transport Division: P Sonveaux
Marketing & Sales Director, Transport Division: J Verraver

Products: Passenger coaches (single and double-deck).

The range of coaches recently supplied to SNCB includes 130 double-deck cars and 95 RIC passenger cars. BN also delivered more than 500 MY-coaches for intercity operations.

As a member of the Euroshuttle Consortium, recent contracts include 126 special single-deck 'tourism'-design shuttle wagons for the transport of private cars on Channel Tunnel services. Delivery of these stainless steel-bodied waggons is scheduled to commence in 1992.

BN is also a member of the TMST Consortium that received an order for 30 18-car high-speed trains. BN is designing and manufacturing 60 central coaches (R9, R10). The Company is also manufacturing body shells for 120 other R7, R8, R11 and R12 coaches.

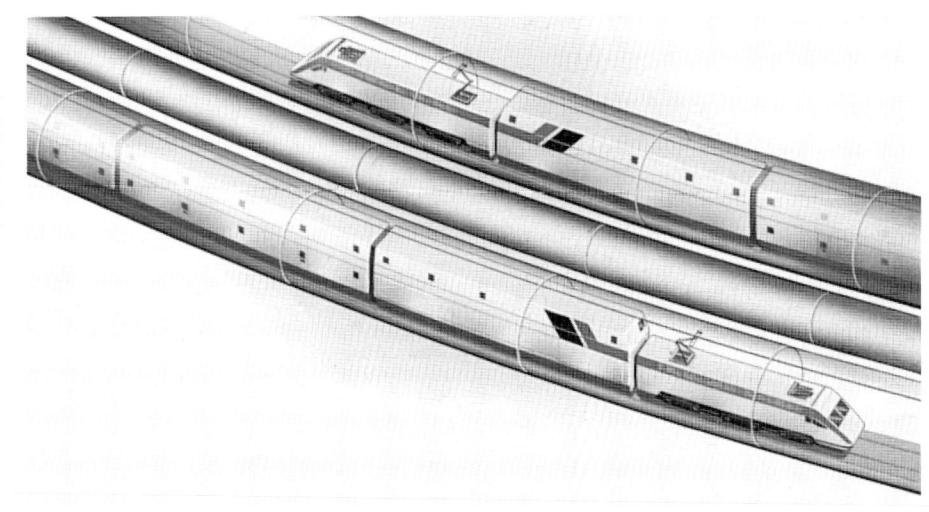

Bombardier Inc
Mass Transit Division

1350 Nobel Street, Boucherville, Quebec J4B 1A1

Telephone: +1 514 655 3830
Telex: 055 61576
Telefax: +1 514 655 4257

Artist's impression of shuttle wagons for the Channel Tunnel by BN

196 MANUFACTURERS / Non-powered passenger vehicles

President: Gilles Bacon
Vice President, Marketing & Sales: Thomas C Owen
Director, Marketing & Sales (Intl): Salem Wahby

Principal subsidiaries: Transportation Group Inc (TGI); ANF-Industrie (France); BN Constructions Ferroviaires et Métalliques (Belgium)

Products: A complete range of rail transit vehicles for urban, commuter and intercity transit; rubber tyred subway cars, steel wheeled subway cars, light rail vehicles, self-propelled gallery commuter cars, commuter train coaches, bi-level transcontinental train coaches, 'PeopleMover'and 'MonoRail' systems and the LRC train (the only high-speed train of North American design).
   For details of recent contracts see **Bombardier Inc** entry in Powered Passenger Vehicles section.

Breda
Breda Costruzioni Ferroviarie SpA

Via Ciliegiole 110/B, 51100 Pistoia, Italy

Telephone: +39 573 3701
Cable: Ferbreda, Pistoia
Telex: 570186 bcf i

Chairman: Giuseppe Capuano
General Manager, Breda Railway Group: Corrado Fici
General Manager, Breda Construzioni Ferroviarie: Roberto Cai

Products: Light alloy stainless steel or carbon steel passenger coaches. The companies of Breda Railway Group design and manufacture LRVs, Rapid Transit Cars, electric train sets, locomotives, trucks and freight wagons.
   Recent products include a prototype stainless steel coach for FS; 99 'Gran Confort' carbon steel coaches for FS; 56 + 56 Mk IV Corten steel coaches for British Railways.

BREL
BREL (1988) Ltd

St Peters House, Gower Street, Derby DE1 1AH, England

Telephone: +44 332 383850
Telex: 377693, 377898
Telefax: +44 332 45737

Chairman: Sir David Nicolson
Deputy Chairman: A R Houseman
Managing Director: Peter J Holdstock
Director, New Construction Group: Christopher V Cook
Director, Manufacture Repair Group: Chris P J Sheppard
Finance Director: C R Wood
Marketing Director: P S Coventry
Personnel Director: I M Forrester

Products: Passenger coaches. Recent contracts include an order from Indian Railways for the supply of over £20 million worth of BREL's 'International' passenger coaches. This is one of the most significant railway coach export orders to be secured by a Western European manufacturer in recent years. The 42 coaches will be built by BREL in its Derby Carriage Works and will run on bogies produced by Fiat in Turin, Italy. They are scheduled to form two high-speed air-conditioned passenger trains on one of Indian Railways' most prestigious routes. The order also includes a technical transfer package which will allow Indian Railways to build BREL-designed International coaches in the new Rail Coach Factory at Kapurthala in the Punjab.

Bremer
Bremer Waggonbau GmbH

Postfach 110 109, Pfalzburger Strasse 251, 2800 Bremen 11, Federal Republic of Germany

Telephone: +49 45 40 11
Cable: Bremer Waggonbau, Bremen
Telex: 024 4423

Mk IV Corten steel coach body for British Railways by Breda Group

Artist's impression of 'International' coach for Indian Railways (BREL)

Managing Director: Peter Müller
Export Sales: Chr Trahm

Products: Passenger coaches.

Constitution: The company was formed in December 1975. The works occupy the site of the former Hansa Waggon AG.

CAF
Construcciones y Auxiliar de Ferrocarriles SA
Member of Servicio de Exportacion de Material Ferroviario

Padilla 17, Madrid 28006, Spain

Telephone: +34 1 435 25 00
Telex: 23197 cafma e
Telefax: +34 1 276 62 63

Export Division

SEMF, Castello 72-1°, 28006 Madrid, Spain

Telephone: +34 1 275 64 03
Telex: 27242 semf e
Telefax: +34 1 276 81 08

Works: Beasain, Zaragoza, Irun

President: José I Cangas
Chairman: Pedro Ardaiz
General Manager: Juan José Anza

Products: Passenger coaches; rolling stock components; all types of bogie.
   RENFE (Spanish National Railways) has ordered CAF 40 sleeping cars of improved comfort. Each vehicle has 13 air-conditioned double compartments each with washstand and shower. Maximum speed is 160 km/h.

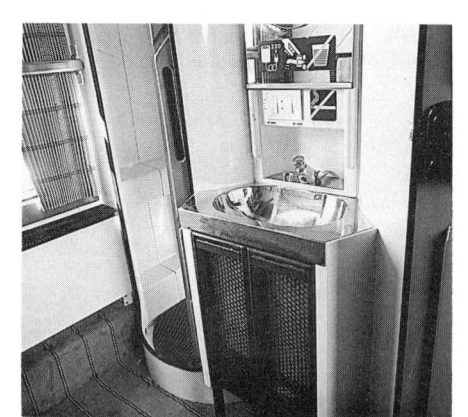

Washstand and shower cubicle of RENFE sleeping car (CAF)

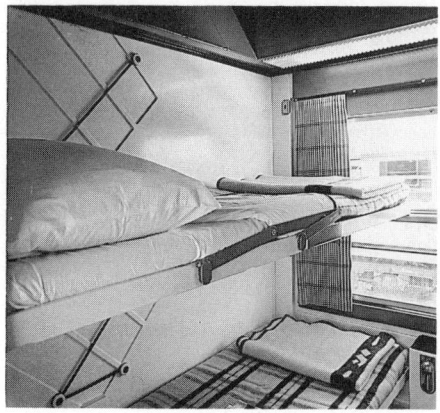

Compartment of RENFE sleeping car (CAF)

Non-powered passenger vehicles / **MANUFACTURERS** 197

Casaralta
Casaralta SpA
A member of the Firema Group

Via Ferrarese 205, 40128 Bologna, Italy

Telephone: +39 51 35 84 54
Cable: Rotabili, Bologna
Telex: 511068 OFFCAS
Telefax: +39 51 363845

President: Giorgio Regazzoni
Managing Directors: Carlo Filippo Zucchini
Carlo Regazzoni

Products: Electric locomotives and railcars; single- and double-deck passenger coaches; freight wagons.
Recent contracts include the Z1 coach for Italian State Railways (FS) (1989); double-deck coaches, trailers and control trailer for FS (1989); Class E 84 electric trainset for ACOTRAL Rome-Italy (1989); double-deck coaches, trailers and control trailer for Nord-Milano Railways, Italy (1990).

Constitution: Founded in 1919, Casaralta has played a leading role in the construction of rail and tram vehicles for the Italian railway network. During the postwar years the company gained prominence with the ALe 601 series of electric railcars and the Class E444 and E656 locomotives. Contracts in recent years with Spoleto-Norcia and Bari-Baletta Railways for electric railcars, together with the double-deck coaches for Nord-Milano Railways, have enabled Casaralta to maintain its market position within the industry. Casaralta is a part of the Firema Group of companies which together offer a fund of skill and experience in the field of rail and tram vehicle building.

CCC
Companhia Comércio e Construcões

Head office: Av Rio Branco 156/22°, Grupos 2233-5, Centro, Rio de Janeiro CEP 20043, Brazil

Telephone: +55 21 262 3312
Cable: Comercon
Telex: 32490 cmct br

Main works: Rua Soldado José Lopes Filho 42, Deodoro, Rio de Janeiro

Telephone: +55 21 390 0760, 1039

Products: Manufacture and repair of passenger cars; repair of locomotives.

Cegielski
Cegielski Locomotive and Wagon Works
Zaklady Przemyslu Metalowego H Cegielski

ul Dzierzynskiego 223/229, 61-485 Poznan, Poland

Telephone: +48 61 212 31
Telex: 0415343

Export sales: Kolmex, 49 Mokotowska, 00-542 Warsaw

Products: Passenger coaches (including couchette cars and bar coaches) for 1435 mm gauge, passenger coaches for 1520 mm gauge.

Constitution: Cegielski is the largest rolling stock works in Poland, building 300 to 400 passenger coaches annually for export alone.

CFC
Costruzioni Ferroviarie Colleferro SpA
A member of the Fiat Group

Via Sabotino, 00034 Colleferro (Rome), Italy

Telephone: +39 6 9781280
Telex: 611434
Telefax: +39 6 9782746

President: Dr C Giancarlo
Delegate Administrator: Ing L Basta
Technical Director: Ing V Travaglini

Double-deck coach for Nord-Milano Railways, Italy (Casaralta SpA)

UIC-Z1 compartment-type 84-seat 46-tonne passenger car for FS, fitted with Fiat F85 A bogies, self-ventilated anti-skid disc brakes and suitable to run at speeds of up to 200 km/h (CFC)

Project Officer: Ing G Clementi
Production Officer: Pl F Cherubini
Production Officer: Ing A Rigon
Import-Export Officer: Rag V Nobilio

Products: Passenger cars, freight cars, refrigerated wagons and containers.
Recent contracts include 45 MDVC cars for Italian State Railways (FS); 90 UIC-Z1 compartment-type cars for FS; 25 UIC-Z1 saloon-type cars for FS; 120 refrigerated wagons for Interfrigo.

Changchun Railway Passenger Car Works

5 Qingyin Road, Changchun, Jilin, People's Republic of China

Telephone: +86 73981
Telex: 83031 cpcf cn

Products: Lightweight passenger coaches for high-speed (160 km/h) operations, sleeping cars.

China National Railway Locomotive and Rolling Stock Industry Corporation

10 Fu Xing Road, Beijing, People's Republic of China

Telephone: +86 45245; +86 42685; +86 44645
Telex: 222218 loric cn

Products: Passenger cars.

Cobrasma SA

Head office: Rua da Estacão 523, Osasco, São Paulo, Brazil

Telephone: +55 11 704 6122
Telex: (011) 71545, 71589
Telefax: +55 11 704 6856

Works: Km 104 Via Anhanguera, Distrito de Hortolândia, Sitio São João, Sumaré, São Paulo, CEP 12170

Telephone: +55 192 65 6000
Telex: (019) 1926

President: Luis Eulálio de Bueno Vidigal
Marketing Director: Alberto Martinez
Export Director: Eduardo Hubert Kirmaier Monteiro

Products: Passenger cars.

Comeng
A division of The ANI Corporation Limited

Frankston Road, Dandenong, Victoria 3175, Australia
Telephone: +61 3 794 2111
Telex: 33253
Telefax: +61 3 792 5817

General Manager: A Connor

Products: Passenger cars. Recent contracts include an order for intercity double-deck cars for SRA of NSW, delivered in 1989.

Costamasnaga
Costamasnaga SpA

Viale 4 Novembre, 22041 Costamasnaga (Como), Italy

Telephone: +39 31 855192
Telex: 380184
Telefax: +39 31 855330

Chairman: Claudio Marina
General Managers: Fabio Magni
Ida Magni

Products: First- and second-class Type MDVC passenger cars for medium-distance working. The MDVC is designed for 160 km/h operation with seating for 72; tare is 37 tonnes and maximum length 26.550 mm. End doorways are at platform level and doors are

198 MANUFACTURERS / Non-powered passenger vehicles

arranged for power operation from a central control point. Bogies are FI type, with self-ventilated disc brakes, and the car features forced-air electric heating and fluorescent lighting powered from autonomous plant. Recent orders from the Italian State Railways include one for a series of 30 MDVC passenger cars.

Czechoslovak Wagon Works
Československé Vagónky
(Member of Strojexport, Foreign Trade Co Ltd, Prague)

Nám Dukelskych hrdinu° 95, 058 01 Poprad, Czechoslovakia

Telephone: +42 25242
Telex: 078 348

Works: Vagónka Studénka, 742 13 Studénka
Vagónka Poprad, 058 80 Poprad
Vagónka Česka Lípa, 470 79 Česka Lípa

Chairman: Stefan Tužinsky
Managing Director: Jan Hlavačik
Sales Director: Karol Kos ik

Products: Passenger cars.

Daewoo
Daewoo Heavy Industries Ltd

PO Box 7955, Seoul, Republic of Korea

Telephone: Seoul +82 2 752 0211. Anyang +82 343 52 6171
Cable: Dhiltdincheon
Telex: 23301/25550
Telefax: +82 2 756 2679

Chairman: Woo Choong Kim
President: Kyung Hoon Lee
Executive Vice President: Oh Jun Kwon
Rolling Stock Executive Director: Won Jai Park
Rolling Stock Export Sales Manager: Soo Hwan Kim

Products: Passenger coaches.

Foreign companies with which Daewoo has technical collaboration arrangements for rail equipment include:
Electric locomotives: 50 c/s Group; ACEC, Belgium; AEG and Siemens, West Germany; Alsthom and MTE, France; BBC, Switzerland
Stainless steel railcars, bogies: Transit America Inc, USA
Electric cars: Hitachi Ltd, Japan
Diesel-hydraulic railcars: Niigata Engineering Co Ltd, Japan
Air-spring bogies, diesel engines: MAN, Federal Republic of Germany
Rubber-spring bogies: Gloucester Railway Carriage & Wagon Co Ltd, England
Barber stabilised bogies: Standard Car Truck Co, USA
Traction motors, motor alternators, design co-operation in electric emu cars: GEC Traction International Ltd, England
Alliance couplers: Amsted Industries Inc, USA

(For affiliated companies, see Daewoo entry, Locomotives section)

De Dietrich
De Dietrich & Cie

Reichshoffen, 67110 Niederbronn-les-Bains, France

Telephone: +33 88 80 25 00
Cable: Dietriwagons
Telex: 870 850
Telefax: +33 88 80 25 12

Sales organisation: De Dietrich & Cie
Railway and Mechanical Division
President: Gilbert de Dietrich
Director, Rolling Stock Division: Maurice Canioni

Products: Passenger coaches; high-speed bogies; coach made of high yield strength steel (special production for French Railways).
Sales since 1985 have included the supply to French Railways (SNCF) of further passenger cars, and Type Y32 high-speed bogies. In 1989 manufacture included TGV-Atlantique train-set cars for French Railways and Z2 emus for Luxembourg National Railways. The manufacture of TAV (Train Alto Velocidad) train-set cars for Spain and for TMST (Transmanche Super Train) began in 1989.

Constitution: Established in 1864, the company commenced railway rolling stock production in the mid-19th century. The company handles manufacture of self-propelled coaching stock, and also manufactures UIC-pattern and other types of passenger car and high-speed bogie for SNCF and railways abroad. In addition to rolling stock, the company makes and markets other railway-related equipment such as special steel-industry wagons and signalling equipment.

Type MDVC passenger car for Italian Railways (Costamasnaga)

Passenger car for Tunisia (Daewoo)

Passenger car for Burma (Daewoo)

Non-powered passenger vehicles / **MANUFACTURERS** 199

Trailer car for French Railways' TGV-Atlantique train-set (De Dietrich)

Presidential saloon for Gabon (De Dietrich)

First-class compartment of car for OCTRA (De Dietrich)

De Dietrich Type C80 metre-gauge bogie for passenger cars

Dimetal
Dimetal SA

Avenida de Castilla 33, San Fernando de Henares, Torrejon de Ardoz, Madrid 28850, Spain

Telephone: +34 1 6751100
Telex: 22332
Telefax: +34 1 6565942

President: Jésus Ruano Alvarez
General Manager: Eugendio Vela Sastre
Railway Products Manager: Antonio Gonzáles del Peral
Railway Products Technical Manager: Santiago González Kaendler
Products: Door equipment. Recent contracts include intercommunication doors for TALGO and external doors for FFVV commuter trains.

Duro Daković
Duro Daković Industries

PO Box 63, 55001 Slavonski Brod, Yugoslavia

Telephone: +38 55 231-011
Cable: Lokomotive, Slavonski Brod
Telex: 23421/23424

Products: Passenger coaches.

Constitution: Duro Daković was founded in 1921 as the first Yugoslav locomotive and wagon manufacturer. Diesel locomotives have been produced since 1954.

Engesa-FNV
FNV Veiculos e Equipamentos S/A
An Engesa Company

Avenida Tucunaré 125/211, 06400 Barueri, São Paulo, Brazil

Telephone: +55 11 421 4711
Telex: 11 71302 enes br
Telefax: +55 11 421 4445

President: José Luiz Whitaker Ribeiro
Vice-President: José Guilherme Whitaker Ribeiro
Directors: Sérgio Antonio Bardella
Armando Ulbricht Junior
Marco Aurelio de Barros Montenegro
Vail Eduardo Gomes
José Carlos Pereira de Carvalho
Marcos Puglisi de Assumpão

Products: Passenger cars.

Ferrostaal
Ferrostaal AG

PO Box 10 12 65, Hohenzollernstrasse 24, 4300 Essen, Federal Republic of Germany

Telephone: +49 201 818 01
Cable: Ferrostaal, Essen
Telex: 0857100

Products: Passenger coaches including special designs; inspection and service trolleys for track and overhead maintenance and track installation; motor and trailer bogies for freight wagons, passenger coaches, locomotives, railcars; components of rolling stock such as wheels, axles, assembled wheelsets, bearings, suspensions, couplers, electrical equipment.

Ferrosud
Ferrosud SpA

PO Box 94, Via Appia Antica Km 13, 75100 Matera, Italy

Telephone: +39 835 222841
Telex: 812525 fersud i
Telefax: +39 835 217137

Chairman: Corrado Fici
Managing Director: Angelo Palmieri
Export Sales: Claudio Mannucci (Breda)

Products: Passenger and service coaches; all types of bogie.
Recent orders have included 70 first-class and 22 second-class air-conditioned cars of Type Z1 for Italian Railways (FS); and 49 body-shells, with an option for a further 36, for Metro-Cammell of the UK, to be delivered between March and October 1990. In December 1989, Ferrosud completed delivery of 32 body shells for Metro-Cammell.

Constitution: Ferrosud was set up in 1963 for the manufacture and marketing of railway and tramway rolling stock. Production began in 1968. Export sales are handled by the company or through Breda Costruzioni Ferroviarie. The company is now wholly owned by EFIM through the Gruppo Ferroviario Breda.

Fiat
Fiat Ferroviaria SpA

Piazza Galateri 4, 12038 Savigliano (CN), Italy

Telephone: +39 172 2021
Telex: 201234 fiatsv
Telefax: +39 172 202 426

Chairman: Renato Piccoli
Managing Director and General Manager: Giancarlo Cozza
Deputy General Manager and Project Manager: Pierantonio Losa
Sales Manager: Andrea Parnigoni

Products: Passenger coaches (sleeping cars, self service cars, restaurant coaches, saloon cars, TEE coaches); bogies and components, wagons (including refrigerated types).
A new kind of passenger coach with modular construction is ready to be tested. Particular characteristics are the reduced weight and manufacturing technology. This car will be coupled to Fiat independent wheeled bogies.
Still continuing at CFC is the construction of a series of medium range passenger cars. Construction has started in consortium with Breda for the shuttles for the Channel Tunnel project; a decision is awaited soon for the bogies.
Recent orders include 33 LHGVLs (Light heavy goods vehicle loaders) to be supplied to TML, in consortium with Breda, plus 18 SDL (Side deck loaders) for TML (Transmanche Link). CFC has been awarded an important order from Interfrigo for 120 refrigerated vans.

Constitution: The activity of Fiat in the field of railway rolling stock began in 1917 with the manufacture of passenger and freight cars. In 1931 Fiat put the first diesel railcars into service before beginning production of diesel multiple-units and locomotives, progressing to the tilting body electric 'Pendolino' train.
By the end of 1975 all the activities of Fiat concerning design and manufacture of railway rolling

MANUFACTURERS / Non-powered passenger vehicles

stock were entrusted to Fiat Ferroviaria SpA, the company which now controls Costruzioni Ferroviarie Colleferro SpA, Rome, and Elettromeccanica Parizzi, Milan.

Firema Consortium

Head office: Corso di Porta Romana 63, 20122 Milan, Italy

Telephone: +39 2 5465708
Telefax: +39 2 5460133

President: Dr Ing Giorgio Regazzoni
Board Members: Avv Dino Marchiorello
Dr Giorgio Fiore
Procurator: Prof Ing Francesco Perticaroli
Export Manager: Dr Ing Maurizio Fantini

For full list of member companies see Firema entry in Locomotives section

Products: Passenger cars.

To improve and increase rail transport facilities during the World Cup competition in mid-1990, Fiore of Caserta has received orders from FS for 33 light alloy Le 763 intermediate trailers which will operate with ALe 582 and ALe 642 electric railcars. Another batch of eight Le 763 trailers has been ordered from OMS of Padua.

In order to improve the capacity of the six two-car E 84 trainsets delivered by FIREMA in 1986–87 and currently in service on the Rome-Prima Porta Railway, ACOTRAL has ordered six intermediate trailers. The car bodies are manufactured by Casaralta of Bologna and the bogies by OMS of Padua. These vehicles also were ordered to improve public transport facilities during the 1990 World Cup.

Twelve two-car Type T 67 articulated LRVs were supplied to ATAN of Naples by Ansaldo Trasporti and FIREMA, to improve the urban transport system in Naples during the 1990 World Cup. Delivery started in the spring of 1990.

In June 1988 Officine di Cittadella delivered to FS a new Press and Conference car. Fully air-conditioned, the car is divided into four areas: reception; lounge with bar and 10 seats; room with table and 22 seats, equipped as press room, conference/meeting hall; and service area with secretarial services, audio-video direction data transmission equipment, lavatory. Equipment includes audio-video system, information process system, telephone and telefax. Power supply is by static converter or diesel-driven electric generator. The body shell is welded in high-performance steel. The car weighs 54 tonnes tare and is designed to operate at up to 200 km/h.

Fuji
Fuji Heavy Industries Ltd
Transport Equipment Division

7-2, 1-chome Nishishinjuku 1-chome, Shinjuku-ku, Tokyo 160, Japan

Telephone: +81 3 347 2436
Telex: 232 2268 fuji j
Telefax: +81 3 347 2117

President: Toshihiro Tajima
Senior Managing Director: Sadasuke Nakazato
General Manager, Transport Equipment Division: Noboru Yuzawa
General Manager, Overseas Business Department: Kinji Hitomi

Products: Passenger coaches; works vehicles.

Constitution: Fuji Heavy Industries stems from the Nakajima Aircraft Company. The Nakajima Company was dissolved in 1945, but in 1953 it was reorganised as Fuji Heavy Industries, specialising in building SUBARU automobiles, buses, rolling stock and aircraft.

Fuji Car
Fuji Car Manufacturing Co Ltd

28 Hachiman-cho, Minami-ku, Osaka 542, Japan

Telephone: +81 6 213 2711
Telex: 5225279 fujosk j

Press and Conference car: meeting room (Firema)

Press and Conference car: bar lounge (Firema)

Type T 67 LRV for ATAN-Naples (Firema)

President: Tetsuhiro Nishi
Vice President: Junichi Takano
Export Sales: Kazuo Okazaki

Products: Passenger cars.

Gallinari
A Gallinari SpA

Viale Ramazzini 37, 42100 Reggio Emilia, Italy

Non-powered passenger vehicles / **MANUFACTURERS** 201

Telephone: +39 522 31 641
Cable: Gallinari, Reggio Emilia
Telex: 530601

Products: Passenger coaches; baggage and mail cars.

Ganz Hunslet
Ganz Hunslet Rt.

Budapest VIII, Vajda Péter u 12, H-1430 Budapest PO Box 29, Hungary

Telephone: +36 1 114 0840
Telex: 22 5575 gmbp
Telefax: +36 1 114 3481

Chief Executive: Harry A Codd
Sales Director: Géza Bereczky
Technical Director: László Süveges

An Anglo-Hungarian joint venture company, associated member to the Hunslet (Holdings) PLC of Leeds. Bearer of goodwill and tradition of the 1844 established Ganz and later Ganz-Mávag companies.

Products: 101 passenger coaches of various saloon configurations including power generating vans for long distance service on both of standard and metre-gauge lines of Tunisian Railway (SNCFT) were supplied in 1985-86.
Order placed by the Hungarian Post Administration for the supply of 23 postal vans suitable for international mail, parcel and postal container transport for 1990 delivery.

GEC Alsthom
Transport Division

Tour Neptune, 92086 Paris La Défense Cedex 20, France

Telephone: +33 1 47 44 9000
Telex: 611 207 alstr f
Telefax: +33 1 47 78 77 55

Works: Belfort, Aytré-La Rochelle, Marly-Les Valenciennes, Le Creusot.

Products: All types of passenger rolling stock and related equipment, including metro cars, suburban and interurban train-sets, double-deck coaches, automatic light rail vehicles (VAL).

Subsidiaries in France
CIMT Lorraine (Compagnie Industrielle de Matériel de Transport)
Tour Neptune, 92086 Paris-La Défense, Cedex 20
Telephone: +33 1 47 44 90 00
Telex: 610 119 F cimtran
Telefax: +33 1 47 44 96 96

Works
70 avenue Jean Jaurès, 59770 Marly-Les Valenciennes
Telephone: +33 27 45 92 20
Telex: 110 803 f
Telefax: +33 27 41 08 59

Products: Metro cars, train-sets, double-deck motor cars and trailer coaches, automated light vehicles (VAL).

CFI (Carel Fouché Industries)
PO Box 86, 27940 Aubevoye
Telephone: +33 32 53 08 40
Telex: 180 665 f
Telefax: +33 32 53 11 49

Products: Stainless steel passenger cars and multiple-units.

ACR (Alsthom Creusot Rail)
PO Box 42, rue Jean-Baptiste Marcet, Porte Magenta, 71202 Le Creusot
Telephone: +33 85 80 70 70
Telex: 800 141 f
Telefax: +33 85 80 70 99

Products: Carrying and motor bogies, 300 to 600 hp diesel engines (Saurer licence), Dispen shock absorbers.

Subsidiaries in USA
For full list see GEC Alsthom entries in Locomotives and Powered Passenger Vehicles sections

GEC Alsthom
Transportation Projects Ltd
(formerly Metro-Cammell Ltd)

PO Box 248, Leigh Road, Washwood Heath, Birmingham B8 2YJ, England

Telephone: +44 21 328 5455
Cable: Metro, Birmingham
Telex: 337601
Telefax: +44 21 327 6430

Managing Director: B S Ronan
Sales Manager: Ken Willis

Products: Passenger cars for surface, sub-surface and underground routes; main contractors for railway mechanical and electrical engineering systems.
A major order from British Rail appointed Metro-Cammell as main contractor for the supply of 31 nine-car trains to a new BR Mk 4 car design, plus spare cars to make the total 283 vehicles, for BR's East Coast Main Line electrification now in progress. All train-sets are for push-pull working, so that each includes a driving trailer (DVT); one DVT is also among the four spares. For the rest, two train-sets will feature three Pullmans, one tourist open, one tourist open with disabled person's toilet, two service vehicles and one tourist end car; the remainder will comprise two Pullmans, three tourist open, one tourist open with disabled person's toilet, one service vehicle and one tourist end car. The remaining spare cars will consist of a tourist open, a service vehicle and a tourist end car. There is an option for the supply of a further 31 tourist open cars.

Constitution: In the latter part of 1966 Metropolitan-Cammell absorbed the railway rolling stock business of Cravens of Sheffield. In 1969 Vickers Ltd relinquished their 50 per cent shareholding and a new company was formed for railway matters under the style of Metro-Cammell Ltd. In 1989 the company was acquired by GEC-Alsthom.

Goninan
A Goninan & Co Ltd

PO Box 21, Broadmeadow, New South Wales 2294, Australia

Telephone: +61 49 69 9250
Cable: Platinum, Newcastle
Telex: A28061
Telefax: +61 49 69 9250

Chairman: D A W Thomson
Chief Executive & Director: John Fitzgerald
General Manager, Railway Products Division: Barry Henshaw
Engineering & Sales Manager, Railway Products Division: Anthony Finnegan

Products: Passenger cars.

Görlitz
VEB Waggonbau Görlitz
Member of VEB Kombinat Schienenfahrzeugbau and of Vereinigter Schienenfahrzeugbau der DDR e V

Brunnenstrasse 11, 8900 Görlitz, German Democratic Republic

Telephone: +37 690
Cable: Waggonbau, Görlitz
Telex: 02 286227

Prototype Type C London Underground Tube train (Metro-Cammell)

Upper level of bi-level car for DR (Görlitz)

202 MANUFACTURERS / Non-powered passenger vehicles

Passenger cars for Indonesia (GOŠA)

Stainless steel sleeping car for USSR Railways (GOŠA)

Lower level of bi-level car for DR (Görlitz)

Export Director: Dieter Falkenberg

Products: Passenger cars; sleeping cars; double-deck coaches; bogies.

Recent deliveries have included 100 second-class double-deck coaches for the commuter and suburban traffic of the German State Railway (DR).

Constitution: After resuming production in 1945 as a manufacturer of special-purpose freight wagons, the plant switched to broad-gauge restaurant and couchette cars in 1949. In 1952 it took up production of double-deck passenger trains and cars and electric and diesel multiple-units, but since 1970 it has specialised in passenger cars, principally in double-deck vehicles and long-distance sleeping cars.

Exports: Schienenfahrzeuge Export-Import Volkseigener Aussenhandelsbetrieb der DDR, Otztaler Strasse 17, 1100 Berlin

GOŠA
SOUR Industrija GOŠA
Rolling Stock Manufacturing Division

Head office: Industrijska 70, 11 420 Smederevska Palanka, Yugoslavia
Sales office: Goša Commerce, Sitnička 39, 11 000 Belgrade

Telephone: +38 26 32 022
Cable: Goša Smederevska Palanka
Telex: 11 684
Telex (sales): 12605

Chairman: Momir Pavlićević
Managing Director: Miodrag Bajčić
Export Sales: Slavko Djorić

Products: Passenger coaches, sleeping, dining and saloon cars; special-purpose coaches.

Hungarian Railway Carriage
Hungarian Railway Carriage & Machine Works

Foreign Trade Department, PO Box 50, 9002 Györ, Hungary

Telephone: +36 96 12 300
Cable: RABA Györ
Telex: 02 4255

Products: Passenger cars.

Bi-level commuter cars for German State Railway (DR); over 4000 such vehicles have been built for various railways by Waggonbau Görlitz

Hunslet TPL
Hunslet Transportation Projects Limited
Member of Telfos Holdings Plc

Dogpool Mills, Stirchley, Birmingham, B30 2XJ, England

Telephone: +44 21 471 1047
Telex: 334269 HTPL-G
Telefax: +44 21 414 1369

Chairman: J Mallins
Managing Director: T M Jefferies
Sales Director: P C Johnson

Associate Companies
Hunslet (Holdings) Plc
Hunslet Engine Works, Leeds, LS10 1BT, England

Telephone: +44 532 432261
Telex: 55237
Telefax: +44 532 420820

Hunslet-Barclay Limited

Caledonia Works, Kilmarnock, Ayrshire, KA1 2QD, Scotland

Telephone: +44 563 23573
Telex: 778497
Telefax: +44 563 41076

Products: Railcars, metro cars, trams, LRVs and coaches.

Constitution: In the early part of 1989, Hunslet-TPL was formed as a project oriented company to co-ordinate the interest of the Hunslet Group in the design manufacture and supply of emu, dmu, metro, tram and LRV vehicles and passenger coaches.

Hyundai
Hyundai Precision & Ind Co Ltd

Head office: Hyundai Building, 140-2, Gye-Dong, Chongro-ku, Seoul, Republic of Korea
Postal address: KPO Box 1677, Seoul, Republic of Korea

Non-powered passenger vehicles / MANUFACTURERS

Interior of metre-gauge second-class car for Bangladesh (ICF)

Interior of metre-gauge third-class day car for Bangladesh (ICF)

Telephone: +82 2 719 0649
Telex: 23238, 23720 hdpic k
Telefax: +82 2 719 0741

Works: 621 Deokjeong-Dong, Changwon, Kyungnam, Republic of Korea
Telephone: +82 551 82-1341/50
Telex: 53744 hdpic k

Chairman: Mong Koo Chung
President: Ki Chyul Yoo
Senior Vice President: Kyung Wook Kim

Products: Passenger coaches.

Affiliated companies
Hyundai Engineering & Construction Co, Ltd
Hyundai Building, 140-2, Gye-Dong, Chongro-ku, Seoul, Republic of Korea
Telephone: +82 2 741 2111/5
Telex: 23111

Products: Design and construction of high-speed railway and underground systems.

ICF
The Integral Coach Factory

Perambur, Madras 600 038, India

Telephone: +91 44 618920, 618091
Cable: Raildib, Madras
Telex: 7390

General Manager: Kuldip Narain

Products: Air-conditioned sleeper and chair cars; pantry cars; metro cars; tourist cars; coaches for inter-city express trains; track recording cars; power cars; and double-deckers.

Imesi
Imesi SpA
(Industrie Metalmeccaniche Siciliane)
A member of the Breda Railway Group

Contada Olivelli Pistone, 90044 Carini, Palermo, Italy

Telephone: +39 91 8668677
Cable: Imesi-SpA, Carini
Telex: 910113 imisi i

Chairman: Giuseppe Capuano
General Manager: Angelo Palmieri

Products: Passenger coaches.
The company's recent output has included driving trailers for the push-pull trains of the Italian State Railways latest medium-distance stock. The vehicles are of two types: one cab for trains hauled by diesel-electric locomotives, the other for use with electric locomotives.

Jenbacher
Jenbacher Werke AG

6200 Jenbach, Austria

Telephone: +43 5244 2291-0

Imesi-built driving trailer for Italian State Railways

Cable: Motor Jenbach
Telex: 053756-7

Managing Director: F Franer
Technical Director: Dr Ebner
Production Manager: Ing Truppe

Products: Passenger coaches.

Constitution: The company was started in 1946 for the manufacture of diesel engines and combined units.

Jessop
Jessop & Co Ltd, Calcutta

63 Netaji Subhas Road, Calcutta 700 001, India

Telephone: +91 33 25 3420/5041
Cable: Jessops, Calcutta
Telex: 021-5054; 021-5298

Works: Jessore Road, Dum Dum, Calcutta, India

Telephone: +91 33 57 2321

Chairman and Managing Director: S R Choudhury
Managing Director: S N Sinha
Director (Engineering): R N Bhowal
Director (Production): D Sen

Products: All types of rolling stock including passenger coaches.

Constitution: Jessop and Co was founded in 1788, one of the oldest engineering firms in India. The works at Dum Dum, which cover 80 acres, comprise six separate units: wagon, coach, structural, road roller, mechanical and paper works. The works at Durgapur, built on 116 acres, manufacture heavy duty iron castings.

Kalmar
Kalmar Verkstads AB

PO Box 943, S-39129 Kalmar, Sweden

Telephone: +46 480 62600
Cable: Kvab, Kalmar
Telex: 43029
Telecopier: +46 480 18975

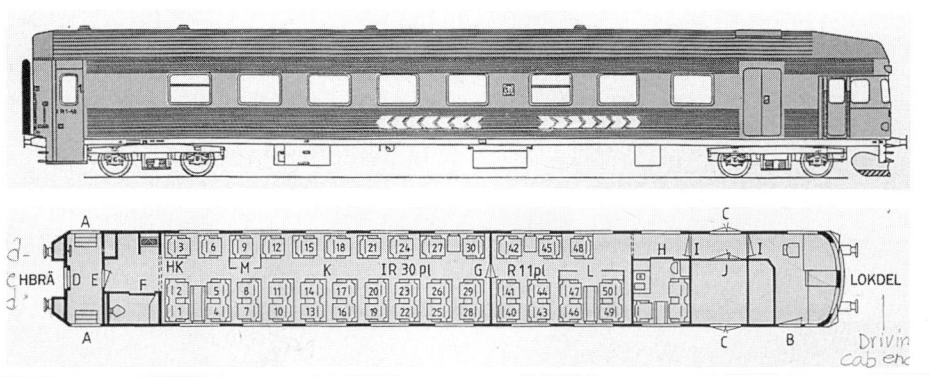

Layout of Type UA 7R driving trailer for Swedish Railways' regional service (Kalmar)

MANUFACTURERS / Non-powered passenger vehicles

Chairman: Sven Arnerius
Managing Director: K Harry Eriksson

Products: Passenger coaches.

Important recent sales have been: 100 passenger coaches for Kenya and Tanzania; 90 saloon, 15 restaurant and three driving trailers for Swedish State Railways (SJ). On order are two office, two conference and two family travel cars for SJ. The family cars include a children's playroom and facilities for the disabled, including a wheelchair lift. In collaboration with ASEA the company is involved in the design and delivery to SJ of 20 Type X-2 tilt-body 200 km/h trainsets.

Development in progress includes sleeping cars.

Constitution: Kalmar Verkstad was founded in 1902 and is Swedish State Railways' (SJ) major supplier of diesel locomotives, railcars and passenger cars. Kalmar Verkstad is a subsidiary of the Kalmar Industries Group.

Kawasaki
Kawasaki Heavy Industries Ltd, Rolling Stock Group

Head office: World Trade Centre Building, 4-1 Hamamatsu-cho 2-chome, Minato-ku, Tokyo 105, Japan

Telephone: +81 3 435 2589
Telex: (NTT) 242-4371
Telefax: +81 3 435-2157

Works: 1-18 Wadayama-dori 2-chome, Hyogo-ku, Kobe 652, Japan
Telephone: +81 78 682 3133
Telex: (NTT) 5622-115
Telefax: +81 78 671 5784

Chairman: Kenko Hasegawa
President: Hiroshi Ohba
Executive Vice Presidents: Motoo Okada
Yoshio Nakai
Director (Rolling Stock): Shozo Shimoura

Products: Electric and diesel railcars and locomotives, passenger coaches and freight cars

Kinki Sharyo
The Kinki Sharyo Co Ltd
Kinki Rolling Stock Manufacturing Co Ltd

Head office and Tokuan factory: 3-9-60 Inada-Shinmachi, Higashi Osaka City, Osaka 577, Japan

Telephone: +81 6 746 5240
Cable: Kinsha Fuse
Telex: 5278911
Telefax: +81 6 745 5135 (GIII)

Tokyo office: 527 Nippon Bldg, Ohtemachi, Chiyoda-ku, Tokyo 100, Japan

Telephone: +81 3 270 3431
Telex: 222 3105
Telefax: +81 3 245 0238 (GIII)

Stainless steel first-class cars for Korean National Railroad by Korea Shipbuilding & Engineering

President: Seihei Katayama
Executive Vice President: Akira Kitamori
Senior Managing Director: Hisatsugu Sugano
Managing Director: Yasuji Yukawa
Export Sales Director: Takumi Ono

Products: Passenger cars.

Kolmex
Foreign Trade Enterprise Co Ltd
Mokotowska 49, 00-542 Warsaw, Poland

Telephone: +48 22 28 22 91
Cable: Kolmex, Warsaw
Telex: 813270; 813714
Telefax: +48 22 295879

Managing Director: Aleksander Gudzowaty
Sales Directors: Aleksander Kociszewski
Wieslaw Husarski
Tomasz Suprowicz

Products: Passenger coaches.

Korea Shipbuilding & Engineering
Korea Shipbuilding & Engineering Corporation

Head office: 1, 1-Ka Jongro, Jongro-ku, Seoul, Republic of Korea
CPO Box 1520, Seoul, Republic of Korea

Telephone: +82 2 739 5577
Telex: 23669; 23415 ksecs
Telefax: +82 2 733 8113

Pusan factory: 370-6 Tadae-dong, Saha-ku, Pusan
PO Box 74, Pusan, Republic of Korea

Telephone: +82 51 204 0541
Telex: 53613 ksecs
Telefax: +82 51 204 0626

Chairman: Ryun Namkoong

President: Ho Namkoong
Executive Director: Jong-Chul Mun
Sales Director: Jun Kil Suh

Products: Passenger cars, special-purpose rolling stock, bogies, couplers.

In recent years, KSEC has delivered over 5000 units of various kinds of rolling stock to Korean National Railways and to Malaysia, Saudi Arabia, Indonesia, Sudan, Thailand, Argentina, New Zealand and elsewhere.

La Maquinista
La Maquinista Terrestre y Maritima, SA

Fernando Junoy, 2-64, 08030 Barcelona, Spain

Telephone: +34 3 345 57 00
Telex: 54539 maqui e
Telefax: +34 3 345 69 58

President: D Miguel Saenz de Viguera y Aispurua
Commercial Director: D Pedro Sole Raventos
Export Director: D Javier Masoliver y de Marti

Products: Passenger cars.

Macosa
Material y Construcciones, SA

Head office: Plaza de la Independencia 8, Madrid 28001, Spain

Telephone: +34 1 522 4787
Cable: Material, Madrid
Telex: 22168

Works: Herreros 2, Barcelona
Telephone: +34 3 307 05 00; Telex: 52286
San Vicente 273, Valencia
Telephone: +34 6 377 39 00; Telex: 62452
Marqués de Mudela 10, Alcazar de San Juan
Telephone: + 34 54 1124
Telex: 23692

Series 10800 cafeteria car for RENFE (Macosa)

Saloon of Series 10800 cafeteria car for RENFE (Macosa)

Non-powered passenger vehicles / **MANUFACTURERS**

German Federal Type Bxf control trailer (MAN GHH)

Driver's console of Type Bxf control trailer (MAN GHH)

President: Eduardo Santos
Vice President: Pedro Nueno

Products: Passenger cars.

MAN GHH
MAN Gutehoffnungshütte Aktiengesellschaft

Bahnhofstrasse 66, PO Box 11 02 40, 4200 Oberhausen 11, Federal Republic of Germany

Telephone: +49 208 692 1
Telex: 856691 oghhd
Telefax: + 49 208 6922887

Main works: MAN GHH Railway Rolling Stock Division, Frankenstrasse 150, PO Box 44 01 00, 8500 Nürnberg 44, Federal Republic of Germany

Telephone: +49 911 18 2632
Telex: 622 291 mn d
Telefax: +49 911 18 2375

Vice President of Railway Rolling Stock Division: Heinz Hennig
Senior Department Sales Manager: Wolfgang Knörle
Senior Department Design Manager: Gerhold Sames

Products: Passenger coaches, luggage vans, with carbodies fabricated in steel, light metal or stainless steel (Nirosta); bogies, powered and non-powered, especially with air suspension and also for high-speed transport; vehicle components; technology transfer; product service.

In 1988 MAN GHH completed manufacture of bi-directional control trailers for the push-pull suburban services of the German Federal Railway in the Rhine-Ruhr and Nuremberg regions. The trailers of series Bxf are equipped with the integrated driver's console adopted by the German Federal Railway.

The German Federal Railway placed an order with a consortium including MAN GHH for the manufacture of 123 centre cars of the Bvmz series for the IC Express trains which will come into service from 1991 onwards on the new high-speed lines of the German Federal Railway.

Materfer
Materfer SA

Suipacha 1109, Pisos 2° and 5°, 1008 Buenos Aires, Argentina

Telephone: +54 1 313 0870/1296/0900/0927
Telex: 25175 catmg ar
Telefax: +54 1 331 5491

Works: Fábrica Materfer SA
Ruta 9, Km 694, 5000 Ferreyra, Córdoba, Argentina

Telephone: +54 51 97 2730/32/34
Telex: 51300 mat sa

Telefax: +54 51 97 2489

Trailer cars for Argentine Railways' Roca Line emus under construction (Materfer)

Interior of Roca Line emu trailer (Materfer)

MANUFACTURERS / Non-powered passenger vehicles

Chairman: Ing Enzo Filipelli
President: Lic Eduardo Jorge Nava
Vice-President: Dr Edgardo Héctor Iriarte
General Manager: Ing Enzo Nicolás Filipelli
Commercial Director: Antonio Maltana

Group companies: Centro de Actividades Termomécanicas SA (CAT), Grandes Motores Diésel SA (GMD) and Ingesa SA.

Products: Passenger coaches (with or without air-conditioning); metro cars; mail vans.

In 1988, Materfer gained an order from Argentine Railways to manufacture 34 coaches to be used as a fourth trailer in the 25 kv emus of the Roca Line suburban service.

Since 1979, Materfer has engaged in rebuilding activity and has overhauled 1095 passenger coaches, all with over 20 years service. In 1989 a three-year passenger coach rehabilitation contract was obtained from Argentine Railways, covering complete overhaul of their fleet.

Bi-level cars for Japan Rail (JR) Group Series 211 1067 mm-gauge commuter emu (Nippon Sharyo)

MBB
Messerschmitt-Bölkow-Blohm GmbH
Transportation Technology Division

PO Box 1353, 8850 Donauwörth, Federal Republic of Germany

Telephone: +49 906 711
Telex: 51843 mbb d
Telefax: +49 906 71898

General Manager: Dieter v Hummel

Products: Rail vehicles in lightweight construction for underground and rapid transit commuter services, main-line passenger coaches for short-haul and long-haul services, sleeping cars, dining cars and saloon cars.

Constitution: Formerly trading under the name of WMD (Waggon-und Maschinenbau Donauwörth).

Mecanoexportimport

10 Mihail Eminescu Street, Bucharest, Romania

Telephone: +40 0 1198 55
Cable: Mecanex, Bucharest
Telex: 10 269
Telefax: +40 0 106650

Products: Passenger coaches.

Miner Railcar Services Inc

PO Box 2208, East Cherry Street, New Castle, Pennsylvania 16102, USA

Telephone: +1 412 658 9061
Telefax: +1 412 658 9061

Vice President and General Manager: R M Giallonardo
Vice President: Gabe Kassab

Associated companies
Miner Railcar Services
Garrett Railroad Car Parts Corporation
PO Box 34, Darlington, Pennsylvania 16115, USA
Telephone: +1 412 827 8121
Telefax: +1 412 827 2961

Products: Railcars for transit authorities.

Nippon Sharyo
Nippon Sharyo Ltd

Head office: 1-1 Sanbonmatsu-cho, Atsuta-ku, Nagoya, Japan

Telephone: +81 52 882 3315
Cable: Nishiya, Nagoya
Telex: 447 3411
Telefax: +81 5 882 3337

Tokyo office
Telephone: +81 3 668 3330
Telex: 252 2095
Telefax: +81 3 669 0238

Works: Toyokawa

President: Osamu Shinohara
Senior Vice President: Eiichi Okumura
Managing Director (Chief of Export Division): Kenji Nishimura
General Manager (Rolling Stock Divison, Overseas Dept): Kazuhiko Iwadare

Products: Passenger cars.

OFV
Officine Ferroviarie Veronesi SpA

Lungadige A Galtarossa 21, 37100 Verona, Italy

Telephone: +39 45 595022
Telex: 481017

President: Giacomo Galtarossa

General Manager: Adriano Mattalia

Products: Passenger cars. Recent production has included the latest types of medium-distance, long-distance and suburban passenger cars adopted by the Italian State Railways.

OMECA
OMECA SpA

Works: Reggio Calabria, Italy

Products: Passenger coaches of all types.

Constitution: The OMECA plant is jointly owned by Fiat Ferroviaria and Aviofer Breda (EFIM).

OMS
Officina Meccanica della Stanga
Member of Firema Consortium

Corso Stati Uniti 3, 35100 Padua, Italy

Telephone: +39 49 8700866
Cable: OMS, Padova
Telex: 430218 omspd i
Telefax: +39 49 76 06 82

Chairman: Dr Dino Marchiorello
Vice-Chairman: Ing Aldo Iaia
Managing Director: Dr-Ing Ugo Soloni

Products: Passenger cars; freight wagons.

Recent contracts have included: 30 light alloy control trailer cars, 10 Gran Confort inter-city cars for Italian State Railways (FS). The inter-city control trailer for the FS features a body entirely formed of aluminium-alloy extruded profiles and welded with MIG/TIG processes. Tare weight is 35 tonnes and max operating speed 140 km/h.

Recent contracts include an order for eight light alloy control trailers for FS.

Second-class compartment coach with 80 seats, tare weight 40.4 tonnes, max speed 140 km/h, for CFR (Mecanoexportimport)

Type Le 562 control trailer for Italian Railways' emu operation by OMS

'Gran Confort' intercity car for FS by OMS

Pafawag
FW Pafawag

Fabryka Wagonow Pafawag, ul Pstrowskiego 12, 53-609 Wroclaw, Poland

Telephone: +48 71 56 21 11
Telex: 0712431

Engineering Manager: R Gappert
Commercial Director: K Krzyczmonik

Export sales: Kolmex, 49 Mokotowska, 00-542 Warsaw, Poland

Products: Passenger and service cars, bogies.

Pakistan Railway Carriage
Pakistan Railway Carriage Factory

PO Box 286, Rawalpindi, Islamabad, Pakistan

Telephone: +92 51 860253, 860349
Cable: Carfac, Rawalpindi
Telex: 54135 prcfi pk

Works: Sector 1-11, Khayaban-e-Sir Syed, Islamabad

Chairman: S M Jafar Wafa
General Manager, Railway Manufacture: Vacant
Chief Mechanical Engineer, Railway Manufacture: Zaki Ahmad Siddiqui
Chief Officer, Carriage Factory: Mohammad Fahiem-ud Din

Products: Passenger coaches.
The main design features of the factory's standard second-class carriages are welded construction with pre-fabricated steel structure framing, to the following dimensions:
  Track gauge: 1676.4 mm
  Length over buffers: 22 606 mm
    over headstocks: 21 332 mm
  Width: 3251 mm
  Height above rail level: 3899 mm
  Maximum seating capacity: 88 passengers
  Bogies: Type BG 64 with welded and riveted frame with all coil spring for primary and secondary suspension
  Max speed: 120 km/h
  Weight of bogie unit: 6 tons
  Tare weight of vehicle: 37 tonnes

For economy-class travel on Pakistan Railways, the Carriage Factory has manufactured Type WACCP air-conditioned lower-class parlour cars and power vans for head-end auxiliary power supply, also air-conditioned sleeping cars of two types: one has a self-contained diesel alternator for current generation, the other draws current from a power car included in its train. The main feature of these cars is an air-conditioning facility at a comparatively cheap cost.

PEC
The Projects & Equipment Corporation of India Ltd
A Government of India Enterprise

Hansalaya, 15 Barakhamba Road, New Delhi 110 001, India

Telephone: +91 11 3313542, +91 11 3313356, +91 11 3314419
Cable: Pecoind
Telex: 31 65199, 31 65256
Telefax: +91 11 331 5279

Chairman: S N Malik
Executive Director: R Khosla
Chief Marketing Manager (Railway Equipment Division): C Chatterji

Products: Passenger coaches of any type and design for various gauges. Spares for coaches for export.
Over 470 coaches manufactured in India are currently operating in Taiwan, Zambia, Philippines, Burma, Bangladesh, Mozambique, Nepal, Nigeria, Sri Lanka, Tanzania, Uganda and Viet-Nam. Most recent export has been 61 metre-gauge cars to Bangladesh.

Constitution: PEC was formed in 1971 as a corporation under the Indian Ministry of Commerce to handle and boost the export of railway equipment and engineering goods.
The Indian coach building industry comprises the Integral Coach Factory, Madras (an Indian Railway unit), BEML, Bangalore (a unit under the Ministry of Defence) and Jessop & Co Ltd with a combined annual capacity of approximately 1700 units. These companies also regularly supply Indian Railways.

Pu Zhen
Pu Zhen Rolling Stock Works

Nanjing, Kiangsu, People's Republic of China

Telephone: +86 686786
Cable: 6611

Products: Passenger coaches; roller bearings; axle boxes; brake cylinders.

Constitution: Originally a locomotive repair yard, now a passenger coach repair and manufacturing works.

Reggiane
Officine Meccaniche Italiano SpA

PO Box 431, 27 Via Vasco Agosti, 42100 Reggio Emilia, Italy

Telephone: +39 522 5881
Telex: 530665
Telefax: +39 522 588243

Chairman: Dr Giuseppe Ivan Bonora
General Manager: Vincenzo Giuliano

Products: Passenger, pilot, dining, sleeping, saloon cars; rolling stock components.

Constitution: Reggiane has been engaged in railway locomotives and rolling stock since 1905.

RFS
RFS Engineering Ltd

PO Box 192, Hexthorpe Road, Doncaster DN1 1PJ, England

Telephone: +44 302 340700
Telex: 547296
Telefax: +44 302 340693

Managing Director: P Page
Technical Director: D W Theyers
Finance Director: B J Pierce
Director: L Harrison
Commercial Manager: M Rowe

Products: Conversion/overhaul and repair of non-powered passenger vehicles and equipment.
Recent contracts include the conversion of Mk 2F coaches for British Railways (September 1989); coach overhaul for Flying Scotsman Services (November 1989); conversion of Mk 2D coaches (March 1989); conversion of special coaches for Schering (March 1989).

RPS
Rail Passenger Services Inc

PO Box 26381, Tucson, Arizona 85726, USA

Telephone: +1 602 747 0346

Vice President: Robert B Stout

Products: Heavy passenger car rebuilding and modernisation. The company specialises in one-off customised passenger car refurbishments for private owners, corporations and railroads.

Scandia Randers
ABB Scandia A/S

Toldbodgade 39, PO Box 200, 8900 Randers, Denmark

Telephone: +45 6 425300
Telegrams: Scandia, Randers
Telex: 65145
Telefax: +45 6 415700

Export Manager: Kjeld Hvid

Products: Passenger coaches.

Schienenfahrzeuge Export-Import
Volkseigener Aussenhandelsbetrieb der DDR
Member of VEB Kombinat Schienenfahrzeugbau and of Vereinigter Schienenfahrzeugbau der DDR e V

Ötztaler Strasse 5, 1100 Berlin, German Democratic Republic

Telephone: +37 2 48040
Telex: 114372

Products: Passenger coaches; rail vehicle equipment; railway cranes.

Constitution: Sole exporter of all rail vehicles and rail vehicle equipment built in the German Democratic Republic.

Bi-level passenger car (Pu Zhen)

208 MANUFACTURERS / Non-powered passenger vehicles

Refurbished lounge of 'Arizona' car (RPS)

Refurbished 1940s bedroom-lounge car 'Arizona', built originally by Pullman for the Northern Pacific Railroad (RPS)

Schindler
Schindler Carriage & Wagon Co Ltd

4133 Pratteln, near Basle, Switzerland

Telephone: +41 61 825 91 11
Cable: Schindlerwagon, Pratteln
Telex: 968010
Telefax: +41 61 825 9205

Managing Director: P Piffaretti
Technical Director and Director of Works: H Knecht
Sales Manager: R Meury

Products: Passenger cars.
  The company has participated in construction of first-and second-class cars of the new Mk IV type for Swiss Federal Railways and has itself developed and built 19 Mk IV restaurant-kitchen cars.
  In 1990 the first double-deck coaches in Switzerland were put in service on Zurich's regional express system (RER). The shuttle-service train-sets are composed of a locomotive, two intermediate cars and a driving car, with a total length of about 100 m. Up to three such train-sets can be coupled together. A first order to the company included 36 second/class cars, 30 first-/second-class cars and 24 second-class driving trailers. The first coach was delivered in 1988. A further 90 cars were ordered in 1989.

SBB Mk IV restaurant car

Interior of Zurich RER bi-level car

Schindler Waggon Altenrhein
Schindler Waggon Altenrhein AG

9423 Altenrhein, Switzerland

Telephone: +41 71 43 43 43
Telex: 881530 swa ch
Telefax: +41 71 43 44 45

Chairman: Pierino Pittaretti
President: Hans Kubat
Sales Director: Robert Séquin

Products: Passenger cars, driving trailer, dining cars, of lightweight steel and aluminium alloy design for

Bi-level intermediate car of Zurich RER

all gauges. Special constructions for all purposes; designs; under-structure; modification; and individual components and sub-assemblies.

The company is one of two groups involved in manufacture of Swiss Federal Railways' (SBB) Mk IV passenger cars for internal intercity service. Fully air-conditioned, the vehicles are built to standard UIC 26.4 m length in welded all-steel on an orthodox underframe meeting UIC end-loading specifications. Weight is 43 tonnes, seating capacity 60 and a new design of SIG bogie, equipped with disc and electro-magnetic rail brakes, fits the vehicle for speeds up to 200 km/h.

Electro-pneumatically-operated sliding plug doors are of an 800 mm wide single-leaf Kiekert-pattern type. The automatic air-conditioning demands up to 35 kW of power for cooling and 42 kW for heating, but economises on energy by mixing fresh air with recirculated air from non-smoking seating areas.

Constitution: The company was founded in 1925 as Flug-und Fahrzeugwerke AG Altenrhein (FFA). During 1931–35 the first funiculars and suspension cars were built, and the rail carriage department began in 1945–47. At the start of 1987 FFA was taken over by the Schindler company and in the following June its railway vehicle building and general engineering were separated from its aircraft manufacture, the former activities taking the new title of Schindler Waggon Altenrhein AG. The company supplies rolling stock for the SBB (Swiss Federal Railways) as well as for a large number of private and municipal railway undertakings.

SCIF
Société Cherifienne du Matériel Industriel et Ferroviaire

PO Box 2604, Allée des Cactus, Aïn Sebaa, Casablanca, Morocco

Telephone: +212 35 3911, 35 1093
Telex: 26802 m

Products: Passenger cars. Passenger car production for the Moroccan Railways began in 1984.

SEMAF
Société Générale Egyptienne de Matériel des Chemins de Fer

Ein Helwan, Cairo, Egypt

Telephone: +2 2 782358; +2 2 782177; +2 2 782716; +2 2 782306; +2 2 630097; +2 2 782623
Cable: SEMAF, Ein Helwan
Telex: 23342 semaf un
Telefax: +2 2 788413

Chairman: Eng T El-Maghraby
Works Manager, Coach & Metro: Dr Eng L Melek
Works Manager, Wagon & Bogie: Eng S El-Sherbiny
Technical Manager: A Rahik
Administrative Manager: D Maged
Financial Manager: A Farid

Products: Passenger cars; first, second and third class air-conditioned and normally ventilated, post and baggage cars, air-conditioned cars with two package units or seven roof units, perishables and parcels vans and hospital coaches; power cars, tram and metro units; broad, standard, narrow and metre-gauge freight cars.

Recent contracts include 36 power, first, second and third class cars for Sudan Railways (1990); 27 second class air-conditioned coaches with buffet compartment for Egyptian National Authority (1990); 40 air-conditioned sleeper coaches for Egyptian National Authority (1991).

SGI
Società Gestioni Industriali SpA

48 Via Adriano Cecchetti, 62012 Civitanova Marche, Italy

Telephone: +39 733 72 918/770 555
Cable: Rotabili, Civitanova Marche
Telex: 560 896
Telefax: +39 733 761538

Model of the Swiss Federal Railways (SBB) panorama carriage by Schindler Waggon

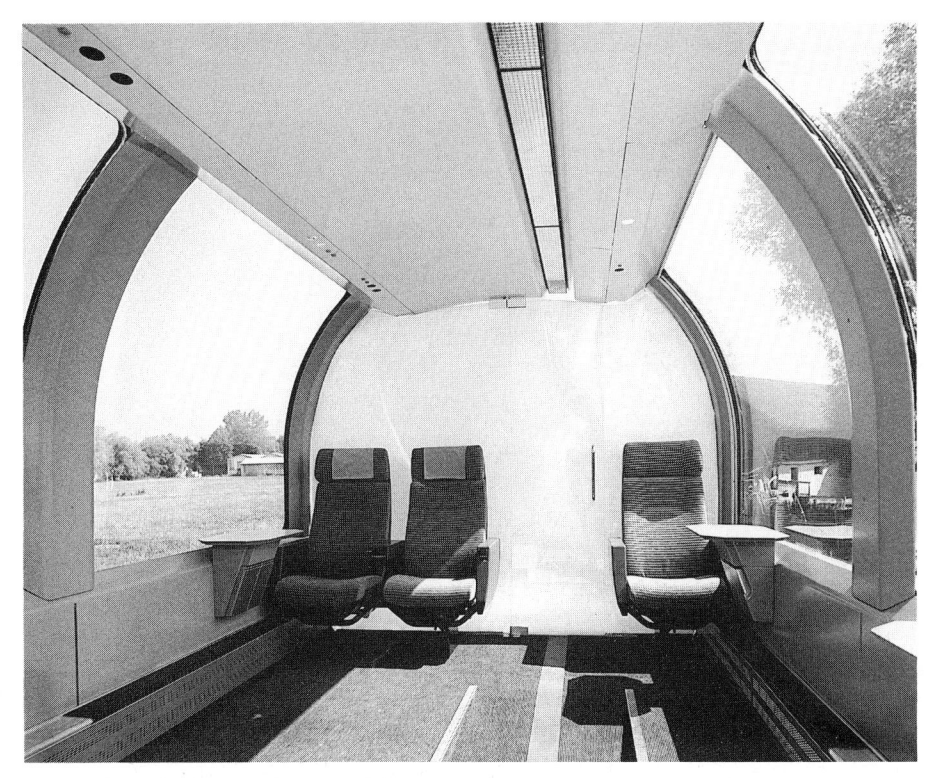

Interior view of SBB panorama carriage mock-up

Air-conditioned second class buffet coach (SEMAF)

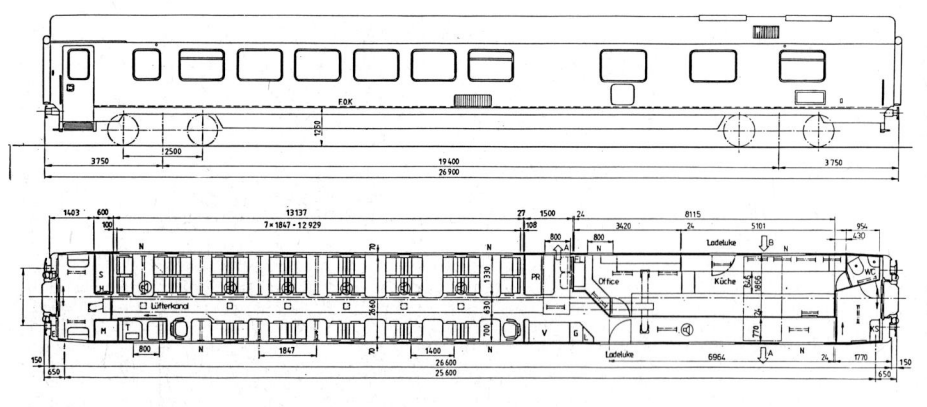

MANUFACTURERS / Non-powered passenger vehicles

General arrangement of Type WRmz restaurant car for Austrian Federal Railways' (ÖBB) international series. Note passenger telephone booth (T), space for Minibar wagon (M) and staff compartment (PR). Tare weight: 54 tonnes (S-G-P)

Interior of Type WRmz restaurant car (S-G-P)

General Manager: Dott Ing Giorgio Caputo
Sales Manager: Dott Attilio Iezzi (Administration)

Products: Passenger cars.

Constitution: In 1957 SGI took over the business of Costruzioni Meccaniche A Cecchetti, which had been wound up previously, having been operating since 1892.

S-G-P
Verkehrstechnik Gesellschaft mbH

Head office: PO Box 103, Brehmstrasse 16, 1110 Vienna, Austria

Telephone: +43 1 22 7469
Cable: Esgepe, Vienna
Telex: 131891, 132574
Telefax: +43 1 22 745148

Main works
Simmering Works, Leberstrasse 34, 1110 Vienna, Austria
Graz Works: Eggenbergerstrasse 31, 8021 Graz, Austria

General Manager: Dr Herbert Ziegler
Sales Director: Dipl Ing Heinz Butz
Technical Director: Dipl Ing Roland Himmelbauer

Products: Passenger coaches, service coaches, sleeper and couchette coaches, ambulance cars, metro and suburban rolling stock, double-deck cars.

Siemens
Siemens AG
Transportation Systems Group

Werner von Siemens Strasse 50, PO Box 3240, D-8520 Erlangen, Federal Republic of Germany

Telephone: +49 9131 724157
Telex: 6291508 si d
Telefax: +49 9131 726840

Group President: W O Martinsen
Mainline Rolling Stock Division: R Stubenrauch
Passenger Coaches Dept: P Lueftenegger

Products: Passenger coaches, electrical equipment

Socimi
Società Costruzioni Industriali Milano SpA

Head office: Via Varesina 115, 20156 Milan, Italy

Telephone: +39 2 30091
Telex: 323564
Telefax: +39 2 3085161

Main works
Via Enrico Fermi n 25, 20082 Binasco (Milan)
Telephone: +39 2 9055605/6/7/8

Via Donatori del Sangue n 100, 20010 Arluno (Milan)
Telephone: +39 2 9017666, 9017803

Viale Porto Torres, Reg Zentu Figghi, 07100 Sassari
Telephone: +39 79 260206

Via I Maggio, 21045 Gazzada Schianno (Varese)
Telephone: +39 332 461313

Chairman: Dr Eng Alessandro Marzocco
Managing Director: Dr Eng Pierino Sacchi
Assistant to Chairman: Dr Eng Corrado Landolina

Products: Passenger cars of all kinds.

SOFER
SOFER—Officine Ferroviarie, SpA

Via Miliscola 33, Pozzuoli (Naples), Italy

Telephone: +39 81 5262522
Cable: SOFER, Pozzuoli
Telex: 710048
Telefax: +39 81 5262288

Chairman: Dr Ing Corrado Fici
General Manager: Dr Ing Giovanni Alfano

Products: Passenger coaches of all types and classes; luggage and mail vans.
Recent contracts include Breda-built cars for Washington and Los Angeles Metros.

Sorefame
Sociedades Reunidas de Fabricações Metálicas, SA

Board of Directors: Av Antonio Augusto de Aguiar, 163, 3° Dto, 1000 Lisbon, Portugal

Telephone: +351 1 976051
Telex: 12608 sorfam p

Head office: Rua Vice-Almirante Azevedo Coutinho, PO Box5, 2701 Amadora Codex, Portugal

Telephone: +351 1 976051
Cable: Sorefame, Amadora
Telex: 12 608 sorfam p
Telefax: +351 1 977210

Works: Amadora

Chairman: Rui Vilares Cordeiro
Rolling Stock Division Manager: M Andrade Gomes

Products: Passenger cars and car-shells.
Sorefame supplies carbody shells according to its own or the client's design. The self-supporting shells are in stainless steel. All sheets and profiles, visible or not, used in the structure of the shell are in stainless steel except the end underframes which are built in low alloy, high tensile steels. Stainless steel profiles are obtained in draw-bench machines from strip coils. For Portuguese Railways (CP), Sorefame has supplied main-line coaches in stainless steel, the engineering of which is adapted from the existing Corail concept of GEC Alsthom, keeping the VTU-78/3 design of the Federal Railways Corail coaches.

Soulé
Soulé SA

PO Box 1, 65200 Bagnères-de-Bigorre, France

Telephone: +33 62 95 07 31
Cable: Soulé, Bagnères de Bigorre
Telex: 530 179
Telefax: +33 62 95 55 65

Chairman: Arnaud de Boysson
Executive Vice-President: Guy Thomas

Products: Passenger cars; postal vans.
Developed for tropical areas, the company's range of passenger cars offers interior day, restaurant, sleeping berth and couchette layouts within a standard 22.32-metre body-shell of semi-stainless steel, at tare weights ranging from 28 to 35.5 tonnes. The company also offers passenger cars of 17.5- or 20-metre lengths, at tare weights ranging from 19 to 23 tonnes.
The car bogies are also manufactured by Soulé. Two types are available, the Y500 for a maximum axleload of 10 tonnes, and the Y600 for a maximum of 13 tonnes.

Constitution: Founded in 1862.

Strojexport Company Ltd

Vàclavské n 56, 11326 Prague 1, Czechoslovakia

Telephone: +422 2357565
Cable: Strojexport, Prague
Telex: 121671, 122604
Telefax: +422 2323084, +422 2323092

General Director: Ing Josef Regner
Deputy General Director: Ing Stanislav Urabec
Commercial Director: František Forgàcs
Products: Strojexport handles all transactions for the export of passenger and freight rolling stock built by Czechoslovak wagon works. The principal passenger car product is a second-class design, as well as diesel railcars and diesel locomotives.

Strømens
A/S Strømens Vaerksted

PO Box 83, 2011 Strømen, Norway

Telephone: +47 6 809600
Cable: Verkstedet, Strømen
Telex: 71 551
Telefax: +47 6 809601

Managing Director: P Hauan
Technical Director: J Jacobsen

Products: Passenger cars of all types.

Constitution: The company was established in 1873 for the manufacture of railway rolling stock and is now the only car builder in Norway.

Non-powered passenger vehicles / **MANUFACTURERS**

First-class day coach for Gabon State Railways (OCTRA)

Soulé Type Y625 bogie for Cameroon coaches

Tafesa
Construcción y Reparación de Material Ferroviario

Carretera de Villaverde a Vallecas 16, Madrid 28041, Spain

Telephone: +34 1 798 0550
Telex: 42283 tran e
Telefax: +34 1 798 0961

General Manager: M A Simón Langarica

Products: Passenger cars.

Constitution: The group comprises the Tafesa, Fabesa, Transervi, Ifasa and Imedexsa companies.

Double-deck commuter cars for Netherlands Railways (NS) (Talbot)

Talbot
Waggonfabrik Talbot

Postfach 1410, Jülicherstrasse 213-237, 5100 Aachen, Federal Republic of Germany

Telephone: +49 241 18210
Cable: Talbot, Aachen
Telex: 08 32 845
Telefax: +49 241 1821214

Products: Passenger carriages; double-deck passenger cars.
Recent passenger rolling stock orders have included the supply to Netherlands Railways (NS) of bi-level cars comprising 12 driving trailer seconds, 24 second-class and 28 composite-class trailers.

Interior of NS double-deck car, upper floor (Talbot)

Talgo
Patentes Talgo SA

Montalbán 14, Madrid-14, Spain

Telephone: +34 1 222 28 44, 222 74 50
Cable: Talgo
Telex: 22184

Products: Lightweight, low centre-of-gravity high-speed passenger equipment employing a patent Talgo system of vehicle suspension and wheel guidance to permit higher curving speed without passenger discomfort or undue wear of track. Each vehicle (except end-cars of a train-set) is carried on a single pair of half-axles with independent wheels. At present the equipment is used exclusively by Spanish National Railways (RENFE). The latest Talgo designs include equipment with automatically adjustable axles for easy through running between Spain and France, and equipment with pendular suspension introduced to revenue service in 1980 (see also under Spanish National Railways).

212 **MANUFACTURERS** / Non-powered passenger vehicles

Tokyu
Tokyu Car Corporation

Head office: 1 Kamariya-cho, Kanazawa-ku, Yokohama, Japan
Sales and Export Department: 2-7-2, Yaesu, Chuo-ku, Tokyo, Japan

Telephone: +81 3 272 8091/3
Cable: Tokyucarcorp Tok
Telex: 0222 2020
Telefax: +81 3 272 3656

Chairman: Ihaho Takahashi
President: Kiyoshi Yasuzumi
Executive Vice-Presidents: Hikaru Honda
Hiroshi Hotta

Products: Stainless steel cars with bogie, passenger cars with bogie, bogies of various types.

Constitution: The company was formed in 1948, its predecessors being the Yokohama Plant of the Tokyo Electric Express Railway Co. It built the first stainless steel train-set in Japan following technical agreement with the Budd Company of USA in 1960. Merging Teikoku Car & Manufacturing Co of Osaka into its organisation in 1968, the company is now the largest Japanese supplier of rolling stock to home and overseas railways.

Turnu-Severin
Mecanoexportimport supplier

3 B-dul Dunării, 1500 Drobeta Turnu Severin, Romania

Telephone: +40 978 12078
Telex: 42233

Products: Passenger cars.

Constitution: Member of the Wagons Manufacture Enterprises Group.

Union Carriage
Union Carriage & Wagon Co (Pty) Ltd

Marievale Road, Vorsterkroon, Nigel 1490, Transvaal, South Africa

Telephone: +27 11 739 2411
Cable: Unicarwag
Telex: 750524 unicar
Telefax: +27 11 739 5156

Chairman: G S E Coucourakis
Managing Director: R Bingham
Commercial Manager: A A M Lyle
Technical Manager: J J R Watten

Products: Locomotive-hauled passenger coaches.

UTDC
UTDC Inc

PO Box 70, Station A, Kingston, Ontario, Canada K7M 6P9

Telephone: +1 613 384 3100
Telex: 066 3357
Cable: URBANTRANS KGTN
Telefax: +1 613 389 6382

President and CEO: David Pattenden
Senior Vice President, Marketing: Herb Goldman
Vice President, Sales & Proposals: Richard Giles

Main works: Thunder Bay and Kingston, Ontario

Products: Intercity rapid transit and suburban rail coaches (bi-level and single-level); frame-braced and steerable axle bogies.

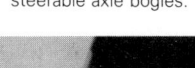

Bi-level commuter car lower level (UTDC)

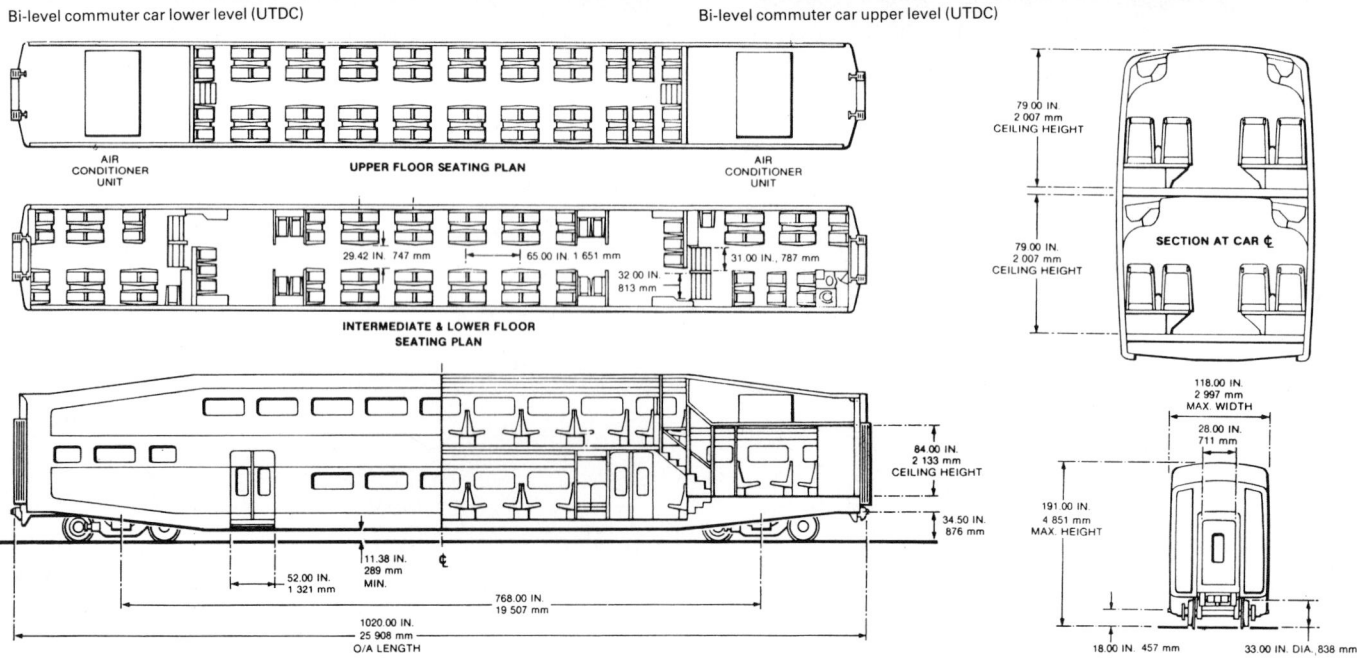

Bi-level commuter car upper level (UTDC)

Layout of bi-level passenger car for GO Transit (UTDC)

Recent orders include 60 bi-level (double-decked) commuter cars for GO (Govt of Ontario) Transit's regional commuter service, and 16 automated transit vehicles for the Vancouver SkyTrain.

Extensive research into the limitations of standard rail freight bogies led UTDC to develop a frame-braced bogie for freight cars. Simple bracing and cushioning modifications to a standard three-piece bogie improve performance considerably while lowering operating and also maintenance costs, by significantly reducing both wheel and track wear. Tested and used successfully by several North American railroads, the frame-braced bogie's increased stability allows bulk and intermodal cars to operate at higher train speeds, even with very heavy loads.

Constitution: UTDC is a leading supplier of ground transportation systems, equipment and services. In addition to transportation systems research and development, UTDC offers complete services to develop, train, operate and maintain efficient revenue services on behalf of clients. UTDC is owned 85 per cent by Lavalin, a wholly-owned Canadian Corporation. In addition to advanced research and development, UTDC offers complete lifecycle support offering turnkey services – planning, designing, building and maintaining its own systems. The company also assembles original financial packages for clients that sometimes include equity participation by the company.

Valmet
Valmet Corporation, Railway Division

PO Box 387, 33101 Tampere, Finland

Telephone: +358 31 658111
Telex: 22112
Telefax: +358 31 657044

General Manager: Esko Määttänen
Marketing Manager: Olavi Kivimäki

Bi-level commuter cars of GO Transit at Toronto (UTDC)

Products: Passenger cars; rapid transit cars; coaches for special purposes.

Recent orders include one for 20 passenger cars for Finnish State Railways, to be delivered in 1989–91.

Waggon Union
Waggon Union GmbH

PO Box 2240, 5902 Netphen 2, Federal Republic of Germany

Telephone: +49 271 702 1

Cable: Waggonunion, Siegen
Telex: 08 72843

General Manager: Dipl-Ing Hans-Richard Hippenstiel

Products: Passenger cars, tramways, underground trains; double-deck buses and fabricated bogies for freight cars and passenger coaches.

THE CLASS 158 BY BREL

Passenger coaches/coach equipment

First of a new generation of advanced diesel multiple units for the 1990's.

BREL Limited has won orders for over 1,500 extruded aluminium rail vehicles for customers including British Rail, London Underground Limited and the State Railways of Thailand.

For details of these and other BREL products please contact:

Marketing Director, BREL Limited, St. Peter's House, Gower Street, Derby DE1 1AH
Tel: (44) 332 383850, Ext 4204. Telex: 377693/377898 BREST PG. Fax: (44) 332 292001

BREL LIMITED

Luwa – THE Specialist for Air Conditioning and Shock Wave Protection Systems in High Speed Trains

*Railway companies all over the world rely on the experience and know-how of Luwa.
The proof: More than 2.000 coaches in all continents are equipped by Luwa.
Luwa's diagnostic systems lead to considerable savings in maintenance and repair.*

Come to Luwa for comfort, reliability and savings

Branch offices, licensees and representatives in over 60 countries.

Luwa

*Luwa GmbH · Railway Airconditioning Division
Hanauer Landstrasse 200 · D-6000 Frankfurt/Main 1
Tel. 069/4035-0 · Telex 411775 · Fax 069/4035-307*

Passenger coach equipment

ARGENTINA
SIAM 225

AUSTRALIA
SMC 225
Stone McColl 226

AUSTRIA
IFE 221

BELGIUM
ACEC 216
Manta 222

BRAZIL
Fresinbra 219

DENMARK
Semco 225

FINLAND
EKE Group 218
Nesite 222

FRANCE
AIF 216
Carrier Khéops Bac 217
EFF 217
Equip Rail 218
Faiveley 218
Ferraz 219
Halais 220
Klein 221
Sable 224
SAFT 225
Sofanor 226

GERMANY, DEMOCRATIC REPUBLIC
FAGA 218

GERMANY, FEDERAL REPUBLIC
ABB 216
AEG 216
Belz 217
GEZ 220
Kuckuck 221
Luwa 221
Phoenix 223
Pintsch Bamag 224
Schaltbau 225
Siemens 225

HUNGARY
Kismotor és Gépgyár 221
Nikex 222

INDIA
Central Engineering 217
Cimmco 217
Stone India 226

ITALY
Socimi 226

JAPAN
Alna Koki 217
Hitachi 221
Nippon Air Brake 223
Nippon Signal 223
Toshiba 227
Toyo Denki 227
Yusoki Kogyo 229

NETHERLANDS
Tebel 226

SOUTH AFRICA
Conbrako 217
Wispeco Widney 229

SPAIN
Macosa 221
Stone Ibérica 226

SWEDEN
EVAC 218

SWITZERLAND
SIG 225

UK
Bayham 217
Beclawat/Bode 217
Deans Powered Doors 217
GEC Transmission & Distribution Products 220
Graviner 220
Henshall 220
Howden Sirocco 221
Insulation Equipments 221
Mealstream 222
Middleton 222
Permali 223
Siemens 225
Stone 226
Stone Transportation 226
Stuart Turner 226
Temperature 226
Thorn EMI 227
Triplex 227
Westinghouse Door Systems 228
Young 229

USA
Adams & Westlake 216
AEG Westinghouse 216
Delaware Car 217
Ellcon-National 218
Microphor 222
Monogram Sanitation 222
Research Products/Blankenship 224
Stone Nycal 226
Stone Safety 226
Vapor 228

216 MANUFACTURERS / Passenger coach equipment

ABB
ASEA Brown Boveri
Transportation Business Segment

ABB BTM, PO Box 100163, Gottlieb-Daimler-Strasse 6, 6800 Mannheim, Federal Republic of Germany

Telephone: +49 621 468 200
Telex: 462411220
Telefax: +49 621 468 298/9

President: Eric Kocher
Executive Vice President: Åke Nilsson
Vice President, Marketing: Peter Albexon

(For a full list of ABB companies, see ABB entry in Locomotives section)

Products: Development, design, engineering, sales, production, installation, maintenance and after-sales service of rolling stock systems and equipment for all railway types, systems and track gauges, including complete range of electrical equipment, electric subsystems and complete climatisation equipment for all rail vehicles; mechanical systems and components; and service, minor equipment and spare parts.
Recent contracts have included:
Germany, Federal Republic
For many years ABB air-conditioning systems have equipped passenger cars circulating all over Europe. ABB has also supplied almost 600 air-conditioning systems to Egyptian Railways.
In production for the German Federal Railway (DB) in 1989 were: 492 air-conditioning aggregates and 311 power converters for their compressors within an industry consortium for the DB ICE train series; 120 sets of air-conditioning aggregates and power converters for IC passenger cars type BVmZ (second-class); 24 sets of air treatment and electrical equipment for Interregio second-class passenger cars.
For all the above cars ABB is supplying its MICAS Type L micro-processor and diagnosis system.
Switzerland
All new SBB passenger cars of Type EWE 4 include ABB air-conditioning and electrical equipment. ABB microprocessor control and diagnosis supervise and regulate the performance of all equipment. Within this equipment, the latest ABB realisations of electronic on-board power converters include GTO thyristors. This modular BUR-type series permits combinations for many applications.
ABB is also providing complete air-conditioning and electrical equipment with microprocessor control, diagnosis and BUR converters for additional passenger, dining and parlour cars of Type EW 4 in production for the SBB. The 70 RIC (International Circulation) passenger cars of SBB Type EW 4 for Euro-City trains have the four-system type BUR modular on-board power converter combination. This can take its primary supply from four different train line dc or ac voltages within the range 800–4000 V. The four-system BUR power converter combination has the following features:
 Automatic circuit adjustment when the train line changes from one to another supply;
 Supply of three secondary systems. Apart from the three-phase ac voltage (3 × 380 V/50 Hz), it delivers regulated 36 V dc for battery charging and for loads at battery voltage level. In open saloon cars this on-board converter also feeds a third three-phase system with variable frequency and voltage; and
 microprocessor control of the complex functions.
The 12 panoramic cars which SBB has ordered to the Type EW 4 design will also get ABB air-conditioning and electrical equipment with the BUR on-board converter combination.
In partnership with the Swiss car builders Schindler and SIG, ABB has provided the air-conditioning and electrical equipment for all SBB Type EW 4; this includes the ABB Type KUR on-board power converter for lighting and air-conditioning. At the end of 1988 the SBB operated 441 Type EW 4 cars, comprising: one saloon car, 174 first-class, 262 second-class, and four dining cars.
The BLS (Bern-Loetschberg-Simplon) Railway also has 18 Type EW 4 cars with ABB electrical and air-conditioning equipment.
ABB air treatment and electrical equipment is being supplied for the series of 180 double-deck rail passenger cars for the Zurich regional express service (S-Bahn).

ABB modular Type BUR control

Solid state converter for Metro car

ACEC
Transport Department

PO Box 4, 6000 Charleroi, Belgium

Telephone: +32 71 44 57 99
Telex: 51 227 acec b
Telefax: +32 71 43 78 34

General Director: Ch Jauquet
Commercial Director: D Hausman

Products: Dc, ac and multi-voltage solid-state converters specially designed for the supply of rolling stock auxiliary (ac and dc), such as air-conditioning, heating and ventilation units and battery charging.

Adams & Westlake
Adams and Westlake Ltd

940 North Michigan Street, Elkhart, Indiana 46514, USA

Telephone: +1 219 264 1141
Telefax: +1 219 264 1146

President: L F Ott
General Sales Manager: P E Gingerich

Products: Luggage racks, car hardware, lamps, lanterns and curtains, diaphragms, vestibule curtains.

AEG
AEG Westinghouse Transport-Systeme GmbH

Nonnendammallee 15–21, D-1000 Berlin 20, Federal Republic of Germany

Telephone: +49 30 3305 0
Telefax: +49 30 3305 21 69

General Manager, Train Equipment and Railway Automation Systems: Dr H H Dubenkropp
Manager Commercial Affairs: G Mayer

Products: Train equipment including heating, lighting, information systems and power supply.

AEG Westinghouse
AEG Westinghouse Transportation Systems Inc

1501 Lebanon Church Road, Pittsburgh, Pennsylvania 15236-1491, USA

Telephone: +1 412 655 5335
Telex: 866267
Telefax: +1 412 655 5860

President: J R Tucker
Vice Presidents, Commercial: D R Marcucci
 Engineering: R T Betler
 Manufacturing Operations: T Jost

Products: Train equipment and auxiliary systems (power converters, lighting inverters, couplers, passenger information and ticketing systems).

AIF
Air Industrie-Faiveley
Subsidiary of the Faiveley Group

93 rue du Docteur Bauer, 93407 Saint Ouen Cedex, France

Passenger coach equipment / MANUFACTURERS

Telephone: +33 1 42 64 1260
Telex: 290 653
Telefax: +33 1 46 06 0001

President: Alain Bodel
General Manager: Maurice Babin
Marketing Manager: Setha Nex

Subsidiary company: Faiveley Corporation, 14d World's Fair Drive, Somerset, New Jersey 08873, USA

Telephone: +33 1 201 560 9390
Telex: 833 412
Telefax: +33 1 201 560 9278

Products: Air-conditioning, ventilation and heating equipment.

Recent deliveries have included air-conditioning equipment for the French TGV trains, air conditioning or ventilating equipment for rolling stock on the Paris Metro, the Mexico City Metro, Santiago de Chile Metro, the Rio de Janeiro pre-metro, Caracas Metro, Cleveland LRVs, Barcelona Metro, and on Algerian, Moroccan, Portuguese, and People's Republic of China railways. Heating and ventilating equipment has also been supplied for French Railways' Type Z6400, Z7300, Z2N, XR6000, X2100, VR2N and RER multiple-unit cars.

Alna Koki
Alna Koki Co Ltd

4-5 Higashi Naniwa-cho 1-chome, Amagasaki 660, Japan

Telephone: +81 6 401 7283
Telex: 5242782 alnosk
Telefax: +81 6 401 6168

President: Jitokuro Sakai
Managing Director, Production: Yoshinobu Sugimoto
Chief Engineer, Director: Kiyoyuki Yamagami
Managing Director, Sales & Marketing: Masahiro Higuchi

Main works
Aluminium window sash: Yoro Factory
Sawada, Yoro-cho, Yoro-Gun, Gifu-Prefecture 503-12
Honeycomb sandwiches aluminium door: Ibuki Factory 808, Osa, Tarui-cho, Fuwa-gun, Gifu-Prefecture 503-21

Products: Various types of aluminium window sash, power windows, unit-type large-sized single glass drop aluminium window sash; honeycomb sandwiched aluminium doors and panels for electric railcars and passenger coaches.

Bayham Ltd

Daneshill West, Basingstoke, Hampshire RG24 0PG, England

Telephone: +44 256 464911
Telex: 858318
Telefax: +44 256 464366

Managing Director: R C Laule
Sales Director: E A Salter

Subsidiary company: The Ranger Instrument Co Ltd

Products: R & G direct and remote reading fuel and coolant tank gauges, together with those for drinking water and lavatory flush tanks on passenger carriages; combination indicators and switches to give continuous level indication plus warning of low liquid level and automatic shutdown in the event of catastrophic coolant loss.

Recent introductions include toilet flush water level checking gauges to UIC specification. Mounted both inside and outside the carriage, each indicator consists of a vertical strip of five lights marked 0 to 1, the lowest of which, when illuminated alone, shows also that the operating circuit is alive. An optional weatherproof press button on the indicator prevents battery drainage when the gauge is out of use. These indicators are operated from a four-switch Minidee unit in the roof tank. A version of this set is incorporated in the restaurant car drinking water tank on the British Rail Engineering International Train.

Beclawat/Bode
Beclawat/Bode (UK)

Tickford Street, Newport Pagnell, Buckinghamshire MK16 9BE, England

Telephone: +44 908 211110
Telex: 825572
Telefax: +44 908 210882

Director & General Manager: C J Kean
Sales & Marketing: R Shakespeare

Products: Windows, doors, door systems and sliding door gear.

Belz
August Belz Apparatebau GmbH

Postfach 12 25, 7990 Friedrichshafen 1, Federal Republic of Germany

Assistant General Manager: Willi Gottner
Export Manager: Manfred Carl

Products: Sapor solid and cream soap dispensers; towel cabinets; waste paper towel bins; solid and cream soap.

The company's Standard model of solid soap dispenser, manufactured in die-cast aluminium alloy to withstand vandalism, has been supplied to most European railways for washroom/toilet installation.

Carrier Khéops Bac

PO Box 3, Boulevard Pierre-Le Faucheux, 72024 Le Mans Cedex, France

Telephone: +33 16 43 86 02 81
Telex: 720021
Telefax: +33 16 43 75 15 66

Chairman and Managing Director: G de Vienne
Commercial Manager: D Plantey

Products: Electrical plugs and sockets; connectors, cable couplers for train lines, on-board equipment connection, and external power supply (quay to coach); Public address coupler according to UIC 568; and heating coupler according to UIC 552.

Central Engineering
Central Engineering Works

Gandhi Park, Malkajgiri, Secunderabad 500 047, India

Telephone: +91 78328/9
Cable: Gangway

Principal Proprietor, Technical and Financial: G Ramjiwan Rao

Products: Design, modification and manufacture of gangways, flexible gangways and vestibule bellows; and arrangement of footplate for metre-gauge and broad-gauge passenger coaches. The company specialises in maximum possible utilisation of locally available material, weight and cost reduction and ease of maintenance by the user without loss of performance.

Cimmco
Cimmco International

Prakash Deep, 7 Tolstoy Marg, New Delhi 110 001, India

Telephone: +91 11 3314381-5, 3310814
Telex: 31 65148, 31 62294

Products: Underframes for passenger cars and components.

Conbrako
Conbrako (Pty) Ltd

PO Box 14010, 167 Tedstone Road, Wadeville 1422, Transvaal, South Africa

Telephone: +27 11 827 3421
Telex: 4 29206

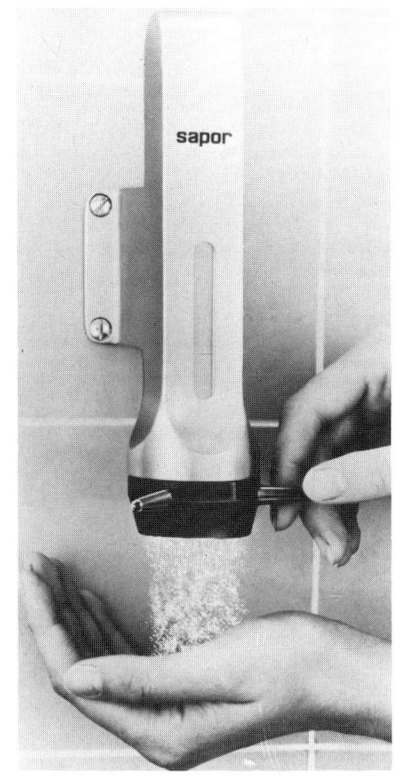

Standard Sapor soap dispenser in die-cast aluminium

Products: Sliding doors; electro-pneumatic door mechanisms; coach windows.

Deans Powered Doors
Deans Powered Doors Ltd

PO Box 8, Grovehill, Beverley, North Humberside HU17 0JL, England

Telephone: +44 482 868111
Telex: 592551
Telefax: +44 482 881890

Chairman: S G Leavesley
Managing Director: F Cawood
Directors: J Borwick
R C Robinson

Products: Powered doors (electric and pneumatic) and door operating mechanisms; seating stanchions, handrails and windows; aluminium sand and gravity die castings for rail and bus application.

Delaware Car
Delaware Car Company LP

PO Box 233, 2nd & Lombard Streets, Wilmington, Delaware 19899, USA

Telephone: +1 302 655 6665
Telefax: +1 302 655 7126

President: Harry E Hill
Vice President and General Manager: Thomas J Crowley

Products: Refurbishment, repair and assembly of railway passenger cars.

EFF
French Association of Railway Equipment

12 Rue Bixio, 75007 Paris, France

Telephone: +33 1 45 56 13 53
Telex: 200576 fedrail

Chief Officer: Jehan Guenael Poulain

Products: All equipment for rolling stock, collection systems, engineering and design.

MANUFACTURERS / Passenger coach equipment

Portable ticketing terminals and microcomputer system by EKE

EKE Electronics

Engineering Office, Bertel Ekengren Oy, EKE Electronics, Westendintie 1, SF 02160 ESPOO, Finland

Telephone: +358 0 42031
Telex: 125492 eke sf
Telefax: +358 0 427184/425300

Chairman: Bertel Ekengren
Head of Electronics Division: Kari Knosmanen
Sales Manager: Ari Hakala

Associate company
EKE GmbH, Robotersysteme, Tegernseer, Landstrasse 161, D-8000 Munchen 90, Federal Republic of Germany

Telephone: +49 89 69779-0
Telex: 5214039 eke d

Products: EKE-Trainnet has been developed in co-operation with Finnish State Railways and provides all the electronics needed in coaches in one package. This includes heating control, diagnostics and fault registration, loudspeaker systems and videotape control, microcomputer for maintenance and updating of destination and information boards and coach numbers, over a local area network.

The new portable ticketing system allows ticket purchase by credit card. The inbuilt microprocessor can forward information regarding passengers, transactions and tickets direct to the depot, and can also access up-to-date information for the conductor from the depot. The hand terminal has a graphic display with an alphanumeric keyboard and also has a ticket stamping attachment. Battery charging and data transfer takes place in the depot microcomputer system.

Ellcon-National
Ellcon-National Inc

30 King Road, Totowa, New Jersey 07512, USA

Telephone: +1 201 256 7110
Telex: 130154

President: E P Kondra
Vice President, Engineering: C F Roselius
Vice President, Sales: R A Nitsch
General Manager: J A Testa
Treasurer: J P Gilson

Products: Hand brakes, window sashes, impact-resistant glass, stanchions, grab handles, windscreens, luggage racks.

Licensees: South Africa: Conbrako Ltd, Tedstone Road, Wadeville, Transvaal

Sales Representatives: Canada: Beclawat Ltd, 345 Bell Blvd, Box 884, Belleville, Ontario K8N 5B5

Mexico: Dinamica SA, Avenida Madero 40, Mexico 1DF

Equip Rail
12 Rue Bixio, 75007 Paris, France

Telephone: +33 1 45 56 13 53
Telex: 200576 fedrail

General Manager: Jehan Guenael Poulain

Products: Automatic doors; windows; air conditioning; train heating; tachometers; pantographs; electrical and electronic equipment; brakes; seats; lighting and signalling equipment; accessories.

EVAC
EVAC AB

PO Box 140, S 29500 Bromolla, Sweden

Telephone: +46 456 28000
Telex: 48191 evac s
Telefax: +46 456 27972

Managing Director: Lennart Von Sydow
Business Area Manager, Trains: Rolf Terve

Subsidiaries: Envirovac Inc, 1260 Turret Drive, Rockford, Illinois 61111 USA

Telephone: +1 815 654 8300
Telefax: +1 815 654 8306

EVAC SAED SA, Zac de Bellevues, PO Box 98, F-95613 Cergy-Pontoise, France

Telephone: +33 1 3421 9988
Telefax: +33 1 3464 3900

Products: Vacuum toilet and sewage handling systems.

The flushing of toilet soil from trains directly on to the track is becoming increasingly unacceptable from environmental, aesthetic and hygienic viewpoints. Problems such as the soiling of rolling stock and airborne soil dispersion are accentuated with high-speed trains. At the same time, there is less willingness to accept restrictions on the use of toilets while trains are standing at stations. The EVAC Vacuum Toilet System for trains solves these problems while maintaining a high standard of sanitary facilities.

Components of the EVAC System comprise: toilet bowl(s); pipework; ejector; discharge (interface) unit; and control equipment. When not in use, the system is completely passive and uses no energy. Pressing the flush button on the toilet causes the ejector to start, creating vacuum in the piping within a few seconds. The discharge valve at the rear of the toilet then opens at the same time as fresh water is admitted to the bowl by the feeder valve. The vacuum in the piping evacuates the bowl and the discharge valve closes after about two seconds. The feeder valve stays open a little longer to restore a pool at the bottom of the bowl, but the total amount of water admitted does not exceed 1.2 litres. When the soil enters the discharge (interface) unit, the gate is opened by a pneumatic cylinder and allows the soil to pass to the holding tank under atmospheric pressure. The system is then ready again for use.

The toilet bowl may be of vitreous china or of plain or Teflon-coated stainless steel. Both floor and wall-hung models are available. The compressed-air ejector and the discharge unit require very little space and may be placed wherever convenient. The holding tank may also be freely located, since the system is independent of gravity: pipes may be run upwards if required. A single system can serve toilets at both ends of a coach. The very low consumption of water, and the small amount of sewage generated, mean that, even with moderate-sized tanks, servicing intervals are much extended.

Recent contracts include vacuum toilet systems for Sweden's X2 high-speed trains (1989); BUMZ coaches for DB (1989); B-Wagen for ÖBB (1990).

FAGA
VEB Fahrzeugausrüstung Berlin
Member of VEB Kombinat Schienenfahrzeugbau and of Vereinigter Schienenfahrzeugbau der DDR e V

Andreastrasse 71/73, 1017 Berlin, German Democratic Republic

Telephone: +37 2 2700921
Telex: 112295

Exports: Schienenfahrzeuge Export-Import, Volkseigener, Aussenhandelsbetrieb der DDR, Ötztaler Strasse 5, 1100 Berlin

Products: Ac and dc generators; rectifier sets; single and multi-voltage heating plants; single and multi-voltage transformers; devices for autonomous and central power supply plants; electronic control and diagnostic devices; switch cabinets.

A recently developed product is the individual transistor inverter for feed of fluorescent tube lighting in coaches and traction stock with on-board voltages of 110 V dc. This transistor inverter conforms to the latest technical requirements of UIC leaflet 555-1.

Faiveley
Faiveley SA
Transportation Department

93 rue du Docteur Bauer, 93407 Saint-Ouen Cedex, France

Telephone: +33 1 4264 12 60
Telex: 290653
Telefax: +33 1 4606 0001

Chairman: Alain Bodel
Manager, Transportation Department: Jean Chapoutier
Export Manager: Denis Calando

Main Works
Doors
Les Yvaudières-ZI, Avenue Yves Farges, 37700 St-Pierre-des-Corps
Telephone: +33 47 44 52 71
Telex: 750742 f
Telefax: +33 47 44 80 24

Electromechanics & Pantographs
ZI-1, rue des Grands Mortiers, 37700 St-Pierre-des-Corps
Telephone: +33 47 44 56 15
Telex: 750025 f
Telefax: +33 47 44 80 24

Electronics
ZI-37270 Montlouis-sur-Loire
Telephone: +33 47 45 04 45
Telex: 751295 f

International companies
Faiveley Española SA
Head office: Puerto Rico 5, BC, 28016 Madrid, Spain
Works: Autovia Reus Km 5, Apartado 525, 43080 Tarragona, Spain
Telephone: +34 77 54 85 06
Telex: 56656

Faiveley Italia SpA
Via della Meccanica N 21, Zona Industriale de Bassone, 37139 Verona, Italy
Telephone: +39 45 98 94 11
Telex: 43–481062

Faiveley Corporation
14 d World's Fair Drive, Somerset, New Jersey 08873, USA
Telephone: +1 201 560 93 90
Telex: 833412
Telefax: +1 201 560 92 78

Passenger coach equipment / MANUFACTURERS

Faiveley (Canada) Inc
376, boulevard Guimond, Longueil, Québec J4G 1R1, Canada
Telephone: +1 514 651 33 10
Telex: 05–267341
Telefax: +1 514 670 18 68

Faiveley do Brazil Ltda
Rua Libero Badaro N° 377.22 and 01139, São Paulo, Brazil
Telephone: +55 11 32 02 59
Telex: 1135217 faibr

Equipfer Ltda (Works)
Rua Ach Orlando, Curtolo 636, Parque Industria Thomas Edison, 01139 São Paulo, Brazil
Telephone: +55 11 825 02 00
Telex: 1123372 fvbr br

Faiveley Industry (Pty) Ltd
Allied Building, Cor Rissik and Bree Sts, PO Box 3844, Johannesburg 2001, South Africa
Telephone: +27 11 23 21 45
Telex: 485334–488375

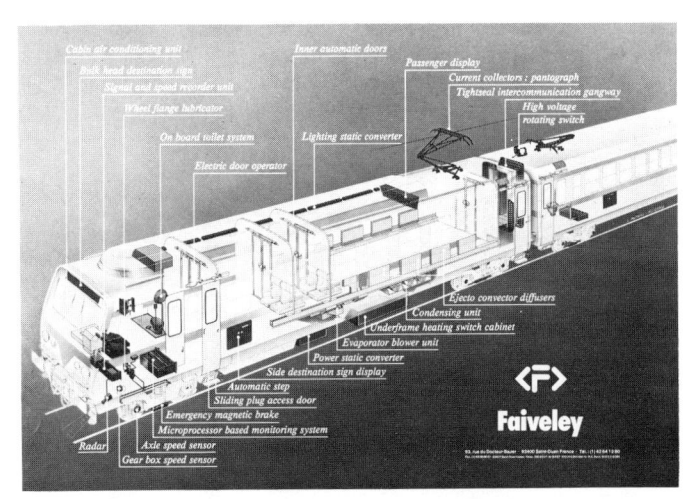

Faiveley equipment in a French Railways Type Z2 electric multiple-unit

Faiveley sliding plug-in door with folding step fitted to French Railways (SNCF) TGV train-set

Faiveley external sliding door on French Railways (SNCF) double-deck commuter car

Products: A complete range of on-board equipments and systems, including: manually-operated doors; electro-pneumatic doors and door gear; electric and electro-pneumatic door control fittings; electric and electronic control fittings for heating equipment; miscellaneous electronic equipment.

With a background of 50 years' experience in automatic door operating systems, the company co-operates with car-builders by assuming the entire responsibility for the design, development and production of all components of a door equipment; several alternative models are on offer for each sub-assembly. The company aims to assist the vehicle builder by minimising the interface to obtain rapid installation on the car body; and, assuming the entire responsibility for the correct operation of the automatic door equipment, guarantees the highest level of reliability and trouble-free maintenance and secures the highest degree of safety and comfort. Faiveley offers the widest range possible for rail passenger vehicles, from simple hinged doors for toilets to electrically-operated sliding plug-in doors, via pneumatic sliding doors for mass transit systems. It has executed 300 000 door equipment installations in 20 countries spread over five continents.

Ferraz SA

28 rue St Philippe, 69003 Lyon, France
PO Box 3025, 69391 Lyon CEDEX 03

(See also entries in Electrical traction, Bogies and suspensions, and Fixed electrification equipment sections)

Marketing Manager: M Renart
Export Sales Manager: H Behr

Products: Earth return current units to prevent current flowing through bearing of axle boxes and associated resistors; dc protistor fuses with very high breaking capacity for dc/ac converter protection and for heating circuits protection.

Contracts include supply to major builders.

Earth return current unit fastened to the axlebox of a bogie (Ferraz)

Fresinbra
Fresinbra Industrial SA

Rua Laureano Fernandes Junior, 10-Vila Leopoldina CEP-05089, São Paulo, Brazil

Telephone: +55 11 260 3122
Telex: 83263
Telefax: +55 11 831 6035

Engineering Manager: Sergio Ulian

Marketing Manager: Affonso Galvao Buenho Filho

Works: Rua Lauriano Fernandes Jr 10, São Paulo, Brazil

Railway signalling (ranging from optic signals to CTC, ATC and cab signal systems) and braking systems.

Recent contracts include an order from FEPSA, Brazil, for special hydraulically operated crossing gates.

MANUFACTURERS / Passenger coach equipment

GEC Transmission & Distribution Projects Limited

PO Box 27, Stafford, ST17 4LN, England

Telephone: +44 785 57111
Telex: 36203
Telefax: +44 785 52540

Managing Director: K J Ralls
Sales Director: E G Nolan

Products: Auxiliary convertors and battery chargers for locomotives, coaches and multiple-unit stock.

GEZ
GEZ Gesellschaft für elektr Zugausrüstung mbH

Flinschstrasse 20/51, 6000 Frankfurt/Main 60, Federal Republic of Germany

Telephone: +49 69 420906-0
Telex: 417155
Telefax: +49 69 420906-13

Export Manager: R Hentrich

Products: Low-voltage equipment and electrical components for coaches, especially train lighting equipment, control panels, alternators, inverters.

Alongside the familiar stationary diagnostic technology, a new micro-processor-controlled version has now been developed which is installed in the vehicle to provide continuous monitoring of the system. The master diagnostic system uses a data bus to which all sub-systems are connected. Apart from the display of irregularities, a status report can be called up and the connected sub-systems can also be diagnosed via an interface.

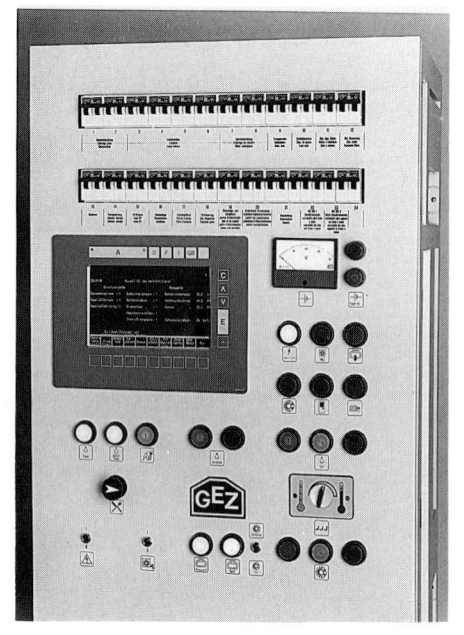

Graviner
Graviner Ltd

Poyle Road, Colnbrook, Slough, Berkshire SL3 0HB, England

Telephone: +44 753 683245
Telex: 848124
Telefax: +44 753 685126

Genenral Manager: H B Maughan
Financial Director: N J Coleman
Marketing Manager: D J V Smith
Sales Manager: C H Maddock

Products: Design, development and production of fire, smoke and explosion detection and suppression systems; repair and refurbishing of products.

Graviner equipment includes a wide range of detectors, each designed to react to a specific fire or overheat condition: in the case of overheat/fire, a localised or point detector (high speed re-setting switch, HSRS), a continuous pyrotechnic detector (Pyrocord) or continuous electrical detector (Firewire); in the case of flame, optical detectors (ultra-violet or infra-red); and smoke detectors. The detectors are linked to a control panel in the locomotive cab or any appropriate staff compartment in the train. The control panel can be designed to give warning lights, audible alarms, and information on the position of the fire, or overheat condition, to enable manual operation of extinguishers, and/or to activate the appropriate extinguisher system automatically. The control unit stabilises the power fed to the system, and can also provide continuous system monitoring.

Recent developments include a smoke detection and coach alarm system for sleeping cars; and an auto/manual fixed fire extinguisher valve.

The advanced smoke detectors used in British Rail's Mk III sleeping cars are of the latest ionisation/chamber type which detects smoke in the early stages of combustion from the change of impedance in the chamber. Detectors are fitted in each berth, the attendant's compartment, the end vestibules, each toilet and in the inlet and outlet ducts of the air-conditioning module.

All detectors in each car are supervised by an electronic central control unit which monitors their outputs continuously and also for smoke and for serviceability of the system. In the event of a smoke indication or a fault, audible and visual warnings are given. There is a warning horn in each sleeping berth, each vestibule and all attendant's compartments. Red smoke warning lights are built into each detector unit and are also located on the bulkhead outside each berth and on the panel of the control unit. To differentiate between smoke and fault alarms, the horn sounds a continuous high-pitched note for smoke and an intermittent note for an equipment fault. The visual alarm for a fault signal is an amber indicator lamp.

Each control unit is housed in a glass-fronted cabinet in the vestibule of the sleeping car. A remote indicator panel is mounted in the attendant's compartment and in addition to providing a visual check that the system is operational also incorporates controls which allow the horns in the car to be muted, silenced or sounded manually.

The control units are also interlinked to provide an integrated detection system for the whole train. In the event of smoke being detected, or a fault, the appropriate alarm note is sounded in the attendants' cabins along the train and also in the vestibules. Alarm warning lights on the control panels identify the source and nature of the alarm. If the source is in the sleeping area, the berth responsible is indicated by the warning light on the corridor bulkhead. Inside the berth the warning light on the detector unit is illuminated and the warning horn sounds.

Halais
Georges Halais

13-15 rue Sedaine, 75011 Paris, France

Telephone: +33 1 48 05 62 75
Telex: 240282

Products: Stainless steel interior fitments for passenger cars.

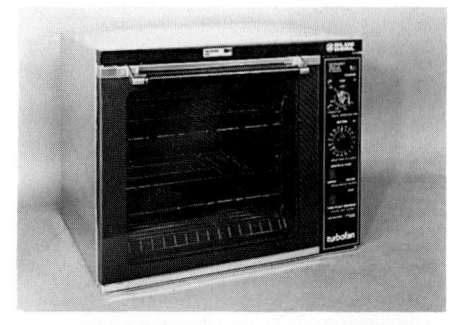

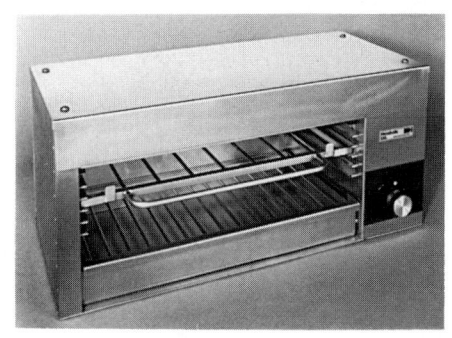

Switchboard with control screen and operating panel for diagnostic system by GEZ

Henshalls equipment to common modular dimensions of 600 × 750 × 300 mm supplied for British Rail Engineering's International catering car

Henshall
Henshalls Ltd

Abbot Close, Oyster Lane, Byfleet, Surrey KT14 7JT, England

Telephone: +44 9323 51011
Telex: 928460 whs g
Telefax: +44 9323 52792

Chairman and Chief Executive: J C Smith
Managing Director: L J Rogers
Technical Director: V J Chennell
Commercial Director: B P Bartlett
Financial Director: M J Davis

Products: Catering equipment for rolling stock; ticket office equipment; Micro-aire cookers. Recent sales have included a new range of catering equipment, principally of stainless steel welded construction, for the High Speed Trains of British Rail and supply of ticket office equipment to the same organisation.

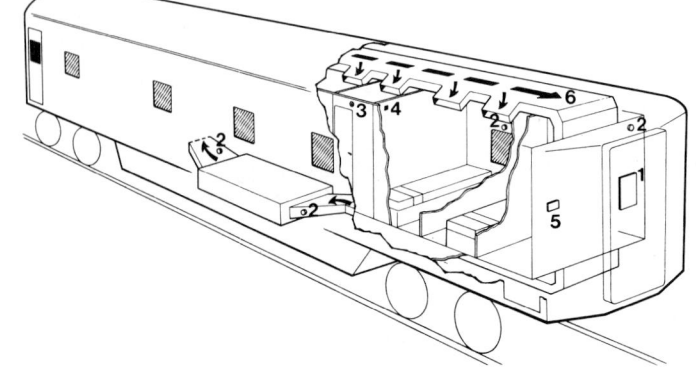

Typical Graviner sleeping car protection and alarm system (1) control units (2) smoke detectors (3) corridor warning lights (4) horn (5) flashing arrows (6) air-conditioning duct

Hitachi
Hitachi Ltd

6 Kanda Surugadai 4-chome, Chiyoda-ku, Tokyo 101, Japan

Telephone: +81 3 258 1111
Cable: Hitachy, Tokyo
Telex: 22395, 22432, 24491, 26375 hitachy

Products: Air-conditioning equipment.

Howden Sirocco
Howden Sirocco Ltd

195 Scotland Street, Glasgow G5 8PJ, Scotland

Telephone: +44 41 429 2131
Telex: 77439
Telefax: +44 41 429 0612

Managing Director: J N Allison

Products: Railcar air-conditioning fans, ceiling-mounted ventilator fans, main engine cooler groups, braking resistor cooling fans, electronics cooling fans, mixed flow fans, small brushless dc fans.

IFE
IFE Industrie-Einrichtungen Fertigungs-Aktiengesellschaft

3340 Waidhofen/Ybbs, Patertal 20 Austria

Telephone: +43 7442 2545
Telex: 19 244
Telefax: +43 7442 2545 213

Sales Director, Export and Marketing: Ing Ewald Ginzler
Managing Director: Dr Helmut Prinz

Products: Sliding plug doors with electro-pneumatic drive for light rail vehicles, metro, suburban trains and intercity coaches. Swing plug doors with pneumatic or electro-drive for light rail vehicles, railbus, suburban trains and buses. IFE also manufactures external sliding doors, pocket doors, inside swing doors, moveable steps, door control equipment and microprocessors.

IFE doors are designed for most exacting conditions. They are used by ÖBB, SJ, NSB, DSB, SNCB, NS, BR and local authorities.

Insulation Equipments
Insulation Equipments Ltd

Salop Road, Oswestry, Shropshire SY11 2RR, England

Telephone: +44 691 652351
Telex: 35424
Telefax: +44 691 658033

Managing Director: Dr P J Crook
Sales Director: J O Hebditch
Technical Sales Manager: J D Hemming

Products: Interior trim panels, doors, windshields, partitions, luggage racks, exterior end caps, window surrounds.

Recent contracts include drivers' and guards' consoles for Brush Electric Machine Co Ltd, Hong Kong Metro, Rome Metro, British Rail, Kowloon Canton Railway, Dallas Fort Worth People Movers, Berlin Underground, Washington Metro, Los Angeles Metro, London Underground Ltd.

The company specialises in the design and supply of prefabricated decorative linings, lightweight panel systems and bonded structures for vehicles and associated public buildings. Panels are supplied for new buildings, for refurbishment and prefabricated for international KD assembly. Full export sales and service facilities are available together with ability to meet existing and anticipated international safety standards, particularly smoke emission and fire resistance. Consultancy services are available on panel design and installation techniques. Materials manufactured include Phenolic GRP, laminates bonded to aluminium or steel together with sandwich honeycomb panel, all formed and fabricated for easy installation.

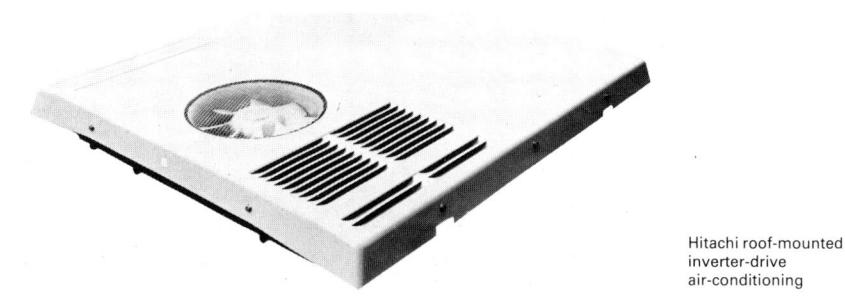

Hitachi roof-mounted inverter-drive air-conditioning

Registered tradenames are Metalite, Melaminium, Melasteel and Melaform. Recent contracts have included provision of fire-resistant Melaminium, Melasteel and Melaform.

Kismotor és Gépgyár

Fehérvári ut 44 (RB), Budapest XI, Hungary

Telephone: +36 1 667 644
Telex: 22 4384

Products: Door and window gear.

Klein
Etablissements Georges Klein

36 rue Boussingault, 75013 Paris, France

Telephone: +33 1 45 89 58 96
Telex: 270 507
Telefax: +33 1 45 89 04 74

President: Jean Pierre Ulmann
Director General: Dominique Lemarchand

Products: Hera-type window balancing and operating devices; all types of aluminium windows and windscreens.

Kuckuck
Kuckuck GmbH & Co KG Bau Strömungstechnischer Apparate

An der Weide 39/40, Postfach 103 931, 2800 Bremen, Federal Republic of Germany

Telephone: +49 421 321303
Telefax: 244479
Telefax: +49 421 328400

Managing Director: G Eggers

Products: Electric-powered fans and ventilators for rail vehicles, buses and trucks, including ventilators powered by three-phase motors with three-phase converters.

The company supplies the German and Austrian Federal Railways, the Danish State Railways, many European metro systems and several railways in the Middle East and elsewhere in the world.

Luwa
Luwa GmbH

PO Box 101 437, 6000 Frankfurt am Main 1, Federal Republic of Germany

Telephone: +49 69 4035 229
Telex: 411775
Telefax: +49 69 4035 385

Managing Director: U Zimmermann
General Manager, Railway Division: C Hattingberg
Sales Manager, Railway Division: C Hattingberg

Products: Air-conditioning, heating and ventilating equipment for locomotives and all passenger, multiple-unit and rapid transit stock; split systems; unitary equipment; underfloor-mounted, ceiling-integrated or roof-top installation. Microprocessor-based electronic controls for HVAC-equipment with integrated diagnostic and control features for all pneumatic and electrical components of a coach.

Luwa pioneered the induction system in air-conditioned rail passenger cars and invented the single-duct reheat principle.

The company's latest development is the air-conditioning system for the ICE, the German Federal Railway's (DB) high-speed train of the future. Designed for an operating speed of 250 km/h and a maximum speed of 350 km/h, the ICE is subjected to abnormal shock waves (+8000 Pa, −6000 Pa), since on the DB's new high-speed lines it will travel 30 per cent of the time through tunnels. Special features incorporated in the air-conditioning system protect passengers and crews from any hazardous air pressure variation.

Macosa
Material y Construcciones SA

Plaza de la Independencia 8, Madrid 1, Spain

Telephone: +34 1 222 47 87
Telex: 22168

Products: Sliding and plug doors, vertical sliding windows for passenger cars.

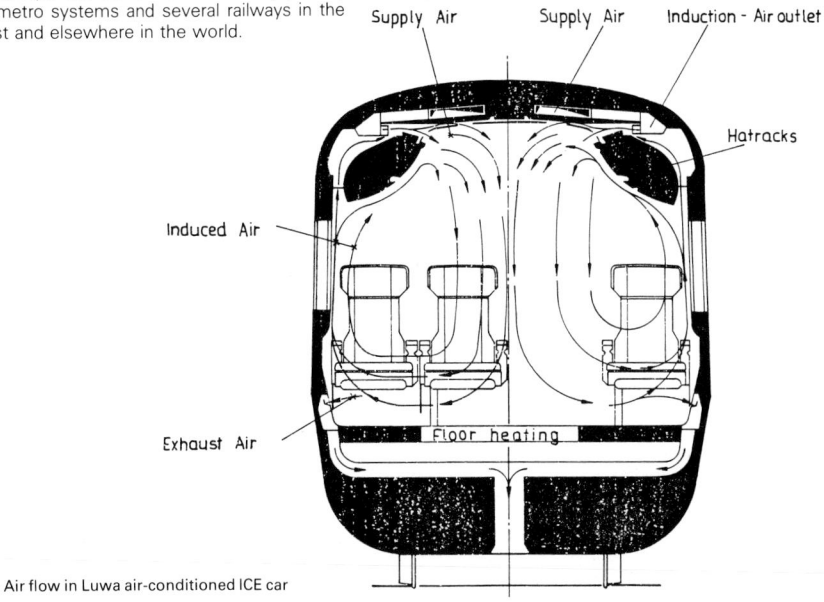

Air flow in Luwa air-conditioned ICE car

MANUFACTURERS / Passenger coach equipment

Manta
NV Manta SA

Neerstraat 58, 9170 Waasmunster, Belgium

Telephone: +49 52 47 86 31
Telex: 21695

Products: Air-conditioning, heating and ventilation systems.

Mealstream
Mealstream (UK) Ltd
AIM Group Company

Manufacturing and Service Division: Fleming Way, Crawley, West Sussex, England

Telephone: +44 293 546161
Telex: 928460
Telefax: +44 293 562280

Managing Director: B J Reeve
Technical Director: J L Hayes

Products: Micro-aire ovens, microwave ovens, coffee-pot warmers supplied to British Rail for use in the catering vehicles of High Speed Trains and APT intercity trains.

Microphor
Microphor Inc

PO Box 1460, 452 East Hill Road, Willits, California 95490, USA

Telephone: +1 707 459 5563
Telefax: +1 707 459 5563

President: J M Mayfield Jr
Sales, Railroad Division: J Johnson
Marketing Manager: Ross C Beck

European offices:
2 South Street, Hythe, Southampton SO4 6EB, England
Telephone: +44 703 849495
Telex: 47288 pcsupp g
General Manager: Ken Bassham

Microphor Europe GmbH, PO Box 80 03 59, Huttenstrasse 45, 4320 Hattingen, Federal Republic of Germany
Telephone: +49 23 24 29 5546
Telex: 8229974 thh d
General Manager: Peter Lukemann

A Siliani Spa (Licensee)
Via P Fanfanin 21, 5027 Florence, Italy
Telephone: +39 55 412 171 2 2
Telex: 572418 sil fi i
Contact: Angelo Siliani

Products: Sewage treatment systems for locomotives, passenger cars and cabooses; Microflush half-gallon flush toilets; refrigerators for locomotives; low temperature protection systems for locomotives; plastic injection moulding of special components.

In the Microphor toilet and sewage treatment system, treatment tank (or tanks) can be mounted inside the car or engineered to fit under the car, depending on space available, and can be insulated and electrically heated to prevent freezing in winter. Heating also maintains the biological action within the treatment tank. The Microphor toilet is flushed by depressing the integral or wall-mounted lever or button. This supplies a compressed air signal to shift the air and water sequence valve so as to allow water to start flowing into the toilet bowl and the flapper to open to accept waste into the lower evacuation chamber. The flapper stays open for approximately six seconds, then closes and hermetically seals off the lower evacuation chamber. Thereupon the chamber is pressurised with air and waste is evacuated into the treatment tank. While this action is taking place the toilet bowl level is replenished with two quarts of fresh water for the next use.

Once the waste and liquids have entered the treatment tank the liquids are gravity-filtered through a series of fibre filter columns mounted in a dam in the lower portion of the treatment tank. The liquid then passes through the chlorinator unit where it is chlorinated by solid chlorine tablets. From there it flows into the secondary treatment tank.

In the secondary tank the chlorinated liquid flows through a series of baffles, thus allowing the chlorine time to reduce the coloform bacteria count to O, before being allowed to drain onto the trackbed via a drain port on the bottom of the tank.

The solid waste still remaining in the treatment tank is broken down bacteriologically by microbes, which live within the treatment tank, to a liquid (which drains off as described above) and to carbon dioxide which escapes through the tank vent port.

Microphor onboard sanitation systems can be adapted to a full range of applications including locomotives, cabooses, passenger cars, maintenance-of-way equipment and executive cars. The company offers standard-sized plastic tanks, but also manufactures steel tanks in custom sizes with extra heavy coal tar epoxy coating on interior surfaces. Other options include double-walled, insulated tank construction with heating system for cold weather protection. Toilets are available in abuse-resistant stainless steel or high-fired vitreous china. The flush mechanism can be mounted internally or remotely. Discharge can be from back or bottom in some models.

The Model LF-210 vitreous china bowls are available in stock colours of white bone and grey, to which 14 special colours have been added. The Models LF-310 and LF-320 stainless steel bowls are available in standard or electro-polished surfaces. Optional powder coatings in white are also available.

Middleton
Middleton Sheet Metal Co Ltd

Spring Vale Works, Middleton, Manchester M24 2HS, England

Telephone: +44 61 643 2462
Telex: 667607 msmgrp g
Telefax: +44 61 643 3490

Chairman and Chief Executive: F Pedley
Managing Director: J D Pedley
Director and Company Secretary: I Warrington

Principal subsidiaries
Middleton Welders Ltd
Aircraft Tanks Ltd
Cooper Webb Jones & Co (1967) Ltd

Products: Glycol reservoirs and louvred windows; fuel tanks.

Monogram Sanitation

800 West Artesia Blvd, Compton, California 90224-9057, USA

Telephone: +1 213 638 8445
Telex: 69-1243
Telefax: +1 213 638 8458

European office: Monogram Sanitation, PO Box 49, 8470 De Panne, Belgium

Telephone: +32 58 41 38 72
Telex: 81883
Telefax: +32 58 41 45 23

President: G Yanuck
Vice-President, Sales & Marketing: J Durso
Sales Manager: W I Mercer

Products: On-board water flush, vacuum transfer waste collection systems for all types of passenger rail cars. Pneumatically operated retention recirculating toilet equipment in many configurations including remotely located flushing urinal systems.

Recent contracts include 240-car retrofit toilet programme for Taiwan Rail Administration (TRA); toilet-urinal system for Hitachi-Tokyo Car, 55 MU cars for TRA (1990); Tokyo Car, bi-level commuter cars for Long Island Railroad (1990).

Microflush toilet Model LF-210 elongated half-gallon per flush, supplied to British Railways

Narita Seisakusho
Narita Seisakusho Manufacturing Ltd

20-12 Hanaomote-cho, Atsuta-ku, Nagoya 456, Japan

Telephone: +81 52 881 6191
Telex: 59500 nag 139
Telefax: +81 52 881 6196

Chairman: Hayashi Narita
President: Masatoshi Narita
Technical Adviser: Hiroshi Morimoto

Products: Vestibule diaphragms, gangways, rubber bellows; door leaves; fuel and water tanks; and interior accessories and parts in carbody. The company claims a Japanese railway market share of nearly 98 per cent for its diaphragms (gangways). Features of the product are light weight, soundproofing, thermal insulation, snow and waterproofing, fireproofing, long life and automatic connection and disconnection, and interior panelling for enhanced safety and comfort.

The company's door leaves, for which a Japanese market share of almost 30 per cent is claimed, include sliding, folding, hinged and emergency types with skeleton and honeycomb structures.

Recent sales include products for Type TEC-100 Shinkansen electric cars for Japan Railways Group; for UIC-type electric cars for MARTA, USA and for PJKA in Indonesia; for other types of electric and passenger cars for two authorities in USA: for the Los Angeles CTC LRVs built by Nippon Saryo; for passenger cars for PJKA in Indonesia; and for electric cars for the authorities of Brazil and Taiwan. The company has also supplied diaphragms with interior panels for MRT electric cars for Singapore.

Constitution: The company was founded in 1938. It has supplied various types of its products for electric cars of JNR Shinkansen lines, passenger and subway, passenger and diesel cars delivered by Japan's car-builders to JNR; the main cities including Tokyo, Osaka, Yokohama, Kyoto and Nagoya; more than 40 private railway corporations in Japan; and to many users in other countries including USA, Mexico, Brazil, Argentina, Chile, Indonesia, Thailand, Malaysia, the Philippines, Taiwan, Hong Kong, China, Korea, New Zealand, Zambia, Nigeria, Burma and USSR.

Nesite
Nesite Industri Finland Oy

Lahnalahdentie 5, SF-00200 Helsinki, Finland

Telephone: +358 0 682 1870
Telefax: +358 0 387 829

Marketing Director: Kaj Lännenpää

Products: Toilet flush systems

Nikex
Hungarian Trading Company for Products of Heavy Industry

48/54 Mészáros utca, Budapest I, Hungary 1016

Telephone: +36 1 560122, 564737, 565449
Telex: 224971, 226406 nikex h
Telefax: +36 1 755131

Passenger coach equipment / **MANUFACTURERS** 223

General Manager: Mihály Petrik
Deputy General Manager: Hugo Szücs
Export Sales: Csaba Jonas

Main Works
Jarmü Works for Vehicle Parts
Ságvári Endre ut 14, 1153 Budapest

Kismotor és Gépgyár
Fehérvári ut 44, 1119 Budapest

Products: Window frames, windows and fittings for passenger coaches.

Nippon Air Brake
Nippon Air Brake Co Ltd

Head office: Sannomiya Building, Nishikan 1-12, Goko-dori 7-chome, Chuo-ku, Kobe 651, Japan

Telephone: +81 78 251 8101
Telex: 5622 143

Products: Door operating equipment; windshield wiper engine equipment.

Nippon Signal
The Nippon Signal Co Ltd

Head Office: 3-1, Marunouchi 3-chome, Chiyoda-ku, Tokyo, Japan

Telephone: +81 3 287 4500
Telex: 222 2178
Telefax: +81 3 287 4649

Works: Yono Factory, 13-8, Kamikizaki 1-chome, Urawa City
Utsunomiya Factory, 11-2, Hiraide Kougyo Danchi, Utsunomiya City

Associated companies: Nisshin Industrial Co, Ltd
Nisshin Electrical Installation Co, Ltd
Nisshin Electronics Service Co, Ltd

President: H Takeuchi
Executive Vice President: T Oki
Managing Director, Electronics Information & Control Systems: I Fujiwara

Products: Magnetic card key system for compartments. When a passenger purchases a ticket a magnetic card is encoded for his designated compartment and handed to the passenger. The card becomes invalid at the time of disembarkation and the passenger can retain it as a souvenir. For the next passenger a new card will be encoded and issued. This system is the same as that now used in many hotels.

Permali
Permali Gloucester Ltd

Bristol Road, Gloucester GL1 5SU, England

Telephone: +44 452 28282
Telex: 43293
Telefax: +44 452 507409

Products: Composite panels for passenger carriages; 'Permatred' densified wood locomotive flooring.

Phoenix
Phoenix AG

PO Box 90 08 54, 88 Hannoversche Strasse, 2100 Hamburg 90, Federal Republic of Germany

Telephone: +49 40 76 67 1
Telex: 2 173 611 pxhh d
Telefax: +49 40 76 67 211

Products: Rubber sealing profiles for windows and doors; rubber floor coverings; air spring bellows.

Gangway and sliding door of emu car for Chicago South Shore & South Bend RR by Narita Seisakusho

Partition unit and door of LRV for Niagara Frontier Transportation Authority by Narita Seisakusho

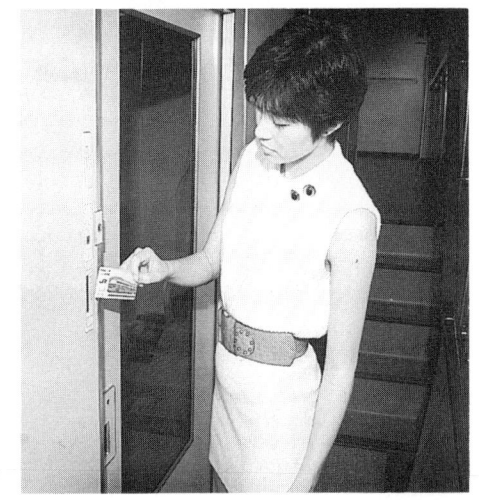

Magnetic card key for Shinkansen train-set compartments, Japanese National Railways by Nippon Signal

MANUFACTURERS / Passenger coach equipment

Pintsch Bamag
Pintsch Bamag Antriebs-und Verkehrstechnik GmbH

Postfach 10 04 20, 4220 Dinslaken, Federal Republic of Germany

Telephone: +49 21 34 602–0
Telex: 8551938
Telefax: +49 21 34 602266

Products: Power supply equipment, inverters for train lighting, electronic door controls and air-conditioning equipment, tail lights.

Recent developments include a new system for the control and supervision of folding, hinged and sliding coach doors which features fault diagnosis and is adaptable to all types of car. Its salient features are: fully electronic, short-circuit-proof control with microcomputer; centralised arrangement of all functional groups in a 19-inch modular framework; closure, locking and control of all doors of a coach; identification of faults during operation and memorisation of them; indication of operational condition by means of a three-digit luminescent diode; on interrogation, indication of all faults registered in a three-second rhythm; memorisation of up to 98 faults and irregularities in the operational procedure; routine checking of the overall system.

Advantages for the car designer include: uniform modular groups for all coach types; instantaneous adaptation to modified service conditions by simple re-programming; increased service reliability through minimisation of components; greater economy due to reduced storekeeping, simpler maintenance and low-cost repair.

Research Products/Blankenship Corporation

2639 Andjon Drive, Dallas, Texas 75220, USA

Telephone: +1 214 358 4238
Telex: 730161

Managing Director: E Bayne Blankenship

Products: 'Incinolet' electric incinerating toilet for diesel locomotives.

Sable
Sable Sièges Industrielles

Beaulieu, 42230 Roche la Molière, France

Telephone: +33 77 90 03 31
Telex: 330 126
Telefax: +33 77 90 35 10

Sales office: 81 rue Irène et Frédéric Joliot-Curie, 93170 Bagnolet, France

Telephone: +33 1 48 70 12 12
Telex: 232 030
Telefax: +33 1 48 70 10 40

Products: Passenger and driver seats for railway equipment and other public transportation. The company is one of the main suppliers of French Railways (SNCF) and the Paris bus operation of RATP.

Foreign markets include Federal Republic of Germany, Italy, Belgium, the Netherlands, Luxembourg, Portugal, Algeria, Egypt, Switzerland and Sweden.

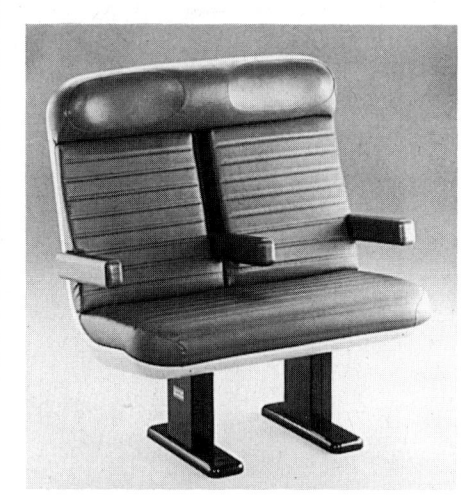

Second-class seat for French Railways open-layout Corail car

First-class seat for French Railways inter-urban emu, adjustable for attitude; tubular frame with aluminium armrests

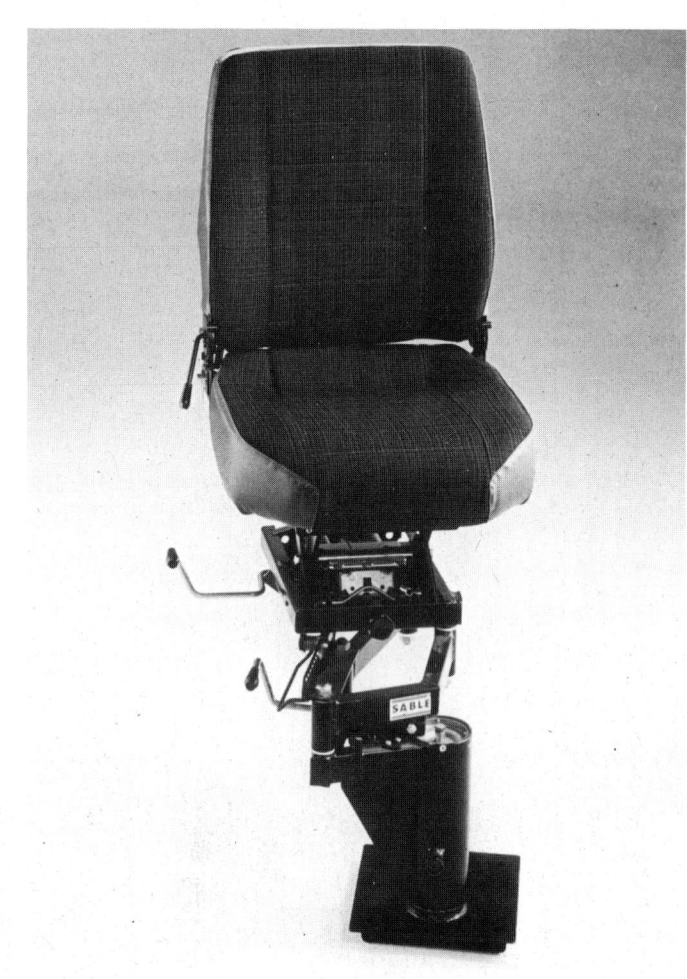

Driver's seat for French Railways TGV or locomotive, with fore/aft, height and backrest adjustment capability, mounted on 360° swivelling plate

First-class seat, pressed steel frame, with multi-position attitude adjustment, for French Railways TGV

SAFT

156 avenue de Metz, 93230 Romainville, France

Telephone: +33 1 48 43 93 61
Telex: 235566
Telefax: +33 1 49 42 34 00

Chairman: Claude Darmon
Managing Director, Industrial Battery Department: François Putois
Sales Manager, Industrial and Railway Batteries: Philippe Ulrich

Products: Nickel-cadmium batteries, pocket plates or sintered types for starting diesel passenger cars, emergency supply, security, etc. The company supplies railways in 56 countries covering Africa, Central and South America, Australia, Bangladesh, Belgium, Bulgaria, Burma, Canada, Czechoslovakia, Finland, Federal Republic of Germany, Hungary, Indonesia, Iraq, Iran, Italy, Republic of Korea, Netherlands, New Zealand, Norway, Pakistan, Poland, Portugal, Romania, Spain, Taiwan, Turkey, United Kingdom, USA and Yugoslavia.

Subsidiaries: Australia, Belgium, Canada, China, Federal Republic of Germany, Finland, Italy, Japan, Korea, Singapore, Spain, Sweden, United Kingdom and USA.

Schaltbau
Schaltbau GmbH

Klausenburger Strasse 6, 8000 Munich 80, Federal Republic of Germany

Telephone: +49 89 93005-0
Telex: 523 156
Telefax: +49 89 93005 350

General Manager: Dr Heinz Ludwig Schmitz
Div Manager Rail: Manfred John
Export Manager: Sigfried Hohm

Subsidiary companies in Federal Republic of Germany
Pintsch Bamag Antriebs- und Verkehrstechnik GmbH, Hünxer Strasse 149, 4220 Dinslaken
GEZ, Gesellschaft für Elektrische Zugusrüstung mbH, Flinschstrasse 20, 6000 Frankfurt/Main 63
Carl Brose GmbH, Uellendahler Strasse 437, 5600 Wuppertal 1

Products: High-voltage equipment for coaches; electrical equipment for diesel-hydraulic railcars; electrical components for locomotives and mass transit trains.

Semco
Semco Odense A/S

PO Box 20, Svendborgvej 226, 5260 Odense S, Denmark

Telephone: +45 9 95 77 55
Telex: 5 999 1
Telefax: +45 9 95 73 75

Products: Semvac vacuum toilet system. In this system transport from ventricle to tank is effected by air pressure, which makes it possible to install the tank within as well as below the carriage floor. Rinse water is transported by vacuum; the water tank can be placed in or below the carriage floor as desired. Flushing of toilet takes place at high pressure (four bar) with a small amount of water (approx 1 litre). There are no mechanical parts in the system so no regular service is needed. A thoroughly tested electronic control system is adaptable to the mechanical and electrical systems of the vehicle.

SIAM
SIAM SA
Electrodomestic and Electromechanical Division

Cnel Molinedo 1600, 1870 Avellaneda, Buenos Aires, Argentina

Telephone: +54 1 208 5421
Telex: 24181 siam ar

Export Manager: Lic Norberto Panizza

Products: Absorption refrigerators, kerosene, gas or electric-operated; electric refrigerators and air-conditioners.

Siemens
Siemens AG
Transportation Systems Group

Werner von Siemens Strasse 50, PO Box 3240, D-8520 Erlangen, Federal Republic of Germany

Telephone: +49 9131 724157
Telex: 6291508 si d
Telefax: +49 9131 726840

Group President: W O Martinsen
Mainline Rolling Stock Division: R Stubenrauch
Passenger Coaches Dept: P Lueftenegger

Products: Electrical components for passenger coaches; complete vehicles.

Siemens
Siemens AG
(Formerly Plessey Controls Limited)

Sopers Lane, Poole, Dorset BH17 7ER, England

Telephone: +44 202 782000
Telex: 41272
Telefax: +44 202 782331

General Manager: D G Hornby
Marketing Manager: A J Rose
Product Manager: B J Watkins
Sales Manager: M T Deem

Products: Sophisticated control and monitoring systems for the control of traction, braking and auxiliary function on diesel or electric multiple-units. Controls initiated by the driver are distributed at high speed to all coaches of the train. Technical and operational information gathered throughout the train is concentrated and analysed in the operative cab and either stored or displayed. Detailed displays may be presented to the maintenance engineer showing the present and recorded state of the train system. The information presented to the driver is restricted to essential information and includes advice in fault situation.

SIG
Swiss Industrial Company

8212 Neuhausen Rhine Falls, Switzerland

Telephone: +41 53 21 61 11
Telex: 896023

Chairman: U Baumberger
Managing Director: U Dätwyler
Director: Peter Gsell

Member of Export Association of Swiss Rolling Stock Manufacturers

Products: Completely closed, airtight and noise damping SIG inter-car gangways, suitable for railway rolling stock with screw-, semi-permanent or automatic couplers.
More than 500 SIG inter-car gangways have been delivered for underground railway cars of the Hong Kong Mass Transit Railway Corporation. These are the MT-IA type (automatic) for automatic couplers and the MT-I SP type (semi-permanent) for rod-couplings. Type MT-IA is suspended on the upper side and guided by the actual coupler; it can be coupled and separated automatically. Type MT-I SP is suspended on the upper side, symmetrically supported and guided on the rod-coupling; these gangways can be coupled and separated only in depots.

SMC
SMC Pneumatics (Australia) PTY Ltd

Transport Division Head Office: 161 Showground Road, Castle Hill, New South Wales 2154, Australia

Telephone: +61 2 680 3222
Telex: 7123152
Telefax: +61 2 634 7764

High voltage equipment for 1 kV/ 1.5 kV dc/ 1.5 kV ac/ 3 kV dc power supply to passenger cars of DB by Schaltau.

SIG inter-car gangway for Hong Kong Mass Transit Railway

Manufacturing facilities: Australia, England, Federal Republic of Germany, Japan, Hong Kong, New Zealand, Singapore, USA

Branches: Italy, Malaysia, Netherlands, Switzerland, UK

Products: Door systems, electro-pneumatic door-operating equipment, including control valves, cylinders and pressure and flow control valves; air dryers, filters and automatic drain valves; EP valves, door operating cylinders, special railway test equipment.

Socimi
Società Costruzioni Industriali Milano SpA

Head office: Via Varesina 115, 20156 Milan, Italy

Telephone: +39 2 30091
Telex: 323564

Main works
Via E Fermi n 25, 20082 Binasco (Milan)
Telephone: +39 2 9055605/6/7/8

Via Donatori del Sangue n 100, 20010 Arluno (Milan)
Telephone: +39 2 9017666, 9017803

Viale Porto Torres, Reg Zentu Figghi, 07100 Sassari
Telephone: +39 79 235056

Chairman: Dr Eng A Marzocco
Managing Director: Dr Eng P Sacchi
Assistant to Chairman: Dr Eng C Landolina

Products: Automatic doors.

Sofanor

94 rue Valériani, 59920 Quiévrechain, France

Products: All types of passenger coach equipment.

Stone
Stone International plc
FKI Rail Equipment Division
An FKI Babcock Company

Headquarters: Tom Cribb Road, Thamesmead, London SE28 0BH, England

Telephone: +44 81 854 9663
Telex: 87132 g
Telefax: +44 81 316 6952

Managing Director: D Dunbar

Member companies: See below.

Stone Ibérica
Stone Ibérica SA
FKI Rail Equipment Division

Antonio Maura 8, 28014 Madrid, Spain

Telephone: +34 1 531 3907
Telex: 23245 Stone E
Telefax: +34 1 522 7697

General Manager: Nicolás Fúster
Sales Director: Ignacio Fuster
Technical Director: Julio Rey

Overseas subsidiaries: Stone Safety (USA), Stone Argentina, Stone-Safety (Canada), Stone Bennett Corp (USA), Stone India

Products: Air-conditioning equipment, both conventional type and the new system with a reversible heat pump, as dispersed and package units, with air discharge by roof or by inductor units; air discharge by roof or by inductor units; power static converters and inverters; inverter ballast for fluorescent lamps; train lighting equipments; speed static regulators for asynchronous motors; electronic and micro-electronic controls; ticket-issuing machines.
The company has supplied air-conditioning equipment for 3500 cars for mail line, urban and metro systems; also train lighting equipments and regulators for Spanish National Railways (RENFE) and other

Socimi automatic door systems on Milan metro car

operators; P40 equipment for Cuba; UP37 unit with heat pump for British Railways; roof-mounted package unit for Hong Kong Underground; other equipment for the Italian Railways and United States; and 102 car sets of equipment for Taipei (Taiwan); equipment for RENFE high-speed train and bi-level cars.

Stone India
Stone India Limited
FKI Rail Equipment Division

16 Taratalla Road, Calcutta 700 088, India

Telephone: +91 33 773077
Telex: 0217249 stone in
Telefax: +91 33 776886

Managing Director: V K Parashar

Products: Train lighting, dynamo and dc spares, train air-conditioning, turbo-generators; air brakes; locomotive valves; slack adjusters; train lighting; pantographs.

Stone McColl
Stone McColl Pty Ltd
FKI Rail Equipment Division

PO Box 540, Baulkham Hill, New South Wales 2153, Australia

Telephone: +61 2 674 4411
Telex: 70073
Telefax: +61 2 624 6010

Managing Director: G Sills

Products: Alternators, inverters, converters, alarms, air-conditioning equipment, door operators, toilets, destination indicators, train lighting equipment, anti-vandalism seats, folding bellows for articulated vehicles.

Stone Nycal
Stone Nycal Corporation
FKI Rail Equipment Division

240 South Main Street, South Hackensack, New Jersey 07606, USA

Telephone: +1 201 489 0200
Telex: 134497

Vice President: V Mirandi

Products: Manufacture of metro car door opening systems; overhaul complete air-conditioning systems; overhaul complete air and freon compressors. Distributors for Stone Safety spare parts.

Stone Safety
Stone Safety Corporation
FKI Rail Equipment Division

PO Box 798, Wallingford, Connecticut 06492, USA

Telephone: +1 203 265 7131
Telex: 963454
Telefax: +1 203 284 0835

President: C Vanderweele
Vice President, Sales and Marketing: D E Burt
Vice President, Engineering: W A Sackman

Products: Air-conditioning, heating and temperature controls, static converters, voltage and power regulators, electric motors, motor generators, motor alternators, battery monitors, battery chargers; motor repairs. Recent contracts include equipment for PATH; NYCTA R-62, R-62A and R-68 cars; BART, San Francisco; MBTA, Boston.

Stone Transportation
Stone Transportation Ltd
FKI Rail Equipment Division

Tom Cribb Road, Thamesmead, London SE28 0BH

Telephone: +44 81 854 9663
Telex: 87132 g
Telefax: +44 81 316 6952

Managing Director: D J Kiddie
Commercial Manager: M J Murray

Products: Air-conditioning (including heat-pump type) for all rail rolling stock, heating and ventilating equipment for all forms of rolling stock; axle-driven alternators, static converters and inverters for auxiliary power supplies; powered doors; door operating equipment; door control systems; and specialised door-leaf construction for all types of railway operation and chemical toilets for vehicles.
Equipment has lately been provided for British Rail suburban stock; CIE (Ireland); Stockholm; Hong Kong MRT and KCR trains; Tuen Mun LRT and Lille Metro (VAL).

Stuart Turner
Stuart Turner Ltd

Market Place, Henley-on-Thames, Oxon RG9 2AD, England

Telephone: +44 491 572655
Telefax: +44 491 573704

Products: Pressurised water system for passenger coaches.

Tebel
Tebel Pneumatik BV

Zwettestraat 32, Post Box 515, 8901 BH Leeuwarden, Netherlands

Telephone: +31 58 973 333
Telex: 46045
Telefax: +31 58 128800

Managing Director: J Groenenboom
Manager, Rolling Stock Division: Jacobus P Mast
F & A Manager: Ben J M te Wierik

Products: Air-operated and electric swing-plug, sliding-plug and sliding doors; windscreen wiper systems; pantograph control units; complete control units for pneumatic and electro-pneumatic systems for rolling stock applications.
The proven principle of over-centre locking, which has been patented in several countries, is a Tebel feature. The driving mechanism for swing-plug doors as well as for swing-plug systems are always secure when closed. Many years of experience with swing-plug doors developed for railway cars and installed in streetcars have proved this.
Tebel has fitted its existing swing-plug sliding door system with an electric drive, using many of the proven dynamic components. When open, the doors project less than 80 mm from the sidewall.

Temperature
Temperature Ltd

Newport Road, Sandown, Isle of Wight, England

Telephone: +44 983 402221
Telex: 86288

Products: Unit air-conditioning for all passenger stock and locomotives; heating and ventilation units for

Passenger coach equipment / **MANUFACTURERS** 227

Tebel electric double-leaf swing-plug-sliding door system for new Amsterdam Tramways vehicles with an entrance width of 1200 mm, during prototype testing at Tebel Pneumatiek's research centre

multiple-unit stock; refrigeration units for kitchen and dining cars.

Recent production has included air-conditioning units with a nominal cooling capacity of 18 kW and 6 kW of heating for British Rail's Mk III sleeping cars.

Other current products include roof-mounted air-conditioning units for lightweight emu cars for the Kowloon-Canton Railway, Hong Kong.

Temperature Ltd was awarded a contract to manufacture and supply heating and ventilating units for the eleven trains of the Docklands Light Railway, London.

Thorn EMI
Thorn EMI Lamps and Components Ltd, Smart & Brown Division

Miles Road, Mitcham, Surrey CR4 3YX, England

Telephone: +44 81 640 1221
Telex: 25534 telc g
Telefax: +44 81 685 9625

Business Manager: Nick Langman

Distribution in Federal Republic of Germany:
Glühlampenfabrik Jahn GmbH, Carl-Zeiss-Strasse 15, Postfach 1509, 4460 Nordhorn

Telephone: +49 5921 17723
Telex: 98216 jahn d
Telefax: +49 5921 17733

Managing Director: Dirk Weniger

Products: Lighting components for rail vehicles; inverter ballasts for fluorescent lighting 24 V, 36 V, 50 V, 70 V, 110 V dc, ac; ballast for various voltages; lampholders and other lighting accessories including luminaires and sub-assemblies of standard or special types; ac and dc converters for low voltage tungsten halogen lamp for 12 V reading lights and locomotive head lamps; a wide variety of lamp types for most applications; illumination, indication, heating.

Recent developments include a range of new inverter ballasts for fluorescent lamps to the European standard, and luminaires using compact fluorescent lamps.

The company has equipped most British and Swedish trains, and exports to many European and Far Eastern countries.

Toshiba
Toshiba Corporation
Railway Projects Department

Toshiba Building, 1-1 Shibaura 1-chome, Minato-ku, Tokyo 105, Japan

Telephone: +81 3 457 4924
Telex: 22587 toshiba j
Telefax: +81 3 457 8385

Products: Air-conditioning equipment; exhaust fans; orbit fans; heaters; refrigerators; water coolers; beer coolers; lighting equipment; alternators; static GTO inverters.

Over 80 000 air-conditioning units have been delivered to a number of railways, including Japanese National Railways, rapid transit systems in Tokyo, Osaka, Kobe, Nagoya, Fukuoka and Seoul, New South Wales State Rail Authority, Philippine National Railways, New Zealand Government Railways, Chilean State Railways, Korean National Railroad, Chinese People's Republic Railways, Soviet Union Railways, Malayan Railway Administration and New York Transit Authority.

Typical air-conditioners with hermetic compressors include:

Package types: RPU-1500: 4500 kcal/h, 10 m³/minute, 2 refrigerating cycles, 2.1 kW, 1240 × 930 × 400 mm, 120 kg; RPU-2200J: 8000–8500 kcal/h, 3.7 kL, 21 m³/minute, 1 cycle, 1720 × 1100 × 370 mm, 180 kg; RPU-3000J: 10 500 kcal/h, 27 m³/minute, 2 cycles, 4.6 kW, 2034 × 1100 × 346 mm, 225 kg; RPU-6000: 2000 kcal/h, 50 m³/minute, 2 cycles, 7.5 kW, 1930 × 1880 × 295 mm, 430 kg; RPU-11 000: 42 000 kcal/h, 120 m³/minute, 2 cycles, 20.6 kW, 3660 × 2000 × 5300 mm, 760 kg. Split type 25 000 kcal/h unit: 25 000 kcal/h, 2 cycles, compressor condenser unit 2380 × 1180 × 630 mm, 470 kg; evaporator blower unit 920 × 1850 × 500 mm, 230 kg.

Overseas offices
North America: Houston, New York, San Francisco, Vancouver
Latin America: Bogota, Buenos Aires, Caracas, Mexico City, Rio de Janeiro
Europe: Athens, West Berlin, London, Vienna
Africa: Cairo, Tehran, Baghdad, Dubai, Jeddah
Asia: Bangkok, Beijing, Hong Kong, Jakarta, Manila, Taipei, Shanghai, Guangzhou, New Delhi
Oceania: Sydney

Toyo Denki
Toyo Denki Seizo KK

Yaesu Mitsui Building No 7-2, Yaesu 2-chome, Chuo-ku, Tokyo, Japan

Telephone: +81 3 271 6374
Telex: 222 4666

Products: Door operating equipment.

Triplex
Triplex Aircraft & Special Products Ltd

Eckersall Road, Kings Norton, Birmingham B38 8SR, England

Telephone: +44 21 451 3901
Telex: 333463 tasp
Telefax: +44 458 6880

Marketing Director: R W Wright
Technical Director: R S Bruce
Manufacturing Director: W L Belshaw
Managing Director: Dr R D King

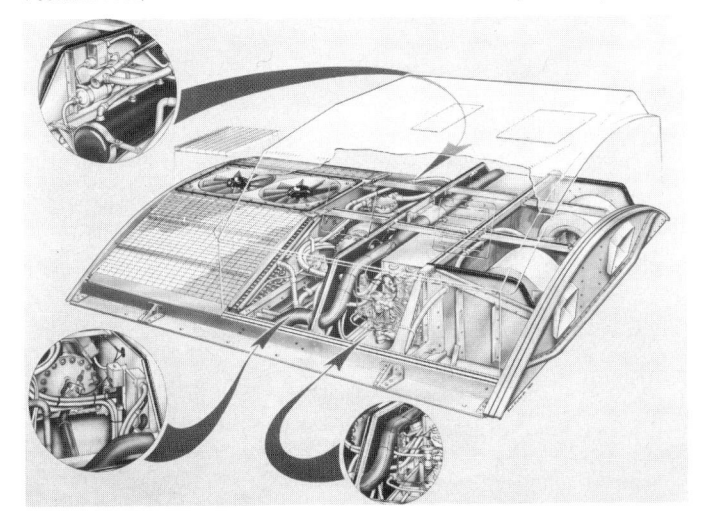

Air-conditioning unit supplied for Kowloon-Canton Railway cars, roof-mounted at each end of vehicle by Toshiba

Cars equipped with Toshiba air-conditioning in Malaysia

MANUFACTURERS / Passenger coach equipment

Products: Design and manufacture of heated/unheated, curved/flat, framed/unframed impact-resistant transparencies for railroad and transit industries.

Among the company's products are multi-laminate glass/plastic windscreen assemblies for locomotives and rolling stock, incorporating high impact-resistant performance, integral electrical de-icing system and fully bonded aluminium alloy frames. British Rail's HST power cars are among units which have been so equipped.

Vapor
Vapor Corporation
A Brunswick Company
Railroad Products Division

6420 West Howard Street, Chicago, Illinois 60648-3394, USA

Telephone: +1 312 631 9200
Telex: 210314 vapn-ur
Telefax: +1 708470 7800

President: G I S Patterson
Vice-President: J A Machesney
Manager, Marketing Services: J R Pearson

Associated companies: Vapor Canada Inc, 10655 Henri Bourassa West, Ville St-Laurent, Quebec H4S 1A1
Vapor International, Holland BV, Atoomweg 496, 3542 AB Utrecht, The Netherlands

Products: Passenger car heating and temperature controls; electronic speed indicators and recorders, inverters/converters and battery chargers, relays and contactors.

Westinghouse Door Systems
Westinghouse Brakes Ltd
A subsidiary of Westinghouse Brake & Signal Co Ltd
A member of the Hawker Siddeley Group

PO Box 74, Chippenham, Wiltshire SN15 1HY, England

Telephone: +44 249 654141
Telex: 449411/12
Telefax: +44 249 655040

Chairman: H R Grant
Managing Director: J R C Boulding
Finance Director: S R Crook
Marketing Director: E J Widdowson
Manufacturing Director: M C Colyer

Subsidiaries
Westinghouse Brake and Signal Co (Australia) Pty Ltd
PO Box 120, PO Concord West, New South Wales 2138, Australia
Westcode Ltd
3688 Nashua Drive, Unit 'F', Mississauga, Ontario L4V 1M5, Canada

Italian Railways' high-speed train, the ETR 500 uses complex windows supplied by Triplex

Vapor Corporation's floor-mounted automatic door operator

Westcode Incorporated
90 Great Valley Parkway, Great Valley Corporate Centre, Frazer, Pennsylvania 19355, USA

Products: Power-operated door equipment comprising electric and electro-pneumatic door operators suitable for mounting within the vehicle structure at cantrail, waist or floor levels; electric and electro-pneumatic door control systems inclusive of various interlocking features; lightweight door leaves profiled to match the vehicle bodyside; station platform edge door screens, with electric and electro-pneumatic operated sliding doors arranged to align with the train doors and to open and close automatically.

The company supplies door equipments to rail systems world-wide including London Transport underground and surface lines, British Railways, Glasgow Underground, Tyne and Wear Metro, New Zealand Government Railways, Calcutta Metro, Seoul Subway, Southeastern Pennsylvania Transit Authority, Long Island Rail Road, Danish State Railways, Toronto Transit Commission, Northern Ireland Railways, New York City Transit Authority, Taiwan, Stockholm Metro, Massachusetts Bay Transportation Authority, Hong

Westinghouse bi-parting doors fitted to British Rail emu and dmu stock

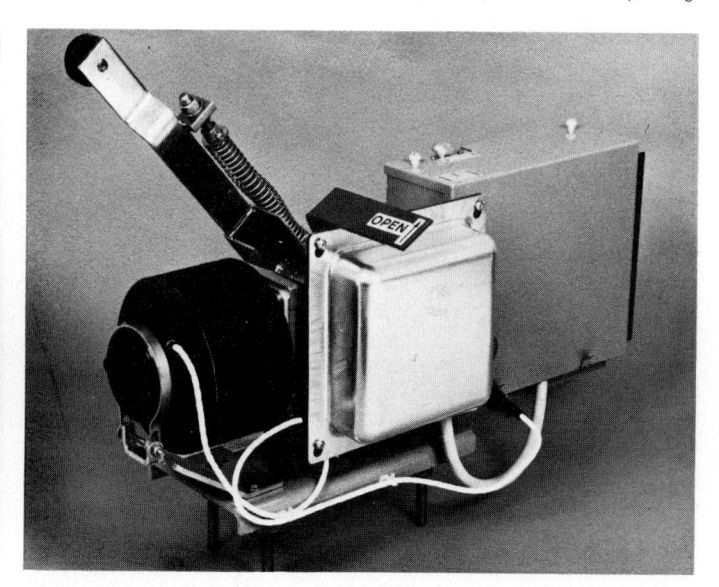

Westinghouse floor-mounted electric door operator as supplied for USA

Kong Mass Transit Railway Corporation and Singapore Mass Rapid Transit Corporation.

Wispeco Widney
A division of Wispeco (Pty) Ltd

Head office: PO Box 3886, Alrode 1451, South Africa

Telephone: +27 11 864 4945
Telex: 748529
Telefax: +27 11 864 7221

Main works: 678 Potgieter Street, Alrode Ext 9, Transvaal, South Africa

Managing Director: I Wood
General Manager: E Rousset

Products: Windows (all types), sliding hopper and double-glazed; door operating gear; doors (all types) for locomotives and passenger (suburban and mainline) rolling stock; locks and general carriage fittings.

Young
Young Commercial Windows Ltd

Claydon Works, Millbank Road, Wishaw ML2 0JD, Scotland

Telephone: +44 698 372557
Telex: 779150
Telefax: +44 698 356422

Managing Director: S H Magnus

Products: Constant balance half-drop windows; fixed windows and full-drop windows.

Licensing agreements: The company has agreements with Macosa (Spain) and Sorefame (Portugal).

Yusoki Kogyo
Yusoki Kogyo KK

102 Kamihamacho, Handa, Aichi 475, Japan

Telephone: +81 569 21 3311
Telex: 4563 605

Products: Door panels.

Freight vehicles

HOW MANY SPECIAL RAILWAY WAGONS DO WE STILL HAVE TO DESIGN TO GET YOU ON AN AEROPLANE?

Since 1986 we have manufactured railway wagons for over ten different companies in five different countries. In total, over 9000 units.

Since 1986 we have patented over 20 technical innovations.

Since 1986 we have developed and manufactured 18 entirely new wagon types. No other European wagon manufacturer can say the same.

How many more wagons do we have still to make to show that our young, design-orientated and probably the most up to date wagon works in Europe can provide a service which the most developed and unbiased transportation companies have specifically demanded?

We are ready for just as many examples of our work as is necessary; we are continuously developing new solutions for our clients' needs. Still we hope that 18 will be sufficient to get you on a plane. Aren't you interested in finding out what these 18 are?

RAUTARUUKKI

Transtech Division
P.O.Box 217, SF-90101 Oulu, Finland
tel. +358 81 327 711, tlx 32109 steel sf
fax +358 81 327 196

England Rautaruukki (UK) Ltd, Merevale House, Parkshot, Richmond, Surrey TW 9 2 RW, tel. +44 1 948 8177, tlx 295743 steel g, fax +44 1 948 5716 BRD Rautaruukki (Deutschland) GmbH, Grafenberger Allee 87, D-4000 Düsseldorf 1, tel. +49 211 682 616, tlx 172114075 rruukki d, fax +49 211 689 842

Freight vehicles

ARGENTINA
- AFNE 232
- Bautista Buriasco 233
- Betran Hnos 233
- Callegari 237
- Cometarsa 238
- Comsal 238
- Prati-Vazquez Iglesias 252

AUSTRALIA
- Centurion 237
- Comeng 238
- Goninan 243
- Moss 249
- Perry 251

AUSTRIA
- S-G-P 257

BELGIUM
- BN 234
- BREC 235

BRAZIL
- CCC 237
- Cobrasma 237
- Engesa-FNV 241
- Mafersa 248
- Santa Matilde 256
- Soma 258

CANADA
- Alcan 233
- Hawker Siddeley 244
- National Steel Car 249
- Procor 253

CHINA
- Chian An Rolling Stock 237
- China National Railway Corporation 237
- Dalian Locomotive 239
- Qiqihar 253

CZECHOSLOVAKIA
- Czechoslovak Wagon Works 239
- Strojexport 258

DENMARK
- ABB Scandia A/S 232, 256

EGYPT
- SEMAF 257

FRANCE
- ABRF 232
- AFR 232
- Cadoux 236
- Orval 251
- Remafer 255
- SFC-Daval 257
- SNAV 258
- Soulé 258

FINLAND
- Rautarruukki Oy 254

GERMANY, DEMOCRATIC REPUBLIC
- Dessau 240
- KSFB 247
- Niesky 250
- Schienenfahrzeuge Export-Import 256

GERMANY, FEDERAL REPUBLIC
- Badische Waggonfabrik 233
- Bremer 236
- BWR 236
- Ferrostaal 242
- Graaf 243
- Krupp Maschinentechnik 247
- MAN GHH 248
- O & K 250
- Peiner 251

INDIA
- Talbot 259
- Waggon Union 264
- Bharat Wagon & Engineering 233
- Braithwaite 235
- Burn Standard 236
- Cimmco International 237
- KT Steel 247
- PEC 251

IRELAND
- Liebherr 247

ITALY
- BP-Battioni & Pagani 234
- Casaralta 237
- CEFF 237
- CFC 237
- Costamasnaga 238
- Ferrosud 242
- Fiat 242
- Firema 243
- Imesi 245
- Keller 246
- OFV 250
- OMS 250
- Reggiane 255
- SGI 257

JAPAN
- Alna Koki 233
- Fuji Car 243
- Kawasaki 245
- Kinki Sharyo 246
- Nippon Sharyo 250
- Wakamatsu Sharyo 264

KOREA
- Daewoo 239
- Hyundai 245
- Korea Shipbuilding & Engineering 246

MEXICO
- CNCFSA 237
- Concarril 238

MOROCCO
- SCIF 256

MOZAMBIQUE
- Cometal 238

NETHERLANDS
- Nelcon 250

NEW ZEALAND
- A & G Price 253

NORWAY
- Finsam 242
- Strømmens (NEBB) 259

PAKISTAN
- Pakistan Railways Carriage 251

POLAND
- Kolmex 246
- Konstal 246
- Zastal 264

PORTUGAL
- Metalsines 248

ROMANIA
- Arad 233
- Mecanoexportimport 248

SOUTH AFRICA
- Hudson 245
- RSD 256

SPAIN
- Babcock & Wilcox 233
- CAF 237
- CAT 237
- Herederos de Ramon Mugica 244
- Inta-Eimar 245
- Macosa 247
- Maquinista 248
- Tafesa 259

SWEDEN
- Ageve 232
- Kalmar 245
- Lagab 247

SWITZERLAND
- Cattaneo 237
- Schindler 256
- Stag 258
- Tuchschmid 263
- VeVey 264

USSR
- Altai 233
- Energomachexport 241

UK
- Blatchford 233
- W H Davis 240
- Howden 245
- Oleo 250
- Powell Duffryn 251
- Procor Engineering 253
- Ray Smith 254
- RFS Engineering 255
- Trailer Train 261

USA
- ACF 232
- Amherst 233
- Anbel 233
- Bethlehem Steel 233
- Briggs & Turivas 236
- Difco 240
- Dorsey 241
- Greenville Steel Car 243
- The Gregg Company 243
- Gunderson 243
- Kilo-Wate 246
- Letourneau 247
- Miner Railcar 249
- Ortner 251
- Portec 251
- Pullman Standard 253
- RoadRailer 255
- SM-Strick RailTrailer 258
- Strick 258
- Taylor 260
- Thrall 260
- Trailer-Rail 261
- Transcisco Industries Inc 260
- Transcisco Rail Services Co 261
- Transit America 262
- Trinity Industries 262
- Union Tank 263

YUGOSLAVIA
- Bratstvo 235
- GOŠA 243
- Kraljevo 247

ZIMBABWE
- More Wear 249

232 MANUFACTURERS / Freight vehicles

ABB Ageve
AB Gävle Vagnverkstad

PO Box 655, 801 27 Gävle, Sweden

Telephone: +4626 115890
Telex: 47106 ageve s
Telefax: +4626 187832

Products: General and special-purpose freight wagons.

ABB Scandia A/S
See entry on page 256

ABRF
Atelier Bréton de Réparation Ferroviaire

PO Box 19, ZI rue Lafayette, 44141 Châteaubriant Cedex, France

Telephone: +33 40 81 19 20
Telex: 710075 abr f

Products: Freight wagons, including 'Easiloader' curtain hood wagon for general merchandise.

ACF
ACF Industries, Incorporated

Head office: 3301 Rider Trail South, Earth City, Missouri 63045-1393, USA

Telephone: +1 314 344 4500

President: J C O'Hara
Vice-President, Sales and Leasing: R D Wynkoop
Senior Vice President, Manufacturing: D E Reese

Products: Freight cars and car parts, piggyback trailer hitches and mixing bowls. Recent products include the ACF Pressureaide covered hopper car, which has been developed specially for the transport of flour and similar commodities. A pressure differential car with a capacity of 141.6 m^3 (5000 ft^3), it operates with internal pressures of up to 14.5 psi, which allows both faster unloading of the product, and also unloading at a greater distance from receiving bins than with previous models.

AFNE
Astilleros y Fabricas Navales del Estado

Corrientes 672, 1043 Buenos Aires, Argentina

Telephone: +54 1 7031/39
Cable: AFNE
Telex: 17924

Products: Ride control bogies for freight wagons manufactured under licence from Amsted.

AFR
Arbel Fauvet Rail

Head office: 40 Boulevard Henri Sellier (92156), Suresnes CEDEX, France
Works: 194 Boulevard Faidherbe, 59506 Douai CEDEX, France

Telephone: +33 27 93 39 39
Telex: 130036
Telefax: +33 27 87 06 32

Other works at Lille and Arras

President: Francois Perreau-Saussine
Managing Director: Bernard Delhomme
Commercial Directors: Henri Caijo
Georges Carbonnières

Products: In addition to conventional types, AFR develops, designs and builds covered and open freight wagons, tank wagons, wagons for bulk transport of powdered chemicals, mineral wagons and container wagons; bogies of various types; tank semi-trailers; ISO tank containers.
New orders booked since 1989 include 196 bogie tank wagons for washing soda, slurry, adipic acid and chemicals; 150 twin units, short-coupled double deck car carriers; 20 flat wagons for swap bodies and

Type Sdms piggyback wagon by ABB Ageve

Type Smmnps wagon for carriage of steel ingots by ABB Ageve

Bogie tank wagon for transport of slurry (AFR)

High-sided gondola with tilt cover (AFR)

containers; 50 gondola wagons and 74 hopper wagons for transport of aggregates.

During 1989 a licence agreement was signed with Road Railer USA and since then the system has been adapted by AFR to meet the European requirements. The prototype AFR Road Railer was first shown and demonstrated during INTERMODAL 90 at Brussels and then started intensive testing with SNCF.

Constitution: In September 1985, Arbel-Industrie and Fauvet-Girel merged their railway equipment activities into a common subsidiary, called Arbel-Fauvet-Rail (AFR).

The factories at Douai, Arras and Lille belonging to Arbel-Fauvet-Rail manufacture the widest range of goods rolling stock, shunting locomotives, ISO containers and the semi-trailers for which the company has a wide reputation both in France and abroad.

Alcan
Alcan Canada Products Ltd

Box 269, Toronto-Dominion Centre, Toronto, Ontario M5K 1K1, Canada

Telephone: +1 416 366 7211
Cable: Alcan, Toronto
Telex: 06-22641

Products: More than 30 years of experience designing lightweight aluminium rolling stock for freight service. Supplies aluminium sheet, plate, and extrusions for rail transport applications of all kinds.

All-aluminium LRC locomotives and cars in service with VIA Rail Canada are designed jointly by Alcan, Bombardier–MLW and Dofasco.

A total of 2424 aluminium covered hopper cars for grain are in service in Canada for the Canadian Wheat Board: tare, 20.2 tonnes; payload, 79.6 tonnes; cubic capacity, 125 m^3. Construction: 7004, 6351 extrusions; 5083 plate, steel stub sills and bolsters.

Alna Koki
Alna Koki Company Ltd

Head office and works: No 4-5, Higashinaniwa-cho, 1-chome, Amagasaki-City, Hyogo Pref, Japan

Telephone: +81 6 401 7283
Telex: 5242782 alnosk
Telefax: +81 6 401 6168

President: Jitokuro Sakai
Managing Director, Production: Yoshinobu Sugimoto
Chief Engineer & Director: Kiyoyuki Yamagami
Managing Director, Sales & Marketing: Masahiro Higuchi

Products: General purpose freight wagons; low floor wagons; tank wagons; dump wagons.

Altai
Altai Wagon Works

Head office: Altai, USSR
Exports: Energomachexport, Deguninskaya Str 1, Korp 4, 127486 Moscow, USSR

Telephone: +7 095 147 21 77
Telex: 7565

Products: Freight wagons.

Amherst
Amherst Industries, Inc

Port Amherst, Charleston, West Virginia 25306, USA

Telephone: +1 304 925 1171

President: Charles T Jones

Products: Freight wagons; interior linings for tank and hopper wagons.

Anbel
The Anbel Group

2323 South Voss Road, Houston, Texas 77057, USA

Telephone: +1 713 977 9737
Telex: 910 881 1168

Alcan aluminium grain hopper

President: Kenneth Roy Nichols
Vice-President: Alan R Cripe
Administration Manager: F J Demme
Field Services: H Rendon
Plant Manager: H M Tillman

Products: Freight wagons.

Arad
Intrepinderea de Vagoane

Avenue Aurel Vlaicu 41-43, 2900 Arad, Romania

Telephone: +40 66 37292
Cable: Vagoane Arad
Telex: 76256

General Manager: Mihai Surany
Technical Manager: Ioan Pantea
Export Sales Manager: Sandu Albulescu

Products: Sleeping and dining cars; first-, second- and third-class coaches; train-heating cars; brake and luggage vans; power-generating cars; mail vans; observation and conference saloons; lounge coaches; four- and multi-axled freight cars, covered high-board open, flat with or without side and front walls and stanchions, tipping of 40 or 25 m^3, gondola, grain transport, pellet, etc; four- and six-axle dumpers; flat cars on four, six, 10, 12 or 20 axles for heavy transport; ore transport cars, sliding-roof or side-wall cars, etc, for any gauge from 900 to 1676 mm.

Special equipment for metallurgical and siderurgical plants as flat cars for ingots; incandescent, coke operating cars; liquid transport transportable pot on railway car; equivalent cars for slag etc.

Recent contracts include USSR side-dumping cars for 1520 mm gauge – 105 to capacity; USSR grain hopper wagons 1520 mm gauge – 72 to capacity; Eaos Gondola wagons; coal transportation wagons – Fals type; ore transportation wagons 1435 mm gauge – 120 to capacity.

Constitution: Mecanoexportimport supplier.

Babcock & Wilcox
Babcock & Wilcox Española

Galindo, (Vizcaya), Spain

Telephone: +34 4 4966011, +34 4 4957011
Telex: 32235, 32544 bw fbe
Telefax: +34 4 4956676

Main works
Alameda Recalde 27, 48009 Bilbao
Lagasca, 88, 28001 Madrid

Executive President: Manual Fernández García

Products: Freight cars, railway rolling stock for steel industries, railway slewing cranes.

Badische Waggonfabrik
Badische Waggonfabrik GmbH

Werkstrasse 2, 7550 Rastatt, Federal Republic of Germany

Telephone: +49 7222 7790
Telex: 786620

Sales Manager: M Ansorge

Products: Rebuilding and overhaul of passenger and freight cars.

Bautista Buriasco
Bautista Buriasco E Hijos Ltda SA

Av Bautista Buriasco s/n, 2445 Maria Juana, Province Sante Fe, Argentina

Telephone: +54 42 91 214/414

Products: Freight wagons; welded steel bogies.

Bethlehem Steel
Bethlehem Steel Corporation

Bethlehem, Pennsylvania 18016, USA

Telephone: +1 215 694 2424

Chairman, President and Chief Executive Officer: W F Williams
Executive Vice President, Sales: S D Arnot

Products: Freight wagons; components; axles; rails and track accessories.

Betran Hnos
Betran Hnos y Cia SACI

Don Bosco 1505, 8000 Bahia Blanca, Argentina

Telephone: +54 91 20335/8

Products: Freight wagons.

Bharat Wagon & Engineering
Bharat Wagon & Engineering Co Ltd
A Government of India undertaking

Mokameh, 803 302 Bihar, India

Telephone: +91 Mokameh 25, 51, 89

General Manager: S P Singh

Products: Freight wagons.

Blatchford
Ralph Blatchford & Co

West Road, Midsomer Norton, Bath, Avon BA3 2AB, England

Telephone: +44 761 412281

Products: The Linercrane. self-propelled by a Rolls-Royce C6 220P 190 hp engine, the 22.46 metre-long, 66-tonne Linercrane is a container transfer vehicle mounted on Gloucester RC&W GP525 bogies. It can deal with the majority of ISO container types up to 40 feet long, top-lifting boxes and corner-lifting flats. Hydraulic legs are extended for support when container transfers are being made. The two transverse container lifting gantries can be folded flat on the vehicle's central platform, within loading gauge, for inter-terminal movement, which can be at up to 120 km/h when the Linercrane is hauled by other traction. Within yards the Linercrane can also move about under its own power at up to 25 km/h carrying a container of up to 30 tonnes glw on its platform. Lifting capacity is also 30 tonnes. The prototype Linercrane is designed for operation on standard gauge with 3.4 to 4.25 metre track centres, but versions for different track parameters are planned. Transfer can be as swift as with an orthodox gantry crane, but the Linercrane's productivity is maximised when selecting containers at random from a long train.

234 MANUFACTURERS / Freight vehicles

Blatchford Linercrane with gantries folded for inter-terminal movement

Blatchford T-Lift mounted on highway trailer

Linercrane in container transfer operation

T-Lift with transfer equipment retracted

A railhead and general purpose ISO container hauling and handling system called the T-Lift has been devised in two versions. One is embodied in a highway-type semi-trailer that can be pulled by in-service articulated tractor units. The other version is in the form of a hamper that can be attached to selected rigid truck chassis; the choice of axle and drive configurations can be 8 × 4, 8 × 6, 8 × 8 or 10 × 8 depending upon the degree of site mobility required. Both versions have lifting frames with powered twistlocks for toplifting the containers. This feature, allied with an entirely new and patented structural geometry, gives the Blatchford system the capability to take a 20 ft container from any standard rail or road vehicle even when containers are grouped close together, eg 3 × 20 ft containers on a rail wagon, or 2 × 20 ft containers on a 40 ft semi-trailer; and also to haul an 8 ft 6 in (2591 mm) high container on the highway and still comply with the European height limit of 4000 mm. On front axle-drive rigid chassis versions only 8 ft (2440 mm) high containers can be hauled in this way. For railhead transfer operations machines are of dual-sided construction so that containers can be lifted from, say, a train on one side and be transferred direct on to a road vehicle, or to the ground on the other side. When progressing alongside a train productivity is in the order of 10 transfers per hour. The special geometry of the main structures enables working beneath power cables over rail tracks.

All machines are available in an alternative single-sided and lightweight form when the prime requirement of the equipment is the highway delivery of containers out of railheads and depots. On all semi-trailer versions there is a choice of either tandem or tri-axel rear bogies. Additionally the spacing between individual axles, and the outer axle spacings can be set to have optimum compliance in most countries with local laws, so that in many cases full payloads can be legally carried on public highways. All machines are controlled from a control box on a wanderlead. For those mounted on rigid vehicles the driver can stay in the truck cab. The machines have low axle weight which means they can operate on existing surfaces as used by conventional road vehicles. When mounted on 8 × 8 or 10 × 8 chassis, containers can be hauled and handled across country, across beaches etc.

Three 20-ton semi-trailer-mounted machines for 20 ft ISO containers and flatracks were bought in 1984 by the Ministry of Defence and trialled in the UK and British Army of the Rhine as part of the DROPS project. The machines have proved highly successful and others have been sold on the civilian market. An austere version of the MoD machine is offered on the civilian market in two sizes: 20-ton, for 20 ft containers only, made as a skid unit which the customer can either fit to a rigid heavy duty 8 × 4 or 8 × 8 truck chassis, or make into a semi-trailer by setting a tandem axle running gear beneath; or 30-ton for 20 ft–40 ft containers. The pair of T-Lifters with telescopic spreader are set on a proprietary semi-trailer that has a trombone chassis. At extra cost both machines can be arranged to handle 9 ft-high containers and stack them two-high on both sides.

BN
Constructions Ferroviaires et Métalliques
Formerly La Brugeoise et Nivelles SA

Avenue Louise 65, 1050 Bruxelles, Belgium

Telephone: +32 2 535 55 11
Telex: 61 736 Brunag
Telefax: +32 2 539 10 17

Managing Director: M Simonart
Executive Director, Transport Division: P Sonveaux
Marketing & Sales Director, Transport Division: J Verraver

Products: Freight vehicles. Recent wagon export orders have included 100 bogie covered wagons for Zambia and 100 wagons for Zaïre. In 1989, 50 container waggons were ordered by CFL (Luxemburger Railways).

BP-Battioni & Pagani
BP-Battioni & Pagani SpA

Località Croce, 43058 Sorbolo (Parma), Italy

Telephone: +39 521 604141/2
Telex: 530081 bapag i
Telefax: +39 521 604252

BP SL35 side-loader for handling 20/30 ft containers of 8 ft or 8 ft 6 in height

Freight vehicles / MANUFACTURERS 235

BP SL55, biggest in Battioni & Pagani's side-loader range

Chairman: Pagant Gianfranco
Vice-President: Battioni Amilcare

Products: A complete range of side-loaders, including container handling machines up to 55 tons capacity and heavy machines fitted with telescopic top spreaders and special top clamps for intermodal transport movements; a range of heavy-duty forklift trucks of 4 to 38 tons capacity including machines fitted with spreader attachments for container handling.

Braithwaite
Braithwaite & Co Ltd
(A Government of India Undertaking)

Head office: 5 Hide Road, Calcutta 700 043, India

Telephone: +91 33 45 9901 08
Cable: Bromkirk, Calcutta
Telex: CA 21-8116

Branch office: Competent House (3rd floor), F-14 Connaught Place, New Delhi 110 001

Telephone: +91 11 331 0111
Telex: 031 66204 bwte in

Works: Clive Works, 5 Hide Road, Calcutta 700 043
Angus Works, Angus PO, Hooghly, West Bengal

Projects office: 59B Chowringee Road (4th Floor), Calcutta 700 019

Telephone: +91 33 44 0695 43 1782
Telex: 21 3288 bwt in

Managing Director: P K Rath
Director, Finance: D K Sen
Director, Production & Control: S Roy
General Manager, Clive Works: S S Ahmed
General Manager, Angus Works: Dr P K Dey
General Manager, Corporate Planning: S S Mathur
General Manager, Projects: S Banerjee
General Manager, Personnel: D C Sinha
Chief of Public Relations: S Krishnan

Products: Railway wagons, bridges, buildings for factories, power houses and steel plants, overhead electric travelling cranes, wharf cranes, railway breakdown cranes, container cranes, portal cranes, tower cranes, hammerhead cranes, diesel-electric cranes, trailers, coal and other material handling plants, jute mill machinery, pressed steel tanks, iron castings, steel forgings.

Constitution: Braithwaite is a Government of India undertaking and a subsidiary of BBUNL and has successfully executed orders for equipment from undertakings abroad in Bahrain, Burma, Ghana, Hong Kong, Iraq, Republic of Korea, Kenya, Kuwait, Malaysia, Maldives, Nepal, New Zealand, Philippines, Sudan, Sri Lanka, Taiwan, Uganda, the United Arab Emirates, Viet-Nam, Yugoslavia and Zambia.

Bratstvo

24106 Subotica-Aleksandrovo, Ilindenska 46, Yugoslavia

Telephone: +38 23 762
Telex: 15138 yu vagoni
Telefax: +38 37 124

General Manager: Gajodi Antal
Technical Manager: Sefcic Djordje
Sales Manager: Rasovic Dragan

Products: Two, three and four-axle freight wagons for all gauges, general and bulk goods, as well as car transporters and special wagons in large, medium and small sizes. Industrial repair and modernisation of all freight wagons. Production of spare/exchange parts and assemblies such as buffers, drawgear, spring leaves and spring suspensions.

Recent contracts include various products for Yugoslav Railways (JZ) (1989-90); contracts with JZ for repair of freight wagons (1990).

BREC
Belgian Railway Equipment Company NV

Avenue Huysmans 53, B-1660 Beersel (Lot), Belgium

Telephone: +32 2 378 05 10
Telex: 21 357 brec b
Telefax: +32 2 378 11 09

General Manager: J Sambre
Sales & Logistics: R Peeters
J Ostyn

Products: All types of freight wagon and bogies for wagons and passenger coaches.

Since 1981, the following freight wagon orders have been executed:
Belgium
Belgian National Railways: 750 high-sided open goods wagons; 250 covered box wagons with sliding doors, Type Hbis; 100 coal wagons, Type Fals; and 100 container flat wagons Type Sgss.
CAIB:
38 flat wagons for the transport of semi-trailers and containers; and 23 flat wagons for the transport of trailers-containers (or semi-trailers)
INTRANS:
50 coal wagons, Type Fals.
Benguela
Benguela Railways: 10 low-sided flat wagons.
Guinea
Compagnie des Bauxites de Guinée, Guinea: 10 bodies completely welded, without accessories; and 20 complete ore cars.

Eight-wheeler 20/32-tonne axle load BG bogie Type BOXN open wagon (Braithwaite)

BREC 40 m³ capacity tank wagon for SEP, Zaïre

236 MANUFACTURERS / Freight vehicles

Saudi Arabia
Saudi Government Railways Organisation: 50 gondola cars.
Sudan
Sudan Railways Corporation: 69 double-deck sheep wagons.
Zaïre
Société Nationale des Chemins de Fer Zaïrois: 175 coal wagons; and 100 low-sided container flat wagons.
Gécamines-Exploitation: 307 bottom-door discharge hopper cars.
SEP Zaïre: 50 tank wagons for the transport of petroleum products.
Zambia
Zambia Railways: 25 flat wagons for the transport of containers.

Bremer
Bremer Waggonbau GmbH

Postfach 110 109, Pfalzburger Strasse 251, 2800 Bremen 11, Federal Republic of Germany

Telephone: +49 421 45 40 11
Cable: Bremer Waggonbau, Bremen
Telex: 024 4423

Managing Director: Peter Müller
Export Sales: Chr Trahm

Products: Freight wagons, in particular repair and renovation.

Constitution: The company was formed in December 1975. The works occupy the site of the former Hansa Waggon AG.

Briggs & Turivas
Briggs & Turivas, Inc

Box 270, 310 Grant Street, Dennison, Ohio 44621-0270, USA

Telephone: +1 614 922 5994

President: Vacant
Secretary/Treasurer: G Kaswinkel

Products: Freight wagons.

Burn Standard Co Ltd
A Government of India Enterprise

Head office: 10-C Hungerford Street, Calcutta 700 017, India

Telephone: +91 33 1067, 1762, 1772, 1788
Cable: Burnwagon Calcutta
Telex: 021 4034

Works: Howrah, Burnpur, Jellingham and Raniganj, Durgapur, Ondal, Gulfarbari, Jabalpur, Niwar and Salem

Chairman and Managing Director: S R Chowdhury

Products: Railway rolling stock and components; centre buffer couplers and components; points and crossings; crossing sleepers; casting-steel, grey iron, S G iron and alloy steel; forging, stamping and pressing; railway sleepers and fishplates; springs for railway and automotive industry; automatic bottom-door discharge wagons; tramcars; high-tensile couplers.

Constitution: Burn Standard Company Ltd, a Government of India undertaking, is successor to Burn and Co Ltd and The Indian Standard Wagon Co, Ltd. The company came into existence following the nationalisation of the undertakings of the two companies in 1975. The company has two engineering units located at Howrah and Burnpur in West Bengal and seven refractory and ceramic units spread over different parts of the country.

Established in 1874, the Howrah Works of the company was the first manufacturer of rolling stock in India and pioneer in foundry practice and structural steel fabrications of a wide range including bridge construction. The Works have extensive facilities for manufacture of railroad equipment such as crossing sleepers, switches and crossings. The Burnpur Works manufactures prototypes of almost all new types of wagon introduced by the Indian Railways and has guided the Railway Board in design and manufacture of wagons for use in the country and also for export. It specialises in production of springs for coaches, locomotives, wagons and automobiles and for various other uses. The Burnpur Works also deals in heavy die forgings, material handling structurals and equipment for the mining industry.

The company has produced about 201 000 wagon units for Indian Railways and exported more than 1300 wagons.

Bottom-discharge hopper wagon for the transport of copper concentrates for Gécamines-Exploitation, Zaïre, by BREC

Type Hbis wagon with aluminium sliding doors for Belgian National Railways by BREC

BWR
BWR Bizerba Werkstoffsysteme und Fahrzeugbau GmbH

Werkstrasse 2, 7550 Restatt, Federal Republic of Germany

Telephone: +49 7222 599-0
Telex: (17) 7222 5602
Telefax: +49 7222 599 185

Sales Manager: M Ansorge

Products: Rebuilding and overhaul of passenger and freight cars.

Cadoux
Cadoux International

7 rue Galilée, 75116 Paris, France

Telephone: +33 1 4723 61 52
Telex: 610091

Products: Freight wagons. The company's latest products include a bogie container flatcar, of which 100 have been supplied or are on order. Mounted on Type Y25Css bogies, it has a tare weight of 18.5 tonnes and is designed for load capacities of up to 61.5 tonnes; it can traverse a minimum curve radius of 75 m.

Clinker wagon for Ghana, tare weight 16.8 tonnes, load capacity 27 m³ and 40.2 tonnes

Metre-gauge car transporter for RAN by Cadoux

Freight vehicles / **MANUFACTURERS** 237

CAF
Construcciones y Auxiliar de Ferrocarriles SA
Member of Servicio de Exportacion de Material Ferroviario

Padilla 17, Madrid 28006, Spain

Telephone: +34 1 435 25 00
Telex: 23197 cafma e
Telefax: +34 1 276 62 63

Export Division

SEMF, Castello 72-1°, 28006 Madrid, Spain

Telephone: +34 1 275 64 03
Telex: 27242 semf e
Telefax: +34 1 276 81 08

Works: Beasain, Zaragoza, Iran

President: José I Cangas
Chairman: Pedro Ardaiz
General Manager: Juan José Anza

Products: Freight wagons.

Recent contracts have included an order from RENFE (Spanish National Railways) for 225 air-braked bogie flat wagons for the transport of steel products: maximum payload 55 tonnes and maximum speed 120 km/h.

Callegari
José Callegari E Hijos

Rivadavia y Peru, Zarate, Prov Buenos Aires, Argentina

Telephone: +54 1 2800 3228

President: Pablo A A Callegari
Director General: Clara Mandelli Vda de Callegari
Sales and Export Director: Eduardo Rivas

Products: Freight wagons.

Casaralta
Casaralta SpA

Via Ferrarese 205, 40128 Bologna, Italy

Telephone: +39 51 35 84 54
Cable: Rotabili, Bologna
Telex: 511068

President: Giorgio Regazzoni
Managing Directors: Carlo Filippo Zucchini
Carlo Regazzoni

Products: Freight wagons.

CAT
Compañia Auxiliar de Transportes SA

Avenida José Antonio 20, Apartado 358, Madrid 14, Spain

Telephone: +34 1 2 22 0414
Cable: Autrans, Madrid

Works: Carretera du Andalucia, Villaverde

Telephone: +34 797 91 00

President: D Miguel Igartua Losa
Sales Director: D José Ma Oteiza

Products: Freight wagons.

Cattaneo
Ferriere Cattaneo SA

6512 Giubiasco, Switzerland

Telephone: +41 09227 31 31/32/33/34
Cable: Ferrum
Telex: 84 6375
Telefax: +41 09227 69 55

Managing Director: Aleardo Cattaneo

Products: Freight wagons, carbon and alloy steel die forgings.

Constitution: Established 1870.

CCC
Companhia Comércio e Construções

Head office: Av Rio Branco 156/22°, Grupos 2233–5, Centro, Rio de Janeiro CEP 20043, Brazil

Telephone: +55 21 262 3312
Cable: Comercon
Telex: 32490 cmct br

Main works: Rua Soldado José Lopes Filho 42, Deodoro, Rio de Janeiro

Telephone: +55 21 390 0760, 1039

Products: Manufacture and repair of cars and freight wagons. The company's two freight manufacturing plants, in Deodoro and Cruzeiro (São Paulo state), have the capacity to produce 1500 vehicles annually.

CEFF
Costruzioni Elettromeccaniche Ferroviarie Fiorentine di Patrizia Pecchioli & C S as

Via Petrosa 11/13/15, Sesto Fiorentino, Florence, Italy

Telephone: +39 55 449 1241
Telex: 580475 ceff i

Products: General freight wagons, refrigerator wagons.

Centurion
Centurion Industries Ltd
(formerly Tomlinson Industries)

GPO Box U1973, Perth, Western Australia 6001, Australia

Telephone: +61 9 361 2055
Telex: AA 92280
Telefax: +61 9 361 0724

General Manager: R E Modolo
Contracts Manager: A Loh
Controller: P Wright

Products: Freight rolling stock.

CFC
Costruzioni Ferroviarie Colleferro SpA
A member of the Fiat Group

Via Sabotino, 00034 Colleferro (Rome), Italy

Telephone: +39 6 4680
Telex: 611434

Products: Freight cars, refrigerated wagons with fibreglass-reinforced polyester resin bodies and refrigerated containers.

Recent production for Italian State Railways (FS) has included the Type Vrtz rail-transporter train. This consists of eight wagons mounted on Y25CS2 bogies with a total tare weight of 164 tonnes and length of 144 m. Load carrying capacity is 36 rails up to a maximum weight of 311 tonnes. The rails can be unloaded from either end of the train. Among freight wagons built for the FS are bogie vans of Types Gabs and Habis (with sliding walls). The company has also constructed refrigerated vans compatible with the British Rail loading gauge for Interfrigo and Transfesa.

Chiang An Rolling Stock
Chiang An Rolling Stock Plant

Chiang An, Wuhan, Hubei, People's Republic of China

Products: Freight wagon and passenger coach repairs.

China National Railway Locomotive and Rolling Stock Industry Corporation

10 Fu Xing Road, Beijing, People's Republic of China

Telephone: +86 45245; +86 42685; +86 44645
Telex: 222218 loric cn

Products: Box cars, gondola cars, flat cars, and various kinds of special freight car. Recent export contracts include an order for 65 metre-gauge wagons for Burma Railways Corporation.

Cimmco International
Cimmco Ltd

Prakash Deep, 7 Tolstoy Marg, New Delhi 110 001, India

Telephone: +91 11 3314383-5, 3310814
Cable: Cimwag, New Delhi
Telex: +91 11 31-62294, 65148

Head office: Birla Nagar (Gwalior)

Main works: (Wagon Division), Bharatpur (Rajasthan)

Chairman: D P Mandelia
Chief Executive President, Cimmco International: D K Goyal
Vice President: S K Sharma

Products: Design and manufacture of freight vehicles including special-purpose wagons; wagon components and spares. The company has pioneered the Indian development of bottom-door discharge hopper wagons for the transport of coal in connection with the country's Super Thermal Power projects; these vehicles have been built under licence from Ortner Freight Car Co and are similar to the US company's well-known 'Rapid Discharge' wagons. The company has also devised lineside apparatus to trigger the opening and closing of the hopper doors, thus permitting automatic discharge to any pre-programmed sequence.

CNCFSA
Constructora Nacional de Carros de Ferrocarril

San Lorenzo 925 5° Piso, Colonia del Valle, 03100 Mexico, DF, Mexico

Telephone: +52 688 52 33
Telex: 1771738 cncf me

General Manager: Ing Mateo Treviso
Sales Director: Ing Pablo Boeck
Technical Director: Ing Vincente Ramos

Works: Ciudad Sahagún, Hidalgo

Products: Box cars of 70-tons capacity for 5000 ft^3 with 10 ft sliding door, outside post, nailable steel floor and fixed corrugated ends; covered hopper cars of 70- or 100-ton capacities for 2200–5750 ft^3 for general service and up to four discharges; open-top hopper gondola of 70- or 100-ton capacities for 2500 ft^3 with corrugated sides and fixed ends; 70-ton capacity dump cars; tank cars of 100-ton capacity to carry 20 000 or 26 000 gallons for general service with top and bottom discharges or steam coils and insulation; top cupola cabooses equipped with oil heaters, kitchen, toilet and standard factures; 72/84 seat passenger coaches with air-conditioning (optional), heating system and toilets; rehabilitation and modernisation of freight cars, passenger coaches and 2000/3000 hp diesel-electric locomotives.

A major contract held in 1987 covered 530 freight cars including box cars, piggyback, flat and hopper cars, 175 passenger coaches and modernisation of 12 2000 hp diesel-electric locomotives.

Cobrasma SA

Head office: Rua da Estação 523, Osasco, São Paulo, Brazil

Telephone: +55 11 704 6122
Telex: +55 11 71545, 71589

Works: Km 104 Via Anhanguera, Sitio São João, Distrito de Hortolândia, Sumaré, São Paulo

President: Luis Eulálio de Bueno Vidigal
Marketing Director: Alberto Martinez
Export Director: Eduardo Hubert Kirmaier Monteiro

Products: Freight wagons.

238   MANUFACTURERS / Freight vehicles

Comeng
A Division of The ANI Corporation Limited

Frankston Road, Dandenong, Victoria 3175, Australia

Telephone: +61 3 794 2111
Telex: 33253
Telefax: +61 3 792 5187

General Manager: A Connor
Commercial Manager: G Daniels

Products: Freight wagons; containers; wagon handlers and placers; shunters.

Cometal
Cometal-Mometal SARL

PO Box 1401, Maputo, Mozambique

Telephone: +258 752124/5/6/7/8
Cable: Cometal, Maputo
Telex: 6-267 vagao mo

Products: Freight wagons; baggage vans; inspection cars; harbour and overhead cranes.

Cometarsa
Cometarsa SAIC

LN Alem 1067, Piso 25, 1001 Buenos Aires, Argentina

Telephone: +54 1 31 6277
Cable: Cometarsa, Baires

Works: Campana, Prov Buenos Aires

Products: Freight wagons.

Comsal
Comsal LTDA

8520 San Antonio Oeste, Rio Negro, Argentina

Products: Freight wagons.

Concarril
Constructora Nacional de Caros de Ferrocarril SA

San Lorenzo No 925, Col del Valle, CP 03100, Mexico

Telephone: +52 5 688 5233
Telex: 1771738 cncf me
Telefax: +52 5 688 8482

General Manager: Lic Jorge Tamayo
Commercial Subdirector: Lic Ignacio Riva Palacio
Technical Director: Ing Juan Ollivier f

Works: Ciudad Sahagun, Edo de Hidalgo, Mexico

Products: Box cars; covered hopper cars; open-top hopper gondolas; dump cars; tank cars; cabooses; passenger coaches; refurbishment and modernisation of freight cars, passenger coaches and diesel-electric locomotives.
   A major contract held in 1989 covered 100 freight cars including modernisation of box cars and manufacturing of flat cars, manufacturing of 20 special class coaches and modernisation of 12; rebuilding of three 2000 hp diesel-electric locomotives.

Costamasnaga
Costamasnaga SpA

Viale 4 Novembre, 22041 Costamasnaga, Como, Italy

Telephone: +39 31 85 51 92
Telex: 380184
Telefax: +39 31 855330

Chairman: Claudio Marina
Directors, General: Fabio Magni
                      Ida Magni

Subsidiary company: ASTRIDE Srl
Via Euripide, 9, 20145 Milan

Telephone: +39 2 490177/4392289
Telex: 380161 pplcc
Telefax: +39 2 490177

Bogieless ore car for Mount Newman Mining by Comeng; these vehicles are designed for 40-tonne axleloads and have stainless steel bodies and a novel independent suspension system

Costamasnaga auto-carrier

Costamasnaga Type Sdgmnss intermodal wagon

Products: Type Sdgmnss bogie wagon for transport of semi-trailers and ISO and UIC containers. Tare 20 tonnes, max carrying capacity 70 tonnes. Max speed is 120 km/h, bogies are Y25Lssi type. This wagon complies with the latest UIC specifications. The company is supplying 174 Sdgmnss to Italian Railways.
   Double-deck auto-carrier wagon with wagon body designed by Costamasnaga and bogies of Y024 type. Max speed is 160 km/h, length 26.4 m. The wagon complies with the latest UIC specifications. Italian Railways has been supplied with 56 of these vehicles.
   CoPiFer System (rail-freighted modules) for civil defence emergency. The system consists of special railway wagons capable of transporting modules ready

Freight vehicles / **MANUFACTURERS** 239

for occupancy and equipped with primary facilities. A basic train consists of 40 combination special wagon/mobile modules, completely furnished and self-sufficient to set up as a fully-equipped village.

The ASTRIDE bi-modal chassis is a road truck equipped with rail traction, axles, journal boxes, suspensions and braking equipment as used in rail vehicles, all in their own frame. Vehicles can be supplied fitted as normal road trucks with open/closed, dump or tank body, fitted with various equipments for rail track maintenance, for inspecting overhead lines, for towing dead trolley/subway cars, etc.

Czechoslovak Wagon Works
Československé Vagónky
(Member of Strojexport, Foreign Trade Co Ltd, Prague)

Nám Dukelskych hrdinu° 95, 058 01 Poprad, Czechoslovakia

Telephone: +42 25242
Telex: 078 348

Works: Vagónka Studénka, 742 13 Studénka

Works: Vagónka Poprad, 058 80 Poprad
Vagónka Česka Lípa, 470 79 Česka Lípa

Chairman: Stefan Tužinsky
Managing Director: Jan Hlavačik
Sales Director: Karol Kos ik

Products: Freight wagons of types Faccs, Falls, Es, Eas, Gbgkks, Res, Zacs, Zags, Zagkks and Zae.

Daewoo
Daewoo Heavy Industries Ltd

PO Box 7955, Seoul, Republic of Korea

Telephone: Seoul +82 2 752 0211.
Anyang +82 343 52 6171
Cable: Dhiltdincheon
Telex: 23301/25550
Telefax: +82 2 756 2679

Chairman: Woo Choong Kim
President: Kyung Hoon Lee
Executive Vice President: Oh Jun Kwon
Rolling Stock Executive Director: Won Jai Park
Rolling Stock Export Sales Manager: Soo Hwan Kim

Products: Freight wagons.

Foreign companies with which Daewoo has technical collaboration arrangements for rail equipment include:
Electric locomotives: 50 c/s Group; ACEC, Belgium; AEG and Siemens, West Germany; Alsthom and MTE, France; BBC, Switzerland
Stainless steel railcars, bogies: Transit America Inc, USA
Electric cars: Hitachi Ltd, Japan
Diesel-hydraulic railcars: Niigata Engineering Co Ltd, Japan
Air-spring bogies, diesel engines: MAN, Federal Republic of Germany
Rubber-spring bogies: Gloucester Railway Carriage & Wagon Co Ltd, England
Barber stabilised bogies: Standard Car Truck Co, USA
Traction motors, motor alternators, design co-operation in electric emu cars: GEC Traction International Ltd, England
Alliance couplers: Amsted Industries Inc, USA

Dalian Locomotive and Rolling Stock Works
Member of China National Machinery Import and Export Corporation

Dalian, Liaoning, People's Republic of China

Costamasnaga ASTRIDE bi-model chassis

Costamasnaga CoPiFer rail-freighted module

Tank wagon for Burma by Daewoo

Covered wagon for Burma by Daewoo

MANUFACTURERS / Freight vehicles

Cable: Dallocwks, Dalian
Telex: 86414 daloc cn

Products: Freight wagons.

Davis
W H Davis Ltd

PO Box 3, Langwith Junction, Mansfield, Nottingham NG20 9SA, England

Telephone: +44 623 74 2621
Telex: 37657

Chairman and Managing Director: D Sharpe
Sales Director, Rolling Stock: M S Burge

Products: Freight wagons; containers.

Constitution: The company was formed in 1984 following a management buy-out of W H Davis & Sons Ltd.

Dessau
VEB Waggonbau Dessau
A member of VEB Kombinat Schienenfahrzeugbau and of Vereinigter Schienenfahrzeugbau der DDR e V

Joliot-Curie-Strasse 48, 4500 Dessau, German Democratic Republic

Telephone: +37 7510
Telex: 0488241

Exports: Schienenfahrzeuge Export-Import Volkseigener Aussenhandelsbetrieb der DDR
Ötztaler Strasse 5, 1100 Berlin

Products: Mechanical refrigerated wagons and trains; ice-cooled wagons; freight wagons.
The production programme includes two- and four-axle ice-activated refrigerator wagons, independent mechanically-refrigerated cars, insulated wagons, and five-and nine-car refrigerated trains. In 1988 more than 48 000 refrigerator wagons from Dessau were in service with 14 railway administrations.

Constitution: The works began special-purpose goods wagon manufacture when it resumed production in 1945. In 1948 it began construction of ice-cooled wagons and from 1951 mechanically-refrigerated vehicles. It had produced its 51 500th vehicle during 1989.

Difco
Difco Inc

PO Box 238, Findlay, Ohio 458390, USA

Telephone: +1 419 422 0525
Cable: Difco, Findlay
Telefax: +1 419 422 1275

President and Managing Director: Wayne S Westlake
Vice-President, Sales: Robert J Ward

Products: Air-operated side-dump wagons, air operated drop-end side-dump cars, Ballaster.
Patented Difco Air Side-Dump Cars are specially designed to haul huge tonnages of bulk material economically and to dump it cleanly and clearly on target away from tracks. The low height of these big-capacity cars saves loading time and allows for larger loads.
In addition, Difco cars are readily adaptable to waste disposal of sewer sludge, scrubber sludge, bottom ash and many other abrasive and resistant waste products, simplifying operations by dumping waste directly on landfill, saving energy and reducing operating costs.
Difco cars are constructed from Tri-Ten Steel to withstand constant load shocks and abrasive action. They dump to either side with equal facility and raise to a self-cleaning 50-degree angle to facilitate the dumping of ash, sludge and other bulk materials. The automatic down-folding doors assure maximum load

Dalian C62A(N) weather-resistant steel open-top 21.7-tonne wagon

102-tonne glw aggregates hopper with rapid mobile discharge by W H Davis

Insulated wagon for the Soviet Railways (SZD) by VEB Waggonbau Dessau

Electric generator car for Chinese Railways by VEB Waggonbau Dessau

cast accuracy. Their all-welded construction and double fulcrum design assures complete stability.

Bogies are AAR ride control and roller bearing-equipped and feature a long-travel spring arrangement. A maximum capacity spring package consisting of 63 mm travel outer, 95 mm travel inner and 86 mm travel helper springs is available as an option for heavy industrial mining applications.

The company's new 'Ditcher Train' adds drop-end doors to standard air dump cars, so that a conventional excavator can drive through the train. The excavator can clean ditches on either side, backing up while filling cars, closing end doors as it goes. After the last car is filled, the excavator backs onto a flat car for the trip to the dump.

The 11,000 lb 15-tonne capacity spot maintenance Ballaster is an all-steel, fully welded construction, axleless truck assembly which assures parallel alignment when placing on rail, and rugged construction which permits loading from trucks or front-end loaders. Special doors for third rail clearance are available for transit systems. One-man operation of this truck places ballast inside and outside rails and the discharge door regulates ballast to any desired depth, from the top of the rail to the top of the tie in one operation.

Recent contracts include 22 used 50 cu yd 100-tonne air dumps for Burlington Northern Railroad (1988); two stainless steel 50 cu yd 77-tonne air dumps for Ohio Edison Company (1988-89); repair 28 50 cu yd 77-tonne air dumps (1989); two Ballasters for Island Creek Corporation (1990).

Constitution: Founded in 1915 for the production of heavy and light industrial railway rolling stock and mine haulage equipment.

Dorsey
Dorsey Trailers, Inc

Corporate office: 100 Paces West, Suite 1200, 2727 Paces Ferry Road, Atlanta, Georgia 30339, USA

Telephone: +1 404 438 9595

Sales office: 1409 Hickman Street, Elba, Alabama 36323

Telephone: +1 205 897 5711
Telex: 62884173
Telefax: +1 205 897 5345

President & CEO: Marilyn R Marks
Vice President, Sales: Joe B DeVane

Products: Trailers, incorporating Road-Railer systems; piggyback trailers; vans platform trailers, reefers, dumps, and drop-frame vans.

Energomachexport
V/O Energomachexport

Deguninskaja Str 1, Korp 4, 127486 Moscow, USSR

Telephone: +7 095 487 31 82/87
Cable: Energoexport
Telex: 411965

100-ton, 50 yd³ payload capacity Difco air side-dump wagon by Difco

Difco 15-tonne capacity spot maintenance Ballaster

President: V Pavlov
Vice President: N Evteev
Sales Directors: V Slabejko
V Tsvetkov

Products: Soviet exports of freight wagons; railway interlocking equipment; signalling and block systems; track machines and mechanisms.

Constitution: The company was formed to handle all railway equipment exports from the Soviet Union. Principal partners include the Ludinovo, Novocherkassk, and Voroshilovgrad locomotive works.

Engesa-FNV
FNV Veiculos e Equipamentos S/A
An Engesa Company

Avenida Tucunaré 125/211, 06400 Barueri, São Paulo, Brazil

Telephone: +5511 421 4711
Telex: 11 71302 enes br
Telefax: +5511 421 4445

Main works: PO Box 23, Rua Dr Othon, Barcellos 83, Cruzeiro, São Paulo, Brazil

President: José Luiz Whitaker Ribeiro
Vice-President: José Guilherme Whitaker Ribeiro
Directors: Sérgio Antonio Bardella
Armando Ulbricht Junior
Marco Aurelio de Barros Montenegro
Vail Eduardo Gomes
José Carlos Pereira de Carvalho
Marcos Puglisi de Assumpção
International Sales Manager: Antonio Cleubis de Campos

Products: Freight wagons. Barber stabilised bogies; draftgears; couplers; cast steel wheels and components.

Metre-gauge hopper wagons for grain transportation, 80 m³ capacity, 80 tons glw, delivered to CVRD, Brazil, in 1984-85 by Engesa-FNV

Tank car for gasoline and alcohol transportation, 83.7 m³ capacity, 100 tons glw, delivered to Fepasa, Brazil, in 1987 by Engesa-FNV

242 MANUFACTURERS / Freight vehicles

Constitution: The company was formed in 1943 to manufacture freight wagons and has diversified to include production of couplers, yokes, bogies, and cast steel-wheels among its railway industry range. The plant covers an area of over 100 000 m².

Ferrostaal
Ferrostaal AG

PO Box 101265, Hohenzollernstrasse 24, 4300 Essen, Federal Republic of Germany

Telephone: +49 201 818 01
Cable: Ferrostaal, Essen
Telex: 0857100

Directors: Dr Hans Singer
Dr F Graf von Ballestran
Helmut Julius
Dr Klaus von Menges
Heinz Staudinger
Gerhard Thulmann

Products: Freight wagons, including special designs; inspection and service trolleys for track and overhead maintenance and track installation; bogies for freight wagons, rail-mounted cranes and special trolleys; components of rolling stock such as wheels, axles, assembled wheelsets, bearings, suspensions, couplers.

Ferrosud
Ferrosud SpA

PO Box 94, Via Appia Antica Km 13, 75100 Matera, Italy

Telephone: +39 835 222841
Cable: TF222841 Ferrosud
Telex: 812525 fersud i
Telefax: +39 835 217137

Chairman: Corrado Fici
Managing Director: Angelo Palmieri

Export Sales: Claudio Mannucci (Breda)

Products: Freight wagons; all types of bogie; intermodal and bi-modal systems.

Recently the company obtained from Italian Railways (FS) contracts covering: 240 hopper wagons of 70 m³ capacity; 50 Type Saadkms low-floor wagons; and 150 low-floor articulated wagons (Alpin Express) in course of delivery in 1990-91.

Other recent contracts have included orders from Intercontainer and RENFE for, respectively, 260 and 100 two-axle transcontainer flat wagons to operate at up to 120 km/h on Spanish broad-gauge and standard gauge track.

Pursuing its research into intermodal systems the company has developed and designed an 'amphibian' vehicle which it terms Sistema Bimodale. This consists of a road semi-trailer which is mounted on a standard Type Y25 Lssi bogie for rail movement. The coupled ends of the adjoining trailers are carried on a single bogie when units are formed into a train. The system has been improved (second generation) to automate the coupling operation which now takes only 3 minutes per unit. The prototype set of five vehicles, delivered to FS in July 1987, has been converted to second-generation standard and is in service operation. The company recently obtained from RENFE an order for 20 Bimodale units, built to the Spanish gauge.

Constitution: Ferrosud was set up in 1963 for the manufacture and marketing of railway rolling stock and production began in 1968. Export sales are handled either directly by the company or through Breda Construzioni Ferroviarie. The Company is 100 per cent owned by EFIM through the Gruppo Ferroviario Breda.

Fiat
Fiat Ferroviaria SpA

Piazza Galateri 4, 12038 Savigliano (CN), Italy

Telephone: +39 172 2021
Telex: 201234 fiatsv
Telefax: +39 172 202 426

Chairman: Renato Piccoli
Managing Director and General Manager: Giancarlo Cozza
Deputy General Manager and Project Manager: Pierantonio Losa
Sales Manager: Andrea Parnigoni

Principal subsidiaries: Costruzioni Ferroviarie Colleferro
Elettromeccanica Parizzi

Products: Freight wagons; bogies and components.
Recent contracts include an order for 120 refrigerated vans from Interfrigo.

Finsam
A/S Finsam International Inc

Bygdoey Allé 23, PO Box 3065, 0207 Oslo 2, Norway

Telephone: +47 2 441860
Telex: 78050
Telefax: +47 2 558705

Wood-chip containers by Finsam

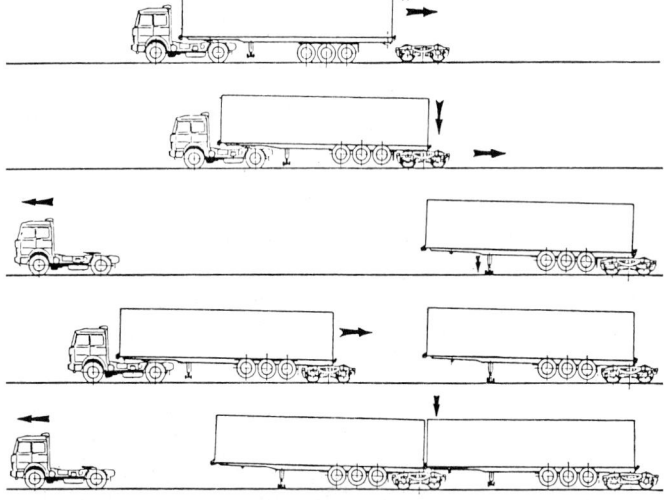

Operating principle of Ferrosud 'Sistema Bimodale'

'Sistema Bimodale' units in rail mode

'Sistema Bimodale' unit in road mode

Type Saagss articulated intermodal unit by Ferrosud

Freight vehicles / **MANUFACTURERS** 243

President: P R Samuelsen
Export Director: K E Jensen

Products: Refrigerated containers, refrigerated swap-bodies, wood-chip and reefer containers, refrigeration and heating systems.

Firema Consortium

Head office: Corso di Porta Romana 63, 20122 Milan, Italy

Telephone: +39 2 5465708
Telefax: +39 2 5460133

President: Dr Ing Giorgio Regazzoni
Board Members: Avv Dino Marchiorello
                   Dr Giorgio Fiore
Procurator: Prof Ing Francesco Perticaroli
Export Manager: Dr Ing Maurizio Fantini

(For full list of member companies, see Firema entry in Locomotives section)

Products: Freight cars.

Fuji Car
Fuji Car Manufacturing Co Ltd

28 Hachiman-cho, Minami-ku, Osaka 542, Japan

Telephone: +81 6 213 2711
Telex: 5225279 fujosk j

President: Tetsuhiro Nishi
Vice President: Junichi Takano
Export Sales: Kazuo Okazaki

Products: Freight cars, ladle cars, bogies, road trailers and tank lorries.

Goninan
A Goninan & Co Ltd

PO Box 21, Broadmeadow, New South Wales 2294, Australia

Telephone: +61 49 69 9250
Cable: Platinum, Newcastle
Telex: A28061
Telefax: 049 69 9250

Chairman: D A W Thomson
Chief Executive & Director: John Fitzgerald
General Manager, Railway Products Division: Barry Henshaw
Engineering & Sales Manager, Railway Products Division: Anthony Finnegan

Products: Freight wagons; and fabricated rail bogies.

GOŠA
SOUR Industrija GOŠA
Rolling Stock Manufacturing Division

Head office: Industrijska 70, 11 420 Smederevska Palanka, Yugoslavia
Sales office: Goša Commerce, Sitnička 39, 11 000 Belgrade

Telephone: +38 26 32 022
Cable: Goša Smederevska Palanka
Telex: 11 684
Telex (sales): 12605

Chairman: Momir Pavlićević
Managing Director: Miodrag Bajčić
Export Sales: Slavko Djorić

Products: Tank wagons; refrigerated cars; and special-purpose wagons.

Graaff
Graaff Kommanditgesellschaft

Postfach 160/180, 3210 Elze 1, Federal Republic of Germany

Telephone: +49 5068 18 204
Cable: Graffwaggon, Elze

Goninan 76-tonne payload Austen steel coal car for SRA New South Wales, designed using finite element analysis; mounted on GPS 25-tonne axleload rigid frame bogies manufactured under licence from Gloucester C & W, UK

Greenville aluminium-bodied hopper car

Telex: 927168, 927251
Telefax: +49 5068 18 197

Managing Director: Dipl Ing Wolfgang Graaff
Sales and Marketing Director: Dipl Ing Dieter Matthies
Sales Director, Rolling Stock: Ing Eberhard Miehlke

Products: Containers; railroad rolling stock; road vehicles; plywood van bodies; sandwich panels.

Constitution: Founded in 1914.

Greenville Steel Car Company
Subsidiary of Trinity Industries Inc

60 Union Street, Greenville, Pennsylvania 16125, USA

Telephone: +1 412 588 7000
Cable: Greencar

Vice President, Freight Car Sales: W C Newby
Manager, Sales: A C Snyder

Products: Railroad freight cars of all types, with coal and auto-rack cars a speciality.

Constitution: Formed in 1910 as the Greenville Metal Products Co, the present name was adopted in 1914 when the company first undertook repair of freight wagons. In 1916 the first new wagons were built and this has been the major activity since, combined with extensive repair work and supply of replacement parts.

In December 1986 the company's manufacturing facilities were acquired by Trinity Industries Inc.

The Gregg Company, Ltd

15 Dyatt Place, PO Box 430, Hackensack, New Jersey 07602, USA

Telephone: +1 201 489 2440
Cable: Greggcar Hackensack NJ
Telex: 219216; 134320
Telefax: +1 201 592 0282

Main works: Gregg/Metalsines (Companhia de Vagões de Sines), SARL, 7521 Sines Codex, Portugal

Chairman: R T Gregg
President: H Ross

Products: Covered and open wagons, mineral wagons, refrigerator wagons, tank wagons, wagons for transport of road vehicles, container wagons, bulk powder wagons, flat wagons, ballast and aluminium wagons, conventional and self-steering bogies for freight and passenger vehicles.

Gunderson
Gunderson Inc

4350 Northwest Front Avenue, Portland, Oregon 97210, USA

Gunderson Maxi-Stack III

244 MANUFACTURERS / Freight vehicles

Telephone: +1 503 228 9281
Telex: 36 0672
Telefax: +1 503 242 0683

COB: C Bruce Ward
President: William A Furman
Chief Engineer: Gary S Kaleta

Products: Freight cars. A principal product is the Maxi-Stack III which utilises the 125-ton truck articulated stack-car configuration. The Maxi-Stack III can handle 20, 24, 40, 45 or 48 ft containers in all wells, and any size container from 40 to 53 ft on the top level.

Another product is the Twin-Stack container car, an articulated five-platform vehicle for double-stacked COFC operation. The lightweight platforms, each approximately 35 000 lb, are formed of deep computer-designed side sills braced by floor trusses on which the containers rest. Adapting devices at each bulkhead, easily operated by personnel from ground level, allow containers of 48 ft as well as 40 and 45 ft to be stacked securely on the upper level. The lower level can accommodate a single 40 ft or two 20 ft containers.

Leading particulars of Twin-Stack
Length overall of 5-unit car: 265 ft 1½ in
Width overall: 9 ft 11½ in

Gunderson Twin-Stack car for double-stack COFC operation

Hawker Siddeley
Hawker Siddeley Canada Inc

Head office: 7 King Street East, Toronto, Ontario M5C 1A3, Canada
Main works: Trenton Works Division, Trenton, Nova Scotia
Marketing office: PO Box 130, Trenton, Nova Scotia B0K 1X0

Telephone: +1 902 752 1541
Cable: Hawsidcan, Toronto
Telex: 019 36510

Chairman: Peter Baxendell
President: R F Tanner
Director of Marketing (Freight Wagons): R C Frost

Products: Railway freight and tank cars of all types; wheels and axles; bogies; railway castings.

Constitution: Hawker Siddeley Group plc, UK, has a 59 per cent interest in the company; the remaining interest is held by public shareholders.

Herederos de Ramon Mugica
Herederos de Ramon Mugica SA

Barrio de Ventas s/n, PO Box 14, 20300 Irún, Spain

Telephone: +34 43 62 90 22
Cable: Herem
Telex: 36 195
Telefax: +34 43 62 26 79

Chairman: Juan O Ohlsson
Director: José R Jusué
Sub Directors: Luis Múgica
Iñigo Saldãna

Export Sales: Juan O Ohlsson
José R Jusué

Products: Tank wagons for liquefied gases and any kind of chemicals and alimentary liquids; hopper wagons for granulated chemical products and cereals; bulk powder wagons with compressed air discharge system; tank containers; standard type wagons such as container flats, high-sided wagons etc; welded construction Y 21 L bogies, 22.5-tonne axle-load prepared for 1435 mm and 1668 mm gauges with interchangeable axles.

Recent contracts include 120 90-tonne wagons for bulk cement; 30 bulk powder wagons for RENFE; 27 30 ft tank containers for styrene; 200 articulated three-bogie passenger vehicles for RENFE; 20 Gran Confort-

5800 ft³ plastic pellet car for CGTX/Dow

Type Y21L bogie, 22.5 tonnes axleloading, prepared for 1435–1668 mm-gauge interchange of axles by Ramon Mugica

Tank wagon with insulation and internal heating for caustic soda transport

90-tonne soda carbonate hopper wagon

Freight vehicles / **MANUFACTURERS** 245

Spoil wagon for use with Channel Tunnel boring machines by Howden

Two-axle piggyback car for Trailer Train, USA by Hyundai

type bogies for RENFE passenger vehicles; 400 Type Y 21 L bogies (22.5-tonne axle load) for RENFE wagons; six tank wagons for chloro; one prototype automatic discharge hopper wagon for coal.

Howden
James Howden & Co

Old Govan Road, Renfrew, Scotland PA4 0XJ

Telephone: +44 41 886 6711
Telex: 778929
Telefax: +44 41 886 7578

Managing Director: M C H Penfold

Products: Special-purpose wagons.

Hudson
Robert Hudson SA (Pty) Ltd

Van Dyk Road, Benoni 1500, PO Box 299 Benoni 1500, South Africa

Telephone: +27 11 915 2410/13, 915 3410/13
Cable: Raletrux
Telex: +27 11 75 0329
Telefax: +27 11 915 2413

Chairman: W R Hudson
Managing Directors: M E Adams, H A Brooke, P J M Hoeben (Sales)

Products: Surface and underground ore transportation wagons.
  Hudson surface ore hopper wagons are used extensively in the South African gold, platinum and coal industries where the need for rapid discharge is a high priority. Special wagons for the transportation of limestone, iron ore, chrome ore and pulp tank wagons are designed and manufactured to customers' requirements.
  Wagons from 1 to 30 tonnes for the transportation of ore underground offer continuous loading and automatic continuous discharge, combined with low tipping forces and strength of design.

Hyundai
Hyundai Precision & Ind Co Ltd

Head office: Hyundai Building, 140-2, Gye-Dong, Chongro-ku, Seoul, Republic of Korea
Postal address: KPO Box 1677, Seoul

Telephone: +82 2 719 0649
Telex: 23238, 23720 hdpic k
Telefax: +82 2 719 0741

Works: 621 Deokjeong-Dong, Changwon, Kyungnam
Telephone: +82 551 82-1341/50
Telex: 53744 hdpic k

Chairman: Mong Koo Chung
President: Ki Chyul Yoo
Senior Vice President: Kyung Wook Kim

Products: General freight wagons, special freight wagons.

Imesi
Imesi SpA
(Industrie Metalmeccaniche Siciliane)
A member of the Breda Railway Group

Contada Olivelli Pistone, 90044 Carini, Palermo, Italy

Telephone: +39 91 8668677
Cable: Imesi-SpA, Carini
Telex: 910113 imisi i

Chairman: Giuseppe Capuano
General Manager: Angelo Palmieri

Products: All types of freight wagons.

Inta-Eimar
Industrias de transdportes y almacenamientos

General management and commercial department: PO Box 5059, Poligono Industrial de Malpica, Calle D, Zaragoza 50016, Spain

Telephone: +34 76 57 17 85, 57 28 92
Telex: 58 055 conte e
Telefax: +34 76 57 20 91

Products: Dry cargo containers of box, open-top, side-door, high-cube, half-height and many other types to CSC, UIC and TIR specifications. Reefer and insulated containers with or without clip-on clip-off system to CSC, UIC, TIR and ATP specifications. Steel and stainless steel tank containers with or without insulation to meet CSC, UIC, TIR, ADR, RID and IMCO specifications, and for all kinds of hazardous products. Gantry cranes for railway yards, container cranes, general loading port cranes, bulk unloading cranes, slewing deck cranes, portal deck cranes, special crane bridges and all kinds of spreaders. Road trailers (insulated and reefer) and chassis.

Kalmar
Kalmar Verkstads AB

PO Box 943, S-39129 Kalmar, Sweden

Telephone: +46 480 62600
Cable: Kvab, Kalmar
Telex: 43029
Telecopier: +46 480 18975

Chairman: Sven Arnerius
Managing Director: K Harry Eriksson

Products: Freight wagons, special wagons (eg for installation and maintenance of overhead wiring).

Kawasaki
Kawasaki Heavy Industries Ltd, Rolling Stock Group

Head office: World Trade Centre Building, 4-1 Hamamatsu-cho 2-chome, Minato-ku, Tokyo, Japan

Telephone: +81 2867 3 0022
Cable: Kawasaki Heavy, Tokyo
Telex: 22672, 26888, (domestic) 242-4371

40-ton container park crane by Inta-Eimar

Inta-Eimar spreader

MANUFACTURERS / Freight vehicles

Type 425 R tank wagon for liquid chlorine by Kolmex

Kolmex Type 416 V ballast wagon for Polish State Railways (PKP)

Type 623Z six-axle 12-wheel flat wagon by Kolmex

Works: 1/18 Wadayama-Dori 2-chome, Hyogo-ku, Kobe
Telephone: +81 78 671 5021

2857-2, Naka Okamoto, Kawachi-cho, Kawachi-Gun, Tochigi Pref
Telephone: +81 3 435-2589

Chairman: Zenji Umeda
President: Kenko Hasegawa
Executive Vice Presidents: Renzo Nihei
Yutaki Onishi
Director (Rolling Stock): Masahiko Ishizawa

Products: Freight cars; containers.

Keller
Keller SpA

Via Francesco Guardione, 3, 90139 Palermo, Italy

Telephone: +39 91 586322
Telex: 911062 kelldg i
Telefax: +39 91 582784

Chairman: Dr Ing Giovanni Salatiello
Managing Directors: Dr Maurizio Salatiello
Dr Alfonso De Simone
Dr Graziella Viale

Main works: Via Maltese 147/149, Palermo
Via della Ferrovia 2/A, Palermo
Via Ugo La Malfa 61, Palermo

Associated company: Keller Meccanica SpA, Villacidro (Cagliari), Italy

Products: Freight cars of all types; bogies for freight cars; overhead line installation, maintenance and inspection cars; special purpose vehicles.

Kilo-Wate
Kilo-Wate Inc

A subsidiary of Georgetown Railroad Company

PO Box 798, Georgetown, Texas 78627-0798, USA

Telephone: +1 800 531 5006
Telex: 025 776 445 tcs kilowt

Products: The Legaloader III weigh-as-you-load device.

Kinki Sharyo
The Kinki Sharyo Co Ltd
Kinki Rolling Stock Manufacturing Co Ltd

Head office and Tokuan factory: 3-9-60, Inada Shinmachi, Higashi Osaka City, Osaka 577, Japan

Telephone: +81 6 746 5240
Cable: Kinsha Fuse
Telex: 5278911
Telefax: +81 6 745 5135 (GIII)

Tokyo office: 527 Nippon Bldg, Ohtemachi, Chiyoda-ku, Tokyo 100

Telephone: +81 3 270 3431
Telex: 222 3105
Telefax: +81 3 245 0238 (GIII)

President: Seihei Katayama
Executive Vice President: Akira Kitamori
Senior Managing Director: Hisatsugu Sugano

Managing Director: Yasuji Yukawa
Export Sales Director: Takumi Ono

Products: Refrigerator cars; freight cars; industrial wagons and equipment.

Kolmex
Foreign Trade Enterprise Co Ltd

Mokotowska 49, 00-542 Warsaw, Poland

Telephone: +48 22 28 22 91, 28 39 06
Cable: Kolmex, Warsaw
Telex: 813270; 813714
Telefax: +48 22 295879

Managing Director: Aleksander Gudzowaty
Sales Directors: Aleksander Kociszewski
Wieslaw Husarski
Tomasz Suprowicz
Elbieta Zaleska

Products: Freight wagons; containers.

The Polish rolling stock industry has the capacity and experience to manufacture all types of freight wagon, including special-purpose vehicles. Among those presently manufactured is the Type 420 V four-axle, self-discharging wagon for granular foodstuffs, particularly cereals. Loading is through a top filling hatch, which is closed by flap covers, and unloading through eight bottom-discharge ports, which are manually opened. The opening and closing mechanisms of the discharge ports are at the car side; each pair of covers is individually controllable.

The Type 418 V self-discharging dump car has air-operated, 45-degree body tilting to either side of the track. Tare weight is 28 tonnes and payload capacity 51 tonnes or approximately 31 m³. Car length between coupling faces is 12.52 m, bogie wheelbase 1.8 m and distance between bogie pivot centres 7.5 m. Maximum operating speed is 100 km/h and minimum curve radius negotiable 75 m.

The Type 431 R tank wagon is designed for transport of liquefied sulphur. Its construction is in conformity with the UIC, OSShD, RIV, and PKP regulations. The pressureless tank is of all-welded construction. In its upper part, placed at its transversal axis, there is a manhole of 500 mm diameter for filling and top-discharge, but discharge through a three-way draining cock is also possible.

The Type 425 R tank wagon for transport of liquid chlorine has a capacity of 47 m³ and payload of 55 tonnes. Filling and unloading of the tank is carried out from the top by means of two automatic valves with 40 mm nominal diameter. The tank conforms to UIC and RIV prescriptions.

The Type 416 V ballast wagon is designed for the transport of crushed stone ballast at a speed of 100 km/h and for measured discharge, which can be interrupted at any time. The ballast may be discharged either between the rails or across the whole width of the permanent way. The mechanisms for metering and spreading the discharge are pneumatically-operated from a panel located on the wagon platform. The wagon is equipped with two automatic blockage systems to avoid an ill-timed discharge of ballast.

The Type 419R concentrated nitric acid tank wagon is 12.34 m long over buffers, with a bogie wheelbase of 2 m and distance between bogie pivot centres of 6.8 m. The aluminium tank has a capacity of 49 tonnes or 41 m³. Tare weight is 23.5 tonnes. Maximum operating speed is 100 km/h and the minimum curve radius negotiable 75 m.

Constitution: Kolmex acts as sole exporter of railway motive power and passenger and freight stock manufactured in Poland, and purchaser of imported equipment. Between 1947 and 1989 Kolmex export production has totalled 2356 locomotives and other traction units, 9250 passenger coaches and emus, 201 374 freight wagons and 33 377 containers. Kolmex has exported rolling stock units and containers to 44 countries.

Konstal
Steel Construction Works Konstal

ul Metalowcow 7, 41-501 Chorzów, Poland

Export sales: Kolmex, 49 Mokotowska, 00-542 Warsaw

Telephone: +48 22 411051-58
Cable: Konstal, Chorzów
Telex: 0312451

Products: Electric and storage battery mine locomotives and special-purpose freight wagons; heavy-duty well cars and platforms.

Korea Shipbuilding & Engineering
Korea Shipbuilding & Engineering Corporation

Head office: 1, 1-Ka Jongro, Jongro-ku, Seoul, Republic of Korea
CPO Box 1520, Seoul

Telephone: +82 2 739 5577
Telex: 23669; 23415 ksecs
Telefax: +82 2 733 8113

Freight vehicles / **MANUFACTURERS** 247

Busan factory: 370-6 Tadae-dong, Saha-ku, Busan
PO Box 74, Busan

Telephone: +82 51 204 0541
Telex: 53613 ksecs
Telefax: +82 51 204 0626

Chairman: Ryun Namkoong
President: Ho Namkoong
Executive Director: Jong-Chul Mun
Sales Director: Jun Kil Suh

Products: Freight cars, special-purpose rolling stock, bogies, couplers.

Kraljevo
Fabrika Vagona Kraljevo

Kraljevo, Yugoslavia

Telephone: +38 36 21 455
Telex: 17652

Products: Freight wagons of all types.

Krupp Maschinentechnik GmbH

Helenenstrasse, 149, D–4300 Essen 1, Federal Republic of Germany

Telephone: +49 201 363–0
Telex: 857767-0 km d
Telefax: +49 201 32 44 49

Chairman: Dr Ing Gerd Weber
Vice-Chairman, Mechanical Engineering: Dipl.-Ing. Günter Kaes
General Manager, Railway Engineering: Dipl.-Ing. Heinrich Gerdsmeier
Manager, Marketing: Dipl. Vw Horst Boege

Products: Multi-axle heavy-load carriers, e.g. Schnabel cars up to 800 tonnes payload, torpedo ladle cars and other special cars for steel mills.

KSFB
VEB Kombinat Schienenfahrzeugbau
Member of Vereinigter Schienenfahrzeugbau der DDR e V

Adlergestell 598, GDR 1183 Berlin

Telephone: +37 68100
Telex: 112267

Products: General management of all wagon and equipment manufacturers which belong to the VEB Kombinat Schienenfahrzeugbau.

K T Steel
K T Steel Industries Pvt, Ltd

Directors office: 9 Altamount Road, Bombay 400 026, India

Telephone: +91 22 36 35 03
Cable: Metticorail, Bombay
Telex: 11 75649 rail in

India's largest wagon, built in 42 days by K T Steel for conveyance of a Urea reactor: load capacity, 220 tons

Chairman: T K Gupta
Executive Director: V R Gupta

Products: Rolling stock. In addition to supplying wagons for the home market, K T Steel Industries has built mineral wagons for Iranian State Railways and supplied wagon spares to the Sri Lanka Government Railway. The company now specialises in manufacture of special-purpose wagons.

Lagab
Lagab AB

PO Box 209, S-312 01 Laholm, Sweden

Telephone: +46 430 12820
Telex: 38121 lagab s
Telefax: +46 430 12710

Products: Rail-road container transfer system, developed in conjunction with British Rail, which avoids need of cranage; latest development employs 20 ft containers, and is branded MaxiLink by BR, but extension to use of 40 ft containers of all types is possible. A specially-designed road transfer vehicle is fitted with two hydraulic sledges with air bags built in. When positioned parallel to the rail track, the sledges are extended and locked on to locating pins on the container-carrying subframe of a rail wagon. The air bags are inflated to lift the container clear of the railwagon twistlocks. The container is then hydraulically retrieved, and the air bags deflated to position it on the twistlocks of the lorry. Load sensing controls on the lorry adjust the suspension to maintain constant platform height.

Letourneau
Marathon Letourneau Company
Subsidiary of Marathon Manufacturing Company, Longview Division. Marathon Manufacturing is a wholly-owned subsidiary of Penn-Central Corporation

PO Box 2307, Longview, Texas 75606, USA

Telephone: +1 214 236 6500
Telex: 730 371

President: Paul Glaske
Vice President, Sales: Mel Kangas

Products: Gantry cranes and the 'Letro Porter' handling equipment for containers and piggyback trailers.

Liebherr
Liebherr Container Cranes Ltd

Head Office: Killarney, Co Kerry, Ireland

Telephone: +353 64 31511
Telex: 73946 lbhr ei
Telefax: +353 64 31602/32735

UK sales office: Liebherr Great Britain Ltd, Travellers Lane, Welham Green, Hatfield, Hertfordshire AL9 7HW, England

Telephone: +44 7072 68161
Telex: 261271
Telefax: +44 7072 61695

Directors: K Noelke
R Geiler
Secretary: H Brunner

Products: Liebherr Container Cranes Ltd manufactures and sells rail-mounted container handling cranes for ship-to-shore terminals, railway and trucking terminals and storage yards. Sizes, speeds and safe working loads to meet all international tenders and specific customers' requirements.

Macosa
Material y Construcciones, SA

Head office: Plaza de la Independencia 8, Madrid 28001, Spain

Telephone: +34 1 522 4787
Cable: Material, Madrid
Telex: 22168

Works: Herreros 2, Barcelona
Telephone: +34 3 307 05 00; Telex: 52286
San Vicente 273, Valencia
Telephone: +34 6 377 39 00; Telex: 62452
Marqués de Mudela 10, Alcazar de San Juan
Telephone: +34 54 1124; Telex: 23692

President: Eduardo Santos

Lagab MaxiLink container on container flat wagon (*G Freeman Allen*)

Volvo truck with in-built hydraulic transfer sledges for MaxiLink (*G Freeman Allen*)

248 MANUFACTURERS / Freight vehicles

Vice President: Pedro Nueno
Managing Director: Emilio Daroca
Financial Director: José Miguel Olabarria
Rolling Stock Director: Andrés Soler
Export Director: José Sanz

Products: Freight cars.

Mafersa
Sociedade Anönima

Av Raimundo Pereira de Magalhães 230, CEP 05092, São Paulo, SP, Brazil

Telephone: +55 11 261 8911
Cable: Mafersa
Telex: +55 11 83862

Works: Contagem Industrial Works, Rua das Industrias, Parque Sao Joae, CEP 32340, Contagem, Minas Gerais, Brazil.

Chairman: Marcos Ferraz Miranda
Commercial Director: Carlos Roberto Doll
Financial Director: Jose Wellington M de Arauja
Industrial Director: Seijió Ogusku
Commercial Manager: Sergio Mendes Chieco
Export Dept Chief: Edgar Toledo

Products: All-purpose freight cars; underframes for railway cars and steel welded trucks.
Recent contracts include 40 tank cars for CVRD (1990); 50 frameless tank cars for Fepasa (1990).

MAN GHH
MAN Gutehoffnungshütte GmbH
Aktiengesellschaft

Bahnhofstrasse 66, PO Box 11 02 40, 4200 Oberhausen 1, Federal Republic of Germany

Telephone: +49 208 692 1
Telex: 856691 oghhd
Telefax: +49 208 6922887

Main works: MAN GHH Railway Rolling Stock Division Frankenstrasse 150, PO Box 44 01 00, 8500 Nürnberg 44

Telephone: +49 911 18 2632
Telex: 622 291 mn d
Telefax: +49 911 18 2375

Vice President of Railway Rolling Stock Division: Heinz Hennig
Senior Department Sales Manager: Wolfgang Knörle
Senior Department Design Manager: Gerhold Sames

Products: Freight cars, especially open versions and also high-capacity designs; vehicle components; technology transfer; product service.

Maquinista, La
La Maquinista Terrestre y Maritima SA

General offices, technical bureaux and works: Calle Fernando Junoy 2-64, PO Box 94, 08030 Barcelona, Spain

Telephone: +34 3 345 5700
Cable: Maquinista, Barcelona
Telex: 54539 maqui e
Telefax: +34 3 345 6958

President: D Miguel Sãenz de Viguera y Aizpurua
Commercial Manager: Pere Solé Raventós
Export Manager: D Javier Masoliver y de Marti

Products: Bogies and freight wagons.

Constitution: Since 1855 La Maquinista has specialised in production of railway equipment. Largest shareholder is the Instituto Nacional de Industria (INI).

Mecanoexportimport

10 Mihail Eminescu Street, Bucharest, Romania

Telephone: +40 0 1198 55
Cable: Mecanex, Bucharest
Telex: 10 269
Telefax: +40 0 106650

Tank wagon by Mafersa

Frameless tank wagon by Mafersa

Products: Freight wagons.
Mecanoexportimport is the export sales company for the Romanian railway supply industry. Freight wagons are manufactured by Arad, Caracal and Drobetu Turnu Severin Works.

Metalsines
Companhia de Vagoes de Sines SARL

Apart 18, 7521 Sines Codex, Portugal

Telephone: +351 69 633081/4
Telex: 13814 metals p
Telefax: +351 69 633090

Commercial Director: F Barroso
Technical Director: C Dias

Products: Freight wagons of various types to AAR or UIC standard, or to client's railway specification, for any gauge or loading. Components available with Metalsines rolling stock or separately include the Gregg/Barber-Metalsines stabilised bogie and the self-steering Gregg/Scheffel-Metalsines bogie. Recent contracts executed have comprised ballast wagons, two-deck car-carrier wagons, flat wagons (curtain-sided) and hopper wagons.
Recent products include a 'speedy discharge' bottom-door hopper wagon. The wagon can be supplied with a choice of four methods of door operation.

Metalsines 'speedy discharge' hopper wagon

The doors are operated by a beam mounted in the wagon's centre sill. Automated discharge of wagons on the move at speeds up to 10 km/h is possible by use of a wayside device to activate a pneumatic control on the wagons; or, at a lower speed, the wagon doors' air control can be manually activated. Alternatively, the door-opening air mechanism can be connected to a land supply. Finally, the doors can be arranged for manual operation.

Miner Railcar Services Inc

PO Box 2208, East Cherry Street, New Castle, Pennsylvania 16102, USA

Telephone: +1 412 658 9061
Telefax: +1 412 658 9061

Vice President and General Manager: R M Giallonardo
Vice President: Gabe Kassab

Associated companies
Miner Railcar Services
PO Box 34, Darlington, Pennsylvania 16115
Telephone: +1 412 827 8121
Telefax: +1 412 827 2961

Products: Custom-designed steel mill and railroad speciality equipment; freight wagon reconstitution and repairs.

Constitution: The company is comprised of two divisions. The Railroad Car Division engages in the manufacture of new freight cars and remanufacture and contract repair of used equipment. Miner Railcar Services Parts Corporation remanufactures freight car parts and has available all types of new and used freight car components.

More Wear
More Wear Industrial Holdings Ltd

PO Box 2199, Harare, Zimbabwe

Works: 53 Plymouth Road, Southerton, Harare, Zimbabwe

Telephone: +263 4 67802
Telex: 24110 MORWER ZW
Telefax: +263 4 67807

(For personnel and subsidiary company information, see entry in Powered Passenger Vehicles section)

Products: Freight cars, high-sided wagons, tankers, flat-deck container wagons, box wagons, Gloucester rubber suspension bogies, ride control bogies, and railway spares.
Recent products have included:
For Tanzania-Zambia Railway Authority: 25 fuel tank wagons (1988); For the National Railways of Zimbabwe: 100 HSI wagons (1990); For Uganda: 300 covered wagons (1989); and for Malawi: 22 fuel tank wagons (1990).

Moss
George Moss Ltd

PO Box 136, Mount Hawthorn 6016, 461 Scarborough Beach Road, Osborne Park 6017, Western Australia, Australia

Telephone: +61 4468844
Cable: Gemco, Perth
Telex: 92645
Telefax: +61 4463404

Products: Mineral wagons.

National Steel Car
National Steel Car Ltd

Head office and works: PO Box 2450, 602 Kenilworth Avenue, North Hamilton, Ontario L8N 3J4, Canada

Telephone: +1 416 544 3311
Telex: 061 8255
Telefax: +1 416 544 7614

Stand alone double-stack well car by National Steel Car

Lightweight spine car by National Steel Car

MANUFACTURERS / Freight vehicles

Telescopic hood, twin-unit wagon with hoods open by Niesky

Twin-unit Type Laadks flat wagon for Transwaggon AG, Switzerland by Niesky

Sales office: Suite 1011, 1155 Boulevard Rene-Levesque, Montreal, Quebec H3B 2J2

Telephone: +1 514 866 7461
Telex: 052 4488
Telefax: +1 514 866 1692

President and Chief Executive Officer: R W Cooke (Hamilton)
President & Chief Operating Officer: J W Nelham
Vice President, Sales: A E Kallio (Montreal)
Vice President, Finance: M G Nichols (Hamilton)
Vice President, Operations: A van Halderen (Hamilton)
General Sales Manager: A Wilson (Hamilton)

Products: Freight cars of all types; industrial, mining and speciality cars and car parts.
  Current car equipment includes a lightweight design of spine car with the capacity to carry two fully loaded 20 ft containers on each platform. Platforms are connected into a five-unit car by articulated connectors with shared bogies.
  Also available a 'stand-alone' design of well car for double stack service of fully loaded containers. Wells are designed to accommodate up to a 49 ft container with a 53 ft container on top. Units are complete with an individual brake system, complete set of bogies and are connected by solid drawbars.
  Recent development has included a two-compartment 2900 cu ft capacity cylindrical covered hopper car with sparger unloading system in slurry service.
  National Steel Car's design and manufacturing capabilities are well suited to the production of all standard freight cars as well as the development of custom designs to suit specific applications.

Constitution: National Steel Car Ltd has been building railway cars since 1913 and is a wholly-owned subsidiary of Dofasco Inc, Hamilton, Ontario.

Nelcon
Nelcon BV

Doklaan 22, PO Box 5303, 3008 AH Rotterdam, Netherlands

Telephone: +31 10 297955
Telex: 28003
Telefax: +31 10 297955

Managing Director: Ir T E M Kocken
Export Manager: W G Van Seters

Products: Ship-to-shore container gantry cranes, container stacking cranes (rail-mounted and rubber-tyred), barge loading container cranes, container ship-to-shore cranes for feeder vessels, rail/road container transfer cranes, straddle carriers stacking two-, three- and four-high, multi-purpose cranes, mobile cranes, railway rescue cranes. Recent orders have included deliveries to the Netherlands and Belgium.

Niesky
VEB Waggonbau Niesky
Member of VEB Kombinat Schienenfahrzeugbau and of Vereinigter Schienenfahrzeugbau der DDR e V

18-20 Strasse der Befreiung, 8920 Niesky, German Democratic Republic

Telephone: +37 40
Telex: 26516

Products: Open and covered goods wagons, flat wagons with and without stanchions, double-deck auto-carrier wagons, special-purpose brown coal wagons for the iron and steel industry, bogies.

Constitution: The plant took up repair of passenger, post and baggage cars in 1946, but since 1950 has specialised in freight wagon construction, a sector in which it currently offers more than 100 different types.

Exports: Schienenfahrzeuge Export-Import Volkseigener Aussenhandelsbetrieb der DDR, Oetztaler Strasse 17, 1100 Berlin

Nippon Sharyo
Nippon Sharyo Ltd

Head office: 1-1 Sanbonmatsu-cho, Atsuta-ku, Nagoya, Japan

Telephone: +81 52 882 3315
Telex: 447 3411
Telefax: +81 52 882 3337

Tokyo office
Telephone: +81 3 668 3330
Telex: 252 2095
Telefax: +81 3 669 0238

Works: Nippon Shanyo Toyokawa-Warabi, 2-20 Honohara, Toyokawa City, Aichi Prefecture

President: Osamu Shinohara
Senior Vice President: Eiichi Okumura
Managing Director, Chief of Export Division: Kenji Nishimura
General Manager (Rolling Stock Division, Overseas Dept): Kazuhiko Iwadare

Subsidiary companies
Nissha Washino Steel Co Ltd
Nippon Sharyo USA Inc

Products: Freight cars of all types including tank cars, containers, tractors and trailers.

O & K
O & K Orenstein & Koppel AG

Head office: Karl-Funke-Str 30, 4600 Dortmund 1, Federal Republic of Germany

Telephone: +49 231 1760 1
Cable: Orenkop, Dortmund
Telex: 822 222
Telefax: +49 231 1725 03

Main works: West Berlin, Butzbach, Dortmund, Ennigerloh, Hattingen, St Ingbert-Rohrbach, Kissing, Lauf, Lübeck, Déols and Sarreguemines (France), Keighley (England), Batavia (New York, USA), Contagem (M.G., Brazil)

Chairman: Dr Karl-Friedrich Golücke
Personnel Director: Dr Heiko Körnich
Marketing Director: Friedrich Kreigenfeld

Principal subsidiary: O & K Orenstein & Koppel Ltd, Watford, Northampton NN6 7XN, England

Products: Goods wagons; bi-modal excavators (rail and road); fork-lift trucks; escalators and autowalks.

OFV
Officine Ferroviarie Veronesi SpA

Lungadige A Galtarossa 21, 37100 Verona, Italy

Telephone: +39 45 595022
Telex: 481017

President: Giacomo Galtarossa
General Manager: Adriano Mattalia

Products: Freight wagons.

Oleo
Oleo Pneumatics Ltd (UK)
Oleo International Holdings Ltd (Overseas)

Walcote, Blackdown, Leamington Spa, Warwickshire CV32 6QX, England

Telephone: +44 926 421116/8
Telex: 311458
Telefax: +44 926 450273

Managing Director: F M Thompson
Sales & Marketing Director: R W Elliott
Technical Director: D G Williams

Products: Freight cushioning units for sliding sill or sliding platform wagons. The Oleo Type 18 long-stroke hydraulic unit is widely used in Europe. Located in a centre pocket of the flat wagon, protection is afforded over a wide container weight range keeping decelerations to less than 2 g at 15 km/h. The Oleo Type 18 conforms to UIC 529.

OMS
Officina Meccanica della Stanga
Member of Firema Consortium

Corso Stati Uniti 3, 35100 Padua, Italy

Telephone: +39 49 8700866
Cable: OMS, Padova
Telex: 430218 omspd i
Telefax: +39 49 76 06 82

Oleo Type NC908 hitch cushion

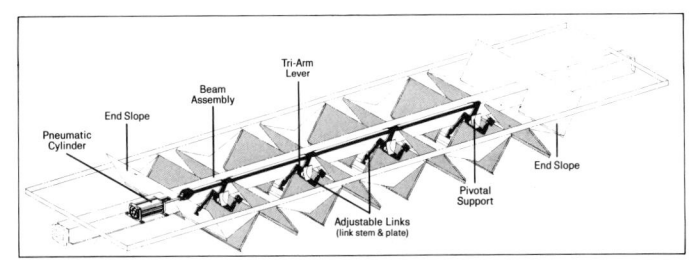

Ortner RD II single-lever bottom door discharge system

Ortner RD II aluminium coal car

Chairman: Dr Dino Marchiorello
Vice-Chairman: Ing Aldo Iaia
Managing Director: Dr-Ing Ugo Soloni

Products: Freight wagons. Recent deliveries have included 49 Type Hbillns wagons for Italian Railways.

Ortner
Ortner Freight Car
An affiliate of Trinity Industries Inc

PO Box 640, 5300 Dupont Circle, Suite A, Milford, Ohio 45150, USA

Telephone: +1 513 248 0300

President: John Lowry
Director of Sales: Robert C Ortner Jr

Products: Freight cars and components, with coal cars a speciality.

Constitution: In November 1986 Trinity Industries Inc reached agreement with Avondale Industries Inc for acquisition of the manufacturing facilities of Ortner Freight Car.

Orval
Ateliers d'Orval SA

Route de l'Ombrée, BP 64-18202 Saint-Amand-Montrond CEDEX, France

Telephone: +33 48 96 07 39
Telex: 760428
Telefax: +33 48 96 50 97

President: Jean Magonty
General and Commercial Manager: André Potier

Products: Freight wagons of all types, mobile brake testing equipment.

Pakistan Railways Carriage
Pakistan Railways Carriage Factory

PO Box 286, Rawalpindi, Islamabad, Pakistan

Telephone: +92 51 860253, 860349
Cable: Carfac, Rawalpindi
Telex: 54135 prcfi pk

Works: Sector 1-11, Khayaban-e-Sir Syed, Islamabad

Chairman: S M Jafar Wafa
General Manager, Railway Manufacture: Vacant
Chief Mechanical Engineer, Railway Manufacture: Zaki Ahmad Siddiqui
Chief Officer, Carriage Factory: Mohammad Fahiem-ud Din

Products: Freight wagons of all types for any gauge.

PEC
The Projects & Equipment Corporation of India Ltd
A Government of India Enterprise

Hansalaya, 15 Barakhamba Road, New Delhi 110 001, India

Telephone: +91 11 331 3542, 331 4419, 331 3356
Cable: Pecoind
Telex: 31 65199, 31 65256
Telefax: +91 11 331 5279

Chairman: S N Malik
Executive Director: R Khosla
Chief Marketing Manager (Railway Equipment Division): M Chatterji

Products: Freight wagons of any type and design for various gauges; spares for export.
PEC has also exported over 8500 wagons to various countries such as Uganda, Tanzania, Zambia, Hungary, Sri Lanka, Burma, Bangladesh, South Korea, Malaysia, Nigeria, Poland, Sudan, East Africa, Iran, Yugoslavia, Hungary, and Viet-Nam. Most recent contracts have been 300 wagons for Uganda Railway and 100 wagons for Zambia Railway.

Constitution: PEC was formed in 1971 as a corporation under the Indian Ministry of Commerce to handle and boost the export of railway equipment and engineering goods. The Indian wagon industry, with companies such as Burn Standard Co Ltd, Braithwaite & Co Ltd, Texmaco Ltd, Cimmco Ltd and Jessop & Co Ltd, has a combined manufacturing capacity of 25 000 wagons per annum and is a regular supplier to the Indian Railways.

Peiner
Peiner Port Equipment & Cranes
Division of Noell GmbH

PO Box 1649, 3012 Langenhagen, Federal Republic of Germany

Telephone: +49 5 11 77 04-0
Telex: 9 24 682
Telefax: +49 5 11 77 04-302

Products: Container stacking cranes (either rail-mounted or rubber-tyred); straddle carriers; spreaders; harbour cranes for handling general cargo and bulk material; shipyard cranes; tower cranes.

Perry
Perry Engineering
Boral Johns Perry Industries Pty Ltd

Railway Terrace, Mile End South, South Australia 5031, Australia

Postal address: Box 1838, GPO Adelaide, South Australia 5001

Telephone: +61 8 352 1777
Cable: Sperry, Adelaide
Telex: 82493
Telefax: +61 8 234 1896

Sales Manager: W J Baker
Market Development Manager: F T Howlett

Products: Railway rolling stock.

Constitution: Perry Engineering is an engineering operation of Boral Ltd. In 1986 Johns Perry became part of the Boral Group, one of Australia's largest and most diversified companies.

Portec
Portec Shipping Systems Division

300 Windsor Drive, Oak Brook, Illinois 60521, USA

Telephone: +1 708 573 4600
Telefax: +1 708 573 4604

General Manager, Shipping Systems Division: George A McLean

Products: Rail car tie-down systems and intermodal and freight car components; standard COFC container pedestals with optional positive locks for transportation of HAZMAT; special container locks and pedestals for TOFC/COFC skeleton (spine) railcars; portable and permanent bridge plates for TOFC and auto racks; winches, chain, cable and webbing tie-down components for railroad flat cars and autoracks.

Powell Duffryn Standard Ltd
(Formerly Gloucester Railway Carriage & Wagon Co Ltd)

Cambrian Works, Maindy, Cardiff CF4 3XD, Wales

Telephone: +44 222 626000
Telex: 4 97233
Telefax: +44 222 692174

Managing Director: R E Morgan
Director and General Manager: A B Harding
Sales Director: R A Clark

Products: Freight wagon designs; bogies; suspension systems; Miner doorgear.

Peiner tubber-tyred container stacking crane

252 MANUFACTURERS / Freight vehicles

51-tonne pressure-discharge wagon for powders by Powell Duffryn Standard

102-tonne wagon for steel coil by Powell Duffryn Standard

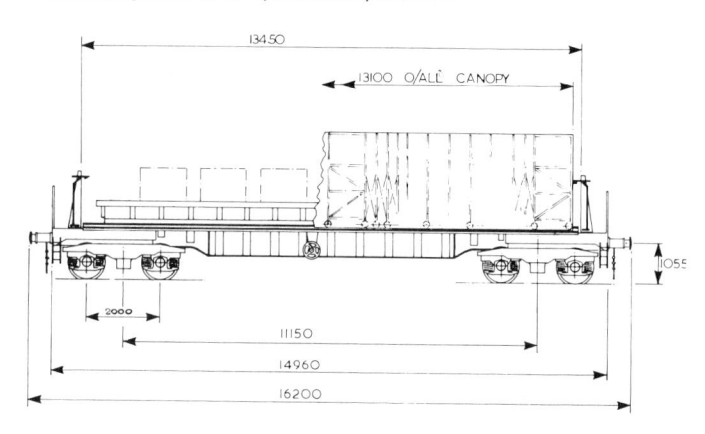

General arrangement of 102-tonne steel coil wagon

Constitution: First known as the Gloucester Wagon Co Ltd, the company was formed in 1860 and two years later built the first iron wagon in the United Kingdom. Since 1969 the company has concentrated on the design of railway wagons and the design and manufacture of bogies and vehicle suspensions. Gloucester is a licensee for Miner Enterprise Inc for discharge door mechanisms and Tecspac elastomeric springs. From April 1990, the company has been trading as Powell Duffryn Standard Ltd although the bogies previously produced by the Gloucester Railway Carriage & Wagon Company will have the trade name of Gloucester.

Powell Duffryn Standard Ltd
(Formerly Powell Duffryn Wagon Company Limited)

Head office: Cambrian House, Maindy, Cardiff CF4 3XD, Wales

Telephone: +44 222 621 621
Cable: Wagons, Cardiff
Telex: 497233
Telefax: +44 222 692 174

Main works: Cambrian Works, Maindy, Cardiff CF4 3XD

Chairman: W J Franklin
Managing Director: R E Morgan
Engineering Director: D Hughes
Financial Director: T D B Rosser
Works Director: J C Dymock
Sales Director: R Buttigieg

Principal subsidiary: Gloucester Railway Carriage & Wagon Co (qv)

Products: Manufacture, maintenance and repair of railway rolling stock, bogies and primary suspension units.
Since April 1990 the company has been trading as Powell Duffryn Standard Ltd.

Powell Duffryn Standard Ltd
(Formerly The Standard Railway Wagon Co Ltd)

Head office and main works: Green Lane, Heywood, Lancashire OL10 1NB, England

Telephone: +44 706 64135/9
Cable: Wagons, Heywood
Telex: 63327
Telefax: +44 706 624213

Chairman: W A Gamble
Managing Director: L T Reddy
Director and General Manager, Commercial: R E Parker

Products: Freight cars of all types.

Constitution: The works at Heywood have been building railway wagons for over a century. In 1989 the company was acquired by Powell Duffryn and from April 1990 has been trading as Powell Duffryn Standard Ltd.

Prati-Vazquez Iglesias
Prati-Vazquez Iglesias SA

B Rivadavia 4402, 1822 Valentin Alsina, Prov Buenos Aires, Argentina

Telephone: +54 1 241 4101/4186
Telex: 122586

Products: Freight wagons for bulk commodities and piggyback.

102 tonnes glw in-line tipper wagon by Powell Duffryn Standard

102 tonnes glw Class A tank car by Powell Duffryn Standard

Freight vehicles / MANUFACTURERS

Procor plastic pellet hopper of 5838 ft³ capacity

102 tonnes glw open wagon for Trans-Manche Link by Procor

FNA nuclear flask transporter wagon for CEGB/BR by Procor

Price
A & G Price Ltd

Private Bag, Thames, Auckland, New Zealand

Telephone: +64 9 399 526
Cable: Priceco, Thames
Telefax: +64 9 392 819

Chief Executive Officer: D Gatland
Resident Manager: T W Just
Production Manager: B J O'Sullivan

Products: Freight wagons.

Constitution: This company stems from a foundry and workshop set up at Onehunga near Auckland in 1868 by two brothers, Alfred and George Price.

Procor
Procor Ltd, Rail Car Division

2001 Speers Road, Oakville, Ontario L6J 5E1, Canada

Telephone: +1 416 827 4111
Telex: 06 98 2241
Telefax: +1 416 827 0800

Chairman: S H Bonser
President and Chief Executive Officer: Gordon C Mills
Vice President, Operations: M C Parker
Vice President, Marketing: A Stremecki
Manager, Maintenance Services: J S McKechnie
Chief Engineer: S Wong
Fleet Manager: G Mancini

Products: Tank and special-purpose freight cars.

Procor Limited designs and manufactures tank cars and freight cars for a great variety of products, for lease to shippers in Canada. Procor operates and maintains the largest fleet of privately-owned railway freight and tank cars (over 17 000) in Canada.

Procor plastic pellet hopper of 5838 ft³ capacity

Procor Engineering
Procor Engineering Ltd
A member of the Marmon Group

Horbury, Wakefield, West Yorkshire WF4 5QH, England

Telephone: +44 924 271881
Telex: 556457
Telefax: +44 924 274650

Managing Director: Ralph W J Bennett
Financial Controller: Keith R Brown
Sales & Marketing Manager: Alan E Andrews

Products: Railway freight rolling stock.

The company designs, manufactures and refurbishes a complete range of railway freight rolling stock, manufacture passenger coach bodyshell assemblies, road tankers, Class 1 pressure vessels, and high quality stainless and mild steel fabrications. It has gained quality assurance approvals to British Standard 5750 Parts 1 and 2, and can offer a full design and manufacturing service to these standards.

Recent and ongoing major rail contracts have included 128 passenger dmu bodyshells (1987-89); 100 Class 60 locomotive body shells for Hawker Siddeley Brush (1989-91); 34 FNA nuclear flask carrying wagons for the Central Electricity Generating Board/BR (1988-89); 22 102-tonne aggregate hopper wagons for ARC Ltd (fitted with low track force bogie) (1990).

Pullman Standard
Division of Trinity Industries

200 South Michigan Avenue, Chicago, Illinois 60604, USA

Telephone: +1 312 322 7336

Vice President, Marketing: Gerald F Lahey
Vice President, Fleet Operations: Mitchell R Gillenwater
Vice President, Sales: Alan G Eades

Products: Freight cars.

Constitution: In 1979 Pullman announced its withdrawal from the railroad passenger car business, devoting its business to freight cars and parts. Pullman Incorporated was purchased by Wheelabrator-Frye Inc, which established Pullman Transportation Co in 1981.

In 1983 the Pullman Transportation Co sold its car-building facilities, including workshops at Butler, Pennsylvania, and Bessemer, Alabama, and also use of the title 'Pullman Standard Manufacturing', to Trinity Industries of Dallas. Trinity Industries now has an exclusive licence to manufacture and market Pullman intermodal car designs in the Americas, but Pullman Transportation Company has retained car manufacturing rights in Europe and Asia.

Qiqihar
Qiqihar Rolling Stock Works

Zhonghua East Road, Qiqihar, Heilongjiang 161002, People's Republic of China

Telephone: Qiqihar +86 52981
Telex: 87126 qrsw cn

General Manager: Wei Minghai
Chief Engineer: Qiu Shiyu
Sales & Marketing: Wu Jingyu

Products: Freight wagons, chiefly Type C62A open and Type P62 box cars, both with roller bearings, for Chinese Railways.

The Type C62A open wagon is for use in transporting coal, coke, mine ore, machinery, steel, timber and goods packed in bags. The wagon body is a welded

Type C62A open wagon

254 MANUFACTURERS / Freight vehicles

fabrication of low carbon steel (corrosion-resisting steel can be used to the customer's requirement. The brake system is conventionally comprised of: a GK triple valve; a 356 mm × 254 mm brake cylinder; a double-acting automatic slack adjuster; a 'load and empty', manually-regulated brake device; and a chain-type, single-shoe vertical hand brake. Drawgear consists of top-operating automatic couplers with AAR contour and expansion ring friction draftgears. The cast steel bogie has a constant friction damping device and rolling bearings.

The Type P62 box car has a body of welded fabrication from low carbon steel (corrosion-resisting steel may be adopted if required) with top wood shielding. Brake system, drawgear and bogies are the same as on the Type C62A open wagon.

Recent and ongoing contracts include the construction of 7 7600 new wagons and 46 cranes; 43 cranes repaired for the Chinese railway system (1989); 200 hopper wagons for Botswana and spare parts for East Germany.

Rautaruukki Oy
Transtech Division

Head office: Kiilakiventie 1, PO Box 217, SF-90101 Oulu, Finland

Telephone: +358 81 327 711
Telex: 32109
Telefax: +358 81 327 196

Main works: SF-88200 Otanmäki, Finland

Chairman and President: Mikko Kivimäki
Vice President, Transtech Division: Seppo Sahlman
Executive Manager, Product Design and Development, Transtech Division: Jorma Lukkari
Executive Marketing Manager, Transtech Division: Veli-Matti Nopanen

Principal subsidiary companies
Rautaruukki (UK) Ltd
Merevale House, Parkshot, Richmond, Surrey TW9 2RW, England
Telephone: +44 81 948 8177
Telex: 295743
Telefax: +44 81 948 5716

Rautaruukki (Deutschland) GmbH
Gragenberger Allee 87, D-4000 Düsseldorf 1, Federal Republic of Germany
Telephone: +49 211 682616
Telex: 172114075
Telefax: +49 211 689 842

Products: Various types of special-purpose freight wagons; covered, open, mineral, tank, intermodal and wagons for automobile transport. Recent sales include container flat wagons, intermodal, multi-purpose, mineral fertiliser, timber, liquid sulphur and automobile transport wagons. So far Rautaruukki Oy Transtech Division has delivered its products to the USSR, the home market and other West European countries.

Constitution: The activity of Rautaruukki Oy, one of the leading steel firms in Scandinavia, in railway rolling stock began in 1985, when the highly automated and mechanised works specially designed for wagon production was inaugurated. The factory has a production capacity of 3000 freight wagons annually and it employs more than 1000 people. The first deliveries were to meet the growing demand for special freight wagons of the USSR. Today Rautaruukki's Transtech Division is increasingly engaged in the design and manufacture of special freight wagons for Western markets. In addition to rolling stock, Rautaruukki Transtech Division manufactures a wide range of special containers and other transportation equipment for intermodal traffic, ports and terminals.

Ray Smith
Ray Smith Demountables Ltd

Botolph Bridge, Oundle Road, Peterborough PE2 9QP, England

Telephone: +44 733 63936
Telefax: +44 733 47090

Type P62 box car

Liquid sulphur tank wagon

Multi-purpose intermodal wagon

Covered auto-transporter

Freight vehicles / **MANUFACTURERS** 255

Chairman: R W B Smith
Sales Director: D J Browning

Products: Low-cost container handling equipment for low-volume sites, consisting of four hydraulic jack legs, operated by four independent manual pumps; a four-man team is needed to lock the legs in position and operate the pumps simultaneously.

Demountable bodies carried on truck-trailer outfits in which the DAF towing truck has a high-stow variation of cantilever tail-lift, are the key items of a high-productivity transport package put together by the Ray Smith Group for the national pallet-supply organisation of GKN Chep. The outfits are contract-hired from BRS Northern and can be transported by rail.

Reggiane
Officine Meccaniche Italiano SpA

PO Box 431, 27 Via Vasco Agosti, 42100 Reggio Emilia, Italy

Telephone: +39 522 5881
Cable: Reggiane
Telex: 530665
Telefax: +39 522 588243

Chairman: Dr Giuseppe Ivan Bonora
General Manager: Vincenzo Giuliano

Products: Freight wagons; rolling stock components.
Reggiane has been engaged in railway locomotives and rolling stock since 1905. Present capabilities include: the construction of special wagons and crane equipment for railborne vehicles and manufacture of machines for the removal and laying of track.

Remafer
Société de Construction et de Réparation de Matériel Ferroviaire

Head office & works: rue d'Alger, BP 23, 51051 Reims CEDEX, France

Telephone: +33 26 07 96 68
Telex: 830645
Telefax: +33 26 02 21 38

Chairman & Managing Director: Gérard Bouthelou
Commercial Manager: Joachim Lagall

Subsidiary company: Marly Industrie
AFD (Ateliers Ferroviaires de Dakar)
CAT (Compagnie Africaine de Transports)

Products: Special-purpose, small and medium series of freight wagons, including cement tank wagons with fluidised and pulsed-air discharge; automatic-discharge coal wagons; and heavy-load 20 axle wagons. The company also engages in engineering studies.

RFS Engineering
RFS Engineering Ltd

PO Box 192, Hexthorpe Road, Doncaster DN1 1PJ, England

Telephone: +44 302 340700
Telex: 547296
Telefax: +44 302 340693

Managing Director: P Page
Technical Director: D W Theyers
Finance Director: B J Pierce
Director: E Harrison
Commercial Manager: M Rowe

Products: Manufacture, repair, conversion and service of freight rolling stock and components.

Recent and ongoing contracts include the conversion of MEA wagons for British Railways Board (BRB) (1989); wagon repair for British Industrial Sand (1989); wagon repair for MoD (1989); new wagon design/build for RMC (1990); establishment of in-field service support for NACCO (1990); rebody HAA wagons for BRB (1990); design/build prototype steel-carrying wagons for BRB (1990); bogie test vehicles RFSP for TML and GEC Alsthom (1990).

Ray Smith demountable bodies carried on truck-trailer outfits

Prototype 19 m steel-carrier for BRB by RFS Engineering Ltd

Norfolk Southern 'Triple Crown' RoadRailer train

RoadRailer
A subsidiary of Duchossois Industries Inc and an affiliate of Thrall Car Manufacturing Co

Head Office: 26th and State Streets, Chicago Heights, Illinois 60411, USA

Telephone: +1 312 757 5880

Marketing Office: 60 Arch Street, Greenwich, Connecticut 06830, USA

Telephone: +1 203 629 4692

MANUFACTURERS / Freight vehicles

Vice-President, International Marketing:
B L Hedrick

Products: The RoadRailer family of intermodal freight vehicles. RoadRailers are bi-modal vehicles capable of being pulled over the highway by a conventional road tractor or operated in railway unit trains pulled by a locomotive.

Recently, RoadRailer designed a new addition to its product line named RefrigerRailer. The RefrigerRailer is a 48 ft × 8 ft 6 in Mark V trailer featuring a refrigeration unit with a 75-gallon fuel tank to operate the cooling unit. With 3136 ft^3 of capacity and payloads in excess of 45 000 lb, the prototype RefrigerRailer will be the first truly intermodal 'reefer'-type trailer available to shippers of perishable goods.

In 1988 the Burlington Northern Railroad was demonstrating a Mk V dump trailer known as a DumpRailer. The 40 ft unit has a 52 yd^3 capacity and was specifically designed for use in hauling bulk commodities.

In 1988 the company unveiled a new rail transition vehicle named the CouplerMate. It provides a method of joining RoadRailer trailers with their unique coupling system to railroad equipment equipped with conventional couplers. Previously the transition was supplied only by the 45-ft AdapterRailer. The new unit's compact 16 ft length offers simplicity and versatility at a lower cost greatly enhancing Road-Railer terminal operations.

RoadRailer has opened a new facility in Harvey, Illinois, to provide fast distribution of spare parts to customers. This facility also houses a new assembly line dedicated to Mk V high performance rail bogies.

Testing has begun to explore the feasibility of operating RoadRailer trailers behind trains of articulated, low-slack conventional equipment such as double-stack cars. The testing has been performed at the AAR test facility at Pueblo, Colorado, under the principal sponsorship of Burlington Northern Railroad. Initial results appear favourable.

In addition to producing the RoadRailer vehicles, the RoadRailer organisation offers a complete support capability for the operation of the RoadRailer system, including operation of the rail/highway terminals, and maintenance of the equipment.

Through its subsidiary, RailFreight Systems, New Zealand Railways has signed a licensing agreement for the production of Mark V trailers and high performance rail bogies. RoadRailer's engineering group is working with their counterparts at RailFreight to modify the RoadRailer technology to meet New Zealand's rail and highway requirements. An initial fleet of 20 units was to appear in 1989. The New Zealand pact marked RoadRailer's first international licensing agreement. Negotiations were underway for similar arrangements with freight carriers and equipment builders in Europe, the Far East, and other regions, and in 1989 the first European licensing agreement was concluded with Arbel-Fauvet-Rail of France.

RSD
A Division of Dorbyl Ltd

PO Box 229, Boksburg 1460, South Africa

Telephone: +27 11 52 8276
Cable: Dorlonsa, Johannesburg
Telex: 4-29576
Telefax: +27 11 52 5714

Chairman: M J Smithyman
Marketing Manager: D L Cope

Products: Freight wagons, guards' vans, steam heat vehicles.

A South African Transport Services (SATS) requirement for special-purpose wagons of low tare and high payload ratio has led to several new designs. One example is the covered and lengthened Type FP-1 wagon with modular constructed body sides, using pressed corrugated panels, with joints covered by pressed stanchions. The self-powered refrigeration unit circulates air at fixed temperature through ducting in the newly designed mechanical refrigeration wagon.

The emphasis is now on bulk handling wagons of all-welded design which will also meet the Association of American Railroads (AAR) Standard. One of the specifications is that the underframe horizontal forces be roughly twice that of previous requirements. The first of these wagons, Type OZL, is for conveyance of palletised boxes of fruit for export. To facilitate loading and unloading, four sliding plug doors are provided per side, exposing any quarter of the wagon at one time.

A major breakthrough in payload/tare ratio is the iron ore gondola wagon, Type CR-1; this has a ratio of almost 4:1, whereas previous wagons normally had a ratio of 2:1. It has Scheffel High Stability (HS) bogies and air brakes, so that it is possible for the first time in South Africa to run unit trains of up to 220 wagons. It is designed with a minimum axleload of 25 tonnes, where previously the maximum was 18 tonnes.

Other recent productions are: frameless tank wagons of the parallel cylinder type and of jumbo type, which is enlarged in the centre to reduce length, while keeping the centre of gravity low; a covered grain hopper capable of discharging a 40-tonne load in 20 seconds; a motor car transporter capable of transporting eight vehicles per wagon; a bulk sugar wagon with payload capacity of 52 tonnes; a refrigerated meat/fish wagon, which is the largest covered freight vehicle in use in South Africa; and bulk powder wagon, Type XBJ-12, with three pots, capable of discharging approximately 2 tonnes of cement per minute by pneumatic discharge.

Constitution: The company is a subsidiary of Dorbyl Ltd, which was established in South Africa as Wade & Dorman Ltd, Structural Engineers in 1909. The manufacture of rolling stock was begun in 1944.

Santa Matilde
Cia Industrial Santa Matilde

Export sales and head office: Av Koeler 260, Petrópolis 25.685, Rio de Janeiro, Brazil

Telephone: +55 21 242 43 8656
Telex: +55 21 36694/5/6 cism br

Products: Freight wagons; bogies.

Constitution: Companhia Industrial Santa Matilde, founded in 1916 was initially engaged in mining manganese ore. In 1926 it began repairing railway passenger and freight cars. Manufacture of rolling stock and electric train units began in 1946.

Scandia-Randers A/S
ABB Scandia A/S

Toldbodgade 39, DK 8900 Randers, Denmark

Telephone: +45 6 86 425300

Type SCL-4 motor vehicle transport wagon; tare 25.24 tonnes, load 11.36 tonnes

Bolster wagon mounted on four bogies for the transport of 24.4 m lengths of material by RSD

Telex: 65 145 scanas dk
Telefax: +45 6 86 415700

President: Henning Balle Kristensen
Vice President: Ragnar Sjöström
Export Manager: Kjeld Hvid

Products: Freight wagons.

Schienenfahrzeuge Export-Import
Volkseigener Aussenhandelsbetrieb der DDR

Member of Vereingter Schienenfahrzeugbau der DDR e V

Ötztaler Strasse 5, 1100 Berlin, German Democratic Republic

Telephone: +37 48040
Telex: 114372

Products: Freight wagons; rail vehicle equipment; railway cranes.

Constitution: Sole exporter of all rail vehicles and vehicle equipment built in the German Democratic Republic.

SCIF
Société Cherifienne du Matériel Industriel et Ferroviaire

PO Box 2604, Allée des Cactus, Aïn Sebaa, Casablanca, Morocco

Telephone: +212 35 3911, 35 1093
Telex: 26802 m

Products: Freight wagons. The company's freight car production, which includes special-purpose types to UIC specifications, now exceeds 4500 units.

Schindler
Schindler Carriage & Wagon Co Ltd

4133 Pratteln, near Basle, Switzerland

Telephone: +41 61 825 91 11
Telex: 968010
Telefax: +41 61 825 9205

Managing Director: P Piffaretti
Technical Director and Director of Works: H Knecht
Sales Manager: R Meury

Products: Freight cars.

SEMAF
Société Générale Egyptienne de Matériel des Chemins de Fer

Ein Helwan, Cairo, Egypt

Telephone: +20 2 782358; 782177; 782716; 782306; 630097
Telex: 23342 semaf un
Telefax: +20 2 788413

Chairman: Eng T El-Maghraby
Technical Director: Eng A Rahik
Commercial Manager: A Farid
Administrative Manager: D Maged
Works Manager, Coach & Metro: Dr Eng L Melek
Works Manager, Wagon & Bogie: Eng S El-Sherbini

Products: Freight wagons of all types. Recent output has included 134 65-tonne covered hopper wagons for the bulk transport of grain for Egyptian National Railways; also 60-tonne container flat cars, power cars, passenger cars, second class air-ventilated air-conditioned cars with two side package units or seven roof units, rail car trailers, trams and metro cars. Recent output has included metro units for Heliopolis, trailer cars for Egypt's National Authority for Tunnels; power cars, first, second and third class coaches for Sudan Railways.
Recent contracts include 40 air-conditioned sleeper coaches for Egyptian National Railways to be supplied in 1991.

SFC-Daval
Société Francaise du Conteneur

Main office and factory: Z I de Grévaux Les Guides, 59750 Feignies, France

Telephone: +33 27 62 99 75
Telex: 160 136

Marketing and sales: Immeuble Elysees La Défense Cedex 35, 92072 Paris La Défense

Telephone: +33 1 4767 83 83
Telex: 614 850 daval

Chairman: Gérard Hillion
Marketing and Sales Director: Bruno Chabert
Sales Manager: Jean Richard

Products: Dry cargo and refrigerated ISO containers in steel and aluminium dry and refrigerated vans; TIR tilt-platform trailers for intermodal movements; TIR tilt cargo and refrigerated swapbodies or inland containers (UIC Class II and III).

SGI
Società Gestioni Industriali SpA

48 Via Adriano Cecchetti, 62012 Civitanova Marche, Italy

Telephone: +39 733 72 918/770 555
Cable: Rotabili, Civitanova Marche
Telex: 560 896
Telefax: +39 733 761538

General Manager: Dott Ing Giorgio Caputo
Sales Manager: Dott Attilio Iezzi

Products: Freight cars of all types, pressure tank cars for compressed gas and acids; refrigerator cars; special tanks for motor vehicles.

Constitution: In 1957 SGI took over the business of Costruzioni Meccaniche A Cecchetti, which had been wound up previously, having been operating since 1892.

Articulating bogie of 12-axle low-platform 'Rollende Landstrasse' piggyback wagon by S-G-P

S-G-P Verkehrstechnik GmbH

Head office: PO Box 103, Brehmstrasse 16, 1110 Vienna, Austria

Telephone: +43 1 222 7469
Cable: Esgepe, Vienna
Telex: 131891, 132574
Telefax: +43 1 222 745148

General Manager: Dr Herbert Ziegler
Sales Director: Dipl Ing Heinz Butz
Technical Director: Dipl Ing Roland Himmelbauer

Products: Freight wagons, special goods wagons, low-platform wagons; tramways, underground railway stock and suburban trains; high capacity goods wagons, sliding wall wagons, flat wagons for transporting tracked vehicles, rotary slide side-discharge wagons, silo wagons, tank wagons, saddle-bottomed self-discharge coal wagons, pocket wagons for semi-trailers and containers, carrier trucks for transporting wagons of a different gauge.
The company's range includes several types of low-platform piggyback wagons with small-wheeled, four-axle bogies and movable headstocks allowing roll-on/roll-off loading over end ramps.
A recent addition to the range is the 12-axle low-platform wagon for Transalpine piggyback traffic. It is an articulated, two-sectional vehicle incorporating three 4-axle bogies and is able to carry trucks and tractor/trailer units with a total weight of up to 44 tons plus 10% overload, a maximum width of 2600 mm, and a height of up to 4 m. Hinged headstocks that can be swung aside enable ro/ro loading and discharge over end ramps.

Constitution: S-G-P Verkehrstechnik comprises two works: one in Vienna and one in Graz. They are an enterprise within Austrian Industries Maschinen-und Anlagenbau Holding AG.

SM-Strick RailTrailer
Strick Corporation

US Highway No 1, Fairless Hills, Pennsylvania 19030, USA

Telephone: +1 215 949 3600
Telex: 84 3412
Telefax: +1 215 949 4778

Sambre Et Meuse, SA
Division Grande Exportation
Tour Aurore, 92080 Paris La Défense Cedex, France

Telephone: +33 1 47 76 44 07
Telex: 620161
Telefax: +33 1 47 78 61 85

US office: S M Industrial Metal Products, Inc, 227 East 56th Street, New York, NY 10022, USA

Products: RailTrailer bi-modal vehicle. The RailTrailer is a highway trailer with detachable rail bogie assembly. It is adaptable to any trailer length, from 20 to 53 and even 57 ft, though the companies are initially promoting 48 and 53 ft dry vans. RailTrailer is being marketed by a new Strick subsidiary, Strick Lease Intermodal.

SNAV
Société Nouvelle des Ateliers de Venissieux

40 Boulevard Henri Sellier, 92150 Suresnes, France

Telephone: +33 1 45 06 15 74
Telex: 611468

Works: 4 Chem du Génie, 69631 Venissieux

Telephone: +33 78 00 86 44
Telex: 340603F

Products: Freight wagons, mineral wagons, wagons for transport of road vehicles, tank wagons, container flats; containers.

Soma
Soma Equipamentos Industries SA

Head office: Parque Industrial Mariano Ferraz, Avenida Soma 700, Sumaré, São Paulo, Brazil

Telephone: +55 11 192 73 1000
Telex: 019 1923
Telefax: +55 11 192 73 2472

President: Victorio Walter dos Reis Ferraz
Executive Vice President: Victorio Mariano Ferraz
Vice President Operations: Guilherme Marcondes Ferraz

258   MANUFACTURERS / Freight vehicles

Commercial: Carlos Marcondes Ferraz
Products: Freight cars; tank cars; refrigerator cars; ore cars; ingot cars; hopper cars; car building, repairing, maintenance and leasing.

Constitution: The company was founded in 1929 and was the first company in South America to manufacture freight cars. It has specialised in the development of refrigerator cars and tank cars which are leased to various transport concerns.

Soulé
Soulé SA

PO Box 1, 65200 Bagnères-de-Bigorre, France

Telephone: +33 62 95 07 31
Cable: Soulé, Bagnères de Bigorre
Telex: 530 179
Telefax: +33 62 95 55 65

Chairman: Arnaud de Boysson
Executive Vice-President: Guy Thomas

Products: Insulated and mechanically refrigerated wagons; postal vans.

Stag
Stag AG

Industriequartier, 7304 Maienfeld, Switzerland

Telephone: +41 85 9 19 02
Telefax: +41 85 9 59 77

Managing Director: J Küttel

Principal subsidiary: Stag GmbH, D-6636 Felsberg, West Germany

Products: Bulk transport wagons with pneumatic discharge.
    Recent contracts include orders from Swiss Federal Railways and Portuguese Railways.

Strick
Strick Corporation
Strick Lease Intermodal Co

225 Lincoln Highway, Fairless Hills, Pennsylvania 19030, USA

Telephone: +1 215 949 3600
Telex: 84-3412
Telefax: +1 215 949 4778

President, Manufacture: Frank Katz
President, Intermodal Leasing: Charles Willmott

Products: Full range of dry freight containers, piggyback trailers and container chassis.

Strojexport
Strojexport Company Ltd

PO Box 662, Václavské náměstí 56, 113 26 Prague 1, Czechoslovakia

Telephone: +42 2 2131
Telex: 121 671, 122 604
Telefax: +42 2 2323084, 2323092

General Director: Ing Josef Levora
Deputy General Director: Stanislav Vrabec
Commercial Director: Ing František Forgács

One of 75 wagons supplied to Swiss Federal Railways in 1988 by Stag

Type Eaos wagon for bulk commodity transport by Strojexport

Products: Strojexport handles all transactions for the export of freight rolling stock built by Czechoslovak wagon works, also components such as Y25 bogies, couplings, etc.
    Czechoslovak-manufactured freight wagons have been delivered to customers in Europe, Africa, Asia and America. At present Czechoslovak wagon works' main production lines are manufacturing an extensive series for Czechoslovak Railways and for railways in the German Democratic Republic, Poland and Hungary. The wagons are mostly bulk and merchandise carriers. Depending on design complexity, 7000 to 10 000 wagons are manufactured each year. Some types have been manufactured in great quantity. Production of Type Fals self-tipping wagons with 75 m^3 capacity has reached more than 14 000 units; of Type Gags covered wagons more than 6700; and of Type Es two-axle wagons more than 7500. Output of Type Eas high-sided wagons has passed 11 000 units and a further 10 000 will be manufactured before 1990. Deliveries to Polish Railways (PKP) have been headed by 5250 four-axle wagons of Type Eaos for transportation of coal, ore etc; and 300 wagons of the same type were delivered to Hungary for MÁV in 1989. In parallel with the above production other wagon types are manufactured in smaller series for foreign clients.
    Production of wagon parts is an important part of production in Czechoslovak Wagon Works. In the wagon factory in Poprad a modern workshop specialises in production of two-axle bogies of Type Y25, which are manufactured on automatic machines. This enables output of 10 000–12 000 bogies yearly.

Strømmens (NEBB)
A/S Strømmens Vaeksted

PO Box 83, 2011 Strømmen, Norway

Telephone: +47 6 809600
Cable: Verkstedet, Strømmen
Telex: 71 551
Telefax: +47 6 809601

Managing Director: P Hauan
Technical Director: J Jacobsen

Products: Freight cars of all types.

Constitution: The company was established in 1873 for the manufacture of railway rolling stock and is now the only car builder in Norway. It took over the rolling stock building activities of A/S SKABO in 1960 and A/S HOKA in 1968. In 1979 the company became a subsidiary of NEBB, the Norwegian company of the ASEA-Brown Boveri Group.

Tafesa
Construcción y Reparación de Material Ferroviaria

Carretera de Villaverde a Vallecas 16, Madrid 28041, Spain

Telephone: +34 1 91 798 0550
Telex: 42283 tran e
Telefax: +34 1 91 798 0961

General Manager: Michel Magermans Lange

Products: All types of freight rolling stock; special containers; bogies; covered wagons; cars transportation wagons; dual-purpose container carrying; piggyback wagons; air discharge cement wagons; ventilated wagons with sliding doors; spheroidal graphite cast; power line masts; vans.

Constitution: The group comprises the Tafesa, Fabesa, Transervi, Ifasa and Imedexsa companies.

Talbot
Waggonfabrik Talbot

Postfach 1410, Jülicherstrasse 213-237, 5100 Aachen, Federal Republic of Germany

Telephone: +49 241 18210
Cable: Talbot, Aachen
Telex: 08 32 845
Telefax: +49 241 1821214

High-capacity, aluminium sliding-wall wagon, loading volume 158.7 m^3, loading clearance area 11 × 2.8 m with one half-wall withdrawn, tare 29 tonnes

Products: Freight vehicles. In addition to conventional stock, Talbot develops, designs and builds goods wagons with special features, such as: high-capacity wagons; sliding wall wagons with or without movable partitions, wagons with spread-type hoods and wagons with swivelling or rolling roof; self-discharging wagons for transport of bulk materials, eg saddle-bottomed wagons, wagons with rotary slide valves and bottom self-dischargers (for the transport of bulk material sensitive to moisture these wagons can be equipped with a swivelling roof); intermodal wagons for transport of road vehicles, swop or demountable bodies and containers, such as low-level 'Rolling Highway' wagons, 'pocket' wagons and cushioned container carriers; special wagons for steel mills and mines, such as wagons with or without telescopic hoods for transport of coils, wagons for transport of plates, wagons for transport of glass panes, garbage vans, mail and luggage vans, service wagons for building, ballasting and maintenance of tracks; containers and swop or demountable bodies with folding side walls.

The company's recent production has included two-axle wagons capable of operation at 140 km/h. Recent development work, with impending German Federal completion of high-speed new lines for use with mixed-traffic in mind, has included production of designs for disc-braked bogie covered wagons capable of operation at 160–200 km/h.

Taylor
Taylor Machine Works Inc

Louisville, Mississippi 39339, USA

Telephone: +1 601 773 3421
           +1 201 722 4442 (international)
Telex: 6858111
Telefax: +1 601 773 9646

Products: Container and trailer handling trucks, offering a wide range of lift attachments: top pick; side pick; top and bottom pick; bayonet; twistlocks; fork-mounted; carriage mounted or suspended by chains; for use with 20 ft to 44 ft empty or laden containers, conventional or refrigerated. Attachments range from 12 500 lb to over 90 000 lb capacity. The truck is designed specifically as a container or container/trailer handler.

Thrall
Thrall Car Manufacturing Co

PO Box 218, Chicago Heights, Illinois 60411, USA

Telephone: +1 312 757 5900
Telex: 721476 duchind ud

Bi-level auto transporter by Tafesa

Chairman: C J Duchossois
President: J C Leath
Vice President, Marketing and Sales: L B Sis
Vice President, International Sales: B L Hedrick

Products: Freight cars.

Thrall is one of the leading designers and manufacturers of freight cars in the US. Its products are used by railroads and shippers to provide low-cost transportation for a wide variety of commodities. In addition, Thrall has entered into a number of technology transfer agreements to allow other rail systems outside the US to benefit from its technology.

Constitution: Thrall Car is a wholly-owned subsidiary of Duchossois Industries, Inc. The company acquired the entire car product line of Whitehead & Kales in 1982, the former United American Company, Cartersville, Georgia in 1983 and the railcar-building business of Portec, Inc in 1984. The latter's car manufacturing plants at Clinton, Illinois and Winder, Georgia were part of the transaction. All plants now operate under Thrall Car's control resulting in a carbuilding capacity of 10 000 cars per year at five plants having eight production lines.

Trailer-Rail
Trailer-Rail Inc

Suite 1306, 680 North Lake Shore Drive, Chicago, Illinois 60611, USA

Telephone: +1 312 642 8338

President: Hugh W Foster

Products: Trailer-Rail, a highway trailer and container piggyback system designed specifically to enable North American railroads to compete for truck hauls of less than 500 miles, was undergoing revenue-earning tests on the Iowa Interstate Railroad in 1987-88. The prototype rail vehicles were built by Thrall Car Manufacturing.

The system uses the highway trailer body or container to connect drop-platform railcars. The front end of one trailer or container and the rear end of another forms a continuum of trailer, railcar, trailer, railcar, etc, making a 15 trailer-length train. Any conventional highway trailer from 28 to 60 ft in length can be carried. A chocking system secures the trailer wheels to the first car and a fixed trailer hitch secures the king pin to the second. Conventional container tie-downs secure the various length containers. A flexible hose continues the standard air brake line between cars. A low-cost ramp is used for loading trailers on or off the railcar drop deck. No expensive lifting equipment or lifting operators are required.

The system's components are completed by the Tractor-Railer, a highway tractor equipped with retractable steel railroad wheels that can both load and unload the trailers and pull a Trailer-Railer train. The cars are equipped with standard railroad couplers and brake system, and can also be pulled by a locomotive or at the end of a regular freight train.

Pocket wagon for top-loading of containers, swap bodies or highway trailers: tare 20 tonnes

MANUFACTURERS / Freight vehicles

Side-discharge flaps of a Type FL wagon are operated by a drill-type machine with friction clutch; the wagon can be fitted with hydraulic or pneumatic-powered operation of the flaps

Type Fal saddle-bottomed wagon with Talbot crankshaft locking gear for bulk transport: load volume 75 m³, tare 25 tonnes

Trailer Train
Trailer Train Ltd

Alliance House, 12 Caxton Street, London SW1H 0QS, England

Telephone: +44 71 1 222 7692
Telex: 916201
Telefax: +44 71 1 222 3736

Transcisco Industries Inc

555 California Street, Suite 2420, San Francisco, California 94104, USA

Telephone: +1 415 477 9700
Telefax: +1 415 788 0583

Chairman & CEO: Mark C Hungerford
Vice-President: Marvin B Hughes
Vice-President: John E Carroll Jr
Chief Financial Officer: Timothy P Carlson
Senior VP, Marketing & Sales: George A Tedesco

Principal subsidiaries:
Transcisco Rail Services Company
Transcisco Trading Co International
Transcisco Tours

Shock absorber-equipped container wagon, tare 20.5 tonnes, with load area length of 14.6 m

Chemical products tank wagon, capacity 66 m³, tare 25.1 tonnes, by Talbot

Products: UNITEMP heating element for tank wagons; UNIFLO unloading device for high-density dry bulk products; Car-Pur state-of-the-art cleaning system for tank wagons and tank lorries; freight and passenger car maintenance and repair.

Recent and ongoing contracts include a joint venture with leasing company Soufinamtrans based in Moscow, USSR. The partnership includes Ministry of Rail and Petrochemicals, Haka Öy of Finland and Transcisco Industries Inc. Soufinamtrans leases UNITEMP-equipped tank wagons in the USSR and Eastern/Western Europe.

Double-stack APL Linertrain unit by Thrall Car

Freight vehicles / **MANUFACTURERS** 261

Alstar 110 short-ton aluminium coal car for unit train operation by Thrall Car

Tri-level auto rack by Thrall Car

107 short-ton aluminium auto-unload hopper car

Lightweight centre-beam lumber products car

Transcisco Rail Services Company
A division of Transcisco Industries Inc

601 California Street, Suite 1301, San Francisco, California 94108, USA

Telephone: +1 415 397 1010
Telefax: +1 415 788 0583

President: John E Carroll Jr
Senior Vice President, Sales: Robert W Gruber
Vice President Engineering: Paul G Hayes
Vice President Operations: William C McDowall

Products: Transcisco Industries is an industrial services company engaged in the maintenance, manufacturing and retrofitting of railroad car equipment. Transcisco's railcar maintenance operation is the largest non-railroad-owned operation of its kind in the US.

Many major railcar owners are looking at refurbished and retrofitted cars as an alternative to new equipment acquisition. Transcisco Rail Services Company (formerly Railcar Maintenance Company-RMC) converts steel coal cars to aluminium bodies. These converted cars have both a higher payload and weigh less than the cars they replace, thus producing economies for the customer.

Transcisco's Uni-Temp technology, which is the basis of a joint venture in the USSR, allows quicker and more uniform heating of temperature sensitive commodities. Uni-Flo technology is applied to covered hopper cars, and expedites unloading of dry commodities, such as flour, starch and sugar.

Reflecting Transcisco Industries' expansion into the cruise train industry, Transcisco's newest activity is in passenger railcar retrofitting and maintenance.

Transit America
Transit America Inc
Freight Car Products Operation

One Red Lion Road, Philadelphia, Pennsylvania 19115, USA

Telephone: +1 215 934 3100

Telex: 834 551 transit am pha
Telefax: +1 215 671 9227

Vice President: Larry H Fort
Manager: Michael J Pavlick
Marketing and Sales: Charles S Vogan

Products: Specialised freight car design.

Trinity Industries
Trinity Industries Inc

2525 Stemmons Freeway, Dallas, Texas 75207, USA

Telephone: +1 214 631 4420
Telex: 5101001867
Telefax: +1 214 689 0501

Vice-President and Director, New Railcar Sales: L Clark Wood

Prototype Trailer-Rail vehicle carries the rear wheels of a 48 ft highway trailer secured to the car by a special chocking system; the rail vehicle (right) carries both the front end of the trailer through the king pin and a 20 ft container secured by conventional container tie-downs

Trailer Train vehicles in road mode, awaiting tractors

MANUFACTURERS / Freight vehicles

Trailer Train vehicles in rail mode (*G Freeman Allen*)

Hi Cube 2000 hopper car

Products: Freight cars of all types, principally hopper, gondola, intermodal, tank and speciality cars. The company's manufacturing facilities (located in Bessemer, Alabama; Greenville, Pennsylvania; Mt Orab, Ohio; Oklahoma city, Oklahoma; and Forth Worth and Longview, Texas) are highly automated, from computer-assisted drafting in the engineering stages to advanced fit-up and welding techniques during manufacture. Trinity Industries, Inc has the greatest capacity in the USA to produce all types of railcars including flats, gondolas, covered hopper and open-top hopper, automobile racks, tank cars, pressure discharge and speciality cars.

Trinity Industries, Inc, headquartered in Dallas, Texas, is a major manufacturer of heavy-metal products within its established business segments of railcars, structural products, marine products, pressure and non-pressure containers and a variety of metal components and other metal products.

'Backpacker' articulated five-well platform unit for container double-stacking and highway trailer carriage

Tuchschmid
Tuchschmid AG

Kehlhofstrasse 54, CH-8500 Frauenfeld, Switzerland

Telephone: +41 54 26 11 11
Telex: 7 64 63 tuag
Telefax: +41 54 22 28 38

Manager: Richard Nägeli
Manager, Transport Systems: Carl Ruch
Sales Manager, Transport Systems: Willi Rossi

Products: Translift system of container transfer, developed in conjunction with Swiss Federal Railways and road hauliers. The system dispenses with independent transfer machines and enables the driver of a road vehicle to achieve a road-rail transfer or vice-versa on his own. The system employs special flat wagons surmounted by rotatable guideways and road chassis equipped with a tilting frame and chain mechanism to slide the containers on and off the wagons.

Power-Flo pressure discharge car

Union Tank
Union Tank Car Co
A member of The Marmon Group of companies

111 West Jackson Boulevard, Chicago, Illinois 60604, USA

Telephone: +1 312 431 3111
Telex: 910 221 4213
Telefax: +1 312 431 5003

President: Sidney H Bonser
Senior Vice President, Marketing: William L Snelgrove

Poly-Flo hopper car

Freight vehicles / **MANUFACTURERS** 263

Trinity Spine Car

Rapid Discharge II aluminium coal car by Trinity Industries

Vice President, Operations: Louis A Kulekowskis
Vice President, Fleet Management: Kenneth P Fischl
Vice President, Sales: Douglas E Edmonds

Products: Steel, stainless steel, and aluminium tank cars carrying liquids, compressed gases; covered hopper cars for plastic pellets and resins.

VeVey
VeVey Engineering Works Ltd

Railway Division: 1844 Villeneuve

Telephone: +33 21 960 42 51
Telex: 453 105 vey ch
Telefax: +33 21 960 42 56

Sales Manager: Fritz Hess

Products: Freight cars, bogies, patented transporter bogies for conveyance of standard-gauge vehicles over narrow-gauge tracks.

Translift container transfer

Waggon Union
Waggon Union GmbH

PO Box 2240, 5902 Netphen 2, Federal Republic of Germany

Telephone: +49 271 702 1
Cable: Waggonunion, Siegen
Telex: 08 72843

Products: Freight cars of all types, covered, open, mineral, tank, refrigerated, and for transport of road vehicles and containers, and fabricated bogies for freight cars.

Constitution: This company was formed in 1971 as a result of the merger between SEAG Waggonbau (of Rheinstahl Transporttechnik) and DWM Deutsche Waggon-und Maschinenfabrik GmbH. Plants are sited at Siegen and West Berlin. Passenger coaches, type ET420 electric trains, underground trains, articulated tramcars and double-deck buses for urban traffic are built in West Berlin, tank wagons, articulated wagons for the automobile industry, ore wagons and bogie well wagons are among the major products manufactured in the Siegen works.

General-purpose 25 000-gallon tank car

High-capacity wagon with sliding roof-and-wall units by Waggon Union

264 MANUFACTURERS / Freight vehicles

Wakamatsu Sharyo
Wakamatsu Sharyo Co Ltd

1 Kitaminato machi, 6-chome, Wakamatsu-ku, Kitakyushu 808, Japan

Telephone: +81 93 761 2331
Telefax: +81 93 761 2335

Products: Freight wagons, specialised steelworks vehicles.

Zastal

ul Sulechowska 4a, 65-119 Zielona Gora, Poland

Telephone: +4868 4241
Telex: 0432101 zas pl
Telefax: +4868 22869

President: Czeslaw Fedorowicz
Vice-President, Engineering: Janusz Kapala
Director, Finance: Mikolaj Kapala
Director, Admin & Materials: Mieczyslaw Marciniak
Director, International Trade: Henryk Nowak
Deputy Director, International Trade: Janina Krol

Export sales: BHZ Zastal, ul Sulechowska 4a, 65-119 Zielona Góra
Kolmex, ul Mokotowska 49, 00-542 Warsaw

Products: Twelve-wheel open dump cars for 1520 mm gauge operation in USSR; covered four- and eight-wheel wagons, eight-wheel high-sided coal wagons, eight-wheel open dump cars, eight-wheel self-dumping wagons for cereals transport, and eight-wheel flat wagons for 1435 mm gauge; and spare parts for above-mentioned wagons.
Recent contracts include 1700 Type 904 V 12-wheel dump cars for Soviet Railways (1989); 40 Type 418 V 8-wheel dump cars for Czechoslovakian Railways (1989); 1700 Type 414 W 8-wheel coal wagons for China Export-Import Corporation (1989-90); 207 Type 418 V 8-wheel dump cars and 400 Type 412 W 8-wheel coal wagons for Polish Railways (1989).

Constitution: The Zastal works is one of Europe's biggest freight car builders with an annual production of over 2000 wagons. Biggest buyers are Polish State Railways (PKP), Soviet Railways (SZD), and China National Machinery Import and Export Corporation.

5800 ft^3 capacity covered hopper car for plastic pellets and powders by Union Tank Car

Type Laadkmmss 605 transporter for piggybacking of road trailers by Waggon Union

Type 418 V open dump car by Zastal

WESTINGHOUSE - WORLD LEADERS

For more than a hundred years Westinghouse Brake & Signal has provided braking and signalling systems for the worlds railways. This experience has made the company a world leader in controlling suburban, urban mass transit and intercity systems as well as single lines for heavy haul freight.

RAIL SYSTEMS
▼

- Braking ■ Rail doors
- Architectural doors ■ Platform screens
- Air conditioning ■ Signalling
- Passenger information ■ Revenue Control
- Automatic train control
- Telecommunications ■ Panel processing
- Traction power supply telecontrol
- Plant supervisory and monitoring
- Centralised traffic control
- Radio electric token block

HAWKER SIDDELEY

Westinghouse Brake and Signal

Westinghouse Brake and Signal Limited
A subsidiary of
Westinghouse Brake and Signal Holdings Limited
P.O. Box 74, Foundry Lane, Chippenham,
Wiltshire, England SN15 1HY.
Tel: Chippenham (0249) 654141 Telex: 449411.
Telefax: (0249) 655040

Brakes/bogies/bearings/components

Brakes and drawgear

ARGENTINA
SIAM 277
SKF Argentina 277

AUSTRALIA
Bradken 266
Comeng 268
Comsteel 268
SMC 277

AUSTRIA
Stabeg 277

BELGIUM
Buhlmann 268

BRAZIL
Cobrasma 268
Cobreq 268
Fresinbra 270
Suecobras 278

FINLAND
Saalasti Oy 275

FRANCE
Couplomatic 268
Domange-Jarrett 269
Forges de Fresnes 270
Paulstra Hutchinson 274
Reservoir, Le 275
Sambre et Meuse 277
SEE 277
Valeo 279
WABCO Westinghouse 280

GERMANY, DEMOCRATIC REPUBLIC
BBW 266

GERMANY, FEDERAL REPUBLIC
BSI 267
Jurid 270
Knorr-Bremse 270
Newag 273
Ringfeder 275
Scharfenberg 277
Textar 278
WABCO Westinghouse 280

INDIA
Bharat 266
Cimmco International 268
Greysham 270
Stone 278

ITALY
Socimi 277
WABCO Westinghouse 279

JAPAN
Mitsubishi 273
NABCO 273
Nippon Signal 273
Sumitomo 278
Tokyu Car 278

MEXICO
Miner y Mendez 273

NETHERLANDS
SAB WABCO 275

POLAND
Kolmex 271

PORTUGAL
LDA 272

ROMANIA
Mecanoexportimport 272
Uzinexportimport 279

SOUTH AFRICA
Conbrako 268
Matrix 272

SPAIN
Dimetal 269
Frenos Calefaccion y Señales 270
Macosa 272

SWITZERLAND
BBC-Sécheron 266
Oerlikon Brakes 274

SWEDEN
Dellner-Malmco AB 269

USSR
Energomachexport 270

UK
Atlas Copco 266
Avon 266
Davies and Metcalfe 268
Gresham and Craven 270
Litton 272
Lloyd 272
Lucas Girling 272
Oleo 274
RFS Engineering 275
SAB Brake Regulator 276
TBL 278
Westinghouse Brakes 280

USA
Abex 266
Amsted 266
ASF 266
Buckeye 267
Buffalo Brake Beam 267
Cardwell Westinghouse 268
Cobra Brake Shoes 268
EFE North America 269
Ellcon-National 269
FM Industries 270
Graham-White 270
Griffin 270
Miner 272
Multi-Service Supply 273
NYAB 274
Purdy 275
Triax-Davis 279
WABCO 279
Walton 280

YUGOSLAVIA
Fabrika Vagona Kraljevo 270
MZ Tito-Skopje 273

266 MANUFACTURERS / Brakes and drawgear

ABC Rail Corporation
Abex
(Formerly Abex Corporation)

200 S Michigan Avenue, Chicago, Illinois 60604, USA

Telephone: +1 312 322 0360
Telex: 756108
Telefax: +1 312 322 0377

Chairman & CEO: Glenn E Stinson
President: Donald W Grinter
Vice-President, Marketing: Paul E Dunn
Manager, Export Sales: John D Rayan

530 Fifth Avenue, New York, New York 10036
Telephone: +1 212 560 3200
Telex: 126605

European sales office: Karl W Kever, Manager
Augustinergasse 2, D-5100 Aachen, Federal Republic of Germany
Telephone: +49 241 33003
Telex: +49 241 29453
Telefax: +49 241 832849

European works: Frendo-Sud SpA, 83100 Avellino, Italy
Telephone: +39 825 626808/626811

Products: Normal and high phosphorus cast iron shoes (patented), composition and sintered brake shoes and disc brake pads.

Amsted
Amsted Industries International
A division of Amsted Industries Inc

200 West Monroe Street, Chicago, Illinois 60606, USA

Telephone: +1 312 372 5386
Telex: 254187
Telefax: +1 312 346 3373

Amsted Industries International handles all business, licensing and sales of American Steel Foundries (ASF) and Griffin Wheel Company, which are divisions of Amsted Industries Inc.

ASF
American Steel Foundries
A division of Amsted Industries Inc

3600 Prudential Plaza, Chicago, Illinois 60601, USA

Telephone: +1 312 645 1746
Telex: 254187

Products: Automatic couplers and yokes. ASF designs the Alliance coupler system. This knuckle-style coupler system covers a range of styles suitable for applications from small mine cars to the largest freight cars and passenger cars. Alliance couplers can include provision for rotary dumping, interlocking and slack control. A full range of accessories such as yokes, drawbars and transition systems is included. One recent development is the Ultra Capacity Alliance Coupler, which although able to couple freely with other knuckle-style couplers has a capacity far in excess of the standard couplers. Another recent development is ASF's Articulated Connector, which provides a proven means to fully exploit the articulated car or train principle.

All inquiries should be directed to Amsted Industries International, 200 West Monroe Street, Chicago, Illinois 60606. Telephone: +1 312 372 5386. Telex: 254187

Atlas Copco
Atlas Copco (Great Britain) Ltd

PO Box 79, Swallowdale Lane, Hemel Hempstead, Hertfordshire, HP2 7HA, England

Telephone: +44 442 61201
Telefax: +44 442 214106

Products: GAR series of rotary screw railway brake compressors for electric and diesel locomotives, railcars, LRVs and tramcars.

Avon
Avon Industrial Polymers Ltd

Bradford-on-Avon, Wiltshire BA15 1AA, England

Telephone: +44 2216 3911
Cable: Industrial, Bradford-on-Avon
Telex: 44856

Sales Manager: G M Lewis
Technical Manager: J R K Parry

Products: Draftgear, drawgear, buffers, rubber-to-metal bonded components and suspension systems, and air suspension systems.

BBC-Sécheron
BBC-Sécheron SA

14 avenue de Sécheron, 1202 Geneva 21, Switzerland

Telephone: +41 22 3941 11
Cable: Electricité, Genève
Telex: 22130
Telefax: +41 22 3421 94

Products: Automatic couplers, which are of three main parts: the mechanical coupler; pneumatic coupler and the low contact resistance of the strip-type plug contacts.

BBW
VEB Berliner Bremsenwerk
A member of VEB Kombinat Schienenfahrzeugbau and of Vereinigter Schienenfahrzeugbau der DDR e V

Hirschberger Strasse 4, 4 Berlin, GDR-1134

Telephone: +37 55740
Telex: 0112408

Products: Pneumatic brake equipment for rolling stock, tramcars and road vehicles, KE-distributor valves, driver's brake valves, brake cylinders, hydraulic shock absorbers.

Exports: Schienenfahrzeuge Export-Import, Ötztaler Strasse 5, Berlin, DDR-1100

Bharat
Bharat Brakes and Valves Ltd
A Government of India undertaking

22 Gobra Road, Calcutta 700 014, India

Telephone: +91 33 44 1754
Telex: 021 2545

Products: Vacuum brake equipment; rotary-type high vacuum exhausters (28in Hg), air-cooled; air brake valves and reservoirs; vertical turbine pumps.

Bradken
Bradken Consolidated

22 O'Riordan Street, Alexandria, Sydney, New South Wales, Australia

Telephone: +61 2 699 3000
Telex: aa 21512
Telefax: +61 2 698 1559

Products: Friction draftgear, couplers, yokes, centre plates, strikers and other general castings, including bogies.

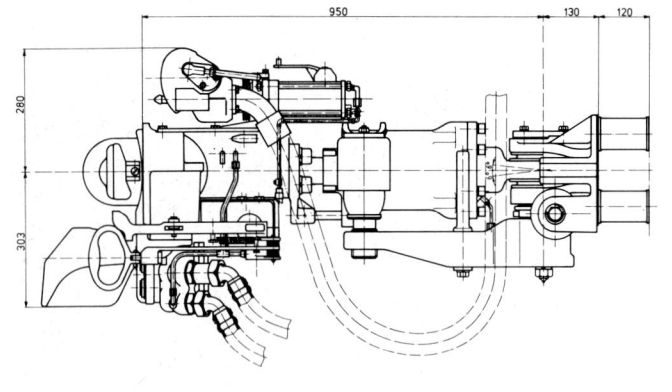

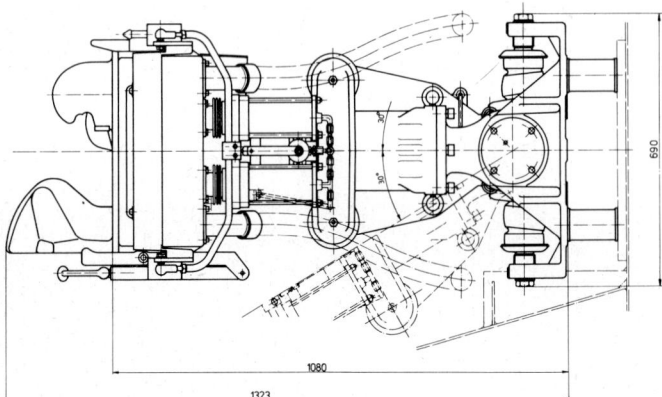

Arrangement of BBC-Sécheron automatic central buffer coupler for suburban and standard-gauge railways

BBW axle-mounted disc brake

Brakes and drawgear / **MANUFACTURERS** 267

BSI
Bergische Stahl-Industrie
A member of Thyssen Guss AG

PO Box 100165, 5630 Remscheid 1, Federal Republic of Germany

Telephone: +49 21 91 150
Telex: 8513858
Telefax: +49 21 91 152215

Mülheim works: Oberhausener Strasse 1, PO Box 011507, 4330 Mülheim/Ruhr

Telephone: +49 208 771
Telex: 856589

Products: A large range of special components for all classes of rail vehicles: railway brake systems and equipment: disc brake with high reliability, low wear, and high capacity; different designs of wheel-, axle- or flange-mounted brake discs meeting all demands with enforced recooling by self-ventilation, special low-energy ventilation for use at very high speeds or arrangement on fast-turning gear or motor shafts; complete disc brake rigging including brake pads and actuators for pneumatic, electro-hydraulic or spring force application, spare parts and incomplete components; BSI or SAB brakes; brake indicator devices; BSI electromagnetic brakes and their supporting devices, actuator cylinders, switching devices and auxiliar equipment; automatic centre-buffer couplers of the COMPACT type and semi-permanent couplers for commuter trains, subway, rapid transit and tramway vehicles; special semi-permanent couplers for high-speed ICE trains, automatic shunting couplers for UIC drawgear equipment of Type RK 900; resilient SAB-V-wheels; railway axle drives for longitudinal and parallel-arranged motors in a large range of power classes and different executions; fully integrated drives including motor bearings and brake systems; special arrangements of drives and brakes for low-floor mass transit vehicles; elastic shaft couplings.

The essential assemblies of a COMPACT coupler – that is, the coupler head with air and electricity connections; the drawbar, possibly with an overload protection (shock release) feature and spring systems; and the draftgear – are offered in variable configurations to suit individual users. The coupler head comes in two sizes and is made of cast steel in a variety of tensile strengths, also in corrosion-protected alloys. It is thus consistent with any demands in terms of resistance to tensile and compressive forces and climatic conditions.

The electric coupling can be arranged on top, underneath or at the side, and the compressed air connection on top or at the bottom of the coupler head. The drawbar and draftgear form a self-contained unit, depending upon the type of equipment. If the drawbar and draftgear are used with pre-stressed rubber elements, they may be complemented with a vertical adjustment system and overload protection feature with a shock-release member. The draftgear consists simply of an articulated or joint bearing to follow the horizontal and vertical motions between vehicles if the drawbar is joined with a spring system. The spring systems connected with the drawbar can be made of frictional steel springs, metal-rubber springs or hydro-mechanical components at the user's option. Such an arrangement can also be provided with a compressive overload protection feature.

In these combinations of draftgears, spring systems and drawbars, the overall unit will follow all motions and take up all tensile and compressive stresses between the vehicles. A re-adjusting or resetting device retains the idle coupler in its rest position. The coupler can be operated manually, pneumatically or electrically. The main assemblies in a COMPACT coupler are detachably interlocked and each may also be used in other coupler brands. All types within this coupler system have low-wear and reduced-maintenance design features.

BSI components for rail vehicles are known and applied in all five continents. Light rail, metro, suburban and long-distance railway systems as well as very high-speed trains such as the French TGV, the British HST and the German ICE make use of BSI couplers, brakes or motor gears. Recent important sales include couplers for the new metro system at Medellin (Columbia), LRT in Monterrey (Mexico) and other cities, diesel-powered multiple-units of British Rail.

Disc brakes and magnetic track brakes are supplied or are on order for ICE trains and IC cars of DB; for long-distance and suburban trains of BR (including the Class 91 locomotive), SNCB, SBB, ÖBB, FS, NSB, SJ, NS, MÁV, BDZ (Bulgaria), SNCF, RENFE, Amtrak (USA), VIA Rail (Canada) and for many regional traffic services, such as KCR Hong Kong, MBTA, BVG Berlin (suburban trains) and others.

Axle drives for LRV and metro use are designed and produced at the Mülheim/Ruhr works of BSI. Latest designs are integrated drive and brake units in combination with high speed ac motors to fit the most advanced light rail and mass transit vehicles with extreme low-floor height.

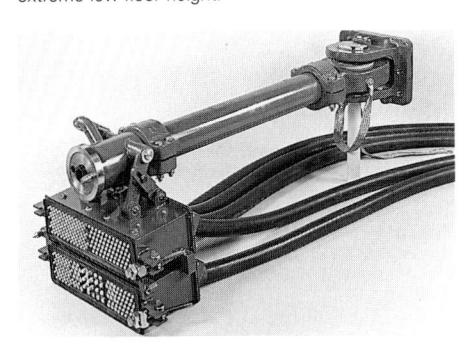

BSI semi-permanent coupler with integrated pneumatic and electrical connections

BSI semi-permanent coupler head for DB high-speed InterCity Express (ICE)

BSI-COMPACT coupler standardised for British Rail diesel multiple-units

BSI disc brake in SIG motor bogie

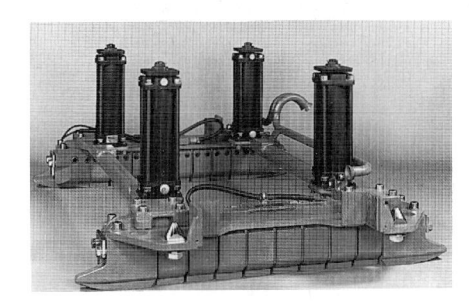

Buckeye
Buckeye Steel Castings Co

2211 Parsons Avenue, Columbus, Ohio 43207, USA

Telephone: +1 614 444 2121
Telex: 810 482 1757

President: R W Armbruster
Vice-President: W C Buffington
Director, Product Engineering and Mass Transit: J R Downes

Products: Automatic couplers, draft yokes, centre plates, sill centrebraces, draft sill ends, passenger and freight bogies.

Buffalo Brake Beam
Buffalo Brake Beam Co

400 Ingham Avenue, Lackawanna, Buffalo, New York 14218, USA

Telephone: +1 716 823 4200
Telefax: +1 716 822 3823

Chairman: Walter S Crone
President: Richard G Adams
Vice-President & Treasurer: Garold L Stone Jr

BSI double brake disc for SNCF TGV-A high-speed train-set

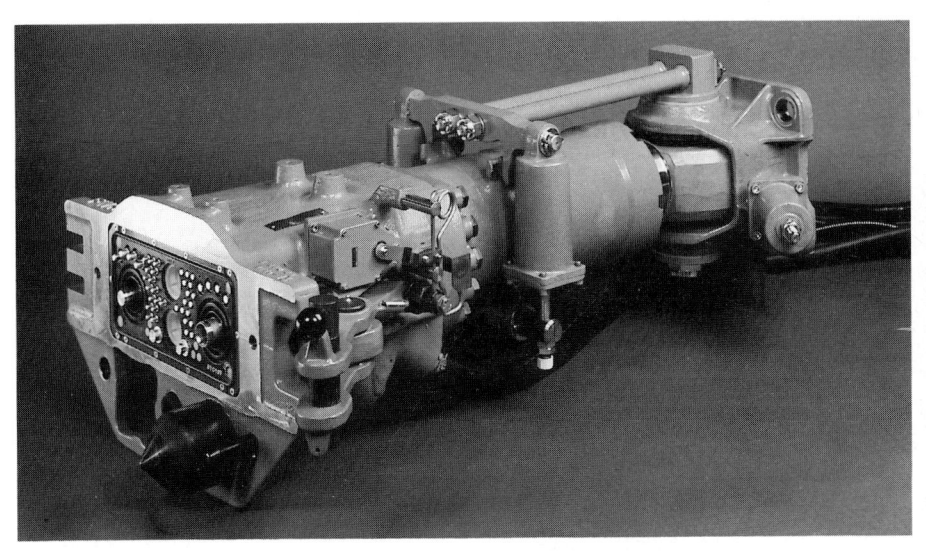

BSI electro-magnetic track brake for high-speed passenger cars

268 MANUFACTURERS / Brakes and drawgear

Vice-President, Marketing: James E Orr Jr
Director of Sales: Eugene J Jacob

Principal subsidiary: Buffalo Railroad Equipment Corp

Products: Railcar brake beams, unit side frame wear plates, brake rod connectors, railcar steel ladders and brake shoe keys.

Agent: Canada-Davanac Industries Ltd, 135 Montee de Liesse, Montreal, Quebec H4T 1V2, Canada

Buhlmann
Buhlmann SA

Rue des Coteaux 249, 1030 Brussels, Belgium

Telephone: +32 2 216 20 30
Telex: 61 134
Telefax: +32 2 241 96 02

Chairman: Walter Buhlmann
Director: Marcel Givel

Products: Railway and mass transit brake equipment, pneumatic, hydraulic, electro-pneumatic and electro-magnetic; electronic wheel spin and slide detection; automatic couplers; high-pressure air-starting equipment for diesel locomotives; point operating mechanisms for Vignoles and grooved rails in all gauges; track circuit equipment and accessories; level crossing gates, barriers and warning signals.

Cardwell Westinghouse
An American-Standard Company

332 South Michigan Avenue, Chicago, Illinois 60604, USA

Telephone: +1 312 427 5051
Cable: Cardwell
Telex: 25 4210
Telefax: +1 312 483 9302

Vice-President and General Manager: James L Duffy
Mechanical Operations: Vern S Danielson
Administration and Control: William C Davis
Vice President, Engineering and Product Development: William D Wallace

Products: Friction, rubber-friction and hydraulic-friction draftgear; hand brakes; automatic slack adjusters.

Licence agreements
Argentina: Siam di Tella Ltd, Division Electrodomestica, Tucman 633, Buenos Aires
Australia: Bradken Consolidated Ltd, 22 O'Riordan Street, Alexandria, Sydney, New South Wales
Belgium: Acieries de Haine-Saint-Pierre & Lesquin, 7160 Haine Saint Pierre
Brazil: Cobrasma SA, PO Box 8225–ZP-1, São Paulo
Portugal: Engenharia e Comercio LDA, Rua da Alegria, 61 R/C, Lisbon 2

South Africa: Sturrock (South Africa) Ltd, 91 Commissioner Street, PO Box 2863, Johannesburg

Cimmco International
Division of Cimmco Ltd

Prakash Deep, 7 Tolstoy Marg, New Delhi 110 001, India

Telephone: +91 11 3314383–5, 3310814
Cable: Cimwag
Telex: 31 65148, 31 62294

Products: Vacuum brake equipment and components, Alliance couplers, AAR standard-type Alliance couplers, MCA couplers, screw couplings.

Cobra Brake Shoes
Railroad Friction Products Corporation

Wilmerding, Pennsylvania 15148, USA

Telephone: +1 412 825 1106
Telex: 866467

Acting President: W B West
Vice President and General Manager: J L Duffy
Marketing Manager: E W Kojsza

Products: Composition brake shoes and disc pads.

Agent: Cobra Canada Inc, PO Box 2050, Hamilton, Ontario L8N 3T5, Canada

Cobrasma
Cobrasma SA

Rua da Estacao, 523 Osasco, São Paulo, PO Box 969, Brazil CEP 06090

Telephone: +55 11 704 6122
Telex: (011) 71545/71589
Telefax: +55 11 704 6856

President: Luis Eulalio de Bueno Vidigal
Marketing Director: Alberto Martinez
Export Director: Eduardo Hubert K Monteiro

Works: Via Anhanguera Km 104, Distrito de Hortolândia, PO Box 151 Municipio de Sumaré, São Paulo, CEP 13170

Telephone: +55 192 65 6000
Telex: (019) 1926

Products: Couplers and draftgear.

Cobreq
Cia Brasileira de Equipamentos

Praia do Flamengo, 200–9° andar, Caixa Postal 16219, 22.210 Rio de Janeiro, Brazil

Telephone: +55 21 285 2233
Telex: 021 21632

Director-President: Engr Ali El Hage
Export Sales Director: Engr Rodolfo Luiz Darigo

Exclusive distributor: Fonseca Almeida Comércio e Indústria SA

Praia do Flamengo, 200–9° andar, 22.210 Rio de Janeiro

Telephone: +55 21 285 2233
Telex: 021 21632

Products: Non-metallic composition brake shoes and brake pads for railroad vehicles.

Comeng
Comeng (Equipment and Spares)
A division of The ANI Corporation Limited

Unit 1, Bankstown Blvde, 332-350 Edgar Street, Bankstown, NSW 2200, Australia

Telephone: +61 2 772 4166
Telex: 170511
Telefax: +61 2 774 3619

General Manager: Ted Parr

Products: Miner RF-170, RF-185, RF-361, RF-444 and SL-76 draftgear; Miner handbrakes.

Comsteel
Commonwealth Steel Co Ltd

PO Box 14, Maud Street, Waratah, New South Wales 2298, Australia

Telephone: +61 49 68 0411
Telex: 28115

Products: Automatic couplers and drawgear.

Conbrako
Conbrako (Pty) Ltd

PO Box 4018, Luipaardsvlei 1743, Transvaal, South Africa

Telephone: +27 11 762 2421
Telex: 4 21283
Telefax: +27 11 762 6535

Products: Air and vacuum brakes; drawgear; snubbers.

Couplomatic

25 rue des Bateliers, PO Box 165, 93404 Saint-Ouen Cedex, France

Telephone: +33 1 40 10 64 22
Telex: 290317 alssig f
Telefax: +33 1 40 10 61 00

Products: Automatic couplings.

Davies and Metcalfe
Davies and Metcalfe plc

Injector Works, Romiley, Nr Stockport, Cheshire SK6 3AE, England

Telephone: +44 61 430 4272
Telex: 668801 dmltd g
Telefax: +44 61 494 2828

Chairman: Richard Metcalfe
Sales Director: E Mulryan

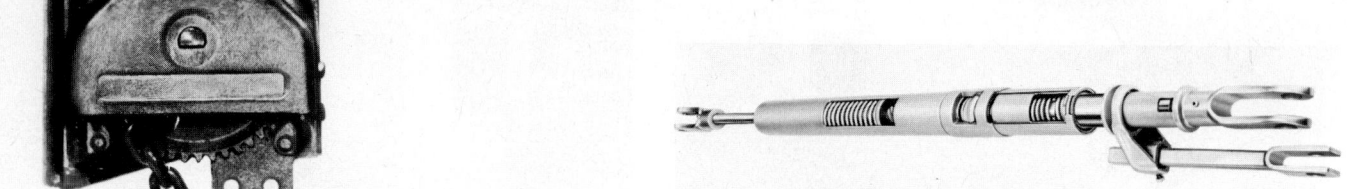

Cardwell-Universal Model 2420 lever-type hand-brake

Cardwell-Universal Model DJ 2300 cone-clutch design, automatic two-way slack adjuster

Principal subsidiaries: Davies & Metcalfe (Services) Ltd, Leek, England
Davies & Metcalfe Engineering Ltd, Sydney, Australia
Davies & Metcalfe Rail Products Ltd, Bramley, S Africa
Davies & Metcalfe Financial Services Ltd

Products: Electronic, pneumatic and electro-pneumatic brake control systems; air compressors and accessories; air dryers; electronic overspeed protection equipment; electronic and electro-mechanical vigilance systems; wheelslip detection and correction equipment; disc brakes; automatic couplers; brake rigging regulators; brake cylinders; distributor valves; load proportional brake equipment; spring and hydraulic parking brakes; sanding equipment; passenger emergency systems.

Continuous development of the Metcalfe range of products allows the company to offer a complete range of equipment specifically designed for mass transit rail systems. Practically the whole of the British Rail High Speed Train fleet is equipped with Metcalfe Type E70 brake control equipment and the 2A115D air compressors. All the BR Class 58 locomotives built by British Rail Engineering have Davies & Metcalfe equipment fitted. Some 405 sets of Metcalfe Type EPB/1 brake equipment have been supplied for the latest Class 455 electric multiple-units built by British Rail Engineering at York, and the same type of equipment is fitted to the Railbus fleet built jointly by British Rail Engineering and Andrew Barclay. All BR Class 142 Railbuses and the Intermediate diesel multiple-units of BR Class 150 and 151 also have the Metcalfe/BSI multi-function auto-coupler; a version of this type of coupler is also fitted to the Tyne and Wear Metro cars manufactured by Metropolitan-Cammell. A recent success in an overseas market for Brush Electrical Machines has been for the building of 22 25 kV ac locomotives for New Zealand Railways; these have the Davies & Metcalfe P85 brake control system with the Type 2A320 air compressor. The Davies & Metcalfe P85 brake control system is also fitted to 146 25 kV electric locomotives built by Comeng and Clyde/ASEA-Walkers in Australia for Queensland Railways. Metcalfe/BSI compact multi-function auto couplers are fitted to over 400 cars built by Metropolitan-Cammell for the Hong Kong Mass Transit System. These cars are also equipped with the Metcalfe Type 2A115D air compressors.

Recent contracts obtained include: 400 Metcalfe/BSI double-reduction transmission gear boxes for Brush Electrical Machines Ltd for fitting to the new BR Class 465 emus; 26 vehicle sets of Metcalfe Type EBC/5 electronic brake control equipment and Metcalfe/Hydrovane Type TB11 rotary vane compressors for GEC Alsthom for fitting to Manchester's Metrolink LRVs; eight sets of Metcalfe/Emergency air brake equipment for Clayton Equipment to be fitted to 10-tonne diesel-hydraulic locomotives at Konkola Copper Mines in Zambia; 14 sets of air brake equipment for Clayton Equipment for 12-tonne 500 V dc trolley wire locomotives for use in China; 180 car sets of Metcalfe/BSI Compact multi-function couplers for BREL Ltd to fit to the BR Class 165 dmu; automatic air brake equipment for dmus on the State Railway of Thailand; air brake control equipment for wagons supplied under British Aid for operation on Kenya Railways; 300 sets of Metcalfe Graduable Release Automatic Air Brake Equipment for More Wear Industries of Zimbabwe; brake control equipment, disc brakes and automatic couplers for BR Class 319, 320, 456 and 321 emus, and Class 158 dmu (the total quantity of EPB/1 brake control systems now ordered for British Railways board's rolling stock exceeds 1900 sets; 75 complete sets of Automatic Air Brake Equipment for railway wagons to be built by ZECO Ltd of Bulawayo, Zimbabwe.

Dellner-Malmco AB

Vikavägen 144, 791 95 Falun, Sweden

Telephone: +46 23 70220
Telex: 8425012
Telefax: +46 23 70588

President: Clas Nicolin
President, Coupler Division: Dieter F Ernst
Marketing Director, Coupler Division: A Philip Pastouna
Marketing Director, Scandinavian Coupler Division: Tomas Westbom

OB lightweight high-performance Dynaglide current collectors as supplied for the Los Angeles (California) Metro

Principal subsidiaries: Dellner Kupplungen GmbH, Adlerstrasse 74, D-4000 Düsseldorf 1, West Germany
Telephone: +49 211 3677 210
Telex: 8588321
Telefax: +49 211 3677 211

Dellner Couplers Inc, 237 Asylum Street, Bridgeport, Connecticut 06610, USA
Telephone: +1 203 579 7742
Telex: 06 43969
Telefax: +1 203 334 8261

Products: Couplers; fully automatic and semi-automatic couplers designed for rapid transit vehicles to streetcars and other vehicle types.

Recent and ongoing contracts have been obtained from: DPM Vancouver, Canada; DSB (Danish State Railway); BSC Redcar and BSC Scunthorpe (British Steel); FS (Italian State Railway), LRV Naples, Metro Naples; NSB (Norwegian State Railway); LRV Gothenburg, SJ High Speed Train (Swedish State Railway); LRV Istanbul; LRV San Diego, LRV Baltimore, USA; LRV Cologne, DB (German State Railway).

Dimetal
Dimetal SA

Avenida de Castilla 33, San Fernando de Henares (Torrejon de Ardoz), Madrid 28830, Spain

Telephone: +34 1 6751100
Telex: 22332
Telefax: +34 1 6565942

President: Jesús Ruano Alvarez
General Manager: Eugenio Vela Sastre
Railway Products Manager: Antonio Gonzáles del Peral
Railway Products Technical Manager: Santiago González Kaendler

Products: Brake equipment and antislip/antislide equipment; brake discs; electronic equipment for brake control, blending, etc; tread brake units with or without spring parking brakes; electromagnetic rail brakes; PPC (Printed Pneumatic Circuit) panels.

Recent contracts executed and obtained include: Design, building and installation surveillance of new air brake equipments in RENFE wagons equipped with vacuum brakes (1987–91); brake control equipments for 100 RENFE train units of Type 446 (1990); air brake equipment for 50 locomotives; dual brake equipment for 28 locomotives; air delivery equipment for high-speed locomotives; 252 sets of brake equipment for RENFE wagons; brake equipment for 10 articulated LRVs for Valencia Metro.

Domange-Jarrett

198 avenue des Grésillons, PO Box 251, 92602 Asnières Cedex, France

Telephone: +33 1 47 90 62 72
Telex: 620798
Telefax: +33 1 47 90 03 57

OB coupler in service on the Washington Metro

General Manager: Philippe Domange
Export Manager: Pierre Serbinenko

Products: Buffers; shock absorbers for automatic couplers; buffer stops.

Advantages claimed for the company's shock absorbers for couplers and end-of-track stops include: increase in impact speed avoiding car damage up to 25 km/h; automatic and instant recovery of the shock absorber's operational capacity; and high reliability of the Jarret cartridge, which remains maintenance- and adjustment-free over many years. Applications include high-speed trains, inter-city trains, commuter trains, metro and light rail units.

EFE North America Inc
OB Transit Products

380 North Main Street, Mansfield, Ohio 44903-1319, USA

Telephone: +1 419 522 7111
Telex: 987414
Telefax: +1 419 522 7069

President: John F Harkness
Vice President, Marketing and Sales: Terry W Duffy
Product Manager, Car Equipment: T G Tarantino
Product Manager, Traction Distribution: Michael P Bitsora

Products: Transit car coupling and braking systems.

The compatibility of OB transit coupler systems, combined with an enviable record of performance and dependability, has led to their integration with the designs of car manufacturers in many areas of the world, including Germany, Canada, Italy, Mexico and Japan. The latest contract provides for 30 car sets of heavy rail couplers and 120 third-rail current collectors to Breda of Italy, builder of the heavy rail vehicles for Southern California Rapid Transit District's Metro cars. A recent new product development is an energy absorption system for transit couplers that utilises a lightweight replaceable cartridge.

Six high-activity light rail markets are the latest customers for OB light rail coupler systems. On track and compiling favourable service records are OB light rail coupler systems in Boston, Massachusetts; Cleveland, Ohio; Pittsburgh, Pennsylvania; and San Jose, California. Soon to join them will be light rail couplers for Guadalajara, Mexico; and Los Angeles, California.

The latest overhead distribution contracts involve new light rail or trolley electrification projects in Monterrey, Mexico; Vancouver, Canada; San Diego, Sacramento and San Francisco, California; Boston, Massachusetts; New Orleans, Louisiana; Seattle, Washington.

Ellcon-National
Ellcon-National Inc

30 King Road, Totowa, New Jersey 07512, USA

Telephone: +1 201 256 7110
Telefax: +1 201 256 3275

President: Douglass E Kondra
Chairman: Emil P Konda
Vice President, Sales: R A Nitsch
General Manager: J A Testa

Products: Hand brakes, empty/load device, change-over valve, sash impact-resistant glass, stanchions,

MANUFACTURERS / Brakes and drawgear

grab handles, windscreens, luggage racks, locomotive slack adjusters, slack adjusters, pellet gates, bogie-mounted brakes.

Sales Representatives
Mexico: Dinamica SA, c/o GVH Construcciones, Navarra No 210, Dept 202, Colonia Alamos Del Benito Juarez, CP-03400, Mexico DF
Canada: Davanac Inc, 135 Montée de Liesse, Montreal, Quebec H4T 1V2
USA: Gregg Car Co, PO Box 430, Hackensack, NJ 07502 (including Gregg Car Co representatives in Europe, the Middle East, and Australia)
Taiwan: Sunrise Trading Corp Ltd, PO Box 51–25, Taipei, Taiwan 105

Energomachexport
V/O Energomachexport

25 A, Bezbozhny per, 129010 Moscow, USSR

Telephone: +7 095 288 84 56
Telex: 411965
Telefax: +7 095 288 79 90

Director General: Vladimir I Filimonov
Deputy Director General: I Lapytko
Director: Transmash

Products: Type SA-3 automatic coupling.

Fabrika Vagona Kraljevo

Postanski FAH 90, Kraljevo, Yugoslavia

Telephone: +38 36 333455
Telex: 17625
Telefax: +38 36 339919

General Manager: Rodoljub Petrovic
Manager, Economic Affairs: Veljo Nedeljkovic
Technical Manager: Milivoje Slovic
Manager of Institute: Radoslav Lesevic

Main works: Pajsijeva 1, 11000 Beograd

Products: Draftgear; buffers under licence from Miner; brake equipment; automatic couplers.

FM Industries Inc
(Formerly trading as FreightMaster)

8600 Will Rogers Boulevard, PO Box 40555 Fort Worth, Texas 76140, USA

Telephone: +1 817 293 4220
Telefax: +1 817 5515801

President & CEO: O E Seay
Vice-President, Sales & Marketing: T W Howe
Vice-President, Engineering: R N Hodges
Vice-President, Manufacturing: M S Dew

Products: FreightMaster brand end-of-car cushioning units; electronic training simulators.
FMI offers a complete line of FreightMaster Hydraulic Cushioning Devices in both mechanical and pressurised nitrogen gas return. All devices incorporate a slack action control system, as well as proven impact performance during yard switching. A sight glass to verify the hydraulic fluid level is provided in all new and reconditioned devices. This equipment can be used on all types of cars for protection of equipment and sensitive cargos.
FreightMaster's Train Dynamics Analyzer 4000 is now available with many standard and optional features: multi-training stations, custom design cabs, test and customer-proven user-friendly software, realistic train sounds, laser disc video, full motion base, in-cab defaults, trainee grading package, on-screen signals plus realtime dynamic force and train brake system displays, time plot displays of user-chosen items, record/playback and others.

FreightMaster Train Dynamics Analyzer 4000

Forges de Fresnes

80 rue Pasteur, 59970 Fresnes sur Escaut, France

Telephone: +33 27 25 92 22
Telex: 810 122 f
Telefax: +33 27 26 17 27

Manager: J M Deramaux

Products: Forged brake beam assemblies and other forgings for railway industry bogies, coaches and freight wagons.

Frenos Calefaccion y Señales
Sociedad Española de Frenos, Calefaccion y Señales SA

C/Nicolas Fuster 2, 28320 Pinto (Madrid), Spain

Telephone: +34 1 6910054
Telex: 46399 sefr e
Telefax: +34 1 6910100

General Director: Nicolás Fúster Junquera
Commercial Director: José Miguel García Ponte
Technical Director: Miguel Angel Martin Jiménez
Manufacturing Director: Jésus Martín Jiménez

Products: All products related to compressed air brakes, vacuum brakes and high-voltage heating; compressed air production and treatment; all types of brake control units; electronic anti-skid, anti-spin and brake control (analogue and microprocessor); bogie equipment such as cylinders, discs, block brake units; hydraulic brakes, magnetic track brakes, etc.
Recent contracts include many equipments for RENFE units, for Madrid Metro and for the Medellin Metro, Columbia.

Fresinbra
Fresinbra Industrial SA

Rua Laureano Fernandes Junior, 10-VilaLeopoldina, CEP-05089, São Paulo, Brazil

Telephone: +55 11 260 3122
Telex: 11 83263
Telefax: +55 11 831 6035

Engineering Manager: Sergio Ulian
Marketing Manager: Affonso Galvão Bueno Filho

Works: Rua Lauriano Fernandes Jr 10, PO Box 24065, São Paulo 05089

Products: Brake equipment for freight cars, locomotives and passenger cars; electro-pneumatic door equipment for rail vehicles; railway signalling equipment.

Girling
Lucas Girling Ltd
Member of Lucas Industries Ltd
(see under Lucas Girling Ltd)

Graham-White
Graham-White Manufacturing Co
Graham-White Sales Division

PO Box 1099, 1242 Colorado Street, Salem, Virginia 24153-1099, USA

Telephone: +1 703 387 5620
Telefax: +1 703 387 5639

President: J Spencer Frantz
Vice President of Sales: W Stewart Bruce Jr
General Sales Manager: Roger Caudill

Products: Pneumatic and electro-pneumatic devices for locomotives and powered passenger vehicles, such as air dryers, locomotive sanding systems, air filters, automatic drain valves, air check valves (one- and two-way), solenoid valves, horn valves, coalescers, bell ringers, air gauges, air test fittings for air gauges and pressure switches, electric timers, mirror and windshield wing combinations, locomotive cab awnings and ventilators for locomotive cabs.

Gresham & Craven
Gresham and Craven Ltd

PO Box 74, Chippenham, Wiltshire SN15 1JD, England

Telephone: +44 249 654141
Telex: 449411/12

Sales Director: S J Pursey

Products: Complete vacuum brake equipments for locomotives, carriages, wagons and breakdown cranes; rotary exhausters; static and portable vacuum brake test sets; pneumatic fittings for the control of engines, gearboxes, hopper doors and dump cylinders.

Greysham
Greysham (International) Pvt Ltd

4-B Vandhna, 11 Tolstoy Marg, New Delhi 110 001, India

Telephone: +91 11 2523746, 2523989, 3313518, 3312969
Telex: 031 63202 grey in
Telefax: +91 11 3310952

Managing Director: Govind Singh

Products: Complete vacuum brake equipment including vacuum cylinders 'E' and 'F' types, D A valves, couplings, release valves, rubber hoses, reservoirs and piping system; Greysham slack adjusters for wagons and coaches; semi-automatic locks for flat wagons; air brake equipments for wagons and coaches, manufactured under licence from Davies & Metcalfe, UK.

Griffin
Griffin Wheel Co
A division of Amsted Industries Inc

200 West Monroe St, Chicago, Illinois 60606, USA

Telefax: +1 312 372 8230

Products: The company has developed and manufactures in the USA and Canada lead and asbestos-free 'Anchor' high-friction composition brake shoes for all railroad applications.
All enquiries should be directed to Amsted Industries International, 200 West Monroe Street, Chicago, Illinois 60606, USA. Telephone: +1 312 372 5386. Telex: 254187.

Jurid
Jurid Werke GmbH

Postfach 1249, 2057 Reinbek/Hamburg, Federal Republic of Germany

Telephone: +49 40 7271-0
Telex: 0217834 jurh d
Telefax: +49 40 7271 2408

Chairman: Dr Schroiff
Managing Director: Dipl-Ing C-H Glanz
Sales Director: S Hackländer

Products: Composition brake blocks; disc brake pads; friction plates; sintered brake blocks and disc brake pads for heavy-duty rail brakes; data acquisition equipment and complete test and measurement instrumentation for rail brake system evaluation; opto-electronic-laser systems for engineering measurement.

Knorr-Bremse
Knorr-Bremse AG

Moosacher Strasse 80, 8000 Munich 40, Federal Republic of Germany

Telephone: +49 89 3547-0
Telex: 524228
Telefax: +49 89 3547 2767

Brakes and drawgear / MANUFACTURERS

Knorr-Bremse brake disc and pressure-applied hydraulic brake caliper with spring-applied parking brake actuator

Motor bogie of German Federal ICE 350 km/h trainset equipped with three brake discs of high temperature-resistant material, mounted to each hollow drive-shaft, and abrasion-free eddy-current brakes

Microprocessor electronic control unit (with anti-skid control incorporated) for electro-pneumatic and electro-hydraulic brake systems by Knorr-Bremse

Chairman Heinz-Hermann Thiele
Directors: Peter Riedlinger
Egon Werner
Dr H Ziegler

Associated companies:
Foundry Volmarstein
Vogelsanger Strasse 50, 5802 Wetter/Ruhr
Telephone: +49 2335 631-1
Telex: 823235
Telefax: +49 2335 631 260

Carl Hasse & Wrede
Mohriner Allee 30-42, 1000 Berlin 47
Telephone: +49 30 7034085
Telex: 46399
Telefax: +49 30 700908-11

Aldersbach Works
Josef-Prex-Strasse 10, Aldersbach
Telephone: +49 8543 818
Telefax: +49 8543 3375

Subsidiaries:
Knorr Electronic GmbH
Moosacher Strasse 80, 8000 Munich 40
Telephone: +49 89 3547-0
Telex: 524228
Telefax: +49 89 3547 2856
Director: Dr Gerd Kessel

Australia: Knorr Brake Australia Pty Ltd
119 Willoughby Road, Sydney/Crows Nest, New South Wales 2065
Telephone: +61 2 439 5488
Telex: AA 25468
Telefax: +61 2 439 8531
Director: Dr Dieter W Haseke

Austria: Knorr-Bremse GmbH
Steinfeldergasse 12, 2340 Mödling
Telephone: +43 2236 23651
Telex: 79245
Telefax: +43 2236 23651 12
Director: K Skach

Knorr-Bremse Holding GmbH
Steinfeldergasse 12, 2340 Mödling
Telephone: +43 2236 23651
Telex: 79245
Telefax: +43 2236 23651 12
Director: K Skach

Dr Techn Josef Zelisko
Fabrik für Elektrotechnik und Maschinenbau GmbH
Steinfeldergasse 12, 2340 Mödling
Telephone: +43 2236 23651
Telex: 79175
Telefax: +43 2236 23651 12
Director: K Skach

Brazil: Industria Freios Knorr Ltda
Caixa Postal 7679, CEP 01000 São Paulo
Telephone: +55 11 5480211
Telex: 1135348
Telefax: +55 11 2468954
President: Thomas P Wagner

Canada: Knorr Brake Ltd
385 Watline Avenue, Mississauga, Ontario L4Z 1P3
Telephone: +1 416 890 1550
President: A A Wachsmuth

France: Knorr-Dahl Frainga SA
31 rue Ferdinand Daulne, 14140 Lisieux
Telephone: +33 31 321000
Telex: 171796 f
Telefax: +33 31 3162 0820
President: Georges Castelnaü

Italy: Knorr-Bremse Italia SpA
Via Milano, 5, 20068 Peschiera Borromeo/Milan
Telephone: +39 2 547 5221
Telex: 352283
Telefax: +39 2 547 5182
Director General: Dr Olivares

South Africa: Knorr-Bremse SA Pty Ltd
PO Box 2411, Kempton Park 1620
Telephone: +27 3943120/28
Telex: 742348
Director: A W Adlkofer

Spain: Sociedad Espanola de Frenos Calefaccion y Señales SA
Antonio Maura 8, Madrid 14
Telephone: +34 1 2226546
Telex: 742348
Telefax: +34 1 2227697
General Manager: Nicolás Fúster Conrado

Sweden: Svenska Knorr-Bremse AB
Sprintgatan 4, 21124 Malmö 6
Telephone: +46 40 291040
Telex: 33078
General Manager: G Hambitzer

USA: Knorr Brake Corporation
PO Box 1905, Rockville, Maryland 20850
Telephone: +1 301 424 5500
Telex: 898 398
Telefax: +1 301 840 1089
President: A A Wachsmuth

Affiliated companies:
Brazil: MWM Motores Diesel Ltd
PO Box 7679, CEP 01000 São Paulo
Telephone: +55 11 548 0211
Telex: 1121571
Telefax: +55 11 523 5822
President: Kuno Frank

Switzerland: Facto AG
Ringstrasse 31, 4600 Olten
Telephone: +41 62 210580
Telex: 68799
President: R Gunthart

Products: Single and two-pipe brake systems; graduated-release air brakes complying with UIC rules; direct-release air brakes complying with AAR rules; air brakes convertible for direct/graduated release; electro-pneumatic brake systems complying with UIC rules for main-line vehicles; brake systems for all types of rapid transit, metro and light rail vehicles; microprocessor brake control systems with anti-spin/slide function incorporated; electro-pneumatic brake systems; microprocessor-controlled electro-hydraulic brake systems; equipment for ATC/ ATO; screw-type compressors and reciprocating compressors; air dryers; door closing and sanding equipment; disc brake and tread brake equipment; vacuum brakes, vacuum-controlled air brakes, pneumatically-controlled vacuum brakes; load-controlled brake systems; high-power brakes; electro-magnetic rail brakes; eddy-current brakes; spring-loaded brakes; air supply equipment; driver's brake valves and driver's brake valve systems; direct and graduated-release distributor valves; mechanically-controlled anti-skid systems; electronically- and microprocessor-controlled anti-skid and anti-spin systems; mechanically- or pneumatically-operated emergency brake equipment; 'empty-load' changeover devices; slack adjusters; brake cylinders, also with incorporated slack adjuster; hydraulic brake cylinders and caliper units; electric and pneumatic equipment for automatic train operation (ATO); pneumatic and vacuum equipment for automatic train control (ATC); deadman and vigilance devices; control equipment for air suspension systems; pneumatically-controlled unloading, tipping and associated ancillary equipment; pneumatic and electro-pneumatic door closing equipment; pneumatic and electro-pneumatic engine and transmission controls; monitoring equipment for brake operation; indicating devices for pad wear; brake testing equipment and remote-controlled terminal testing equipment; Vebeo fittings; and automatic centre buffer couplers.

Kolmex
Foreign Trade Enterprise Co Ltd

PO Box 236, 00-950 Warsaw 1, Poland

Telephone: +48 22 28 22 91; 29 92 41
Telex: 813270; 813714
Telefax: +48 22 295879

Products: Brake equipment and components.

MANUFACTURERS / Brakes and drawgear

LDA
Engenharia e Comercio LDA

Rua da Alegria, 61 R/C, Lisbon 2, Portugal

Products: Brake equipment and friction draftgear.

Litton
Litton Interconnection Products

72 Whitecraigs Road, Glenrothes, Fife KY6 2RX, Scotland

Telephone: +44 592 774018
Telex: 727208
Telefax: +44 592 774143

General Manager: E J McCartin
Sales & Marketing Director: A O'Connor

Products: Large veam power B connectors; all types of electric and electronic connectors.

Lloyd
Lloyd (ABC Couplers) Ltd
A subsidiary of F H Lloyd Holding plc

James Bridge Steel Works, PO Box 5, Wednesbury, West Midlands WS10 9SD, England

Telephone: +44 21 526 3121
Telex: 339502

Chairman: L Robertson
Director and General Manager: C Higgs

Products: Automatic couplers; semi-rigid bar couplers; draftgear; side buffers; carbon and alloy steel castings for the railway industry.

Lucas Girling
Lucas Rail Products

Thermal Road, Bromborough, Wirral, Merseyside L62 4TR, England

Telephone: +44 51 334 4040
Telex: 627020
Telefax: +44 51 334 7243

Director and General Manager: B G Cousins
Marketing Manager, UK and Scandinavia: D Donnell
Manager UK Passenger Sales: M T Tamagni

Products: Wheel-mounted disc brakes, transmission disc brakes, solid and ventilated steel discs for high-temperature applications with sintered pad materials, axle-mounted disc brakes, with air or hydraulic actuation for all rail applications; complete electrical hydraulic systems; track brakes for LRV applications; wheel-slide prevention equipment; automatic mechanical and electric couplers; third-rail current collection devices and overhead current equipment.

Lucas Rail Products has supplied brakes for the majority of the disc-braked commuter stock operated by British Rail. The division's recent orders for disc brake equipment include the supply of brakes for the Class 158 dmus and supply of brakes for the Mk IV intercity coaches. Other recent orders cover the supply of brakes for the second tranche of London Docklands light rail vehicles; the first tranche of vehicles commenced passenger-carrying service in August 1987.

The range of high-duty axle-mounted discs, successfully introduced into the European market for main-line vehicle stock, has been successfully adapted for LRV and tram applications. The disc can be supplied with a complete or a split annulus, the latter enabling in-service disc replacement while retaining the original hub, and without the need to remove wheels.

The Lucas Girling ADB catalogue for ventilated axle-mounted discs has been supplied on request to railway vehicle engineers in over 40 countries. This catalogue is intended to assist in the early stages of vehicle design by identifying the performance and spatial requirements of brake systems for a wide range of applications. The brake-testing facility includes two computer-controlled dynamometers, the advanced control system which can simulate the effects of gradients, vehicle rolling resistance, blended supplementary braking, drag braking and air flow on the brake at speeds up to 300 km/h. These machines offer an inertia range of 200–7900 kg/m^2 and a maximum speed of 2000 rpm.

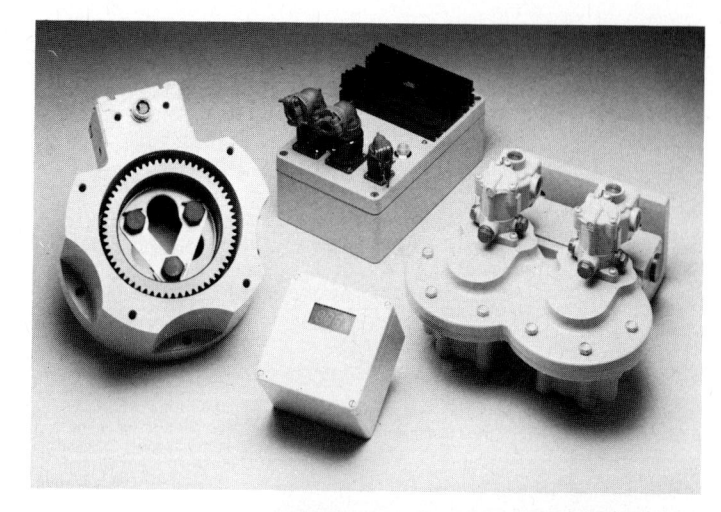

Adhesion-enhancing wheel slide protection equipment by Lucas Girling

Macosa
Material y Construcciones, SA

Plaza de la Independencia 8, Madrid 1, Spain

Telephone: +34 2 22 47 87
Telex: 22168

Products: Draftgear; buffers.

Matrix
A Division of Matrix Industrial Company (Pty) Ltd
(Formerly Sturrock (South Africa) Ltd)

1st Floor, Gallo House, Hood Avenue, Rosebank, South Africa

PO Box 1885, Parklands 2121, South Africa

Telephone: +27 788 1970
Telefax: +27 788 2780

Main works: 19 Maclean Street, Chamdor Industrial Township, Krugersdorp

General Manager: J B Ebden
Commercial Manager, Sales/Marketing: M K Appelblom
Technical Manager, Engineering: W S A Wyszkowski
Manufacturing Manager, Production: S J Pawlowicz

Principal subsidiary company
Matrix Industrial Co (Pty) Ltd
19 Maclean Street, Chamdor, Krugersdorp
P O Box 4093, Luipaardsvlei, 1743

Products: Locomotive and freight car braking equipment; mass transit car braking equipment; friction and rubber draft gear; brake automatic slack adjusters; friction snubbers; hand brake units.

An order worth R12.5 million has been received from SATS for 5000 ABDW Valves over 40 months.

Mecanoexportimport

'23 August' Works, 73428 Bucharest, Romania

Telephone: +40 0 28 30 10; 28 20 10
Telex: 10 344

Products: Brakes built under licence from Knorr-Bremse; drawgear equipment for locomotives and rolling stock.

Miner
Miner Enterprises Inc
International Division

PO Box 471, 1200 East State Street, Geneva, Illinois 60134, USA

Telephone: +1 312 232 3000
Telex: 190186; 720442
Telefax: +1 312 232 3123

Solid steel disc by Lucas Girling

President: C R Barney
Vice President M L McGuigan
Marketing Manager: C Vanbutsele

Products: Draftgear; buffers; snubbers; hand brakes; discharge systems for bulk commodities; TecsPak compression springs.

Amongst recent Miner products, TecsPak is a heavy-duty elastomeric spring package based on Hytrel, claimed to be up to ten times as durable as rubber. In endurance trials, a TecsPak buffer spring remained in excellent condition after seven consecutive UIC tests, while a comparable rubber spring suffered complete destruction of its lower half after a single UIC test. All buffers and traction springs in wagons built after the end of 1984 must meet new UIC standards. TecsPak completely satisfies the requirements for buffers with a minimum dynamic capacity of 30, 50 or 70 kJ (UIC-526-1), and for traction springs with a minimum capacity of 20 kJ (UIC-520), and does so with the use of existing buffer housings. TecsPak offers the simplicity of an all-elastomer spring combined with the high-performance previously obtained only from complicated designs. Several European railway administrations have already placed TecsPak buffers and traction springs in service in anticipation of the new UIC requirements.

The Miner SL-76 draftgear, developed for use in 24⅝-inch standard pockets, is approved in accordance with AAR Specification M-901E-82. It offers 44 980 ft-lb of capacity, the highest for an all-steel draft gear. The Crown SE is engineered for heavy-unit train applications with cars up to and including 100 short tons weight. The full pocket rectangular alloy steel housing and heat-treated steel components ensure toughness and durability.

The Miner TF-880 draft gear is the lightest weight, high-capacity draft gear available. The official capacity is 45 520 ft-lb in a gear weighing only 274 lb. The one-piece alloy housing and Miner's proven friction clutch concept assure a minimum of wear on draft attachments. The TecsPak elastomer spring provides optimum capacity in a lightweight, durable package.

Miner Constant Contact Side Bearings are engineered to reduce bogie hunting on cars ranging from lightweight articulated intermodal cars with 13 700 lb car bodies, up to heavy freight cars with 96 000 lb car bodies. The side bearings use the patented TecsPak elastomer spring to retain resilience and preload capabilities over a wide temperature range, assuring bogie hunting control under severe climatic conditions.

The AutoMEC air cylinder-activated hopper door

Brakes and drawgear / **MANUFACTURERS** 273

mechanism is adaptable for 8 to 20 door openings; and compressed air actuation can be specified as either a hand-operated four-way valve or side-mounted electrical pick-up shoe for in-motion discharge.

Foreign licensees

Argentina: Aceros Especiales SAIyC, Sarmiento 767, Buenos Aires

Australia: Comeng (Spares), a division of ANI Corporation Ltd, Private Bag 28, Post Office, Bankstown, New South Wales 2200

Brazil: Engesa-FNV, Avenida Tucunare 125/211, 06400 Barueri, SP

France: Usines et Acieries de Sambre et Meuse, Tour Aurore, 92080 Paris-Défense Cedex 5

India: Burn Standard Co Ltd, 10-C Hungerford Street, PO Box No 191, Calcutta 700 017

Mexico: Miner y Mendez de Mexico SA, Insurgentes Sur 2462, Villa Alvaro Obregon, 01070

South Africa: Conbrako (Pty) Ltd, PO Box 4018, Luipaardsvlei 1743

Spain: Material y Construcciones SA, Herreros, 2 (PN), Barcelona 19

Construcciones y Auxiliar de Ferrocariles SA, Padilla 17, 28006 Madrid

Switzerland: Georg Fischer Limited, 8201 Schaffhausen

United Kingdom: Gloucester Railway Carriage & Wagon Co Ltd, Cambrian Works, Maindy, Cardiff CF4 3XD

Yugoslavia: Fabrika Vagona Kraljevo, Postanski FAH 90, Kraljevo

Foreign sales agents

Argentina: D G Cormick SRL, Casilla de Correo 5260, Buenos Aires

Austria: Stabeg AG, Reinlgasse 5-9, 1140 Vienna

Chile: Peoro T Orellana M and Guillermo Campana T, Los Profetas 3629, Nunda-Santiago

China: HLK Services Ltd, 16th Floor, Shacombank Bldg, 666 Nathan Road, Kowloon, Hong Kong

Colombia: Quinteros Limitada, Apartado Aereo 4308, Bogota

Egypt: El Tahawy Foreign Trade, PO Box 33, El Mohandeseen, Cairo

Italy: GERA, Piazza Ludovico Antonio Muratori 3, 50134 Florence

Korea: Yu Jin Ki Kong Mfg Co Ltd, 82-22, 3-KA, Munrae-Dong, Young Deung Po-Ku, Seoul

Mexico: Mexican Railway Appliance Company, Insurgentes Sur 2462, Villa Alvaro, Obregon 01070

Peru: Restesa SRL, Casilla 804, Lima

Thailand: Borneo Tech Ltd, 231/2 South Sathorn Road, Bangkok 10120

Miner y Mendez
Miner y Mendez de Mexico SA de CV

Av Insurgentes Sur 2462, CP 01070 Mexico DF

Telephone: +52 550 8377
Telex: 17 72 503 stmme
Telefax: +52 550 6915

President: Felipe Zirion Quijano
Vice President, Marketing: Cesar Mota Aguilar
Sales Executives: Manuel Fernandez E, Ramon Ibarra G, Raul Peña Garza

Products: Miner TF-880 and 22-XL draftgears under licence from Miner Enterprises Incorporated; Flopack lubricators.

Mitsubishi
Mitsubishi Heavy Industries Ltd
Mitsubishi Electric Corporation

2-3 Marunouchi 2-chome, Chiyoda-ku, Tokyo 100, Japan

Telephone: +81 3 218 2637
Telex: 24532
Telefax: +81 3 218 2641

Products: Air brake systems and components for various locomotives, Shinkansen trains, other electric cars, diesel cars, freight cars, passenger cars, light rail vehicles, automated guideway transit and monorail.

Mitsubishi motor-driven air compressor

Mitsubishi electronic brake control unit

Low weight air compressors; air dryers; master controllers; brake control valves; brake operating units; blending units of electric and air brakes; brake cylinders; tread brake units; slip/slide protecting devices; testing devices.

Multi-Service Supply
Multi-Service Supply Division
Buncher Co

Leetsdale, Pennsylvania 15056, USA

Telephone: +1 412 741 1500
Telefax: +1 412 266 8631

President: Ralph L Coffing
Vice-President & General Manager: Timothy Crone
Director, Marketing: Larry Blair

Products: Air brake systems and components, repair and reconditioning.

MZ Tito-Skopje

Komerc-III, Mak Brigada BB, 91000 Skopje, Yugoslavia

Telephone: +38 91 220 033
Telex: 51700
Telefax: +38 91 233 252

Works: Ul Pero Nakov BB, 91000 Skopje, Yugoslavia

Principal subsidiaries: Hepos, Skopje; Mikron, Prilep

Manager: Sokole Ivanovski
Export Organiser: Branko Georgievski

Products: Brake regulators; brake cylinders; disc brakes; parking brake equipment; load brake equipment; weighing valves; slack adjusters; pipe connectors.

Contracts have been received recently from USSR, E Germany, Romania, Belgium, Turkey, Austria, Bulgaria and Poland.

NABCO
Nippon Air Brake Co Ltd

Head office: Sannomiya Building, Nishikan 1-12, Goko-dori 7-chome, Chuo-ku, Kobe 651, Japan

Telephone: +81 78 251 8101
Telex: 5622 143
Telefax: +81 78 251 8090

Tokyo office: Kokusai Hamamatsucho Bldg, 9-18, Kaigan 1-chome, Minato-ku, Tokyo 105

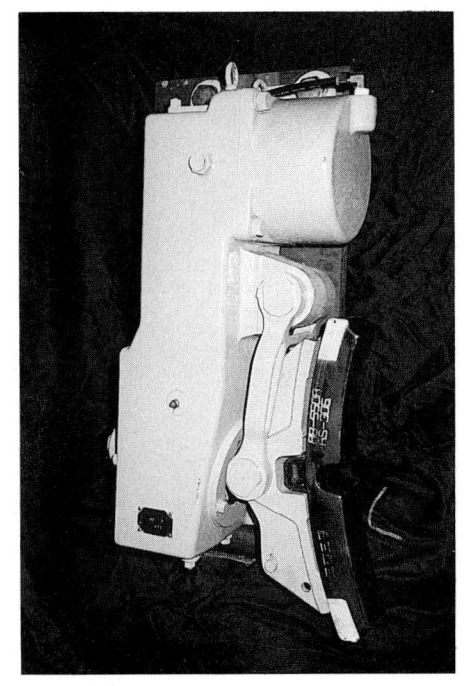

Mitsubishi tread brake

Telephone: +81 3 5470 2401
Telex: 242 2855
Telefax: +81 3 5470 2418

Works: Kobe, Seishin, Konan, Yokosuka, Tokyo

President: Masayuki Tsuchimoto
Managing Director: Yasuyuki Mashimo
Export Sales Manager: Shigeaki Hagihara

Products: Various air brake systems; NABCO shoe automatic slack adjusters; door operating equipment; windscreen wiper motors.

NABCO brake systems are operating on over 35 000 emu cars of various Japanese authorities and on the Shinkansen train-sets of Japanese National Railways. NABCO has also equipped the automated, rubber-tyred people mover systems of Osaka and Kobe, Japan.

Newag
Newag GmbH & Co

PO Box 101201, 4100 Duisburg 1, Federal Republic of Germany

Telephone: +49 203 33 40 61
Telex: 0855526

Products: Composition brake shoes, shoe carriers, disc brake pads.

Hitherto composition brake shoes have had the disadvantage of having a high content of asbestos. Normally the percentage of crystal and thus hazardous asbestos fibres which are dissipated into the environment is very small since the heat formed during braking converts crystalline fibres into an amorphous and thus non-hazardous state. Nevertheless, particularly in closed systems such as subways or metro tunnels, the remaining crystalline fibres can become a health hazard by slowly forming a concentration. Hence Newag has developed a range of non-asbestos composition brake shoes and can now supply appropriate friction materials with friction coefficients between $\mu = 0.15$–0.35 for any desired brake shoe. The same applies to Newag disc brake pads, which can be supplied with friction coefficients between $\mu = 0.25$–0.35.

Nippon Signal
The Nippon Signal Co Ltd

Head Office: 3-1 Marunouchi, 3-chome, Chiyoda-ku, Tokyo, Japan

Telephone: +81 3 237 4500
Telex: 222 2178

274 MANUFACTURERS / Brakes and drawgear

Works: Yono Factory, 13-8, Kamikizaki 1-chome, Urawa City
Utsunomiya Factory, 11-2, Hiraide Kougyo Danchi, Utsunomiya City

Associated companies: Nisshin Industrial Co Ltd
Nisshin Electrical Installation Co Ltd
Nisshin Electronics Service Co Ltd

President: H Takeuchi
Senior Managing Director, General Sales: T Oki
Managing Director, Foreign Trade: S Naganuma

Products: Synthetic resin brake shoes for high or low friction; grinding brake shoes; lining for disc brakes; brake shoe aline plates; anti-friction resin plates.

NYAB
New York Air Brake Co
Member of the General Signal group

Starbuck Avenue, Watertown, New York 13601, USA

Telephone: +1 315 782 7000
Telex: 937 304

President: P Owen Willaman
Vice President, Marketing: James C Pontious
General Manager, Railroad Sales: Michael C May
General Manager, New Product Development: Thomas H Engle
Vice President, Engineering: Bruce W Shute

Products: Brake systems for all types of rail vehicles including freight wagons, locomotives, transit and passenger stock. Freight systems are of the AAR type; other systems are pneumatic, electro-pneumatic, hydro-pneumatic or pure hydraulic designs. Transit products include ac or dc rotary screw-unitised (RSU) compressor and a complete line of cab-type single T-handle master controller (MC) propulsion and brake control devices.

Oerlikon Brakes
Machine Tool Works Oerlikon-Bührle Ltd

Birchstrasse 155, 8050 Zurich, Switzerland

Telephone: +41 1 316 22 11
Telex: 822031 obrech
Telefax: +41 1 311 57 51

Director: J Gysi

Products: Air brakes for automatic and direct systems, distributors, electro-pneumatic and pneumatic brake control valves, electronic anti-wheel spin and skid systems, automatic load brake devices and weighing valves, for any type of wagon, passenger car, locomotive, railcar, tramway, suburban train or metro.

Oerlikon Brakes, a department of Machine Tool Works Oerlikon-Bührle Ltd, produces complete control systems for automatic and direct air brakes as well as electro-pneumatic systems. The UIC-approved Oerlikon systems have been employed in many countries since the 1940s. Current products include:
The Type FVE 700 driver's brake valve, designed for use in railcar trains for control of the Oerlikon UTB electro-pneumatic and automatic air brake. Both systems are actuated in the same control sector of the operating lever;
The UTB universal railcar distributor valve, which can be controlled either by a seven-step electrical binary code or by the brake pipe of the automatic brake system;
The Oerlikon multi-functional electronic system, covering automatic EP-control, anti-skid, anti-wheel spin, speed-activated switches for track brake, door-operating, pressure step, etc and odometer;
Oerlikon brake panels containing complete pneumatic, electro-pneumatic and electronic devices for the brake control of train-sets, locomotives and coaches;
The Oerlikon EBO-1, a kit-principle system for passenger coaches and goods wagons which can be used to activate automatic air brake, automatic load-proportional braking with or without R/RIC changeover, automatic empty/load braking, two-step R brake or electro-pneumatic brake.

Recent contracts have included brake systems for: electric locomotives for Turkish State Railways (TCDD), built by Toshiba; AE locomotives for Netherlands Railways (NS), built by MAK; AM 86 train-sets for Belgian State Railways (SNCB); and NPZ train-sets for Swiss Federal Railways (SBB).

Oerlikon EBO-1 brake system for freight wagons, with one relay valve per bogie for load-dependent brake

Oleo
Oleo Pneumatics Ltd (UK)
Oleo International Holdings Ltd (Overseas)

Walcote, Blackdown, Leamington Spa, Warwickshire CV32 6QX, England

Telephone: +44 926 21116/8
Telex: 311458
Telefax: +44 926 450273

Managing Director: F M Thompson
Sales & Marketing Director: R W Elliott
Technical Director: D G Williams

Products: Oleo International is the leading supplier of hydraulic side buffers to major European railways. It has recently introduced specialised Long Stroke side buffers. By increasing the stroke from the traditional 105 mm to 150 mm, the energy capacity is increased by up to 50 per cent. The new Type 5SC-150 has been developed to meet the requirements of provisional UIC 526-3. Long Stroke hydraulic side buffers give additional flexibility in accommodating wide variations in wagon weights.

Also widely available are the standard Type 4EC-80-105 and 5SC-105 (high static resistance) side buffers which meet UIC 526. Where very high slow-closure resistance is required, the company offers the Type 3RCA in combination with a friction spring, supplied by Ringfeder.

The Oleo Hydraulic Draft Gear Type DA 4463 (Hycon) has an energy absorption capacity of 300,000 ft lb compared with a typical non-hydraulic alternative having an energy absorption capacity of 61,000 ft lb. The unit is designed to fit standard AAR 2458 in coupler pockets, and has been tested by the AAR and approved to M-901-K.

New products include the Oleo Draw Hook Snatch Damper, an adaptation of the well-proven Oleo side buffer capsule to protect draw hooks from snatch damage, particularly on long trains. The unit, designated HB804, is a direct 'drop-in' replacement for the rubber draw spring pack on those wagons equipped with standard UIC draw gear.

Also new is the energy-absorbing Anticlimber Side Buffer for passenger stock and is specified for the latest train sets (eg: BR Class 465). Used in conjunction with centre couplers, the Oleo series of anticlimbers is designed to meet two important functions: to absorb energy generated during an accident and to prevent coaching stock from climbing and 'piling up'.

Paulstra Hutchinson
Railway Department

61 rue Marius Aufan, 92305 Levallois-Perret, France

Telephone: +33 1 40 89 53 31
Telex: 613990 antiv f
Telefax: +33 1 47 57 44 20

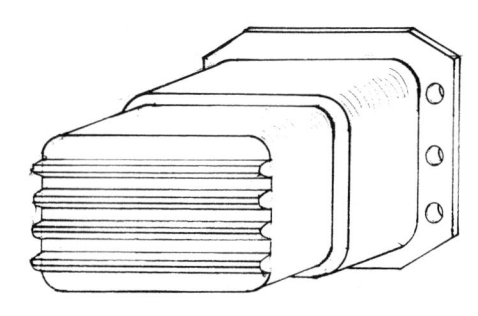

Oleo Anticlimber Side Buffer

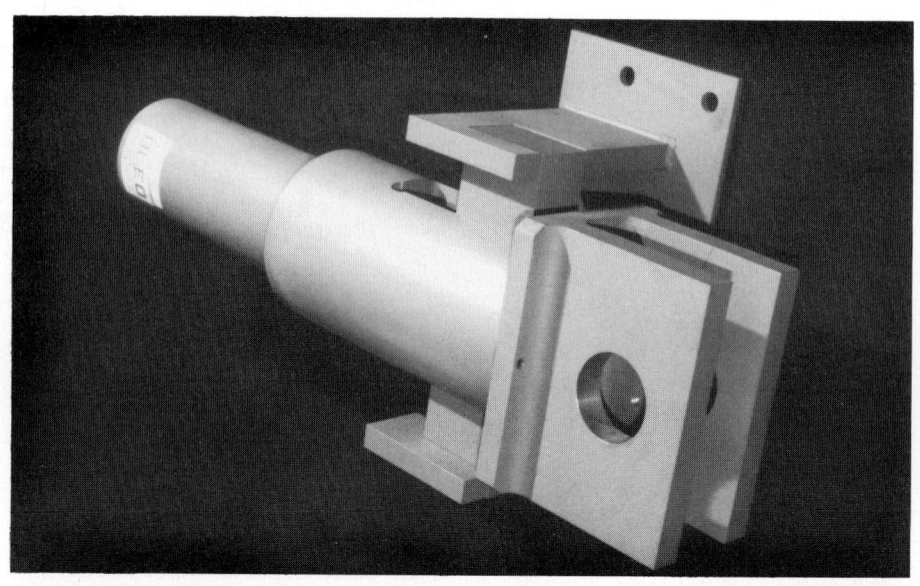

Oleo Draw Hook Snatch Damper

Products: Buffers; elastic couplings; primary and secondary suspension springs, bushes and oil seals.

Purdy
Purdy Co

2400 West 95th Street, Chicago, Illinois 60642, USA

Telephone: +1 312 239 4200

Products: Brake equipment.

Réservoir, Le
La Société le Réservoir

Rue Jean Henri Fabre, 03103 Montlucon, France

Telephone: +33 70 05 39 74
Telex: 390 675

Products: Brake reservoirs and cylinders.

RFS Engineering Ltd

PO Box 192, Hexthorpe Road, Doncaster DN1 1PJ, England

Telephone: +44 302 340700
Telex: 547296
Telefax: +44 302 340693

Managing Director: P Page
Technical Director: D W Theyers
Financial Director: B J Pierce
Director: L Harrison
Commercial Manager: M Rowe

Products: Accredited repair and overhaul of all brake and drawgear equipment with numerous contracts from both British Railways Board and the private vehicle producers, owners and operators.

Ringfeder
Ringfeder GmbH

Duisburger Strasse 145, Postfach 486, 4150 Krefeld-Uerdingen, Federal Republic of Germany

Telephone: +49 2151 450-1
Telex: 853846
Telefax: +49 2151 450 214

Managing Directors: Dipl Kfm Carl-Fr Krumm
Dipl Ing Horst-Dieter Schäfer
Dr Theo Wichterich

Subsidiary companies:
Ringfeder Ltd
Unit E 2, Forum Drive,
Midland Industrial Estate, Rugby, Warwickshire CV21 1NT, England

Ringfeder Corporation
165 Carver Avenue, PO Box 691, Westwood, New Jersey 07675, USA

Products: Side buffers, draw and buffing gear for automatic central coupling, drawgear.

Saalasti Oy

Arinatie 4, 00370 Helsinki, Finland

Telephone: +358 0 557 775
Telex: 124 694 insa sf
Telefax: +358 0 550 780

Products: Shunting couplers, multi-couplers, drawgears.
 Saalasti Oy has delivered over 600 automatic multi-couplers to the Finnish State Railways and to the private industry in Finland and Sweden. With this Vapiti multi-coupler it is possible to couple the locomotive to both the draw hook and to the central buffer. The latest model, Vapiti 90, is now also available, and it is especially suited for hauling passenger wagons due to its patented tensioning method.

Vapiti multi-coupler by Saalasti Oy

SAB WABCO

Head Office:
SAB WABCO NV, PO Box 3176, NL-2001 DD, Haarlem, Netherlands

SAB WABCO NV Coordination Centre
Imperia Straat 6, 1930 Zaventem, Belgium

Telephone: +32 27 59 79 12
Telex: 25395 sabnife b
Telefax: +32 27 59 32 45

President: Lennart Sjöstedt
Vice-President, Manufacturing & Product Development: Brian Cousins
Vice-President, International Operations: Roger Kemp
Vice-President, Finance & Administration: Keith Morrell

Principal subsidiaries:
BELGIUM
SAB WABCO NV, Walenberg 73, B1930 Zaventem

Telephone: +32 27 59 79 12
Telex: 25395 sabnif b
Telefax: +32 27 59 32 45
Managing Director: Lennart Kjellberg

BRAZIL
Suecobras Industria & Comercio Ltda, Rua Cachambi 713, CEP 207 80 Rio de Janeiro-RJ

Telephone: +55 21 201 4552
Telex: 21 23702, 21 33988 suic br
Telefax: +55 21 261 4266
Managing Director: Kristjan Laks

FRANCE–Office
Société SAB, 5 Avenue Caroline, BP 29, 92215 St-Cloud CEDEX

Telephone: +33 1 47 71 91 01
Telex: 250935 sabnife f
Telefax: +33 1 47 71 22 46
Directeur Commercial: Bruno Guillaumin

FRANCE–Works
Société SAB, Zone Industrielle, 80046 Amiens CEDEX

Telephone: +33 22 43 70 44
Telex: 140944 sabnife f
Telefax: +33 22 52 10 54
Directeur d'Usine: Pierre Majoni

SAB WABCO bogie brake panel, SNCF locomotive

MANUFACTURERS / Brakes and drawgear

SAB WABCO hydraulic disc brake for GEC Alsthom

SAB WABCO Type BF2L FPX tread brake unit with integrated parking brake

SAB WABCO brake disc for TGV Atlantique

FRANCE–Office & Works
WABCO Westinghouse Equipements Ferroviaires, 4 Boulevard Westinghouse, 93270 Sevran

Telephone: +33 1 43 32 14 20
Telex: 23151
Telefax: +33 1 43 32 02 66
Managing Director: Alain Pautonnier

GREAT BRITAIN–Office & Works
EFE (UK) Ltd, Thermal Road, Bromborough, Merseyside L62 4TR

Telephone: +44 51 334 4040
Telex: 627020
Telefax: +44 51 334 7243
Managing Director: J Mason

GREAT BRITAIN–Works
SAB Brake Regulator Co Ltd, Howden Way, Aycliffe Industrial Estate, Newton Aycliffe, Co Durham DL5 6HR

Telephone: +44 325 312666
Telex: 58416 sabnic g
Telefax: +44 325 310530

ITALY–Main Office & Works
WABCO Westinghouse SpA, via Volvera 51, 10045 Piossasco, Turin

Telephone: +39 11 90 44 1
Telex: 221340 wabco i
Telefax: +39 11 90 41 017
Managing Director: Victorio J Novelli

SAB Sistemi SpA, via P Petrocchi 24, 1501 27 Florence

Telephone: +39 55 43 98 91
Telex: 571496 sab i
Telefax: +39 55 41 36 55

SAB Ricerche Progetti Srl, via P Petrocchi 24, 1501 27 Florence

Telephone: +39 55 43 98 91
Telex: 573455 sabsil i
Telefax: +39 55 41 36 55

SPAIN
SAB Iberica SA, Avda Llano Castellano 13, E-280 34 Madrid

Telephone: +34 1 729 34 77/3950
Telex: 23108 sabni e
Telefax: +34 1 729 29 97
Managing Director: Bengt Ahlberg

SWEDEN-Office & Works
SAB Nordic AB, PO Box 515, S-261 24 Landskrona

Telephone: +46 418 162 80
Telex: 72416 sabife s
Telefax: +46 418 106 90
President: Lars Arnup

Related companies:
FRANCE
Faiveley Transport SA, 93 rue du Docteur-Bauer, 93407 Saint-Ouen CEDEX

Telephone: +33 1 40 10 35 00
Telex: 234653
Telefax: +33 1 40 12 00 93
(See separate entry)

ITALY
SAB Siliani SpA, via P Petrocchi 24, 1-501 27 Florence

Telephone: +39 55 43 98 91
Telex: 573455 sabsil i
Telefax: +39 55 41 36 55

USA
Westinghouse Air Brake Company, Wilderming, PA 15148-0001

Telephone: +1 412 825 1084
Telex: 199118
Telefax: +1 412 825 1158
(See separate entry)

Products: Complete range of braking systems for all types of locomotives, passenger and freight vehicles, including LRVs and guided vehicles with rubber tyres; UIC and AAR approved automatic air brakes to the requirements of most railway administrations; electropneumatic, electrohydraulic and all electric brake systems; vacuum and combined brake systems; air supply equipment, reciprocating and screw compressors, air treatment devices and accessories; air brake control devices of all types; automatic slack adjusters, variable load devices; friction brake devices, tread brakes, brake discs, caliper assemblies, disc brake actuators with options spring, hydraulic or mechanically operated parking; friction materials; electromagnetic track brakes in simple and segmented forms; UIC approved microprocessor controlled wheelslide protection devices, anti-slip and speed controls; data transmission systems, event recorders and monitoring devices; automatic test equipment for brake controls; air suspension control equipment; resilient wheels for mainline vehicles, noise reducing V wheels for LRVs; climate control equipment, air conditioning, heating and ventilating for locomotive cabs, passenger cars and LRVs; power supplies, multivoltage power supplies, static inverters for auxiliary on-board services and battery chargers; fluorescent lighting equipment; doors and door controls, complete range of sliding, folding and plug door systems for mainline metro and LRV applications; automatic computer controlled systems for marshalling yards; transit car coupling systems; vehicle current collectors; overhead power distribution systems.

Recent contract successes include:
HIGH SPEED TRAINS-TGV Atlantic (France), TAV (Spain), TMST (Channel Tunnel) complete brake control system for 144 trains plus disc brakes, tread brakes and parking brakes. ETR500 (Italy)-brake actuators and disc brakes. ICE (Germany)-brake actuators.
BILEVEL CARS-(France) 166 Z2N Paris suburban cars and 103 V2N middle distance cars. Complete air brake systems and disc and tread brakes as specified.
DMUS & EMUS-disc brakes for 500 BR Class 158, 165 and 465 units.
INTERCITY & LONG DISTANCE TRAINS-(Italy) air conditioning or heating equipment for 100 vehicles, door equipment for 136 vehicles, antiskid equipment for 90 vehicles, 45 kW power supplies for 72 vehicles.
EUROTUNNEL 252 SHUTTLE WAGONS-complete brake systems with monitoring, antiskid and air suspension system. Sliding plug-type emergency doors.
METRO CARS-nine trains, MF88 new generation cars, RATP Paris complete air brake system; 20 cars, Milan Metro, air brake system.
LRVs-VAL system. 91 trains for Orly, Toulouse (France) and Taipei. Complete air brake or electrohydraulic brake system as specified, air suspension system. Disc brakes for 95 LRVs for London Docklands, St Etienne (France), and Bern (Switzerland). Electrohydraulic brake systems for 45 vehicles for Rome and Naples (Italy); resilient wheels for Naples vehicles.
FREIGHT-air brake systems for 1450 wagons for Portugal, Algeria and Morocco, complete systems for 200 high speed disc-braked wagons for France, and 180 low-track force and small wheel wagons (UK).
LOCOMOTIVES-air brake equipment for 78 locomotives for France, Netherlands and Morocco. Rotary compressors for Italy and Metro North (USA). Cab air conditioning for 60 locomotives for Italian Railways.

Sambre et Meuse
Usines et Acieries de Sambre et Meuse

Tour Aurore, 92080 Paris-Défense Cedex 5, France

Telephone: +33 1 47 78 61 62
Telex: 620 161

President: Pierre Boissier
Sales Director: Jeanne-Pierre Jomeau

Products: Drawgears, buffers, UIC-type couplers, etc.

Scharfenbergkupplung GmbH

PO Box 411160, 3320 Salzgitter, Federal Republic of Germany

Telephone: +49 5341 214292
Telex: 954430 skud
Telefax: +49 5341 214202

General Managers: V Waldstätten
H J Jabs
Commercial/Sales Director: Dr Horn

Principal licensees
France: Alsthom-Atlantique, Paris
Netherlands: Noord-Nederlandsche Machinefabrick, Winschoten
India: Escorts Ltd, Faridabad
Italy: ABB Tecnomasio, Milan
Spain: CAF
Australia: Voith Australia Pty Ltd, Perth

Products: Automatic multi-function couplers and semi-permanent couplers for light rail rapid transit, tramways, subways, commuter rail systems, motor cars, passenger cars, freight cars, locomotives, automated guideway transit, mountain railways; special couplers for shunting vehicles, ladle cars, cranes; transition couplers.

SEE
Société Européenne d'Engrenages

5, rue Henri Cavallier, PO Box 110, 89104 Sens Cedex, Saint-Denis-Les-Sens, France

Telephone: +33 86 640688/953450
Telex: 800121 f seesens
Telefax: +33 86 951378

Commercial Director: Jean-Claude Prugne

Products: A complete range of disc brakes suitable for rail vehicles. Discs are made of cast iron moulded on a flexible high-grade steel member. Self-ventilation is obtained by specially-designed cooling passages. Discs are available in different versions: direct mounting on axle or wheel; bolted or flanged on the wheel; or split discs for easier replacement. Such discs equip railway coaches, trams, LRT, subways in France, Belgium, Austria, Portugal, Netherlands, USA, Philippines, Morocco.

SEE designed and manufactured the high-performance disc brake mounted on the French Railways (SNCF) TGV-Atlantique high-speed train (300 km/h speed in service). Thanks to the unique experience gained in this project, SEE has built several computer programmes for the calculation of disc performances and their mechanical characteristics especially for high-speed applications.

The company has introduced a new model of wheel flanged disc brake provided with flexible steel wheel fixation.

SEE has supplied all disc brakes for the 160 km/h cargo wagons purchased by the SNCF.

Constitution: SEE was created in 1981 as a joint venture of Pont-à-Mousson SA of France and Renk AG of West Germany (qv).

SIAM
SIAM, SA
Electrodomestic and Electromechanical Division

Cnel Molinedo 1600, 1870 Avellaneda, Buenos Aires, Argentina

Telephone: +54 1 208 5421
Telex: 24181 siam ar

Products: Standard and direct brake equipment and brake block travel adjusters for railroad cars.

SKF Argentina
SKF Argentina SA

Postal address: Casilla de Correo 197, 1000 Buenos Aires, Argentina
Head office: Perú 545, 1068 Buenos Aires

Telephone: +54 1 331 3061/8
Telex: 9203
Telefax: +54 1 331 8622/5280

Chairman: Göran Malm
Managing Director: Jimmie Holmberg

SKF Industriel SA
(Address as above)

Chairman: Tommy Karlsson
Managing Director: Raúl Horacio Gaspar

Products: Ball and roller bearings, axle boxes and mounting tools.

SMC
SMC Pneumatics (Australia) PTY Ltd

Transport Division head office: 161 Showground Road, Castle Hill, New South Wales 2154, Australia

Telephone: +61 2 680 3222
Telex: 7123152
Telefax: +61 2 634 7764

Manufacturing facilities: Australia, New Zealand, England, Federal Republic of Germany, Japan, Hong Kong, Singapore, USA, People's Republic of China, Thailand, France, Austria, Argentina, Chile and Venezuela

Branches: Italy, Malaysia, Netherlands, Switzerland, UK

Products: Air dryers and filters, drain valves, pressure and flow control valves, EP valves, door operating cylinders, special railway test equipment.

Recent contracts have included supply of pneumatic door operating equipment and current collection pantographs for the Hong Kong KCRC LRV project, SRA of NSW suburban, interurban and XPT passenger cars and 25 kV pantographs for Queensland Rail heavy haulage locomotives.

Socimi
Società Costruzioni Industriali Milano SpA

Via Varesina 115, 20156 Milan, Italy

Telephone: +39 2 30091
Telex: 323564

Main works
Via E Fermi n 25, 20082 Binasco (Milan)
Telephone: +39 2 9055605/6/7/8
Via Donatori del Sangue n 100, 20010 Arluno (Milan)
Telephone: +39 2 9017666/9017803
Viale Porto Torres, Reg Zentu Figghi, 07100 Sassari
Telephone: +39 79 235056

Chairman: Dr Eng Alessandro Marzocco
Managing Director: Dr Eng Pierino Sacchi
Assistant to Chairman: Dr Eng Corrado Landolina

Products: Disc brakes under BSI licence, electromagnetic track brakes, automatic couplers.

Stabeg
Stabeg Apparatebaugesellschaft GmbH

Reinlgasse 5-9, 1140 Vienna, Austria

Telephone: +43 1 92 23 57
Teletex: 0047 613222223

Products: Complete air brake equipment for locos, coaches, freight wagons; air springs; drawgear; buffer and drawgear; side buffers.

Trailer bogie disc brake supplied to Ferrovie Nord Milano (FNM) by Socimi

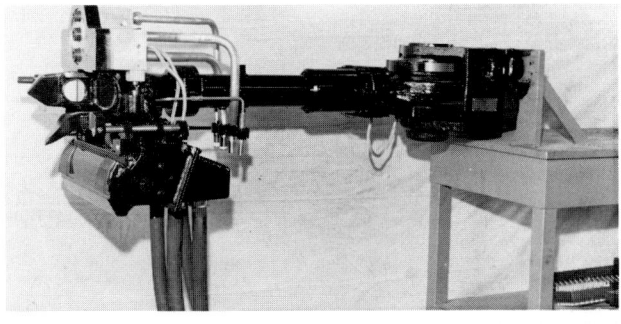

Automatic coupler produced for Rome Metro by Socimi

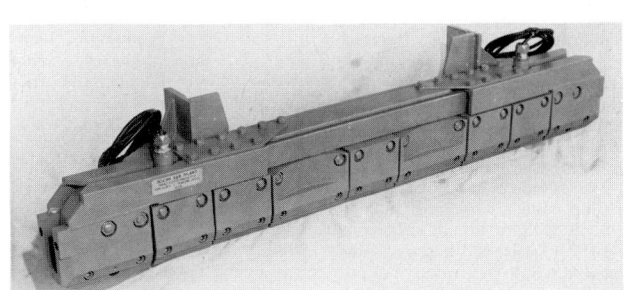

Electro-magnetic track brake by Socimi

MANUFACTURERS / Brakes and drawgear

SAB Type RK2 automatic slack adjuster for locomotive applications

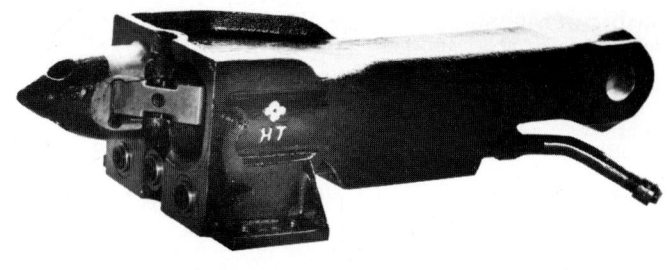

Sumitomo rotary key-block type of tight-lock automatic coupler for Shinkansen train-sets, Japanese National Railways

Stone
Stone India Ltd

16 Taratalla Road, Calcutta 700 088, India

Telephone: +91 33 77 3077
Telex: 021 7249

Chief Executive: V K Parashar

Products: Air brakes, locomotive valves, slack adjusters, train lighting, pantographs, superheaters.

Suecobras
Suecobras Indústria e Comércio Ltda
A company of SAB NIFE AB

Rua Cachambi 713, PO Box 20780, Rio de Janeiro, Brazil

Telephone: +55 21 201 4552
Telex: 21 23702 suic br
Telefax: +55 21 261 4266

President: Dr Eduardo Caio da Silva Prado
Managing Director: Kristjan Laks
Managing Director: Barry Bystedt
Railway Manager: Eduardo José Gomes Gonçalves

Products: Brake regulators; disc brakes; parking brake equipment; load brake equipment; weighing valves; axleboxes; automatic and semi-permanent couplers.

Sumitomo
Sumitomo Metal Industries Ltd
Ote Center Building, 1-1-3 Otemachi, Chiyoda-ku, Tokyo 100, Japan

Telephone: +81 3 282 6111
Telex: J22865
Telefax: +81 3 282 6764

General Manager, Sales: K Koshida
Senior Manager, Railway Products/Equipment Sales: Y Hirano

Products: Couplers; draftgear and steel castings for the railway industry.

TBL
TBL Limited
A BBA Group Co

11 Emery Road, Bristol BS4 5PF, England

Telephone: +44 272 710261
Telex: 44665
Telefax: +44 272 714298

Managing Director: I P Smith
Sales and Marketing Director: S Tearle
Technical Director: P Fitton
Rail Product Manager: D Brunskill

Products: High-and low-friction asbestos-free composite blocks for passenger and freight vehicles; asbestos-containing or asbestos-free disc pads for freight use; asbestos-free disc pads for passenger vehicle use; oil-immersed brake or clutch components.

The company is a major supplier of composite friction materials to British Rail and London Underground with other applications around the world. The BBA Group is the largest friction material manufacturing group in Western Europe. Created around a non-asbestos composite matrix, the brake block range includes TBL 800 series high-friction products which

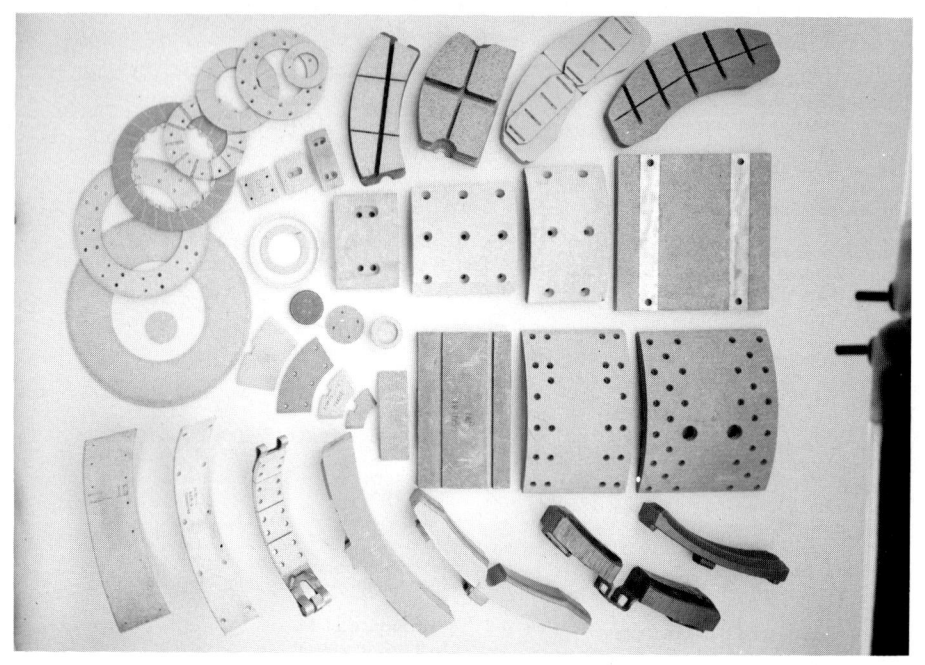

TBL products

have approvals for 25-tonne axleload freight braking, mass transit and multiple-unit intensive services, and are now finding applications in Inter-City stock for operations up to 200 km/h. Similarly, TBL 700 series disc brake pads have been developed for freight and Inter-City use, and low-friction TBL 900 series brake blocks offer a range of friction coefficients designed to allow direct replacement of cast-iron blocks. Tread brakes of composite materials are claimed to have at least twice the life expectancy of cast iron.

Recent contracts executed include one for London Underground. Environmentally friendly brake blocks with greatly extended life have been introduced during 1990, dramatically reducing brake dust and reducing cost per km for the blocks.

Licensees: Rane Brake Linings Ltd, India
Mintex-Don Marketing Pty Ltd, South Africa
Erka, Turkey
Bendix-Mintex Pty Ltd, Australia

Textar
Textar GmbH Brems-und Kupplungsbeläge

Jägerstrasse 1-25, 5090 Leverkusen 1, Federal Republic of Germany

Telephone: +49 214 540-0
Telex: 8510803

Products: Conventional and asbestos-free synthetic brake linings. Special materials have been developed for different types of vehicles and braking systems, as well as for different types of operation. The company's products are now used as standard equipment by Cologne's public transport company (KVB), Berlin's commuter system, the RATP Métro in Paris and STIB Métro in Brussels, Stockholm's Underground, the public transport systems of Basle, Grenoble, Göteborg and Prague, as well as Hong Kong's MTRC, and other well-known systems throughout the world.
Products include:
T 535 asbestos-free friction material for high-speed intercity service at speeds up to 200 km/h and commuter service where equipment is subjected to excessive heat build-up. Used in conjunction with cast iron and steel, the coefficient of friction is exceptionally stable, and at the same time the counter-material is subjected to minimum wear. Material: rubber and synthetic resin-bound metals, oxides and sulphates. Average coefficient of friction: 0.35.
T 536 asbestos-free friction material for commuter and local underground service at speeds up to 100 km/h and average thermal conditions. A constant coefficient of friction is claimed under all service and weather conditions, with no glazing (long-term fading) under low load in stopping or blending operation. For shunting locomotives the material demonstrates very high impact strength in shunting operation with considerable reversing. No noise development. Material: rubber and synthetic resin-bound metals, oxides and sulphates. Average coefficient of friction: 0.34.
T 539 asbestos-free friction material for streetcar and commuter service with disc or shoe brakes. Material: rubber and artificial resin-bound metals, oxides and sulphates. Average coefficient of friction: 0.30.
T 541 asbestos-free friction material for locomotives. Synthetic lining material with constant coefficient of friction, even when exposed to humidity and snow. Material: rubber and artificial resin-bound metals, oxides, sulphates and silicates. Average coefficient of friction: 0.20-0.25.

Tokyu Car
Tokyu Car Corporation

1 Kamariya-cho, Kanazawa-ku, Yokohama 236, Japan

Telephone: +81 45 701 5151
Telex: 3822 392
Telefax: +81 45 781 7962

Products: Disc brakes.

Triax-Davis
(Formerly Davis Brake Beam Co)

PO Box 338, Johnstown, Pennsylvania 15907, USA

Telephone: +1 814 535 1595

President: Bob Jackson
Plant Manager: Gordon L Jacobs

Products: Solid-truss brake beams and bogie-mounted braking system manufactured under the trade-name, Truc-Pac.

By providing simultaneous control of piston stroke and lever angularity, the Truc-Pac system is claimed to overcome deficiencies inherent in most of the compact bogie braking systems that have eliminated body-mounted rigging. These are that, without piston stroke control, the piston stroke tends to lengthen to compensate for wheel or shoe wear; or that with reliance solely on stroke control, there may be an increase in lever angularity. In both cases a reduction of braking force ensues.

Through extensive testing, Triax-Davis found that diagonal 'binding' of the unit end extension in the side frame guide pockets causes major brake beam problems with wear on the unit end extensions. Other designs, in order to eliminate binding, allow the entire beam to sag, which in turn puts undue wear on the shoes, rigging and truck components. This in turn causes the brake shoe to make contact with the wheel at an angle that causes uneven wear. Triax-Davis claims to have solved these problems with a new unit brake beam that has a one-piece head and a completely redesigned support extension.

At the heart of this design is a unique contour which eliminates diagonal corner contact without diminishing either the overall thickness or length of the support extension. The result is a brake beam that has smooth travel in the guide pockets, prohibits sagging and allows the brake shoe to meet the wheel on a level plane for uniform wear.

Triax-Davis's design and production procedures make brake head replacement easy and inexpensive. Strong, secure two-piece rivets eliminate cutting and welding. Identically matched holes in the head and truss automatically put the brake beam into AAR gauge, eliminating costly labour and jigging equipment.

Uzinexportimport

Calea Victoriei 133, Bucharest, Romania

Products: Brake regulators; disc brakes; parking brake equipment; load brake equipment; weighing valves.

Valeo
Va Leo

64 avenue de la Grande Armée, 75017 Paris, France

Telephone: +33 1 574 96 96
Telex: 280 844

Products: Automotive components.

WABCO
Passenger Transit Division

PO Box 11, Spartanburg, S Carolina 29304, USA

Telephone: +1 803 439 5400
Telex: 1561192 wabco
Telefax: +1 803 439 0856

Vice President & CEO: W E Kassling
Vice President & General Manager: J Meister
Manager, International Marketing: J R Raspet

Products: Friction brake systems for light rail, heavy rail, commuter and passenger rail vehicles; pneumatic, electronic and hydropneumatic equipment couplers, disc and tread brake units, compressors, dryers and accessory devices.

WABCO
Locomotive and Rubber Products Division

Wilmerding, Pennsylvania 15148, USA

Telephone: +1 412 825 1000
Telex: 199118 wabco ut
Telefax: +1 412 825 1019

Vice-President & CEO: W E Kassling
Vice-President & General Manager: H J Bromberg
Manager, International Marketing: J R Raspet

Products: Locomotive braking equipment including air brake control equipment with engineer's brake valve, control valve, relay valves, safety control valves, brake cylinders, air flow indicators, air compressors (new and remanufactured). Also rubber parts such as O-rings, seals, gaskets etc, and rubber maintenance kits for air brake components.

WABCO
Westinghouse Air Brake Division

Wilmerding, Pennsylvania 15148, USA

Telephone: +1 412 825 1000
Telex: 199118 wabco ut
Telefax: +1 412 825 1019

Vice-President & CEO: W E Kassling
Vice-President, Marketing: J Duffy
Manager, International Marketing: J R Raspet

Products: Freight wagon air brake control equipment including control valves (ABDW/ABDX/ABDX-L), brake cylinders, retaining valve, combined dirt collector and cut-out cock, reservoirs and angle cocks; Cobra high friction composition brake shoe and disc pads, bogey mounted WABCOPAC and WABCOPAC II brake assemblies and empty and load equipment.

WABCO Westinghouse
Compagnia Freni SpA

Head office and main works: Via Volvera 51, 10045 Piossasco, Turin, Italy

Telephone: +39 11 9044 1
Telex: 221340 wabco i
Telefax: +39 11 904 1017

Vice-President, Managing Director and General Manager: V J Novelli

Products: Braking systems: air compressors and air treatment devices, self-lapping control valves, brake cylinders with or without automatic slack adjuster, electro-magnetic track brakes, brake units for disc and shoe brakes, tread brake units with or without parking brake, antiskid, antislide and electronic speed control systems.

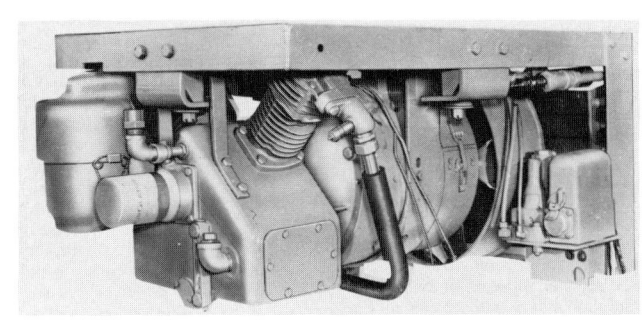

WABCO D-4 two-stage, two-cylinder, single-acting, air-cooled compressor

WABCO 30-CDW piloting-type, console-mounted brake valve for compact cab installation

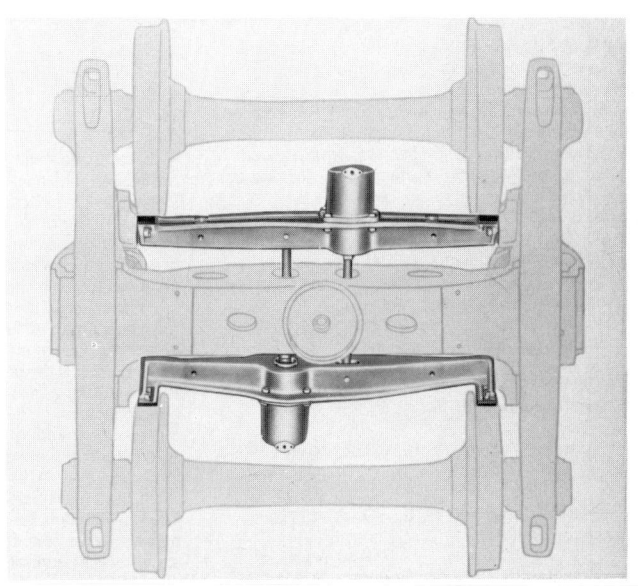

WABCOPAC brake assembly combining brake cylinder and brake beam functions

MANUFACTURERS / Brakes and drawgear

Climate control: underroof and/or underframe-mounted heating and ventilating equipment for passenger coaches, air-conditioning systems for long-distance, sleeping and dining cars as well as for locomotives and metro cabs.

Power supply: multivoltage power supply, static inverters for auxiliary on-board services and battery chargers.

Doors and door controls: complete range of sliding, folding and plug door systems for metro and railway passenger vehicles.

Fluorescent lighting: ceiling single lights, luminous rows, ballasts.

WABCO Westinghouse
WABCO Westinghouse Equipements Ferroviaires SA

4 boulevard Westinghouse, 93270 Sevran, France

Telephone: +33 1 43 32 14 20
Telex: 231514 f
Telefax: +33 1 43 32 02 66

Managing Director: Alain Pautonnier
Commercial Director: B de Malberck

Products: Complete air supply equipment for rolling stock; complete braking system (air-vacuum) for all types of traction, passenger and freight vehicles; marshalling yard automatisation.

Recent contracts executed include complete brake control system for TGV-A high-speed trains of SNCF; 800 braking equipments for freight cars in Morocco; Gevrey and Miramas marshalling yard automatisation for SNCF.

WABCO Westinghouse
**Steuerungstechnik GmbH & Co
Railway Division**

Bartweg 13, PO Box 911270, 3000 Hanover 91, Federal Republic of Germany

Telephone: +49 511 2136-0
Telex: 921 415 63 wawe d

Managing Director and General Manager: H Kedzierski

Products: Air brake equipment including:
Compressors and accessories; safety valves; check valves; air dryers.
Control and regulation devices; driver's brake valves; control valves for pneumatic and electropneumatic systems; all-electric brake systems.
Change-over devices; two or more-stage relays; variable relay valves.
Effort-producing devices: cylinders with or without slack adjuster for shoe brake or disc brake or without slack adjuster for shoe or disc brake systems; tread brake unit with or without parking brake.
Mass transit brake equipment, motive power control for diesel-hydraulic vehicles. Vacuum brake equipment: Effort-producing devices: cylinders; diaphragm actuators.
Dual brake equipment: air pressure brake on locomotive and air or vacuum brake on the train.
Electronics:
Marshalling yard automation: retarder and complete range of devices for target-shooting system.
On-board signalling repetition for max speed of 300 km/h; speed control systems, anti-skid and anti-slide systems.
Power supply equipment: Static inverters; battery chargers.
Climate control equipment: Heating and air conditioning equipment.
Lighting equipment: Fluorescent ceiling lighting units; continuous luminous rows; ballasts.
Doors and door control equipment.

Walton
Walton Products Inc

868 Sussex Boulevard, Broomall, Pennsylvania 19008, USA

Telephone: +1 215 544 8410
Telefax: 328 5489

Vice President & General Manager: W R Rorer
Marketing Manager: S W Madeira

Products: Automatic couplers, including mechanical coupler assemblies, and electro-pneumatic system, designed and manufactured by Walton Electric Coupler Inc. Diaphragms, toilets, body-end doors, etc, manufactured by Walton Products Inc.

Westinghouse Brakes
Westinghouse Brakes Ltd
A subsidiary of Westinghouse Brake and Signal Co Ltd
A Hawker Siddeley Company

PO Box 74, Foundry Lane, Chippenham, Wiltshire SN15 1HY, England

Telephone: +44 249 654141
Telex: 449411
Telefax: +44 249 655040

Chairman: H R Grant
Managing Director: J R C Boulding
Finance Director: S R Crook
Marketing Director: E J Widdowson
Manufacturing Director: M C Colyer

Products: Electro-pneumatic brakes for suburban and rapid transit trains; UIC-approved graduable release automatic air brakes for locomotives, carriages and wagons; AAR-approved direct-release automatic air freight brakes; dual air and vacuum brakes; spring-applied brakes; parking brakes; wheelslide correction equipment; automatic warning systems; automatic train operating equipment; disc brakes and friction materials; air compressors; air dryers; air flow measuring equipment; vigilance and deadman's systems; uncouplers; air suspension equipment; brake equipment test racks and portable test trolleys.

Complete systems available include:
UIC-approved graduable release automatic air brakes for passenger carriages and freight wagons. These include Type P4a series distributors, with variable load feature if required. Control of the pressure in the automatic brake pipe may be pneumatic by means of a self-lapping driver's brake valve or electro-pneumatic by means of a small brake controller in the driver's desk and an associated control unit elsewhere. The latter system is adaptable for control by manual push buttons or automatic electrical circuits.

AAR-approved direct-release air brake equipment for freight vehicles. The Z1AW control valve included in these equipments is compatible and interchangeable with AB, ABD and ABDW control valves, and makes use of the same standard pipe bracket. Also available is the Z1A control valve for use when an accelerated application feature is not required.

Vacuum brake equipment for passenger carriages and freight wagons. This equipment is marketed under the name Gresham and Craven.

Dual vacuum/air brake equipment for locomotives, for use by railways that decide to change over from the vacuum brake to the automatic air brake and require locomotives that are capable of operating trains fitted with either type of brake during the period of transition.

Air brake equipment for locomotives (suitable for operation with any class of train). This includes straight air brakes and straight air with emergency brakes for shunting (switching) locomotives; vacuum-controlled straight air brakes for locomotives that haul vacuum-braked trains; and straight air and automatic brakes for locomotives that haul trains fitted with air brakes, whether of the direct-release or graduable-release type.

Electro-pneumatic brake equipments for suburban passenger and rapid transit trains. These include the Westcode ep brake with digital control, in which the electrical control circuits usually comprise three or more train wires that are connected throughout a train and are energised and de-energised by means of switches to apply and release the brake on all vehicles simultaneously. This form of control permits the brake to be graduated on and off in steps and may be used when the brake is to be operated from either a separate driver's brake controller or a combined traking and traction controller. Alternatively, the electro-pneumatic brake may have analogue control, in which the electrical control is usually by means of a wire connected throughout a train to form a continuous loop, to which a variable current or a pulse width modulated (pwm) signal is applied. This arrangement affords a stepless control of the brake and is particularly suitable when the traction equipment requires the same type of control and the two systems are to be operated from a combined braking and traction controller. Both types of electro-pneumatic brake are suitable for use with automatic train operation equipment. A recent addition to the suburban and rapid transit product range has been an electro-pneumatic straight air brake system designated type WE2.

Graduable-release automatic air brakes for railcars including type P5 distributors, ep brakes and straight air with emergency brake equipment.

Air brake equipment for industrial and mines locomotives and rolling stock, railcranes, special purpose rail vehicles etc. The traditional brake for mines vehicles is the straight air and emergency system. This is manufactured in brass and ferrous materials for use in coal mines. A spring-applied air-released brake system is also available.

Deadman's and vigilance control systems.

Wheelspin and/or slide control systems. The equipment includes electronic control units, frequency generators and brake cylinder blowdown devices, and is arranged so that if a condition of incipient wheel sliding develops while the brake is applied, the braking force on the affected axles is reduced to allow them to regain speed. Alternatively, if the acceleration of an axle begins to exceed a predetermined level while tractive power is being applied, tractive power may be arrested at its existing level, or reduced, as required.

Remote-operated parking brake equipment. Parking brakes may be of the air-released spring-applied type. Alternatively, electro-pneumatic or electro-hydraulic parking brakes may be provided in which pneumatic or hydraulic pressure is exerted to apply the brake initially, and is then relaxed to leave the brake blocked on mechanically by a nut and clutch mechanism in each actuator. The brake is released by re-exerting the pressure to disengage the clutch.

Air suspension control equipment.
Automatic warning equipment.

Special on-vehicle equipments offered include:
Mechanically-driven air compressors, air-cooled machines with capacities ranging from 221 to 1416 litres/minute free air delivery, at pressures up to 9.65 bar.

Electrically-driven air compressors (for normal traction auxiliary voltages, either ac or dc), which are air-cooled; motors may be totally enclosed, screen-protected or pipe-ventilated depending upon operating conditions. Capacities range from 283 to 1487 litres/minute free air delivery, at pressures up to 10.34 bar.

Regenerative type dryers in which an adsorptive desiccant is used to remove water from moist air and is regenerated by a purge of dry air. The dryer is installed in the air delivery pipe from the air compressor and includes a timer to ensure that, as the compressor stops and starts during its normal operating cycle, the correct drying sequence is resumed whenever the compressor is restarted.

Air flow measuring equipment for use with locomotive air brakes, comprising an air flow measuring valve for fitting between the main air storage reservoirs and the driver's brake valve, and an indicator for mounting in the instrument panel on the driver's desk. The indicator is connected to the valve and has a scale which is directly proportional to the mass air flow through the driver's brake valve into the brake pipe, and so provides an indication of the amount of brake pipe leakage that is taking place.

Brake cylinder and slack adjusters.
Tread brake units.
Disc brake actuators.
Rail diesel engine control devices.

Driver's combined traction and braking controllers, ranging from small brake controllers containing only a few cam-operated switches, through combined controllers affording control of braking and traction by means of a single handle, to complete driver's desks specially designed to blend with the interior of the cab and containing traction controls and other apparatus as well as brake control equipment.

Subsidiaries
Australia: Westinghouse Brake & Signal Co (Aust) Pty Ltd, PO Box 120, PO Concord West, New South Wales 2138
Canada: Westcode Ltd, 3688 Nashua Drive, Unit 'F', Mississauga, Ontario L4V 1M5
USA: Westcode Incorporated, 90 Great Valley Parkway, Great Valley Corporate Center, Frazer, Pennsylvania 19355

Bogies and suspensions, wheels and axles

ARGENTINA
Forja 285

AUSTRALIA
Bradken 283
Comsteel 284

BELGIUM
Braine-le-Comte 283
Cockerill Forges & Ringmill 284

BRAZIL
Mafersa 287

CANADA
Invar 287

FRANCE
ANF-Industrie 282
Ascometal Valdunes 283
De Dietrich 285
Ferraz 285
GEC Alsthom 286
Sambre et Meuse 290

GERMANY, DEMOCRATIC REPUBLIC
FWZ 286
Görlitz 286
LEW 287
Rafil 290

GERMANY, FEDERAL REPUBLIC
Ferrostaal 285
Krupp Brüninghaus 287
MAN GHH 288
Phoenix 289
Ruhfus 290
Wegmann 293

HUNGARY
Ganz 286
Nikex 288

INDIA
Cimmco International 284
Wheel & Axle 293

ITALY
Fiat 285
Socimi 291
Terni 293
TIBB (BBC Brown Boveri) 293

JAPAN
Sumitomo 292

NETHERLANDS
Koni 287

POLAND
Pafawag 288

ROMANIA
Arad 283

SOUTH AFRICA
Ringrollers 290
RSD 290

SPAIN
Macosa 287
Talleres de Amurio 292

SWEDEN
ABB 282
SAB NIFE 290

SWITZERLAND
BBC-Sécheron 283
SIG 290

USSR
Energomachexport 285

UK
ABB British Wheelset 293
Avon 283
BREL 284
HDA Forgings 286
International Metal Service (UK) 286
Metalastik 288
Powell Duffryn Standard 289
RFS Engineering 290
Silentbloc 291
Specialist Rail Products 292
Wickham 293

USA
ABC 282
Adirondack 282
ASF 283
Beall 283
Buckeye 284
Griffin 286
GSI 286
Lord 287
National Castings 288
Penn 289
R W Mac 290
Standard 292
Stucki 292

MANUFACTURERS / Bogies and suspensions

ABB
ASEA Brown Boveri Transportation

(For full details of all ABB companies see ABB entry in Locomotives section.)

Products and services–Sweden:
Some 20 years ago ABB engineers began to develop models for computer-aided mathematical analysis of bogie behaviour. With these programmes it is now possible to define characteristics and running performance already at the design stage. The aim was to increase the speed on existing tracks without running into stability problems and also to reduce wear of wheels and rails.

Rubber chevrons have been traditionally used for the primary suspension in all ABB bogies. The computer programmes provided the basis for design of these chevrons with carefully calculated stiffness in the vertical, lateral and longitudinal directions and also for definition of how and where the necessary damping should be applied in the system. Steering of the wheel-set is achieved exclusively by the conicity of the wheel treads in combination with creep forces between wheel flange and rail.

A passenger coach bogie was developed for Swedish State Railways (SJ) and measurements prove that the wear is reduced by about 80 per cent on curved tracks. A large number of such passenger coach bogies are in use in several countries.

ABB has extended its railway bogie programme with a new freight car bogie with the radially self-steering quality, resulting in low track forces, significant reduction of wheel and track wear and improved running performance of the car.

The company has a long and wide experience in using rubber elements for the primary suspension and wheel-set guidance to obtain the self-steering capability. A similar design concept has been used on the freight car bogie. For secondary suspension and damping a design utilising the advantages of rubber components has again been used. By an optimised combination of springing and damping the car will maintain its running properties independent of load. This combination includes rubber springs, friction wedges and friction damping. The rubber springs carry the bolster and are located in the spring pocket of the side frame. The springs are designed for a progressive characteristic. The spring stiffness is proportional to the vertical load both in vertical and lateral directions. The yaw damping is achieved by the centre plate and vertical and lateral damping by a friction wedge acting on the side frame. The vertical damping is proportional to the vertical load, while the lateral damping is independent of the load. The bogie has been substantially tested both in Australia (1067 mm version) and in Sweden. The tests have been carried out at speeds up to 170 km/h, on different track standards and with different loads up to 22.5 metric tonnes. Conclusions of the test results are claimed to be that track shifting forces are well below limits under all conditions; that the ride index (Wzg) both laterally and vertically is good and well below limits under all conditions (as an example, Wzg increases from 2.7 at 120 km/h to 3.0 at 170 km/h on a good Swedish mainline track); and that the radial self-steering ability operates well even during brake application. The bogies have been in revenue service under a number of freight cars on Swedish State Railways since 1988.

Recent contracts include bogies of a special design for tilting car bodies in curves, and are in production for the Swedish X2 high-speed trains.

ABC
ABC Corporation
Railroad Products Group

200 South Michigan Avenue, Chicago, Illinois 60604, USA

Telephone: +1 312 322 0360
Telex: 756108
Telefax: +1 312 322 0377

President: G E Stinson
Vice President, Operations: J F Hinel
 Marketing: P E Dunn
Export Marketing Manager: J D Rayan

Products: Cast steel wheels, composition and metal brake shoes.

Bogie for car of Swedish State Railways' Type X2 high-speed train by ABB

ABB passenger car bogie with radial self-steering characteristics

ABB's newly-developed freight car bogie with radially self-steering wheel-sets

Adirondack
Adirondack Steel Casting Co Inc

Watervliet, New York 12189, USA

Products: One-piece, cast steel bogies.

ANF-Industrie
Société ANF-Industrie

Tour Aurore, 92080 Paris-Défense Cedex 5, France

Telephone: +33 1 47 78 62 62
Telex: 610 817 anf courb
Telefax: +33 1 47 78 62 66

Chairman: Michel de Lambert de Boisjean
Sales Manager: Jean-Claude Viche

Works: Place des Ateliers, BP No 1, 59154 Crespin, Blanc-Misseron, France

Products: Power and trailer bogies of all types for passenger equipment.

Among recent orders from SNCF are 332 Type Y401 power bogies for Z2N double-deck power cars; 442 Type Y36 P2A carrier bogies for double-deck trailer cars and 500 carrier bogies for TGV-R.

ANF-Industrie type Y36P bogie for French Railways bi-level emu cars

Prototype bogie with steerable axles for new generation of Paris Metro cars by ANF-Industrie

ANF-Industrie motor bogie for French Railways Type X2200 diesel railcar

Bogies and suspensions / **MANUFACTURERS**   283

Arad
Intrerrinderea de Vagoane

Calea Aurel Vlaicu 41-43, 2900 Arad, Romania

Telephone: +40 966 37292
Telex: 76256

General Manager: Mihai Surany
Technical Manager: Ioan Pantea
Export Sales Manager: Sandu Albulescu

Products: Bogies for passenger and special-purpose cars.

Constitution: A member of the Car Building and Rolling Stock Trust.

Ascometal Valdunes

Immeuble Elysées La Défense, 29 le Parvis, 92072 Paris-La-Défense 4, Cedex 35, France

Telephone: +33 1 47 67 91 17
Telex: 61 4623 asfor
Telefax: +33 1 47 67 91 11

Chairman: Bernard Rogy
Chief Sales Director: Claude Vidal

Products: Wrought solid wheels; straight axles; mounted wheel-sets.

ASF
American Steel Foundries
A division of Amsted Industries Inc

3700 Prudential Plaza, Chicago, Illinois 60601, USA

Products: Ride Control bogies. The ASF Ride Control bogie snubbing system is a built-in design that maintains constant control of spring action. The ASF side frames and bolsters exceed AAR strength requirements and can be furnished either as grade B or grade C steel castings. The pressure between the friction shoes and the side frame friction plates provides the necessary loadings to exercise optimum control. This pressure is generated by the ride control springs which force the friction shoes up the inclined ledges and outwardly against the friction plates. These ride control springs are compressed during assembly, and this amount of compression is not changed by varying bolster loads or truck spring movements, thus maintaining damping and alignment control at the light car condition. ASF is also a major producer of coil load bearing springs for all railway applications.
  A recent development is the Super Service Ride Control AR-1 bogie. This incorporates a rugged, dependable and proven steering capability to insure high-speed stability, and radial curving of wheel-sets to dramatically reduce wheel flange-rail interaction, with corresponding reduction in wear and rolling resistance.

Exports: All inquiries for supply outside the USA should be addressed to Amsted Industries International, 200 West Monroe Street, Chicago, Illinois 60606, USA. Telephone: +1 312 372 5386. Telex: 254187.

Avon
Avon Industrial Polymers Ltd

Bradford-on-Avon, Wiltshire BA15 1AA, England

Telephone: +44 2216 3911
Telex: 44856
Telefax: +44 2216 3780

Sales Manager: G M Lewis
Technical Manager: J R K Parry

Products: Suspension systems, including air springs, chevrons and primary/secondary suspension bondings; sealing sections; drawgear packs/buffing springs and special requirement rail pads.

Trailer wheel-sets with disc brakes for French Railways TGV train-sets by Ascometal Valdunes

ASF ride control AR-1 bogie

BBC-Sécheron
BBC-Sécheron SA

Avenue de Sécheron 14, 1211 Geneva 21, Switzerland

Telephone: +41 22 39 41 11
Telex: 22130
Telefax: +41 22 34 21 94

Products: All-electric wheel flange lubricator, particularly suited to vehicles without incorporated compressed air supply, as is often the case on underground railways and tramways. The WFL all-electric lubricator has been specially designed for reduction: of wheel flange and rail wear; of rolling resistance, for traction power savings; and of friction coefficient, to eliminate risk of derailment and also wheel squealing. Other wheel flange lubricators (Type Lausanne and GB 80), which are air-operated, are available.
  Recent contracts include supply of the all-electric Type WFL to Public Transport Geneva (TPG) and the Bern-Solothurn Railway (RBS).

Beall
Beall Manufacturing inc

112 North Shamrock, PO Box 70, East Alton, Illinois 62024, USA

Telephone: +1 618 259 8154
Telefax: +1 618 259 7953

President: M Speciale
Sales Manager: A Rahn
Engineering Manager: C Jorgenson

Products: Elliptic leaf springs for locomotives and cabooses; trackwashers.

Bradken
Bradken Consolidated

22 O'Riordan Street, Alexandria, Sydney, New South Wales 2015, Australia

Telephone: +61 2 699 3000
Telex: 21512 aa
Telefax: +61 2 698 1559

Chief Executive Officer: I Bonnette
Executive Manager, Transport Division: R Hunter
Manager, Transport Sales: D Cummings

Products: Passenger, freight and locomotive bogies, wheels, drawgear and other general castings.

Braine-le-Comte
Ateliers de Braine-le-Comte et Thiriau Reunis SA

Rue des Frères Dulait 14, 7490 Braine-le Comte, Belgium

Telephone: +32 67 56 02 11
Telex: 046 57458
Telefax: +32 67 56 12 17

Sales Manager: André Lejeune
Commercial Railway Division: Richard Brohée

Products: Wagons; metallic welded bogies and three axle bogies; rail-road vehicle; maintenance of wagons and equipment; crane wagons and ladle wagons.

MANUFACTURERS / Bogies and suspensions

Recent contracts include 100 container wagons for Railway Company of Zaire (1988); 13 crane wagons for Belgian Railway Company (1990); nine casting cars-smelt metal transport for Belgian iron and steel industry (1990); FIAT bogies for carriages for Belgian Railway Company (1991).

BREL
BREL (1988)

St Peters House, Gower Street, Derby DE1 1AH, England

Telephone: +44 332 383850
Telex: 377693/377898 brestp g
Telefax: +44 332 45737

Bogie Business Manager: K W Pennington (Headquarters)
Sales Manager (Bogies): A Brown (Factory: Telephone: +44 332 383737 Ext 4906; Telex: 37421 bredlo)

Products: BREL manufactures a complete range of bogies suitable for high-speed train-sets, diesel and electric locomotives, rapid transit and suburban railcars, and all types of freight vehicles.

The dedicated bogie production facility at the company's Derby factory incorporates some of the most up-to-date machinery and processes in the fields of fabrication and heavy machining. Equipment includes plasma cutting, robot welding and heavy CNC machining centres. Much of the design work utilises the most modern computer aided design (CAD) and mathematical modelling techniques.

Buckeye
Buckeye Steel Castings
A Worthington Industries company

211 Parsons Avenue, Columbus, Ohio 43207, USA

Telephone: +1 614 444 2121

President: R W Armbruster
Vice President: W C Buffington
Director, Product Engineering and Mass Transit: J R Downes

Products: Cast steel four-wheel bogie side frames, bogie bolsters, wagon couplers, draft yokes, centre plates, sill centre braces, draft sill ends, six-wheel bogies, span bolsters, and other castings for railroad wagons. Undercarriages for railroad passenger cars and mass transit rail vehicles. Buckeye Steel Castings is a major supplier to railroads, railcar builders, and railcar repair shops.

BREL's Series 4 high-speed passenger bogie

In addition, Buckeye manufactures steel castings and cast weldments, both machined and unmachined, for heavy industrial and earthmoving equipment, and armour steel castings for military vehicles.

Cimmco International
A Division of Cimmco Ltd

Prakash Deep, 7 Tolstoy Marg, New Delhi 110 001, India

Telephone: +91 3314 383-5, 3310814
Telex: 31 65148, 31 62294

Products: Cast steel bogies.

Cockerill Forges & Ringmill SA

PO Box 65, B-4100 Seraing 1, Belgium

Telephone: +32 41 377777
Telex: 046 41225
Telefax: +32 41 377902

Chief Executive Officer: Fred Goddard
Executive Vice-President, Marketing & Sales: Urbain Roggen
Sales Supervisor: Marie-Anne Bovy

BREL steered rapid transit bogie for prototype London Underground stock

Products: Axle forgings for wheelset assemblies to international standards.

Comsteel
Commonwealth Steel Company Limited

PO Box 14, Maud Street, Waratah, New South Wales 2298, Australia

Telephone: +61 49 68 0411
Telex: 28115

General Manager: G A Burrell
Marketing Manager (Acting): R Brown

Principal subsidiary: Commonwealth Steel (Moorooka) Proprietary Limited, Newman Road, Moorooka

Products: Rolled steel wheels and tyres; axles; assembled sets; bogies and other railway castings. The company is a major supplier to all Australian rail systems and to export markets, especially India.

The company has recently completed a second-stage re-tooling programme to upgrade production of railway wheels with the commissioning of one of the world's most modern wheel machining systems at the Waratah plant.

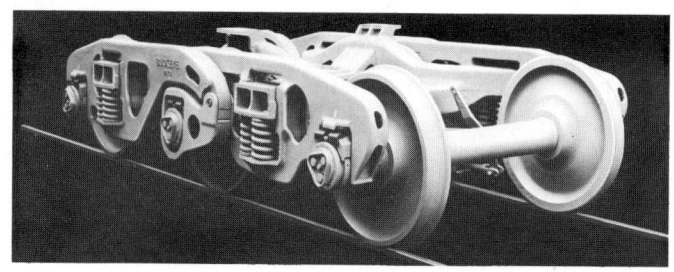

Six-wheel equalised load bogie for wagons of 150 tons or greater capacity by Buckeye

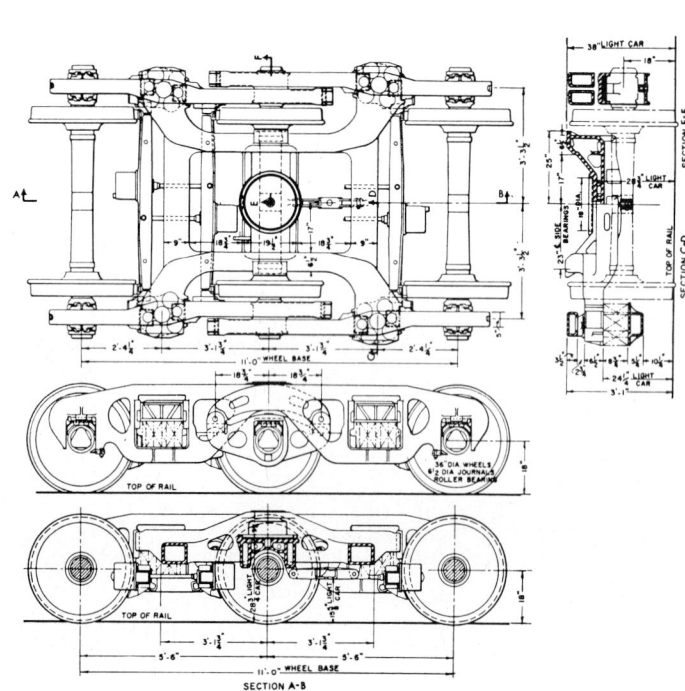

General arrangement of Buckeye six-wheel elasto-cushion bogie, embodying Barber S-2 stabilising with standard Barber friction wedges, wear plates and friction springs

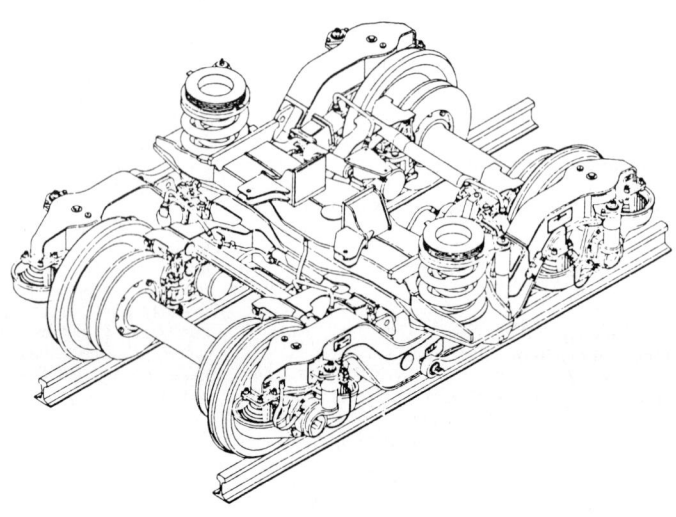

New Type CL136 bogie designed for the North American market by CLRT: first application will be for the Amtrak passenger car prototype programme

Bogies and suspensions / **MANUFACTURERS** 285

De Dietrich
De Dietrich & Cie

Reichshoffen, 67110 Niederbronn-les-Bains, France

Telephone: +33 88 80 25 00
Telex: 870 850
Telefax: +33 88 80 25 12

Sales organisation: De Dietrich & Cie
Railway Rolling Stock Division

President: Gilbert de Dietrich
Director, Rolling Stock Division: Maurice Canioni

Products: Y32 series 1435 mm-gauge bogies, with steel or air secondary suspension springs; and C80 series narrow-gauge (950-1067 mm) bogies, also with steel coil or air secondary suspension.
Having manufactured the first Y32 prototype bogies in 1973, De Dietrich participated in the engineering, development and promotion of the Y32 bogie on the foreign market. This bogie was originally engineered to equip the Corail coaches of the SNCF. De Dietrich has manufactured more than 4000 of these bogies, of which approximately 1000 have been exported to Belgium, the Netherlands, Portugal, Morocco and Gabon. De Dietrich has also granted manufacturing licences to foreign countries, such as Belgium and Portugal (in this latter country the bogie has been adapted to the broad gauge, and adaptation was facilitated by the bogie chassis conception). Early in 1989 the company signed a licensing agreement with Turkish Railways (TCDD) and Morocco (SCIF) for manufacture of Type Y32 bogies.

Energomachexport
V/O Energomachexport

pr Kalinina 19, 121019 Moscow, USSR

Telephone: 7 095 203 15 71
Telex: 411 965, 411 003

Products: Full range of bogies; primary and secondary suspension units; wheels; wheel-sets; bearings.

Ferraz SA
(For full details see Ferraz SA entry in Electric Traction Equipment section.)

Products: Earth current units to prevent current flowing through bearing of axle boxes and its associated resistors; current collecting device on live rail and its associated shoe fuse box.
Recent contracts include earth return current units for TGV-A (SNCF), ICE (DB), and TAV (RENFE); current collecting devices for SEPTA and LACTC (USA), and for LRVs at Orly and Toulouse, France.

Ferrostaal
Ferrostaal Aktiengesellschaft

(For full details see Ferrostaal entry in Locomotives section.)

Products: Motor and trailer bogies for all types of traction, passenger and freight vehicles, wheels, axles, assembled wheel-sets, bearings, suspensions.

Type Y32 MS bogie for Morocco (SCIF)

Fiat
Fiat Ferroviaria SpA

Piazza Galateri 4, 12038 Savigliano (CN), Italy

Telephone: +39 172 2021
Telex: 210234 fiatsv i
Telefax: +39 172 202 426

Chairman: Renato Piccoli
Managing Director & General Manager: Giancarlo Cozza
Deputy General Manager & Project Manager: Pierantonio Losa
Sales Manager: Andrea Parnigoni

Principal subsidiaries: Costruzioni Ferroviairie Collefero
Elettromeccanica Parizzi

Products: Fiat Ferroviaria produces a complete range of bogies for all types of tractive units and towed vehicles. A major feature common to all bogies is the low degree of rail wear they impose, combined with a high level of ride comfort for passengers.
All bogies incorporate integral flexicoil suspensions which eliminate friction and make for simplified construction with consequently reduced maintenance. This solution has been adopted for the various types of suspensions, including coil spring, air spring and rubber spring versions. Significant applications to date include:
Monomotor and twin-motor bogies for locomotives
Passenger car bogies
Motor and trailer bogies for light vehicles (tram and metro cars)
Bogies for diesel and electric railcars with underframe suspended motors.
Latest developments include high-speed bogies (up to 300 km/h), self-steering independent wheel bogies, and high-speed freight bogies (up to 140 km/h). The company has been awarded a contract to design prototype bogies for Eurotunnel's Channel Tunnel road vehicle shuttle trains.
Latest developments include independent wheel bogies for passenger cars, a modern solution due to the reduced weight and competitive costs, and for the running quality and flange wear reduction.
High-speed bogies are already running at over 300 km/h under the ETR500. Bogies up to 160 km/h were ordered from SNCB as preproduction for exiting emus. A decision is expected concerning TML shuttle bogies following the development prototypes. Fiat signed the contract with DB for bogies and tilting components for diesel electric railcars VT610, made with a German consortium.
Recent orders include 8 plus 40 bogies for SNCB to replace existing emu bogies. Forty bogies plus tilting devices for DB as part of an order for 10 tilting diesel trains.

Forja
Forja Argentina SACIF

Diagonal Colomprea 1240, 5012 Cordoba, Argentina

Telephone: +54 51 731912/1952, 732312/2243
Telex: 51713 forco ar

President: Eng Cesar Albrisi
Vice-President: Acc Florencio Escribano
Chief of Marketing: Eng Wenceslao Haliska

Products: Wheels and wheel-sets; tyres and axles.
Recent orders include 101 wheelsets for Cuba; 486 wheels for Peru; 900 tyres for Kenya; 240 wheelsets/300 wheelsets for Turkey; 2324 tyres, 1800 wheels, and 5000 wheels (new order 1990), for India.

Motor bogie for Italian State Railways Class ETR 500 high-speed electric train-set by Fiat

200 km/h independent wheel bogie by Fiat

MANUFACTURERS / Bogies and suspensions

Power bogie with disc brake by Ganz

Trailer bogie with disc brake by Ganz

FWZ
VEB Federwerk Zittau
Member of VEB Kombinat Schienenfahrzeugbau and of Vereinigter Schienenfahrzeugbau der DDR e V

Äussere Weberstrasse 86 b, 8800 Zittau, German Democratic Republic

Telephone: +37 2457
Telex: 0284231

Products: Leaf, conical, ring and helical springs for rail vehicles and other industrial applications.

Exports: Schienenfahrzeuge Export-Import Volkseigener Aussenhandelsbetrieb der DDR, Ötztaler Strasse 5, 1100 Berlin

Ganz
Ganz Locomotive and Railway Carriage Works

PO Box 28, VIII Könyves Kálmán krt 76, Budapest 1967, Hungary

Telephone: +36 1 335 950, 140 840
Telex: 22 5575/6
Telefax: +36 1 143481

General Director: József Balogh
Commercial Director: Ferenc Tordai

Products: Bogies.
The fundamental characteristic of the Ganz standard bogie design is the combination of flexi-coil springs and laminated rubber springs in the secondary suspension system. This arrangement is being patented in many countries. Main features of this design are: elimination of the traditional pendulum-type bolster mechanism; elimination of all friction elements subject to wear; low turning resistance in curves, but sufficient transverse return force; achievement of appropriate oscillation characteristics for good riding quality both vertically and transversally even at high speed; high standardisation of parts in a bogie series which covers all gauges, any known type of drive or axle-hung traction motor and all types of brake used on railway rolling stock, either tread or disc; a suspension system which is maintenance-free and maintains its ride parameters for a long time.
Ganz air-suspended bogies are produced in two versions: a motored bogie driven by two traction motors and a trailer bogie. The two bogie versions are built according to the same design principles with the use of largely similar structural members. Primary suspension and the central pivot arrangement are of standard Ganz design.
Both types of bogies are fitted with torsional air springs, which are manufactured in a light metal casting design. This type of air spring ensures in addition both vertical and transversal suspension of the carbody as well as the turning of the bogie in relation to the carbody when negotiating a curve. The bogies are equipped also with anti-roll stabiliser bar. Vibrations are damped with vertical and lateral hydraulic shock absorbers. The trailer bogies are fitted with disc brakes and the motored bogies with tread brake units with composite brake shoes.

GEC Alsthom
Transport Division

Tour Neptune, 92086 Paris La Défense, Cedex 20, France

Telephone: +33 1 47 44 90 00
Telex: 611 207 alstr f
Telefax: +33 1 47 78 77 55

Plant: le Creusot

Products: Bogies, such as Type Y21 Rse for 20-tonne axleload wagons running at up to 100 km/h, and with special devices for quick axle-change at break of gauge; Type Y27 for 16-tonne axleload wagons on metre gauge; a three-axle bogie for 25-30-tonne axleload vehicles in iron industry use; the Y25 Rst/Lst bogie standardised by the UIC for 20/22.5-tonne axleload wagons; and the Y32B helical-spring, disc-braked bogie for 16-tonne maximum axleload passenger cars running at up to 200 km/h.

Görlitz
VEB Waggonbau Görlitz

Brunnenstrasse 11, Görlitz, German Democratic Republic 8900

Telephone: +37 55 690
Telex: 286227

Products: Bogies. The Type GP 200 bogie is a joint development with the Scientific Research Institute for Rail Vehicles in Prague, Czechoslovakia, the German and Czechoslovak State Railways. It may be equipped with disc brake, additional tread brake or with electro-magnetic rail brake. The bogie is suitable for 200 km/h and, under the terms of UIC leaflet 515, can be fitted to all kinds of passenger car.

Griffin
Griffin Wheel Co
A division of Amsted Industries Inc

200 West Monroe Street, Chicago, Illinois 60606, USA

Telefax: +1 312 346 3373

Products: Steel wheels using the unique controlled-pressure pouring system into graphite moulds. These wheels are AAR-approved for all locomotive, passenger and freight applications. Griffin is the largest North American manufacturer of steel railroad wheels and is further expanding its production facilities. Griffin pressure-poured steel wheels are also manufactured under licence in many countries. The company has additionally developed and manufactures 'Anchor' high-friction composition brake shoes.
All inquiries should be directed to Amsted Industries International, 200 West Monroe Street, Chicago, Illinois 60606. Telephone: +1 312 372 5386. Telex: 254187.

GSI
GSI Engineering
A division of Buckeye Steel Castings

2211 Parsons Avenue, Columbus, Ohio 43207

Manager of Engineering: Eugene L Benner
Manager, Product Development: R B Polley

Products: Design of cast steel rapid transit, coach and locomotive bogies.

Constitution: GSI was founded in 1904 by General Steel Castings Corp and became Castings Division, GSI, in 1964, and Engineering Division in 1973. In July 1989, GSI was sold to Buckeye Steel Castings.

HDA Forgings
HDA Forgings Ltd
A Hawker Siddeley Company

Windsor Road, Redditch, Worcestershire B97 6EF, England

Telephone: +44 527 64211
Telex: 337773
Telefax: +44 527 60818

Dugdale Street, Birmingham B18 4JA

Telephone: +44 21 558 1261
Telefax: +44 21 565 1983

Products: Hand and die forged components in aluminium alloys for railway rolling stock.

International Metal Service (UK) Ltd

Centre City Tower, 7 Hill Street, Birmingham B5 4UP

Telephone: +44 21632 4252
Telex: 337947
Telefax: +44 21643 8762

Managing Director: H Smith
Director, Railway Materials Sales: N M Tristram

UK and Eire agent for:

Valdunes (France): wheels, axles, wheelsets, circular forgings. Approved supplier to BRB, SNCF, AAR.

Cockerill Forges & Ringmill (Belgium): tyres, ring rolled products; forged axle blanks, wheelset repairs; approved suppliers to BRB, SNCF, AAR, SNCB.

Talleres de Amurrio (Spain): finish machined railway castings (main drive motor frames, axle boxes, suspension tubes); railway trackwork-switches and crossings, insulated joints; suppliers to RENFE.

Forges de Courcelles-Centre (Belgium): finish machined railway forgings; UIC drawhooks, drawbars, screw couplings, centre pivots, side bearers, buffing gear.

Recent contracts obtained include: Talleres de Amurrio has been for many years a supplier of motor magnet frames to Brush Electrical Machines Ltd for use in their locomotives for domestic and export markets. The most recent contract has been for the Brush-built Class 60 freight locomotives for BRB. Cockerill Forges & Ringmill have a bi-annual contract to supply tyres to BRB.

Invar
Invar Manufacturing Ltd
A subsidiary of Linamar Machine Ltd

1 Parry Drive, Batawa, Ontario, Canada K0K 1E0

Telephone: +1 613 398 6106
Telefax: +1 613 966 7932

Vice President and General Manager: Brian R Riden
General Sales Manager: Maurice Mainville
Controller & Asst General Manager: Neville Miles
Regional Sales Manager: Cam Nardocchio

Products: Bogie components, wheel-sets and assemblies for urban transit vehicles.
Recent contracts obtained include an order for 32 truck assemblies for UTDC/Lavalin (1990).

Koni
Koni BV

Langeweg 1, PO Box 1014, 3260AA Oud-Beijerland, Netherlands

Telephone: +31 1860 12500
Telex: 21181
Telefax: +31 1860 12117

Chairman and Managing Director: J J Gielen
Sales and Product Manager: P A Maarleveld

Products: Primary and secondary dampers; shock absorber testing equipment. In addition to the normal range of vertical and horizontal dampers Koni has developed the yaw damper which is designed to control small amplitude sinusoidal rotational movements and enable vehicles to operate at higher speeds.

Koni adjustable damper as fitted to SNCF 270 km/h TGV train-sets

Krupp Brüninghaus GmbH

Plettenberger Strasse 12, PO Box 1760/1780, 5980 Werdohl, Federal Republic of Germany

Telephone: +49 2304 6890
Telex: 8 229 615
Telefax: +49 2304 689129

Main Works
Krupp Brüninghaus GmbH
Brüninghaustrasse 1, PO Box 32 40 5840 Schwerte 3

Managing Directors: Klaus Bölling
                              Eckart V Estorff
Sales Director: Günther Neumann

Subsidiary company
Mure SA, Apartado 1423, E-48080 Bilbao, Spain

Products: Werdohl works: parabolic leaf springs. Mure works: coil springs.

Lord V Springs (chevron)

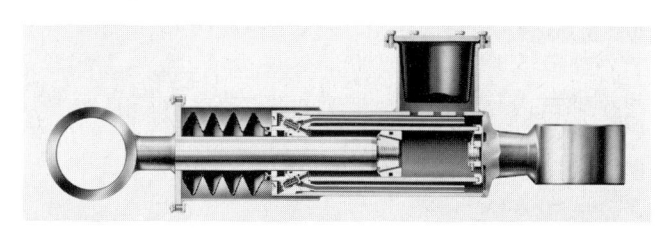

Koni adjustable damper as fitted to SNCF 270 km/h TGV train-sets

LEW
VEB Lokomotivbau-Elektrotechnische Werke 'Hans Beimler'

1422 Hennigsdorf, German Democratic Republic

Telephone: +37 50
Telex: 0158 531

Products: Power and trailer bogies for passenger stock and locomotives. Among latest developments by LEW is a Series 277 powered bogie for use with electric multiple-units. With slight modifications the same bogie can be used for non-powered applications.

Lord
Lord Corporation
Industrial Products Division

1952 West Grandview Blvd, PO Box 10040, Erie, Pennsylvania 16514–0040, USA

Telephone: +1 814 868 5424
Telex: 291935
Telefax: +1 814 8689 3109

Products: LC-Pads for roller bearing adapters. Designed to reduce lateral forces, accommodate motion without wear, reduce rail wear and eliminate adapter crown wear, on self-steering railroad trucks.
V Springs (chevron springs) for the primary suspension system. An engineered elastomeric spring to control spring rate in all directions, equalise wheel load, provide maximum tractive force, isolate noise, reduce wear compared to metal suspensions and control lateral and longitudinal motion. Applications include primary suspension for rapid transit bogies, locomotive bogies, mining cars and railroad maintenance equipment.
Bolster mounts to accommodate lateral movement of locomotive bolsters; these are more economical than conventional mechanical links.
Dyna-Deck for lading shock protection. Designed to absorb longitudinal shock and deflects up to 12 in, it is easily installed on new or existing cars and isolates vibration in all directions. Applications include protection for shipping automobiles, transformers, nuclear components, aircraft fuselage and wing sections, containers, M/W personnel homes, piggy-back nitches and electrical equipment.

Lord Dyna-Deck

Macosa
Material y Construcciones, SA

Plaza de la Independencia 8, Madrid 1, Spain

Telephone: +34 2 22 47 87
Telex: 22168

Products: Bogies and springs.

Mafersa
Mafersa SA

Ave Raimundo Pereira de Magalhaes 320, CEP 05091, São Paulo, SP, Brazil

Telephone: +55 11 261 8911
Telex: (11) 83862
Telefax: +55 11 832 4671

President: Marcos Ferraz Miranda
Administrative & Financial Director: José Wellington Marques de Araújo
Industrial Director: Seijio Ogusku
Commercial Director: Carlos Roberto Fodor
Export Dept Chief: João Carlos Martins

Products: Wrought and rolled carbon steel railway wheels; turned machine axles.
Recent contracts obtained include 25000 wheels (1989) and 14800 wheels (1990) for India; 11900 wheels for Mauritania (1989); 390 wheels for USA (1990); 500 axles (1988), 10300 wheels (1989) and 5900 wheels (1990) for UK.

Bolster mounts to accommodate lateral movement of locomotive bolsters more economically than conventional mechanical links

288 MANUFACTURERS / Bogies and suspensions

MAN GHH
MAN Gutehoffnungshuette GmbH

Head office: PO Box 110240, Bahnhofstrasse 66, 4200 Oberhausen 1, Federal Republic of Germany

Telephone: +49 208 692 1
Telex: 856691 oghhd
Telefax: +49 208 692 2887

Main works: MAN GHH Railway Rolling Stock Division
Frankenstrasse 150, PO Box 44 01 00, D-8500 Nüremberg 44

Telephone: +49 911 18 2632
Telex: 622 291 mn d
Telefax: +49 911 18 2375

Vice President, Railway Rolling Stock Division: Heinz Hennig
Senior Department Manager, Sales: Wolfgang Knörle
Senior Department Manager, Design: Gerhold Sames

Products: Bogies (trucks) powered and non-powered, especially with air suspension and also for high-speed transport. Vehicle components; technology transfer; product service.

The company has received an order for the development of an air-suspension bogie for 160 km/h and 22-tonne axleload for Eurotunnel vehicles to ferry road transport through the Channel Tunnel. From the German bidders Transmanche-Link (TML) selected only MAN GHH. Delivery of the air-suspension bogies for trial operation commenced in the summer of 1989.

Metalastik
Metalastik Vibration Control Systems, Dunlop Ltd

PO Box 98, Evington Valley Road, Leicester, Leicestershire LE5 5LY, England

Telephone: +44 533 730281
Telex: 34397
Telefax: +44 533 735698

Director General, Engineering: D B Kenyon

Products: Rubber-bonded-to-metal springs for primary and secondary suspension systems; air spring systems; anti-vibration mountings; flexible bearings.

National Castings
National Castings Incorporated

1403 South Laramie Avenue, Cicero, Illinois 600650, USA

Telephone: +1 708 863 4800
Telex: 980177
Telefax: +1 708 717 0707

Vice-President & General Manager, International Division: Jack R Long

Corporate office: Suite 107, 2325 Cabot Drive, Lisle, Illinois 60532

Products: Coupler systems for locomotives, passenger coaches, rail wagons and mine wagons including AAR knuckle-type and Willison. Models for rotary wagons, Tightlock for passenger coaches, Sharon 10-A, and AAR standard designs. Product group also includes drawbars, articulated connectors and miscellaneous cast steel components.

Super C-1 Wedgelock Bogie for heavy haul service and Swing Motion Bogie for safe operation at speeds of 120 km/h.

Both designs feature maintenance-free operation of 1.5 milion km. For special wagon designs, Unitruck III single axle suspension for 120 km/h speeds with low maintenance.

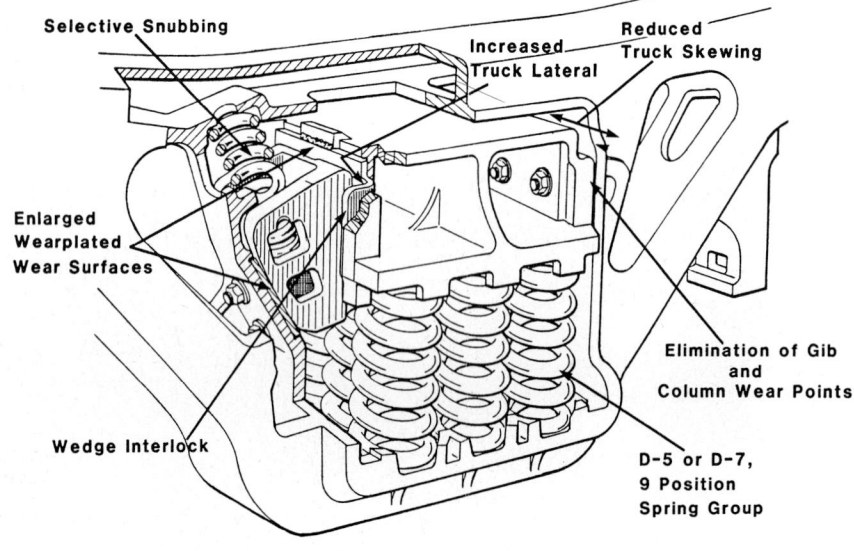

MAN GHH Type DA87 air-suspension bogie for Munich U-Bahn trains

Coupling-frame bogie for German Federal Railway Intercity Experimental (ICE) vehicle by MAN

Nikex
Nikex Hungarian Trading Co for products of Heavy Industry

Head office: Meszaros utca 48-54, H-1809 Budapest, Hungary

Telephone: +36 1 560 122, 564 737, 565 449
Telex: 224971, 226406 nikex h
Telefax: +36 1 755131

Main works
Lenin Metallurgical Works, 3540 Miskolc
Diósgyör Machine Factory, 3544 Miskolc
Hungarian Steel Commodities Factory, Váci ut 95, 13900 Budapest XIII

General Manager: Mihály Petrik
Deputy General Manager: Hugó Szücs
Export Sales: Csaba Jonas

Products: Tyres, helical volute and leaf springs and tyred wheels and wheel-sets.

Pafawag
FW Pafawag

Fabryka Wagonow Pafawag, ul Postrowskiego 12, 53-609 Wroclaw, Poland

Telephone: 48 71 56 21 11
Telex: 0712432

Export salesa: Kolmex, 49 Mokotowska, 00-542 Warsaw

Engineering Manager: R Geppert
Commercial Director: K Krzyczmonik

Products: Bogies, including the 2TN two-axle bogie for freight wagons, which is a modified version of the UIC/ORE standard Type Y25Rm bogie. Track gauge 1435 mm, wheelbase 1800 mm, wheel diameter 840 mm, maximum speed 100 km/h, maximum weight

National Super C-1 Wedgelock truck

per axle 21 tonnes. The bogie is adapted for wagons with automatic coupler. The braking system has levers symmetrically divided along the longitudinal member of a frame with single inserts, braking the wheels from both sides.

Penn
Penn Machine Company

Head office and main works: 106 Station Street, Johnstown, Pennsylvania 15905, USA

Telephone: +1 814 288 1547
Telefax: +1 812 288 2260

Pittsburgh office: 505 E Main Street, Carnegie, Pennsylvania 15106
Telephone: +1 412 279 4460
Telefax: +1 412 279 4465

President: William Baker
Vice President, Sales: E L Van Sickel
Vice President, Manufacturing: H K Wiegand
Sales Manager: R E Trail
Manager, RR Sales: R Harvilla

Products: Resilient wheels; axles; pinions; gears; journal boxes and gear box components.

Recent sales have included resilient wheels for ABB Traction for the Baltimore LRV; Duewag for Sacramento, San Diego and St Louis, and San Francisco LRVs.

Phoenix
Phoenix AG

Hannoversche Strasse 88, 2100 Hamburg 90, Federal Republic of Germany

Telephone: +49 40 76 67 594
Telex: 2 17 611 pxhh d
Telefax: +49 40 76 67 211

Products: Rubber/metal axle springs; pneumatic air bellows.

Powell Duffryn Standard
(Formerly Gloucester Railway Carriage & Wagon Co Ltd)

Cambrian Works, Maindy, Cardiff, Wales CF4 3XD

Telephone: +44 222 626000
Telex: 437173, 497233
Telefax: +44 222 692174

Managing Director: R Jasinski
Director and General Manager: A B Harding
Sales Director: R A Clark
Engineering Director: D Hughes

Products: Freight bogies (primary sprung rigid frame, cast steel bogies with Metalastik rubber or helical steel spring suspension), suspension systems (including floating axles for two-axle wagons) and Miner doorgear.

The company's cast steel bogie with Metalastik rubber suspension is of springplankless type in three-piece form, but without sliding bolster guides; the connection between the bolster and the sideframe is made positively yet resiliently through inclined rubber chevron springs acting in combined shear and compression. The spring elements act as the main suspension in shear and compression and also maintain the relative positions of the moving parts of the bogie without metal wearing contacts, to a degree determined by the design of the spring and not by a 'slop' allowance.

This controlled flexibility allows for wheel drop on undulating track with an inherent restoring force in all flexures. The spring units are symmetrically angled in the frame so that the required characteristics can be obtained in all planes.

Careful design of the sideframe uses the induced reactions of these springs to relieve stresses at the centre of the frame. This allows reduced casting section and weight at this point.

Another feature of the design is that the sideframe weight for any given axleload is less than that of a conventional cast steel bogie; moreover, sideframes and springs do not have to be 'threaded' on to the bolster ends. This bogie is currently operating satisfactorily in 22 countries, and has been manufactured under licence in the USA and Canada.

The Gloucester floating axle suspension for two-axle wagons has been developed to combine efficient running at high speeds with low maintenance costs. It is designed not only for new vehicles but also for existing vehicles; on the latter, relatively simple and economic conversion from laminated to coil spring suspension can be carried out using existing wheelsets complete with roller bearing axleboxes. When used for new vehicles, the unit will accept a modern cartridge roller bearing and will accommodate the variety of solebar heights at present planned for modern vehicles.

The design aim has been to provide fairly low natural frequencies in both the vertical and lateral planes, together with reliable load sensitive friction damping characteristics. The suspension unit incorporates a bearing adapter fitted over the roller bearing unit, on which two inclined rubber pads are mounted. The saddle casting is supported by these pads and houses the suspension spring nests.

The bearing adapter (available in versions to accept modern cartridge or existing roller bearing axleboxes) positively locates the axlebox and is carried within the saddle. This has a spring platform incorporating a nest of coil springs each side of the axlebox to provide a two-or three-rate suspension characteristic.

The pedestal frame consists of the horn guides, which house the friction damper assembly, and the spring top platform. The damper unit selected has operated successfully on the Gloucester Primary Suspension range of bogies (GPS 20 and GPS 25). The friction damping is achieved by fitting an inverted pot over one spring nest per unit. This pot has inclined

Type YCss bogie exported by Pafawag to Switzerland

Gloucester two-axle pedestal suspension unit, available in versions up to 25-ton axleloads

Gloucester low track force bogie

Gloucester 520 mm diameter-wheel bogie for low-floor intermodal wagon

290 MANUFACTURERS / Bogies and suspensions

faces on its sides which locate against inclined guides on the pedestal, thus transferring a percentage of the vertical load into horizontal load. This load, via a damping pad, creates a frictional damping force proportional to the load carried by the wagon.

The company is a licensee for Miner Enterprise Inc in respect of discharge door mechanisms and 'Tecspak' elastomeric springs.

Rafil
VEB Radsatzfabrik Ilsenburg
Member of VEB Kombinat Schienenfahrzeugbau and of Vereinigter Schienenfahrzeugbau der DDR e V

Schmiedestrasse 16/17, 3705 Ilsenburg, German Democratic Republic

Telephone: +37 261
Telex: 088434

Products: Wheel-sets with monobloc and tyred wheels for tractive stock, passenger cars and freight wagons. A new development is a lightweight monobloc wheel, now proved in German State Railway (DR) service. It has a wheel-load carrying capacity of 12.5 tonnes, is capable of a maximum speed of 200 km/h, has permissible brake power of 50 kW (for 30 minutes continuous braking), gauge stability of up to 1 mm at 50 kW and a tare weight of 260 kg.

Exports: Schienenfahrzeuge Export-Import Volkseigener Aussenhandelsbetrieb der DDR, Ötztaler Strasse 5, 1100 Berlin

RFS Engineering

PO Box 192, Hexthorpe Road, Doncaster DN1 1PJ

Telephone: +44 302 340700
Telex: 547296
Telefax: +44 302 340693

Managing Director: P Page
Technical Director: D W Theyers
Finance Director: B J Pierce
Director: L Harrison
Commercial Manager: M Rowe

Products: Repair, overhaul and production of suspensions, wheels and axles. Recent contracts have included: new wheelsets for British Steel (1990); BR Class 60 wheelsets for Brush (1989); BR Class 86 wheelsets for BRB (1990); continuous bogie overhaul programme for BRB; wheelset overhaul for BRB and private wagon sector; continuous damper repair programme for BRB.

Ringrollers of South Africa
A Division of Metkor Industries (Pty) Ltd

Dorbyl House, 4 Skeen Boulevard, Bedfordview 2008, South Africa

Telephone: +27 11 56 0741
Telex: 74 6508
Telefax: +27 11 815 2805

Chairman: P A Olivier
Chief Executive: I J Cumming

Products: Railway steel tyres

RSD
A Division of Dorbyl Ltd

PO Box 229, Boksburg 1460, South Africa

Telephone: +27 52 8276
Telex: 4 29569
Telefax: +27 52 5714

Chairman: M J Smithyman
Executive Director, RSD: C J O Rehder

Products: Various types of bogies under licence, including the Scheffel High Stability bogie.

Where axle loads are low the HS bogie augments rail and wheel life over 20 times; with 26-ton axle load life is increased 10 times before reprofiling of wheels. As there is no flange wear, wheels can be profiled three or four times before the same amount of metal has been removed as in one reprofiling of a wheel subject to flange wear. HS bogies are used exclusively on the South African Transport Services ore line between Sishen and the harbour at Saldanha Bay. Well over 150 million gross tons had been carried on this line by trains of 25 tons axle loading, but the track has remained in excellent condition, flange wear on wheels has been negligible and wheel treads are generally lasting for more than 450 000 km between reprofilings. At that distance reprofiling is usually required only to restore wheel treads and not flanges. It has been found that on certain applications the standard bogie is only able to travel 30 000 to 50 000 km between profilings, with most of the wear on the flange, thus causing extensive damage to the rail.

Ruhfus
August Ruhfus GmbH Federn-Hydraulik

Budericher Strasse 7, PO Box 10 12 63, 4040 Neuss, Federal Republic of Germany

Telephone: +49 2101 26116
Telefax: +49 2101 24996

Managing Director: Ulrich Ruhfus

Products: Leaf, buffer and helical springs; hydraulic cylinders; cylinder tubes; hard-chromed piston rods.

R W Mac
R W Mac Co

PO Box 56, Crete, Illinois 60417, USA

Telephone: +1 312 672 6376/81
Telex: +1 312 672 9883

President: R W MacDonnell
Vice President, Sales & Exports: J K MacDonnell

Products: Car-safe freight car bolster supports; locomotive bogie bolster supports; EMD and GE Journa box wear plates (steel); freight car door safety supports; freight car hand holds; sill steps and ladders; air hose supports; RR cane all-car lifters; trailer door hinges; locomotive coupler wear plates; freight car coupler wear plates; draft gear wear plates; custom-made locomotive or freight car parts.

SAB NIFE
SAB NIFE AB

Instrumentgatan 15, PO Box 515, S-261 24 Landskrona, Sweden

Telephone: +46 418 16280
Cable: SAB NIFE, Landskrona
Telex: 72416 sabnife s
Telefax: +46 0418 106 90

Products: Resilient and low-noise V-wheels.

SAB rubber-cushioned resilient wheels used on street cars, subway cars, coaches and heavy locomotives have led to considerable reductions of wear and maintenance costs of track and vehicle thanks to the radial, tangential and lateral flexibility of the wheels. SAB wheels are also claimed to achieve considerably improved running characteristics and to increase comfort and reduce noise. The SAB Resilient wheel, is contrary to common belief, compatible with tread brakes. These wheels have recently been supplied in considerable quantity for street cars in Belgium, the Netherlands and Toronto, Canada.

Sambre et Meuse
Usines et Acieries de Sambre et Meuse

Tour Aurore, 92080 Paris-Défense Cedex 5, France

Telephone: +33 1 47 76 44 07
Telex: 620 161
Telefax: +33 1 47 78 61 85

General Manager: André-Jean Pommellet
Deputy General Manager: Jean-Pierre Jomeau
Sales Manager: Charles-Henri Pin

Products: Design, testing and manufacture of bogies for all gauges, including the UIC Y25 type and its derivatives; wheels and wheel-sets; drawgear and buffer, couplers.

SIG
Schweizerische Industrie-Gesellschaft
Swiss Industrial Company

8212 Neuhausen Rhine Falls, Switzerland

Telephone: +41 53 21 61 11
Telex: 896023 sig
Telefax: +41 53 21 66 07

Chairman: U Baumberger
Managing Director: U Dätwyler
Director: Peter Gsell

Products: Motor powered and trailing bogies for all applications, developed on the SIG building-block concept, which covers a number of types of motored, powered and trailing bogies for a wide range of railway systems.

A new design was developed by SIG in 1980 as a standard type for motored and trailer bogies of new vehicles of the Swiss Federal Railways (SBB) and the Netherlands Railways (NS). Good riding performance is combined with a lower noise level and lower maintenance cost, and the trailer bogies are suitable for high-speed performance; they have been proved at up to 280 km/h. Already more than 300 motor and 1200 trailer bogies are in operation. The Finnish State

Trailer bogie for Swiss Federal Railways Mk IV inter-city car by SIG

Bogies and suspensions / **MANUFACTURERS**

Trailer bogie for SBB Type NPZ driving trailer of Swiss Federal Railways by SIG

Trailer bogie for British Rail Mk 4 coach by SIG

Railways (VR) have ordered this type and 500 trailer bogies will be built under SIG licence.

The latest contract concerns nearly 600 trailer bogies, which were delivered to Metro-Cammell for the Mk 4 coaches of British Rail's East Coast Main Line. Although the type of operation for all these vehicles is very different, the similarity between their bogies is obvious, because all bogies are based on the same constructional elements, according to the SIG building block concept. With the application of modular technology on bogies, this concept offers a maximum performance capacity for each special case at lowest life-cycle-costs (LCC). It is applicable to motor-powered and trailing bogies for a wide variety of different railway systems.

The trailer bogies for the SBB Type IV and NBZ emu trailers, and for VR broad-gauge cars, have coil springs seated between spherical rubber culottes in the secondary suspension. Other features are: axle-mounted disc brakes; electromagnetic rail brake and parking brake; roll stabilisation; lateral stops dependent upon track radius; block brake units and yaw damping, decoupled; and rail guards upon demand. Details are as follows:
Gauge: 1435/1524 mm
Wheelbase: 2500 mm
Wheel diameter (new): 920 mm
Weight: 6700 kg
Static load on bogie: 200 kN
Max speed: 250 km/h

A variation of this trailer bogie with air-spring suspension has been supplied for the Type SGM-2 electric suburban train-sets, the Type ICM electric intercity train-sets and the Type DD double-deck coaches of the NS. Further applications are to the SZU driving trailers, the Type NPZ driving trailers, the Type ZSB double-deck coaches and the Type EW IV restaurant cars of the SBB.

Axle guides and coil springs figure in the primary suspension, air springs in series with stratified rubber springs in the secondary suspension. Other features are: axle-mounted disc brakes; electromagnetic rail brake and parking brake; block brake units; roll stabilisation; lateral stops dependent upon track radius; yaw damping, decoupled; and rail guards upon demand.

Main data:
Wheelbase: 2500 mm
Wheel diameter: 920 mm
Weight: 6700 kg
Static load: 200 kN
Max speed: 250 km/h

The two-axle trailer bogie with air-spring suspension for the Mk 4 coaches of BR has axle guides and coil springs in the primary suspension; air springs in series with stratified rubber springs in the secondary suspension; axle-mounted disc brakes; parking brake, spring applied; yaw damping; and rail guards and magnets for the automatic train stopping device at the guiding bogie, for driving trailers only.
Main data:
Wheel base: 2500 mm
Wheel diameter: 920 mm
Weight: 6850 kg
Static load: 200 kN
Max speed: 160 km/h

A bi-motor bogie with parallel drive and rubber coil suspension is used for the electric shuttle train motor cars of the Bodensee-Toggenburrg Railway and the Type NPZ shuttle train motor cars of the SBB. The design has axle guides and coil springs in the primary suspension; coil springs mounted between stratified rubber springs in the secondary suspension; propulsion by BBC-rubber drive in connection with K-series traction motors and spur gearing; brake equipment with wheel-mounted disc brakes and block brake units, spring-applied; roll stabilisation; wheel flange lubrication; lateral stops dependent upon track radius; magnets for automatic train stopping device; pneumatic load weighing system upon demand.
Main data:
Wheelbase: 2700 mm
Wheel diameter: 950 mm
Weight: 12 800 kg
Static load: 275 kN
Max speed: 160 km/h
One-hour rating, per motor: 425 kW

The SIG bi-motor bogie type with parallel drive and air spring suspension supplied for the Type ICM electric intercity train-sets of the NS has axle guides and coil springs in the primary suspension, coil springs in series with stratified rubber springs in the secondary suspension. Propulsion is by hollow shaft drive with disc clutch and spur gearing. Brake equipment comprises wheel-mounted disc brakes and block brake units. Other features include: roll stabilisation; yaw damping, decoupled; lateral stops dependent upon track radius; rail guards; and parking brake upon demand.
Main data:
Wheelbase: 2700 mm
Wheel diameter: 950 mm
Weight: 12 100 kg
Static load: 235 kN
Max speed: 160 km/h
One hour rating per motor: 202 kW

Silentbloc
Silentbloc Ltd
Subsidiary of BTR Ltd

Manor Royal, Crawley, West Sussex RH10 2QG, England

Telephone: +44 293 27733
Telex: 87177

Director/General Manager: J Anderson
Technical Director: G Sarosi

Products: Rolling rubber bush primary suspension units, as fitted to British Rail Class 317 and 455 emu power car bogies and Class 58 diesel freight locomotive bogies; axle guide bushes; Alsthom links, bushes and thrust pads; damper end mountings; traction links; centre pivot bushes; engine mountings (locomotive and railbus); resilient couplings; and numerous other rubber-to-metal components.

In the rolling rubber bush suspension the coil spring supports the major proportion of the load and the rolling bush provides the plan view stiffness. Relative movement in the vertical direction between the axlebox and the bogie frame is effected by the rubber bush rolling rather than sliding as in a conventional axle guide. The elimination of lubricated sliding surfaces means that the rolling rubber bush is maintenance-free during the life of the rubber toroid, which is anticipated at being at least 10 years. The initial development bogie sets have now completed over 1.12 million km on British Rail HST trailer cars.

Socimi
Società Costruzioni Industriali Milano SpA

Via Varesina 115, 20156 Milan, Italy

Telephone: +39 2 30091
Telex: 323564

Type FW trailer bogie by Socimi

Socimi Fast-Ride Type 14KR-DB-TB body-tilting system bogies for Korean National Railways

MANUFACTURERS / Bogies and suspensions

Main works
Via E Fermi n 25, 20082 Binasco (Milan)
Telephone: +39 2 9055605/6/7/8

Via Donatori del Sangue n 100, 20010 Arluno (Milan)
Telephone: +39 2 9017666/9017803

Viale Porto Torres, Reg Zentu Figghi, 07100 Sassari
Telephone: +39 79 235056

Chairman: Dr Eng Alessandro Marzocco
Managing Director: Dr Eng Pierino Sacchi
Assistant to Chairman: Dr Eng Corrado Landolina

Products: Bogies.

Specialist Rail Products Limited

PO Box 76, Hexthorpe Trading Park, Doncaster DN4 0EH

Telephone: +44 302 328080
Telex: 548208
Telefax: +44 302 329911

Managing Director: Andrew Lezala
Director, General Manager-Bogie Division: Keith Pennington
Business Development Manager: Paul Forrest
Engineering Director: Eddie Searancke
Quality Manager: Paul Dunton

Products: Advanced specification bogies and suspension systems.

Recent contracts include the design and prototype manufacture of a new lightweight Advanced Suburban Bogie for British Rail (1990); replacement of 565 bogies on London Underground 'C' Stock vehicles (1990); new anti-roll systems for BR Class 317 and 455 vehicles (1989).

Standard
Standard Car Truck Co

845 Busse Highway, Park Ridge, Illinois 60068, USA

Telephone: +1 312 692 6050
Telex: 27 0651

Chairman: Robert S Russell
President: William W Sellers
Manager, Operations: Robert P Geyer
Secretary: John A Walker

Products: Barber stabilised and self-steering Radial bogies.

Features of the Barber Radial bogie include: patented wedge clamp connection between roller bearing adapters and subframe that makes the connection rigid, substantially eliminating dynamic load on the fasteners; resilient bushings connecting the cross-braces to the subframe, which effectively eliminate high impact loads within the subframe system; shear pads to apply longitudinal and transverse restraint are conveniently housed directly above the roller bearing adapters, and provide low yaw constraint in curves; mounting of the subframe inside the side frame, instead of above or outside, which utilises existing space between the wheels and side frames of the classic three-piece bogie; and high-stiffness cross-braces that stabilise the bogie and bring it into trapezoidal configuration for curving.

Advantages claimed for the Barber Radial bogie include: increased wheel life expectancy by a factor of up to three; reduced rolling resistance in curves, up to 70 per cent; high critical bogie hunting speed, more than 80 mph empty; subframe resistance to high longitudinal loads in excess of 100 000 lb imposed by dumper restraint systems; high longitudinal stiffness for firm, reliable brake application, so that slack adjusters are not overworked; and reduction of wheel-set changeouts caused by tread shelling by as much as 90 per cent.

The company also produces the Accutrak mileage indicator for railroad and transit cars.

Fast-Ride motor bogie for Taiwan emu car by Socimi

Fast-Ride bogie for V/Line, Australia, manufactured by Vickers Australia Ltd under Socimi licence

Components of the Barber Radial self-steering bogie

Stucki
A Stucki Company

2600 Neville Road, Pittsburgh, Pennsylvania 15225, USA

Telephone: +1 412 771 7300
Telefax: +1 412 771 7308

Chairman: W S Hansen
President: J G Faryniak
Vice-President: W G Hansen
Manager, Sales and Service Engineering: D Rhen

Products: Hydraulic truck stabilisers, HS-7, HS-7-100 and HS-10, designed to control harmonic rocking and vertical bounce in 50-, 70- and 100-ton freight cars; single and double roller steel bogie side bearings; resilient constant contact side bearings conventional and metal-capped, to control light car bogie hunting; body side bearing wear plates and wedges for 50-, 70- and 100-ton freight cars; resilient-padded friction wedges for elimination of bolster wear in Ride Control or Barber bogies.

The HS-10 is a single-acting compression damper that reduces resonant rocking and vertical bounce reactions to safe operating levels. The cast housing of the HS-10 has the same diameter as a standard AAR bogie spring, so that it can be installed in the spring nest of virtually all conventional freight car bogies.

Stucki Elastowedge resilient friction elements

Sumitomo
Sumitomo Metal Industries Ltd

Ote Center Building, 1-1-3 Otemachi, Chiyoda-ku, Tokyo 100, Japan

Telephone: +81 3 282 6111
Telex: J22865
Telefax: +81 3 282 6764

Manager: Y Hirano
General Manager, Sales: K Koshida
Senior Manager, Export Section: H Watatani
Senior Manager, Railway Products/Equipment Sales: Y Hirano

Products: Bogies, bogie components, wheels and wheel-sets, axles, coupler and draft gear, gear units.

Talleres de Amurio SA

Maskuribai 10, Amurrio, Alava, Spain

Telephone: +34 45 891600
Telex: 32218
Telefax: +34 45 892480

General Manager: J M de Lapatza Urbiola
Foundry Director: L M de Lapatza Urbiola
Director of Engineering: V R Gonzalez
Technical Manager: R F Guereñu
Export Sales Manager: J M Gutierrez Pinedo

Products: wheels, wheeljets, buffers, bogies, axleboxes, pivots and other rolling stock parts.

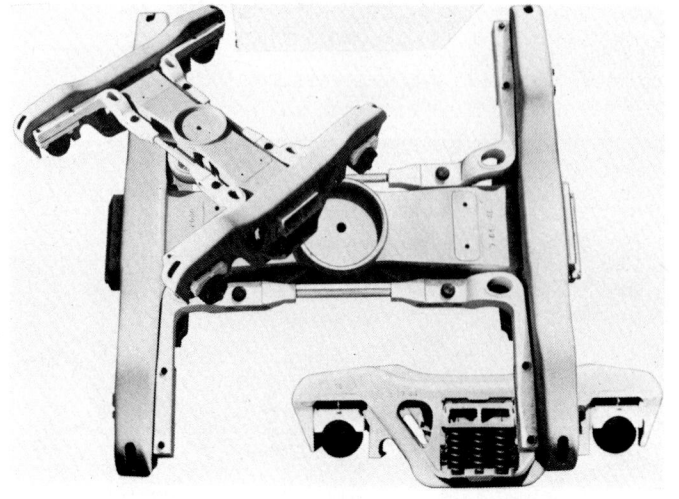

Components of the Barber Radial self-steering bogie

Sumitomo Type SS bolsterless bogie

Terni
Terni SpA
A member of the IRI Group

Via G Paglia 45, 24065 Lovere (BG), Italy

Telephone: +39 35 960 010
Telex: 300125 terlov i

Products: Wheels, wheel-sets, tyres and axles.

TIBB
Tecnomasio Italiano Brown Boveri SpA
Transport Division
A company of the ASEA Brown Boveri Group

Casella Postale 10225, 20137 Milan, Italy

Telephone: +39 2 5797.1
Telex: 310153

Products: Single and double-motor bogies for locomotives, motor-coaches, undergrounds and trams of standard-and metre-gauges; trailer bogies.

Wegmann
Wegmann & Co GmbH

Head office: August-Bode-Strasse 1, 3500 Kassel, Federal Republic of Germany

Telephone: +49 561 1050
Telex: 99 859

Works: Kassel-Rothenditmold (rolling stock construction)
Kassel-Bettenhausen (fittings, frames and castings)

Directors: Dr M Bode
Dr W Zimni
R A J Bode
W Bode

Products: Motor and trailer bogies for railway passenger cars; subway cars etc; electrically and pneumatically-operated doors for buses and railway passenger cars.

The distinctive feature of the Wegmann bogie is its patented torsionally flexible fabricated frame. Because of the torsional elasticity the frame absorbs, without stress, nearly all displacements which are caused by transitions, misalignments of track etc. The primary spring elements do not affect this load equalisation. Torsionally flexible frames are supplied either as H-frames or as frames with end transoms; both feature the same performance advantages. Axle guidance is achieved by wear and maintenance-free primary spring elements with variable elasticity in the x-, y- and z-direction depending on the application. The x-elasticity enables the wheel-sets to line up in curves, reducing wear and the forces between wheel and rail. The self-damping effect of the primary spring elements is sufficient; axle shock absorbers are not necessary.

The secondary suspension can be coil-spring or air. The roll behaviour of the car body is solely controlled by the roll stabiliser. The relatively high air consumption of most air suspension systems has been greatly reduced with the Wegmann two-point levelling system, in which the levelling valve does not respond to roll motions but only to changes in floor height.

The Wegmann Modular System can adapt to individual customer needs at minimum cost. It consists of axle guidance, bogie frame, roll stabiliser, hunting suppression, longitudinal linkage, magnetic track brake, wheel disc brake, axle disc brake, and block and supplementary block brake.

Constitution: The company was established in 1882 and has specialised in bogie design and construction.

Wegmann motor bogie

Wheel & Axle
Wheel & Axle Plant, Indian Railways

Yelahanka, Bangalore 560 064, India

Telephone: +91 812 343749, 341745
Telex: 845 2547 wap in

General Manager: N Rao
Chief Engineer: C Srinivasan

Products: Wheels and axles, under licence from Griffin (USA), GFM (Austria) and Farrels (USA).

Wickham
D Wickham & Co Ltd

Crane Mead, Ware, Hertfordshire SG12 9QA, England

Telephone: +44 920 462491
Telex: 81340
Telefax: +44 920 460733

Joint Managing Director: D S Holden
Joint Managing Director: T H Bailie
Sales Director: P Redfern
Technical Director: A P Mott

Products: Design and construction of bogies using radius arm located axlebox suspension for railcars and coaches of all gauges, and manufacture of other conventional types to specification.

Addendum
ABB British Wheelset Ltd

A member company of the Asea Brown Boveri Group

Trafford Park Works, PO Box 14, Ashburton Road West, Trafford Park, Manchester M17 1GU

Telephone: +44 61 872 0492
Telex: 668973
Telefax: +44 61 872 2895

Products: Precision manufacture, assembly and repair of wheelsets, wheels and tyres for locomotives and other rolling stock.

Bearings

ARGENTINA
SKF Argentina ... 298

AUSTRIA
Miba ... 297

GERMANY, DEMOCRATIC REPUBLIC
AWS ... 296

GERMANY, FEDERAL REPUBLIC
FAG ... 296

JAPAN
Koyo Seiko ... 296
Nachi-Fujikoshi ... 297
NSK ... 297
NTN Toyo ... 297

SWEDEN
SKF ... 298

UK
Railko ... 297
RHP ... 298

Timken ... 298

USA
American Koyo ... 296
Brenco ... 296
Comet ... 296
FAG ... 296
General Standard ... 296
Magnus ... 297
Multi-Service Supply ... 297
Stucki ... 298
Timken ... 298
Unity ... 298

MANUFACTURERS / Bearings

American Koyo Corporation
Division of KCU Corporation of USA

29570 Clemens Road, Westlake, Ohio 44145, USA

Telephone: +1 216 835 1000
Telefax: +1 216 835 9347

General Manager: Yoshio Yabuno
Vice President, Sales: Ray Normandin
OEM Sales Manager: Roger Lewis
After Sales Manager: Don Kishton
OE Industrial Marketing Manager: Dale Neumann

Products: ABU-type journal roller bearings.

AWS
VEB Achslagerwerk Stassfurt
Member of VEV Kombinat Schienenfahrzeugbau and of Vereinigter Schienenfahrzeugbau der DDR e V

An der Liethe 5, 3250 Stassfurt, German Democratic Republic

Telephone: +37 2282
Telex: 088826

Products: Roller bearings for locomotives, railcars, passenger cars and freight wagons according to UIC and GOST, such as roller bearings for the standard Type Y 25 freight bogie and for passenger car bogies without pedestal.

Exports: Schienenfgahrzeuge Export-Import Volks-eigener Aussenhandelsbetrieb der DDR, Ötztaler Strasse 5, 1100 Berlin

Brenco
Brenco Inc

PO Box 389, Petersburg Industrial Park, Petersburg, Virginia 23804, USA

Telephone: +1 804 732 0202
Telex: 828300
Telefax: +1 804 732 2531

President: J Craig Rice
Executive Vice-President: Jacob M Feichtner
Manager, Customer Service: Hilda W Mosbey

Products: Locomotive and freight car bearings and components; forgings.

Comet
Comet Industries Inc

4800 Deramus Avenue, Kansas City, Missouri 64120, USA

Telephone: +1 816 245 9400
Telefax: +1 816 245 9461

Chairman: R O Johnson
President: E O Johnson
Vice-President, Finance: R L Johnson

Works:
4800 Deramus Avenue, Kansas City, MO 64120
4504 Macks Drive, Bossier City, LA 71111
5401 Mills Road, Carson City, NV 89706

Products: Roller bearings.

FAG
FAG Kugelfischer Georg Schäfer KGaA

PO Box 1260, 8720 Schweinfurt 1, Federal Republic of Germany

Telephone: +49 9721 91-0
Telex: 67 345-0 fag d
Teletext: 9721823 fag d
Telefax: +49 9721 91 3435

Products: Axleboxes (cast steel, ductile iron, light metal); journal roller bearings and package units (AAR standard and metric); gearbox bearings; traction motor bearings and complete suspension units.

FAG participated in developing the bearings for the ICE which will enter service in 1991. FAG supplies tapered roller bearing units for the power cars, tapered roller bearings with housings for the coaches and bearings for the hollow shaft drives of the traction motors.

The company has manufacturing plants in Austria, Brazil, Canada, Federal Republic of Germany, Italy, Portugal, Switzerland and the USA.

FAG
FAG Bearings Corporation

Stamford, Connecticut 06904, USA

Products: Journal roller bearings, traction motor bearings, axle box bearings.

General Standard
General Standard Company

805 Golf Lane, Bensenville, Illinois 60106, USA

Telephone: +1 312 236 3526, +1 708 860 9677
Telefax: +1 708 595 0646

President: Robert S Grandy

Products: Roller bearing adapter castings; hand brakes; bearing master (diagnostic tool for inspection of roller bearings); miscellaneous freight car parts.

Koyo Seiko
Koyo Seiko Co Ltd

5-8 Minamisemba 3-chome, Chuo-ku, Osaka 542, Japan

Telephone: +81 6 245 6087
Telex: 63040
Telefax: +81 6 244 0814

President: Uzuhiko Tsuboi
Senior Executive Director: Hiroshi Inoue

Products: Axlebox, sealed journal roller bearings (ABU type); roller bearings, ball bearings, needle roller bearings, pillow blocks.

Koyo tapered roller bearings, cylindrical and spherical roller bearings, and ball bearings are produced with an exclusive, patented hardening process known as 'upset rolling and forging' which makes for continuous metal grain flow. As a result Koyo bearings are claimed to be tougher and to absorb heavier loads over long periods with high reliability. Available in all standard types and sizes, Koyo NFL type journal bearings need no relubrication for eight years or 800 000 km. Koyo bearings have been approved for use by the Association of American Railroads after undergoing a series of rigorous tests. They are fully interchangeable with other AAR-approved makes. Koyo journal tapered roller bearings have been adopted for the metro cars of the New York City Transit Authority.

Associated companies
Koyo Corporation of USA
29570 Clemens Road, PO Box 45028, Westlake, Ohio 44145, USA
Telephone: +1 216 835 1000
Telex: 0985461 amkoy wlke
Telefax: +1 216 835 9347

Koyo Canada Inc
5324 South Service Road, Burlington, Ontario L7L 5H5, Canada
Telephone: +1 416 827 7182
Telex: 618777 cankoy bur
Telefax: +1 416 827 7676

Australian Koyo Ltd
PO Box 205, Unit 7, 907 Bourke Street, Waterloo, New South Wales 2017, Australia
Telephone: +61 2 699 4211
Telex: 120405 auskoyo AA 25019
Telefax: +61 2 319 1421

Koyo Singapore Bearing Pte, Ltd
24 Pasir Panjang Road, 08-33 Psa Multi Storey Complex, Singapore 0511
Telephone: +65 274 2200
Telex: 33854 koyo sp
Telefax: +65 274 1164

Europa Koyo BV
Lekdijk 187, PO Box No. 1, Nieuwport (Z-H), 2965ZG, Netherlands
Telephone: +31 1843 1238
Telex: 3 2118 koyo nl
Telefax: +31 1843 2572

Koyo (UK) Limited
4 Northfield Drive, Northfield, Milton Keynes MKL15 0DQ, England
Telephone: +44 908 664422
Telex: 825611 koyouk g
Telefax: +44 908 607971

Koyo de Mexico SA
Av. 1 de Mayo N 153 col San Andres Atoto, 53500 Naucalpan, Mexico
Telephone: +52 358 0077, 0944
Telex: 1773174 koyo me
Telefax: +52 358 0325

Koyo de Panama SA
Apartado 6-1797, Estafeta El Dorado, Panama
Telephone: +507 64 0921/1816
Telex: 2249 (TRT), 3250 (INTEL)
Telefax: +507 64 2782

Roller bearing for Type Y 25 freight bogie by AWS; max axleload 20 tonnes, max speed 120 km/h

Roller bearing for carriage bogies by AWS

Bearings / **MANUFACTURERS** 297

Type NFL tapered roller bearing by Koyo Seiko

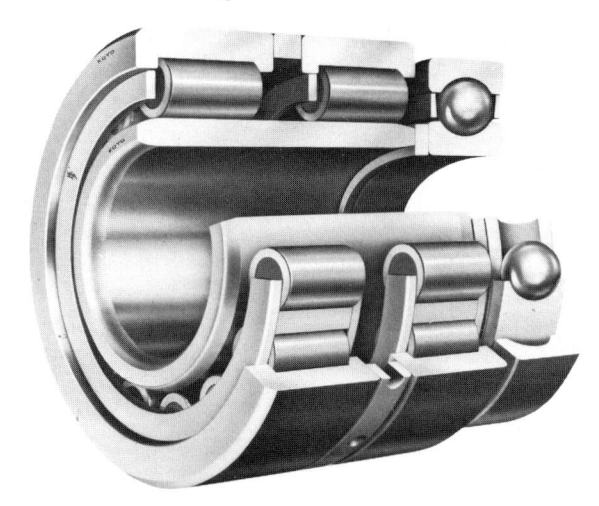

Cylindrical roller bearing with ball bearing by Koyo Seiko

Thai Koyo Co Ltd
464-466, Siam Square 4, Rama 1 Road, Bangkok 10500, Thailand
Telephone: +66 2 251 5190
Telex: 82371 koyo th
Telefax: +66 2 251 5189

Koyo Kullger Scandinavia AB
Kanalvagen 1, 19461 Upplands-Väsby, Sweden
Telephone: +46 760 34185
Telex: 14300 koyo s
Telefax: +46 760 30969

Deutsche Koyo Walzlager Verkaufs GmbH
Bargkoppelweg 4, Postfach 73 0660, Hamburg 73, Federal Republic of Germany
Telephone: +49 40 67 9090 0
Telex: 213138 koyo d
Telefax: +49 40 67 92 03-0

Koyo France SA
8 rue Guy Moquet, ZI, 95100 Argnteuil, France
Telephone: +33 1 3982 7371
Telex: 605974 koyo frc
Telefax: +33 1 3981 5206

Koyo Española SA
Alfonso Gomez, 23 Madrid 28037, Spain
Telephone: +34 1 754 1068/204 9783
Telex: 45249 koyo e
Telefax: +34 1 754 1034

Koyo Fabrica Brasileira de Rolamentos Ltda
Rua Silva Vale 577-ZC-12, Rio de Janeiro, RJ, Brazil
Telephone: +55 21 289 5244
Telex: 2123339 koyo br

Overseas works
Koyo Corporation of USA
PO Drawer 967, Highway 601, Orangeburg, South Carolina 29115, USA
Telephone: +1 803 536 6200
Telefax: +1 803 534 0599

Koyo Fabrica Brasileira de Rolamentos Ltda
Rua Silva Vale 577-ZC-12, Rio de Janeiro, RJ, Brazil
Telephone: +55 21 289 5244
Telex: 2123339 koyo br

Magnus
A Farley Industries Company Inc

South Bell & Viaduct, Fremont, Nebraska 68025, USA

Telephone: +1 402 721 9540

President: S S Coleman
Marketing: L M Hepler

Products: High-leaded bronze bearings for traction motor application; tin bronze bearings and special analyses; solid journal bearings; proprietary centrifugal castings, horizontal and vertical; babbit bearing linings, centrifugal, static and plated; statistical process control (SPC); robotic material handling and integrated machining; electric induction furnaces; spectrographic analysis; and automated green sand molding.

Miba
Miba Gleitlager AG

Dr Mitterbauer Str 3, PO Box 1, A-4663 Laakirchen, Austria

Telephone: +43 7613 2541
Telex: 24648
Telefax: +43 7613 4257

Subsidiaries
Miba American Corporation
258N Witchduck Road, Suite 206D, Virginia Beach, Virginia 23462
Telephone: +1 804 490 6053
Telefax: +1 804 490 7360

Miba Vertriebs GmbH
Wolfgangweg 29, D-7997 Immenstaad, W Germany
Telephone: +49 7545 2222
Telefax: +49 7545 6975

Miba Far East Pty Ltd
35 Selegie Road 10-10, Parklane Shopping Mall, Singapore 0718
Telephone: +65 3395422/3/4

Products: Miba specialises in research and development, design and manufacture of white metal, lead bronze and aluminium bearings for heavy-duty diesel engines. For increased performance and longer service life in modern engines, Miba developed the globally-patented Miba-Rillenlager. Miba's programme covers the major manufacturers in the US and European locomotive engine industry.

Multi-Service Supply
Multi-Service Supply Division
Buncher Co

Leetsdale, Pennsylvania 15056, USA

Telephone: +1 412 741 1500
Telefax: +1 412 266 8631

President: Ralph L Coffing
Vice-President & General Manager: Timothy Crone
Marketing Director: Larry Blair

Products: Roller bearings; couplers; yokes, draft gears; wheel and axle assemblies.

Nachi-Fujikoshi
Nachi-Fujikoshi Corporation

World Trade Centre Building, 4-1 Hammamatsucho 2-chome, Minato-ku, Tokyo 105, Japan

Telephone: +81 3 345 5111
Telex: 24327; 26877

Products: Ball bearings, roller bearings, linear ball bearings.

NSK
Nippon Seiko KK

Nissei Building 6-3, Ohsaki, 1-chome, Shinagawa-ku, Tokyo 141, Japan

Telephone: +81 3 779 7120
Telex: 02228328
Telefax: +81 3 779 7433

President: T Arata
Executive Vice President: M Hosoda

Products: Axleboxes, journal bearings, sealed clean roll-chock bearings, tapered roller bearings, cylindrical and spherical roller bearings, ball bearings and pillow units.

NTN Toyo
NTN Toyo Bearing Co Ltd

3-17 chome, Kyomachibori, Nishi-ku, Osaka, Japan

Telephone: +81 6 443 5001
Telex: 63750, 63806, 63973

Tokyo office: TOC Building, 6th Floor, 22-17, 7-chome, Nishi-Gotanda, Shinagawa-ku, Tokyo

Telephone: +81 3 494 2821

Overseas works
NTN Kugellagerfabrik (Deutschland) GmbH
Goldzack-Strasse 1, 402 Mettmann, Federal Republic of Germany
Telephone: +49 2104 12016
Telex: 8581 135

NTN Bearing Mfg Canada Ltd
6740 Kitimat Road, Mississauga, Ontario L5N 1M6, Canada
Telephone: +1 416 826 5500
Telex: 06 979597

American NTN Bearing Mfg Corporation
9515 Winona Avenua, Schiller Pasrk, Illinois 601076, USA
Telephone: +1 312 671 5450
Telex: 253294

NTN Elgin Corporation
1500 Holmes Road, Elgin, Illinois 60120, USA
Telephone: +1 312 741 4545
Telex: 722472

Products: Journal roller bearings of all types.

Railko
Railko Ltd
A BBA Group Company

Boundary Road, Loudwater, High Wycombe, Buckinghamshire HP10 9QU, England

Telephone: +44 6285 24901
Telex: 848406
Telefax: +44 628 810761

MANUFACTURERS / Bearings

Traction and transmission bearings for railway drive systems by SKF

Tapered bearing unit (TBU) by SKF

SKF light-alloy axlebox and bearings for mass transit cars

Sales & Engineering Director: R S Holmes
UK Sales Manager: C Bisp

Products: Plastics bearings, including the Railko centre pivot liner developed to replace greased metal on UIC Y25C type bogies.

Recently added to the Railko range of non-metallic bearing materials are Railko NF and JL non-asbestos reinforced thermosetting materials, particularly suitable for railway bogie centre pivot liners, side bearer liners and anti-roll bar bearings.

Railko JLX75 is a PTFE coated material especially suitable for bearing pads in air springs. Railko PV80 grade is an oil-filled acetal copolymer giving low-frictional properties. Where quantities permit, injection mouldings can be produced cheaply.

Recent contracts include air-sprung pads and anti-roll bar bearings for BR Class 320 emus (1989); high-capacity wagon pivot bush maintenance (1990).

RHP Bearings
RHP Industrial

PO Box 18, Newark, Nottinghamshire NG24 2JF, England

Telephone: +44 636 605123
Telex: 377652
Telefax: +44 636 605000

Managing Director: A J Bowkett
Engineering Director: E Godson
Sales Director: P S Wheeldon

Products: Ball and roller bearings and bearing units for traction motors, transmissions and suspensions.

SKF
Aktiebolaget SKF

415 50 Gothenburg, Sweden

Telephone: +46 31371000, 371432
Telex: 2350
Telefax: +46 31372832, 372441

Rail Business Manager: Egon Ekdahl

Products: Ball and roller bearings; axleboxes and tapered bearing units (TBUs) for all kinds of railway vehicles; light-alloy axleboxes for mass transit, LRVs and metro cars; motor suspension units (MSUs) for reliable power transmission; special traction motor bearings; slewing bearings for articulated car bogies; and plain bearings for bogie linkages.

SKF is an international organisation comprising 200 companies with 70 factories together operating in more than 130 countries. The SKF sales organisation is backed up by 200 branch sales offices and over 10 000 distributors and dealers. Worldwide availability of SKF bearings is supported by a comprehensive technical advisory service.

To assist a customer in mounting, dismounting and maintenance service, SKF has developed a range of special equipment such as a fully automatic bearing washing machine for axleboxes with spherical roller bearings; a semi-automatic wheel dismounting machine using the oil injection method; and a hydraulic press for the mounting and dismounting of tapered bearing units. Also included in the range are hydraulic and mechanical tools such as oil injection systems, self-centering extractors, impact wrenches and hook spanners. Induction heaters, heating rings and portable monitoring equipment such as digital thermometers and tachometers are also available.

SKF also provides equipment such as hydraulic presses, induction heaters, thermometers, etc for application and maintenance of roller bearings and surrounding parts in the mass transit administrations. For more than 70 years SKF have supplied roller bearings to mass transit systems such as London Transport, Berlin, Paris, Hong Kong, Montreal and Pusan Metros, Washington Metropolitan Area Transit, Canadian LRC and Australian suburban rail systems.

SKF Argentina
SKF Argentina SA

Postal address: Casilla de Correo 197, 1000 Buenos Aires, Argentina
Head office: Perú 545, 1068 Buenos Aires

Telephone: +54 1 331 3061/8
Telex: 9203
Telefax: +54 1 331 8622

Chairman: Göran Malm
Managing Director: Jimmie Holmberg

Products: Ball and roller bearings, axle boxes and mounting tools.

Stucki
A Stucki Company

2600 Neville Road, Pittsburgh, Pennsylvania 15225, USA

Telephone: +1 412 771 7300

Products: Roller and resilient side bearings; hydraulic bogie stabilisers.

Timken
The Timken Co

British Timken, Division of The Timken Company, Duston, Northampton NN5 6UL, England

Telephone: +44 604 752311
Telex: 317411 timken g
Telefax: +44 604 586635

US sales office: Canton, Ohio 44706, USA

Vice-President, Bearings, Europe, Africa and West Asia: M J Amiel
Director, Marketing, Europe, Africa and West Asia: K Schulze
Managing Director, British Timken: I W Tucker
General Manager, Sales, British Timken: M G Clements
Market Manager, Rail, EAWA: P C Vials
Account Manager: R G Lorist

Subsidiaries: Manufacturing plants in Australia, Brazil, Canada, France, South Africa, United Kingdom and the USA.

Products: Tapered roller bearings; AP* and SP* tapered roller bearing cartridge units; and complete axleboxes and motor suspension units.

The Timken Company serves the railway industry world-wide with their expertise in the design, manufacture and supply of tapered roller bearings and ancillary equipment covering transmissions, axleboxes, traction motor suspension units and other equipment, such as cooling fans and screw compressors. This expertise has resulted in contracts from Hitachi Ltd for complete motor suspension units to be used in locomotives for Indian Railways, Australia and Pakistan Railways.

Timken bearings have been selected for the transmission of the BR Class 91 locomotives, the journals

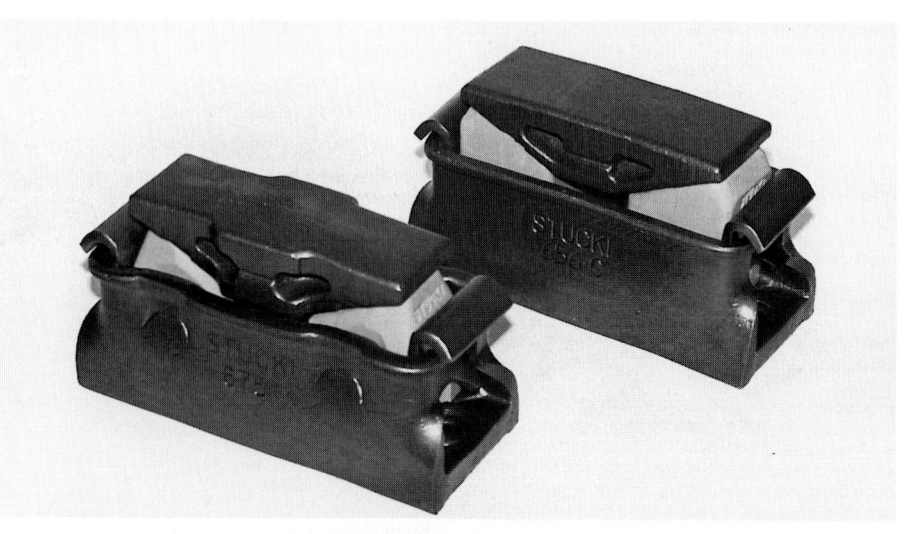

Stucki metal-capped resilient side bearings, Models 675-RL and 656-CRH

of which are also equipped with Timken 150 mm SP bearings. For the Mk IV Pullman and tourist passenger cars, service vehicles and driving van trailers which make up each Class 91 train-set, some 2000 Timken SP 130 mm journal bearings are being supplied. These are to the new higher ratings in accordance with the international UIC 515 standard.

The reliability of the Timken SP bearing has been further endorsed by an order from SNCF for over 4000 150 mm bearings for TGV-Atlantique train-sets. Over 9 million Timken cartridge bearings of various sizes have been manufactured and are used by railways in over 100 countries. The Timken SP bearing is used extensively throughout the United Kingdom on electric multiple-units, diesel multiple-units and freight cars.

*Trademark of The Timken Company

Unity
Unity Railway Supply Co, Inc

805 Golf Lane, Bensenville, Illinois 60106, USA

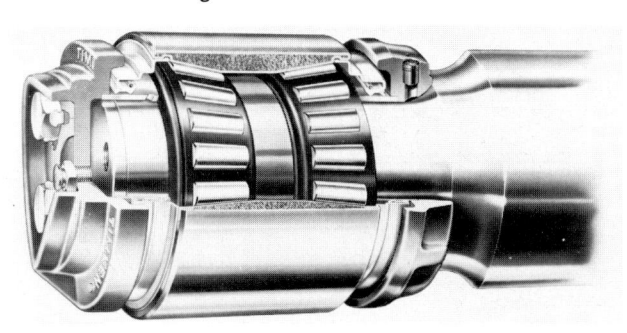

Timken AP (all-purpose) bearing, over 9 million of which are in worldwide rail application

Telephone: +1 708 595 4562
Telefax: +1 708 595 0646

President and Chairman: H R O'Connor
Vice President, Sales: Robert S Grandy
Executive Vice President, Financial: Robert Holden

Products: Journal lubricators, journal stops, journal box rear seals and lid seals, safety warning lights, safety grating (brake steps, end platforms and running boards), air brake shipping covers, wear liners, pedestal liners, side bearing wear liners.

Signalling/telecommunications/ fare systems

Pole lines down again? Leave 'em down!

Pole line elimination is a working goal of Harmon Industries.

We're not simply out to rid the landscape of these familiar trackside symbols. We want to eliminate the ongoing problems: Constant maintenance. Rising prices of copper wire. Growing scarcity of quality poles. High labor costs. And, primarily, the loss of efficiency and performance that results when pole lines are down.

The industries of Harmon have created an integrated family of products that allow you to achieve pole line elimination on a location-by-location basis, within your own time frame and budget.

Harmon's PMD and HXP stand-alone motion detectors eliminate line requirements for highway crossing circuits.

Electro Code solid state coded track circuitry eliminates line wire from wayside signalling control points.

Signals that once travelled the wires for supervisory control of CTC territory can now be transmitted by Harmon voice/data radios.

System by system, Harmon components add up to safer, more efficient train operation. And complete independence from the headaches of pole lines.

The end of the pole line is in sight. Contact Harmon today.

HARMON INDUSTRIES, INC.

1300 Jefferson Court
Blue Springs, MO 64015
(816) 229-3345 • (800) 825-3178
Telefax (816) 229-0556

Canada: Vale/Harmon Enterprises • (514) 636-1026
Australia: Henkes/Harmon Ind. Pty. Ltd. • 61-3-723-1128

TRANSPORTATION TECHNOLOGY WORLDWIDE

Signalling and telecommunications systems

AUSTRALIA
EB Signal 306
Fischer 307
GEC Alsthom 308
Kenelec 311
Teknis 318

AUSTRIA
Futurit 307

BELGIUM
Orlians 313
SAIT 315

BRAZIL
Fresinbra 307

CANADA
BG Checo 303
DSL 305
Motorola Canada 312
SCC 315
SEL Canada 316

CHINA
China Railway Signal 303

DENMARK
DSI 305

FRANCE
CSEE 303
GEC Alsthom 308
Interelec 311
Matra 311
Mors Techniphone 311
Siferdec 317
Silec 318

GERMANY, FEDERAL REPUBLIC
Deuta 304
Hanning & Kahl 309
Krauss-Maffei 311
Pintsch Bamag 313
SB 315
SEL 316
Siemens 316

HUNGARY
Budavox 303
Electroimpex 306
Ganz Electric 307

INDIA
WSF 321

ITALY
Ansaldo Trasporti 302
IBR 311
Parisini 313
SASIB 315
WABCO Westinghouse 321

JAPAN
Kyosan 311
Nippon Signal 312
Toshiba 319

NETHERLANDS
NKF KABEL 312
Philips 313

POLAND
Elektrim 306

SOUTH AFRICA
Telkor 319

SPAIN
Dimetronic 304

SWEDEN
EB Signal 306
SRT 318

SWITZERLAND
Ascom 302
Hasler 310
Integra Signum 311

UK
BP Solar 303
Craswell Scientific 303
Drallim Telecommunications 304
EB Signal 305
EMX International 306
Ferranti 307
Field & Grant 307
GEC-General Signal 308
GPT 309
HWD 310
Motorola 312
Pirelli General 313
Plessey 313
SEMA 316
STC 318
Telemotive 319
Telephone Cables 319
Thorn EMI 319
Vaughan 320
Westinghouse Signals Limited 321

USA
Ametek 302
Amtech 302
Antenna Specialists 302
Aydin 303
Burle Industries 303
Chrysler 303
Cragg Railcharger 303
Dixie Precast 304
Dowty RFL 304
Erico 307
GNB 309
GRS 309
Harmon 309
Harris 310
Maxon 311
OTP Rail and Transit 313
Pulse 313
Railfone 313
Rockwell 313
Safetran 314
SCI 316
Servo 316
Transcontrol 319
Union Switch & Signal 319
Vapor 320
Westinghouse Electric 321

302 MANUFACTURERS / Signalling and telecommunications

Ametek
Ametek Panalarm Division

7401 North Hamlin Avenue, Skokie, Illinois 60076, USA

Telephone: +1 312 675 2500
Telex: 72 4436
Telefax: +1 312 675 3011

General Manager: Larry Froman
Sales Manager: Frank Knopf
Export Sales Manager: John Cundiff
Transportation Marketing Manager: Donald Paul

Products: Panalarm Mosaic Tile Graphic Displays, available in illuminated and non-illuminated form, and capable of printing with any symbols to customer requirement: incorporating push-button or switch controls, indicator lights, digital read-out displays as required; annunciators; event recorders.

Amtech Corporation

4514 Cole Avenue, Suite 1100, Dallas TX 75205, USA

Telephone: +1 214 520 6900
Telefax: +1 214 526 1267

Chairman: Michael R Corboy
President: G Russell Mortenson
Vice-President, Marketing: Dr Thomas L McDaniel
Vice-President, World: Philippe Larue
Vice-President, Intermodal: Fred Krueger
Controller: Randall Guillot
Chairman, Finance Committee: Kenneth W Anderson
Chairman, Executive Committee: David P Cook
Manager, Rail: Thomas Levine

Principal subsidiaries:
Amtech Technology Corporation (Mfg Plant), 2530 Camino Entrada, Santa Fe, NM 87505, USA

Amtech Paris, 63 Boulevard Bessieres, 75017 Paris, France

Products: automatic vehicle identification systems, automatic train control systems.

Recent contracts have been obtained from SNCF; Norfolk Southern, Burlington Northern, Florida Power, Kerr McGee Corp, USA; Canadian National Railroad.

Ansaldo Trasporti
Ansaldo Trasporti SpA
A member of the Ansaldo Group

Head office: 425 Via Argine 80147 Naples, Italy
Works: 260 Via Nuova delle Brecce, 80147 Naples, Italy

Telephone: +39 81 7810111
Telex: 710131 ans na i
Telefax: +39 81 7810698-699

Other offices:
336 Viale Sarca, 20126 Milan, Italy

Telephone: +39 2 64451
Telex: 331279
Telefax: +39 2 6438032

25 Corso Perrone, 16161 Genoa, Italy

Telephone: +39 10 65511
Telex: 271274
Telefax: +39 10 495044

Chairman: Giovanni Nobile
Vice President and Managing Director: Emilio Maraini
General Director: Francesco Granito
General Co-Director: Alberto G Rosania
Technical Director: Salvatore Bianconi
R & D and Commercial Director: Carlo Rizzi

Products: Automation and signalling for railway, underground and surface transport systems, and components for power and signal electronics; all relay and solid state interlocking; automatic block system; electronic track circuit and continuous cab signalling equipment; microcomputer-based automatic train operation apparatus; remote control equipments; CTC; train describer and automatic line supervision systems; level crossing automation; traffic control systems for industrial railways.

Recent contracts include signalling systems for the Staten Island line (New York City Transit Authority), the Boston Blue line (Massachusetts Bay Transit Authority), the Los Angeles-Long Beach line (Los Angeles County Transit Council) and the Surabaya-Kertosono line (Indonesia).

Antenna Specialists
Antenna Specialists Co

Head office: 30500 Bruce Industrial Parkway, Cleveland, Ohio 44139–3996, USA

Telephone: +1 216 349 8400
Telex: 4332133
Telefax: +1 216 349 8683

Driver's cab equipped with train radio supplied by Ascom

Products: Two-way communications antenna systems; personal security devices.

Ascom
Ascom Radiocom Ltd

Feldstrasse 42, CH-8036 Zürich 4, Switzerland

Telephone: +41 1 248 13 13
Telex: 813 368 apo ch
Telefax: +41 1 248 12 02

Main works
Ascom Radiocom Ltd,
Ziegelmattstrasse 1, CH-4500 Solothurn

Ascom Radiocom Ltd,
CH-5300 Turgi

General Manager: Dr Peter Affolter

Principal subsidiary companies
Ascom Teletron GmbH, Frankfurt, Federal Republic of Germany
Ascom Autophon Ges.mbH, Vienna, Austria
Autophon SA, Levallois-Perret/Paris, France
Autophon Radio Communications Ltd, Camberley, Surrey, England
Ascom Autophon NV-SA, Brussels, Belgium
Ascom Teletron BV, Nieuwegein, Netherlands
Ascom Autophon A/S, Oslo, Norway
Ascom Radiocom SpA, San Giuliano Milanese, Italy
Tateco Radiocom AB, Göteborg, Sweden

Products: Complete track-to-train radio systems including dispatcher units, base stations, locomotive stations; voice-only or voice and data transmission; radio systems for railway station and shunting yard

Solid state interlocking by Ansaldo Trasporti

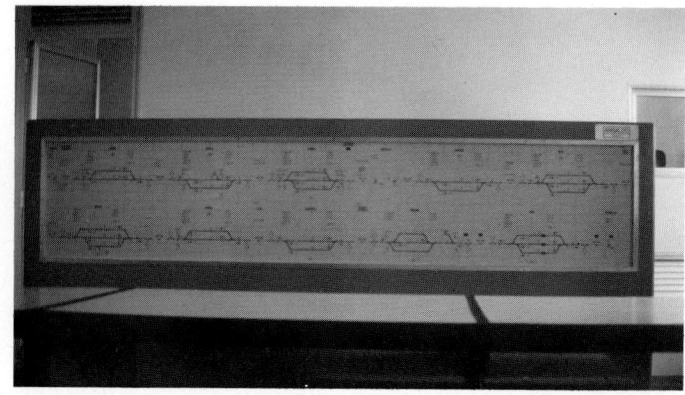

Mimic panel of Cervaro-Potenza CTC, Italian State Railways, by Ansaldo Trasporti

communications; rugged handheld VHF/UHF transceivers for shunting yard communications.

The company's radio systems and products are in operation or being installed on various national and private railways in Europe and abroad:

SBB, Switzerland
Radio communication system compatible with UIC in the 457-468 MHz band. It is capable of handling data, and is to be extended to tunnel antenna systems for public on-train telephone application. The full system will cover 2117 km of radio-served routes, 400 base stations, five operation control centres, 42 remote control centres, 1000 mobile stations, 200 portable stations and 50 tunnel antenna systems.

SNCF, France
Integrated control system for transmitting speech. Can be used wherever data are to be transmitted among different systems and for different transmission media such as wire, radio or optical fibres.

NS, Netherlands
Country-wide speech communications network including 2000 locomotive mobiles and 200 base stations with automatic channel switching to the nearest control centre.

SJ, Sweden, and NSB, Norway
Radio communication system for parallel speech and data in a time division operation interconnecting to track-to-train, maintenance and shunting radio systems and for communication with the guard.

BR, United Kingdom
Track-to-train radio communication system base stations for continuous communications between drivers and signal men.

CP, Portugal
Radio communication system compatible with UIC in the 460 MHz range for speech.

Other countries
Various speech communication systems including microwave multi-channel link systems along the track and to railway stations.

Aydin
Aydin Corporation

700 Dresher Road, PO Box 349, Horsham, Pennsylvania 19044, USA

Telephone: +1 215 657 7510
Telex: 6851211 aydin uw
Telefax: +1 215 657 3830

Main works: Philadelphia, Pennsylvania; San Jose, California.

Products: Communications systems and equipment. In 1989, Aydin completed a major programme to supply a telecommunications network for train traffic control on Egyptian Railways.

BG Checo
BG Checo International Limited

110 Cremazie Blvd West, Montreal, Quebec H2P 1B9, Canada

Telephone: +1 514 382 3030
Telex: 05–827615

Manufacturing Division: BGI/Automatec, 7700 De Lamartine Blvd, Montreal, Quebec H1J 2A8

Telephone: +1 514 353 8940
Cable: Checo Mfg

President, Chief Executive Officer: Joel Pavec
Executive Vice-President, Chief Operating Officer: J Corej

Products: For railway signalling: survey engineering, case wiring, field installation, turnkey systems, automatic train control, wayside signalling and crossing protection systems.

BP
BP Solar International Ltd
(A subsidiary of British Petroleum plc)

Solar House, Bridge Street, Leatherhead, Surrey KT22 8BZ, England

Telephone: +44 296 26100
Telex: 838867 bpsol g
Telefax: +44 296 436241

Main works
BP Solar Systems Ltd
Aylesbury Vale Industrial Park, Stocklake, Aylesbury, Buckinghamshire HP20 1DQ

General Manager: Richard Ely
Marketing Executive, Railway Signalling & Telecommunications: Mark Hammonds

Principal subsidiary companies
BP Solar Espanga SA
BP Solar Australia Pty Ltd
BP Thai Solar Corporation Ltd
BP Solar East Africa Ltd (Kenya)
BP Solar Pakistan

Products: Solar electric (photovoltaic) power systems to supply railway signalling and telecommunications systems.
Recent contracts have been executed for Nigeria Railways, Zambia Railways, Ghana Railways, Indian Railways and Mozambique Railways.

Budavox
Budavox Telecommunication Foreign Trading Co Ltd

Budafoki ut 79, POB 267, 1392 Budapest, Hungary

Telephone: +36 1 868 988
Cable: Budavox, Budapest
Telex: 22 5077

Managing Director: László Nyiredy
Directors: József Benkö
Dr Tamàs Németh

Products: Telecommunications equipment such as dispatcher-type electronic centralised telephone exchanges, data teleprocessing equipment, vhf radiotelephones, complete telecommunications systems etc.

Burle Industries
Robot Access Control Hardware

7041 Orchard Street, Dearborn, Michigan 48126, USA

Telephone: +1 313 846 2623
Telefax: +1 313 846 3569

General Manager: J Kane
Product Manager: B Sparling

Products: Power signalling apparatus; level crossing gates; barriers and warning signals; centralised traffic control and remote control systems.

China Railway Signal & Communication Company

111 Zao Jia Cun Fengtai, Beijing, China

Telephone: +86 1 816289/8641556
Telex: 22780 crsc cn

President: Yu Xiao-Mang
Technical Director: Lu Jiasheng
International Director: Lu Delian

Products: All-relay interlockings, automatic and tokenless block, atc equipment, ctc, cab signalling equipment, track circuits, relays, point machines, communications and telephone systems.

Chrysler
Chrysler Military-Public Electronics Systems (MPES)
A Division of the Chrysler Corporation

1100 Connecticut Avenue NW, Washington DC 20036, USA

Telephone: +1 202 862 5435

Products: Supervisory Control and Data Acquisition (SCADA) systems.

Cragg Railcharger

1433 Energy Park Drive, St Paul, Minnesota 55108, USA

Telephone: +1 612 646 7473
Telefax: +1 612 646 5018

President: Harold M Cragg
Vice-President, Export & Marketing: Robert P Degel

Products: Automatic battery chargers for signal applications.

Craswell
Craswell Scientific Limited

Unit 11, Orchard Trading Estate, Toddington GL54 5EB, England

Telephone: +44 242 621534
Telex: 437 283 vacuum g
Telefax: +44 242 621529

Products: Platform mirrors for surveillance in driver-only operation. An aid to safety in providing rearward visibility from the driver's cab.

CSEE-Transport

Head office: 99 avenue Aristide-Briand, 92542 Montrouge Cedex, France

Telephone: +33 1 40 92 02 03
Telex: 631 604 csee
Telefax: +33 1 40 92 05 04

Chairman: Jean-Claude Pelissolo
Executive Vice President, Transport Division: G Dubot
Sales Manager, Transport Division: P Henric

ZI De la Vigne aux Loups, rue Denis Papin Bp 105, 91380 Chilly Mazarin, France

Telephone: +33 1 64 54 54 54
Telex: 603437
Telefax: +33 1 64 54 54 55

Main works:
Etablissement de Perigueux
ZI de Périgueux Boulazac, 24000 Perigueux, France

Etablissement de RIOM
Atelier Dombrowski, Atelier des Varennes, 15, av A Despérouses, 63203 Riom Cedex, France

Principal subsidiary companies:
Signaltechnik, Federal Republic of Germany
Sinelbras, Brazil
Ecosen, Venezuela
TDC, USA

Products: Transponders, hot box and wheel detectors, CTC systems, power supply, Automatic Train Control, Automatic Train Protection for railways and subway (SACEM), jointless track circuits, electronic treadles, switch machines (electric) and failsafe relays.
CSEE is the sole French manufacturer of track-to-train transmission (ATC) for the Paris-Lyon and Paris-Bordeaux high-speed TGV routes of French Railways and supplied the ATC (SACEM) for Paris RER Line A, commissioned in early 1989.

304 MANUFACTURERS / Signalling and telecommunications

Cab signal display in TGV driving cab by CSEE

Deuta
Deuta-Werke GmbH

Paffrather Strasse 140, PO Box 200260, 5060 Bergisch Gladbach 2, Federal Republic of Germany

Telephone: +49 2202 1006-26
Cable: Deutawerke Berggladbach
Telex: 887725 dewe d
Telefax: +49 2202 100645

Products: Recording equipment for railed vehicles: tacho-generators, analog indicators, variable resistors for adjustment of speed indicators to wheel diameters, electronic data storage units, SIFA vigilance equipment, odometers, clocks, etc.

Dimetronic
Dimetronic SA

Sierra Morena 28-34, Pol Industrial San Fernando II, Torrejón de Ardoz, Madrid, Spain

Telephone: +34 75 42 12, +34 75 17 96
Telex: 46638
Telefax: +34 56 21 15, +34 76 06 56

Products: Power colour-light signalling, relay interlockings, geographical circuit interlockings, automatic block control systems, centralised traffic control (CTC) systems, automatic train supervisory (ATS) systems, automatic train operation (ATO) systems, automatic train protection (ATP) systems, solid state interlocking (SSI) systems, computer-based train description and automatic train control systems, cab signalling and automatic train stop systems, level crossing protection, automatic fare collection, ticket vending machinery and supervisory systems, positive train identification, passenger information, remote control and data acquisition for rail traffic and electrical energy control systems, radio electronic token block (RETB) systems, supervisory systems for urban transport. Nearly all of these systems are designed on computer-aided design (CAD) equipment, tests and quality control being carried out by computers.
Products manufactured include colour-light signals, position-light shunt signals, ground signals and accessories, point machines for both ac and dc working together with the connecting rods, clamp lock mechanism and detection equipment. Relays to BR specification 930, printed circuit board assemblies, mosaic mimic control and indication consoles, apparatus cases, track circuits of ac, dc and the jointless types, fare collection equipment and turnstiles.
Most of the projects contracted are of a turnkey nature and are designed and engineered to customers requirements. Usually the central control offices are equipped with mosaic mimic control and indication consoles supplemented by VDUs, keyboards and printers.
Dimetronic has been an associate company of Westinghouse Brake and Signal Company since 1979 and is within the Hawker Siddeley Group.

Dixie Precast
Dixie Precast Inc

4170 Angelette Drive, Austell, Georgia 30001, USA

Telephone: +1 404 944 1930

President: A M Angelette

Products: Pre-cast sectional foundations for railroad signals and cantilever masts.
Contracts have been obtained from Norfolk Southern, Conrail and CSX (1990/91/92).

Dowty RFL
Dowty RFL Industries Inc

Powerville Road, Boonton, New Jersey 07005-0239, USA

Products: Pressurisation equipment for telephone cables and waveguides; microprocessor telephone network alarm monitoring systems for pressurised cables and security alarm systems.

Deuta ZEV microprocessor-based speed and distance recorder rack

Telephone: +1 201 334 3100
Telex: 215071 drfl ur
Telefax: +1 201 334 3863

President: David S Seabury
Vice President, Sales & Marketing: Roger Eblovi
International Sales Manager: A L Vnencak
International Sales: Peter Stolpe

Products: Model 9850 FSK programmable tones combine digital signal processing (DSP) technology with a second microcontroller co-processor to yield a high-performance communications product compatible with existing channels and flexible enough to handle higher speed requirements for future applications.
Compact Model 9000 fibre-optic TI carrier system offers wide-ranging compatibility with the convenience of modular construction. Digital multiplexer encodes 24 voice channels into a 1.544 mbps digital signal. Offers drop-and/or-insert capability, flexibile channel assignments, etc.
Series 6500 selective calling telephone unit is a telephone communications system designed to provide two-way selective dialling between standard dual-tone multi-frequency (DTMF) push-button dial telephone.
Model 6515w SSB carrier provides an economical approach to the assembly of carrier systems over open-wire or static-line facilities.

Drallim Telecommunications
Drallim Telecommunications Ltd

Brett Drive, Bexhill-on-Sea, East Sussex TN40 2JR, England

Telephone: +44 424 221144
Telex: 95285
Telefax: +44 424 216636

President: A W Millard
Group Chairman: H Pratt
Director: R Bedford
Marketing Director: M F Dawson

DSI
Dansk Signal Industri A/S

Stamholmen 175, 2650 Hvidovre, Denmark

Telephone: +45 1 490333
Telex: 16503

Managing Director: A Wiuff

Products: Signal safety systems; interlocking systems for stations based on free-wired relays, modular relay sets (geographical) or microprocessor-based; block systems, automatic and tokenless; track circuits, relay-based or solid state; level crossing protection (fully automatic warning equipment, or fully automatic equipment with half-barrier or double-barrier); control and supervisory systems, such as internal train control (push-pull trains) and microprocessor remote control and supervision; wayside equipment, including multi-aspect colour-light signals, shunting signals, gate

Signalling and telecommunications / **MANUFACTURERS**

machines, impedance bonds and track circuits; public and staff information systems, comprising computerised systems for a single station or to cover a whole region, with automatic visual presentation of information on boards, train indicators, colour video units and audible transmission via strategically-placed loudspeakers.

DSL

DSL
Dynamic Sciences Limited

359 St Croix Blvd, Montreal, Quebec, Canada H4N 2L3

Telephone: +1 514 744 5571
Telex: 05 825803
Telefax: +1 514 744 0053

President: John T Wilson
Vice-President, Marketing & Sales: James W Johnson

Products: The DSL product line includes the DIGITRAC transponder based train location system, the DIGITAIR end-of-train data telemetry system, a crashworthy on-board event recorder unit featuring solid state memory and computer compatible download. DSL's turnkey systems include advanced locomotive training simulators for driver/engineer training.

The DIGITRAC transponder-based train location system utilises a passive transponder attached to the track structure which provides unique identification codes at critical locations along the right-of-way. The system is comprised of the fixed transponder units in communication with vehicle-mounted antenna and electronic reader units. In operation, a 200 Khz field from the vehicle antenna energises the transponder, which transmits a 64-bit unique message on a 27 Mhz carrier. An error-correcting data acquisition process in the reader provides exceptional identification accuracy at speeds from zero to beyond 160 km/h. Compliant with ATCS specification 335, serial outputs via RS422 link are provided to on-board computers. Optional are HDLC protocol, or RS232C data link. Each component of DIGITRAC is ruggedly constructed to withstand the extremes of temperature, weather, and vibration encountered in railroad and transit system environments.

The DIGITAIR end-of-train telemetry system includes a coupler-mounted Sense and Transmit Unit (STU) attaching to the last car in the train and a Receive and Display Unit (RDU) attached to the locomotive engineer's control console. The information sensed at the end of the train includes the air brake trainline pressure, the motion of the last car, including forward or reverse indication on starting, on/off condition of an attached flashing and highly visible marker (HVM) light, and condition of the rechargeable batteries which power the STU. The STU is extremely rugged in design and operates in the –40° to +70°C temperature range.

The system utilizes UHF transmission at 457 Mhz. In addition to displaying the end-of-train data, the RDU provides a resettable odometer for determining when the train has progressed a full train length past CTC block limits or level crossings. Critical alarms are monitored with audible alert on loss of air pressure, and battery weak or fail (discharged) condition. DIGITAIR is seen to be an essential safety device for cabooseless operation.

The DIGITAIR II system introduced by DSL in 1987 includes all of the above features but, in addition, it allows the locomotive engineer to demand that an emergency brake application initiate at the last car in the train. This added safety feature is provided through two-way communication between RDU and STU.

The DSL crashworthy on-board Event Recorder is a rugged data collection and recording system for use on locomotives and transit vehicles. It collects data from numerous analogue, digital and pulse signal sources. Operating only while the train is moving, the Event Recorder will store about 48 hours of recorded data in its solid state memory. Record of the occurrence of specified discrete events can be retained indefinitely with a time stamp. The recorded information can be retrieved by downloading to a lap-top computer in the cab, transmitting through a radio link, or by removing the memory module. The DSL Event Recorder can be configured with different input cards to change the number of analogue, discrete, and pulsed signals on record. It interfaces with DSL train location and end-of-train devices, as well as ATCS compatible devices from the manufacturers.

DSL offers a complete range of locomotive simulator systems for training engineers or drivers. Full-scale replica units, representing every detail of the locomotive cab, complete with sound and motion cues, are in service in Europe and N America. These are equipped with high resolution colour visual presentations of the down-track scenario based on multiple video discs.

EBA SIGNAL

EB Signal
EB Signal (UK) Ltd

Estover Close, Plymouth, Devon PL6 7PU, England

Telephone: +44 752 702525
Telex: 45383 ebsig g
Telefax: +44 752 701643

President: R Kuvas
Managing Director: R A Haines
Contracts Director: A D Wilson
Technical Director: E Sidebotham
Sales Manager: J Rose

Forward View Visual System Monitor and Graphic Data Display

Alternate Event Visual Video Disc players and report printer

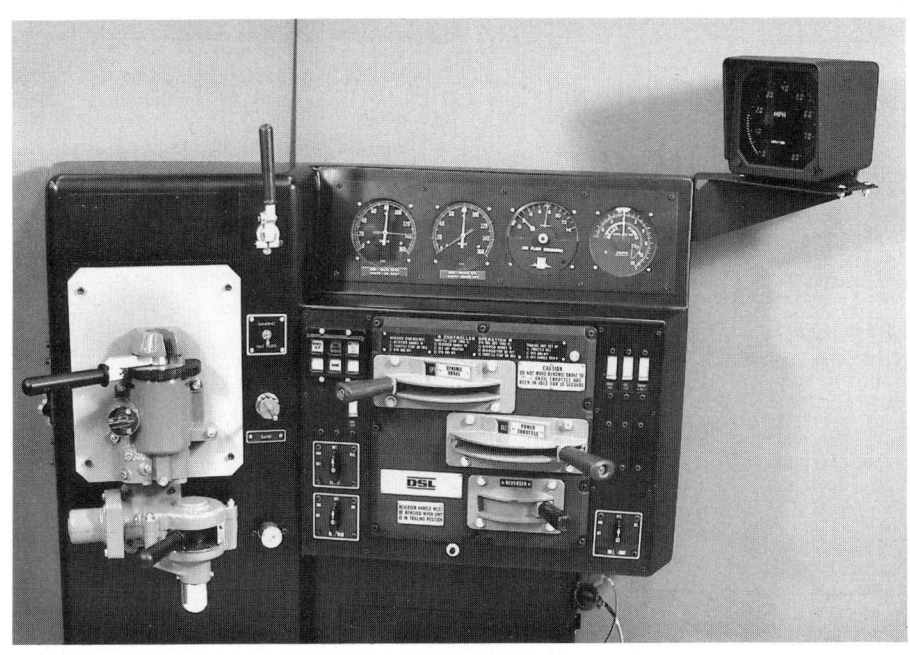

Simulator control stand

MANUFACTURERS / Signalling and telecommunications

Products: Specialists in turnkey projects comprising design, supply, installation and commissioning of railway signalling and telecommunication schemes. Lineside and automatic signalling, relay-based or electronic. Integrated comprehensive control systems, combining total signalling operation, train describers, non-vital and vital data transmission, passenger information, automatic route setting, mimic or VDU display.

Specialist products include interference-immune audio-frequency jointless track circuits, radio block signalling, fibre-optic signals.

Worldwide operations include Far East, Australia, New Zealand, plus Waterloo area resignalling, currently the largest UK resignalling scheme.

The company's recent contracts have included provision of signalling and SCADA monitoring and control for the construction phase of the Channel Tunnel.

EB Signal AB

PO Box 42505, S-126 12 Stockholm, Sweden

Telephone: +46 8 72620000
Telex: 10442 ericj s
Telefax: +46 8 7262300

Managing Director: Olle Andersson
Fimance & Accounting: Ingemar Mellgren
Safety & Control Systems: Hans Borgnas
Automatic Train Control Systems: Lennart Dock
Trackside Materials & Conventional Systems: Lars Rask

Principal subsidiaries:
EB Signal Pty Ltd, Australia
Telephone: +61 7 3693111
Telefax: +61 7 3699366

EB Signal A/S, Denmark
Telephone: +45 36 390100
Telefax: +45 31 495750

EB Señal SA, Spain
Telephone: +34 1 4678700
Telefax: +34 1 4678766

EBFATME SpA, Italy
Telephone: +39 6 4111462
Telefax: +39 6 4111629

EB Scarfini SpA, Italy
Telephone: +39 6 4111462
Telefax: +39 6 4111629

EB Likenne Oy, Finland
Telephone: +358 0 5061177
Telefax: +358 0 5061210

EB Lehmkuhl AS, Norway
Telephone: +47 2 841000
Telefax: +47 2 843300

EB Signal (UK) Ltd, England
Telephone: +44 752 702525
Telefax: +44 752 701643

Products: Railway interlocking systems, automatic train control systems, control and supervisory systems, signalling materials.

Recent contracts include computerised remote control of the Stockholm remote area for Swedish State Railways; automatic train control for Finnish State Railways and Portuguese State Railways.

EB Signal
EB Signals Pty Ltd

1st Floor, South Tower, John Oxley Centre, 339 Coronation Drive, Milton, Queensland 4064, Australia

Telephone: +61 7 369 3111
Telex: 473684901
Telefax: +61 7 369 9366

Managing Director: Robert C Kull
General Manager: Urban Johansson
Marketing Manager: Raymond Black

Products: Power signalling and communications equipment, including signals, point machines, relays and relay racks, trackside cupboards, track circuits and all associated specialised railway signalling equipment. Total turnkey projects, covering full contract services, including designs, supply, installation, testing and commissioning. Specialists in automatic train control (ATC) with EBICAB 700; computerised interlocking systems with EBILOCK 850; remote control and supervisory systems with EBICOS 715; and wagon identification and monitoring systems.

Major works recently completed include:
Queensland Railways: resignalling of Brisbane metropolitan and suburban rail network, with the introduction of 25 kV ac electrification (approximately 150 route-km with 400 point machines and 600 signals).
SRA, New South Wales: signalling with CTC on the North Coast line (over 600 km with 52 field stations) and between Junee-Albury (over 160 km with 12 field stations).
Victoria: remote control and supervision of the Melbourne metropolitan rail network, including the Melbourne Rail Loop. Providing automatic route-setting, train description, train management, passenger information etc. The EBICOS 715 installed provides facilities for controlling approximately 250 field stations.

Major works currently being undertaken include: resignalling associated with Stage 4 of Queensland Railway's main-line electrification project; and ATC installation for Queensland Railways' North Coast line (about 500 km).

Electroimpex
Electroimpex Hungarian Foreign Trading Co

PO Box 296, 1392 Budapest 5, Hungary

Telephone: +36 1 328 300
Cable: Elektro, Budapest

Products: Signalling equipment, CTC, train describers, level crossing apparatus.

Elektrim

Polish Foreign Trade Company for Electrical Equipment Ltd

ul Chalubinskiego 8, PO Box 638, Warsaw, Poland

Telephone: +48 22 301000, 302000
Telex: 814351 pl
Telefax: +48 22 300841/2

Publicity Officer: Rita Wrzesniowska

Products: Interlockings, signals, automatic block, track circuits, level-crossing protection, electromechanical systems, marshalling yard mechanisation and automation.

British Rail Leicester area resignalling scheme by ML Engineering

EMX
EMX Corporation Ltd

8 Warren House, Gatehouse Way, Aylesbury, Buckinghamshire HP19 3DB, England

Telephone: +44 296 435566
Telex: 83374 gchemx
Telefax: +44 296 392404

Contact: M Glynne Jones

EMX Incorporated
3570 Warrensville Center Road, Shaker Heights, Ohio 44122, USA

Telephone: +1 216 662 9240
Telefax: +1 216 662 9250

Contact: J Rozgonyi

Products: Rail and road identification systems for automatic vehicle identification, train annunciation, automatic train stopping, vehicle priority systems, traffic control, electronic signposting, automatic toll debiting.

EMX rail and road systems have been installed in Australia, Africa, Europe, the Far East and North America, with a further system due for installation in eastern Europe. In Australia the EMX priority system for trams is being further expanded. The rail and road ID systems are being enhanced by the addition of variable code transponders that allow variable data from the drivers cab to be included in the transponder message.

The Track 7000 system provides the means to identify, monitor and record the movements of rolling stock over all types of rail systems, from large interstate railway systems down to smaller private rail systems. Each vehicle has fitted to its undercarriage a uniquely coded 64-bit passive transponder, which is read at strategically positioned reader (interrogator) sites. The reader interprets the train's direction, reads the codes of all the transponders fitted, adds date, time and location data and stores the message pending the control computer's request for all current information. Information on up to 500 vehicles can be stored in the trackside buffer unit.

Reversing the system, ie, mounting the transponders between the rails and the reader on the locomotive, provides the basis of automatic train control (ATC), automatic train stopping (ATS) and train location systems.

The Track 7000 has also been successfully integrated with a dynamic weighing system in order to log each unique weighing event relating to each particular rail vehicle.

Erico
Erico Products Inc

34600 Solon Road, Solon, Ohio 44139, USA

Telephone: +1 216 248 0100
Telefax: +1 216 248 0723

General Manager: R B Savage
Marketing Manager: A Weisel
Product Manager: E Lynch

Products: Power and signal bonds and track circuit connections; copper-based exothermic welding (Cadweld process).

Subsidiary companies
Brazil: Erico do Brasil Com E Ind Ltda, Avienda Santa Marina, Nd 1588–LAPA, CEP 05036, São Paulo SP
Telephone: +55 11 872 5444 Telex: (11) 22410
Telefax: +55 11 65 7185

United Kingdom: Erico Europa (GB) Ltd, 59/61 Milford Road, Reading, Berkshire, England
Telephone: +44 734 588386
Telefax: +44 734 594856

Netherlands: Erico Europa BV, Jules Vernweg 75, 5015 BG Tilburg, Netherlands
Telephone: +31 13 360045 Telex: 52182
Telefax: +31 13 351615

Mexico: Mexerico SA, Recursos Hidraulicos 1, Tlalnepantla Estado de Mexico
Telephone: +52 905 398 0033 Telex: 172644

Canada: Erico Canada Inc, 46 Ingram Drive, Toronto, Ontario M6M 2L6
Telephone: +1 416 249 3363 Telex: 06969656
Telefax: +1 416 249 5488

France: Erico France, SARL, rue Benoit Fourneyron, PO Box 31, Zone Industrielle Sud, 42160 Andrezieux-Boutheon
Telephone: +33 77 365656 Telex: 307205
Telefax: +33 77 365998

Hong Kong: Erico-Cadweld (Asia) Ltd, Room 1005, 10th Floor, Heng Ngai Jewellery Centre, Hok Yuen Street, Hunghom, Kowloon
Telephone: +852 3 7648808 Telex: 41274
Telefax: +852 3 764 4486

Ferranti International
Ferranti International Signal plc

Bridge House, Park Road, Gatley, Cheadle, Cheshire SK8 4HZ, England

Telephone: +44 61 428 3644
Telex: 666326
Telefax: +44 61 428 3644 Ext 2230

Products: Telecommunications equipment, computer systems.

Constitution: The company results from the merger of Ferranti plc and International Signal & Control plc.

Field & Grant
Field & Grant Ltd
(Incorporating Tyer and Zone Controls)
A member of the Adwest Group

Pensnett Trading Estate, Kingswinford, West Midlands DY6 7PN, England

Telephone: +44 384 270171
Cable: Controls, Brihill
Telex: 338359

Managing Director: E Jones
Chief Sales Director: B R Whiting
Production Director: R F Yates
Financial Director: R D Brown

Products: Miniature plug-in relays and plug boards to British Rail specification; shelf relays; circuit controllers; key token equipment; colour-light signals; shunt and subsidiary signals; stencil route indicators; Toton indicators.

Fischer
Fischer Industries Pty Ltd

23 Dickson Avenue, Atarmon, New South Wales 2064, Australia

Miniature plug-in relay from comprehensive range to British Rail specifications by Field & Grant

Control desk for a large railway station by Ganz

Telephone: +61 2 436 0611
Telex: 176942 aa
Telefax: +61 2 438 2435

Marketing Director: P Fischer

Products: AWS systems; vigilance equipment; wheel-slide equipment; speed and distance recorders; end-of-train detection apparatus.

Fresinbra
Fresinbra Industrial SA

Head office: Rua Laureano Fernandes Junior, 10-Vila Leopoldina, CEP-05089, São Paulo, Brazil

Telephone: +55 11 260 3122
Telex: (11) 83263
Telefax: +55 11 831 6035

Engineering Manager: Sergio Ulian
Marketing Manager: Affonso Galvão Bueno Filho

Works: Rua Lauriano Fernandes Jr 10, PO Box 24065, Sao Paulo CEP 05091

Telephone: +55 11 260 3122
Telex: +55 11 83263

Products: Railway signalling (ranging from optic signals to CTC, ATC and cab signal systems) and braking systems, under licence of Westinghouse Air Brake Co.

Futurit
Futurit Werk AG

Altmannsdorferstrasse 329, 1232 Vienna, Austria

Telephone: +43 1 222 678521
Telex: 13 3876 fwag
Telefax: +43 1 672266

Products: Railway lanterns with 200, 160 and 125 mm diameter lens; level crossing signals with 200 and 300 mm diameter lens; fibre-optic signs for display of different messages, including speed restrictions, fibre optic signals for tunnels.

Ganz Electric

Lövóház u 39, Budapest H1024, Hungary

Telephone: +36 1 175 3322
Telex: 22 5363 gvm bp
Telefax: +36 1 156 2989

General Manager: Gábor Kara

Products: Signalling and interlocking equipment; complete traffic control systems.

308 MANUFACTURERS / Signalling and telecommunications

GEC Alsthom
Société Générale de Constructions Electriques et Mécaniques Alsthom
Transport Division

Tour Neptune, Cedex 20, 92086 Paris la Defense, France

Telephone: +33 1 47 44 90 00
Telex: 611 207 alstr f
Telefax: +33 1 47 78 77 55

Signalling Systems
33 Rue des Bateliers, PO Box 165, 93404 Saint-Ouen Cedex
Telephone: +33 1 40 10 63 35
Telex: 234 317 f
Telefax: +33 1 40 10 61 00

Products: Signalling activities for complete railway and mass transit systems include Vital relays; light signals; point machines; automatic level crossing barriers; track circuits; wheel detectors; axle counters; visual display panels; microwave communication systems; fail safe data teletransmission; relay block and interlockings; radio-electronic token block signalling; solid state interlocking; computer-based centralised traffic control; train describer; automatic route setting; automatic graph systems; train information systems; automatic train control systems; computer-aided maintenance systems; marshalling yard equipment.

Central control room of SNCF TGV-PSE high-speed line

GEC Alsthom Australia Ltd
Railway Signals & Communications Division

373 Horsley Road, Milperra, New South Wales 2214, Australia

Telephone: +61 2 772 7444
Telex: 120807 aa
Telefax: +61 2 774 4838

Divisional Manager: F J Baker
Sales Manager: R J Perrin
Engineering Manager: C Burton

Products: Complete signalling systems, including CTC solid state interlockings, power and mechanical equipment, track circuits, train describers, platform displays, point machines, modular signals, level crossing equipment; transport control systems.
Signalling contracts recently awarded include:
State Rail Authority of New South Wales, completed in 1989, value $4 million: Port Kembla Inner Harbour Grain Loader, a new balloon loop, around the extremities of the existing coal loader balloon loop, and including re-signalling of the Coniston triangle, connecting with the recently-completed Illawarra electrification scheme.
Metrail (Victoria), completed in 1989, value $3.3 million: design, supply and installation of a solid state interlocking (SSI) with computer-based route setting at Epping Yard. The data preparation and engineering for this contract is being carried out by Australian engineers with co-operation from GEC-GS of the UK.
A contract has recently been awarded by the State Rail Authority of New South Wales for the renewal of cabling and signalling systems between Macarthur and Picton, due for completion in late 1990.

GEC-General Signal
GEC-General Signal Ltd

Borehamwood Industrial Park, Rowley Lane, Borehamwood, Hertfordshire WD6 5PZ, England

Telephone: +44 81 953 9922
Cable: Railsigko, Borehamwood
Telex: 916129 gec gs
Telefax: +44 81 207 5905

Managing Director: M L Boden
Engineering Director: W E Alderson
Export Sales Director: J S Sheldon
European Sales Director: M L Evans

Products: Power signalling equipment (including route relay and solid state interlocking, geographical circuitry and electro-mechanical point machines); electrical control systems; track circuit equipment and accessories; level crossing protection equipment; automatic train control; information and train describing systems; centralised traffic and remote control systems for rapid transit and personalised transit systems. As a part of turnkey projects undertakes responsibility for telecommunications systems including cab-to-control radio (free radiation, leaky feeder and/or carrier wave), special secure telephone systems and CCTV.
Recent technical developments include:
Solid state interlocking systems, using both triplicated or single microcomputers. A pilot scheme involving a triplicated system, the result of a tripartite development with British Rail, was commissioned at Leamington Spa in 1985. Since the successful commissioning, several contracts for SSI systems have now been obtained, as described below.
In Britain: Inverness, Yoker, Docklands, Wick-Thurso, East Anglia, West Highland, Chiltern Lines, Aberdare, Newcastle, Willesden, Dorchester-Weymouth. Elsewhere: in Botswana, on Danish State Railways (DSB), Badli Indian Railways, and at Paldang (KNR), Xiao Li Zhuang (China) and Epping yard (Metrail, Australia).
Radio electronic token block system operated from one signalbox which is in contact by radio with trains under its area of control. Commands are displayed by suitable messages on the vdu in the train driver's cab. Trains cannot proceed into a particular section of single-track until the electronic token is received and its receipt acknowledged by the train driver.
Contracts current at the end of 1989 included:
British Rail, Eastern Region: SSI at Newcastle.
British Rail, Scottish Region: Yoker SSI.
British Rail, Western Region: SSI for Chiltern Line.
British Rail, Southern Region: SSI for Slade Green Depot.
British Rail, Midland Region: SSI for Northampton.
Docklands Light Railway (London): City Extension to Bank Station and upgrading of automatic signalling and driverless, fully automatic train control.
Docklands Light Railway: Beckton 1. Automatic Train Protection for P89 and B90 stock.
London Underground: Dot matrix interface units for passenger information, and dot matrix indicators, as part of current contracts.

Manchester Metrolink: SSI and SIGNET train information systems.
RFFSA Brazil: Signalling between Jaceaba and Saudade (Ferrovia do Aco-Steel Line).
Soviet State Railways: SIGNET train information system between Moscow and Kalinin (176 km).
Indian Northern Railway: Train and passenger information system for Delhi.
Indian Northern Railway: SSI for Badhli.
Danish State Railways (DSB): SSI system at Ringsted.
Ministry of Railways (China): SSI at Xioa-Li Zhuang station.
Royal State Railways of Thailand: Fail-safe interlockings and colour-light signals over 921 km.

Developments: Control and indication equipment utilising keyboard/trackerball and vdus.
SIGNET microprocessor-based train describer using distributed processing techniques. Each function of a train describer is embodied in a separate microcomputer. Any number of these units can be joined together in a set of interconnected rings to provide train describers of varying power and complexity.
Remote control systems and panel processors built up from a family of electronic units which can be put together in different ways. The indications processor is a microprocessor-controlled system for driving panel indications that eliminates many non-vital relays, while the controls processor eliminates many of the non-vital circuits normally included in interlockings.
A coded continuous automatic train control system which ensures driver obedience to lineside signal aspects and associated maximum permitted speeds, both of which are shown on cab displays and result in automatic application of the locomotive brakes where necessary.
This system can be superimposed on both single or double rail-jointed track circuits and also jointless track circuits, in electrified or non electrified areas. New fibre-optic indicators developed for alphanumerical illumination.
Transportation process control systems, using a microprocessor-based computer to regulate the movement of vehicles, as carried out by drivers with the aid of cab display messages transmitted over radio links. Location of the vehicle in the area of control is transmitted to the control centre from vehicle identifiers in the track.

GNB
GNB Industrial Battery Company

2010 Cabot Boulevard West, Suite 1, Langhorne, Pennsylvania 19047, USA

Telephone: +1 215 750 2600
Telex: 4761219 gnblahn
Telefax: +1 215 750 2717/44

Director, International Sales: B C Brooks

Products: Independent power systems for signals and communications: the GNB Absolyte spillproof, leakproof and explosion-resistant battery and the Absolyte Charge Regulator.

GPT
GEC Plessey Telecommunications Ltd
Network Systems Group

PO Box 53, Coventry CV3 1HJ, England

Telephone: +44 203 452152
Telex: 31361 gptel g
Telefax: +44 203 448416

Managing Director: R G Reynolds
Group Director: G W Head
Sales Director: K J Kerton

Products: GPT offers a comprehensive range of primary and intelligent multiplex equipment together with associated optical fibre cable, microwave-radio, pcm, and 2 Mbit/s line systems. They are all tailored to railway communication systems requirements and can incorporate private telephone exchanges, telephone instruments and automatic cross-connect equipment.

Constitution: GEC Plessey Telecommunications Limited is a telecommunications company jointly owned by the General Electric Company plc and the Plessey Company plc.

Two GPT 16 × 2 Mbit/s optical fibre terminals

GRS CenTraCode system circuit board module

GRS
General Railway Signal Company

PO Box 600, Rochester, New York 14602–0600, USA

Telephone: +1 716 783 2000
Cable: Genrasig, Rochester, NY
Telex: 978317

President of GRS Company: G E Collins

Affiliates and associates
GEC-General Signal Ltd, Borehamwood, Hertfordshire, England
Algemene Sein Industrie BV, Utrecht, Netherlands
GRS Trading Corporation, Rochester, New York, USA
Representatives and licensees throughout the world

Products: Centralised traffic control; route-type interlockings; automatic block signalling; level crossing warning signals and gates; overlay track circuits; hot journal detection systems; automatic gravity marshalling yard systems; automatic train control; train stops and rapid transit control systems.

Hanning & Kahl
Hanning & Kahl GmbH & Co

Frachtstr 19, PO Box 3725, 4800 Bielefeld 1, Federal Republic of Germany

Telephone: +49 521 5839 0
Telex: 932426
Telefax: +49 521 583929

Products: Track circuits, mass detectors, point control systems.

Harmon
Harmon Industries Inc
(Formerly SAB Harmon Industries Inc)

Corporate Office and Main Works: 1300 Jefferson Court, Blue Springs, Missouri, USA

Telephone: +1 816 229 3345
Telex: 42 6398
Telefax: +1 816 229 0556

Other manufacturing facilities:
Kansas City, Kansas (Cedrite Technologies subsidiary)
Waycross, Georgia (Consolidated Associated Management Company Inc)
Riverside, California (Electro Pneumatic Corporation)
Grain Valley, Missouri (Harmon Electronics Inc)
Warrensburg, Missouri (Harmon Electronics Inc)
Louisville, Kentucky (Modern Industries Inc)
Jacksonville, Florida (Modern Industries Inc)
Griffin, Georgia (Modern Industries Inc)
Phoenix, Arizona (Phoenix Data Inc)
Englewood, Colorado (Phoenix Data Inc)

Chairman & Chief Executive: R E Harmon
President & Chief operating Officer: Bjorn E Olsson
Vice President, Marketing & Sales: R G Clawson
Director, International Sales: Ernest E Knight

Products: Harmon Industries and its subsidiaries are the largest suppliers in the US market of electronic

Harmon HXP Highway Crossing Processor

Trackstar III cab radio by Harmon Electronics

coded dc track circuit signalling apparatus; microprocessor-based analysers to process inspection data from passing trains; supervisory control systems; dc-dc converters; digital recorders; constant voltage battery chargers; surge protection; high-security audio frequency track circuits; electronic timers.

Constitution: In June 1985 51.1 per cent of the shares of SAB Harmon Industries Inc were redeemed by the corporation from a unit of Wilhelm Sonesson AB of Malmö, Sweden. Thereafter the company conducted business as Harmon Industries Inc. In December 1985 Harmon announced intention to purchase from the Ensun Corporation of Houston, Texas, their Railroad Fuel Management System and Train Data System product lines. Earlier in 1985 West Bend Radar Systems was acquired by Harmon and are now being manufactured by EPC.

Harris
Harris Corporation
Controls and Composition Division

PO Box 430, Melbourne, Florida 32901, USA

Telephone: +1 407 242 4121

Director of Marketing: E Fred Routledge

Products: Locotrol radio remote control equipment for mid-train electric and diesel-electric locomotives. Locotrol II, the latest version, is microprocessor-based. Its use reduces drawbar stresses, controlling distributed tractive effort and increasing brake pipe response by as much as 300 per cent. The operator console provides for the display of many of the remote traction consist's operating parameters. The remote consist may be operated in concert with the front consist or it may be operated independently to control slack and run-in sometimes encountered in difficult terrain. Used on trains from 30 up to 300 cars in length, Locotrol II permits maximum utilisation of track loading.

The company's products also include PROBE (Programmable Recording On-board Evaluation), a system to provide real-time dynamic and historic data for predictive maintenance programmes. PROBE may be implemented on electric and diesel-electric locomotives. Data on diesel engine parameters including compression, as well as various pressure temperature and vibration readings are recorded. Generator and traction motor voltages and currents and related horsepower are available for local display or retained in memory for off-board analysis. Trip histories in hard copy with events tied to 0.1 mile are also provided by the off-board computer analysis system.

The Harris Advanced Train Control System (ATCS) provides a proven enforcement of speed and movement authorities, as well as a high-security data link. The system's versatility allows its use with multiple locomotive types, dispatch schemes and railroad operating practices. Harris ATCS expertise has been tested and proven in current applications on an active railroad.

Complete ATCS functions are targeted for development in the Harris system. The Harris data link is ATCS specification 200 compliant and is designed to provide error-free, two-way data communications between a dispatcher and a locomotive engineman. Data transmissions include train movement authorities, speed enforcement, crew identification, work orders, train speed and location, end of authority enforcement, acknowledgement by a crew of movement authorities and clearances, and management information data.

Farinon Division

1691 Bayport Avenue, San Carlos, California 94070-5307, USA

Telephone: +1 415 594 3000
Telex: 34 8491

Products: Advanced analog and digital microwave and lightwave communication systems. The company also offers a full planning, engineering, construction and testing service for individual system installations, through its Systems Construction Service.

Hasler
Hasler AG

Belperstrasse 23, 3000 Berne 14, Switzerland

Harmon Electro Code 4 microprocessor-based unit

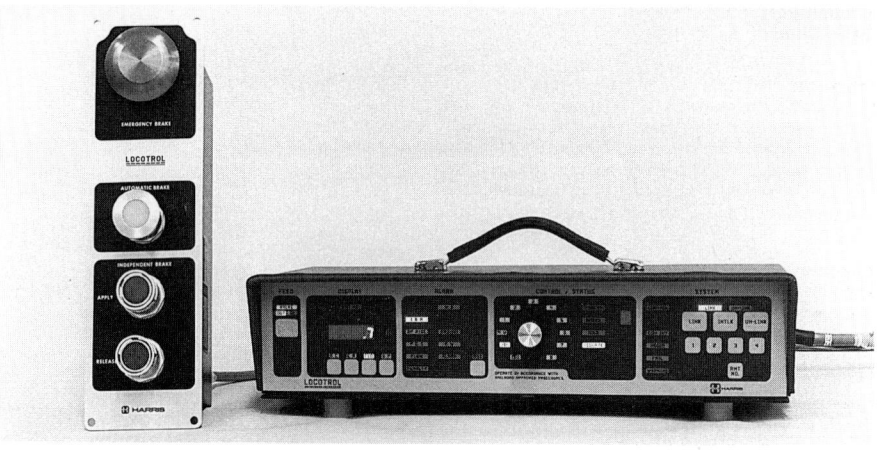

Locotrol II air brake console and operator console

Telephone: +41 31 65 21 11
Telex: 32413

Group companies
Hasler Ltd, Berne
Hasler Installations Ltd, Berne
Hasler Signal Ltd, Berne
Autelca Ltd, Gümligen-Berne
Favag SA, Neuchâtel

Products: Equipment and systems for road and rail vehicles including tachographs, tachometers, remote tachometers, remaining distance recorders, electronic speed and distance measuring and recording systems for locomotives and suburban transport, electronic anti-skid systems, axlebox mileage counters.

Equipment and systems for stations and bus/tram stops including Autelca ticket vending, printing and cancelling systems, Autelca coin checking, measuring and storage systems with or without self-refilling change-return facilities, Favag precision, crystal-controlled time distribution systems, Favag public address systems for passenger announcements and service instructions, Hasler fully automatic fee-collecting systems for garages and car parks.

Communications equipment and systems for commercial and administrative applications including private branch exchanges, radio-paging systems, telex switching centres, teleprinters for automatic telex networks and for private networks, transmission systems and power supply systems, Autelca coinbox telephones.

Henry Williams Electrical Ltd

Dodsworth Street, Darlington, Co Durham DL1 2NJ, England

Telephone: +44 325 462722
Telex: 58421
Telefax: +44 325 381744

Managing Director: R A Thompson
Marketing Director: C Potts
Works Director: N Dodsworth
Finance Director: P J Morris

Products: Mosaic mimic diagram and signalling panels under license from Integra Ltd of Zürich; silec electromechanical treadle switches; level crossing protection systems.

Recent orders include mosaic mimic diagram overview panel for Moscow, Russia; mimic diagram panels for Newcastle resignalling.

Hasler Teloc-2000 electronic speed and distance recorder for traction units

Signalling and telecommunications / **MANUFACTURERS** 311

IBR
Ingg Battaglia Rangoni SpA

PO Box 147, Via del Lavoro, 93 40033 Casalecchio di Reno (Bologna), Italy

Telephone: +39 51 758185
Telex: 511863 elbar i

Products: The MARKER 60, a flexible system for event acquisition and chronological recording, specially created for railway applications. The system synthesises specific experience and know-how gained in railway signalling. It may be applied in railway stations, underground railways and in rail transport in general. Features include: programmable and may be personalised through program keyboard; selectable graphic output (graphic, alphanumeric or mixed); basic 60 input (or 120 double-event) version may be expanded to a maximum of 480 in modules of 120 events each; capacity to operate as central data collection unit with telephone line transmission from remote peripherals (eg from cabins); two RS 232 serial outputs for connection to external units (pc, printers, modem) for storage and further processing of collected data.

Integra Signum
Integra Signum Ltd

Head office: Industriestrasse 42, CH-8304 Wallisellen, Switzerland

Telephone: +41 1 832 32 32
Telex: 826 260 isag
Telefax: +41 1 832 36 00

General Manager: Dr J Leimgruber
Divisional Manager: Dr U Betschart
Departmental Manager: H Wahl

Products: Domino control panels, modular design (Domino is the registered trade mark of Integra for their control panel and is also the brand-name for Integra railway signalling systems and equipment); Integra safety relays; solid state and computer-based equipment; point machines and point locks; signals with optical systems adjustable for optimum performance; fibre-optic signals; and cable accessories as required in railway signalling installations.

Most currently-used components and products are manufactured within the companies belonging to the Integra group.

Systems on offer are: Domino signalling control and indication panels; Domino interlocking systems for various applications; lock-and-block, the modern substitute for token block systems for safe train operation on single-line or multi-track railways with reversible working by means of dc or audio frequency transmission of block information, including track clearance check devices such as last-vehicle detection, track circuits, axle counters, etc; automatic train control and train stop (the Integra system is based on rugged, simple components and a modular structure); and data processing and data transmission systems. Solid state and microcomputer-based systems for applications in CTC, such as remote control and train describer equipment are available, as well as appropriate equipment for keyboard operation.

Interelec
Interelec

53 rue du Commandant Rolland, 93350 Le Bourget, France

Telephone: +33 1 838 92 06
Telex: 210 190

Chairman: Marcel Mas
General Manager: Georges Kayanakis
Commercial Manager: Gerard Estournet
Marketing and Sales Manager: Jean-Michel Bouet

Principal subsidiaries: IMCA, Mercaderes 37, Mexico 19 DF
Promocab, France

Products: Electronic signalling and telecommunications, automatic control (ATP-ATO) and safety systems; fail-safe track-to-train/train-to-track transmission systems; train identification systems; Theseus monitoring system for mass transit surface systems; microprocessor-controlled tachometers.

Kenelec
Kenelec (Aust) Pty Ltd

48 Henderson Road, Clayton, Victoria 3168, Australia

Telephone: +61 3 560 1011
Telex: 35703

Products: CTC systems, signals, jointless and impulse track circuits.

Krauss-Maffei
Krauss-Maffei Aktiengesellschaft

Krauss-Maffei-Strasse 2, D-8000 Munich 50, Federal Republic of Germany

Telephone: +49 89 88 99-0
Telex: 05 23 163-91
Telefax: +49 89 88 99 3336

Director: Dipl Ing Werner Görlitz
Director: Wolfgang Harttrumpf
Sales Director: Walter Tichy

Products: Two-way radio specially developed for hump locomotives at Deutsche Bundesbahn's Mannheim yard.

Kyosan
Kyosan Electric Manufacturing Co Ltd

Head office: 4-2, Marunouchi 3-chome, Chiyoda-ku, Tokyo, Japan

Telephone: +81 3 214 8131

Telex: 2223178
Telefax: +81 3 211 2450

Chairman: C Okawa
President: Y Tanaka
Managing Director, Export Sales: S Orimo
General Manager, Overseas Dept: Y Mitani

Works: 29-1 2–chome, Tsurumi-ku, Yokohama City

Subsidiary companies
Taiwan Kyosan Co Ltd, Taichung, Taiwan

Products: Total traffic control equipment (computer-aided CTC); train describers; programmed train control equipment; relay interlocking equipment; solid state interlocking equipment; automatic block signalling equipment; tokenless block instruments; power switch machines and relays; cab signal and cab alarm equipment; automatic train control equipment; automatic route setting; highway crossing signal and crossing gates; ac and dc automatic voltage regulators; silicon rectifiers; power supply switching devices.

Railways equipped by the company include the New Transit Port Island Line in Kobe, Japan, where the control system provides for fully unmanned operation; new transit systems for Rokko Island (Kobe) and Kanazawa Seaside Line (Yokohama); and the South link line of Taiwan Railway Administration.

Recent contracts include relay interlocking equipment for Pingtung Line, Taiwan Railway Administration due for delivery in 1990.

Matra
Matra Transport SA
ATC and ATO Department

2 rue Auguste Comte, 92170 Vanves, France

Telephone: +33 1 45 29 29 29
Telex: 205079
Telefax: +33 1 45 29 29 08

(For details of chief officers see Matra entry in Locomotives and Rolling Stock section)

Products: Electronic signalling and telecommunications, automatic control (ATP-ATO) and safety systems; fail-safe track-to-train/train-to-track transmission systems; train identification systems.

Telesupervisory Department
The Telesupervisory Department, which became part of Matra Transport in early 1986, is a unit in the Matra Group which has been designing and producing telesupervisory and control centre systems since 1970. The Department designs, builds and installs SCADA systems for geographically distributed process with a particular emphasis on control centres for transit systems, especially for those on which Matra Transport is the system supplier (VAL and ARAMIS systems).

Maxon
Maxon Electronics

10828 NW Airworld Drive, Kansas City, Missouri 64153, USA

Telephone: +1 816 891 6320
Telefax: +1 816 891 8815

Products: Heavy duty VHF and UHF portable two-way radios, compact VHF and UHF portables, compact 30-watt UHF mobile radio, FM transceivers for automatic hands-free communication.

Mors Techniphone

2-4 rue Isaac Newton, ZI du Coudray, 93152 Le Blanc Mesnil CEDEX, France

Telephone: +33 1 49 39 42 00
Telex: 232 480
Telefax: +33 1 48 65 10 18

President: Eric Patry
Sales & Export Manager: Francois Helaine
Marketing Manager: Nicole Gicquel

Products: Railway relays, electronic left-luggage lockers, remote control systems.

Swiss Federal Railways (SBB) signal box and CTC at Arth-Goldau, showing Domino mimic display panel and control desks for keyboard operation by Integra Signum

MANUFACTURERS / Signalling and telecommunications

Motorola
Motorola Communications and Electronics Inc
A subsidiary of Motorola Inc

UK works: Jays Close, Viables Industrial Estate, Basingstoke, Hampshire, England

Telephone: +44 256 58211
Telex: 858823
Telefax: +44 256 469838

General Manager: Peter Tanner
Marketing Director: John Okas
Sales Director: David Hope

Products: Two-way radios; portables; mobiles; paging; secure radios; radio communications systems.
Recent contracts have involved the supply of communication systems for London Underground and Channel Tunnel.

Motorola Canada
Motorola Canada Ltd
Communications Division

3125 Steeles Avenue East, North York, Ontario M2H 2H6, Canada

Telephone: +1 416 499 1441

Products: Two-way portable radios; the PHD 5000 Trackside Communications Network, a self-contained and integrated voice and data system interconnecting management, control offices, field staff and vehicles on the move.

Nippon Signal
The Nippon Signal Co Ltd

Head office: 3-1 Marunouchi, 3–chome, Chiyoda-ku, Tokyo, Japan

Telephone: +81 3 287 4500
Cable: Signal, Tokyo
Telex: 222 2178
Telefax: +81 3 287 4649

Works: Yono Factory, 13 1-chome, Kamikizaki, Urawa City
Utsunomiya Factory, 2-11 Hiraide Kougyo Danchi, Utsunomiya City

President: H Takeuchi
Executive Vice President: T Oki
Managing Director, Foreign Trade: S Naganuma

Associated companies: Nisshin Industrial Co Ltd
Nisshin Electrical Installation Co Ltd
Nisshin Electronics Service Co Ltd

Products: Centralised traffic control (CTC); relay interlocking; electronic interlocking equipment; electronic tokenless block system; automatic block signalling; level crossing signals and automatic gates; overlay track circuits; automatic train control (ATS, ATC); automatic train protection (ATP); remote control equipment (Rc); programmed route control equipment (PRC); automatic announcing system; inductive type wireless remote control equipment; electrical, electro-pneumatic point machines; various kinds of traffic control equipment; various kinds of relays for signalling; integrated traffic control system by computer (ITC), combining automated route-setting, train recording, train announcing and information display, and operational adjustment of train working; micro-electronic track relays (MER); three-colour LED indicators; LED flashing light; LED destination indicator; wheel detectors; crossing obstruction detectors; transponders; level crossing monitor systems.

NKF KABEL BV
Telecom Projects Division

PO Box 85, Noordkade 64, 2740 AB Waddinxveen, Netherlands

Telephone: +31 1828 18122
Telex: 20585 nkft nl
Telefax: +31 1828 13081

General Sales Manager: H Straver

Motorola KDT840 portable data terminal

Products: Design, supply and installation of integrated telecommunications systems; automatic telephone systems; data communication; optical fibre transmission systems; mobile and track-to-train radio systems; signal and communication cabling.

The company applies a systems approach to telecommunications business. A small-scale approach would be involvement limited to supply only of, for example, cables, network materials, communication equipment, and/or measuring-instruments. The extreme of a large-scale approach might be a turnkey commitment to solving a client's telecommunication needs, ie a dedicated communication network designed, engineered and installed in order to operate a SCADA system, have communication and command facilities for its staff, inclusive of mobile radio, be assured of local and standby power supply, whether conventional or other, and to have the staff trained thoroughly on system knowledge.

As turnkey contractor, the company's involvement would entail the system design, engineering, manufacturing and procurement, supply and delivery of goods to site, installation, supervision and co-ordination of the various subcontractors, including civil works, acceptance testing, and finally handing over of the completed dedicated communication network and its documentation. Additionally training and the maintenance will be carried out.

Emphasis of the company's product range is on the application of optical fibre cables in dedicated communication networks. Optical fibre cables are now cost-effective compared to other systems, eg microwave or conventional cable. Furthermore, optical fibre cables are insensitive to electrical interference, can be manufactured to cope with various aggressive environmental conditions. Furthermore, systems using optical fibre cables are easily expanded and reliable.

In January 1990, the NOKIA Corporation of Finland acquired a 51% share in NKF Holdings. Close co-operation between NOKIA and NKF in dedicated networks is anticipated in the future.

Motorola MX 1000 series portable radio

Computer-based CTC centre of Tohoku and Joetsu Shinkansen lines, Japanese National Railways by Nippon Signal

Orlians
Orlians & Co NV

Populierendreef 35, 2800 Mechelen, Belgium

Telephone: +32 15 21 85 85
Telex: 25587
Telefax: +32 15 21 20 64

Products: Multi-aspect colour-light signals with associated speed restriction or route-indicating displays; ground colour-light signals; wall-mounted underground railway signals; warning signals for crossing gates; signal lanterns for electric railways.

OTP Rail and Transit
Oregon Technical Products

380 Quarry Road, Belmont, California 94002, USA

Telephone: +1 415 595 2700
TWX: 910 376 3290

Manufacturing Manager: W R Rice
Marketing Manager: R L Burkdall

Products: Trackside/train integrity management systems; voice digital hot-box analysers; voice synthesisers; mini talkers; electronic locomotive and component test meters.

Parisini
L Parisini SpA

Alcatel Face Group

Via di Corticella, 315, 40128 Bologna, Italy

Telephone: +39 51 322012
Telex: 216857
Telefax: +39 51 325712

Products: Complete range of systems for signalling, safety and automation of railway lines and installations on local and long-distance railway networks, underground railways and high-speed railways. Products include interlocking systems and automatic block equipment of all kinds; level-crossing systems; remote control systems, supervision and automation systems for traffic regulation; on-board assisted or automatic driving systems; and electronic computer-based interlocking systems.

Philips
Philips Telecommunicatie Industrie BV

PO Box 32, 1200 JD Hilversum, Netherlands

Telephone: +31 35 899111
Cable: Philitel, Hilversum
Telex: 43712

Products: Telecommunications (carrier, telephone and telegraph), exchanges, data systems, vehicle and train identification systems, traffic control systems.

Other products in the Philips Group
Intercommunication and
public address systems   NV Philips
Fire alarm and electric   Gloeilampenfabrieken,
clock systems   Eindhoven
Interlocking signalling
systems, automatic block
systems, CTC systems,
wagon and train
identification systems   TRT, Paris
Telemetering equipment   MBLE, Brussels

Pintsch Bamag
Pintsch Bamag Antriebs-und Verkehrstechnik GmbH

Postfach 10 04 20, 4220 Dinslaken, Federal Republic of Germany

Telephone: +49 2134/602-0
Cable: Pintschbamag, Dinslaken
Telex: 8851938
Telefax: +49 2134/60 22 66

Directors: Dipl-Ing Helmut Otte
Dipl-Wirtsch-Ing Wolfgang Kaerger (Str)

Products: Electrical and electronic power supply, lighting, heating and air-conditioning equipment for rail vehicles; level crossing protection equipment (hand-operated or rail-actuated) with flashlights and luminous signals, with barrier guarding and radar obstacle detection; train approach indicator for gang warning; fibre-optic luminous signal indicators; electric gas-operated infra-red and oil-fuelled circulation, compact-type point heating equipment; solid state snow detectors; train pre-heating equipment; test sets for electrical installations on rail vehicles.

Pirelli General
Pirelli General plc

PO Box 4, Southampton, Hampshire SO9 7AE, England

Telephone: +44 703 634366
Cable: Pigekaybel Ston
Telex: 477976 pirgen g
Telefax: +44 703 332754

Managing Director: F Gonzalez
Divisional Manager, Power Cables: A W Dawes
Divisional Manager, General Wiring: J J Siney
Divisional Manager, Telecom Cables: C Massagrande
Divisional Manager, Special Cables: P Cattaneo
Buying Manager: T J Murray Cox
Chief Engineer: S R Norman

Products: Power and telecommunications cables. Pirelli General makes a wide range of power cables, from track feeder cables to high voltage cables for track power supplies. The company has introduced low-smoke zero halogen cables for power, signalling and communication purposes. The new cables, designated LSOH (Low Smoke Zero Halogen), were specifically designed for railway subway systems and were developed in close collaboration with London Transport. LT has been supplied with optical fibre communication cables sheathed with LSOH material for in-tunnel use, and with X-Flam 15 for use above ground.

Telecommunication cables for railway use include a full range of multi-pair designs to British Rail specifications, specially screened designs for use with 25 kV ac overhead systems and optical fibre cables.

Plessey
Plessey Controls Ltd

Sopers Lane, Poole, Dorset BH17 7ER, England

Telephone: +44 202 675161
Telex: 41272
Telefax: +44 202 782331

General Manager: D G Hornby
Marketing Manager: A J Rose
Product Manager: B J Watkins
Sales Manager: M T Deem

Products: Secure radio systems providing high-integrity speech and data communication between signalmen, train crew and passengers with automatic message routing facilities, automatic channel changing and emergency message facilities.

Transponder-based systems for train location, identification, control, in cab signalling and automatic route-setting. Communication can be in either direction and transponders may be battery powered or passive.

High-speed data communication systems on trains provide the backbone of of train-integrated management systems for the multiplexed control and monitoring of traction, brakes, doors, ventilation, information and auxiliary systems.

Pulse
Pulse Electronics Inc

5706 Frederick Avenue, Rockville, Maryland 20852, USA

Telephone: +1 301 230 0600
Telex: WUI 650 221 8919
Telefax: +1 301 230 0606

General Manager: James E McClaine
Customer Services Manager: Richard E Fisher
Director, International Marketing: Andrew Duncan

Products: Research, development and design of electronic equipment for the railway and transit industry including, but not limited to, speed indicating and locomotive event recording equipment. Pulse Electronics has also developed an engineman alertness device, Train Sentry, which issues an automatic train stop if the engineer is disabled in any way and unable to respond. The company is supplying equipment to most major railroads in the USA as well as to those of Canada, Mexico, Brazil and New Zealand.

The solid state Pulse Locomotive Data Recorder, which works off existing sensing points in a locomotive, uses a closed-loop magnetic tape cartridge of computer-grade material. Old data is continuously self-erased when recording, and the instrument will record continuously for up to 48 hours. Depending on model, it will produce a range of event data from speed, distance, elapsed time and traction motor current to such items as brake pipe reductions and reverser movement. Playback equipment supplied by the company includes a portable unit and a playback-duplicator unit for interfacing with the microprocessor-based Data Pack Scanner, which will generate reports for mechanical and operating departments.

The Pulse speedometer embodies a calibrator so that it can be set for a different wheel size within 2 minutes; it is also compatible with most electrical axle drives.

The most recent development is TRAINLINK, an end-of-train monitoring system for cabooseless train operation. The coupler-mounted rear unit continuously monitors brake pipe pressure, motion, and marker light and battery status. This information is transmitted to the front unit where it is displayed to the driver. Newer models incorporate remote emergency brake actuation at the end of a train.

Railfone
Railfone Inc
A subsidiary of Airfone Inc

2809 Butterfield Road, Oak Brook, Illinois 60522, USA

Telephone: +1 312 572 1800
Telex: 280730 airfone oakr

Products: On-train public telephone installations operating by radio through commercial cellular systems in the vicinity of rail routes.

Rockwell
**Rockwell International
Railroad Electronics**

Mail Station 108-166, 400 Collins Road NE, Cedar Rapids, Iowa 52498, USA

Telephone: +1 319 395 2951
Telex: 464 421 collengr cdr
Telefax: +1 319 395 5429

Director, Railroad Electronics: Ronald C McGraw
Manager, Marketing and Support: Gary E Ryker

Pulse TRAINLINK head-end display module

MANUFACTURERS / Signalling and telecommunications

Rockwell ATCS Systems Integration Laboratory

Products: Advanced Train Control System (ATCS).

The company's advanced electronic guidance and communications technology applied to air and space transportation has now been adapted into the Rockwell Advanced Train Control System, to provide railroads with the capability for real-time communications and safe and accurate command and control of any unit in the rail network.

The Rockwell system contains seven integrated but modular sub-systems: Rail Operations Control; Train Location System; Data Management System; Locomotive Analysis and Reporting System; Train Control Computer System; On-Board Display System; and Wayside Interface System.

Benefits of cost, capability, and efficiency not possible with any other electronics system available are claimed. These include:
Knowledge of train position and speed to within ± 150 feet and ± 1 mph;
On-board delivery of and display of train orders, wayside alerts, and other data;
Reduced fuel consumption;
Increased dispatcher productivity;
Increased capacity of existing radio channels;
Increased track capacity;
Knowledge of locomotive performance and fuel status;
Reduced locomotive maintenance expense;
Automated crew time and payroll system;
Knowledge of hy-rail vehicles and track maintenance equipment locations to within ± 150 feet.

All these benefits are obtained without dependence on the CTC blocking and signalling systems or major additions to the along-track installations.

The Rockwell ATCS sub-systems are as follows:

The Rail Operations Control System (ROCS) is an advanced control and dispatching system that generates orders, monitors safety, determines compliance, optimises traffic flow, and implements controller decisions.

From an advanced work station with multiple-colour, touch-sensitive CRT displays, the dispatcher/ sector controller calls up displays on track configuration and colour-coded representation of track status. The position of each train operating within the sector, along with its identity, speed, and current clearance authority limit, is displayed at the controller's station and on the system-wide display. Colour-coded warnings and alerts are appropriately prioritised and annunciated based on the severity of the situation.

The Train Control System determines, via an on-board receiver, highly precise train location and speed from in-track transponder devices and/or signals from multiple Navstar satellites. Train position and speed are displayed on CRTs both on the locomotive and in the Rail Operations Control System centre. Accurate train positioning information enables better utilisation of track capacity, effectively eliminating the need for the geographically fixed block system.

At the heart of the Rockwell system is the Data Communications System. The main element in this subsystem is a proven on-board data management processor that provides for integration and automation of information exchange among the on-train systems as well as the interface to the ground-based ARES system. By utilising digital data communications, the data management system reduces vhf congestion by replacing many voice conversations; establishes a computer controlled data path that includes unique addresses for each control element, automatic message checking and, if required, retransmission; and provides message display and/or hard copy printouts.

The data management processor also provides for: orders/restrictions/clearances/control commands; order/speed limit adherence; and wayside device status; intra-train information; setouts and pickups; crew identification and time reporting; and remote intervention.

Most messages from the train to ground control are automatic, with position, direction, speed, and similar types of messages sent without need for human input.

The Locomotive Analysis and Reporting System (LARS) monitors the health and efficiency of an equipped locomotive by utilising a cost-effective mix of unique sensors and typical locomotive discrete signals. By monitoring those locomotive systems which cause the greatest number of over-the-road problems, LARS can warn of impending failures as well as assess the ongoing performance efficiency of each locomotive.

The LARS computer makes these warnings available to the crew through the Train Situation Indicator, or TSI. At the same time, this data is transmitted, via the ARES data system, directly to the dispatcher and the maintenance repair/power management facility. In either case, LARS stores the history of incidents in which locomotive system values have exceeded the normal range.

Availability of this historical data, and current performance values as well, can greatly reduce maintenance troubleshooting time by eliminating unnecessary equipment removal, identifying the real causes for a 'not loading' write-up, and by differentiating between the various problems which trigger common warning lights, buzzers or bells. The LARS also provides real-time fuel system monitoring including current quantity on-board, low fuel warning, and history of refuelling stops with the time, date and quantity added.

The Train Control Computer provides for energy-efficient control of the train consistent with all requirements for safety and schedule performance. The system is supplied with data on track profile, speed limits, schedules, consist profile, motive power, and special conditions such as slow orders, and then determines what amount of energy is required to meet the schedule at the lowest cost (fuelburn) consistent with good handling techniques.

The Train Control computer constantly assesses the track for the next ten miles to determine whether a hill, curve, or speed restriction should be considered to alter the present energy balance. This judgment is based on a trade-off between energy costs and time costs and is calculated in real time by the on-board computer.

Computed throttle and brake outputs are sent directly to the train situation indicator and displayed as commands to the engineer. Also displayed on the TSI are speed, system mode status, and position of train relative to the track profile. If full available power is not required, the system uses a power allocation mode to idle the least efficient locomotive.

For train crews, the interface to the overall system is the on-board Train Situation Indicator (TSI), a colour cathode ray tube display with touch-screen input control. The Display System conveys information about train status, conveys commands and warnings, and allows crew input to the ATCS system. The normal operating display consists of a train symbol overlaid on a moving map. Warnings are presented in yellow or red depending on the action required by the crew.

The On-Board Display is the primary means of control and interface to other ATCS sub-systems for the train crew. It embraces user-friendly concepts of display flexibility and easily-understood control inputs; only currently required information is displayed.

The On-Board Display is designed to operate in the rugged railroad environment with severe shock and vibration and temperature extremes.

Collins Transmission Systems Division

PO Box 10462, Dallas, Texas 75207-0462

Telephone: +1 214 996 5340

Products: Digital, lightwave, analog and video transmission systems; analog ancillary equipment; operational support systems; multiplex systems.

Service applications include short-, medium-, and long-haul voice message, record message, and video transmission. Also included are special purpose communications, such as radar relay and wide-band telemetry. The company markets a wide range of microwave radios in the 2-to 18-GHz frequency spectrum. A full complement of related products exists, including state-of-the-art frequency-division, single sideband (SSB) multiplex, and digital multiplexer-demultiplexers. Through the company's new MDR-2000 digital radio series, which uses 16-or 64-QAM techniques, Collins introduces an economic means for long-distance transmission of thousands of channels of digital traffic.

Safetran
Safetran Systems Corporation

Head office: 4650 Main Street NE, Minneapolis, Minnesota 55421, USA

Telephone: +1 612 572 0466
Telex: 510 600 7684 (International)
Telefax: +1 612 572 0144

President and Chief Executive Officer: Paul L Wheeler
Vice President, Marketing, Sales and Service: Philip E Pierce
Vice President, Finance: George L Kline
Vice President and General Manager, Electronics Division: Noel B Smith
Vice President and General Manager, Louisville Division: Robert W Kennedy
Vice President and General Manager, Electro-mechanical Division: Michael L Keefe

Works: Safetran Systems Corporation, 7721 National Turnpike, Louisville, Kentucky 40214; 4650 Main Street, NE, Minneapolis, Minnesota 55421; 9271 Arrow Highway, Cucamonga, California 91730

Products: Wayside and level crossing signals and control systems; communications components and systems; transit signal and control systems; maintenance-of-way machines and tools; contract engineering; construction and installation of signal and communication systems.

For control of remote radio base stations, Safetran's Centralised Dispatcher Radio Control System (CDRC II), with FSK, is a new, inaudible frequency shift keying data scheme that transmits data quickly and quietly. A single two-wire or four-wire line may be used with up to 32 bridged control units for base stations. The control unit will interface with virtually any available radio unit. Data and voice transmissions can be handled simultaneously without risking interference with the dispatcher radio or loss of important dispatcher communications. CDRC II's receiver voting option reports only the mobile call-in with the stronger RF signal, eliminating the chance of selecting a fading signal. The frequency scanning option gives access to all calls, preventing missed call-ins. Where multiple territories overlap, the need for expensive, multiple base stations can be avoided with CDRC II's dual wayside option, allowing shared control of a base station for more flexible operations.

Safetran Systems Corporation's Model 660ND offers a new cost-effective alternative in electronic grade crossing warning. The 660ND is a stand-alone system that can provide either motion sensitive or constant warning time operations. Because it can be upgraded from a motion sensor to a grade crossing predictor, the system is an ideal choice for installations where increased or variable speed traffic is anticipated. The dual configuration, the 660ND2, provides a back-up unit in a single case with an automatic transfer module. The 660ND2 is much more economical and requires less space than using multiple units with a separate changeover unit. The system is easily installed with a four-wire connection to the rails. Two leds indicate when the unit is properly adjusted for quick, positive set-up.

The 660ND Motion Sensor/Grade Crossing Predictor is available in complete system packages. Packages include built-in surge protection for both track and battery connections, plus all necessary terminating shunts.

In 1986 the Corporation became wholly owned by the Hawker Siddeley Group.

SAIT
SAIT Electronics
Systems Group

Chaussee de Ruisbroek 66, 1190 Brussels, Belgium

Telephone: +32 2 370 53 11
Telex: 21601 sait bb
Telefax: +32 2 376 6873

Products: Turnkey implementation of HF, VHF, UHF, SHF fixed and mobile telecommunication networks; communication and control systems for public transport, including use of radio in underground and other difficult environments; real time supervisory and control software systems; passenger information display systems under control of central processing units.

SASIB
SASIB SpA
Signalling Division

Via di Corticella 87/89, 40128 Bologna, Italy

Telephone: +39 51 529111
Cable: Sasib, Bologna
Telex: 510020 sasib i
Telefax: +39 51 529436

General Manager: Guiseppe Bonfigli
Sales Manager: Antonio Altobelli

Subsidiary company
Sasib Hellas SA
Solomou Street 53, 10432 Athens, Greece

Telephone: +30 1 523 8625
Telex: 214422 rc gr

General Manager: J Korialos

Products: Route control electrical interlocking systems, push-button- or keyboard-controlled; steady and coded current automatic block; automatically-controlled level crossing protections; continuous and intermittent cab signalling and speed control; centralised traffic control (CTC); automatic car classification systems; train describer systems; train-to-wayside communication systems (TWC); electro-mechanical and electronic equipment for signalling installations, such as electric switch machines, dc and ac safety relays, impedance bonds, level crossing gate mechanisms and control panels with mosaic-type illuminated diagrams etc.

Relay room at Chiusi, on FS Rome-Florence *Direttissima* line by SASIB

Control room of Milan Central, the largest interlocking in Italy, equipped by SASIB; the six operating positions, each with alpha-numerical route-setting keyboards, are all under control of a Chief Dispatcher (extreme right)

SB
Scheidt & Bachmann GmbH

132 Breite Strasse, PO Box 20 11 43, 4050 Mönchengladbach 2, Federal Republic of Germany

Telephone: +49 2166 266 0
Telex: 0852818
Telefax: +49 2166 266 475

Sales Manager: Dipl-Ing Heinz Laumen

Products: Power signalling apparatus; level crossing gates; barriers and warning signals; microcomputer-controlled level crossing techniques; microcomputer-controlled maintenance-free track detector; and centralised remote control systems.

SCC
Signalcom Canada Corporation

6 Indell Lane, Brampton, Ontario L6T 3Y3, Canada

Telephone: +1 416 791 9550
Telex: 06 988595
Telefax: +1 416 791 1199

Vice-President and General Manager: William R Mountain
Director, Engineering: Robert W Tiernay

Products: MITAP (Mobile Information Terminal and Processor) replaces the conventional locomotive voice radio control head and adds two-way, 1200 or 4800 bps data communications capability along with on-board computing power. Interface to the engine-man is by a two-line × 40-character alphanumeric display and a 4 × 4 numeric and function keypad.

ALCAM (Advanced Locomotive Controller and Monitor) is a locomotive control system which allows distribution of motive power throughout the train. Communicating over redundant 4800 bps serial train-lines (or optional radio link), up to four remote locomotives can be controlled from the lead unit. All on-board electronics and brake interface packages are identical. The lead unit is identified by a portable console with a 6 × 40 alphanumeric display and numeric-function keypad. The base system includes an event recorder, speed control system, and real-time monitoring of numerous locomotive functions from the lead unit.

PC Office is an IBM-pc based central control office for railway signalling systems. The system includes multiple high-resolution graphics monitors, entrance/exit route selection or unit-lever control by mouse or keyboard, and track blocking with multiple permits per section. Non-vital office logic utilises Union Switch and Signal's GENISYS development system which allows future modifications by railway personnel. Communication to field locations uses GENISYS protocol. Conversion to most standard code systems can be made with a US&S Programmable Remote Code to Computer (RCCI) unit.

Signalcom has been involved in efforts by the AAR and RAC to develop Advanced Train Control systems. Products currently under development include: radio-based signal enforcement systems; vital on-board computers; and vital wayside interface units using

MANUFACTURERS / Signalling and telecommunications

US&S MICROLOK. Signalcom has the in-house engineering capability to design and supply conventional railway signalling systems and to develop new systems utilising vital microprocessor interlockings with locomotive data radio interface for switch control and manual block operation.

Recent contracts have included:
Central control and monitoring system for CP Rail's new tunnel under Rogers Pass in the Canadian Rockies; placed in revenue service in December 1988.
Central control office for Southern Pacific in Houston, Texas: in revenue service February, 1989.
Over 600 MITAP units had been placed in revenue service with CP Rail by December 1989.

Constitution: Signalcom Canada Corporation was formed in 1985 by Union Switch & Signal (US&S) and RMS Industrial Controls of Port Coquitlam, British Columbia. One of the charters of SCC is to combine the radio data communications technology of RMS with the train control and signalling technology of US&S for development of new systems for the railway industry worldwide.

SCI
Speciality Concepts Inc

9025 Eton Avenue, Suite A, Canoga Park, California 91304, USA

Telephone: +1 818 998 5238
Telex: 662914 sci cnpk ud

Products: Charge regulators, load management controllers and other monitoring equipment for photovoltaic and solar-powered equipment.

SEL
Standard Elektrik Lorenz AG

Head office: Lorenzstrasse 10, 7000 Stuttgart-Zuffenhausen, Federal Republic of Germany

Telephone: +49 711 8211
Cable: Stanlor, Stuttgart
Telex: 72 526-0

Works: 20 locations in Federal Republic of Germany

Chief Officer: Dr H Lohr
Managing Director, Transport: James N Sanders
Export Manager: P Schnabel

Products: Geographic relay interlocking systems; solid-state interlocking systems; automatic block equipment; computerised traffic control and traffic supervision systems; computerised automatic train operation (ATO); train control (ATC) and train stop (ATS) systems; mosaic-tile control panels and desks; fail-safe microprocessor equipment (SELMIS); computerised button processors and train describers; centralised traffic control systems (CTC); computerised remote control systems (vital and non-vital); colour-light signals; electro-hydraulic switch machines; electronic axle counters; electronic track circuits (jointed and jointless); signalling relays (vital and non-vital); signalling and telecom cable; fibre-optic cable; and line terminal equipment.

SEL Canada
SEL Canada
A Division of Alcatel Canada Inc

101 Valleybrook Drive, Don Mills, Ontario M3B 3M5, Canada

Telephone: +1 416 445 8600
Telex: 06 986112 selcan tor
Telefax: +1 416 441 3438

General Manager: Karl U Dobler
Marketing Director: Walter Friesen

Products: Turnkey signalling systems for streetcars, subways, AGT systems and heavy rail. SEL Canada designs/manufacturers and installs all major components, eg: centralised traffic control systems; SELCOM remote control systems (vital and non-vital); INTERSIG microprocessor-based interlocking systems; SELTRAC automatic train control systems, which employ track-mounted transponders and radio transmission for continuous transfer of data between ground control and the on-board computers carried by trains equipped to work with the system; SELTRAIN advanced train control systems; transponders, IDTS inductive transmission systems; VIDAC vital communications controllers; wheel counters; automatic train stops; switch machines and decentralised LRT control logic for automatic routeing, pre-emptive signalling and gate crossing control.

Work position in central office of SEL's computer-based traffic supervision for Austrian Federal Railway's Vienna Schnellbahn, with colour vdus reproducing train graph projections and track/signalling status

SEMA
SEMA Group UK

143/149 Farringdon Road, London EC1R 3AD, England

Telephone: +44 71 831 6144
Telex: 267152 capind g
Telefax: +44 71 278 0574

Director, Communications & Signalling:
S McCarthy
Sales Manager: P Bartlett

Affiliated companies:
Sema Group SA, Montrouge Cedex, France
Sema Group Information BV, Weesp, Netherlands
Sema Group (Suisse) SA, Geneva, Switzerland
Sema Group Belgium, Brussels, Belgium
Sema Group GmbH, Cologne, W Germany
Sema Group SAE, Madrid, Spain
Sema Information Systems Pte Ltd, Singapore
Yard Limited, Glasgow, UK
Yard USA Inc, Virginia, USA

Products: Design and supply of computer systems and electronic signalling equipment; centralised traffic control systems; passenger information systems; consultancy services.

The most recent product is the Integrated Electronic Control Centre (IECC). The IECC is the next generation of signalling control system and is now being incorporated into all major resignalling schemes in the UK. Initial prototype work was undertaken by the R & D Division of BR, and Sema Group has just completed the standard IECC for use throughout BR.

Recent contracts: Sema Group UK has recently (May 1989) been awarded another major signalling contract by BRB. The contract is for two further IECCs on BR's Anglia Region 'Great Eastern' line. This contract will bring the total number of IECC signalling control systems supplied by Sema Group to BR to nine, the company having previously executed BR signalling control contracts for IECCs at Liverpool Street, Waterloo, York, Glasgow North and Newcastle.

Servo
Servo Corporation of America

Headquarters: 111 New South Road, Hicksville, New York 11802, USA

Telephone: +1 516 938 9700
Cable: Servogram
Telex: 516 938 9644

President: S A Barre
Senior Vice President, Transportation Division:
W W Weeden Jr
Vice President, International Division: G P Crispano

European sales office: Chemin Du Cap 1-3, 10006 Lausanne, Switzerland

Telephone: +41 21 299873
Telex: 454420 servo ch
Telefax: +41 21 299 874

Director, European Operations (EUMEA): V Liardet

Products: Automatic train inspection stations, including hot box and hot wheel detectors, load profile detectors and grade crossing control systems. Recent developments include SYSTEM 9000, in addition to the well-established SERVOTRIM, SERVOTALK, SERVOPRINT and ISO-CLAMP rail-mounted scanners.

The ISO-CLAMP Rail Mounted Hot Bearing Detector Scanner can be mounted directly to the baseplate, significantly reducing maintenance and improving reliability. Additional features include improved optics with rotary lens focusing, a simplified and more responsive shutter mechanism and replaceable cover heaters.

The new Acoustical Bearing Defect Detection and Management System incorporates both acoustic and infrared defect detection technologies to provide early warning of bearing defects before overheating and serious bearing failures occur. The system utilises trackside acoustical sensors to capture the wide range of bearing signatures corresponding to cup, cone or roller defect frequencies and transmits them to an acoustic signal processor (ASP) for processing. The ASP processes a wide range of bearing frequency signatures allowing positive identification of bearing damage. It is a rack-mounted chassis with a self-contained power supply. Plug-in circuit boards are dedicated to 28, 33 and 36-inch wheels with Class E and F type bearings. ASP output signals are applied to alarm circuits with adjustable threshold levels.

Siemens
Siemens AG
Transportation Systems Group

Ackerstrasse 22, PO Box 33 27, 3300 Braunschweig, Federal Republic of Germany

Telephone: +49 531 706201
Telex: 952 495 si d
Telefax: +49 531 706398

Servo Bearing Defect Detection and Management System

Modules of Siemens SIMIS microcomputer interlocking for Gemeinschaftbetrieb Eisenbahn und Häfen, Duisburg

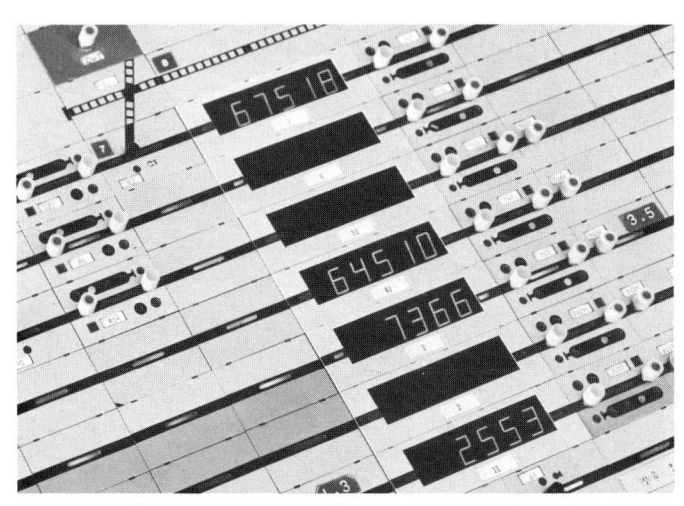

Six-digit signalling panel displays of Siemens microcomputer-controlled train describer system

Transmitting and receiving coils of Siemens ZUB100 train control system

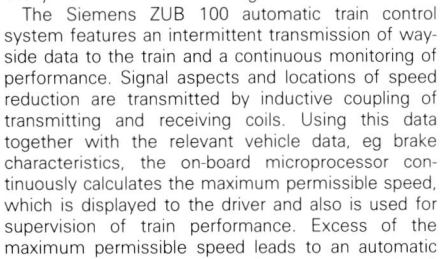

Transportation Systems Group, Vice President: M Czeguhn
Railway Signalling & Safety Systems Division: D Baum
Control Systems Division: D Kupper

Products: Power signalling (all-relay interlocking); geographical circuitry (Spoorplan) interlockings; microcomputer interlockings; block systems; ac and dc track circuits; jointless AF track circuits; axle counters; electric point machines; colour-light signals; level crossing protection systems with lifting barriers and warning signals; centralised traffic control (CTC); computerised traffic and operational control; train describer systems; automatic vehicle identification for control and supervisory purposes; automatic train control (ATC), continuous automatic train control (CATC) for long-distance and rapid transit systems; marshalling yard automation equipment, retarders and retarder control.

By means of the geographical-type Siemens modular interlocking system MIS 801, interlockings of varying sizes, layouts and signalling requirements can be built up. To each route, signal and set of points is assigned a particular relay unit and these units are interconnected according to the track layout. For switching purposes, the K50 relay is used which, together with a new circuitry concept, guarantees the safety and reliability of the interlocking system. New design and manufacturing principles and new materials have created an improved package. Two- or three-row relay units of the 19-inch format are mounted on racks above which are area grids supporting the interconnecting cables.

The microcomputer system MES 80 has been developed by Siemens especially for use under difficult environmental conditions, such as on railways. It is insensitive to vibration, air contamination and aggressive steam, and operates safely in the temperature range of –40 to +85°C.

The microcomputer system SIMIS specially combines the functional units of the MES 80 with fail-safe operating hardware, so that whatever the error, a switch-off prevents further commands which might damage or prejudice the process control. With the SIMIS system, fail-safe data processing is possible in operations which require supreme safety, such as control and supervisory operations in railway signalling or in energy supply systems.

The SIMIS also forms the foundation of the company's latest development, an all-electronic interlocking system which is completely controlled by microcomputers. By early 1990 twenty-seven such interlockings had been ordered or commissioned by 13 railway administrations for service on long-distance, rapid transit and industrial networks.

The Siemens microcomputer-controlled automatic train describer system displays six-digit train numbers on seven-segment gas-discharge displays. The displays have a low heat generation, are sturdy and can be easily inserted in the track diagrams.

The Siemens ZUB 100 automatic train control system features an intermittent transmission of wayside data to the train and a continuous monitoring of performance. Signal aspects and locations of speed reduction are transmitted by inductive coupling of transmitting and receiving coils. Using this data together with the relevant vehicle data, eg brake characteristics, the on-board microprocessor continuously calculates the maximum permissible speed, which is displayed to the driver and also is used for supervision of train performance. Excess of the maximum permissible speed leads to an automatic brake application. When the train passes a stop signal, it is automatically halted by the emergency brake. Dual transmission with data and supervisory circuits ascertain the necessary transmission safety. The design of the on-board microcomputer allows a highly flexible adaptation to be made to existing signal and operation systems.

Siemens
Siemens AG
Building Automation & Video Systems

PO Box 211261, Siemensallee 84, 7500 Karlsruhe, W Germany

Telephone: +49 721 595 2611
Telex: 7825564
Telefax: +49 721 595 6541

Director: Dipl-Ing P Hay

Products: Closed-circuit television systems for crowd control and train monitoring.
CCTV systems have been installed on the rapid networks in Rotterdam, Amsterdam, Brussels and Hong Kong.

Siferdec
Railway signalling company of De Dietrich and Cogifer

Head office: 40 Quai de l'Ecluse, 78290 Croissy-sur-Seine, France

Telephone: +33 1 34 80 02 82
Telex: 695120
Telefax: +33 1 34 80 03 08

Engineering and sales office: PO Box 32, 16 route de Strasbourg, Reichshoffen, 67110 Niederbronn-les-Bains, France

Silec information sensor for vehicle mounting on bogie or below body

318 MANUFACTURERS / Signalling and telecommunications

Silec Cautor Series 69 electro-mechanical detector

Telephone: +33 88 80 25 35
Telex: 880 651 ferdecr
Telefax: +33 88 80 25 36

Products: Computerised signalling systems, safety devices. The company's customers include: the SNCF, RATP and Lille VAL in France; SNCB and Brussels Metro in Belgium; the FS in Italy; SNTF in Algeria; SNCFT in Tunisia; ONCF in Morocco; Regifercam in Cameroon; CFCO in Congo; RAN in Ivory Coast; and RNCF in Senegal.

Silec
Société Industrielle de Liaisons Electriques

69 rue Ampère, 75017 Paris, France

Telephone: +33 1 42 67 20 60
Telex: 280748
Telefax: +33 1 46 22 89 08

Chairman: C Barberot
Managing Director: J P Malaquin
Sales Director: J Fiaud

Products: Electro-mechanical treadles, safety relays, track-to-train transmission systems, on-board signal repetition devices, dead-man's handles, solid state talking units, processing units.

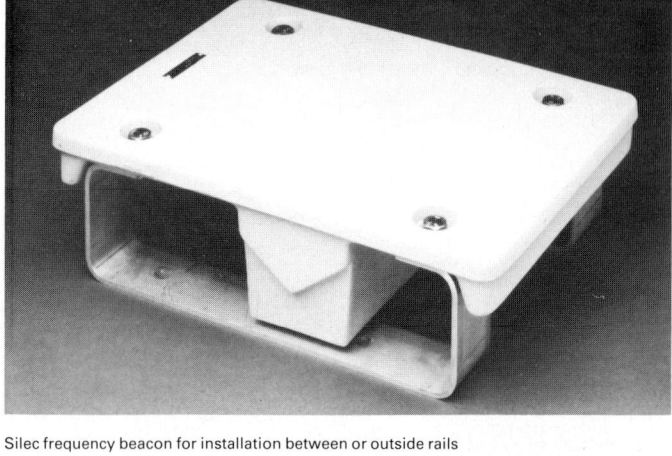

Silec frequency beacon for installation between or outside rails

Telemotive remote radio control of British Steel Corporation locomotive

SRT
Standard Radio & Telefon AB

Box 501, Siktgaten 11, 162 15 Vällingby, Sweden

Telephone: +46 8 73 000
Telex: 178 50 srt s
Telefax: +46 8 739 4478

President: P O Svensson
Marketing Director: F Nordlander

Products: Automatic Train Control (ATC) systems as supplied to Swedish State Railways and contracted for WestRail, Australia. The L10000 ATC system provides a high-capacity data link between track and vehicles. Information from signals and speed boards are transmitted to the vehicle via encoders and transponders between the rails. An on-board computer system processes information from trackside and vehicle. Relevant information is then displayed to the driver and if neglected by the driver the ATC takes over the control of the train. Also information systems for commuters and underground trains and station platforms; hot box and hot-wheel detector systems.

STC
STC plc

STC House, 190 Strand, London WC2R 1DU, England

Telephone: +44 71 836 8055
Cable: Relay, London WC2
Telex: 22385

Chairman: Lord Keith of Castleacre
Chief Executive: A S Walsh

Products: Coaxial line and optical cable systems, pulse code modulation equipment and frequency division multiplex equipment for railway communication networks; telephone exchanges and instruments, office intercom systems, telephone instruments, remote control and telemetry systems; teleprinters and message switching systems for teleprinter network, data terminal and modems; control and communication cables.

Teknis
Teknis Consolidated Pty Ltd

PO Box 54, Philips Crescent, Hendon, South Australia 5014

Telephone: +61 8 268 6122
Telex: 88841 aa
Telefax: +61 8 268 6487

Managing Director: R P Stevens
Systems Manager: M Menadue
Marketing Manager: R T Peirce

Products: CTC systems; hot box, hot-and flat-wheel detection systems; electronic systems; public address systems including digitised voice announcements.

Driving cab equipment with SRT's ATC system

Telemotive
Telemotive UK Ltd

Riverdene Industrial Estate, Molesey Road, Hersham, Walton-on-Thames, Surrey KT12 4RY, England

Telephone: +44 932 247511
Telex: 884751 telmot g

Products: Remote radio control systems for locomotives, cranes and associated equipment.

Telephone Cables
Telephone Cables Limited

Chequers Lane, Dagenham, Essex RM9 6QA, England

Telephone: +44 81 592 6611
Telex: 896216 drycor g
Telefax: +44 81 592 3876

Managing Director: M J Spoor
Commercial Director: D A Hollick
International Marketing Manager: E J R Seville

Products: Copper and fibre-optic cables for telecommunications systems.

Recent contracts executed and obtained include a £12 million contract to provide Bangladesh Railways with a modern communications system for covering 80 per cent of the existing railway network. The 1700 km long optical fibre system provides an automatic telephone service between railway subscribers and includes lineside telephones as part of a sophisticated train control system.

In the UK, TCL has worked closely with British Rail since the early 1970s to help bring the latest optical technology to the railway network. An example of the current work being undertaken is the installation of a £3 million digital communication system for British Rail's Eastern Region which will link busy centres such as Cambridge and Stowmarket, and York and Harrogate.

Telkor
Telkor Signalling Co (Pty) Ltd

185 Katherine Street, Sandton 2148, Transvaal, South Africa

Telephone: +27 11 804 3015/3000
Telex: 4 22171 sa
Telefax: +27 11 804 3041/3046

Chairman: A J Ellingford
Chief Executive: D W King
General Manager: R Middlemass
Group Marketing Manager: A D Smith

Products: Power control cubicles; track circuit equipment (jointed and jointless track circuits); rotary inverters; axle counters; hot box detectors; mimic desks and diagrams; electronic interlocking systems; relay-based modular interlocking systems; train number systems; train time printers and graph plotters; centralised traffic control installations; automatic vehicle identification system; point machines and detectors; level crossing protection equipment; material handling safety equipment; and dedicated mining signalling systems.

Thorn EMI
Thorn EMI Electronics Limited, Computer Systems

Wookey Hole Road, Wells, Somerset BA5 1AA, England

Telephone: +44 749 72081
Telex: 44254
Telefax: +44 749 79363

Managing Director: M T Penery
Business Manager: W S Denman
Product Manager: P L Spencer

Products: Turnkey digital microwave communication systems, point-to-point links and full point-to-multipoint systems, frequencies, 1.56 GHz to 226 GHz, bit rates, 704 Kbit/s to 34 Mbit/s voice and data; public information systems.

Thorn EMI Electronics Limited, Automation Division

PO Box 4, Rugeley, Staffordshire WS15 1DR, England

Telephone: +44 889 585151
Telex: 36135
Telefax: +44 889 578209

Managing Director: G P Hough
Industrial Products Manager: B Carr

Products: The Automation Division of Thorn EMI Electronics has extensive experience in handling traction rectifier contracts for main-line and suburban railways. Many comprehensive contracts include transformers, rectifiers, ac and dc switchgear, supervisory control and auxiliary equipment. Recent installations include power supply equipment for London Underground Ltd, British Rail Southern Region, the Tyne and Wear Metro and the Channel Tunnel Project in the UK, and major extensions to the Mexico City Metro.

A new electronic unit at less than £2000 that protects low-frequency ac signalling systems from the effects of the loss of ac power to traction rectifier equipment has recently been launched. The loss of conduction in a rectifier, whether a phase loss or arm loss, causes an increase in the ripple content of the dc output, which can have a seriously detrimental effect on low-frequency signalling systems operating on or near the conductor rails.

Known as OCAD, this new unit continuously monitors the rectifier and on loss of conduction provides an output to trip the ac supply to the rectifier at a speed which avoids signal malfunction. It is an intelligent unit that discriminates between a spurious, transient condition and a genuine fault, thus avoiding unnecessary trips. Also it has fast operational speed to suit present day requirements.

Toshiba
Toshiba Corporation
Railway Projects Department

Offices: Toshiba Building, 1–1 Shibaura 1–chome, Minato-ku, Tokyo 105, Japan

Telephone: +81 3 457 4924
Cable: Toshiba, Tokyo
Telex: J22587 toshiba
Telefax: +81 3 457 8385

Products: Automatic train control equipment; automatic train stop equipment; electrical indicating and train describing equipment; centralised traffic control and remote control systems; marshalling yard equipment, including retarders, etc.

Transcontrol
Transcontrol Corporation
A member of the Ansaldo Group

180 Keyland Court, Bohemia, New York 11716, USA

Telephone: +1 516 563 0404
Telex: 645117
Telefax: +1 516 563 0419

President and Chief Executive Officer: Edward Riddett
Vice President/General Manager: Gerry Erno
Marketing Director: Dale Logan

Products: Systems: centralised traffic control; wayside and car-borne signalling; interlocking consolidation; classification yard automation; manual yard control; highway crossing warning.

Apparatus: control machines; vital signal relays built to AAA standards; time element relays; overload relays; transformers; inverters; rectifiers; solid state switch operating units.

Recent contracts include equipment for San Jose LRV, Long Beach-Los Angeles LRV, Baltimore LRV, San Diego LRV and Boston Blue Lines 1 and 2.

Transit Control Systems

2641 Walnut Avenue, Tustin, California 92680, USA

Telephone: +1 714 669 9940
Telex: 910 595 2644 transit tstn
Telefax: +1 714 669 0460

Products: Complete command, control and communication systems and their components; end-of-train marker lights.

Transit Control Systems has produced on-board electronics and equipment for San Francisco's BART, Washington DC's WMATA, Amtrak, the track-air-cushion vehicle transit systems, Atlanta's MARTA, Chicago CTA and RTA, Boston MBTA, Philadelphia SEPTA and for the cities of Baltimore and Miami.

Union Switch & Signal
Union Switch & Signal Inc
A member of the Ansaldo Group

PO Box 420, Pittsburgh, Pennsylvania 15230, USA

Telephone: +1 412 366 2400, +1 800 351 1520
Telex: 86 6448
Telefax: +1 412 369 2399

President and Chief Executive: Arthur W Ticknor
Vice President and Chief Operating Officer: Walter Alessandrini
Vice President, Systems: James A Ausefski
Vice President, Marketing and Sales: Allen F O'Rourke
Vice President, Manufacture: Kevin Riddett
Vice President, R&D: Robert C Kull

US&S automatic electronic identification system components for routeing and control of heavy rail and transit vehicles

US&S Microlok microprocessor-based vital interlocking system

320 **MANUFACTURERS** / Signalling and telecommunications

Products: Electronic and electro-mechanical signalling and control systems for railway and rail rapid-transit operations. Included are: coded wayside signalling systems; highway grade-crossing barriers and warning equipment; classification-yard equipment and retarders; cab-signalling devices; computer-aided dispatching systems and other computerised systems for automatic train control, centralised traffic control, automatic car and train identification and two-way locomotive data radio communications.

Manufacturing and Distribution Facilities: Augusta, Ga; Batesburg, SC, Ga.

Field Sales Offices: Chicago, Ill; Jacksonville, Fla; Kansas City, Kan; Montreal, Que, Canada; New York, NY; Omaha, Neb; Philadelphia, Pa; Pittsburgh, Pa; Roanoke, Va; and Topeka, Kan.

International Operations
Brazil: WABCO Westinghouse de Sinalizacao, PO Box 24039, Rua Lauriano Fernandes Jr 168, 05089 São Paulo
Canada: Signalcom Canada Corp, 6 Indell Lane, Brampton, Ontario L6T 3Y3
Chile: WABCO-Chile Ltda, Casilla 10344, Santiago
India: Sundaram-Clayton Ltd, Railway Products Div, Harita Hosur 635109, Tamil Nadu
Ireland: WABCO Westinghouse Ltd, Mona Valley Industrial Estate, Upper Rock Street, Tralee, County Kerry

Vapor
Vapor Corporation
Transportation Products Group

6420 West Howard Street, Chicago, Illinois 60648-3394, USA

Telephone: +1 312 631 9200
Telex: 210314 vapn ur
Telefax: +1 708/470 7800

President: G I S Patterson
Vice-President, Sales & Marketing: J A Machesney
Manager, Marketing Services: J R Pearson

Associated companies:
Vapor Canada Inc, 10655 Henri-Bourassa West, Ville St Laurent, Quebec H4S 1A1
Vapor International Holland BV, Atoomweg 496, 3542 AB Utrecht

Products: ATCS-Advanced Train Control System: Vapor's line of components is designed especially for integration into a fully specification-compliant ATCS system. The system provides extremely accurate position information for use in train control and signalling. Transponders can be placed at crucial locations such as track switches to provide immediate position information to the on-board system. In addition, transponders can be used to update on-board tracking systems.

Vaughan
Vaughan Systems and Programming Ltd

The Maltings, Hoe Lane, Ware, Hertfordshire SG12 9LR, England

Telephone: +44 920 462282
Telex: 81516
Telefax: +44 920 460702

Managing Director: A St Johnston
Director, Engineering: G W Monk
Director, Production: M T C Morley
Director, Marketing: R E Beadle

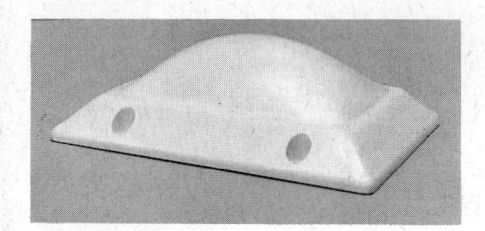

Vapor ATCS Transponder

US&S installation of the most extensive US video-projected track diagram at Union Pacific CTC centre, Portland, Oregon

Products: Train Describer equipment; staff and passenger information systems; train reporting systems; timetable creation and control systems; network management systems.

Late 1989 saw the launch of a new train describer hardware and software package which places great emphasis on the data preparation function. It provides an economic implementation of all sizes from the small with one OCU and up to 60 berths through the normal size TDs of up to 200 berths, and thence to large TDs of virtually any size.

A Time Division Multiplexer (TDM) System has now been added to the range of products. This is housed in a single crate at both office and field ends and enables a total of 704 inputs or outputs to be controlled. It is designed to operate with normal 50 V signalling relays and includes the necessary power supplies for the interface.

In 1989 Vaughan Systems was appointed to supply and commission an integrated electronic control centre (IECC) for British Rail's Chiltern lines (from Marylebone to Aylesbury and Banbury). The IECC is a new signalling control system concept developed by BR with the assistance of a software house. It provides full signalling control and indication functions, replacing large mimic panel-based systems. Although developed using Motorola hardware, it is intended also to operate with other compatible hardware. Vaughan Systems is the first contractor, outside the development team, to be awarded an IECC contract by BR.

Vaughan Systems also received three contracts totalling over £350 000 to supply British Rail with train describers for installation in the Midland Region areas of Stoke, Nuneaton and Manchester. They replace obsolescent equipment in each of the three areas, and link up with existing train describers in Rugby and Crewe.

Train describers are an essential part of modern signalling enabling individual trains to be tracked through the rail network taking information on the presence of trains from trackside interlocking equipment and passing data to and from train describers in adjoining areas as trains pass between them. Train movement information produced by the train describers is distributed to other systems providing information to passengers and staff.

The links to Crewe also provide movement information to an automatic train reporting (ATR) system extending its coverage of the West Coast Main Line (London-Carlisle).

The three contracts employ a mixture of single-processor 'main train describers', based on the dual-

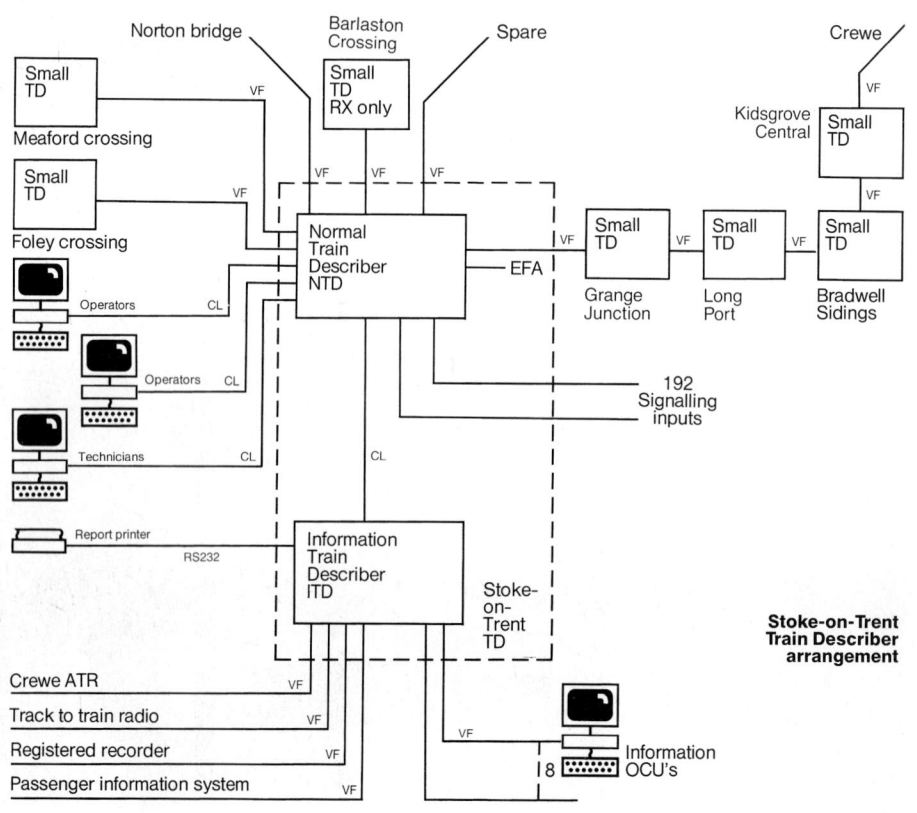

Stoke-on-Trent Train Describer arrangement

Stoke-on-Trent train describer arrangement by Vaughan

processor system recently installed in the Willesden suburban signal box, and 'small train describers' in service at various other locations in the London Midland Region.

WABCO-Westinghouse
Compagnia Italiana Segnali SpA

Head office: Via Volvera 50, 10045 Piossasco (Turin), Italy

Telephone: +39 11 90241
Telex: 211356 wabco
Telefax: +39 11 9066500

Managing Director: Giancarlo Lombardi

Main works: Piossasco (Turin), Tito (Potenza)

Products: Cab signalling and overspeed control systems; automatic block for train separation; computerised centralised traffic control; train description systems; automatic level crossing protection; relays and microprocessed station interlocking systems; electric substation remote supervision; marshalling yard retarders, equipment and automation systems; train and vehicle identification systems; automation and signalling for mass transit; vital equipment and systems for train operation.

Westinghouse Electric
Westinghouse Electric Corporation

1501 Lebanon Church Road, Pittsburgh, Pennsylvania 15236-1491, USA

Telephone: +1 412 655 5335
Telex: 866267
Telefax: +1 412 655 5860

President: J R Tucker
Vice-President, Commercial Operations: D R Marcucci
Vice-President, Engineering: R T Betler
Vice-President, Manufacturing Operations: T Jost

Products: Advanced automatic control systems for mass rapid transit applications, including car-carried, station, wayside and central control equipment.

Westinghouse Signals Limited
A subsidiary of Westinghouse Brake and Signal Co Ltd
A Hawker Siddeley Company

Head office and works: PO Box 79, Chippenham, Wiltshire SN15 1JD, England

Telephone: +44 249 654141
Cable: Westinghouse, Chippenham
Telex: 44618
Telefax: +44 249 652322

Chairman: H R Grant
Managing Director: G Howell
Director, Equipment Division: P J Buttery
Director, Contracts Division: A C Howker
Finance Director: S C Balfour

Products: Systems available include colour-light signalling, relay block for single and double lines, automatic block, radio electronic block, centralised traffic control (CTC), relay interlockings, solid state interlockings, automatic train control, train describers,

BART Central Control Room (Westinghouse Electric)

passenger information systems, traction power supply telecontrol and station plant monitoring and surveillance systems.

Products include colour-light signals, position-light junction route indicators, multi-lamp and stencil route indicators, position-light shunt signals, electric point machines, jointed and jointless track circuits, apparatus cases, control panels, vdus, remote control and indication and data acquisition equipment, and safety plug-in relays.

Control panels and illuminated diagrams (model boards) are supplied to customer requirements in both mosaic and plain forms for a wide variety of applications, ranging from major control centres to monitoring and emergency control panels. Vdu displays are also available either as an alternative to hard-wired panels, or in combination with them. The emphasis is on versatility to provide whatever combination of display and control devices is best suited to a particular application.

Westronic System Two is a microprocessor-based data handling and transmission system designed specifically for railway applications. It is a modular system that can be configured to provide any specific combination of signalling, train control or supervisory facilities, such as CTC, train description, traction power telecontrol, station plant supervision and monitoring, panel processing etc. Standardisation on Westronic System Two for these diverse applications reduces spares inventories and streamlines training and maintenance procedures.

Westinghouse Signals undertakes system design for railway telecommunication facilities including telephone exchanges, transmission systems, public address, closed circuit television, centralised clock systems, optical fibre transmission and fixed and mobile radio. The company manufactures a high security signal post telephone system.

For urban mass transit railways, Westinghouse Signals provides automatic train protection (ATP), automatic train operation (ATO) and automatic train supervision (ATS) systems. Equipment immune to interference from traction equipment is available for both ac and dc electrified areas.

A full range of services including design, manufacture, installation, testing, setting to work, training, maintenance and project management is provided.

Computer-aided design is used for production of circuits and wiring diagrams, for design of control panel layouts and printed circuit cards and for train running simulations

WSF
Westinghouse Saxby Farmer Ltd

Head office: 17 Convent Road, Entally, Calcutta 14, India

Telephone: +91 33 24–7161
Cable: Interlock, Calcutta
Telex: 2348

Works: Above and 24 Canal South Road, Calcutta 15

Managing Director: K L Mukhopadhyay

Products: Mechanical and electrical signalling equipment; point layouts and mechanism; relays; point and signal machines; ball and tablet token instruments; reversers; electric control panels and illuminated diagrams; colour light signals and route indicators; wagon retarders; hump yard equipment; vacuum and air brake equipment for wagons, coaches, locomotives, compressors and slack adjusters; pneumatic, hydraulic and combined road brake equipment; electronic equipment for road traffic signals and control.

Westinghouse Saxby Farmer Ltd is a joint enterprise of Westinghouse Brake & Signal Co Ltd of London, England, and the State Government of West Bengal, India.

---

craswell
scientific ltd.
MIRROR TECHNOLOGY

MANUFACTURERS OF PLATFORM MIRRORS AN AID TO SAFETY BY PROVIDING REARWARD VISIBILITY FROM THE DRIVER'S CAB.

UNIT 11, ORCHARD TRADING ESTATE,
TODDINGTON, GLOS, UK. GL54 5EB
Tel: 0242 621 534
Telex: 437283 Fax 0242 621529

Passenger information systems

AUSTRALIA
Stone McColl ... 327
Teknis ... 327

BELGIUM
SAIT ... 326

CANADA
BG Checo ... 324
Signarail ... 326

DENMARK
ScanAcoustic ... 326

FRANCE
CERCI ... 324
GEC Alsthom ... 324

Seitu ... 326
Silec ... 326

GERMANY, FEDERAL REPUBLIC
ANT ... 324
Brose ... 324
BTS ... 324
Neumann ... 325

ITALY
ME ... 325
Solari ... 326

SWITZERLAND
Omega ... 325

UK
Cartner Display Systems ... 324
Dowty ... 324
Eurosystems Datacol ... 328
Evershed & Vignoles ... 324
IGG ... 324
Klüssendorf ... 324
Krone ... 324
Racal ... 325
RCL ... 326
Ripper ... 326
Siemens Plessey Controls ... 326
Thorn EMI ... 327
Vaughan ... 327
Vultron ... 327
Westinghouse ... 327

USA
AS & I ... 324
Midwest ... 325

MANUFACTURERS / Passenger information systems

ANT
ANT Nachrichtentechnik GmbH

Gerberstrasse 33, 7150 Backnang, Federal Republic of Germany

Products: Passenger information systems.

AS&I
American Sign & Indicator Corporation

PO Box 2727, 2310 Fancher Way, Spokane, Washington 99220, USA

Telephone: +1 509 535 4101
Telex: 510 773 1839

Sales: Tim Connolly
Transportation: Les Bohush
Jim Duthie
Marketing: Steve Hodson

Products: Information display systems.

Constitution: In 1983 AS&I became the subsidiary of the BRAE Corporation, a diversified financial service company with major commitments in the leasing and manufacturing industries. The merger included the addition of Integrated Systems Engineering (ISE), a sister company to American Sign. The consolidation of the three companies will be titled BRAE Communications Incorporated.

BG Checo
BG Checo International Limited

110 Cremazie Blvd West, Montreal, Quebec H2P 1B9, Canada

Telephone: +1 514 382 3030
Telex: 05-827615

Manufacturing Division: BGI/Automatec, 7700 De Lamartine Blvd, Montreal, Quebec H1J 2A8

Telephone: +1 514 353 8940
Cable: Checo Mfg

President, Chief Executive Officer: Joel Pavec
Executive Vice-President, Chief Operating Office: J Corej

Products: Products include the ACSA system, a speech synthesiser-based system for automatic in-car station announcements.

Brose
Carl Brose GmbH

Uellendahler Strasse 437, 5600 Wuppertal 1, Federal Republic of Germany

Telephone: +49 202 7095-0
Telex: 8591511
Telefax: +49 202 7095-102

Managing Director: F Kharand
Sales Manager: H Spahn

Products: Passenger information systems for buses and trains; components for suburban road and rail traffic systems.
The FZG 200 remote-control unit generates, stores and transmits data for the information of driver, passengers and ground-based central control. It can be operated either as an autonomous control and information system or as part of a computer-controlled central control system. Separate input and output channels are available for data exchange: the vehicle bus for flow of data inside the vehicle; the train bus for communication between cars of a multiple-unit train; and a radio interface for communication with the computer-controlled ground centre.
The company's LED full matrix indicator for vehicle interior display of stopping points allows 98 items of information with a total of 2040 letters. The unit is supplied with the names of stopping points via an IBIS remote-control unit.

BTS
BTS Broadcast Television Systems GmbH

Robert Bosch-Strasse 7, PO Box 11 02 61, D-6100 Darmstadt, Federal Republic of Germany

Products: Passenger information equipment.

Cartner Display Systems
Cartner Engineering Ltd

1 Forward Place, Wealdstone, Harrow, Middlesex HA3 8NT, England

Telephone: +44 81 861 4488
Telex: 8954468
Telefax: +44 81 861 2026

Managing Director: D A Watchman
Technical Director: P S Weaver
Sales Director: D J Cockarill

Products: Complete passenger information systems employing LED, LCD, dot-matrix, long-line public address and Solari flap indicators.

CERCI
Compagnie d'Etudes et de Realisations de Cybernetique Industrille

56 rue Roger Salengro, 94126 Fontenay-sous-Bois, France

Telephone: +33 1 48 76 12 20
Telex: 670785

Products: Passenger information systems.

Dowty
Dowty Electronics Ltd
Communications Division

419 Bridport Road, Greenford Industrial Estate, Greenford, Middlesex UB6 8UA, England

Telephone: +44 81 578 0081
Telex: 934512
Telefax: +44 81 578 2320

Sales Manager: F Archer

Products: Passenger information systems.

Evershed & Vignoles Ltd

Acton Lane, London W4 5HJ, England

Telephone: +44 81 994 3760
Telex: 22583
Telefax: +44 81 994 5246

Managing Director: E A Ward
Sales Director: J K Witney
Technical Director: B Pajak

Products: Remote-controlled destination indicators.

GEC Alsthom
Transport Division

93404 Saint Ouen POB 165, 33 rue des Bâteliers, Paris La Défense, France

Telephone: +33 1 40 10 63 35
Telex: 234317 f
Telefax: +33 1 40 10 61 00

Products: Remote-controlled display systems.

IGG
IGG Systems Limited

Seahawk Building, Bilton Business Park, Eastern Road, Portsmouth PO3 5RF, England

Telephone: +44 705 669009
Telex: 86819 igg sys
Telefax: +44 705 679800

Managing Director: Dennis Lockwood
Finance Director: Michael Blackburn
Sales Manager: Roger Smith
Sales Executive, Transport: Tim Dempster
Technical Manager: Steven Greenwood

Principal subsidiary company:
IGG Systems Inc
Suite D, 1017 West Ninth Avenue, King of Prussia, Pennsylvania 19406, USA

Products: Design and manufacture of LED display systems for passenger information systems (platform and on-train) and large area displays for concourses. Displays also suitable for headboard and destination indicators.
Recent contracts executed include London Underground platform signs for passenger information. The company has tendered for passenger information systems for British Rail's Networker Project.

KLÜSSENDORF
Automation Technology for Service Industries

Klüssendorf
Klüssendorf AG

Zitadellenweg 20D-F, 1000 Berlin 20, Federal Republic of Germany

Telephone: +49 30 332030
Telex: 182820
Telefax: +49 30 332 0382 41

Products: Ticket issuing machines and validators/cancellers, including microprocessor-based units; counter ticket printers; information systems.

Developments: Multi-functional automatic ticket machine UniVend MTS 2000.

Krone
Krone (UK) Technique Ltd

Runnings Road, Kingsditch Trading Estate, Cheltenham GL51 9NQ, England

Telephone: +44 242 584900
Telex: 43350 krone g
Telefax: +44 242 578349

Products: Passenger information systems, split flaps, video, LDC, automatic control and specialised interfaces. The company's passenger information systems are installed in over 70 British Rail stations throughout the UK. Also lineside and exchange telecommunication cabinets and telecommunication equipment, including the industry standard termination system LSA-Plus (BT Rapide).

ME
Mischiatti Elettronica SpA

Via Muggiasca 217, 20099 Sesto SG (Milano), Italy

Telephone: +39 2 2487650, 2472605
Telex: 350688 misel i

Products: Electronic information display systems. The ME system connects a computer to a variable number and variety of interfaces (split-flap modular boards, TV monitors, printers, etc). Features of the ME system include: simple two-wire connections for data transmission to displays; low power consumption but rapid and simultaneous change of displayed data; opto-electronic encoder to ensure correct flap positioning and activate read-back control.

Midwest
Midwest Electronic Industries, Inc

4945 W Belmont Avenue, Chicago, Illinois 60641, USA

Telephone: +1 312 685 3500

Vice President, General Manager: H D Vicinus
Product Sales Manager: C L Madonia
National Sales Manager: J Rusick
Chief Engineer: L T Chmiel

Products: On-board communications system; public address and intercom systems.

Neumann
Neumann Elektronik GmbH & Co KG

PO Box 101462, Bülowstrasse 104-110, D-4330 Muelheim a d Ruhr 1, Federal Republic of Germany

Telephone: +49 208 44 34 0
Telex: 856 823
Telefax: +49 208 44 34 203

UK office: Neumann Communications Systems Ltd, Lea Industrial Estate, 151 Lower Luton Road, Harpenden, Hertfordshire AL5 5EQ, England

Telephone: +44 5827 67011
Telex: 826638
Telefax: +44 5827 5082

Director: D Neumann (West Germany)
Project Manager: C D Evans (UK)
Sales Manager: R T Clarke (UK)

Products: Public address and intercom equipment, loudspeaker systems for passenger trains; multiplex remote control systems for station announcements, emergency call, control of clocks, ticket machines, etc; weatherproof and vandalproof loudspeakers and call stations; explosion-proof systems.

Omega Electronics SA

PO Box 6, rue Stampfli 96, Biel/Bienne 4, CH-2500, Switzerland

Telephone: +41 32 42 97 18
Telex: 931207 oe
Telefax: +41 32 41 33 21

GEC Alsthom remote-control display at St Etienne, SNCF

Managing & Technical Director: H M Laumann
Sales Director: D Hopkins

Principal subsidiary: Omega Electronics Ltd, Unit 15, Shakespeare Business Centre, Hathaway Close, Eastleigh, Hants SO5 4SR, UK

Products: Passenger information display systems.
Recent contracts include S-Bahn Zurich (completed 1990) and S-Bahn Vienna (completed 1989).

Racal
Racal Acoustics Ltd

Waverley Industrial Estate, Hailsham Drive, Harrow, Middlesex HA1 4TR, England

Telephone: +44 81 427 7727
Telex: 926288
Telefax: +44 81 427 0350

Managing Director: D L MacDonald
Marketing Director: Dr P D Wheeler
Sales Manager: M Hallows
Publicity Manager: A J Wilson

Products: A wide range of on-board communications equipment. Specialising in led-electromagnetic flip-dot technology, Racal Acoustics provide complete automated or manually-controlled indicator systems specifically designed for train environments. Microprocessor-controlled audio annunciators can be configured to provide automatic messages such as next station, interchange and destination information. The announcements can be in any language or dialect, since words are recorded individually, then programmed into the system and assembled into phrases electronically.

Racal Acoustics has a range of high-quality weatherproof telephones ideal for trackside, siding, tunnel and platform use. Weatherproof telephones are available for DTMF/Loop, CB or Magneto communications systems and can be wall or pole-mounted.

Racal Microelectronic Systems Ltd

Worton Drive, Worton Grange Industrial Estate, Reading, Berkshire RG2 0SB, England

Telephone: +44 734 868601
Telex: 847043
Telefax: +44 734 752300

Products: The Racal SIGNBOARD information display system. The modular construction of the SIGNBOARD system allows information panels to be configured for a wide range of applications.

Its use of advanced guest-host lcd technology results in a highly visible light character on a dark background. A characteristic of this technology is the

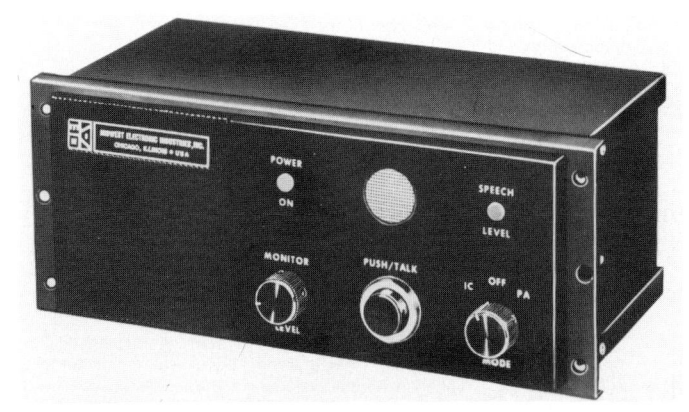

Midwest Model 330 communications control unit for locomotives or mu cars with built-in monitoring speaker, microphone, mode selector and speech-level indicator

The Racal LCD display at London's Euston station

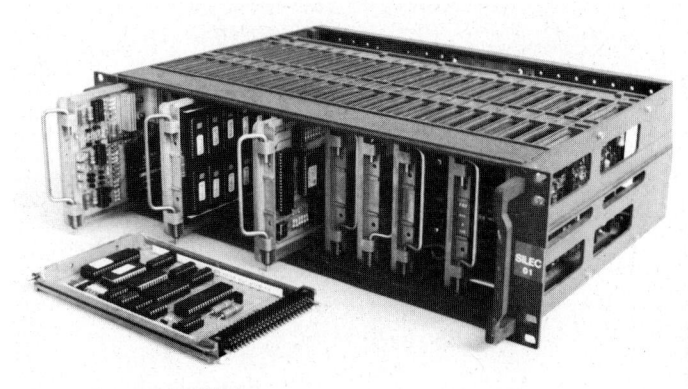

MANUFACTURERS / Passenger information systems

Silec on-train message synthesiser

Solari integrated audio-visual display at Florence SMN station: a public announcement synthesis system allows broadcast of information in four languages

very wide viewing angle not normally attainable using older liquid-crystal technologies. Display modules are available in both 7 × 5 and 9 × 7 dot matrix variants and each can be supplied in two sizes. The 9 × 7 matrix allows an enhanced upper and lower case character set to be implemented, whereas the 7 × 5 matrix provides a cost-effective approach to all applications where upper case only is adequate.

Installation for British Rail include the world's largest lcd public information display, 22.5 m long and 2.71 m deep, at London's Euston station, and displays at other London termini including Kings Cross, Paddington, Charing Cross and Victoria.

RCL

Unit 1, Moreton Hall Industrial Estate, Bury St Edmunds, Suffolk IP32 7BX, England

Telephone: +44 284 752126
Telefax: +44 284 706866

Sales Manager: A C Dean

Products: Audio and visual passenger information systems; on-train communications systems; automatic on-board announcement systems; on-train multiplex and data systems; health monitoring and data recording systems.

Ripper
Ripper Systems Division
Dowty Electronics Ltd

281 Bedford Road, Kempston, Bedfordshire MK42 8QB, England

Telephone: +44 234 854080
Telex: 826276
Telefax: +44 234 852511

General Manager: D Wylde
Technical Manager: I McCullough
Sales Manager: M A Lambert

Products: Audio and visual passenger information systems; on-train communications systems; automatic on-board and lineside announcement systems; on-train multiplex and data systems.

SAIT
SAIT Electronics
Systems Group

Chaussee de Ruisbroek 66, 1190 Brussels, Belgium

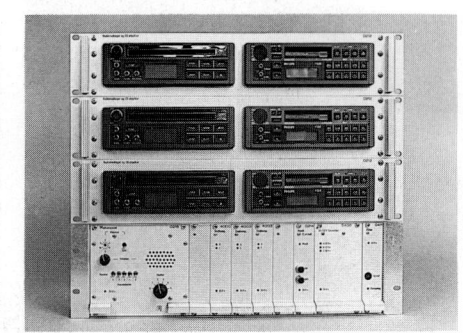

Telephone: +1 322 370 53 11
Telex: 21601 sait bb
Telefax: +1 322 376 68 73

Manager: R Landrie

Products: Passenger information display systems under control of central processing units.

ScanAcoustic AS

Industrivaenget 39, 3400 Hilleroed, Denmark

Telephone: +45 42 25 50 22
Telefax: +45 42 25 20 60

President: J V Andersen
Chief Engineer: T Krogh
Sales & Marketing: P Ronberg

Products: PA systems for passenger coaches (UIC and non-UIC standards); train entertainment systems; train intercom, custom-designed and UIC standard; PA systems for railway stations, remotely controlled from railway control centres or from trains.
Recent contracts include PA and entertainment systems for Danish State Railways' (DSB) IC3 trains (1986-89); 35 remote control PA systems for DSB (1982-89); railway station PA systems for Norwegian State Railways (NSB) (1987-89); railway station remote control PA systems for NSB (1987-89).

Seitu

29 rue Georges Guynemer, 92600 Asnieres sur Seine, France

Telephone: +33 1 47 93 01 08
Telex: 611 425 seitu
Telefax: +33 1 47 93 06 26

President: G Tronel
Technical Director: L Matignon
Sales Manager: M Benoist

Products: Passenger information systems, including the SITU journey planner, a microprocessor-based instrument for station installation on which an arriving traveller can key in the postal address or activity he wishes to reach in the town/city; the required directions will be supplied on a visual display and also on a small takeaway print-out.

Siemens Plessey Controls Ltd

Sopers Lane, Poole, Dorset BH17 7ER, England

Telephone: +44 202 782000
Telex: 41272
Telefax: +44 202 782331

General Manager: D G Hornby
Marketing Manager: A J Rose
Product Manager: B J Watkins
Sales Manager: M T Deem

Products: Provision of integrated passenger information systems for groups of stations with central computer control. Services include project management, system design, installation, commissioning and maintenance. Projects undertaken range from large termini to large groups of stations under central control. On-train passenger information systems include the displays in the passenger saloons, the data transmission system along the train and intelligent controllers in the cab.

Signarail
Signarail Canada Inc
A member of the Alsthom Group

5650 Dessaint St Laurent, Quebec H4S 1A66, Canada

Telephone: +1 514 332 6890
Telex: 05824507

General Manager: P Moscovici

Products: Automatic on-board and station announcement systems.

Silec
Société Industrielle de Liaisons Electriques

69 rue Ampère, 75017 Paris, France

Telephone: +33 1 42 67 20 60
Telex: 280748
Telefax: +33 1 46 22 89 08

Chairman: C Barberot
Managing Director: J P Malaquin
Sales Director: J Fiaud

Product: On-train message synthesiser, for automatic announcement to passengers at the appropriate juncture of a journey of such items as: the next stop; arrival at a station; connections; arrival at the terminus; and procedure in the event of an incident.

Solari
Solari Udine SpA
A member of the Pirelli Group

Via Gino Pieri 29, Udine, Italy

Telephone: +39 432 43241
Cable: Solariudine
Telex: 450155
Telefax: +39 432 480160

General Manager: Ing Angelo Mignoli
Director, System Sales: Edi Tosolino
Systems Division Manager: Aurelio Folladori
Director, System Sales: Edi Tosolino
Marketing Manager: Gianni Vincenzi

Products: Passenger and staff information display systems; master and slave clocks; automatic announcement systems; time attendance systems.
With more than 1000 orders completed, Solari claims the majority of the airport and railroad market in passenger/staff information processing and display

Entertainment rack for passenger trains by ScanAcoustic

Passenger information systems / MANUFACTURERS

systems. The company undertakes turnkey contracts covering in particular: analysis and definition of the specifications, with costs and performance optimisation; selection of the components; supply of the equipment; certification of the system; organisation and implementation of the installation; system commissioning and start-up; operator and technical staff training; and organisation of maintenance.

Stone McColl
Stone McColl Pty Ltd

1/1A Gibbon Road, Baulkham Hills, New South Wales 2153, Australia

Telephone: +61 1 674 4411
Telex: 70073 aa
Telefax: +61 2 624 6010

Managing Director: G R Sills
Engineering Manager: J Walsh
Sales & Marketing Manager: M Ward

Products: On-board information display equipment.

Teknis
Teknis Consolidated Pty Ltd

Philips Crescent, Hendon, South Australia 5014, Australia

Telephone: +61 8 268 6122
Telex: 88841 aa
Telefax: +61 8 268 6487

Managing Director: R P Stevens
Systems Manager: M Menadue
Marketing Manager: R T Peirce

Products: Long-line public address systems; digitised voice announcement equipment.

Thorn EMI
Thorn EMI Electronics Ltd
Computer Systems Division

Penleigh Works, Wookey Hole Road, Wells, Somerset BA5 1AA, England

Telephone: +44 749 72081
Telex: 44254

Managing Director: M T Penery
Business Manager: W S Denman
Sales and Marketing Manager: S Wright

Products: Passenger information systems.

Vaughan
Vaughan Systems and Programming Ltd

The Maltings, Hoe Lane, Ware, Hertfordshire SG12 9LR, England

Telephone: +44 920 462282
Telex: 81516
Telefax: +44 920 460702

Managing Director: A St Johnston
Director, Engineering: G W Monk
Director, Production: M T C Morley
Director, Marketing: R E Beadle
Director, Software: A N St Johnston

Staff Information System terminal for British Rail Southern Region by Vaughan

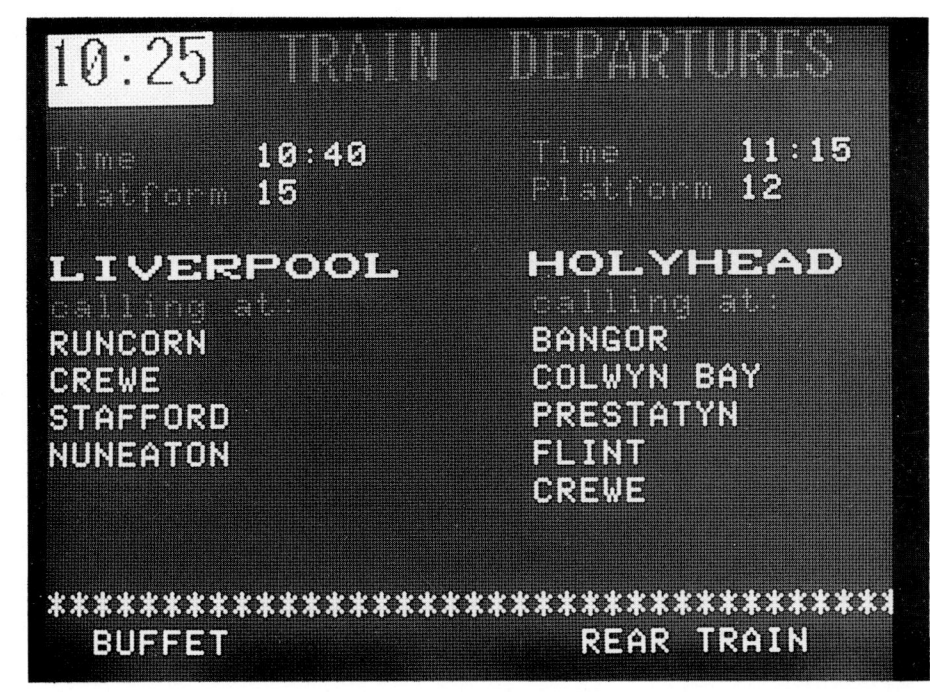

The Solari LDB range of displays uses modules with three-colour LEDs (red, green and yellow) as well as single-colour modules in green and red

Products: Passenger information systems; train describer equipment; staff information systems; train reporting systems; timetable creation and control systems; network management systems.

Vaughan Systems supply a number of information systems to meet the particular requirements of British Rail. These include the Station Information VDU System for Southern Region's staff. This system provides maps giving train locations, route-set information and enquiry facilities using rugged industrial VDUs which may be monochrome or colour. Designed to be capable of catering for the whole of the Southern Region with hundreds of terminals, the initial installation has 50 terminals which will cover the Waterloo control area as a part of the Waterloo Area Resignalling Scheme (WARS).

Stand-alone passenger information systems using high-quality character generators are available and provide both monochrome and colour CRT displays. Large displays of any type, split-flap, electromechanical dot matrix, LCD and LED are incorporated in the bigger systems.

Special interface units are provided to interface to obsolescent equipment. A good example is the Reading Customer Information System. This provides high-resolution map displays on colour monitors to the information system operator. These maps are generated by a train describer-like system interfaced to the relay-based TD.

Recent contracts include the provision of TRUST data converters for ScotRail, East Coast Main Line and Anglia Regions. These systems are based on that installed at Crewe for the West Coast Main Line. They obtain train movement data from the local ATR system or direct from train describers and store, convert and forward it to the TOPS train running system, updating its train location database. The ScotRail system includes special logic to create standard BR messages from the ScotRail train describer format.

A replacement Master Timetabling System (MTS) is being provided to British Rail Southern Region. This system will provide timetabling for any system-passenger information, train reporting, automatic code insertion, route-setting. The MTS will now take timetable data from BRB's new Common (Timetable) Interface-CIF.

A ATR/CIS system is being installed at York to provide train reporting and staff information systems employing the same principles as the SIVS project mentioned above. Similar systems are now being provided to Liverpool Street station with map terminals and to Tyneside with map and report terminals.

Vultron
Vultron International Ltd

Vultron House, High March, Daventry, Northants NN11 4HB, England

Telephone: +44 327 703344
Telex: 317345
Telefax: +44 327 79217

In 1990 Vultron International secured a major contract for the supply of liquid crystal display (LCD) platform indicators and special notice displays for British Rail's Liverpool Street station. The contract, worth some £500,000, provides for 18 indicators of a variety of sizes, the largest measuring 5m × 1m × 300mm. The indicators are housed in polished stainless steel-clad enclosures featuring stainless steel platform numbers with a blue halo effect. The platform indicators comprise anti-reflective, glazed apertures containing 12 lines of 25 characters each with character height of 38mm. The LCD characters are brightly transmissive, yellow on a black background.

The special notice indicators contain ten lines of 40 characters each with character height of 40mm. The LCD characters on these displays are reflective, black on a grey background.

Vultron Incorporated

2600 Bond Street, Auburn Heights, Michigan 48057, USA

Telephone: +1 313 853 2200
Telex: 810 2324114
Telefax: +1 313 853 7571

Products: Digi-Dot information displays. The company's train departure/arrival display for British Rail's Glasgow Central station is one of the world's largest dot matrix boards. Measuring over 66 ft long by 19 ft high it contains 4460 4½ in characters and the whole board is capable of updating in 3½ seconds. The station averages 1500 train movements daily.

Vultron 'Clearsign' liquid crystal displays have been recognised as an ideal medium for platform and on-board passenger information systems. The unique 5 × 3 matrix subdivided into triangular segments produces a bold character set. Character heights of 29, 38, 50 and 65 mm are readable to over 40 metres. The new 'Wessex Electric' Class 442 emus are one of three new British Rail multiple-unit types to be fitted with 'Vultron Clearsign' 12 character 50 mm lcd destination indicators.

Westinghouse
Westinghouse Brakes Ltd
Rail Systems Division

PO Box 74, Foundry Lane, Chippenham, Wiltshire SN15 1HY, England

Telephone: +44 249 654141
Telex: 449411
Telefax: +44 249 655040

MANUFACTURERS / Passenger information systems

Cab-to-cab public address communication logic control unit including passenger emergency talkback feature for New South Wales 'Tangara' emu by Westinghouse

Marketing Director: E J Widdowson

Products: On-train communication equipment for cab-to-cab, public address and passenger emergency talkback.

Train management systems consisting of voice and data multiplex systems and data highways for remote locomotive control, push-pull train working, vehicle health monitoring diagnostics and logging, sub-systems control and passenger information. Train management facilitates rationalisation of sub-systems control and simplification of train wiring and sub-systems interfacing (sub-systems of Westinghouse Brakes supply include brake, door and air-conditioning).

Integrated audio and visual passenger information systems including station-borne communications control systems with facility for interface to signals supervisory control centre, automatic message generation, visual information display and radio link interface to the vehicle-borne passenger information system. Vehicle-borne passenger information over train management voice and data communication links with facility for automatic generation, interface to the station-borne communication system and manual intervention.

Programmable logic controllers which interface with the signalling system and generate or interpret control logic for the traction, service brake, or passenger information.

Recent contracts include: communication system for the Tangara emus in New South Wales, Australia; communication equipment for London Underground Ltd 1986 prototype tube stock; re-equipment of autodriver boxes for London Underground Ltd Victoria Line; and passenger information systems for British Rail.

Addendum
Eurosystems Datacol
8 Portland Place, Pritchard Street, Bristol B52 8RH, England

Telephone: +44 272 232808

Associated companies:
bellomi telecomunicazioni

Via dell'Elettronica, 17/19, 37139 ZAI Basson Verona, Italy

Telephone: +39 45 8510177

cis 84

Via dell'Elettronica, 17/19, 37139 ZAI Basson Verona, Italy

Telephone: +39 45 8510078

DATACOL

Via dell'Elettronica, 17/19, 37139 ZAI Basson Verona, Italy

Telephone: +39 45 8510084

iCELTE

Via Portogallo, 13, 90100 Palermo, Italy

Telephone: +39 91 516638

iTAL EAST ENGINEERING

Via dell'Elettronica, 17/19, 37139 ZAI Basson Verona, Italy

Telephone: +39 45 8510177

Ribali

Viale Piemonte, 63, Cologno Monzese (MI), Italy

Telephone: +39 2 2543904

Scitel

Iskola u.8, H-1011 Budapest, Hungary

Telephone: +36 361 351–120

Sicontraf

Via Ponte di Veja, 37034 Quinto (VR), Italy

Telephone: +39 45 550866

Products: Integrated systems of data collection, processing and display equipment.

Automatic fare systems

BELGIUM
ACEC 330
Automatic Systems 330
Prodata 333

DENMARK
Scanpoint 333

FRANCE
Camp-Alcatel 330
Compagnie Générale d'Automatisme 330
Crouzet 331
Electronique Serge Dassault 331
Klein 332
Schlumberger 333

GERMANY, FEDERAL REPUBLIC
AEG Westinghouse 330
Elgeba 331
Laakmann 332
Makomat 332
Scheidt & Bachmann 333

ITALY
MAEL Computer 332

JAPAN
Nippon Signal 332
Omron 333
Toshiba 334
Toyo Denki 335

SWITZERLAND
Xamax 335

UK
Almex Control Systems 330
Magnordata 332
Modulex Systems 332
Thorn EMI 334
Westinghouse Cubic 335

USA
Cubic Western 331
GenFare International 332

MANUFACTURERS / Automatic fare systems

ACEC
Ateliers de Constructions Electriques de Charleroi SA

BP 211, 6000 Charleroi 1, Belgium

Telephone: +32 71 44 57 99
Telex: 51227 acec b
Telefax: +32 71 43 78 34

General Director: C Jauquet
Commercial Director: D Hausman

Products: Engineering and installation of fare collecting systems.

AEG Westinghouse
AEG Westinghouse Transport-Systeme GmbH

Nonnendammallee 15-21, 1000 West Berlin 20, Federal Republic of Germany

Telephone: +49 30 3305
Telefax: +49 30 3305 2169

Products: Ticket machines; ticket cancellers; ticket vending machines; data recording ticket machines; automatic multiple service ticket machines.

Almex Control Systems
Almex Control Systems Ltd

Love Lane, Cirencester, Gloucestershire, GL7 1YG, England

Telephone: +44 285 651441
Telex: 43120 almex g
Telefax: +44 285 3944

Managing Director: J Jacobson
General Sales Manager, Manufacturing: W K Cameron
General Manager, Print: A C Lindsey

Principal subsidiary companies:
ACS (Inc), (USA)
Bell Punch Co Ltd
Automaticket Ltd
Setright Registers Ltd
Control Systems Ltd
Almex Ticket M/CS Ltd

Products: Ticket-issuing machines; booking office equipment; computerised polling and ticket-issuing systems; Microfare hand-held ticket-issuing machine; fare collection and management data systems.

Automatic Systems
Automatic Systems SA

Avenue Mercator 5, 1300 Wavre, Belgium

Telephone: +32 10 23 02 11
Telex: 59089
Telefax: +32 10 23 02 02

Managing Director: Yves Le Clercq
General Manager: Michel Coenraets
Export Manager: Michel Meli
Market Development Manager: Daniel Wautrecht

Products: Design and manufacture of vehicle and pedestrian access control equipment, including automatic rising barriers, tripod turnstiles, automatic gates type NO or NC, safety rotating drums, ticket vending machines.
In the railway industry the company has provided access controls for the Brussels Metro, the Antwerp Metro and Belgian State Railways. The Manila Metro and the Paris Eastern Network of SNCF have also been equipped with the company's turnstile equipment.
It has recently obtained new contracts from Metropolitana Milanese and Italian State Railways between Rome and Leonardo da Vinci airport at Fiumicino.
The Spanish subsidiary of the company has obtained a contract for access control systems to the Medellin underground network worth 140 million Belgian francs.

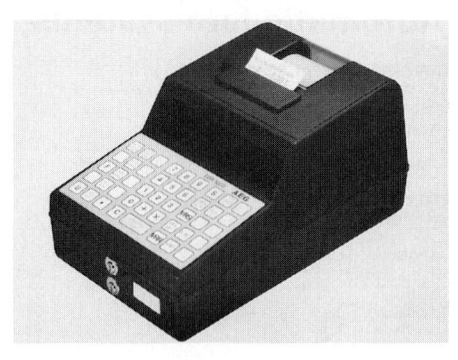

Type EDR1003 electronic print and record unit by AEG

Camp-Alcatel

8 rue de Torcy, 75018 Paris, France

Telephone: +33 1 42 01 46 27
Telex: 240166 afccamp
Telefax: +33 1 42 38 27 88

President: Gilbert Weill
Managing Director: Pierre Lereboullet
Commercial Director: Franklin Zagury

Products: Automatic fare collection equipment.
For metro systems a new generation of equipment has been developed in association with CGA-HBS. Based on magnetic tickets, the range includes a reversible control gate equipped with a double reader and printer which enables the processing or printing of tickets in any position.
The gate can be remote-controlled for entry or exit. Booking office machines can print, encode and count all types of tickets and season cards and feed data to a central computer. The range of ticket vending machines can cope with up to seven coins, 128 destinations and ten classes of passenger with coin cycling and recirculating provisions.
DATAMAG, a magnetic validator equipment, designed for railway stations, is also suitable for bus-metro transfer control and can be installed on board buses, being able to process magnetic tickets in a cycle of less than one second. These tickets may be single or multi-journey tickets, stored value tickets and season passes, and of two formats (Edmonson or credit card). This equipment can be operated either as a stand-alone unit, or connected to a remote control unit capable of driving up to eight validators. Main functions of the remote control unit are transmission of messages to the whole group of validators (date, current time, on/off orders, printing information) and reception of alarm information. Each magnetic ticket is recorded in DATAMAG internal memory units; a special plug-in memory module can also be connected inside to increase records possibilities. Its content can be downloaded into a personal computer, giving all facilities to obtain ridership and revenue statistics. This module is also used to enter data relative to the fare structure and escalation. DATAMAG is fully compatible with RADIOPARC, an on-street parking payment device accepting both coins and magnetic debit cards and manufactured by CGA-HBS Alcatel.
Camp-Alcatel has also developed DIGIPLUS-an electronic ticket issuing machine. This allows up to 40 categories of tickets and is a system serving management and operation, mainly for intercity bus lines, with a full data collection and processing capability which can be calculated from three tariff grids (near each line). Ticket are fully readable and are issued in less than one second by thermal printing. At the beginning of a shift, a 'start of shift ticket' is issued, enabling the operator to know the total revenue collected during the former shifts. In the same way an 'end of shift ticket' is generated by the machine detailing per category the revenue collected. A plug-in module contains full data relative to route structure and tariffs grids. This module also stores all of the transactions allowing, through a personal computer, a complete data processing to obtain ridership statistics and revenue audit.
DATAPUCE is a fare collection system involving smart cards. A personalised smart card is delivered to each subscriber as a transport contract with a programmed period of validity. The characteristics of each journey are recorded on the smart card; at the end of its contract, the customer has to go to a payment terminal installed in public areas (or this operation can be effected from a home personal reader connected to a data transmission network) to pay his bill. The terminal displays a detailed accountancy for the last period; the customer agrees by keying his personal individual number. Debit of his account and credit of transport company's account are simultaneously performed. Then the customer revalidates his transport contract for a new period. The operations are achieved through a processing centre which also stores subscriber's files.
DAGOBER is a new generation of automatic ticket vending machines accepting both coins and credit card for payment. Tickets are fully printed from roll of thermal paper bearing the logotype of the company. This vending machine can include an encoding device and thus can issue magnetic tickets. The available formats are Edmonson, credit card and IATA.
Recent main contracts:
Douai, La Rochelle, Salon and Toulon (France) transit systems are equipped with DATAMAG. São Paulo (Brazil) also has contracted with DATAMAG.
30 regional organisations in France and also Venice (Italy), Canary Islands and Casablanca (Morocco) are using DIGIPLUS ticket-issuing machines.
DATAPUCE is implemented in Blois (France).
DAGOBER has been selected by Lille and Lyon transit systems and by the SNCF (French National Railways).

Microfare portable electronic ticket-issuing machine by Almex

Compagnie Générale d'Automatisme
CGA-HBS/CAMP

Head office: 12 rue de la Baume, 75008 Paris, France

Telephone: +33 1 69 88 52 00
Telex: 601 262 f
Telefax: +33 1 60 84 28 61

Works: Le Plessis-Pâté, 91220 Bretigny-sur-Orge

Telephone: +33 1 60 84 95 40
Telex: 691262 cga

CGA-CAMP TVM 90 ticket-vending machine

Automatic fare systems / MANUFACTURERS

Chairman & CEO: M Gerard
General Manager: J-P Bourdeau
Deputy Managing Director: G Weill
Strategy Director: P Rottembourg
Marketing & Sales Director: J-P Talvard
Export Sales Director: P Blanchard

Subsidiaries: Société Camp and HII (France)
Alta Technology Inc (USA)
Sogima (Italy)
South Korea branch
Egypt branch

Products: Automatic fare collection equipment; stand-alone microprocessor-based equipment for issue of and controlling magnetically encoded tickets; automatic gates with reversible ticket transport; automatic vending machines; ticket office machines; data collection equipment; automatic vehicle monitoring and control systems for buses and tramways (voice and data radio transmission, priority at intersections, statistics, vehicle location, passenger information, etc).

Recent contracts for Automatic Fare Collection systems include Taipeh Subway (1989); SNCF (1987 and 1989); Cairo Subway (1986); Seoul Subway (1984); Caracas Subway (1980).

Other customers include the subways of Paris, Lille, Lyons and Marseilles (France); Montreal, New York, Boston, Pusan, Hong Kong, Toronto, Baltimore, Rio de Janeiro, Sao Paulo, Santiago, Stockholm and Madrid.

Crouzet
Crouzet SA
Terminals and Systems Division

25 rue Jules Védrines, 26027 Valence Cedex, France

Telephone: +33 75 55 41 00
Telex: 345 272
Telefax: +33 75 55 89 22

President and Managing Director: Roger Champt
Export Manager: Gabriel Hanis

Subsidiary companies: Italy, England, Spain, Netherlands, West Germany, Switzerland, Belgium, USA, Mexico, Australia

Products: Automatic fare collection systems including:
Automatic ticket-vending machines with payment by coins, bank notes, multi-service card or credit card: user dialogue by keyboard and display unit.
Small-and large-capacity booking office machines for ticket sales by transport authority clerks.
Access controllers with turnstile or with on-board or fixed ticket validator.
Built-in circuit board for processing statistical and accounting data.

Crouzet's fare collection systems are designed for use with magnetic tickets of Edmonson (30 × 60 mm) or credit card formats or with integrated circuits cards.

The systems are capable of handling all types of ticket: single-ride, pre-pay (stored value) cards, multi-ride tickets, time-based tickets, and a wide variety of user categories: season ticket holders, occasional users, students, reduced rates, and of adapting to any fare structure.

The system can be set up on line with real-time data processing or be associated with portable memory units for deferred processing of data.

Equipment has been supplied for the Paris, Lyons, Lille, Marseilles, Mexico City, Rio de Janeiro, Seoul, Baltimore, Glasgow and Tyne and Wear metros, as well as for the Paris RER, French Railways and Irish Railways.

Cubic Western
Cubic Western Data
A member of the Cubic Corporation

5650 Kearny Mesa Road, San Diego, California 92111-1380, USA

Telephone: +1 619 268 3100
Cable: Cubic
Telex: 68 31138
Telefax: +1 910 335 1550

Chairman: Raymond L de Kozan
Marketing Director: Steve Shewmaker

Products: Automatic fare collection equipment, microprocessor-operated, modular design comprising all components or subsystems, including ticket vendors, entry/exit gates, change makers, addfare machines (excess fares), ticket analysers, sorter/encoders, intermodal bus/rail transfer capability, maintenance-free electronic coin acceptors, interactive centralised computer data acquisition system providing two-way communications; credit card-operated self-service ticket vendors.

Electronique Serge Dassault

55 quai Marcel Dassault, 92214 Saint-Cloud, France

Telephone: +33 1 49 11 80 00
Cable: Electrodassault
Telex: 250787

Products: The Self Service Terminal (TLS 220) can be used either as an automatic vending machine for tickets or as an information service. Payment is made using bank cards. The TLS automates verification of magnetic cards for the purpose of identification or for payment for any of the services offered by the operator of the machine.

The Passenger Operated Ticket Vending Machine (TVM 624) is designed for issuing long-distance tickets on a self-service basis. Its most significant features are encoding, alphanumeric and graphic printing to issue any type of ticket having an ATB/IATA format; it accepts all types of payment, ie: notes, coins and credit cards and, when appropriate, renders change in notes and coins; ease of use facilitated by its touch screen user-friendly menus.

The Boarding Pass Printer (BPR 600) is designed for processing ATB documents or magnetic boarding passes at check-in desks and occasionally at the ticketing counter. The BPR 600 is also able to process validation and can read, encode or re-encode, print and issue ATB documents or magnetic boarding passes.

The DAM 128 ticket vending machine integrates high-performance sub-assemblies which include cash-processing system, bank card payment module, ticket printer and control and monitoring electronic circuitry.

Elgeba
Elgeba Gerätebau GmbH

Postfach 6140, Eudenbacher Strasse 10-12, 5340 Bad Honnef 6, Federal Republic of Germany

Telephone: +49 224 80048
Telex: 885 223

General Director: Bodo Faber

Crouzet AFC equipment

The Boarding Pass Printer BPR 600 by Electronique Serge Dassault

Cubic Western Data exit gates for Hong Kong MTRC

Cubic Western Data turnstiles for Washington DC Metro, USA

MANUFACTURERS / Automatic fare systems

Products: Ticket cancelling, vending and issuing machines. The company's recent contracts have covered urban transport in Cologne, Düsseldorf and Munich, Amsterdam, The Hague, Prague and cities in Africa and Canada.

GFI GenFare International
A Unit of General Signal Corporation

751 Pratt Boulevard, Elk Grove Vilage, Illinois 60007, USA

Telephone: +1 708 593 8855
Telefax: +1 708 593 1824

President: James A Pacelli
VP, Marketing: Norman Diamond
Marketing Director: Kim Richard Green

Products: Design, manufacture, sales, installation and maintenance of all types of fare collection equipment; revenue and passenger controls; fully integrated data systems for bus, light rail and heavy rail applications.
Recent contracts include 4,000 electronic fareboxes for New York City Transit Authority; 2,500 electronic fareboxes, 550 turnstiles, token vending machines and central data system for Chicago Transit Authority; 200 VENDSTAR ticket vending machines and central data system for Los Angeles County Transportation Commission; 400 turnstiles with magnetic card ability, 200 coin-operated transfer issue machines and central data system for SEPTA Philadelphia; 270 turnstiles with stored ride magnetic card ability, 110 change machines, 70 VENDSTAR ticket vending machines and central data system for Port Authority of NY and NJ; 150 turnstiles with magnetic card and token processing ability for Toronto Transit Commission.

Klein
Etablissements Georges Klein

36 rue Boussingault, 75013 Paris, France

Telephone: +33 1 45 89 58 96
Telex: 270 507
Telefax: +33 1 45 89 04 74

President: J-P Ulmann
Managing Director: D Lemarchand

Products: AFC turnstiles and gates.

Laakmann
Laakmann Karton GmbH & Co KG

Bonsfelderstrasse 1-4, 5620 Velbert-11-Langenberg, Federal Republic of Germany

Telephone: +49 2052 603-0
Cable: Laakmann, Langenbergrheinland

MAEL X50 self-service ticket system

Telex: 8516863 laak d
Telefax: +49 2052 603-81

Managing Directors: H J Schwering
Dr W R Roloff
Export Sales: R Mollenkott
Sales Manager: W Anstett

Products: Railway tickets and ticket reels for automatic vending machines.

MAEL
MAEL SpA
A member of the Olivetti group

Viale Lo Antoniniano 13, 00153 Rome, Italy

Telephone: +39 6 7003733
Telex: 624428 maelnk i
Telefax: +39 6 7002711

Main works: Via Turanense Km 415, 67061 Carsoli

Managing Director: Mario Giacobbo Scavo
Marketing Manager: Sante Marcheselli

Products: Electronic ticket systems, for which the company is the official supplier to Italian State Railways. Main items of the company's range are: the MAEL 400 series, which are portable battery-operated microcomputers for ticket-issue on trains and buses and of which 500 have been supplied, mainly to railway and bus companies; and the MAEL 401 series, which are counter minicomputers for ticket-issue and seat reservation, with off-on line communication capability, and of which 1200 machines have been supplied, mainly to Italian State Railways, Ferrovie Nord Milano, Yugoslavian Railways and Italian travel agencies.

Magnordata
Magnordata Security Printing
A Division of Norprint International Ltd

Boston, Lincolnshire PE2 9HZ, England

Telephone: +44 205 65161
Telex: 37578
Telefax: +44 205 64825

Manager: Colin Lever

Products: Magnetic striped products for various markets, including passenger tickets.
Magnordata supplies British Rail with PORTIS tickets and magnetics; also London Regional Transport and Docklands Light Railway.

Makomat
Makomat Automaten-und Maschinenbau GmbH

PO Box 10 12 28, Frankfurter Strasse 74, 6050 Offenbach/Main, Federal Republic of Germany

Telephone: +49 69 88 80 81
Telex: 4 152 709
Telefax: +49 69 800 4509

Products: Microprocessor-controlled, self-printing automatic ticket-issuing machines; automatic bill and coin changers; hand ticket stampers.

Modulex Systems Ltd

10 North Portway Close, Round Spinney, Northampton NN3 4RQ

Telephone: +44 604 494222
Telefax: +44 604 491035

Managing Director: W R Powell
Divisional Manager: P M Dowling
Export Manager: B Serup

Products: Computer-based passenger information systems. Modulex offers a turnkey project management and systems capability in the supply of high-quality visual information systems. Products include LCD panels and TV monitor displays.
Recent contracts include multiple station system for Danish State Railways; airport systems for Hamburg, Bergen, Copenhagen and Frankfurt airports.

VENDSTAR ticket vending machine by GFI GenFare International

Nippon Signal
The Nippon Signal Co Ltd

Head office: 3-1, Marunouchi 3-chome, Chiyoda-ku, Tokyo, Japan

Telephone: +81 3 287 4500
Cable: Signal, Tokyo
Telex: 222 2178
Telefax: +81 3 287 4649

Works: Yono Factory, 13-8, Kamikizaki 1-chome, Urawa City
Utsunomiya Factory, 11-2, Hiraide Kougyo Danchi, Utsunomiya City

Associated companies: Nisshin Industrial Co, Ltd
Nisshin Electrical Installation Co, Ltd
Nisshin Electronics Service Co, Ltd

Nippon Signal automatic passenger gates

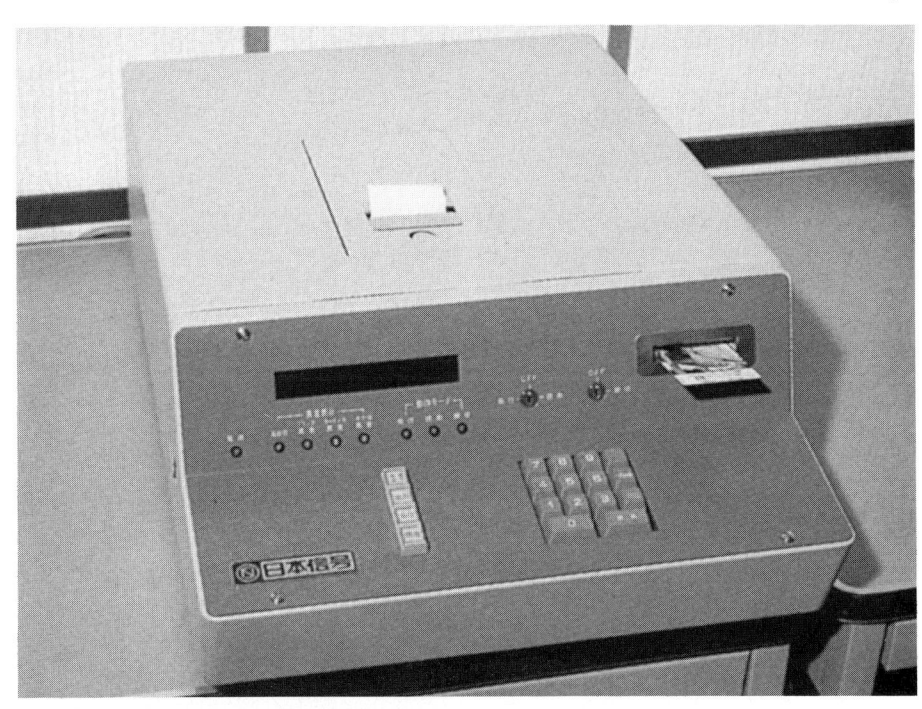

Automatic fare systems / **MANUFACTURERS**

Nippon Signal pre-paid card-issuing machine

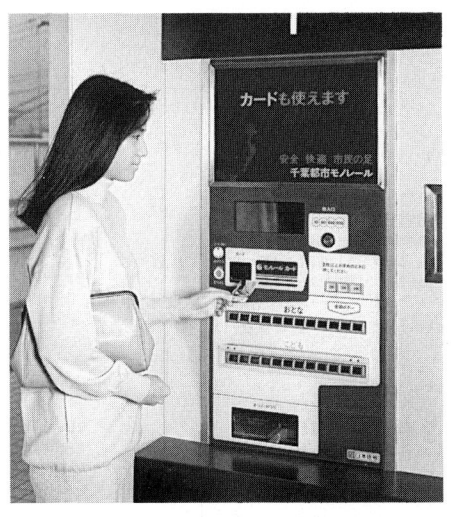

Nippon Signal ticket vending machine

President: H Takeuchi
Executive Vice President, General Sales: T Oki
Managing Director, Electronics Information & Control Systems: I Fujiware

Products: Automatic fare collection equipments such as bill changer, ticket vending machine, gate controller, passenger gate, automatic fare adjusting machine, season ticket issuing machine, multi-function booking office machine, ticket-issuing machine for station staff, data processing machine, visual display, visual magnetic card system (VISMAC); pre-paid card systems.

Omron
Omron Tateisi Electronics Co

Head office: 10, Tsuchido-cho, Hanazono, Ukyo-ku, Kyoto, 616 Japan

Telephone: +81 75 463 1161
Telex: 5422889
Telefax: +81 75 464 2607

Main works: Omron Tokyo Building, 4-10 Toranomon, 3-chome, Minato-ku, Tokyo 105

Telephone: +81 3 436 7186
Telex: 2424086
Telefax: +81 3 436 7223

Manager Director: H Masuda
Sales Division Manager: I Minami

Products: Automatic fare collection system including money changers, coin/bill-operated ticket vendors (also with transfer ticket readers), ticket checking and collecting gates, ticket-issuing machines, automatic fare adjuster, season ticket-issuing machines. Suppliers to Japanese National Railways, numerous private Japanese railways and the Korean National Railroad.

Prodata

Leuvensesteenweg 540, B-1930 Zaventem, Belgium

Telephone: +32 2 722 87 11
Telex: 62054
Telefax: +32 2 725 06 28

Vice-President, Prodata Ticketing: Walter Raffo

Products: Fixed or on-board ticketing machines, automatic ticket-vending machines, window ticket machines and turnstiles. Recent customers have included Algerian and Tunisian Railways (1990).

Scanpoint AS

Vibeholms Allé 22, 2605 Bröndby, Denmark

Telephone: +45 43 43 39 99
Telefax: +45 43 43 34 88

Managing Director: Morton Solling
Marketing Manager: Karsten Thormod

Products: Electronic fare collection systems based on the use of magnetic stripe plastic cards conforming to ISO standards. Product range includes fare computers, card readers, vending machines, data transmission systems, software packages and plastic tickets.
  Scanpoint fare collection systems are installed in the major cities of Scandinavia.

Scanpoint stationary card validator

Scheidt & Bachmann
Scheidt & Bachmann GmbH

132 Breitestrasse, Postfach 20 11 43, 4050 Mönchengladbach 2, Federal Republic of Germany

Telephone: +49 2166 266 0
Telex: 0852818
Telefax: +49 2166 266 475

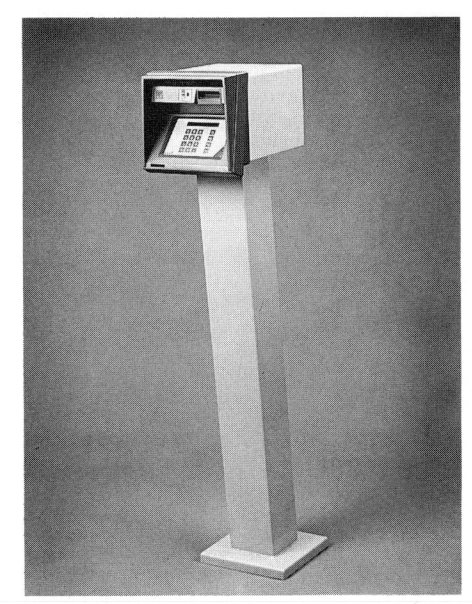

Prodata OV2000 system

Sales Manager: Dipl-Ing Erich Horn

Products: Automatic fare collection and ticket-vending machines for stationary and mobile application; electronic ticket printers for buses and ticket offices; central computer systems for accounting and data provision.

Schlumberger
Schlumberger Industrie
Urban Terminals and Systems

PO Box 620-04, 50 avenue Jean Jaurès, 92542 Montrouge Cedex, France

Telephone: +33 1 47 46 67 80
Telex: 632 391 f
Telefax: +33 1 47 46 67 82

General Manager: Patrick Berthon
Commercial/Sales Director: Louis Casado
Technical Director: Jean-Louis Bezin
Marketing Director: M Fillod
Communications Director: H Myngers

Main works: 32 rue de Terre Rouge, PO Box 1275, 25005 Besançon, France

Telephone: +33 81 51 21 21
Telex: 361 273
Telefax: +33 81 52 76 38

Scanpoint stationary card validator

MANUFACTURERS / Automatic fare systems

Products: The TRANSMAG system, able to process, centralise and implement several items of information. The ticket which looks like a magnetic card is managed electronically. TRANSMAG works with a magnetic card and permits different rates to be applied according to the user's request. It implements the different information generated by each user (time, date, rate, place) so as to establish statistics on the traffic of the lines and timetables, and manages the amount collected (sharing of receipts between operators or modes of transport). For the user each transaction is entered at the back of his card. In this way TRANSMAG does away with any fraud and possible dispute.

The TRANSPUCE system has the same functions as those provided by TRANSMAG, but uses smart cards.

New developments include an infrared connection to transfer data from the validators to a computer to facilitate statistical analysis.

Thorn EMI
Thorn EMI Electronics Limited, Computer Systems Division

Wookey Hole Road, Wells, Somerset BA5 1AA, England

Telephone: +44 749 72081
Telex: 44254 emi w
Telefax: +44 749 79363

Managing Director: M T Penery
Business Manager: W S Denman
A & RCS Sales & Marketing Manager: S Wright

Products: Ticket-issuing equipments and systems; automatic revenue collection systems and equipments; passenger control barriers; ticket preparation equipments; management control systems; data capture and retrieval systems and equipments; total system studies. The company has developed and supplied to British Rail clerk-operated (booking office) ticket machines, portable ticket machines and passenger-operated ticket vendors.

The company has supplied British Rail with one of the largest orders of its type placed anywhere in the world. The contract, worth over £30 million, was for the supply of Accountancy and Passenger Ticket Issuing Systems (APTIS) and Portable Ticket Issuing Systems (PORTIS). Thorn EMI's Computer Systems Division's contract with British Rail was to supply 2871 APTIS and 1750 PORTIS together with supporting equipment which includes 500 hand-held verifiers to read magnetic encoding on the APTIS tickets. The first systems were delivered in early 1985.

In December 1987 British Rail placed an order for a new generation of 'super' portable machines, termed SPORTIS, incorporating a credit card and encoded ticket magnetic reader, plus a greatly expanded data store. Thorn EMI are to supply British Rail with 2300 of these units, and also to retrofit the existing PORTIS machines to the same standard.

APTIS, a desk-top machine for use in booking offices, is a completely self-contained system. Details of the 24 most common destinations can be stored in the system's memory and recalled for printing on blank tickets by a single command. Up to 2500 other destinations can be accessed by keying the first four letters of the destination names; fares to all destinations are stored in the machine's memory. The system offers high security of operation with the ability to store all transaction data and accept sundry station account entries which can be transferred to a centrally-based computer over a telephone line. The central computer can also communicate back to the outstation to pass updated information, such as revised train fare structures.

Thorn EMI DATATECH Type 2424 medium-speed modems have been supplied to British Rail to form the vital data communications link in the APTIS network. The modem, a full duplex 2400 bit/s model with a serial autodialler, features digital signal processing and an active line monitor which automatically downspeeds a link to 1200 bit/s should line quality fall. The DATATECH modems will connect 2300 ticket and booking terminals to BR's central computer at Nottingham.

SPORTIS is a particularly compact battery-operated, microprocessor-based, portable machine printing tickets from blank stock that ensures individual accountability of the operator and maximum security of revenue. It can issue tickets to and from up to 99 locations using a two-digit code which is sufficient for the station name to be printed out. The system has a fares memory which includes an adequate number of boarding and alighting points to cover all normal pay-train routes. The equipment is of rugged and lightweight construction. SPORTIS can also be supplied as a low-cost booking office ticket-issuing system with an optional stand and mains adaptor. Two ancillary devices, a data retrieval unit (DRU) and a portable memory unit (PMU), are available to allow SPORTIS to download data to a central computer or to update its stored fares and destination details.

An interface unit for SPORTIS brings computer-controlled ticket-issuing within the reach of small transport operators by enabling it to link to commercial desk-top computers. The custom-designed opto-interface, with its associated software, provides a two-way link between SPORTIS and a microcomputer which enables data on fare transactions to be transferred to the computer and new data, such as fare changes, to be fed back into SPORTIS's memory. Customised computer software provides complete data preparation and management facilities.

The Hand-Held Verifier, a portable device for checking magnetically-encoded journey information on tickets, has been developed for supply to British Rail as part of a £30 million programme to computerise its ticket-issuing system. Intended for use mainly by inspectors on board trains and passenger-carrying vehicles, the verifiers are likely to prove most useful on routes where different modes of transport are used for each different stage. Journey and fare information, recorded on the ticket, is displayed on a two-line alphanumerical LCD. Powered by standard batteries, the verifier has a manual card stripe reader to handle credit card-size tickets.

Thorn EMI Electronics is one of the largest British-based groups involved in the design, manufacture and supply of ticket-issuing machines and allied products. The company's extensive experience as a supplier to the passenger transport industry has been augmented by involvement in all stages of the British Rail London commuter area ARC project and as lead contractor in the associated government-sponsored joint study group, in co-operation with British Rail, London Regional Transport and the Department of Industry.

The company's range of ticket-issuing equipments offers a variety of facilities which cater for particular situations, systems, or individual company preferences. The range includes clerk-operated systems, portable ticket-issuing systems and self-service vendors. Features include operationally compatible data capture media, microprocessor control systems and a range of tickets and ticket materials.

Toshiba
Toshiba Corporation
Automation Systems Group: Electronic Systems Department

1-1, Shibaura 1-chome, Minato-ku, Tokyo 105, Japan

Telephone: +81 3 457 3249
Cable: Toshiba, Tokyo
Telex: J22587 toshiba
Telefax: +81 3 456 6943

Overseas offices
North America: Houston, New York, San Francisco, Toronto, Tustin (California), Vancouver
Latin America: Bogota, Buenos Aires, Caracas, Mexico City, Rio de Janeiro, São Paulo
Europe: Athens, West Berlin, London, Vienna
Africa: Cairo, Johannesburg
Middle East: Baghdad, Dubai, Jidda, Kuwait, Tehran
South-east Asia: Bangkok, Beijing, Hong Kong, Jakarta, Manila, Taipei
Australasia: Sydney, Wellington

Products: Automatic fare collection systems.

Customers include: Japanese National Railways, Teito Rapid Transit Authority, Sapporo Municipal Transportation Bureau, Tokyu Corporation, Osaka Municipal Transportation Bureau, Kinki Nippon Railway, Odakyu Electric Railway, Seibu Railway, Tobu Railway, Nagoya Municipal Transportation Bureau, Hankyu Corporation, Nankai Electric Railway, Keihin Express Electric Railway, Keihan Electric Railway, Hanshin Electric Railway, Nagoya Railroad, Transportation Bureau Tokyo Metropolitan Government, Kobe Rapid Transit Railway, Keisei Electric Railway, Kobe Municipal Transportation Bureau, Nishi Nippon Railroad, Kyoto Municipal Transportation Bureau, Fukuoka Municipal Transportation Bureau, Japan Travel Bureau and Kobe New Transit Railway.

Products include:

Season ticket renewal machine, which is operated by a passenger by inserting the old season ticket to duplicate the original and destination station and depressing a button to specify the duration of validity; the fare is calculated and displayed automatically and upon insertion of exact money by coins and/or bank notes, the new season ticket is issued.

Ticket-vending machine, including change dispenser. The fare button is a variable fare display type. Upon a fares revision a change of fare indication on the fare button can be effected easily by replacing software. A thermal-dot print system is employed and a microcomputer is used for the processing unit; thus printing can be completely controlled with the software. A bill-processing unit can also be installed and sales data can be recorded.

Multi-function booking office machine, which issues season tickets and single journey, return or tour ticket including express or limited express charge. With on-line data transmission, the single journey or return ticket can be issued with seat booking. The attendant depresses buttons to specify the original station, destination station, intermediate station, duration of validity and discount rate. For season ticket issue the attendant has also to insert an application form, filled in by the patron to transcribe the patron's signature on to the season ticket. Configuration consists of control units, destination select switch board, function keyboard, fare display, magnetic disc drive, magnetic tape cassette unit, and cash drawer in main cabinet and ticket printing unit in separate cabinet.

Automatic flap-door-type gate, available in three models: entry, exit, and reversible. The equipment is provided with a four-flap door, human detector, and ticket pooling mechanism: processing capacity is up to 60 passengers/minute. A belt transport system mini-

Thorn EMI APTIS desk-top machine

Thorn EMI SPORTIS machine.

Toshiba portable ticket issuing machine

Automatic passenger gates installed at Tower Hill Underground station, London by Westinghouse Cubic

Automatic passenger-operated machines by Westinghouse Cubic

Booking office ticket-issuing machine by Westinghouse Cubic

mises ticket jamming. A microcomputer is built into each unit, giving a positive check on every passenger: modifications in routes or fares can be covered by revised software.

A new portable ticket issuing machine replaces the time-consuming process of issuing train tickets by hand. Tickets of any type can be issued in any amount quickly and accurately and the sales data of each transaction is readily transferred to a station computer for exact revenue control.

Toyo Denki
Toyo Denki Seizo KK

7-2 Yaesu 2-chome, Chuo-ku, Tokyo 104, Japan

Telephone: +81 3 271 6374
Cable: Yohden, Tokyo
Telex: 222-4666

Products: Season ticket issuing machine, automatic ticket gate equipment.

Westinghouse Cubic
Westinghouse Cubic Ltd

177 Nutfield Road, Merstham, Surrey RH1 3HH, England

Telephone: +44 7374 4921
Telex: 9419634
Telefax: +44 7374 3693

15-17 Long Acre, London WC2E 9LH, England

Telephone: +44 71 240 9821
Telex: 8950475
Telefax: +44 71 240 4932

Managing Director: P L Clayton
Projects Director: D M Wanless
Marketing Director: P Ellwood

Products: Passenger-operated ticket machines accepting coins, notes, credit cards and stored value cards (tickets issued either with or without magnetic encoding); booking office ticket machines; automatic passenger gates; computerised audit control and management reports.

Westinghouse Cubic systems ensure full and correct fare collection on public transport systems with minimum inconvenience to passengers. Token vending machines for public utilities are secure and vandal-resistant. Automated cash collection on buses, toll roads, bridges and parking sites speeds passenger flow. Equipment can handle cash, including notes, magnetic cards, or debit cards all for highly flexible operation.

Westinghouse Cubic provides a total system from cash accepting and ticket-issuing devices to computer hardware and software, communications networks, installation, lifetime maintenance and support. A modular approach means that systems can be based on proven packages and tailored quickly and effectively to user requirements. Magnetically-encoded ticket systems provide management information and control. Detailed accountability and a full audit trail aid fraud prevention. Operating information can be made available to management in real time.

London Underground chose Westinghouse Cubic to completely re-equip all 274 stations with station computers, control units and printers linked to central computer systems. More than 1400 passenger-operated and booking office ticket machines speed ticket-issuing and cut queues; on-line management information increases operating efficiency and reliable fare collection holds down operating costs.

In 1989, Strathclyde PTE placed an order with Westinghouse Cubic for the supply, installation and commissioning of revenue control equipment for the Glasgow Underground Railway. The equipment covers 24 booking office machines, 35 ticket vending machines, 43 entry gates and the refurbishment of 36 exit gates, together with a central computer control system.

Westinghouse Cubic is also producing 43 ticket vending machines for Docklands Light Railway. These machines will isue tickets with full compatibility with the barrier/gates on the London Underground system. They accept coins and notes with full change giving capability and are linked back to the DLR Operations Centre and WCL supplied central management and revenue control system.

Xamax
Xamax Systems Ltd

Birchstrasse 210, 8050 Zürich, Switzerland

Telephone: +41 1 311 23 22
Telex: 823 258 xsys ch
Telefax: +41 1 311 08 18

General Manager: H Küllmar
Sales Manager: D Stehli
Production Manager: F Linhart

Products: Ticket-vending machines incorporating advanced micro-processor control with interfaces for connection to a central computer, diagnosis of errors with display, possibility of remote status supervision, quick, unlimited change of rates, electronic single-slot coin monitor for six or nine coins, automatic print-out of accounting and statistical data, printing of desired data on tickets, multi-issue potential, paper stock for up to 15 000 tickets, cash vault of 6 litres content, local and remote burglary alarm and, optionally, change return and bank note acceptor. Recent clients have included Athens Metro (Greece), Calgary (Canada), Linz (Austria), Ludwigshafen (West Germany), Lugano (Switzerland), Malmö (Sweden), Sacramento (USA) and Zug (Switzerland).

Electrification/permanent way/yard/terminal/workshop equipment

Fixed electrification equipment

AUSTRALIA
Ampcontrol 339
Barclay 340
Broken Hill 341
Plasser 343
SM 345
Westinghouse Electric 346

BELGIUM
ACEC 339

BRAZIL
Sigla 345

CANADA
Siemens Electric 344

CZECHOSLOVAKIA
Strojexport 345
Technopol 345

FINLAND
Electric Rails 341

FRANCE
CGE 341
Ferraz 341
GEC Alsthom 341
Geismar 342
SAFT 344
SPIE Batignolles 345

GERMANY, DEMOCRATIC REPUBLIC
Görlitz 342

GERMANY, FEDERAL REPUBLIC
ABB 338
AEG Westinghouse 339
SET Schadt 344
Siemens 344

HUNGARY
Ganz 341

INDIA
Greysham 343
SAE (India) 344

ITALY
Ansaldo Trasporti 339
Ercole Marelli 341
SAE Sadelmi 344
Siette 345
TIBB (ASEA Brown Boveri) 345

JAPAN
Fuji Electric 341
Hitachi Cable 343
Toshiba 345

POLAND
Elektrim 341

ROMANIA
Contransimex 341

SWITZERLAND
ASEA Brown Boveri-Sécheron 338
Furrer & Frey 341
Groupement 50 Hz 343

UK
Allied Insulators 339
Balfour Beatty 340
BICC 340
Brecknell, Willis 340
Delta 341
GEC Transmission and Distribution Projects ... 341
GEC Transportation Projects 342
Hawker Siddeley 343
Lucas Automotive 343
Pirelli 343
Powernetics 343
Thorn EMI 345
Transmitton 345
Whipp & Bourne 346
Wickham 346

USA
AEG Westinghouse 339
EFE North America 341
General Electric Co (USA) 342
Siemens Energy & Automation 345

MANUFACTURERS / Fixed electrification equipment

ABB
ASEA Brown Boveri

Head office: ABB Transportation Management and Systems Development (ABB BTM)

Gottlieb Daimler-Strasse 6, PO Box 100183, 6800 Mannheim 41, Federal Republic of Germany

Telephone: +49 621 468 200
Telex: 462411220 abd memo
Telefax: +49 621 468 298/9

President: Erich Kocher
Executive Vice President: Åke Nilsson

Group companies: For full list and addresses see ABB entry in Locomotives section

Development, design, engineering, sales, production, installation, maintenance and after-sales service of fixed installations as follows:
Traction power supply systems: complete ac or dc power supply stations, sub-systems for power supply. Complete catenary systems including installation for voltages from 1 to 50 kV and train speeds to 250 km/h; special overhead contact lines for underground and industrial railways; components.
Complete third-rail systems including their cables for voltages from 750 to 1.5 kV and train speeds to 100 km/h; components.
Service, minor equipment and spare parts.
Large project management and consultancy.
 Recent contracts include:
Germany, Federal Republic
Rectifier systems for Berlin West (S-Bahn): five, total 20 MW, 750 V.
Catenaries for German Federal Railway (DB) high-speed main-line electrification (engineering, supply and installation of 15 kV, 16⅔ Hz systems) and S-Bahn systems in Nuremberg, Munich and Düsseldorf. Catenary developments include designs of new aluminium overhead line components, corrosion-proof and maintenance-free.
Italy
Two complete dc sub-stations for the FS Rome-Florence *Direttissima* line, each with three 5400 kW rectifier groups.
 Medium voltage switch-gear and transformers for six power sub-stations 1.5 kV dc, each with either two or three 3800 kW rectifier groups, of Milan Metro Line 3.
Portugal
Metro Lisbon: dc switchgear for two rectifier sub-stations.
Sweden
Rectifier systems for Stockholm (underground): three total 13.5 MW, 750 V.
United Kingdom
British Rail, Southern Region: 132 dc panels with HSCB Type UR 36 and microprocessor protection unit PCU for 18 rectifier sub-stations and 14 track-parallel huts.
USA
33 dc traction sub-stations with power between 750 to 6000 kW and with 650 to 1000 V dc; five units for Washington Metro (WMATA); three units for Boston (MBTA); 14 units for Chicago (CTA), in two contracts; two units for South Eastern Pennsylvania (SEPTA); three units for San Francisco Bay Area Rapid Transit (BART); and six units for Metro Seattle.
In early 1988, a contract was obtained for the engineering, manufacture and supply of the overhead line/catenary assemblies for the Long Beach-Los Angeles 35 km light rail line of the LACTC (Los Angeles County Transport Community), now under construction by the main contractor Comstock, Los Angeles.
Brazil
Cia do Metropolitano de São Paulo: two rectifier sub-stations, primary voltage 22 kV, power rating 4250 kW.
Egypt
For the Cairo-Helwan line: modification of the overhead line/catenary systems and supply of three rectifier sub-stations.
France
Lille, for automatic light Metro (VAL) line Ibis: six rectifier sub-stations.
Turkey
Istanbul Metro, prime power supply and catenary system.

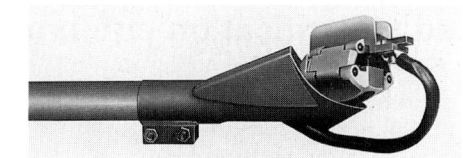

Type T3501 current collector by ABB-Sécheron

ABB
ASEA Brown Boveri-Sécheron Ltd
Member of the ASEA Brown Boveri Group

14 avenue de Sécheron, 1211 Geneva 21, Switzerland

Telephone: +41 22 39 41 11
Telex: 22130
Telefax: +41 22 34 21 94

Products: Transformers for railway electrification, dc traction substations. Rectifiers and circuit breakers, line protection devices for dc traction networks.
 The company is actively involved in the design and supply of complete rectifier substations for dc traction networks. For example, in 1987, in collaboration with British Brown Boveri, Telford, the company manufactured and delivered to British Rail Southern Region an order for supply of dc traction switchgears to the latter's Bournemouth-Weymouth regional line. The ABB high-speed circuit-breaker, Type UR, and a high performance electronic Protection Control Unit (Type PCU), are important items in the company's product line.
 The BR Bournemouth-Weymouth line contract comprised 49 track feeder cubicles in draw-out trolley design, with dc high-speed circuit breakers of Type UR, and the PCU electronic control units mounted inside transportable enclosures. The microprocessor-based PCU continually monitors the track feeder supply by measuring voltage and current and calculating the corresponding line impedance. This is particularly important in the event of a distant fault, which carries the risk that because of high line impedance the short circuit current might remain below the trigger setting of the circuit breaker, and the fault would not be cleared. The PCU detects such a condition with a greater precision than the electro-magnetic protection devices used so far, which respond to the so-called 'dropping voltage characteristic'.
 The Type ADTE automatic microprocessor-based diagnostic and test equipment is specifically designed to test complex electronic control systems. The ADTE itself is controlled by a mini-computer. ADTE architecture is modular and therefore provides the flexibility needed to adapt optimally to the electronic system it is required to monitor. For example, it is possible to test electronic printed circuits, electronic control systems, complete contactor or chopper design vehicles. ADTE signals are routed to the system under test via connecting cables fitted with multiple connectors. The various test sequences are displayed on the micro-computer screen in the form of a menu. Test time is reduced by 50-70 per cent. On completion, the test result is displayed.
 The Type T3501 current collector for electric vehicles has a simple and rugged base, which may be fitted with a special device allowing complete rotation. The lightweight fibreglass pole is capable of horizontal pivoting 0 to 10°. The trolley head has a special trapezium suspension which minimises risk of de-wiring, reduces wear on the contact elements, and permits the vehicle speed to be increased especially in curves and when crossing line equipment.

ACEC
ACEC Transport
ACEC Transport is a subsidiary of GEC Alsthom

BP4211, 6000 Charleroi, Belgium

Telephone: +32 71 44 54 11
Telex: 51227 acec b
Telefax: +32 71 43 72 35

Managing Director: Ch Jauquet
Operations Managing Director: R Pellichero
Commercial Director: D Hausman

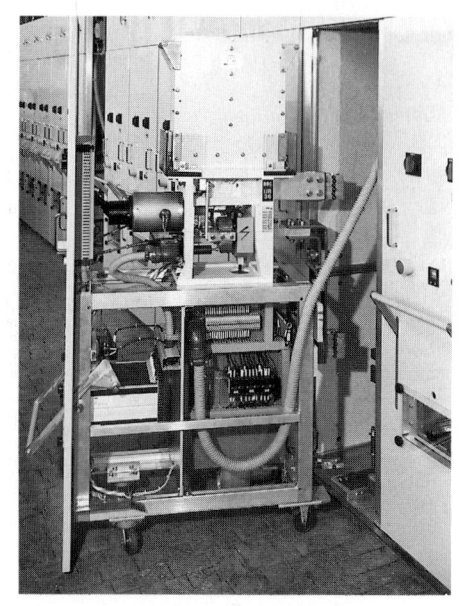

Draw-out trolley with high-speed circuit breaker Type UR36 rated 3600 A/750 V dc and electronic protection control unit Type PCU 2001 for British Rail by ABB-Sécheron

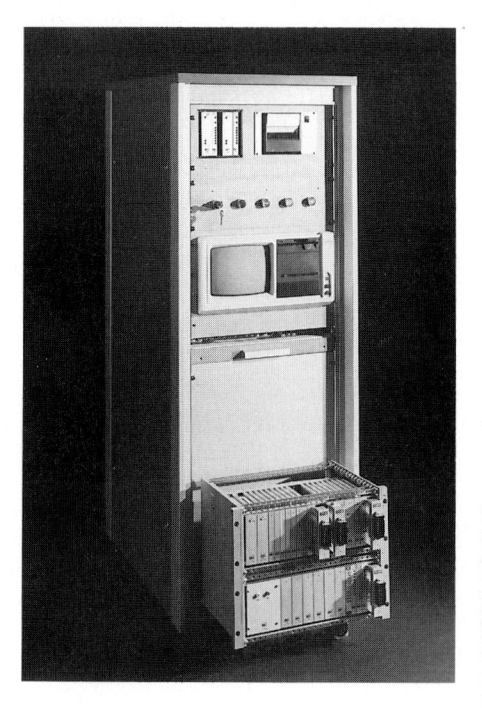

ADTE diagnostic and test equipment by ABB-Sécheron

Products: Remote control, high-speed and ultra-fast DHR circuit breakers.
 The DHR is a new type of ac circuit breaker and offers definite advantages in breaking energy and the facilities offered by the use of microprocessors fault recording, remote control etc.

AEG Westinghouse
AEG Westinghouse Transport-Systeme GmbH

Mainzer Landstrasse 351-367, D-6000 Frankfurt 1, Federal Republic of Germany

Telephone: +49 69 7507 550
Telefax: +49 69 7507 555

General Manager, Power Systems: Dipl Ing A Piel

Fixed electrification equipment / **MANUFACTURERS** 339

DHR ultra-fast dc circuit-breaker by ACEC

Products: Complete railway electrification equipment and systems; engineering and project management; traction power supply, including substations and remote control equipment; catenary equipment for overhead line or third-rail operation; electrical equipment for locomotives and railcars or multiple-units for main-line and branch-line service, mining and industrial locomotives; electrical equipment for rapid transit trains, urban and underground railways, tramways and trolleybuses; traction auxiliaries and special equipment (train lighting and heating).

AEG Westinghouse
AEG Westinghouse Transportation Systems Inc

1501 Lebanon Church Road, Pittsburgh, Pennsylvania 15236-1491, USA

Telephone: +1 412 655 5335
Telex: 866267
Telefax: +1 412 655 5860

President: J R Tucker
Vice Presidents, Commercial Operations: D R Marcucci
Engineering: R T Betler
Manufacturing Operations: T Jost

Products: Power supply and distribution systems (sub-stations, switchgear and protection equipment, transmission lines, catenary, third-rail distribution, power stations and remote control systems) for railroads, heavy and light rail, commuter rail and automated vehicle systems.

AEG Westinghouse Transportation Systems Inc

1501 Lebanon Church Road, Pittsburgh, Pennsylvania 15236-1491, USA

Telephone: +1 412 655 5335
Telex: 866267
Telefax: +1 412 655 5860

President: J R Tucker
Vice-President, Commercial Operations: D R Marcucci
Vice-President, Engineering: R T Betler
Vice-President, Manufacturing Operations: T Jost

Products: Electric ac and dc propulsion equipment (cam, chopper, ac inverter, traction motors/gears) for heavy and light rail vehicles and trolley buses; complete range of after-sales products and services including manuals, on-site training, traction motor remanufacturing, equipment rehabilitation and repair.

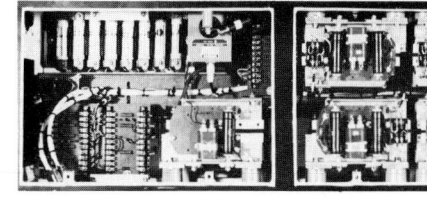

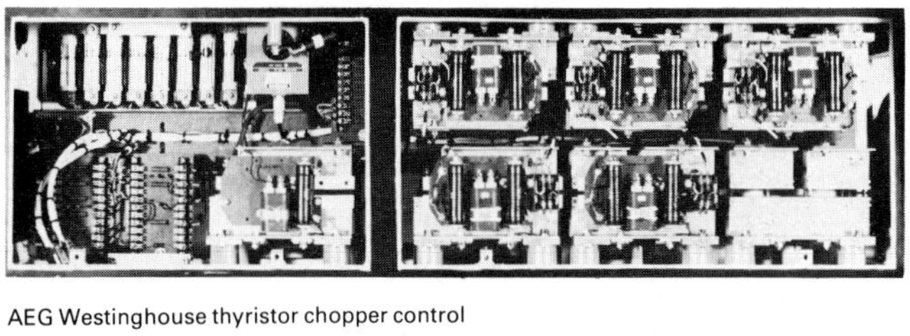

AEG Westinghouse thyristor chopper control

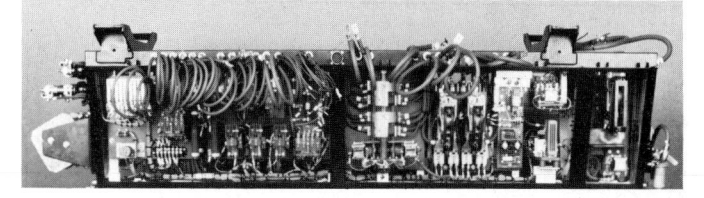

Self-ventilating traction rectifiers in power block design with high overload capacities for dc railways by AEG Westinghouse

Tunnel section of DB Rhein-Main route equipped with overhead contact wire by AEG Westinghouse

Allied Insulators
Allied Insulators Ltd
The Insulator Division of Fairey Group

PO Box 17, Milton, Stoke-on-Trent, Staffordshire ST2 7EE, England

Telephone: +44 782 534321
Telex: 36495
Telefax: +44 782 545804

Managing Director: J A Meighan
Commercial Director: R G Shenton
Technical Director: F Liptropp

Products: Insulator assemblies for feeder transmission, tracked overhead transmission, third-rail systems, pantograph support and switching apparatus.

Ampcontrol
Ampcontrol Pty Ltd

PO Box 163, Broadmeadow, New South Wales 2292, Australia

Telephone: +61 49 693122
Telex: 28158 aa
Telefax: +61 49 622980

Sales Director: N Sawyer
Engineering Director: P Cockbain

Products: Sub-stations for ac or dc traction

AEG Westinghouse electric cam control

Ansaldo Trasporti
Ansaldo Trasporti SpA
A member of the Ansaldo Group

Head office: 425 Via Argine 80147 Naples, Italy
Works: 260 Via Nuova delle Brecce, 80147 Naples, Italy

Telephone: +39 81 7810111
Telex: 710131
Telefax: +39 81 7810698/699

Other offices
336 Viale Sarca, 20126 Milan, Italy

Telephone: +39 2 64451
Telex: 331279
Telefax: +39 2 6438032

25 Corso Perrone, 16161 Genoa, Italy

Telephone: +39 10 65511
Telex: 271274
Telefax: +39 10 495044

Chairman: Giovanni Nobile
Vice President and Managing Director: Emilio Maraini
General Director: Francesco Granito
General Co-Director: Albert G Rosania
Technical Director: Salvatore Bianconi
R & D Commercial Director: Carlo Rizzi

Products: Power supply ac and dc plants for electrified transport with centralised control of electrification networks; high-speed circuit breakers; rectifiers; static converters for ac and dc substations; design, supply and erection of feeder lines and substations; electronic converters and controls, auxiliary apparatus; sales, installation, start-up, service.
  Electrification of the Sardinia line, the first in Italy with a 25 kV 50 Hz line voltage, was in course of installation in 1988. The Tunisian National Railways has awarded Ansaldo Trasporti a new contract for ac electrification of the second section, Monastir-Moknine-Mahdia, of the Metro Léger di Sahel. Electrification of the Sousse-Monastir section is already in operation.

Balfour Beatty
Balfour Beatty Power Construction Ltd
Traction and General Division

PO Box 12, Acornfield Road, Kirkby, Liverpool L33 7UG, England

Telephone: +44 51 548 5000
Cable: Bicalcon, Kirkby
Telex: 627249
Telefax: +44 51 548 5320

Director and Commercial Manager: J A Turner
General Manager: F Rodgers

Products: Consultancy engineering studies, design, supply and installation and maintenance for electrification and trackwork worldwide. Turnkey projects undertaken demonstrating total capability in transport systems. Modern design and analysis techniques are utilised to provide optimum performance from the equipment. This is a system, developed by Balfour Beatty, which ensures before any design stage or even, if desired, at the tender stage, that the equipment proposed will give smooth, spark-free running. Design and quality assurance expertise ensure maximum utilisation of the electrified system with the minimum of maintenance.

MANUFACTURERS / Fixed electrification equipment

With over 80 years of experience, Balfour Beatty have electrified some 23,500 km of railways and have won design, supply and installation contracts in every continent of the world.

Recent contracts have included: trackwork and electrification at 750 V dc on the Tuen Mun LRT and the Eastern Harbour Mass Transit projects in Hong Kong, the electrification of Istanbul's LRT and design, supply and installation of trackwork on the Singapore Mass Rapid Transit project. Electrification at 3,000 V dc on the Recife Metro and Ferrovia do Aco lines in Brazil and 25 kV in Zimbabwe between Harare and Dabuka.

Balfour Beatty is currently electrifying British Rail's high-speed East Coast Main Line between London and Newcastle, designing the power systems in the Channel Tunnel and installing trackwork on the Docklands LRT and Stansted Airport high-speed link.

Barclay
Barclay Brothers Ltd

PO Box 1063, North Sydney, New South Wales 2060, Australia

Telephone: +61 2 922 7244
Telex: 72615 aa
Telefax: +61 2 922 4723

Products: Complete main-line and LRT electrification schemes, ac or dc.

BICC
BICC plc
Formerly British Insulated Callender's Cables

Devonshire House, Mayfair Place, London W1X 5FH, England

Telephone: +44 71 629 6622
Telex: 23463 bicc g
Telefax: +44 71 409 0070

Chairman: Sir William Barlow
Chief Executive: R A Biggam
Executive Directors: E Clark
  D W Cawthra
  R A Henderson
  H Schell

Principal subsidiaries
Balfour Beatty Power Construction Ltd
PO Box 12, Acornfield Road, Kirkby, Liverpool L33 7UG
Balfour Beatty Railway Engineering Ltd
Osmaston Street, Sandiacre, Nottinghamshire NG10 5AN

Products: Electric cables and conductors of all types and their associated accessories and fittings. Consultancy, design, supply and installation of civil, mechanical and electrical engineering for projects on a worldwide basis. Total capability in transport systems, specifically trackwork, electrification, power supply and distribution, telecommunications, SCADA and power remote control.

For recent contracts see Balfour Beatty entry in this section.

Sub-station of Mexico-Irapuato 25 kV 60 Hz line by Ansaldo Trasporti

Mobile sub-station for 25 kV ac Sardinia system by Ansaldo Trasporti

Brecknell, Willis
Brecknell, Willis & Co Ltd
Member of the Fandsten Electric Group

Chard, Somerset TA20 2DE, England

Telephone: +44 460 64941
Telex: 46518
Telefax: +44 935 79140

Chairman: Lord Tanlaw
Managing Director: Tony Hobbs

Marketing & Projects Manager: Tony White

Products: A complete range of current collection and power distribution equipment for all applications in the transportation sector. These include a range of pantographs for railways, tramways, metros and light rail systems.

Also complete third rail systems for railway and metro applications covering design, manufacture, supply and installation of third rail electrification systems.

Automatic gas tensioning equipment. Brecknell Willis supplies automatic gas tensioning equipment for

East Coast Main Line electrification by Balfour Beatty

750 V dc catenary for Tuen Mun LRT system, Hong Kong by BICC

better tensioning control in catenary and contact wire systems. A range of spring boxes is also available.

Broken Hill
Broken Hill Pty Co Ltd
Long Products Division

PO Box 521, Steelworks, Whyalla, South Australia 5608

Telephone: +61 96 40 4444
Telex: 80270 aa
Telefax: +61 86 40 4790

Products: Rolled and galvanised steel masts for catenary support.

CGE
Compagnie Générale d'Electricité

54 rue de la Boétie, 75382 Paris Cedex 08, France

Telephone: +33 1 40 76 10 10
Cable: Electricité, Paris 8
Telex: 280953

The companies within the CGE Group covering electrical contracting are: CGEE Alsthom; Comsip Entreprise; and Controle Bailey.

Products: Communications, electrical and electronic equipment and construction.
The Group has been concerned with numerous metro constructions in France and abroad, including those of Lyons, Marseilles, Montreal, Santiago, São Paulo, Mexico City, Rio de Janeiro, Caracas, Lisbon and Cairo.

Contransimex
Contransimex

PO Box 2006, 38 Dinicu Golescu Boulevard, Bucharest, Romania

Telephone: +40 0 180042
Cable: Ctrix, Bucharest
Telex: 11 606

Products: Railway construction and complete electrifications.

Delta
Delta Crompton Cables Ltd

Mill Marsh Lane, Brimsdown, Enfield, Middlesex EN3 7QD England

Telephone: +44 81 804 2468
Telex: 261749
Telefax: +44 81 804 7505

Managing Director: M W Horwood
Commercial Manager: I G Cummings
Marketing Manager: R A Hills
Export Manager: D Hayes

Products: Elastomer insulated railway signalling and track feeder cables; also a wide range of power, control and instrumentation cables insulated with various materials.
Regular suppliers to British Rail of signalling cables, track feeder cables and cables for traction vehicles and rolling stock. Cables for similar usage have been supplied to other customers including Hong Kong Mass Transit Railway Corporation.

EFE North America Inc
OB Transit Products

380 North Main St, Mansfield, Ohio 44903-1319, USA

Telephone: +1 419 522 7111
Cable: Electric
Telex: 987414
Telefax: +1 419 522 7069

President: John F Harkness
Vice President Marketing and Sales: Terry W Duffy
Product Manager, Car Equipment: T G Tarantino
Product Manager, Traction Distribution: P Bitsura

Products: Design, supply and installation of traction power distribution subsystems for catenary and trolley: catenary and trolley subsystem equipment and components; transit car electrical and electromechanical equipment, coupling and collection.
The company's latest overhead distribution contracts involve new light rail or trolley electrification projects in: Monterrey, Mexico; Vancouver, Canada; San Diego, Sacramento and San Francisco, California; Boston, Massachusetts; New Orleans, Louisiana; Seattle, Washington.
One recent new product development is a unique tunnel insulator to provide soft suspension of overhead contact wire in tunnels and under bridges.

Electric Rails
Electric Rails Ltd

PO Box 123, 00181 Helsinki 18, Finland

Telephone: +358 0 694 6501
Telex: 125550 finre
Telefax: +358 0 694 4975

Managing Director: J Salmivaara
Technical Director: S Saarinen

Products: Design, supply and installation of overhead equipment, supply installation of power lines.

Elektrim
Foreign Trade Company for Electrical Equipment, Poland

PO Box 638, Chalubinskiego 8, Warsaw, 00-950, Poland

Telephone: +48 22 30 10 00, 30 20 00
Telex: 814 351 pl
Telefax: +48 22 30 08 41/2

Products: Substations, overhead line equipment, dc switchgear, high-speed circuit breakers, signalling and telecommunications equipment, engineering and commissioning of signalling and telecommunications projects.

Ercole Marelli
Ercole Marelli Trazione SpA

Corso di Porta Romana 63, 20122 Milan, Italy

Sales office and works: Via le Edison 110, PO Box 17136, 20099 Sesto S Giovanni, Milan, Italy

Telephone: +39 2 24941
Telex: 302575 emtrfaz
Telefax: +39 2 248 8905

General Manager: U Lugo

Products: Converter and feeder sub-stations.

Ferraz SA
(See entry in Electric Traction Equipment section for full details.)

Products: Ac protistor fuses for the internal protection of the ac/dc and/or ac/dc/ac converters of substations, for large power filters and for auxiliary circuits; disconnectors to isolate sub-station converters; automatic fast-acting earthing device with large short-circuit capability, which can be either bi-or uni-directional.
Recent contracts include the supply of protistor fuses for converters and large filters for Swedish State Railways.

Fuji Electric
Fuji Electric Co Ltd

New Yurakucho Building 12-1, Yurakucho 1-chome, Chiyoda-ku, Tokyo 100, Japan

Telephone: +81 3 211 7111
Telex: 22331, 26374
Telefax: +81 3 214 2744

Products: Power supply equipment: remote supervisory control equipment with computer, freon cooling silicon rectifier, SF6 gas circuit breakers and mini high-speed circuit breakers; moulded transformer; total control systems including electric power management, station office apparatus control, data management and disaster prevention management.

Furrer & Frey

PO Box 3000, Thunstrasse 35, Berne 6, Switzerland

Telephone: +41 31 44 26 26
Telex: 912121 ff ch
Telefax: +41 31 4426 46

Products: Design and installation of overhead current supply equipment for electrifications up to 25 kV ac.

Ganz
Ganz Electric Works

PO Box 63, Lövóház utca 39, 1024 Budapest, Hungary

Telephone: +36 1 753 322
Telex: 225363
Telefax: +36 1 562 989

Products: Power supply equipment including: rotating machines, generators and converters. Substation equipment: transformers, switchgear, and complete sub-stations.
Heavy-current electronics equipment: rectifiers, choppers, inverters etc. and electronic controls.

GEC Alsthom Transmission and Distribution Projects
GEC Alsthom Transmission and Distribution Projects Ltd

PO Box 27, Stafford ST17 4LN, England

Telephone: +44 785 57111
Telex: 36203
Telefax: +44 785 52540

Managing Director: K J Ralls
Sales Director: E G Nolan

France
GEC Alsthom, Transport Division, 93404 Saint Ouen POB 165, 33 rue des Bâteliers

Telephone: +33 1 40 10 63 35

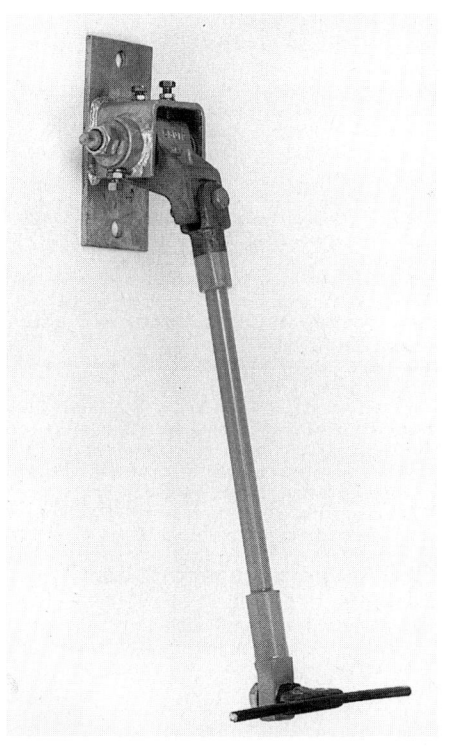

The new OB tunnel insulator supports and insulates overhead wire in tunnels and under bridges while its unique rubber torsion spring works to eliminate hard spots, increasing collector or pantograph life

342 MANUFACTURERS / Fixed electrification equipment

Telex: 234 317 F
Telefax: +33 1 40 10 61 00

Products: Comprehensive dc traction power supply systems comprising indoor or outdoor sub-stations including rectifiers, transformers, ac and dc switchgear, battery chargers and cabling; ac and dc power system studies.

Recent contracts executed include:
1986-90: transformers, rectifiers, ac and dc switchgear and power system study for Docklands Light Rail System and extension in the UK.
1988: rectifiers and dc sub-station equipment for extensions to Hong Kong MTR; truck-mounted rectifiers, transformers, dc switchgear and battery chargers for Hong Kong Tramways.
1988: rectifiers and switchboards for trolleybus system in Mexico City.
1988: replacement 1500 V dc arc chutes for Victoria State Transportation Authority, Australia.
1989-90: modular substations including transformers, rectifiers, ac and dc switchgear for the refurbishment of the London Underground Central Line.
1990: transformers, rectifiers, ac and dc switchgear for the new light rail Metrolink system in Manchester.

GEC Alsthom Transportation Projects
GEC Alsthom Transportation Projects Limited

Head office: PO Box 134, Manchester M60 1AH, England

Telephone: +44 61 872 2431
Telex: 665451
Telefax: +44 61 875 2131

Products: Main contractor for the supply, installation and project management of composite electric railway systems. (See also under Consultancy Services).

Geismar
Société des Anciens Etablissements L Geismar

113 bis avenue Charles de Gaulle, 92200 Neuilly-sur-Seine, France

Telephone: +33 1 47 47 55 00
Telex: 620 700
Telefax: +33 1 46 40 71 70

Products: Geismar provides equipment to build or maintain 25 kV ac, 1500 or 3000 V dc, 750 V dc catenary lines, including contact wire and catenary suspension grips and clips; contact wire splice clamps; ending sleeves; splice sleeves; feeder suspension clamps; electric power supply terminal plugs; automatic tension equipment; section insulators; ceramic insulators; composite insulators; disconnectors; overhead line erection, maintenance and servicing vehicles; catenary inspection gang cars; catenary inspection trailers.

Vancouver, Canada, linear motor-powered LRV incorporating GEC Alsthom 'Transidrive' power conversion units

Recife Metro, Brazil, for which GEC Alsthom designed and installed the power supply

General Electric Co (USA)

570 Lexington Avenue, New York, New York 10022, USA

Telephone: +1 212 750 3515
Cable: Ingeco, New York

Products: Sub-station equipment and automation.

Görlitz
VEB Waggonbau Görlitz

Brunnenstrasse 11, 8900 Görlitz, German Democratic Republic

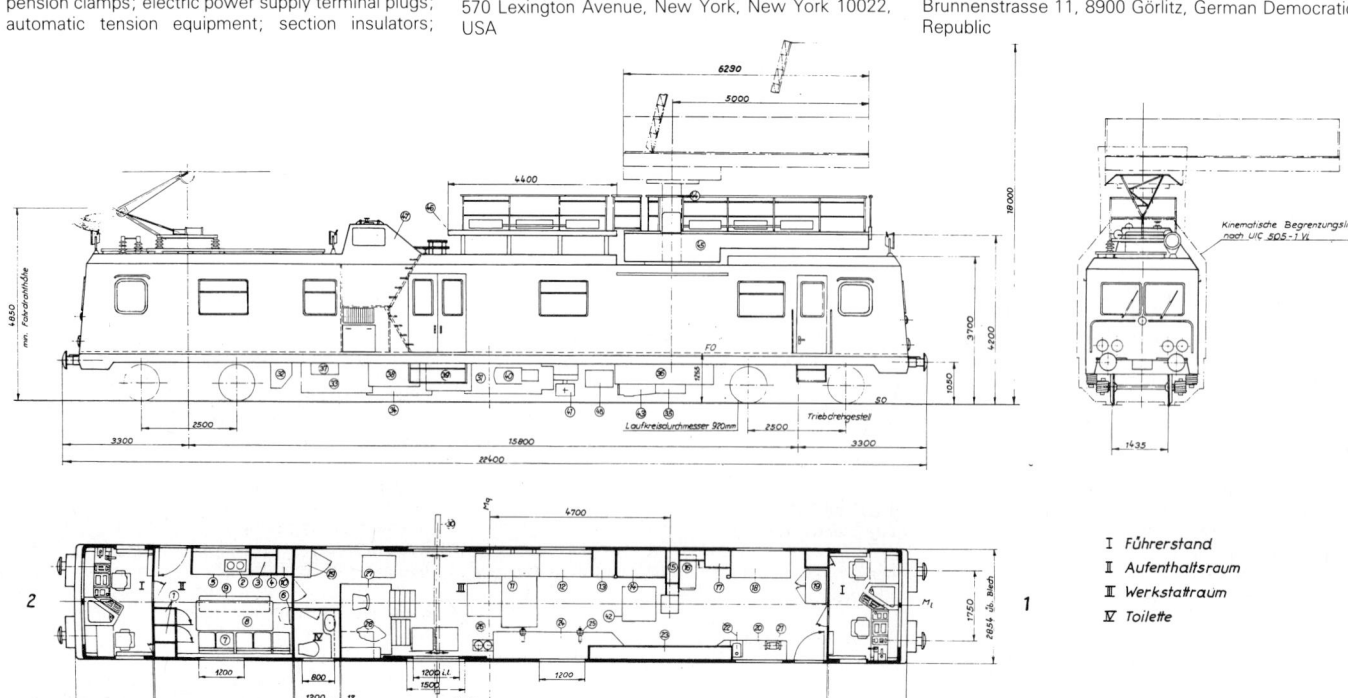

ORT catenary inspection railcar: general arrangement (Görlitz)

I Führerstand
II Aufenthaltsraum
III Werkstattraum
IV Toilette

Fixed electrification equipment / MANUFACTURERS

Telephone: +37 690
Cable: Waggonbau Görlitz
Telex: 02 86227

Export Director: Dieter Falkenberg

Product: Catenary inspection railcar (ORT) for electric railway operation.

The ORT has been developed for regular control and servicing of electrified lines as well as for short-time elimination of averages and failures occurring at the contact wires. The vehicle is provided with a diesel-hydraulic drive unit rated for a maximum running speed of 100 km/h, while the inside is sub-divided into a roomy workshop and rest area. The ORT railcar is equipped with a fixed and a swivellable working platform which can be lifted hydraulically. Operations at the catenary suspension in heights ranging from 8 to 18 m are achieved by means of a telescopic ladder. The glazed dome arranged on the roof ensures a good all-round view of the contact wire system and working platform.

The ORT recently won a design award from from the Industrial Design Office of the GDR.

Greysham
Greysham (International) Pvt Ltd

4-B Vandhna, 11 Tolstoy Marg, New Delhi 110 001, India

Telephone: +91 11 2523746, 2523989, 3313518, 3312969
Cable: Greyshamco
Telex: 031 63202 grey in
Telefax: +91 11 3310952

Managing Director: Govind Singh

Products: Overhead fittings for railway electrification projects.

Groupement 50 Hz
50 c/s Group

Baumackerstrasse 46, PO Box 8524, 8050 Zurich, Switzerland

Telephone: +41 1 312 46 80/81
Cable: Coordinat, Zurich
Telex: 823 854 sehz ch
Telefax: +41 1 312 3968

Products: Provision of complete electrifications including planning, design, technical co-ordination and installation.

Electrifications completely furnished by the Group have included: the Lisbon-Oporto line of Portuguese Railways (CP); Jung Ang, Tae Baeg and Yeong Dong lines of Korean National Railroad (KNR); and the Linea Bananera of Ferrocarriles de Costa Rica (FECOSA).

Constitution: The Group comprises ACEC Transport of Belgium, GEC Alsthom of France and UK, AEG Westinghouse and Siemens AG of the Federal Republic of Germany.

Hawker Siddeley
Hawker Siddeley Rail Projects

PO Box 319, Foundry Lane, Chippenham, Wiltshire SN15 1EE, England

Telephone: +44 249 654141
Telex: 445743 hsrp g
Telefax: +44 249 443165

Managing Director: W B Tait
Director: W B Johnston

Products: Complete electrification projects for main line, suburban, mass transit and light rail systems.

Hitachi Cable
Hitachi Cable, Ltd

ORT catenary inspection railcar (Görlitz)

Head office: Chiyoda Building, 2-1-2 Marunouchi, Chiyoda-ku, Tokyo 100, Japan

Telephone: +81 3 216 1611
Cable: Hitachicable, Tokyo
Telex: 222-2771 hitcbl j
Telefax: +81 3 213 0402

Main works: 5-1, Hitaka-Machi, Hitachi-City, Ibaraki-Pref 319-14

President: Hiroji Hashimoto
Executive Vice President: Kyoji Hikino
Director and General Manager, Overseas Division: Yoshiro Sadayuki

Subsidiary companies
Hitachi Cable (S) Pte Ltd, Singapore
Hitachi Cable America Inc, New York, USA
Hitachi Bangkok Cable Co Ltd, Thailand
Hitachi Shin Din Cable Ltd, Hong Kong

Products: Trolley wires, high-voltage low impedance coaxial feeders for ac electrification, Leaky coaxial cables, electro-magnetic induction-proof signal/communication cables, fiber-optic cables for use in monitoring and control system in electric train cars, superconducting wires for magnetic levitation vehicles, rubber pads, buffers and vibration isolators.

Recent contracts include 59 km of Leaky coaxial cables for China (1987); 24 km of Leaky coaxial cables for Australia (1989-90).

Lucas Automotive
Lucas Automative Ltd

Thermal Road, Bromborough, Merseyside L62 4TR, England

Telephone: +44 51 334 4040
Telex: 627020
Telefax: +44 51 334 7243

General Manager: P L Quinn
Manager, UK Sales: M T Tamagni
Manager, Overseas Sales: M D Evans

Products: Overhead catenary equipment and current collection apparatus.

Pirelli
Pirelli Construction Co Ltd

PO Box 6, Leigh Road, Eastleigh, Hampshire SO5 5YE, England

Telephone: +44 703 644522
Telex: 47615
Telefax: +44 703 642662

Managing Director: J Lewis
Director, Finance: A Atkinson
Commercial Manager: P Brooks

Business Manager, Special Projects: I Ellis
Business Manager, Telecommunications: N Hart
Business Manager, HU Power Projects (UK): B Nettleship
Business Manager, HU Power Projects (Overseas): J Bessey
Chief Engineer: H W Holdup

Products: Design, provision and erection of railway overhead and third rail electrification equipment; provision and installation of all types of power, signalling and communication cables; design and provision of specialised installation plant; design, provision and erection of towers for floodlights, radio, and tv surveillance; civil and electrical engineering.

Recent contracts include East Coast Main Line (ECML) Edinburgh-Chathill ac electrification (1988-89); ECML Cramlington-Chathill/Carstairs-Edinburgh ac electrification (1989-90); Guildford-Fratton optical and copper cable systems (British Telecom) (1988-89); Scotrail, Yoker scheme optical and copper cable systems (British Telecom) (1988-90).

Plasser
Plasser Australia Pty Ltd

PO Box 537, 2 Plasser Crescent, St Marys, New South Wales 2760, Australia

Telephone: +61 2 623 9033
Telex: 24140 aa
Telefax: +61 2 623 6502

Manager: H Hofstadler

Products: Vehicles and equipment for installation, inspection, monitoring and maintenance of overhead contact wire.

Powernetics Ltd

Jason Works, Clarence Street, Loughborough, Leicestershire LE11 1DX

Telephone: +44 509 214153
Telex: 34306
Telefax: +44 509 262460

Managing Director: Satish Chada
Export Manager: Margaret Foggon
National Sales Manager: Chris Smith
Production Manager: Chris Gilbert
Quality Manager: Alan Reilly
Chief Engineer, dc: Ken Woolston
Chief Engineer, ac: Kader Boukari

Products: Dc-dc converters, switch mode power supplies, battery chargers (RIA 12 and 13 approval); uninterruptable power supplies; static inverters; frequency changers.

Recent contracts include dc-dc converters for British Rail driver radio communications ((1989); UPS and dc

MANUFACTURERS / Fixed electrification equipment

Powernetics dc-dc converter

Catenaries for high-speed system of the Intercity Express (ICE)

systems for Channel Tunnel on behalf of ML Engineering (1989); 42 UPS systems for Hong Kong Mass Transit on behalf of Cable & Wireless (1988).

SAE Sadelmi
SAE Sadelmi SpA

Head office: Via Gustavo Fara 26, 20124 Milan, Italy

Telephone: +39 2 67591, 67721
Cable: Saemilan
Telex: 310188, 311094 saemil i
Telefax: +39 2 6759447, 67722415

Main works: Lecco (Como)

Chairman: Ing Achille Colombo
Managing Director: Ing G Orsi
Railway Electrification Engineering Director: Ing Claudio Masi

Products: Masts, structures and fittings for railway electrification and construction of overhead contact lines of any voltage in both dc and ac systems.
Recent contracts include 25 kV ac schemes in Sardinia (Italy) and Mexico, and 3 kV dc projects for Italian (FS) and North Milan (FNM) Railways.

SAE (India)
SAE (India) Limited

Head office: 29-30, Community Commercial Centre, Basant Lok, Vasant Vihar, New Delhi 110 057, India

Telephone: +91 11 675425 (8 lines)
Cable: Saelines, New Delhi
Telex: 31 62514 saer in, 31 65278 saer in
Telefax: +91 11 6873963

Main works: Deori, PO Panagar, District Jabalpur (MP)

Telephone: (Panagar) 24/5
Cable: Saelines Jabalpur
Telex: 765 221 sae in

Director and General Manager: F Sias
Assistant to Director and General Manager: M Dutta

Products: Design, supply and erection of 3 kV dc, 25 kV and 2 × 25 kV ac 50 Hz overhead equipment, traction sub-stations, switching stations, HT sub-stations and booster transformer stations for railway electrification. The company has equipped 5800 km of Indian Railways track for both 3 kV and 25 kV traction. The company also engages in telecommunications and signalling activity connected with ac traction.

Remote control centre by Siemens on Munich U-Bahn

SAFT

156 avenue de Metz, 93230 Romainville, France

Telephone: +33 1 48 43 9361
Telex: 235566
Telefax: +33 1 49 42 3400

Chairman: Claude Darmon
Managing Director: Francois Putois
Sales Manager: Philippe Ulrich

Products: Nickel-cadmium batteries, with pocket or sintered plastic bonded electrodes for supplying energy to all fixed electrification equipment.
These batteries are used by Singapore Metro, Pakistan Railways, CP Rail and DB (Germany).

SET Schadt
SET Schadt Elektrotechnik GmbH

Siemens VT 324, Bruckwiesenstrasse 5, 6700 Ludwigshafen, Federal Republic of Germany

Telephone: +49 621 571 841
Telex: 464746

Products: Overhead line and contact equipment, insulators.

Siemens
Siemens Aktiengesellschaft

Werner-von-Siemens Strasse 50, PO Box 3240, 8520 Erlangen, Federal Republic of Germany

Telephone: +49 9131 721807
Cable: Siemens Erlangen
Telex: 62921 508 si d
Telefax: +49 9131 721807

Transportation Systems Group President: W O Martinsen
Turnkey Systems Division: H Wittmann
Traction Power Supplies Department: R Mades

Products: Ac and dc traction power supply equipment; network automation, transmission lines, catenaries; complete projects for railway electrification schemes.
Recent turnkey contracts have covered: traction power supply and catenary systems for light rail systems in Portland, Oregon and San Jose, California, Tunis, Guadalajara and Medellin; process computerised control and supervisory systems for several cities worldwide and for Danish, South African and Italian Railways.

Siemens Electric
Siemens Electric Ltd

1180 Courtney Park Drive, Mississauga, Ontario L5T 2P2, Canada

Telephone: +1 416 673 1995
Telex: 06 968980

Manager, Traction Systems: H Franzen

Products: Power supply, distribution equipment for overhead wire or third-rail systems.

Fixed electrification equipment / MANUFACTURERS

Siemens Energy & Automation
Siemens Energy & Automation Inc
Transportation Industry

150 Hembree Park Drive, CS 100150, Roswell, Georgia 30077-7150, USA

Telephone: +1 404 751 3180
Telex: 543281
Telefax: +1 404 664 0672

Segment Manager: Werner Katerkamp

Products: Dc substations and catenary: design, supply and installations.

Siette
Alcatel Face Group

Viale Belfiore 26, 50144 Florence, Italy

Telephone: +39 55 4790
Telex: 570118
Telefax: +39 55 4790

Main works: Via Provinciale Lucchese 33, 50019 Osmannoro, Sesto Fiorentino, Florence

Telephone: +39 55 352061
Telefax: +39 55 352061

Overseas offices
Egypt
4 Midan Hiet B1 Tadriss, Dokky, Cairo
Telephone: +20 701444
Telex: 93121

Mozambique
Rua Don Sebastiao, 100 Sommershield, Maputo
Telephone: +258 743145
Telex: 6602

Zaire
Avenue Masikita 219 binza, IPN, Kinshasa
Telephone: +243 12 80064

Products: Siette designs and supplies the following on a turnkey basis: contact lines; primary lines (high voltage); telecommunications systems; co-axial cable and optical fibre transmission systems for video, voice and data.

Sigla
Sigla Equipamentos Electricos Ltda

Av Brigadeiro Faria Lima 2003, 14o Andar, 01451 São Paulo SP, Brazil

Telephone: +55 11 210 3299
Telex: 011 83171
Telefax: +55 11 813 0943

Director, Branch Transportation: Massimo Andrea Giavina-Bianchi

Products: Traction substations.

SM
SMC Pneumatics (Australia) Pty Ltd
Transport Division

161 Showground Road, Castle Hill, New South Wales 2154, Australia

Telephone: +61 2 680 3222
Telex: 7123152
Telefax: +61 2 634 7764

Products: Current collection pantographs and carbon wear strips for ac and dc power supply.
Recent contracts have included supply of pneumatic door operating equipment and current collection pantographs for the Hong Kong KCRC LRV project, SRA of NSW suburban, interurban and XPT passenger cars and 25 kV pantographs for Queensland Rail heavy haulage locomotives.

SPIE Batignolles
SPIE-Batignolles Trindel
Catenary group

Parc Saint-Cristophe, Edison 3, 95861 Cergy-Pontoise Cedex, France

Telephone: +33 1 34 22 50 50
Telex: 699538 p

Products: Catenary equipment.

Strojexport Company Ltd

PO Box 662 886, Václavské n 56, Prague 1, Czechoslovakia

Telephone: +42 2 2131
Cable: Strojexport, Praha
Telex: 121671, 121604
Telefax: +42 2 23 23 084, 23 23 092

General Director: Ing Josef Regner
Deputy General Director: Stanislav Vrabec
Commercial Director: Frantisek Forgdas

Products: Railway electrification equipment.

Technopol
Foreign Trade Corporation

Bratislava, Czechoslovakia

Products: Complete railway electrification projects.

Thorn EMI
Thorn EMI Electronics Ltd
Automation Division

PO Box 4, Rugeley, Staffordshire WS15 1DR, England

Telephone: +44 889 585151
Telex: 36135
Telefax: +44 889 578209

Managing Director: Geoffrey P Hough
Industrial Products Manager: Barry Carr

Products: Traction rectifier equipment.
Much equipment is supplied as part of a comprehensive contract involving transformers, rectifiers, ac and dc switchgear, supervisory control and auxiliary equipment. Modernisation with silicon rectifier replacements for ageing mercury arc equipment have also been undertaken.
Recent installations include power supply equipment for London Regional Transport, British Rail, the Tyne and Wear Metro and Channel Tunnel Project in the UK, and major extensions to the Mexico City Metro.
Under a contract from British Rail to supply power conversion equipment for BR Southern Region's Bournemouth to Weymouth and Sanderstead to East Grinstead electrification schemes, the company will move away from traditional brick-built substations and deliver complete packaged power supplies, each capable of supplying 1.5 MW at 750 V dc. Since each containerised substation will be delivered fully equipped, requiring only securement to a prepared concrete base and electrical connection, installation times and costs (and disruption to timetables) will be considerably reduced.

TIBB
Tecnomasio Italiano Brown Boveri SpA
Company of the Brown Boveri Group

CP 10225, 20137 Milan, Italy

Telephone: +39 2 5797 1
Cable: Tecnomasio, Milano
Telex: 310153

Products: Static and rotary converters for auxiliary services; dc and ac generators; single-arm pantographs and electromagnetic rail brakes; substations for dc traction.
Recent contracts have included one for four Type A140 mobile substations of 3600 kW-150 kV/3–6 kV dc for the Italian State Railways.

Toshiba
Toshiba Corporation
Railway Projects Department

Toshiba Building, 1-1 Shibaura 1-chome, Minato-ku, Tokyo 105, Japan

Telephone: +81 3 457 4924
Cable: Toshiba, Tokyo
Telex: J22587 toshiba
Telefax: +81 3 457 8385

Overseas Offices: Buenos Aires, São Paulo, Rio de Janeiro, Mexico, Colombia, Caracas, Vienna, Athens, Berlin, Johannesburg, Cairo, Teheran, Jeddah, Kuwait, Dubai, Baghdad, Bangkok, Taipei, Manila, Hong Kong, Jakarta, Beijing, Wellington

Toshiba International Corporation: San Francisco, Houston, Tulsa, Vancouver

Toshiba International Corporation Pty Ltd: Sydney

Toshiba International (Europe) Ltd: London

Products: Dc and ac railway substation equipment; supervisory control systems; transformers; rectifiers; circuit breakers; arresters.

Transmitton
Transmitton Ltd
A BICC company

Smisby Road, Ashby-de-la-Zouch, Leicestershire LE6 5UG, England

Telephone: +44 530 415941
Telex: 341628 traind g
Telefax: +44 530 411484

Managing Director: S N Hicks
General Manager, Industrial Division: D Moore

Products: The Mocrotel 700 System provides a comprehensive control of monitoring system featuring a computer masterstation with colour graphics and wall mimic overview. The outstations are microprocessor-based.
Supervisory control projects for various electrified

Supervisory control system with two TOSBAC computers controlling 26 substations of Kinki Nippon Railway, Japan, by Toshiba

lines have been delivered and installed, including the first phase of the East Coast Main Line. The supervisory control equipment for the final phase of the line was being designed and manufactured at the Transmitton factory in Ashby-de-la-Zouch at the start of 1988.

Westinghouse Electric Australasia Ltd

PO Box 13, Villawood, New South Wales, 2163, Australia

Telephone: +61 2 724 7322
Telex: 22763 aa
Telefax: +61 2 7269757

General Manager, Australia: Stan Elias
General Manager, NSW: Michael Sharkey
Marketing Manager, Australia: David Norris

Products: Electric traction equipment; dc and ac traction motors; on-board transformers and reactors; compressor motors; replacement equipment.

Whipp & Bourne Ltd
An FKI Company

Switchgear Works, Castleton, Rochdale OL11 2SS, England

Telephone: +44 706 32051
Telex: 63442 whipps g
Telefax: +44 706 345896

Managing Director: P J Stott
Export & Marketing Director: P R Thompson

Products: dc switchgear and circuit breakers.

Wickham
D Wickham & Co Ltd

Crane Mead, Ware, Hertfordshire SG12 9QA, England

Telephone: +44 920 462491
Cable: Wickham, Ware
Telex: 81340
Telefax: +44 920 460733

Joint Managing Director: D S Holden
Joint Managing Director: T H Baillie
Sales Director: G P Redfern
Technical Director, Railway Products: A P Mott

Products: Overhead line inspection cars.

Permanent way equipment

ARGENTINA
- Artimsa 349
- Famatex 359

AUSTRALIA
- Amatek 349
- BHP 351
- Electrologic 358
- Gemco 361
- Holland 363
- Humes 363
- McKay 368
- Mitchell Equipment 369
- Moss 369
- Sonit 380
- Tamper-Holland Welding 382

AUSTRIA
- Getzner 361
- Linsinger 366
- Plasser 372
- Semperit 378
- Sola 379
- Vöest-Alpine 385

BELGIUM
- Buhlmann 354
- Jambes-Namur 364
- Lauwaert 366

BRAZIL
- Cobrasma 355
- Jaragua 364
- Premesa 374
- Thebra 383

CANADA
- Algoma 348
- CXT 356
- Kershaw 365
- Modern Track Machinery 369
- Nortrak 370
- Sydney Steel 382
- Tipco 383
- Woodings Railcar 386

CHINA
- Zweiweg-Fahrzeug 386

FINLAND
- Rauma-Repola 376

FRANCE
- Aluminothermique 348
- Boulonnerie de Thiant 352
- CFF 354
- Coborail-Extrapo 354
- COGIFER 355
- Dehé 356
- Delachaux 356
- Desquenne et Giral 356
- D'Huart 357
- FAO 359
- Framafer 360
- Geismar 360
- Matériel de Voie 367
- Matix-Industries 367
- MIO 369
- Pouget 374
- Sateba 378
- SECEMM 378
- Spie Batignolles 381
- Stedef 382
- SYCAFER 382
- TSO 384

GERMANY, FEDERAL REPUBLIC
- Arneke 349
- Atlas Weyhausen 350
- Beilhack 351
- Bomag 352
- Bruckner & Thomas GBR 353
- Butzbacher 354
- Cemafer 354
- Clouth 354
- Elektro-Thermit 358
- EXIM 358
- Ferrostaal 359
- Gottwald 362
- Hoesch Rothe Erde-Schmiedag 363

- Klockner-Werke 365
- Koehring 366
- Krautkrämer 366
- Newag Eurorail 369
- Phoenix 371
- Pintsch Bamag 371
- Plastica 373
- Rawie 376
- Robel 376
- SATO 378
- Thyssen Engineering 383
- Turk & Hillinger 385
- Vossloh-Werke 385
- Windhoff 386
- WTB 386

INDIA
- Cimmco 354
- HDC 363
- Richardson & Cruddas 376

ITALY
- Donelli 357
- ILVA 363
- IPA 364
- Italsider 364
- ITI/CLM 364
- Matema 366
- Matisa SpA 367
- SICFA 379
- SILF 379

JAPAN
- Daido 356
- Mitsukawa 369
- Nippon Kido Kogyo 369
- NKK 369
- PS Concrete 374
- Tetsudo Kiki 383
- Tokyo Keiki 383
- Toyo Kizaii 384
- Yamato Kogyo 386

LUXEMBOURG
- KIHN 365

MEXICO
- Monterrey 369

NETHERLANDS
- AKZO 348
- Kloos Railway Engineering 366
- Noord-Ned 369
- Strukton Spoorwegbouw 382

SOUTH AFRICA
- Bain 350
- Conbrako 355
- Grinaker Precast 362
- Trackmaster 384

SPAIN
- Ferrovias y Siderurgia 359
- Talleres de Amurrio 382

SWEDEN
- Abetong 348
- Berema 351
- Centro-Maskin 354
- ESAB 358
- GCE 360
- GIA 362
- Scania 378
- SRS 381

SWITZERLAND
- BBR 350
- EWEM 358
- Intramatic 364
- KAGO 365
- Matisa 367
- Rail-Wel 375
- Rolba 377
- Schlatter 378
- Speno 380
- Von Roll 385

USSR
- Energomachexport 358

UK
- Abtus 348
- Atlas Copco 349
- Atlas Hydraulic Loaders Ltd 349
- Balfour Beattie 350
- Bance 350
- British Steel Track Products 352
- Bruff 353
- BTR 353
- BTR Permali 354
- Colebrand 355
- Cooper & Turner 355
- Costain 355
- Cowans Boyd 356
- Dow Mac 357
- Edgar Allen 357
- Euro-Trac 358
- Fairfield-Mabey 358
- Ferotrack 359
- Findlay, Irvine 359
- Grant Lyon Eagre 362
- Grove Coles 362
- GTC 363
- Hunslet 363
- HWD 363
- Jakem 364
- JW 364
- Kango 365
- Lamp 366
- Lindapter 366
- McGregor 368
- Oleo 370
- Pandrol 371
- Permali 371
- Permaquip 371
- Portec (UK) 374
- Sika 379
- Skelton 379
- Sonatest 379
- Tempered Spring 383
- Thermit Welding 383
- Thomas Robinson 383
- VAI 385
- Wells-Krautkramer 385
- Wickham 385
- Zwicky 386

USA
- ABC 348
- A & K 348
- Aldon 348
- Allegheny 348
- American Railroad Curvelining Corporation 349
- Atlantic Track 349
- Bethlehem Steel 351
- BHP 351
- Burro Crane 354
- Bylin 354
- CF&I Steel 354
- Chemetron 354
- Cobra-X 354
- CXT 356
- Fairmont 358
- Ferrostaal 359
- Foss 360
- Foster 360
- Holland 363
- International Track Systems 364
- Jackson Jordan 364
- Kershaw 365
- Koppers 366
- Loram 366
- Lord 366
- Midwest Steel 368
- Moore & Steele 369
- Nordco 369
- Orton 370
- Osmose 370
- Pettibone 371
- Plasser 372
- Portec Inc 373
- Racine 374
- Rails Co 375
- Raychem 376
- Salient 377
- Schramm 378
- Sigmaform 379
- Sperry 381
- Swingmaster 382
- Szarka 382
- Tamper Corp 382
- Templeton 383
- True Temper 384
- Unit Rail Anchor 385
- Western-Cullen-Hayes 385

MANUFACTURERS / Permanent way equipment

Abetong
Abetong AB

PO Box 24, 351 03 Växjö, Sweden

Telephone: +46 470 10010
Telex: 52145 abetong s
Telefax: +46 470 160 81

Main works: Vislanda

Managing Director: Jan-Erik Håkansson
Technical Director: Stefan Westberg
Marketing Director: Stig Thim

Subsidiary: Swedish Rail System AB SRS, Solna

Products: Concrete sleepers for main-line and turnouts in main lines, sidings etc; LRT sleepers; grade crossings; technical services for manufacture and design of concrete sleepers.

Some 150 000 main-line sleepers per year are made for Swedish State Railways (SJ) at Vislanda, as well as sleepers for turnouts, prefabricated crane tracks and concrete elements for level crossing systems. The present plant produces prestressed reinforced monolithic sleepers designed for 22-ton axleloads at 200 km/h. The company has supplied its knowhow to some 15 different factories worldwide; together these plants have now produced and supplied over 20 million sleepers.

The company has designed for the Hamersley Iron Ore Railway of Western Australia, for Canadian National Railways and Conrail (USA) concrete sleepers for heavy duty switches to suit traffic specifications of 37 tonnes maximum and 30 tonnes nominal axleloads at up to 80 km/h, and annual gross train tonnages of more than 50 million.

ABC
ABC Rail Corporation

200 South Michigan Avenue, Chicago, Illinois 60604, USA

Telephone: +1 312 322 0360
Telex: 756108
Telefax: +1 312 322 0377

Products: Trackwork products.

Abtus
Abtus Co

PO Box 35, Ascot, Berkshire SL5 7LE, England

Telephone: +44 990 24312

Works: 4 Rookwood Way, Haverhill, Suffolk CB9 8PB

Products: Power and manual bond drilling machines, track aligners, measured packing equipment, gauges.

A & K
A & K Railroad Materials Inc

PO Box 30076, Salt Lake City, Utah 84130, USA

Telephone: +1 801 974 5484
Telex: 713789466

Chairman: K W Schumacher
President: M H Kulmer

Products: Complete switches, frogs, anchors, bolts, spikes, lockwashers, gauge rods, sleepers, hand track tools.

AKZO Industrial Systems BV

PO Box 9300, Velperweg 76, 6800SB Arnhem, Netherlands

Telephone: +31 85 662615
Telex: 45204
Telefax: +31 85 662070

Manager, Geotechnics: Wim Voskamp

Products: Reinforced sleeper beds, track components.

Aldon
The Aldon Co

3410 Sunset Avenue, Waukegan, Illinois 60087, USA

Telephone: +1 312 623 8800

Products: Lightweight straddle-type rerailers; track levellers; track gauges; track jacks; safety derailers; rail benders.

Algoma
The Algoma Steel Corporation Ltd

Suite 900, Four Robert Speck Parkway, Mississauga Ontario L4Z 1S1, Canada

Telephone: +1 416 276 1400
Telex: 06965531
Telefax: +1 416 276 1452

President and Chief Executive Officer: Peter M Nixon
General Manager, Marketing & Sales: Ian E Williams
Executive Vice-President: Gary S Lucenti
Asst General Manager: Alex Stewart
Sales Manager: Edward M Small
Marketing Manager: C Gerald Hutchinson

Products: Three main grades of steel rails: standard carbon, intermediate and premium alloy. Carbon and intermediate rails are produced to AREA and international specifications, whereas chromium alloy rails are produced to Algoma's proprietary specifications.

Algoma Steel has recently completed a C$40 million upgrading of its rail facilities and is now the only fully integrated steel producer on the North American continent to continuously cast all its steel-making capability.

A new in-line head-hardening unit is under evaluation to provide a new standard of high-performance rails. The process involved has been patented by Algoma under the trade name of AWC.

Allegheny
Allegheny Rail Products
A division of TASA Corp

Suite 990, Two Gateway Center, Pittsburgh, Pennsylvania 15222, USA

Algoma Steel's upgraded rail manufacturing plant; rail can be produced to a maximum length of 25 m

Manganese switch diamond weld by L'Aluminothermique

Telephone: +1 412 391 2141
Telefax: +1 412 391 2147

Sales Manager: Wayne D Dash
Vice-President: W Bary Colins
Vice-President & General Manager: Robert O Walter

Products: Insulated rail joints, epoxy bonded and 'Toughcoat'.

The Allegheny D bar-bonded rail joint uses the company's Temprange epoxy to bond the full contact, high-strength steel joint bars and rails together, freeze them into position and prevent movement. The epoxy adhesive fills all voids. Epoxy-bonded joints stay tight and in combination with specified rail end hardness (363-401 BHN) can be maintained and perform as cwr. Insulated or non-insulated kits are available. Standard fasteners include structural high-strength bolts and pin bolts. Insulated joint field kits include two insulated bars, epoxy, fasteners and insulating components. Plug assemblies are available in any shipping lengths.

Allegheny 'Toughcoat' insulated rail joints are designed for heavy duty rail locations. Designs are available for 90 lb RA and most other rail sections of 100 lb and heavier. Core bars are first sandblasted to bright metal, followed by an adhesive-primed coating, and total encapsulation in polyurethane to a controlled thickness. The core bars are full rail contact style. Six- and four-hole bars are produced. Joint kits include insulated core bars, washer plates, end post, bushings and fasteners for field installation. Double rail joints are also available.

Aluminothermique
L'Aluminothermique

ZI du Bas Pré, 59590 Raismes, France

Telephone: +33 27 25 55 55
Telex: 110 832
Telefax: +33 27 36 72 98

General Manager: François Gibert

Overseas distributors
USA: Du Wel, 360 Scott Street, Elk Grove Village, Illinois 60007
BRW (USA) Inc, 26 Interstate Drive, PO Box 69, Napoleon, Ohio 43545

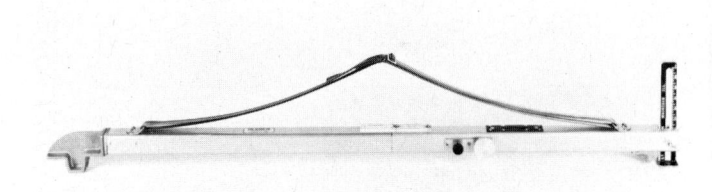

Aldon adjustable combination track level and gauge, easily portable and weighing only 9 lb

Canada: Rail Alu, 5610 Bois Franc, St Laurent, Quebec H4S 1A9
Hong Kong
Australia: BRW Ltd, Unit 1, Dennis Court, 8 Dennis Road, Springwood, Queensland 4127

Products: Rail welding equipment. The company specialises in the Boutet processes of aluminothermic welding for all rail profiles, and for manganese switch diamonds. Other speciality: fixed and mobile welding yard.

Amatek
Amatek Limited

Head office: 6-8 Thomas Street, PO Box 295, Chatswood, New South Wales 2067, Australia

Telephone: +612 411 9611
Telex: 126673 aa
Telefax: +612 411 1777

Managing Director: G J Ashton
General Manager, Concrete Products Division: J F Kelly
Manager, Structural Components (Sleepers): C E Williamson

Associated companies:
BTR Nylex
Lone Star Monier Concrete Tie Co, 701 W 47th Avenue, Denver, Colorado 80216 USA
Telephone: +1 303 296 3500
Telefax: +1 303 297 2255

Associated Concrete Products (M) Sdn Bhd, Wisma APMC, Level 3, No 2 Jalan Kilang, 46050 Petaling Jaya, Selangor, Malaysia
Telephone: +603 791 8788
Telefax: +603 791 7309

Resource Development Corporation
10 Jalan Gali Batu, Off 19 km, Woodlands Road, Singapore 2367
Telephone: +65 769 8832
Telefax: +65 769 4101

Products: Concrete sleepers; plant and equipment for manufacture of prestressed concrete sleepers.

Amatek has developed an efficient and economical method of producing prestressed concrete sleepers adaptable to a wide range of plant capacity requirements. The system is available for licence.

Other products manufactured by Amatek include pre-cast level crossings, box culverts, concrete pipes, prestressed concrete piles and bridge girders, spun concrete transmission and lighting poles and many other products used in engineering and building construction industries.

Amatek has developed the Multilok System which is a fastening system used in conjunction with Pandrol or Mackay 'Safelok' resilient fasteners or 24 mm diameter bolts to permit lateral or rotational adjustment of fasteners in track. The system is suitable for slab track, turnouts and gauge conversion in main line tracks.

Recent contracts have included a $A40 million order for concrete sleepers for Australian National involving supply of one million sleepers over five years.

Amatek has manufactured over six million prestressed concrete sleepers throughout the world including Canada, America, Singapore and Australia and has manufactured in broad, standard, metre and narrow gauge track.

American Railroad Curvelining Corporation

137 Hollywood Avenue, Douglaston, Long Island, New York 11363-1110, USA

Telephone: +1 718 224 1135
Telefax: +1 718 631 3304

Chief Executive Officer: R A Fichter
President: J M Flechter
Subsidiaries: Bondarc Division
Marine Division

Products: Track geometry analysis; curve lining computers; roll ordinators; Trakchek; Trakanalyzer. Recent products include the Archimedes high memory, graphic display curveliner. Archimedes stores practically unlimited volumes of information. Using the latest video technology, it displays the middle ordinate diagram in full size, while identifying the diagram of original ordinates, in one colour, the corrected diagram in another and the super elevation in a third colour. The system automatically highlights the area currently being worked on in a fourth colour. It can be supplied in a set of separate components, and can be interfaced with IBM-PC and other systems. The high capacity built-in memory can give the division engineer complete control of all maintenance work in the division. Versines are fed directly from the Roll-Ordinator III to Archimedes or to Archimedes programme on the division PC.

Arneke
Heinrich Arneke & Co

Seelze, Hannover, Federal Republic of Germany

Telephone: +49 511 5137818

Products: Sleeper placing machines and tracklaying equipment.

Artimsa
Artimsa SAIC

25 de Mayo, 12th Floor, 1002 Buenos Aires, Argentina

Telephone: +54 31 3054/56

Products: Rail fastenings, fishplates, creep anchors.

Atlantic Track
Atlantic Track and Turnout Co

270 Broad Street, Bloomfield, New Jersey 07003, USA

Telephone: +1 201 748 5885
Telex: 138049 attrack
Telefax: +1 201 748 4520

Chairman: G L Morrow
Chief Executive: R H Dreesen
President & Chief Operating Officer: A P Engel

Cobra self-contained tamper by Atlas Copco

Export Sales Director: P A Hughes
Domestic Sales Director: J L Schafer
Plant Operations Director: J R Jones

Products: All ASCE, AREA, ARA-A, ARA-B rail sections currently produced; full line of relay rail and special trackwork; track accessories including switch materials and maintenance tools.

Atlas Copco
Atlas Copco (Great Britain) Ltd

PO Box 79, Swallowdale Lane, Hemel Hempstead, Hertfordshire HP2 7HA, England

Telephone: +44 442 61201
Telefax: +44 442 214106

Products: Portable and stationary compressors, self-contained power tamper/drill and pneumatic equipment, pumps, tampers.

Atlas Hydraulic Loaders Ltd

Wharfedale Road, Euroway Estate, Bradford, West Yorkshire BD4 6SE, England

Telephone: +44 274 686827
Telex: 51404 atsale g
Telefax: +44 274 687889

General Manager: Ulrich Weter
Sales Manager: Martin Stafford

Products: Road/rail excavators.

Atlas road/rail excavators have been on permanent way work for the world's railroads since the mid-1960s. AB 1302 DK and AB 1602 DK wheeled excavators are the most frequently selected models for rail use, since these short-deck versions keep clear of the loading gauge of adjacent tracks during many of the operations they are called upon to perform. Alternatively, their excavator superstructures can be mounted on other rail vehicles or operated as stationary units. The German Federal Railway specification for these Atlas excavators uses four large-section tyres running on the sleeper heads outside the rails, so

MANUFACTURERS / Permanent way equipment

Atlas AB 1602 DK excavator

that the tyres cannot be damaged. The excavator's normal steering lock angle is sufficient to drive it away from the rail track without effort, or cross points. An additional dozer and support blade gives the excavators extra load capacity, particularly along the line of the chassis.

Atlas Weyhausen GmbH

PO Box 1844, Stedinger Str 324, 2870 Delmenhorst, W Germany

Telephone: +49 4221 4910
Telex: 249238
Telefax: +49 4221 491213

Chairman: Dipl Ing Günter Weyhausen
Marketing Director: Gerhard Brünjes

Products: Road/rail excavators and loading cranes.

Bain
William Bain & Co

PO Box 132, Boksburg, Transvaal, South Africa

Telephone: +27 11 892 2920
Telex: 74 1029
Telefax: +27 11 521 932

Managing Director: W C Ebersohn
Export Director: R Morgan
Marketing & Sales Director: J H Laurens

Products: Rail, points, crossings, track components and forgings.

Bance portable impact wrench

Balfour Beatty
Balfour Beatty Railway Engineering Ltd

Osmaston Street, Sandiacre, Nottinghamshire NG10 5AN England

Telephone: +44 602 390125
Telex: 37256
Telefax: +44 602 390000

General Manager/Director: R A Gray
Manufacturing Director: D M Ingham
Contracting Director: B Waterhouse
Commercial Director: N J Duffy

Products: Comprehensive trackwork service including consultancy, design, manufacturing, contracting, maintenance and spare parts; manufacturing includes switches and crossings, turnouts, lever boxes, sliding buffer stops, steel sleepers, turntables, cast products and other ancillary equipment; the services can be provided as discreet items or as a package and cover narrow gauge applications, LTR/Metro projects and main line schemes.

Contracts recently completed include the mass transit and Tuen Mun LRT projects in Hong Kong; the Singapore Mass Transit and the Stansted Airport Link, UK.

Current contracts include extensions to the London Docklands light railway, supply of construction track equipment for the Channel Tunnel and supply of switches and crossings around the world for both light rail use and heavy haul including British Railways, USA, India, Tunisia and Iraq.

Balfour Beatty have recently acquired the railway interests of Henry Boot Railway Engineering Ltd.

Bance
R Bance & Co Ltd

Cockcrow Hill House, St Mary's Road, Surbiton, Surrey KT6 5HE, England

Telephone: +44 81 398 7141
Telex: 928280

Products: Tapered rail joint shims for maintaining jointed track; portable impact wrenches; track spanners; ballast forks; slewing bars; chisels; fish-bolts and nuts; screwspikes; rail clips; shunting equipment including radio-controlled shunters.

BBR
Bureau BBR Ltd

Rieschachstrasse 57, PO Box CH-8034 Zurich, Switzerland

Telephone: +41 1 383 1910
Telex: 816418 staz ch
Telefax: +41 1 383 6640

Atlas 1304 railway excavator

Eastern Harbour Crossing, Hong Kong, supplied and installed by Balfour Beatty Railway Engineering

Permanent way equipment / **MANUFACTURERS** 351

Pionjär combination drill, breaker and ballast tamper for sleeper tamping (Berema)

Chairman: P-Ing A Brandestini
Vice-Chairman: P-Ing G Zenobi
Managing Director: P-Ing F Speck
Managing Director, Export: P-Ing N Winkler

Products: Prestressed concrete sleepers system BBR-THOSTI and BBR-Hibond.
 Contracts include orders from India, Indonesia and Sri Lanka.

Beilhack
Martin Beilhack GmbH

Postfach 160, 8200 Rosenheim 2, Federal Republic of Germany

Telephone: +49 80 31 4033
Telex: 05 25840

Products: Light, demountable ploughs with clearing width of 3.15 metres; heavy, special snow ploughs, model PB600 with adjustable clearing width of 3 to 6 metres; demountable snow blowers with approximately 2.5 tonnes per hour clearing capacity; snow blowers with adjustable clearing head, clearing width of 3 to 6 metres; self-propelled and pushed special snow removal machines, reversible for clearing operations in both directions, with a clearing capacity of up to approximately 14 tonnes per hour.

Berema
Berema AB
A company in the Atlas Copco Group

Box 1286, Svetsarvägen 20, S171 25 Solna, Sweden

Telephone: +46 8 627 3300
Telex: 105 32 berema s

Press Officer: Mrs Anita Wunderman

Products: Pionjär self-contained petrol-powered combination drill, breaker and ballast tamper for construction, maintenance and permanent way work. It switches from drilling to breaking in seconds. With a wide number of tools and accessories the combination machine can be used for ballast tamping, digging trenches, compacting refill, breaking concrete, splitting rock, driving signposts, hammering spikes and drilling holes in rock or concrete. A simpler version exclusively for ballast tamping can also perform normal breaking, digging and compacting jobs. The machines weigh from 21 to 26 kg depending upon model, and deliver 70 000 ft/lb (9500 J) of work per minute, sufficient for effective ballast tamping. Compared to manual methods, for example in digging cable trenches, the Berema machine reduces manpower costs by over 50 per cent and increases speed and efficiency of work.

Bethlehem Steel
Bethlehem Steel Corporation
Shape and Rail Products Division

Industry Marketing, Room 1343, SGO Building, Bethlehem, Pennsylvania 18016, USA

Telephone: +1 215 694 2424

Main works: Steelton, Pennsylvania 17113
Telephone: +1 717 939 8011

Chairman: Walter F Williams
Export Manager: John Palmer
Manager, Sales and Marketing (Steelton office):
 Elden D Johnson

Products: Rail, fabricated trackwork, baseplates, joint bars.
 80 ft-long rails are now manufactured in Bethlehem Steel's plant located in Steelton, Pennsylvania. Produced from continuous cast steel, the rails offer superior internal cleanliness, weldability and surface quality. The head, web and base of every rail is ultrasonically inspected to ensure conformance with the ordered quality level. The long rails are offered in three grades: fully heat-treated, medium hardness and standard.

BHP
BHP Long Products Division

PO Box 21, Whyalla, South Australia 5600, Australia

Telephone: +61 86 40 4569
Cable: Hematite, Whyalla
Telex: 80270
Telefax: +61 86 40 4790

Rail Products Manager: Don McKenzie

Products: Rail (including head-hardened), steel sleeper section, rolled steel masts for catenary support.

Prefabricated movable-point crossing assembly, available in rolled-steel rail, railbound or solid manganese-steel knuckle rail, by Bethlehem Steel

Prefabricated double slip switch assembly, by Bethlehem Steel

BHP Rail Products
BHP Rail Products Inc

1400 Centrebank Boulevard, Suite 870, West Palm Beach, Florida 33401, USA

Telephone: +1 407 687 7593
Telefax: +1 407 687 7597

President: Michael L DeBonny

Main works: BHP Rail Products (Canada) Ltd, 39601 Galbraith Road, Squamish, BC V0N 3G0, Canada

Products: Steel railroad ties (sleepers), turnout steel tie sets, resilient rail fasteners, rail insulation pads. Steel sleepers and turnout bearers; Trak-Lok, resilient fasteners and insulation pads; fishplates and other track components.
 The Trak-Lok S-193 is a resilient rail fastener designed for high-stress, high-wear sections. The single-piece, clip-style fastener is ideal for curves and other high stress areas. It can be used on wood, steel or concrete sleepers, is adaptable to sleeper plates, and suitable for all sizes of rail, and accommodates most insulated rail joints. The low profile facilitates the use of existing equipment.
 In conjunction with the S-193 resilient fastener, Trak-Lok's steel sleepers provide a strong, durable, economical system, which tests have demonstrated will consistently outperform wood sleepers. This combination has also proved superior to wood in the

MANUFACTURERS / Permanent way equipment

Trak-Lok S-193 resilient fastener

Trak-Lok steel sleepers

areas of twisting, superelevation, alignment and surface. Steel sleepers, with their long life span, are resistant to buckling, provide greater gauge control and are economical. Insulation of steel sleepers is perhaps the greatest area of concern, but Trak-Lok insulated steel sleepers have never caused a signalling problem due to pad failure. A new two-piece high-density polyethylene pad is proving to have two to three times longer life span.

Recent contracts include 45,000 ties and 16 turnouts for BC Rail (1989-90); 5,000 ties for Alaska Railroad (1990); 1,000 ties and 5 turnouts (1989) and 4,000 ties (1990) for Burlington Northern; 1,000 ties and 2 turnouts for TSX Transportation (1989).

Bomag GmbH

PO Box 1180, Industriegebiet Hellerwald, D-5407 Boppard/Rhein, Federal Republic of Germany

Telephone: +49 6742 1000
Cable: Bomag, Boppard
Telex: 4 263 16
Telephone: +49 6742 3090

President: Anton Schwarzinger
Senior Vice-President, Finance: Wilfried Reinelt
Senior Vice-President, Manufacturing: Lothar Wahl
Senior Vice-President, Engineering: Gülertan Vural
Vice-President, Sales: Dr Arnd Julius

Principal subsidiaries:
Austria
BOMAG GmbH, Porchestrasse 9, PO Box 73, A-1234 Wien-Siebenhirten
Telephone: +43 2 22 693 6170
Telex: 133 535
Telefax: +43 2 22 69 4051

Canada
BOMAG (Canada), 1300 Aerowood Drive, Mississauga, Ontario L4W 1B7
Telephone: +1 416 625 6611
Telex: 06 96 1250
Telefax: +1 416 625 4403

France
BOMAG SAF, PO Box 34, ZA des Cochets, F-91220 Bretigny-sur-Orge
Telephone: +33 1 60 84 95 30
Telex: 601 370
Telefax: +33 1 60 84 18 66

Great Britain
BOMAG (Great Britain) Ltd, Sheldon Way, Larkfield, Maidstone, Kent ME20 6SE
Telephone: +44 622 716611
Telex: 965 787
Telefax: +44 622 718385

Japan
Nippon BOMAG Company Ltd
Kowa Building, 4th Floor, 39-10, Higashiueno 3-chome, Taito-ku, Tokyo 110
Telephone: +81 3 8 358765
Telex: 072 28519

Jordan
BOMAG GmbH, PO Box 5269, Amman, Jordan
Telephone: +962 6 827096
Telex: 21065 boma jo
Telefax: +962 6 827436

Singapore
BOMAG GmbH, 545 Orchard Road, 08-11 Far East Shopping Centre, Singapore 0923
Telephone: +65 734 6233
Telex: RS 33482 bomadi
Telefax: +65 734 7296

USA
BOMAG (USA), 1210 Kenton Street, Springfield, Ohio 45501-0959
Telephone: +1 513 325 8733
Telex: 4 33 3073
Telefax: +1 513 323 1526

Products: Vibratory tampers, vibratory plate compactors, single-drum vibratory rollers, trench compactors, slope compactors, double vibratory rollers, tandem vibratory rollers, single-drum wheel drive vibratory rollers, towed vibratory rollers, tandem static rollers, asphalt recyclers, soil stabilisers, sanitary landfill compactors, pneumatic-tyred rollers, combination rollers, multi-purpose hammers, Terrameter and Omegameter.

Bomag produces over 10 000 machines every year in a range of over 100 different models. Subsidiaries and specialist services in 120 countries ensure availability through an effective distribution and service network.

The company has lately developed the Terrameter BTM, which operates according to a dynamic measuring principle and can determine the actual state of compaction continuously while rolling is in progress.

Other recent additions to the range of machines include: two vibratory tampers, the BT 58 and BT 68; two vibratory plate compactors, the BP 10/36 and BP 15/45; a single-drum vibratory roller, the 55 E; two small tandem vibratory rollers, the BW 75 ADL and BW 90 ADL; a middle-sized tandem vibratory roller, the BW 130 AD; a large tandem vibratory roller with two split drums and hydrostatic drive to each of the four drum sections, the 144 AD; three heavy tandem vibratory rollers, the BW 161, 164 and 202 AD; six combination rollers with operating weights between 2 and 8 tonnes, the BW 100 AC, BW 120 AC, BW 141 AC, BW 144 AC, 154 AC and BW 164 AC; three single-drum wheel drive vibratory rollers with pad-foot drum and dozer blade, BW 142 PDB, BW 172 PDB and BW 213 PDB; two single-drum wheel drive rollers in the 12-tonne class, BW 214 D and BW 214 PD; two heavy single-drum wheel drive vibratory rollers in the 17-tonne class, the BW 217 D and BW 217 PD; four tandem static rollers, the BW 4 AS, BW 6 AS, BW 10 AS and BW 12 AS; a pneumatic-tyred roller BW 12 R; and two pneumatic-tyred rollers, the BW 16 R and BW 12 R, the sanitary landfill compactor 3C 601 RB and three new trench compactors, the BU 650T, BW 850T and BW1050T.

Boulonnerie de Thiant

94 rue Saint-Lazare, 75442 Paris Cedex 09, France

Telephone: +33 1 285 47 23
Telex: 650 842 f

Products: Rail fastenings for wooden, concrete or steel sleepers. The company has been registered as a supplier of the SNCF and of many foreign railway systems for many years. Main specialities include bolting screws, screwspikes with standard or variable threads and various rail fasteners.

British Steel Track Products

Moss Bay, Derwent Howe, Workington, Cumbria CA14 5AE, England

Telephone: +44 900 64321
Telex: 64147
Telefax: +44 900 64800

Director: A V L Williams
Commercial Manager: Stuart W Askew
Works Manager: J P Guerin

Products: Heavy and light railway track rails (from 9.88 kg/m to 67.57 kg/m; steel sleepers; rolled steel baseplates; fishplates; bridge and crane rails; electric conductor rails; special turnout rails.

A full range of rail grades is manufactured from 800N/mm^2 to heat treated grades at 1250N/mm^2 tensile strength. High strength rails are produced by both an off-line reheating process and an in-line treatment process.

Recent contracts in 1989-90 included contracts with British Railways Board for its major requirements for rail track, and in the export market with Indian Railways Board, Tanzanian Railways Corporation,

BSC rail entering mill hardening unit for transformation to Hi-Life quality

Permanent way equipment / **MANUFACTURERS** 353

New BSC Type W400 steel sleeper with welded-on baseplate and lug for Pandrol clip, fully insulated, for industrial track with axleloadings of up to 64 tonnes

Prototype Bruff grading machine

Bruff Road Rail Rescue vehicle in rail mode

Bruff Road Rail Rescue vehicle changing mode

Quebec North Shore & Labrador Railroad Canada, Iranian State Railways, Portuguese Railways, Spanish National Railways, and CSX Railroad, USA.

Considerable emphasis has been placed on sophisticated automatic inspection equipment to ensure internal and geometric standards for both heavy haul and high-speed track.

Major capital expenditure has improved steel sleeper handling and the range of sleepers available.

Bruckner & Thomas GBR

Karlstrasse 9, D-8900 Augsburg 1, Federal Republic of Germany

Telephone: +49 821 512989
Telex: 533279 ctt a
Telefax: +49 821 515874

Products: Prestressed concrete sleepers; technical and design services in establishment or modernisation of concrete sleeper manufacturing plant.

Bruff
Bruff Rail Ltd

Suckley, Worcester WR6 5DS, England

Telephone: +44 8864 333
Telex: 336331 bruff g
Telefax: +44 8864 418

Managing Director: M C Kukla
Commercial Director: D C Oldroyd

Products: Road/rail conversions, track machines, lasers.

A comprehensive range of road/rail conversions to tractors, excavators, and commercial vehicles, including the Bedford-based Road Rail Rescue vehicle. Other variants on the Bedford have been purchased by Blackpool Tramway system and British Rail for overhead current wire inspection. Uses under evaluation include shunting, rail welding, scrub clearance and general maintenance. The company is also supplying four road/rail conversions of the Mercedes 307D for personnel carrying and maintenance duties.

Bruff have extensive applications experience in the use of single-line and rotating laser systems. This service is now to be extended to cover the company's Rail Division in the use of lasers to improve performance on ballast cleaners, tampers, etc.

Bruff Rail Ltd is a joint venture company, between Bruff Manufacturing Co Ltd and the Tamper Corporation, USA. Bruff Rail Ltd has therefore the capability of supplying tamping machines, ballast regulators, permanent way maintenance units and track renewal trains to suit the European market.

BTR
BTR plc

Silvertown House, Vincent Square, London SW1P 2PL, England

Telephone: +44 71 834 3848
Telex: 22524 btrldn g
Telefax: +44 71 834 1395

Main works
BTR Rail Fasteners Division
PO Box 4261, Luipaardsvlei 1743, South Africa

BTR Rail Fasteners (Zimbabwe) PVT Ltd
PO Box 8034, Belmont, Bulawayo, Zimbabwe

BTR Rail Fasteners Inc
1581 Stone Ridge Road, Stone Mountain, Georgia 30083, USA

BTR Rail Fasteners (Australia) Pty Ltd
2 Pine Road, Yennora, New South Wales 12161, Australia

Fist do Brasil Fixocoes Ltda
Caixa Postal 049, Barueri, São Paulo, CEP 06400, Brazil

Products: FIST-BTR elastic rail fasteners for concrete sleepers.

FIST-BTR elastic rail fasteners installed on Richards Bay coal line, South African Transport Services

MANUFACTURERS / Permanent way equipment

BTR Permali
BTR Permali RP Ltd

Bristol Road, Gloucester, GL1 5TT, England

Telephone: +44 452 28282
Telex: 43546
Fax: +44 452 507409

Products: GRP compression moulded scab shells; GRP track baseplates.

Buhlmann
Buhlmann SA

Rue des Coteaux 249, 1030 Brussels, Belgium

Telephone: +32 2 216 20 30
Telex: 61 134
Telefax: +32 2 241 96 02

Director: Marcel Givel
Administrative Delegate: Walter Buhlmann

Products: Point-operating machines for Vignoles and grooved rails, all gauges; track circuit equipment and accessories; self-regulating electrical switch-point heating; level crossing gates, barriers and warning signals.

Burro Crane
Burro Crane Inc

1300 South Kilbourn Avenue, Chicago, Illinois 60623, USA

Telephone: +1 312 521 9200

President: R L McDaniel
Sales Manager, Cranes: C G Edwards
Sales Manager, Materials Handling: G Buchik

Products: Rail threaders, panel track lifters, multiple rail lifters, locomotive and other cranes.

Butzbacher
Butzbacher Weichenbau GmbH

PO Box 305, Wetzlarer Strasse 101, Industriegebiet Nord, 6308 Butzbach, Federal Republic of Germany

Telephone: +49 6033 8920
Telex: 418 4691
Telefax: +49 6033 892 113

Sales Manager: K Meusel

Products: Points and crossings, swing-nose crossings, welded frogs.

Bylin
Bylin Heating Systems Inc

837 Second Avenue, Redwood City, California 94063, USA

Telephone: +1 415 365 6112

President: Robert O Bylin

Products: Design and manufacture of switch, trip stop and third-rail heating systems.

Cemafer
Cemafer Gleisbaumaschinen und Gerate GmbH

Ihringer Landstrasse 3, Postfach 1327, 7814 Breisach, Federal Republic of Germany

Telephone: +49 7667 585
Telex: 7722524
Telefax: +49 7667 1008

Products: Power wrenches, coach-screwing machines, rail drills, rail saws, sleeper drills, sleeper adzing and drilling machines, rail grinding equipment, rail benders, light tampers, inspection trolleys, trailers, portal cranes, hand tools, electric generators (portable), gauges, jacks, rail cutting machines, rail stripping machines, sleeper boring machines, sleeper placing machines, spanners, spike drivers and extractors, track laying equipment, wrenches.

Centro-Metalcut Type VE carbide-tipped cut-off machine by Centro-Maskin for single-operation precision rail sawing and boring of up to 0.005 in accuracy enabling one operator to deal with a rail in 35 s

Centro-Maskin
Centro-Maskin AB

Head office: PO Box 35076, Sodra Gubberogatan 6, S-400 24 Gothenburg, Sweden

Telephone: +46 31 25 03 40
Telex: 20977 centro s
Telefax: +46 31 25 07 11

President: Larry J Flodin
Marketing Manager: Ove Lein
Technical Manager: Lars-Gunnar Stenström

Subsidiary
ALT Industrial Services Inc
3312 Crosby Street, Rockford, Illinois 61107

Products: Carbide-tipped saws; carbide-tipped drill units; grinders for reconditioning of rail. Suppliers to rail manufacturers and to Canadian National and Belgian National Railways.

CFF
Compagnie Française de Forges et Fonderies
Groupe Usinor

Immeuble Ile de France, 92070 Paris La Défense Cedex 33, France

Telephone: +33 1 767 10 10
Telex: 614 730 f

Products: Frogs in 12 and 14 per cent manganese steel, 2.5 to 10.5 m long in size with weights ranging from 150 to 4000 kg, in UIC and AREA norms.

CF&I Steel
CF&I Steel Corporation

PO Box 1830, Pueblo, Colorado 81002, USA

Telephone: +1 303 561 6000
Telex: 45 2446

President: F J Yaklich
Manager, Railroad Sales: R T Binder

Products: Rails, sleeper plates, rail anchors and track spikes.

Chemetron
Chemetron Railway Products Inc

177 West Hintz Road, Wheeling, Illinois 60090, USA

Telephone: +1 312 520 5454
Telex: 5106002541
Telefax: +1 312 520 6373

President: P J Cunningham
Vice President, Sales & Marketing: G D Schmolke

Products: Contract welding of continuous rail of 25 to 82 ft (7.62–25 m) lengths into quarter-mile lengths; TRANS/PORTABLE mobile flash-butt welding plant; spot polisher; rail straightener; rail pusher; abrasive saw.

Chemetron rail welding machines are available in both ac or dc operation. Systems are capable of welding rail in excess of ¼ mile in length in any of the standard, alloy or head-hardened rails. Machines are solid state and can be programmable-controlled. Eight automatic clamps evenly distribute the clamping forces throughout the weld area. High-speed hydraulics integrated with two-speed alignment systems provide rail geometry. Rail can be manually or automatically aligned while fully clamped with the broadest range of crown adjustment in the industry. After clamping, alignment and welding cycles are completed, the upset metal is sheared in the machine under full upset pressure while the weld is hot, resulting in smooth, clean welded areas. This allows special quenching operations of heat-treated rail with minimal delay in productivity.

Chemetron Railway Products, Inc operates plants in the United States and Canada; provides technical advice to Mexico; and its equipment is in use in Asia, South America and Australia.

Cimmco
Cimmco International

Prakashdeep, 7 Tolstoy Marg, New Delhi 110 001, India

Telephone: +91 3314383–5, 3310814
Cable: Cimwag
Telex: +91 31 65148, 31 62294

Products: Permanent way materials.

Clouth
Clouth Gummiwerke AG
Military and Moulded Articles Division

PO Box 600229, Niehler Strasse, 5000 Cologne 60, Federal Republic of Germany

Telephone: +49 221 77 73-1
Telex: 8 885 376 cl d

Products: Vibration-damping ballast mats, developed to reduce vibrations in new track and to reconstruct switches and crossings in existing track where particularly heavy impact forces occur.

Coborail-Extrapo

36 avenue Hoche, 75008 Paris, France

Telephone: +33 1 45 63 87 69
Telex: 649478

Products: Timber sleepers.

Cobra-X
Railroad Friction Products Corporation

Wilmerding, Pennsylvania 15148, USA

Telephone: +1 412 825 1106
Telex: 866467

Acting President: W B West
Vice President and General Manager: J L Duffy
Marketing: E W Kojsza

Products: Cobra-X prefabricated crossing modules.

Agents: Cobra Canada Inc, PO Box 2050, Hamilton, Ontario L8N 3T5, Canada

Permanent way equipment / **MANUFACTURERS** 355

Cobrasma
Cobrasma SA
Trackwork Specialities Plant

Head office: PO Box 969, Rua da Estação no 523, Osasco, São Paulo, CEP 06090, SP, Brazil

Telephone: +55 11 704 6122
Telex: (011) 71545, 71589
Telefax: +55 11 704 6856

Works: Km 1045, Via Anhanguera, Sítio São João, Municipiode Sumaré SP, PO Box 13170

Telephone: +55 192 65 6000
Telex: (019) 1926

President: Luis Eulálio de Bueno Vidigal
Marketing Director: Alberto Martinez
Export Director: Eduardo Hubert Kirmaier Monteiro

Products: Turnouts, switches and frogs.

COGIFER
Compagnie Générale d'Installations Ferroviaires

40 quai de l'Ecluse, 78290 Croissy-sur-Seine, France

Telephone: +33 1 34 80 02 82
Telex: 695121 f
Telefax: +33 1 34 80 03 31

President: Gérard Testart
Vice President: Jacques Darre
Managers, Industrial Division: René d'Ambrieres
  Works Division: Henri Dehé

Subsidiaries in USA
COGIFER Inc
5038 Beech Street, Cincinnati, Ohio 45212

Telephone: +1 513 631 3440
Telex: 810 461 2781
Telefax: +1 513 631 3682

President & CEO: George Voorhees
Vice-President, Sales: Jacques Galicher
Operations Manager: Serge Baumert
Controller: Glen Napolitano

Nelson Iron Works
2203 Airport Way, South Suite 205, Seattle, Washington 98134

Telephone: +1 206 623 3800

Products: COGIFER specialises in the manufacture of points and crossings as well as the equipment, laying and maintenance of all types of railway (main line, metros, tramways, VAL Systems, industry and harbour networks, rack-system railways, cable funiculars).
  COGIFER's Industrial Division has two plants in France and subsidiaries in Luxemburg (KIHN) and in the USA (COGIFER Inc and Nelson). The Division specialises in the design and manufacture of points and crossings. It also runs COGIFER's 50 per cent investment in the SOCAREC (manganese welded frogs) and SIFERDEC (railway signalling) companies.
  COGIFER's Works Division is in charge of railway track laying and maintenance works, and operates through a network of regional branches and agencies throughout France as well as a few subsidiaries abroad (SOLUXTRAFER, SOGAFER, ETC).
  The COGIFER Group benefits from more than 80 years' experience and has supplied national railway networks in more than 60 countries; metros in a great number of capital cities (such as Paris, Brussels, Cairo, Caracas and Santiago); tramways in Nantes, Grenoble, Calcutta, Manila, Portland, and Santa Clara; VAL systems in Lille, Chicago, Jacksonville; and the cable car system in San Francisco.
  In April 1989 Cogifer took over the 100-year-old company DEHE which specialises in railway engineering. Among its existing contracts are the laying of new track for Algeria and Mozambique; renewal of over 20,000 km of track for SNCF.

Colebrand STU on Docklands Light Railway

Colebrand
Colebrand Ltd

Colebrand House, 20 Warwick Street, Regent Street, London W1R 6BE

Telephone: +44 71 439 1000
Telex: 261495
Telefax: +44 71 734 3358

Managing Director: K N Tusch
Chief Executive: Rear-Adm R I T Hogg
Sales Manager: J R Harrison

Main works: CXL Factory, Goodshawfold Road, Rosendale, Lancashire BB4 8QF

Products: The Colebrand Level 2000, an instrument of advanced levelling technology. Accurate readings of level, angle and tilt are shown instantly on the digital display of the device, which consists of a rugged electronic sensor, custom VLSI circuitry and liquid crystal display.
  The Colebrand Shock Transmission Unit (STU) is fitted to structures such as bridges which must resist the braking and traction forces from rail traffic while allowing for thermal expansion/contraction as well as possible shrinkage and creepage. Colebrand STUs have recently been successfully incorporated into the Docklands Light Railway where they have been used to strengthen the overhead sections carrying the existing track.

Conbrako
Conbrako (Pty) Ltd

PO Box 14010, 167 Tedstone Road, Wadesville 1422, Transvaal, South Africa

Telephone: 27 11 827 3431
Cable: Conbrako
Telex: 4 29206

Products: Track jacks.

Cooper & Turner range of fastenings

Cooper & Turner

Sheffield Road, Sheffield S9 1RS, England

Telephone: +44 742 560057
Telex: 54607
Telefax: +44 742 445529

Directors: P N Cook
  K Wragg

Products: Fish bolts, track bolts, screw spikes, crossing bolts, Renlock locknut, insulated fishplates.

Costain
Costain Concrete Co Ltd

Rye House, Hoddesdon, Hertfordshire EN11 0EW, England

Telephone: +44 992 463037
Telex: 894396
Telefax: +44 992 444297

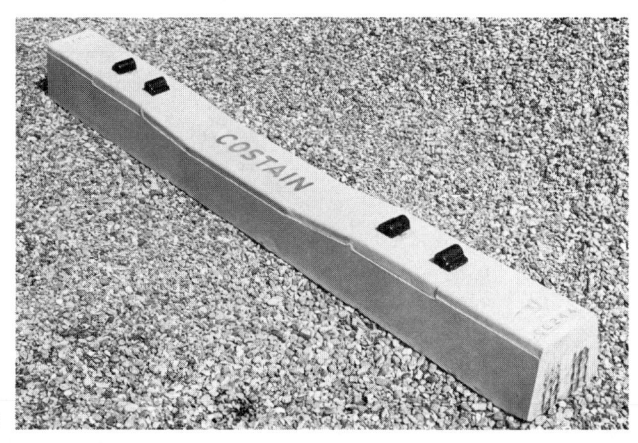

Costain prestressed concrete sleeper

MANUFACTURERS / Permanent way equipment

Hydraulic lightweight re-railing equipment with full range of lifting jacks by Cowans Boyd

Cowans Boyd ballast regulating machine for British Rail

Cowans Boyd track panel laying gantry

Managing Director: David B Scott

Products: Prestressed concrete sleepers, turnout and crossing sleepers.

NOTE: Company now part of Costain Dow Mac Ltd

Cowans Boyd
NEI Clarke Chapman Ltd

Works: PO Box 9, Carlisle Enterprise Centre, James Street, Carlisle, Cumbria CA2 5BJ, England

Telephone: +44 228 24196
Cable: Cowans Carlisle
Telex: 64136
Telefax: +44 228 24795

General Manager: F J Gilroy
Marketing Manager: S Whitfield
Product Manager: J E Steele

Products: Track maintenance equipment, including long-welded rail trains for laying continuously welded rail, twin line tracklaying machines, single-line track panel laying cranes, side-mounted rail loading cranes, heavy diesel breakdown cranes, ballast regulating machines, lightweight hydraulic re-railing equipment. Railway workshop equipment including traversers, turntables.

CXT (formerly Genstar Costain)
CXT Ltd

North American head office: North 2420 Sullivan Road, PO Box 14918, Spokane, Washington 99214, USA

Telephone: +1 509 924 6300
Telefax: +1 509 926 8312

President: John G White

US Works: CXT Inc, North 2420 Sullivan Road, PO Box 14918, Spokane, Washington 99214, USA

Telephone: +1 509 924 6300
Telefax: +1 509 927 0299

President: John G White
Vice-President: Derek Firth

Canadian works: CXT Ltd, 12707 170 Street, PO Box 3618, Stn 1, Edmonton, Alberta T5L 4J6, Canada

Telephone: +1 403 447 2025
Telefax: +1 403 447 1277

President: John G White
Vice President and General Manager: Anders Eriksson

Products: Prestressed concrete sleepers for both track and turnouts. CXT designs and manufactures sleepers for specific applications.

Daido
Daido Steel Co Ltd

Kogin Bldg 11-18, Nishiki 1-chome, Naka-ku, Nagoya, Japan

Telephone: +81 52 201 5111
Cable: Steel Nagoya
Telex: 442 2243

Tokyo office: Daido Bldg 7-13, Nishishinbashi, 1-chome, Minato-ku, Tokyo

Telephone: +81 3 501-5261
Cable: Steel
Telex: 222 2079

Products: High manganese cast steel frogs and crossings. Recent developments include a movable-nose frog for slab track.

Dehé
Société des Entreprises A Dehé

40 quai de l'Ecluse, 78290 Croissy-sur-Seine, France

Telephone: +33 3976 53 54
Telex: 690817
Telefax: +33 3976 16 33

Products: Track construction and maintenance equipment.

Delachaux
C Delachaux SA
Welding Division

119 avenue Louis-Roche, 92231 Gennevilliers, France

Telephone: +33 1 47 90 61 20
Telex: 620 118
Telefax: +33 1 47 90 64 52

Products: Aluminothermic rail welding equipment and mechanised equipment for high-activity worksites.

Desquenne et Giral
Desquenne et Giral Group

Head Office: 9 rue Friedland, 75008 Paris, France

Telephone: +33 1 42 89 80 63
Telefax: +33 1 42 89 80 58

Director General: C M Moreau

Delachaux self-propelled aluminothermic welding machine

Permanent way equipment / MANUFACTURERS

Desquenne et Giral mobile gantry with girder for sleeper spacing laying TGV-A track

Desquenne & Giral SPRO machine

Desquenne et Giral guiding and positioning machine unloading long-welded rails on TGV-A formation

Principal subsidiaries: SECO/Desquenne et Giral, Nanterre; RCFC, Lens.

Products: Mechanised railway track construction and track maintenance work, supported by manufacture of specialised equipment. This machinery includes: SPRA *(Satellite pour rails et attaches)*; SPRO *(Satellite pour récupération optimale du ballast)*; ballast cleaning machines; ballast conveyors; twin crane assembly, track-laying, gantry cranes; torque-controlled coach-screwing machines.

The company has been responsible for high-productivity tracklaying (over 1000 m/day) on French Railways' TGV-PSE and TGV-A high-speed lines; and for the STEDEF 'direct' tracklaying method on the Paris RER Line C Montmorency-Ermont-Invalides extension.

D'Huart
Jean D'Huart et Cie

3 rue de l'Industrie, 57110 Yutz, France

Telephone: +33 8 256 34 81
Telex: 860006

Products: Rail, steel and timber sleepers, fishplates, other track components.

Donelli
Donelli, SpA

Via Romana 69, 42028 Poviglio, Reggio Emilia, Italy

Telephone: +39 522 689046
Cable: Donelli, Poviglio
Telex: +39 522 530320

Products: Ballast regulators, hydraulic cranes, jacks, sleeper placing machines, track aligners, track laying equipment, track lining machines.

Prestressed concrete turnout by Dow Mac

Other products: complete range of light and heavy duty gang cars; brushwood cutters; workshop trailers; weedkiller spreading trailers; overhead catenary line erection; maintenance and servicing vehicles; catenary inspection gangcars; catenary inspection trailers; rail road loaders; hi-rail cranes.

Dow Mac
Dow Mac Concrete Ltd

Head office and works: Tallington, Stamford, Lincolnshire, England
Telephone: +44 778 342301
Telex: 32206
Telefax: +44 778 348041

Works: Eaglescliffe, Cleveland
Telephone: +44 642 781811
Telex: 32206
Telefax: +44 642 784011

Dow Mac sleeper plant for New Railways Implementation Authority, Iraq

Quedgeley, Gloucestershire
Telephone: +44 452 720428
Telex: 43343
Telefax: +44 452 720187

Atlas Works, Lenwade, Norwich
Telephone: +44 603 872291
Telex: 975097
Telefax: +44 603 871123

London office: 210 High Holborn, 6th Floor, London WC1V 73P
Telephone: +44 71 242 6921, +44 71 430 1458

Chairman: J Matthews
Managing Director: A S Darroch
Marketing Director: J A D Morgan-Giles

Products: Dow Mac prestressed concrete sleepers; building and civil engineering components.

The company's supply of pre-tensioned sleeper production technology world-wide steadily increases and to date has involved development in Australia, India, Norway, USSR, Belgium, Iraq, Northern Ireland, Republic of Ireland, Zambia, South Africa, Hong Kong, North America and the Dominican Republic. Services offered cover sleeper design, factory design, construction of factory, supply of plant, commissioning of plant, training of engineers and operatives, complete operation of factory, management of factory and quality assurance, all of which can be provided individually or together.

NOTE: Company now merged with Costain as Costain Dow Mac Ltd

Edgar Allen
Edgar Allen Engineering Limited
Engineering Division of Aurora plc

PO Box 42, Shepcote Lane, Sheffield S9 1QW, England

Telephone: +44 742 446621
Cable: Alleneng, Sheffield
Telex: 547111
Telefax: +44 742 426826

MANUFACTURERS / Permanent way equipment

Managing Director: R Connelly
Technical Director: D R Pendleton
Commercial Director: P Sutcliffe

Products: Design and manufacture of railway switches and crossings for railways, mass transit systems, tramways, docks and harbours and steelworks; manganese steel wearing parts for locomotive and axlebox manufacturers and railway maintenance workshops.

The company is a major supplier to British Rail of manganese steel switches and crossings. It also supplies trackwork to North America to AREA specifications and to other countries to UIC specifications.

Electrologic
Electrologic Pty Ltd

24-33 College Street, Gladesville, New South Wales 2111, Australia

Telephone: +61 2 816 1515
Telex: 72385 aa
Telefax: +61 2 816 5978

Managing Director: B Heij

Products: Continuous non-contact, optical, track geometry measurement system; continuous non-contact, optical railshape measurement system; rail thermometers; digital laser guidance system for resurfacing curves and straights; survey data base systems.

Elektro-Thermit
Elektro-Thermit GmbH

Postfach 10 10 43, 4300 Essen 1, Federal Republic of Germany

Telephone: +49 201 17303
Cable: Elektrothermit
Telex: 857 1715 tgd
Telefax: +49 201 173 2694

Managing Directors: Dr Hans Guntermann
Johann Hugo Wirtz

Products: Thermit rail welding equipment and materials, rail de-stressers, rail grinding machines, glued insulated rail joints. Contract welding: joint and build-up welding of flatbottom and grooved rails; special techniques for urban transport systems to counter the effects of rail corrugation, side cutting and flange squeal.

Energomachexport
V/O Energomachexport
(Export company for all Soviet-built railway products)

Deguninskaja Str 1, Korp 4, 127486 Moscow, USSR

Telephone: 7 095 487 31 82
Cable: Moscow Energoexport
Telex: 411965

Products: Ballast cleaning machines; tamper-leveller-liner machines; track-laying cranes and gantries; snow ploughs; snow clearing and removal equipment; rail welding equipment; portable powered machines for tamping, rail cutting-drilling-grinding and spike driving-pulling; electronic and ultrasonic fault finding equipment; inspection cars; gang and maintenance railcars and trailers.

ESAB
ESAB AB

PO Box 106, 69501 Laxa, Sweden

Telephone: +46 0 584 81000
Telex: 73374 esabeng s
Telefax: +46 0 584 11721

Managing Director: C Palm
Divisional Manager: L G Eriksson
Marketing & Sales Manager: J Björkman

Products: Flash butt welding machines for rails; equipment for welding automation in rolling stock production; equipment for building-up welding of wheels.

Euro-Trac
Euro-Trac Ltd

Flockton House, Audby Lane, Wetherby, West Yorkshire LS22 4FD, England

Telephone: +44 937 64548
Telex: 557472

Managing Director: R Kerr

Products: Excavators, inspection cars, road-rail cranes, scrub cutters, track vacuum cleaning equipment.

EWEM AG CH 8500 FRAUENFELD
EWEM
Everts & van der Weyden Exploitatie Maatschappij
EWEM BV

Head office: Thundorferstrasse 58, CH-8500 Frauenfeld, Switzerland

Telephone: +41 52 352122
Telex: 896 238 gmd ch
Telefax: +41 52 351639

Managing Director: A A G van Hees

Licence-holders for DE Clips: Bonem SA, Medellin, Colombia; Arte Tecnica SA, Porto Alegre, Brazil; Kloos-Kinderdijk BV, Kinderdijk, Netherlands

Products: DE elastic railfastener and DE system, which includes springclip and sleeper plate or shoulder cast in concrete sleeper.

The system, which exerts a clamping force of 2500 Kp (5500 lb) per rail seat, compensates for the heavy vertical, lateral and longitudinal thermal and dynamic stresses caused by modern, high tonnage traffic. It does not disturb the relationship between plate and sleeper. Rail changes are made by removing the clip, taking out the old rail, putting in new rail and replacing the clip. Gauge is held firmly and spike killing is eliminated. The DE Springclip develops practically no metal fatigue and is reusable. It can be used on both wood and concrete sleepers. With wood sleepers a special rolled steel base plate or cast iron clip holder is used, depending on the type of traffic. Reinforced or prestressed concrete sleepers use cast-in clip holders. The company's Brazilian plant now produces ribbed sole plates in nodular cast iron, which by comparison with rolled plates save 15 per cent in both weight and cost, without sacrifice of physical qualities.

Major users of the DE fastener are the Netherlands Railways (NS), which has 3600 km of track equipped with DE clips and has an annual requirement for 2 to 2.5 million clips, mainly for UIC 54 rails. Other users include the municipal tramway lines of The Hague and Rotterdam; Rheinische Braunkohle; Köln; Thyssen Edelstahl Krefeld and Thyssen Weichenbau; Norwegian State Railways (NSB); Soviet Railways; Suriname Railways; Compania de Vale de Rio Doce (Brazil); AT&SF, USA; National Railways of Colombia (FNC); and Madrid Metropolitan Railway; Carajas Railroad (EFC) and FEPASA, Brazil; PJKA, Indonesia; RFF SA, Brazil.

EXIM
EXIM Aussenhandels GmbH & Co

PO Box 1406, D-3550 Marburg 1, Federal Republic of Germany

Telephone: +49 6421 81001
Telex: 482389 exim
Telefax: +49 6421 85353

Sales Director: J Heyden

Products: Rails, turnouts, sleepers, fastenings, glued joints, welding equipment, machinery for workshops.

Fairfield-Mabey
Fairfield-Mabey Limited

Chepstow, Gwent NP6 5YL, Wales

Telephone: +44 2912 3801
Telex: 497019 fm ltd g
Telefax: +44 2912 5453

Chairman: B G Mabey
General Manager: G Hammond
Sales Director: C M Booth

Products: Temporary and permanent bridging; heavy steel plate fabrication including plate and box girders.

Fairmont
Fairmont Railway Motors
A division of Harsco Corporation

415 North Main Street, PO Box 415, Fairmont, Minnesota 56031-0415, USA

Hydraulic lightweight ZB-M rail shear with double-stroke hand pump and long lasting shear blades, by Elektro-Thermit

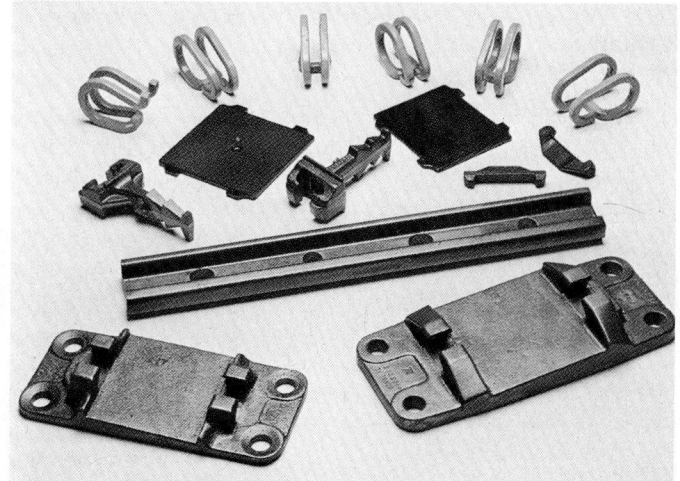

EWEM DE system components

Telephone: +1 507 235 3361
Telex: (910) 565 2122
Telefax: +1 507 235 9048

President: G Robert Newman
Vice President, Marketing: Robert C Kramer
Export Sales Manager: Stephen Byers

Products: HY-RAIL highway/railway guide wheel units; maintenance-of-way work equipment for sleeper and rail renewal gangs; rail grinding machines; motor cars; push cars and trailers; wheels, axles, and bearings; overhead and tunnel maintenance aerial lifts; utility cranes; small grinders for rail maintenance;; in-track rail welding accessories; hand-held hydraulically powered tools; hydraulic power units; bridge jacks and maintenance tools; and contract rail grinding services.

Famatex
Famatex SRL

Aviendia San Martin 7910, 1650 San Martin, Province of Buenos Aires, Argentina

Telephone: +54 1 755 0352

Products: Inspection cars, light and heavy gangers' trollies.

FAO
Fonderies et Aciéries d'Outreau

PO Box 119, 62230 Outreau, France

Telephone: +33 21 30 58 00 (factory)
+33 1 341 72 83 (sales)
Telex: 110 915 f

Products: FAO is the sole supplier of cast cradles for movable point crossings installed by French Railways (SNCF) on the Paris-Lyon TGV track, which is operated at 270 km/h. FAO produces more than 4000 monobloc crossings in manganese steel according to AREA and UIC specifications and frog centre castings according to AREA specifications.

Ferotrack
Ferotrack Engineering Ltd

Head office: 332 Kilburn High Road, London NW6 2QN, England

Telephone: +44 81 624 0103
Telex: 8812198 bstog

Works: Duck Mill Lane, Bedford MK40 0AX

Telephone: +44 234 211151

Products: Electric pad point and crossing heaters; cartridge heaters; clamp lock heaters; control cabinets; plus a major range of 996 Type Ni-Cad rechargeable batteries with integral electronic charger.

Ferotrack Electric Pad Heaters prevent not only snow and ice compacting between the switch blades and fixed rail, but also grease and/or water freezing on the baseplate. They are easily installed on existing or new track, and designs can be for a single switch or a complete marshalling yard.

Ferrostaal
Ferrostaal AG

PO Box 10 12 65, Hohenzollernstrasse 24, 4300 Essen, Federal Republic of Germany

Telephone: +49 201 818 01
Cable: Ferrostaal, Essen
Telex: 0857100

Directors: Dr Hans Singer
Dr F Graf von Ballestrem
Helmut Julius
Wilhelm Lüttenberg
Dr Klaus von Menges
Gerhard Thulmann

Products: Permanent-way materials: rails of all grades, light and heavy vignole rails, crane rails, grooved rails; wooden, concrete and steel sleepers; rail fastening systems and individual components for ballasted and slab tracks, ie resilient and rigid clips, sole plates, sleeper screws, spring washers, anticreep rail anchors, sleeper anchoring devices; switch and crossing systems of various types, expansion joints, insulated joints; turntables; sliding buffer stops; rail welding materials; plastic components, ie screw dowels, plastic dowels for reconstruction of wooden and concrete sleepers, rail pads; elastomers for reducing ground-borne noises, ie ballast mats, bearings for floating and slab tracks, resilient pads; and rolling stock materials.

Ferrostaal
Ferrostaal Corporation

One Maritime Plaza, San Francisco, California 94111, USA

Telephone: +1 415 781 3237
Telex: 470883

Products: Vossloh rail fastening systems.

Ferrovias y Siderurgia SA

Cedaceros 4, Madrid 14, Spain

Telephone: +34 1 231 9752

Products: Points, switches and crossings.

Findlay, Irvine
Findlay, Irvine Ltd

Bog Road, Penicuik, Midlothian, Scotland

Telephone: +44 968 72111
Telex: 727502
Telefax: +44 968 72596

Chairman: James S Findlay
Managing Director: John A Irvine
Sales Manager: J S S Macdonald

Products: Points heating controller; thermostats.

The Icelert Model 162 points heating controller is suitable for controlling electric or gas points heating and a special temperature and moisture probe assembly has been designed for this particular application. It controls on a temperature and moisture detection basis and only when the temperature set point (usually 1°C) is reached and moisture is detected at the probes will a relay be activated. This gives a better degree of control than the normal thermostat working on a temperature basis only. The heated moisture probe with its snow arrester is normally fixed to a 3-inch diameter vertical pole beside the track. The temperature sensor can either be sited on this pole or clamped to the rail itself. Simple spring clamps are available for easy fixing to the rail. The temperature level at which the instrument is set to bring on heat in wet conditions is usually 3°C, to prevent the accumulation of wet snow. A setback control can be used to prevent the rails becoming very cold even when dry, and therefore slow to rise to above freezing point. Another control knob is provided to enable the selection of a second operating point at a number of degrees below the normal operating level. The heaters will be switched on when the ambient temperature falls to this level and moisture and snow are not detected. A single controller can cover a number of points, for example in a marshalling yard.

The Icelert 287 points heating control has been developed to fulfil a general requirement for a small controller which operates to bring on heating when conditions are near freezing and snow or moisture is present. There are three main parts to the system: the control unit; the snow probe; and the temperature sensor. They operate together to sense the rail temperature and precipitation. When the sensed conditions reach preset levels on the control unit a relay is energised which causes the main contactor within the cubicle to energise and provide power to the electric heaters that are fitted to the railway track switches. Since the temperature sensor is fitted to the rail by means of a suitable rail clamp supplied with the system, it detects the rise of temperature of the rail and switches off at a preset value, thus thermostatically controlling the rail temperature at the set point if wet, or at the set point minus set back if dry.

The Icelert Type 307 control unit has been developed to fulfil a general requirement for a controller which operates when its sensors detect near freezing or snow and ice conditions. Various sensors are available for use with the unit which makes it a suitable choice for many different applications in one of its three forms: Type 307A, B or C. For example, the control of heating to prevent gutters, railway points, footpaths, car ramps etc from becoming snow-bound or frozen. By providing a signal, a warning of imminent or dangerous conditions is also possible or a heating contactor could be controlled by the output relay.

A low-voltage 24 V 50 Hz supply is provided by the unit to run some types of external sensors. In the case of surface sensors, for example, the supply feeds a heater in the sensor and this enables the measurement of conductivity between two surface elements when snow or ice is present. By combining this with the measurement of unheated elements and temperature it is possible to give various control options which may be set by the front panel controls.

The new Icelert 307 Model D has been specially designed for use with switch heating and features two temperature sensors; two-level switch on and switch off control; operation with either a precipitation sensor or a low-level track-mounted snow detector, or both; excellent visual indication by LEDs indicate when set point temperatures have been reached and precipitation is detected; time delay circuit to ensure that all switches have reached the proper temperature before the heating is switched off; self-checking facilities.

Fairmont RG-8 rail grinder

360 MANUFACTURERS / Permanent way equipment

Foss
Foss Manufacturing Company Inc
Construction Products Division

231 Neck Road, PO Box 277, Haverhill, Massachusetts 01830, USA

Telephone: +1 617 374 0128
Telex: 94 7116

Products: GEOMAT polyester non-woven geotextiles and GEOMAT Switch-Pack.

Foster
L B Foster Co

Foster Building, 415 Holiday Drive, Pittsburgh, Pennsylvania 15220, USA

Telephone: +1 412 928 3400

Vice-President, Rail Products: D A Frenz

Products: Rail and track accessories, frog and switch material crossings, railroad ties, steel mine ties and track tools; mass transit conductor rail track fastening systems and coverboards.

Transit Products Division

PO Box 47367, Doraville, Georgia 30362, USA

Telephone: +1 404 448-4211

Works: 1864 Sullivan Road, College Park, Georgia 30337

General Manager: W R Harper Jr
Bid Manager: J D McCollum
Administration: N Snyder

Products: Direct fixation rail fasteners; special trackwork; composite and co-extruded conductor rail; insulator chairs for conductor rail; concrete and wood sleepers; resilient rail fasteners for heavy haulage; catenary equipment test laboratory for track components.

Constitution: The company, formerly Transit Products Inc, was purchased by L B Foster in September 1983.

Framafer
Société Française de Construction de Matériel Ferroviaire

77 rue de la Gare, 57803 Bening-les-Saint-Avold, France

Telephone: +33 87 81 4554
Telex: 860243
Telefax: +33 87 81 5063

Products: Automatic track levelling, tamping and lining machines, ballast cleaners and ballast regulators, track relaying systems, sleeper changing machines, brush-cutters, ditch-cleaners, track measuring cars, flash-butt welding machines.

Foss GEOMAT Switch-Pack, reinforced at high loading areas, placed as a one-piece unit ready to receive the prefabricated track section

GCE
GCE Gas Control Equipment AB

Box 21004, 200 21 Malmö, Sweden

Telephone: +46 40 188100
Telex: 8305162
Telefax: +46 40 290791

President: Claes Wessberg
Sales Manager: Hans Ohlin

Products: Bright-Bond pin brazing system; signal and power bonds; track circuit and connectors for protective earthing; clamps and short circuit devices; heating devices for rail.
 The Bright-Bond technique is based on electric-arc brazing with a specially designed pin brazing unit. The hollow pin contains brazing material and flux. The specially designed connectors consist of lengths of copper, or galvanised steel wire fitted with a lug at each end. Advanced measuring units have revealed the exceptionally low resistance of a Bright-Bond connector. For example, a Type 278 190 069 connector consists of 145 mm copper wire with a section area of 25 mm^2. It has been shown that the total resistance of this connector is only 130 microhms. The cable itself accounts for 120 microhms. Thus the transition resistance in each brazed joint is only 5 microhms.

Geismar
Société des Anciens Etablissements L Geismar

113 bis avenue Charles de Gaulle, 92200 Neuilly sur Seine, France

Hydraulic rail threader by Geismar

Telephone: +33 1 47 47 55 00
Telex: 620700
Telefax: +33 1 46 40 71 70

Works: 5 rue d'Altkirch, 68006 Colmar Cedex
Telephone: +33 89 41 48 83
Telex: 880953
Telefax: +33 89 79 78 45

Products: Track laying, handling and transport equipment: self-propelled tracklaying gantries; rail and sleeper positioners; ballast regulators; ballast compactors; hydraulic rail threaders; thermit weld shears; rail heaters; point heaters; rail loaders; rail pullers; rail changers; sleeper loading machines; tamping and slewing jacks; track slewing and lining machines; ballast tamping units.
 Trolleys (1 to 200 tons); inspection trolleys; light and heavy-duty gang cars; brushwood cutters; workshop trailers; weedkiller spreading trailers; rail-road loaders; hi-rail cranes.
 Machines and track maintenance equipment: Rail saws; rail drills; coach-screwing machines; fishbolt fastening machines; plug drivers; spike pullers and drivers; rail profile grinding machines; rail grinding machines; sleeper drilling machines; chamfering machines; sleeper adzing machines; heavy-duty sleeper changing machines; hydraulic rail benders;

Adjustable TPI Type H17 fastener for heavy-haul railroads by Foster

Foster TPI Type H-10 fastener

hydraulic rail joint straighteners; rail tensors; rail lubricators; illumination plants; track warning devices; electronic train warning device for gangs working on the track; electronic train loading gauge control device; ultrasonic rail checking equipment.

Tools and measuring instruments: Complete range of hand tools; measuring instruments; fishplate lubricators; sleeper banding machines; equipment for sidings; oscillation testing and track recording equipment.

Factories and workshops: Rail flash-butt welding plants; rail reclaiming plants; wooden sleeper manufacturing plants; reconditioning of steel sleepers; foundries; maintenance workshops.

Gemco
George Moss Ltd

461 Scarborough Beach Road, Osborne Park, PO Box 136, Mount Hawthorn, Western Australia, Australia

Telephone: +61 9 446 8844
Cable: Gemco, Perth
Telex: 92645
Telefax: +61 9 446 3404

Managing Director: F Quilty
Manager, Railways Division: H R Geddes

Products: Hydraulic controlled track machines for sleeper extraction and replacement, track lifting, levelling, ballast scarifying, sleeper boring, spike pulling and bolt renewal; rubber crossings; Teletamp tamping tines; rail flaw detection, speed weigh, light slice track recording equipment and track management systems. Also Australian agents for Geismar rail maintenance machines.

Getzner
Getzner Chemie GmbH

PO Box 159, Herrenau 5, 6700 Bludenz-Bürs, Austria

Telephone: +43 5552 6 33100
Telex: 3552300 syl a
Telefax: +43 5552 66864

Export Manager: Dipl-Kfm Julius Fahrensteiner

Subsidiary company
Getzner Mutter & Cie GmbH
Nördliche Münchner Strasse 27, D-8022 Grünwald/München, Federal Republic of Germany

Telephone: +49 89 6492195

Products: Complete programme for protection from vibration and noise using Sylomer ballast mats, elastic resilient pads, elastic bearings for track slabs and mass-resilient systems, elastic bases for grooved rails, grooved track fillings for crossings and industrial sidings and passive vibration insulation.

Light tamping machine by Geismar

Bridge inspection vehicle by Geismar

Sylomer resilient pads elastically carry rails or sleepers

Sylomer mats in Munich U-Bahn new line construction

MANUFACTURERS / Permanent way equipment

GIA
GIA Sparteknik AB
Company of Athena (Cardo)

Box 1512, 271 00 Ystad, Sweden

Telephone: +46 411 13820
Telex: 33235
Telefax: +46 411 11742

Director: Alf Göransson
Export Manager: Pher Lundgren

Products: Design, laying and maintenance of shunting yards, industrial tracks, mine tracks, crane tracks, etc; design and production of switch points, crossings, temporary points, signalling material etc; supply of track material such as standard rails, grooved and crane rails, sleepers, Värnamo protective strips and blocks, buffer stops, point locks, accessories, etc, rails from Svenskt Stål AB, Domnarvet and concrete sleepers from AB Strängbetong; project work on and installation of safety installations with rail/road crossing barriers, light and acoustic signals and automatic control systems; sales of locomotives, rolling stock, wheels and wheel-sets, track laying machinery, lubricators, electric switch drives, leasing of machinery and equipment for railways.

Gottwald GmbH

PO Box 130329, D-4000 Düsseldorf 13, Federal Republic of Germany

Telephone: +49 211 79 56 0
Telex: 858 2638

Managing Director: W Philipp
Sales Director: R Koos

Products: Tracklaying and maintenance equipment.

Grant Lyon Eagre
Grant Lyon Eagre Ltd
A subsidiary of British Steel Plc

Scotter Road, Scunthorpe, South Humberside DN15 8EF, England

Telephone: +44 724 862131
Telex: 527215
Telefax: +44 724 280262

Chairman: A V L Williams
Managing Director: D W Schafer

Products: Manufacture and supply of a comprehensive range of railway switches and crossings to UIC and National Standards for a wide range of railway systems. Also manufacturers of technically advanced narrow gauge switches and crossings to meet high speed and heavy haul requirements.

Temporary points by GIA

Crane rail layouts are produced and a comprehensive variety of castings, forgings, pressings and fabrications are available. The installation and maintenance of the above types of track and components is a major activity. A comprehensive design service for all types of railway track construction is available.

Recent work includes supply of switches and crossings to British Rail, further work on the extension of the Docklands Light Railway, London, and for a range of major industrial clients.

Expert work includes supply of switches and crossings to Middle East and Far Eastern clients. An extensive range of track maintenance equipment and associate plant available for hire or leasing.

Grinaker Precast
Grinaker Precast (Pty) Ltd

PO Box 75084, Gardenview 2047, Transvaal, South Africa

Telephone: +27 11 615 6401
Telex: 425721 SA
Telefax: +27 11 622 3718

Chairman: E J Sadie
Managing Director, Sleeper Division: J C Havinga

Products: Prestressed concrete railway products including sleepers, level crossing slabs, turnouts and electrification masts.

Grove Coles
Groves Coles Ltd
International Sales and Marketing

Head office: Pallion, Sunderland SR4 6TT

Telephone: +44 91 565281
Telex: 53484/5 cranes g
Telefax: +44 91 5640442

Sales: Telford Road, Bicester, Oxfordshire OX6 OT2, England

Telephone: +44 869 246800
Telex: 837447 cranes g
Telefax: +44 869 246965

Standard-gauge turnout in 90A rail with manganese crossing for a Middle East dock installation by Grant Lyon Eagre

Grove Manlift MZ76, maximum working height 23.2 m, platform capacity up to 272 kg

Grove TMS 250EB truck crane, 30 tonnes maximum capacity, conforming to European road regulations

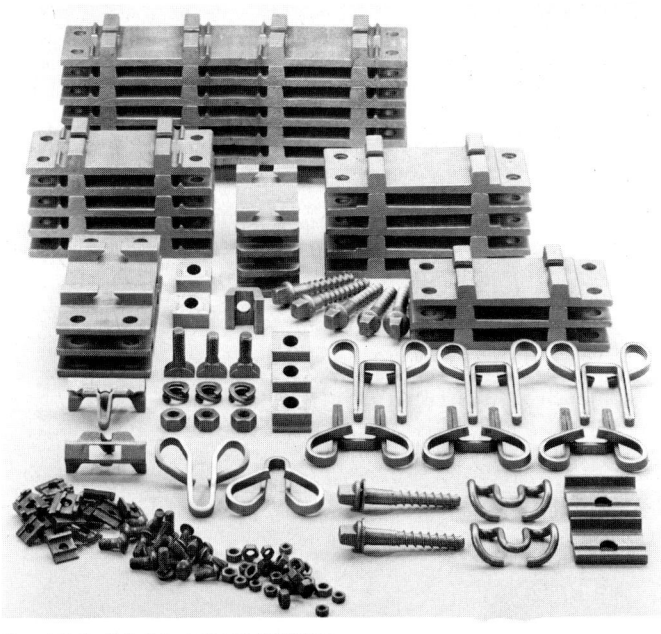

Permanent way equipment / **MANUFACTURERS** 363

Hoesch Rothe Erde-Schmiedag product range

Holland MobileWelder

Director of International Sales & Marketing: M Lamb
Sales Director, Cranes: W Lawson
General Manager, Marketing: N Day
Director, UK Sales & Service: P Allison

Principal subsidiary: Grove Coles France SA, 16 Chaussee Jules-Cesar, 95520 Osny, BP 203, 95523 Cergy-Pontoise Cedex, France

Products: Grove mobile hydraulic telescopic cranes: truck-mounted, all-terrain and rough-terrain, lifting capacities from 8 to 127 tonnes; Grove Manlift self-propelled aerial work platforms: scissor lift, telescopic boom and articulated telescopic boom, lifting capacities from 227 to 907 kg.

GTG
Greenside Hydraulics Ltd

Belgrave House, 58 Belgrave Road, Sheffield S10 3LN, England

Telephone: +44 742 308033
Telex: 547938

Chairman: J W Thompson
Directors: Guy Lees Thompson
Margaret Thompson

Products: Rail tensors for tensioning continuous welded rail; rail support arms and rollers; rail welding jigs; track lifting machines; rail joint straightening machines; rail manipulators; rail lifting bars; lightweight trolleys; rail curving machines.

HDC
Hindustan Development Corporation Ltd

Kanchenjunga 7th Floor, 18 Barakharaba Road, New Delhi 110001, India

Telephone: 91 11 3312201
Cable: Hidevol
Telex: 031 62989/63149

Products: Points, crossings, steel sleepers, bogies.

Hoesch Rothe Erde-Schmiedag
Hoesch Rothe Erde-Schmiedag AG

Tremoniastrasse 5-11, 4600 Dortmund 1, Federal Republic of Germany

Telephone: +49 231 186 0
Cable: Rotheerde Dtd TW 245
Telex: 17 231 302 hrs d
Telefax: +49 231 186 500
Teletex: 23 1302

Technical Director: Jürgen F Eysel

Commercial Director: Dr Jürgen Remmerbach
Controlling Director: Herbert Stippel

Products: Permanent way material for wood, concrete and steel sleepers, meeting the technical conditions of delivery of railway companies worldwide; ribbed base plates for track and switches, coach screws and hook bolts, clip plates, elastic rail spikes, tension clamps, angular guide plates, elastic rail clips etc.

Holland
John Holland International

PO Box 199C, Melbourne, Victoria 3001, Australia

Telephone: +61 3 268 0209
Telex: 30774

Products: Trackwork, track materials, concrete sleepers.

Holland
Holland Co

1020 Washington Avenue, Chicago Hts, Illinois 60411, USA

Telephone: +1 708 756 0650
Telex: 6974773 hol co
Telefax: +1 708 756 2641

President: Philip C Moeller
Senior Vice President, Marketing & Sales: Joseph F Sloat
Vice President, International Sales: René A Hunziker
Engineering Manager: George K Clem
Secretary & Treasurer: Steven M Kuehn

Products: Sales and contracting of electric flash-butt welding personnel and equipment; rail and road mobile welders, portable on-site welding plants and fixed plant management/production services. Holland can supply all support equipment or provide a turnkey operation.
Recent contracts include Monterrey Mexico Light Rail Transit; Robe River, Australia; Canadian National; Conrail USA; Burlington Northern, USA; Metro North Transit, USA; Trailer Train, USA.

Humes Ltd
Concrete Division

World Trade Centre, PO Box 3005, Corner Flinders & Spencer Streets, Melbourne 3005, Australia

Telephone: +61 3 611 3311
Telex: 38015

Products: Concrete sleepers.

Hunslet
The Hunslet Engine Company Ltd

Hunslet Engine Works, Leeds LS10 1BT, England

Telephone: +44 532 432261
Cable: Hunslt, Leeds
Telex: 55237
Telefax: +44 532 420820

Sales Manager: D H Townsley

Products: Self-propelled six-foot and shoulder ballast cleaning machines; rail mounted drainage trenchers.

HWD
Henry Williams Ltd

Dodsworth Street, Darlington, Co Durham DL1 2NJ, England

Telephone: +44 325 462722
Cable: Williams, Darlington
Telex: 58421
Telefax: +44 325 381744

Managing Director: R A Thompson
Marketing Director: C Potts
Works Director: N Dodsworth
Financial Director: P J Morris

Products: Forged and fabricated railway engineering components: rail fish plates, switch levers, switch clamps, buffer stems, signal posts and gantries, adjustable track gauges, dog spikes, rail anchors, luggage lockers, signalling apparatus cases.
Recent contracts have been received from British Rail, Kowloon Railway, Tyne & Wear Metro, BREL, GEC General Signal, Westinghouse, London Underground, Toronto Transit Commission.

ILVA
ILVA SpA

Via Corsica 4, 16128 Genoa, Italy

Telephone: +39 10 55181
Telex: 270069
Telefax: +39 10 594073

MANUFACTURERS / Permanent way equipment

Main works
Viale Resistenza 2, 57025 Piombino, (Li)
Via Torino 19, 10055 Condove (To)

Products: Cast steel rails and rolled section for track work manufactured by computer-controlled process.

International Track Systems
International Track Systems Inc and Railroad Rubber Products

PO Box 857, 620 West 32nd Street, Ashtabula, Ohio 44004, USA

Telephone: +1 216 992 9206/992 6752

Managing Director: H L Reiter
Sales Director: B F Baker

Products: Rubber products for railway track such as butyl rubber shock barriers for use between the base of rails and steel tie plates and between the plates and sleepers; window and door glazings for transit cars.

Intramatic SA

28 Avenue du Leman, CH-1005 Lausanne, Switzerland

IPA
Industria Prefabbricati E Affini

via Provinciale per Trescore, 24050 Calcinate (BG), Italy

Telephone: +39 35 841291
Telex: 301285 creber i
Telefax: +39 35 841040

Products: Pre-fabricated concrete sleepers.
IPA is currently involved in the reconstruction of the railway between Gemona and Pontebba on the Udine-Tarvisio line in northern Italy. It is planned to extend the work to the Austro-Italian border near Tarvisio.

Italsider
Italsider SpA

Via Corsica 4, Genoa, Italy

Telephone: +39 10 5999
Cable: Italsider, Genoa
Telex: 270690

Products: Permanent way equipment including baseplates, fishplates, clips, switches and crossings.

ITI/CLM
Impianti Tecnici Industriale SpA

Via Nazionale 69, 33042 Buttrio, Italy

Telephone: +39 432 298651
Telex: 450618 iticlm i
Telefax: +39 432 298656

Managing Director: F Mancini
Sales Director: G Comelli

Products: Track maintenance machinery, including ballast cleaners and graders; rail fastening equipment.

Jackson Jordan
Jackson Jordan Inc

General sales office: 1699 East Woodfield Road, Schaumburg, Illinois 60173, USA

Telephone: +1 312 843 3995
Telefax: +1 312 569 2667

Works: Ludington, Michigan

Chairman: J O'Laughlin
President: D J Donahue

Products: Complete line of tie tampers, automatic with or without liners (curve and tangent one unit); non-automatic switch tampers; surfacing light beam fits all manufacturers' tampers; hand tampers; Jackson/Jordan spreader-ditcher/snow plough; flaw detection; corrugation measurement; switch and crossing grinding.

IPA slab track system turnouts, Rome-Fiumicino airport connection

Jakem
Jakem Timbers Ltd

The Old Malt House, 125 High Street, Uckfield, East Sussex BN22 1EG, England

Telephone: +44 825 768555
Telex: 95670
Telefax: +44 825 768483

Directors: R A Helyar
G E Davies

Products: Hardwood sleepers, crossing and bridge timbers.

Jambes-Namur
Jambes-Namur, SA des Ateliers de Construction

5100 Jambes, Belgium

Telephone: +32 81 30 18 51
Cable: Jamur, Jambes
Telex: 59127

General Manager: Etienne Offergeld
Director, Assistant General Management: Louis Warolus
Head Engineer, Technical Department: Raymond Olivier
Head, Sales Department: Paul De Groote
Head, Fabrication Department: Pol Gueret
Head, Erection Department: Louis Piret
Head, Mechanical Department: Werner Schank
Head, Research Steel Constructions: Jean Rulmont
Pressure Vessels: Marc Francois
Head, Financial Department: Jean Leurquin

Products: Bridges of all kinds.

Jaragua
Jaragua SA, Industries Mecanicas

Av Mofarrej 840, 05311 São Paulo, Brazil

Telephone: +55 11 260 4011

Product Manager: S Coscia

Products: Switches, crossings and components.

JW
James Walker & Co Ltd

Lion Works, Woking, Surrey GU22 8AP, England

Telephone: +44 483 757575
Telex: 859221
Telefax: +44 483 755711

Technical Director (Trackelast): L B Goulding
Projects Manager: H M Kenyon
Customer Service Manager: D W Aves

Products: Resilient track support materials for all types of permanent way construction; the resilient cork-elastomer materials are made without grooves or profiles with low to high stiffness characteristics to suit all types of track support construction. Product range includes: rail seat pads for concrete or timber sleepers; baseplate pads; under-sleeper pads for reducing ground-borne vibration; ballast mats for reducing ground-borne vibration; continuous rail support material for slab track; and specialised resilient materials and pre-fabrications for unconventional track support systems. Additional products include specialised adhesives and grouts used in permanent way applications.

Overseas companies
James Walker Australia Pty Ltd, Lion Works, 32

Permanent way equipment / **MANUFACTURERS** 365

Kershaw Type 46 ballast regulator

Kershaw Type 47 sleeper replacer

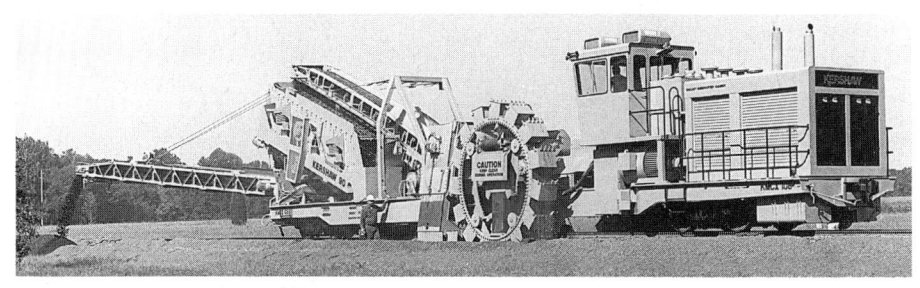

Kershaw Type 90 ballast undercutter/cleaner

Clapham Road, Regents Park 2143, PO Box 13, Sydney, New South Wales, Australia

James Walker Belgium NV, 't Serclaesdreef 8, 2220 Wommelgem, Antwerp, Belgium

James Walker Ireland Ltd, 17a Goldenbridge Industrial Estate, Inchicore, Dublin 8, Ireland

James Walker France sarl, 1/7 rue Edouard Branly, Zone Industrielle de la Garenne, BP 73, 93602 Aulnay-sous-Bois, France

James Walker Nederland BV, Röntgenstraat 7-9, 3261 LK Oud-Beijerland, PO Box 1506, 3260BA Oud-Beijerland, Netherlands

James Walker Italiana srl, via Pontevecchio 2/4, 120127 Milan, Italy

James Walker New Zealand Ltd, Rostrevor House, Corner of Marion & Vivian Streets, PO Box 11-055, Wellington C1, New Zealand

James Walker Iberica SA, Santa Lucia 8/10, Bilbao 4, Spain

James Walker Mfg Co, 511 West 195th Street, PO Box 467, Glenwood, Illinois 60425, USA

KAGO
A Kaufmann AG

Pilatusstrasse 3, 6300 Zug, Switzerland

Telephone: +41 42 216700
Telefax: +41 41 823701

Products: Specialist engineering for railways, including: complete range of non-screwed rail clamps and rail connectors for various rail profiles and sections of 4 to 240 mm^2; various fastenings along rail tracks for cables, wires, etc; special welding electrodes for copper welding; special earthing connectors; complete range of welding connectors in 35 and 50 mm^2.

Kango
Kango Ltd

Hanger Lane, London W5 1DS, England

Telephone: +44 81 998 2911
Telex: 937021
Telefax: +44 81 991 0132

Chairman: L I H Dacey
Sales and Marketing Director: M J Harrison

Products: Portable electric ballast tampers; generators; hand-held stone blowers; general power tools.

Kershaw
Kershaw Manufacturing Company, Inc

PO Box 17340, Montgomery, Alabama 36117-0340, USA

Telephone: +1 205 271 1000
Telex: 593416
Telefax: +1 205 277 6551

President: Royce Kershaw
Sales & Marketing Manager: John Whitaker
Sales Representative (Europe): Alain Sigfrit

Products: Ballast regulators, ballast undercutter/cleaners, railroad cranes, equipment for sleeper and rail replacement, sand and snow removal, vegetation control and various other maintenance operation.

Kershaw ballast undercutter/cleaners are high production machines that excavate and clean total track sections, shoulders and turnouts, and which are operational after 15 minutes upon arrival at job site. The undercutter operates with minimum disturbance to existing track line and surface, eliminating the need for track raising and lining devices. Five models are available with outputs of up to 750 m of track per hour, and shoulder cleaning up to 1600 m per hour.

The Kershaw mobile rescue cranes are heavy duty lifters, specifically designed for handling the railroad's toughest and heaviest lifting jobs. They feature a heavy duty carrier specially designed by Kershaw for maximum lifting utilisation. These cranes are capable of travelling over the road or on the rail with equal ease and are designed to handle locomotive wagon panel track sections and containers. Eight models are available with lifting capacities from 78 to 135 tons, equipped with lattice and hydraulic telescopic booms.

The Kershaw ballast regulators perform ballast shaping, shoulder profiling and a variety of other functions. They feature a one-pass transfer plow, hydraulically controlled reversible wings and a broom attachment. The one-pass transfer plow is hydraulically controlled from the operator's cab. The unit can plow in or out, and all plowing operations can be performed in either direction of travel. Eight models are available from 70 hp to 250 hp with optional integrated hopper, snow and sand equipment.

Kershaw
Kershaw Manufacturing Canada Ltd

3300 Marleau Ave, PO Box 1929, Cornwall, Ontario K6H 6N7, Canada

Telephone: +1 613 938 6104
Telex: 05 811571
Telefax: +1 613 933 8766

Manager: Rene Lalonde

Regional Sales Office: Winnipeg

Products: Complete range of self-propelled machines for mechanised track, switch and yard maintenance; ballast regulator and ballast broom-snow switch cleaner-brushcutter attachment; brush-type cribber; track broom; yard cleaner; dual-sleeper saw and end remover; sleeper bed scarifier and sleeper inserter; sleeper-end remover; sleeper injector; sleeper, bridge, and bundle cranes; crawler adzer; track and switch liner; clear way brushcutter and snow blower, undercutter and ballast cleaner, portable set off.

KIHN
Ateliers de Constructions KIHN Sarl

17 rue de l'Usine, L-3701 Rumelange, Luxembourg

Telephone: +352 56 47 71-1
Telex: 1728 kihn lu
Telefax: +352 56 58 54

Manager: Jean-Pol Braquet
Export Sales Engineer: Thiery Kayser

Products: Engineering and supply of turnouts, points and crossings, crossovers and junctions, trackwork combinations, monobloc and welded frogs, diamond crossings, expansion joints, glued insulated joints and special layouts for urban transport systems, main-line railways and industrial network. After-sales service.

Klöckner-Werke
Klöckner-Werke AG

Georgsmarienwerke, Postfach 2780, 4500 Osnabrück, Federal Republic of Germany

Telephone: +49 541 3221
Telex: 09 4742

Works Director: Dr Otto Mehner
Sales Director: Hans-Heinrich Niebaum

Products: Flat-bottom rail; fishplates; special slewing fishplates; fishplates for insulated joints; inserts for insulated fishplates; tongue rails; full-web rails; guard rails; flangeway sections; conductor rails; heavy crane rails; Herkules rails and components; grooved rails; thick-web rails; ribbed soleplates; points; crossings; complete track system of flat-bottom or grooved rails; points for permanent railway without ballast bed; points with movable frogs; paving points and track of the special 'Herkules' profile; hard-surfacing of switch rails; scarfed joints; stop block devices; bonded insulated rail joints for the German Federal Railway (DB), tramways and underground railways, secondary lines and local railways, foreign state and private railways, owners of private sidings and all industrial railways; powered and idle wheel-sets; wheel-sets of light construction; wheel-sets for heavy loads; wheel-sets for gauge changes; sound-proofed wheel-sets; rubber-suspended wheel-sets; bond-shrunk wheel-

MANUFACTURERS / Permanent way equipment

sets; axles; hollow axles; solid wheels; wheel centres; tyres, and crane wheels.

Kloos Railway Engineering
Kloos Kinderdijk BV

PO Box 3, 2960 AA Kinderdijk, Netherlands

Telex: 29382

Products: Switches, crossings, turnouts and frogs; rail fastenings; rail shunter and shunting systems; crane rails and chairs.

Koehring
Koehring GmbH-Bomag Division

Postfach 180, 5407 Boppard/Rhein, Federal Republic of Germany

Telephone: +49 6742 2051
Cable: Bomag, Boppard
Telex: 04 263 16

Products: Tamping compactors, reversing vibratory plate compactors, trench compactors, double vibratory rollers, single-drum vibratory rollers, double vibratory slope compactors, tandem vibratory rollers, towed vibratory rollers, sheepsfoot rollers, pneumatic-tyred rollers, soil stabilisers, refuse compactors.

Koppers
Koppers Industries Inc

1650 Koppers Bldg, Pittsburgh, Pennsylvania 15219, USA

Telephone: +1 412 227 2396

Marketing Manager: Dale Beachy

Products: Crossties and switchties, grade crossing panels, EZ panel grade crossings.

Krautkrämer
Krautkrämer GmbH

Robert Bosch Strasse 3, PO Box 1363, 5030 Hürth 5, Federal Republic of Germany

Telephone: +49 2233 601 0
Cable: Impulsschall, Hürth
Telex: 8881643 echo d
Telefax: +49 601402

Products: Stationary rail testing installations, rail testers, rail test cars.

Lamp
Lamp Manufacturing & Railway Supplies Ltd

Signal House, Stanbridge Road, Leighton Buzzard, Beds LU7 8JH, England

Telephone: +44 525 377477
Telex: 826014 lamp g

Chairman: F A Barnes
Technical and Sales Director: A P Bale
Chief Sales Engineer: D Farrington

Products: Oil and electric lamps for a variety of railway applications; switch heaters, including the Planlite

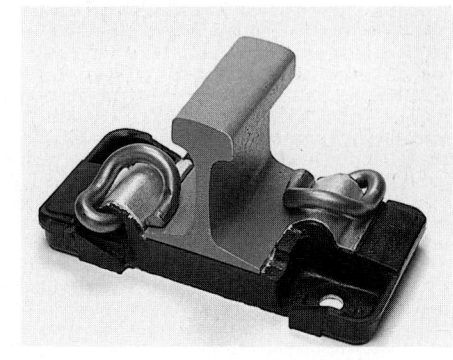

Lord direct fixation fastener

Loram 88-stone rail grinder, with three individually-monitored 20 hp grinding modules per grinding carriage

5000 designed to allow mechanical tamping machines to operate without the need to remove the switch heater from the points; terminal blocks, fuseholders and lightning arresters. Lamp has yearly contracts for its products and spare parts with British Rail.

Lauwaert
Lauwaert & Cie SA

Havenstraat, 1800 Vilvorde, Belgium

Telephone: +32 2 251 20 20
Telex: 25438

Managing Director: G Herpoel

Products: Supply, installation and maintenance of track.

Lindapter
Lindapter International Ltd

Lindsay House, Canal Road, Bradford, West Yorkshire BD2 1AL, England

Telephone: +44 274 370717
Telex: 51147
Telefax: +44 274 370766

Managing Director: H R Hassell
Sales Director, Home & Export: D B Thompson
Export Sales Manager: J Kaznowski
Marketing Manager: E J Lesniak

Subsidiary company
Tecner Lindapter Sarl
79 rue du Fossé Blanc, 92230 Gennevilliers, France
Telephone: +33 1 40 85 07 37
Telex: 641 155 (ext 732)
Telefax: +33 1 40 85 03 10

Products: Holdfast adjustable rail clips: two-piece rail clip giving stepless lateral adjustment of up to +/−11.5 mm, depending on the diameter of the holding bolt used. The 'soft' clip allows rail to lift to cater for rail wave; the 'hard' clip holds rail down tightly and the spring clip incorporates an elastomer 'spring' to hold the rail down and also cater for rail wave. Type LR: provides adjustment to accommodate a flange of any thickness. Type BR: suits flat bottom or bridge rails from 5° to 10° slope.

Linsinger
Linsinger Maschinenbau GmbH

Dr Linsinger Strasse 24, A-4662 Steyrermühl, Austria

Telephone: +43 7613 2411-0
Telex: 24645
Telefax: +43 7613 2441-38

Managing Director: Ing H Riepl
Technical Manager: D I Pomikacsek
Marketing: Hermann Pamminger

Products: Mobile rail milling machine with post grinding and measuring equipment.

Loram
Loram Maintenance of Way, Inc

PO Box 188, 3900 Arrowhead Drive, Hamel, Minnesota 55340, USA

Telephone: +1 612 478 6014
Telex: 29 0391
Telefax: +1 612 478 6916

Vice-President, Marketing: G A Farris
International Marketing Manager: D A Powell

Principal subsidiary company
Loram Pty Ltd

Corner of Kangan & Munda Way, Wedgefield, PO Box 2492, South Hedland, Western Australia, 6722, Australia

Telephone: +61 92 72 3111
Telefax: +61 91 72 3412

Products: Self-propelled rail grinders of 16, 24, 32, 44, 72 and 88 stones; self-propelled shoulder ballast cleaners; self-propelled ditch cleaners; rail corrugation analyser; and various undertrack equipment.

Lord
Lord Corporation
Industrial Products Division

1952 West Grandview Blvd, PO Box 10040, Erie, Pennsylvania 16514-0040, USA

Telephone: +1 814 868 5424
Telex: 914438
Telefax: +1 814 868 3109

Chief Executive: Donald M Alstadt
President: Robert E Brooker Jr
Marketing Managers: Ray Misjan
                          Alan Gregg
Communications Specialist: John J Buchna

Products: Elastomeric direct fixation fasteners. Manufactured in a variety of designs for new and existing transit systems, they are installed at grade, below grade and on elevated structures, and are fully tested and qualified by user transit authorities. The mid-range direct fixation fastener vertical spring rate ranges from 100 000 to 300 000 lb/in, the low-range (soft) direct fixation fastener from 60 000 to 90 000 lb/in, and the mid-range special trackwork fastener's vertical spring rate is comparable to that of the mid-range direct fixation fastener. Rail clamping systems are available for aerial and rigid installations. Lord fasteners, placed between the rail and the track support structure, reduce the transmission of noise and vibration with controlled rail motion.

Matema
Matema Materiali Meccanici SpA

Via Ardeatina Km 21, 00040 S Palomba, Rome, Italy

Telephone: +39 6 919112
Cable: Matistal, Pomezia
Telex: 68150

Chairman: R Blomqwist
Managing Director: R Naggar
Chief Sales Director: F Vittori
Export Sales Director: G Uccelli

Products: Track recording trolleys; automatic track levelling, tamping and lining machines; ballast cleaners; ballast regulators; heavy and light gang cars; sleeper boring machines; rail power saws; wrenches and drills; continuous-rail welding machines and grinding machines; electric generators (portable); gauges; handfacing equipment; jacks; screwing machines; sleeper placing machines; spike drivers and extractors; track laying equipment.

Permanent way equipment / **MANUFACTURERS** 367

P 91 UMD track renewal train adapted to German Federal Railway requirements

Matériel de Voie
Le Matériel de Voie SA

Cedex 35, 92072 Paris-La Défense, France

Telephone: +33 1 47 67 96 00
Telex: 612550 matvoi
Telefax: +33 1 47 67 96 50

Products: Rails, fishplates, baseplates.

MATISA

Matisa
Matériel Industriel SA

Head office: Matisa Matériel Industriel SA, Case Postale, 1001 Lausanne, Switzerland

Telephone: +44 21 634 99 34
Telex: 454 447 mat ch
Telefax: +44 21 634 37 52

Works: Crissier (Lausanne), Santa Palomba (Rome)

Subsidiaries: Italy, France, Federal Republic of Germany, Spain, Japan

Products: Spot tampers; automatic tamper-leveller-liners for plain track and switches; track renewal trains; new track-laying trains; ballast cleaners; ballast regulators; service vehicles; track-measuring cars and analysing equipment.

Matisa SpA
Matisa SpA

Via Ardeatina km. 21, 00040 Pomezia S Palomba (Rome), Italy

Telephone: +39 6 9194112
Telex: 622144
Telefax: +39 6 9194083

Chairman: H P Wyder
Managing and Sales Director: R Naggar
Financial Director: A Fantoni
Export Sales Director: G Uccelli
Technical Director: F Marconi

Products: Track recording trolleys; ballast regulators; heavy and light gang cars; switch-laying equipments; sleeper boring machines; rail power saws; wrenches and drills; screwing machines.
Sale of all equipments of Matisa Matériel Industriel SA, Crissier, Switzerland, including automatic tamping and lining machines; ballast cleaners; ballast compactors; track laying equipments; track recording cars and coaches.

Matix-Industries
Société Matix Industries

59 rue Saint-Lazare, 75009 Paris, France

Telephone: +33 1 42 80 65 55
Telex: 650672

Marketing Manager: M Chevrery

Products: Design and supply of rail reclaiming and welding plants on a turnkey basis. Matix has also developed specific equipments and machines such as: ultrasonic testing stands; straightening presses; reprofiling machines; welding and stripping machines; grinding machines; and rail handling equipment.
The company additionally supplies ultrasonic testing systems.

Type R 20 LS ballast regulator and recuperator

Type B 50 D continuous tamper

Type C 90 L ballast cleaner

Type MPV 8 track recording railcar

Electronic control panel of Matix ultrasonic testing car MXUS 30 40 MAI

368 MANUFACTURERS / Permanent way equipment

McGregor
McGregor Paving Ltd

Turnoaks Lane, Birdholme, Chesterfield, Derbyshire
S40 2HB, England

Telephone: +44 246 276791
Cable: McGregors, Chesterfield
Telex: 547467
Telefax: +44 246 207680

Managing Director: J M Brown

Products: In collaboration with British Rail's Research and Development Division, Robert McGregor developed PACT — the Paved Concrete Track system. PACT is an alternative to conventional ballasted track and is virtually maintenance free.

The system consists of a continuously reinforced concrete slab which provides a continuous support to the rails through a resilient rail pad. The main advantages of the system are its shallow depth of construction and that it ensures that the track geometry remains within tolerance over long periods with negligible maintenance.

The PACT system has been in service for over 18 years throughout the world. A recent contract involved the installation of PACT through the 14 km-long Rogers Pass tunnel, the longest rail tunnel in North America.

McKay
McKay Rail Products
(A division of McKay Australia Ltd)

44-80 Hampstead Road, Maidstone, Victoria 3012, Australia

Telephone: +61 317 8961
Cable: Agridisc
Telex: 31538
Telefax: +61 318 6369

Main works: Maidstone, Victoria
Port Wakefield Road, Gepps Cross, South Australia

Chairman: L T McKay
Chief Executive: T R B Threlfall
Director & General Manager: A P McCall
International Sales Manager: L A Sheppard

Subsidiaries: Ralph McKay (Canada) Limited
Ralph McKay (USA) Limited

Products: McKay 'Safelok' concrete rail fastening system; timber and steel sleepers; rail anchors for most sizes of rail.

The contract for 525,000 concrete sleeper sets of McKay Safelok Fastenings for Australain National has just been completed. The contract with Burlington Northern for 3.5 million concrete sleeper sets of McKay is at the halfway point as is the Robe River mining contract for 316,000 concrete sleeper sets. A large proportion of Union Pacific's fastening requirements are now McKay Safelok. Norfolk Southern: a substantial test section will be installed in 1990 and negotiations are continuing with a major European railway.

Midwest Steel
A Division of Midwest Corporation

PO Box 271, 1012 Kanawha Blvd East, Charleston, West Virginia 25321, USA

Telephone: +1 304 343 8874
Telefax: +1 304 346 0624

President: Joseph Guilfoile
Assistant VP: John Wilhoit
Director of Purchasing: Bill Kenny
National Sales Manager: Hank Ortwein
General Manager, Trackwork Sales: Jim Mihailoff
District Manager, International Sales: David Hayes
General Trackwork Superintendent: Pete Mumber
Director, Corporate Communications: Penny Ellis

Installation of PACT track by McGregor

McKay Safelok for concrete sleepers

Switch stand by Midwest Steel

Products: Rail, new and relay; crane rail; rail accessories; trackwork, light and heavy; turnouts; frogs; switches; switch stands; crossings; guard rails; twin-tie plates; braces; heel blocks; track tools; crossties; bumping posts; gauge rods; bolts/spikes.

MIO
Manoir Industries Outreau

PO Box 119, 62230 Outreau, France

Telephone: +33 21 30 58 00
Telex: 214709

Sales Manager: F Sudol

Products: Manganese steel monobloc crossings to AREA and VIC specifications.

Mitchell Equipment Corporation

16 Ballantyne Road, Kewdale, Western Australia 6105

Telephone: +61 9 350 6363
Telefax: 451 4516

Managing Director: A G Evans
Marketing Manager: G R Birkbeck
Sales Engineer: P A N Hayes

Principal subsidiary: Mitchell Equipment Corporation, Toledo, Ohio, USA

Products: All road/rail vehicular conversion equipment; insulated fishplate joints, switchblade slide pads; specialised track insulation etc.
Current contracts include vehicles for Vic Rail, West Rail (Australia), New Zealand Railways and equipment for Royal State Railways (Thailand).

Mitsukawa
Mitsukawa Metal Works Co Ltd

21 Harima-cho-nijima, Kako-district, Hyogo Pref, Japan

Telephone: +81 794 35 2288

Products: Rail fastenings, steel sleepers and forged crossings.

Modern Track Machinery
Modern Track Machinery Canada Ltd

5926 Shawson Drive, Mississauga, Ontario L4W 3W5, Canada

Telephone: +1 416 564 1211
Cable: Momack
Telex: 06 960140
Telefax: +1 416 0 564 1217

President: C Geismar
Sales Manager: B Pingel
International Sales Manager: M J Byrne

Products: Railway track maintenance machines and tools with after-sales service.

Monterrey
Monterrey Industrial Ferroviaria SA de CV

Insurgentes Sur 2462, Villa Alvara Obregón 01070, Mexico DF

Telephone: +52 550 4605/8377, +52 548 9470
Telex: 1772 503
Telefax: +52 550 6915

President: Felipe Zirion
Vice President, Marketing: Cesar Mota
Manager: Alberto Elias

Products: Turnout sets for all rail sections, solid manganese or assembled frogs, switch-points, guard rails, plates, heel plates and switch stands.

Moore & Steele
Moore & Steele Corporation

PO Box 189, Owego, New York 13827, USA

Telephone: +1 607 687 2751
Telefax: +1 607 687 3914

President S M Lounsberry

Products: Rail lubrication systems.

Moss
George Moss Ltd

PO Box 136, Mount Hawthorn 6016, 461-465 Scarborough Beach Road, Osborne Park, Western Australia 6017, Australia

Telephone: +61 9 446 8844
Cable: Gemco, Perth
Telex: 92645
Telefax: +61 9 446 3404

Managing Director: F A Quilty
Technical Manager: A Small
Railway Sales Manager: N R Geddes

Products: Track maintenance machinery, such as resleepering machines, rail-handling cranes, sleeper-handling machines, ballast scarifiers (linear), spike pullers, track jacks etc; track layers; rail flash-butt welding equipment.
The company can now offer rail flaw detection, speed weigh, light slice track recording equipment and track management systems.

Newag Eurorail
Newag GmbH & Co KG

Ripshorster Strasse, Tor 73, 4200 Oberhausen-Osterfeld, Federal Republic of Germany

Telephone: +49 208 865 030
Telex: 17208 383
Telefax: +49 208 86503 20

Managing Director: C Kohl
Technical Director: E Fiaccadori
Sales Director: G Halfmann

Products: Track motor cars; gauger's and platform trolleys; multi-purpose and custom-built cars and trolleys; special purpose trains, e.g. ballast and dirt handling trains for ballast cleaners, mobile concrete plants built on wagons for foundation work on bridges, tunnels and for electrification; Hyrail rail and road-vehicles and cranes; remanufacture of tampers, levellers and liners for all gauges, ballast regulators and cleaners, gantries, rail positioners, rail lifters and threaders.

Constitution: An associate company of Gleismac Italiana SpA.

Nippon Kido Kogyo
Nippon Kido Kogyo Co Ltd

21-1 Nishi Shinjuku 1-chome, Shinjuku-ku, Tokyo 100, Japan

Telephone: +81 3 343 8321
Telefax: +81 3 349 8705

Managing Director, Chief of Marketing: Masuzo Ida

Products: Pre-cast concrete slab for level crossings, concrete sleepers, rail fastenings.

NKK
NKK Corporation

1-2, 1-chome, Marunouchi, Chiyoda-ku, Tokyo, Japan

Telephone: +81 3 217 2248
Cable: Kokannk, Tokyo
Telex: 222 2811 nkk j
Telefax: +81 3 214 8417

Chairman: Minoru Kanao
President: Yoshinari Yamashiro

Products: Rails to meet all internationally recognised specifications including AREA, ASTM, UIC, BS, JIS and others.
NKK has developed special heat-treated premium rails with high wear and fatigue resistance properties for heavy axleload and heavy curvature rail applications. NKK currrently produces two types of premium rails: New Head-Hardened (NHH); and Low Alloy Head-Hardened (AHH). The heads of these rails are slack-quenched in order to impart a fine pearlitic structure to improve wear resistance.
The top surfaces of NKK NHH and AHH rails feature Brinell hardness (H_B) values of 341 to 388, and H_B 351 to 405, respectively. AHH rails show little change in hardness even after flash welding, and have increased resistance to end batter. The steel is produced by a continuous casting machine including a vacuum degassing process, which results in very clean steel with low non-metallic inclusions and very low sulphur and hydrogen content. NKK has recently developed heat-treated rails, designated THH, with high toughness for low temperature service down to 60° C.
NKK NHH and AHH rails have been supplied to major railway companies in the USA, Canada and other countries.
NKK also has extensive experience in providing rail welding technology, both for hardware and software, and welding services. The enclosed arc welding repairs of high-speed Shinkansen track are performed chiefly by NKK. The company has developed an automatic rail welding machine, the Rail Welding Robot, for the field welding of rail. This machine has been realised by applying the high-speed rotating arc welding method to enclosed arc welding. The arc time per joint is about one-third that of the manual enclosed arc welding. Welding quality is claimed to be more stable than that of aluminothermic welding.

Noord-Ned
Noord-Nederlandsche Machinefabriek BV

St Vitusstraat 81, PO Box 171, 9670 AD Winschoten, Netherlands

Telephone: +31 5970 15225
Telex: 53096

Sales Manager: P E A Nankmann

Products: The multi-purpose Noordned railhopper for track and overhead contact wire maintenance units.
The railhopper is a self-powered rail vehicle fitted with steel crawlers, which make it a cross-country vehicle capable of moving itself on and off the rails. Once on the rails it runs on four wheels. It moves up to the rails at right angles. As soon as the vehicle starts crossing the first rail a support comes out at the rear, which puts the vehicle in a level position. At the front a slide arm is pushed across the second rail to prevent the crawlers from dropping between the rails. Two position hooks block the railhopper as soon as its railwheels are in a position above the rails. When the wheels are lowered the support, the slide arm and the position hooks automatically return to their original position. Maximum speed on rails is 40 km/h. When it is operated from its aerial platform, however, its rail running speed is automatically limited to 5 km/h. The aerial platform can be raised to a maximum height of 9 metres above the rails without any extra support being necessary. The assembly is insulated up to 1500 volts. The diesel engine is 49 hp and the drive hydrostatic.

Nordco

Export sales head office: 182 W Oklahoma Avenue, Milwaukee, Wisconsin 53207, USA

Telephone: +1 414 769 4600
Telefax: +1 414 481 3199

President: Don Himes
Marketing Manager: Steve Wiedenfeld

Licensee: Micon Pty Ltd, PO Box 310, Kingswood, Adelaide, South Australia 50

Nordberg Ride-On Adzer

370 MANUFACTURERS / Permanent way equipment

Products: Trackliners, switchliners, self-propelled adzers, rail drills, surf-rail grinders, heavy-duty rail grinders, utility grinders, spike hammers, hydraulic spike pullers, spike straighteners, tie drills, self-propelled spike pullers, hydraulic powerjacks, dun-rite gauging machines, hydra-spikers, line indicators, E-Z lifts, tie spacers, rail gang spikers, X-level indicators, track inspectors, one-man scarifier inserters and sleeper removers/inserters.

Nortrak Ltd

16160 River Road, Richmond, British Columbia, Canada V6V 1L6

Telephone: +1 604 273 3030
Telefax: +1 604 273 8927

President: A J Tuningley
Sales Manager: R A Fraser
Railroad Sales: G S Weatherly

Products: A full line of trackwork products specialising in high-solidity manganese products such as RBM and SSGM frogs as well as diamond crossings. Supplier of a full line of new and relay track materials.

Recent contracts include Grand Island NE triple diamond crossing (1989); two-year RBM and SSGM frog contract with BN (1989); Potash Corp of Saskatchewan, 28 turnouts and 7 miles of track (1989).

Oleo
Oleo International

Walcote, Blackdown, Leamington Spa, Warwickshire CV32 6QX, England

Telephone: +44 926 421116
Telex: 311458
Telefax: +44 926 450273

Products: A wide range of long-stroke hydraulic buffers suitable for mounting on fixed or sliding end-stops. Applications include freight yards, steelworks and passenger terminals.

On sliding friction end-stops the need for continual re-setting of the friction elements is eliminated, and the hydraulic buffers absorb all of the impact energy at low speeds. Typically a 400-tonne train may be arrested by a pair of 800 mm stroke buffers at 6 km/h without causing the end-stop to slide. Initial and final jerk forces are also eliminated. These buffer units are available for all types of rail operation from LRVs to heavy freight.

Orton
Orton McCullough Crane Company

Oakbrook Executive Plaza, 1211 West 22nd Street, Oakbrook, Illinois 60521, USA

Telephone: +1 312 573 1695
Cable: Orcrane

Products: Cranes and heavy lifting gear.

Osmose
Osmose Railroad Division

PO Box 8276, Madison, Wisconsin 53708, USA

Telephone: +1 608 221 2292, +1 800 356 5952
Telefax: +1 608 221 0618

Vice-President: Ken Norton
Product Manager: David Ostby

Products: NONFLAM spray-on fire retardant coating with a 15-year lifespan. Easy application up to 600 lineal ft per day; available in 55-gallon drums; environmentally safe. ADZ-LIFE wood sleeper preservative for in-place preservative treatment of the sleeper plate area. Especially useful for recycled sleepers; can be pumped to facilitate large production methods; available in 5- and 55-gallon containers. ADZ-PAD preservative sleeper pad wafer designed especially for rail relay. Environmentally safe and employee-friendly; proven results on North American railroads; low cost; high productivity. Services: in-place preservative treatment of timber bridges; complete inspection and repair of concrete, steel and timber bridges.

Nordberg 'Grabber' dual rail spike puller by Nordco

Nordberg Super B automatic spiking machine by Nordco

Oleo Type 24 hydraulic buffers fitted to sliding friction end-stops

Permanent way equipment / **MANUFACTURERS**

Pandrol
Pandrol International Ltd

63 Station Road, Addlestone, Weybridge, Surrey KT15 2BH

Telephone: +44 932 850666
Telex: 21474
Telefax: +44 932 850858

Group Managing Director: J A Pool
Managing Director, Fastenings Division: G M Lodge
Marketing Director, Fastenings Division: J Beal-Preston

Principal subsidiaries:
Pandrol UK Ltd, Worksop, Notts
Pandrol Incorporated USA, Bridgeport, New Jersey
Pandrol North America, Ludington, Michigan
Dapco Industries Inc, New Jersey, USA

Products: Design and manufacture of rail fastening systems, and allied products including 'Pandrol' brand rail fastenings, lockspikes and elastic rail spikes; Pandriver rail fastening installation machines; 'Panloggers' Pandrol Timbershield rods and Pandrol resilient railpads; ultrasonic testing equipment; rail grinders; tamping equipment.

Built around the well-proven Pandrol rail clip, the range of track fastenings offered by Pandrol is suitable for all applications on concrete, timber and steel sleepers and slab track and for use under every type of traffic from simple crane rails, sugar-cane railways and LRT to heavy haul freight.

With the introduction of the Pandrol Gauge-Lock the successful range of Pandrol track-fastening systems has been expanded to include a low-cost resilient fastening for use on lightly-used railways.

Permali
Permali Gloucester Ltd

Bristol Road, Gloucester GL1 5SU, England

Telephone: +44 452 28282
Telex: 43293
Telefax: +44 452 507409

Product: Glued rail joints, densified wood fishplates.

Permaquip
Permanent Way Equipment Co Ltd

Giltway, Giltbrook, Nottingham NG16 2GQ, England

Telephone: +44 602 384004
Telex: 37254 permaq g
Telefax: +44 602 384821

General Manager: Michael D Bailey
Marketing Director: M J Hudson
Sales and Marketing Manager: Paul Bancroft

Products: A wide range of on-track machines including:
Ballast Packer: a tough, durable, heavy-lifting, soft packing, off-trackable machine which produces good level top and can be worked with laser levelling equipment or sighting board system.
Permaclipper: this has a rail clip driving rate of 3000 per hour and clip removal at 20 000 per hour; it is reliable even with old clips.
Overhead machine: this enables inspection, maintenance and conversion work to be carried out on electrification equipment, bridges, tunnels and any location that requires overhead access quickly and safely.
PCT: a Mobile Welder's Workshop, providing all power functions for welding and related work, which carries the men, all materials and equipment and provides for full weather protection for in situ welding work.
BREV: enlarged version of the PCT, which carries four rail lengths each up to 9 m long; it is a completely self-contained emergency workshop capable of travel speeds up to 80 km/h for rapid response.
Inspection Saloon/Personnel Carrier: a high-speed, self-powered, 'quality ride' vehicle with all round

Dapco Industries ultrasonic flaw detection wheel probes

HCT on overhead wire inspection (Permaquip)

visibility and immediate driver control, accommodating 10 men.
HCT (High Capacity Trolley): recently introduced and suitable for all overhead work on tunnels, bridges, overhead electrification equipment and track side structures, it incorporates a very large high lift platform with wide outreach. The vehicle is totally stable on all track and has free travel speed options from 55 to 100 km/h. Operational control is from the sizeable working area platform. The vehicle has capacity to propel heavily laden trailers and OLE. British Rail has lately ordered 16 of these trolleys, use of which will enable appreciable reduction in use of diesel-powered work trains in electrified areas.
Rastic: straightens welded joints (and removes other rail dips) accurately to 0.15 mm SD and quickly at 80 operations per hour.

In addition, a complete range of track tools, including weld trimmers and hydrostressors is available.

Advances in productivity, safety, optimisation of track possessions and quality/integrity of work are claimed for all Permaquip machines.

Pettibone
Pettibone Corporation
Railroad Products Group

5401 W Grand Avenue, Chicago, Illinois 60639, USA

Telephone: +1 312 745 9496
Telex: 6871485
Telefax: +1 312 237 3763

Main works: Pettibone Ohio
6917 Bessemer Avenue, Cleveland, Ohio 44127, USA

President: Larry Klumpp
General Manager: T E Hitesman

Products: Switches, switch points, frogs, crossings, switch stands, guard rails, rail fasteners, compromise joints, switch plates, mobile maintenance-of-way and material-handling equipment.

Phoenix
Phoenix AG

Hannoversche Strasse 88, PO Box 90 08 54, 2100 Hamburg 90, Harburg, Federal Republic of Germany

Telephone: +49 40 76 67–1
Telex: 217 611 pxhh d
Telefax: +49 40 76 67 211

Managing Director: K Ellegast
Technical Manager: B Meister
Sales Manager: K Wankel

Products: Elastomer track bed matting: CentriCon and Megiflex rail fastener; rubber groove-sealing sections for safety of rails in workshops and other pedestrian areas.

Phoenix's engineers, physicists and chemists have been concerned for years with the problems of reducing vibration in machines and vehicles, and have developed a wide range of elastomer products for vibration and noise attenuation on the railways.

Pintsch Bamag
Pintsch Bamag Antriebs- und Verkehrstechnik GmbH

Postfach 10 04 20, 4220 Dinslaken, Federal Republic of Germany

Telephone: +49 2134 602/0
Telex: 0855 1938
Telefax: +49 2134 160 2266

Products: Automatic propane-fuelled infra-red and electric point heating equipment and solid state snow detectors.

MANUFACTURERS / Permanent way equipment

Plasser Continuous Action Tamper 09-CAT

Plasser
Plasser American Corporation

2001 Myers Road, PO Box 5464, Chesapeake, Virginia 23324-0464, USA

Telephone: +1 804 543 3526
Telex: 82 3662

Products: Automatic track tamping, levelling and lining machines; switch tamping, levelling and lining machines; ballast compacting machines; ballast regulators; ballast brooms; ballast cleaning machines; crib cleaning machines; track recording cars; railway motor cars; railway maintenance and crane cars; speciality track maintenance machines.

Plasser
Plasser & Theurer

Head office: Johannesgasse 3, A-1010 Vienna, Austria

Telephone: +43 1 515 72-0
Cable: Bahnbau, Vienna
Telex: 1/32117 a plas a
Telefax: +43 1 222 513 18 01

Main works: Pummererstrasse 5, 4021 Linz Donau

Principal subsidiaries:
Australia
Plasser Australia Pty Ltd, 2 Plasser Court, PO Box 537, St Marys, NSW
Telephone: +61 62 39 033
Telex: 24 140; 92366 plasser aa
Telefax: +61 900612/623 6502

Brazil
Plasser do Brasil Ltda, Rua Campo Grande, 3050 Campo Grande, 23000 Rio de Janeiro
Telephone: +55 21 39 43 032
Telex: 21 22 523 pbcr br
Telefax: +55 21 9005521/39 47 721, 9005521/27 35 998

Canada
Plasser Canada Inc, 2705 Marcel Stret, Montreal H4R 1A6, Quebec
Telephone: +1 3363 274
Telex: 05824513 plas rail mtl

Denmark
Plasser Scandinavia, Svejgardsvej 29, 2900 Hellerup
Telephone: +45 1 62 98 70
Telex: 19670 plasca/dk
Telefax: +45 1/62 24 10

France
Framafer, 90 rue de la Gare, 57801 Bening les St Avoid
Telephone: +33 81 45 54
Telex: 860243 framafer f
Telefax: +33 87 81 50 63

W Germany
Deutsche Plasser Bahnbaumaschinen GmbH, Spare parts & customer service: D-8000 Munich 81, Friedrich-Eckart Strasse 35
Telephone: +49 89 93008-0

Plasser Motor Car PMC-30

HUZ 2000-Q high-capacity relaying train

RM 80 high-capacity ballast cleaning machine with material conveyor and MFX 40 hopper units

Telex: 524693 dplas
Telefax: +49 89 930080151
Works: D-8228 Freilassing, Industriestrasse 31

Telephone: +49 86 3031
Telex: 56634 dplass
Telefax: +49 86 543020

UK
Plasser Railway Machinery (GB) Ltd, Manor Road, West Ealing, London W13 0JF
Telephone: +44 81 998 4781
Telex: 262160 plas gb
Telefax: +44 81 997 8206

Hong Kong
Plasser Far East Ltd, 11th Floor, Sing Pao Centre, 8 Queens Road, Central, Hong Kong
Telephone: +852 52 17 391
Telex: 84162 plas fhx
Telefax: +852/58610477

India
Plasser India Private Ltd, Factory: Mathura Road, 13th Milestone Gurukul, Indraprastha Estate, Faridabad (Haryana State)
Telephone: +91 54 91/5383
Telex: 343310

Registered office: c/o Mohinder Puri & Co, C-37, Atma Ram House, Connaught Place, New Delhi 110001
Telephone: +91 33 29 829
Telex: 313025
Telefax: +91 9009 111/64 10 504

Italy
Plasser Italiana Srl, Sales Dept, Service, Workshop. Spare Parts: Piazzale Stazione FS, 00049 Velletri (Rome)
Telephone: +39 96 26 387, 96 26 204, 96 26 155
Telex: 62 16 578 plasrm i
Telefax: +39 406/96 26 155

Japan
Nippon Plasser KK, 26-11, Kasuga, 2-Chome Bunkyo-ku, Tokyo
Telephone: +81 30 561
Telex: 26 957 niplass
Telefax: +81/38 16 1550

Spain
Plasser Espanola SA, Posterior Occidental 8, Madrid (33)
Telephone: +34 1 41 54 103
Telex: 22910 plaes
Telefax: +34 1/25 34 059

USA
Plasser American Corporation, 2001 Myers Road, Chesapeake, Virginia 23324-3231
Telephone: +1 54 33 526
Telex: 823662 plasrail chpk
Telefax: +1 901804/54 34 330

Products: Automatic track tamping, levelling and lining machines; universal points and crossing tamping machines; ballast consolidating machines; ballast regulators; ballast cleaning machines; formation rehabilitation machine; track (re)laying machines; gantry cranes; rail rectification machines; track recording cars; railway motor vehicles; railway cranes and lightweight equipment for track maintenance.

The Plasser & Theurer 08 and 09 Series of tamping machines covers a range for the most varied conditions and demands.

To suit the demands of customers a wide range of special machines for track maintenance and track works is supplied, including all kinds of motor vehicles and one- or twin-jib heavy railway cranes as well as lightweight track maintenance equipment.

Plastica
Plastica Kunststoffwerk GmbH

Ambrosius-Brand Strasse 20, PO Box 1452, 5828 Ennepetal 1, Federal Republic of Germany

Telephone: +49 2333 7891/92
Cable: Plastica Ennepetal
Telex: 0823 382

Managing Director: Bernd Konrad

Products: Resilient rail fastenings and insulating elements.

Portec Inc
Railway Maintenance Products Division

PO Box 38250, Pittsburgh, Pennsylvania 15238–8250, USA

Telephone: +1 412 782 6000
Telex: 866145

Senior Vice-President: John S Cooper
Manager, Sales, Service & Engineering: Richard J Jarosinski

Products: Standard, compromise, and insulated rail joints; rail joint insulation; rail and flange lubricators; Weld-Mate safety strap; Curv Bloc anti-rail tipping device.

Among recent products, the Protector Electronic Lubricator features solid state electronics which eliminate all high-impact parts and provide fast, easy installation with no-grind wiping bars. Finger-tip controls allow fine-tuned adjustments for easy and effective grease flow regulation. The Protector's pumping action is activated via a passive magnetic wheel detector. This electronic lubricator is suited to heavy-haul/main-line track or high-speed operations where electrical power is available.

The Protector Multi-Track lubricator eliminates the need to maintain a complete lubricator for each of two tracks. It incorporates sophisticated electronics designed with separate magnetic wheel sensors to trigger the control box to begin pumping grease to the appropriate track. Building on the electronics, one or two-way directional control is available. This allows the railroad the option of not lubricating the rail when equipment is being pulled back up the hump and through the retarders in classification yards. The electronic controls allow selective lubrication of either the 2nd, 4th, 8th or 16th wheel only. These options, along with the finger-tip grease controls, allow the customer to fine tune and apply exactly the right amount of grease for the individual location's needs.

This unit is designed for both unit train/heavy-haul territory and transit applications. Tunnels where clearances are also restricted are also well suited to the Protector's 12 V dc or 110 V ac electronically-controlled operation. Solar power packages are also available.

The MC-2 Mechanical Lubricator offers the no-grind wiping bar, allowing faster installation on any rail size. The 42-gallon round tank reduces the number of refills required.

The Weld-Mate with insulation offers protection against the hazards caused by broken field welds or detected rail defects. Made from high-strength steel, this bar can be installed on most currently used rail sections. It is designed with a forged offset that fits around the weld and holds securely until repairs can be made. Insulation for the Weld-Mate provides even greater rail safety through signal indication. Available in kits for both retrofit and new Weld-Mate installations.

MTW 100 catenary maintenance and inspection car by Plasser & Theurer

Portec bonded joint

Protector lubricator by Portec

Portec Weld-Mate with insulation

374 **MANUFACTURERS** / Permanent way equipment

Portec (UK)
Portec (UK) Ltd

Vauxhall Industrial Estate, Ruabon, Wrexham, Clwyd LL14 6UY, Wales

Telephone: +44 978 820820
Cable: Tracman, Wrexham
Telex: 61369 portec g
Telefax: +44 978 821439

Managing Director: Derek J Joy
Commercial and Marketing Manager: Idwal R Leese
Sales Engineer, Railways: Chris Maddock

Products: Track-mounted rail and flange lubricators, mechanical and electrical; rail and flange lubricant; Switchglide; insulated rail joints; rail anchors; two-way rail benders; Mack switch protectors.

Portec electric lubricator does not require wheel contact to activate the lubrication system; the machine is recommended for high-speed vehicle applications. Portec rail and flange lubricant is specially designed for use in all Portec machines and gives superior lubrication to both rails and wheels.

Portec Switchglide units support the tongue rail so that during switch movement the tongue slides on the low friction material. The Switchglide is spring-loaded to transfer wheel load onto the baseplate. Four, six or eight Switchglides are used for each switch, depending on the switch length. Portec Research Centre has tested the Switchglide to more than 30 000 cycles with no indication of pad wear; in the event of pad damage it can be replaced by removing one screw. There are in excess of 4000 Switchglides now in use in Europe and USA.

Pouget

BP 69, 6 Allee du Val du Moulin, 93240 Stains, France

Telephone: +33 1 4826 62 12
Cable: Motovoipouget Stains
Telex: 236813 f pouget
Telefax: +33 1 48 22 37 15

Products: Track laying gantry cranes, coach-screwing machines, fish-bolting machines, sleeper drills, rail saws, rail cutting machines by disc, rail drills, portable vibrating tampers, rail grinders, rail loaders, sleeper adzing-drilling machines, light ballast cleaners, ballast profiling and regulator, lorries, jacks, hand tools, Type 'Y' rail for heavy loads and BIBLOC steel sleepers.

Recent products include the TR-4-14 abrasive rail cutter which allows cutting of all standard rails in situ with complete security (for 60 kg/m rail the time of cut is 2 minutes). This machine is equipped with a STIHL petrol engine of 6.5 hp.

Premesa
Premesa SA Industrio e Comercio

Av Nossa Senhora do O, 565-Limão – São Paulo, Brazil

Telephone: +55 11 266 8188
Telex: (011) 30204 psai br
Telefax: +55 11 210 6031

General Manager: José Luiz Martins
Sales Superintendent: Luiz da Costa

Products: Turnouts, crossings, switches, points, frogs, track components.

P S Concrete
P S Concrete Co, Ltd

Head office: 4-1, Marunouchi 3-chome, Chiyoda-ku, Tokyo, Japan

Telephone: +81 3 216 1981
Cable: PS Concrete, Tokyo
Telex: 2224691 pscon j
Telefax: +81 3 184 0361

Main works
Nanao
59 Hobu, Yatashin-machi, Nanao-shi, Ishikawa-ken

Kamonomiya
370, Nakashinden, Odawara-shi, Kanagawa-ken

Zenibako
206, 3-chome Zenibako, Otaru-shi, Hokkaido

Mizushima
6, 2-chome Kaigandoori, Mizushima, Kurashiki-shi, Okayama-ken

Itami
1, aza Tanokuchi, Aramaki, Itami-shi, Hyoogo-ken

Minakuchi
6236, Ooaza Minakuchi, Minakuchi-cho, Koogagun, Shiga-ken

Kurume
1200, Shirakuchi Araki-cho, Kurume-shi, Fukuoka-ken

Kitagami
426 14 Chiwari, Aza Murasakino, Iitoyo-cho, Kitagami-shi, Iwate-ken

Jinmachi
1-62, 2-chome, Jinmachi Nishi, Higashine-shi, Yamagata-ken

Chairman: Marekata Kondo
President: Masanari Nakada
Managing Directors
 Business Development: Kiyotachi Mouri
 General Affairs: Akira Mogi
 Technical: Kaoru Yambe

Subsidiaries: Japan Consultant Co, Ltd
 Hatano Seisakusho Co, Ltd

Products: Prestressed concrete sleepers; concrete track slabs; construction of prestressed concrete railway bridges.

Recent contracts include construction of JABOTABEK Railway Project Track Elevation Segments A4 and B1 (Jakarta, Indonesia).

Pouget Type TR-4-14 abrasive rail cutter

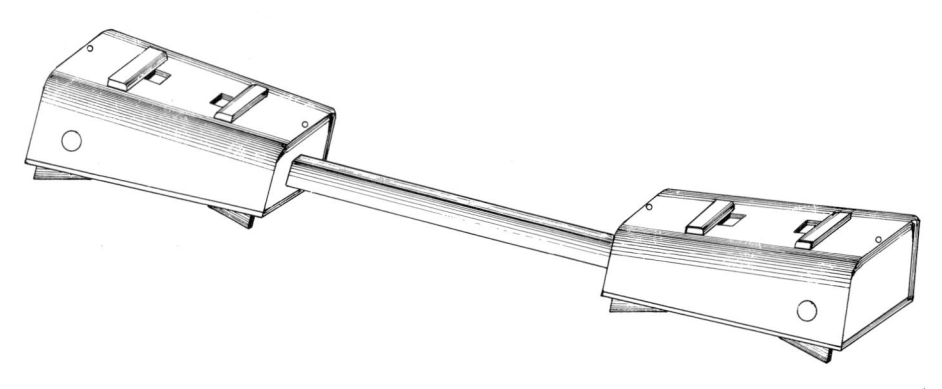

BIBLOC-Pouget steel sleeper

Racine
Racine Railroad Products Inc

PO Box 4029, 1524 Frederick Street, Racine, Wisconsin 53404, USA

Telephone: +1 414 637 9681

Chairman and Chief Executive Officer: G W Christiansen, Sr
Vice-Chairman and Treasurer: Robert C Schrimpf
President: George W Christiansen, Jr
Executive Vice-President: George S Sokulski
Vice President, Sales: R Zukowski

Racine Rail Profile Grinder, recently upgraded and, with flex shaft attachment, capable of universal use as a utility grinder

Service Manager: R L Turner
Manager of Engineering: Jeff S Hon

Products: Anchor applicators, spreaders and adjustors; rail clip applicators; rail vibrators; spike hole filling material and applicators; portable track measuring device; regauge adzer; abrasive rail saws; reciprocating hack saws; rail profile grinder; rail drills; and stationary multi-bore rail drill.

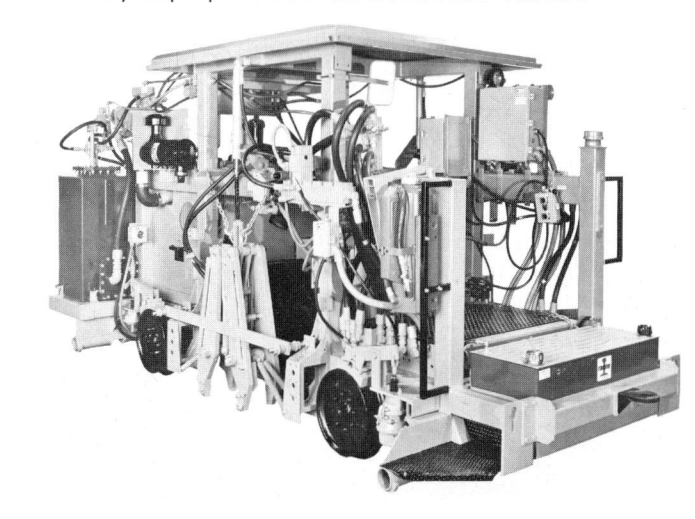

Rails Co
The Rails Company

101 Newark Way, Maplewood, New Jersey 07040, USA

Telephone: +1 201 763 4320
Telefax: +1 201 763 2585

President and Export Sales Director: G N Burwell

Products: Rail anchors, switch point locks, switch heaters (propane and natural gas), snow detectors.

An improved electric HAB switch heater is now available. Designated the HAB-HP-2000 Electric, it features new high-velocity heat distribution nozzles that provide increased effectiveness in protecting switch parts from freezing. As in previous HAB electric switch heaters, a high pressure blower forces air around the combustion chamber and through the duct work, assuring even transfer and distribution of heat. The new high-velocity nozzles permit air to pass through more slowly, so that it is heated more and then ejected under higher pressure which dislodges snow further down the track. All the heat energy is distributed to the snow between point and stock rail and relatively little is used for heating the rail and tie plates. Warm air can be directed to the tie spaces as well. The positive action of the forced air system and the high capacity blower that delivers up to 1200 cubic feet per minute of hot air minimise losses due to cold air movement over the rail. This operating efficiency permits reductions in kW requirements or added effectiveness for the same kW output. The HAB-HP-2000 measures 24¾ × 28⅜ inches at the base. Its 2 hp motor runs at 3450 rpm on 240 volts ac, but it can also be supplied at 480 and 600 volts, three-phase ac. The heating element is adjustable to provide a selection ranging from 6.5 to 52 kW for three-phase power systems.

Rails Company also offers HAB switch heaters utilising oil, natural gas or propane as well as Type RTS propane gas, Type LP low-pressure natural gas and Type TH tubular electric switch heaters.

The company's latest model of snow detector features an aluminium head that incorporates rim heating for wet snow conditions. The detector is a fully automatic, transistorised device that senses snow, freezing rain, hail or ice and instantaneously activates switch heaters or transmits an alarm signal to maintenance crews. It shuts off automatically when the precipitation stops. An independent temperature control prevents the detector from being accidentally activated by rain that is not cold enough to turn into ice. By providing local control of switch heaters at remote points, the snow detector eliminates the need for supervision by dispatchers and for CTC modifications.

A new automatic switch point lock, featuring a vandal-proof foot pedal, is now available. When in 'lock' position, the foot pedal folds up and tucks under the web of the rail, leaving nothing exposed to vandals.

Rails' Type PL automatic track lubrication system consists of a high-pressure pump (supplied with drum cover and hoses for connection to air supply and grease lines), an electrical air control system, a tripper that automatically delivers a measured amount of lubricant to wiping bars on the rail at the passage of each wheel, and necessary wiping bars, hoses and fittings. Lubricant is delivered from the original factory drum (110 lb or 55 gallons) directly to the track. As many as ten separate tracks may be serviced from one pump. The air control system provides automatic shut-off when the drum is empty or in case of pipeline damage. Initial cost is low and installation requires no drilling of the rail.

Racine Anchor-Tight anchor adjusting machine

Rail-Wel
Rail-Wel Inc

PO Box 180, 1025 St-Sulpice, Switzerland

Telephone: +41 21 35 42 65/66
Telex: 26294 rail ch
Telefax: +41 21 35 44 43

Representatives
Du Wel Steel Products Co, 360 Scott Street, Elk Grove Village, Illinois 60007, USA
Telephone: +1 312 439-3630

Rail-Alu Inc, Baie d'Urfe PQ H9X 2MB, Canada
Telephone: +1 514 457-5141
Telex: 058-5925585

Products: Boutet rail welding process: track maintenance machinery; including the Boutet rail weld shear (standard and compact models); rail drilling and cutting machines; sleeper drilling machines; tampers; and grinders.

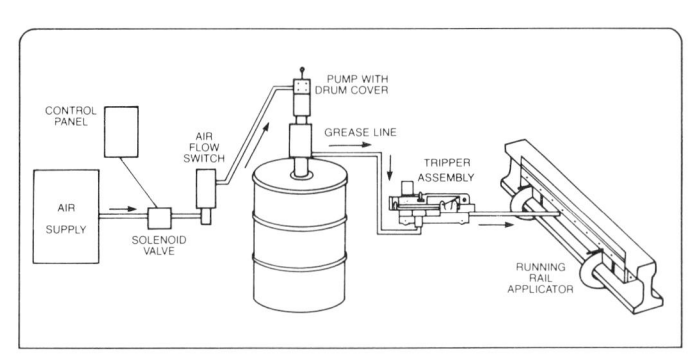

Layout of Rails' Type PL automatic track lubrication system

Rails Co Hot Air Blower (HAB) point heater

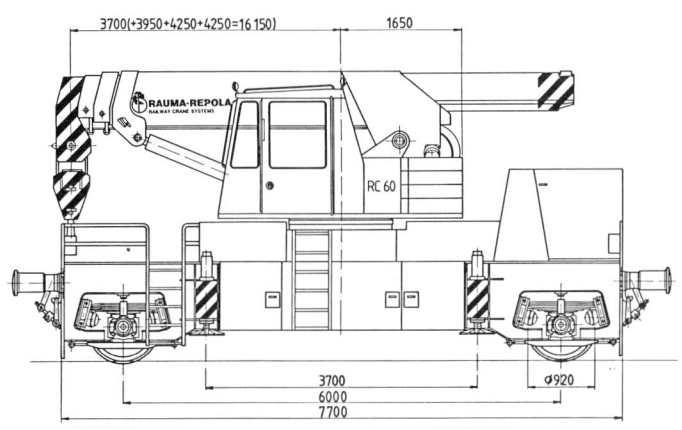

Rauma-Repola Type RC60

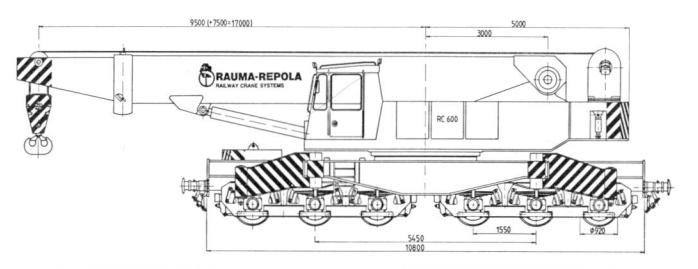

Rauma-Repola Type RC600

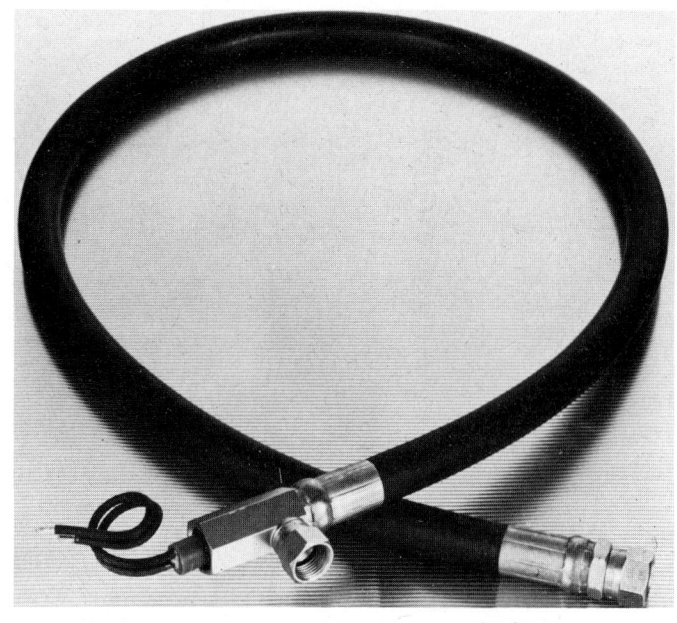

MANUFACTURERS / Permanent way equipment

Raychem Thermoline diesel fuel line heater (suitable for dmu vehicles)

Raychem Thermospace cabinet heater

Rauma-Repola
Rauma-Repola Oy Parkano Engineering

SF-39700 Parkano, Finland

Telephone: +358 33 1151
Telex: 244 1033024 rrpno sf
Telefax: +358 33 81984

Sales Manager: E Venäläinen

Products: Rail-mounted cranes, either from the company's standard range or designed and built to individual customer specification. Rauma-Repola railway cranes are currently operational in Europe, Africa and Asia. All are equipped with computer-based control systems to guarantee safe lifting in all conditions.

The company's standard range of diesel-hydraulic rail cranes currently comprises three main types and sizes: Type RC60: a 15-tonne/4 m crane with high tractive effort and travel speed of 40 km/h for maintenance and light construction work; Type RC200: a medium-sized 36-tonne/6 m crane for construction and tracklaying; Type RC600: a heavy 100-tonne/6 m rescue crane, suitable also for heavy construction work and freight handling.

Constitution: Rauma-Repola, a diversified metal and wood-processing enterprise, was founded in 1951. Active in the shipbuilding, offshore, engineering, pulp and paper, and mechanical wood-processing industries, the company exports 70 per cent of its output and is one of Finland's biggest industrial concerns.

Rawie
A Rawie GmbH & Co

PO Box 3529, Dornierstrasse 11, D4500 Osnabrück, Federal Republic of Germany

Telephone: +49 541 12 50 81
Telex: 94649

Products: Friction element buffer stops.

Raychem
Raychem Corp

Transportation Division, USA: 300 Constitution Drive, Menlo Park, California 94025

Telephone: +1 415 361 6227
Telex: 34 8316
Telefax: +1 415 361 2113

Chairman: Paul M Cook
Vice-Chairman: Robert M Malperin
President & CEO: Robert J Saldich
Electronics Manager: Barbara Fruhwirth

Raychem Ltd

Transportation Division, Europe: Faraday Road, Dorcan, Swindon, Wiltshire SN3 5JA, England

Telephone: +44 793 528171
Telex: 449409
Telefax: +44 793 482516

Transportation Division Manager, Europe: Mike Jones

Products: Wire and cable offering high performance, lightweight and low fire hazard properties as well as good handling characteristics for easy installation. Newly introduced Type 99T wire has been designed to meet the stringent low fire hazard performance now being specified by many transit authorities, including London Underground and the Channel Tunnel. Complete harness systems offered using Raychem wire, heat-shrinkable tubing and moulded shapes, Soldersleeve interconnection devices and TMS computerised, permanent identification system. Ruggedised databus interconnection systems give excellent EMI protection and minimum signal distortion for critical multiplex train control and data processing systems. Telecommunications and power distribution cable accessories. Self regulating heaters for brake and diesel fuel lines; interconnection devices; cable marking sleeves; telecommunication cable splices; signal cable splices; high- and medium- voltage joints and terminations; power distribution splices; electrical harnesses; switchpoint heaters; contact rail heaters; anti-condensation heaters (electrical/electronic cabinets); air brake pipe heaters; sandpipe heaters; passenger comfort heaters; vibration sensing cable; PTC current switching devices.

Richardson & Cruddas
Richardson & Cruddas (1972) Limited

P Box No 4503, Sir J J Road, Bombay 400 008, India

Telephone: +91 22 866832-39
Cable: Ironworks, Bombay 400 008
Telex: 011 75662

Managing Director: S C Duggal

Products: Manufacture of railway points and crossings; pressed steel turnout sleepers; steel track; sleepers; slide chairs, etc; fabrication of overhead structures for railway electrification.

Robel
Robel GmbH & Co

Thalkirchnerstrasse 210, D-8000 Munich 75, Federal Republic of Germany

Telephone: +49 89 72491-0
Cable: Robelco, Munich
Telex: 5 23012
Telefax: +49 89 7249150

Products: Powered ganger's trolleys with hydraulic tipping platform and crane, trailers, stationary and mobile machines for processing sleepers and rails, equipment for loading and unloading long-welded rails, rail drilling machines, rail saws, power wrenches, rail

Robel Type 68.05 emergency fishplate connector

Robel Type 43.32 rail threader with freely adjustable wheel-sets for smooth travel while adjusting rail gauge during relaying

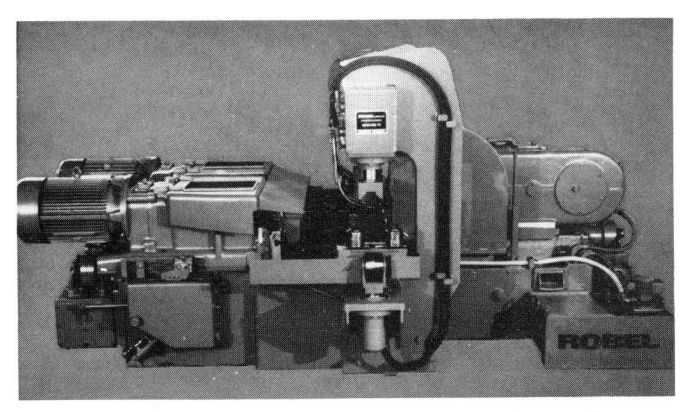

Permanent way equipment / **MANUFACTURERS** 377

Robel Type 02.03 rail-saw and drilling machine cuts rails up to a maximum tensile strength of 110 kg/mm^2 into standard lengths and simultaneously drills fishbolt holes on either side of the cut

Robel 30.83 combined power wrench and drilling machine

grinders, hydraulic rail benders, ratchet track jacks and spanners, gauges, portal cranes etc.

Recent products include:

The powered ganger's trolley, Robel Type 54.17, normally supplied with a six-cylinder 167 hp diesel engine. For the Norwegian State Railways it has been equipped with a magnet-type rail brake, arranged between the axles of the rear pivoted bogie. Axles have maintenance-free rubber suspension and guidance, with shock absorbers, and the frame can accept buffing loads of up to 120 tons. The cabin accommodates nine including the driver.

At the lower end of the wide Robel range of personnel cars, the recently-introduced Type 56.27 small track trolley can be supplied with a variety of cabins, including full, air-conditioned enclosure. It has a load-carrying capacity of 2000 kg. Tare weight is 1000 kg, platform length/width 2750/1800 mm and maximum speed 55 km/h. Hydraulic disc brakes are fitted to each axle. The vehicle is normally supplied with an 11 or 12 kW, 3000 rpm diesel engine, but other types can be fitted on request.

The Type 40.61 rail loading equipment facilitates quick and economical loading and unloading of 30 long-welded rails, up to a length of 240 metres each, on straight sections as well as in curves, also providing transport of these rails over long distances. Loading or unloading time per pair of rails is 2 to 5 minutes. More than 120 of these rail loading equipments are in operation in the world.

The Type 05.48 sleeper planing and drilling machine is a complete machining centre for fully automatic treatment of wooden sleepers.

The Type 68.05 emergency fishplate connector, which makes emergency fishplating possible using only one clamp; the device is obstructionless, so that it cannot be damaged by ballast levelling machines, track tamping machines etc.

The Type 30.82 power wrench for all track bolting jobs is equipped with two-speed gear, reverse gear; metal cone clutch and hydraulic torque adjuster. This power wrench may also be delivered in parallelogram design, so that all vertical drilling jobs can be performed as well.

Rolba
Rolba AG

Zürcherstrasse 51, CH-8620 Wetzikon, Switzerland

Telephone: +41 1 933 6111
Telex: 875404
Telefax: +41 1 933 6666

Products: Rotary snowploughs from 10 to 2000 hp.

The Rolba RR-6000 COP-D-S high-performance rotary snowplough employs a single turbo-charged diesel engine for propulsion of the purpose-built carrier vehicle as well as to drive the cutter assembly. Fully hydrostatic transmission guarantees adjustment to the clearing of any kind of snow. Two variable axial piston pumps as well as the two variable axial piston motors allow maximum use of propulsion power, with infinitely variable speeds for forward and reverse motion. The rotary plough head can clear snow up to a height of approximately 3.2 metres in one run, the casting distances varying from approximately 10 to 35 metres depending on the gear selected. The rotary head can be hydraulically lifted and lowered by approximately 600 mm. A powered hydraulic device which raises the complete unit 100 mm above rail level enables it to be turned through 360 degrees under one operator's control without a turntable.

Type RR-2/200 fitted with hydraulic mechanism by which a Rolba snowplough can be turned without a turntable

Salient
Salient Systems Inc

4140 Tuller Road, Suite 101, Dublin, Ohio 43017, USA

Telephone: +1 614 792 5800
Telefax: +1 614 792 5888

President: Harold Harrison

Products: Salient manufactures state-of-the-art microprocessor-based wayside monitoring and detection instrumentation for monitoring track/train dynamics at selected wayside sites. Salient's Mk II Wheel Impact Load Detector system has been designed in anticipation of the future where all detectors will be integrated at any one location for more cost effective installation and co-ordinated readout of reports to remote centres, thereby reducing both total installation costs and the

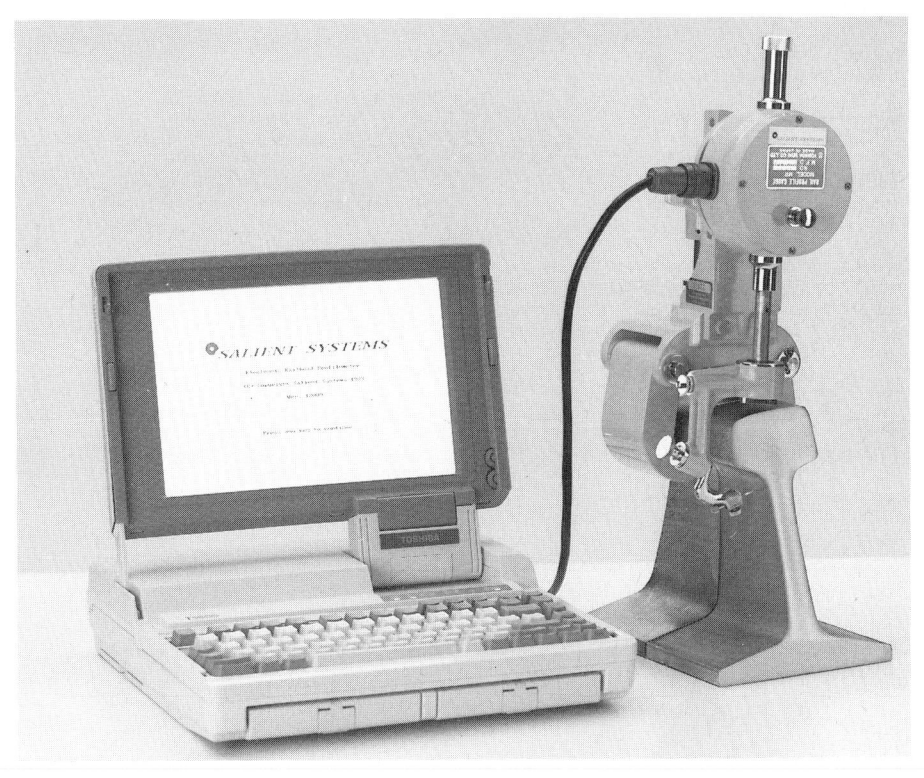

Salient's Railhead Profiler

MANUFACTURERS / Permanent way equipment

Scania Motortralla 112 motor maintenance trolley

daily operating cost of wayside detectors.

The Overload Car Detector is an option available for the Wheel Impact Load Detector Subsystem. Load data of each wheel is processed and the total vehicle weight is then estimated from 80 separate load estimations.

The Skewed/Hunting Bogie Detector Subsystem utilises the same front-end processors as the Wheel Impact Load Detector Subsystem. The sampled and digitised vertical and lateral load values are sent across the optically isolated bus to the Site Master where the data is formatted and processed to identify the skewed or hunting bogies.

Saliant's Electronic Longitudinal Wheel Profiler allows a railroad to determine independently how many hotbox alarms and/or burnoffs are caused by 'thumpers', as well as to verify the runout on wheelsets that are alarmed on the Wheel Impact Load Detector.

The Tribometer is one of Saliant's new precision instruments that measures rail friction and calculates the coefficient of rail friction for the purpose of improving the railroad's field lubrication inspection.

Saliant's new Railhead Profilometer produces automated railhead profiling capabilities which are captured on an integral laptop in a format that can be transferred directly to the railroad's existing database.

Sateba
Sateba International

262 boulevard St-Germain, 75007 Paris, France

Telephone: +33 1 4705 71 18
Telex: 200808
Telefax: +33 1 47 53 7927

Managing Director: Claude Cazenave
Commercial Manager: Denis Vallet

Main works: Chalon-sur-Saone (Saone et Loire); La Fleche (Sarthe)

Principal subsidiaries
Sotradest, Charmes (Vosges), France
American Concrete Ties Corporation, California, USA

Products: Various types of concrete sleeper for all types of track and gauges: very high speed; heavy haul (axleloads of 30 tonnes); metro; LRT; tramway; secondary lines. Technical studies. Sleeper factory design and installation, supply of machinery, personnel training and technical assistance.

SATO
SATO Bahnsysteme

Stahlwerke P + S, Werk Peine, PO Box 41 11 80, 3320 Salzgitter 41, Federal Republic of Germany

Telephone: +44 5171 50 1
Telefax: +44 5171 50 2373

Product: Y-form steel sleepers for plain track and turnouts.

Scania
Saab-Scania AB, Scania Division

151 87 Södertälje, Sweden

Telephone: +46 755 810 00
Telex: Scania 10200
Telefax: +46 755 83180

Products: Motor maintenance trolleys based on components from the new Scania T112 truck models. The new vehicles are designated Motortralla 112. In winter the vehicles, equipped with front and side plough blades and track-clearing units, are used for snow clearance. The extended cab can accommodate six people, including the driver. Equipment also includes a two-way communications radio and a 6-tonne-metre loading crane. Overall weight is 21 tonnes and top speed about 80 km/h. The trolley is equipped with a turntable device and the entire vehicle can be quickly turned on the track. Export sales are handled exclusively by Swedish Rail System AB SRS.

Schlatter
Schlatter AG HA

Bandstrasse 24, CH-8952 Schlieren, Switzerland

Telephone: +41 1 732 7111/732 7200
Cable: Elektropunkt Schlieren
Telex: 827 790 has ch
Telefax: +41 1 730 9476

Product Manager: Klaus Nebel

Products: Dc railwelder Type GAAS 80 with automatic rail-end alignment and inbuilt upset-removing device; stationary or portable railwelder Type AAS 50.

Schramm
Schramm Inc

800 East Virginia Avenue, West Chester, Pennsylvania 19380, USA

Telephone: +1 215 696 2500
Telex: 83 5455
Telefax: +1 215 696 6950

Schlatter AAS 50 portable rail welding machine, with welding range of rail cross-section up to 15 in^2, production capacity of up to 20 welds/h; dimensions of 13 ft × 4 ft 8 in × 4 ft 4 in, weight 30 000 lb

Marketing Manager: Robert V Edwards

Products: Pneumatractors; high pressure air compressors; Rotadrills; Pneumagopher. The HT300C Pneumatractor can be fitted with four flanged wheels to permit its use in track maintenance and construction; its 325 cubic feet/minute rotary screw compressor can power heavy-duty drills, torque wrenches, spike drivers and tampers.

SECEMM
Société d'Etudes et de Constructions Electriques, Mécaniques et Métallurgiques

15/17 rue Chabrol, 75480 Paris Cedex 10, France

Products: Track maintenance and inspection equipment, including rail grinding units of several types, lateral deburring machines, rail heaters, rail de-scaling machines, electrode ovens, and rail butt-end cutters.

Semperit
Semperit Technische Produkte GmbH
Industrial Technology Division

Modecenterstrasse 22, A 1031 Vienna, Austria

Telephone: +43 1 222 78 00-0
Telex: 131889
Telefax: +43 1 222 7800 606

Division Manager: G Beidl
Sales Manager: H Stastny

Products: Rubber and plastics track items, including rail pads, elastic support of sleepers, fastening parts made of plastics.

Type GAAS 80 automatic railwelder by Schlatter

SikaRail
Rail Fixing Systems

- LOAD BEARING
- LOW MAINTENANCE
- NOISE REDUCTION
- VIBRATION REDUCTION
- ELECTRICAL INSULATION

Permanent way equipment / **MANUFACTURERS** 379

LRT turnout using RI60 girder rail, Calgary, Canada

LRT turnout using RI60 girder rail, Calgary, Canada

SICFA
SICFA SpA

PO Box 987-16100, Viale Brigate Bisagno 2, Genoa 16129, Italy

Telephone: +39 10 543941
Cable: sicfaferro genova
Telex: 270457 sicfa i

Deltasider SpA
Divisione Piombino

Export sales: SICFA SpA, FER Department

Telephone: +39 10 54941
Telex: 270201/2 sdx ge i

Products: Railway rails from 33 to 60 kg/m.

Divisione San Giovanni Valdarno
Piazza Matteotti 13, 52027 San Giovanni Valdarno (AR), Italy

Telephone: +39 55 9204
Telex: 570119

Products: Permanent way materials (baseplates, clips and fishplates), switches, points and crossings.

Sigmaform
Sigmaform Corporation

2401 Walsh Avenue, Santa Clara, California, USA

Telephone: +1 408 727 6510
Telex: 346335
Telefax: +1 408 727 8417

President: David Plummer
Director of Marketing: Andy Moshier

Sigmaform UK Ltd
Sywell Road, Park Farm Industrial Estate, Wellingborough, Northants NN8 3XD

Telephone: +44 933 674866
Telex: 312421
Telefax: +44 933 679962

Products: Self-regulating heating systems. Sigmaform's range of self-regulating heaters offer a wide range of applications: switchpoint, contact and tramway rail heating; concrete track (under surface) and deck/platform, ice-protection; cabinet heaters (anti-condensation). The self-regulating switchpoint rail heater has been installed on the London Docklands Light Railway.

Sika Ltd

Watchmead, Welwyn Garden City, Herts AL7 1BQ

Telephone: +44 707 329241
Telex: 269428 sikash g
Telefax: +44 707 329129

Managing Director: B Baggarsgaard
Sales & Marketing Director: M Moore
Specialist Engineer: R J Barton

Products: Sikarail KC 330 elastic rail fixing system is a highly durable chemical formulation of elastomeric resin and compressible fillers that provides both high efficiency in absorbing vibration, and consistency in load bearing characteristics in conditions of the most eccentric loading.

SILF Srl

Via Romagnosi 60, 29100 Piacenza, Italy

Telephone: +39 523 27885, 36377, 36966
Telex: 530122 rotaia
Telefax: +39 523 385124

President: Luisa Co

Works: SS 10, Via Emilia Pavese 98, Sarmato (PC), Italy
Telephone: +39 523 847575, 847543

Products: Light and heavy rail sections; crane rails and grooved rails for tramways; guard rails; wooden, concrete and steel sleepers; plates; clips; nuts and bolts; spikes; anchor bolts; screwspikes; fishplates and baseplates; buffer stops; frogs; points and crossings; turnouts.

Skelton
H J Skelton & Co Ltd

9 The Broadway, Thatcham, Newbury, Berkshire RG13 4JA, England

Telephone: +44 635 65256
Telex: 884920 sklton g
Telefax: +44 635 65710

H J Skelton (Canada) Ltd
165 Oxford Street East, London, Ontario N6A 1T4, Canada

Telephone: +1 519 679 9180
Telex: 064 7241 skeltoncan
Telefax: +1 519 679 0193

Chairman:(Canada): P S W Fraser
Directors (Canada): G C Richey
(UK): J W G Smith

Products: Special trackwork in all types of railway and crane rails to North American, British and European standards; sliding rail expansion joints for both longitudinal and vertical expansion; swing nose crossings; resilient grout by SIKA for direct fixation for discrete pads or continuous support for embedded rail; Vossloh rail clips for all conditions; friction buffer stops by A Rawie, also wheel stops and fixed stops; friction buffer supplied to Balfour Beatty for Docklands Light Railway.

Sola
Ing Guido Scheyer

Unteres Tobel 25, 6840 Gotzis, Austria

Telephone: +43 5523 2344-0
Telex: 52488
Telefax: +43 5523 2344-10

Managing Director: Dr Walter Hörburger
Sales & Marketing Manager: Dr Alois Gabriel

Products: Track gauge and superelevation measuring equipment; measuring devices for lower clearance.

Sonatest Plc

Dickens Road, Old Wolverton, Milton Keynes, Buckinghamshire MK12 5QQ, England

Telephone: +44 908 316345
Telex: 826131 sonamk g
Telefax: +44 908 321323

Managing Director: M Reilly
Sales Director: J Whyte

Products: Ultrasonic flaw detectors, ultrasonic thickness gauges and industrial X-ray equipment for examination of welds, components, structures, etc.
Sonatest also supplies ultrasonic thickness meters,

MANUFACTURERS / Permanent way equipment

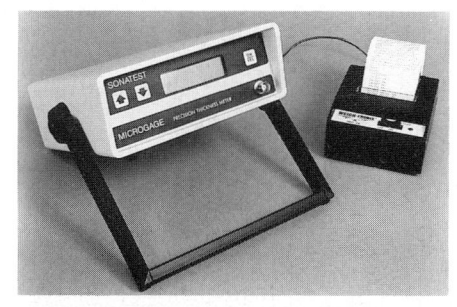

Sonatest thickness meter

ultrasonic transducers, X-ray equipment, eddy current equipment and small systems for other non-destructive testing applications, including the dryscan ultrasonic technique.

Sonit
Sonit Pty Ltd

PO Box 152, 46 Clavering Road, Bayswater, Western Australia 6053, Australia

Telephone: +61 9 272 6166
Telex: 92020 aa
Telefax: +61 9 272 2409

Managing Director: George W Browne
Technical Director: Harold W G Lowe

Products: Crossings and switches, electric point detection machines.

The company is owner and manufacturer of the dual stockrail system of crossings and switches which provides full rail section through the turnout and achieves significant reduction in maintenance costs.

Speno
Speno International SA

PO Box 16, 22-24 parc Château-Banquet, 1211 Geneva 21, Switzerland

Telephone: +41 22 732 84 07
Telex: 23921 speno ch
Telefax: +41 22 731 52 64

General Manager: J J Méroz
Deputy General Manager: J Cooper
Commercial Manager: D Arvet-Thouvet
Technical Manager: J P Jaeggi
Operation Manager: J C Schaffner

Principal subsidiaries:
Speno Rail Maintenance (Australia) Pty Ltd
11 Robinson Street, Belmont, Western Australia 6104, Australia

Telephone: +61 9 479 14 99
Telex: 94079
Telefax: +61 9 479 13 49

Nippon Speno KK
Room 613, Aios Gotanda Building, 1-10-7 Higashi-Gotanda, Shinagawa-ku, Tokyo 141, Japan

Telephone: +81 3 440 85 33 or 34
Telex: (072/032) 42 37 36
Telefax: +81 3 4408532

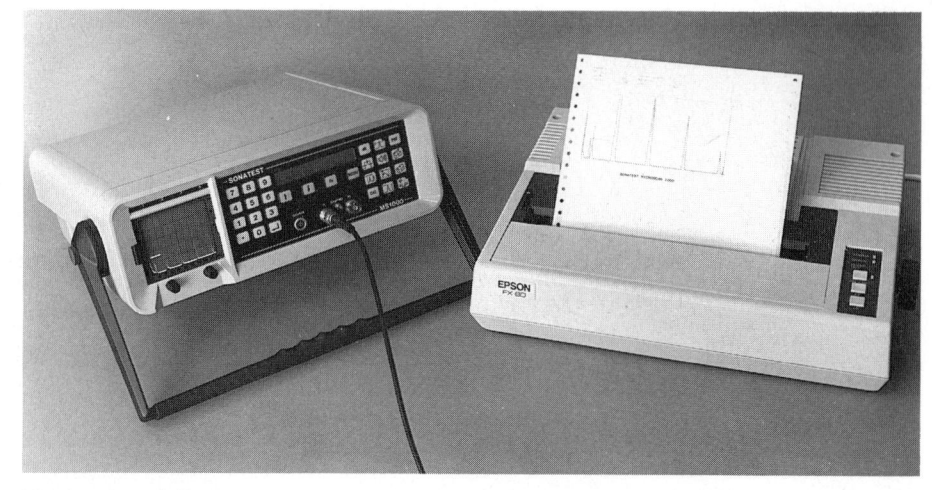

Microscan ultrasonic flaw detector

Sonit crossing installation

Products: Specialised machines for in-track rail rectification, rail surface measurement and rail flaw detection.

Latest developments include:

URR 48/4 grinding train:
This consists of 48 reprofiling units, each of 20 hp, mounted on four cars. About 70 m (230 ft) long and weighing 230 tonnes, the machine has a working speed of 6-8 km/h (3/5-5 mph) and a travelling speed of more than 80 km/h (50 mph). The URR 48/4 features a number of advanced facilities including: remote-controlled grinding angle adjustment (variable by up to ± 75 degrees with respect to the axis of the rail) with automatic selection of any of 30 patterns according to the state of the rail running surface and whether conventional or asymmetric grinding is required; automatic grinding load control; microprocessor-controlled obstacle monitor; surface fault measuring and recording facility, also enabling the rail head cross-profile to be displayed in the form of 10-column bar graph. This worldwide exclusive Speno feature allows precise reprofiling with no wasted metal.

In 1987 a URR 48/4 used by British Railways achieved 8300 km of grinding passes, or about 1700 km of finished track, in 273 working days.

RR 16 P/D switch and crossing grinder:
The RR 16 P/D was specially developed to meet the particular requirements of switch and crossing grinding. Eight grinding units are provided for each rail: six for the running surface and two for the gauge corner. The six running surface units are equipped with 130 mm grinding stones; the two conical stones for grinding the gauge corner are 260 mm in diameter and are suitable for use throughout the entire switch and crossing including the checkrail area.

The grinding units, grouped in pairs, can be angled as desired within broad limits, thereby making it possible to remove running-surface defects while at the same time restoring the cross-profile of the rail

Speno RR 32m grinding train

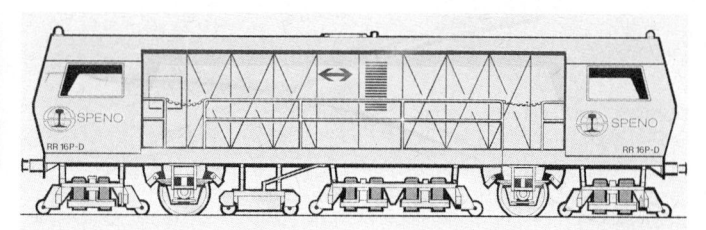

Speno RR 16P-D switch and crossing grinder

SRS Over/Under Bridge Inspection and Maintenance Vehicle

SRS Stormobil road/rail vehicle, with hydraulic, pneumatic and other tools, manoeuvring on to its rail wheels

head. All grinding units are angled and positioned under the control of the on-board computer. Programmed in advance for several different angle patterns, the computer calls them up as required and monitors them continuously. The machine operator decides the grinding procedure to be followed according to the state of the rails. The grinding units can be raised and lowered in succession to clear obstacles or critical areas which are not to be ground such as the crossover from the stock rail to the frog. This operation is likewise controlled by the on-board computer, which also monitors the preselected grinding load. When required, each rail can be ground separately. Surface defects are detected, measured and recorded electronically.

This new Speno technique makes it possible to grind several switch and crossing sets, including double crossings, in succession at a speed of 3 km/h (1.80 mph). Ten to 25 passes are necessary to restore a switch to its ideal profile, depending on the nature and extent of the defects present.

SM 775 self-propelled recording car:
The measuring facilities installed in Speno grinding trains can also be used to check the condition of the rail running surface over relatively short distances at a speed of about 10 km/h (6 mph). However, for drawing up major grinding programmes covering hundreds or even thousands of kilometres, railway administrations turn to the SM 775 self-propelled recording car. This vehicle measures and records all running surface defects, for example, corrugations, short and long waves and rail joint irregularities, at a speed of 80 km/h (50 mph)–30 km/h (20 mph) in switches and crossings. The measuring system relies on four accelerometers for each rail and is accurate within a few hundredths of a millimetre. The chart recorder plots the faults with wavelength and amplitude. The machine is also equipped with a digital analyser which classifies the defects in each section of each rail string according to size. This computer also has a second function: it assesses the quality of the track inspected each day by the SM 775, thereby furnishing the basing data for the grinding budget.

VUR 505 ultrasonic flaw detection car:
The Speno VUR 505 rail inspection car (Matix system) was developed specially to detect all internal rail flaws by ultrasonic testing.

The machine is fitted with a probe carrier containing eight probes for each rail string as follows: one 0 degree probe to detect horizontal cracks; four 70 degree probes to detect transverse flaws in the entire rail head section; one 55 degree probe for longitudinal vertical cracks in the rail head; two 35 degree probes to detect bolthole cracks. This system therefore detects all dangerous flaws invisible on the surface of the rail.

The vehicle also includes frog detectors (which automatically raise the probe holder), and bolthole detectors. A continuous film of water is injected between the probes and the surface of the rail to maximise transmission of the ultrasonic waves and their echoes. The capacity of the water tank is sufficient for an operating range of 150 km (95 mi) without any further attention. The information provided by the probes is processed and interpreted by the electronics which convert it into immediately usable data. The electronics are housed in a console which also contains a simulation module that can be used to check the operational status of all equipment items when the vehicle is at a standstill. The incoming signals are continuously displayed on a monitor screen and a pilot lamp lights up each time a flaw is detected. The operator console also houses all the pneumatic and hydraulic controls. Presumed defect sites are paint-marked by an automatic spray gun. The monitor display is augmented by analog and digital records. The analog record is produced by a chart recorder and is also displayed on a video screen. In addition, the probe information is interpreted by a computer which provides a hard-copy printout of the data on an extra-high-speed printer, listing the defects according to type, size and kilometric location in the track.

The VUR 505 is a twin unit with an overall weight of 80 tonnes. One part of the vehicle contains the laboratory and the other the crew's quarters. The unit is operated by a four-man crew. The water tanks for the probe-to-rail contact have a capacity of 4000 litres. Working speed is approximately 40 km/h (25 mph), making it possible to inspect 100–150 km (60–95 mi) of track a day, or 15 000–20 000 km (9000–12 500 mi) per year with an extremely high degree of reliability.

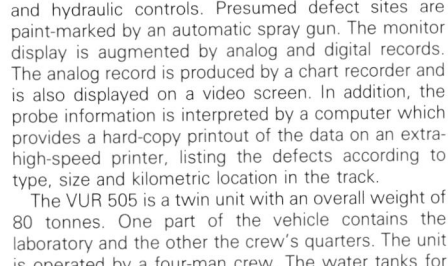

Sperry
Sperry Rail Service
Division of Sperry Rail Inc, a unit of Penn Central Corporation (NYSE)

Head office: 46 Shelter Rock Road, Danbury, Connecticut 06810, USA

Telephone: +1 203 791 4500
Telefax: +1 203 797 8417

President: T F de Joseph
Director, Quality Service: J J Blodgett
Director, Operations: D D McCoy
Director, Customer Service: R J Rice

Sperry owns and operates a fleet of 26 induction-ultrasonic cars and five all-ultrasonic cars.

Spie Batignolles
Société Spie Batignolles (Service Voies Ferrées)

Parc Saint-Cristophe, Edison 3, 95861 Cergy-Pontoise Cedex, France

Telephone: +33 1 34 22 50 02/3
Telex: 609542

Products: Track welding and maintenance equipment.

SRS
Swedish Rail System AB SRS

Framnäsbacken 18, PO Box 1031, 171 21 Solna, Sweden

Telephone: +46 8 830 660
Cable: Railsystem, Stockholm
Telex: 104 06 rail s
Telefax: +46 8 270 250

Managing Director: Ingvar Svensson

Products: Concrete sleepers; Hambo rail fastenings; machines developed for the mechanical mounting of sleepers and fastenings; gantry cranes; rail threaders; hydraulic track lifters; switch exchanger; Stormobil hi-rail vehicles; Clicomatic rail lubricators.

The SRS Clicomatic rail lubricator consists of a steel cabinet and a grease gun housing connected by a grease hose. All components are mounted in the cabinet, except the grease gun with nozzle, solenoid valve, and the vibratory sensor, which are installed in the grease gun housing. The Clicomatic is driven by compressed nitrogen gas and controlled by an electronic control unit, powered by a standard 9-volt battery. Gas pressure is reduced by a regulator applying a constant pressure on the grease in the container right through the grease hose to the grease gun. Passing trains create vibrations in the track which are monitored by the vibratory sensor in the grease gun housing. A signal then activates the electronic control unit, which opens the solenoid valve at preset intervals, activating the grease gun. The grease is then ejected through a four-hole nozzle, hitting the rail flange with four drops. The intervals between the impulses can be preset for different times. This means that while the sensor is registering vibrations either one or several grease shots can be released during a train passage, depending on the preset intervals. This allows optimal lubrication fully adapted to various local conditions, such as train speeds, axleloads, length of trains etc. Swedish State Railways (SJ) has 1800 units in use and reports considerable resultant reduction in wear on wheel flanges and rail heads.

The SRS Stormobil is in daily use on SJ as a rail/road catenary inspector for overhead work. SJ has 41 SRS Stormobils operational. The Stormobil's lift chassis is provided with a hydraulically-operated wheel carriage which supports and guides the front end, at the same time locking the front axle. A driving bogie which pivots through ± 100 degrees is mounted at the rear. The rear of this bogie has hydraulic vertical adjustment. The bogie incorporates a drive unit which powers all four wheels. Both front and rear arrangements are spring-suspended. The drive unit in the bogie is fed from an external power source connected to the power take-off on the vehicle gearbox. The drive can be controlled from the cab for forward/reverse speeds of 0–70 km/h and from the working platform for forward/reverse speeds of 0–5 km/h. Gear changing takes place in the planetary gearbox on the bogie. All travelling wheels are provided with brakes which can be operated both from the cab and working platform.

The design has recently been modified in the following respects: the front end rail wheel assembly has been moved in front of the front road axle; total weight of vehicle is now 11 tonnes; the working speed controlled from the platform is 7.25 km/h in both directions; there is no limitation on platform slewing radius in superelevated curves up to 10 degrees; the clearance height from rails to bottom of working platform is 8 metres, giving a working height of about 9.5 metres; the load capacity on the platform is now

382 MANUFACTURERS / Permanent way equipment

Nabla RNTC spring fastener by Stedef for concrete sleepers, twin- or monobloc, as used on French Railways' high-speed TGV/LGV

C-Series Model C254ESDAL switch production tamper by Tamper

350 kg; and fully equipped, the SRS Stormobil can load additionally 2250 kg.

The SRS Over/Under Bridge Inspection and Maintenance Vehicle is a further development of the SRS Stormobil.

Stedef

320 bureaux de la Colline, 92213 Saint-Cloud Cedex, France

Telephone: +33 1 4602 56 00
Telex: 200 888 rail f

General Manager: J P Dervaux
Export Managers: Patrick Cathou, Jean-Jacques Roger

Products: Track materials and equipment including elastic fastenings; Stedef ballastless track, with sleepers supported by elastic boots and microcellular pads to dampen vibration.

Strukton Spoorwegbouw
BV Strukton Spoorwegbouw

PO Box 1025, Westkanaaldijk 2, 3600 BA Maarssen, Netherlands

Telephone: +31 30 466911
Telex: 40275 nl

Products: Complete range of railway construction services: track, ballast bed, points, overhead conductor system supports and conductors.

For over 60 years Strukton Spoorwegbouw has been The Netherlands' largest railway contractor. The company builds new railway and carries out renewal and maintenance work in close co-operation with Netherlands Railways.

Swingmaster Corporation

11415 Melrose Avenue, Franklin Park, Il 60131, USA

Telephone: +1 708 451 1224
Telefax: +1 708 451 1247

President: Dan A Grammatis
Vice-President: Jerry Rakowski
General Manager, Manufacturing: John Noga

Products: On and off track, rough terrain loaders, excavators and cranes.

SYCAFER
Syndicat de la Voie

100, avenue Albert 1^2e^2r, 92500 Rueil-Malmaison, France

Telephone: +33 1 47 49 67 91
Telex: 632 191

Products: SYCAFER is a French track suppliers association including several large French companies designing and manufacturing equipment for urban, suburban and main lines railway, transport, trams, VAL systems, ports and mines.

Sydney Steel
Sydney Steel Corporation

PO Box 1450, Sydney, Nova Scotia B1P 6K5, Canada

Telephone: +1 902 564 7900
Telex: 019 35197
Telefax: +1 902 564 7903

Chairman: M H Cochrane
President: Dr J A Strasser
Director, Marketing: L A Hicks

Products: Railroad rails; sleeper plates. A major supplier of rails to Canadian National Railways and world markets.

Sydney Steel manufactures rails to all major national and international specifications, including AREA, ASTM, BSS, CNR, CPR, ISO and UIC. Sydney rails are produced in carbon, intermediate, and premium alloy grades. Sections range from 70 to 136 lb/yd (37 to 70 kg/m). According to the specifications required, rails may be either control cooled to ensure diffusion of hydrogen from the steel or produced from vacuum degassed steel. When specified, the top end rail surface is end-hardened to reduce wear at rail joints. Standard rail length is 78 ft, although rails 39 to 82 ft (12 to 25 m) are produced.

A new head hardening unit has been installed for the production of premium wear-resistant head-hardened rails.

Szarka
Szarka Enterprises, Inc

PO Box 2027, Livonia, Michigan 48151, USA

Telephone: +1 313 427 5535

President: Paul J Szarka
Vice-President: John O'Brien

Products: Fab-Ra-Cast rail/road grade crossing surface. Special features include: pre-fabricated metal end ramps, which prevent damage usually associated with 'dragging' equipment, and restrict expansion/ contraction throughout the limits of the crossing; a poured-in-place rubber-resin flange-way filler encapsulates the crossing against penetration by ice, snow, rain, dirt and debris, aids drainage at the crossing location, makes the crossing safe for small-wheeled vehicular, as well as pedestrian traffic, and eliminates damage to vulnerable products such as glassware, electronic parts, etc, by creating smooth passage; boiled linseed oil and mineral spirits treatment, plus broom finish surface prevents skidding, hydroplaning, eliminates spalling or scaling, and provides resistancy to salts, the elements, as well as car drippings; the product is removable, interchangeable and relocatable without loss of materials; immediate delivery for tangent and curved crossings.

All crossings are unconditionally guaranteed and installed under manufacturer's supervision.

The company's proprietary rubber-resin flange-way filler material is offered for use in all types of open flange-ways at crossings, and/or adjacent highway expansion joints. Fab-Ra-Filler consists of cryogenically-processed rubber and moisture-cured polyurethane, which is field-mixed and 'poured-in-place' into the open flange-ways or expansion joints. The filler material contours exactly to any configuration, sets in two hours and is ready for traffic in eight hours. The material has a unique recovery capability when depressed by rail or vehicular traffic. The resultant crossing is impervious to ice, snow, rain, dirt or debris, as well as to salts, fuels, caustic materials, etc and safe for small-wheeled vehicles and pedestrian traffic. The filler ensures the integrity of signal and communication systems and provides guaranteed assurance that the adjacent crossing panels cannot encroach against the track rails. At least one side of the open flangeway or expansion joint must have some type of contour similar to the track rail shape to provide a positive locking feature for the filler material.

Talleres de Amurrio SA

Maskuribai 10, Amurrio, Alava, Spain

Telephone: +3445 891600
Telex: 32218
Telefax: +3445 892480

General Manager: J Urbiola
Director of Foundry: L Urbiola
Engineering Director: V Gonzalez
Technical Manager: R Guerenu
Export Sales Manager: J Pinedo

Products: Points, crossings, crossovers, turnouts, expansion joints, insulated rail joints, turntables, buffers, height gauges, re-railers.

Tamper Corp
Tamper Corp
Division of Canron Corp

2401 Edmund Road, West Columbia, South Carolina 29171-0020, USA

Telephone: +1 803 822 9160
Telefax: +1 803 822 8710

President & COO: D Bozic
Senior VP, Sales & Marketing: C L Coy
International Manager: K Outred

Products: Tamper manufactures a complete line of railway track maintenance of way equipment including tampers for levelling and lining, ballast equalisers, tie exchangers, ballast undercutters, rail inspection equipment, rail change out units, track renewal units, snow blowers, grinders, drills, wrenches, lubricators, tie cranes and rail welder.

Tamper-Holland Welding Services

4 Strathwyn Street, Strathpine, Queensland, Australia 4500

Telephone: +61 07 205 6500
Telex: 40560
Telefax: +61 07 2057369

Sales Manager: K Harley
Contract Manager: P Hibberson

Permanent way equipment / **MANUFACTURERS** 383

Tamper UTV with flat car and third-rail ice scraper

Liteslice rail profile measuring vehicle (Tamper)

Products: Mobile flash butt rail welding, sales, leasing, contracting.
Recent contracts include 25 k, new construction for BHP Iron Duke, Whyella, South Australia (1989); defect elimination, Robe River Iron Associates, Western Australia (1989).

Tempered Spring Co
A unit of T & N Plc

Park Works, Foley St, Sheffield S4 7W5, England

Telephone: +44 742 720031
Telex: 54103
Telefax: +44 742 731413

Sales Manager: M L Martin

Products: Elastic rail fastenings, including BTREC system and CS-Springlock for concrete sleepers, KTG for K-type baseplates and KT for switches and crossings.

Templeton
Templeton, Kenly and Co

2525 Gardner Road, Broadview, Illinois 60153, USA

Telephone: +1 708 865 1500
Cable: Temkenco, Broadview, Illinois
Telex: (WUI) 6871027
Telefax: +1 708 865 0894

President: Peter Coster
Vice President, Sales: Dan Bemi
Manager, Export Sales: Mike Wlezen

Products: Mechanical trip/track jacks, hydraulic rail puller and expanders, hydraulic rerailing system, portable air/hydraulic jacks for car shop maintenance.

Tetsudo Kiki
Tetsudo Kiki Kaisha Ltd

Yaeso, 1-5-5 Chuo-ku, Tokyo 103, Japan

Telephone: +81 3 271 5341

Products: Points and crossings, expansion and glued insulated joints.

Thebra
Thebra do Brazil

Rua Antonio Austregesilo 360, Rio de Janeiro GB, Brazil

Telephone: +55 21 280 473
+55 21 260 4234

Products: Thermit in-track welding equipment and rail grinders.

Thermit Welding
Thermit Welding (GB) Ltd

87 Ferry Lane, Rainham, Essex RM13 9YH, England

Telephone: +44 4027 22626
Telex: 291380
Telefax: +44 4027 53806

Directors: Dr J J Guntermann
F W Geiger
Dr D C Lamb
V K Saith

General Manager: A J Key
Commercial Manager: P A Bright

Products: Portable rail welding equipment; welding consumables; insulated rail joints.
Recent business secured by the company has included: for Singapore Mass Rapid Transport Corporation, a sub-contract to supply Thermit rail welding materials for Phase II (1988-89); and for supply of rail-welding equipment and consumables to the Ghana Railway Corporation and National Railways of Zimbabwe (1989).

Thomas Robinson
Thomas Robinson & Son plc

Railway Works, Fishwick Street, Rochdale, England

Telephone: +44 706 47811
Telex: 635321

Chairman: D W Povey
Managing Director: I Davis
Director and Chief Executive: C Heap

Subsidiaries
Northern Woodworking Machinery Co Ltd, Rochdale, Lancashire
S S Stott Ltd, Haslingden, Rossendale, Lancashire
Thomas Robinson & Son Pty Ltd, Revesby, New South Wales, Australia
Thomas Robinson & Son Pty Ltd, Johannesburg, South Africa

Products: Sleeper inciser; sleeper adzing and boring, chair/sleeper screwing machines.

Thyssen
Thyssen AG vorm August-Thyssen Hütte

Kaiser-Wilhelm Strasse 100, Postfach 1100 67, 4100 Duisburg 11, Federal Republic of Germany

Telephone: +49 203 52–1
Telex: 85543

Products: Permanent way material: heavy rails, including highly wear-resistant THS 11 special grade; light rails; fishplates for light and heavy rails; light and heavy sleepers; guide rails.

Thyssen Engineering
Thyssen Engineering GmbH

Werk Klönne Dortmund, Körnebachstrasse 1, Postfach 269/270, 4600 Dortmund 1, Federal Republic of Germany

Templeton Kenly portable jack

Telephone: +49 231 5480 1
Telex: 822186
Telefax: +49 231 5480 444

Products: Bridge construction: trough and deck bridges of the plain girder, truss and bascule type; switches and crossings according to West German and foreign standards (including German Federal Railway) of rails S 41, S 49, S 54, UIC 54, UIC 60 and foreign standard sections of strengths from 680 to 1080 N/mm^2; curve points and small curve points for radii of up to 100 metres; tramway switches; point devices with inner stock rail bracing and brace point locks of the latest design; cross frogs of welded and high-strength friction grip block construction; cross frogs of monobloc type, of special alloys (among other things, with 12 to 14 per cent manganese content); cross frogs with resilient-mobile ends; scarfed joints; drag shoe ejectors; small curve switches; loose sets of steel or wooden sleepers with fasteners; transition rails; insulated rail joints according to the latest regulations; rail surface hardening, austenitic and pearlitic, for tensile strengths from 1180 to 1570 N/mm^2; structural steel buildings; elevated structures for off-station track area, station platform roofs, halls.

Tipco
Tipco Inc

1 Coventry Road, Bramalea, Ontario L6T 4B1, Canada

Telephone: +1 416 791 9811
Telex: 06 97799

President: J J Tickins

Products: Flat beaded track bits.

Tokyo Keiki
Tokyo Keiki Co, Ltd
Industrial Division

Sales office: Nishi-Gotanda 1-chome, Shinagawa-ku, Tokyo 141, Japan

Telephone: +81 3 490 0821
Telex: 246 6193/4; 246 8252

Director and Division Manager: Toru Mizuno
General Sales Manager: Yukio Numakura

Products: Ultrasonic flaw detector, Model UM and SM series and accessories; portable rail flaw detector, Model PRD II; portable rail tester, model RT-101; and ultrasonic thickness meter, Model UTM 100. The company has also supplied an ultrasonic rail flaw detector car for the Tohoku Shinkansen of Japanese

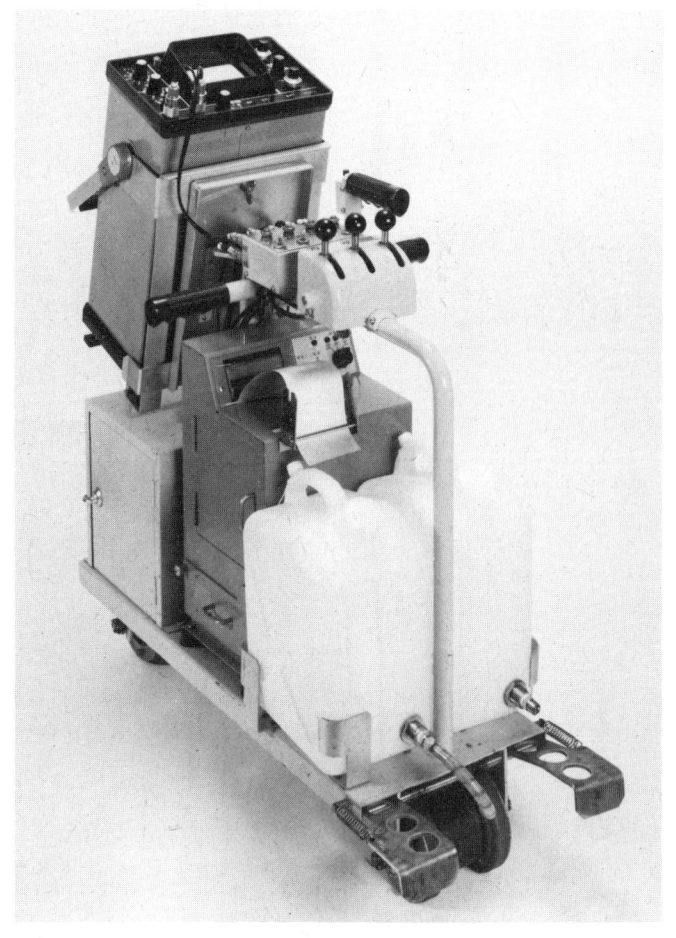

384 MANUFACTURERS / Permanent way equipment

Model PRD-II-R ultrasonic rail flaw detector by Tokyo Keiki

Toyo Kizai double elastic fastener for prestressed concrete sleepers

Toyo Kizai double elastic fastener for wooden sleepers

detector car for the Tohoku Shinkansen of Japanese National Railways (JNR), in addition to two already in use on the Tokaido and Sanyo Shinkansen between Tokyo, Osaka and Hakata.

Toyo Kizai
Toyo Kizai Co Ltd

Head office: PO 100, 6-7, Marunouchi 3, Chiyoda-ku, Tokyo, Japan

Telephone: +81 3 214 6871

Main works: PO 254, 10-12, Amanuma, Hiratsukashi, Kanagawa Pref

Managing Director: N Sasaki
Technical Manager: M Fukuda
Director, Export Department: Tsugio Murayama

Products: Rail fastenings such as sleeper tie-plates, spring clips, bolts, nuts, spikes and sleeper pads.

The company's new Type U resilient spring clip for timber sleepers has unique shape and mounting method for which patents have been applied. High resistance to canting of rails is claimed. This clip has dispensed with fine adjustment of screw spike tightening torque which is needed to provide a given rail fastening torque in conventional types of fastenings; it has a smaller number of component parts and is therefore easy to handle.

Trackmaster
Trackmaster (Pty) Limited

Head office: 4 Davey Road, Industria North, PO Box 80017, 1701 Ridgeview, South Africa

Telephone: +27 11 27 5171
Cable: Mecantrak, Maraisburg
Telex: 4-25876

Main works: 4 Davey Road, Industria North, PO Box 80017, 1701 Ridgeview, South Africa

Chairman: F J Douwes
Directors: N C Segal
P B Morgan
J F Pretorius

Products: Railway track construction and maintenance machinery and equipment including rail saws/ friction cutter, drills, grinders, creep adjusters, changers, destressing device, transporters/trolleys, loaders, benders, sleeper drills; powered railcars and trucks, track gauges and various hand tools including spanners, jacks, slewing bars etc.

True Temper
True Temper Railway Appliances Inc

177 West Hintz Road, Wheeling, Illinois 60090-6078, USA

Telephone: +1 312 565 5435

Vice President and General Manager: R S Jones

Products: Channeloc rail anchors; Trueloc spring anchors; Lineloc low-profile fastening system.

Lineloc is specially designed for concrete crossties, providing a low-profile fastening system that is flush to the track and therefore minimises the need to modify existing track maintenance equipment. The shoulder has a back-off stop to ensure that the 'S' clip stays in place. A one-piece, glass-reinforced nylon insulator distributes forces through a radius that offers a greater contact surface and helps eliminate high stress concentration.

TSO
Travaux du Sud-Ouest SA

Chemin du Corps de Garde, Zone Industrielle, BP 8, 77501 Chelles Cedex, France

Telephone: +33 1 60 20 9010
Telex: 691025 f
Telefax: +33 1 64 26 3023

President: Loïc Perron
Export Manager: Claude Petit
France Manager: Christian Boscher
Equipment: Jean-Marie Delpy

Products: Turnout laying equipment; construction and adaptation of track equipment; track maintenance. The company has been engaged in TGV high-speed line tracklaying for French Railways.

Recent contracts include track-laying in the Ajaokuta steel works, Nigeria; tracklaying in the CIMAO project, Togo; track doubling on a turnkey basis for the Greater Cairo Regional Metro; technical assistance in Saudi Arabia (track re-laying and doubling) and Gabon (new track laying).

TSO has been involved in TGV—A high speed line tracklaying for French Railways

Permanent way equipment / **MANUFACTURERS** 385

Turk & Hilinger GmbH

Föhrenstrasse 20, D 7200 Tuttlingen, Federal Republic of Germany

Telephone: +49 7461 70140
Telex: 762692
Telefax: +49 7461 78218

Products: Electric point heating systems.

Unit Rail Anchor
Unit Rail Anchor Company

High Point Plaza Suite 340, 4415 W Harrison, Hillside, Illinois 60162, USA

Telephone: +1 708 449 3040
Telefax: +1 708 449 5640

President: Douglas C Trites
International Sales: Patricia Veremis

Products: Unit rail anchors, spring and drive-on; reclamation and remanufacturers of rail anchors.

VAI
Verson Ai Limited

Seafield Road, Longman Industrial Estate, Inverness IV1 1LZ, Scotland

Telephone: +44 463 239381
Telex: 75271
Telefax: +44 463 225445

Managing Director: P Cook
Marketing Director: D A MacKenzie

Products: Alternative designs of rail-welding machines to handle either continuous welded rail or combined programmes of continuous welded rail, switches and crossings. These machines are supplied with either ac or dc welding systems and incorporate special features for de-twist and aligning the rail ends prior to commencement of the welding operation in order to meet the tolerances and specifications demanded by major railway organisations which are designing their track systems for operating at speeds of up to 250 km/h. The machines incorporate control and post-heating systems to enable the welding of wear-resistant steels to be carried out. In addition to the design and manufacture of rail welding and ancillary machines, VAI supplies complete rail-welding depot installations including rail handling and cranage systems.

The company's latest product is its Mk IV combined rail welder and stripper, supplied to British Rail, Queensland Railways and Indian Railways. Design is based on the Mk II and hydraulically-operated Mk III models, which have been performing successfully throughout the world railroads since the early 1960s. The Mk IV incorporates the latest developments and features to provide facilities for welding a wide range of rail steels including the chrome wear-resistant steel; automatic de-twist and alignment of the rail ends in the area of the weld joints; data on welding current, time, force and velocity and also equipment utilisation and kWh per weld; electronic weld control unit incorporating feedback systems controlling velocity; pressure, energy and displacement; and integral weld upset removal unit.

The company can also supply complete rail welding installations including conveyor systems, gantry cranes, rail straightening presses, etc.

Vöest-Alpine
Verkauf Eisenbahnsysteme

Floragasse 7, 1040 Vienna, Austria

Telephone: +43 222 501 08
Telex: 75312553 vaew a
Telefax: +43 222 501 08 222

President, Rail Systems: Edmund Auli

Products: Rails, turnouts, frogs, fishplates, soleplates, steel and plastic sleepers.

Von Roll
Von Roll Ltd
Machinery and Handling Systems Division

PO Box 2701, 3001 Berne, Switzerland

Telephone: +41 31 231444
Telex: 911880 rolb ch
Telefax: +41 31 244946

Director: Dr Eckehard Hanert
Vice Director: Kuno Schnider
Export Sales: W Peter

Products: Rail fastenings, points, crossings; racks and rack turnouts for cog-wheel railways; turnouts; turntables and transfer tables.

Vossloh-Werke
Vossloh-Werke GmbH

Postfach 1860, Steinwerthstrasse 4, 5980 Werdohl 1, Federal Republic of Germany

Telephone: +49 2392 520
Cable: Vosslohwerke
Telex: 826 444
Telefax: +49 2392 52375

Managing Director: Ulrich Rieger
Sales Manager: F G Heisler

Products: Resilient rail fastenings including: Tension Clamp Skl 1 on concrete sleepers with lateral angled guide plates; Tension Clamp Skl 12 on timber sleepers with ribbed plates.

Wells-Krautkramer

Blackhorse Road, Letchworth, Hertfordshire SG6 1HF, England

Telephone: +44 4626 78151
Telex: 82329

Managing Director: C D Wells
Sales Director: C Brook

Products: Inspection cars, ultrasonic rail flaw equipment, track recorder analysis equipment, track recording trolleys, eddy current crack detection equipment.

Western-Cullen-Hayes
Western-Cullen-Hayes Inc

2700 West 36th Place, Chicago, Illinois 60632, USA

Telephone: +1 312 254 9600
Cable: Wesrailsup, Chicago
Telex: 253206

President: R L McDaniel
Sales Director: J P Schaefer

Products: Switch point guards, derails, track liners, rail benders, power drills, hand drills; 'Western' (formerly Buda) hydraulic, journal and mechanical jacks, 100 models from 3 to 100 tons capacity; bumping posts, derails, vehicle warning lights, automatic blue flags.

Western-Cullen-Hayes is a consolidation of the Western Railroad Supply Co, and the Hayes Track Appliance Co.

Wickham
D Wickham & Company Ltd

Crane Mead, Ware, Hertfordshire SG12 9QA, England

Telephone: +44 920 462491
Cable: Wickham, Ware
Telex: 81340 wickhm g
Telefax: +44 920 460733

Western-Cullen-Hayes compromise rail joint

Western-Cullen-Hayes switch point guard in manganese steel, preventing derailment on worn points

MANUFACTURERS / Permanent way equipment

Joint Managing Director: D S Holden
Joint Managing Director: T H Bailie
Sales Director: G P Redfern
Technical Director: A P Mott

Products: A range of self-propelled railway track and overhead line inspection cars, crane cars, maintenance gang trolleys, a range of road/rail vehicles, and other special-purpose vehicles; also hand and push cars and track tools.

The Wickham road/rail tamper, incorporating a Vibratool tamping unit, is mounted on the rear end of a Ford Cargo lorry chassis and is hydraulically powered by the vehicle's 6.2 litre engine. A hydraulic motor provides a rail speed of 30 km/h. Also hydraulically operated is a central jacking turntable which facilitates tracking and off-tracking on level crossing surfaces. Optional variations include a laser or wire reference system for levelling and lining, and laterally movable tamping heads for use at points and crossings. Other vehicles in the road/rail range are an undercarriage inspection unit and a loader equipped with a hydraulic crane.

Windhoff
Rheiner Maschinenfabrik Windhoff AG

Hovestrasse 10, Postfach 1160, 4440 Rheine, Federal Republic of Germany

Telephone: +49 5971 580
Telex: 981 643

President: Dr Bernd Windhoff
Managers: Heinz Lörfing
Franz-Josef Cramer
Christoph Wessels
Herbert Bucksch
Export Manager: Helmut Pühs

Products: Overhead line inspection and maintenance cars, multi-purpose track maintenance machines with extensive attachments programme, rail crane trucks, crib ballast removers, light track motor trailers.

Woodings Railcar
Woodings Railcar Ltd

PO Box 1540, Prescott, Ontario K0E 1T0, Canada

Telephone: +1 613 925 2847
Telefax: +1 613 925 3893

Managing Director: D N Noseworthy
Sales Director: J J Reid

Products: Rail-mounted inspection cars, personnel trailers, small motorised personnel/tool/equipment carriers, portable and non-portable track trollies.

WTB
WTB Walter Thosti Boswau Bauaktiengesellschaft
Prestressed concrete sleeper department

PO Box 102547, Boeheimstrasse 8, 8900 Augsburg, Federal Republic of Germany

Telephone: +49 821 5582-389
Telex: 53847, 533273

Products: Prestressed concrete sleepers to international standards and suitable for any type of rail fastening.

Yamato Kogyo
Yamato Kogyo Co Ltd

380 Kibi Otsu-ku, Himeji, Hyogo Pref, Japan

Telephone: +81 792 73 1061

Manager: S Ichimura

Products: Rails, sleeper plates, fishplates, standard and special turnouts, welded frogs, expansion joints, glued insulated joints, compromise rails, rack rail, steel sleepers, etc.

Zweiweg-Fahrzeug
Zweiweg-Fahrzeug GmbH & Co Vertriebs-KG

Innlände 18, 8200 Rosenheim, Federal Republic of Germany

Telephone: +49 8031 15031
Telex: (17) 8031 822
Telefax: +49 8031 15899

Director: Adolf Löw

Products: Track-guidance rollers which convert a road vehicle into a rail vehicle. Besides its use in creating a shunting unit (the resultant tractive power equals about that of a 20-ton locomotive) the device also permits use of the Daimler-Benz Unimog on rails as a working unit with various supplementary equipment.

A Zweiweg Unimog model ZW 82S provided with a steam-jet can be employed for points cleaning, for example; another unit equipped with a loading crane (and at the same time as a shunting unit) can haul up to 25 laden wagons. For winter operation a rotary snow plough or a drum-type snow plough can be fitted, permitting effective snow removal on rails as well as on the road.

Two special units are available for the construction and maintenance of catenary: a Zweiweg Unimog with hydraulic lifting platform and the Zweiweg road-railer with working platform which was initially constructed for the Netherlands Railways. The Zweiweg Unimog vehicles are also available for broad-gauge lines.

The Kremer-Tremo all-purpose vehicle Model A-52S equipped with guidance device ZW 52S is available for demonstrations on narrow-gauge lines.

Fitted with Type ZW MB 3 track-guidance rollers, the Zweiweg-Mercedes Benz Transporter Type 308 has been passed by German Federal Railway (DB) for rail operation at up to 70 km/h and is adaptable to a variety of uses, from personnel transport to weed-killing, firefighting and, fitted with an overhead platform, catenary maintenance.

The Loctrac 150S has been approved by the German Federal Railway for up to 1200 tonnes wagonloads after extensive evaluating trials. This heavy-duty shunting unit is based on the Daimler-Benz MB Trac 1500 with an engine output of 110 kW and a total gross weight of 14 tonnes. On rails it is a shunting unit with 1200 tonnes capacity, and on the road, a traction unit for 120 tonnes payload.

Independently controlled track guiding devices allow quick on-and off-tracking with audio-visual indicators for safe operation. The air receivers of the railway wagon air braking system are automatically maintained at the correct working pressure by a pressure valve compensator. The articulated buffer system allows negotiation of particularly tight curves and is easily demountable to facilitate the fitting of, for instance, a snow plough, a road sweeper, a crane or other implements depending on individual requirements.

Several city metros in different countries have made use of Zweiweg vehicles for inspection, traction and maintenance purposes, and recently a series of such special vehicles has also been delivered to Metro Montreal, Canada, which is a rubber-tyred system. Each metro has individual characteristics, which must be taken into consideration when these auxiliary machines are planned and constructed. The only common feature is the basic vehicle, a Daimler-Benz MB-trac 1500 of 110 kW/150 hp capacity with torque converter transmission for high-starting performance, a Mercedes-Benz six-cylinder direct injection diesel engine with exhaust turbo-charger, and the Zweiweg track-guidance roller device.

The Zweiweg metro vehicle has a total weight of 12 tons, which is 2 tons less than the standard Loctrac 150S. Equipped with seven gears, the vehicle achieves a speed of approximately 32 km/h at an engine speed of 2400 rpm, on road as well as on rails. Great importance has been attached to low noise level, which under load is approximately 87 db(A).

The Zweiweg ZW 120S track-cleaning vehicle based on the Unimog 1250 is used by the Rome Metro, Italy, and the Caracas Metro, Venezuela. It has a power of 92 kW/124 hp and a permissible total high load weight of 11.5 tonnes, which is due to the installation of an air-suspended trailing axle. Equipment comprises: four pneumatically-tiltable suction nozzles, adjustable to the side; front-mounted suction apparatus, hydraulically adjustable, for cleaning the tunnel walls; a dirt-collecting container with a capacity of 3 m^3, which is tiltable to the rear for draining purposes; an access door on the side of the aggregate compartment to facilitate maintenance; and a water tank with a capacity of 1000 litres.

The Type 62S, 82S and 150S shunting vehicles for trailing loads of up to 1200 tonnes can be equipped for radio remote control. The portable transmitter operates via a 2 m band with a frequency range of 138 to 173 MHz. Transmitter performance is 50 to 500 MW. An NC battery provides the power supply. The receiver is mounted in a stable, shock-resistant aluminium steel-cast housing in the vehicle. Test equipment is via light-emitting diodes.

Zwicky
Zwicky Engineering Limited
Skyhi Division
A member of EIS Group plc

Molly Millars Lane, Wokingham, Berkshire RG11 2RY, England

Telephone: +44 734 771331
Telex: 848852
Telefax: +44 734 774856

Directors: P J K Haslehurst
P F Drewitt
J J Hobbs
B H Wormsley
M K Wood
F E Bing
Sales Director: F E Bing

Products: Track and wagon hydraulic jacks; jack test rigs; rail benders; air-draulic power packs; Track Aliner tools.

The Skyhi Track Aliner has been designed for the aligning and slewing of track, including points and crossings. When positioned in the ballast its low profile makes it obstructionless, so that it may be used during traffic intervals and left in the track. Its horizontal action slides the sleepers through the ballast with minimum disturbance of the 'top' of the track.

Constructed in mild steel, it weighs 23 kg and has a safe working load of 8.128 tonnes. There are two main parts: a hydraulic ram unit having a 152 mm (6-inch) stroke mounted on to a base designed to provide a firm anchorage in the ballast. The swivel head has been designed so that it can be positioned against the web of any rail and on the foot of flat bottom rails as required.

Freight yard and terminal equipment

AUSTRALIA
Clyde 390

BELGIUM
ACEC 388
Jambes-Namur 394

FINLAND
Kone 394
Saalasti 395
Valmet 398

FRANCE
Caillard 389
Chemico 389
De Dietrich 391
Domange-Jarret 391
GEC Alsthom 392

GERMANY, DEMOCRATIC REPUBLIC
TAKRAF 397

GERMANY, FEDERAL REPUBLIC
ABB 388
AEG Westinghouse 388
Dickertmann 391
Haacon 392
Hauhinco 392
Hoesch 393
Peiner 395
SEL 395
Siemens 395
Thyssen 397
Vollert 399
Windhoff 399
Zagro 400

HUNGARY
Hungarian Crane 393

IRELAND
Liebherr 394
Unilock 398

ITALY
Ansaldo Trasporti 389
BP-Battioni & Pagani 389

JAPAN
Kyosan 394
Mitsubishi 394
Nippon Signal 394
Toshiba 397

NETHERLANDS
Noord Ned 395

SPAIN
Babcock & Wilcox 389

SWEDEN
Ericsson 392

SWITZERLAND
Integra Signum 394

UK
Allen 388
Cowans Boyd 390
Dawson-Aquamatic 390
EKA 391
FKI Godwin Warren 392
Hyster 393
Jones 394
Kalmar 394
Oleo 395
Sika Ltd 395
Smith Bros & Webb 395
Steele 396
Stothert & Pitt 396
Strachan & Henshaw 396
Teklite Lighting 397
Ultra Hydraulics Ltd 398
Warrington Tractors 399
Westinghouse Signals 399

USA
Abex 388
Aldon 388
Allis-Chalmers 389
Central Maufacturing 389
CE & MCO 389
Diversey Wyandotte 391
Durbin-Durco 391
Fergusson 392
Godwin Warren Engineering 392
GRS 392
Holmes 393
Impco Products Inc 393
Kershaw 394
Letourneau 394
Modern Industries 394
Penetone 395
Ross and White 395
Safetran 395
Trackmobile 398
Tysol 398

MANUFACTURERS / Freight yard and terminal equipment

ABB
ASEA Brown Boveri Transportation
Group headquarters: ABB BTM, PO Box 100163, 6800 Mannheim, Federal Republic of Germany

Telephone: +49 621 468 200
Telex: 462411220 abd btm gmbh
Telefax: +49 621 468 298/9

(For full list of ABB companies, see ABB entry in Locomotives section)

Products: ABB Traction has developed a hydraulic retarder with self-regulating braking power for use in railway marshalling yards. The spiral-type retarder consists essentially of a steel cylinder bolted to the rail. As each wagon wheel passes the retarder it runs on a spiral cam, which under hydraulic resistance forces the cylinder to rotate one revolution, thus braking the wheel. Each time the cylinder rotates it starts an internal hydraulic pump, which yields an oil flow proportional to the wheel speed. At the pre-set value the oil flow is shut off and is not released again until the oil pressure corresponds to a braking force of 10 kNm. The wagons will therefore be braked smoothly and precisely. Retarders working according to this principle do not require any measuring device or computer control.

Abex
ABC Rail Corporation
Railroad Products Group

65 Valley Road, Mahwah, New Jersey 07430, USA

Telephone: +1 201 529 3450
Telex: 642415

Products: Yard control systems.

ACEC
Transport Department

PO Box 211, 6000 Charleroi 1, Belgium

Telephone: +32 71 44 57 99
Telex: 51 227 acec b
Telefax: +32 71 43 78 34

General Director: C Jauquet
Commercial Director, Transport Department: D Hausman

Products: Engineering, manufacture and installation of yard control systems.

AEG Westinghouse
AEG Westinghouse Transport-Systems GmbH

Nonnendammallee 15-21, D-1000 Berlin 20, Federal Republic of Germany

Telephone: +49 30 3305 0
Telefax: +49 30 3305 2169

General Manager, Train Equipment and Railway Automation Systems: Dr H H Dubenkropp
Commercial Manager: G Mayer

Products: Marshalling yard equipment; automatic humping control; control panels and desks; point machines; electronic interlocking systems and components; identification systems.

AEG Westinghouse supplies up-to-date equipment and systems covering train splitting and combining, running distance or target braking, rail brake control and transport equipment controls and the remote control of marshalling locomotives, for marshalling yards, both new and to be extended.

Aldon
The Aldon Company

3410 Sunset Avenue, Waukegan, Illinois 60087, USA

Telephone: +1 312 623 8800/1

Products: Wheel blocks, wheel chocks, warning signs, portable friction rail skids, car stops, bumping posts, electric and pneumatic car shakers, winch-type car pullers, electric car haulers, power car movers, portable grip-pull car movers, car door wrenches and pullers, automatic bulk car gate openers and retarders.

Marshalling yard equipped with ABB hydraulic retarders, Gothenburg, Sweden

ABB hydraulic retarders in Gothenburg marshalling yard

A new line of winch-type railroad car pullers consists of four electrically-driven pullers with 5 to 15 hp motors and starting pull capacities from 10 000 to 30 000 lb. Haulage capacity is up to six loaded heavy-class freight cars as far as 700 ft in one direction, or half that distance in two-way movements. The operator can control the car puller from a sheltered location. These car pullers are specifically designed for the industrial firm that has to load or unload multi-car trains frequently and wants its own independent means of moving freight cars.

The company has recently developed the AL-122 Track Level for Hi-Rail Vehicles that can be used on any rail-riding truck or track geometry equipment to check level condition of track. Mounted on the dashboard the level can be easily seen from the driver's seat. It consists of a rugged electronic sensor, custom VLSI circuitry and LCD. Display is in inches and tenths of an inch. There is no limit on elevation reading on curves. For very accurate reading, the vehicle must be stopped on curve; it takes 2 seconds for the display to settle.

Allen
Allen Cranes (N'pton) Ltd

Baird Court, Park Farm Industrial Estate, Wellingborough, Northamptonshire NN8 3QJ, England

Telephone: +44 933 677833

Telex: 312665 pbsuk
Telefax: +44 933 678385

Crane Sales Manager: S Austin

Products: Goliath-type rail-mounted container cranes. Capacity up to 40 tonnes for road to rail transfer operations. Electric overhead travelling container cranes associated with refuse, disposal compaction stations.

Allis-Chalmers

Industrial Truck Division, 21800 South Cicero Avenue, Matteson, Illinois 60443, USA

Telephone: +1 312 747 5151

General Manager: Ronald Burns
Marketing Manager: A V DeCola
General Sales Manager: John S Pink Jr
International Marketing Manager: Fred G Owen

Products: Heavy-duty side-loaders and front-loading forklift trucks.

Ansaldo Trasporti
Ansaldo Trasporti SpA
A member of Ansaldo SpA

Head office: 254 Via Argine, 80147 Naples, Italy
Works: 260 Via Nuova delle Brecce, 80147 Naples, Italy

Telephone: +39 81 7810111
Telex: 710131 ans na i
Telefax: +39 81 7810698 699

Other offices:
336 Viale Sarca, 20126 Milan, Italy

Telephone: +39 2 64451
Telex: 331279
Telefax: +39 2 6438032

25 Corso Perrone 16161 Genoa, Italy

Telephone: +39 10 65511
Telex: 271274
Telefax: +39 10 495044

Chairman: Giovanni Nobile
Vice President and Managing Director: Emilio Maraini
General Director: Francesco Granito
General Co-Director: Alberto G Rosania
Technical Director: Salvatore Bianconi
R & D and Commercial Director: Carlo Rizzi

Products: Yard control equipment and yard layout design; power signalling apparatus; geographic relay interlocking; remote control equipment; level crossing automation.

Babcock & Wilcox
Babcock & Wilcox Espan ola SA

Alda de Recalde 27, Apdo 294, Bilbao 9, Spain

Telephone: +34 4 4415700
Cable: Babcock
Telex: 32776 bwbil e

Products: Mechanical handling equipment; container cranes; portal cranes; dockside cranes; shipyard portal cranes; giant shipyard portal cranes; polar cranes for nuclear power facilities; overhead travelling cranes of all kinds; ingot mould stripper and foundry ladle cranes; ship discharging machinery; wagon tipplers, etc.

BP–Battioni & Pagani
BP–Battioni & Pagani SpA

Località Croce, 43058 Sorbolo (Parma), Italy

Telephone: +39 521 604141-2
Telex: 530081
Telefax: +39 521 698742

Products: A complete range of side-loaders, including container handling machines up to 55 tons capacity and heavy machines fitted with telescopic top spreaders and special top clamps for intermodal transport movements; a range of heavy-duty fork-lift trucks of 4 to 38 tons capacity including machines fitted with spreader attachments for container handling.

Aldon AL-122 Digital Hi-Rail vehicle Track Level

Caillard

BP 1368, Place Caillard, 76065 Le Havre Cedex, France

Telephone: +33 35 25 81 31
Telex: 190616
Telefax: +33 35 25 11 41

Director: P Schwarzmann
Sales Manager: A Herrmann

Products: Breakdown cranes up to 150 tons capacity for railways; rail- and pneumatic tyre-mounted gantries for container handling; mobile cranes; all kinds of gantry cranes, unloaders and jib cranes for general cargo, container or bulk cargo; and mobile port cranes for ports and railways.

Recent contracts include railway breakdown crane for Malawi (1988).

Central Manufacturing Inc

4116 Dr Greaves Road, Grandview, Missouri 64030, USA

Telephone: +1 816 767 0300
Telefax: +1 816 763 0705

Vice President and General Manager: Jack Highfill
Director of Marketing: Tom Connel

Products: Re-railing cranes 130- to 150-ton road/rail; railcar movers of 24 000 to 40 000 lb drawbar pull; maintenance of way equipment; road-to-rail conversion units.

CE & MCO
Coast Engineering and Manufacturing Company

13085 West Seaway Access Road, Gulfport, MS 39503 USA

Telephone: +1 601 896 1010
Telex: 58 9924
Telefax: +1 601 896 4257

President & CEO: Robert A Spoerl
Director, Marketing & Sales: Gary B Lipely
Sales Manager, Material Handling: Charles I Melaney

Products: Among recent deliveries of PACECO Transtainer rubber-tyred 40-ton lift capacity yard gantry cranes by US licensee Coast Engineering and Manufacturing Company (CE & MCO) are a total of three units built for American President Intermodal (API) at its new intermodal terminal at South Kearny, New Jersey, delivered mid-1989.

Six further Transtainers have been delivered to Virginia Ports Authority.

Coast Engineering has delivered two 40 long ton capacity PACECO Transtainer Cranes to Maryland Port Administration (MPA) for use at the new dockside rail yard.

Chemico
Société des Établissements Roger Brillié SA

25 rue de la Victoire, PO Box 45, 93151 Le Blanc Mesnil Cedex, France

Telephone: +33 1 48 65 30 76

Caillard 100-tonne crane for Zaire Railways (SNCZ)

390 MANUFACTURERS / Freight yard and terminal equipment

Paceco rail-mounted Transtainer crane with 110 ft span, rotating trolley and 50 short-ton lifting capacity

Shuttle railcar mover, equipped with 205 or 210 hp engine by Central Manufacturing; can be supplied with UIC draft gear

Telefax: +33 1 48 67 30 18

President: J N Vassipoulos

Products: Design, manufacture and installation of washing machines to customer specification. Customers include SNCF (sole supplier, including special apparatus for TGV train-sets), RATP, DB, BR, RENFE, SNTF, SNCFT, CFCO and various metro and light rail systems.

Clyde
Clyde Engineering Co Pty Ltd
Motive Power Division

Factory Street, Granville, PO Box 73, New South Wales 2142, Australia

Telephone: +61 2 637 8288
Telex: 72636 aa
Telefax: +61 2 636 8735

Products: Yard control equipment, including retarders.

Cowans Boyd
NEI Clarke Chapman Ltd

PO Box 9, Carlisle Enterprise Centre, James Street, Carlisle, Cumbria CA2 5BJ

Telephone: +44 228 24196
Cable: Cowans, Carlisle
Telex: 64136
Telefax: +44 228 24795

General Manager: F G J Gilroy
Marketing Manager: S Whitfield
Product Manager: J E Steele

Products: Cranes: diesel-hydraulic, diesel-electric and diesel-mechanical railway breakdown and general purpose cranes, capacity 5–250 tonnes, with telescopic or lattice booms; carriage designs to suit all rail gauges and all wheel-loading conditions.

Dawson-Aquamatic
A Barry-Wehmiller International Company

Gomersal Works, Gomersal, Cleckheaton, West Yorkshire BD19 4LQ, England

Telephone: +44 274 873422
Cable: Dawgom, Cleckheaton
Telex: 51347 dawgong
Telefax: +44 274 874930

Managing Director: B J Turner
Divisional Manager: P Barnett

Products: Design, manufacture and installation of drive-through washing and brushing systems for railcars, ranging from the simplest detergent/water wash-up to fully automatic installations for daily detergent washing and periodic removal of oxides and staining by acidic solutions; supporting control systems, water storage, effluent treatment and water re-cycling systems; railway workshop cleaning plant including bogie washing installations.

Dawson-Aquamatic has supplied combined regular washing and acid cleaning plants to British Rail, Chingford, Clacton and Southend for emu trains, and a dual line machine at Wimbledon. London Transport uses machines at its Stonebridge Park, Hainault, Morden and Ruislip depots. Washing and acidic units are operating in Hong Kong at MTRC and KCR and also

Cowans Boyd 12-tonne general-purpose crane for British Rail

80-tonne capacity diesel-hydraulic breakdown crane supplied to Zambia Railways

60-tonne capacity low-axleload diesel-hydraulic breakdown crane with relieving bogies supplied to Tanzanian Railways

140-tonne capacity diesel-hydraulic breakdown crane with lattice boom for Indian Railways; 12 have been ordered

Freight yard and terminal equipment / **MANUFACTURERS** 391

Dawson-Aquamatic dual-line train wash plant for Wimbledon emu depot, British Rail

Dawson-Aquamatic bogie washer at London Transport's Acton works

Mule haulage system for railway yards by De Dietrich

Autoloc Locotractor with remote control by De Dietrich

at Caracas Metro (two phosphoric-foam plants), and on Seoul Metro.

Dawson-Aquamatic bogie washers are installed at the British Rail, Derby, York and Glasgow depots, and at London Transport, Acton and on the Seoul Metro.

Recent and current contracts include carriage washing equipment for British Rail at Cardiff, Colchester, Swansea, Reading, Inverness, Kings Lynn, Shrewsbury and Stockport.

De Dietrich
De Dietrich & Cie

Reichshoffen, 67110 Niederbronn-les-Bains, France

Telephone: +33 88 80 25 00
Cable: Dietnwagons
Telex: 870 850
Telefax: +33 88 80 25 12

Sales organisation: De Dietrich & Cie
Railway and Mechanical Division

President: Gilbert de Dietrich
Director, Rolling Stock Division: Maurice Canioni

Products: Autoloc remote-controlled shunter.

Dickertmann AG

PO Box 2109, Hakenort 47, D-4800 Bielefeld 1, Federal Republic of Germany

Telephone: +49 521 3039-0
Telex: 932750 gedi d
Telefax: +49 521 3039-40

President: Dipl-Ing Günther Kelle-Emden

Products: Lifting jacks, underfloor lifting plants, bogie lifting stands, lifting trucks and tables, shunting vehicles, dismantling devices for wheelsets and bogies, mobile handling equipment, turning platforms, maintenance platforms, auxiliary bogies, lifting equipment for complete trains.

Recent contracts include lifting installations for railways and municipal transport services in more than 30 countries.

Diversey Wyandotte
Diversey Wyandotte Corp

1532 Biddle Avenue, Wyandotte, Michigan 48192, USA

Telephone: +1 313 281 0930

Products: General maintenance and overhaul cleaning compounds; degreasers; rust removers; paint strippers; locomotive and car-washing products.

Domange-Jarret

198 Avenue des Grésillons, PO Box 251, 92602 Asnières Cedex, France

Telephone: +33 1 47 90 62 72
Telex: 620798 f
Telefax: +33 1 47 90 03 57

General Manager: P Domange
Export Manager: P Serbinenko

Principal subsidiary: Jarret GmbH, PO Box 11 02 48, Feldstrasse 36A, D-4200 Oberhausen, W Germany

Products: Shock absorbers for end-of-track stops.

Durbin-Durco
Durbin Durco Inc

8659 Olive St Road, PO Box 8396, St Louis, Missouri 63132, USA

Telephone: +1 314 993 4750
TWX: 910763-0798 Durbinder STL
Telefax: +1 314 993 2099

President: M Durbin
Executive Vice-President: T J Durbin

Products: Tie down hooks and hook assemblies; R-hooks, grab hooks; winches, ratchets; re-work chain assemblies.

EKA
EKA Ltd

Valkyrie House, 38 Packhorse Road, Gerrards Cross, Buckinghamshire SL9 8EB, England

Telephone: +44 753 889818
Telex: 847659 eureka g
Telefax: +44 753 880004

Products: The new EKA 'Stevedore' side-loading semi-trailer, ideally suited to handling ISO containers at lightly-used road/rail transfer yards where the cost of

392 MANUFACTURERS / Freight yard and terminal equipment

Dismantling device for wheelsets and bogies by Dickertmann

Friction buffers and retarders as supplied to British Rail (BR) by FKI Godwin Warren

expensive fixed gantries or heavy forklift trucks is not justified. There is also no need for separate vehicles for transporting containers by road. With the 'Stevedore', one man can collect a container at a transfer yard and deliver to a destination where it can be grounded for ease of emptying or stacking for storage. Four individually-controlled hydraulic stabilisers ensure total stability and ease of levelling. There are versions for 20 and 40 ft-long ISO containers weighing up to 30 tonnes.

EB Signal AB
(Formerly Ericsson Signal Systems AB)

Box 42505, 126 12 Stockholm, Sweden

Telephone: +468 7262000
Cable: Ericsignal
Telex: 10442 ericj s
Telefax: +468 7262300

Products: Yard communications and signalling control equipment.

Fergusson
Alex C Fergusson Company

Spring Mill Drive, Frazer, Pennsylvania 19355, USA

Telephone: +1 215 647 3300
Telex: 173233

Products: Cleaners, sanitisers and lubricants.

FKI Godwin Warren
FKI Godwin Warren Ltd

Brearley Works, Lyddendenfoot, Halifax, West Yorkshire HX2 6JB, England

Telephone: +44 422 882383
Telex: 517249
Telefax: +44 422 884021

General Manager: A D Garritty

Director, Sales & Marketing: M J Brimble
Rail Project Engineer: P Notter

Products: Friction buffers, retarders and wheel stops; level crossing barrier systems; automatic wagon locators. The automatic wagon locator is designed to secure wagons or tankers during loading and discharge; it is normally custom-manufactured to specific order. Fold-out wheel stops and retarding buffers are employed to provide added protection for the system, especially where complicated rail movements are involved.

GEC Alsthom
Transport Division

PO Box 165, 33 rue des Bateliers, 93404 Saint-Ouen, France

Telephone: +33 1 40 10 63 35
Telex: 234317 f
Telefax: +33 1 40 10 61 00

Godwin Warren Engineering
Godwin Warren Engineering Inc

400 Stenton Avenue, Plymouth Meeting, Pennsylvania 19462, USA

Telephone: +1 215 834 0232
Telex: 4761066

Chief Executive: D J Simpson
President: M T Strange
Treasurer: J G Jeffrey
Marketing Manager: P M Franklin

Products: Frictionally-controlled buffer stops, mine car arresters and level crossing barrier systems.

The Godwin Warren bumper post is mounted on the track in such a way that it slides under impact. However, the speed of sliding can be adjusted by means of specially designed friction shoes clamped to the rail. The shoes are set at a predetermined pressure to insure stopping within a designated distance. The friction bumpers uniquely incorporate a device which ensures rapid dissipation of heat energy so that bumpers do not stick or weld to the rails. The unit is not significantly affected by rust, dirt or oil. Maintenance is minimal, involving only periodic torque setting of the shoes. The friction bumpers can be hinged midline or third rail.

GRS
General Railway Signal Co

PO Box 600, Rochester, New York 14602-0600, USA

Telephone: +1 716 436 2020
Cable: Genrasig, Rochester, New York
Telex: 978317

President: G E Collins

Products: Yard control systems.

YARDS 2000 is an advanced application of distributed microprocessor technology to marshalling yard operations. Key functions formerly performed in a central minicomputer are distributed to dedicated microprocessors for switch and retarder control, distance-to-couple control, and crest detection and cut characterisation.

Using a building block approach, YARDS 2000 can computerise a yard in phases as a customer's needs grow, with expansion usually requiring only added circuit board modules. Each module has self-diagnostics and user-indicated diagnostics for rapid detection and isolation of failures to reduce maintenance costs, and the system interfaces with most existing field equipment. Consisting of six function modules, the system is ideal for the initial step-by-step automation of yards, the replacement of obsolete analog retarder control, upgrades of relay switching systems, and as a complete control system for new yards.

SPEED FRATE is a GRS equipment package especially developed for smaller yards. It provides substantial benefits in car handling speed, damage control, work simplification, and in customer satisfaction. With the SPEED FRATE system, a small yard can marshall four to five cars a minute, with one person handling all car speed control and routeing. Equipment cost and earth moving too are of modest proportions: for example, less than 2.1 m hump is ample for up to 18 tracks. GRS ground equipment for the system includes: Type F4 weight-responsive hydraulic car retarders; Speed-Frater high-speed electric point machines; control panel and colour-light signals.

GRS ground equipment for the GRS yard system includes: Type E160 heavy-duty car retarders, available in either electric or hydraulic operation, Type F5 weight-responsive hydraulic retarders for tangent tracks, Type F4 hydraulic skating retarders, Model 6 high-speed trailable electric switch machines, dragging equipment detectors, radar speed detectors, and colour-light hump and trim signals.

Haacon
Haacon Hebetechnik GmbH

Josef Haaman Strasse 6, 6982 Freudenberg/Main, Federal Republic of Germany

Telephone: +49 9375 84-0
Telex: 689224
Telefax: +49 9375 8466

Managing Director: L H Klein
Export Sales Director: C Cappellaro

Products: Winches for platforms of car-transporter wagons; container handling equipment; jacks for shifting screens inside freight wagons.

Hauhinco
Hauhinco Maschinenfabrik G Hausherr Jochums GmbH & Co KG

Zweigertstrasse 28/30, PO Box 10 16 61, 4300 Essen 1, Federal Republic of Germany

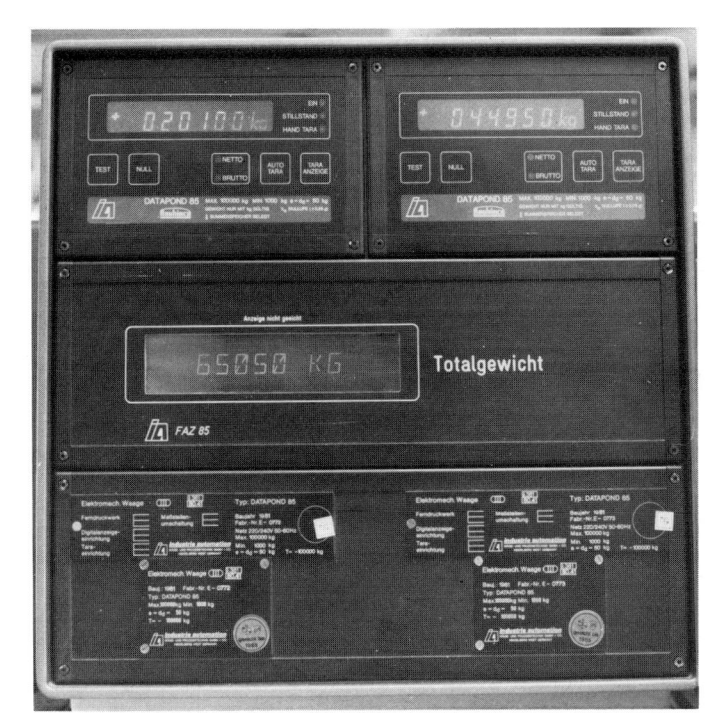

Hauhinco Fahrtwäger digital display

Telephone: +49 201 771071
Cable: Hauhinco, Essen
Telex: 857 834

Products: Wagon shunting equipment for classification and sorting tracks at marshalling yards and industrial sites; railway weighing systems.

The latest addition to the company's automatic systems is a device that overcomes the operating handicaps of static wagon weighing equipment. The Hauhinco in-movement weigher, the Fahrtwäger, weighs wagons by the axle or bogie with the accuracy of static weighers while they are in motion during marshalling. A special filtering process has been developed jointly with Industrie-Automation, Heidelberg, and the Kaiserslautern University, with support from the state of Nordrhein-Westphalia, to eliminate from the weighing results by complex algorithm any distortions arising from the wagon's movement; this requires the use of sophisticated microprocessors to be economically viable. The Fahrtwäger closes the one major gap in a fully automated shunting process.

Hoesch
Hoesch Maschinenfabrik Deutschland AG

Borsigstrasse 22, PO Box 274, 4600 Dortmund 1, Federal Republic of Germany

Telephone: +49 231 84 910
Cable: Deutschland Dortmund
Telex: 822269 mfd d
Telefax: +49 231 84 91333

Products: Hydraulic rerailing systems of special aluminium alloy, especially designed for portable use; hydraulic equipment for rapid track clearing after serious accidents; combined road and rail vehicle with rerailing equipment on board for fast and efficient use.

Holmes
Holmes International Inc

2505 East 43rd Street, Chattanooga, Tennessee 37377, USA

Telephone: +1 615 867 2142
Telex: 5584092 holmes
Telefax: +1 615 867 2145

President: Walter Lock
Export Director: Paul A Becksvoort

Products: Automotive towing and recovery cranes (breakdown cranes).

The Holmes PT2208 8.5-ton twin-winch wrecker blends an 8-ton extendable boom, two 8,500lb Holmes winches and a six-function fully hydraulic wheel lift system into a powerful performing unit.

Hauhinco Fahrtwäger track installation

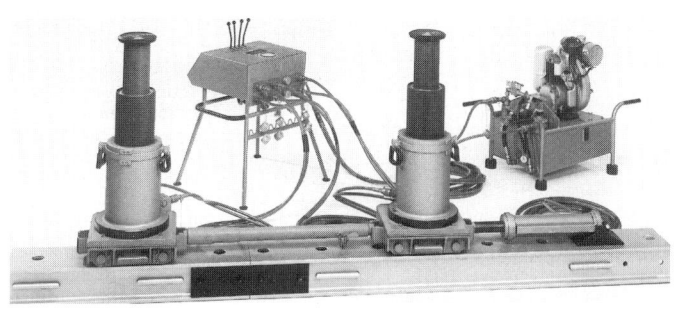

Hoesch rerailing equipment

Hungarian Crane
Hungarian Shipyards and Crane Factory

Vaci ut 202, Budapest XIII, Hungary

Telephone: +36 1 496 370
Telex: 22 5047

Products: Container gantry cranes.

Hyster
Hyster Europe Ltd

Berk House, Basing View, Basingstoke, Hampshire RG21 2HQ, England

Telephone: +44 256 461171
Telex: 858384

Managing Director: David Pollock
Marketing Director: Graham Lovatt

Products: Lift trucks for handling loads from 1 to 48 tonnes, including 20, 30 and 40 foot ISO containers.
Recent orders include one from Swiss Railways in 1988-89 for 1.25-tonne capacity trucks, and a maintenance contract with Irish Rail.

Impco Products Inc

PO Box 2783, Airport Road & Adams Lane, Allentown, Pennsylvania 18001, USA

Telephone: +1 215 266 9060

President: Philip von Funk

Jones' 20RT 20-tonne capacity crane

394 MANUFACTURERS / Freight yard and terminal equipment

Products: Locomotive sand towers with pneumatic sand-conveying unit and automatic control; mobile sand supply trailers.

Integra Signum
Integra Signum Ltd

Industriestrasse 42, CH-8304 Wallisellen, Switzerland

Telephone: +41 1 832 32 32
Cable: Integra, Wallisellen
Telex: 826 260 isag
Telefax: +41 1 832 3501

General Manager: Dr J Leimgruber
Divisional Manager: Dr U Betschart
Departmental Manager: H Wahl

Products: DOMINO unit construction panels for marshalling yard control systems; alpha-numerical keyboard control.

Jambes-Namur
Ateliers de Construction de Jambes-Namur SA

Rue de la Gare Fleurie 16, 5100 Jambes, Belgium

Telephone: +32 81 30 18 51
Cable: Jamur-Jambes
Telex: 59127

Managing Director: Etienne Offergeld
Chief of sales: Paul de Groote

Products: 'Locopulseur Pulso' shunting machine. The Locopulseur Pulso shunting machine is a single- wheel vehicle capable of moving freight cars weighing 160 to 200 tons on straight level track. It can also move cars in curves, split a line of cars and handle a car on a turntable.

Jones
GCM 600 Ltd
Member of The 600 Group Plc

Avenue One, The Business Park, Letchworth, Herts SG6 2HB, England

Telephone: +44 462 682360
Telex: 82112 g
Telefax: +44 462 684226

Managing Director: K Hancox
Deputy Managing Director: S Fitton
Financial Director: G Satterthwaite
Sales Director: G Patient
Parts & Services Director: D Sleeman

Products: Jones diesel-hydraulic and diesel-mechanical road/yard mobile cranes with lifting capacities from 8 to 45 tonnes; HIAB lorry, rail, truck and ship-mounted hydraulic loaders with capacities from 0.7 to 45 tonne/m.

Kalmar
Kalmar UK Ltd

Kalmar House, Sandy Lane, Coventry CV1 4DX, England

Telephone: +44 203 555355
Telex: 312414
Telefax: +44 203 229417

Managing Director, Sales & Marketing: A D R Sproul
Managing Director, Manufacture: T D Gray

Products: Lift trucks (1.25–80 tonnes), reach trucks and side loaders.

Kershaw
Kershaw Manufacturing Co, Inc

PO Box 17340, Montgomery, Alabama 36117-0340, USA

Telephone: +1 205 271 1000
Telex: 593416
Telefax: +1 205 277 6551

President: Royce Kershaw Jr
European Sales: Alain Sigfrit
Manager, Sales & Marketing: John Whitaker

Products: Rubber-tyred/rail-mounted yard cleaners, track brooms, on/off track snow and sand removers: rubber-tyred and rail-mounted cranes equipped with lattice or hydraulic telescopic booms for handling locomotives, wagons or containers of up to 135 tons: road/rail wagon movers with optional mounted crane.

Kone
Kone Cranes

PO Box 6, 05801 Hyvinkáá, Finland

Telephone: +358 14 271
Cable: Kone
Telex: 15-122 or 15-320
Telefax: +358 14 273100

President: Gerhard Wendt
Director, Crane Division: Stig Gustavson
Manager, Marketing: Eero Keihari

Products: Railway terminal gantry cranes, container handling dockside cranes, multi-purpose cranes, cargo and container handling gantry cranes, container storage cranes, overhead travelling cranes for containers and other loads.

Kyosan
Kyosan Electric Manufacturing Co Ltd

Head office: 4-2 Marunouchi 3-chome, Chiyoda-ku, Tokyo, Japan

Telephone: +81 3 214 8131
Cable: Signalkyosan Tokyo
Telex: 222 3178
Telefax: +81 3 211 2450

Main works: 29-1 Heian-cho, Tsurumi-ku, Yokohama

Telephone: +81 45 501 1261

Chairman: C Okawa
President: Y Tanaka
Managing Director: S Orimo
General Manager: Y Mitani

Products: Automatic car haulage systems. Overseas installations of yard systems have included projects in Brazil, India and Thailand.

Letourneau
Marathon Letourneau Company
Subsidiary of Marathon Manufacturing Company, Longview Division. Marathon Manufacturing is a wholly-owned subsidiary of Penn-Central Corporation

PO Box 2307, Longview, Texas 75606, USA

Telephone: +1 214 236 6500
Telex: 730 371

President: Paul Glaske
Vice President, Sales: Mel Kangas

Products: Gantry cranes.

Kone type CT4 40 tonnes container crane loading for Swedish State Railways (SJ)

Liebherr
Liebherr Container Cranes Ltd

Head office: Killarney, Co Kerry, Ireland

Telephone: +353 64 31511
Telex: 73946 lbhr ei
Telefax: +353 64 31602

UK sales office: Liebherr Great Britain Ltd, Travellers Lane, Welham Green, Hatfield, Hertfordshire AL9 7HW, England

Telephone: +44 7072 68161
Telex: 261271

Directors: K Noelke
R Geiler
Secretary: H Brunner

Products: Liebherr Container Cranes Ltd manufactures and sells rail-mounted container handling cranes for ship-to-shore terminals, railway and trucking terminals and storage yards. Sizes, speeds and safe working loads to meet all international tenders and specific customers' requirements.

Mitsubishi
Mitsubishi Heavy Industries Ltd

5-1 Marunouchi, 2-chome, Chiyoda-ku, Tokyo, Japan

Telephone: +81 3 212 3111
Telex: 22282

Products: Straddle carrier and gantry cranes.

Modern Industries
Modern Industries Inc

PO Box 14287, Louisville, Kentucky 40214, USA

Telephone: +1 502 361 1113
Telefax: +1 502 361 7925

Products: Yard control equipment.

Nippon Signal
The Nippon Signal Co Ltd

Head office: 3-1 Marunouchi, 3-chome, Chiyoda-ku, Tokyo, Japan

Telephone: +81 3 237 4500
Cable: Signal, Tokyo
Telex: 222 2178
Telefax: +81 3 287 4649

Works: Yono Factory, 13-8, Kamikizaki 1-chome, Urawa City
Utsunomiya Factory, 11-2, Hiraide Kougyo Danchi, Utsunomiya City

Associated companies: Nisshin Industrial Co, Ltd
Nisshin Electrical Installation Co, Ltd
Nisshin Electronics Service Co Ltd

President: H Takeuchi
Executive Vice President, General Sales: T Oki
Managing Director, Foreign Trade: S Naganuma

Products: Automatic freight car control system for marshalling yards, automatic self-gravity car-retarder equipment and various indication control boards for passengers.

Noord Ned
Noord-Nederlandsche Machinefabriek BV

St Vitusstraat 81, PO Box 171, 9670 AD Winschoten, Netherlands

Telephone: +31 5970 15311
Telex: 53096

Products: Road/rail range of Trackmobile shunting units.

Oleo
Oleo Pneumatics Ltd (UK)
Oleo International Holdings Ltd (Overseas)

Walcote, Blackdown, Leamington Spa, Warwickshire CV32 6QX, England

Telephone: +44 926 21116/8
Telex: 311458
Telefax: +44 926 450273

Managing Director: F M Thompson
Sales & Marketing Director: R W Elliott
Technical Director: D G Williams

Products: Type 23 and Type 24 long-stroke hydraulic buffers available for mounting onto either rigid or sliding stop structures, providing effective emergency impact protection for passenger trains at termini, also used in marshalling yards and steelwork railway complexes.

Peiner
Peiner Port Equipment and Cranes
Division of Noell GmbH

PO Box 1649, 3012 Langenhagen, Federal Republic of Germany

Telephone: +49 511 77 04-0
Telex: 9 24 682
Telefax: +49 511 77 04-302

Products: Container stacking cranes (either rail-mounted or rubber-tyred); straddle carriers; spreaders; harbour cranes for handling general cargo and bulk material; shipyard cranes; tower cranes.

Penetone
Penetone Corporation

74 Hudson Avenue, Tenafly, New Jersey 07670, USA

Telephone: +1 201 567 3000

Products: Cleaning and maintenance products.
The range includes Penetone solvent emulsion degreasers, safety solvents and cleaning products that rapidly penetrate tenacious deposits, such as iron pyrites and silica soils, and remove them from exterior rolling stock surfaces. Operations covered include: exterior locomotive body cleaning; bogie cleaning; stainless steel and painted exterior car body cleaning; interior diesel locomotive cleaning; diesel engine overhaul; journal box cleaning and repair; machine shop, locomotive maintenance; hot and cold tank cleaning; electrical equipment maintenance; steam cleaning operations (both ferrous and non-ferrous metals); pit and ramp maintenance; pre-paint treatment; and rust prevention and protective coating application.

Ross and White
The Ross and White Company

50 West Dundee Road, Wheeling, Illinois 60090, USA

Telephone: +1 312 537 0060

President: Jeffery A Ross
Vice President, Marketing and R & D: R W Burrill
Vice President, Engineering: Roy A Schuetz

Products: Railway sand handling equipment including cleaning, drying, storage and delivery of sand to locomotives; Buck Cyclone Cleaners for rail passenger coach interiors incorporating high-pressure, high volume hand guns; brush scrubbing systems for passenger coach exteriors; pressure washing equipment for locomotives.
Recent activity has included installation of a state-of-the-art washing facility for METRA bi-level commuter cars in Chicago.

Saalasti
Saalasti Oy

Arinatie 4, 00370 Helsinki 37, Finland

Telephone: +358 0 557 775
Telex: 124 694 insa f
Telefax: +358 0 550780

Products: Diesel shunting locomotives; road/rail shunting tractors; rail repair locomotives; shunting couplings; snow ploughs.

Saalasti Oy 'Little Bear' road-rail shunting tractor

Safetran
Safetran Systems Corporation

4650 Main Street NE, Minneapolis, Minnesota 55421, USA

Telephone: +1 612 572 0466

Products: Marshalling yard communication systems; despatcher communication systems.

SEL
Standard Elektrik Lorenz AG

Lorenzstrasse 10, 7000 Stuttgart-Zuffenhausen, Federal Republic of Germany

Telephone: +49 711 8211
Telex: 72 526-0

Products: Automatic humping control; yard control equipment.

Siemens
Siemens AG
Transportation Systems Group

Marshalling yard at Nuremberg (Siemens AG)

PO Box 3327, Ackerstrasse 22, D-3300 Braunschweig, Federal Republic of Germany

Telephone: +49 531 70 61
Telex: 952 495, 952 858
Telefax: +49 531 706398

Group Vice-President: M Czeguhn
Control Systems Division: Dieter Kupper
Freight Traffic: Jochen Schmidt

Products: Planning, control and monitoring of humping operations in marshalling yards.
Multi-microcomputers, in hot standby operation, are used to acquire technical and operating data of arriving trains, and to plan, control and monitor train splitting and formation in accordance with the timetable. The MSR 32 multi-microcomputer system, employed for humping operation control, is of modular design, high reliability and easy handling. It is designed to suit individual operational demands, and guarantees a high rate of throughput in the distribution area and a target-accurate slowing-down even on curved classification tracks.
Recent major installations/modernisations include: Hamburg-Maschen (DB); Vienna (ÖBB); Zürich (SBB); Bologna (FS); Sentrarand (SAR); Nuremberg (DB). Orders on hand include: Munich (DB); Villach (ÖBB); and Antwerp.

Sika Ltd

Watchmead, Welwyn Garden City, Herts AL7 1BQ

Telephone: +44 707 329241
Telex: 269428 sikash g
Telefax: +44 707 329129

Managing Director: B Baggarsgaard
Sales & Marketing Director: M Moore
Specialist Engineer: R J Barton

Products: Sikarail KC 330 elastic rail fixing system is a highly durable chemical formulation of elastomeric resin and compressible fillers that provides both high efficiency in absorbing vibration, and consistency in load bearing characteristics in conditions of the most eccentric loading.

Smith Bros & Webb
Smith Bros & Webb Ltd

Britannia Works, Arden Forest, Industrial Estate, Alcester, Warwickshire, England

Telephone: +44 789 763222
Telex: 338212
Telefax: +44 789 400231

Chairman: D Edwards
Managing Director: K H Harrison
Service Director: J Ziegler
Technical Manager: R Wood
Contracts Manager: M W Patterson

Products: Britannia fully-automatic train washing system. Operators which have selected Britannia equipment include British Rail (over 40 systems) for its Inter-City and HST operations; the Tyne and Wear PTE; the Piraeus Metro in Greece; the Lisbon Metro system; and the Western Australian Government.
The company has wide experience in designing rail washing systems for unusual geographic locations, to meet extremes of temperatures, arid and wet climates and in situations where space constraints have been extremely limiting. SB&W's own trained engineers are available to supervise installations anywhere in the world.

MANUFACTURERS / Freight yard and terminal equipment

British Rail HST passing through typical Britannia train washing system; note roof brush in operation

Locopulsor shunting machine by Steele

Recent contracts include train washing installation for Kowloon Canton Railway Co, Hong Kong (1989); five train washing installations for Egyptian National Railways (1988).

Steele
E G Steele & Co Ltd

25 Dalziel Street, Hamilton, Lanarkshire ML3 9AU, Scotland

Telephone: +44 698 283765
Cable: Mountings, Hamilton
Telex: 77454
Telefax: +44 698 891550

Managing Director: J G Steele
Export Director: D A Steele

Products: Locopulsor shunting machines.
The company is UK agent for Trackmobile road/rail shunting equipment. It thus offers a range of shunters capable of moving from to 10 to 2000 tonnes.
Recent contracts include 18 Locopulsor shunting machines for Indian Railways.

Constitution: E G Steele & Co Ltd are the sole manufacturers of the Locopulsor shunting machine, which they supply worldwide. They are also rolling stock contractors and hirers of tank wagons. They have the only private wagon repairing works in Scotland and undertake the supply of wagon spares to other repairers; they supply a rewheeling service for railway wagon wheels and axles.

Stothert & Pitt
A business unit of NEI Clarke Chapman Ltd

PO Box 25, Bath, Avon BA2 3DJ, England

Telephone: +44 225 314400
Cable: Stothert, Bath
Telex: 44311
Telefax: +44 225 332529

General Manager: J D Gittins
Sales Manager: P G Anderson

Products: Telescopic spreader beams, twin lift spreader beams, automatic or manual fixed-length spreader beams; bridge cranes for container marshalling and for loading on road/rail transport; quayside transporter cranes for loading container vessels; jib cranes for container handling.

Strachan & Henshaw

PO Box 103, Ashton Works, Ashton Vale Road, Bristol BS99 7TJ, England

Telephone: +44 272 664677
Telex: 44170
Telefax: +44 272 662605

Chairman: J H Floyd
Managing Director: J R Parker
Director, Handling Division: M J Miller
Sales & Marketing Manager, Handling Division: P A Denning

Products: Wagon tipplers (car dumpers), random wagons or rotary-coupled unit trains; train movers (indexers, chargers, positioners) for use with wagon tipplers and at loadout stations; 'Beetle' haulage systems and wagon traversers.
Systems are individually designed to meet specific plant requirements, with all wagon movements, whether of random wagons, rakes, or complete coupled trains, precisely controlled and integrated with loading and unloading plant operations. With all

Two Strachan & Henshaw train tandem tipplers at Richards Bay coal terminal, South Africa

First Rotaside XL tippler for installation in India during assembly by Strachan & Henshaw

Tandem Crescent tippler at Port of Qinhuangdao, China, the first to be installed in that country by Strachan & Henshaw

Freight yard and terminal equipment / **MANUFACTURERS** 397

movements thus integrated, speeds and timings are optimised to minimise loads on machinery and risk to personnel. With appropriate use of interlocks and automatic sequence control, a complete installation for unloading a unit train of over 10 000 tonnes in under two hours can be operated by one person from a remote panel.

As top-unloading wagons can show valuable operating economies compared with bottom-dump hopper wagons, demand for tippler installations for new terminal developments is very active and Strachan & Henshaw has recently supplied new high-throughput plants to terminal operators in USA, Canada, Mexico, South Africa, Australia and the People's Republic of China. Strachan & Henshaw wagon marshalling systems also provide useful economies and improve plant efficiency at installations of all sizes and levels of complexity, including where the rate of working is less intensive and movements irregular.

TAKRAF
TAKRAF Export/Import

Mohrenstrasse 53/54, 1080 Berlin, German Democratic Republic

Telephone: +37 2 4887 0
Cable: Ahb tk Berlin
Telex: 112347/8, 115027/9
Telefax: +37 2 4827 705, +37 2 4828 295

Export Director: Gerald Ludwig
Sales Manager: Uwe Schumberg

Products: Railway cranes of 20 to 250 tons lifting capacity (net), for operation on all tracks. Special features available: telescopic/lattice or any type of boom; electric/hydraulic drive system; travelling speed of 100/120 km/h; high lifting capacities free-on-rails; crane movable with suspended load; operation with external current supply or emergency power; suitable for operation in all climates.

Teklite Lighting
Clark Masts Teksam Ltd

Unit 54, Pocklington Industrial Estate, Pocklington, York YO4 2NR, England

Telephone: +44 759 305665
Telex: 86686
Telefax: +44 759 305679

Managing Director: A N Clark
UK Sales Manager: R M Smith

Products: The TF600S series of portable floodlighting units provides a quick and reliable means of temporary illumination wherever a 110-volt or 240-volt power supply is available.

The TF610S models are designed to be easily portable and quick to deploy in any situation. The masts are manually extended and locked by means of a simple collar. Used widely for railway track nighttime repair work.

The TF620 and TF640 models feature pneumatic masts which are quickly extended to 6 m by means of attached handpumps.

The Teklite 6500 lighting system uses an energy convertor which converts 12 or 24 V direct current from an automobile battery into the electrical energy form needed to power a high-pressure sodium lamp.

Thyssen
Thyssen Umform-technik

Werk Wanheim, Friemersheimer Strasse 40, Postfach 28114, 4100 Duisburg 28, Federal Republic of Germany

Telephone: +49 203 732-0
Telex: 855 861

Products: Marshalling yard retarders and wagon-moving equipment. The company has equipped with retarders more than 60 shunting yards of the German Federal Railway (DB), of West German industry and of railway companies abroad. The Hamburg-Maschen shunting yard alone incorporates as many as 136 Thyssen retarders.

Teklite TF610S mast unit, mounted on rear of road vehicle

Teklite TF600 Economy unit fully extended on stand

Teklite TF610S/3/2 erected for nighttime track maintenance

Toshiba
Toshiba Corporation
Railway Projects Department

1-1, Shibaura 1-chome, Minato-ku, Tokyo 105, Japan

Telephone: +81 3 457 4924
Cable: Toshiba Tokyo
Telex: 22587 toshiba
Telefax: +81 3 457 8385

TAKRAF Type EDK 750 crane

TAKRAF Type EDK 2000 crane

398 MANUFACTURERS / Freight yard and terminal equipment

Products: Yard control equipment including retarders; and automatic car vehicle identification (ACI) systems employing vehicle-mounted transponders and track-mounted interrogators. Toshiba ACI showed reliability and performance in a field test at Hokkaido (Northern Japan) conducted by Japanese National Railways from November, 1969 to July, 1970 with 60 transponders and an interrogator under severe environmental conditions such as low temperature (−30°C) and thick snow which covered the interrogator to a depth of 150 mm or more.

Trackmobile Inc
A member of the Marman Group

1602 Executive Drive, La Grange, Georgia 30240, USA

Telephone: +1 404 884 6651
Telex: 510 100 1554
Telefax: +1 404 884 0390

President: Richard Lich
Vice Presidents, Marketing: Jack Kennedy
International Sales: James Codlin

Products: A range of road-rail rail car movers with drawbar pull of up to 40 000 lb. Features include automatic weight transfer couplers.

Tysol
Tysol Products Inc

919 N Michigan Avenue, Chicago, Illinois 60611, USA

Telephone: +1 312 642 4823

President: Edward M Johnson
Purchasing Agent: Alan S Johnson

Products: Rolling stock cleaning equipment.

Ultra Hydraulics Ltd
(Formerly Dowty Group plc)

Arle Court, Cheltenham, Gloucestershire GL51 0TP, England

Telephone: +44 242 221155
Telex: 43176
Telefax: +44 242 533004

Managing Director: D Burton
Director: R J Scarborough
Sales Manager: C R G Ellis

Principal subsidiary: Ultra Fluid Technologies Inc, PO Box 30809, Columbus, Ohio 43230-0809, USA
Telephone: +1 614 759 9000
Telefax: +1 614 759 9046

Products: Dowty retarders and booster/retarders are speed-sensitive units simply bolted to the inside of the rails at strategic intervals along the track. Retarders can be installed on the hump, in the switching area and in the classification tracks to provide the required wagon speed control. Booster/retarders can be used in yards with shallow or level gradients, thereby avoiding the need for track laying with steeper gradients, through use of a pneumatically-operated cylinder which provides additional gravitational height to maintain wagon speed.

The retarder unit is pre-set during manufacture to the required speed control conditions of a particular marshalling yard. Installed in the tracks, it provides a continuous speed control system suitable for low, medium and high throughput yards achieving optimum and economic yard performance.

Retarder units are available with a retraction facility for use in yards where operations require considerable resorting of trains in the marshalling programme.

Dowty's continuous speed control systems are operating in a wide variety of conditions in marshalling yards in the United Kingdom, Federal Republic of Germany, Switzerland, Hungary, Finland, Norway, USA, Canada, Japan, India, Australia and South Africa. A total of 42 000 Dowty high-capacity retarders and 18 000 booster retarders are now employed in the 64-track Sentrarand Yard, South Africa. Dowty systems are used in the high throughput yards in Austria at Vienna Central and Villach Süd where a total of 75,000 Dowty retarders are installed.

High-capacity retarders for continuous wagon speed control the Cordoba marshalling yard in Spain. A total of 44 000 high-capacity retarders are working in the Nuremberg marshalling yard of the German Federal Railway.

The new Trackmaster unit is being tested in working marshalling yards in four countries and results to date are very successful. First production orders have been received for Trackmasters which now complement the proven High Capacity unit range.

To date Ultra has supplied or received orders for the supply of almost 300 000 units.

Unilok
Unilokomotive Ltd
Subsidiary of Killeen Investments (Ireland) Ltd

Mervue Industrial Estate, Galway, Ireland

Telephone: +353 91 57034
Telex: 50113 ulok ei
Telefax: +353 91 51373

Sales Director: Michael Lalor

Product: The Unilok range of shunting/switching locomotives available in three basic configurations: C-series for rail only duty; D-series for road/rail (smooth terrain); and E-series for road/rail (rough terrain).

During 1989 machines were delivered to Pakistan, UK, Germany, Syria, Holland and Iran.

Valmet
Valmet Corporation
Materials Handling Equipment Division

PO Box 387, 33101 Tampere, Finland

Telephone: +358 31 658 111
Telex: 22140
Telefax: +358 31 656 220

Chief Executive, MHE Division: P Heikkilä

Products: Container stacking straddle carriers, up to three-high stacking of 9 foot 6 inch high containers; mobile gantry cranes of 22 to 35 tons lifting capacity; fork-lift trucks of 12 to 42 tons capacity; industrial

Unilok E-105 with snowplough for USSR

Dowty high-capacity hydraulic retarders in Vienna Kledering yard, Austrian Railways

Close-up of Dowty high-capacity hydraulic retarders

Freight yard and terminal equipment / **MANUFACTURERS** 399

Valmet snowplough fitted to permanent way maintenance trolley

Windhoff Tele-Trac shunter for railway maintenance workshop

straddle carriers of 13 to 60 tons capacity; special equipment for ro-ro ships, etc; container handling reach stackers; log stackers.

Railway Division

PO Box 387, 33101 Tampere, Finland

Telephone: +358 31 658 111
Telex: 22112
Telefax: +358 31 657 044

General Manager: Esko Määttänen
Marketing Manager: Olavi Kivimäki

Products: Snowploughs for railways. Valmet has designed a snowplough that will fit on to any locomotive model. It comprises two identical units which are fitted to the buffer plates at each end of the locomotive; mounting takes about 30 minutes. Valmet's snowplough is standard equipment of the Finnish State Railways (VR) and used also in Norway.

Vollert
Hermann Vollert KG Maschinenfabrik

7102 Weinsberg/Wurtt, Federal Republic of Germany

Telephone: +49 7134 52228
Telex: 728736
Telefax: +49 7134 52202

Products: Shunting equipment of various types; wagon transfer cars, radio-controlled diesel, battery or electric robot shunters of varying sizes and power including models capable of moving 5000-tonne trains in temperatures as low as −15°C; remote-controlled functions include disengagement of couplings and infinitely variable traction speed for accurate wagon positioning at discharge points, etc.

Warrington Tractors

Winwick Road, Warrington, Cheshire, England

Telephone: +44 925 36122
Telefax: +44 925 36042

General and Sales Manager: W Bennell
Sales Engineer: D A Banks

Products: Mersey rubber-tyred shunting tractor, 80 to 180 hp.

Westinghouse Signals
Westinghouse Signals Ltd
A subsidiary of Westinghouse Brake & Signal Co Ltd
A Hawker Siddeley Company

Head office and works: PO Box 79, Chippenham, Wiltshire SN15 1JD, England

Telephone: +44 249 654141
Telex: 44618
Telefax: +44 249 652322

Products: Yard control equipment.

Windhoff
Rheiner Maschinenfabrik Windhoff AG

Hovestrasse 10, Postfach 1160, 4440 Rheine, Federal Republic of Germany

Telephone: +49 5971 580
Telex: 981 643

President: Dr Bernd Windhoff
Managers: Heinz Lörfing
 Christoph Wessels
 Herbert Bucksch
Export Manager: Helmut Pühs

Products: Tele-Trac shunting vehicle with tractive forces up to 40 000 daN, diesel or electro-hydraulically driven, control of shunting course and coupling operations by radio or by interlinking with loading programme; marshalling yard equipment; turntables and traversers; screw jacks for lifting locomotives, wagons and other heavy loads; lifting equipment for complete trains.

Vollert robot shunter in desert environment

Vollert robot shunter servicing refuse-processing power plant

MANUFACTURERS / Freight yard and terminal equipment

Zagro
Zagro Bahn und Baumaschinen GmbH

Muhlstrasse 13, 6927 Bad Rappenau-Grombach, Federal Republic of Germany

Telephone: +49 7266 458/1030
Cable: Zagro
Telex: 782381 zagro d
Telefax: +49 726 2855

Director: Werner Zappel
Director: Wolfgang Zappel

Products: Daimler-Benz Unimog and MB-trac railroad vehicles with Zagro track guiding equipment, for standard-, broad- and narrow-gauge railways, with working units for servicing, maintenance and transport.
Zagro fork-lift shunters for shunting railway wagons on standard-, broad- and narrow-gauge tracks, hauling capacity 300 tonnes.
Zagro Mini-Shunter for shunting operation on level track systems, tractive force 100 tonnes. The Mini-Shunter can be driven by a petrol or gas engine. The required thrust force is transmitted from its wheel flanges to the wagon wheel. This and the continuously-controlled hydraulic drive ensure safe braking of wagons. Wagons can be shunted in both directions without removing the machine.

Zagro rail-road shunter

Zagro fork-lift shunter

Sika

SikaRail
Rail Fixing Systems

- LOAD BEARING
- LOW MAINTENANCE
- NOISE REDUCTION
- VIBRATION REDUCTION
- ELECTRICAL INSULATION

Workshop, repair and maintenance equipment

DENMARK
GC-Hydraulik 403

FRANCE
SEFAC 405

GERMANY, FEDERAL REPUBLIC
AEG Westinghouse 402
Alzmetall 402
Dickertmann 403
Hegenscheidt 403
Hoesch 404
Hywema 404
Probat 405
Wagner 407
Windhoff 408

HUNGARY
Nogradi Szenbanyak 408

INDIA
Cimmco 403

ITALY
Ranzi-Legnano 405

JAPAN
Sumitomo 406
Toshiba 407

UK
Aabacas 402
Atlas 402
Brown & Root Vickers 402
Casaire 408
Stratos Ventilation Products 406
Telemotive 406

USA
CAM Industries 403
Portec 404
Proceco 405
Railquip 405
Simmons 405
Whiting 407

MANUFACTURERS / Workshop repair and maintenance equipment

Aabacas
Aabacas Cranes Ltd
Member of the Marthill Group

Kelvin Road, Wallasey, Merseyside L44 7DN, England

Telephone: +44 51 638 5932
Telex: 628690
Telefax: +44 51 666 1346

Operations Manager: K Rainford
Erection Manager: A Smith
Works Manager: K Grundy

Products: Electric wire rope hoists up to 20 tons swl capacity; single and double girder overhead electric travelling cranes (standard and custom-built designs, capacities up to 30 tons and spans up to 25 metres); overhead cranes; Goliath and Semi-Goliath cranes; jibs; gantries.

Aabacas offers a fully metricated standard range of portal building cranes which are based on double girder construction, warren-braced on the top section with an eight-wheel in-running crab with hoist supported within the girders. The best possible side hook approaches are assured and a hook height is kept at approximately gantry rail level, with the crane girders a minimum of 300 mm above the hook position, to secure substantial overhead clearance for stacked workpieces etc, and obtain high side walls beneath the gantry. An addition to the Aabacas range is a fully metricated arrangement of single girder underhung electric travelling cranes.

AEG
AEG-Westinghouse Transport System GmbH

Nonnendammallee 15-21, D-1000 West Berlin 20, Federal Republic of Germany

Telephone: +49 30 3305 0
Cable: Elektronbahnen, Berlin
Telex: 1 85 498
Telefax: +49 30 3305 2169

Production Director: Dr-Ing P Gold
Sales Director: Dipl-Ing U Voss

Products: Electric equipment for electric motors; generator and control equipment; repair shops; spare parts.

Alzmetall
Machine Tool Factory and Foundry Friedrich & Co

Postfach 1169, 8226 Altenmarkt/Alz, Federal Republic of Germany

Telephone: +49 8621 881
Telex: 5 63124

Products: Drilling machines, boring mills.

Atlas
Atlas Engineering Company

12 Croydon Road, Caterham, Surrey CR3 6QB, England

Telephone: +44 883 47635
Telex: 8951847
Telefax: +44 883 45662

Sales Director: P J Hines

Products: Mobile railway lifting jack (up to 35 tons capacity); wheel profile trueing machines; crank axle turning machines; jacks; screwing machines; underfloor wheel trueing machines; double wheel lathes; hydraulic wheel presses.

A new range of axle conversion machinery is designed for conversion of plain axle journals ready for the fitting of roller bearings. This entails cutting the axles to length, drilling new centre holes, drilling and tapping fixing holes for the bearing end-plate, turning the journals to their new form, and finally grinding to a very fine tolerance for the new bearings. The various operations can be tackled in a variety of ways, depending on specific requirements, the output required, and the customer's budget. The company claims these machines to be unique both in character and in their level of accuracy.

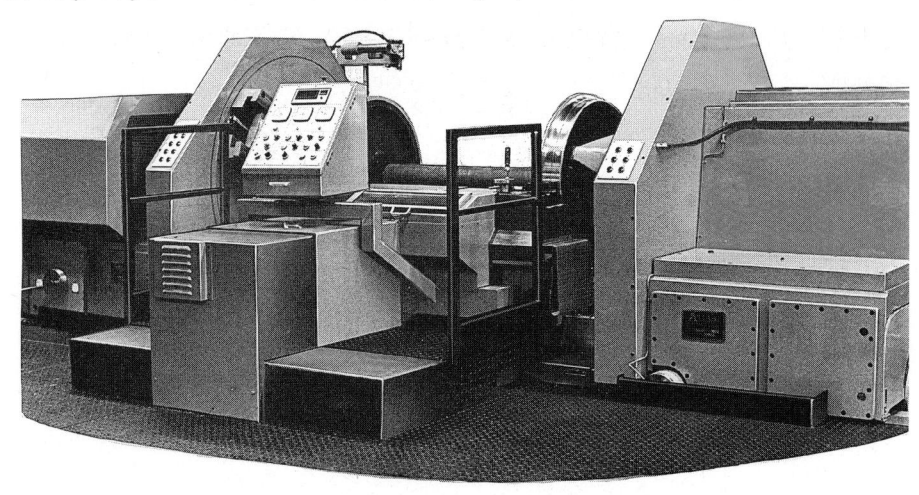

Atlas Engineering wheel lathe

Atlas CDT axle cutting, drilling and tapping machine

Atlas ATG axle turning and grinding machine

Brown & Root Vickers
Brown & Root Vickers Ltd

Wessex House, Market Street, Eastleigh, Hampshire SO5 4FD, England

Telephone: +44 703 619722
Telex: 477313 brveas g
Telefax: +44 703 619808

Technical Director: C J Ray
Projects Director: A R Feely
General Manager, Sales: R R Vye

Products: Design, supply and setting to work of all equipment needed to overhaul, maintain, repair and clean rail vehicles and their components for metro, main-line and suburban railway systems; provision of design and consulting services for workshop layouts and special-purpose equipment design; design and supply of diagnostic test equipment for rail vehicles; supply of maintenance equipment for trackwork and signalling and all fixed systems.

Major completed contracts include the workshops for London Docklands Light Railway, and Caracas and Seoul Metros; maintenance equipment for Tuen Mun Light Transit Railway, Hong Kong, and Istanbul LRT.

Current contracts include consultancy studies for maintenance depots and facilities at Hainault and Ruislip, and the supply of maintenance equipment for the Manchester Metrolink project including layout design of workshop complex.

London Docklands Light Railway workshop by Brown & Root Vickers

CAM Industries
CAM Industries Inc
Peerless Tool Division

215 Philadelphia Street, PO Box 227, Hanover, Pennsylvania 17331, USA

Telephone: +1 717 637 5988
Cable: Cam
Telex: 840470 cam hnvr

President: Charles A McGough Jr

Products: Machinery and equipment for use in the manufacture and repair of dc motors and generators; electric traction motor and generator repair shops for railway workshops; engineering service for planning and equipping electric traction departments of railway workshops.

CAM offers services in planning and equipping electric motor shops ranging from a running maintenance operation to a general maintenance and repair shop and a complete rewinding shop. Three basic types of specialised machine cover maintenance, repair, and rewinding of traction motors and generators: multi-purpose, for all major repairs on armatures; single-purpose, or fully automatic and semi-automatic machines designed for a specific task; and auxiliary or accessory units for adaptation to existing shop machines. Other machines for use with either universal multi-purpose or single-purpose machines fall into two categories: job-related units, for performing required operations in the assembly, disassembly, handling and repair, and maintenance of traction motors and generators; and test equipment. In addition to the standard machines, which include undercutters, banding machines, test equipment, tig welders, and seasoning machines, the company has developed a new line of handling equipment which can be integrated into the shop line and used with specialised automatic and semi-automatic machines at various stations to assist in the disassembly, repair and maintenance, assembly, and testing of motors and generators as they proceed through the shop. This line of equipment consists of motor and armature upenders, traction motor frame machines, armature extractors for traction motor and generator armatures, and upenders for handling generator and alternator frames. The single-purpose machines include armature banding machines with devices for tensioning wire or glass tape, and a special tension device for rerolling with the wire bands in order to pull the coils down and properly seat them.

The company has active projects with Turkish Railways, Korean Railways, Pakistan Railways, Bangladesh Railways, Egyptian Railways and Long Island Railroad.

CAM supplies specialised dc electric motor shop equipment, helps upgrade shops, and provides training in current methods.

Peerless Type DJM Universal Armature repair machine with automatic undercutting, commutator turning and tape/wire banding capabilities

Cimmco
Cimmco International

Prakash Deep, 7 Tolstoy Marg, New Delhi 110 001, India

Telephone: +91 11 3314383-5, 3310814
Cable: Cimwag
Telex: 31 65148, 31 62294

Products: Machinery and equipment for manufacture and maintenance of rolling stock.

Dickertmann
Gebr Dickertmann Hebezeugfabrik AG

PO Box 2109, Hakenort 47, 4800 Bielefeld, Federal Republic of Germany

Telephone: +49 521 323021
Telex: 09 32 750

Products: Spindle lifting jacks, underfloor elevators, bogie lifting platforms, various types of hoist.

GC
GC-Hydraulik A/S
A member of the Grevenkop-Castenskiold group

Nordkranvej 2A, DK-3540 Lynge, Denmark

Telephone: +45 2 18 89 88
Telex: 42175 kroll dk
Telefax: +45 2 18 88 07

Chairman: Gert Grevenkop-Castenshiold
Division Manager: Frants Oldenburg

Products: Lifts for bogies; lifts for locomotives; arrangement for lifting and dismantling bogies; pull-off machine for train wheels.

The loco-lift is used for service and repairs to locomotives up to 160 tonnes but it has a permissible capacity of 80 tonnes point load in the centre. The lift is built as a welded-up frame with the rails as a part of the load-carrying construction. The frame is raised and lowered by use of four hydraulic cylinders. The locomotive is held in position by four wheel locks and the frame cannot be raised unless these are activated. When the lift is in bottom position the frame is lowered into the floor so that the rail top and the frame are level with the concrete floor. The lift can be held in all positions between 0 and 1500 mm.

The device for lifting and dismantling train bogies is built as a frame which is lifted by four hydraulic cylinders, driven by four hydraulic motors which are connected to secure synchronised oilflow. In the topside of the lift are tracks with eight lowerable parts, used to position and hold the bogie in relation to the work cylinders. In the centre of the platform is a cylinder, which is used to pull the swing balk on the bogie down, to enable removal of the laminated springs. In both sides of the platform are cylinders which are used to press the swing balk bearings upwards, to enable the shackles between the bearing and the balk to be removed.

The 600 kN pull-off machine is used to dismount train wheels from axles. It consists of a main frame, on which a revolving table is mounted. This is used to fix the axle after which a hydraulic cylinder and matching backstop can be positioned and pull wheels, brakes and gear wheels off the axle. The hydraulic cylinder is mounted horizontally on a carriage, on which are also mounted two backstops, which are turned in around the subject that is to be pulled off. The revolving table has a vertical axle and the wheel-set is positioned horizontally. In this way it is possible, by turning the revolving table, to work on both ends of the axle. A pedal-operated pawl secures the revolving table in the chosen position.

Hegenscheidt
Wilhelm Hegenscheidt GmbH

Bernhard-Schondorff-Platz, Postfach 1408, D-5140 Erkelenz, Federal Republic of Germany

Telephone: +49 2431 86-0
Telex: 8329 865 heg d
Telefax: +49 2431 86 470

404 MANUFACTURERS / Workshop repair and maintenance equipment

Hegenscheidt Type 106CNC heavy-duty underfloor wheel lathe with CNC-controlled tool slides for reprofiling wheel sets in situ

Affiliated companies
Hegenscheidt Corporation
1070 Livernois Ave, Troy, Michigan 48083, USA
Telephone: +1 313 585 77 04
Telex: 23 1172 hegencorp trmi

Hegenscheidt (Pty) Ltd
PO Box 995, 99 York Street, Sydney, New South Wales 2000, Australia
Telephone +61 2 290 2844
Telex: 27 585
Branch office: 96 Wellington Parade, East Melbourne, Victoria 3002
Telephone: +61 3 417 4961
Telex: 135033 flerex aa

Products: Machines, plant and planning of systems for maintenance of railway wheel sets, eg: wheel lathes for wheel set reprofiling in portal or flat bed design, including options for rim and brake disc turning and axle machining; universal wheel lathes for profile turning of wheel sets, hub boring, tyre turning, journal turning and roller burnishing, turning of rims and brake discs; underfloor wheel lathes for reprofiling of wheel sets in mounted condition; cleaning equipment for bogies, wheel sets, bearings, axleboxes; measuring and testing machines for worn wheel sets; automatic in-track wheel set inspection equipment; planning and modernisation of wheel shops with integrated automatic wheel set conveying systems.

Machines, plant and planning of systems for machining of railway wheels, eg: vertical turning and boring machines for machining of railway wheels, wheel tyres and wheel discs; vertical turning and boring machines for machining of railway wheel hub bores; measuring and testing equipment for railway wheels; automatic and integrated loading equipment for railway wheels, wheel tyres and wheel discs for vertical turning and boring machines; planning of workshops for machining of railway wheels.

Hoesch
Hoesch Maschinenfabrik Deutschland AG

Borsigstrasse 22, PO Box 10 16 62, 4600 Dortmund 1, Federal Republic of Germany

Telephone: +49 231 84 91-0
Cable: Deutschland Dortmund
Telex: 822269 mfd d
Telefax: +49 231 84 01-333

Managing Director: M Henniag
Chief of Division: G Lades

Products: Machines for railway and LRT workshops: CNC-controlled wheel lathes for universal machining jobs around the wheel set, including roller-burnishing of bearing seats; CNC heavy-duty wheel lathes, roll-through type, for reprofiling of wheel sets, including turning of brake discs and rims. Underfloor wheel lathes. Hydraulic wheel mounting and demounting presses, inductive tyre heaters for fitting tyres on wheel centres; tyre stripping devices for removing tyres from the wheel centres. Hydraulic rerailing systems of special aluminium alloy for portable use.

Portec Inc
Railway Maintenance Products Division

PO Box 38250, Pittsburgh, Pennsylvania 15238-8250, USA

Telephone: +1 412 782 6000

Senior Vice-President: John S Cooper
Manager – Sales, Service & Engineering: Richard J Jarosinski

Products: Portec Spot Car and Locomotive Repair Systems allow for repair of cars and locomotives in an efficient central area, with car-handling achieved by 'rabbits' under push-button control. The systems include integrated jacking, job cranes, hose reels and other accessories. The systems operate on the basic principle of moving the cars to the men and materials, rather than have men carry materials to cars needing repairs. Advantages claimed include increased labour efficiency, reduction in per diem costs, and savings of 50 to 90 per cent in switch engine hours.

Hywema
Hywema Lifting Systems

134-148 Wuppertaler Strasse, D-5650 Solingen 1, Federal Republic of Germany

Telephone: +49 212 59891-95
Telex: 8514822
Telefax: +49 212 592951

General Manager: H Henn
Sales Director: D Paul

Products: Type FL/N mobile vehicle lift system for

Hywema FL/VN 48 000 kg capacity mobile lifts for LRV in the workshop of Würzburg City Transport

A pair of 75-ton side jacks is raised to allow removal of the bogie and repair of under car members

locomotives and for standard, articulated and multi-articulated railcars. Independent operation in all workshop areas. Synchronisation of all lifts is by a microprocessor-controlled electronic system.

Recent contracts have been obtained from Vienna Tramway (1989); EVA-Brühl/Cologne (1989); Deutsche Plasser, D-Freilassing (1989); Indian Railways (1989).

Probat
Probat-Werke

4240 Emmerich/Rhein, Federal Republic of Germany

Telephone: +49 2822 2561
Cable: Probat, Emmerich
Telex: 8 125 154

Products: Spring testing machines for coil, leaf and torsion springs; hardness testers; tensile, compression and bending test systems; microprocessor control equipment for testing machines.

Subsidiary: Tarno Grocki, Tarnotest Prüfsysteme GmbH
Resser Strasse 94, Postfach 1220, 4240 Emmerich 1
Telephone: +49 2822 70060
Telex 08125154

Proceco
Proceco Inc

1020 East 8th Street, Jacksonville, Florida 32206, USA

Telephone: +1 904 355-2888

Proceco Industrial Machinery Ltd

1243 rue Dorion, Montreal, Quebec H2K 4A2, Canada

Telephone: +1 514 527 1335
Telex: 055 62262

Products: Locomotive bogie washer, bolster and side frame washer, car bogie washer, gear case washer, locomotive wheel set washers, car wheel set washers, car axle wet brushing machine, journal box washer, car and locomotive roller bearing washer, air brake valves washer, spring test device, draft gear testing device, heat treating furnace for draft gear and truck frames.

Locomotive engine washer (assembled, engine block, oil pan, other components), engine rotating fixtures, cylinder head washer, cylinder liner washer (cylinder jacket for GE engines), washer for all other power assembly components, piston phosphating system, cylinder head assembly and disassembly device, valve guide press, leak test devices for heads and liners, wrist pin bolt torqueing device, piston regrooving lathe, complete power assembly shop, Dynavane washer, radiator cleaning, heat treating furnace for engine blocks.

Locomotive traction motor and main generator (alternator) spray washing and vacuum drying system, vacuum-pressure impregnating devices, traction motor stripping and assembly device, traction motor remanufacturing transfer line.

Railquip
Railquip Inc

3731 Northcrest Road, Suite 6, Atlanta, Georgia 30340, USA

Telephone: +1 404 458 4157
Telex: 700546 wu
Telefax: +1 404 458 5365

President: H Schroeder
Sales Manager: D Whisenhunt
Treasurer: M Schroeder

Products: Portable hydraulic rerailing equipment for locomotives and cars; hydraulic aluminium alloy jacks (telescopic and single-piston); screw lifting systems; pneumatic lifting devices; self-propelled wash racks for passenger cars and metro systems; axle lathes; wheel lathes; truing machines; wheel presses; shunting vehicles; rail fastening systems; and hydraulic track jacks; general railway tools.

Recent contracts include five Fleetcleaner wash units for Amtrak (1989); one Fleetcleaner wash unit for New York City Transit Authority (1989); two sets of eight each Spindle-type jacks for Servicio de Transportes Electricos del Distrito Federal, Mexico City.

Ranzi-Legnano
Ranzi-Legnano SRL

20025 Legnano, Italy

Telephone: +39 331 548754
Cable: Ranzi Legnano

Products: Hydrodynametric reversible brakes for the test of any type and power motors.

SEFAC
SEFAC Equipment

28 rue d'Assas, 75006 Paris, France

Telephone: +33 1 45 44 88 16
Telex: 200 847
Telefax: +33 1 45 44 88 66

Chairman: Bernard Despas
Export Manager: Anne de Montluc

Principal subsidiaries: SEFAC Lift & Equipment Corp (USA), 9050 Red Branch Road, Columbia, MD 21045

SEFAC Espagne, Avda Menéndez Pelayo, 28009 Madrid, Spain

Products: Electromechanical lifting systems with mobile or fixed columns, partially or totally in ground, capacity per unit from 5 tons up to 40 tons per column. SEFAC lifting systems allow the lifting of railway power cars, LRT permitting maintenance work under vehicles, train-sets, wagons; lifting platforms allowing maintenance of bogies and undercarriage; bogie drop for bogie maintenance without uncoupling cars.

Lifting systems have been supplied to TLM, Dover, UK; De Dietrich, France; NS, Holland; RENFE, Spain; DSB, Denmark. Bogie drop: TML, France.

Simmons
Simmons Machine Tool Corporation

1700 No Broadway, Albany, New York 12204, USA

Telephone: +1 518 462 5431
Telex: 592999 simmons
Easylink: 62798084
Telefax: +1 518 462 0371

Chairman and Chief Executive: H J Naumann
President: T H Smith
Vice President, Finance: D A Simonian
Vice President, Operations: D W Davis
Manager, Wheelshop Equipment Sales: F A Pascazio

Subsidiary: Simmons-Stanray Wheel Truing Machine Corporation
7345 Calumet Avenue, Hammond, Indiana 46324
Telephone: +1 219 933-0333
Telex: 51060 06081 stanray
Easylink: 62909395

Products: The corporation is a worldwide supplier in the layout, design and manufacture of complete, automated railway and transit wheel shops, including automatic material handling and integrated computerised control systems.

The Simmons-Niles and Simmons-Farrel product lines offer above-floor and underfloor wheel tread contouring lathes, axle lathes, axle/journal turning and burnishing lathes, car wheel borers, locomotive wheel borers with loading and unloading manipulators, axle-measuring stations and all types of presses for mounting and/or demounting of wheels or roller bearings to/from the axle.

The Simmons-Stanray product line consists of underfloor wheel-truing machines for machining wheel sets while assembled in railroad locomotives and transit cars.

Simmons equipment can be furnished with conventional controls or with high technology systems, including computer numerical controls (CNC).

Worldwide installation supervision and start-up assistance can be provided as well as the necessary service and spare parts.

Railquip Fleet Cleaner mobile car wash unit

SEFAC jacks raise a Franch Railways TGV power car.

Simmons-Niles fully automatic car and locomotive demount press for automatic removal of wheels and gear

MANUFACTURERS / Workshop repair and maintenance equipment

Simmons-Farrel underfloor wheel truing machine for mounted wheel sets on locomotives or transit cars

Simmons-Niles CNC fully automatic wheel machining centre with robot manipulator; handles two wheels simultaneously

Stratos Ventilation Products Ltd

Southam Drive, Southam,
Leamington Spa, Warwickshire CV33 0FA, England

Telephone: +44 92681 3232
Telex: 317385
Telefax: +44 92681 4546

Managing Director: D G Gilbey
Sales Director: J C Ellard
Contract Director: W A Herbert
Company Secretary: P Cox
Divisional Manager: K Mezzone

Principal subsidiary: Stratos/Fläkt (a part of the Asea Brown Boveri Group)

Products: Industrial ambient air curtains, air handling units, heat recovery, workshop heating, ventilation and air-conditioning systems.

Sumitomo
Sumitomo Metal Industries Ltd

Ote Center Building, 1–1–3 Otemachi, Chiyoda-ku, Tokyo 100, Japan

Telephone: +81 3 282 6111
Telex: J22865
Telefax: +81 3 282 6764

General Manager, Sales: K Koshida
Senior Manager: H Watatani
Senior Manager, Railway Products and Equipment Sales: Y Hirano

Works: Osaka Steelworks, Shimaya, Konohana-ku, Osaka 554

Products: Bogie rotation testing stand, bogie vibration testing stand, gear unit testing stand, wheel stress testing machine, axle fatigue testing machine, creep force testing machine, etc.

Sumitomo Metal has developed various types of testing and inspecting equipments for rolling stock, using their designing and manufacturing technology achieved in the manufacture of rolling stock equipment.

Telemotive
Telemotive UK Ltd

Riverdene Industrial Estate, Molesey Road, Hersham, Walton-on-Thames, Surrey KT12 4RY, England

Telephone: +44 932 247511
Telex: 884751 telmot g

Products: Radio remote control systems for cranes and associated equipment. Telemotive radio crane

Shinkansen high-speed bogie on bogie rotation testing stand by Sumitomo

CHD variable direction air curtain, installed at factory main access door by Stratos Ventilation Products Ltd

Radio control of two 50–ton overhead cranes with Telemotive UK equipment at Derby workshops of British Rail Engineering

Workshop repair and maintenance equipment / **MANUFACTURERS** 407

Battery-powered car body transporter by Toshiba

Multi-purpose test equipment for traction motors by Toshiba

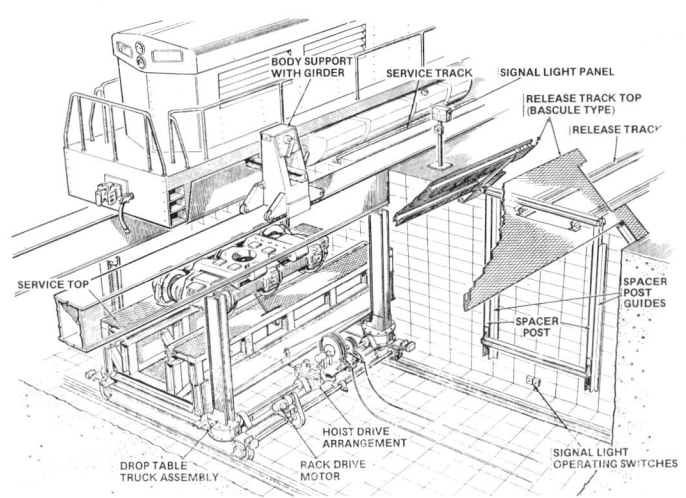

Whiting car hoist, 25 tons capacity

Arrangement of Whiting bogie drop table

controls allow overhead cranes to be operated from either a hand-held push-button controller weighing 0.7 kg, or a rugged joystick controller weighing less than 3 kg and worn on a belt. The company claims that railway workshop cranes with Telemotive radio controls have improved productivity and increased the safety of crane operation, compared with the original cab controls, by giving crane control to a single crane driver/slinger who can situate himself in the ideal position to see the load and its clearances. Telemotive radio has particularly aided productivity in congested rolling stock workshops, where drivers in crane cabs could not see the load and so relied on hand signals relayed along a chain of operators on the shop floor.

Toshiba
Toshiba Corporation
Railway Projects Department

Toshiba Bldg, 1–1, Shibaura 1–chome, Minato-ku, Tokyo 105, Japan

Telephone: +81 3 457 4924
Cable: Toshiba, Tokyo
Telex: 22587 toshiba
Telefax: +81 3 457 8385

Products: Multi-purpose test equipment for traction motors; automatic test equipment for silicon rectifiers; battery trucks for transporting car bodies; battery tractors interchangeable with both steel and rubber-tyred wheel sets for moving car bodies in shops or yards.

Wagner
Gustav Wagner Maschinenfabrik

PO Box 2942, 7410 Reutlingen, Federal Republic of Germany

Telephone: +49 7121 2081
Telex: 0729846
Telefax: +49 7121 38909

Products: Rail sawing and drilling machines.

Air cushion platform by Windhoff

Whiting
Whiting Corporation

15700 Lathrop Avenue, Harvey, Illinois 60426, USA

Telephone: +1 312 468 9400
Telex: 2 53274
Telefax: +1 312 785 0755

President: R E Gibson
Executive Vice President and Chief Financial Officer: J L Kahn
Director International Marketing: C T Bourtsos

Products: Workshop systems design and equipment including metro car hoists, body hoists, turntables, transfer tables, overhead bridge cranes, car progression systems and train washers, drop tables, jacks and sanding systems for locomotive power.

MANUFACTURERS / Workshop repair and maintenance equipment

Windhoff
Rheiner Maschinenfabrik Windhoff AG

Hovestrasse 10, Postfach 1160, 4440 Rheine, Federal Republic of Germany

President: Dr Bernd Windhoff
Managers: Heinz Lörfing

Gunter Knieper
Franz Josef Cramer
Christoph Wessels
Herbert Bucksch
Export Manager: Helmut Pühs

Telephone: +49 5971 580
Telex: 981643

Telefax: +49 5971 58209

Products: Spindle lifting jacks; hydraulic wheel-set and bogie lifts; bogie changing systems.

Addenda

Casaire Ltd

Raebarn House, Northolt Road, Harrow, Middlesex HA2 0DY, England

Telephone: +44 81 423 2323
Telefax: +44 81 864 2952

Chairman: R T Roberts
Managing Director: M K Campbell
Technical Director: C H Hickson
Sales Director: G C Hayday
Publicity Manager: I J Clarke

Products: Direct-fired gas space heating systems.

Nogradi Szenbanyak

P.O. Box 377, 1394 Budapest, Hungary

Telex: 22 4571

Products: Repair of dc traction motors and manufacture of their main components; welded stator casings for electric motors; fully-assembled rotors and stators, main and auxiliary poles and rotor ld windings.

Casaire heating seen at high level at British Rail's Chart Leacon Depot, Ashford, Kent

There's A New Gang In Town That Won't Hold Up Your Trains.

Holdup men on horseback, barricading tracks and robbing trains, make great scenes for old west movies. But M-O-W equipment blocking tracks, holding up schedules and robbing your profits are a maintenance manager's nightmare.

The CAT Rail Gang to the rescue. Fast, mobile, maintenance-of-way machines specifically designed to work on—and around—the track. Each with Caterpillar's proven dependability plus parts and service support. Each designed to enter or exit the rail at any point along the track to eliminate traffic delays.

The IT28B with Swingboom—The workhorse of The Rail Gang. Change from swingboom with rail tongs or magnet to bucket or parallel-lift forks in seconds. One Integrated Toolcarrier can do the work of many special purpose machines—even a railcar mover.

The 518 Railcar Mover—The muscle of The Rail Gang. The 518 Railcar Mover travels up to 20 mph, moves up to eight cars and is the first to move onto or off of the tracks anywhere along the line—clearing the way for freight traffic.

The 416 Backhoe Loader—The speed of The Rail Gang. Traveling at 20 mph, the full suspension Mitchell Hi-Rail keeps the 416 Backhoe Loader moving smoothly. Load it up with hydraulic tools and it becomes the perfect mobile spot-tie replacer.

Put the CAT Rail Gang to work on your railroad, and increase productivity and availability of your maintenance-of-way equipment. Get CAT quality, reliability and unequalled service. Call your CAT® dealer today for more details on The New Rail Gang.

CAT® Rail Gang

CATERPILLAR®

Leasing/associations/consultants

Private freight car leasing companies

WAGON LEASING

EUROPE

Algeco SA

16 avenue de l'Opera, 75040 Paris, France

Telephone: +33 1 42 96 10 21
Telex: 239758 algeco paris

Vehicles: Tank and special-purpose wagons; ISO tank containers for hazardous products.

Armita
Armita Nederland BV

Apollolaan 109, 1077 AN, Amsterdam, Netherlands

Telephone: +31 20 736117
Telex: 12147
Telefax: +31 20 735857

Manager: Dr Arnold W Endstra

Vehicles: Tank cars 720 open wagons 132

Ausiliare
Ausiliare SpA

Via Leopardo 32, 20123 Milan, Italy

Telephone: +39 2 439 0041
Telex: 330483 ausimi i
Telefax: +39 2 463 221

Managing Director: R M Engeler
Sales Director: L Rampinelli

Vehicles: 2070 comprising double-deck automobile transporters and wagons for palletised freight, liquid and powder chemicals

CAIB
Groupe CAIB
A member of Brambles Europe SA

18 Square de Meeus, B-1040 Brussels, Belgium

Telephone: +32 2 507 75 00
Telex: 24295
Telefax: +32 2 507 75 10

Managing Director: J F Weerts
Technical Director: A Leclercq
Finance Director: P Penninckx
Marketing Director: F Boehlen

Vehicles: Approx 40 000, of which a quarter are for petroleum products, a quarter for chemicals, a quarter for dry bulk loads and the remainder comprise gas, high cube and transporter wagons.

Group CAIB covers the wagon hiring and maintenance activities through a network of national representatives and is the largest European railway wagon-owning group and is managed by Hans Groote and Herve Thoumyre.

Brambles Europe also owns the Brambles UK Division under the leadership of Bob Penman; the Eurotainer tank container hiring business under the management of Raymond de Blegiers; the Multilog Division under the direction of Jean Louis Laurent which encompasses the multi-modal logistic activities of Cargotainer and System B; and the Eurolev Division which will consolidate the crane and lifting activities recently acquired in a new division under the responsibility of Jacques Guerin.

CAIB UK
CAIB Uk Ltd

Dukes Court, Woking, Surrey GU21 5BH, England

Telephone: +44 483 755556
Telex: 858829
Telefax: +44 483 755150

Managing Director: Robert J Penman

CAIB UK Ltd combines four existing companies: Storage and Transport System Ltd; Marcroft Engineering Ltd; Railcall Ltd; and Traffic Services Ltd. Each now trades as a division of the new company. In 1988 the company took over the rental business of Procur (UK) and its 2600 freight wagons, bringing the total fleet to over 3500 wagons, together with Marcroft Engineering's repair network with 40 repair facilities spread throughout the UK.

Charterail
Charterail Ltd

Abinger House, Church Street, Dorking, Surrey RH4 1DF, England

Telephone: +44 306 741626

Charterail Ltd, a joint private sector (78 per cent) – British Rail (22 per cent) venture, has been formed to offer a total distribution service based on the latest intermodal techniques. The company is initially promoting use of two types of vehicle: the bi-modal RoadRailer and the Tiphoook swing-well piggyback wagon, with compatible Tiphook semi-trailers (see also Tiphook entry, this section).

Convoy
Convoy-Contigas BV

Apollolaan 109, 1077 AN Amsterdam, Netherlands

Telephone: +31 20 629333, 6623443
Telex: 12147
Telefax: +31 20 735857

Director: Dr Arnold W Endstra

Vehicles: 180 tank wagons

ETRA
Eisenbahn-Transportmittel AG

Lavaterstrasse 40, 8027 Zurich, Switzerland

Telephone: +41 1 202 5135
Telex: 815588 etra ch
Telefax: +41 1 202 5142

General Manager: Dr C. Grunig

Vehicles: 1100, comprising tank, hopper and powder wagons

EVA
Eisenbahn-Verkehrsmittel GmbH

Schillerstrasse 20, 4000 Dusseldorf 1, Federal Republic of Germany

Telephone: +49 211 67 02-0
Telex: 8 586848 eva d
Telefax: +49 211 670 2110

Managing Director: H Vossen

Vehicles: Tank, powder and high-cube wagons: 10,056 owned and 2,889 managed

Fert & Cie

PO Box 2364, 1211 Geneva 2, Switzerland

Telephone: +41 22 34 88 00
Telex: 412183
Telefax: +41 22 733 19 50

Vehicles: 270 wine tank wagons

Invatra
Industrial de Vagones y Transportes SA

Poligone Industrial Alces, Alcazar de San Juan, Ciudad Real, Spain

Telephone: +34 26 511113

Vehicle: 58 tank wagons

Liga de Proprietarios de Vagones de España

Juan Alvarez Mendizábal, 30-4° Centro, Madrid 28008, Spain

Telephone: +34 1 2 47 82 86

President: D Santiago Muñoz Valero (SALTRA)

Members
Cementos Alfa, SA, Calderón de la Barca, 4, 39002 Santander
Cementos Portland de Morata de Jalon, P° de María Agustín 4 and 6, 50004 Zaragoza
Cargill España SA, Muelle Castilla, 43080 Tarragona
Elosua, SA, P° de Salamanca 13, 24009 Leon
Ensidesa, Transportes Terrestres Exteriores, Factoría de Avilés, Oviedo (Asturias)
Fertilizantes Españoles, SA, Villanueva 24, 28001 Madrid
Gas Madrid, SA, Marqués de Cubas 8, 28014 Madrid
Herederos De Ramon Mugica, SA, Apartado 14, Irun (Guipúzcoa)
Ivexa, SA, Alberto Alcocer 46, 6° B, 28016, Madrid
Metransa, Doctor Esquerdo 138, 6° Dcha, 28007 Madrid
Protran, SA, Alberto Alcocer 46, 7° A, 28016 Madrid
Salaverria, Gomara, y Cia, SRC, Apartado 3, Fuenterrabia (Guipúzcoa)
Saltra, SA, Doctor Esquerdo 138, 6° dcha, 28007 Madrid
Savesa, Oquendo 5, 4° A, 20004 San Sebastian
Semat, Capitán Haya 48, 2°, 28020 Madrid
Seostris, P° de la Castellana 131, 1°, 28046 Madrid
Talleres Meleiro SA, Avda Industrial 9, Barco de Valdeorras (Orense)
Tramesa, Oquendo 5, 4°, 20004 San Sebastian
Transfesa, Bravo Murillo 38, 2°, 28015 Madrid
Tudela Veguin, SA, Melquiades Alvarez 1, 33002 Oviedo
Luciano Vaño Giner, Gran Vía Ramón y Cajal 2, 46007 Valencia
Vda de Simon Parareda, Santo Tomás 12, San Martin de Ruideperas (Barcelona)
Vda de A Fernandez E Hijo SA, Almagro 24, 28010 Madrid

Metransa
Manipulaciones Especiales y Transportes SA

Telephone: 467 2700
Telex: 42081

Vehicles: 158 tank wagons

Mineral Haul
Mineral Haul Ltd

5th Floor, Alliance House, 12 Caxton Street, London SW1H 0QS, England

Telephone: +44 71 222 7692
Telex: 916201
Telefax: +44 71 222 3736
TOPS Lata: K191500

Sales Manager: B Wellmore

Products: Financiers, hirers, owners and operators of

Tiger 53 hopper wagon operated by Mineral Haul

specialised rail wagons and terminals: for the in-bulk movement and distribution throughout the United Kingdom and Continental Europe of industrial minerals, construction materials and aggregates and solid chemical and allied products in bulk granular form.

Vehicles: 25 Tiger 53 hopper wagons, supplemented as required by 50–60 box wagons and Polybulk hopper wagons

OEVA
Oesterreichische Eisenbahn-Verkehrs-Anstalt GmbH

Volksgartenstrasse 3, 1010 Vienna 1, Austria

Telephone: +43 222 033 621
Telex: 133430 oeva a
Telefax: +43 222 931 555

Managing Director: Dr A Ulrich

Vehicles: 678 owned and 720 managed

SATI

38 Station Road, Cambridge CB1 2JH, England

Telephone: +44 223 324261
Telex: 817044
Telefax: +44 223 351784

Vehicles: 6500 comprising wagons for a wide range of liquid chemicals, gases, including cryogenics; hoppers, and Debach Vit heavy-duty wagons

Savesa SA

Oquendo 5, 4° A, 20004 San Sebastian, Spain

Telephone: +34 43 424208, 428568
Telefax: +34 43 276214

Managing Director: José Luis Gómara

Vehicles: 200 bogie tank wagons

SEWAR
Société Exploitation de Wagons Reservoirs

43 rue de Provence, 75009 Paris, France

Telephone: +33 1 874 5508
Telex: 280564

Vehicles: 1650 wagons for foodstuffs transport

SGTL
Société Générale de Transport de Liquides

43 rue de Provence, 75009 Paris, France

Telephone: +33 1 874 5508
Telex: 280564

Vehicles: 200 tank wagons

SGW
Société de Gerance de Wagons Grande Capacité
A subsidiary company of French Railways

163 bis avenue de Clichy, 75017 Paris, France

Telephone: +33 1 47 30 81 30
Telex: 281703

Chairman: Maurice Auroy
General Manager: Christian de Fournoux
Marketing Manager: Alain Keck

Products: SGW caters exclusively for unit train movement of bulk freight suitable for open-wagon conveyance, such as coal, coke, ores, sand, stones and ballast, throughout Europe. So far as coal and ores are concerned it operates principally in the north and east of the continent and in southern West Germany, where heavy industry is concentrated. Its business in other commodities is widespread. It does not own wagons, but markets and manages the deployment of a pool of some 12 000 special-purpose vehicles on behalf of wagon manufacturers, national and private industries, and private wagon leasing companies. Between 50 and 60 million tonnes a year, or about a quarter of French Railways' total freight tonnage, is moved in SGW vehicles. The company offers a total rail transport service, including advice on loading and discharge facilities, and prospecting for branches and sites suitable for establishment of unit-train discharge facilities in the case of short-term construction activity.

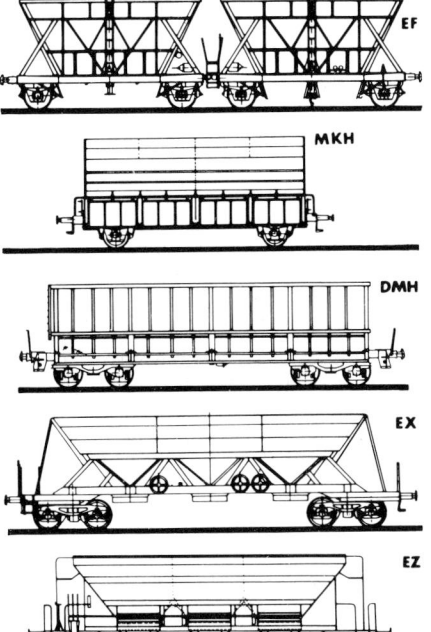

SGW works in close co-operation with the Société Auxiliaire de Déchargement et Manutention (SADEMA), which specialises in the establishment (and, where required, financing) of private sidings and special-purpose loading and discharge facilities.

Wagon types: Bottom-door hopper wagons with power-operated automatic discharge of Types EF two-axle, with capacity of 38 m^3 or 29.4 tonnes (single) or 76 m^3 and 58.5 tonnes (permanently- coupled pairs); and EF bogie, with capacity of 75.5 m^3 and 58 tonnes;
Side-door discharge hopper wagons, manually operated, of Types MKH, with payload capacity of 61 m^3 and 28.2 tonnes; and DMH, with payload capacity of 55 m^3 and 58.65 tonnes;
Controlled-discharge bottom-door hopper wagons with three outlets of Type EX with payload capacity of 58 m^3 and 61.3 tonnes;
Three-hopper wagons with individual side- or bottom-door discharge of Type EZ, with payload capacity of 48 m^3 or 58 tonnes.

Constitution: SGW was formed by government decree in 1941, originally to pool high-capacity hopper wagons in such a way as to prevent them being sequestrated by the wartime German administration.

Simotra SA

36 rue Guersant, 75017 Paris, France

Telephone: +33 1 45 74 98 39
Telex: 280256 f
Telefax: +33 1 45 74 36 39

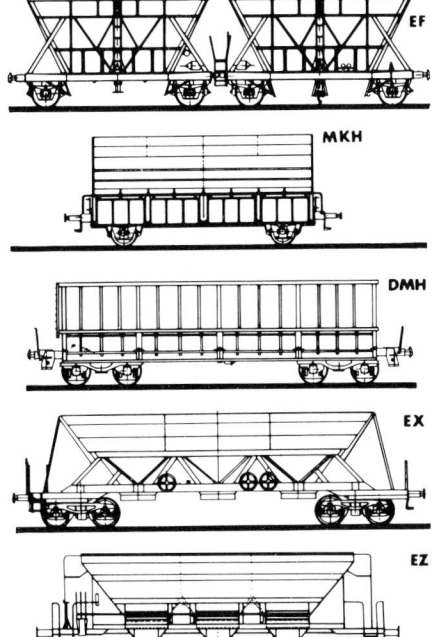

Types of wagon operated by SGW, France

Managing Director: C Courau
Sales Director: G Desserne

Vehicles: 13 000 of all types

Steele
E G Steele & Co Ltd

25 Dalziel Street, Hamilton, Lanarkshire ML3 9AU, Scotland

Telephone: +44 698 283765
Cable: Mountings Hamilton
Telex: 77454
Telefax: +44 698 891550

Managing Director: J G Steele
Export Director: D A Steele

Vehicles: 95 45-tonne tank wagons chiefly for petroleum products, 32 100-tonne wagons for petroleum products and sulphuric acid

E G Steele 45-tonne Class A tank wagons for methanol

TVA
Société de Transports de Vehicules Automobiles

14 rue Ferrus, 75683 Paris Cedex 14, France

Telephone: +33 1 45 89 89 09
Telex: 270 306/7/19
Telefax: +33 1 45 81 02 71

Commerical Director: J Henry

Vehicles: Automobile transporters

Tiger Rail Ltd

Fifth Floor, Alliance House, 12 Caxton Street, London SW1H 0QS, England

Telephone: +44 71 222 7692
Telex: 916201
Telefax: +44 71 222 3736
TOPS Lata: K191500

Marketing and Sales office: Second Floor, Office Suite B, Brunswick Square, Oldham OL1 1DE, Lancashire

Telephone +44 61 627 2765

Chief Executive: B K Pettit
International Director: J A C Evans
Technical Director: B R Ellis
Financial Director: R C Angus
Sales & Marketing Manager: B W Ellmore
Chief Engineer: N Green

Products: Tiger Rail operate a modern railcar fleet incorporating a wide range of railcar types specially designed and constructed for the transportation of goods such as liquid chemicals, gases, bulk powders, aggregates, clays, slurries and steels, as well as a wide range of finished products.

Tiger Rail have recently introduced a new fleet of international 90-tonne stainless steel insulated railcars for the carriage of clay slurries as used by the paper manufacturing industry.

A full range of long-, medium- and short-term hire or fully payout leasing is offered, with all cars provided on a fully maintained basis. Part of the service includes advice, planning, specifying and financing all rail-related activities.

In addition to hiring, Tiger offers a fully inclusive

E G Steele 45-tonne Class A tank wagons for methanol

WAGON LEASING

46-tonne open-top box wagon for UK operation by Tiger Rail

Tiphook curtain-roofed platform wagon by Arbel-Fauvet-Girel

Tiphook aggregate hopper wagon

Tiphook swing-well piggyback car showing loaded platform swung out for trailer discharge

railfreight service throughout the UK and Europe, extending from terminal-to-terminal deliveries, collections through to door-to-door deliveries.

Vehicles: 800

Tiphook
Tiphook Rail Ltd

Chelsea House, 26 Market Square, Bromley, Kent BR1 1NA, England

Telephone: +44 81 460 6060
Telex: 927294
Telefax: +44 81 466 1556

Managing Director: J Emms
Marketing Director: R Walker
Technical Director: M Ord
Finance Director: D S M Hatton

Products: Short-, medium-, long-term rental of freight wagons in the United Kingdom and Continental Europe; development of intermodal systems for international traffic.

The company is a member of Tiphook plc, an internationally-operating group that embraces container rental (approx. 480 000 TEU), trailer rental (approx 22 000 TEU) and container manufacture.

Following the acquisition of Railease in 1989, Tiphook Rail's fleet is in excess of 1750 wagons and consists of container-carrying flat wagons, covered flats, steel coil carriers, Class A and stainless steel tank wagons, aggregate hoppers and box wagons, bulk powder wagons and specifically built tank wagons for various commodities.

The development of the Tiphook Piggyback intermodal system has continued and 100 4-axle bogie versions of the wagon have been ordered. These vehicles will commence service in the UK in 1990-91.

Trailer Train Ltd

Alliance House, 12 Caxton Street, London SW1H 0QS, England

Telephone: +44 71 222 7692
Telex: 916201
Telefax: +44 71 222 3736

Vehicles: Bi-modal road/rail trailers for international haulage (see also entry in Freight Vehicles section)

Tramesa
Transportes Mixtos Especiales SA

Head Office: Avda Pablo Garnica, 20 Torrelavega, Cantabria, Spain

Telephone: +34 942 893000
Telex: 35873
Telefax: +34 943 276214

Main works: Oquendo 5, 4° B, San Sebastian

Telephone: +34 943 424208, 943 428568

General Manager: Gerardo Gómara Hernandez

Subsidiary company: Savesa (Soc Agrupadora de Vagones Especiales SA), Oquendo 5, 4A°, San Sebastian (Guipuzcoa)

Vehicles: 200 chemical tank wagons

Transfesa
Transportes Ferroviarios Especiales SA

Bravo Murillo 38 2, 28015 Madrid, Spain

Telephone: +34 1 448 89 00
Telex: 27745, 22632
Telefax: +34 1 593 28 76

President: José Manuel Otero Novas
Executive Director: Emilio Fernandez Fernandez
Managing Director: José Ma Fernandez Sanz

Products: The company promotes freight transport between Spain and other countries in its privately owned wagons fitted with interchangeable axles to negotiate the break of gauge at the Franco-Spanish border.

The company owns a fleet of over 7000 wagons.

WAGON LEASING

Tramesa petroleum products tankers

Tramesa chemical liquid tanker

Unit train of VTG 107 m³ capacity pressurised gas tank wagons on Swiss Bern-Lötschberg-Simplon Railway

128 m³ capacity bulk-freight wagon for coal dust transport

VTG sliding-hood wagon for steel coil and other heavy freight transport

VTG tank wagon for caustic soda

Vagones Frigorificos SA

Marques de Valdeiglesias 8, Madrid 4, Spain

Telephone: +34 1 231 71 04
Telex: 44081

Vehicles: 97 refrigerated cars; 151 hopper wagons

VTG
VTG Vereinigte Tanklager und Transportmittel GmbH
Member of the Preussag Group

Neue Rabenstrasse 21, Postfach 30 55 70, 2000 Hamburg 36, Federal Republic of Germany

Telephone: +49 40 44 19 1-0
Telex: 2 17008-0 vtd
Telefax: +49 40 44 19 14 28

Managing Directors: Roelf J Janssen (rail tank cars)
Dr Klaus-Jürgen Juhnke (tank terminals)
Heinrich Sikora (offshore)

Principal subsidiaries: VTG (UK) Limited, Hitchin, England; VTG GmbH Vienna; VTG AG, Basle; VTG Benelux BV, Rotterdam; ALGECO SA, Paris; VTG Benelux BV, Brussels; OSA Marine Services GmbH, Bremen

Products: VTG is Europe's leading hiring company for tank wagons and special-purpose freight cars. VTG handles the products of the chemical and petrochemical industries, from liquid chemicals through pressurised gases to dry goods in bulk. VTG Ferry-wagons offer straight-through transportation via the train ferries for goods to and from the UK. VTG Tanktainers are available for intermodal transportation of chemicals, gases or foodstuffs door-to-door.

VTG is Germany's leading independent tank operator, with fully equipped modern installations at key positions and seaport terminals in Hamburg and Amsterdam. Facilities are available for the temporary or longer term storage of mineral oil and chemical products. The company offers a total service covering top security, product treatment, handling and local distribution.

The French Group Algeco SA, Paris, is not only one of the largest French companies hiring out tank wagons, but at the same time an important supplier of multipurpose prefabs and industrial buildings in Europe.

Vehicles: 2000 tank and special-purpose wagons

VTG (UK)
VTG (UK) Limited
A subsidiary of VTG Vereinigte Tanklager und Transportmittel GmbH

Manor Court, 26b Bancroft, Hitchin, Hertfordshire SG5 P1JW, England

Telephone: +44 462 55411
+44 462 36696 (Ferry wagon)
+44 462 37502 (Tanktainer)
Telex: 826956 vtguk g
826949 vtgfw g (Ferry wagon)
826942 vtgtt g (Tanktainer)
Telefax: +44 462 37739

Manager: Dr Gerd Slotta

Vehicles: As a wholly-owned subsidiary of VTG GmbH, Hamburg, VTG (UK) has 23 000 rail wagons available for lease for transportation of bulk liquid and powder products, most of which are hazardous. VTG (UK) also offers high-capacity rail wagons and specialised wagons for steel coils for domestic and international transit which can include an all-in forwarding service. P900 VTG tank containers are available for hire for door-to-door movements.

NORTH AMERICA

American Refrigerator Transit Co

1416 Dodge Street, Omaha, Nebraska 68179, USA

Telephone: +1 402 271 5198

President: R J Dunne Jr

Vehicles: 295

Anbel
Anbel Leasing Corporation
A member of the Anbel Group

Suite 450, 2323 S Voss Road, Houston, Texas 77057, USA

President: K R Nichols

Products: Leasing of all types of rolling stock

CGTX Inc

16th Floor, 1600 Blvd René Lévesque Ouest, Montreal, Quebec H3H 1P9, Canada

Telephone: +1 514 931 7343
Telex: 05 267562
Telefax: +1 514 931 5534

Chairman: R D Cole

President and Chief Executive Officer: J C Leger
Vice President and Treasurer: John D Buckley
Vice President, Marketing and Sales: R A Podsiadlo
Chief Engineer: Geoff Sinclair
Mechanical Superintendent: J Harris

Products: Lessors of railway rolling stock in Canada: tank cars and freight cars. The company has maintenance workshops at Montreal, Red Deer and Moose Jaw.

Vehicles: 6876

Chicago Freight Car Leasing Co
Chicago Freight Car Leasing Co

One O'Hare Centre, Suite 5010, 6250 N River Road, Rosemont, Illinois 60018, USA

Telephone: +1 708 318 8000

President: F R Sasser
Vice President, Marketing and Sales: T F Kuklinski

Products: New and rebuilt freight wagons of all types; leasing services.

Vehicles: 3200

FGE
Fruit Growers Express Co

3220 Duke Street, Alexandria, Virginia 22314, USA

Telephone: +1 703 370 7300
Telex: 62893325

President: Edward H Latchford
Vice President, Marketing and Sales: John E Chapman
Vice President, Operations: Clair E Smithers

Products: Insulated cars and refrigerator cars. Refrigerator car service on several railroads.

Vehicles: 7241 RBL insulated cars; 1885 RPL type cars, mechanical refrigeration.

GATX
General American Transportation Corp
A subsidiary of GATX Corporation

120 South Riverside Plaza, Chicago, Illinois 60606, USA

Telephone: +1 312 621 6200
Telex: 25 3623

President: Kenneth A Krick
Senior Vice President Sales and Marketing: Robert E Lynch
Vice President and Chief Financial Officer: W C Andrews

Products: Railcar leasing, repair, maintenance and fleet management services. GATX operates the world's largest independent railcar fleet, numbering over 52 000 cars, 88 per cent of which are tank cars. Over half of the tank car fleet is employed in chemicals traffic. The GATX tank car fleet includes the TankTrain system, a series of tank cars interconnected with flexible hoses that allow the entire string to be loaded and unloaded from one connection. Advantages of the TankTrain system include lower facility capital costs, reduced loading and unloading times, less manpower, and safer handling for the crew, commodity and environment.

GATX offers tank cars of every size for handling any liquid commodity transported by rail. The tank car fleet includes general service, pressure, stainless steel, aluminium and commodity-specific tank.

The milling and baking industry had used the GATX Airslide as its railcar standard for the past 33 years. The Airslide car is ideal for transporting and unloading finely

FGE mechanical refrigerated box car

GATX Power-Flo car

GATX Airslide car

GATX Cascade coal car

Flexible hose linking TankTrain cars

divided bulk chemical and food products such as talc, flour, sugar, starch and carbon black. For shippers who require pneumatic unloading of their dry bulk commodities, GATX now complements its Airslide car by offering the Trinity-designed Power-Flo car. The 15 psi, 5125 ft^3 covered hopper is claimed to offer shippers easy unloading, loading and cleaning.

For coal shippers, GATX offers its Cascade car, claimed to be the lightest-weight steel fast-discharge hopper car on the market. With an estimated tare weight of 62 300 lb, the Cascade car can carry a full 100 tons of coal. It discharges its load in three to seven seconds.

Through its Professional Administrative Car Services (PACS), GATX offers full fleet management services to railcar owners as well as lessors. PACS's services include AAR auditing, defect card billing, mileage accounting, UMLER reporting, preparation of car taxes, regulatory reports, and managment analyses for budgeting and forecasting. Special services are available for tailoring the programme to specific customer needs. Car repair, maintenance and inspections are also available on a contract basis.

Vehicles: 52 000

General Electric Railcar Services Corp
A subsidiary of General Electric Credit Corp

33 W Monroe Street, Chicago, Illinois 60603, USA

Telephone: +1 312 853 5000
Telex: 255222

President: A F Barber
Vice Presidents,
  Sales and Marketing: G D Birmingham
  Operations: G Reynolds

Subsidiary: Quality Services Railcar Repair Corp

Products: Railcar leasing and management services; 12 full service repair facilities in US, one in Canada; two wheel shops; mobile repair facilities in US and Canada.

Vehicles: 62 000

Itel
Itel Railcar Corporation

303 W Madison Street, Suite 2075, Chicago, Illinois 60606, USA

Telephone: +1 312 781 1880
Telefax: +1 312 781 1883

President, Itel Rail: Desmond P Hayes
Vice President, Marketing: E Lloyd Manasco
Sales Manager: Darel Albin

Products: Primarily operating leases of general purpose boxcars and other equipment to US railroads and shippers. Leases are for varying periods and are either fixed or variable. The variable lease provides for payments of rentals solely from a portion of car rentals received by the lessee for the period the leased equipment is on the tracks of other railroads. At the start of 1988 Itel Rail's fleet numbered approximately 36 000 units, consisting of boxcars, flatcars, gondolas, hopper cars and 3000 intermodal trailers.

More than doubling its size in December 1987, with the acquisition of substantially all of the assets of Evans Transportation Company, Itel Rail not only consolidated its position in the industry but also added a new range and diversity to its customer base. In addition, new opportunities to service Itel's expanded customer base were provided by the acquisition of the four maintenance shops which will not only ensure the availability of equipment but will also complement Itel's programme to rebuild or modify equipment to meet customer's specifications as an alternative to the high cost of new construction.

Northbrook
Northbrook Corporation Rail Division

900 North Michigan Avenue, John Hancock Center, Chicago, Illinois 60611, USA

Telephone: +1 312 915 2900
Telefax: +1 312 915 2999

President: E L Freeman
Vice President, Sales: R M Dwyer
Vice President, Market Operations: D L Amick

Products: Comprehensive fleet management service for wagon owners: approx 3800 freight cars currently under management, for several Class I railroads as well as coal, mining, public utility and other companies.

Procor Ltd
Rail Car Division

2001 Speers Road, Oakville, Ontario L6J 5E1, Canada

Telephone: +1 416 827 4111
Telex: 06 982241
Telefax: +1 416 827 0800

President and Chief Executive: G C Mills
Fleet Manager: G Mancini
Vice President, Operations: M C Parker
Vice President, Marketing: A M Stremecki
Vice President, Mechanical Services: J McKechnie

Products: Leasing of tank and special-purpose freight cars.

Vehicles: 16 500

Pullman Leasing Co

200 South Michigan Avenue, Chicago, Illinois 60604, USA

Telephone: +1 312 322 7070
Telex: 254036

President: E J Whalen
Vice President, Sales: N G Johnson

Vehicles: 32 398

Railbox Co
A subsidiary of Trailer Train Co

101 North Wacker Drive, Chicago, Illinois 60606, USA

Telephone: +1 312 853 3223
Telex: 206274

President: R C Burton

Vehicles: 13 300

Railgon Co
A subsidiary of Trailer Train Co

101 North Wacker Drive, Chicago, Illinois 60606, USA

Telephone: +1 312 853 3223
Telex: 206274

President: R C Burton

Vehicles: 1200

Trailer Train
Trailer Train Company

101 North Wacker Drive, Chicago, Illinois 60606, USA

Telephone: +1 312 853 3223
Telex: 206274

President: R C Burton Jr
Vice President, Equipment: R S Hulick
Senior Vice President, Fleet Management: H V Logan

Products: The company acquires, finances and maintains, for US railroads, pools of flatcars including 38 800 intermodal, 32 800 for carrying automobiles and 13 300 special-purpose flatcars. Its capital stock is owned by 14 operating railroads. It has two wholly owned subsidiaries: Railbox Company, which operates 13 300 boxcars; and Railgon Company operating 1200 general-service gondola cars.

Of the company's 38 800 intermodal cars, 20 200 are for road trailer piggybacking only; 14 300 are dual-purpose trailer- or container-carrying; and 4300 are suitable for container transport only. Over the past several years the company has modified its most recently built 89ft 4in all-purpose and standard piggyback flatcars to carry two of the 45 ft long road trailers now heavily employed in US intermodal transport. At the end of 1989 there were 24 820 cars in the fleet.

As of the end of 1989, Trailer Train had in service 1997 five-unit articulated double-stack, well-type container cars for use between major seaports and inland points or for transcontinental moves. The company has developed a five-unit articulated single-stack container car to supplement the double-stack car in corridors with less dense container traffic and/or clearance restrictions. This so-called 'Spine Car' utilises rebuilt material released from the retirement of 85 ft intermodal cars. During 1989 the company put into service an all-purpose version of the 'Spine Car' which is capable of carrying various combinations of highway trailers and/or containers of various sizes.

At the end of 1989 a total of 519 'Spine Cars' were in service.

Vehicles: 85 000

Transcisco
Transcisco Industries, Inc.

555 California Street, Suite 2420, San Francisco, California 94104, USA

Telephone: +1 415 477 9700
Telex: 62817554
Telefax: +1 415 788 0583, 477 0599

Chairman and Chief Executive Officer: Mark C Hungerford
Vice President, Finance: Timothy P Carlson
Senior Vice-President, Marketing: George A Tedesco
President, Transcisco Rail Services: John E Carroll Jr
President, Transcisco Trading: Marvin B Hughes

Products: Transcisco is engaged in the manufacture, retrofitting and maintenance of railcars. Its railcar maintenance operation, Transcisco Rail Services company, is the largest non-railroad owned railcar maintenance operation in the USA.

Transcisco has formed two new subsidiaries, Transcisco Tours Inc and Transcisco Trading Company.

Transcisco Tours has announced plans to enter the luxury 'cruise train' market. Transcisco Tours is considering to operate on the San Jose-Oakland-Truckee-Reno route, and service is expected to begin late in 1990. Also being considered is the route between Los Angeles and Las Vegas, and service is anticipated to begin in 1991.

Transcisco Trading was formed upon the company's success with its joint venture SOVFINAMTRANS. The partners in this venture are the Soviet Ministries of Rail and Petrochemicals, and Haka Corporation in Finland. Transcisco's patented and proprietary Uni-Temp heating system is the catalyst which brought about the formation of SOVFINAMTRANS, in which Transcisco holds a 20% ownership. All international activities will be conducted by Transcisco Trading Company.

Trinity Industries Leasing Co
A subsidiary of Trinity Industries Inc

PO Box 10587, Dallas, Texas 75207, USA

Telephone: +1 214 631 4420
Telex: 73 0250

Conventional Trailer Train TOFC flatcar modified to carry three 28 ft trailers of the type now popularly moved in US 'double-bottom' highway trucking

WAGON LEASING

Trinity Industries twin covered hopper

Trinity Industries sulphuric acid tank car

Executive Vice President: Richard G Brown
Vice President, Sales: Clark Wood

Products: Tank cars are leased to companies in the chemical, petroleum, foods, minerals and fertiliser industries. Freight cars are leased to railroads, chemical, minerals and fertiliser companies. Trinity's tank cars are designed for the maximum load permitted on US railroads (263 000 lb glw) for specific commodities according to Department of Transportation (DoT) and Association of American Railroads (AAR) specifications. Typical optimum tank car sizes and specifications in Trinity's fleet are:

Chlorine	71 368 gal
Carbon dioxide	20 110 gal
Propane	34 000 gal
Propylene	33 600 gal
Caustic soda	16 664 gal
Corn syrup	17 574 gal
Sulphur	13 818 gal
Sulphuric acid	13 946 gal
Clay slurry	14 428 gal
Alcohol	29 947 gal
General purpose	20 413 gal

Cars are leased for varying periods of time from one to 20 years. The majority of new car leases are for 10-year terms. Trinity Leasing offers cars on full service leases which provide lessees with a complete management package including administration, mileage accounting, insurance, filing and paying property taxes, auditing and paying AAR repair bills, negotiating wreck settlements with the railroads, and providing maintenance and repairs for the cars. Trinity also offers a net lease to customers who are staffed to perform these administrative chores in house; net leases generally are for 10- to 15-year terms.

Vehicles: 7831

Union Tank
Union Tank Car Co
A member of the Marmon Group of companies

111 West Jackson Boulevard, Chicago, Illinois 60604, USA

Telephone: +1 312 431 3111
Telex: 910 221 4213

Union Tank general-purpose car of 23 500 US-gallon capacity

Main works: 151st & Railroad Avenue, East Chicago, Indiana 46312

President: Sidney H Bonser
Senior Vice President, Marketing: William L Snelgrove
Senior Vice President & Controller: Stephen G Dinsmore

Products: Steel, stainless-steel, and aluminium tank cars carrying liquids, compressed gases, and granular solids.

Vehicles: 43 000 for lease in the US and Mexico.

Operators of international rail services in Europe

EUROPEAN RAIL OPERATORS

PASSENGER

International Sleeping Car Company (CIWLT)
Cie Internationale des Wagons-lits et du Tourisme

40 rue de l'Arcade, 75381 Paris Cedex 08, France

Telephone: +33 1 4268 24 00
Cable: Wagolits, Paris
Telex: 643 241
Telefax: +33 1 42 68 22 08

Vice-President: Jacques-Bernard Dupont
Chief Executive: A Veil
Director General: François Boyaux
Finance Director: Daniel Convent
Director, Personnel and Social Relations: Guy Pallaruelo
Director, Legal and Estates Division: Jean-Pierre Martinaud
Director, Railway Services Division: Wilhelm Scheiff
Director, Travel Division: Hervé Gourio
Director, Hotels Division: Jean Darras
Director, Computer Services: Yves Lamache
Director, Development: Vincent Mercier
Director, Restaurants: Xavier Fontanet
Head of Public Relations: Françoise Toursaint

German Rail Service Company (DSG)
Deutsche Service-Gesellschaft der Bahn mbH
(formerly Deutsche Schlafwagen und Speisewagen GmbH)

18-22 Guiollettstrasse, 6000 Frankfurt am Main, Federal Republic of Germany

Telephone: +49 69 71 64-1
Cable: Speisewagen ffm
Telex: 4 11 918

Chairman: Hemjö Klein
Directors: Heinz Streichardt
Alexander Bautzmann

Intraflug
Intraflug AG

Forchstrasse 149, 8132 Egg b Zurich, Switzerland

Telephone: +41 1 984 25 50
Telex: 828 518
Telefax: +41 1 984 07 05

President: Albert Glatt
Chief Executive Officer: Edy Züger

Organisme Repartiteur Central du Pool-TEN (Trans-Europ-Nacht)

20 rue de Rome, 75008 Paris, France

Telephone: +33 1 4008 92 47
Telex: 097
Telefax: +33 1 40089258, 40089258

Chief of Organisation: H Kunze

SSG
Schweizerische Speisewagen-Gesellschaft

PO Box 1760, Neuhardstrasse 31, 4601 Olten, Switzerland

Telephone: +41 62 31 85 85
Telex: 981682
Telefax: +41 62 26 45 88

Director: S Sadok

VSOE
Venice-Simplon-Orient-Express Ltd
A division of Orient Express Hotels Inc

Sea Containers House, 20 Upper Ground, London SE1 9PF, England

Telephone: +44 71 928 6969
Telex: 8955803

President: James B Sherwood
Vice-President and Treasurer: D J O'Sullivan
Chief Executive: John Jac Roozemond

FREIGHT

Intercontainer
Company for International Transport by Transcontainers
Société Internationale pour le Transport par Transcontainers

Margarethenstrasse 38, 4008 Basle, Switzerland

Telephone: +41 61 45 25 25
Cable: Transcofer, Basle
Telex: 962 298 a itc ch
Telefax: +41 61 452445

Chairman: Dr Max Lehmann
Vice-Chairmen: Heinrich Sittler, Andras Ambrus and Werner Remmert
General Manager: Claude Durand
Manager, Operating Department: Nicholas Crama
Finance and General Affairs: Conrad Löffel
Commercial Service: Peter Schmelter
Technical Service: Giovanni Sempio
Marketing Services: Jan de Haan
Organisation and Data Processing Department: René Christe

Interfrigo
(International railway-owned company for refrigerated transport)

General management: Wettsteinplatz 1, PO Box 341, 4005 Basle, Switzerland
Registered office: 85 rue de France, 1070 Brussels, Belgium

Telephone: +41 61 695 33 33
Cable: Interfroid Basle

Telex: 962 231; 963 372
Telefax: +41 61 691 08 81

Board of Directors
Chairman, Deputy General Manager, French National Railways: Roger Gerin
Vice-Chairmen, Deputy General Manager, Italian State Railways: G de Chiara
Member of the Board of Management, German Federal Railway: H Wiedeman
Members
Director, Freight, British Railways Board: C J Driver
Director, Marketing Freight, Swiss Federal Railways: Dr M. Lehmann
Director, Transport Department, Belgian State Railways: A Martens
Chief Co-ordinator, Freight Traffic, Netherlands Railways: C J W Bos
Deputy General Manager (Honourable), Danish State Railways: E Rolsted Jensen
First Deputy General Manager, Hungarian State Railways: Dr B Szemök
Secretary
Chief Legal Adviser to the Belgian State Railways: J Biére
General Management
Managing Director: Wolfgang Gritz
Operating Manager: Georg Schick
General Studies and Data Processing Manager: Pierre Bombois
Administrative and Financial Manager: Christian Röthlisberger
Commercial Director: Henning Nygaard
Head of Department, Deputy Administrative and Financial Manager: Fritz Schultheiss

Transfesa
Transportes Ferroviarios Especiales

Bravo Murillo 38-2°, Madrid 3, Spain

Telephone: +34 1 448 89 00
Telex: 27745, 22632

President: José Fernandez Lopez
Executive Director: E Fernandez Fernandez
Managing Director: M Salis Balzola

UIRR
International Union of Road-Rail Transport Companies

Viale Manzoni 6, CH 6830 Chiasso, Switzerland

Telephone: +41 91 43 60 47/8
Telex: 84 20 42
Telefax: +41 91 43 93 83

Link office: Gare de l'Ouest, rue A Vandenpeereboom, B-1080 Brussels, Belgium
Telephone: +32 2 425 62 51
Telex: 24 82 9
Telefax: +32 2 424 20 82

Chairman: Pietro Ris
Secretary: Theo Alleman

Member companies:
Belgium
TRWSA
Gare de l'Ouest, rue A Vandenpeereboom, B-1080 Brussels
Telephone: +32 2 425 62 51
Telex: 24829
Telefax: +32 2 424 20 82

Federal Republic of Germany
Kombiverkehr KG
Breitenbachstrasse 1, D-6000 Frankfurt/Main 93
Telephone: +49 69 79 50 50
Telex: 416399
Telefax: +49 69 70 87 58

Denmark
Kombi Dan Amba
Thorsvej 8, Posboks 87, DK-6330 Padborg
Telephone: +45 4 67 41 81
Telex: 52670
Telefax: +45 4 67 08 98

France
Novatrans SA
21 rue de Rocher, F-75365 Paris Cedex 08
Telephone: +33 1 43 87 41 79
Telex: 650625
Telefax: +33 1 45 22 45 25

Italy
Cemat SpA
Via Vattellina 5-7, I-20159 Milan
Telephone: +39 2 6682110
Telex: 325045
Telefax: +39 2 66800755

Netherlands
Trailstar NV
Boezembocht 31, PB 3017, NL-3003 AA Rotterdam
Telephone: +31 10 413 47 20
Telex: 23371
Telefax: +31 10 404 61 32

Austria
Ökombi
Nordwestbahnhof, Taborstrasse 95, A-1200 Vienna
Telephone: +43 1 222 35 01 05-08
Telex: 114507

Switzerland
Hupac SA
Viale R Manzoni 6, CH-6830 Chiasso
Telephone: +41 91 43 60 47/48
Telex: 842042
Telefax: +41 91 43 93 83

Sweden
S-Combi AB
PO Box 528, S-10127 Stockholm
Telephone: +46 8 23 43 00
Telex: 10550
Telefax: +46 8 723 01 94

Subsidiaries
Kombi UK Ltd
10 Old Bond Street, London W1X 4EN, England
Telephone: +44 71 491 8973
Telex: 25671

Novatrans UK Ltd
49 Queen Victoria Street, London EC4N 4SB, England
Telephone: +44 71 236 0851
Telex: 883836

Hupac Italiana SpA
Via Torcello 2, I-20126 Milan
Telephone: +39 2 255 19 49
Telex: 330519

Novatrans Italia
Via Toffetti 90, I-20139 Milan
Telephone: +39 2 569 37 46
Telex: 325471

International
railway associations and agencies

INTERNATIONAL

International Union of Railways (UIC)
Union Internationale des Chemins de Fer

14 rue Jean-Rey, 75015 Paris, France

Telephone: +33 1 4273 01 20
Telex: 270835
Telefax: +33 1 4273 01 40

President: V Pavlov (Bulgarian State Railways)
Secretary General: J Bouley
Assistant Secretary General: K Ebeling
Communications Manager: P Veron

Office for Research and Experiments—ORE
Oudenoord 500, 3513 EV Utrecht, Netherlands
Telephone: +31 30 314646

Central Clearing House
49A ave Fonsny, Section 31, 1060 Brussels, Belgium

International Railway Congress Association (IRCA)
Association Internationale du Congrès des Chemins de Fer

36 rue Ravenstein, 1000 Brussels, Belgium

Telephone: +32 2 513 92 80

Management Committee
President: E Schouppe, Director General, Belgian National Railways
Vice-Presidents: E Osmotherly, Deputy Secretary, Public Transport, Department of Transport (Great Britain); K Reimers, Mitglied des Vorstandes der Deutschen Bundesbahn
Secretary General: A Martens, Directeur Transport, Belgian National Railways

International Union of Public Transport (UITP)

19 avenue de l'Uruguay, B-1050 Brussels, Belgium

Telephone: +32 2 673 61 00
Telex: 63916
Telefax: +32 2 660 10 72

President: J Ossewaarde, Amsterdam
Vice-Presidents: J K Isaac, Birmingham
M Robin, Paris
H-J Sattler, Bochum
G Y Villafanez, Barcelona
J Zahumenszky, Budapest
General Secretary: Pierre Laconte

Intergovernmental Organisation for International Carriage by Rail (OTIF)
Secretariat: Central Office for International Carriage by Rail (OCTI)

Thunplatz, 3006 Berne, Switzerland

Telephone: +41 31 43 17 62
Cable: OCTI, Berne
Telex: 912 063 octi ch
Telefax: +41 31 43 11 64

Chairman of Administrative Committee: Not yet appointed
Director-General: C Mossu

International Association of Rolling Stock Builders
Association Internationale des Constructeurs de Matériel Roulant (AICMR)

12 rue Bixio, 75007 Paris, France

Telephone: +33 1 4705 36 62
Telefax: +33 1 4705 29 17

President: Conrad Bernstein (France)
Delegate General: R de Planta (Swiss)

International Container Bureau (BIC)
Bureau International des Containers

14 rue Jean Rey, 75015 Paris, France

Telephone: +33 1 4734 68 13
Telex: 270 835 uninfer (attention BIC)
Telefax: +33 1 4273 01 40

General Secretary: P Fournier

International Organisation for Standardisation (IOS)
Organisation internationale de normalisation

Case postale 56, 1 rue de Varembé, 1211 Geneva 20, Switzerland

Telephone: +41 22 734 12 40
Cable: Isorganiz
Telex: 4122 05 iso ch
Telefax: +41 22 733 34 30

President: Roy Phillips (Canada)
Vice-President: Helmut Reihlen
Treasurer: Guy Waldvogel
Secretary General and Chief Executive Officer: Lawrence D Eicher

International Rail Transport Committee (CIT)

Managing Railway: General Management of the Swiss Federal Railways, Legal Division, Mittelstrasse 43, CH-3030 Berne, Switzerland

Telephone: +41 31 60 25 65/27 94/28 06
Cable: Fervojocit Bern
Telex: 99 1212
Telefax: +41 31 60 40 07

President and Chairman: Hans Eisenring
Secretary: Eric Bertherin

International Union of Private Railway Wagon Owners' Associations (UIP)
Union Internationale d'Associations de Propriétaires de Wagons de Particuliers

General Secretary, Via F Zorzi 10, Case Postale 142, 6902 Lugano-Paradiso, Switzerland

Telephone: +41 91 54 52 14, 54 52 15
Telex: 844 370
Telefax: +41 91 54 57 73

Secretary General: Walter Suter

International Union of Railway Medical Services (UIMC)

85 rue de France, 1070 Brussels, Belgium

Telephone: +32 2 525 25

President: Dr Jack Quinn (IR)
Treasurer: D N Nordvik (SNCB)

Organisation for the Collaboration of Railways (OSShD)

Hoza 63/67, Warsaw, Poland

Telephone: +48 22 216154
Cable: Komtrans

Committee Chairman: Dr Rvszard Stawrowski
Secretary: Stefan Vala

CONTINENTS

Arab Union of Railways (UACF)

PO Box 6599, Aleppo, Syria

Telephone: +963 21 220302/3
Cable: Arabsikket Alep
Telex: 331 009 sy

Chairman: Dr Abdalla Haroun El Djazi
Deputy Chairman: Saleh Khaled Ammar
Secretary-General: Eng Mourhaf Sabouni

Latin American Railway Association

Avda Córdoba 883 6° piso, 1054 Buenos Aires, Argentina

Telephone: +54 1 311 9463; 312 5151
Cable: Amerail, Buenos Aires
Telex: 22507 buefa ar

General Secretary: Gen Emiliano A S Flouret
Administrative Secretary: Felipe Muniain
International Transport Department: Alberto Paolini
Accounting Department: Dres Basagña, Matarrese Asociados
General Co-ordinator of ALAF Magazine: Dr Jorge Gutracht
Training and Technical Assistance: Ing Angel Ceci
Economic Adviser: Ing Ignacio Echevarria
Technical Adviser: Ing Justo Baliño
President of the Information Systems: Ing Francisco Gorostiza
Standards Department: Atilio Sanguinetti

Pan American Railway Congress Association (ACPF)
Asociación del Congress Panamericano de Ferrocarriles

Av 9 de Julio 1925, Piso 13, 1332 Buenos Aires, Argentina

Telephone: +54 1 38 4625/8911
Cable: Panriel
Telex: 22507 buefa ar

President: Major General Eng Juan Carlos De Marchi
1st Vice-President: General Senen Casas Regueiro, Member of the Political Bureau & Vice-President Minister of Transport, Cuba
2nd Vice-President: Eng Ozires Silva, Minister of Infrastructure, Energy & Transport Communications of Brazil
General Secretary: Eng Cayetano Marletta Rainieri
Treasurer: Dr Ricardo S Tawil
Special Adviser: Ambassador Victor E Beauge (Director General, International Organisation, Ministry of Foreign Affairs, Argentina)

ASSOCIATIONS AND AGENCIES   423

Union of African Railways (UAR)

Avenue Tombalbaye 869, PO Box 687, Kinshasa, Zaire

Telephone: +243 12 23861
Telex: 21258

President: Adama Diague (Senegal)

Vice Presidents
North Africa: Sudan Railway Corporation
West Africa: Ghana
East Africa: Djibouti-Ethiopia Railways
Central Africa: Cameroon
Southern Africa: Zaire
General Secretariat (staff)
  Secretary-General: Robert G Nkana

Administration & Finance: Canute Peter Shengena
Documentation & Information: Vacant
Translations: Stephen Tettey
Economic Studies & Transport: Girma Woldeyes
Permanent Way, Signalling & Telecommunications: Benoit Nguimbi Moulangou
Technical Studies: Nda Ezoa Joseph

EUROPEAN

Association of European Railway Component Manufacturers (AFEDEF)
Association des Fabricants Européens d'Equipements Ferroviaires

12 rue Bixio, 75007 Paris, France

Telephone: +33 1 4705 3662
Telefax: +33 1 4705 2917

President: A Bodel (France)
Delegate General: R de Planta (Swiss)

Community of European Railways

rue de France 85, B 1070 Brussels, Belgium

Telephone: +32 2 525 30 50
Telefax: +32 2 525 40 45

Chairman: Sir Robert Reid

European Company for the Financing of Railroad Rolling Stock (EUROFIMA)

Rittergasse 20, 4001 Basle, Switzerland

Telephone: +41 61 287 33 40
Telex: 962 999
Telefax: +41 61 23 41 05

General Manager (CEO): Heinz Weber

European Conference of Ministers of Transport (ECMT)

19 rue de Franqueville, 75775 Paris Cedex 16, France

Telephone: +33 1 45 24 82 00
Telex: 611040 cemt paris
Telefax: +33 1 45 24 97 42

Council of Ministers
Chairman: S Andersson, Minister of Transport, Sweden
First Vice-President: C Tuncer, Minister of Transport and Communications, Turkey
Second Vice-President: G Noutsopoulos, Minister of Transport, Greece
Committee of Deputies
Chairman: R Wiberg, Director, Ministry of Communications, Sweden
ECMT Secretariat
Secretary-General: Dr Jan C Terlouw

European Diesel and Electric Locomotive Manufacturers' Association
Constructeurs Européens de Locomotives Thermiques et Electriques (CELTE)

12 rue Bixio, 75007 Paris, France

Telephone: +33 1 4705 36 62
Telefax: +33 1 4705 2917

President: B G Sephton (United Kingdom)
Delegate General: R de Planta (Swiss)

European Freight Timetable Conference

Czechoslovak State Railways, Na příkopě 33, 110 05 Prague, Czechoslovakia

Telephone: +42 2 2122/3029
Cable: Domini Praha CEM/EGK
Telex: 121096

President: Ing Ladislav Štros
Secretary: Ing Pavel Vopálka

European Passenger Train Timetable Conference
Conférence Européenne des Horaires des Trains de Voyageurs (CEH)

c/o Direction Générale des Chemins de Fer Fédéraux Suisses, Hochschulstrasse 6, 3030 Berne, Switzerland

Telephone: +41 31 60 11 11
Telex: 99 11 21

President: H Eisenring, Swiss Federal Railways

European Wagon Pool (Europ Agreement)
Communauté d'Exploitation des Wagons Europ (Convention Europ)

Société Nationale des Chemins de Fer Belges, Frankrijkstraat 85, 1070 Brussels, Belgium

Telephone: +32 2 525 41 30
Telex: 24607 railib b
Telefax: +32 2 525 21 38

Eurotunnel
London
The Channel Tunnel Group Ltd

Victoria Plaza, 111 Buckingham Palace Road, London SW1W 0ST, England

Telephone: +44 71 834 7575
Telex: 915539
Telefax: +44 71 821 5242

Chairman: P A Bénard
Chief Executive: R A Mason
Project Chief Executive: G Neerhout

Paris
France Manche SA

Tour Franklin, 100 Terrasse Boieldieu, Puteaux Cedex 11, 92081 Paris La Défense, France

Telephone: +33 1 47 76 4260
Telefax: +33 1 47 74 5429

Union of European Railway Industries
Union des Industries Ferroviaires Européennes (UNIFE)

12 rue Bixio, 75007 Paris, France

Telephone: +33 1 4705 3662
Telefax: +33 1 4705 2917

President: O J Bronchart (Belgium)
Delegate General: R de Planta (Swiss)

United Nations Economic Commission for Europe

Palais des Nations, 1211 Geneva 10, Switzerland

Telephone: +41 22 734 60 11
Telex: 28 96 96
Telefax: +41 22 734 98 25, 733 98 79

Executive Secretary: G Hinteregger
Deputy Executive Secretary: A Ornatski
Director Transport Division: G Dente

ASSOCIATIONS & AGENCIES

NATIONAL

ARGENTINA

Chamber of Railway Industries
Cámara de Industriales Ferroviarios

Alsina 1607, Buenos Aires

Telephone: +54 1 40 5063 5571 4967

President: Eng E G Nottage
Secretary: J C Bietti

AUSTRALIA

The National Committee on Railway Engineering

11 National Circuit, Barton, ACT 2600

Telephone: +61 62 73 3633
Cable: Enjoaust Canberra
Telex: aa 62758

Chairman: M D O'Rourke, Railways of Australia, Melbourne, Victoria
Members: J C B Adams, Australian National Railways, Adelaide, South Australia
F R Bell, Queensland Railways, Brisbane
B W Hall, State Railway Authority, New South Wales
I Duncan, ACET Perth, Western Australia
I J McElwee, Australian National Railways, Launceston, Tasmania
P E Jenkins, ELRAIL Consultants Pty Ltd, Brisbane, Queensland
D J Ferris, State Transport Authority, Victoria
G D Erdos, State Transport Authority, South Australia
G C Venn-Brown, Railway Project Engineering Pty Ltd, Sydney, New South Wales

Railways of Australia Committee

4th Floor, 85 Queen Street, Melbourne 3000

Telephone: +61 3 608 0811
Telex: 31109 aa
Telefax: +61 3 670 8808

Chairman: R M King
Executive Director: M C G Schrader
Secretary: B P Williams

Rail Track Association of Australia

14-32 Greenoaks Avenue, Cherrybrook, New South Wales

Telephone: +61 2 875 3344
Telex: 37484

President: H N Walker
Secretary: J H Foxton

AUSTRIA

Federation of Private Railways
Fachverband der Schienenbahnen

PO Box 172, Wiedner Hauptstrasse 63, 1045 Vienna

Telephone: +43 1 65 05 3165

Directors: E Gollner
           Dipl Ing I Stern
Manager: Dr V Schlaegelbauer

Federation of Cable Railways
Fachverband der Seilbahnen

PO Box 172, Wiedner Hauptstrasse 63, 1045 Vienna

Telephone: +43 1 65 05 3165

President: Dr Franz Baldauf
Manager: Dr Viktor Wagner

CANADA

National Transportation Agency of Canada (NTA)

Ottawa, Ontario K1A QN9

Telephone: +1 819 997 0677

Chairman: The Honourable Erik Nielsen
Vice Chairman: Micheline Beaudry
Members: Ed Weinberg, Jim Mutch, Ed O'Brien, Nicolle Forgat, Keith Pennier, Craig Dickson, Kenneth Ritter
Executive Director: Keith Thompson, QC
Director General, Dispute Resolution: Amelita Armit
Director General, Market Entry and Analysis: Gavin Currie
Director General, Transportation Subsidies: Mike Parry
Director General, Corporate Management & Regional Operations: Doug Rimmer
General Counsel: Marie-Paule Scott
Secretary: Suzanne Clément

The Railway Association of Canada

1117 Ste Catherine Street West, Suite 721, Montreal, Quebec H3B 1H9

Telephone: +1 514 849 4274
Telefax: +1 514 849 2861

Chairman: R E Lawless
Vice-Chairman: R S Allison
President: R H Ballantyne

Member companies
Algoma Central Railway
Southern Railway of British Columbia
BC Rail Ltd
Burlington Northern Railroad
Burlington Northern (Manitoba) Ltd
Canadian National Railways
CP Rail
CSX Transportation
Norfolk Southern Corporation
Ontario Northland Transportation Commission
Consolidated Rail Corporation (Conrail)
Toronto, Hamilton & Buffalo Railway Co

Associate members
Canada Gulf Terminal Railway Co
Essex Terminal Railway Co
VIA Rail Canada Inc
Napiervelle Junction Railway
Roberval and Saguenay Railway Co
Wisconsin Central Ltd

Canadian Institute of Guided Group Transport

Queens University, Kingston, Ontario K7L 3N6

Telephone: +1 613 545 2810
Telex: 066 3202
Telefax: +1 613 545 3856

Executive Director: W Gregory Wood

Canadian Railway & Transit Manufacturers Association

1 Yonge Street, Suite 1400, Toronto, Ontario M5E 1J9

Telephone: +1 416 363 7261 ext 231/217
Telex: 065424693
Telefax: +1 416 363 3779

President: R B Winsor
Manager: Alex C Dick

Canadian Urban Transit Association

55 York Street, Suite 1101, Toronto, Ontario M5J 1R7

Executive Vice-President: A Cormier

DENMARK

Institution of Railway Signal Engineers
Telfon-og Sikringsteknisk Forening

40 Sølvgade, Copenhagen K

Chairman: U Hass Andersen

FRANCE

Railway Industries Association
Fédération des Industries Ferroviaires (FIF)

12 rue Bixio, 75007 Paris

Telephone: +33 1 4556 1353
Telex: 200 576 fedrail
Telefax: +33 1 4705 2917

President: P Sudreau

GERMANY, FEDERAL REPUBLIC

German Locomotive Industry Association
Verband der Deutschen Lokomotivindustrie

Lyonerstrasse 16, 6000 Frankfurt (Main) 71

Telephone: +49 69 6666 741
Telefax: +49 69 6701 018

President: Dr Gerd Weber
Director: G Morsey-Picard

Railway Rolling Stock Industry Association
Verband der Waggonindustrie eV

Lindenstrasse 30, 6000 Frankfurt (Main)

Telephone: +49 69 72 72 44
Telefax: +49 69 72 72 44

Chairman: Dipl-Ing Peter Koch
Director: Dipl-Volksw Ivo Wolz

Rolled Steel Association Long Products Division/Railway Material
Walzstahl Vereinigung Fachgruppe Oberbau

Breitestrasse 69, 4000 Düsseldorf

Telephone: +49 211 829 314
Telex: 858 18116
Telefax: +49 211 829 231

Secretary: H Müller

Switch and Crossing Manufacturers Association
Fachverband Weichenbau

PO Box 927, Schwerterstrasse 149, 5800 Hagen

Telephone: +49 2331 61070

Director: W Jentzsch

Private Railways Association of German Federal Republic
BDE Bundesverband Deutscher Eisenbahnen, Kraftverkehre und Seilbahnen

Hülchrather Strasse 17, 5000 Cologne 1

Telephone: +49 221 73 0021

Chairman: Dieter Ludwig
Executive Director: M Montada

ITALY

ANIE
Italian Association of Electrotechnical and Electronics Industries

Via Algardi 2, 20148 Milan, Italy

Telephone: +39 2 3264 1
Telex: 321616 anie
Telefax: +39 2 3264 212

College of Italian Railway Engineers
Collegio Ingegneri Ferroviari Italiani

Via G Giolitti 34, 00185 Rome

Telephone: +39 6 462129

President: Dr Ing L Misiti
Secretary: Dr Ing M Perilli

JAPAN

Japan Railway Construction Public Corporation (JRCC)

Sanno Grand Building 2-14-2, Nagata-cho, Chiyoda-ku, Tokyo

Telephone: +81 3 506 1845
Cable: Tetsudokodan-Tokyo
Telefax: +81 3 506 1890

President: Hiroshi Okada
Vice-President: Yasushi Tamahashi

Japan Railway Electrification Association Inc

Toho Building, 1-19-23 Shibuya-ku, Tokyo 150

Telephone: +81 3 449 9471
Telefax: +81 3 449 9472

President: Tadashi Miyoshi
Managing Director: Tsutomu Sakaguchi
Director: Nagao Sakakura

Japan Private Railways Association

Kotsukosha Building, 1-6-4 Marunouchi, Chiyoda-ku, Tokyo

Telephone: +81 3 211 1401

President: S Hirata

Japan Railway Engineers Association

SNK Building, 2-20-7, Misaki-cho, Chiyoda-ku, Tokyo 101

Chairman: Dr-Eng Masao Nagahama
Deputy Chairmen: Ryoichi Mohri, General Manager, Nippon Steel Corporation
Tatsuo Hashikura, Director, Teito Rapid Transit Authority
Executive General Manager: Masahiro Shintaku

Japan Rolling Stock Exporters Association

Tekko Building, 8-2 Marunouchi 1-chome, Chiyoda-ku, Tokyo

Telephone: +81 3 201 3145
Telefax: +81 3 214 4717

President: Z Umeda
Senior Managing Director: T Koizumi

Materials & Information Office: Yaesu 1-chome Bldg, 1-6-2, Yaesu, Chuo-ku, Tokyo

Telephone: +81 3 278 0360

Japan Society of Mechanical Engineers

Sanshin Hokusei Building, 4-9 Yoyogi 2-chome, Shibuya-ku, Tokyo

Secretary: H Haraguchi

UNITED KINGDOM

Crown Agents for Overseas Governments and Administrations

St Nicholas House, St Nicholas Road, Sutton, Surrey SM1 1EL

Telephone: +44 81 643 3311
Cable: Crown, London
Telex: 916205
Telefax: +44 81 643 8232

Senior Crown Agent and Chairman: Sir Peter Graham OBE
Crown Agent and Deputy Chairman: D Probert
Crown Agents: P F Berry
H R J Human
A L Kingshott
Dr A I Lenton
K Taylor
Mrs D L Wedderburn
Executive Committee
Managing Director and Chairman: P F Berry
Director of Technical Services: W Bowyer
Director of Business Development: D V Moule
Director of Procurement: A M Slater
Director, Financial Services: H Dale
Financial Controller: N V C Jackaman
Corporate Secretary: K G White
Head of Transport Branch: J A Wrighton

Association of Consulting Engineers

Alliance House, 12 Caxton Street, Westminster, London SW1H 0QL

Telephone: +44 71 222 6557
Telex: 265871 monref g (ref 83 ice 001)
Telefax: +44 71 222 0750

Chairman: G H Coates
Secretary: Brigadier H C Woodrow
Deputy Secretary: Col J C Peacey

Association of Independent Railways Ltd

85 Balmoral road, Gillingham, Kent ME7 4QG

Telephone: +44 634 52672

Chairman: Ian Allan
Vice-Chairman: A C W Garraway
Secretary: Malcolm Burton

Member companies
Bala Lake Railway
Bluebell Railway Co
Bodmin and Wadebridge Plc
Bo'ness & Kinneil Railway
Bowes Railway
Brecon Mountain Railway
Bure Valley Railway
Colne Valley Railway
Dart Valley Light Railway plc
Dean Forest Railway
East Lancashire Railway
East Somerset Railway
Fairbourne Railway Ltd
Festiniog Railway Co
Foxfield Light Railway
Gloucester Warwickshire Steam Railway plc
Great Central Railway
Gwili Railway
Isle of Man Railways
Isle of Wight Railway
Keighley & Worth Valley Railway
The Kent & East Sussex Railway
Lakeside & Haverthwaite Railway Co Ltd
Leighton Buzzard Narrow Gauge Railway
Llanberis Lake Railway
Llangollen Railway
Market Bosworth Light Railway
Mid Hants Railway
Middleton Railway Trust
Midland Railway Centre
Mull & West Highland Railway
National Railway Museum
Nene Valley Railway
North Norfolk Railway
North Yorkshire Moors Railway
Pleasurerail Ltd
Railway Preservation Society of Ireland
Ravenglass & Eskdale Railway
Romney Hythe & Dymchurch Railway
Severn Valley Railway
Sittingbourne & Kemsley Light Railway
Snowdon Mountain Railway
South Tynedale Railway
Steamtown Railway Museum Ltd
Strathspey Railway Co
Swanage Railway Co
Talyllyn Railway
Welsh Highland Railway
Welshpool & Llanfair Light Railway
West Somerset Railway
West Yorkshire Transport Museum
Yorkshire Dales Railway

Association of Private Railway Wagon Owners

26 Mayfield, Rowledge, Farnham, Surrey GU10 4DZ

Telephone: +44 252 254358

Chairman: J M B Gotch
Secretary: K J Rose
Treasurer: G Pratt

Association of Wagon Builders and Repairers

26 Mayfield, Rowledge, Farnham, Surrey GU10 4DZ

Telephone: +44 252 254358

Chairman: P Page
Vice Chairman: T Head
Secretary: K J Rose

Chartered Institute of Transport

80 Portland Place, London W1N 4DP

Telephone: +44 71 636 9952
Telefax: +44 71 637 0511

President: G T P Conlon
National Chairman, UK: A D Jones
Director General & Secretary: R P Botwood
Director, Professional Activities: L F Aldridge
Director, Education, Training & Membership: A M J Pomeroy
Director, Finance & Administration: J M Feore

Federation of Civil Engineering Contractors

Cowdray House, 6 Portugal Street, London WC2A 2HH

Telephone: +44 71 404 4020
Telefax: +44 71 242 0256

Institution of Civil Engineers

Great George Street, London SW1P 3AA

Telephone: +44 71 222 7722
Telefax: +44 71 222 7500

President: Prof P Stott
Secretary: J C McKenzie

Institution of Diesel and Gas Turbine Engineers

18 London Street, London EC3R 7JR

Telephone: +44 71 481 2393

Secretary: K S Edmanson

ASSOCIATIONS & AGENCIES

Institution of Electrical Engineers

Savoy Place, London WC2R 0BL

Telephone: +44 71 240 1871
Telex: 261176
Telefax: +44 71 240 7735

Secretary: Dr J C Williams

Institution of Mechanical Engineers Railway Division

1 Birdcage Walk, London SW1H 9JJ

Telephone: +44 71 222 7899
Telex: 917944 imeldn g
Telefax: +44 71 222 4557

Chairman: Dr M G Pollard
Manager: A T H Tayler

Institution of Railway Signal Engineers

Telephone: +44 626 888096

Hon General Secretary: R L Weedon, The Cutting, 1 Badlake Close, Dawlish, Devon EX7 9JA

Permanent Way Institution

27 Lea Wood Road, Fleet, Hampshire GU13 8AN

Telephone: +44 252 613643

Hon General Secretary: L J Harris

Railway Industry Association

6 Buckingham Gate, London SW1E 6JP

Telephone: +44 71 834 1426
Telex: 297304
Telefax: +44 71 821 1640

Director: David Gillan
Assistant Director and Training Manager: Steven Kercher

UNITED STATES OF AMERICA

American Association of Railroad Superintendents

18154 Harwood Ave, Homewood, Illinois 60430

Telephone: +1 708 799 4650

President: David K Barnes
Secretary: P A Weissmann

American Public Transit Association (APTA)

1225 Connecticut Avenue NW, Washington DC 20005

Telephone: +1 202 898 4000
Telefax: +1 202 898 4070

Chairman: Daniel T Scannell
Vice Chairman: Alan F Kiepper
Executive Vice President: Jack R Gilstrap
Secretary-Treasurer: Richard J Simonetta

American Railroad Truck Lines Association

422 West Chase, Springfield, Missouri 65803

President: R O Nall (Director Maintenance, Missouri Pacific Truck Line)
Secretary: M Strope

American Railway Car Institute

Governors Office Park V, 19900 Governors Highway, Suite 10, Olympia Fields, Illinois 60461

Telephone: +1 708 747 0511
Telefax: +1 708 747 0793

Chairman: L Clark Wood (Trinity Industries Inc)
President, Secretary and Treasurer: Elwyn T Ahnquist
Vice President: William L Snellgrove (Union Tank Car Company)

American Railway Development Association

233 N Michigan Avenue, Chicago, Illinois 60601

President: Frank L Thompson
Vice Presidents: Robert E Mortensen
G A McArdle
Secretary-Treasurer: E G Tyckoson Jr

American Railway Engineering Association

50 F Street NW, Washington DC 20001

Telephone: +1 202 639 2190

President: D E Turney Jr
Executive Director: L T Cerny

American Short Line Railroad Association

2000 Massachusetts Ave NW, Washington DC 20036

Telephone: +1 202 785 2250

President: William E Loftus
Vice-President and General Counsel: Thomas C Dorsey
Treasurer: Kathleen M Cassidy
Traffic Department
 Vice President: K G Ozburn (Atlanta)
 Vice President: W F Gralewski (Chicago)
 Vice President: M B Reilly
Regional Vice-Presidents
 Crosett, Arkansas: S R Tedder
 San Francisco, California: W J Herndon
 Meridian, Mississippi: M V Dendy
 Westfield, Massachusetts: M P Silver
 Green Bay, Wisconsin: S P Selby

American Society of Mechanical Engineers Rail Transportation Division

Chairman: V T Hawthorne, PE, Programme Director-Engineering Analysis, LTK Engineering Services, 1500 Chestnut Street, Philadelphia, Pennsylvania 19102
Secretary-Treasurer: T E Schofield, 376 Mallard Point, Barrington, Illinois 60010
Manager, Division Affairs: G H Arrasmith, 1228 Camellia Drive, Munster, Indiana 46321. Telephone: +1 219 924 0474

Association of American Railroads

American Railroads Building, 50 F Street NW, Washington DC 20001

Telephone: +1 202 639 2100

Transportation Test Center: PO Box 11130, Pueblo, Colorado 81001
Telephone: +1 303 545 5660

President and Chief Executive Officer: William H Dempsey
Executive Vice-President: Richard E Briggs
Vice President and General Counsel: J Thomas Tidd
General Solicitor: Hollis G Duensing
Vice Presidents
 Information and Public Affairs: Daniel L Lang
 Legislative Department: Joseph L Carter
 Economics and Finance Department: Dr Harvey A Levine
(Railinc Corp): Henry W Meetze

Research and Test Department: George H Way
Operations and Maintenance Department: Harvey Bradley
Secretary and Treasurer: David B Barefoot
Controller: Joseph C Slattery

Association of Railroad Advertising and Marketing

3706 Palmerston Road, Shaker Heights, Ohio 44122-5016

Telephone: +1 216 751 9673

President: Kenneth F Key
Executive Secretary: J D Singer

Association of Railway Communicators

50 F Street NW, 4304 Washington DC 20001

President: Robert B Hoppe
Vice-Presidents: Richard E Bussard
Rebecca A Burcher
Secretary-Treasurer: J Ronald Shumate

Membership: 52 organisations in the USA, Canada
94 individual members.

High Speed Rail Association

206 Valley Court, Suite 800, Pittsburgh, Pennsylvania 15237

Telephone: +1 412 364 9306
Telefax: +1 412 364 6113

Chairman: Paul H Reistrup (President, Monogahela Railway)
Vice-Chairmen: Robert Pattison (Vice President, Parsons-Brinckerhoff)
Pike Powers (Fulbright & Jaworski)
President: Dr Anthony Eastman (Professor, Queen's University
Vice President: Richard I Kilroy (International President, Transportation and Communications Union)
Vice President of Membership: Henry C Schrader (Vice President, URS Consultants)
Secretary/Executive Director: Robert J Casey
Treasurer: Mark R Dysart (Transportation and Communications Union)

Locomotive Maintenance Officers' Association

3144 Brereton Ct, Huntington, West Virginia 25705

Telephone: +1 304 523 7276

President: D H Propp
Secretary: L Koerner

National Mediation Board

1425 K Street NW, Suite 910, Washington DC 20572

Chairman: Joshua M Javits
Members: Patrick J Cleary, Walter C Wallace
Executive Director: Charles R Barnes
General Counsel: Ronald M Etters
Hearing Officers: Roland Watkins, Mary L Johnson

The National Railroad Construction and Maintenance Association Inc

10765 Woodwatch Circle, Eden Prairie, Minnesota 55347

Telephone: +1 612 942 8825, +1 800 544 4672
Telefax: +1 612 942 8947

President: Larry Goorlsen
Executive Vice-President: Daniel D Foth
1st Vice-President: Jon Schaefer
2nd Vice-President: Philip Stout

National Railroad Intermodal Association

4515 Kansas Avenue, Kansas City, Kansas 66106

ASSOCIATIONS & AGENCIES

President: R A Muellner (Assistant Vice-President, International Marketing and Pricing, Burlington Northern Railway)
Secretary: T A Murphy (Director Intermodal Operations, Santa Fe Railway)

National Railway Labor Conference

Suite 500, 1901 L Street NW, Washington DC 20036

Telephone: +1 202 862 7200

Chairman: C I Hopkins, Jr

National Transportation Safety Board

800 Independence Avenue SW, Washington DC 20594

Chairman: James L Kolstad
Acting Vice Chairman: Susan Coughlin
Members: John K Lauber
James E Burnett Jr
Acting General Counsel: Ron Battocchi
Acting Managing Director: Lloyd Miller

Railroad Personnel Association

American Railroads Building, 50 F Street NW, Washington DC 20001

Telephone: +1 202 639 2151

President: Neil D Mann
Chairman: Kenneth A Wood
Secretary: Penny L Prue

Railroad Public Relations Association

50 F Street NW, Washington DC 20001

Telephone: +1 202 639 2552
Telex: +1 202 639 5546

Secretary: Carol B Perkins

Railroad Retirement Board

844 Rush Street, Chicago, Illinois 60611

Telephone: +1 312 751 4500

Chairman: Vacant
Members: J D Crawford
C J Chamberlain
Chief Executive Officer: K P Boehne

Railway Engineering-Maintenance Suppliers Association Inc (REMSA)

6955 W North Avenue, Oak Park, Illinois 60302

President: J Schumaker
Secretary: G A Farris
Executive Secretary: J James Stallmann

Railway Progress Institute

700 N Fairfax Street, Alexandria, Virginia 22314-2098

Telephone: +1 703 836 2332

President: R A Matthews
Chairman: Richard Barney
Vice-Chairman: Robert E Harmon

Railway Supply Association Inc

1150 Wilmette Avenue, Office No 3, Wilmette, Illinois 60091

Telephone: +1 708 251 5476

President: W R Galbraith (The Greenbrier Companies)
Vice President: G S McNally (Thrall Car Mfr Co)
Executive Director: W J Burrows (Railway Supply Association, Inc)

Railway Systems Suppliers, Inc

561 Middlesex Avenue, Metuchen, New Jersey 08840

Telephone: +1 201 494 2910

Chairman and President: Al F O'Rourke
Executive Vice President: Robert P DeMarco
Executive Director, Secretary and Treasurer: W Edward Rowland

Regional Railroads of America

324 Fourth Street NE, Washington DC 20002

Telephone: +1 202 543 0038

Chairman: David Hughes (Bangor & Aroostook RR)
Vice-Chairman: Allan E Kaulbach (Providence & Worcester RR)
Secretary-Treasurer: Bruce Flohr (San Diego & Imperial Valley RR)

Roadmasters and Maintenance of Way Association of America

Cary Building, 18154 Harwood Ave, Homewood, Illinois 60430

Telephone: +1 708 799 4650

President: A K Pottorff
Secretary: P A Weissmann

Consultancy Services

AUSTRALIA
ACET Ltd	430
Colston, Budd, Wardrop & Hunt	434
Elrail Consultants Pty Ltd	438
Fluor Daniel Australia Ltd	439
Gutteridge Haskins & Davey Pty Ltd	440
Hyland Joy & Associates Pty Ltd	443
Kuttner, Collins Group	446
Maunsell Consultants Pty Ltd	447
Queensland Railways Consulting Services	453

BELGIUM
Transurb Consult	458

CANADA
CANAC International Inc	433
Canadian Pacific Consulting Services Ltd	433
Cole, Sherman & Associates Ltd	433
Delcan Corporation	435
International Rail Consultants	443
Reid Crowther	453
Transurb Inc	459

DENMARK
DanRail Consult	434
KAMPSAX International A/S	444

FRANCE
Groupe Design MBD	440
Interinfra	444
SGTE	454
Sodetag-TAI	455
Sofrerail	455
Sofretu	455

GERMANY, FEDERAL REPUBLIC
BVC Berliner Verkehrs-Consulting GmbH	431
De-Consult	435
Hamburg-Consult	441
Light Rail Transit Consultants GmbH	446

HONG KONG
Charles Haswell & Partners (Far East)	442

INDIA
Rail India Technical & Economic Services Ltd (RITES)	453

ITALY
Ansaldo Trasporti SpA	430
Transystem SpA	459

JAPAN
Japan Transportation Consultants Inc	444
Japan Railway Technical Service (JARTS)	444

NEW ZEALAND
Datarail	435

SWEDEN
Swederail Consulting AB	456

SWITZERLAND
Electrowatt Engineering Services Ltd	438

UK
Accent Marketing & Research	462
ACER Consultants Ltd	430
Aston Martin Tickford Ltd	431
W S Atkins & Partners	431
Coopers and Lybrand Deloitte	434
Design Triangle	436
C H Dobbie and Partners	437
Ewbank Preece Consulting Group	439
W A Fairhurst & Partners	439
GEC Alsthom Transportation Projects Ltd	439
Sir Alexander Gibb & Partners	439
Sir William Halcrow & Partners Ltd	441
Charles Haswell & Partners	442
Hawker Siddeley Rail Projects Ltd	442
Kennedy Henderson Limited	445
London Transport International Services Ltd	446
Maunsell Consultancy Services Ltd	447
Merz and McLellan	448
Mott MacDonald Group	450
The MVA Consultancy	451
Peregrine and Partners	452
Planning Research & Systems plc	452
P W Consulting	453
Rendel, Palmer & Tritton Ltd	454
RFS Projects Ltd	454
Roundel Design Group	454
Steer, Davies & Gleave Ltd	456
Transmark	457
Transportation Planning Associates	458
Transport Design Consortium	458
Travers Morgan International Ltd	460
Trevor Crocker & Partners	460

USA
ALK Associates Inc	430
American Transit Corp (ATC)	430
Ammann & Whitney	430
Arinc Research Corporation	431
Michael Baker Jr Inc	431
R L Banks & Associates, Inc	431
Barton-Aschman Associates, Inc	431
BBN Laboratories Inc	431
Bechtel Corporation	432
BJLJ Engineers	432
Blauvelt Engineers PC	432
Booz, Allen & Hamilton Inc	432
CAM International Inc	433
Carr Smith Associates	433
Century Engineering Inc	433
Clough, Harbour & Associates	433
Terence J Collins Associates Inc	434
Comsul Ltd	434
Daniel, Mann, Johnson & Mendenhall	434
De Leuw, Cather & Company	435
DKS Associates	437
Dubin, Dubin and Moutoussamy	437
Thomas K Dyer Inc	437
EG & G Dynatrend Inc	437
Edwards & Kelcey Inc	437
EMJ Engineers Inc	438
Envirodyne Engineers Inc	438
Fleming Corporation	439
Foster Engineering Inc	439
Gannett Fleming	439
Gellman Research Associates Inc	439
Gibbs & Hill Inc	440
Greiner Engineering Inc	440
Delon Hampton & Associates	441
Harbridge House, Inc	442
Harris Miller Miller & Hanson Inc	442
Harza Engineering Co	442
HDR Engineering Inc	443
Hill International Inc	443
Iffland Kavanagh Waterbury PC	443
Ilium Associates, Inc	443
IIT Research Institute	443
Bernard Johnson Incorporated	444
Kaiser Engineers Inc	444
A T Kearney Inc	445
Laramore, Douglass and Popham	446
Lester B Knight & Associates Inc	446
J W Leas & Associates Inc	446
LTK Engineering Services	447
Maguire Group Inc	447
Modjeski & Masters	449
M,orrison-Knudsen Company, Inc	449
Morrison-Knudson Engineers Inc	449
Peter Muller-Munk Associates	451
National City Management Company	452
Parsons Brinckerhoff Centec International Inc	452
Pullman Technology Inc	453
Ralph M Parsons Company	452
Railway Systems Design Inc	453
Real Estate Research Corp	453
Schimpeler Corradino Associates	454
STV Engineers Inc	454
Simpson and Curtin	455
Smith & Egan Associates, Inc	455
Wilbur Smith Associates	461
Sundberg-Ferar Inc	456
Sverdrup Corporation	456
Syscon Corporation	457
TAMS Consultants Inc	457
Temple Barker & Sloane Inc	457
Transit & Tunnel Consultants Inc	457
Transportation and Distribution Associates, Inc	458
Tudor Engineering Co	461
Urbitran Associates	461
URS Company	461
URS Consultants Inc	461
Wallace, Roberts and Todd	461
Harry Weese & Associates	461
William Nicholas Bodouva & Associates PC	461
Wilson, Inrig & Associates	461
ZT	461

CONSULTANCY SERVICES

Acer Consultants Ltd

Acer House, Medawar Road, The Surrey Research Park, Guildford, Surrey GU2 5AR, England

Telephone: +44 483 35999
Telex: 859393 acerg g
Telefax: +44 483 35051

Director: G S Daniel

Associated companies: Halcrow Fox & Associates

Regional offices: Bath, Bristol, Birmingham, Cardiff, Dolgellau, Edinburgh, Isle of Man, Liverpool, London, Maidstone, Plymouth, Stevenage, and Wetherby.

Overseas offices: Australia, Denmark, Eire, France, Hong Kong, Malaysia, India, Indonesia, Japan, Kuwait, Pakistan, Qatar, Saudi Arabia, Singapore, Thailand, Turkey, United Arab Emirates, USA and Yemen.

Capabilities: Project management; preliminary planning and feasibility studies; detailed planning; design, cost estimation and preparation of complete contract documents; contractor selection and construction supervision. Experience in the following fields: urban and inter-urban highways, mainline railways, light rail systems, metros, development and transportation planning.

Projects: Principal rail projects currently in hand or undertaken since 1980 are: Baghdad Metro
The firm is a principal member of the British Metro Consultants Group (a consortium of British consultants) which was retained by the Baghdad Rapid Transit Authority for planning and supervision of design and construction of the Baghdad Metro. The Group's work covers all civil engineering, architecture and electrical and mechanical engineering. Advice is also offered on training programmes and implementation procedures. The first stage comprises two lines totalling 32 km with 38 stations, depots and workshops.
Hong Kong Mass Transit Railway
The firm's work on this system began in 1966 with the Hong Kong Transport Study and continued uninterrupted through the planning and construction stages of the Initial System (Kong Kow and Kwung Tong lines) and the Tsuen Wan extension completed in 1982. In 1982-83 the firm finished the elevated section including station design of the Island Line that connects with the Kong Kow line at Admiralty station. The firm's connection with the MTR continued with the civil, electrical and mechanical engineering design of the road and rail Eastern Harbour crossing, opened in 1989. In association with other consultants, the firm has been undertaking the Airport Rail Link Study in Hong Kong.
Taipei Metro
Acer was the leading firm in British Mass Transit Consultants (BMTC) retained by the Ministry of Communications in Taiwan. BMTC completed a detailed and comprehensive study of the technical economic and financial feasibility of the proposed system and completed the preliminary engineering of the priority line.
Tuen Mun LRT System, Hong Kong
Since 1985 Acer Freeman Fox (Far East) has been working in joint venture with another consulting firm on the design and construction supervision of a light rail transit system to serve the western New Territories. The initial phase scheduled for completion in 1992 includes 22.5 km of double track, 41 stops, three termini, two interchanges, two substations, 10 rectifier stations and a depot.
Hong Kong Tramways
The firm participated in the engineering assessment of modernisation plan options for the Hong Kong Tramways.
Docklands Light Railway, London
In 1984 a study was undertaken to assess the potential and optimum route for the second phase of the Docklands Light Rail System, linking Central London with the former dockland area.
Jubilee Line Extension
The firm has been involved with the system options aspects of this extension to the London Underground from the East London Rail Study to the preparation of the Parliamentary Bill.

ACET
ACET Limited

22-24 Hasler Road, Osborne Park, Western Australia 6017, Australia

Telephone: +61 9 445 3766
Telex: AA 95314
Telefax: +61 9 446 9090

Chairman: Professor D J F Allen-Williams
Managing Director: Dr J R Blair
Directors: Dr D H Steven
Professor A T Morkel
W R Fahey

Capabilities

ACET Limited (Applied Computing & Engineering Technology) is a specialised project engineering, research, development and manufacturing organisation based in Perth Western Australia, with the ability to design, manufacture, test, assemble and support specialised equipment to operate in harsh environments. Expertise and equipment have been developed for simulation; process control; the design of dynamic systems and projects involving high-speed data acquisition, analysis and display.
The research project which led to the establishment of ACET was a study of longitudinal train dynamics on the heavy-haul iron-ore railroads of Mount Newman Mining Company Ltd and Hamersley Iron Pty Ltd in the Pilbara region of Western Australia. Both companies remain major clients, and railway studies for them and for Robe River Iron Associates continue to be a major part of ACET's activities in the area of the application of advanced technology to train management and rail operations and maintenance.
ACET has a current staff of 75 people, of whom about 40 are highly qualified engineers.

Projects

ACET's current operations cover a range of other mining, resources and manufacturing industries, but the primary emphasis remains on railways.

ALK Associates Inc

1000 Herrontown Road, Princeton, New Jersey 08540, USA

Telephone: +1 609 683 0220

Senior Vice President: Mark A Hornung

Capabilities

Transportation strategic planning; rail fleet management; distribution modelling and simulation; intermodal analysis; customised software design; traffic flowgraphics and computer mapping.

Projects

ALK is currently designing and coding a Motive Power Information and Management Support System for Canadian National Railways. This consists of an array of five workstations and 12 video projection screens and will be used to support motive power control. The system tracks trains and power as they move across the railway, aids power supply planning, and alerts the controllers to various important events.
ALK Associates has developed and installed a Locomotive Distribution System for the Burlington Northern and Union Pacific Railroads, USA. This customised software programme assists a power distributor in assigning locomotives to trains in real time, optimising assignment by looking at demands in the next seven-day period.
In a project sponsored jointly by the Association of American Railroads and the Federal Railroad Administration, ALK has developed software to optimally distribute empty containers and vans to reloading points. The software will be used on a daily basis to guide the decisions of equipment distributors.
ALK is providing support and enhancements for the Service Planning Model, a railroad simulation and costing model for evaluating operating plans and setting origin-to-destination service standards. Currently in use in the USA at Grand Trunk Western, Burlington Northern, CSX, Norfolk Southern and ATSF railroads, and Union Pacific Railroads, and at Canadian National Railways, the model has helped these carriers demonstrate significant financial savings in performance of site-specific unit-based costing, evaluation of system-wide regional operating plans, and proposed line and yard closings.
ALK's Princeton Transportation Network Model/Graphics Information System (PTNM/GIS) is a network, data, and geographic mapping programme leased to seven large USA railroads and government agencies and accessible via timesharing by three others. The PTNM/GIS is used by these clients for a variety of operations, marketing, and strategic applications.

American Transit Corporation
A subsidiary of Chromalloy American Corporation

120 South Central Ave, St Louis, Missouri 63105, USA

Telephone: +1 314 726 9200

Vice-President: Paul J Ballard

Capabilities

Professional transit-management; maintenance/operations analysis; consulting and planning services. ATC currently manages 22 transit systems at 19 locations in 15 US states.

Ammann & Whitney

96 Morton Street, New York, New York 10014, USA

Telephone: +1 212 524 7200
Telex: 127978

Partners: Edward Cohen
Edward Laing
Harold Birnbaum
Samuel Weissman
Marketing Director: Douglas Hebard

Capabilities

Engineering of new rail facilities; inspection and rehabilitation of existing rail facilities. Design of bridges, stations and civil engineering.

Projects

Reconstruction of trackage, one swing bridge, eleven fixed bridges and design of new Providence, Rhode Island station for the Northeast Corridor improvement Project (three projects, $50 million); design of Lindbergh and Avondale multi-modal, at-grade mass transit stations, including control buildings and parking lots, for MARTA, Atlanta, Georgia ($32 million); design of Lechmere elevated mass transit station for MBTA, Boston, Massachusetts ($40 million); design of two stations and 5.24 km of tunnel for SCRTD (Southern California Rapid Transit District), Los Angeles, California ($180 million); relocation of three miles of the Frankford Elevated Railroad, including new trackwork, signals, bridges, a 1400-ft tunnel and two new stations, for SEPTA, Philadelphia, Pennsylvania ($50 million); study to determine requirements to rehabilitate all rail systems in the United States for the US Department of Transportation; rehabilitation and modernisation of two historic underground transit stations for SEPTA, Philadelphia, Pennsylvania ($13 million).

Ansaldo Trasporti
Ansaldo Trasporti SpA (Ansaldo Group)

Head Office: 425 Via Argine, 80147 Naples, Italy

Telephone: +39 81 7810111
Telex: 710131 ans na
Telefax: +39 81 7810698-699

Other offices: Viale Sarca, 20126 Milan

Telephone: +39 2 64451
Telex: 331279
Telefax: +39 2 6438032

25 Corso Perrone, 16161 Genoa

Telephone: +39 10 65511
Telex: 271274
Telefax: +39 10 495044

Chairman: Giovanni Nobile
Vice President and Managing Director. Emilio Maraini
General Director: Francesco Granito
General Co-Director: Albert G Rosania
Director, R & D and Commercial: Carlo Rizzi
Technical Director: Salvatore Bianconi

CONSULTANCY SERVICES 431

Capabilities
Main contractors, project managers and system engineers for long-distance railways, suburban, metro and mass transit systems.

Projects
Principal projects in the last two years have been, in Italy, the light rail system for Genoa and Naples (where the company is involved in the municipality's traffic project); the metro system for Naples, the Sardinian ac electrification system for Italian State Railways, and a comprehensive study of the technical, economic and financial feasibility of a mass transit system in the Bologna province. For Colombian Railways Ansaldo Trasporti has studied the Valle Cauca transport system; and in Ethiopia a feasibility study of a transportation system for Addis Ababa has been executed.

Arinc Research Corporation

2551 Riva Road, Annapolis, Maryland 21401, USA

Telephone: +1 301 266 4717

Manager, Surface Transportation and Distribution Group: Gary Pruitt

Capabilities
Advanced train control systems; communications systems; information systems; maintenance engineering/management; new technology applications; system integration; and training.

Aston Martin Tickford Ltd

Tickford House, 8 Tanners Drive, Blakelands North, Milton Keynes MK14 5BH, England

Telephone: +44 908 614688
Telex: 826983

Managing Director: J Thurston
Engineering Director: D S Burnicle

Capabilities
Interior design of rail passenger vehicles.

W S Atkins Consultants Limited

Woodcote Grove, Ashley Road, Epsom, Surrey KT18 5BW, England

Telephone: +44 372 726140
Telex: 266701
Telefax: +44 372 740055

Director: P A Brown
Director: R D Jarvis
Head of Transportation Engineering Division: R C French
Head of Infrastructure Planning Division: D S James
Technical Directors: J S Dawswell
  P J Williams
  N M Aspinall
  R H Cuthbert

Capabilities
Atkins is a multi-discipline consultancy with over 2000 staff and can provide comprehensive consultancy services to the railway industry. Capabilities include feasibility studies, traffic forecasts, cost estimates, detailed design of trackwork, rolling stock and depots, civil and structural engineering, architectural design, signalling/communications and systems engineering and supervision of construction. Studies devoted to the socio-economic aspects of a project, route assessment, environmental impact analysis – including noise and vibration, rationalisation of services, operating methods, future strategy, inventories of facilities and asset valuations are also undertaken.

Projects
Current major railway projects include:
Manchester Metrolink: design on new light rail network for GMA group, including city centre street-running and re-use of British Rail track.
Hammersmith Depot: study and preparation of schemes to improve depot for London Underground Ltd.
Cambridge, England: LRT feasibility study.
Channel Tunnel as *Maître d'oeuvre*, in a joint venture with SETEC: responsible for monitoring the activities of the design and construction contractors for the 50 km-long triple-bore tunnel. Duties include approval of programming and technical design, monitoring of construction progress, supervision of quality assurance activities and certification of payment;
Docklands Light Railway, London: design of upgrading the system to take double- and triple-unit trains following the successful start of operation in 1987;
British Rail Midland main line: study of options for upgrading and improving the line from London to Nottingham and Sheffield (240 km);
Iraq: W S Atkins is a major contributor to the British Metro Consultants Group for the Baghdad Metro.
Other current projects include congestion studies of underground stations, accident assessment, evaluation of operational efficiency, system upgrading and investment analysis, funding studies, railway industry marketing studies and design and implementation of a quality assurance system for depots.

Michael Baker Jr Inc

4301 Dutch Ridge Rd, Beaver, Pennsylvania 15009, USA

Telephone: +1 412 495 7711

420 Rouser Road, Coraopolis, Pennsylvania 15108, USA

Telephone: +1 712 269 4200

Principals: George D Ehringer, Vice President, Coraopolis office
Chuck Russell, Manager, Beaver office

Capabilities
Rail transit planning and design.

Projects
Section III of Southwest Transit Project, Chicago, Illinois.
Maintenance shop rehabilitation, Chicago South Shore and South Bend Railroad, Michigan City, Indiana.
Randolph Street commuter station, Illinois Central Gulf Railroad, Chicago, Illinois
METRA/CNW trainshed rehabilitation, Chicago, Illinois
Section EHB, Northeast Corridor Improvement Project.
Terminal bulk storage facility, Chessie System, Pittsburgh, Pennsylvania.

R L Banks & Associates Inc

900 17th Street NW, Washington DC 20006, USA

Telephone: +1 202 296 6700

President: Robert L Banks

Capabilities
Economic analysis, cost ascertainment, planning and policy development, concept engineering and railway engineering.

Projects
Recent and current projects include:
Examining the feasibility of rail commuter service (100 km) installation on the Soo Line Railroad between Chicago and northwest suburbs;
Examining the feasibility of establishing rail commuter service between Seattle and Tacoma, Washington (80 km) on the Burlington Northern Railroad;
For the Northern Virginia Transportation Commission, providing professional economic and engineering services for installation of rail commuter service (200 km) between Washington, DC, and suburban Northern Virginia over four railways;
Advising the US Department of Justice as to the viability of proposed divestitures to accompany the sale of Consolidated Rail Corporation to Norfolk Southern Corporation;
For the Federal Railroad Administration, investigating a number of railroads to determine financial viability with regard to government rehabilitation loans;
For several banks and other investment concerns, performing due diligence and investment examinations for a number of railroads existing or to be acquired;
Assisting the Mass Transit Administration of Maryland with various aspects of establishing a 50 km light rail system to serve Baltimore and its suburbs;
Assisting Japan Coal Development Company to assess economic characteristics of American railroads;
Providing advisory services to North American railway and transit industries of Hyundai Corporation;
On behalf of Halifax-Dartmouth Port Development Commission, analysing economics of rail container movement between Halifax and inland ports;
Analysing socio-economic aspects of proposed high-speed ground transportation between Las Vegas and Los Angeles;
Developing operating plans, railcar specifications, cost-optimisation computer software and assisting Intermountain Power Agency in negotiating contracts with railroads for unit train movements of 4 m per year.

Barton-Aschman Associates, Inc

820 Davis Street, Evanston, Illinois 60201, USA

Telephone: +1 708 491 1000; +1 202 775 6069
Telex: 270258 EXPRSTLX CGO
Telefax: +1 708 475 6053; +1 202 775 6080

Senior Vice-President: Michael A Powills, Jr
Director of International Marketing: H T Scott Gibbons
Director, Transit Operations Consulting: Thomas N Black

Projects
Alternatives analysis and draft environmental impact statement for a new rapid transit line in Miami; light rail alternatives analyses in Minneapolis and St Louis; general planning and demand analysis for Wilshire Subway line in Los Angeles; statewide high-speed rail feasibility study for Florida Department of Transportation; patronage estimate for Los Angeles-Las Vegas high-speed rail facility; rapid transit planning for Seoul, Republic of Korea; rapid rail access study, suburban Washington DC; commuter rail access study, Tri-County region, South Florida; multi-modal transit study, suburban Atlanta.

BBN Laboratories Inc

125 Cambridge Park Drive, Cambridge, Massachusetts 02140 USA

Telephone: +1 617 499 8000
Telex: 921470

Senior Environmental Consultant: R M Letty

Capabilities
Noise and vibration engineering design for new systems; noise and vibration control for existing facilities; environmental impact assessments.

Projects
Proposed Florida high speed rail system (technical advisor, noise and vibration); MBTA Southwest Corridor Project (transit train noise and vibration study); MBTA South Station Project (air-quality commuter modelling and physical modelling study).

BVC
Berliner Verkehrs-Consulting GmbH
Subsidiary of BC Berlin-Consult GmbH

Ernst-Reuter-Platz 10, PO Box 12 58 47, 1000 Berlin 10, Federal Republic of Germany

Telephone: +49 30 34 001 387/8
Telex: 181 284

Managing Director: Rainer Lehmitz
Key consultants: Dipl-Ing Goetz Klingbeil
  Stefan Dunskus
  Dipl-Ing Hasko Theis

Capabilities
BVC-Berlin traffic and transport consultants is a subsidiary of BC Berlin-Consult GmbH and has concluded an exclusive contract of co-operation with Berlin Transport Corporation (BVG), which operates about 1500 buses, 230 suburban S-Bahn and 1000 U-Bahn cars carrying 2.5 million passengers a day. The U-Bahn network covers 105 km, the S-Bahn 77 km and the bus network more than 1000 km. The firm's activities cover feasibility studies, traffic and transportation engineering, architecture, communications, electrical and mechanical engineering, management and financial studies, network design, operational planning and training. BVC-Berlin can call on the expertise of about 270 engineers, economists and administration staff of BVG.

CONSULTANCY SERVICES

Projects

Transportation studies: BVC performs transportation studies, regionally as well as nation-wide, covering transport survey, analysis and forecast of traffic demand, network design, and economic evaluation. Recently studies have been conducted in Trinidad and Tobago and Gambia (nation-wide), in Kingston, Jamaica, in Conakry, Guinea and in Mendoza, Argentina.

Integration and intermodalism were the topics of a study initiated by the revitalisation of the West Berlin suburban S-Bahn system. Based on a traffic survey, the study aims at restructuring the bus network in order to feed into the S-Bahn.

BVC is participating in the preparation of a long-term development plan for Berliner Verkehrs-Betriebe (BVG) (Berlin Transport Corporation), covering network development, tariff system and marketing strategies.

Metro systems: BVC participated in feasibility studies for metro systems planned in Rio de Janeiro (Brazil), Lima (Peru), Lisbon (Portugal) and Baghdad (Iraq). BVC activities covered: traffic analysis and forecast, recommendations for an integrated transportation system, determination of design criteria and route location; recommendations for Rapid Transit System operation; design of the energy supply system (high and low tension), signalling and control system (CTC, ATC, ATO) and the telecommunication and information system; planning of the feeder bus system, recommendations on bus operation and design of bus workshop facilities; cost estimates and proposals for implementation programmes; proposals for organisation, tariffs and training programmes.

BVC is participating in the detailed design of the first stage of the Baghdad metro, which covers the first section of about 5 km tunnel with seven stations, a depot and the main workshop, and planned Madrid Metro's main workshop.

BVC participated in the development of a new S-Bahn car featuring the latest developments in car-construction, electrical equipment, etc.

For light rail systems in West Germany BVC experts carry out acceptance tests according to BOStrab (West German statutory regulations on construction and operation of rapid transit systems) on signalling systems and safety installations. Such tests have been performed for the systems in Essen, Mülheim, Bochum and Gelsenkirchen.

In technical assistance and training, projects normally cover the preparation and implementation of training programmes in technical, operational, economic and managerial aspects. Such projects have been performed with Public Transport Service Corporation (PTSC) Trinidad and Tobago, National Transport Corporation (NTC) Zambia, and Traffic Police San José, Costa Rica. Analyses of public bus companies in this respect and programme preparation have been performed for various public transport undertakings in African countries, eg in Ghana, Sierra Leone, The Gambia, Zaire, Nigeria.

On behalf of the Federal Ministry of Research and Technology (BMFT), BVC manages research projects in the field of public transport. These include:

Installation of an automatic train control system, SELTRAC, on the West Berlin U-Bahn.

Specification and documentation of acceptance procedures of the ATO/ATC system for the State Supervisory Authority.

Feasibility study and detailed study on the installation of an Automated Guideway Transit (AGT) system in West Berlin.

Expertise on safety aspects, specification of the operational concept and preparation of a concept to deal with technical and operational disturbances for the Berlin M-Bahn (maglev AGT) system.

Operational test of the use of alcoholic fuels in public bus transport.

Development of a Hydraulic Hybrid Propulsion Bus featuring energy recovery.

Construction management projects on a turnkey base have been conducted for the introduction of storage facilities for oil and tyres for BVG, facilities for handling and shipping of 1.3 million tons of rubbish per year in the Berlin-Spandau harbour and a central electricity workshop for BVG. BVC was further commissioned with the rehabilitation and extension of the depot covering maintenance and repair of the S-Bahn rolling stock. Works cover planning, design, supervision of construction and commissioning of the entire complex.

Bechtel Corporation

50 Beale Street, San Francisco, California 94105, USA

Telephone: +1 415 768 4476
Cable: Wateka- SF, Ca
Telex (international): 184907 bechtel sfa (domestic): 34783
Telefax: +1 415 768 0952

Associated companies
Bechtel Power Corporation (same address)
Bechtel Inc
Bechtel National Inc

Capabilities

Bechtel has over 90 years of experience in all aspects of rail and transit projects. From its headquarters in San Francisco, California and regional offices in 70 countries worldwide, Bechtel offers a broad spectrum of services including feasibility and environmental studies, architectural/engineering design, project management, engineering management, construction management, start-up and operations, and financial planning in addition to engineering, procurement, and construction.

Bechtel Civil Company, the entity in the Bechtel group of companies responsible for transportation projects, is staffed by over 2000 specialists, of whom 1000 are familiar with technical transportation issues and have recent experience in railroads, rapid transit, and people-mover systems.

Bechtel's transportation experience includes 13 modern urban transit systems and more than 2200 miles of railroads. The company has been involved in virtually every new transit project in the US (Washington Metro; Boston rapid transit; San Diego light rail; Banfield light rail; Atlanta MARTA; San Francisco BART; Baltimore Rapid Transit; and the Los Angeles Metro) as well as in key international transit projects, such as the Caracas Metro, the São Paulo Metro, and Taipei Rapid Transit.

BJLJ Engineers
A Minority Business Enterprise

1225 Franklin Avenue, Garden City, New York 11530, USA

Telephone: +1 516 741 2222, +1 212 772 0270

President: Andrew C P Wong
Vice-Presidents: Benjamin B Tue
Joseph R Jenal

Capabilities
Professional services in mechanical, electrical and structural engineering and architecture.

Projects
Since 1982 BJLJ has designed renovations for 100 buildings, including subway stations, bus depots, movable bridges and public buildings, under contracts aggregating US$75 million in value.

Blauvelt Engineers PC

1 Park Ave, New York, New York 10016, USA

Telephone: +1 212 481 1600

Executive Vice President: Louis C Ripa

Capabilities
Rail transit facilities design; construction and operating inspection.

Projects
Vienna Line ($60 million) for Washington Metropolitan Area Transit Authority (WMATA).

Booz, Allen & Hamilton Inc
Transportation Consulting Division

USA
4330 East West Highway, Suite 8 South, Bethesda, Maryland 20824
Telephone: +1 301 907 4020
Telefax: +1 301 907 4333

1700 Market Street, Philadelphia, Pennsylvania 19103
Telephone: +1 215 496 6800
Telefax: +1 215 496 6801

523 West Sixth Street, Los Angeles, California 90014
Telephone: +1 213 620 1900

Senior Vice President, Managing Officer: John F Wing

United Kingdom
100 Piccadilly, Mayfair, London W1V 9HA
Telephone: +44 71 493 9595
Telefax: +44 71 629 3560

Vice President: William R Steinmetz

Capabilities

Booz, Allen & Hamilton has conducted numerous assignments for a diverse group of passenger and freight railways spanning a broad range of functional areas and issues. Clients have retained Booz, Allen for assistance in: strategic planning; operations and productivity improvement; vehicle engineering studies; and reliability, maintainability and safety systems.

Projects

Strategy planning. For several US railroads, Booz, Allen has carried out strategy studies, using various data bases and analytical tools developed by Booz, Allen including the Freight Flow Data Base and Shipper Cost Model (to evaluate the potential to expand intermodal revenues), analyses of carload diversions (to predict the traffic resulting from various rail industry mergers, acquisition scenarios, or various regulations), and the Rail Network Simulation Model and detailed revenue/cost analysis (to predict the expected financial impact of various restructuring options).

For the New Zealand Railways, Booz, Allen provided a comprehensive operations review, including an assessment of various alternative operating strategies utilising Booz, Allen's Rail Network Simulation Model and detailed revenue cost analysis process.

Operations and productivity improvement. For the US Federal Railroad Administration, Booz, Allen carried out an analysis of railroad terminal productivity in major terminals on four US railroads, to assist in improving their productivity.

Booz, Allen assisted Conrail in conducting a productivity improvement and cost reduction programme in 20 large rail terminal areas. The study scope covered most aspects of terminal operations, including rationalisation of terminal management control systems and clerical productivity improvements.

For London Transport, Booz, Allen recently completed a management study of administrative functions and is currently assisting preparation of a productivity programme for engineering activities.

For a railway in Brazil, Booz, Allen conducted a study of yard operations. Crew productivity was analysed and work plans were developed to improve productivity.

Vehicle engineering studies. For the Greater Cleveland Regional Transit Authority, Booz, Allen is providing technical assistance with the procurement of 60 new stainless steel heavy rail cars. The three-year project includes such technical activities as design review and inspection, management support in subcontractor monitoring and document control.

Booz, Allen has been retained by San Francisco MUNI to manage its Equipment Maintenance Division's equipment engineering section. The work includes analysis and evaluation of rolling stock, development of methods to improve vehicle performance, evaluation of new products, formulation of procurement specifications and evaluation testing of new and prototype equipment.

Reliability, maintainability and safety systems. Booz, Allen is providing the Southern California Rapid Transit District's 18-mile Metro Rail Project with system management and analysis. Booz, Allen's main task is to assist in maintaining effective management and control of the project. Responsibilities involve a number of technical areas, system simulation modelling, safety planning, RAMD programmes, up-dated operating planning, design criteria, life-cycle costs and fare collection system design.

For the new Baltimore Rapid Transit System, Booz, Allen developed management plans in the areas of safety, system assurance and document control.

Modelling capabilities. Booz, Allen has conducted alternative analyses using advanced modelling and simulation techniques. Booz, Allen utilised its SPORT II (Sketch Planning of Rapid Transit) programme to evaluate rail alternatives in California and Pennsylvania. In another assignment, demand estimation for various commuter rail lines serving the New York Metropolitan

Area were developed to establish a prioritised programme of improvements.

Booz, Allen's rail network models have supported the strategic analysis of some of the world's largest freight and passenger railways. Booz, Allen's financial model predicts change in ridership and revenue based on the application of an arc elasticity measure. Route planning models permit the user to vary headways, vehicle types, load factors and other operating parameters and assess financial and service implications. Booz, Allen's cost allocation models allocate. systemwide cost to the route level. Other costing tools Booz, Allen has developed include a labour cost model used to estimate the impact of change in any number of contract terms relative to driver cost components, and a marginal costing model which measures the cost effect of a change in service.

CAM International Inc

215 Philadelphia Street, PO Box 227, Hanover, Pennsylvania 17331, USA

Telephone: +1 717 637 5988
Cable: CAM
Telex: 840-470 cam hnvr
Telefax: +1 717 637 9329

Capabilities
Planning and equipping of railway electric shops, including methods development in traction motor and generator-repair and maintenance, equipment specification, machine commissioning and operator training.

Projects
The company has active projects with British Rail, Turkish Railways, Indian Railways, Long Island Rail Road, Pakistan, Bangladesh, Tazara, Egyptian, Indonesian, Chinese and Saudi Arabian Railways, Zambia Railways, Algerian Railways and Morocco Railways.

CAM supplies specialised dc electric motor shop equipment, helps upgrade shops, and provides training in current methods.

CANAC International Inc
Subsidiary of Canadian National Railways

PO Box 8100, Montreal, Quebec H3C 3N4, Canada

Telephone: +1 514 877 4816/3500
Cable: Condiv, Montreal
Telex: 055 60753
Telefax: +1 514 399 8298

President and Chief Executive Officer: M L De Pellegrin
Vice President and General Manager (with responsibility for international services): J L Marchard
Vice President, North American Services: J P Vilagos
Vice President, Sales (railway equipment and spare parts): J Garrish

Capabilities
Provides comprehensive management (administration, planning, information systems, costing, project control), engineering, procurement, training and other consulting services in relation to the design, construction, operation, direct management and maintenance of new or existing surface transport facilities including railway, water and intermodal transport networks as well as telecommunications. Specialises in direct or consultative management of any aspect of existing railway operations or design and construction of new rail lines (including signalling and telecommunications) and railway facilities. Recently added CANAC services include provision of spares for Canadian-manufactured rail equipment; and coastal and inland container terminal design and construction supervision. Since 1971 CANAC has undertaken over 300 projects in some 60 countries on every continent.

Projects
One of CANAC's early contracts in Africa is still in progress. In Guinea CANAC is providing expertise for Halco (Mining) Inc, Compagnie des Bauxites de Guinée and l'Office d'Aménagement de Boké in all areas of management and operations on the Chemin de Fer de Boké.

Elsewhere in Africa, the Nigerian Railway Corporation has contracted CANAC for technical assistance in locomotive rehabilitation, while in Mali modernisation of the railway's administrative procedures, management and rolling stock is under study.

In Asia, a CANAC team is implementing Canadian National's traffic reporting and control system (TRACS) on the Indian Railways. This consultancy work commenced in New Delhi in November 1985.

In Latin America and the Caribbean, CANAC is active in Brazil, Nicaragua, Cuba and Jamaica. In Brazil a CANAC specialist is designing and locating the new Acailandia-Brasilia Railroad; and a four-man team is implementing a management information system on the national railways of Brazil.

Railway equipment is being sold to Nicaragua and Cuba, while in Jamaica technical assistance is being given for the establishment of an economical and efficient railway operation.

Canadian Pacific Consulting Services Ltd
Subsidiary of Canadian Pacific Ltd

740 Notre Dame Street West, Suite 760, Montreal, Quebec H3C 3X6, Canada

Telephone: +1 514 876 1900
Telex: 055-60147
Telefax: +1 514 875 1023

Branch offices:
16-00 Route 208, Fair Lawn, New Jersey 07410, USA
Telephone: +1 201 7947224
Suite 317, 205 9th Avenue SE, Calgary, Alberta, Canada T2G 0R4
Telephone: +1 403 234 0700
Telefax: +1 403 265 0886

President and Chief Executive Officer: G T Fisher
Vice Presidents: H Bedikian
D H Page
J D Spielman
P L Eggleton
Assistant Vice Presidents: N Gurd
P Eggleton
Assistant Vice President and Treasurer: A Kostanuick

Capabilities
Canadian Pacific Consulting Services Ltd (CPCS), the international and domestic consulting arm of the Canadian Pacific group, is a broadly-based transportation management, engineering and economic consulting organisation. Founded in 1969, CPCS provides technical and advisory services to governments and the private sector in the planning, engineering, operating, marketing and maintenance of transportation and telecommunications systems. Since its inception, CPCS has undertaken a variety of assignments in 64 countries throughout the world.

Representative projects in 1989-90
Algeria: Study of the eastern mining line to decide whether to upgrade existing 3000 dc line, to convert it to 25 kV ac or to abandon electric operation and use diesels.
Bangladesh: Implementation of the preventive maintenance system and associated inventory management.
Brazil: To carry out the pre-engineering and obtain financing for a 250 km privately-owned railway in the State of Parana.
Preliminary planning and feasibility studies of a privately owned railway, Ferronorte, to move agricultural products from the state of Mato Grosso to the port of Santos near Sao Paulo.
Canada: Feasibility study and implementation plan for a private tour train operator for a transcontinental luxury train service.
Congo: To prepare costing studies and rate-setting methods and to provide training for ATC railways and marine operations.
Malaysia: Implementation of a microcomputer-based railway costing system for the establishment of tariffs.
Sudan: Technical assistance to SRC in all railway departments involving 30 consultants working 63 manyears. Integral component of Railway Emergency Recovery Program.
Tanzania: Preparation of a 10-year development programme for TRC covering all major activities, ie railways, lake and road transport and hotels.
USA: Design and turnkey installation of an automatic vehicle identification system for the Green Line of the Massachusetts Bay Transport Authority.

Carr Smith Associates
A Schimpeler-Corradino Associates Company

4055 NW 97th Avenue, Suite 200, Miami, Florida 33178, USA

Telephone: +1 305 594 0735
Telefax: +1 305 594 0755

Chairman: Joseph C Corradino
President: Brian J Mirson
Secretary/Treasurer: Charles C Schimpeler

Capability
Carr Smith Associates has the capabilities for environmental studies, roadway design, structural design, traffic engineering, surveying/mapping, transportation planning and construction management. It has provided civil, structural and traffic engineering, environmental studies, surveying, GIS and construction inspection services to a wide variety of roadway, transit and subdivision projects in south Florida and other areas of the USA. It has also provided complete architectural design services to numerous clients within the state of Florida, including structural, electrical and mechanical support services.

Projects
Recent and current work includes the 120th Street/turnpike interchange environmental study and final design services, Dade County, Florida ($14 million); East 10th Avenue Corridor Improvement master plan, final design and construction management services, Hialeah, Florida ($9 million); Brandon/Chaffee road Toll Facility main line barrier, ramp plazas and administration building design, Jacksonville, Florida ($4 million); bridge design and inspection services for 30 structures in various subdivisions, Charlotte and St Lucie Counties, Florida ($2 million); Miami Metrorail structural engineering, environmental studies and construction support service, Dade County, Florida ($1.1 billion).

Century Engineering Inc

32 West Road, Towson, Maryland 21204, USA

Telephone: +1 301 823 8070

Vice-President: Robert G James

Projects
Baltimore North Corridor Transportation alternative study.
Baltimore Busway.
Baltimore Mass Transit Systems: Section C.

Clough, Harbour & Associates

III Winner's Circle, Albany, New York 12205, USA

Telephone: +1 518 453 4500

Partner: William A Harbour

Capabilities
Light and heavy rail rapid transit design and operation; automatic fare systems; complete project management.

Cole, Sherman & Associates Limited

2025 Sheppard Avenue, East Willowdale, Ontario M2J 1W3, Canada

Telephone: +1 416 491 4503
Cable: CSAInc, Tor
Telex: 06 966647
Telefax: +1 416 491 0137

President: R J Cole
Vice-Presidents: T J Sherman
D E C Wicks

Capabilities
Cole, Sherman & Associates Ltd, was founded in 1954 and is a Canadian company wholly-owned and operated by its principals and partners. With its head offices in Toronto, the company has been providing engineering services to railway clients including Canadian Pacific Ltd, Canadian National Railways, VIA Rail, GO Transit, and Ontario Northland Railway. The company also has offices in the US and in 1988 was

providing services to authorities in three states, and to the Burlington Northern Railroad. Assignments have included track layout and geometric improvements to accommodate high-speed inter-city travel, the development of signalling systems, the design of various types of grade separations and the redevelopment of complex rail corridors. Other completed projects include diesel locomotive repair shops; light and heavy freight car repair facilities; component rebuild shops; passenger coach shops and high-speed and standard servicing facilities. These projects have been undertaken both as separate entities within operating yards and as components of an overall assignment for a total yard, including inspection, servicing and maintenance buildings, together with feed, release and storage track and the associated operational studies.

Cole, Sherman has specialist staff in planning and research, providing services on such subjects as policy analysis, feasibility planning, corporate planning, economic analysis, technology analysis and management systems development.

Projects
Technical co-ordination of VIA Rail's nation-wide $300 million servicing and maintenance programme.
Complete engineering and architectural design and construction management of the $100 million Toronto Maintenance Centre for VIA Rail.
System-wide study of maintenance-of-way operations for CP Rail. Scope of work includes review of systems, procedures and physical facilities and requires future recommendations in these areas.
Complete engineering and architectural design of $28 million maintenance-of-way equipment maintenance and operations centre for CP Rail.
The Technology Assessment component of a study for Transport Canada of the rail transportation of dangerous goods through the Metropolitan Toronto area.
A study on behalf of Illinois Department of Transportation to determine the feasibility for the development of a passenger rail corridor between Chicago and Milwaukee. The study includes market research, route comparison and the analysis of available technology options.
Development and implementation of a track management system for Burlington Northern Railroad to assist the railroad in making capital and maintenance investment decisions based on track quality as measured by track geometry cars.
Railroad performance and capacity review for Exxon and Carbocal in Colombia, South America. Development of the plan for the rehabilitation of the Colombian National Railways. Assistance to Canadian Pacific Railway in developing its Track Management Advisory System (TMAS), including the development of a set of rail/wear and defect prediction relationships based on LIGHTSLICE and defect analyses car outputs.

Terence J Collins Associates, Inc

Woodfield Lake Office Court, 953 North Plum Grove Road, Suite B, Schaumburg, Illinois 60173-4704, USA

Telephone: +1 312 843 7300

President: Terry Collins

Projects
Project management of a transit radio system upgrade project for the Municipality of Metropolitan Seattle (Metro). This system is to meet Metro's communication needs through 1990, including a 40 per cent expansion of the active vehicle fleet along with a projected 50 per cent increase in services offered. The system must also ensure reliable communications throughout Metro's service area, including such rugged terrain as through the Snoqualmie Pass, into the Auburn Valley and across to neighbouring Vashon Island. In addition, the Municipality has selected full, system-wide automatic vehicle monitoring (AVM), integration with Metro's existing data collection systems and novel control arrangements for system operation. Involvement included establishment of a 'Prime Data Base' detailing the existing system and future requirements, leading to performance specification development. It now comprises reviews of the vendors' bid proposals. Five vendors' bid proposals were evaluated, with recommendations provided, which resulted in contract award; system design and premanufacturing meetings with the contractor have been held; and control centre design has been completed. Future activities include equipment and system installation monitoring, computer software reviews, acceptance testing, development of training programmes, and recommendations on formal acceptance. Contract value: $7 million.

For the Municipality of Metropolitan Seattle (Metro), system design, specification preparation, bid reviews and complete project management for the radio communications system for the Downtown Seattle Transit Project (DSTP), a 1.6-mile tunnel under the central business district of Seattle. This system, comprising multiple below-ground transmitter and receiver sites and operating over a radiating lossy line antenna, will be completely compatible with the transit radio upgrade project system. Control of the below-ground equipment will be via fibre-optic cable and a dedicated T1 carrier system. Contract value: $2 million.

For the Municipality of Metropolitan Seattle (Metro), system design, specification preparation, bid reviews and complete project management for the radio communications system for the new North Operating Base facility. Contract value: $750 000.

For the Fort Worth Transportation Authority (FWTA) Texas, a complete fleet-wide Automatic Vehicle Monitoring system and radio/data communications system. Developed specifications, reviewed bids, and provided a recommendation on contract award. Provided complete project management services during system implementation for this 800 MHz, colour graphic AVM system. System acceptance testing will be conducted, with a recommendation provided on same. Contract value: $1.5 million.

For the San Mateo County Transit District (SMCTD) system design and specification preparation for a computerised Management Information System (MIS) and radio/data/AVM communications system. Reviewed bids and provided recommendation on contract award. MIS system currently installed, with the radio/data/AVM system undergoing installation. Providing complete project management services for all phases of the project. Radio/data/AVM system provides for Automatic Vehicle Monitoring, collection of fare categories over the radio/data system, and supplying real-time information to the Telephone Information Center. Additonally prepared specification, reviewed bids and provided recommendations on contract award for the automatic fare collection (AFC) system. Contract value: $4.5 million.

For the Metropolitan Atlanta Rapid Transit Authority (MARTA), conducted a needs analysis, and developed specifications for a radio/data/AVM and automated scheduling system, including real-time interfaces to the MARTA MIS computer system. Future involvement includes proposal reviews, development of final-bid technical requirements, review of final and best offers, and complete project management for this 800-vehicle fleet system. Contract value: $7.5 million.

For the San Francisco Municipal Railway (MUNI), developed System Acceptance test plans and procedures, and conducted these tests for the approximate 1000 vehicle fleet radio/data/AVM system. Tests included computer polling response and display times for the AVM system, as well as vehicle location accuracy per type of vehicle (included diesel coaches, electric trolleys, and light rail vehicles). Evaluated data collected and provided recommendation on System Acceptance, including recommendations on outstanding issues. Future involvement includes development of equipment reliability and system availability quantities, for the purpose of establishing operating costs for maintenance of this system (personnel, parts and test equipment).

For the Denver Regional Transportation District (RTD), evaluation of the existing 450 MHz radio/data system, including recommendations on reuse of existing equipment in a new system. System design and specification development for a radio/data/AVM system (including MIS system interfaces), bid reviews and recommendations on contract award are included. Contract value: $7.5 million.

For OMNITRANS, evaluation of the existing system components for both the fixed route and demand response systems, specification development, bid reviews, recommendation on contract award, and complete project management are included for this radio/data/AVM system. The system will utilise the LORAN C vehicle location system. Contract value: $1.5 million.

Colston, Budd, Wardrop & Hunt

Suite 71, Chatswood Village, 47 Neridah Street, Chatswood, New South Wales 2067, Australia

Telephone: +61 2 411 7922
Telefax: +61 2 411 2831

Capabilities
Railway operating consultancy; modelling of system performance; proving of computerised schedules; traffic optimisation.

Comsul Ltd

353 Sacramento Street, San Francisco, California 94111, USA

Telephone: +1 415 989 6700
Telex: 278697 cmsl ur

President: Peter B Valentine
Vice-President and Chief Executive Officer: James D Posner

Projects
Providing engineering services in the planning, design, testing and review of the combined communications network for San Francisco Municipal Railway.

Coopers & Lybrand Deloitte

Plumtree Court, London EC4A 4HT, England

Telephone: +44 71 822 4743
Telex: 887470
Telefax: +44 71 822 4652

Director, Rail Transport Consultation: Christopher Castles

Capabilities
Coopers Deloitte provides management consulting and accounting services to a wide range of clients in the public and private sectors. Coopers Deloitte is the UK firm of Coopers & Lybrand International practising in 102 countries through 580 offices. The firm provides broadly-based consulting services in strategic planning, organisation and management, finance, information systems and human resources development for railways throughout the world.

Recent representative projects
British Rail
Advisers on overall restructuring and management control processes (1990); privatisation advice to BRB, analysis of structural options, financial viability, regulation and subsidy issues (1989); Network SouthEast strategic review (1990); accounting development (1988).
Docklands Light Railway
Strategic planning (1989).
London Underground
Management information systems (1986-87).
West Midlands PTA
Financial evaluation of LRT system (1986).
Moroccan Government
Financial feasibility of a fixed link between Spain and Morocco (1987).

Daniel, Mann, Johnson, & Mendenhall

3250 Wilshire Blvd, Los Angeles, California 90010, USA
(other offices world-wide)

Telephone: +1 213 381 3663
Telex: 910 321 3058

Vice-President and Director, Transportation: Gerald W Seelman

Projects
Management and design of Vancouver, British Columbia, advanced light rail transit system ($850 million).
Management and design of Los Angeles metro rail system for Southern California Rapid Transit District.
Management and design of Baltimore Transit System ($998 million), Extension B under construction ($150 million) and Extension C under design ($350 million).
Management, design and construction of Long Beach-Los Angeles Light Rail Transit System ($700 million).

DanRail Consult

Soelvgade 40, 1349 Copenhagen, Denmark

Telephone: +45 33 14 04 00 (ext 13001)
Telex: 22225
Telefax: +45 33 14 04 00 (ext 12110)

CONSULTANCY SERVICES

Chairman: Peter Langager

DanRail Consult is a group formed by the Danish State Railways (DSB) and two private engineering consultancy companies all with comprehensive experience within railway systems.

Capabilities
DanRail's fields of activity include feasibility studies, design, planning, financing and economic studies, supervision, procurement services, turnkey projects and staff training for railway systems.

Projects covered by DanRail Consult include those in the areas of electrification, traction, rolling stock, signalling, remote control systems, telecommunications, permanent way, workshops and depot facilities, ferry systems including landing facilities and booking systems.

Datarail

Progeni, PO Box 44107, Lower Hutt, New Zealand

Telephone: +64 4 666-014

New Zealand Railways
Private Bag, Wellington

Telephone: +64 4 725-599

Capabilities
Datarail is a joint venture between NZ Railways and Progeni, a New Zealand computer company, established to market NZ Railways Traffic Monitoring System (TMS) overseas. Datarail will provide railway and computer consultants to install TMS on any overseas rail network.

The Datarail organisation also helps users in the practical aspects of traffic monitoring beyond system commissioning and staff training.

Projects
TMS was initially created to record the location, status and scheduled movement of rail wagons, locomotives and guards vans and was established by NZ Railways nation-wide in 1980. Now fully operational it has enabled NZ Railways to expand freight-carrying service while significantly reducing the number of wagons in its fleet. TMS will also provide further continuing financial benefit through helping to minimise future capital expenditure on new wagons.

The system has performed to expectations and further developments, which will eventually provide real-time automatic vehicle identification and electronic way-billing for individual wagonloads, are being implemented in a continuing programme. In Australia NZ Railways TMS is being used by the railways of New South Wales and as the basis of the computerised wagon control system under development by Australian National Railways.

DE-Consult
Deutsche Eisenbahn Consulting GmbH

Postfach 700 254, 6000 Frankfurt (Main) 70, Federal Republic of Germany

Telephone: +49 69 6319-0
Cable: Deconsult, Frankfurtmain
Telex: 4 14 516

Supervisory Board: C Wreth
P Münchschwander
K Steves
General Managers: F W Möller
G F Scheller
B Ziller
Manager, Project Development: Dr K L Haucke
Manager, Production: K Grossmann
Manager, Planning: E Wendt
Commercial Administration: D Christofzik
Personnel: M Senne
Civil Engineering: H Schmidt
Electrical and Mechanical Engineering: Dr Hans
Traffic and Transport: D Lehnert
Transportation Economics: U Kloss
Modern Technology: Dr W Henn
Project Management: E Grosser
Regional Managers: Dr Schuler, R Schmitt

Capabilities
DE-Consult, an international consulting enterprise, carries out planning and consultancy work in the transport sector all over the world. The main accents in such activities are placed upon national and municipal railway networks. The firm was founded in 1966 by the Federal German Railways and the Deutsche Bank AG, which are the only shareholders.

At present, DE-Consult employs over 300 engineers and economists. As DE-Consult operates a staff exchange scheme with the German Federal Railway, both the home office staff and the expert teams working abroad can be quickly supplemented to meet current requirements.

Associated offices: DE-Consult has offices in: Algiers, Algeria; Atbara, Sudan; Bangkok, Thailand; Chittagong, Bangladesh; Douala, Cameroon; Kinshasa and Lubumbashi, Zaire; Taipei, Taiwan; Copenhagen, Denmark; Nalukolongo, Uganda; Maputo, Mozambique; Kuala Lumpur, Malaysia; Ankara, Turkey; Dar es Salaam and Tabora, Tanzania; Cairo, Egypt; Nairobi, Kenya; Medellin, Colombia.

Projects
DE-Consult has executed or is at present executing projects in the following countries:
Algeria, Angola, Argentina, Australia, Bangladesh, Benin, Bolivia, Botswana, Brazil, Burkina Faso, Burma, Cameroon, Canada, Columbia, Congo, Costa Rica, Ecuador, Egypt, West Germany, Ghana, Greece, Guinea, India, Indonesia, Iran, Iraq, Ivory Coast, Jordan, Kenya, South Korea, Liberia, Luxembourg, Nigeria, Madagascar, Malawi, Malaysia, Mali, Mozambique, Pakistan, Paraguay, Peru, Portugal, Ruanda, Saudi Arabia, Senegal, Singapore, Sri Lanka, Syria, Sudan, Switzerland, Taiwan, Tanzania, Thailand, Togo, Tunisia, Turkey, Uganda, USSR, USA, Venezuela, Viet-Nam, Yugoslavia, Zaire, Zambia and Zimbabwe.

Projects (civil engineering) for DE-Consult

Country	Client	Description of project	Completion
Algeria	Société Nationale des Transports Ferroviaires	Detailed engineering for rehabilitation and new construction of lines	1989
Egypt	Egyptian Railways	Detailed engineering and site supervision for rehabilitation of permanent way	1990
Germany, Federal Republic	German Federal Railway (DB)	High speed railway line Mannheim-Stuttgart, computer-controlled supervision of construction	1990
Taiwan	Engineering Office of Taipei Underground Project (TRUPO)	Preliminary and final design tendering and site supervision for underground system construction in Taipei City	1990
Egypt	Egyptian National Railways	Rehabilitation of the Baharia line	1990

Projects (electrical and mechanical)

Country	Client	Description of project	Completion
Tanzania	Tanzania Railway Corporation	Technical assistance for maintenance of diesel locomotives	1989
Turkey	Turkish State Railways (TCDD)	Divrigi-Iskenderum electrification: staff training and supervision of works	1991
Zaire	German Society for Technical Co-operation	Management and technical assistance for maintenance services with SNCZ	1990
Bolivia	Kreditanstalt für Wiederaufbau	Rehabilitation of locomotives	1989
Cameroon	Regifercam	Supervision of modernisation of brakes	1992

Projects (signalling, telecommunications)

Country	Client	Description of project	Completion
Kenya	Kenya Railways	Detailed engineering and supervision of telecommunications project	1989
Tanzania	Tanzania Railway Corporation	Modernisation of the communication system	1990

Miscellaneous projects

Country	Client	Description of project	Completion
Colombia	MAN, Nuremburg	Engineering services for Metro Medellin	1991
Germany, Federal Republic	Ministry of Transportation, Bonn	State of the art of rail/wheel technology	1990
Singapore	MRT, Singapore	Engineering services for permanent way, third rail and workshop	1989
Zaire	ONATRA	Supervision of works for urban railway system	1990
Egypt	Egyptian National Railways	Training in the workshops	1991
Cameroon	Regifercam	Assistance in marketing	1991
Tanzania	Tanzania Railway Corporation	Training in the workshops	1992
Uganda	Uganda Railway	Training in the workshops	1991
Thailand	State Railway of Thailand	Management assistance	1990
Sudan	Sudan Railway	Recovery programme	1992

Delcan Corporation

Eastern Region

133 Wynford Drive, North York, Metropolitan Toronto M3C 1K1, Canada

Telephone: +1 416 441 4111
Telex: 06 9666 89
Telefax: +1 416 441 4131

Senior Vice-President Operations: P J Boyd

Prairie Region

1217 Centre Street North, Calgary, Alberta T2E 2R3

Telephone: +1 403 276 9861

Manager: A A Vandertol

Pacific Region

Suite 300, 604 Columbia Street West, New Westminster, British Columbia V3M 1A6

Telephone: +1 604 525 9333
Telefax: +1 604 525 9458

Vice-President Operations: John C Collings

Capabilities
Railway and rail transit planning and engineering; trackwork, electrification, communications, maintenance facilities, stations and civil engineering.

De Leuw, Cather & Company

1133 15th Street NW, Washington DC 20005-2701, USA

Telephone: +1 202 775 3300
Telex: 440413 delcawsh
Telefax: +1 202 775 3422

Offices: Baltimore, Boston, Buffalo, Chicago, Dallas,

Denver, East Hartford, Edison, Fairfax, Fort Lauderdale, Fresno, Gaithersburg, Los Angeles, New York City, Orlando, Pasadena, Phoenix, Provo, Raleigh-Durham, San Francisco, San Jose and District of Columbia, Seattle and Tustin. Various overseas offices including Abu Dhabi, Accra, Bandung, Bangkok, Islamabad, Istanbul, Izmir, Jakarta, Khartoum, Kuwait, La Paz, London, Mbabane, Sarawak, Singapore and Taipei

President: D S Gedney
Executive Vice President, De Leuw, Cather International: V P Lamb
Senior Vice-Presidents
   Manager, International Regions: M D Coleman
   Manager, Eastern Region: R S O'Neil
   Manager, Western Region: G M Randich
   Manager, Business Development: G E Griggs
   Manager, Project Services: L A Dondanville
   General Counsel: J C Lockwood
Treasurer/Financial Manager: C J Blase
Vice-Presidents
   Engineering Management Services:
   R F Fergerstrom
   Manager, Rail Projects: R P Howell
   Manager, Corporate Services: C C Eby
Controller: P Thompson
Manager, Business Development Services:
W C Nevel

Capabilities
Services undertaken by De Leuw, Cather include: feasibility studies, preliminary and final design, site development, surveys, soils investigations, specifications and cost estimates, contract documents, construction supervision, construction management.

Projects
De Leuw, Cather was retained in 1989 to furnish management and technical assistance for the rehabilitation and upgrading of the Swaziland Railway. Funded by the United States Agency for International Development, services include review of management concerns, accounting procedures, operations and marketing strategies and provision of management training for rail personnel. The program will be completed in 1993.

A 120-mile rail corridor for moving high-level nuclear waste between Yucca Mountain, Nevada, and rail line connecting points is under study by De Leuw, Cather in an assignment for Science Applications International Corporation. The access study includes identification, development and evaluation of rail options, socio-economic impacts, alignments and implementation plan; it is scheduled for completion in 1990.

De Leuw, Cather, in association with the Ralph M Parsons Company, is providing engineering, economic and railway operations advisory services to the syndicating banks for the rail tunnel under the English Channel. The team submitted a report to the banks in early 1987 covering project management, cost control procedures, risk analysis, and rail operations. De Leuw, Cather has participated in feasibility studies for the project since the 1960s.

Construction work on the Northeast Corridor Improvement Project, valued at $2200 million, was essentially complete after the opening of the Stamford (Connecticut) station in November 1987. The entire 456-mile rail corridor from Washington, DC to Boston has been rehabilitated and upgraded under the project, which was authorised by the US Congress in 1976. De Leuw, Cather/Parsons services have included systems engineering, design, construction supervision, inspection, administration, and procurement of long lead items throughout the project. During the course of this project, the De Leuw, Cather/Parsons joint venture successfully managed a total of 304 contracts including 87 of the 120 construction packages. The DCP-managed projects resulted in construction work in place of more than $500 million. Two design/furnish signal contracts valued at $140 million were successfully closed out in 1987. The Centralised Electrification and Traffic Control (CETC) system project was completed in 1988.

The programme included the rehabilitation or replacement of over 1200 miles of track structure; the reconfiguration, installation or removal of some 50 interlockings; the rehabilitation of over 200 bridges including five movable bridges, and the replacement of two movable and five fixed bridges; the construction of three new stations, renovation of seven stations including six classified as landmark structures; rehabilitation of the century-old B&P Tunnel in Baltimore and improvements in the tunnels serving New York City; installation of Centralised Electrification and Train Control (CETC) in the high-density territories between Washington and Wilmington and the Boston terminal area; catenary improvements in electrified territory and final design of catenary poles and foundations for the future extension of electrification from New Haven to Boston, Massachusetts; the elimination of at-grade crossings in much of the corridor; and the fencing of high-risk areas of the right-of-way. Four maintenance-of-way bases were constructed to provide facilities for continuing protection of the programme's investment in upgraded fixed facilities. New maintenance of equipment facilities are in Washington, Wilmington, New York, New Haven, and Boston.

In Florida, De Leuw, Cather engineers furnished full design and construction supervision services on the newest US commuter rail line, the 70-mile Tri-County System between West Palm Beach and the Miami International Airport. The system including rehabilitated locomotives and new bi-level coaches was placed in revenue service in January 1989. One of its 15 stations is a direct link with Miami's Metro Rail rapid transit system.

De Leuw, Cather is now in the fourth year of the firm's open-ended contract with the Burlington Northern Railroad, furnishing professional services on a task order basis throughout the 25 000-mile system. Approximately 150 task orders have been issued by client departments for work including civil, structural, mechanical, electrical, architectural, and environmental engineering, in one of the first contracts of its kind in the railroad industry.

New assignments in 1988 included design and construction services for New York's Metro-North Commuter Railroad maintenance of way base in North White Plains; inventory and recommendations for improvements for the Alaskan Railway's Whittier tunnels; and special trackwork for the Bethlehem Steel Corporation, Bethlehem, Pennsylvania.

De Leuw, Cather was selected in joint venture to provide services for a new high-capacity transit system to serve the Seattle, Washington metropolitan area. Another recent assignment was selection of De Leuw, Cather by the Ramsay County (Minnesota) Regional Transportation Authority to perform alternative analyses of the northeast corridor of the proposed St Paul, Minnesota, transit system.

In the heavy rail transit field, De Leuw, Cather was retained in joint venture to manage the construction of Chicago's new southwest transit line, and to design the second of two central area subway sections of the new Taipai Mass Rapid Transit System. Continuing assignments include the general engineering consultancy for the Washington DC Metro system and construction management of the Los Angeles Metro subway.

An intermodal facility will link the Los Angeles Metro system with the historic Union Station Terminal Building, major western terminus for transcontinental passenger trains. The Union Station Metro terminal is scheduled for completion in 1992 and operation in late 1993.

New contracts have also included design services for improvements to Long Island Rail Road and New York City Transit Authority facilities at the intermodal Atlantic Avenue Terminal Complex in Brooklyn; and detailed feasibility studies for the potential relocation of Rock Island commuter terminal facilities to the Chicago Union station.

Construction of a new Exchange Place Station designed by De Leuw, Cather for the Port Authority Trans-Hudson Corporation (PATH) was completed in 1989. The multi-storey transit structure overlooks the Hudson River and serves New York commuters. Facilities include a fare collection concourse, second-storey substation, 75-ft deep escalatorway, and passageways to the PATH rapid transit line below. The existing PATH station and 100-year-old train tunnels below remained fully operational at all times during construction of the new station.

Main line relocations, extension, consolidations and improvements: Major projects have been completed in California, Georgia, Illinois, Indiana, Iowa, Massachusetts, Michigan, Minnesota, Nebraska, Nevada, New Jersey, Pennsylvania, Texas, and Wisconsin as well as Canada, Indonesia, and Turkey.

Railroad grade separations and related studies: Assignments involving a variety of disciplines have been completed in 15 US states, Australia, and Jordan.

In Illinois, structural engineering is under way on a 2300 ft four-lane viaduct over the Norfolk Southern main line and railroad yard. The viaduct, which also spans a major industrial complex, is being built using incremental or push launch construction; this method, where the superstructure is formed in segments behind an abutment and pushed across the bridge piers, minimises disruption of railroad operations at ground level.

Railroad appraisals, inventories and operational studies: Engineering and economic analyses; revenue studies; operational studies; valuation appraisals; and condition reports for major railroad facilities in the United States, Canada, Philippines, Jamaica, Venezuela, Chile, Turkey, Kuwait, Saudi Arabia and China; feasibility studies for Bosphorus Railway Tunnel.

In California, De Leuw, Cather is heading a team studying rail access and transportation requirements for Terminal Island, serving the container and bulk cargo business of the Port of Los Angeles. In the New York metropolitan area, assignments have involved the performance of annual engineering audits for the Metropolitan Transportation Authority's commuter rail system revenue bond financing; the programme is funding capital improvements for the Long Island Rail Road and the Metro-North Commuter Railroad.

Railroad signalling and communications: Projects have included automatic interlocking circuits; remote control interlocking; electrification; design of signal and communication systems or modifications to existing facilities; and automatic crossing protection.

Yards, shops, and terminal facilities: Modernisation of existing facilities or construction of new facilities in 13 states, Kuwait, Thailand, and Venezuela. Design of Norfolk and Western Landers intermodal facility.

In 1986, De Leuw, Cather completed final design for the Carbondale Railroad Relocation Project, a 2-mile depression of the Illinois Central Gulf Railroad mainline tracks through central Carbondale, Illinois. Two facilities in the demonstration project are already built: the US Route 51 overpass; and a pedestrian-utilities overpass for Southern Illinois University.

Design Triangle
The Maltings, Burwell, Cambridge CB5 0BH, England

Telephone: +44 638 743070
Telefax: +44 638 743066

Associated Company:
   Davis Associates, Cambridge, England
   Secoinfo, Madrid, Spain
   Peter Bayly Assoc., Melbourne, Australia

Partners: Siep Wijsenbeek
         Andrew Crawshaw
         Andrew Clark

Capabilities
Specialist design for the transport industry. Design Triangle is an independent company of industrial designers, engineers and ergonomists. The integrated service encompasses:

design, combined with ergonomics and engineering, for operators and manufacturers of public transport and specialist vehicles;
industrial design for manufacturers of products connected with transport;
design management consultancy for public transport operators.

Design Triangle places equal emphasis on excellence in design, ergonomics and engineering. This unified approach has enabled the company to provide successful solutions for clients worldwide and it is from this that its practice has grown. The scientific training and industrial management background of the partners of Design Triangle provide both the discipline and freedom to unleash the creativity of the group. Talented designers are supported by full CAD systems and Finite Element Stress Analysis capability, ensuring both the quality and accuracy of all design proposals.

Recent projects
Before establishing Design Triangle, Siep Wijsenbeek instigated and for 20 years was responsible for co-ordinating the Design and Corporate Identity Programme for the Netherlands Railways. Design management consultancies followed for clients worldwide on corporate design programmes, uniforms, rolling stock, terminals and public transport systems.

Other partners have many years experience in the motor industry. They are skilled in aerodynamic design and in product development and testing. Design Triangle has successfully undertaken the design and engineering of railway carriages and LRV exteriors and

CONSULTANCY SERVICES

interiors as well as aircraft interiors and designs for buses, coaches and trucks.

Design Triangle's ergonomists undertake major studies relating to passenger safety and comfort, driver work-stations, traffic control rooms, passenger access and movement studies. These have resulted in improved passenger handling times and ultimately in major savings for operators on equipment and in capital investment.

Recent projects include:
BR: Design Management: Rolling stock. Design Management: Uniforms.
DB & SBB: Advanced carriage design concepts.
DSB: Ultra lightweight seat design, engineering and prototype build. Corporate Image consultancy.
FS: Design and engineering development of seats for ETR 500 and UIC Z1 Salone in conjunction with Bianchi & Compin SpA.
KCRC: Industrial Design and driver and passenger ergonomics for the Tuen Mun LRV.
OBB: Corporate Design consultancy.
RENFE: Luxury seat design, engineering and prototype build for high speed train.
SRA of NSW: Design concepts for HPT high speed train (in association with Peter Bayly Assoc Melbourne).

DKS Associates

1956 Webster, Suite 300, Oakland, California 94612, USA

Telephone: +1 415 763 2061
Telefax: +1 415 268 1739

President: Richard T Sauve

Capabilities
Urban transport planning; light rail transit system design; at-grade LRT traffic signal design; transit centre design; maintenance facility design; traffic operations and transportation planning models.

Dobbie and Partners

17 Lansdowne Road, Croydon, Surrey CR9 3UN, England

Telephone: +44 81 686 8212
Telex: 917220
Telefax: +44 81 686 2499

Projects
Station buildings including Birmingham International station serving National Exhibition Centre; Harecastle tunnel and line diversions; sidings; carriage washing plants; wagon repair shops, overhead electrification foundations for Kowloon-Canton Railway, Hong Kong; maintenance shop at Sha Tin, Hong Kong; signal boxes, computer centre and telephone exchanges, over 400 bridges for British Rail; survey and design for new railways in Guinea and Liberia.

Dubin, Dubin and Moutoussamy

455 East Illinois Street, Chicago, Illinois 60611, USA

Telephone: +1 312 836 7750

Contacts: Claude L Moutoussamy
Peter A Dubin

Projects
Dubin, Dubin and Moutoussamy is an established architectural engineering firm (1914) with a general practice which includes transportation projects largely financed by local, state, and Federal agencies.

Current assignments include:
General architectural consultant with Raymond Kaiser Engineers, Inc and Envirodyne Engineers, Inc, a joint venture, for the design of the Southwest Transit Project (estimated value $496 000 000), a new 14.8 km-long elevated rail rapid transit line connecting the Chicago central business district with Midway Airport on the southwest side of the City of Chicago. The new line, which contains eight stations and an 88 000 ft^2 maintenance facility, connects with the existing Chicago Transit Authority (CTA) Dan Ryan line at 18th Street. The Southwest Transit Project is being developed by the Department of Public Works, City of Chicago, Illinois, and will be operated by the Chicago Transit Authority (CTA). Scheduled completion is 1992. Partner-member of the Southwest Transit Group, a joint venture with The Ralph M Parsons Company, De Leuw, Cather, & Company, William E Brazley & Associates, Ltd, and C F Moore Construction Company: the construction management team for the Southwest Transit Project (described above), Chicago, Illinois. The project is being developed by the Department of Public Works, City of Chicago, Illinois and will be operated by the Chicago Transit Authority (CTA);
Architectural consultant for the new Evanston Transportation Center (estimated value $8 400 000), Evanston, Illinois with Envirodyne Engineers, Inc. The new rail rapid transit complex is being developed by the City of Evanston for operation by the Chicago Transit Authority (CTA) and includes bus interchange with NORTRAN/PACE and the CTA.
Architectural consultant for the new Skokie Swift rail rapid transit terminal (estimated value $2 000 000), Skokie, Illinois. The new terminal is an intermodal transportation center for use by passengers on the Chicago Transit Authority (CTA) rail rapid transit and buses, NORTRAN/PACE buses, and private automobiles. The Skokie Swift terminal is being developed by the Village of Skokie, Illinois, for operation by the Chicago Transit Authority (CTA);
Architectural consultant with Envirodyne Engineers, Inc for the reconstruction of the Wells Street Viaduct, and the Merchandise Mart station, Chicago, Illinois (estimated value $13 180 000) a new rail rapid transit station and track relocation located in downtown Chicago at the Merchandise Mart on the loop elevated line. The Wells Street station is being developed by the Department of Public Works, City of Chicago, Illinois, for operation by the Chicago Transit Authority (CTA).
Architectural consultant with the joint venture of Gannett-Sih, section designer, for the new Addison Street station and track relocation, Chicago, Illinois (estimated value $8 000 000). The new facility improves passenger flow and accommodates crowds from nearby Wrigley Field, home of the Chicago Cubs baseball club.
Architectural consultant for the Winnetka and Hubbard Woods commuter rail stations (estimated value $1 500 000) for operation by Metra Rail/Chicago and North Western Railway. The project includes the rehabilitation of existing facilities, including station buildings, stairs, pedestrian overpasses, trackside platforms, trackside passenger shelters, and the design of two new freestanding elevator towers for the elderly and handicapped at Winnetka.
Architectural consultant with Envirodyne Engineers, Inc for the Route 59 station, Naperville, Illinois (Cost NA) a new commuter rail station for the Burlington Northern Railroad/Metra Rail.
Architectural consultant with Envirodyne Engineers, Inc for the restoration of the historic Stone Avenue commuter rail station, La Grange, Illinois (estimated value $350 000) for the Burlington Northern Railroad/Metra Rail.

Thomas K Dyer Inc

762 Massachusetts Avenue, Lexington, Massachusetts 02173, USA

Telephone: +1 617 862 2075
Telefax: +1 617 861 7766

President: Charles L O'Reilly Jr
Vice-Presidents: Glenn E Hartsoe
David F Jones

Capabilities
DYER provides planning, engineering, design, valuation, construction inspection, research, and computer services to the rail transportation industry in the disciplines of signal and train control systems, communications, track and right-of-way, electric traction (sub-stations, catenary and contact rail) and civil engineering.

Projects
Provide signal, train control, communications and central control engineering and design services for a 20-mile long LRT system and a 14-mile long commuter rail system for Dallas Area Rapid Transit (DART); completion is scheduled for 1996 ($40 million).

Provide general design consult services for system-wide equipment for development of a fixed guideway system for Houston's Metropolitan Transit Authority (METRO).

Provide designs for rehabilitation of track, signals, communications, fixed span bridges, draw bridges and passenger stations for some 30 miles of MBTA's Eastern Route Main Line Commuter Rail Rehabilitation project in Boston, Massachusetts; Completion is scheduled for 1990 ($75 million).

Identified transit system alternatives and specified technical criteria for track and right of way, preliminary station concepts, signal and train control systems, communications, and the electric traction system for the Kaohsiung Municipal Government in Taiwan, completion was due in 1989 ($7300 million).

EG & G Dynatrend Inc

21 Cabot Road, Woburn, Massachusetts 01801, USA

Telephone: +1 617 935 3960

Vice President: Rudolph G DiLuzio

Capabilities
Light rail, rapid rail, and commuter rail technologies. Track structures safety analysis.

Projects
Urban transportation systems planning, management, and operations. Evaluation and development of management systems for application in urban transit-systems. Client is the Urban Mass Transportation Administration. Value approximately $200 000.

Rail modernisation planning for the Urban Mass Transportation Administration to identify the methods currently used by the US rapid rail industry for planning capital project improvements and develop analytical techniques which may be applied to the project planning and selection process.

Technical information support services for the Transportation Systems Center (US DOT). Provide information/data research, analysis, documentation and technical reference services for transportation and logistics systems. The technical and management disciplines include operations research, systems engineering, transportation systems analysis and planning, information sciences, safety and security, and logistics management. Value approximately $32 500 000.

Dynatrend Inc was acquired by EG & G Inc in 1989 and is now a wholly-owned subsidiary of EG & G Inc.

Edwards and Kelcey
Edwards and Kelcey Inc
Edwards and Kelcey Engineers, Inc

Central office: 70 South Orange Avenue, Livingston, New Jersey 07039, USA

Projects: DKS Associates

Project Name and Location	For	Completion Date Actual or Estimated
Long Beach-Los Angeles Rail transit: Traffic analysis and traffic control devices design	Los Angeles Co Transportation Comm, 403 West 8th Street, Suite 500, Los Angeles, California 90014-3069	1990
Guadalupe Corridor LRT Traffic analysis and traffic signal system design	Santa Clara Co Transportation Agency, 1555 Berger Drive, San Jose, California 95112	1988
Mission Valley LRT Extension Establishment of plan and profile for LRT extension for Old Town to Jack Stadium	Metropolitan Transit Development Board, 620 C Street, Suite 400, San Diego, California 92101-5368	1987
Sacramento LRT Design Traffic analysis and traffic signal system design	Regional Transit, 1400 29th Street, Sacramento, California 95810	1987
Fremont South Bay AA/EIS/EIR Analysis considering nine alternatives including LRT and BART rail options	Metropolitan Transportation Commission, Metrocenter, 101 8th Street, Oakland, California 94607	1989

CONSULTANCY SERVICES

Telephone: +1 201 994 4520
Telex: 138807
Telefax: +1 201 994 7176

Regional offices
The Schrafft Center, 529 Main Street, Boston, Massachusetts 02129
Telephone: +1 617 242 9222

7401 Metro Boulevard, One Corporate Center, Minneapolis, Minnesota 55435
Telephone: +1 612 835 6411

53 Park Place, New York, New York 10007
Telephone: +1 212 619 5300

2300 East Katella Ave, Suite 355, Anaheim, California 92806
Telephone: +1 714 634 9212

Capabilities
Rail planning and design; vehicle and maintenance facilities; rail transit and commuter operations and facilities; railroad management and operations; merger, acquisition and control studies; financial analyses and evaluations; cost and rate structures; short line feasibility and operations studies; logistics management.

Projects
Planning, environmental studies, evaluations, operations, management, design and construction management for railways, terminals, tunnels and bridges, transportation companies, shippers, insurance companies, bankers and law firms.

North Jersey Coast Line electrification and modernisation design and construction management, Matawan to Long Branch, New Jersey, 16 miles of double-track commuter rail, for NJ Transit; estimated construction cost is $145 million.

Montclair Rail Connection conceptual design, alternatives analyses and environmental impact statement in Montclair, NJ, for the New Jersey Transit Corporation, Newark, NJ.

IRT Broadway/7th Avenue Line station rehabilitation, New York, NY: design of the rehabilitation of five stations.

Secaucus Transfer station, Secaucus, New Jersey: design of two miles of track and signal improvements to Amtrak's northeast corridor for a rail transfer station to link the Northeast Corridor and NJ Transit commuter lines to serve NYC-bound workers, and serve a large-scale office/commercial complex.

Soo line railroad bridges final design, Minnesota; design of single-span and two-span replacement bridges; high-level platform study, NJ Transit Authority; feasibility study for prototype high-level platforms on the commuter rail system.

Electrowatt Engineering Services Ltd

Bellerivestrasse 36, 80342 Zurich, Switzerland

Telephone: +41 1 385 22 11
Telex: 815115 ewi ch
Telefax: +41 1 252 22 46

Managing Director: P Könz
Technical Director: Heinz Saxer

Capabilities
Feasibility studies, modelling and data processing, economic assessment; consulting, planning and engineering of all rail systems; specifications, tender documents, bid evaluations; supervision of manufacture and installation; project management; consultancy in all aspects of railways.

ELRAIL
ELRAIL Consultants Pty Ltd

Head Office:
135 Wickham Terrace, Brisbane, Queensland 4000, Australia

Telephone: +61 7 839 4950
Telex: 42238 elrail
Telefax: +61 7 832 4081

Sydney Office:
15 Blue Street, North Sydney, New South Wales 2060, Australia

Telephone: +61 2 959 4577
Telefax: +61 2 929 0997

Director & CEO: Paul E Jenkins
Director, Power Systems: Grahame D Anthon
Director, Catenary Systems: David Germain
Chairman & Non-Executive Director: William A Sampson

Capabilities
Elrail Consultants is a private professional consulting engineering practice working in the principal areas of engineering including civil, electrical and mechanical, with particular railway related skills in power supplies, catenary, traction, communications, signalling and control systems. It has undertaken a number of specialist commissions in these areas. The Company provides professional services for feasibility studies, investigations, design, specification and construction management.

Projects
Elrail Consultants has current and completed assignments for most of the railway systems in Australia and New Zealand. Principal railway systems and projects on which work was done in 1989 include:
State Rail Authority of New South Wales: Preliminary investigation of route options, operating requirements, costs and benefits for a rail link from the Sydney CBD to Kingsford Smith Airport.

Work has continued on the SRA's programme for improvement of the suburban system overhead catenary traction equipment by conversion of the 1500 V dc system from fixed termination to constant tension.

A study of maintenance practices for traction overhead equipment, transmission lines and power cables.
Queensland Railways: Detailed analysis of performance of the 25 kV ac traction power system of the Brisbane Suburban electric Railway and a projection of performance under growing traffic volumes to the year 2000.
Western Australian Government Railways Commission (Westrail) and Metropolitan Transport Trust (Transperth):
Perth-Joondalup Railway – Northern Suburbs Transit System: Technical input and co-ordination for the preparation of the $220 million Northern Suburbs Railway Master Plan. This Master Plan is for a co-ordinated passenger transport system serving the northern suburbs of Perth with bus services linking widely spaced stations at which passengers will transfer to rapid transit rail services.
25 kV ac Perth Urban Rail electrification Project: Elrail's responsibilities (as part of an international joint venture) include the detailed design, specification and implementation of the electric traction power and overhead system design and performance analysis; earthing and bonding procedures; interference studies and negotiations with telecommunications authorities; train control and passenger information systems; design and specification of power transformers, 25 kV switchgear, traction overhead equipment (145stkm), supervisory control system and train radio facilities.
Public Transport Commission of Victoria (The Met): Provision of overhead equipment (1500 V dc) design assistance for rehabilitation and extensions of the system and in preparation of the introduction of double-deck passenger rolling stock.
VFT (Very Fast Train) Project: Participation in the preliminary feasibility studies of the projected Sydney-Melbourne 350 km/h Very Fast Train (VFT) proposal.

Elrail continued the work of further definition studies for feasibility purposes and has participated in the operations aspects of the FFT Project (Fast Freight Train) investigation for V/Line.

VFT Feasibility Study – Investigation of Power Supply System: This 1990 commission covers the investigation and development of options for the power supply for the VFT and the preparation of estimates and a preliminary implementation/construction programme.

EMJ
EMJ Engineers Inc

Suite 209, 6525 Belcrest Road, Hyattsville, Maryland 20782, USA

Telephone: +1 301 779 6868
Telex: 898387
Telefax: +1 301 699 1164

Subsidiaries
EMJ/Electrack Inc
6525 Belcrest Road, Suite 209, Hyattsville, Maryland 20782, USA

EMJ/McFarland-Johnson Engineers Inc
171 Front Street, Binghamton, New York 13902, USA

EMJ UK Engineering
PO Box 12, Acornfield Road, Kirkby, Liverpool L33 7UG, England

ELRAIL Consultants Pty Ltd
135 Wickham Terrace, Brisbane, Queensland 4000, Australia

Telephone: +61 7 839 4950
Telex: 42238 elrail
Telefax: +61 7 832 4081

President: Gordon E Woodhead

Capabilities
Rail electrification, power engineering, rail systems, railroad engineering, signalling and communications, construction services.

Projects
Electrack: Rehabilitation design for Amtrak railroad bridges in Maryland and Pennsylvania. Value $500 000.

Southeastern Pennsylvania Transportation Authority: two contracts in connection with the refurbishment of the catenary and traction power system in the Philadelphia area. Value $7 million.

Century Freeway LRT Project for the Los Angeles County Transportation Commission, Los Angeles: Subconsultant performing conceptual and detailed design to the 30 per cent level for traction power supply and catenary distribution system. Completion date 1986. Value $10 million.

North Jersey Coast Line Project, New Jersey Transit Corporation, Newark: Subconsultant providing design, engineering and construction management services for electrification of the North Jersey Coast Line from Matawan to Long Branch (26.5 km of two-track, commuter railroad with storage yard). Completion date 1988. Value $22.75 million.
Elrail: North Island Main Trunk Railway Electrification, New Zealand Railways Corporation: traction overhead design. Detail design work for the catenary traction overhead system. Value NZ$15 million.

Perth Rail Electrification Project, Government of Western Australia: ELRAIL, as part of a joint venture, helped prepare the Master Plan for the development and completion of the electrification project covering details of the work to be carried out; technical criteria to be adopted; programme of work and related cash flows; and a management plan with the direction and control of the project including requirements for expenditure and manpower. Value A$300 000.

Envirodyne Engineers Inc

168 N Clinton Street, Chicago, Illinois 60606, USA

Telephone: +1 312 648 1700

Senior Vice President: Marshall Suloway

Capabilities
Complete engineering services for heavy and light rail transit. In-house expertise in corridor planning, track layout, industrial engineering, elevated and subway, station and line section design. Offices in principal cities throughout the United States.

Projects
General engineering consultants for a new, 14.5 km heavy rail transit line in Chicago ($496 million); expansion and modernisation of the 14th St Railyard and new maintenance shop for the Burlington Northern Railroad and Regional Transportation Authority in Chicago ($38 million); modernisation of the Aurora Hill Yard for the Burlington Northern Railroad in Aurora, Illinois ($14 million); rehabilitation and modernisation of the Western Avenue Railyard and new shop facility for the Regional Transportation Authority in Chicago ($38 million); design of two new transit service and inspection shops for the Washington Metropolitan Area Transit Authority ($22 million); design of a movable single-track railroad bridge over Reynolds Channel for the Long Island Railroad ($4 million);

design of a new heavy rail transit station and replacement of 600 ft of elevated transit line in Chicago for the City of Chicago ($13 million); rehabilitation of four stations for the New Jersey Transit System ($4 million); rehabilitation and expansion of the 13-acre Howard Yard transit facility for the Chicago Transit Authority ($27 million); evaluation, design and construction management for rehabilitation of Park Avenue tunnel, New York City, for Metro-North Commuter Railroad ($75 million); planning and design of new heavy repair shops for Metra commuter rail fleet at 47th Street, Chicago, for Metropolitan Rail ($80 million); planning and design of new multi-model transportation centre for city of Evanston, Illinois ($7 million).

Ewbank Preece Consulting Group

Prudential House, North Street, Brighton, East Sussex BN1 1RZ, England

Telephone: +44 273 724533
Telex: 878102 eplbtn g
Telefax: +44 273 200483

Director: T Wiltshire

Capabilities
Engineering specialists in power supply, traction, rolling stock, signalling, communications and automatic fare collection.

W A Fairhurst & Partners

Cragside House, Heaton Road, Newcastle upon Tyne NE6 1SN, England

Telephone: +91 265 7112
Telex: 53440 for Fairhurst
Telefax: +91 265 8819

Projects
Fairhurst was responsible to the Tyne and Wear Passenger Transport Executive for the following projects which are part of the Tyne and Wear Metro: 350-metre long steel truss bridge across the Tyne between Newcastle and Gateshead; installation of overhead line equipment throughout the 56 km length of Metro, including design of all structural elements, procurement of components and supervision of installation; design of the depot for all equipment installed in the Metro; inspection of 40 existing bridges that cross or carry the Metro together with design and contract supervision where necessary. The Metro came into full operation in 1982; Fairhurst are retained by the Executive to carry out periodic detailed maintenance inspections of the Queen Elizabeth Bridge over the Tyne and the Howdon Viaduct.

Fleming Corp

400 Olive Street, St Louis, Missouri 63102, USA

Telephone: +1 314 241 9550

President: Charles E Fleming

Capabilities
Transportation planning, rail alignment, right-of-ways, utility relocation, maintenance facilities, and station design.

Fluor Daniel Australia Limited

616 St Kilda Road, Melbourne, Victoria 3004, Australia

Telephone: +61 3 520 4444
Telex: 30062
Telefax: Gp3 +61 3 520 4244

Chairman: R J Harden
Specialist Engineer, Railways: D J O'Grady (Perth Office, Western Australia)

Associated companies
All Fluor/Fluor Daniel entities including Civil & Mechanical Maintenance Pty Ltd (CMM). Civil & Mechanical Maintenance Pty Ltd is the Railway Upgrading and Maintenance Division of the company, based in Perth, Western Australia.

Office
22 Mount Street, Perth, Western Australia 6000

Telephone: +61 9 322 3600
Telex: 92139 aa
Telefax: +61 9 322 5841

General Manager: R M Wright
Manager Technical Services: D J O'Grady
Resident Manager, Hamersley Iron Project: N W Prince

PO Box 222, Dampier, Western Australia 6713

Telephone: +61 91 436455
Telefax: +61 91 436496

Capabilities
Feasibility and operational studies; financial planning; engineering; procurement; construction and project management for railway or integrated multi-discipline projects. Capabilities cover general and heavy haul trackwork, earthworks, structures, electrification, rail grinding, flaw detection, track geometry measurement.

Associated divisions offer railway construction, upgrading and maintenance services.

Projects
Upgrading and maintenance (including rail profile grinding and track renewal with concrete sleepers): Hamersley Iron Railway from Paraburdoo to Dampier, Western Australia. This maintenance contract has been running since 1968.

Concrete resleepering, upgrading and designated maintenance on the Cliffs Robe River Railway from the Pannawonica iron ore mine to Cape Lambert port, Western Australia, scheduled for completion in September 1992.

Foster Engineering, Inc

847 Howard Street, San Francisco, California 94103, USA

Telephone: +1 415 543 1193

President: H A Foster

Projects
Design, management, construction administration for various rail transit projects for Bay Area Rapid Transit District (BART) and Systems Integration/Operations Consultant for Sacramento Light Rail Project.

Gannett Fleming Inc

PO Box 1962, Harrisburg, Pennsylvania 17105, USA

Telephone: +1 717 763 7211
Telex: 842375 gfcc hbg
Telefax: +1 717 763 8150
Cable: Ganflec

President: Maurice A Wadsworth

Capabilities
Transport systems analysis and planning; feasibility studies, preliminary and final designs for light rail, rapid rail, intercity rail and automated guideway systems; design of rail and tracked vehicle maintenance facilities; comprehensive construction management, depreciation studies; and litigation support services.

Projects
Final design and construction services for Long Island Rail Road yards and shops ($250 million); final design manager for Detroit central automated transit system ($210 million); feasibility studies and preliminary design for the Philadelphia to Pittsburgh high speed rail passenger system ($8000–10 000 million) for PA HSR Commission; Phase 2 preliminary engineering and design ($130 million) for the Miami Downtown People Mover for the Metropolitan Dade County, Florida; feasibility study and final design for a bayside line extension of the San Diego LRT ($20 million); final design of the Los Angeles County light rail El Segundo line extension ($25 million); final design of the 3000 ft aerial viaduct for the Los Angeles-Long Beach LRT ($25 million); final design and construction management for the US$30 million Automated Skyway Express, Jacksonville, Florida; feasibility study for a US$280 million AGT system linking Newark and Elizabeth, New Jersey, with Newark International Airport; final design for the $200 million MBTA (Boston) Commuter Rail maintenance facility; light rail feasibility study for the Seattle metropolitan area; final design for the service and inspection facility for the Dallas light rail system; Tri-County Commuter Rail Study from West Palm Beach to Miami, Florida; and rehabilitation of the former Reading Railroad Ninth Street Mainline Branch for SEPTA in Philadelphia ($175 million).

Intercity travel demand forecasts for VIA Rail, Canada; demand forecast study for Rapid Rail between Santa Fe and Albuquerque, New Mexico; and depreciation consulting and tax litigation support services for Burlington Northern and other Class 1 railroads.

GEC Alsthom Transportation Projects Ltd

PO Box 134, Manchester M60 1AH, England

Telephone: +44 61 872 2431
Telex: 667152, 665451
Telefax: +44 61 848 8710

Managing Director: B S Ronan

Capabilities
Main contractors, project managers and system engineers for composite main-line, suburban, metro and mass transit railway systems.

Projects
Docklands Light Railway, London: A design and construct, turnkey contract was placed with GEC-Mowlem Railway Group covering a complete light railway to serve London's Docklands. Public service started in mid-1987 (some 2½ years later) and a further contract is now in hand both to extend the existing systems eastwards into the City of London and also to increase the capacity of the existing system to handle the vast increase in traffic which has been created by the railway itself.
Channel Tunnel: GEC-TPL is currently working with French and Belgium manufacturers as well as other British manufacturers on the Very High Speed Trains – now known as Trans Manche Super Trains or TMST – (for international through services). In the case of the TMSTs GEC-TPL is co-chairman of the joint venture management committee and is co-ordinating the activities of all the UK participants.

Gellman Research Associates Inc

115 West Avenue, Suite 201, Jenkintown, Pennsylvania 19046, USA

Telephone: +1 215 884 7500
Telex: 834653

President: Aaron J Gellman
Principals: Frank Berardino
Richard Golaszewski
Associate: W Bruce Allen

Capabilities
Preparation and presentation of expert testimony; financial planning; asset valuation analysis and asset disposition; rehabilitation and acquisition financing; forecasting; traffic analysis and costing; reorganisation economics; revenue division analysis; high speed rail feasibility studies.

Projects
Current GRA projects include:

Economic impact assessment for the New York State Department of Transportation and the Vermont Agency of Transportation to analyse the urban and regional impacts of a very high speed rail system; work for the creditors' committee of a bankrupt railcar leasing firm, in addition to three private car management firms, to identify and evaluate various alternatives for the reorganisation of the company; for a major US transportation company, an evaluation of the existing and historical freight car weighing policies of its rail system with provision of expert witness testimony which estimates maximum rates for coal movements involving three railroads, these maximum rates are based upon the Maximum Competitive Contribution Methodology (MCCM).

Sir Alexander Gibb & Partners

Earley House, 427 London Road, Earley, Reading, RG6 1BL, England

440 CONSULTANCY SERVICES

Telephone: +44 734 61061
Telex: 848061 gibb rg
Telefax: 44 734 64088

Chairman: G H Coates
Group Chairman: J G F Dawson
Group Directors: B G Dent
T J W King R St H Cox
Rail Division Directors: D G Drake
B M Gren

Capabilities
Sir Alexander Gibb & Partners Ltd is an independent firm of consulting engineers with 80 years' experience in the design and execution of a wide range of engineering projects.

The Railway Division of the firm has the capability of carrying out all types of railway projects ranging from very high speed railways, main line and urban systems to metro and light railway planning and engineering. The Division is backed by the worldwide resources of GIBB and the Law Group of Companies, providing the services of approximately 3500 staff including civil, structural, mechanical and electrical, signalling and telecommunications engineers, economists, geologists, architects, surveyors, scientists and environmental specialists.

In addition to the 15 offices in the UK and Europe, offices are established at 60 locations worldwide, with particular concentration in the USA, Africa, the Middle East and Australasia.

Projects
Work undertaken includes: engineering design management of the high speed rail link between the Channel Tunnel and London; GIBB ia also undertaking the detail design of the 28 km Folkestone-Ashford section of the route.

London Underground Ltd has appointed GIBB to investigate and recommend new track designs suitable for existing and proposed new underground lines.

GIBB recently provided a senior railway team in Madrid to assist staff from RENFE to produce a full project justification statement for the proposed 600 km Madrid-Barcelona high speed railway.

In Africa GIBB provided railway, port and airport engineering and operations study input to the Moroccan National Transport Study which was carried out by a multinational team.

A review of track maintenance activities on TAZARA, the Tanzania-Zambia railway was completed, with particular reference to how rail burn welding repairs were being carried out.

A review of the transport infrastructure of Namibia was carried out by an international team of consultants. GIBB provided the specialist railway and ports engineering and operating inputs to this study which identified the areas where assistance would be required after the country gained independence.

In Australia, working in association with JARTS, initial and then detailed traffic surveys were undertaken to establish the projected passenger and freight traffic in the period 1992–2015, for the 870 km Sydney-Melbourne line which it is proposed will operate trains at speeds up to 350 km h.

A study in Pakistan examined the transportation of petroleum products between marine and refinery terminals and up country consumers with the intention of realising economies from the increased use of rail in conjunction with a major pipeline.

Station Planning
GIBB was appointed to plan the International Passenger Terminal in Waterloo Station which will be built for the Channel Tunnel trains. The Terminal has been designed to handle 14 million rail passengers forecast in the year 2003.

GIBB was appointed to compare the benefits of Kings Cross and Stratford as alternative sites for the second London terminal for the Channel Tunnel Rail Link and following BR's selection of Kings Cross the consultancy was further appointed to prepare evidence to support BR during the subsequent Parliamentary enquiry.

GIBB has also been appointed to carry out final planning of the proposed International Passenger Terminal at Ashford which is required to handle up to 2.7 milion passengers per year.

In connection with the new high speed rail link to London's Heathrow Airport, GIBB has been appointed by BR and BAA to identify a layout of facilities at Paddington that will cope with the road traffic and pedestrian flows generated when the Heathrow Express link is introduced.

Gibbs & Hill Inc

11 Penn Plaza, New York, New York 10001, USA

Telephone: +1 212 216 6725
Cable: Gibbshill, New York
Telex: 177199, 428813

Branch and subsidiary offices
Gibbs & Hill Inc, 80 Boylston Street, Boston, Massachusetts 02116
Telephone: +1 617 542 6968
Gibbs & Hill Inc, 226 Airport Parkway, San Jose, California 95110
Telephone: +1 408 291 2700
Gibbs & Hill Inc, 1225 19th Street NW, Washington DC 20036
Telephone: +1 202 785 1901
Gibbs & Hill Inc, One Oliver Plaza, Pittsburgh, Pennsylvania 15222
Telephone: +1 412 566 3000
Gibbs & Hill Inc, 70 East Lake Street, Chicago, Illinois 60601
Telephone: +1 312 372 5671
Gibbs & Hill Española, SA, Magallanes, 3 Planta 9, Madrid 15, Spain
Telephone: +34 447 2800 Cable: Gandhesa, Madrid
GIBSIN Engineers Limited, 6th Floor, Sinotech Building, 171 Section 5/Nanking East Road, Taipei, Taiwan
Telephone: +886 2 531-4250
Cable: Gibsin, Taipei, Taiwan
Telex: 785 26350

President: Roy H Gordon
Vice Presidents
  Planning and Development, International: S Hull
  Planning and Development, Domestic: D K Mazany
  Transportation and Transmission Division: J S Silien
Assistant Vice President Arch/Urban Development Division: R Stultz
Director, Business Development: K E Vought

Capabilities
Gibbs & Hill was founded in 1911 to provide engineering and design services for the then new field of railway electrification. The company has designed the electrification systems for over 70 per cent of all ac rail systems in the United States. Following incorporation in 1923, the firm began diversifying into a number of related fields, including power engineering, now the major source of company business.

Overall, Gibbs & Hill has a staff of more than 500 professional and support personnel, providing a variety of vital services.

The Transportation and Transmission Division operates as an integrated group with a permanent technical staff of over 100, together with all necessary supporting personnel. Assignments in the transportation field have comprised: engineering and economic feasibility reports; system planning studies; alternative transportation mode studies; preliminary design and cost estimates; environmental impact studies and reports; preparation of project loan applications; site and right-of-way investigations; comprehensive investigations and appraisals of available hardware and rolling stock. Additionally, actual detailed engineering and design services have been furnished for: railroad and rapid transit electrification, including traction power supply and transmission facilities, substations, and overhead catenary or third-rail distribution systems; signalling and train control; communications; automation; operations analysis and computer simulation; shops, yards and terminals; vehicle procurement; waste treatment and disposal facilities; steam generation; and all ancillary and supporting facilities.

Projects
Washington Metropolitan Area Transit Authority (WMATA), Washington DC: Engineering and design of automatic computerised train control signal and communications system for the fully automated transit system of Washington DC. The system provides for 90-second headway with top speeds of 120 km/h and features capability for automatic schedule maintenance by a central computer system. The communication system includes a private automatic branch exchange (PABX) of 2000 lines, an emergency and maintenance telephone system, a public address system in each station, train and yard fire and intrusion alarm system, a teleprinter network, a mobile radio system, a closed circuit television system to monitor station areas and a centralised technical control centre.

New York City Transit Authority: Gibbs & Hill has provided engineering services for the surveillance of construction for 325 of the Authority's R62 cars being manufactured by Kawasaki and 825 R62A cars manufactured by Bombardier of Canada. Working in joint venture, Gibbs & Hill is responsible for review of construction drawings for electrical components, including controls, all motors and hotel amenities on the Kawasaki cars, and engineering and inspection for similar components on the Bombardier cars.

MTA, Metro-North Commuter Railroad and Connecticut Department of Transportation: Gibbs & Hill is providing engineering management and construction surveillance of 76 push-pull commuter cars.

New York City Transit Authority: In joint venture Gibbs & Hill is providing engineering and design services for the upgrading of the complete communications facilities on the Fourth Avenue Line between Whitehall Street Station in Manhattan and 95th Street Station in Brooklyn.

Florida High Speed Rail Transportation Commission: Technical consultant to the Commission to assist them in evaluating proposals from applicants competing for the franchise to build a high-speed rail system that will link Tampa, Orlando and Miami. Work is being performed in joint venture with Kaiser Engineers Inc.

Greiner Engineering Inc

Suite 1900, LB-44, 909 E Las Colinas Blvd, Irving, Texas 75039 USA

Telephone: +1 214 869 1001

President and Chief Executive Officer: Frank T Callahan

Projects
Coney Island Main Repair Facilities inspection of construction (rehabilitation of existing facilities) for the New York City Transit Authority. This facility will become the largest rail maintenance facility in the United States when completed in 1990 ($80 million); Fort Totten station construction services ($25 million) for the Washington Metropolitan Area Transit Authority; design for new three-track bridge over Fort Point Channel for Massachusetts Bay Transportation ($8 million).

Groupe Design MBD

11 rue Victor Hugo, 93177 Bagnolet Cedex, France

Telephone: +33 48 57 30 00
Telex: mbd rvpa 231 821 f
Telefax: +33 48 57 41 31

Marketing Manager: Yves Domergue
Engineering Process Manager: Alain Domergue

Capabilities
Group Design MBD accepts commissions by network authorities and rolling stock manufacturers for both long and short-term railway transportation projects.

Projects
Design studies have been undertaken for the Paris suburban Z2N double-deck train; SYBIC locomotive for SNCF; MF88 for Paris Metro.

Gutteridge Haskins & Davey Pty Ltd

Principal offices: 39 Regent Street, Railway Square, New South Wales 2000, Australia

Telephone: +61 2 690 7070
Telefax: +61 2 698 1780

97 Franklin Street, Melbourne, Victoria 3000

Telephone: +61 3 665 0222
Telefax: +61 3 663 4867

15 Astor Terrace, Brisbane, Queensland 4000

CONSULTANCY SERVICES

Telephone: +61 7 831 7955
Telefax: +61 7 832 4592

Projects:

Project	Client	Value
Queensland main line electrification	Queensland Railways	1050 million

Stages 1, 2 and 3. Project management services: electrification Gladstone to Emerald and Mines, Hay Point and Dalrymple Bay Systems (680 km). Stage 4. Project management services: electrification Gladstone to Brisbane (500 km)

Halcrow
Sir William Halcrow & Partners Ltd

Vineyard House, 44 Brook Green, London W6 7BY, England

Telephone: +44 71 602 7282
Telex: 916148 halcro g
Telefax: +44 71 603 0095

Chief Executive, Geotechnics, Transportation & Tunnelling: D Buckley

Directors: R W Rothwell
M S Fletcher
G D Hillier
N A Trenter
J Weaver
R N Craig
C T K Heptinstall
A J Madden
R S Gray
D S Kennedy P Jenkin

Principal subsidiaries
Halcrow Fox and Associates
Vineyard House, 44 Brook Green, London W6 7BY

Telephone: +44 71 603 1618
Telex: 8811763 halfox g
Telefax: +44 71 603 5783

Halcrow Gilbert Associates
Burderop Park, Swindon, Wiltshire SN4 0QD

Telephone: +44 793 814756
Telex: 44844 halwil g
Telefax: +44 793 815020

Projects: Sir William Halcrow & Partners

Location	Project	Consultancy services*					Date	Client
United Kingdom								
London	Crossrail feasibility of fast routes		PG	PE			1988 ongoing	London Underground Ltd
London	Docklands Light Railway extension to Lewisham			PE			1988 ongoing	London Regional Transport
London	Heathrow Express		PG	PE			1988 ongoing	British Airport Services Ltd
London	Waterloo to Greenwich line	AY					1988 ongoing	Department of Transport
London	SE London rail study			PE			1988 ongoing	Private/Department of Transport
London	King's Cross development		PG	PE			1987 ongoing	London Regeneration Consortium
London	Victoria station congestion relief			PE			1987 ongoing	London Underground Ltd
UK	Stansted Airport rail link				DD	CS	1986 ongoing	British Rail
London	Docklands Light Railway – 3 consultancies	AY	PG	PE			1986, 88 ongoing	City of London (2), Contractor
London	Silvertown tunnel refurbishment		PG	PE			1985, 88 ongoing	London Docklands DC
UK	Channel Tunnel	AY				CS	1985 ongoing	Eurotunnel
London	London Underground future power supplies			PE	DD		1985 ongoing	London Underground Ltd
UK	Rail market survey	AY					1988	Private
London	Greenwich Peninsula LRT		PG				1988	Private
London	Jubilee Line extension		PG				1979, 88	London Underground Ltd
London	Waterloo station redevelopment			PE			1987-88	British Rail
London	Liverpool Street Central Line station upgrading			PE			1986-87	London Underground Ltd
London	Waterloo and City Line re-equipping			PE			1986-87	British Rail/UTDC
London	East London Line extension			PE			1986	Private
London	Piccadilly Line to Heathrow Terminal 4	AY					1986	London Regional Transport
London	London Underground track conversation	AY					1985	London Regional Transport
Birmingham	West Midlands rapid transit study		PG	PE			1983	West Midlands County Council
Overseas								
Greece	Athens Metro Project				GC		1986 ongoing	Government of Greece
Brazil	São Paulo Metro	AY					1986 ongoing	Contractor
Iraq	Baghdad Metro Project				GC		1981 ongoing	Government of Iraq
Denmark	Copenhagen Metro and light railway			PE			1987-88	Danish State Railways
Taiwan	Taipei Mass Transit System		PG	PE	GC		1985-87	Government of Republic of China
Singapore	Contract 200(D)					DD	1985-87	Government of Singapore
Denmark	Gt Belt Crossing			PE			1983-87	Government of Denmark
Singapore	North-East Sector MRT Study		PG	PE			1985-86	Government of Singapore
Singapore	Contract 102(D)					DD	1983-84	Government of Singapore
Singapore	System Design and Project Staging (SDPS)		PG	PE			1983-83	Government of Singapore
Taiwan	Taipei Mass Transit Study		PG	PE			1981-83	Government of Republic of China
Singapore	Preliminary engineering design Phase III		PG	PE			1979-80	Government of Singapore

* AY advisory, PE preliminary engineering, DD detailed design, PG planning, GC general consultancy, CS construction supervision

Hamburg-Consult
Gesellschaft für Verkehrsberatung und Verfahrenstechniken mbH

Steinstrasse 20, PO Box 102720, 2000 Hamburg 1, Federal Republic of Germany

Telephone: +49 40 30 1007-0
Cable: Hochbahn hc
Telex: 2-162 277
Telefax: +49 40 30 1007-77

Parent company: Hamburger Hochbahn Aktiengesellschaft (Hamburg Public Transport Company)

Chairman: Prof Dipl-Ing Hans-Hermann Meyer
Managing Director: Fritz Pasquay
Vice Directors: Arnold Mies
Walter Keudel

Capabilities
Hamburg-Consult is a subsidiary of the public transport company, the Hamburger Hochbahn Aktiengesellschaft (HHA), and works in close connection with the management of the parent company as well as other affiliated local railroad companies.

Consulting services are based to a large extent on the operational experiences of the HHA. Combined with the experience gained from a large number of national and international projects successfully executed in the past, Hamburg-Consult (HC) can offer comprehensive services for any future project. Hamburg-Consult (HC) employs at present about 70 engineers and economists. Because of the close co-operation with the HHA its staff can be quickly extended by HHA experts for specific projects, if necessary.

Main consulting activities are:
Urban and regional transportation and development studies, planning of integrated transport systems, routes and networks.
Feasibility studies for transport projects, cost/benefit investigations for individual projects and entire systems.
Preliminary design for urban rail and bus systems including functional design for all structures, installations and equipment.
Detailed design for urban rail and bus systems including tender documents and procurement as well as supervision of construction, installation and start of operation.
Design and engineering of signalling and telecommunication systems, automatic train control and bus control systems.
Workshop and depot layout and design as well as management of maintenance and repair facilities.
Management investigations of operation and administration of public transport companies.
Introduction of EDP-systems for public transport services.
Training of personnel for operation and workshops.

Projects
Radiotelephone system for West Berlin in conjunction with AEG-Telefunken; planning Dusseldorf U-Bahn; optimum routing for Munich tunnel sections; construction advice on Vienna and Baghdad metros; wheel rail investigations for Lisbon metro; fire investigations on the rubber-tyred Montreal metro; transit system reliability study for Denver, Colorado, USA; several investigations of rail transit operation without personnel; automatic train operation by data processing techniques; development of the failure monitoring system BEFUND to detect and evaluate vehicle defects and to store failure data (the system is controlled by a microprocessor and data from this unit is transmitted to an operational central control); investigations of an integrated transport system rail transit-taxi (INTAX); investigations of subway vehicles with small profile and of different sizes; checking signalling project for the Bielefeld municipal railway; feasibility study for small profile train in Karlsruhe; specification for an international tender on subway vehicles for Athens metro; investigation of means to benefit from coefficient of adhesion with dc and three-phase current propulsion; studies of reliability and maintenance of modern metro vehicles.

Delon Hampton & Associates

111 Massachusetts Avenue, Suite 400, Washington DC 20001, USA

Telephone: +1 202 898 1999

President: Delon Hampton

Capabilities
Design, planning and inspection of rapid transit and light rail system.

CONSULTANCY SERVICES

Projects
Prime consultant for design of two stations and 10 000 ft of tunnel sections for Southern California Regional Transit District's heavy rail system; sub-consultant for design of Section E-7a of the Washington Metropolitan Area Transit Authority's heavy rail transit system; sub-consultant for the Howard-Dan Ryan rail extension for the Chicago Transit Authority; prime consultant for station and section design of the Southwest Transit project, Chicago, Illinois; prime consultant for aerial structure design of the Long Beach-Los Angeles Light Rail Transit System for the Los Angeles County Transportation Authority.

Harbridge House, Inc

11 Arlington Street, Boston, Massachusetts 02116, USA

Telephone: +1 617 267 6410

Chairman: George J Rabstejnek

Offices: Boston, New York, Washington DC, Chicago, London

Capabilities
Management consulting, education, and research; specialising in transport, financial services, and economic analysis.

Projects
Projects have included:
Boston & Maine Railroad study: For the Massachusetts Port Authority, and in co-operation with the Massachusetts Bay Transit Authority, the Commonwealth of Massachusetts Office of Transportation and Construction, and the New England Regional Commission, Harbridge House developed and analysed alternative viability plans for the Boston & Maine Railroad. Topics covered were: provision for substantial commuter traffic; the financial feasibility of the freight system; a physical freight-flow model; a right-of-way valuation; methods for improving the efficiency of operations; and pertinent labour-management questions.
New England regional rail study: Harbridge House was selected by the New England Regional Commission (NERC) to conduct a comprehensive study of all the New England railroads. The study was designed to: identify, define, and assess the socio-economic and environmental importance of various levels of rail service to the New England region; evaluate the economic viability of the various New England railroads and major segments thereof; analyse various possible alternative physical and institutional configurations of the New England rail system; and provide an analytic methodology which will be available to public decision-makers on a continuing basis. Basic research incorporated data findings on revenue, freight flow and capacity, and configuration of the New England rail system.
Wisconsin State rail plan: For the Wisconsin Department of Transportation, Harbridge House has engaged in a large-scale effort to develop and implement a comprehensive rail plan. The plan covers both freight and passenger (intercity and commuter) services. Harbridge House collected and analysed data in various categories, including costs and revenues of existing services, developed demand forecasts, performed economic and operational analysis, identified alternatives to existing rail operations, and determined the relative costs and benefits of these alternatives.
Amtrak planning and consulting: For Amtrak, Harbridge House has provided business planning assistance, focusing on the national climate and competitive environment facing the client. Planning objectives included: defining the role of Amtrak within the US transport system as a whole; evaluating its performance to date; defining its objectives, and strategies for achieving them; and anticipating potential opportunities and risks, and planning appropriate responses.
Study of rail passenger service: For the US Railway Association (USRA), Harbridge House conducted a study of rail passenger service in the north-east and mid-west regions of the United States. The research effort for this study included:
A survey of existing rail passenger service in terms of scope (routes, stops, frequency, and passenger traffic) and quality (condition of track and facilities, and passenger satisfaction);
Identification of potential additional passenger rail services. This has involved review of Amtrak and Department of Transportation plans, ICC hearings on rail service, and plans of state and local transportation planning bodies, including evaluation of demand forecasting methodologies;
Identification of passenger rail services which would be considered by USRA in its plan to restructure rail service in the regions;
Identification of potential interfaces between desirable levels of passenger service and the overall rail system in the regions.
Northeast Corridor project study: For the Office of Policy and Planning of the US Department of Transportation, Harbridge House conducted an evaluation of passenger demand forecasts for the proposed Northeast Corridor (NEC) improved high-speed rail (IHSR) system;
Study of high-speed rail impact on other transport modes: For the US Department of Transportation, Transportation Systems Center, Harbridge House analysed selected impacts of high-speed passenger rail service (HSRS) legislation on alternative transport modes (specifically, auto, air, and bus) in the Northeast Corridor.
Training programme in joint labour-management problem solving: For the US Federal Mediation and Conciliation Service, Harbridge House developed and conducted a two-day training programme designed to help labour-management committees in the railroad industry to develop the key skills necessary for resolving problems of common interest and concern. The programme is based on recently developed techniques for problem analysis, negotiation, and conflict resolution.
BN senior management needs assessment: For Burlington Northern, Inc (BNI), Harbridge House interviewed 50 senior level and mid-level BNI executives to assess the development needs of the company's senior managers in relation to changing expectations for their performance. The interviews served to identify the changing strategic directions of the company and managers' reactions to those changes, emerging success profiles for senior managers of the future (including accountabilities, skills, and activities), and educational/developmental needs. As a result of the needs analysis, Harbridge House provided recommendations for specific developmental activities and developed detailed curricula for educational programmes for two levels of management.
Study of market demand for rail freight facility: For New York State Urban Development Corporation and the New York City Office of Economic Development, Harbridge House conducted a study of the market demand for a rail freight facility at a 60th St yard. The primary focus of the study was to assess the potential demand for intermodal (TOFC/COFC) rail services at 60th St. This involved the identification of intercity traffic flow throughout the New York City metropolitan area as well as a geographic and modal breakdown of traffic. It also involved the conduct of direct interviews with and mail surveys of shippers for the purpose of identifying the shipping activities and practices of firms in areas likely to use a 60th St facility. Based on the survey/interview findings, forecasts of future intercity traffic demand and future TOFC/COFC traffic volumes were developed as alternative scenarios. An assessment of the design and operating considerations for a 60th St TOFC site was also included, as well as an evaluation of the economic impact and key marketing considerations.
Transcontinental freight shipment analysis: For a Washington DC law firm and in support of the cross-examination of expert witnesses appearing on behalf of the proposed Missouri Pacific-Union Pacific merger, Harbridge House prepared analyses of impacts of the economic and strategic position of transcontinental markets in selected key materials, notably coal and trona (soda ash).

Harris Miller Miller & Hanson Inc

429 Marrett Road, Lexington, Massachusetts 02173, USA

Telephone: +1 617 863 1401

Co-ordinator of Rail Transportation Services: Dr Carl E Hanson PE

Capabilities
Noise and vibration control.

Projects
Environmental noise and vibration assessment for the new Taipei Rapid Transit System in Taiwan as part of the URS International team.
Noise and vibration control for the assessments and design of light rail transit projects in Los Angeles, including the Long Beach-Los Angeles line, the San Fernando Valley alternatives study and the Century Freeway/E1 Segundo Extension. Consulting fees are approximately $200 000 for these projects.
Noise and vibration assessments and preliminary engineering for several Massachusetts Bay Transportation Authority projects, including the Bowdoin/Charles Connector Project and the Old Colony Railroad Rehabilitation Project serving Boston. Consulting fees are approximately $100 000 for these projects.

Harza Engineering Company

150 South Wacker Drive, Chicago, Illinois 60606, USA

Telephone: +1 312 855 7000

Senior Vice-President: John A Scoville
Project Manager, Transportation, Mass Transit and Underground Projects: Konstanyn Hrechniw
Associate and Manager, Government Agency Services, US/Canada: Walter D Linzing

Projects
Chicago, Illinois: Howard Dan Ryan rapid transit tunnel connection for the City of Chicago. Services include structural, civil, mechanical and electrical design of approximately one-quarter of a mile of subway.
New York, New York: concrete technology consultant to the New York City Transit Authority. Services include review and recommendations for updating concrete standards and specifications, and input on projects requiring state-of-the-art concrete technology.

Charles Haswell & Partners (Far East)

3/F KA Cheong Building, 2-4 Sunning Road, Causeway Bay, Hong Kong

Telephone: +852 5 8909211
Telex: 83152 chafe hx
Telefax: +852 5 8906343

Managing Director: J G Campbell
Director (Hong Kong): R Clarke

Charles Haswell & Partners Ltd
99 Great Russell Street, London WC1B 3LA

Telephone: +44 71 580 2412
Telex: 299544
Telefax: +44 71 631 4602

Capabilities
International consulting engineers for civil and structural engineering work and geotechnic work. Specialists in driven tunnel works for heavy and light rail rapid transit systems. Capable of handling all aspects of projects from concept through feasibility, design, tender documentation and assessment stages to supervision of construction for driven tunnel/cut and cover stations and running line sections. Also offering advice on asessment of alternatives, contractual matters, claims assessment, litigation and arbitration.

Hawker Siddeley Rail Projects Ltd

PO Box 319, Foundry Lane, Chippenham, Wiltshire SN15 1EE, England

Telephone: +44 249 654141
Telex: 445743 hsrp g
Telefax: +44 249 443165

Chairman: H R Grant
Managing Director: W B Tait

Capabilities
Hawker Siddeley Rail Projects co-ordinates all the

railway activities of the Hawker Siddeley group and markets and manages turnkey railway projects. The group includes such companies as Brush Electrical Machines, Brush Transformers and Westinghouse Brake & Signal. The rail project company is controlled by directors of the various constituent railway-orientated companies. Services extend from advice and assistance in the preparation and presentation of a preliminary study, co-ordination of several contracts with individual Hawker Siddeley companies within a single contract, to management of complete turnkey railway projects, including provision of financial arrangements. Hawker Siddeley companies have experience of urban transport projects in London, Toronto, Hong Kong, New York and Boston, and of rail electrification projects in Australia, New Zealand and the UK.

HDR Engineering Inc

8404 Indian Hills Drive, Omaha, Nebraska 68114-4049, USA

Telephone: +1 402 399-1000

Assistant Vice-President: William M Dowd

Capabilities
Railroad structures design and inspection; railroad trackwork design and inspection; construction administration services; rail rapid transit (line and station) designs; terminal and transfer facilities design; and light rail and people mover design.

Projects
Engineer-of-record and provided construction administration services for the upgrading and new construction associated with 160 km of spur connector in eastern Wyoming ($100 million) for the Chicago & North Western and Union Pacific Railroads; plans and specifications for 2.6 km of line and one station ($25 million), for Metropolitan Atlanta Rapid Transit Authority (MARTA); plans and specifications, 4 km of line, and four stations ($30 million) for Washington Metropolitan Area Transit Authority (WMATA); plans and specifications for 2.66 km of line, including a major aerial guideway for Dade County Rapid Transit System; plans and specifications for six truss, deck plate and through-plate girder bridges on the system of the Union Pacific Railroad; plans for yard lighting and microwave towers at five sites on the Union Pacific system; rehabilitation of existing canal siphons at Gering, Nebraska, for Union Pacific Railroad; plans and specifications for numerous highway/railroad grade separation structures for city, county and state agencies across the US.

Hill International Inc

One Levitt Parkway, Willingboro, New Jersey 08046 USA

Telephone: +1 609 871 5800/+1 800 222 0127

President & Chief Operating Officer: Peter A Russo

Capabilities
Engineering consultancy; project management oversight; project management; productivity and cost containment consulting.

Projects
Projects include: Istanbul, Turkey, high speed line (project management, claims management); Frankford elevated project, Norristown high speed line, Philadelphia, USA; Los Angeles Metro Rail, USA.

Hyland Joy & Associates Pty Ltd

11th Floor, 157 Liverpool Street, Sydney, New South Wales 2000, Australia

Telephone: +61 2 261 8700
Telefax: +61 2 264 8126

Director: David Hyland
Director: Stewart Joy

Capabilities
All aspects of railway systems planning; operations analysis; patronage pricing and revenue forecasting; organisational design; electrical systems analysis.

Iffland Kavanagh Waterbury PC

1501 Broadway, New York, New York 10036, USA

Telephone: +1 212 944 2000

President: Jerome S B Iffland

Capabilities
Rail transit station, line section (tunnelling, cut-and-cover, sunken tube, at grade, elevated) and maintenance facilities design; construction management.

Projects
F Route Section 3 for Washington Metropolitan Area Transit Authority, Washington DC: Final design of four major construction contracts consisting of 4085 feet each of double shield-driven soft earth tunnel and one station (Navy Yard station) and cross-over box involving 1000 feet of cut-and-cover construction. Estimated construction cost $135 million.

Ilium Associates, Inc

500 108th Ave. N.E., Suite 2450, Bellevue, Washington 98004, USA

Telephone: +1 206 6466525

President: Carolyn Perez Andersen
Vice President: Robert M Prowda

Capabilities
Consumer research and analysis; preparation of marketing strategies and plans; project planning, graphic design of signage systems, corporate identities including vehicle graphics and uniforms; brochures, posters and map design.

Recent projects
Signage system design and specification for light rail systems in Sacramento and Portland; transit malls in Rochester, Tampa, Nashville, Long Beach and Portland; corporate identity system for DART in Dallas; consumer research and evaluation studies in Hartford, Dallas, Indianapolis, Savannah, Lansing, Tampa, Spokane and Contra Costa County; design and preparation of Marketing Manual for Community Transit Operators.

IIT Research Institute

10 W 35th Street, Chicago, Illinois 60616, USA

Telephone: +1 312 567 4459
Telex: 282472 iitricgo
Telefax: +1 312 567 4608

Manager: Charles E Radgowski

Capabilities
IITRI specialises in cost-effective, realistic operator training for drivers and management. Training usually includes use of an advanced locomotive simulator, either on IITRI premises or available separately. Clients have found that simulator training saves fuel, decreases the need for train and track time, and lowers property damage. Students gain a wide range of hands-on experience in a short time and can practise hazardous situations at no risk to life or property.

IITRI's full-function Research and Locomotive Evaluator/Simulator (RALES) is permanently located in Chicago. It features a full-scale, completely furnished SD 40-2 locomotive cab mounted on a six-axis motion base. The system includes dual 35 mm projectors and a synchronised sound system. Together, these features allow RALES to simulate the sights, sounds and motion of an actual train in operation.

Operating conditions are created by three mainframe computers, IITRI-developed software and other peripherals. The software allows customisation of train makeup, equipment configuration, performance monitoring, and data display and recording.

From a separate control room, supervisors view the cab's interior, controls and indicators on closed circuit TV. They can also specify the events of the training run and add special effects such as a malfunction. Throughout the simulation, the student's reactions are videotaped and the effects on the train are recorded. Objective, computerised performance evaluations measure proficiency and identify students who need more training.

Computer graphics display all aspects of the simulation, including brake and force effects on the train. The system will also process physiological and psychological data to explore human factors of operation, such as long work cycles or night shift operation.

RALES specifications: simulates trains of more than 200 cars (lengths, loads and empty weights of cars can be specified); handles one to 10 power units at the head of the train and one to five power units as a remote consist, either helper or Locotrol-controlled; contains an AAR-105 control stand and 26L brake equipment; simulates AB, ABD and ABDW 26C, 26F brake valves, retainer valve settings, various shoe types and rigging efficiencies; utilises a motion base with six degrees of freedom (vertical, lateral, longitudinal, roll, pitch, yaw) to recreate movements experienced at various speeds and track classes, and the effects of slack run-in and run-out; handles alternate events selection and multi-reel runs with dual 35 mm projectors or video disc system; operates in real-time; can simulate composite cab signal/speed control system and Plus One Alerter; replicates sounds including cab/diesel engine operation, air brakes and window sounds such as horn, crossing bells and trailing units.

For clients who prefer to work at their own location, IITRI offers a choice of two simulators that can be purchased as part of a consulting arrangement.

The TS-2 is a room-size, transportable simulator that contains many of the capabilities found in RALES, including air brake and dynamic simulation, programmable conditions, and computerised performance evaluations. The basic TS-2 equipment includes a TS-2M control stand, complete graphics displays, computer hardware and software, and synchronised forward view projector and screen. The system can also be upgraded with a number of available sub-systems, including sound.

The TS-3 is a complete, full-function simulator including full-size cab (carrier's choice of design used), separate control room and performance evaluation software. Like RALES, it provides the closest possible simulation of the sights, sounds and motion of a real locomotive.

Projects
IITRI has been providing research and development services to industry and government since 1936. Each year, the Institute conducts more than 500 research projects for US and international clients, for an annual volume of about $100 million. Since 1985, IITRI has provided an average of 1500 training hours per year for major railroads, equipment suppliers and government agencies.

International Rail Consultants

1190 Hornby Street, Vancouver, British Columbia V6Z 2H6, Canada

PO Box 8770, Vancouver, British Columbia V6B 4X6

Telephone: +1 604 984 5019, 684 9311

Capabilities
In 1985 British Columbia Rail Ltd and Swan Wooster Engineering Ltd, of Vancouver, British Columbia, formed this joint transportation consulting services venture. International Rail will market consulting services from pre-feasibility through feasibility assessment to engineering design, procurement, construction, construction management and implementation of projects. It also will offer consulting expertise in management, operation, fixed plant, rolling stock and systems analysis. Swan Wooster was founded in 1925 as a firm of consulting engineers and transportation economists. Along with its affiliates, it operates throughout the Americas, Africa, Asia and the Middle East.

BC Rail is Canada's third largest railway. It operates exclusively in Canada's province of British Columbia, with interline connections to all rail-served points in North America. The railway operates 2150 km of trackage with a fleet of 130 locomotives, both electric and diesel-electric powered. BC Rail also operates a fleet of 10 000 freight cars.

International Rail is equipped to offer consulting services in large project management and control systems for construction and operation of new facilities, as well as: railway management and control;

444 CONSULTANCY SERVICES

computerised train control and dispatch; microwave communications; freight and passenger operations; all railway engineering and construction matters; railway systems analysis; rolling stock and motive power procurement, maintenance and reconstruction; personnel and labour relations functions; data processing acquisition and operation; and marketing, car lease and tariff compilation.

In 1987 International Rail was involved in projects in Africa and Indonesia.

Interinfra

16 rue de la Baume, 75008 Paris, France

Telephone: +33 1 45 61 96 01
Telex: 642829 f
Telefax: +33 1 42 25 26 54

Marketing Manager P Blanic

Capabilities
Project management and general contractor for mainline and rapid transit schemes.

Japan Transportation Consultants Inc

Tadokoro Building, 5-2 Nishi Kanda 2-chome, Chiyoda-ku, Tokyo 101, Japan

Telephone: +81 3 263 9470
Telefax: +81 3 263 9472

Manager, Overseas Services: E Kurakawa

JARTS
Japan Railway Technical Service

TSK Building, 2nd and 3rd Floors, 8-13 Hongo 4-chome, Bunkyo-ku, Tokyo 113, Japan

Telephone: +81 3 5684 3171-79/81-84
Cable: Railwaytechs, Tokyo
Telex: 25254
Telefax: +81 3 5684 3170/80

Chairman: Yutaka Takeda
President: Misao Sugawara
Senior Executive Vice President: Hotsumi Harada
Executive Vice Presidents: Sadaaki Kuroda
    Koji Terado
    Takeshi Nagashima
    Ichiro Mitsui
Senior Technical Counsellor: Hideo Shima
Counsellors: Tatsuya Ishiaha
    Saburo Okita
    Fumio Takagi
    Sohei Nakayama

Capabilities
JARTS was established for the express purpose of co-operating with the international community in the development of urban, suburban, and main line railways, operating under the guidance of Japan's Ministry of Transport and in co-operation with the Japan Railways Group (formerly Japanese National Railways), the Japan Railway Construction Public Corporation and the Teito Rapid Transit Authority.

Fields of activity include: studies, surveys, and projects, and management relating to railways, subways and monorails; construction of new lines; modernisation and improvement of railway track; electrification; dieselisation; modernisation of rolling stock; automatic train control and centralised traffic control; seat reservation systems; and marshalling yard automation; holding of overseas seminar, making PR films, introducing Japanese railway technology and training of personnel.

Projects
Projects have included:
Argentina: consulting services for the electrification of the Rocaline of the Argentine Railways (1973–74, 1975) and supervision (1981–86);
Australia: investigation of Very Fast Train Project between Sydney and Melbourne (1986–88);
Bangladesh: Feasibility study of the construction of a rolling stock plant for Bangladesh Railway (1984–85);
Bolivia: engineering services (detailed design) on the national railway (East Line) rehabilitation project and supervision of construction (1982–88);
Brazil: technical co-operation services to RFFSA for the improvement of railway operations (1980–84); special technical services for the Carajas Railway wagon project for CVRD (1983);
Chile: recommendation and advice to the Chilean State Railways on the improvement of freight-car control and information system (1982-83);
China: feasibility studies of double-tracking and electrifying the railway line between Hengyang and Guangzhou, and electrifying the double-track line between Zhengzhou and Baoji (1983-84); consulting services for and studies of the construction of an integrated station-building complex in Beijing for Ministry of Railways (1985-86); feasibility study of the first stage of the Shanghai subway project for Shanghai Municipal Science and Technology Commission (1985-86); consultancy service in soil investigation (1986-87); feasibility study for the construction of commuter railway between Tianjin and Tanggu in People's Republic of China (1989-90);
Egypt: pre-feasibility study of the rapid transit system between Cairo and the Tenth of Ramadan city, Cairo and Sadat city, Alexandria and New Ameriyah city (1987);
India: investigation into the management of the Indian Railways, for the International Bank for Reconstruction and Development (1981); feasibility study of raising train speed on Delhi-Kampur main line; study on development plan for the New Delhi railway station (1988-89); 2 × 25 kV ac electrification of Indian Railways (1988 ongoing);
Indonesia: establishment of the master plan for development of railway transportation in the metropolitan area of Jakarta (JABOTABEK) (1980-81); feasibility study of the improvement of the Kampung Bandan station area for Indonesian State Railways (1984–85); feasibility study of electrification and overall upgrading of the railway system in Java for Indonesian State Railways (1984–86); consulting and management-related services for the development of railway transportation in the JABOTABEK region for Indonesian State Railways, PMS-1 (1984–89), PMS-2 (1990 ongoing). The study on integrated transportation system improvement by railway and feeder service in JABOTABEK area (1989–99); Iran: preliminary survey of the upgrading and rehabilitation of Iran National Railway (1989–90); Korea, Republic: consulting services for the NATM for Seoul Metropolitan Subway Corporation (1982–84); technical service for the subway Line 1 construction project for the Busan City government (1983–85); consulting service for Seoul Metropolitan Subway construction Line 5 (1989 ongoing);
Myanmar: feasibility study of electrification of the circular railway line in Rangoon for the Burma Railways Corporation (1984–85); feasibility of track, telecommunication and signalling improvement (1986);
New Zealand: consulting service for the electrification project of the North Island Main Trunk of the New Zealand Railways (1981–88);
Pakistan: consulting services for constructing a locomotive manufacturing factory for the Pakistan Railways (1984–91); study of national transport plan for the seventh five-year plan (1987–88); preliminary study on electrification of the Pakistan Railway;
Philippines: study of the Manila metrorail network extension project (1987–88);
Sudan: fuel transportation project for power schemes (1988–90);
Taiwan: advisory service for the construction of High Speed Underground Railway in Taipei (1986 ongoing); technical advisory service for West Taiwan High Speed Railway feasibility study (1989 ongoing);
Thailand: study on the Rama VI Bridge rehabilitation project for RSR (1982); preliminary study for elevating the railway lines in the Bangkok Metropolitan area (1983–84); study of railway yards improvement in the Kingdom of Thailand (1985–86);
Turkey: preliminary study of high-speed train operation between Istanbul and Ankara by constructing a new railway line between Arifiye and Sincan (1987);
USA: consulting services for the Northeast Corridor Improvement Project between Boston and Washington, for the Federal Railroad Administration, DOT, in conjunction with De Leuw, Cather/Parsons (1977–79); consulting services for the Ohio High-speed Intercity Rail Passenger Plan, for the Ohio Rail Transportation Authority, in conjunction with Dalton-Dalton-Newport Inc (1979–80); consulting services for the preliminary design of the passive tilt system of Amcoach, for the Federal Railroad Administration, DOT (1980–81); consulting services for the high-speed rail test track plan, for the Ohio Rail Transportation Authority, in conjunction with Dalton-Dalton-Newport Inc (1981–82); feasibility studies for the high-speed railway construction project in the states of California, Florida and in the Chicago region (1981–85); consulting services for constructing a Shinkansen line between Los Angeles and San Diego, for the American High-Speed Rail Corporation (1983–84);
Zaire: feasibility study of new railway construction between Kinsenso and Kinban-seke (1986–87).

Bernard Johnson Incorporated

5050 Westheimer Road, Houston, Texas 77056, USA

Telephone: +1 713 622 1400

Executive Vice President: Ronald W Kilpatrick

Capabilities
Transit systems planning and engineering; railcar and locomotive maintenance facilities; trackwork, yards and bridges.

Kaiser Engineers Inc

1800 Harrison St, PO Box 23210, Oakland, California 94623 USA

Telephone: +1 415 268 6000
Telex: 335326

Vice President, Transportation: Steven K Kauffmann

Capabilities
Programme management; planning and design; systems engineering; construction management for light rail, metros, commuter rail and automated guideway transit systems.

Projects
Taipei Metro (general consultant, technology transfer); Chicago Southwest corridor (co-ordinating consultant, new rail link to Midway Airport); Exchange Place station, New Jersey; Park Avenue tunnel rehabilitation, New York (construction management).

KAMPSAX International A/S

Dagmarhus, Raadhuspladsen, 1553 Copenhagen V, Denmark

Telephone: +45 1 14 14 90
Cable: Kampsax, Copenhagen
Telex: 15508

Subsidiary and associate companies
KAMPSAX (Nigeria) Ltd, PO Box 5810, Lagos, Nigeria
KAMPSAX-PACIFIC Ltd, 9th Floor, Centre Point Building, 181-185 Gloucester Road, Hong Kong
Geoplan A/S, Dagmarhus, 1553 Copenhagen V (aerial photography and mapping)
Geodan, Stamholmen 112, 2650 Hvidovre (soils survey, geotechnical engineering)
Geodata A/S, Dagmarhus, 1553 Copenhagen V (computer services)

Parent company
KAMPSAX A/S, Dagmarhus, 1553 Copenhagen V

Deputy Managing Director: Ulf Blach
Chief Railway Engineer: Jan Svendsen

Capabilities
Founded in 1917 as a general Danish civil engineering firm, the firm entered the international market as consulting engineers in 1927. In Denmark, the firm provides complete engineering services including construction.

As consultants, the company has the capacity and experience to undertake a wide range of projects. Transport and communications have been the most important KAMPSAX activities, with major projects covering all modes of transport. One of the earliest tasks was the consulting services related to the Trans-Iranian Railway, a major international engineering undertaking between the World Wars.

The company undertakes design and supervision, and covers planning, maintenance, and training activities as well. In recent years KAMPSAX has performed preliminary investigations, preparation of countrywide and regional long-term transport development and investment programmes, and project feasibility studies, and has provided technical assistance for improvement of maintenance, and for administration and management of public sector transport agencies.

Projects
On assignment by the Danish and Swedish Development Agencies, KAMPSAX is undertaking special studies and provides technical support to the Meeting of Railway Administrations convened by the SATCC Countries (Angola, Botswana, Lesotho, Malawi, Mozambique, Swaziland, Tanzania, Zambia and Zimbabwe) with the objective of furthering transport collaboration between these states.

For the Danish International Development Agency (DANIDA), the company has completed an outline design of a locomotive and wagon maintenance depot for Mahalapye, Botswana. After assistance with tendering, KAMPSAX has supervised construction and is providing a management team for the operation of the depot. For DANIDA a study on rehabilitation of the Tanzania Railway's link line is being carried out.

Under a contract with DANIDA, KAMPSAX assists the Beira Corridor Authority in Mozambique, financed by the Danish, Finnish, Norwegian and Swedish Development Agencies in the implementation of transport projects including railway installations. The corridor links Zimbabwe and the other landlocked countries to the Indian Ocean. Technical assistance consists in supplying the Beira Corridor Authority with a series of experts acting as a so-called Core Unit in the administration.

In Uganda, KAMPSAX under a contract with DANIDA is conducting a feasibility study concerning a wagon ferry terminal at Port Bell, as well as replacement and realignment of the Port Bell-Kampala rail link.

A T Kearney Inc

222 S Riverside Plaza, Chicago, Illinois 60606, USA

Telephone: +1 312 648 0111

Vice-President Transportation: John Throckmorton

Capabilities
Kearney's rail practice began in 1945 with studies for several Midwestern railroads. This early work consisted of developing data and recommendations to improve operations, maintenance, purchasing and stores, traffic cost analysis, organisation and staffing, management development and training of personnel, abandonment studies and a wide range of railroad policy decisions. Since 1955, Kearney's consulting services to the railroad industry have expanded rapidly. Kearney has worked for over 20 client railroads, and a similar number of clients in industries peripheral to the rail industry. In addition, Kearney has worked for a number of federal and state agencies in the rail area such as the Federal Railroad Administration, the Interstate Commerce Commission, and the United States Railway Association; and also for the Association of American Railroads.

Kearney has also been retained to aid many railroads in the management of their trucking operations and intermodal yards, analysis of corporate strategy, implementation of marketing and cost-based pricing strategies, development of management information systems, improvement of rail terminal operations, and studies of facilities consolidation. Kearney's railroad engagements have also encompassed many other phases of management and innovation, such as programmes to benefit from the unit train concept; development of standard cost systems, rates and divisions, economic analysis, tariff qualifications, administrative and clerical controls, profit and productivity improvement studies; development of new freight-handling techniques, facility and equipment improvements; development of specifications for freight cars, yard modernisation, freight car utilisation, container handling systems, work measurement and labour standards, cost reduction studies of yards and maintenance shops; and selection and training of personnel for new innovative activities, such as industrial engineering and marketing. Such engagements often require the use of simulation and systems design techniques coupled with industrial engineering expertise.

Projects
Assignments covered by Kearney deal with: railroad corporate strategy; marketing and pricing strategies; unit train economic feasibility; simulation and systems design; truckline subsidiary analysis; terminal operations; intermodal terminal operations; intermodal planning and operations; industrial engineering and methods; railroad research and technology; facilities consolidation; forecasting; productivity improvement; railcar leasing strategy; railroad service assessment; cost analysis; government rail research; and regulatory policy analysis.
Clients have included:
Railroads: Burlington Northern; Canadian National; Canadian Pacific; Chessie System; Chicago and North Western; Denver and Rio Grande Western; Detroit Toledo and Ironton; Grand Trunk Western; Illinois Central Gulf; Kansas City Southern; Missouri Pacific; Norfolk and Western; St Louis-San Francisco; Santa Fe Industries; Southern; Southern Pacific; Union Pacific; Western Pacific
Railroad suppliers and car leasing companies: AFC Industries; General American Car; North American Car; Pullman, Inc; Union Tank Car Company
Governmental agencies and organisations: Amtrak; California Department of Transportation; Central Illinois Public Service Commission; Federal Railroad Administration; Interstate Commerce Commission; United States Railway Association

Kennedy Henderson Ltd

A member of the Kennedy & Donkin Group

Westbrook Mills, Godalming, Surrey GU7 2AZ, England

Telephone: +44 4868 25900
Telex: 859373 kdhog
Telefax: +44 4868 25136

Directors: J M Booth
R H Busby
G D Macfarlane
J B Gaskell J R Springate

Overseas offices: Kennedy & Donkin International Ltd, 13th Floor, New Town Tower, 8-18 Pak Hok Ting Street, Shatin, Hong Kong NT

Telephone: +852 06010822

Managing Director: R H Busby

Other overseas offices: Austria, Botswana, Cyprus, Iraq, Italy, Jordan, Malawi, Switzerland, United Arab Emirates, West Germany, Yemen Arab Republic, Zimbabwe.

Capabilities
Kennedy Henderson offers services to railway administrations and transit authorities covering feasibility studies, system design and engineering and advice on organisation, operation and maintenance, and training. The Company's expertise in electrical and mechanical disciplines includes traction and rolling stock, signalling and train control, communication, power supply, automatic fare collection equipment, environmental control, depot and workshop equipment, station services including escalators, lifts, container handling and freight transfer.

Civil and structural services are also offered including design of stations; workshops and depots, cut-and-cover tunnels, bridges, viaducts etc, route alignments, permanent way and earthworks.

Projects
Trans-Kalahari Railway: The Government of Botswana appointed the Company to undertake a feasibility study for the 1200 km Trans Kalahari Railway. The railway is required to transport coal for export from new mines in eastern Botswana, across the Kalahari and through Namibia, to a new coal terminal to be constructed on the west coast of Africa. The first phase of the study examined the alternative routes for the railway and alternative locations for the port/coal terminal. The second phase comprises a detailed engineering financial and economic appraisal of the preferred route.
Nigerian Railway Corporation: Revitalisation study funded by the World Bank to review all aspects of management and operations.
European rail study: KH was appointed by the Department of Trade and Industry to carry out a study of the European market for railway components. The aim of the study was to identify market opportunities for the UK manufacturers particularly post-1992. The study was broadly based both in market terms and product coverage. It included both mechanical and electrical components used in railway locomotives and rolling stock, trackwork and maintenance. The study was designed to meet DTI objectives of highlighting market-led opportunities under the Enterprise Initiative.
British Rail, locomotives and rolling stock: The Company was appointed by British Rail to report on the capability and capacity of the private sector to build new locomotives and rolling stock and to provide heavy maintenance services in competition with British Rail Engineering Ltd. The Company visited all the major UK manufacturers and reviewed their works before preparing the report, which concluded that tenders could advantageously be sought from the private sector.
Hong Kong, Eastern Harbour Crossing: The Eastern Harbour Crossing Project will provide a second mass transit railway link between Kowloon and Hong Kong Island. Kennedy Henderson were appointed by Freeman Fox and Partners in 1987 to provide engineering services in the fields of signalling, power supply and overhead conductors systems. The scope of the work included the preparation of design specifications, the approval of designs, tender assessment, negotiations with equipment suppliers and site supervision and co-ordination.
Hong Kong KCR: The Company was appointed as consultants to carry out a feasibility study on the Kowloon-Canton Railway Corporation for modernisation, electrification and development of the system, with a view to maximising the operational capability of the KCRC to meet both the traffic demands postulated by the Hong Kong government's population redistribution plans and the potential freight traffic from mainland China.
Hong Kong Tuen Mun LRT: In association with Scott Wilson Kirkpatrick and Partners the company undertook a planning study in 1986 to determine the engineering and economic feasibility of extending the LRT system between Tuen Mun and Yuen Long. A second part of the study was concerned with possible connections to the main line and mass transit railways. As a result of the study findings, design contrcts for four of the regional links were awarded in 1987 to a group comprising Kennedy & Donkin International, KH and Scott Wilson Kirkpatrick. KH is providing the project management, design specifications and contract documents for alignment and permanent way, power supplies, overhead line equipment, radio and telephone systems, public address, vehicle information systems and fare collection.
Hong Kong Island LRT: Kennedy Henderson participated in a study of a new LRT system to link the central business district of Hong Kong Island to the developing southern side. Engineering, operational and financial feasibility were studied and an appropriate type of system recommended. KH's specific tasks related to the system design including rolling stock, signalling, power supplies communications, fare collection, trackwork and operations. The study was commissioned by Hong Kong and Shanghai Hotels Limited and is being managed by Maunsell Consultants Asia Limited.
Hong Kong, Victoria Peak Transportation Scheme: Kennedy Henderson through Kennedy & Donkin International (Hong Kong) were appointed in 1987 by the Hong Kong and Shanghai Hotel Group to carry out a study for replacing the historic Peak Tram with a fast, modern people-mover system. The study required a technical evaluation of alternative systems capable of ascending and descending the slopes of up to 50 per cent for part of the route and for near horizontal grade on other sections.
Singapore MRT: KH was appointed by the successful tenderer for the supply and installation of the trackwork for the Singapore MRT, Henry Boot, to carry out the detailed design on their behalf. The basic system comprises two lines, an east-west line 33 km long with 24 stations and north-south line, 14 km with 12 stations. Detailed drawings for the switch and crossing layouts as well as fabrication and component drawings have been prepared.
Greece, Athens Metro: In September 1986 British Mass Transit Consultants, of which KH is a member, were appointed to implement the priority line, Line B, of the extended metro. KH is responsible for the engineering of the track and all electrical and mechanical systems for the railway, its tunnels and stations. The first stage of the work involved advice on the design, specification and contract conditions for a 1 km tunnel contract, which will be followed by a turnkey contract for the rest of Line B.
Iraq, Baghdad Metro: As a member of the British Metro Consultants Group KHL is retained for the design of the major contracts of the Baghdad Metro. KH is responsible for all electrical and mechanical work

CONSULTANCY SERVICES

and trackwork on the planned ultimate 65 km system, the first 32 km of which, with 38 stations, was due to open in 1990, but is currently delayed due to the war.
Taiwan, Taipei Metro: KH is a member of the British Mass Transit Consultants consortium, retained by the Tawain Ministry of Communications to provide consultancy services for the proposed Taipei mass rapid transit system. KH was responsible for the E & M design and specifications.
London Docklands Light Railway: KH advised on the planning, engineering, operations and implementation of the project. The work included reviewing available systems; studying operations; determining an alternative route to a terminus at Stratford; planning the Operations and Maintenance Centre; investigating the merits of alternative trackforms; preparing specifications, advising on tendering strategy and adjudicating returned tenders. The Company is involved in the planned western extension which will link Tower Hill with the London Underground at Bank station, bring the new Enterprise Zone into the heart of the City, and the Eastern extension to Beckton.
Docklands Railway, Beckton Extension: In 1987 KH was appointed to prepare alignment and trackwork design together with the specifications for all the electrical and mechanical work for the Beckton extension including rolling stock, power supplies, signalling, communications, depots and automatic fare collection equipment.
Avon Light Rail System: KH was commissioned in 1987 to review demand forecasts previously prepared for the Advanced Transport for Avon LRT network and to develop them for two initial routes from Yate to the centre of Bristol and from the centre to Portishead. KH was also appointed to prepare preliminary plans for the first stage of implementation. This is a 14 km section from Portishead to Wapping Road in the centre of Bristol. The plans support the Bill deposited in November 1987.
Croydon Light Rail study: KH and other consultants were commissioned jointly in 1987 by British Rail and London Regional Transport to consider the potential for a light rail network centred on Croydon. This involves use of BR tracks for part of the system with street running through the central area of Croydon.
Nottingham LRT: KH is part of a group consultant appointed to study the potential for a LRT system in the Greater Nottingham area. The first stage of the study identified 14 possible routes and selected one of them as being the most suitable as the initial line of the network. A further study is under way to examine alternative on-street routes through the city centre.
Sheffield Supertram: The Company was appointed by the South Yorkshire Passenger Transport Executive as lead consultants for the LRT project proposed for Sheffield. The project team is providing consultancy to the SYTPE in support of the application for a Section 56 Grant following Parliamentary approval of Line 1. Preliminary design work on some of the more critical civil engineering aspects and on the rolling stock specifications is proceeding in parallel.
Maglev: Working with the People Mover Group (led by GEC Transportation Projects) KH prepared civil engineering design and specifications for the Birmingham Airport magnetic levitation (maglev) transit link with the nearby railway station. The link consists of small, automatically controlled vehicles running on their own segregated elevated guideway. It is the first maglev system of its kind to be operated in public service.
Heathrow surface access study: With Howard Humphries and the MVA Consultancy, KH has been retained by the UK Department of Transport to study alternative means of providing improved access between Heathrow Airport and central London.
Channel Tunnel: During 1985 KH was appointed by the Channel Tunnel Group in support of their bid to government. The Company is now retained by Transmanche-Link JV for design studies covering terminals, ferry wagons and locomotives, control and signalling systems, maintenance requirements, track form, service tunnel vehicles, hot axlebox and derailment detection. KH is currently responsible for the preparation of the performance specifications for the special rolling stock and locomotives which will form the shuttle trains.

Lester B Knight & Associates Inc

549 W Randolph Street, Chicago, Illinois 60606, USA

Telephone: +1 312 346 2100
Telex: 254622
Telefax: +1 312 648 1085

Vice Presidents: Benjamin F Svoboda
Dominick J Gatto
Lee A Hoyt

Capabilities
Transport and environmental studies; railroads and rapid transit systems planning, design and construction, engineering and management; operations and maintenance.

Kuttner, Collins Group
(with affiliated offices)

Head office: 61 Lavender Street, Milsons Point, New South Wales 2061, Australia
Telephone: +61 929 7411
Cable (all offices): Calculus
Telex: 27987
Telefax: +61 957 6914
276 The Avenue, Parkville, Victoria 3052
Telephone: +61 387 2622
Telefax: 387 2767
117 Queen Street, Brisbane, Queensland 4000
Telephone: +61 7 229 3322
40 Marcus Clark Street, Canberra, ACT 2608
Telephone: +61 62 48 8988
31 Hay Street, Subiaco, Western Australia 6008
Telephone: +61 381 7899
60 Wyatt Street, Adelaide, South Australia 5000
Telephone: +61 223 7433
PO Box 783, Bandar Seri Begawan, Brunei
Telephone: +673 3370
190 Middle Road, 11-01 Fortune Centre, Singapore 0718
Telephone: +65 339 2611
8A Persiaran Za'aba, Taman Tun Dr. Ismail, Kuala Lumpur, Malaysia
Telephone: +60 3 790077
KC-Romaho, PO Box 4483, Jakarta, Indonesia
Telephone: +62 21 815712
Citybank Building, Apt 903, Batha Street, Riyadh, Saudi Arabia
Telephone: +966 1 403 5812
50 Road No 5, Dhanmondi Residential Area, Dacca, Bangladesh
Telephone: +880 506201

Principal: G A Collins
Additional Directors (Victoria): M J Smyth, J G Flather
Associate Directors: I Stewart, J Colquhoun, J Y Fok, G R Hislop
Associated Consultants: W L Kuttner, F S Hespe, H G Wallace, B Spencer

Capabilities
Railway works constitute a specialised sub-division within the general scope of the firm's civil engineering practice.

Laramore, Douglass and Popham

332 South Michigan Ave, Suite 400, Chicago, Illinois 60604, USA

Telephone: +1 312 427 8486
Telefax: +1 312 427 8474

1120 Avenue of the Americas, New York, NY 10036, USA

Telephone: +1 212 302 1480

President: Robert H Steinberger
Vice President: Richard T Harvey

Capabilities
Design and Project Management for electrified rapid transit and electric railroad traction power supply and distribution systems.

Projects
Power supply and substation improvements ($80 million) for Massachusetts Bay Transportation Authority (MBTA); dc distribution for Howard-Dan Ryan Project ($3 million), City of Chicago; addition of five rectifier substations for Chicago Transit Authority ($9 million); Green Line extension, traction power ($15 million) for Washington Metropolitan Area Transit Authority (WMATA); and third annual traction power maintenance evaluation (study) for Metropolitan Atlanta Rapid Transit Authority (MARTA).

J W Leas and Associates Inc

910 Potts Lane, Bryn Mawr, Pennsylvania 19010, USA

Telephone: +1 215 525 1952

President: J Wesley Leas

Capabilities
Fare collection system studies, fare structure analyses, fare collection equipment specifications and revenue control procedures for rapid and mass transit operations.

Current Projects
Phased implementation plan for a multi-operator pass to serve the needs of BART, AC Transit, MUNI and CCCTA systems in San Francisco area; system recommendation, equipment requirements, cost analysis and preparing technical specifications for the self-service fare collection (SSFC) system for Los Angeles-Long Beach LRT; station design to accommodate possible future fare collection needs for downtown Seattle Transit project; recommend fare structure and fare collection system features and specify the equipment and fare media for SSFC system for DART's planned LRT network in Dallas; develop system alternatives for ferry fare collection system for the proposed Trans-Hudson ferry service between Hoboken, New Jersey and Manhattan, New York; prepare specifications for electronic registering fareboxes with Pass Reader interface for the MARTA, Atlanta bus system; revenue security and accountability audit of Santa Clara and Portland bus systems.

Light Rail Transit Consultants GmbH

Oskar-Sommer-Strasse 15, D-6000 Frankfurt/Main 70, Federal Republic of Germany

Telephone: +49 69 6319 300
Telex: 414516 decon d
Telefax: +49 69 6319 295

Managing Director: Helmut Gerndt

Capabilities
Comprehensive planning of light rail and other transit systems; design of light rail vehicles and stationary equipment; management assistance and training of personnel.
The company is a subsidiary of Rhein-Consult GmbH, Deutsche Eisenbahn-Consulting GmbH, Hamburg-Consult GmbH and Transport und Technolgie Consult GmbH.

Projects
Guadalajara, Mexico, and Konya, Turkey (system engineering, alignment, workshops, depots, trackwork, stations, operational planning); Monterrey, Mexico (feasibility study, alignment).

London Transport International Services Limited

A wholly-owned subsidiary of London Regional Transport

55 Broadway, Westminster, London SW1H 0BD, England

Telephone: +44 71 227 3777/3685
Telex: 8812227 intran
Telefax: +44 71 222 1142

Chairman: J Telford Beasley
Managing Director: D T Coughtrie

Subsidiary company
LTI Consultants Inc, Suite 1000, 1611 N Kent Street, Arlington, Virginia 22209, USA

Telephone: +1 703 522 9253
Telefax: +1 703 524 8977

President: D T Coughtrie
Executive Vice President: R Lindsell

Capabilities
As a wholly-owned subsidiary of London Transport (which is responsible for 10 Underground lines, the Docklands Light Railway and 350 bus routes), London

CONSULTANCY SERVICES 447

Transport International is able to call on the knowledge and expertise of London Transport's staff and, by agreement, on the staff resources of other UK networks to advise clients on a wide range of aspects including operating, planning and maintaining bus and rail rapid transit systems.

Specialist Consultancy
Transportation and economic planning; passenger marketing and publicity; commercial advertising and concessions; architecture and design; stores and supplies management; capital investment analysis and prioritisation; fares and ticketing systems; revenue control; graffiti and vandalism prevention.

Bus Consultancy
Privatisation; operations and organisation; route planning and scheduling; automated bus control systems; vehicle overhaul and maintenance procedures, including computerised maintenance; garage and workshop design and layout; real-time passenger information; vehicle design and services for the disabled.

Rapid Transit & Light Rail Consultancy
Planning and construction; safety monitoring and security; real-time passenger information; workshop and depot design; quality control; signalling and communications; rolling stock design and maintenance; operations and organisation; station modernisation and design.

Training
LTI arranges training programmes in rapid transit, light rail and buses within the UK and overseas, for personnel from other transport undertakings. Trainees may join standard courses but more usually a programme of attachments is arranged specifically to meet the needs of an individual. Training facilities are offered to all levels of staff and in all different spheres of operation.

Projects
LTI has carried out several varied assignments in 60 cities around the world. LTI's latest projects have included:
United Kingdom: LTI has been assisting with the Channel Tunnel Project since 1986. The mixture of heavy rail technology, train weights and size with projected metro style headways and passenger loadings has made this a particularly challenging project. LTI's knowledge and experience of metro operations has been called on to provide advice on dealing with potential incidents where access is difficult. LTI specialists have helped to review operational procedures, safety arrangements control systems and the service tunnel transport system. LTI provided technical advice on the signalling system, permanent way and operational and safety aspects of the terminal at Folkestone.
Singapore: London Transport has been involved in the development of public transport since the formulation of proposals for a mass transit system in 1966. A team of consultants played a vital role in the planning and outline design of the system. LTI provided consultants to plan the revenue service and to assist with training of local personnel in railway control, train and station operations and maintenance procedures. Training continued following the opening of the system in 1988.
Sydney & Melbourne: In 1988 LTI undertook an audit of the State Rail Authority's signalling system in Sydney. LTI subsequently assisted on a cable replacement programme. In Melbourne a similar audit was undertaken for the Metropolitan Transit Authority. Attention was paid to the integrity of the system and to safety. A review was also undertaken of the effectiveness of signalling maintenance methods.

Taipei: LTI was part of a consortium carrying out a comprehensive design for a metro in Taipei in 1985/86 and is currently engaged to undertake the operating and maintenance planning of the metro in its final design and construction phase.
Hong Kong: LTI arranged training for local MRT staff during the commissioning of rolling stock and the start of passenger operations.
India: LTI has developed training programmes for personnel from Indian Railways. Attachments have been arranged for senior managers in various aspects of railway management.

LTK Engineering Services
A member of the Klander Group

1200 Pennsylvania Building, 1500 Chestnut Street, Philadelphia, Pennsylvania 19102, USA

Telephone: +1 215 563 2570
Telex: 83 4783
Telefax: +1 215 563 2570, Ext 200

President: J Richard Tomlinson
Vice President: John R Vollmar

Capabilities
LTK Engineering Services offer a wide variety of engineering, managerial and planning services designed specifically for the transport field. Based in Philadelphia, Pennsylvania, since founding in 1921, the firm has provided professional and technical assistance to numerous clients throughout the United States and Canada, as well as in Australia, Brazil, Japan, New Zealand, People's Republic of China and Spain.

Projects
Latest assignments undertaken by LTKES include assistance in the following electric rolling stock purchases:

For Metro-North Commuter Railroad LTKIS is to carry out engineering, inspection, testing and acceptance services in connection with remanufacture of ten FL-9 locomotives and conversion to ac traction system (1987–91).

The firm has also assisted in the purchases of 776 locomotive-hauled passenger cars, 61 multiple-unit electric cars and two three-unit articulated gas-turbine trains for intercity passenger services since 1965.

Maguire Group Inc

225 Foxborough Blvd, Foxborough, Massachusetts 02035, USA

Telephone: +1 508 543 1700

President: Vincent M Cangiano

Projects
Vermont Avenue Station design ($30 million) for Los Angeles Metro Wilshire Line; tunnel ventilation shafts ($9 million) for Massachusetts Bay Transportation Authority (MBTA); Red Line extension tunnel section ($110 million) with an associate firm, for Massachusetts Bay Transportation Authority (MBTA); Section E2 tunnel design ($75 million) for Washington Metropolitan Area Transit Authority (WMATA); and five-year improvement rail and drainage study (5.2 miles of rail) for ER Dupont de Nemours & Co Inc; Study and report of the Spine Line Alternative Analysis/Environmental Impact Analysis, Port Authority of Allegheny County, Pennsylvania (estimated cost of construction: $500 million); Airport Busway Transitional Analysis Study and Report, Port Authority of Allegheny County, Pennsylvania (estimated cost of construction: $115 million); Parkway West Multi-Modal Transportation Study and Report, Southwestern Pennsylvania Regional Planning Commission (estimated cost of construction: $472 million).

Maunsell Consultants Pty Ltd

6 Claremont Street, South Yarra, Victoria 3141, Australia

Telephone: +61 3 249 1234
Telex: 31067 maunciv
Telefax: (Gp 2/3) +61 3 240 8636

Chief Executive: P G Sands
Principals: J B Laurie
　　　　　　　D J Lee
　　　　　　　S A Kubaisi
　　　　　　　R K Grieve
　　　　　　　D M A Hook
　　　　　　　J W Downer
　　　　　　　J G Clayton
　　　　　　　J A Leslie
　　　　　　　P H N Norman
　　　　　　　B Richmond
　　　　　　　H B James
　　　　　　　P H Gray
　　　　　　　E V Jenkins
　　　　　　　G Forrest-Brown
　　　　　　　A E Churchman
　　　　　　　K S Miles
　　　　　　　P J Jarvis
　　　　　　　L M Elliss
　　　　　　　A Symmons
　　　　　　　D C Gregory
　　　　　　　D R H Maher
　　　　　　　A J Herbert
　　　　　　　M J Worrall
　　　　　　　D J Macleod
　　　　　　　F S Y Bong
　　　　　　　D N Odgers
　　　　　　　G S Cowie
　　　　　　　R M Stone

Associated companies
G Maunsell & Partners
London, England
Contact:

Managing Director: D M A Hook
Yeoman House, 63 Croydon Road, Penge, London SE20 7TP
Telephone: +44 81 778 6060
Telex: 946171
Telefax: (Gp 3) +44 81 659 5568
Also offices in Birmingham, Swansea, Manchester and Witham

Maunsell & Partners Pty Ltd
Melbourne, Australia
Contact:

Managing Director: J A Leslie
6 Claremont Street, South Yarra, Victoria 3141
Telephone: +61 3 249 1234
Telex: 31067 maunciv
Telefax: (Gp 2/3) +61 3 240 8636
Also offices in Perth, Sydney, Canberra, Hobart, Brisbane, Adelaide and Darwin

Maunsell Consultants Asia Ltd
Kowloon, Hong Kong
Contact:

Managing Director: F S Y Bong
1 Kowloon Park Drive, Kowloon, Hong Kong
Telephone: +852 3-695251
Telex: 44458
Telefax: (Gp 3) +852 3 722 4070

Sindhu Maunsell Consultants
Bangkok, Thailand
Contact:

Resident Manager: R H Ashburner
Chongkolnee Building, 56 Surawong Road, Bangkok
Telephone: +66 2 253 0002/3
Telex: 20251

Maunsell Consultants (Malaysia) Sdn Bhd
c/o ESAS

LTK Engineering Services

Year	No of cars	Car type	Owner
1978-86	316	Commuter	Metropolitan Transportation Authority of the State of New York (for Metro-North and LIRR service)
1978-92	466	Rapid transit	Washington Metropolitan Area Transit Authority
1981-87	26	Light rail	Tri-County Metropolitan Transportation District of Oregon
1982-89	50	Light rail	Santa Clara County Transportation Agency
1982-87	26	Light rail	Sacramento Transit Development Agency
1982-90	54	Commuter	Metro-North Commuter Railroad (for New Haven Line service)
1982-90	100	Light rail	Massachusetts Bay Transportation Authority
1985-87	95	Rapid transit	Port Authority Trans Hudson
1985-89	248	Rapid transit	Port Authority Trans Hudson (overhaul inspection)
1985-90	54	Light rail	Los Angeles County Transportation Commission
1985-93	120	Rapid transit	Dallas Area Rapid Transit
1988-91	250	Rapid transit	Shanghai Metro Corporation
1989	48	Commuter	Metro-North Commuter Railroad
1989-92	96	Commuter	Massachusetts Bay Transportation Authority
1989-93	50	Light rail	Los Angeles County Transportation Commission

CONSULTANCY SERVICES

Contact:
Aziz bin Hassan
362 Jalan Rubber, 1st Floor, 93400 Kuching, Sarawak
Telephone: +60 82 427 575

Maunsell Consultants PNG
Port Moresby, Papua New Guinea
Contact:
Resident Manager: J Walls
Defence Force Building, Corner Hunter Street and Champion Parade, Port Moresby
Telephone: +675 212955
Telex: 23394
Telefax: +675 212930

Maunsell Consultants (Singapore) Pte Ltd
Singapore
Contact:
Resident Manager: A Agnew
151 Chin Swee Road, Suite 08-08, Manhattan House, Singapore 0316
Telephone: +65 733 8622
Telex: 51150
Telefax: +65 733 5706

Maunsell SARL
Paris, France
Contact:
Resident Manager: K Marlow
262 rue de Faubourg, Saint Honoré, 75008 Paris
Telephone: +33 1 475 35498
Telex: 643977
Telefax: +33 1 476 67172

Maunsell Consultants Ltd
Muscat, Oman
Contact:
Resident Manager: P Sockett
PO Box 5980 Ruwi, Muscat, Sultanate of Oman
Telephone: +968 564 499
Telex: 5293
Telefax: +968 564 498

Maunsell Consultants
Japan
Contact:
Resident Manager: H Angel
Fujimi-Machi, Konoma, Nagano-Ken 399-02, Japan
Telephone: +81 2666-2-5458
Telex: 3362-519 angel j

Capabilities

The International Maunsell group operates from centres in the United Kingdom, Australia and Hong Kong and through regional offices and associated companies in Europe, the Middle East, South East Asia and Australasia to provide civil and structural engineering consultancy services throughout the world. Over the years the group has undergone steady sustained growth resulting from its diversification and expansion into new geographic areas. It now employs over 1000 members of staff throughout the world.

It has always been Maunsell policy to establish close connections with professionals in the countries in which the group is active. In many cases this has led to the establishment of associated firms which usually take the form of partnerships between professional engineers established in the particular country and suitably qualified expatriates from Britain and Australia. It follows that the best possible service can then be rendered and maximum understanding achieved of local conditions and the requirements of local clients.

Links within the group are close and members of staff from each main office are available to whichever Maunsell firm may need their particular knowledge or skills. This co-operation in the technical sphere ensures that the strength and wide experience of the whole group can be readily drawn upon for the benefit of any one client.

The group is registered with bodies concerned with world-wide developments, such as the International Bank for Reconstruction and Development, the United Nations Industrial Development Organisation, the Asian Development Bank, the World Bank, etc.

Some of the range of services offered are:

Engineering: The group can provide co-ordinated planning and control of a project from its inception to final completion. Particular aspects of this work are: Feasibility studies and report estimates.
Detailed design, preparation of working drawings, contract documents, etc.
Evaluation of tenders and placing of contracts.
Supervision of construction and certification of interim and final payments to contractors.
Full contract management services, with computer back-up for major multi-discipline engineering contracts.
Land survey: A comprehensive and fully experienced land survey section, employing the latest techniques and equipment, is available to undertake work anywhere in the world. Electronic equipment is available to facilitate accurate linear measurement over any terrain.
Ground exploration: The group employs qualified personnel fully experienced in soil mechanics, foundation engineering and geology and it arranges and supervises contracts for ground exploration.
Transport studies: A traffic engineering department was established in 1963 and is able to undertake transport studies of all kinds together with the associated economic and cost benefit analyses, route location, traffic management and studies of environmental effects.
Town and regional planning: One of the individual consultants in the group is a past president of the Town Planning Institute and additionally, there are strong links with architects, landscape architects, building quantity surveyors and others so that the group is able to handle assignments involving town or regional planning.
Environmental and health engineering: The Health Engineering section designs and supervises the construction and installation of water supply systems, sewage treatment plants and solid waste disposal facilities. The group has been particularly active in the field of solid waste disposal and undertakes comprehensive studies which cover economic appraisal and management aspects. The group is well equipped to advise on liquid waste disposal problems. Expansion of the Group's activities in the fields of irrigation and major water supply schemes has been recently accomplished.

The organisation is active in the field of environmental engineering and carries out surveys to evaluate and appraise pollution of all forms including noise and gaseous emissions.
Economic studies: When the scope of the work so demands, the group associates with various specialist firms or individuals who are experts in the field of economics.
Computing: Comprehensive computer facilities are available for the solution of problems in engineering design, traffic engineering, and land and marine surveying while specialised programmes for use with the foregoing have been developed by the group's engineers and applied mathematicians.

Merz and McLellan

Amberley, Killingworth, Newcastle-upon-Tyne NE12 0RS, England

Telephone: +44 91 216 0333
Telex: 53561 amber g
Telefax: +44 91 216 0019

Other UK offices: London, Birmingham, Paisley, Manchester and Aberdeen

Overseas offices: Australia, Botswana, Chile, Singapore, Sudan, Zambia and Zimbabwe

Associated Firm: Merz Australia Pty Ltd, Brecon 47 Colin Street, West Perth, Western Australia 6005, Australia

Telephone: +61 9 322 2433
Telex: 92311
Telefax: +61 9 325 5972

Current projects for Maunsell Consultants Pty Ltd

Expected completion date	Client	Project description	Country	Value US$ million (when built)
1992	Metropolitan Transit Authority, Victoria	Jolimont Decentralisation Project: Programme planning and implementation of the relocation of maintenance and stabling facilities for the metropolitan train fleet to suburban locations*	Australia	280
1991	State Rail Authority, NSW	Rail bridge over the Cordeaux River gorge to be the largest arch rail bridge in Australia	Australia	4
1988	Mass Rapid Transit Corp, Singapore	Mass Transit Railway-Phase 2B: 17 km railway viaduct, 8 elevated stations, stabling sidings and depot*	Singapore	180
1990	Mass Rapid Transit Corp, Singapore	Mass Transit Railway Phase 2C: 2 km railway viaduct plus station	Singapore	10
1988	Very Fast Train	Feasibility study of structures and alignment for proposed new high-speed line from Sydney to Melbourne via Canberra	Australia	n/a
1988	Perisher Skitube, NSW	Perisher Skitube Railway: Cog rail link being constructed beneath Kosciusko National Park from below the snow line to the centre of the Perisher Valley ski resort	Australia	33
1987	KCR Corp	Kowloon-Canton Railway: design and supervision of 7 stations	Hong Kong	70
1987	State Transport Authority of South Australia	Remodelling of all track approaches to Adelaide station	Australia	2.3
1987	KCR Corp	Remodelling study of Hung Hom goods yard, reclamation and development	Hong Kong	n/a
1987	Perth Urban Electrification Steering Committee	Development of a master plan for the introduction of electrificaton to the 80 km Perth suburban passenger rail system	Australia	n/a
1987	State Rail Authority, NSW	Stanwell Park Bridge: Investigation and repair to a 66 year-old rail brick viaduct bridge standing 65 m above Stanwell Creek	Australia	4
1987	Mt Newman	Marshalling yard improvements and extensions at Port Hedland and the Mt Newman mine to allow for trains of up to 300 car lengths/ 37 000 gross tonnes	Australia	10.5
1987	State Rail Authority, NSW	Georges River East Bridge: First incrementally-launched rail bridge in Australia	Australia	4
1987	KCR Corp	Kowloon-Canton Railway: Trackwork study for redesign of existing maintenance facility at Sha Tin*	Hong Kong	n/a
1987	Docklands Light Railway	Feasibility study, tender design and documentation for extension of the railway westwards	England	n/a
1988	West Midlands Council/West Midlands Passenger Transport Executive	West Midlands Light Rail Transit: Alignment review of proposed 60 km route with sections underground Birmingham city centre	England	n/a

* With Parsons Brinkerhoff

Also Sydney, Melbourne, Brisbane and Darwin

Associates and Agencies: Bolivia, Brazil, Ecuador, India, Indonesia, Malaysia, Peru, Saudi Arabia and Venezuela

Partner involved in Transportation Projects:
Dr Malcolm W Kennedy
Transportation Projects Manager: Paul H Dawkins
Head of Marketing: Ian P Burdon

Established: 1899
Staff: 620

Capabilities
The firm's capabilities are associated with the fixed and mobile electrical and mechanical components of transport systems. Current activities include system and engineering feasibility studies and specifications of passenger transport vehicles, power supply and distribution systems including overhead line equipment, signalling, communications and SCADA systems, and fare-collection equipment. Other components of transport systems covered by the firm's expertise include lifts, escalators and baggage-handling equipment. In addition the firm offers a comprehensive service in the engineering and design of electrical and mechanical fixed systems such as environmental control and building services in passenger, maintenance and office facilities and tunnel ventilation and pumping systems.

Projects
Current or recent activities include: assisting British Rail with tender evaluation of rolling stock and locomotive procurement contracts; the engineering of a tramway operation on an old railway route; system studies and engineering of passenger transport systems for the 1990 and 1992 Garden Festival Sites; the outline design and specification of the infrastructure and trolleybuses proposal for Bradford; the engineering feasibility of a leisure and tourist tramway in Gateshead; promotion of LRT schemes in UK.

Modjeski & Masters

PO Box 2345, Harrisburg, Pennsylvania 17105, USA

Telephone: +1 717 761 1891
Telefax: +1 717 761 1032

Partner: C F Comstock

Capabilities
Rail structures; design, inspection and rail layout.

Projects
Norfolk Southern Corporation: Design replacement movable bridge, involving transfer of existing bridge at Florence, Alabama, to Hannibal, Missouri, and rehabilitation, design and inspection of construction, systemwide, for bridges and tunnels.
Southern Pacific Transportation Company: Systemwide steel bridge inspections, bridge rehabilitations and emergency on-call services.
New Orleans Public Belt Railroad: Annual inspection and rehabilitation plans, Huey P Long Bridge, New Orleans, Louisiana.
New Orleans Dock Board: On-call emergency services and periodic inspections and repairs for four combination railway and highway movable bridges crossing Inner Harbor Navigation Channel, New Orleans, Louisiana.
New England District, US Army Corps of Engineers: Electrical, mechanical and structural rehabilitation designs, Buzzards Bay Bridge, Cape Cod, Massachusetts.
Vicksburg District, US Army Corps of Engineers: Design replacement movable bridge, for Union Pacific Railroad at Alexandria, Louisiana.
Burlington Northern Railroad Company: Load history, bridge on four routes of system.
Louisiana Department of Transportation and Development: Design railroad bridge, Kansas City Southern/Mid-South crossing of Interstate 20.
Terminal Railroad Association of St Louis: Inspection, rehabilitation, system-wide bridges.

Morrison-Knudsen Company, Inc

Morrison-Knudsen Plaza, PO Box 7808, Boise, Idaho 83729, USA

Telephone: +1 208 386 5398
Telex: 368439

President, Manufacturing Group: J G Fearon
Director, Railroad Construction & Services Division: Rinaldo Monteferrante

Capabilities
Morrison-Knudsen ranks as one of the largest and most widely experienced railroad engineering and construction operations in the world. Design/engineering work for the railroad industry is performed by Morrison-Knudsen's Railroad Division. Morrison-Knudsen has been engaged in the design of various heavy civil engineering projects, including railroads and their associated facilities since 1915. Comprehensive programmes for increasing the safety, speed and economy of railroad services have evolved from extensive studies and economic evaluations determining the size, capacity, location and disposition of various elements making up a railroad system.
  In the design of railroads and maintenance facilities, M-K's staff is experienced in field reconnaissance, site and route surveys, preparation of economic studies, quantity and cost estimates, yard trackage layouts and facilities design. A partial inventory of M-K's railroad engineering accomplishments totals well over 22 000 km of overland railways.
Construction services: Morrison-Knudsen's services include the capabilities to construct both surface and underground railroads throughout the world. The services include the furnishing of all materials, equipment, support services, management, technical and hourly labour necessary for completion of the project. Construction activities are performed on an individual basis or as part of the turnkey, design/construct agreement. The Morrison-Knudsen organisation recently finished the design, procurement and construction of the 144 km Cerrejon Coal Haul Railroad in Columbia. This project included 30 major bridge structures, railroad shop facilities, signal system, loading and unloading trackage, main-line trackage, yards and sidings, optimisation of track structure components, rolling stock and operational and maintenance analysis. In addition to construction Morrison-Knudsen also provides construction management services from supplementing client's existing staff to complete management of total construction contracts.
Rehabilitation and maintenance services: Morrison-Knudsen's services include all aspects of track and structure rehabilitation and maintenance. This includes on-site inspection and appraisal of condition, recommendations on improvements, specifications for rehabilitation, construction management or actual rehabilitation and recommended maintenance plans after rehabilitation. Morrison-Knudsen has performed these services for numerous railroads, government and industrial clients as well as on railroads operated by Morrison-Knudsen.
Operations and maintenance: Morrison-Knudsen is also experienced in railroad operations. The Wabash Valley Railroad Company, a subsidiary of Morrison-Knudsen, formerly operated short-line railroads in Kansas and Illinois. M-K has operated and maintained other railroads in the USA and overseas. These include Vermont Northern Railroad in Vermont and the Black Mesa-Lake Powell Railroad in Arizona; the Hamersley Iron Railroad, the Mount Newman Railroad and the Robe River Railroad, all in Australia; the Quebec North Shore and Labrador Railroad in Canada; the Orinoco Railroad in Venezuela; the Southern Peru Copper Railroad in Peru; and the Burlington Northern Railroad at Libby, Montana. Work with these and other railroads has included maintenance of trackage, signal systems, rolling stock and locomotive remanufacturing, and a comprehensive programme of personnel training.
Procurement: Morrison-Knudsen also offers a capable and experienced organisation for the procurement of railroad materials, equipment, supplies, subcontracting and the appropriate expediting services to complement the procurement. This service is the responsibility of M-K's Railroad Division and supported by the Procurement Department.
Consulting services: Morrison-Knudsen has considerable experience in the development of comprehensive transport analysis, where its services cover a wide range of modes, commodities and objectives. Morrison-Knudsen has conducted comprehensive analysis of railroad operations, electrification studies and design equipment appraisals, costing of services developed rail costing and investments, examined carrier traffic and revenue patterns, developed comprehensive long-term forecasts, projections and operating plans, constructed extensive railroad reorganisation programmes, developed variable cost studies, investigated freight rates and divisions thereof, conducted alternative rail route evaluations, and developed the necessary information for clients to make intelligent and well-informed decisions about the feasibility of mergers and acquisitions.

Morrison-Knudsen Engineers Inc

180 Howard Street, San Francisco, California 94105, USA

Telephone: +1 415 442 7300
Telex: 470040 (ITT)
  278362 (RCA)
  34376 (WUD)
  677058 (WUI)

Capabilities
Morrison-Knudsen Engineers Inc (MKE) perform systemwide engineering, procurement and construction management of railroads, transit systems and associated facilities. Engineering services include feasibility and planning studies; conceptual, basic and detailed design; equipment selection; cost estimating; operations planning; maintenance programming; complete bid documentation; material procurement; construction management and inspection; testing and commissioning; and personnel training.
  MKE's engineering capabilities cover the following railroad and transit facilities and systems: alignment and trackwork; electrification; signalling and communications; maintenance facilities; yards and terminals; bridges and tunnels; and rail operations. Support is also offered in related activities, such as geotechnical, hydrological, and structural engineering. An inventory of MKE's railroad and transit engineering work totals well over 24 000 track-km worldwide.
  MKE is among world leaders in the development and design of high-voltage railroad electrification systems. The firm has completed 2400 track-km of electrification design, and has prepared feasibility studies for an additional 7000 route-km of systems. MKE has been the principal designer or a primary participant in the design of all five of the only 50 kV railroad electrification systems operating in the world today.
  MKE has developed a complete set of computer programmes for use in design and analysis of electrified rail systems. These programmes include train simulation, pantograph dynamic simulation, catenary performance analysis, and traction power system analysis, among many others.
  MKE is a wholly-owned subsidiary of the worldwide construction-engineering-development firm of Morrison Knudsen Corporation. As such, MKE has access to the full resources of its parent firm, which has over four decades of experience in railroad construction, operation, and facility maintenance.

Projects
Examples of current MKE projects include the following:
Cerrejon Coal-Haul Railroad, Colombia: MKE prepared preliminary and final design of the complete 160 km railroad system for this new $2000 million mine-railroad-port complex in Colombia. MKE also provided project procurement and construction management services. Design included railroad alignment, gradient and bridges; a locomotive and wagon maintenance shop; yard trackage at the export facility and at the mine; train operations scheduling and control; an organisation structure of the railroad; and track and equipment maintenance and inspection programmes.
Erie-Lackawanna Railroad Electrification, USA: MKE provided construction management, testing and commissioning services, for rehabilitating and conversion of the catenary system and substations from 3 kV dc to 25 kV ac. The 107 km route provides commuter service from New Jersey to New York City.
East Hills-Campbelltown Connection, Australia: This new two-track line near Sydney is 8 km long and designed for 160 km/h operation. The electrification is at 1500 V dc. MKE's work for the NSW State Rail Authority included verification of the proposed catenary design for 160 km/h speed and possible recommendations for design improvements, followed by layout design, preparation of materials list and specifications, and construction supervision.

450 CONSULTANCY SERVICES

Metro North Railroad Traction Conversion: The Connecticut Department of Transportation is rehabilitating the traction power supply system on 76 route-km of this commuter line serving New York City. Three supply substations and 12 autotransformer stations are being converted from 11 kV 25 Hz to 13.2 kV 60 Hz operation, at a cost of approximately $6 million. MKE is providing construction management services for the conversion, including scheduling, inspection, testing and commissioning.

Seoul Metropolitan Subway, South Korea: This project involved system design verification studies for electrification of 56 route-km of new transit lines in Seoul, costing approximately $40 million. MKE also provided general technical support in traction power systems and detailed design documentation for both substations and overhead contact system, plus construction support and training of electrification staff.

Guadalupe (San Jose) Light Rail Transit, USA: MKE is performing final design of trackwork installation and overhead contact system for this new 32 km light rail transit system in San Jose, California. Estimated cost of the track and electrification is $30 million.

Sacramento Light Rail Transit, USA: MKE was engaged to perform preliminary and final design of the electrification system for Sacramento's light rail transit starter line. The line is 30 km long, in two corridors: the Folsom Corridor and the I-80 Corridor. MKE is also providing construction support for the electrification system, which is estimated to cost approximately $13 million.

Los Angeles-Long Beach Light Rail Transit, USA: For this new 23-mile light rail line MKE has been contracted to design the overhead contact system, both on the main line and in the vehicle maintenance facility. Estimated cost of the overhead system is approximately $12 million.

Transit Tunnel, Seattle, Washington, USA: A 2.1 km downtown transit tunnel for electric trolley buses. MKE prepared preliminary and final design of traction power system in tunnel; and determined design requirements for conversion to light rail transit. The cut-and-cover structure will relieve traffic congestion in the central business district.

Metro-Dade Transit System, Miami, Florida, USA: This $1 billion project involves construction of 34 km of elevated guideway for electrically-propelled stainless steel trains, and 20 stations approximately 1.5 km apart. As construction management oversight consultant, MKE reviewed owner's and contractor's quality control programmes, design drawings and changes, and material tests reports, and made equipment selection.

Meadows Yard Maintenance Facility, Kearny, New Jersey, USA: MKE, with a joint venture partner, provided electrification system engineering and full construction management services on this major rail maintenance facility for the New Jersey Transit Corporation. The $130 million facility will service 1000 commuter rail vehicles in the New Jersey area.

North Jersey Coast Line Testing and Commissioning, USA: Testing and commissioning services for electrification of 27 km of existing commuter railroad on the heavily-travelled corridor between Matawan and Long Branch. Total project cost through 1988 is estimated to be $96 million. Facilities to be supplied include a new overhead contact system, power supply station, supervisory control and signal systems.

Hudson/Harlem Contact Rail, Mount Vernon, USA: MKE provided full construction management services on this project to replace an existing contact rail. The contact rail is over 346 km long, including yards, sidings and spurs. The $36 million project also included installation of ancillary equipment and a new system for activation and control of snow melters at turnouts.

Los Angeles-San Diego (LOSSAN) Rail Corridor Study, USA: The study will develop a programme for the incremental upgrading of the existing rail line to increase passenger service. MKE is providing the existing condition assessment, current and proposed operations analysis, and capital cost estimates.

Baltimore Light Rail Transit, Baltimore, Maryland, USA: MKE and a joint-venture partner have been assigned as the general engineering consultant for the proposed $290 million light rail project that includes a 27.5-mile-long route, both elevated and at grade, and 35 passenger stations. The consultants will be responsible for conceptual planning/ engineering; preparing environmental documentation; preparing preliminary engineering design and final design of civil, trackwork, and other facilities; and providing certain construction management services.

Jamaica Station Complex Improvements, Long Island, New York, USA: MKE is providing construction management services for the improvements to Jamaica station, one of the busiest commuter rail stations in the USA. The $350 million project involves rebuilding and renovating the station. MKE is providing programme management, inspection, contract administration, co-ordination of railroad force accounts, scheduling, estimating, project control, safety and quality assurance/control.

Mott MacDonald Group

Headquarters: St Anne House, 20/26 Wellesley Road, Croydon, Surrey CR9 2UL, England

Telephone: +44 81 686 5041
Telefax: +44 81 681 5706

UK Group offices

16 Albert Street, Aberdeen AB1 1XQ
Telephone: +44 224 641348
Telefax: +44 224 642640

15 Wellington Park, Belfast BT9 6DJ
Telephone: +44 232 661916
Telefax: +44 232 660420

Canterbury House, 85 Newhall Street, Birmingham B3 1LZ
Telephone: +44 21 2361638
Telefax: +44 21 2362634

Demeter House, Station Road, Cambridge CB1 2RS
Telephone: +44 223 460660
Telefax: +44 223 461007

23 Cathedral Yard, Exeter, Devon EX1 1HB
Telephone: +44 392 210804
Telefax: +44 392 214512

77 Church Street, Inverness IV1 1ES
Telephone: +44 463 239323
Telefax: +44 463 224951

Trident House, Dale Street, Liverpool L2 2HF
Telephone: +44 51 2271457
Telefax: +44 51 2363515

Pearl Assurance House, New Bridge Street, Newcastle upon Tyne NE1 8BH
Telephone: +44 91 2610866
Telefax: +44 91 2326326

St Nicholas Chambers, Amen Corner, Newcastle upon Tyne NE1 1PE
Telephone: +44 91 2618333
Telefax: +44 91 2323472

Capital House, 48/52 Andover Road, Winchester SO23 7BH
Telephone: +44 962 66300
Telefax: +44 962 63224

International Group offices

Headquarters: Mott MacDonald International Ltd
Demeter House, Station Road, Cambridge CB1 2RS, England
Telephone: +44 223 460660
Telefax: +44 223 461007

Connell Group
60 Albert Road, South Melbourne 3205, Victoria, Australia
Telephone: +613 6978333
Telefax: +613 6978444

PO Box 194, 122 Gulshan Avenue, Dhaka, Bangladesh
Telephone: +8802 607341
Telefax: +8802 883393

2401 Sun Hung Kai Centre, 30 Harbour Road, Wanchai, Hong Kong
Telephone: +852 575 7108
Telefax: +852 834 5523

PO Box 236/KBY, J1 Kemang Raya 2, Jakarta, Selatan, Indonesia
Telephone: +6221 7997715
Telefax: +6221 7998648

PO Box 4329, Maputo, Mozambique
Telephone: +2581 428171
Telefax: +2581 1743961

PO Box 2201, Kathmandu, Nepal
Telephone: +977 415534
Telefax: +977 414184

PO Box 3587, Ruwi, Muscat, Oman
Telephone: +968 696242
Telefax: +968 603265

32-I/D, Block 6, Pechs, Karachi 29, Pakistan
Telephone: +92 21 437107
Telefax: +92 21 542751

15 Hoe Chiang Road, 09-04 to 06 Sanford Building, Singapore 0208
Telephone: +65 2253988
Telefax: +65 2254710

PO Box 996, Mogadishu, Somalia
Telephone: +252 1 80307

444C Galle Road, Ratmalana, Colombo 3, Sri Lanka
Telephone: +94 1 722962
Telefax: +94 1 547972

PO Box 7094, Abu Dhabi, United Arab Emirates
Telephone: +971 2 725526
Telefax: +971 2 722805

Suite No. 107 The Schrafft Center, 529 Main Street, Charlestown, Maryland 02129, USA
Telephone: +1 617 241 8850
Telefax: +1 617 241 9378

Jordan Jones & Goulding International Inc
2000 Clearview Avenue NE, Suite 200, Atlanta, Georgia 30340, USA
Telephone: +1 404 4558555
Telefax: +1 404 4557391

Transit & Tunnel Consultants Inc
6215 Sheridan Drive, Buffalo, New York 14221-4884, USA
Telephone: +1 716 6327200
Telefax: +1 716 6327209

Site offices and local representation also in: Algeria, Denmark, Egypt, Ethiopia, Ghana, Gibraltar, Guinea Bissau, Guyana, Lesotho, Libya, Morocco, Philippines.

Group Main Board Directors: J A Turnbull
R Beresford
G M Fenton
T J Thirlwall
J F Robson

Divisional Directors, Railways & Transportation Division: E A Cruddas
R A Vickers
R T Masters
G J D Porter
M Wallwork
T J Thirlwall

Capabilities

The Mott MacDonald Group is one of the UK's leading multi-disciplinary engineering consultancies with a worldwide staff resource of over 3000 including chartered engineers, transportation planners, computer specialists, environmental scientists and support staff. The group has been associated with public transport since the beginning of the century when it undertook design work for the London Underground railway system. More recently it has taken part in studies/project management of many forms of public transport such as bus, tramway, light rail, heavy mass transit and suburban and mainline railways. Recent light rail studies have included those in Leeds, Manchester, the Midlands and the London Docklands. The Group's major design projects include the Channel Tunnel and the Great Belt Crossing in Denmark.

Capabilities of the group in the field of transportation cover investigations, studies and technical feasibility reports, project definition, financial and environmental appraisal; preliminary and detailed design, contract preparation and tendering supervision, project scheduling, specification and procurement, quality control, cost and budget control, project implementation and construction management. It also includes management and operational planning in the areas of traffic engineering, bus routeing and scheduling, rail and transit operation and management related to different modes, inspection and testing of equipment during manufacture; investment planning, including development of transport models, traffic forecasting, evaluation techniques on economics, financial, technical and environmental grounds and modal choice techniques.

The Channel Tunnel: Mott MacDonald are the principal consulting engineers to Transmanche Link (TML), the Channel Tunnel contractors, for the preliminary and detailed design of the civil engineering for the British section of the Channel Tunnel scheme and for certain of the mechanical services throughout the tunnel. The firm's appointment includes design of: the British tunnels and associated underground structures; the ventilation system; the railway trackwork within the UK tunnels and terminal road links to the Folkestone terminal from the M20 motorway; major

Current recent projects (Mott MacDonald Group)

Project	Completed or current	Details
Brussels Metro section 4	1985	Study, design and supervision of construction: two-level station 300 m long including 100 m of tunnelling
Perth Railway Electrification, Australia	1985	Study to assess the proposal to electrify three suburban lines
Buffalo light rail rapid transit system, USA	1986	Design and construction management of 5.6 km underground section of light rail rapid transit, including five stations
Rail freight study, Hong Kong	1988	Study to review requirement for an expanded rail freight handling depot including reassessment of traffic forecasts marshalling and holding requirements of alternative options and financial and economic analyses
Edinburgh rapid transit system	1988	Engineering feasibility study for an alignment of a north-south underground line. Preparation of budget costs for a wide range of transport modes for the whole network
Manchester light rail system	Current	Feasibility study and detailed design for the entire system including the preparation of Parliamentary Plans for Phase I from Bury to Altrincham and the feasibility of extending the system through Salford Quays. Feasibility of extensions into Rochdale town centre and the Trafford Park development area
Docklands Light Rail, City extension	Current	Feasibility study followed by technical assistance on all disciplines including tunnelling, mechanical and electrical engineering and building services as well as specialist expertise in trackwork and alignment matters and inspection and quality assurance auditing
Limpopo railway rehabilitation, Mozambique	Current	Rehabilitation of track, material supply and maintenance facilities for existing railway, including rehabilitation of a concrete sleeper factory and quarry
Singapore mass rapid system	Current	Study, preliminary design of entire system; detailed engineering of major tunnelled and elevated sections
Gezira light rail system	Current	Study of existing rail system and recommendations for renovations
Channel Tunnel	Current	Preliminary and detailed design of the civil engineering, ventilation systems and railway trackwork for the British section of the Channel Tunnel project (on behalf of TML)
Midlands metro	Current	Network overview: tunnels study for Birmingham city centre section; preparation of Parliamentary plans
Great Belt Crossing, Denmark	Current	Preliminary and detailed design of 8 km of rail tunnel to link Sprogø to Zealand beneath the Eastern Channel of the Great Belt
London Underground: Chelsea–Hackney line	Current	Feasibility study for new underground railway route from south-west to north-west London
Channel Tunnel rail link	Current	Engineering design, to submission of Parliamentary Plans, for London tunnels section from Kings Cross to Swanley
Heathrow Express	Current	Civil enginering design for 12 km of tunnel (plus open cut-and-cover works) with two underground stations serving Heathrow from Paddington BR Station. Co-ordination of other disciplines.

tunnel and bridge structures within the terminals; and a new 1.5 km sea wall at Shakespeare Cliff to contain tunnel spoil. The total value of the works amounts to some £1000 million.

Preliminary work undertaken during 1986/87 included analysis of all the results of previous geological investigations in the Channel undertaken during the 1960s and 1970s. To complement this, a major geophysical survey and borehole investigation was undertaken by TML, for which the firm has acted as technical adviser for the British section.

In the short length of the tunnel built in 1975 under the previous scheme, Mott, Hay & Anderson supervised a series of loading tests to measure the performance of the existing tunnel linings. Concrete durability studies were undertaken by the firm's Special Services Division as part of the development of new linings for the Tunnel.

The British section of the fixed link extends 25 km to mid-Channel and involves some 80 km of tunnels; these consist mainly of the two running tunnels and a smaller service tunnel being driven as the pilot tunnel. At regular intervals a series of cross-passages will provide for emergency access, maintenance and ventilation along the route. Other cross-tunnels will serve as pressure relief ducts to reduce the aerodynamic drag from the high-speed trains. Two large scissor crossovers will be provided in large under-sea caverns, one in the UK section, one in the French; these will link the main running tunnels beneath the Channel, and allow for operations to continue if a section should need to be closed temporarily. A further crossover arrangement near the British portal will be built by cut-and-cover. This section is located in the environmentally important area between Castle Hill and Holy Well, and is to be fully landscaped after completion. The design of the trackform in the tunnel covers both the plain line, in non-ballasted and ballasted track, and switches and crossings.

At the point where the tunnel emerges to the west of Castle Hill, high-speed turnouts connect the tunnel tracks with the new terminal at Folkestone. This will house customs and interchange facilities for the rail shuttles. The railway layout will take the form of a loop, with three arrival lines and twin departure lines serving initially 10 parallel platform tracks where vehicles will drive on and off the shuttles. The track layout is designed to permit future expansion to 16 platforms. Nearly 54 km of ballasted and non-ballasted track will be required in the final layout with upwards of 100 turnouts, including stabling and maintenance sidings. Thirty-two km of track drains will also be provided. A separate through line comprising triple and quadruple tracks, linked with a series of crossovers, connects the tunnel with British Rail's main London route and will carry BR and SNCF International through trains at speeds up to 200 km/h. At a point where a new double junction in the British Rail Charing Cross to Dover main line at Dolland's Moor, new freight sidings and locomotive interchange facilities will be provided.

The new road transport network in Kent will include links with the M20 London to Dover motorway and the local A20 trunk road. Construction of seven new bridges and viaducts will be required, each designed to allow for maintenance of motorway traffic flow – during construction. Environmental disturbance to local villages will be minimised with the incorporation of sound-retention barriers and extensive landscaping.

Peter Muller-Munk Associates
Division of Wilbur Smith & Associates

2100 Smallman Street, Pittsburgh, Pennsylvania 15222, USA

Telephone: +1 412 261 5161

Director: Paul R Wiedmann

Projects
Advanced concept train (ACT-1) for AiResearch/Urban Mass Transit Administration (UMTA);
Australian Urban Passenger Train (AUPT) for Ministry of Transport, Australia;
Station signage system for Greater Cleveland Regional Transit Authority.

The MVA Consultancy

MVA House, Victoria Way, Woking, Surrey GU21 1DD, England

Telephone: +44 483 728051
Telex: 859079 mva uk
Telefax: +44 483 755207

115 Shaftesbury Avenue, London WC2H 8AD
Telephone: +44 71 836 9381
Telefax: +44 71 240 0750

27 York Place, Edinburgh EH1 3HP
Telephone: +44 31 557 5533
Telefax: +44 31 557 5596

26th Floor, Sunley Tower, Piccadilly Plaza, Manchester M1 4BT
Telephone: +44 61 236 0282
Telefax: +44 61 236 0095

Overseas office: 710 East Town Building, 41 Lockhart Road, Hong Kong

Telephone: +852 5 297037
Telex: 63440 mva hk
Telefax: +852 5 278490

Associated Company: MVA Systematica

Managing Director: Martin G Richards
Directors: David Ashley
Fred Brown
Geoff Copley
Prof Tony May
Hugh Neffendorf
Mick Roberts
Dan Samter
John Wicks
Andrew Last
Bill Wyley

Divisional Director: Martin Dix

Directors (MVA Asia): Fred Brown
Graham Bodell
Terry Bowker
Peter Brown

Capabilities
The MVA Consultancy is an independent British company providing services in the planning, operation, management and marketing of transport systems and related facilities. The Consultancy also provides services in computing, economics, mathematical modelling and statistics, and social and market research. Founded in 1968 as the British company of Alan M Voorhees and Associates Inc, MVA became wholly-owned by its Executive Management in 1983.

MVA has a professional staff of 160 with skills which encompass a wide range of disciplines including computing, economics, engineering, mathematics, operations research, planning, psychology, social science and statistics.

The scope of MVA's services relating to rail systems includes policy and planning studies; demand forecasting; economic and financial studies; market research and marketing; fare systems and fare collection, and computer-assisted scheduling.

In addition to its consultancy services, MVA markets and supports computer program systems for the planning and operational management of transport systems. TRIPS, MVA's comprehensive package of transport planning programs, is widely used around the world, with some 250 installations in more than 30 countries. MVA has the exclusive rights in the UK and Hong Kong for the VIPS computer-aided public transport service planning system developed by VTS Transportation Systems, and the British and Australian rights to HASTUS, the computer-assisted vehicle and crew scheduling system developed by Montreal-based GIRO.

Projects
One of MVA's earliest assignments led to the development of plans for the Tyne & Wear Metro, and MVA remained closely involved in the progress of those

CONSULTANCY SERVICES

plans through to implementation; more recently, MVA has advised the Tyne & Wear PTE on the extension of Metro to Newcastle Airport.

Since its formation 20 years ago, MVA has undertaken a wide variety of studies concerned with rail transport; urban, intercity and rural; passenger and freight. Clients for such commissions included: British Rail, East Sussex County Council, London Docklands Development Corporation, Cheshire County Council, Greater Manchester Passenger Transport Executive (PTE), the London Planning Advisory Committee, London Regional Transport, South Yorkshire PTE, Strathclyde PTE, Tyne and Wear PTE, West Midlands PTE, the UK Department of Transport, the Netherlands Ministry of Transport, Netherlands Railways, Karachi Development Authority, the Singapore Mass Rapid Transit Corporation, the Kowloon and Canton Railway Corporation, and New Zealand Railways.

British Rail is one of the Consultancy's major clients for rail studies, including the management of the Provincial Passenger Monitor. The Monitor is a continuous programme of on-train interviews which enable the provincial business sector to assess passenger responses to their services. Other projects MVA has been engaged in for BR are concerned with quality of service on Network SouthEast, market opportunities associated with major service improvements on the West Coast Main Line, research on Railcards and Red Star Parcels services, and market studies for a number of lines in both England and Scotland. Advice continues to be given on the use and further development of the passenger demand forecasting model for Channel Tunnel service which MVA developed and installed for BR.

Prospects for improved freight services between the North-west and Continental Europe, following the opening of the Channel Tunnel, are the subject of a study undertaken for the Borough of Crewe and Nantwich. The possible effects of the Channel Tunnel are one of the aspects covered by MVA's study of potential service improvements on the Crewe-Holyhead line (undertaken for the counties of Cheshire, Clwyd and Gwynedd); MVA are now studying in greater detail certain options identified through the original project.

The London transportation studies, operated by MVA under contract to the Department of Transport, are a major source of demand information for the central London rail study being undertaken jointly by the Department, British Rail and London Regional Transport. MVA is also advisor to the London Planning Advisory Committee, representing all the local authorities within Greater London, on the transport components of a review of the development strategy for London.

British Airports and BR have agreed to jointly finance and operate the 'Heathrow Express', following acceptance by the government, British Rail and British Airports of the recommendation of the Heathrow surface access study that a new rail link should be built into Heathrow to enable a direct, non-stop, service to be operated between Paddington and Heathrow. MVA are now providing advice to BAA and BR on demand forecasts for both the original scheme and studies of an extension to serve a possible fifth terminal at Heathrow.

For Docklands Light Rail, DLR, MVA undertook the third annual survey of passengers, following up the first such survey which MVA also undertook.

MVA has continued to play a leading role in the development of a number of light rail schemes in the UK, helping those which are most advanced through the Parliamentary Bill stage giving the necessary powers to build and operate. For South Yorkshire Passenger Transport Executive, MVA provided much of the technical evidence required to facilitate the passage of the Sheffield Supertram Bill through to the grant of Royal Assent. MVA also managed the studies which identified the route of Line 2 through the Don Valley and advised on the preparation of submissions for government grants for both lines.

As already noted, MVA advised Tyne & Wear PTE on the proposed extension of Metro to Newcastle Airport. In Manchester, MVA updated patronage forecasts for MetroLink Line 1, examined the key issues relating to in-street running in the city centre, and lead the team identifying and appraising options for additional lines. MVA was also leader of the team undertaking an initial study of a people-mover scheme for Southampton. Elsewhere in Hampshire, working for the County Council, MVA undertook studies of possible light rail schemes in the Portsmouth-Gosport area, and for Berkshire MVA examined the potential for light rail schemes in the Reading area. To assist in the planning of the Midland Metro light rail scheme, West Midlands PTE used the VIPS network planning software provided by MVA.

In Continental Europe, MVA continued to advise the Netherlands Ministry of Transport on passenger demand for the proposed Paris-Brussels-Cologne/Amsterdam high speed line.

In Karachi, MVA is a member of an international team of consultants undertaking a World Bank funded mass transit study.

In Singapore, following the MVA study undertaken for the principal bus operator SBS to assess the potential effects of the mass rapid transit system, the two bus operators (SBS and TIBS) and SMRT (the mass rapid transit operator) have formed a joint company, TransitLink, to develop an integrated network, and to manage the implementation and operation of the common through, ticketing system; the common ticket will be magnetics based and available for use on all bus and MRT services. MVA is advising TransitLink on planning for, and the management of, integration.

In Hong Kong, MVA designed and supervised the implementation of the traffic-LRV control system for the 56 at-grade street crossings of the first phase of the Tuen Mun LRT system, opened in September 1988, and is now preparing the traffic/LRV control system for Phases II and III scheduled for opening between 1990 and 1992. For the government, MVA is undertaking studies for new rail links in the MTRC and KCRC systems to serve large land areas being reclaimed from Hong Kong Harbour. For Hong Kong Tramways, MVA have prepared an investment strategy which covers the renewal of their stock of 162 double-deck vehicles, as well as fares, operating practices, traffic management measures. For other private sector interests, MVA is examining the potential for medium-capacity systems serving the tourist areas of Tsim Sha Tsui and the south of Hong Kong Island.

In Auckland, MVA advised New Zealand Railways on the redevelopment of their large Central Railyards site, including an investigation of future options for the various NZR rail and road services which currently use the site.

National City Management Company

9720 Town Park Drive, Suite 109, Houston, Texas 77036, USA

Telephone: +1 713 772 1272

President/General Manager: Stan Gates Jr

Projects
Management contracts with West Palm Beach, Florida; Shreveport, Louisiana; Colorado Springs, Colorado; Spokane Transit System, Spokane, Washington.

Parsons Brinckerhoff Centec International Inc

460 Spring Park Place, Herndon, Virginia 22070, USA

Telephone: +1 703 478 0070
Telex: 89 9493 centec mcln

Technical Director: R K Pattison

Offices: New York, Boston, Atlanta, Pittsburgh, Chicago, Philadelphia, San Francisco, Santa Ana, Cairo, Hong Kong, Istanbul

Projects
Joint venture with others for location and design of 850 km line in Morocco;
Study of rehabilitation and upgrading of the Sudan Railway system;
Joint venture with others for the design of highway and rail tunnel under the Bosphorus;
Mechanical and electrical engineers for tunnel ventilation in Hong Kong;
Rogers Pass Tunnel, Canadian Rocky Mountains;
Design of tunnel ventilation, Denver & Rio Grande Western Railroad;
Design of marine facilities in Port of Suez; Somalia; Groton, Connecticut; and Newport News, Virginia;
Studies for High Speed Rail, States of Pennsylvania, Washington, Texas, and Ohio;
Design of transit systems and light rail: Atlanta-MARTA; Los Angeles-Long Beach; Wilshire Boulevard, Los Angeles; Guadalupe Corridor, Santa Clara County, California; and Pittsburgh Light Rail System;
Design of track, signal and bridge rehabilitation for the Massachusetts Bay Transportation Authority.

PARSONS
Ralph M Parsons Company

100 West Walnut, Pasadena, California 91124, USA

Telephone: +1 818 440 2000, 2439
Telex: 675336
Telefax: +1 818 440 2630

Chairman: W E Leonard
President: Robert B Sheh
Senior Vice President and Manager, Systems Division: Edward Cramsie
Vice-President and Manager, Business Development: Richard J Begley

Projects
Southern California Rapid Transit District: Construction management, heading a consortium which includes De Leuw, Cather & Company, of the $3.75 billion Los Angeles Metro Rail project, a 17.3-mile subway system.
Channel Tunnel Arranging Banks Group: Parsons-De Leuw, Cather, a division of The Ralph M Parsons Company Ltd, has been selected as leader of the Technical Adviser Team (TAT) by the banks arranging the F5 billion financing for the 60 km Channel Tunnel Program.
Federal Railroad Administration, US DOT: Overall program management in a joint venture with De Leuw, Cather & Co completing the final segments of the eight states 1350 track miles rail system between Washington DC and Boston.
City of Chicago Department of Public Works: Construction management, heading a joint venture with De Leuw, Cather & Company, of the Southwest Transit Project to build a new 9-mile, double-track transit line from downtown Chicago to Midway Airport, with eight stations sized to accommodate eight-car trains. The $410 million project is scheduled for completion in late 1992.

Additional rail project information is listed under De Leuw, Cather & Company, which is a wholly-owned subsidiary of The Parsons Corporation.

Peregrine and Partners

PO Box 3, Royston, Hertfordshire SG8 7BU, England

Telephone: +44 763 42384
Telex: 817178

Principal: E P Peregrine

US associates: H K Friedland and Associates, PO Box 893, Solana Beach, California 92075
Telephone: +1 619 481 9339
Gianotti Associates, 380 Station Road, Bellport, New York 11713
Telephone: +1 516 286 9492

Capabilities
Established in 1950, the firm has an international practice in mechanical engineering design, manufacture and commissioning of prototypes and working machinery for governments, universities, consulting firms and major industry; invention; arbitration.

Planning Research & Systems plc

Premier House, 44-48 Dover Street, London W1X 3RF, England

Telephone: +44 71 409 1635
Telex: 23442
Telefax: +44 71 629 0221

Chairman: John Martin

Planning Research & Systems plc is a business consultancy specialising in prime mover, component and related equipment research and consultancy. The company maintains electronic databases covering automotive engine and equipment production and market data. PRS operates mainly from a London base

CONSULTANCY SERVICES 453

although in 1984 PRS Consulting Group Inc was established as a fully functional business consultancy operation in Darien, Connecticut, USA, and PRS Asia Pacific was set up in 1987. All three companies form part of PRS Consultancy Group operating in London, Tokyo and the USA.

Staffing is mainly business graduates, principal disciplines include economics and engineering as well as fluency in the main commercial languages.

Principal services provided include:
Strategy Planning Services. In particular, marketing and product strategies and the development of new earnings (including acquisition).
Data Services. Prime mover databases customised for individual clients.
Business Publications. Automotive and engine publications, yearbooks and forecasts.
Automotive news service (European, US and technology tracking).

Main business area specialisations are automotive and industrial equipment; machine tools and manufacturing systems business; printing and publishing.

Pullman Technology Inc

16412 Lathrop Avenue, Harvey, Illinois 60426, USA

Telephone: +1 708 339 8600
Telex: 887894
Telefax: +1 708 339 8607

Capability
Full range of consulting services, design and engineering, manufacturing engineering, quality control and testing, engineering analysis, spare parts, technical publications, specification documentation, customer engineering representation, and computer aided design (CAD), relating to commuter, rapid transit and tour train operations.

Projects
A brief list of recent clients includes: Alaska Railroad Corporation; Bombardier; China National Machinery & Equipment Import & Export; Daewoo Corporation, Korea; General Electric Company; Goninan, Australia; GOSA, Yugoslavia; Morrison-Knudsen; New York City Transit Authority; Nippon Sharyo Ltd; Southeastern Pennsylvania Transportation Authority; Tillamook Railcar Repair Inc; Transcisco; Westinghouse Electric Company.

PW Consulting
Rail Transport Group

St James' Chambers, St James' Square, Newport PO30 1UX, England

Telephone: +44 983 822444
Telefax: +44 983 822479

Principal: T A Wood

Capabilities
The Rail Transport Group of PW Consulting offers completely independent and impartial advice which embraces all aspects of railway engineering, operations and maintenance. The practice specialises particularly in the UK private rail freight sector and has accumulated considerable experience in trainload bulk commodities such as steel, petroleum, chemicals and minerals as well as in general merchandise traffics involving the latest developments in intermodal thinking, particularly in the context of the Single European Market and the Channel Tunnel.

Projects
In 1989, PW Consulting undertook major feasibility studies which considered the location and capacity of projected Euroterminal freight facilities; the impact of the advent of high-capacity freight locomotives on the economics of rail movement of petroleum products; and the proposed remodelling of the rail layout of a major UK refinery and the implications that would have for safety and for the economics of railcar and locomotive utilisation.

Construction projects completed in 1989 for which the practice was responsible included the rehabilitation and expansion of an important China clay handling terminal; the construction of a new timber handling rail terminal including factory expansion and warehouse expansion aspects; the remodelling of steel scrap handling facilities; the remodelling of hazardous chemical terminal facilities.

The company also operates as a specialist railway sub-consultancy to lead consultants and project consortia: in this capacity the practice has worked on the Channel Tunnel Rail Link; on Euroterminal feasibility studies; on infrastructure developments in Africa, the Middle East and the Far East and on LRT projects.

Queensland Railways Consulting Services

305 Edward Street, Brisbane, Queensland Australia 4000
PO Box 1429, Brisbane 4001

Telephone: +61 7 225 1700
Telex: AA41514
Telefax: +61 7 225 1305

Assistant Commissioner (Projects): Robin G Read

Capabilities
Queensland Railways offers expertise in all areas of railway operations from the feasibility and planning stages through to project management commissioning operating and maintenance. These areas include: railway transport optimisation studies; railway feasibility studies; route selection and subsequent detailed design including track, bridges and all major civil works; all aspects of high voltage ac electrification rolling stock design, including features required for heavy-haul and developments in mid-consist remote locomotive operation for heavy-haul; communications and signalling facilities including radio system; data systems, microwave and pcm equipment; fibre-optics.

With all of these disciplines a comprehensive project management and operating and maintenance training package is also available.

Rail India Technical & Economic Services Ltd (RITES)

New Delhi House, 27 Barakhamba Road, New Delhi 110 001, India

Telephone: +91 331 4261-64
Cable: Ritesrail, New Delhi
Telex: 031-62596/66863 rites in
Telefax: +91 331 5286

Chairman: A N Wanchoo
Managing Director: M Seshagiri Rao
Director, Technical: S K Dikshit

Rail India Technical and Economic Services Ltd, a Government of India Enterprise under the Ministry of Railways, is a multi-modal transport and infrastructural consultancy organisation geared to execute projects through all stages from concept, commissioning to successful implementation. RITES provides complete and comprehensive services to various transport systems such as railways, roads and highways, ports and harbours, inland water, urban transport, airports, aerial ropeways and tramway systems. RITES employs high technology with computer informatics, geotechnology and aerial photogrammetry facilities. RITES has a decade of experience in transportation technology in India and abroad with operational experience in over 29 countries.

Capabilities
Project identification, feasibility studies, market survey and analysis, detailed planning, designing and scheduling, cost estimates and cash flow specification, bid evaluation, contract assistance, detailed project engineering, technical and managerial support, site supervision, implementation and commissioning services, training and human resource development, economic and financial evaluation, efficiency and optimisation studies, quality assurance and quality control, project monitoring etc.

Projects
Currently being undertaken in the following countries: Angola, Bangladesh, Botswana, Bhutan, Ethiopia, Ghana, India, Iraq, Jordan, Mozambique, Mexico, Sri Lanka, Zambia and Zimbabwe.

Railway Systems Design Inc

105 Hagley Building, Concord Plaza, 3411 Silverside Road, Wilmington, Delaware 19810, USA

Capabilities
Design and construction management of railroad and transit signalling, communications and electric traction power systems.

Real Estate Research Corp

1101 17th St NW, Washington DC 20036, USA

Telephone: +1 202 223 4500

Vice-President: C H Broley

Projects
People-movers for US Department of Transportation.

Reid Crowther

7410 Blackfoot Trail SE, Calgary, Alberta T2H 1M5, Canada

Telephone: +1 403 253 3301
Telex: 03 822780
Telefax: +1 403 255 3189

Principals: John M Atkinson
Edward A Tahmazian

Capabilities
With almost 100 rail-related projects completed or under way and an inter-disciplinary team of engineers, scientists and technicians, the company has shown it can provide a comprehensive range of services to railways, governments and industry. Services embrace: project management, contract administration and procurement, rail and highway alignment, bridges and other structures, grade separations, yard facilities, rehabilitation and relocation studies, waste management and environmental projects.

Projects
Monterrey, Mexico: Reid Crowther is providing engineering services for design and procurement of 18.5 km of trackwork for the Metrorrey transit project. The system includes direct-fixation trackwork as well as turnouts crossings and crossover units installed on an elevated segmental beam system. Value: US $275 million.

Vancouver, Canada: Reid Crowther in association with Parsons Brinkerhoff Centec were responsible for design, procurement and construction of the first 21 km of trackwork in the city's Skytrain system. Value: US $800 million.

A further 3.25 km is currently under construction for which Reid Crowther provided engineering services in design, procurement and construction of trackwork and guideway elements. This phase also included all trackwork systems as well as linear induction motor (LIM) rail, power rails and automatic train control (ATC) cables. Reid Crowther in association with Bush Bohlman were responsible for design and construction of a 616 m long cable-stayed bridge (340 m mainspan) including all trackwork and guideway elements. This is the world's first cable-stayed bridge designed specifically for Light Rail Transit. Value: US $179 million.

Calgary, Canada: Reid Crowther was prime consultant and provided trackbed, trackworks and general civil engineering design for the 5 km south extension of the city's LRT system. They were also responsible for some of the civil works on the Northwest LRT project, which included a cut-and-cover tunnel section. Value: US $7 million.

Projects (RITES)

Country	Client	Description	Completion
Thailand	State Railways of Thailand	Conversion of passenger train lighting system	1988
Sarawak	John Holland Constructions Pty Ltd	Feasibility study for a 200 km log railway in Sarawak	1988
India	Olex Cables	Design, supply and construction of optical fibre and radio communications systems for the Indian Government Railway	1988

CONSULTANCY SERVICES

Rendel Palmer & Tritton Ltd

61 Southwark Street, London SE1 1SA, England

Telephone: +44 71 928 8999
Telex: 919553 rendel g
Telefax: +44 71 928 5566

UK Regional Offices: Glasgow, Newport (Gwent), Newcastle, Birmingham, Bristol, Darlington, Warrington, Bath, Newport Pagnell, Wantage, York

Overseas Offices: Bahrain, Bangladesh, Brazil, Hong Kong, Indonesia, Libya, Malaysia, New Zealand, Singapore, Taiwan, United Arab Emirates, USA

Associate companies
Economic Studies Group
61 Southwark Street, London SE1 1SA
Telephone: +44 71 928 4222
Telex: 266664

Transportation Planning Associates Ltd
191 Corporation Street, Birmingham B4 6RP
Telephone: +44 21 236 6204

High-Point Schaer
King Edward House, New Street, Birmingham B2 4QJ
Telephone: +44 21 632 4561

Rendel Planning
61 Southwark Street, London SE1 1SA
Telephone: +44 71 928 6690

B R Wood Associates
Bank Chambers, 764/6 Fishponds Roads, Bristol BS16 3UA
Telephone: +44 272 653 6641

Rendel Mechel
The Old Tannery, Kelston, Bath BA1 9AN
Telephone: +44 272 327751

Bangladesh Consultants Ltd
4 Dhanmondi RA, Road 14, Dhaka 9, Bangladesh

Planave SA
Rua Costa Ferreira 106, Rio de Janeiro, Brazil

PT Indulexco
Jalan Abdul Muis 42, Jakarta Pusat, Indonesia

Chairman: R V Wharton
Directors: D W Hookway
R J Day
T Walsh
D E Bingham
R B Claxton
P J Clark
J M Dawson
J R Hyde
D V Hattrell
R G Tappin

Capabilities
Rendel Palmer & Tritton has had wide experience of railway planning, design, manning, operation and maintenance; and prior to joining RPT, the firm's railway specialists have had extensive hands-on technical and managerial experience with railways of various gauges and axle loads in Europe and Africa. The firm has carried out numerous railway assignments in Africa, Asia, Australasia, Europe and South America, the range of activities encompassing: feasibility studies; economic studies; survey, design and supervision of construction of railways; specification and inspection for motive power, rolling stock, maintenance installations and equipment, signalling and telecommunications; reconstruction, upgrading or rehabilitation of railway infrastructure; modernisation programmes for motive power, rolling stock and other equipment; layout and equipping of container and freight terminals; layout and equipping of loading and unloading installations for bulk mineral and ore traffic; sidings and ports, mines, power stations and industrial areas; setting-up and equipping of railway workshops and training centres.

Projects
Railway consultancy projects currently under way include:
Salisbury and Axminster, UK: Design and supervision of construction of road/rail bridges associated with new road by-passes.
Southampton, UK: Design of railway extension and sidings layout to serve the proposed coal-fired Fawley 'B' power station.
Barking, UK: Design of new highway bridges to span seven railway tracks with overhead electrification at 25 kV.
Tanzania/Zambia, Study of accident prevention on the 1800 km-long Tazara Railway. Formulation and supervision of a railways staff training programme.
Tanzania: Specification and inspection of 100-tonne breakdown crane for the Tanzanian section of the Tazara Railway.
Bangladesh: Preparation of design and specifications for tendering for a 4.8 km long road/rail bridge across the river Jamuna.
Channel Tunnel, UK: Consultants to Eurorail who has been selected by British Rail as joint venture partner for the Channel Tunnel Rail Link.

RFS Projects Ltd

Strutt House, Bridgefast, Belper, Derbyshire DE5 1XZ, England

Telephone: +44 773 821051
Telex: 378514
Telefax: +44 773 821045

Capabilities
Rail vehicle design consultancy offering a total supporting design service for major projects. Capabilities include concept generation, specifications, detail engineering, project management and technical documentation support.

Roundel Design Group

7 Rosehart Mews, Westbourne Grove, London W11 3TY, England

Telephone: +44 71 221 1951
Telefax: +44 71 221 1843

Managing Director: Michael Denny
Director: John Bateson
Director: Harold Batten
Associate Director: Vivien Edwards
Associate Director: Chris Bradley

Member of the Transport Design Consortium. Other member companies are Jones Garrard, Industrial Designers, RFS Projects, Engineering Design and Tilney Lumsden Shane, Interior Designers & Architects.

Capabilities
Design of new corporate identities.

Projects
Implementation and ongoing associated promotional and literature projects for British Rail and British Rail–Railfreight; signing programme for Docklands Light Railway.

Schimpeler Corradino Associates

200 South Fifth/300N, Louisville, Kentucky 40202, USA

Telephone: +1 502 5877221
Telefax: +1 502 587 2636

Managing Principal: Joseph C Corradino
Principal for Special Transit Projects: Dr Charles C Schimpeler

433 South Spring Street, Suite 1004N, Los Angeles, California 90013

Telephone: +1 213 6130937

Managing Principal: Dr Charles C Schimpeler

Technical Directors
Transit System Design: R W Moore
Transit Systems Analysis: K D Kaltenbach, Dr P L Mokhtarian
Planning and Urban Design: Dr D A Ripple
Public Information and Involvement: D J Ridings
Financial and Economic Analysis: Dr W C Vodrazka
Transit Planning: D C Kelly
Environmental Analysis: T Stone

Major Offices
Los Angeles; Miami; Dallas; Jeffersonville, Indiana (S K Wilson Division)

Capability
Capabilities include civil engineering (design and construction management); systems and management planning; tranportation and environmental engineering; and land use and urban design. Has provided project planning and design covering a wide range of civil and transportation projects, including mass transit and airport improvement projects throughout the continental United States. It has also provided urban planning, environmental assessment, and transportation modelling services.

Projects
Recent and current projects include: Metro Rail, a multi-billion dollar underground rail transit system under construction in Los Angeles for the Southern California Rapid Transit District; Project management of the Louisville Kentucky Airport Improvement Project which will involve realignment of two runways in a constrained urban environment; the Dade County Rail Rapid Transit System in Miami, a 21-mile elevated transit system serving the Greater Miami area; major transportation corridor studies in San Antonio, Cincinnati, Columbus (Ohio) and several other major American cities.

SGTE
Société Générale de Technique et d'Études

Tour Anjou, 33 quai de Dion Bouton, 92814 Puteaux Cedex, France

Telephone: +33 1 47 76 43 43
Telex: 613591 getud f
Telefax: +33 1 47 76 28 34

Chairman and Chief Executive: Claude Pradoo
Commercial Manager: Antoine Massabki

Capabilities
Project design, planning, engineering and supervision of rail and rapid transit systems.

STV Engineers

STV Engineers

11 Robinson Street, Pottstown, Pennsylvania 19464, USA

Telephone: +1 215 326 4600
Telex: 84-6430

STV/Seelye Stevenson Value & Knecht

225 Park Avenue South, New York, New York 10003, USA

Telephone: +1 212 777-4400
Telex: 64-9081

Chairman: R L Holland
Key rail staff: C E Defendorf
F G Fisher
D M Servedio
C Stark
K Bossung
E Allen
W F Matts

Capabilities
Transport planning; system and facility design; rolling stock engineering; operations and maintenance analysis.

Projects
Massachusetts Bay Transportation Authority
North station improvements and Green Line relocation (joint venture). Estimated construction costs: $160 million
Boston engine terminal, Boston (sub-consultant). Estimated construction costs: $360 million
Lynn Central Square Phase III, bridge replacement, and garage and station modifications, Lynn (sub-consultant). Estimated construction costs: $16 million
Design of interim and permanent maintenance facility: South station, Boston. Estimated construction costs: $8 million
Bowdoin-Charles Street station connector, feasibility study for connecting MBTA Red Line subway with Blue Line subway, Boston.
Red Line rapid transit car fleet modernisation and

procurement. Estimated construction costs: $138 million
Equipment engineering services for acquisition, rebuilding and upgrading passenger locomotives and coaches. Estimated construction costs: $75 million
Service and inspection facility, Boston. Estimated construction costs: $35 million
New Hampshire branch railroad rehabilitation, Boston to Tynsboro. Estimated construction costs: $75 million
New York City Transit Authority
Power Department training manuals development and job evaluation, New York.
Engineering and inspection services for 425 R-68 IND/BMT rapid transit cars. Estimated construction costs: $427 million
Modernisation of Grand Central station IRT, New York. Estimated construction costs: $12 million
R-68 rapid transit car support engineering services. Estimated construction costs: $43 million
Metropolitan Transportation Authority/Long Island Rail Road
LIRR line improvements, Part B, Section IA, and Ronkonkoma yard design, Long Island (sub-consultant). Estimated construction costs: $100 million
Port Jefferson storage yard design and Port Jefferson and main lines stations study (sub-consultant). Estimated construction costs: $6.5 million
Holban/Hillside yard and shops renovation and design (sub-consultant), Queens, New York. Estimated construction costs: $170 million
Mineola station/main line improvement program, Mineola, New York. Estimated construction costs: $70 million
Ronkonkoma storage yard welfare facility, Ronkonkoma, New York. Estimated construction costs: $1.5 million
Metro-North Commuter Railroad
Port Jervis, Harmon and North White Plains storage yards design, New York. Estimated construction costs: $30 million
Connecticut Department of Transportation
Southeastern Pennsylvania Transportation Authority
Illinois Department of Transportation
Statewide engineering support for rail rehabilitation and improvement program.
California Department of Transportation
Preliminary design of rail maintenance shop to serve Caltrain commuter rail service between San Francisco and San Jose.
Los Angeles County Transportation Commission
Feasibility study for light rail route through Lincoln Heights-El Sereno area, California.
Urban Mass Transportation Administration
St. Charles streetcar line refurbishment project management oversight project. Estimated construction costs: $43 million
Denver Rio Grande Western Railroad Co: Review and analyse the Southern Pacific Transportation company's rolling stock and facilities.
Northern Virginia Transportation Commission: Acquisition of 10 locomotives and 38 cars for commuter lion.
SEPTA, Philadelphia: New maintenance facilities at Frazier for electric locomotives & commuter cars Value, $25 million.

Simpson and Curtin
Division of Booz, Allen & Hamilton, Inc

400 Market Street, Philadelphia, Pennsylvania 19106, USA

Telephone: +1 215 627 5450

President: Michael G Ferreri

Projects
Commuter rail contract management study for the Massachusetts Bay Transportation Authority;
Organisation and management development assistance to the Long Island Rail Road;
Car maintenance management assistance to the Long Island Rail Road;
Performance audit of the Bay Area Rapid Transit District;
Organisation and management study for the Chicago Transit Authority;
Management and organisation study for the Louisiana Department of Transportation;
Management and organisation study for the West Yorkshire County Council.

Smith & Egan Associates, Inc

1127 11th Street, Suite 1003, Sacramento, California 95814, USA

888 16th Street NW, Suite 600, Washington DC 20006, USA

Telephone: Sacramento: +1 916 444 5433
　　　　　　Washington DC: +1 202 223 5133

President: Tim Egan (Sacramento)

Capabilities
The firm serves as lobbyist for those transit authorities and suppliers desiring assistance in the US. The company also assists foreign companies to organise and gather information affecting their US operations and future business opportunities.

Sodeteg-TAI

Route de la Minière 238, ZI Nord, 78530 Buc, France

Telephone: +33 1 39 56 80 60
Telex: 698 138 f

Marketing Manager, Transportation Division: Robert Fillier

Capabilities
Study and construction of transport systems; metro train control, power control and communications; light rail transit systems; marshalling yard automation.

Sofrerail
Société Française d'Etudes et de Réalisations Ferroviaires

3 avenue Hoche, 75008 Paris, France

Telephone: +33 1 42 67 97 08
Cable: Sofrerail, Paris
Telex: 280084
Telefax: +33 1 47 66 55 94

President: Philippe Roumeguère
Managing Director: Pierre-Louis Rochet
Marketing Director: Christian Bret
Financial Director: Guy Lambert

Capabilities
Sofrerail is a private company, founded in 1957, the first of its kind to supply consultancy services for all fields of railway activity.
Overall studies involve: reorganisation of rail networks, preparation of investment plans, construction of new lines and electrification projects. Special studies cover very diverse sectors: analysis of transport costs, tariff reform, containerisation, maintenance of rolling stock, modern track maintenance, signalling and telecommunications systems and adaptation to traffic and town planning projects. Technical assistance is carried out by teams of specialists and technicians for the application, down to working level, of the resulting recommendations.
Sofrerail is backed up by the important knowledge and know-how potential of high-level engineers, economists and managers, as well as technicians of the French National Railways (SNCF).
Sofrerail has carried out numerous railway and transport studies in more than 80 countries on behalf of governments, international agencies and railway administrations.

Projects
Australia: Study of passenger traffic demand for Very Fast Train project between Sydney, Canberra and Melbourne (1987–1988).
Brazil: Setting up of a railway costs evaluation system for RFFSA (1987–1988).
Cameroon: setting up of a staff management service (1987–1988).
Channel Tunnel: Technical advices and various studies (1987–1988).
Congo: Technical assistance in Comilog Railway,
Gabon: Supervision and control of the construction of the Transgabonese Railway (Owendo-Booué-Franceville). Technical assistance for maintenance (1979–1988).
Jordan: Participation in studies of the economic feasibility of developing shidiyah rock phosphate deposit (1984–1987).
Luxembourg: Study of reorganisation of CFL suburban traffic (1987).
Madagascar: Assistance to Malagasy Railways in the fields of permanent way, ballast production, staff management, training (1984–1988).
Mauritania: Technical assistance to SNIM iron ore railway.
Mozambique: Co-ordination and supervision of the works of rehabilitation of the Nacala-Entrelagos line (1983–87). Setting up of a railway training scheme at Inhambane Railway School, in association with SEDES (France) and NORMA (Portugal) (1984–1989).
Saudi Arabia: Study of Holy Area-Djeddah railway transportation system (1987–1988).
Spain: Participation in supervision of High Speed Railway line construction works (NAFA Project) (1988).
Swaziland: Assistance to staff training school (1986–1988).
Turkey: Technical assistance to TCDD for rolling stock maintenance. (1988).
USA: Participation in modernisation study of Jamaica station in New York suburban area for Long Island Railroad (1988–1989).
Zaïre: Technical assistance to SNCZ (1987–1989). Study of signalling and telecommunications system modernisation for ONATRA (1988).

Sofretu
Société Française d'Etudes et de Réalisations de Transports Urbains

38, boulevard Henri IV, 75004 Paris, France

Telephone: +33 1 42 71 22 62
Cable: Sofretu, Paris
Telex: 210120
Telefax: +33 1 42 71 06 62

Chairman and Chief Executive Officer: Paul-André Bolgert
Executive Vice President, Technical: J F Bougard
Commercial Manager: F Guittonneau

Associate company: Sofretu & Associés

Subsidiary companies: LS Transit Systems Inc, USA
　　　　　　　　　　　SITUS, Italy

Capabilities
Sofretu is the consulting subsidiary of the Paris metro and bus authority Regie Autonome des Transports Parisiens (RATP). Sofretu's main function is exporting urban transport know-how based on RATP experience. Capabilities include: technical, economical and financial studies dealing with transportation planning, traffic flow estimates, selection of transportation system (bus, light rail, heavy rail and subways), layout of networks, financial plan for investment; basic and detailed design, including functional and technical specifications; assistance in construction, including analysis of contractors' and suppliers' tenders, assistance in drawing up contracts, work supervision and manufacturing quality control, and supervision of acceptance tests. In commissioning a system, Sofretu offers assistance in establishing the operation company, starting staff recruiting and training programmes, drawing up operating rules and maintenance instructions and providing technical assistance during the first months of operation. Sofretu offers assistance to existing companies in administrative, technical and financial organisation, improvement of operational and maintenance methods, modernisation of stock and equipment and staff training.
In 1984, Sofretu created a consortium with six French groups, Sofretu & Associés, which includes the SCET consultancy, the Lyons and Nantes transport undertaking consultancy consortium METRAM, the Marseilles Transport Authority RTM, the Marseilles Metro undertaking SMM, the contract management company CGFTE, which manages transport in several French cities, and Via Transtec which manages transport through its subsidiary Transexel.
In 1985, Sofretu, in joint venture with the American group Combustion Engineering, created a subsidiary in New Jersey, LS Transit Systems. This subsidiary

provides mass transit consulting and contracting capabilities on the North American market.

In 1986, Sofretu established, with Italian partners, a subsidiary in Rome, SITUS.

Projects
France
Saint-Etienne: Modernisation study of two railway tunnels (1981).
Europe
Channel Tunnel: Consultancy services for the Channel Tunnel project (1987–91).
Barcelona: Technical assistance to the railway company for design manufacturing, commissioning and maintenance of rolling stock (1982–88). Consultancy services for high-speed train operation (1986).
Africa
Abuja: Transportation planning, feasibility study and basic design for railway network (1980–81).
Abidjan: Basic and detailed design for an urban railway service line (1978–87).
Algiers (1986): Analysis of mass transit alternatives on dedicated right-of-way, utilising the existing railway infrastructure.
Cairo: Transportation planning, technical assistance to the Egyptian National Railways (1979–81). Engineering services for the Greater Cairo Regional Metro construction, work supervision, operation and maintenance technical assistance (1982–90). Staff training for the Cairo Transport Authority (1983–85).
Asia
Ahmedabad (1985): Feasibility study of a commuter rail line.
Jakarta: Jabotabek project, feasibility study of the urban railway lines' modernisation, basic and detailed design (1982–88).
Jakarta (1988–92): Project management, factory control and work supervision of the Serpong line single-track improvement programme.
Shanghai (1988–89): Feasibility study of a north-south commuter rail link.
South America
Caracas: Preliminary design for 'Caracas Littoral' suburban railway and Tuy railway line project (1987).
New York, USA: (1986–88) Penn station, design of access improvements for New Jersey Transit; (1988–89) Jamaica station, Long Island Railroad, design of complex improvements.

Steer, Davies & Gleave
Steer, Davies & Gleave Ltd

11 Worple Way, Richmond, Surrey TW10 6DG, England

Telephone: +44 81 940 0275
Telex: 932905
Telefax: +44 81 948 5014

Managing Director: Jim Steer
Directors: David Hollings
Robert Sheldon
Peter Twelftree
Luis Willumsen

Consultants: Hugh Inwood
Roy Noble (Freight and Distribution)
Charles Russell
Pam Ventham-Smith
Peter Warman

Associated and subsidiary companies
Barnes Associates
Cleverdon Steer
Hague Consulting Group

Managing Director: John Davies

Capabilities
Steer Davies & Gleave Ltd was formed in 1978. A member of the British Consultants Bureau, it undertakes a wide range of assignments concerned with LRT and heavy rail in the UK and overseas. The scope of the assignments undertaken for railway administrations includes: investment appraisal planning; management services; and marketing and market research.

The range of commissions is wide because the senior staff embrace several disciplines such as engineering (civil and mechanical), planning, economics, computing services, forecasting, operational research, social and market research, marketing, and advertising and promotion. The practical experience of the staff includes multi-modal projects and some have held senior management positions within the passenger and freight fields.

UK clients include: British Railways Board (Director InterCity, Director Railfreight and the General Managers of the five Regions), London Regional Transport, London Docklands Light Railway, Northern Ireland Railways, Greater London Council, Greater Manchester Council, West Midlands County Council and Passenger Transport Executive, Mid-Wales Development Board, Wales Tourist Board and Grampian Regional Council. European clients include the state rail operations of the Republic of Ireland, Netherlands, Denmark, France, Belgium and Federal Republic of Germany. Assignments on a subcontract basis have been undertaken for the governments of Hong Kong, Maharashtra (Bombay, India), Chile, Indonesia, Mozambique, Republic of Korea and the Federal Railroad Administration (USA).

The consultancy has been heavily involved in major passenger transport planning and investment projects in Ireland, Bombay, Hong Kong and Australia. It has also supplied modelling and evaluation techniques for freight projects in Africa, South Korea and the Philippines. Its current orientation is substantially towards business strategies incorporating existing, modified or expanded networks. These strategies relate to the retention and development of existing markets, the attraction of new ones and the strengthening of the competitive thrust.

Projects
Recent projects have included investment priority studies for a number of European railways involving passenger evaluation of rolling stock, station facilities and quality of service features. This has resulted in the consultancy providing advice on rail product development and improving the commercial practices of railway operators.

Since its inception the consultancy has participated in over 100 projects concerned with the planning and operation of rail systems. Many of these studies have been of an international nature. In the UK work is currently being undertaken on a profile study of the Anglo-Irish rail market for British Rail. Other projects are related to airport access. The consultancy evaluated the viability of a direct rail link for Manchester International Airport in conjunction with a major study for the airport providing long-term passenger traffic forecasts.

The company was appointed as the Transportation Planners for the Canary Wharf development with the consultancy working in an advisory capacity for the developers, planners and government departments. The extension of the Docklands Light Railway into the city is critical to the Canary Wharf development; the consultancy have made a full evaluation of the options for its extension.

The 70 projects undertaken exclusively for British Rail cover a wide range of assignments. The consultancy assisted in formulating the recent InterCity strategy and subsequently have worked closely with senior management in implementing the various marketing, financial and operational measures in the strategy.

Access to the rail network is a further major issue. New park-and-ride stations, car parking provision and interchanges have been evaluated to determine the commercial benefits attributable to new and existing facilities.

Steer, Davies & Gleave Ltd have undertaken a number of projects for BR Railfreight over the last three years focusing upon strategies and operations to increase Railfreight competitiveness in the freight transport market in the UK and Northern Europe. These have included a study of opportunities for door-to-door freight movements to Scotland from the Midlands and the South, a specific study of the movement of lubricating oil by rail, a study of trends in UK palletised freight movement and a project to forecast cross-Channel movements of freight by train ferry.

The company are currently advising BR on new product development projects aimed at developing new commercial initiatives as well as evaluating the opportunities of new technological innovations.

The complex relationship between journey time, service frequency and fares was successfully identified for British Rail and subsequent assignments have been undertaken for Netherlands Railways and Danish Railways. Fares, both standard and promotional, have been studied in great depth in respect of their financial performance, their success as competitive measures and in generating new rail travellers.

The public acceptability of new and existing type of rolling stock has been assessed for British Rail management. The rolling stock studies embrace the spectrum from the Advanced Passenger Train, through British and Continental main-line rolling stock to various forms of potential replacement for the diesel multiple-units which operate commuter, secondary and branch line services.

Other passenger service and sales related topics have included catering, reservations and sleeping car facilities. In respect of the open station design, the consultants were asked to assess passenger reactions and identify the effects on the passengers and other station users. Included in the study was a review of the consequent effect upon station and on train staff. Of a more general character were the studies related to quality of service throughout the journey process, including the planning by the passengers and the activities of Travel Centres and travel agents. The consultancy participated in the programme which inaugurated BR's Customer Care.

Sundberg-Ferar Inc

27777 Franklin Road, S-1548 Southfield, Michigan 48034-2376, USA

Telephone: +1 313 356 8600

President: Richard A Heck

Projects
Dallas Area Rapid Transit (DART): vehicle design.

Sverdrup Corporation

13723 Riverport Drive, Maryland Heights, Missouri 63043, USA

Telephone: +1 314 436 7600
Telex: 9107611085
Telefax: +1 314 298 0045

Chairman: Brice R Smith Jr
Executive Vice-President: James C Uselton
Vice-President: Gordon R Pennington

Projects
Over 80 miles of the Old Colony Railroad System will be restored, once again providing residents in the South Shore areas of Boston with commuter rail service. The project consists of 51 railroad bridges, 21 passenger stations, and parking lots along three lines, and a new 2-track bridge to be built across the Neponet River.

To permit Amtrak passenger trains to operate directly from Canada and upstate New York to Penn Station in New York City, Sverdrup is providing construction management for the West Side Connection.

Using a design/build approach, Sverdrup completed a new $21.5 million centralised dispatching facility for CSX Transportation of Jacksonville, Florida. The round 18 000 sq ft theatre-like building handles the dispatch and crew call activities for CXST train operations for the eastern half of the USA.

The Port of Tacoma's South Intermodal Yard – a high-volume near dock intermodal container facility – was completed on a fast-track, 4-month schedule. The innovative use of roller-compacted concrete in the rail yard's loading areas provided 25% savings in paving costs.

Swederail Consulting AB

105 50 Stockholm, Sweden

Telephone: +46 8 762 37 80
Cable: Statsbanan, Stockholm
Telex: 19410
Telefax: +46 8 21 27 69

President: Per-Erik Olson

Swederail Consulting is a subsidiary of the Swedish State Railways SJ and the consulting arm of SJ and the newly established entity, Swedish National Rail Administration, which is responsible for all rail infrastructure and fixed installation in Sweden as of 1989. It is independent of any industrial, construction or banking interest.

CONSULTANCY SERVICES

Projects
Feasibility study and preliminary engineering for rehabilitation and electrification of railways in Southern Mozambique and Swaziland; the study covers a railway network of almost 1000 km of prime economic strategic importance for transport of merchandise of various kinds from major countries in Eastern Africa to the Indian Ocean.

Feasibility study design and final construction of electrification of Tumbler Ridge coal line of British Columbia Railways in Western Canada; the project included studies and design of 50 kV 60 Hz electrification in an area of very severe climate conditions. The railway is designed for heavy hauls.

Study of railway rolling stock in the SADCC states of Africa. The objective of this study is mainly to prepare a detailed inventory of the existing railway stock in the nine SADCC states and to collect information regarding existing maintenance and repair facilities for formulation of a policy for standardisation of rolling stock and maintenance.

Other recent projects have included: trainworking and telecommunication systems including installation, operation and training responsibility for Botswana Railways; and for Tazara a 10-year plan participation in product co-operation for civil engineering and commissioning of freight wagons supply.

Syscon Corporation

1000 Thomas Jefferson Street NW, Washington DC 20007, USA

Telephone: +1 202 342 4000
Telex: (710) 822 0103

Vice President: Robert Kidwell

Capabilities
Syscon Corporation is engaged principally in the business of providing systems engineering, computer systems, facilities management, technical services and software products for the US Government, primarily the military. In addition, Syscon has developed software products and services for state and municipal governments, and commercial enterprises. The company is engaged in the development, limited production and marketing of microprocessor-based products.

TAMS Consultants Inc
Tippetts-Abbett-McCarthy-Stratton

655 Third Avenue, New York, New York 10017, USA

Telephone: +1 212 867 1777
Telex: ITT 422188, RCA 223055
Telefax: +1 212 697 6354

President: Austin E Brant, Jr
Corporate Vice Presidents: Dana E Low
　　　　　　　　　　　　　　Patrick J McAward, Jr
　　　　　　　　　　　　　　Philip Perdichizzi
　　　　　　　　　　　　　　Lyle H Hixenbaugh
　　　　　　　　　　　　　　Edward C Regan
　　　　　　　　　　　　　　Mario Asin
　　　　　　　　　　　　　　Anthony H Dolcimascolo
　　　　　　　　　　　　　　G Barrie Heinzenknecht
　　　　　　　　　　　　　　Ronald H Axelrod

Capabilities
TAMS Consultants Inc, founded in 1942, offers international services in engineering, architecture, and planning. The firm has worked in more than 80 countries, providing comprehensive services for major ports, highways, railroads, bridges, airports, dams, agricultural and regional development, waste management, and urban planning projects. Headquartered in New York City, TAMS has branch offices world-wide and throughout the United States.

TAMS has broad experience in the planning, design, and inspection of railroad facilities, ranging from the engineering of more than 4000 km of railroads throughout the world to the design of major tunnels and stations. Projects include planning new lines through jungle or desert and rapid transit systems in US cities. Services provided by TAMS include location and alignment, trackwork, bridges, tunnels, and marshalling yards. The firm has also provided track location and development studies at: Wilmington, Delaware; Philadelphia, Pennsylvania; Providence, Rhode Island; and other locations. Rapid transit facilities have been planned and designed for Boston, New York, Baltimore, Washington DC and Atlanta, Georgia.

Projects
Recent projects have included:
Transgabon Railroad, West Africa: TAMS, in association with the firms of BCEOM and Sofrerail of France, Electroconsult of Italy, GERI and Gauff of the Federal Republic of Germany, and Tecsult of Canada, was retained by OCTRA, the Transgabon Railroad Authority, to provide engineering services in connection with the design review and supervision of construction of the Transgabon Railroad. Services included the review of designs prepared by the contractors and supervision of the construction of all works below the ballast level from Libreville to Franceville, totalling approximately 730 km of railroad.

Metro subway, Washington DC: TAMS provided final design and technical inspection of construction services for the 750-metre-long Section A-2 of the Washington Metro. The engineering involved design of 670 metres of twin-bore and mixed-face tunnel, a section of cut-and-cover construction, one fan shaft, and the underpinning of two major buildings. The firm also engineered the 2.3 km-long Section F-003 of the Metro. Its services, in association with other consultants, have included all engineering and architectural design for a centre-platform air-conditioned station, station ancillary areas, three vent shafts, two fan shafts, the underpinning of 11 structures in the Washington DC Navy Yard, soil stabilisation of four major sewers, underpinning of the South Capitol Street Underpass, and 1.9 km of twin-bore earth tunnel.

Long Island Rail Road, Pennsylvania Station, New York City: Rehabilitation and expansion of the commuter facility; the project involves new and extended platforms and entrances, the installation of escalators and lifts, and air-conditioning. Estimated construction cost is $70 million.

At Pennsylvania Station, new Amtrak and New Jersey Transit ticket counters have opened on the Eighth Avenue side of the B level concourse. TAMS designed the facilities as part of a two-phase design/build redevelopment project at the station for the general contractor. The ticket counters are the first phase of a plan to redesign the entire Amtrak passenger concourse. Phase 1A also includes back-up offices for support personnel, new escalators and stairs with glass railings, column covers, architectural finishes, communications equipment, air conditioning, and lighting.

SCRTD-Union Station, Los Angeles, California: TAMS provided engineering services for the final design of the Union Metro station in Los Angeles. A prior TAMS assignment involved preliminary engineering services for 16 rapid transit stations of this system, all of which are located underground.

Temple Barker & Sloane Inc

33 Hayden Avenue, Lexington, Massachusetts 02173, USA

Telephone: +1 617 861 7580

Transit and Tunnel Consultants Inc

6215 Sheridan Drive, Buffalo, New York 14221-4884, USA

Telephone: +1 716 632 7200
Telefax: +1 716 632 7209

Capabilities
Transit and Tunnel Consultants Inc was formed in 1972 to bring together a broad range of disciplines related to transit and tunnel technology. Founders of the firm, Hatch Associates Ltd of Toronto, and Mott, Hay and Anderson International Ltd of London, both affiliates of Transit and Tunnel Consultants Inc, have played major roles on numerous large transit projects. Activities cover: feasibility studies: examining the viability of the project as a whole, alternative methods of fulfilling requirements, basic concepts and standards, costs entailed and benefits to be derived; surveys and preliminary designs; detailed designs, drawings and specifications, and bid documents; preparation, awarding, financial control, and final settlement of contracts; project management; construction management.

The firm's wide experience in tunnelling includes design and construction management in all types of ground from water-bearing silts and sands to rock. Under difficult tunnelling conditions, techniques such as compressed air, ground treatment and freezing have been employed. The ground conditions, together with the type and location (urban or rural) of the facility, form the major constraints on design. T & TC and its affiliates have carried out projects in both soft ground and rock involving full-face and part-face excavators, tunnelling shields, and conventional drill-and-blast methods. Tunnel linings have been developed to suit the specific requirements of the project and have ranged from segmental linings in cast iron, steel and precast concrete to cast-in-place concrete.

On many projects, both planning requirements and construction costs result in the selection of cut-and-cover methods rather than a tunnelled solution. T & TC is highly experienced in the design of cut-and-cover structures in both rock and soft ground, employing the full range of available techniques for ground support.

Projects
Design and construction management of Buffalo light rail rapid transit 5.6 km twin rock tunnel including five stations ($174 million) for Niagara Frontier Transportation Authority.

Final design of 5.6 km twin rock tunnel through Santa Monica Mountains ($117 million) for Los Angeles Metro rail transit consultants to Southern California Rapid Transit District.

Transmark
Transportation Systems and Market Research Limited

Enterprise House, 169 Westbourne Terrace, London W2 6JY, England

Telephone: +44 71 723 3411
Telex: 8953218 britmk g
Telefax: +44 71 258 1938

Parent company: British Railways Board, Euston House, 24 Eversholt Street, PO Box 100, London NW1 1DZ

Chairman: R J Withers
Managing Director: H M Jenkins
Deputy Managing Director: J S Bell
Directors: K B Hampton
　　　　　　W Turner
　　　　　　A H Wickens

Capabilities
Transmark is a wholly-owned subsidiary of the British Railways Board, formed in 1969 to undertake transport consultancy, give technical advice and carry out market research throughout the world. It operates under the name of Cole Sherman Transmark in Canada and GHD Transmark Australia in New South Wales and Queensland.

Transmark consultants are drawn from all departments and disciplines of British Rail and bring extensive experience of BR's techniques to projects overseas. Having completed more than 800 overseas contracts in 80 countries from every continent, Transmark is able to offer expertise both on high technology/sophisticated railway systems and on the railways of developing nations. Some 2000 senior managers and specialist engineers from British Rail can also be called upon to augment Transmark's permanent staff with their own particular managerial or technical expertise which ranges from civil engineering and computers to planning and marketing. Indeed, Transmark has the backing of all the resources of the British Railways Board, including the latter's world-renowned Railway Technical Centre as well as associated companies, which have interests as diverse as shipping, containers, catering, rolling stock construction, property development and advertising.

A wide variety of projects has been undertaken, ranging from major studies covering all railway disciplines and technical assistance programmes to short visits by a single railway specialist. Training is an important element in many projects and is undertaken both in the UK and overseas. Clients include national and state governments, international lending agencies, national and privately-owned railways and many industrial and commercial organisations.

Typical projects
Australia: High Speed Train (HST) licence agreement with Comeng for New South Wales' State Rail Authority; design and construction supervision of Brisbane's suburban railway system for Queensland Railways; electrification and associated works on the

CONSULTANCY SERVICES

Illawarra line for New South Wales' State Rail Authority; train operations study for Mt Newman Mining Company.
Bangladesh: Technical assistance to Bangladesh Railways at Saidpur and Pahartali railway carriage and wagon workshops.
Botswana: Provision of railway management support for Botswana Railways.
Brazil: Technical consultancy and training in connection with the Ferrovia do Aco Railway, Belo Horizonte-Volta Redonda for GEC.
Canada: Laying of slab track in Rogers Pass for CP Rail.
Egypt: Cairo Metro, in-house consultancy for National Authority for Tunnels.
Hong Kong: Modernisation, electrification and construction supervision for the Kowloon-Canton Railway.
Iraq, Kuwait: Basra-Kuwait border railway study for the Ministry of Transport and Communications/Municipality of Kuwait.
Kenya: Technical assistance to Kenya Railways.
Malaysia: Containerisation study for Malayan Railway Administration.
Middle East: Arabian Gulf railway study for the Cooperation Council for the Arab States of the Gulf.
New Zealand: North Island main-line electrification: technical consultancy for New Zealand Railways.
Northern Ireland: Centralised traffic control, feasibility and design studies, for Northern Ireland Railways.
Pakistan: World Bank studies concerning purchasing/stores control and track machinery maintenance for Ministry of Railways.
Portugal: Review of Portuguese Railways' parcels services.
Singapore: Inspection of equipment for Singapore Metro.
Sri Lanka: Technical assistance to Sri Lanka Government Railways.
Sudan: Grain train project (rail transportation of food to Kordofan and Darfur) for Sudan Railway Corporation.
Tanzania: Tabora railway training college design and equipment acquisition for Tanzania Railway Corporation.
Thailand: Signalling and telecommunications, technical assistance for the State Railway of Thailand.
Turkey: Technical feasibility study for electrification on Turkish State Railways.
UK: Parcel's business machine training for British Rail; Battersea Leisure Centre project.
USA: Engineering and design services for signal improvements at Grand Central Terminal, New York.
Uruguay: Analysis of railways' improvement programme for Ministry of Transport and Public Works.
Zimbabwe: Provision of training adviser and specialist instructors for the National Railway of Zimbabwe.

Transport Design Consortium

5 Heathmans Road, London SW6 4TJ, England

Telephone: +44 71 731 8190
Telefax: +44 71 736 3356

116 Regent Road, Leicester LE1 7LT
Telephone: +44 533 542390

Strutt House, Bridgefoot, Belper, Derbyshire DE5 1XZ
Telephone: +44 773 821051

7 Rosehart Mews, Westbourne Grove, London W11 3TY
Telephone: +44 71 221 1951

Industrial Design: Roger Jones
Corporate & Graphic Design: Michael Denny
Environmental Design (Rolling Stock & Interiors):
  Marvin Shane
Engineering Design: Andrew Lezala
Engineering Design: Paul Robinson

Transport Design Consortium is an association of four specialist design companies: Jones Garrard Ltd, RFS Projects, Roundel Design Group, Tilney Lumsden Shane.

Capabilities
Styling, industrial design, environmental design, engineering design, graphic design, corporate identity and project management for the rail industry.

Projects
Recent ongoing projects include corporate identity, implementation and ongoing associated projects for British Rail and British Rail–Railfreight (1987); design of the front end, driver's cab and catering vehicle interior for the Channel Tunnel High Speed Train (1988); refurbishment of 1967–72 stock for London Underground Ltd (1989); refurbishment of 1973 stock and Heathrow service for London Underground Ltd (1989).

Transportation and Distribution Associates, Inc

A subsidiary of Day & Zimmermann, Inc

1818 Market Street, Philadelphia, Pennsylvania 19103, USA

Telephone: +1 215 299-8080
Cable: Dayzim
Telex: 845192

President: Alan B Buchan

Projects
Rehabilitation and modernisation of track, signal, and traction power facilities at Cleveland's Union Terminal as part of a multi-million dollar Tower City redevelopment project.
Identification and evaluation of impacts on Boston commuter rail operations caused by the construction of I90/I93 highways.
Industrial engineering and signal design for Massachusetts Bay Transportation Authority's light rail maintenance shop and a Port Authority Trans-Hudson (PATH) main repair facility and yard at Harrison, New Jersey.
Chemical, metallurgical, and physical testing services through TSD Inc.
Project management oversight of design and construction of new segments of Washington Metrorail System for the Urban Mass Transportation Administration.
Construction management of Long Island Rail Road's Jamaica station.
Engineering audit of the New York Metropolitan Transportation Authority's inspection, maintenance, and repair programmes and budgets for its commuter rail operations.
Grade crossing protection device design and maintenance for short lines and regional railroads.

Transportation Planning Associates

61 Southwark Street, London SE1 1SA, England

Telephone: +44 71 928 6690
Telex: 919553
Telefax: +44 71 928 5566

UK Regional Offices: Glasgow, Newport (Gwent), Darlington, Warrington, Birmingham, Bath.

Overseas Offices: Australia, Bahrain, Brazil, Hong Kong, Indonesia, Kuwait, Libya, Papua New Guinea, Philippines, Singapore, United Arab Emirates, USA, Dhaka.

Associated companies
Rendel Palmer & Tritton Ltd
61 Southwark Street, London SE1 1SA, England
Telephone: +44 71 928 8999
Telex: 919553
Telefax: +44 71 928 5566
RPT Economic Studies Group Ltd
61 Southwark Street, London SE1 1SA, England
Telephone: +44 71 928 4222
Telex: 266664
High-Point Services Group plc
King Edward House, New Street, Birmingham B2 4QJ, England
Telephone: +44 21 632 4561
Telex: 339110
Telefax: +44 21 643 6024
Rendel Scott Furphy
390 St Kilda Road, Melbourne, Australia
Planave SA
Rua Costa Ferreira 106, Rio de Janeiro, Brazil

Chairman: T M Mulroy

Directors: B J Blunt
R Cathcart
H A Collis
E J Fearon
I S Findlay
D W Hookway
M P McCrory

Capabilities
Transportation Planning Associates have extensive experience of multi-modal transportation planning at a regional and local level. Capabilities include the overall planning of transport systems, the development of econometric models for predicting transportation demand, economic and operational evaluation of transport proposals, market research and the planning of rail terminal and interchange facilities for both passengers and freight. The consultancy maintains its own comprehensive transportation software package T-PACK. In association with civil engineering consultants, Rendel Palmer & Tritton and Merz & McLellan, TPA are able to provide a full planning and design package particularly for urban light rail and mass transit systems. Additional specialist civil engineering, economic, management and financial consultancy services are provided in association with other High-Point Rendel Group companies.

Projects
Railway consultancy projects under way in 1988 included:
London Docklands Development Corporation and London Regional Transport: Docklands Light Rail study. TPA are responsible for the transportation planning aspects of studies of extensions to the Docklands Light Railway (DLR) system. During 1988 work on this study included a review of passenger demand forecasts on the existing DLR system and passenger demand forecasting for the proposed Lewisham extension.
Trafalgar House and British Rail Engineering: Manchester Metrolink study. TPA in consortium with Merz and McLellan and Transurb are advising this consortium on their bid for the contract to construct and operate the Manchester Metrolink.
Channel Tunnel Rail Link study: TPA carried out a pre-feasibility study of a high-speed rail link between the Channel Tunnel and Central London.
Leeds City Council and Coopers and Lybrand: Leeds light rapid transit study. TPA provided transportation planning input to a pre-feasibility study of alternative LRT routes in Leeds.
British urban development: Greenwich Peninsula study. TPA carried out pre-feasibility studies for light and heavy rail options to link this major development site with London's main rail network.
Hereford and Worcester County Council: Worcester Parkway study. TPA carried out a feasibility study for an international freight terminal and a new parkway station on the outskirts of Worcester.
West Midlands Passenger Transport Executive and British Railways: Rail survey methodology study. TPA developed a new rail passenger survey methodology for the West Midlands Region.
Greater Manchester Passenger Transport Authority: Greater Manchester Channel Tunnel freight study. In association with Coopers and Lybrand, TPA are assessing the demand for international freight in Greater Manchester and the capability of existing rail infrastructure to handle this freight.
Northern Ireland Railways: Belfast Great Victoria Street scheme, technical audit. TPA are carrying out a technical audit of previous feasibility studies for the reopening of the Belfast Great Victoria Street terminus.
World Bank/UNDP: Jamuna Bridge study, Bangladesh. TPA developed rail and bus passenger traffic forecasts for the Jamuna multi-purpose bridge.

Transurb Consult

2–4 rue des Colonies, 1000 Brussels, Belgium

Telephone: +32 2 512 3047/5847/1881
Telex: 62413
Telefax: +32 2 513 9419

President: J Groothaert
General Manager: Pierre M De Smet

Transurb Consult was formed in 1973 to bring together for world-wide deployment the various aspects of Belgian transport technology. Its capital is equally apportioned between Belgian Railways (SNCB),

CONSULTANCY SERVICES

Current contracts (Transurb Consult)

Country/client	Duration of Assignment	Assignment
Algeria National Company of Railway Transports (SNTF)	1985–89	Control and works supervision for the construction of the railway connection Jijel-Ramdane Djamal (125 km)
Burkina Faso Economic Community of West Africa (CEAO)	1988	Actualisation of the feasibility study and site study of the Fabrique Communautaire de Wagons FACOWA in Bobo Dioulasso.
Ethiopia Djibouti-Ethiopian Railway. Montan Engineering	1987–88	Training programme for the rehabilitation of a maintenance workshop.
France/UK Channel Tunnel	1987–93	Control and supervision of the rolling stock and fixed electro-mechanical equipment for a railway connection under the Channel.
Gabon Transgabonese Railway Company (OCTRA)	1983–89	Technical assistance for the operation of the Transgabonese Railway by secondment of 18 experts in different railway techniques.
	1985–89	Turnkey project of a railway training centre in Franceville, including design, technical studies, training programmes, engineering works, construction, equipment supply, assembly and assistance of Gabonese instructors for two years.
Greece Railway Company of Greece (OSE)	1988	Training of track engineers.
Hong Kong KCRC (Kowloon-Canton Railway Corporation)	1985–88	Control management and follow-up for the construction of a 23 km light rail transit in Tuen Mun.
India Ministry of Urban Development	1987	Pre-feasibility study for the introduction of LRT system in New Delhi.
Indonesia Indonesian State Railways (PJKA)	1988–91	Technical assistance and training project for PJKA.
Iraq Baghdad Rapid Transit Authority (BRTA)	1986–88	Execution study for section 015 of the Baghdad metro network (including 5 stations, single-track twin-bored tunnels, part of the route under River Tigris).
Jordan Aqaba Railways Corporation	1986–87	Development and implementation of new financial, accounting and management information systems and training of accounting staff.
Kenya Ministry of Transport, Ministry of Local Government and City Council of Nairobi	1985–86	Preliminary study of urban transport needs in Nairobi conurbation (first stage).
	1988–89	Study of urban transport needs in Nairobi conurbation (second stage) and definition of a light rail transit line and bus system.
Mali Railway Authority of Mali (RCFM)	1988	Studies related to the elaboration of an investment plan for RCFM.
Mexico Covitur	1985–86	Technical assistance in the maintenance organisation of light rail vehicles in Mexico City.
Nigeria Nigerian Railway Corporation (NRC)	1987	Preliminary study for the improvement of locomotive maintenance in NRC depots.
Peru Invermet	1987–89	Complementary studies related to the urban development plan of metropolitan Lima and El Callao.
Tanzania Tanzania-Zambia Railways (Tazara)	1988	Wheel-sets reprofiling lathes appraisal mission.
Thailand State Railways of Thailand (SRT)	1987–90	Technical assistance for Management Information Systems (MIS).
Zaïre National Railway	1985–87	Technical assistance for the installation of CTC between Tenke and Likasi.
Company of Zaire (SNCZ)	1987–88	Renewal of the main line between the stations of Kapolowe and Likasi; training of 37 SNCZ experts.
	1987–89	Technical assistance to the SNCZ technical and operation divisions.
	1988–89	Study related to low-traffic density route sections.
Zambia Zambia Railways	1987–89	Training of Zambian staff and technical assistance in the design, construction and repair of wagons.
Zimbabwe National Railways of Zimbabwe (NRZ)	1988	Identification mission in the field of locomotive maintenance.

Luxembourg Railways (CFL), the Société Nationale des Chemins de Fer Vicinaux (SNCV), the Brussels Public Transport Company (STIB), the public transport companies of Antwerp (MIVA), Ghent (MIVG), Charleroi (STIC), Liège (STIL) and Verviers (STIV), and the ministries of the Brussels, Flemish and Walloon Regions. The private sector is mainly represented by TRACTEBEL, a major holding company in Belgium, and by specialised private research offices dealing with all aspects of transportation. Transurb Consult's experience derives from its members' operation of over 4000 km of national railway, mainly electrified, with more than 2000 locomotives and transport units; of an urban public transport network comprising 35 km of metro, with 49 stations, 62 km of LRT and 261 km of bus lines; and from its consulting departments.

Transurb Consult has international experience in the design, construction and operation of metro systems, covering more than 200 km in Belgium (Brussels, Antwerp, Charleroi, Seacoast) and 100 km abroad (Singapore, Manila, Kuala Lumpur, Hong Kong, Tunis, Baghdad, Buenos Aires). Transurb Consult has executed approximately 400 km of rail line construction or reconditioning projects; 10 km of mass transit systems; 60 km of light rail systems; and maintenance workshops for vehicles aggregating 150 000 m² in area.

Capabilities

The main skills of Transurb Consult are in the following areas: passenger traffic (urban, suburban, intercity and international) and goods (collection, forwarding and delivery); railway, underground, tram, trolleybus, bus and all intermodal transport catering for transport of goods or passengers from door to door, mine to plant or supplier to user (rail-road, rail-shipping, etc); all town planning involved in the improvement of transport.

Transurb provides for its clients a particularly wide range of services, as the company combines the capabilities of: a consulting and engineering bureau dealing with expert reports, feasibility studies, detailed engineering studies, conditions of the contract, invitations to tender, drafting of contracts, supervision of working sites, commissioning; a commercial agent, bringing the potential purchasing public authorities in contact with the building contractors; a contractor of turnkey infrastructures (in this case, Transurb is not acting as a general contractor solely responsible for the project, but generally operates within the framework of temporary joint ventures with building contractors, manufacturers and consultants); an assistant body in the field of operation and management, with assignments ranging from staff training (on site and/or in Belgium) to technical assistance, maintenance of rolling stock, permanent way and equipment; and a supplier of transport equipment to networks with which Transurb has privileged commercial relations.

Since 1973 Transurb Consult has acted in Algeria, Argentina, Australia, Bangladesh, Brazil, Cameroon, Canada, Central African Republic, Chile, China, Congo, Egypt, El Salvador, Ethiopia, France, Gabon, Greece, Guinea, Hong Kong, India, Indonesia, Iraq, Ivory Coast, Jordan, Kenya, Lebanon, Malaysia, Mali, Mauritania, Mauritius, Mexico, Morocco, Netherlands, Niger, Nigeria, Peru, Philippines, Saudi Arabia, Senegal, Singapore, Sudan, Thailand, Togo, Tunisia, Turkey, Burkina Faso, United States, Venezuela, Zaire and Zambia.

Active in 5 continents, Transurb is presently conducting more than 40 projects located in 25 different countries.

Transurb Inc

85 Saint Catherine Street West, Montreal, Quebec, Canada H2X 3P4

Telephone: +1 514 871 0178
Telex: 055 61161
Telefax: +1 514 397 9750

President and General Manager:
　Claude Archambault
Vice-President: Guy Fournier
Directors: Paul Saint-Jacques
　　　　　　Paul T Beauchemin
　　　　　　Denis Thibeault
　　　　　　Yves Pigeon

Capabilities

Comprehensive mass transit studies; rail-based transit studies and design; planning and design of ancillary services; planning, design and construction management of railways and maintenance facilities.

Transurb is owned by two consulting engineering firms of Montreal: Beauchemin-Beaton-Lapointe Inc and Tecsult Inc.

Projects

Valparaiso-Limache (Chile): Suburban rail modernisation study (1989).
Granby (Canada): Public transit operational plan (1988–89).
Montreal, Canada: Public transit services in large multi-functional park (1987–88).
Montreal, Saint-Jean, Brossard and Longueuil (Canada): Suburban bus terminals (1985–89).
Montreal (Canada): Via Rail's maintenance centre, planning, design and construction management (1983–89).

Transystem SpA

Via Giulini 3, 20123 Milan, Italy

Telephone: +39 2 86 05 46
Telex: 334211 transy i

460 CONSULTANCY SERVICES

Telefax: +39 2 87 65 41

Managing Director and General Manager: Gabriele Testa
Manager Technical Director: Georgio Beltrami
Marketing Manager: Alberto Mirri

Capabilities
Transystem offers consultancy services and comprehensive capabilities in railway engineering, including general planning, economical and financial evaluation, feasibility studies, general to detailed design, project start-up, operation and maintenance consultancy. It operates in the field of infrastructural design and erection, permanent way, signalling, automation and computerised train control, overhead and third-rail contact line, power supply, auxiliary installation, workshops and depot yard. Transystem also produces and uses models and original package programmes for planning and design activities.

Projects
Italian State Railway master plan (1985).
New railway section 'Klong 19 project' for Thailand State Railway: preliminary and final design (1987).
Egypt, Alexandria transport master plan and preliminary design for the first mass transit line (1988).
Light rail transit line for Naples, final design (1988).
Study for the complete restructure of the Italian State Railway network in the Campania Region (1988).

Travers Morgan International Ltd

Mead House, Cantelupe Road, East Grinstead, West Sussex RH19 3DG, England

Telephone: +44 342 327161
Telex: 957009 rtmegd g
Telefax: +44 342 313500/315927

Other offices
Travers Morgan Pty Ltd
83 Mount Street, PO Box 1162, New South Wales 2059, Australia
Telephone: +61 2 922 1999
Telex: 22003 tmasyd aa
Telefax: +61 2 959 5706

Salahuddin Travers Morgan
PO Box 111, Manama, Bahrain
Telephone: +973 253663
Telex: 8368 arch bn
Telefax: +973 240199

Travers Morgan Wong Ltd
6a Hung On Building, 2 Kings Road, Causeway Bay, Hong Kong
Telephone: +852 5 667211
Telefax: +852 5 807 0492

Travers Morgan Malaysia Sdn Bhd
Lot 12.08, 12th Floor, Wisma Stephens, Jalan Raja Chulan, 50200 Kuala Lumpur, Malaysia
Telephone: +60 3 2489898
Telefax: +60 3 2486326

Uhimwen Travers Morgan
1 Efosa Street, Uzebu, Benin City, Nigeria (PO Box 597)
Telephone: +234 240535
Telex: 41152 bel ng

R Travers Morgan (Oman) Ltd
PO Box 5212, Ruwi, Sultanate of Oman
Telephone: +968 564459/60
Telex: 5624 sedfor on
Telefax: +968 564461

Travers Morgan International Ltd
PO Box 14628, Doha, Qatar
Telephone: +974 852098
Telex: 4397 aplan dh
Telefax: +974 853465

Directors: P P A Brogan
M A B Boddington
L R Cooke
M R Tull
M I Shenfield
R H Stewart
S J Tranter

Capabilities
The Travers Morgan Consulting Group is one of the UK's leading multi-disciplinary consultants with a long and enviable track record in the evaluation and design of major infrastructure projects. The Group was founded as Travers Morgan & Partners in 1929, initially providing services in civil and structural engineering from London. The Group has grown to a total of over 850 staff worldwide, providing a wide range of expertise including: route feasibility studies; economic modelling and evaluation; railway engineering; infrastructure engineering; transport planning and regional and national planning.

Projects
Argentina
National Transport Plan: In consortium with Coopers & Lybrand Associates, responsible for key policy contract on this three-year project covering all modes of transport for both passengers and freight. Responsible for the development and testing of transport policies for inter-urban transport, and review of the administrative structure in the transport sector. This included an examination of tariff structures and taxation policies, and an assessment of the economic and financial cost of transport mode. Responsible also for the development of cost analyses of all modes in a form suitable for computer modelling of test policy options. Client: Ministry of Economy and IBRD.
Buenos Aires Metro: Development of demand and modal split forecasts for the planned expansion of the five-line Buenos Aires metro system, which serves an urban population of 8 million. Client: Consorcio Subtes Rio de la Plata.

Australia
Railway systems: Railways pricing study for each of the five major railway systems of Australia. Carried out an investigation and assessment of the pricing policies of each system, considering freight, suburban and inter-urban passenger traffic. In each case assessed the effects of contractual arrangements, government influence, the extent of competition from road transport and coastal shipping and the availability of market intelligence. Client: Australian Railway Research and Development Organisation.
Analysis of rail freight cost in New South Wales: Commissioned to identify the sources of cost in rail freight operations and to compare costs and revenues for different types of traffic. Analysed the railway's accounts and identified joint and wholly attributable costs. Developed the RAILCOST suite of computer programs used as a strategic planning tool to investigate operating and investment strategies. Client: Public Transport Commission of New South Wales.
Sydney-Melbourne electrification: In association with Elrail and Sofrerail, studied the economic costs and benefits of electrification of 1000 km of main-line railway. The study also included a technical assessment of various electrification options as well as an improved diesel railway. Responsible for economic and financial appraisals including demand forecasting, train service simulation, modelling and costing. Client: Australian Department of Transport.
Capacity and operations modelling: Assessed the capability of the rail network to handle coal exports through Port Kembla. Developed computer models TOURING and PATHING to model the train and signal system and find paths for coal trains, and interfaced these with a port simulation model developed separately. In other work developed schedule proving models for metropolitan timetable verification. Client: State Transport Study Group of New South Wales.
Railway operating plan: Extensive involvement in the development and implementation of INTRANS, the Railways of Australia Intersystem Transport Operating Plan. Retained to assist the study of wagon movement delays and traced the principal causes of delay using sample wagons. Also carried out analysis of the Port Pirie bogie exchange. Later provided advice on a manual wagon monitoring system and the design and implementation of a computerised system. Client: Railways of Australia.
Management Information Systems: Introduced MIS systems for traffic financial performance. Client: Australian National Railways Commission.
Container Services: Developed business strategies for all interstate railway container services: Client: National Freight Group, Railways of Australia.

Botswana
Trans-Kalahari Railway feasibility study: In consortium with the Henderson Busby Partnership, appointed to examine proposals for a new 1400 km rail link across Botswana and Namibia, including the provision of new port facilities on the Atlantic Coast, to enable the exploitation of coal deposits at Serowe. Study activities include demand analysis and forecasting for coal and other bulk goods, route investigation and evaluation, and a full technical, economic and financial appraisal of the project. Client: Ministry of Mineral Resources and Water Affairs.
Locomotive procurement: In connection with the taking over of the railway from Zimbabwe National Railways, advised on the procurement of locomotives, including the financial evaluation of supply officers. Client: Botswana Railways.

Brazil
Commissioned to direct studies of the demand and economic evaluation for a high-speed rail link between Rio de Janeiro and São Paulo. Client: Government of Brazil.

Malaysia
Malaysian Railway privatisation: Undertook an economic and operational evaluation of the total railway system with the objective of privatisation. Analysis included demand forecasting of freight and passenger levels. Assessment of engineering, track, maintenance and workshops also carried out.

New Zealand
Reviewed the operational and financial performance of all suburban rail lines in Auckland and Wellington. Carried out investment evaluation of future capital programmes. Undertook social cost-benefit analysis to recommend optimum strategies for the future of the lines.

Uruguay
National rail study: In association with Transmark, Mott, Hay and Anderson and local consultant CTEA for this study to produce an investment and action plan for the next five years. World Bank funded. Client: Ministry of Transport and Public Works.

United Kingdom
London Docklands study: Carried out, for the urban regeneration of a 2250-hectare site, an appraisal of various forms of public transport provision including extension of the London Transport underground railway and feeder bus services as well as a new light rail route. Client: Greater London Council and the Department of the Environment.
Manchester International Airport rail link: Assessed the likely patronage and revenue for different scenario for linking this major airport into the rail network. Client: British Rail.
Docklands Light Railway: Examination of alternative routes for an extension to the DLR. Engineering and passenger forecasting work was undertaken. Client: London Borough of Newham.
Strategic planning model of British Rail operations: Appointed as consultants to Committee which reviewed finance, administration and policy for the 16 000 route-km UK national rail network. Part of work involved development of a financial model of the various passenger and freight services and evaluation of different options for the development of the network according to various possible policies. Client: Committee for the Review of Railway Finances.
Channel Tunnel Rail Link: Commissioned to advise British Rail on the work they need to undertake and the resources which need to be committed to enable a Parliamentary Bill to be submitted in respect of the above link. Client: British Rail.

Trevor Crocker & Partners

Priory House, 45/51 High Street, Reigate, Surrey RH2 9RU, England

Telephone: +44 7372 40101
Telex: 942153

Capabilities
Trevor Crocker & Partners carries out feasibility and economic studies for new railway facilities, transport and traffic studies, route location studies, bridges, railways, workshops and ancillary facilities, preparation of specifications and tender documents, supervision of construction.

Recent projects
Prestressed concrete bridge carrying six rail tracks over Romford inner ring road, for British Rail Eastern Region.
Two prestressed concrete bridges to carry six tracks and a siding line over proposed inner ring road at

Preston for British Rail London Midland Region.
Continuous two-span steel box girder bridge with composite RC deck carrying railway over dual three-lane A42 Ashby by-pass for British Rail London Midland Region.
Preliminary designs for the reconstruction of 20 bridges for overhead electrification of the Bedford to Corby line for British Rail London Midland Region.
Preliminary designs for the reconstruction of 25 bridges for overhead electrification of suburban lines in the Birmingham area for British Rail London Midland Region.
Feasibility studies and detailed design of railway trackwork and installations for major colliery surface works for British Coal in UK, including bridgeworks and automatic weighing and loading facilities.
Inspection and assessment of 34 road bridges over railway tracks and feasibility studies for reconstruction for London Underground Ltd.
Route assessment and outline design for 7 km rail connection to major new coal mine for British Coal.

Tudor Engineering Co

301 Mission Street, San Francisco, California 94105, USA

Telephone: +1 415 543 9820

President: Thomas J O'Neill

Projects
Rapid transit system ($2500 million) for MARTA, Atlanta;
Rapid transit system planning for Metro de Caracas, Venezuela ($1000 million).
Extension to BART transit system, San Francisco ($30 million).

Urbitran Associates

15 Park Row, Suite 2610, New York, New York 10038, USA

Telephone: +1 212 267 6310

President: Dr Robert B Lee
Executive Vice-President: Dr Michael Horodniceanu

Projects
Reconstruction of the subway station of Woodhaven Blvd in Queens, New York, ($3.5 million) for New York City Transit Authority.
Construction and inspection of the Oak Point rail yard ($80 million) for New York State Department of Transportation.
42nd Street light rail study for NYCDOT.
Downtown Brooklyn light rail study for Brooklyn Economic Development Corp.
Oyster Bay light rail transit study for the Long Island Railroad.

URS Company

3605 Warrensville Center Road, Cleveland, Ohio 44122, USA

Telephone: +1 216 283 4000

Senior Vice-President: Frederick J Richardson

Projects
Ohio High Speed Rail Programme.

URS Consultants Inc

One Penn Plaza, Suite 610, New York, New York 10119-0118, USA

Telephone: +1 212 736 4444

President: Irwin Rosenstein
Executive Vice-President: Martin S Tanzer

Projects
Glenmont Section for WMATA; Mondawin station for Baltimore.
Metro-North: bridge inspection and rehabilitation; Grand Central Terminal expansion joint replacement; 125th Street station rehabilitation.
NYCTA: substation replacement.

Wallace, Roberts and Todd

260 South Broad Street, Philadelphia, Pennsylvania 19102, USA

Telephone: +1 215 732 5215
Telefax: +1 215 732 251

Partners: David A Wallace
William H Roberts
David C Hamme
Richard W Huffman
Charles B Tomlinson
Richard W Bartholomew
Gilbert A Rosenthal
John E Fernsler
Barbara A Maloney

Projects
System-wide environmental impact and route selection studies ($2.3 million) for the Washington Metropolitan Area Transit Authority.
Atlantic City Amtrak rail terminal and convention centre.
Guadelupe Corridor Light Rail Transit station design, Santa Clara County, California.

Harry Weese & Associates

10 W Hubbard Street, Chicago, Illinois 60610, USA

Telephone: +1 312 467 7030

President: Stanley N Allan

Projects
Washington Rapid Rail Transit System: general architectural consultant for 103-mile (160 km), 86-station system.
Southern California Rapid Transit District: general architectural consultant for a 20-mile, 20-station rail system.

Wilbur Smith Associates

1301 Gervais Street, Columbia, South Carolina 29201, USA

Telephone: +1 803 7380580
Cable: Wilsmith
Telex: 573439
Telefax: +1 803 2512064

President: Robert A Hubbard

Projects
Texas: analysis of rail branch lines for Texas Railroad Commission.
Rail Corridor Acquisition Assistance, for Florida Department of Transportation.
Georgia Statewide Rail System Plan, for Georgia Department of Transportation.
Norfolk, Virginia Beach Light Rail Study: feasibility study for Tidewater Transportation District Committee.
Honolulu Hali 2000 Rail Corridor Concept, planning study for Oahu Metropolitan Planning Organization (OMPO).
San Diego Bayside line extension feasibility study for Metropolitan Transit Development Board (MTDB).
Los Angeles-San Diego Rail Corridor Study for CALTRANS.
Anchorage, Alaska commuter rail study for the city.
LRT extension study for the Kowloon-Canton Railway Corporation, Hong Kong in association with Scott Wilson Kirkpatrick and Partners.
Sacramento light rail project: cost analysis for California Transportation Commission (CTC).
BART station area planning and development services for BART.
State of California: analysis of annual capital costs and funding needs for all rail projects approved for state funding support including rail projects programmed by BART, San Francisco MUNI, San Diego MTDB (East Line), Santa Clara County, Caltrans (Caltrain Peninsula Commuter Service), and Sacramento Transit Development Agency for CTC.
Vancouver, Canada: Rail (and roadway) system access planning relating to Metro Town for private developer.
Singapore mass transit system for Mass Rapid Transit Corporation: final design of Section 2A with DCI for new rapid transit system.
Idaho State Railroad Plan: a rail freight study for Idaho Transportation Department.
Washington, Idaho Regional Rail Study: a regional grain study for rail needs for Idaho Department of Transportation.
Sandag I-5 LRT Alignment Study for San Diego Association of Governments.

William Nicholas Bodouva & Associates PC

11 Pennsylvania Plaza, Suite 242, New York, New York 10001 USA

Telephone: +1 212 563 5655
Telefax: +1 212 967-2315

Capabilities
Rapid transit station design; rail maintenance facilities; station rehabilitation.

Wilson, Inrig & Associates

5776 Broadway, Oakland, California 94618 USA

Telephone: +1 415 658 6719

President: George Paul Wilson

Capabilities
Acoustical design of stations, line sections and facilities; vehicle noise, vibration and ride quality evaluation; assessment and prediction of ground-borne vibration; track fastener design, testing and specification; noise and vibration criteria development.

ZT
Zeta-Tech Associates Inc

1060 Kings Highway N, PO Box 8407, Cherry Hill, New Jersey 08002, USA

Telephone: +1 609 779 7795
Telefax: +1 609 779 7436

President: Allan M Zarembski
Director of Costing and Pricing: Randolph R Resor
Manager, Analytical Engineering: Joseph T A Masih

Zeta-Tech Associates is a technical consulting and applied technology company directed at the railway and transportation industries.

Capabilities
Track and track systems
Rail/rail failure/rail maintenance: prediction of failure, definition of acceptable criterion, maintenance and maintenance planning.
Fasteners and fastener systems: conventional and non-conventional fastener systems for heavy freight systems, high-speed railway, transit, commuter and special problem areas. Performance evaluations, specification, system design, and test definitions.
Sleepers: design, development, specification, maintenance planning.
Track strength: vehicle and track interaction from the point of view of the strength of the track structure. System design and development, specifications, evaluation, test definition.
Track buckling: theory and application, maintenance practices to prevent track buckling, development of design and maintenance standards, failure investigations.
Track maintenance: planning and standards, integration of track data for use in maintenance planning, development of maintenance standards, performance standards, maintenance practices and equipment.
Track geometry: measurement and interpretation, measurement systems, conventional and non-conventional, analysis of data, integration of data with data bases, maintenance planning.
Vehicle/track interaction
Track and vehicle dynamics, interaction of vehicular and track systems to predict the behaviour of either the track or the vehicular system. Modelling of track and vehicle systems.
Freight car systems
Design, analysis, and test of conventional and non-conventional freight cars and systems; fatigue analysis and design of freight car systems, fatigue life prediction, test design.

CONSULTANCY SERVICES

Inspection and measurement systems
Conventional and non-conventional inspection systems, such as track geometry, track strength and track modulus. Development of inspection and maintenance standards, planning, and implementation.

Fatigue design and analysis of structures
Fatigue design and analysis of structures to include bridge and overhead structures.

Applied economics
Economic analysis of railroad systems and subsystems. Engineering economic analysis on the effects of maintenance or design changes on economic performance for railroad systems and sub-systems. Development of analytical and user-orientated computer models.

Technical marketing
Development and preparation of technical marketing aids and tools. In-depth technical presentations as well as short technical and performance summaries. Interaction with engineering, research, marketing and management on technical marketing programmes. Development and implementation of seminars and training programmes.

Computer simulation and modelling
Development of custom software for railroad and rail rapid transit applictions, including: maintenance planning; data base management; processing of track geometry car and similar data; simulation of vehicle performance and energy consumption. Engineering economic analysis of alternative operating strategies equipment types, and routes. Modelling of the economics of alternative track and vehicle component choices.

Transportation cost analysis
Regression-based and deterministic cost modelling for railroads and rail rapid transit operators. Allocation of common costs among traffics. Identification of incremental costs resulting from changes in operating strategies. Economic analysis of the costs and benefits of alternative vehicle and track component choices. Life-cycle costing.

Addenda

Accent Marketing and Research

Gable House, 14-16 Turnham Green Terrace, Chiswick, London W4 1QP, England

Telephone: +44 81 742 2211
Telefax: +44 81 742 1991

Managing Director: Rob Sheldon
Directors: Tim Grosvenor
David Hollings
Hugh Inwood

Consultant: Roy Noble (Freight & Distribution)

Capabilities

Accent provides specialised Marketing consultancy and research services directly to railway operators and also in association with transport and planning consultancies. The staff has undertaken several hundreds of railway projects embracing passenger, parcels and freight operations. Its experience is enriched by an equivalent range of projects for other modes of transport and for the tourism and distribution sectors. They are a leading exponent of the stated preference research technique in the fields of mode choice, demand forecasting and quality of service assessments.

The firm has particular consultancy strengths in the areas of marketing strategies, rolling stock design assessments, passenger terminal and on-board facilities, new product development in the passenger and freight sectors, competitive profitable pricing and, in general, the designing of responses to changing market needs.

Projects

A selection of typical studies and projects is illustrated below.

Channel Tunnel related Studies: Accent was a significant participant in studies concerned with the business and leisure markets for the through rail services. Commissioning clients were BR, DB, NS, SNCB and SNCF.

In association with Halcrow Fox and Associates, a series of studies has been undertaken concerned with the markets for and viability of, strategic multi modal tranship facilities in the context of the Tunnel and the Single European Market.

On behalf of Eurotunnel plc, Accent has undertaken studies related to the markets for the shuttle trains and the factors, including future on-board and terminal facilities, which would influence route choice.

Parcels Study: In August 1990, Accent was commissioned to undertake a marketing strategy study by the Parcels Group of British Rail.

Freight Studies: The range of studies extends from a review of the Europewide market for swapbodies and demountables to the identification of northbound flows for P & O Containers.

Rolling Stock Design related Studies: Passenger and public reactions to existing, prototype, refurbished and potential new designs of rolling stock are a particular specialism of Accent's project experience. They acted as research advisors to Stockholm Transport, recently undertook a study for BR InterCity and has, to date, undertaken over 20 studies for London Underground.

Pricing Studies: Projects have included a Business Travel Price Elasticity Study for BR InterCity, a review of pricing policy related to the main rail market sectors in the North East of England, assessments of railcards, travel cards and season tickets for the BR Board, for Network SouthEast and for London Transport. There have also been numerous studies related to price based travel promotion offers.

Passenger Catchment Areas and traveller profiles: Accent's survey capability has been enlisted in several capacities. N.S. was the client for the capture of data to establish the trip rates and catchment and to model the travel demand for various services. The InterCity and Regional Sectors of BR required on and off train research in pursuit of marketing strategies and London Transport and BR are the clients for a very large scale project involving the placement and analysis of several thousand travel diaries.

Stated Preference Studies: Accent performs the roles of executor, designer and advisor in the use of the stated preference technique in respect of railway services. It has undertaken several projects related to the planning of new regional rail services e.g. in Belfast and Edinburgh. It has also applied the technique for operators such as British Rail and London Underground Ltd. It has undertaken designs for applications in France and Germany. It provided a Pan European review of the applications of the technique for SJ and coordinated a survey for NSB as an input into its assessment of long distance rail travel markets.

A-TRAIN A/S

Strandvænget 22, 2100 Copenhagen East, Denmark

Telephone: +45 39 27 15 55, +45 39 27 18 88
Telefax: +45 39 27 30 35

President: Niels Tougaard Nielsen

Capabilities

A-TRAIN was established in 1990 as a R & D company in the ABB group, covering design, research and development and supporting R & D activities in ABB-railway companies, in DSB (Danish State Railways), and for other railway companies.

A-TRAIN develop new solutions in railway techniques and design, aiming for cheaper and lighter railway systems through the use of the newest technologies, modulised layouts and by use of standard components and systems, by implementation from other modes of transport. They have access to all R & D resources within DSB and ABB worldwide.

Automatic train systems

CAT (City Automatic Trainsystem) using lightweight carbodies combining aluminium extrusions and sandwich elements, modulised axle systems for rail and rubber solutions, usage of mass produced electrical equipment for electrical propulsion.

Metro systems

DART (dynamic automatic rail transportation), lightweight carbodies, single axle driven bogies, giving new dimensions for capacity (similar to double-deckers in one level solutions) and new standards for performance and economy.

Regional and intercity dmu's and emu's

Unconventional solutions for design and specifications, train system evaluations, timetable analyses, energy, noise and environmental effects, implementation of standard elements, models for maintenance and reliability, project management.

Freight car systems

Design, analyses for bi-modal freight systems; signalling, positioning and information systems; analyses and specifications for Automated Trains Control Systems (ATCS) based on digital radio transmissions, satellite based positioning, and station and on-board radio-based information systems.

Railway systems

Above: Hitachi's Inverter-Controlled Electric Locomotive (Type EF200)
Below: The world renowned shinkansen train (Series 300)

Stay Ahead with Advanced Railway Technology from Hitachi.

Trains rolling off the line today at Hitachi represent the future of railway engineering. The latest in technological advancements are incorporated into every phase of our production process, from design and manufacturing to testing and maintenance. At Hitachi, we're combining expertise gained through sixty-five years of producing entire railway systems — from rolling stock to bogies and electrical equipment — with daily advancements at our ten different R&D facilities, in order to bring you the very best in railway technology.

HITACHI

For More Information, Please Contact: Hitachi, Ltd. Transportation and Building Systems Dept. (XL) 6, Kanda Surugadai 4-chome, Chiyoda-ku, Tokyo 101, Japan
Telephone: Tokyo (03) 258-1111   Telex: J22395, J22432, J24491, J26375 (HITACHY)   Cable: HITACHY TOKYO

Railway Systems

Country	Page
Afghanistan	464
Albania	464
Algeria	464
Angola	467
Argentina	468
Australia	469
Austria	490
Bangladesh	498
Belgium	499
Benin	505
Bolivia	506
Botswana	507
Brazil	508
Bulgaria	517
Burkina Faso	518
Burma (Myanmar)	518
Cameroon	519
Canada	520
Chile	536
China, People's Republic	539
Colombia	543
Congo	544
Costa Rica	545
Cuba	545
Czechoslovakia	547
Denmark	549
Dominican Republic	554
Ecuador	554
Egypt	555
El Salvador	556
Ethiopia	557
Finland	557
France	561
Gabon	574
Germany, Democratic Republic	575
Federal Republic	577
Ghana	590
Greece	591
Guatemala	593
Guinea	593
Honduras	594
Hong Kong	594
Hungary	596
India	599
Indonesia	610
Iran	613
Iraq	614
Ireland	616
Israel	618
Italy	620
Ivory Coast	632
Jamaica	632
Japan	633
Jordan	657
Kampuchea	658
Kenya	658
Korea, Democratic People's Republic	660
Korea, Republic	660
Lebanon	662
Liberia	663
Libya	664
Luxembourg	664
Madagascar	665
Malawi	667
Malaysia	667
Mali	669
Mauritania	670
Mexico	670
Mongolia	672
Morocco	672
Mozambique	674
Namibia	674
Nepal	675
Netherlands	675
New Zealand	679
Nicaragua	681
Nigeria	681
Norway	682
Pakistan	685
Panama	688
Paraguay	688
Peru	689
Philippines	690
Poland	691
Portugal	695
Romania	698
Saudi Arabia	699
Senegal	700
South Africa	700
Spain	705
Sri Lanka	713
Sudan	715
Swaziland	716
Sweden	716
Switzerland	722
Syria	740
Taiwan	741
Tanzania	742
Thailand	744
Togo	748
Tunisia	748
Turkey	749
Uganda	752
Union of Soviet Socialist Republics	753
United Kingdom	757
United States of America	765
Uruguay	805
Venezuela	805
Viet-Nam	806
Yugoslavia	806
Zaïre	809
Zambia	810
Zimbabwe	811

Afghanistan

In May 1982 the first railway tracks appeared in Afghanistan with completion, after three years' work by Afghan and Soviet labour, of an 816 metres-long combined rail and road bridge over the Abu Darja river, the border with the USSR, and the projection over it of a rail link from the Buehara-Tashkent line of Soviet Railways (SZD) near Termez to Hairaton in Afghanistan. This penetration was to be continued into Afghanistan, beginning with a 200 km line to Pali-Khumri, some 160 km north of Kabul, but progress was blocked by the mountainous terrain, the long annual periods in which the area is blanketed by heavy snow, and the Soviet occupation of the country.

Before the Soviet incursion into Afghanistan the then govenment had endorsed plans drafted by the French consultants Sofrerail for a rail system of 1815 km connecting Kabul with Kandahar and Herat; with Pakistan Railways at Chaman; and with Iranian State Railways at Islam Quala and Tarakun.

Albania

Albanian Railways (HRPSSh)
Hekurdhë Republika Popullore Socialiste e Shqipërisë

Drejitoria e Hekurudhave, Tirana

Minister of Transport: Luan Babameto
Director of Rail Transport: M Dizdari
Director, Railway: V Caprazi

Railway construction has been made difficult by the predominantly mountainous terrain, with 70 per cent of the territory at elevations of more than 328 metres (1000 feet). The remainder of the country consists of a lowland on the Adriatic coast through which the main Vlorë-Fier-Progozhinë-Laç-Shkodër line runs. Tirana, the capital and principal city, terminates a branch leaving this north-south main line at Vorë. All means of transport are state-owned.

During the Italian occupation of Albania the first plans for a public railway from Durrës to Tirana were drawn up and some minor construction work carried out. Full construction was not completed until after the Second World War, when the New Communist Party government of Albania undertook a vast industrialisation programme, calling for extensive railway building. The first section of Albanian Railways from Durrës to Pequin (42 km) was opened in 1947 and this line was extended 30 km to Elbasan in 1950. In the meantime, another line from Durrës to Tirana, 38 km long, was completed in 1949. Building then continued at a much slower pace.

There is a short length of narrow-gauge industrial line which is not operated by the Albanian State Railways. This 950 mm gauge runs from Vlorë, on the Adriatic, 8 km to the bitumen mine at Selenicë with a 4 km branch to Mavrove.

Traffic
Railway freight traffic is mainly bulk transport with chrome and nickel from the Pogradec area, phosphates from Laç and Fier, asphalt from Vlorë, and cement from Vlorë and Elbasan the main commodities. Much of this is for shipment through the port of Durrës. Projection of rail connections to new traffic sources, especially industrial plants, now has a priority in the country's investment.

New lines
In April 1979 an agreement was signed between Albania and Yugoslavia, under which standard-gauge line was to be built connecting a new Albanian railhead at Shkodër with Yugoslav Railways' recently completed Belgrade–Bar line at Titograd. This is now Albania's first rail link with a foreign railway. The line carries chromite and nickel ore mined in Albania into East Europe, while Yugoslav raw materials and finished goods flow south into the terminal at Tirana. Construction from Laç in Albania began in November 1979 and completion to the Yugoslav border at Hani Hotit was marked by a formal inauguration in January 1985. On the Yugoslav side, construction of the 25 km from Titograd to the frontier did not start until January 1985, but completion was achieved in early 1986 and formal inauguration followed in August.

Initially, one train a day each way sufficed to carry the meagre traffic offering. This, plus Albanian shortage of motive power and insistence that locomotives and train crews be changed at the frontier, led to Yugoslav disinclination to continue the link's operation. But in 1989 disagreements were resolved; Yugoslav locomotives now work beyond the border to Shkodër, and conversely Albanian locomotives travel through to Titograd.

In Albania an extension from Pogradec east to the Yugoslav border, then south to Korcë, a distance of 39 km, was finished in 1987. In addition a new 63 km line from Milot, on the Laç-Shkodër route, has been under construction up the Mat river valley to Klos, in the heart of the country. This project is employing concrete sleepers for the first time in Albania. Despite crossing difficult terrain, the first 25 km were finished in 1987; completion throughout was expected in 1990. The line will tap major sources of chrome. Also under construction is a 70 km line from Balish to Girokaster. Further main-line extensions of the Albanian system now under consideration include lines to Shëngjin port in the north; also under study is double-tracking of the Tirana-Rrogozhina main line.

Locomotives and rolling stock
For years Albania had no railway industry, so all equipment, especially rolling stock and motive power, had to be imported. Some steam locomotives came from Chrzanow works in Poland, whose engines were similar to PKP's Tkt-48 class standard general-purpose superheated 1D1 (2-8-2) tank type. Some second-hand engines seem to have found their way from Poland to Albania. Residual steam power is now confined mostly to switching work. In 1958 Albanian Railways bought their first two diesel-mechanical class BN 150 shunting locomotives from CKD Praha, followed by two more of the same type and two 750 hp Bo-Bo diesel-electric road locomotives of CSD's T 435.0 class in the next year. Czechoslovak-built locomotives now make up the whole diesel locomotive fleet, which totals 80 units and comprises chiefly Czech Types T435.0 and T458.1 Bo-Bos, and T669.1 Co-Cos. In 1989 five redundant German Federal (DB) Class 221 diesel-hydraulic B-B locomotives were delivered following refurbishment by the Regental Railway's workshops in Bavaria.

Passenger cars are mostly of Chinese construction, but in the late 1980s 43 French Railways Type B10t cars were acquired. The SNCF has also supplied 350 freight wagons, and the DB 250. Freight stock further includes modern bogie wagons of Chinese, Czech, Hungarian or Yugoslav manufacture, and the railway's proportion of obsolescent two-axle wagons is thus reducing. Moreover, Albania has lately begun to build its own freight wagons. Total freight vehicle stock is believed to be around 2 500.

Signalling
Modern signalling equipment has been imported from Poland.

Track
Rail: 38, 43, 48, 49 kg/m in 12 to 24 m lengths
Sleepers: Wood
Minimum curve radius: 300 m
Max axleload: 21–24 tonnes
Max speed: 60 km/h

Algeria

Ministry of Transport

Algiers

Minister: El-Hadi Khediri
Secretary-General: A Salah-Bey
Director, Infrastructure and Rail Transport: A Zahi

Algerian National Railways (SNTF)
Société Nationale des Transports Ferroviaires

21-23 boulevard Mohamed V, Algiers

Telephone: +213 61 15 10
Telegrams: Cefafer, Algiers
Telex: 66 484 sikek dz

Director General: Châabane Derouiche
Commercial Director: Bouifrou Tahar
Operating Director: Abdelkader Mekrebi
Director of Personnel: Rachid Harrati
Director of Rolling Stock: Abdelhamid Lalaimia
Director of Projects, Planning and Computer Systems: Fouad Arab
Director of Fixed Equipment: Abdelhamid Moudjebeur
Director of Finances: Mokrane Haddad
Inspector General: Layachi Douibi

Gauges: 1432 mm; 1055 mm
Route length: 2649 km; 1138 km
Electrification: 299 km at 3 kV dc

The network at present consists primarily of two standard-gauge coastal lines running east and west from Algiers: about 550 km westward to the railhead at Oujda (where a connection with Moroccan Railways, broken in 1976, was reactivated in 1989), and about 370 km eastwards to a connection with the 520 km north-south line at Od Rahmoun. In addition to standard-gauge spur lines, a 300 km (partly electrified) 1435 mm gauge line runs parallel with the Tunisian border (providing international connecting services at Souk-Ahras with Tunisian National Railways–SNCFT) from the port of Annaba to Djebel Onk. Major narrow-gauge lines run from Mohammadia (on the Algiers-Oujda line) to Kenadsa and Blida to Djelfa.

None of SNTF's main lines were built to handle present passenger and freight traffic volumes, which trebled in the course of the 1980s. The government is committed to a heavy investment in SNTF to fit rail transport for the demands both of new industry and of the agricultural development now accorded considerable priority. Importance is also attached to enlargement both of long-haul and suburban rail passenger capacity. Since 1979 the Algerian government and the SNTF administration have engaged consultancy teams from Austria, Belgium, France, the Federal Republic of Germany, Italy and India to aid SNTF improvements.

Capacity enlargement
Besides lengthening existing passing loops on single-track routes to permit operation of trains up to 1200 metres long instead of the previous 800 metres maximum, and also laying in additional loops, SNTF has launched some large-scale projects to double-track single lines which are quite inadequate for latter-day industrial development. The first such undertaking was formally set in motion by President Chadli Bendjedid in February 1980 between Ramdane-Djamal, 67 km north of Constantine, and El-Gourzi, 38 km south of Constantine. This vital link between Algiers and the petro-chemical port of Skikda as well as Annaba was previously double-track only for 18 km between Constantine and El-Khroub, was handicapped by gradients as steep as 1 in 50 and curves sharper than 200 metres radius in its negotiation of the Constantine mountains. With an axleload limit of 18 tonnes it could carry only 9000 tonnes of freight a day. Under a scheme estimated to cost DA 2200 million and managed by Cogifer and Italconsult, the line is being doubled throughout the 64.8 km from Ramdane-Djamel to Constantine and the 20.6 km south from El-Gourzi to El Khroub, along with realignments. The task involves laying 233 km of new track, constructing 34 bridges, including the 650 metre-long Beni-Brahim viaduct, and boring three tunnels aggregating 4206 metres in length. In many places the line has been

completely rebuilt to iron out curves and avoid treacherous ground.

In conjunction with the installation of heavier UIC 54 continuously welded rail on concrete sleepers of SL Type U (1722 per km), this scheme will on completion raise permissible freight speed from 60 to 90 km/h and wagon axleloadings from 18 to 28 tonnes. The next phase of the work will be installation of modern automatic signalling. When that is commissioned the line's train operating capacity should be doubled and a throughput of 7 million tonnes a year should be possible.

To create a relief route between Constantine and Annaba, resuscitation of the 95 km El Khroub-Guelma connection, abandoned in the 1950s, has been decided. In 1989 local contractors began the double-tracking of 65 km between Khemis Miliana and Oued Fodda; and a six-year upgrading has been put in hand between Mohammadia and Bechar.

Resignalling and a complete renewal of its tele-communications network ranks high in SNTF's current modernisation activity. Among other things, the railway aims to make track-to-train radio communication a standard feature on its principal routes. In late 1989 ACEC Transport of Belgium won a Dinars 70 million contract to modernise signalling in the Annaba area; the contract included commissioning and local staff training as well as equipment supply and installation.

West of Constantine some double-track already exists on the littoral main line to Algiers and Oran, and the creation of more is among the projects which are utilising a $477 million loan obtained from Austria for infrastructure modernisation in July 1981. The credit was for drawing over a period of 15–20 years. A 16-company Austrian group including Simmering-Graz-Pauker, Jenbacher Werke, Plasser & Theurer and Voest-Alpine, is one of the largest concerns collaborating in SNTF modernisation.

The first double-tracking scheme to be undertaken with these funds, supervised by Deutsche Eisenbahn Consult, covered the 43.5 km from El Harrach, on the outskirts of Algiers, to Thenia. The double-tracking is to be projected from El Harrach, junction of the Oran and Constantine routes, to Blida. A further $157 million contract provides for reconstruction planning of 350 km of trunk routes from Thenia eastward to Setif, and between Skikda and Annaba.

In 1986 Indian Railway Construction Co was given the contract to upgrade the 80 km from Thenia east towards El Esnam. Threading the foothills of the Atlas Mountains, this section is imposing some substantial tunnelling on the realignments planned as part of the upgrading. The scheme, which is part-financed by India's Export-Import Bank, includes the remodelling of three marshalling yards for prospective enlargement.

In 1988 SNTF received loans of US $47 million from Japan Export-Import Bank and of US $143 million from the World Bank towards its current US $430 million upgrading programme.

In 1990 Transurb was contracted to provide technical assistance. The World Bank would fund a management training centre at Algiers, where Transurb would help to set up senior staff training courses.

GM-built 3300 hp Co-Co at Ghardimaou, on the Tunisian border (*Marcel Vieugels*)

In 1980 a series of agreements with India led to a contract with RITES, the Indian Railways consultancy, for provision of technical, management assistance and staff training services in the period up to 1985. A further US $20 million contract was signed with RITES in 1988. A joint Algerian-Indian study group was formed to plan a first section of the High Plateau route, the 146 km from Ain-Touta, on the line south from Constantine to Biskra, to M'Sila, where a new aluminium plant was in urgent need of rail service. A 60 km line from M'Sila to the existing east-west transversal at Bordj Bou Arreridj was also committed to study. In June 1982 President Chadli Bendjedid inaugurated the works between Ain-Touta and M'Sila.

Construction of a 160 km line from further northeast on the Constantine-Biskra route, at Ain-M'Lila, to Tebessa was subsequently added to the forward programme. Work on this scheme was entrusted to French companies and began in 1988. RITES is supervising the Ain Touta-M'Sila operation, but the Ain-M'Lila scheme is being overseen by EIF and EST, the infrastructure and signalling/telecommunications subsidiaries among a number lately formed by SNTF to free the railway's management for full attention to transportation.

The other subsidiaries created include: EMF, covering rolling stock modernisation; Infrarail, tracklaying; Informatique Service, computerisation; Restau-Rail, on-train catering; Rail-Express, small freight consignments door-to-door; and Rail-Export, a consultancy marketing SNTF expertise.

The Ain Touta-M'Sila line is being engineered for 160 km/h with long-welded 54 kg/m rail on twin-block sleepers, the latter manufactured in a plant established at Ain Touta. The Ain M'Lila-Tebessa section is being engineered for 150 km/h.

In 1983 Bouygues of France secured a contract to construct a new 137 km railway from Ramdane Djamel to the new port of Jijel-Djendjen, west of Skikda (the line was also to serve a new steel works of El Milea, halfway to the port, but construction of this plant has been deferred). Tracklaying began in October 1987 and completion with installation of signalling and telecommunications was forecast for 1990. The project has entailed construction of 70 bridges and eight tunnels, including one of 2.8 km length, and a 22-track marshalling yard 14 km from Jijel-Djendjen. Ruling gradient is 0.17 per cent and minimum curve radius is generally 800 m, exceptionally 500 m in a few difficult locations.

SNTF contemplates extension of its standard-gauge system across the heart of the Sahara, looping southward from Touggourt, in the south-east, through Ouargla then north-west via Ghardaia and Laghouet to Ain Quessara, on the projected High Plateau route. Deutsche Eisenbahn Consult was commissioned to design the first section of this project, from Touggourt via the oil region of Hassi Messaoud and Ouargla to Ghardaia, and eventually to draft tender documents for construction.

Following its acquisition of a Rs 350 million turnkey contract to construct 23 km of 1055 mm-gauge railway

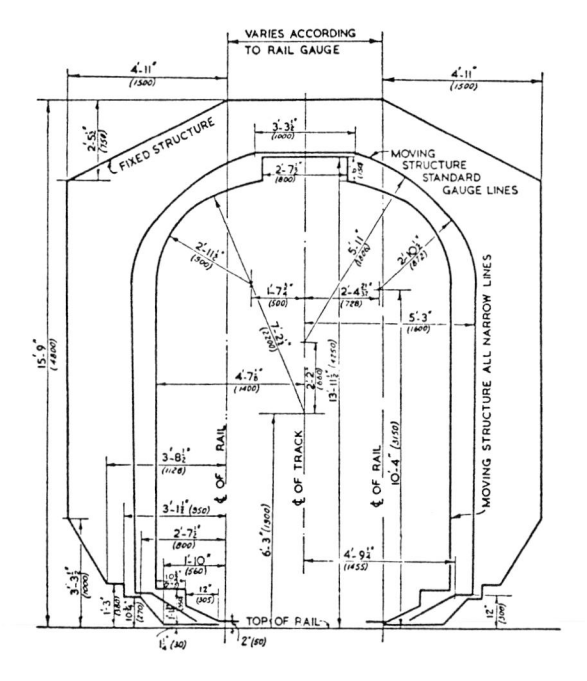

Traffic	1984	1986	1987
Total passenger journeys (000)	35 700	NA	43 296
Total passenger km (million)	1835	NA	1972
Total freight tonnes (000)	11 400	12 500	12 816
Total freight tonne-km (million)	2631	2947	2941

New railways

The El Hadjar steel complex gets its ore in 1500-tonne trains from mines at Quenza and Bou Khedra, about 190 km south of Annaba (whence the imported coal for its coking plant is also ferried by unit train). The ore line was electrified at 3 kV dc before the Second World War and most of the ore trains, plus trains of phosphates from the mines at Djebel Onk further south, are powered by 32 2700 hp electric locomotives procured from the East German builders LEW in the early 1970s. As the rail input and output at El Hadjar grows, SNTF is concerned to avoid choking the approaches to Annaba and the rail area in the port itself. That prompted the first steps toward construction of Algeria's biggest long-term rail construction project, a second east-west transversal line deep inland, the so-called High Plateau route from the area of the phosphate deposits in the east to Sidi Bel Abbes, south of Oran. The total distance involved is over 800 km.

near Saida, between Mohammadia and Kenadsa, to serve a cement works, which was finished in 1985, the Indian Railway Construction Company (IRCON) in 1983 secured a US $81.2 million contract to build a 22 km connection on standard gauge from Ain Témouchant to the port of Beni Saf, west of Oran. The project involved viaducts aggregating 2.2 km in length. The Export-Import Bank of India has provided loan support.

Algiers Urban Railway

Passenger and freight traffic growth has seriously outstripped capacity in the four principal cities and ports, above all in Algiers. The main Algiers Maritime station is a terminus, hemmed between the port and the cliffs which the city surmounts, so that the station cannot be enlarged.

SNTF's aim by the 1990s is to convert the terminus into a branch leaving a new cross-city suburban line at Place Emir Abdel Kader. The cross-city line is being created by driving a line underground westward beneath the densely populated Casbah to Bab el Oued. The tunnelling is a delicate job, because of the high water table in the area. New stations will be built on the extension. This suburban SNTF extension will parallel and be integrated with Line 1 of the Algiers metro.

At the same time SNTF intends to divert traffic from the centre of Algiers by creating a rail-road passenger interchange at Dar el Beida, in a thriving development area to the south, with a branch to the adjacent Houari Boumedienne airport. The works at Dar el Beida, which is to become Algiers' main passenger station with nine island platforms and a five-storey passenger facility, will also open a route for east-west freight traffic via the existing transversal that will give it a through run avoiding the centre of Algiers between Thenia and Blida. Inter-city trains on the Oran-Constantine axis will transfer Algiers passengers to and from local trains at Dar el Beida. Further relief for Algiers Maritime station will be obtained by constructing a new station in the city's downtown business area at Tafourah. A new chord line will enable through running between Tafourah and Blida via Dar el Beida, and new lines are also to connect Tafourah and Dar el Beida with residential development north-east of the city around Ain Charb. SNTF plans to accompany these developments by redeveloping installations in the port area and shifting the centre of freight handling and train marshalling from Agha to a new yard and depot further east at Rouiba, near Dar el Beida. Completion of the entire Algiers network development is not expected until the next century.

Traffic

In 1988 SNTF recorded 44.86 million passenger journeys and 2439 million passenger journeys, but by mid-1989 traffic was 18 per cent up on levels at the same period of 1988. Couchette revenue was up fourfold following introduction of new services of this kind between Algiers and both Annaba and Oran.

Since the mid-1989 restoration of rail communication with Morocco, a daily service has been launched between Algiers and Casablanca, but it entails a change of train at Morocco's frontier station of Oujda. However, the interval at Oujda is limited to 20 minutes, as immigration and customs formalities are conducted on the trains. It has been agreed that by 1992 the change of trains will be eliminated, with a Moroccan train running through to Algiers and an Algerian to Casablanca. The two railways and that of Tunisia have planned that by 1995 they will operate a combined Trans-Maghreb service, with connections in Algiers, including sleeping and couchette cars. For the longer term North African railways are considering the feasibility of a new 6000 km, 200 km/h railway connecting Morocco, Algeria and Tunisia with Libya and Egypt.

Freight traffic, grossing 12.98 million tonnes and 2 799 million tonne-km in 1988, was receding in the first half of 1989. Reasons cited were a deterioration in wagon availability ratios, the effects of inadequate operating capacity: and, in consequence, the drift of some important customers to other modes.

Traction and rolling stock

SNTF has been spending heavily to continue the well-advanced expansion and modernisation of its traction and rolling stock. At the end of 1982, following purchase of 60 second-hand coaches from the German Federal Railway, a Fr 2500 million order was placed with French industry for 400 stainless steel cars to effect an almost complete renewal of the coaching stock. Delivery was completed in the summer of 1987. The order comprised 100 cars for suburban use, 200 day and 50 couchette cars for standard gauge, and 41 day cars and nine baggage-generator cars for metre-gauge cars.

In 1989 delivery began of 20 diesel locomotives from General Motors of Canada; a further 60 were to be supplied in kit form for assembly in Algeria under a technology transfer deal. A Canadian loan was expected to fund purchase of a further 10 main-line units and 10 diesel shunters.

At the start of 1990 SNTF invited bids for the supply of 15 2400 kW electric locomotives.

Algeria now has its own freight wagon producing plant, Ferovial, at Annaba, with capacity to produce for export as well as SNTF demand. Recent contracts have included 150 wagons, for Iraq, 500 for the German Democratic Republic and orders from several African countries.

Some freight trains are operated with the Locotrol system in which a slave locomotive in the middle of the train is controlled by radio from the lead locomotive. The system is being used primarily to increase the length and carrying capacity of unit phosphate trains.

On 1432 mm gauge SNTF operates 24 electric and 145 diesel locomotives and 28 twin-unit Fiat diesel railcars. Coaching stock totals 631 cars and freight stock 6066 vehicles. Narrow-gauge traction comprises 32 diesel locomotives; narrow-gauge coaching stock totals 50 vehicles and freight stock 3785 wagons. The narrow-gauge locomotives are capable of change of bogie for 1432 mm-gauge operation.

Electrification

Algeria has only one electrified line running 256 km (single-track) between Tébessa and Annaba at 3000 volts dc. No new electrification is planned thanks to cheap home-produced oil.

Signalling

Electrically-operated mechanical signals are gradually being replaced by colour-light signal displays throughout the system. On new lines and upgraded tracks automatic signalling is being installed. SNTF has signed an agreement in principle with Siemens for formation of a joint company to manufacture and install signalling equipment.

In 1990, with World Bank funding, bids were sought for resignalling the 373 km Thenia-El Gourzi and 114 km Annaba-Ramdane Djamel-Skikda lines.

Diesel locomotives

Class (Railways own designation)	Manufacturer's type	Wheel arrangement	Transmission	Rated power kW	Max speed km/h	Total weight tonnes	No in service 1988	Year first built	Builders Mechanical parts	Engine	Transmission
Standard gauge											
060 DD	GT 26 W	Co-Co	Elec	2400	120	120	27	1971	GM	GM	GM
060 DF	GT 26 W	Co-Co	Elec	2400	120	120	25	1973	GM	GM	GM
060 DG	GT 26 W	Co-Co	Elec	2400	120	120	14	1976	GM	GM	GM
060 DN	GT 22 W	Co-Co	Elec	1600	120	120	24	1976	GM	GM	GM
060 DL	GT 26 W	Co-Co	Elec	2400	120	120	25	1982	GM	GM	GM
060 WDK	GL 18 M	Co-Co	Elec	800	100	78 T	5	1977	GM	GM	GM
040 YDA	GL 18 M	A1A-A1A	Elec	800	100	72 T	25	1977	GM	GM	GM
060 DJ	U 18 C	Co-Co	Elec	1400	100	96 T	25	1977	GE	GE	GE
1050 mm gauge											
060 DG	GT 22 W	Co-Co	Elec	1600	80	N/A	25	1977	GM	GM	GM

Diesel railcars

Class	Manufacturer's type	Cars per unit	Motor cars per unit	Motored axles per motor car	Transmission	Rated power (kW) per motor	Max speed km/h	Weight tonnes per unit	Total seating capacity per car	Length per unit mm	No in service 1988	Year first built	Builders Mechanical parts	Engine type and transmission
ZZN 200	ALN 668	2	2	2	Mechanical	143	120	77·4 T	83	46 990	56	1972	Fiat (Iveco)	Fiat (Iveco)

Electric locomotives

Class	Wheel arrangement	Line current	Rated power hp	Tractive effort Continuous at kg	km/h	Max speed km/h	Wheel dia mm	Total weight tonnes	Length mm	First built	Builders Mechanical parts	Electrical equipment
6CE	Co-Co	3 kV dc	2000	24 600	30	80	1350	130	18 640	1972	LEW	Skoda

Angola
Ministry of Transport & Communications

PO Box 1250-C, Luanda

Telephone: +244 1 70061/73270
Telex: 3108 Mitrans AN

Minister of Transport: B de Sousa

Caminhose de Ferro de Angola

PO Box 1250-C, Luanda

Telephone: +244 1 70061/73270
Telex: 3108 Mitrans AN

Director: A de S E Silva
Deputy Technical Director: R M da C Junior

Gauge: 1067 mm; 600 mm
Route length (four railways combined): 2798 km; 154 km

Portuguese colonialists developed an extensive transport and communications network until Angola became independent in 1975, since when civil war has seriously disrupted both highway and rail services. Four previously independent railways are now amalgamated in a national system, the Caminhos de Ferro de Angola, but because of the country's guerilla warfare the four railways have so far been unable to integrate operation fully or handle international traffic consistently.

Traction and rolling stock
The four railways combined operate 120 steam and 114 diesel locomotives, 25 railcars, 243 passenger cars and 4011 freight cars. In 1987 serviceable traction was reported to be 57 steam and 10 diesel locomotives only. General Electric of Brazil delivered six shunting locomotives for use in Lobito port in 1987-88. Recently, 259 kits of wagon parts were ordered from Cobrasma and CCC of Brazil for local assembly; they would be used on the Benguela Railway.

Namibe Railway

Caixa Postal 130, Sá de Bandeira, Moçâmedes

General Manager: L de M G Cipriano
Deputy General Manager: Renato da Silva Ferreira

Gauge: 1067 mm
Route length: 899 km

The Namibe Railway consists of an 858 km line running from Moçâmedes on the west coast to Menongue in the interior via Lubango, Matala and Entrocamento; spur lines connect at Lubango (running 150 km south-east to Chibia) and Dongo (running 109 km south to Cassinga). Ore branch lines from Cassinga North (16 km) and Cassinga South (94 km) carried 6 million tonnes of ore annually to Moçâmedes when the railway was operating normally.

A rehabilitation programme was announced in the spring of 1990. Besides track work, the intention was to restore 11 locomotives, 59 passenger and 50 freight cars for use. There was also hope of purchasing 30 new passenger cars.

Luanda Railway
Porto e Caminhos de Ferro de Luanda

PO Box 1250-C, Luanda

Telephone: +244 1 70061; 73270

Director: J M Ferreira do Nascimento

Gauge: 1067 mm; 600 mm
Route length: 505 km; 31 km

Founded in 1886 the Luanda State Railway runs 496 km from the port of Luanda east to Malange serving an iron, cotton and sizal producing region. Rehabilitation of the line is in progress; it was again operational between Luanda and Ndalatando in late 1988.

Amboim Railway
Caminho de Ferro do Amboim

Puerto Amboim

General Manager: A V Ferreira

Gauge: 600 mm
Route length: 123 km

Founded in 1922 the railway operates a single line between the port of Amboim and the coffee growing region at Gabela. A priority is replacement of steam with diesel traction and a new telecommunications system is to be installed.

Benguela Railway
Caminho de Ferro de Benguela

PO Box 32, Lobito

Telephone: +244 22645
Telex: 8253 cf bang anv

President: vacant
Vice President: Eng F M Falcão
Director-General: C Silinge

Gauge: 1067 mm
Route length: 1394 km

The Benguela Railway should be a major traffic route to the sea for Zambian and Zaire copper, but the connection from the port of Lobito across Angola to the Zaire border at Dilolo, where it is connected with Zaire National Railways, has been disrupted by guerrilla action since 1975. The section of the line from the central highlands to the Zaire border has been unusable since 1982, and the 380 km from the port of Lobito to Huambo carries almost all traffic that is still operated.

The Benguela Railway is one of the routes to the sea, the rehabilitation and safeguarding of which from sabotage are urgently needed by the landlocked southern African states, eager to end their dependence on South Africa's railway, SATS, for export/import traffic movement.

Agreements were reached in May 1987 to rehabilitate the connection between Zaire and Lobito, but without follow-through because of continued Unita activity. New attempts to raise some US $280 million to reconstruct the railway (a six-year task, according to a Sofrerail expert) were made in the early summer of 1989. At present 90 per cent of Benguela stock is held by DY Tanks Consolidated Investments plc, a fully-owned subsidiary of the Société Generale de Belgique, which in late 1988 agreed to finance an engineering study of the railway's reopening, providing the engineers' safety could be guaranteed. In late 1989 this study was begun by the Belgian consultancy Tractebel.

Meanwhile, as a first step rehabilitation of the railway's workshops at Lobito and Huambo was begun in 1989.

Traffic	1986	1987
Total freight tonnes	249 491	191 869
Total freight tonne-km (million)	27·302	13·961
Total passenger-km (million)	98·84	85·184
Total passenger journeys (million)	4·118	3·549

Finance (kz 000)		
Revenue	**1986**	**1987**
Passengers and baggage	138 499	122 835
Freight, parcels and mail	148 082	139 281
Other income	25 991	29 046
Total	312 572	291 162
Expenditure	**1986**	**1987**
Staff/personnel	595 024	609 552
Materials and services	226 677	249 352
Depreciation	30 540	30 540
Financial charges	660 778	715 387
Total	1 513 019	1 604 831

Traction and rolling stock
The railway owns 34 line-haul and 12 switcher diesel locomotives, but the serviceable proportion is much smaller and variable. The line-haul units are exclusively General Electric Type U20C. The 47 passenger cars include 4 sleeping and 4 restaurant cars. The railway owns 2015 freight wagons.

Type of coupler in standard use: AAR-10A
Type of braking in standard use: Vacuum
Track
Rail: BS-30, 40 and 45
Sleepers: Wood 2000 × 250 × 140 mm, spaced 1460/km in plain track, 1600/km in curves
Fastenings: Elastic spike
Minimum curve radius: 100 m
Max gradient: 2%
Max axleload: 15 tonnes

Caminho de Ferro de Benguela

Benguela Railway diesel locomotives

Wheel arrange-ment	Trans-mission	Rated power hp	Max lb (kg)	Tractive effort Continuous at lb (kg)	mph (km/h)	Max speed mph (km/h)	Wheel diameter in (mm)	Total weight tonnes	Length ft in (mm)	No in service 1988	Year first built	Builders Mechanical parts	Engine & type
C	Hyd	425	24 000 (10 890)	9000 (4080)	12 (19)	17 (27)	40 (1016)	40	28'5½" (8680)	1	1960	North British	Paxman 8RPHXL
C	Hyd	425	24 000 (10 890)	9000 (4080)	12 (19)	17 (27)	40 (1016)	41	28'5½" (8680)	1	1972	Andrew Barclay	Paxman 8RPHXL
Co-Co (U20C)	Elec	2150	59 520 (27 000)	50 400 (22 800)	12 (19)	67.7 (109)	36 (914)	90	55'0" (16 764)	8	1972	General Electric	General Electric 7FDL12
Bo-Bo	Elec	600	39 000 (17 690)	25 600 (11 612)	26 (42)	36 (94)	41 (12 500)	60		6	1987	General Electric	2 × Cummins NT855L4

Argentina

Secretariat of Works & Public Services

Avenue de Julio 1925, 1322, 1002 Buenos Aires

Telephone: +54 1 38 8911

Minister: José R Dromi
Secretary: Dr Osvaldo Pritz
Secretary for Transport: Miguel d'Alessandro

The Secretariat, a constituent of the Ministry of Economy, determines the policy and provision of all forms of public and privately-owned transport in Argentina.

Argentine Railways (FA)
Ferrocarriles Argentinos

Avenida Ramos Mejia 1302, 1104 Buenos Aires

Telephone: +54 1 312 1746/9528/9168
Telex: 22507

Trustee: Ing Julio César Savón
Assistant Trustee: Ing Fernando Frediani
Chief Executive, Operating: Ing José Donzelli
Departmental Directors
  Mechanical: Edgardo Moya
  Way and Works: Eduardo Alfredo Miotti
  Commercial: Homero Marinari
  Finance: Horacio Gamero
  Economics & Finance: Alberto Varesi
  Technical & Administration: A Barletta Blumetti
  Communications: Edgardo Galli
  Purchasing: Jorge Piltz
  Systems & Computers: Jorge Inagaki
  Transportation: Efrain Schumovich
  Electrification: Eugenia Giles
  Planning: Luis A Gutierrez
Divisional Managers:
  Mitre: Vacant
  San Martin: Heliberto Feuske
  Urquiza: Ing Conrado Bataglia
  Belgrano: Vacant
  Roca: Ing Juan Legnazzi
  Sarmiento: Ing Efraim Schumovich
Administration of Suburban Railways
  Manager, Technical & Operations: Ing Agustin Pigliacampo
  Manager, Northern Zone: Ing José Propato
  Manager, Southern Zone: Ing J Castaños Saenz

Gauge: 1000 mm; 1435 mm; 1676 mm
Route length: 34 172 km

Electrification: 169 km at 600 and 800 V dc; 40 km at 25 kV 50 Hz

Divisions	Gauge
Roca	1676 mm
	750 mm
Mitre	1676 mm
San Martin	1676 mm
Sarmiento	1676 mm
Urquiza	1435 mm
Belgrano	1000 mm

Railway in decline

Since 1965, when the FA network extended for almost 68 500 route-km, there has been drastic pruning of lightly-trafficked lines, with a concurrent reduction of the work-force by almost 50 per cent.

FA's already grievous financial difficulties were aggravated in 1985 by the Alfonsin government's cut of the railway's subsidy by 45 per cent. FA's assets have been decaying to the extent that 90 per cent of its track is over 10 years old, over half its locomotives more than 20 years old (and little more than half of them unusable for lack of adequate maintenance) and a great deal of signalling more than half-a-century old. At the same time freight traffic has been declining.

During 1986 the Alfonsin government did authorise investment in FA to a value of some US $700 million. This was to provide for rehabilitation of about 1200 km of track. Priority, however, was accorded the construction of 210 2450 hp diesel-electric locomotives by the Argentina-based General Motors Interamericana over the 1986–89 period, to keep the local industry in production.

However, the Directorio de Empresas Publicas (DEP), a new organisation created by the Alfonsin regime to oversee Argentina's state enterprises and set about reducing public sector deficits, soon ruled that the state was incapable of funding FA's massive investment needs. In a first move towards privatisation, the government in February 1987 invited bids for private enterprise operation of eight FA routes, among them the 702 km line from Embarcacion to Formosa. The private operators were expected to furnish their own rolling stock and pay rental for use of the existing infrastructure. The first privatisation was effected in late 1987, when the privately-owned Ferrocarriles del Sur took over the 140 km La Cocha branch in Tucumán province, using three reconditioned Ganz railcars hired from FA.

But this privatisation scheme made little further headway. The plan had proposed the licensing of three private companies to run main-line, urban passenger and freight services on payment of rental for use of infrastructure. However, it was soon apparent that on these terms, and without freedom to dispense with superfluous FA staff (who fiercely resisted any move for redundancies), the private operators would be incapable of offering competitive tariffs. The few private operators who did take over branch lines either failed to run trains as pledged, or withheld their rental payments.

Menem orders drastic cuts and privatisation

Following his election to the national presidency in 1989, Carlos Menem made FA one of the first targets in his plans to 'restructure the state'. An intervenor, or trustee, lawyer Dr Alberto Trezza, was appointed to take charge of FA affairs. He soon pronounced the railway's financial state so dire that he would, he said, declare FA bankrupt by the year's end unless some improvement were detectable.

All of FA's divisions except the Sarmiento promptly had their managers replaced. FA's state subsidy was limited to making good its staffing costs; all other expenditure, including investment had to be recouped from revenue. Some 8000 administrative staff were made redundant, partly by merging the four broad-gauge railways into two, the San Martin/Mitre and Roca/Sarmiento; and 40% of FA's long-distance

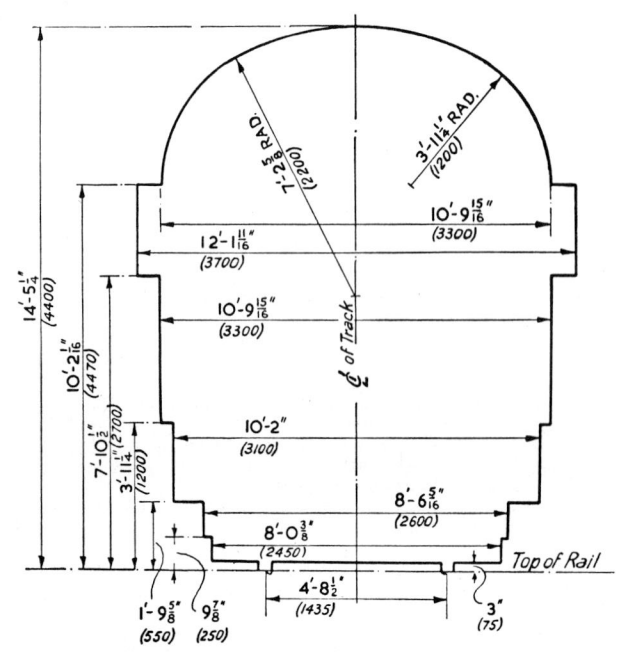

Argentinian General Roca train-set by Toshiba

Northwest Region-standard gauge

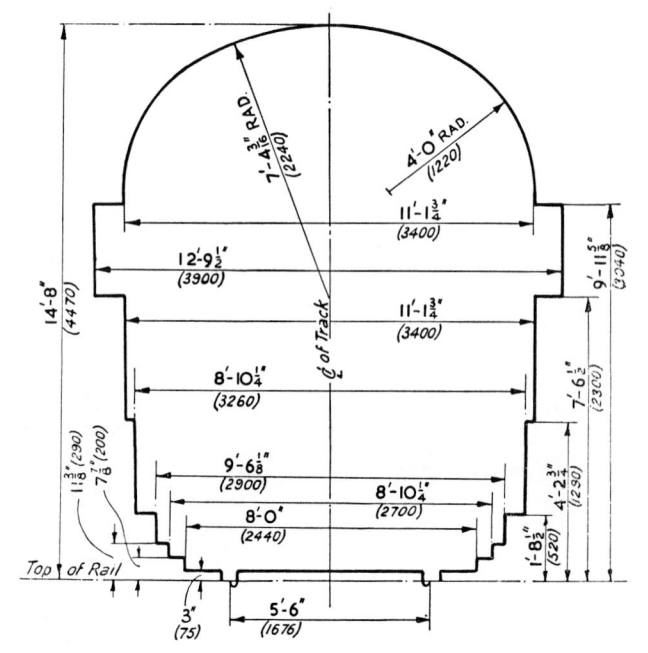

Central and Southwest Regions-1676 mm gauge

passenger services were withdrawn. The latter economy did not spare some significant services out of Buenos Aires, notably those to Bahia Blanca, Mendoza, Posadas and Bariloche; numerous surviving services were reduced from daily to once or twice weekly. Finally, the President ordered new plans for privatisation to be drafted.

This last order sparked a fresh crisis. While the Public Works Ministry and Dr Trezza busied themselves with the drafting of terms for bidders to take over some 5200 route-km of lines forming grain corridors to the port of Bahia Blanca, the Ministry of Economy toyed with a proposal from Citibank that the latter should manage a sale of FA to its staff. This scheme envisaged a break-up of FA into almost a score of small companies. Unaware of this parallel negotiation until it was revealed in the press, Dr Trezza resigned in December 1989 and was succeeded by a former Federal Commissioner of Railways, Ing Julio César Savón.

By mid-1990 the Bahia Blanca scheme had been severely cut back to 1750 km of route in use and an option to reopen a further 365 km. This left only two bidders interested in the proposal, which included hire of six locomotives and 500 wagons from FA.

Suburban railways hived off
In 1990 the Buenos Aires suburban passenger operation was segregated under a new subsidiary, the Adminstration of Suburban Railways (AFS). The aim was that the system should in future be funded by the city authority and the 19 districts of the Buenos Aires province. AFS is in charge of a 184-station network that covers the electric services of the Sarmiento, Mitre, Urquiza and Roca Divisions, and diesel-powered workings of the Belgrano, San Martin and Roca Divisions.

Link with Paraguay
A connection with the railways of Paraguay was forged in March 1990 when the first Urquiza Division train crossed the newly completed San Roque González de Santa Cruz bridge over the Paraná river. There was a formal opening attended by the Presidents of both countries in April.

Workshops privatisation
Privatisation of FA's workshops was among plans at the start of 1990. It was claimed that amongst other things this would improve the very poor availability of FA locomotives. The expectation was that Materfer would be involved in a new company to take over plant in Cordoba province for maintenance of FA's Alco and GE units. GM-EMD units would be cared for at the Bahia Blanca shops by a company including GM's local subsidiary. The local subsidiary of Ganz Mavag was in mind for management of the Mendoza workshops.

New line plans
In 1986 parliament set up a committee to study the feasibility of building a 1980 km line through Patagonia from the 750 mm gauge outpost of Esquel south to Rio Turbio-Gallegos industrial railway near the Chilean frontier. A 200 km branch from this projected line at Gobernador Gregores to the South Atlantic port of San Julian was to be considered.

In December 1987 the Argentine, Bolivian and Peruvian governments agreed to create an Argentina-Peru rail link by 1990. The connection involves a break of gauge at the Peru-Bolivia border. The Argentine part of the scheme is the Belgrano railway.

Electrification
The long-delayed electrification of the Roca line serving Buenos Aires suburbs began in December 1981. The main contracts were secured by a Japanese consortium led by Marubeni Corporation and including Toshiba, Mitsubishi Electric and Hitachi; local companies involved are Fabricaciones Militares, SIAM and Materfer for some rolling stock items, and Desaci, Techint, Ecofisa, Sade and Impresit-Sideco for the civil engineering and installation works; the track is being renewed integrally with the electrification and automatic signalling installed.

The US $450 million first stage of the electrification, which is at 25 kV 50 Hz, runs from Plaza Constitución to Temperley and thence on the lines diverging to Glew (29 km) and Ezeiza (32 km). This was ready for full public service in November 1985. The second stage, under way in 1988–89, covers the Plaza Constitución-La Plata line and its links with the first stage line, a total of 83 km. A branch to Buenos Aires' Ezeiza airport is now planned also.

The first stage service employs 52 twin-sets of three-car emus, of which an initial order of 40 was constructed in Japan, the remainder by local industry.

At the end of 1984, in a deal embracing co-operative development of a new 25 kV 50 Hz catenary by FA and Spanish National Railways (RENFE), a Spanish-Argentinian consortium, with the support of RENFE consultants, was contracted to undertake electrification of a further 93 route-km of the General Mitre suburban system. Financial support was to come from Spanish sources, but no physical progress with this project has been reported. Meanwhile the 92 cars of the existing General Mitre emu fleet have been undergoing thorough renovation by Emepa.

Early in 1986 tenders were sought for electrification of the General San Martin suburban line from Retiro to Pilar and Mercedes. At the end of the year this 25 kV 50 Hz electrification was authorised by the then government. The work, which would involve upgrading of some 50 route-km and 120 km of track and its resignalling, was entrusted to a USSR organisation. USSR industry would also supply 28 electric locomotives for operation of a push-pull service with the line's existing cars refurbished and retrofitted with air brakes instead of their present vacuum. The deal had USSR financial backing, but here again no progress has been reported.

Buenos Aires Metropolitan
The Metropolitan railway was added to FA's divisions in 1979, to co-ordinate the commuter services previously managed independently by the other six railways within the national rail system. Metropolitan's authority will eventually cover 518 route-km on all sides of the city. Several new stations have been opened since the division's creation; and 130 Japanese-built emus of the 1956–62 period have been refurbished.

Traction and rolling stock
FA has been rationalising its previously diverse fleet and concentrating on units of either General Motors, General Electric or Alco/Bombardier manufacture, to eliminate difficulties in spares procurement. Shortage of funds has inhibited purchase of new locomotives, but in 1989 a local company was manufacturing 30 Alco 251-C engines under Bombardier licence to repower FA's MLW Type RSD-30 locomotives.

In 1988 orders were placed with the Muriasco Group of Spain for 2600 freight cars and spares. The contract, supported by Spanish funding, was valued at US $120 million. Other contracts, with Materfer and Fabricaciones Militares, covered provision of 52 cars for the General Roca railway commuter service; supply of 250 hopper wagons by Bautista Buriasco; and of 119 box cars by Mecanoexportimport of Romania.

At the end of 1988 FA owned 1003 diesel-electric, 129 diesel-hydraulic and eight electric main-line locomotives, 808 emu cars, 215 diesel railcars, 1973 passenger cars and 39 780 freight cars.

Signalling
Considerable CTC extensions have been in hand. Routes involved include: 370 km of single track between Buenos Aires and Mar del Plata; from Jose C Paz to Pilar, on the San Martin commuter line from Retiro; the 102 km between Beazley and La Paz; and the busy four-track, 6 km section of the General Mitre system between Retiro and Maldonado Junction, where Siemens and Desaci are installing computer-aided apparatus. Outdated telephone networks are also being renewed.

Track-to-train radio and CTC is being installed over the 398 km between Buenos Aires and Mar del Plata by Sicom, an Italian subsidiary of Motorola.

Diesel-electric locomotives

	Power rating
1000 mm	
General Electric 4 GE 756	735
General Electric CGE 756	1000
General Electric U 12 C	1000
Alco M RSD 35	1000
Fiat Transfer	735
General Motors G 22 CU	1200
General Motors GT 22 CU	1820
Werkspoor	440

	Power rating
1676 mm	
Baldwin LH	1200
Cockerill O	1290
Gaia 1350	1000
Gaia 1050	770
General Electric U 13 C	1045
General Electric U 18 C	1460
General Electric GG 731	1125
Alco RSD 16	1435
Alco M PPD 7	1435
Alco M RSD 35	1000
General Motors GT 22 CW	1820
General Motors GR 12 W	1045
General Motors G 12	1045
General Motors GA 8	625
Werkspoor 600	440
General Motors G 22 CW	1200

	Power rating
1435 mm	
General Electric U 12 C	970
General Electric U 13 C	1045
General Motors G 22 CW	1200

Australia

Department of Transport and Communication

PO Box 594, Myuna Complex, Corner Northbourne and Cooyong Streets, Canberra City, ACT 2600

Telephone: +61 62 687111
Telex: 62018
Telefax: +61 62 572505

Minister, Transport & Communication: Ralph Willis
House of Representatives, Canberra, ACT 2600
Telephone: +61 62 777200

Minister, Land Transport & Shipping Support: Bob Brown
House of Representatives, Canberra, ACT 2600
Telephone: +61 62 777440

Australian National Railways

Australian National House, 1 Richmond Road, Keswick, South Australia 5035

Telephone: +61 8 217 4111
Telex: 88445
Telefax: +61 8 217 4544

Chairman: Dr D G Williams
Deputy Chairman: J W McArdle
Managing Director: R M King
Manager Tasrail: Dr N Otway (Acting)
General Manager, Corporate Affairs: Dr F N Affleck
Human Resources: C R Hall
Passenger & Travel: G J Templer (Acting)
Freight: B T Conroy
Financial Services: R G Greatrex
Technical Services: A Neal
Manager, Corporate Planning: K T Norley
Chief Mechanical Engineer: L C Smith
Chief Civil Engineer: J D Mullen
Signals & Communications Engineer: W B B Johnston
Manager, Operations: R A Robertson
Manager Public Relations: P S Bramwell
Manager, Purchasing and Supply: C M Kiley

Gauges 1435 mm; 1067 mm; 1600 mm
Route length: 3530 km; 1740 km (of which 840 km in Tasmania); 1788 km

RAILWAY SYSTEMS / Australia

Constitution

AN is responsible for the management and operation of railways owned by the Commonwealth government and provides a key link in the chain of inter-system rail transport operating round Australia. It is a statutory authority under the Australian National Railways Act operating as a commercially-oriented business enterprise.

In 1988 the Federal Minister for Transport and Communications put through a reform package for Government Business Enterprises. The effect of this package was to strengthen AN's emphasis on commercial business management, long-term planning and accountability for results. Relaxation of some government controls allowed faster response to market developments.

AN comprises:
Standard-gauge (1435 mm; main lines from Broken Hill (NSW) via Port Augusta (South Australia) to Kalgoorlie (Western Australia) (2173 km). Connecting standard-gauge line from Crystal Brook to Adelaide (197 km).
Central Australia Railway (1435 km) from Tarcoola to Alice Springs (831 km).
Branch lines from Port Augusta to Telford (Leigh Creek) (251 km) and Whyalla (75 km).
Broad-gauge (1600 km) main line from Adelaide to Melbourne (307 km to Victorian border), with various branches (1540 km). Isolated narrow-gauge (1067 mm) networks on Eyre Peninsula (South Australia) (718 km) and in the island State of Tasmania (AN Tasrail-840 km).

Operating offices

Adelaide, South Australia; Port Augusta, South Australia, Launceston, Tasmania

Commercial offices

Sydney, New South Wales; Melbourne, Victoria; Perth, Western Australia

Finance

In 1978 the Australian National Railways Commission embarked on an ambitious plan to achieve break-even from commercial operations by 1988. This was achieved in FY 1987–88, when AN's commercial freight business earned a surplus after all expenses (including interest and depreciation) of A$0.7 million. The improvement was sustained in FY 1988–89 with a surplus of A$9.1 million in AN Freight, which is AN's biggest business segment.

AN's non-commercial or Community Service Obligation business segments and certain costs associated with public ownership incurred losses in FY 1988-89 of A$50.6 million, a reduction of 72% compared with deficits under these heads in the late 1970s. Community Service Obligations are services and other activities which the Federal government has requested AN to continue operating. They comprise mainland passenger operations and AN Tasrail, for both of which AN receives a revenue subvention. The total cash revenue supplement paid to AN in FY 1988–89 was A$41.9 million.

Finance (A$ million)

	1985/86	1986/87	1987/88
Revenue	283.3	283.3	306.5
Expenditure	352.8	352	358.4

Passenger traffic

Competition has severely eroded ANR passenger business in the 1980s. Airlines now hold about 65 per cent of the interstate market, road coaches 25 per cent and rail only 10 per cent. However, the long-term decline in interstate and country passenger services has been arrested and lost ground is now being recouped.

Following enhancement of facilities on the 'Ghan' by the introduction of the Entertainment Car, complete with poker machines, video movies and games, a shop, a games room and a hairdressing salon, a thorough refurbishing of this train's equipment was carried out in 1989. The refurbished cars are repainted externally in a new and distinctive 'Ghan' livery. The renovated train, now first class only, has attracted such an increase of passengers that in 1990 AN invited proposals for a similar treatment of the 'Indian Pacific'.

Adelaide-Melbourne 'Overland', including motorail facility for accompanied autos, headed by Clyde-built 2240 kW Class BL diesel-electric with GM-EMD electronic creep control

Passenger traffic (000)

	1985/86	1986/87	1987/88
Passenger journeys	322.3	328.9	352.7
Passenger-km	2485.6	2381.1	NA

Freight traffic

Bulk commodities account for only a third of AN's tonnage, because the system does not serve mineral or coal sources to anything like the extent of the neighbouring State railways. Consequently AN's main freight effort, commercially, is directed to the general merchandise market, where it faces fierce and near-unregulated road competition. Traffic under this heading generates over 40 per cent of AN's freight tonne-km and a third of its freight income. Its main elements are piggyback; export deep-sea containers; and the groupage traffic of freight forwarders, in containers or covered wagons, for which AN has been making a particular play.

In FY 1988-89 AN's freight business increased 5.9 per cent in tonne-km terms, spurred by significant growth in the intermodal sector. Expansion of the Superfreighter system boosted inter-state traffic, and competitive edge in the market was sharpened by new hardware developments.

Complete trains of articulated, skeletal-frame Five-Pack container cars, hauled by new Class Dl locomotives, began service in FY 1988/89. The cost reductions obtained from this technology, which were passed on to customers, led AN to expect to win a significant volume of new business from competitors operating to Western Australia. Customers would soon be able to lease sets of these wagons, to be operated as express Five-Pack trains between Adelaide and Perth.

During the year a well-frame derivative of the Five-Pack, designed and manufactured in AN's own workshops, proved its ability to double-stack full-height containers without clearance infringement. As a result a trial fleet of 13 five-platform well units was put in hand for use on routes to Perth and Alice Springs. Another success has been a refrigerated container service using generator cars to supply power. To handle the growth in intermodal traffic, a major upgrading of the Islington Freight Centre has begun. This will include provision of broad-gauge access from the south, so that Superfreighters to and from Melbourne can use the yard without shunting.

In late 1989 AN tabled a A$550 million scheme to create a standard-gauge route throughout from Adelaide to Melbourne. The scheme would involve

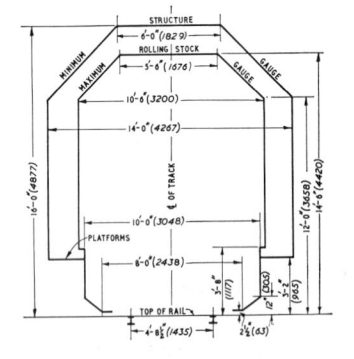

AN 1435 mm gauge (former Commonwealth Railways)

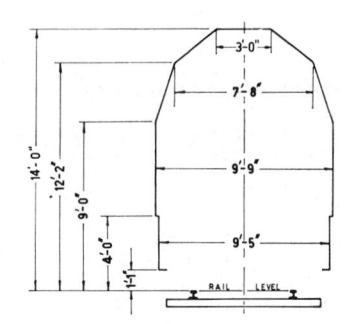

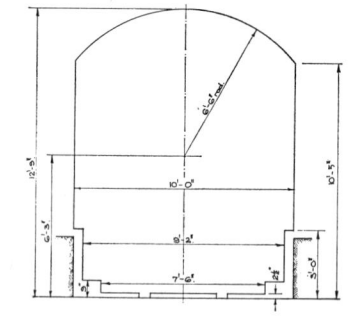

AN 1067 mm gauge lines in Tasmanian Region (former Tasmanian Government Railways)

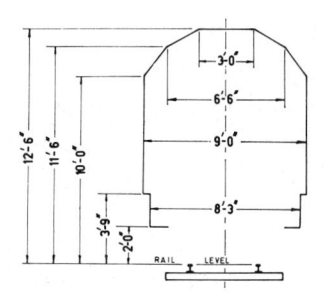

AN loading gauge for former South Australian Railways (left) 1600 and 1435 mm lines and (right) 1067 mm line

new infrastructure from AN's Crystal Brook line at Two Brooks to Murray Bridge, and re-gauging from there to Melbourne. In 1987-88 AN set a haulage record of 2 562 521 tonnes for coal transported from the Leigh Creek coal fields to the Electricity Trust of South Australia's Port Augusta power stations. In FY 1988-89 the record rose higher still. Modifications to ETSA's loading facilities and modifications to AN's coal wagons have markedly improved rolling stock utilisation, with net wagon loads increased from 48 to 60 tonnes. In FY1988-89 trains were doubled in length from 80 to 160 coal cars, the biggest operated on any Australian government-owned railway.

AN is to introduce RoadRailer freight services to Australia, under an exclusive Australian manufacture, sale and operating licence from the RoadRailer division of the Chamberlain Group of Illinois. The first units were available in early 1990 for trial service, which the Federal government is backing with a A$1.4 million grant. AN proposes to operate RoadRailer on a national basis with emphasis on the busy East Coast corridor. RoadRailer will compete successfully for loading presently handled by road hauliers and should have a significant impact on highway safety.

Train running has been further improved by the introduction of movement managers with responsibilities, on a 24-hour basis, for the operating performance of each freight business group's loadings. Increasing train lengths to 1800 metres (up to 6000 gross tonnes) west of Dry Creek to both Alice Springs and Perth has ensured that loading is not detached en route due to length or tonnage restrictions. General freight trains in excess of 4000 gross tonnes are regularly scheduled to Western Australia and the Northern Territory. AN has continued to implement two-person crew operation wherever possible. In the automotive traffic sector, 31 car-carrier wagons have been converted from double-to triple-deck.

Computer-based information services continue to expand AN's Traffic Information Management System (TIMS), providing on-line information about wagon location, train location, loads, running details, track conditions and maintenance requirements. TIMS provides statistical information and is being extended to assist yard and freight terminal management. Customers will be given direct access (with full data security) to TIMS. A pilot programme is being developed with Fujitsu Australia to apply knowledge-based systems technology to maximise locomotive roster efficiency. This joint-venture artificial intelligence project is known as Expert Rostering of Locomotives (EROL).

Freight traffic (million)

	1985/86	1986/87	1987/88
Tonnage	13.05	12.9	13.629
Tonne-km	7080	6866	7647

Signalling and telecommunications
AN has contracted to purchase two fibres in the optical fibre cable being laid by the Australian Telecommunications Commission (Telecom) for 1700 km alongside the Trans Australian Railway between Port Augusta and Kalgoorlie. This development, which became operational in October 1989, provides modern digital communications and train control systems on the route. All trains are in direct contact with central control via radio base stations established in conjunction with the optical fibre cable.

Automatically normalising electric switches required for the operation of two-person crew trains were installed at 41 locations on the Trans Australian and Central Australia Railways, so as to have automatically normalising switches in place coincidentally with the installation of the optical fibre communications system. The equipment is suitable for operation in conjunction with a future ATCS system while having a minimum amount of redundant equipment.

AN has signed an A$11.5 million contract with the Adelaide, South Australian company, Teknis Systems, to design an advanced train control system for AN to be known as AUSTRAC. Priority will be given to installation of automatic switches and improved driver/controller communication on the Trans Australian Railway (Port Augusta to Kalgoorlie) and on the Central Australian Railway (Tarcoola to Alice Springs). The system will also allow train fault detection. AUSTRAC will have considerable export potential.

Tasrail
The worn-out railway system taken over from Tasmania in 1978 is being rehabilitated by investment of assets with a replacement value of over A$50 million. Few if any traffics carried in Tasmania cover their own direct costs, a result in part of concessionary contracts inherited from the State.

AN entered into a contract with the Federal government whereby the latter provided A$52.4 million to support operation of the Tasmanian rail system, now given the business name of Tasrail, from 1985/86 to 1987/88. The contract has since been extended for a further five years. AN aims to achieve break-even point by the mid-1990s.

Traction and rolling stock
A major locomotive replacement programme amounting eventually to 100 units was begun with an order for 15 Class DL 3000 hp units from Clyde Engineering. These have all been delivered. The 3000 hp Co-Co locomotives, built by Clyde Engineering to a GM-EMD design and intended primarily for heavy freight trains of up to 6000 tonnes, incorporate the latest innovations in diesel technology, including microprocessor controls, self-diagnostic fault finders, increased fuel effiency and improved tractive effort. They can operate at speeds of up to 150 km/h and will achieve significant fuel savings.

AN has also ordered from Goninan 14 Class EL locomotives, a derivation of the General Electric Dash-8 series in the US, for east-west intermodal freight haulage.

At the start of 1990 ANR was operating 254 diesel locomotives, 22 diesel railcars and trailers, 206 passenger cars and 5875 freight cars.

Type of coupler in standard use: Alliance
Type of braking in standard use: Air (vacuum on some narrow-gauge vehicles).

A$20.5 million has been allocated to the upgrading of major workshop areas. New equipment will include production line handling equipment and computer-controlled, high-speed wheel boring machines, locomotive cleaning equipment, robotic welding machines and modern presses and guillotines. A 'one-spot' repair workshop at Dry Creek, South Australia, has been completed for the daily maintenance of wagons.

Civil engineering
AN's major programme to convert the Trans Australia Railway entirely to minimum-maintenance concrete-sleepered track continued during 1988-89.

To accelerate the replacement of wooden with concrete sleepers, a new SMD-80-AN machine has

New 'Five-Pack' intermodal well wagon allows container double-stacking

AN conference car

The first of AN's new Class DL diesel locomotives

RAILWAY SYSTEMS / Australia

Diesel locomotives

Class (Railways's own designation)	Gauge	Wheel arrangement	Transmission	Rated power (kW)	Max speed km/h	Total weight tonnes	No in service 1988	Year first built	Builders Mechanical parts	Builders Engine & type	Builders Transmission
Mainland											
500	1600, 1435	Bo-Bo	Elec	410	64	56.8	22	1964	SA Railway	Eng Elec 4 SRKT	EE 548/2A
600	1435	Co-Co	Elec	1450	120	112.8	7	1965	Goodwin	Alco 251C	GE 752
700	1600	Co-Co	Elec	1600	112	111.6	6	1971	Goodwin	Alco 251C	AEI 165
800	1600	Bo-Bo	Elec	558	97	73.2	8	1956	Eng Elec	Eng Elec 6 SRKT	EE 526/39
830	1600, 1435, 1067	Co-Co	Elec	725	120	71.4	45	1959	Goodwin	Alco 251	GE 761
930	1600, 1435	Co-Co	Elec	1305	112.6	105.9	26	1955	Goodwin	Alco 251 B	GE 761
AL	1435	Co-Co	Elec	2460	155	132	8	1976	Clyde	EMD 16/645	EMD D77
BL	1600, 1435	Co-Co	Elec	2460	115	128	10	1983	Clyde	EMD 16/645	EMD D77B
CL	1435	Co-Co	Elec	2460	155	128.5	17	1970	Clyde	EMD 16/645	EMD D77
DL	1435	Co-Co	Elec	2360	153	121.5	6	1988	Clyde	EMD 710G3	EMD D87
GM (F)	1435	AIA-AIA	Elec	1230	143	108	5	1951	Clyde	EMD 16/567B	EMD
GM (S)	1435	Co-Co	Elec	1450	143	116	32	1955	Clyde	EMD 16/567B	EMD
NJ	1067	Co-Co	Elec	1230	106	72	6	1971	Clyde	EMD 12/645E	EMD CD-36
NT	1067	Co-Co	Elec	970	80	70.3	2	1965	Tulloch	Sulzer 6LDA28C	AEI 253AZ
Tasrail											
Y	1067	Bo-Bo	Elec	595	72	59	8	1961	Tasmania Government Railway	EE 6SRKT	Eng Elec
Z	1067	Co-Co	Elec	1530	97	97.5	4	1972	GEC	EE 12CVST Mk II	Eng Elec
ZA	1067	Co-Co	Elec	1900	97	97.5	6	1973	GEC	EE 12CVST Mk III	Eng Elec
ZB	1067	Co-Co	Elec	1454	96	91.5	16	1987	GEC	EE 12CVST Mk III	Eng Elec

Diesel railcars or multiple-units

Class (Railway's own designation)	Gauge	Cars per unit	Motor cars per unit	Motored axles per motor car	Transmission	Rated power (kW) per motor	Max speed km/h	Weight tonnes per car (M-motor T-trailer)	Total seating capacity per car (M-motor T-trailer)	Length per car mm	No in service 1988	Year first built	Builders Mechanical parts	Builders Engine & type	Builders Transmission
CB	1435	1	1	2	Hyd	205	137	50 (M)	84	25908	3	1951	Budd	GM 6/110	Allison
250	1600, 1435	1	1	2	Hyd	224	112	61 (M)	51	22860	11	1954	SA Railway	Cummins NT-855-R2	Twin-Disc
280	1600	1	1	2	Hyd	224	112	53 (M)	Baggage car	21410	2	1958	SA Railway	Cummins NT-855-R2	Twin Disc
100	1600, 1435	1	-	-	-	-	-	43.2 (T)	68 (T)	23850	7	1955	SA Railway	Cummins NT-855-R2	Twin Disc

been purchased from Plasser. It will eventually be used to complete the Trans Australia Railway re-sleepering programme. AN will use concrete sleepers on all lines by 1994.

Track
Standard rail: Flat bottom throughout, weighing 53, 47, 40, 31.2, 30, 25 kg/m
Joints: Fishplates, bolts and welding
Rail fastening: Dog spikes, Pandrol and McKay Safelok elastic rail spikes
Cross ties (sleepers): 1600 mm gauge: impregnated hardwood 2600 × 250 × 125 mm; 1435 mm gauge: treated and untreated hardwood 2500 × 230 × 115 mm; CR2 prestressed concrete 2514 × 264 × 211 mm; AN3 prestressed concrete 2500 × 264 × 211 mm; 1066 mm gauge: treated hardwood 1900 × 200 × 115 mm
Spacing: 1600 to 1300 per km
Filling: Crushed stone and gravel ballast
Minimum curve radius: 14.5°
Max gradient: 2.5%
Max axleload: 23 tonnes

ALICE SPRINGS-DARWIN RAILWAYS

In February 1981 the Commonwealth government authorised the survey, design and preliminary planning of a standard-gauge railway link between Alice Springs and Darwin. In January 1983 the then Prime Minister, Malcolm Fraser, approved construction of the 1420 km line for completion in 1988-89. It was to be funded with A$500 million of Federal finance. In 1984, however, the project was suspended. Following a government statement in 1983 that the Northern Territory must underwrite 40 per cent of the capital cost, an official enquiry reported in 1984 that the line's traffic potential could not justify the anticipated construction cost of A$578 million.

During 1985, however, the project resurfaced. A re-examination by Canadian Pacific Consulting Services concluded that a 1500 km line could be built for A$500 million by adopting more of the alignment of the narrow-gauge Darwin-Birdum railway closed in 1976, and by recourse to less exacting track parameters that would adequately serve prospective traffic. The consultants also suggested that revenue projections of the earlier study were understated. The Northern Territory government believed that on these terms, subject to some Federal aid, the project could be privately capitalised and the completed line operated at a profit. In 1987 it set about forming a privately financed consortium to undertake the project.

In 1988 a joint venture group, Rail-North Pty Ltd, was formed by the Northern Territory government, Australian companies and Japanese construction, engineering and banking interests to undertake a further feasibility study.

SYDNEY-CANBERRA-MELBOURNE VFT (VERY FAST TRAIN)

VFT Joint Venture, a group comprising BHP, Elders-IXL, TNT Transport Group and Japanese construction company Kumagai-Gumi is financing studies of a new 360 km/h standard-gauge, electrified line of 870 km length to connect Sydney, Canberra and Melbourne. The double-track line would carry high-value merchandise traffic as well as passenger trains. Intermediate stations would be served, also motorists' railheads on the periphery of Melbourne and Sydney, and Sydney's main airport. A ruling gradient of 3.5 per cent is envisaged to minimise earthworks.

Comeng has produced draft rolling stock designs to the VFT specification. Passenger train-sets would be of six cars plus, at each end, a three-phase ac motor power car with a 4000 kW rating to allow for the ruling gradient and achieve a 0.75 m/s rate of acceleration. The high-speed freight car design allows for a 53 tonnes payload within a gross laden weight of 80 tonnes. A subsequent Sydney-Brisbane high-speed route is possible.

State Railway Authority/SRA (New South Wales)

Transport House, 11–31 York Street, PO Box 29, Sydney, New South Wales 2000

Telephone: +61 2 219 8888
Telex: 25702 nswtc

Minister of Transport: Bruce Baird
Chairman and Chief Executive: Ross Sayers
Finance Director: F Morrison

COMMUTER SERVICES GROUP: CITYRAIL

Group General Manager: Rob Schwarzer
General Manager, Engineering: Brian Lanyon
General Manager, Operations: Peter Niven
Commercial Services Manager: Barry Garnham
Finance Manager: Paul Slater
Strategy Manager: Chris Ailwood

FREIGHT AND COUNTRY PASSENGER

Group General Manager: Vince Graham
Financial Manager: Gary Pedersen
Commercial Services Manager: Gareth Grainger
Engineering Manager: Bill Newton
Workshops Manager: Bill Goodwin
Business Manager, Coal & Minerals: Terry Kearney
Grain: Vince O'Rourke
Express Rail: Lucio Di Bartolomeo
CountryLink: Faye Powell
Trackfast: Gary Camp

Gauge: 1435 mm
Route length: 9917 km
Electrification: 618 km at 1.5 kV dc overhead

Reorganisation for economy

A new state Transport Administration Act that became effective in January 1989 had as main aim reduction of government subsidy for SRA's activity. The Transport Minister retained authority for transport policy, but under a new Board of Directors, and a new Chairman and Chief Executive, SRA was given full commercial authority.

SRA's management structure was slimmed down and split into two business groups. CityRail is responsible for the network and all passenger operations in an area around Sydney extending to Lithgow in the west, Muswellbrook/Dungog in the north, Nowra on the south coast, and Moss Vale in the Southern Highlands. The Freight and Country Passenger Group competes in a completely deregulated market for inter- and intra-state freight traffic, and for country and inter-state passenger business. SRA has been relieved of its common carrier obligation and set to run its freight business on strictly commercial lines.

Drastic Freight & Country Group rationalisation
In the autumn of 1989 SRA accepted many of the recommendations for its Freight and Country Passengers Group put up in a study commissioned from consultants Booz Allen & Hamilton. The consultants' advice that SRA should get out of country and inter-state passenger service altogether was not accepted, despite support from one Sydney newspaper. Nor were its drastic freight rationalisation plans in full. The consultants estimated that were their recommendations fully implemented, SRA would within 10 years show a profit of A$466 million on its freight services, instead of a prospective accumulated deficit of A$2663 million if no action were taken. The government preferred action forecast to trim the expected loss at the end of the 1990s to A$501 million.

SRA's plan has three main threads. In both freight and passenger services, the emphasis will be on bulk movement by rail, road service for other work. Thus wagonload traffic will be cut by 60 per cent, but hopefully without reduction of total freight volume. The passenger service is being reshaped as Country-Link, integrating XPT trains on key routes with modern road coaches, branded XPCs, at upgraded rail-road interchanges. The aim is to confine passenger operations to the XPTs, which will entail closure of overnight sleeping-car operations; that will cut the rail passenger services' need of staff by 72 per cent. The XPTs are being repainted in a newly-adopted CountryLink style of blue, grey and aquamarine, with touches of white.

It was announced in the 1989 autumn that SRA would invest A$40 million in more XPT train-sets for its own routes, and subject to Victorian agreement to shared funding, further units for extra Sydney-Melbourne services. However, SRA's Chief Executive returned in the 1990 spring from a European visit with the view that ABB's X2 tilt-body train-set for Swedish Railways had significance for his system.

Over A$600 million will be invested in the course of the 1990s' first half in strategic areas such as new locomotives, new technology, communications and upgrading of terminals.

The group's staff is being cut by 45 per cent over four years, which should result in a 70 per cent rise in productivity. Before the economies staff costs accounted for 70 per cent of the group's direct railway operating expenses. Plans include introduction of driver-only train crewing.

Freight tariffs are being revised to economic levels. The price for wool movement was expected to double.

Three lines have already lost their rail freight services. Others were under review in early 1990.

CityRail economies
The CityRail staff is being reduced from 13 200 to 7600 over a period of five years in parallel with a A$2000 million investment in this system.

Under the second head the Transport Minister in 1990 approved a 28km extension of the Illawarra line's electrification from Wollongong to Shellharbour. The further 43km of the line to Nowra is to be upgraded, but will have its through services from Sydney superseded by a diesel train shuttle to and from Wollongong. A consortium including the Qantas airline has proposed to fund construction of a branch from the Illawarra line to Sydney Airport.

Bids have been invited for the concentration of the Sydney metropolitan system's signalling and traffic control in one centre. This would be the centrepiece of a A$400 million outlay on signalling modernisation. In a pilot scheme a computer-based interlocking is to be installed in the Liverpool area.

Other investments planned or in progress include accelerated installation of concrete sleepers in the course of track improvements; renovation of the pre-Tangara bi-level emu fleet cars, some of which are now 25 years old; modification of the traction current feeder system to accommodate the higher power

XPT train-set, Comeng-built version of British Rail's InterCity 125 HST, passes Bowral on 'Riverine' service to Albury. *(Leon Oberg)*

Class 86 electric locomotives in special Australian Bicentennial livery head the 'Indian Pacific' through the Blue Mountains.

Tangara double-deck suburban emu

demands of the new Tangara train-sets (see below); and refurbishment of 250 stations.

Finance
Despite industrial problems in the coal industry and reduced demand for grain transport, plus higher-than-forecast national wage increases. the total government subsidy for FY1988-89 was held at the budgeted figure of A$1067 million. The main reason was a 10 per cent cut in the workforce, the largest for 25 years, which lowered direct operating costs by A$140 million.

Freight traffic
Haulage of export coal is a major component of SRA traffic. SRA haul up to 150 000 tonnes of coal a day from mines to the ports of Newcastle, Sydney and Wollongong. There are some 20 mines, opencast as well as underground, in the Hunter Valley. On routes from the Hunter Valley to Newcastle coal loaders four double-length trains were in circuit operation in 1989. Each comprises 84 100-tonne gross coal wagons hauled by four Class 81 3000 hp diesel locomotives. The Class 81 is being progressively equipped with 'Speedmaster' slow-speed control for loading and discharge of these trains on the move. In 1989 a feasibility study of electrification for the coal route from Muswellbrook to Newcastle was under way.

Longer trains with greater capacity have also been a key element in the efficient movement of record NSW wheat harvests. The introduction of more powerful locomotives has allowed bigger trains to operate between sub-terminals and terminals. These consist of 39 NGTY-type wagons with a capacity of 2340 tonnes net. The trains are 50 per cent bigger than those previously operated, and obtain more productive use of vehicles and train crews.

In 1990 SRA beat stiff road haulage competition to a contract with the Australian Wheat Board that gives the railway exclusive title to movement of the state's export wheat for the next three years. Another important development in early 1990 was the opening of the Port Kembla Grain Terminal. To cater for this project SRA has invested in track upgrading, a balloon loop, resignalling and the reconstruction of 350 grain cars with automatic discharge apparatus.

Intermodal services
Overnight container trains operate to and from approximately 25 NSW country locations, running as standardised units, picking up and dropping off wagons en route. Superfreighter container services operate to and from Melbourne, Adelaide, Perth, Brisbane and other interstate locations, and have proved a key factor in the recapture of interstate traffic lost to road since the 1950s. Road pick-up/delivery are provided in country and metropolitan areas.

Two maritime container terminals, served by rail, are located at Sydney. The Balmain or White Bay Terminal which, owned by the Maritime Services Board, is operated under lease by Seatainer Terminals Ltd, and the Glebe Island Terminal, also owned by the Maritime Service Board, is operated as a 'common user' terminal under lease by a consortium, Glebe Island Terminals Pty Ltd. Each is also served by road. At Newcastle, container ships call at No 1 Throsby Wharf and No 4 Western Basin Wharf, each of which is serviced by rail.

Further rail-served container complexes are located at Homebush and Yennora, 26 km and 29 km from Balmain and Glebe Island respectively, specialising mainly in containerisation of export wool.

In March 1989 SRA published proposals to upgrade the Sydney-Melbourne line as a fast freight corridor, with trains running at up to 160 km/h so as to maintain a 9-hour schedule for the 960 km between the two centres. In both suburban areas the freight trains would have dedicated tracks. Cost of the project was put at A$1000 million.

Traction and rolling stock
At the close of 1989 SRA was operating 99 electric and 526 diesel locomotives, 51 diesel train-sets (including 73 XPT power cars and trailers), 1995 passenger cars (including 1027 double-deck emu cars) and 9209 freight wagons.

January 1988 saw the debut of the first of 450 double-deck cars to a completely new design, brand-named the 'Tangara' (aboriginal word for 'go'). DCA Design Consultants of England won the commission to style the new equipment. Features include: solid state traction power control; microprocessor-based diagnostic system; modular equipment design; passenger-operated power doors of plug-type; internal

Artist's impression of new bi-level inter-city emu ordered from Comeng

Two Class 81 diesel locomotives head a 'Superfreighter' inter-city container train.

and external public address for the guard, for control of passengers on platforms; video surveillance of passenger saloons by the guard; regenerative braking; and increased seating capacity. The specification provided for:

Design speed: 130 km/h
Acceleration (on level track): 0.8 m/s^2
Acceleration (fully loaded on 1 in 30 grade): 0.6 m/s^2
Service deceleration: 0.9 m/s^2
Emergency braking (on dry level track): 1.2 m/s^2
Length, four-car train: 80.88 m
  eight-car train: 161.76 m
Tare weights: motor car 50 tonnes; trailer 42.3 tonnes
Max axleload (car fully loaded): motor car 16.9 tonnes; trailer 14.5 tonnes
Total train seating capacity:

	Tangara	Previous double-deck design
Four-car set	1040	972
Eight-car	2080	1944

The construction contract, worth A$498 million, was won by Goninan and the traction contract by Mitsubishi Electric, which provided four-quadrant chopper control of motors with GTO thyristors. As sub-contractors Clyde Engineering furnished the motor bogies and traction motors, Comeng the trailer bogies. Delivery has proceeded at the rate of one train-set a month.

A A$48 million order for 30 double-deck inter-urbans went to Commonwealth Engineering (NSW) Pty Ltd and was in addition to a previous order for 80 interurban carriages scheduled that was completed in 1987. Both the new interurbans and the additional 16 double-deck suburban carriages, which have been ordered from Goninans of Newcastle, are fitted with chopper control. The extra 16 suburban cars were in addition to a previous A$113 million order which Goninan had to build 100 double-deck suburban carriages; this latter was completed in 1987.

In 1988 Comeng received an order to build an initial 14 double-deck emu cars of a new design, embodying much of the Tangara technology, for inter-city operation between Sydney and Newcastle, Lithgow and Wollongong. Delivery began in March 1989. There was an option for a further 36 cars.

In 1990 tenders were to be sought for 50 4000 hp and 30 medium-power diesel locomotives.

Traffic	1982/83	1983/84	1984/85	1985/86	1986/87	1988/89
Freight tonnage (million)	41.358	46.6	48.0	54.0	54.6	50.2
Passenger journeys (million)	207.7	223.9	200.2	218.6	224.2	249.3

Revenue (A$ million)	1981/82	1982/83	1983/84	1984/85	1986/87
Passengers and baggage	168.131	193.674	213.686	281.86	13.02
Freight, parcels and mail	451.373	452.626	559.876	736.79	739.25
Trading and catering	11.908	23.243	24.652	31.32	34.90
Rents	10.582	13.360	15.196	–	
Other	10.222	11.916	9.645	18.7	34.02
Government supplement	387.409	448.267	394.948	32.41	305
Total	1050.625	1143.086	1218.003	330.0	1412.39
				1303.6	1426.9

Expenditure (A$ million)	1981/82	1982/83	1983/84	1984/85	1986/87
Staff/personnel expenses	688.752	716.040	730.393	782.7	NA
Materials and services	361.873	427.046	487.61	520.9	NA
Total	1050.625	1143.086	1218.003	1412.6	1446.13

Australia / **RAILWAY SYSTEMS**

Electrification deferred
A final Sydney suburban electrification over the 15 km between Richmond and Riverstone was to have been completed in 1989, but this scheme was postponed under the state government's economy drive. However, in late 1989 the government announced that it would now finance the project for completion in 1991-92.

Signalling and telecommunications
The Ericcson ATC system is being evaluated in conjunction with a resignalling scheme between Liverpool and Campbelltown.

Track
Rail
Type to AS1085
30 kg/m: 2600 km approx
35 kg/m: 700 km approx
40 kg/m: 1200 km approx
46 kg/m: 1550 km approx
53 kg/m: 3700 km approx
60 kg/m: 150 km

Cross ties (sleepers)

Type	Thickness	In plain track and curves
Hardwood	120 mm minimum	1660/km
Concrete	165 mm minimum (200 mm at rail seat)	1660/km*
Steel	9 mm	1660/km

* 1820/km in curvature of less than 400 m radius

Fastenings
Dog spikes and lock spikes: in timber sleepers
Resilient fasteners: in some timber sleepers
Resilient fasteners: in concrete and steel sleepers

Minimum curvature radius
Branch lines: 100 m (90 m very seldom)
Main lines: 240 m (110 m very seldom)

Max gradient
Branch lines: 3% (4% one line only)
Main lines: 3% (2.5% more frequent)

Max axleload: 25 tonnes

Max gradient, compensated
Main lines: 2.3% = 1 in 30 (electric traction on City Railway). 1.5% = 1 in 66 elsewhere
Branch lines: 4.4% = 1 in 25 and 3.3% = 1 in 30

Max gradient, uncompensated
Main lines: 3.5% = 1 in 40, but there is a 30.5 km electrified length of 1 in 30 to 1 in 33 on the Blue Mountains.
Branch lines: 3.3% = 1 in 30 and 2.5% = 1 in 40

Longest continuous uniform gradient: Werris Creek to Binnaway Branch, 13 km of 1% grade, 75% curved with radii varying from 282 to 1207 m (6.2° to 1.45°) with average of 503 m (3.5°). Compensated grade, single track, no tunnels

Worst combination of curvature and gradient: On Batlow Line: radius of 90 m (19.3° curve) on 4% (1 in 25) compensated grade

Max altitude: 377 m on main Northern Line, 645 km from Sydney

Diesel locomotives

Class	Wheel arrangement	Transmission	Rated power kW	Max speed km/h	Total weight tonnes	No in service 1988	Year first built	Builders Mechanical parts	Engine & type	Transmission
422	Co-Co	Elec	1492	124	110	20	1969	Clyde Eng	EMD 16-645 E	EMD
44	Co-Co	Elec	1342	121	108	30	1957	A E Goodwin	Alco 12-251 B	GE/AEI
44	Co-Co	Elec	1342	129	112	37	1965	A E Goodwin	Alco 12-251 C	AEI
442	Co-Co	Elec	1491	120	115	34	1971	A E Goodwin	Alco 12-251 C	GE/AEI
442	Co-Co	Elec	1491	120	115	6	1973	A E Goodwin	Alco 12-251 C	Mitsubishi
45	Co-Co	Elec	1342	120	112	39	1962	A E Goodwin	Alco 12-251 C	GE/AEI
47	Co-Co	Elec	678	113	85	15	1972	A Gonian	Caterpillar D399	Hitachi
48	Co-Co	Elec	708	120	75	163	1959	A E Goodwin	Alco 6-251 B	GE/AEI
49	Co-Co	Elec	652	124	81	17	1960	Clyde Eng	EMD 8-567 C	EMD
73	B-B	Hyd	484	64	50	45	1970	Walker	Caterpillar D379	Voith
80	Co-Co	Elec	1492	130	121	50	1978	Comeng	Alco 12-251 CE	Mitsubishi
81	Co-Co	Elec	2237	115	129	80	1982	Clyde Eng	EMD 16-645E3 B	EMD
X100	B	Hyd	69	24	18	1	1962	NSWGR	Bedford 300	Allison
X200	B	Hyd	194	51	30	15	1963	NSWGR	Cummins NHRS-6-B1	Allison

Electric multiple-units (1.5 kv dc)
Single-deck suburban

Class	Cars per unit	Trailer cars per unit	Control trailer cars per unit	Motor cars per unit	Motors per car	Rated output per motor kW	Max speed km/h	Tare weight tonnes	Seating capacity per car	Length over coupling faces mm	Acceleration m/s^2	Year first built	No in service 1988	Builders Mechanical parts	Electrical equipment
Motor car 1923	4	2*	—	2	2	205	—	51	71	19 399	NA	1925	14	Leeds Forge	Metropolitan Vickers
Motor 1927	4	2*	—	2	2	205	—	50.4	71	19 399	NA	1926	21	Govt Dockyard	Metropolitan Vickers
Trailer car 1927	4	2	2*	—	—	—	—	35.5	79	19 399	—	1926	14	Govt Dockyard	—
Motor car 1927	4	2*	—	2	2	205	—	50.4	76	19 399	NA	1928	17	Clyde Engineering	Metropolitan Vickers
Motor car 1927	4	2*	—	2	4	120	115	50.4	76	19 399	NA	1927	8	Clyde Engineering	Metropolitan Vickers & AEI
Motor car 1940	4	2*	—	2	2	205	—	50.2	64	19 757	NA	1941	17	Tullochs	Metropolitan Vickers
Motor car 1940	4	2*	—	2	4	120	115	50.2	64	19 757	NA	1951	3	Tullochs	Metropolitan Vickers & AEI
Trailer car 1940	4	2	2*	—	—	—	—	34	72	19 755	—	1940	5	Tullochs	—
Trailer car 1950	4	2	2*	—	—	—	—	34	72	19 755	—	1952	47	Tullochs	—
Motor car 1950	4	2*	—	2	4	120	115	50.8	56	19 757	NA	1952	41	Tullochs	Metropolitan Vickers & AEI
Motor car 1955	4	2*	—	2	4	123	115	52.5	59	19 856	NA	1957	32	Comeng	Metropolitan Vickers
Trailer car 1955	4	2	2*	—	—	8	115	33.7	70	19 856	—	1956	29	Comeng	—

* These cars do not belong to the class concerned
† Includes 9 parcels vans

Electric locomotives

Class	Wheel arrangement	line voltage	Rated output (kW) continuous one-hour	Max speed km/h	Weight tonnes	No in service 1988	Year first built	Builders Mechanical parts	Electrical equipment
46	Co-Co	1.5 kV dc	2533/2816	115	114	39	1956	Beyer Peacock	Metropolitan Vickers
85	Co-Co	1.5 kV dc	2700/2880	130	123	10	1979	Comeng	Mitsubishi
86	Co-Co*	1.5 kV dc	2700/2880	130	119	50	1983	Comeng	Mitsubishi

* One locomotive is Bo-Bo-Bo

RAILWAY SYSTEMS / Australia

Double-deck suburban electric multiple-units

Class	Cars per unit	Trailer cars per unit	Control trailer cars per unit	Motor cars per unit	Motors per car	Rated output per motor kW	Max speed km/h	Tare weight tonnes	Seating capacity per car	Length over coupling faces mm	Acceleration m/s²	No in service 1988	Year first built	Builders Mechanical parts	Builders Electrical equipment
Trailer car T4801-T4920	4	2	–	2*	–	–	–	32.5	132	20 218	–	119	1964	Tullochs	–
Motor car C3805-C3857	4	2*	–	2	4	135	115	45.4	112	20 218	0.8	52	1971	Comeng	Mitsubishi
Motor car C3858-C3911	4	2*	–	2	4	135	115	45	112	20 219	0.8	53	1973	Comeng	Mitsubishi
Control trailer D4011-D4020	2	–	1	1*	–	–	–	33.8	126	29 219	–	9	1973	Comeng	–
Trailer car T4921-T4962	4	2	–	2*	–	–	–	33.6	130	20 219	–	41	1973	Comeng	–
Motor car C3912-C3986	4	2*	–	2	4	135	115	45.4	112	20 219	0.8	75	1976	Comeng	Mitsubishi
Control trailer D4021-D4070	2	–	1	1*	–	–	–	33.8	114	20 219	–	50	1976	Comeng	–
Trailer car T4963-T4987	4	2	–	2*	–	–	–	33.6	130	20 219	–	25	1976	Comeng	–
Motor car C3001-C3080	4	2*	–	2	4	135	115	45	113	20 216	0.8	80	1978	A Goninan	Mitsubishi
Trailer car T4101-T4170	4	2	–	2*	–	–	–	33.6	130	20 217	–	70	1978	A Goninan	–
Motor car C3741-C3765	2	–	1*	1	4	135	115	45	112	20 219	0.8	25	1978	Comeng	Mitsubishi
Control trailer D4071-D4095	2	–	1	1*	–	–	–	33.8	114	20 219	–	25	1978	Comeng	Mitsubishi
Air-cond motor car C3501-C3504-& 3550	2	–	1*	1*	4	135	115	46.9	108	20 385	0.8	5	1981	A Goninan	Mitsubishi
Air-cond cont trailer D4096-D4099 & 4216	2	–	1	1*	–	–	–	41.2	108	20 385	–	5	1981	A Goninan	Mitsubishi
Force-ventilated motor car C3505-C3549/51-80	4	2*	–	2	4	135	115	46.9	106	20 385	0.8	75	1981	A Goninan	Mitsubishi
Forced ventilated trailer car T4171-T4215/17-46	4	2	–	2*	–	–	–	41.2	118	20 385	–	75	1981	A Goninan	Mitsubishi
Motor car C3581-3608 chopper	4	2	–	2	4	150	115	48.5	105	20 385	0.8	28	1985	A Goninan	Mitsubishi
Trailer T4247-74	4	2	–	2	–	–	–	40	116	20 385	–	28	1985	A Goninan	Mitsubishi
Tangara Chopper/GTO	4	–	2	2	4	170	115	M50 DT42.3	M116 DT106	20 220	0.6	450*	1988	A Goninan	Mitsubishi

* These cars do not belong to the class concerned

Double-deck interurban electric multiple-units

Class	Cars per unit	Trailer cars per unit	Control trailer cars per unit	Motor cars per unit	Motors per car	Rated output per motor kW	Max speed km/h	Tare weight tonnes	Seating capacity per car	Length over coupling faces mm	Acceleration m/s²	No in service 1988	Year first built	Builders Mechanical parts	Builders Electrical equipment
Trailer car DMT9201-DMT9211	4	2	–	2	–	–	130	40	92	23 965	–	11	Converted from motor car by NSW SRA in 1981-82		
Trailer car DFT9212-DFT9215	4	2	–	2*	–	–	130	40	96	23 965	–	4	Converted from control trailer by NSW SRA in 1981		
Motor car DCM8021-DCM8036	2	–	1*	1	4	140	130	59	88	23 968	0.65	15	1977	Comeng	Mitsubishi
Control trailer DCT9031-DCT9044	2	–	1	1*	–	–	130	39	94	23 968	–	14	1977	Comeng	Mitsubishi
Motor car DIM8037-92	4	2*	–	2	4	140	130	59	96	23 968	0.65	56	1980	Comeng	Mitsubishi
Trailer car DIT9101-38	4	2	–	2*	–	–	130	39	112	23 828	–	38	1980	Comeng	Mitsubishi
Motor car DOM8093-chopper	4	2	–	2	4	140	130	61	96	23 968	31	0.65	1986	Comeng	Mitsubishi
Trailer car DIT 9139-	4	2	–	–	–	–	130	44	112	23 828	34	–	1986	Comeng	Mitsubishi

* These cars do not belong to the class concerned

Single-deck interurban electric multiple-units

Class	Cars per unit	Trailer cars per unit	Control trailer cars per unit	Motor cars per unit	Motors per car	Rated output per motor kW	Max speed km/h	Tare weight tonnes	Seating capacity per car	Length over coupling faces mm	Cars in service 1988	Acceleration m/s²	Year first built	Builders Mechanical parts	Builders Electrical equipment
Motor car CF5001-CF5040	4	2*	–	2	4	123	115	50	52	20 574	36	–	1958	Comeng	Metro-Vickers
Trailer car TF6001-TF6020 ETB6021-ETB6040	4	2	–	2*	–	–	–	30	64	20 574	38	–	1958	Comeng	Metro-Vickers

* These cars do not belong to the class concerned

Diesel railcars or multiple-units

Class	Cars per unit	Motor cars per unit	Motored axles per motor car	Trans-mission	Rated power (kW) per motor	Max speed km/h	Weight tonnes per car (M-motor T-trailer)	Total seating capacity (M-motor T-trailer)	Length per car mm (M-motor T-trailer)	No in service 1988	Year first built	Builders Mechanical parts	Engine & type	Transmission
600/700	2	1	2	Hyd	114 × 2	101	M 30 T 22	M 32-60 T 50-50	19 380	4	1949	NSWGR	GM 6081	Allison
620/720	2	1	2	Hyd	164 × 2	105	M 38 T 26	M 48 T 54	19 380	2	1961	NSWGR	Rolls-Royce C8SFLH	Rolls-Royce
620/720	2	1	2	Hyd	186 × 2	116	M 38 T 26	M 28-48 T 54	19 380	7	1961	NSWGR	GM 62806	Allison
620/720	2	1	2	Hyd	212 × 2	122	M 38 T 26	M 28-48 T 54	19 380	3	1961	NSWGR	Cummins NTA855R4	Twin Disc
620/720	2	1	2	Hyd	227 × 2	122	M 39 T 26	M 48 T 54	19 380	5	1961	NSWGR	Cummins NTA855R4	Voith
660/760	2	1	2	Hyd	212 × 2	122	M 38 T 22	M 28-52 T 50-50	19 380	5	1973	NSWGR	Cummins NTA855R2	Twin Disc
900	3 or 4	2	2	Hyd	186 × 2	116	M 41 T 28	M 39-24 T 36-55	M 19 380 T 18 340	4	1951	NSWGR	GM 62808	Allison
900	3 or 4	2	2	Hyd	250 × 2	122	M 42 T 28	M 39-24 T 36-55	M 19 380 T 18 340	9	1951	NSWGR	Cummins NTA855R4	Nigata
900	3 or 4	2	2	Hyd	250 × 2	122	M 42 T 28	M 39-24 T 36-55	M 19 380 T 18 340	3	1951	NSWGR	Cummins NTA855R4	Voith
100	4 or 5	1	2	Hyd	186 × 4	121	M 64 T 25	M 0 T 41-52	M 19 775 T 17 488	3	1937	NSWGR	GM 62400	Allison
XPT	7							M 0 T 30-72	M 17 335 T 24 200	15	1981	Comeng	Paxman Valenta	Brush

Queensland Government Railways

Railway Centre, PO Box 1429, 305 Edward St, Brisbane, Queensland 4000

Telephone: +61 7 237 1947 (Transport Ministry)
+61 7 235 2222 (Railways)
Telex: AA 41514 gldrail
Telefax: +61 7 225 1799 (Transport Ministry)
+61 7 235 1799 (Railways)

Minister of Transport: David Hamill
Acting Director General of Transport: D G Stevenson
Acting Commissioner for Railways: R G Read
Assistant Commissioner, Projects & Planning: W J Adamson
Director, Planning & Development: D H Kane
Director of Projects: A M Drake
Chief Workshops Engineer: K W Wood
Assistant Commissioner, Commercial: K E Neil
Assistant Commissioner (Traffic Operations): E K Thomas
Southern Division
General Manager: B D Doyle
Central Division
General Manager: F C Simmonds
Northern Division
General Manager: K McElligott
Assistant Commissioner (Engineering): I M Nibloe
Chief Mechanical Engineer: B M Stephens
Chief Civil Engineer: F R Bell
Chief Signal and Telecommunications Engineer: T J Ellis
Chief Electrical Engineer: R J Galvin
Assistant Commissioner (Corporate Services): R J Mullins
Asistant Commissioner, Finance & Administration: R E Scheuber
Director of Administration: G Aitken
Acting Chief Financial Accountant: C T Henry
Chief Supply Manager: H W Smith
Assistant Commissioner, Special Duties: T J Parminter

Gauge: 1435 mm (inter-state line); 1067 mm
Route length: 111 km; 9983 km
Electrification: 1707 km of 1067 mm-gauge at 25 kV 50 Hz ac

Queensland Railways are the second longest in route-km in the British Commonwealth and are state-owned, serving the whole of the north-east part of Australia. The 1435 mm inter-state line connects Brisbane with Sydney, New South Wales.

Finance
Revenue earnings for 1988/89 totalled A$1 107.13 million, a new record and 11.7 per cent higher than the previous year's gross. Income from coal was at a record level of A$779.51 million, and revenue from agricultural produce was up 23.7 per cent on FY 1987-88.

All passenger services generated increased revenue. A rise of 18 per cent in Brisbane suburban income was largely attributable to World Expo 88 traffic.

Freight traffic
The aggregate of goods and livestock carried in 1988/89 was 80.51 million tonnes, an increase of 7.1 per cent or 5.34 million tonnes on the record haulage established during FY 1986-87. The commodity having the greatest impact was again coal, the haulage of which rose by 4 million tonnes compared to the previous year. Operation of the rising tonnage has been facilitated by extension of electrification and completion in 1989 of the delivery of 166 electric locomotives, the main task of which is to haul an average of over 1 million tonnes of coal weekly in Central Queensland. A quarter of the railway is now electrified and this moves 75 per cent of the gross freight tonnage and 99 per cent of the railway's passenger traffic.

In 1989 the state government took a controversial decision on future policy concerning rail transport of coal. In future concessionary pricing will be limited to new coal mines or major expansions of existing pits. The pill was sugared by the government's assumption of most of the costs in laying rail access to new mines, previously covered wholly by mineowners, but there was provision to claw back some of the cost in the event of a rise in coal prices.

Queensland Railways continues to respond to market demands and increased road transport competition by arranging for pick-up and delivery to customers' premises, where appropriate, to hold cost-effective business.

Container transportation has been a rapid growth business for Queensland Railways in recent years.

Brisbane suburban emu. *(Leon Oberg)*

Freight traffic

	1985/86	1986/87	1987/88	1988/89
Freight train-km million	26.003	25.739	24.4	23.2
Freight revenue earnings (A$ million)	905.5	960.95	910	1021.3
Freight tonnage (million)	73.599	75.169	74.9	80.5
Freight net tonne-km (million)	20 450	20 871	20 676	20 884
Average haul per tonne (km)	276.9	276.85	276.08	259.4
Average train load (tonnes)	1427	1487	1638	901

Containerised movement has been fostered particularly for exports of such commodities as cotton, seeds, grain, fruit and meat. As a result, 160 Type PCO skeletal container wagons have been acquired; these have an improved payload/tare ratio and higher speed capability than existing container wagons.

Upgrading of freight facilities continues. Major projects include the relocation of Roma Street Freight Terminal in 1991, a new marshalling yard at Portsmith near Cairns, and A$110 million investment in infrastructure, including signals and telecommunications.

Passenger traffic

Passenger journeys during 1988/89 totalled 50.94 million, yet again a record, exceeding the previous year by 10.2 per cent. While World Expo 88 stimulated much of the rise, there was a satisfying upward trend in long-distance travel.

The railway's flagship train, the 'Queenslander', running the 1 681km betwen Brisbane and Cairns, continues to impress international as well as Australian tourist travellers.

Electrification of the Brisbane-Rockhampton corridor spurred a 90 per cent upsurge in patronage. This was largely due to the new 'Spirit of Capricorn' train, which reduced journey times by a quarter.

Traction and rolling stock

The stock of locomotives in service at the end of February 1990 comprised 166 main-line electric, 410 diesel-electric and 71 diesel-hydraulic. There were 20 031 wagons in service at the end of February 1990, once more a substantial reduction compared with the previous year.

The number of carriages at the close of February 1990 had dropped further to 376, compared with 561 at June 1987 and 499 in February 1989. The decrease was brought about by the ongoing withdrawal from service of long-distance wooden passenger carriages.

A fleet of 88 three-car electric multiple-units was in use on the metropolitan passenger network. The 20 new cars for electric long-distance inter-city emus (ICE) were all operational by the end of February 1990.

Brisbane suburban electrification

The A$480 million 25 kV ac electrification of the metropolitan rail network was completed in February 1988, following commissioning of the link between Eagle Junction and Eagle Farm, a northside branch. The system covers 360 single-track km throughout Brisbane and surrounding areas.

Work will start in 1992 on a new 12.4 km branch from Petrie to Kippa-Ring in northeast Brisbane.

Passenger traffic

		1985/86	1986/87	1987/88	1988/89
Revenue (A$ million)	Country	13.54	12.70	13.8	N/A
	Suburban	26.987	31.59	43.32	49.94
Journeys (million)	Country	1.278	1.332	1.275	1.44
	Suburban	40.246	43.002	44.953	49.51

Main line electrification

Queensland Railways' A$1050 million, four-stage mainline electrification project was completed on schedule in July 1989. It involved the wiring of 2100 single-track km for the haulage of coal and grain in Central Queensland and of mixed freight and passenger services along the North Coast line between Rockhampton and Brisbane.

The lines have been electrified with a 25 kV ac 50 Hz overhead traction system slightly different to that adopted for the Brisbane suburban electrification, in order to allow greater spacing between feeder stations. Existing overhead communications routes have been replaced with an optical fibre-based underground communications system, used for both voice and data transmission. This is backed up by a microwave standby system for use in emergencies. Signalling has been updated and immunised.

The locomotives are 3000 kW Bo-Bo-Bos with a maximum axleload of 18 tonnes, featuring microprocessor control and Locotrol II equipment for remote radio control of slave units. The operating plan is based on 100 wagon-minimum trains, but provides for maximum gross loads of 148 wagons, hauled by up to five electric locomotives, three of which are 'slaves' marshalled mid-train and remotely controlled by radio from the driver in the leading locomotive. Of the 166 locomotives ordered, 39 have been equipped as Locotrol 'Command' units.

In 1990 consultants commissioned to study the matter recommended that the electrification be extended a further 1 042km, from Rockhampton to Cairns, and from Ipswich to Toowoomba.

Driver-Only operation

Driver-Only Operation (DOO) was introduced on electrically-powered trains between Brisbane and Rockhampton in October 1989. Extension to other areas was planned from early 1991. Tests are being conducted with single-manning of marshalling yard locomotives.

In association with the DOO project, CTC and ATP contracts for the Rockhampton-Mackay section were to be awarded in April 1990. CTC and ATP would be installed from Mackay to Townsville, and Ipswich to Toowoomba by early 1993.

Gold Coast Railway

Queensland Railways obtained government approval in November 1985 to proceed with a 160 km/h electric rail link from Brisbane to the Gold Coast, a thriving tourist centre 89 km by rail south-east of the capital. Detailed design and preliminary construction works began in 1990.

The line, to be built at an estimated cost of A$240 million, will be commissioned in 1994. It will run from the existing Brisbane suburban terminus of Beenleigh to a new station near Broadbeach on the Gold Coast, with four intermediate stations. The 85 km journey from Brisbane Central to Robina will take 65 minutes at a maximum speed of 160 km/h, which will entail upgrading part of the existing Brisbane-Beenleigh line; in addition, the 1435mm-gauge inter-state line betwen South Brisbane and Yeerongpilly will be dual-gauged to accommodate 1067mm-gauge Gold Coast trains. The new line will be electrified at 25 kV ac 50 Hz similarly to the existing Brisbane suburban system. A service frequency of 30 minutes in peak periods and one hour off-peak is proposed.

In 1990 tenders were invited for supply of 10 high-performance three-car emus for the new line. The design will be based on that of Brisbane's current suburban emus, but modified for higher performance and longer journeys.

Other projects

Mackay Railway relocation – Central Queensland: A 6.2 km long relocation of the North Coast Railway out of Central Mackay will eliminate 16 level crossings. It includes a new bridge over the Pioneer River, construction of the new Mackay station and the relocation of diesel servicing and wagon repair and goods handling facilities out of Mackay. Completion is set for early 1992. Total cost: A$54 million.

Stanwell Power Station Balloon Loop – Central East Queensland: A new 2.1km passing loop at Warren and a 5.1km balloon loop to cater for coal suply of the power station. Construction was scheduled to commence in July 1990 and finish by February 1992. Total cost: A$8.4 million.

Cook Colliery project – Central Queensland: The Cook Colliery is located approx 20 km south of Blackwater. Railway facilities are being upgraded to cater for an

Electric railcars

Class	Wheel arrangement	Line current	Rated output kW	Max kg	Tractive effort (full field) Continuous at		Max speed km/h	Wheel diameter mm	Total weight tonnes	Length mm	No in service 1989	Year first built	Builders Mechanical parts	Electrical equipment
					kg	km/h								
1979 emu	2 axle bogie	25 kV 50 Hz single phase	1080 (8 driving axles per set)	14 276	8668	50	100	840	Tare DM 40.74 M 42.22 DT 34.54	23 050	68	1979	Walkers Ltd	ASEA
1982 emu	2 axle bogie	25 kV 50 Hz single phase	810 (6 driving axles per set)	14 276	8668	50	100	840	DM 37 M 42 T 34.5	23 050	20	1983	Walkers Ltd	ASEA
1988 emu long distance	2 axle bogie	25 kV 50 Hz single phase	1080 (8 driving axles per two-car set)	10 700	6422	62	120	840	DM 30 M 47 T 36	23 050	6 + 2 trailers	1988	Walkers	ASEA

Electric locomotives

Class	Wheel arrangement	Line voltage (kV) 50 Hz	Rated output kW	Max kN	Tractive effort Continuous at		Max speed km/h	Wheel diameter mm	Total weight tonnes	Length mm	No in service 1989	Year first built	Builders Mechanical parts	Electrical equipment
					kN	km/h								
3100	Bo-Bo-Bo	25	2900	375	260	40	80	1067	109.8	20 396	86	1986	Comeng	Hitachi/GEC
3500	Bo-Bo-Bo	25	2900	375	260	40	80	1100	109.8	20 016	50	1986	ASEA/Walkers	ASEA/Clyde
3900	Bo-Bo-Bo	25	2900	300	210	50	100	1100	109.8	20 018	30	1988	ASEA/Walkers	ASEA/Clyde

Australia / **RAILWAY SYSTEMS**

expansion of export mining operations from 0.8 to 1.8 million tonnes per annum. Work has included double-tracking of 17 km of the North Coast Railway between Gladstone and Rockhampton, the acquisition of four electric locomotives and 92 90-tonne coal wagons and a new weighbridge at the mine. The project was finished in October 1989. Total cost: A$34 million.
Blair Athol Railway expansion project – Central West Queensland: Facilities are to be upgraded to cater for an expansion of export mining operations from 5 to 8 million tonnes per annum. Work includes the purchase of additional rolling stock (seven electric locomotives and 150 90-tonne wagons) and the carrying out of various track and railway facilities improvements. Work has commenced and is due for completion in late 1991; rolling stock will be delivered by May 1993. Total cost: A$52 million.
Ebenezer/Jeebropilly mines rail spur project – 56 km west of Brisbane: A new 8.4 km-long rail spur has been constructed to service the Ebenezer and Jeebropilly coal mines near Rosewood to cater for an initial maximum haulage of 2.2 million tonnes/year to the port at Fisherman Islands. The work was finished in January 1990. Total cost: A$12 million.
Cairns station redevelopment – North Queensland: Work involves the redevelopment of the existing Cairns Station site to include a shopping complex and new station facilities. The railway workshops and marshalling yard are being relocated in the suburb of Portsmith. Construction of station facilities was scheduled to commence in mid-1990 for completion in mid-1991. Total cost of Queensland Railways work: A$28 million.

Signalling, traffic control and communications

A continuing programme for the modernisation of signalling systems throughout the State has been undertaken in recent years. The 175 route-km of the Brisbane Metropolitan area have been completely resignalled and are now wholly operated from a central signalling complex at Mayne. This complex houses a 31 metre-long entrance-exit push-button signalling diagram console which incorporates a computer-based train describer system. In association with a double-track project of 22km betwen Kuraby and Beenleigh an IECC approach is to be progressively implemented at Mayne, together with a new PC-based train describer.

The remainder of the State railways are mainly single line, of which 4973 km is operated under train order regulations, 1249 km by a staff-and-ticket system, 1044 km by an electric train staff system, 1970 km by six computer-based CTC systems. The 250 km is double line operated by automatic colour-light signals or block telegraph signalling. Ericsson's Ericab 700 system of intermittent ATP is operative over 589km of the North Coast line between Caboolture and Rockhampton.

The six CTC systems govern predominantly single-track route. In 1990 design of two more, at Rockhampton and Mackay, was progressing in conjunction with the railway's DOO programme. This will lead to virtual extinction of electric staff and staff/ticket systems.

QR commissioned its first PC-based local traffic working scheme at Cairns marshalling yard in January 1990. All operator actions are initiated by use of PC mouse and colour VDU.

Use of dragging equipment detectors (DED) is being extended in the Rockhampton CTC area. Except for one paddle-type on trial, all are of the frangible bar kind. Nine of the new sites employ solar-powered radio telemetry links between DED and the nearest relay room.

In association with the electrification project significant improvements to the Department's telecommunication network have been achieved. This includes the latest optical fibre-based systems employing digital branching techniques and digital microwave radio systems. Microwave radio systems now cover some 2100 km, a significant portion of which parallels some of the above optical fibre-based systems. Both systems will be considerably extended over the next three years.

Radio is used extensively, with a UHF system on suburban electric stock providing continuous driver-to-control communications, VHF for driver wayside communications in country areas, a variety of UHF yard systems for shunting applications in major

New intercity emu on 'Spirit of Capricorn' service

Diesel locomotives

Class	Wheel arrangement	Transmission	Rated power hp (kW)	Tractive effort Max lb (kg)	Tractive effort Continuous at lb (kg)	Tractive effort Continuous at mph (km/h)	Max speed mph (km/h)	Wheel diameter in (mm)	Total weight tons	Length ft in (mm)	No built (in service 3.90)	Year first built	Builders Mechanical parts	Builders Engine & type	Builders Transmission
1170	A-1-A+ A-1-A	Elec	640 (477)	26 880 (12 200)	19 750 (8960)	9.6 (15.4)	50 (80)	36 (914)	60	41'6" (12 649)	12 (4)	1956	Walkers (Aust)	Cooper Bessemer (USA) FWA-6T	Australian Electrical Industries
1460 (1460-1501)	Co-Co	Elec	1310 (977)	54 432 (24 700)	50 820 (23 050)	7.5 (12.1)	50 (80)	40 (1016)	90	53'1⅜" (16 189)	42 (41)	1964	Commonwealth Eng (under sub-contract to Clyde Eng)	General Motors EMD (USA) 12-567C	General Motors EMD (USA) & Clyde Eng (Aust)
1502 1530	Co-Co	Elec	1500 (1119)	60 480 (27 430)	50 820 (23 050)	8.8 (14.1)	50 (80)	40 (1016)	90	52'7½" (16 034)	29 (29)	1967	Commonwealth Eng (under sub-contract to Clyde Eng)	General Motors 12-645 E	General Motors EMD (USA) & Clyde Eng (Aust)
1550 2400 2450 2470	Co-Co	Elec	1500 (1119)	60 480 (27 430)	50 820 (23 050)	8.7 (13.9)	50 (80)	40 (1016)	90	59'2¼" (18 040)	107 (105)	1972	Commonwealth Eng (under sub-contract to Clyde Eng)	General Motors EMD (USA) 12-645 E	General Motors EMD & Clyde Eng (Aust)
1600	Co-Co	Elec	838 (625)	41 500 (18 800)	30 000 (13 600)	7.8 (12.6)	50 (80)	37.5 (952)	61.5	44'2" (13 462)	18 (15)	1963	English Electric (Aust)	English Electric (UK) 6-CSRKT	English Electric (Aust and UK)
1620	Co-Co	Elec	838 (625)	41 500 (18 800)	30 000 (13 600)	7.8 (12.6)	50 (80)	37.5 (952)	62.5	45'5" (13 843)	34 (33)	1967	English Electric (Aust)	English Electric (UK) 6-CSRKT	English Electric (Aust and UK)
1700	Co-Co	Elec	875 (652)	39 650 (18 000)	33 600 (15 250)	7.1 (11.4)	50 (80)	37.5 (952)	59	43'10" (13 360)	12 (11)	1963	Commonwealth Eng (under sub-contract to Clyde Eng)	General Motors EMD (USA) 8-567CR	General Motors EMD (USA) Clyde Eng (Aust)
1720	Co-Co	Elec	1000 (746)	39 650 (18 000)	33 600 (15 250)	8.4 (13.5)	50 (80)	37.5 (952)	62.5	43'11⅜" (13 395)	58 (56)	1966	Commonwealth Eng (under sub-contract to Clyde Eng)	General Motors EMD (USA) 8-645E	Clyde Eng (Aust)
2100 2130 2150 2170 2141	Co-Co	Elec	2000 (1492)	64 500 (29 256)	50 820 (23 050)	11.5 (18.5)	50 (80)	40 (1016)	96	59'2¼" (18 040)	102 (101)	1970/72	Commonwealth Eng (under sub-contract to Clyde Eng)	General Motors EMD (USA) 16-645E	General Motors EMD (USA) Clyde Eng (Aust)
2600	Co-Co	Elec	2200 (1640)				50 (80)	38 (965)	96	62'3⅜" (18 894)	13 (13)	1983	Goninan	General Electric FDL12	General Electric
DH	B-B	Hyd	465 (347)	25 000 (11 350)	18 000 (8150)	6 (9.7)	50 (50)	36 (914)	40	36'5" (11 100)	73 (71)	1968 1970	Walkers Ltd (Aust)	Caterpillar D355 Series E	Voith L42 or U2 (West Germany)

480 RAILWAY SYSTEMS / Australia

marshalling yards, and VHF and UHF car-to-base systems. Electric and almost all diesel locomotives are at least VHF train radio-fitted and thereby have direct access with train controllers while en route. Because of the heavy demand on the VHF system, a dedicated UHF radio system is now being implemented for 'dark territory' operation beyond CTC limits.

Track
Standard rail: Flat bottom 60, 53, 50, 47, 41, 40, 31, 30 and 20 kg/m rail has been used throughout the State, dependent on line class. New construction has been standardised to 60 kg/m rail for heavy-haul lines, 50 kg/m as the normal main line standard and 41 kg/m for lighter trafficked lines
Joints: 6-hole bar fishplates
Welded rail: Rails are purchased in 27.4 m lengths and flashbutt welded at depot into lengths up to 110 m. Long-welded rails are laid in lengths up to 220 m on unplated track and to unrestricted lengths in plated track. Heavy-haul lines are continuously welded. Site welding is generally by the thermite process though extensive work using a mobile flash-butt welding machine has been undertaken
Tracklaying: Relay of track is predominantly carried out by tracklaying machine
Sleepers: Mostly unimpregnated local hardwood timber 2150 × 230 × 115 mm or 150 mm thick on the older heavy-haul lines. Prestressed concrete sleepers are used extensively for new construction including heavy-haul lines. Steel sleepers have been installed on central west and other branch lines. Extensive installation of treated timber sleepers has also been undertaken in recent years.
Sleeper spacing: Normally 610 mm in main line or heavy haul tracks for timber, 685 mm for concrete and steel
Fastenings: Normal standard 16 mm square dogspikes and springspikes with 115 mm thick timber sleepers. 19 mm square dogspikes used with 150 mm thick timber sleepers and indirect fasteners on curves used on older heavy-haul lines. The use of elastic rail spikes has now been discontinued. Indirect fastenings are used with concrete and steel sleepers
Ballast: Mainly crushed rock in new work but river gravel used on some branch lines
Max curvature: Generally minimum radius of 100 m though new construction to 300 m radius at least
Max gradient: Generally not exceeding 1 in 50
Max altitude: 925 m near Cairns, North Queensland
Max permitted speed: General freight and heavy-haul unit trains, 60 km/h. Long-distance passenger traffic, 100 km/h for the premier 'Queenslander' service and 80 km/h for the 'Sunlander'. 80 km/h for fast freight, but 100 km/h under consideration in 1990; 100 km/h for electric multiple-units operating on the Brisbane suburban rail network. Interurban emus operate at 120 km/h between Brisbane and Rockhampton.
Max axleload: 22.5 tonnes on some mineral wagons
Bridge loading: All bridges on important lines can carry loading equivalent to Coopers E25-E30. Many equivalent to Coopers E35 and most new construction to this standard. Heavy-haul mineral lines have bridges built to carry Coopers E50 loading

Interior of new intercity emu

The 'Queenslander', electrically hauled, leaves Brisbane Transit Centre on its 1681km run to Cairns

Diesel railcars

Class	Wheel arrangement	Transmission	Rated power hp (kW)	Max speed mph (km/h)	Wheel diameter in (mm)	Total weight tons (tonnes)	Length ft in (mm)	No built (in service 3.90)	Year first built	Builders Mechanical parts	Builders Engine & type	Builders Transmission
1900	2 axle bogie	2 off epicyclic 4 speed gearbox	2 × 125 (2 × 93)	50 (80)	33 (838)	40 (40.64)	57'8" (17 577)	2 passenger luggage (1)	1956	Commonwealth Engineering under licence to Budd Car Co	AEC 9.6 litre horizontal	Self Changing Gears Ltd Type R14
2000	2 axle bogie	Epicyclic 4 speed gearbox	150 (112)	50 (80)	33 (838)	25 (25.4)	56'9" (17 297)	40 passenger	1956	Commonwealth Engineering	AEC 11-38 12.5 litre horizontal: four cars re-engined with Rolls Royce C6 150 HR	Self Changing Gears Ltd Type R14

Australia / **RAILWAY SYSTEMS** 481

South Australia State Transport Authority

PO Box 2351, 136 North Terrace, Adelaide, South Australia 5001

Telephone: +61 8 218 2200
Telex: 87115 stadel
Telefax: +61 8 211 7614

Chairman: J D Rump
General Manager: John V Brown
Director, Operations: Bob Heath
  Engineering: H Kong Ng
  Finance: Ian Fitzgerald
  Human Resources: Philip Bedford
  Corporate Services: Adrian Gargett
Train Operations Manager: Jim Kewley
Operational Planning Manager: Dick Gleeson
Supply Manager: Lindsay Lugg
Chief Mechanical Engineer: Dean Phillips
Electrical Engineer: George Erdos
Permanent Way Engineer: Ian Domleo
Signals Engineer: Lee Tran

Gauge: 1600 mm
Length: 127 route-km

Since the 1978 transfer of the country railway system of the State to the Australian National Railways, the Authority controls only the metropolitan railway system of Adelaide. This is used by freight services to and from the country system as well as by suburban rail services, which are integrated with the bus and tram services also run by the Authority in the city.

New 3000/3100 class railcars

Interior of 3000 class railcar

Passenger journeys (000)

	1985/86	1986/87	1987/88
Full fare	3317	3144.5	1802·4
Discount fare	2842	2636.8	2680·8
Concession fare	4511	5467.1	4103·6
Free	2229	550	64·2
Total	12 899	11 798.4	8651·0

Diesel railcars or multiple-units

Class (Railway's own designation)	Cars per unit	Motor cars per unit	Axles per motor car	Transmission	Rated power (kW) per motor	Max speed km/h	Weight tonnes per car (M-motor T-trailer)	Total seating capacity per car (M-motor T-trailer)	Length per car mm	No in service 1989	Year first built	Builders Mechanical parts	Builders Engine & type	Builders Transmission
300 motor (driving)	2	2	2	Hydraulic torque convertor/	163.4 × 2	90	M10.7	M86	20 013	26	1955	S Aust Railway W/shops, Islington	GM 6.71	Twin Disc
				Direct drive	170.8 × 2	90	M42.7	M86	20 015	6	1959		RR C65FLH	
					156.7 × 2	90	M41.9	M84	20 015	12	1968		GM 6.71	
400 motor (driving)	1	1	2	Hydraulic torque convertor/	163.4 × 2	90	M42.6	M80	20 015	17	1959	S Aust Railway W/shops, Islington	GM 6.71	Twin Disc
				Direct drive	156.7 × 2	90		M78		17	1968			
2300 motor (driving)	3	2	2	Hydraulic torque convertor/ Direct drive	163.4 × 2	90	M45.8	M96	20 015	2	1955	Rebuilt S.T.A.	CM 6.71	Nigata
2500 Trailer (non-driving)	3	2	—	—	—	—	T39	T39	16 980	1	1949	Rebuilt S.T.A.	—	—
2000 motor (driving)	1 × 2000 with 1 or 2 × 2100	1	4	Hydraulic torque convertor two-stage	360 × 2	110	M68	M64	2550	12	1980	Comeng Aresco	MAN 03050 HM7U	Voith
2100 Trailer (driving)	1 or 2 × 2100 with 1 × 2000	1	—	—	—	—	T42	T106	2550	18	1980	Comeng Aresco	—	—
3000 motor (driving)	1	1	2	Elec	354 × 1	100	M48.2	M105	20 174	8	1987	Comeng Sth Aust	Mercedes Benz OM444LA	Stromberg
3100 motor (driving)	2	2	2	Elec	354 × 1	100	M46·8	M113	25 737	12	1988	Comeng Sth Aust	Mercedes Benz OM444LA	Stromberg

482 RAILWAY SYSTEMS / Australia

Finances (A$000)

Revenue	1985/86	1986/87	1987/88
Passengers and baggage	10 053	11 143	11 374
Other income	4504	3289	3996
Total	14 557	14 437	15 370

Expenditure	1985/86	1986/87	1987/88
Staff/personnel	27 380	28 073	31 759
Materials and services	15 990	12 999	12 198
Depreciation	2858	3239	4017
Financial charges	7486	9121	12 309
Total	53 714	53 432	60 283

Ticketing
A new automatic fare collection system by Crouzet, electronically-based and using magnetic-striped tickets that encode conditions of ticket validity, was commissioned in September 1987. Two main ticket types, single-journey cash fare and ten-journey multi-strip, are sold. Within set time limits the tickets allow transfer between vehicles anywhere in the system.

Traction and rolling stock
The Authority operates four steam locomotives and 29 historic passenger cars (for historic/special purposes only), 112 diesel railcars and 19 trailers. All railcars are equipped both with public address and for uhf radio communication with Adelaide Train Control. In peak traffic periods, cars are formed into two power and three trailer car formations; maximum load for two power cars is four trailers.

In 1988 Comeng (SA) completed delivery of 20 Class 3000/3100 diesel-electric railcars, comprising eight single and six twin-units, all air conditioned. The cars have Mercedes engines, Strömberg transmissions and Linke-Hofmann-Busch fabricated bogies. At the end of 1989 Comeng (SA) was awarded a A$142.9 million contract to supply 50 more cars compatible with Class 3000/3100 for delivery over a seven-year period. They will replace the elderly 'Red Hen' cars.

The Class 2000 railcars are being equipped with 'Metromiser' units, a development by STA and Techsearch Pty Ltd, which advises drivers on the best driving strategy to minimise fuel consumption.

Engineering
Resignalling of the whole of the Adelaide metropolitan rail system, commenced in 1985, continued at an estimated total cost of A$43 million. The first stage of the work, involving two routes and including remote control, was commissioned in November 1986. The second stage, which includes a solid state interlocking system (SSI) for Adelaide station yard, the first of its kind in Australia, was completed in late 1988. The SSI system was supplied by Westinghouse Brake & Signal Co (UK) as sub-contractor to the Joint Venture group.

The Joint Venture Group of O'Donnell Griffin of South Australia and ML Engineering has the resignalling contract for the third phase, covering two lesser routes.

Westinghouse Brake & Signal Co (Aust) have been awarded a contract for the computerised train describer/passenger information/remote control systems which will provide real-time train information using synthesised voice announcements.

The remote control and train describer components are operational on the already resignalled lines. The Management Information System should be completed at the same time as the third phase of the resignalling.

Coupler in standard use: Knuckle automatic; and Scharfenberg fully automatic

Track:
Rail: Australian Standard 47, 53 and 60 kg/m rail
Cross ties (sleepers): Hardwood timber 2600 × 260 × 130 mm; steel (BHP M7-5 section) 2595 × 260 × 98 mm
Spacing: 1400/km plain track and curves
Fastenings: 19 mm^2 dogspike with sleeper plates. Elastic fastenings on steel sleepers, points and crossings
Minimum curvature radius: 200 mm
Max gradient: 2.22%
Max axleload: 23 tonnes

The Emu Bay Railway Co Ltd
A subsidiary of Pasminco Ltd

PO Box 82, Wilson Street, Burnie, Tasmania 7320

Telephone: +61 4 30 4211
Telex: 59034
Telefax: +61 4 30 4230

Chairman & Chief Executive: P C Barnett
Manager, Operations: L Beaumont

Traffic

	1984/85	1985/86	1986/87
Freight tonnage	371 240	395 637	428 432
Freight tonne-km	43 234 622	44 927 022	49 282 643
Average net freight train load (tonnes)	1547	1583	NA
Passenger-km	6104	5194	2700
Passenger journeys	53	46	22

Gauge: 1067 mm
Route length: 133 km (143 track-km)

Traction and rolling stock
The company operates 12 diesel locomotives and 99 vacuum-braked freight wagons

Track
Rails are 31 and 41 kg/m, permitting a 14.5 tonnes maximum axleload. Sleepers are untreated wood of 130 mm thickness, spaced 1640/km and rails are fastened with elastic spikes. Maximum gradient is 1 in 33 and minimum curvature 100 metres.

Diesel locomotives

Class	Wheel arrangement	Transmission	Rated power kW	Max speed km/h	Total weight tonnes	No in service 1988	Year first built	Builders Mechanical parts	Engine & type	Transmission
21	D	Hyd	480	40	44	1	1953	North British	Paxman 12YHXL	Voith L37V
10	B-B	Hyd	480	48	53	4	1963 & 1966	Walkers	Paxman 12YHXL or Caterpillar D398B	Voith L37ZUB
11	B-B	Hyd	530	48	55	7	1970-71	Walkers	Caterpillar D398B	Voith L27ZUB

Victoria Public Transport Corporation

Transport House, 589 Collins Street, Melbourne, Victoria 3000

Telephone: +61 3 619 1111
Telex: 33801
Telefax: +61 3 619 2343

Chief Executive, Public Transport Authority: Ian Stoney
General Manager, Project Resources: F Wagner
  Industrial Relations & Personnel: B Shaw
  Information Technology: E Atkinson
  Corporate Strategy: C Malan
  Corporate Services: L Harkin
  Budget & Finance: P C Wade
  Workshops: J Barry
  Development Projects: G Spring
Chief Engineer: G Swift
Manager, Special Projects: G Carkeek
Chief General Manager, V/Line: T Mulligan
  General Manager, Freight: F Tait
    Passenger: J Hearsch
    Infrastructure: A Hurse
Chief General Manager, The Met: R Terrell
  General Manager, Commercial: N Walker
    Trains: D Watson
    Works & Services: G Brover

Two Class C Co-Cos and empty Sydney-Melbourne auto carrier train *(Hugh Ballantyne)*

Australia / **RAILWAY SYSTEMS** 483

In July 1983 the State government disbanded the State's eight existing transport authorities, including VicRail, and replaced them with four new authorities: a Metropolitan Transit Authority for urban and suburban train, tram and bus services; a State Transport Authority for all non-metropolitan public transport; a road safety and licensing authority; and a road construction authority. Further legislation in 1989 abolished the Metropolitan Transit and State Transport Authorities and from July 1989 the Public Transport Corporation became their successor in law. However, V/Line and The Met continue as trading names and as separate divisions of the Public Transport Corporation.

V/Line

Gauge: 1600 mm; 1435 mm
Route length: 5047 km; 330 km

V/Line is responsible for the provision, maintenance and operation of the network of rail lines that serve the State of Victoria and its interstate services.

Traffic	1986/87	1987/88	1988/89
Freight tonnes (million)	10.597	10.901	9.95
Freight tonne-km (million)	3216	NA	NA
Passenger journeys (million)	5.22	5.478	5.825

Finance
Operating revenue in FY1988-89, at A$294.2 million, was 0.9 per cent down on the previous year. Passenger income was up 6.3 per cent, but a poor grain harvest and depressed consumer demand combined to cut freight revenue by 5.6 per cent. Operating expenses rose by A$153.6 million; abnormal rises in pensions liabilities were responsible for 83.5 per cent of this increase. Capital expenditure totalled A$96.9 million, A$2.3 million less than in the previous year.

Finance (A$ million)

Revenues	1986/87	1987/88	1988/89
Passengers and baggage	42.63	41.54	46.13
Freight, parcels and mail	174.73	163.2	153.56
Other income	28.89	391.78	413.47
Total	246.25	596.53	613.16

Expenditure	1986/87	1987/88	1988/89
Staff/personnel	124.57	295.98	253.64
Materials and services	128.03	23.26	25.74
Depreciation	18.99	26.49	30.09
Financial charges	65.38	20.55	11.99
Total	320.84	326.28	321.46

Freight services
Freight services have been progressively rationalised and now a network of 25 regional freight centres, known as Freightgates, is served from Melbourne by Fast Track overnight freight trains and road vehicles. Highway trucks deliver and collect freight from the centres privately under contract. Freight is palletised as much as possible. FY1988-89 was marked by a 33 per cent increase of Fast Track less-than-carload traffic, sharply reversing a decline in this business throughout the earlier 1980s. Over the Fast Track sector as a whole there was a 9 per cent growth.

Grain comprises around 24 per cent of annual freight revenue, as V/Line is one of the few Australian railways which lacks large bulk coal or mineral traffic. Other important freights include industrial raw materials and finished goods railed over the inter-state trunk routes linking Melbourne with Sydney and Adelaide. Moving in trainloads over relatively long hauls, this traffic represents 46 per cent of V/Line's annual freight. It is subject to fierce road competition, but the 1982 repeal of the State Transport Authority's (STA) common carrier duty now makes possible a more flexible and selective response. Heavy industrial traffic hit a budgeted FY1988-89 financial target that was set 16 per cent above the previous year. Performance was particularly strong in conveyance of slab steel, cement and motor vehicles, thanks to the buoyancy of these industries; contracts won included a Ford deal for transport of vehicles to Sydney and Brisbane.

Strongest performer in FY1988-89 was intermodal traffic, which has exhibited real growth for five successive years and now contributes 27 per cent of V/Line freight revenue. Container traffic produced 28 per cent more revenue than in the previous year. An important factor in this intermodal success has been the development of dedicated Superfreighter train service between state capital cities. This was further expanded with a second daily Melbourne-Adelaide working in late 1988, and with a second Melbourne-Sydney train operating three times a week. V/Line's fleet of container cars is to be progressively renewed with a new design of articulated three-pack wagon. Four prototypes were operational in 1989.

New Class G 2237kW locomotive on unit aggregates train. *(Leon Oberg)*

Dimboola-Melbourne train of new air-conditioned cars headed by a 1715kW Class N locomotive. *(Leon Oberg)*

Class T locomotive re-engined by Clyde Engineering as Class P *(Colin Underhill)*

Passenger services

During FY 1988/89 the total number of passengers carried by V/Line road and rail services rose for the seventh successive year to a new post-1955 record of 5.8 million. In seven years patronage has risen by close on 65 per cent.

The seven-year traffic growth on commuter services has been still higher, at 78 per cent. As a result, six new passenger cars were taken into service and bids invited for supply of 24 new diesel railcars, planned to enter service in 1992-93. The Transport Minister said in the 1989 summer that V/Line might adopt a design derived from British Rail's 'Sprinter' dmus.

Motive power and rolling stock

Diesel locomotives 287; diesel railcars 10; diesel trailers 4; passenger coaches, wholly owned or jointly owned with ANR and SRA/NSW: 255 (including 32 buffet, 5 restaurant and 61 sleeping cars); freight wagons 4236.

In December 1986 an order was placed with Clyde Engineering for 11 Class G locomotives and a subsequent order was placed for seven more. Ten of these units were delivered in 1989 to supersede withdrawn Class S and T locomotives.

Signalling and telecommunications

In 1988 a specification was drafted for an A$20 million Computerised Absolute Block System (CABS). This now provides a radio-controlled electronic train order system throughout the railway's low-density routes.

Other works recently executed include power signalling installations at Rockbank, Melton and Melbourne terminal; power signalling was then to be installed in Bendigo and Ballarat yards.

An integrated Service Digital Network (ISDN) has been extended to all major Regional centres to interconnect local PABX systems and provide in-house direct dial facilities throughout the State.

Track

Standard rail: Flat-bottomed 47, 53 and 60 kg/m rail rolled in 13.72 m lengths
Cross ties (sleepers)
Timber: Non-treated Australian hardwoods (Red Gum, Ironbark, Box Stringbark and Messmate)
Dimensions: 1600 mm gauge 2705 × 250 × 125 mm; 1435 mm gauge 2590 × 250 × 125 mm
Spacing: 685 mm centres
Concrete: Prestressed concrete with cast-iron shoulders to take Pandrol rail clips
Dimensions: 2670 × 275 × 145 mm at midspan (208 mm deep at ends). Rail seat canted at 1 in 20
Spacing: 670 mm centres

Fastenings

Timber: Most track fastened with dogspikes. Sleeper plates used on all tracks except 60 lb/yd branch lines, double shouldered and canted at 1 in 20. 'Fair' deep bow one-piece rail anchors used instead of pads. Approx 150 km of track relaid in 60 kg/m rail on rolled double-shoulder sleeper plates with Pandrol clips and 3 lock spikes per rail foot
Concrete: Pandrol rail clips, rail pads and insulators used on 53 and 60 kg/m rail laid on concrete sleepers
Ballast: Generally broken stone, usually volcanic basalt, but granite, rhyodicite and diabase also used. For rail lengths up to 27 m, 250 mm bearing depth with 50 mm shoulder width. For long or continuously welded rail, 300 mm deep with 405 mm shoulder width

Max gradient

Main line: 2.08% = 1 in 48
Branch line: 3.33% = 1 in 30
Trackwork design standards: Curves of less than 2400 m radius transitioned. Main-line curves for 100 km/h traffic to be 830 m radius minimum, while for 50 km/h main-line traffic minimum radius should be 400 m
Max altitude: 591.3 m near Wallace, Melbourne-Serviceton line
Welded rail: Standard 13.72 m rail lengths welded into 27.5–82 m lengths at the central flashbutt welding depot, Spotswood. Once laid, rails thermit-welded into 328 m lengths or continuously welded rail. Stress control measures taken during field welding to ensure the continuously welded rail is in an unstressed condition within the temperature range of 33–38°C
Max axleload: 22.36 tonnes on Class C diesel-electric locomotives

Diesel locomotives

Class	Mfr's type	Wheel arrangement	Transmission	Rated power kW	Max speed km/h	Total weight tonnes	Length mm	No in service 1.1.90	Year first built	Builders Mechanical parts	Builders Engine & type	Builders Transmission
A	AAT22C-2R	Co-Co	Elec	1840	133	121	18 542	11	1983*	Clyde	GM 12-645E3B	GM
B	ML-2	Co-Co	Elec	1190	133	123	18 542	12	1952	Clyde	GM 16-567B	GM
C	GT26C	Co-Co	Elec	2460	133	134	20 573	10	1977	Clyde	GM 16-645E3B	GM
G	JT26C-255	Co-Co	Elec	2460	115	127	20 684	33	1984	Clyde	GM 16-645E3B	GM
H	G188	Bo-Bo	Elec	820	100	81	13 386	5	1968	Clyde	GM 8-645E	GM
N	JT22C HC-2	Co-Co	Elec	1840	115	124	20 034	25	1985	Clyde	GM 12-645E3B	GM
P	G18HB-R	Bo-Bo	Elec	826	100	77	14 554	13	1984*	Clyde	GM 8-645E	GM
S	A-7	Co-Co	Elec	1450	133	123	18 567	14	1957	Clyde	GM 16-567C	GM
T	G88	Bo-Bo	Elec	710/826	100	69	13 386	67	1959	Clyde	GM 8-567CR or 8-645E	GM
X	–	Co-Co	Elec	1450/1640	133	118	18 364	24	1966/74	Clyde	GM 16-567E or 16-645E	GM
Y	–	Bo-Bo	Elec	480	64	68	13 182	73	1963	Clyde	GM 6-567C or 6-645E	GM

* Rebuilt

Diesel railcars

Class	Cars per unit	Motored axles per unit	Transmission	Rated power kW	Max speed km/h	No of seats (M-motor T-trailer)	Total weight tonnes	Length mm	No in service 1.1.90	First built	Builders Mechanical parts	Builders Engine	Builders Transmission
DRC	1	2	Hyd	400	140	56	60	18 339	4	1971	Tulloch	Two Cummins NT 855R	Voith T113R
DERM	1	2	Elec	185	110	34/54/61	45	24 105	4	1928	VicRail	Twin Detroit 6-71	GE 239 TM

Electric railcars or multiple-units

Class	No of cars per unit	Line voltage (dc)	Motor cars per unit	Motored axles per motor car	Rated output (kW) per motor	Max speed km/h	Weight tonnes per car (M-motor T-trailer)	Total seating capacity per car (M-motor T-trailer)	Length per car mm (M-motor T-trailer)	No of sets in service 1.9.90	Year first built	Builders Mechanical parts	Builders Electrical equipment
Hitachi	6	1.5 kV	4	4	112	115	52M 36T	88M 96T	M&T 22.9	58	1972	Martin & King	Hitachi
Comeng	6	1.5 kV	4	4	137	115	50M 34T	98M 106T	M&T 22.9	95	1981	Comeng	GEC
Rebuilt Harris	4	1.5 kV	2	4	107	115	39M 34T	65M 80T	M&T 18.63	4			

The Met

60 Market Street, Melbourne 3000, Victoria

Telephone: +61 3 610 8888
Telex: AA 151929
Telefax: +61 3 610 8140

Gauge: 1600 mm
Route length: 330 km
Electrification: 330 km at 1.5 kV dc

The Met is Australia's largest integrated public transport undertaking. About a third of the 306 million passenger journeys it registers annually are on rail.

A feature of The Met's 15-route system is the four-track, three-station underground loop beneath Melbourne's commercial centre. Each of the four tracks (all of which are reversibly signalled) is associated with a suburban service group. Combined with the six tracks threading Flinders Street and Spencer Street main stations, the loop establishes a circuit affording access to or from any route in the suburban system. Two short routes to Port Melbourne and St Kilda were converted to standard-gauge LRT in 1987-88, and are

Australia / **RAILWAY SYSTEMS** 485

operated by 20 LRVs. A similar conversion of the Upfield line is now under study, together with adoption of a new design of low-floor LRV.

Signalling and traffic control
The loop and the greater part of the suburban network is under the unitary control of a computer-based signalling centre located near Flinders Street, known as Metrol, which has train describer apparatus by L M Ericsson; Metrol operators work with individual control panels and vdu displays of track state and occupation. Emu power cars are being progressively equipped for radio communication with Metrol.

The bulk of the network is double-track which is automatic-signalled for left-hand running with coloured light or searchlight signals.

Rolling stock
The suburban services have been re-equipped with Comeng-built stainless-steel bodied six-car emus under an A$108.5 million order covering 95 sets of 380 power cars and 190 trailers. The order was completed in June 1989. The Met's suburban fleet is presently completed by 58 Hitachi emus, but acquisition of a stock of new bi-level emus for the Ringwood and Dandenong lines was under study in 1989-90.

Emu maintenance is being decentralised from the Jolimont yard to four new depots, of which Epping was ready in 1989. The outcome will be creation of four separate emu fleets.

MTA (Victoria) air-conditioned emu by Comeng

Track
Existing
Rail: 53 kg to AS 1085 Part 1-1981
Cross ties (sleepers): Timber
Thickness: 125 mm
Spacing: 1500/km plain track and curves
Rail fastenings: Dogspike

New (introduced 1980)
Rail: 60 kg to AS 1085 Part 1-1981
Cross ties (sleepers): Concrete
Thickness: 200 mm
Spacing: 1500/km plain track and curves
Rail fastenings: Pandrol clips

Minimum curvature radius: 9.7° (180 m)
Max gradient: 3%
Max axleload: 22 tonnes

Western Australian Government Railways (Westrail)

Westrail Centre, West Parade, East Perth, Western Australia (PO Box S1422, GPO Perth, WA 6001)

Telephone: +61 9 326 2222
Telex: 92879
Telefax: +61 9 326 2589

Minister of Transport: Mrs Pam Beggs
Commissioner: Dr J Gill
Executive Director, Urban Rail Development: J F Hoare
General Manager, Business Development: J R Sutton
 Finance: R D Collister
 Engineering: T Field
Director, Rail Operations: M G Baggott
 Marketing: R Drabble
Manager, Human Resources: L A Leeder
Secretary for Railways: F D Munyard

Gauge: 1067 mm; 1435 mm; dual gauge
Route length: 4169 km; 1212 km; 172 km

Westrail is the trading name of the Western Australian Government Railways Commission, a statutory authority. Its primary activity is rail freight, but the changing nature of the freight industry is making Westrail more flexible in use of complementary modes.

Passenger services are provided by interstate and country trains, and by country road coaches. The Perth metropolitan rail service is owned by Westrail and operated for Transperth under contract.

Performance
Financial year 1988/89 continued Westrail's progress. The commercial deficit was wound back for the fifth successive year, this time from A$17.2 million in the previous year to A$6.0 million. Total revenue was up A$40.4 million thanks to significant improvement in results from the agricultural sector, interstate freight and coal.

The conventionally reported result (which includes community services) decreased by A$44.4 million to A$32.9 million prior to adjustment for an extraordinary item of A$1690 million, which was related to accrued costs of superannuation.

Freight
Westrail's dominant business, freight, raised tonnage by 9 per cent to 24.3 million in 1988/89, when the railway carried more than at any time in its history. Achievements included an all-time weekly record grain haulage of 202 000 tonnes, and high or even record levels of fertiliser, minerals and interstate freight were also recorded. Real growth was experienced in all

The 'Prospector' heads for Kalgoorlie

Class DB and N locomotives with unit alumina train of Type XF wagons loading at Alcoa refinery, Pinjarra; unit trains are now worked with two-man crews

business segments. This was attributed to the sustained high prices obtainable for most internationally-traded commodities, which prompted local producers to maximise output or even expand their production capacity.

Of a total state grain harvest of 5.8 million tonnes,

RAILWAY SYSTEMS / Australia

Westrail carried 4.5 million. Westrail has been required under a five-year Grain Agreement to achieve competitive freight rates; in conformity with this provision there was an average 3.2 per cent cut which conferred a benefit of some 11 per cent on farmers consigning their grain by rail.

In bulk commodity markets large quantities of raw and refined materials and consumables are conveyed by rail between mines, processing plants and ports. Industrial revival in the international economy created a strong demand in virtually all areas of this business segment.

The alumina industry performed at or close to capacity. Westrail services the industry's processing plants at Kwinana, Pinjarra, Wagerup and Worsley.

Coal tonnage rose substantially because coal-fired power stations were meeting more of the domestic energy need following large export sales of the State Energy Commission's surplus of natural gas. Further growth was anticipated.

There was an unprecedented number of enquiries for transport specifications as inputs to feasibility studies for prospective resource projects in the south of the state. Several of these were expected to yield Westrail major bulk hauls in the 1990s.

Passenger operations

The total number of passenger journeys on interstate and country trains and country road coaches rose 8 per cent in FY 1988/89.

The 'Australind' train operating between Perth and the south-west city of Bunbury was regularly required to run with all five railcars during holiday periods. The Perth-Kalgoorlie 'Prospector' also attracted new traffic, to the extent that at times it had to be supplemented by road coaches. Passenger numbers on the trans-continental 'Indian Pacific' and 'Trans Australian' were up by 5 per cent.

The 'Australind' is run by a formation of five new Comeng-built diesel-hydraulic railcars each powered by a 496 hp Cummins under-floor engine driving through Voith transmission and operating at up to 110 km/h. Each car weighs 46 tonnes.

Suburban passenger numbers during 1988/89 were 9.6 million. This was a small decrease on the previous year.

Perth suburban electrification

In February 1988 the government announced its intention to proceed with electrification of Perth's suburban passenger services and work commenced. The first line to be wired is the Armadale, which will be followed by lines to Midland and Fremantle. Electric operation (at 25 kV ac) was to be ready for launch on the first converted route during 1990 and on the other two by mid-1991.

Walkers-ASEA Pty won a A$66 million order for 21 air-conditioned emus, to be delivered by end-1990. In

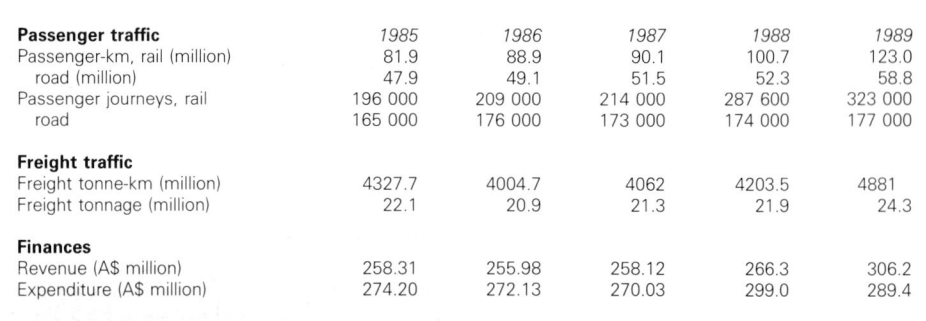

	1985	1986	1987	1988	1989
Passenger traffic					
Passenger-km, rail (million)	81.9	88.9	90.1	100.7	123.0
road (million)	47.9	49.1	51.5	52.3	58.8
Passenger journeys, rail	196 000	209 000	214 000	287 600	323 000
road	165 000	176 000	173 000	174 000	177 000
Freight traffic					
Freight tonne-km (million)	4327.7	4004.7	4062	4203.5	4881
Freight tonnage (million)	22.1	20.9	21.3	21.9	24.3
Finances					
Revenue (A$ million)	258.31	255.98	258.12	266.3	306.2
Expenditure (A$ million)	274.20	272.13	270.03	299.0	289.4

Goninan-built Type ADL diesel-hydraulic railcars in Transperth livery on Perth suburban service

1990 the order was extended by 22 sets, delivery to be completed in late 1992.

In December 1988 a second project of equal magnitude, the construction of a new 25 km line to Joondalup, Perth's northern suburbs, was announced. Westrail is responsible for executing both projects, which will cost A$250-300 million in all.

In 1990 the Transport Minister moved for a further new line construction south of the city, from Rockingham to Mandurab.

Motive power and rolling stock

The end of FY 1988/89 saw the locomotive fleet standing at 82 narrow-gauge and 32 standard-gauge diesel-electric main-line units, along with 36 shunters.

A contract for the supply of 16 1967mm-gauge Class P 2000kW main-line locomotives (the makers' designation is CM25-8) was awarded to A Goninan and delivery began in December 1989, thereafter continuing at the rate of one unit a month. Destined to replace 21 old locomotives, the new units are the first General Electric 'Dash 8' narrow-gauge locomotives in Australia. They incorporate the latest proven microprocessor control and diesel engine technology, and feature automatically-adjusted wheel-slip control.

Westrail operates 41 diesel railcars and 35 trailers, and 5848 freight wagons.

Communications and signalling

The year's work programme included significant support infrastructure for the planning and design of the Perth's suburban electrification.

Main-line diesel locomotives: 1067 mm gauge

Class	Wheel arrangement	Transmission	Rated power kW	Max kN	Tractive effort Continuous at kN	km/h	Max speed km/h	Wheel dia mm	Total weight tonnes	Length mm	No in service January 1990	First built	Builders Mechanical parts	Engine	Transmission
A	Co-Co	Elec	1063/977	240	226	12	100	1016	89.16	15 036	14	1960	Clyde Eng Co	EMD 12-567C	EMD D25-D29
AA	Co-Co	Elec	1230/1120	240	226	14	100	1016	96	15 036	5	1967	Clyde Eng Co	EMD 12-645E	EMD D25-D29
AB	Co-Co	Elec	1230/1120	240	226	14	100	1016	96	15 496	6	1969	Clyde Eng Co	EMD 12-645E	EMD D32-D29
C	Co-Co	Elec	1145/1035	240	200	14.5	96	1016	90.42	15 088	3	1962	English Electric	English Electric 12 SVT	EE 822 6C-548
D	Co-Co	Elec	1640/1490	—	245.3	18	90	1016	107.85	17 044	5	1971	Clyde Eng Co	EMD 16-645E	EMD D32-D29
DA	Co-Co	Elec	1640/1490	—	245.3	18	90	1016	96.72	17 044	7	1972	Clyde Eng Co	EMD 16-645E	EMD D32-D29
DB	Co-Co	Elec	1640/1490	—	244.5	17.7	90	1016	110	18 000	13	1982	Clyde Eng Co	EMD 16-645E	EMD AR6-D29
G	Co-Co	Elec	768/708	240	191.2	9.5	90	952	76.2	12 496	2	1963	English Electric	English Electric 8 SVT	EE 819/7E-548
N	Co-Co	Elec	1940/1790	371	241	21	105	952	103.46	17 000	7	1977	Comm Eng Co	Alco type	5GTA11B4-761 AS
NA*	Co-Co	Elec	1940/1790	371	241	21	105	952	103.46	17 000	4	1977	Comm Eng Co	Alco type	5GTA11B4-761 AS
P	Co-Co	Elec	2000/1830	380	292	18.6	90	955	100.5	19 800	1	1989	Goninan	GE 7 FDL 12	5GMG 191A1 GE 761 F1
R	Co-Co	Elec	1454/1338	275	226.9	17.5	96	952	96	15 240	5	1968	Comm Eng Co	English Electric 12 CSVT	EE 822/16J-548
RA	Co-Co	Elec	1454/1342	298	226.9	17.5	96	952	96	16 306	11	1969	Comm Eng Co	English Electric 12 CVST	EE 822/16J-548

* Locomotive converted from 1067 mm gauge Class N unit in 1982

Shunting diesel locomotives: 1067 mm gauge

Class	Wheel arrange-ment	Trans-mission	Rated power kW	Max kN	Tractive effort Continuous at kN	km/h	Max speed km/h	Wheel dia mm	Total weight tonnes	Length mm	No in service January 1990	First built	Builders Mechanical parts	Engine	Transmission
M	B-B	Hyd	522/484	–	109	9.6	53	1016	49.66	10 961	2	1972	Walkers Ltd	Cummins VTA 1710-L	Voith L4r4U2-G
MA	B-B	Hyd	522/484	–	109	9.6	53	1016	44.8	10 955	3	1973	Walkers Ltd	Caterpillar D379B	Voith L4r4U2-G
T	0-6-0	Elec	492/447	111.2	69	18.6	65	1016	37.35	7569	4	1967	Tulloch	Cummins VT-12-825	Brush TG 78-43 TM 68-46
TA	0-6-0	Elec	492/447	111.2	69	18.6	65	1016	38.1	7569	10	1970	Tulloch	Cummins VTA-1710-L	Brush TG-78-43 TM 68-46
Y	Bo-Bo	Elec	306/280	102.3	40	18.5	72	915	38.8	10 020	6	1953	British Thompson Houston	Paxman 12 RPHL	RTB 8944- BTH 124 PV

Diesel locomotives: 1435 mm gauge

Class	Wheel arrange-ment	Trans-mission	Rated power kW	Max kN	Tractive effort Continuous at kN	km/h	Max speed km/h	Wheel dia mm	Total weight tonnes	Length mm	No in service January 1990	First built	Builders Mechanical parts	Engine	Transmission
K	Co-Co	Elec	1454/1338	298	198	19	130	1016	114.3	16 764	8	1966	English Electric	English Electric 12 CSVT	EE 822/16J-538
KA*	Co-Co	Elec	1454/1342	298	226.9	17.5	96	952	99	16 306	1	1969	English Electric	English Electric 12 CSVT	EE 822/16J 548
L	Co-Co	Elec	2386/2162	337.2	311.4	21	134	1016	134	19 355	25	1967	Clyde Eng Co	EMD 16-645E3	EMD AR10-D77
H	Bo-Bo	Elec	708/641	240	167.7	10	100	1016	72.38	12 952	5	1965	English Electric	English Electric 6 CSRKT	EE 819/8F-538
J	Bo-Bo	Elec	485/447	159.2	117.8	11.2	100	1016	66.64	13 004	3	1966	Clyde Eng Co	EMD 6-567C	EMD D25-D29

* Locomotive converted from 1067 mm gauge Class RA unit in 1974

Diesel railcars

Class	Wheel arrange-ment	Trans-mission	Rated power kW	Max speed km/h	Wheel dia mm	Total weight tonnes	Length mm	No in service January 1990	First built	Builders Mechanical parts	Engine	Transmission
1067 mm gauge												
ADG	1A-A1	Hyd	112	80	800	30.99	19 050	14	1954	Cravens	AEC A 219	Voith DIWA 501
ADH	1A-A1	Hyd	112	80	800	30.99	19 050	3	1963	Cravens	AEC A 219	Voith DIWA 501
ADK	1A-A1	Hyd	195	85	800	33.28	20 254	10	1968	Comm Eng Co	Cummins NHHTO-6-B1	Voith DIWA 501
ADL	B-B	Hyd	212	80	838	42.97	20 260	10	1982	A Goninan	Cummins	Voith T211R
ADP	B-B	Hyd	350	120	840	52	21 160	3	1987	Comm Eng Co	Cummins KTA 19R	Voith T311R
ADQ	B-B	Hyd	350	120	840	52	21 160	2	1987	Comm Eng Co	Cummins KTA 19R	Voith T311R
1435 mm gauge												
WCA	1A-A1	Hyd	283	144	940	68.22	20 076	5	1972	Comm Eng Co	MAN D 3650 HM 6U	Voith T113R

Westrail's 1067 mm loading and structural gauge

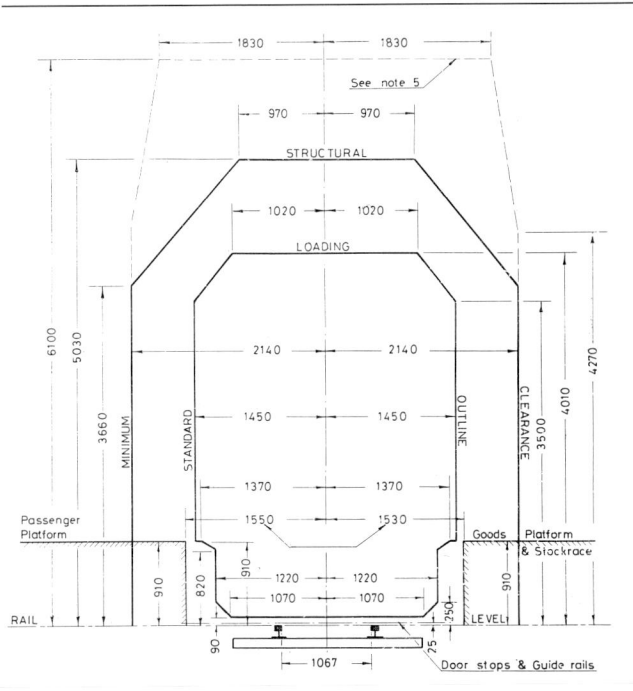

Westrail's 1435 mm loading and structural gauge

RAILWAY SYSTEMS / Australia

Track
Standard rail: Flat-bottom in 13.72 and 27.4 m lengths, weighing 46.6, 40.61 and 60 kg/m; and older material of varying weights
Joints: Fishplates; but in relaying the lengths are flashbutt-welded to 274 and 109.5 m, then thermit-welded into 439 m lengths or into continuous rail
Rail fastenings
Concrete sleepers: Fist BTR fastenings or Pandrol fastenings
Timber sleepers: Dogspikes or Pandrol fastenings
Cross ties (sleepers)
Concrete: Standard-gauge: 2600 × 300 × 205 mm
Dual gauge: 2600 × 300 × 210 mm; 2600 × 300 × 190 mm
Timber: (local hardwood jarrah, wandoo etc)
Standard-and dual-gauge: 2500 × 225 × 150 mm; 250 × 225 × 130 mm
Narrow gauge: 2100 × 225 × 130 mm; 2100 × 225 × 115 mm
Spacing: Standard-gauge: concrete 1493/km, timber 1640/km
225 × 115 mm
Narrow gauge: 1320/km (steel and timber)
Ballast: 38 mm crushed rock ballast on main lines. Iron stone gravel on minor branch lines
Minimum curvature radius
Main lines: 242 m = 7.25 curve
Branch lines: 141 m = 12.5° curve
Max gradient: 1 in 40 = 2.5%
Max altitude: 500 m Wallaroo
Axleloading: 1067 mm gauge main lines, 20.5 tonnes; branch lines, 16 tonnes
1435 mm gauge main lines, 24 tonnes; branch line, 21 tonnes

Grain train in the port of Albany

New 'Australind' diesel train-set for Perth-Bunbury service
(Colin Underhill)

Western Australian ore railways

Goldsworthy Railway

Head office: 197 St Georges Terrace, Perth, Western Australia

Telephone: +61 9 3221788

Railway: PO Box 2570, South Hedland, Western Australia 6722

Telephone: +61 91 469000
Telex: 99542
Telefax: +61 91 469173

Gauge: 1435 mm
Route length: 182 km

Traffic	1985/86	1986/87	1987/88	1988/89
Freight tonnage (million)	5.084	5.468	4.68	6.7
Average net freight train load (tonnes)	4264	4368	4320	NA

Railway Manager: M G Howe

Traffic
Iron ore reserves were exhausted and mining operations closed at the Goldsworthy mine site in December 1982. Mining operations were concentrated at Shay Gap until October 1988 when new reserves at Nimingarra were developed. The majority of railing is now from Nimingarra to Finucane Island (Port Hedland) over a route length of 170 km.

Rolling stock: 7 English Electric 1950 hp and 2 English Electric 950 hp diesel locomotives, 234 ore cars. A new Type JT42C Clyde-GM 3000hp diesel locomotive was to be delivered in April 1990.

Type of brake: Air
Type of coupling: Alliance automatic

Track
Rail: 50.4 kg/m (PS)
Cross-ties (sleepers): Jarrah (timber)
Thickness: 127 mm
Spacing: 1670/km
Fastenings: Dogspikes
Minimum curvature radius: 3°
Max gradient: 1.04%
Max axleload: 24 tonnes

Diesel locomotives

Class	Wheel arrangement	Transmission	Rated power kW	Max speed km/h	Total weight tonnes	No in service	Year first built	Builders Mechanical parts	Engine & type	Transmission
H	Bo-Bo	Elec	708	128	70	2	1965	English Elec	English Elec	English Elec
K	Co-Co	Elec	1452	128	120	6	1966	English Elec	English Elec	English Elec

Hamersley Iron Ore Railways

PO Box 21, Dampier, Western Australia 6713

Telephone: +61 91 436000
Telex: AA 99529
Telefax: +61 91 435109

General Manager: I J Williams
Principal Technical Advisor: N D Perkins
Manager, Railway Operations: G J Murdoch
  Rolling Stock Maintenance: H Doddrell
  Track, Signals and Communications: A J Attenborough

Gauge: 1435 mm
Route length: 389 km

Hamersley operates over a distance of 386 km from Paraburdoo through Mount Tom Price to Dampier. The main line is predominantly single-track with passing sidings at approximately 20 km intervals. Heavy-duty rail, continuously welded, is used throughout with alloy and head-hardened steels utilised for high-wearing curve sections.

The Mount Tom Price to Dampier section of the railway has been progressively upgraded by improvements to the track structure and associated drainage. Replacement of the original timber sleepers with concrete sleepers, using a P811 unit, was completed in June 1988.

Trains consist of three diesel-electric locomotives hauling 206 wagons each of 100 tonnes nominal capacity. This results in gross train weights of 26 000 tonnes. Wagons are coupled in pairs by a solid drawbar with rotary couplings connecting each pair. A train is approximately 2 km in length and is the heaviest and longest employing head-end locomotive power operating anywhere in the world. The main line configuration permits following train movements at 15 minutes headway.

The maximum opposing grade to loaded trains on the Mount Tom Price to Dampier section is 0.33 per cent whilst empty trains returning to the mine negotiate a maximum adverse grade of 2 per cent. These grades and the gross loads of trains permit an exact balance of locomotive power. On the Mount Tom Price to Paraburdoo section, there is constant compensated grade of 0.42 per cent against the loaded trains. Six head-end locomotives are required by loaded trains for the 100 km journey between Paraburdoo and Mount Tom Price to overcome this adverse grade. At Dampier, trains are unloaded in rotary dumpers at either the Parker Point or Ell terminal. At Parker Point pairs of wagons are uncoupled from the train prior to dumping.

Rolling stock
47 diesel locomotives, 2400 ore wagons, 126 other vehicles.

Communications
A centralised traffic control (CTC) system utilising motorised switch operations and block signalling is used for control of all traffic from the mine terminals to the ports. Radio communication is maintained with train crews and track maintenance personnel and provides an emergency back-up service for the CTC system.

The communications system consists of a microwave bearer and uhf mobiles.

A locomotive data logging capability has been developed to monitor and record various locomotive performance parameters and driver control functions. Integrated in this system is a vdu display in the cab to communicate information to the driver.

Track
Rail: 68 kg/m
Cross ties (sleepers): Concrete, 2590 × 263 × 150 mm
Spacing: 1640/km
Max speeds:
Loaded train 80 km/h
Empty train 70 km/h
Freight train 80 km/h
Passenger train 80 km/h
Light engines 100 km/h

Traffic:

	1985	1986	1987	1988	1989
Freight tonnage (million)	40.5	38.3	39.1	33.9	41.3
Average net freight train load (tonnes)	18 935	19 230	20 200	20 610	20 440

Diesel locomotives

Class	Wheel arrangement	Transmission	Rated power (kW)	Max speed (km/h)	No in service	Year built	Builders
30	Co-Co	Elec	2685	80	12	1968	Alco
40	Co-Co	Elec	2685	80	27	1971	Alco
50	Co-Co	Elec	2685	80	3	1978	GE
60	Co-Co	Elec	2610	80	5	1982	GM/Clyde

Hamersley ore train hauled by GM-EMD Type SD-50 locomotives employing 'Super Series' adhesion control and built by Clyde Engineering

Max gradients:
Against empty 2.03%
Against loaded ex-Tom Price 0.33%
Against loaded ex-Paraburdoo 0.42%

Mt Newman Railroad

PO Box 231, Nelson Point, Port Hedland, Western Australia 6721

Telephone: +61 91 73 6888
Telex: Hemore 99271

Chief Executive Officer: G Freeman
Area Manager, Hedland: W D Wallwork
Railroad Manager: A L Neal
Superintendents, Track & Signals: R Mitchell
Operations & Rolling Stock: W A Walker
Signals and Communications Engineer: A Nicholls

Gauge: 1435 mm
Route length: 423 km

The railway is owned by Mt Newman Mining Co Pty Ltd, which manages the Mt Newman Iron Ore Project on behalf of members of the Mt Newman Joint Venture and which is a wholly-owned subsidiary of The Broken Hill Proprietary Co Ltd (BHP). Mining operations were inaugurated in January 1969. The railway, which runs from Mt Newman to Port Hedland, on the north coast, allows 32.5 tonne average axleloadings, one of the highest figures in the world. The company is experimenting with special alloy wagon wheels as a measure to permit further increases in axleloads.

The company normally runs trains of 192 and 240 car lengths, but has operated trains of up to 270 cars.

The single-track route has one 1.64 km and 11·3 km passing loops. It is lately scheduled to carry six trains a day, three of which are 240-car Locotrol trains and three 192-car banked trains. In 1988-89 seven Locotrol sets were in use. Maximum speed of a fully loaded train is generally 65 km/h, but coasting at up to 75 km/h is permitted over some sections. The sophisticated facilities at the Mt Newman railhead allow a train to be fully loaded, in only 70 minutes, so that a train-set can be turned, loaded and re-manned within 114 minutes. Each return journey over the 426 km route from Port Hedland to Mt Newman and back is scheduled to average 19½ hours; ore dumping at the port takes 2 hours and 3 hours are allowed at Port Hedland for locomotive servicing.

Early in 1986 BHP increased its share in the Mt Newman project to 85 per cent. To make the investment worthwhile, it became necessary to lift the performance of the project substantially. The effect on the Mt Newman Mining Company Railroad is that certain development work has been undertaken and further expansion is being evaluated. Significant current and future projects are the upgrading of the Port Hedland terminal and the railhead at the mine (Newman); the purchase and upgrading of locomotives for superior performance to those currently in service; and continued investment in Locotrol equipment.

Construction is possible of a 30 km branch to serve BHP ore workings at Yandicoogina, which were coming to full production in 1989.

The object of these projects is in harmony with the Mt Newman Railroad trend towards further increases both of train length and axleloadings. Holding capacity at the terminals has been augmented by the addition of new sidings at the mine and port yards with sufficient length to accommodate trains of from 200 to up to 300 cars (representing train lengths from 2.1 to 3.3 km). This is the largest civil engineering project undertaken since the construction of the railroad in the late 1960s.

Traction and rolling stock
The company operates 56 diesel locomotives and 2066 ore cars, 120 other freight cars and one lounge/dining car. A 'loco logger' has been developed to monitor performance of engines (in 16 parameters) and other components while a locomotive is in use on the track, as a diagnostic aid to maintenance. Fitting of all locomotives with this apparatus continues.

The locomotive fleet replacement programme has continued and by early 1988 eight 2800 kW GE 'Dash 7' rebuilds were in main-line service. Four new 2984 kW GE 'Dash 8' locomotives were delivered by Goninan in 1988. The 'Dash 8' locomotives have microprocessor-based control and diagnostic systems which are expected to result in less maintenance

Diesel locomotives

Class	Wheel arrangement	Transmission	Rated power kW	Max speed km/h	Total weight tonnes	No in service 1988	Year first built	Builders Mechanical parts	Builders Engine & type	Builders Transmission
Alco C636	Co-Co	Elec	2680	112	190	10	1966	Goodwin	Alco 2515	GE
Alco M636	Co-Co	Elec	2680	112	190	37	1971	Goodwin/Comeng	Alco 2515	GE
GE C36-7M*	Co-Co	Elec	2800	112	190	8	1986	GE	GE 7FDL 216	GE
GE C39-8	Co-Co	Elec	2984	112	195	4	1988	Goninan	GE 8FDL-16	GE

* Rebuilt from C636

downtime as well as greater tractive effort. Rebuilding of the Alco locomotives using the 'Dash 8' technology is currently under investigation.

Seven experimental ore cars, incorporating different body and bogie designs, are being evaluated. The cars are designed for a nominal 40-tonne axleload at 90 km/h with reduced wind resistance.

Signalling

The railway is operated by CTC, supplemented by track-to-train radio, from a control centre at Port Hedland. Interlockings can function automatically in the event of any failure in the CTC telemetry.

A computerised CTC control centre was installed in 1988. This includes the use of computer-aided dispatching.

The Hedland yard is also worked using a combination of radio instructions and remotely-operated switches. Eight hot box detectors, three hot wheel detectors and 39 dragging equipment detectors are used on the main line.

Automatic car identification (ACI) transponders are fitted to each ore car and readers are located at two positions on track.

An existing 24-channel analogue uhf radio link between Port Hedland and Newman and wayside vhf equipment would be replaced in 1988/89 by a 2 Mbit digital microwave link with improved vhf wayside coverage.

Track

A total of 170 000 steel sleepers are now installed, representing 26 per cent of main-line track. Rerailing with head-hardened rail continues at a rate of 40 km of rail per annum. Rail maintenance is assisted by use of rail grinding and ultrasonic flaw detection in order to manage the rail most economically.

Rail: 66 and 68 kg/m continuous welded rail (standard carbon on tangent and head-hardened on curves and some tangents)
Cross ties (sleepers): Timber, 228 × 152 × 2600 mm; steel, 120 mm deep × 9 or 10 mm thick
Spacing: Timber 1875/km; steel 1515/km
Fastenings: AREA plate and dog spike; Omark Traklok 1 and 2; Pandrol PR Series
Minimum curvature radius: 582 m
Max gradient: 1.5% (empty); 0.5% (loaded)
Max axleload: 32.5 tonnes (nominal)

Traffic

	1984/85	1985/86	1986/87	1987/88
Freight tonnes (million)	28.2	27.7	31.7	34.5*
Freight tonne/km	6.2	6.2	6.0	6.2*
Average net train load (tonnes)	18 600	18 600	18 500	20 300*
Average wagon load (tonnes)	104	103	101	103*

* Forecast

Robe River Railroad
Cliffs Robe River Iron Associates

PO Box 21, Wickham, Western Australia 6720

Telephone: +61 91 87 1001
Telex: AA 99058
Telefax: +61 91 1650

Manager, Rail: B D Oliver
Superintendent, Operations: E E Girdler
  Locomotive Workshops: K Hodges
General Foreman, Track Maintenance: D G Higgins

Gauge: 1435 mm
Route length: 189.4 km

Traffic

Freight tonnage has lately amounted to between 15 and 18 million tonnes a year. Average net freight train load is around 13 000 tonnes.

Rolling stock: 18 diesel locomotives, 762 wagons, 22 service vehicles.

Couplers in standard use: Fixed and rotary
Braking in standard use: Westinghouse air

Track

Standard rail: Head-hardened 1130 mpc 68 kg/m
Cross ties (sleepers): Timber, 2700 × 225 × 125 mm; Concrete 2600 × 280 × 235 mm
Spacing: Timber 1860/km, concrete 1538/km
Fastenings: Timber tie plates, spikes on tangent, Pandrol on curves. Concrete, McKay Safelock
Minimum curvature radius: 3°
Max gradient: Loaded 0.50%, empty 1.29%
Max axleload: 35 tonnes

Diesel locomotives

Class	Wheel arrangement	Transmission	Rated traction power kW	Max speed km/h	Total weight tonnes	No in service 1990	Year first built	Builders Mechanical parts	Engine & type	Transmission
Alco C36R	Co-Co	Ac-dc	2682	110	190	2*	1968	Alco	Alco 251F 16 cylinder	General Electric
Alco M636	Co-Co	Ac-dc	2682	110	190	14	1971	Alco	Alco 251F 16 cylinder	General Electric
GE Dash-8 C408M	Co-Co	Ac-dc	2983	110	190	6	—	GE	GE 7 FDL 16 16 cylinder	General Electric

* Including two rebuilds of Conrail locomotives

Austria

Ministry of Transport

Radetskystrasse 2, 1030 Vienna

Minister: Dr Rudolf Streicher
Heads of Division: Dr K Halbmayer
                    Dr K Bauer

Telephone: +43 1 756501/757631
Telex: 111800
Tedlefax: +43 1 730326

Austrian Federal Railways (ÖBB)
Österreichische Bundesbahnen

Elisabethstrasse 9, 1010 Vienna

Telephone: +43 222 5650/5011
Telex: 1377

President: Dkfm Dr Alfred Weiser
Vice-President: Franz Hums
Director General: Dr Heinrich Übleis
Deputy Director General: Dipl-Ing Helmut Hainitz
Chief of Finance and Accounts: Dr Heinz Berger
Chief of Revision: Dr Herbert Schmidt
Manager, Finance: Fritz Proksch
Administrative Director: Dr K Hellweger
Personnel Director: Dr F Piskaty
Financial Director: Dr Heinz Berger
Operating Director: Erich Lüftner
Sales Director: Heinrich Sittler
Chief Engineer: Dipl-Ing Gottfried Kubata
Director, Construction and Electrical Engineering:
  Dr tech Joseph Ebner
Purchasing Director: Dr Max Posch
Chief Public Relations Officer: Dr Gerd Kern

ÖBB Type 4010/6010 inter-city emu: refurbishing and re-livery of these units has begun

Gauge: 1435 mm; 1000 mm; 760 mm
Route length: 5297 km; 15.5 km; 338.5 km
Electrification
  1435 mm: 3152 km at 15 kV 16⅔ Hz ac; 2.2 km at 3 kV dc
  760 mm; 84 km at 6.5 kV 25 Hz ac

Financial restructure

The government has long dealt separately in its annual budgeting with the investment requirements of ÖBB's commercial and socially necessary but essentially unremunerative services. This segregation became wide-ranging from the start of 1987. The government now denominates and specifically subsidises the total costs of the ÖBB services regarded as a social obligation, which the railway runs under contract to the state. All other ÖBB services, including wagonload freight and long-haul (more than 70 km) passenger operation, and bus and road freight activity, must cover running costs out of revenue. However, in this latter commercial sector ÖBB pays for track use only a toll equivalent to three-eighths of total maintenance costs; the government has assumed financial responsibility for all infrastructure renewal. The state also makes a contribution to capital investment in the railway's commercial sector.

Under the new regime the socially necessary services are individually accounted for support and not covered by a block grant. The new arrangement has relieved ÖBB of financial responsibility for upkeep of, and investment in approximately 2800 route-km of its system.

New financial targets beaten

In both 1987 and 1988 ÖBB improved on the financial objectives it was set under the new arrangements. Compared with a projected 1987 surplus in its commercial sector of Sch 100 million the railway actually recorded Sch 530 million. In the following year this was increased to Sch 630 million. At the same time requirement of state support for the social railway sector was lowered from Sch 16.8 billion in 1986 to Sch 13.8 billion in 1988. Both passenger and freight traffic volumes were increased in 1988-89; but the improving financial performance was attributable mainly to substantial staff reductions accruing from productivity measures such as drastic rationalisation of less-than-wagonload freight business and concentration of freight marshalling on the first of ÖBB's automated yards, at Vienna Kledering.

Managerial restructure

In March 1990 the Transport Minister and the railway's directorate announced a major organisational restructure to be completed during the year. Below Directorate level, and excluding central functions such as human resources, the undertaking would be regrouped in Commercial and Infrastructure sectors.

The Commercial sector would cover passenger and freight business, timetable planning, operation and mechanical/electrical engineering: in other words, sales, marketing and the means of production to fulfil demand. Functions concerned with upkeep, construction, electrification and planning of the infrastructure would be concentrated in the other sector.

A primary aim of the reorganisation is to decentralise, create specific responsibilities, eliminate a great deal of previous overlaps in decision-making, and thereby expedite action.

Traffic

Gross freight traffic rose 1.3 per cent to 55.4 million tonnes in 1988, but this was outclassed in 1989 by a 5.7 per cent increase to a new annual record of 58.6 million tonnes. Because of fierce competitive pressure on rates, revenue growth has been proportionately much smaller.

Outstanding 1989 performance was logged in intermodal transport, up 22.3 per cent overall. Within that total 'Rolling Highway'(ROLA) piggyback put on no less than 34 per cent, swap bodies 8 per cent and containers 11 per cent. Conventional wagon traffic rose by 3.4 per cent, despite a recession in bulk commodity freight, especially incoming from abroad. Import freight in general bucked the upward trend in other categories, declining by 0.9 per cent.

Despite addition of over 500 trains to the passenger timetables in 1988-89, growth in this sector has been less marked. There was a rise in passenger journeys of 0.8 per cent in 1988, and of just over 1 per cent in 1989, the latter to a total of 162 million. But passenger revenue at Sch 4037.3 million was 5.1 per cent higher than in 1988. A notable feature was a big rise in accompanied auto traffic, up from some 60 000 vehicles in 1988 to 90 000 in 1989. To this three new routes contributed strongly.

'New Railway' Plan

In June 1985 ÖBB management took the initiative of commissioning US consultants Arthur D Little to evaluate the economic feasibility of creating a core 'high-performance' ÖBB network. The American's report was delivered in September 1986.

The consultants endorsed the case for development of the Vienna-Linz-Salzburg Westbahn for 200 km/h; and, for that objective, three major realignments, one between Melk and Ybbs, another from Haag to St Valentin and the third and most grandiose, from central Vienna to St Pölten, 53 km out via the present main line.

The report also favoured the long-cherished, 24 km-long Semmering base tunnel on a ruling 1 in 150 gradient, aligned for 200 km/h, to bypass the stiffly-graded historic Semmering route, which is beset by curves that limit much of the distance from Gloggnitz to Mürzzuschlag to speeds of 50–80 km/h. This, in conjunction with more modest works to allow 160 km/h elsewhere on the Sudbhan, could cut 45 min from the present Vienna-Graz passenger timing of over 2½ h, accelerate freights still more, and not least eliminate much of the present freight double-heading over the Semmering Pass.

The consultants further supported concentration of all Vienna's main-line passenger traffic, presently handled at considerable cost by four separate terminals, in a single new station. This would need new infrastructure from St Pölten to the projected central station via Tullnerfeld.

In the spring of 1987 the ÖBB published a Sch 60 000 million *Neue Bahn* ('New Railway') plan based on the consultants' recommendations. To the 200 km/h upgrading of the Vienna-Salzburg route this added upgrading of the Arlberg route from Wörgl via Innsbruck to the Swiss border for 180 km/h. But for the next century it proposed new construction of a shorter 200 km/h line from Salzburg to Wörgl, cutting out the present detour via the Rosenheim curve. On the Sudbahn route, besides reiterating the need of 200 km/h upgrading from Vienna to Wiener Neustadt, the plan suggested a new 207 km line from there to Graz via Oberwart as an alternative to upgrading the present route via Bruck and Mur for a maximum 180 km/h. Either option would demand a new base

Class 1044.5 rebuild of a standard Class 1044 Bo-Bo, for a 220 km/h test programme

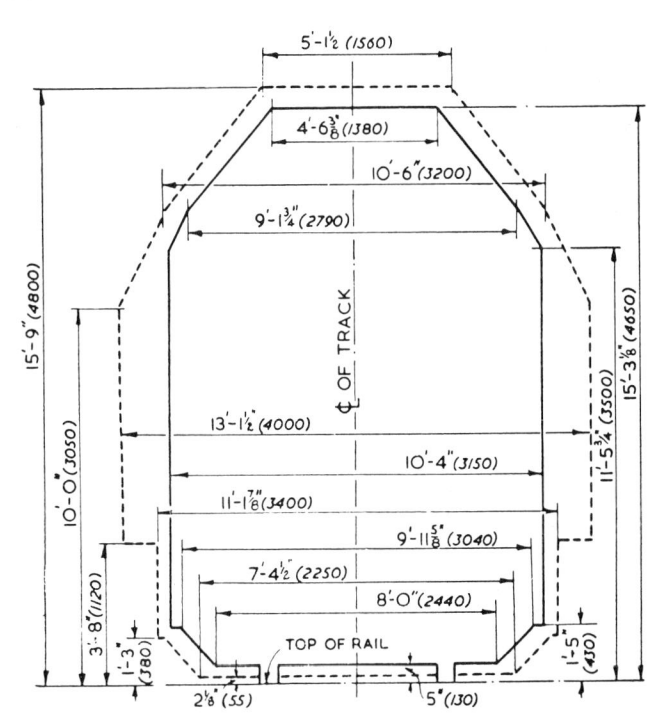

ÖBB structure and clearance gauge

tunnel under the mountains to replace the existing Semmering Pass tunnel. A new 200 km/h line from Graz to Klagenfurt and Villach was advocated to complement the Wiener Neustadt-Graz new line scheme.

To encourage international transit traffic, upgrading of the north-south Linz-St Michael, Salzburg-Villach and Kufstein-Innsbruck-Brenner routes was advocated, in the first two cases for maximum speeds of 180 and 160 km/h respectively.

Neue Bahn: first phase

By the end of 1987 the *Neue Bahn* plan was approved in principle by the government and in March 1989 Parliament approved execution and funding of the first phase. Of a total of Sch 43 billion needed in the period up to 1998, the railway expected to have committed Sch 31 billion by the end of 1992. A third of the latter total is being put up by the state, a sixth by Eurofima, and the rest is being raised by banks in similar fashion to the capitalisation of the country's motorway construction.

In April 1989 a new company, Eisenbahn-Hochleistungsstrecken-AG (HL-AG) was created to manage the planning and execution of the 'Neue Bahn' new infrastructure and upgrading projects. The state owns all shares in HL-AG, which was launched with a capital of Sch 6 million.

In addition to the projects which the Plan originally embraced, the ÖBB began in 1989 construction of a Sch 3.2 billion Innsbruck bypass, mostly comprising a 12.7 km tunnel. This project is a key item of the Brenner Corridor capacity enlargement scheme (see below). Set for completion in 1993, the bypass is estimated to double Brenner route capacity to 100 trains daily each way. The tunnel is being generously proportioned to admit piggybacking of the largest road vehicles in standard use. Its northern part will serve as the start of the hoped-for new Brenner base tunnel (see below).

The railway is spending a further Sch 2.3 billion on continued Arlberg Route double-tracking between St Anton and St Jakob, and on local realignments on this vital international route. An operating capacity increase of 20 per cent is the objective.

Work has also begun on the 200km/h transformation of the Vienna-Linz-Salzburg transversal between St Pölten and Attnang Puchheim. This embraces upgrading of 94 km of existing route and new construction of 66 km, plus resignalling and level crossing elimination. In 1989 outlay on this project totalled Sch 133 million. By 1992 enough should have been done to achieve a cut of 15 minutes in 1989's best 2¾-hour Vienna-Salzburg timing. The ultimate objective is a Vienna-Salzburg journey time of less than 2 hours.

Nationwide regular-interval timetable

A main objective of 'Neue Bahn' investment is progressive creation of a Swiss-style interval timetable that integrates train and bus operations nationwide. The first phase is to be introduced in May 1991 and completion is set for the year 2000. The final version is expected to add over 7300 train-km to the ÖBB timetables and to expand passenger traffic by at least 50 per cent.

Schober Pass scheme

Provision of operating capacity for the regular-interval timetable, and also to hoist the route's scope for freight throughput from 90 to 150 trains daily, motivates extensive double-tracking, realignment and resignalling of the largely single-track south-to-north, Schober Pass-Ennstal lines. Construction of a loop at Selzthal to save Graz-Salzburg trains reversal there will also contribute to prospective saving of 25 min on their present 2 h 40 min timing between Leoben and Bischofshofen. Total cost, including level crossing elimination, is put at Sch 2.9 billion, of which Sch 93 million was spent in 1989.

Tauern route improvements

The Sch 600 million assigned to the Tauern transalpine route for the remainder of this century continues its double-tracking, now on the northern side of the tunnel, and also covers improvements between Salzburg and Schwarzach St Veit, and between Spittal-Milstattersee and Rosenbach. Realignments where feasible will lift maximum speed from 90 to 120 km/h. The aim is to raise daily freight train throughout capability from 110 to 150 workings.

In November 1988 work was ceremonially begun on enlargement of the 280 m-long Untersberg Tunnel near Schwarzach/St Veit. This Sch 46 million scheme, to be finished in 1990, will allow Tauern route piggybacking of 4 m-high road vehicles. A start of construction was expected in 1989.

Station schemes

Sch 650 million is being spent on 32 stations, to create public transport interchanges, parking space and station garages, and a wide range of other passenger services and amenities. Planning of the new central station in Vienna, too, is in hand. The aim is to drive a tunnel from the Salzburg main line near St Pölten to the Graz main line in Vienna's outskirts and create a through station, which the ÖBB want to have on the site of the present Vienna Sud station. The

Traffic (rail only) (million)	1985	1986	1987	1988	1989
Freight tonnes (excluding parcels)	58.2	55.07	54.7	55.4	58.61
Freight tonne-km (excluding parcels)	11 903	11 273	11 114	11 212.8	11 849.1
Passenger journeys	158.1	158.3	158.9	160.3	163
Passenger-km	7290.4	7331.9	7362.9	7783.4	8100

Signalling centre at Linz Hbf

Class 1044.2 Bo–Bo and Euro-City train

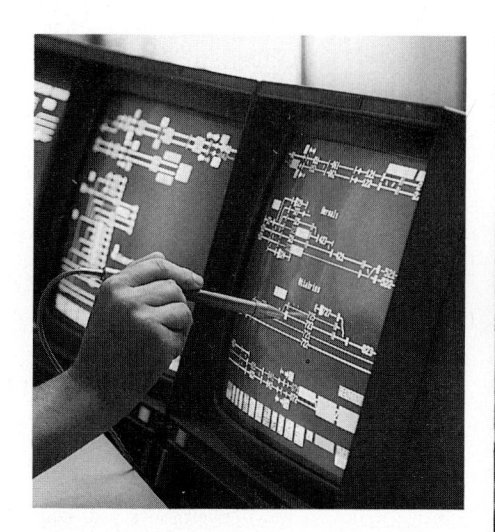

VDUs in new Heiligenstadt signalling centre

whole scheme is estimated to cost Sch 5200 million.

Elsewhere in the environs of Vienna the partly single-track Pottendorf line between the city and Wiener Neustadt is to be upgraded and have its length of double track extended, partly because of its new-found significance as an access to Vienna's recently completed central marshalling yard at Kledering. Furthermore, after additional improvements in the 1990s, the line will be able to carry an effective local train service that will relieve pressure on the Vienna-Wiener Neustadt main line via Baden.

Freight proposals
Freight terminal improvements are allocated Sch 800 million in the 'Neue Bahn' plan, with particular emphasis on: closure of those minimally-used and concentration on fewer, well-equipped depots; provision for intermodal traffic; and ability to offer customers a full logistics service. The last is bound up with a Sch 575 million investment in computer-based data transmission systems for both passenger and freight traffic.

Neue Bahn: rolling stock projects
The first phase of 'Neue Bahn' investment earmarks Sch 1600 million for new traction and rolling stock (but over the whole period of 'Neue Bahn' development forecast expenditure in this area totals Sch 12 500 million). Most of the first-phase money is going on development and evaluation of new 200 km/h passenger car prototypes with sophisticated amenities. The ÖBB eventually aims to have train-sets capable in international service of using the 300 km/h new lines of neighbour railways.

Tilt-body equipment ordered
Tilt-body rolling stock is included in forward plans. In the course of 1988 ÖBB procured sample Talgo Pendular vehicles from RENFE and the Fiat 'Pendolino' Class ETR 401 prototype unit from the FS for trials of automatic body-tilt systems on its own tracks. In spring 1989 ÖBB contracted Simmering-Graz-Pauker to build three six-car sets with Fiat bogies and the Fiat tilting system. Electrical equipment will be furnished by ABB. To be delivered in 1992-93, the units will have the inner axle of all bogies motored to reduce maximum axle loadings. Each set will seat 249 passengers and include a buffet car. ÖBB subsequently lodged an enquiry with Fiat for nine more train-sets, and also for a dual-voltage version for Vienna-Budapest operation.

With the German and Swiss Federal Railways the ÖBB is working up a 'Hotel Train' concept for international overnight services. These trains will feature bi-level cars exploiting the innovatory layout possibilities of such vehicles to offer three types of overnight accommodation: De Luxe, with a toilet, shower and other amenities such as a minibar for each two-berth compartment; Comfort, which will reproduce the facilities of a current sleeping car compartment; and Sleeperette, with generously reclining seats. A service car will provide a reception area, restaurant and bar.

Prototype bi-level 'Hotel Train' sets are not expected to be operational until 1994. The three railways are therefore considering, as an interim step, the 1992 introduction of Talgo Pendular sleeping-car sets on three routes. These Spanish train-sets include 'Gran Clase' cars in which each compartment has its own shower and toilet. The ÖBB Talgo sets would run between Vienna and Cologne; Swiss sets would ply between Basel and Vienna.

Business cars
An innovation in the 1990-91 timetable was the provision of business accommodation in several EuroCity services between Vienna, Innsbruck, Basel and Zurich. Ten of ÖBB's latest first-class cars have one of their compartments fitted up with typewriter, telephone and power points for personal computers.

Class 1064 Bo-Bo with three-phase motors for heavy yard shunting at hump of new Vienna Central yard

Finance (Sch million)

Revenues	1985	1986	1987	1988
Passengers and baggage	8379	8260	8439	8170
Freight, parcels and mail	11 857	11 385	10 877	11 009
Other income	7195	8277	14 734	10 069
Total	27 431	27 922	34 050	34 655

Expenditure	1985	1986	1987	1988
Staff/personnel	21 378	22 490	22 634	21 698.5
Materials and services	3215	3260	3029	NA
Depreciation	3577	3817	4000	4561.9
Financial charges	3966	3928	4018	NA
Total	32 136	33 495	33 681	33 884

Investment in Eastern European links
Following the political upheavals in Czechoslovakia and Hungary, and the easing of movement to and from those countries, the ÖBB announced in 1990 plans to develop cross-border rail links. On the Austrian side, the proposals would entail a total investment of Sch 4000 million, additional to 'Neue Bahn' requirements. Government financial support was being sought for measures costing Sch 500 million, which would be put in hand immediately.

The routes into Czechoslovakia for which major investment is sought are: Vienna-Gmünd-Ceske Velenice-Prague: ÖBB electrification from Sigmundsherberg to Gmünd to be started in June 1990, together with other infrastructure upgrading, at a total cost of Sch 900 million. The objective is a Vienna-Prague journey time of 3½–4 hr, instead of about 6 hr at present.
Vienna-Retz-Satov-Znojmo-Prague: At present a freight route, to become a major trunk. Electrification to be begun in June 1990 from Hollabrunn to Satov, at a cost, with other works, of Sch 480 million.
Vienna-Parndorf-Kittsee-Bratislava: At present a freight route, to be upgraded as a trunk route; work to include a new 2.5 km stretch of infrastructure between Kittsee and the frontier. Finalisation of plans awaits further discussion with CSD and the city of Bratislava. A Vienna-Bratislava journey time of 1 hr is the objective.

An added stimulus to development of links with Hungary is the major World Expo to be mounted jointly by Vienna and Budapest in 1995. The cross-border route for which major investment is planned in this case is Vienna-Hegyeshalom-Budapest. It will be upgraded, with realignments, for a maximum speed of 140 km/h, so as to cut Vienna-Budapest journey time from 2 hr 48 min to 2¼hr. Total cost, Sch 800 million, of which Sch 220 million to be invested in 1990.

Intermodal drive to relieve roads
Following its earlier imposition of a transit tax on international road freight vehicles crossing the country, the government announced in 1985 another major move to ease the pressure on its transalpine roads.

Graz-Regensburg *Rollende Landstrasse* piggyback train

Betwen 1984 and 1989 it would put up Sch 22 000 million to stimulate piggyback traffic over the Brenner Pass route (where the parallel autobahn now carries 3000 of the 3500 road freight vehicles that cross Austria each working day), over the Tauern Pass route and between Passau and Spielfeld. At the same time the government announced a 67 per cent cut in previously planned building of new autobahns.

In December 1989 the Transport Minister took a still more stringent action against road transport by barring all freight vehicles of more than 7.5 tonnes, domestic as well as foreign, from night-time travel on Austrian roads. Fierce reaction included a retaliatory Federal German government ban on Austrian heavy lorries travelling German roads by night.

A major Austrian anxiety is the ecological harm caused by road vehicle exhaust emissions. In the Tyrol destruction of trees is now reckoned to be 2 per cent and the rate of mere damage as high as one-third. The Austrian government aims to halve the 18.5 million tonnes currently moving through the Brenner Pass by road.

In the past few years the ÖBB has done a good deal to enlarge operating capacity on the Austrian side of the Brenner, which is the steeper approach to the Pass. The greater part of its 37 km is on the ruling grade of 1 in 38.5, whereas on the Italian slope the ruling grades are 1 in 43.5 and 1 in 45.5, though they affect the whole of its final 41.8 km apart from an easier stretch before Vipiteno/Sterzing. The ÖBB's Brenner traction current supply system has been reinforced, elderly Class 1110 and 1020 Co-Cos modified to match the modern Class 1044 Bo-Bos in dynamic braking capability, and means of inter-locomotive radio communication provided, all so that maximum freight trainloads of 1500 tonnes can be worked up and down the hill with two locomotives up front, and one in the rear.

Modification of the route's tunnel and other structures' clearances to accept ROLA-piggybacked road vehicles of up to 4.05 m height was finished in 1989. Enlargement of tunnel clearances on the Italian side of the Brenner, however, will not be completed until at least 1992.

Other measures being undertaken on the ÖBB sector of the route are the Innsbruck bypass described above; installation of automatic block signalling and reversible working on each track of the northern ramp; and provision for increased trainloads. The 12.7 km Innsbruck cut-off, begun in 1989, will run mainly in tunnel from Baumkirchen, east of the Hall-in-Tyrol marshalling yard, to Gärberbach, 4 km up the Brenner route out of Innsbruck. As the bypass will skirt the Hall yard, a small yard for attachment or detachment of Brenner pilot/banking locomotives is planned at Baumkirchen.

Austrian, Italian and West German governments agree that the present route over the Brenner Pass must be replaced by a deep-level base tunnel. Who pays is one problem; and how long the tunnel should be is another. The Austrians and Germans want a tunnel some 65 km long from Innsbruck's outskirts to Fortezza, about 40 km into Italy. That would minimise curvature and gradients. Because of the political sensitivity of their presence in the South Tyrol the Italians are loath to see border formalities removed so far from the Brenner. They insist that the tunnel must surface 23 km below the Pass at Vitipeno/Sterzing, which would result in less direct routeing and considerably reduce the scope for gradient easing.

New Class 2068 diesel-hydraulic shunter

'Rolling Highway' piggyback growth

'Rolling Highway' (ROLA) carryings have risen from 24 081 road units in 1980 to over 85 000 a year. These are the drive-on, drive-off services for road freight vehicles or rigs complete, which employ low-floor, ultra-small-wheel well cars that form an uninterrupted driveway from end to end of a train.

ROLA services on the Brenner route were further increased at the end of 1989 to offset the government's new restrictions on nocturnal highway freight. At the same time rates for the ÖBB component of piggyback transits, both ROLA and unaccompanied trailer, were significantly reduced for a six-month period. The German Federal and Italian Railways were not prepared to cut rates for their proportions of international transits.

After just two months' work to create a terminal in the Brenner pass, a five times-daily shuttle was launched between Brennersee and Ingolstadt (Bavaria) for vehicles up to 4.05m high that could not be railborne beyond the pass because of unmodified Italian clearances. For 3.6m-high road vehicles three ROLA trains ran daily each way between Munich and Verona. Intermodal services over the Brenner were completed by 26 trains for containers. swapbodies and unaccompanied semi-trailers. Another response to the Austrian government's nocturnal HGV ban was Inter-container's launch of two new Mondays-Fridays Trans-Europe-Container Express (TECE) between Munich Johanneskirchen and Verona's inland port, Quadrante Europa.

Further work on Arlberg Tunnel clearances to allow through ROLA trains with 4.05m-high vehicles to use that route from Germany will not be finished until the mid-1990s. As a stopgap, and again in response to the night-time road prohibition, the ÖBB in March 1990 launched a domestic ROLA shuttle between Wels, Lower Austria, and initially a temporary Tirolese terminal at Schönwies; from November the service was moved to a new, permanent terminal at Wörgl.

A major contribution to ROLA traffic growth has been the success of the Graz-Regensburg operation, launched in October 1984 with a single pair of trains and since expanded by demand to a five times daily each way service. A considerable volume of traffic to and from Yugoslavia, Hungary, Greece and Turkey has been attracted to this government-sponsored service, which completes the 470 km Graz-Passau-Regensburg transit in 9 hours. Each train has space for 18 heavy road freight vehicles or lorry-and-trailer rigs, and includes one of 10 couchette-saloon-kitchen cars which ÖBB has had specially built to accommodate the road vehicle crews. .

Elsewhere ROLA operations were expanded in December 1989 by introduction of two services between a newly-created Franz Welz terminal in Salzburg and Ljubljana (Yugoslavia). Further ROLA trains plied regularly between Vienna and Regensburg, Munich and Ljubljana, and Wels and Mainz.

Plans for 1990-91 include new intermodal services between Scandinavia and Bologna/Southern Italy, and Munich and Milan. In subsequent years new services between North Germany and Verona, Vienna and Verona/Bologna are projected.

To permit ROLA piggybacking of 48-tonnes glw road rigs, Simmering-Graz-Pauker have developed an articulated wagon mounted on three four-axle bogies, with 360 mm diameter; five prototypes were delivered to the ÖBB in April 1989. ÖBB was also evaluating three prototype free-standing, 10-axle small-wheel flatcars with 42-tonne payload capacity built by Waggon Union. A further 100 units were added to ÖBB's stock of 372 low-floor wagons of existing types in January 1990.

Since July 1983 the piggyback component of ÖBB intermodal traffic has been entrusted managerially to a separate company, Okombi GmbH & Co KG, in which some 70 forwarding agents and road hauliers have a minority interest.

In 1989 Hungarian Railways contracted with Okombi for extension of piggyback services to Debrechen, Szeged, Szolnok and Pecs in Hungary.

ÖBB was in 1990 considering evaluation of Road-Railer bi-modal techology.

Passenger service developments

Service developments in 1989 included, from mid-December, launch of the first long-haul train service to Vienna's Schwechat airport. The latter was previously served only by Vienna S-Bahn trains. Initially running on Fridays and Saturdays only, the Salzburg-Schwechat

New Class 5090 railcar for narrow-gauge lines

Class 1146 dual-voltage Bo-Bo, for through operations to Hungary

Class 5047 diesel-hydraulic railcar

'Vie Airport Express' was designed to cater for the numerous weekend charter flights into and out of the Vienna Airport. In January 1990 the S-Bahn service was modified to include experimentally some non-stop services between central Vienna stations and Schwechat. The possibility of providing for Inter-City train service of Schwechat is being considered in the planning of Vienna's new central through station and its connections with the Sudbahn and Westbahn trunk routes.

With the May 1989 timetable change 160 km/h top speed was scheduled on the Vienna-Salzburg main line for the first time. The sole train concerned was the 'Philharmoniker', and as a result its time for the 317 km between the two cities was cut to 2 hours 48 minutes. Allegedly because the ÖBB Class 1044-1 had been found detrimental to track at high speed, the 160 km/h train was powered by one of the DB Class 103 Co-Cos which cover a proportion of the through workings from Munich to Austria. Also in May 1989, following satisfactory trial operation in 1988 on the Bregenz-Vienna 'Symphoniker', Class 4010 inter-city emus were passed to run at up to 150 km/h on three Vienna-Salzburg and four Vienna-Graz/Villach services.

Other 1989 innovations included a summer train service between Vienna and Passau specifically for cyclists and including vans specially equipped to stack their machines. From July two restaurant cars rebuilt with a six-seat Video compartment showing a continuous film programme were in experimental service on the Vienna-Graz, Graz-Linz, Vienna-Villach and Vienna-Salzburg routes.

In 1989 ÖBB ordered from Simmering-Graz-Pauker 15 new Type Arnz first-class cars incorporating an office instead of a tenth compartment. The number of daily trains offering coin-in-the-slot telephone service was increased in 1989 from 82 to 107.

The first of a new build of 16 restaurant cars from Simmering-Graz-Pauker began service in 1988. The 40-seater cars, mounted on German-type MD52 bogies, are pressure-sealed and fitted with vacuum toilets to permit their through working over the German Federal *Neubau* routes. The ÖBB, following DB's example, now offers at-seat service of light refreshments to first-class passengers by the train's conductors on its inter-city services.

Bi-level train-set plans
In early 1990 the ÖBB borrowed three of the Swiss Federal's Zurich S-Bahn bi-level cars for trial initially on its Vienna Franz-Josefs terminus-Tulln suburban service. The vehicles were then to be evaluated in the Innsbruck area and in Steiermark. OBB plans to apply diesel-powered bi-level units to some of its regional services and has commissioned Jenbacher Werke to design a bi-level diesel-electric power car with three-phase drive.

Electrification
To relieve pressure on the Brenner route, electrification of the 110 km Lendorf (Spittal-Millstätersee)-Lienz line linking Carinthia with Italy was accorded new priority in 1984 and work began in 1985, a year earlier than previously planned. The electrification was completed and energised in December 1988. It has been complemented by Italian Railways' electrification of their Puster Valley line from the border to the southern slope of the Brenner route at Fortezza.

Further electrification has now yielded priority to the renewal of existing catenary and other works on trunk routes undergoing 'Neue Bahn' redevelopment. The only new schemes envisaged in the short term concern short stretches of connections between Vienna and the Czechslovak system. The two railways are planning to revive the route between Vienna and Bratislava.

Traction and rolling stock
Delivery began in 1989 of a new series of 15 Class 1044.2 locomotives built by Simmering-Graz-Pauker with electrical equipment from ABB, Elin and Siemens. The new batch, designated Class 1044.2, has a restyled exterior and is geared for 180 km/h top speed, compared with the 160km/h of previous examples.

A final order for 25 Class 1044 is expected. Its successor in the later 1990s is to be an 82-tonne, 6000kW Class 1012 Bo-Bo featuring GTO thyristor inverter drive of three-phase motors, and designed for a top speed of 230km/h. Traction motors will be bogie-mounted with a hollow cardan shaft drive. The Class 1012 will be equipped with the German Federal's LZB inductive train control to fit them for through running over West Germany's high-speed lines.

Following satisfaction with the two dual-voltage Class 1146 Bo-Bos rebuilt from Class 1046 units for throughout haulage of the Vienna-Budapest Euro-City train, a 72-tonne dual-voltage 3500kW Class 1014 with 160km/h capability is to be ordered. Mechanical parts will be derived from Class 1044 and electrical equipment from Class 1146. An order for 18 is likely to be placed with SGP-Elin in 1992.

For through freight working between Germany and Italy via the Brenner the ABB-Siemens-SGP consortium is to deliver in 1991 five prototypes of dual-voltage (15kV ac/3V dc) 82-tonne Class 1822 Bo-Bo with a 4300kW rating. Top speed will be 140km/h.

For standard-gauge service 20 Class 5047 diesel-hydraulic railcars of DB VT627 type have been supplied by Jenbacker Werke. Seating 62, each railcar is powered by a Daimler Benz 440 kW engine with Voith hydraulic transmission. Seating capacity has proved inadequate on some services, compelling renovation of three railbus trailers to work with the cars.

Although the ÖBB has opted for electric locomotives (the three-phase Classes 1063/4) to work its new main yards (see below), it has also taken on a new 820 kW four-axle diesel-hydraulic type, Class 2068, for marshalling work elsewhere. The first example was delivered by Jenbacher-Werke in November 1989.

At the start of 1990 ÖBB owned 721 electric, 488 diesel and 18 steam locomotives, 223 emus and 97 dmus, 3396 passenger cars (including 25 restaurant, 11 sleeping and 120 couchette cars) and 30 270 freight wagons.

Vienna and Villach yards
The automated Villach Süd yard, with 13 arrival tracks and a 40 track sorting and departure complex, was completed in May 1990; its 49 tracks can process 3400 wagons daily. A major multi-function goods transhipment terminal is to be set up close to it by Austrian Cargo Port in association with the ÖBB.

Remote radio control of humping is already in practice with the new Class 1064 asynchronous motor electric Co-Co shunters at the Vienna Klesering automatic yard and will also be the practice at Villach. The locomotives are under driver control for collection of trains from reception sidings. When humping is to begin, the driver is directed by the control tower to switch his locomotive to remote operation by the computer-based apparatus that switches the wagon 'cuts' below the hump and calculates ideal humping speed for each 'cut'.

Double-tracking
On the Vorarlberg route, double-tracking proceeds in the Feldkirch-Bludenz sector, for completion by 1992.

Another important route improvement is in progress through the Schober pass, on the line from Selzthal to St Michael that connects the western provinces including Linz with the industries of upper Styria. Besides double-tracking the project includes station reconstruction, installation of modern reversible signalling and track-to-train radio, abolition of some 80 level crossings and realignment for maximum speed of 120 km/h overall, but up to 140 km/h in places.

Track
Standard rail
Standard gauge: 53.81, 49.43, 44.35 kg/m
Narrow gauge: 26.15 kg/m
Length
Standard gauge: 30 and 60 m
Narrow gauge: 20 m
Cross ties (sleepers)
Standard gauge: impregnated wood 2600 × 260 × 160 mm
also steel and concrete
Narrow gauge: impregnated wood 1600 × 200 × 130 mm
Cross ties spacing
Standard gauge: 600–700 mm (1540 per km)
Narrow gauge: 810 mm (1235 per km)
Rail fastening
Standard gauge: resilient fastening, ribbed slabs, clips and bolts, keyed plates and bolts. Pandrol (spring U-bolt) and Macbeth (spring grip spike)
Narrow gauge: base plates and spikes
Filing
Standard gauge: broken stone ballast
Narrow gauge: broken stone ballast
Thickness under sleepers
Standard gauge: 200–300 mm
Narrow gauge: 150 mm
Minimum or sharpest curvature
Standard gauge: 9.7° = minimum radius of 180 m
Narrow gauge: 29.1° = minimum radius of 60 m
Max gradient compensated
Standard gauge: 1 in 22 (4.6%)
Narrow gauge: 1 in 40 (2.5%)

RAILWAY SYSTEMS / Austria

Max gradient uncompensated
Standard gauge: 7.4%
Max combination of gradient and curvature
Standard gauge: 1:46 with 125 m curve radius
Narrow gauge: 1:40 with 100 m radius
Gauge width with max curvature
Standard gauge: 20 mm

Narrow gauge: 20 mm
Max super elevation
Standard gauge: 160 mm
Narrow gauge: 60 mm
Max axleload
Standard gauge: 20 tonnes
Narrow gauge: 12 tonnes

Max permitted speeds
Passenger trains, standard gauge: 140 km/h
 narrow gauge: 50 km/h
Freight trains, standard gauge: 120 km/h
 narrow gauge: 40 km/h

Principal electric locomotives

Class	Wheel arrangement	Line voltage	Rated output (kW) continuous/one hour	Max speed km/h	Weight tonnes	Overall length mm	No in service 1.1.90	Year first built	Builders Mechanical parts	Builders Electrical equipment
1010	Co-Co	15 kV 16⅔ Hz ac	3260/3990	130	110	17 860	20	1955	SGP	ABES
1110	Co-Co	15 kV 16⅔ Hz ac	3260/3990	110	110	17 860	29	1956	SGP	ABES
1018	1-Do-1	15 kV 16⅔ Hz ac	2950/3340	130	110	16 920	4	1939	Lofag	AEG, S
1020	Co-Co	15 kV 16⅔ Hz ac	2910/3186	90	119	18 600	39	1940	Krauss/Lofag	AEG, S
1040	Bo-Bo	15 kV 16⅔ Hz ac	1980/2020	90	80	12 920	16	1950	Lofag	ABES
1041	Bo-Bo	15 kV 16⅔ Hz ac	1980/2020	90	83	15 320	23	1952	SGP	ABES
1141	Bo-Bo	15 kV 16⅔ Hz ac	2100/2400	110	80	14 260	30	1955	SGP	ABES
1042	Bo-Bo	15 kV 16⅔ Hz ac	3336/3600	130	84	16 220	60	1963	SGP	BES
1042	Bo-Bo	15 kV 16⅔ Hz ac	3808/4000	150	84	16 220	195	1966	SGP	BES
1043	Bo-Bo	15 kV 16⅔ Hz ac	3600/4000	135	83	15 580	10	1971	ASEA	ASEA
1044	Bo-Bo	15 kV 16⅔ Hz ac	5000/5310	160	84	16 000	132	1974	SGP	BES
1044	Bo-Bo	15 kV 16⅔ Hz ac	5000/5310	220	84	16 000	1	1987	SGP	BES
1045	Bo-Bo	15 kV 16⅔ Hz ac	930/1105	60	61	10 400	3	1927	Lofag	ELIN
1145	Bo-Bo	15 kV 16⅔ Hz ac	1070/1260	70	71	11 880	4	1930	Krauss/Lofag	ELIN
1245	Bo-Bo	15 kV 16⅔ Hz ac	1504/1780	80	83	12 920	32	1934	Lofag	ABES
1046	Bo-Bo	15 kV 16⅔ Hz ac	1360/1550	125	67	16 330	19	1956	Lofag	ABES
1146	Bo-Bo	15 kV 16⅔ Hz ac/ 25kV ac 50 Hz	2400	140	73	16 330	2	1987	Lofag	ELIN
1061	D	15 kV 16⅔ Hz ac	525/700	40	55	9890	4	1926	Lofag	AEG
1161	D	15 kV 16⅔ Hz ac	545/725	40	56	10 500	13	1928	Lofag	AEG
1062	D	15 kV 16⅔ Hz ac	775	50	68	10 820	12	1953	Lofag	AEG, S
1063	Bo-Bo	15 kV 16⅔ Hz ac/ 25kV 50 Hz ac	1520/2000	100	80	15 560	37	1983	SGP	BES
1064	Co-Co	15 kV 16⅔ Hz ac	1520	100	113	18 000	8	1985	SGP	BES
1067	C	15 kV 16⅔ Hz ac	440	70	48	10 500	2	1962	JW	ELIN
1080	E	15 kV 16⅔ Hz ac	815/990	50	77	12 750	6	1923	Krauss	S
1180	E	15 kV 16⅔ Hz ac	970/1260	50	81	12 750	5	1926	Krauss	S
760 mm gauge										
1099	C-C	6{929}5 kV 25 hZ	310/405	45	50	11 020	15	1911	Krauss	S

Electric railcars or multiple-units

Class	No of cars per unit	Line voltage	No of motor cars per unit	No of Motored axles per motor car	Rated output (kW) per motor	Max speed km/h	Weight tonnes per car (M-motor T-trailer)	Total seating capacity per car (M-motor T-trailer)	Length per car mm (M-motor T-trailer)	No in service 1.1.90	Rate of acceleration m/s²	Year first built	Builders Mechanical parts	Builders Electrical equipment
4010	6	15 kV 16⅔ Hz ac	1	4	620	150	M=72 T=40	264	M=17 000 T=26 000	29	0,18	1964	SGP	BBC
4020	3	15 kV 16⅔ Hz ac	1	4	300	120	M=63 T=34	184	M=23 000 T=23 000	120	0,32	1978	SGP	BES
4030	3	15 kV 16⅔ Hz ac	1	4	250	100	M=68/59 T=33/36	210	M=23 000 T=23 000	72	0,26/0,2	1956	SGP	BES
4130	3	15 kV 16⅔ Hz ac	1	4	315	120	M=70 T=37	158	M=23 000 T=23 000	2	0,26	1958	SGP	Siemens

Diesel locomotives

Class	Wheel arrangement	Trans-mission	Rated power (kW)	Max speed km/h	Total weight tonnes	No in service 1.1.90	Year first built	Builders Mechanical parts	Engine and type	Transmission
1435 mm gauge										
2043	B-B	Hydr	1120	110	70	76	1964	JW	JW 400 (01–4) LM 1500 (5+)	Voith
2143	B-B	Hydr	1120	110	68	76	1965	SGP	SGP T 12c	Voith
2045	Bo-Bo	Elec	750	90	68	11	1952	SGP	SGP (2x) S12a	Elin
2050	Bo-Bo	Elec	1140	100	75	18	1958	Henschel	GM 12-567c	GM
2060	B	Hydr	140	30/60	27	95	1954	JW	JW 200	Voith
2062	B	Hydr	290	40/60	32	65	1958	JW	JW 400	Voith
2066	C	Hydr	147	40	32	1	1954	-	SGP R 8	Voith
2067	C	Hydr	440	65	49	111	1959	SGP	S 12a/S12na	Voith
2068	B-B	Hyd	820	50/100	68	1	1989	JW	JW 480D	Voith
760 mm gauge										
2090	Bo	Elec	90	40	13	1	1930	SGP	Saurer BXD	Syst. Gebus
2190	Bo	Elec	110	45	13	1	1934	SGP	SGP SU8	Syst. Gebus
2091	1-Bo-1	Elec	160	50	22	10	1936	SGP	SGP R 8	Syst. Gebus
2092	C	Hydr	100	20	17	4	1943		Deutz ABM 517	Voith
2093	Bo-Bo	Elec	160	40	29	1	1926	SGP	SGP R 8	Syst. Gebus
2095	B-B	Hydr	450	60	32	15	1958	SGP	S 12a	Voith

Graz-Köflach Railway
Graz-Köflacher Eisenbahn- und Bergbau-Gesellshaft (GKB)

Grazbachgasse 39, 8010 Graz

Telephone: +43 316 8001
Telex: 311318 gkb g
Telefax: +43 316 832570

Director: Dr Arnold Plankensteiner

Gauge: 1435 mm
Total route-km: 96.5

The railway, which since the Second World War has been a subsidiary of the Alpin-Montan group though it is operated as an autonomous entity, heads south from its own station at Graz to Lieboch, where it branches north-west to Köflach and south to Wies. In addition the company operates 28 bus routes in West Steiermark.

Traffic
Regular passenger service is provided chiefly by diesel railcars, but the company also maintains steam locomotives of Classes 29, 56 and 50 for special charter train operation.

Traffic	1988	1989
Total fright tonnes:	650 592	620 254
Total freight tonne-km (million)	17.577	17.119

GKB Type VT70 diesel railcars at Graz (*Graham Scott-Lowe*)

Revenues (Sch million)
Passengers and baggage:	84,1
Freight, parcels and mail:	53,2
Other income:	24,6
Total	161,9

Total passenger-km (million)	53.347	50.920
Total passenger journeys (million)	2.068	1.950

Expenditure (Sch million)
Staff/personnel:	262,3
Materials and services:	71,2
Total	333,5*

* State subsidy covers depreciation, financial charges and revenue shortfall

Modernisation
In 1988 a modernisation plan was formulated. Its main aims were: double-tracking; a lift of maximum speed to 100 km/h; introduction of track-to-train radio; signalling renewal; acquisition of bi-level passenger cars; and electrification from Graz to Köflach and Lieboch to Wies/Eibiswald.

Rolling stock
The company operates 3 steam locomotives, 15 diesel locomotives, 13 diesel train-sets, 7 diesel railcars and 20 trailers, 40 passenger cars, 1 buffet car and 254 freight wagons. Its latest railcars are 13 Type VT70 articulated twin-units with MTU engines and Brown Boveri electric transmissions, built by Simmering-Graz-Pauker to Linke-Hofmann-Busch design under licence.

Diesel line-haul locomotives

Class	Wheel arrangement	Trans-mission	Rated power kW	Max speed km/h	Total weight tonnes	No in service	Length mm	Years built	Builders Mechanical parts	Engine & type	Transmission
1500	B-B	Hyd	1103	100	64-72	6	12 000	1975/78	Jenbach/Henschel	Jenbach LM1500	Voith L720rU2
750	C	Elec	550	60	48	3	9500	1964/69	JAM Zeltweg	MAN and MTU	BBC dc-dc
700	C	Hyd	515	48	6	1	9860	1977	MaK	MaK	Voith L4r4U2
600	C	Hyd	441	60	48	3	10 660	1973	Jenbach	Jenbach JW600	Voith L26StV
390	C	Hyd	294	60	38	1	9440	1955	Henschel	Jenbach JW400	Voith L37U2
360	C	Hyd	265	60	36	1	9460	1940	MBA	Jenbach JW400	Voith L37U2

Diesel railcars

Class	Cars per unit	Motor cars per unit	Motored axles per motor car	Trans-mission	Rated power (kW) per motor	Max speed km/h	Weight tonnes per car	Total seating capacity	Length per unit mm	No in service	Year first built	Builders Mechanical parts	Engine & type	Transmission
VT70 (Bo-2-Bo)	2	2	2	Elec	228	90	54	104	30 186	5	1980	SGP/LHB	Büssing BTYUE	BBC ac-dc
VT70 (Bo-2-Bo)	2	2	2	Elec	237	90	54	106	30 186	8	1985	SGP/LHB	Büssing D2866 LUE	BBC ac-dc
VT50	1	1	1	Mech	110	90	20.2	62	12 750	2	1952	Uerdingen	Büssing U10	ZF-Gmeinder
VT10	1	1	2	Mech	2 × 110	90	24	61	13 298	7	1953/1968	Uerdingen	Büssing U10	ZF-Gmeinder

RAILWAY SYSTEMS / Austria—Bangladesh

The railway was expected in 1991 to order 15 bi-level passenger cars. Which of the existing European models it would adopt, and whether the cars would be imported or built in Austria under licence, remained to be decided. Seven passenger cars were acquired from the ÖBB in mid-1989.

Signalling
The railway's next major investment is expected to be installation of track-to-train radio communication.

Type of coupling: UIC-coupler, railcars and railbuses excepted.
Type of braking: Compressed air

Track
Rail: (B) (S49) 49.43 kg/m; Xa 35.65 kg/m
Cross ties (sleepers): Wood, thickness 160 mm
Concrete, thickness 200 mm

Spacing: 1538/km plain track and curves
Fastening: Rippenplatte and Pandrol
Minimum curvature radius: 181.25 m
Max gradient: 0.015%
Max axleload: Rail B (S49) 20 tonnes; Rail Xa 16 tonnes

Bangladesh

Ministry of Communications
Dhaka

Minister: Anwar Hossain
Inspector, Railways: M S Zaman

Bangladesh Railway (BRB)

Rail Bhaban, Dhaka
Telephone: +880 31 416665
Cable: Transrail Dhaka

Railway Building, Chittagong
Telephone: +880 31 500120/39
Telex: 66200 Crbbj

Director General: Manzoor-ul-Karim

EAST ZONE

General Manager: A K M Zainul Abedin
Additional General Manager: M S Zaman
Chief Commercial Manager: M T Hossain
Chief Mechanical Engineer: K M A Rab
Chief Engineer: M A Manaf
Chief Signals & Telecommunications Engineer: A Khaleque
Chief Electrical Engineer: M Saifur Rahman
Chief Operating Superintendent: M Rashidul Alam
Chief Accounts Officer: A I M Habibur Rahman
Stores Controller: K G Ahmed

WEST ZONE

General Manager: L Rahman
Additional General Manager: M A Rahim
Chief Commercial Manager: K Anowar
Chief Operating Superintendent: M A Alim
Chief Accounts Officer: B A M A Sattar
Stores Controller: S Islam
Chief Engineer: A K M Saiful Alam
Chief Mechanical Engineer: S Habibullah
Chief Signals & Telecommunications Engineer: A M M Yahia
Chief Electrical Engineer: M M R Khandaker

PROJECT MANAGEMENT

General Manager: A I Chowdhury
Chief Engineer: A H Khan
Chief Mechanical Engineer: S C Das
Director, Telecommunications: M Rahman
Financial Adviser: M Roushanuzzaman

Gauge: 1676 mm; 1000 mm
Total route length: 923 km; 1822 km

The previous unitary Railway Board was dismantled in June 1982. The system is now under the overall control of a Director-General who heads the Railway Division of the Ministry of Communications. For day-to-day operational management the railway is partitioned into two administrative zones. The West Zone is mainly broad gauge, the East metre.

Zones to be connected
At present the only link between East and West is a metre-gauge freight wagon ferry across the Jamuna River. The crossing adds 18 hours to transits.

In 1988 BR moved to construct a 105 km metre-gauge rail connection between the two zones, from Bogra on its Santahar-Bonarpara line to Bausi on the Jamalpur-Jagannathganj Ghar branch. Centrepiece will be a 4.8 km road-rail bridge over the Jamana river. Completion is forecast for 1994.

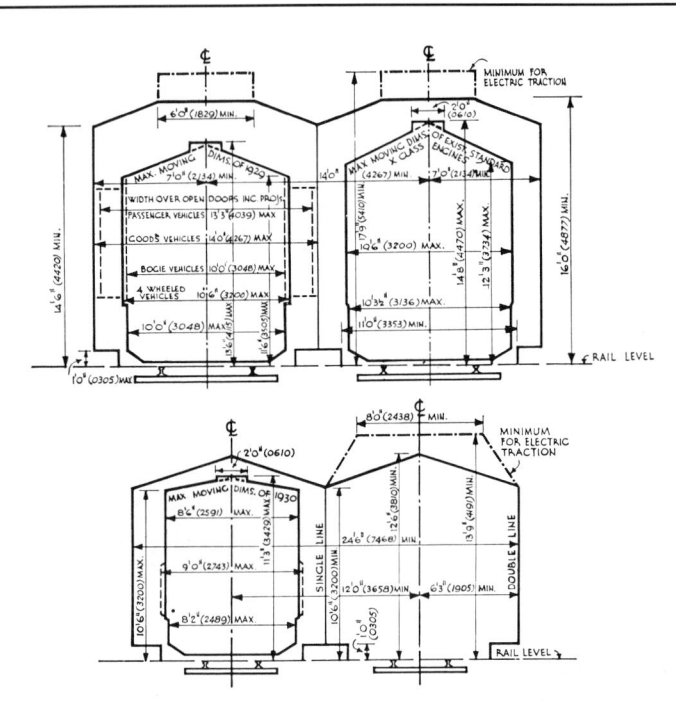

Loading and structure-design diagrams for Bangladesh Railways showing (top) for broad-gauge trucks and (bottom) for metre-gauge

Diesel-hydraulic six-wheeled 368 kW locomotive by Ganz Mávag (manufacturer's Type DHM-9)

Freight traffic
In 1988, the latest period for which statistics are available, carryings were 2.5 million tonnes and 678 million tonne-km. Container transport has begun between the Port of Chittagong, on the Gulf of Bengal, and a new terminal at Dhaka, using box wagons converted into flatcars. In early 1990 the railway was about to invite bids for supply of 69 metre-gauge bogie flatcars for conveyance of 40ft containers.

Passenger traffic
Passenger traffic rose from 89.3 million journeys in 1980/81 to 105.6 million in 1982/83, but had slumped drastically to 53 million in 1988. Passenger-km in 1988 totalled 5052 million. Effort is increasingly concentrated on long-haul business and BR's 30 daily inter-city trains account for a third of its passenger income.

Motive power and rolling stock
In 1988 BRB was operating 291 diesel locomotives. The diesel locomotive fleet includes units of British, Canadian, US, Hungarian and Japanese manufacture. BRB also operated seven single-unit diesel railcars. Recent additions have been 38 368 kW shunters from Ganz-Mávag of Hungary.

The stock of 1794 passenger cars includes 11

metre-gauge coaches recently built in BRB's own workshops, 62 cars from Pakistan Railways' Islamabad works, 70 cars from Projects & Equipment Corporation of India including five dining cars, and 60 cars from Hyundai of South Korea.

Freight wagon stock totals 19 524 vehicles. Equipment of wagon stock with vacuum brakes is a high priority, with the immediate objective of continuously braking at least half the vehicles in all freight trains, which average 1000 tonnes of payload on the metre-gauge and 1200 tonnes on the broad gauge.

Infrastructure
Under the third Five-Year Plan starting in 1985 14 major junctions have been equipped with relay interlockings and a microwave network set up for inter-divisional communication (see below).

In connection with this third plan the government approved a US$70 million investment programme that would be substantially supported by foreign finance. A major item was creation of a workshop for heavy maintenance and repair of diesel locomotives at Parbatipur. With Swedish aid new signal interlockings would be provided at three key stations. Rehabilitation of track and bridges on the 475 km Khulna-Parbatipur line was to be undertaken, also attention to a considerable proportion of the passenger car and wagon fleet.

In 1988 a monobloc prestressed concrete sleeping manufacturing plant was completed by Indian Railway Construction Co with Indian financial aid.

Feasibility studies for three new lines and for a bypass of Dhaka have been completed.

Signalling and communications
In 1986 Telephone Cables Limited (TCL), a subsidiary of Britain's GEC, gained a contract worth £12 million for a turnkey optical fibre communications system for Bangladesh Railway. The project, which is being funded by the Norwegian Government, was the first optical fibre system within Bangladesh.

The 1700 km-long optical fibre system has been constructed along routes connecting the East and West zones of the railway with a radio link across the River Jamuna. The contract included the supply and installation of digital automatic telephone exchanges and telephone instruments. This provides an automatic telephone service between Bangladesh Railway subscribers located through the railway network from Chittagong to Lalmonirhat. In addition, the contract included a train control system for telecommunication between trains and railway stations, civil engineering work, installation, training and maintenance

Track
Rail types and weight: 75 lb 'A', 90 lb 'A' FF BSS rails, 50 lb 'R', 60 lb 'R', 90 lb 'R' FF BSS rails, 50 NS, 50 ISR and 80 lb

Cross ties (sleepers)
Thickness: wooden sleeper BG 5 in; steel through sleeper BG ½ in, cast iron CST/9 block; wooden sleeper MG 4½ in; steel through sleeper MG 11/32 in; cast iron sleeper CST/9 (block)
Spacing: N + 1, N + 2, N + 3, N + 4, N + 5
Rail fastenings: Fishplates, fish boxes, dog spikes, bearing plates, anchor bearing plates, round spikes, steel keys and steel jaws and rail anchors of different sizes
Signal and train control installations: Relay and mechanical interlocking

Railway-owned shipping services, train and road vehicle ferries
Routes served
(i) Jagannathganj-Serajganj ghat (passenger ferry services)
(ii) Bahadurabad-Tistamukh ghat (passenger and wagon ferry services)
Vessels employed: 1 steamer, 6 tugs, 9 barges

Belgium
Ministry of Communications

62 rue de la Loi, 1040 Brussels

Telephone: +32 2 237 6711

Minister: Jean-Luc Dehaene
Secretary-General: R Baelde

Société Nationale des Chemins de fer Belges (SNCB)
Nationale Maatschappij der Belgische Spoorwegen (NMBS)

85 rue de France, 1070 Brussels

Telephone: +32 2 525 2111
Telex: 25035 rail cb (Marketing and Sales)
20424 berail b (General Services)
21526 rail rb (Transportation)
Telefax: +32 2 525 4045

President, Board of Administration: D Reynders
Chief Executive: Etienne Schouppe
Assistant General Manager: J Cornet
General Manager's Office
 International Affairs: L Verberckt
General Services Group
 Co-ordination, General Inspection: M Page
 Legal Affairs: J Bière
 Business Economics: J de Greef
 External Relations: W Van Gestel
 Personnel: M Bouquiaux
 Research and Safety Development: F Freys
 Information Systems: J Surmont
 Purchasing: F Moraux
Rolling Stock Department Manager: R Soenen
Infrastructure Department Manager: J P Van Wouwe
Marketing & Freight Sales: Francis de Pooter
Finance Manager: B de Closset
Transport Department Manager: A Martens

Gauge: 1435 mm
Route length: 3568 km
Electrification: 2207 route-km at 3 kV dc

All standard-gauge lines are operated by the SNCB. All metre-gauge light railways, in addition to bus services, have hitherto been under the aegis of the Société Nationale des Chemins de Fer Vicinaux (SNCV). But in 1990, in deference to Belgium's new federal statutes, SNCV was to be divided into separate Flemish and Walloon territory organisations.

Management structure
The post of Chief Executive was created in 1987. The SNCB General Manager and his Deputy report to the Chief Executive.

The five activities reporting directly to the General Manager are: transport; rolling stock and equipment; infrastructure; finances; and marketing and sales. Other administrative functions, such as data processing, purchases and co-ordination, are segregated as a General Services Group to which General Management has access, but whose direct responsibility is to the Chief Executive.

Alongside the Chief Executive are three committees, two of which assemble general management, department and district heads in co-ordinating and inter-communicating roles. The third, with limited Board of Administration, Chief Executive and General/Deputy General Manager membership, has an executive role, with power to authorise expenditure on a scale previously reserved to Ministerial decision.

SNCB is partitioned into five operational districts.

Turnround in 1988
Results of the drastic managerial restructure and subsequent rationalisation measures were beginning to show through in 1988. After years of deficit (even with account taken of subsidies that in sum exceeded total passenger and freight revenue), SNCB recorded a modest surplus of Bfr406 million. The budget had provided for a loss of Bfr4300 million. The turnround was secured despite the government's cut of support for passenger services, so that only half instead of two-thirds of their operating costs are subsidised. Accumulated debt, too, was reduced to Bfr83 900 million, a drop of almost 17 per cent in three years.

Contributing to the improved financial result was an extraordinary gain of Bfr875 million from a rolling stock sale-and-lease-back exercise. Another important development, introduced in 1988, is that state contributions to infrastructure and rolling stock renewals are now treated as additions to SNCB capital.

The labour force has been cut from 68 000 in 1982 to 47 000. Other important economies have come from rationalisation of rolling stock maintenance, leading to greatly extended periods between basic routines and a cut of maintenance sites from 115 to 79; from a decision to persist with a 140 km/h top speed except where complete track renewal is required, as SNCB services' short distances and frequent stops prevent a worthwhile return on the cost of upgrading for 160 km/h; and from freight service rationalisation (see below).

STAR 21
In the autumn of 1989 SNCB published a development plan for the next century titled, in a Flemish acronym, STAR 21. This assumes that by the year 2000 Belgian people's mobility will have increased by 35 per cent; and consequently that the railway's traffic will by then have risen 17 per cent.

SNCB therefore seeks to restructure its passenger services. Their centrepiece would be the Paris-London-Brussels-Amsterdam-Cologne high-speed trains over new infrastructure (see below). On the domestic front a limited-stop IC-Plus network of trains between main cities would be superimposed on SNCB's present IC system. Where feasible, SNCB seeks to accelerate journeys by infrastructure work, including elimination of some bottlenecks. Where this is not practicable, it envisages resort to tilt-body train-set technology; routes in mind in that context include Lille-Liége and Basel-Brussels.

STAR 21 proposes the restructuring of suburban services in Brussels, and subsequently in Antwerp and

Eupen-Ostend InterCity headed by Class 27 electric locomotive. (Marcel Vleugels)

Liége, on regional express metro principles. It is also anxious for approval of a scheme to convert the presently terminal Brussels Zaventem Airport branch into a loop for service by through IC trains. The branch would be projected north of the airport to a junction with the Brussels-Antwerp line south of Mechelen; and its junction with the Brussels-Liége line would be made triangular to allow through Liége-Antwerp service via the airport station.

STAR 21 foresees SNCB's 1989 freight gross of 66.2 million tonnes scaling 92.6 million by year 2010. A slight loss of domestic freight is anticipated, so achievement centres on lifting annual international traffic to 67.6 million tonnes. This will be founded on a new framework of fast, daily direct train links between Belgian ports and some 30 trunk Continental axes, running at 120 km/h and scheduled to obtain next-morning delivery over transits of up to 1500 km. The resultant shortening of many current freight transits by 12 hours is reckoned to be worth a 30 per cent increase of traffic. This rejuvenated service will be comprehensively supported by electronic data interchange and traffic monitoring systems.

Maximisation of intermodal potential is vital. SNCB believes that 55 per cent of its freight traffic other than bulk commodities is apt for one or other intermodal system.

Full implementation of STAR 21 is calculated to require investment in the railway to jump from the present annual figure of some Bfr 7000 million a year to around Bfr 25.900 million a year for the next three decades. The high-speed infrastructure and rolling stock elements of the 30-year plan would absorb a third of the expenditure. SNCB also calls for more evenhanded fiscal treatment of rail and road transport. It expects regional and local authorities to contribute financially to domestic passenger service projects.

Passenger traffic

Belgium's dense road system, which includes over 1600 route-km of motorway (in relation to land area, this represents four times more motorway coverage than in neighbouring France), conduces to the 88.5 per cent private motoring share of all Belgian travel. SNCB claims only 9.7 per cent. Only a third of all rail travel, moreover, is on standard fares: discounted period tickets account for almost 40 per cent, reduced-price tickets for the remainder.

A regular-interval timetable interlocks InterCity (IC) and Inter-Regional (IR) routes. The service is one of the most intensive in Europe. Brussels and Bruges, for example, are linked daily by 44 pairs of trains, which beyond Bruges continue alternately to Ostend and Knokke. Brussels and Namur are connected by 32 pairs of trains daily, Brussels and Tournai by 20 pairs.

In 1989 SNCB recorded a modest 0.8 per cent rise in passenger-km and a 2.7 per cent increase in passenger revenue. Continued recession in commuter income was offset by a substantial resurgence of international travel to and from neighbouring countries.

Freight traffic

In 1989 freight traffic volume rose 1 per cent to 66.22 million tonnes. Ores were up 10 per cent and aggregates 5.5 per cent, but there were declines of 4.5 to 17 per cent in volumes of fuels, petrochemical products and agricultural freight. Steel plants' input and output contributed 19.6 million tonnes, a drop of 1.2 per cent compared with 1988, but this was less than the steel industry's own output reduction of 2 per cent.

Intermodal traffic climbed 12 per cent to 5.9 million tonnes. Container transport was up 6.6 per cent, piggyback of highway trailers and swap bodies up 26 per cent. Piggyback now constitutes almost a quarter of SNCB's intermodal traffic, just over 80 per cent of which is international.

In a short-term programme SNCB aims by 1995 to capture 20–30 per cent more maritime container business, and to double its international piggyback traffic. Supporting investments that are going ahead include clearance enlargement of a Montzen area tunnel on the Antwerp-Aachen axis to ease restrictions on container and swapbody sizes that have hitherto compelled the routeing via the Netherlands of some traffic to Germany, Austria, Eastern Europe and Scandinavia.

In 1989 container traffic between Antwerp and Germany was up 44 per cent, fuelled partly by the MCN scheme for unified North Sea port-German terminal tarification and marketing, and partly by the plugging of Antwerp into the DB's KLV Europa expansion of its KLV 88 network of overnight inter-

Finances (Bfr million)

Revenue	1983	1984	1985	1986	1987
Passengers and baggage	10 289.7	10 701.7	11 578.1	11 164.8	11 300.1
Freight					
Wagonloads	11 425.7	13 362.9	14 279.3	12 500.3	12 165.2
Less-than-wagonloads	3337.8	3451	3409.1	3004.7	3196.4
Other income	2321.6	2423.3	2908.2	2847.2	2904.3
Financial income	350.3	485.3	696.1	706.2	337.6
State compensation in respect of social tariffs and track maintenance	20 885.5	23 367	22 865.2	22 868.3	19 654.4
Total	48 610.6	53 791.2	55 736	53 085.5	49 554.7

Expenditure					
Administration	1613.4	1781.7	1888.5	2123.5	1993.6
Infrastructure upkeep	6387.5	7405.3	7276.1	7302.2	6986.9
Signalling, telecommunications, electrification, fixed assets	6340.5	7145.8	6543.1	6459.9	6379.9
Traction	22 934.2	24 958.9	25 021.4	23 689.3	22 854.3
Terminals	17 503.8	19 210.4	18 801.1	19 026.8	18 801.3
Road transport, publicity, etc	868.8	1028	1007.1	1059.3	1107.3
Renewals (State-financed)	–	–	–	–	–
Insurance	334	592.4	423.1	306.6	160.1
Financial charges	8598.6	8770.8	9530	10 481.4	3075.6
Less rationalisation costs	316.2				
Other	-	1461	766.6	1060.9	1154.0
Total	64 264.6	72 354.3	71 257	71 502.9	68 543.0
Less state compensation to equalise terms of competition and to cover financial charges	15 598	18 245.9	15 689.2	15 455.7	14 947.9
Total	48 666.6	54 108.4	55 567.8	56 046.2	53 565.1

Class 20 electric locomotive and Basle-Brussels 'Iris' EuroCity train (*John C Baker*)

Class AM86 suburban emu

modal trains between key centres. This move forged direct connections between Antwerp and eight DB intermodal hubs.

SNCB investment planned for the first half of the 1990s includes acquisition of 300 intermodal wagons; fettling up of international intermodal train routes for 120 km/h in general, 140 km/h for lightly-loaded wagons on some routes; and improvement of access to several intermodal terminals, renewal of transshipment equipment, and in some cases terminal expansion.

The SNCB also proposes to reform its intermodal business in two companies. One, Rail Terminals, in which the SNCB as majority shareholder would partner piggyback company TRW and the rail container groupage company Railtrans, would manage the terminals. Interrail, in which the SNCB share would be 49 per cent, would market the services.

Under SNCB's 1986 TOP-Plan, aimed to improve the quality of its offer for higher-rated traffic, wagonload traffic is concentrated on six yards, at Antwerp North, Hasselt, Merelbeke, Kinkempois, Monceau and Saint-Ghislain, which are interconnected by unit trains. These six surviving yards are interlinked by at least two direct trains each way daily. As a result, 97 per cent of freight moving between a pair of Belgian terminals now gets overnight delivery. The recent introduction by European railways of the Trans-Euro-Freight (TEF) scheme has in effect extended the TOP concept to international traffic. TEF is focussed on 120 yards in 23 countries and interlinks them with the SNCB through the medium of 145 daily TEF trains. It has secured 24-hour transits to and from most of Federal Germany, 48-hour transits to a further area bounded by northern Italy, Austria, Czechoslovakia and the German Democratic Republic.

The long-awaited Bfr3842 million modernisation of Antwerp Nord marshalling yard nears completion. The yard, which processes a quarter of all SNCB freight traffic, covers an area 5.5 km by 2 km with 140 km of track. Main items of the modernisation are installation of fully automated sorting and braking control, electrification of additional trackage, enlargement of the sorting yard dealing with incoming traffic from inland by 14 sidings to a total of 56 and similarly that of the yard which handles outgoing traffic.

In 1990 the SNCB was negotiating a new contract with the government. One result was expected to be greater freedom for railway management to set its own freight tariffs.

Paris-Brussels-Cologne high-speed line

The government approved SNCB's choice of route for the projection of the French TGV-Nord into and through Belgium in January 1990. As discussed below, it then remained for the country's three regional administrations to endorse the proposed alignments.

From the French border new 300 km/h infrastructure is planned over the 71.3 km to Brussels Midi, where TGVs will use platforms 1 to 6. The new route would cross the frontier west of Tournai, and from near Ath to Enghien parallel the existing Tournai-Halle tracks. From Halle into Brussels the existing layout will have two extra 3kV dc-electrified tracks added for the TGVs. A burrowing junction may be built at Halle to provide TGV access to the existing tracks into Brussels.

The Lille-Baisieux-Tournai line is to be electrified for use by some Liège-Mouscron trains, which will be re-routed to make connection with TGVs at Lille.

A choice has yet to be made between alternative routes from Brussels to Leuven. In one concept, a pair of 200 km/h tracks would be added to the existing route via Haren. The other would lay new tracks alongside the E40 motorway and afford 300 km/h infrastructure most of the way to a junction with the existing Brussels-Liège route at Bierset. Beyond Liège new 200/250 km/h infrastructure, on a ruling 2.5 per cent gradient, will include a single-track 7 km tunnel beyond Chênée to return the route to a further partnership with the E40 motorway up to Welkenraedt; there trains would join the existing route into Germany via Aachen.

If the maximum amount of new infrastructure is built, journey time for the 71.3km from the French border to Brussels Midi will be 26 minutes; from Brussels Midi to Liège, 100 km, 37 minutes; and from Liège to Aachen, 41.5km, 18 minutes.

The existing exit from Brussels to Antwerp will be upgraded for 160 km/h by TGVs. From Berchem, on the outskirts of Antwerp, a 3 km line tunnelling under that city has been proposed. It would serve en route a two-platform underground station beneath Antwerp Central. Emerging from the tunnel, TGVs would use

First-class compartment of Class AM86 suburban emu

Four Type AM03 'Break' emus form Luxemburg-Brussels InterCity at Jemelle. (*Marcel Vleugels*)

Driving trailer and trailers of Type M5 ('Duo') bi-level commuter stock

RAILWAY SYSTEMS / Belgium

the existing route to the Dutch frontier via Essen and Roosendael.

TGV route not ready until 1995
Within Belgium the high-speed project is highly controversial. A consequence is that the new infrastructure from Lille to Brussels will not be available until 1995, two years after the opening of the Channel Tunnel and the SNCF's inauguration of its TGV-Nord. The works involved in extending the route from Brussels to Liège, Aachen and Cologne will not be complete until 1997-98.

One problem has been Belgium's ability to finance its share of the project. That was covered to some extent, following a démarche by the five Transport Ministers concerned in the high-speed scheme, by the EEC's December 1989 grant of a Bfr4950 million loan towards the cost of the Belgian works between Lille and Brussels, and a further Bfr1.100 million for works on the other side of Brussels.

Crucial, however, is the sharply differing attitude of Flemish-speaking Flanders and French-speaking Wallonia. The Wallonians, in the south of the country, oppose the surrender of farming land for a railway that will have no stations in their territory and demand that they must be compensated by an upgrading of their west-east transversal to plug Namur, Charleroi and Mons into the Paris-Brussels high-speed axis. Flanders will be far less affected by construction of new route, and flatly refuses to contribute through taxes for satisfaction of the Walloons' demands. Following Belgian government approval of the TGV route in January 1990, under the country's new federal provisions it was then up to the Flemish, Walloon and Brussels regional administrations to endorse the proposed alignments in their territory and permit the SNCB to begin construction.

Antwerp-Brussels upgrading
At the end of January 1987 a major upgrading programme was launched on the key SNCB route between Antwerp and Brussels. Completion was expected in 1990. Components are: complete track renewal, including increase of inter-track space to 2.25 m to simplify mechanised maintenance and later increase of permissible speed to at least 160 km/h; resignalling for reversible working and accompanying installation of crossovers; and renewal of electric traction current supply system. The opportunity is being taken to lay a fibre-optics communications cable.

Electrification
Electrification was completed over the 28km from Namur to Dinant early in 1990. As a result the Gent-Namur IC route was extended to Dinant in May 1990.

Locomotives and rolling stock
A batch of 35 M + T two-car emus classified AM 86 was delivered in 1988-89. The design employs the modular construction technology of BN's suburban emu prototype (see BN entry), but the SNCB units have been arranged for IC and IR service. One car in each two-car unit is powered with four ACEC thyristor chopper-controlled 171.5 kW motors. Maximum speed is 120 km/h (but could be uplifted to 140 km/h if desired later), weight of each set 126 tonnes and its total seating capacity 136.

A further 17 AM 86 were ordered in 1989, and at the same time 68 trailers to convert the fleet to three-car units.

A new fleet of two-car postal emus has been created by a complete reconstruction of 15 units from the Class 54 passenger emus of 1954. The units, now windowless except for their cabs, have been flamboyantly liveried in scarlet overlaid on one car by 'POST 90' in white characters that extend the full depth of the bodyside, and on the other by broad lateral stripes of white. The units, adapted internally to load and carry Post Department containers, convey these between Brussels and regional centres at Gand, Liège, Antwerp and Charleroi. Each set can carry up to 86 postal container trolleys.

Type 08 emu at Mons (*Marcel Vleugels*)

Class 53 diesel locomotive (*John C Baker*)

Class 54 diesel locomotive (*John C Baker*)

Locomotives and rolling stock January 1989
Locomotives	
electric	381
diesel	674
Railcars	
electric train-sets	672
diesel railcars	26
Passenger coaches	1911
Freight wagons	31972

Traffic	1984	1985	1986	1987	1988
Freight tonnes (million)	70.8	72.4	63.1	64	66.22
Freight tonne-km (million)	7905	8254	7423	7266	7694
Passenger-km (million)	6444	6572	6069	6230	6348
Passenger journeys (million)	149.9	150.3	139.1	142.2	143.1

Signalling and telecommunications

The SNCB is progressively installing a track-to-train radio system, employing equipment supplied by Bell Telephone, a member of the ITT group. Incorporating state-of-the-art technology, the system conforms to the UIC 751-3 specification. Because of the country's dual language and the need for drivers to use the system with facility in both French- and Flemish-speaking territory, the system uses illuminated cab displays of pictogram codes rather than telephonic speech communication between control centre and train crew.

The major single item on the signalling investment list is a new route-relay centre for Brussels Midi, to oversee the entire layout on the city's southern side plus the key north-south links, a network covering about 120 route-km in total and carrying some 2000 scheduled train movements daily.

The three Brussels main line stations, Midi, Central and Nord, have been equipped by ACEC with computer-controlled passenger announcement systems. Designated SES, the system relies not on synthesised speech production, but on formation of the required announcements by selection from some 4000 words pre-recorded by feminine voices picked for their attractiveness as well as their clarity. The announcements are automatically triggered by approaching trains through the signalling's train describers, but there is a facility for intervention by a local supervisor in the event of service disruption. In time this facility will become superfluous, as a new electronic traffic regulation system, SER, will be able to direct SES automatically in the event of temporary train service adjustments.

The SNCB is in course of replacing its traditional ATC system, based on contact between brushes mounted beneath traction units and track-mounted 'crocodiles', with an inductive transponder system known as 'Train-Balise-Locomotive' (TBL).

Track

Standard/rail: Flat bottom, 50 and 60 kg/m main lines, 50 kg/m secondary lines
Length: Main lines: 243 m rails long-welded. Secondary lines 27 m
Joints: 6-hole fishplates
Rail fastenings: Soleplates and screws for wood sleepers. Type RN flexible fastenings on RS concrete sleepers, rigid clips on FB concrete sleepers, Pandrol fastenings on Type DMD and VDH concrete sleepers (see below). Pads are inserted under the rail when concrete sleepers are used. Pandrol fastenings are used in tunnels.
Cross ties (sleepers): Generally oak, 2600 × 280 × 140 mm. Sections of welded-rail track have been laid with three types of concrete sleeper: Type RS (two blocks joined by a steel bar) with Type RN flexible rail fastenings; Type VDH (two blocks joined by a steel bar) with Pandrol fastenings; and Type DMD (monobloc prestressed) with Pandrol fastenings.

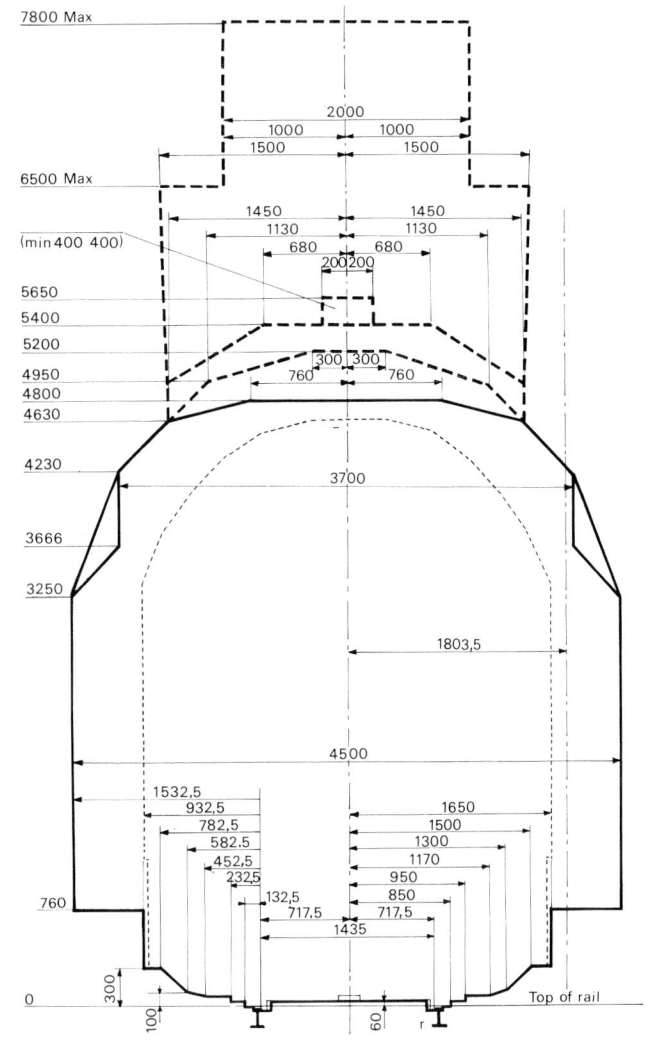

Spacing: 1667/km main-line track; 1370–1590/km secondary routes
Filling: Broken stone or slag
Minimum curvature radius
Main line: 2.18° = 800 m
Secondary line 3.5° = 500 m
Running lines: 8.75° = 200 m
Sidings 11.7° = 150 m

Max gradient: 2.5%
Max altitude: 536 m at Hockai on Pepinster-Trois Ponts line
Max permitted speed: 140 km/h on major main lines. 120 km/h on all other main lines
Max axleload: Certain locomotives have axleload of 24 tonnes. Except for certain bridges they can operate anywhere on the system, subject to speed restriction.

SNCB loading and structure gauge

Electric locomotives

Class	Wheel arrangement	Line current	Rated output (kW) continuous/one-hour	Max lb (kg)	Tractive effort (full field) Continuous at lb (kg)	mph (km/h)	Max speed mph (km/h)	Wheel dia in (mm)	Total weight tonnes	Length ft in (mm)	Year built	Builders Mechanical parts	Electrical equipment
20	Co-Co	3000 V dc	5130/5150	70 100 (32 000)	52 100 (23 600)	50 (78)	100 (160)	49½ (1250)	110	63'11¾" (19 500)	1975-78	Brugeoise et Nivelles	ACEC Charleroi
22	Bo-Bo	3000 V dc	1740/1880	44 000 (20 000)	27 600 (11 500)	32 (51)	81 (130)	49⅝ (1262)	87	59'0¾" (18 090)	1954	Brugeoise et Nivelles	ACEC Charleroi SEM Ghent
23	Bo-Bo	3000 V dc	1740/1880	44 000 (20 000)	27 560 (12 500)	32 (51)	81 (130)	49⅝ (1262)	93.3	59'0¾" (18 000)	1955-57	Atel Metallurgiques de Nivelles	ACEC Charleroi SEM Ghent
25	Bo-Bo	3000 V dc	1740/1880	44 000 (20 000)	27 600 (12 500)	32 (51)	81 (130)	49⅝ (1262)	83.9	59'0¾" (18 000)	1960	Brugeoise et Nivelles	ACEC Charleroi SEM Ghent
25.5	Bo-Bo dual current	3000/ 1500 V dc	1740/1880	44 000 (20 000)	21 600 (12 500)	32 (51)	81 (130)	49⅝ (1262)	85	59'0¾" (18 000)	modified 1973	Brugeoise et Nivelles	ACEC Charleroi SEM Ghent
26	B-B monomotor bogies	3000 V dc	2240/2355* 2470/2590	52 910 (24 000)	35 270 (16 000)	30.7 (49.5)	81 (130)	49¼ (1150)	82.4	56'5" (17 280)	1964/ 69/72	Brugeoise et Nivelles	ACEC Charleroi
28	Bo-Bo	3000 V dc	1620/1985	44 000 (20 000)	27 780 (12 600)	32 (51)	81 (130)	495 (1262)	85	56'4½" (17 180)	1949	Baume-Marpent	ACEC Charleroi SEM Ghent
15	Bo-Bo triple-current	25 kV 50 Hz 3000/ 1500 V dc	2620/2780	38 400 (17 400)	22 000 (10 000)	56 (91)	100 (160)	49¼ (1250)	77.7	58'3" (17 750)	1962	Brugeoise et Nivelles	ACEC Charleroi

RAILWAY SYSTEMS / Belgium

Electric locomotives (continued)

Class	Wheel arrangement	Line current	Rated output (kW) continuous/ one-hour	Tractive effort (full field) Max lb (kg)	Continuous at lb (kg)	mph (km/h)	Max speed mph (km/h)	Wheel dia in (mm)	Total weight tonnes	Length ft in (mm)	Year built	Builders Mechanical parts	Electrical equipment
16	Bo-Bo quadri-current	25 000 V 50 Hz / 15 000 V 16 Hz / 3000 V dc / 1500 V dc	2620/2780	44 000 (20 000)	23 590 (10 700)	52 (84)	100 (160)	49¼ (1250)	82.6	54'7¾" (16 650)	1966	Brugeoise et Nivelles	ACEC Charleroi Siemens
18	C-C quadri-current	25 000 V 50 Hz / 15 000 V 16⅔ Hz / 3000 V dc / 1500 V dc	4320/4450	37 300 (17 000)	26 500 (12 000)	81 (130)	112 (180)	49⅓ (1100)	113	72'5⅓" (22 080)	1973-74	Brugeoise et Nivelles	Alsthom
27	Bo-Bo	3000 V dc	4150/4250	52 910 (24 000)	36 815 (16 700)	56 (90)	100 (160)	49¼ (1250)	85	61'2¼" (18 650)	1981-84	Brugeoise et Nivelles	ACEC Charleroi
21	Bo-Bo	3000 V dc	3140/4500	52 910 (24 000)	33 070 (15 000)	46.6 (75)	100 (160)	49¼ (1250)	84	61'2¼" (18 650)	1984-88	Brugeoise et Nivelles	ACEC Charleroi
11	Bo-Bo	3000 V dc 1500 V dec	3125/3310	52 910 (24 000)	33 070 (15 000)	46.6 (75)	100 (160)	49¼ (1250)	84	61'2¼" (18 650)	1985-86	Brugeoise et Nivelles	ACEC Charleroi
12	Bo-Bo	3000 V dc 25 000 V 50 Hz	3125/3310	59 910 (24 000)	33 070 (15 000)	46.6 (75)	100 (160)	49¼ (1250)	84	61'2¼" (18 650)	1986	Brugeoise et Nivelles	ACEC Charleroi

* First five locomotives only

Electric railcars or multiple-units

Class	Cars per unit	Line current	Motor cars per unit	Motored axles per motor car	Rated output kW per motor car	Max speed km/h	Weight tonnes per set	Total seating capacity	Length per car mm (M-motor T-trailer)	Rate of acceleration m/s²	Year first built	Builders Mechanical parts	Electrical equipment
09/2	2	3000 V dc	2	4	155	120	109	(Postal)	44 970	0.42	1935	NMBS, CW Mechelen	ACEC Charleroi, SEM Ghent
00/2	2	3000 V dc	2	4	155	130	93	170	44 402	0.57	1950-54	La Brugeoise, Nicaise et Delcuve AS, Energie-Marcinelle	ACEC Charleroi SEM Ghent
00/2	2	3000 V dc	2	4	160	130	93	170	44 402	0.47	1954	SA Energie-Marcinelle	SA Ercole Marelli, Milan
00/1	2	3000 V dc	2	4	155	130	84	171 + 17	45 280	0.54	1954	La Brugeoise, Ragheno Mechelen, Germain et Famillereux	ACEC Charleroi SEM Ghent
00/1	2	3000 V dc	2	4	155	130	85.5	173 + 8	45 680	0.54	1956	Ateliers de la Dyle Anglo Franco-Belge-Forges UF Haine St Pierre	ACEC Charleroi SEM Ghent
00/1	2	3000 V dc	2	4	155	130	79.5	171 + 17	45 280	0.49	1956	La Brugeoise Nicaise et Delcuve	ACEC Charleroi SEM Ghent
00/3	2	3000 V dc	2	4	155	130	101	180	46 575	0.47	1962-65	BN Bruges Ragheno Mechelen	ACEC Charleroi
05	2	3000 V dc	2	4	170	140	104	180	46 575	0.46	1967-71	BN Brugge Ragheno Mechelen, Les Usines de Braine-le-Comte, Ateliers Belges Réunis	ACEC Charleroi
05 Airport	2	3000 V dc	2	4	170	140	104	118	46 575	0.46	1970	BN Ragheno Mechelen, Les Usines de Braine-le-Comte, Ateliers Belges Réunis	ACEC Charleroi
Benelux	2	3000 V dc 1500 V dc	2	4	155	125	115	98	50 420	0.36	1957	Werkspoor	ACEC Charleroi SEM Ghent
06	2	3000 V dc	2	4	170	140	106	178	46 615	0.46	1973-80	BN Const Ferrov du Centre Famillereux	ACEC Charleroi
08	4	3000 V dc	2	8	170	140	217	358	99 028	0.47	1975-78	BN	ACEC Charleroi
03 ('Break')	2	3000 V dc	1	4	310	160	106	171	50 850	0.75	1981-85	BN	ACEC Charleroi

Diesel locomotives

Class	Wheel arrangement	Transmission	Rated power hp	Tractive effort Max lb (kg)	Continuous lb (kg)	Max speed mph (km/h)	Wheel dia in (mm)	Total weight tons	Length ft in (mm)	Year first built	Builders Mechanical parts	Engine & type	Transmission
51	Co-Co	Elec	1950	61 200 (27 750)	37 250 (16 900)	75 (120)	49¾ (1010)	117	66'1¾" (20 160)	1961	Cockerill-Ougrée	Cockerill-Ougrée	ACEC-SEM
59	Bo-Bo	Elec	1750	44 000 (20 000)	37 500 (17 000)	75 (120)	44 (1118)	87	53'1" (16 180)	1955	Cockerill; Baume et Marp	Cockerill (licence Baldwin)	ACEC (licence Westinghouse)
52-53	Co-Co	Elec	1720	55 000 (25 000)	35 500 (16 100)	75 (120)	39¾ (1010)	108	61'10" (18 850)	1955	Anglo-Franco-Belge	GM (USA)	GM (USA) Smit
54	Co-Co	Elec	1720	55 000 (25 000)	35 500 (16 100)	75 (120)	39¾ (1010)	108	61'10" (18 850)	1957	Anglo-Franco-Belge	GM (USA)	GM (USA) Smit
55	Co-Co	Elec	1950	61 200 (27 750)	38 000 (17 250)	75 (120)	39¾ (1010)	110	64'2⅜" (19 550)	1961	Brugeoise et Nivelles	GM (USA)	ACEC-SEM (licence GM)

Diesel locomotives (continued)

Class	Wheel arrangement	Transmission	Rated power hp	Max lb (kg)	Tractive effort Continuous lb (kg)	Max speed mph (km/h)	Wheel dia in (mm)	Total weight tons	Length ft in (mm)	Year first built	Builders Mechanical parts	Engine & type	Transmission
60	Bo-Bo	Elec	1400	44 000 (20 000)	24 250 (11 000)	75 (120)	39¾ (1010)	85.4	56'11" (17 350)	1961	Cockerill-Ougrée	Cockerill (licence Baldwin)	ACEC
62 Bogie Flexicoil	Bo-Bo	Elec	1425	47 600 (21 600)	24 250 (11 000)	75 (120)	39¾ (1010)	80	55'1" (16 790)	1961	Brugeoise et Nivelles	GM (USA)	GM (USA)
62 Bogie BN	Bo-Bo	Elec	1425	47 600 (21 600)	24 250 (11 000)	75 (120)	39¾ (1010)	81.6	55'1" (16 790)	1961	Brugeoise et Nivelles	GM (USA)	ACEC (licence GM)
75	B-B	Hyd	1460	42 978 (19 500)	(P)25 350 (11 500) (F)27 500 (17 000)	(P)75 (120) (F)51 (82)	44 (1118)	79	55'1" (16 790)	1965	Brugeoise et Nivelles	GM-2 speed Type 12-567DI	Voith
71	B-B	Hyd	900	39 700 (18 000)	25 300 (11 500) 41 800 (19 000)	(P)50 (80) (F)31 (50)	39¾ (1010)	74	43'9½" (13 350)	1962	ABR	Anglo-Belgian Corp (ABC)	Voith L217
91	B	Hyd	335	22 000 (10 000)	(S)21 560 (9800) (L)10 340 (4700)	13 (21) 28 (45)	49⅝ (1262)	36	21'9" (6625)	1961	Cockerill Brugeoise et Nivelles ABC	GM HM	Twin-Disc Q Cockerill
92	C	Hyd	350	(S)33 000 (15 000) (L)20 700 (9400)		(S)17 (29) (L)28 (45)	49⅝ (1262)	50.55	34'1½" (10 400)	1960	Brugeoise et Nivelles	SEM	Voith L37
84	C	Hyd	550	(S)35 300 (16 000) (L)33 000 (15 000)		(S)20 (33) (L)31 (50)	49⅝ (1262)	55.8	34'11¼" (10 650) 33'3½" (10 150)	1955	ABR; Baume et Marpent	ABC Type 6 DUS	Voith L 37U
85	C	Hyd	550	(S)35 300 (16 000) (L)33 000 (15 000)		(S)20 (33) (L)31 (50)	49⅝ (1262)	58.5	32'10" (10 000)	1956	Forges, Usines et Fonderies Haine St Pierre	ABC Type 6 DXS	Turbo-transmission Voith L37U Inverseur-réduct SEMt.B.122
83	C	Hyd	550	(S)35 300 (16 000) (L)33 000 (15 000)		(S)20 (33) (L)31 (50)	49⅝ (1262)	57	35'3¼" (10 750)	1956	Cockerill-Ougrée	Cockerill-Ougrée (lic Hamilton) 695 SA	Turbo-transmission Voith L37U Invers-reduct
80	C	Hyd	650	(S)38 800 (17 600) (L)28 400 (12 900)		(1g)24 (38) (2g)49 (78)	49¼ (1250)	52.1	34'0" (10 360)	1960	Brugeoise et Nivelles; ABR	Maybach GTO 6A	Voith L 37
70	Bo-Bo	Elec	700	44 000 (20 000)	34 000 (15 400)	31 (50)	42⅛ (1070)	83	39'10¼" (12 150)	1954	Baume et Marpent	ABC	ACEC (licence Westinghouse)
82	C	Hyd	650	42 978 (19 500)		37 (60)	49⅝ (1262)	57	36'7¾" (11 170)	1965/6	Brugeoise et Nivelles; Atel Belges Réunis	ABC Type DXS 6 cyl	Voith L217U
73	C	Hyd	750	47 386 (21 500)		37 (60)	49⅝ (1262)	56	36'7¾" (11 170)	1965/8	Brugeoise et Nivelles	Cockerill-Ougrée 24 000 6-cyl	Voith L217U
74	C	Hyd	750	47 386 (21 000)		37 (60)	49⅝ (1262)	59	36'7¾" (11 170)	1977	Brugeoise et Nivelles	ABC Type 6 DXC	Voith L217V

Benin

Ministry of Equipment and Transport

PO Box 16, Cotonou

Minister: G Gado

Organisation Commune Benin-Niger des Chemins de Fer et des Transports (OCBN)

PO Box 16, Cotonou

Telephone: +229 31 33 80
Cable: Orcodani Cotonou
Telex: 5210

Director-General: René Loko
Director of Motive Power and Rolling Stock: Antoine Tchibozo
Director of Way and Works: A Tamou-Tabe
Director of Operations: M da Silva
Director of Supplies: J Hinson
Director of Finance: O Tinni

Gauge: 1000 mm
Route length: 578 km

OCBN operates, on behalf of Niger and Benin, a single-track metre-gauge railway consisting of: Northern line: from Cotonou to Parakou via Pahou 438 km

Cotonou station (*Wilhelm Pflug*)

Two Alsthom Series 600 diesel locomotives head a Parakou-Cotonou main-line freight (*Wilhelm Pflug*)

Eastern line: from Cotonou to Pobè 107 km
Western line: from Pahou to Ségboroué 33 km
From Parakou freight traffic is transported by road to the Niger capital of Niamey.

A cherished project is the extension of the Northern line from Parakou to Niamey, Niger's capital, a distance of 650 km. At present Niger traffic has to be road-hauled to Parakou. An agreement was signed in 1976 between Niger and Benin for the construction of a rail link, since three-quarters of Niger's exports are channelled through Cotonou, and construction was started in 1978 but made scant progress. Finance remains the major problem. The World Bank has not been forthcoming, nor any other agency.

OCBN has also been seeking external finance for modernisation of the Cotonou-Pobé Eastern line and its extension to a cement factory at Onigbulo with a projected output of 500 000 tonnes a year. Half the output would be for Nigeria, and Belgian finance has been offered for construction of a railway from the cement plant to Ilaro, north-west of Lagos, in Nigeria.

Traffic

A sharp 1982–84 decline of passenger traffic from 188 to 138 million passenger-km has been reversed. In 1988 the figure was 141 million. Freight has receded since a 1986 figure of 194 million tonne-km, to 184 million in 1988. However, the railway has been in the black financially since 1984; it finished 1987 with a surplus of Fr 9.4 million.

Motive power and rolling stock

Number of locomotives in operation in 1988 totalled eight Alsthom BB500 and 12 Alsthom BB600 diesel-electrics, seven shunting tractors. Soulé railcars totalled eight and other stock consisted of 43 Soulé passenger coaches and trailers and 360 freight cars.

Bolivia

Ministry of Transport and Communications

Cewntro de Comunicaciones, Av Mcal, Santa Cruz esq Oruro

Minister: Willy Vargas Vacaflor

Bolivian National Railways
Empresa Nacional de Ferrocarriles (ENFE)

Estacion Centrale, Plaza Zalle, Casilla 428, La Paz

Telephone: +591 2 327401/ 354756
Telex: 2405 bv enfe la paz

General Manager: Ing Rafael Echazú B
Deputy General Manager: Abraham Monasterios C
Director, Planning: Lic Lilia D de Aguirre
Manager, Operations: Ing René Chávez J
Manager, Administration: Ing Arturo Zurita C
Manager, Commercial: Lic Valentín Quiroga S
Head of Finance Department: Mario Veizaga O
Head of Traffic Department: Juá Aramayo P
Head of Traction Department: Ing Walter Medina G
Manager, Industrial Relations: Alfredo Gómez García

Eastern Line
(Santa Cruz de la Sierra)
Manager: Ing Jorge E Gonzáles A
Deputy Manager: Ing Jorge Capobiando R
Manager, Operations: Ing Leopoldo Quiroga F
Director, Planning: Lic Willian Saenz
Manager, Administration: Lic Jorge Rivera S
Manager, Commercial: Ing Hugo Muñoz L

Gauge: 1000 mm
Route length: 3652 km (of which 1377 km is Eastern Line)

Bolivia is a landlocked country and lack of communications has made virtually impossible the sort of economic development which the country needs. The railways are of major importance as a means of access to ports on the Pacific and Atlantic Oceans via the neighbouring countries. These international railway connections, some of which have fallen into disrepair, are as follows:
with Chile to the Pacific ports of Arica and Antofagasta;
with Argentina to the Atlantic ports of Rosario and Buenos Aires;
with Brazil to the Atlantic port of Santos;
with Peru (by ship across Lake Titicaca to Puno) to the Pacific port of Matarani.

Empresa Nacional de Ferrocarriles (ENFE) consists of two separate rail systems: Andean, operating 2275 km of route; and Eastern, operating 1377 km of route. There is presently no connection between them, but in May 1983 the President asked the country's Congress to endorse procurement of foreign finance to the value of US$600 million towards construction of a 390 km connection running from Aiquile to Santa Cruz. Connection of the Andean and Eastern networks would be the final link in a 3952 km line from Brazil's Atlantic port of Santos to Chilé's Pacific port of Arica.

Finance

(000 million pesos)	1987	1988	1989
Income	103.289	99.69	108.05
Expenditure	101.266	97.28	116.03

International links

In 1989 an International Development Association loan was secured by the goverment, the greater part of which would be applied to improving the railway's links with neighbouring systems, and thus access to Atlantic and Pacific ports. The government, exercised to develop economic transportation to stimulate the country's exports, also sought a strengthening of ENFE's market orientation and development of the railway's container transportation capability.

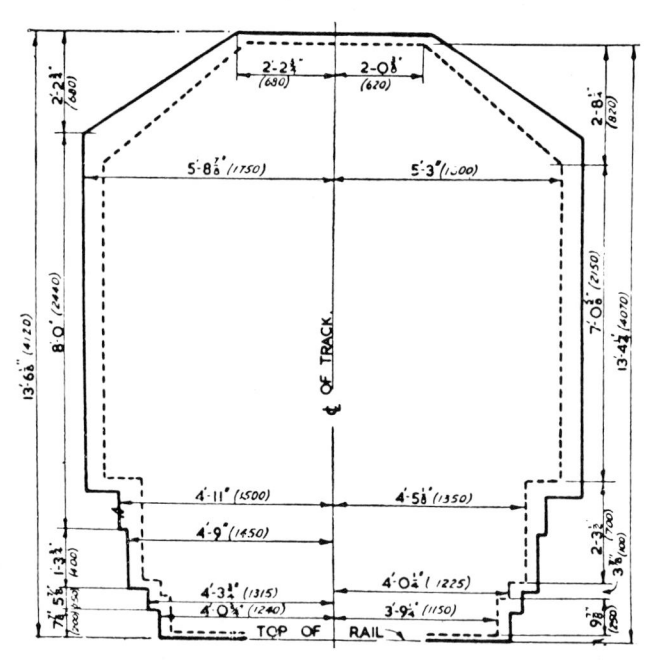

ENFE loading and structure gauge

To the west, the La Paz-El Alto-Charana line to the Chilean border would be treated to two realignments to ease its ruling gradient from 2.3 to 1.3 per cent. The La Paz freight terminal would be redeveloped. To the east, the Santa Cruz-Corumba line to the Brazilian border would be fully rehabilitated and a new freight terminal would be built at Santa Cruz.

In December 1987 the governments of Bolivia, Argentina and Peru agreed to move for an unbroken 3425km Atlantic-Pacific Ocean rail route interconnecting their countries. It would be known as the 'Corredor Interoceánico de los Libertadores'. The main Bolivian contribution, rehabilitation of the 65km from Guaqui to Viacha, was in hand in 1990.

SLM-built, MTU-engined 1180 kW locomotive taken over from COMIBOL

Rehabilitation programme

A Railway Rehabilitation Programme has been in progress since 1973 with the aid of funds from the World Bank and other countries, but progress has been governed by the delicate state of Bolivia's economy. In 1987, with inflation tamed, further World Bank credits totalling US$18.5 million were granted to allow start of a fourth phase of the programme in 1988. In late 1989 the Transport Minister announced that the World Bank and Japanese sources would fund a further US$87 million outlay on railway upgrading schemes up to 1993.

Work so far completed has covered the 315km from Viacha to Challapata, and from the frontier at Ollagüe

Traffic	1986	1987	1988	1989
Freight tonnage (000)	933.9	981.4	873.24	1031.7
Freight tonne-km (million)	470.5	503.1	426.5	512.6
Passenger-km (million)	657.1	503.5	368.9	381.6
Passenger journeys (000)	1885.3	1396.96	1050.8	1081.4

to Julaca. Besides Guaqui-Viacha (see above), 1990 activity was centred on the 69km from Alto Comanche to La Paz. Sections still to be dealt with were Challapata-Uyuni (202km) and Uyuni-Villazoñ (289km).

Extension of the line north from Santa Cruz has proceeded. By 1989 this work was complete over 204 km as far as Yapaceni and continued over 85 km thence to Rio Grande. Further extension to Trinidad was under study.

Future projects
In 1990 a one-year study, funded by the Japanese International Cooperation Agency, was in progress to consider the modernisation of the railway and the drafting of a development plan for the period up to year 2020.

Besides the Aiquile-Santa Cruz connection, ENFE hopes in the 1990s to build a new line from Motacucito through Mutun to Puerto Busch at a cost of US$76 million, and another from Vallegrande to Zudanes. To assist the soya bean industry a branch from Santa Cruz to Puerto Quijarro has been proposed.

To cater for population growth in La Paz, ENFE also plans to create an electrified commuter operation over the 19 km between the city centre and El Alto airport.

Purchase of five two-car emus is envisaged. Total cost is put at US$15 million plus US$4.5 million for the emus.

Traffic
Passenger and freight traffic volumes have been seriously reduced as a result of the country's economic difficulties. But it was hoped that the new economic policies of the government would soon reverse the downturn.

Investment
For 1990 ENFE planned investment of US$19.214 million, of which US$18.61 million would come from external credits. Included in the provisions were purchases of 12 container wagons and intermodal transshipment cranage, and re-engining of 19 MAN-motored locomotives.

Motive power and rolling stock: 1990
Locomotives, diesel	67
Railcars, diesel	14
Passenger cars	127
Freight wagons	2030

With the takeover of the Bolivian Mining Corporation railway ENFE added to its locomotive fleet two 1180 kW diesel-electric Bo-Bo locomotives with MTU396 engines built by SLM of Switzerland for COMIBOL and delivered in 1986.

In 1989 ENFE was still awaiting government authority to order 14 diesel locomotives from Mitsubishi, ten 250 kW diesel railcars and trailers from Materfer of Argentina, 30 passenger cars from Santa Matilde of Brazil and 400 freight wagons. One of the latest World Bank credits worth US$8 million was for rehabilitation of existing locomotives.

Track
Rail: ASCE 29.76, 37.2 and 39 kg/m
BSS 32.24 and 37.2 kg/m

Cross ties (sleepers): Wood and steel
Spacing: 1400–1640/km
Minimum curvature radius: 15°
Max gradient: 3% compensated on curves
Max axleload: 18 tonnes

Diesel locomotives

Class	Wheel arrangement	Transmission	Rated power kW	Max kg	Tractive effort Continuous at kg	km/h	Max speed km/h	Wheel dia mm	Total weight tonnes	Length mm	No in service 1989	Year first built	Builders Mechanical parts	Engine & type	Transmission
950	Bo-Bo-Bo	Elec	970	20 400	9200	28	70	1000	81.6	16 800	9	1968	Hitachi Mitsubishi	MAN VGV 22/30 ATL	Hitachi Mitsubishi
1000	Bo-Bo-Bo	Elec	1550	22 000	10 150	42	100	1000	90	17 800	7	1978	Hitachi Mitsubishi	MTU 12 V 956TB 11	Hitachi Mitsubishi
521	Bo-Bo	Hyd	280	5000	2700	25	25	910	30	14 000	1	1968	Hitachi	MAN RGV 18/12 TL	Hitachi
841	Bo-Bo	Hyd	395	–	–	–	40	910	55	–	1	1980	Hitachi Mitsubishi	MTU V396 TC 12	Hitachi
U 20C	Co-Co	Elec	1550	34 000	11 000	40	103	1016	89.9	17 000	6	1977	General Electric	FDL 12 GE	General Electric
U 10B	Bo-Bo	Elec	590	25 000	5500	40	103	914	50.8	13 000	7	1977	General Electric	D 398 Caterpillar	General Electric
980	Bo-Bo	Elec	551	–	–	–	60		66.5	15 400	1	1987	Sulzer	MTU	Sulzer
846	Bo-Bo	Electro-mech	480	–	–	–	60		66.4	15 400	2	1950	Sulzer	Sulzer	Sulzer

Diesel railbuses

Cars per unit	Motor cars per unit	Motored axles per motor car	Transmission	Rated power (hp) per motor	Max speed km/h	Weight tonnes per car (M-motor T-trailer)	Total seating capacity	Length per car mm	No in service 1989	Year first built	Builders Mechanical parts	Engine & type	Transmission
2	1	2	Mech	340/240	80	19.8/15.1	44/54	13 757	8	1967/78	Ferrostaal	Cummins NHHRTO-6	Zahnfabrik
2	1	2	Hyd	335/240	90	26/21	32/40	13 500	3	1978	Ferrostaal	Cummins	Voith T 211 R

Botswana

Ministry of Works, Transport and Communications, Gaborone

Telephone: +267 31 358500
Telex: 2743 works bd
Telefax: +267 31 313303

Minister: C J Butate
Permanent Secretary: M C Tibone
Deputy Permanent Secretary: A V Lionjanga

Botswana Railways (BR)

Private Bag 00125, Gaborone

Telex: 2980 rails bd
Telefax: +267 31 312305

Chairman: M C Tibone
Vice Chairman: L E Serena
General Manager: F W Markham
Chief Traffic Manager: O S Thobega
Operations Manager: O S Molebatsi
Commercial Manager: O S Mogopa
Chief Finance & Supplies Manager: C K Ramachandra
Supplies Manager: P M Mmereki
Chief Civil Engineer: D R Ballinger
Chief Mechanical Engineer: W W Gordon
Chief Signal Engineer: L Johansson
Chief Personnel Manager: M S Maoto
Information Technology Manager: S S Koopile

Gauge: 1067 mm
Route length: 713 km

The country, formerly the British Protectorate of Bechuanaland, is traversed by 640 km of main line between Ramatlabama (north of Mafeking, South Africa) and Bakaranga (south of Plumtree, Zimbabwe) with two branch lines, from Serule to Selebi-Phikwe (56 km) and Palapye to Morupule (9 km), formerly managed by National Railways of Zimbabwe. Botswana Railways took over the operation of the railway system in December 1986, to be followed, in 1987, by the formal takeover of the assets and supporting administrative services. In 1990 RITES was engaged to advise on the organisation and management structure of the railway.

Rehabilitation
China has provided financial and technical aid for track rehabilitation on the main line with long-welded 50 kg/m rail, laid on concrete sleepers, in a phased programme. The southern sector, between Gaborone and Mafeking, was finished in October 1987, and the northern end between Bakaranga (the border) and Francistown in March 1989. Branch line renewal commenced in 1989 using serviceable 40 kg/m rail on steel sleepers recovered from the main line. Sweden has helped fund the modernisation of telecommunications by Ericsson.

Traffic
	1987/88	1988/89
Total freight tonnes (million)	2.08	2.03
Total freight tonne-km (million)	800	771
Total passenger journeys	443 680	425 314

508 RAILWAY SYSTEMS / Botswana—Brazil

Finance (million Pula)

Revenue	1987/88	1988/89
Passengers and baggage	4.9	6.6
Freight, parcels and mail	39.7	43.5
Other income	1.6	2.78
Total	46.17	52.89

Expenditure	1987/88	1988/89
Staff/personnel	15.07	17.49
Materials and services	32.61	33.98
Depreciation	4.30	5.94
Financial charges	4.69	4.96
Total	56.67	62.37

Freight
Plans include the construction of two container terminals, capable of early conversion into dry ports, and it was hoped these would be operational in late 1991. As part of the further development of the country's mineral resources of salt and soda ash a 175 km branch line between Francistown and Sua Pan is being constructed by Cooperativa Muratori & Cementisti of Ravenna, Italy, and should be completed by April 1991.

Trans-Kalahari project
Plans have been formulated for a Trans-Kalahari line of 1400 km length, of which 850 km would be in Botswana, to channel Botswana coal from the Kgaswe coalfield to Walvis Bay, Namibia, on the west coast, for export shipment. A preliminary route study by consultants Henderson Travers Morgan has been agreed by the government. The scheme would involve construction of 800 km of single track from the coalfield to Gobabis, where it would connect with the railway system of Namibia. The 600 km on to Walvis Bay would be upgraded. Throughput of the Trans-Kalahari Railway could be as high as 15 million tonnes a year.

Computer developments
A network of micro-computers has been installed in the headquarters of Botswana Railways using Novell Netware. Currently more than 60 computers at the headquarters are linked to the network; 12 at local offices in Gaborone, Francistown and Mahalapye are connected by modems and multiplexors. The system uses proprietary software for payroll, nominal ledger, revenue accounting, asset register and word processing. In addition a vehicle control system has been written 'in house', primarily to calculate vehicle hire charges and produce operational statistics.

In 1990 a stock control system and the first phase of a personnel management system was implemented. During the year systems to monitor vehicle utilisation, schedule preventive maintenance and automate the daily operating diary would be developed 'in house' as an adjunct to the vehicle control system. It was also planned to install a small network of computers in Mahalapye, linked to the headquarters network by a communications bridge.

Signalling
In May 1989 a Radio Electronic Token Block system supplied by GEC-General Signal of the UK was installed over the 698km of the Plumtree-Rakhuna main line and the Selebi Phikwe branch.

Traction and rolling stock
Botswana Railways owns 12 Krupp diesel-electric locomotives and 20 Type GK22LC diesel-electric locomotives, delivered in 1986 by GM Canada. In 1989 wagon stocks totalled 813, following use of a Japanese loan to fund purchase from Zeco of 160 high-sided, 230 drop-sided, 90 aluminium box and 80 oil tank wagons. Denmark donated 20 container wagons and 40 refrigerated containers.

A depot for basic traction and rolling stock maintenance and repair has been built at Mahalapye with Danish IDA assistance and is fully operational.

Tenders were sought in 1989 for the supply of 330 wagons for salt soda ash traffic over the Sua Pan line (see above), and coal haulage from Morupule; for 41 passenger cars to launch a Francistown-Gaborone service in late 1991; and for 10 shunting and short-haul freight locomotives. The wagon contract was awarded to China National Machinery Import & Export Corporation, the passenger car contract to Mitsui, and the locomotive contract to General Electric. All deliveries would start and be completed in 1991.

Type of coupler in standard use
Freight cars: Automatic

Type of braking in standard use, locomotive-hauled stock: Vacuum

Track
Rail type and weight: Flat-bottom 30, 40, 50 kg/m. By end-1988 approx 200 km of route was 50 kg/m cwr on concrete sleepers, approx 60 km 40 kg/m cwr on steel/wood sleepers, and the remainder 36 kg/m jointed on steel/wood sleepers

Sleepers: Concrete/steel/wood, spaced 1430 km in cwr, 1450/km in jointed trade

Fastenings: Fist/clip bolt/Pandrol

Minimum curvature radius: 250 m

Max gradient: 1.25%

Max permissible axleload: 17 tonnes

Diesel locomotives

Class	Type	Wheel arrangement	Transmission	Rated power kW	Max speed km/h	Total weight tonnes	No in service 1988	Year first built	Builders Mechanical parts	Engine & type	Transmission
BD 1	UM 22	Co-Co	Elec	1604	103	96	12	1982	Krupp	GE 7FDL 12	GE
BD 2	GT22C-2	Co-Co	Elec	1846	107	96.16	20	1986	GM	GM 645E3B	GM

Brazil

Ministry of Infrastructure
Esplanada dos Ministérios, Bloco 9, 70 062 Brasilia DF

Telephone: +55 61 321 8886
Telex: 0611096, 0611689, 0612262 mntr br

Minister: Ozires Silva

Rede Ferroviaria Federal SA (RFFSA)

Praça-Procópio Ferreira 86, Rio de Janeiro

Telephone: +55 21 223 5795/3945
Cable: Referro
Telex: 021 21372 rffsa br
Telefax: +55 21 263 3128

President: Martiniano Lauro Amaral de Oliveira
Vice-President: Vincente Vanni Nardelli
Director, Planning: Eng Fernando Limeira de França
  Marketing: Eng Dyrno Jurandyr Pires Ferreira
  Development: C F Sirotsky
  Administration: A Braga
  Procurement & Maintenance: Francisco Mário Chiese
  Mechanical: E S Alves
  Electrical: N Goncalves Damasio
  Permanent Way: R S S Lucas

Gauge: 1600 mm; 1000 mm; 762 mm
Route length: 1397 km; 20 657 km; 13 km
Electrification: 828 km at 3 kV dc (including systems of CBTU subsidiary)

GE Type U20C diesel-electric Co-Co

New Presidential approach
Privatisation of RFFSA, wholly or in part, was under continuing consideration in the final years of President Sarney's regime, as the only solution to meeting the railway's need of substantial investment. The topic is being pursued under new President Fernando Collor de Mello, who was elected in November 1989. President Collor has reorganised the oversight of the country's land and sea transport, putting it, along with communications, energy and mining, in the charge of a Ministry of Infrastructure. The Minister, Ozires Silva, also heads TAVSA, the company contracted to seek finance for a Rio de Janeiro-São Paulo high-speed line (see below).

President Collor de Mello seeks to interest private companies in running their own trains over RFFSA infrastructure in return for their financial contribution to modernisation projects.

New modernisation funds
In total, RFFSA aimed to invest US$225 million in 1988-90. Toward this total RFFSA secured in 1988 a

World Bank loan of US$100 million, plus US$67 million from BNDES. The main objective of the expenditure was to raise the operating capacity of the railway in the export corridors of Goias, Minas Gerais and Paraná states.

Early in 1990, while imposing draconian economic measures to combat the country's relapse into horrendous inflation, President Collor de Mello was seeking means to invest US$2000 million in RFFSA. The money would be devoted to purchase of 100 locomotives and 2500 freight cars, to rehabilitation of existing traction and rolling stock, and to renewal of 4500km of track. But in the spring the government froze all investment in RFFSA until inflation was curbed.

Passenger trains not wanted

RFFSA's new president appointed in 1988, Jorge Fernando Fagundes Netto, soon made known that he intended to be rid of passenger business because of heavy losses and withdrawal of subsidy for passenger trains in 1989. Private interests and local authorities were approached for possible interest in taking over RFFSA's few surviving long-haul services. The fate of the remaining urban services not taken over by CBTU (qv) was unclear.

RFFSA's long-haul passenger busines is negligible, amounting to only 0.5 per cent of the national market in total and totalling about 5 million journeys a year. Passenger trains are confined chiefly to routes devoid of bus competition, and for which RFFSA hitherto counted on government subsidy as a social service.

Steel Railway

The first 397 km section of a projected 740 km ore-carrying line was begun in the spring of 1975 and then programmed for opening in September 1978, at a cost, at the time, of over US$100 million. This first stage was to connect Belo Horizonte, Jeceaba and Itutinga with the big steelworks complex at Volta Redonda; a second stage would project the line into the state of São Paulo. The project was halted in 1978, but resumed in 1979, then suspended once more in 1982.

The Steel Railway's projected route follows a difficult path through mountainous terrain in Minas Gerais and Rio de Janeiro provinces. No less than 135 million cubic metres of earthworks were incurred, together with boring of 70 tunnels grossing 50 km in length and erection of 95 bridges and viaducts with a total length of 27 km. The longest tunnel is one of 8.7 km beneath the Serra de Mantequiera, which was constructed with the New Austrian Tunnel-Driving Method (NATM); the longest viaduct is 761 metres, with 24 spans; and the highest, 81.8 metres above ground. It was originally to be double-track throughout, with a ruling 1 per cent gradient, minimum 900 m curve radius, and constructed for 30 tonnes axle-loadings.

The line was to be electrified at 25 kV 60 Hz and signalled by GEC Transportation Projects Ltd. It would employ 35 180-tonne 3500 kW Co-Co locomotives with thyristor control built locally by Equipamentos Villares SA to a GEC design and embodying electrical equipment supplied from the UK. The originally planned capacity was 28 daily pairs of trains loading to a maximum of 7000 tonnes northbound, permitting an eventual annual throughput of over 50 million tonnes; the initial annual total was expected to be 24 million tonnes, primarily of ore, steel, limestone and cement.

The inland extremity of the project, from Belo Horizonte to Jeceaba, was abandoned in the cause of economy before the end of the 1970s. When government funding was withdrawn at the start of 1984 from the rest of the project after some US$1700 million had already been spent, earthworks elsewhere were virtually finished, but little or no track had been laid.

In February 1987 Azevedo Antunes, the industrial group controlling the prospective mining users of the line, agreed to share with the National Bank for Economic & Social Development (BNDES) the cost of finishing the Steel Railway infrastructure to a junction with the existing RFFSA at Barra Mansa, on the Rio-São Paulo line near the Volta Redonda plant. As part of the deal, Azevedo Antunes' mining company, which sends some 16 million tonnes of ore a year over the existing line from Belo Horizonte to the coast, would enjoy a 60 per cent discounted tariff for its first 10 years' use of the completed Steel Railway.

Additional funds of US$136 million therefore became available in March 1987. Later that year engineering contracts were concluded, but for only half the route from Jeceaba, as far as Saudade, 296 km. Moreover, the line would be finished as a non-electrified single track, though the finance did allow for telecommunications and installation of CTC. (Electrification would have cost a further US$395 million.) Loaded trains would use the single-track Steel Railway to descend to the coast, returning empties the existing Rio-Belo Horizonte line, to avoid problems from hard-working diesel locomotive exhausts in the new line's many tunnels which were, of course, planned with electrification in view. Even so, an annual capacity of 15 million tonnes was predicted.

The 296 km of single track from Jeceaba to Saudade were completed and formally inaugurated by President Sarney at the end of May 1989. By the end of that year the line was carrying an average of 12 90-wagon, 8 200-tonnes gross weight trains daily, each hauled by a quartet of 3000 hp diesel locomotives. Over-engineered for its ore-carrying purpose, the Steel Railway's economics are now made worse by contraction of global demand for steel.

Production Railway: no progress in 1989

Access to the port of Paranagua is needed by the fast-growing soya industry in eastern Parana and southern Mato Grosso. In 1982 a project to achieve a 1340 km route from Asuncion in Paraguay to Paranagua was stalled by a World Bank decision to defer loan finance for it, but in 1985 CVRD undertook a fresh feasibility study at the request of the Paraná state government.

In June 1986 then President José Sarney announced the government's full backing for construction of the project, now developed on slightly different parameters to the original scheme and known as the Production Railway. Start of the Production Railway will be the existing 490 km from Paranagua through Curitiba to the present railhead at Guarapuava; this will be upgraded, possibly at the cost of some new infrastructure before Curitiba, where the line encounters some sharp curves and a 3.9 per cent ruling gradient in the climb to the central Brazilian plateau that hampers other rail routes heading inland from the ports. In 1988 RFFSA was to seek bids for large-scale installation of CTC and telecommunications in the Paranagua area.

From Guarapuava 270 km of new railway, dotted with bulk cereal transshipment terminals, will be built to the initial target, Cascavel. The ultimate objective is to move on to Guaira, and from there to drive one line northwest to Miranda, another southwest into Paraguay as far as Asuncion. In mid-1987 the Paraná state government commissioned Canadian Pacific Consulting Services to conduct financial feasibility study of the Production Railway.

In 1988 it was announced that the first 270 km of the railway, from Guarapuava to Cascavel, would be built by Ferroeste, a company headed by Osiris Guimaraes, the former RFFSA president dismissed in 1987 for opposing the North-South Railway project. Construction would be funded 80 per cent by some 30 companies, 26 of them Brazilian and including Canadian Pacific, Fiat and Volvo; 12.5 per cent by Paraná state; and 7.5 per cent by the Federal government.

By early 1990, however, financial arrangements were still incomplete. Consequently construction work had not begun and Canadian Pacific Consulting Services, engaged to assist in the project, had slimmed down their local organisation.

North-South Railway

The so-called North-South Railway, a 1600 km line extending from the Carajas Railway at Acailandia to Anapolis, 115 km south-west of Brasilia, was approved by then President Sarney in the spring of 1987. Starting in Maranhão state, it would thread the sparsely-populated agricultural state of Goias en route to the vicinity of the national capital, Brasilia. The aim of the project was to open up the neglected interior and provide a rail route to the northern ports for the agriculture, principally soya beans and maize, which the venture would foster in Goias.

The project was quickly enveloped in scandal. It was hotly criticised, first of all, as an ill-timed extravagance. Total cost was put at US$2400 million, of which US$540 million had been provided in the country's 1987 budget in order to start work in that year. Former Transport Minister Alfonso Camargo Netto was reported to have condemned the project as 'nothing to do with transport. It doesn't have economic viability and is going to generate more inflation.' Other assailants forecast that it would prove as valueless as the Trans-Amazonian Highway, built at massive cost from the far northwest of the country to Brasilia by the National Roads Department, but which has diverted very little traffic from Amazon river transport. The Brazilian business community also pointed out that huge investment in irrigation would be needed to develop the 20 million tonnes of crops a year the railway was promised to generate in its territory.

Politically, the scheme was embarrassed by the fact that President Sarney came from Maranhão state. But that was overshadowed by revelations that Valec, a dormant state company reactivated to supervise the project and draw up contract specifications, had begun parcelling out contracts to 18 major companies before bids had been opened. Federal police were called in and a parliamentary commission was appointed to investigate; meanwhile the offending contracts were annulled. But in November 1987 the President himself opened the first construction office, and with fresh contractors organised construction was started in 1988.

At first the line was to be metre-gauge, which would have matched the RFFSA system at the Brasilia end, but complicated the connection with the 1600 mm-gauge CVRD route to Sao Luis port from Acailandia. Now, to reduce operating costs, the North-South Railway is 1600 mm gauge. This will permit 30-tonne axleloads and operation of 8000-tonne trains with two locomotives. The line of route involves scarcely any major civil engineering works.

President Sarney opened the first 105 km from Acailandia to Imperatriz, in the north, in March 1989. But with presidential elections pending in November 1989, and the country's relapse into rampant inflation, work on the second 110 km stretch of the railway ground to a halt. There was then considerable scepticism that under new President Collor de Mello the project would ever be completed.

New Chapeco railway scheme

Yet another new railway project surfaced in 1988, in this case a private venture *ab initio*. The private interests involved have studied an 860 route-km scheme to the south of the Production Railway, from the city of Chapeco near the Argentinian border to the port of Sao Francisco do Sul. The US$300 million scheme would entail taking over and upgrading 730 km of RFFSA track and tacking onto it 130 route-km of new line to Chapeco. A Federal German bank was reported to be interested in furnishing up to half the finance under a Brazilian debt-to-equity conversion

GE Type U23C diesel-electric Co-Co

510 RAILWAY SYSTEMS / Brazil

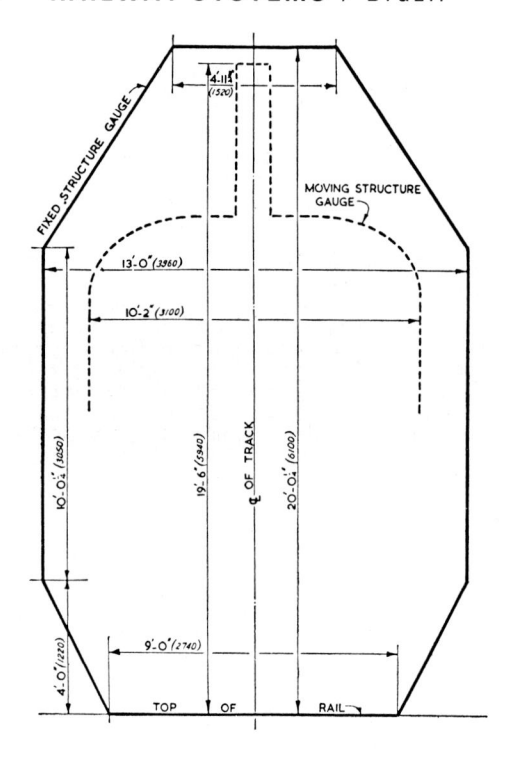

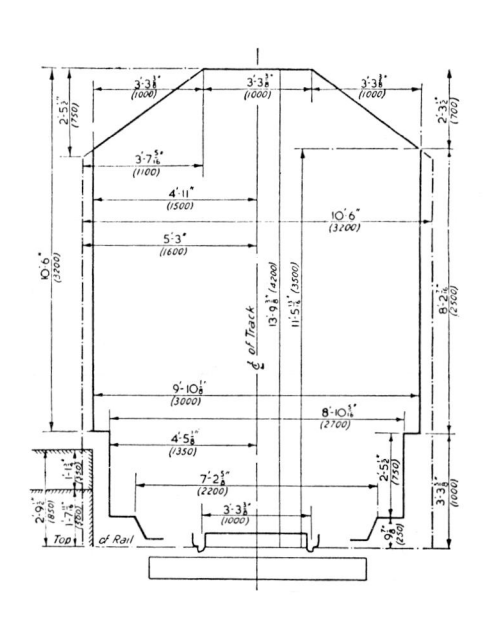

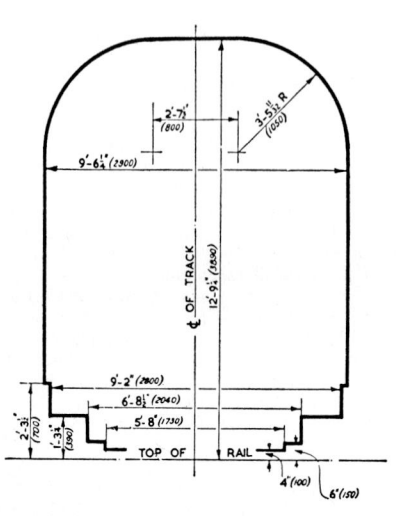

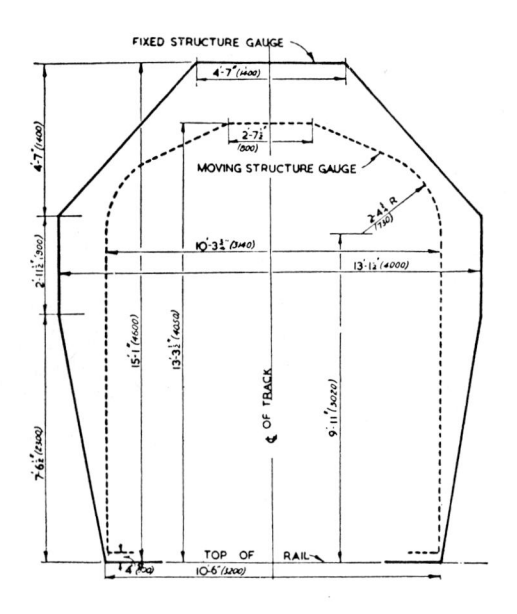

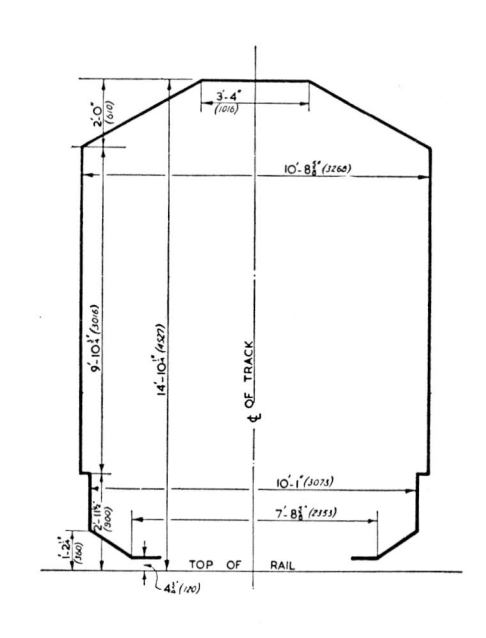

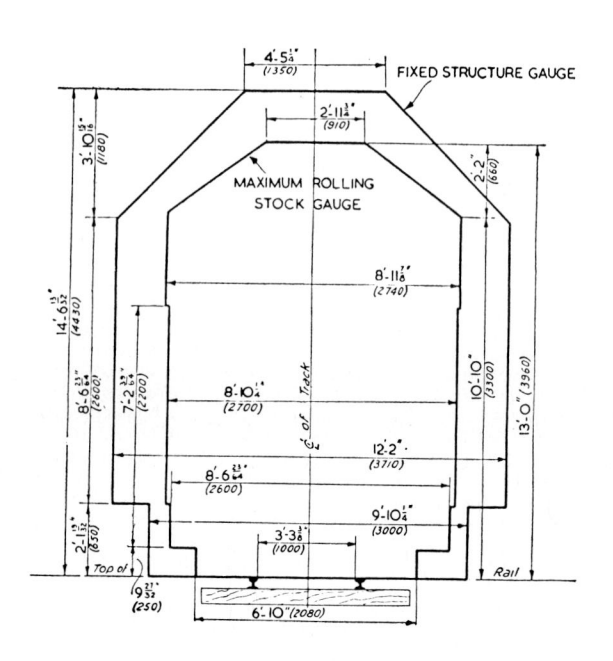

Six types of loading and structural gauge employed on Brazil's railway lines

Brazil / RAILWAY SYSTEMS

scheme. This latter process, which Brazil is promoting as means to reduce its huge external debt, is encouraging foreign agencies to consider involvement in other current Brazilian rail development projects. Nothing was heard of this scheme in 1989.

Transnordestina Railway
A further new line projected is the Transnordestina Railway. As its name suggests, this would traverse the country's far northeast inland, linking up three metre-gauge lines that head inland from the Atlantic coastal line between Salvador and Recife. The single-track line would extend some 350 km from Petrolina through Crato and Salgueiro to Missao Velha, making access to Salvador and Fortaleza much simpler for inland cities in this area. In 1988 USSR assistance in construction was secured under an agreement providing for export of Brazilian railway technology to the USSR. But no move to build was reported in 1989.

Brasilia-Belo Horizonte cut-off
In 1990 RFFSA was seeking bidders agreeable to organise the finance for, then build a 40 km cutoff to bypass a steeply-graded and severely-curved stretch of the Brasilia-Belo Horizonte line that severely limits the latter's throughput. The likely cost would be US$89 million.

Rio-São Paulo high-speed line
Moves to further the scheme for a high-speed passenger link between Rio and São Paulo have been confused. In late 1988 the World Bank funded a feasibility study of the project, for which options under consideration ranged from use of British-type HST or Spanish Talgo equipment, diesel-powered, on existing, upgraded infrastructure to a new French TGV-style railway. At the same time Fepasa was partnering the São Paulo Technological Institute in a study of the case for means to run trains over the 105 km of electrified Fepasa route from São Paulo westward to Campinas in 50 minutes.

Abruptly, with neither of these exercises complete, the Transport Ministry in March 1989 invited build-and-operate bids for a new railway achieving 2-hour transits between Rio and São Paulo (some 400 km apart, probably, by a new line) and 30-minute journeys between São Paulo and Campinas.

Later in the year a new company, Trens de Alta Velocidade (TAVSA) was formed under the chairmanship of Ozires Silva, former president of the country's aircraft manufacturing company, Embraer, to pursue the project. This concern, which was registered in the Bahamas but has a US owner, Pharoah Holdings, was the only respondent to the invitation to tender and signed a contract with the Ministry of Transport in June 1989. The hope is that the investment in the high-speed line can be found from some of the country's foreign creditors agreeable to converting their liabilities into local currency to fund the railway's construction.

Freight traffic
Since the start of 1985 RFFSA has been charged by government decree to adjust its freight rates so that direct costs are covered. In 1988 the railway was given rate-making freedom, and its freight operations are subsidised only where the government deems service to be a socio-economic necessity, even at a loss.

Steel industry input and output accounts for 55 per cent of RFFSA's total tonnage, coal, alcohol and petroleum products for 15 per cent, agricultural and fertiliser products for 20 per cent, and cement and building materials for 10 per cent. Almost half the total tonnage is moved over the 1600 mm gauge network. New wagon orders are concentrating on high-capacity vehicles for unit train working.

An example of private sector involvement is a proposal by several companies and the Rio de Janeiro state administration to finance the upgrading and dual-gauging of a route, at present part 1000mm and part 1600mm gauge, from the Cantagalo region to Rio. This would encourage the addition of substantial tonnages of cement, paper and steel products to the route's currently limited freight traffic – mainly sugar – because of the transshipment entailed at changes of gauge.

Traction and rolling stock
RFFSA operates 1517 diesel, 35 electric and 24 steam locomotives; 6 four-car dmus and 20 diesel railcars; 13 emus; 603 passenger cars (including 127 sleeping cars and 65 restaurant cars); and 40 032 freight wagons.

Track
Rail type and weight: 25.68 kg/m
Cross ties (sleepers)
Timber: 160/180 mm thickness spaced 1666/1850 per km in plain track, 1750/km in curves
Concrete: 220/240 mm thickness spaced 1666/1750 per km in plain track, 1750/km in curves

RFFSA traffic	1982	1983	1984	1985	1988
Freight tonnes (million)	69.828	69.774	76.938	82.4	80.562
Freight tonne-km (million)	31 686.8	29 633	33 526	37 100	36 104

RFFSA electric locomotives

Gauge mm	Wheel arrangement	Line current	Rated output hp	Max kg	Continuous at kg	Continuous at km/h	Max speed km/h	Wheel diameter mm	Weight tonnes	Length mm	First in service	Builders Mechanical parts	Builders Electrical equipment
1000	B-B	3000 V	1000	9080	–	–	80	1092	50	12 040	1951/60	Metropolitan Vickers	Metropolitan Vickers MV188
1600	B-B	3000 V	3000	–	15 600	–	100	1257	110	16 270	1959	Siemens-Schuckert	Siemens Schuckert VB320/22
1600	B-B	3000 V	3780	38 560	–	–	45	1118	106	16 760	1972/80	Hitachi	Hitachi DES 100-701-762 EFFZO-HGO
1600	C-C	3000 V	4400	–	21 120	27.2	117	1168	123	16 857	1963	General Electric	General Electric GE-729
1600	2C + C2	3000 V	4470	–	17 000	58	117	1168*	165	23 539	1947/48	General Electric Westinghouse	Westinghouse 375-A General Electric GE-729-B1
1600	C-C	3000 V	3000	25 850	–	–	100	1219	127	20 520	1949/55	English Electric	English Electric EE 514A
1600	2C-C2	3000 V	4470	–	17 000	58	117	1168*	165	23 539	1948/49	Westinghouse	Westinghouse 375-A-5

* Guide wheel diameter: 914.4 mm

RFFSA diesel locomotives: 1600 mm gauge

Class	Wheel arrangement	Transmission	Rated power hp	Max kg	Continuous at kg	Continuous at km/h	Max speed km/h	Wheel dia mm	Total weight tonnes	Length mm	First built	Builders Mechanical parts	Builders Engine & type	Builders Transmission
RS-1	B-B	Elec	1650	–	19 250	17.7	104	1016	108	15 697	1948/49	Alco-GE	Alco-12-244	GE-752E1/ GT-564-C1
RS-1	B-B	Elec	1100	–	15 400	12.8	96	1016	109.7	16 909	1945	Alco-GE	Alco-539	GE-731D3/ GT-553-C3
RS-1	B-B	Elec	1100	22 680	–	–	96.6	1016	109.7	17 303	1945	Alco	Alco-539	5GE731-D3/ GT-553-C3
RS-3	B-B	Elec	1750	–	23 835	15.2	104	1016	109	16 990	1946/52	Alco (Montreal Locomotive Works)	Alco-12 244	GE-5GE752E1
RSD-12	C-C	Elec	1950	–	36 013	9.4	104	1016	163.4	17 721	1962/63	Alco	Alco-12 251	GE-752PC4/ GT582-A2
Baldwin A-608	C-C	Elec	1750	–	32 950	11.2	55	1066.8	147.5	17 678	1952	Baldwin Westinghouse	Baldwin-Lima Hamilton 608-A	Westinghouse 370DEZ/471BZ
–	B-B	Elec	720	15 400	–	–	88	914.4	64/80	11 278	1955	General Electric	Cooper-Bessemer FWL-6T	GE-5-761A1/ 5GT-571-C3
U-5B	B-B	Elec	600	–	15 422	6.2	64	914.4	51.3	11 403	1961	General Electric	Caterpillar D-379	GE-761-A1/ GT-601
U-6B	B-B	Elec	700	–	15 200	7.9	64	914.4	57	11 073	1967	General Electric	Caterpillar D-379B-V8	GE-761A5/ 5GT-601-C1
U-23C	C-C	Elec	2500	–	34 686	13	120	1016	165	20 497	1976	General Electric	GE-7-FDL-12	GE-752E8-A/ GT-586

RAILWAY SYSTEMS / Brazil

RFFSA diesel locomotives: 1600 mm gauge (continued)

Class	Wheel arrangement	Transmission	Rated power hp	Max kg	Tractive effort Continuous at kg	km/h	Max speed km/h	Wheel dia mm	Total weight tonnes	Length mm	First built	Builders Mechanical parts	Engine & type	Transmission
U-23C	C-C	Elec	2500	–	34 686	13	120	1016	175	20 497	1976	General Electric	GE-7-FDL-12	GE-752E8-A/GT-586
U-23C	C-C	Elec	2500	–	38 900	11.6	112.6	1016	180	20 497	1972/76	General Electric	GE-7-FDL-12	GE-752E8-A/GT-586
SD-18	C-C	Elec	1950	–	35 174	10.5	104	1016	163.4	18 504	1962/63	General Motors Corp	GM-16-567-D1	GM-EMD-D47E1/EMD-D22C
SD-38	C-C	Elec	2200	–	37 235	10.6	96.8	1016	163	18 550	1967	General Motors Corp	GM-16-645-E	GM-EMD-D77/EMD-D32
SD-40	C-C	Elec	3300	–	37 235	17.7	113	1016	163	18 590	1967	General Motors Corp	GM-16-645-E	GM-EMD-D77/EMD-AR10-D14
SD-40-2	C-C	Elec	3300	–	–	13.7	104.5	1016	180	20 980	1980	General Motors Corp	GM-16-645-E-3	GM-EMD-D77/EMD-AR-10-D14
–	B-B	Elec	1050	–	14 740	12.1	104.5	–	115	16 760	1980	Hitachi Ltd	Alco-6-251-B	–
U-20C	C-C	Elec	2150	–	–	–	104.5	–	120	–	1981	GE	GE-7-FDL-12	–

RFFSA diesel locomotives: metre-gauge

Class	Wheel arrangement	Transmission	Rated power hp	Max kg	Tractive effort Continuous at kg	km/h	Max speed km/h	Wheel dia mm	Total weight tonnes	Length mm	First built	Builders Mechanical parts	Engine & type	Transmission
6GE-761	C-C	Elec	1750	–	–	–	96	–	96	–	1953	Ge-General Electric	Alco 244E	–
RS-8	B-B	Elec	900	–	–	–	95	914.4	62.6	13 802	1958	Alco Products, Inc	Alco-251	GE-761 GE-5, 584-D3
RSD-8	C-C	Elec	900	–	–	–	95	914.4	68.1	13 802	1958/59	Alco Products, Inc	Alco-251 B	GE-761, GE5GT-584-D3
MX-620	C-C	Elec	2150	–	21 120	21.3	103	914.4	96	17 634	1980	Emaq-Eng Emaq SA	Alco-251-CE	GE-761 PA14/GT581P51/GY27PF1
U-5B	B-B	Elec	600	12 500	9200	17	64	914.4	49.5	11 402	1961/62	GE-General Electric	Caterpillar D-379	GE-5, GE-761-A1/B1, GT-601-B1, GAG-146-B, GM-601-B1
U-6B	B-B	Elec	700	–	–	–	64	–	57	–	1957	GE	Caterpillar-D-379B78	GE-761-A5/5, GT601-C1
U-8B	B-B	Elec	900	13 625	–	–	96	914.4	54.5	11 380	1961	GE-General Electric	Caterpillar-VD3988B	GE-761 & GT601
U-9B	B-B	Elec	990	16 600	–	–	96	914.4	66	15 144	1957	GE-General Electric	Cooper-Bessemer FWB-6	GE-5GE761-A1, GE-5GT599-A1
U-10B	B-B	Elec	1050	15 200	–	–	96	914.4	60	11 380	1971/72	GE-General Electric	Caterpillar-D398B	GE-761, GT601-B1
U-12B	B-B	Elec	1320	17 500	–	–	96	914.4	70	15 144	1958/59	GE-General Electric	Cooper-Bessemer FVBL-8T	GE-761-A1
U-12C	C-C	Elec	1320	20 000	–	–	96	914.4	80	15 144	1958	GE-General Electric	Cooper-Bessemer FVBL-8T	GE-761-A1/GT581
U-13B	B-B	Elec	1420	17 500	–	–	96	914.4	70	15 144	1963	GE-General Electric	General Electric 7-FDL-8	GE-761-A3/GT581-C
U-20C	C-C	Elec	2150	–	22 800	19	103	1016	108	16 947	1974/77	GE-General Electric	General Electric 7-FDL-12	GE-761-A9/10, GT581-C11
B-12	B-B	Elec	1125	–	–	24	97	1016	68	13 563	1953	General Motors Corp	GM-12-567-B	GM-D-19/GM-D15 & 8078909
G-8	A1A-A1A	Elec	950	–	12 720	15	72	1016	71.7	14 336	1958	General Motors Corp	GM-8-567-C	GM-T-29, GM-D15E
G-8	B-B	Elec	950	–	12 720	15	72	1016	68.9	14 336	1958/60	General Motors Corp	GM-8-567-C	GM-T-29, GM-15DE
G-12	A1A-A1A	Elec	1425	–	15 180	20	100	1016	78.2	13 106	1957	General Motors Corp	Gm-12-567C	GM-D-29/D-12F
	B-B	Elec	1425	–	15 180	15	72	1016	72.4	14 336	1958/60	General Motors Corp	GM-12-567C	GM-D-29, D-12E/F, AH159A1/2
G-22U	B-B	Elec	1650	–	15 540	21.7	97	1016	73	15 493	1971/74	GM-EMD	GM-645-E	GM-D-29 GM-D-32T
G-22CU	C-C	Elec	1650	–	21 500	14	97	1016	92	15 970	1970/71	GM-EMD	GM-645-E	GM-D-29/32T
GT-22CU	C-C	Elec	2450	–	–	–	105	–	108	–	1982	Villares	GM-645-E3B	GM-D-31
G-26CU	C-C	Elec	1650	–	–	–	97.2	1016	108	15 764	1974/75	Macosa-GM-EMD	EM-645-E	GM-D-29/D-321
GL-8	A1A-A1A	Elec	950	17 010	15 370	–	100	1016	68	13 584	1962	General Motors Corp	GM-8-567-C	GM-D29/GM-D25E
GL-8	B-B	Elec	950	17 010	15 370	–	100	1016	59.2	12 344	1960/62	General Motors Corp	GM-567-C	GM-D29/GM-D25-E

Companhia Brasileira de Trens Urbanos (CBTU)

Estrada Velha de Tijuca, 77-Usina, Rio de Janeiro, RJ
CEP 20531

Telephone: +55 21 288 1992
Telex: 021 22793 tren br

President: Issac Popoutchi
Director, Planning: H O B Neves
  Technical: Nestor Rocha
  Administration: Carlos Aloisio Rabello
  Operations: R F Schoppa

Personnel: W de Souza Vieira

Gauge: 1600 mm; 1000 mm
Route length: 800 km; 410 km
Electrification: 815 km at 3 kV dc

Regionalisation planned

CBTU is at present the urban transit management subsidiary of RFFSA. At the start of 1988 the then government announced proposals to break up CBTU and pass control of its urban railways to the relevant state governments. It did not implement the proposal, but the idea has been espoused by new President Collor de Mello. He has indicated that if the transfer were achieved, he would seek in consort with the local authorities to invest US$3500 million in development of CBTU services. In the interim he proposed in March 1990 complete withdrawal of state financial support for CBTU, which in 1989 had been granted only a quarter of the US$670 million it requested.

CBTU operations cover some 1500 train services carrying over 1 million passengers daily, three times the volume of 1975. Passenger journeys total annually over 450 million. Since 1975 over US$1000 million has been spent on rehabilitation of track with 57 kg/m welded rail, on capacity enlargement and on new equipment, including CTC. Train formations have been enlarged from six to eight cars, with platforms lengthened to match, and may go to 12 cars.

Developments have included:

Rio de Janeiro: MAN has supplied 60 new four-car emus with GEC Traction power equipment; construction was shared with Santa Matilde. In 1989 Cobrasma and Mafersa were contracted to refurbish 62 cars of the 1954 Series 200 emu stock. By 1990 the Rio system was in bad state, with some 250 emu cars unserviceable and as a result service frequency reduced from 10 to 20 minutes. In 1990 CBTU was preparing to order from Materfer of Argentina 22 four-car dmus for the metre-gauge line to Fundo de Baía.

Belo Horizonte: A Franco-Brazilian group headed by Francorail won a contract worth Fr900 million to establish the first 14.5 km Belo Horizonte Central-Eldorado stage of a 3 kV dc, 1600 mm-gauge, electrified suburban system that will eventually total 111 km.

A consortium led by Cobrasma and Francorail furnished 25 stainless-steel four-car emus, supply of which was facilitated by a French government loan. Train control is by CTC and ATC featuring cab signalling and track-to-train radio.

Porto Alegre: Under management of a CBTU subsidiary, Trensurb, a 42.4 km, 21-station electrified line has been established from the northern suburbs to the city centre, at a cost of Cr 862 million. A contract for 25 four-car air-conditioned emus was won by a Japanese consortium of Hitachi, Nippon Sharyo, Seizo Kaisha and Mitsui financed by a World Bank loan. The trains operate at 4–5 minute headways under ATC and CTC control.

Recife: An electrified network is being created. Works have included conversion to 1600 mm gauge of the 20 km Recife Central-Jaboatão line and a metre-gauge freight bypass from Lacerda to Prezeres. For this and the Belo Horizonte scheme 25 four-car emus incorporating electrical equipment by GEC Traction and Equipamentos Villares were supplied by Brazilian manufacturers. GEC-General Signal won the resignalling contract and GEC Transmission and Distribution Projects Limited an order to the value of £3.9 million to supply a power system.

CBTU and RFFSA set up an urban passenger transport authority, Metrorec, to operate the modernised suburban system; however, Metrorec now reports only to CBTU.

Fortaleza: Signalling modernisation and some double-tracking was proposed in this area, but Japanese interests have recently recommended that electrification and replacement of the present four-car diesel trains by eight-car emus would be more cost-effective. CBTU adopted this recommendation in 1987 and began planning a two-route system of 42 route-km converging on the city's Joao Felipe terminus from south and west.

São Paulo: The governor of São Paulo state has sought to convert some of the CBTU system in the city into surface metro lines. The line initially proposed for transmutation is the eastern, from Roosevelt to Mogi das Cruzes.

Recife, Natal, João Pessoa and Maceió: In 1990 CBTU was planning to buy for the non-electrified routes in these areas 15 four-car dmus from Materfer.

Constitution

CBTU now covers the suburban systems of:

City	Route length (km)	Rolling stock
Rio de Janeiro	165	45 diesel locos
		237 emus
		319 electric railcars
		360 trailers
		73 diesel railcars
São Paulo (excluding those of FEPASA)	191	8 diesel locos
		139 emus
		164 electric railcars
		274 trailers
Belo Horizonte	12.5	10 emus (20 to order)
Porto Alegre	42.2	2 diesel locos
		25 emus
		8 diesel railcars
		14 trailers
Recife	electric 20.5 diesel 32	25 emus
		8 diesel locos
		51 trailers
Natal	56	2 diesel locos
		18 trailers
Joao Pessoa	30	2 diesel locos
		18 trailers
Salvador (GETUS)	13.6	6 emus
		6 electric railcars
		2 trailers
Fortaleza (GETUF)	42	6 diesel locos
		45 trailers
Maceio	32	1 diesel loco
		7 trailers

In total, these systems recorded 34 million passenger journeys in 1987, an increase of 3 million on the previous year.

CBTU electric multiple-units

Class	No of cars	Voltage	Motor cars per unit	Motored axles per motor car	Output per motor	Max speed km/h	Weight per car kg (T-trailer, M-motor)	Passenger capacity per car (T-trailer, M-motor)	Car length (mm)	No in service 1987	Rate of acceleration m/s²	Date first built	Builders Mechanical parts	Builders Electrical equipment
Rio de Janeiro														
200	3	3000	1	4	237	85	T 35 923 / M 60 135	T 76 / M 79	22 000	96	0.55	1954	Metropolitan Vickers	Metropolitan Vickers
400M	3	3000	1	4	315	90	T1 45 000 / M 58 000 / Tc 40 000	T 61 / M 70	22 000	63	0.57	1964	FNV-Cobrasma CISM	Hitachi/Toshiba
400	3	3000	1	4	255	90	T 40 900 / M 63 080	T 70 / M 74	22 000	27	0.47	1964	FNV/Cobrasma CISM	General Electric
500	4	3000	2	8	315	90	T 43 500 / M 58 000	T 61 / M 70	22 000	30	0.80	1977	Japanese consortium	Hitachi/Toshiba
700	4	3000	2	8	315	90	T 37 000 / M 57 000	T 61 / M 70	22 000	48	0.80	1980	Mafersa	Hitachi/Toshiba
800	4	3000	2	8	280	90	T 35 500 / M 55 400	T 61 / M 70	22 000	60	0.80	1980	Santa Matilde Cobrasma	GEC
900	4	3000	2	8	279	90	T 40 400 / M 60 200	T 61 / M 70	22 000	60	0.80	1980	Cobrasma	MTE
São Paulo														
101	3	3000	1	4	306	100	M 63 830 / Tc 40 900 / Ts 41 670	94	25 907	21	0.47	1957	Budd	General Electric
401	3	3000	1	4	343	100	T1 40 990 / M 61 900 / Tc 40 050	T1 98 / M 92 / Tc 92	25 907	21	0.5	1976	Mafersa	General Electric
431	3	3000	1	4	343	100	T1 40 990 / M 59 800 / Tc 39 500	T1 98 / M 92 / Tc 96	25 907	27	0.47	1977	Mafersa	General Electric
EC	3	3000	1	2	259	90	T1 28 000 / M 48 000 / Tc 32 000	T 64 / M 52	T 20 000 / M 20 400	30	0.65	1980	Mafersa	ACEC
Belo Horizonte														
BH	4	3000	2	8	315	90	T1 44 000 / M1 58 000 / Tc 43 500	T 72 / M 60	22 000	5	0.80	1985	Cobrasma	MTE
Porto Alegre														
100	4	3000	2	8	315	90	T 43 500 / M 58 000	T 60 / M 54	22 000	25	0.80	1984	Nippon Sharyo Hitachi-Kawasaki	Japanese Consortium
Recife														
REC	4	3000	2	8	276	90	T 43 500 / M 58 000	–	22 000	25	0.8	1984	CISM/MAN	GEC
Salvador														
ACF	1	3000	1	4	574	90	M 52 100	50	15 240	18	0.8	1962	ACF	GE

514 RAILWAY SYSTEMS / Brazil

Ferrovia Paulista SA (FEPASA)

Praça Júlio Prestes 148, São Paulo CEP 02218

Telephone: +55 11 223 7211
Telex: 011 22724

President: Antonio Carlos Rios Corral
Assistant Director: Benedicto Jose Pinheiro Ribiero
Director, Administration: Sergio Lorena de Mello
  Finance: Norberto Stensen
  Law: Frederico Pegler
  Planning: Manuel Rocha Carvalheiro
  Transportation: João Rinaldo Ribiero
  Technical: Paolo Antonio Bonomo
  Metropolitan Transport: Osmar Luiz Geddes
Superintendents:
  Commercial: J M M Hoffman
  Planning: O L Guedes
  Rolling Stock: W Z Filho
  Suburban Services: A Sergio Fernandes
  Terminals: J A R Peres
  Permanent Way: H Romiti
  Works: J F de Araujo
  Contracts: W G Fernandes

Gauge: 1600 mm; 1000 mm; mixted 1600/1000 mm
Route length: 1590 km; 3408 km; 74 km
Electrification: 1532 km at 3 kV dc

FEPASA was formed in 1971 to consolidate the operation of five railways owned by the State of São Paulo. There are three divisions: First (the former Paulista and Araraquara); Second (the former Sorocabana); Third (the former Morgiana and São Paulo-Minas).

Traffic

Drastic action in 1976 rid the railway of most of its long-distance passenger and general freight traffic. Thereafter FEPASA concentrated on haulage of a dozen major commodities in bulk, headed by oil, agricultural produce, phosphates, cement and alcohol.

In recent years, however, FEPASA has reinvigorated its long-distance passenger business. Cars have been refurbished, train schedules accelerated by limitation of stops to key towns, and on-board services improved with restaurant cars and stewardess service at seats. Another development has been creation of tourist trains for incorporation in travel agency packages. Passenger journey totals advanced 9.5 per cent in 1988 to 7.6 million and revenue was increased by 50 per cent (even though passengers aged more than 65 travel free). In 1990 FEPASA was studying the feasibility of upgrading its 90km São Paulo-Campinas route for schedules of no more than 50 minutes; current timing for the journey is 90 minutes.

Despite increasingly aggressive and efficient competition from road transport, which will be intensified still more by a São Paulo state 4000 km, four-year road-building programme (the state also contemplates authority for 73 tonnes glw road trains), FEPASA has managed to improve its freight tonnage in the 1980s. This development owes a great deal to creation of total transportation packages, for example throughout from non rail-served soya bean source to mill or shipment port. Petroleum and grain rail movement has been concentrated in unit train haulage from a few terminals, with significant results in traffic increases. New planning techniques are ensuring prompt supply of wagons to clients and better relating service to port activity. The number of privately-owned rail-served transshipment terminals is increasing.

The biggest partnership with private enterprise to date involves a soya bean company, Cutrale-Quintella. The latter is to invest US$30 million in acquisition of seven GE 'Dash-7' locomotives, track work, terminals and FEPASA staff training so as to run its own trains to Guarujá port, near Santos, from Colombia, 700km away to the northwest. The company will provide 300 of its own freight cars to supplement 950 refurbished vehicles from FEPASA's fleet, and FEPASA will also repair and reserve 14 2000 hp locomotives for the company's exclusive use. In a similar deal, FEPASA is overhauling 12 locomotives and 200 wagons for an 848 km bauxite haul to the order of the Votorantim mining company. The deals barter discounted freight tariffs for the companies' investment in new and refurbished FEPASA rolling stock.

Container train services have been revived, along with establishment of intermodal terminals at key centres. A through container train service to Argentina is operational. In 1990 FEPASA was studying creation of new container terminals outside São Paulo and at Campinas for traffic to and from Santos port.

A computerised wagon control system is being progressively commissioned, with aid from the Brazilian National Bank for Social and Economic Development.

Suburban passenger modernisation

From a total of 56 million passenger-journeys in 1982, volume in this sector has now scaled 99 million following further extension of the suburban network.

FEPASA has undertaken a sizeable programme to replace metre-gauge services on the western side of São Paulo with a high-capacity broad-gauge operation. Tracks are renewed, stations rebuilt, mixed gauge laid, the electrification modernised, and the existing CTC replaced with a new cab-signalling and speed-control form of ATC; bi-directional operation on multi-track sections has also been provided.

To serve the new system a total of 138 three-car chopper-controlled and stainless-steel bodied emus have been procured. Two-thirds have been furnished by a Franco-Brazilian group comprising Francorail, Cobrasma, Industria Electrica Brown Boveri of Brazil, CEM-Oerlikon and Jeumont-Schneider, the remaining third, which have Budd bodies and Pioneer bogies, by a consortium of ACEC, Mafersa, Villares and Sorefame. Existing Japanese-built Series 5800 emus have been comprehensively renovated with power-operated doors, better seating and lighting and public address.

The state government has been looking for loan finance to establish a commuter rail service in the city of Campinas. The scheme involves the development of FEPASA double-track that crosses the city north to south from Bova Vista to Vinhedo.

Traction and rolling stock

In 1988 FEPASA operated 146 electric and 363 diesel locomotives, 140 power and 284 trailer emu cars, 4 diesel railcars, 273 other passenger cars, and 14 060 freight wagons.

Ferronorte railway project

A soya farming magnate (without world peer in that respect, according to some sources) in the provinces of Mato Grosso and Goias who also fronts one of the country's major banks, Olacyr Francisco de Moraes, has formed a company, Ferronorte, to build a line from Fepasa at Santa Fe do Sul, northwest of São Paulo, into Mato Grosso. The new railway would eventually be two-pronged, forking at Cuiaba (Mato Grosso) into lines heading northwest to Porto Velho and north to Santarem, on the Amazon. The objective is movement of rice, soya and grain for export to the Atlantic ports of Santas, below São Paulo, and Rio.

Tenders to build the first stage were called in March 1989 and would be evaluated by the Transport Ministry, though the government will not provide any financial support for the project. However, half the cost is expected to come from the Amazon Development Authority, Sudam. Length of the first stage alone

GE Type U20C diesel-electric Co-Co

São Paulo 1600 mm-gauge emu on mixed-gauge trackage

will be 1038 km, from Santa Fe do Sul to Cuiaba, where the line would fork as described above. Construction cost has been estimated as US$1700 million. The successful bidder would have 90 years' exclusive development rights throughout a 200 m-wide corridor adjoining the railway. The Ferronorte prospectus envisages a fleet of 147 2630 kW diesel locomotives used in pairs on 6700-tonne trains formed from a stock of 3232 wagons. Ruling gradients would be 1–1.3 per cent.

Electrification

FEPASA is working to improve and extend its electrified route-length of 1158 km. A two-stage plan was started under financial arrangements with French, Swiss and German Federal Republic banking concerns, which together put up US$106 million, while Brazilian credit concerns funded a further US$214 million.

The first priority has been FEPASA's prime export freight route, the metre-gauge line carrying 50 per cent of its total freight traffic, from the interior at Uberaba southward to the port of Santos, a distance of 710 km, which bypasses São Paulo. A US$250 million turnkey contract for this project was secured by a Franco-Brazilian consortium, led by Alsthom and including the 50 c/s Group in July 1976. The corridor was also being streamlined by realignments, other track works and in particular construction of a new 79 km Mayrink-Helvetia bypass to eliminate 100 metre-radius curvature and a 2.1 per cent ruling gradient. This new line, which has been constructed on a ruling gradient of 1 per cent with 600-metre minimum radius curves, is built to mixed-gauge. The project was protracted by lack of funds, but completed in 1988.

The whole section from Boa Vista to Santos is being relaid to mixed gauge in order to re-route 1600 mm-gauge freight away from the congested São Paulo metropolitan area.

In the late 1970s the original intention to adopt 25 kV ac for the electrification was dropped in favour of 3 kV dc, as the advantages of compatibility with the system already existing from the Mayrink area into São Paulo were deemed conclusive. This would be more costly, and for that reason wiring of the northern 218 km from Uberaba to Ribeirao Preto was deferred. In 1980 a fresh US$322 million contract was concluded with the 50 c/s Group that limited 3 kV dc electrification to some 600 track-km between Ribeirao Preto and Mayrink. By early 1988 it was anticipated that 165 route-km of this section, from Campinas to Casa Branca, would be energised during 1989.

Two locomotive contracts have been signed, one for 70 metre-gauge units, a second for 10 broad-gauge units, but both cover the same design, and all 80 units will be adaptable to either gauge. The chopper-controlled design is a derivative of the Class 1600 Bo-Bo built by Alsthom for Netherlands Railways. Weighing 100 tonnes, it has a continuous rating of 2480 kW, a one-hour rating of 2600 kW, and is equipped for mixed regenerative-rheostatic braking. Up to four units can be driven in multiple.

Two of the locomotives were shipped complete by Alsthom, the remainder to be assembled in Brazil by Emaq. The French-built pair were eventually shipped, together with components for 30 more, in October 1987. Difficulties at Emaq prevented any start on the locally-assembled locomotives until 1987.

Track

Rail
Type: TR 37, TR 45, TR 50, TR 55, TR 57, TR 68
Weight: 37, 45, 50, 55, 57, 68 kg/m
Cross ties (sleepers)
Wood: 1000 mm gauge 200 × 220 × 160 mm; 1600 mm gauge 2800 × 240 × 170 mm
Spacing: 1000 mm gauge 1600/km; 1600 mm gauge 1667/km
Rail fastenings: GEO or K; ML
Concrete block: 1000 mm gauge 680 × 290 × 211 mm; 1600 mm gauge 680 × 290 × 239 mm
Spacing: 1500/km
Fastenings: FN
Concrete (monoblock): (1000 mm gauge only) 2000 × 220 × 210 mm to 2000 × 320 × 242 mm
Spacing: 1500/km
Fastenings: RN
Minimum curve radius: Main lines 150 m; branches 90 m
Max gradients: Main lines 2%; branches 3%
Max axleload: 1000 mm gauge 20 tonnes; 1600 mm gauge 25 tonnes

Diesel-electric locomotives

Class	Wheel arrangement	Rated power kW	Tractive effort Continuous at kg	km/h	Max speed km/h	Wheel diameter mm	Total weight tonnes	Length mm	Year first built	Builders* Mechanical parts	Engine & type	Transmission
3100	C + C	447	9934	14	80	838	64	11 785	1948	GE	CB	GE
3200	B – B	894	15 422	17	138	910	71.2	14 970	1957	GE	CB	GE
3500	C – C	671	11 200	18	95	1050	68.1	14 232	1957	Ge	Alco	GE
3600	B – B	652	13 370	13	100	1016	56.7	12 344	1961	GM	GM	GM
3600	B – B	652	15 370	13	100	1016	60.5	11 300	1960	GM	GM	GM
3650	B – B	976	16 300	18	100	1016	74.9	14 429	1957	GM	GM	GM
3700	B – B	574	12 650	14	90	1050	70	14 500	1969	LEW	SACM	LEW
3750	B – B	835	12 650	20	100	1050	74	14 500	1968	LEW	SACM	LEW
3800	C – C	1491	22 800	19	103	914	108	16 990	1974	GE	GE	GE
7000	B – B	1304	19 600	20	105	1016	110.6	17 120	1958	GM	GM	GM
7050	B – B	976	18 160	16	124	1016	80	14 589	1958	GM	GM	GM
7760	B – B	574	12 600	14	90	1050	74	14 500	1967	LEW	SACM	LEW
7800	C W C	1491	22 800	19	103	914	108	16 990	1977	GE	GE	GE

* GE = General Electric
GM = General Motors
LEW = LEW Henningsdorf
SACM = Société Alsacienne de Constructions Mécaniques de Mulhouse
CB = Cooper Bessemer

Electric locomotives

Class	Wheel arrangement	Line current	Rated output kW	Tractive effort Continuous at kg	km/h	Max km/h	Wheel diameter mm	Weight tonnes	Length mm	No in service 1984	Year first built	Builders* Mechanical parts	Electrical equipment
2000	1 – C + C – 1	3000 V dc	1729	12 450	12	90	1118	130	18 590	25	1943	GE	GE
2050	1 – C + C – 1	3000 V dc	1729	12 750	17	90	1118	130	18 590	121	1943	West	West
2100	B – B	3000 V dc	1371	11 800	22	90	1117	72.7	13 942	30	1968	GE	GE
6100	2 – C + C – 2	3000 V dc	2846	–	–	145	–	165	–	5	1982	West	rebuilt FEPASA
6150	2 – C + C – 2	3000 V dc	2846	–	–	145	–	165	–	5	1982	West	rebuilt FEPASA
6350	C – C	3000 V dc	3269	22 800	20	134	1168	144	18 339	10	1967	GEBSA	GEBSA
6370	2 – C + C – 2	3000 V dc	2846	14 600	22	145	1168	165	23 101	22	1940	GE	GE
6410	C + C	3000 V dc	1134	13 600	9	65	1015	107	15 291	6	1927	West	West
6450	2 – D + D – 2	3000 V dc	3470	35 000	9	110	1200	242.6	27 076	5	1951	GE	GE
6500	B – B	3000 V dc	341	6890	8.5	64	1016	55.5	12 649	9	1924	GE	GE
6510	B – B	3000 V dc	341	6890	8.5	65	1016	55.5	12 649	8	1947	GE	GE
EC362	B – B	3000 V dc	2480	–	–	90	–	100	16 200	80 on order	1984	50 c/s Gp	50 c/s Gp

* GE = General Electric   West = Westinghouse   GEBSA = General Electric do Brasil

Diesel railcars

Class	Cars per unit	Motor cars per unit	Motored axles per motor car	Transmission	Rated power per motor	Max speed	Weight per car	Total seating capacity	Length per car	No in service 1984	Year first built	Builders
5000	1	1	2	Hyd	81 kW	90 km/h	41.1 tonnes	56	18 745 mm	2	1962	Budd
5010	1	1	2	Hyd	81 kW	90 km/h	42.9 tonnes	48	18 745 mm	2	1962	Budd

RAILWAY SYSTEMS / Brazil

Electric multiple-units

Class	Cars per unit	Line voltage dc	Motor cars per unit	Motored axles per motor car	Rated output (kW) per motor	Max speed km/h	Weight tonnes per car (M-motor T-trailer)	Total seating capacity	Length per car mm (M-motor T-trailer)	No in service 1984	Rate of acceleration m/s^2	Year first built	Builders
4000	3	3000	1	4	130	90	M 44.5 T 25.8 T$_2$1 25.1	270	M 17 300 T 17 300	2	–	1943	Pullman Standard Car
4100	3	3000	1	4	168	80	M 40 T 30 T$_2$1 30	270	M 18 300 T 18 300	30	–	1957	Kawasaki Rolling Stock Ltd
5000	3	3000	1	4	207	90	M 49.8 T 32 T$_2$1 29	270	M 21 000 T 24 000	98	0.7	1978	Cobrasma IE Brown Boveri MTE, TCO
5500	3	3000	1	4	250	90	M 48 T 32 T$_2$1 28	270	M 22 000 T 27 000	10	0.65	1978	Mafersa Villares Sorefame, ACEC

Companhia Vale do Rio Doce (CVRD)

CVRD, the biggest producer of iron ore in the world, owns the Vitoria a Minas Railway (EVFM) and since 1977 has been in sole control of the Carajas mining development and the Carajas Railway (EFC) built to serve it.

Vitoria a Minas Railway (EVFM)
Estrada de Ferro Vitória a Minas

CP 155, 29000 Vitoria, Espirito Santo
Telephone: +55 27 226 0656/0762
Telex: 0272161
Telefax: +55 27 226 0093

Superintendent: J C Marreco
General Managers, Operations: A F Passos
  Administration: A Pippi
  Permanent Way: J G Mattos
  Mechanical Maintenance: A B Gomes
  Signals & Telecommunication: M A Basilio
  Industrial Engineering: J Encarnação

Gauge 1000 mm
Route length: 799 km

CVRD ore train crossing the Calupara River, Maranhão, hauled by two GE C30-7 and two GT-26 locomotives

The railway's principal role is to transport ore from mines at Itibara to Port Tubarão, Vitoria. The normal ore train comprises 160 cars of 100 tonnes glw hauled by a pair of 3600 hp diesel locomotives; usually 20 trainloads and their return empties are operated daily. The railway's existence has attracted other industrial development to the area, including two steel mills and pulpwood plants, as a result of which EVFM now operates additionally an average of 14 general freight trains daily. A 50 km branch to cater for pulpwood sources was completed in 1982. Passenger traffic, too, has developed, and a daily service of four passenger trains has built up an annual traffic of almost 3 million journeys; 32 new passenger cars were recently acquired from Romanian suppliers.

Traffic	1987	1988
Total freight tonnage (million)	87.06	97.07
Total freight tonne-km (million)	63 810.8	71 412.5
Average net freight train load (tonnes)	4974	5061
Total passenger-km (million)	454.8	378.4
Total passenger journeys (million)	2615	2096

Finances (Cz$ million)		
Revenue	*1987*	*1988*
Passengers and baggage	54.877	608.415
Freight, parcels and mail	5370.9	51 358.6
Other income	844.0	11 383.1
Total	6269.8	63 350.2
Expenditure	*1987*	*1988*
Staff/personnel	4651.8	39 137.9
Materials and services	2098.7	15 268.2
Depreciation	828.9	4308.1
Financial charges	1220.0	9019.0
Total	8799.5	67 733.4

Signalling
The railway is double-tracked and bi-directionally signalled on each track by CTC, with reproduction of signal aspects in locomotive cabs. Each signal block has the added protection of derailment detectors; these are being supplemented by hot box and broken wheel detectors.

Traction and rolling stock
EVFM operates 195 diesel locomotives, 64 passenger cars (including five buffet and three baggage cars) and 13 135 freight wagons.
  In 1989 EVFM was testing a locomotive rebuilt with two Caterpillar 3612 engines arranged to work on a mixture of diesel and fuel oil. EVFM also aims to refit a locomotive with ABB three-phase motors for trials.

Coupler in standard use: E/F (AAR)
Braking in standard use; Locomotives, 26L (AAR) Hauled stock, ABD mechanical empty/load

Track
Rail: 68 kg/m AREA, carbon steel heat treated and alley
Cross ties (sleepers): Wood, thickness 170 mm, and steel
Spacing: 1851/km
Fastenings: Elastic (Denik)
Minimum curvature radius: 202 m
Max gradient: 0.3% export-bound
  0.5% import-bound
Max axleload: 25 tonnes

Carajás Railway (EFC)
Estrada de Ferro Carajás

Praia do Boqueirão, BR1355, km 10 Itaqui-Pedrinhas, CEP 65000, São Luis-Maranhão

Telephone: +55 98 221 3714/5388
Telex: 098 2138

General Manager: Romildo Coelho Vello
Executive Managers,
  Operations: S B da Silva
  Transportation: M G Serpa
  Permanent Way: A J Oliveira
  Mechanical and Electrical: R B Vieira F

Gauge: 1600 mm
Route length: 890 km

Reserves of high-quality iron ore estimated at almost 18 000 million tonnes were discovered in the Serra dos Carajás, in the far north of the country, in 1967 and subsequently deposits of manganese, copper, nickel and bauxite were also revealed. The recession delayed exploitation, but engineering of an 890 km railway to transport the ore to a new Atlantic port of Ponta da Madeira, near São Luis, was begun in 1978. In 1982 CVRD was granted a US$304 million loan from the World Bank and obtained a further US$123 million loan from West German interests towards the cost, which is now estimated to total US$4100 million. A further loan of US$600 million was negotiated with the European Economic Community.
  The pace of construction was stepped up in 1984 to achieve completion in March 1985, a year earlier than originally budgeted.
  The 1600 mm-gauge railway crosses mostly flat terrain, so that maximum gradients can be restricted to 0.4 per cent for loaded and 1 per cent for empty trains, and curvature observes a minimum 860 metres radius. It is eventually to be electrified at 50 kV 60 Hz·ac, but not yet for financial reasons. There are no tunnels and the most significant engineering work is a 2.3 km viaduct over the Tocatins river at Maraba. Construction of a 200 km branch to a bauxite mine is contemplated.

More recently CVRD has been considering a 1000 km extension of its rail system into the grain-producing Cerrado area to the south-east.

Traction and rolling stock
At the start of 1990 the locomotive stock comprised 29 GM-EMD SD40-2, 41 GE C30-7B and 4 recently-delivered GE C40-8. Deliveries of 16 more units were expected during 1990, including 6 GE B40-8. Freight cars totalled 2538, dominated by 1446 ore hoppers of 100 tonnes glw, 89 tonnes maximum payload, built by Cobrasma, FNV, Santa Matilda, Marfesa, Convap and CIC.

Orders were placed with South American builders in 1989 for 200 more freight cars, and with Romanian industry for 20 passenger cars. In 1990 CVRD invited bids for supply of 20 bi-modal wagons, to be employed primarily in delivery of new autos, and orders were placed with General Electric do Brasil for the first 1600 mm-gauge version of the GE 'Dash-8' diesel locomotive.

Signalling
Ansaldo Trasporti of Italy gained the contract to equip the line with a comprehensive CTC and ATC system (all locomotives are ATC fitted), controlled from a centre at Ponta de Madeira.

Tracks
Rails: 68 kg/m long-welded
Fastenings: Pandrol or Denik
Cross ties (sleepers): Timber, creosote-treated, thickness 170 mm, spaced 540 mm between centres
Minimum curve radius: 860 m
Max gradient: 0.4% loaded trains, 1% empty trains
Max axleload: 30 tonnes

EVFM diesel locomotives

Class	Wheel arrangement	Transmission	Rated power (kW)	Max speed km/h	Total weight tonnes	No in service 1988	Year first built	Builders Mechanical parts	Engine & type	Transmission
G-12	B-B	Elec	964	97	76	29	1956	GM	EMD 12-567C	EMD
G-16	C-C	Elec	1325	100	100.7	38	1961	GM	EMD 12-567C	EMD
GT-26 CU2	C-C	Elec	1987	90	120.6	34	1973	GM	EMD 16-645E3	EMD
GT-26 CU2	C-C	Elec	2208	100	138	6	1982	Villares	EMD 16-645E3B	EMD
DDM-45	D-D	Elec	2650	85	162	82	1969	GM	EMD 20-645E3	EMD
GE-U26C	C-C	Elec	1914	105	120	6	1981	GE (Brazil)	GE 7FDL12	GE (Brazil)

Bulgaria
Bulgarian State Railways (BDZ)

Iwan-Wazov Str 3, Sofia 1080

Telephone: +359 2 873045
Telex: 22423 Bulfer Sofia

Minister: Trifon Paschov
General Manager, Railways: S Ferdov
Deputy General Managers: Entcho Velinov, A Petkov
Traffic Manager: Atanas Tonev
Traction Engineer: Guenadi Kolev
Signalling and Telecommunications Manager: I Covatshev
Infrastructure Manager: G Detchev
Rolling Stock Manager: Dimitre Mantchev
Electrical Engineer: Ivan Kovatchev
Commercial Director: Simeon Hhristov

Gauge: 1435 mm; 760 mm
Route length: 4055 km; 245 km
Electrification: 2588 km at 25 kv 50 Hz ac

Rail transport has taken an increasingly important role in Bulgaria's communications network following the government's 1980 decision to freeze highway-hauled transport volumes.

The systematic development of the different modes of transport, including railway transport, and the national distribution of goods between these modes is the responsibility of the national Transport Authority which oversees all the modes, including road transport.

Traffic
In 1988 passenger traffic amounted to 107.77 milion journeys and 8 143 million passenger-km. Freight traffic totalled 82.5 milion tonnes and 7 842 million tonne-km.

In May 1990 a twice-weekly sleeping-car service was inaugurated between Sofia and Thessaloniki, Greece.

Motive power and rolling stock
Main-line diesels have been built in Romania and the Soviet Union with Hungary and the German Democratic Republic supplying shunters. The Czechoslovak Skoda works has supplied BDZ with all its electric locomotives.

The structure of the wagon fleet has been greatly improved by the modernisation of existing wagons and the introduction of heavy-duty and specialised goods wagons for carrying a variety of goods at speeds of 100 to 120 km/h.

Electrification
Electrification of most of the principal railways lines has now been completed, using single-phase 25 kV 50 Hz ac. The whole of the 1700 km 'Great Ring', encircling the country from the capital to the Black Sea on a Sofia-Mezdra-Gorna-Orjahovitza-Dybovo-Karlovu-Sofia route is now under wires. The 67 km between Karlovu and Plovdiv, a north-south link between the key Sofia-Varna and Sofia-Burgas routes, were energised early in 1986.

Further lines scheduled for electrification were: Mezdra-Vidin-Lom; Sofia-Radomir-Petricn-Kulata (on the Greek frontier); Sofia-Dragoman (on the Yugoslav border, beyond which there will be wiring through to Nis on the Yugoslav Railways; in 1990 BDZ and JZ were negotiating a joint venture); and Plovdiv-Svilengrad (on the Turkish frontier). This totalled 511 route-km.

Sofia-Plovdiv CTC
A CTC installation covering the whole 156 km, double-track and electrified Sofia-Plovdiv main line was completed in July 1987. It was supplied by Iskra of Yugoslavia. A Sofia centre remotely controls 18 of the line's 26 intermediate stations. The Iskra contract included automation of level crossings and of yards at each end of the route. The line was next to be equipped with ground-to-train radio and ATC.

Permanent way and installations
On key routes BDZ aims, after double-tracking, for speeds of 140 to 160 km/h for passenger trains and from 100 to 120 km/h for freight trains by perfecting vehicle design, permanent way and signalling techniques.

On high-density lines 60 kg/m rail is laid. Rail of 49 kg/m is used elsewhere, laid on Bulgarian pre-stressed concrete sleepers secured with K-type fastenings. Track is built for an axleload of 20 tonnes nation-wide and 23 tonnes on a few selected sections. About one-quarter of the main-line system has continuous welded rail and this is being extended.

Following Romania's refusal to allow construction of a broad-gauge railway across her territory to simplify access for Soviet traffic, the number of train ferries plying the Black Sea between Varna and Ilychevsk (USSR) has been doubled to eight by 1990.

BDZ Clas 5100 4600 kW electric Co-Co, built by Electroputers of Romania

Burkina Faso

Burkina Faso Railway

Société des Chemins de Fer du Berkina

PO Box 192, Ouagdougou, Burkina Faso

Telephone: +237 306048/9
Telex: 5433 dirano

Director General: Gregoire Babore Bado

Gauge: 1000 mm
Route length: 495 km

The country was for long served by the Abidjan-Niger Railway under a joint arrangement with the Ivory Coast (qv). In 1986, following a disagreement over the wisdom of embarking on the 375 km Tambao extension in Burkina Faso, it was announced that the railway would be split. In early 1988 it appeared that the two countries had healed their differences, but by March the split was reaffirmed, because potential aid donors were unconvinced that the railway could be efficiently run as a whole, given the scale of differences over such matters as the Tambao extension.

Construction of the Tambao extension has begun, with the aid of credits, under the aegis of the Office General des Projets de Tambao. The government has bought 6000 tonnes of used main-line rail from Canadian National. By the end of 1988 the first 104 km had been laid from Ouagadougou to Kaya. In the following year funds were obtained from the UN Development Programme for engagement of consultants to manage and advise on completion of this section, and the Burkina Faso government advanced CFA6 250 million for construction of the remaining 271km from Kaya to Tambao.

In 1988 Canac International, a subsidiary of Canadian National, won a C$2.3 million turnkey contract to supply and install a telecommunications network over the new line. Completion was scheduled for December 1989. The work includes installation of five microwave sites between Ouagadougou and Kaya. In addition, a VHF/FM communications network would be installed to link train stations and train crews.

A deal has been agreed with Projects & Equipment Corporation of India for launch of local freight car production. The Indians will set up a manufacturing plant at Bobo Dioulasso, get it going with supply of wagon kits for assembly, then oversee transition to local manufacture from scratch.

Burma (Myanmar)

Burma Railways Corporation (BRC)

PO Box 118, Bogyoke Aung San Street, Rangoon

Telephone: +95 1 14455
Cable: Rheostat

Managing Director: Colonel Win Sein
General Manager: U Saw Clyde
Deputy General Manager: U Kyaw Hlang
Chief Traffic Manager: U Kenneth Shein
Chief Mechanical & Electrical Engineer: Vacant
Deputy Chief Mechanical Engineer, Locomotives: U Hla Mint
  Carriages and Wagons: U Kyaw Mint
  Operations: U Tin Shwe
Chief Engineer: U Tun Thein
Deputy Chief Engineer, Planning: U Thin Tu
  Signals & Communications: U Kyi Nyut
  Track: Vacant
Controller of Stores: U Aye Mu
Controller of Accounts: U Kan Tun

Gauge: 1000 mm
Route length: 3137 km

Burma has a metre-gauge network comprising a main section and two short isolated sections of railway. The most important line connects the two principal cities, Rangoon the capital, and Mandalay 619 km to the north, BRC has no connections with neighbouring railways. Extension of the Pegu-Martaban line over the Salween river and into Thailand at Phisantouk has been studied, but is not seen as a priority. The government seeks to expand public transportation and thus asked BRC to stress passenger services in its 1986-90 development.

The latest reports available indicate traffic totalling over 3700 million passenger-km and 560 million tonne-km of freight annually. Principal freight constituents are timber, rice, sugar cane and aggregates. The three daily passenger trains between Rangoon and Mandalay include an overnight sleeping-car service.

Investment projects
Foreign aid has been sought to allow execution of several major projects. One is conversion of Rangoon's orbital commuter line to an electrified system operated by 19 locomotives and 105 passenger cars, the total cost of which is put at US$86.7 million. A second is the first stage of relaying the Rangoon-Mandalay main line and its equipment with a VHF communications system. A third proposal is for a new line, Pakkoku to Yinmabin, in the north of the country.

Motive power and rolling stock
Since 1956 BRC's diesel locomotive purchases have been almost exclusively from Alsthom. Most have been double-cabbed 1200 hp B-B-Bs, but 45 1600 hp B-B-Bs with dynamic braking have been supplied, principally to supersede 2-8-2 + 2-8-2 Beyer-Garratts on the mountain lines. The French manufacturer has also provided new engines, spares and advisers to superintend the refurbishing of immobilised diesel locomotives in BRC's Insein workshops. A further 15 2000 hp B-B-Bs were ordered from Alsthom in 1985, together with equipment and assistance in rehabilitating 26 existing units. The new order raised BRC's total of Alsthom locomotives to 154. Also in 1985, however, BRC ordered seven 375 kW diesel-hydraulic locomotives from Kawasaki and Sumitomo of Japan, five of the units were to be assembled in Burma. In 1987 BRC took delivery of the first of 19 1100 hp diesel-hydraulic locomotives by Krupp.

In 1984 Daewoo of South Korea was awarded a US$13 million contract to provide 71 passenger cars and 100 freight wagons under a technology transfer arrangement, whereby Daewoo would set up a factory at Mandalay and train Burmese engineers for local assembly of 51 passenger cars and 75 freight wagons of the order. The plant was later to produce 60 passenger cars and 120 freight cars a year. Daewoo has also supplied a 280 hp diesel-hydraulic shunting locomotive.

280 hp diesel-hydraulic shunter by Daewoo

At the latest report operating stock comprised:
Steam locomotives	140
Diesel locomotives	227
Diesel railcars	13
Passenger coaches	960
Freight wagons	7234

Track
Standard rail: Flat bottom BS
Main line: 75 and 60 lb (37.2 and 29.8 kg) in 39 ft lengths

Alsthom-built 2000 hp diesel-electric locomotive and train of Daewoo-built passenger cars

Main branches: 60 lb (29.8 kg)
Other branches and sidings: 50 lb (24.9 kg)
Joints: Suspended; joint sleepers 14 in centres. Rails joined by fishplates and bolts
Welded track: 117 ft (35.7 m) lengths. Thermit welded in situ
Cross ties (sleepers): Hardwood (Xylia Dolabriformis) and creosoted soft wood, 8 in × 4½ in × 6 ft (203 × 115 × 1829 mm)
Spacing
Main line: N × 3

Branch line: N × 2
(N = length of rail in linear yards)
Rail fastening: Dog spikes, elastic rail spikes
Filling (ballast): Broken stone, 2¾ in (50.8-19.1 mm), single on branch lines
Thickness under sleeper: 6 in (150 mm)
Max curvature
Main line: 6° = radius of 955 ft (291 m)
Branch line: 17° = radius of 338 ft (103 mm)
Max gradient
Main line: 0.5% = 1 in 200 compensated

Branch line: 4.0% = 1 in 25 compensated
Max permitted speed
Main line: 30 mph (48 km/h)
Branch line: 20 mph (32 km/h)
Max axleload: 12 tons on 75 and 60 lb rail
Bridge loading: Indian Railway Standard ML

Cameroon

Ministry of Transport

PO Box 1608, Yaoundé

Telephone: +237 23 22 36

Minister: André-Bosco Cheuwa
Director of Land Transport: M Mundi Kengnjisu

Regie Nationale des Chemins de Fer du Cameroun (Regifercam)

PO Box 304, Douala

Telephone: +237 42 60 45/42 71 59
Cable: Regifercam, Douala
Telex: 5607 kn

Director General: Samuel Minko
Assistant Director: Paul Djoko Moyo
Technical Adviser: René Kamo
Operating Director: J C Nana
Commercial Director: E Ngankou
Administrative Director: Soulemanou Danbaba
Financial Director: S Beloa Forcha
Manager, Traction and Rolling Stock: G Wamal
Director, Way and Works: Jean-Marie Mbida
Director, Planning: G Monayong
Vice-Director, Purchases & Stores: I Ntjono
Vice-Director, Computer Technology: S Ebata

Gauge: 1000 mm
Route length: 1104 km

The Cameroon system consists of two single-track lines: the West line running 160 km from Bonaberi to Nkongsamba operated by Regifercam; and the Transcameroun line opened in 1974 between Douala-Ngaoundéré (885 km). Ngoumou-Mbalmayo (37 km), and Mbanga-Kumba (29 km).

Traffic	1986	1987	1988
Passenger journeys (million)	2.3	2.268	2.414
Passenger-km (million)	443.7	443.68	469.57
Freight tonnes (million)	1.4	1.416	1.381
Freight tonne-km (million)	674.9	675.85	595.45

First-class passenger car by De Dietrich

Finance (FCA Fr million)		
Revenue	*1987*	*1988*
Pasengers and baggage	4 751.24	5 384.57
Freight, parcels and mail	16 895.63	15 607.17
Other income	22 325.58	11 790.15
Total	43 975.45	32 781.89
Expenditure	*1987*	*1988*
Staff/personnel expenses	16 188.11	14 518.78
Materials and services	7 553.08	12 135.86
Depreciation, financial charges	3 077.48	3 564. 00
Total	40 729.89	40 222.60

Traffic
Freight traffic, which had been diminished since the 1985 opening of a highway from Douala to Yaoundé, rebounded with an increase of 21 per cent in FY 1988-89. Passenger traffic has grown by 14 per cent since FY 1985-86.

Civil engineering
Following completion of the Transcameroun line to Ngaoundéré (935 km from Douala) it was decided to re-align the Douala-Yaoundé section to match the standard of the Yaoundé-Ngaoundéré extension. The Transcameroun Railway Authority (Office du Chemin de Fer Transcamerounais) has undertaken the task, with the support of funds from Kreditanstalt für Wiederaufbau (Frankfurt/Main), the German Federal Government, Canada, European, Saudi and African Development Funds, and Fonds d'Aide et de Cooperation. The work has been phased in four stages.

The most difficult stretch, the 27 km from Eséka to Maloumé, which has entailed construction of three tunnels aggregating 3295 metres in length and five viaducts with a total length of 875 metres, has taken longer than expected. In 1989 it was heading for completion, and with that the end of the whole project. The works are expected to double the line's train operating capacity to 40 services a day, raise single-locomotive trainloads to 1000 tonnes and increase annual throughput potential to over 14 million tonnes. Solar-powered colour-light signalling, with interlockings at intermediate stations, and track-to-train radio are being installed.

Foreign credits have been sought for purchase of track maintenance equipment, to re-sleeper the Yaoundé-Nagaoundéré extension and to realign an 8 km section of it. Sofrerail has signed a personnel management contract aimed to train local staff.

New export line
A new port is to be built at Grand Batanga, and in 1988 the Transcameroun Authority. commissioned from French consultants a feasibility study of a 136 km freight line from the Regifercam main line near Eseka

Diesel locomotives

Class	Wheel arrangement	Transmission	Rated power (kW)	Max speed km/h	Total weight tonnes	No in service 1989	Year first built	Builders Mechanical parts	Engine & type	Transmission
3600	BB-BB	Elec	2100	80	132	5	1070-77	MTE	AGO V16 SACM	Alsthom
2200	CC	Elec	1460	100	102	30	1080-83	Bombardier	Alco	General Electric
1200	BB	Elec	870	70	56	10	1968-73	Alsthom	MGO V16 SACM	Alsthom
1100	BB	Elec	650	60	68	20	1981	Alsthom	MGO V12 SACM	Alsthom/MTE
1000	BB	Elec	580	60	68	7	1978	Moyse	MGO V12 SACM	Moyse
300	BB	Elec	530	70	54	8	1951	Alsthom	MGO V12 SACM	Alsthom

Diesel railcars

Class	Cars per unit	Motored axles per motor car	Trans-mission	Rated power (kW) per motor	Max speed km/h	Weight tonnes per car	Total seating capacity	Length per car mm	No in service 1989	Year first built	Builders Mechanical parts	Engine & type	Transmission
ZE	1	2	Elec	360	85	45	26	23 600	4	1964-68	Soulé	MGO V8 SACM	Alsthom

to Grand Batange and Kribi, on the coast some 20 km north of the new port's site. Kribi is the starting-point of a proposed 1100 km new line running east to the Central African Republic.

Motive power and rolling stock

In 1989 Regifercam operated 92 diesel locomotives, 17 locotractors, four diesel railcars, 104 passenger cars and 1953 freight vehicles. Deliveries of 29 passenger cars from France have been completed. They comprised: 16 second-class from Soulé; and 8 first-class, one restaurant and four baggage-generator cars from De Dietrich. Conversion from vacuum to air braking is beginning under a four-year CFAFr 2290 million programme.

Track
Rail: Vignole 30 and 36 kg/m

Cross ties (sleepers): Timber and steel, thickness 130 mm
Spacing: 1500/km plain track; 1714/km curves
Fastenings: Sleeper screw (stiff); sleeper screw and Nabla (elastic)
Minimum curvature radius: 120 m
Max gradient: 19%
Max axleload: 20 tonnes

Canada

Transport Canada

Place de Ville, Ottawa, Ontario K1A 0N5

Telephone: +1 613 998 2690
Telex: 053 3130
Telefax: +1 613 993 5146

Minister: Benoit Bouchard
Minister of State (Transport): Shirley Martin
Assistant Deputy Minister, Policy and Co-ordination: Ken A Sinclair
Chairman, National Transportation Agency: Erik Nielsen
Surface Policy and Programs Directorate Director General: Suzanne Hurtubise

A new era in Canada's transportation history was ushered in on New Year's Day 1988 with the coming into effect of the National Transportation Act, 1987. The emphasis of the Act is on greater inter- and intra-modal competition, less regulatory intervention and more innovative transportation services. A new National Transportation Agency has replaced the former Canadian Transport Commission.

In the area of rail freight transport, the Act reshapes the freight rate negotiating framework for shippers, who now have greater access to competing railways. Shippers have extended interswitching limits and can also seek competitive line rates from other railways in that area. Shippers can also bring rate disputes to the National Transportation Agency for mediation or arbitration. Rail line abandonment procedures have also been streamlined.

The Rail Freight Policy Branch is responsible for providing railway expertise and policy advice for Federal interests in the various fields of railway activity. The Branch monitors, analyses and evaluates rail freight issues and the impact of the new regulatory reforms and overall transportation legislation on carriers, shippers, provinces and regions. As part of the Branch mandate, it also develops, maintains and provides expertise and information on rail infrastructure and operational capacity; capital investments; rail service availability and its utilisation; rail freight rates and costing; railway economics and carriers' financial performance; rail technology and systems concepts; energy and alternate fuels for railways; and environmental objectives.

The Rail Freight Programs Branch is responsible for management of certain Federal expenditure programmes in respect of freight facilities and services. The Branch is expected to manage the Federal involvement in any new projects involving the emergence of short line or regional roads or the installation of alternative transportation facilities which may occur as the result of increased rail line abandonments under the National Transportation Act, 1987. The Rail Freight Programs Branch also has the responsibility for programme delivery in respect of the federal involvement in grain transportation and handling. The Branch Line Rehabilitation Program is slated to continue through to March 1990 and is anticipated to involve further expenditures of approximately C$70 million.

The Rail Passenger Branch is responsible for evaluating and providing policy advice on the operating, capital, and legal requirements of rail passenger services in Canada within the context of overall government objectives. In the course of 1989, a major review by government of the long-term direction of rail passenger services was to take place. Particular focus would be on VIA's equipment renewal and associated funding needs. The work of the branch is carried out in conjunction with VIA Rail and, to a lesser extent, CN and CP Rail.

Algoma Central Railway

PO Box 7000, 289 Bay Street, Sault Ste Marie, Ontario P6A 5P6

Telephone: +1 705 949 2113
Telex: 067 77254
Telefax: +1 705 949 8722

Chairman: Henry N R Jackman
President and Chief Executive Officer: Leonard N Savoie
Secretary: W S Vaughan
Vice-President, Rail: Stanley A Black
Finance: R G Topp
Comptroller, Rail: J A Campbell
Manager, Traffic: J F Ross
  Materials: J E Norton
  Freight Marketing: J M Hogg
  Passenger Marketing: J K White
  Data Services: R J Cook
Superintendents, Transportation: N L Mills
  Mechanical Services: R M Zettler
  Motive Power: R M Zettler
  Signals & Communications: M G Ross
Chief Engineer: K J Coventry
Engineer, Maintenance of Way: H M Hamilton

Gauge: 1435 mm
Route length: 518 km

Incorporated in 1899, the company operated for many years chiefly as a wilderness railroad transporting iron ore and forest products out of Northern Ontario. Since 1960 it has become a diversified transport company moving cargo by water, rail and road. Its main line runs 474.7 m north from Sault Ste Marie and serves the natural resource, manufacturing and tourist industries of the Algoma region, operating a regular thrice-weekly passenger train each way and seasonal tourist trains, of which the best known is the Agawa Canyon service, as well as providing a freight service. The Agawa Canyon train frequently calls for a consist of 20 cars and has been known to demand as many as 27. Besides ex-CP Rail cars of late 1940s vintage, the Algoma Central fleet includes a number of ex-US streamliner cars, among them some former Central of Georgia and Illinois Central vehicles.

Developments include the 1988 commissioning of a reservation system for tour passengers and installation of a microwave communication system, the latter to be completed in 1989.

The company also sails a fleet of 18 dry bulk cargo vessels, principally on the Great Lake and the St Lawrence Seaway. It has developed commercial real estate complexes in Sault Ste Marie and Elliot Lake, in addition to the 850 000 acres it owns, inclusive of mineral and timber rights, in the Algoma region.

In 1989 the National Transportation Agency of Canada (NTA) rejected a proposed agreement to transfer the Rail Division of Algoma Central Railway to a separate and wholly-owned company on the grounds that the conveyance would not be in the public interest. The NTA said that separating the railway from

Algoma Central's Agawa Canyon tour train, headed by four GP38-2 locomotives

Traffic	1984	1985	1986	1987	1988
Freight tonnage (million)	2.857	3.204	2.563	2.755	3.0
Freight tonne-miles gross (million)	1252.3	1197.3	1005.4	1105.6	1065.3
Passenger-km (million)	45.619	47.448	40.484	46.319	46.0
Passenger journeys	249 560	258 213	255 506	253 840	251.514
Average net freight train load (tonnes)	3271	1899	1725	NA	NA

Finances (C$ million)				
Revenue	1983	1984	1985	1987
Passengers and baggage	2.691	3.108	3.363	3.75
Freight, parcels and mail	24.095	25.104	27.068	21.435
Other income (government subsidy, lands and forests, switching, demurrage)	4.543	4.073	4.785	3.682
Total	32.139	32.285	35.216	28.867
Expenditure				
Staff/personnel expenses	14.315	14.788	16.492	15.938
Materials and services	9.313	10.467	12.745	8.201
Depreciation	2.642	2.826	2.317	2.268
Total	26.270	28.081	31.554	26.407

ACR's marine and real estate divisions to create Algoma Central Railway Inc (ACR Inc) was cause for concern because the new company would lack the size and diversity of operations which presently exists. The situation would make the new company 'susceptible' to failure if it faced serious economic or financial adversity. Although ACR Inc would be a wholly-owned subsidiary of ACR, the Agency concluded it would be 'a financially weaker company'.

Traction and rolling stock
The company owns 27 locomotives, comprising nine EMD 3000 hp Type SD-40, six EMD 2000 hp Type G38-2, 10 EMD 1500 hp Type GP-7 and two diesel-electric switchers. Its rolling stock consists of 40 passenger cars, which include business and restaurant cars, and 1104 freight cars.

Coupler in standard use
  Passenger cars: AAR Type E, F, H
  Freight cars: AAR Type E, F, H
Braking in standard use, locomotive-hauled stock: Air Type 26

Track
Rail type: 115 RE, 100 RE, 85 CPR, 80 ASCE
Sleepers: Wood 7 in × 9 in × 8 ft
Spacing: 1822/km
Fastenings; Splice bars
Minimum curve radius: 1°
Max gradient: 1.7%
Max axleload: 30.4 tonnes

BC Rail

BC Rail Centre, 221 West Esplanade, North Vancouver, PO Box 8770, British Columbia V6B 4X6

Telephone: +1 604 986 2012
Telex: 04 352752 bcol sales vcr
Telefax: +1 604 984 5004

President and Chief Executive: Paul McElligott
Vice-Presidents, Finance and Information
  Services: J Roger Clarke
  Real Estate & Administration: Walter Young
  Human Resources, Engineering & Communications: Brian Foley
  Operations & Maintenance: J Charles Trainor
  Marketing & Sales; Wayne Banks
  Strategic Planning & Business Development: Vacant
Manager, Corporate Information: M B Wall
Chief Mechanical Officer: George L Kelly
Chief Engineer: Valentin W Shtenko
Manager, Operations and Maintenance; L Beaulieu
Manager, Materials: David Anstee
Chief of Transportation: Barry M McIntosh

Gauge: 1435 mm
Route length: 2846 km
Electrification: 129 km at 60 kW 60 Hz

BC Rail Ltd is the operating subsidiary of British Columbia Railway Company. BC Rail was organised in June 1984 when it acquired the railway operating assets of BCRC. It is 25 per cent owned by BCRC, a provincial Crown corporation, and 75 per cent owned by BCR Properties Ltd. BCR Properties is wholly-owned by BCRC and owns the non-operating real estate assets of the group.

The economic significance of the British Columbia Railway can be gauged from the fact that some 20 per cent of net rail freight tons loaded in British Columbia originates on the BC Rail line. The railway services approximately 700 carload shippers in the province, including 70 planer and sawmills, six veneer and plywood giants and seven pulp mills. With railway connections at North Vancouver, Prince George and Dawson Creek, BC Rail's freight service extends to all corners of North America. The two national railways of Canada and two major US carriers form a network which links BC Rail with major points on the continent.

The railway's principal yard facilities are at North Vancouver, Squamish, Lillooet, Williams Lake, Quesnel, Prince George, Fort St James, Mackenzie and Fort St John. Industrial Parks are situated at Williams Lake, Prince George, Mackenzie, Fort St John, Dawson Creek, Fort St James and Fort Nelson for the benefit of rail-oriented industries.

Traffic and Finance
Its recently-developed coal hauling activity apart, BC Rail is principally engaged in transporting British Columbia's forestry products from the central interior and northern parts of the Province. One major market is the eastern USA. Bulk commodities dominate the total traffic volume.

At the start of 1990 a substantial managerial restructure was carried out with the prime objective of strengthening the railway's market orientation. As a result of deregulation on both sides of the 49th Parallel, BC Rail has been losing business to road-rail services organised by US carriers and based on transshipment at Vancouver railheads.

Operating income was raised by 3.8 per cent in 1989, but improvements since 1985 have not matched the rate either of inflation or of growth in the national economy. Return on investment in 1989 was 7 per cent, an improvement on the 4 per cent figure of the previous year.

Dease Lake write-off
Amongst assets taken over from the British Columbia Rail Company by BC Rail were the costs of a projected extension from Fort St James northwest to Dease Lake, construction of which was halted in 1977. In 1989 it was decided to write off those costs, and as a result BC Rail sustained an extraordinary loss for the year's operations. At the same time BC Rail was considering a resumption of operation over the first, completed 200km of the line as far as Sustut River.

Investment
Investment totalling C$121 million was budgeted for 1990, of which C$46 million would go on new locomotives (see below). A five-year programme of upgrading on the Fort Nelson programme would be completed.

Traction and rolling stock
In 1989 BC Rail was operating seven electric and 114 diesel locomotives, nine Budd diesel railcars and 9 914 freight cars. The freight stock was augmented in 1988 by 200 centre-beam bulkhead flatcars for lumber assembled at BC Rail's Squamish plant from Korean-manufactured kits and components from the USA, Brazil, Mexico and Canada.

In the spring of 1990 BC Rail was taking delivery of 22 4 000hp GE Dash 8-40 CM locomotives, to replace 29 of the system's Alco 3 000hp locomotives. The new units are being equipped with Locotrol II radio control equipment from Harris Corporation of the US.

The nine Budd railcars have undergone a C$3.4 million upgrading that included new seating and air conditioning, and provision for on-train catering through installation of microwave/convection ovens. The provincial government financed the project.

TMACS system
All nine Budd cars and 98 BC Rail diesel locomotives have been equipped with a Microfuel Train Monitoring and Control System (TMACS) developed by BC Rail and Microfuel Systems of Nanaimo. TMACS is a combination event recorder and reset/safety device. The event recorder is computerised and has a storage memory so that information can be down-loaded into a computer later. If an engineman becomes incapacitated and no control activity is sensed by the

Budd diesel railcars

Traffic

	1985	1986	1987	1988
Freight tonnes gross (million)	16.18	16.20	16.03	15.73
Freight tonne-km (million)	10 698.4	11 400.5	11 006.6	11 670.9
Average net freight train load (tonnes)	1575	1409	1301.5	1227.3
Passenger journeys	79 122	80 183	78 907	95 748
Passenger-km (million)	NA	16.904	18.159	24.873

Finances (C$ 000)	1985	1986	1987	1988
Revenue				
Passengers and baggage	1246	1484	1619	2202
Freight, parcels and mail	252 000	272 175	281 710	286 612
Rent from equipment	31 354	42 499	38 885	NA
Other rents, land sales and miscellaneous	1844	–	–	–
Total	296 444	316 158	322 214	319 710
Government assistance	7077	9151	9890	7284
Expenditure				
Staff/personnel	99 160	108 365	105 691	NA
Materials and services	86 654	89 672	97 577	NA
Depreciation	30 425	32 359	34 870	35 853
Financial charges	18 442	13 687	11 839	NA
Total	234 681	244 083	249 976	242 709

RAILWAY SYSTEMS / Canada

device within a set time limit, the reset safety device will apply the train's brakes.

The event recorder scans several different functions such as brake pipe pressure, brake cylinder pressure, radio functions, and many others. It can store up to 30 hours of Budd railcar data and about 120 hours of locomotive data. A collision recorder is similar to the event recorder but records all functions at a 1-second rate, allowing approximately 33 minutes of data storage. The recording starts when locomotive speed rises over 0.2 mph and ceases 10 seconds after the locomotive speed drops below that level. An operations recorder compiles statistical data on a daily basis. It monitors throttle duty cycle and speed ranges; penalty brake applications are noted, and on the Budd cars, power braking levels are recorded.

In addition to these three functions, the TMACS unit can display, on a computer screen, all of the functions being monitored, and changes can be observed instantly. This feature has the potential for a permanent cab display unit that would indicate speed, odometer, air brake pressures, and motor currents in a digital manner. By expanding the memory capacity, the unit can provide a total engine health monitoring system.

Tumbler Ridge electrification

The development of British Columbia's north-east coalfields prompted construction of BC Rail's 129 km Tumbler Ridge branch line to the coalfield area. The branch was completed a month ahead of schedule and carried its first coal train, diesel-hauled, in November 1983. Full electric working started in June 1984.

The Tumbler Ridge branch is the fourth line in the world to be electrified at 50 kW ac. Seven Type GF6C 4400 kW Co-Co electric locomotives were procured from General Motors of Canada, which applied to them the ASEA technology to which GM has access under licence; all electrical equipment apart from traction motors was supplied by ASEA, which adopted thyristor control in the design. The units are fitted with EMD's HTC high-adhesion bogie and radar speed measurement devices for slip control. They normally operate in back-to-back pairs. Rheostatic braking is provided. Each train consists of 98 118-tonne hopper cars, of which 913 have been built for the Tumbler Ridge project by CN Rail. BCR owns a quarter of the wagon fleet.

CN Rail is involved because the Tumbler Ridge coal is for export to Japanese steel producers via the deep-water port at Ridley Island, near Prince Rupert. Roughly two-thirds of the 720 km run to Ridley Island is over CN Rail tracks. At Tacheeda Junction (Anzac), the BC Rail electric locomotives hand the 13 000-tonne trains over to CN Rail diesels, which are manned by BC Rail crews as far as Prince George, then by CN Rail crews for the rest of the journey to Ridley Island. Here, as at the Quintette and Teck loading terminals at Tumbler Ridge, the rail layout is a continuous loop. The

Lumber train in Howe Sound, 15 miles from North Vancouver

Prince George maintenance shop

Diesel locomotives

Class	Wheel arrangement	Transmission	Rated power hp	Max speed km/h	Total weight tonnes	No in service 1988	Year first built	Builders Mechanical parts	Engine & type	Transmission
RS18	Bo-Bo	Elec	1800	105	111.6	29	1957	MLW	MLW Alco 251/IV	General Electric
RS20	Bo-Bo	Elec	2000	105	112.5	8	1973	MLW	MLW Alco 251-IV	General Electric
RS20B	Bo-Bo	Elec	2000	105	112.5	8	1975	MLW	MLW Alco 251-IV	General Electric
RS25	Bo-Bo	Elec	2500	105	119.3	9	1962	Alco	Alco 251-16	General Electric
RS30	Co-Co	Elec	3000	105	174.6	29	1969	MLW	MLW Alco 281-16	General Electric
GF30	Co-Co	Elec	3000	105	176	30	1980	GM	EMD 645-16	EMD
SW10	Bo-Bo	Elec	1000	96	113.4	3	1959	MLW	MLW Alco 25-76	General Electric
Slug	Bo-Bo	Elec	1600	105	109	10	1981	MLW	-	General Electric

Diesel railcars

Class	Cars per unit	Motored axles per motor car	Transmission	Rated power hp per motor	Max speed km/h	Weight tonnes per car	Total seating capacity	Length per car mm	No in service 1988	Year first built	Builders Mechanical parts	Engine & type	Transmission
RDC1	1	2	Torque converter	350	129	53.5	82	25 908	3	1956	Budd	Cummins	Twin Disc
RDC3	1	2	Torque converter	350	129	54.9	45	25 908	3	1956	Budd	Cummins	Twin Disc
RDC1 (leased)	1	2	Torque converter	300	129	55.3	91	25 908	3	1962	Budd	CM-6/110	Allison

Canada / **RAILWAY SYSTEMS** 523

Electric locomotives

Class	Wheel arrangement	Line voltage	Rated output kW Continuous/one-hour	Max speed km/h	Weight tonnes	Length mm	No in service 1987	Year first built	Builders Mechanical parts	Electrical equipment
GF6C	Co-Co	50 kV	4400/6480	90	178	20 980	7	1983	GMC	ASEA

wagons have rotary couplers to allow individual dump-discharge without need of dismantling a train, and thus train-sets can run in continuous circuit between mine silos and Ridley Island. The operating plan provides for nine trains to be in use, each on a 75-hour cycle for the round trip.

Two-way microwave radio communication between despatcher and train crews is operative throughout the Tumbler Ridge branch. Amplifiers spaced at intervals in the two major tunnels, Table and Wolverine, link with transmitters just outside the bores and maintain secure communications under ground.

Track
Rail: 50, 60 and 68 kg/m
Cross ties (sleepers): Softwood, 17 × 228 × 2400 mm
Steel, 130 × 300 × 2500 mm
Spacing: 1969/km
Fastenings: Cut spikes and anchors on timber sleepers, elastic clips on steel sleepers
Minimum curve radius: 120 m
Max gradient: 2.2%
Max axleload: 29.9 tonnes

Following trials of 520 Australian-made experimental steel sleepers over a 1000 ft section that includes a 12-degree curve and a 2.2 per cent grade, 28 000 of this type were to be installed through curves in a 1990 track renewal.

Two Type GC6C electric locomotives haul coal down the Tumbler Ridge branch

Canadian National (CN Rail)

935 de la Gauchetière Street, Montreal, Quebec H3B 2M9

Telephone: +1 514 399 5430
Telex: 055 61497
Telefax: +1 514 399 5586/5479

Chairman: Brian R D Smith
Vice-Chairman: B O'N Gallery
President and Chief Executive Officer: R E Lawless
Senior Vice President and Chief Operating Officer: J H D Sturgess
Senior Vice-President, Western Canada: R A Walker Sr
Operations: J P Kelsall
Marketing: P A Clarke
Financial Planning & Administration: Y-H Masse
Vice-President, Public Affairs and Advertising: B E Ducey
Secretary: D P MacKinnon
Employee Relations: J P Laroche
Purchasing and Materials: Don Parsons
Law: R Boudreau
Information Systems: A R Pozniak
Government Affairs: D E Todd
Intermodal: A J Gillies
Accounting and Comptroller: R D McGrath
Prairie Region: F D Campbell
Great Lakes Region: A E Deegan
St Lawrence Region: J R Lagacé
Atlantic Region: M A Blackwell
Treasurer: G C Church
President & General Manager, TerraTransport: J H Easton
President, Canac International Inc: M L De Pellegrin
Chief of Transportation: D H Grant
Chief of Motive Power and Car Equipment: V H Mizrahi
Chief Engineer: P R Richards
Chief Mechanical & Electrical Engineer: R W Radford

Gauge: 1435 mm
Route length: 35 242 km
Electrification: 29 km at 2.7 kV dc

CN container train in New Brunswick, hauled by two Type MF-32A locomotives

Canadian National is a major transportation distribution company owned by the Canadian government. The company includes the Grand Trunk Corporation, which connects the Canadian railway system through CN-owned railways to major markets in the US. Non-rail activities include real estate, mineral and petroleum resource development and international consulting.

CN's rail operations in Canada service nine of the 10 provinces and the two northern territories and provide access to the country's rich natural resources. Railway operations on the island of Newfoundland were terminated in September 1988. However, CN remains active in the Newfoundland freight market, providing intermodal service through two gateways: Halifax-St John's; and North Sydney-Port aux Basques.

Finance
Corporate net income for 1989 was around C$200 milion, compared with C$282.7 million in the previous year. This was primarily due to recession in the national economy, especially in natural resource markets, which dented rail revenue. Overal rail traffic was some 10 per cent lower than in 1988, with the largest decreases occurring in the export grain, coal, sulphur, potash, lumber, pulp and paper groups.

However, the company improved its financial state because of its success in reducing its long-term indebtedness, mainly through divestiture of non-rail assets. From C$3 500 million in 1986 total indebtedness had been cut by end-1989 to C$1 800 million.

Since recapitalisation of the company in 1978, CN

524 RAILWAY SYSTEMS / Canada

has been responsible for sustaining its own financial self-sufficiency. Its capital needs have been met solely through commercial borrowings, earnings, and sale of surplus assets. Capital needs during the period following recapitalisation were unusually high, mainly because of heavy expenditure required to expand railway capacity in Western Canada and performance of a number of imposed public duties for which the company received no compensation from the government. As a result, CN was compelled to borrow heavily at a time when interest rates were at their peak.

Closure threat
The company established a planning unit early in 1988 to design the rail network CN will need for the future. With two-thirds of CN's trackage carrying just 10 per cent of its traffic, some pruning of the network is clearly necessary. The unit is developing a plan for orderly disposition of non-viable rail lines through sale, transfer to other operators, or abandonment.

The new National Transportation Act debars CN from abandoning track at a rate greater than 4 per cent per annum of its total extent. The move to contract results from the combined pressures of the new Canadian Act's transport deregulation, competition from US railroads, and the increasing weight of CN's overhead costs and accumulated debt.

Finance (rail only)
Results (C$ million)

	1987	1988	1989
Revenue	3732.3	3792.1	3528.3
Expenditure	3618.6	3571.4	3403.3
Income/(loss)	113.7	220.7	125.0

Traffic

	1987	1988
Total freight short tons (million)	111.5	128
Total freight tonne-km (million)	260 703	NA

Intermodal activity
CN Rail's current focus is to become a total transportation distribution system for as wide a variety of goods as practicable. To the end, the company has been shifting its emphasis to the operation of a trunk line rail system, with road service to and from the main line organised through strategically-located hub centres. At these hub centres, traffic is transferred between the road and rail modes.

The company currently operates six such hubs, in Moncton, Montreal, Toronto, Winnipeg, Vancouver and Edmonton, with satellite terminals at Halifax, Windsor, Saskatoon and Calgary. The network will be completed with the 1991 commissioning of a new C$19 million intermodal terminal at Port Mann, near Vancouver. This will replace two installations in downtown Vancouver which are nearing capacity and have no room for expansion to handle forecast growth. With completion of the new Vancouver terminal, all CN Rail hub terminals will be equipped for toplift loading.

CN's transcontinental Supertrains, and the Laser trains operating between Moncton, Montreal, Toronto, and Chicago, continue to set standards in fast, reliable service. Halifax to Montreal and Toronto is CN's highest-volume container corridor.

The Montreal-Toronto Laser service to Chicago employs low-deck Five-Pak cars to enable operation through the tunnel under the St Clair River between Sarnia and Port Huron, which is too constricted for conventional piggyback equipment. The low-deck cars can handle tri-axle trailers with a gross vehicle weight of 90 000 lb. With existing weight/dimension regulations in Central and Eastern Canada, this is a requirement if CN is to complete on an equal footing with trucks.

In 1989 CN Rail's Transcona plant was entrusted with construction of 40 articulated five-car intermodel platforms, commonly referred to as Five Paks, each one 49 ft 3 in long and capable of carrying trailers as well as single-stacked or double-stacked containers. A further 60 Five Paks were ordered from Trenton Works Lavalin, Nova Scotia. The design features which allow the freight cars to carry trailers as well as double-stacked containers make them unique in North America. Entry into service began in January 1990.

CN Rail has been discussing with Norfolk Southern the case for extending that US railroad's RoadRailer network from Detroit to Toronto.

CN was initially loth to invest in double-stack COFC trains because, first, individual train capacity was not generally a problem. Second, CN's major movements are oriented towards the East Coast where the

Low-deck Five-Pack car in Laser service

Unit export grain train threads Thompson River Canyon en route to Vancouver

Monterm Intermodal yard, Montreal

generally heavier container weights than experienced on the US West Coast are not well suited to fully productive double-stacking. However, in February 1989 CN Rail launched a Vancouver-Montreal/Toronto double-stack train for deep sea traffic from the Pacific Rim countries, which is being driven upward by imports of Japanese car kits for assembly in Canadian plants. In July 1989 Maersk Line inaugurated a weekly double-stack train service for Far Eastern traffic between Tacoma, Washington, on the US Pacific coast and Toronto/Montreal via Union Pacific to Chicago, Norfolk Southern thence to Buffalo, NY, and CN Rail to the Toronto Brampton and Montreal Montport terminals. In 1990 the railway's first double-stack service exclusively for domestic traffic was to be launched between Toronto and Moncton.

CN has been among the pioneers in the introduction of computer-based technology to streamline its operations and satisfy the needs of its customers. Included have been:

TRACS, the company's on-line real-time Traffic Reporting and Control System;
WIN, Waybill Information Network;
CARLOC, Car Location Information System;
BLADE, Bill of Lading Data Exchange System; and
UNLOC, introduced recently, an electronic information access system for intermodal shipments.

Customer Information Services is CN's latest development. Using Customer Information Services, customers can electronically handle all their accounting information with CN through the complete business cycle, from bill of lading to freight bill to remittance advice.

Signalling and telecommunications

In conjunction with a consortium led by the SEL Division of Alcatel Canada Inc and including Motorola Canada and Vapor Canada, CN Rail is engaged in an Advanced Train Control Systems pilot project valued at more than C$14 million. In 1991 this will culminate in commissioning of an ATCS system over 301 km of the railway's North Division between Harvey, British Columbia, (west of Jasper, Alberta) and Prince George, British Columbia. To prove the equipment a prototype installation was put under test on the Hagersville Subdivision in January 1990.

The BC North Line project will provide computer-assisted dispatching, radio-monitored and controlled switches, and computer-assisted train movement and track occupancy authorities. Export grain traffic on this line has grown, and more modern train control systems are warranted. To that end, the railway will progressively upgrade the Harvey to Prince George section to an intermediate level of ATCS functionality. It has already introduced computer verification of train movement authorities.

By the spring of 1990, remote-controlled power switches were installed at sidings, and computer equipment allowing the driver to operate had been fitted to 54 locomotives. Phase II, to be complete by the end of 1990, would see a direct data communication link between the dispatching office and locomotive, replacing the current verbal communication of movement authorities by radio.

The Federal government's Department of Industry, Science and Technology has contributed C$4.1 million to help offset start-up costs for the railway and the consortium of Canadian suppliers who are providing the computer hardware and software.

Alcatel Canada Inc, SEL Division, is developing the software and hardware for the on-board computer used in ATCS operations. The data communications network and the mobile communications packages installed on the locomotives are provided by Motorola Canada. Vapor Canada has developed the computer screen for use in the locomotive cab, the wayside transponders which monitor locomotive position, and the on-board transponder interrogators.

A Railway Electronic Identification System (REIS) is already operational systemwide. REIS is a monitor of train movements based on ground-sited interrogators working with transponders on locomotives. Some 2200 locomotives have been fitted with the transponders. Groups of interrogators are periodically scanned by microcomputer devices, which transmit the data they collect to displays in yard offices.

Motive power and rolling stock

In March 1988 CN Rail placed locomotive orders worth more than C$180 million over the following three years. General Motors of Canada would manufacture 60 of its SD-60F 3800 hp freight locomotives. Twenty were delivered to the railway in the fourth quarter of

New GM Type SD50 locomotive

Unit hopper train near Clearwater, British Columbia

526 RAILWAY SYSTEMS / Canada

1988, and the remainder in the first half of 1989. General Electric delivered 30 of its 4000 hp Dash-8 freight locomotives to CN in the first quarter of 1990. This was CN's first purchase of GE locomotives.

CN Rail expects in the foreseeable future to place orders for 200 to 300 high horsepower and about 150 medium horsepower locomotives.

Pursuing its policy of in-house locomotive remanufacture for branch-line and yard service, the company's Pointe St Charles shops in Montreal were commissioned in mid-1989 to refurbish 18 locomotives and 150 traction motors.

In April 1989 CN Rail placed orders worth C$35 million with National Steel Car Company in Hamilton, Ontario, for 500 new box cars specially designed to meet the needs of an expanding woodpulp industry, most of which is concentrated in western Canada. The new 50 ft cars are equipped with plug doors rather than sliding doors, are vented and have steel linings and floors, and each will load up to 100 tons of freight.

At the end of 1989 CN Rail operated 1774 diesel locomotives, 14 electric locomotives, 85 passenger cars and 67 895 freight cars. Acquisitions in 1989 totalled 70 locomotives and 874 freight cars.

Rail: Current sections being bought are 136 CN (a special section for head-hardened rail used only in curves), 136 RE, 132 RE and 115 RE. Balance is 31 different older sections 130 to 50 lb/yard.

Welded rail
Electric pressure flash-butt welded into lengths of about 1480 ft (451 m) in central plants. After unloading at laying site rail may be electric pressure flash-butt field welded by portable plants into longer lengths before laying, or welded by aluminothermic process after laying.

ETIS head-on locomotive cab display; besides registering tail-end brake air pressure it also maintains the distance the train travels and indicates when the last car is moving and in which direction, enabling the head-on crew to ensure that the main track is clear at sidings and that level crossings are not blocked

Cross ties (sleepers)
Thickness
Wood: Main lines 7 or 6 in (180 or 150 mm)
  Branch lines: 6 in (150 mm)
Concrete (CN 60B): 8 in (200 mm) at rail seat
Spacing
Wood: Main lines: 1932/km
Concrete: 1640/km

Rail fastenings
Wood: 6 or 5½ × ⅝ in (150 or 140 × 16 mm)
Concrete: Pandrol

Grand Trunk Corporation
The Grand Trunk Corporation is the holding company for CN's three wholly-owned US railways. For details of results and railroads see US Class I railroads section.

Diesel locomotives

Class	Builder and model		No in service 1989	Year built	Year modified	Rating hp	Max speed mph	CN-rated continuous tractive effort lb	Weight in working order	
									On drivers lb	Total lb
Road										
GR-12n	GM	GMD-1	6	1958		1200	65	30 000	159 000	239 000
GR-12t	GM	GMD-1	3	1959		1200	65	30 000	160 000	239 000
GR-12w	GM	GMD-1	10	1959		1200	65	30 000	160 000	239 000
GR-12z	GM	GMD-1	8	1960		1200	65	30 000	159 000	238 000
GR-12zc	GM	GMD-1	4	1959		1200	65	30 000	158 000	237 000
GR-12m	GM	GMD-1	13	1958	1983-88*	1200	65	40 000	248 000	248 000
GR-12s	GM	GMD-1	3	1959	1983-88*	1200	65	40 000	248 000	248 000
GR-12t	GM	GMD-1	9	1959	1983-88*	1200	65	40 000	248 000	248 000
GR-12w	GM	GMD-1	8	1959	1983-88*	1200	65	40 000	248 000	248 000
GR-12z	GM	GMD-1	2	1960	1983-88*	1200	65	40 000	248 000	248 000
GR-12zc	GM	GMD-1	1	1959	1986*	1200	65	40 000	248 000	248 000
GR-12d	GM	SW-1200RS	11	1956		1200	65	40 000	225 000	225 000
GR-12d	GM	SW-1200RS	3	1956		1200	65	40 000	246 000	246 000
GR-12f	GM	SW-1200RS	16	1956		1200	65	40 000	225 000	225 000
GR-12h	GM	SW-1200RS	14	1956-57		1200	65	40 000	226 000	226 000
GR-12k	GM	SW-1200RS	10	1957		1200	65	40 000	226 000	226 000
GR-12k	GM	SW-1200RS	1	1957		1200	65	40 000	246 000	246 000
GR-12l	GM	SW-1200RS	12	1958		1200	65	40 000	225 000	225 000
GR-12r	GM	SW-1200RS	28	1958		1200	65	40 000	223 000	223 000
GR-12u	GM	SW-1200RS	16	1959		1200	65	40 000	223 000	223 000
GR-12y	GM	SW-1200RS	30	1960		1200	65	40 000	222 000	222 000
GR-12e	GM	SW-1200RS	5	1955-56		1200	65	40 000	246 000	246 000
GR-612a	GM	GMD-1A	15	1988 (Rebuilds)		1200	65	30 000	160 000	240 000
MR-14b	MLW	RSC-18	6	1959	1975-76†	1400	65	30 000	160 000	240 000
MR-14c	MLW	RSC-18	22	1960	1975-76†	1400	65	30 000	160 000	240 000
GRG-12n	GM	GMD-1	4	1958		1200	65	40 000	246 000	246 000
GR-12n	GM	GMD-1	13	1958-59		1200	65	40 000	246 000	246 000
MR-18e	MLW	RS-18	6	1959		1800	80	44 000	230 000	230 000
MR-18e	MLW	RS-18	7	1959		1800	80	44 000	235 000	235 000
MR-24c	MLW	C-424	2	1967		2400	75	49 000	260 000	260 000
MR-20a	MLW	M-420	28	1973	1986-87‡	2000	65	47 000	248 000	248 000
MR-20b	MLW	M-420	28	1974	1986-87‡	2000	65	47 000	248 000	248 000
MR-20c	MLW	M-420	19	1976	1986-87‡	2000	65	47 000	248 000	248 000
MR-20d	MLW	HR-412	10	1981	1986-87‡	2000	65	50 000	248 000	248 000
MR-18b	MLW	RS-18	29	1957		1800	75	47 000	246 000	246 000
MR-18c	MLW	RS-18	12	1957-58		1800	75	47 000	246 000	246 000
MR-18d	MLW	RS-18	4	1958		1800	75	47 000	247 000	247 000
MR-18f	MLW	RS-18	3	1959		1800	75	44 000	233 000	233 000
GR-418a	GM	GP-9RM	12	1981-82 (Reman'fd)	1987‡	1800	65	49 000	248 000	248 000
GR-418b	GM	GP-9RM	10	1982-83 (Reman'fd)	1987‡	1800	65	49 000	248 000	248 000
GR-418c	GM	GP-9RM	15	1984 (Reman'fd)	1987‡	1800	65	49 000	248 000	248 000
GR-418d	GM	GP-9RM	17	1984 (Reman'fd)		1800	65	47 000	246 000	246 000
GR-17n	GM	GP-9R	12	1957		1750	65	44 000	232 000	232 000
GR-17q	GM	GP-9R	7	1958		1750	65	44 000	232 000	232 000
GR-17t	GM	GP-9R	11	1958		1750	65	44 000	230 000	230 000
GR-17u	GM	GP-9R	34	1959		1750	65	44 000	229 000	229 000
GR-17z	GM	GP-9R	8	1959		1750	65	44 000	229 000	229 000
GR-17p	GM	GP-9R	3	1957		1750	89	33 000	238 000	238 000
GR-17p	GM	GP-9R	6	1957		1750	65	44 000	236 000	236 000
GR-17y	GM	GP-9R	4	1959		1750	65	44 000	235 000	235 000

Diesel locomotives (continued)

Class	Builder and model		No in service 1989	Year built	Year modified	Rating hp	Max speed mph	CN-rated continuous tractive effort lb	Weight in working order	
									On drivers lb	Total lb
GR-17a	GM	GP-9R	14	1955		1750	65	44 000	248 000	248 000
GR-17f	GM	GP-9R	19	1955-56		1750	65	44 000	247 000	247 000
GR-17g	GM	GP-9R	4	1956		1750	65	44 000	240 000	240 000
GR-17h	GM	GP-9R	14	1956-57		1750	65	44 000	247 000	247 000
GR-17m	GM	GP-9R	7	1957		1750	65	44 000	247 000	247 000
GR-17r	GM	GP-9R	6	1957-58		1750	65	44 000	248 000	248 000
GR-17za	GM	GP-9R	4	1957		1750	65	44 000	248 000	248 000
GR-17zb	GM	GP-9R	2	1958-60		1750	65	44 000	248 000	248 000
GR-420b	GM	GP-38-2	37	1972-73	1982-83‡	2000	65	57 000	248 000	248 000
GR-420c	GM	GP-38-2	47	1973-74	1982-83‡	2000	65	57 000	248 000	248 000
GR-430a	GM	GP-40	9	1966		3000	65	57 000	260 000	260 000
GR-430b	GM	GP-40	3	1967		3000	65	57 000	259 000	259 000
GR-430b	GM	GP-40	2	1967		3000	65	-50 000	259 000	259 000
Road Freight										
MF-30a	MLW	C-630	2	1967		3000	75	74 000	386 000	386 000
MF-30b	MLW	C-630	42	1967-68		3000	75	74 000	388 000	388 000
MF-32a	MLW	HR-616	20	1982		3000	65(1)	74 000	390 000	390 000
MF-36a	MLW	M-636	12	1970		3600	75	74 000	388 000	388 000
MF-36b	MLW	M-636	17	1971		3600	75	74 000	388 000	388 000
GF-30c	GM	SD-40	8	1967		3000	65	85 000	389 000	389 000
GF-30d	GM	SD-40	65	1967-68		3000	65	85 000	388 000	388 000
GF-30e	GM	SD-40	48	1969		3000	65	85 000	389 000	389 000
GF-30h	GM	SD-40	48	1969-71		3000	65	85 000	389 000	389 000
GF-30k	GM	SD-40	50	1971		3000	65	85 000	389 000	389 000
GF-30m	GM	SD-40	15	1971		3000	65	85 000	388 000	388 000
GF-30n	GM	SD-40-2	20	1975		3000	65	85 000	385 000	385 000
GF-30p	GM	SD-40-2	17	1975		3000	65	85 000	385 000	385 000
GF-30q	GM	SD-40-2	15	1976		3000	65	85 000	387 000	387 000
GF-30r	GM	SD-40-2		1978		3000	65	85 000	384 000	384 000
GF-30s	GM	SD-40-2		1979		3000	65	85 000	384 000	384 000
GF-30t	GM	SD-40-2	30	1980		3000	65	85 000	387 000	387 000
GU-30u	GM	SD-40-2	10	1980		3000	65	85 000	387 000	387 000
GF-636a	GM	SD-50F	40	1985-86		3600	65	94 000	390 000	390 000
GF-636b	GM	SD-50F	20	1987		3600	65	94 000	390 000	390 000
GF-638A	GM	SD-50AF	4	1986		3800	65	94 000	395 000	395 000
GF-620a	GM	SD-38-2	4	1976		2000	65	71 000	373 000	373 000
GFB-17b	GM/CN	F-7A/B	4		1983	1750	65	44 000	246 000	246 000
GFB-17b	GM/CN	F-7A/B	4		1984	1750	65	44 000	246 000	246 000
GFA-17a	GM/CN	F-7A	12		1972-74	1750	65	44 000	229 000	229 000
GFA-17a	GM/CN	F-7A	7		1972-74	1750	65	44 000	240 000	240 000
GFB-17a	GM/CN	F-7B	3		1972-73	1750	65	44 000	240 000	240 000
GF-430a	GM	GP-40-2L	33	1974		3000	80	49 000	263 000	263 000
GF-430a	GM	GP-40-2L	56	1974		3000	65	57 000	263 000	263 000
GF-430b	GM	GP-40-2L	40	1974		3000	65	57 000	263 000	263 000
GF-430c	GM	GP-40-2L	102	1975		3000	65	57 000	263 000	263 000
GF-430d	GM	GP-40-2	35	1977		3000	65	57 000	260 000	260 000
Switchers										
MH-10r	MLW	DL-411A	1	1959	1978§	1000	40	49 000	258 000	258 000
MHL-410a	MLW/CN	DL-411RB	4	1982-85 (Rebuild)		1000	40	49 000	258 000	258 000
MHT-410a	MLW/CN	DL-411RB	3	1984 (Rebuild)		1000	40	49 000	258 000	258 000
MY-10r	MLW	DL-411A	7	1959	1981§	1000	40	47 000	253 000	253 000
GY-9d	GM	SW-900	1958	1980§		900	40	36 000	253 000	253 000
GY-12d	GM	SW-1200RS	2	1956	1980§	1200	65	40 000	246 000	246 000
GS-418a	GM/CN	GP-9RM	14	1985 (Reman'fd)		1800	65	49 000	257 000	257 000
GS-413a	GM/CN	SW-1200RM	2	1986 (Reman'fd)	1987	1350	65	45 000	246 000	246 000
GS-413b	GM/CN	SW-1200RM	6	1987 (Reman'fd)		1350	65	45 000	246 000	246 000
GY-418a	GM/CN	GP-9RM	14	1985-86 (Reman'fd)		1800	65	49 000	257 000	257 000
GY-418b	GM/CN	GP-9RM	18	1986 (Reman'fd)		1800	65	49 000	257 000	257 000
GY-418c	GM/CN	GP-9RM	9	1987 (Reman'fd)		1800	65	47 000	248 000	248 000
GY-418d	GM/CN	GP-9RM	8	1988 (Reman'fd)		1800	65	47 000	248 000	248 000
GS-412a	GM/CN	SW-1200RB	18	1987 (Rebuild)		1200	65	47 000	246 000	246 000
GS-8a	GM	SW-8	2	1951		800	40	36 000	232 000	232 000
GH-20b	GM	GP-38-2	24	1973	1977-85	2000	65	47 000	257 000	257 000
GS-12a	GM	SW-9	6	1952		1200	40	36 000	247 000	247 000
GS-12e	GM	SW-1200	9	1956		1200	40	36 000	246 000	246 000
GS-12f	GM	SW-1200	3	1957		1200	40	36 000	246 000	246 000
GS-12g	GM	SW-1200	1	1959		1200	40	36 000	246 000	246 000
GS-9a	GM	SW-900	10	1953-54		900	40	36 000	229 000	229 000
GS-9c	GM	SW-900	6	1957		900	40	36 000	232 000	232 000
GS-9d	GM	SW-900	2	1958		900	40	36 000	233 000	233 000
MS-10q	MLW	DL-411	14	1959		1000	40	36 000	233 000	233 000
MS-410a	MLW/CN	DL-411RB	12	1983-85 (Rebuild)		1000	40	49 000	258 000	258 000
Boosters										
MH-00a	CN		8	1964-65		—	40	36 000	259 000	259 000
GY-00b	GM	YBU-4M	10	1980	1985-86	—	65	49 000	258 000	258 000
GY-00c	GM/CN	YBU	4	1986 (Reman'fd)		—	65	49 000	258 000	258 000
GY-00d	GM/CN	YBU	18	1986 (Reman'fd)		—	65	49 000	257 000	257 000
GY-00e	GM/CN	YBU	9	1987 (Reman'fd)		—	65	47 000	248 000	248 000
GH-00a	GM	HBU-4	19	1978		—	65	57 000	258 000	258 000
GH-00b	GM	HBU-4	4	1980		—	65	57 000	258 000	258 000
MY-00a	CN	8	4	1964-66		—	40	36 000	253 000	253 000
GH-00c	GM	HBU-4M	2	1980	1986	—	65	57 000	258 000	258 000
GY-00m	MLW-CN	8	2	1964-66	1986	—	65	40 000	254 000	254 000

* Rebogied from AIA-AIA to B-B
† Rebogied from b-b to AIA/AIA
‡ weight reduced
§ Booster cabling for hump and flat yard service

RAILWAY SYSTEMS / Canada

CP Rail
Canadian Pacific Limited

Head office: PO Box 6042, Station A, Montreal, Quebec H3C 3E4

Telephone: +1 514 395 5151
Telex: 0523130
Telefax: +1 514 395 7754

Chairman and Chief Executive Officer: I B Scott
President: R J Ritchie
Executive Vice-President & Chief Financial Officer: A S Lanyi
Vice-Presidents
  Systems Operations: J A Linn
  Industrial Relations: R Colosimo
  Administration: R Klein
  Public Affairs: R A Rice
  Computers and Communications: G F Sekeley (Toronto)
  Purchases and Materials: F Wallace
  Legal Services: Ms K F Braid (Toronto)
Assistant Vice-Presidents
  Industrial Relations: D V Brazier
  Advanced Train Control Development: R A Shea
  Government and Industry Affairs: M D Apedaile
Chief Mechanical Officer: G W Bartley
Chief of Transportation: M A Lypka
Chief Engineer: E J Rewucki

HEAVY HAUL SYSTEMS

Granville Square Square, 9th floor, Vancouver, British Columbia V6C 2R3
Telephone: +1 604 665 3250

Executive Vice-President: E V Dodge
Vice-Presidents:
  Marketing and Sales: R A Sallee
  Operation and Maintenance: L A Hill
Assistant Vice-President, Grain: W H Somerville (Winnipeg)

INTERMODAL FREIGHT SYSTEMS

Union Station, Toronto, Ontario M5J 1E8
Telephone: +1 416 863 8026

Executive Vice-President: G R Mackie
Vice-President, Operation and Maintenance: G A Swanson
Assistant Vice-President, Grain: W H Somerville (Winnipeg)

CANADIAN ATLANTIC RAILWAY

790 Dever Road, Saint John, New Brunswick E2M 4X2
Telephone: +1 506 635 2200

General Manager: F J Green

Gauge: 1435 mm
Length: 23 944 km

CP Rail, a unit of Canadian Pacific Limited, serves all Canadian provinces except Newfoundland and Prince Edward Island, with lines passing through the US State of Maine and extending into the State of Vermont. The railway employs some 23 000 staff and in 1989 transported 93 200 million revenue tonne-km of freight.

Soo Line takeover
In April 1990 Canadian Pacific completed the merger of Soo Line Corporation after acquiring the majority of outstanding interest in this US railroad company (qv, US systems section).
  Based in Minneapolis, USA, Soo Line is the 10th largest US railroad, operating in 12 Mid-Western states. The merger will permit development of more competitive rail service for Canada-US traffic that is expected to grow following the Free Trade agreement between the two countries.

Bid for Delaware & Hudson
In 1990 CP Rail was also seeking to acquire the US Delaware & Hudson Railroad, which was in course of bankruptcy proceedings. One condition of the bid was that Conrail would grant trackage rights over its line from Harrisburg, Pennsylvania, to Hagerstown,

CP Rail's 60-acre Obico intermodal terminal, Toronto

Westbound CP Rail coal train at Wakely Siding, Rogers Pass

Maryland, for access to southern US markets and connections. Conrail immediately said it would not agree.

Organisation

CP Rail's operations are structured as two business units: one, Heavy Haul Systems (HHS) in western Canada; and the other, Intermodal Freight systems (IFS), in the east. Each business unit has a nationwide mandate and the resources to respond to significant changes in the transport market resulting from regulatory reforms and changing business patterns in Canada and internationally.

Based in Vancouver, HHS is reponsible for all heavy-haul traffic, which includes grain, coal, export sulphur, fertilisers, chemicals, gases and acids. Most of this traffic originates or terminates in western Canada. Much of the tonnage is carried in unit trains.

Toronto-based IFS is responsible for all modal-competitive traffic base, such as consumer goods, pulp and paper, semi-processed materials, automobiles and auto parts. This traffic is moving between east and west, as well as to and from the United States.

CP Rail's lines in Nova Scotia, New Brunswick and the US state of Maine, where operations are financially unsatisfying, are segregated as a business unit within IFS named the Canadian Atlantic Railway (CAR). Based in Saint John, NB, CAR is consolidating and rationalising services to meet competitive conditions in the Maritimes, especially the growing dominance of truck transportation in the long-haul market.

The new National Transportation Act, which came into effect at the start of 1988, has brought fundamental change into Canadian railway operations. The new law disallows collective rate-making, permits confidential rate contracts between railways and shippers, and allows certain shippers served by only one railway to ship to the nearest interchange with a connecting carrier at prescribed rates. In addition, the Act introduced final offer arbitration to settle disputes between carriers and shippers.

Investment

CP Rail lifted its annual expenditure on repair and upkeep of roadbed and rail equipment from C$709 milion in 1985 to C$770 million in 1989. During this period, maintenance expenditure represented 32.8 per cent of CP Rail's annual operating costs on average. In addition CP Rail committed an average of C$386 million a year to capital investment projects during the same period.

Intermodal services

CP Rail Intermodal Services (IMS), which began in 1957, was designed to counteract the inroads truckers were making into the railway's regular carload traffic by combining highway and rail transport to carry containers and trailers. IMS now moves more than 400 000 loaded containers and trailers a year via a coast-to-coast network of terminals. The largest terminals are at Montreal, Toronto, Winnipeg, Calgary, Edmonton and Vancouver.

IMS now has approximately 2200 89 ft flatcars for container-on-flatcar (COFC) service, 1500 piggyback flatcars for trailer-on-flatcar (TOFC) serice, 2000 domestic containers, 1100 high-way trailers, 1400 highway chassis for pick-up-and-delivery of domestic and marine containers, and 45 pieces of lifting equipment.

Developments in 1990 included construction of a C$30 million intermodal terminal at Vaughan, near Toronto. This will be the most advanced containerised freight facility in Canada, featuring four 609m-long working tracks, six storage and make-up tracks of similar length and three electrically-powered gantry cranes. Completion was expected in the spring of 1991. The Vaughan terminal will handle western Canadian domestic traffic as well as maritime containers to and from west coast ports, and will improve links between Ontario and markets in western Canada and Pacific Rim countries. Another CP Rail Toronto area intermodal terminal, Obico, will continue to handle overseas container traffic to and from east coast ports, plus domestic business for eastern Canada and the US.

Maritime and domestic container handling is integrated at CP Rail's intermodal terminals. This leads to better utilisation of cars and equipment, faster turn-round of containers, flatcars and highway chassis, and reduced costs.

Domestic containerisation equipment includes: temperature-controlled, insulated, and heated con-

Finances (C$million)	1986	1987	1988	1989
Revenues	2573.6	2794.6	2730.5	2476.3
Expenditures				
Maintenance	700.5	740.2	752.5	769.6
Transportation	863.7	915.3	929.2	854.0
General and administrative	482.1	487.3	494.5	481.3
Depreciation and amortisation	137.5	136.8	139.0	148.5
Interest expense	100.3	100.1	87.9	82.5
Income taxes	156.8	220.9	160.4	69.4
Total	2440.9	2600.6	2563.5	2405.2

Pact-Track concrete roadbed with Pandrol fastenings in Albert Canyon

tainers and highway trailers used for carrying perishable commodities; and stake-and-rack containers and trailers for lumber and steel. Trains dedicated to Intermodal Services run daily between: Saint John and Montreal; Montreal and Toronto; Montreal and Chicago; Montreal and Western Canada; and Toronto and Western Canada.

In 1990 the COFC fleet was being reinforced with 100 articulated five-platform 'spine' cars built by National Steel Car and leased from CGTX and Alberta Intermodal Services. These cars can carry either two maximum-load 20ft containers or one 40 ft, 48ft or 49ft container on each platform.

CP Rail has also begun using 48 ft dry-van containers on its domestic services instead of its 44ft 3in containers, which will be gradually phased out. The 48ft module is the maximum currently permitted on all North American highways. The new containers are fully lined with plywood walls to limit load damage and prevent condensation. Laminated hardwood floors provide extra strength for blocking and bracing shipments.

Unit train operation

CP Rail now secures impressive productivity in its unit train operation. Cars ferrying Japan-bound coal from the Selkirk mines to the Roberts Bank terminal on the west coast, for instance, achieve a 2240 km round trip in 132 hours for an annual gross of around 110 000 miles per car. That reflects attention to precisely scheduled maintenance, which CP Rail has recently stressed by a C$50 million investment in a dedicated coal car workshop at Golden, British Columbia. These coal trains are also witness to CP Rail's achievement in train-crew productivity, since at no time are they worked by more than three men. Further important gains have been achieved on the traction side for instance, by modifications that cut a line-haul locomotive's fuel consumption by up to 10 per cent without diminishing its performance. Gross ton-miles logged per gallon has been lifted 9.8 per cent to 692.9 since 1980.

Safety record

For the seventh successive year CP Rail gained the title in 1989 of safest major railroad in North America, with a record, based on US FRA criteria, of 1.93 accidents per million train-miles. Particular attention has been paid to training and precautions in the movement of dangerous commodities. CP Rail has 12 strategically-located emergency response centres across Canada equipped for immediate reaction and mobile deployment to any incident affecting such freight.

Computer links with customers

Some 500 customers are linked to CP Rail's electronic mail system (Merlin) and EDI facilities. Merlin enables customers, for a minimal fee, to trace their cars and containers, or receive daily reports on the location of their cars and containers. Customers can also use pre-formated forms to send information about tracing and ordering rail equipment, releasing and redirecting shipments. New information can be sent instantly to one or more recipients. It saves customers from having to use Telex for car tracing or the phone to obtain rates.

EDI is best for transmitting large volumes of formated information between CP Rail's and its customers' computers, such as bills of lading, freight invoices and freight claims. EDI has many benefits which include paperless business transactions, faster filling of orders, reduced clerical staffing, fewer errors, enhanced productivity and better inventory control.

Rogers Pass Tunnel

The Rogers Pass project was completed and formally inaugurated early in May 1989. Construction of a new single line for westbound trains has featured construction of the 14.66 km Mount Macdonald Tunnel in the Selkirk Mountains of British Columbia, North America's longest tunnel and the centrepiece of a massive grade reduction and double-tracking project. The scheme also included a 1.85 km tunnel (the Mount Shaughnessy Tunnel) under the Trans-Canada Highway, the 1229m-long John Fox viaduct and 17.31 km of new surface route, for a total of 33.82 km of new track.

The tunnel design includes a unique ventilation system that purges the tunnel of locomotive exhaust quickly, so that a train can pass through it every 30 minutes. In addition, the tunnel houses a 'Pact-Track' concrete roadbed which eliminates the need for sleepers and ballast. It is the first time this railway roadbed system has been used in North America. The most modern engineering techniques have been used in both design and construction, which allows for future electrification if required.

Completion of the Rogers Pass project has tripled operating capacity in this area of the main line. The existing route through the Connaught Tunnel, with its ruling 2.2 per cent gradient, is used by eastbound trains. The heavily-loaded westbound commodity trains, taking the new line with its 1 per cent ruling grade, no longer need the aid of six banking locomotives. That saves the one hour it took to attach them to each train, and also the C$18 million a year incurred by that operation and the local stationing of 12 locomotives purely for pusher service.

Unhappily, opening of the new tunnel coincided with a serious downturn in traffic, largely because of a recession in grain traffic.

Planned maintenance schemes

CP Rail is expanding the planned maintenance concept successfully inaugurated in 1987 at the C$50 million coal car shop at Golden, BC. Here the average of bad order cars per train has been cut from 6 to less than 2; and distance between coal inspections raised, since planned maintenance, from 69 000 to 160 000km. The principle is to be extended to all important freight car types by 1991.

To complement the planned maintenance programme, a C$12 million automated system was installed in October 1989 at the Weston shops in Winnipeg. Known as the Flexible Manufacturing System (FMS), it reconditions used bogie side frames and bolsters, and obtains more consistent quality than previous manual methods, with resultant gains in wheel, bearing and rail wear and also train economy in fuel consumption through better performance.

Towards Advanced Train Control (ATCS)

CP Rail operates 20 000–22 000 trains a month across Canada. A computer-assisted train dispatching system known as CMBS (Computerised Manual Block System) helps control traffic over more than 80 per cent of CP Rail lines not covered by CTC. It provides dispatchers with computer verification to prevent issue of conflicting occupancy authorities. Radio communicates authorities to train crews and verifies that they have been correctly received.

Development of Advanced Train Control Systems (ATCS) continues. In 1989 specifications were completed and detailed design work begun, including negotiations with equipment suppliers. In 1990 a pilot area was to be established for progressive installation and testing of systems, and to provide a foundation for more advanced levels of control: for example, those which would permit automatic override in the event of a train crew failing to comply with their operating authorities.

CMBS computer programs are being used as a basis for the software design, with the communications used being shifted from voice to data network. Data network security is guaranteed by use of sophisticated checking routines, both in the office and on board trains.

All present and future CP Rail signalling and traffic control development is being designed for compatibility with prospective achievement of ATCS. For instance, the connection of hot freight car axlebox detectors to the central computers has begun. CP Rail is now progressively installing the latest type of detector that is equipped with a transmitter which radios the data direct to the train's cab in synthesised speech.

Caboose-less trains

CP Rail began operation of caboose-less trains in November 1989 and expected to have largely standardised the practice by the end of 1990. Such trains are equipped with a train information braking system (TIBS), an electro-mechanical device that monitors brakepipe pressure, can apply brakes from the train end, and also provides information on movement at the train's rear. With TIBS the caboose's crew can be relocated to the train's lead locomotive.

Articulated 'spine' cars and new 48ft containers

CP Rail's dispatch control centre in Winnipeg

As an alternative to weed control by conventional herbicide, CP Rail has developed a prototype vegetation control car that kills weeds with high-temperature steam

Motive power and rolling stock
In 1988 CP Rail took delivery of the first of 25 3000 hp GM-Canada SD40F locomotives. For renewal of its 1250-strong main-line fleet, which is formed almost 50 per cent by GM 3000 hp SD40-2 units, CP has selected the 3850 hp GM SD60 with advanced microprocessor control and diagnostic systems. However, it has engaged in research with Bombardier and Brown Boveri by trying out an MLW six-axle prototype, the 4744, in which only four axles are powered, each with 1000 hp three-phase motors. Since 1980 259 units have been remanufactured from the frame up.

At the start of 1990 CP Rail operated 1288 diesel-electric locomotives and 34 352 revenue freight cars.

Cartier Railway
Cie de Chemin de Fer Cartier

Port Cartier, Duplessis County, Quebec G5B 2H3

Telephone: +1 418 766 2321 Telex: 05186422 ptcr

President: Giorgio Massobrio
Comptroller: Andre Le Bel
General Superintendent, Transport: Gaston Gendreau
Divisional Superintendent, Maintenance & Rail Operations: Serge A Michaud
Divisional Superintendent, Mechanical: Jean Paul Leveque
Director, Materials Management and Business Development: Alan H Ketterling

Gauge: 1435 mm
Route length: 416 km

The 191-mile (307.4 km) railroad built to convey iron ore concentrate from Lac Jeanine (mine and concentrator site) to Port Cartier (harbour site) was completed in 1960. In 1972 an 86-mile (138.4 km) railroad extension was built to Mt Wright where a second concentrator was being built for another iron ore mine exploitation.

In 1975/76 a 3-mile (4.8 km) bypass was constructed to transport crude ore from Fire Lake (which was opened to compensate for the closing of the Lac Jeannine mine). However, Fire Lake mining ended in 1985 and today only Mt Wright workings are exploited.

The ore is worked in unit trains of 150 cars operated with three 3600 hp locomotives on the head end in summer, and two 3600 hp locomotives on the head end and a third at the rear under Locotrol remote control during the winter, when ambient temperature can drop to −40°C. Trains are operated with a two-man crew of engineman and conductor without cabooses. The railroad normally operates five such trains daily throughout the year to match the concentrator production, this format was standardised after experiments with various train-sizes up to 298 cars with six 3600 hp locomotives.

The present size best matches the cycle time of the fixed installations, which provide continuous loading and discharge at the port, the latter by a double-car Strachan & Henshaw rotary dumper which works at the rate of 3800 tons an hour.

Computerised control has been superimposed on the CTC system, which is supplemented by centrally-controlled hot box detectors and switch point heaters. Radio communication with crews is employed for despatch of train orders.

Traffic

	1983/84	1984/85	1985/86	1986/87
Freight tonne-km (million)	581.8	961.7	6032	5934.2
Average net freight train load (tonnes)	13 650	14 136	13 357	14 285
Average freight wagon load (tonnes)	91	93	93	93
Total net freight tonnes (million)	NA	7.73	9.658	14.3

Main-line track is entirely cwr, employing 132lb rail until 1988, but since then 136lb has been adopted as the standard rail.

Motive power and rolling stock
Total fleet consists of 42 diesel-electric line-haul locomotives and 1333 freight wagons.

Track
Rail: Std carbon, head hardened and ⅜ chrome 132 and 136lb
Cross ties (sleepers)
Type: Hardwood 2590 × 228 × 177 mm
Spacing: 1851/km
Fastenings: Cut spikes and Trak-lok clips on test section
Minimum curvature radius: 250 m
Max gradient: 1.35% against empty trains; 0.4% compensated against loaded trains
Max axleload: 31 tonnes
Type of braking: Wabco 26L
Type of coupler: CF70HT

Diesel locomotives

Class	Wheel arrangement	Transmission	Rated power hp	Tractive effort continuous lb (kg)	Max speed mph (km/h)	Wheel dia in (mm)	Total weight tons	Length ft in (mm)	Year first built	Builders Mechanical parts	Builders Engine & type	Builders Transmission
RS	Bo-Bo	Elec	1750	60 000 (27 216)	65 (104.6)	40 (1016)	130	56'2" (17 120)	1960	GM (London)	GM V-16	GM
RS	Bo-Bo	Elec	1800	64 900 (29 439)	65 (104.6)	40 (1016)	129	56'11¾" (17 367)	1960	MLW (Montreal)	Alco 251 V-12	MLW
RS	Co-Co	Elec	3000	103 000 (46 721)	65 (104.6)	40 (1016)	195	69'6" (21 298)	1966	Alco (New York)	Alco 251-EV-16	Alco
RS	Co-Co	Elec	3600	104 000 (47 174)	65 (104.6)	40 (1016)	186	69'10" (21 298)	1970-3	MLW (Montreal)	Alco 251-FV-16	MLW
RS	Co-Co	Elec	3600	108 000 (48 989)	65 (104.6)	40 (1016)	194.2	69'6" (21 184)	1968	Alco (New York)	Alco 251 V-16	Alco
RS	Co-Co	Elec	3600	108 000 (48 989)	65 (104.6)	40 (1016)	200	69'10" (21 285)	1975	MLW (Montreal)	Alco 251-FV-16	MLW

GO Transit
Government of Ontario Transit

1120 Finch Avenue West, Toronto M3J 3J8

Telephone: +1 416 665 9211
Telex: 06 217508
Telefax: +1 416 665 9006

Chairman: Louis H Parsons
Managing Director: Thomas G Smith
Executive Directors, Operations: James A Brown
  Engineering, Development and Plant: R C Ducharme
  Planning, Finance and Administration: David A Sutherland

Gauge: 1435 mm
Route length: 356 km

Government of Ontario (GO) Transit, set up in 1967, was Canada's first inter-regional transport system created and funded by a Provincial government. Since 1974 it has been under the control of the Toronto Area Transit Operating Authority, a body on which five regional municipalities are represented as well as Toronto the Province of Ontario (which appoints the chairman). GO Transit serves a territory of over 8000 square km with a population of 4 million, which is steadily growing. It runs an integrated bus and rail

Flyunder at western approach to Toronto Union station with GO Transit's Bathurst North storage yard on left

passenger network with a total annual ridership of more than 30million.

Finance
Operating cost recovery ratio was 68.5 per cent in 1987-88 fiscal year, the best performance in GO Transit's history. For the first time the organisation's target of 65 per cent was bettered.

Operations
Starting with a single rail route along Lake Ontario, GO Transit now operates six lines, with Toronto's Union station as the system's hub. Train services are run under contract over Canadian National and Canadian Pacific tracks by CP and CN crews to GO Transit specification. CN also maintains GO Transit rolling stock under contract at the GO Transit-owned Willowbrook depot in west Toronto.

In December 1987 CN and GO Transit concluded a new operating agreement which for the first time provided operating performance incentives for the railway.

Traffic
In FY1988-89 trains carried over 19.7 million passengers, about two-thirds of GOP Transit's total traffic. In calendar year 1989 the trains carried 21 per cent more passengers than in 1988. During the year services underwent significant expansion. Some peak-hour trains on the Lakeshore line were doubled in length to 12 cars and the timetable on some other routes was intensified.

Lakeshore route extension
The 15km Lakeshore extension of GO Transit from Pickering eastward to Whitby was inaugurated in December 1988. It featured GO Transit's first use of concrete sleepers.

Traction and rolling stock
The 1990 survivors of GO Transit's initial traction fleet comprised 11 3000 hp GP40-2 of 1973-75, seven units of 1966-67 remanufactured as 3000 hp GP40-M2 and six 3000 hp FP40H of 1978. The fleet also included 14 GM-EMD FP7 diesels with traction plant removed which were re-equipped to serve as 600 kW auxiliary units to power train electrical supplies (which the GP40-2 locomotives cannot feed); 11 of these auxiliary units were also equipped to serve as driving trailers for push-pull working. The FP7s were acquired second-hand from the Ontario Northland, Milwaukee and Burlington Northern Railroads.

In 1988 GO Transit took delivery of 16 F59PH diesel-electric locomotives and spare parts from General Motors of Canada. The F59PH was specially developed with GO's requirements in mind and its design was evolved jointly by General Motors and GO's engineers. Delivery of a second order for 12 F59PH began at the end of 1989; and a third order for 14 was to be delivered in the autumn of 1990. The aim is to standardise passenger train operation on the F59PH.

To cope with its rapidly rising ridership (see above), GO Transit is greatly enlarging its fleet of UTDC-built bi-level cars, a proportion of which are control trailers for push-pull working of bi-level sets. A fourth order, for 60 cars, was delivered during the 1989-90 winter, lifting the total stock to 274 cars. A fifth order would have 60 more cars arriving between May 1990 and April 1991.

Coupler in standard use (passenger cars): H-tight-lock
Braking in standard use (locomotive-hauled stock): 26L, 26LUM and 26C

Montreal Urban Community Transport Commission
Société de Transport de la Communauté Urbaine de Montreal (STCUM)

159 rue St-Antoine West, Montreal, Quebec H2Z 1H3

Telephone: +1 514 280 5150
Telex: 05 825570
Telefax: +1 514 280 5193

Route length: 91 km
Electrification: 27 km at 2.4 kV dc

Chairman: Robert Perreault
President and General Manager: Louise Roy
Senior Executive Officer, Resources & Quality Development: Francis Therrien
Executive Director, Finance: Claire Monette
  Planning & Commercial: Xavier Ceccaldi
  Metro & Commuter Rail: Roger C Choquette
  Construction & Maintenance: Jacques Rompré
Secretary & Manager, Legal Dept: Daniel Robert

Besides the Montreal Metro, STCUM supports CN Rail commuter operations from Montreal Central to Deux-Montagnes under a 10-year contract signed in July 1982. A major renovation programme for this route was likely to be approved in 1990. In October 1982, after STCUM had bought the necessary material from CP Rail, a 10-year contract for commuter operations from the city's Windsor station over 64km to Rigaud was signed with CP Rail. The two routes together recorded 8.4 milion passengers in 1989. As part of a plan to modernise the Rigaud line, 24 new cars, seven

Ex-CP Rail bi-level push-pull control trailer used on Rigaud line

Diesel locomotives

Class	Wheel arrangement	Transmission	Rated power hp	Max speed km/h	Total weight tonnes	No in service 1987	Year first built	Builders
F7A	B-B	Elec	1500	114	113	1	1951	GM
F7A	B-B	Elec	1500	114	113	6	1952	GM

Electric locomotives

Class	Wheel arrangement	Line voltage dc	Rated output kw	Max speed km/h	Weight tonnes	Overall length mm	No in service 1987	Year first built	Builders Mechanical parts	Builders Electrical equipment
Z1a	B-B	2400	932.5	88	78.7	11 379	6	1914	GE English Electric	GE
Z4a	B-B	2400	932.5	80	91.4	12 192	5	1924		GE
Z5a	B-B	2400	932.5	97	77.9	13 052	3	1950	GE	GE

Electric railcars

Class	Cars per unit	Line voltage	Motor cars per unit	Motored axles per motor car	Rated output (kW) per motor	Max speed km/h	Weight tonnes per car (M-motor T-trailer)	Total seating capacity per car (M-motor T-trailer)	Length per car mm (M-motor T-trailer)	No in service 1987 (M-motor T-trailer)	Year first built	Builders Mechanical parts	Builders Electrical equipment
P-59-A	2-6	2400 dc	1-2	4	62	105	M 71 T 42	M 84 T 88	M 21.5 T 21.5	M 5 T 11	1952	CCF	GE

of them control trailers, were delivered by Bombardier in late 1989. The Corporation was also to acquire four renovated Type GC-418 locomotives and seven emu cars, and to modernise 41 of its hauled cars for a total of almost C$44 million.

In 1989 STCUM was operating 14 electric and seven diesel locomotives, five electric railcars, 10 trailers and 132 passenger cars.

Ontario Northland Railway

555 Oak Street E, North Bay, Ontario P1B 8L3

Telephone: +1 705 472 4500
Telex: 067 76103
Telefax: +1 705 476 5598

President & Chief Executive Officer: P A Dyment
Vice President, Rail Services: K J Moorehead
  Passenger Services: E Marasco
  Administration: K J Wallace
  Telecommunications & Computer Services: R S Hutton
Chief Mechanical Officer: R G Leach
Superintendent, Train Operations: D K Hagar
Chief Engineer: G A Payne

Gauge: 1435 mm
Route length: 926 km

Ontario Northland, a component of the mult-modal Ontario Northland Transportation Commission's operations, lies at the eastern rim of the province. It runs from North Bay, where it is intersected by CN and CP Rail routes westward from Ottawa to Moosonee on James Bay, the southward-probing neck of Hudson Bay. Freight, chiefly lumber, pulp, newsprint and ores, is the backbone of its business, but it runs two significant passenger services into and out of Toronto Union station, travelling 228 miles of CN Rail track between there and the fringe of Ontario Northland territory at North Bay.

The railway operates 21 line-haul and 6 switching diesel-electric locomotives, 46 passenger cars and 668 freight cars. A stock of 20 single-level commuter cars has been acquired from GO Transit and renovated as first-class cars in Ontario Northland workshops. This conversion from commuter to intercity use has employed state-of-the-art technology in reconstructing the cars, interiors, sub-systems, electrical heating systems and air-conditioning systems. Also acquired were seven redundant un-cabbed diesel locomotives for conversion to auxiliary power units to operate with the refurbished cars as head-end electrical services supply. The total cost of the conversion project is expected to be about C$24.5 million.

The 'Polar Bear Express', headed by two FP7-A units, which is operated from late June to early September by Ontario Northland

Ontario Northland Type SD40-2 unit

Track
Rail: 125.77 kg/m
Cross ties (sleepers)
Wood: Thickness 180 mm
Spacing: 1886/km

Fastenings: 4 spikes per sleeper on tangent, 8 spikes per sleeper on curves
Minimum curvature radius: 300 m
Max gradient: 1.5%
Max axleload: 29.5 tonnes (65 000 lb)

Diesel locomotives

Class	Wheel arrangement	Transmission	Rated power kW	Max kg	Tractive effort Continuous at kg	km/h	Max speed km/h	Wheel dia mm	Total weight tonnes	Length mm	No in service 1989	Year first built	Builders Mechanical parts	Engine & type	Transmission
SD40-2	C-C	Elec	2237.1	42 676	32 727.4	17.87	104.6	1016	170.7	20 980	8	1973	GM	645E3	GM Main Gen
GP38-2	B-B	Elec	1492.5	28 803	25 151.6	16.9	104.6	1016	115.67	18 034	10	1974	GM	645E	GM Main Gen
FP7-A	B-B	Elec	1118.55	29 283	18 160	17.8	104.6	1016	117.1	16 662	9	1951	GM	567BC	GM Main Gen
GP-9	B-B	Elec	1304.97	29 337	22 700	16.9	104.6	1016	117.34	17 120	6	1956	GM	567C	GM Main Gen

Quebec North Shore and Labrador Railway

PO Box 1000, Sept-Iles, Quebec G4R 4L5

Telephone: +1 418 968 7400
Telex: 051 84102
Telefax: +1 418 968 7451

President and Chief Operating Officer: M D Walker
Vice-President: A Ouellet

Secretary, Treasurer: G Hamelin
Comptroller: S Levesque
General Manager, Sept-Iles Division: Yvan Bellevance
Manager, Rail Operations: G Hétu
Manager, Materials and Services: John Turnbull
Superintendent, Transportation and Traffic: John Nadeau
Equipment Maintenance: B Gagnon
Maintenance of Way: Tom McElroy

Supervisor, Signals and Communications: Paul Gauthier

Gauge: 1435 mm
Route length: 638.77 km

Begun in 1950 by its then newly-formed owners, the Iron Ore Company of Canada (IOC), with the shareholding support of several US steelmakers, the 356-mile (573 km) main line of the Quebec North Shore &

Diesel locomotives

Class	Wheel arrangement	Transmission	Rated power hp	Tractive effort Continuous at lb (kg)	mph (km/h)	Max speed mph (km/h)	Wheel diameter in (mm)	Total weight tonnes	Length ft in (mm)	No in service 1988	Year first built	Builders Mechanical parts	Engine & type	Transmission
SD40-2	C-C	Elec	3000	84 000 (38 000)	11.1 (17.86)	71 (114.26)	40 (1016)	174	68'10" (20 980)	44	1972	GM	GM	GM
GP-9	B-B	Elec	1750	48 000 (22 000)	11.1 (17.86)	71 (114.26)	40 (1016)	109	56'7" (17 247)	8	1954-60	GM	GM	GM

534 RAILWAY SYSTEMS / Canada

Labrador Railway runs from Schefferville south to Sept-Iles on the St Lawrence. Schefferville, the railhead for the Ungava ore tract in the Labrador peninsula, is just inside the Quebec border, but otherwise the northern half of the route is enclosed by Newfoundland. Within this section a 36-mile (57.9 km) branch was run from Ross Bay westward to Labrador City in 1960.

IOC stopped mining in the Schefferville area in 1982, but still serves the railhead as there are no roads north of Sept-Iles. Mining is now concentrated in the Carol Lake area, at the extremity of the Labrador City branch.

Despite the savage winters in the region, QNS&L functions all year round. However, in winter it moves only processed ('benefiated') ore in pellets, because of 'raw' ore's propensity to freeze.

QNS&L runs loaded ore trains varying from 117 to 265 cars in length; the latter trail about 2.06 miles (3.3 km) behind their lead locomotives and gross over 33 700 tons, but a 117-car train weighs at least 14 000 tons. Normal power is two 3000 hp GM-EMD SD40s from the railroad's 50 unit-strong fleet at the front end, but when a train is made up to 165 cars or more mid-train helper units, radio-controlled by the Locotrol system from the lead locomotive, are added. The whole line is traffic-controlled by CTC from Sept-Iles. The railway was the first in Canada to gain Canadian Transport Commission authority to dispense entirely with end-of-train cabooses.

Electrification study
The Transport Departments of Quebec and the Federal government have shared the C$400 000 cost of a study by CP and CANAC consultancies into the value of electrifying both the Cartier and QNS&L ore railways as a means of making their mining output more competitive in world markets.

Motive power and rolling stock
The fleet at the end of 1988 consisted of 52 diesel-electric locomotives, 2641 freight wagons and 23 passenger coaches.

Track
Rail: 65.5 kg/m
Cross ties (sleepers)
Treated hardwood: 177.8 × 228.6 × 2743.2 mm
Spacing: 2080/km
Fastenings
Standard track, 165 mm (5½ in)
Minimum curvature radius: 220 m
Max gradient: 1.32%
Max axleload: 32.5 tonnes

QNS&L loaded ore train headed by three GM-EMD SD40 locomotives (above) with remotely Locotrol-operated SD40 mid-train (below)

Traffic	1984	1985	1986	1987
Freight tonnage (000)	19 049	20 188	19 469	18 441
Freight tonne-km (million)	7513	7991	7751	7298
Average net freight train load (tonnes)	24 020	24 020	20 374	NA
Passenger-km (million)	10.338	8.444	8.215	NA
Passenger journeys	-	25 982	25 277	18 705

VIA Rail
VIA Rail Canada Ltd

2 Place Ville-Marie, Suite 400, PO Box 8116, Montreal, Quebec H3B 2G6

Telephone: +1 514 871 6000
Telex: 05 268530
Telefax: +1 514 393 1519

Chairman: Lawrence Hanigan
President & Chief Executive Officer (Part-time): Ronald Lawless
Senior Vice-President & Chief Operating Officer: W Morin
Vice-President, Marketing & Sales: Murray Jackson
  Equipment & Facilities: R Béchamp
  Human Resources: J-R Boivin
  Corporate Planning: J Roche
  Transportation: R J Guiney
  Finance: Nicole Beaudoin-Sauvé
General Manager, Marketing: Paul G Coté
General Manager, Public Affairs: Marc-André Charlebois
General Manager, On-board Services: D Carmichael
General Manager, Equipment Maintenance and Engineering: W Gelling
Senior Director, Public Affairs: M-A Charlebois
  Operations: M Gregoire
  Engineering: R M Vadas

Total route operated: 18 500km

Constitution

Originally incorporated as an independent subsidiary of Canadian National in 1977, VIA Rail Canada Inc became an autonomous Crown Corporation in April 1978. At that date it took over management of all rail passenger services previously operated by GN and CP

GM-EMD Type FP40H-2 locomotive

LCR power car and trailers

Rail, except commuter services.

VIA contracts with the Federal government for the provision of those rail passenger services specified by the Minister of Transport. In turn, VIA contracts with railway companies for the operation of these services and with non-railway companies for the provision of incidental goods and services.

Initially, no statutory requirement was laid on the railroads to publish the formulae which assigned VIA a share of the total costs of the infrastructure and assets used by the passenger trains, as well as the latter's avoidable operating costs. Nor was VIA given authority to query the changes.

Some of these uncertainties were addressed in the National Rail Passenger Transportation Act of 1986. This entrusted VIA with decision-making on levels of service, subject to VIA's satisfaction of financial objectives set by the government. The latter required VIA to operate within a subsidy envelope which was to be progressively reduced from C$505 million in 1986 to C$400 in 1990; and to cover fully all avoidable costs of service in the Quebec-Montreal-Toronto-Windsor corridor, 60 per cent of transcontinental services' avoidable costs, and 40 per cent of regional trains' avoidable costs. The act also revised VIA's relationships with CN and CP Rail; the railroads would have to provide detailed accounts of all charges and be debarred from billing VIA later than two months from a year's end. When the existing contracts with the railroads expired at the end of 1987, new agreements were negotiated that provided for the transfer of CN and CP operating and maintenance staff involved in passenger service to VIA.

VIA's difficult life

Throughout the 1980s VIA's operating costs were burdened with the average 25 years' age of 90 per cent of the steam-heated car fleet it inherited from CN and CP Rail, or bought secondhand from US railroads,

VIA's new Montreal maintenance facility

Traffic	1983	1985	1986	1987
Passenger journeys (000)	6960	7034	6286	5865
Passenger-miles (000)	1 531 420	1 542 869	1 405 033	1 300 296
Train-miles operated (000)	12 200	12 954	13 042	12 172
Average occupancy rate (%)	51.7	51.2	50.3	51.6
Average passenger-miles per train-mile	123	119	108	107

Diesel locomotives

Class	Type	Wheel arrangement	Transmission	Rated power (kW)	Max speed km/h	Total weight tonnes	No in service 1988	Year first built	Builders Mechanical parts	Engine & type	Transmission
GPA 30 a	F40 PH2	Bo-Bo	Elec	2238	145	118	20	1986	GMD	16-645E3C	GMD
GPA 30 b	F40 PH2	Bo-Bo	Elec	2238	145	118	10	1987	GMD	16-645E3C	GMD
GPA 30 c	F40 PH2	Bo-Bo	Elec	2238	145	118	(29 on order)	1989	GMD	16-645E3C	GMD
LRC 2	MPA 27	Bo-Bo	Elec	2760	166	115	20	1978	B/MLW	16 CYL 251-F	CGE
LRC 3	MPA 27	Bo-Bo	Elec	2760	201	115	10	1982	B/MLW	16 CYL 251-F	CGE
GPA-418A	FP 9-A	Bo-Bo	Elec	1342	143	112	5	1954 Rebuilt 1983	GMD	EMD 16-645	EMD
GPA-418B	FP 9-A	Bo-Bo	Elec	1342	143	118	10	1954 Rebuilt 1984	GMD	EMD 16-645	EMD
GPA-17	FP 9-A	Bo-Bo	Elec	1305	143	116	25	1954	GMD	EMD 16-567	EMD
GPB-17	FP 9-A	Bo-Bo	Elec	1305	143	117	34	1954	GMD	EMD 16-567	EMD
MPA-18	FPA-4	Bo-Bo	Elec	1342	148	117	15	1958	MLW	MLW-ALCO 12-251	CGE
MPB-18	FPB-4	Bo-Bo	Elec	1342	148	117	5	1958	MLW	MLW-ALCO 12-251	CGE
GS-10	SW 1000	Bo-Bo	Elec	746	97	104	4	1966	EMD	EMD 8-645E	EMD

GMD General Motors Diesel (Canada)
EMD Electromotive, GM (USA)
MLW Montreal Locomotive Works
CGE Canadian General Electric
B/MLW Bombardier/Montreal Locomotive Works

Diesel railcars

Class	Type	Cars per unit	Motor cars per unit	Motored axles per motor car	Transmission	Rated power (kW) per motor	Max speed km/h	Weight tonnes per car	Total seating capacity per car	Length per car mm	No in service 1988	Year first built	Builders Mechanical parts	Engine & type	Transmission
RDC-1	RDC-1	1	1	2	Hyd	254	145	55	76-64	25908	2	1957	Budd	Cummins NTA 855R	Voith
RDC-1	RDC-1	1	1	2	Mech	254	145	55	76/64	25908	41	1949	Budd	Cummins	Twin Disc
RDC-1	RDC-1	1	1	2	Hyd	205	145	55	76	25908	2	1956	Budd	GM 6-110	Allison
RDC-2	RDC-2	1	1	2	Mech	254	145	55	60/48	25908	21	1955	Budd	Cummins NTA 855R	Twin Disc
RDC-2	RDC-2	1	1	2	Hyd	205	145	55	60	25908	2	1956	Budd	GM 6-110	Allison
RDC-4	RDC-4	1	1	2	Hyd	205	145	52.5	—	22860	1	1955	Budd	GM 6-110	Allison

Higher No: All passenger
Lower No: With snack bar

and the shortcomings of its equally secondhand GM-EMD FPA4, FP7 and FP9 diesel locomotives. Its only modern equipment for many years was 31 LRC power cars and 100 LRC tilt-body trailer cars.

In June 1985 the then government at length authorised purchase of 20 GM-EMD FP40H-2 locomotives immediately and 10 more in 1986.

Later in the year the government allowed VIA to seek construction bids for 130 bi-level cars of similar style to the US 'Superliners' of Amtrak, for use of transcontinental services. In May 1987, however, that authority was withdrawn and VIA was made to accept instead a C$119 million refurbishing programme for 190 existing cars. A key item of this rehabilitation project, to be executed in 1988–90, was conversion from steam to electric auxiliary power, which would not only eliminate many winter freeze-up problems and cut maintenance costs, but permit more aggressive train scheduling, because stops purely to replenish water supplies would be obviated. The government also released C$63 million for 26 more FP40H-2 locomotives, raising the stock of these units to 56; C$176 million for fixed structure projects, including additional maintenance depots and renovation or replacement of some 165 stations; and C$3 million for evaluation of railcar prototypes to supersede the Budd RDC cars.

Train service is halved

In November 1988 a Conservative government gained re-election. Despite the fact that a plank in the platform on which the party had won the previous election had been a better deal for VIA — and then the Conservatives had forced through revival of some withdrawn VIA services — the 1988 administration quickly took a scythe to VIA's operations.

Drastic action began in May 1989. Although 1988 had seen improved results, with passenger journeys up 10 per cent and revenue up 13 per cent (though cost recovery from revenue was still no better than 28 per cent), VIA's president was dismissed and replaced on a part-time basis by the head of CN Rail, Ron Lawless. Simultaneously, it was announced that over the next four years VIA's subsidy would be cut from C$600 to C$250 million by FY 1993-94. For FY 1989-90 the support was reduced by C$105 million to C$531 million.

As 1989 progressed the government tightened the financial noose. Originally told to cut its costs by C$500 million over four years, VIA found the demand hoisted to a saving of C$1 300 million over the same period.

In October 1989 the Transport Minister announced service cuts that would reduce weekly VIA service from 405 trains to 191. Despite widespread protest, the reductions were made in mid-January 1990. Their most important effect was to leave only 63 trains a week running outside the Windsor-Quebec corridor. The most conspicuous casualty was the Montreal/Toronto-Vancouver 'Canadian', abandoned in favour of a thrice-weekly Toronto-Vancouver service following a circuitous route through northern Ontario via Winnipeg, Saskatoon, Edmonton and Jasper. Ironically, VIA improved in 1989, increasing revenues by 11 per cent, load factors from 52 to 59 per cent, and cutting costs.

Bombardier revives high-speed scheme

The savage VIA surgery of 1989-90 seemed at first to have buried hopes of the high-speed inter-city link between Montreal, Ottawa and Toronto that had been projected and studied in the 1980s. But in February 1990 they were revived by Bombardier's Transportation Equipment Group, whose President announced that partners were being sought to develop a 300km/h French TGV operation in the Quebec-Windsor corridor. In 1987 Bombardier had acquired the North American TGV manufacturing and marketing rights from GEC-Alsthom, who made known their full support for the Canadian company's 1990 initiative.

A full feasibility study had yet to be executed, but Bombardier claimed that preliminary work had shown a scheme offering 2 hr 45min Montreal-Toronto rail journey time to be economically viable. Total cost of the project was put at C$5 300 milion for infrastructure and C$650 milion for train-sets.

ABB subsequently entered the arena with a proposal based on the use of its tilt-body X2 on existing tracks.

Traction and rolling stock

In 1989 VIA Rail was operating 125 diesel-electric line-haul locomotives, 30 LRC power cars, 69 Budd RDC diesel railcars, 67 steam generator and three electric generator units and 642 passenger cars.

Chile

Ministry of Transport and Telecommunications

Amunategui 139, Santiago

Minister of Transport: German Correa Diaz

Chilean State Railways (EFE)
Empresa de los Ferrocarriles del Estado de Chile

Av Libertador Bernado O'Higgins, 3322 Casilla 124, Santiago

Telephone: +56 2 763869/790707
Telex: 242290 fcs cl
Telefax: +56 2 762609

Director-General: Ignacio Echevarria
Inspector General: Indalicio Gallardo S

Traffic	1985	1986	1987	1988
Freight tonnes (000)	12 800	12 958	6093*	6300
Freight tonne-km (million)	1804	1814	1601	1763
Passenger journeys (000)	8900	6233	7233	6800
Passenger-km (million)	1555	1271	1174	996

* 1987 figures exclude approx 7 million tonnes of ore carried in 1986, but over lines that passed into private ownership in 1987.

Finances (C$ million)				
Revenue	1985	1986	1987	1988
Passengers and baggage	3085.6	2889.4	3508	3054
Freight	6845.5	7229.3	10 208	11 306
Other	1985.7	1033	2046	4657
Total	11 916.8	11 151.7	15 762	19 017
Expenditure				
Personnel	5354.7	5222.9	7136	7640
Materials and services	6309.8	5226.6	6836	7069
Depreciation	2606.1	2262.6	12 489	12 589
Financial charges	3964.9	2607.4	3332	2842
Other	517.9	457.5	2944	2172
Total	18 753.4	15 777.0	32 737	32 312

Diesel locomotives

Class	Type	Wheel arrangement	Transmission	Rated power (kW)	Max speed km/h	Total weight tonnes	No in service 1988	Year first built	Builders Mechanical parts	Builders Engine & type	Builders Electrical equipment
D-18 000	DL-541-RSD-20	C-C	Elec	1342	130	107.3	10	1961	Alco	Alco 251-C	General Electric USA
D-16 000	253/253	C-C	Elec	1193	120	114.5	16	1954/57	GE	Alco 251-C	General Electric USA
Dt-13 100	U-13-C	C-C	Elec	984	95	85	8	1967	GE	GE FDL-8	General Electric USA
DT-13 000	UGR-12	C-C	Elec	969	100	87.7	14	1962	GM-EMD	General Motors	Delco-Remy
Dt-12 000	U-12-C	C-C	Elec	932	80	80	2	1961	GE	Cooper-Bessemer FVBL-8-ST	General Electric USA
Dt-12 100	DL-535-RSD-30	C-C	Elec	887	80	85	5	1962	Alco	Alco 251-D	General Electric USA
Dt-9000	U-9-C	C-C	Elec	671	80	775.	3	1958	GE	Cooper-Bessemer FVBL-6T	General Electric USA
D-7100	0440	B-B	Elec	559	90	72	30	1963	Brissoneau et Lotz	SACM-MGO 12V-175-ASH	Various European builders
D-6100	148/148	B-B	Elec	492	88	74	11	1957	GE	Cooper-Bessemer FWL-6T	General Electric USA
Dt-6000	140/140	C+C	Elec	447	40	64	12	1954	GE	Cooper-Bessemer FWL-6T	General Electric USA
D-6000	146/146	B-B	Elec	431	80	66.3	8	1951/54	GE	Cooper-Bessemer FWL-6T	General Electic USA
D-5100	U-5-B	B-B	Elec	402	70	54.5	16	1963	GE	Caterpillar D-379	General Electric USA

Chile / **RAILWAY SYSTEMS** 537

Director, Administration: Aminodow Feller N
Director, Financial and Budget: Patricio Yunis J
Director, Human Resources: Teresa de la Carrera
General Manager, Infrastructure: Jorge Max O
General Manager, FC del Sur: Rolando Zúniga
General Manager, FC del Norte: Fernando Kaiser O
General Manager, FC de Arica: Fernando Ibarra
General Manager, Valparaiso Regional Metro (MERVAL): Manual Salinas C
Passenger Manager, VIA Sur: Jorge Echevarría

Gauge: 1676 mm; 1000 mm
Route length: 3974 km; 2914 km
Electrification: 1865 km (1676 mm gauge) and 80 km (1000 mm gauge) at 3 kV dc

Restructure

During 1987 EFE was involved in a major restructure to the dictates of a government plan formulated by several Ministries in conjunction with EFE's Director-General. EFE was required to seek eventual amortisation of its accumulated debt of US$120 million by a reorganisation involving identification of a viable route system, sale of some activities to private enterprise, and the drafting of an operational and investment plan that was realistic in relation to forecast demands for rail transportation. With much of its infrastructure, traction and rolling stock in need of renovation or repair, EFE was unable to satisfy all demands for freight service.

The future EFE network was eventually delineated as: the section of the Arica-La Paz line within Chile, which is an outlet for Bolivian exports; the metre-gauge Northern railway, now almost entirely traversed by mineral freight; and the 1676 mm-gauge Southern railway.

Following the reorganisation, ECE now comprises five administrations reporting to the Director-General. FC del Norte (Northern Railway), the core of which is the Central Northern line, extending from Calera, near Valparaiso, to Iquique.

FC del Sur (Southern Railway), which extends from Santiago south to Puerto Montt, on 1676 mm gauge with branch lines of metre and 1676 mm gauge. Most of the FC del Sur is electrified.

Since 1986 the FC del Sur has taken over from the FC del Norte; the 71 km Transandine Railway, of which stretches totalling 21 km are rack-assisted, from Los Andes to Caracoles, where it connects with Argentine Railways; and the line from Santiago to Valparaiso, which is 1676 mm gauge.

FC Regional de Arica, which is diesel-operated and extends from Arica to Visviri (206 km), linking with Bolivian Railways and rising from sea level to 3733 metres within 39 km on a 6 per cent gradient. At 183 km the line reaches its maximum height of 4257 m.

Because of its difficult mountain route, FC Arica reflects one of the most remarkable examples of railway engineering. In turn it represents 'the shortest route from the Pacific to Bolivia', (its own slogan), covering 440 km between the port of Arica in Chile to the Bolivian capital city of La Paz.

Metro Regional de Valparaiso (MERVAL): A new administration for commercial exploitation of suburban passenger services in the Valparaiso region. In 1989 the latter comprised 56 daily trains providing a 17-stop service over the 43 km between the city and Limache; and four daily trains running the 140 km from Valparaiso to Los Andes.

VIA Sur: A new administration to manage passenger services between Alameda (Santiago) and Puerto Montt.

Class D5100 diesel recently renovated with World Bank loan aid.

Long-distance emu by Kawasaki at Cabrero intermodal passenger station

Emu of MERVAL, the Valparaiso region passenger authority

New track authority

Decentralisation of management to the five administrations outlined above and moves to sell off dispensable operations were intensified in 1988. In March 1989 a new subsidiary Ferrovia, was established to take over responsibility for the upkeep of infrastructure, including electrification, signalling, communications and traffic control. Ferrovia would draw appropriate rental from the train-operating administrations, or from any privately-owned train operators.

Northern Railway heads for privatisation

EFE's proposal that FC del Norte should be hived off as a limited company was accepted by the government. In January 1989 it was taken over by Ferronor, a joint organisation of the Public Works Corporation and private interests. The line carries no passenger traffic.

No operating subsidy

Drastic rationalisation, including closures of 500 km of route and a severe staff reduction to 9500 compared with 28 000 in 1973, had earlier followed a government requirement of 1978 that EFE eliminate its need of a state operating subsidy, which was terminated in 1979, along with assistance for the servicing of internal and external debts. At the same time EFE was granted commercial freedom to set its own rates and to recruit or dispense with labour.

Passenger traffic

Many passenger services are operated at a loss. Between Santiago and Valparaiso (186 km) the 1676 mm gauge trains take over three hours, but rival bus services have use of a motorway. EFE had drafted plans for a 46 km la Dormide bypass, 16 km of it in tunnel under the Barriga mountains, which would reduce the distance to 121 km and journey time from 2½ hours to 50 minutes if maximum speed were 125 km/h. The deviation would be electrified at 3 kV dc, for compatibility with existing electrification, and the line would be engineered with a ruling gradient of 1.5, as against the present 2.5 per cent and a minimum curve radius of 1500 metres.

Construction of the La Dormida bypass remains a long-range aspiration for lack of resources. It has become a still more remote prospect because at the end of 1987 the government set up an organisation to plan a new 106 km high-speed line between Santiago and Valparaiso. No less than 26 km would be in tunnel. At the close of 1988 the Transport Minister issued a fresh call for international finance to build the line.

Alameda station, Santiago, is the first to be treated

under a station remodelling plan. Other recent developments have included the launch of an accompanied car-carrying train service. Some trains now feature video as well as bar facilities, in pursuance of EFE policy to upgrade regular and second-class services to fast express and de luxe status, and some sleeping cars have been refurbished. Computerised seat reservations is in process of extension.

Freight traffic
The principal traffic has been iron ore, from mines in the north to the ports of Chanaral, Caldera, Huasco and Coquimbo, but several branches on which this traffic originates have been privatised under the new order. However, container and piggyback traffic is developing, and forestry products haulage have boomed to a gross of 1.5 million tonnes. With commercial freedom, EFE now endeavours to strike individual pricing contracts with its principal customers.

Investment
Expenditure planned in 1989 would cover track work, locomotive overhauls, refitting of freight wagons for copper transport, bridge repairs, new telecommunications on the FC del Sur and signalling and telecommunications improvements on the FC de Arica

a La Paz. In the longer term ambition is at present confined to extensions of welded rail, more improvement of track and communications and renovation of freight wagons.

Major investments planned in the short and medium term under the latest reorganisation plan include: track improvements between Santiago and the south, US$1700 million; traction and rolling stock rehabilitation, and acquisition of spares, US$3000 million; signalling and communications improvements between Santiago and the south, US$170 million; metre- to 1676 mm-gauge conversion of the branches from Talca to Constitucion (90 km) and Los Andes to Saladillo (38 km), US$800 million; realignment between Curanilahue and Los Alamos (22 km), US$3200 million; and procurement of 415 wagons for forestry product transport, US$1700 million.

Traction and rolling stock
In 1989 the railway's equipment status was:

Locomotives Total	Diesel	105
	Electric	45
Multiple-units		
	Diesel	2
	Electric	25
Passenger cars		390*
Freight cars		5418

*Including 17 dining, 5 video bar and 17 sleeping cars

In 1990 EFE was to spend US$70 million, partly World Bank-financed, on renovation of 10 electric and 23 diesel locomotives, 3 emus, 23 passenger and 350 freight cars.

Couple: Automatic
Braking: Air

Track Rails (kg/m)	Lengths laid 1988 (km)
60	551
50	1041
40	1964
30	2091

Cross ties (sleepers): Wood
Cross-section: 250 × 150 mm
Spacing: 1800/km
Minimum curvature radius, main lines: Metre gauge, 80 m; 1676 mm gauge, 180 m
Max gradient: Adhesion, 6% rack, 8%
Max permissible axleloading: 18 tonnes (metre gauge), 25 tonnes (1676 mm gauge)

Electric railcars or multiple-units

Class	Cars per unit	Line voltage	Motor cars per unit	Motored axles per motor car	Rated output (kW) per motor	Max speed km/h	Weight tonnes per car	Total seating capacity per car	Length per car mm	No in service 1988	Rate acceleration m/s²	Year first built	Builders Mechanical parts	Builders Electrical equipment
AEZ	4	3000	2	4	305	160	75 63	64-72 36-80	25 100 25 100	6	0.7	1973	Kawasaki	Toshiba
AMZ	4	3000	2	4	315	130	64 40	200	23 000 21 120	3	0.53	1961	Breda	Ansaldo-Marelli
AEL	4	3000	2	4	305	130	72 57	88-88 92-88	25 100 25 100	5	0.7	1973	Kawasaki	Toshiba-Hitachi
AES	4	300	1	4	190	130	67 56	79 83	25 230 25 230	12	0.84	1977	Fiat-Concord	Standard-Electric Siam di Tella
AML	4	3000	2	2	315	130	58 36	340	23 000 22 260	2	0.53	1962	Breda	Ansaldo-Marelli

Electric locomotives

Class	Wheel arrangement	Line voltage	Rated output (kW) continous/ one-hour	Max speed km/h	Weight tonnes	Overall length mm	No in service 1988	Year first built	Builders Mechanical parts	Builders Electrical equipment
E-32	C-C	3000	2700/3350	130	136	21 440	19	1962	Breda	Marelli
E-30	B-B	3000	1650/2200	130	96	17 700	18	1962	Breda	Ansaldo-Marelli
E-29	2-C+C-2	3000	3300/2650	120	210	23 060	2	1949	Baldwin-Westinghouse	GE
E-28	1-C+C-1	3000	1360/1700	100	115	17 828	2	1922	Westinghouse	Westinghouse
E-24	B-B	3000	1060/1230	80	70	12 763	4	1949	GE	GE
E-23	B-B	3000	290/410	56	62	12 192	4	1922	Baldwin-Westinghouse	
E-17	B-B	3000	1300/1750	90	76	13 300	20	1973	Breda	Ansaldo-Marelli
E-100*	1-C+C-1	3000	1150/1400	40	85	16 070	1	1926	Brown-Boveri	Brown-Boveri
E-200	B-B	3000	930/1060	60	60	13 470	-	1961	Brown-Boveri	Brown-Boveri

*Rack-equipped

Diesel railcars or multiple-units

Class	No of cars per unit	Motor cars per unit	Motored axles per motor car	Transmission	Rated power (kW) per motor	Max speed km/h	Weight tonnes per car (M-motor T-trailer)	Total seating capacity per car (M-motor T-trailer)	Length per car mm (M-motor T-trailer)	No in service 1988	Year first built	Builders Mechanical parts	Builders Engine & type	Builders Transmission
D-200	2	1	2	Hydr-Mech	134	80	M23.75 T18.80	M50 T40	M13 460 T12 037	1	1962	Ferrostaal 1548-MT	MAN D-DIWABUS	Voith
D-250	2	1	2	Hydr-Mech	134	80	M23.75 T18.80	M50 T40	M13 460 T12 037	3	1962	Ferrostaal	MAN D-1548-MT	380 U+S Voith DIWABUS 380 U+S
D-2000	2	1	2	Hydr-Mech	138	80	M24.5 T21.5	M46 T54	M14 280 T14 280	5	1970	Ferrostaal	MAN D-2556 HM5-US	Voith DIWA 501
ADZ	1	1	4	Hydr	134 (2)	75	33.6	32	19 600	7	1955	Schindler Waggon	A Saurer BDX-SL	A Saurer 8 speeds
ADI	1	1	4	Hydr	134 (2)		33.0	40	19 600		1955	Schindler Waggon	A Saurer BDX-SL	A Saurer 8 speeds

Antofogasta (Chile) & Bolivia Railway plc (FCAB)
Ferrocarril de Antofogasta a Bolivia

Bolivar 255, Casillas S-T, Antofogasta

Telephone: +56 83 215 700
Telex: 325002 fcab ck
Telefax: +56 83 221206

London address: 5 London Wall Buildings, Finsbury Circus, London EC2M 5NT, England

Telephone: +44 71 588 7456
Telex: 8954284 Anrail g

General Manager: Francisco Courbis G
Operations Manager: Patricio Manzor P
Administration & Financial Manager: Guillermo Delgado O
Traffic Manager: Mario Quinteros V
Marketing Manager: Carlos Acuña C
Engineering & Development Manager: Miguel Sepulveda
Technical Manager: H Parez R
Chief Mechanical Engineer: E Ewertz V

Gauge: 1000 mm
Route length: 728 km

After Bolivia's 1964 takeover of the railway's route-mileage in that country, FCAB, which is entirely self-supporting financially, deteriorated badly through lack of investment. But since 1981 a drastic reorganisation of management and method, which also included a halving of staff, has both restored solvency and effected a substantial modernisation. The railway now runs from the Pacific port of Antofogasta to the Argentinian frontier at Socompa on one route, to the Bolivian border at Calam and Ollague on the second.

Traffic	1985	1986	1987
Freight tonnage (million)	1.339	1.347	1.4
Freight tonne-km (million)	359.606	352.688	NA
Passenger-km (million)	3.549	1.248	NA
Passenger journeys	9716	6177	NA

The railway now hopes for important growth coming mainly from two markets. First, at the Codelco Chuquicamata copper mine a new sulphuric acid plant was to go on stream producing 200 000 tonnes per annum. Additional capacity planned for start-up in 1989 was to boost production to 600 000 tonnes. The port for shipping is Antofagasta, 270 km distant, and in 1987 FCAB acquired 80 new wagons to transport the copper sheet for export (see below). Second, through an important marketing effort, agricultural traffic from north-west Argentina has already doubled. FCAB foresees a mid-term potential of 400 000 tonnes a year and a long-range potential of over 1 million.

Investment
Recent capital investment has been oriented towards improving the service of copper transportation provided for Codelco. Until recently this service was provided with old cars of a low payload to tare weight ratio. Due to the large inventory of cars required both operational and maintenance expenses were very high. FCAB has now developed a car designed both for greater capacity (45 tonnes versus 20 to 25 tonnes of the older cars) and to ease loading and unloading operations. The 80 new cars have been built using the structure and rolling equipment of 217 secondhand ore cars purchased by FCAB during 1985-86. The braking system of these cars has been improved to incorporate the latest technology and roller bearings have replaced friction bearings. For quicker turnaround of the equipment FCAB has built a transfer yard close to the shipping port, where the copper will be transferred to smaller cars or stocked on the ground until the date of shipment.

Signalling and traffic control
The company's original train control system was changed to radio VHF system in 1984. This covers the full 751 km of the railroad system (main line and branches). All trains, including yard shunting locomotives, are provided with the radio system for route control.

Data processing capabilities are mainly oriented to the administrative area (accounting, budgeting, inventory control, invoicing, purchasing management, etc) and some information systems to support maintenance plans, car interchange, traffic statistics, etc.

Traction and rolling stock
At the start of 1988 FCAB operated 21 diesel locomotives, 6 diesel train-sets, and 2600 freight wagons.

During the year FCAB bought from Canadian National 10 diesel locomotives, 200 freight wagons and 3000 tonnes of rail made redundant by CN Rail's closure of its 1067 mm-gauge Newfoundland system.

Coupler in standard use, freight and passenger cars: enricot and Sharon.
Braking in standard use, locomotive-hauled stock: 26L and 65L with straight control.

Track
Rail: 25 kg/m, 86 km; 32 kg/m, 420 km; 37 kg/m, 245 km
Cross ties (sleepers): Wood (oak) 188 × 254 × 127 mm
Spacing: In plain track: 1422/km; in curves: 1422 km
Fastenings: Wood screw
Minimum curvature radius: 180 m
Max permissible axleload: 15 tonnes
Max gradient: 3%

Diesel locomotives

Manufacture	Model	Rated output hp	Max speed km/h	Year built	No in service 1987
Davenport Dessler		500	55	1958	3
General Motors	GA 18	1100	57	1969	1
General Motors	GA 8	950	55	1965	3
General Motors	GA 18U	1100	96	1977	1
General Motors	GR 12U	1425	95	1961	10
General Motors	GR 12	1425	95	1962	2
General Motors	GR 22CU	1650	97	1969	1

China, People's Republic

Chinese People's Republic Railways (CPPR)

Ministry of Railways, 10 Fuxin Men, Beijing

Telephone: +86 1 864 2845
Telex: 22483 mifra cn

Minister of Railways: Li Sen Mao
Vice-Ministers: Zhang Xin Tai
  Selon Tu Yourui
  Sun Yong Fu
Chairman: Li Kefei
General Manager: Feng Yu Ting
Deputy Director, Railway Construction: Li Wen Yi
  Finance: Tan He-Quan
Chief Engineer, Railway Construction: Tan Bao Xian
  Operations: Wu Feng

Gauge: Almost entirely 1435 mm, some 750 mm
Route length: 54 000 km approx
Electrification: 5000 km approx at 25 kW 50 Hz ac

The Ministry of Railways at present administers 13 CPRR railway bureaux throughout China, as well as most of China's 33 locomotive and rolling stock factories via the Locomotive and Rolling Stock Factories Department.

At the start of 1986 the new politico-economic policy of devolved responsibility and incentives was applied to the national railway. In principle the Ministry of Railways was made financially autonomous. It was set performance standards and development objectives by central government, then required to fulfil the targets and finance construction and other projects from its own resources after paying to the state a 5 per cent tax on its turnover and another of 0.3 per cent on its assets. Among the resultant changes was introduction of staff payment on the basis of results: in other words, the money available for wages would henceforward be related to tonne-km performed. The new policy is being progressively applied by devolution to individual railway regions.

A separate administration, the Guangshen Railway, runs the Chinese section of the Kowloon-Canton Railway, the 147 km line from Guangzhou (Canton) to the Hong Kong border's end-on junction with the British section (see under Hong Kong). Its capacity has been increased by two phases of double-tracking completed in January 1987 in the course of which stations were rebuilt and two more added, following which electrification was planned.

Type DFH3 diesel-hydraulic locomotive and long-distance train at Wong Gung, in Northern China (*Marcel Vleugels*)

540 RAILWAY SYSTEMS / China, People's Republic

Local railways
The government now encourages local authorities to build and operate their own railways of up to 2000 km length, where such investment would stimulate regional economic development. Such local railway systems operate in 11 of the country's provinces. The two biggest are in Henan and Hebei.

In the past 30 years over 6300 route-km of local railway have been built. Much of this construction was subsequently absorbed in the national railway system as the latter's new line construction made junction contact with local development. Naturally, this was especially the case where local lines had been built to 1435 mm gauge. Nevertheless local railways have had to meet set parameters of gradient, curve radius, maximum permissible axleloading, etc, to be eligible for a national railway takeover.

Local railway construction continues on a considerable scale and route length was forecast to reach 15 000 km by 1990. In 1989 plans were active for 40 new lines aggregating some 2000 route-km.

1989-90 Five-Year Plan
Capital investment equivalent to US$8100 million in railways under the country's 1986-90 Five-Year plan has been focused, so far as infrastructure is concerned, on the central eastern area of China, which was allocated a fifth of the total funds. As described below, new line construction to establish modernised alternative routes to the coastal area around Shanghai is a feature of the proposals.

Passenger traffic
Relentlessly rising demand for passenger and freight transportation outstrips both infrastructure and rolling stock capacity. In 1988, the most recent for which detailed figures are available, the railways recorded 1215.95 million passenger journeys and 325 731 million passenger-km. A new record for a single day's passenger movement was set in May 1988, when 3.96 million journeys were recorded.

Between 1968 and 1989 passenger traffic quadrupled, whereas the number of trains run rose by only 1.7 per cent. Consequently severe overcrowding was common, inability to buy a ticket likewise in some major cities.

To stop this congestion fares were abruptly doubled in September 1989. As a result the daily average of passenger journeys dropped sharply from 3.5 million to 2.7 million.

To cope with demand, passenger trains of 20 to 25 cars are operated on some key routes, such as Beijing-Guangzhou. The aim is to standardise 20-coach trains on other lines, such as Beijing-Shanghai and Beijing-Dalian, but progress is dependent on the rate at which station accommodation can be enlarged. Meanwhile management has to resort to such expedients as substituting day coaches for sleeping cars and trolley refreshment service for restaurant cars to increase train capacity; and, on the Nanjing-Qiqihar section, to running 26-car trains formed of two self-contained 13-car consists, into which the formation is split for separate platforming at each intermediate stop. Such a train normally includes five sleeping, two restaurant and two dining cars, and can accommodate 2300 passengers.

In another move to ease pressure a prototype 16-car bi-level train-set was introduced to Shanghai-Nanjing service in 1989. Built by the Puzhen works in Nanjing, the air-conditioned train-set can seat over 3000 and can operate at 120km/h.

In 1990 Vice-Minister Selon Tu Tourui revealed that opinion was tending to belief that separation of passenger and freight traffic was the only solution to congestion on prime rail axes. Consequently studies had begun of a pilot scheme for a 200 km/h line reserved to passenger trains. The two routes under review for the experiment were Beijing-Tinajin (137km) and Guangzhou to the Hongkong border at Shenzhen (143km).

Freight traffic
Freight tonnage has been rising with similar rapidity. Over 70 000 wagons a day are being despatched under load. In 1988, the most recent for which detailed figures are available, rail freight movement grossed 1405.5 million tonnes, 40 per cent of it coal, and 986 019 million tonne-km. Here too, there is shortage of capacity, and consequent inability to supply raw materials regularly to some manufacturing plants, driving them to temporary closure.

Canadian National has signed an agreement to assist in the computerisation of freight operations.

Dong Feng 4C diesel locomotive

CANAC Consultants Ltd, a subsidiary of CN, will introduce Canadian National's Yard Inventory System (YIS). Included in the package is the Canadian software needed to implement the system, technical assistance to adapt YIS for Chinese railway conditions, some CN-designed hardware and staff training. The technology transfer involves setting a pilot project in which Chinese Railways can evaluate hardware and software alternatives and plan future development and implementation strategy.

The Ministry of Railways aims to raise individual train weights by a third, to a norm of 3000–4000 tonnes, which by 1989 had been achieved on nine trunk routes. The development has been fraught with several problems, such as yard siding and loop capacities, and not least the limitations of most of the existing wagon stock. These are largely fitted with plain bearings and restricted to maximum speeds of 60 km/h. To accelerate development of a more modern fleet, a roller bearing works has been established to speed conversion of existing wagons as well as to supply new wagon construction.

Motive power
The pace of traction and rolling stock production by China's factories is phenomenal. In 1989 industry was budgeted to turn out 214 electric, 520 diesel and just 20 steam locomotives.

Steam locomotive production at Datong works was terminated in December 1988. Until then it had been necessary since vigorous expansion of diesel traction and electrification was inadequate to match traffic demand. Modest construction of the Class JS 2-8-2 continued elsewhere in 1989, but the railway's stock was set to reduce by about 3000 units in the 1990s.

The railways now operate a large fleet of the locally-built 2640 kW Dong Feng 4 freight Co-Co diesels. Over 4000 are expected to be in use by the century's end. Other standard Chinese-built types are the Beijing passenger locomotive and the Tangshan-built Dong Feng 5, a heavy shunter which also deals in local passenger and freight haulage. A 4000hp Dong Feng 6 has been developed for freight haulage by Dalian works, and a Dong Feng 8 version for freight haulage is reported.

In recent years imports have developed rapidly, both of diesel and electric units. In 1983 General Electric (USA) was given a contract to supply 220 of its Type C36-7 4000 hp Co-Co diesel-electrics for freight haulage. Deliveries were completed in 1984. Chinese staff were trained at GE's Erie plant, and GE sent technical staff to China to assist in the servicing of the locomotives. A repeat order for 200 more C36-7s, designated Class ND5 in China, was then placed with GE.

In 1989 Electroputere of Romania, already the supplier of close on 300 diesel and 45 5400kW Co-Co electric locomotives, was contracted to supply 20 more diesel locomotives of similar design to those the Romanian factory has supplied in great quantity to its home railway. Price per unit was reported as a modest US$ 800 000.

To serve newly-electrified lines, Chinese builders have supplied new 138-tonne Shaoshan SS3-type electric locomotives, a development of the preceding SS1 and SS2 designs offering enhanced adhesion and equipped with single-arm pantographs. Most of the Shaoshan series have a one-hour rating of 4200 kW at 44.6 km/h (continuous rating 3780 kW at 45.9 km/h) and employ silicon rectifiers with tap-changer control of power, but the latest version is rated at 4800 kW and, though still equipped with silicon rectifiers, has thyristors to regulate motor excitation. All have a maximum speed of 95 km/h.

A Shaoshan 4 Bo-Bo + Bo-Bo development of the Shaoshan 3 Co-Co is now in series production at the Zhizhou plant in Human province. With thyristor control, the new type weighs 184 tonnes, is rated at 6490 kW and has a top speed of 100 km/h. It will be the standard traction of the new Daqin Coal line (see below), hauling 6000-tonne trains single-handed or 10 000-tonne trains in tandem. In prospect for the 1990s is evolution of a three-phase motor design employing Federal German technology.

Dong Feng 5 diesel locomotive

In March 1985 the 50 c/s Group, with French industry the chief protagonist, secured an order for 150 6400 kW, 184-tonne B-B + B-B electric locomotives valued in French currency at Fr2600 million. The contract provided for 10 locomotives of the order to be assembled in China as a preliminary to technology transfer for future construction of complete locomotives to the 50 c/s design in China. Execution of the order was shared by AEG, Siemens, ACEC and BBC Brown Boveri, but 130 of the locomotives were assembled in France, mostly by Alsthom at Belfort, where their mechanical parts were chiefly manufactured; and whence the first complete locomotives of the order were shipped in 1986. The contribution of the other group members was principally electrical equipment. Delivery of the second half of the order was temporarily delayed in the summer of 1987 while teething difficulties encountered in China with the first 60 or so twin-units were resolved.

In April 1986 a contract, funded under a Japanese line of credit, was signed with a consortium of Sumitomo, Kawasaki and Mitsubishi Electric for 80 micro-processor-equipped, thyristor-controlled, 138-tonne 4800 kW Co-Cos to haul Zhengzhou-Baoji coal traffic. Delivery was executed in full in 1987-88. The locomotives are classified 6K. China is also buying 100 electric locomotives from the USSR.

At the start of 1990 traction stock comprised 7117 steam, 4734 diesel and 1197 electric locomotives.

Rolling stock

The country's four coach manufacturing plants have lately been manufacturing about 1450 vehicles a year. In 1985 the World Bank aided a quest for a new standard vehicle design with which China's major carbuilding plant, at Changchun, could be adapted to raise its annual output from 900 to 1500 vehicles a year. Seven companies submitted propositions: Alsthom of France; BREL of England; Linke-Hofmann-Busch of the Federal Republic of Germany; UTDC of Canada; Tokyu Car of Japan; Schindler of Switzerland; and the Indian Railways Integral Coach Factory. As a result, in 1986 BREL secured an initial contract worth almost £5 million with the China National Technical Import Corporation (CNTIC) on behalf of the Chinese Ministry of Railways. The contract was for the design and supply of three prototype passenger coaches based on BREL's International design and for assistance in the modernisation of the Changchun factory. The coaches would be delivered in 1988. In addition, industry in the German Democratic Republic was commissioned to deliver 250 sleeping and 50 day cars in 1988-89; and BN of Belgium, 146 freight wagons.

At the start of 1989 rolling stock comprised 24 725 passenger cars (including 1427 restaurant and 4233 sleeping cars) and 338 644 freight cars.

World Bank loan

In the autumn of 1989 the Chinese press reported that a fifth World Bank loan of at least US$300 million was in course of negotiation. The four previous long-term loans from this source, granted from 1984 onwards, had totalled US$885 million. The new loan would be devoted to improvements of infrastructure and rolling stock in the east of the country.

Electrification

Electrification at 25 kV 50 Hz has been a high priority throughout the 1980s. By the end of 1988 at least 5000 route-km were under wires and forward targets were 9000 route-km by 1990, almost 20 000 route-km by the century's end. By 1989, electric traction was responsible for 13.3 per cent, diesel traction for 46.9 per cent and steam traction for 38.8 per cent of the railways' gross tonne-km haulage.

The 1986–90 electrification programme covered eight routes, one of which, the 296 km from Zhengzhou to Sanmenxia, was finished at the end of 1986. By 1989 these wires had been extended over the 234 km from Sanmenxia to Baoji, there linking up with the already wired stretch to Lanzhou in the west so as to complete an unbroken east-west electrification of 1187 km.

Top priority has been to complete wiring of the double-track coal line from Datong, the key coal railhead in Shanxi province, to the port of Qinhuangdao (see below). On another coal route, the 355 km from Datong south to a junction with the electrified east-west transversal at Taiyuan, wiring was complete and electric haulage inaugurated in August 1989.

Other schemes are in the centre and southern half of the country. In pursuit of electric traction over the whole length of the 2313 km north-south corridor from Beijing to Guangzhou, close to Hong Kong, the wires are being erected over the 547 route-km from Zhengzhou to Wuhan, with the backing of a World Bank loan. This scheme embodies CTC, fibre-optic cabling, jointless track circuits and computerised interlockings. Further south Guiyang is the focus of three schemes: the 902 km eastward to Zhouzou, the 463 km north to Chongqing, and the 395 km from Shuicheng to Kunming. On this last route energisation of a further 132km at the end of 1989 had carried the wires from Guiyang to Xuanwei.The eighth project covers the 694 km from Vingtan southward to Xiamen port, in the southeastern Fujan province.

Plans for subsequent electrification include the 1462 km route from Beijing to Shanghai.

New lines

New line is being added to the system every year, partly to relieve pressure on the heavily occupied trunk routes in the east of the country, where the bulk of the network is concentrated, partly to extend railways into the western provinces which are almost without rail transport. The target is an 80 000 route-km system by the end of the century.

The most daunting project, construction of a 2200 km line from Xining, in Tsinghai province, to the Tibetan capital, Lasa, remains halted at Golmud, 835 km out. The rest of the route lies almost entirely at 4000 metres or more above sea level, up to a peak of 5000 metres at the Tangla pass, in a region where not only is the terrain permanently frozen to a depth of several metres and ambient temperature below –20°C for six months of the year, but seismic disturbance is also a chronic difficulty. These conditions have demanded exhaustive research into durable track structures before construction can continue. No date has yet been set for this. The thinness of the air will demand pressurised passenger car interiors and special designs of diesel locomotive with two-stage turbo-charging.

China's busiest artery is the north-south route of 2313 km from Beijing via Zhengzhou to Guangzhou (formerly Canton), and in the country's east a recent priority has been this line's relief by the construction of links between other existing routes to its east and west so as to create two additional and parallel trunk lines from north to south. The main line itself is now double track throughout since the 1987 completion of 514 km from Hengyang to Guangzhou by a labour force of 60 000 working round the clock. This project included construction of China's longest double-track tunnel, 14.3 km, through the Dayas mountain on the Guangdong-Hunan border.

In 1988 the World Bank agreed a US$200 million loan towards double-tracking 489 km in Hubei and Henan provinces from Yueshan, northwest of Zhengzhou, through Luoyang and Nanyang to Xiangfan, in the south; this should be finished in 1993. The 119 km from Yueshan to Luoyang will be electrified. The enlarged route will serve to relieve the Zhengzhou north-south main line.

Double-tracking of the 296km route from Taiyuan south to Houma was finished in August 1989. During the year plans were published to complete double-tracking of the southwestward transversal route from Shanghai as far as Hangzhou by the end of 1990, and of the 944km from Hangzhou on to Zhuzhou, junction with the north-south Zhengzou-Guangzhou trunk, by 1994. Other double-tracking, expected to be finished in 1990, covered the 360 km

Alsthom-built 6400 kW B-B+B-B electric locomotive

Prototype 4000kW Dong Feng 6 diesel locomotive

RAILWAY SYSTEMS / China, People's Republic

from Ji'nan to Qingdao, and the 220 km from Xuzhou to Lianyungang.

To the east a new single-track 539 km railway from Wuhu, south of Nanjing, to Guixi was opened in 1984; this addition made the Beijing-Shanghai line a route to Jiangxi province also. A 125 km line from Fuyang, south east of Zhengzhou, to Hainan, on the Xuzhou-Hefei-Wuhu route, has provided further north-south relief and has subsequently been developed by construction of new feeder lines from the northwest (see below). Much further north, another recent achievement was the 220 km Handan-Changzhi line across the Taihang mountains to link Hebei and Shanxi provinces; its construction involved 49 tunnels and 108 bridges.

Austrian co-operation
In 1989 the government concluded co-operation agreements with the Austrian railway industry. Advice on passenger coach design and manufacture would be furnished by Simmering-Graz-Pauker and Jenbacher Werke. Elin Union would help with electrification.

Coal route expansion
In both new line construction and electrification, expansion of coal-carrying capacity is of paramount importance. China's domestic energy needs are 70 per cent met by coal and at the same time exports rise steadily; from one coalfield alone, the Shanxi province, where reserves are put at almost 200 000 million tonnes, shipments abroad are expected to top 150. The country's principal coalfields are found in Shanxi, Inner Mongolia, Henan, Shandong, Ningxia, Guizhou, Anhui and Heliongjiang provinces. Coal flows are predominantly north-to-south and west-to-east, and form over half the traffic on some main lines, such as Beijing-Shanhaiguan, Beijing-Baotou, Beijing-Guangzhou, Harbin-Dalian and Tianjin-Nanjing.

The Ministry of Railways is embarked on a 10-year programme aimed to raise rail coal-carrying capacity to over 600 million tonnes a year. It involves the upgrading of 12 existing coal routes and the construction of eight more, plus a lift of maximum trainloads on key routes from 3500 to 6000–10 000 tonnes. The requirements of the coal traffic dominated the double-tracking, new line building and electrification executed in the 1980s. Five lines have already been completed primarily to serve the coal industry: Baotou-Lanzhou; Yuanping-Beijing; Jiaozuo-Xiangfan; Taiyan-Jiaozuo; and Changzhi-Handan.

In the north the west-to-east coal route has been electrified from Baotou and Datong to the outskirts of Beijing, where, from Fengtai, a 281 km new line was completed in December 1984 to the major coal shipment port of Qinhuangdao. Double-tracking of the whole 423km from Datong to Batou was finished in March 1990.

From Ji'ning, north of Datong, a new 948km single line is soon to be started to Tongliao. Completion of this line, which is to improve coal distribution in northeast China, is forecast for 1993.

The Qinhuangdao port facilities are being expanded, since the route from Baotou is set to carry China's heaviest coal trains. Construction to this port of a 630 km direct line from Datong via Huairou, north of Beijing, known as the Daqin line, began in April, 1986, to lift operating capacity over both routes to a combined total of 100 million tonnes a year. In December 1988 a further section of the 25 kV 50 Hz ac electrified line was formally opened, bringing into full use 410 km of route from Datong through Huairou, north of Beijing, to Dashizhuang. The residual 220 km to Qinhuangdao should be finished by 1991. Canadian Pacific Consulting Services has been contracted to study the feasibility of North American-type unit train working between the Shanxi coalfield and Qinhuangdao. The Fengtai-Qinhuangdao project is one of three for which the aid of the Japanese International Cooperation Agency has been enlisted. A second is upgrading of the line from Beijing south-east to Tianjin, the route to Shanghai.

Another new route is being created out of the great Shanxi coalfield by construction of a new electrified, double-track line 270km eastward from Shenmu, south of Baotou, to Shuoxian, on the main north-south route from Datong to Taiyuan. Completion is expected in 1992. The aim is then to continue for a further 500km eastward to a new coal port at Huanghua. Forecasts are that the completed route will be carrying 50–60 million tonnes of coal a year in the late 1990s.

The first of the 80 Japanese-built 4800 kW electric locomotives

Elsewhere in Shanxi a 170 km coal-carrying branch is being built from Yan'an south to Tongchuan, for access to the Baoji-Zhengzhou transversal in the area of Xi'an.

A further new west-to-east coal route of some 800 km is being assembled in the south. It involves new construction, started in 1987, from Houma to Yueshan (246 km), from where there is already a lateral line to Xinxiang. More new construction will project the route 150 km from Xinxiang to the existing railway linking Heze with the heart of the Shandong coalfield at Yanzhou. As already mentioned, a direct line from Yanzhou to Shijiuso is now operational.

The whole of the 1800 km lateral route from Lanzhou to Lianyungang is to be double-tracked and electrified. As remarked above, electrification work has been on its central section between Xi'an and Zhengzhou, to the east of which two new lines are being built for the benefit of the coalfields in western Henan, around Zhoukou. A further coal input to the Lianyungang port route will be soon operational, a 315km line from Yan'an, in the north of Shanxi, south to X'ian. A 143 km cut-off from Luohe, on the main line south of Zhengzhou, eastward to Fuyang, was opened in 1989.

A 173 km link between Shangqui, east of Zhengzhou, and Fuyang was also completed in 1989. This is part of the development of an alternative 1000 km

Diesel locomotives

Class	Wheel arrangement	Transmission	Rated power kW	Max speed km/h	Total weight tonnes	Year first built	Builders Mechanical parts	Engine & type	Transmission
DF	Co-Co	Elec	1350	100	126	1958	Dalian	10E207	ZQFR 1350
DF2	Co-Co	Elec	750	95.3	113	–	Dalian	6E207	–
DF3	Co-Co	Elec	1350	120	126	1972	Dalian	10E207	ZQFR 1350
DF4	Co-Co	Elec	2680	100/120*	138	Dalian	16 240 Z/ZA	TQFR 3000†	
DF5	Co-Co	Elec	1230	100	–	1976	Tangshan	8240Z	†
DF7	Co-Co	Elec	1500	–	–	1981	Beijing February 8	12 240Z	†
DF8	Co-Co	Elec	3000	120	–	1987	Qishuyian	–	–
DFH1	B-B	Hyd	1350	140	84	–	Qingado	2 × 12 175Z	2 × SF 2010
DFH2	B-B	Hyd	750	50	60	–	Qingdao	12 180Z	SF 2010
DFH3	B-B	Hyd	2000	120	84	–	Qingdao	2 × 12 180ZL	2 × SF 2010Z
DFH5	B-B	Hyd	930	40/80	84	–	Qingdao	12 180ZL	SF 2010
DFH	B-B	Hyd	450	35/72	–	1964	Qingdao	–	–
BJ 3000	B-B	Hyd	2000	120	92	1075	Beijing February 7	12 240Z	EQ 2027
BJ 6000	D-D	Hyd	4000	–	–	1969	Beijing February 7	2 × 12 240Z	2 × EQ 2027
ND2	Co-Co	Elec	1540	100	120	1974	Electroputere	Sulzer 12LDA288	Electroputere
ND4	Co-Co	Elec	2945	100	138	1973	Alsthom	AGO 240V16 ESHR	MTE†
ND5 (C36-7)	Co-Co	Elec	2980	120	210	1984	General Electric	GEFDL16	General Electric
ND15	Bo-Bo	Elec	450	80	62	1958	Ganz-Mávag	16 JV 17/24	Ganz
NY5	C-C	Hyd	2760	160	130	1966	Henschel	2 × MB 839B6	2 × Voith L830rU
NY6	C-C	Hyd	3200	120	138	1972	Henschel	2 × MB 16V 652	2 × Voith L820
NY7	C-C	Hyd	3740	120	138	1972	Henschel	2 × MA 12V 956	2 × Voith L820
NY14	B-B	Hyd	690	100	65	1973	VEB LEW	MJW 12 KVD 21 A111	GRS 30/57
NY16	B-B	Hyd	870	110	68	1975	23rd August, Romania	Sulzer 6LDA 28B	TH2

* Nos 2001 onwards † Alternator

Electric locomotives

Class	Wheel arrangement	Line voltage	Rated output kW continuous	Max speed km/h	Weight tonnes	Length mm	Year first built	Builders Mechanical parts	Electrical equipment
SS1	Co-Co	25 kV	4200	95	138	20 400	1958	Zhouzhou	–
6Y2	Co-Co	25 kV	4800	100	138	21 332	1960	Alsthom	Alsthom
6G5O	Co-Co	25 kV	5600	110	138	21 330	1972	Alsthom	Alsthom
SS3	Co-Co	25 kV	4800	100	138	21 680	1975	Zhouzhou	–
SS45	Bo-Bo + Bo-Bo	25 kV	6400	100	184	32 900	1986	Zhouzhou	–
6G1	Co-Co	25 kV	5400	110	126	19 010	1971	Electrputere, Romania	ASEA
8K	Bo-Bo + Bo-Bo	25 kV	6400	100	184	2 × 16 746	1986	50 c/s Group	50 c/s Group
6K	Bo-Bo-Bo	25 kV	4800	100	138	NA	1987	Kawasaki	Mitsubishi

north-south route to the Shanghai area (see below). The Lanzhou-Lianyungang route is set to take on more coal traffic, as construction began in 1987 of a new 490 km railway through the mountains southward from Zhongwei, on the Lanzhou-Baotou route to Baoji, to develop the Gansu and Ningxia coalfields. Provincial governments are sharing the investment in this scheme, which is designed to benefit their coalfields. The first 132 km from Baoji to Ankou were ready in late 1989.

It is now proposed to develop the Shangqui-Fuyang new line, mentioned above, as the start of an alternative trunk route more than 1000 km long to the Shanghai area, to the further benefit of Shanxi coal output. The single-track line from Fuyang to Hefei and Yuxikou will be upgraded. The outstanding item of the project occurs in the next section of the route; that is supersession of the present train ferry crossing of the great Yangtze river to Wuhu with a bridge that will rival the Shanghai main line's 12 km spanning of the river further east at Nanjing for scale. Construction began in late 1987 and spans three years. Completion of the new route to the port of Hangzhou, southwest of Shanghai, involves upgrading of existing single-track lines from Wuhu to Xuancheng, and from Hangzhou northwestward to Niutoushan; and closure of the gap between them with a new 125 km line around the mountains. Further up the Yangtse, a link is being built from Daye to Jiujiang to shorten the distance from Wuhan, extremity of the southward electrification from Zhengzhou (see above) to Nanchang.

In the southeast, a coastal line of 250 km is under construction from Xiamen (the former Amoy) to Shanjou (formerly Swatow); and, further west, another link of 320 km from Sanshui, west of Guangzhou, to Moaming.

In 1985 a major new scheme was added to the agenda. It concerns a new Jitong line of some 850 km from Jining, north of Datong, through Inner Mongolia to a rich mineral area around Tongliao, in the north-east.

In the far north-west, in Xinjiang province, a 236 km line from the provincial capital, Urumqi, to Usu was finished in September 1987 and in late 1988 an extension of 224 km from Usu through the Alatau Pass to Lankol in the USSR was begun. Eager for completion of this connection, the USSR has supplied rail to accelerate the project, completion of which was expected in October 1990. Besides opening up Xingjiang province's considerable mineral resources, which include 35 per cent of China's coal reserves and also oil, this line may also develop as a landbridge between the Far East and Europe. For Japanese industry there will be direct access to the international route via the Chinese ports of Linayungang or Shanghai.

Also in the far north, Harbin's former link with the USSR that has been derelict since the 1940s, the 303 km Bei'-an-Heihe line, is being rehabilitated.

Signalling and communications
Elin of Austria is supplying a track-to-train radio system embracing some 600 route-km south of Beijing. The country's first solid state interlocking is being supplied by GEC-General Signal; it will be installed at Xiao Li Zhang, on the Zhengzhou-Wuchang line.

Permanent way
Standard rails are 50 kg/m, with 43 kg/m on less busy routes. These two types account for the bulk of the system's track, but 60 kg/m has been applied to key routes radiating from Beijing since 1978. Continuously welded, with elastic fastenings, prestressed concrete sleepers and hard rock ballast, 60 kg/m rail is regarded as adequate for all foreseeable operating requirements. Sleepers are spaced 1760 per km. Track maintenance is now 50 per cent mechanised.

Colombia

Ministry of Public Works and Transport

Bogotá

Minister: Luis Fernando Jaramillo Correa
Deputy Minister: Ernesto Felipe Velasquez Salazar

National Railways of Colombia (FNdeC)
Ferrocarriles Nacionales de Colombia

Calle 13 No 18, 24 Bogotá

Telephone: +57 2 77 5577
Cable: Ferrocarriles

Chairman: J Arias R
General Manager: Sergio Hugo Amaya Córdoba
Special Adviser: G M Mario Ballesteros
Technical Manager: Victor Solano Duran
Finance Manager: Herbert Cabrera Martinez
Commercial Manager: Jorge Rojas Martinez
Legal Adviser: T Sanchez
Systems Adviser: Heriberto Zarate Olarte
Secretary General: Rodrigo Toledo Zamora
Directors, Accounts: Luis Hernando Morales
  Maintenance of Way: R Dueñas
  Finance: Luis Uriel, Palacio Torres
  Materials: Hernan Copete
  Marketing: Aldolfo Cortes Torrado
  Personnel: German Dario Hernandez Vera
  Transportation: Guillermo Villamarin Eslara
  Workshops: Affif Nassas

Gauge: 914 mm
Route length: 3236 km (1989: 2611 km only in use)

Traffic	1983	1984	1985	1987	1988
Freight tonnes (million)	1.247	1.268	1.333	1.058	1.2
Freight tonne-km (million)	641.6	725.6	774.4	565.155	694
Passenger journeys (million)	1.295	1.445	2.6	1.48	1.5
Passenger-km (million)	175.066	192.789	237.8	176.768	181.0

Financial crisis
In recent years FNdeC has lost traffic through poor availability of traction and rolling stock, and also through numerous interruptions of service by lowland floods and landslides in the rugged Andean valleys. The Andean routes are marked by gradients as steep as 4 per cent and curves as sharp as 80 m radius, which are a further brake on freight operating capability. Of late the railway has been working at only a quarter of its capacity, and its national market share of freight has slumped to 4 per cent.

By 1987 FNdeC was in so critical a condition, both physically and financially, that the Public Works Minister and the railway's management were locked in a struggle with other Ministries and the legislature to prevent complete abandonment of the railway. Apart from the lapse into disuse of 700 route-km of the system, 80 per cent of the remainder was in poor condition and by 1988 only a fifth of the railway's locomotives and fewer than half its freight cars were reported usable.

In 1986 FNdeC gained offer of a World Bank loan of US$77 million towards a proposed US$177 million rehabilitation programme spread over the period to 1992. It was to cover reconstruction of some 900 km of track, overhaul of some 140 locomotives and 1400 freight wagons, purchase of eight locomotives and 200 wagons, and signalling and telecommunications work. But more than half this credit was withdrawn in February 1987 because the government failed to fulfil a commitment to provide additional funds for emergency repair work.

In late 1987 the government received a study of the railway's condition and needs by a Colombo-Spanish consortium. This gloomily reported that 90 per cent of the infrastructure needed attention. An immediate cash infusion of US$615 million was needed, as much as US$2000 million in the medium term alone.

By the end of 1988 the railway was US$60 million in debt and still without promise of curing its alleged inefficiency and over-staffing. Independent analysts believe staff could be halved. However, the government is determined to preserve a rail system. Early in 1988 it framed new legislation setting a period of 18 months for a restructure and rehabilitation of the system. Liquidation of the state railway system as at present constituted looks certain. In its place a state corporation will be set up to manage the infrastructure; another company, hopefully combining public and private sector, will run the trains and the railway's workshops. It is possible that this new order will restrict the railway to freight operation. Given annual investment of around US$50 million a year, it was hoped that the railway could lift its present annual freight gross of 1.2 million tonnes, which represents a national market share of only 4 per cent, to 4.5 million tonnes by the end of the century.

Oil industry development is forecast to generate up to 11 000 tonnes of freight a day in the northeast of the country by the end of the 1990s and local state governors have joined with commercial interests in pressing for rehabilitation of the 258 km line from Bogota to Belencito. The oil industry also wants US$2 million spent to renovate the 618 km south-north line from workings at Neiva to Barrancabermeja, whence oil could be piped to a Caribbean port. Moreover, the country now has a major coal export trade.

New lines
FNdeC cherishes two long-planned new line schemes. Construction of a cut-off between Ibague and Armenia that would obviate the circuitous journey from Bogota to the west coast of Buenaventura via Puerto Berrio was abandoned in 1930. The project has since been revived, but on a shorter 85 km route between the two points that entails driving a 22 km-long tunnel. Its achievement, likely to take five years, would reduce the rail distance from Bogota to Buenaventura by no less than 500 km.

The other project concerns a 180 km link between Saboya and Puerto Carare, known as the Carare Railway. This line would provide a new connection between the northern and Atlantic lines and cut the transport distance between Santa Marta and Bogota

Diesel locomotives

Type	Wheel arrangement	Transmission	Rated power hp	Max speed km/h	Wheel dia mm	Weight tons	Length mm	Year first built	No in service 1985	Manufacturers Mechanical	Manufacturers Transmission
GE-U6B	Bo-Bo	Elec	750	80	914	53	10 211	1960	8	GE	GE
GE-U8B	Bo-Bo	Elec	850	80	914	58	10 211	1961	7	GE	GE
GM GA-8	Bo-Bo	Elec	850	85	838	54.5	10 823	1964	2	GM	GM
GE U10-8B	Bo-Bo	Elec	1050	80	914	60	11 171	1969/73	74	Alco-GE	GE
Alco	Co-Bo-Co	Elec	1600	48	833	114.7	17 323	1953	5	GE	GE
GE U12C	Co-Co	Elec	1300	80	914	88	13 903	1958	18	GE	GE
GE U13C	Co-Co	Elec	1400	80	914	88	13 903	1958	6	GE	GE
GM GR-12	Co-Co	Elec	1425	85	1016	91	14 427	1963	24	GM	GM
GE-U20 C	Co-Co	Elec	2050	80	914	90	15 926	1964	10	GE	GE

by 350 km. Ruling gradient would be 2.4 per cent, minimum curve radius 200 metres. Rails would be 56 kg/m to sustain 20-tonne axleloads in moving coal traffic from the Checua and Lenguazaque deposits.

The project would involve lifting a line from 100 m above the sea level to an altitude of 2560 m at Saboya. Construction would involve some 90 tunnels aggregating over 30 km in length and about 50 significant bridges or viaducts. The line's completion would shorten the rail transit between the country's central coalfields and the Caribbean port of Santa Marta by some 300 km and quadruple the operating capacity of the route's core.

Also under consideration has been resurrection on a new 93 km alignment of the Cali-Medellin line's section between La Pintada and Caldas, derelict since flooding and landslides in 1976; and construction of 240 km of new railway to connect the northern ports of Cartagena and Barranquilla with the Santa Marta line at Fundación.

In 1988 a Japanese technical mission was working with the Colombian government to examine the feasibility of an Atlantic-Pacific link consisting of a motorway, railway and oil pipeline. The project would involve construction of a new port on the Gulf of Cupica on the Pacific coast which would be connected with Colombia's Atlantic coast by road, rail and pipeline. Japan's foreign aid budget is funding the study, though that does not mean that Japan will necessarily contribute to the cost of the project if and when it is carried out. The technical mission is operating at a time when fresh uncertainties exist concerning Panama Canal capacity and plans to build a second canal alongside the first.

Motive power and rolling stock
Motive power in ownership in 1989 comprised six steam locomotives, 153 diesel-electric locomotives, 16 diesel railcars and 22 trailers. Four GE U18-C locomotives were procured in 1986. Total number of passenger train coaches owned in 1989 was 164 (including 6 sleeping, 19 restaurant, 1 bar car and 14 luggage vans); freight wagons, 4111.

Track
Rail: 55, 60 and 75 lb/yd
Cross ties (sleepers): Wood
Thickness: 150 mm
Spacing: In plain track 1666/km in curves 1700/km
Minimum curvature radius: 80 m
Max gradient: 3.8%
Max speed: 62 km/h
Max axleload: 15 tonnes
Max altitude: 2900 m

El Cerejon Coal Railway

Gauge: 1435 mm
Route length: 150 km

Constructed by Morrison Knudsen in several months less than the originally scheduled time-scale, this new railway was built at a cost of US$300 million for Carbocol, the national coal-mining corporation, and Intercor, an Exxon affiliate. These two organisations have jointly developed South America's biggest coal-producing project in an opencast operation in the north-eastern province of Guajira. By the end of the 1980s it was expected that the new railway would be carrying 15 million tonnes of coal annually from the El Cerejon complex to a new coal shipment port close to the Venezuelan border at Bahia de Portete.

The line has been laid with 61.8 kg/m rail (supplied by the British Steel Corporation), continuously welded, on timber sleepers. The route is through scrubland, which has helped to restrict ruling gradients to 0.3 per cent against loaded trains, 1 per cent in the reverse direction. At the mine, where trains are overhead-loaded from a pair of 10 000 tonnes-capacity silos, and at the port, where the 91-tonne coal wagons are bottom door-discharged, track lay-outs are in loop form to allow merry-go-round operation of the trains. Thus each 93-wagon train is planned to achieve three return trips within the 24 hours.

The hopper wagons have been supplied by Ortner. The locomotives are General Electric Type B36-7 2685 kW Bo-Bos.

Congo

Ministry of Transport & Civil Aviation

Brazzaville

Minister: R D Ngollo

Chemin de Fer Congo-Océan (CFCO)

PO Box 651, Pointe Noire

Telephone: +242 94 25 63
Cable: Congoocéan
Telex: Cfco 8231 kg

General Manager: Noël Bouanga
Technical Manager: M Louchart
Chief, General Sept: A Yalouca-Gama
Chief Operating Superintendent: A Moussayandi
Chief of Motive Power: Jean Zoungani
Chief Civil Engineer: Jacques Koutoundou
Chief of Supplies: Joseph Yongolo-Tchizinga

Gauge: 1067 mm
Route length: 517 km

Congo is served by the Congo-Ocean Railway which extends 509 km from Pointe Noire to Brazzaville, between which points there is no paved road. A 285 km branch line, built by the Compagnie Minière de l'Ogooue (Comilog) connects Mort-Belo station (200 km from Pointe Noire) with M'Binda and public service over this line is now provided by the Congo-Ocean Railway. The Comilog railway shifts some 2 million tonnes of manganese per annum.

The CFCO is a department within the Agence Trans-congolaise des Communications (ATC).

Traffic
Freight traffic was reviving after a severe drop in 1981, but in 1987 the railway's traffic was again diminished, this time as a result of the country's economic problems caused by falling export oil prices. The government consequently trimmed investment in the railway.

Passenger carryings slumped 15 per cent, but freight was down by over 20 per cent in containers and general merchandise, by as much as 45 per cent in raw materials. However, recovery began in 1988, with passenger traffic rising by 5 per cent and freight volume by 6.5 per cent.

Motive power and rolling stock
CFCO operates 54 diesel-electric locomotives, 25 diesel shunters, five diesel railcars, 107 passenger cars and 1682 freight wagons.

In 1985 CFCO took delivery of 15 4200 hp Co-Co locomotives (eight from GM Canada and seven from Alsthom) and five 400 hp locotractors. Its previous main-line locomotive stock comprised eight 3600 hp 18 1800 hp and 13 1000–1100 hp units.

New air-conditioned cars procured from British Rail Engineering are employed in an overnight service, the 'Train Bleu', between Pointe Noire and Brazzaville.

Route realignment
The first 91 km realignment of the Pointe Noire-Brazzaville line, between Loubomo and Bilinga, was completed in August 1985. At the cost of three tunnels, one 4623 m long, construction of 19 major bridges and almost 16 million m^3 of earthworks, it eases the ruling gradient in the area from 2.7 to 1.5 per cent and raises the minimum curve radius from 90 to 300 m. As a result speed ceilings were raised to 60 km/h for freight and 80 km/h for passenger trains, and transit times were reduced by an hour for passenger trains, two hours for Comilog manganese trains and three hours for other freight. This scheme, which was funded by the World Bank and over a dozen other agencies, has achieved quicker transits and also raises the line's freight operating capacity beyond its previous 21 trains daily to 31. Total cost of the project trebled compared with initial 1970 estimates, reached CFA Fr107 000 million at its conclusion.

Following studies by Tecsult International of Canada, further realignment and track with welded 46 kg instead of 30 kg rail has progressed between Bilingua and Tahitondi. In the long term it is hoped to bridge the Congo river and connect CFCO with the Kinshasa-Matadi line of Zaire. Tecsult has studied a combined road-and-double-track rail bridge. The plan includes double-tracking of 33 km between Loubomo and Mont Belo, where the 285 km Comilog line diverges to the border of Gabon; and between M'Filou and Brazzaville.

Costa Rica

Ministry of Public Works and Transport

San José

Telephone: +506 26 00 03
Telex: 2493 mop

Minister: Dr Guillermo Constenia Umaña
Director, Transport Division: Lic Luis Ramirez
Director-General, Railways: Ing Juan Abrahams Vargas

Ferrocarriles de Costa Rica (INCOFER)

Apartado Postal No. 2, 1009 F E al P Estacion, Zona 3, San José

Telephone: +506 26 00 11
Telex: 2393 fecosa cr
Telefax: +506 275197

President: Ing José Fco Nicolás Alvarado
Vice-President: M F Calvo C
Administration Manager: Roberto Quirós Calvo
Operations Manager: Ing Miguel A Mata Solano
Projects Director: Ing Oscar Brenes Alpizar
Transport Director: Ing Cilliam Barrantes
Financial Director: S Guillen S
Maintenance of Way Director: Francisco Muñoz Hernández
Chief Electromechanical Engineer, Atlantic Division: Leonel Altamirano Larios
Chief Electromechanical Engineer, Pacific Division: Ing Carlos Ceciliano Camacho

Gauge: 1067 mm
Route length: 700 km
Electrification: 128 km at 15 kV 20 Hz, 109 km at 25 kV 60 Hz

The country's two principal railways, the National Atlantic and the Pacific, were merged under the title of Ferrocarriles de Costa Rica in 1977.

Traffic
Bananas form a substantial part of the traffic on Incofer's Atlantic route with about 700 000 tonnes (40 million crates) exported annually through the port of Limón.

	1986	1987	1988
Total freight tonnes	768 891	885 174	974 081
Total passenger journeys	2 007 324	1 891 923	1 300 000

Electrification
The former Pacific Railway running 128 km from San José to Puntarenas was electrified at 15 kV 20 Hz in 1929-30. Under the 1977 decree which created FECOSA, modernisation and electrification of the Atlantic Railway was put in hand. As a result, the 132 km Limón-Rio Frio main line was completely relaid with 43 kg/m long-welded rail on concrete sleepers under the supervision of Canadian Pacific Consulting Services, new yards were installed at both ends, bridges strengthened for 16-tonne axleloads, and electrification at 25 kV 60 Hz executed by the 50 c/s Group under the leadership of AEG-Telefunken. Electric working was inaugurated in February 1982.

The Group also supplied 12 dual-voltage, 62-tonne 1200 kW Bo-Bo electric locomotives which are adaptable either to the new Atlantic Railway system or to the 15 kV 20 Hz system of the Pacific Railway. The latter is ultimately to be converted to 25 kV 60 Hz when its generating plant falls due for renewal. In the meantime a 58 km extension of the Pacific Railway from El Roble, near Puntarenas, to a new cement factory at Colarado will be electrified at 15 kV 20 Hz, but the works will be designed for easy conversion to the higher voltage.

Modernisation plan
As part of a move to develop a co-ordinated national transport policy, an Institute of Railways (INCOFER) was created in 1985 to plan and supervise modernisation of the rail system. Given the country's hydro-electric resources, further electrification was to be considered wherever practicable. In 1987 Incofer took over the 250 km Ferrocaril del Sur system and its rolling stock, including 13 diesel locomotives and some 500 freight wagons, formerly operated by the Compania Bananera del Costa Rica.

Incofer's first step was to initiate a changeover from vacuum to air braking, which the government approved. The Federal German government agreed to advance DM65 million for construction of a main workshop in the La Moin-Limon area.

A concrete sleeper plant has been set up to assist upgrading of some 170 km of secondary lines in the banana-producing regions. Subject to availability of finance, construction of a number of new branches in these areas is to be undertaken.

The outstanding project, talked of for some time past, is achievement of an effective link between the Atlantic and Pacific railways, which are at present connected only by a steeply-graded line through the streets of San José. The proposal is to resurrect and then electrify a 42 km line threading a corridor between Alajuela and Cartago that would run through the centre of San José. At Alajuela, close to the country's International Airport, Atlantic and Pacific lines are only 3 km apart and this gap would be bridged by a connection. The interurban line would initially be single track, but provision would be made for later double-tracking. The scheme involves some 6 km of elevated infrastructure. Cost of the work and of rolling stock for a suburban passenger service is put at a total of US$70 million.

In 1989 the Transport Ministry disclosed that planning was in progress of a 300km rail connection between new Atlantic and Pacific coast ports. The objective would be container movement, to create short landbridge competition for shipping too large to take the Panama Canal.

Traction and rolling stock
Incofer has recently obtained three locomotives of 1067 mm gauge secondhand from Canadian National, which used them in Newfoundland. Incofer has built two 14-tonne railbus prototypes with 200 hp Cummins engines in its own workshops and has also converted a Romanian-built diesel-hydraulic B-B shunter to a 15 kV 20 Hz electro-hydraulic unit.

The initial 15 kV 20 hz electric system is operated by AEG locomotives of 1929 and Siemens locomotives of 1956. The diesel locomotive fleet is chiefly General Electric, with the latest 825 and 1100 hp units dating from 1979, but includes some 950 hp diesel-hydraulic units supplied by the 23 August works of Romania in 1971.

Motive power

Electric locomotives	19
Diesel locomotives	40
Steam locomotives	1
Electric train-sets	15
Diesel train-sets	30
Diesel railcars	41

Rolling stock

Passenger coaches	83
Freight wagons	757

Type of coupler: Standard
Type of braking in standard use: Westinghouse

Signalling
A current priority is to install automatic block signalling throughout both Pacific and Atlantic Railway main routes and on the Alajuela branch. A new operating control centre is also planned. At present a radio despatching system is in use.

Track
Rail: ASCE 42.5
Sleepers: Wood or concrete spaced 1600/km
Fastenings: Pandrol, Nabla RN, spikes
Minimum curve radius: 80 m
Max gradient: 4.25%
Max permissible axleload: 18 tonnes

Cuba

Cuban National Railways (FdeC)
Ferrocarriles de Cuba

Ave Independencia y Tulipan, Havana

Director-General: Vacant
Director, Western Division: Simon Escalona
Director, Central Division: P Perez Fleites
Director, East-Central Division: J Castellanos Torres
Director, Camilo Cienfugos Division: J R Delgado Alvarez
Director of Locomotives and Rolling Stock: Juan Reverster Carrata la
Director, Finance: M Hernández Padua
Director, Traffic: A Mesa Muniz
Director, Permanent Way: Ing O González Penichet
Director, Supplies: E Veláquez
Director, Investment: Mercades Mustelier

Gauge: 1435 mm
Route length in public service: 5053 km
Electrification: 151.7 km at 1.2 kV ac

Traffic

	1985	1986	1987
Freight tonnes (million)	14.97	13.579	13.238
Freight tonne-km (million)	2796.7	2155	2105.7
Passenger journeys (million)	23.2	25	23.64
Passenger-km (million)	2257	2200	2189

Civil engineering
Reconstruction of the Havana-Santiago de Cuba line should now be finished in 1990. This is five years later than once planned, because of delays enforced by the country's economic recession. Total length of the new track being installed is 1170 km, comprising 837 km of main line, 224 km of sidings and passing loops and 109 km of feeder branch lines. The line has been laid with Soviet-supplied Type P50 (50-48 kg/m) rail in 12-5-metre lengths; sidings are being laid with 43 kg/m rails, also from the Soviet Union. Sleepers are pre-stressed monobloc concrete.

The project involves reconstruction of 400 bridges, 511 km of re-alignment, which will reduce distance by 15 km, and closure of over 50 small stations. The ruling gradient will be 1.2 per cent, except for a short section of 2 per cent on the exit from Santiago. The aim is to run trains of up to 1800 tonnes gross initially, but later of 2600 tonnes, with maximum speed raised to 100 km/h for freight trains, 140 km/h for passenger. In a second phase, FdeC is aiming for 200 km/h passenger train speed. Completion of the infrastructure works should see the present best Havana-Santiago passenger train schedule of 14¾-hours cut to 10 hours.

New Five-Year Plan
At the end of 1989 the Transport Ministry issued a 1991–95 investment plan for FdeC. From USSR, East German and Hungarian industry it proposed to import 110 diesel locomotives, 2144 freight cars, 15 diesel railcars and 40 other passenger cars. Cuban industry would manufacture 40 diesel train-sets under Hungarian licence and 150 other passenger cars. Hopes of fulfilling the proposed imports were inevitably coloured by the reducing level of Soviet financial aid for the country.

FdeC was targeted to expand its freight traffic by 43 per cent to 19million tonnes a year, and its passenger traffic by no less than 80 per cent, from 23 million to 44 million journeys a year.

Traction and rolling stock
FdeC operates 411 diesel and 12 electric locomotives, 65 diesel and 15 electric railcars, 580 passenger cars and 9016 freight cars.

FdeC diesel traction is an eclectic assortment of British, French, Canadian, East German, Hungarian, Canadian and more recently Soviet types. The Canadian machines are 20 Bombardier-MLW Type MX 624 supplied in the mid-1970s. Dominant model is the

Soviet 1912 kW Type TE-114 Co-Co, of which the stock is 99, and of which more are likely to be procured. In 1988 a further 12 Type TGM-8K diesel locomotives were ordered from the USSR.

In 1986 Cenemesa of Spain was contracted to recondition the electrical power plant of 40 GM and Ganz-Mávag-built locomotives. The diesel railcars are mostly a Fiat design with 409 kW engines, built in the mid-1970s by Concord of Argentina under licence. In the same period Concord also supplied 100 main-line passenger cars and 20 restaurant cars. A local company, Empresa Productora de Equipos Ferroviarios de Cardenas, has begun supply of diesel railbuses based on the Ganz-Mávag design. The plant's first 85 passenger cars have been delivered to FdeC. RENFE of Spain has shipped to FdeC 150 passenger cars of its 5000 and 6000 series, refurbished and re-gauged by Spanish industry.

In 1988 FdeC was seeking to have 20 of its diesel railcars renovated by Materfer, and to procure from the same firm 19 buffet and 15 mail/baggage cars.

Signalling and telecommunications

On the main Havana-Santiago da Cuba line it was hoped by 1990 to have replaced the almost exclusive manual point and block-telephone operation (only nine of some 100 stations have central point working and one short section is equipped with track-to-train radio) with modern signalling. A semi-automatic block system of USSR manufacture and relay interlockings are being installed between Havana and Santa Clare (207 km); extension to Santiago de Cuba was to follow.

In 1989 Iskra of Yugoslavia was contracted to supply equipment for the resignalling of key junctions in the Havana area.

Sugar railways

The numerous railways serving the sugar plantations and factories are in sum of greater extent than FdeC and together carry six times FdeC's present freight traffic. They total 7742 km, of which some 65 per cent are standard gauge, and serve 131 of the island's 154 sugar plants. These railways employ around 900 locomotives, 380 of them steam, and over 30 000 wagons. Of the diesel fleet, 144 locomotives are of US origin, and 376 of USSR derivation, in three types, delivered since 1960.

Cuba intends to increase its sugar production to 10 million tons in the next few years and to modernise the railway network simultaneously, as well as using it for the transport of other agricultural products and minerals.

Type of coupler in standard use: Air (50% Matrosov, 30% Westinghouse, 20% Dako)

USSR-built Type TE114K diesel locomotive, of which FdeC has a considerable number

Track
Rail: 46.7 kg/m
Sleepers: Prestressed concrete: 2460 mm, spaced 1520–1840/km;
Timber: 2750 mm, spaced 1520–1840/km
Fastenings: Elastic and rigid with track rails and screw bolts
Minimum curvature radius: 150 m
Max gradient: 30%
Max permissible axleload: 23 tonnes

Diesel locomotives

Class	Manu-facturer's type	Wheel arrange-ment	Transmission	Rated power kW	Max speed km/h	Total weight tonnes	No in service 1987	Year first built	Builders Mechanical parts	Builders Engine & type	Builders Transmission
TE-114	TE-114K	Co-Co	Elec	1912	120	121	102	1978	Rev October Voroshilov-grad	5049	Const. Máq Jaricov
MLW	MX-624	Co-Co	Elec	1912	135	112	44	1975	Born Sadler	Alco 251E	General Electric Canada
M62	M62-K	Co-Co	Elec	1234	100	120	17	1974	Rev October Voroskilov-grad	14D4DT2	Kharkov
Alco	(FA-2) y (RSC-3)	Co-Co	Elec	1176	105	100	0	1951	Alco	Alco 244	General Electric, Canada
TEM-4	TEM-4	Co-Co	Elec	735	100	120	35	1965	Bransk	PDIT	Kharkov
TEM-2	TEM-2TK	Co-Co	Elec	757	100	120	58	1974	Bransk	PDITM	Kharkov
Ganz-Mavag	DVM-9	Bo-Bo	Elec	735	90	76	63	1969	Ganz-Mavag	16VCE17/24	Ganz Electric
CMC	6-8	Bo-Bo	Elec	662	124	72	33	1955	Gral Motor	IM8-5667-8	Gral Electric
MaK	600D	D	Hyd	625	80	64	0	1956	MaK	MaK-301-AK	MaK
Brissonneau et Lodz	BB63000	Bo-Bo	Elec	606	90	72	13	1965	Brissonneau et Lodz	M60V12BSH	Brissonneau et Lodz
Brissonneau et Lodz	040-DE	Bo-Bo	Elec	588	90	70	3	1955	Brissonneau et Lodz	Sulzer GLDA 22	Brissonneau et Lodz
TGM-25	TGM-25	C	Hyd	294	50	46	12	1970	—	—	—

Electric railcars or multiple-units

Class	Cars per unit	Line voltage	Motor cars per unit	Motored axles per motor car	Rated output (kW) per motor	Max speed km/h	Weight tonnes per car	Total seating capacity per car	Length per car mm (M-motor T-trailer)	No in service 1987	Year first built	Builders
Brill	1	1200	1	4	55	70	28	50	M15036	16	1923	General Electric

Czechoslovakia

Czechoslovak State Railways (ČSD)
Ceskoslovenské Státni Dráhy

Na příkopě 33, 110 05 Prague 1

Telephone: +42 2 2122
Cable: Domini, Praha
Telex: 121096 domi c
Telefax: +42 2 236 8379

Minister of Transport: Jiri Nezval
First Vice-Minister: J Jira
Vice-Ministers: I Laška
R Chovan
Director General: I Malina
Deputy Directors General: V Stareček
J Těmin
S Rimár
General Manager: V Fukan
Department Directors
  Finance: K Dlabač
  International: J Ondroušek
  Personnel: J Dostál
  Movement and Traffic: J Novotny
  Traction: Ing K Sellner
  Track: Ing V Mazel
  Telecommunications and Signalling: Ing K Koška
  Rolling Stock: Ing J Hlaváč
  Research and Development: M Glos
  Electrical Engineering: M Vaňásek
  Long-range Planning: J Gazda
  Information Systems: A Vechet
  Public Relations: M Kozák

Gauge: 1435 mm; 1520 mm; various narrow gauges
Route length: 12 855 km; 102 km; 146 km
Electrification: 1559 km at 25 kV 50 Hz; 2146 km at 3 kV dc; 87 km at 1.5 kV dc.

The ČSD system is divided into four administrative regions each of which is largely autonomous:

Railway	Headquarters
Eastern	Bratislava
Midland	Olomouc
North-Eastern	Prague
South-Western	Plzeň

Traffic
ČSD is the country's principal means of transport for heavy freight, notably the coal and lignite output of Bohemia and Moravia, imports from the USSR and the industries of Slovakia.

More than two-thirds of ČSD's freight moves over 17 per cent of its route-mileage, comprising chiefly the two east-west transversals: from Cheb, in western Bohemia near the West German border, to the USSR frontier at Cierna and Tisou, in the far east of Slovakia, a distance of 1290 km; and from Cheb via Plzeň, Prague, Kolin, Brno and Bratislava to the Hungarian border at Stúrovo on the Danube, a distance of 753 km. The first of these routes is 95 per cent electrified at 3 kV dc, double track throughout and signalled with automatic colour-lights. The second, which interconnects 15 per cent of the population and is a key passenger route, is 86 per cent double-tracked and presently electrified with two systems. From Cheb it is 25 kV ac, to the start of Prague's 3 kV dc network at Králův Drůr, but 25 kV ac is resumed at Kutná-Hora, near Kolin, for the remainder of the route.

From a peak of 21 600 million passenger-km in 1961, volume in this sector has receded to 19 408 million. That reflects the simultaneous rise of private car ownership from 6 to about 45 per cent of Czechoslovak households.

Prague area modernisation
A major investment programme has been under way in the Prague area. It includes modernisation of the Vrsovice and Liben yards, and creation of an automated control centre for the city's northern area.

Prague-Brno high-speed project
In 1988 ČSD unveiled a scheme to build a new high-speed route between Prague and Brno. The existing route, 257 km long, threads the Moravian hills and would be difficult economically to adapt for higher pace. The proposed new route would reduce the distance by some 50 km and be engineered for 200–

Dual-voltage Class ES499.0 4000kW Bo-Bo (*Jaromir Pernička*)

Two Class S489 25kV 50Hz ac Bo-Bos cross viaduct near Dolní Loučky with freight (*Jaromir Pernička*)

Type T754 1460kW diesel-electric locomotive at Brno (*Jaromit Pernička*)

RAILWAY SYSTEMS / Czechoslovakia

250 km/h, so that it would entail major civil engineering works to negotiate the Moravian environment.

The scheme would be the centrepiece of a plan to upgrade the key trunk passenger routes of ČSD. From Brno onward to Breclaw, Bratislava and the Hungarian frontier the existing line of 276 km would be upgraded for 140 to 160 km/h so as to reduce Prague/Bratislava journey time from the present 5 hours 20 minutes to 2½–3 hours. Other upgradings were proposed on the Prague-Zilina, Zilina-Bratislava and Prague-Pilzen routes, also for the ČSD segments of the routes between Warsaw and Vienna, and between Berlin and Vienna. In all the plan touched over 11 per cent of ČSD's total route-km.

The cost of the Prague-Brno high-speed alone would equal ČSD's total investment in the second half of the 1980s. However, it was claimed that the whole plan would amortise its cost within 19 years.

Class T457.0 600kW diesel-electric shunter

Traffic (million)	1985	1987	1988
Freight (tonnes)	293.5	290.4	293.93
Freight tonne-km	73 590	67 901	69 430
Passenger journeys	419.5	415.8	415.37
Passenger-km	19 839	20 029	19 408

Computerisation

The KOMPAS system for automation of yard sorting is being developed and gradually introduced. The last Five-Year Plan provided for installation of KOMPAS 3 at Ceské Budějovice, Usti nad Labem, Praha Liboň and Žilina Toplička.

New data processing developments include the spread of the BEVOZ system for real-time surveillance of all wagons of foreign railways as well as ČSD wagons on the ČSD network, supervision of train running, balance of wagons between regions and dissemination of advanced information on the running of trains and wagons. Service trials have begun of a German Democratic Republic computerised system (ARES) for reservation in coaches with reclining couchettes, in sleeping cars and others at the time of ticket purchase.

An automated information system of traffic control is operative at transhipment points in eastern Slovakia. Traffic on the Prague-Kralupy nad Vlt section is now supervised by computer-aided traffic control.

Electrification

Electric traction is now available over 26 per cent of ČSD route-mileage and hauls 69 per cent of all traffic. The north operates at 3 kV dc, the south at 25 kV ac. There are three junctions of the electrification systems; at Kutná-Hora, 77 km east of Prague; Králův Drůr in western Bohemia; and Nedakonice in central Moravia.

A fully electrified transversal was achieved in 1987 with energisation of the 113 km between Prague and Pilsen.

The 1986–90 Five-Year Plan programme was electrification of a further 370 route-km, with the objective of raising the proportion of electrically-powered traffic to over 80 per cent. It is hoped by the end of the century to have 35 per cent of total ČSD route-km under wires.

One of the latest schemes increases the electrified proportion of the north-south route from the German Democratic Republic frontier at Decin to Ceske Budejvicé, close to Austria's northern border. Sections of this lately wired are the 48 km between Benesov and Tabor and the 27 km from there to Veseli and Luznici. This establishes uninterrupted catenary for 167 km from Prague to the south. Further east the 158 km from Bratislava northwestward to a junction with the line from Prague at Puchov is being wired.

Track and signalling

Main lines are generally laid with 49 kg/m rail, secondary lines with 30 to 40 kg/m. However, almost 10 per cent of all route-km is now relaid with 65 kg/m rail, since the lines concerned, carrying freight trains of increasing weight, are recording 60 to 80 million tonne-km of traffic a year. Most of the system allows maximum axleloads of 20 tonnes.

ČSD planned to install automatic block over a further 170 km of route in the 1986–90. Attention currently focusses on the north-south route.

Traction and rolling stock

In 1988 ČSD operated 1513 electric locomotives, 108 emus, 3008 diesel locomotives, 3491 diesel railcars and trailers, 7421 other passenger cars and 134 052 freight wagons. Principal supplier of passenger cars are the Bautzen and Görlitz plants in the German Democratic Republic. Almost 80 000 units of the freight car fleet are now four-axle, operable at 100 km/h.

In 1991 ČSD was to receive 60 sleeping cars from Waggonbau Görlitz.

Diesel locomotives

Class	Wheel arrangement	Transmission	Rated power (kW)	Max speed km/h	Total weight tonnes	No in service	Year first built	Builders Mechanical parts	Builders Engine & type	Builders Transmission
T211.0	B	Mech	118	40	22	54	1959	ČKD	Tatra 11A/6	ČKD
T212.0	B	Mech	147	40	24	56	1968	ČKD	Tatra 930-51	ČKD
T334.0	C	Hydrodynamic	300	60	39.7	90	1961	ČKD	ČKD 12V 170 DR	ČKD
T426.0	D	Hydrodynamic	800	50/20	62.8	4	1961	SGP	SGP T 12 b	Voith
T435.0	Bo-Bo	Elec	551	60	61	145	1958	ČKD	ČKD 6S 310 DR	ČKD
T444.0	B-B	Hydrodynamic	515	70	56	202	1961	ČKD	ČKD K 12 170 DR	ČKD
T444.1	B-B	Hydrodynamic	515	70	56.6	101	1963	ZTS Martin	ČKD K12 170 DR	ČKD
T457.0	Bo-Bo	Elec	600	80	68.4		1985	–	ČKD K6S 230 DR	
T458.1	Bo-Bo	Elec	551	80	74	221	1963	ČKD	ČKD 6S 310 DR	ČKD
T466.0	Bo-Bo	Elec	926	90	64	298	1973	ZTS Martin	ZTS 12PA 4 185	ČKD
T466.2	Bo-Bo	Elec	883	90	64	403	1977	ČKD	ČKD K6S 230 DR	ČKD
T478.1	Bo-Bo	Elec	1102	100	75	230	1966	ČKD	ČKD K6S 310 DR	ČKD
T478.2	Bo-Bo	Elec	1102	100	74	82	1969	ČKD	ČKD K6S 310 DR	ČKD
T478.3	Bo-Bo	Elec	1325	100	73.2	408	1968	ČKD	ČKD K12V 230 DR	ČKD
T478.4	Bo-Bo	Elec	1460	100	74.4	86	1978	ČKD	ČKD K12V 230 DR	ČKD
T669.0	Co-Co	Elec	993	90	114.6	108	1966	ČKD	ČKD K6S 310 DR	ČKD
T669.1	Co-Co	Elec	993	90	115.8	195	1968	SMZ Dubnica	ČKD K6S 310 DR	ČKD
T678.0	Co-Co	Elec	1215	100	111	17	1962	ČKD	ČKD K8S 310 DR	ČKD
T679.0	Co-Co	Elec	1215	100	114	27	1962	ČKD	ČKD K8S 310 DR	ČKD
T679.1	Co-Co	Elec	1435	100	116	574	1966	KMZ	VSZ 14 D 40	CHZE

Diesel railcars or multiple-units

Class	Motored axles per motor car	Transmission	Rated power (kW) per motor	Max speed km/h	Weight tonnes per car	Total seating capacity	Length per car mm	No in service	Year first built	Builders Mechanical parts	Builders Engine & type	Builders Transmission
M 152.0	1	Hydro-mech	156	80	20	55	13 970	678	1975	Vagonka Studénka	Praga 2M70	ČKD Praha
M 240.0	2	Hydrodynamic	206	70	31.6	56	18 500	120	1963	Vagonka Studénka	Tatra T 930-4	ČKD
M 262.0	2	Elec	301	90	46.7	56	21 236	238	1949	Vagonka Studénka	ČKD 12V 170 DR	ČKD
M 286.0	2	Hydrodynamic	515	110	50.2	48	24 790	52	1964	Vagonka Studénka	ČKD K12 170 DR	ČKD
M 286.1	2	Hydrodynamic	588	110	50.3	48	24 790	37	1967	Vagonka Studénka	ČKD K12 170 DR	ČKD
M 296.1	2	Hydrodynamic	588	120	50.3	48	24 790	35	1969	Vagonka Studénka	ČKD K12 170 DR	ČKD

Electric locomotives

Class	Wheel arrangement	Line voltage	Rated output (kW) continuous/one-hour	Max speed km/h	Weight tonnes	No in service	Year first built	Builders Mechanical parts	Builders Electrical equipment
E 422.0	Bo-Bo	1.5 kV dc	360/440	50	48	4	1956	Škoda	Škoda
E 426.0	Bo-Bo	1.5 kV dc	400/960	50	64	6	1973	Škoda	Škoda
E 458.0	Bo-Bo	3 kV dc	800/960	80	72	52	1972	Škoda	Škoda
E 458.1	Bo-Bo	3 kV dc	760	80	72	35	1981	Škoda	Škoda
E 469.1	Bo-Bo	3 kV dc	2032/2344	90	88	85	1960	Škoda	Škoda
E 469.2	Bo-Bo	3 kV dc	2040/2340	90	85	55	1967	Škoda	Škoda
E 469.3	Bo-Bo	3 kV dc	2040/2340	90	85	30	1971	Škoda	Škoda
E 479.0	Bo-Bo	3 kV dc	2040/2340	100	85	40	1977	Škoda	Škoda
E 479.1	Bo-Bo + Bo-Bo	3 kV dc	2 × 2240/2 × 2500	100	170	50	1980	Škoda	Škoda
E 499.0	Bo-Bo	3 kV dc	2030/2340	120	80	100	1953	Škoda	Škoda
E 499.1	Bo-Bo	3 kV dc	2032/2344	120	84	61	1959	Škoda	Škoda
E 499.2	Bo-Bo	3 kV dc	4000/4200	140	84	27	1978	Škoda	Škoda
E 499.3	Bo-Bo	3 kV dc	3060	120	88		1981	Škoda	Škoda
E 669.1	Co-Co	3 kV dc	2790/3000	90	120	150	1960	Škoda	Škoda
E 669.2	Co-Co	3 kV dc	2790/3000	90	120	168	1963	Škoda	Škoda
E 669.3	Co-Co	3 kV dc	2790/3000	90	120	43	1971	Škoda	Škoda
S 458.0	Bo-Bo	25 kV 50 Hz	880/984	80	72	74	1973	Škoda	Škoda
S 489.0	Bo-Bo	25 kV 50 Hz	3080/3200	110	88	110	1966	Škoda	Škoda
S 499.0	Bo-Bo	25 kV 50 Hz	3080/3200	120	85	206	1968	Škoda	Škoda
S 499.1	Bo-Bo	25 kV 50 Hz	3080/3200	120	85	25	1970	Škoda	Škoda
S 499.2	Bo-Bo	25 kV 50 Hz	3060	120	85	NA	1984	Škoda	Škoda-ČKD
ES 499.0	Bo-Bo	3 kV dc/ 25 kV 50 Hz	4000/4200	160	87	20	1974	Škoda	Škoda
ES 499.1	Bo-Bo	3 kV dc/ 25 kV 50 Hz	3060	120	85	NA	1980	Škoda	Škoda-ČKD

Electric railcars or multiple-units

Class	Cars per unit	Line voltage	Motor cars per unit	Motored axles per motor car	Rated output (kW) per motor	Max speed km/h	Weight tonnes per car (M-motor T-trailer)	Total seating capacity	Length per car mm (M-motor T-trailer)	No in service	Rate of acceleration m/s²	Year first built	Builders Mechanical parts	Builders Electrical equipment
EM 475-1	4	3 kV dc	2	4	165/190	100	M 59 T 33	300	M 24 597 T 23 348	62	0.7	1964	Vagonka Studénka	MEZ Vsetin
EM 488.0	5	3 kV dc	2	4	250/270	110	M 64 T 35	336	M 24 500 T 24 500	43	0.8	1974	Vagonka Studénka	MEZ Vsetin
SM 488.0	5	25 kV 50 Hz	2	4	420/465	110	M64 T 37	336	M 24 500 T 24 500	17	0.7	1968	Vagonka Studénka	MEZ Vsetin

Series production of 100 dual-voltage 3 kV dc/25 kV ac locomotives to the prototype ES499.1 Bo-Bo design began in 1984, followed by that of the companion 3 kV dc Class E 499.3 for domestic ČSD operation; both have thyristor chopper control of traction motors. A dual-voltage 3 kV dc/15 kV 16⅔ Hz ac Class ES499.2 for through working into the German Democratic Republic has also emerged and ČSD is testing a Škoda 3000 kW Bo-Bo with asynchronous three-phase motors.

ČSD intends to introduce bi-level emus on Prague suburban routes in the 1990s. A prototype unit has been built by Ceskoslovenske Vagonky at Poprad for evaluation on the Prague Railway Research Institute's Velim test track and subsequent trail on several Prague services. Construction of a production series of 50 units is set to begin in 1991.

Each set will comprise a 1104 kW single-deck power car with all axles motored and four bi-level trailers. The latter will each have seats for 70 on the upper and 56 on the lower deck, plus room for 188 standees. The power car will seat 64 and have space for 97 standees.

ČSD has a fleet of over 500 lightweight Type M-152 diesel railcars. Built by Studénka in Moravia, powered by a Škoda 154 kW engine, seating 55 with standing room for 40, and with a maximum speed of 80 km/h, these vehicles monopolise passenger operations over more than 2250 route-km of ČSD.

The 1986–90 Five-Year Plan budgeted for acquisition of 280 electric and 210 diesel locomotives, 730 passenger cars, 163 diesel railcars, 12 suburban emus and 20 454 freight wagons.

Denmark

Ministry of Transport

Frederiksholms Kanal 27, 1220 Copenhagen K

Telephone: +45 33 923355
Telex: 22 275 trami dk
Telefax: +45 33 123893

Minister: Knud Østergaard
Permanent Under-Secretary of State: J L Halck

Danish State Railways (DSB)
Danske Statsbaner

Sølvgade 40, 1349 Copenhagen K

Telephone: +45 33 140400
Telex: 22 225 dsbadt dk
Telefax: +45 33 140400 ext 12110

Managing Director: Peter Langager
Directors
  Commercial and Operations: Hans Winther
  Technical: Eigil Koop
  Personnel, Administration: Peter Elming

Superintendents
  Traffic: Henrik Nørgaard
  Way & Works: P Jensen
  Passenger: Svend E Pedersen
  Freight: Søren B Rasmussen
  Finance: Jesper Hansen
  Signalling and Telecommunications: Knud Abildgren

Gauge: 1435 mm
Route length: 2025 km
Electrification: 1.66 route-km at 1.5 kV dc
  78 km at 25 kV 50 Hz ac

DSB accounts for 95 per cent of total Danish passenger rail traffic and 99 per cent of the total freight rail traffic. The remainder is carried out by 13 smaller private railway companies with a total length of 483 route-km. These are also state-supported, by an annual amount of over DKr150 million. Together these 13 railways record some 12 million passenger journeys and 350 000 tonnes of freight per annum. All have standardised a Duewag diesel railcar design for their passenger traffic.

DSB is a government department with staff having the status of civil servants; the General Manager has the status of a Permanent Under-Secretary of State. DSB is subject to government control, staff redundancies are not normally permitted and staff reductions are obtained through wastage. Quantity licensing for road hauliers is in force in Denmark, affording some protection to rail.

Management decentralisation
A major restructure implemented at the start of 1990 established four self-contained regions: North Jutland based in Aarhus; South Jutland/Fünen based in Fredericia; Seeland based in Naestved; and Copenhagen. Each Region has been given bottom-line responsibility for commercial performance, with considerable autonomy, and has its own sales and production departments: passenger, freight, operation, track, construction and electrical, corresponding to those at headquarters.

Great Belt fixed link agreed
The long-cherished scheme for a fixed crossing of the 19 km-wide Store Baelt (Great Belt) water-way, which interrupts communications between Copenhagen and the rest of the country, is going ahead. This means that for three or four years in the mid-1990s Danish State Railways (DSB) will have a competitive advantage unique among Western European railways. After September 1993 its trains alone will have the benefit of a Great Belt fixed link. It will be 1996 before a fixed highway link is added to save road transport a ferry crossing of the waterway.

From Halsskov, northwest of the present Zealand

RAILWAY SYSTEMS / Denmark

train ferry terminal, Korsør, the railway will cross the Great Belt's 60 m-deep eastern channel to Sprogø island in tunnel. Contracts to bore twin single-track tunnels under the waterway were let to a Danish-led multi-national consortium by Storebaeltsforbindelsen A/S (Great Belt Link Ltd) in November 1988. These rail tunnels, each 8 km long, will be bored to a diameter of 7.7 m. That slightly exceeds the girth of the Anglo-French Channel Tunnel, though as yet there is no intention to run any but standard DSB trains through them. Like the Channel Tunnel, the two Great Belt bores, 25 m apart, will be connected by lateral passage-ways spaced 250 m apart. The rail tunnels will have raised trackside walk-ways on which passengers from an incapacitated train can be evacuated via a cross passage through the service tunnel to a train in the other tunnel.

On Sprogø the railway will surface to cross the 27 m-deep western channel on a combined rail-road bridge. But whereas the structure's rail tracks are to be finished by mid-1993, its highway will not open until 1996; consequently contracts to build a highway bridge over the eastern channel are not to be signed until 1991.

DSB is not directly involved in the fixed rail link's cost. Initially its trains will pay rent for use of the rail crossing. When that has amortised the investment, ownership will pass to DSB.

Fixed link with Sweden

In August 1987 the governments of Denmark and Sweden received expert reports on the preferred character of fixed link between the two countries. Chiefly on environmental grounds, the previously favoured rail solution of a Helsingør-Helsingborg tunnel under the Oresund was rejected in favour of a combined rail-road crossing between Malmö and Copenhagen. This option had the further benefit of serving Copenhagen's Kastrup airport, which has a terminal function for a wide area of Scandinavia.

The scheme recommended by the government-appointed working parties called for a high-level bridge over the shipping lanes carrying a four-lane motorway and a double-track electrified railway. Copenhagen's Kastrup airport would be directly served by an underground station. It was envisaged that the link would be built and financed in the same way as the Great Belt fixed link, with users, including the railways, paying tolls for its use. However, in the autumn of 1987 the project was stalled because of environmental objections by a powerful faction in Sweden's ruling Social Democratic party, which pressed for reversion to the Helsingør-Helsingborg rail-only tunnel scheme.

A Danish-Swedish link government working party studied alternatives for the Malmö-Copenhagen link in 1988. In February 1989 it presented the two governments with evaluated cases for three options: a bored underwater rail-only tunnel; a rail-road tunnel; or a two-stage variant, beginning with a rail link and adding a highway later.

In early 1990 the Danish parliament voted by a big majority to continue discussions with Sweden on the fixed link. The Swedish government responded that it cannot respond until completion of environmental and regional impact studies in 1991.

Plan 2000

The government has broadly approved a 10-year DSB development and investment strategy tagged Plan 2000, through which the railway intends to maximise its mid-1990s window of opportunity.

The plan aims for a total takeover of inter-city services, in three stages, by a fleet of IC/3 train-sets. It is hoped to have 85 sets available by the completion of the Great Belt fixed link. DSB seeks to launch a two-hourly-interval Copenhagen-Hamburg service in early 1990.

Siemens ZUB100 automatic train control should be widely installed by 1993 (see below), enabling the IC/3s to operate at up to 180 km/h. Consequently, journey times will be drastically cut – by an hour, for instance, between Copenhagen and Aarhus. New IC/3-based emus are included in the plan (see below), as the 25 kV ac electrification should have crossed the Great Belt and reached Odense by 1993, but IC/3 trains will work to and from Copenhagen under wires.

A completely new regular-interval timetable, with departures from main termini on the hour or half-hour, will be introduced for the IC/3 service in 1993. Operation will then centre on Odense, as it will be the changeover point from electric to diesel traction pending further extension of the wires. A new west-to-south curve is to be laid at Fredericia to obviate reversal there by trains between Esbjerg and Copenhagen.

ME three-phase motor diesel and Inter-city train at Glostrup

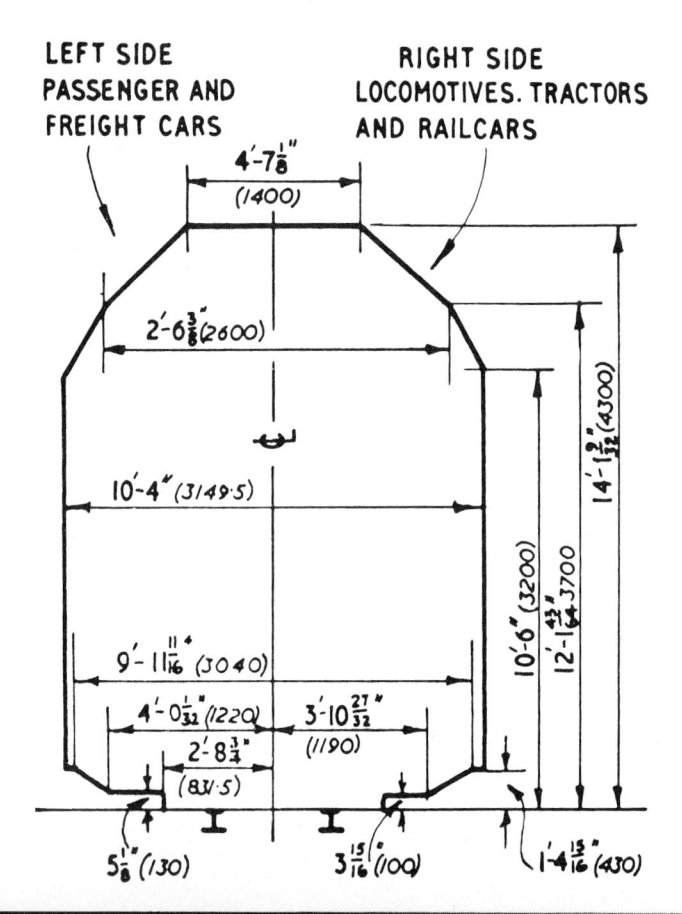

Leased British Rail Mk III sleeping cars provide overnight service between Copenhagen and Jutland

In Copenhagen a second cross-city S-train route is planned, to be fully open by the end of the century. It will run from Frederiksberg to the island of Amaget.

Plan 2000 predicates increased state investment funding until 1992 and tolerance of a rising DSB deficit until the Great Belt fixed link is opened. But DSB forecasts that by 1994 the deficit will be cut to its lowest level for over a decade and that there will be reduced need for subsidy as the investment takes effect.

In early 1990 DSB was negotiating a DKr 2 350 million loan from the European Investment Bank. This would meet half the cost of an investment plan embracing 85 diesel-powered IC3 train-sets, 17 four-car emus, development of an ATCS system (see below), electrification from Nyborg to Odense and construction of a Fredericia cutoff.

Finance

For the first time ever, Parliament has determined an economic framework for a state enterprise spanning several years. The DSB's subsidy has been fixed for the years 1990–93. The DSB was also given more freedom of commercial judgement notably in fixing tariffs. The contract assumed a halving of the cash grant for running expenses and a productivity improvement (train km-per-working hour) of almost 30 per cent over the four years. Rolling stock acquisitions required by additional traffic projections has been made possible. On the other hand, investment opportunities were reduced in other areas.

Passenger traffic

DSB's passenger traffic is influenced by the fact that Denmark is divided into a number of islands and pensinsulas. Moreover, the relatively short distances and the location and size of Copenhagen (population of Greater Copenhagen: 1.735 million) also influence the traffic pattern. The traffic structures east and west of Store Baelt do not have a great deal in common. On Zealand the daily commuting in the metropolitan area dominates traffic patterns with S-trains alone accounting for almost 75 per cent of DSB's total rail passenger journeys. Local train traffic west of Store Baelt is of more modest proportions.

The east-west main line runs from Copenhagen to Aarhus, supplemented by an alternative route from Copenhagen to Kalundborg which connects with a ferry service to Aarhus.

DSB's regional services are fixed-interval. Departures from Copenhagen for Elsinore and Roskilde are scheduled every half-hour; for Holbaek, Ringsted, Sorø, Slagelse, Kalundborg, Nykøbing and Naestved every hour. In Jutland and Fünen all regional and local services are now covered by the new Type MR diesel railcars.

At the end of 1989 DSB had on loan two French Railways Paris suburban bi-level emus to evaluate passenger reaction to this form of vehicle on services between Helsingør, Copenhagen and Roskilde.

New inter-city train-sets

February 1988 saw completion of the first of 23 three-car articulated IC3 diesel train-sets for inter-city operation. Unfortunately, deliveries and entry into service were then retarded for at least a year mainly owing to problems with the trains' electrical systems from a sub-contractor. The delay severely embarrassed the IC3's main supplier, which had to submit to a financial reconstruction; it is now Scandia-Randers A/S, partially owned by ABB.

The first trains eventually entered revenue service in mid-January 1990. All 23 trains of the initial order were expected to be available by the close of 1990. The DSB plan to procure a total of about 100 trains of this type before the Great Belt Fixed Link opens in 1993. A further 35 were ordered from ABB-Scandia Randers in March 1990.

Each unit has two power cars enclosing a trailer. Each power car has two KHD-Deutz 294 kW motors underfloor-mounted between the bogies; drive from a motor to its adjacent bogie axle is by ZF hydro-mechanical gearbox and Kaeble-Gmeinder final drive. The power plant achieves a high acceleration rate of 1–1.3m/s^2, desirable because of the low average distance between stops on DSB's inter-city routes. Extensive application of modular principles allows prompt repair by replacement of any components. All equipment is monitored by an electronic diagnostic system, Stella, devised by ABB.

Body shells are welded from extruded aluminium profiles, a prime factor in confining total weight of a three-car set to 89 tonnes. Car lengths have been limited to 20.533 m for the power cars, 17.733 m for the trailer, because of constraints imposed by use of the Nyborg-Korsør train-ferry decks. Internal fittings are modular-based and accommodation is entirely open saloon, providing 16 first- and 128 second-class seats. The trailer includes a catering compartment from which trolley service is purveyed throughout the unit.

Up to five units can be operated in multiple, permitting several destinations to be served by one departure from Copenhagen. To facilitate assembly and disassembly of mu formations the centrally-sited driver's console in each power car has been made movable; it can be swung to one side when not operative, to allow free passenger movement between adjacent three-car units. The automatic couplers are by Deliner of the German Federal Republic.

Passenger appointments include a children's play area, at-seat radio facilities and train telephone. Toilets are vacuum, by Semco. An electronic information system by Focon features interior displays of seating details and of the train service the unit is operating, including the side of the train on which to alight at the next stop.

Class EA 25 kV 50 Hz ac electric locomotive on Helsingør-Copenhagen service. A further 12 locomotives have been ordered *(John C Baker)*

New IC/3 diesel train-set for inter-city service

Traffic	1985	1986	1987	1988	1989
Freight tonnes (000)	7414	7436	7232	7371	7656
Freight tonne-km (million)	1756	1791	1699	1639	1678
Passenger-km (million)	4716	4704	4782	4726	4649
Passenger journeys (million)	145 482	145 241	145 760	140 181	140 071
Finances (DKr million)					
Revenue					
Passengers and baggage	2254	2273	2436	2613	2664
Freight, parcels and mail	1070	1071	989	976	978
Ferry operations	825	940	994	1025	2042
Other sources	702	776	685	800	
Total	4851	5060	5104	5414	5684
Expenditure					
Staff	5856	5994	6172	6565	6706
Materials and services					
Depreciation	708	798	858	904	1288
Financial charges	932	1019	1084	1167	1194
Total	7496	7811	8114	8636	9188

Initially the IC/3s will operate at a top speed of 160 km/h, but following ATC installation (see below) this will be raised to 180 km/h; a further lift to 200 km/h is under study. This and the units' acceleration from stops will permit an average 25 per cent saving in present inter-city overall timings.

New emus planned

With the opening of the Great Belt fixed link and electrification of the line to Odense in 1993, the DSB plans to introduce 25 kV ac emus known as Type ER on the Helsingør-Odense-Copenhagen route. An order for 17 units was placed with ABB-Scandia in March 1990. They will be 80 m long and each comprise four articulated coaches on the same principles as the IC/3, with which they will be multiple-unit-compatible. The units, employing three-phase ac motors, will be delivered between mid-1992 and mid-1993.

For international service DSB is working up an IC Nord concept based on an overnight version of the IC/3. DSB envisages a multiple-unit train running intact from Copenhagen to Hamburg, and splitting there into two separate emu trains. One would comprise three units for the Netherlands, Brussels and Paris, which

552 RAILWAY SYSTEMS / Denmark

would part from each other at Osnabruck and Liège. The second would separate Basle-Milan and Munich-Rome units at Fulda. Each unit would combine two-berth sleeping and couchette compartments with a limited seating section and four compartments adaptable to either family accommodation or luxury format. For long itineraries an IC Cat emu is proposed, in which a centre car would offer provide a restaurant, cafeteria and bar.

Over the next 15–20 years, further electric trains will be required to supplement and renew the rolling stock for the regional traffic in the eastern area.

The DSB also planned in 1990 to invite tenders for 26 1.6 kV dc emus to supplement the rolling stock of the Copenhagen S-train network. These units will be 87.5 m long, made up of five articulated coaches. Tenders would be invited for alternative formats, including designs with single-axle bogies. In this connection the DSB was to carry out some tests of their own with single-axle bogies in 1990; these tests would be made with Professor Frederich from the Technical University of Aachen as consultant. It has been decided to renovate 260 cars of the current S-train fleet, and renew the other and older half of the fleet.

Freight

The small size of Denmark and its industrial structure, which offers little bulk traffic, limits DSB's freight potential. Moreover, a good road network and the incidence of waterway crossings favour road competition, which is strong. These factors and the country's economic difficulties have had DSB's freight traffic on a downward trend for some time. International traffic constitutes 60 per cent of DSB's tonnage, with Swedish-West German transit traffic via the DanLink Copenhagen-Helsingbord-Rødby-Puttgarden route an important component. Transit traffic represents nearly 40 per cent of the total.

Domestic traffic has now been revived through the development of swapbody, intermodal and palletised parcel traffic, which has shown a substantial growth. Substitution of intermodal packages for conventional freight wagonload business is one of the themes of Plan 2000 (see above). Another is elimination of paperwork in favour of EDI wherever possible.

DSB currently moves some 7.4 million tonnes of freight a year. Of that just over 2.1 million tonnes uses the Great Belt train ferries. But by the mid-1990s DSB expects that fixed link will be carrying on rail almost as much tonnage as its whole network does at present.

In its domestic market DSB is hopeful of substantial new non-bulk business from the novel '+ Box' container system it was introducing nationally in 1989. DKr35 million has been invested in the equipment, developed in conjunction with HMK Truck A/S and submitted to four years of R&D before acceptance.

The containers, manufactured in steel-lined aluminium, are 3.34 m long, 2.55 m wide and 2.67 m high; internal load area is 17 m^3 and payload capacity 6.8 tonnes. Each end is a roller shutter door; and when rolled back the two doors mesh with each other below the roof so that the box is completely open-ended for ease of loading or discharge.

Security is a key selling point of '+ Box'. Each container is fitted with a microcomputer that monitors interior humidity and temperature, also shocks and vibrations. It also governs by changeable codes the infrared light system that controls the container's doors. The microcomputers signal to DSB's mainframe system in Copenhagen. Thus the railway's freight management not only monitors in real time each container's transit, but is promptly alerted to any potentially damaging circumstance affecting its cargo, including attempts at theft.

The highway trucks and trailers completing the '+ Box' system are equipped with hydraulic devices that slide the containers from road vehicle to rail flat wagon or vice versa. The system has been launched with 300 containers.

Particularly in the post-1992 single European market DSB sees international traffic as offering its best hopes of expanding freight business. One method already paying dividends is partnerships with private carriers or forwarding agents that exploit the trunk-haul economy of a dedicated train: examples include a twice-weekly charter service to Dijon, France, and the Mahe charter service to and from Paris. Intermodal traffic to and from Italy has quadrupled since 1986.

The Scandinavian railways have combined to create more opportunities for long-haul dedicated train operation. The Nordic European Railway Unit (NERU), formed of the Norwegian, Swedish, Finnish and Danish State Railways, opened its account in May 1989 with through container/swapbody trains to Bochum Langendreer in the Ruhr. These trains, assembled for their through journey at Helsingborg and Copenhagen, take the Danlink route to West Germany.

NERU programmes similar operations to Italy in May 1990, to France and Spain in 1991 and to Benelux in 1992. Quite possibly NERU will become a free-standing subsidiary of the railways, with the resources to market total door-to-door packages. Meanwhile, Intercontainer has been improving the Spanish connections of all container terminals served by DSB. The latter are located at Copenhagen, Esjberg, Odense, Aarhus, Albor, Herning, Skive, Slagelse, Naestved, Nykobing F and Fredericia.

DSB is working with its NERU partners in evaluation of various bi-modal designs, so as to arrive at a choice of type common to all NERU systems and acceptable also to the German Federal and Netherlands Railways. In 1990 two RoadRailer vehicles were to be evaluated.

Danlink differences

Relations with SJ have been somewhat strained by SJ's plans to launch two jumbo train ferries on a Malmö-Lubeck/Travemünde route in 1994. SJ transit traffic presently accounts for a third of DSB's Danlink route tonnage for Germany. The SJ view is, first, that post-1992 traffic will far outstrip the Danlink ferries' capacity; and, second, that even when the Great Belt fixed link is finished, routeing via Denmark is an unacceptably long detour. This latter view could be changed if the political and industrial pressure mounted in north Germany in early 1990 for an underwater tunnel to replace the Puttgarden-Rødby ferries were successful. This would create an uninterrupted Hamburg-Copenhagen rail route of 360 km, compared with 550km via Padborg, Fredericia and the Great Belt.

Intermodal business forms 30 per cent of DSB's international traffic, spearheaded by a tenfold upsurge in swapbody movement to over 40 000 units a year since 1985. In 1989 DSB ordered 50 bogie container wagons from Rautaruukki Oy of Finland, with an option on 25 more.

Airport link studies

In 1987 DSB commissioned feasibility and engineering studies of a 10-station S-Bane or light rail line from Copenhagen's Fredriksberg station to the city's Kastrup airport. Some 10 km of tunnel would be involved. The Greater Copenhagen Council has contributed DKr5 million to the studies' cost.

Electrification

The segregated Copenhagen suburban S-Bane system operates on 1500 volts dc overhead supply. This system was extended by 24 km from Ballerup to Frederikssund in May 1989.

A 25 kV ac main-line electrification is in progress. Main-line electric trains began operating between Copenhagen and Helsingør in March 1986 and from Copenhagen to Roskilde in May 1988.

It was originally planned to complete 25 kV ac electrification on Zealand before any wiring on Funen or Jutland, but policy has been revised with the firm decision to build the Store Baelt fixed link and renewed hope of a fixed link with Sweden. The objective now is to project the catenary to Odense in time for the expected 1993 opening of the Store Baelt fixed link. Thereafter catenary will probably be erected to the German frontier or Padborg, to achieve electric traction of transit freight. However, as described above, there is a possibility that the Germans will go for a fixed Puttgarden-Rødby link across the Fermen sound.

Motive power and rolling stock

Motive power and rolling stock operated by DSB in 1989 were: 10 line-haul electric locomotives; 181 line-haul diesel locomotives; 176 shunting diesel locomotives; 759 passenger coaches; (including 17 sleeping, 3 conference and 25 couchette cars); 4303

Air-conditioned second-class saloon of IC/3 train-set

DSB ferry services		km
Korsør-Nyborg	passenger and rail ferries	26
Halsskov-Knudhoved	passenger and car ferries	19
Kalundborg-Samsø	passenger and car ferries	41
Bøjden-Fynshav	passenger and car ferries	14
Helsingør-Helsingborg (Sweden)	passenger, rail and car ferries	5
Copenhagen-Helsingborg (Sweden)	rail freight ferry	39
Rødby Faerge-Puttgarden (W Germany)	passenger, rail and car ferries	19
Gedser-Warnemünde (E Germany)	passenger, rail and car ferries	48
Kalundborg-Aarhus	passenger and car ferries	89
Esjberg-Fanoe	passenger and car ferries	3.5
The above services are operated by 27 DSB ferries, 1 motor boat and 4 foreign ferries		
In co-operation with the Swedish State Railways (SJ), DSB runs:		
Dragør-Limhamn (Sweden)	passenger and car ferries	17
Copenhagen-Helsingborg (Sweden)	passenger hydrofoils and catamarans	36
In co-operation with SAS, DSB runs:		
Kastrup-Malmö (Sweden)		

freight wagons; 49 mail and 14 baggage cars; 299 electric train-sets (598 cars) for Copenhagen suburban lines. DSB also operates 586 buses.

In 1990 DSB ordered 12 more Class EA electric locomotives. Electrical equipment will be by ABB, with assembly by ABB Scandia.

In 1989 orders were placed with Cockerill Mechanical Industries of Belgium for 20 Class MJ diesel-hydrostatic shunters. To be powered by Caterpillar Type 3408 BTA 525 hp/2100 rpm engines with Sauer hydrostatic transmissions, and equipped with BSI automatic couplers and for remote radio control, the 40-tonne, two-axle units would be delivered between end-1990 and early 1993.

With the delivery by early 1990 of 15 new IC/3 train-sets, the diesel-hydraulic Type MA 'Lyntog' train-sets were withdrawn.

Signalling

In 1984 DSB began installation in Copenhagen of a new operating centre (DC) to control all trains running east of the Great Belt. It will be fully computer- and microprocessor-based, embodying numerous automatic functions. A network-wide information system (EMPS) will be linked with the DC, automatically providing staff and public with up-to-date information on train running in relation to schedule via tv screens and flap-type train indicators. In the DC controllers will be able to extract instantaneously from the computer system revised train plans when operating non-conformity with timetable is detected; DSB has not yet decided whether to extend this facility to automatic implementation of a revised plan (in the rearrangement of loop meets by trains on single line, for example), when working gets out of course.

After a careful analysis of five different tenders to equip the DC project, a contract was signed with Siemens. The contract covers CTC equipment, automatic train describers, automatic routeing, public information equipment, and equipment for remote control of the traction current. Commissioning began in late 1985. The whole line between Klampenborg north of Copenhagen and Roskilde west of Copenhagen, a total of 45 km, was taken into use in May 1990. Installation would continue westward so that when the Great Belt fixed link opens in 1993 the new system will cover the line all the way to Fredericia. Smaller parts of lines around Fredericia were taken into use in 1989.

Under DSB's 'Plan 2000' maximum speed will be increased from 140 to 180 km/h on most of the DSB's main lines. This is a prerequisite for the planned

Diesel-hydraulic railcars on Fredericia-Svendborg service leave Årup (*John C Baker*)

interval timetable system. The level of safety must also be increased, since the DSB has at present no simple AWS system. Therefore at the end of 1988 the DSB signed contracts for the Siemens ZUB 100 system. The total investment (including installation) of the contracts amounted to DKr470 million. The DSB's aim is to have ATC on all lines by 1996-97, for a total investment of some DKr700 million.

The 1988 orders covered 267 vehicle and 3220 trackside equipments. Additional orders were expected. It was planned to start operations with a prototype system at the end of 1989; the entire project was scheduled for completion by late 1992.

The ZUB 100 system for DSB utilises the maximum message length of 96 information bits plus eight code security bits. As a result, it is possible not only to transmit DSB's highly complex signalling system in its entirety but also to include an indication of the following signal, and thus provide for running speeds of 160 to 180 km/h without modifying the entire signalling system at considerable expense.

ZUB 100 is able to transmit the signalling information via additional trackside loops located from about 300 m ahead of the signal; this improves the headway on signal approach. DSB has adopted a further refinement in certain station areas. This involves the ZUB 100 message being transmitted via continuous conductors laid in the track to an additional receiver antenna on the locomotive. Thus, lower-cost intermittent control will be combined with the more sophisticated continuous control in situations where overall economies can be achieved.

In late 1989 DSB invited bids for supply and installation of an Advanced Train Control System (ATCS) on the 70km Struer-Thisted line in north Jutland. The system will provide for radio data link transmission of movement authority from the line's computerised signalling centre to trains, and return data on train location prompted by track-mounted transponders.

Track
Rail: Flat-bottom, 60, 45 kg/m
Cross ties (sleepers)
 Twin-block concrete: SL AND S/5 255 × 2327.5 mm

Diesel locomotives

Class	Wheel arrangement	Transmission	Rated power kW	Max speed km/h	Total weight tonnes	No in service 1989	Year first built	Builders Mechanical parts	Engine & type	Transmission
MZ 1401-1426	Co-Co	Elec	2270	143	120	26	1967	Nydqvist & Holm, Frichs	GM 16-645-E3	Thrige
MZ 1427-1446	Co-Co	Elec	2865	165	121-126	20	1972	Nydqvist & Holm, Frichs	GM 20-645-E3	GM
MZ 1447-1461	Co-Co	Elec	2865	165	123	15	1977	Nydqvist & Holm, Frichs	GM 20-645-E3	GM
MX 1001-1045	AIA-AIA	Elec	1015	133	89	32	1960	Nydqvist & Holm, Frichs	GM 567C, 12 cyl	Thrige
MY 1101-1159	AIA-AIA	Elec	1395	133	102	51	1954	Nydqvist & Holm, Frichs	GM 567C, 16 cyl	GM, Thrige
MT 151-167	Bo-Bo	Elec	361	90	52	17	1958	Frichs	MTU MB 12V 493 AZ1	Titan
MH 201-203	C	Hydr	323	60	45	3	1957	Henschel	MAN-W 8V 17-5/22A	Voith
MH 301-420	C	Hydr	323	60	41	98	1960	Frichs	MAN-W 8V 17-5/22A	Voith
ME 1501-1537	Co-Co	Elec	2270	175	115	37	1981	Thyssen-Henschel, Scandia	GM 16-645-E3B	BBC
Tractor 101-116	B	Mech	123	60	28	3	1951	Ardelt-Werke	MAN-W 5V 17-5/22A	Ardelt
Tractor 117-146	B	Mech	123	60	28	15	1955	Frichs	Frichs 4185 CA	Ardelt
Tractor 251-290	B	Hydr	94	45	17	40	1966	Frichs	Leyland UE 680	Voith

Diesel railcars or multiple-units

Class	Cars per unit	Motor cars per unit	Motored axles per motor car	Transmission	Rated power kW per motor	Max speed km/h	Weight per car mm (M-motor T-trailer)	Total seating capacity	Length per car mm (M-motor T-trailer)	No in service 1989	Year first built	Builders Mechanical parts	Engine & type	Transmission
MR/MRD	2	2	2	Hydr	191	130	34.5	128	22 500	97	1979	Duewag/Scandia	KHD F12L413F	Voith
MA	8	2	2	Hydr	647 (traction) 218 (auxiliary)	160	M 51 T 26-29	257	M 20 800 T 18 250-18 400	5	1963	MAN/Wegmann/Link Hofmann	Maybach MD 650/1 (traction) MWM TRHS 518A (auxiliary)	Voith
ML/FL	3	2	2	Hydr	132	80	M 27 T 18	160	M 17 530 T 17 450	3	1984	Duewag/Scandia	Daimler-Benz OM 407H	Voith
MFA/FF/MFB	3	2	2	Hydr/Mech	250	180	M + T + M 90	M 36/44 T 46	M 20 533 T 17 733	50*	1988	Ascan-Scandia/Duewag	KHD BFBL-513-CP	ZF 5HP600

* On order for 1990/91 delivery

Electric locomotives

Class	Wheel arrangement	Line voltage	Rated output (kW) continuous	Max speed km/h	Weight tonnes	No in service 1989	Year first built	Builders Mechanical parts	Builders Electrical equipment
EA	Bo-Bo	25 kV 50 Hz	4000	175	80	10	1985	Thyssen-Henschel/ Scandia	BBC

Electric multiple-units (Copenhagen suburban lines)

Class	Cars per unit	Line voltage	Motor cars per unit	Motored axles per motor car	Rated output kW per motor	Max speed km/h	Weight tonnes per car (M-motor T-trailer)	Total seating capacity	Length per car mm (M-motor T-trailer)	No in service 1989	Rate of acceleration m/s²	Year first built	Builders Mechanical parts	Builders Electrical equipment
MM/FS	2	1.5 kV dc	1	4	147	100	M 42 T 28	130	M 20 270 T 20 270	145	0.75	1968	Scandia	GEC
MM/FU/ MU/FS/	4	1.5 kV dc	2	4	147	100	M 42 T 29 M 43 T 28	260	M 20 270 T 20 340 M 20 340 T 20 270	65	0.75	1975	Scandia	GEC
FC/MC/ MC/FC	4	1.5 kV dc	2	4	210, 218	120	M 46 T 34	250	M 20 100 T 20 790	4	0.90	1979	Scandia	ASEA, GEC
FC/MC/ MC/FC	4	1.5 kV dc	2	4	150	100	M 48.5 T 34.5	240	M 20 580 T 20 765	8	0.90	1986	Scandia	ASEA

Monobloc concrete: S89 224 × 2500 mm
Thickness: 224 mm
Spacing: 1600/km
Fastenings: Nosslok w/SKL 1
Minimum curvature radius: 300 m
Max gradient: 1.25%
Max axleload: 22.5 tonnes

After 30 years' standardisation of French-type twin-block concrete sleepers, DSB has now switched to monobloc. A monobloc manufacturing plant at Fredericia began deliveries in March 1989.

Ferry services
The geography of the country makes ferries a necessity; DSB operates ten routes with a total of 31 ferries and other vessels either alone or in conjunction with the Swedish State Railways (SJ), the Deutsche Bundesbahn (DB) and the Deutsche Reichsbahn (DR). Three of the routes are served by rail/road ferries.

Dominican Republic

Ministry of Public Works and Communications

Avenida San Cristobal, Santo Domingo

State Secretary: Ing Pedro Delgado Malagón

Central Romana Railroad

Central Romana, La Romana

President: C Morales T
Vice-President and General Superintendent: R J Rivera
Director, Purchases: B R Grullon

Gauge: 1435 mm
Route length: 375 km

The railroad operates 16 locomotives and 950 freight cars.

Dominica Government Railway

Santo Domingo

Gauge: 588, 762 and 1067 mm
Route length: 142 km

The railway operates five locomotives and 70 freight cars.

Ecuador

Ministry of Public Works

1184 Avenida 6 de Diciembre y Wilson, Quito

Telephone: +593 2 242 666
Telex: 2353

Minister: J A Neira Carrasco
Under-Secretary: J Lanas Silva
Director-General: L Gallardo Roman

State Railways of Ecuador (ENFE)
Empresa Nacional de los Ferrocarriles del Estado

PO Box 159, Calle Bolivar 443, Quito

Telephone: +593 2 216 180
Telex: 2663 miopq
Cable: Chimborazo

Director: Jorge Bastidas
Traffic Manager: Vicente Cevallos Cazar
Director Administration: Arg Bayardo Tobar
Supervisor: Ing José Guevara G
Chief of Finance: Lic Rommel Illesacas
Director Technical Dept: Ing César F Noboa U
Diesel Maintenance Engineer: Marcelo Flores
Transport and Telecommunications Engineer: Luis Zapata G
Motive Power Superintendent: César Rodriguez
Permanent Way Engineer: Marco Redrobán A
Manager, FC Quito-San Lorenzo: Col P Garcia

Gauge: 1067 mm
Route length: 965.5 km

Railway	Gauge	Length
FC Guayaquil-Quito	1067 mm	446.7 km
*FC Quito-San Lorenzo	1067 mm	373.4 km
FC Sibambe-Cuenca	1067 mm	145.4 km

*The FC Quito-San Lorenzo is operated as a separate railway.

Ecuador, 275 000 square km in area, is bordered by the Pacific Ocean on the west, Colombia on the north, and Peru on the south and east.

The principal line, 446.7 km long, connects Guayaquil, the main port and largest city of the country, with Quito, which lies at some 2800 metres altitude in the Sierra of the Andes. From Durán the line runs across low lying plains for 87 km to Bucay, at the foot of the western slopes of the Andes. Over the next 79 km the line climbs 2940 metres at an average grade over the whole section of 3.7 per cent (1 in 27). The line strikes many sharp curves, and several stretches are laid on a grade of 5.5 per cent (1 in 18), including a double reversing zig-zag which was required to negotiate a particularly awkward mountain outcrop known as the Nariz del Diablo (Devil's Nose). Once the summit of this section is reached at Palmira, 3238 metres in altitude and 166 km from Durán, the line remains in the high Sierra, never falling below 2500 metres, and rising to 3609 metres at the overall summit of Urbina, 264 km from Durán.

There has been no through service between Durán and Quito since catastrophic floods of 1982-83 cut the line in several places. Damage was aggravated by a landslide in 1984. Restoration of this section is ENFE's top priority. A 20 km realignment in one affected area, between Bucay and Palmira, was recently completed.

The two remaining lines of the system link Quito with San Lorenzo, on the north-west coast of Ecuador near the Colombian border; and Sibambe, 131 km from Durán on the main line, with Cuenca, an important provincial capital in the southern part of the country. The San Lorenzo line was finally completed, with the aid of French backing, in 1957.

New President backs rehabilitation
Soon after his accession to power in August 1988, the country's President Rodrigo Borja Cevallos affirmed that he considered the train 'a vital necessity for the country, especially for the poorest. . . .the symbol of my government's philosophy.' His problem has been to find the finance to recoup years of neglected investment.

In July 1989 a new statute imposed an annual tax on all imported autos to finance a railway modernisation and development fund, which would also gain a US$3.5 million credit from the InterAmerican Development Bank.

Apart from infrastructure repair renewal, there was hope of financing acquisition of 19 diesel-electric locomotives of 1200–1400 hp, 18 passenger cars and 150 freight cars, including 26 flatcars. Also sought was modernisation of signalling and substitution of radio dispatching for an antique telegraphic system.

French offer aid
Following a visit to Ecuador by President Mitterand in October 1989, France offered a gift of FFr4.2 million and a credit of FFr165 million for rehabilitation of the railway. On this basis GEC-Alsthom were in 1990 putting up proposals for supply of nine locomotives, and Sofrerail offers of assistance in betterment of the rail system.

New line
The principal ambition of ENFE is to build a new north-south axis connecting the oil port of Esmeraldas, in the north of the country on the Pacific coast, with Machala, the inland centre of banana plantations south of Guayaquil. It would not entail difficult civil engineering. There would be a case for up to three branches to the line, one to serve a major economic development area based on prawn farms at Manta.

Traffic

	1986	1987
Total freight tonnes	37 100	36 800
Total freight tonne-km (000)	5679.4	5597.0
Total passenger-km (000)	36 817.4	20 901.0
Total passenger journeys	2 084 400	1 642 200

Motive power and rolling stock

Locomotives	
diesel-electric	13
steam	6
Railcars	31
Passenger coaches	50
Freight wagons	308

The diesel locomotives are a mix of Alco DL535B Co-Cos and Alsthom 960 hp B-B-Bs. Of late only six of the former and four of the latter have been in use.

Type of coupler in standard use: Automatic
Type of brake in standard use: Air

Track
Rails: 35, 30, 27.5 and 22.5 kg/m
Sleepers: Wood, 2000 × 2000 × 180 mm
Spacing: 1700/km
Minimum curve radius: 20°
Max gradient: 5.5%
Max axleload: 15 tonnes

Egypt
Ministry of Transport Communications and Shipping

Cairo

Minister: Soliman Metwalli

Egyptian Railways (ER)

Station Building, Ramses Square, Cairo

Cable: Railways, Cairo
Telex: 92616 astrod un

Chairman: H Gado
Deputy Chairmen
  Operation and Regions: Eng A S Fayed
  Track and Structures: Dr Eng Fathy Kames
  Technical and Engineering: Eng M Hasan El Sahn
  Planning and Projects: Dr A Kader Larheen
General Manager: A Abu Mawash
General Manager, Rolling Stock: William Naseef
Deputy General Manager, Permanent Way:
  N Saddik

Gauge: 1435 mm
Route length: 4548 km
Electrification: 42 km at 1.5 kV dc

The railways in Egypt are mainly confined to the more fertile area of the Nile Delta, with a line following the course of the Nile southward to Shâllal, just below Aswân.

Egyptian Railways, which forms the largest system in the country, extends from the Mediterranean down the Nile Valley, serving the Nile Delta, Cairo, Alexandria, Port Said, Ismailia, Suez and connecting at Shâllal, its southernmost point, with the river steamers of Sudan Railways. From El Quantara, on the Port Said-Ismailia line, a branch runs east following the coast and connects with Israel Railways.

Traffic
In modern times ER has always been primarily a passenger railway, recording four to five times as many passenger-km as freight tonne-km. In terms of passenger-km, now at a level of some 3 000 million annually, volume has more than doubled since 1970. ER has correspondingly expanded train lengths substantially, with the aid of 700 new main-line day cars and 605 new suburban cars acquired since the mid-1970s; the suburban stock has supplanted some 340 diesel railcars. Freight too has advanced, though ER has only a 12 per cent national market share. Current levels are some 9 million tonnes and 2900 million tonne-km a year. The main constituent is 2 million tonnes of ore a year on the Baharia-Helwan line (see below), with wheat and oil next in importance.

New five-year investment plan
In November 1987 the Transport Minister disclosed a new five-year development plan. Its main components were: double-tracking from Sohag to Qena on the north-south main line, from Dekernis to Matarya, and from El Marg to Shebin; upgrading of the Imbaba-Itay el Barud, Cairo-Qalyub, Benha-Alexandria and Giza-Beni Suef sections; and resignalling and telecommunications modernisation. ER has difficulty in financing its development from its own resources because of the low level at which its tariffs are contained.

Turbotrains
Three ten-car turbotrain sets built by ANF-Industrie provide prime service over the 208 km between Cairo and Alexandria. The trains' current best timing is 2 hours 45 minutes, inclusive of two intermediate stops. It is hoped eventually to exploit this equipment's 160 km/h capability to achieve a Cairo-Alexandria transit in 1½ hours, with each of the train-sets completing three round trips daily. Initially, however, the turbotrains have been confined to a limit of 140 km/h, and that only over certain sections. In the Cairo area speed cannot exceed 60 km/h for some 25 km distance.

Carrying up to 150 trains an hour in the Cairo and Alexandria suburban areas and 60 to 80 on the intervening main line, the route is being resignalled by French industry. Six control centres of the entrance-exit route relay type with associated train describers are being established at the line's main centres in conjunction with four-aspect colour-light signalling. The route is already equipped with the Siemens system of ATC.

Rolling stock
Coaching stock purchases have been given priority over freight vehicles because of the passenger fleet's lack of substantial enlargement since the early 1960s, since when rail passenger journeys per annum have trebled.

Luxury air-conditioned overnight trains formed from a fleet of 60 sleeping cars, 12 club cars and 12 generator cars built by Messerschmitt-Bölkow-Blohm operate on the Cairo-Luxor-Aswan route. These cars are deployed in seven-car units each comprising five sleeping cars, a club car and a generator car. Running is non-stop between Cairo and Luxor in either direction. Pre-prepared meals are served to passengers in their compartments from galleys in each sleeping car.

Recent deliveries have been dominated by an order for 300 air-conditioned cars, including bar facilities, placed with Francorail and supported by a French government loan of E£34 million. For lower-class accommodation cars ER has relied primarily on local builders Semaf, who have provided 120 air-conditioned second-class cars mounted on Ganz-Mávag bogies. Equipment of the Cairo and Alexandria suburban systems with bi-level cars is under consideration.

In 1989 Semaf gained an order to build a further 40 luxury sleeping cars for the Cairo-Luxor-Aswan service, adopting the previous MBB design under licence.

At latest report, rolling stock totalled 805 diesel locomotives, 143 diesel shunters, three turbo-trains, 21 dmus, 100 emus, 2321 passenger cars, 17 railcars and 15 845 freight wagons.

Traffic

	1986/87
Freight tonnage (million)	8.616
Freight tonne-km (million)	2896
Passenger-km (million)	28 339.7
Passenger journeys (million)	612

Thyssen-Henschel Type AA22T 3000 hp Co-Co locomotives with GM engines

Club car of Cairo-Luxor luxury train, with air-conditioning by BBC Brown Boveri

Finance (E£ million)

	1986/87
Revenue	
Passenger and baggage	82.854
Freight, parcels and mail	34.267
Other income	28.912
Total	146.033
Expenditure	
Staff/personnel	129.449
Materials and services	52.093
Depreciation	66.216
Financial charges	187.178
Total	433.936

Western desert rehabilitation

The Transport Ministry has authorised a E£30 million rehabilitation of the Alexandria-Mersa Matruh line to promote tourism and foster development in the western desert. The line is to be double-tracked and its 43 stations rebuilt. Also being double-tracked is the Nile route to Aswan.

In October 1989 the Presidents of Egypt and Libya signed an agreement extending this project across the border between them. Rehabilitation would be continued beyond Mersa Matruh to El Salloum, and from there a new 150km line would be built to Tobruk.

Another priority is renovation of the 350 km line built shortly after the Second World War with Soviet aid from Helwan to Baharia, which is primarily an ore-and coal-carrier. The present alignment is prone to interruption by drifting sand at several points and needs rerouteing. With German loan finance contracts for the work were let in 1988. Semaf is to build new ore wagons for the line. Revival of passenger traffic is planned after the route's rehabilitation.

To the east, ER now plans to restore to use the whole of the line between Suez and Ismailia. Since destruction of a bridge in the Six-Day War of June 1967 the line has been cut short at El Rassoua. The Transport Minister approved the E£3 million scheme in 1986.

New control organisation

A new Central Operations Control System (COCS) is based on seven Regional offices and a co-ordinating office at headquarters. Regional controllers now have direct radio communication with many correspondingly-equipped locomotives.

Signalling

French industry has resignalled the 48 km between Benha and Cairo, a route recently quadruple-tracked, and a French consortium has a Fr460 million contract for the supply of resignalling telecommunications and CTC between Giza and Beni Suef. Siemens has a contract to install ATC on the Alexandria-Cairo-Assiut route. A 13 km section at the approach to Alexandria has been converted from two-to four-track and resignalled. Other CTC centres are to be established at Alexandria, Assyout, Luxor, Mersa Matruh, Tanta and Zagazig. Tokenless block working is to be installed between Sohag and Nag Hammadi.

France is helping financially to fund resignalling around Alexandria, and Alsthom has been bidding against Ansaldo of Italy to resignal 120 km of the north-south line between Beni Suef and Minya.

Double-tracking to Aswan

It was announced in 1988 that double-tracking was to be completed throughout the Cairo-Luxor-Aswan main line. The work involves renewal of 107 km of existing track and laying of 88 km of new track.

New lines

The infrastructure of a 70 km line from Port Said to the Nile Delta has been completed from Mansura to Matareyya, and is in operation over 24 km to Dikernis, but the final 24 km into Port Said entails a crossing of the Manzala lake and that is taking time to execute.

The most important new railway in hand, because of its freight potential, is a 590 km line which will span the Nile and connect phosphate mines at Tartour in the western desert with a new Red Sea port at Safaga, intersecting the Cairo-Aswan line and using it between Qena and Nag'Hammadi.

In 1983 the Hollandse Constructie Group won a E£16 million contract to build the 1.2 km bridge over the Nile at Nag'Hammadi and it was anticipated that completion of this would soon be followed by a start of work on the western 363 km of the new line, from Qena to Abu Tartour. The track of the new railway is being laid with 60 kg/m rail on concrete sleepers with K fastenings.

The 227 km from Qena, on the north-south main line, to Safaga nears completion. Pending completion of the western section, the line will convey bauxite from Safaga port to an aluminium plant near Nag'Hammadi and finished products in the reverse direction. For this traffic five 3600 hp diesels and 94 wagons will be required. After commissioning of the western section the line will initially convey some 7 million tonnes a year of phosphates from Abu Tartour, for which ER will need 26 3600 hp diesel locomotives and 770 freight cars. The ultimate output from the phosphate workings is expected to double the early figure; that will necessitate purchase of an additional 31 locomotives and 680 wagons.

Also envisaged is the southward extension of the north-south railway and its present limit at El-Sadd El-Aali to the Sudanese border at Wadi Halfa.

Diesel locomotives

Class	Wheel arrangement	Transmission	Rated power (hp)	Max speed km/h	Total weight tonnes	No in service 1987	Year first built	Builders Mechanical parts	Engine & type	Transmission
JT22MC	Co-Co	Elec	3000	140	111	45	1983	GM-EMD	645E3-12	GM-EMD
AA22T	Co-Co	Elec	3000	140	121	21	1983	Henschel and GM-EMD	645E3-12	GM-EMD
AA22T	Co-Co	Elec	3000	120	121	203	1975–84	Henschel and GM-EMD	645E3-12	GM-EMD
G26CW	Co-Co	Elec	2900	140	98	32	1973–76	GM-EMD	645E-16	GM-EMD
G22W/AC	Bo-Bo	Elec	2200	105	80	228	1980	GM-EMD	645E-12	GM-EMD
G22W	Bo-Bo	Elec	2200	105	80	32	1978	GM-EMD	645E-12	GM-EMD
AA22T/DB	Co-Co	Elec	3000	80	122	29	1979	Thyssen-Henschel and GM-EMD	645E3-12	GM-EMD

El Salvador

Ministry of Public Works

1a Avenida sur 630, San Salvador

Minister: L Lopez Ceron

El Salvador National Railways (FENADESAL)

Ferrocarriles Nacionales de El Salvador

PO Box 2292, Avenida Peralta 903, San Salvador

Telephone: +503 715672
Telex: 20-194 Area 301
Telefax: +503 241355

President (CEPA): M Suarez Barrientos
General Manager (CEPA): Jose Ricardo Hernandez Platero
Operations Manager: J A Nunez B
Chief Purchasing Agent: E Wilfredo Ciudad Real
Chief Finance: M A Flint
Chief Transportation: Ing Luis Alfredo Carballo R
Traffic Manager: Andre s Escoto
Chief, Rolling Stock and Equipment: J Fernando Pineda
Chief Maintenance of Way: Manuel Ortiz

Gauge: 914 mm
Route length: 601.6 km

Ferrocarriles Nacionales de El Salvador (FENADESAL) was formed from two railways which were formerly the property of overseas companies: the Salvador Railway, which passed to the state in 1965 under the name of Ferrocarril de El Salvador (FES); and the International Railways of Central America (IRCA), a railway undertaking that includes the railway system and port at Cutuco, which was nationalised in 1974 under the name of Ferrocarril Nacional de El Salvador (FEN-ASAL).

The two undertakings were merged under state control in May 1975, together with the port of Cutuco, and renamed Ferrocarriles Nacionales de El Salvador (FENADESAL). The railway is administered by the Commission Ejecutive Portuaria Autonoma (CEPA).

FES and FENASAL are divided into three districts: District No 1 which comprises San Salvador (the capital) to the port of Cutuco, Department of La Union (East Zone of the country), (252 km).

District No 2 which runs from San Salvador to the frontier of El Salvador with Guatemala (146 km), and a branch to Ahuachapan, in the west of the country (60 km).

District No 3 which runs from San Salvador to the port of Acajutia, on the Pacific Ocean (104 km), and includes a branch from Sitio del Nino to Santa Ana in the west (40 km).

Diesel locomotives

Class	Wheel arrangement	Transmission	Rated power kW	Max speed km/h	Total weight tonnes	Year first built	Builders Mechanical parts	Engine & type	Transmission
GA-8	Bo-Bo	Elec	595	57	61	1965	GM	GM 567 CR	EMD
4GE747	B-B	Elec	280	60	47	1956	GE	Caterpillar D-397	GE
4GE764	B-B	Elec	630	57	65	1956	GE	Caterpillar D-398	GE

Traffic	1987	1988
Freight tonnage	353 344	319 880
Freight tonne-km (000)	39 500	36 100
Passenger-km (000)	5600	6000
Passenger-journeys (000)	364	389.7

Traffic
The country's political unrest has had a severe impact on the railway's business. Passenger traffic in particular has slumped more than 75 per cent since 1980. International traffic, principally exported coffee and imported fertiliser, makes up well over half the railway's freight business.

Motive power and rolling stock
Diesel-electric locomotives	17
Steam locomotives	4
Railcars	2
Passenger coaches	57
Freight wagons	550

Track
Rail: ASCE 54-60-6570 and 75 lb/yd
Sleepers: Hardwood 7 ft
Fastenings: Standard, spike and angle bar 54/75 lb per yard
Spacing: 1667/km
Minimum curvature radius: 80 m on main lines, 60 m elsewhere
Max gradient: 3.6%
Max axleloading: 17.5 tonnes

Ethiopia

Chemin de Fer Djibouti-Ethiopien (CDE)

PO Box 1051, Addis Ababa

Telephone: +251 1 44 7250
Cable: Djibeba, Addis Ababa
Telex: 21414

President, Administrative Council: Y Ahmed
General Manager: T Tamerou
Technical Director: F Badar

Gauge: 1000 mm
Route length: 781 km

Rail and highway traffic and development have been severely affected by guerilla activity since the 1970s. There are two separate railways: the larger is the metre-gauge CDE Railway running from the port of Jibuti to Addis Ababa, a route length of 781 km of which 100 km are in Jibuti; the other is the 950 mm gauge Northern Ethiopia Railway, 306 km long, running from the Red Sea port of Massawa inland to Agordat, but this has been out of action since 1978.

Since 1982 the railway has been under joint control of the republics of Jibuti and Ethiopia, but with its headquarters remaining in Addis Ababa. The Transport Ministers of the two countries occupy the positions of President and Vice-President.

Since 1987 a rehabilitation programme has been under way with aid from several European countries, notably Italy. It features relaying with 36 kg/m rail over 80 km, with the aim of raising maximum axle-loadings to 17.2 tonnes, increasing maximum freight train speeds to 70 km/h and improving traffic regulation (at present effected by telephonic despatching). Before this work was begun only the first 171 km of the route were laid with 30 kg/m rail; the objective now is to install 36 kg/m over 300 route-km.

The government contemplates a new 860 km railway from Addis Ababa to the Red Sea port of Assab. In 1987 RITES secured a contract to pursue an engineering design study of this project. However, the estimated cost represents a quarter of the country's GNP and the scheme was not favoured by the World Bank, which regarded the RITES traffic forecasts of 4.5 million tonnes of freight per annum as extremely optimistic. Nevertheless, in October 1987 agreements were signed with the USSR and seven other Comecon countries, including Cuba, whereby the Comecon group would substantially support the project, with a start of work set for 1989.

The railway stands to benefit from a current development of Djibouti port, which will double its container throughput capability. A substantial share of the inland movement of the port's container traffic is by rail.

Rolling stock
Diesel locomotives	25
Locotractors	4
Diesel railcars	6
Passenger cars	58
Freight wagons	842

Locomotive stock is dominated by 15 Alsthom 1200 hp, three Alsthom 1050 hp and five Alsthom 675 hp diesel locomotives. Three SLM Type AIA-AIA 600 hp units of 1950 survive and CDE hopes to renew their diesel-generator plant for further service; also still active are two of four Alsthom C-Cs of 1967, now derated from 2400 to 1850 hp, but these are restricted in use because of their damage to the track.

The resources are completed by four Fauvet-Girel locotractors. Passenger traffic is monopolised by six 600 hp Soulé diesel railcars, each of which normally operates with three trailers.

Aid was sought from France and the EEC in 1987 for procurement of eight locomotives, two railcars and eight trailers, and 200 wagons. In 1987-88 Zeco of Zimbabwe was delivering an order of 76 freight wagons.

Track
Rail type: 20 kg, 25 kg, 30 kg
Sleepers: Metalbloc
Fastenings: Clips and bolts
Max axleloading: 13.7 tonnes

Finland

Ministry of Communications

Etela Esplanadi 16, 00130 Helsinki

Telephone: +358 0 17361
Telex: 125472 limin sf
Telefax: +358 0 173 6340

Minister: M Puhakka
Secretary-General: V S Rauvanto
Head of Railway Affairs: J Pohjola

Finnish State Railways (VR)
Valtionrautatiet

Vikhonkatu 13, 00100 Helsinki
Mailing address: PO Box 488, 00101 Helsinki

Telephone: +358 0 7071
Telex: 12301151 vr
Telefax: +358 0 707 3700

Director General: Eino Saarinen
Deputy Director General: Panu Haapala
Directors
  Freight Services; Henri Kuitunen
  Passenger Services: Juhani Kopperi (Acting)
  Transport Services Production: Erkki Nieminen
  Permanent Way: Erkki Tattari
  Economy: Veikko Vaikkinen
  Administration: Juhani Kopperi

Gauge: 1524 mm
Route length: 5863 km
Electrification: 1636 km at 25 kV 50 Hz ac

The railway network was shaped for a large part in the last century, when the railways were the most important form of transport in long-distance traffic. Only a few lines have been built since the Second World War, during a period of rapid changes in the economy and the social structure of the country. In the last few decades, the railway network has been considerably improved, so that 22.5-tonne axleloads are now permissible on main lines. The maximum permissible speed for passenger trains has been raised to 140 km/h.

Type Sr 1 locomotive stock now totals 110 units

State takes over infrastructure costs
From the start of 1990 the full cost of the railway's fixed asset upkeep, renewal and new construction, signalling and safety systems included, was transferred to the state. For use of the infrastructure VR will pay tolls at rates set annually to reflect national transport policy rather than cost factors.

In contrast to the Swedish restructure of the same kind, VR retains ownership of its infrastructure as well as managing any work upon it. But new projects such as major upgrading, new lines and electrification will require Ministerial approval.

Commercial mandate
Under the new legislation, VR becomes a fully commercial enterprise, mandated to have eradicated its annual loss and to be covering all costs of its non-social operations out of revenue by 1993. For any unremunerative activity that it is required to continue for social reasons the state will meet the loss. Parliament and the Council of State will also retain a voice in determining overall service and performance objectives.

Only 70 per cent or so of VR's recent average annual loss wil be recouped from the transfer of infrastructure costs. The rest of the saving needed for financial equilibrium must come chiefly from further cuts in staff, whose costs currently run at 85 per cent of total revenue. VR may also get a state grant to meet its

RAILWAY SYSTEMS / Finland

investment needs before it reaches solvency in 1993.

The reform clarifies decision-making regarding rail services. Previously the railway had to decide many matters which fall into the sphere of general transport policy. This included the maintenance of certain unprofitable services.

Freight traffic

Freight traffic, already accounting for nearly 75 per cent of annual traffic receipts, is regarded as the best business growth area. In 1989 volume again rose, by 2 per cent to 33.6 million tonnes, a record for the second successive year. The national timber and paper industries made a strong contribution to the rise.

VR's freight business is organised in three sectors: Domestic, International and Transpoint Services.

Industrial Services, the biggest Domestic component, offers customers comprehensive service, including loading, unloading, transport, area rentals, storage, link traffic and data services. Special emphasis has been placed on developing services for the forest, engineering, metal and chemical industries.

In recent years structural changes in the metal and engineering industries have been clearly reflected in VR's freight business. Recent mine closures in Finland have shifted the flow of ore carryings from mines to seaports and imported ore; thanks to new short-distance transport tasks, the total volume has not declined significantly, even though the change in terms of tonne-km has been considerable.

Transpoint is a country-wide transport system for intermodal and part-load freight, run in co-operation with VR's road haulage subsidiary, Pohjolan Liikenne Oy. Its traffic in 1989 was up for the fifth successive year, rising 15 per cent. New terminals were opened in Helsinki and in the industrial centre of Tampere. However, Transpoint's ISO container and piggyback traffic as yet totals only some 1.5 million tonnes a year; the gross is divided equally between containers and semi-trailers. To expand intermodal business Transpoint was restructured at the start of 1990; it is now partnered in this respect by the Finnlines Group.

In the future VR is to concentrate more intensely on those areas in which it is most competitive. The goal is to develop effective comprehensive services in which transfer work and other costly and time-consuming measures are minimised. Traditional wagonload traffic will shift towards regularly scheduled two-way services on the most important links, with the aim being to market capacity so as to reduce empty wagons. The division into domestic and international freight business will grow less distinct as the railway offers customers comprehensive services including both.

International freight traffic

International traffic accounts for 40 per cent of VR's tonnage. Just over 90 per cent of it is with the USSR, or via the USSR with other Eastern European countries and via Hungarian Railways with Italy, Austria and Southeast Europe.

Capacity to exchange traffic with Western Europe is steadily expanding thanks to new train ferry routes and availability of more wagons with interchangeable axles to negotiate the disparity in rail gauge. At present 60 per cent of the Western European freight traffic moves via the Hanko-Travemünde (West Germany) ferry route of Oy Railship Ab. The latter has installed a third ferry on this crossing and simultaneously raised its stock of over 1000 changeable-axle freight cars by 400.

In June 1989 SeaRail, an Oy Railship subsidiary, opened a Turku-Stockholm train ferry route backed with a stock of changeable-axle wagons. In October 1989, again with the support of a changeable-axle wagon fleet, another ferry route was established by Finnlink from Uusikaupunki, a new terminal some

VR has converted 11 second-class cars to provide for family travel

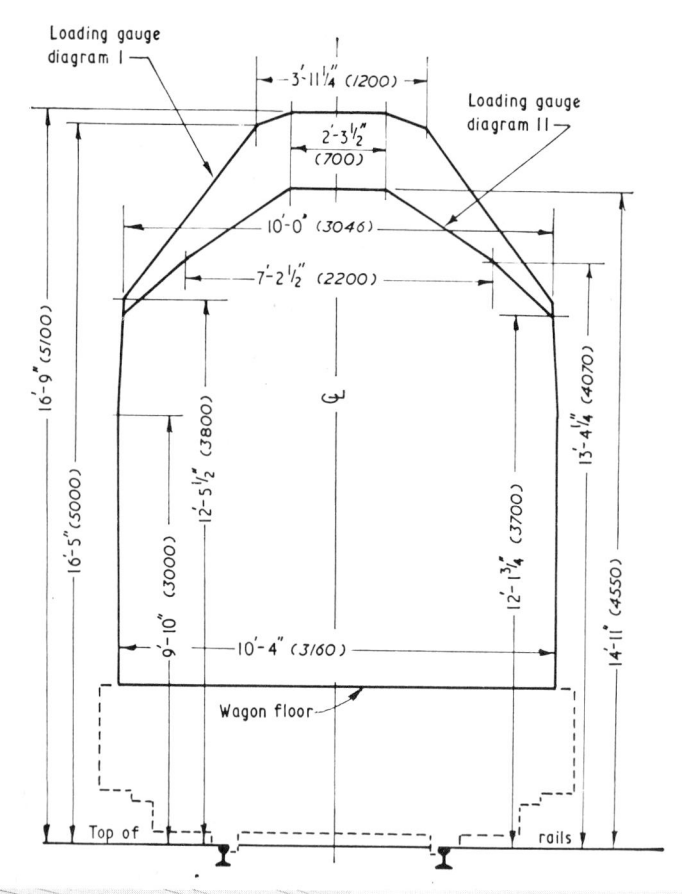

VR operates regular piggyback services from Rovaniemi and Oulu to Helsinki; 80 per cent of VR's network has clearance for this type of operation

Type Dr 16 asynchronous motor diesel locomotive and type Sim wagons with two-section sliding roof and side walls

Finland / RAILWAY SYSTEMS

65km northwest of Turku, to Hargshamm, about 100km north of Stockholm.

Passenger traffic
VR's passenger business is divided into long-distance services and local services in the Helsinki area. Local services outside the Helsinki area are included in long-distance services.

Passenger business in 1989, totalling more than 44 million journeys, improved by 2 per cent on the record figure of 1988. There was 10 per cent growth in patronage of the InterCity trains, introduced in 1988 primarily for business travellers. These are in operation on the Helsinki-Vaasa, Helsinki-Imatra and Helsinki-Tampere-Jyväskylä routes. Significant improvement was also recorded on services to the USSR, with Helsinki-Leningrad travel up 25 per cent and accompanied auto traffic to Moscow up 16 per cent.

VR has begun negotiations to start a EuroCity link from Helsinki to Hamburg via Turku, Stockholm and Copenhagen; and also to include trains from Helsinki to Leningrad and Moscow in EuroCity traffic. Acquisition of automatic tilt-body train-sets with 200 km/h capability is under consideration.

A prerequisite for a lift of maximum speed from the present 140 km/h is installation of automatic train control. That began in 1989. In addition, a great deal of further infrastructure work, including level crossing elimination, signalling alterations and modification of overhead wiring, is needed before VR can achieve its immediate aim of lifting top speed from 140 to 160 km/h on key routes.

New-generation passenger coaches for VR
VR took delivery in 1989 of 13 more new-generation passenger coaches for long-distance service. The series comprises Class Cx first-class, Class Ex second-class and Class Rx restaurant cars. Coach livery is light grey, red and black.

VR's medium-term plan includes the construction of 80 new-generation coaches by 1991. The entire series will comprise 50 second-class and 18 first-class day coaches plus 12 restaurant cars.

New vestibule and entrance door designs feature less steep steps, larger doorways and push-button plug-sliding doors. Fully-adjustable seats have a mechanism which returns the back and seat to an upright position when the seat is vacated. Armrests incorporate a hinged table for each seat. Integrated in an armrest of each first-class seat is a radio receiver system with sockets for stereo headphones; four programmes can be called up from a control panel in the armrest. Interiors have electrically-controlled destination panels, which show the name of the train, its destination, larger stations on the route and scheduled times of arrival. A microcomputerised device in the guard's compartment automatically updates the displays once it has been fed with the train's timetable number. All coaches have public address, located near doorways, for announcements to passengers on the platform. This can be set to purvey pre-recorded information.

The second-class coaches have a large centre-aisle open compartment for non-smokers and a 15-seat smaller compartment with separate ventilation arrangements for smokers. Seating is arranged 2 + 2, giving a total of 83. In open compartments the seats in each half of the coach face the centre. The first-class car combines an open compartment with seats laid out 1 + 2 and six compartments, each seating six passengers.

The new dining cars incorporate a self-service buffet and a restaurant with full waiter service at tables. More than 50 passengers can be served at a time, with 30 seated in the restaurant and 25–30 seated in the self-service section. The restaurant car also has a small compartment for train crew. This houses an information counter, where passengers can buy rail tickets, inquire about connections and make table reservations etc. A public coin telephone booth is located next to this compartment.

The new-generation coaches are designed for speeds up to 160 km/h. They run on SIG bogies and have air-operated disc brakes of type KE-PR; some will have magnetic rail brakes. An anti-skid device is microprocessor-based. Each vehicle is 26.4 m long overall and 18.3 m between bogie centres. The coach body is 26.1 m long and 3.09 wide with floor height 1.25 m above the rail. Inter-communication gangway arrangements are of a new and improved type by SIG.

Traffic	1986	1987	1988	1989
Freight (000 tonnes)				
Wagonload	27 028	29 112	31 873	NA
Part-load	755	996	1133	NA
Total	27 783	30 108	33 006	33 600
Tonne-km (million)	6952	7403	7815.9	7958
Passenger traffic				
Long-distance journeys (000)	8743	10 160	10 600	NA
Local journeys	27 458	31 208	33 146	NA
Total	34 763	41 368	43 746	45 500
Passenger-km (million)	NA	NA	3147	3208

Finances (FMk million)		
Revenue	1988	1989
Freight traffic	1923·5	1954
Passenger traffic	7·3	978·3
Other	251	229·8
Total	3092·1	3162·1

Expenditure					
Transport operations	1988	1989	Track maintenance costs	1988	1989
Staff/personnel		1928·7	Staff/personnel		378·4
Other staff costs		643·8	Other staff costs		142·1
Other expenditure		904·1	Other expenditure		631·3
Production for own use		−555·6	Production for own use		−578·9
Total	2946·0m	2921·0	Depreciation		333·6
			Total	762·5m	906·6

New Type Ex and Cx cars; the digital destination displays are microcomputer-controlled by the guard

Compartment of Type Cx car with stereo radio at seats

Traction and rolling stock
In 1989 VR operated 110 electric, 254 line-haul and 110 shunting diesel locomotives, 100 emus, 10 diesel railcars, 947 passenger cars (including 122 sleeping and 48 restaurant/buffet cars) and 15 722 freight cars.

RAILWAY SYSTEMS / Finland

Video car rebuilt from second-class car

Destination display control in guard's compartment of Type Cx car

Track
During 1989 a total of 53 km of track laid with UIC 54.45 kg/m rail was replaced with UIC 60 kg/m rail on the Riihimäki-Turenki and Luumäki-Kaipiainen sections in southern Finland.

Signalling and telecommunications
In 1990 EB Signal AB of Sweden, a member of the ABB group, gained a contract to supply Automatic Train Protection (ATP) equipment to VR over the period up to 1996. The first installations would be made in the Helsinki area. A total of 425 traction units are to be equipped.

Siemens has been commissioned to equip the stations of Piek-sämäki and Jyväskylä with microcomputer interlockings. These two stations, about 300 km north of Helsinki, have relatively heavy traffic.

Electrification
Electrification of the industrial line from Kerava to Sköldvik (36 track-km) was scheduled for completion before the end of 1990.

In 1989 VR gained government approval to electrify a further 1234 route-km. The plan is that, following the 1990 wiring of the Kerava-Sköldvik branch, teams would move straight on to the Helsinki-Turku line and complete electrification from Kirkkonummi to Turku by 1994. Also to be electrified is the Tampere-Jyväskylä-Piek:sämäki route, throughout by 1995. Both routes

Saloon of Type Ex second-class car

Diesel locomotives

Class	Wheel arrangement	Transmission	Rated power kW	Tractive effort Max lb	Continuous at lb	mph	Max speed km/h	Wheel dia mm	Total weight tons	Length mm	No in service 1989	First built	Builders Mechanical parts	Engine & type	Transmission
Dr 12	Co-Co	Elec	1400	28 000	12 800	30	120	1180	121.8	18 560	10	1959–63	Lokomo Oy, Valmet Oy	Tampella-MAN V8V 22/30 mAuL	Strömberg-BBC
Dr 13	Co-Co	Elec	2060	28 300	19 400	30	140	950	98.1	18 576	48	1962–66	Alsthom, Lokomo Oy under licence by Alsthom	Tampella-MG0 (two engines)	Strömberg
Dv 12	B-B	Hyd	1000	17 000	12 600	20	125	1000	60.8	14 000		1964–66	Lokomo Oy, Valmet Oy	Tampella-MG0 V 16 BSHR	Voith L 216 rs
Dv 12	B-B	Hyd	1000	17 000	12 000	20	125	1000	69	14 000	192	1974–79	Valmet Oy	Tampella-MG0 V 16 BSHR	Voith L 216 rs
Dv 12	B-B	Hyd	1000	18 700	12 600	20	125	1000	65.6	14 000		1965–68, 1971–72	Lokomo Oy, Valmet Oy	Tampella-MG0 V 16 BSHR	Voith L 216 rs
Dv 15	D	Hyd	620	18 800	14 300	10	75	1180	60	11 930	58	1958–61	Lokomo Oy, Valmet Oy	Tampella-MAN WBV 22/30 AmA	Voith L 217 U
Dv 16	D	Hyd	700	18 800	14 850	10	85	1270	60	11 930	28	1962–63	Lokomo Oy, Valmet Oy	Tampella-MAN W8V 22-30 AmAuL	Voith L 217 U
Dr 14	B-B	Hyd	875	24 100	21 900	5	75	1050	86	14 000	24	1969–72	Lokomo Oy	Tampella-MAN B8V 22/30 ATL	Voith L 2C6 rsb
Dr 16	Bo-Bo	Elec/ac	1500	NA	NA	NA	140	1250	84	17 600	2	1987	Valmet Oy	Wartsila Vasa 8 V22	Strömberg
Dr 16	Bo-Bo	Elec/ac	1677	NA	NA	NA	140	1250	84	17 600	2	1987	Valmet Oy	Pielstick 12 PA4-V-200	Strömberg

will be prepared for 200 km/h. VR is considering resort to self-powered electric tilting-body train-sets by ABB, with which Helsinki-Turku journey time could cut from the present 2 hours 20 minutes to 1½ hours after electrification (the deposed Sr1 locomotives would be devoted to freight haulage). Other routes covered by the proposals are the 235 km across country from Tampere to Piek-sämäki, the 135 km from Tampere to Pori, the 128 km from Turku to Toijala and, in the north, the 475 km from Iisalmi to Oulu and Rovaniemi.

Type of coupler in standard use: screw
Type of braking in standard use, locomotive-hauled stock: KE-GP, KE-GPA, KE-GP + Mg, Ke-PR + Mg

Track
Rail type: K 43 (43.367 kg/m)
K 60 (59.74 kg/m)
UIC 54 (54.43 kg/m)
UIC 60 (60 kg/m)
Sleepers: concrete 16%; wood 84%; 2700 × 240 × 160 mm; spaced 1640/km
Fastenings type: Pandrol, Hey-back
Minimum curvature radius: 300 m
Max gradient: 1.25%
Max permissible axleload: 25 tonnes Soviet wagons, 22.5 tonnes, Finnish wagons

Club car with buffet and disco facilities, rebuilt from second-class car

Electric locomotives

Class	Wheel arrangement	Rated power kW	Max lb	Continuous at lb	mph	Max speed mph	Wheel dia mm	Weight tons	Length mm	No in service 1989	Builders Mechanical parts	Electrical equipment
Sr 1	Bo-Bo	3100	57 400	39 700	44	87	1250	83	18 960	110	Energomachexport (Novocherkassky Works) USSR	Strömberg

Diesel railcars or multiple-units

Class	Cars per unit	Motor cars per unit	Motored axles per motor car	Transmission	Rated power (kW) per motor	Max speed km/h	Weight tonnes per car (M-motor T-trailer)	Total seating capacity (M-motor T-trailer)	Length per car mm (M-motor T-trailer)	No in service 1989	Year first built	Builders Mechanical parts	Engine & type	Transmission
Dm 7	1		1A + 1A	Mech	130	95	M 19.4	M 63	M 16 600	2	1951	Valmet Oy	Valmet 815D	Wilson R11
Dm 7 Trailers			—	—	—	—	T 14.7/14.9	T 46/76		2		Valmet Oy	—	—

Electric railcars or multiple-units

Class	Cars per unit	Line voltage	Motor cars per unit	Motored axles per motor car	Rated output (kW) per motor	Max speed km/h	Weight tonnes per car (M-motor T-trailer)	Total seating capacity (M-motor T-trailer)	Length per car mm (M-motor T-trailer)	No in service 1989	Rate of acceleration m/s²	Year first built	Builders Mechanical parts	Electrical equipment
Sm 1	2	25 kV 50 Hz ac	1	4	215	120	M 58.6 T 35.6	M 90 T 97	M 25 900 T 25 900	50	0.88	1968	Valmet Oy	Strömberg
Sm 2	2	25 kV 50 Hz ac	1	4	155	120	M 46.5 T 29.5	M 102 T 98	M 25 900 T 25 900	50	1.12	1975	Valmet Oy	Strömberg

France

State Transport Secretariat, Ministry of Public Works, Housing, Transport and Maritime Affairs

l'Arche, 92055 Paris La Défense Cedex 04

Telephone: +33 1 40 81 21 22
Telex: 610 835
Telefax: +33 1 40 81 39 59

Minister (Transport): Michel Delebarre
Director of Cabinet: Jean Cyril Spinetta
Deputy Director of Cabinet (International Affairs): Jean-Marie Delarue
Chief of Cabinet: Gilles Bardou
Director, Land Transport: Claude Gressier
Councillor to the Minister: Paul Mingasson
Technical Advisers:
  Jacques Colliard
  Dario d'Annunzio
  Thierry Kerisel
  François Brousse
Press Relations: Veronique Brachet

French National Railways (SNCF)
Société Nationale des Chemins de Fer Français

88 rue Saint-Lazare, 75436 Paris Cedex 09

Telephone: +33 1 42 85 60 00
Telex: 290936 sncf dg

President: Jacques Fournier
Director General: Jean Costet
Deputy Director General: Michel Fève

Chiefs of Support Services:
  Law: R Viricelle
  Safety: J-L Meyer
  Communications: M Merlay
  Audit & General Inspection: Y Roussier
  Central Organisation: P Lupo
  International Affairs: P Monserie
Assistant Director General, Operations: Roger Gerin
Business Directors:
  Passenger: Jean-Marie Metzler
  Freight: Alain Poinssot
  Ile-de-France Passenger: J Berducou
  Regional Services: J Chauvineau
  Sernam: J Peter
Production Managers:
  Traffic: Francis Taillanter
  Rolling Stock: F Lacote
  Fixed Installations: Philippe Roumeguère

562 RAILWAY SYSTEMS / France

Supplies: J-M L'Hopitalier
New Line 2 (TGV-A): Etienne Chambron
New Line 3 (TGV-N): Jean-Pierre Pronost
Marketing: P Lachaze
Assistant Director General, Economics & Finance: J-F Bernard
Department Managers
  Budget: J Bornet
  Finance: P Lubek
  Real Estate: G Verrier
  Data Processing: André Bouzy
Assistant Director General, Social Affairs & Human Resources: Jean-François Colin
Department Managers
  Personnel: J Pourdieu
  General Administration: R Dormieux
Assistant Director General, Development: Michel Walrave
Manager, Studies: J Pellegrin
Heads of Equipment Departments
  Track Design and Research: Serge Montagné
  Signalling: Jean Paul Guilloux
  Electrical Installations: Charles Gourdon
  Buildings: Jean-Marie Duthilleul
  Civil Engineering: Jacques Gandil
  General Studies and Projects: Jean-Yves Taillé
Heads of Rolling Stock Departments
  Traction Maintenance: Edmond Bissey
  Rolling Stock Maintenance: Alain Bernheim
  Construction: Gérard Coget
  Testing: Alain Moreau
  Investment: Pierre Tachet
  Laboratories and Control: Alain Moreau
Head of Press Service: Richard Angé

Gauge: 1435 mm; 1000 mm
Route length: 34 322 km; 99 km
Electrification: 5847 km at 1.5 kV dc; 6473 km at 25 kV 50 Hz ac; 63 km at 850 V dc; 35 km at 750 V dc; 4 km at 750 V dc (third-rail); 12 km (1000 mm-gauge) at 650/700 V dc (third-rail).

Managerial reorganisation
A major restructure of top management was announced in the spring of 1990. It followed a study by consultants. Their findings were that as previously constituted, management of the railway's activity had become diffused, leading to development of 'empires' within the organisation, a debilitation of top-level direction and consequently a production-led approach to many operations that did not take full account of their profitability.

The new structure reinforces the top-level directorate, which has a group of support services, and reorganises the next level of management on a basis of traffic businesses and production, financial, data processing, personnel and other resource services. There are five businesses – Passenger, Freight, Ile-de-France Passenger (ie, covering the local network of Paris and its suburbs), Regional and Sernam (the intermodal small freight consignment subsidiary) – each of which has its own budget and bottom-line responsibility.

Each Business Director will contract with the other departments for the means of production and back-up services. However, the British Rail concept of dedicating specific traction, rolling stock and fixed asset resources to each business has been rejected as too disruptive of existing arrangements. On the other hand, the SNCF alternative will require considerable development of data processing systems for effective allocation of costs to each business.

The new post of Deputy Director-General has the primary task of gearing the SNCF and its subsidiaries to changing market conditions. He is also charged with developing synergies within the SNCG group.

New State contract
A new contract with the State for the 1990–94 period differs from its five-year predecessor in specifying the means required to achieve its objectives.

On the vexed question of the SNCF's accumulated deficit of some Ffr100 000 million, the government is to transfer to a special fund Ffr38 000 million, the amount incurred since a change of the SNCF's status at the start of 1983, at the rate 10 per cent per annum, plus an increment for inflation, starting at the beginning of 1991. This amount will be separated from the SNCF's balance sheet while it is being paid off. At the same time the State's recent annual subvention to assist amortisation of the deficit will be discontinued from the start of 1991; there would be a payment of Ffr 3763 million for 1990. The SNCF will put up Ffr1100 million annually towards elimination of the remaining debt.

The contract requires the SNCF to balance its accounts annually, inclusive of statutory supports. Under the revised methods of calculation prescribed in the new contract, these supports for 1990 were to be, in FFr million:
Infrastructure 10 381
Pensions 13 895
Compensation for socially reduced tariffs 1618
Regional passenger services 3667

On means, the contract provides for investment in the SNCF of some FFr 100 000 million within the 1990–94 period. In its detail this was controversial, especially with the railway trades unions, because as much as Ffr 45 500 million of the total was allocated to TGV extensions, provoking complaints from areas not affected by TGV plans that this hinted at development of a 'two-speed' SNCF.

In sum, the investment provision is 55 per cent more than expenditure under the previous plan. The TGV figure is two-and-a-half times more; and there is also provision for doubling the investment in the greater Paris suburban system to FFr 15 700 million, as the contract places particular emphasis on the role of the railway in daily life. The State is to share in development of intermodal transport, which the contract sees doubling in volume to 13 300 milion tonne-km by the end of the plan's period. The SNCF has undertaken to get its freight business out of loss by the end of the decade.

The new contract, while maintaining a high level of State support for regional passenger services, envisages that there may be more substitution of bus service for poorly-used trains.

SNCF 1990–94 Plan
The SNCF's 1990–94 Plan assumes an annual 2.5 per cent rate of national economic growth. With the high-speed network extensions due for completion during the year (see below), TGVs are expected by 1994 to be carrying over half of the SNCF's inter-city passenger passengers, compared with 22 per cent in early 1990. Some rationalisation of overnight services is probable as TGVs extend the practical range of day travel; over longer distances, especially cross-border, overnight TGV service will be studied as a long-term possibility. Total inter-city passenger travel is expected to grow from 48 800 million to 62 100 million passenger-km by 1995.

In the Ile-de-France region of greater Paris there will be investment totalling Ffr 15 700 million in the connection of RER Line D and the SNCF's southeast Paris network, by tunnelling from the present terminal subterranean Gare de Lyon station to Châtelet; and in the EOLE project to connect the Est and Saint-Lazare stations by a main-line gauge tunnel (see below).

To reverse the decline of freight traffic, the SNCF is to concentrate to a greater extent on traffic axes where the economy of the rail mode can be optimised, particularly in more extensive operation of unit trains. In less productive areas the required traffic concentra-

Lyon-Paris TGV-PSE train near Cluny (John C Baker)

TGV-Atlantique train-set

Two generations of Paris Type Z2N suburban bi-level emu: the latest asynchronous motor type on the left, earlier dc motor type on the right

France / RAILWAY SYSTEMS

tion and cost reduction may be achievable without loss of competitivity by less-than-daily frequency of service; but some random wagonload traffic will be discarded. Full logistics capability is to be developed, both with external partners and foreign railways as well as within the SNCF group.

As mentioned above, the aim is to double inter-modal traffic to 7 600 million tonne-km by 1994. Techniques to be developed are described in a later section. During the plan's currency investments are planned of Ffr 503 million in terminals, of Ffr 505 million in enlargement of clearances on the main north-south axes and on routes to Le Havre, Dunkerque and Marseilles.

Investment 1990–94
The 1990–94 SNCF-State contract makes the following financial provisions for capital investment:
Historic system: SNCF, Ffr37 600 million; the State, other authorities or third parties, FFr 5 500 million (including support for Poitiers-La Rochelle and Paris-Caen-Cherbourg electrifications)
TGV infrastructure and rolling stock: SNCF, Ffr 43 500 million; the State, other authorities or third parties: Ffr 2 000 million.
Greater Paris suburban system: SNCF, 10 300 million (including loans); the State, other authorities: Ffr 5 400 million.

Investment 1990
Including outlay on the Paris suburban system and shipping, the SNCF planned for 1990 new investments totalling Ffr 22 098 million. Payments on projects in hand would total Ffr 16 342 million.

New investment in TGV and Channel Tunnel-related infrastructure would total Ffr 10 312 million, payments under this head Ffr 5 915 million. New investment in TGV rolling stock would amount to Ffr 3 929 million, payments Ffr 3 098 million. TGV train-set orders in 1990 would comprise 12 TGV-Nord, 12 Interconnection, 4 Paris-London-Brussels, and four additions to the TGV-PSE fleet to cover that route's extension to Valence via the Lyon bypass.

New investment in the historic or 'classic' network would aggregate Ffr 5 201 million, payments Ffr 5 494 million. Almost a quarter of these sums would be absorbed by the SNCF's major signalling and safety programme (see below).

Bearing in mind lead times of two to three years, orders were likely to be placed for new locomotives. Estimations were that, assuming normal life expiry. 305 new electric locomotives would be needed by the start of 1995 and the first 22, a new batch of Class BB26000 'Sybics'. would be ordered in 1990. Further electrification would eliminate need of more main-line diesel locomotives, but a further 30 Class Y8000 locotractors would be ordered in 1990. No need was foreseen of main-line passenger cars before 1995, and only a modest requirement of 500 freight wagons.

Performance in 1989
Passenger-km outside the Paris suburban area were up 1.9 per cent on the previous year in 1989, and were 20 per cent ahead of the 1979 total, just before the TGV-PSE opening. TGV-PSE passenger-km again rose significantly in 1989, by 4.7 per cent, to 11 000 million; growth continues to be greater in first-than in second-class (8.8 compared with 3.4 per cent in 1989).

Assisted by an upturn in industrial production, the freight sector managed to resist still keener competition and a weak consumer market to register a 1.9 per cent increase in total tonne-km. Perishables traffics were down by as much as 20 per cent. International traffic was up 4.1 per cent on the preceding year.

Finance: balance is won
The target of the 1985–1989 contract with the State was achieved with attainment in 1989 of a modest surplus of just over Ffr 200 million, as against a loss of Ffr 563 million in 1988. With passenger receipts exclusive of the Paris suburban system up by Ffr1 500 million and freight revenue up Ffr 1000 million in 1988, the operating surplus before depreciation and financial charges was Ffr 9 600 million, as against Ffr 9 000 million in 1988.

Channel tunnel
To avoid duplication of text, details of the Channel Tunnel fixed link under construction by British and French Railways, and of the Eurotunnel and Anglo-Belgian-French joint-venture rolling stock which will operate its through services, are included in the United Kingdom entry only.

Finances (Fr million)					
Revenue	*1984*	*1985*	*1986*	*1987*	*1988*
Passenger traffic	21 576	23 779	23 863	24 596	26 370
Freight traffic	18 799	19 157	18 246	17 606	17 441
Postal services	668	720	612	615	626
Other activities	3988	4483	4624	4798	5148
Own work capitalised	2580	2654	2807	3117	4913
State and local authority support	14 262	14 705	15 345	15 893	14 626
Reversal of provisions	676	642	634	890	790
Total	62 549	66 140	66 131	67 515	69 914
Expenditure	*1984*	*1985*	*1986*	*1987*	*1988*
Materials, supplies and services	17 474	18 195	17 809	17 724	18 185
Staff costs	38 471	39 844	39 511	39 224	39 793
Taxes and similar charges	1831	1831	2035	2045	2149
Depreciation and amortisation	4105	4852	5095	5469	5608
Total	61 881	64 722	64 450	64 462	65 735
Operating income	668	1418	1681	3053	4179

TGV-Atlantique 'Club' interior arrangement in first-class

TGV-Paris Sudest (TGV-PSE)
Services on France's first high-speed line, TGV-PSE, logged their 100 millionth passenger in March 1989, after 7½ years of operation. By then the high-speed line was showing a return of 15 per cent on the investment in it, 3 per cent more than the best estimates when it was inaugurated.

The 1989–90 timetable scheduled 11 TGV-PSE services daily to run the 427.2 km from Paris Lyon to Lyon Part-Dieu non-stop in 2hr at an average of 213.6 km/h, and three the 427.9km in the reverse direction in the same time at an average of 214 km/h. Fastest train on this route was a service scheduled over the 363.4 km from Paris to Mâcon in 1 hr 40 min, average 218 km/h.

In 1989 the TGV-PSE registered 22 million passenger journeys, 4.7 per cent more than in 1988; average daily load was 55 600 passengers, average occupancy factor of the trains 76 per cent.

The Pasilly turnout for Dijon was replaced in 1989 with new prototype pointwork allowing the speed of divergent trains to be raised from 220 to 230 km/h (after installation it was test-negotiated at a maximum of 245 km/h). The new pointwork has blades lengthened from 38.13 to 58.14 m. No adjustment of the catenary contact wires was necessary.

A new Paris outer suburban railhead station is to be built on the TGV-PSE at the new town of Melun-Sénart, close to the TGV's divergence from the historic main line at Lieusaint.

TGV Rhône-Alpes
Work began in 1990 on construction of a 300 km/h Lyons bypass that will extend new high-speed infrastructure to the outskirts of Valence. The project is known as TGV Rhône-Alpes. Total cost will be Fr 5040 million.

The 115 km cut-off will diverge from the existing TGV-Sud-Est at Montanay, at first routed through a cut-and-cover alignment, then in tunnel under the urban zone of Rillieux as it sweeps to the east of Lyons, serving a station close to Lyons' Satolas Airport. Soon afterward, at St-Quentin-Fallavier, it will cross the Lyons-Grenoble/Chambéry line and make a double junction with it, so that trains for Grenoble/Chambéry can avoid Lyons, and also that trains into and out of Lyons can use the high-speed bypass to and from the south. The bypass will rejoin existing infrastructure at St-Marcel-les-Valence, close to Valence on the route to that city from Grenoble. Completion of the bypass should cut TGV journey times from Paris to Grenoble and to Valence and points south by between 20 and 30 minutes.

To cater for the 1992 Winter Olympics at Albertville, the first 9km from Satolas airport to St-Quentin-Fallavier are to be ready by January 1992. At the end of that year the section from Montanay to Satolas is to be inaugurated. The remaining 70km are scheduled to be operational for the summer of 1994.

TGV-Atlantique
Construction of the 25 kV 50 Hz ac TGV-Atlantique was formally inaugurated in February 1985 and the first stage was opened to service in September 1989.

The scheme involved construction of approximately 280 km of new track in the shape of a lateral 'Y'. Starting from a Paris terminus at the Gare Montparnasse, the new line forks at Courtalain, 130.6 km out. From here its 51.5 km western branch joins the existing Paris-Brest main line between Connerre and Point de Gennes. This was the part opened in 1989.

The south-western branch, opened for service in September 1990, proceeds for 86.9 km to the Montlouis area, near its crossing of the Loire river, where it forks into a connection with the Orléans-Tours main line and a Tours bypass of 16.9 km that joins the Bordeaux main line about 8 km south of Tours. The Tours bypass is electrified at 1.5 kV dc and is accessible to and from the Orléans-Tours main line, so that it can be used by classic passenger and freight trains not having business at Tours or St Pierre-des-Corps, which relieves pressure on installations at the latter of these centres.

The SNCF is holding in reserve for the present a plan to create a similar bypass of Le Mans, likewise open to classic trains, which would regain the Brest main line some 10 km beyond Le Mans. If this were built, a second flying junction with the historic Paris-Le Mans main line would be constructed at Connerre.

In 1985 construction costs of the TGV-A were put at Fr 9430 million, 30 per cent of which has been advanced by the government. In 1990 the EEC Commission advanced a loan of Ffr 577 million towards the project.The capital cost has been contained by the availability of the formation created for an aborted suburban Paris-Chartres suburban railway via Gallardon for the new line's negotiation of suburban Paris.

Beyond Le Mans and Tours considerable distances of the historic main lines to Nantes and Bordeaux respectively have been upgraded for 220 km/h by TGV trains. Sub-station capability has also been increased. Consequently major reductions in journey times between Paris and provincial cities will be attainable even though the TGV will extend only partway from the capital.

The new line branches from the existing railway almost 3 km out from Paris Montparnasse at Malakoff. Expected by 1995, after five years of TGV-A operation, to be handling 59 million passengers a year, the comprehensively rebuilt Paris Montparnasse station will become the busiest station in France. The cost of the works in the station and at its approaches is being met by large-scale commercial development of the site and its environs, in which a Japanese group has a Fr 2500 million involvement.

In the 8.5 km through the Paris suburbs from Bagneux to Massy-Palaiseau the line is largely cut-and-covered for environmental reasons and, where it is in the open, flanked by noise-deadening screens. At local authority request the path of the line is twinned with creation of a 'green corridor' of foot and cycle paths and, in some locations, parks or other leisure facilities. This section includes two continuous tunnels, one of 475 m and the other of 800 m. A TGV-A station, motorists' railhead and interchange with Paris RER Lines A and B was to be opened at Massy-Palaiseau in 1991.

The line's major tunnel, a twin bore some 5000 m long, is necessary beyond Massy-Palaiseau, where the Gallardon formation has been taken over for roadways. From Massy to Courtalain TGV-A shares a path with the A10 autoroute over some 20 km and later appropriates ground reserved for it; over a further 40 km it generally parallels the existing line to Tours via Vendôme. TGV-A's south-western branch has the new line's other intermediate station at Vendôme, beyond which it tunnels under the Vouvray vineyards before it enters the Loire valley.

Like the TGV Paris Sud-Est, the new TGV has been engineered for 300 km/h but in this case it operates at that speed, a few areas excepted. Out of Paris the limit is 200 km/h for the first 15 km, rising through 270 km in the 500 m Villejust Tunnel to the start of 300 km/h 25 km out. The Courtalain divergence has been engineered for 300 km/h for south-west branch trains, 200 km/h for trains to the west. The Vouvray tunnel is also limited to 270 km/h. The junctions at Connerre and between the Tours bypass and Bordeaux main line south of Tours are designed for 220 km/h in each direction.

With the exception of some 3200 radius bends on the Tours bypass the minimum curvature radius is 4000 m. Easier terrain than that traversed by the TGV-PSE has allowed a ruling gradient of 1.5 per cent, exceptionally steepening to 2.5 per cent, compared with 3.5 per cent on the Paris Sud-Est. As on the latter, the new line has two-way signalling on each track, the same system of cab-signalling and automatic speed control, and supervision from one centre, in this case at Paris Montparnasse.

The 1.5 kV dc Tours bypass is the first stretch of line shared by TGV's at close to their maximum speed (270 km/h, as opposed to 300 km/h until they diverge from the new Atlantique line) and mixed traffic, including freight. It will also be the first use of 1.5 kV dc at such pace. This has required special catenary arrangement and also a superimposition of the TGV cab-signalling system on conventional lineside signalling for non-TGV traffic. The latter has been achieved by relating the TGV system's staged automatic speed control to the block sectioning of the orthodox signalling over the bypass. When a TGV's control has

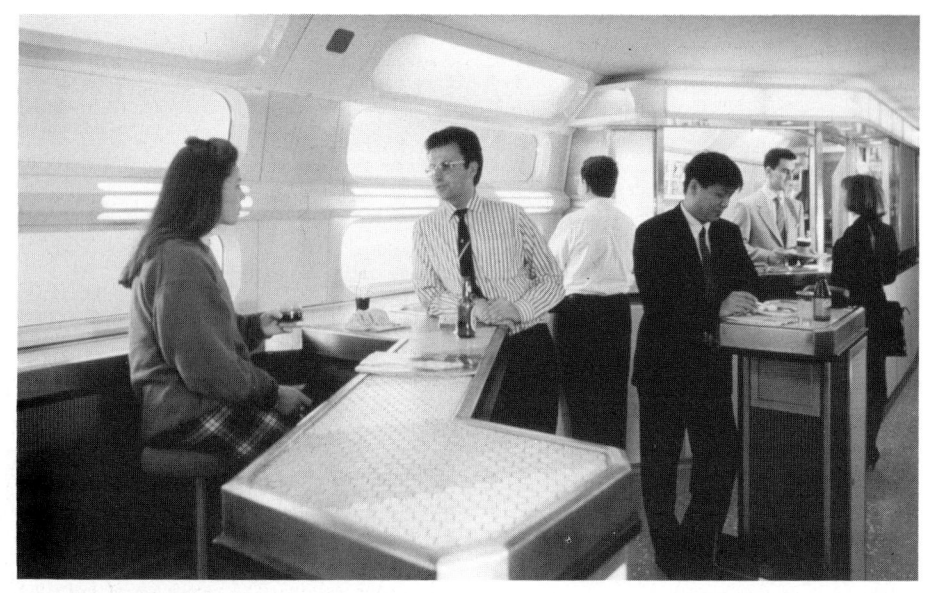

TGV-A bar car interior

Meals-at-seat service in TGV-PSE first-class

brought speed down to the 160 km/h mark on the cab display, its driver will get an indication instructing him to adhere to lineside signalling until he is cleared to resume 160 km/h-plus speed.

Service over the Brittany branch was begun at the end of September 1989, initially limited by problems with the electronics of the TGV-A train-sets which at first prevented operation of two sets in multiple; and also pending energisation of electrification to Brest (see below). The new route nevertheless took the palm for the world's fastest scheduled service, with four trains daily set to run the 201.6 km between Paris Montparnasse and Le Mans in 55 min, average 219.9 km/h. A new fare scheme applied to the service excited considerable controversy, but by mid-January 1990 the 2 millionth passenger had been registered. From the end of January the weekday service comprised 11 trains each way between Paris and Nantes, a few of them extended beyond Nantes to St-Nazaire and Le Croisic; and 11 trains each way between Paris and Rennes, four of them extended over the newly electrified tracks to and from Brest.

Service over the south-western branch was to begin in September 1990. The fastest transit between Paris and Bordeaux would then be 2 hours 58 minutes, compared with 4 hours 4 minutes in the previous timetable; and to Pau, 4 hours 54 minutes compared with 6 hours 35 minutes, to quote just two examples of TGV acceleration. Introduction of some services between Brittany and southeastern France via the Paris Grande Ceinture was planned for mid-1991.

Bordeaux, where the St Jean station has undergone a Fr 130 million renovation in preparation for TGV service, expects a long-haul passenger traffic growth of over 40 per cent as a result of high-speed service. The possibilities for raising line speed between Bordeaux and Toulouse are limited, not least because of a profusion of level crossings. It remained to be decided, given that only 50 at most of the initial 73 TGV-A sets would be operational by mid-1990,whether in that year to concentrate the initial service on 15 daily pairs of Paris-Bordeaux trains and defer service of Toulouse.

TGV signalling

Each TGV is controlled from a centre in Paris that houses both current and train describer-aided traffic controllers in the same room. There are no active lineside signals; drivers are guided entirely by the TVM 300 system of continuous and automatic cab signalling, which provides 10 aspects covering freedom to proceed at maximum line speed, warnings of reduction to 220, 160 or 80 km/h in ensuing sections, instruction to proceed within either of the speeds mentioned, and requirement to stop or proceed on sight at a maximum of 30 km/h. The signalling is linked to automatic speed-check and braking systems.

Block sections, of a standard 2100-metre length, are indicated by markers serving as either absolute stopping positions (lettered) or stop-and-proceed positions. Each block is covered by a CSEE UM71 voice frequency jointless track circuit capable of 18 rates of frequency shift, which are picked up by each train-set through inductive coils, one of which is located ahead of each end axle of the unit. An additional discrete transmission system employing track-mounted cable loops and offering up to 14 frequencies supplies further information to trains, for example to activate or deactivate the cab signalling on entrance to or exit from the new line. Lineside sensors linked to PAR watch for hot boxes.

TVM 300 permits a four-minute headway between TGV-A trains at their full 300 km/h speed. A TVM 400 development to be applied to the TGV-Nord (see below) will allow a three-minute headway.

TGV train-sets orders

The first TGV-A order was for 95 TGV-A train-sets. In addition to 300 km/h capability on the new line, the TGV-A sets had to be apt for operation at 220 km/h on stretches of existing infrastructure beyond high-speed line limits limits between Le Mans and Nantes, and between Tours and Bordeaux. In January 1990 a further 10 sets were ordered

For the TGV-A sets a new livery was selected: basically silver white, with grey roof, and a window-enclosing band of blue that is interrupted by a parallelogram around each entrance door in red, green or yellow, these latter signifying respectively first-class, second-class and bar cars.

Each TGV-A set comprises two power cars enclosing 10 trailers. A major difference by comparison with the TGV-PSE sets is the use of synchronous three-phase motors, each with a 1100 kW continuous, 1300 kW one-hour rating, as against the 535 kW continuous rating of each dc motor in a TGV-PSE set. This, coupled with the easier gradients of the Atlantique line, means that only the power car axles of a TGV-A set need be motored, despite the greater number of trailers (two axles of a TGV-PSE trailer unit are additionally motored). Maximum axleloading, nevertheless, does not exceed 17 tonnes. Like the TGV-PSE units, the TGV-A are dual-voltage, 1.5 kV dc and 25 kV ac; working off the latter, the eight body-mounted synchronous motors provide a continuous 8800 kW (11 800 hp) to move a tare train-set weight of 490 tonnes. Other technological advances in the power plant include use of GTO thyristorised inverters, freon cooling of choppers, and extensive application of microprocessors both for controls and diagnostics; in the latter case they report to a visual display in the driving cab and, interrogated from the ground, radio-transmit data to maintenance shops 45 minutes ahead of arrival at destination, so that work schedules and provision of any necessary spares can be pre-planned. Conversely, some pre-service preparations, such as start-up of air-conditioning and refrigerated catering apparatus, can be radio-activated from the ground.

TGV-A sets have a new design of pantograph, the GPU, which operates with a simpler, unstitched catenary than that on the PSE line, and ride on a new Type Y237 trailer bogie design, differing notably from the Y231 under TGV-PSE sets in the absence of rubber elements in its primary suspension. Redesigned air suspension with four longitudinal shock absorbers gives a steadier ride at 220 km/h on historic infrastructure as well as at high speed on new line. Braking systems employ a new design of non-ventilated steel disc combined with microprocessor-controlled anti-locking devices.

The trailers of a TGV-A set comprise three first-class cars, one including a telephone kiosk, separated by a full-length bar car from six second-class cars, one including a telephone kiosk. Two of the three first-class cars are each arranged in what is designated 'club style' with, on one side of an off-centre gangway,

Class BB15000 leaves Bettembourg on the Paris-Luxembourg 'Robert Schumann' EuroCity train (*John C Baker*)

TGV route comparisons

	Paris-Sud-Est	Atlantique	Nord (Paris-Brussels-Cologne-Amsterdam)	Est*
Route length	417 km	283 km	716 km (321 km in France)	384 km
Ruling gradient (%)	3.5	2.5	2.5	3.5
Infrastructure construction costs (Fr million, 1986 values)	8500	9400	18 000 (of which 12 000 in France)	10 400
TGV train-set costs (Fr million, 1986 values)	6.4	7	4 (6 for France)	3
Composition of train-sets	M + 8R + M	M + 10R + M	M + 8R + M	M + 8R + M
Traffic, actual or projected (passenger journeys, million)	in 1984	in 1990	in 1992	in 1995
without TGV	13.4	18	12.7	8.1
with TGV, including that on historic route	19.4	24	17.5	11.9
TGV traffic only	14.3	20	15.5	11.8
Rate of return on investment	15%	12%	7% (15% for France)	4%
Fastest TGV journey time from Paris (fastest time by classic train)	Lyons 2 hours 50 minutes (3 hours 50 minutes)	Le Mans 1 hour (1 hour 37 minutes)	Lille 1 hour (2 hours)	Rheims 42 minutes (1 hour 26 minutes)
	Geneva 3 hours 31 minutes (5 hours 42 minutes)	Nantes 2 hours 5 minutes (2 hours 53 minutes)	Brussels 1 hour 20 minutes (2 hours 27 minutes)	Metz 1 hour 30 minutes (2 hours 40 minutes)
	Marseilles 4 hours 40 minutes (6 hours 40 minutes)	Bordeaux 2 hours 58 minutes (4 hours 4 minutes)	Cologne 2 hours 30 minutes (5 hours 8 minutes)	Strasbourg 2 hours 12 minutes (3 hours 48 minutes)
	Grenoble 3 hours 12 minutes (5 hours 31 minutes)	Brest‡ 4 hours 16 minutes (5 hours 37 minutes)	Amsterdam 3 hours 10 minutes (5 hours 23 minutes) London 3 hours (5 hours 12 minutes)	Nancy 1 hour 43 minutes (2 hours 34 minutes)

* Assuming Paris-Rheims-Vosges route passing between Metz and Nancy is chosen
‡ After electrification of Rennes-Brest section

TGV train-sets

	TGV-PSE Dual-voltage dual-class	TGV-PSE Dual-voltage first-class	TGV-PSE Tri-voltage dual-class	TGV-A Dual-voltage dual-class	TGV-R Dual-voltage dual-class	TGV-R Tri-voltage dual-class
Length over couplers	200.19 m	200.19 m	200.19 m	237.6 m	200.19 m	200.19 m
Tare weight in working order	386 tonnes	384 tonnes	386 tonnes	490 tonnes	383 tonnes	385 tonnes
Weight available for adhesion	194 tonnes	194 tonnes	194 tonnes	136 tonnes	136 tonnes	136 tonnes
Continuous power rating						
At 25 kV 50 Hz	6450 kW	6450 kW	6450 kW	8800 kW	8800 kW	8800 kW
At 1.5 kV dc	3100m kW	3100 kW	3100 kW	3880 kW	3880 kW	3880 kW
At 15 kV 16⅔ Hz	–	–	2800 kW	–	–	–
Max speed	270 km/h	270 km/h	270 km/h	300 km/h	300 km/h	300 km/h
Seating capacity						
1st class	111/108*	287	111/108*	116	120	120
2nd class	275/250*	–	275/260*	369	257	257

* After modifications, principally enlargement of buffet-bar area, now in progress.

six doorless semi-compartments with seat pairs in sofa-form around a table, and on the other, six open pairs of seats each with its own table. The third, outermost first-class car is entirely open, but with an eight-seat saloon for group use at one end. In the second-class section, one car has a 16-place section where seating can be removed to create a children's playing area; and two other cars have sections specially arranged for family travel.

With the TGV-Interconnection (see below) in mind, orders were placed with GEC-Alsthom in January 1990 for 80 TGV-R (Réseau, or Network) sets suitable for use throughout the TGV system, the Channel Tunnel link excepted, with an option for 30 more. Of the initial 80 units, 50 would be dual-voltage 1.5kV dc/25kV 50Hz ac; and 30 would add a third voltage, 3kV dc, for through running to Belgium.

The TGV-R power cars will repeat the TGV-A design, but as the units must be capable of working over the steeper TGV-PSE ruling gradient of 3.5 per cent, there will be only eight trailers. The main trailer differences by comparison with TGV-A units will centre on full pressure sealing, to cope with the tunnels found necessary on later TGV projects; and enlarged luggage room, for the benefit of travellers to and from Paris Charles de Gaulle airport. TGV-R units will be able to multiple with all other types of TGV train-set.

The 1989 train-set orders, as for 80 per cent of the initial TGV-A order, were placed on a financial basis of lease over a period of years. The sets would become SNCF property after progressive pay-off of the capital cost.

A state-subsidised contract with GEC-Alsthom for the latter's development work on a third-generation TGV design has a Ffr 85 million provision for study of automatic body-tilting, should this be found desirable for extension of the train-sets' scope for international service. The government is contributing Ffr 170 million and the SNCF Ffr 95 million to the Ffr 445-530 million four-year development programme, objectives of which include standardisation of 350 km/h top speed.

TGV-Nord

In October 1987 the French government approved construction of the TGV-Nord line from Paris to Lille, branching in a triangular junction there to the Channel Tunnel and to the Belgian border. The Belgian government simultaneously authorised the line's continuation to Brussels. Construction began in 1989, with completion set to coincide with inauguration of the Channel Tunnel in 1993. In early 1990 work was progressing at 12 locations and ground for 60 per cent of the route had been secured. The project involves in all 333 route-km of new infrastructure.

The 225 route-km of new route from the Paris outskirts to Lille will start 15 km out from Paris Gare du Nord at Villiers le Bel. The decision also taken in October 1987 to build around the east of Paris a high-speed TGV-Interconnection (see below) welding together all TGV routes, altered the initial plans for TGV service of Charles de Gaulle Airport at Roissy. That will now have its TGV station on the Interconnection. North of Roissy the Interconnection will make a triangular junction with the TGV-Nord.

The TGV-Nord will cross the River Oise in the vicinity of Verberie. Then, as planned two decades ago when this was conceived as France's first TGV, it will parallel the A1 motorway for much of the remaining distance to Lille.

Arras will have a short spur, but controversially the TGV-Nord will serve neither Amiens nor St Quentin directly. Each of these centres will be about 30 minutes road time from a station named TGV-Picardy on the new line, to be located at the intersection of the Paris-Lille and Amiens-St Quentin motorways. However, a second TGV line to the Channel Tunnel via Amiens figures in the long-term TGV network plan published in 1990 (see below).

The city of Lille has agreed to put up half the high cost of threading the new line through the city centre. The TGV will have its own subterranean station close to the city's present main station. Beyond it the TGV will briefly parallel and make connection with the historic main line.

At the approach to Lille there will be a triangular junction between the line from Paris and a TGV line of 108 km in length running to Fréthun, on the southwestern outskirts of Calais at the mouth of the Channel Tunnel.

The Boulogne-Calais-Dunkerque line has already been diverted to the site of a new passenger station being built at Fréthun. Non-TGV traffic will mostly reach Fréthun over the line from Hazebrouck, which is being modernised and electrified. Beyond Fréthun will be a triangular junction, formed by tracks heading for the tunnel, tracks heading to freight yards and Calais, and tracks leading from these areas to the tunnel. On the coastal side of the triangle will be a big complex of road transport terminals and intermodal installations.

Accommodation of TGV-Nord trains in Paris demands a further massive rebuilding of the Gare du Nord and its approaches. Platforms in the main station are being extended to TGV train-set length and from January 1990 all remaining suburban services were displaced from the main train-shed either to the ground-level annexe for local services or to the sub-surface platforms leading to the Paris RER. Two of the main station platforms will be set aside for Channel Tunnel TGVs, as the British authorities require their accommodation to be segregated for airport-style immigration controls and baggage examination. The extensive works at the station's approaches include substantial layout reorganisation and creation of a TGV maintenance depot at Landy.

Type X4500 diesel railcars in Basse-Normandie regional livery

Interior of second-class RER trailer

Class Z11500 25kV 50Hz ac emus in Forbach-Metz service (John C Baker)

As described in the section on Belgium, because of political and financial problems in that country the Belgian continuation of high-speed infrastructure from the frontier to Brussels will not be available until 1995. Upgrading and new infrastructure beyond Brussels to the German border will not be finished until 1997-98.

Four types of high-speed train are likely to use the TGV-Nord. One will be the 30 so-called 'Three Capitals' or 'Trans-Manche Super-Trains' (TMST) train-sets working between London and Paris/Brussels (for details see United Kingdom entry in this section). A second participant will be the TGV-R sets ordered in 1989 (see above). The third type, yet to be ordered in early 1990, would be 24 TGV-Paris-Nord de la France train-sets, each comprising two power cars and eight bi-level trailers with a total seating capacity of 550. Resort to aluminium bodywork and other weight-saving ploys will enable the bi-levels to observe the SNCF's maximum TGV axle-loading of 17 tonnes, even with articulation of adjoining cars.

A final type, tagged PBKA and not yet in approved design in early 1990, will be four-voltage units for through working from Paris to Brussels, Amsterdam and Cologne. A need is foreseen of 39 sets, each comprising two power cars and eight trailers. These units will not need to be capable of more than 200 km/h beyond the limits of French 25 kV ac. But completion of Germany's projected 300 km/h Cologne-Frankfurt new line, requiring that speed ability under DB 15 kV 16⅔ ac wires, might prompt need of a fifth type of train for through Paris-Frankfurt service.

TGV-Interconnection

In October 1987 the government approved construction, simultaneously with the TGV-Nord, of a TGV-Interconnection skirting the east of Paris. To be engineered for 270 km/h, the 102 km line will interlink the Nord, Sudest, Atlantique and putative Est TGVs, serving en route a Charles de Gaulle station for the airport of that name at Roissy, and another at Marne-la-Vallée in the heart of the EuroDisneyland now under construction. Cost of TGV-Nord construction is put at Fr 7600 million (which the SNCF is largely raising itself, with some support from the Paris Airports Authority and EuroDisneyland); usage at some 6.5 million cross-country and 5 million Parisian travellers a year; and the return on the investment at 14 per cent.

As mentioned above, the Interconnection will make a triangular junction with the TGV-Nord north of Roissy and tunnel under Charles de Gaulle Airport for its first 5 km, serving a Roissy TGV underground station in the process. There is provision for a second triangular junction, at Claye-Souilly, to connect with the prospective TGV-Est, which is planned to leave the historic Paris Gare de l'Est route at Chelles (see below).

In a final triangular junction at Coubert the Interconnection will fork. One arm will head for a junction with the TGV-PSE northeast of Melun, at Moisenay; the other, making partial use of former Paris-Bastille-Marles en Brie line infrastructure (now a freight-only route, in which capacity it will be closed), will run west through Villecresnes and connect with the Paris Grande Ceinture at Valenton, so that trains can reach the TGV-Atlantique at Massy-Palaiseau. The Coubert triangle will allow interchange via its base between TGV-PSE and TGV-Atlantique, and also afford TGV-PSE trains an alternative route out of Gare de Lyon that will let them to run up to top speed within 9 km of their city-centre start.

The Charles de Gaulle station will be sited between the airport's No 2 (Air France) terminal and its future No 3 terminal. The Paris RER Line B is to be extended to its own two-track, island-platform station in the same complex. The TGV station will have six tracks, four of them paired athwart island platforms, and the other two through tracks engineered for passage at 230km/h by non-stopping trains. The total TGV station cost of Ffr 1 330 million is being borne 68.6 per cent by the SNCF, the rest by the Paris Airports Authority (ADP). The cost of the RER extension wil be met by the Ile-de-France regional authority and a tax on airport users.

Roissy TGV is seen as a key interchange, both between air and TGV and between TGV routes. Units will couple and uncouple here to cover service of more than one TGV route with a single TGV-Nord cross-country service. When both TGV-Nord and Interconnection are operational some of the forecast journey times from Roissy (and thus Charles de Gaulle Airport) are: London 3 hours; Brussels 1½ hours; Lille 53 minutes; Lyons 1 hour 58 minutes; Marseilles 4 hours 8 minutes; and Bordeaux 3 hours 28 minutes.

'Sybic' Class BB26000 with three-phase synchronous motors

Class 67000 diesel-electric B-Bs at Geneva on a Nice train (*John C Baker*)

The Marne-la-Vallée station will have two through high-speed tracks and three platformed tracks, the latter providing interchange with Paris RER Line A.

The double-track route will be bi-directionally signalled and engineered for 270 km/h maximum speed. There will be three tunnels each of 1.5-1.6 km, one under Charles de Gaulle airport.

The TGV-Interconnection project gained its declaration of public utility in June 1990. Construction began soon afterward so that the northeast-southeast axis of the line can open for public service in May 1994. Work on the south-east-to-west branch was expected to begin in 1991, for opening in 1995.

TGV-Est

The TGV-Est scheme gained impetus in 1989 with the Transport Minister's March appointment of a former SNCF president, Philippe Essig, to produce a report on feasibility. Key issues to resolve were the project's profitability, which at 4.3 per cent was falling well short of the 8.2 per cent minimum return on investment set by the SNCF for new TGV schemes; and the line of route. The latter concerned not only a path through France, but also points of connection with the German Federal Railway's emergent high-speed network and the balance of investment either side of the frontier involved in each routeing option.

Published in April 1990, the Essig report estimated construction costs at Ffr 22 000 million for 430km of new infrastructure and Ffr 6 300 milion for TGV trainsets. To overcome the financial problem the report recommended that the State should put up Ffr 6 600 million, roughly the same 30 per cent of infrastructure costs as contributed to TGV-A; that the four French regions traversed should together put up Ffr 4 000 million, to which Alsace, Lorraine and Champagne-Ardennes readily agreed, leaving a response to some only from the Ile-de-France around Paris; and that apart from a possible EEC contribution, the balance of the required capital should be raised in thirds by the SNCF, the principal contractor and the construction firms employed, which in association would lease the completed line to the SNCF. The SNCF would pay off the cost out of revenue over a period of 30 years and then take ownership of the line.

The proposed route from Paris, diverging from the historic Strasbourg main line at Chelles, would make a junction with the TGV-Interconnection and then head via a Champagne-Ardennes station southwest of Rheims, a Lorraine station midway between Metz and Nancy and a tunnel under the Vosges mountains to Strasbourg. Beyond Strasbourg trains would initially use existing cross-border tracks to connect with the German Federal high-speed network and reach Mannheim or Stuttgart.

It has been forecast that a fleet of between 35 and 50 train-sets would be needed for purely SNCF service, plus 35–50 multi-voltage sets for through working into Germany, Luxembourg and Switzerland.

The ultimate TGV network plan

In January 1989, with an increasing number of areas pressing for TGV service, the SNCF was bidden by the Transport Minister to produce by the year's end a master plan for an ultimate TGV route system. The report was published in the spring of 1990. In June the government accepted it as the basis of a TGV Master Plan. Reading anti-clockwise from the TGV-Nord, these routes are added by the Master Plan to those already in existence or under construction in 1990 (prospective journey times from Paris in brackets):

- TGV Picardie, 165 km: Paris-Amiens (40 min) and Calais/Channel Tunnel
- TGV Normandie, 169 km: Paris-Rouen (40 min) and Caen
- TGV Bretagne, 156 km: TGV-A Brittany branch extended to Rennes (1hr 26 min)
- TGV Aquitaine, 508 km: TGV-A southern branch extended via Poitiers and Angoulême to Bordeaux (2 hr 6 min)
- TGV Midi-Pyrénées, 177 km: a branch from the TGV Aquitaine near Libourne to Toulouse (2 hr 48 min)
- TGV Grand-Sud, 184 km: comprising new line from Carcassone to Narbonne, upgraded route thence to Toulouse and a new connection from it to Bordeaux
- TGV Provence-Côte-d'Azur, 344 km: continuing the

TGV Rhone-Alpes southward from Valence to a station at Aix-en-Provence, to the northeast of which a triangular junction would throw off a branch to the historic main line at the approach to Marseille (3hr) while the main route, titled the TGV Mediterranée, would head southeastward to rejoin the historic and upgraded main line near St Raphael for TGV trains' continuation to Nice (4hr).

- TGV Languedoc-Roussillon, 323 km: branching from the TGV-Côte d'Azur just northeast of Orange, heading via the outskirts of Nîmes to Montpellier (3 hr) and from the border at Perpignan prospectively using a new Spanish high-speed line to Barcelona (4 hr 30 min).
- TGV Interconnexion-Sud, 49 km: a link on the Paris outskirts between the TGV Sud-Est at Melun-Sénart and TGV Atlantique near Vaugrigneuse.
- TGV Limousin, 192 km: upgrading from Paris to Vierzon, new line thence to Limoges (2 hours).
- TGV Auvergne, 249 km: chiefly upgrading of existing route to Clermont Ferrand (2 hr 32 min).
- TGV Transalpin, 189 km: from the TGV Rhone-Alpes in the area of Valence to Chambéry and Modane, with the possibility of projection via a transalpine tunnel (which would require Italian collaboration) to Turin (3 hr 05 min) and Milan (4 hr 15 min), and extension over Italian high-speed lines to Venice (6 hr) and Rome (7 hr 20 min).
- TGV Rhine-Rhône, 425 km: comprising extension of the TGV-PSE's branch from Pasilly for Dijon to full TGV status through Dijon and Besançon (1 hr 35 min), Belfort and Mulhouse for service to Basel (2 hr 25 min) and Zurich (3 hr 15 min); and also a connecting TGV line from north of Lyon to Besançon.
- TGV-Est, 430 km: from Paris to Strasbourg (1 hr 50 min) to a link-up with the German Federal high-speed network for access to Frankfurt (3 hr 10 min), Stuttgart (2hr 45 min) and Munich (4 hr 25 min).

New world speed record 515.3 km/h

Yet again the world rail speed record was raised by TGV equipment on 14 December 1989, when 482.4 km/h was touched by a slightly modified TGV-A unit on the opening stretch of the TGV-A line's southern branch, at that date not yet in public service. For the record attempt TGV-A unit No 325 was reduced in length to two power cars and four trailers, one of the latter equipped as a laboratory, for a total weight of some 300 tonnes. The power cars had their 920mm wheels replaced by ones of 1050mm diameter, and their normal 1100kW motor rating raised to 1500kW (making the unit's total rating 12000kW). Traction current voltage was raised from 25kV to 28kV.

The following May 18 the record was hoisted to 515.3 km/h. For this exploit set 325 was reduced to five cars, tare 260 tonnes. Power car wheels were of 1090 mm diameter current voltage was increased to 29.5 kV and the set had some aerodynamic modifications.

1989–1993 Paris suburban plan

In February 1989 the government announced a 1989-1993 Paris suburban development plan priced at Ffr 7000 million. Of this sum 40 per cent would be furnished by central government (exploiting in part an increase to 2.2 per cent in the transport payroll tax levied on central Paris employers), 40 per cent by the Ile-de-France authority of Greater Paris, and 20 per cent by loans from this authority to the SNCF and RATP.

A major item, costing Ffr 1550 million, is the boring of two extra single-track RER tunnels of 2.5km length in mid-town between Gare de Lyon and Châtelet-Les Halles. This will go far to solve the problems created by the incessantly rising traffic on the east-west RER Line A. That has so far prevented the addition to the trains of Line A and the north-south Line B of a through RER Line D service between SNCF's northern and south-eastern networks via the subterranean, presently terminal Gare de Lyon platforms. It is from the latter that the new tunnels will begin; they will debouch into the centre platforms of Châtelet-les-Halles. Completion of the new tunnels is foreseen in 1995.

Some immediate relief for the core RER section has been secured by adoption of the SACEM signalling system, which has enabled reduction of peak-hour train headway to 2 minutes (for details see Paris entry in Urban Transit Systems section). The need of major capacity enlargement in the heart of Line A has become the more urgent because by 1992 it will have been extended eastward beyond Torcy to serve the EuroDisneyland at Marne-la-Vallée. A refined version of SACEM is now under study for wider application; a prototype of this is likely to be installed on RER Line C in 1992.

The latest Paris plan provides further relief for Line A in EOLE (East-West Liaison Express), a new SNCF underground, main line-clearance line that will abstract some of the Gare de l'Est local trains and route them via new subterranean Gare Nord-Est and Saint-Lazare-Condorcet stations to a temporary Pont-Cardinet terminus. Cost of this first stage is put at Ffr 3 900 million.

Westward extension to the commercial complex of La Défense is envisaged in a second phase of the project. In a third phase the Nord-Est and Saint-Lazaire-Condorcet stations would have their two tracks doubled to four. This move, for which provision will be made in the project's first phase, will raise the line's peak capacity to 70 000 passengers each way per hour. Its completion will raise the total EOLE cost, exclusive of rolling stock, to Ffr 8 000 million.

Total SNCF investment in its Ile-de-France network in the course of the 1989-93 Paris suburban plan is set at some Ffr 5000 million, twice that spent under the previous plan. Other major schemes to be undertaken include:

- Connections to create direct service from the new town of Saint-Quentin-en-Yvelines to La Défense. Cost: Ffr 446 million
- Restoration of passenger service over two stretches of the orbital Grande Ceinture line, to Noisy-le-Roi and to Sant-Germain-en-Laye. Cost of first stage: Ffr 300 million

At the start of 1990 the SNCF's Parisian suburban system covered 935 route-km, since 1988 totally electrified, serving 318 stations and carrying up to 2 million passengers daily, for a total of 500 million passenger journeys annually (compared with 432 million in 1980). Train-to-ground radio communication now covers 85 per cent of the network.

Passenger service developments

A new first-class travel facility is planned for Paris-Strasbourg and Paris-Brive services. Titled 'Haut de gamme' (Top Rank), it will offer first-class cars with the interior configurations of the TGV-A sets; meal service at seats but dish by dish, not in airline tray fashion, under the direction of an on-board chief steward; telephone facility; and fully-equipped business sections. A stock of 53 'Grand Confort' locomotive-hauled cars is being appropriately rebuilt as they became due for overhaul.

In March 1989 SNCF signed a contract with American Airlines for adoption of the latter's highly-reputed Sabre technology (already used by Amtrak in the US) in creating a new electronic reservation system. Named Socrate, this is to be in full operation by the inauguration of the TGV-Nord in 1993. It will be able to handle over 1000 transactions a second, so that it can deal with reservations ancillary to the principal bookings of train space.

Regional passenger services

The concept of partnership between the SNCF and local authorities for development of local passenger services derives from France's establishment in the early 1970s of 25 autonomous Regional Councils, to whom a substantial amount of decision-making capability was delegated from central government. Central government continues to provide basic financial support for local transport services throughout the country, but the Regional Councils have the power and resources to supplement that in developing passenger transport systems within their respective Regions as they judge will best suit local social and economic development need.

Multi-annual Regional schemes contracted with the SNCF's *Service de l'Action Regionale* (SAR) take existing rail service as a guaranteed base and are concerned with its variation and/or expansion, which

'Fret Chrono' 160 km/h freight cars; livery of these high-speed wagons is bright green

Traffic (million)

	1985	1986	1987	1988	1989
Freight tonnes-km	55 800	51 700	51 330	52 280	53 300
Freight tonnes	162	146	142	144.9	146.5
Passenger-km	62 100	59 800	60 040	63 300	64 500
of which Paris suburban	8470	8610	8650	8910	9130
Passenger journeys	777	778.7	782	818	824
of which Paris suburban	475	481.9	482.1	499	511

Class BB 7200 and Chronofroid refrigerated swapbody train

alone involves the Regional Council in any financial obligation. Computerised data sifting systems enable the SNCF to provide a Regional Council with quarterly, line-by-line statements of receipts, so that a Council can assess precisely the outcome of its initiatives. Agreements have included fare innovations. Most of the contracts have featured initial Regional funding of extra rolling stock, which has been distinctively liveried to mark its Regional affinity. Such acquisitions have included examples of the SNCF's latest Type Z2 emu.

Two new types of equipment were applied to TER service in the late 1980s. One is the Type RRR push-pull unit of stainless steel-bodied vehicles, similar in character to the Type RIB sets of the Paris suburban network. The RRR are produced in sets of three or four cars each, and in alternative rural and outer-suburban internal seating configurations. Capable of operation in up to three-car sets coupled, they are designed for top speeds of 140 km/h hauled and 120 km/h propelled. The initial order for RRRs comprised 201 regional and 132 outer-suburban cars. They are unpainted stainless steel below window level, and around the windows and at each end green, red, yellow or blue according to the choice of the Region in which they operate.

The other newcomer is the Type X2200 diesel railcar with matching Type XR6000 trailers. The X2200 design is closely derived from the 400 kW X2100, the main differences being relocation of the first-class section away from mid-body position above the motor to one end of the car, and a redesigned cab end and Z2 emu-style livery.

With signature of agreements by Lorraine and Rhône-Alpes in 1989, the number of regions to have completed contracts with the SNCF rose to 19. An agreement with Poitou-Charentes was expected in 1990.

Freight traffic

At 142.5 million tonnes, freight carryings in 1989 were 1.1 million tonnes up on 1988. Best performing sectors were minerals and metals, up 9.3 per cent; fuels, up 6.5 per cent; piggyback, up 4.1 per cent; and containers, up 3.2 per cent. Prime factor in the rising tonnage was continued growth in international traffic. The SNCF has relaunched its freight sector under the brandname of 'Fret'. This followed the SNCF's loss of a third of its gross tonne-km in 15 years and the reduction of its national market share of domestic traffic in tonnage terms to 9 per cent.

Great store is set by intensified use of computers; on the one hand, for communication with clients, to eliminate the laborious paperwork that has been deterrent to use of 'Fret'; and on the other, to quicken yard processing of wagons and closely monitor their performance in transit.

From November 1989, via Edi Fret, a joint subsidiary of the SNCF and France Télécom, customers became able to obtain real-time information on the status of their consignment, and were automatically advised of selected events in its movement, via telex, telefax or compatible PC communication. The scope of EDI Fret is being extended to other activities such as invoicing and provision of data for private wagon owners.

On the operating front, all freight trains now run at a top speed of at least 100 km/h where track alignment permits. All SNCF main lines are passed for axle-loadings of 22.5 tonnes, so that four-axle wagons can gross up to 90 tonnes, which means wagon payloads can reach at least 60 tonnes.

Marshalling yard strategy has been revised to secure better train loadings and more through main yard-to-main yard unit train operation. Siding-to-siding unit trains now account for half the SNCF's freight operation, random wagonloads for 35 per cent.

A new freight strategy under the acronym ETNA exploits computerised techniques for tighter control of wagons in transit. As a result the post-1946 RA (Régime Acceléré) and RO (Régime Ordinaire) grading of traffic and its corollary of separate yard dedication to either RA or RO work, has been abolished. The new strategy substitutes three grades of transit. The first, Fretexpress, is equivalent to RA performance, and minimises inter-train transfer en route so as to ensure next-day or day-after delivery. The second, Fretrapide, permits up to 24 hours additional transit time, but is an improvement on RO and offers considerably greater assurance of delivery time. The third, Freteco, allows up to six days in transit. Tariffs are scaled accordingly. Through a central computer at Lyons and mini-computers at each major yard, the latter linked to terminals at key points in a yard, the yards are informed in advance of the consist of incoming trains so that they can pre-plan their classification according to the priorities of the traffic arriving trains are carrying.

In terms of offering 'just-in-time' service, great interest attached to the summer 1987 launch of Europe's first scheduled 160 km/h freight train service, running between Marseilles and Lille overnight each way. A second such service, aimed at the produce growers of Roussillon, was inaugurated between Perpignan and the Paris Rungis market in the following winter.

The Marseilles-Lille trains were each formed two-thirds of covered vans, one-third of container flats. The vehicles were existing types modified with completely new electro-pneumatic braking embodying double brake shoes, their Y25 bogies fitted with dampers and extra weight, and repainted in distinctive green livery.

Now branded Fretchrono, overnight 160 km/h trains have been extended to three other routes: Paris-Avignon; Paris-Bordeaux-Toulouse; and Avignon-Valenton (Paris), this last for refrigerated swapbody traffic conveying fresh produce to the capital's Rungis market.

Chronodis, launched in February 1990, offers a total distribution service for palletised traffic between Paris and the Rhone delta in the south. Road collection and delivery is provided by Sceta's Tautliner trucks; the rail component is a 120km/h overnight train of H96 sliding-wall vans betwen Paris Villeneuve-Saint-Georges and Avignon.

To lift possible axle-loading of 160 km/h wagons to 18 tonnes and the cant deficiency restraint on their speed to 160 mm, the SNCF has developed a new Type Y37 bogie. On test prototype Y37s not only satisfied the revised 160 km/h specification, but have been run successfully up to a maximum of 224.5 km/h, in all probability a world record for freight car speed. The recently-introduced low-platform Multifret wagons for container/swapbody traffic have variants of the Y37 bogie.

To meet customer demand for heavier trainloads of imported ore and aggregates, the SNCF has developed a radio control for slave locomotives. As a result, it was planning in 1990 to begin operation of trains grossing 5600 or even 6000 tonnes. It had already satisfactorily worked a 5200-tonne train of aggregates from Caffiers to Dunkerque.

In the spring of 1990 the SNCF was carrying out a field trial of an automatic vehicle identification system (AVI) on some 400 wagons employed in the 160 km/h Lille-Marseilles/Avignon freight service. The system employs vehicle-mounted transponders and trackside interrogators. The latter were installed at the entrances and exits of yards in the three terminal areas of the train service, and at the terminals of some major customers using it, such as Novatrans, CNC and groupage companies.

Intermodal

Intermodal traffic now accounts for 15 per cent of total traffic. Domestic traffic is marketed by two companies, Novatrans and SNCF's CNC subsidiary, but with the swapbody figuring in the business of both the piggyback/container distinction between them is

Chronofroid swapbody on 160 km/h Multifret wagon (G Freeman Allen)

Semi-Rail bi-modal trailer in highway mode (G Freeman Allen)

no longer wholly valid. The critical difference now is that CNC is open to all users, while Novatrans deals exclusively with road hauliers.

CNC operates some 40 terminals in France and 5500 flatcars. In 1989 it reported some 6 million tonnes of traffic, a 5 per cent rise on the previous year. Its international traffic increased 10 per cent, but domestic traffic only 3 per cent.

Novatrans, 60 per cent owned by road haulage interests, 40 per cent by the SNCF, also registered significant international traffic growth in 1989. Of the 265 700 semi-trailers piggybacked, 104 000 were on cross-border transits, 6.9 per cent more than in 1988. Of 200 100 swapbodies transported, 75 500 were on international transits, 13.6 per cent more than in 1988. Domestic piggyback was down in 1988, and domestic swapbody movement up only 4.2 per cent.

During the currency of the new contract with the State (see above), the SNCF aims to double its intermodal traffic to 15 000 million tonne-km a year, representing 30 per cent of its total freight business. To that end it will be investing Ffr1500 million in its intermodal sector.

At least one bimodal system will be included in the intermodal sales portfolio. In conjunction with the SNCF, Remafer and Fruehauf have devised the Semi-Rail, three trailers of which went into trial revenue service on the 140 km/h Lille-Lyon train in the spring of 1990. Semi-Rail is similar in concept to the RoadRailer, for which Arbel-Fauvel-Rail has a French licence, the main difference being that in the rail mode Semi-Rail supports each of a coupled pair of trailer bodies independently on a connecting Y25LD bogie surmounted by standard highway tractor hitches. Given satisfactory experience, two rakes of at least 15 Semi-Rail trailers each would be put into daily service on the Lyon-Lille route in 1991. Subject to satisfactory trial of three Road-Railer prototypes, it was planned to operate these commercially between Paris and Marseilles in 1991.

The Avignon-Rungis Fretchrono service inaugurated a Chronofroid programme by which the SNCF aims to recover some of the 50 per cent (2 million tonnes) of refrigerated perishables traffic it has lost to road since 1980. The SNCF itself invested Ffr 33 million in 50 low-platform Multifret wagons, 75 refrigerated swap bodies and road chassis to fulfil the programme. Chronofroid recorded 120 000 tonnes of traffic in 1989. In the course of 1990 the SNCF planned to introduce further services between Avignon/Lyon and Lille, Perpignan and Rungis, and Avignon and Nancy.

In 1990 SNCF was developing with its subsidiaries a similar swapbody operation for chemical products, in this case with international service as an objective. Hence its title of Transeurochem. To be inaugurated with a stock of 40 swapbodies, the project was expected to deploy 100 and to be moving 200 000 tonnes a year in 1991.

Commutor terminal project
For focal points in its intermodal network the SNCF plans a new form of terminal that will substitute exchange of loads between connecting intermodal trains for exchange of wagons, and that will accelerate loading/discharge at centres dealing in originating/terminal traffic only. The project, named 'Commutor', aims to effect a train's take-up and discharge of loads–semi-trailers as well as containers and swapbodies–within 15 min.

An interchange terminal (Commutor 2) would have a single electrified running line spanned by up to nine semi-gantry cranes alongside a storage area. The catenary will be retractable when the cranes are operating. The cranes will be computer-programmed with advance data on a train's consist, so that they are ready-positioned for the loads to be handled when the train arrives. In the storage area, loads will be craned on to individual transfer platforms, for shuffling by robotic devices to a place appropriate for the reloading on to a connecting train.

The SNCF aims to have a prototype Commutor 1 terminal, the version limited to originating/terminating traffic, active by 1992, and a Commutor 2 interchange by 1994.

Electrification
Electrification of the Paris-Massif Central main line was completed with energisation of the final 65km from Saint-Germain-des-Fossés to Clermont-Ferrand in March 1990. From September 1990 the fastest transit for the 420km from Paris to Clermont-Ferrand would be 3hr 08min. The line has been electrified at 1.5 kV dc to a point south of Montargis, but at 25 kV ac

Arbel-Fauvet-Rail RoadRailer in rail mode (*G Freeman Allen*)

thereafter. Retention of dc as far as Montargis, to a point 104.7 km from Paris Gare de Lyon, preserves a common system within the outer limit of Paris Gare de Lyon outer surburban operation.

The Britanny electrification was extended a further stage over the 148km from Saint-Brieuc to Brest in September 1989, allowing the inauguration of TGV-A service from Paris to Brest. Scheduled dates for completion of the remaining stages were: Rennes-Vannes (1991); and Vannes-Quimper (1992).

In January 1989 the SNCF gave the go-ahead for electrification of the 147 km from Poitiers to La Rochelle for a total cost, including signalling modernisation, of Ffr 700 million. The work will be supplemented by purchase of two more TGV-A train-sets and five electric locomotives. A completion target date of late 1991 has been set.

The Tarentaise line from Saint Pierre-d'Albigny to Bourg-Saint Maurice (80 km) was wired throughout by the winter of 1988/89, in readiness for Albertville's staging of the Winter Olympics in 1992. This electrification is dual-mode: 1.5 kV dc to Albertville, where trains for Bourg St Maurice must reverse, and 25 kV ac from Albertville over the remaining two-thirds of the distance. It has been considered preferable to allow 1.5 kV dc locomotives to work unchanged from the Paris-Chambéry main line to the Albertville reversal, rather than to go for the savings of 25 kV fixed installation throughout.

Late in 1987 the government approved electrification from Paris to Caen and Cherbourg, together with the branch from Lisieux to Trouville-Deauville, which will be single-tracked. The project will include track upgrading for 200 km/h with the consequent suppression of 106 level crossings. The total cost of some Ffr 2000 million will be shared by the SNCF, the state and Regional authorities (who pressed for the 200 km/h upgrading). Completion by 1995 is possible.

Other recent additions to the electrification programme, all of them under way in 1990: are Savernay-Redon (42 km), a 25kV ac scheme connecting Nantes with Rennes and southern Brittany, set for energisation in May 1991; La Ferté-Alais–Malesherbes, on the outer suburban fringes of Paris between Montargis and Corbeil; and, in Northern France in the hinterland of the Channel Tunnel, Calais-Boulogne, Douai-Cambrai, Hazebrouck-Calais and Lille-Baisieux.

Traction and rolling stock
At the end of 1989 the SNCF was operating 2221 electric, 1904 diesel and 1423 tractor locomotives. 14 four-car Type ETG and 38 five-car Type RTG gas turbine train-sets were in use. Emu motor cars and trailer cars totalled 1075 and 1606 respectively (108 TGV sets excluded), diesel railcars and trailers respectively 715 and 760, and there were 9664 hauled passenger cars. Freight stock totalled 96 400 SNCF-owned and 71 500 privately-owned.

In late 1989 orders were placed with the GEC-Alsthom group for 104 non-powered bi-level cars, among them 14 driving trailers, for long-haul Paris commuter operation. An option was taken on 47 more cars, including a further six driving trailers. Deliveries were to begin the spring of 1991. Services in mind for the equipment include those to Paris from Rouen, Amiens, Château-Thierry and Laroche-Migennes.

Orders were also placed in late 1989 for 104 more Type Z20500 five-car bi-level dual-voltage emus. Of these, 62 would be delivered between October 1991 and mid-1994 for the prospective RER Line D service from Orry-la-Ville via Gare de Lyon to Melun/Evry. In addition, 35 bi-level trailers were ordered to bring the 35 four-car emus of the same type already operating betwen Orry and Châtelet up to five-car length. The remaining 42 emus ordered were to reinforce the fleets on the southeast and northern suburban sectors,

Class 63500 diesel-electric Bo-Bo

France / RAILWAY SYSTEMS

in view of developments such as the revived Grande Ceinture operation and RER extensions other than Line D. Total value of these emu orders for 387 vehicles is about Ffr 3 000 million.

Rather than order new heavy electric shunters, the SNCF decided to have Alsthom completely renovate the 12 1.5 kV dc Class CC1100 locomotives, built between 1938 and 1948, with new GTO thyristor, microprocessor-controlled traction equipment. The first rebuild emerged for trials in February 1989.

In the line-haul electric locomotive sector a new dual-voltage 5600 kW 'Sybic' class, the BB26000, has introduced a fresh SNCF locomotives outline. GEC-Alsthom began delivery of an order for 44 Type BB26000 in the spring of 1988. However, it was not until March 1990 that the first examples of the class based at Dijon, for through working via Dôle to Vallorbe, took up revenue-earning service. Deliveries were some way behind schedule because initial problems with the TGV-A train-sets' electronics were absorbing the manufacturers' attention.

A further order for 30 Type Y8000 locotractors, for mid-1990 delivery, was placed with Arbel-Fauvet-Rail in 1988, with an option for two further series of 30 units apiece. All are being equipped for remote control by radio.

All Corail passenger cars are to be progressively modified, principally by addition of anti-wheelslide devices, for 200km/h operation. In 1989 stock available for this speed comprised 408 'Corail' cars, 18 Grill-Express cafeteria cars and 101 'Grand Confort' cars. Of the last-mentioned, which also have electro-magnetic brakes, 53 cars are undergoing internal reconstruction to offer a special grade of first class accommodation on services from Paris to Strasbourg and to Brive (see above).

Signalling and traffic control
Following a sequence of serious accidents earlier in the year that aroused public anxiety, the SNCF announced in October 1988 a Ffr 4100 million, five-year programme of expenditure on signalling and safety measures. Half the sum is to go on a version of the L M Ericsson automatic train and speed control (ATP) system developed jointly with MTE-Alsthom. It is to be operative on all electrified main lines by 1994. The system, employing track-mounted transponders, will identify temporary speed restrictions as well as signal aspects. Another measure, motivated by a bufferstop collision at Paris Gare de l'Est, is equipment of all traction units and driving trailers with a device that automatically cuts off power when brakes are applied. A major accident at Paris Gare de Lyon has led to the substitution of passenger intercommunication on suburban emus with the driver for passenger ability to activate emergency brake application. New automatic devices will protect the approaches to terminal platforms in Paris. Driver training is being reorganised and backed by new equipment, including simulators.

In the course of the next decade the SNCF plans to install a system of computerised real-time control of train movement described by the acronym ASTREE. Total cost of the project is estimated at between Ffr 8000–10 000 million. The principle of the concept is radio-telephone communication between on-board train microprocessors and a central control.

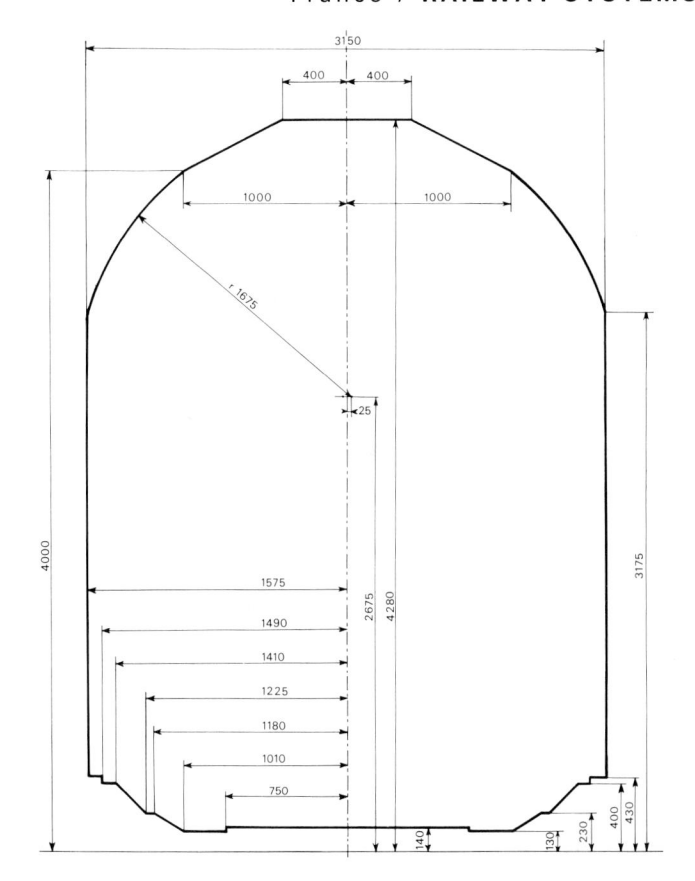

Traction units will be fitted with Doppler radar apparatus that will both compute a train's speed and establish its location to an accuracy of ± 0.1 per cent. This information will be associated with data pre-fed into an on-board computer concerning the train's consist destination, weight, braking capacity and other commercial data derived from intelligent systems on each of the train's vehicles. The results will be radio-transmitted to a control centre via a new national network of the French Post Office, scheduled to cover 85 per cent of France by 1990. Later, perhaps, signals may be transmitted via geostationary satellites in space.

The control centre, equipped with a computer-banked map of the entire SNCF operational trackage, will computer-process the data received from moving trains and determine the desirable headway to be maintained between those on the same line of route or on converging paths and thus the speed at which they should move. This will be transmitted and received as driving commands on visual displays in traction unit cabs.

The first field trial of ASTREE technology was instituted in the spring of 1990 on the 8km part-single, part-double track Bondy-Aulnay line in the Parisian suburbs. Ten Class BB16500 locomotives on the line's push-pull service were equipped for the trials.

The SNCF's first fully solid state interlocking is on trial at Chateauroux on the Paris-Toulouse main line.

By the end of 1989 over 6500 km of route had been equipped for ground-to-train radio communication, and about 3500 electric tractive units were fitted to use the system.

Track
Rails: 60 kg/m where traffic exceeds 30 000 tonnes per day; 50 km/h elsewhere
Sleepers: Wood (oak or tropical wood) of 150 mm thickness
Concrete (mono-or duo-block) of 220 mm thickness
Spacing: 1600 to 1722/km
Fastenings: Wooden sleepers; rigid or screw or elastic (Types NR and NABLA); Concrete sleepers: elastic or NR or NABLA type.
Minimum curve radius: 150 m (in depots)
Max gradient: 4 per cent
Max axleloading: (on selected routes): 22.5 tonnes

Electric locomotives: principal classes

Class	Wheel arrangement	Line current	Rate output hp (kW)	Max lb (kg)	Continous at lb (kg)	mph (km/h)	Max speed mph (km/h)	Wheel dia in (mm)	Weight tonnes	Length ft in (mm)	No in service 1.1.90	Year built	Mechanical parts	Electrical equipment
BB-8100	Bo-Bo	1500 V dc	2815 (2100)	67 000 (30 400)	36 000 (16 300)	25.8 (41.5)	65 (105)	55* (1400)	92	42'5" (12 930)	165	1949	Alsthom	Alsthom
BB-8500 (2 gear ratios)	B-B	1500 V dc	3940 (2940)	44 300 (20 100) 73 850 (33 000)	28 200 (12 800) 46 700 (21 200)	51.3 (82.5) 30.6 (49.2)	93 (140) 56 (90)	43¼ (1100)	78	48'3"-51'1" (14 700-15 570)	146	1963	Alsthom	Alsthom
BB-7200	B-B	1500 V dc	5845 (4360)	66 100* (30 000)	30 400* (13 800)	60* (97)	112* (180)	49¼ (1250)	84	57'4¼" (17 480)	239	1977	Fives-Lille Francorail	Francorail
BB-9200	Bo-Bo	1500 V dc	5160 (3850)	58 500 (26 500)	32 600 (14 800)	58 (93)	100 (160)	49¼ (1250)	82	53'2" (16 200)	91	1957	MTE	MTE
BB-9300											40	1968		
BB-9400	B-B	1500 V dc	2965 (2210)	60 600 (27 500)	34 800 (15 800)	31 (50)	81 (130)	40* (1020)	59	47'3" (14 400)	101	1959	Fives-Lille	CEM
CC-6500 (2 gear ratios)	C-C	1500 V dc	7910 (5900)	64 700 (29 347)	60 400† (27 397)	38.5† (62)	62 (100) 137 (220)	45 (1140)	115	66'3" (20 190)	74	1970	Alsthom MTE	Alsthom MTE
CC-7100	Co-Co	1500 V dc	4680 (3490)	58 500 (26 500)	34 600 (15 700)	49.5 (79.5)	93 (150)	49¼ (1250)	105	62'1" (18 922)	49	1951	Alsthom Fives-Lille	Alsthom MTE
BB-12000	Bo-Bo	25 kV 50 Hz	3310 (2470)	79 400 (36 000)	41 900 (19 000)	29.5 (47.5)	75 (120)	49¼ (1250)	83	49'10½" (15 200)	137	1954	MTE	MTE

572 RAILWAY SYSTEMS / France

Class	Wheel arrangement	Line current	Rate output hp (kW)	Tractive effort (full field)			Max speed mph (km/h)	Wheel dia in (mm)	Weight tonnes	Length ft in (mm)	No in service 1.1.90	Year built	Builders	
				Max lb (kg)	Continous at lb (kg)	mph (km/h)							Mechanical parts	Electrical equipment
BB-13000	Bo-Bo	25 kV 50 Hz	2680 (2000) 2855 (2130)	55 100 (25 000)	26 000 (11 800)	40.5 (65)	65 (105) 75 (120)	49¼ (1250)	84	49'10½" (15 200)	26	1954 1956	MTE	MTE
BB-16000	Bo-Bo	25 kV 50 Hz	5540 (4130)	69 500 (31 500)	33 500 (15 200)	53 (85)	100 (160)	49¼ (1250)	84	53'2" (16 200)	60	1958	MTE	MTE
BB-15000	B-B	25 kV 50 Hz	5485 (4360)	64 000* (29 000)	33 000 (15 000)	62* (100)	112 (180)	49¼ (1250)	88	57'4¼" (17 480)	62	1971	Fives-Lille Alsthom, MTE	Alsthom MTE
BB-16500 (2 gear ratios)	B-B	25 kV 50 Hz	3460)2580)	72 700 (33 000)	24 900 (11 300) 42 300 (19 200)	51 (82) 30 (48)	93 (150) 56 (90)	43¼ (1100)	74	47'3" (14 400)	294	1958	Alsthom	Alsthom
BB-17000 (2 gear ratios)	B-B	25 kV 50 Hz	3940 (2940)	44 300 (20 100) 73 850 (33 000)	28 200 (12 800) 46 700 (21 200)	51.3 (82.5) 30.6 (49.2)	87 (140) 56 (90)	43¼ (1100)	78	48'3"-49' (14 700-19 940)	105	1964	Alsthom	Alsthom
CC-14100	Co-Co	25 kV 50 Hz	2495 (1860)	94 700 (43 000)	51 200 (23 200)	17.7 (28.5)	37 (60)	43¼ (1100)	126	62'0" (18 890)	34	1954	Alsthom Five-Lille	Alsthom CEM
BB-20200 (2-current) (2 gear ratios)	B-B	25 kV 50 Hz 15 kV 16⅔ Hz	3940 (2940) 2225 (1660)	–	–	–	56 (90) 93 (150)		80	47'6½" (14 490)	13	1969	Alsthom	Alsthom
CC-21000 (2-current) (2 gear ratios)	C-C	25 kV 50 Hz 1.5 kV dc	7910 (5900)	–	–	–	62 (100) 137 (220)		122	66'3" (20 190)	4	1969	Alsthom-MTE	Alsthom-MTE
BB-22200 (2-current)	B-B	25 kV 50 Hz and 1500 V dc	5845 (4360)	66 100* (30 000)	30 400* (13 800)	60* (97)	112‡ (180)	49¼ (1250)	89	57'4¼" (17 480)	202	1977	Francorail	Francorail
BB-25100 (2-current)	Bo-Bo	25 kV 50 hz and 1500 V dc	5540 (4130) 4560 (3400)	81 600 (37 000)	39 000 (17 700)	52 (83.5)	81 (130)	49¼ (1250)	84	53'3" (16 200)	70	1963	MTE	MTE
BB-25200	Bo-Bo	25 kV 50 Hz and 1500 V dc	5540 (4130) 4560 (3400)	68 300 (31 000)	32 600 (14 800)	62 (99.5)	99 (160)	49¼ (1250)	84	53'2" (16 200)	51	1964	MTE	MTE
BB-25500 (2-current) (2 gear ratios)	B-B	25 kV 50 Hz and 1500 V dc	3940 (2940)	44 300 (20 100) 73 850 (33 600)	25 100 (11 400) 41 900 (19 000)	51 (82) 30 (48)	93 (140) 56 (90)	43¼ (1100)	78	53'3"-51'1" (14 700-15 570)	194	1963	Alsthom	Alsthom
CC-40100 (4-current) (2 gear ratios)	C-C	25 kV 50 Hz 15 kV 16⅔ Hz 3000 V dc 1500 V dc	6000 (4480) 6000 (4480)	32 000 (14 500) 44 500 (20 200)	19 000 (8600) 27 000 (12 000)	95.4 (153.5) 68 (110)	149 (240) 99 (160)	42½ (1080)	108	72'3¼" (22 030)	10	1964	Alsthom	Alsthom
BB-26000	B-B	25 kV 50 Hz 1500 V dc	7500 {5600}	–	–	–	125 (200)	–	90	–	2	1988	GEC-Alsthom	GEC-Alsthom

* Some units re-geared for higher tractive effort and 100 km/h maximum
† Low gear
‡ Some units geared for 220 km/h (136.7 mph) maximum

Electric multiple-unit power cars: principal classes

Class	Cars per unit	Line voltage	Motor cars per unit	Motored axles per motor car	Rated output kW per unit	Max speed km/h	Weight tonnes	Total seating capacity	Length of unit mm	No in service 1.1.90	Rate of acceleration under normal load	Year first built	Builders	
													Mechanical parts	Electrical equipment
Z5300	4	1.5 kV dc	1	4	1180	130	154	387	102 800	145	0.7 m/s² 0 to 50 km/h	1965	Fives-Lille CFL-CIMT de Dietrich	Jeumont
Z5600	4	1.5 kV dc	2	4	2700	140	216	550	98 760	104	0.9 m/s² 0 to 50 km/h	1982	ANF-CIMT	TCO
Z7100	4	1.5 kV dc	1	2	940	130	139	275	94 170	32	0.47 m/s² 0 to 50 km/h	1960	Decauville de Dietrich	Jeumont Oerlikon
Z7300 Z7500	2	1.5 kV dc	1	4	1275	160	103	151	50 200	86	0.5 m/s² 0 to 50 km/h	1980	Francorail	MTE
Z6100	3	25 kV 50 Hz	1	2	615	120	113	273	74 450	82	0.45 m/s² 0 to 40 km/h	1964	SFAC-CFL de Deitrich	CEM-SW Alsthom
Z6300	3	25 kV 50 Hz	1	2	615	120	105	173	60 100	35	0.5 m/s² 0 to 40 km/h	1965	CFL-Fives Lille de Dietrich	CEM-SW Alsthom
Z6400	4	25 kV 50 Hz	2	4	2350	120	189	264	92 430	150	1 m/s² 0 to 50 km/h	1976	CFL	Alsthom TCO
Z8100	4	1.5 kV dc 25 kV 50 Hz	2	4	2500	140	212	312	104 160	102	0.9 m/s² 0 to 50 km/h	1979	SFB-ANF	TCO
Z8800	4	25 kV 50 Hz	2	4	2800	140	224	534	98 760	116	0.9 m/s² 0 to 50 km/h	1985	Alsthom ANF-CIMT	TCO
Z9500 Z9600	2	1.5 kV dc 25 kV 50 Hz	1	4	1275	160	115	151	50 200	54	0.5 m/s² 0 to 50 km/h	1982	Francorail	MTE
Z11500	2	25 kV 50 Hz	2	4	1275	160	115	151	50 200	22	NA	1987	Alsthom	Alsthom

France / RAILWAY SYSTEMS

Class	Cars per unit	Line voltage	Motor cars per unit	Motored axles per motor car	Rated output kW per unit	Max speed km/h	Weight tonnes	Total seating capacity	Length of unit mm	No in service 1.1.90	Rate of acceleration under normal load	Year first built	Builders Mechanical parts	Builders Electrical equipment
Z20500	4	25 kV 50 Hz 1.5 kV dc	2	4	2800	140	224	386	10 300	40	0.9 m/s^2	1988	GEC-Alsthom ANF	GEC-Alsthom
TGV-PSE 2300	10	25 kV 50 Hz 1.5 kV dc	2	12	6450 3100	270	418	386	200 190	99	0.5 m/s^2 0 to 50 km/h	1978	Alsthom Francorail	Alsthom Francorail
TGV-PSE 3300	10	25 kV 50 Hz 15 kV 16⅔ Hz 1.5 kV dc	2	12	6450 3100 2800	270	419	386	200 190	9	0.5 m/s^2 0 to 50 km/h	1981	Alsthom Francorail	Alsthom Francorail
TGV-A		25 kV 50 Hz 1.5 kV dc	2	8	8800 3880	300	485	485	237 560	39	0.44 m/s^2 0 to 50 km/h		GEC-Alsthom ANF De Dietrich	GEC-Alsthom

Diesel locomotives: principal classes

Class	Wheel arrangement	Transmission	Rated power hp (kW)	Max lb (kg)	Tractive effort Continuous at lb (kg)	Tractive effort Continuous at mph (km/h)	*Max speed mph (km/h)	Wheel dia in (mm)	Total weight tons	Length ft in (mm)	No in service 1.1.90	First built	Builders Mechanical parts	Builders Engine & type	Builders Transmission
68000	A1A-A1A	Elec	2225 (1660)	67 000 (30 400)	39 700 (18 000)	19 (30.6)	81 (130)	49¼ (1250)	106	58'8½" (17 920)	83	1963	CAFL	Sulzer 12LVA 24	CEM
68500	A1A-A1A	Elec	2205 (1645)				81 (130)		105		24	1963	CAFL	SACM-AGO V12 DSHR	CEM
65500	Co-Co	Elec	1300 (970)	56 200 (25 000) 37 500 (17 000)	32 800 (14 900) 19 000 (8600)		75 (120)	41¼ (1050)	112	65'0" (19 814)	20	1956	Alsthom CAFL	SACM MGO V12SH	Alsthom
72000 mono-motor bogies (2 gears)	C-C	Elec	3020 (2250)	19 300 (36 400) 81 600 (37 000)	30 900 (12 400) 51 800 (23 500)	34.7 (65) 21.5 (34.5)	100 (160) 53 (85)	44⅞ (1140)	110	66'3¼" (20 190)	91	1967	Alsthom	SACM-AGO V16 ESHR	Alsthom
63000	Bo-Bo	Elec	480 (355)	37 500 (17 000)	231 000 (10 500)	6 (10)	50 (80)	41¼ (1050)	68	48'2" (14 680)	108	1953	Brissonneau et Lotz	Sulzer 6LDA22C	Brissonneau et Lotz
63100	Bo-Bo	Elec	585 (435)	37 500 (17 000)	24 200 (11 000)	8 (13)	50 (80)	41¼ (1050)	68	48'2" (14 680)	142	1957	Brissonneau et Lotz	Sulzer 6LDA22D	Brissonneau et Lotz
63400/ 63500	Bo-Bo	Elec	605 (450)	37 700 (17 100)	28 400 (12 900)	7.5 (12)	50 (80)	41¼ (1050)	68	48'2" (14 680)	623	1956	Brissonneau et Lotz	SACM MGO V12 SH	Brissonneau et Lotz
66000	Bo-Bo	Elec	1115 (830)				75 (120)		70	48'10½" (14 898)	390	1959	Alsthom	SACM-MGO V16 BSHR	CEM
66600	Bo-Bo	Elec	1195 (890)				75 (120)		71	48'10½" (14 898)	11	1962	Alsthom	SEMT 12PA4	CEM
67000 mono-motor bogies (2 gears)	B-B	Elec	1930 (1440)	45 400 (20 600) 68 300 (31 000)	26 500 (12 000) 39 700 (18 000)	26 (42) 17.4 (28)	56 (90) 56 (90)	45¼ (150)	80	56'1" (17 090)	192	1963	Brissonneau et Lotz MTE	SEMT-Pielstick 16PA4	MTE
67400	B-B	Elec	2045 (1525)	63 934 (29 000)	31 746 (14 400)	23 (37)	87 (140)	49¼ (1250)	83	56'1" (17 090)	230	1969	Brissonneau et Lotz	SEMT-Pielstick 16PA4	MTE
Y7100	B	Hyd	175	16 300 (7400)			34 (54)	41¼ (1050)	32	29'4" (8940)	200	1958	Billiard Decauville	Poyaud 6PYT	Voith
Y7400	B	Mech	175				37 (60)	41¼ (1050)	32	29'4" (8940)	489	1963	Decauville De Dietrich	Moyse/Poyaud 6 PYT	BV Asynchro
Y8000 (2 gears)	B	Hyd	290	13 600 (6750)	2750 (1247)	20 (32)	37 (60)	41¼ (1050)	36	33'9" (10 140)	390	1977	Arbel-Fauvel Rail	Poyaud Y12-520NS	Voith

Diesel and gas turbine multiple-units

Class	Cars per unit	Motor cars per unit	Motored axles per motor car	Transmission	Rated power kW	Max speed km/h	Weight tonnes per car	Total seating capacity (M-motor T-trailer)	Length per car mm (M-motor T-trailer)	No in service 1.1.90	Year first built	Builders Mechanical parts	Builders Engine & type	Builders Transmission
T1000 (EGC*)	4	2	2	Hyd	1115	180	146.7	188	M 22 840 T 20 750	14	1969	ANF	SFAC, Saurer SDHR Turboméca Turmo IIIH	Voith
T2000 (RTG*)	5	2	2	Hyd	1970	200	225	280	M 26 230 T 25 510	39	1973	ANF	Turboméca Turmo IIIH Turmo XIIC	Voith
X2100 X2200	1	1	2	Hyd	440	140	42	65.54	22 400	49 57	1980	ANF	SFAC, Saurer SJS-S 1DHR	Voith
X2800	1	1	2	Hyd-Mech	426	120	53	62	27 730	118	1957	Decauville RNUR	SACM-MGO V12 SH	Maybach
X4300 X4500	2	1	2	Mech	295	120	M 34 T 23	141	M 21 240 T 21 240	268	1963	ANF	Poyaud or SFAC, Saurer SDHR	De Dietrich
X4630	2	1	2	Hyd	295	120	M 37 T 23	141	M 21 240 T 21 240	113	1971	ANF	SFAC, Saurer SDHR	Voith
X4750	2	1	2	Hyd	440	140	M 37 T 23	135	M 21 240 T 21 240	47	1975	ANF	SFAC, Saurer S1DHR	Voith
X4900	3	2	2	Hyd	590	140	M 37.5 T 24.5	154	M 21 240 T 21 240	28	1975	ANF	SFAC, Saurer SDHR	Voith

* Gas turbine

Gabon

Ministry of Transport & Communications

Libreville

Minister: G Rawiri

Gabon State Railways (OCTRA)
Office du Chemin de Fer Transgabonais

PO Box 2198, Libreville

Telephone: +241 22478/20974
Telex: 5307, 5663 go

President: Charles Tsibah
General Manager: Richard Damas
Director of Administration: Anselme Rokissi
Director, Technical: Firmin Gorra
Director, Finance: Marie-Therèse Ngoundji
Manager, Fixed Installations: Ferdinand Mbo-Edou
  Operations: Joël Engone
  Rolling Stock: Paul-Christian Renamy
  Signalling and Telecommunications: Suzanne Mengome
  Data Systems: Joseph Aoumbou
  Commercial: Guillaume Opaga
  Purchases: Claude Dovy

Gauge: 1435 mm
Route length: 668 km

The Gabonese government announced the decision to construct the first section of the 648 km Trans-Gabon Railway from Libreville/Owendo to Boué in 1972. Construction work started in 1974 and the first section between Owendo and N'Djolé (183 km) opened to traffic in January 1979.

The OCTRA plans originally called for construction first of the main Owendo-Boué section, and later extensions south to Franceville and north to iron ore fields at Belinga. However, the economic case for continuous construction of the Boué-Franceville line was found to be overwhelming, as there are large deposits of manganese at Moanda in the Haut-Ogooué as well as extensive reserves of timber. Hitherto, a manganese output of only two million tonnes a year had been transported from Moanda by a 75 km aerial ropeway across the border into the Congo at M'Binda, and thence by the Comilog and Congo-Ocean railways to Pointe-Noire for export.

A contract for construction of the 311 km Boué-Franceville section was signed with the Eurotrag consortium in 1982. The first sleeper was formally placed by President Mitterrand of France during his visit to Gabon in January 1983. At the same time train services were inaugurated over the 162 km from N'Djolé to Boué, which was finished at the end of 1982. The Boué-Franceville section was completed in December 1986 and formally inaugurated by President Omar Bongo of Gabon.

Transfer of some manganese exports from Moanda to rail began in 1988 and in 1989 was expected to gross 1.35 million tonnes. OCTRA stands to handle an even larger volume of freight with the start of operations at hitherto untapped iron deposits in the northern part of the country, providing a spur is built between Belinga and Boué. According to traffic forecasts, some 250 000 passengers and about 3 million tonnes of freight could be carried each year over the new line. A deep water mineral port is under construction at Owendo and OCTRA's manganese terminal there was formally opened by President Bongo in December 1988.

The 230 km branch northwards to Belinga, where vast iron ore and manganese deposits are awaiting exploitation, will not be built until there is an upturn in world demand for manganese. Forecasts of mineral shortage in the 1990s promoted OCTRA to launch surveys in 1984, and the government to seek means of financing a start of construction, but in 1985 further action was shelved.

Finance
OCTRA is burdened by serious debt, attributable to a number of factors, ranging from the costs of its construction to high operating costs as a result of climactic conditions, and its obligation to carry out social projects that are not strictly railway-related. As a result, there is a backlog of investment in track and rolling stock.

Traffic
Over 80 per cent of OCTRA's income is derived from freight, which has been increasing rapidly. In 1988 freight traffic totalled 829 000 tonnes, three times the volume of 1980; freight tonne-km grossed 250 million. Passenger journeys, at 118 353, and passenger-km, at 48 million, were up close on 19 per cent over the previous year, but still below the 1985 figure, partly because of rolling stock shortage and partly due to economic recession.

Timber is the principal freight traffic, generating half the railway's revenue. But in the past two years the most spectacular growth has been in container movement.

Motive power and rolling stock
Diesel locomotive stock comprises 12 Bombardier 2685 kW MX636, designated locally CC200; 22 Alsthom BB100; six Krupp-MaK 760 kW diesel-hydraulic locomotives based on the company's Type G1203, but with Cummins engines; six 760 kW diesel-hydraulic locomotives from Cockerill; five Brush Electrical Machines 90-tonne 820kW Bo-Bos with Cummins engines and Brush alternator transmission; and 12 other diesel shunters, including a pair from Hyundai of South Korea.

Passenger cars total 37. These include 10 second-class part-couchette compartment, part-saloon passenger coaches from BREL (1988) based on the latter's International design. De Dietrich has delivered four first-class passenger cars, six first-class couchette cars and two presidential saloon cars; and Soulé of France three first-class and two restaurant-bar cars. Freight wagon suppliers include British Rail Engineering, Hyundai and companies in Brazil, France, Japan, Morocco and Romania; in 1989 stock totalled 883 wagons.

Infrastructure
In 1989 the Ansaldo group gained a L20 000 million order to resignal the system's western and central routes.

Similar track standards have been devised for both sections of the Trans-Gabon. Rail is 50 kg/m throughout, laid on 1670 wood sleepers per km in 25 cm of ballast; maximum axleload is 23 tonnes. Steepest gradient against coast-bound trains is 1 per cent between Franceville and Boué, and 0.5 per cent onwards to Owendo. Eastbound, the maximum grade is 1.5 per cent throughout.

Krupp-MaK diesel-hydraulic B-B on newly-completed Boué-Franceville section near Latoursville

First-class couchette car by De Dietrich

Alsthom Type BB100 2800 hp diesel-electric alternator B-B (Wilhelm Pflug)

Presidential saloon by De Dietrich

Germany (Democratic Republic)

Ministry of Transport

Vossstrasse 33, 1086 Berlin

Telephone: +37 2 232 3881
Telex: 11 2250

Minister: Horst Gibner

German State Railway (DR)
Deutsche Reichsbahn

Vossstrasse 33, 1086 Berlin

Telephone: +37 2 232 3881
Telex: 11 2250 mfv in dd

General Manager: Hans Klemm
Department Heads
  Traffic Operating: Dipl-Ing P G Kienast
  Mechanical and Electrical: Dipl-Ing G Ruppert
  Infrastructure: E Moras
  Motive Power and Rolling Stock: M Gürges
  Safety Installations and Telecommunications: Dipl-Ing H Klemm
Chief Operations Officer: Dipl-Ing oec H Krüger

Gauge: 1435 mm; narrow gauge
Length: 13 733 route-km; 274 km
Electrification: 3721 km at 15 kV 16⅔ Hz ac; 26 km at 25 kV 50 Hz ac; 2 km at 3 kV dc; 1.2 km at 600/800 V dc

Aftermath of political change

The drastic political change in the country in November 1989 had a considerable impact on the railway. The migration to West Germany that followed the opening of the border with that country seriously disrupted freight traffic, of which the railway has a 75 per cent national market share, not only because of the many extra passenger trains required, but also through the presence of some 3500 railwaymen amongst the crowds leaving for the West. Between 11 November and 4 December 2150 extra passenger trains were run.

By early 1990 attention was concentrated on the development of existing links with the German Federal Railway (DB) and the reopening of others closed since Germany's partition.

Of the 37 potential cross-border links, nine only were operational at the start of 1990. With the opening of the frontier scheduled passenger service over the available routes was immediately doubled, not without some strain on coaching stock resources. A first step in restoration of historic inter-city route was the reconnection for the summer 1990 timetable of the Eichenburg-Arenshausen stretch between Kassel and Halle, the route from the Ruhr to Leipzig and Breslau, for five daily passenger trains each way. The 1990 timetable inaugurated DB IC service between Frankfurt and Leipzig, and Inter-Regio (IR) services between Munich/Nuremburg and Leipzig, and between Cologne and Berlin; after trials at the DB's Munich test centre it was proved that the DR Type 132 diesel locomotive could be equipped to produce the auxiliary power needed by DB air-conditioned IC cars and the Bistro-Cafe cars used in the DB's IR trains, though initially pairs of DB Class 218 locomotives were used. Intermodal freight services directly connecting DB and DR services were to begin in the autumn of 1990.

Other immediate aims listed by the DB were: double-tracking of the Lübeck-Herrnburg and Büchen-Schwarzenbek sections; infrastructure development and reinstatement of the south curve at Bebra by the DB; electrification of the Helmstedt-Magdeburg, Bebra-Neudietendorf (Erfurt), Probstella-Camburg and Hof-Reichenbach cross-border routes; and, above all, upgrading of the Hannover-Berlin route to the highest standards, so as to gather Berlin into the DB's IC network (see below).

The DR and DB planned in 1991 to launch a two-hourly IC service between Cologne, Hannover and Berlin, interchanging on the DB with the latter's IC Line 5 service. At the same time, DR and DB would issue a joint timetable. In the spring of 1990 the DB was negotiating to hire back for five years from the Leichtenstein company Lenka to which they had been sold the DB's three VT601 ex-Trans-Europ Express five-car diesel-hydraulic train-sets. These have lately been refurbished in Italy for their present owners. The aim was to operate them in 1991 as a modern version of the pre-war 'Fliegende Hamburger' between Hamburg and Berlin, but in mid-1990 the idea was abandoned because the refurbishment had discarded so much equipment essential for DB operation.

Subsequent IC routes planned included Cologne-Helmstedt-Leipzig, Düsseldorf-Kassel-Halle-Leipzig/Dresden; Karlsruhe-Stuttgart-Nuremberg-Dresden; and Leipzig-Frankfurt.

In the expectation that Berlin will again become a major hub of international passenger services, the city's Senate is reconsidering historic plans to connect the former Lehrter and Potsdamer stations by an underground link, which would fuse north-south and west-east traffic flows and pass them through a new subterranean North-South station in the Lehrter station area. Such a move would relieve the overtaxed Stadtbahn and avoid some circuitous routeing at present necessary in East Berlin. Connection of the southern route from Dresden, Halle and Leipzig to the proposed link would involve tunnelling from the area of the onetime Potsdamer station. Meanwhile work has begun on restoring through S-Bahn routes in Berlin and the first reconnection was ready in the spring of 1990.

The DR's former political executives' train has been made available for charter. Its accommodation includes saloons, conference rooms, video cinema, restaurant, two sleeping cars and a car convertible to disco or auto-carrying use.

Hannover-Berlin high-speed project

A joint subsidiary has been set up by the DR and DB, headed by former DR General Manager Herbert Keddi, to oversee development of an electrified high-speed route from Hannover to Berlin, agreed in principle by

Skoda-built Class 230 3 kV dc/15 kV ac dual-voltage electric locomotive

Class 243 electric Bo-Bo and train of new air-conditioned inter-city cars

New inter-city first-class air-conditioned car

RAILWAY SYSTEMS / Germany (Democratic Republic)

the two countries' heads of state in December 1989. The route will be via Stendal and Obisfelde. New stretches of infrastructure wil be engineered for 250 km/h top speed. It was hoped to start construction in 1992.

Traffic
With 131 route-km of railway per 1000 km^2, the German Democratic Republic is Europe's most densely rail-served country after Belgium.

In 1989 freight grossed 339.2 million tonnes. For the first time in years the inexorable upward trend in tonnage was slightly reversed, chiefly because of a clement winter that reduced demand for solid and liquid fuels. Underlying this change was also the fact that the balance of the country's output is veering away from bulk commodities to high-rated merchandise, for which there is powerful road competition by road haulage. As a result the previously 75 per cent DR share of the national freight market is expected to decline by 30 or even more per cent in the 1990s.

Electrification
From 1986 to 1990 the DR aimed to average 300 route-km of electrification a year. Besides the greater efficiency of operation with electric traction, the DR has the stimulus of liberal resources of lignite coal, the means of 60 per cent of its current generation, which make electric traction 40 per cent cheaper to run than diesel. In 1989 a further 320 km went over to electric traction.

The 1986–90 programme embraced in total 1259 route-km. Its main components were: Berlin eastward to Frankfurt/Oder; Stendal-Wittenberge-Wismar/Güstrow, to complete a route north from Magdeburg to Rostock; Berlin-Angermünde-Züssow-Stralsund-Sassnitz port; Berlin southeastward to Cottbus. Other conversions planned were Frankfurt/Oder-Cottbus-Ruhland (133 km); Ruhland-Lutherstadt-Wittenberge (104 km); and Elsterwerda-Karl Marx Stadt (89 km).

Major stretches newly energised in 1989 were: Eilenburg-Falkenberg/Elster-Cottbus (137km); Stralsund-Sassnitz-Mukran (55km); Jüterbog-Falkenberg/Elster (49km); and Lübbenau-Cottbus (40km). At the end of the year 52 per cent of all DR trains were electrically powered.

It had been hoped in 1990 to complete these major projects: (Berlin)-Erkner-Frankfurt/Oder; Frankfurt/Oder-Guben-Cottbus; Cottbus-Senftenberg; and Riesa-Karl Marx Stadt. But depletion of staff following the political upheaval, financial problems, and new urgency to improve links with the DB were likely to change plans. To close east-west catenary gaps priority was now expected to be electrification from Wittenberge to Wustermark, on the Hamburg-Berlin artery; and Halle-Nordhausen, en route to Kassel.

Traffic (million)	1987	1988	1989
Total freight tonnes	338.0	345.3	339.2
Total freight tonne-km	58 823	60 429	59 030
Total passenger-km	22 563	22 285	23 170
Total passenger journeys	603.5	599.9	592

The wiring gap of 14.5 km between the DR and Czech electrified networks at Schöna (DR) and Decin (ČSD) was closed at the end of 1986. Škoda has developed the ČSD Class ES 499.2 dual-voltage 15 kV 16⅔ Hz and 3 kV dc 3000 kW locomotive to enable through running between Berlin and Prague via Bad Schandau. The DR is getting 20, which are designated its Class 230 and based at Dresden for through running between that city and Prague. Top speed is 120 km/h and maximum axleloading 21 tonnes.

Civil engineering
In the past few years available funds have been concentrated on capital improvements, notably electrification, and infrastructure maintenance has not been adequate to absorb the constantly rising volume of freight without strains. As a result, DR has been engaged in a rehabilitation programme termed 'network stabilisation'. The Berlin-Halle route was given priority, followed by other routes together connecting the system's key marshalling yards and bearing about a third of its freight. The latter are: Berlin to Erfurt, Sassnitz, Blankenheim, Dresden and Bad Schandau; Halle to Wittenberge, lately electrified; Elsterwerda to Karl-Marx Stadt; Bitterfeld to Leipzig and Werdau; Halle to Delitsch; Jüterborg to Zossen; Dresden to Werdau; the Berlin outer ring; and the Leipzig freight ring.

The DR's heavy civil engineering programme has been complicated by a high incidence of alkali damage in its concrete sleepers. The cause is the addition in manufacture of gypsum to quicken the hardening of the concrete. The resultant product tends to become porous, leading to failures that risk safety. The only feasible solution is immediate replacement of the defective sleepers. In 1989 this was completed over almost 1000 km of track.

Traction and rolling stock
In August 1989 the 500th Class 243 electric locomotive was taken into use. The 82.5-tonne unit has 120 km/h top speed and a tractive effort of 280 kN. Originally intended as the freight version of the design the 243 has taken over virtually all DR inter-city passenger haulage. A further 110 locomotives were

New inter-city second-class car

expected in 1990, to bring the class total to 654 units, all built since 1984. The 234 built in 1988-89 and those to come in 1990 are equipped for multiple operation in freight traffic.

The DR is preparing to adopt three-phase ac traction technology. Like its DB neighbour, the DR will employ the asynchronous motor. A first step was expected to be the creation of a 1000 kW electric shunting/light haulage electric locomotive prototype, designated Class 208. The main objective, however, is a main-line locomotive with similar characteristics to the DB's Class 120, to be known as DR Class 255.

Diesel locomotives are being fitted with microprocessor devices to aid the driver in energy-economical use of power.

The DR is to persist with locomotive-hauled trainsets of its bi-level cars for S-Bahn operation. In the 1970s a four-car commuter emu, Type 280, was developed by the DR in conjunction with the VEB Hans Beimler works in Henningsdorf. Two prototypes were

Principal electric locomotives

Type	BR 250	BR 211	BR 242	BR 243	BR 251
Service weight	120 tonnes	82 tonnes	82 tonnes	82.5 tonnes	126 tonnes
Wheel arrangement	Co-Co	Bo-Bo	Bo-Bo	Bo-Bo	Co-Co
Length over buffers	19 600 mm	16 320 mm	16 320 mm	16 640 mm	18 640 mm
Max width (over car body/hand rails)	2970/3090 mm	3050 mm	3050 mm	-	3065 mm
Height above top of rail with pantograph lowered	4650 mm	4530 mm	4530 mm	-	4585 mm
Distance between bogie pivots	11 200 mm	7800 mm	7800 mm	8500 mm	9800 mm
Minimum curve radius	140 m	140 m	140 m	140 m	140 m
Rated power (one-hour rating)	5400 kW	2920 kW	2920 kW	3720 kW	3660 kW
Tractive effort at rated power	17.5 Mp	10.4 Mp	14.4 Mp	13 Mp	32 Mp
Speed at rated power	102 km/h	98 km/h	72 km/h	102 km/h	38 km/h
Max service speed	125 km/h	120 km/h	100 km/h	120 km/h	80 km/h
Max tractive effort on starting	47.4 Mp	21.3 Mp	25.2 Mp	28.55 Mp	45.5/54 Mp

Principal diesel locomotives

Class	Wheel arrangement	Transmission	Rated power hp	Max speed mph (km/h)	Wheel dia in (mm)	Length ft in (mm)	Year first built	Builders Mechanical parts	Builders Engine & type	Builders Transmission
106	D	Hyd	650	19 (30)	43.2 (1100)	35'8½" (10 880)	1964	VEB Lokomotivbau-Elektrotechnische Werke "Hans Beimler"	12 kV D 18/21	VEB Strömungsmaschinen Pirna
114	B-B	Hyd	1500	63 (100)	39.9 (1000)	45'9" (13 940)	1969	VEB Lokomotivbau-Elektrotech-	12 kV D 18/21 A-4	VEB Strömungsmaschinen Pirna
111	B-B	Hyd	1000	40 (65)	39.3 (1000)	45'9" (13 940)	1981	Nische Werke "Hans Beimler"	12 kV D 18/21 A-3	
118	B-B	Hyd	1800	75 (120)	39.3 (1000)	63'10" (19 460)	1962	VEB-Lokomotivbau "Karl Marx"	12 kV D 18/21 A-I / 12 kV D 18/21 A-II	VEB Strömungsmaschinen Pirna
119	C-C	Hyd	2600	75 (120)	39.3 (1000)	63'10" (19 460)	1978	Bucharest, Romania		VEB-Strömungsmaschinen Pirna; Voith
120	Co-Co	Elec	2000	63 (100)	41.3 (1050)	57'7" (17 550)	1966	Voroshilovgrad USSR	14 D40	Charkov Works USSR
130	Co-Co	Elec	3000	87 (140)	41.3 (1050)	67'8" (20 620)	1970	voroshilovgrad USSR	5 D49	Charkov Works USSR
131	Co-Co	Elec	3000	63 (100)	41.3 (1050)	67'8" (20 620)	1973	Voroshilovgrad USSR	5 D49	Charkov Works USSR
132	Co-Co	Elec	3000	75 (120)	41.3 (1050)	67'8" (20 820)	1973	Voroshilovgrad USSR	5 D49	Charkov Works USSR

built and plans formulated to mass-produce the design for the Halle, Magdeburg, Leipzig and Dresden areas, but these have been discarded because of the overriding need to pursue electrification and electric traction development for long-haul operation.

The latest bi-level cars of Type DBmtru from Waggonbau Görlitz 26.8 m long, 44 tonnes tare and with 124 seated (119 in the 50 control trailers) and 210 standee passenger capacity per car, are in red and cream livery. By the end of 1988 DR had taken delivery of 200, principally for Berlin area service. Polish industry has been contracted to supply 260 passenger cars in 1991-92.

In mid-1987 Waggonbau Görlitz completed for evaluation a four-axle diesel-hydraulic railcar with a single 330 kW motor. It was reported at the time that this might presage a production series to replace the DR's fleet of two-axle railbuses. By early 1990, however, it seemed more likely that the DR would take a run-on of a German Federal Railway order for more of the latter's VT628 dmus, for construction of which East German builders were among the bidders.

At the start of 1989 DR owned (including museum units and units scheduled for withdrawal) 424 steam, 4482 diesel and 1209 electric locomotives, eight emus and 155 diesel railcars, 538 emus and six electric railcars, 8251 passenger cars (including 19 buffet, 92 restaurant, 81 sleeping and 138 couchette cars) and 168 392 freight wagons.

Additions to stock in 1989 included 180 passenger cars and 1700 freight wagons, the latter including 420 self-discharge coal hoppers.

Passenger services
The DR has overcome its initial hesitance to place a series order after experience with its first air-conditioned inter-city cars from VEB Waggonbau Bautzen. A rake of three first-class and seven second-class open saloon cars, built to the UIC Type Z specification and designed for 200 km/h operation, was together with a restaurant car from a recently-built series of 25 cars installed on a Berlin-Prague service in 1986. Subsequently it was reported that the maintenance requirements of these cars, with their automatic power-operated doors, air-conditioning and other refinements, had proved financially unacceptable. But any misgivings have been overcome by the need of high-quality cars for international services. DR's General Manager announced at the 1990 Leipzig Spring Fair that orders had been placed for 500 air-conditioned cars, deliveries to begin in 1991.

In conjunction with VEB Kombinat Robotron a computerised seat reservation system has been commissioned at 105 main stations. Some 400 stations are now equipped with microprocessor-based ticket-issue machines.

Signalling
The equipment of the DR has been further improved with rational safety and telecommunications technology by the introduction of more efficient push-button signalboxes and relay interlocking systems, modern track crossing safety installations, as well as the construction of automatic train stopping devices and an automatic block system.

All trunk routes and selected secondary lines are being equipped with ground-to-train radio. It was applied to a further 350 route-km in 1989. Under development are solid state interlocking, electronic track circuits and microprocessor-controlled axle counters.

Ferries
Following a June 1982 agreement between the Soviet and German Democratic governments there is now a high-capacity train ferry link between the two countries. The service is operated by five giant double-deck ferries, three German and two Soviet, each with a capacity of 103 broad-gauge wagons. They provide three sailings every 24 hours over the 500 km passage between Klaipeda, in the USSR, and a new port at Mukran, south of Sassnitz. The facilities at Mukran include a gauge-changing installation.

A new DR train ferry was launched on the Sassnitz-Trelleborg route in March 1989.

Germany (Federal Republic)

Ministry of Transport

Kennedyalle 72, Postfach 20 0100, 5300 Bonn 2

Telephone: +49 228 3001
Cable: Bundesverkehrsministerium, Bonn
Telex: 885700

Minister: Friedrich Zimmermann
Secretary of State: Dr Wilhelm Knittel
Parliamentary Secretary: Dr Dieter Schule
Railways Department Manager: Peter Reinhardt

German Federal Railway (DB)
Deutsche Bundesbahn

Friedrich-Ebert-Anlage 43-45, 6000 Frankfurt (Main)

Telephone: +49 69 265-1
Telex: 04 414 087 dbd
Telefax: +49 69 265 6480

Chairman of the Board: Hans Wertz
Directorate
  Chairman: Vacant
  Freight Traffic: Wihelm Pällmann
  Passenger Traffic: Hemjö Klein
  Personnel: Rudi Kobilke
  Planning: Dr Lothar Dernbach
  Production: Dipl-Ing Johann Wiedemann
  Technical: Dipl-Ing Knut Reimers
  Deputy Member: Dipl-Ing Peter Münchschwander
  Director Secretary: Helmut Sattler

International Affairs: Dr jur Peter Häfner
Chief of Public and Press Relations: Elmar-Haass
HQ Departmental Managers
  Passenger Sales: Dr Wolfgang Zoller
  Freight Sales: Günter Lorent
  Freight Marketing and Planning: Roland Heinisch
  Buses: Dr Friedrich
  Production: Dipl-Ing Manfred Scheerer
  Operational Infrastructure Planning and Systems Technology: Dipl-Ing Peter Spiess
  Mechanical Engineering: Dipl-Ing Peter Molle
  Workshops: Dipl-Ing Hermann Wolters
  Civil Engineering: Dipl-Ing Helmut Maak
  New Railways: Dipl-Ing Wilhelm Linkerhägner
  Personnel: Siegfried Klippel
  Finance and Administration: Werner Rusceweyh

Law: Dr jur Rudolf Eiermann
Purchasing: Dipl-Ing Wolfgang Gemeinhardt
Planning: Dr jur Wolfgang Stertkamp
Accounts: Stefan Gade
Research and Procurement, Minden (Westphalia): Dipl-Ing Johann-Peter Blank
Research and Procurement, Munich: Dipl-Ing Theophil Rahn

Gauge: 1435 mm
Route length: 27 278 km
Electrification: 11 609 km at 15 kV 16⅔ Hz ac

The total network of DB is sub-divided into 10 regions for which regional headquarters are responsible. These are: Essen; Frankfurt (Main); Hamburg; Hanover; Karlsruhe; Cologne; Munich; Nuremberg; Saarbrücken; and Stuttgart.

State to take over infrastructure costs
The DB's finances will obtain some relief in 1991, when the Federal government is at last to write off some DM 12 600 million representing loans to the DB for its immediate post-World War II rehabilitation and on which it has had to pay interest ever since. That interest currently amounts to about DM 900 million a year.

The Federal government has also moved to free the DB's balance sheet of total responsibility for infrastructure costs. The DR was mandated by the end of 1990 to produce a detailed separation of its direct operating and track costs, which will then be turned into a draft for legislation by an expert commission representing the Federal, provincial and local governments, and also industry. The Transport Minister made clear that he expected an appropriate share of infrastructure costs to be assumed by provincial and local administrations.

The special commission is required to report to the government by the end of September 1991. Any fresh legislation that report engendered would be presented to parliament in 1992.

In the interim DB management was moving in 1990 to develop bottom-line responsibilities in its passenger and freight departments and create separate infrastructure and technical services divisions.

Finance
In 1989 performance was better than forecast. The deficit of DM 3880 million was some DM 600 million less than anticipated and an improvement of DM 65 million on the 1988 loss. This was inclusive of state support under all heads of DM 13 700 million. Passenger revenue was DM 130 million up on the previous year and freight revenue came in more than DM 150 million above budget. Income from all sources was 4.7 per cent above budget, but expenses were only 1.1 per cent above forecast, though total costs of DM 28 400 million compared with total revenue of DM 24 530 million. Accumulated debt rose by DM 1 200 million to close on DM 44 000 million.

Passenger traffic: IC and Interregio
With the completion of the 93.3 km Fulda-Würzburg stretch of the Hannover-Würzburg new line, saving 21 km by comparison with the historic route, all Hamburg-Basle IC services were routed over the new track from the start of the 1989-90 timetable. As a result their overall schedules were accelerated by 24 minutes. However, speed through the new lines' tunnels was initially restricted to 160 km/h pending availability of more cars either built new or rebuilt with full pressure sealing and closed WC systems.

By the end of 1990 106 existing first-class IC cars would have been modified. The DB aims to acquire 240 of the Type Bvmz 185 design of air-conditioned second-class IC car with full sealing and chemical toilets that was introduced in 1988. This has an innovative interior design that mixes conventional compartments at each end of the vehicle with a central area combining open single seats on one side of the gangway with, on the other, multi-seater compartments having fully glazed walls on their gangway side. However, placement in late 1989 of an order for 50 to

Class 120 Bo-Bo and IC train at Würzburg

follow the first 120 of these cars was delayed by concern over the construction price quoted by the country's supply industry.

Introduced in May 1989, the 'Hamburger Clipper' IC, leaving Hamburg Altona at 06.23, non-stop through Bremen and Osnabrück, and reaching Cologne at 10.15, with a balancing 06.00 from Cologne reaching Altona at 10.00, was the forerunner of a new element of IC service offering limited-stop, early morning trains between key centres with arrival around 10.00 at the latest. Launch of a comparable Munich-Frankfurt service, the 'Frankfurter Flair', in 1990 had to be deferred because of shortage of suitable locomotives and rolling stock.

In May 1989 the DB and its subsidiary, the DSG (Deutsche-Service-Gesellschaft der Bahn mbH), introduced the first realisation of the 'hotel train' concept discussed by European railways in a new night express 'Luna'. Consisting of three couchette cars and three sleeper cars, one of which is a Type T2S, plus a former 'Rheingold' club car service coach, it operates between Münster and Munich. The train also includes a car carrier so that passengers can change to their cars at destination.

In 1994 the DB, OBB and SBB plan to combine in a launch of 'hotel' trains with new designs of bi-level car. Full-size mock-ups of vehicle interiors unveiled by Waggonfabrik Talbot in early 1990 displayed spectacular innovations. Upper-level de luxe compartments with individual WC/shower and facilities including a minibar are arranged longitudinally each side of a central corridor, so that in daytime format the two occupants have an armchair rotatable to face outwards to a window curving into the roof, or inwards to a table between the chairs. Pending availability of the new vehicles the DB planned to acquire sleeping-car sets of Talgo Pendular equipment (see below).

In May 1989 a hairdressing service was experimentally offered in specially equipped first-class cars on two IC trains circulating between Dortmund and Munich. A Wolfsburg hairdressing company shared in the cost of modifying the coaches used.

Waggon Union has been converting to a new Type WRmz 137 all 40 of the DB's unpopular Type WRbumz 'Quickpick' self-service cars. The conversion has included air-conditioning and body sealing for *Neubau* line operation. One half of the car becomes a classic restaurant and kitchen, of almost equal length: and beyond the dining saloon the bar of the 'Bistro' section has its own limited kitchen equipment, since its wares include some hot dishes. Ten more cars are being built to this new specification, which is designated 'Bord-Restaurant'.

The D-train long-haul system is being progressively converted into an improved product branded 'Interregio'. The quality criteria for 'Interregio' are that, like IC, it will operate over specific routes that interconnect for easy passenger interchanges between trains; and on each route, service will be fixed at no worse than two-hourly intervals. All Interregio trains will be locomotive-hauled and include a 'Bistro-Cafe' catering car separating first- and second-class sections; second-class is being furnished by an improved car design.

Interregio must be capable of 200 km/h where that is permissible, not less than 140 km/h elsewhere; average end-to-end speed must be at least 90 km/h (which is 20 per cent higher than the norm of today's D trains). Intermediate stops will be patterned, like those of the IC network: will be restricted to two minutes except where connectional, reversal or other circumstances preclude: and will never be less than 30 km apart.

The first IR route to be created was Hamburg-Gottingen-Fulda/Kassel, which was inaugurated with existing rolling stock in September 1988. That was followed by Kassel-Konstanz in May 1989; and, in February 1990, as introduction of the new-style second-class rolling stock began, by Duisberg-Bebra. Saarbrücken-Stuttgart had also been planned for launch in 1990, but network development had by early that year became uncertain, partly because of delayed delivery of rolling stock owing to heavy workload at the Munich plant supplying 200 km/h-equipped bogies, but above all because of the unexpected need to accelerate incorporation of East Germany in IR planning (see Deutsche Reichsbahn entry).

For the 'Interregio' network the DB is mainly rebuilding existing second-class cars to a layout following that of the latest IC second-class vehicles, installing air-conditioning, and modifying their running gear with extra bogie dampers and electro-magnetic brakes. This is a large-scale project, as the 18 projected 'Interregio' routes need 1200 second-class cars. Of this total 962 will be rebuilds, 238 new vehicles; for a total cost of some DM 1200 million.

On cost grounds, only the new cars will have the full protective sealing which the DB has found essential for 200 km/h operation through the long tunnels of its *Neubaustrecke*. So the new second-class cars only will be able to cover Interregio services taking in these high-speed cut-offs.

DB ticket offices and agencies selling DB tickets through START, a central computer-based system, now have access to a computer-based timetable information system (EVA). This holds all the data for some 36 million routeing permutations. Within six seconds a counter clerk can obtain a fully detailed trip programme for an enquiring customer, including alternative routeings and timings, which can be supplied to the client in printout if desired. EVA's capability is to be extended via interfaces with other railways' systems to cover travel on Swiss, Austrian, French, Belgian and Danish railways.

In 1991 the DB plans to restructure its long-haul passenger fares. The new tariffs will not be strictly related to distance. Account will be taken on each route of rail's competitive speed in relation to road, not only as influenced by the grade of train travelled but also as affected by the characteristics of the infrastructure.

Interior of new second-class Type Bvmz IC car

Tilt-body developments

A stock of 10 tilt-body-equipped diesel train-sets is in production for Nuremberg-Bayreuth services in Bavaria. The Bavarian Land government is contributing to the DM 65 million cost. In mid-1989 Bonn set aside DM 68.5 million for a further 16 units for Bavaria; and by the end of the year options had been placed on 15 more sets as a result of interest from the Baden-Württemberg and Rhineland-Pfalz Land governments.

Classified VT610 by the DB, the new trains will adopt Fiat bogies and the Fiat body-tilting system. A prototype was to be completed for trials in 1990, and delivery of the first 10 was to be finished in 1991 in time for full service launch coincidentally with that year's IC timetable restructure after full commissioning of the Hannover-Würzburg and Mannheim-Stuttgart *Neubaustrecke*. VT610 construction project leader is MAN, with support from Duewag and MBB. Siemens, ABB and AEG share the electrical equipment. Each car of a twin-unit will have an MTU 485 kW engine powering asynchronous motors. To limit axleloading to 13 tonnes, one bogie will be non-powered. Tilt will be limited to 8 deg to allow a body width of 2.85 m.

The DB has also commissioned a feasibility study by Fiat of an eight-car electric tilt-body train-set, in both single and dual-voltage versions. A tranche of 16 to 20 such sets is under consideration.

Prototype Bistro car for Interregio service (G Freeman Allen)

Following late 1988 trials of a set of Talgo Pendular cars from Spain, the DB was set from the summer of 1992 to operate 14-car sets of this equipment on the day Munich-Zurich service. The five train-sets, each costing roughly DM 8 million, will be bought by Siemens and leased to the DB for 17 years, after which the DB will take the equipment over at its depreciated value. Class 218 diesel locomotives will power the trains over the route's non-electrified Munich-Lindau section.

A further five Talgo Pendular day sets are likely to be procured for the Stuttgart-Zurich day service. Over this fully electrified route the likely traction would be Class 120 electric locomotives fitted with a new design of cross-braced, steerable-axle bogie, to avoid trouble in curving at the Talgo equipment's higher permissible speed.

In the spring of 1990 the DB was also negotiating acquisition of four Talgo Pendular sleeping-car train-sets. Each set would be formed of 12 cars with four-berth compartments, 12 *Gran Clase* cars in which each two-berth compartment has its own shower/wc (see Spanish Railways entry), a restaurant and a baggage car. Intended initially for Hamburg-Frankfurt-Munich overnight service and later for operation into Austria and Switzerland, these Talgo units would be fore-runners of the 'Hotel' concept of overnight train to be introduced in 1994 (see above). They would be procured through Siemens in the same way as the Talgo day sets, but even so Ministerial approval for the deal was needed. DB's partners in the 'Hotel' enter-prise the Swiss and Austrian Federal, were each acquiring two Talgo sleeper train-sets.

Passenger services: local
The summer 1989 timetable introduced new acro-nyms. Besides IC (InterCity), EC (EuroCity), the schedules now indicate IR (Interregio), RSB (Regional-schnellbahn: top-grade regional trains), RB (the general run of regional trains) and CB (CityBahn, the top-grade urban services with refurbished cars and buffet).

The Regionalschnellbahn concept, inaugurated in Schleswig-Holstein in the autumn of 1986 between Kiel and Flensburg, embraces upgrading station facil-ities, improving passenger information, raising line speed and introducing a market-orientated regular-interval timetable. Co-operation with local bus oper-ators is also an objective, not least to limit intermediate stops by the trains. An important tool is the latest VT628/928 one-man-operated diesel railcar twin-set, of which 150 units were built in the initial series.

The City-Bahn concept of higher-quality suburban service has been further developed in the Hamburg, Munich, Saarbrucken, Hanover, Cologne and – most recently – Bremen areas.

Rail-air links
In April 1990 DB and the national airline Lufthansa formed a joint subsidiary, Airport-Express GmbH, to develop the co-operation initiated by Lufthansa's char-ter operation of DB ET 403 intercity-emus as the 'Airport Express' four times a day between Düsseldorf and Frankfurt Airports. The aim is to develop an 'Airport Express' network that substitutes the train for plane on domestic feeder routes of international flights that are less than 400km in length.

The ET 403 'Airport Express' service calls inter-mediately at Düsseldorf Hbf, Cologne-Deutz, Cologne Hbf and Bonn stations, and end-to-end travel time between airports is 155 minutes. The timetables are geared to flight-passengers arriving 45 minutes prior to take-off or departing 45 minutes after landing.

The 'Airport Express' may only be used by pas-sengers in possession of a flight ticket. Meals at seats and drinks are included in the price. Each coach has a luggage compartment, where flight baggage is checked in during the journey and transported by the staff to the plane for owner reclaim at the flight destination. Lufthansa booking terminals are now installed on the trains to link them with the reservation centre in Frankfurt Airport via radio; thus passengers can be issued their boarding cards on the train and avoid having to go to the booking desk at the airport.

New moves in 1990 included the May launch of a locomotive-hauled 'Airport Express' twice daily each way between Frankfurt Airport and Stuttgart via Darmstadt (to be doubled in frequency in 1991); and of IC connections providing early morning arrivals at Frankfurt Airport from Cologne and Mannheim/Ludwigshafen, with corresponding late-evening return workings, using the Class 141 two-car push-pull sets that provide the Wiesbaden-Mainz IC connection during the day. A planned extension of the ET 403 service from Düsseldorf to Dortmund was deferred. Lufthansa, Japan Airlines and Cathay Pacific tickets for domestic journey legs are now available for use on IC trains. From 10 stations on IC Line 5, Düsseldorf-Cologne-Frankfurt-Würzburg-Munich, a pilot scheme has been launched under which international passen-gers flying Lufthansa or the charter airline Condor can consign their baggage direct to their destination airport. A Lufthansa check-in has been opened at Munich Hbf.

The DB is expected to develop an IC connection with Munich's second airport, due to open in the northeast of the city in 1991. At present a 19 km extension of S-Bahn Line 3/5 is being built from Ismanning to a dead-end terminus at the airport. But the airport's predicted traffic now leads, at Transport Ministry request, to DB consideration of additional S-Bahn access in orbital form, serving through platforms, so that continuous service between city centre and airport will be possible. This would be achieved by a 25 km link between S-Bahn Line S1 (at Neufahrn) and Line S6 (at its present Erding terminal) that would pass beneath the Airport. A short spur between the main line west of Munich Hbf at Pasing and S-Bahn Line S1 at Moosach would enable IC trains from the Augsburg direction to reach the Airport station and, if required, to serve Munich Hbf as well by completing the S-Bahn orbit to arrive in the city centre from the east.

A second station is to be built at Frankfurt Airport (see below).

DB: Federal financial support 1988

	1988
Compensations for social services (DM million)	
Local rail services	3334.5
Long-distance rail services	35.0
Bus services	302.7
Infrastructure maintenance	34.6
Subsidised tariffs	–
Intermodal development	80.0
Equalisation of terms of competition	
Level crossing upkeep	327.0
Total social, medical and training provisions	4699.2
Federal obligations as DB owner	
Interest on loans and capital	940.2
Amortisation of loans	–
Investment of grants	3977.3
(of which for route improvement)	(2333.0)
Liquidity assistance	–
Miscellaneous	
S-Bahn development	335.4
Fuel tax rebates	13 935.2

DB finances (DM million)	
Revenue	1988
Passengers (rail and bus)	5940
Freight (rail and road)	8650
Other	4580
Federal contribution	28 020
Expenditure	
Personnel	20 400
Materials	6120
Depreciation	2360
Financial charges (net)	1980
Other	1070
Total	29 950
Deficit	3930

IC-Express order
Translation of the high-speed technology developed for the five-car IC-Experimental unit into production IC-Express units for *Neubaustrecke* route service has been chequered. With the latter needed by 1990-91, there was no time to develop a pre-production proto-type; and Treasury approval for construction of the 41 IC-Express units which the DB regarded as its minimum requirement for launch of high-speed service on the Munich-Würzburg Hamburg and Hamburg-Frankfurt-Stuttgart-Munich routes in the spring of 1991 was not granted until the late summer of 1987.

Priority was production of the power cars. Mechan-ical parts were ordered from Krupp, Thyssen-Henschel and Krauss-Maffei, with the first-named as project leader. Siemens led an electrical equipment team including AEG and ASEA Brown Boveri. Deliveries began in late 1989.

Options on a further 19 IC-Express train-sets needed for launch of a Hamburg-Frankfurt-Basel high-speed

New Class 628/928 diesel railcar sets

Class 103 Co-Co and Milan-Dortmund EuroCity train (*John C Baker*)

RAILWAY SYSTEMS / Germany (Federal Republic)

service in 1993 expired in July 1989. Up to the spring of 1990 Ministerial approval for this second tranche was still wanting, despite DB pressure, but on the assumption that the sets must be needed the manufacturers had begun work on their power cars.

Of the aluminium-bodied trailers Duewag and Waggon Union are building the first-class cars, Linke-Hofmann-Busch, MAN and MBB the second-class and Waggon Union the catering cars. AEG lead a consortium providing the electric and air-conditioning equipment. The first of the 492 trailers required emerged in mid-1990, and it was hoped to have a train available for a test programme by August 1990. However, running at up to 280 km/h would not begin until the end of the following November, after verification of the braking systems. The first of the catering cars (see below) would not be available until January 1991.

IC-Express train-sets will have power cars at each end capable together of sustaining 250 km/h with intermediate trailer formations of up to 12 cars. Running and brake gear are designed for at least 280 km/h and with potential for 300 km/h development. Power cars basically follow the technology of those in the IC-Experimental unit, employing three-phase traction with asynchronous motors. Main differences are: continuous rating of each car lifted to 4800 kW; enlarged cab and redesigned driving console to make use of latest information display techniques; no 15 kV through-train cable connection between power cars, since the train length will pose no problems of running with both power cars' pantographs raised; a second pantograph on each power car for use under Swiss catenary; two cast-steel brake discs per axle instead of three; increased microprocessor control of apparatus groups; and revised pressure sealing. The whole train-set will have its equipment monitored by elaborate diagnostic apparatus.

The trailer order comprises 146 Type Avumz first-class cars; 305 second-class cars, of which 41 will include a segregated conference room; and 41 restaurant-bistro cars. Telephone kiosks will feature in 41 of the first-class and in the 41 conference-room equipped second-class cars. But the conference rooms themselves will have cordless telephones, also telefax machines. The problem of keeping this equipment usable in the new lines' long tunnels is being solved by lining the bores with special cables to serve as aerials. This will also maintain continuity of public broadcasting service to the headphone terminals at all passenger seats, some of which will have seatback video screens. Area per seat will be more generous than in the SNCF TGV; 1.2 m^2 compared with 0.9 m^2 in first-class, 0.9 m^2 against 0.6 m^2 in second-class. Body width will be 3.02 m, for improved seating comfort.

Dividing first- and second-class sections of a set will be a service car with a slightly raised roof, aerodynamically faired off at each end; this was originally conceived to create a spacious interior ambience, but has since been exploited for convenient housing of some equipment. In this car a central kitchen will serve a 'Bistro' bar on one side, a 24-seater restaurant on the other. The kitchen will also, if required, serve at seats in the first- and second-class cars on each side of the service vehicle.

The seating trailers will be of modular interior construction and include two second-class types of car. The standard second-class car will be open saloon, but there will also be a special second-class car embodying crew quarters, telephone kiosk, family compartments and an orthodox saloon. Wardrobes will feature in saloon configurations.

The target was to have available 164 first-class, 287 second-class and all 41 catering cars available to form 25 trains for the May 1991 change of timetables.

The price of the order has been controversial. Approval for the investment was originally based on the DB's 1986 estimate of DM 1500 million. But that was struck before experience with the IC-Experimental and other vehicles on the first completed section of the Hanover-Würzburg new line had shown that high-speed passage of trains in the long Neubaustrecke tunnels demanded considerable reinforcement of every component contributing to insulation of vehicle interiors (and also redesign of vehicle sanitary fitments). The necessary modifications, claimed the manufacturers, raised the price of each far beyond the original estimate.

The contracts were eventually signed for a total figure 33⅓ per cent above the 1986 estimate: DM 700 million for 82 power cars and DM 1300 for 492 trailers. As a result the DB has had to scale down its projected train format from 14 to 12 trailers.

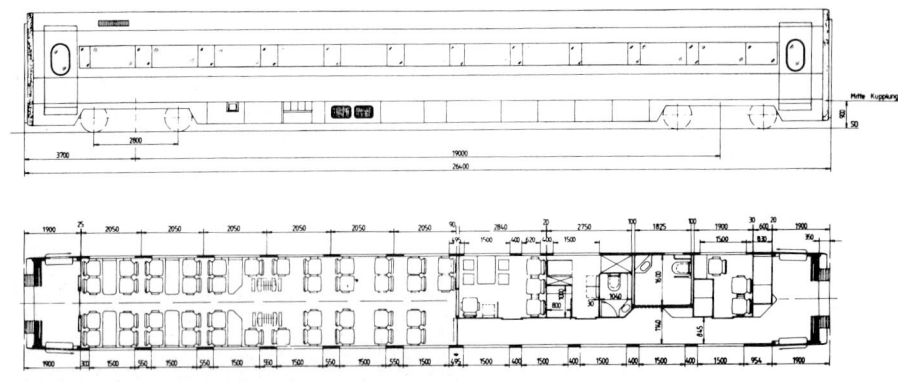

Proposed layout of InterCity-Express second-class car with conventional saloon and special compartment configuration

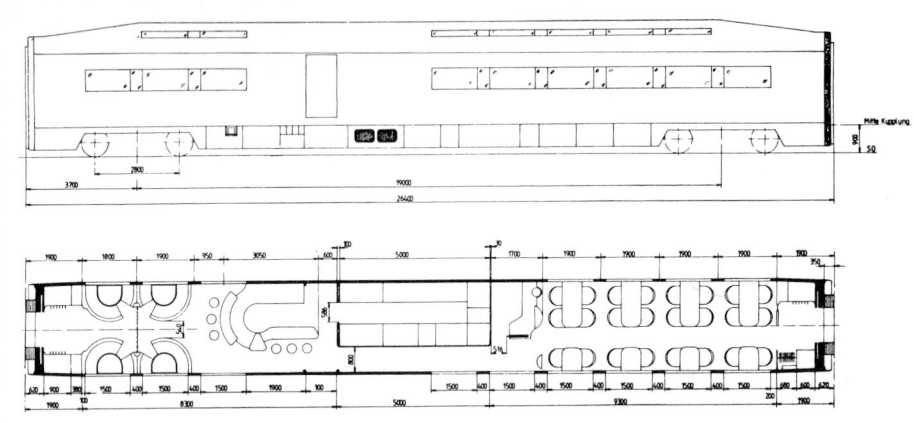

Proposed layout of InterCity-Express service car

The IC-Express units will encounter a good deal of trackwork with wooden sleepers off the Neubaustrecke, and their use of eddy current brakes, by their lifting of rail temperature, may risk track buckling. But although, for this reason, eddy current brakes will not be standardised on the IC-Express sets, five will have them to allow research in this form of braking to continue.

Because of the restricted timescale, the first train-set series will repeat several technical features of the Experimental unit. Thus trailer bogies will be the metal-sprung Type MD522. Later series will have air-spring bogies.

The 41 IC-Express train-sets will be maintained in a DM 250 million depot that is being purpose-built on the site of a former freight yard at Hamburg-Eidelstadt. The depot will be 430 m long and have eight levels. Also being prepared to maintain the trains is the diesel locomotive repair works at Nuremburg.

Multi-voltage IC-Express

Early in 1989 the Transport Minister approved development work on an order for seven sets of a four-voltage version of the ICE, designated IC-M and DB Class 411 for the power cars, 811 for the trailers. In the spring of 1990 the three electrical companies, AEG Westinghouse, ABB and Siemens, were invited to bid as project leaders for complete train-sets, a departure from the procedures followed for the IC-E contracts.

The DB envisaged production of between two and seven prototype train-sets by the end of 1993, followed by series production of between 25 and 40 train-sets. Initially the DB is reluctantly adhering to the French TGV stipulation of 17 tonnes maximum axleload, but not to French TGV bodywidth parameters. Bodywidth will be 3.02m, and the first Series 410/810 sets are therefore likely to operate services on an Amsterdam-Brussels-Cologne-Frankfurt axis with extensions into Switzerland and Austria.

The axleload limit restricts power car output to 3600kW ac/2500 kW dc. Set format will therefore be two GTO thyristor-controlled asynchronous motor power cars enclosing six trailers, one of which will house a restaurant in one half of its body. But provision will be made for two sets to operate in multiple. Maximum designed speed will be 300 km/h under ac current, 220 km/h under dc.

1991 timetable restructure

The long-haul passenger timetable and its connecting services are to be completely revised with the summer availability of the first two new lines and of IC-Express units. The core of the operation will be an IC-Express Line 6 extending from Hamburg via Hannover, Kassel, Frankfurt, Mannheim and Stuttgart to Munich. A second IC-Express route from Hamburg via Würzburg to Munich will be launched in September 1991.

IC-Express and ICM technical data

	IC-E	IC-Express
Max speed	300 km/h (ac) 220 km/h (dc)	280 km/h
Overall length	200 m	367 m
Seats		
1st class	112	192
2nd class	258	567
Power car		
Tare weight	68 tonnes	78 tonnes
Length over couplings	19 160 mm	20 510 mm
Max width of car body	3020 mm	3080 mm
Height of roof top	3840 mm	3840 mm
Continuous rating motors	3600 kW	4800 kW
Max tractive effort on starting	2 × 133 kN	200 kN
Trailer cars		
Vehicle length over couplings	26 400 mm	26 400 mm
Max width of car body	3020 mm	3020 mm

S-Bahnen

Investment in new and extended S-Bahn systems continues at a rate of some DM 600 million a year. The Cologne area's third stage, which focussed on creating a dedicated S-Bahn route through the city centre, via Cologne Hbf, has included addition of two tracks to the four crossing the famous Hohenzollern Bridge over the Rhine at the Hbf approach.

Completion of segregated S-Bahn tracks throughout the distance from Cologne via Langenfeld to Düsseldorf and the Rhine-Ruhr S-Bahn network was accelerated because of the planned intensification of long-distance traffic in 1991. Besides more IC trains the fast tracks will be carrying Interregio services and a planned hourly-interval EuroCity service between Amsterdam and Cologne; they are being upgraded for 200 km/h in preparation. The core tracks through the city centre were ready for use by Bergisch Gladbach-Neuss trains in May 1990.

In the Rhine-Ruhr network a second S-Bahn route has been created between Dortmund and Duisburg. The new 58 km Line S2 runs via Herne, Gelsenkirchen, Essen-Altenessen and Oberhausen; almost all of the project's total cost of DM 155 million was spent on new line construction in the first 8 km between Dortmund Hbf and Mengede. In 1990 Line S9 from Haltern through Bottrop and Essen to Wüppertal was added to the Ruhr network, at a cost of DM 60 million chiefly for electrification of an 88 km route previously operated by diesel locomotive-powered push-pulls. From May 1990 Düsseldorf Airport had direct access from the Duisburg/Essen direction as well as from Düsseldorf; to that end the Duisburg-Düsseldorf suburban tracks have been remodelled and a new northern curve laid in to the Airport branch, allowing introduction of an S-Bahn service from the airport to Duisburg and Dortmund.

The 2.1km of tunnelling involved in projecting the Rhine-Main S-Bahn from its temporary terminus under Frankfurt city centre to the DB's South station and Mühlberg, with later extension of S-Bahn service to Darmstadt and Hanau in view, has been completed. S-Bahn service through Frankfurt South to Stresemanallee could thus start in May 1990.

Eight years of negotiations culminated early in 1987 in agreement between the DB, the Land, city and other local communities involved to finance the Frankfurt-Langen-Darmstadt and Frankfurt-Offenbach-Hanau extensions. Inclusion of the lines on from Offenbach to Ober Roden and Dietzenbach is possible, provided they can meet the Federal government's S-Bahn extension proviso that the resultant new train operations do not inflate public subsidy of operating costs. Federal obligation under the Municipal Transport Finance Act of 1967 to apply part – presently 5.4 pfennigs per litre – of its oil tax to providing 60 per cent of the cost of locally approved and financially guaranteed urban transport infrastructure improvements remains unaltered; it applies to the Darmstadt and Hanau extensions.

In Stuttgart boring of the 5.5 km Hassenberg tunnel, a critical phase in projecting the city's core underground line to Böblingen and eventually to Stuttgart airport, was completed in October 1983, and the extension was opened to traffic as far as Böblingen in September 1985, adding 18 km to the network, which now totals around 150 route-km. Continuation to an underground station at the airport would be completed in 1990. A new branch from the existing system at Herrenberg to Nagold is under study.

Construction of the first phase of the Nuremberg S-Bahn, the 17 km from Nuremberg Hbf to Lauf, was finished and service inaugurated in September 1987. A second route was being prepared in 1990, but further extensions had struck cost snags in discussions with the local authorities.

Following planning agreement, extension of the Munich S-Bahn from Ismaning to an underground station at the city's Munich II airport at Erdinger Moos was begun in 1986. Completion is forecast for 1991.

In 1989 the DB was test-running on the Munich S-Bahn's Geltendorf-Ebersberg route a train of four bi-level cars borrowed from the Netherlands Railways with Class 120 locomotives front and rear providing push-pull power. Expansion of the Munich S-Bahn network is threatening to choke the system's crosstown underground section and there is no possibility of boring a second route. Consequently to secure extra capacity the DB meditates use of three-car bi-level emus on a route from an interchange with IC and IC-Express services at Munich-Pasing via Ismaning to the forthcoming Munich II airport.

Munich's S-Bahn network records some 630 000 journeys each working day on average, and carries 40 per cent of the public transport traffic within the city's integrated transport fare system territory.

Plans are taking shape for a first S-Bahn route in the Hanover area, running east to west between Lehrte and Wunstorf. Also under discussion in 1990 was an S-Bahn service, using ET430 emus, in the Rhine-Neckar area on the Neustadt/Speyer-Ludwigshafen-Mannheim-Heidelberg-Bruchsal/Eberbach axis.

At government request, S-Bahn systems are being suitably equipped for one-man train operation. Initially it has been agreed only for working with single Type 420 emus or three-car push-pull trains, but trials have been in progress on the Munich and Stuttgart networks to secure its extension to larger formations on all S-Bahn networks. Push-pull working with locomotives is now the preferred S-Bahn technique, because of the high cost of the Class ET420 emus.

Freight traffic

Fuelled principally by an upturn in the country's iron and steel industry, freight tonnage advanced quite strongly in 1989 and freight revenue came in some DM 150 million above budget.

An international extension of DB's *Kombinierter Ladungsverkehr* (KLV) network of dedicated intermodal trains interconnecting key economic regions and port areas began in 1989. The first services were launched each way between German centres and north Italy, France and Vienna. The German centres covered by KLV are: Hamburg; Bremen-Bremerhaven; the eastern Ruhr; Düsseldorf; Cologne; Frankfurt; Mannheim; Stuttgart; Munich; and Nuremberg. Within this 10-centre network domestic KLV service offers next-morning delivery before 0700 for consignments submitted up to 2000 the previous evening. But connecting services promise delivery by 0800 to 19 other terminals in centres such as Augsburg, Basle, Hannover and Kiel. Some routes have more than one nightly train.

Following Austria's imposition of nocturnal restrictions on highway freight movement, new KLV services were launched between Nuremberg and Verona, and between Munich and both Verona and Milan, raising the daily total of trains for unaccompanied semi-trailers between Germany and North Italy to 13 each way. *Rollende Landstrasse* services for accompanied road rigs were also expanded (for details see Austria entry).

Intermodal traffic grossed 23.3 million tonnes in 1989 and was forecast to scale 32 million tonnes by 1994, 50 million tonnes by the end of the decade.

KLV's concentration of the majority of DB intermodal traffic on efficient, fast corridors is, however, causing an overload of the major terminals. Expansion and new construction cannot keep up with traffic increases. In all, DB is currently operating 57 terminals, with its subsidiary Transfracht operating an additional 17.

Electronic data processing is expected to contribute significantly to efficient use of these facilities. The new computer-supported DISK dispositioning-and-control system allows the DB to track container movement. Vehicle registration points have been installed in all terminals to speed up handling time.

A new KLV strategy under discussion in 1989 it was emerging that the most efficient and competitive system would be concentrated on no more than 40 terminals originating and receiving traffic. These would be interconnected by direct trains. In addition the network should have a number of strategically-located hubs equipped for easy exchange of loads between trains assembling or distributing other areas' traffic,

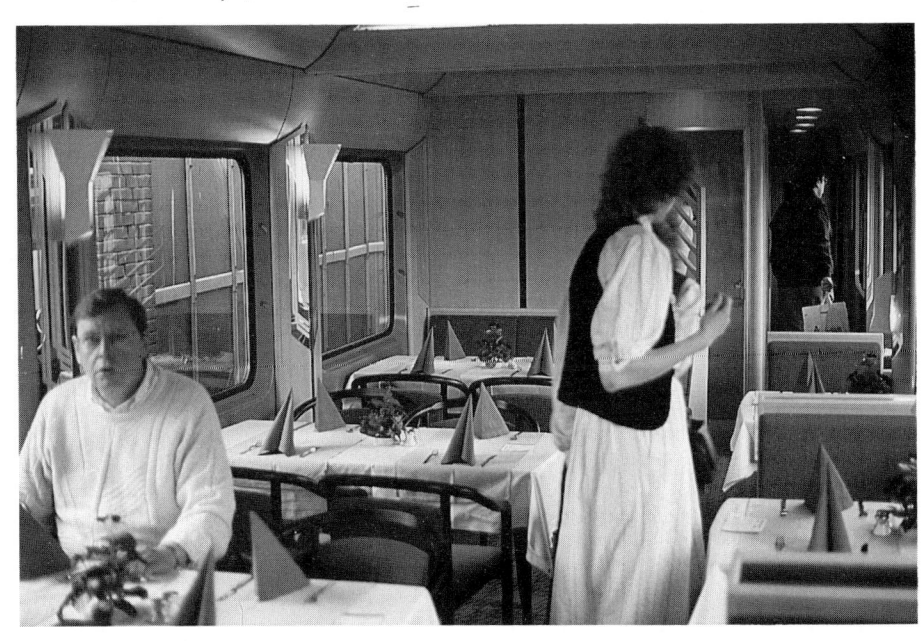

'Bord Restaurant' car has a Bistro on one side of the central kitchen (*G Freeman Allen*)

At the other end of the 'Bord Restaurant' car is a dining section (*G Freeman Allen*)

and trains feeding such traffic into and out of the key terminal network.

The DB is also studying bi-modal technology. In 1990 it was to pursue trials of RoadRailers built by the US company's German licence-holder.

The first EurailCargo train service was launched in May 1990. This is a scheme in which DB is collaborating with other railways to establish, on key international traffic axes, through trains for wagonload traffic offering cargo acceptance up to 1600 on Day and readiness for collection by 0900 on Day C for transits of up to 1500km, 0900 on Day D for transits of more than 1500 km. The first service runs from Wels, Austria, to the Kifhoek yard, Rotterdam, with no intermediate stop for commercial purposes. Further planned routes are between north Italy and north Germany, south Germany and Helsingborg/Malmö, Sweden, and Austria and north Germany.

In collaboration with neighbouring railways, inter-train exchanges of other traffic and border formalities are being rationalised to shorten frontier delays. Transit interruptions at Basel have been cut by an hour to 30 minutes by concentration of Swiss and French wagonload traffic processing on Mannheim, and of KLV traffic between Italy, Switzerland, Ruhr, North German and Netherlands terminals on Frankfurt East.

In a major strengthening of its service of the auto industry, the DB would from the summer of 1990 be carrying 85 per cent of the inter-works movement of Audi-Volkswagen materials. This deal, more than doubling rail's previously 40 per cent share of the group's traffic, was an important gain from road freight.

With full availability of the Hannover-Würzburg and Mannheim-Stuttgart new lines, the DB planned to launch two overnight 160 km/h freight routes, Hamburg-Munich and Bremen-Stuttgart, in May 1991. Each train-set would comprise up to 20 wagons for intermodal traffic and up to five for grouped less-than-wagonload traffic. Intermodal traffic will be carried on a version of the Type Sgns 694 flatcar with redesigned bogies, electro-pneumatic disc brakes and anti-wheel slide protection, allowing a payload of 49 tonnes maximum at 160 km/h. For the small-consignment traffic the wagons will be two-axle Type Hbis 306 sliding-wall vans with similar braking modifications, each able to accept up to 18 tonnes payload for 160 km/h operation. Off the new lines the trains will be limited to 140 km/h, except where LZB continuous speed control is operative, as between Augsburg and Munich.

Almost half the DB's freight traffic is generated by about 3 per cent of its 40 000 clients. Consequently management of the rail freight business of these major customers, numbering about 150, is now centralised at DB headquarters under a 'Key Account Management' system. The system does not assign a single manager to each account, but has five teams each concerned with a specific commodity or group of related commodities: coal; iron and steel; oil, chemicals and fertilisers; manufactured goods; and natural resources, from agriculture to stone and minerals. Each team has responsibility for major clients' business in all its aspects, from strategy to performance, and for maintenance of close contact with the customer.

The DB's freight business gained a competitive boost from July 1990, when the Federal Government introduced a new tax on all heavy freight vehicle operation, domestic as well as foreign, in the country. The move was intended to prod the EEC into enforcing full harmonisation of heavy road freight taxation and attribution of infrastructure costs throughout the Community when the Single Market becomes operative after 1992. At present there are wide discrepancies – notably, from the German viewpoint, between the modest tax on the vehicles of the Netherlands' busy road freight industry and the levies on German lorries. The new German tax is paid in the form of purchase of a disc, obtainable abroad as well as in Germany, the cost of which reflects vehicle weight, number of axles and period of validity desired.

More than 230 Class 260/261 and 170 locotractors have been equipped for radio remote control. These robot locomotives are reclassified respectively 360/361 and 333.

Rail traffic (million)	1987	1988	1989
Passenger journeys	994	1009	1016
Passenger-km	39 174	41 664	41 213
Freight tonnes	266.2	270.8	278.8
Freight tonne-km	57 122	57 957	61 233

The IC-Experimental prototype on the Hanover-Würzburg new line

Modern DB signalling centre at Essen Hbf

Traction and rolling stock

At the end of 1988 the DB's traction stock stood at 254 electric, 1838 line-haul diesel and 1640 shunter/tractor locomotives; 1586 electric mus; 72 battery-electric mus, 328 diesel mus; and 157 diesel railbuses. Total coaching stock at the year's end was 12 185, that of freight wagons 220 927. Just over 50 000 privately-owned wagons were also operating over the DB.

Deliveries in 1990 were expected to include 55 IC-E power cars (the first 11 were completed in late 1989) and an unspecified number of IC-E trailers; 100 IC second-class cars; the remaining 20 of the final order (for the Stuttgart S-Bahn) for Class ET420 emus; six Bistro-Cafe and 120 rebuilt cars (to add to 144 delivered in 1989) for IR services; 59 cars refurbished for City Bahn services; and some 1200 new and 1100 rebuilt freight wagons. Principal items in the freight car deliveries would be 450 Falns 183 automatic discharge hoppers, 350 Shimms sliding-hood wagons and 250 Hbbillns 305/306 two-axle covered wagons.

It was expected that authority for a second built of Class 120 would be sought in the early 1990s. This would almost certainly embody important changes – for instance, resort to GTO thyristor technology and a flexible instead of a fixed bogie-mounted drive; as a result the successors would likely become a new Class 121. Meanwhile, the first series was giving some cause for concern in early 1990. According to local press reports, availability was only some 70 per cent because of increasing problems of damage in the mechanical parts of the power train after 300 000–500 000km running. It was suggested that these were being overtaxed by the universal role of the Class 120 as a projected successor to the Class 103 IC passenger and Class 151 heavy freight Co-Cos.

In 1990 the DB put its requirement for a second series of VT628/928 diesel railcar twin-sets out to international tender. Respondents were five German companies and nine foreign firms, the latter including BREL(1988) and builders in Hungary and Yugoslavia. The DB was likely to place a firm order for 85 sets, but options and add-ons for the country's local railways and possibly the DR could take the total to 130 sets. The original batch was powered by a single Daimler-Benz 410 kW motor, with a Voith transmission, and had a top speed of 120 km/h. The second batch is likely to have a recently-developed Daimler-Benz 485kW engine, for a top speed of 140km/h. Micro-processor-controlled anti-slip equipment supports air brakes on both cars and there is also magnetic track brake; bogies, built by Waggon Union and Wegmann, are of a new air suspension type. Construction of the first DM 340 million, 150-unit order was shared between Duewag (project leader), Linke-Hofmann-Busch and MBB, and provision of electric equipment between AEG and BBC.

Earlier Class 624/924 and 634/934 diesel railcar sets are being modernised to City Bahn standards.

Three prototype Krupp-MaK diesel-electric locomotives began trials in Schleswig-Holstein in late 1989 (for details of the design, see Krupp-MaK entry). The units remain Krupp-MaK property, but the DB has given them the 240 designation in its own classification.

Equipment of traction to work with the LZB 80 continuous ATP system of the *Neubaustrecke* has included 86 Class 151 heavy freight Co-Co and the 25 dual-voltage Class 181.2 electric locomotives, the latter so that they can work trains from France over the Mannheim-Stuttgart new line.

The NBS/ABS programme

The last revision of the Federal German Transport Plan (BVWP) in 1985 accepted all the DB's submissions for further *Neubau* and *Ausbau* (NBS and ABS) trunk-route development. These were assigned a total of DM 23 286 million for construction over a ten-year period. The planning groundwork on schemes to follow after 1995 was allocated a further DM 4170 million.

A prime objective of the new high-priority NBS/ABS schemes is greatly improved rail communication between the country's two biggest population and industrial conglomerations, Rhine-Ruhr and Rhine-Main, to secure a bigger share of a huge market which at present DB only skims because of its tortuous, speed-limiting Rhine Valley route south of Cologne. Also important is to carry the improvement right through to Munich via the Mannheim-Stuttgart NBS from the Rhine-Main area.

Consequently the biggest single project endorsed by the BVWP was an NBS between Cologne and the Rhine-Main area. This was at first conceived for exclusive use by 250 km/h passenger trains, which would have simplified its civil engineering, but in 1990 it was evidently being planned, like the other new lines, for mixed traffic. Line of route was finally fixed in 1989 (see below).

One important NBS/ABS project of the previous BVWP has only recently been put in hand. Not until late 1984 was the requisite local authority agreement secured to the siting of an extra pair of 250 km/h-engineered tracks alongside the present north-south double-track between Karlsruhe and Offenburg. Approval to begin a combined NBS/ABS project between Karlsruhe and Basle was given by the Transport Minister at the start of 1987 and work commenced at the end of that year (see below).

The thrust of the overall NBS/ABS programme is to develop four high-speed IC corridors: Fulda-Basle; Münster-Cologne-Stuttgart-Munich; Dortmund-Kassel-Nuremberg-Munich; and Saarbrücken-Ludwigshafen-Karlsruhe-Stuttgart-Nuremberg (though the latter is not a priority until plans for a TGV-Est from Paris into Germany are finalised). Thus, almost as much weight is attached to developing an eastern high-speed axis from the Ruhr and beyond to the south, as to a western route via the projected Rhine/Ruhr-Rhine/Main NBS.

The biggest scheme in this context is ABS over the 215km from Dortmund, in the Ruhr, via Hamm and Paderborn to a junction with the Hanover-Würzburg NBS at Kassel. With the aid of several major curve re-alignments the DB aimed originally to create 250 km/h capability over almost 90 per cent of the distance from Dortmund to Kassel, but economy has watered the scheme down to creation of 200 km/h capability over 98 km of the distance from Dortmund to Paderborn, and of 160 km/h wherever possible over the topographically unfavourable stretch from Paderborn to Kassel. Work began in late 1989 and by 1997 should be finished. Dortmund-Kassel journey time will then be cut from 2½ hours to 1 hour 50 minutes. Total cost will be DM 1630 million.

Another costly project in the new BVWP is continuation of the high-speed IC system beyond the extremity of the Mannheim-Stuttgart NBS to Munich, bypassing the severe and very sinuous grades of the present route between Stuttgart's outskirts and the area of Ulm. Up to 1990 it had not been decided whether to build an NBS (much of it in tunnel under the uplands) all the way from Plochingen, 40 km out of Stuttgart, to Günzburg, 9 km beyond Ulm; or whether to triple-track the existing line from Plochingen under an ABS scheme for 27 km to Sussen and start the NBS there, which would trim the bill. An ABS scheme already underway covers the stretch from Günzburg to Augsburg, beyond which the present main line is already 250 km/h territory to Munich. Also at issue is whether the improved route should pass through or avoid the centre of Ulm. East of Munich an ABS scheme to Freilassing, near the Austrian border, en route to Salzburg, was approved in 1989 (see below).

Other new ABS schemes on the 1986–95 action agenda covered trunk route stretches from Fulda to Frankfurt; Münster to Cologne; Mainz to Mannheim; and Hamburg, Harburg to Rothensburgsort. As described below, most of these are now in progress. During 1990 the DB expected to clear the procedures for improvement of the link between Nuremberg and Munich (see below).

In the freight sector the new BVWP assigned DM 716 million to further development of the DB's intermodal operations, in furtherance of the government's concern to get as much long-haul tonnage as it can off the roads and into containers or the piggyback mode.

Another DM 2200 million was assigned to main marshalling yard development. Main items were to be new automated yards at Munich North, Regensburg, Kassel and Dortmund; the rest was for improvement of existing installations. Construction of Munich North, a DM 700 million project to rival Hamburg's Maschen yard, was long delayed by local environmental objections. The blocks were finally dismantled by the Transport Minister and the work started in the spring of 1987, for part-opening in 1991 and completion by 1992.

Hanover-Würzburg, Mannheim-Stuttgart new lines

Both Hanover-Würzburg and Mannheim-Stuttgart new high-speed lines, or *Neubaustrecke*, are being Federally-financed with interest-free grants. Their combined cost has lately been cut from DM 15 500 million to DM 14 700 million thanks to rationalisation of various aspects of the work and encouragement of keener bidding by contractors. The Hanover-Würzburg line is absorbing DM 11 100 million of the total.

The two DB lines thread more intensively populated territory than the French TGV-PSE. Average population density along the French high-speed route is only 70/km^2, whereas between Hanover and Würzburg it is 240/km^2, between Mannheim and Stuttgart 300/km^2. The Hanover-Würzburg *Neubaustrecke* in particular cuts through a tract of mountains and deep valleys with no parallel on the French high-speed line, which, coupled with the West German requirement to engineer to more demanding parameters for mixed traffic operation, has incurred a great deal of costly tunnelling and bridging.

Topography was not strictly responsible for all the tunnelling. On the Mannheim-Stuttgart line the 5.38 km Pfingstberg Tunnel, in the suburbs of Mannheim, is essentially a covered trench set in flat terrain. Despite the proximity of a busy *autobahn*, environmental agitation forced the DB into this concealment of the railway. No less than 10 per cent of the capital cost of the two *Neubaustrecke*, or almost DN 1500 million, is attributable to deviations from the most practical lines of route or to other measures not dictated by any technological considerations, such as noise-absorbing barriers, each side of the track in many locations.

Principal track parameters: DB Neubaustrecke

Ruling gradient	1 in 80
Minimum curve radius (standard)	7000 m
Minimum curve radius (exceptionally)	5100 m
Designed max speed	250 km/h
Max speed (exceptionally, at one location)	200 km/h
Max speed through turnouts	160 km/h
Average double-track formation width	13.7 m
Distance between tracks	4.7 m
Tunnel cross-section straight/curved track	81/86.5 m^2

Only 93 of the Hanover-Würzburg line's 327 km is not in tunnel, in cutting or on bridgework. Its 62 tunnels

Krupp-MaK prototype Class 240 diesel locomotive on trial in Schleswig-Holstein

Class 218 diesel-hydraulic B-B and City-Bahn train leaves the widened Hohenzollern bridge at Cologne (John C Baker)

aggregating 116 km include several of more than a mile's length: the 5.5 km Mühlberg Tunnel south of Gemünden, where the line is driving through the hills to the Markheidenfeld plateau around Rohrbach; the 5.33 km Hainroder and 7.34 km Ditershan Tunnels, two of a close succession between Kassel and Fulda; and south of Fulda, the 10.75 km Landrücken Tunnel, the longest in the country, and which succeeds a 7 km climb to the line's highest point, 386 m above sea level. The bridges have a total length of 34 km. Other railways are crossed by 109 of them, roads by 97, but the outstanding structures are the 61 which swing the line across intersecting valleys. Longest is a 1315 m crossing of the Main river at the approach to Würzburg.

Besides being threaded through the existing (but suitably remodelled) stations at towns and cities like Göttingen, Kassel, Fulda and Gemünden, where there are connections with the historic DB network, the new line is studded with a number of *Uberholungsbahnhöfe*, or 'overtaking stations'. The same applies to the Mannheim-Stuttgart *Neubaustrecke*. These not only have crossovers between the two main tracks but also loops for priority regulation of traffic. They are the only areas of the line controlled by lineside signals. Elsewhere the only form of signalling is the LZB80, the DB's system of continuous automatic train control which was previously confined to the 200 km/h tracts of the IC network and to the locomotives rostered to work ICs at that pace.

Of the 99 km of new infrastructure constructed for the Mannheim-Stuttgart *Neubaustrecke*, only 4 km is at ground level. The 28 tunnels aggregate 29 km, bridges 5 km, deep cuttings 39 km and embankments 22 km. The tunnelling and bridgework falls mostly in the final 55 km or so, after the line has interconnected with Mannheim-Karlsruhe and Heidelberg-Karlsruhe main lines near Bruchsal, and is launched on the gradual climb that lifts it to the plateau around Stuttgart. The longest tunnel on this new line is the 6.63 km Freudenstein.

The DB had the first substantial section of the Mannheim-Stuttgart line, the 35 km between its two junctions with the Mannheim-Karlsruhe main line at Hockenheim station and at Graben-Neudorf, ready for scheduled use by IC passenger and fast freight trains in May 1987. Target date for commissioning of the whole route is 1991. The same year is set for inauguration of the complete Hanover-Würzburg *Neubaustrecke*, but its Fulda-Würzburg section was available for use from the end of May 1988. The 37.2 km section from Fulda to Kirkheim became usable in late 1989 and a further 9km to Göttingen in February 1990.

With both lines in full use, IC journey time between Hanover and Würzburg will be cut from 213 to 122 minutes, and between Mannheim and Stuttgart from 84 to 40 minutes. Thus the Hamburg-Munich IC journey time, for example, should be trimmed in the 1990s to 5½ hours for a journey of 820 km, inclusive of intermediate stops. One of those will be the city of Kassel, hitherto isolated from the framework of IC lines and accessible only by D- or E-train connection with the IC system at Bebra or Göttingen.

Emergency aid trains
Precautions against fire within *Neubaustrecke* tunnels include the mustering of elaborately-equipped rescue trains (TUHI). A TUHI is formed in two sections, each with a Class 212 diesel locomotive, so that in an emergency one section can remain at the site of the incident, and the other is available to remove people from the site or bring additional aid. Each section includes surgery, equipment, fire-fighting, control and compressed air-supply vehicles. The last-mentioned is to supply the diesel locomotive, whose driver has the aid of ultra-red sensors to help him discern any people who may have wandered on to the track. The first two TUHI for the Fulda-Würzburg sector have been equipped by Talbot.

Fulda-Frankfurt-Mannheim Ausbau
The DB is undertaking an *Ausbau* upgrading of the 103 km main line from the Hanover-Würzburg new line at Fulda to Frankfurt, and of the 79 km Riedbahn line from Frankfurt to Mannheim. The Fulda-Frankfurt line has to thread difficult country to gain the Rhine-Main plain and over the first 25 km or so IC speed is limited at present to 110 km/h. The *Ausbau* work will make 200 km/h possible over 55 km of the rest of the route.

The scheme involves boring a new 3.5 km Schlüchterner Tunnel, because of the existing tunnel's deterioration. Repair would need the latter's reduction to single-track use only for eight to ten years, which is operationally unacceptable. All level crossings must be eliminated before 200 km/h is permissible. Work on the Riedbahn involves installing a third track to allow overtaking at eight locations, elimination of 27 level crossings and realignments at 11 points to permit 200 km/h over 62 km of its distance. It is hoped to have significant stretches of both upgradings finished by May 1991.

The biggest item in the scheme is enlargement of the underground Frankfurt Airport station facilities; and to the east of the station, construction of a new triangular junction with the Riedbahn, so that trains from the Airport station can proceed direct to Mannheim without entering and reversing in Frankfurt Hbf.

The original plan was to thread a fourth track through the existing Frankfurt Airport station, but by 1990 traffic forecast growth had dictated construction of a second station exclusively for IC traffic, leaving the existing station exclusively to S-Bahn services. The existing station is already used by 7.5 million a year. It is hoped to complete the new station, to be built east of the present one, by 1997. The DB then aims to route three of its IC-Express routes through the Airport. The prospective Cologne-Frankfurt high-speed line will have direct access to Frankfurt Airport station.

Increased capacity on Austria route
Prospective post-1992 growth of north-south EEC freight traffic and Austria's recent restrictions on transiting highway trucks have made enlargement of cross-border capacity urgent. Following the Austrian clampdown 31 extra daily freight trains were immediately scheduled betwen Munich and the Brenner in December 1989. The Transport Minister at the same time approved a start on the 120km Munich-Markt Schwaben-Mühldorf-Freilassing *Ausbau* scheme. This project includes electrification and will create a fully valid relief for the heavily-taxed main route from Munich to Freilassing via Rosenheim. Mühldorf's considerable commuter traffic to Munich will also benefit from the electrification. The total cost is likely to be some DM 1000 million.

Rastatt-Offenburg new line
In January 1987 Transport and Finance Ministers approved a start on the part-*Neubau*, part-*Ausbau* improvement of the 193 km Karlsruhe-Offenburg-Basle main line. Completion is expected by the early 1990s. This is one of Europe's foremost international rail arteries, uniting at Rastatt the main lines from Mannheim and Heidelberg, and channelling into Switzerland traffic from the whole of north-west Europe. In the Offenburg area the Black Forest line to the Lake Constance region and the connection to Strasbourg and France drain off some traffic.

The priority is a *Neubau* scheme over the 49.1 km between Rastatt and Offenburg. The new double-track line is starting on the Karlsruhe side of Rastatt and almost the whole way to Offenburg runs alongside the present main line; it is being engineered throughout for 250 km/h, whereas the limit on the existing main line is 160 km/h.

From Offenburg on to Basle the DB was at first content, in an *Ausbau* project, to add a third track to the existing pair and to realign the latter for a maximum speed of 200 km/h, though it left open the possibility of fitting some sections at least for 250 km/h. However, an extra pair of tracks is now being laid because of the additional growth to be expected from Swiss schemes to increase greatly transalpine rail freight capacity.

An imponderable in early 1990 was whether the French TGV-Est high-speed line would be built: and, if this were projected into Germany, where and how it would be connected with the Rastatt-Offenburg-Basle route.

Nuremburg-Munich Neubau
A decision on the route of the Nuremberg-Munich *Neubaustrecke* was expected in 1990. It would probably favour a 171 km course via Ingolstadt, but at the start of the year it was uncertain whether the route would bypass or thread the city of Ulm. Only 76 km of new 250 km/h infrastructure would be built; the remainder would be existing route upgraded for 200 km/h.

Cologne-Frankfurt Neubau
At their April 1988 meeting, the Transport Ministers of the Federal Republic, France and Benelux countries were informed not only that the Germans had settled the route of a high-speed link from the Belgian frontier at Aachen to Cologne, and would have it prepared by 1993 (upgrading for 220 km/h was begun in 1990), but also that a high-speed, passenger-only Cologne-Frankfurt link was now considered an integral part of the TGV-Nord project.

Choice of route has been particularly controversial, because the most direct excites environmental objections and also avoids major cities including the West German capital. In July 1989 the Federal government opted for the most direct route, through the hills (and nature reserve) to the east of the Rhine. A third of the route will be in tunnel and for much of the distance it will parallel a motorway. It will serve stations at Cologne-Bonn Airport, Bonn-Vilich or Siegburg (to cater for Bonn) depending on route selected immediately south of Cologne, and Limburg. Estimated cost is DM 4900 million and entry into service is now expected in 1998.

Freight use of the line seems likely to be restricted to high-speed merchandise trains. Since it will be primarily a passenger axis, used by up to five IC routes, and because of alignment constraints, it is to be built to more demanding parameters than the other new lines, with a ruling gradient of 4 per cent and minimum curve radius of 3500m.

Maglev scheme
In late 1989 the government at length approved construction of a demonstration Transrapid Maglev line over the 35 km between Düsseldorf and Cologne-Bonn Airports. However, means of financing the DM 3600 million cost of the project remained to be settled. Also to be overcome were the strong objections of local residents and environmentalists to the development.

Electrification
The DB has raised its economic criteria for electrification. Schemes must now show a 15 per cent annual return on investment, not merely avoid worsening the railway's financial situation.

As a result Provincial government aid is now sought to continue electrification. The first government to agree was Baden-Württemberg, which put up some DM 15 million towards closure of the last catenary gap between Stuttgart and Zurich, the 20 km from Schaffhausen to Singen, which was finished in 1989. In that

Two 6000 kW Class 151 Co-Cos and 'double train' of ore from Duisburg to the Saar (*John C Baker*)

Germany (Federal Republic) / **RAILWAY SYSTEMS**

year agreement was reached with the Niedersachsen administration over aid for electrification of the 55 km from Oldenburg to Leer, to close a catenary gap in a route of importance to InterRegio service development in north Germany.

Also agreed was electrification of 21 km of the Bretten-Heilbronn line in south Germany, funded entirely by the Federal and Baden-Württemberg governments and local communities. The line is to be used jointly by DB and Karlsruhe Stadtbahn trains.

Signalling

Nuremberg is the first hub on the historic system to commission a computer-aided traffic control centre (RZu). Similar installations are being completed at Frankfurt and Karlsruhe by Standard Electric Lorenz, which supplied the Nuremberg apparatus, and at Cologne and Hannover by Deutsche Philips. Total cost of these projects is DM 126 million. In an RZu train movements are monitored by train describer apparatus and VDUs in the control centre depict graphically their performance against schedule. In the light of their realtime progress the computer will propose individual train priorities for optimal adherence to the timetable.

In 1990 AEG would complete electronic signalling installations at Dieburg, in Hessen, and on the new high-speed lines at Kirchheim North and Orxhausen.

Siemens would commission two more electronic interlockings, at Essen-Kupferdreh and Overath; this company would also be working on its tenth such DB project, at Elmshorn, a junction 35km northwest of Hamburg, for early 1992 completion. Electronic signalboxes of Standard-Elektrik-Lorenz type would become operational at Husum and Itzehoe in 1991.

SIG L 90, a new signalling system evolved jointly by the DB and Standard Elektrik Lorenz for lightly-trafficked single lines, was inaugurated on the 50 km Nagold Valley line between Pforzheim and Hochdorf in 1989.

Track

Standard rail: Type S49, weighing 49.5 kg/m, type S54, 54.5 kg/m and type S64, 64.9 kg/m. Lengths generally 30–120 m
Type of rail joints: 4- and 6-hole fishplates
Cross ties (sleepers): Wood; steel; reinforced concrete
Wood sleepers impregnated beech, fir or oak, 2600 × 260 × 160 mm
Steel, 2600 × 9 mm weighing 86.3 km
The latest type of RC sleeper (Spannbetonschwelle B58) weighs 235 kg, is 2400 mm long, 190 mm thick under rails, 280 mm wide at bottom and 136 mm at top

Spacing: 650–800 mm
Rail fastenings: Baseplates and bolts, clips and spring washers with thin rubber or wood (poplar) pad between rail and plate; resilient rail spikes with wood and concrete sleepers and resilient rail clips with steel sleepers.

Max gradient: Main lines: 2.5% = 1 in 40
Secondary lines: 6.6% = 1 in 16.5

Max curvature
Main lines: 9.7 = minimum radius 180 m
Secondary lines: 17.5° = minimum radius 100 m

Max superelevation: 150 mm on curves of 180 m radius and under
Rate of slope of superelevation: Generally 1:10V (V = speed in mph). On occasion this may be increased to 1:8V up to 1 in 400. On reverse curves the permissible limit is 1:4V up to 1 in 400
Max altitude: Main line: 967 m between Klais and Mittenwald. Highest station Klais, 933 m
Secondary line: 969 m between Bärenthal and Aha on the Titisee-Seebrugg line
Max axleloading: 22.5 tonnes

Diesel locomotives: principal classes

Class	Wheel arrangement	Transmission	Rated power hp	Max speed km/h	Length over buffers mm	Total weight tonnes	No in service 1988	Year first built	Engine & type
211	B-B	Hyd	1100	90/100	12 100	62	159	1958	MTU MD 12 V 538 TA MTU MB 12 V 493 TZ
213	B-B	hyd	1350	100	12 300	63	378	1962	MTU MB 12 V 652 TA MAN V 6 V 18/21 TL
215	B-B	Hyd	1900	140	16 400	77.5	149	1968	MTU MB 16 V 652 TB MAN V 6 V 23/23 TL
217	B-B	hyd	1900	120	16 000	75.5-77	224	1960	MTU MB 16 V 652 TB MTU MD 16 V 652 TB
218	B-B	Hyd	2500	140	16 400	80	418	1968	MTU MA 12 V 956 TB MTU V 6 V 23/23 TL
360	C	Hyd	650	60	10 450	46.3-49.5	539	1956	MTU GTO 6 MTU MB 12 V 493 AZ
361	C	Hyd	650	60	10 450	53	288	1955	MTU GTO 6/6A
290	B-B	Hyd	1350	70*/80	14 000 14 320	77*/77.8	407	1964	MTU MV 12 V 652 TA
291	B-B	Hyd	1100-1400	90	14 320	76-90	103	1965	MaK 8 M 282 AK

* Nos 290 001-20 only

Electric railcars or multiple-units

Class	Cars per unit	Line voltage	Motor cars per unit	Motored axles per motor car	Rated output (kW) per unit	Max speed km/h	Unit weight tonnes	Total seating capacity	Unit length mm	No in service 1988	Year first built	Builders Mechanical parts	Builders Electrical equipment
403	4	15 kV	4	4	3840	200	235.7	183	109 220	6	1973	LHB, MBB, MAN	AEG, BBC, SSW
420/421	3	15 kV	3	4	2400	120	138	194	67 400	1162		MBB, MAN	AEG, BBC, SSW
470*	3	1200 V	2	4	1280	100	107	200	65 520	90	1959	MAN, Wegmann	BBC, SSW
471*	3	1200 V	2	4	1160	80	131.2	202	62 520	135	1940	LHW, Wegmann MAN	BBC
472*	3	1200 V	3	4	1500	100	114	196	65 820	124	1974	LHB, MBB	BBC, SSW
515	1	†	1	2	200	100	49/56	59.86	23 400	156	1957	Rathgeber, O & K Waggon Union Wegmann, AFA	SSW

* Hamburg-S-Bahn third-rail dc system
† Battery-powered

Diesel railcars or multiple-units

Class	Cars per unit	Motor cars per unit	Motored axles per motor car	Transmission	Rated power (hp) per motor	Max speed km/h	Weight tonnes per unit	Total seating capacity	Length per unit mm	No in service 1988	Year first built	Builders
614	3	2	2	Hyd	450	140	124.5	158	79 460	84	1972	—
624/634*	3	2	2	Hyd	450	120	115.5-118.1	238/256	79 420/ 79 460	84	1961	MAN, Waggonfabrik Uerdingen
627	1	1	2	Hyd	390	120	36	64	22 500	13	1974	—
628	2	1	2	Hyd	550	120	64	136	44 350	139	1974	Duewagm KGB, MBB
628.2	2	1	2	Hyd	550	120	—	122	—	85	1987	Duewag, LHB, MBB
798†	1	1	2	Mech	150	90	20.9	58	13 950	157	1953	MAN, Waggonfabrik Uerdingen, WMD

* Type 624 rebuilt with air suspension bogies
† Two-axle railbus: works as required with non-powered trailers, but not in permanent set formations

RAILWAY SYSTEMS / Germany (Federal Republic)

Electric locomotive: principal classes

Class	Wheel arrangement	Rated output (kW) continuous/one hour	Max speed km/h	Length over buffers mm	Weight tonnes	No in service 1988	Year first built	Builders Mechanical parts	Builders Electrical equipment
103	Co-Co	5950/6420* 7440/7780	200 250†	19 500* 20 200	110# 114	145	1965# 1970	Henschel	Siemens
110	Bo-Bo	3620/3700	140	16 490 16 440**	86.4 86**	377	1956 1963**	Krauss-Maffei, Henschel, Krupp	Siemens, AEG, BBC
111	Bo-Bo	3620/3700	160	16 750* 83		226	1974	Krauss-Maffei	Siemens
112/114	Bo-Bo	3620/3700	140	16 440	86	31	1962	Krauss Maffei, Henschel	Siemens
120	Bo-Bo	4400/5600	160## 200	19 200	84	42	1979	Krauss-Maffei, Krupp-Thyssen-Henschel	BBC
139††	Bo-Bo	3620/3700	110	16 490	86	30	1957	Krauss-Maffei, Krupp Thyssen-Henschel	AEG, BBC, Siemens
140	Bo-Bo	3620/3700	110	16 490	83	847			
141	Bo-Bo	2310/2400	120	15 660	67	429	1956	Henschel	BBC
150	Co-Co	4410/4500	100	19 490	126/128	193	1957	Krupp, Henschel, Krauss-Maffei	AEG, BBC, Siemens
151	Co-Co	5982/6288	120	19 490	118	169	1973	Krupp, Krauss-Maffei	AEG, BBC, Siemens
181 (dual-frequency 15 kV 16⅔ Hz 25 kV 50 Hz)	Bo-Bo	3000/3240	150	16 950	84	27	1968	Krupp	AEG
181.2 (dual-frequency 15 kV 16⅔ Hz, 25 kV 50 Hz)	Bo-Bo	3200/3300	160	17 940	83		1975	Krupp	AEG

* Nos 103.001-4 and 103.101-215   # Nos 103.001-4 only   † No 103.118 only
** Nos 110.288 onwards, which are Class 110.3; remainder are Class 110.1
Nos 120.001-4 only
†† The principal difference between Classes 139 and 140 is that the former has rheostatic braking for heavily graded routes

Other principal public railways

Albtal Railway
Albtal-Verkehrs-GmbH (AVG)

Tullastrasse 71, 7500 Karlsruhe

Telephone: +49 721 599-1
Telex: 7 82 978 avg d
Telefax: +49 599 5899

Manager: Dipl-Ing Dieter Ludwig

Gauge: 1435 mm
Route length: 56.8 km
Electrification: 55.6 km at 750 V dc

Located in Baden-Württemberg, the railway runs from Karlsruhe to Bad Herenalb, in Ettlingen, Karlsruhe to Linkenheim and from Busenbach to Karlsbad. It owns two diesel locomotives, 19 eight-axle and one four-axle railcars and 15 light rail.

Traffic	1987	1989
Passenger journeys (million)	15·23	17·20
Passenger km (million)	93·48	104·30
Freight (tonnes)	48 238	53 022
Freight tonne km	230 294	474 985

Altona-Kaltenkirchen-Neumünster Railway
Eisenbahngesellschaft Altona-Kaltenkirchen-Neumünster

Grusonstrasse 31, 2000 Hamburg 74

Telephone: +49 40 733 341
Telex: 215197

Directors: H H Meyer
Josef Hoffstadt

Gauge: 1435 mm
Route length: 216 km

The company operates a group of local railways: Hamburg-Eldelstedt-Neumünster; Tiefstack-Glinde; Hamburg-Bergdorf-Geesthacht; the Alsternordbahn; and Elmshorn-Barmstedt. Their combined operating stock comprises 14 diesel-hydraulic locomotives, 16 diesel-electric two-car multiple-units, 14 diesel rail-buses and five trailers.

Track
Rail: 49.4 kg/m; 50 kg/m
Sleepers: Hardwood, 160/240 mm thickness, spaced 1539/km
Minimum curve radius: 100 m
Max gradient: 2.15%
Max axleload: 20/22.5 tonnes

Bentheim Railway
Bentheimer Eisenbahn AG

Bahnhofstrasse 24, Postfach 72, 4444 Bad Bentheim

Telephone: +49 5922 75-0
Telex: 98 935 d
Telefax: +49 5922 7555
Director: Peter Hoffmann

Gauge: 1435 mm
Route length: 91 km

The Bentheim Railway is the principal system, but the company also manages the Ahaus-Alstätter Railway. Rail traffic is almost entirely freight, which on the Bentheim Railway totalled 590 500 tonnes and 27.1 million tonne-km in 1989. Passenger operation is mainly by road. The Bentheim Railway owns 12 diesel-hydraulic locomotives, three passenger cars, two baggage cars and 37 freight wagons.

The railway has recently opened a container terminal inside Dutch territory at Coevorden. In the summer of 1989 it inaugurated a daily service from this installation to Verona, Italy, saving users customs formalities and charges at the Dutch-German border. The success of

Bentheim Railway's Coevorden terminal in Netherlands. (*Marcel Vleugels*)

the venture led to the launch of a Moscow service in February 1990, and to a Dm 7 million investment in development of the Coevorden terminal.

Germany (Federal Republic) / **RAILWAY SYSTEMS** 587

Cologne-Bonn Railways
Köln-Bonner Eisenbahnen AG (KBE)

Scheidtweilerstrasse 38, Postfach 45 06 47, 5000 Cologne 41

Telephone: +49 221 54 71
Telex: 8 881 701 kvb e d

Directors: Dipl-Ing Klaus-Dieter Bollhöfer
Dr-Ing Wolfgang Meyer
Hans Schoessler
Chief Engineer: Dr-Ing Wolfgang Meyer
Engineering Manager: H Köhler

Gauge: 1435 mm
Route length: 82.8 km
Electrification: 67.4 km at 750 and 1200 V dc

In 1974 the Köln-Bonner Eisenbahnen, Kölner Verkehrs-Betriebe (KVB) and Stadtwerke Bonn Verkehrsbetriebe were fused as the Stadtbahn Rhein-Sieg organisation, to integrate local tracked transport in the Cologne-Bonn region. In 1978 the systems were physically integrated to create a through 44 km light railway between the city centres of Bonn and Cologne, at a cost of DM 81 million. The resultant Stadtbahn welds together the KBE main lines and the U-Bahn and tramway systems of Cologne and Bonn. In Cologne the Stadtbahn LRV train-sets share tracks with the local tram services, to permit which the traction current systems of all the companies involved were standardised at 750 volts dc during the conversion process.

The Stadtbahn route runs along the west banks of the Rhine via Wesseling (the Rheinuferbahn) and also, since November 1986, over a second connection via Brühl (the Vorgebirgsbahn). Freight working on the Stadtbahn route is restricted to the latter's Wesseling-Hersel section. KBE freight for the Wesseling Rhine quays can reach this by a branch from Kendenich via Brühl.

KBE operates 17 diesel and three electric locomotives, 14 'Köln'-type LRVs, 41 other cars and 596 freight wagons. The stock now includes five MaK 1320 kW diesel-electric locomotives with BBC three-phase transmission.

Modernised Brühl Mitte station on Stadtbahn Line 18 from Bonn to Cologne

MaK 1320 kW diesel-electric locomotive in Cologne-Niehl yard

KBE's new microprocessor-based signal centre in Hurth-Kendenich yard

Cologne-Frechen-Benzelrather Railway
Köln-Frechen-Benzelrather Eisenbahn (KFBE)

Scheidtweilerstrasse 38, Postfach 45 06 29, 5000 Cologne 41

Telephone: +49 221 5471
Telex: 08 881 701 kvb e d

Chairman: Dipl-Ing Klaus-Dieter Bollhöfer
Directors: Dr-Ing Wolfgang Meyer
Hans Schoessler
Manager: Dr-Ing Wolfgang Meyer

Gauge: 1435 mm
Route length: 47.2 km
Electrification: 12.5 km at 800 V dc

The railway is operated by the Kölner Verkehrsbetriebe AG (KVB) and part of its route is electrified to permit through running; it owns no electric traction units, only nine diesel locomotives, and its passenger services are operated by KVB equipment.

Dortmund Railway
Dortmunder Eisenbahn GmbH

Speicherstrasse 23, Postfach 465, 4600 Dortmund 1

Telephone: +49 231 84901

Directors: Dipl-Ing Joachim Riemer
Reiner Woermann
Manager: Dipl-Ing Joachim Riemer

Gauge: 1435 mm; 837 mm
Route length: 20.3 km (for public traffic)

The freight railway operates 42 1435 mm-gauge diesel locomotives, three narrow-gauge diesel locomotives and 1165 freight wagons. Its public traffic totals some 15 million tonnes and 130 million tonne-km, but in all the system moves around 40 million tonnes a year.

East Hanover Railway
Osthannoversche Eisenbahnen AG (OHE)

Biermannstrasse 33, Postfach 436, 3100 Celle

Telephone: +49 5141 276-0
Telex: 925 058 ohe
Telefax: +49 5141 35036
Director: Dr jur Hans Wilhelm Wolff
Transport Manager: Dr rer pol Jens Jahnke

Gauge: 1435 mm
Route length: 326.2 km

The company also operates the 14.8 km Buxtehude-Harsefelder Railway.

The railway's principal business is freight, with maximum trainloads operated reaching 1800 tonnes. Gross tonnage in 1989 was 1.735 million, for a total of 89.394 million tonne-km.

With support from the Federal and Lower Saxony governments OHE has embarked on a DM 30 million expenditure principally concerned with renewal of 191 km of its route. Half of this work will be carried out with Y-form steel sleepers. Some locomotives are to be equipped for remote radio control.

In May 1990 the railway was to take over from the DB freight working between Gifhorn and Wittingen. The DB would retain passenger operation.

The railway owns 28 diesel-hydraulic locomotives, two diesel railcars and 54 baggage and freight wagons.

Track
Rail: 49.3 kg/m
Cross ties (sleepers): Oak, thickness 200 mm; spacing 1540/km
Fastenings: Spring clips
Minimum curvature radius: 190 m
Max gradient: 1.7%
Max permissible axleload: 20 tonnes

Elbe-Weser Railway
Eisenbahnen and Verkehrsbetriebe Elbe-Weser GmbH

Bahnhofstrasse 67, Postfach 1550, 2730 Zeven

Telephone: +49 4281 2232/3252

Director: Dipl-Ing Heinz Badke

Gauge: 1435 mm
Route length: 111.2 km

Operating in Niedersachsen Land, the company runs the former Bremervörde-Osterholzer and Wilstedt-Zeven-Tostedter Railways. It owns four diesel locomotives, two diesel railcars, two baggage cars and six freight wagons.

In 1989 agreement was reached for the company to take over DB lines from Bremerhaven to Stade, and from Bremervörde to Rotenburg.

Hersfeld Railway
Hersfelder Eisenbahn GmbH

Heinrich-Börner-Strasse 10, Postfach 44, 6430 Bad Hersfeld

Telephone: +49 6621 740 34

Manager: Dr Valentin Jost

Gauge: 1435 mm
Route length: 30 km (26.1 km owned)

The railway runs from Bad Hersfeld to Heimsboldshausen in Hessen. It owns three diesel locomotives, four diesel railcars and nine trailers.

In 1988, the railway took delivery of two new MaK Type DE 1002 diesel-electric locomotives, to replace its two ex-DB diesel-hydraulic Class V160 and V320 prototypes of the 1960s. Its third locomotive is of the DB Type V100 B-B design.

Hohenzoller Provincial Railway
Hohenzollerische Landesbahn AG (HzL)

Hofgartenstrasse 39, Postfach 1104, 7450 Hechingen

Telephone: +49 7471 6026/7

Director: Dipl-Kfm Günter Zeiger

Gauge: 1435 mm
Route length: 114.8 km

The railway runs principally from Sigmaringen and Sigdorf to Eyach and Kleinengstingen. The company also operates bus routes aggregating 848 km.

Rolling stock comprises two 1135 kW, four 956 kW, one 860 kW, one 698 kW, one 250 kW and one 176 kW diesel locomotives, seven twin-engined diesel railcars of 228–282 kW total power, four control, and five intermediate trailers.

Minden Local Railways (MKB)
Mindener Kreisbahnen GmbH

Karlstrasse 48, PO Box 1147, 4950 Minden

Telephone: +49 517 39 94-0
Telex: 97966 mkbd

Directors: Dietmar Schweizer
Dr Günter Linkermann

Gauge: 1435 mm
Route length: 57.1 km

The chiefly freight-hauling railway runs from Minden, in Nordrhein-Westfalen, to Todtenhausen, Hille and Kleinenbremen. The company also operates widespread road passenger and freight services. Railway rolling stock comprises three diesel locomotives, nine passenger cars and seven freight wagons.

Niederrhein Railway
Niederrheinische Verkehrsbetriebe Aktiengesellschaft (NIAG)

Homberger Strasse 113, Postfach 1940, 4130 Moers 1

Telephone: +49 2841 205-0
Telex: 8121198 niag d

President: Rudolf Erberich
Manager: Dipl-Ing Manfred Diehl

Gauge: 1435 mm
Route length: 35.8 km

Sited in Nordrhein-Westfalen, the railway runs from Moers to Sevelen and Rheinberg. It operates four diesel locomotives, two diesel tractors, two diesel railcars and 95 freight wagons. Its passenger operation is primarily road.

Oberrhein Railway
Oberrheinische Eisenbahn-Gesellschaft, AG (OEG)

Käfertaler Strasse 9-11, 6800 Mannheim 1

Telephone: +49 621 330860

Directors: Dr Karl Wimmer
Dipl-Ing Eduard Stephan

Gauge: 1000 mm
Route length: 61 km
Electrification: 651 km at 600/750 V dc

The railway operates between Mannheim and Heidelberg and Käfertal and Heddesheim in Baden-Württemberg. It owns 31 eight-axle, four six-axle and five four-axle LRVs, 13 trailers, and one 95 kW diesel-hydraulic locomotive.

Type of coupler in standard use
Passenger cars: Scharfenberg Gt8 + Tw 4; BSI Gt6 + Bw 4
Freight cars: Scharfenberg
Type of braking in standard use, locomotive-hauled stock: Knorr

Track
Rail: S 41 (41 kg/m); Ri 60 (60 kg/m)
Cross ties (sleepers): Wood; thickness 160–180 mm; spacing 1538/km

Minimum curvature radius: 40 m
Max gradient: 3%
Max. permissible axleload: 10 tonnes

OEG six-axle LRV

Peine-Salzgitter Transport
Verkehrsbetriebe-Peine-Salzgitter GmbH (VPS)

Postfach 100670, Am Hillenholz 28, 3320 Salzgitter 1

Telephone: +49 5341 211
Telex: 954481-0 sgd
Telefax: +49 5341 212727

Manager: Dipl-Ing Karl-Joachim Bunte

Gauge: 1435 mm
Route length: 69.8 km

This heavy industrial freight system comprises two systems, the 31.6 km Peine Railway and the 38.2 km Salzgitter Railway. The former moves some 6.5 million tonnes a year, the latter some 28 million. Rolling stock comprises 65 diesel locomotives, of which 50 can be remote-controlled by radio, and 110.0 freight wagons.

Regental Railway
Regentalbahn AG (RAG)

Bahnhofsplatz 1, Postfach 1320, 8374 Viechtach

Telephone: +49 9942 570
Telex: 69430
Telefax: +49 9942 5728

Manager: Dr-Ing Willi Höppner

Gauge: 1435 mm
Route length: 63 km

The railway operates three Bavarian lines, from Lam to Kötzing, Deggendorf to Metten, and Gotteszell to Blalbach. It owns two diesel locomotives, eight diesel railcars and four trailers, two battery-electric railcars (which in 1990 were undergoing conversion to diesel-electric traction for a takeover of two DB passenger services), three passenger cars and two freight wagons.

South-West German Railways
Südwestdeutsche Eisenbahnen AG (SWEG)

Friedrichstrasse 59, Postfach 2009/10, 7630 Lahr

Telephone: +49 7821 27020
Telex: 754809 sweg d
Telefax: +49 7821 270267

President: Dipl-Kfm Hansjörg Kraft

Gauge: 1435 mm; 750 mm
Length: 158 km; 39.2 km

The group was created in 1972 and now operates nine railways and bus services covering a 5000 km network of routes in the province of Baden-Württemberg. A financial surplus has been continuously achieved on operations since the group's formation.

The Group operates one steam locomotive (used only for special trips sponsored by private organisations over three stretches of its system), 13 diesel locomotives, 27 diesel railcars and 42 passenger cars and 34 freight cars.

MaK Type G1203 locomotives of SWEG

Teutoburger Wald Railway
Teutoburger Wald Eisenbahn-Aktiengessellschaft (TWE)

Mainzer Landstrasse 41, Postfach 160253, 6000 Frankfurt (Main) 1

Telephone: +49 69 273 40
Telex: 4 14860

Directors: Dr-Ing Karlheinz Geuckler
Willi Ries
Josef Sowa

Gauge: 1435 mm
Route length: 103.2 km

Situated in Nordrhein-Westfalen, the railway operates in the area of Gütersloh, Brochterbeck and Harsewinkel. It operates seven diesel locomotives, one diesel railcar, four passenger cars, one baggage car and 19 freight wagons.

In 1989 TWE took over from the Hersfeld Railway the ex-DB Class V320 4000 hp diesel-hydraulic C-C prototype of 1962. The V320 was needed for TWE's 1600-tonne steel train haulage from Emsland to Paderborn.

Wanne-Bochum-Herner Railway
Wanne-Bochum-Herner Eisenbahn

Wanne-Herner Eisenbahn und Hafen GmbH, PO Box 20 04 63, Am Westhafen 27, 4690 Herne 2

Telephone: +49 2325 770 71-75

General Manager: Dipl-Kfm Richard Görl

Gauge: 1435 mm
Length: 13.7 km (12.4 km owned)

The railway is operated by 14 diesel locomotives and owns 83 freight wagons.

Track
Rail: 49.43 and 54.54 kg/m
Sleepers: Oak, thickness 1667/1385 mm
Minimum curve radius: 140 m
Max gradient: 1 in 38
Max axleload: 22.5 tonnes

Diesel locomotives

Type	Transmission	Power rating kW	Max speed km/h	Weight tonnes	Year first built	No in service 1986	Builder	Diesel engine
D	Hyd	882	66	80	1961	3	MaK Kiel	MaK/Ma 301 FAK
B-B	Hyd	809	40	80	1968	2	MaK Kiel	MaK/6M AK
B-B	Hyd	1180	80	90	1972	4	MaK Kiel	MaK/8M 282 AK
B-B	Hyd	860	40	88	1979	1	MaK Kiel	MTU/12 V331
G	Hyd	1120	60	88	1983	2	MaK Kiel	MTU
DE 502	Elec	560	45	66	1984	2	MaK Kiel	–

Westphalian Provincial Railway
Westfälische Landes-Eisenbahn GmbH (WLE)

Krögerweg 11, Postfach 8809, 4400 Münster

Telephone: +49 251 618 02-0
Telefax: +49 251 618 02 34

Director: Dr-Ing Eberhard Christ
Operating Manager: Dipl-Ing Uwe Spillner

Gauge: 1435 mm
Route length: 125 km

The lines operated are in Nordrhein-Westfalen. They were reduced at the end of January 1988 by closure of the last surviving section in West Münsterland. Passenger services were abandoned in 1975. Traffic in 1988 amounted to 1.04 million tonnes and 59.9 million tonne-km. Tracks have a maximum axleloading of 22.5 tonnes and a minimum curve radius of 140 metres; rail weight varies from 33 to 60 kg/m. The railway owns 14 diesel locomotives, three locotractors and 67 freight wagons.

Wurttemberg Railway
Württembergische Eisenbahn GmbH (WEG)

PO Box 10 54 27, Mönchhaldenstrasse 26, 7000 Stuttgart 10

Telephone: +49 711 25008-0
Telex: 722145
Telefax: +49 711 25008-35

General Managers: Dr Karlheinz Geuckler
Willi Ries
Günther Zobel

Waggon Union standard diesel railcars for local railways, in use on the WEG's Strohgäubahn (Wilhelm Pflug)

Gauge: 1435 mm
Length: 108 km

The WEG comprises the main Württembergische Eisenbahn, with seven lines aggregating 108 route-km of 1435 mm gauge.

The organisation also operates 359.6 km of bus routes.

On 1435 mm-gauge rolling stock comprises 16 railcars, 23 trailers and one freight wagon.

Ghana

Ministry of Transport and Communications

PO Box M38, Ministry Branch Post Office, Accra

Secretary: J A Danso
Chief Director, Administration: B O Antwi

Ghana Railway Corporation (GRC)

PO Box 251, Takoradi

Telephone: +233 31 2181, 2505
Cable: Railways
Telex: 2297 rail gh accra; 2437 tk

Managing Director: Amponsah Ababio
Deputy Managing Director
 Engineering: J A K Baidoo
 Administration & Operations: M K Arthur
Financial Controller: W D Asaam
Administrative Manager: J E Buah
Chief Civil Engineer: S K Agboletey
Chief Mechanical and Electrical Engineer:
 Raymond Afeke (Acting)
Chief Signalling and Telecommunications
 Engineer: Dr Y Devadas
Traffic Manager: D Y Hagan
Controller of Supplies: E L Wayoe
Chief Internal Auditor: E Y Yankson (Acting)
Principal, Central Training Institute: S Barnes
Project Manager, Rehabilitation (Eastern and Central Lines): Emmanuel Opoku

Gauge: 1067 mm
Route length: 953 km

The railway network is in the form of a letter 'A', the apex being at Kumasi and two feet at the port of Takoradi and at Accra; the chord connects Huni Valley and Kotoku on the two legs. Branch lines run to Sekondi, Prestea, Kade Awaso and Tema.

In the 1960s and 1970s the railway was unable to obtain finance and foreign currency even for normal renewals. The resultant decline of service quality, exacerbated by loss of demoralised staff in the higher grades, contrasted with a simultaneous, uncontrolled growth of heavy road transport. Consequently the railway today carries only a third of the passengers and a fifth of the freight tonnage it recorded in the early 1960s.

The railway has completed a rehabilitation project on the western Kumasi-Takoradi line (including the Awaso branch), which is the main export trunk route. Foreign exchange inputs for the project, totalling US $45 million, came mainly from the World Bank and African Development Bank, but also from donor countries (Switzerland, United Kingdom and France). The project covered track rehabilitation, replacement of signalling (using solar power) and telecommunication equipment, rehabilitation of locomotives and rolling stock, equipment of wagons with roller bearings, workshop modernisation, setting up of a Central Training Institute, institution building and staff training.

In 1988 the Italian government granted US$30 million towards similar rehabilitation of GRC's central and eastern lines, and also towards a microwave radio network. Preliminary studies were completed by RITES of India, who were consultants for the western line project, and with additional World Bank support of US$9 million work on the 306 km eastern line from Accra to Kumasi was started. The available funds also provided for attention to the 182 km Kotoku-Huni Valley section of the central line from Accra to Takoradi. The works should be complete in mid-1992.

Ghana's railway network has excessive curvature in several sections, and this tends to reduce line capacity. For example, between Kumasi and Takoradi there are 504 curves in a section of 270.48 km. Realignment of the permanent way on these sections has increased minimum curve radius to 335 metres, improving train speeds and lessening the risk of derailments and damage to property. Also under way is replacement of existing 39.7 kg/m rail by 45 kg/m rail, and a ballasting programme to provide for a depth of 15.7 cm of ballast on existing track and 23.6 cm on track which is relaid.

With completion of signalling works (see below), the improvement in operating capability is forecast to see passenger traffic doubled and freight traffic quadrupled in the later 1990s.

New lines

In the long term GRC is hopeful of building three new lines. One would run from Accra, where GRC wants to build a new multi-function station, to Akosombo, to link the Volta lake region with the north of the country. The other lines, from Awaso to Sunyani, and Bosuso to Kibi, would have exploitation of bauxite deposits as their objective.

Traffic

The railway's freight traffic is mainly export-orientated and its main commodities are cocoa, timber, bauxite and manganese. It is also engaged in haulage of petroleum products, cement and other imports from the coast to the interior, as well as agricultural produce from sources to marketing centres.

Terminal facilities are being established at Fumisua, near Kumasi, for movement of container traffic from Takoradi and Tema ports.

Signalling and telecommunications

Under the World Bank project, the GRC has changed from the previous semaphore system to colour-light signals powered by solar panels in all 42 stations on the western rail line. Between stations the western line is worked on the tokenless block system, with end-of-train detectors. There is station-to-station communication, section control telephones, deputy control telephones and administrative trunk telephones. The section control at GRC headquarters in Takoradi connects the section controller to all stations and important operating points on the section. The equipment consists of an operator's console with single push-button selective calling facilities. Group calls and all-station calls are also possible. Digital automatic telephone exchanges with instantaneous direct dialling facilities between the exchanges have

Brush 523 kW Bo-Bos, employed both for main-line haulage and shunting, are among GRC's latest locomotive acquisitions

New GRC second-class sleeping car by VEB Görlitz, German Democratic Republic

Berth of new second-class sleeping car

been provided at Takoradi, Location, Tarkwa, Dunkwa, Awaso and Kumasi.

The contract for the installation of the system was awarded to Aydin Monitor System of USA, with subcontracts to Wabco of Italy for the signalling and tokenless block, Harris for telephones and BP Solar Systems of the UK for solar power. The project was commissioned in February 1988. In 1990 similar modernisation of signalling and telecommunications on the eastern and central lines was to begin, for completion by the spring of 1991.

Motive power and rolling stock
At the close of 1989 the GRC operated:
Diesel locomotives, diesel-hydraulic shunters 63
Passenger train coaches 194
Freight train cars 1736

Delivery of 130 passenger cars from the German Democratic Republic has been completed. The order included buffet cars, first- and second-class day and sleeping cars and an inspection saloon. Orders were placed in 1988 for a further 30 cars from the same source.

Type of coupler in standard use: No 2 Alliance/ABC type
Type of brake in standard use: Locomotives, air; carriages and wagons, vacuum

Traffic	1986	1987	1988	1989
Total freight-tonnage	609 271	638 895	743 400	760 200
Total freight-tonne-km (million)	102.29	108.67	125.77	141.51
Average net freight train load (tonnes)	580	580	25.6	25.6
Total passenger-km (million)	200.69	345.66	321.35	330.0
Total passenger journeys (million)	2.2	3.3	3.36	3.3

Finance (¢ million)
Revenues

	1986	1987	1988	1989
Passengers, luggage and parcels/mail	262.55	453	793.06	953.27
Freight	460.87	654	1005.45	1430.60
Other income (rents)	7.59	16		
Finance and miscellaneous	4.52	5	–	–
Total	735.53	1128	1798.51	2383.87

Expenditure

	1986	1987	1988	1989
Staff costs	889.91	1119	1450	1768.40
Materials and services	836.33	619	823	1012.13
Depreciation	15.0	15.0	25	156.00
Financial charges	5.66	6	7	14.16
Total	1746.9	1759	2305	2950.69

Track
Standard rail, type and weight
Western Line
Takoradi-Manso: RBS 39.7 kg/m
Manso-Huni Valley: BSA 44.7 kg/m
Huni Valley-Kumasi: RBS 39.7 kg/m
Eastern Line
Kumasi-Konongo: BS 29.8 kg/m
Konongo-Juaso: BA 'A' 39.7 kg/m
Juaso-Osino: RBS 39.7 kg/m
Osino-Tafo: BS 29.8 kg/m
Tafo-Accra: RBS 29.8 kg/m
Central Line
Huni Valley-Nyinase: RBS 39.7 kg/m
Nyinase-Twifu: BS 'A' 39.7 kg/m
Twifu-Akenkausu: BS 29.8 kg/m
Akenkausu-Achiasi Junction: BSA 39.7 kg/m
Achiasi Junction-Kotoku Junction: RBS 39.7 kg/m
Prestea branch line: RBS 29.8 kg/m
Awaso branch line: ASCE 37.2 kg/m
Joints: 4-hole fishplates
Cross ties (sleepers): Standard steel; and wood 127 × 254 × 1981 mm
Spacing: 1365 per km steel, 1602 per km wood
Rail fastenings
Wood sleepers: Dog spikes, Macbeth spike anchors, Type T3 (UK) elastic rail spikes. Elastic rail spikes Type ES18 and DS18 (West Germany)
Steel sleepers: Keys, ABK clips
Filling: Mainly crushed granite, some gravel
Max curvature
  Takoradi-Kumasi 8° 40' = radius of 202 m
  Kumasi-Accra 8° 40' = radius of 202 m
  Central line 8° 40' = radius of 202 m
  Prestea branch 17° = radius of 103 m
  Awaso branch 6° = radius of 291 m
Max gradient: 1.25% = 1 in 80; except Prestea branch 2.5% = 1 in 40
Longest continuous gradient: 10 km with ruling grade of 1.25% and max curves of 8° 40'
Max altitude: 286 m near Kumasi
Permitted speeds
  Freight trains 40 km/h
  Passenger trains 56 km/h
  Except Prestea branch:
  Freight trains 24 km/h
  Passenger trains 40 km/h
Max axleloading
  Takoradi-Kumasi-Accra 16 tons
  Central line 16 tons
  Prestea branch 13½ tons
  Awaso branch 16 tons
Gauge widening on sharpest curve: 12 mm
Superelevation on sharpest curve: 89 mm
Rate of slope of superelevation: 13 mm per rail length

Diesel locomotives

Class	Wheel arrangement	Transmission	Rated power kW	Max speed km/h	Total weight tonnes	No in service 1989	Year first built	Builders Mechanical parts	Engine & type	Transmission
1851	Co-Co	Elec	1380	96	84	10	1969/70	English Electric	English Electric 12CVST	English Electric
1651	Co-Co	Elec	1232	96	85	10	1978/79	Thyssen-Henschel	General Motors 645E	Thyssen-Henschel
1401	Co-Co	Elec	1045	99	81.6	10	1959/60	Henschel	General Motors 567C	Henschel
751	Bo-Bo	Elec	560	88	53.2	7	1954/55	English Electric	English Electric 6 SKRT	English Electric
721	Bo-Bo	Elec	426/450	65/80	56	4	1986	Daewood	MTU 8V396TC12	Toshiba SE-223
701	Bo-Bo	Elec	523	64	59	6	1982/83	Brush	Rolls-Royce DV8TCE	Brush
541	C(0-6-0)	Hyd	404	45	42-6	12	1975/76	Thyssen-Henschel	Henschel 12V 1516A	Voith L4, 4V2
501	C(0-6-0)	Hyd	374	34	39	3	1960/61	Henschel	Henschel 12V 1416A	Voith L4, two convertors

Greece
Ministry of Mercantile Marine, Transport and Communications

Xenofontos Street 13, 10557 Athens

Telephone: +30 1 325 1211-9
Telex: 216369 ysyg gr
Telefax: +30 1 323 9039

Minister: J Charalambous
Secretary: A Rousopoulos

Hellenic Railways Organisation (OSE)
Organismos Sidirodromon Ellados

1-3 Karolou Street, 10437 Athens

Telephone: +30 1 522 5561
Telex: 215187 ceha

Director-General: H Karapanos
Deputy Directors-General: Manolis Lalakakis
    Eleftherios Manolas
    George Charamis
    Evagelos Crinis

Directors
Personnel: El Xenos
Operation: A Tsamourtzis
Traction: A Varvarigos
Track: K Kouparoussos
Organisation Design and Planning: K Kochilas
Modernisation & Development: G Andritsos
Supplies: Kh Michalopoulos
Commercial: A Alexandros
Finance: D Tserpes
Workshops Manager: D Tassonis
Regional Management
Athens: A Papanicolaou
Thessaloniki: A Georgiadis
Peloponnesus: E Zographakis

RAILWAY SYSTEMS / Greece

Gauge: 1435 mm; 1000 mm; 750 mm
Route length: 1565 km; 892 km; 22 km

The railway from Athens to the Peloponnese, serving Patras and southern Greece, is metre-gauge.

Modernisation
The principal project in hand is doubling and realignment of the Inoi-Tithorea (95 km) and Domokos-Larissa (60 km) and Larissa-Plati (134 km) sections of the Athens-Thessaloniki main line and relaying with UIC54 continuously welded rail on two-block concrete sleepers, with minimum curve radius of 2000 metres. Doubling of the Inoi-Tithorea and Domokos-Larissa sections was completed by early 1988. Completion of the 134 km between Larissa and Plati was anticipated in 1990. Automatic block signalling is being extended to the whole route and is already operational between Athens and Inoi, Plati and Thessaloniki, and Tithorea and Domokos (122 km); it was nearing completion over the Inoi-Tithorea and Domokos-Larissa sections in 1989.

Another work in progress is conversion of the 80 km Paleofarsalos-Kalambaka metre-gauge line to 1435 mm-gauge.

These projects are being financed by the country's Public Investment Programme, the EEC and loans from the European Investment Bank and other banks.

Key objectives remain:
Infrastructure upgrading throughout the Athens-Thessaloniki route, except for the difficult, 65 km/h-limited mountain section between Tithorea and Domokos which is unlikely to be finished before the mid-1990s;
A new north-west Athens marshalling yard and freight centre catering for both gauges, to be located at Thriassio Pedio;
Private siding connection of major industries;
Installation of automatic colour-light signalling on the Thessaloniki-Promachon (143 km) and Plati-Aminteo-Kozani-Florina (220 km) lines. Promachon is the frontier station with Bulgarian Railways.
Modernisation of the Peloponnese network. The scheme to convert from 1000 to 1435 mm-gauge remained shelved in 1990.

Electrification
The long-discussed 25 kV 50 Hz ac electrification of the 587 km Athens-Thessaloniki-Idomeni main line, along with its upgrading, is approved in principle. The originally-planned order of work has been changed and the 76 km of single line from Thessaloniki to the Yugoslav border at Idomeni, where track is being renewed and curvature eased, is now the priority. This route carries three times the freight of the Athens-Thessaloniki line. Electrification of the remainder of the route to follow in stages, the order of the latter dependent on completion of their civil engineering improvements. In 1987 SASIB was contracted to resignal between Thessaloniki and Idomeni, and set up a subsidiary company in Greece, SASIB Hellas, to design and manufacture the equipment.

The hope is that, with the benefit of route alignment where possible for 200 km/h, the Athens-Thessaloniki passenger journey time will eventually be reduced from the accelerated schedule of 6 hours 50 minutes, operative from May 1988, to 3 hours 40 minutes after completion of the whole project, including double-tracking throughout the Tithorea-Domokos section.

Rolling stock	1435 mm-gauge	narrow-gauge
Diesel locomotives	171	43
Diesel railcars	52	67
Trailers	13	4
Diesel train-sets	47	59
Passenger cars	324	143
Baggage cars	136	32
Freight wagons	8898	1687

The 20 redundant Class 221 diesel-hydraulic B-Bs purchased from the German Federal Railway had all completed their renovation by an Italian company at Bergamo at the end of 1989 and were ready for shipment to Greece. In preliminary trials of one example in Greece it had been shown that the type could haul 500-tonne passenger and 790-tonne freight trains over the Athens-Thessaloniki main line. From the same railway OHE has also acquired a batch of couchette cars.

In 1986 the government signed agreements with MAN of the German Federal Republic, Schienenfahrzeuge Export-Import of the German Democratic Republic and Hellenic Shipyards, for a joint venture manufacture of 12 air-conditioned four-car and 25 single-car diesel railcar units for 1435 mm-gauge, 10 air-conditioned three-car and 10 two-car diesel railcar units for metre-gauge, 56 passenger and 446 freight cars.

The first of the four-car inter-city units was handed over in November 1989. They have been built by VEB Kombinat Schienenfahrzeugbau of the German Democratic Republic with traction and ancillary equipment by AEG-Westinghouse.

Each of two power cars in a four-car set has an MTU Type 12V396TC13 995 kW 1800 rpm engine driving via a Siemens three-phase synchronous alternator to AEG traction motors. Bogies are the German Type GPG and GP200S. Two sets can be operated in multiple-unit formation. Designed for 160 km/h, these units will be assigned to Athens-Thessaloniki service.

Prototypes of the other three new dmu types will be completely built by MAN at Nuremberg; series production will be completed by Hellenic Shipyards in Greece.

Class DEL 4000 hp diesel-electric Co-Co built by Electroputere, Romania

Traffic (000)	1984	1985	1986	1987	1988
Freight tonnage	4017	4151	4164	3800	4216
Freight tonne-km	769 579	733 009	702 366	599 000	618 000
Passenger journeys	10 989	11 156	11 660	11 800	11 834
Passenger-km	1 651 519	1 731 806	1 950 000	1 973 000	1 963 000

The freight car order mentioned above was subsequently expanded to 1260 vehicles. In 1989 Hellenic Shipyards was completing wagons at the rate of one vehicle a day.

In the spring of 1990 the railway was preparing to order 10 Alco-engined 3600 hp diesel locomotives from Electroputere of Romania. Also contemplated was an order for 66 air-conditioned long-haul cars, including 10 restaurant and 14 sleeping cars, this to be placed with the Hellenic Shipyards-East German industrial consortium.

Coupler in standard use: 1435 mm-gauge, UIC 520-521
Brake in standard use: Air, mostly Knorr

Track
Rail: 1435 mm-gauge, UIC 50, 54; narrow-gauge, 31.6 kg/m
Sleepers: 1435 mm-gauge, reinforced concrete and steel (Vagneux type); narrow-gauge, steel and timber

A pair of new diesel-electric inter-city train-sets built in East Germany with AEG-Westinghouse electrical and traction equipment

Fastenings: 1435 mm-gauge, RN and Nabla for concrete sleepers; direct fastenings for wood or steel
Minimum curve radius: 1435 mm-gauge, 300 m; narrow-gauge, 110 m

Max gradient: 1435 mm-gauge, 2.8%; narrow-gauge, 2.5%
Max permissible axleload: 1435 mm-gauge, 20 tonnes; narrow-gauge, 14 tonnes

Max permissible speed: 90–100 km/h; 120 km/h parts of Athens-Thessaloniki main line

Diesel locomotives

Class	Wheel arrangement	Transmission	Rated power hp	Max speed km/h	Total weight tonnes	No in service 1987	Year first built	Builders Mechanical parts	Engine & type	Transmission
1000 mm-gauge										
CC AD 1600 A1	Co-Co	Elec	1600	90	80	10	1967	Alsthom	Pielstick 12 PA 4V 185	
DL 537	Co-Co	Elec	1350	96	80·3	12	1965	Alco	Alco 251 D	
48 BB HI	B-B	Hyd	2 × 322·5	90	48	20	1967	Mitsubishi	GM 71N	Niigata
1435 mm-gauge										
DHM 7-9	B-B	Hyd	1800	103	66	11	1982	Ganz-Mávag	Ganz-Mávag 12 PA 4V-185	Ganz-Mávag H 182-11
DEL 4000	Co-Co	Elec	3880	145	123	10	1982	Electroputere	Electroputere 16 R 251	
MX 636	Co-Co	Elec	3550	149	124	10	1974	MLW Canada	Alco 251 F	
MX 627	Co-Co	Elec	2700	149	120	20	1973	MLW Canada	Alco 251 F	
2000 HP	Co-Co	Elec	2000	120	108	10	1966	Siemens	Maybach MD 870	
CC AD 2100 CI	Co-Co	Elec	2100	105	89·4	26	1967	Alsthom	Pielstick 16 PA 4V 185	
DL543	Co-Co	Elec	2000	120	107	7	1966	Alco	Alco 251 C	
DL500C	Co-Co	Elec	1800	120	107	10	1963	Alco	Alco 251 B	
KM 10B	Bo-Bo	Elec	1065	109	63·5	13	1973	General Electric	Caterpillar D398B	
DL 532B	Bo-Bo	Elec	1050	105	64·6	10	1962	Alco	Alco 251 B	
LDH 70	B-B	Hyd	700	70	48	12	1973	FAUR 23 August	Maybach-Mercedes 820 Bb	Voith
Y60	C	Hyd	650	60	51	30	1962	Krupp	Maybach GT06A	Voith

Guatemala

Guatemala Railways
Ferrocarriles de Guatemala (FEGUA)

9a Ave, 18-03 Zona 1, Guatemala City

Telephone: +50 2 83037
Cable: Ferrocarril

Manager: Fernando A Leal Estévez
Deputy General Manager: Otto rene Celada Corzo
Directors:
 Planning: Ing Carlos A Moino González
 Finance: H Annibal Bonilla
 Operations: O A Peralta Aytala
 Manager, Mechanical: S M Rivas
 Engineering: A Boerseth de V
 Permanent Way: C Camey
 Transport: J César Cordón
 Commercial: A Mérida Pedralta

Gauge: 914 mm
Route length: 782 km

Traffic	1987	1988
Total freight tonnes	581 779	425 847
Total freight tonne-km (million)	78.86	48.18
Total passenger-km (million)	16 249	9 094

Finance (Quetzaks million)	1987	1988
Revenue	17.471	17.608
Expenditure	16.015	17.226

The company, which became state-owned under its present title in 1968, operates 30 diesel and 14 steam locomotives, five three-car diesel railcar sets, 53 passenger cars and 1527 wagons. Recent additions are 10 Type MX620 2000 hp locomotives from Bombardier. The remainder of the locomotives are General Electric built, 15 of 900 hp and five of 400 hp, all with Caterpillar engines.

Commuter line study
In 1988 FEGUA was studying creation of a 28 km commuter line in Guatemala City. The scheme would involve construction of a 10 km cross-town link between existing sections of the railway. Service by railbuses is proposed. Cost of the scheme is estimated to be US$70 million.

Track
Rail: 60 lb/yd
Sleepers: Timber 72 × 8 × 7 in, spaced 1800/km in plain track, 1000/km in curves
Minimum curve radius: 0.25°
Max gradient: 3%
Max permissible axleload: 20 tonnes

Bandegua Railway
Cia de Desarrollo Bananero de Guatemala Ltd

Edificio La Galeria 5° Nivel, 7 Avenue 1444, Zone 9, Guatemala City

Telephone: +502 2 478 026
Manager: Mario O Mena
Director of Engineering: Luis A Martinez V
Transportation Superintendent: Ramiro Arriaga
Mechanical Superintendent: Dionisio Badillo

Gauge: 914 mm
Route length: 102 km

The company operates 11 diesel locomotives, 17 railcars, 18 passenger cars and 106 freight wagons.

Guinea

Chemin de Fer de la Guinée (ONCFG)

PO Box 581, Conakry

Cable: Ofergui

Director: M K Fofana

Gauge: 1000 mm
Route length: 662 km

The railway from Conakry to the River Niger joins the limits of navigability of the Upper Niger (Kouroussa) with the sea port of Conakry on the coast of Guinea. The railway was opened from Conakry as far as Kouroussa in 1910. In 1914, it was extended as far as Kankan, on the River Milo, a tributary of the Niger.

The railway, which crosses the Fouta Djalon mountains on gradients as steep as 2.9 per cent, and with curves of 100–150 m radius, was lightly laid, without ballast, and has consequently deteriorated badly with rising axleloads. Renovation of track and rolling stock under French guidance and with French material began in 1977, but two years later was checked by the second world oil crisis.

Studies had been completed and initial earthworks started on a new 1400 km Trans-Guinea line which would link new bauxite deposits at Tougue and Dabola and the agricultural region of Nimba with the port of Conakry. This, too, was shelved in 1979.

However, with the aid of a credit from CCCE the new government has now ordered a resumption of the rehabilitation, based on 1983 studies by Sofrerail and Transurb Consult. At last report traffic was no higher than 41.5 million passenger-km and 7.3 tonne-km of freight.

Motive power and rolling stock
At last report the motive power fleet included 30 mainline diesel locomotives and 16 diesel railcars. Rolling stock numbered about 20 passenger coaches and 500 freight wagons. However, no recent figures are obtainable and much equipment is reported unserviceable.

Industrial railways
There are three other lines in operation, all serving bauxite deposits. Guinea is the world's second largest exporter of the mineral.

The CF de Friguia, opened in 1960, carries the products of the bauxite mine and aluminium plant at Friguia to the port of Conakry. It is of metre-gauge, 145 km long single-track; laid with 46 kg/m continuous welded rail on metal sleepers. Three Alsthom 1100 hp diesel-electric locomotives hauling 50-tonne load wagons transport some 700 000 tonnes of export per year. Freight car stock totals 61 wagons.

The Boké Railway of the Compagnie des Bauxites de Guinée is a mineral ore line, running 136 km from mines at Boké and Sangaredi to Port Kamsar on the northern coast of Guinea. Built by a consortium of European contractors, the line was inaugurated in 1973.

The first half of the line runs through the coastal sea plain while the upper half reaches into the foothills of the Fouta Djalon mountains. The line is standard gauge with 60 kg/m continuously welded UIC profile rail laid entirely on steel sleepers. The line currently transports some 12 million tonnes annually. Rolling stock comprises 15 US-built diesel locomotives, 425 ore wagons, 39 other freight cars and three passenger cars.

In 1974, with technical and financial assistance from the USSR, the Kindia Bauxites office built a 105 km 1435 mm-gauge line running almost parallel to ONCFG's Conakry-Kankan line. The former moves 2.5 million tonnes a year to a new mineral quay at Conakry.

Honduras

Honduras National Railway (FNH)
Ferrocarril Nacional de Honduras

1 calle O, No 2, PO Box 496, San Pedro Sula

Telephone: +504 53 3230/4080

General Manager: E Vitanza Funez
Assistant Manager: J A Vaquero
Supply Manager: A Suazo Matute
Chief of Commercial Services: J Blas Mayen
Trainmaster: J D Rosales
Superintendent: L Miranda
Director of Operations and Maintenance:
  A Escobar Sandoval

Gauge: 1067 mm; 914 mm
Length: 318 km; 277 km

FNH operates 318 km of its 1067 mm-gauge system and the 190 km railway formerly operated by Tela R R Co. The 914 mm system's operation by the Standard Fruit Co terminated at the end of 1983, when FNH took over control.

Traction and rolling stock on the 1067 mm-gauge comprises two steam, eight diesel-hydraulic and 24 diesel-electric locomotives, 37 passenger cars, 22 railcars or railbuses and 1960 freight cars. The 914 mm-gauge is operated with 19 diesel-electric and four diesel-mechanical locomotives, 25 passenger and 751 freight cars.

New lines
In 1983 the government agreed to a major enlargement of the 1067 mm-gauge system, likely to cost US$100 million. Its central features are new lines from Puerto Castilla on the Caribbean to Sonaguera and from Arenal to Bonito Oriental on the Pacific, a total of some 350 route-km. The existing line between Sonaguera and Arenal is to be upgraded to match the extensions.

The end result will be a new coast-to-coast railway, which the government hopes can be built on terms that will remunerate the contractors' costs out of revenue. The contractors will be required to supply 12 locomotives and undertake staff training and operation. A good deal of the new line's traffic will be the Standard Fruit Company's now containerised banana exports.

Construction of a further new line of 97 km, from the banana traffic centre of San Pedro Sula to Yoro, on the route of the projected new Arenal-Bonito Oriental line, was started in 1983.

FNH is also anxious to develop short suburban lines in Tegucigalpa and San Pedro Sula.

Tela Railroad Company

Apartado Postal No 30, San Pedro Sula, Cortes

Telephone: +504 56 2018
Telex: 8305 trr co ho
Telefax: +504 56 2435

General Manager: K F Koch
Operations Manager: Miguel Chock
Controller: A J De Cicco
Superintendent: Gustavo Collart
Manager, Technical Services: C Fúnez
Purchases: J S Hernandez

Gauge: 1067 mm
Route length: 190 km

The railway is operated with 28 diesel locomotives, 18 railcars, 70 passenger cars and 1324 freight wagons. Rail installed is ASCE 50, 60, 70, 75 lb, minimum curve radius 3 degrees, maximum gradient 0.62 per cent and maximum axleloading 6.82 tonnes.

Traffic in 1989 totalled 1.069 million tonnes of freight and 771 600 passenger journeys.

Hong Kong

Kowloon-Canton Railway (British Section KCR)

KCR House, Sha Tin, New Territories, Hong Kong

Telephone: +852 0 6069333
Cable: Hongrail
Telex: 51666 kcrc hx
Telefax: +852 0 6951168

Chairman: H M G Forsgate
Directors
  Managing: Kevin Hyde
  Heavy Rail: A I McPherson
  Planning and Freight: Clement B T Chiu
  Light Rail: Jonathan H G Yu
Managers:
  Property: Dominic Lau
  Buses: David Hassey
  Human Resources: Richard Alves
  Corporate Affairs: Samuel Lai
  Public Affairs: Barry Choi

Gauge: 1435 mm
Route length: 34 km
Electrification: 34 km at 25 kV 50 Hz ac

The British Section of the Kowloon-Canton (Guangzhou) Railway (KCR), built in 1910, links Kowloon with the Chinese frontier city of Shum Chun (Shenzhen). It is basically a suburban railway catering mainly for internal commuting needs, but it also serves millions of passengers crossing the border at Lo Wu and boarding the Guangzhou-bound trains at Shenzhen. Mail and freight are conveyed across the border without transhipment.

The Kowloon-Canton Railway Corporation is a statutory body wholly owned by the government, but required to operate on full commercial principles. In 1990, following some controversy, the government decided to exercise greater control. It was announced that when the terms of office of the Chairman and Managing Director expired at the end of 1990, they would be replaced by a full-time Chairman acting as Chief Executive and reporting to the Hong Kong Transport Secretary.

Since July 1983 the whole line has been served by electric trains, following the substantial completion of the five-year, HK$3500 million modernisation and electrification programme which comprised double-tracking and electrification of the entire length and redevelopment and/or remodelling of all the stations. The KCR interchanges with the underground Mass

KCR emu by Metro-Cammell with GEC Traction power equipment at Lo Wu, the Chinese border terminal

Interior of KCR emu

Transit Railway at Kowloon Tong station, forming the backbone of the territory-wide mass transport network.

Traffic
Since the introduction of electric train service passenger traffic has increased from about 40 000 journeys a day prior to electrification of the first stage in May 1982 to some 511 000 daily. It is projected that traffic will reach 500 000 daily in the early 1990s.

About 24 freight trains operate daily, 12 in each direction. Freight traffic is exclusively conveyed in wagons belonging to China.

Following completion in China of double-tracking of the main line between Beijing and Guangzhou in November 1988, opportunity for expansion of freight traffic is envisaged in the coming years. Container traffic growth has been stimulated by acquisition of a superstacker for Kowloon yard.

Rolling stock
All passenger service on the railway, with the exception of through train service to Guangzhou, is operated by emus. During the morning and evening peak periods, trains run at 4-minute intervals to Tai Po Market, at 5-minute intervals to Sheung Shui and at 15-minute intervals to Lo Wu. Journey times have been roughly halved since electrification, so that the 34 km run from Kowloon to Lo Wu takes 37 minutes.

The through train service between Kowloon and Guangzhou is operated in conjunction with the Guangzhou Railway Administration. Its diesel-hauled trains provide air-conditioned soft-seating. Four trains are operated each way daily, and the journey takes about 2¼ hours from Kowloon to Guangzhou.

Rolling stock in 1989 consisted of 85 three-car electric multiple-units. Trains are of either nine- or 12-car formation.

Delivery began in late 1989 of a further batch of 54 cars to form six-car emus, all supplied by the Metro-Cammell arm of GEC-Alsthom at a cost of HK$360 million. By comparison with earlier units these have fewer seats and more standing room, so that their carrying capacity is 10 per cent greater; all earlier cars are now to be similarly modified. The latest deliveries, raising the emu car total to 309, lift KCR's overall passenger carrying capacity by a further 25 per cent. In mid-1989 it was decided to exercise KRC's option on a further 42 new cars, costing $350 million, for delivery by end-1992.

The system also operates 12 diesel locomotives and 70 freight wagons.

To cope with the large increases in rolling stock and to more effectively undertake maintenance work, a HK$ 1000 million redevelopment of the workshop and depot facilities at Ho tung Lau was commenced in 1989.

Possible extension
In 1989 a feasibility study was conducted into extension of the railway from Hung Hum across the harbour to create through service from the New Territories and Kowloon to Hong Kong Island without intermediate change of transport mode.

Signalling and telecommunications
A modern electronically-controlled and fully track circuited colour-light signalling system is in use, operated from a combined signalling and electrical control centre at Kowloon station. The system incorporates remote control of outlying interlocking installations, train describer equipment and an automatic warning system (AWS) operating on all locomotives and electric trains. The train describer operates a platform indicator system for passenger information. Trains are one-man-operated, with the back-up of train-to-control centre radio communication. The control centre can also broadcast to passengers on board, while passengers can speak to the driver in emergency through an intercom.

Light Rail Transit System
The Corporation has also constructed and now operates a light rail transit (LRT) system in the Northwestern New Territories (for further details see Rapid Transit section).

Emu maintenance depot

Finance (HK$000)	1986	1987	1988	1989
Revenue from operations	733 992	964 186	1 195 617	1 359 000
Operating profit before depreciation and interest charges	306 706	465 458	595 545	604 000
Depreciation	110 508	115 027	165 398	207 000
Interest charges	82 068	74 378	106 308	112 000
Profit after charging interest and depreciation	117 130	276 053	323 839	285 000
Profit on property development	—	—	238 853	1
Profit for the year	117 130	276 053	562 692	286 000
Accumulated profit/(loss) at 31 December	(47 445)	228 608	791 300	1 077 300

Traffic	1986	1987	1988	1989
Freight tonnage (000)	4203	4580	4528	4500
Freight tonne-km (million)	133.996	145.440	144.498	140 188
Passenger-km (million)	1907.7	2190.5	2284.0	2402.3
Passenger journeys (million)	116.0	136.5	152.6	171

Coupler in standard use
Passenger cars: AAR coupler between units; bar coupler between cars
Freight cars: AAR coupler

Braking in standard use, locomotive-hauled stock:
Air

Track
Rail: UIC 54 (54 kg/m)
Cross ties (sleepers): Prestressed concrete, 203 mm thick, spaced 700 mm centre to centre
Rail fastenings: Pandrol rail clip, Type PR429A with Pandrol glass reinforced nylon insulators
Minimum curvature radius: Main line 200 m
  Sidings 140 m
Max gradient: 1 in 100
Max speed: 120 km/h throughout
Max axleload: 25 tonnes

Diesel-electric locomotives

Manufacturer's type reference	Wheel arrangement	Transmission	Rated power (kW)	Max speed km/h	Total weight tonnes	No in service 1989	Year first built	Engine	Builders
Clyde-GM Model G12-1125	Bo-Bo	Elec	843	100	71	2	1954	EMD 12-567C	The Clyde Engineering Co Pty Ltd, Australia
Clyde-GM Model G12-1310	Bo-Bo	Elec	983	100	72	3	1957	EMD 12-567C	The Clyde Engineering Co Pty Ltd, Australia
General Motors Model G-16-1800	Co-Co	Elec	1350	100	98.3	3	1961	EMD 16-567C	Electro-Motive Division, General Motors Corporation, USA
General Motors Model G-18-1950	Co-Co	Elec	1463	100	98.5	1	1965	EMD 16-567C	The Clyde Engineering Co Pty Ltd, Australia
G-26-CU-2000	Co-Co	Elec	1500	100	98	1	1973	EMD 16-645E	Electro-Motive Division, General Motors Corporation, USA
G-26-CU-2200	Co-Co	Elec	1650	100	98	2	1976	EMD 16-645E	Electro-Motive Division, General Motors Corporation, USA

RAILWAY SYSTEMS / Hong Kong—Hungary

Electric railcars or multiple-units

Class	Cars per unit	Line voltage	Motor cars per unit	Motored axles per motor car	Rated output (kW) per motor	Max speed km/h	Weight tonnes per car (M-motor T-trailer)	Total seating capacity per car (M-motor T-trailer)	Length per car mm (M-motor T-trailer)	No of sets in service 1989	Rate of acceleration m/s²	Year first built	Builders Mechanical parts	Builders Electrical equipment
Type A (tap-changer control)	3	25 kV 50 Hz, single phase	1	2	228 kW 700 V 350 A 2092 rpm	120	Tare mass MC 52 DT 33 BDT 35	MC 78 DT 66 BDT 66	Over couplers MC 24 136 BDT-DT 24 481	37	0.5	1981	Metro-Cammell	GEC Traction
Type B (tap-changer control)	3	25 kV 50 Hz single phase	1	2	228 kW 700 V 350 A 2092 rpm	120	Tare mass MC 52 DT 33 BDT 35	MC 78 DTC 56 BDT 66	Over couplers MC 24 136 DTC/BDT 24 481	23	0.5	1981	Metro-Cammell	GEC Traction
Type C (thyristor-control)	3	25 kV 50 Hz single phase	1	2	228 kW 700 V 350 A 2092 rpm	120	Tare mass MC 52 DT 33 BDT 35	MC 78 DT 66 BDT 66	Over couplers MC 24 136 BDT/DT 24 481	43	0.5	1987	Metro-Cammell	GEC Traction

Hungary

Ministry of Transport, Communications & Construction

PO Box 87, Dob utca 75-81, Budapest 1400

Telephone: +36 1 22 0220
Telex: 225 729 h
Telefax: +36 1 22 8695

Minister of Transport: András Derzsi
Department Head, Transport: G Kalman
  International: P Bánhalmi
  Technical: A Katona

Hungarian State Railways (MÁV)
Magyar Államvasutak

Népköztársaság utja 73-75, 1940 Budapest VI

Telephone: +36 1 22 0660
Telex: 224342 mavvi
Telefax: +36 1 42 8596

President & General Manager: Dipl Ing Lajos Urbán

Chief Assistant General Manager: Béla Szemök
Assistant General Manager, Finance:
  András Ambrus
  Operations: András Mészáros
  Technical: László Tóth
Chief of Secretariat: J Németh
Chief of International Section: Dr Gábor Bessenyei
Departmental Managers
  Economics: M Bodor
  Technical: B Maráz
  Operating: Z Rigò
  Construction and Track Maintenance: J Pàl
  Traction and Rolling Stock: I Tongori
  Signals and Telecommunications: L Fülöp
  Commercial: I Egri
  Financial: A Benczédi
  Organisation: K Árva
  Personnel: G Dobos
  Administration: Dr I Jánosi
  Supplies: L Alberti

Gauge: 1524 mm; 1435; 760 mm
Route length: 35 km; 7408 km; 176 km
Electrification: 2129 km at 25 kV 50 Hz ac

Centred on Budapest, railway lines radiate to all sectors of Hungary, providing international connections with Austria, Czechoslovakia, Soviet Union, Romania and Yugoslavia.

At the start of the 1970s MÁV analysis showed that some 2300 route-km of the system then existing was carrying only 3 per cent of passenger and 1 per cent of freight traffic and by 1982 about 1700 km of the lines concerned had been shut. At that juncture plans for further closures were rescinded on ecological and energy conservation grounds, also because of

Class V63 electric locomotive and inter-city train alongside new BDv emu

Interior of special first-class 'comfort' car, buit by MÁV workshops in 1987 and employed on EuroCity trains

restricted investment in highways. Scarcely any new lines have been built since 1945, except to serve industrial premises.

Traffic

A downward trend in MÁV passenger traffic, notably in short-haul journeys, which have dropped by more than 150 million a year since 1970, was arrested in 1989. But in the first half of 1990 MÁV was hit hard by the inflationary aftermath of political change. With traffic down by 15 per cent on the same period of 1989 and an annual loss of 1500 million forints (largely due to uneconomic passenger fares) aggravated by bad debts totalling 6500 million forints, MÁV discontinued 300 daily passenger and freight trains at the end of May.

MÁV joined the Western European EuroCity system with the May 1988 conferring of this status on the Vienna-Budapest 'Lehar'. A second EC link was forged in May 1989 by creation of the Dortmund-Budapest 'Franz Liszt'. Each service features MÁV special-category cars offering a parlour-type service.

Train catering on MÁV is performed by Utasellato, a company created in 1948, which in 1990 became a division of MÁV. It operates 29 restaurant, 64 buffet, 29 sleeping and 48 couchette cars. Utasellato also runs 295 station restaurants and buffets.

In the freight sector imports, exports and transit traffic together represent 56 per cent of all MÁV tonne-km, which are about half the national freight total. Private sidings generate 53 per cent of all tonnage and almost 40 per cent of the total moves in unit trains.

To offset the drop in heavy industrial traffic, the main cause of a downward trend in tonnage, rail container movement is being fostered both by discounted MÁV tariffs and by national bank aid for terminal mechanisation. It was expected to have container handling facilities at 66 stations in 1990.

MÁV opened its first piggyback terminal at Szeged in 1987 and the *Rollende Landstrasse* operations between Germany and Austria was extended into Hungary in 1988.

A new marshalling yard with Dowty hydraulic retarders has been created at Székesfehérvár. However, a speed-control system by Elin-Union of Austria has been installed at Budapest Ferencvaros yard, the Hungarian hub of the Trans-Europ Express Marchandises (TEEM) system.

Profitability study

With deregulation of the country's road transport in prospect, and stagnant demand for transport, MÁV in 1989 commissioned Western European consultants to advise on measures to make the railway financially self-supporting. At present MÁV has no rate-making freedom. As a result its passenger services cover only 40 per cent of their costs. That is the chief factor in the deficit and lack of investment resources. MÁV wants not only commercial freedom but also a state takeover of its infrastructure with responsibility for cost and investment, and a clear determination of state responsibility for financing unprofitable passenger services that are considered a social necessity.

A new top-level management was to be appointed in August 1990. It would be charged to carry out a five-year reorganisation, aimed to adjust MÁV to the new economic environment.

Investment

In the 1980s MÁV investments were limited. Available funds were used to modernise tracks for greater axleloads and to upgrade former secondary routes which have international significance, such as Hatvan-Szolnok-Lökösháza and Kiskunfélegy-Háza-Kiskunhalas; to install more safety equipment, such as telecommunications, as this enlarged the capacity of the railway and saved labour; for a start on reconstruction of several large marshalling yards and junctions; to extend electrification and eliminate steam traction; to extend the use of computers, first at border stations; and to take a major step in freight containerisation.

Much of the MÁV funding under the railway's 1986–90 plan went towards rebuilding, modernising and automating the Ferencvaros East yard in Budapest, to end some of the present diffusion of work among several yards in the capital. The Budapest yard, its operating capacity now raised by 50 per cent, processes 90–110 trains a day through its 32 sorting sidings.

Five container terminals were modernised under the 1986-90 plan and the rest of the money spent chiefly on track maintenance equipment, track renewals and traction maintenance. A prime objective of the programme was to enhance the railway's capability to deal competitively with international transit freight traffic and to develop intermodal freight (see above).

MÁV is concerned in the 1990s to become compatible with the latest techniques, technologies and capabilities of western European rail operation. Key objectives are electrification of the whole trunk line network, totalling about 4000 route-km; elimination of operational bottlenecks; development of signalling and traffic control; and connection with the electronic data transmission systems of other railways. Additional passenger transport capacity is required for the Expo 95 which Vienna and Budapest are jointly mounting.

To obtain hard currency for faster modernisation, MÁV has been urging Western European interests to invest in its manufacturing subsidiaries. The railway is getting a share of a second World Bank loan for development of Hungary's transport.

Part of this World Bank aid is going towards a computerised management information system. This is to provide real-time data on traction and vehicle movements, marshalling yard operation and wagon distribution as well as fulfil cost accounting functions. Some 800 terminals throughout the railway will be linked to it.

New Type BDv emu with asynchronous motors built by Ganz-Hunslet in 1988; unit comprises a power car and three trailers

Budapest Ferencváros East yard under reconstruction

Finance (million forints)
Revenues

Passengers and baggage	10 594	12 374
Freight, parcels and mail	30 996	34 303
Other income	8 062	9 395
Total	49 652	56 072

Expenditure

Staff/personnel	16 817	20 527
Materials and services	22 080	23 491
Depreciation	7 402	7 596
Financial charges	3 213	4 107
Total	49 512	55 721

Traffic (million)	1985	1986	1987	1988	1989
Pasenger journeys	232	230	227	223.7	225
Passenger-km	11 093	11 106	11 206	11 395	11 762
Freight tonnes	116.9	118.5	114.8	111.3	104.2
Freight tonnes-km	21 929	22 213	21 387	20 737	19 528

RAILWAY SYSTEMS / Hungary

Electrification

Under its 1986–90 electrification plan MÁV planned to wire almost 400 route-km more, with electrification of the sections from Börgönd to Pusztaszabolcs, Budapest to Balatonszentgyörgy (by November 1989 wires had reached Fonyod, not far from the objective), Gyékényes to Dombóvár, and Sárbogárd to Komárom. Budapest-Balatonszentgyörgy is the first step in electrifying the main line from Budapest throughout to Nagykanisza and Gyékényes, in the south-west, near the Yugoslav border, where the wires should reach in 1990. East of Budapest, electrification is planned to Hidasnémeti and Somoskoújfalu (on the Czechoslovak border), and to Biharkeresztes (on the Romanian frontier). After 1990 lines in the west of the country will be the focus of electrification work, forecast to cover a further 1000 km.

Civil engineering

Under the 1986–90 programme about 1000 km of track was being upgraded for axleloads of more than 20 tonnes. Five main lines were the priority: Budapest-Hegyeshalom; Budapest-Miskolc; Budapest-Szolnok-Zahony; Szolnok-Békéscsaba; and Budapest-Pusztaszabolcs. All new rails are 54.3 kg/m laid on prestressed concrete sleepers with a ballast depth of 500 mm. Minimum curve radius is 1300 metres and normal top speed is 140 km/h.

Major renovation work was recently completed on the line from Budapest to Hegyeshalom on the frontier with Austria, involving modernisation of seven stations between Nagyszentjanos and Hegyeshalom. As part of the same exercise, the 60 km stretch was relaid and new safety equipment installed to allow for 140 km/h operation.

A major remodelling scheme was begun at Budapest Kelesti station in 1987 and completed in 1989. Traffic has outpaced the station's passenger handling and train operating capacity. Platforms have been lengthened and the number of tracks raised from 11 to 12; a single signalbox, employing computer technology, has replaced two Siemens electro-mechanical installations of 1924 vintage. Of the city's four main stations, only Budapest-Nyugati remains to be modernised.

Traction and rolling stock

A new version of the Type V63 Co-Co electric locomotive is now expected to emerge in 1992-3. The 50 examples built by Ganz-Mávag since 1975 have been 3600 kW machines of only 100 km/h maximum speed. Later examples have had thyristor control. The new model developed by Ganz-Mávag and Ganz Electric will have three-phase asynchronous motors, weigh only 80 tonnes, be rated at 5000 kW, and have a maximum speed of 160 km/h.

Hitherto MÁV has relied entirely on push-pull practice in its suburban passenger operations, but a change is now in prospect.

Ganz-Mávag was commissioned by Ganz-Hunslet Ltd in 1987 to produce a prototype outer suburban emu, and two prototypes, classified BDVmot, were turned out for trial service in 1988. Each consists of a 25 kV ac power car with a 1520 kW rating, two intermediate trailers and a control trailer; maximum speed is 120 km/h, total weight 191 tonnes and seating capacity 356. The power car has two body-mounted asynchronous three-phase motors with thyristor control driving one bogie via a cardan shaft transmission, and has regenerative braking. In August 1988 the Transport Minister announced that the company would build up to 200 emus for MÁV. A first batch of 60 sets would be built for Budapest local services, and 20 of these were to be delivered in 1990.

A 160 km/h inter-city emu is under development and a prototype is expected to emerge in 1992.

Coaching stock standardisation is now complete. The fleet comprises compartment cars built in Poland or the German Democratic Republic, open cars built locally by Györ or Dunakeszi and employed in push-pull sets, 42 Ganz-built six-car push-pull sets used on intercity services and known as *Piroska* ('red hats') by virtue of their livery, Ganz five-axle railcars and two-axle Tatra-Studenka diesel railbuses and trailers.

At the end of 1989 MÁV was operating 467 electric locomotives, 1063 diesel locomotives, 4 emus, 248 dmus, 4512 hauled passenger cars (including 93 buffet/dining, 77 sleeper/couchette, 29 special and 262 baggage cars) and 69 340 freight cars.

ELIN-Thyssen hydraulic retarders in Budapest Ferencváros East yard

Control console of Budapest Ferencváros East yard

Diesel locomotives

Class (Railway's own designation)	Manufacturers type reference	Wheel arrangement	Transmission	Rated power kW	Max speed km/h	Total weight tonnes	Length mm	No in service 1989	Year first built	Builders Mechanical parts	Builders Engine & type	Builders Transmission
M28	Rába M033	B	Mechn	100	30	20	7 390	25	1955	Rába	Ganz	Rába
M31	DHM2	C	Hyd	330	60	45	9 830	38	1958	Mávag	Ganz	Voith
M32	DHM6	C	Hyd	260	60	36	9 510	55	1973	Mávag	Ganz	Ganz
M40	DVM6	Bo-Bo	Elec	440	100	75·6	13 590	77	1966	Mávag	Ganz	Ganz Elec. W.
M41	DHM7	B-B	Hyd	1320	100	66	15 500	114	1973	Mávag	Pielstick/Ganz	Voith/Ganz
M43	LDH45	B-B	Hyd	330	60	48	11 460	161	1974	Aug 23	Aug 23	Brasso Hydrom.
M44	DVM2	Bo-Bo	Elec	440	80	62	11 290	188	1956	Mávag	Ganz	Ganz Elec. W.
M47	LDH70	B-B	Hyd	520	70	48	11 460	111	1974	Aug 23	Aug 23	Brasso Hydrom.
M61	M60	Co-Co	Elec	1430	100	108	18 900	16	1963	Nohab	GM	GM
M62	M62	Co-Co	Elec	1470	100	120	17 560	272	1965	Lugansk	Kolomna	Charkov
M63	DVM10	Co-Co	Elec	2200	130	120	19 540	6	1971	Mávag	Pielstick	Ganz Elec. W.

Signalling

Almost 27 per cent of the system is equipped with automatic colour-light signalling and modern Integral signalling centres have been installed at numerous stations. Track-to-train radio is operational on 1400 km of the radial routes from Budapest. CTC has been installed on the busy 50 km single line from Szerencs to Nviregyháza and is being applied to the 67 km from Budapest to Székesfehérvar. In the 1986–90 plan automatic block was extended to a further 400 km and CTC to an additional 400–500 km. Elin Union of Austria has been contracted to resignal the Ferencváros area of Budapest, work on which began in 1987.

Track

Rail: 54 or 48 kg/m, in some places lighter
Sleepers: concrete and timber. Length, 242cm; height, 19cm; width, base, 28cm; width, top, 20cm.
Minimum curve radius: 1300m for 140 km/h top speed; 1700m for 160 km/h top speed
Maximum gradient: 1.7% **Maximum permissible axleload:** 24 tonnes.

Diesel railcars or multiple-units

Class (Railway's own designation)	Manufacturer's type reference	No of cars per unit	No of motor cars per unit	No of motored axles per motor car	Transmission	Rated power (kW) per motor	Max speed	Weight tonnes per car (M-motor T-trailer)	Total seating capacity per car (M-motor T-trailer)	Length per car mm (M-motor T-trailer)	No in service 1989	Year first built	Builders Mechanical parts	Builders Engine & type	Builders Transmission
Bz mot	Bz mot	2	1	1	Hydro-mech	140	70	M19 T15	M55 T55	M13970 T13970	206	1977	Vagonka Studenka	Rába Man	Praha
MD mot†	MDa	5	1	4	Hydro-mech	590	100	M41 T30	M-T80	M15520 T22400	42	1969	Mávag	Ganz	Ganz

† Power units of *Piroska* sets

Electric locomotives

Class (Railway's own designation)	Manufacturer's type reference	Wheel arrangement	Line voltage AckV	Rated output kW continuous/one-hour	Motor and control type	Max speed km/h	Weight tonnes	Overall length mm	No in service 1989	Year first built	Builders Mechanical parts	Builders Electrical equipment	Remarks special features
V43	VM14	B-B	25	2200	dc. tr.	130	80	15 700	366	1964	Mávag	Ganz Elec. W	
V46	VM16	Bo-Bo	25	800	dc. tr.	80	80	14 440	45	1983	Mávag	Ganz Elec. W	
V63	VM15	Co-Co	25	3680	dc. tr.	130	116	19 600	56	1975	Mávag	Ganz Elec. W	

Electric railcars or multiple-units

Class (Railway's own designation)	Manufacturer's type reference	No of cars per unit	Line voltage	No of motor cars per unit	No of motored axles per motor car	Rated output (kW)	Motor and control type	Max speed km/h	Weight tonnes per car (M-motor T-trailer)	Total seating capacity per car (M-motor T-trailer)	Length per car mm (M-motor T-trailer)	No in service 1989	Rate of acceleration m/s²	Year first built	Builders Mechanical parts	Builders Electrical equipment
BDV	BDV	4	25	1	4	722	Three Phase Ac. Drive	120	65/41	64/96	24 600 26 400	4	0·6	1988	Ganz-Hunslet RT	Ganz Elec. W.

Györ-Sopron-Ebenfurt Railway (GySEV)
Györ-Sopron-Ebenfurti-Vasut

Szilágyi Dezsö-tér 1, Budapest 1011 1

Telephone: +36 1 388 103/144/536/548/720/977

General Manager: László Oroszváry
Deputy General Manager: Dr József Szigeti

Managers
Finance: Dr Lászlo Fehérváry
Commercial and Operating: Dipl-Ing Dr Géza Bódy
Engineering: Dipl-Ing Csaba Siklós

Gauge: 1435 mm
Route length: 84 km (Hungary), 82 km (Austria)
Electrification: 166 km at 25 kV 50 Hz ac

The Austrian and Hungarian components of this international link are under separate operational management. The railway own 2 steam, 12 electric and 19 diesel locomotives, 61 passenger cars and 466 freight wagons.

Traffic

The railway handles some 5 million tonnes of freight a year, 70 per cent of it international. Key freight centre is Sopron, where the recently modernised yard processes 500 wagons daily and there is a big container terminal. The railway, now electrified throughout, can accept wagons of 25 tonnes maximum axleload.

India

Indian Railway Board (IR)
Rail Bhavan, Raisina Road, New Delhi 110 001

Telephone: +91 388931-41
Cable: Railways, New Delhi
Telex: 031 3561

Minister of Railways: George Fernandes
Chairman: Madhavan Narayan Prasad
Railway Board Members
  Engineering: Y P Anand
  Electrical: V C V Chenulu
  Mechanical: Anup Singh
  Traffic: C M Khosla
  Staff: N Mitra
  Finance: S K Mitra

Advisers
  Industrial Relations: Vacant
  Metro Transport Projects: S S Narayan
  Finance: R M Vakil
Executive Directors
  Electrical Engineering: K R Vij
  Mechanical Engineering: M K Rao
  Finance: S S Goyal
  Traffic, Commercial: M S Bhandari
  Transportation: C M Khosla
  Stores: Dr J P Char
  Railway Electrification: A S Sant
  Management Services: M Kapoor
  Planning: H K L Jaggi
  Signalling and Telecommunications: O P Jain
  Telecommunications Development: P S Sampathkumaran
  Civil Engineering: J S Mundrey
  Statistics and Economics: S M Puri
  Accounts: S K N Nair
  Workshops: P L Rawal
  Works, Projects: V S Dutta
  Track: Y V Aswathanarayara
  Track Procurement: B S Agarwal
  Track Modernisation: S P Singh
  Traction: S Ramanathan
  Rolling Stock Engineering: O F H Jung
  Rolling Stock Modernisation: H P Mittal
  Coaching: K K Arora
  Operations Information Services: R D Saklani
Manufacturing Units
  Chittaranjan Locomotive Works: V K Fondekar
  Diesel Locomotive Works: R C Sethi
  Integral Coach Factory: Satish Bahl
  Wheel and Axle Plant: Vacant
Research, Design and Standards Organisation
  Director General: D N Singh

RAILWAY SYSTEMS / India

Chief Officers
 Workshops Modernisation: R K Sabharwal
 Diesel Component Works: R C Sethi
General Managers, Construction Units
 Calcutta Metro: A S Argarwal
 Railways: M R Ranganath
 Central Organisation, Electrification:
  V Ramaswamy

Gauge: 1676 mm; 1000 mm; 762 mm; 610 and 762 mm
Route length: 33 831 km; 23 898 km; 4246 km
Electrification: Total 8900 km; on 1676 mm-gauge 8249 km at 25 kV 50 Hz ac, 405 m at 1.5 kV dc; 166 km of 1000 mm-gauge at 25 kV 50 Hz ac

Indian Railways, organised as a central government undertaking, is Asia's largest and the world's second largest state-owned railway system under unitary management.

The railway is made up of nine zonal systems: Central, Eastern, Northern, North Eastern, Northeast Frontier, Southern, South Central, South Eastern, and Western.

Demand unchecked
IR confronts serious problems of adjustment to rising demand for efficient rail transport, undertaking just over two-thirds of all Indian freight movement. The crux is that its cash and physical resources cannot cope with the need for capacity expansion throughout its network and in its ancillary services, such as workshops.

Electrification, track doubling and resignalling on key routes are priorities to augment operating capacity. Since 1950 doubling has been carried out over almost 10 000 route-km.

About 85 per cent of IR's total originating freight is moved on 1676 mm-gauge lines, so there is no economic case for a massive programme of gauge conversion. Moreover, it now costs 75 per cent of the bill for a new line, so it is ordered only where break-of-gauge transhipment is heavy, or traffic is overtaxing the narrower-gauge lines. Elsewhere narrow-gauge tracks are being reinforced to withstand 12–14 tonne axleloads. It is also hoped to raise maximum metre-gauge speed to 120 km/h.

For the 1985–90 period of the seventh five-year plan IR was allowed more than double the capital spending budgeted under the previous plan, RS 123 000 million as against RS 50 000 million. The figure for FY 1988-89 was RS 38 500 million.

The actual growth of traffic during the first two years of the seventh plan was higher than anticipated. On a mid-term review, it was expected that the originating loading in 1989–90 might reach 348 million tonnes with an average haul of 730 km against 340 million tonnes and 680 km. But in the event the 1989–90 budget set targets of 316 million tonnes and 252 000 million tonne-km. Increase in loading was expected for most commodities, the maximum being in the case of coal.

In the original seventh plan document, it had been stipulated that in view of the scarce resource position, priority would be given to freight traffic: passenger traffic demand should be contained. Thus provision was made for a modest growth of 2 per cent per annum only in respect of non-suburban passengers. Actual growth of traffic was, however, much higher during the first two years of the plan.

Investment plans cut back
IR had prepared a Corporate Plan for 1985–2000 providing for traffic levels by the century's end of: 370–400 000 million net freight tonne-km; 310–330 000 million non-suburban passenger-km; and 105–110 000 million suburban passenger-km. The Plan, which had been costed at Rs 461 500 million, had been approved by the Gandhi government's Railways Minister. Most of the money was earmarked for traction and rolling stock.

IR expected to generate just over half the total from its own resources. The plan envisaged acquisition of 4000 locomotives, 38 000 passenger cars and 310 000 freight wagons; track renewal of over 54 000 km by 1995; workshop modernisation; and more gauge conversion to 1676 mm and double-tracking.

In pursuance of these objectives IR submitted a 1990–95 Five-Year Plan to the newly-elected National Front coalition government proposing a Rs 414 000 million investment. However, asserting a tightness of funds, the Railways Minister cut this proposed outlay back to Rs 365 000 million. Acquisition of new traction and rolling stock would remain a priority, and a further 12 000 km of track would be renewed.

Class WCAM-1 dual voltage Co-Co

Traffic	1984/85	1985/86	1986/87	1987/88
Freight tonnes (million)	264.8	286.4	277.75	319
Freight tonne-km (million)	182 161	205 904	223 097	230 000
Passenger journeys (million)	3333	3433	3580	0
Passenger-km (million)	226 582	240 614	256 468	268 000

Revenues

(Rs million)	1984/85	1985/86	1986/87
Passengers and baggage	14 750.7	19 301.4	22 344.4
Freight, parcels and mail	37 659.2	43 763.8	51 332.4
Other income	12 416.5	1215.8	1379.8
Total	53 656.4	64 428.1	75 056.6

Expenditure	1984/85	1985/86	1986/87
Staff/personnel, materials and services	40 933	46 529.5	53 005.6
Depreciation	8500	9200	12 500
Financial charges	6179.3	6876.3	NA
Total	55 612.3	62 605.8	NA

Finance
IR's 1990-91 budget estimated a surplus of Rs 1860 million. The government's support of expenditure would be 28.4 per cent, the lowest share yet. Achievement of the surplus would be facilitated by a rise in freight tariffs and first-class passenger fares. Freight generates 70 per cent of IR's traffic revenue.

Traffic
Since 1950 IR's passenger traffic, measured in journeys, has jumped over 70 per cent. Assessed in passenger-km of non-suburban rail travel, the growth during the same period has been as much as 200 per cent, almost all of it in second-class, as first-class passengers have gravitated to other modes since the mid-1960s. This prompted the new Railways Minister in early 1990 to require IR to build exclusively second-class cars after its outstanding orders for first-class vehicles had been fulfilled. Length of journey, too, has steadily increased. Though the efficiency of other modes has substantially improved and their competition has become much keener in recent years, IR still commands 40 per cent of the total national passenger travel market and analysts expect that the railway's passenger-km will rise to 300 000 million by the end of the century.

Passenger services
Lack of line capacity has become an acute problem on key routes, such as parts of that between Delhi and Bombay where the annual gross is some 20 million tonnes a year. This problem has been tackled by increasing many express and mail train loads to 21–24 cars with, in some cases, double-heading.

The capacity problem has also been attacked by raising vehicle seating and berth space. Bi-level day cars offering 146 seats each were introduced successfully between Bombay and Pune in 1983 and have been subsequently approved for more widespread use.

The flagship twice-weekly 'Rajdhani Express' between Bombay and New Delhi was India's first fully air-braked, air-conditioned passenger train. Accelerated by half-an-hour at the start of 1990, following electrification throughout the route, it now covers the 1384 km in 16 hours 15 minutes. The latest WAP-1 3000 kW Co-Co electric locomotives featuring Flexicoil bogies and axle-hung, Alsthom-designed motors can be operated at a maximum speed of 130 km/h. The general limit on the Bombay-Delhi route the limit is 120 km/h, but over most of the IR 1676 mm-gauge network speed is restricted to 110 km/h.

With the back-up of AWS, IR has lately raised the limit to 140 km/h on the Delhi-Jhansi section and has ordered a 160 km/h electric train-set for trial between Delhi and Kanpur. An air-conditioned chair car design for this speed has been completed. The Japanese International Corporation Agency has been commissioned to conduct a feasibility study of a high-speed line in the Delhi-Agra-Kanpur corridor. On the Southern Railway, maximum metre-gauge passenger train speed has been lifted from 100 to 110 km/h. The metre-gauge limit generally is 75 km/h, however.

In FY 1987–88 IR logged 3792 million passenger journeys and 269 389 million passenger-km.

To augment existing passenger car production, construction of a new factory planned ultimately to turn out 1100 cars a year has been completed at Karpurthala, in the Punjab. Two prototype cars with 200 km/h operational capability have already been built and new designs evolved at Kapurthala may well be conceived for 225 km/h.

IR is building new passenger terminals in the key cities. They will be at Kurla and Bandra in Bombay; Shalimar in Calcutta; and Nizamuddin in Delhi.

Freight services
The chief measures taken to enlarge freight operating capacity (and also to enhance productivity and efficiency) are recourse to more unit train working, block train segregation of high-capacity, roller bearing-equipped wagons and pursuit of as many 4500-tonne

trainloads as are feasible within existing passing loop parameters. Between 90 and 100 per cent of all coal, ore and petroleum product traffic moves in unit trains.

Locotrol II systems, which provide microprocessor-based control of distributed locomotive power, have been supplied by Harris Corporation of the USA to increase train tonnages and alleviate traffic density problems on the North East Frontier and South Eastern Railways. The equipment includes communications and air brake systems for interface with two different locomotive models.

In North Eastern territory, trains use the Locotrol systems with vacuum air brakes, but the systems shipped to the South Eastern Railway, which hauls mainly coal and iron ore, are for air-braked trains. Both installations are equipped with 300 MHz radios for communication between the lead and remote locomotives. PC-based simulators are also included to test electronics modules, which are part of the Locotrol system.

In 1986-87 IR crossed the 300 million-tonne mark for the first time. In 1987-88 the total moved was 318 million tonnes, for a gross of 231 241 million tonne-km. Recent growth is unparalleled in the system's history.

Domestic container service operates between 16 pairs of terminals. For ISO container traffic, Inland Container Depots (ICDs) function at Bangalore, Guntur, Anaparti, Coimbatore, New Delhi, Amingaon (Guwahati) and Dhandari Kalan (Ludhiana). In addition besides the Container Freight Station (CFS) at Patparganj, Delhi serves for consolidation and dispersal of LCL cargo.

Since the container traffic handled at New Delhi ICD (Pragati Maidan) is growing fast, it was decided to set up a full-fledged ICD at Tughlakabad, which was likely to be commissioned during 1990. It is proposed to set up a further ICDs at Hyderabad, Ahmedabad, Varanasi and Narainpur Anant.

A Container corporation of India has been set up under the administrative jurisdiction of the Ministry of Railways. This Corporation is responsible for the development of ICDs/CFSs in the country and will develop multi-modal transportation of containers between gateway ports and inland destinations.

Indian Railways are developing a computerised freight operation information and control system which will improve efficiency and productivity of the railways to a large extent. For this purpose a registered society known as 'Centre for Railway Information Systems' has been set up. Training of personnel has since been initiated and a detailed project report has been prepared. Tenders to fulfil the World Bank-funded US$850 million programme are likely to be called in 1990.

Initially, the freight operation and information system (FOIS) will be implemented in the Northern Railway with phased cut-overs; after successful implementation on Northern Railway, the system will be extended to the rest of the zonal railways. It is expected that all the broad-gauge division of Indian Railways will be covered under the system by the end of 1993.

Technology drive

A Rs 2800 million, 10-year Technology Development Programme was announced by the Railways Ministry in 1988. Objectives include: faster operation of 4500-tonne freight trains and ability to run 160 km/h passenger trains on mixed-traffic routes; means to run 200 km/h passenger trains on dedicated routes; and ability to operate 18 000-tonne freight trains at up to 75 km/h. Ways to upgrade the metre-gauge systems are to be explored, also linear motor technology and systems for train and traffic control via satellite transmissions.

Electrification

All recent extensions have been at 25 kV 50 Hz. The 405 km of 1.5 kV dc are confined to the Bombay area. In the course of the seventh five-year plan, which covered the 1985–90 period, the aim was to electrify 3500 km at an average rate of 500 to 800 km each year. In the 1988-89 financial year the total achieved was 743 route-km.

Focus of work in the later 1980s was the Western Railway's Bombay-Delhi main line. Completion was achieved early in 1988, and through electric working between the two cities via Vadodora (1384 km) was inaugurated in February that year. By 1990 it is hoped to have 75 per cent of Western Railway traffic electrically hauled.

Delhi-Calcutta was the first key inter-city route electrified throughout. The primary objective is to interlink these two cities and Bombay and Madras in an electrified network, then to spread catenary from this framework as desirable to minimise traction changes.

Wiring of the 298 km between Itarsi and Nagpur in December 1989 completed electrification of the 2194 km north-south route between Delhi and Madras. The remaining 178 km gap in the catenary of the 1968 km east-west Bombay-Calcutta route was wired and commissioned in March 1990. A second fully electrified route between Bombay and Delhi, over the Central Railway, would become available in March 1991 with wiring of the final side of the Itarsi-Nagpur-Bhusawal triangle. It was hoped to energise throughout between Madras and Bombay, and between Madras and Calcutta, before the 1990s were out.

In the course of the 1990s IR hoped to electrify a further 6500 route-km, starting with 3625 route-km in the course of the 1990–95 Plan. The planned total for the decade would have wires over about half the broad-gauge system. If achieved, this would have some 80 per cent of IR's freight tonne-km and 60 per cent of its passenger-km powered by electric traction. However, in 1990 the plan was under review by the country's National Planning Commission against projections of the country's electricity generation resources.

Track

Extension of mechanised track maintenance is a priority. The World Bank is financing substantial purchases of equipment. IR calculates that it has 19 500 km arrears of track renewal to recover.

Signalling

At Delhi, the hub of seven 1676 mm-gauge and one metre-gauge routes, GEC-General Signal was in 1989 installing its new SIGNET electronic signalling and traffic control, embodying automatic route-setting. The SIGNET centre will take over control from 17 relay interlockings and govern the whole area of the capital's railways, including its ring railway, except that existing signalboxes will remain to govern local operation in the city's Main and New Delhi stations. This installation is seen as a model for 23 other key traffic centres of IR.

IR plans its first ground-to-train radio installation between Delhi and Mughalsarai, where IR has one of its biggest freight marshalling yards. Solid state

Class WAP-1 25 kV ac passenger Co-Co

Class WAG-5A 25 kV ac freight Co-Co

RAILWAY SYSTEMS / India

interlocking (SSI) is to be provided between Mughalsarai and Sonengar.

Traction and rolling stock
For its future electrification schemes IR seeks a 4475 kW Co-Co electric locomotive of 123 tonnes to haul 4500-tonne trains, with tractive efforts of some 32 000 kg continuous and 45 000 kg maximum.

To arrive at a model for Indian mass manufacture under a technology-transfer deal, IR applied part of its 1984 World Bank loan to 1985 orders for 18 electric locomotive prototypes. Of these 12 are Bo-Bo-Bos. ASEA gained a contract to supply six 4015 kW 123-tonne units, delivery of which was completed in 1988, and the other six were built by Hitachi, which also provided six Co-Co units. IR forecasts a need of 100 such locomotives a year, later examples of which would be built at Chittaranjan works. IR is also seeking three-phase drive units and is borrowing from Japan's Import-Export Bank and the Asian Development Bank to support this development.

In 1989 tenders were obtained for supply of 40 4475 kW locomotives with ac motors, 10 to be arranged for passenger and 30 for freight haulage. Supply of 20 high-power 25 kV ac electric locomotives from the USSR was also a possibility, under an Indian-USSR agreement on co-operation in railway technology that was signed in October 1988.

But in early 1990 there were moves to curtail imports of locomotives.

A similar call for prototype offers on which to base future diesel locomotive construction at Indian plants had been made in 1986; the prospective order would be for 45 to 50 4000 hp units, up to half to be assembled locally. Bidders had been whittled down to three – GE and GM from the US, and a Krupp-Thyssen-Henschel consortium – but in 1990 the country's National Planning Commission vetoed order placement.

IR had also gone overseas to choose models for series production at the new Kapurthala works (see above); and here again a prospective deal has fallen through. A fleet of 42 air-conditioned passenger coaches mounted on Fiat bogies was to be supplied from the UK by BREL (1988), based on the latter's modular 'International' design. Associated with the contract was a technology-transfer package under which the 'International' coach to be built at Kapurthala. But the British company was subsequently confronted with contractual conditions which led it to withdraw from the deal in 1989.

Finally, in the same vein, bids have been sought world-wide for the supply of 25 new types of wagon, of better payload/tare characteristics and less injurious to track and running gear than IR's existing vehicles.

At the end of FY 1988-89 Indian Railways operated 4950 steam, 3182 diesel and 1366 electric locomotives, 2988 emu vehicles, 35 009 other passenger cars and 354 018 freight cars.

Type of coupler in standard use: Passenger cars, screw; freight cars, screw and centre buffer

Type of brake in standard use: Vacuum, except for air in 'Rajdhani Express' and Box 'N', Box 'Y' and BCN freight wagons.

Communications and data transmission
The long-discussed computerisation of IR management systems and modernisation of communication systems is getting under way. It had become possible in the early 1980s, when the World Bank approved a US$600 million line of credit for its achievement.

In mid-1985 Canadian National won a keenly contested contract worth almost US$25 million for installation of a state-of-the-art traffic control system. The contract covers a seven-year period, with a two-year extension option, and involves introduction by CN's subsidiary, CANAC Consultants, of CN's Traffic Reporting and Control (TRACS). The package includes software, technical assistance in adaptation of TRACS to IR need, and staff training. Both hardware and software are being imported.

In February 1986 a parallel turnkey contract for a telecommunications and data transmission network worth Rs3200 million was handed to a European consortium headed by Detecon, a Federal German organisation under the wing of that country's post and telegraph office and linked with Norwegian suppliers. A completion date of 1991 is now forecast.

Central Railway

Victoria Terminus, Bombay 400001

Telephone: +91 22 2621551
Telex: 011 73819 crst in

General Manager: A N Shukla
Additional General Manager: O P Jain
Senior Deputy General Manager: M D Navatny
Deputy General Manager: V V Kathavate
Chief Administrative Officer, Construction:
  V S Subramanian
Chief Planning Officer: Dalip Kumar
Chief Electrical Engineer: G S Chauhan
Chief Commercial Superintendent: G S Ganguly
Chief Operating Superintendent: M B Taly
Chief Engineer: G S Koppikar
Chief Mechanical Engineer: S B Mohindra
Financial Adviser and Chief Accounts Officer:
  P V Kawthalkar
Chief Signal and Telecommunication Engineer:
  B G Kale
Chief Stores Controller: P C Oak

Gauge: 1676 mm; 762 mm; 610 mm
Route length: 5806 km; 737 km; 303 km
Electrification: 1426 km at 25 kV 50 c/s ac; 349 km at 1500 V dc

Central Railway is an amalgam of the former GIP Railway, Gwalior Light Railway and Dholpur State Railway. It serves six states: Maharashtra, Madhya Pradesh, Uttar Pradesh, parts of Rajasthan, Haryana and Karnataka, and has divisional headquarters at Bombay, Bhusawal, Nagpur Jabalpur, Solapur, Jhansi and Bhopal.

By virtue of its central location, Central Railway is of pivotal importance to the Indian Railway network, connecting North and South India and East and West India. Besides carrying heavy transit traffic, it has a high loading potential of its own.

Passenger traffic
Central Railway transports nearly 2.76 million passengers daily between its 718 stations and 7084 on Indian Railways as a whole, running about 1350 passenger trains every day. Passenger-km on Central Railway constitute 20.6 per cent of the Indian Railways total and are the highest amongst the nine zones in which IR is divided.

The Bombay area suburban services account for nearly 81 per cent of the total originating passengers and about 31 per cent of total passenger-km, with an average trip length of 20.6 km. Suburban traffic has grown from 452 million originating passengers to 669 million since 1970. Central Railway runs 1015 suburban trains every day. The network is also being extended by an 18 km double-track line across Thane Creek to a satellite city, New Bombay, on the mainland to absorb population from the overcrowded Bombay island.

In 1988-89 originating passenger journeys on Central Railway totalled 859 million, a reduction over the previous year, of which suburban traffic accounted for 669 million (76.7 per cent) and non-suburban 155 million (23.3 per cent) on the broad-gauge system. The balance of 5 million passengers were carried on narrow-gauge lines. The growth-rate of passenger traffic in the four most recent financial years was:

Passengers carried
(millions)	1984-85	1988-89	Growth rate per year (%)
Total	935	1015	1.97
Suburban	754	817	2.08
Non-suburban	181	198	2.4

Future planning is based on an annual growth rate of 4 per cent for suburban and 3 per cent non-suburban traffic. To cater for the rise in suburban traffic, the suburban network in the Bombay area is being expanded, and a new Belapur-Mankhurd suburban line was to be finished by March 1991. Additional emu rakes are being introduced and necessary signalling works are under way. It is expected that the headway

Class WAM-4 25 kV ac mixed traffic Co-Co

of suburban services during peak hours, currently 5 minutes, will be progressively reduced to 4 minutes within three or four years, and eventually to 3 minutes.

Central Railway has one of the two new terminal stations being built in Bombay. This was progressing in 1989 at Kurla, on the city's outskirts. Its five platforms are of a length to accommodate the 26-car trains which IR now seeks to develop. A new station is also being built at Habibganj.

Central Railway claims to run IR's fastest train. This is the air-conditioned 'Shatabdi Express' which, with licence to run at up to 140 km/h in parts of the Delhi-Bhopal route and the benefit of a route equipped with AWS, averages 104 km/h over the 104 km from Delhi to Agra and reaches Bhopal, Madhya Pradesh, in 7 hours 40 minutes for the 705 km distance.

Freight traffic
Freight traffic consists chiefly of bulk commodities such as coal, cement, fertiliser, petroleum products, foodgrains, raw material to steel plants. Originating traffic totals about 35 million tonnes. The gross tonne-km of Central Railway are the highest of the Indian Railways.

The growth of freight traffic in the four most recent financial years has been:

India / RAILWAY SYSTEMS

Freight

(million tonnes)	1984-85	1988-89	Growth rate yearly (%)
Originating traffic	27.22	34.86	7.04
Tonnes carried	71.01	88.00	5.98
Net tonne-km	31 698	37 677	4.72

The trend will be maintained. To meet the increased demands, extensive electrification works, doubling of tracks, track renewals, improved signalling, etc, are in various stages of completion. Higher capacity electric locomotives are also to be ordered. Freight trains with trailing loads of 4700 tonnes are already running on the system and their number is being progressively increased.

An increase in ISO container traffic was anticipated from the 1989 opening of Jawaharlal Nehru Port at Nhava Sheva in New Bombay. This is served by an offshoot of the new suburban line across Thane Creek.

Traffic (million)

	1986-87	1987-88	1988-99
Total freight tonnes	84.36	86.29	88
Total freight tonne-km	70 627	71 496	70 597
Total passenger-km	53 837	57 695	54 425
Total passenger journeys	997	1076	1076

Revenue (Rs million)

	1986-87	1987-88	1988-89
Passengers and baggage	4172	4506	5262
Freight, parcels and mail	8519	9473	10 290
Other income	229	246	333
Total	12 920	14 225	15 885

Expenditure (Rs million)

	1986-87	1987-88	1988-89
Staff/personnel	4486	5413	5913
Materials and services	3176	3187	3504
Depreciation	1720	1872	2076
Financial changes*	1251	1493	1732
Total	10 633	11 965	13 225

* Pension fund and payment to general revenue

Electrification

A massive electrification programme is under way. In 1988-89, an additional 432 route-km were energised, electrification works on 782 route-km were in progress and targeted to be completed by March 1991. The Delhi-Madras route would be fully electrified during 1990, and the Bombay-Itarsi-Delhi and Bombay-Calcutta routes likewise in the following year.

In 1990 electrification works were proceeding throughout the following sections:
Bhusawal-Itarsi, on the Bombay-Delhi route (301 km)
Bhusawal-Badnera-Wardha, on the Bombay-Calcutta route (314 km)

New lines

Besides double-tracking and electrification, moves to raise operating capacity include three major new line projects. Of these the biggest is a 348 km Guna-Gwalior-Etwah bypass of Jhansi, where routes to the south from Delhi and Lucknow converge: the first 50 km of this project were opened by 1990. Southeast of this a 50 km line is being built from Satna to Rewa; and not far from and to the southwest of Delhi, a 119 km line to Alwar from Mathura, on the electrified Bombay-Delhi main line.

Signalling

Signalling advance includes installation of AWS in the Bombay suburban area, to complete the plan for train headway reduction. The emphasis of other development is on panel interlocking, route-relay interlocking, track circuiting and block proving by axle counters, plus a survey for track-to-train radio communication in the Bombay-Agra area.

Computerisation

A computerised passenger reservation system has been installed at Bombay VT at a cost of Rs170 million. On average, 45 000 passengers are dealt with at this centre every day. The centre is connected to 160 terminals located in Bombay and on the Western Railway at Ahmedabad. Additional terminals are proposed in the Bombay suburbs and at Pune.

Computerisation of passenger reservation has also been installed at Bhopal station and connected to the

WAP3 electric locomotive and 'Shatabdi Express' at Bhopal

Rush hour at Bombay VT suburban station

Class WDM-2 diesel and inaugural train on newly-opened Miana-Badarwas section of the 348km Guna-Gwalior-Etawah line under construction

604 RAILWAY SYSTEMS / India

Delhi computer system. Provision of this facility in the cities of Nagpur, Indore and Vadodara is planned.

Traction and rolling stock

Central Railway aims to eliminate its remaining steam locomotives by 1995. In FY 1989-90 the system took delivery of 20 electric, 24 diesel locomotives and two emus.

At the start of 1990 the railway operated 166 ac and 125 dc electric locomotives, 647 diesel locomotives (of which, 35 narrow-gauge), 87 emus, 2217 passenger cars (including 759 sleeping and 20 buffet/restaurant cars) and 77 776 freight cars.

Coupler in standard use

Passenger cars: Screw, Schabau (emus); enhanced screw, Majex, Alliance (emus)
Freight cars: CBC AAR-type screw; CBC alliance II– four-wheeled stock

Braking in standard use

Locomotive-hauled stock: Vacuum
Emus: Air

Track

Rail: 60 and 52 kg/m MFF
Cross ties (sleepers): Concrete, wooden, steel, CST9; varying thickness; spaced 1660 or 1540/km
Fastenings: Keys, elastic fastenings such as Pandrol clip
Minimum curvature radius: 8° (in yards only)
Max gradient: 2.7%
Max permissible axleload: 22.9 tonnes

Eastern Railway

17 Netaji Subhash Road, Calcutta 700 001

Telephone: +91 33 236811-24
Cable: Purail

General Manager: R D Kitson
Additional General Manager: J Kumar
Senior Deputy General Manager: G S Ganguli
Chief Planning Officer: Dr C M Kulshreshtha
Financial Adviser & Chief Accounts Officer: S E H Shah
Chief Electrical Engineer: C P Gaurishankar
Chief Electrical Loco Engineer: Dr K R Dorairaj
Chief Rolling Stock Engineer: A Biswas
Chief Engineer: Vacant
Chief Engineer (Construction): R K Garg
Chief Mechanical Engineer: V Viswanathan
Chief Signal & Telecommunications Engineer: J M Sharma
Controller of Stores: K Veeraraghavan
Chief Workshop Engineer: R K Shukla

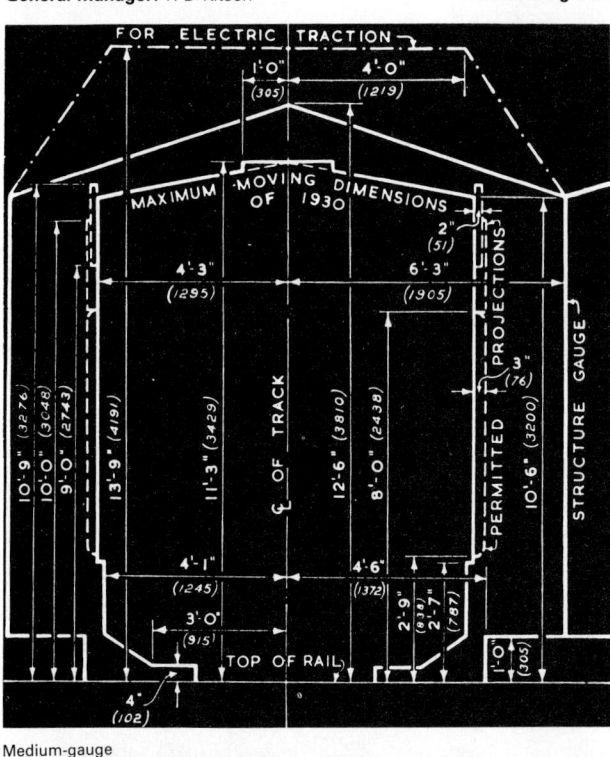

Medium-gauge

Class WDS-8 diesel-electric shunter

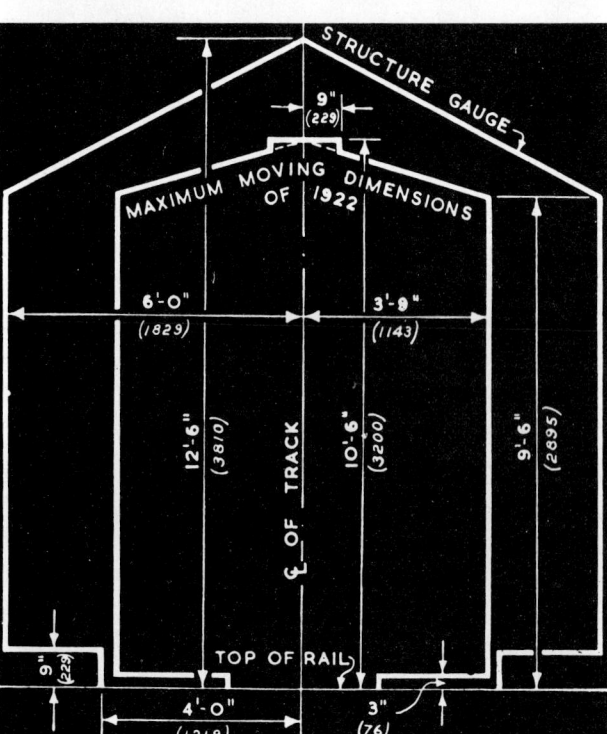

Narrow-gauge

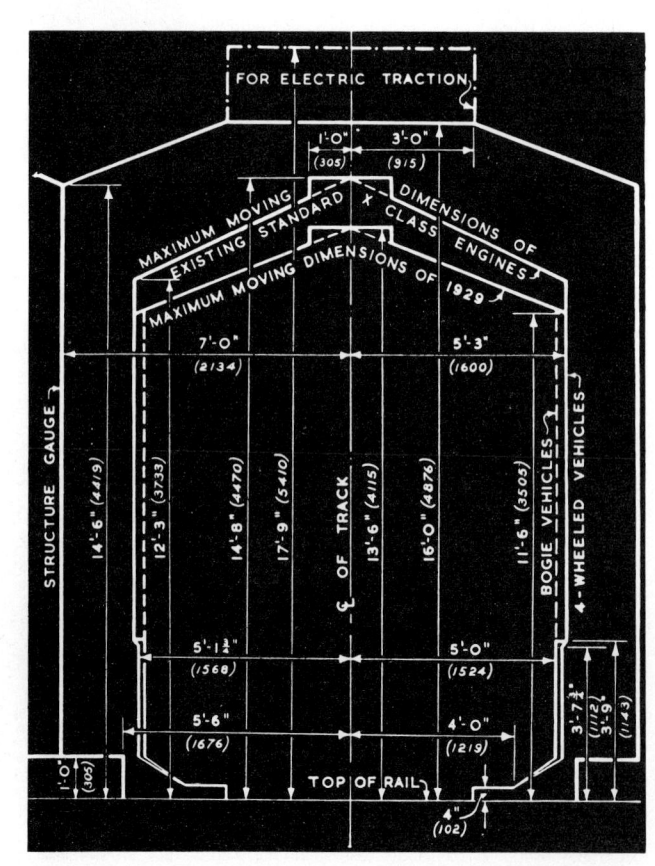

Broad-gauge

India / RAILWAY SYSTEMS

Gauge: 1676 mm; 762 mm
Route length: 4138 km; 132 km
Electrification: 1231 km at 25 kV 50 Hz ac

The Eastern Railway is among India's biggest zonal railways, running mainly in the states of West Bengal and Bihar, and also in parts of Uttar Pradesh and Madhya Pradesh. It was formed in 1952 from the Bengal-Nagpur Railway and parts of the East Indian Railway, but in 1955 the Bengal-Nagpur was transferred to the new South Eastern Railway zone.

Eastern Railway originates over 53 million tonnes of coal traffic a year, which accounts for over 80 per cent of freight traffic emanating from its territory.

Almost all main-line passenger services are operated by electric locomotives. A fleet of 296 motor and 730 trailer emu cars is operating on the suburban system as three-car sets and more than 700 trains run daily from Calcutta's passenger terminal at Howrah and Sealdah. Around 1.4 million passager journeys are recorded daily, two-thirds of them suburban.

Developments
Improvements are under way on the Calcutta-New Delhi line to raise speeds from a present maximum of 130 km/h to 160 km/h.

A Rs 3300 million programme to develop service of the Karanpura coalfield has been launched. It involves electrification between Sonenagar ansd Patraju, provision of a third electrified track between Sonenagar and Mughalsarai, and double-tracking of the 93 km Garwa Road-Sonenagar line.

Under a 1985–89 Rs 9000 million investment programme, a microwave communications system is being installed. A new 474 km railway is being constructed from Lakshmikantapur to Namkhana, and double-tracking of some 200 route-km of line around Khalari is in progress to cope with rising coal output. Also well under way is construction of a Calcutta orbital line, 10.5 km of which was operational in 1989.

Traction and rolling stock
At the start of 1989 the railway operated, on the broad-gauge: 567 steam, 294 electric and 373 diesel locomotives, 3497 passenger cars, 974 emu cars, 59 605 freight cars; and on the narrow-gauge: 9 steam locomotives, two diesel railcars, 72 passenger cars and 9 freight cars.

Coupler in standard use
Passenger cars: Drawbar with screw coupling
Freight cars: Centre buffer coupler; CBC with transition coupling; drawbar with screw coupling
Braking in standard use: Locomotive-hauled stock: Air and vacuum brake

Track
Rail: 52 and 60 kg/m
Cross ties (sleepers): CST-9; thickness: M + 4 to M + 7; spacing 1562/km
Fastenings: Key
Max gradient: 1.25%
Max permissible axleload: 22.5 tonnes

Northern Railway

Baroda House, Kasturba Ghandi Marg, New Delhi 110 001

Telephone: +91 11 387227
Telex: 3166329

General Manager: S M Vaish
Chief Engineer: Y P Anand
Chief Mechanical Engineer: A N Shukla
Chief Electrical Engineer: C P Gupta
Chief Signal & Telecommunications Engineer: R K Nair

Gauge: 1676 mm; 1000 mm; 762 mm
Route length: 7502 km; 3215 km; 259.6 km
Electrification: 874 km of 1676 mm-gauge at 25 kV 50 Hz ac

The railway was created in 1952 from parts of the Eastern Punjab Railway, of the East Indian Railway, and of the Western Railway, together with the Jodhpur and Bikaner Railways. Its territory extends from Delhi through the Punjab, Haryana Delhi, Himachal Pradesh and parts of Jammu, Kashmir, Rajasthan and Uttar Pradesh States.

At the start of 1988 the railway operated 238 electric, 465 diesel and 739 steam locomotives; 1200 emus, 12 electric and 4 diesel railcars; 5761 passenger cars; and 43 157 freight wagons. The electric locomotive fleet consists of Types WAP-1, WAM-4, WAG-5, WAG-4 and WAM-1. Line-haul diesel locomotives are Types WDM-2, WDM-4 and YDM-4.

A massive new re-gauging project was approved by the government in late 1989. At a cost of Rs 5000 million it proposes to create a broad gauge route from the Gujarat coast at Kandla, on the Western Railway, northeast to Bhatinda Junction, in the Punjab on the Northern Railway. The scheme involves building new line from Kandla to Viramgam, and re-gauging from Viramgam to Bhildi, and from Bikaner to Sadulpur.

Traffic 1986-87
Total freight tonnage (million)	78.24
Total freight tonne-km (million)	37 363.4
Total passenger journeys (million)	420.38
Total passenger-km (million)	44 489.6

North Eastern Railway

Gorakhpur 273 012, UP

Telephone: 3234
Cable: Upurail, Gorakhpur

General Manager: Gauri Shankar

Gauge: 1676 mm; 1000 mm
Route length: 862 km; 4301 km

Increases of population and economic development now exert extreme pressure on the predominantly narrow-gauge network of the NER, which consists of part of the Assam and one-time Mobay, Baroda & Central India Railways and Oudh Tirhut Railway. It covers Bihar and Uttar Pradesh from Achnera in the west to Katihar in the east. In 1984 the railway completed enlargement to 1676 mm-gauge of its key Samastipur-Barabanki route (587.3 km). Similar conversion of the 180 km Barauni-Katihar line ensued in 1985, followed by enlargement of the 158 km Bhatni-Varanasi line. The first of these projects achieved conversion throughout NER's trunk route and also connection with the newly extended 1676 mm network of the Northeast Frontier Railway, thereby creating much improved rail access to Assam from all parts of India. The second simplified freight interchange with the Central, Eastern and Northern Railways. Gauge conversion continues on other routes, such as Moradabad-Ramnagar (77.5 km) and Lucknow-Kanpur-Anwarganj (75 km).

At last report NER operated, on metre gauge, 592 steam and 68 diesel locomotives, 2099 passenger cars, and 19 780 freight cars; and, on broad gauge, 47 diesel locomotives, 5 diesel railcars, 2099 passenger cars and 267 freight cars.

Northeast Frontier Railway

Maligaon, Gauhati 781 011, Assam

Telephone: +91 361 88422, 28393
Telex: 031 0235 336

General Manager: S K Mitra
Additional General Manager: Jagdish Chandra
Chief Commercial Superintendent: M M P Sinha
Chief Engineer: R B A Ajgaonkar
Chief Electrical Engineer: R Srinivasan
Chief Mechanical Engineer: M C Das
Chief Operating Superintendent: E A Khan
Controller of Stores: C P Subramanian
Chief Personnel Officer: Mahinder Singh
Chief Signal and Telecommunication Engineer: D P Joshi
Chief Accounts Officer: A Dasgupta
Senior Deputy General Manager: A K Jain

Gauge 1676 mm, 1000 mm, 610 mm
Route length: 764 km; 2911 km; 88 km

The NFR was hived off from the North Eastern Railway in 1958. It serves the whole of Assam and North Bengal, parts of North Bihar, the states of Arunachal, Manipur, Meghalaya, Mizoram, Nagaland, Tripura. Its 610 mm-gauge component is the world-famous Darjeeling-Himalaya Railway, still worked by 19th century steam power, which takes 7 hours for the scenic journey of 87 km from New Jaipalguri to Darjeeling, and is now approved for rehabilitation by the government. This narrow-gauge railway records some 33 million passenger journeys and 5 million tonnes of freight a year.

The 3763 km Northeast Frontier Railway (NFR) is the smallest of the nine zonal railways of India. Besides playing a vital role in the transport of people and essential commodities for the entire region, NFR is also of strategic importance, since the region is practically enveloped by international borders. NFR covers one of the most picturesque regions of the country, overlooked by the Himalayas. Apart from serving well-known tourist centres like Darjeeling, Shillong and the wild-life sanctuaries of Kaziranga, Manas and Jaldapara, it also covers the vast tea-garden belts of North Bengal and Assam, from Darjeeling to Dibrugarh. Several stretches of NFR are prone to damage by floods or landslides during monsoons. To maintain this vital communication link with the least interruption has always been a challenging task for the railwaymen serving in this region.

Direct mail/express trains link Guwahati with such important cities as Delhi, Calcutta, Madras, Patna, Lucknow, Kanpur, Varanasi, Allahabad and Trivandrum. In 1988 NFR was running a daily total of 192 mail/express trains (44 broad- and 148 metre-gauge).

Inward freight traffic consists mainly of essential commodities such as foodgrains, salt, sugar, cement and steel. Outward traffic, which is smaller in volume, comprises petroleum products, coal, bamboo, timber, jute, tea, dolomite etc.

Since 1979 NFR has had an independent construction organisation which has given a boost to the development of the railway network in the North Eastern Region, with an annual outlay of about Rs 8000 million. Four new railways have been under

Diyang viaduct on the Lumching-Badarpur hill section

606 RAILWAY SYSTEMS / India

construction. Two of them, metre-gauge lines from Balipara to Bhalukpung (35 km) and from Silchar to Jiribam (49 km), were opened at the end of 1989. The following spring was to see completion of a 48 km metre-gauge line from Lalbazar to Bhairabi. The fourth line is an extension from Balipara to Agartala, near the Bangladesh frontier.

Signalling work has been dominated by installation of tokenless block over 423 km between Kumedpur and New Jalpaiguri. In 1990–92 the railway was to resignal its Gauhati-Lumding line for a maximum speed of 100 km/h.

Traffic	1986	1987	1988
Total freight tonnage (million)	4.754	5.277	5.385
Total freight tonne-km (million)	4724.4	5278.6	5827.4
Total passenger-km (million)	5027.7	5542	NA
Total passenger journeys (million)	34.2	30.67	NA

In 1988 NFR was operating 169 diesel and 261 steam locomotives, 1676 m-gauge diesel locomotives comprising 32 WDM2 and seven WDS6, narrow-gauge 115 YDM4 and 11 YDM4A.

Type of coupler in standard use: Passenger cars, screw; freight cars, CBC/screw type
Type of braking in standard use: Vacuum

Track
Rail: Flat-bottom 52, 44.61, 37.13, 29.76, 24.8 kg/m
Cross ties (sleepers): Wood, steel trough, cast iron
Thickness: Wood: BG, 127 mm
MG, 114 mm
NG, 114 mm

Spacing
Main lines: BG, 1540/km
MG, 1596/km
NG, 1230/km
Branch lines: BG, 1309/km
MG, 1344/km

Fastenings: Wooden sleepers: CI/MS bearing plates and rail screws; steel trough sleepers: loose jaws with keys; cast iron sleepers: keys
Minimum curvature radius: BG 5°; MG 16°; NG 115°
Max gradient: BG 0.64%; MG 2.7%; NG 4.44%
Max permissible axleload: BG 22.9 tonnes; MG 12.7 tonnes; NG 7.6 tonnes

The famous Batagia loop on the Darjooling-Himalaya Railway

Southern Railway

Park Town, Madras 600 003

Telephone: +91 44 564141
Cable: Freight Madras

General Manager: S P Jain
Additional General Manager: V Viswanathan

Gauge: 1676 mm; 1000 mm; 762 mm
Length: 2309 km; 4299 km; 148 km
Electrification: 432 km of 1676 mm-gauge at 25 kV 50 Hz ac; 166 km of 1000 mm-gauge at 25 kV 50 Hz ac

Formed in 1951 from the previous Madras & Southern Mahratta, Mysore and South Indian railways, the Southern extends from Mangalore on the west coast and Kanya Kumari in the south to Renigunta in the north-west and Gudur in the north-east. Electrification is concentrated in the Madras suburban area on the main line from Madras to the fringe of South Central Railway territory at Vijayawada.

Traffic
Freight traffic amounts to some 35 million tonnes a year. Container traffic is expanding fast.

Passenger traffic grosses about 300 million journeys a year. Recent innovations have included a train with the longest itinerary in India, Trivandrum to New Bongaigaon in Assam, 3800 km.

Infrastructure
Gauge conversion has been completed on the 269 km Guntakal-Bangalore route to open up through 1676 mm-gauge running between Bangalore and Bombay. Now Tutocorin port, previously confined to metre-gauge service, is being connected to the core of the broad gauge by a combination of gauge conversion and new 1676 mm-gauge construction throughout a 328 km route from the coast to Karua. The second stage of the scheme, the 74 km from Karua to Dindigul, was formally inaugurated by then Prime Minister Rajiv Gandhi in August 1988. The two remaining stages, totalling some 200 km, will fill the gap between those now completed. The third stage, which was proceeding in 1989, covers 64.3 km between Dindigul and Madurai.

New works include a 1676 mm-gauge coastal line of 57 km from Ernakulam south to Aleppey, in Kerala state, which was opened in October 1989. The line is now being projected further south for 43km to Kayankulam. It is hoped in the later 1990s to continue further through Quilon to Trivandrum.

Track renewals on 1676 mm gauge are being executed with 52 kg/m rail, concrete sleepers and elastic clips. Extension of microwave communications proceeds.

Electrification
Creation of a rapid transit system in the Madras metropolitan area proceeds. Two bottlenecks have been opened out by four-tracking and associated electrification. Current projects include construction of a station near Madras Airport on the electrified Madras-Villupram line.

Electrification of the 176km Jolarpet-Erode line should be completed in 1991.

Traction and rolling stock
At last report the railway operated on 1676 mm- gauge 16 steam and 211 diesel locomotives, 42 emu power cars and 124 trailers, 2464 passenger cars and 21 193 freight cars; and on the narrow-gauge 364 steam, 69 diesel and 20 electric locomotives, 45 emu power cars and 143 trailers, six diesel railcars, 2025 passenger cars and 7443 freight cars.

Steam traction has now been cleared from the 1676 mm-gauge system and electric traction caters for most of the mail and express services between Madras, Gudur and Arakkonam. The 4300-tonne ore trains between Arakkonam and Madras port are also electrically-powered. Steam has also been ousted from express train haulage on the metre-gauge.

South Central Railway

Rail Nilayam Secunderabad 500 371, Andhra Pradesh

Telephone: +91 842 73583

General Manager: R Narasimhan

Gauge: 1676 mm, 1000 mm
Route length: 3820 km, 3314 km
Electrification: 514 km of 1676 mm-gauge at 25 kV 50 Hz ac

The South Central Railway (SCR) was set up in 1966 from portions of the Southern and Central Railways. It covers the states of Andhra Pradesh and Goa, north-west Karnataka and south-west Maharashtra.

Traffic
Principal raw material moved is coal, which accounts for more than 40 per cent of originating freight. Coal movements are expected to increase dramatically by 1992, when the Singareni collieries in Andhra Pradesh may be producing 25 million tonnes annually and numerous new coal-fired generating plants will have come on stream. The other major bulk freight flow is iron ore from the Hospet-Bellary region to Madras for export, which the railway moves in 4500-tonne unit trains. Many new industries are arising in SCR territory, including steelworks, 21 cement plants and a fertiliser plant at Kakinada, which promise considerable traffic growth. Annual freight tonne-km gross over 22 000 million.

SCR has no considerable suburban traffic, relying mainly for passenger growth on improved inter-city services. Traffic is around 22 000 million passenger-km annually.

Developments
The railway's forward corporate plan envisages building 269 km more of new lines at a cost of Rs 649 million, track doubling over 177 km at a cost of Rs 420 million, conversion of 244 km of metre-gauge route to 1676 mm-gauge at a cost of Rs 649 million and enlargement of several principal passenger stations.

Electrification has been completed over SCR's 295 km (Gudur-Vijayawada) section of the Madras-Gudur-Vijayawada line; its operation is shared with the Southern Railway, which has electrified the 136 km southern section to Madras. Forward electrification plans aim to extend the Gudur-Vijayawada wiring by 543 km, from Vijayawada to Balharshah and between Secunderabad and Kazipet.

Traction and rolling stock
In 1988 the railway operated 192 steam, 113 electric and 277 diesel locomotives; 1573 passenger cars and 22 611 freight cars on 1676 mm-gauge, 278 steam and 105 diesel locomotives, 1017 passenger cars and 9109 freight cars on metre-gauge.

India / RAILWAY SYSTEMS

South Eastern Railway

11 Garden Reach Road, Kipperpore, Calcutta 700 043

Telephone: +91 33 45 1741
Cable: Dapujan
Telex: 021 2417 cosy

General Manager: Vacant

Gauge: 1676 mm; 762 mm
Route length: 5635 km; 1479 km
Electrification: 2866 km at 25 kV 50 Hz ac

SER was created in a 1955 partition of the Eastern Railway and comprises the lines of the former Bengal-Nagpur Railway centred on Calcutta.

Traffic

The South Eastern Railway handles one third of Indian Railways' total freight; 85 per cent of the railway's earnings come from freight traffic, which grosses over 43 000 million tonne-km a year. The mainstay of its traffic is generated by steel, coal and cement and movement of export ore to Visakhapatnam and Paradip ports.

New lines

Several major construction schemes were progressing in 1989. To serve the new Visakhapatnam steelworks a 174 km line was being built from Koraput to Rayagada, for access to Visakhapatnam port. This project, also serving an aluminium plant, should be finished in 1991. Access to Paradip port is being improved by a bypass between Sambalpur and Talcher. An 87 km line from Tamluk to the coast at Digha will benefit the tourist trade in West Bengal.

A new station at Calcutta reserved for South Eastern trains is being built at Shalimar, across the Hooghly river from the city's Howrah station. The city is also gaining a new freight terminal 10 km from Howrah, at Sankrail.

Traffic	1987-88
Freight tonnes (million)	100
Freight tonne-km (million)	43 200
Passenger-km (million)	16 366
Passenger journeys (million)	192

Class ZDM-4A narrow-gauge diesel locomotive

Class WAG-1 25 kV ac freight Bo-Bo

Diesel-hauled ore train in the Kuppavalasa gorge, between Kottavalasa and Kirandul

Traction and rolling stock

At the start of 1988 SER was operating on its 1676 mm-gauge 354 electric, 366 diesel and 300 steam locomotives, 51 emus, 2802 passenger cars, 101 980 freight cars; and on its 762 mm-gauge 45 diesel and 102 steam locomotives, 426 passenger cars and 3659 freight cars.

In 1988-89 the South Eastern Railway was the arena of 9000-tonne freight train trials with the new electric locomotives from ABB and Hitachi. The railway was also evaluating freight wagon bogies of French, West German, Australian and US design.

Track
Rail: 60, 52, 44.6 kg/m
Cross ties (sleepers): Wooden, concrete, steel CST/9
Thickness
Wooden: 125 mm
Concrete: 200 mm
Steel: 106 mm
CST/9: 112 mm
Spacing
On straight track: 1540/km
On curves (less than 4% (438 m)); 1617/km
Fastening: Elastic on cwr, conventional elsewhere
Minimum curvature radius: 176 m
Max gradient: 0.02%
Max axleload: 22.86 tonnes

Western Railway

Churchgate, Bombay 400 020

Telephone: 22 298016
Cable: Pasbandha

General Manager: K Subramanian
Senior Deputy General Manager: M P Srivastava
Chief Engineer: Y K Patwardhan
Chief Engineer, Survey & Construction: Raj Kumar
Chief Mechanical Engineer: D P Joshi
Chief Rolling Stock Engineer: P Kumar
Chief Motive Power Engineer: K Damor
Chief Signal & Telecommunications Engineer: N Krishnan
Financial Adviser and Chief Accounts Officer: R P Oberoi
Controller of Stores: Kanti Swaroop
Chief Planning Officer: E A Khan

Gauge: 1676 mm; 1000 mm; 762 mm
Route length: 3632 km; 5493 km; 1100 km
Electrification: 876 km at 25 kV 50 Hz ac; 63 km at 1.5 kV dc

Formed in 1951, the railway comprises the former Bombay, Baroda & Central India, Jaipur State, Gaekwar of Baroda's, Cutch State, Saurashtra and Rajasthan Railways.

Traffic

The railway is IR's busiest passenger carrier and its

RAILWAY SYSTEMS / India

most profitable component, with an operating ratio close to 80 per cent. WR covers the commuter network of Bombay, running 764 emu commuter trains daily and bringing a morning peak flow of almost 250 000 passengers into the city's Churchgate terminal, where trains arrive at 2.1-minute intervals. A new seven-platform terminal is now under construction at Bondra; two of its platforms were available in 1989 and full opening was forecast for 1993.

Since 1960 Bombay's population has doubled and Western Railway's suburban passenger journeys have soared from 236 million to 840 million a year, but it has not been possible to raise the number of trains operated in proportion. Consequently some peak-hour trains, with a seating capacity of only 900 or so, carry 3000–3500 commuters each.

The railway's daily total of 43 Mail and Express trains on the broad-gauge includes IR's prestigious 'Rajdhani Express' (see above).

WR was the first of the Indian railways to cater for container traffic in 1966, and its current services include dedicated ISO container trains from Bombay to the New Delhi dry port at Pragati Maidan. WR also operates a guaranteed transit Bombay-New Delhi wagonload service under the title 'Speed-Link Express'. Most of WR's bulk commodity unit trains, like three of the country's other major bulk-hauling railways, are now made up to 4500-tonne formations of BOX-N wagons with double-headed locomotive power.

Infrastructure
The major construction project to date has been a new broad-gauge line of 166 km from Kota to Chittogarh and Nimach, due for completion in 1989. It should tap traffic amounting to 4.6 million tonnes a year, principally in coal input to and output from cement plants and a zinc smelter.

Traction and rolling stock
At last report the railway was operating, on its 1676 mm-gauge: 121 electric, 62 diesel and 264 steam locomotives, 585 emu cars, 2563 hauled coaching stock cars and 37 208 freight cars; on the metre-gauge: 149 diesel and 520 steam locomotives, 2480 coaching stock cars and 16 168 freight cars; and on the 762 mm-gauge: 85 steam locomotives, 289 coaching stock cars and 1064 freight cars.

Telecommunications
STC Telecommunications of Britain has gained a Rs 31.1 million contract to install between Bombay and Virar Indian Railways' first optic-fibre-based communications system.

Type YDM-4 1400 hp 1000 mm-gauge Co-Co diesel electric

Coupler in standard use
Passenger cars: Screw
Freight cars: Centre buffer couplers and screw coupling

Braking in standard use
Locomotive-hauled stock: Vacuum and air

Indian Railways track
Rail, types and weight

Broad gauge	Type/specification
Flat bottom	
65 kg steel rails	Gost 8160 & 8161.56
Wear-resistant rails	
60 kg/m	UIC 860/0 grade 'C'
Wear-resistant rails	
52 kg/m	UIC 860/0 grade 'B'
Medium manganese	
flat bottom 60, 52 and 44.6 kg/m	IRS speen T12

Metre gauge	
Medium manganese	
44.6, 37.1 and 29.7 kg/m	IRS speen T12

Sleepers: Wooden, cast iron, concrete and steel sleepers. The standard now adopted for high-speed trunk routes is concrete or steel trough

Concrete: Monobloc, thickness at centre 180 mm, thickness at rail level 210 mm, length 2750 mm. With elastic rail clips

Wooden
1076 mm-gauge 2750 × 250 × 130 mm
1000 mm-gauge 1800 × 200 × 115 mm
762 mm-gauge 1500 × 180 × 115 mm

Steel
Cast iron: CST-9 for 1676 and 1000 mm-gauge

Spacing: 1660/km high-speed routes; 1310 to 1540/km other routes

Rail fastenings
Fish plates and bolts and nuts to suit rail type, viz 60 kg, 52 kg
Fittings for concrete sleepers:

	Drawing No
Concrete	
Elastic clips	RDSO/T-1892

Electric railcars

Class	Cars* per unit	Motor cars per unit	Motored axles per motor car	Line current	Rated output per motor kW	Max speed km/h	Wheel dia mm	Total seating capacity per car (M-motor T-trailer)	Year first built	Builders Mechanical parts	Builders Electrical equipment
1500 V dc BG emus											
WCU5	3	1	4	1500 V dc	100.8	104	914.4	M 100 T 102	1956	Breda Feroviaria Milomo Hitachi	English Electric Co
WCU6	3	1	4	1500 V dc	104.6	104	914.4	M 110 T 102	1957	Hitachi	Hitachi
WCU7	3	1	4	1550 V dc	104.6	104	914.4	M 110 T 102	1958	NSSK	NSSK
WCU8	3	1	4	1500 V dc	137.7	104	952	M 100 T 102	1958/59	MAN	AEG
WCU10	3	1	4	1500 V dc	102.3	104	914.4	M 110 T 102	1959	Breda/ Ansaldo	Ansaldo San Georgio
WCU12	3	1	4	1500 V dc	158.8	104	952	M 87 T 104	1961	Jessop	AEI
WCU13	3	1	4	1500 V dc	135.9	105	952	M 87	1964	Jessop	Jessop AEI
WCU14	3	1	4	1500 V dc	135.9	105	952	M 98 T 114	1969 1986	Jessop	BHEL TDK
WCU15	3	1	4	1500 V	135.9	105	952	M 86	1970	ICF	BHEL
25 KV ac/dc BG											
WAU-2 (conv)	3	1	4	25 kV ac	158.8	104	952	M 100 T 102	1959/60	SIG	AEI
25 kV ac BG											
WAU-3 (Hitachi)	4	1	4	25 kV ac	160.6	96	915	M 114 T 114	1963	ICF	Hitachi
WAU-4	4	1	4	25 kV ac	167.3	105	952	M 114 T 114	1967	ICF	BHEL
25 kV ac MG											
YAU-1	4	1	4	25 kV ac	128.5	90	MC 838 TC 725	M 82 T 82	1966	ICF	M/s Nichoman, Japan

* Length of all cars 20 272 mm except Class YAU-1, 19 500 mm

India / RAILWAY SYSTEMS

Glass-filled nylon-66 liners	RDSO/T-2505	
Grooved rubber pads	RDSO/T-2052	
Fittings for steel trough sleepers:		
Fittings for wooden sleepers:		
Mild steel or cast iron bearing plates	IRS spn T5 and T7	
Plate screw, rail screw	IRS spn T-16	
Round spikes, dog spikes		
Keys	IRS spn T2, BG T405 (M) & MG T413 (M)	
Spring steel loose jaws	IRS spn T17	
MS Keys (for high speed tracks)	IRS spn T8	
Double shank elastic spike	BG RD50/T-3358, MG RD50/T-3474	
Elastic clips	RDSO/T-1892	
Grooved rubber pads	RDSO/T-2059	
Fittings for cast iron sleepers:		
Tie bars	BG T404 (M), MG T433 (M)	
Modified loose jaws	RDSO/T-1801	
Grooved rubber pads	RDSO/T-2058	
Elastic clips	RDSO/T-1892	

Standard method of welding: New rail is flash butt welded in workshops into 3, 5 or 10 rail bar lengths, carried to site on specially designed wagons then alumino-thermic welded into cwr lengths after laying in position.

Max curvature: 5° to 6° on 1676 mm-gauge trunk routes (approx. 300 m radius)
Max gradient: 0.66%
Max axleload: 22.9 tonnes on 1676 mm-gauge

Electric locomotives

Class	Wheel arrangement	Line voltage	Rated output (kW) continuous	Max speed km/h	Weight tonnes	Overall length mm	Year first built	Builders Mechanical parts	Builders Electrical equipment
WAM1	Bo-Bo	25 kV ac	2113	112.5	74	15 892	1960	50 c/s Group	50 c/s Group
WAM2	Bo-Bo	25 kV ac	2083	112.5	76	15 000	1961	Mitsubishi	
WAM3	Bo-Bo	25 kV ac	2083	112.6	76	15 000	1964	Mitsubishi	
WAM4	Co-Co	25 kV ac	3640	120	112.8	18 974	1971	CLW, India	CLW/BHEL, India
WAM4A	Co-Co	25 kV ac	3640	80	112.8	19 974	1971	CLW/RDSO	BHEL/CLW
WAP1	Co-Co	25 kV ac	2837	130	108.3	18 794	1979	CLW, India	CLW/BHEL, India
WAG1	B-B	25 kV ac	2165	80	85.2	17 092	1963	50 c/s Group/CLW, India	50 c/s Group, CLW India
WAG2	B-B	25 kV ac	3450	80	85.2	16 882	1964	Hitachi	Hitachi/Mitsubishi
WAG3	B-B	25 kV ac	2352	80	87.32	17 092	1965	50 c/s Group	50 c/s Group
WAG4	B-B	25 kV ac	2352	80	87.6	17 216	1967	CLW	CLW/BHEL
WAG5A	Co-Co	25 kV ac	3850	80	118.8	19 974	1983	CLW	CLW/BHEL
WAG5B	Co-Co	25 kV ac	2837	80	118.8	19 974	1979	CLW	CLW/BHEL
WCAM1	Co-Co	25 kV ac / 1500 V dc	1971/2187	110	112.8	20 950	1975	CLW	BHEL/CLW
WCM1	Co-Co	1500 V dc	3170	120.5	123.98	20 834	1955	EE Co Ltd & Vulcan Foundry	
WCM2	Co-Co	1500 V dc	2810	120.5	112.8	20 066	1957	EE Co Ltd & Vulcan Foundry	
WCM3	Co-Co	1500 V dc	2460	120.7	113.0	19 583	1961	Hitachi	
WCM4	Co-Co	1550 V dc	3280	120.5	125.0	20 000	1961	Hitachi	
WCM5	Co-Co	1500 V dc	3170	120.5	124.0	20 168	1961	CLW	
WCG2	Co-Co	1500 V dc	3640	80	132	19 974	1971	CLW	HEIL, India
YAM1	B-B	25 kV dc	1217	80	52	13 150	1965	Mitsubishi	

Diesel locomotives

Class	Wheel arrangements	Transmission	Rate power hp	Max kg	Tractive effort Continuous at kg	Tractive effort Continuous at km/h	Max speed km/h	Wheel dia mm	Total weight tonnes	Length over headstocks mm	Year first built	Builders Mechanical parts	Builders Engine & type	Builders Transmission
1676 mm gauge														
WDM1	Co-Co	Elec	1800	27 900	19 300	19	104	1016	112	16 777	1958	Alco, USA	Alco 12-cyl V251B	GE, USA
WDM2	Co-Co	Elec	2400	30 450	24 600	18	120	1092	112.8	15 580	1962	DLW, India	Alco 16-cyl V251B	BHEL, India
WDM3	B'-B'	Hyd	2500	High-speed 22 000	14 000	28	120	1092	76	14 800	1970	Henschel, West Germany	MD-108 oz 20-cyl	Myu, West Germany
		Hyd-Mech		Low-speed 20 080	20 000	18.5								
WDM4	Co-Co	Elec	2636	28 200	20 600	24	120	1092	113	17 270	1962	GM, USA	GM567D3 16-cyl	GM, USA
WDM6	Bo-Bo	Elec	1200	—	—	—	75	—	70	—	1981	DLW	DLW 6-cyl in-line, 4 stroke 251D	BHEL
WDS1	Bo-Bo	Elec	193	11 550	5000	10	56	965	46	9061	1945	GE, USA	Caterpillar D-17000-8-cyl	GE, USA
WDS2	C	Hyd	440	High-speed 9200	7300	7.55	54	1092	51	7265	1945	Krauss-Maffei, West Germany	MAN W 8V-17-5/ 22A 8-cyl	Voith L37 V
				Low-speed 15 420	14 750	3.86	27.6							
WDS3	C	Hyd	618	High-speed 10 400	7500	12	65	1092	57	9430	1961	MaK, West Germany	Maybach MD-435 8-cyl	MaK, West Germany
				Low-speed 1700	18 000	4								
WDS4	O-C-O	Hyd or Hyd-Mech	700	High-speed 11 500	8500	13	65	1092	60	9730	1969	MaK/CLW, India	MaK/CLW 6M282A(k) 6-cyl	Kirkoskar, India
				Low-speed 18 000	16 900	5.5	27							
WDS4A WDS4B	O-C-O	Hyd	660 700	High-speed										
WDS4D			600	16 700	12 400	8	65	1092	60	9730	1968 1969	CLW, India	MaK, West Germany	Voith, L4r2u
				Low-speed 18 000	17 000	5					1988		6M282A(k) 6-cyl	
WDS5	Co-Co	Elec	1065	31 500	32 300	3.2	109	1092	126	15 400	1967		Alco 251-B 6-cyl	GE, USA
WDS6	Co-Co	Elec	1400	34 000	30 300	6.9	62.5	1092	126	15 290	1977	DLW	Alco/DLW 251D	BHEL

Diesel locomotives continued

Class	Wheel arrangements	Transmission	Rate power hp	Max kg	Tractive effort Continuous at kg	km/h	Max speed km/h	Wheel dia mm	Total weight tonnes	Length over headstocks mm	Year first built	Builders Mechanical parts	Engine & type	Transmission
1000 mm gauge														
YDM1	B-B	Hyd	634	10 920	8230	12	88	864	44	10 630	1955	MaK/CLW	MaK/CLW 6M282A 6-cyl*	Voith, UK
YDM-2	B-B	Hyd	700	14 400	–	–	75	865 new 795 min	48	11 000	1986	CLW, India	CLW/MaK 6M282A(k) 6-cyl	Voith Hydraulic
YDM3	1B-B1	Elec	1390	14 300	10 300	24.5	80	Driving 865 Carrying 762	58.5	12 350	1961	GM, USA	GM 12 567c 12-cyl	GM, USA
YDM4	Co-Co	Elec	1400	18 935	19 200	15.65	96	965	72	13 818	1961	Alco/DLW, India	Alco 251-D 6-cyl	BHEL, India
YDM4A	Co-Co	Elec	1400	18 935	19 200	11.6	96	965	67	13 818	1964	MLW, Canada	MLW/251-D 6-cyl	GE, Canada
YDM5	C-C	Elec	1390	21 792	11 250	22.35	80	865	69	13 260	1964	GM, USA	GM 12 567c 12-cyl	GM, USA
610/762 mm gauge														
NDM1	B'-B'	Hyd	145	8790	7500	5	33	700	29	8400	1955	Arn Jung, West Germany	MWM TRHS 518 S 6-cyl	Voith, L33 U
NDM5	B-B	Hyd	490	–	–	–	50	–	22	–	1987	CLW, India	Cummins KTA 1150L	Voith L2r2zu2
ZDM2	B'-B'	Hyd-Mech	700	10 560	8500	12.5	50	700	32	9120	1964	MaK, West Germany	Maybach MD 435 8-cyl	MaK, West Germany
ZDM3	B'-B'	Hyd-Mech	700	10 500	9800	6.4	32	700	35	10 300	1971	CLW, India	CLW/MaK 6M282A(k) 6-cyl	Kirloskar
ZDM4A	1B-B1	Hyd	700	7800	–	–	50	700 new 640 min	38.5	10 300	1984	CLW, India	CLW/MaK 6M282A(k) 6-cyl	Voith L4r2u2

* Re-engined

Indonesia

Department of Communications

Departemen Perhubungan, 8 Jalan Merdeka Barat, 10110 Jakarta Pusat

Telephone: +62 21 351596/361308
Telex: 44310 dephub ia

Minister: Azwar Anas
Secretary-General: Dr D Hadisumarto

Indonesian State Railways (PJKA)
Perusahaan Jawatan Kereta Api

Jalan Perintis Kemerdekaan, 1, Bandung 40113, Java

Telephone: +62 22 58001-6
Cable: Qdirutka BD
Telex: 28263 bandung

Chief Director: Ir Soeharso
Corporate Secretary: Ir Soetarno
Director Personnel: Ir Soegiarto
Director of Finance: Imam Rustadi
Director of Traffic and Commerce: Ir Soernarno
Director of Operations: Ch N Latief, SH
Director, Traction Rolling Stock and Workshops: J T Situmorang
Director of Fixed Installations: Ir Koestomo
Chief of Planning Centre: Amir Harbani
Chief of Research and Development Centre: Eddy Buslani
Chief of PT Inka (Rolling Stock Plant): Ir Soetijanto
Chief of Education Training Centre: Soerono Martosewojo
Chief Auditor: Abdullah Sani

Gauge: 1067 mm; 750 mm
Route length: 5961 km; 497 km
Electrification: 125 km at 1.5 kV dc

The railway network in Indonesia is confined to the islands of Java, where the main system of some 4900 km is located, and Sumatra, where there are three separate systems totalling about 1900 km, including the whole 750 mm trackage. The system was built up to its present size during the 70 years prior to the Second World War, at which time 40 per cent of the network was owned privately. Nationalisation took place in the 1940s and 1950s.

Traffic

Indonesian Railways (PJKA) draws almost two-thirds of its income from a passenger business that has steadily increased since the 1970s. But annual freight carryings have soared more strikingly still, from 800 million tonne-km in 1982-83 to some 1600 million. PJKA management estimates that traffic apt for rail movement amounts to an extra 3500 million tonne-km a year, which at present eludes the railway for several reasons. One is government control of pricing. Another is that PJKA remains statutorily a common carrier, obliged to carry all freight offered whether or not it is profitable cargo. However, as things are the railway is overtaxed. It is short of rolling stock, with only a quarter of its passenger vehicles reported serviceable at the start of 1990; there are arrears of track renewal and resignalling; and more staff training

Japanese-built four-car emu for Jabotek system

is needed. In 1988 a World Bank loan of US$28 million was secured primarily for management improvement schemes, including introduction of a computer-based data transmission system.

PJKA has lately scored an important gain from road on its 180 km main line between Bandung and Jakarta. That is American President Lines' charter of a weekly unit train for its maritime containers. The new World Bank loan mentioned above will provide some money for development of container handling, which PJKA is keen to expand. A recent addition to this mode has been a service between Cigading port and Bekasi.

Electrification

The electrified system in Java covers the line between Jakarta and Bogor and some sections around the city of Jakarta. It is being expanded under the Jabotabek scheme into a regional network of nine lines and some 220 km envisaged as catering for 20 million people by the end of the century.

Financial difficulties have retarded progress, but consultancies have been committed to studies of the whole project, estimated to cost a total of R$ 643 000 million. JARTS of Japan (whence some multiple-unit sets have already been supplied for the Jakarta-Bogor line) has been engaged in the central area of the scheme, Sofretu of France in the west, and a British group, financed by the British Overseas Development Administration, in the east.

Besides provision of extra tracks where the suburban traffic will be intensive, and transfer of some sections to elevated rights of way, the project embraces two new orbital lines and construction of two new freight lines aggregating 80 km in length. These last will provide for the coal feed from Serpong of a new cement works at Cibinong, and the despatch of the plant's output to the port of Tanjungpriok. New workshops and depots will be needed to cater for a suburban emu fleet that may total up to 700 cars.

So far work has chiefly concerned track renewal, double-tracking and installation of some new halts and signalling improvements. Electrification proceeds on the western line from Jakarta to Tanahabang and Manggarai and is operational between Bogor and Tanahabang.

Investment and new line

Canadian Pacific Consulting Services assisted in a US$1300 million project to upgrade the 410 km 1067 mm-gauge route in Sumatra for the 40-wagon unit train movement of 2.5 to 3 million tonnes of coal a year from the Bukit Asam field to a new south coast port of Tarahan for shipment to an electricity generating station near Merak in West Java. Parts of the route are also used by other bulk freight flows. The works raised maximum permissible axleloadings from 13 to 18 tonnes and line speed to 60 km/h for freight and 90 km/h for passenger trains. Mechanical signalling is being retained, but traffic control by single-line token has been superseded by radio control through a new uhf/vhf radio network. A US$26 million contract for telecommunications equipment was awarded to International Aeradio of Canada. Hawker Siddeley Canada supplied 265 rotary-tippler wagons for the unit coal trains and General Motors of Canada 15 2000 hp diesel locomotives to haul them.

The Bukit Asam-Tarahan port coal haul could eventually gross 12 million tonnes a year. The investment needed and the operational economics of quadrupling the scheme's present design capacity have been under investigation by the Canadian consultancy.

Elsewhere, the port of Meneng has been rail-connected under a US$42.6 million project. The 22 km line's main purpose will be fertiliser transport in unit trains from a plant at Meneng.

There is a possibility of another substantial bulk flow of coal, destined for a cement works at Cibinong in West Java. Its capture would involve track renewal, signalling modernisation and telecommunications installation throughout the 120 km line from the port of Cigading to Serpong. The coal input could be balanced by rail transport of around 1.5 million tonnes of cement clinker output.

In West Sumatra new line construction has been mooted from Solok south to Indarung, east of Padang: and in North Sumatra, from Besitang through Langsa to Daaceh.

Intermodal terminal creation is on the agenda, exploiting railway-owned land wherever possible. PJKA is also pondering installation of a train ferry link between Java and Sumatra.

Traction and rolling stock

Upgrading of PJKA's rolling stock to modern standards and customer need is gathering pace. Almost a quarter of the diesel locomotive fleet is formed of 112 machines bought since 1980, chiefly from US and Canadian builders. Over 100 older locomotives will be thoroughly rehabilitated and in some cases re-engined.

In September 1989 PT Inka, BN of Belgium and Holec of the Netherlands signed an agreement for joint production of seven four-car emus for the Jakarta suburban network. The first three trains will be assembled by BN in Belgium and probably delivered in late 1991. The remainder will be assembled by PT Inka, which is expected subsequently to build a further tranche of 40 units. The deal followed a call for tenders for emus embodying chopper control and VVF inverter transmission.

At the end of 1989 PJKA was about to award a contract for rehabilitation of 96 of its Japanese-built diesel railcars. Contenders were three Japanese groups and an alliance of RENFE and two local companies.

PT Inka was initially established to manage a big programme of air-braked freight wagon assembly, chiefly from kits supplied by Japanese manufacturers, at the Madiur workshops. PJKA badly needs to rebuild its freight wagon fleet, which is inadequate on several counts: number of vehicles, because new construction has been outpaced by scrapping of antiques; incompatibility of some wagon types, since they do not have similar couplers; and lack of purpose-built vehicles for certain present-day traffics, specifically those from the steel industry.

At last report PJKA was operating 35 steam, and 518 diesel locomotives, 25 four-car emus, 415 dmus, 146 diesel railcars, 1145 passenger cars and 14 052 freight wagons.

Signalling

Over 2580 route-km are now equipped with Siemens & Halske mechanical tokenless block, located at some 300 centres in Java and 45 in Sumatra. All-relay interlockings on operational at numerous traffic centres.

Recent contracts issued included one to Ansaldo Trasporti for the 73 km from Surabaya to Kertosono, part of the southern main line to Yogyakarta; the installation would include centralised interlocking at 12 stations. Alkmaar of the Netherlands is resignalling the 135 km route in Java between Cikampek and Cirebon; interlockings are being supplied by Algemene Sein Industrie. LSE Technology of Australia is supplying a microwave telecommunications network with funding from the Australian Trade Commission.

Track
Standard rail
R54 54-43 kg/m; R50 50.4 kg/m; R14A 42.59 kg/m; R14 41.52 kg/m; R3 33.4 kg/m; R2 25.75 kg/m
750 mm-gauge: R10 16.4 kg/m
600 mm-gauge: ID 12.38 kg/m
Cross ties (sleepers)
Wood, thickness 130 mm
Concrete, thickness 195 mm
Steel, thickness 100 mm
Spacings: 1666/km plain track, 1700/km curves
Rail fastening: Rigid: dog or screw spike for R2 rail; Klem plate KI/KK for R42 rail; Klem plate KE/KF for R2 rail; Dorken spike; double elastic spring clip F type with rubber pad; double elastic Pandrol clip and rubber pad; single elastic Pandrol clip
Max gradient: 2.5%; 7% (rack sections)
Minimum curvature radius
Main line: 300 m
Max altitude: 1246 m near Garut, Java
Max axleload
Main line: 14 tons

Class BB303 1000 hp diesel-hydraulic B-B by Thyssen-Henschel

Ferrostaal diesel railcars at Yogyakarta (Marcel Vleugels)

612 RAILWAY SYSTEMS / Indonesia

Diesel locomotives

Class	Wheel arrangement	Transmission hp	Rated power	Max kg	Tractive effort Continuous at kg	km/h	Max speed mm	Wheel dia mm	Total weight tons	Length mm	Year first built	Builders Engine & type	Transmission	Repowering
CC 200	Co-Co	Elec	1600	21 623	14 074	15	90	908	96	17.00	1951	GE 12V 244E		Alco 12V 250 (4 locos)
CC 201	Co-Co	Elec	1950		11 825	12.7	100	952	82	14 133	1976	GE 7 FDL 8		
BB 200	A1A-A1A	Elec	875				120	1016	74.8	14 006	1956	GM 8567CR		
BB 201	A1A-A1A	Elec	1310	21 810			120	1016	78	14 026	1964	GM G12 567C		
BB 202	A1A-A1A	Elec	1000	21 810			100	1016	65	12 900	1968/71	GM GL8 645E		
BB 203	A1A-A1A	Elec	1730				100	904	78	14 133	1978	GE 7 FDL 8		
BB 204	B-2-B	Hyd	1000	–	–	–	60 20*	–	55	–	1982	MTU 12V 396 TC 12	Voith hydrostatic	
BB 300	B-B	Hyd	680	10 100			75	909	36	11 890	1956	MB 820 B		
BB 301	B-B	Hyd	1500	15 800	11 700	19	120	904	52	13 380	1962/69	MTU 12V 652 TR 11	L630 r U2	MB 12V 652 TB11 (23 locos)
BB 302	B-B	Hyd	1100	14 520 12 500	12 500	15	80	904	44	12 180	1969	MTU 12V 493	L520 r U2	
BB 303	B-B	Hyd	1150	14 100	11 500	15	90	904	44	12 320	1971/77/78	MTU MB12V 493	L52 r U2	
BB 304	B-B	Hyd	1500	17 150	11 700	20	120	904	52	13 380	1974	MTU 12V 652	L720 r U2	
BB 306	B-B	Hyd	857	–	–	–	75	–	40	–	1983	MTU 8V 396TC 12	L4 r 42 U2	
C 300	C	Hyd	350	9800	9250	4.5	30	904	30	8020	1964	MB 836 B	L203 U	
D 300	D	Hyd	340	10 200		5	50	904	34	9279	1956	MB 836 B	2WIL1.15	GM 8V92 (40 locos) GM 8V71 (6 locos) GM 12V 71 (6 locos) MWM TD 232V12 (13 locos)
D 301	D	Hyd	340	8400		5	50	904	28	8980	1960	MB 836 B/2	2WIL1.5	

* When working on rack

Electric railcars or multiple-units

Class	Cars per unit	Line voltage	Motor cars per unit	Motored axles per motor car	Rated output per motor (kW)	Max speed km/h	Weight tonnes per car (M-motor T-trailer)	Total seating capacity (M-motor T-trailer)	Length per car mm	Year first built
MCW 5	4	1500 dc	2	4	230	120	M 49.4 T 41.5	M 82 T 92	20 000	1976
VCW 8	4	1500 dc	2	4	230	120	M 49.4 T 41.5	M 51 T 82	20 000	1978

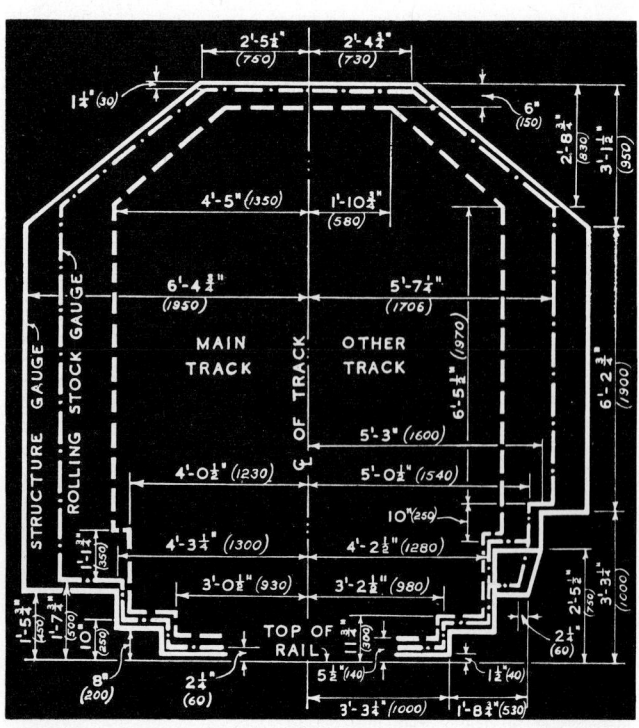

Loading gauge: main lines

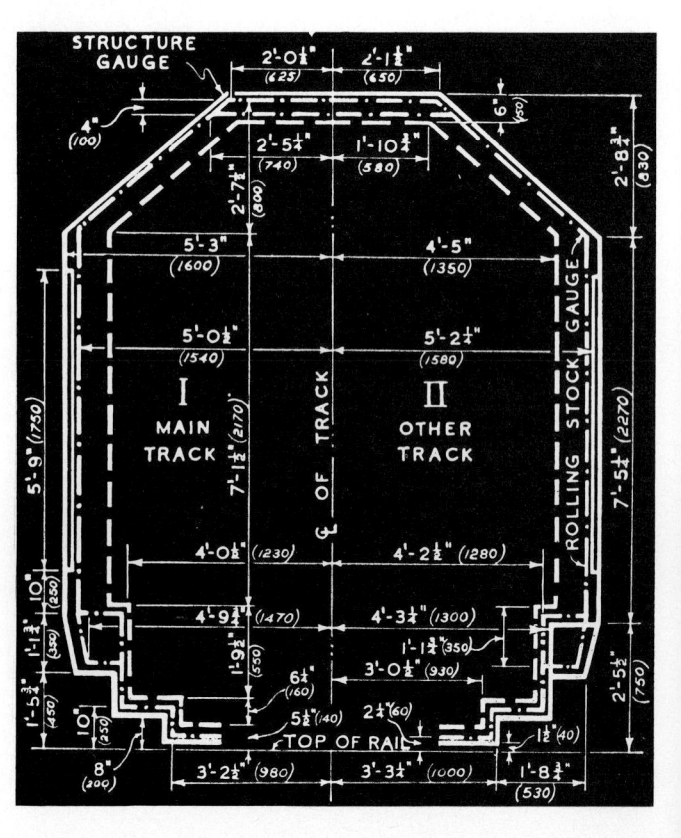

Loading gauge: secondary lines

Diesel railcars or multiple-units

Class	Cars per unit	Motor cars per unit	Motored axles per motor car	Transmission	Rated power per motor (hp)	Max speed km/h	Weight tonnes per car	Total seating capacity per unit	Length per car mm	Year first built	Builders Engine & type	Transmission
MCDW 300/ MCW 300	1	1	4	Hyd	215	90	36	200	19 640	1964	8V 71	DIWABUS US
MCW 301	2	2	2	Hyd	180	90	45	200	20 000	1976	DMH17H	TC 2A
MCW 302	2	2	2	Hyd	290	90	46	200	20 000	1978	DMH17SA	TCR 2-5

Iran

Ministry of Roads & Transportation

49 Taleghani Avenue, Tehran

Telephone: +98 21 646770, 664157

Minister: Eng Mohammad Saeedi Kia

Islamic Iranian Republic Railways (IIRR)

Rahe-Ahan Square, Tehran

Telephone: +98 21 555120
Cable: Rahan
Telex: 213103 rai ir

President: Eng Sadeq Afshar
Vice-Presidents
  Technical and Operating: Eng N Pourmirza
  Finance: A Sohrabian
  Planning: H Mehrazma
  Construction: Eng V Jamshidi
Managing Director: Sadeq Afshar
Directors
  Traction: P Alivand
  Electrical: Eng S A Jaafari Motlagh
  Technical Studies: F Sharifi
  Communications and Signalling: A Shikh-Mohammad
  Operations: S Parsania
  Track and Construction: S R Lèsani
  Purchasing: A Saidi
  Accounting: A A Saberi Pirouz
  Planning: M Daghighi

Gauge: 1435 mm; 1676 mm
Route length: 4573 km; 94 km
Electrification: 145 km at 25 kV 50 Hz ac

IIRR's key routes run from the ports of Bandar Khomeini and Khorramshar on the Persian Gulf to Tehran; and from the capital northwest to Razi on the Turkish and Djolfa on the USSR border. Teheran also radiates lines northeastward to Bandar Turkhman and Mashdad, and southeastward to Bafgh and Kerman. Further to the southeast is an isolated 94 km, 1524 mm-gauge line from Zahedan to the Pakistan border at Mirjaveh.

The electrified part is the final 146 km of the route to the USSR, from the junction of Tabriz to Djulfa. The electrification was undertaken by Technoexport of the USSR and the traction is furnished by eight 3600 kW locomotives based on Swedish Railways' Rc4. Built by SGP of Austria, the units have ABB electrical equipment.

Traffic

In its 1988-89 Islamic year IIRR recorded 12.509 million tonnes of freight and 6.799 million passenger journeys. Passenger-km grossed 4661 million, freight tonne-km 8047 million. The principal flow of international freight is with the USSR through Djulfa.

A drive has been mounted to lift international traffic with Turkey. The presidents of IIRR and Turkish Railways (TCDD) recently agreed to meet at six-monthly intervals to co-ordinate action; liaisons have been formed with exporters and importers; and competitive tariffs have been introduced. Creation of a Mediterranean-Persian Gulf landbridge by use of Syrian ports is an objective.

Restructure

In 1988 conversion of the railway into a government company, with greater freedom for management to apply modern techniques and equipment, was in progress. Some authority is being devolved to divisional management. Market orientation is a key principle of the restructure and quality of service is getting special attention. In the freight sector this is marked by development of door-to-door arrangements with improved intermodal transshipment: thus Kerman, the present extremity of the line southeast from Teheran, is now the railhead for truck deliveries to a wide area of southern Iran, including the port of Bandar Abbas on the Strait of Hormuz, with its access to the Indian Ocean.

Other priorities include improved facilities for staff training, adoption of computer-based data transmission systems for strict vehicle control, and investment in mechanised track maintenance equipment.

New lines

Construction of a new 709 km line from Bafgh to Bandar Abbas, to connect the port of Shahid Rajai and the iron mines of Golegohar to the existing railway network, began in 1983. It was anticipated that 350 km would be completed and become ready for operation from Bafgh to Golegohar in 1989.

Initially laid as single track, the line will eventually be double-track, electrified and CTC-controlled. A fleet of 1200 axle wagons of large capacity are being delivered by Wagon Pars Works for use on this line which, apart from connecting the port of Rajai to the network, will also be used for the transportation of iron ore from the inland mines to the steel complex of Mobarekeh in Isfahan.

IIRR aims next to connect Kerman with Zahedan. A study of the route has been completed and a building programme drafted. Construction will be undertaken when the volumes of transport are determined to be sufficient to justify the outlay.

Following discussions between the USSR and Iran, the latter announced early in 1988 that it contemplated

GM-EMD Type GT26CW locomotive

Hitachi 1050 hp diesel locomotive for IIRR

construction of an 800 km line north from Bafq to Meshdad and the USSR frontier at Sarakhs. Tenders to build were invited in late 1988. The national budget for 1989-90 provided US$380 million for infrastructure work, including construction of 1956 track-km.

The country's 1990–94 Five-Year Plan issued in the spring of 1990 proposed an investment of US$6800 million in IIRR infrastructure and rolling stock.

Other infrastructure projects

Construction of marshalling yards at Ghom and Aprin, and of bypasses at Ghom and Tehran, was under way in 1989. So was a programme of private siding construction at industrial plants within reach of the railway but not using it.

Doubling of track on lines where limits of capacity have been reached proceed. Of late this has concerned the Tehran-Ghom (180 km) and Ahwaz-Bandar Khomeini (120 km) sections.

To improve the availability of wagons and locomotives, a locomotive repair shop has been constructed at Bafgh.

To increase the reliability of signalling and communications system, a project for replacement of overhead cables by co-axial cables has been implemented on the

RAILWAY SYSTEMS / Iran—Iraq

330-km long Ghom-Sistan line. Radio communcation with trains is being introduced.

Traction and rolling stock
In 1989 IIRR's motive power fleet consisted of 523 diesel-electric and eight electric locomotives, and four Turbotrains from ANF-Frangeco, France.

Standard diesel locomotives have been provided by General Motors and more recently, to the GM-EMD design, by Hyundai of South Korea. Ninety more locomotives were ordered in 1988-89. For heavy shunting, IIRR has 38 Hitachi locomotives.

In 1989 IIRR had a fleet of 12 420 freight wagons, and operated 925 passenger cars, including 60 restaurant and 140 couchette cars. A number of secondhand passenger cars have been acquired from the German Federal Railway.

In 1987 Simmering-Graz-Pauker of Austria signed a technology-transfer contract to supply 400 air-conditioned passenger cars, partly couchette vehicles, in 1988–94. The first 10 were shipped complete from Austria, the next 65 in kit form for local assembly by Wagon Pars in the latter's Arak plant, which has been modernised and enlarged with SGP help. The first of the latter were rolled out in mid-1989. The residue of the order would be built by Wagon Pars with a steadily dwindling Austrian content. The conclusion of the order, in 1993, will be wholly built by Wagon Pars.

Purchase of 2750 freight cars was planned in the 1985–90 Five-Year Plan, and by 1989 more than 2000 wagons of different types had already been delivered by the Wagon Pars company. The majority were constructed under a licensing and technology transfer contract with Waggon Union of West Germany.

Track
As investment in track upkeep was inadequate before the 1979 Revolution 1400 km of track were found to be in need of complete renovation. Of this total, 700 km have already been renovated with the use of continuously welded UIC-60 rails and 'K' type fastenings. Renovation of the remainder continues.

With the increase of the length of trains and of their tonnage the loops of all stations on the Tehran-Ghom, Tehran-Mashad, Andimeshk-Ahwaz and Tehran-Tabriz lines have been lengthened.

Standard rail
Type U33 46 kg/m
Type IIA, 38.4 kg/m in 12.5 m lengths
Type III, 33.5 kg/m in 12 m lengths
UIC 50 kg/m in 12.5 m lengths
UIC 60 kg/m in 18 m lengths (Zahedan-Mirjaveh)
Rail joints: 4 and 6-hole fishplates; and welding
Cross ties (sleepers): Creosote impregnated hardwood, steel and concrete. Wood 2600 × 250 × 150 mm. Steel 2400 × 300 × 70 mm. Concrete sleepers under welded rail

Spacing
1680 per km
Rail fastenings
Wood sleepers: sole plates, screws and bolts
Steel sleepers: clips and bolts
Filling: Part broken stone, and part river ballast; minimum 200 mm under sleepers
Max curvature: 7.9° = minimum radius 220 m
Longest continuous gradient: 16 km of 2.8% (1 in 36) grade between Firouzkouh and Gadouk
Max altitude: 2177 m near Nourabad station
Max axleloading: 20 tonnes (25 tonnes Bafgh-Bandar Abbar)
Max permitted speed
Freight trains: 55 km/h
Passenger trains: 80 km/h

Principal diesel locomotives

Class	Wheel arrangement	Transmission	Rated power (kW)	Max speed km/h	Total weight tonnes	No in service 1989	Year first built	Builders
GT26CW	C-C	Elec	2235	120	120	263	1973	GM-EMD Hyundai
G22W	B-B	Elec	1118	114	80	42	1975	GM-EMD
G-18	B-B	Elec	820	100	80	2	1958	GM-EMD
G-16	C-C	Elec	1350	100	120	20	1957	GM-EMD
G-12	B-B	Elec	980	100	82	135	1958	GM-EMD
G-8	B-B	elec	715	100	78.5	13	1958	GM-EMD
HD10C	B-B	Elec	798	100	80	38	1961	Hitachi

Electric locomotives

Class	Wheel arrangement	Line voltage	Rated output (kW)	Max speed km/h	Weight tonnes	Overall length mm	No in service 1989	Year first built	Builders
40-700RC4	Bo-Bo	25 kV-50 Hz	3500	100	80	151 582	8	1982	SGP/ASEA

Iraq

Ministry of Transport & Communications

Kanat Street, Baghdad

Minister: M H Al-Zubaidi

Iraqi Railways

Central Station, Damascus Square, Baghdad

Telephone: +964 1 537 0011
Cable: Transrail Baghdad
Telex: 212272 railway ik

Director General; Mohammed Yunis Al Ahmad
Directors
  Traffic and Operations: Ing Akram M Owaid
  Mechanical and Electrical Engineering: A Nabeel
  Civil Engineering: E Jibrail
  New Projects: Ing Hashim H Sarsam
  Administration and Finances: Mouaid M Khatab
  Planning: Ing Ghassan Z Rushdi
  Stores and Purchasing: Ing Saleem Yousif Shammou
  Signalling and Telecommunications: Ing Mohammed H Tahir

Gauge: 1435 mm
Route length: 3081 km;

New lines
The war with Iran did not deter Iraq from pressing ahead with its grandiose plan to invest the equivalent of US$20 000 million, largely obtained from oil, minerals and other state industry profits, in 2700 km of new railways. The New Railways Implementation Authority (NRIA) was established in September 1980 to co-ordinate the construction activity. In 1987, however, NRIA was wound up and its functions assumed by a new organ, the State Enterprise for Implementation of Transport and Communications Projects.

The first of the new projects, completed in the 1980s, was a 404 km line from Baghdad via Radi and Haditha to the Syrian border at Husaiba, with a 115 km branch from Al Qaim to the phosphate mines at Akashat in the west, so as to link the latter with a fertiliser plant at Al Qaim, in the Euphrates valley. Like all new IRR lines, the Baghdad-Husaiba was engineered

Thyssen-Henschel 2485 hp diesel-electric Co-Co, delivered in 1984

for 250 km/h, partly for ease of maintenance in the forseeable future, when speeds will be limited to 140 km/h for passenger and 100 km/h for freight. Track specifications called for UIC 60 kg/m rail fastened by Pandrol clips to prestressed concrete monobloc sleepers, with ballast depth of 350 mm. The main contractor for the Baghdad-Husaiba line's colour-light signalling and CTC was WSSB of the German Democratic Republic; the National Buildings Construction Corporation of India won the Rs 630 million contract for the line's stations and traction depots and workshops.

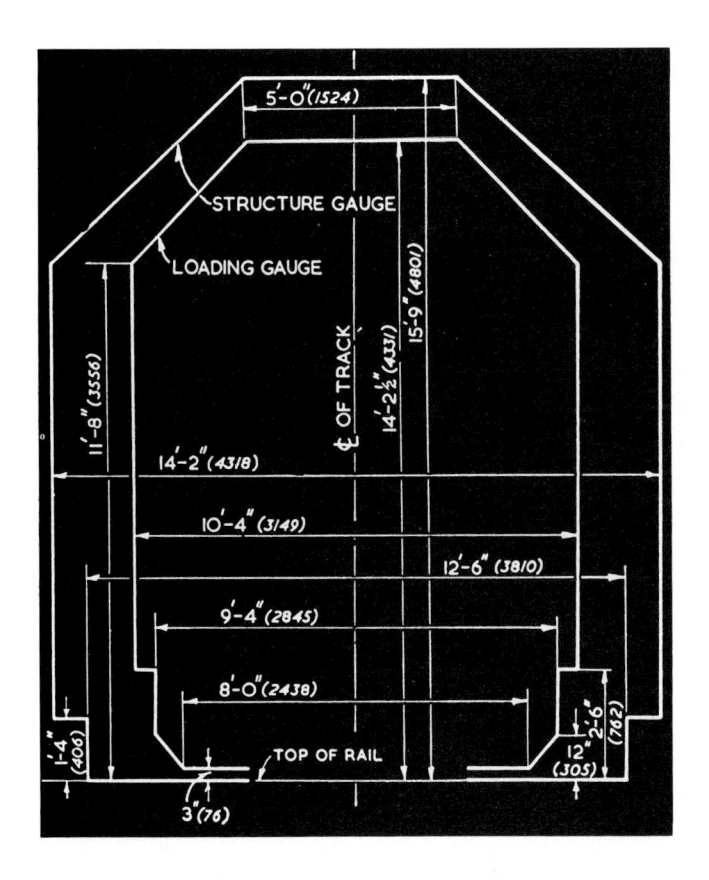

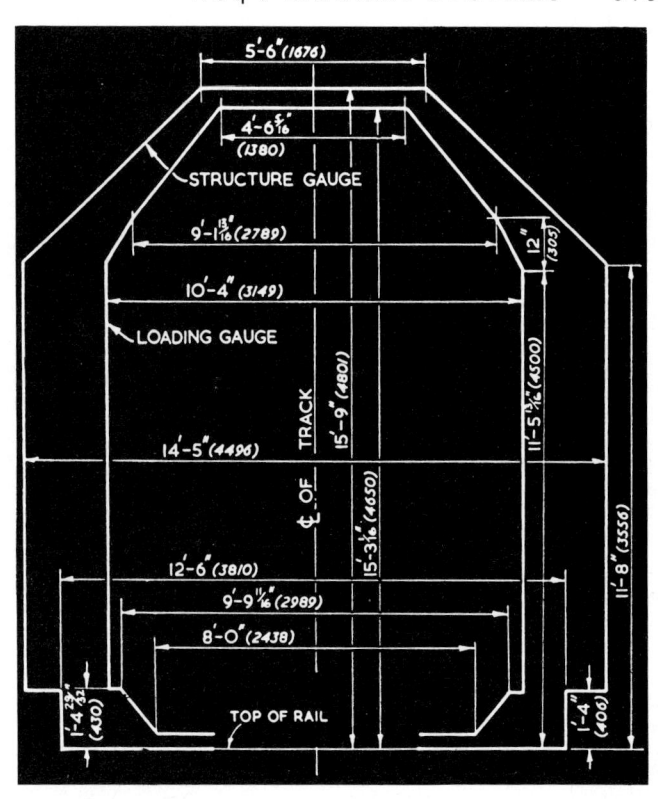

Management, operation and maintenance of the 519 km Baghdad-Al Qaim railway for a five-year term was put on contract offer. RITES was eventually selected and also took over the Akashat branch. Revenue-earning operation was begun in May 1988. However in 1990, with the war over, many demobilised soldiers seeking employment, and the country suffering foreign exchange problems as a consequence of the conflict, the contract with RITES was cancelled in mid-term. RITES had some 1500 staff working on the railway.

From Haditha on this route a 252 km transversal, built initially as single-track with provision for later doubling, has been completed via Baiji to Kirkuk. This project involved bridging the Euphrates, Tigris and Therthar rivers. Consultants for the scheme, which included a new marshalling yard and passenger terminal at Kirkuk, were DEConsult. The work was executed by Hyundai Engineering and Namkwang Construction under project management by DE-Consult and its subcontractors, China Railway Foreign Service Corporation. Completion was achieved in November 1987. This route, too, was put out to international tender for management, operation, maintenance and staff training. The line is CTC-controlled with the complement of track-to-train radio and hot box detectors; this contract was secured by GEC-General Signal of Britain. An 80 km extension was planned from Kirkuk to Sulaymaniya, but the latter's proximity to the Iranian border caused the scheme's original consultants, Sofrerail, to withdraw in 1984.

The metre-gauge line from Baghdad via Khanaqin to Kirkuk and Erbil has been closed and IRR no longer operates any metre gauge. The intention has been to substitute a new 480 km standard-gauge line from Baghdad to Mosul on a more direct route, with a branch to Khanaqin (which until peace was out of the question because of proximity to the war zone) and a 160 km extension to beyond Mosul to Zakho on the Turkish border. Sofrerail were consultants for the preliminary study of the Baghdad-Mosul scheme, Henderson Busby for the continuation to Zakho. This scheme now has a low priority, because for the present Kirkuk is adequately served by the new line east from Baiji.

The largest single project in the original network plan embraces a new 910 km double-track route south from Baghdad to the port of Um Qasr. This is presently the first priority so as far as new trunk route building is concerned, because of traffic pressure on the historic Baghdad-Basra route, the infrastructure characteristics of which are inferior to those of the recently-built lines. At Kut the new line would split, the primary arm making for Basra via Nasiryah, the secondary arm taking the Tigris route via Amara. This new route would be constructed with a ruling gradient of 0.5 per cent and a minimum curve radius of 5000 metres. The scheme envisages a new marshalling yard at Shuiaba. Engineering design has been undertaken by Henderson Busby but no construction contracts have as yet been placed. In 1982 Transmark, British Rail's consultancy, was commissioned to undertake an upgrading design study, including an electrification assessment, for the existing 543 km route between Baghdad and Basra via Diwaniya (together with similar work on the 425 km metre-gauge line from Baghdad to Kirkuk and Erbil).

A line already achieved south of Baghdad is a 38 km double-track bypass of Samawa. This was to be the beginning of a new 242km line to the west of the present Basra-Baghdad line, rejoining the latter south of Baghdad at Mussayab. Besides relieving the existing route, the loop would serve new cement plants.

Other recent construction has embraced several lengthy branches to industrial plants. One such, built by IRCON, was a 32 km branch from Samawa to a cement plant at Al Muthana, which was formally opened in January 1988.

Sotecni have been the consultants for a prospective 130 km line from Karbala to Ramadi, to provide access to the north for cement plants at Karbala.

A key component of the new main-line plans, and currently the first priority for completion, is a Baghdad Belt Line of 112 km, from which the new trunk routes would sprout in flying or burrowing junctions. This scheme, involving three major river bridges and a 7.5 km tunnel, is also motivated by anxiety to separate Baghdad area passenger and freight traffic to the maximum extent. Sotecni are the main consultants, with Sofrerail of France as sub-consultants. Freight handling is to be concentrated on a new yard, depot and workshop complex at Yousifia, in south-west Baghdad, and a new passenger terminal in the east of the city to complement the present Baghdad West.

Other new line projects include a 150 km line from Salman Pak, south-east of Baghdad on the putative route of the new Baghdad-Kut line, to Khanaqin; and a 95 km branch from Basra to the port of Fao, on the Shatt al Arab waterway. The first of these, for which Sofrerail are the consultants, has been low in priority because of the hostilities with Iran. Henderson Busby completed a feasibility study of the second.

In March 1988 the Transport Minister announced ambition to construct a 1280 km line from Baghdad to Amman and Aqaba (Jordan) and Cairo (Egypt). A route to Aqaba, starting on IRR at Haditha, northwest of Baghdad, was subsequently agreed with Jordan, but that country's shortage of resources braked progress. During the war with Iran, Iraq made considerable use of Aqaba as an export-import gateway, to avoid use of the Persian Gulf.

Agreement was also concluded between Iraq and Turkey to renew studies of a direct link between the two countries' rail systems, to avoid a 70 km transit of Syrian territory between Kurtalan and Mosul. However, all this predated the Middle Eastern crisis sparked by Iraq's August 1990 invasion of Kuwait.

Traffic 1988

Total passenger-km (million)	1570
Total freight tonne-km (million)	2079

Traction and rolling stock

Huge orders for locomotives and rolling stock have already been placed in connection with the network expansion programme. Placement of contracts supervised by Henderson Busby, in partnership with Guthrie and Craig, of the UK, entrusted Francorail-MTE with an order for 72 3600 hp diesel-electric locomotives for the Baghdad-Husaiba line, Prago-invest with one for 21 1100 hp diesel shunters, Kolmex with one for 2505 freight wagons, ANF-Industrie with one for 260 special-purpose freight wagons and Invest-Import of Yugoslavia with one for 78 passenger cars and 1960 freight vehicles. Bombardier of Canada was commissioned to supply spares worth US$14.5 million for the 61 2000 hp Type MXS620 diesel locomotives which the company delivered in 1975-76. Thyssen-Henschel has been fulfilling an order worth DM250 million for 82 2485 hp mixed-traffic diesel-electric locomotives. In 1982 ANF-Industrie was contracted to supply a total of 236 air-conditioned passenger cars including 25 luggage-generator coaches, 70 first-class couchette cars, 10 restaurant cars, 25 sleepers, 100 second-class day cars and six special cars for VIP travellers.

At latest available report, in 1988, the railway was operating 436 diesel-electric locomotives, 496 passenger cars (including 28 restaurant and 386 couchette cars) and 12 836 freight wagons.

Track-to-train radio

A £2 million contract for track-to-train radio operation has been placed with Marconi Communications of Great Britain.

Ireland

Department of Tourism & Transport

Kildare Street, Dublin 2

Telephone: +353 1 789522
Telex: 93478
Telefax: +353 11 763350

Minister: Seamus Brennan
Secretary: Donal O'Mahony

Iarnród Éireann
Irish Rail

Connolly Station, Dublin 1

Telephone: +353 1 363333
Telex: 31638
Telefax: +353 1 364760

Chairman: G T P Conlon
Directors: E J O'Connor
 S Feely
 T A Tobin
 J Daly
 J McCullough
Managing Director: E J O'Connor
Manager, Business Development (Passenger): J B Mooney
Manager, Business Development (Freight): D Looney
Manager, Operations: C D Waters
Manager, Human Resources: J P Walsh
Manager, Finance and Accounting and Company Secretary: J A Watters
Chief Civil Engineer: P O Jennings
Chief Mechanical Engineer: R P Grainger
Manager, Media and PR: Cyril Ferris

Gauge: 1600 mm
Route length (open to traffic): 1947 km
Electrification: 36.92 km at 1.5 kV dc

Restructure

Following passage of the Transport (Reorganisation of Coras Iompair Éireann) Act in December 1986, Iarnród Éireann (Irish Rail), Bus Éireann (Irish Bus) and Bus Atha Cliaith came into being in February 1987. CIE is now a holding company, of which the three transport concerns are subsidiaries.

Irish Rail is responsible for all rail services in the state including the Dublin Area Rapid Transit. It is also responsible for all rail and road freight services, for catering services, and for the operation of Rosslare Harbour, which caters for sailings to Fishguard and the Continent.

The subvention formula introduction in 1983 and requiring an annual reduction of 2.5 per cent in real terms in rail expenditure was extended for one year to 1989. In addition, the 1984 expenditure on main line maintenance, renewals and depreciation was required to be reduced by 25 per cent between 1985 and 1989 (ie 5.6 per cent per annum including the 2.5 per cent reduction already imposed in 1983).

Freight traffic

The 1989 results were seen as very encouraging, generating an overall revenue increase on 1988, and were denied further growth by a continuing decline in the fertiliser market. Parcels, groupage and unit load revenues were all up on the previous year's totals, despite intense road competition from local and international hauliers. Cement, mineral ores and beet revenues were also up on the 1988 returns, but fertiliser and beet revenues were down.

Significant gains have been flow of bulk coal from Dundalk to Dublin and Arklow; and distribution of Ford vehicle parts from Daventry, England, for next-day delivery by passenger train nationwide. Successful fulfilment of this latter contract resulted in the securing for IE's freight train operation of Ford stock order business in open tender against international operators.

Besides developing almost 600 000 tonnes of container business annually with Bell Lines, CIE has adapted containerisation to most other traffics, notably coal and grain. Parcels traffic is palletised and then

IE GM-built Class 071 2250 hp diesel and inter-city train of BREL-built cars based on British Rail's Mk III design

IE Dundalk-Dublin push-pull set of Mk III coaches

Class B diesel-electric Bo-Bo and Waterford-Dublin unit container train for Bell Lines

Ireland / **RAILWAY SYSTEMS** 617

containerised for trainload movement nightly between Dublin and 30 centres in the country.

Passenger services
In 1988 IE completed construction of 22 Mk III push-pull coaches, five of them driving trailers. These are now operated in four- or six-car rakes on the suburban service between Dublin and Dundalk.

IE has lifted maximum speed from 120 to 145 km/h over sections of its Dublin-Cork main line. As a result it aims now to raise the ceiling from 110 to 145 km/h on the Dublin-Belfast route, and to standardise a limit of 130 km/h on other key routes.

Dublin Area Rapid Transit (DART)
Dublin's rapid transit rail system operates over 38 route-km electrified at 1.5 kV dc from Bray, south of Dublin Connolly station, to Howth, in the north. The 40 two-car emus that run the service were built by Linke-Hofmann-Busch, with thyristor chopper-controlled traction and regenerative braking equipment by GEC Traction; they have air suspension and passenger-operated sliding doors. Up to three units can be operated in multiple.

The emus share the route with diesel locomotive-hauled trains, for which lineside signalling has been retained. The emus are fitted with Automatic Train Protection (ATP) equipment, activated by coded currents passed through the running rails, detected by coils on the emus and processed on board.

The locomotives are fitted with a Continuous Automatic Warning System (cab signalling). Both emus and locomotives are fitted with AEG-Telefunken train radio allowing two-way transmission of fixed message telegrams communication with the controlling signalman at the appropriate CTC centre (suburban or main line).

Signalling and telecommunications
The Dublin suburban line is controlled from a computer-based vdu console at Connolly station. The system utilises automatic route-setting and optimisation of public road level crossing closures, the latter being supervised by closed-circuit television. The CTC building also houses a similar console for control of 408 route-km of main line railway. The system permits operation of cab signalling equipment fitted to all locomotives, as well as train radio, and is being extended to cover further lines.

Motive power and rolling stock
IE's motive power fleet at the start of 1990 consisted of 126 diesel locomotives. Freight wagons totalled 1878, passenger coaches 267, including 24 buffet/restaurant cars, 40 emus and 74 vans.

Type of coupler in standard use: Passenger cars, screw; freight cars, buckeye or Instanter
Type of braking: Locomotive-hauled stock, vacuum or air

Track
Standard rail: Flat bottom; 113, 95, 92 and 85 lb/yd, 54 kg/m, 50 kg/m. Bullhead; 95, 90, 87 and 85 lb/yd
Cross ties (sleepers): Timber, 2590 × 255 × 125 mm; concrete, 2475 × 220 × 188 mm
Spacing: Concrete 144/km straight, 1556/km curved track; timber, 1313/km straight, 1422/km curved track
Rail fastenings: Timber sleepers, CI chairs and sole-

Traffic	1985	1986	1987	1988	1989
Freight tonnage (000)	3379	3126	3014	3010	3067
Freight tonne-km (million)	600.1	574.4	563.1	544.6	559.9
Passenger-km (million)	1023.4	1085.6	1196	1180.3	1220.2
Passenger journeys (000)	20 090	21 735	24 895	24 043	24 718

Finances (I£ 000)					
Revenue	1985	1986	1987	1988	1989
Passenger	37 513	38 771	42 153	45 190	47 317
Freight	23 990	24 462	24 410	24 151	24 634
Other	—	—	—	—	—
Total	61 503	63 223	66 563	69 341	71 951
Expenditure					
Staff	32 958	NA	83 731	85 553	84 891
Materials and services	94 392	NA	44 788	46 727	43 044
Depreciation	9895	NA	10 109	10 425	10 458
Financial charges	23 558	NA	26 182	18 768	19 218
Total	160 803	162 470	164 810	161 473	157 611

Two-car emu by Linke-Hofmann-Busch for Howth-Bray electrification

Diesel locomotives

Class	Wheel arrangement	Transmission	Rated power hp	Tractive effort Max lb (kg)	Tractive effort Continuous at lb (kg)	Tractive effort Continuous at mph (km/h)	Max speed mph (km/h)	Wheel dia in (mm)	Total weight tons (tonnes)	Length ft in (mm)	No in service 1989	First built	Builders Mechanical parts	Builders Engine & type
071	Co-Co	Elec	2475/2250	65 000 (29 484)	43 264 (19 625)	16.4 (26.39)	89 (143.2)	40 (1016)	99 (100.6)	51' 0" (15 545)	18	1976	GM	GM12-645 E3
AR (00)*	Co-Co	Elec	1325/1250	54 000 (24 494)	18 000 (8165)	21.5 (34.6)	75 (120.7)	38 (965)	82 (83.3)	51' 0" (15 545)	39	1955/56	Metro-Cammell	GM12-645 E
AR (00)	Co-Co	Elec	1650/1500	43 300 (19 656)	22 415 (10 166)	21.5 (34.6)	75 (120.7)	38 (965)	82 (83.3)	51' 0" (15 545)	5	1956	Metro-Cammell	GM12-645 E
B (121)	Bo-Bo	Elec	950/875	36 000 (16 330)	30 400 (13 789)	8 (12.9)	77 (123.9)	40 (1016)	64 (65)	39' 10" (12 141)	15	1961	GM	GM
B (141)	Bo-Bo	Elec	950/875	36 000 (16 330)	27 500 (34 304)	9 (14.5)	77 (123.9)	40 (1016)	67 (68)	40' 0½" (13 424)	37	1962/63	GM	GM 8-645 CR
B (181)	Bo-Bo	Elec	1100/1000	37 500 (17 010)	24 400 (11 975)	11 (17.7)	89 (143.2)	40 (1016)	67 (68)	44' 0½" (13 424)	12	1966	GM	GM 8-645 E

* Uprated

Electric multiple-units

Class	Cars per unit	Line voltage	Motor cars per unit	Motored axles per motor car	Rated output (kW) per motor (continuous)	Max speed km/h	Weight tonnes per car (M-motor T-trailer)	Total seating capacity	Length per car m	No in service 1989	Rate of acceleration m/s²	Year first built	Builders Mechanical parts	Builders Electrical equipment
8101	2	1500	1	4	130	100	M 42 T 29	144	21	40	0.9	1983	Linke-Hofmann-Busch	GEC Traction

plates with fangbolts; concrete sleepers, H-M fastenings generally, Pandrol on crossings
Minimum curvature radius
Running lines: 140 m

Sidings: 80 m
Max gradient: 1 in 40
Longest continuous gradient: 8.45 km, with 1% (1 in 100) ruling gradient

Max altitude: 165 m at Stagmount, Co Kerry
Max axleloads: 17 tonnes for locomotives, generally 15.75 tonnes for wagons, but 18.8 tonnes for specific traffics on bogie wagons

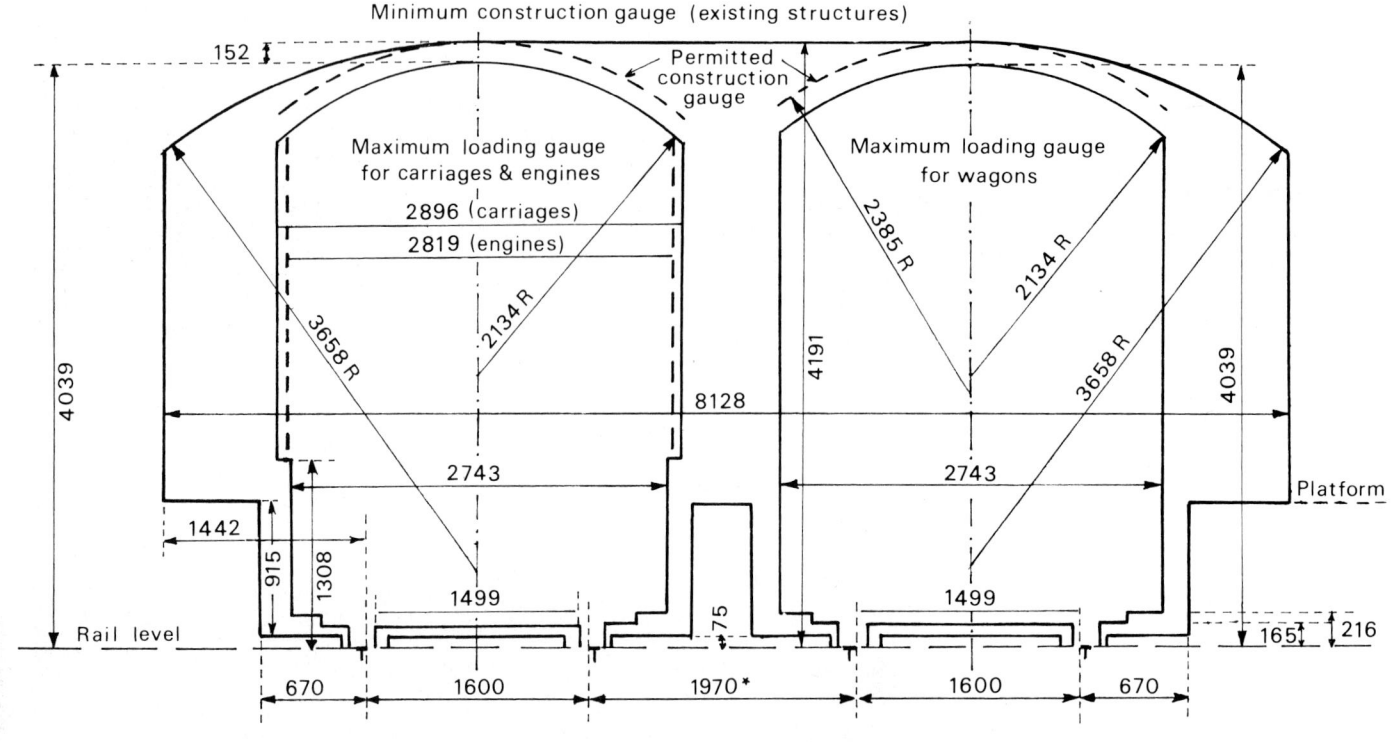

Minimum construction gauge (existing structures)

Notes *1870 in isolated cases
All dimensions subject to curvature additions as follows
End throw $\frac{21440}{R}$ Centre throw $\frac{22480}{R}$
Vehicles may drop 38 mm with wheel wear and under load
R Radius in metres

Israel

Ministry of Transportation

97 Jaffe Road, Jerusalem

Telephone: +972 2 229211

Minister: Moshe Katzav
Director General: Jacki Even

Ports & Railways Authority

74 Petach Tikva Road, Tel Aviv
Telephone: +972 3 5121905

Chairman: Zvi Keynan
Director General: Ing Shaul Raziel

Israel Railways (ISR)

Central Station, PO Box 18085, Tel Aviv

Telephone: +972 3 5421401
Cable: Rakevet
Telex: 46570 iral il
Telefax: +972 3 258176

Director General: Eliahu Barak
Deputy Director General (Technical): Leon Heyman
Managers:
  Northern Division: Bobi Solonicov
  Southern Division: Ezra Erez
  Traffic & Commercial: Yaacov Abitbol
  Finance: Eliahu Nakar
  Traction and Rolling Stock: Michael Bar-Noy
  Signalling and Telecommunications: Meier Lozar
  Railway & Civil Engineering: Kalman Slutsker

Development: Pinhas Ben Shaul
Legal Adviser: Doron Ravel
Public Relations: Ilan Falkov

Gauge: 1435 mm
Route length: 520 km

Change of Status

Israel State Railways was for long operated as a separate economic enterprise by the Ministry of Transport, but from September 1988 the system became part of a new public enterprise, the Ports and Railways Authority. One objective was to reallocate some of the former Ports Authority's accumulated funds to railway investment, since government policy for the past few years has been to renovate the railway, principally as regards its passenger operations, as an attractive alternative to the rising volume of motor transportation. Another aim of the change was to allow the railway more commercial freedom to react to changing market conditions.

Traffic (million)	1985/86	1988-89	1989-90*
Passenger journeys	2.8	2.495	2.313
Passenger-km	205	161.25	152.66
Freight tonnage	6.04	6.59	6.65
Freight tonne-km	942.2	1034.5	1037.6

* Estimated

Passenger traffic development plan

At present only 224 route-km are operated by passenger trains, because of the strong national competition from Dan-Egged bus services, which cover a 10 000 route-km network with some 5000 vehicles. The railway's share of the national travel market, in terms of passenger-km, is less than 5 per cent. But the railway's development plan, recently updated to the end of the next century's first decade, envisages passenger service of an additional 126 route-km.

In a first step, the railway was in 1990 renovating 28 passenger cars, restyling them internally and decking them externally with a new azure blue livery instead of the traditional brown and tan. The refurbished cars, which include eight British Rail Mk II bought second-hand in 1977, have had their seating density reduced and their use will incur a supplementary fare. A train-set will divide such cars from those not modified with a modernised buffet car, including a pay-telephone kiosk.

Passenger service development will be facilitated when the long-awaited 4.5 km Aylon rail connection between the two terminals in Tel Aviv is completed. That will make a wide range of attractive cross-country services possible. A new Tel Aviv Central station was opened in the Ayalon area in May 1988. In the summer of 1987 the Transport Minister authorised upgrading of the 97 km Tel Aviv-Jerusalem line to revive the line's passenger service, abandoned in face of invincible bus competition. The scheme includes a major realignment that will shorten the severely-graded route by 8 km and cut transit time to 60–65 minutes, on a par with that of the competing buses.

Revival of passenger service is planned between Tel Aviv and Beersheva, possibly as far as a new station in the centre of Beersheva; and between Tel Aviv, Ashdod and Ashkelon. Realignment to shorten the distance between Tel Aviv and Ashdod is proposed, also the relocation of Ashkelon station in the town centre. It is hoped to trim Haifa-Tel Aviv journey time from today's 60–68 minutes to 45 minutes.

The core of the future passenger system is seen as electrified double track. Freight traffic, principally in the south, will remain diesel-powered.

By the year 2010, Israel Railways envisage a business of some 117 million passenger journeys a year, 77 per cent of the total suburban. The prospective timetables will integrate suburban and longer-haul services.

Haifa and Tel Aviv suburban plans

The Ministry of Transport has endorsed plans to launch rapid transit in Haifa and Tel Aviv. In Haifa the first move planned is upgrading of the 11.8 km Haifa-Krayot line to permit increase of its Haifa-Nahariya trains and a cut of their transit time from today's 45–60 minutes to 26–38 minutes.

Construction of 9km of new track is planned to start a Haifa-Kiryat Ata service, and of 13 km for a new Tel Aviv-Herzliya-Ra'anana-Kfar Saba service. A Tel Aviv-Petah Tikva service will require upgrading of 9 km of existing track and a new segment of 2 km. A 5 km branch to Ben Gurion Airport is planned, and construction of 13 km, 6 km of it associated with the new Tel Aviv-Ashdod alignment (see above), for a Tel Aviv-Rishon Letzion service.

In total these schemes are foreseen to require a fleet of 100 three- or four-car diesel or electric trainsets.

In 1990 work in connection with these projects included station improvements and resignalling over 9km of the Haifa-Motzkin line.

Freight

In contrast to passenger traffic, the volume of freight has doubled since 1972. It is expected to reach between 14.5 and 16.5 million tonnes annually by the next decade. In this sector the railway's current market share is 20 per cent. About 70 per cent of the tonnage is potash from the Dead Sea and phosphates from Oron and Har Zin, which are conveyed over the Negev lines to the port of Ashdod in unit trains of up to 4000 tonnes hauled by two GM Type G26CW 2200 hp Co-Co diesel-electrics in multiple. Some goes to chemical plants on Haifa Bay. For the rest, ISR's freight is chiefly bulk movement of containers, grain and oil.

In 1987 a new rail terminal was completed at Tzefa, to which a conveyor belt of 18 km length delivers increased quantities of potash from Sedom on the Dead Sea. The potash is carried by rail from Tzefa mainly to the port of Ashdod (155 km), but some for domestic purposes is taken to the industrial area north of Haifa (270 km).

In late 1990 a new power station located at Ashkelon, 42 km south of Ashdod, would be opened. IR will carry 2.5 m tons of coal per annum from the port of Ashdod to the new power station site on the merry-go-round unit train principle. The coal will be conveyed in five daily trains each of 30 self-discharging hopper wagons (60 tonnes payload) hauled by two 3000 hp diesel-electric locomotives, the most powerful so far operated by IR, equipped with slow speed control for moving train discharge. The wagon fleet will total 69 (see below).

Finances (INS million)

	1988/89	1989/90*
Revenue		
Passenger	7.873	8.435
Freight	46.031	57.497
Other income	12.094	3.310
Total	65.998	69.242
Expenditure		
Staff	35.010	50.668
Materials & services	36.521	44.600
Depreciation & interest	3.511	19.584
Total	1.056	
Deficit	75.971	110.256

* Estimated

Eilat line in suspense

In 1984 the government approved a start on the Galilee-Eilat project, but this was subsequently postponed. A start was once again authorised in 1987, but there was no follow-through.

In 1988 the government attempted to negotiate a turnkey contract for the Eilat line's construction with White Industries of Australia, which had offered to raise the necessary finance. Total cost is asssssed within a wide range of US$180 to US$500 million, dependent on the extent of infrastructure work at Eilat that is embodied in the final plan.

The first phase would be a 17 km extension eastward to Hazera of the southern arm of ISR, currently terminating at Zin. Next a 30 km line would be projected from this extension northward to Sedom, at the southern end of the Dead Sea. Finally, a 156 km line would be built to Eilat from the initial extension near Hazeva. It has been forecast that together these new lines could double ISR's current freight carryings, principally in movement of potash from Sedom, of containers and imported coal shipped through Eilat, and of fertiliser from the Zin area for export. Eilat's tourist trade could add sizeable passenger traffic. Rolling stock requirements for the completed extensions have been put at 24 locomotives, 20–30 passenger cars and about 400 freight cars.

Hopes have also been voiced that the new line could transmute Israel Railways into a Red Sea-Mediterrean landbridge for Far Eastern/Australasian-European traffic that would surpass the parallel Suez Canal for speed.

New Kalmar T44 diesel locomotive and renovated cars; the front end of the leading car houses a 220 hp diesel-generator set for hotel power supplies

Interior of refurbished buffet car

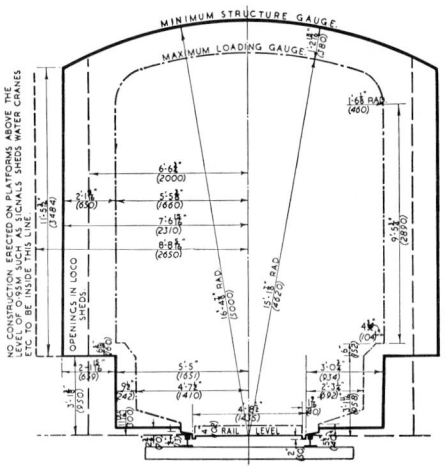

Structure and loading gauge for 1435 mm standard-gauge track

Traction and rolling stock

Diesel locomotive stock at the start of 1990 comprised 52 units. Coaching stock totalled 73 vehicles, including 8 buffet cars. Freight stock totals 1400 vehicles, including 500 privately-owned.

In 1989 two locomotives were acquired: a GM-EMD 3000 hp GT26CW2 for the Ashdod port-Ashkelon power station coal haul; and a Kalmar 1650 hp Type T44 Bo-Bo from Kalmar, originally planned for freight use, but found on delivery to be apt for mixed traffic employment. The year also saw the arrival of 69 hopper cars for the coal flow from Ashdod Port, which was expected to begin at the end of 1990. Four GM G12 diesel locomotives, formerly 1400 hp, were rebuilt with new 1650 hp engines.

Type of coupler in standard use: Screw
Type of brake in standard use: Air

Track
Rail: 54 kg/m
Cross ties (sleepers): Concrete monobloc, 300 kg, and timber

Diesel locomotives

Class	Wheel arrangement	Transmission	Rated power hp	Max speed km/h	Total weight tonnes	Year built	No in service 1989	Builders Mechanical parts	Engine & type	Transmission
AFB	Bo-Bo	Elec	1125	105	84	1952	3	Société Franco-Anglo-Belge	GM 567B	GM
G12	Bo-Bo	Elec	1400	105	76	1954-66	22	GM	GM 12-567C	GM
G16	Co-Co	Elec	1950	124	107	1960/61	3	GM 567C	GM 16-567C	
G26CW	Co-Co	Elec	2200	124	99	1971-79	9	GM	GM 16-645E	GM
G26CW-2	Co-Co	Elec	2200	124	116	1982-86	6	GM	GM 16-645E	GM
GT26CW-2	Co-Co	Elec	3000	124	119	1989	1	GM	GM 16-645E3	GM
T44	Bo-Bo	Elec	1650	105	76	1989	1	Kalmar	GM 645E3	GM
G8	Bo-Bo	Elec	850	105	70	1956	1	GM	GM 8-567C	GM
V60 Shunting	0-6-0	Hyd	650	70	54	1956-58	6	Esslingen	MTU 8 V 331 TC10	Voith-Gmeinder

Spacing: 1670/km, concrete; 1720/km, timber
Fastenings: tension clamp

Minimum curvature radius: 140 m; 600m minimum, new projects

Max gradient: 2.2% (compensated)
Max permissible axleload: 22.5 tonnes

Italy
Ministry of Transport

Piazza della Croce Rossa, 00100 Rome

Minister: Carlo Bernini

Italian Railways (FS)
Ente Ferrovie dello Stato

Piazza della Croce Rossa, 00100 Rome

Telephone: +36 6 8840724
Telex: 610089 mintra i
Telefax: +36 6 8831108

Special Commissioner: Lorenzo Necci
Director General: Vacant
Vice-Director Generals: Valentino Zuccherini
 Ing Giuseppe Massaro
Directors of Departments
 Production: Ing Antonio Lagana
 Marketing & Sales: Giuseppe Pinna
 Re-equipment & Development: Dr Ing Giovannino Caprio
 Organisation: Ing Cesare Vaciago
 Finance & Property: Dr Franco Capanna
 Management Control: Prof Giovanbattista Di Miceli
Directors, Autonomous Headquarters:
 High Speed System: Ing Maurizio Cavagnaro
 Legal Affairs: Dr Giovanni Maricchiolo
 Information Systems: Dr Mario Miniaci
 Communications & Public Relations: Dr Carlo Gregoretti
 Purchasing: Ing Rocco Testa
Divisional Managers
 Ancona: Dr Cesare Cingolani
 Bari: Dr Luca Barbera
 Bologna: Ing Gian Pietro Monfardini
 Cagliari: Ing Errico Laneri
 Florence: Dr Ing Giovanni Bonora
 Genoa: Ing Paolo Enrico De Barbieri
 Milan: Dr Ing Silvio Rizzotti
 Naples: Ing Riccardo Augelli
 Palermo: Ing Mario La Rocca
 Reggio Calabria: Dr Antonio Mazzuca
 Rome: Ing Carlo Gino Ianniello
 Turin: Dr Luigi Di Giovanni
 Trieste: Ing Vincenzo Volpe
 Venice: Ing Giovanni Stabile
 Verona: Ing Dario Manaresi

Gauge: 1435 mm
Route length: 16 030.2km
Electrification: 9376.9 km at 3 kV dc

New state corporation status
New legislation of May 1985 transformed the Italian State Railways (FS) from its previous status as a government department into a state corporation, Ente FS, with effect from the start of 1986. FS remains under the tutelage of the Transport Ministry, but has become owner of all its assets and answerable for its accounts and finances. It retains all its previous rail, marine and road services. However, the government has held on to control of internal rail passenger fares (the lowest in Western Europe), but not of fares for international journeys; and though the railway has been granted commercial freedom in freight tariff fixing, even here certain limitations have been imposed.

The railway has the responsibility for maintenance and renewal of its assets, for which it can resort to borrowing or issue of state-guaranteed bonds, subject to the approval of the Ministers both of Transport and Finance. The railway is required to produce an annual balance sheet providing for depreciation and financial charges. The new constitution includes a committee of auditors which will supervise financial management.

Crises of status, development and retrenchment
The crises detonated by the so-called 'golden sheet scandal' of late 1988 rumbled on into the spring of 1990. Determined to reduce FS' massive calls on public money, the then Transport Minister had in December 1988 brought in Dr Mario Schimberni from the private sector to head FS with the temporary title of Special Commissioner. Dr Schimberni had behind him the achievement of turning the country's Montedison chemicals group from a decade's accumulated loss of US$1600 million into the black, so that it could then sell off the government's residual shareholding and become a fully private enterprise.

Dr Schimberni quickly ignited antipathy on several fronts. In February 1989 he came up with a choice of three five-year plans to trim the FS subsidy. All had themes that ran roughshod over powerful interests.

Already fractious trades unions were aghast at a threat to dispense with perhaps 50 000 of FS' 226 000 staff. The national railway supply industry, heavily reliant on FS orders to sustain its excessive capacity, was shocked on two counts: first, by Dr Schimberni's determination to get rid of cosy FS-manufacturer relationships; and second, by his conviction that measures to increase freight traffic and advance FS efficiency generally were the priority, not the AV high-speed passenger network.

On the supplier front, all contracts were ordered to be renegotiated with the objective of cutting prices by up to 20 per cent. Resort to external companies for maintenance work was to be cut to ensure optimal use of internal resources. Social benefits were to be ignored in evaluating investment cases.

In mid-April 1989 Dr Schimberni crossed swords with Ministers already nervous at the impact of his plans on the railway unions, and with a Transport Minister unhappy at his disinterest in the AV project. A new FS reform bill framed by the government included provision for joint public-private sector involvement in railway construction and operation. This was anathema to Dr Schimberni, who insisted that unitary

Class 447 Bo-Bo and Inter-City train on Rome-Florence Direttissima

Type E633 Bo-Bo-Bo electric locomotive

management of the FS network must not be compromised. He was equally emphatic that the government must abandon its historic control of fares and allow FS freedom to market price.

These objections were reinforced by resignation threats both from Dr Schimberni and his new FS Director-General. But an uneasy peace was arranged.

In May the Transport Minister of the by then caretaker government, following a parliamentary defeat, accepted the most expensive of three ten-year development plans proffered by Dr Schimberni. Costed at L 48 500 million this was, however, far less expansive than the plan advanced by the disgraced FS Board he superseded. The agreed plan effectively preserved part of the projected AV network (see below) by providing for four-tracking from Florence to Milan, and from Turin through Milan to Venice and Trieste. The Minister pressed for this work to proceed immediately, whereas Dr Schimberni had deferred it to the second half of the plan's period.

The plan set FS some exacting economic targets: a 43 per cent lift of freight tonnage by 1994 and of 53 per cent by 1999; a 24 per cent reduction of operating costs by 1994, so that in conjunction with rising revenue FS would by that year recover 56 per cent of its costs from traffic; and that recovery to reach 73 per cent by 1999, so that by then subsidy of FS would be 89 per cent less than in 1988.

But a new government's Transport Minister refused to accept this compromise. In the late summer of 1989 Dr Schimberni was forced to accept private sector investment in new infrastructure projects.

In September 1989 Dr Schimberni produced a revised 10-year investment plan costed at L 52 000 000 million, of which L 30 000 000 milion, it was proposed, should be laid out in the first five years. Against only 32 per cent coverage of costs from revenue in 1988, the new plan forecast 53 per cent coverage in 1993 and 84 per cent by 1998, when costs themselves would have been trimmed by 30 per cent. Some of the improvement would come from a predicted 50 per cent rise in freight traffic by the close of the plan period, and from at least a 6 per cent growth in passenger traffic. The investment proposals provided for FS infrastructure development to match increased Austrian and Swiss transalpine capacity. As for AV schemes, construction of two new 300 km/h tracks from Bologna to Milan was retained; on the Turin-Milan-Venice transversal such improvement would be limited to three segments of the route.

Sporadic railway union strikes in the spring of 1990 followed issue by Dr Schimberni of a revised staff rationalisation plan. This sought immediate reduction of at least 29 000 full-time staff through a combination of early retirement, transfer to other public services or switch to part-time employment. In addition, many other staff would be required to relocate or switch to lower-grade work, in the latter case to permit reduction of resort to external contractors.

Early in 1990 Transport Minister Bernini trumped the new Schimberni investment plan by pushing through Parliament a bill to furnish FS with L 86 127 000 million of state money up to 1998. The major additional monies by comparison with the Schimberni plan included: L 5 000 000 million for the AV programme, to allow reinstatement of the Rome-Naples-Battipaglia scheme; L 4 877 000 million for intermodal freight; L 4 054 000 million for international links; L 4 660 000 million for commuter services; and L 7 321 000 million for general upgrading projects. Provision was also made for completion of the Sardinian electrification project (see below), which had been slowed down as an extravagance under the Schimberni regime.

Political agreement was not reached, however, on the vexed issue of private sector involvement. A cabinet proposal for a division of FS into an asset-owning company with responsibility for policy and investment, and a purely operating company, made no headway. It was strongly resisted by the railway unions and the political left.

In June 1990 Dr Schimberni resigned, along with the FS Director-General, reportedly because the government would not accept full privatisation. At that stage the government seemed to be favouring a structure of FS as a state-owned holding company, with its tracks available to privately-operated train services.

Finance

State financial input to the Italian Railways is now theoretically confined to: compensations for social service obligations; grants for research and technical development; contribution to infrastructure upkeep and renewals. Major projects can if politically desirable be financed, as before, under special government programmes.

Finances (L million)

Revenue	1987	1988
Passengers and freight	2 875 551	3 178 614
Other	1 749 758	1 964 752
Compensations and subsidies	11 538 572	12 273 603
Total	16 163 881	17 416 979

Expenditure	1987	1988
Personnel	8 562 681	8 859 842
Materials and services	3 712 690	3 944 369
Depreciation	2 416 753	3 281 237
Financial charges	1 853 929	2 192 796
Total	16 546 053	18 278 231

Closure of loss-making lines halted

Roughly half the route-km of the FS network are classified as commercially viable. Of the remainder, the government has subsidised 364 route-km as socially necessary in a national context. Among the residual loss-making and sparsely-used lines, 40 aggregating 1937 route-km were in 1987 safeguarded indefinitely by the Transport Ministry pending studies of whether continued rail operation is justified or whether road service should be substituted. The initial purport of those studies, revealed in the spring of 1988, was that 1271 route-km should retain their rail service provided that their operating costs could be reduced to a level not exceeding that of alternative modes. The residue looked best suited to road transport replacement.

Closure of the financially most debilitating lines has been halting. Eight grossing 233 route-km were shut in January 1986, but thereafter only one further line of 49 km was closed, in February 1987. The Transport Ministry had planned to shut 17 lines aggregating 569 route-km in June 1986, but three of these lines were later upgraded to the category of government-subsidised retention and the fate of the rest was twice deferred. In the spring of 1988, in face of pressure from regional administrations and trade unions, the FS was given until March 1989 to study how their operation of these 14 lines might be made less financially demanding, and thus more likely to attract the financial support of the relevant regional authorities or other local bodies.

The closures effected have included the last 71.6km of FS' narrow-gauge tracks, in Sicily.

Integral plan

In December 1980 an Integral Plan (Piano Integrativo) was approved by the Transport Commission of the Chamber Deputies and in September 1981 the necessary decree was signed by the then government. This budgeted for FS a total of L 12 450 000 million over the period to 1985. It was recognised, however, that even this sum would be inadequate to execute all urgently needed works and in 1983 the sum was lifted to L 18 850 000 million. FS was granted a further L 15 900 million in 1984 (almost all to cover rolling stock acquisition) and thereafter the total was been topped up annually by an amount reflecting the annual rate of inflation. By 1989 the Plan's funding was almost fully committed.

Operating capacity enlargement

A considerable amount of four- and double-tracking was scheduled in the 1980 Integral Plan, the former chiefly to segregate urban commuter traffic, the latter in a number of cases to enlarge the capacity of some important routes, such as Genoa-Ventimiglia, Ancona-Bari-Lecce (with the addition of electrification), Caserta-Foggia, Bologna-Verona, Terni-Falconara, Bari-Taranto and Udine-Tarvisio. Between 1985 and the end of 1989 a total of 175 route-km were double-tracked, raising the double-track total to 5 649 route-km and leaving 10 378 route-km single track.

In 1990 double-tracking and upgrading was chiefly

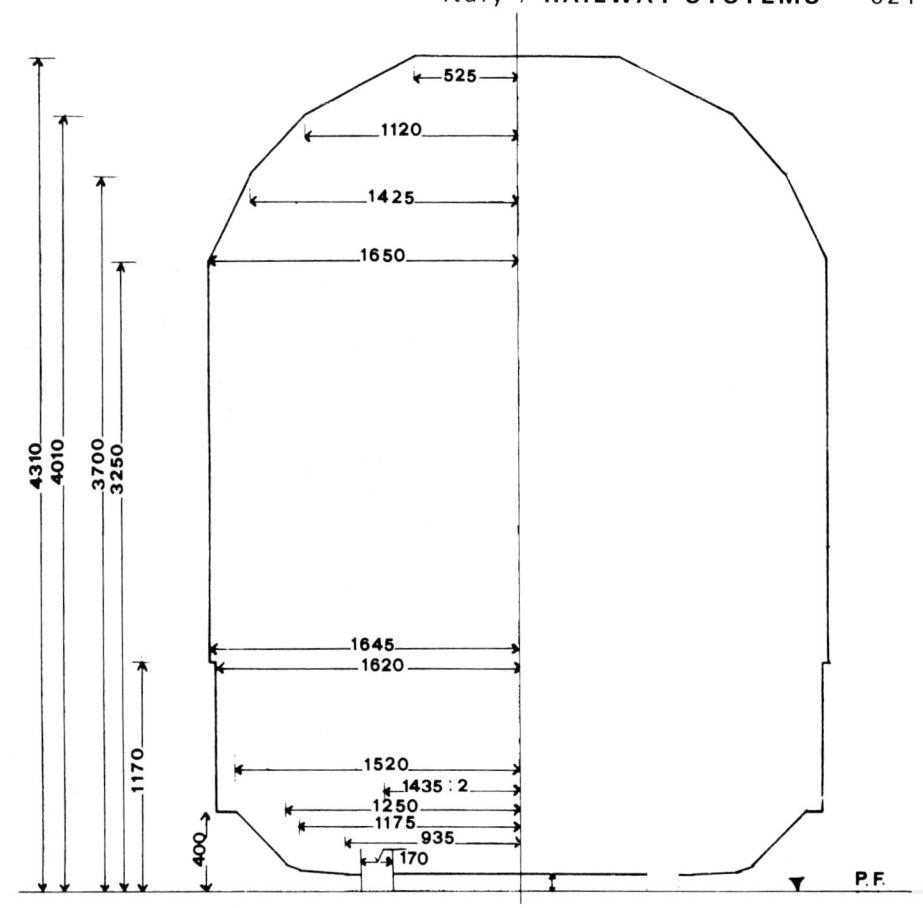

Minimum lateral clearance between loading gauge (above) and fixed gauge varies according to the radius of curvature eg:

Radius of curve	Clearance inside of curve	Clearance outside of curve
250 m	150 mm	150 mm
200 m	200 mm	210 mm
150 m	283 mm	310 mm
100 m	676 mm	706 mm
70 m	1177 mm	1211 mm

RAILWAY SYSTEMS / Italy

concentrated in the south and in Sicily, where single track is predominant on main lines. Considerable doubling work was proceeding in and around Naples, and on the Adriatic coast.

The doubling of the difficult Bari-Taranto line, heading for completion in the 1990s, is combined with some substantial realignments that will reduce its distance from 115 to 103 im. They will ease the minimum curve radius from 500 to 1100 m and the ruling gradient from 1.6 to 1.2 per cent. These works have entailed driving 5 km of new tunnels and 2 km of bridgework. The outcome will also be improvement of the line's speed limit from 115 to at least 150 km/h and probably to 180 km/h by suitable rolling stock, to the benefit of passenger traffic that has climbed commensurately with the growth of freight, chiefly agricultural produce.

Among new works lately contracted has been double-tracking of two lengths of the La Spezia-Parma and Fidenza line, with associated resignalling, at a cost of L 901 398 million, including a new yard at S Stefano di Magra and junction work at La Spezia.

Traffic (million)	1986	1987	1988
Passenger journeys	393.2	394.2	410
Passenger-km	40 500	41 395	43 343
Freight tonnes	57	59.2	64.4
Freight tonne-km	17 410	18 427	19 567

Poliennale plan

In March 1987 the then Transport Minister approved the FS *Poliennale* plan for a total investment of L 41 000 000 million up to 1995. Its main provisions: Improvements at the traffic hubs of Turin, Milan, Domodossola, Verona, Vicenza, Trento, Venice, Padua, Cervignano, Ventimiglia, Genoa, Modena, Ravenna, Ferrara, Bologna, Florence, Civitavecchia, Rome, Pescara, Naples, Bari, Brindisi and Palermo: L 8 200 000 million;

Double-tracking (start of, or completion) of the sections Calolziocorte-Carnate Usmate, Udine-frontier, Cormons-Redipulgia, Novi San Bovo-Tortona, Ventimiglia-Genoa, Castelbolognese-Ravenna, Bologna-Verona, Parma-La Spezia, Rome-Ancona, Certaldo-Granaiolo, Bologna-Lecce, Cancello-Sarno, Naples-Bari, Bari-Taranto, Villa San Giovanni-Reggio Calabria, Messina-Palermo, Messina-Catania and Decimomannu-San Gavio: L 13 500 000 million;

Completion of Rome-Florence Direttissima (see below) and upgrading of main line from Rome to Naples and the south: L 1 050 000 million;

Electrification of the lines Mestre-Castelfranco Veneto-Padua, Verona-Mantua-Monselice, Metaponto-Sibari-Cosenza, Reggio Calabria-Melita Porto Salvo, Roccapalumba-Agrigento, Palermo-Trapani: L 450 000 million;

Upgrading with realignments of the lines Milan-Chiasso, Treviso-Portogruaro, Venice-Trieste, Empoli-Siena, Terontola-Foligno, Rocca d'Evandro-Venafro, Matera-Ferrandina, Lamezia Terme-Catanzaro Lido; L 1 150 000 million;

First phase of Brenner route upgrading (see below) and feasibility study of Splügen tunnel line into Switzerland (since rejected by the Swiss): L 650 000 million;

Intermodal development: L 3 650 000 million;

Telecommunications and track-to-train radio: L 500 000 million;

Level crossing suppression: L 7 000 000 million.

Investment in international links

Pending agreement to build a Brenner Pass base tunnel (see Austrian Railways entry) and to complement investment on the Austrian side of the Pass, a previous Italian government agreed investment of L 450 000 million to improve the existing Brenner route on the Italian side. A new tunnel is being bored between Ponte Gardena and Campodazzo to facilitate an 8 km realignment of the route. Italian Railways has also put in hand some realignments for 160 km/h between Bolzano and Colle Isarco. Completion is unlikely until 1991/92. A new customs depot will be set up near Vitipeno. Associated with these improvements is double-tracking between Verona and Bologna, and the recently completed container terminal within Verona's Quadrante Europa inland port.

The Puster Valley single line has been electrified to provide a relief route to the Brenner, in association with ÖBB electrification of its Lienz-San Candido line between Fortezza (FS) and Spittal-Milstättersee (ÖBB). During the electrification Fortezza-San Candido line clearances were modified to accept CI loading-gauge traffic and the track was strengthened for 22.5 tonne axleloads.

'Sleeperette' car for overnight travel

First-class interior of 'Sleeperette'

The first of the production series of Class E402 Bo-Bo

With Swiss contributions in grant and loan totalling SwFr 60 million the Monte Olimpino tunnelling project has pierced an improved freight bypass of Como. Besides easing the ruling gradient from the previous main freight route's 1.8 to 0.8 per cent and raising the maximum permissible speed to 120 km/h, the replacement project has created a tunnel to Class C1 loading-gauge parameters, which has enabled extension of DB-SBB *Rollende Landstrasse* piggyback trains beyond Chiasso to Milan. Completion of the tunnel was achieved and the new 9 km bypass opened in 1989.

The so-called Pontebbana route between Villach, Austria, and Trieste/Venice via the Tarvis Pass and Udine already carries 11 per cent of FS international traffic, almost the same as the Brenner route, and is heading for major growth of its freight traffic. Its single line and outdated electrification have consequently become more of a burden year by year, prompting the FS to launch a major programme of double-tracking, track rebuilding for heavier axleloads, realignment and grade easement, re-electrification and resignalling with automatic block for reversible working on each track. The track renewal includes some resort to slab track. New tunnelling is involved in obtaining an alignment for the second track over 85 per cent of the route. The first 19 km of renewal were completed in 1985, a further 18 km (including the slab track sections) was in hand in 1989, and 54 km then remained to tackle. Completion is expected during the 1990s.

As a result of rising traffic on the recently reopened Ventimiglia-Cuneo line via Tende, the Vievola-Ventimilia section is being electrified and a 24 km section of the Ventimiglia-Genoa line, between Mara and Ospedaletti, is being doubled. A new freight terminal, linked to the main coastal trunk road by a tunnel under the town, is to be constructed at Ventimiglia.

A feature of the Integral plan is marshalling yard modernisation. A major new yard, Domodossola II, is being built to complement the widening of the BLS Lötschberg route through Switzerland to the Simplon Tunnel; it will absorb all wagonload traffic sorting so that the existing Domo I yard can be devoted to unit train servicing. Other yards on the modernisation programme have included Milan, the Bologna San Donato (which in 1987 became the first fully-automated FS yard), Marcianise and the new Turin Orbassano yard, one of Europe's largest, which has 79 km of track.

Orbassano has 20 reception tracks, two humps, a 40-siding main yard, two sets of departure tracks, one of 12 and the other of 33 tracks, a 10-siding yard for Fiat traffic, and intermodal and Customs yards. In 1990 it was processing around 1500 wagons daily and dealing with 50–60 incoming and the same number of outgoing trains. Completion of signalling schemes would see capacity rise to 2000 wagons daily by 1991. Turin Smistamento yard has been switched to passenger rolling stock storage, and the activity of other yards in the region reduced.

Rome-Florence Direttissima

The last segment of the Rome-Florence Direttissima between Arezzo South and Figline was heading for completion in late 1990. The original line of route north of Arezzo had to be discarded because of geological difficulties complicating the prospective construction of a 14.5 km tunnel and a new 44 km alignment adopted between Arezzo South and Figline. In 1989, 193.8 route-km of the Direttissima were operational.

There remains the question of entry into the city of Florence. In December 1986 the FS and local administrations of Florence and the Tuscany Region signed agreements covering a wide range of transport developments prompted by imminent completion of the Direttissima. It remained thereafter for the proposals to be agreed by the assemblies of the local authorities involved.

The signatories agreed to a direct tunnel link under the city between Rovezzano, the Direttissima's junction with existing infrastructure after it has negotiated the San Donato tunnel, and Prato, on the Bologna main line on the other side of the city. It remained to select one of two options. Under one, a tunnel would run via Champ-de-Mars and below the city's Santa Maria Novella main station to a new complex of freight yards and passenger stock maintenance tracks at Peretola-Osmannoro. This alternative would serve both passenger and freight traffic. The other option, a tunnel the whole way from Rovezzano to beyond Prato, would be essentially passenger traffic-oriented. Both possibilities envisage a subterranean through-station below the Santa Maria Novella surface terminus.

Type ETR450 tilt-body train-set

Interior of ETR450 saloon

Passenger traffic

Total passenger journeys in 1989 rose 8.1 million to a total of 418.1 million. Passenger-km increased from 43 343 million in 1988 to 44 443 million. The year was marked by a 5.8 per cent reduction of local and little-used rural services, but a 3.3 per cent increase in long-haul services. At the same time costs were reduced some 10 per cent by a combination of measures, including extension of coach maintenance on an intact train-set basis.

New legislation of 1988 authorised FS to raise fares by up to 20 per cent a year until parity with the passenger tariffs of other Western European railways was attained. In 1989 and 1990 the full permissible increase was not applied. FS has the problem that a high proportion of its passengers get a sharply discounted fare, either on various social grounds or as commuters. Close on 51 per cent of all passenger journeys are made on commuters' season tickets.

Very conscious that acceptability of higher fares depends on improved quality and reliability of service, the FS, though harassed by strikes, took several measures to raise standards in 1989. They included a rebate of InterCity supplement, usable for the passenger's next fare purchase, in the event of arrival more than 29 minutes late. Following a scandal concerning hygiene in catering cars at the start of the year, a new on-board catering contract was concluded with Ristofer.

RAILWAY SYSTEMS / Italy

By the start of 1990 14 Class ETR450 eight-car tilt-body train-sets were in service. The FS had originally commissioned Fiat to build ten 11-car and four five-car ETR 450 sets, each exclusively first class, with the odd car in each unit a non-powered trailer providing catering and other on-train services. That role of the non-powered car was dropped in favour of preprepared tray meals-at-seat service from galleys in the powered units, and not until late 1989 was it decided to fit out the body shells of these cars with orthodox seating, reduced in quantity by comparison with others to make room for pay-telephone kiosks. Also abandoned was the the five-car train-set concept.

The decision to standardise the ETR 450 format left two motored two-car units of the original order spare. At the end of 1989 an order was placed with Fiat for two more motored twin-sets and a trailer. With completion of this order and of the 14 trailers in the original order, the ETR450 fleet would be stabilised as 15 nine-car sets.

The ETR450 reproduces the shape and much of the technology of the four-car ETR401 tilt-body prototype which Fiat Ferroviaria Savigliano handed to FS for evaluation in 1974. The aluminium-bodied ETR450 has all vehicles bar one trailer powered on each bogie by an Ercole Marelli 625 kW chopper-controlled motor. The motors are body-mounted, each driving a bogie's inner axle via a cardan shaft drive. The powered vehicles are arranged as electrically and operationally inseparable two-car units with a gross weight of 93 tonnes tare, half of which is available for adhesion: but for sustained contact and avoidance of arcing only two twin-units in each ETR450 have pantographs, which, as in the ETR401, are mounted on bogie-supported frame for immunity to the car bodies' change of posture.

At 2450 mm the ETR450's bogie wheelbase is almost a third shorter than that of a French TGV's distinctive articulating bogie. The former's Fiat bogie, which has an articulated frame, is designed to curve without bringing its primary coil spring suspension into play. An oscillating cross-member, with a set of coil springs at each end, is interposed between bogie frame and body. This arrangement obtains both vertical and transverse suspension, the latter through lateral coil spring flexibility, which permits the bogie to veer independently of the cross member at the onset of a curve. The amount of relative movement between body and cross member is restricted to the minimum required to compensate for transverse acceleration by hydraulic servos that are governed by the electronic control of the tilt system.

In the ETR401 prototype, each of the four cars' tilt was independently actuated. The ETR450's electronically-controlled system, which utilises processed gyroscope and accelerometer signals, has sensors operating solely on the lead vehicle. These transmit impulses down a train-line databus to modules on each following car, which relate the messages to the position of their own vehicles in the formation and command their cars' hydraulic tilt mechanisms accordingly. Body tilt is hydraulically powered, through two cylinders per bogie that are inserted between the bogie crossmember and anchors in the body frame.

FS currently accepts uncompensated lateral acceleration of 0.8 m/s^2. An ETR450 is designed for a body tilt of up to 10°, which, added to 6° of track cant, compensates for a further 2.8 m/s^2. The unit's resulting total tolerance of 3.6 m/s^2 is reckoned to permit it roughly 30 per cent greater curving speed than non-tilting FS cars. In practice tilt has been restricted to 8° and with that the speed gain through curves to 20 per cent.

The ETR450's maximum design speed is 250 km/h, which it exploits on the Rome-Florence Direttissima. Parts of the historic, predominantly straight main line from Bologna over the plains to Milan have been cleared for ETR450 traversal at 200 km/h. ETR450 braking is disc and rheostatic, the latter with a maximum 1900 kW power at the wheel rim at 200 km/h. The driver has the support of a comprehensive equipment monitoring and diagnostic apparatus.

In the summer of 1990 ETR450 sets were providing the following services each way (number per day in brackets): Rome-Milan (3. of which one non-stop); Milan-Turin (2); Rome-Naples-Salerno (1); Rome-Naples (1); Rome-Venice (2); Rome-Bologna (1); Florence-Milan (1); Rome-Florence-Pisa-Genoa(1); Rome-Bari (1). The ETR450's timing of 3 hours 58 minutes on the 632km non-stop Rome-Milan service is 1 hours 5 minutes faster than the previous best with locomotive-hauled rolling stock. Rome to Turin via Milan (785km) by ETR450 takes 5 hours 30 minutes, as against 6 hours 45 minutes for the 661 km from Rome via Genoa to Turin by conventional train.

In 1989 Fiat Ferroviaria was engaged on a second-generation ETR450 development programme. Its main items: use of inverter transmission with asynchronous motors of greater installed power, to allow of more unpowered trailers per set; simplification of components for reduced maintenance and extended life; improved diagnostics; and a completely restyled driving cab with more modern characteristics.

There was further extension of the regular-interval timetable concept in the summer 1989 timetable to Turin-Milan, Milan-Venice and Turin-Rome InterCity services.

A through Madrid-Milan overnight service via Modane employing Talgo Pendular equipment with variable axle gauge was launched in the 1989-90 winter timetable. Named 'Pau Casals' and categorised a EuroCity service, the train includes a portion for Zurich detached at Chambéry, France. Four other services were added to FS' Euro-City quota in 1989, raising the latter to 21 daily out-and-back pairs.

The Gran Confort bodyshell has been adopted for a recently addition to FS' portfolio of overnight travel facilities on internal routes: open first-class saloons branded 'Sleeperette' in which the 55 seats are reclinable to a back angle of at least 45°. A companion second-class version has 66 reclining seats. Use of either incurs no surcharge on the standard fare.

The FS share of the domestic travel market in 1989 was 11.75 per cent. Including the concessionary systems, rail share was 12.49 per cent, compared with 13.83 per cent for interurban buses and 1.51 per cent for air.

Freight

The downward trend in freight traffic has been reversed and for the third successive year there was growth in 1989, when tonne-km rose 6 per cent to 20 851 million. Intermodal traffic, which grossed 16.29 million tonnes, a quarter of the railway's total, again showed a strong increase of 12.74 per cent in container and of 13.5 per cent in piggyback movement. The number of unit trains operated was lifted by 13 per cent.

In domestic freight transport FS' market share improved slightly to 12 per cent, though this was still well below its 17 per cent share in the early 1970s. However, almost two-thirds of FS freight traffic is international. In the latter realm there were considerable gains in traffic to and from Germany as a result of the extra trains scheduled following new Austrian restrictions on transit road freight (for details see Austria entry).

Improvements in 1989 included a move from 100 to 120 km/h operation of intermodal trains on the north-south trunk route from Milan and a general 3 per cent advance in the commercial speed of such services. There was emphasis on the betterment of connections between Italian ports and other countries, on the one hand, and the inland ports of Bologna, Padua, and Verona's Quadrante Europa on the other.

As an intermodal operator, FS is essentially a wholesaler of track space and train operation. Its intermodal terminals are mostly managed by CEMAT (which runs 23 of them), or else privately owned; domestic rail container transits are organised and marketed by big forwarders such as Intermodale Italia, INT, Sogestir and TCF. International rail container transits are managed and marketed by Intercontainer, which is represented in Italy by INT.

In late 1988 FS was promised EEC finance of 14 million ecu for clearance enlargement to create a piggyback route from Modane via Turin, Bologna and Ancona to Bari.

Notable success in generating new international traffic has been achieved with the 'Tres' system of dedicated trains for high-value merchandise. The offer is restricted to clients who can load at depots within direct and convenient feeder-train range of a main marshalling yard, from which the trains are run without further remarshalling to destination areas. Tres was inaugurated in 1981 with services from Venice, Bologna and Pisa into France, since complemented by return services from France to Verona, Venice, Vicenza and the Yugoslav border; domestic services between the north and south of Italy, services from the Emilia Romagna, Venice and Florence areas to Federal German, Austrian and Swiss destinations via both Brenner and Gotthard routes; and a four times-weekly unit train operation between Lombardy, including the Milan/Brescia area, and Normandy.

CCR (*Controllo Centralizzato Rotabili*), a central real-time and computer-based data transmission system, now monitors freight operation through input via 400 terminals of activity at all 2800 freight-generating and reception points on Italian Railways.

A regrettable gap as yet in Italian rail preparation for post-1992 rail landbridge opportunities is any funding for the plan to improve access to Genoa port. That is currently handicapped by the historic Turin/Milan rail route's steep climb out of the city, and by bottlenecks and junction conflicts of traffic flows.

Six years ago the FS and local government agreed the route for a new but expensive direct link from the Ventimiglia to the Turin/Milan line that would keep traffic to and from the new Voltri container terminal clear of the city's junctions. But the scheme is still confined to paperwork.

In 1989 FS launched a guaranteed 24-hour service for less-than-30 kg packages between its 11 principal stations. The tariff includes road delivery to consignee. The rail component is provided by small containerisation of the packages for transport in the baggage cars of InterCity trains.

Electrification

Ansaldo Trasporti was appointed the main contractor for the 25 kV 50 Hz ac electrification of the Cagliari-Porto Torres and Olbia lines in Sardinia, which was

IPA slab track installed betwen Gemona and Pontebba in course of reconstructing the 55.3 km from Udine to Tarvisio; the route has 39.2 km of tunnels and 6.08 km of bridges

undertaken to provide an ac electrification shop window for Italian industry. Ansaldo is responsible for the supply of vehicles, automation and signalling apparatus, power supply and central control. The project includes track doubling between Cagliari and Decimomannu, enlargement of two tunnels and upgrading for maximum speeds of 125–140 km/h south of Oristano.

Three prototype E491 Bo-Bo locomotives have been built for the Sardinian scheme. Weighing 88 tonnes, with a 2950 kW continuous and 3230 kW one-hour output, the E491 is designed for 140 km/h maximum speed and is capable of sustaining 60 km/h up a 2.5 per cent gradient with a 500-tonne train. A further 22 were under construction in 1988.

Further 3 kV dc electrification under way in 1989 included the following lines: Metaponto-Potenza-Battipaglia, not likely to be finished until 1992 because of need for tunnel reconstruction; Lamezia Terme-Catanzaro L; Faenza-Russi-Ravenna.

Regional schemes, Milan and Turin

In May 1982 the then Prime Minister Spadolini formally launched construction of a new cross-Milan line as the first step toward creation of an integrated Milan conurbation rail and road transport system. Extending 13.2 km from Rogoredo to Certosa, on the main line to Turin, the new link's centrepiece will be a 5.9 km double-track tunnel between the city's Porta Garibaldi and Porta Vittoria stations, with five new stations below ground. Besides interconnecting the main lines to and from the south (Genoa), east (Piacenza and Treviglio, by a 3.3 km-long branch from Porta Vittoria) and north-west (Turin and Domodossola), the link will throw off a connection to the Ferrovie Nord Milano system at Bovisa, enabling integration of ENM and Italian Railways services. It will have four interchanges with the Milan metro. Operation of the tunnel line with a proportion of bi-level train-sets is planned to achieve a peak-hour capacity of 36 000 passengers/hour each way. The Milan car-sleeper terminal has been moved to San Cristoforo station from Porto Vittoria. The new terminal will be situated in an area with good road connections to the city centre and main trunk roads. FS' investments associated with the scheme include four-tracking from Milan to Treviglio and to Molegnano, on the Bologna route; and upgrading of an orbital line on the city's north-east quadrant interconnecting interchange stations at Certosa, Bovisa, Lambrate, Porta Vittoria, Rogoredo and Porta Romana. The cross-city tunnel should be finished in 1991.

In 1983 Italian Railways signed an agreement with the Turin city authorities aiming to establish a similar regional rail system. This also features construction of a 3.3 km cross-city tunnel, through Zappata, to create a through axis between Lingotto, Porta Susa, Dora and Stura (Porta Nuova terminus will remain the city's main station for long-haul trains). The scheme involves the quadrupling of 15–20 route-km between Porta Susa and Dura. Porta Susa will be the starting-point of a putative link with Caselle airport, 15 km from the city centre, over the independent Torino-Ceres Railway, which is embraced in the proposed regional scheme and will abandon its Ponte Mosca terminal. The Ceres Railway will be connected to the cross-city line at Dora.

Early in 1985 agreement on a go-ahead was reached, with the city set to advance L 84 000 million of the projected cost of the first phase, including the Zappata tunnel and the quadrupling, and the first contracts for design and construction were let. Since then, however, disagreements have arisen and progress has been halting. The project was at a standstil in early 1990.

Palermo regional metro

Agreements were signed in 1987 for transmutation of FS lines in the Palermo area into a 30 km cross-city metro. The scheme involves 18 km of new construction to separate metro and main-line traffic.

Airport links

A 2.3 km double-track branch to Rome's Leonardo da Vinci airport at Fiumcino was opened in May 1990. It diverges from the Ponte Galeria-Fiumcino branch and is built on an elevated structure. The track is 60 kg/m rail set in a concrete base. The airport service is provided at 10-minute intervals by push-pull sets of Class E424 locomotives and five low centre-floor cars slightly modified for increased baggage room. This terminates at Rome Ostiense, officially because of inadequate capacity for additional traffic at Rome Termini, but reportedly because of pressure by Rome's taxicab industry.

As far as Ponte Galeria the line from Ostiense is the historic main route for trains to Pisa and Genoa, but for the latter a new route has been created by adopting an existing single-track path from Trastevere to St Peters for a new double-track electrified line, which from St Peters turns west to join the Pisa main line at Maccarese. Between St Peters and Maccarese this bypass will be joined (in its 3.3 km Aurelia Tunnel) by a new orbital link with the Rome-Florence main line; the latter will thread a 4.6 km tunnel, the Monte Mario, in its progress through Rome's northern suburbs. In all, 10.8 km of the 29 km of new route under construction will be in tunnel.

Also under construction in 1989 was a link of 2 km from the Palermo-Trapani line in Sicily to Palermo's Punta Raisi airport. The ultimate aim is to create a new underground link in the centre of Palermo and launch a regional express service between city and airport.

High Speed Inter-City Network (AV)

In June 1986 a high-speed network plan (Alta Velocita, or AV) was adopted by the FS Board and an AV project group established.

By October 1987 the group's work had progressed sufficiently for the FS Board to invite tenders for first-phase civil engineering of a new Rome-Naples line that would form part of a 250/300 km/h 'T'-shaped network extending north-south from Milan to Battipaglia, south of Salerno, and west-east from Turin to Venice. In the more distant future the north-south line was planned to reach not only to Reggio Calabria, but beyond, over the Messina Straits suspension bridge, to Palermo and Catania in Sicily; and from the Cassino area south of Rome to throw off a cross-country prong to Foggia and Bari. This system would embrace almost half the Italian passenger travel market: the north-south trunk yields 30 per cent of FS passenger traffic.

As outlined earlier, the Schimberni regime sought during 1989 to have the AV plan cut back to new high-speed infrastructure between Florence and Milan, and to three stretches aggregating some 90–100 km betwen Turin, Milan and Venice. But in early 1990 a new financial package initiated by Transport Minister Bernini provided for reinstatement of the Rome-Naples-Battipaglia high-speed infrastructure scheme.

The Transport Minister also indicated interest in a private consortium's scheme to build a 250 km/h Milan-Genoa high-speed line and operate it for 40 years before ceding it to state ownership. But union opposition to private sector involvement made immediate progress to negotiations unlikely.

Between Milan and Bologna the two new AV tracks would start at Melegnano, 21 km south of Milan Central, and parallel the north-south motorway to

The ETR X 500 300 km/h power car and trailer

Push-pull train of MDVC cars

Bologna's outskirts. En route, spurs would diverge to service Piacenza, Fidenza, Cremona, Parma and Modena. A choice had yet to be made of three possible trans-Apennine mountain routes between Bologna and Florence; the most direct would entail 13 tunnels with an aggregate length of 39 km and 18 viaducts, one of them 2 km long.

ETR500 300 km/h AV train-sets

AV track parameters, dictated by need to make the new lines usable by fast freight as well as passenger trains, obviate need of body-tilt in the Type ETR500 train-set design for dedicated AV operation that has been entrusted to a Breda-led consortium. Other companies involved are: Fiat, partnering Breda in the mechanical elements, with Breda responsible for the car bodies and interior design, Fiat for the bogies and transmissions; and Ercole Marelli, Ansaldo Trasporti and TIBB caring for the electrics. Pininfarina, renowned Italian exponent of high-performance auto styling, has been recruited both for the external aerodynamic shaping of the ETR500, and also for a contribution to the internal decor and furnishing scheme. The ETR500 will have 300 km/h capability, but initially AV top speed will be 270 km/h.

ETR500 format reverts to power concentration in front and end vehicles, which are streamlined, single-cabbed derivations of the Class E402 double-cabbed locomotive already constructed in a pre-production batch of five units. The ETR500 version is designated Class E404.

The E404 is a three-phase asynchronous motor 4250 kW Bo-Bo of 72 tonnes, steel-framed with a cladding of aluminium and fibre composite to keep its centre of gravity as low as possible. Each bogie's pair of chopper inverter-fed motors, though located within the bogie frame, is suspended from the body by a linkage which permits them to pivot with the bogie when train speed is low. At high speed, preloaded springs keep the motors centrally stabilised. Flexible drive takes the form of a quill system in which two concentric tubes enclosing the axle transmit the output from the gearcase via flexible bushes and links. This concept, it is claimed, ensures smooth transfer of power when tubes and axle are not in perfect alignment, and also protects gearcase and motor from lateral shocks sustained by the axle. Some transmission components are of weight-saving aluminium or titanium.

Trailer consists between each pair of E404s are to vary as traffic potential dictates, up to a maximum of 12. Each ETR500 set's format will normally remain constant from one day's operation to another, but to allow reshuffles no trailers will be articulated. Aluminium-bodied, each trailer weighs around 40 tonnes tare. Some first class-only ETR500s are possible, but the great majority will be dual-class.

A single E404 power car and trailer, designated the ETRX500, emerged in April 1988 to road-test innovative features of the design, and 38 km of the Modena-Mantua line between San Pancrazio and Suzzara are being fettled up for the prototypes' full-speed testing. The latter work had scarcely begun before it was suspended in late 1988 because of doubt about the future of the AV project, but resumption a year later was expected to lead to completion in 1991. Meanwhile, tests of ETRX500 on the Rome-Florence Direttissima reached 316 km/h in 1989.

ETRX500 was followed in May 1990 by two ETRY500, each comprising two E404 power cars and 10 trailers, which would submit the passenger accommodation to public evaluation. There were not ready in time for sampling, as hoped, by visitors to the 1990 World Cup soccer finals in the country.

Because of the AV network cutback, the extent to which FS would pursue ETR500 and ETR450 tilt-body development was uncertain in early 1990. It was anticipated, however, that 42 train-sets based on the ETR500 design would eventually be ordered.

Diesel locomotives

Class	Wheel arrangement	Trans- mission	Rated power kW	Tractive effort Max kg	Tractive effort Continuous at kg	Tractive effort Continuous at km/h	Max speed km/h	Wheel dia mm	Total weight tonnes	Length in mm	No in service 1989	Year first built	Builders Mechanical parts	Builders Engine & type	Builders Transmission
D341	Bo-Bo	Elec	970	18 500	7850	26	100*/110	1040	66·5*/67/70·4	14 480*/14 540	14	1957	Fiat, Reggiane, OM, OCREN, Imam, Breda, Ansaldo	Fiat 3212.SF or Breda-Paxman 12 YLX†	Brown Boveri, OCREN
D343	B-B (monomotor bogies)	Elec	995	19 000	11 000		130	1040	60	13 240	75	1967	Fiat, OM, Sofer, Omeca, Breda	Fiat 218 SSF (Nos 1001-40) or Breda-Paxman 12YJC (Nos 2001-35)	TIBB generator, 2 traction motors Breda-Elettromeccanica, OCREN
D443	B-B (monomotor bogies)	Elec	1400	22 000	14 000		130	1040	72	14 100	50	1966	Fiat, OM, Sofer, Imam, Reggiane	Fiat 2312 SSF (Nos 1001-30) or Breda-Paxman 12YLC (Nos 2001-20)	ASG generator, 2 traction motors Breda-Elettromeccanica, OCREN
D345	B-B	Elec	995	19 000	11 270	25·1	130	1040	61	13 240	145	1974	Breda, Sofer, Savigliano	Fiat A 218SSF	TIBB, Marelli, Italtrofo
D445	B-B	Elec	1560	22 000	14 500	23·5	130	1040	72	14 100	149	1970	Fiat, Omeca	Fiat A 2112SSF	Ansaldo
D141	Bo-Bo	Elec	515	–	–	–	80	–	64	13 240	29	1963	TIBB, Reggiane	Fiat MB 820B	TIBB
D143	Bo-Bo	Elec	420	–	–	–	70	–	64	13 250	49	1964	TIBB, OM	OM	TIBB
D145	Bo-Bo	Elec	850	25 500	–	–	100	1040	72	15 240	93	1982	Fiat, TIBB	BRIF ID 36 SS12V Fiat 8297.22	TIBB-Parizzi three-phase
235	C	Hyd	280	14 600	9000	7·4	50	1070	39	9540	45	1957	Badoni	BRIF 1D36 N8V	Voith
225	B	Hyd	190	9800	7000	4·2	50	900	30	8322	149	1955	Breda, Jenbach, Greco, Sofer, Imam	Breda, Jenbach, Deutz	Breda, Voith
245	C	Hyd	370	14 000	11 000	6·5	65	1040	43	9240	411	1962	Reggiane, OM CNTR, Breda, Imam, Ferraro, Greco	MB820-Fiat D26N12V BRIF JW 600 CNTR OM-SEV	BRIF-Voith L24
214	B	Hyd	95	5700	4000	4	35	910	22	7158	494	1964	Badoni, Greco, Simm CNTR	Fiat 8217-02,001	BRIF-Voith L33

* First series of 19 units and second series Nos 2018-32
† Nos 2003-35

Traction and rolling stock

Pre-production prototypes of a new 3600 kW design, the Class E453 for freight and a Class E454 passenger counterpart, emerged in 1989-90. These are single-cab designs: the E454 intended to work medium-distance trains push-pull, a unit at each end, at up to 160 km/h; the E453 to work in back-to-back pairs, at a maximum of 120 km/h. Pininfarina was commissioned to style the E453/4 outline. Construction of the first examples (two Class E453, and three Class E454) was entrusted to Breda's Sofer plant in Naples. The locomotives will have wide operational availability, as total weight is set at 79 tonnes. It was thought likely that E454 pairs would be applied to heavy international trains on the Brenner route.

The first Class E402 Bo-Bo was outshopped in 1988. This is an 84-tonne, 5600 kW locomotive designed for 250 km/h, with a tractive effort of 180 kN at 102 km/h and of 92 kN at 200 km/h. Early in 1985 the FS placed an order for a pre-production batch of five. Construction of mechanical parts was entrusted to OMI Reggiane: Ansaldo Trasporti has been project leader for the electrical components in a consortium also including Breda, Fiat Ferroviaria and TIBB. These three-phase traction locomotives were required to have haulage capability of 140 km/h with 900 tonnes on a 0.8 per cent gradient and to sustain 200 km/h with 10 cars on level tangent track. In March 1989 the first of the E402 quintet was tested at up to 230 km/h on the Rome-Florence Direttissima.

The FS was allocated the finance in 1987 to place a further large-size batch of traction and rolling stock orders. The list was headed by 80 Class E652, a new higher powered version of the E632 electric Co-Co-Co locomotive. Other motive power would comprise 30 Class 255 diesel-hydraulic shunters and 120 electric railcar-and-trailer sets. Coaching stock orders would embrace 70 first-class cars of Gran Confort type, 350 air-conditioned Eurofima Type Z1 cars of both classes, 450 open-saloon medium-distance cars, 130 Type MU bi-levels, 45 sleeping cars (equipped for 200 km/h) 10 restaurant cars and 120 baggage cars, of which 40 would be arranged for 200 km/h running. By 1989 orders had been placed for all the foregoing. The first Class E652 were rolled out during the year and were given their first trials on the Brenner route.

Traction and rolling stock orders standing to be completed at the start of 1990 included 60 Ale642, 40 Le764, 20 Le682 and 41 Le763 emu cars; 45 Type MU sleeping cars, 10 restaurant cars, 70 Gran Confort InterCity cars, 535 Type Z InterCity cars in various configurations (these are now being liveried in lined two-tone grey), 468 Type MDVC medium-distance cars in various configurations, 120 baggage cars amd 130 bi-level cars.

The Class E444 Bo-Bo electric locomotives are being rebuilt with new cabs of similar pattern to those

Diesel railcars

Class	Motored axles per motor car	Transmission	Rated power (kW) per motor	Max speed km/h	Weight tonnes per car	Total seating capacity	Length per car mm	No in service 1989	Year first built	Builders Mechanical parts	Builders Engine & type
ALn64	2	Mech	136	80	41	64	20 670	6	1955	Fiat	Fiat
ALn668	2	Mech	150	120	36	68	22 110	778	1956	Omeca, Breda, Fiat Savigliano	Fiat
ALn773	2	Mech	140	110	43	73	25 400	69	1956	OM	OM
ALn873	2	Mech	220	110	50	73	25 400	19	1963	OM	OM
ALn880	2	Mech	315	130	44	80	27 000	12	1950	Breda-OM	Breda
ALn990	2	Mech	355	130	49	88	28 000	57	1950	Fiat-OM	Fiat
ALn663	2	Mech	170	130	40	63	23 540	97	1983	Fiat Savigliano	Fiat
ALn556	2	Mech	80	110	23	56	19 000	13	1937	Breda	Breda
ALn772	2	Mech	110	130	37	72	24 500	101	1940	Fiat-OM	Fiat-OM

Electric train-sets

Class	Cars per unit	Line voltage	Motor cars per unit	Motored axles per motor car	Rated output (kW) per motor	Max speed km/h	Weight tonnes per set	Total seating capacity	Length per set mm	No in service 1989	Rate of acceleration m/s^2	Year first built	Builders Mechanical parts	Builders Electrical equipment
ETR200	4	3000	2	4	250	160	164	154	87 550	15	0·5	1936	Breda	Breda
ETR250	4	3000	2	4*	250	180	181	146	97 250	4	0·5	1960	Breda	Breda
ETR300	7	3000	3	4	250	180	310	190	165 500	3	0·6	1952	Breda	Breda
ETR401	4	3000	2	4	260	250	161	175	105 900	1	0·8	1976	Fiat	Fiat
ETR450	11	3000	10	2	315	250	540	460	285 000	11	0·8	1987	Fiat	Marelli

* Plus two further motored axles on trailers

Intercity Electric locomotives

Class	Wheel arrangement	Line current	Rated output continuous/ one-hour kW	Tractive effort (full field) Max kg	Tractive effort (full field) Continuous at kg	Tractive effort (full field) Continuous at km/h	Max speed km/h	Wheel dia mm	Weight tonnes	Length mm	No in service 1989	Year first built	Builders Mechanical parts	Builders Electrical equipment
E626	Bo-Bo-Bo	3000 V dc	1890/ 2100	22 800 26 200	11 800 13 700	52 45	95	1250	93	14 950	310	1928	Savigliano, CGE, Brown Boveri, Elettromeccaniche Saronno, Breda, OM, Ansaldo, CENSA Saronno, Reggiane, Fiat	Marelli, Savigliano CGE, Brown Boveri, Elettromeccaniche Saronno, Breda, OM, Ansaldo, CENSA Saronno
E428	2-Bo-Bo-2	3000 V dc	2520/ 2800	20 000 22 000	10 500 11 500	77 71	130	1880	135	19 000	13	1934	Breda, Ansaldo, Reggiane, Fiat, Brown Boveri,	Breda, Ansaldo, Marelli, Brown Boveri
E424	Bo-Bo	3000 V dc	1500/ 1660	19 500	9500	55	100	1250	73	15 500	152	1943	Breda, Savigliano, Ansaldo, Reggiane, Brown Boveri, OM	Breda, Savigliano, Ansaldo, Marelli, Brown Boveri, CGE
E444	Bo-Bo	3000 V dc	4000/ 4440	23 600	12 800	105	200	1318	81	16 840	116	1967	Savigliano, Breda, Casaralta, Fiat	OCREN, Asgen, Savigliano
E636	Bo-Bo-Bo	3000 V dc	1890/ 2100	22 000	11 500	52	110	1250	101	18 250	460	1941	Breda, Brown Boveri, Savigliano, OM, Reggiane, Pistoiesi	Breda, Brown Boveri, Savigliano, CGE, Ansaldo S Giorgio
E645	Bo-Bo-Bo	3000 V dc	3780/ 4320	29 200	16 800	72	120	1250	110	18 290	97	1958	Breda, Brown Boveri, Savigliano, OM, Reggiane, Pistoiesi, IMAM	Breda, Brown Boveri, Savigliano, CGE, Marelli, Ansaldo S Giorgio, OCREN
E646	Bo-Bo-Bo	3000 V dc	3780/ 4320	23 800	13 500	92	145	1250	108	18 290	198	1958	Breda, Brown Boveri, Savigliano, OM, Reggiane, Pistoiesi, IMAM	Breda, Brown Boveri, Savigliano, CGE, Marelli, Ansaldo S Giorgio, OCREN
E656	Bo-Bo-Bo	3000 V dc	4200/ 4800	24 900	13 100	103	160	1250	120	18 290	427	1975	TIBB	TIBB
E632	B-B-B	3000 V dc	4350/ 4900	23 150	16 215	95	160	1040	103	17 800	66	1980	Fiat, TIBB, Sofer	Ansaldo, Marelli, TIBB
E633	B-B-B	3000 V dc	4350/ 4900	28 350	19 680	77·8	130	1040	103	17 800	151	1980	Fiat, TIBB, Sofer	Ansaldo, Marelli, TIBB
E321	C	3000 V dc	190	9000	5000	20·5	50	1310	36	9280	20	1960	FS, Verona	Brown Boveri, TIBB
E322	C	3000 V dc	190	9000	5000	20·5	50	1310	36	9280	20	1961		
E323	C	3000 V dc	190	11 700	8400	11	65	1040	46	9240	20	1966	TIBB	TIBB
E324	C	3000 V dc	190	11 700	8400	11	65	1040	45	9240	10	1966	TIBB	TIBB

RAILWAY SYSTEMS / Italy

Electric multiple-units: power cars

Class	Cars per unit	Line voltage	Motor cars per unit	Motored axles per motor car	Rated output (kW) per motor	Max speed km/h	Weight tonnes per power unit	Total seating capacity	Length per car mm	No in service 1989	Rate of acceleration m/s²	Year first built	Builders Mechanical parts	Builders Electrical equipment
ALe 540	1	3000	1	4	180	150	62	54	27 400	30	0·4	1957	OCREN, Stanga	OCREN, Stanga, Sacfem
ALe 582	1	3000	1	4	280	140	67	58	25 800	70	1·0	1987	Breda	Marelli; Ansaldo
ALe 601	1	3000	–	4	250	200	62	60	27 400	65	0·6	1961	Casaralta	Casaralta, OCREN
ALe 660	1	3000	1	4	180	150	62	77	27 400	15	0·3	1955	OCREN	OCREN
ALe 790	1	3000	1	4	100	115	39	79	27 667	18	0·3	1938	Marelli, Savigliano	CGE, Ansaldo
ALe 803	3*	3000	1	4	250	130	240*	240*	75 430*	53	0·4	1961	Stanga, Savigliano, IMAM	Savigliano, Sofer
ALe 840	1	3000	1	4	180	130	58	84	28 000	67	0·4	1950	OCREN, OM, OTO	OCREN, OM
ALe 880	1	3000	1	4	100	115	37	88	26 800	55	0·3	1938	Breda, Ansaldo, Savigliano	Breda, CGE, Marelli
ALe 801	4†	3000	2	4	250	140	220†	390†	81 140†	130	0·5	1976	Stanga, Fiore, Aetal, Lucana, Sofer	Marelli, Stanga, Fiore, Lucana, Sofer
ALe 940	4†	3000								130				
ALe 883	1	3000	1	4	180	110	56	88	28 767	23	0·4	1944	Breda	Marelli
ALe 644	2	3000	1	4	280	140	67	64	50 300	6	0·8	1980	Breda	Breda
ALe 724	2	3000	1	4	280	140	67	72	24 780	90	1·0	1982	Breda	Marelli, Ansaldo
ALe 804‡	2	3000	1	4	250	140	84‡	92‡	50 300‡	6	0·8	1980	Breda	TIBB

* Including two Type Le 803 trailers   † Including two Type Le 108 trailers   ‡ Including Type Le 884 trailer

of the latest E402 type. Rebuilds are also being similarly liveried to the E402.

Orders were placed in April 1988 for 60 ALe 642 emu power cars plus matching trailers, 20 of them with control cabs. The ALe 642 is a variant for local services, and hence with increased seating, of the 90 recently delivered. Class ALe 582, a new design with matching trailers for cross-country service in the south and in Sicily. The ALe 582 cars have aluminium alloy bodies and the motor cars front ends of polyester reinforced fibreglass.

In diesel traction, delivery of a further 70 Class D145 three-phase motor shunting/trip Bo-Bos, 42 from TIBB and 28 from Fiat-Parizzi, was completed in 1989.

A total of 10 coaches are being built to evaluate Fiat's new design of independent-wheel bogie. The first, a Type MDVC medium-distance car, was delivered for trials by Colleferro in late 1989. The residue would comprise four more MDVC, two Type Z InterCity cars built by Ferrosud, and three cars of new modular structure design evolved by Fiat with support from the National Research Council.

Total FS rolling stock resources at the start of 1989 comprised 171 steam (in reserve), 2075 main-line, 70 shunting electric, 486 main-line and 758 shunting diesel locomotives, 31 permanent electric train-sets, 730 electric and 1150 diesel motor cars, 8 diesel train-sets, 14 211 hauled passenger, railcar trailer, postal and baggage cars, and 99 226 freight wagons.

Track

Monoblock prestressed concrete sleepers are being used almost exclusively in current track upgrading and doubling projects (though a test installation of slab track was recently completed). Length of sleeper is 2.3 metres, but for new track where speeds may exceed 160 km/h, a new design with a length of 2.6 metres is being adopted. Ballast is crushed stone chips with a minimum depth of 35 cm below the sleeper base. In new construction a sub-ballast consisting of a granular mixture with 3 per cent cement content is being laid to a depth of 20 cm. For rail renewals, and all new lines, UIC 60 (60 kg/m) rails are being used, fastened with K-type clips. Italian Railways installs about 850 km of new track each year. At the end of 1989 60 kg/m rail was installed over 12 700 km, 50 kg/m over 6000 km, 46 kg/m over 1800 km and 36 kg/m over 300 km.

Signalling

For speeds above 150 km/h, automatic block with coded current cab repetition is being adopted. Cab repetition is integrated with automatic speed control. For speeds up to 250 km/h on the Rome-Florence Direttissima the following speeds are encoded (km/h): 250-230-200-150-100-60-30.

In 1988 the Telettra microprocessor-based ground-to-train radio telephone system was proven devoid of interference with the electronics of the latest traction, provided only that some modifications were made to the circuitry of the ETR450 tilt-body train-sets. The attraction of the system is that it affords selective train communication with a wide range of ground installations and also with the national telephone network. It is now to be installed throughout the Milan-Naples-Reggio Calabria and Bologna-Venice routes. This will allow installation of public telephones on board trains.

Arezzo Railways
Societa La Ferroviaria Italiana (LFI)

Via Concino Concino 2, Arezzo

Gauge: 1435 mm
Route length: 85 km
Electrification: 85 km at 3 kV dc

Director: Marcello Grillo

The railway operates nine electric and two diesel locomotives, 10 electric railcars, 19 trailers and 33 freight wagons.

Bari-Nord Railway
Ferotranviaria SpA
Managed by Government Commission, Rome

Head Office: Piazza G Winckelmann, 12 Rome

Executive Office: Piazza Moro 50B, Bari
Telephone: +39 80 213577

Operating Manager: Dr Ing N Nitti

Gauge: 1435 mm

Route length: 70 km
Electrification: 70 km at 3 kV dc

The railway operates two electric locomotives, three diesel locomotives, 12 electric railcars, 16 passenger cars and 16 freight wagons. The Ministry of Transport is financially assisting modernisation.

Benevento-Naples Railway
Ferrovia Benevento-Napoli
Managed by Government Commission, Rome

Via Torre della Catena, Benevento

Telephone: +39 824 24961, 29902

Director: D Perrotta

Gauge: 1435 mm

Route length: 48 km
Electrification: 48 km at 3 kV dc

The railway operates one diesel and two electric locomotives, 12 electric train-sets, 15 passenger cars and seven freight wagons.

Brescia North Railway
Ferrovia Brescia Nord

Via Mier 27B, Iseo

General Manager: Dr Ing P Gamba

Gauge: 1435 mm
Route length: 108 km

The railway operates 12 diesel locomotives, 10 diesel railcars (which include Fiat ALn 668 of recent build) and 16 trailers and passenger cars, and 63 freight wagons.

In 1987 the government allocated the railway L 96 000 million for modernisation. Following the end of the Brescia-Iseo-Edolo Railway's concession in mid-1987, it was reformed as the Brescia North Railway. Two passenger cars were obtained secondhand from the Swiss Federal Railway in 1988.

Italy / **RAILWAY SYSTEMS** 629

Calabria-Lucana Railways
Ferrovie Calabro-Lucane
Managed by Government Commission, Rome

Viale del Caravaggio 105, Rome

Government Commissioner: Ing U Quaranta
Director-General: Dr-Ing V De Luca

Gauge: 950 mm
Route length: 418 km

The railway operates 12 diesel locomotives, 62 diesel railcars and 75 trailers, and 100 freight wagons. Recent additions are six Type M300 railcars built by Ferrosud and based on the FS Type ALn 663. Five more have been ordered and the first was delivered in 1989. The Ministry of Transport is financing modernisation.

In December 1989 the railway inaugurated a new line, with two intermediate stations in the city's outskirts, to a central terminus in Cosenza.

Circumvesuviana Railway
Managed by Government Commission, Rome

Corso Garibaldi 387, 80142 Naples

Telephone: +39 81 779 2111
Telex: 772156
Telefax: +39 81 779 2450

General Manager: Dr Ing Ulisse Paci
Operating Director: Dr Ing Carmine Sergio
Finance Director: Dr Fernando Origo
Works and Maintenance Manager: Dr Ing Ugo Pulerà
Traction Manager: Dr Ing Michele di Matteo
Electric Installations Manager: Dr Ing Antonio Pesce
Traffic Manager: Dr Ing Antonio Sarnatoro
Personnel Manager: Dr Gaetano Febbraio

Gauge: 950 mm
Route length: 144 km
Electrification: 144 km at 1.5 kV dc

The Circumvesuviana Railway serves an extensive territory to the east of Naples stretching to Baiano, situated on the border of the province of Avellino, and to Sarno in the province of Salerno, with four lines: Naples-Barra-Torre Annunziata-Poggiomarino (42.9 km); Naples-Barra-Torre Annunziata-Castel (42.9 km); Naples-Barra-Torre Annunziata-Castellammare di Stabia-Sorrento (42.5 km); and Naples-Pomigliano d'Arco-Nolo-Baiano (38.7 km), with a branch to Pomigliano/Alfa Sud (2.7km). The Sorrento branch, completed in 1947, is largely in tunnels, one of which is 4.8 km long with a station inside the bore.

In 1990 the railway was completing a new double-track section from S Giorgio to Cremano-Volla-Casoria, and at work on double-tracking the line from Poggioreale to Pomigliano d'Arco for a distance of 11km. The railway records almost 645 milion passenger-km a year.

The service is furnished by 85 three-car emus and the company also operates three diesel and four electric locomotives, and 42 freight wagons. In 1989 the railway took delivery of 11 new Series 200 three-car articulated emus, built by Sofer of the Breda group with Ansaldo Trasporti electrical equipment. Each unit is powered by two 350kW motors and tares 56 tonnes, seating 120 with standing room for 276.

The signalling is automatic block under control of route-setting signalboxes, the latest supplied by Ansaldo Trasporti.

In 1986 management of the railway was taken over by the state authority controlling a number of local Italian lines, the Commission for Government Management.

Track
Rails: 36 and 50 kg/m
Cross ties (sleepers): Vagneaux, timber or cement

New Circumvesuviana articulated emu by Sofer of the Breda group

Dimensions: 1800 x 240 x 140 mm
Spacing: 1500/km
Fastenings: Indirect K; RN and Nabla (for Vagneux)

Minimum curvature radius: 100°
Max gradient: 3%
Max permissible axleload: 15 tonnes

North Milan Railway (FNME)
Ferrovie Nord Milano Esercizio SpA

Piazzale Cadorna 14, 20123 Milan

Telephone: +39 2 85 111
Telex: 325643 minord i
Telefax: +39 2 85 11708

Operations Director: Dr Ing Arnaldo Siena
Modernisation Director: Giorgio Picchi
Director, Electrical Plant and Signalling: Dr Ing Vincenzo Celentano
Purchasing Director: Dr Gianfranco Fusetti
Director, Traction and Rolling Stock: Dr Ing Luigi Legnani

Gauge: 1435 mm
Route length: 231 km, of which 200 km in use
Electrification: 200 km at 3 kV ac

The railway serves the north Milan suburbs with a main double-track route from Milan Nord to Como and to Laveno on Lake Maggiore; the latter has a branch from Saronno to Novara. A further double-track route runs from Milan to Seveso, beyond which single-track reaches to Canzo-Asso.

Traffic
FNME's originating freight traffic, has suffered a serious decline, leading to closure of several private sidings and of the long Valmorea branch, and this trend was accelerated in 1989. Passenger traffic, on the other hand, still rises.

Modernisation plan
In 1984 the government approved execution of a L 260 000 million modernisation plan. The main item is 17 km of quadrupling on FNME's Como main line, between Bovisa and Saronno, accompanied by level crossing elimination and station reconstruction, plus installation of two new stations, which was launched in July 1985. Completion will halve Milan-Como journey time to 30 minutes. This development is germane to the integration of FNME and Italian Railways in the Milan regional rail transport system (for details see under Italian Railways). In 1978 the government allocated FNME L 400 000 million for level crossing suppression and four-tracking from Bovisa to Cadorna and for more new rolling stock.

The 4 km from FNME's present Milan terminus to Bovisa, which is common to all FNME services, presently carries over 300 trains a day and roughly two-thirds of that sum continues on to Saronno. Quadrupling beyond Bovisa will enable separation of fast and slow services.

The Milan Regional scheme provides for a connection from the FNME at Saronno to the Italian Railways line from Rho to Porta Garibaldi, which will enable FNME trains to share use of the projected cross-city tunnel with Italian Railways. Still awaiting formal Transport Ministry authorisation is a L 420 000 million scheme to cater for Milan's Malpensa airport by doubling 20.5 km of the Saronno-Novara branch and constructing from it an airport link; dedicated airport train service would be furnished by four-car, chopper-controlled emus. Completion of these projects and of the cross-city tunnel, through which FNME would run 12 of the 20 planned peak-hour trains each way, is forecast to boost FNM daily train working to almost 500 services. Cross-city FNME services envisaged include Malpensa airport-Treviglio and Seveso-Pavia.

In late 1989 work began on reconstruction of FNM's Milan North station. The layout is being expanded from nine to ten tracks, which will be of IPA's prefabricated slab track type. Completion was anticipated in 1992.

Traction and rolling stock
Rolling stock at the start of 1990 comprised two usable steam locomotives (for special events only), 15 electric locomotives, seven diesel-electric tractors, 70 emu power cars, 211 trailers and passenger cars, of which 175 are formed in 79 semi-permanent formations and 82 freight wagons. The latest electric power car arrivals are 10 Type E750 chopper-controlled 1120 kW units built by Breda, of similar design to the Italian Railways ALe 724, which work both with 42 French-pattern bi-level trailers and with 28 cars delivered by Socimi in 1982. Other recent deliveries include 47 open, centre-aisle coaches bought second-hand from the Swiss Federal Railway.

Signalling
Automatic block controls 77 route-km, of which 69.8 km is double-track. FS-type semi-automatic block controls 16.8 km, including 12.8 km of double-track. There are 161 signal-protected level crossings on the system. FNME's eleventh push-button route-setting signalbox was recently commissioned, and in 1990 five more were in course of installation. FNME has been testing an experimental track-to-train radio installation between Milan and Saronno.

Track
Rails (percentage in use): RA 36 kg/m (5.2%); FS 46 kg/m (2.46%); UNI 50 kg/m (92.34%)
Sleepers: Timber, FS concrete monobloc and bi-bloc
Size: Timber 260 × 26 × 15 mm
Monobloc 230 × 30 × 19 mm
Bi-bloc 230 × 26.3 × 21.7 mm
Spacing: 1500 km
Fastenings: Type K for FS 46 and UNI 50; Type RN and Nabla for bi-bloc sleepers
Minimum curve radius: 250 m
Max gradient: 3%
Max permissible axleload: 20 tonnes

Traffic	1985	1986	1987	1988	1989
Freight tonnes	62 620	56 300	50 215	30 009	23 652
Freight tonne-km	905 530	814 280	726 108	414 597	337 857
Passenger-km (million)	716.786	715.096	731.93	749.74	772.377
Passenger journeys (million)	35.163	34.990	35.758	36.564	37.405

Finance (L million) Revenues	1985	1986	1987	1988	1989
Passengers and baggage	26 544.6	29 404.5	30 542.7	31 360.5	35 864.54
Freight, parcels and mail	762.4	755.4	696.5	564.4	578.29
Other	1431.0	1563.0	1632.2	1679.2	3359.78
Total	28 738.0	31 723.9	32 871.4	33 604.1	39 802.61

Expenditure	1985	1986	1987	1988	1989
Staff/personnel	91 802.1	98 304.2	109 774.7	113 825.9	128 391.4
Materials and services	46 276.9	49 977.3	50 020.9	52 764.0	53 562.8
Depreciation	1036.1	1113.3	3999.3	4497.4	6021.5
Financial charges	3993.0	7676.6	8660.8	10 018.3	12 910.7
Total	143 108.1	157 071.4	172 455.7	181 105.6	200 886.4

Electric locomotives

Class	Wheel arrangement	Line voltage	Rated output kW	Max speed km/h	Weight tonnes	No in service 1989	Year first built	Builders Mechanical parts	Builders Electrical equipment
600	Bo + Bo	3000	1030	75	63	5	1928/30	OM	CGE
610	Bo + Bo	3000	1030	75	61	4	1949	Breda	CGE
620	B + B	3000	2250	130	72	6	1985	TIBB (Fiat bogies)	Ansaldo

Electric railcars

Class	Line voltage	Motored axles per motor car	Rated output (kW) per motor	Max speed km/h	Weight tonnes per car	Total seating capacity	Length per car mm	No in service 1989	Year first built	Builders Mechanical parts	Builders Electrical equipment
700	3000	4	183	80	55	57/90	20 600	23	1928/32	OM	TIBB
730	3000	4	272	80	57	78	20 600	3	1932	Tallero	TIBB
740	3000	4	272	80	57	87	20 600	5	1928/30	Tallero	CGE
740	3000	4	272	80	52	100	22 720	11	1953/55	Breda	CGE
740	3000	4	272	80	52	80	23 320	8	1957	Breda	CGE
750	3000	4	280	130	53	72	24 900	18	1982	Breda	Ansaldo, Marelli

Diesel locomotives

Class	Wheel arrangement	Transmission	Rated power (kW)	Max speed klm/h	Weight tonnes per car	No in service 1989	Year first built	Builders Mechanical parts	Builders Engine & type
500	Bo-Bo	Elec	383	75	47	5	1971	TIBB	Fiat
510	A-A	Elec	103	30	18	2	1966	TIBB	Fiat

Padane Railways
Ferrovie Padane
Managed by Government Commission, Rome

Via foro Boario 27, 44100 Ferrara

Telephone: +39 532 941 78

Via Clementini 33, 47037 Rimini

Telephone: +39 541 25474

Parma-Suzzara Railway
Ferrovia Parma-Suzzara
Managed by Government Commission, Rome

Largo Europe 16, Padua 35130

Manager: Gino Zarotti

Gauge: 1435 mm
Route length: 52 km

In 1989 the railway recorded 546 000 passenger journeys, 6·95 million passenger-km, 47 000 tonnes of freight and 1·917 million freight tonne-km.

The railway operates five diesel locomotives, 12 diesel railcars, 10 trailers and 10 other passenger cars.

Telephone: +39 49 38541

Operating Manager: U Polettini

Gauge: 1435 mm
Route length: 44 km

The stock includes two secondhand 2200 hp V220 diesel-hydraulic locomotives from the German Federal Railway and passenger cars from the Swiss Federal Railways. In 1988 the railway was studying modification of this equipment to form push-pull train-sets with central control of passenger car door closure. The remaining diesel locomotives are three 300 hp diesel-hydraulics built by OM in 1942. Railcars comprise seven Fiat ALn 668 with eight trailers, and two ALn 772 and three ALn 773 with two trailers, all by OM.

Maximum permissible axleload is 20 tonnes.

The railway operates five diesel locomotives, three diesel railcars, 15 passenger cars and 13 freight wagons. The railway has recently acquired two German Federal Type V220 diesel-hydraulic B-Bs and 11 FS cars to operate peak-hour students' trains between Ferrara and Codigoro.

San Severo-Peschici Railway
Ferrovie del Gargano Srl

Via Don Minzoni 101, 71016 San Severo

Telephone: +39 882 21414

Operating Manager: Ing F Stea

Gauge: 1435 mm

Route length: 79 km
Electrification: 79 km at 3 kV dc

The railway operates four electric locomotives, six electric railcars, nine passenger cars and 28 freight wagons.

Sangritana Railway
Ferrovia Adriatica Sangritana

Piazzele della Stazione, 66034 Lanciano

Telephone: +39 872 45147
Telefax: +39 872 45144

Managing Director: Dr Ing Antonio Bianco

Gauge: 1435 mm
Route length: 102 km
Electrification: 102 km at 3 kv dc

In 1987 the railway recorded 896 251 passenger journeys, 17.925 million passenger journeys, 54 271 tonnes of freight and 1.09 million freight tonne-km. The railway operates four 400 kW Bo-Bo electric and two 397 kW Bo-Bo diesel locomotives, 11 railcars, nine passenger cars and 35 freight wagons. Maximum permissible axleload is 18 tonnes.

Sardinian Railways
Strade Ferrate Sardegna SpA

Head Office: Piazza G Winckelmann 12, Rome
Local Office: Via Sicilia 8, Sassari

Operating Manager; Ing A Aromando

Gauge: 950 mm
Route length: 196 km

The railway operates five diesel locomotives, 11 diesel railcars, 32 passenger cars and 162 freight wagons.

Sardinian Minor Railways
Ferrovie Complementari della Sardegna SpA

Head Office: Piazza G Winckelmann 12, Rome
Local Office: Viale Bonaria, Cagliari

Operating Manager: Ing A Aromando

Gauge: 950 mm
Route length: 435 km

The railway operates 15 diesel locomotives, 20 diesel railcars, 41 passenger cars and 428 freight wagons.

Sassuolo-Modena Railway
Azienda Transporti Consorziale de Modena

Piazza Manzoni 21, 41100 Modena

Telephone: +39 59 308011

General Manager: Dr Ing Giancarlo Della Casa

Gauge: 1435 mm
Route length: 16 km
Electrification: 16 km at 3 kV dc

The railway operates two Breda-built 440 kW Bo-Bo electric locomotives of 1932 construction and eight emus (five Firema Type E126 of 1984/85, three of them three-car and the other pair two-car; and three Breda three-car units of 1932); six other passenger cars and 10 freight wagons.

South Eastern Railway
Ferrovie del Sud-Est
Managed by Government Commission, Rome

Head Office: Via Edoardo D'Onofrio 212, 00155 Rome

Telephone: +39 6 456 8513
Telex: 621564
Telefax: +39 6 621567

Executive offices:
Via G Amendola 136, 70126 Bari

Telephone: +39 80 583222
Telefax: +39 80 339844

Viale Oronza Quarta 38, 73100 Lecce

Telephone: +39 832 41931

Director-General: Dr Carlo Bombrini
Executive Office Director; Ing Armando Pastore

Gauge: 1435 mm
Route length: 473 km

In 1984 the Ministry of Transport announced financial aid for the modernisation of this system. Double-tracking from Bari to Murgivacca and this section's provision with new signalling was completed in late 1986.

The railway took delivery in 1989 of three 1220 kW diesel-electric locomotives from IMPA of Catania, with Breda engines and Jeumont-Schneider electrical equipment, to supplement its previous fleet of 14 diesel locomotives (all but one diesel-hydraulic), five diesel-hydraulic shunters, 56 diesel railcars, 69 trailers or passenger cars, and 209 freight wagons. Signalling includes a push-button route-setting installation.

In 1986 the railway's management was taken over by the Commission for Government Management, a state organisation which controls a number of Italian local railways.

Traffic	1986	1987
Total freight tonnes	211 315	190 314
Total freight tonne-km	8838 060	7657 345
Total passenger-km (million)	159.25	151.9
Total passenger journeys	6972 855	6788 552

Finance		
Revenues (L million)	1986	1987
Passengers and baggage	4842	4668
Freight, parcels and mail	1297	1221
Other income	824	794
Total	6963	6683

Expenditure	1986	1987
Staff/personnel	79 268	NA
Materials, services, depreciation and financial charges	22 801	NA
Total	102 069	NA

Diesel locomotives

Class	Wheel arrangment	Transmission	Rated power (kW)	Max speed km/h	Total weight tonnes	No in service 1988	Year first built	Builders Mechanical parts	Engine & type	Transmission
BB 151-63	Bo-Bo	Elec	600	80	52	13	1959	Reggiane	Man Reggiane	Marelli
BB 101-05	B	Hyd	185	55	26	5	1959	Greco	Deutz	Voith

Suzzara-Ferrara Railway
Ferrovia Suzzara-Ferrara SpA

Via Cesare Battisti, 29 Ferrara

General Manager: Dr Ing L Puccetti

Gauge: 1435 mm
Route length: 82 km

The railway operates three diesel locomotives, 22 diesel railcars, 27 other passenger cars and 19 freight wagons. The railway has recently acquired 12 ex-Swiss Federal lightweight passenger cars, and in 1990 took delivery of three new Fiat diesel railcars.

Trento-Male Railway
Societa per Azioni Ferrovia Elettri Trento-Male

PO Box 530, Via Secondo da Trento N7, 38100 Trendo

Telephone: +39 461 824181/823671

Telex: 401144 tremal i
Telefax: +39 461 820256

General Manager: Dr Ing Daniele Cozzini

Gauge: 1000 mm
Route length: 56 km
Electrification: 56 km at 3 kV dc

The railway recorded 4892 passenger journeys and 39.8 million passenger-km in 1987. It operates one 800 kW electric locomotive, five three-car train-sets of 1964-build, five railcars and two trailers.

Turin-Ceres Railway
Torinese Trasporti Intercommunali SpA

Corso Turati 19/6, 10100 Turin

Telephone: +39 11 521 2266

General Manager: R Notor

Gauge: 1435 mm
Route length: 152 km
Electrification: 43 km at 4 kV dc

The railway operates one diesel and five electric locomotives, seven diesel railcars, 23 passenger cars and 28 freight wagons. Its unusual 4 kV electrification was re-energised in November 1986 after 18 months' disuse while the equipment was overhauled.

Umbria Railway
Ferrovia Centrale Umbra (FCU)
Managed by Government Commission, Rome

Largo Cacciatori delle Alpi 8, Perugia

Telephone: +39 75 239457

Telefax: +39 75 65257

Manager: Ing P Angeloni

Gauge: 1435 mm
Route length: 43 mm
Electrification: 152 km at 3 kV dc

The railway operates three electric and five diesel locomotives, 16 railcars, 16 other passenger cars and 65 freight wagons. In 1989 three more Fiat ALn 776 railcars were procured and FCU also purchased three Class D341 locomotives from FS.

Ivory Coast

Ivory Coast Railways
Société Ivoirienne des Chemins de Fer (SICF)

01 PO Box 1394, Abidjan 01, Ivory Coast

Telephone: +225 32 02 45
Telex: 3564 ferdia abidjan
Telefax: +225 32 39 62

President: P Y Kouakou
Director-General: Karim-Jacques Budin
Deputy Director-General: Oumar Diawara
Director Rolling Stock and Traction: Ousseyni Diarra
Director Track and Structures: Privat Noël Kla
Financial Director: Christophe Yesso
Commercial Director: Gbon Coulibaly
Traffic Director: André Balma
Planning Director: Kprêt Bombo
Head of Telecommunication and Signalling Service: Aboubacar Nabilébié Bazie

Gauge: 1000 mm
Route length: 660km

SICF is the Ivory Coast portion of the former Abidjan-Niger Railway that was jointly owned and managed by the Republic of the Ivory Coast and Burkina Faso (formerly the Republic of Upper Volta). In 1986 the partnership broke up. The reasons were partly a change of government in Burkina Faso to one of diametrically contrasting political complexion to that in the Ivory Coast, but more especially a Burkina Faso shortfall of FrCFA 20 000 million in payments to RAN and a divergence of opinion over the wisdom of carrying out the line's extension to Tambao.

In 1982 the then Upper Volta government sought tenders to build the long-cherished 375 km extension to the manganese fields at Tambao in north-eastern Burkina Faso, beyond which the line might eventually extend to Tin Hrassan, near the Mali and Niger frontiers. Until 1985 there was no action of the Tambao project because prospective sources of loan finance were sceptical of its viability, particularly as mining companies were disinterested in working the deposits. The World Bank firmly refused its support, which discouraged other potential sources of finance. In 1985, nevertheless, Burkina Faso unilaterally began construction, appropriating track renewal materials for its purpose, which roused the RAN Director-General to disclaim responsibility for the railway in Burkina Faso.

In February 1988 the countries seemed to settle their differences, but this rapprochement was short-lived, and each country now separately manages its part of the railway.

Formed in June 1989, SCIF was immediately in serious financial difficulty, unable to meet its costs from revenue. Local analysis estimated that the railway was in immediate need of CFA 1200 million to keep going, and of at least CFA 14 000 million for rehabilitation.

Despite a good network of permanent roads the railway is a vital link with Burkina Faso, which particularly relies on it for transport of goods to and from the coast. The railway comprises a principal line which connects Abidjan, capital of Ivory Coast, with Ouagadougou, capital of Burkina Faso, and two branches, one of 12 km from Abidjan to the oil port of Vridi and the other of 14 km from Azaguie to Akebefiat.

Traction and rolling stock
SICF operates 22 diesel locomotives, 14 railcars, 136 passenger cars and 1463 freight cars.

At the break-up SICF and the Burkina Faso system shared resources of 19 GM 2500 hp Co-Cos of 90.7 tonnes acquired in 1979-80, six more 2250 hp Class FT22LC units obtained from General Motors of Canada in 1981, a stud of mostly French-built 1800 hp Bo-Bos, plus 39 diesel shunters. The shunters were chiefly Henschel-built and diesel-hydraulic, mostly obtained in 1979-80 and of 450–750 hp, but including four GM units delivered in late 1981 for Pétroci traffic; nine more Thyssen-Henschel units were delivered in 1983. Of a total of 39 railcars and 30 trailers, the great majority of the railcars were 57-tonne 950 hp vehicles by GIMT. Coaching stock featured 55 air-conditioned stainless steel-bodied cars supplied by Carel-Fouché in 1977–80. Recent acquisitions of 426 vehicles to meet rising traffic demand have built the wagon stock up to 1621 vehicles.

Signalling
21 stations have been equipped with a system of colour-light signalling and power point operation based on French Railways NSI relay system. Installation was by a French subsidiary of ABB.

Track
Rail: 30 and 36 kg/m
Ballast: Granite, 800–1200 litres/m, hard sandstone, 700 litres/m
Sleepers: Metal, 1550 per km; concrete monobloc (Blochet), 1357 per km
Minimum curvature radius: 500 m, being raised to 800 m
Ruling gradient: 10%
Max axleload: 17 tonnes

Diesel railcar for express services by Soulé (Wilhelm Pflug)

GM of Canada Type GT22LC 2250hp diesel locomotive (Wilhelm Pflug)

Jamaica

Ministry of Public Utilities and Transport

PO Box 9000, 2 St Lucia Avenue, Kingston 5

Minister: R D Pickersgill
Permanent Secretary: Dr H I C Lowe

Jamaica Railway Corporation (JRC)

PO Box 489, 142 Barry Street, Kingston

Telephone: +1 809 922 6620/1531
Telex: 2190
Telefax: +1 809 922 7290

General Manager: O D Crooks
Secretary: Phillippa E Hewan
Finance Controller: N Robertson
Chief of Transportation; E Scott

Chief Mechanical Engineer: P Smith
Chief Civil Engineer: A Allen

Gauge: 1435 mm
Route length: 294 km

The island of Jamaica is intersected by 5000 km of main roads, of which about 75 per cent are asphalted, and the railway which is centred on the principal port town of Kingston. The railway has a vital role in transport to the ports of bauxite, of which Jamaica is a major world producer. Annual traffic has lately aggregated some 115 freight tonne-km and 1.2 million passenger journeys.

Shortage of funds has retarded planned track upgrading on key freight routes and reduced traction availablity. In mid-1989 the northern sector of the Kingston-Montego Bay line had to be closed for three months because of its disrepair. However, in 1989 Alcan Jamaica Alumina Bauxite Corporation loaned JRC US$4.25 million towards recouping track maintenance arrears, which are being attacked first on the sector taken by the bauxite trains. Because of timber scarcity, renewals are employing locally-manufactured concrete sleepers.

Motive power and rolling stock
Resources in 1989 comprised 20 diesel locomotives, six diesel railcars, 58 freight cars and 30 passenger cars, some of which are Metro-Cammell-built former diesel railcars; the remainder include 12 Schindler-built cars of 1978 and nine Soulé-built cars of 1982.

In 1982 a contract worth Fr55 million was placed with Alsthom-Atlantique for six 2000 hp Type AD 20B, 68-tonne Bo-Bo diesel-electric locomotives with alternator/dc transmissions and rheostatic braking; deliveries were completed in 1983/84 and a further six locomotives were delivered in 1985/86. The locomotives have a starting tractive effort of 20 900 kg and a maximum speed of 105 km/h.

JRC train of Alco DL-528 locomotive, one Soulé and two Schindler passenger cars (*F Gerald Rawling*)

Japan
Ministry of Transport

1-3, 2-chrome, Kasumigaseki, Chiyoda-ku, Tokyo

Telephone: +81 3 580 3111

Minister: Takami Eto
Deputy Vice-Minister for National Railways Reorganisation: Yasushi Tanahashi
Director-General, National Railways Department: Akira Niwa
Director-General, Private Railways Department: T Hattori

Japan Railways Group (JR)

Japan Rail is the title under which the national railway system was represented from the start of April 1987 for external marketing purposes, but domestically it took the title of Japan Railways Group. At that date, Japanese National Railways (JNR) was statutorily disbanded and its assets, operations and liabilities were distributed among a number of new companies, known as the Japan Railways Group.

The dismemberment legislation provided that the passenger business, its infrastructure and its assets, on JNR's 1067 mm-gauge network be distributed geographically between six companies, three on Honshu island and one each on Hokkaido, Shikoku and Kyushu. On Honshu the frontiers between the three companies' jurisdictions were drawn with the primary objective of avoiding partition of short-haul and commuter systems; as a result the key Tokaido trunk route from Tokyo to Osaka was severed twice.

The eventual aim is that all will become private commercial enterprises, but initially all remain in the public domain. Only the Hokkaido, Shikoku and Kyushu companies started free of any inherited debt liabilities, but all three of these need subsidy of their current operations, which has been provided through government-established Management Stabilising Funds. The island companies take the interest generated by these Funds, which total 1 000 000 million yen. In FY 1988-89 the subsidies to the three companies were budgeted at 93 000 million yen.

At the same time, transfer of rural lines to new local companies continues. The latter are known as third-sector companies, because they are a hybrid of private and local community finance.

Previously Japanese railway business was governed by two sets of statutes, one to regulate JNR, and one covering other railways. This has been superseded by new legislation covering all railway business. It reduces the degree of regulation, with provisos that railway safety and customer services are not impaired. A licence is required to run a railway business and railway facilities are subject to inspection. Furthermore, fares and charges must be approved in advance by the Minister of Transport, although written notice is considered adequate for discounted fares and charges. Finally, train schedules must be submitted to the Ministry in advance of implementation.

East Japan Railway Co (JR-East)

6-5, Marunouchi 1-chome, Chiyoda-ku, Tokyo 100

Telephone: +81 03 215 9649
Telex: 24873 ejr
Telefax: +81 3 213 5291

Chairman: Isamu Yamashita
President: Shoji Sumita
Executive Vice President, Director of Operations and Construction: Shuchio Yamanouchi
Managing Directors
  Administration and Affiliated Enterprises: Wataru Yamada
  Corporate Planning and Personnel: Masatake Matsuda
  Finance: Masami Terada
  Tohoku District: Mizuo Yamaoka
  Development Enterprises: Keisuke Amiya
  Inquiry and Audit: Eiji Tomours
  Tokyo Metropolitan and Marketing: Katsuyoshi Nagao

Route length: 6642.8 km of 1067 mm- and 835.3 km of 1435 mm-gauge (Shinkansen)
Electrification: 2676.9 km of 1067 mm-gauge at 1.5 kV dc and 1889.2 km at 20 kV 50 Hz ac
835.3 km of 1435 mm-gauge at 25 kV 50 Hz ac

The railway runs rail passenger transport and related activities in the Tohoku region and the Tokyo metropolitan region, including the Tohoku and Joetsu Shinkansen.

Traffic (million)	FY 1988-89
Total passenger-km	109 700
Total passenger journeys	5351

Finance
In its second year of operation, the net income of JR-East after corporation taxes rose 50.8 per cent over the previous year. A favourable environment resulting from the strong national economy was behind some of the causes for the advance.

Total passenger-km grew by 5.2 per cent and revenue from diversification into restaurants and stores was sharply up, likewise income from other activities. At the same time, cost-control measures improved the railway operating ratio from 80.5 to 79.8

Series 200 Shinkansen train-set of Tohoku and Joetsu lines

634 RAILWAY SYSTEMS / Japan

per cent, and interest charges were cut 16.4 per cent through a substantial reduction of long-term debt. Return on assets was lifted to 1.1 per cent and on equity to 12 per cent.

JR-East has already established 14 subsidiary companies and plans to develop a corporate group structure with satellite companies surrounding the core railway operation. Subsidiary activity includes well-established advertising and distribution companies. Activity in finance, hotel and restaurant management, real estate, sport and leisure is to be significantly expanded.

Operating revenue

(000 million yen)	1987-88	1988-89
Passengers and baggage	1415.7	1483.3
Other	179.1	216.0
Total	1594.8	1699.3

Operating expenditure

(000 million yen)	1987-88	1988-89
Staff	438.2	431.4
Materials and services	593.6	636.5
Depreciation	237.4	272.3
Financial charges	253.4	270.7
Total	1522.7	1611.0

Services

About 66 per cent of JR-East revenue is generated in the Tokyo metropolitan area, where the railway operates 21 commuter routes. The area has been a focus of considerable investment, one result of which was that by mid-1990 all 21 routes would be operating exclusively air-conditioned rolling stock. During FY 1988-89 JR-East spent 1600 million yen on station improvements in the area.

In the spring of 1991 JR-East expected to start service to and from Tokyo's Narita Airport. A third sector company was in 1990 completing an 8.7 km extension from JR-East's present Narita line and another from the 1435 mm-gauge Keisei Electric Railway (which at present terminates short of the airport) to a new station beneath the airport's passenger terminal, which the two railways will share. The shell of this terminal was built with the airport, in preparation for a planned Shinkansen link that was aborted after completion of the right of way.

With the migration of workers from the Tokyo centre to its outskirts because of the resumed upsurge of land prices and rents in the capital, JR-East has been energetically promoting sales of Shinkansen season tickets, priced roughly 60 per cent per journey below standard Shinkansen fare, for regular travel of 100km or so to and from the city. Extension of the Tohoku and Joetsu Shinkansen routes the final 3.6 km from their temporary terminus at Ueno to Tokyo Central would be completed by March 1991. Joetsu maximum speed was raised to 275 km/h in March 1990.

Following the formal opening in March 1988 of the 53.8 km Seikan Tunnel between Honshu and Hokkaido islands (see below), through express services were inaugurated. From March 1989 these comprised eight daily trains each way between Aomori and Hakodate or Sapporo, two between Morioka and Hakodate, three overnight 'Hokutosei' sleeper trains between Tokyo Ueno and Hokkaido and one between Osaka and Hakodate. The 'Hokutosei' overnight services include a new design of sleeper embodying single-occupancy 'roomettes' with fixed-bed and separate armchair for day use, as well as shower facilities, a bar-lounge car and public telephone kiosk.

In 1989 JR-East introduced bi-level 1067 mm-gauge cars. They have been inserted in Series 211 electric train-sets operating west of Tokyo on the Tokaido line.

Signalling

In FY 1988-89 Programmed Route Control (PRC) was installed over 169.4 m of the Banetsu-To and Echigo lines. In FY 1989-90 it would be completed over 146.3 km of the Nikko, Mito and Agatsuma lines.

Traction and rolling stock

At the start of 1990 the railway was operating 277 electric and 190 diesel locomotives, 9968 electric railcars (including 708 Shinkansen cars) 767 diesel railcars, 1069 passenger cars, including 306 sleeping and eight restaurant cars.

Recent deliveries have included 47 Series 651 seven-car limited-express electric train-sets to work 'Super Hitachi' services between Tokyo and Sendai via Mito and Taira. These are among several limited-express services of the JR Group which, by agreement among the member railways, had their maximum permitted speed lifted from 120 to 130 km/h following

East Japan Railway Series 651 'Super Hitachi' limited express electric train-set for Joban line

'Super Hitachi' Series 651 standard class

Bar-lounge car of 'Hokutosei' overnight Tokyo-Sapporo train via the Seikan Tunnel

trials with a new Series 485 train-set on JR-West. In 1990 trials were being held of a Series 651 unit equipped with eddy current brakes, with a view to raising maximum permissible speed to 140 km/h.

The company has declared its intention to reverse traditional JNR procedure and allow foreign companies equal opportunity in tendering with Japanese firms. An early result has been trial of three Cummins (UK) NTA855R1 engines for diesel railcar repowering in comparison with the products of two domestic manufacturers. On the basis of these trials the company plans to re-engine the greater part of its railcar stock, which will require some 700 engines.

Diesel locomotives

Class	Wheel arrangement	Transmission	Rated power (kW)	Max speed km/h	Total weight tonnes	No in service 1989	Year first built	Builders Mechanical parts	Engine & type	Transmission
DD 51	B-2-B	Hyd	2200	95	84	29	1966	H, Me, K	2 × 1000 hp DML61Z	2 × DWZA
DD 14	B-B	Hyd	1000	70	58	20	1966	K	2 × 500 hp DMF31SB-R	2 × DS1.2/1.35
DD 15	B-B	Hyd	1000	70	55	19	1961	N	2 × 500 hp DMF31SB	2 × DS1.2/1.35
DE 10	AAA-B	Hyd	1350	85	65	68	1969	K, N, H	DML61ZB	DW6
DE 11	AAA-B	Hyd	1350	85	70	14	1970	K, N	DML61ZA, B	DW6
DE 15	AAA-B	Hyd	1350	85	65	33	1970	N	DML61ZB	DW6

Abbreviations: D Daithatsu Motor; F Fuji Heavy Industries Ltd; Fe Fuji Electric; H Hitachi; K Kawasaki Heavy Industries; Kn Kinki Sharyo; Me Mitsubishi Electric; Mh Mitsubishi Heavy Industries; N Nippon Sharyo Seizo; NC Niigata Converter; NT Niigata Engineering; S Shinko Engineering; Se Shinko Electric; T Toshiba; To Toyo Denki Seizo

Electric railcars or multiple-units

Class	Cars per unit	Line voltage	Motor cars per unit	Motored axles per motor car	Rated output (kW) per motor	Max speed km/h	Weight tonnes per car (M-motor T-trailer)	Total seating capacity per car (M-motor T-trailer)	Length per car mm (M-motor T-trailer)	No of cars in service 1989	Rate of acceleration m/s^2	Year first built	Builders Mechanical parts	Electrical equipment
103	10	1500 V dc	6	4	110	100	M 39.7 T 28.8	M 54 T 54	M 20 000 T 20 000	2389	0.64	1964	N, T, H K, Kn	H, T, Me, Fe, To
105	2	1500 V dc	1	4	110	100	M 42.5 T 27.8	M 62 T 62	M 20 000 T 20 000	4	0.56	1980	T	H, T, Me, Fe, To
201	10	1500 V dc	6	4	150	100	M 41.7 T 30.6	M 54 T 54	M 20 000 T 20 000	788	0.69	1979	N, T, H K, Kn	H, T, Me, Fe, To
203	10	1500 V dc	6	4	150	100	M 35.9 T 24.4	M 54 T 54	M 20 000 T 20 000	170	0.92	1982	N, T, H K, Kn	H, T, Me, Fe, To
205	10	1500 V dc	6	4	150	100	M 32.6 T 23.6	M 54 T 54	M 20 000 T 20 000	733	0.64	1984	N, T, H K, Kn	H, T, Me, Fe, To
113	4	1500 V dc	2	4	120	100	M 41 T 34.3	M 76 T 76	M 20 000 T 20 000	1587	0.64	1963	N, T, H K, Kn	H, T, Me, Fe, To
115	4	1500 V ac	2	4	120	100	M 41.6 T 34.3 T 34.3	M 54 T 54 T 54	M 20 000 T 20 000 T 20 000	1176	0.57 0.57	1966 1966	N, T, H K, Kn	H, T, Me, Fe, To
211	10	1500 V dc	4	4	120	110	M 34.1 T 23.9	M 64 T 64	M 20 000 T 20 000	360	0.42	1985	N, T, H K, Kn	H, T, Me, Fe, To
165	3	1500 V dc	2	4	120	110	M 36.7 T 34.6	M 84 T 84	M 20 000 T 20 000	217	0.53	1962	N, T, H K, Kn	H, T, Me, Fe, To
415	4	1500 V dc 20 kV ac	2	4	120	100	M 41.2 T 34	M 72 T 72	M 20 000 T 20 000	255	0.65	1971	N, K, Kn	H, T, Me, Te, To
455	3	1500 V dc 20 kV ac	2	4	120	110	M 42.5 T 34.6	M 84 T 84	20 000 20 000	171	0.50	1962	N, T, H K, Kn	H, T, Me, Fe, To
183	4	1500 V dc	2	4	120	120	M 42.5 T 41.5	M 68 T 68	M 20 500 T 21 000	341	0.33	1972	N, T, K, Kn	H, T, Me, Fe, To
185	4	1500 V dc	2	4	120	110	M 44.2 T 36.2	M 68 Ts 68	M 20 000 T 20 280	227	0.65	1980	N, T, K H, Kn	H, T, Me, Fe, To
485	4	1500 V dc 20 kV ac	2	4	120	120	M 41.7 T 44.7	M 72 T 72	M 20 500 T 21 250	433	0.30	1968	N, T, H, K	H, T, Me, Fe, To
583	4	1500 V dc 20 kV ac	2	4	120	120	M 48.3 T 44.4	M 60 T 60	M 20 500 T 20 503	141	0.28	1968	N, T, H K, Kn	
651	17	1500 V dc 20 kV ac	4	4	120	130	M 39.6 Ts 28.1	M 64 Ts 33	M 20 000 Tc 21 100	88	0.54	1988	K	
200*	12	25 kV ac	12	4	230	240	62	95	25 000	708	0.44	1980	N, T, H, K	H, T, Me, Fe, To, Se

* Shinkansen

Electric locomotives

Class	Wheel arrangement	Line voltage	Rated output (kW)	Max speed km/h	Weight tonnes	Overall length mm	No in service 1989	Year first built	Builders
ED 75	B-B	20 kV 50 Hz	1900	100	67.2	14 300	79	1968	Me, H, T
ED 78	B-2-B	20 kV 50 Hz	1900	100	81.5	17 900	12	1968	H
EF 63	B-B-B	1500 V	2550	100	108	18 050	21	1962	T, Me, K
EF 64	B-B-B	1500 V	2550	115	96	17 900	14	1964	T, K, To
EF 65	B-B-B	1500 V	2550	115	96	16 500	42	1965	T, To, N
EF 71	B-B-B	20 kV 50 Hz	2700	100	100.8	18 500	14	1968	Me, T
EF 81	B-B-B	1.5 kV 20 kV 50 Hz	2550 (dc) 2370 (ac)	115	100.8	18 600	78	1968	H, Me

636 RAILWAY SYSTEMS / Japan

Diesel railcars or multiple-units

Class	Cars per unit	Motor cars per unit	Motored axles per motor car	Trans-mission	Rated power (kW) per motor	Max speed km/h	Weight tonnes per car (M-motor T-trailer)	Total seating capacity per car (M-motor T-trailer)	Length per car mm (M-motor T-trailer)	No in service 1989	Year first built	Builders Mechanical parts	Engine & type	Transmission
28	1	1	1	TCZA	180	95	34.1	84	21 300	79	1961	F, NT	DMH17H D, S, NT	S, NC
58	1	1	1	TCZA	180 × 2	95	39.4	84	21 300	232	1961	F, NT	DMH17H D, S, NT	S, NC
40	1	1	1	DW10	220	95	37.3	66	21 300	117	1977	F, NT	DMF15HSA D, S, NT	S, NC
47	1	1	1	TCZA	220	95	35.9	76	21 300	28	1977	F, NT	DMF15HSA D, S, NT	S, NC
48	1	1	1	TCZA	220	95	36.2	82	21 300	74	1979	F, NT	DMF15HSA D, S, NT	S, NC

Track

Rail type and weight: 50 kg N rail; 60 kg N rail
Sleepers: PC (concrete) sleepers Shinkansen 2400 × 254.6 × 330 mm
Conventional lines 200 × 174 × 240 mm
Wood sleepers Shinkansen 2600 × 150 × 240 mm
Conventional lines 2100 × 140 × 200 mm

Sleeper spacing per km:
1st grade line, PC: 1760 Wood: 1920
2nd grade line, PC: 1560 Wood: 1640
3rd grade line, PC: 1560 Wood: 1560
4th grade line, PC: 1480 Wood: 1480

On sharp curves and sharp gradient sections, the number of wood sleepers shown is increased by 2 per 25 m.

Minimum curvature radius on trunk lines:
More than 300 m to 800 m, depending on train speed and tonnage carried as well as on the numbers of sleepers used.

New bi-level car for East Japan 1067 mm-gauge Tokaido line introduced in 1989

West Japan Railway Co (JR-West)

1-1, Ofuka-cho, Kita-ku, Osaka, 530

Telephone: +81 6 375 8917
Telefax: +81 6 374 6068

Chairman: Tsutomo Murai
President: Tatsuo Tsunoda
Vice-President: Masataka Ide
Managing Directors: Y Kusaki
S Shirakawa
H Ito
R Sato

Route length: 4561 route-km of 1067 mm-gauge, 646 km of 1435 mm-gauge (Sanyo Shinkansen)

Electrification: 646 km of 1435 mm-gauge of 25 kV ac, 60 Hz; 317 km of 1067 mm-gauge at 20 kV ac 60 Hz; 2064 km of 1067 mm-gauge at 1.5 kV dc

The railway runs passenger transport and related activities in the Hokuriku region and western Honshu including the Sanyo Shinkansen. The network totals 51 lines.

Traffic (million)	1987	1988	1989
Total passenger-km	45 782	45 135	48 227
Total passenger journeys (rail only)	1496	1521	1566

Finance (million yen)	1988	1989
Operating revenue	763 100	807 100
Operating expenses	692 300	727 700
Operating surplus	70 800	79 300
Non-operating revenue	8 900	14 200
Non-operating expenses	71 700	76 200
Ordinary profit	8 000	17 200
Pre-tax profit	9 200	18 200
Tax	7 200	13 500
Profit after tax	2 000	4 600

The company has steadily diversified into activities such as the travel trade, restaurants and retail shops.

Type 185 express emu, with eight 120 kW motors per four cars

Series 100N Shinkansen train-set including bi-level cars

In 1989 JR-West introduced to its Hokuriku line, which runs north from Osaka to Kanazawa, four new seven-car electric train-sets to form a 'Super Raicho' limited-express service permitted a maximum speed of 130 km/h, instead of the previous limit of 120 km/h.

On the Tokaido Shinkansen JR-West began running two 16-car Series 100 trains including four bi-level trailers in 1989. Such trains have been denominated 'Grand Hikari'.

Traction and rolling stock
In 1989 the company operated five steam, 61 electric and 148 diesel locomotives (including 4 Shinkansen DLs), 832 electric train-sets (including 61 Shinkansen), 847 diesel train-sets, 864 hauled passenger cars including 290 sleeping and three dining cars, and 392 freight cars.

Signalling
The company installed four electronic interlockings between September 1989 and March 1990, and was to bring the 84km Miyazu line under control of an electronic interlocking in October 1990.

Track 1067mm-gauge lines
Rail: 30 to 60.8 kg/m
Sleepers: Wood 140 x 200 x 2100 mm and concrete 174 x 156-240 x 2100 mm
Sleeper spacing: Wood 1480–1920/km depending on class of route; concrete 1480–1760/km. On Class 2, 3 and 4 track with wooden sleepers, increased by 80 through curves of 600m radius or less.
Fastenings: Wooden sleepers, spike or spring clip with plate and pad; concrete sleepers, spring clip with pad.
Max permissible axleload: 19 tonnes

Upper deck dining saloon of Shinkansen Series 100N bi-level car

Diesel locomotives

Class	Wheel arrangement	Transmission	Rated output hp	Max speed km/h	Total weight tonnes	No in service 1989	Year first built	Builders Mechanical parts	Engine & type	Transmission
DD 14	B-B	Hyd	1000	70	58	3	1965	K	DMF31SB-R D	DS1.2/1.35 S
DD 15	B-B	Hyd	1000	70	55	11	1961	N	DMF31SB D S	DS1.1/1.35
DD 16	B-B	Hyd	800	75	48	3	1971	K	DML61Z S, D	DW2A H, K
DD 51	B-2-B	Hyd	2200	95	84	59	1966	H, Mh, K	DML61Z S, D	DW2A H, K
DE 10	AAA-B	Hyd	1350	85	65	42	1969	K, N, H	DML61ZB S, D	DW6 H, K
DE 15	AAA-B	Hyd	1350	85	65	13	1970	N, K	DML61DZB S, D	DW6 H, K

Abbreviations: D Daihatsu; F Fuji Heavy Industries; GW Goto Workshop; H Hitachi; K Kawasaki Heavy Industries; Ki Kinki Sharyo; Mh Mitsubishi Heavy Industries; Me Mitsubishi Electric; MW Matto Workshop; N Nippon Sharyo Seizo; NC Niigata Converter; NT Niigata Engineering; S Shinko Engineering; T Toshibia; Tk Tokyu Haryo; To Toyo Denki Seizo; Ty Toyo Electric

Diesel railcars

Class	Cars per unit	Motor cars per unit	Motored axles per motor car	Trans-mission	Rated output (ps) per motor	Max speed km/h	Weight tonnes per car (M-motor T-trailer)	Total seating capacity per car (M-motor T-trailer)	Length per car mm (M-motor T-trailer)	No in service 1989	Year first built	Builders Mechanical parts	Engine & type	Transmission
181	3	3	2	Hyd	500	120	44.6	68	21 300	94	1968	F, NT, N D, S, NC	DML30HSE D, S, NC	DW4E S, NC
28	2	2	1	Hyd	180	95	34.3	84	21 300	135	1961	F, NT, N D, S, NC	DMH17H D, S, NC	TC2A, DF115A S, NC
58	2	2	2	Hyd	180 × 2	95	39.4	84	21 300	188	1961	F, NT, N D, S, NC	DMH17H D, S, NC	TC2A, DF115A S, NC
65	2	2	2	Hyd	500	95	42.9	84	21 300	14	1969	F, NT, N D, S, NC	DML30HSD D, S, NC	DW4F S, NC
20	1	1	1	Hyd	180	95	32.2	70	20 000	3	1957	F, NT, N D, S, NC	DMH17C D, S, NC	TC2, DF115 S, NC
23	1	1	1	Hyd	180	95	34.2	76	21 300	40	1966	F, NT, N D, S, NC	DMH17H D, S, NC	TC2A, DF115A S, NC
30	1	1	1	Hyd	180	95	32.4	56	20 000	11	1962	F, NT, N D, S, NC	DMH17H D, S, NC	TC2A, DF115A S, NC
33	1	1	1	Hyd	250	95	34	60	20 000	2	1988	GW NT	DMF13HS NT, S	DF115A
35	2	2	1	Hyd	180	95	32	58	20 000	10	1961	F, NT, N D, S, NC	DMH17H D, S, NC	TC2A, DF115A S, NC
37	2	2	1	Hyd	210	95	31.6	64	20 000	2	1982	NT	DMF13S	
40	1	1	1	Hyd	220	95	36.4	66	21 300	63	1979	F, NT D, S, NC	DMF15HSA D, S, NC	DW10
45	2	2	1	Hyd	180	95	33	84	21 300	38	1966	F, NT, N D, S, NC	DMH17H D, S, NC	TC2A, DF115A S, NC
47	2	2	1	Hyd	220	95	35.5	76	21 300	189	1976	F, NT D, S, NC	DMF15HSA D, S, NC	DW10
48	2	2	1	Hyd	220	95	35.9	74	21 300	5	1971	F, NT D, S, NC	DMF15HSA D, S, NC	DW10
52	1	1	2	Hyd	180 × 2	95	36	76	20 500	13	1962	F, NT, N D, S, NC	DMH17H D, S, NC	TC2A, DF115A S, NC
53	1	1	2	Hyd	180 × 2	95	39.7	73	21 300	9	1966	F, NT, N D, S, NC	DMH17H D, S, NC	TC2A, DF115A S, NC

RAILWAY SYSTEMS / Japan

Electric locomotives

Class	Wheel arrangement	Line voltage	Rated output (kW)	Max speed km/h	Weight tonnes	Overall length mm	No in service 1989	Year first built	Builders Mechanical parts	Builders Electrical equipment
EF 15	1-C-C-1	1500 V dc	1900	75	102	17 000	1	1947	H	H, T, Mh, F, To
EF 58	2-C-C-2	1500 V dc	1900	100	115	19 900	1	1946	T	H, T, Mh, F, To
EF 59	2-C-C-2	1500 V dc	1350	90	106.6	19 920	1	1963	H	H, T, Mh, F, To
EF 60	B-B-B	1500 V dc	2550	100	96	16 500	1	1962	To	H, T, Mh, F, To
EF 64	B-B-B	1500 V dc	2550	100	96	17 900	2	1964	T, K, To	H, T, Mh, F, To
EF 65	B-B-B	1500 V dc	2550	110	96	16 500	23	1969	K, To, T, N	H, T, Mh, F, To
EF 66	B-B-B	1500 V dc	3900	110	100.8	18 200	16	1973	K, To	H, T, Mh, F, To
EF 81	B-B-B	1500 V dc 20 kV ac	2550 (dc) 2370 (ac)	110	100.8	18 600	16	1968	H, Mh	H, T, Mh, F, To

Electric railcars or multiple-units

Class	Cars per unit	Line voltage	Motor cars per unit	Motored axles per motor car	Rated output (kW) per motor	Max speed km/h	Weight tonnes per car (M-motor T-trailer)	Total seating capacity per car (M-motor T-trailer)	Length per car mm (M-motor T-trailer)	No in service 1989	Year first built	Builders Mechanical parts	Builders Electrical parts
101	7	1500 V dc	6	4	100	100	M 42.3 T 32.0	54	M 20 000 T 20 000	14	1957	K, Ki, N	H, T, Me, F, Ty
103	7	1500 V dc	4	4	110	100	M 39.7 T 28.8	54	M 20 000 T 20 000	894	1964	K, Ki, H, N, Tk	H, T, Me, F, Ty
105	2	1500 V dc	1	4	110	100	M 42.5 T 29.8	38	M 20 000 T 20 000	121	1980	Ki, H, Tk	H, T, Me, F, Ty
113	4	1500 V dc	2	4	120	100	M 38.6 T 32.8	76	M 20 000 T 20 000	756	1963	K, Ki, H, N, Tk	H, T, Me, F, Ty
115	4	1500 V dc	2	4	120	100	M 38.7 T 31.6	76	M 20 000 T 20 000	578	1962	K, Ki, H, N, Tk	H, T, Me, F, Ty
117	6	1500 V dc	4	4	120	110	M 43.7 T 35.9	64	M 20 000 T 20 000	144	1979	K, Ki, N, Tk	H, T, Me, F, Ty
165	3	1500 V dc	2	4	120	110	M 39.8 T 34.6	84	M 20 000 T 20 000	57	1962	K, Ki, N, Tk	H, T, Me, F, Ty
201	7	1500 V dc	4	4	150	100	M 41.7 T 23.6	54	M 20 000 T 20 000	224	1981	K, Ki, H, N, Tk	H, T, Me, F, Ty
205	7	1500 V dc	4	4	120	100	M 32.6 T 24.5	54	M 20 000 T 20 000	48	1986	Ks, N	H, T, Me, F, Ty
211	2	1500 V dc	1	4	120	120	M 40.0 T 33.0	40	M 20 000 T 20 000	2	1988	Ki	H, T, Me, Ty
213	3	1500 V dc	1	4	120	110	M 37.3 T 24.1	64	M 20 000 T 20 000	37	1986	K, Ki, H, N, Tk	H, T, Me, F, Ty
381	7	1500 V dc	4	4	120	120	M 36.1 T 34.0	76	M 21 300 T 21 300	189	1978	K, Ki, H, N	H, T, Me, F, Ty
413	3	1500 V dc 20 kV ac	2	4	120	110	M40.5 T 36.0	72	M 20 000 T 20 000	28	1975	MW	H, T, Me, F, Ty
419	3	1500 V dc 20 kV ac	2	4	120	100	M 41.7 T 41.3	66	M 20 500 T 20 500	45	1975	MW	H, T, Me, F, Ty
457	3	1500 V dc 20 kV ac	2	4	120	110	M 42.1 T 35.6	84	M 20 000 T 20 000	85	1969	H	H, T, Me, F, Ty
485	10	1500 V dc 20 kV ac	6	4	120	120	M 44.1 T 33.1	72	M 20 500 T 20 500	433	1968	K, Ki, H, N, Tk	H, T, Me, F, Ty
583	11	1500 V dc 20 kV ac	6	4	120	120	M 43.7 T 35.3	60	M 20 500 T 20 500	60	1968	K, Ki, H, N	H, T, Me, F, Ty

Hokkaido Railway Co (JR-Hokkaido)

Kita-5 jo, Nishi-4-chome, Chuo-ku, Sapporo 060

Telephone: +81 11 222 6123
Telefax: +81 11 222 5676

Chairman: Takei Tojo
President: Yoshihiro Omori
Managing Directors: H Shimizu
S Kebi
K Shoji
M Hio
S Sakamoto
T Obara
S Aoyama
T Takeda

Gauge: 1067 mm
Route length: 3192.8 route-km
Electrification: 431 km at 20 kV 50 Hz ac

The company is responsible for rail passenger transport and related activities in the Hokkaido region. In FY 1987-88 it recorded 3920 million passenger-km.

Finance
In FY 1988-89 the company reduced its loss before grant from the Financial Stabilisation Fund from the previous year's 2223 million to 1200 million yen.

Traction and rolling stock
In 1989 the railway operated 50 electric, 102 diesel locomotives; 186 electric train-sets and 14 spare trailers; 581 diesel railcars; 292 other passenger cars; and 218 freight wagons.

Diesel locomotives

Class	Wheel arrangement	Transmission	Rated power (kW)	Max speed km/h	Total weight tonnes	No in service 1988	Year first built	Builders Mechanical parts	Builders Engine & type	Builders Transmission
DD 51	B-2-B	Hyd	1618	95	84	25	1967	H, M, K	DML61Z S, NT, D	DW2A H, K
DD 14	B-B	Hyd	735	70	58	17	1966	K	DMF31SBR S, NT, D	DS1.2/1.35 NT
DD 16	B-B	Hyd	588	75	48	1	1974	N	DML61Z S, NT, D	DW2A H, K
DE 10	AAA-B	Hyd	993	85	65	23	1973	K, N	DML61ZB S, NT, D	DW6 H, K
DE 15	AAA-B	Hyd	993	85	65	36	1969	N	DML61ZB DML61ZB S, NT, D	DW6 DW6 H, K

Abbreviations: D Daihatsu; F Fuji Heavy Industries; H Hitachi Ltd; K Kawasaki Heavy Industries Ltd; M Mitsubishi Heavy Industries; NC Niigata Converter Co Ltd; NT Niigata Engineering Co Ltd; S Shinko Engineering Co Ltd; Toshiba Corp; To Toyo Denki Seizo KK

Japan / RAILWAY SYSTEMS

Electric railcars or multiple units

Class	Cars per unit	Motored axles per motor car	Trans-mission	Rated power (kW) per motor	Max speed km/h	Weight tonnes per car (M-motor T-trailer)	Total seating capacity per car (M-motor T-trailer)	Length per car mm (M-motor T-trailer)	No in service 1988	Year first built	Builders Mechanical parts	Builders Engine & type	Builders Transmission
27		1	Hyd	132	95	35	84	21 300	37	1962	T, NT, N	DMH17H S, NT, D, JNR	TC2A, DF115A S, NC
		1	Hyd	132	95	35	76	21 300	4	1968	T, NT, N	DMH17H S, NT, D, JNR	TC2A, DF115A S, NC
56		2	Hyd	132	95	38.9 40.2	84	21 300	46	1986	NT	DMH17H S, NT, D, JNR	TC2A, DF115A S, NC
		2	Hyd	132	95	40.2	76	21 300	4	1986	NT	DMH17H S, NT, D, JNR	TC2A, DF115A S, NC
26		1	Hyd	132	95	35	52	21 300	1	1986	T	DMH17H S, NT, D, JNR	TC2A, DF115A S, NC
29	5	1	Hyd	132	95	38.3	52	21 300	1	1985	T	DMH17H S, NT, D, JNR	DF115A NC
59		2	Hyd	132	95	41.4	52 39	21 300	3	1985	NT	DMH17H S, NT, D, JNR	TC2A, DF115A S, NC
29		1	Hyd	132	95	33.8	44	21 300	3	1966	T	DMH17H S, NT, D, JNR	DF115A NC
59		2	Hyd	132	95	42.2	44	21 300	2	1983	NT	DMH17H S, NT, D, JNR	DF115A NC
22		1	Hyd	132	95	32.9	71	20 000	90	1960	F, NT, T, N	DMH17H S, NT, D, JNR	TC2, DF115 S, NC
24		1	Hyd	132	95	34.5	77	21 300	10	1967	N	DMH17H S, NT, D, JNR	TC2A S
40		1	Hyd	162	95	37.6	66	21 300	149	1976	F, NT	DMF15HSA S, NT, D	DW10 S, NC
		1	Hyd	162	95	36.4	63	21 300	1	1985	F	DMF15HSA S, NT, D	DW10 S, NC
46		1	Hyd	132	95	33.2	85	21 300	5	1966	F	DMH17H S, NT, D, JNR	DF115A NC
48-300		1	Hyd	162	95	36.6	74	21 300	4	1982	NT	DMF15HSA S, NT, D	DW10 S, NC
48-1300		1	Hyd	162	95	36.3	82	21 300	3	1982	NT	DMF15HSA S, NT, D	DW10 S, NC
182		2	Hyd	324	100	44.8 42.6	68	21 300	6 48	1979	F, NT	DML30HSI D, S, NT	DW9A S, NC
		2	Hyd	324	100	45.2 44.7	40 32	21 300	1 10	1978	F, NT	DML30HSI D, S, NT	DW9A S, NC
182-500		2	Hyd	405	110	38.8	68	21 300	18	1986	F, NT	DML30HSJ D, S	DW12 S, NC
		2	Hyd	405	110	40.8	32	21 300	8	1986	F, NT	DML30HSJ D, S	DW12 S, NC
183	7	1	Hyd	162	100	47.4	40	21 300	24	1979	F, NT	DMF15HSA D, S, NT	DW10 S, NC
183-100		1	Hyd	162	100	43.8	40	21 300	4	1981	F, NT	DMF15HSA D, S, NT	DW10 S, NC
183-500		2	Hyd	405	110	40.9	60	21 300	7	1986	F, NT	DML30HSJ D, S	DW12 S, NC
183-1500		1	Hyd	184	110	40.3	68	21 300	11	1986	F, NT	DMF13HS NT	DW12 NC
184		1	Hyd	162	100	44.2	52	21 300	7	1981	F, NT	DMF15HSA D, S, NT	DW10 S, NC
		1	Hyd	162	100	46.6	32	21 300	1	1979	F	DMF15HSA D, S, NT	DW10 S, NC
80		2	Hyd	132	100	41.2	72	21 100	5	1965	F	DMH17H S, NT, D, JNR	TC2A, DF115A S, NC
		2	Hyd	132	100	43	32	21 100	3	1964	NT	DMH17H S, NT, D, JNR	TC2A, DF115A S, NC
82	3	1	Hyd	132	100	42	52	21 100	3	1965	F, NT	DMH17H S, NT, D, JNR	TC2A, DF115A S, NC
83		1	Hyd	132	100	41.2	52	21 100	3	1986	NT	DMH17H S, NT, D, JNR	DF1125A NC
84		2	Hyd	132	100	41.2	44	21 100	4	1986	NT, F	DMH17H S, NT, D, JNR	DF115A NC
53		2	Hyd	184	95	42.2	74	21 300	10	1961	NT	DMH17H S, NT, D, JNR	TC2A, DF115A S, NC
54		2	Hyd	184	95	38.7	70	21 300	26	1986	F, NT	DMF13HS NT	TC2A, DF115A NC
		2	Hyd	184	95	39.3	60	21 300	3	1986	F	DMF13HS NT	TC2A, DF115A NC

Electric locomotives

Class	Wheel arrangement	Line voltage	Rated output (kW)	Max speed km/h	Weight tonnes	Overall length mm	No in service 1988	Year first built	Builders Mechanical parts	Builders Electrical equipment
ED 76	B-2-B	20 kV ac	1900	100	90.5	18 400	16	1968	M, T	H, M, T
ED 79	B-B	20 kV ac	1900	100	68	14 300	34	1971	H, M, T	H, M, T

RAILWAY SYSTEMS / Japan

Electric railcars or multiple-units

Class	Cars per unit	Line voltage	Motor cars per unit	Motored axles per motor car	Rated output (kW) per motor	Max speed km/h	Weight tonnes per car (M-motor T-trailer)	Total seating capacity per car (M-motor T-trailer)	Length per car mm (M-motor T-trailer)	No in service 1988	Rate of acceleration m/s²	Year first built	Builders Mechanical parts	Builders Electrical equipment
711	3	20 kV ac	1	4	150	110	M 47.8	M 68	M 20 000	2	0.3	1966	H, T, K	H, T, M, Fe, To
							M 45.6	M 74		9		1968		
							M 45.2	M 74		10		1969		
							M 44.7	M 74		17		1980		
							T 32.2	T 68	T 20 000	36		1968		
							T 32.2			36		1968		
							T 33.5			20		1980		
							T 33.4			18		1980		
781	4	20 kV ac	2	4	150	120	M 48.5	M 56	M 21 250	12	0.4	1978	H, K	H, T, M, Fe, To
							M 46.2	M 68	M 20 500	12		1978		
							T 45.4	T 64	T 21 250	12		1978		
							T 43.1	T 64	T 20 500	12		1978		
481	-	1500 V dc / 20 kV ac	-	-	-	120	T 31.7	T 48	T 20 500	3	-	1972	H, T, K	H, T, M, Fe
							T 32.2	T 48		3		1972		
							T 38.1	T 40		1		1972		
581	-	1500 V dc / 20 kV ac	-	-	-	120	T 35.3	T 60	T 20 500	7		1968	K	H, T, M, Fe

Kyushu Railway Co (JR-Kyushu)

1-1, Chuogai, Hakataeki, Hakata-ku, Fukuoka 801

Telephone: +81 92 474 2501
Telefax: +81 92 474 4805

Chairman: Masasuke Nakagawa
President: Yoshitaka Ishii

Gauge: 1067 mm
Route length: 2101 route-km
Electrification: 1044.7 route-km at 20kV 60Hz ac; 42.6 route-km at 1.5kV dc.
The company runs rail passenger transport and related activities in the Kyushu region.

Finance (million yen)	1987-88	1988-89	1989-90
Operating revenue	129 888	139 619	143 900
Operating expenditure	158 712	168 154	182 200
Operating loss	28 823	28 536	28 800
Non-operating surplus (including Stabilisation Fund grant)	34 004	33 043	32 600
Pre-tax profit	3633	3338	6500
Profit after tax	905	1168	2900

In FY 1989-90 the railway recorded an after-tax profit of 2500 million yen.

Traction and Rolling Stock
At the end of 1989 the company operated 43 electric and 22 diesel locomotives, 959 electric and 468 diesel railcars, 357 other passenger cars and 161 freight wagons.

Signalling
CTC controls 67 per cent of the railway's system and 81 per cent has automatic block signalling.

Track
Rail: 50.4 and 60 kg/m
Sleepers: Prestressed concrete or timber 2100 x 200 x 140 mm spaced 1480, 1560 or 1760/km according to class of route
Fastenings: Elastic
Maximum axle load: 18 tonnes

JR-Kyushu diesel railcars or multiple-units

Class	No of cars per unit	No of motor cars per unit	No of motored axles per motor car	Transmission	Rated power (kW) per motor	Max speed km/h	Weight tonnes per car (M-motor T-trailer)	Total seating capacity per car (M-motor T-trailer)	Length per car mm (M-motor T-trailer)	No in service 1989	Year first built	Mechanical parts	Engine & type	Transmission
65	1	1	1	DW4D	500	95	42.9	84	21 300	35	1969	N, F	DML30HSD	N
58	1	1	2	TC2A DF115A	360	95	39.2	64	21 300	108	1961	Nt, F, N, TE	DMH17H S, N	S, N
28	1	1	1	TC2A DF115A	180	95	33.1	84	21 300	44	1961	Nt, F	DMH17H S, N	S, N
66	2	2	1	DW9	440	95	40.7	62	21 300	15	1975	Nt, F	DML30HSH	S, N
67	2	2	1	DW9	440	95	42.2	64	21 300	15	1975	Nt, F	DML30HSH	S, N
40	1	1	1	DW10	220	95	36.4	66	21 300	36	1978	Nt, F	DMF15HSA	N
47	1	1	1	DW10	220	95	35.5	76, 80	21 300	106	1979	Nt, F	DMF15HSA	N
52	1	1	2	TC2A	360	95	36.6	76	21 300	25	1961	Nt	DMH17HSN	S, N
53	1	1	2	TC2A DF115A	360	95	39.7	73	21 300	4	1968	Nt	DMH17HSN	S, N
45	1	1	1	TC2A DF115A	180	95	33.0	84	21 300	10	1966	Nt, N, F	DMH17HSN	S, N
35	1	1	1	TC2A DF115A	180	95	32.0	58	20 000	6	1966	Nt, N	DMH17HSN	S, N
30	1	1	1	TC2A DF115A	180	95	32.4	56	20 000	17	1965	Nt, N	DMH17HSN	S, N
23	1	1	1	TC2A DF115A	180	95	34.2	76	21 300	3	1965	N, F, Tk, TE	DMH17HSN	S, N
20	1	1	1	TC2 DF115	180	95	32.1	70	20 000	11	1960	N, F, Tk, TE	DMH17HSN	S, N
31	1	1	1	TC2A DF115A	250	95	29.8	38	17 750	20	1987	F, N	DMF13HS	N, F

Nt: Nigata; F: Fuji; N: Nihonsharoyo; TE: Teikoku; Tk: Tokyu

Electric locomotives

Class	Wheel arrangement	Line voltage	Rated output (kW) continuous/one-hour	Max speed km/h	Weight tonnes	Overall length mm	No in service 1989	Year first built	Builders Mechanical parts
EF81	B-B-B	20kV	2550	100	100.8	18 600	6	1968	H
ED76	B-2-B	20kV	1990	100	90.5	18 400	8	1965	T, M, H

T: Toshiba; M: Mitsubishi; H: Hitachi

JR-Kyushu diesel locomotives

Class	Wheel arrangement	Transmission	Rated power (kW)	Max speed km/h	Total weight tonnes	No in service 1989	Year first built	Builders Mechanical parts	Engine & type	Transmission
DD51	B-2-B	Hyd	2200	95	84	1	1966	M	2 × 1100PS DML61Z	DW2A
DD16	B-B	Hyd	800	75	48	2	1971	K	1 × 800PS DML61Z	DW2A
DE10	AAA-B	Hyd	1350	85	65	19	1969	K, N	1 × 1350PS DML61ZB	DW6

K: Kawasaki; M: Mitsubishi; N: Nihon Sharyo

Electric railcars or multiple-units

Class	No of cars per unit	Line voltage	No of motor cars per unit	No of motored axles per motor car	Rated output (kW) per motor	Max speed km/h	Weight tonnes per car (M-motor T-trailer)	Total seating capacity per car (M-motor T-trailer)	Length per car mm (M-motor T-trailer)	No in service 1989	Year first built	Builders Mechanical parts
421	4	20	2	4	100	100	M42.7 T33.2	76	M20 000 T20 000	12	1961	H, Tk, K, TE, R
423	4	20	2	4	120	100	M42.7 T33.2	76	M20 000 T20 000	120	1961	H, Tk, K, TE, R
415	4	20 kV AC	2	4	120	100	M41.2 T34	72	M20 000 T20 000	184	1971	H, N, S, Tk, R
713	2	20 kJ AC	1	4	150	100	M45 T34.7	66	M20 000 T20 500	8	1982	H, Tk
715	4	20	2	4	120	100	M45.7 T34.7	71 53	M20 500 T20 500	48	1985	H, N, S, R
717	2	20	2	4	120	100	Mc40.5 Mc37.7	65 64	Mc20 000 Mc'20 000	6 6	1985	R, S, H
457	2	20	2	4	120	100	Mc42.1 Mc42.5	76 84	Mc20 000 Mc'20 000	11 11	1969	R, S, Tk
475	2	20	2	4	120	100	Mc42.5 M42.5	76 84	Mc20 400 M'20 000	27 27	1965	R
485	4 3	20 kV AC	2	4	120	120	M42.5 T34.6	84	T20 000 T20 000	324	1969	K, Tk, N, R, S
103	3 6	1500 V DC	4	4	110	100	M39.7 T28.8	48	M20 000 T20 000	54	1964	H, R
811	4	20 kJ AC	2	4	150	120	M44.1 T36.3	52 50	M20 000 T20 000	40	1989	H, S

K: Kisha; H: Hitachi; TE: Teikoku; S:Kinkisharyo; R: Kawasaki; N:Nihonsaryo

Central Japan Railway Co (JR-Tokai)

1-4, Meieki 1-chome, Nakamura-ku, Nagoya 450

Telephone: +81 52 564 2316
Telefax: +81 52 564 2331

1-6-5 Marunouchi Chiyoda-ku, Tokyo 100

Telephone: +81 3 214 0216
Telefax: +81 3 5252 7056

Chairman: Shigemitsu Miyake
President: Hiroshi Suda
Senior Executive Directors: Junkei Kowaguchi
Ikuo Murakami (1067 mm-gauge operations)
Executive Director, Corporate Planning: Yoshiyuki Kasai
  Shinkansen Operations: Hiroumi Soejima
  Affiliated Enterproses: Satoshi Fujita

Route length: 1431 route-km of 1067 mm-gauge, 552.6 km of 1435 mm-gauge (Tokaido Shinkasen)
Electrification: 552.6 km of 1435 mm-gauge at 25 kV 60 Hz; 939.2 km of 1067 mm-gauge at 1.5 kV dc

The company runs rail passenger transport and related activities in Nagoya and surrounding areas including the Tokaido Shinkansen. It has diversified into 28 subsidiary companies forming the Central Japan Railway Group, and engaged chiefly in bus services, restaurants and retail shops, commercial development of stations, hotels, construction, advertising and publishing.

Traffic	1987-88	1988-89
Total passenger journeys (million)	403	434
Total passenger-km (million)	41 148	45 085

JR-West 'Akatsuki' overnight express from Shin-Osaka to Nagasaki and Sasebo in Kyushu

Finance (million yen)	1988	1989	1990
Operating revenues		
Railway	868 336	965 924	NA
Other	6 334	2 768	NA
Total	874 670	968 692	100 300
Operating expenses		
Railway	797 257	864 462	NA
Other	5 856	1 785	NA
Total	803 113	866 247	889 400

In FY 1988-89 railway operating revenues increased 11.2 per cent by comparison with the previous year, though rolling stock-km rose by only 2.5 per cent. Cost containment held the rise in operating expenses to 7.9 per cent, despite heavy expenditure on enhancement of services and on new rolling stock. Consequently, operating income improved no less than 43.2 per cent on the previous year.

Services
Centrepiece of the railway's operations is the inaugural 552.6 km Tokaido Shinkansen, running 251 trains daily in 1989. In FY 1988-89 this high-speed line carried 112 million passengers, 10 per cent more than in the previous year. Steady fleet renewal and additions have expanded the car fleet to 1584 vehicles, of which, in 1989, 23 per cent were less than five years old. The additions have included Series 100 train-sets including bi-level cars (see under Shinkansen entry), of which 22 were at work in mid-1989; by March 1990 half the Hikari services were incorporating bi-level cars.

The popularity of the limited-stop Hikari services as opposed to the Kodama, which call at all the line's 16

642 RAILWAY SYSTEMS / Japan

Luxury A-type compartment of JR-West Osaka-Sapporo limited sleeping car 'Twilight Express'

'Salon du Nord' bar of JR-West Osaka-Sapporo 'Twilight Express'

stations, saw the ratio of the two per hour raised to 7 to 4 in March 1989. A further increase to 9 to 4 is planned in future years. The company has formed the Shinkansen Passengers Service Co to manage Tokaido line station and on-board catering and retail operations.

A new Series 300 Shinkansen train-set prototype began trials in 1990. For details see Shinkansen section below. With the Series 300 and a top speed of 270 km/h Hikari timings between Tokyo and Osaka will be cut from the 2 hours 52 minutes of mid-1990 to 2 hours 30 minutes in the spring of 1992.

On the 1067mm-gauge lines passenger journeys rose 7 per cent in FY 1988-89. By the summer of 1989 84 per cent of all cars employed were air-conditioned. It was hoped to make this coverage total by mid-1991.

At 15 of its stations the company has opened travel centres that cover all transport modes, foreign as well as domestic travel, and hotel and restaurant reservations. Rail tickets are also sold in over 1000 stores in the Tokyo metropolitan area.

Traction and rolling stock
In 1989 the railway operated on 1067 mm-gauge 11 electric and 19 diesel locomotives, 109 passenger cars, 287 electric train-sets, 13 diesel train-sets, 64 other electric and 164 diesel railcars, and 24 trailers for the electric power cars. Shinkansen rolling stock comprised 1207 Series 0 and 528 Series 100 cars formed into 109 train-sets and four spare cars. During FY 1988-89 240 Shinkansen and 225 1067 mm-gauge cars were delivered.

Signalling
In 1990 the revision of the Tokaido Shinkansen's ATP system for introduction of 270 km/h operation in the spring of 1992 was under way. The coded track circuit frequencies and the signalling are being adjusted to provide for staged reduction from top speed to 220, 170, 120, 70 and 30 km/h to dead stop. Cost of the changes will be 3 000 million yen.

Track 1067mm-gauge lines
Rail: 30.1 to 60.8 kg/m
Sleepers: Prestressed concrete or timber 2100 x 200 x 140 mm, spaced 1480 to 1760/km according to grade of route, increased in curves where timber is used
Fastenings: elastic or rigid
Minimum curve radius: 200m
Max gradient: 4%
Max axleloading: 17 tonnes

Shikoku Railway Co (JR-Shikoku)

1-10, Hamano-cho, Takamatsu 760

Telephone: +81 878 51 1880
Telefax: +81 878 51 0497

President: Hiroatsu Ito
Senior Adviser: Tsunenori Yamaguchi

Route length: 855.8 km of 1067 mm-gauge
Electrification: 68.1 km at 1.5 kV dc

The company runs passenger transport and related activities in the Shikoku region.

West Japan Series 211 'Marine Liner' electric train-set with high windows for passenger viewing of the Inland Sea on the Seto Bridge crossing into Shikoku island

Series 211 interior

Observation saloon of West Japan's 'Edel Tottori'

Finance (million yen)	1987-88	1989-90
Operating revenue	35 244	43 900
Operating expenditure	50 184	55 500
Operating loss	14 940	11 600
Non-operating surplus (including Stabilisation Fund grant)	17 026	17 700
Pre-tax profit	1054	6100
Profit after tax	264	3600

In FY 1988-89 traffic was significantly inflated by the availability of through trains from Honshu island over the bridges opened in April 1988 and pre-tax profit soared to 5700 million yen.

Electrification
The electrification, completed in October 1987, was in preparation for the formal opening of the Seto bridge complex from Honshu island to Shikoku in April 1988. The catenary runs from Tadotsu to Kanongi, Kotohira and Sakaide; and from Sakaide to Takamatsu. The service of 28 trains each way daily to Shikoku connects with the Sanyo Shinkansen at Okayama. There is also an overnight Tokyo-Shikoku sleeper service.

Traction and Rolling Stock
In 1989 the railway operated 27 diesel locomotives, 50 electric and 82 diesel train-sets, 257 other diesel railcars, 71 passenger cars and 39 freight wagons.

New JR-Shikoku equipment includes three Type TSE-2000 diesel train-sets arranged for a top speed of 120 km/h. They are employed on cross-island services between Okayama and Takamatsu, and Matsuyama and Koshi. They are the world's first diesel-powered vehicles to be equipped with an active body-tilt system, which is designed to raise acceptable curving speed by 20 to 30 per cent depending on curve radius.

Each bolsterless, air-sprung bogie is driven by a body-mounted 330 hp, 2000 rpm Komatsu engine via a ball bearing-type spline shaft transmission. Track-mounted transponders at the approach to curves are detected by microprocessors on the leading car of the set and convey data on which the train's control progressively activates and measures the degree of tilt to be applied to each car body.

Track
Rail: 40 and 50 kg/m
Sleepers: Wood or prestressed concrete spaced 1560/km in plain track, 1640/km in curves
Fastenings: Spike (wood sleeper) or double elastic
Minimum curve radius: 200m
Max gradient: 3.3%
Max axle load: 17 tonnes

Japan Freight Railway Co

6-5, Marunouchi 1-chome, Chiyoda-ku, Tokyo 100

Telephone: +81 3 285 0071
Telefax: +81 3 216 2089

Chairman: Naoshi Machida
President: Masashi Hashimoto

'Edel Tottori' diesel train-set of West Japan Railway with observation saloons at each end

Series 221 commuter emu of West Japan Railway's Yamatoji line

Series ED79 ac electric locomotive of JR Hokkaido in under-sea Seikan Tunnel

RAILWAY SYSTEMS / Japan

JR-Kyushu diesel locomotives

Class	Wheel arrangement	Transmission	Rated power (kW)	Max speed km/h	Total weight tonnes	Length mm	No in service 1989	Year first built	Builders Mechanical parts	Builders Engine & type	Builders Transmission
DE10	AAA-A	Hyd	1250	85	65	14 150	29	1966	K/N/H	DML61ZA DML61ZB NT/S/D	DW6 K/H

JR-Kyushu diesel railcars or multiple-units

Class	No of motored axles per motor car	Transmission	Rated power (kW) per motor	Max speed km/h	Weight tonnes per car	Total seating capacity per car	Length per car mm	No in service 1989	Year first built	Mechanical parts	Engine & type	Transmission
2001	1	TACN 22-1600	330 × 2	120	37.7	46	20 800	1	1989	F	SA6D125-H	K
2101	1	TACN 22-1600	330 × 2	120	37.7	43	20 800	1	1989	F	SA6D125-H	K
2201	1	TACN 22-1600	330 × 2	120	36.9	54	20 800	1	1989	F	SA6D125-H	K
186	1	TC2A DF115A	250	110	35.0	56	21 300	8	1986	NT/F/N	DMF13HS NT	S/NC
185	1	TC2A DF115A	250 × 2	110	39.0	60	21 300	37	1986	NT/F/N	DMF13HS NT	S/NC
181	2	DW4E	500	120	44.2	52	21 300	18	1968	NT/F	DML30HSE NT/S/D	S/NC
180	2	DW4E	500	120	41.4	76	21 300	26	1968	NT/F	DML30HSE NT/S/D	S/NC
65	2	DW4F	500	95	42.9	84	21 300	39	1969	NT/F/N	DML30HSD NT/S/D	S/NC
58	1	TC2A DF115A	180 × 2	95	38.0	84	21 300	49	1962	NT/F/N	DMH17H NT/S/D	S/NC
57	1	TC2A DF115A	180 × 2	95	38.2	84	21 300	2	1961	N	DMH17H NT/S/D	S/NC
54	1	TC2A DF115A	250 × 2	95	37.0	148	21 300	12	1987	NT/F	DMF13HS NT	S/NC
47	1	DW10	220	95	35.5	124	21 300	42	1980	NT/F	DMF15HSA NT/S/D	S/NC
45	1	TC2A DF115A	180	95	33.0	124	21 300	24	1966	F/N	DMH17H NT/S/D	S/NC
40	1	DW10	220	95	36.4	96	21 300	11	1981	NT/F	DMF15HSA NT/S/D	S/NC
32	1	TC2A DF115A	250	95	27.0	106	16 300	21	1987	NT/F	DMF13HS NT	S/NC
30	1	TC2A DF115A	180	95	32.4	128	20 000	2	1966	N	DMH17H NT/S/D	S/NC
28	1	TC2A DF115A	180	95	33.1	84	21 300	33	1961	NT/F/N	DMH17H NT/S/D	S/NC
20	1	TC2A DF115A	180	95	32.1	82	20 000	20	1958	F/N	DMH17H NT/S/D	S/NC

NT: Niigata Tekko   F: Fuji Juko   N: Nippon Sharyo Seizo Ltd   S: Shinko Zouki   D: Daihatsu   NC: Niigata Converter   K: Komatsu Seisakusyo

JR-Kyushu Electric railcars or multiple-units

Class	No of cars per unit	Line voltage	No of motor cars per unit	No of motored axles per motor car	Rated output (kW) per motor	Max speed km/h	Weight tonnes per car (M-motor T-trailer)	Total seating capacity per car (M-motor T-trailer)	Length per car mm (M-motor T-trailer)	No in service 1989	Rate of acceleration m/s^2	Year first built	Mechanical parts	Electrical equipment
111	4	DC 1500 V	2	1	100	100	M37.3 T29.6	M128 T116	M20 000 T20 000	20	0.38	1962	N/K	H/T/M/To/Se
121	2	DC 1500 V	1	1	110	100	M42.0 T27.0	M118 T118	M20 000 T20 000	30	0.52	1986	H/K/Kn/Tk	H/T/M/To

Diesel locomotives

Class	Wheel arrangement	Transmission	Rated power (Ap)	Max speed km/h	Total weight tonnes	No in service 1989	Year first built	Mechanical parts	Engine & type	Transmission
DE 10	AAA-B	Hyd	1350	85	65	150	1967	K, N, H	DML6ZB	DW6 (2000 series)
DE 11	AAA-B	HYd	1350	85	70	4	1979	K, N	DML61ZA, B	DW6
DD 51	B-2-B	Hyd	2200	95	84	137	1966	H, M, K	2 × DML61Z	2 × DW2A

Electric locomotives

Class	Wheel arrangement	Line voltage	Rated output (kW)	Max speed km/h	Weight tonnes	Overall length mm	No in service 1989	Year first built	Builders
EF 64	B-B-B	1500 V dc	2550	100	96	17 900	113	1964	T, K, To
EF 65	B-B-B	1500 V dc	2550	100	96	16 500	205	1964	K, To, T, N
EF 66	B-B-B	1500 V dc	3900	110	100.8	18 200	40	1968	K, To
EF 67	B-B-B	1500 V dc	2850	100	99.6	17 050	3	1981	To
ED 75	B-B	20 kV ac 50 Hz	1900	100	67.2	14 300	83	1963	M, H, T
ED 76	B-2-B	20 kV ac	1900	100	87	17 400	25	1967	H, M, T
EF 81	B-B-B	1.5 kV dc 50 Hz	2550 (dc) 2370 (ac)	110	100.8	18 600	56	1968	H, M

Abbreviations: K Kawasaki Heavy Industries; H Hitachi; M Mitsubishi Heavy Industries; N Nippon Sharyo Seizo; T Toshiba; To Toyo Denki Seizo

Managing Director, Commercial: Masahisa Okada
Corporate Planning & Finance: Hiroo Nakashima
Director, Engineering: Katsuji Iwasa

Freight service is managed and marketed by a single Japan Freight Railway Company nation-wide on the 1067 mm-gauge network. This concern owns its locomotives, wagons and terminals, but hires its track space from the six passenger railway companies. It has no marshalling yards and dedicates itself to bulk commodity and container traffic in trains using rolling stock modified to permit operation at up to 130 km/h. Maintenance is subcontracted to the passenger railways.

Services

JR Freight is a drastically slimmed-down enterprise compared with the freight activity of JNR at its death. Its 12 000 staff are two-thirds fewer than JNR's, so is its stock of locomotives; and its aggregate of freight cars is less than half JNR's final fleet.

The company has withdrawn from a third of the route-mileage served by JNR and is running 40 per cent fewer daily trains. At the same time labour productivity has been almost trebled in terms of tonne-km recorded per employee; and revenue per employee has been hoisted slightly more than three-fold.

The prime reason for the remarkable upturn is that JR Freight has discarded most traffic in individual wagonloads, eliminated marshalling yards and concentrated on business that will make intact trainloads from one terminal to another. Only 350 or so terminals are now served, as against over 2500 in the final years of JNR. In 1988–89 tonnage moved totalled 56.8 million, of which 16.2 million was containerised.

Consequently, almost half JR Freight's annual tonnage is bulk commodities – petroleum, followed by limestone and cement – which are particularly apt for unit train haulage. Paper or pulp, chemicals and coal are the other significant traffics of this kind.

JR Freight's biggest single traffic component is containers. In 1989 220 container trains were running daily over trunk routes extending from Sahikawa and Kushiro in Hokkaido down to Fukuoka, Nagasaki and Kagoshima in Kyushu. One service runs throughout from Fukuoka to Sapporo, a distance of 2130 km. 'Superliner' container trains connecting the main cities such as Tokyo, Osaka, Hiroshima and Fukuoka are permitted a top speed of 110 km/h (68.7 mph). In all, 132 terminals are served by the container train system. Extension of 48 container trains daily into Hokkaido followed the opening in 1988 of the undersea Seikan Tunnel. Shortly afterwards the Seto Bridge's completion enabled extension of container trains to Matsuyama in Shikoku island.

Most container traffic moves in JR Freight's own stock of 63 700 distinctively-sized containers. Width is the difficult dimension rather than height; since 1987 JR Freight has raised the latter from 8 ft to 2.5 m in its own stock. Length was at first a standard 20 ft, but since 1987 JR Freight has also developed a quantity of 30 ft containers with 47 m^3 capacity; that approximates to the cube available in the Japanese trucking industry's most widely-used vehicles. JR Freight deploys refrigerated and live-fish-carrying containers, as well as boxes, tanks, hoppers and open-tops.

Meanwhile, JR Freight is building up a stock of new low-floor flatcars that can carry 40 ft, 8 ft 6 in-high ISO container of 30 tonnes gross weight, or two 20 ft boxes with a total gross weight of 40 tonnes. JNR relied mostly on forklifts for container transshipment, but in view of the trend into bigger box sizes JR Freight is investing in toplift cranage.

Because of its inherited scant terminal cranage, JR Freight partnered lorry manufacturer Izuku to develop

Series 783 inter-city electric train-set of JR Kyushu

Japan Freight piggyback operation

Japan Freight Superliner container train

a craneless transshipment technique for swapbody business. Known as 'Slide Vanbody', this uses a system of electrically-powered winches and rollers with which the move from rail to road vehicle can be effected by one man. Recently perfected, too, is a low-floor flatcar with wheels of 610 mm diameter. That has enabled JR Freight to pursue ro/ro piggyback train service for the smaller size of road freight vans in common Japanese use. Business now amounts to some 150 truck movements daily and is growing. The wagon can also take 9ft 6in-high containers.

JR Freight's business as a whole is growing. At the 1989 change of national rail timetables, the company raised its daily total of scheduled trains from 837 to 864. One consequence is that the company has been compelled to acquire 45 more electric locomotives. Of these, 28 are machines declared surplus at JR Freight's foundation and now rehabilitated, but the rest are brand new. Kawasaki has supplied eight Class EF66-100, a modernised version of the EF66, for the 1.5 kV dc Tokaido-Sanyo route; the others are six Class ED79-50 ac locomotives for Seikan Tunnel route services and the Class EF81-500 dual-voltage ac/dc locomotives. Two 6000 kW inverter-controlled asynchronous motor Bo-Bo-Bo prototypes classified EF200 have also been obtained.

The mainspring of the advance is container traffic – which, moreover, yields around half JR Freight's total revenue because on average the containers travel over four times the distance of other traffic. More growth and the passenger railways could be pressed to accommodate extra container trains on their very busy trunk routes. That possibility has JR Freight studying concepts of mu container flatcar sets.

Main features of first four Shinkansen

	Tokaido Tokyo–Shin Osaka	Shin Osaka–Okayama	Sanyo Okayama–Hakata	Tohoku Tokyo–Morioka	Joetsu Omiya–Niigata
Route length	515 km	161 km	393 km	496 km	270 km
Tunnels	69 km (13%)	58 km (36%)	223 km (57%)	115 km (23%)	106 km (39%)
Bridges	57 km (11%)	20 km (12%)	31 km (8%)	78 km (16%)	30 km (11%)
Viaducts	116 km (22%)	74 km (45%)	86 km (22%)	276 km (56%)	133 km (49%)
Fastest journey time, end-to-end	2 h 56 min	56 min	2 h 19 min	2 h 32 min	1 h 33 min
Max speed	220 km/h	230 km/h	230 km/h	240 km/h	240 km/h
Minimum curve radius	2500 m	4000 m	4000 m	4000 m	4000 m
Max grade	20/1000	15/1000	15/1000	15/1000	15/1000
Minimum longitudinal curve radius	10 000 m	15 000 m	15 000 m	15 000 m	15 000 m
Construction gauge			Height: 7700 mm		Width: 4400 mm
Rolling stock gauge			Height: 5450 mm		Width: 3400 mm
Rail			60.8 kg/m		
			1500 m long-welded rails		
Track gauge			1435 mm		
Formation width	10.7 m	11.6 m	11 m	11.6 m	11.6 m
Distance between track centres	4.2 m	4.3 m	4.3 m	4.3 m	4.3 m
Power system	154 kV or 77 kV 2 lines	275 kV or 220 kV 2 lines		275 kV 2 lines	
Feeder system	25 kV 60 Hz ac single phase booster-transformer	25 kV 60 Hz ac single phase auto-transformer		25 kV 50 Hz ac single phase auto-transformer	
Catenary system	Composite compound	Heavy compound	Heavy compound	Heavy compound	Heavy compound
		ATC (automatic train control)			
		CTC (centralised traffic control)			
		COMTRAC (computer-aided traffic control)			
Opening date	October 1964	March 1972	March 1975	June 1982 (Omiya–Morioka)	November 1982

Traffic (millions)	1987-88	1988-89
Total freight tonnes	56	56.8
Total freight tonne-km	201 000	NA

Finance (million yen)	1987	1988-89
Revenue	172 746	192 100
Expenditure		
Staff	69 557	NA
Materials and services	79 702	NA
Depreciation	10 385	NA
Financial charges	1941	NA
Total	161 385	182 200

Traction and rolling stock

JR Freight owns 569 electric and 295 diesel locomotives and 17 630 freight cars.

Shinkansen Property Corporation

6-5, Marunouchi 1-chome, Chiyoda-ku, Tokyo 100

Telephone: +81 3 211 3580 Telefax: +81 3 240 5640

Chairman: Shoji Ishizuki

Route length: 2101 km

The company leases Shinkansen railway facilities to passenger railway companies.

Generally, railway assets have been transferred at book value. Those taken over by the Shinkansen company, however, were valued at replacement cost and that organisation is required to pay the JNR Accounts Settlement Corporation (see below) by instalments the difference between its assumed long-term liabilities and the replacement value of its assets.

The 1435 mm-gauge Shinkansen system was handed over to the Shinkansen Property Corporation for general management. However, operation and infrastructure upkeep is in the hands of the companies through whose territories the high-speed lines run, as follows for the lines so far in full operation:

JR-East Railway Company:
  Tohoku Shinkansen   Tokyo to Morioka
  Joetsu Shinkansen   Omiya to Niigata

JR-Tokai Railway Company:
  Tokaido Shinansen   Tokyo to Shin Osaka

JR-West Railway Company:
  Sanyo Shinkansen   Shin Osaka to Hakata

The three companies pay rental for use of the network. The aim of this arrangement is to ensure that no company is penalised by limitation to 1067 m-gauge operation while the profits of Shinkansen business in its territory are all pocketed by another organisation, but equally to see that Shinkansen users do not derive inequitable financial benefit from the objective of developing individually viable companies.

Shinkansen services underwent further development in 1988-89. In March 1989 maximum speed on the Joetsu line was lifted to 240 km/h, enabling a cut of 'Super Asahi' schedules from 1 hour 53 minutes to 1 hour 39 minutes. Tokohu speed was also raised to 240 km/h, and a new 'Yamakibo II' service was scheduled to run the 492.9 km between Tokyo Ueno and Morioka in 2 hours 32 minutes, inclusive of one intermediate stop, an end-to-end average speed of 194.6 km/h. Six trains daily were timed over the 171.1 km between Morioka and Sendai in 48 minutes, representing an average speed of 213.9 km/h.

In March 1989 Sanyo line maximum speed was raised to 230 km/h. And in 1990, with emergence of the first Series 300 train-sets, Tokaido speed was to be raised to 275 km/h.

The recent advance in Shinkansen speed resulted from an exhaustive programme of research and high-speed tests begun in the late 1970s. It proved possible to limit lineside noise at 240 km/h to 79 dB(A), the figure previously achieved at 210 km/h to respect the statutory limit of 80 dB(A), largely by increasing the frequency of rail grinding to eliminate surface defects, and by pantograph alterations. As built for the Joetsu and Tohoku lines, the Series 200 train-sets were formed of two-car units; each of the latter had to run with a pantograph operative. The normal 12-car formation now runs with only three pantographs raised and a 25 kV bus-line laid along the tops of the cars distributes the current. Noise has been further curbed by adoption of three-stage pantograph springing to sustain contact with the overhead wire and to minimise the intermittent arcing that has been a perennial cause for environmentalist complaint; and by surrounding the pantograph with shielding, which limits transmission of noise to the lineside. The only significant modification prompted by concerns other than noise suppression arose from need to control the temperature of the resistances in the course of unchecked electric braking from 240 km/h to a stand.

Shinkansen 100 train-set

During the first 20 years after the opening of the Tokaido-Sanyo Shinkansen, rolling stock of essentially the same performance and accommodation was employed. The original cars of this Series 0 have all been replaced, however. Not until 1985 did there appear the prototype of a new Series 100 train-set design, production versions of which now form a substantial Tokaido-Sanyo fleet.

The Series 100 combines pursuit of better aerodynamics, more effective noise control and economy in energy consumption with improvement of passenger comfort and amenities. Earlier Shinkansen train-set types have had all cars powered, but in the Series 100 four of a set's 12 cars are trailers. The powered cars have a 230 kW motor of new, lighter (828 kg) and more compact design on each axle. Compared with a Series 0 set a Series 100, even though two of its four trailers are bi-levels (the other two are the end cars with driving cabs), is lighter – 922 tonnes as against 967 tonnes for 16 cars with a full complement of 1277 passengers. Maximum axleloading, at 15 tonnes, is 1 tonne below that of a Series 0.

Other characteristics of the Series 100 include a balancing speed on level track of 276 km/h. Each of the six pairs of motored cars (which are fed from only three pantographs if the unit is equipped with a 25 kV bus-bar between neighbouring pairs) has a 2510 kVA main transformer, weight 2530 kg. Features of the main rectifier are 4000 V 1000 A thyristors, single-phase four-mixed bridge series connectors and freon-evaporative cooling.

Aerodynamic improvements in the Series 100 include a longer and reshaped noise and closer attention to smooth exterior surfaces, in particular by avoiding recessed windows. The effect has been to reduce drag coefficient by 20 per cent, compared with Series 0, and also noise emission. Moreover, even though the total installed power of a Series 100 (11 040 kW) is less than that of a Series 0 16-car unit the Series 100 has proved 17 per cent more economical in power consumption on a Tokyo-Sanyo 'Hikari' schedule. The 1.6 km/h/s^2 acceleration rate of a Series 100 compares with the 1.0 km/h/s^2 of a Series 0. Nose shaping is a factor in noise control as well as reduction of drag, since the noise emanating from an accelerating train's front end rises at a factor of between the fifth and sixth power of its speed.

Of the two bi-level cars, one has a dining saloon on its upper deck, a kitchen and storerooms on the lower. The other bi-level is a 'Green' or first-class car. Its upper level is an open saloon, but the lower is given over to compartments, of which five are single-seat, three two-seat and one three-seat. In the prototype Series 100 set these compartments were ranged each side of a central corridor, but in the later production sets they have been made more spacious, without loss of capacity, by moving the corridor to one side of the car and laying out the compartments with seats back to, or facing the windows. All compartments are passenger-lockable with magnetic card-type keys; and all single-seat compartments have their own telephone for external calls, and a clock and radio amongst their other amenities.

The second 'Green' car in a Series 100 set is open, with 2 + 2 seating; all seats have a headphone plug-in fixture for personal radio reception. In the standard class cars, 3 + 2 open saloon seating has been retained, but of improved design with increased spacing between seats. In both cases the reclining angle of all seats is adjustable, and all are rotatable. Each pair of cars has at least one passenger telephone booth. Noise level within the train, measured on ballasted track, has been lowered from the 73 dB(A) of a Series 0 to 70 db(A).

By comparison with the earlier Shinkansen train-set types the Series 100 displays significant advances in its electronic systems. A fibre-optic transmission system links all cars with microprocessor-based central control units in each driving cab; the latter include a CRT screen on the driving desk and a recording unit.

A diagnostic system reports on the driver's CRT screen any equipment malfunction and precisely locates it, wherever in the train it occurs, and then the effectiveness of counter measures taken by the driver. The driver can also call up real-time information on such matters as traction motor current, air pressure, overhead current line voltage, rectifier and auxiliary power voltage; in some cases these are displayed in colour or other schematics that identify the individual performances of car pairs in the train-set. Data is automatically recorded and can be immediately radio-transmitted to the ground for the information of ground controllers and maintenance staff.

In the passenger accommodation plasma displays above each saloon-end doorway indicate continuously, in both Japanese and English script, the time, the next station stop and, as it is approached, the distance to it. During station stops the displays identify the train; they also identify main stations which the train passes non-stop. The public address system supplements the displays, but not continuously.

Initially the on-train broadcast service was limited to music on all its five channels. By 1989 the train-to-ground radio link on the Tokaido Shinkansen had been superseded by a leaky coaxial cable (LCX) system, which made it possible to relay FM radio broadcasts on two channels and increase the number of on-board passenger telephones.

With eddy current brakes on its non-motored trailers to complement the regenerative braking of the powered cars, the Series 100 has a superior braking performance to its predecessors.

Shinkansen extensions approved
Laws of the early 1970s prescribing a national Shinkansen network envisaged these new lines:
Hokuriku: from Takasaki on the Joetsu line, forming an arc via Toyama and Komatsu on Honshu's north coast to rejoin the Tokkaido Shinkansen at Osaka;
Tohoku: extension of the existing Shinkansen line from its terminus at Morioka to Aomori;
Hokkaido: to run from the Tohuku Shinkansen at Aomori via the Seikan undersea tunnel to Sapporo in Hokkaido; and
Kyushu: to run from the Sanyo terminus at Hakata to Nagasaki and Kagoshima.

Since completion of the first two Shinkansen, the Tokaido and Sanyo, attitudes to new line building have been adversely coloured by numerous factors. They have ranged from rising costs of construction and more particularly of land, through the strength of environmental reaction that demanded very costly retrospective provision of environmental protections, to the disastrously deteriorating financial state of the former JNR. Furthermore, JNR itself was not eager to take on new Shinkansen that were likely to operate initially at a loss (as the Tohoku and Joetsu did).

Pressure from Western countries to take domestic investment steps that would reduce the country's payments surplus reawakened government interest in Shinkansen schemes in 1987. But there was now the need to arrive at financial arrangements that satisfied the new JR Group companies. In January 1989 agreements were reached that would enable extensions to begin, but in a modest fashion that would tame the construction costs. As before, almost all the extensions will be built by the government-capitalised Japan Railway Construction Corporation. But 10 per cent of the costs will ultimately fall on local governments and 50 per cent on the JR Group companies which will operate the new lines, leaving only 40 per cent to be footed by central government. The JR Group companies will pay by instalments from a pooled share of their receipts from the new lines' services; they will also pay rental to the Shinkansen Leasing Corporation.

The extensions will be of three kinds:
Type 1. To full Shinkansen 1435 mm-gauge standard, engineered for 260 km/h by present equipment, 300 km/h by the next-generation equipment in design.
Type 2. Addition of a third rail to mix existing 1067 mm-gauge, possibly with some realignment. Such extension will demand use of small-profile train-sets, which will be restricted to 130 km/h on the mixed-gauge.
Type 3. Infrastructure to full Shinkansen 1435 mm-gauge standard, but initially laid with 1067 mm-gauge track, engineered for 160-200 km/h.

The application of these concepts to the extensions listed above is to be as follows:

Type KIHA 183 diesel train-set with high-floor first-class car, for improved passenger viewing of scenery (second car); for service in Hokkaido

New Type K1HA 185 diesel train-set for service in Shikoku

The first Series 300 Shinkansen train-set

Hokuriku Shinkansen
  Type 1: Takasaki-Kaurizawa (41 km)
  Type 1 or 2: Karuizawa-Nagano (75 km): choice, which is dependent on choice of a Japanese site for the 1998 winter Olympics, will be made within three years.
  Type 3: Nagano-Kanazawa (89 km)
Tohoku Shinkansen
  Type 2: Morioka-Numakunai and Hachinohe-Aomori (125 km)

648 RAILWAY SYSTEMS / Japan

Type 1: Numakunai-Hachinohe (but dual-gauged for use also by freight trains)
Kyushu Shinkansen
Type 3: Yatushiro-Kagoshima (128 km)
Hokkaido Shinkansen
Not yet approved for construction

Construction work on the Takasaki-Kaurizawa, Morioka-Aomori and Yatushiro-Kagoshima extensions was started in late 1989.

Already set to open in 1992 is a mixed-gauge Shinkansen, constructed for JR-East by the Yamagata JR Through Limited Express Holding Co.

In February 1988 conversion to 1435 mm gauge began of most of the 1067 mm-gauge line running 88 km from the Tohoku Shinkansen at Fukushima to Yamagata. The final 12 km into Yamagata will be mixed-gauge. The Finance Ministry provided 170 million yen of seed money for the first stage. To minimise loading-gauge problems, the dual-gauge line's trains will be a lower-slung and narrower version of the standard Shinkansen design. On the Tohoku Shinkansen they will run at the maximum 240 km/h, but they will be limited to 130 km/h on the extension. A prototype six-car unit was ordered in 1989 for March 1990 delivery, with the aim of evaluation in time for completion of a production series in 1991.

The 3.5 km cross-Tokyo line that will project Tohoku and Joetsu trains from their present Ueno terminus to interchange with the Tokaido-Sanyo trains in Tokyo's central station would be inaugurated in the spring of 1991.

Shinkansen Series 300

Test programmes have demonstrated that speeds up to 300 km/h are feasible on the present track of all Shinkansen. But not with existing train-sets, which at that speed would break both the 80 dB(A) noise limit and also generate unacceptable vibration. Also aerodynamic drag in tunnels would be too high. Consequently a new Series 300 train-set has been designed and the first prototype emerged in late 1989.

The Series 300 is distinguished externally by a dramatically reshaped nose-end and low-slung bodies. Floor level is 1.15m and roof crown 3.6m above rail, compared with 1.3m and 4m respectively for the Series 100. A considerable reduction of weight results from adoption of aluminium alloy body construction and more powerful traction motors. With six of a set's 16 cars non-motored, total weight is 691 tonnes, compared with the 922 tonnes of a Series 100. Maximum axleloading in the bolsterless bogies is 14 tonnes. Like the Series 100, the 300 adds eddy current to its braking systems; a change is that the 300 has regenerative instead of dynamic braking.

Traction is provided by three-phase ac 300kW motors, four per motor car, supplied by a 3000kW pulse-width modulation converter with 4500V 2000A GTO thyristors feeding 1760kVA VVVF inverters. Power/weight ratio is 17.37kW/tonne. Designed top speed is 300 km/h.

The Series 300 is to run a 'Super-Hikari' Tokyo-Osaka service to a schedule of 2½ hours for the 515 km. That would represent an end-to-end average of 206 km/h.

The rump of JNR

What remains of JNR is reorganised as the Japanese National Railways Accounts Settlement Corporation, which retains all the assets and liabilities that are not transferred to successor companies (including the Japan Railway Construction Corporation). Its tasks are:
Reimbursement of long-term liabilities and payment of interest;
Disposal of real estate and other assets in order to raise the necessary money;
Execution of necessary business activities to utilise the rights and meet the obligations transferred to the company from JNR;
Action to achieve re-employment of personnel made surplus by the Reform. Some 93 000 JNR personnel were surplus to the needs of the new companies in April 1987.

After years of refusal by the Treasury to write off any of JNR's historic debt, in preparation for privatisation the government at last agreed in late 1985 to write off 16 700 000 million yen. That still left about 27 100 000 million yen of accumulated liabilities to resolve in 1989. The debt write-off helped all seven Japan group companies to move immediately into profitable operation.

At the start of 1990 the Corporation still had for disposal vast amounts of surplus JNR rolling stock.

Japan's maglev research vehicle MLU-002

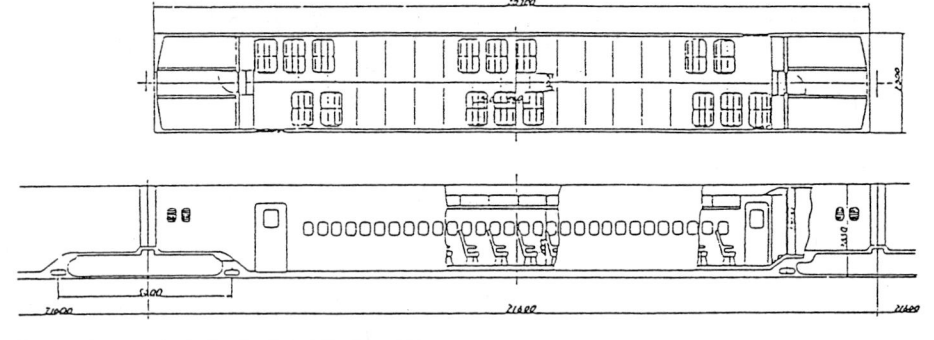

Concept of proposed articulated well-deck Maglev vehicle.

Despite substantial sales and scrapping since 1987, there remained in store some 300 electric and 800 diesel locomotives, 800 railcars, 1400 other passenger cars and almost 15 000 freight cars.

JNR Accounts Settlement Corporation
6-5, Marunouchi 1-chome, Chiyoda-ku, Tokyo 100

Telephone: +81 3 240 5579
Telex: 24873

Director: Takaya Sugiura (former JNR President)

The corporation's function is disposal of the assets and long-term liabilities not transferred to new companies, and promotion of the re-employment of surplus employees.

Railway Telecommunications Co Ltd
6-5 Marunouchi 1-chome, Chiyoda-ku, Tokyo 100

Telephone: +81 3 214 4785

President: Koichi Sakata

Maintenance of railway telecommunication equipment and provision of general telecommunication services.

Railway Information Systems Co Ltd
6-5, Marunouchi 1-chome, Chiyoda-ku, Tokyo 100

Telephone: +81 3 214 4695
Telefax: +81 3 240 5593

President: Ryosuke Muto

Information processing for railway companies, and related computerised information services.

Railway Technical Research Institute
2-8-38, Hikari-cho, Kokubunji, Tokyo 185

Telephone: +81 425 73 7237
Telefax: +81 425 73 7356

Chairman: Masaru Ibuka
President: Masanori Ozeki

Research and development activities to meet the requirements of the railway companies.

Maglev system

The Group has continued development of maglev (magnetically levitated) vehicle technology employing opposed superconductor magnets and linear synchronous motors on a 7 km test guideway near Miyazaki. Test vehicle ML 500 reached a record speed of 517 km/h in December 1979, bringing this series of tests with an inverted T-shaped guideway to a successful conclusion. The guideway then was modified into a U-shaped configuration, and tests were run with a new vehicle, MLU 001, as a single car and as a two-car train.

In 1984, two-car running tests were conducted with the object of safe operation at about 300 km/h, and also with irregularities in coil positioning to collect data on guideway maintenance limitations. Tests in 1985 were directed toward increasing the reliability through an improved cooling system with a helium refrigerator, running a single maglev car at a high speed of about 400 km/h, producing a cycloconverter with circulating-current system, and checking car movements with irregularities in coil positioning during running tests.

In parallel with these field tests, studies were directed toward development of operational concepts for a maglev system and toward technologies for vehicle control at turnouts, power supply, on-board power sources, and emergency braking. Research is also treating vehicle-guideway dynamics and precise measurement of guideway irregularities, reduction of reactive power, performance of associated equipment, and human body reactions to magnetic effects and to high-speed running. The system has also had a fillip from progress in superconductor technology.

These tests culminated in achievement of 400 km/h by the two-car MLU-001 in February 1987.

Since then trials have progressed with a 44-seat MLU-002 vehicle. At the same time development has been pursued of a superconductor maglev system with the objective of 500 km/h operation over a Tokyo-Osaka route of some 500 km, which would be covered in one hour. To further this aim, the government has authorised construction of a 43 km-long test track as a national project, and construction was to start in the Yamanashi Prefecture in 1990. An articulated, well-deck vehicle is under consideration to test the new technology.

Major private and Third Sector railways

Chichibu Railway
Chichibu Tetsudo

1-1, Akebono-cho, Kumagaya-shi 360

Telephone: +81 485 23 3311

Gauge: 1067 mm
Route length: 79.3 km
Electrification: 79.3 km of 1.5 kV dc

President: K Kakihara

The railway operates 27 locomotives, 64 emus and 338 freight cars.

Hankyu Corporation
Hankyu Dentetsu

8-8 Kakutacho, Kita-ku, Osaka 530

Telephone: +81 6 373 5088
Telex: 65617 hankyuco j
Telefax: +81 6 373 5670

Chairman: Sadao Shibatani
President: Kohei Kobayasi
Vice-President: Masatsugu Tanaka

Gauge: 1435 mm
Route length: 146.8 km

Electrification: 146.8 km at 1.5 kV dc

The Corporation was set up in 1907 to construct a 600-volt interurban railway to develop suburban Osaka, and is now a diversified enterprise as well as a railway operator. Since converted to 1.5 kV, the railway serves nine lines with 84 stations and runs over 1000 eight-car trains daily on its Kobe line and to Kyoto, over 700 a day to Takarazuka. The terminal in Osaka, built in the 1970s, has ten platforms and is embodied in a complex including a 17-storey office building and an underground shopping mall; the rail exit from the terminal is six-track. Traffic is CTC-controlled from a centre in Osaka.

In FY 1988-89 passenger journeys totalled 770 million and passenger-km 11 074 million.

The railway owns 723 powered and 550 trailer cars, all air-conditioned and of which the latest employ solid state chopper control. Substations are solid state. An automatic train stop system is combined with speed-control cab signalling.

Track
Rail: 50.4 or 60.8 kg/m
Sleepers: Wood: 230 × 2400 mm; prestressed concrete: 300 × 2400 × 170 mm
Fastenings: Double elastic
Spacing: 1760/km
Minimum curvature radius: 100 m
Max gradient: 4%
Max permissible axleload: 17.78 tonnes

Hankyu electric railcars or multiple-units

Class	Cars per unit	Line voltage	Motor cars per unit	Motored axles per motor car	Rated output (kW) per motor	Max speed km/h	Weight tonnes per car (M-motor T-trailer)	Total seating capacity per car	Length per car mm (M-motor T-trailer)	No in service 1987	Rate of acceleration m/s²	Year first built	Builders Mechanical parts	Builders Electrical equipment
1010	4	1.5 kV dc	2	4	110	110	M 36-38 T 27-29	54, 60	M 19 000 T 19 000	32	0.72	1956	Bodies, Alna Koki Bogies, Sumitomo	Toshiba or Toyo Denki
2000	3, 6, 8	1.5 kV dc	2, 4	4	150	110	M 35-37 T 24-30	54, 60	M 19 000 T 19 000	48	0.72	1960	Bodies, Alna Koki Bogies, Sumitomo	Toshiba or Toyo Denki
2300	4, 6, 7	1.5 kV dc	2, 4	4	150	110	M 35-39 T 25-31	48, 52 54, 60	M 19 000 T 19 000	78	0.72	1960	Bodies, Alna Koki Bogies, Sumitomo	Toshiba or Toyo Denki
2800	7	1.5 kV dc	4	4	150	110	M 34-37 T 27-33	54, 60	M 19 000 T 19 000	56	0.72	1964	Bodies, Alna Koki Bogies, Sumitomo	Toshiba or Toyo Denki
3000	8	1.5 kV dc	4	4	170	110	M 35-38 T 27-28	48, 52 54, 60	M 19 000 T 19 000	114	0.72	1964	Bodies, Alna Koki Bogies, Sumitomo	Toshiba or Toyo Denki
3100	8	1.5 kV dc	4	4	120	110	M 35-38 T 25-28	48, 52 54, 60	M 19 000 T 19 000	40	0.72	1964	Bodies, Alna Koki Bogies, Sumitomo	Toshiba or Toyo Denki
3300	6	1.5 kV dc	4, 6	4	130	110	M 35-36 T 24-26	48, 52	M 18 900 T 18 900	126	0.72	1967	Bodies, Alna Koki Bogies, Sumitomo	Toshiba or Toyo Denki
5000	8	1.5 kV dc	4	4	170	110	M 35-37 T 25	48, 52	M 19 000 T 19 000	47	0.72	1968	Bodies, Alna Koki Bogies, Sumitomo	Toshiba or Toyo Denki
5100	6, 8, 10	1.5 kV dc	4, 6	4	140	110	M 37 T 25-28	48, 52	M 19 000 T 19 000	90	0.72	1971	Bodies, Alna Koki Bogies, Sumitomo	Toshiba or Toyo Denki
5200	6, 8	1.5 kV dc	4	4	170	110	M 36-37 T 26-29	48, 52	M 19 000 T 19 000	25	0.72	1970	Bodies, Alna Koki Bogies, Sumitomo	Toshiba or Toyo Denki
5300	7, 8	1.5 kV dc	4, 6	4	140	110	M 36-37 T 25-26	48, 52	M 18 900 T 18 900	105	0.72	1972	Bodies, Alna Koki Bogies, Sumitomo	Toshiba or Toyo Denki
2200	8	1.5 kV dc	6	4	135, 150	110	M 33-38 T 21-25	50, 56	M 19 000 T 19 000	10	0.72	1975	Bodies, Alna Koki Bogies, Sumitomo	Toshiba or Toyo Denki
6000	6, 8, 10	1.5 kV dc	4, 6, 8	4	140	110	M 36-37 T 25-27	50, 56	M 19 000 T 19 000	130	0.72	1976	Bodies, Alna Koki Bogies, Sumitomo	Toshiba or Toyo Denki
6300	8	1.5 kV dc	4	4	140	110	M 36-37 T 25-27	50, 56	M 19 000 T 19 000	72	0.72	1975	Bodies, Alna Koki Bogies, Sumitomo	Toshiba or Toyo Denki
7000	6, 8	1.5 kV dc	4, 6	4	150	110	M 33-38 T 20-31	50, 56	M 19 000 T 19 000	180	0.72	1980	Bodies, Alna Koki Bogies, Sumitomo	Toshiba or Toyo Denki
7300	8, 10	1.5 kV dc	4, 5	4	150	110	M 32-37 T 21-25	50, 56	M 18 900 T 18 900	64	0.72	1982	Bodies, Alna Koki Bogies, Sumitomo	Toshiba or Toyo Denki

---

Hokuriku Railway
Hokuriku Tetsudo

556, Waride-machi, Kanazawa-shi 920

Telephone: +81 762 37 8111

Gauge: 1067 mm
Route length: 22.7 km
Electrification: 22.7 km at 600 V dc

President: M Yamaguchi

The railway operates two electric and two diesel locomotives and 34 emus.

Iyo Railway
Iyo Tetsudo

4-1, Minatomachi 4-chome, Matsuyama-shi 790

Telephone: +81 899 48 3321

Gauge: 1067 mm
Route length: 33.9 km
Electrification: 24.5 km at 750 V dc and 9.4 km at 600 V dc

President: H Nagano

The railway operates 50 electric multiple-units.

650   **RAILWAY SYSTEMS** / Japan

Izu Express
Izu Kyuko

26-20 Sakuragaoka, Shibuya-ku, Tokyo 150

Telephone: +81 3 464 6751

President: J Yokota

Gauge: 1067 mm
Route length: 45.7 km
Electrification: 45.7 km at 1.5 kV dc

The railway, opened in 1961, serves the eastern coastline of the Izu peninsula from Ito to Izukyu-Shimoda. For the most part this is territory of the Fuji Hakone Izu national park, not far from Tokyo, and at Ito the railway connects with the Japanese National Railways branch from Atami (served by the Tokaido Shinkansen). The railway operates one electric locomotive and 53 emus.

Izu Series 2100 emu

Interior of Series 2100 non-powered trailer

Izu Hakone Railway
Izu Hakone Tetsudo

300, Daiba, Mishima-shi 411

Telephone: +81 559 77 1200

Gauge: 1067 mm
Route length: 29.4 km
Electrification: 29.4 km or 1.5 kV dc

President: K Kato

The railway, which has through running arrangements with JR, operates two electric locomotives and 54 emus.

Joshin Electric Railway
Joshin Dentetsu

51, Tsurumi-cho, Takasaki-shi 370

Telephone: +81 273 23 8066

Gauge: 1067 mm
Route length: 33.7 km
Electrification: 33.7 km at 1.5 kV dc

President: Y Sakurai

The railway operates four locomotives and 25 emus.

Keifuku Electric Railway
Keifuku Denki Tetsudo

3-20, Mibu-kayo-goshomachi, Nakagyo-ku, Kyoto 604

Telephone: +81 75 841 9381

Gauge: 1067 mm
Route length: 59.2 km
Electrification: 59.2 km at 600 V dc

President: T Iwata

The railway operates three locomotives and 63 emus.

Keihan Electric Railway Co Ltd
Keihan Denki Tetsudo

7-24, Otemae 1-chome, Chuo-ku, Osaka 540

Telephone: +81 06 944 2521
Telefax: +81 06 944 2501

Chairman: Hiroshi Sumita
President: Minoru Miyashita
Senior Managing Director, Business Planning & Research: Megumi Shigematsu
  Civil Engineering, New Line Construction: Akio Kimba
  Otsu Branch, Supervision & Research: Toshikazu Uno
  Accounts, Finance, Purchases, Subsidiaries: Yutaka Ogura

Gauge: 1435 mm
Route length: 91.5 km
Electrification: 66.3 km at 1.5 kV (Keihan line); 25.2 km at 600 V dc (Otsu line)

The railway's main Keihan line runs 51.6 km from its Yodoyabashi station in Osaka to the Demachi-yanagi station in Kyoto, with two branches, the Uji and Katano lines. A 2.3km underground extension of this line in Kyoto City was opened in October 1989. The Otsu line is light rail extending 25.2 km from Kyoto Sanjo to Hamaotsu and Sakamoto.

Serving 89 stations, the railway records some 1.07 million passenger journeys each normal working day. The main line is four-track for 11.5 route-km in the Osaka area. In FY 1988-89 passenger journeys totalled 394.46 million and passenger-km 5138.2 million.

The railway generates only 55 per cent of the company's income; the rest is derived chiefly from real estate and department stores.

In December 1983 the railway achieved the considerable feat of converting most of its power system from 600 volts to 1.5 kV dc overnight. The change was

Japan / **RAILWAY SYSTEMS** 651

ordered because increasing traffic was overtaking the lower voltage supply. Rolling stock comprises 601 emu cars on the Keihan line and 61 on the Otsu line.

Future plans include a connection with Kyoto City's Tozai Subway and construction of a Nakanoshima Line westward through Osaka City.

Deliveries in FY 1989 comprised 15 more Series 6000 cars and the first of two new types, 16 of Series 7000 and 12 of Series 8000. Series 7000 has VVVF inverter transmission and is for express and local service. Series 8000 is for limited express service and features on-board video and a telephone booth.

Signalling and traffic control
Commissioning of the ADEC (Autonomous Decentralised Traffic Control System) on the Keihan Line was completed at the end of 1988. ADEC, which links central control and local processors by optic-fibre cable, allows overall traffic control to proceed simultaneously with independent control of an area's operation where that has become irregular.

Coupler in standard use: Tight lock automatic couplers; rotary key-block tight lock automatic couplers; rod couplers

Braking in standard use: Electric command digital and electric pneumatic brake

Track
Rail: Keihan line: 50 kg/m (144.1 km) and 60 kg/m; Otsu line 40 kg/m (47.1 km) and 50 kg/m
Sleepers (cross ties): Keihan: concrete, thickness 170 mm; spacing 1760/km; Otsu; wood, thickness 150–170 mm; spacing 1520/km
Fastenings: Elastic (spring clip or F type)
Minimum curvature radius: Keihan line: 200 m; Otsu line 45 m
Max gradient: Keihan: 3.3%; Otsu: 6.7%
Max permissible axleload: Keihan: 15 tonnes; Otsu: 8–15 tonnes

New Series 8000 limited express train-set

Keihan Electric railcars or multiple units

Class	No of cars per unit	Line voltage dc	No of motor cars per unit	No of motored axles per motor car	Rated output (kW) per motor	Motor & control km/h	Max speed per car	Weight tonnes capacity (M-motor T-trailer)	Total seating mm per car (M-motor T-trailer)	Length per car 1989 (M-motor T-trailer)	No in service	Rate of acceleration m/s²	Year first built	Builders Mechanical parts	Builders Electrical equipment
Keihan Line															
8000	7	1500	4	4	175	DC Phase Control	120	M 33 T22-24	MC 56 M. T 60	MC 18 900 M. T 18 700	12	0.75	1989	Kawasaki Sumitomo Nabco	Toyo Toshiba Mitsubishi
7000	4/6	1500	2/3	4	200	AC (I.M.) VVVF	120	M 32	MC 50	18 700	16	0.75	1989	Kawasaki Sumitomo Nabco	Toyo Toshiba Mitsubishi
6000	7/8	1500	4	4	155	DC Phase Control	120	T 22-24	M. T 56	18 700	106	0.75	1983	Kawasaki Sumitomo Nabco	Toyo Toshiba Mitsubishi
5000	7	1500	4	4	155	DC Rheostatic Control	120	M32 T 22-25	Mc, Tc 48 M. T 54	18 700	49	0.75	1970	Kawasaki Sumitomo Nabco	Toyo Toshiba Mitsubishi
3000	6/7	1500	4	4	175	DC Phase Control	120	M 35 T 27-31	Mc, Tc 56 M. T 64	18 700	58	0.6	1971	Kawasaki Sumitomo Nabco	Toyo Mitsubishi
2600	4/6 7	1500	2/3 4	4	155	DC Phase Control	120			18 700	131	0.75	1978	Kawasaki Sumitomo Nabco	Toyo Toshiba Mitsubishi
2200	7/8	1500	4	4	155	DC Rheostatic Control	110	M 34 T 28	Mc, Tc, 48 M. T 52	18 700	142	0.75	1964	Kawasaki Sumitomo Nabco	Toyo Toshiba Mitsubishi
Otsu Line															
600	2	600	2	4	53	DC Phase Control	70	21	40	15 000	20	0.8	1984	Keihan Sumitomo Nabco	Toyo Toshiba
500	2	600	2	4	60	DC Rheostatic Control	70	24	46	14 900	6	0.8	1968	Kinki Sumitomo Nabco	Toyo
80	2	600	2	4	45	DC Rheostatic Control	65	20	40	15 000	16	1.1	1961	Kinki Nabco	Toyo

Keihin Express Electric Railway
Keihin-Kyuko Dentetsu

20-20, Takanawa 2-chome, Minato-ku, Tokyo 140

Telephone: +81 3 280 9120
Telefax: +81 3 280 9199

President: M Serizawa
General Manager: N Maruyama

Purchasing manager: M Sohno

Gauge: 1435 mm
Route length: 83.8 km
Electrification: 1.5 kV dc

The railway extends from Shinagawa in Tokyo southward to Yokohama and the Miura peninsula, and exercises through running over the Asakasa line of the Tokyo metro. Rail accounts for only 44 per cent of the company's income; most of the residue comes from transport-related activities. In FY1988-89 the railway recorded 425 million passenger journeys and 6080 million passenger-km.

The railway owns 688 emu cars. Its track is laid with 50 kg/m rails on 165 mm thick prestressed concrete sleepers with elastic fastenings, with a minimum curvature of 60 metres radius. Maximum axleloading is 13.7 tonnes.

652   RAILWAY SYSTEMS / Japan

Electric railcars or multiple units

Class	Cars per unit	Line voltage	Motor cars per unit	Motored axles per motor car	Rated output (kW) per motor	Max speed km/h	Weight tonnes per car (M-motor T-trailer)	Total seating capacity	Length per car mm	No in service	Rate of acceleration m/s²	Year first built	Builders Mechanical parts	Builders Electrical equipment
1000	2 4 6 8	1500 dc	2 4 6 8	4	75.9	105	M 35	108 228 348 468	18 000	356	3.5	1958	Kawasaki, Tokyu, Sumitomo, etc	Mitsubishi, Toyo, Koito, etc
800	3 6	1500 dc	3 6	4	100	100	M 35	140 284	18 000	111	3.5	1978	Kawasaki, Tokyu, Sumitomo, etc	Mitsubishi, Toyo, Koito, etc
2000	8	1500 dc	6	4	120	105	M 35 T 29	440	18 000	8	3.0	1982	Kawasaki, Tokyu, Sumitomo, etc	Mitsubishi, Toyo, Koito, etc

Keio Teito Electric Railway
Keio Teito Dentetsu

3-1-24, Shinjuku, Shinjuku-ku 3-chome, Shinjuku-ku, Tokyo 160

Telephone: +81 3 356 3111

President: K Kuwagama

Gauge: 1372 mm; 1067 mm
Route length: 66 km; 12.8 km
Electrification: 75.8 km at 1.5 kV dc

The railway runs northwest from Shibuya in Tokyo and southwest from Shinjuku, exercising through running over the Shinjuku line of the Tokyo metro. The railway, one of 41 companies in the group, generates 57 per cent of the group's income. It operates 488 1372 mm-gauge and 135 1067 mm-gauge emu cars.

Keisei Electric Railway
Keisei Dentetsu

1-10-3 Oshiage 1-chome, Sumida-ku, Tokyo 131

Telephone: +81 3 621 2231

President: Mitsuo Sato
Managing Director, Railway: H Hosokawa

Gauge: 1435 mm
Route length: 104.5 km
Electrification: 104.5 km at 1.5 kV dc

The railway stretches eastward from Ueno in Tokyo to Chiba and to the new station in the International Airport of Narita, to which it operates its 'Skyliner' expresses at half-hour frequency. It has a reciprocal through service with Tokyo metro's Asakasa line. Passenger journeys annually total some 24 million, passenger-km 300 million. Rail revenues forms 48 per cent of the company's gross, the remainder coming from buses and real estate. The company has a half-share in Tokyo's Disneyland, but has no rail connection with the site.

Rolling stock
The railway operates 422 emu cars.

'Skyliner' emu (Type AE) employed in Narita Airport shuttle service

Track
Rail type and weight: 50N 50 kg/m
Cross ties (sleepers): Type K2
Thickness: 172 mm
Spacing: In plain track 1560/km in curves 1680/km
Fastenings: Dog spike (double elastic fastening)
Minimum curvature radius: 160 m
Max gradient: 3.5%
Max axleload: 14.75 tonnes

1.5 kV dc electric railcars

Class	Cars per unit	Motored axles per motor car	Rated output (kW) per motor	Max speed km/h	Weight per car tonnes (M-motor T-trailer)	Total seating capacity (M-motor T-trailer)	Length per car mm	No in service (M-motor T-trailer)	Rate of acceleration m/s²	Year first built	Builders Mechanical parts	Builders Electrical parts
AE	4M 2T	4	140	120	M 38 T 34	M 60 Tc 52	18 000	42	0.69	1972	Tokyu, Nippon	Toshiba, Toyo, Mitsubishi
3600	4M 2T	4	140	120	M 33 T 28	M 54 Tc 50	18 000	M 4 Tc 2	0.92	1981	Tokyu, Nippon	Toshiba, Toyo, Mitsubishi
3500	4M	3	100	120	33	M 54 Mc 50	18 000	M 48 Mc 48	0.97	1972	Tokyu, Nippon, Kawasaki	Toshiba, Toyo, Mitsubishi
3000	4M	4	75	120	29.8	M 56 Mc 50	18 000	M 4 Mc 10	0.97	1958	Nippon	Toshiba, Toyo, Mitsubishi
3050	4M	4	75	120	33	M 56 Mc 50	18 000	M 13 Mc 13	0.97	1959	Nippon, Kisha, Teikoku	Toshiba, Toyo, Mitsubishi
3100	4M	4	75	120	33	M 56 Mc 50	18 000	M 16 Mc 16	0.97	1960	Nippon, Kisha, Teikoku	Toshiba, Toyo, Mitsubishi
3150	4M	4	75	120	M 34 Mc 34	M 56 Mc 50	18 000	M 22 Mc 22	0.97	1963	Nippon, Kisha, Teikoku	Toshiba, Toyo, Mitsubishi
3200	4M	3	100	120	33	M 54 Mc 48	18 000	M 44 Mc 44	0.97	1964	Nippon, Kisha, Teikoku	Toshiba, Toyo, Mitsubishi
3300	4M	3	100	120	33	M 54 Mc 48	18 000	M 27 Mc 27	0.97	1968	Nippon, Kisha, Teikoku	Toshiba, Toyo, Mitsubishi
2100	2M 2T	4	110	100	M 33 Tc 27	M 48 Tc 40	17 150	M 10 Tc 10	0.75	1918	Teikoku, Kisha	Toshiba, Toyo, Mitsubishi

M: Motored car   Mc: Driving motor car   Tc: Driving trailer

* Tokyu: Tokyu Car Corporation
  Nippon: Nippon Sharyo Seizo Kaisha Ltd
  Kawasaki: Kawasaki Heavy Industries Ltd
  Kisha: Kisha Seizo KK
  Teikoku: Teikoku Sharyo Kogyo KK
  Toshiba: Toshiba Corp
  Toyo: Toyo Denki Seizo KK
  Mitsubishi: Mitsubishi Electric Corp

Japan / **RAILWAY SYSTEMS** 653

Kinki Nippon Railway
Kinki Nippon Tetsudo

1-55 Uehommachi Tennojiku 6-chome, Osaka 543

Telephone: +81 6 771 3331

President: Yoshinori Ueyama

Gauge: 1435 mm; 1067 mm; 762 mm
Route length: 405.7 km; 162.4 km; 27.4 km
Electrification: 1.5 kV dc (395.2 km of 435 mm-gauge; 159.1 km of 1067 mm-gauge). 750 V dc (10.2 km of 1435 mm-gauge; 27.4 km of 762 mm-gauge)

Part of the Kintetsu conglomerate with widespread commercial interests, ranging from numerous hotels and construction concerns to bus and taxi companies, like the majority of Japan's private railways, the Kinki Nippon has the most extensive route-mileage of any and lies third in the table of passenger movement, carrying 2 million daily. Extending eastward from Namba to Osaka to Kyoto, Nara, Nagoya and Ise Bay, the railway runs limited expresses throughout the Kinki and Tokai areas. Its main line is inter-city, running 186 km from Osaka to Nagoya, and it also serves Nara, Kyoto and the Ise-Shima National Park (136 km from Osaka). A 10.2 km extension, 4.7 km of it in tunnel, was opened from Ikoma to Nagata in October 1986; at Nagata it makes a junction with the Osaka Metro, over which through service is run to central Osaka.

The Kinki Nippon records over 13 000 million passenger-km annually. It operated computer-based seat reservation as early as 1960 and has since computerised its timetabling. The railway has its own research laboratory and generates 80 per cent of the income of its parent company, Kintetsu.

Rolling stock includes bi-level and vista-dome passenger cars. It comprises 8 electric locomotives (1067 mm-gauge only) and 1445 1435 mm-gauge, 287 1067 mm-gauge and 41 762 mm-gauge emu cars. In 1988 the company installed a new fleet of luxury six-car emus in its non-stop service between Nagoya and Osaka.

Kinki Nippon Series 30 000 limited express emu including bi-level cars

Series 21 000 'Urban Liner' limited-express electric train-set of Kinki Nippon Railway

Kobe Electric Railway
Kobe Denki Tetsudo

1-1, Daikai-dori 1-chome, Hyogo-ku, Kobe 652

Telephone: +81 78 575 2236

Gauge: 1067 mm
Route length: 63.7 km
Electrification: 63.7 km at 1.5 kV dc

President: D Nakada

The railway operates an electric locomotive and 153 emu cars.

Konan Railway
Konan Tetsuda

23-5, Hommachi, Kita-Yanagida, Hiraka-machi, Minami-Tsugaru-gun, Aomori 036-01

Telephone: +81 172 44 2675

Gauge: 1067 mm
Route length: 36.9 km
Electrification: 1.5 kV dc

President: T Tarusawa

The railway operates three electric locomotives; three dmu cars and 43 emu cars.

Nagoya Railroad
Nagoya Tetsudo

1-2-4, Meikei 1-chome, Nakamura-ku, Nagoya 450

Telephone: +81 57 571 2111
Telex: 4424135 ngorrd j
Telefax: +81 52 561 7020

Chairman: K Takeda
President: K Kajii

Gauge: 1067 mm
Route length: 544.5 km
Electrification: 481.2 km at 1.5 kV dc; 63.6 km at 600 V dc

Between 1941 and 1944 the private urban railways of the Nagoya region were knitted into a coherent regional network by conversion of downtown tram tracks into an inter-system connection focussed on a new underground Shin-Nagoya station alongside the Japan Rail station. Since then the system has been rationalised by some closures, but new lines have been laid to cater for fresh suburban development, such as the Chita line in 1980. The network includes 33.9 km of light rail in Gifu Prefecture and a 1.2 km monorail line operating six cars. Besides the Nagoya Railroad, the diversified Meitetsu Corporation also runs bus, taxi, road freight, sea ferry and air-taxi services, hotels, restaurants and travel agencies, but

Nagoya Railroad Series 7000 emu

RAILWAY SYSTEMS / Japan

the railway produces 56 per cent of the total revenue.

The Shin-Nagoya station handles over 800 trains a day, with 25 trains hourly each way on the main route between Shin Gifu/Inuyama and Toyohashi/Tokoname/Kowa. Electrification was progressively standardised at 1.5 kV dc after the unification of the system, but some 600 volts dc survives on lines to the north of Gifu. Passenger carryings annually total 380 million journeys and over 7000 million passenger-km.

Rolling stock includes 14 electric locomotives. Over half the emu fleet of 786 cars is of post-1955 construction, with lightweight bodies, rheostatic braking and fully suspended motors. The company also has 12 diesel railcars.

Coupler in standard use: Passenger cars: tight-lock automatic; freight cars; automatic
Braking in standard use: Electro-magnetic

Track
Rail: 50 kg/m; 37 kg/m
Sleepers (cross ties): Prestressed concrete: 240 × 160 × 2000 mm; wood: 200 × 140 × 2100 mm
Spacing: 1640/km
Fastenings: Tie plate, dog spike
Minimum curvature radius: 160 m
Max gradient: 3.3%

Nankai Electric Railway
Nankai Denki Tetsudo

1-60 Namba 5-chome, Minami-ku, Osaka 542

Telephone: +81 6 644 7120

President: S Yoshimura
Managing Directors: A Sibatini
T Murai
A Ieda
T Domoto

Gauge: 1067 mm

Route length: 166.1 km
Electrification: 151.8 km at 1.5 kV dc; 14.3 km at 600 V dc

The railway operates 618 emu cars. Serving 110 stations, it runs from Osaka to Wakayama and in FY 1989-89 recorded 302 million passenger journeys.

Nishi Nippon Railroad
Nishi Nippon Tetsudo

11-17 Tenjin 1-chome, Chuo-ku, Fukuoka 810

Telephone: +81 92 761 6631

President: Genkei Kimoto

Gauge: 1435 mm; 1067 mm
Route length: 95.2 km; 21 km
Electrification: 116.2 km at 1.5 kV dc

The railway, which owns 481 emu cars, operates from Fukuoka to Omutra, with branches, and has a suburban system in Kitakyushu. Track is laid with 37, 40 and 50 kg/m rails on timber and prestressed concrete sleepers spaced 1560/km and allowing 16 tonnes maximum axleloadings; minimum curvature is 160 metres. Traffic totals some 475 000 passenger journeys daily.

1·5 kV dc electric railcars or multiple units

Class	Cars per unit	Motor cars per unit	Motored axles per motor car	Rated output (kW) per motor	Max speed km/h	Weight tonnes per car (M-motor T-trailer)	Total seating capacity (M-motor T-trailer)	Length per car mm	Rate of acceleration m/s²	Year first built	Builders Mechanical parts	Builders Electrical equipment
1435 mm-gauge												
5000	3	2	4	135	105	M 35/36 T 28	160	19 500	0.8	1975	Kawasaki	Mitsubishi
	4	2	4	135	105	M 33/36 T 28	220	19 500	0.7	1977	Kawasaki	Mitsubishi
2000	6	4	4	135	105	M 34.4/36.2 T 30	348	19 500	0.7	1973	Kawasaki	Mitsubishi
1000	4	4	4	80	105	M 33/32	224	18 500	0.7	1957	Nippon Sharyo Kinki Sharyo	Mitsubishi Toyo Denki
1300	4	2	4	110	105	M 34 T 25	256	18 500	0.6	1961	Nippon Denki	Toyo Denki Kinki Sharyo
600	2	1	4	135	105	M 33.8 T 28.2	112	19 500	0.7	1962	Kawasaki	Mitsubishi
	3	2	4	135	105	M 33.8 T 28.2	168	19 500	0.8	1962	Kawasaki	Mitsubishi
700	4	2	4	135	105	M 34.9 35.2 T 26.4/25.8		19 500	0.7	1972	Kawasaki	Mitsubishi
300	2	1	4	115	80	M 38.3 T 28.5	88	M 18 500 T 18 800	0.6	1948	Kisha-Gaisha	Toshiba
	3	2	4	110	80	M 36.8 T 28.5	156	17 500	0.6	1948	Kisha-Gaisha	Mitsubishi
200	2	1	4	45	65	M 22 T 16.8	80	M 13 600 T 13 900	0.3	M 1937 T 1941	M Kisha-Gaisha T Kinami-Sharyo	Toshiba
	3	2	4	45	65	M 22 T 18.3	120	13 600	0.4	1937	Kisha-Gaisha	Toshiba
	4	3	4	45	65	M 22 T 18.3	160	13 600	0.5	1937	Kisha-Gaisha	Toshiba
1067 mm-gauge												
120	2	1	4	100	65	M 35.8 T 24	100	M 15 700 T 15 700	0.6	1958	Kawasaki	Toshiba
	3	2	4	80	65	M 33/32.1 T 24	162	M 16 700/16 500	0.8	1960	Kawasaki	Mitsubishi
308	2	1	4	100	65	M 39.6 T 29	100	M 18 700 T 19 000	0.7	1948	M Kisha-Gaisha T Nippon Sharyo	Mitsubishi
313	2	1	4	104	65	M 39.2 T 24.1	132	18 700	0.4	1952	Kinki Sharyo	Mitsubishi

Odakyu Electric Railway
Odakyu Dentetsu

1-8-3 Nishi Shinjuku, Shinjuku-ku, Tokyo 160

Telephone: +81 3 349 2291
Telex: 2325060 odakuj Telefax: +81 3 349 2140
President: Tatsuzo Toshimitsu

Gauge: 1067 mm
Route length: 119 km
Electrification: 119 km at 1.5 kV dc

Series 10 000 articulated electric train-set operating between Tokyo and resort areas

The railway runs southwest from Shinjuku, Tokyo, to Odawara, Hakone, the Mount Fuji region and the coast west of Yokohama. It has through service arrangements with the Chiyoda line of the Tokyo metro. In FY1988-89 the railway recorded 669 milion passenger journeys and 10 868 million passenger-km; revenue grossed 75 985 million yen against expenditure of 64 402 million yen. At peak periods its core handles 29 trains each way per hour. It owns four electric locomotives and 940 emu cars which form 163 semi-permanent train-sets.

The railway has adopted ATP based on coded frequency circuitry and a total trafic control system with both relay and electronic interlockings. Track is formed of 50 or 60 kg/m rail on prestressed concrete sleepers spaced 1640/km in plain track, 1760/km in curves; minimum curvature radius is 200m, maximum gradient 2.7 per cent and maximum permissible axleload 16 tonnes.

A 1.1 km, 600-volt dc monorail and a 10 km light rail system, the Enoshima Electric Railway, are also operated by the group, which numbers 100 individual companies and obtains 32 per cent of its income from rail transport.

Odakyu electric railcars or multiple-units

Type	No of cars per unit	Line voltage	No of motor cars per unit	No of motored axles per motor car	Rated output (kW) per motor	Motor & control type	Max speed km/h	Weight tonnes per car (M-motor T-trailer)	Total seating capacity per car (M-motor T-trailer)	Length per car mm (M-motor T-trailer)	No in service 1989	Rate of acceleration m/s²	Year first built	Builders Mechanical parts	Builders Electrical equipment
3000	5	1500Vdc	4	2	100	DC-T/M & Cam Con.	125	M 28.3 T 28.2	M 52 T 36	M 16 150 T 12 700	20	0.44	1957	N,K,Kn	T,M,Te etc.
3100	11	1500Vdc	11	2	110	DC-T/M & Cam Con.	130	M 29.4	M 50	M 16 465	77	0.42	1963	N,K,S	T,M,Te etc.
7000	11	1500Vdc	9	2	140	DC-T/M & Cam Con.	110	M 32.6 T 22.0	M 50 T 32	M 16 390 T 12 500	44	0.56	1980	N,K,S	T,M,Te etc.
10 000	11	1500Vdc	9	2	140	DC-T/M & Cam Con.	110	M 32.7 T 22.6	M 46 T 28	M 16 370 T 12 600	44	0.56	1987	N,K,S	T,M,Te etc.
2600	6	1500Vdc	3	4	117	DC-T/M & Cam Con.	100	M 37.8 T 32.9	M 58 T 58	M 20 000 T 20 000	132	0.78	1964	N,K,Tc,S	M,T,Te etc.
4000	4	1500Vdc	2	4	135	DC-TM & Cam Con.	110	M 39.0 T 32.5	M 58 T 50	M 20 000 T 20 000	32	0.67	1966	N,K,Tc,S	M,T,Te etc.
4000	6	1500Vdc	4	4	135		110	M 39.0 T 31.7	M 58 T 50	M 20 000 T 20 000	60	0.75	1966	N,K,Tc,S	M,T,Te etc.
5000	4	1500Vdc	2	4	135	DC-T/M & Cam Con.	110	M 40.2 T 33.7	M 58 T 50	M 20 000 T 20 000	60	0.67	1969	N,K,Tc,S	M,T,Te etc.
5000	6	1500Vdc	4	4	135		110	M 40.5 T 33.9	M 58 T 50	M 20 000 T 20 000	120	0.75	1978	N,K,Tc,S	M,T,Te etc.
8000	4	1500Vdc	2	4	140	DC-T/M & F-CH	110	M 40.0 T 34.0	M 58 T 50	M 20 000 T 20 000	64	0.67	1984	N,K,Tc,S	M,T,Te etc.
8000	6	1500Vdc	4	4	140		110	M 40.0 T 32.0	M 58 T 50	M 20 000 T 20 000	96	0.75	1982	N,K,Tc,S	M,T,Te etc.
9000	4	1500Vdc	4	4	110	DC-T/M & F-CH	120	M 39.7	M 58	M 20 000	36	0.69	1972	N,K,Tc,S	M,T,Te etc.
9000	6	1500Vdc	4	4	110		120	M 40.0 T 27.6	M 58 T 58	M 20 000 T 20 000	54	0.79	1973	N,K,Tc,S	M,T,Te etc.
1000	4	1500Vdc	2	4	175	I/M & VVVF	120	M 38.2 T 30.1	M 58 T 50	M 20 000 T 20 000	56	0.75	1987	N,K,Tc,S	M,T,Te etc.
1000	6	1500Vdc	3	4	175		120	M 38.1 T 29.3	M 58 T 58	M 20 000 T 20 000	24	0.75	1988	N,K,Tc,S	M,T,Te etc.

Abbreviations:
N: Nippon Sharyo Seizo Ltd.
K: Kawasaki Heavy Industries Ltd.
Tc: Tokyu Car Co.
T: Toshiba Co.
M: Mitsubishi Electric Co, Mitsubishi Heavy Industries Ltd.
Te: Toyo Electric Mfg Co. Ltd.
S: Sumitomo Metal Industries Ltd.
Kn: Kinki Nihon Sharyo Ltd.
Nl: Nihon Lockheed Monorail Co.
W: Westinghouse Electric Co.
Nn: Naka Nihon Co. Ltd.

Omi Railway
Omi Tetsudo

3-1 Daito-cho, Hikone-shi 522

Telephone: +81 7492 2 3301

Gauge: 1067 mm
Route length: 59.5 km
Electrification: 59.5 km at 1.5 kV dc

President: T Kaida

The railway operates 40 emus, 11 electric and three diesel locomotives, five diesel railbuses, 68 wagons.

Sagami Railway
Sagami Tetsudo

2-9-14 Kitsaiwaii, Nishi-ku, Yokohama 220

Telephone: +81 45 319 2111

Gauge: 1067 mm
Route length: 33 km
Electrification: 33 km at 1.5 kV dc

President: K Tsushima

The railway operates 360 emu cars, four electric locomotives, 28 wagons.

Sanyo Electric Railway
Sanyo Denki Tetsudo

1-1, Oyashiki-dori 3-chome, Nagata-ku, Kobe 653

Telephone: +81 78 611 2211

Gauge: 1435 mm
Route length: 63.3 km
Electrification: 63.3 km at 1.5 kV dc

President: T Watanabe

The railway operates 194 emu cars.

Seibu Railway
Seibu Tetsudo

16-15, 1-chome, Minami-Ikeburkuro, Toshima-ku, Tokyo 171

Telephone: +81 3 989 2035

President: Y Tsutsumi

Gauge: 1067 mm; 762 mm
Route length: 175.8 km; 3.6 km (rubber-tyred)
Electrification: 175.8 km at 1.5 kV dc

Part of a multi-faceted corporation that includes hotels, Japan's busiest department store, housing and road transport among its businesses, the railway serves the western suburbs of Tokyo with two main routes radiating from terminals on or near Japanese National Railway's city-centre Yamanote loop, the 43.8 km Ikebukuro and 22.6 km Shinjuku lines. These lines throw off and are in some cases interconnected in the suburbs by 10 branches. The Ikebukuro terminus deals with an average of 700 train workings daily, with departures at 1½ minute headways in the evening peak. There is a reciprocal through service with the Yurakuho line of the Tokyo metro. A subsidiary company has a rail system in the Izu peninsula.

Traffic runs at some 555 million passenger journeys a year, or almost 1.6 million a day, of which 67 per cent are made on season tickets and generate 46 per cent of total receipts. The railway's operating ratio is approximately 87 per cent.

The railway is desperately in need of extra capacity. It seeks to double the size of its Shinjuku line by tunnelling 13 km of double-track below it at a cost of 150 000 million yen. The tunnel tracks would be used by non-stop trains.

Improvements recently completed include construction of a 6 km branch, partly underground, from

RAILWAY SYSTEMS / Japan

Ikebukuro, rejoining the existing line near Nerima, and the quadrupling of the Ikebukuro route for 4.6 km from Nerima to Shakujikoen.

The fleet of 897 emu cars comprises 12 types; most numerous type is the air-conditioned 101 series, dating from 1969, which numbers 330 cars. Six 'Red Arrow' six-car units are used for a supplementary-fare service, including perambulated buffet, on the Ikebukuro line.

The 10 locomotives comprise four ex-JNR Westinghouse-built units of 1922 build and four recent Mitsubishi-built Type E851 96-tonne B-B-Bs of 2250 kW.

Shimbara Railway
Shimbara Tetsudo

7385-1, Bentencho 2-chome, Shimbara-shi 855

Telephone: +81 95 762 2231

Gauge: 1067 mm
Route length: 78.5 km

President: D Shirakuta

The railway operates three diesel locomotives and 23 dmus.

Shin Keisei Electric Railway
Shin-Keisei Dentetsu

16-16 Hatsutomi, Kamagaya-shi 273-01

Telephone: +81 473 84 3151

President: I Fukuda

Gauge: 1435 mm
Route length: 26.5 km
Electrification: 26.5 km at 1.5 kV dc

The railway operates 152 emu cars.

Tobu Railway
Tobu Tetsudo

1-2, 1-chome, Oshiage, Sumida-ku, Tokyo 131

Telephone: +81 3 621 5057

President: Kaichiro Nezu

Gauge: 1067 mm
Route length: 473.4 km
Electrification: 473.4 km at 1.5 kV dc

The railway's main line runs 135 km northward from Asakusa and Ikebukuro in Tokyo to Shimoimaichi and Nikko, with branches to Utsunomiya and Isezaki and through service arrangements with the Hibiya line of the Tokyo metro. Its daily average of just over 2 million passengers ranks second in the table of the busiest private railways in Japan. There are 80 different companies in the group, which takes 57 per cent of its revenue from the revenue. The railway operates 28 electric locomotives, 1474 emu cars and 326 freight cars.

Tobu limited express, air-conditioned and including buffet, on Tokyo-Nikko tourist route

Tokyo Express Electric Railway
Tokyo Kyuko Dentetsu

26-20 Sakuragaika-cho, Shibuya-ku, Tokyo 150

Telephone: +81 3 477 6111
Telex: 2423395

President: Jiro Yokota

Gauge: 1372 mm; 1067 mm
Route length: 5.1 km; 95.6 km
Electrification: 5.1 km, 1372 mm-gauge at 6000 V dc; 95.6 km, 1067 mm-gauge at 1.5 kV dc

The railway is one of 300 companies and eight non-profit institutions within the Tokyu Corporation, which was established in 1922 and now covers real estate enterprises, bus and taxi companies, department stores, supermarkets, construction companies, road freight, railcar building, advertising agencies, construction companies, shipping, airline (Japan Air, the country's third largest carrier) and air freight activity. The rail network is located in the south-west of the Tokyo metropolitan area and runs from Shibuya, Meguro and Gotanda on JNR's Yamanote line to Kanagawa Prefecture and Yokohama. The 9.4 km of route out of Shibuya is effectively a metro, and the

Electric railcars or multiple-units

Class	Cars per unit	Line voltage	Motor cars per unit	Motored axles per motor car	Rated output (kW) per motor	Max speed km/h	Weight tonnes per car (M-motor T-trailer)	Total seating capacity	Length mm (M-motor T-trailer)	No in service 1988	Rate of acceleration m/s²	Year first built	Builders Mechanical parts	Builders Electrical equipment
3450	3	1500 V dc	2	4	94		M 36.1-37.2	140	M 17 040	9	0.61	1931	Nippon Kawasaki Tokyu	Hitachi
3500	3	1500 V dc	2	4	94		M 37.7-39.8 T 26.7-29.0	140	M 17 040 T 17 840	11	0.58	1930	Kawasaki Tokyu Tokyo	Hitachi
3650	3	1500 V dc	2	4	94		M 37.4 T 28.4	140	M 16 960 T 17 680	3	0.58	1942	Kawasaki Tokyu Toyoko	Hitachi
6000	6	1500 V dc	6	4	100-120	95	M 28.0-29.0	364	M 18 000	2	0.89	1960	Tokyu	Toyo
6000	2	1500 V dc	2	4	120	95	M 28.5	108	M 18 000	1	0.86	1960	Tokyu	Toyo
7000	8	1500 V dc	8	4	60	100	M 27.18-28.15	464	M 18 000	7	1.1	1962	Tokyu	Toyo
7000	6	1500 V dc	6	4	60-70	100	M 27.18-28.15	328	M 18 000	9	0.86-1.11	1962	Tokyu	Toyo
7200	3	1500 V dc	2-3	4	110	100	M 32.2-34.0 T 21.0-24.5	152	M 18 000 T 18 000	15	0.86	1967	Tokyu	Hitachi Toyo
7200	2	1500 V dc	1	4	110	100	M 30.1 T 17.9	96	M 18 000 T 18 000	1	0.64	1967	Tokyu	Hitachi
7600	3	1500 V dc	3	4	110	110	M 32.2	144	M 18 000	1	0.89	1986	Tokyu	Toyo
7600	6	1500 V dc	4	4	110	110	M 32.2 T 24.0	288	M 18 000 T 18 000	1	0.89	1986	Tokyu	Toyo
7700	6	1500 V dc	3	4	170	120	M 33.3-33.8 T 26.8-29.8	328	M 18 000 T 18 000	3	0.83	1987	Tokyu	Toyo
8000	7	1500 V dc	4-5	4	130	120	M 32.7-36.3 T 22.5-26.6	432	M 20 000 T 20 000	8	0.75-0.92	1969	Tokyu	Hitachi Toyo Toshiba
8000	8	1500 V dc	6	4	130	120	M 32.7-36.3 T 23.3-26.6	486	M 20 000 T 20 000	6	0.92	1969	Tokyu	Hitachi Toyo Toshiba

Japan—Jordan / **RAILWAY SYSTEMS** 657

Electric railcars or multiple-units

Class	Cars per unit	Line voltage	Motor cars per unit	Motored axles per motor car	Rated output (kW) per motor	Max speed km/h	Weight tonnes per car (M-motor T-trailer)	Total seating capacity	Length mm (M-motor T-trailer)	No in service 1988	Rate of acceleration m/s^2	Year first built	Builders Mechanical parts	Builders Electrical equipment
8000	5	1500 V dc	3	4	130	120	M 32.7-36.3 T 22.5-26.6	304	M 20 000 T 20 000	5	0.78	1969	Tokyu	Hitachi Toyo Toshiba
8090	8	1500 V dc	5	4	130	120	M 31.97-32.57 T 23.9-27.51	420	M 20 000 T 20 000	10	0.83	1980	Tokyu	Hitachi Toyo Toshiba
8500	8	1500 V dc	6	4	130	120	M 31.0-35.8 T 27.3-30.0	496	M 20 000 T 20 000	3	0.92	1975	Tokyu	Hitachi Toyo Toshiba
8500	10	1500 V dc	8	4	130	120	M 31.0-35.8 T 27.3-30.0	556	M 20 000 T 20 000	36	0.92	1975	Tokyu	Hitachi Toyo
3450	1	1500 V dc	1	4	94	120	M 37.5	40	M 17 040	2	0.86	1931	Nippon Kawasaki	Hitachi
9000	8	1500 V dc	4	4	170	120	M 31.8-33.8 T 24.3-26.4	434	M 20 000 T 20 000	4	0.86	1986	Tokyu	Hitachi Toyo
70	2	600 V dc	2	2	48.5		M 19.2-19.3	80	M 13 960	4		1942	Kawasaki	GE
80	2	600 V dc	2	2	74.6		M 21.1-21.2	64	M 13 960	3		1950	Hitachi Tokyu	Hitachi
150	2	600 V dc	2	2	60		M 18.8-18.15	64	M 13 960	2		1964	Tokyu	Toyo

railway also has through service arrangements with the Tokyo metro's Hibiya and Hanzomon lines. With a total of some 895 million passenger journeys a year it is the busiest in the capital's suburban area. Average length of passenger journey is only 92 km.

The company needs extra capacity and plans to lay 15.9 km of additional track from Meguro to Okurayama.

Signalling
On the Tohyoko, Mekama, Ohimachi, Ikegami and Penetoshi lines a total of 81.6 route-km is equipped with a cab signalling ATC system and automatic train stop operated through the track circuiting.

Track
Tokyu employs 50 kg/m rail on prestressed concrete sleepers of 150–160 mm thickness, with double elastic fastenings.

Rolling stock
Tokyu operates 984 emu cars on 1067 mm-gauge, 18 two-car emus on 1372 mm-gauge. The great majority of the vehicles has been built in the Corporation's own workshops. Tokyu Car Corporation is one of the group's subsidiaries.

New Tokyu Corporation Series 1000 emu with VVF inverter control

Toyama Chicho Railway
Toyama Chiho Tetsudo

1-36 Sakuramachi 1-chome, Toyama-shi 930

Telephone: +81 764 32 5111

Gauge: 1067 mm
Route length: 93.3 km
Electrification: 93.3 km at 1.5 kV dc

President: H Ogata

The railway operates 53 emu cars, two electric and six diesel locomotives, three wagons.

Jordan
Ministry of Transport

PO Box 1929, Amman 35214

Telephone: +926 6 41461
Telex: 21541 mot jo

Minister: A Dakhkan

Planning: Fawaz al Twal
Finance: B Debee
Mechanical & Traction: Mohammed Shafa-Amri
Signalling and Telecommunications: Abdulla Malkawi
Traction and Rolling Stock: Khalil Ahmed
Permanent Way: M Z Mulla
Administration: A Maitah

Stores: Naim Al Saoud

HJR Departmental Heads
  Operating and Mechanical: O S Kraisheh
  Traffic: S Rasheed
  Permanent Way: M K Imad Eddeen
  Finance, Stores and Supplies: M A Al-Jukhadar
  Administration: M Y Hidjaz

Hedjaz Jordan Railway (HJR)
Aqaba Railway Corporation (ARC)

PO Box 582 (HJR) and 50 (ARC), Ministry of Transport, Amman

Telephone: + 962 3 32114/32234 (ARC)
        +962 3 895413/4 (HJR)
Telex: 64003 jo arc maan (ARC), 21541 (HJR)

Director-General (HJR): Dr Abdullah Al Djazi
Deputy Director-General (ARC): A A Maitah
Deputy Directors-General (HJR): M K Imad Eddeen, F Rashid

ARC Departmental Heads
  Traffic and Operating: Mohammed Kashmar

GE Type U20C 2000 hp Co-Co of Aqaba Railway Corporation

Gauge: 1050 mm
Route length: ARC: 293 km
HJR: 496 km

ARC

ARC's sole function is haulage of phosphates from mines at Al-Hassa to the Red Sea port of Aqaba over a network of new and reconstructed lines, which are passed for 16-tonne axleloads. Part of the route, from Al-Hassa to Hettiya, is the original Hedjaz Railway rehabilitated; the remainder is new. ARC also connects with HJR at Batn el Ghul.

It was reported in 1989 that the government was minded to pass ARC into the ownership of the phosphate mining company.

In 1982 ARC was extended to serve a further phosphate mine at Wadi el Abyad, north of El Hassa and east of Menzil, the output of which raised its phosphates traffic from 1.63 to 3.15 million tonnes per annum. Phosphate carryings could be trebled by development of a further source at Shediya, 30 km south of Ma'an. In the meantime ARC hopes to break into the maritime traffic of other commodities, including containerised freight, flowing between Aqaba and Amman.

The originally designed capacity of the line was 1.5 million tonnes, but it has carried two-and-a-half times as much. A prime concern has therefore been the limitations of the existing infrastructure, with its curves of as little as 125 metres radius and a 30 km gradient in places as steep as 1 in 37 near Aqaba. That slope restricts train length to 35 wagons of 42 tonnes payload and 64 tonnes gross each. The curvature has dictated adoption of Scheffel cross-braced bogies in recent wagon deliveries from Gregg of Belgium and Samsung of South Korea.

A new Shediya mine is now planned to come into production in 1990-91 and in 1986 the government applied about a quarter of the US$400 million assigned to rail projects under the country's 1986-90 plan for construction of a new line from Aqaba to Shediya. Feasibility studies of a new 1435 mm-gauge, 25-tonne axleload line from Aqaba to Shediya, with branches to Hassa and the Wadi al Abiad mine, were commissioned by the Jordan government.

Meanwhile, 49 kg/m, concrete-sleeper track is being laid in place of 30 kg/m, wooden-sleeper track on the existing route, under a three-phase programme, partly funded by World Bank loan. Completion of the first two phases, covering the 181km from Aqaba to Ma'an, was set for March 1990.

The block signalling between El Hassa and Umran is controlled by uhf radio, employing fail-safe frequency-division multiplex apparatus. In 1983 Westinghouse Signals (UK) secured a £2.7 million turnkey contract to install Westbloc coded block and colour-light signalling at five stations, which was finished by the start of 1988. A vhf radio system, using mobile sets, connects train and station staff with the Ma'an control centre.

ARC's traction comprises 18 GE Type U20C 2150 hp, three GE Type U18C 1850 hp, eight GE Type UL17C 1750 hp diesel-electric locomotives and two hired GE Type U10C 750hp locomotives. Wagon stock totals 500, of which 294 were in service at the end of 1989.

ARC traffic	1985	1987	1988	1989
Total freight (million tonnes)	2.47	2.58	2.24	2.15
Total gross freight tonne-km (million)	1 262	719	621	607

Type of coupler in standard ARC use: AAR Alliance 2
Type of braking in standard ARC use; Air 26 Lavi

ARC Track
Rail: S-49 (49 kg/m); BSS 70A (34.8 kg/m); and S-30 (30 kg/m)
Cross ties (sleepers): Wood and concrete
Spacing: 1666/km, 1755/km in curves less than 300m radius
Fastenings: DS 18 and Pandrol
Minimum curvature radius: 125 m, 13.9°
Max gradient: 2.7%
Max permissible axleload: 16 tonnes

HJR

ARC's expanding traffic has been at the expense of HJR, which currently carries little traffic. Its Amman-Damascus passenger service was ended by the Syrians in 1983. However, freight service was revived with a twice-weekly Amman-Damascus working in October 1985, and in 1987 passenger service was reinstated over the 20 km between Amman and Zarqua. Annual traffic has lately grossed only 31 000 passenger journeys and just under 9000 tonnes of freight. HJR owns five GE Type U10 670 kW Caterpiller-engined diesel-electric locomotives and four oil-fired steam locomotives of German and Belgian build. Passenger rolling stock comprises two diesel railcars and five coaches. Freight wagons total 292.

HJR traffic	1986	1987
Total freight (tonnes)	8814	10 902
Total freight tonne-km	972 142	992 808

The future of the railway has become problematical following Syria's intention, with Soviet assistance, to build a new 1435 mm-gauge line from Damascus to the border at Deraa in place of the 1050 mm-gauge Hedjaz Jordan line in its territory. It is not clear whether the Syrians would keep their part of the 1050 mm-gauge line operational.

Pending a decision whether to rebuild the HJR line from the border to Amman on the 1435 mm-gauge, HJR has been hopeful that the government will put up the comparatively modest track work funds necessary for launch of an oil feed service to the phosphate mines from Zarqa refinery, 20 km north of Amman. HJR would also like to break into grain haulage from Aqaba to Amman, but for that would need four additional locomotives and some 60 freight cars, for which no funds are forthcoming.

Type of coupler in standard use: Screw
Type of braking in standard use: Vacuum (locomotives air and vacuum)

HJR Track
Rail; 12.5 kg/m flat-bottom
Sleepers: Steel fish-type, 1830 mm long × 20 mm thick
Spacing: 1418/km
Fastenings: Angle-type four bolt
Minimum curvature radius: Main line 100 m, turnouts 91.5 m
Max gradient: 2%
Max axleload: 10.5 tonnes

Kampuchea

Cambodia Railways
Chemins de Fer du Cambodge

Railway Headquarters, Phnom Penh

Telephone: 25156
Cable: Fercam, Phnom Penh

President and Managing Director: In Nhel
Deputy Managing Director: Seng Kim Chun
Technical Director: Bou Saman
Chief, Mechanical Engineering: Khalut Thol
Chief, Permanent Way: Youg Sokhon
Chief, Operating: Em Thoul

Gauge: 1000 mm
Route length: 649 km

Because of the country's unchecked internal unrest only a third of the system is reported usable. The newest line on the system, between Phnom Penh and Kompong Som (264 km), opened in 1969, has been closed to traffic since 1970 owing to damage. This is the country's only rail outlet to the sea, other than via Thailand to Bangkok. The 385 km Phnom Penh-Poipet line is believed to be usable only in part.

Motive power
The railway's present operations were at last available report covered by 18 diesel-electric locomotives and nine steam locomotives, all that have so far been made serviceable, along with some 450 freight wagons. Backbone of the diesel-electric fleet were Alsthom-built BB 1200 hp units fitted with MGO-V12 BZSHR engines delivered in 1966/67.

Permanent way and installations
A line linking Phnom Penh and Ho Chi Minh City (formerly Saigon) has been projected for a number of years but consistently cancelled owing to hostilities. The line would fill one of the missing links in the Transasian Railway Project.

Kenya

Ministry of Transport & Communications

PO Box 52692, Ngong Road, Nairobi

Telephone: +254 2 729200
Cable: Transcomm Nairobi

Minister: J Kamotho
Permanent Secretary: P Mwaisaka

Kenya Railways (KR)

PO Box 30121, Nairobi

Telephone: +254 2 21211
Telex: 22254 railways
Telefax: +254 2 340049

Executive Chairman: Prof J K Musuva
General Manager: Eng J Mudhune
Corporation Secretary: Miss R K Muthiga
Chief Personnel & Administration Manager: B C K Tireito
Chief Internal Auditor: C Katambo

TECHNICAL SERVICES DIVISION
Manager: Eng O Alkizim
Chief Mechanical Engineer: Eng J K Njue
Chief Civil Engineer: Ebg G K Guchu
Chief Electrical & Communications Engineer: Eng A Y Hariz
Workshops Manager: Eng A Mbago
Chief Security Officer: C Okelo
Public Relations Manager: E Muthui

FINANCE DIVISION
Manager: John Mbithi
Chief Supplies Officer: N Nyanjom
Data Processing Manager: N Makhulo

BUSINESS & OPERATIONS DIVISION
Manager: A J Kinyua (Acting)
Chief Traffic Manager: S A Meova
Business Manager: D N Odette (Acting)

Gauge: 1000 mm
Route length: 3034 km

Kenya Railways operates the main line from Mombasa through Nairobi, Nakuru and Eldoret to the border of Kenya with Uganda and the branch line joining the Lake Victoria town of Kisumu to the farming centre of

Nakuru. The rest are branch lines linking Nairobi to Nanyuki near Mt Kenya, Gilgil to Nyahururu, Voi to Taveta, Kisumu to Butere, Konza to Magadi and Rongai to Solai. The railway is also responsible for lakes services within Kenya.

Investment
KRC has been considering the application of a fresh US$28 million World Bank loan to partial double-tracking of the Nairobi-Mombasa main line. A £9.6 million grant from Britain has been used chiefly for rolling stock (see below). Together with a US$13.3 million loan from the Overseas Development Association, these moneys have enabled the start of a US$45.5 million-development programme to make the railway more competitive with road transport. KRC has an edge on price, but is often beaten for speed of transit and for reliability, because of traction shortages.

Management restructure
The development programme has been accompanied by a management restructure. This has included delegation of authority to regional managers at Mombasa, Nairobi and Nakuru, who have powers to effect local purchases and thereby reduce non-commercial wagon traffic.

New line projects
A decision was taken in 1981 to proceed with the engineering design of the first stage of a 240 km Kerio valley line northward from Kampiya ya Moto, on the Rongai-Sola line, to Sigor, to cater for the fluorine mineral deposits in the Baringo uplands. Connection with the proposed Sudan Railways line from Wau to Juba on the Upper Nile is the ultimate possibility. Surveys and financial studies were completed in 1982 and in 1984 Sofrerail was contracted to assist in building the line, which would include a 5 km-long tunnel south of Kimwarer. No groundwork had been reported by late 1989, however.

The Transport Ministry has approved feasibility study of a new line from Kipkelion, on the Kisumu-Butere branch, through tea plantation country to Awendo. Also under consideration is a new and shorter 500 km route from Nairobi to Mombasa.

Signalling and telecommunications
The Nairobi-Mombasa telecommunications system has been renewed, incorporating teleprinter exchage, and two new PABX.

Motive power and rolling stock
Fleet numbers at the start of 1990 were: 219 diesel locomotives; 546 passenger coaches (including 29 buffet restaurant and 125 sleeping/couchette cars); 6490 freight wagons.

Under the British aid programme, W H Davis and Powell Duffryn Standard were supplying 44 wagons in 1990; and BREL and GEC-Alsthom were to begin a £2.5 million rehabilitation of five Class 87 and six Class 71 and 72 locomotives.

Taveta, the border station for traffic interchange with Tanzania and other points in Central Africa

Type of coupler in standard use: PH/DA
Brake system: Graduated automatic air

Civil engineering
Mechanised track maintenance equipment has been acquired, including a pair of tamping, levelling and lining machines and four ballast crushers. Continuous rail welding has been developed. Track renewals include easement of curvature.

Track
Rail: 50, 60, 80 and 95 lb FB
Cross ties (sleepers): Steel
Spacing: 1476/km (1558/km in curves)
Fastenings: 'K' type (Pandrol)
Minimum curvature radius: 16°
Max gradient: 2.5%
Max axleload: 18 tons

Traffic	1984	1985	1986	1987/88	1988/89
Freight tonnage (000)	3655	3268.9	3226.7	3200	3080
Freight tonne-km (million)	2034	1859.7	1827.9	1704.44	1826.94
Passenger-km (million)	484	586.8	687	795.56	822.53
Passenger journeys (000)	1709	1920.2	2300	3860	3960

Finance (KES million)	1986/87	1987/88	1988/89
Revenue			
Passengers and baggage	138.2	149.4	162.93
Freight parcels and mail	1600.3	1050.6	1144.51
Other	3.1	103.5	204.2
Total	1741.6	1303.5	1511.64
Expenditure			
Staff	657.9	584.1	662.7
Materials and services	1083.0	1209.87	1200.08
Depreciation	105.0	99.2	99.2
Financial charges	115.4	135.93	151.76
Total	1961.3	1893.17	2113.74

Diesel locomotives

Class	Wheel arrangement	Transmission	Rated power hp	Tractive effort Max lb (kg)	Tractive effort Continuous at lb (kg)	Tractive effort Continuous at mph (km/h)	Max speed mph (km/h)	Wheel dia in (mm)	Total weight tonnes	Length ft in (mm)	No built	Year	Builders Mechanical parts	Builders Engine & type	Builders Transmission
92	1 Co-Co 1	Elec	2550	77 000 (35 000)	43 500 (19 730)	16.5 (26.4)	45 (72)	37½ (953)	113.64	59' 1¼" (18 015)	15	1971	MLW Ind	Alco 251 F	GE Canada
93	Co-Co	Elec	2610	66 138 (30 000)	52 299 (23 700)	13.64 (22)	45 (72)	37½ (953)	98.9	60' 1¼" (18 320)	26	1978	GE (USA)	GE 7FDL12	GE (USA)
94	Co-Co	Elec	2920	–	–	–	–	–	–	–	10	1987	GE (USA)	GE	GE
87 (90)	1 Co-Co 1	Elec	1840	51 600 (23 000)	44 500 (20 180)	11.7 (18.8)	45 (72)	37½ (953)	101.5 (Adhesive)	55' 7¼" (16 948)	10 / 14 / 20	1960 / 1964 / 1967/8	English Electric	EE 12 CSVT	EE
72	1 Bo-Bo 1	Elec	1240	40 000 (18 150)	32 500 (14 750)	10.7 (17.2)	45 (72)	37½ (953)	70.1	43' 9¼" (13 341)	10	1972	GEC Traction	EE 8CSVT	GEC
71 (91)	1 Bo-Bo 1	Elec	1240	40 000 (18 150)	32 000 (14 400)	10.5 (17.7)	45 (72)	37½ (953)	69	43' 9¼" (13 341)	10	1967	English Electric	EE 8CSVT	EE
62	B-B	Hyd	760	27 750 (12 500)	21 825 (9900)	7.8 (12.3)	45 (72)	37½ (953)	38	37' 5" (11 404)	56	1977	Rheinstahl AG	MTU MB 12V 493 T210 (10) MTU EB 12V 396 TC11 (46)	Voith L520-U2
46 (86)	D	Hyd	606 (2 × 303)	32 900 (14 900)			20 (32)	39½ (1003)	48	36' 1¼" (11 007)	22	1967	Andrew Barclay	2 × Cummins	British Twin Disc CF 11500
35	C	Hyd	300	24 460 (11 100)	20 000 (9070)	3.8 (6.1)	17 (27)	39½ (1003)	36	29' 7¼" (9023)	15	1972	Andrew Barclay	Paxman 8 RPHL	Voith L320V
47	D	Hyd	525	35 060 (15 900)	23 590 (10 700)	17.5 (28)		39½ (1003)	52	31' 9¼" (9680)	35	1979	Hunslet Holdings	Rolls-Royce DV8TCE	Voith L2r3ZU

Korea (Democratic People's Republic)

North Korea Railway

Pyongyang

Minister for Railways: Pak Yong Sok

The railway system is known to total over 8500 route-km of 1435 mm-gauge. Electrification at 3 kV dc has been pursued and is believed to cover 2200 km, or more than half the network. The country's Kim Jong Tae factory has begun to produce its own electric locomotives, the latest of which is a 4240kW unit for the railway's severely-graded routes.

An important recent conversion has been the 90 km from Koindong to the vicinity of the Chinese frontier at Manpochin, which besides its strategic value is of importance to the line that has been under construction roughly parallel with the border. The latter, extending 252 km from Hyesan to Manpochin, was completed in 1988. Another recently completed electrification runs from Wonsan to the electrified Pyongyang-Chongjin route at Kowon, which benefits the country's chief coalfield.

Electrification is continuous throughout the 780 km from Pyongyang to Vladivostok, and through passenger car service (involving a bogie change at Tumangang, near Rajin in Korea) between Pyongyang and Moscow was launched in April 1987. There is electrification between Sepo and Pyongyang, on the recently built line between Namdokchon and Toknam. Catenary has been installed between Pyongyang and the nearby port of Chinmanpo, and in 1987 it was extended to the Hari-Kangdong line, east of Pyongyang. In 1988 the Kaechon-Choyang, Tanchon-Mandok and Hari-Kandang lines were wired, and wiring work was started on the Paekan-Musan line.

Other new lines have been built. They include an 80 km railway from Jukchon to Onchon, for more direct access to the port of Nampo, and a 252 km line from Hyesan to Kanggye and Manpo.

Local production of rolling stock has been supplemented by delivery of seven French-built 3600 hp, 132-tonne diesel-electric Co-Cos similar to the type lately delivered to Iraq. A first batch of seven was supplemented in 1987 by five more, built by De Dietrich with Alsthom electrical equipment.

Korea (Republic)

Ministry of Transportation

168, 2ka Bongrae-dong, Chung-ku, Seoul 100162

Telephone: +82 2 392 9801-8
Telex: motrans k24778
Telefax: +82 2 392 9809

Minister: Rhee Bomb-June

Korean National Railroad (KNR)

122, 2ka Bongrae-dong, Chung-ku, Seoul

Telephone: +82 2 392 0078
Telex: 24802 knrail
Telefax: +82 2 313 7105

Administrator: Kim Ha-Kyeong
Deputy Administrator: Shin Young-Kook
Director General, Planning and Business Management: Kang Shin Tae
  Civil Engineering Bureau: Choi Kang-Hee
  Rolling Stock Bureau: Ha Kye-Uk
  Electrical Bureau: Jae Keun Kim

Finance and Accounting: Bang Suk-Ki
Transportation Bureau: Park Hyo Keun
Director, International Co-operation Division: Kim Young-Ki

Gauge: 1435 mm; 762 mm
Route length: 3102 km; 47 km
Electrification: 523 km at 25 kV 60 Hz ac

The backbone of the railway system is the 444 km double-track Gyeongbu line, running between the nation's two principal cities, Pusan on the south-east coast across the Tsushima Straits from Japan and the capital city of Seoul in the north-west. Principal intermediate cities reached by this route include Taegu and Taejon. While it constitutes less than 15 per cent of total KNR route-km, the Gyeongbu line accounts for nearly half of the system's operating revenues. A second north-south route, and a revenue source second only to the Gyeongbu line, is afforded by the Chungang (Central) and Tonghaenambu lines. Diverging to the south-west from the Gyeongbu line at Taejon, the Honam line reaches into the rich agricultural plain of North and South Cholla provinces and the important south-western port of Mokpo. Branching from the Honam line at Iri is the Cholla line, which extends southward to Yosu, an important southern port and the site of a major oil refinery.

Linking these two lines across the south coast of South Korea with the Gyeongbu line near Pusan is the Kyongchon line. The Yongdong line, which links the east coast with the Chungang line at Yongju, was extended northward to the major east coast city of Kangnung. KNR's second route to the east coast was completed through the heart of the Taebaek mountain range late in 1973.

The solitary 762 mm branch was opened in 1937 from Suweon to Songdo.

Traffic

Main road development and growth of coastal shipping have cost KNR its leading role in the nation's transport system and levelled off rapid growth which doubled passenger traffic in the 1970s. At the same time KNR slipped into deficit after 1980, with resultant government pressure for economies, a two-year curb on investment to contain financial charges, and deferral of plans for a new high-speed passenger railway between Seoul, Taejon and Pusan. However, KNR has drastically reduced and almost eliminated its deficit, partly by staff cuts. Operating losses have been cut to to two-thirds since 1983. As a result, in July 1988 legislation was framed to remove KNR from the tutelage of the Transport Ministry, which would give railway management commercial freedom. KNR was contemplating line closures for further economy.

Passenger traffic further improved in 1988, swollen chiefly by long-haul gains, sustaining the unchecked

Diesel locomotives

Manufacturer's type (KNR class)	Wheel arrangement	Rated power hp	Max speed km/h	Wheel diameter mm	Total weight tons	Length mm	No in service	Year first built	Builders Mechanical parts	Builders Engine & type
SW 8 (2000)	Bo-Bo	800	105	1016	94.5	13 420	13	1957	GMC (USA)	8-567 BC
SW 1001 (2100)	Bo-Bo	1000	105	1016	87	13 610	28	1969	GMC (USA)	8-645 E
G8 (3000)	Bo-Bo	875	105	1016	75	14 325	51	1959	GMC (USA)	8-567 CR
Alco (3100)	Bo-Bo	950	105	914	71.5	14 650	6	1967	Alco (USA)	6-251 B
GM (3200)	Bo-Bo	875	105	–	–	–	42	1968	GMC (USA)	–
G12 (4000)	Bo-Bo	1310	105	1016	78.5	14 325	15	1963	GMC (USA)	12-567 C
G12 (4100)	Bo-Bo	1310	105	1016	85	14 325	10	1966	GMC (USA)	12-567 C
G22 (4200)	Bo-Bo	1310	105	1016	88	14 170	22	1967	GMC (USA)	12-567 E
SD9 (5000)	Co-Co	1750	105	1016	141	18 500	29	1957	GMC (USA)	16-567 C
SD18 (6000)	Co-Co	1800	105	1016	147	18 500	14	1963	GMC (USA)	16-567 D
SDP28 (6100)	Co-Co	1800	105	1016	147	18 500	6	1966	GMC (USA)	16-567 E
SDP38 (6200)	Co-Co	1800	105	1016	147	18 500	17	1967	GMC (USA)	16-567 E
SDP38 (6300)	Co-Co	1800	105	1016	148	18 500	23	1967	GMC (USA)	16-567 E
G26CW (7000)	Co-Co	2000	105	1016	99	15 765	8	1969	GMC (USA)	16-645 E
G26CW (7500)	Co-Co	3000	105	1016	132	19 650	96	1972	GMC (USA)	16-645 E3
GT26CW (7100)	Co-Co	3000	150	1016	132	19 650	56	1979	GMC (USA)	16-645 E3
FT36HCW-2	Co-Co	3000	150	1016	120	NA	15	1986	Hyundai	16-645 F3B
GT36HCW-2	Co-Co	3700	150	1016	128	20 347	6	1986	Hyundai	16-645 F3B

Electric locomotives

KNR series	Wheel arrangement	Line current	Rated output hp	Tractive effort continuous at tons	Tractive effort continuous at km/h	Max speed km/h	Wheel diameter mm	Weight tons	Length mm	No built	Year first built	Builders Mechanical parts	Builders Electrical parts
8000	Bo-Bo-Bo	ac, 1ø, 25 kV (60 Hz)	5300	31.3	46	85	1250	132	20 730	90	1972	Alsthom MTE	AEG ACEC

Korea (Republic) / **RAILWAY SYSTEMS**   661

growth since 1980. Freight traffic, too, has risen sharply since 1981 (see table).

Traffic (million)	1986	1987	1988
Freight tonnes	58	59.3	60.7
Freight tonne-km	12 813	12 892	13 784
Passenger journeys	519	525	564
Passenger-km	23 563	24 457	25 978

Investment
World Bank loans are permitting conversion of the Suweon-Songdo 762 mm-gauge line to 1435 mm at a cost of US$13 million, to create a bypass of Seoul for freight to Incheon; and a 20 km electrified double-track line, funded by an industrial development corporation, was completed in October 1988 from the Seoul-Suweon line to the new industrial city of Ansan, on the coast south of Incheon. A new Seoul freight complex is being built at Shihunggun near Bugog, 23 km south of the city, with intermodal and bulk handling facilities, and the existing terminal Seongbug is being enlarged.

In 1987 the Transport Ministry initiated studies of an 80 km cut-off between Chonan and Nonsan, on the route from Seoul to the southwest. This would eliminate the route's present detour via Taejon, where it diverges from the main line to Pusan, and cut as much as an hour from current journey times between Seoul and Kwangju.

With relations between South and North Korea less strained, KNR has resumed planning to revive rail connections severed after the Korean war. Engineering design was to begin in 1989 on restoration of the connection north of Shintani, which was one of two that existed before the war.

Seoul-Pusan inter-city trains
With the future of the prospective Seoul-Pusan high-speed passenger railway uncertain, but with road coach competition as well as the opposition of an hourly air service fierce in the passenger market, KNR counter-attacked in 1985 by lifting the line speed limit from 120 to 150 km/h so as to trim half-an-hour from the schedules of the six premier day trains each way between the two cities. Timing for the 445 km was cut to 4 hours 10 minutes inclusive of two intermediate stops. The first of a fleet of new diesel train-sets with streamlined six-axle locomotives classified Type GT 36HCW-2 and powered by GM-EMD 3700 hp engines entered Seoul-Pusan service under the brand name 'Saemaul-ho' in July 1986.

Four diesel-hydraulic train-sets of new lightweight design, two built by Daewoo and two by Hyundai, were introduced to the Seoul-Pusan service in mid-1987. Seven more of the new train-sets were to be ordered, so that the units could cover two daily Seoul-Kwangju services on the Honam line as well as each day's ten Seoul-Pusan 'Saemaul-ho' workings.

Each new train-set, classified DHC, has two 1180 kW MTU-engined power cars (which include a passenger saloon) enclosing three trailers, one of which is a catering car. Subsequent units are planned to have five trailers and to employ MTU engines uprated to 1476 kW. The Voith transmission is body-mounted, driving the inner axle of the leading bogie via a cardan shaft, but the bogie's two axles are shaft-coupled. Maximum axleload is 17 tonnes, to minimise dynamic track forces at the line's maximum speed of 150 km/h. Bodies are stainless steel-panelled on steel framing; primary suspension is coil spring, secondary suspension air on the Daewoo sets and coil spring on the Hyundai pair.

KNR is showing interest in tilt-body technology. It has imported from Socimi of Italy two of that company's newly-developed equipments for application to existing KNR cars, with an eye to possible series production, at first in Italy but later by Hyundai under licence. The equipment on trial includes four bogies developed from Socimi's Fast-Ride design. Each bogie embodies apparatus that transmits signals to an electronic processor commanding the electronic-hydraulic body-tilting mechanism. Fitted to existing cars the system enables a tilt of up to 6 degrees.

Class 8000 Bo-Bo-Bo electric locomotive and inter-city passenger train

Diesel railcars

KNR series	Wheel arrangement	Transmission	Rated power hp	Max speed km/h	Wheel diameter mm	Total weight tons (M-motor T-trailer)	Length mm (M-motor T-trailer)	No built	Year built	Builders Mechanical parts	Builders Engine & type
600	Bo-Bo	Hydraulic Converter	420	105	864	51	21 500	11	1962	Niigata (Japan)	N-855-R (Cummins USA)
600	Bo-Bo	Hydraulic Converter	420	105	864	51	21 500	32	1963	Kinki (Japan)	N-855-R (Cummins USA)
600	Bo-Bo	Hydraulic Converter	420	105	864	51	21 500	36	1966	Kawasaki (Japan)	N-855-R (Cummins USA)
600	Bo-Bo	Hydraulic Converter	360	105	864	51	21 500	9	1963	Niigata (Japan)	DMH 17 (Japan)
700	Bo-Bo	Hydraulic Converter	420	105	864	51	21 500	12	1966	Niigata (Japan)	N-855-R (Cummins)
700	Bo-Bo	Hydraulic Converter	360	105	864	51	21 500	8	1966	Niigata (Japan)	DMH 17 H (Japan)
160*	Bo-Bo	Hydraulic Converter	210	105	711	25	14 750	6	1965	KNR	N-855-R (Cummins)
100*	Bo-Bo	Hydraulic Converter	360	105	914	33.9	10 400	2	1969	Niigata (Japan)	DMH17C (Japan)
200†	Bo-Bo	Electric	4 × 112	110	—	58.5	21 000	4	1979	Daewoo	Cummins KTA-1150L
DHC	Bo-Bo	Hydraulic‡	2 × 1580	150	860	M68 T38	M23 500 T23 030	4	1987	Daewoo Hyundai	MTU 12V 369TC13

* 762 mm-gauge   † Operates in two five-car units with Type 300 and 400 trailers on long-haul services   ‡ Voith L520r U2

High-speed scheme revived

In 1989 the country's President Roh Tae Woo announced his support for construction of both the 380 km Seoul-Pusan, or Kyongbu, high-speed line and of new electrified lines from Seoul to the east coast, and from Taejon on the Seoul-Pusan line southwest to Mokpo. A 300 km/h capability is sought for the Seoul-Pusan line. Because of the terrain a top speed of 200 km/h is envisaged on the Seoul-east cast line. The maximum in mind betwen Taejon and Mokpo is 180 km/h.

The Seoul-Pusan line is to be built first. Construction was to begin in late 1991 and completion is anticipated in 1998. The state is expected to put up about half the estimated cost US$ 5200 million; the rest will be raised through overseas loans. There are two Seoul-Pusan route options. One would largely follow the course of the existing main line; the other, slightly less expensive, would run via Gyeongju.

The traction and rolling stock technology to be adopted was still an open question in mid-1990, but the objective is a 2-hour Seoul-Pusan timing, demanding a start-to-stop average of close on 200 km/h. A timetable of as many as 140 trains daily is envisaged, running at 5 or 6-minute intervals in peak periods. French, German and Japanese high-speed technologies have been keenly contesting for the project, for which bidding was set to begin in mid-1990.

Three routeing options for the east coast line, known as the Dongsuh, are under consideration. One would extend from Seoul-Chongnyangni through Chunchon and Wontong to Sokkcho; the second would reach Wontong via Yangpyong and Hongchon; and the third, the southernmost, would run from Seoul via Jagokdong and Wonju to Kangnung. Lengths of the three routes range from 240 to 272 km. Extension over the border to Koesong in North Korea is envisaged at a later date.

Electrification

Following agreement to a World Bank loan of US$98 million in 1983, the 64 km extension of electrification from Jecheon to Yeongju was put in hand, and the government subsequently endorsed electrification of the main line south of Seoul from its present limit at Suweon to Chonan by 1990.

In the Seoul metropolitan area the 13 km line from Seongbug to Euijeongbu is being substantially rebuilt, double-tracked and electrified. This project is to be followed by similar work on the 10 km from Yongsan north-west to Susaeg. Further electrification of links between Seoul and its dormitory towns of Kuri, Paju and Songnam is proposed, and a third track is to be installed between Seoul and Kuri. KNR records 282 million passenger journeys annually on its Seoul suburban services, compared with some 160 million on intercity routes.

Motive power and rolling stock

In 1989 the 1435 mm-gauge traction in operation comprised 487 diesel and 93 electric locomotives, 495 emu cars and 142 diesel railcars. Other passenger stock in operation totalled 2172 locomotive-hauled cars and the railway owned 15 489 freight cars.

Track

Main lines are mostly laid with 50 kg/m rail, but since 1981 KNR has rapidly extended continuously-welded 60 kg/m rail to heavily trafficked sections. Some secondary lines have 50 kg/m rail, others 27 kg/m. Sleepers are mostly wood, but more than a quarter are of locally-manufactured concrete.

Signalling

Some 650 km of KNR are equipped with automatic block signalling and 246 km of route CTC-controlled. Over 550 traction units are equipped to work with KNR's automatic train-stop equipment and over 600 have been fitted with track-to-train radio.

KNR's first solid-state interlocking, supplied by GEC-General Signal and remotely-controlled by CTC, was commissioned at Paldang on the Chung-An line in March 1989.

Type GT36HCW-2 3700 hp diesel locomotive

Electric multiple-units

Class	Cars per unit	Line voltage	Motor cars per unit	Motored axles per motor car	Rated output (kW) per motor	Max speed km/h	Weight tonnes per car (M-motor T-trailer)	Total seating capacity (M-motor T-trailer)	Length per car m	No of cars in service	Rate of acceleration km/h/s	Year first built	Builders Mechanical parts	Builders Electrical equipment
Commuter	4	25 kV ac or 1500 V dc		4	160	110	Tc 33.3 M 42.1 M 46.1	—	20	76	—	1974	Hitachi	Hitachi
Commuter	4, 6, 8 or 10	25 kV ac or 1500 V dc	2, 4, or 6	4	120	110	Tc 34.5 M 43.5 M 46.5	T 48 M 54 M 54	20	212	2.5	1976	Daewoo	Daewoo & Hitachi (Japan)
Commuter	4, 6, 8 or 10	1500 V dc	4 or 6	4	150	100	MC 41.5 M1 40.5 M2 40.5	MC 48 M1 54 M2 54	20	32	3.0		Daewoo	Hitachi
Inter-city	10	25 kV ac	6	4	120	100	Tc 43.5 M 51.5 M 51.0 Tb 40.0 Ts 37.5	561	20	20	2.0	1979	Daewoo	Daewoo & Hitachi

Lebanon

Chemins de Fer de l'Etat Libanais (CEL)
et le Transport en commun de Beyrouth et de sa Banlieue (CEL/TCB)

PO Box 109, Souk El-Arwan, Beirut

Telephone: +961 443619
Cable: Assikkat
Telex: 43088 cel tcb

President: Adel Hamiyé
Director General: Emir Abdullah Chehab
Chief of Traffic and Operation: Adnan Ramadan
Chief of Traction and Rolling Stock, Track and Structures: Sayed Aouad
Chief of Finance: Mardiros Djabrayian
Chief of Stores: Emmanuel Barakat

Gauge: 1435 mm
Route length: 222 km

The state took over the railways in January 1961. The system then ran from Tripoli through Hous, Hama and Aleppo to the Turkish frontier and from Nusaybin to the Iraq frontier at Tel Kotchek, also from Makowai to Tripoli. The hostilities that have ravaged the country in the 1980s have naturally affected the railway very severely and major parts of the system have become unusable.

The line from Beirut to Zerghaya is non-existent, its tracks ripped up, its alignments either bulldozed for military purposes or built over by lineside inhabitants. Only 23 km of the Beirut-Nakoura line still have tracks continuously in place, for movement of freight for the Zahrani refinery. The line from Jbeil through Tripoli to the frontier at Akkari is out of use, that from Rayak to

Koussair completely destroyed. In the notorious Bekaa valley the rail infrastructure is totally demolished for a distance of 19km. Some efforts to restore track in the Beirut area have had to be abandoned because of fighting.

Tractions and rolling stock
In early 1990 CEL's resources were four 600hp GM (two of them unserviceable) and three Polish diesel locomotives, four Büssing railcars, four control trailers (one unserviceable) and four other trailers (one unserviceable). The railcar vehicles were all imported from Germany in 1984. Availability of a reported stock of 505 freight wagons was uncertain.

Track
Max axleload: 16 tonnes on standard-gauge lines; 13 tonnes on narrow-gauge lines.
Minimum curvature radius: 1435 mm-gauge; 218 m; 1050 mm-gauge: 100 m
Max gradient: 2% uncompensated; 7% on rack rail section
Max altitude: 1487 m

Liberia

There are three railways in Liberia, all originally constructed for iron ore transports:
(1) Bong Mining Co (from Monrovia to Bong Town), a joint West German and Italian undertaking;
(2) National Iron Ore Co Ltd (from Monrovia to Mano on the Sierra Leone border), an American/Liberian organisation;
(3) Lamco JV Operating Co, set up by the Liberian American-Swedish Minerals Co and Bethlehem Steel Corporation. At the start of 1990 this railway's status was uncertain, as the company decided to cease ore mining at the end of October 1989.

Bong Mining Company

PO Box 538, Monrovia

Telephone: + 231 225222
Telex: 44269, 44569
Telefax: +231 225770

General Manager: H-G Schneider
Technical Manager: H Demmer
Maintenance Mechanical Superintendent: S Abdullai
Railroad Engineer: F Hall
Chief Workshop Engineer: W Faure
Locomotives and Rolling Stock: R Knaut

Gauge: 1435 mm
Length: 78 km

The company operates four diesel-electric and one diesel-hydraulic line-haul locomotives, five diesel-hydraulic shunters, a diesel railcar, three trailers and 222 freight wagons.

Traffic	1987–88
Freight tonnage (million)	7
Freight tonne-km (million)	546
Average net freight train load (tonnes)	2750

Type of coupler in standard use: Scharfenberg centre coupler

Track
Rail: Type S49 and S54
Cross ties (sleepers): Type UIC 28
Spacing: 1588/km
Fastenings: Type K
Minimum curvature radius: 190 m
Max gradient: 1%
Max axleload: 25 tonnes

Diesel locomotives

Class	Wheel arrangement	Transmission	Rated power kW	Max speed km/h	Total weight tonnes	No in service 1987	Year first built	Builders Mechanical parts	Builders Engine & type	Builders Transmission
Line-haul										
01-04	Bo-Bo	Elec	1350	70	100	4	1964	Krauss Maffei	MAN VV 22/30	BBC
05	C-C	Hyd	2 × 588	60	114	1	1957	KHD	T12M 625	Voith L306V
Shunters										
2	B	Hyd	165	30	25	1	1962	Krauss Maffei	MAN 17-5/22	Voith L33YUB
3	C	Hyd	370	30/60	60	1	1969	Henschel	Henschel DHG 500 12V 1416A	Voith L37AB
4	C	Hyd	370	30/60	60	1	1976	Henschel	Henschel DHG 500 12V 1416A	Voith L4r4 SV2
5	B	Hyd	200	30	36	1	1968	Krauss Maffei	KHD BF-12L714	Voith L2R3U
6	C	Hyd	515	30	60	1	1977	Henschel	Henschel DHG 700 12V 1516A	Voith L4r4V2

Lamco Railroad
Lamco JV Operating Company

Roberts International Airport

Telephone: +231 22 11 90
Cable: Lamco, Monrovia
Telex: 44269 (Buchanan); 44293 (Nimba)

Manager, Lamco Railroad: H N Bas Koenen
Railroad Operating Superintendent: Brian Forster
Chief Engineers
  Workshops, Nimba: M Bryan Chesters
  Signals & Telecommunications: K Andersson

Electrical: Sten Henriksson
Railroad: Wayne Peacock
Maintenance Superintendent, Nimba: John W Hart

Gauge: 1435 mm
Route length: 267 km

Lamco, the Liberian American-Swedish Minerals Co, is an iron ore mining company which mined at Nimba and Tokadeh. The railway has served principally to move ore, latterly amounting to some 6.5 million tonnes annually, from these mines to the deep water port in Buchanan. The whole line is CTC controlled.

Signalling
Signalling is by the LM Ericsson JZA 711 system coupled to GRS Traffic Master II MIS. The Farinon radio link system is employed for communication.

Motive power and rolling stock
In 1989 motive power consisted of 24 diesel-electric locos. The number of ore wagons totalled 473, other freight stock, 72.

Diesel locomotives

Class	Wheel arrangement	Transmission	Rated power kW	Max speed km/h	Total weight tonnes	No in service 1985	Year first built	Builders Mechanical parts	Builders Engine & type	Builders Transmission
HG-16	Co-Co	Elec	1342	80	176	14	1962	Henschel	General Motors	EMD, licence-built by AEG
SD-10	Co-Co	Elec	1342	80	176	2	1980	General Motors (remanufactured by ICG)	General Motors	EMD
GP 10	Bo-Bo	Elec	1342	80	120	2	1979	General Motors (remanufactured by ICG)	General Motors	EMD
SW-900	Bo-Bo	Elec	671	80	120	5	1962	General Motors	General Motors	EMD
Ex-BR Class 08	0-6-0	Elec	298	32	49	1	Design 1933 Purchased 1973	British Rail	EE 6KT	English Electric

RAILWAY SYSTEMS / Liberia—Luxembourg

National Iron Ore Co Ltd

PO Box 548, Monrovia

General Manager: S K Datta Ray

Locomotive Superintendent: S Robert
Superintendent, Maintenance of Way: J Albert

Gauge: 1067 mm
Length: 145 km

The railway was opened in 1951. It operates 12 diesel locomotives, 253 ore and 28 other wagons. Annual traffic totals approximately 1 million tonnes.

Libya

Department of Road Transport and Railways

Shawa Esseidi, Secretariat of Communications Building, Tripoli

Telephone: +218 21 605808
Telex: 20401 nasekak ly

Director General: Ahmed Osman Ben Kafo
Director, Railways: Eng Alaeddin Al Wefati

With the dismantling of the British projection of 1435 mm-gauge from Egypt to Tobruk laid in the Second World War, no railways have run in Libya since 1965. Also discarded is the 950 mm system built around Tripoli and Benghazi on the eve of the First World War.

The present government, however, intends to build a new 1435 mm-gauge system from the Tunisian frontier to Tripoli and Misratah, then inland to Sebha, the country's third city, in the heart of a mineral-resource area. In November 1983 an agreement was signed for Chinese construction of the line for 170 km from Ras Jedir, on the border, to Tripoli. Construction would be supervised by Tesco-Uvaterv of Hungary, which has undertaken the engineering design of this project and was also contracted to study a 70 km Tripoli metro system. A longer-term objective is to construct a further, coastal line from Misratah to the Egyptian border via Benghazi and Tobruk. Misratah is the site of a major steel plant which would be fed with raw materials by unit trains from the Sebha area. Service by air-conditioned passenger trains is also planned.

In 1982 the government commissioned Sofrerail to create a new railway administration, define methods of administrative and operating management, plan the administrative buildings and also programme the installation of personnel. A further contract required Sofrerail to draft traction and rolling stock specifications and the relevant tender documents.

By the start of 1990 no progress had been reported on any of these projects. In the previous October Presidents Gaddafi of Libya and Moubarak of Egypt signed an agreement to rebuild the line from the Egyptian frontier at El Salloum to Tobruk.

Luxembourg

Ministry of Transport, Public Works & Energy

1018 Luxembourg

Minister: Robert Goebbels

Luxembourg Railways (CFL)
Société Nationale des Chemins de Fer Luxembourgeois

9 place de la Gare, PO Box 1803, 1018 Luxembourg

Telephone: +352 4 99 01
Telex: 2288 cfl lu
Telefax: +352 4 990 470

President: Jeannot Schneider
General Manager: Romain Kugener
Assistant Director, Technical: Ernest Junck
Operations Manager: Robert Molitor
Traction and Rolling Stock: Charles-Leon Mayer
Fixed Plant and Signalling Manager: Jean Meyer
Personnel Manager: Florent Gilson
Commercial Manager: Fernand Wirion
Financial Manager: Joseph Offenheim
Internal Control Manager: Gilbert Schmit

Gauge: 1435 mm
Route length: 272 km
Electrification: 178 km at 25 kV 50 Hz ac
  19 km at 3 kV dc

CLF is supported by a public service grant, which in 1989 amounted to LFr6931 million, just over three-quarters of the railway's total income.

Traffic

In 1989 CFL benefited from an economic upturn in the country, increasing its freight tonnage by some 6 per cent. The iron and steel industry is the major customer, its output forming 38.7 per cent of freight revenue in 1989. Just under a quarter of CFL's freight moves in unit trains; gross trainload weight averages 950 tonnes.

CFL is adopting the SNCF's ETNA system of freight traffic control (for details see France entry). A computer installation is to be achieved at Bettenbourg yard in 1991-92. Local depot terminals will also be linked with the SNCF's computer database at Lyon.

Passenger traffic contends with the Grand Duchy's heavy and ongoing expenditure on new interurban highways, including a Luxembourg City bypass, and on in-city parking provision, while development of rail services and their equipment has been meagre. Following a Sofrerail study, however, the train service pattern is now to be substantially revised to cater for changing patterns of travel demand.

CFL Class 3600 electric locomotive and Luxembourg-Belvaux train *(John C Baker)*

CFL Class 1800 diesel Co-Co and northbound freight at Bettembourg *(John C Baker)*

Electrification

The decision was taken in November 1981 to electrify and upgrade the only remaining diesel-operated through route, Luxembourg-Trois Vierges, which runs 75 km from north to south and is CFL's second busiest route. To contain cost, the line is being single-tracked for most of the distance between Ettelbrück and Trois Vierges, where there are 18 tunnels. SEL has the complementary resignalling contract between Luxembourg and Ettelbrück. The first stage, from Luxembourg to Ettelbrück and Diekirch, was completed and formally inaugurated in June 1989. The second stage, from Ettelbrück to Kautenbach/Wiltz, has begun and completion throughout is expected in 1993.

There was great concern that up to early 1990 pressure by both government and CFL had not persuaded the Belgians to upgrade and electrify their line from Liège and Gouvy to Trois Vierges. However, rerouting of some ore trains from Antwerp to the Arbed steel plant at Esch-Belval via Trois Vierges has encouraged hope of Belgian action.

Luxembourg station modernisation

The Luxembourg city station has been improved. A fourth island platform has been added and the track

Electric locomotives

Class	Wheel arrangement	Line voltage	Rated output (kW) one-hour	Max speed km/h	Weight tonnes	Wheel diameter mm	Length mm	No in service	Year first built	Builders Mechanical parts	Builders Electrical equipment
3600	Bo-Bo	25 kV	3600	120	84	1250	15 200	19	1958	MTE	MTE

Diesel locomotives

Class	Wheel arrangement	Transmission	Rated power hp	Max speed km/h	Total weight tonnes	No in service	Year first built	Builders Mechanical parts	Builders Engine & type	Builders Transmission
800	Bo-Bo	Elec	875	80	74	6	1954	AFB	GM 8-567B	GM
850	Bo-Bo	Elec	825	105	72	8	1956	B & L	SACM MGO V-12 SH	B & L
900	Bo-Bo	Elec	925	105	72	13	1958	B & L	SACM MGO V-12 SHR	B & L
1600	Co-Co	Elec	1600	120	108	4	1955	AFB	GM 16-567C	GM
1800	Co-Co	Elec	1800	120	110/114	20	1963	BN	GM 16-567C	GM

layout revised to raise the speed limit on some tracks from 30 to 60 km/h. By the end of 1992 a new computerised signalling centre will have replaced the six existing signalboxes.

International services
In February 1990 ageement was reached in principle that, should the French TGV-Est be built, Luxembourg would have four daily TGV services to and from both Paris and Strasbourg in exchange for putting up Ffr450 million towards necessary infrastructure works, including construction of a Beaudrecourt spur. Meanwhile, Brussels–Luxembourg service was raised to regular-interval frequency in May 1990; the SNCF is considering extension of its Nancy–Metz–Thionville 'Métrolor' regional service to Luxembourg; and the DB has a through Frankfurt–Luxembourg service under study.

Motive power
During 1988 CFL operated 19 electric, 24 line-haul and 27 shunting diesel-electric locomotives, 14 diesel tractors, eight two-car dmus, two three-car and six two-car emus, 75 passenger cars (including 12 Corail cars of the SNCF-CFL pool) and 2551 freight wagons.

The traction fleet is now elderly and new acquisitions are planned in the 1990s, with the extension of electrification particularly in mind. The first purchase is of 22 SNCF-type Z2 emus, being delivered by De Dietrich with GEC-Alsthom electrical equipment and ANF bogies between June 1990 and April 1992. For 1993 CFL seeks 14 three-car emus, 10 25 kV ac and three dual-voltage 25 kV ac/3 kV dc locomotives, the latter hopefully for through working into Belgium. In 1997 CFL hopes to buy eight more 25 kV and 11 more dual-voltage locomotives, together with 17 passenger cars.

Track
Rails: UIC 60, 54 and U33
Cross ties (sleepers): Wood
Thickness: 150 mm
Spacing: 1435 mm
Rail fastenings: 'K' fastenings

Traffic (million)	1985	1986	1987	1988	1989
Freight tonne-km	645	604	593	638·9	703·68
Freight tonnage	16·7	15·7	14·8	16·59	17·86
Passenger-km	229	225	214	223	NA
Passenger journeys	NA	10·6	10·3	10·73	NA

Finances (LFr million) Revenue	1985	1986	1987	1988	1989
Passengers and baggage	347·8	359·2	374·3	392·3	394·9
Freight	1595·4	1467·2	1394·8	1500·4	1564·3
Other	153·6	157·7	125·9	161·4	199·4
State subsidies and compensations	5966·7	6226·2	6700·0	6565·0	6931·0
Total	8063·7	8210·6	8629·3	8619·0	9089·6
Expenditure					
Staff/personnel	6299·8	6528·4	6884·1	6991·5	7263·9
Materials and services	784·8	719·3	758·3	675·3	770·1
Taxes	96·6	98·9	57·9	53·2	53·4
Financial charges	281·3	249·0	298·4	244·8	264·7
Depreciation	461·8	545·6	559·2	610·1	657·9
Other	242·6	260·1	270·5	266·3	289·4
Total	8167·1	8401·3	8828·4	8958·8	9299·4
Deficit	103·4	190·7	199·1	222·3	209·8

Signalling and train control
CFL is pursuing a plan to concentrate signalling of each route on a single centre, supported by the new installation at Luxembourg itself.

Installation of AWS equipment in traction units is a major item of recent investment. Now in progress is equipment of all units and the necessary fixed equipment installation for track-to-train radio.

Madagascar

Société d'État Réseau National des Chemins de Fer Malagasy (RNCFM)

PO Box 259, 1 Avenue de l'Indépendance, Antananarivo 101

Telephone: +261 2 205 21
Telex: 222 33 cfm tn mg

General Director: Samuel Razanamapisa
Technical Director: Gilles Richard Rosoamanana
Commercial Director: Cathérine Raasoanirina
Financial Director: Auguste Rajaonarivony
Heads of Departments
  General Affairs: Henri Désiré Rasamimanana
  Finance: Jean Armand Ramamonjisoa
  General Studies: Jean Claude Rajemialisoa
  Supply and Stores: Sébastien Rakotondravao
  Traction and Rolling Stock: Jacky Rambelotsalmanirina
  Operations: Alexis Rabejoel
  Track and Structures: Aimé Victor Mosa
  Building and Domanial Affairs: Noelson Rabefaritra
  Industrial Wood Treatment Centre: Roger Rabetsoa
  Southern Region (FCE): Roger Rajaona
  Training Centre: Denis Razafindrabe
  Equipment: Claude Roger Rajaonarison

Gauge: 1000 mm
Route length: 1054 km

The Malagasy railways system lies mostly in the central-eastern region of the country.

Its northern system comprises three main lines: the TCE (Antananarivo-Eastern Coast) 380 km, connecting Antananarivo in the inland with the port of Tamatave; the MLA (Moramanga-Ambatosoratra), connected to the TCE, which runs between Moramanga and Lake Alaotra, the rice-producing region (180 km); and the TA (Antananarivo-Antsirabé) serving the far southern region of Antananarivo (154km).

The southern system consists of one main line, the FCE (Fianarantsoa-Eastern Coast). This 163·3 km route serves the Fianarantsoa semi-industrial region from Manakara harbour.

Since 1982, the railway has been established as a state-owned society operating under the country's laws governing anonymous societies, which allow some independence in commercial policy-making.

New lines
In the south of the country the mountainous territory has extraordinarily rich and very diverse mineral deposits. RNCFM was expected in 1989 to finish a 27 km extension of the TA to a new cement works 1800 m above sea level in the Ibity mountain massif. The government has lately ordered a feasibility study of an extension almost 900 km long from Antsirabé and Ibity south to Tuléar, through almost uninhabited terrain, to exploit the barely tapped mineral resources of the area.

Rice production is being energetically developed at the northern end of the MLA. In the rainy season road traffic is severely handicapped, so a 35 km rail extension from Ambatosoratra around Lake Alaotra to Imerimandroso was begun in 1986, to facilitate shipment of rice from the territory.

The busiest line is that from Antananarivo to Toamasina, which bears about 85 per cent of RNCFM's traffic but which is now in competition with a newly-

RAILWAY SYSTEMS / Madagascar

completed macadamised road and its encouragement of higher-capacity road freight vehicles. Freight traffic includes a rising component of containers; a terminal at the Indian Ocean port of Toamasina has been complemented by one on the outskirts of Antananarivo at Soanierana.

Finances
Despite the sharpening road competition, RNCFM has lately come close to eliminating annual deficits. This achievement is attributed to operational rationalisation, improved service, and exploitation of pricing freedom.

Signalling and traffic control
With World Bank aid under the Third Railway Project, the MLA line has been equipped with a radio telecommunications system that should greatly improve the efficiency of traffic control and train-set use in the chrome ore export flow to Toamasina and in rice movement.

Motive power and rolling stock

	Number
Diesel locomotives	29
Diesel railcars	9
Passenger coaches	60
Freight wagons	725

In mid-1989 RNCFM took delivery of three more 1600hp Type AD16B diesel locomotives (RNCFM Class BB250) from GEC-Alsthom for use on the southern system. The total of this type is now 27, since 24 were delivered in 1986-87. Future planned purchases include four shunting locomotives, four railcars and 10 passenger cars. Hitherto France has been the exclusive supplier of traction and rolling stock.

Type of coupler in standard use: Freight cars, Willison automatic, Madagascar type; passenger cars, De Dietrich, Soulé

Type of brake in standard use, locomotive-hauled stock: Automatic air; direct air; and vacuum

Track
Rails: S25, 26, 30, 36, 30 US, 30 East, 37 English
Sleepers: Wood 1920 × 220 × 150 mm; Steel 1900 × 294 × 147 mm
Spacing: 166/km wood; 1500/km steel
Fastenings: Screw (wood sleepers); frog (steel sleepers)
Minimum curvature radius: 80 m
Max gradient: 3·5%
Max axleload: 16 tonnes

Type ZE800 diesel railcar supplied by De Dietrich

Type AD16B diesel locomotive from Alsthom, RNCFM Class BB250, and container train on TCE line

Traffic	1986	1987
Freight tonnage	640 000	596 335
Freight tonne-km (million)	221·895	200·925
Passenger-km (million)	200·456	205·076
Passengers (million)	2·525	2·744

Finance (MGF million)		
Revenue	1986	1987
Passengers and baggage	2123	2490
Freight, parcels and mail	9404	9278
Other income	3689	1798
Total	15 216	13 566

Expenditure	1986	1987
Staff/personnel expenses	4852	5275
Materials and services	7068	6235
Depreciation	1993	2000
Financial charges	1224	2805
Total	15 137	16 315

Principal diesel locomotives

Class	Wheel arrangement	Transmission	Rated power hp	Max speed km/h	Length mm	Total weight tonnes	No in service 1987	Year first built	Builders Mechanical parts	Builders Engine & type
BB 200	Bo-Bo	Power-shift	1050	70	13 630	56	4	1965-68	Alsthom/SACM	MGO V12
BB 220	Bo-Bo	Power-shift	1200	70	11 775	58	18	1973-82	Alsthom/SACM	MGO V12
BB 250	Bo-Bo	Power-shift	1600	70	—	64	24	1986-87	Alsthom	UD 30 V16RS

Diesel railcars

Class	Cars per unit	Motored axles per motor car	Transmission	Rated power hp per motor	Max speed km/h	Weight tonnes per car	Total seating capacity	Length per car mm	No in service 1987	Year first built	Builders Mechanical parts	Builders Engine & type	Transmission
ZE 800	1	2	Power-shift	650	70	33	36	18 864	4	1958	De Dietrich	MGO V8	Alsthom
ZE 900	1	2	Power-shift	750	70	39	42	18 830	4	1967	Soulé	Poyaud V12	Alsthom
ZE 700	1	1	Power-shift	900	70	34	34	17 780	1	1983	Soulé	MGO V12	

Malawi

Ministry of Transport and Communications

Private Bag 322, Capital City, Lilongwe 3

Telephone: +265 730122
Cable: Trancom, Lilongwe

Minister: Dalton Katopola
Principal Secretary: J L Kalemera

Malawi Railways Ltd (MR)

PO Box 5144, Limbe

Telephone: +265 640844
Cable: Marailas, Limbe
Telex: 44810

Chairman: Christopher Barrow
Directors: I C Bonongwe
  E B Kadzako
  Dr I A J Nankwenya
  E F W MacPherson
  E B Salifu
  Mrs R R Semu
  Secretary, Transport and Communications or representative (Ex-officio)
  Secretary, Economic Planning and Development or representative (Ex-officio)
  Secretary to the Treasury or Representative (Ex-officio)
General Manager: W L Gillman
Assistant General Manager (Projects): K A Manjolo
Divisional Manager, Rail Service: H T Thindwa (Acting)
Divisional Manager, Engineering & Supplies: E R Limbe (Acting)
Financial Controller: R S Foster-Brown
Chief Personnel Manager: M J Banda (Acting)
Chief Traffic Manager: O Khofi (Acting)
Chief Mechanical Engineer: S L Takomana
Chief Civil Engineer: G J Kavwenje (Acting)
Lake Service Manager: A C Nkana
Supplies Manager: D P Msyani (Acting)
Security Superintendent: A E G Mankhambo
Management Accountant: K Karuna Karan
Internal Auditor: E H Msowoya

Results	1984/85	1985/86	1986/87	1987/88	1988/89
Freight tonnage (000)	543	460·8	550·1	415	347
Freight tonne-km (million)	109·092	99·135	132·17	95·164	70·649
Passenger-km (million)	113·485	121·457	108·388	114·231	111·609
Passenger journeys (000)	1720	1814	1639	1750	1664

Finance (MK 000)

Revenue	1984/85	1985/86	1986/87	1987/88	1989/90
Passengers and baggage	2076	2514	2869	3609	4431
Freight, parcels and mail	8702	9564	13 238	12 115	11 606
Hire of locomotives	560	107	—	—	—
Traffic sundry receipts	950	867	—	—	—
Outside work	308	167	—	—	—
Miscellaneous	3934	3693	4973	5245	5444
Total	16 530	16 912	21 080	20 969	21 481

Expenditure	1984/85	1985/86	1986/87	1987/88	1988/89
Staff/personnel	7004	7089	7953	9259	9217
Materials and services	10 549	10 985	11 667	11 961	13 083
Depreciation	2787	2604	2768	2693	2780
Financial charges	3000	195	272	265	550
Total	22 340	20 873	22 660	24 178	25 630

Gauge: 1067 mm
Route length: 797 m

A single-track line runs from Mchinji near the Zambian border through Lilongwe and Blantyre to the southern border with Mozambique. This line connects with the Mozambique port of Beira. A line from Nkaya to Nayuci on the eastern border with Mozambique connects with the port of Nacala.

In addition to the railway the administration operates passenger and cargo services on Lake Malawi, connecting with the rail system at Chipoka at the south end of the water.

Investment

Approximately MK 7.8 million was provided for 1990/91 by the UK to finance an ongoing rehabilitation programme that includes local concrete sleeper manufacture, upgrading of track and the repair of bridges. A total of MK 34 million has been assigned to this project under a British Aid Phase II programme spread over six years.

Motive power and rolling stock

The locomotive fleet at the end of 1989 comprised 32 main-line diesel-electrics, 11 diesel-hydraulic units and eight diesel-hydraulic shunters. The rolling stock fleet consisted of 814 goods wagons, one diesel railcar and 38 passenger coaches including one restaurant car.

Following 1988 agreement of a USAID grant of US$8 million, the railway was to have its 19 MLW-built diesel locomotives re-engined.

Type of coupler in standard use: AAR 10 Automatic profile.
Type of brake in standard use: Vacuum

Track

Standard rail: BSR 30 kg/m, length 12.2 m
BSA 30 kg/m, length 48·8 m; BSA 40 kg/m, length 48·8 m and cwr
Sleepers
Timber, steel and concrete

Spacing in plain track	Spacing in curved track
Timber 1310/km	1476/km
Steel (30 kg) 1310/km	1476/km
Concrete 1430/km	1640/km

Fastenings: Pandrol clips, coach screws, clips and bolts, elastic rail spikes
Minimum curve radius: 111 m
Max axleload: 15 tonnes

Diesel locomotives

Class	Wheel arrangement	Transmission	Rated power hp	Max speed mph	Total weight tonnes	No in service 1989	Year first built	Builders Mechanical parts	Engine & type	Transmission
Shunter	0-6-0	Hyd	340	24	40·5	2	1962	Bagnall	Rolls-Royce C8 TFL-IV	Twin Disc
Shunter	0-6-0	Hyd	355	25	43	2	1967	Andrew Barclay	Cummins NT400	Twin Disc
Shunter	0-6-0	Hyd	388	16	40	4	1974	Hunslet	Cummins NT400	Twin Disc
Light-line	B-B	Hyd	2 × 380	35	38	2	1967	Nippon Sharyo	Cummins NH-380	Niigata
Light-line	B-B	Hyd	540	35	38	7	1968	Nunslet Taylor	Cummins VT-12	Niigata
Light-line	B-B	Hyd	2 × 380	35	38	4	1972	Nippon Sharyo	Cummins NTA855L	Niigata
Main-line	Co-Co	Elec	1200	50	81	9	1963	Metro Cammell	Sulzer 6 LDA 28B	AEI
Main-line	Co-Co	Elec	1500	64	86	19	1973	MLW	Alco 251 Type E	GE
Main-line	Co-Co	Elec	1400	50	81	4	1965	Metro Cammell	Sulzer 6 LDA 28C	AEI

Diesel railcars or multiple-units

Class	Cars per unit	Motor cars per unit	Motored axles per motor car	Transmission	Rated power (hp) per motor	Max speed km/h	Weight tonnes per car	Total seating capacity	No in service 1988	Year first built	Builders Mechanical parts	Engine & type	Transmission
DRC	1	1	2	Hyd	200	50	33	27	1	1952	Drewry	Leyland RE-902	Sinclair 550

Malaysia

Ministry of Transport

Wisma Perdana, Tingkat 3-9, Jalan Dungun 50490, Damansara Heights, Kuala Lumpur

Telephone: +60 3 254 8122
Telex: 30999 ma
Telefax: +60 3 255 7041

Minister: Dato' Dr Ling Liong Sik
Secretary-General: Dato' R V Navaratnam

Malayan Railway Administration (KTM)
Pertadbiran Keretapi Tanah Melayu

PO Box 100001, Jalan Sultan Hishamuddin, 50050 Kuala Lumpur

Telephone: +60 3 274 9422
Telex: 32925 ktm pb ma
Telefax: +60 3 274 9424

General Manager: Sulaimin bin Hashim
Deputy General Manager, Marketing & Operations: Abdul Rahim bin Osman
Infrastructure & Technical: L J Kee
Director, Personnel: Samat bin Mahat
Finance: Mrs M Johari
Civil Engineering: Chuah Chow Hee

668 RAILWAY SYSTEMS / Malaysia

Mechanical Engineering: Mazlan bin Waad
Freight Traffic: Mohd Zin bin Yusop
Passenger Service: S Apputhurai
Signalling: P Satyamoorthy
Stores Superintendent: Rahiminb Harrish
Chief of Computer Unit: Chan Kim Beng

Gauge: 1000 mm
Route length: 1672 km

Principal route is the 787 km main line from Singapore north through the capital, Kuala Lumpur, to Butterworth, one of Malaysia's principal sea ports on the west coast of the peninsula. Short branches reach sea ports at Port Weld, Telok Anson, Port Kelang and Port Dickson. The other major route is the 528 km east coast line running northwards from a junction with the Singapore-Butterworth main line at Gemas to Kota Baaru and Tum Pat. Both lines are linked with the State Railway of Thailand.

Privatisation progress

In April 1989 Transport Minister King Liong Sik announced that a state-owned public corporation was to be set up to run KTM, though a firm date for the transfer remains to be set.

The government has been seeking to privatise KTM since late 1986, in line with its general objective of contracting the country's public industrial sector. At first it offered virtually to give the system away to any concern willing to operate the railway intact as a commercial enterprise. Mature consideration, however, prompted the commissioning in 1988 of a group of merchant bankers to consider all the implications of a handover and prepare a coherent plan. The bankers' findings have not been published. But it seems likely that they stressed a need to shape KTM as a free-standing enterprise to make it marketable.

Thus, financial independence will be the key characteristic of the new KTM corporation when it takes over. KTM's accumulated deficit is not a privatisation stumbling-block; that was eliminated from any private sector purchaser's liabilities by legislation passed in March 1987.

Management reorganisation

KTM management has already taken significant steps to develop bottom-line responsibility. In 1988 substantial responsibility was devolved from the centre to newly-appointed regional managers based at Johor Bahru, Butterworth, Ipoh, Gemas, Kuala Lumpur and Krai. In 1989 separate budgeting for, and dedication of resources to passenger and freight traffic was being introduced. KTM is also trying to identify the indirect costs incurred by individual traffics.

Passenger traffic

KTM operates a comprehensive network of passenger services over almost all its lines. In addition to ordinary train services, the system operates day and night Singapore-Kuala Lumpur and Kuala Lumpur-Butterworth express trains, and a single daily express between Gemas and Tum Pat on the east coast line. In conjunction with the State Railway of Thailand, KTM runs a daily International Express between Butterworth and Bangkok. An air-conditioned lounge car features in the Butterworth-Kuala Lumpur-Singapore 'Sinaran Express'; KTM plans to add on-board telephone and telex facilities.

Principal passenger trains now carry train managers to improve service to users and ensure prompt attention to vehicle defects.

New Ganz-Ikarus railbuses have entered service between Singapore and Kulasi, and between Butterworth and Ipoh.

Since 1970 long-distance travel has soared spectacularly, lifting annual passenger-km from 620 million to over 1600 million in the mid-1980s and passenger journeys to more than 6·5 million. Passenger revenue now surpasses that of freight.

Computerised ticketing is operational and from 1988 has covered seat reservation.

Freight traffic

Management sees freight as the railway's sector with the greater 1990s promise, not only of expansion but also of profitability.

Container traffic is the mainspring. Begun in 1974, this had become KTM's third biggest freight earner by 1988, when 67 000 TEUs were recorded, and was expected to top the revenue league in 1989, with over 100,000 TEU logged. A significant component of the growth has been containers from southern Thailand, which have a quicker haul across the border at Padang Besar to a Malaysian port than to Bangkok. Around a quarter of southern Thailand's rubber exports are shipped through Butterworth. The current congestion of Bangkok is another deterrent that attracts Thai business to KTM.

In 1989 the Thai government approved development of Port Klang as a gateway for international maritime container traffic to and from Thailand. In view of the prospective traffic growth, KTM sought bids for double-tracking of the branch from Kuala Lumpur to Port Klang.

At present KTM serves Kontena Nasional's Inland Clearance Depots (ICD) at Kuala Lumpur, Ipoh and Prai. KTM was urging the government to budget in its sixth National Plan for creation of five more, at Padang Besar, Ipoh, Alor Star, Tampin, Kluang and Tanah Merah/Wakaf Bharu.

Because KTM is metre-gauge and its tunnel clearances consequently modest, the railway cannot readily accept all container sizes. But its stock of some 800 container flatcars does include a number that permit carriage of 8ft 6in-high boxes.

A programme of bridge strengthening is in hand to permit a lift of maximum permissible freight axle-loading from the present 16 to 20 tonnes. Another move is directed to increasing permissible gross train weight by about 50 per cent, by changing from hook couplers to an automatic knuckle-type, which is now standardised in all new construction. The old-style coupler fixes a ceiling of 1200 tonnes on gross train weight. Though the general limit with the automatic coupler goes up to 1800 tonnes, a recent train-set of wagons for the cement industry is designed for 2400 tonnes gross.

New lines

National economic stresses have perforce shelved a scheme of the mid-1980s for a new east-west, coast-to-coast line, to run for 214 miles from Paka via Kuala Lumpur to Port Kelang, to cater for industrial development anticipated as a by-product of offshore gas and oil exploration.

The only new line project now under consideration is

Class 24 and Class 22 diesel locomotives head Bangkok-Kuala Lumpur international express at Ipoh (Marcel Vleugels)

Ganz-Ikarus railbus on Singapore island (Wilhelm Pflug)

KTM mixed train at Kuala Lipis (Wilhelm Pflug)

Malaysia—Mali / RAILWAY SYSTEMS 669

for a first railway in Sarawak, where indifferent communications hamper both the timber and the tourist industry. The government recently approved feasibility study by the Bintulu Development Agency of a line from Bintulu port to Belaga, in central Sarawak.

Much of the 340 million ringgits that KTM was authorised to invest in the fifth (1986-90) plan has been concentrated on the Singapore-Butterworth trunk.

Except in the taxing mountain pass area between Taiping and Padang Rengas KTM aims to double-track the Singapore-Butterworth line throughout, ease curves to a minimum 100 m radius, install 60 kg/m rail and resignal so that passenger train speeds of up to 130 km/h at least will be possible.

KTM's ambition is by 1995 to run passenger trains over the 245 miles from Kuala Lumpur to Singapore in a flat 5 hours. The fastest schedule in 1988 was 6 hours 40 minutes. The faster running is a more realistic prospect since KTM was enabled in 1988 to place a 1 billion-rupee contract with IRCON for track renewal of virtually the entire Kuala Lumpur-Singapore route.

Investment
With his April 1989 announcement of the new KTM corporation concept, the Transport Minister forecast investment in KTM equivalent to US$645 million. That stilled some apprehension that spending would be curbed pending a private sector takeover. Soon afterwards the promise was elaborated by the country's Deputy Prime Minister, who outlined a big development programme to be completed by 1993.

Double-tracking would take in, besides the Port Klang branch and Subang Airport mentioned above, the sector from Rawang, north of Kuala Lumpur, to Seremban. These moves, besides raising track capacity, would halve Kuala Lumpur-Port Klang journey time to 30 minutes and cut the transit from Rawang to Seremban from 1 hour 30 minutes to 1 hour. Passenger services would be doubled and the upgrading programme would also raise maximum freight train speed from 40 to 60 km/h. The freight service would be supported by a new data transmission network.

KTM was soon afterward authorised to import 30 new sleeping cars to reinforce the well-equipped, air-conditioned rolling stock it already deploys on the through Singapore-Kuala Lumpur and Kuala Lumpur-Butterworth day and night trains.

KTM has submitted a case for purchase of a further 35 main-line diesel locomotives, to reinforce the high-power units bought from Japan in the past four years, and also for signalling modernisation, this last to embrace CTC and new interlockings in the Kuala Lumpur area.

In late 1989 tenders were invited for the supply of 18 three- or four-car air-conditioned diesel train-sets.

In 1990 a US$395 million soft loan was obtained for an upgrading programme from the Japanese Overseas Development Assistance Programme.

Signalling
Siemens is equipping sections of the west coast line with tokenless block and colour-light signalling of stations. KTM intends to install a radio communications system because of the chronic pilfering of the wire of its existing telephone network.

Motive power and rolling stock
The traction fleet in 1987 comprised 144 diesel locomotives. The passenger stock totalled 304 coaches and freight stock 5012 vehicles.

The 25 main-line locomotives recently supplied by Toshiba are designated Class 24. They are powered by 2400 hp SEMT-Pielstick 16PA4-200VG engines from the Alsthom group and have a top speed of 130 km/h.

Ganz-Mávag/Ikarus won a contract to supply five three-car and five five-car two-axle diesel railbus sets powered by Cummins NTA 855R engines with Twin Disc transmissions.

Track
Standard rail: Flat bottom in 40 ft (12·2 m) lengths
  Main line: 40 and 60 kg/m
Rail fastening: Elastic spikes
Cross ties (sleepers): Malayan hardwoods 242 × 127 × 2000 mm
Spacing: 1666/km
Filling: 2½ in limestone ballast to a depth of 6 in under sleepers
Max curvature: 12·25° = radius of 142 m
Ruling gradient: 1% = 1 in 100; except Taiping Pass 1·25% = 1 in 80
Longest continuous gradient: 8·2 km on Prai-Singapore main line, with 1·25% (1 in 80) grade, sharpest curve 12·25° (142 m radius) for a length of 320 m
Max altitude: 137 m near Taiping
Max axleload: 16 tons

Diesel locomotives

Class	Wheel arrangement	Transmission	Rated power hp (kW)	Max speed km/h	Total weight tonnes	No in service 1987	Year first built	Builders Mechanical parts	Builders Engine & type	Builders Transmission
20	Co-Co	Electric	1500 (1119)	96	96	13	1956-57	English Electric	English Electric 12 SVT	English Electric
21	Bo-Bo	Hydraulic	1060 (790)	96	52	24	1968	KSK-Japan	MTU-12VTC 11	Voith
22	Co-Co	Electric	1710 (1276)	96	84	39	1971	—	—	—
23	Co-Co	Electric	2160 (1611)	96	90	15	1983	Hitachi	Pielstick 12PAH-200PG	Hitachi
24	Co-Co	Electric	2400 (1790)	120	90	25	1987	Kawasaki	Pielstick 16PA4-V-200VG	Toshiba

Mali

Ministry of Public Works & Transport

Minister of Transport: Cheikh Oumar Doumbia
Director General: Noumoucounda Savané
Secretary General: Oussouby Soumare

Chemins de Fer du Mali (RCFM)

BP 260, Bamako

Telephone: +233 22 2967/8
Telex: 586 fer mali bamako

Director General: Abdoulaye Mangassy
Deputy Director-General, Planning and Administration: Mamadou Sidibe
Directors, Personnel: Youssouf Sacko
  Investment and Projects: D SOry
  Supplies: Mamadou Bah
  Operations: Daouda Diane
  Commercial: Abdoulaye Bah
  Buffets & Hotels: Abdoulaye Magassy

Gauge: 1000 mm
Route length: 641 km

The former Dakar-Niger Railway starts at Dakar in Senegal and runs inland via Kayes to the River Niger. The present CF du Mali is that portion of the line inside its territory, the remainder being the CF du Senégal. A new line linking Bamako, capital of Mali, with Conakry, capital of Guinea, is planned to give Mali an alternative outlet to the Atlantic with a route length of 800 km, of which 600 km will be in Guinea.

Traffic
Recovery of major international traffic role is a prime management objective and this has been recognised in a new contract with the government. The latter has proclaimed RCFM to be its main means for spurring development in the west of the country. The railway currently records annually some 195 million passenger-km and 200 milion freight tonne-km.

Investment
Under the 1986–90 five year plan the railway undertook renewal of 114 km of track between Kayes and

Soulé diesel-electric railcar (Wilhelm Pflug)

Mahina, also of 60 km between Bamako and Koulikore, reconstruction of Kayes station and telecommunications improvement. Finance was procured for this programme from Canadian, Belgian and Italian sources.

Motive power

RCFM owns a total of 30 line-haul diesel locomotives, two diesel shunters, four diesel-electric railcars, 19 trailers, 19 other passenger coaches and 545 freight wagons. The locomotive fleet includes 11 Alsthom Type BB1100, 12 GM-Canada CC2200 and seven Alsthom CC2400.

In common with RCFS of Senegambia (qv), RCFM was planning in 1989 to acquire and adapt for metre gauge 20 redundant French Railways Type B10t passenger cars of the 'Bruhat' type.

Mauritania

Mauritanian National Railways (TFM-SNIM)

PO Box 42, Nouadhibou

Telephone: 1691
Cable: SNIM-Fer Nouadhibou
Telex: 426 mtn

Minister of Mining & Industry: Ahmed Ould Jiddou
General Manager: Mohamed Saleck Ould Heyine
Director of Harbour & Port: M A Ould Taleb Mohamed
Head of Movement and Traction: Mohamed Khalifa Ould Beyah
Head of Permanent Way: Zeidane Ould Hmeida

Gauge: 1435 mm
Route length: 689 km

The line, completed in 1963, runs from Mouadhibou (ex-Port Etienne) to Tazadit for the transport of iron ore from the mines at F'Derik (ex-Fort Gouraud).

Built and originally operated by Miferma, the line was nationalised in 1974 and is now operated by Société Nationale Industrielle et Minière (SNIM).

Modernisation

In 1987 SNIM was granted a European Investment Bank loan of 10 million ecus, supplementing assistance from other sources to permit a modernisation programme valued at 62 million ecus. Most of this would be assigned to non-railway projects, but the port rail system of Nouadhibou was also to benefit.

Traffic

Principal traffic is iron ore shipments. Average net freight train load is almost 11 000 tonnes. Passenger traffic is slight.

Traffic (million)	1985	1986	1988
Freight tonnes	9·401	9·568	9·515

Motive power and rolling stock

Equipment consists of 30 main-line diesel-electric locomotives, 11 shunting diesel-electrics, 1421 freight wagons and eight passenger-carrying cars.

Track

Standard rail: 54 kg/m UIC
Welded joints: Practically the whole line was laid with long-welded rail: 8 × 18 m railbars were flash-butt welded at the depot into 144 m lengths, which after laying were Thermit welded into continuous rail. Longest individual length of welded rail is 80 km
Cross ties (sleepers): Type U28 steel, weight 75 kg
Spacing: 600 mm
Rail fastening: Clips and bolts to metal sleepers
Max curvature: 1·75° = minimum radius of 1000 m
Max gradient: 0·5% (1 in 200) against loaded trains 1·0% (1 in 100) against empty trains
Max altitude: 350 m
Max axleload: 25 tonnes
Max speed: Loaded trains 50 km/h; empty 60 km/h
Type of signalling: Radio control

Diesel line-haul locomotives

Class	Wheel arrangement	Transmission	Rated power hp	Max speed km/h	Total weight tonnes	No in service 1988	Year first built	Builders Mechanical parts	Engine & type	Transmission
Alsthom	Co-Co	Elec	2500	50/60 (loaded/empty trains)	138	20	1961	Alsthom	SACM MGO V16 BSHR / SACM MGO V12	Alsthom / RVR
GM-EMD	Co-Co	Elec	3000	70	137	10	1982	EMD	EMD 645 E3	EMD
BL (France)	Bo-Bo	Elec	850	80	73	11	1961	Brissonneau et Lotz	SACM MGO V12 ASHR	Brissonneau et Lotz

Mexico

Department of Transport and Communications

Avenida Universidad y Xola, Col Narvarte, 030228 Mexico 12, DF

Telephone: + 52 5 519 7456/9203
Telefax: +52 5 530 1074

Secretary: Lic Andrés Caso Lombardo
Under-Secretary: C P Gustavo Patiño G

Ferrocarriles Nacionales de Mexico (FN de M)

Avenida Central 140, 06538 Mexico City, DF

Telephone: +52 5 177 3999 fnme
1773111 fnme

Chairman: Lic Andres Caso Lombardo
Director General: Ing Carlos Orlozco Sosà
Assistant Directors General
  Finance: Miguel Villaseñor Miranda
  Motive Power and Rolling Stock: J Vargas S
  Operations: Epifanio Viveros Mejia
  Planning and Systems: E Avalos de Leungas
  Purchases and Stores: Lic Gustavo Cortes Fuentes
  Personnel and General Services: E Arroyo S
  New Line Construction: Ing Eduardo Barousse Moreno
  Traffic: Ing Rodolfo Dominguez Calzada
  Maintenance of Communications: Ing Romualdo Ruiz Castro
General Comptroller: Martha Aguirre Simenez

Gauge: 1435 mm; 914 mm
Route length: 20216 km; 90 km

FNM extends from the northern border with the USA from the cities of Matamoros and Nuevo Laredo, Tamaulipas, from Piedras Negras and Ciudad Acuña, Coahuila and from Ciudad Juarez, Chihuahua to the southern border with Guatemala at Ciudad Hidalgo, Chiapas.

On the Gulf of Mexico, it connects with the ports of Coatzacoalcos, Veracruz, and Tampico, and also, as a result of mergers, Campeche and Progreso. On the Pacific Ocean, it serves the ports of Puerto Madero, Salina Cruz, and Manzanillo; and, since the 1980 completion of a line from Coróndiro, the port of Lázaro Cárdenas.

In the interior, it connects the important cities of Mexico City, Querétaro, Leon, Aguascalientes,

First of GE Type E60C 4400 kW electric Co-Cos for FNdeM

Cacatecas, Durango, Toreon, Chihuahua, San Luis Potosi, Saltillo, Monterrey, Ciudad Frontera (Coahuila), Morelia, Guadalajara, Colima, Pueblo, Oaxaco, Jalapa and Orizaba.

In August 1987 Ferrocarril del Pacifico, Ferrocarril Chihuahua al Pacifico and Perrocarril Sonora Baja California were merged with FNM, which completed the latter's absorption of all common carrier railways in Mexico.

Freight traffic
FNM continues to shape more of its freight working of major commodities, principally ore and grain but also fertilisers and cement, into block trains that are not remarshalled en route. With the aim of lifting maximum trainloads to 5600 tonnes on some routes, FNM is adopting the Locotrol system of mid-train 'slave' locomotive control.

A drastic reduction of the points at which less-than-wagonload freight is handled from over 600 to just 42 is in hand, to fit the railway for its prime role as a bulk mover. The railway is keen, though, to expand its merchandise business through piggyback (refrigerated trailers incoming from the US now amount to some 15 000 a year) and containers, and is energetically promoting the construction of private sidings.

In 1990 two double-stack container services were launched across the Mexican-US border. One was running from Southern Pacific's Long Beach terminal in California to Mexico City. In the other, FNdeM combined with the Santa Fe Railway and Rail-Bridge Corp, a subsidiary of the maritime K Line, in an operation branded Azteca and designed for Far East-Mexican trade, between K Line's ITS terminal in Long Beach and Mexico City's Pantaco terminal and Monterrey.

Tight economic conditions are checking increases of traffic. The 1988 results were slightly down on those of the previous year.

Passenger traffic
Commanding only 1 per cent of the national long-haul passenger market, FNdeM has been energetically courting new business on key routes with trains of new or former US railroad cars substantially refurbished and improved on-board service supported by special fare offers, including tickets packaging on-board meal service. A new top tier of train is branded 'Estrella' and equipped with specially furnished cars, including observation-bar cars. These air-conditioned trains are first-class only and rate a supplementary fare. They are run by both day and night in addition to standard trains on the routes they serve.

In February 1990 the government announced intention to build new electrified double-track lines to cater with 120 km/h trains for five satellite towns that are to be created within a 70 km radius of Mexico City, to drain off some of the capital's inexorably rising population.

Finance
FNM managed to get its annual accounts in balance by 1988. This had become a realistic objective following the government's assumption of about half the railway's accumulated debts, and also agreement by the labour unions to staff reductions and job mobility as a result of changed working practices. In 1985 the government had undertaken to shoulder about half of FNM's external debt of US$736 million, which was almost three times the total of the railway's annual expenditure budget.

New lines and line relocations
In January 1989 the government turned over the construction of new railway lines, which were previously the responsibility of the Ministry of Communications and Transportation, to the National Railways. This is now the responsibility of an Assistant Director-General of FNdeM.

With the revival of new line building after the country's resolution of its 1982 external debt crisis, work resumed on the 174 km of new double-track between Huehuetoca, 40 km north of Mexico City and Querétaro, on the core route from the capital to the north and north-west. Engineered for a maximum speed of 160 km/h, with the ruling gradient eased to 0·75 per cent, the new alignment will permit operation of 5000-tonne freight trains. This was opened for operation with diesel power in 1986, but electrification was in progress and the inauguration of electric haulage was set for April 1990.

Construction of a further 120 km of new double-track alignment of this route between Querétaro and Irapuato, where the routes to the west coast and to Aguascalientes and the north diverge was finished in 1989.

Work was also resumed on the new bypasses designed to reduce the rail connection between Guadalajara and Monterrey from 1007 to 881 km. Furthest ahead is the Salinas-Laguna Seca cut-off. A second cut-off will shorten the distance between Guadalajara and Encarnacion.

Other projects reactivated included a direct Cardel-Nautla link along the Gulf coast between Veracruz and Tampico, serving en route the Poza Rica oilfield; and upgrading of the trunk route from Mexico City to Cordoba and Veracruz. The latter traverses mountain country, where new alignments and considerable tunnelling have reduced the ruling gradient from 4·1 to 2·5 per cent and eased the most severe curvature. The final stretch, from Orzaba to Cordoba, features the new 430 m-long, 101 m-high Metlac viaduct, which has taken sixth place in world rankings for height above ground.

Further schemes approaching completion comprised two new cut-offs, Angostura-Juanita and Texistepec-Almagres, at the approach to Coatzacoalcos.

Electrification
The first step to the objective of electrifying the entire core of the FNM system, conveying 80 per cent of its traffic, has been wiring of the new route from Mexico City to Querétaro. Extension beyond Querétaro to San Luis Potosi is to follow.

The line has been electrified at 25 kV 60 Hz and

Mexico City Buenavista station concourse

Traffic (million)	1985	1986	1987	1988
Freight tonnes	60·455	54·4	57·183	56·039
Freight tonne-km	37 536·5	33 300	40 605	38 401
Passenger-km	4014	3800	5870	5658
Passenger journeys	19·831	19·01	22·43	19·373

Finances (million pesos)				
Revenue	1985	1986	1987	1988
Passengers and baggage	4817	9500	34 076	93 203
Freight and mail	183 257	317 000	787 690	3124 818
Other revenue	15 705	47 000	149 718	233 255
Total	203 779	373 500	971 484	3451 276
Expenditure				
Staff/personnel expenses	122 968	NA	601 251	1088 224
Materials and services	36 120	NA	660 163	1404 291
Depreciation	28 471	NA	256 185	460 893
Financial charges	51 313	NA	67 799	63 813
Other	35 233	NA	-	-
Total	274 105	436 700	1585 398	3017 221

Freight train hauled by three 2250 hp General Electric diesel-electric locomotives assembled by Aguascalientes provided with modern signalling and communication systems. It will be fed through nine substations, receiving current at 230 kV 60 Hz. Each substation is provided with two monophasic transformers of 20 MVA capacity and outlet voltage of 27·5 kV. The catenary on the main line is of polygonal design, allowing train speeds up to 160 km/h. The substations and equipment for sectioning the catenary are supervised and remotely controlled from two electric dispatching centres located in Mexico City and Querétaro.

Contracts were assigned to the suppliers of the first stage of the electrification project as follows: General Electric (USA) for the locomotives; Società Anonima Elettrificazióne (Italy) for the catenary; Ansaldo, Società Generale Elettromeccanica (Italy) for the sub-stations; WABCO-Westinghouse International Co (USA) for the signalling; Union Switch and Signal for CTC with computer-aided despatching; and Sumitomo Corp (Japan) for the communications system.

The first of the 39 Type E60C 4400 kW Co-Co locomotives ordered from General Electric were completed in 1982. The parallel-connected motors are thyristor-controlled and all power control circuits are solid state. Maximum starting tractive effort is 520 kN, continuous tractive effort 365 kN and maximum speed 110 km/h. The locomotives are designed for mixed traffic employment.

FNdeM aims to have 2131 route-km of its system under wires by the year 2010. Private sector involvement is sought for this expansion and for other major components of the railway's 1990-94 investment programme.

Signalling
Installation of a modern telecommunications system and of electronic centralised traffic control (CTC) was put in hand in 1975 and areas of the system have been progressively brought within the compass of a new hierarchy of high-capacity microwave links affording up to 120 speech channels, and of a uhf radio system for direct communication between control bases and train and track crews.

The microwave links have been exploited to set up a central, computer-based management data apparatus known as SCINCO and modelled on the TOPS system of the US Southern Pacific Railroad. The microwave equipment has been supplied by Nippon Electric of Japan, the uhf radio apparatus by Motorola of the USA.

CTC installation continues. It was commissioned between Irapuato and Guadalajara in 1987 and would come into use between San Luis and Benjamin Mendez on the Mexico City-Nuevo Laredo line in 1990. It will eventually be operative throughout the routes from Mexico City to Guadalajara and Monterrey.

Motive power and rolling stock
FNM's most recent diesel locomotive purchases have been dominated by the GE Type C-30-7. The GE machines were supplied in kit form and assembled in FNM's Aguascalientes shops.

With the release of some 80 diesel locomotives in the 1990 spring following the start of electric haulage between Mexico City and Querétaro, FNM hoped to initiate an ongoing update and expansion of its diesel traction resources. An extensive rehabilitation programme to reactivate unserviceable locomotives was under way in 1990. No new units have been purchased since 1985. Now FNM seeks to order between 70 and 100 a year, and to renovate 180 of its existing units over a period of five years.

The railway is also formulating new passenger car designs in the hope of ordering at least 200 vehicles a year up to 1994, and about 125 a year thereafter. Considerable associated expansion of workshop and maintenance installations is planned. Meanwhile, orders for 30 first-class cars were placed with Concarril in 1989.

At the start of 1989 FNM owned 1742 diesel locomotives, 1489 passenger cars and 49 988 freight cars.

Diesel-electric locomotives

Horsepower rating	No of units
800	19
900	9
1000	13
1200	1
1310	67
1350	1
1500	85
1600	2
1750	7
1800	186
2000	204
2250	149
2400	105
2500	31
2750	52
3000	664
3600	147
Total	1742

Track
Rail: 40–56 lb/yd (316 km); 60–75 lb/yd (1726 km); 80–90 lb/yd (2265 km); 100–115 lb/yd (11175 km)
Cross ties (sleepers): 7 in × 8 in × 8 ft (178 × 203 × 2438 mm)
Spacing: In plain track 2000/km; in curves 2028/km
Minimum curvature radius: 14°
Max gradient: 4·17%
Max axleload: 22 tons

Acquisition of mechanised track maintenance equipment has high priority in current expenditure plans.

Mongolia
Railways of the Mongolian People's Republic

PO Box 376, Ulan Bator

Gauge: 1524 mm
Route length: 1802 km

General Manager: A I Dolgii
Senior Deputy General Manager: S Bold

The main line of this diesel-operated system extends from the USSR frontier at Sukhe-Bator to the Chinese border at Zamin-Ude, with a branch to Erdent. There is an isolated Choibalsan-Erentsav line in the northeast of the country.

In 1989 the railway recorded 18.8 million tonnes of freight, 5960 million freight tonne-km, 2.7 million passenger journeys and 578 million passenger-km. Of the freight, about 10 per cent was transit between China, the USSR and North Korea.

The stock of 84 diesel-electric locomotives is formed of USSR-built Type 2M62 2 x Bo-Bo and TEM2 Bo-Bo. Passenger cars total 249 and freight cars, 1586.

Track is 50 kg/m rail on wooden sleepers spaced 1840/km in plain track, 2000/km in curves, and minimum curve radius is 297m. Some 1500 route-km have semi-automatic block signalling.

Morocco
Ministry of Transportation

Rabat

Telephone: +212 7 268 01

Minister: Mohamed Bouamoud
Secretary General: Abdelkader Nouini

Moroccan Railways (ONCFM)
Office National des Chemins de Fer du Maroc

Rue Abderrahman El Ghafiki, Rabat-Agdal

Telephone: +212 7 747 47
Telex: 31907, 32711 m
Telefax: +212 7 744 80

General Manager: Moussa Moussaoui
Assistant General Managers:
  Abderrazak Benjelloun
  Driss Kanouni
  Abdellatif Benali
  Zini El Abidine Achour
  Mohammed Aichaoui
  Abrahem Choukroun
Heads of Departments
  Motive Power and Rolling Stock: Abdallah Bouamri

ONCFM phosphates train leaving Casablanca *(Marcel Vleugels)*

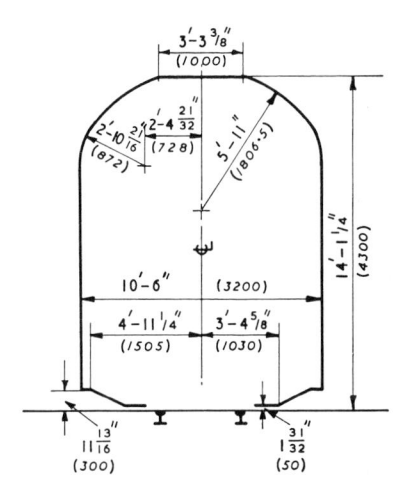

Morocco / RAILWAY SYSTEMS

Permanent Way and Works: Ahmed Tounsi
Supply: Ahmed Raissi
Traffic: Abdeslam El Ghissassi
Computer Services: Mustapha Benmoussa
International Relations: Abdelhamid Benchokroun

Gauge: 1435 mm
Route length: 1893 km
Electrification: 974 km at 3 kV dc

Belgian-built inter-city emus at Rabat station

While an extensive network of well-surfaced highways links all principal Moroccan towns, the railway is growing in importance, particularly for mineral transports. The ONCFM system is at present largely confined to the north-western coastal region.

The railway runs about 220 km south from Tangier to the Sidi-Kacem junction with the north-west coastal line to Rabat. The latter continues to the present railhead at Marrakech via Sidi-el-Aidi and has a spur to Oued-Zem and east to Oujda, via Fez, to link up with Algerian Railways at the frontier. A line running due south from Oujda skirts the Morocco-Algerian frontier as far as the south-east railhead at Bou-Arfa.

The National Railway Corporation is a public industrial and commercial enterprise with its own legal entity and financial autonomy working under the administrative umbrella of the Ministry of Transport.

New contract with government

Following a major 1985 reappraisal (with World Bank participation) of the Moroccan economy in general and the alignment of its production with domestic demand, a new agreement between the government and ONCFM was formulated. This derived from conclusions that ONCFM was capable within five years of generating a cash-flow sufficient to finance its compensations for socially obligatory operations and commercial freedom in other rail activity.

Traffic (million)	1986	1987	1988
Freight tonne-km	4594·1	4725·6	5705·9
Freight tonnage	28·5	28·748	33·088
Passenger-km	1958·6	2069	2092·5
Passenger journeys	11·603	12·154	11·556

Freight traffic

Phosphates are moved for export shipment in 78 three-axle wagon trains of 3900 tonnes payload, 4680 tonnes gross, over the Beni Idir-Khouribga/Sidi Daoui-Casablanca and Sidi Azouz/Youssoufia-Safi electrified routes. In 1988 phosphates tonnage improved sharply by 16.5 per cent to 23·578 million tonnes, though this gross was still below the 25 million tonnes expected when capacity expansion was put in hand in the 1970s.

Passenger traffic

The astonishing growth of passenger traffic continues. Volume has now doubled since the start of the 1970s.

The newly-doubled 90 km main line between Rabat and Casablanca has been upgraded for 140–160 km/h over 76 km and is exploited by a regular-interval service of 14 trains each way daily employing eight new three-car emus built in Belgium by BN and ACEC to a design based on the Belgian State Railways' (SNCB) Type AM80 emu. But whereas the SNCB AM80 has regenerative braking, the Moroccan units have rheostatic. The Moroccan sets operate in multipled pairs. ONCFM ordered six more of these three-car emus from BN at the start of 1990.

Recently-built UIC Type X air-conditioned cars (see below), designed equally for 160 km/h operation, equip named trains between Rabat and Marrakech; Casablanca, Tangier, Fez and Oujda; Tangier to Marrakech; and Oujda and Marrakech.

Recent development has included the marketing of travel packages, such as train travel plus hotel accommodation or car hire. International tourist trade has been courted with an accompanied-auto train including couchettes between Tangier and Oujda, and new quality day trains serving Safi and Oued Zem.

Motive power and rolling stock

The fleet at the start of 1989 consisted of 36 line-haul and 92 shunting diesel locomotives, 100 electric locomotives, eight three-car emus, eight diesel railcars, 591 passenger coaches (including 127 air-conditioned cars, six sleeping and 10 couchette cars) and 8454 freight wagons.

Under an agreement with De Dietrich, UIC Type X air-conditioned cars of side-corridor layout have been built for ONCFM in Morocco. The initial order comprised 79 cars, the first five of which were shipped from France part-assembled; the remainder have been fully built in Morocco by Société Chérifienne du Matériel Industriel et Ferroviaire (SCIF), though some parts are supplied from France. In addition, 52 cars for local service have been acquired secondhand from Belgian Railways (SNCB). A fleet of 80 Corail-type cars, mounted on Y32 bogies supplied by De Dietrich, are being assembled locally by SCIF.

Early in 1989 ONCFM awarded GEC-Alsthom an order for 18 4650 kW electric locomotives closely based on the design of the 7200 and 22 200 series built for the French National Railways (SNCF). The locomotives are being manufactured jointly with Société Chérifienne de Matériel Industriel et Ferroviaire (SCIF). For this contract, pursuing the co-operation initiated with Morocco in 1947, GEC-Alsthom acquired a stake in the capital of SCIF.

Later in 1989 ONCFM placed an order with Brush Electrical Machines for 19 1100hp Cummins-engined Bo-Bo diesel-electric shunters.

New Lines

A 102 km line from Nouasseur to the port of Jorf Lasar was completed in 1986 and subsequently electrified. It has been built initially as single-line, but with provision for later doubling and a 13 km branch from Nouasseur to the nearby Casablanca airport, known as Mohamed V. In 1988 tenders were invited for the design and construction of the airport link, which had the offer of assistance in the African Development Fund's 1989-90 budget.

The African Development Fund has also provided funding for a first step in double-tracking of the Rabat-Fez line, as far as Kenitra. This entails new tunnelling under Rabat and reconstruction of Rabat Ville station. The Casablanca-Rabat-Fez route carries 46 per cent of all ONCFM passenger traffic and 40 per cent of its freight (phosphates excluded).

Construction of a 123 km line from the deep-water port of Beni Enzar southward to join the Oujda-Fez-Rabat line at Taourirt was begun but called off in the 1970s because of uncertain prospects for the Sonasid steelworks, near Selouane, which it would also serve. Following completion of the Nouasseur-Jorf Lasar line (see above), resources were released to reactivate the Beni Enzar-Taourirt scheme, but no progress has been reported subsequently. Construction of a littoral line from Nador westward to Tangier is a longer-term possibility.

A 955 km Marrakech-Laayoun project was formally inaugurated by King Hassan II in April 1981. The prospective route crosses the Atlas Mountains between Marrakech and Agadir, a 272 km segment involving tunnels and bridgework aggregating respectively 27.1 km and 15.8 km in length. Shortly after the inaugural ceremony, ONCFM announced that it planned to extend this line a further 850 km from Laayoun southward to Boujdour, Ad Dakhla and Lagwira, across the frontier from the Nouadhibou port terminus of the Mauritania Railway. However, the project subsequently lapsed for lack of funding. Studies were revived in 1989 with the encouragement of some French interest in the scheme.

Also shelved is a plan for an 800 km line southwestward around the Atlas range from Bouarfa to a junction with the Marrakech-Laayon line near Taroudant, which en route would tap deposits of manganese at Imini, of cobalt at Bou Azzer, and of phosphates at Quarzazate. A third new line proposed but postponed indefinitely is one of 225 km from Guercif, on the Fez-Oujda line in the north, southward to Midelt.

Extension of the Casablanca-Khouribga line to cater for phosphate traffic from Beni Mellal has also been deferred pending an upturn in phosphates demand, but the double-track as far as Khouribga is being upgraded.

Signalling

In 1988 ONCFM was seeking tenders for supply and installation of power signalling between Rabat Agdal and Kenatra, and of CTC between Kentra and Fez, on its Casablanca-Fez line, currently being double-tracked. Multiple-aspect colour-light signalling is to be installed between Casablanca and Nousseur.

Mozambique

Ministry of Transport & Communications

Maputo

Minister: Armando Guebuza

Mozambique Ports & Railways (CFM)

PO Box 276, Maputo

Telephone: +258 24133; 30151–5
Cable: Ferroporto, Maputo
Telex: 6438 cfm ds mo

Rail installations at Maputo

Director-General: Eng Mario Dimande
Deputy Directors-General:
  Eng Rui Fonseca
  Dr Luis Ah-Hoy
Directors, Engineering: Eng Júlio Hingá
  Finance: Oscar Dinis
  Engineering: Eng Julio Hinga
  Commercial: Alberto Elias
  Planning: Francisco Soares
  Southern Railway: Dr Llidio Dinis
  Central Railway: G Mabunda
  North Railway: R P dos Santos
  Zambésia Railway: Dr M Duda Jambo
  Inhambane Railway: A de Andrade
  Human Resources: Roque Fernandes Junior

Gauge: 1067 mm; 762 mm
Route length: 3128 km; 143 km

In 1990 the Mozambique Railways (CFM) were joined with the country's ports of Maputo, Beira and Nacala in a new state corporation, Mozambique Ports & Railways. This changed the status of both activities from government agency to a financially-accountable corporation.

The railway is made up of five distinct systems linking the coastal ports to the hinterland. From north to south of the country these are:

Northern system
Gauge: 1067 mm
Route length: 919 km

This line runs from the port of Nacala, with a branch (presently closed) to Lumbo westward to Cuamba and Lichinga. A recently-built line from Cuambra connects at Entrelagos, on the border, with Malawi Railways and affords Malawi rail access to the port of Nacala.

Central system
Gauge 1067 mm
Route length: 994 km

From the port of Beira the line runs eastwards to connect with Zimbabwe Railways at Machipanda. From Dondo Junction, 29 km from Beira, a line runs northward to connect with Malawi Railways with an extension from Diana to Moatize. In 1989 Brazil's big Companhia Vale do Rio Doce (CVRD) was negotiating with the Mozambique government possible creation of a joint company to exploit coal mining at Moatize. This would involve significant upgrading of the 500km of railway between Beira and Moatize.

A new line 83 km long was built from Inhamitango to Marromeu to replace the old 915 mm-gauge length.

Inhambane system
Gauge: 1067 mm
Route length: 90 km

This consists of the isolated 1067 mm-gauge line from the port of Inhambane to Inharrime

Zambésia system
Gauge: 1067 mm
Route length: 145 km

Also an isolated line, running from the coastal town of Quelimane to Mocuba.

Southern system
Gauge: 1067 mm; 762 mm
Route length: 840 km; 143 km

From the port of Maputo lines run west to connect with South African Railways at Kamatipoort, north to Chicualacuala and south-westwards to connect with Swaziland Railways at Goba.

In the south, there are four railway lines, with the port of Maputo as a railhead:

Goba line (to the Swaziland border)	64 km
Ressano Garcia line (to the South African border)	88 km
Limpopo line (to the Zimbabwe border, at Chicualacuala)	528 km
Xinavane line (domestic service)	93 km
Branch lines (domestic service)	71 km

The first joins up at the border of Swaziland with the Swaziland Railway, which connects the Umbovu Ridge iron-ore complex at Kadake with the port of Maputo. The second continues into the Republic of South Africa. The third line goes through Zimbabwe to Zambia, Botswana and south-east Zaire.

Traffic
In recent years operation has been severely disrupted by hostilities, with serious consequences for neighbouring railways for whom Mozambique's ports provide a shipment outlet.

Creation of a container terminal at Nacala has been facilitated by a US$6 million loan from the Finnish government.

Traction and rolling stock
CFM operates 58 line-haul and 20 shunting steam locomotives, 99 diesel-electric line-haul locomotives, 38 diesel-hydraulic shunters, 19 diesel railcars, 199 passenger cars and 8442 wagons.

Since 1979 the traction fleet has been strengthened by the delivery of 32 Type DH 125 1250 hp diesel-hydraulic shunters from Romania and a further 20 Type U20C 2200 hp locomotives from General Electric do Brasil. In 1987 Zeco of Zimbabwe was renovating nine steam and two diesel locomotives for use on the line to Beira.

An order was placed in late 1989 with GEC-Alsthom for 15 Caterpillar-engined Type AD26C 1850 kW diesel locomotives. They will be employed on the Limpopo line. Finance was provided by France's Economic Co-operation Fund (CCCE).

Rehabilitation
Reconstruction of CFM's deteriorated trunk route tracks is a top priority, in view of the demands for access to the ports of traffic to and from the country's landlocked neighbours. Loans from Canadian, French and Portuguese sources have helped to fund a US$195 million rebuilding of the 538 km Northern line from Nacala to Cuamba with 40 kg/m long-welded rail on concrete sleepers. Under Sofrerail supervision, the first 192km from Nacala to Nampula were finished in 1987. It was expected to finish the remaining 346 km to Cuamba in 1991. Meanwhile, the line has again become usable throughout from the Malawi border at Entrelagos to Nacala port, though not without the protection of Malawi and Mozambique troops against rebel action.

A grant from the UK of US$20 million has supported rehabilitation of the Beira-Machipanda line west of Dondo Junction, starting with the severely-graded 100 km near the Zimbabwe border, where 30 kg/m is being replaced by 40 kg/m rail, curves eased to a minimum radius of 500 metres and ruling gradient from 1·2 to 2·4 per cent. In a subsequent phase the route is to be double-tracked and resignalled for 27 km between Beira and Dondo at a cost of US$22 million.

In 1984 the Italian government agreed to fund the US$18 million rehabilitation of the 300 km Beira-Sena line, to be undertaken by an Italian consortium led by Ansaldo Trasporti.

The Swedish government financed a Swederail Consulting study of requirements for upgrading the 524 km Maputo-Chicualacuala (or Limpopo) line to the Zimbabwe border, for which an annual transit traffic potential of 2·3 million tonnes was foreseen by 1990 if security uncertainties could be eliminated, and of the 140 km line from Maputo to Phuzumoya in Swaziland.

In 1988 improving relations with South Africa limited rebel activity and prospects for rehabilitating the vital Limpopo link between Zimbabwe and the port of Maputo were thus brighter. By the end of 1988 National Railways of Zimbabwe (NRZ) had renewed 143 route-km from the frontier into Mozambique and was advancing further south. British, Canadian, West German Portuguese and Kuwaiti donors have proferred a further US$65 million towards the US$200 million that consultants calculate will be needed to reactivate the Limpopo line fully. A locomotive restoration programme may be separately funded by the USA.

Namibia

TransNamib Ltd
(formerly National Transport Corporation of Namibia/Nasionale Vervoer Korporasie Beperk

Private Bag 13204, Windhoek 900

Telephone: +264 61 298 1111

Telex: 908829
Telefax: +264 61 227984

Managing Director: J Greebe
General Manager: F Uys
Assistant General Managers
  Commercial: S Brink
  Administration: G du Preez
  Finance: J Maree
Infrastructure Engineer: J Steyn
Rolling Stock Engineer: C Havemann

Gauge: 1065 mm
Route length: 2349 km

In July 1988 the Namibian rail, road and harbour services, previously worked by South African Transport Services under contract, were formally handed over to the Namibian body that was renamed TransNamib in 1989. This followed a de facto transfer in May 1985.

The railway operates 128 diesel locomotives, comprising mainly 42 GE U18C1 and 82 GE Type U20C; 187 passenger cars; and 1717 freight cars.

Nepal

Ministry of Works & Transport

Babar Mahal, Katmandu

Minister: Hon H Mahat

Nepal Government Railway (NR)

Birganj

Acting Manager: Devendra Singh
Traffic Officer: Pratap Bahadur

Gauge: 762 mm
Route length: 48 km

There are only two short railways within Nepal, operating in the Terai, a fertile and level strip adjacent to the border with India. The Janakpur Railway (JR) runs from Jaynagar in Bihar State, India, across the Nepal border north and west to Janakpurdam (32 km) and on to Bizulpra (21 km).

The Nepal Government Railway (NR) runs a mere 6 km from Raxaul in the Bihar State across the Nepal border to Birganj. The line was originally built as a key link in the railway-road-ropeway transport system that supplied the mountain-locked valley of Katmandu, closed to the outside world until the early 1950s. The line formerly continued north to the base of the Siwalik Hills at Amlekhganj.

The government is now undertaking to develop Hetauda into a new industrial centre. As part of the scheme, preliminary feasibility studies have been made for the construction of a new rail line from the limit of Indian metre-gauge at Raxaul to Hetauda.

A study by Sofrerail in 1982 suggested construction of two metre-gauge lines, one north-south from Katmandu to the Indian frontier at Birganj (200 km), the other east-west for 570 km across the Terai plain from Dharan and Biratnagar to Butwal and Bhairahwa.

The Nepal Government Railway railway operates seven steam locomotives, 12 passenger cars and 82 freight wagons.

Janakpur Railway (JR)

Jaynagar

Telephone: 82
Cable: Janakrailo

Manager: P PK Poudyal
Traffic Officer: K G D Upadhya
Assistant Engineer: D B Khadka

Gauge: 762 mm
Route length: 48 km

The Janakpur Railway (JR) was originally built as a timber line designed to open the virgin jungle to the north of Janakpurdam. As the forest has long since been cut, the railway now operates primarily to provide access in an area with few roads. Passengers are the main source of revenue with pilgrims to the temples of Janakpurdam forming the bulk of traffic. In 1986 the railway recorded 1·6 million passenger journeys and 22 000 tonnes of freight.

In recent years JR officers have been upgrading track by laying new sleepers and secondhand 16 kg/m rail to replace existing 12·5 kg/m profile. Locomotives (including two Garratts) and wagons released from the Nepal Railway have been rebuilt and pressed into service. Recent stock comprised 10 steam locomotives, 25 passenger cars and 52 freight wagons.

Netherlands

Ministry of Transport & Public Works

Plesmanweg 1-6, PO Box 20901, 2500 The Hague

Telephone: +31 70 516171
Telex: 32562
Telefax: +31 70 517895

Minister: Hanja May Weggen
Secretary General: H N J Smits
Director-General of Transport: B Westerduin

Netherlands Railways (NS)
NV Nederlandse Spoorwegen

Moreelsepark 1, 3511 EP Utrecht

Telephone: +31 30 359111
Telex: 47257 ns ut
Telefax: +31 30 354560

President and Chief Executive: L F Ploeger
Directors, Operating: C H M Clemens
 Development: T Regtuijt
 Commercial: H E Portheine
 Personnel: A M Messing
 Finance: H Streefkerk
Heads of Product Divisions
 InterCity and International Passenger:
  F D Andrioli
 Regional Passenger: P M Ranke
 Freight: C J W Bos
 Special Services: Vacant
Departmental Managers
 Operations: J Schouten
 Stores: K Geveke
 General Secretariat: E M Nikkels
 Rolling Stock and Workshops: C Moolhuyzen
 Infrastructure: G Koppenberg
 Public Relations: P J W Craghs

Gauge: 1435 mm
Route length: 2828 km
Electrification: 1957 km at 1·5 kV dc

Rail services within the Netherlands are run by NS, a limited company with shares held wholly by the state. Freight traffic is operated on an avoidable cost basis, but also subsidised.

'Rail 21'

With urban road traffic increasingly congested, and worse threatened in Amsterdam and Rotterdam particularly through approach highway improvements impossible to match with additional in-town car space, NS published in the 1988 summer a 'Rail 21' programme setting out a rail capacity expansion programme for the next century. The government subsequently accepted the proposals and embodied them in the long-term plans of the Ministry of Transport and Public Works. Total cost of 'Rail 21' is estimated at Fl9000-10000 million. Its funding would require the government to raise its present NS infrastructure subsidy of Fl250 million by some Fl200 million a year.

'Rail 21' enshrines the concept, entertained by NS management for some years past, of a three-category passenger service instead of the present two-level. Another of its themes is improvement of international services. But these and other advances demand substantial investment in infrastructure.

'Plan 21' proposals include construction of one new 200 km/h line direct from Schiphol Airport to Rotterdam and the Belgian frontier, for access to Antwerp; of a second extending the new Flevoland line from Lelystad to Groningen; and of a third from Arnhem to the German border at Emmerich. Extensive four-tracking of existing trunk route is sought to achieve segregation of the new top-level services from an expanded service of multi-stop services and also costly redevelopment of 10 major stations with additional platforms and flying junctions. A typical outcome of these proposals would be an IC route from Amsterdam and Rotterdam to Germany that was four-track the whole way to Emmerich, and partly over new 200 km/h line – Rotterdam to Schiphol and Arnhem to Emmerich. The Schiphol Airport-Rotterdam-Belgian frontier new line would be the NS access to the TGV-Nord, though Belgium now proposes only 160 km/h upgrading of its sector from the border and Antwerp to the TGV's threshold at Brussels.

The top category of the projected passenger service would embrace limited-stop InterCity and EuroCity trains running at up to 200km/h. Several new long-haul EuroCity services are envisaged: for example The Hague to Hamburg, Schiphol to Frankfurt/Main, and Groningen/Amsterdam to London via the TGV-Nord and Channel Tunnel. The network would connect Amsterdam, Rotterdam, The Hague, Utrecht, Schiphol Airport and 15 regional centres.

The remainder of the present NS InterCity service would be redesigned and designated Express Inter-Regional. This network would embrace the country's 65 most significant towns and cities. Its routes would operate half-hour interval timetables and its trains would run at 140–160km/h.

The 'Stop-train' service would be redesigned as the Agglo-Regio network of high frequency, regular-interval through trains interconnecting suburbs astride a main centre, instead of terminating at it. The Agglo-Regio network would be closely integrated with feeder bus services.

Achievement in full of 'Rail 21', claimed the NS, would ensure that the present 35 per cent proportion of urban commuters using rail would rise to 50 per cent. The cost is put at an annual investment of Fl200 million from now until the year 2015.

As an interim measure the NS aims to launch a three-tier service revision from 1995 onwards under the brandname of Prorail. This will not attempt the speeds of 'Rail 21'; the scale and price of its improvements will depend on progress with the elimination of bottlenecks.

The coalition government newly elected in 1989 has asked the NS to consider the feasibility of completing the required investment by year 2005 instead of 2015. The NS has replied that if Fl 3700 million instead of the previously planned Fl 1500 were made available up to 1996 for infrastructure investment, notably in flyovers and extra tracks in the Randstad, implementation of 'Rail 21' could start in 1994.

Higher motoring taxes to fund 'Rail 21'

The country's vulnerability to flooding makes it particularly alive to the consequences of global warming. To that is added concern at the choking of its tightly-knit conurbations in the west by motor traffic. Although one coalition government was brought down in 1989 on the issue of curbing motoring in favour of public transport, the Transport Minister of the replacement coalition announced drastic measures in the spring of 1990.

From November 1990 the petrol tax would be raised by 5 per cent annually. Peak period motoring between the four main conurbations would become permissible only on payment of a 25 per cent car licence surcharge and daily tolls would also be exacted. The proceeds of these measures would be put to public transport development, with NS the principal beneficiary.

Management restructure

In 1990 top NS management was revised. The chairman heads a directorate of five with commercial, development, production, personnel and finance responsibilities. At the next level are four product and marketing departments covering respectively international and intercity passenger services, local passenger services, freight and special services (mail, small consignment goods, etc).

Passenger traffic

The inexorable rise of passenger traffic was maintained in 1989. Rising more than 5 per cent over 1988, total passenger-km scaled a fresh record of almost 10 200 million, and passenger revenue climbed from Fl1209 million to Fl1272 million. Fare increases were kept to 1 per cent in 1989 and for 1990 were to be only 2 per cent, half the national inflation rate, so that a gross of 10 600 million passenger-km was confidently anticipated in 1990.

A doubling of some service frequencies to quarter-hourly was to be effected in May 1990. This would increase pressure particularly on the layout at Utrecht.

RAILWAY SYSTEMS / Netherlands

The NS now believes that infrastructure investment must prepare for an annual gross of 13 000 million passenger-km by 1995 and 15 500 million by the year 2015. That will also entail a coaching stock increase of at least 550 vehicles. A first step was taken in 1989 with orders for 38 locomotives and 116 more bi-level cars (see below).

The Transport Ministry jointly introduced and financed in February 1990 a Train-Taxi scheme. Operative in 30 towns and cities (excluding Amsterdam, The Hague, Rotterdam and Utrecht, because of their adequate public transport), a train traveller can pre-purchase a voucher entitling him to taxi service, in NS-owned and liveried vehicles, from arrival station to destination, subject to some limitation on road distance.

Amsterdam development

Direct connection between the Schiphol Airport-Sloterdijk line and the Hem Tunnel route to North Holland is planned, but priority has been given to the so-called Southern Branch, an extension of the original line through Schiphol from its present Amsterdam RAI terminus through a new two-level station at Duivendrecht, on the Amsterdam-Utrecht line, to a two-way junction with the Amsterdam-Amersfoort line at Diemen. This will be achieved by 1994. The government authorised its construction in April 1986.

All trains on the Amsterdam-Rotterdam axis are now re-routed away from Haarlem and via Sloterdijk and Schiphol to Leiden, so that a train between Schiphol and Amsterdam Central is available at least every five minutes. Trains from North Germany no longer terminate at Amsterdam Central but continue through Schiphol to Hoofdorp, a station south of Schiphol, where tracks have been arranged for their cleaning and turnround. Trains to and from Paris, however, are still routed along with Zandvoort-Amsterdam and Rotterdam-Den Helder trains via Haarlem. Amsterdam RAI continues to be served by a shuttle service to and from The Hague. Schiphol is now accessible by direct train or with only one change of train from 75 per cent of all NS stations.

Despite development pressures on its already constricted space, Amsterdam Central is to remain the city's prime international station. From 1996 it will be receiving TGV-Nord services. The NS has to surrender the site of the present signalbox, and the opportunity will be taken for complete state-of-the-art renewal on a new location by 1995.

Weesp station has been rebuilt and enlarged as a future interchange between Flevoland-Schiphol-The Hague and Amersfoort-Amsterdam InterCity services. That will become possible after completion of the link between Amsterdam RAI and the Utrecht line, and of the complementary spur to the Amersfoort line at Diemen. Also possible in the future is extension of the Flevoland line, engineered for 160km/h, to Groningen.

Freight traffic

A fresh commission appointed by the Transport Ministry to review NS' subsidised freight reported in July 1989 with recommendations not only for investment, but for a state assumption of financial responsibility for freight-related infrastructure. Given annual investment of some Fl100 million in bottleneck easements up to the end of the century, and Fl200 million annually thereafter, the commission believed that the present annual freight tonnage of 20 million might be raised to 75 million by the year 2020.

In a 'Rail Cargo 21' report presented to the Transport Minister early in 1991, NS argued that maintenance of a significant freight service in parallel with its proposed three-tier passenger service development (see above) required a Fl5500 million investment alongside the projected Fl10 000 million expenditure on passenger service in the period up to year 2005. Development will have a strong intermodal bias, founded on between 10 and 20 Rail Service centres. Wagonload service would be confined to some 40 terminals.

The NS seeks as a priority to create by 1995 a 22.5-tonne axleload corridor for 160 km/h intermodal trains between Rotterdam's Europoort and the German border at Venlo. This will require provision of additional tracks and flyovers and cost Fl1000 million. In a second phase, occupying the rest of the decade, a similar corridor would be achieved from Kifhoek yard and Europoort to the border at Emmerich via Geldermalsen. There would be associated improvements at Amsterdam, raising the total cost of this phase to Fl2500 million. Finally, at the start of the next century, new lines would be built from Ijmond south to

Two Class 1600 electric locomotives head international train at Amsterdam Central (Marcel Vleugels)

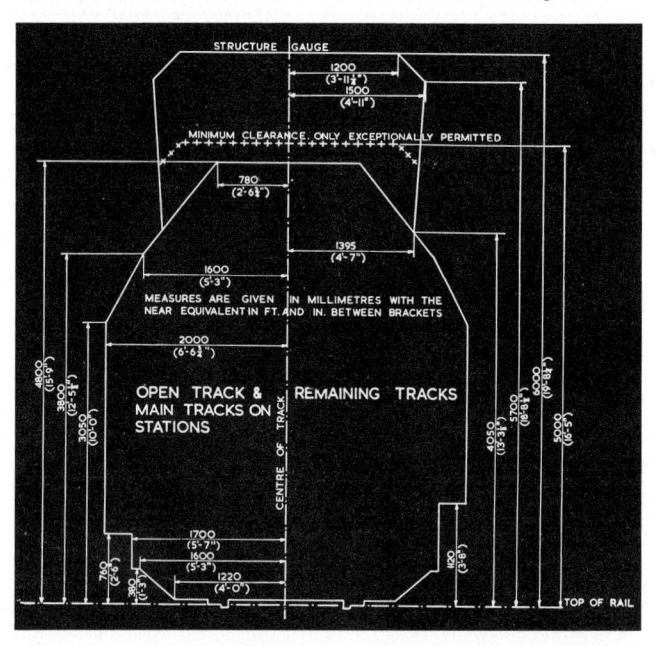

Bi-level push-pull train-set, driving trailer leading, on the ground-level, relocated Amsterdam-Haarlem line at the new Sloterdijk station; encased in glass structure on top level, with road interchanges and booking hall at the centre level, is the new Schiphol-Amsterdam Central link

Gorinchen, the Nijmegen-Roermond line would be upgraded, a bypass laid around Zwolle and a new connection built to Dieren, for a total cost of Fl2000 million.

Meanwhile, double-tracking of the busy Rotterdam dock area line from Botlek to Europoort is under way.

About 73 per cent of NS freight traffic is international and 50 per cent to or from Rotterdam. In bulk commodities the outstanding rail flow is ore from the Rotterdam Maasvlakte terminal, which can accept the largest deep-seat bulk carriers, to Ruhr and Saarland steel plants, though this has lately been losing ground to inland waterway shipping. The majority of the ore trains are 2400 tonnes gross with a 1600-tonne payload, but some are 4000 tonnes gross, of which 2700 tonnes is payload.

In May 1990 Kifhoek yard, Rotterdam, became the terminus of the first EurailCargo service, a direct long-haul train for wagonload traffic from Wels, Austria. With no intermediate stop for commercial purposes, the service offered second-morning delivery at each end of the run.

Container traffic, managed by NS' subsidiary Holland Rail Container, increased from 228 000 to 260 000 movements in 1989. Domestic traffic was up 17 per cent, international 12 per cent. The former benefited from rising interport movement between Amsterdam, Rotterdam and Vlissingen, the latter from diversions as a result of labour troubles at Italian ports. International traffic was further boosted by the German Federal (DB's) extension of its KLV network of dedicated overnight intermodal trains to links between Rotterdam/Amsterdam and eight key German centres.

In March 1988 an alliance of German Federal, Belgian, Netherlands Railways, their container traffic subsidiaries and Intercontainer, inaugurated a scheme to market North Sea port-West Germany container traffic jointly, and without discrimination as regards the port of entry or departure. The new scheme embraces container traffic between Hamburg, Bremen, Bremerhaven, Brake, Nordenham, Kiel, Lübeck, Rotterdam, Vlissingen, Antwerp, Zeebrugge and all terminals (including ports) in Federal Germany. Management of Maritime Container Network (MCN), as the project is titled, is by the DB's container subsidiary, Transfacht. However, staff at its Frankfurt base have been supplemented by a contingent from Intercontainer, whose local agents represent MCN in Rotterdam. MCN offers a range of service modules that can be aggregated into a total package at an inclusive price.

Transfracht's existing 'InGrid' price structure has been expanded to cover traffic to and from the Dutch ports. As its name suggests, InGrid, a computer-compatible system, partitions West Germany into 145 zones; within each zone a common price applies to container transits between any terminal and a given port.

The first part of the Rail Service Centre (RSC) in Rotterdam was inaugurated in April 1989. The strategy behind this development, which will be fully operational in 1993, is to attract more intermodal business, particularly in international container-based transport. The RSC terminal will contribute to the development of international railborne traffic by facilitating organisation of through trains and container groupage operations. The next phase of the project provides for integration of piggyback traffic into the terminal's service package.

Holland Rail Container (HRC) serves the major container transhipment areas in Rotterdam, has its own inland Rotterdam terminal for domestic traffic, and also caters for maritime traffic at Amsterdam and Vlissingen. Within Holland it serves other terminals at Almelo, Heerlen, Leeuwarden, Kempen (privately-owned), Veendam (privately-owned) and two at Venlo, near the German border.

The Dutch piggyback company Trailstar put on almost 50 per cent more business in 1989, handling some 24 000 semi-trailers and swapbodies. This was primarily due to the opening of a new terminal at Ede, which attracted business previously transshipped on the German border at Emmerich. Further improvement was expected from the opening of the Rotterdam Rail Service Centre, with its more convenient Waalhaven terminal than that at Rotterdam North. Trailstar runs daily piggyback trains to and from South Germany, Italy and Austria.

Bottleneck easement

In the early 1980s the NS has identified 10 bottlenecks in its network as a severe handicap to its operation at present and prospective levels of service intensity.

'Sprinter' emu at Almere Central on newly-opened Flevoland line (Marcel Vleugels)

Type IC3 emu passes Amsterdam Lelylaan station on Schiphol Airport-Amsterdam Central line

New Class 6400 three-phase diesel locomotive

A previous centre-left government had agreed to finance work on enlargement of eight; the remainder would be covered by the NS. In mid-1989 eight of the ten pinpointed in 1983 were still unblocked. Progress at that time was:

Layout enlargement at Utrecht, including new flyovers. Cost: Fl380 million. Work in progress for 1990 completion;

Four-tracking between Leiden and The Hague. Cost: Fl150 million. Only preparatory work so far financed;

Flyover at Boxtel and other capacity enlargement between there and Eindhoven. Cost: Fl60 million. Some works finished in 1989, and flyover construction expected in 1990;

RAILWAY SYSTEMS / Netherlands

Replacement of double-track swing with new four-track fixed bridge at Gouda, quadruple tracking from Gouda to Moordrecht Junction, and construction at Moordrecht Junction of a flyover to keep The Hague-Gouda traffic clear of the Gouda-Rotterdam flow. The Gouda-Moordrecht Junction works will almost double the area's operational capacity. The new bridge should be finished in 1992. Cost: Fl210 million;

Amsterdam-Sloterdijk: layout enlargement to six tracks. Cost Fl150 million. Approval for start at end of 1989, for completion in 1997;

Rotterdam: replacement of lift bridge by a four-track tunnel under the Maas river (see below). Cost: Fl770 million. Construction in progress and ahead of schedule; two tracks to be available in late 1993, the other two in the spring of 1995;

The Hague-Rijswijk: four-tracking. Cost: Fl45 million. No progress, but work would hopefully start in 1990 for 1995 completion;

Delfshaven: new Schie bridge. Cost: Fl120 million. In progress for 1993 completion.

The four-track tunnel east of Rotterdam Central will replace two double-track bridges, the Koningshaven and Willemsbrug, over the Nieuwe Maas waterway where the latter flows round the Noorder island. The Konigshaven is a lift bridge that has to be raised for 20 minutes every 2 hours for passage of shipping – a grievous handicap to NS interval timetable planning. The 3 km tunnel will be approached on 2.8 per cent gradients, because it must drop to 18 m below the level of the existing elevated main line. The latter's station of Blaak will be rebuilt inside the tunnel.

On the other side of Rotterdam Central, between that station and Schiedam West, tracks are being elevated and a new lifting bridge installed over the Delftsche Schie Canal to obtain more headroom for shipping and reduce the occoasions when the bridge must be lifted.

Schiphol Airport station enlargement

When the TGV-Nord service from Paris to Brussels is extended to Amsterdam it will be routed via Schiphol Airport, which is itself to extend operations by opening a second air terminal in the early 1990s. NS has therefore begun enlargement of its underground Schiphol station from the present three to six tracks served by three island platforms each long enough to cater for a twin-unit TGV formation.

Electrification

NS has begun to electrify its 49 km single-track line from Dordrecht to Geldermalsen and Elst. Completion is foreseen in 1992. Besides avoiding need to renew the diesel railcars which presently furnish a half-hourly passenger service, the wiring will achieve an additional route for through NS-DB freight trains from Rotterdam that normally travel via Breda and Eindhoven.

Traction and rolling stock

With rising pressure on NS capacity and government backing for 'Rail 21', NS was authorised in 1989 to order 30 four-car ICIII emus and 116 more bi-level cars from Waggonfabrik Talbot, all to be delivered by 1992. The first two series of ICIII emus, totalling 70 sets after delivery of the second series of 47 was completed in early 1990, were three-car. An order for Alsthom-built 38 Class 1700 electric locomotives to supersede Class 1100 followed in July 1989; they would be lower-powered versions of NS's Alsthom-built Class 1600, and would be delivered in 1991-92.

In September 1985 the Transport Minister gave long-awaited approval for renewal of the NS freight diesel locomotive stock. Replacements are 60 Krupp-MaK Type DE1002 1180kW Bo-Bos with BBC three-phase ac traction motors, of which the first was delivered in the spring of 1988. Delivery will be completed in 1992. A second order for 30 has been placed, with an option on a further 30 units.

First of the existing locomotive types to be scrapped will be Class 2400-2500, to become extinct by 1991. By 1992 Class 2200-2300 will have been pared from 123 to 86 units.

The ultimate total of these new diesel locomotives is likely to be 150, to be reached in 1997. The majority will be Class 6400, designed for haulage in multiple of freight trains up to 2400 tonnes weight. Some later examples will be a lower-powered Class 6200, fitted with slow-speed control for shunting assignments. All will be fitted for remote radio control.

In another three-phase motor venture, the NS has in 1989 ordered from Waggonfabrik Talbot nine proto-

Tonnage (million)	1985	1986	1987	1988	1989
Freight tonnage	20·4	19·1	18·6	19·6	19·4
Freight tonne-km	3269	3107	2995	3200	3108
Passenger-km	9226	8919	9396	9664	10 162
Passengers carried	208	215·5	222·5	230	239

Finances (Fl million)		
Revenue	1987	1988
Passengers and freight	1458·668	1517·445
Other	193·988	357·583
State and other supports	1417·093	1427·606
Total	3234·495	3302·634
Expenditure	1987	1988
Staff/personnel	1737·682	1718·589
Materials and services	749·581	806·269
Depreciation	243·489	257·842
Financial charges	433·815	402·365
Total	3164·567	3185·065

Diesel locomotives

Class	Wheel arrange-ment	Trans-mission	Rated power hp	Tractive effort Max lb (kg)	Continuous at lb (kg)	mph (km/h)	Max speed mph (km/h)	Wheel dia in (mm)	Total weight tonnes	Length ft in (mm)	Year first built	Builders Mechanical parts	Engine & type	Transmission
2400 2500	Bo-Bo	Elec	850	36 400 (16 500)	12 830 (5800)	12 (20)	50 (80)	38⅜ (1000)	60	41' 1" (12 500)	1954	Alsthom	SACM, V 12 SHR	Alsthom
2200 2300	Bo-Bo	Elec	900	40 800 (18 500)	27 000 (12 250)	8·7 (14)	62 (100)	37⅜ (950)	74	45' 11½" (14 010)	1955	Allan Schneider	Stork, Schneider (lic Superior) 40 C-LX-8	Heemaf Westinghouse
511-545 601-665	C	Elec	400	32 100 (14 600)	14 436 (6550)	6 (10)	19 (30)	48⅜ (1230)	47	29' 9" (9070)	1949	English Electric	EEC, 6 KT	EEC
200-300	Bo	Elec	72				60 (98)	39⅜ (1000)	21	23' 7½" (7220)	1934-1951	Schneider-Werkspoor	Stork, Hengelo	Heemaf: ETI; Hengelo or Slikkerveer

Principal electric locomotives and emus

Class	Wheel arrange-ment	Line current	Rated output hp	Tractive effort (full field) Max lb (kg)	Continuous at lb (kg)	mph (km/h)	Max speed mph (km/h)	Wheel dia in (mm)	Weight tonnes	Length ft in (mm)	Year first built	Builders Mechanical parts	Electrical equipment
1300	Co-Co	1500 V dc OH	3870	51 000 (23 100)	28 600 (13 000)	31 (50)	84 (135)	49¼ (1250)	111	62' 2" (18 950)	1952	Alsthom	Alsthom
1200	Co-Co	1500 V dc OH	3000	43 500 (19 700)	22 400 (10 200)	31 (50)	84 (135)	43¼ (1100)	108	59' 4" (18 080)	1951	Werkspoor-Baldwin	Heemaf-Westinghouse
1100	Bo-Bo	1500 V dc OH	2580	34 200 (15 500)	14 300 (6500)	31 (50)	84 (135)	49¼ (1250)	80	42' 7½" (12 980)	1950	Alsthom	Alsthom
1600	Bo-Bo	1500 V dc OH	5630				100 (160)	49¼ (1250)	85	57' 9" (17 640)	1981	Alsthom	Jeumont-Schneider
EL2	(2-Bo)+ (Bo-2)	1500 V dc OH					86 (140)	37⅜ (950)	85	170' 3" (52 140)	1966/76	Werkspoor Talbot	Heemaf/Smit
ELD4	(2-2)+ (Bo-Bo)+ (Bo-Bo)	1500 V dc OH					86 (140)	37⅜ (950)	168	331' 7" (101 240)	1964/65	Werkspoor	Heemaf/Smit
SGM II	Bo-Bo	1500 V dc OH	1720				80 (125)	37⅜ (950)	106	171' 3" (52 200)	1975/80	Talbot SIG	Oerlikon Holec
ICIII	Bo-Bo (2-2)+ (2-2)	1500 V dc OH	100				100 (160)	37⅜ (950)	114	264' 5" (80 600)	1977	Talbot Wegmann	Heemaf/Smit TCO

types of the next generation of stopping train emu designated the SM90. These two-car sets will have Holec three-phase ac motors, and will be delivered from mid-1991. The SM90s will be designed with longer and wider bodies than the recent 'Sprinter' emus. This will allow the NS to evaluate the economy of 3 + 2 seating format instead of the 'Sprinter's' 2 + 2 and also to identify any problems involved in operating longer-bodied train-sets. Other features will include a floor 150mm lower than in existing NS emus, and a built-in power lift to aid the embarcation of handicapped passengers.

In the spring of 1988 NS was testing a German Federal Class 628 dmu between Groningen and Leeuwarden.

Further requirements are assessed as 47 push-pull-equipped electric locomotives, 290 bi-level cars for the Agglo-Regio network to be launched in 1994, a production series of SM90 emus, and a diesel-hydraulic version of the SM90 to replace existing diesel railcars.

The Agglo-Regio bi-levels are likely to be produced as three- or four-car 160 km/h emus, not push-pull trailers. They will also differ from the existing short-haul bi-levels in their interior layout, which will afford greater seat leg room and more baggage space. It may be necesary to incorporate a lift so that a refreshment trolley can be perambulated on both levels.

At the beginning of 1990 NS operated 147 electric and 251 diesel locomotives, 127 locotractors, 1531 emu cars, 258 dmu cars, 33 electric postal railcars, 563 passenger cars and 6608 freight wagons.

Signalling
The investment plan envisages a substantial increase of route-km signalled for reversible working, primarily to simplify track maintenance under traffic. The Hague, Haarlem, Utrecht, Amersfoot and Amsterdam have been equipped with central route-relay interlocking signalboxes and automatic train describer apparatus, and NS's first computerised interlocking has been installed at Hilversum. This last was supplied by Siemens. The ultimate objective is to control the entire network from about 20 signalling centres and Siemens has now been contracted to install a microcomputer-based signalling system at Rotterdam. The scheme involves 56 interlockings and was to be commissioned in 1990. At Roosendaal GRS is supplying a microprocessor-based apparatus for electronic route selection.

The NS has ordered an initial batch of ATP equipments from ACEC.

Track
Standard rail, weights
Main lines: 46·9 and 63 kg/m
Branch lines: 38 and 46 kg/m
Standard rail, lengths
Main lines: 24 and 30 m
Branch lines: 15 and 18 m
Rail joints: 4-hole fishplates and bolts; some welding
Cross ties (sleepers): Hard and soft wood, 250 × 150 × 2600 mm
Spacing
Main lines: 1666 per km
Branch lines: 1333 per km
Rail fastenings: Coach screws (on hard wood), coach screws and soleplates (on soft wood), ribbed soleplates and bolts, ribbed soleplates and curved stirrups of spring steel. Elastic fastening with curved stirrups for both wood and concrete sleepers, the clips fitting into a cast iron housing having two pins glued into concrete sleeper or pressed into wood. Cast iron chairs and bolts. Pads under rails are grooved rubber 4 mm thick or wooden wearing plates 4 mm thick.

Experimental sections laid with 'Zig-zag' concrete block and steel tube track construction.
Filling: Gravel or broken stone, 10–80 mm
Minimum thickness under sleeper: 200 mm
Max curvature: 5·8° = minimum radius 300 m
Max gradient, compensated: 2% = 1 in 50 (on Sittard-Hertzogenrath line)
   uncompensated: 1·43% = 1 in 70 (on Sittard-Hertzogenrath line)
Longest continuous gradient: 8·85 km of 1 in 300 grade with three curves of 1500 m radius
Worst combination of gradient and curvature: 1 in 175 (0·57%) gradient with curves of 300 m radius
Gauge widening on sharpest curve: 7 mm
Super elevation on sharpest curve: 120 mm on track in gravel, 150 mm on track in broken stone
Speed higher than V 105 km/h: 1 in 8V
Speed 105 km/h or less: 1 in 1100 with minimum of 1 in 600
Altitude, max: 181·7 mn Simpleveld-West German frontier section
Max axleload: 22·5 tonnes
Max permitted speed
   Passenger trains: 140 km/h
   Freight trains: 60 km/h
   Fast freight trains: 90 km/h

New Zealand

Ministry of Transport

Minister's Office, Parliament Buildings, Wellington C1

Minister of Transport: Bill P Jeffries
Minister of Railways: Richard W Prebble

New Zealand Railways Corporation (NZR)

Railway Station Building, Bunny Street, Wellington

Telephone: +64 4 725 599
Telefax: +64 4 712 491

Railways Corporation Board
Chairman: Murray R Smith
Directors: Sir Allan Wright
          W J Knox
          Jennifer Morel
          P D Bone
          C Mace
          R Congreve
Chief Executive: K O Hyde
Railfreight Systems Group General Manager: Dr A F Small
General Managers, Finance: E D Dunn
  Rail Properties: J Lee
  Passenger Business Group: R J Middleton
  Railfreight Systems: T I Ambler
  Railnet: J T Atkinson
  Inter-island Line: S Voullaire
  Communications Business Group: P G Hunt
  TEEL: A E Blaber

Gauge: 1067 mm
Route length: 4227 km
Electrification: 108 km at 1·5 kV dc, 411 km at 25 kV 50 Hz ac

Rail transport services are governed by the New Zealand Railways Corporation Act 1981, which requires NZR to provide safe, efficient rail and road transport passenger and freight services; operate a safe, efficient inter-island ferry service for freight including carriage of passengers and vehicles; and provide ancillary support services. The Act also requires revenue to exceed expenditure and a return to be secured on capital. Some urban passenger services are operated in accordance with provisions of the Urban Transport Act 1980; NZR now operate these services primarily as a contractor to regional and local authorities which decide services and fares, and also supply finance.

Management restructure
NZR has been passing through a rapid transition from a politicised government department to a commercially-oriented business. Deregulation of New Zealand's road transport industry, which began in 1983, has resulted in increasingly intensive competition from private truck operators. And, like other business, NZR has also been adversely affected by a downturn in the economy.

These are key factors behind the ongoing restructure of NZR. Continuing rationalisation had reduced staff from over 20 000 in 1983 to below 9000 by the end of 1989. The final total may be 7500.

In March 1990 the government introduced a bill to Parliament that provided for privatisation of NZR assets. Sales might be partial, in which event the North Island-South Island train ferries and NZR bus operations were likely candidates, or total. However, the government promised that the core rail network would not be sold off unless its future was seen as secure.

Finance
In FY 1988-89 the operating loss was NZ$40.6 million, compared with NZ$37.3 million in the previous year. The final result was affected by properrty sale adjustments and masked the fact that in the second half of the year a clear trend towards operating profit in the core businesses, particularly Railfreight Systems, was evident.

Real freight rates have been cut by 43 per cent since deregulation in 1983, but NZR's tonne-km volume of freight has remained stable. This owes a great deal to a 20 per cent rise in average train size and a 94 per cent improvement in staff productivity since 1983.

Another key factor in the operating result has been a growing debt burden. This arises not only from legacies of the past, such as the cost of electrification of the North Island main trunk, but from present restructuring through the high cost of severance payments.

Freight
The key to profitable operation is now seen to be provision of fast, frequent and reliable services particularly for full wagonloads over longer distances.

In 1988 agreement was reached with the enginemen's union for single-manning of selected freight trains. The new Class 30 electric locomotives are designed for driver-only operation.

Tailored comprehensive services, to match specific customer needs, are provided by separate, specialised businesses within the Freight Distribution Division.

Railfreight Intermodal, which provides a range of services for manufacturers and distributors, concentrates on products moved in pallet-load or larger units. The division also provides line-haul transport for most New Zealand and freight forwarding companies. Railfreight Intermodal offers door-to-door, terminal-to-door, terminal-to-terminal, or private siding-to-door transport as well as warehousing, order picking and stock control services.

Railfreight Bulkflow, which handles bulk commodity movements of materials such as coal, cement, quarry products, petroleum products, chemicals, grain, flour, metals and fertilisers, is introducing a new generation of bulk product, aluminium bottom-discharge freight cars with Scheffel cross-braced bogies, and open-top containers specially designed to meet the needs of the coal, grain and fertiliser industries.

Railfreight Cargoflow, which provides onshore distribution of shipping companies' containers, moves import/export containers around New Zealand on behalf of shipping companies, exporters and importers or their agents. A container storage service is available.

Primary produce is handled by Railfreight Agriculture. Railfreight Forestry manages the transport and distribution of forest-based products, and in addition to rail-road-sea transport can provide an integrated storage, warehousing and distribution service.

Railfreight Forwarding specialises in freight transport of small consignments of all types of freight. The door-to-door service provides pick-up and delivery throughout New Zealand. Railfreight Removals provides a nationwide agency for household removals and transport of delicate freight such as furniture. Railfreight Container Services provides storage, cleaning, repair and pre-tripping services for shipping containers.

A freightliner express service between Auckland, Wellington and Christchurch is a recent innovation to speed the delivery of freight traffic. The overnight service (two days for inter-island traffic) is used primarily for containers or wagonloads of cargo consolidated at railfreight terminals. The Doorrail door-to-door freight service, which covers the entire country, concentrating movement between about 30 centres, is also proving successful.

Expansion and consolidation of Railfreight terminals

RAILWAY SYSTEMS / New Zealand

is part of the programme to steadily upgrade freight services.

A programme of incorporating stronger coupling hooks and pins on existing drawgear is proceeding. This will allow longer trains and more competitive pricing. Electrification and associated resignalling (see below) will enable NZR to operate longer, heavier freight trains quicker and more economically through the mountainous central section of the North Island.

In 1988 the Railfreight Group acquired an exclusive licence to build and operate RoadRailer vehicles in the country. The first of 10 curtain-sided prototypes appeared in 1989. They will be used between Auckland and Wellington.

Also in 1989 ability to monitor freight consignments was refined by adoption of a customised version of the computerised system used by the US railroad, CSX. The new software additionally facilitates rate quotations.

Passenger business

The Railways Passenger Business Group provides New Zealand's largest passenger transport network. Long-distance rail and coach services provide daily links between all major centres and principal tourist areas. Suburban trains and buses provide commuter and feeder services in accordance with the Urban Transport Act 1980, which established the Urban Transport Council, and centralised responsibility for the allocation of financial assistance for scheduled urban rail and road passenger services. NZR now acts primarily as a contractor to regional authorities which, with local authorities, determine services and fares. Inter-Island ferries provide a frequent service across Cook Strait. The Passenger Group also operates Speedlink, the depot-to-door parcels delivery service which uses NZR's road, rail and sea services together with private operators, including air charter, to reach all parts of New Zealand.

All sectors of the passenger business suffered from depressed market conditions in FY 1988-89.

Finances (NZ$ million)	1987	1988
Revenue	613.6	648.8
Expenditure	690.1	684.1

Motive power and rolling stock

Number of locomotives in service at the end of 1988:
Diesel 323
Electric 22

Passenger stock in service: three Rm 'Silver Fern' and one PW S&E railcars, 194 electric multiple-unit cars, 176 carriages and 279 vans. Freight wagon stock totalled 15 885 vehicles.

Type of coupler in standard use: Passenger cars: Alliance
Freight cars: 'Norwegian' hook and pin
Type of braking in standard use: Air

Electrification

Electrification of the 411 km North Island Main Trunk railway line between Palmerston North and Hamilton was completed and formally inaugurated in late June 1988. Brush Electrical Machines supplied 22 Bo-Bo-Bo locomotives of 4350 kW output with 105 km/h maximum speed. Other companies of the Hawker Siddeley Group involved were: Hawker Siddeley Rail Projects, which provided technical assistance; Westinghouse Signals, covering telecommunications; and Westinghouse Brake & Signal, Australia, which was engaged for the signalling.

Track
Rail
Main line: 50 kg/m; 91 lb/yd; 85 lb/yd
Provincial lines: 91 lb/yd; 85 lb/yd; 75 lb/yd; 70 lb/yd
Branch lines: 70 lb/yd; 55 lb/yd
Longest length continuous welded rail: 8.5 km (through Kaimai tunnel)
Relaid in new rail: 60 km
Welded method: Flash butt in depot, Thermit in field. New rails flash butt welded in depots into 76.8 m lengths and transported to site for laying. Short rail in track may be Thermit welded into similar lengths. Continuous welded rail is formed on straight track by Thermit process with lapped expansion joints at extremities and epoxy glued joints

Cross ties (sleepers)
NZ Pinus radiata (all lines)
Concrete (main lines only)
Spacing
Main line: Timber 650 mm; Concrete 700 mm

Fastenings
Main lines: Timber: Pandrol spring fastenings on bedplates with rubber pads; clips, screw spikes, spring washers on double-shoed bedplates. Spring clips and screw spikes without bedplates.
Concrete: Pandrol spring fastenings with rubber or plastic pads and nylon insulators.
Branch lines: Timber: Elastic spikes, screws and dog spikes cascaded from higher-ranking lines
Laying method: Concrete: By NZR designed and built sleeper-laying machine
Timber: Laid manually either in face or by spotting
Dimensions
Concrete: 254 × 190 × 2134 mm
Timber: 200 × 150 × 2134 mm

Traffic	1985	1986	1987	1988
Total freight tonnes (million)				
rail	10.39	9.63	9.004	8.228
Searail	1.074	1.07	1.14	1.28
Total freight tonne-km (million)	3192	3051	2912	2924
Average rail haul (km)	307	317	323	328
Total passenger journeys (million)				
rail, long-distance	0.834	0.837	NA	NA
rail, suburban	14.36	14.76	NA	NA
road, long-distance	6.69	6.219	NA	NA
road, suburban	10.03	9.707	NA	NA

Class Dc locomotive, rebuilt by Clyde Engineering, with new Freightliner express heading for Tauranga

Diesel locomotives

Class	Wheel arrange-ment	Trans-mission	Rated power gross kW	Rated power net kW	Tractive effort continuous at kN	Tractive effort continuous at km/h	Weight tonnes	Max axle load tonnes	Year into service	Builders Mechanical parts	Builders Engine & type	Total in service 1988	Use
Dbr	A1A-A1A	Elec	709				68	-	1980	GM	8-645C	10	GP
Dc	A1A-A1A	Elec	1230	1020	140	21.2	82.75	15	1977	GM	12-645E	85	GP
Df	Co-Co	Elec	1230	1020	194	16.5	86.6	14.4	1979	GM	12-645E	30	GP
Di	Co-Co	Elec	755	640	132	14.5	63	10.5	1966	EE	6 CSRKT	2	Freight
Dj	Bo-Bo-Bo	Elec	780	585	128	16.9	65	10.9	1968-69	Mitsubishi	CAT D398	31	GP
Dx	Co-Co	Elec	2050	1940	207	27.4	97.5	16.3	1975-77	GE	7 FDL-12	48	GP
Dh	Bo-Bo	Elec	678	2 × 150	150	20	54	13.5	1978	GE	CAT D398 B	6	Shunting
Dsc	Bo-Bo	Elec	2 × 155		46	13.7	41	10.3	1959-67	AEI/NZR	RR C6TFL Cummins NT855	45	Shunting
Dsj	Bo-Bo	Elec	354				52	13	1982	Toshiba	Cummins KTA-1150-L	5	Shunting
Dsg	Bo-Bo	Elec	2 × 354				56	14	1983	Toshiba	2 × Cummins KTA-1150-L	24	Shunting
Dsa	C(0-6-0)	Hyd	235				30.5	10.2	1956-57	Bagnall	CAT D343T	1	Shunting

Railcar										Builders		Total in service 1988	Use
Class	Wheel arrangement	Transmission	Rated power gross kW	Rated power net kW	Tractive effort continuous at kN	Tractive effort continuous at km/h	Weight tonnes	Max axle load tonnes	Year into service	Mechanical parts	Engine & type		
Rm		Elec	750	650	39	55	111	14·2	1973	KHI Toshiba	CAT D398	3	
Electric locomotives													
Eo	Bo-Bo		960		101	33	55	13·7	1968	Toshiba		5	5 Freight
30	Bo-Bo-Bo		4350		—	—	—	—	1986	Brush		22	Freight
*Delivery 1986/87													
Electric multiple-units													
DM/D			450		38	42·6	42·4	10·7	1936-47	EE		30/50	Suburban passenger
EM/ET			400				72·1	12·9	1982	Ganz-Mávag		44/44	Suburban passenger

Nicaragua

Nicaragua Railway
Ferrocarril de Nicaragua

Apartado Postal No 5, Managua DN

Telephone: +505 22160; 22802-3
Telex: 1239 nicarril

General Manager: S Aguirre Solis
Deputy General Manager Operating: S Cordoba Zamuria
   Technical and Administration: C Altamirano Perez
Directors
   Way and Works: D Parras Ordenana
   Operations: A Tijerino Solis
   Rolling Stock Maintenance: D Araica Martinez
   Finance: G Pena Cortez

Chief Engineer: M Ramos

Gauge: 1067 mm
Route length: 300 km

The railway running from Corinto to Granada with branches to Rio Granda and Puerto Sanohio, operates 16 diesel locomotives (including seven lately acquired secondhand from Canada), eight petrol and four trailers, two diesel railcars, seven passenger cars and 80 freight wagons. Track is laid with 20, 25 and 30 kg/m rails, maximum permissible axleloading is 13.5 tonnes, minimum curve radius 157 metres and maximum gradient 2.5 per cent. Traffic amounts to some 3.5 million passenger journeys and 2.5 million tonnes of freight a year.

New 1435 mm-gauge line
Because of severe hurricane damage in 1982 to the 138 km, 1067 mm-gauge line between the port of Corinto and Granada, it had been reported that construction of a new 1435 mm-gauge line was to be put in hand between Corinto, on the Pacific coast, and the capital city of Managua. This was depicted as the first stage of a line eventually extending some 400 km across the country to the Caribbean port of El Bluff, for a further outlay of US$300 million, and which might ultimately be electrified. However, finance could not be organised and ambition has been limited to rebuilding the worst-affected section of the existing line, the 56 km from Corinto to Leon, by 1993. Loss of this section has been costing the railway 5 million tonnes of import/export freight a year.

In its 1986–91 plan the railway aimed to procure 10 diesel-electric locomotives with the help of Spanish credits; and 10 diesel railcars and 20 trailers with assistance from the German Democratic Republic. Meantime, six locally-constructed petrol railbuses have been taken into use, and two existing but disused diesel railcars have been rebuilt with Perkins KP3 engines and returned to service.

Nigeria

Ministry of Transport and Aviation

1 Joseph Street, Marina, Lagos

Telephone: +234 1 652120

Minister: Lt Gen Alani Akinrinade
Permanent Secretary: T A Anumudu

Nigerian Railway Corporation (NRC)

PMB 1037, Ebute Metta, Lagos

Telephone: +234 1 834300
Telex: 26584 eb rail ng

Administrator: Dr Samuel O Ogbemudia
Secretary: U A Uduma
Directors, Administration: M Dange
   Operations: J C Machie
   Civil Engineering: J N E Maduekwe
   Mechanical and Electrical Engineering: S R M Wilcox
   Finance: Mrs F O Fadipe
   New Lines: A Bakare
Assistant Directors, Loco: C E Okoye
   Running: P T Makyur
   Operations: L O Badamosi
   Research & Development: B U Chine
   Carriages & Electrical: H C Uche
   Track: C A Odumodu
   Works: A G I Nwokedi
   Signals and Communications: M O Sokoya
   Finance: H O Sanusi
   Commercial: N O Ndukwe
   Materials Management: P I A Ricketts

Gauge: 1067 mm
Route length: 3505 km

Hitachi 1870 hp I-B+B+B-I diesel-electric locomotive

Nigeria has the most extensive highway and railway networks in West Africa. The Federal government has responsibility for 30 000 km of primary and secondary highways as well as NRC. The former Nigerian Government Railways was converted to a statutory corporation by Act of Parliament in 1955.

The entire network, apart from the departments based at Lagos headquarters, is managed in six divisions.

Neglect
NRC has suffered severely from the country's earlier oil boom, which fed an explosive road transport development in the 1970s, and Nigeria's more recent financial difficulties. With road transport enjoying an oil price subsidy and the railway badly run down, NRC has only a 5 per cent share of the transport market. After the departure of a RITES management team in 1982, NRC's freight tonnage halved and its passenger traffic dropped to some 10 million journeys from a peak of 15.3 million.

Bankruptcy and recovery
In November 1988 NRC was driven to declare bankruptcy. That was inevitable when the government blocked further subsidy until NRC could show that the money was not being frittered away. The government peremptorily ordered the sacking without compensation of a quarter of NRC's staff, whereupon the remainder stopped work because, with NRC's subsidy

682 RAILWAY SYSTEMS / Nigeria—Norway

cut off, they could not be paid. Thereafter few if any trains ran until spring 1989, when a new administrator was appointed. His brief was to set up an emergency programme of traction and rolling stock overhaul, get trains running again, but at the same time to reduce NRC's labour costs. The new appointee was also bidden to make more money from NRC's property.

By mid-1989 some short-haul passenger services were back in regular operation and long-haul passenger and freight services were working as sporadically as drastically limited availability of serviceable locomotives allowed. At the same time reorganisation of staff arrangements and negotiations for a new relationship with the government were put in hand.

At the start of 1990 the Transport Minister announced intention to legislate more commercial freedom for the railway. The latter would be restructured to place infrastructure under a separate authority, and new passenger and freight divisions would be created. It was also disclosed that the World Bank had agreed a US$20.8 milion loan for rehabilitation of 75 diesel locomotives, chiefly with spares from General Electric of the USA.

Motive power and rolling stock
At last report NRC owned 189 main-line diesel locomotives, 54 diesel shunters, 480 passenger cars and 4917 freight wagons. Only some 40 locomotives were reported servicable in 1989.

In 1989 an order was placed with Samsung of Korfea for 36 passenger cars.

Standard-gauge project
In 1981 the government engaged Sofrerail to undertake a detailed engineering study of the first planned stage of a new standard-gauge system; a 463 km line from Port Harcourt to Makurdi; and a 217 km line from Oturkpo to the new steelworks at Ajaokuta being built by the USSR. Early in 1982 the first three of the six segments into which the construction has been divided were under contract. Later in the year, however, the US$2500 million scheme had to be postponed indefinitely. Because of the receding world demand for oil and its declining price, it proved impossible to finance two of the six contracts, besides which the country had to curb imports. The future of the branch to the Ajaokuta steelworks, already begun, looked for a time uncertain, but in 1987 Julius Berger Nigeria Ltd, subsidiary of a Federal German company, was in 1987 awarded a contract to complete and equip with rolling stock this 51.2 km iron ore line from Itakpe to the steelworks. Completion was set for January 1990 with opening to traffic in the following June.

Signalling
In 1983 Westinghouse Brake & Signal Co gained a N5.5 million contract to install colour-light power-operated signalling. The 420 km Offa-Minna section of the Lagos-Kano line and over 156 km of the Port Harcourt line from Kaduna to Kafanchan are now controlled by panel interlockings and tokenless block instruments.

Track
As much as 80 per cent of NRC track is reported in need of overhaul
Rail: BS60R 29.8 kg/m; BS70A 34.7 kg/m; BS80R, 80A 39.7 kg/m
Cross ties (sleepers): Steel, 130 × 7.5 mm
Fastenings: Pandrol: K Type

Norway
Ministry of Communications

Møllergaten 1-3, Oslo

Telephone: +72 2 349090
Telex: 21439 sdepn
Telefax: +47 2 349570

Minister: William Engseth
Under-Secretary of State: Bjørg Simonsen
Secretary-General: Karin Brazelius

Norwegian State Railways (NSB)
Norges Statsbaner

Storgaten 33, 0184 Oslo 1

Telephone: +47 2 368000
Telex: 71 168 nsbdc n
Telefax: +47 2 415581

Director General: Tore Lindholt (Acting)
Managers: Human Resources: Lars Haukaas
Labour Relations: Ole M Drangsholt
Special Projects: Yngve Pedersen
Pubic Relations: Reidar Skaug Høymork
Work Environment and Social Services: Ivar Ødegaard
Passenger Traffic: Rolf Bergstrand
Freight Traffic: Rolf Gillebo
Infrastructure: Magne Paulsen
Rolling Stock and Workshops: Per Bøyum
Engineering: Kjell Moi
Property: Jan Runesson
Road Traffic: Narve Breili
Travel Agencies: Tore Helland

Gauge: 1435 mm
Route length: 4044 km
Electrification: 2422 km at 15 kV 16⅔ Hz ac

1990–93 investment plan
In June 1989 Parliament set a capital investment limit of NOK 5400 million on the NSB's 1990–93 Plan, which was NOK 900 million less than the NSB had requested. However, Parliament restored a NOK 150 million cut in NSB's 1990 investment which the government had proposed. Thus the principle of progressive annual increase in NSB's investment during the Plan's currency was respected.

In the passenger sector, NSB aims to concentrate on high-usage services, which will mean in particular a bias to the short- and medium-distance intercity operations, such as Oslo-Ski and Oslo-Halden. Considerable extra traffic is expected from the projected line to Oslo's new Hurum airport (see below).

In the freight sector, investments totalling NOK 1700 million were sought in the Norwegian parts of the Oslo-Göteborg and Oslo-Stockholm lines, to plug NSB effectively into the Scandinavian Railways'

Class El 17 electric locomotive and B7 cars forming Oslo-Trondheim 'Dovesprinten'

New aluminium-bodied sleeping car

developing Scanlink network of unit train links with Western European railways. NSB aims to standardise 100 km/h speed for freights with 22.5-tonne axleloads, and 160 km/h for intermodal trains with 14-tonne axleload wagons. In mind is establishment of 11 strategic centres for interconnection by direct fast trains under the brandname of 'InterCity Gut'.

State takes over infrastructure costs

Parliament also approved in mid-1989 a new NSB budgetary system, which came into operation from the start of 1990. It separates financially the infrastructure and business activity of the railway. Infrastructure management remains within the NSB organisation, but Parliament will fix annual appropriations for operating and upkeep expenses and for investment. NSB accounts will no longer have to include investments in infrastructure.

Parliament will determine annually the toll to be paid by NSB for use of the infrastructure. The level of toll will reflect long-term marginal costs and in that respect may differentiate between different types of rail traffic. The level of toll will also take account of environmental factors and of parity with other modes. It was therefore probable that passenger trains would be exempt, since road passenger transport pays no specific infrastructure tax. Since an objective of the new arrangements is that NSB become self-financing as a purely transport operator, it was expected that socially neceassry passenger services would be state- or locally-subsidised.

Finance

Financially, 1989 was a satisfying year. Total operating revenues were up 3.6 per cent on 1988, but operating expenses by only 2.6 per cent. The final result was NOK 83.7 million above budget.

Passenger traffic

Passenger traffic on intercity and medium-distance routes continued its growth in 1989, rising by a further 5.9 per cent in terms of journeys. Passenger-km were up 1.2 per cent. Since the national passenger travel market generally was stagnant, this represented a gain of market share. Concentration of all Oslo's traffic on the new Central station was one stimulus. Another was the Kundekort introduced in 1988. Costing Kr295, this card entitles holders up a 30 per cent discount on the full fare on Fridays and Sundays and a 50 per cent discount during the rest of the week. More than a third of its purchasers are reckoned to have been non-railway users previously.

The 1994 Winter Olympics are being staged at Lillehammer, 184 km north of Oslo. To cater for the extra passenger traffic anticipated NSB wants to install five new passing loops on its line and to extend others. Its working party studying need of rolling stock has advocated acquisition of three four-car medium-distance and 15 three-car local service emus by 1994. Further rolling stock would be borrowed from other railways. Up to the start of 1990, however, government approval for the investment was stil awaited.

200km/h tilt-body proposal

In May 1990 NCB unveiled a plan branded 'Tog 2004' (the year 2004 will be the 150th anniversary of the country's first railway) to develop four routes for operation at up to 200 km/h by tilt-body train-sets. The routes in mind are: Oslo-Halden-(Göteborg-Copenhagen); Oslo-Skien; Oslo-Lillehammer-Trondheim; and Oslo-Bergen, including the Ringeriksbanen. It was estimated that with such development Oslo-Bergen journey time could be cut from 6 hours 35 minutes to 2 hours 50 minutes, and Oslo-Trondheim time from 6 hours 40 minutes to 3 hours 45 minutes. Copenhagen would become only 4 hours 15 minutes travel time from Oslo instead of 9 hours 30 minutes, Stockholm 3 hours 30 minutes away instead of 6 hours 20 minutes. Total investment required for the four routes would be NOK 55000 million, but for NOK 7000 million a pioneer scheme could be completed between Oslo and Lillehammer.

Freight traffic

In the second half of 1989 a further decline in the first half was reversed and the end-result for the year as a whole was a rise of 6.2 per cent in tonne-km. Ore traffic on the Ofoten line rose 6.1 per cent. The turnround was ascribed partly to increased demand from some customers, partly to new traffic, in particular exports of fresh and frozen fish. But the financial state of the rail freight business continues to cause concern.

On the Ofoten line a major investment in new transshipment facilities was in progress at Narvik. Completed, it will enable a 4200-tonne train to be discharged on the move within 30 minutes.

In conjunction with EB Strømmens Verksted, NSB has concluded an agreement with Tiger Europe to exploit the latter's bi-modal TrailerTrain. Prototype vehicles were given a midwinter evaluation on the NSB in early 1990.

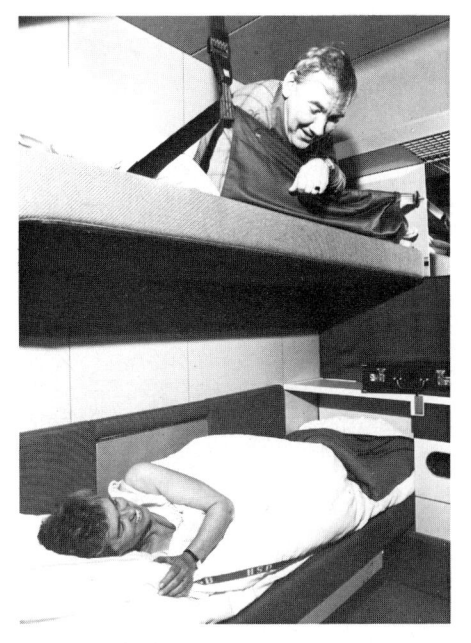

Berth of new sleeping car

Broad corridor of sleeping car makes room for seats and tables

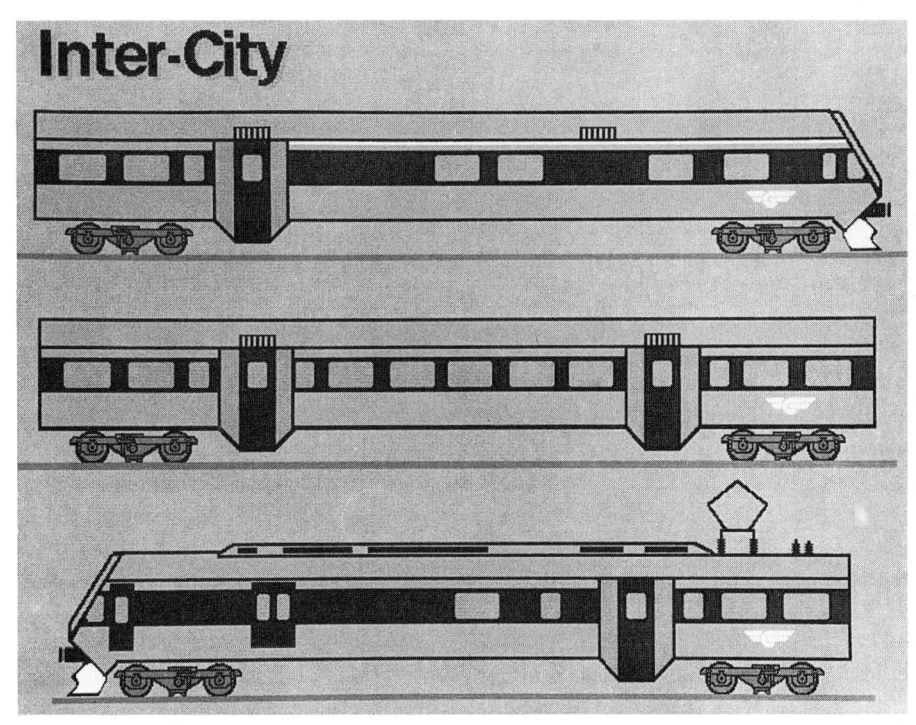

Artist's impression of new intercity electric train-set

Traffic	1987	1988	1989
Freight tonnage	23.6	22.7	23.7
Freight tonne-km	2822	2617	2780.3
Passenger journeys	36.7	34.1	33.8
Passenger-km	2187	2110	2136
Finances (NOK million)	1987	1988	1989
Total revenues	3158	3153	3201*
Operating expenses	4380	4601	4719
Depreciation and interest	786	663	729
Total deficit	2008	2111	

* In addition there was NOK 2331 million of revenue through social services operated under contract

Infrastructure

Re-routing of the track between Voss and Bulken on the Bergen line started in 1988. NSB is carrying out this work in co-operation with the Public Roads Administration. NSB has pressed for provision in the 1990–93 Plan for a start on the 11.8 km cut-off, including a 10.2 km tunnel, in the Finse summit area of the Oslo-Bergen line. This project was aborted in 1988 by government curbs on NSB's capital investment.

Work to renew the overhead contact line and safety system on the Østfold line between Oslo and Ski was completed during 1988. In December 1989 the first section of the line's double-tracking from Ski to Moss was completed between Tveter and Vestby, and the Vestby-Rustad segment was ready for the summer traffic of 1990. The entire line will be doubled by 1996. NSB wanted to accelerate the work, but the government saw no reason to provide for an earlier completion in the 1990–93 plan.

Branch line closures

From 1 January 1989 onwards the 26km Kragerø line was closed down. Passenger traffic ceased on the 107

RAILWAY SYSTEMS / Norway

km Valdres and 92km Numedal lines, but on these latter goods traffic continues on certain sections. Traffic on the Flekkefjord line was to continue until the end of 1990.

Hurum Airport line
A major project initiated in 1988 will create a rail link to the new national airport at Hurum. NSB has planned an orbital line, which will cross the Oslo fjord and link the Østfold line and the Drammen line together at Hurum. NSB is cooperating in the scheme with the Civil Aviation Administration's project management division and the Directorate of Public Roads. The first segment is expected to be ready in 1995.

North Norway project shelved
Feasibility studies for the construction of a line from Fauske to Narvik, and Tromsø, to connect these ports directly with the rest of the NSB network, were completed in 1981, but there has been no further action. The proposed route was 476 km long and much of the 183 km from Fauske to Narvik would have had to be tunnelled through the mountains enclosing a succession of fjords in its path. NSB now regards the scheme as shelved indefinitely in favour of other infrastructure investments.

Instead, a joint intermodal service has been developed with the Tollpost-Globe coastal shipping line, which plies between Bodø and Tromsø, where an NSB freight centre has been set up. The service is for swap-bodies, which are transshipped to ship at Bodø, or at Fauske for onward road haulage to the far north.

New carriage maintenance depot at Lodalen

Traction and rolling stock
In 1989 NSB's motive power park consisted of 154 electric locomotives, 101 diesel locomotives, 129 electric railcars and emu vehicles, 36 diesel railcars and 95 locotractors. Rolling stock included 777 passenger coaches and 6086 freight wagons.

EB Strømmens Verksted, an ABB Group company, is the main contractor for nine new electric intercity train-sets ordered in 1988 by NSB for routes in eastern Norway. Production began in the second half of 1989, and deliveries would be completed by September 1992.

Each of the nine, 232-seat sets is made up of a motor coach, two intermediate coaches and a driving trailer. The motor coaches will contain luggage compartments, family compartments and second-class accommodation. The intermediate coaches will have second-class accommodation and space for taking skis. The driving trailers will contain first-class seating arranged so that it is suitable for conferences, second-class accommodation, telephones and catering facilities for serving hot and cold food and drinks. The trains will also have provision for handicapped passengers. These intercity trains are intended for a maximum speed of 160 km/h. They will be built using extruded aluminium profiles and fitted with asynchronous traction motors.

The contract also includes two alternative options for further deliveries. The first is for five complete sets. The second option is for the supply of nine to 14 intermediate coaches. These would be identical to those included in the first nine train-sets. If this latter option were taken up, this part of the delivery could be completed before 1994, enabling the coaches to enter service in time for the Winter Olympics in Lillehammer.

To extend Oslo stopping train services, five more Type 69D three-coach units were ordered for delivery in 1990.

NSB hopes to order 10 more diesel locomotives with asynchronous three-phase motors. A choice of power plant remains to be made between the latest GM engine or two MWM engines. In the longer term NSB aims to buy 60-80 universal electric locomotives, classified E18, with asynchronous motors and six axles, possibly with radial steering. These mixed traffic units would supersede NSB's older types.

Signalling
EB Lehmkuhl a.s., a company in the ABB Group, received an order from NSB for a new computer-controlled, electronic interlocking system, the first of its kind in Norway. It was to be installed at NSB's Alnabru goods yard in Oslo.

Track
Rail: S 54 kg/m S 49 kg/m
Cross ties (sleepers): Concrete 2400 × 280 × 196 mm; wood 2500 × 250 × 140 mm
Spacing: 1667/km
Rail fastenings: On main lines the principal fastenings to wood sleepers are Hey-Back and Deenik. Pandrol fastenings have been adopted as standard fastenings on concrete sleepers. On the Bergen-Tunestveit line, and in long tunnels where UIC54 and 864 rails are used, the fastening is elastic double-shaft railspikes on hardwood sleepers without base-plates.
On branch lines the fastenings consist mainly of dog spikes, wedge plates and Hey-Back
Pads under rails: With Hey-Back fastenings a thin, 1.25 mm rubber pad is inserted between rail and base-plate.
With Pandrol fastenings a 5 mm thick plastic pad is inserted between rail and concrete sleeper.
As a general rule pads are not used under rails except with Hey-Back fastenings

Minimum curve radius: 130 m (branch)
    180 m (main line)
Max gradient: 5.5% (branch)
    2.5% (main line)
Max axleload: 22.5 tonnes

Electric locomotives

Class	Wheel arrangement	Line current	Rated output kW	Max lb (kg)	Tractive effort (full field) Continuous at lb (kg)	mph (km/h)	Max speed mph (km/h)	Wheel dia in (mm)	Weight tonnes	Length ft in (mm)	No in service 1989	Year built	Builders Mechanical parts	Electrical equipment
El 10	C	15 kV 16⅔ Hz	515	23 400 (10 600)	11 700 (5300)	17 (27)	28 (45)	43¼ (1100)	47	31'6" (9600)	8	1949-52	ASJ, Thunes	ASEA, PK
El 11	Bo-Bo	15 kV 16⅔ Hz	1676	32 280 (14 300)	17 640 (7800)	44 (71)	62 (100)	40⅜ (1025)	62	47'5" (14 450)	40	1951-64	Thunes	Norsk Elektrisk; Brown Boveri
El 12	1-D+D-1	15 kV 16⅔ Hz	2398	99 200 (45 000)	8157 (3700)	31 (60)	47 (75)	52⅛ (1350)	180	82'4" (26 490)	7	1954-57	Motala	ASEA
El 13	Bo-Bo	15 kV 16⅔ Hz	2648	41 900 (19 000)	28 700 (13 000)	43 (69)	62 (100)	53⅛ (1350)	72	49'2½" (15 000)	37	1957-66	Thunes	Norsk Elektrisk; Brown Boveri
El 14	Co-Co	15 kV 16⅔ Hz	5076	77 200 (35 000)	47 619 (21 700)	41 (76)	75 (120)	50 (1270)	105	58'5" (17 740)	31	1968-73	Thunes	Norsk Elektrisk; Brown Boveri
El 15	Co-Co	15 kV 16⅔ Hz	5406	171 600 (78 000)	111 480 (53 400)	44 (71)	75 (120)	49¼ (1250)	132	130'4" (19 900 + 19 900)		1967	Thunes	ASEA-Per Kure
El 16	Bo-Bo	15 kV 16⅔ Hz	4440	72 311 (32 800)	45 194 (20 500)	48 (78)	87 (140)	51 (1300)	80	50'11" (15 520)	17	1977-78/83	Strømmens, Nohab, Hamjern	ASEA
El 17	Bo-Bo	15 kV 16⅔ Hz	3400 3400	52 911 (24 000)			93 (150)	43¼ (1100)	64	53'6" (16 300)	12	1981	Henschel	NEBB, BBC Mannheim

Diesel locomotives

Class	Wheel arrangement	Transmission	Rated power hp	Max lb (kg)	Tractive effort Continuous at lb (kg)	mph (km/h)	Max speed mph (km/h)	Wheel dia in (mm)	Total weight tonnes	Length ft in (mm)	No in service 1989	First built	Builders Mechanical parts	Engine & type	Transmission
Di 2	C	Hyd	575 600	30 600 (13 900)	26 500 (12 000)	3.7 (6)	50 (80)	49¼ (1250)	45	32'10" (10 000)	46	1958	Thunes	BMV-LT6	
Di 3a	Co-Co	Elec	1775	48 500 (23 000)	37 900 (17 200)	14 (23)	65 (105)	40 (1016)	102	61' (18 950)	31	1954-69	Nohab	GM 16-567C	GM-ASEA
Di 3b	A1A	Elec	1775	37 478 (17 000)	30 864 (14 000)	11 (26)	81 (143)	40 (1016)	104	62' (18 900)	3	1959	Nohab	GM 16-567C	GM-ASEA
Di 4	Co-Co	Elec	3300	39 365 (17 860)			87 (140)	43¼ (1100)	113.6	68' (20 803)	5	1981	Henschel	GM 16-645E 3B	GM-BBC
Di 5	C	Hyd	650	-	-	-	27 (60)	-	54	-	16	1959*	MaK	MTU GTU 6	Voith

* Bought secondhand from DB 1985/87

Diesel railcars or multiple-units

Class	Cars per unit	Motor cars per unit	Motored axles per motor car	Transmission	Rated power (kW) per motor	Max speed km/h	Weight tonnes per car (M-motor T-trailer)	Total seating capacity per car (M-motor T-trailer)	Length per car mm (M-motor T-trailer)	No in service 1989	Year first built	Builders Mechanical parts	Engine & type	Transmission
BM 86	2	1	2	Mech	2 × 156 = 312	100	M:31 T:19	M:70 T:68	21 500	8	1940	Strømmen	2 × Rolls Royce C6SFLH	SCG SE4
BM 89	1	1	2	Mech	145	115	19	47	17 550	5	1957	Linköping	Scania Vabiz D 815	Wilson R11B
BM 91	2	1	2	Mech	2 × 156 = 312	100	M:31 T:19	M:64 T:24	21 500	1	1954	Strømmen	2 × Rolls Royce C6 SF1H	SCG SE4
BM 92	2	1	2	Elec	2 × 357 = 714	140	M:58 T:38	M:68 T:68	24 725	15	1984	Duewag	2 × Daimler-Benz OM 424A	BBC

Pakistan

Ministry of Railways

Islamabad

Telephone: +92 51 872650
Telex: 5714 mrail pk

Minister: Zafar Ali Khan Leghari
Secretary: Muhammad Ashraf Sheikh

Pakistan Railway (PR)

Shara-E-Sheikh Abdul Hameed Bin Badees, Lahore

Telephone: 306186/7, 67424
Cable: Pakrail Lahore
Telex: 44672 prh pk

Chairman, Railway Board: Muhammad Ashraf Sheikh
Board Members
  Mechanical Engineering: S M Waheeduddin
  Traffic: S Zahoor Ahmad
  Civil Engineering: M A Shaikh
  Finance and Budget: M A Khan
Federal Government Inspector, Railways: Raji Abdul Razzaq
General Manager: Zafarullah Qureshi
Deputy General Manager: S H Shah
Chief Operating Superintendent: Lal Din Tarar
Chief Traffic Manager: Iqbal Samad
Chief Traffic Manager, Dry Port: I S Khan
Chief Marketing Manager: Hadi Iqbal Hussain
Chief Commercial Manager: M Aslam
Chief Controller of Stores: M Sarwar
Chief Controller of Purchase: M A Qadeer Khan
Chief Personnel Officer: A Rehman
Chief Electrical Engineer: Dr A F Hamdani
Chief Engineer, Way & Works: Mohammed Ashiq
Chief Engineer, Planning: S Akhtar Ali Shah
Chief Mechanical Engineer: Muhammad Zia Ullah
Chief Mechanical Engineer/C&W: M Z Mozaffar
Chief Engineer, Surveys and Construction: R Mahmud
Chief Engineer, Signals: M A Mahfooz Khan
Chief Engineer, Telecom: Maghfoor Khan
Director, Management Information System: Mohammad Ashraf Bhatti
Financial Adviser and Chief Accounts Officer: K Rashid
Director, Land Management: A R Chaudhry
Director, Research and Training: S A Kazim
General Manager, Railway Manufacture: K A Khurshid
Joint Director, Civil Engineering: A M Mian
Joint Director, Commercial: Nazir Ahmad
Joint Director, Traffic: M Saeed Pervez
Chief Engineer, Manufacture: S R A Rizvi
Chief Mechanical Engineer, Manufacture: Z A Siddiqui

Gauge: 1676 mm; 1000 mm; 762 mm
Route length: 7718 km; 446 km; 611 km
Electrification: 293 km of 1676 mm-gauge at 25 kV 50 Hz ac

The PR system comprises the whole of the North-Western system of the former British India rail network with the exception of lines in the south-western Punjab. The main routes connect Karachi with Hyderabad, Multan, Lahore, Rawalpindi, Peshawar,

A GE-built diesel brings a Kundian–Multan train into Sher (Hugh Ballantyne)

Quetta and Zahidan. It was known as Pakistan Western Railway from 1961 to 1974.

Privatisation

The now deposed government of Ms Benazhir Bhutto sought to privatise state industry. For the railway, the first step proposed was a trial privatisation of operation on PR's narrow-gauge lines, though the state would retain ownership of the infrastructure.

The broad-gauge system would be divided into two networks under overall Ministry control. The part in Punjab and the Northwest Frontier province would become Pakistan Northern Railway; that in Sind and Baluchistan would become Pakistan Southern Railway.

In 1990 the Railways Ministry invited prequalification bids from consultants for a study of hiving off the railways' workshops and manufacturing units as independent organisations. That apart, no positive move to change the railways' status was reported in 1989.

Investment

For FY 1989-90 PR's investment was cut 28 per cent

below the previous year's amount, to Rs 572.4 million. Moreover, close on half the 1989-90 amount was earmarked for a controversial locomotive manufacturing plant's construction at Risalpur. This project has been strongly criticised as an extravagance, given the limited new locomotive requirements of PR from year to year. The case for local assembly of kits rather than importation of finished locomotives is certainly persuasive. But critics assert that at far less cost existing PR plant could have been be developed to fully meet PR's needs.

By the spring of 1990, however, government attitudes appeared to be changing. The Ministry of Railways announced that in conjunction with the World Bank it had drafted a Rs11 650 million five-year programme for PR, encompassing all the items in the railway's own plan (see below) and furthermore budgeting more generously for the proposals.

Seventh Five-Year Plan

Pakistan Railways has launched a development programme with a tentative outlay of Rs 8480 million which is covered by the government's seventh Five-Year Plan from 1988-93. The main objectives are to enable the railway to carry its due share of passenger and freight traffic to achieve self-sufficiency; and to ensure a proper communication system for better utilisation of assets and to improve railway operation.

PR's national freight market share has slipped from 49 to 25 per cent since the early 1970s. But the freight operations cover their cost, whereas the passenger business meets only 47 per cent of its expenses.

Major items of expenditure include an outlay of Rs 1525 million for the rehabilitation of 101 Alco diesel-electric locomotives and Rs 1345 million for the local manufacture of 440 passenger carriages, including procurement of 15 high-speed passenger coaches. In 1989 four companies pre-qualified for the Alco locomotive re-engining, which the Canadian International Development Agency and the World Bank are supporting financially. Rs 72 million has been earmarked for the manufacture of 100 bogie tank wagons for the transportation of POL products while rehabilitation and procurement of 250 traction motors would be carried out through an allocation of Rs 361 million.

The plan also proposes rehabilitation of 310 km of track with 50 kg rails/PSC sleepers, 200 km of sleeper renewal with PSC sleepers on primary A section, 265 km of complete track renewal with 45 kg rails/RCC sleepers on primary B section and 475 km each of rail and sleeper renewal with SS rails and new RCC sleepers on secondary/tertiary sections.

Another major project is the electrification of 91 km of single track and 27.35 km of double track of the Khanewal-Samasata section via the Chord line (see below). It is also intended to move for transfer of technology in various fields: for track in the manufacture of RCC sleepers for points and crossings; and for rolling stock in the manufacture of high-speed carriages. The Islamic Development Bank has loaned US$6 million for acquisition of 15 vehicles under a technology transfer deal (see below).

On the Lahore-Karachi main line, the speed of mail and express trains has been lifted from 95 to 120 mph. Action is under way to improve the existing speeds of passengers and goods trains on other sections.

Under the World Bank-sponsored eleventh Railway Project, expansion of Lahore Dry Port has almost been completed with adequate facilities for handling container traffic, which is fast increasing. The first dedicated ISO container train has been inaugurated for American President Lines between Karachi and the Lahore Dry Port.

Trials of a 2500-tonne freight train equipped with a new type of air brake have proved the feasibility of raising freight train speed.

Signalling and traffic control

A major improved signalling project comprising both conventional and modern signalling works, such as provision of colour-light signals on the double-track main line between Lahore and Raiwind and of tokenless block on other important railway sections, starting with Lodhran-Khanewal-Faisalabad and Sangla Hill-Wazirabad, is programmed. Following a call for international tenders, orders for design, supply and installation of the equipment were placed with Siemens of Federal Germany. Bids for installation of automatic block signalling over the 101km Bin Qasim-Meting sector of the Karachi-Kotri section were called in 1989.

A modern train and traffic control system has been installed on the Rawalpindi-Peshawar Cantt section of main line over a length of 173.59 km. The equipment

Class HBU 20 Hitachi-built diesel Co-Co leaves Ratanabad with a Hyderabad-Mirphur Khar train (*Hugh Balantyne*)

PR electric locomotives at Khanewal (*Hugh Ballantyne*)

was supplied by Aydin Monitor System of the USA.

Provision of modern telecommunications to replace the existing open-line network was begun in 1981 with World Bank assistance. The core of the system is a microwave link between Karachi and Rawalpindi, with branches to Quetta, Multan and Lahore, which was completed in 1986. Outlying areas are served by uhf links, while vhf radio is being provided at about 80 base stations and in 500 locomotives, giving voice communication between controllers and moving trains. Axle counters are installed at 68 locations between Lodhran and Hyderabad. The project was delayed by a dispute with the US contractor, but was resumed by Daewoo of Korea in 1984. The new system is a 960-channel microwave network in the 7 GHz band interconnecting 44 sites between Karachi and Rawalpindi via the Khanewal-Faisalabad-Lahore route and spurs on the Sukkur-Shaheed Allah Bakhsh-Rojhan-Liaquatpur, Sangla Hill-Hafizabad-Wazirabad and Khanewal-Multan-Kot Adu and on Bandhi-Dadu routes.

Finances (Rs 000)

Revenue	1986/87	1987/88
Passengers and luggage	1 586 161	1 988 126
Freight, parcels and mail	3 044 340	3 357 357
Other	80 016	93 597
Total	4 710 517	5 439 080
Expenditure		
Operation	4 073 378	4 405 904
Depreciation	845 475	845 475
Total	4 918 853	5 251 379

Traffic	1987	1988
Freight tonnage (million)	11.646	11.639
Freight tonne-km (million)	7819.82	8033.23
Passenger-km (million)	16 919.8	18 541.5
Passenger journeys (million)	78.141	81.239

Motive power and rolling stock

At the start of 1989 PR disposed of 137 steam locomotives, 566 diesel-electric locomotives, 29 electric locomotives, 11 railcars, 2500 passenger cars and 35 596 wagons on its broad-gauge system. Metre-gauge stock comprised 25 steam locomotives, 71 passenger cars and 609 freight cars; and narrow-gauge (762 mm gauge) stock, 35 steam locomotives, 92 passenger cars and 301 freight wagons.

In 1989 PR was seeking offers for supply of 15 passenger cars under a technology transfer arrangement, with two to be shipped complete, three part-finished and the residue in kit form for local assembly at Islamabad. The Islamic Development Bank was backing the deal.

In March 1988 PR's Moghalpura works at Lahore completed its first diesel locomotive. This was a 3000 hp Co-Co similar to the HGMU-30 type supplied by Thyssen-Henschel to a GM-EMD design, but built for about 80 per cent of the cost of an imported example. PR has a licence to build to GM-EMD design, and aims to develop series production of 15-20 locomotives a year in the course of the Seventh Five-Year plan. The Bhutto government was against further importation of complete locomotives, and would sanction only purchase of components incapable of local manufacture.

Electrification

In order to get full benefits of electric traction and to remove operational bottlenecks, further extension of electric traction up to Samasata both via Chord and Loop is considered essential. It will eliminate the operating handicaps of engine changing, duplicate maintenance facilities for electric and diesel traction and rest facilities for crew and supervisory staff at Khanewal. Extension of electric traction up to Samasata via the Chord section of the main line has, therefore, been given priority over the Loop line. The project, involving 90.1 km of single and 27.4 km of double track has been included in the seventh Five-Year Plan at an estimated cost of Rs 657.9 million, which on completion is expected to result in an annual approximate saving of Rs 74.90 million. Tenders to execute the electrification were called in late 1989.

Track doubling
Doubling of track for 50 km from Multan Cantt to Khanewal has been included in the seventh Five-Year Plan at an anticipated cost of Rs 191.0 million. This will be an extension of doubling from Sher-shah to Multan Cantt which has been functioning since the end of 1980. At present 27 trains each way are running on this section against the nominal capacity of 19 trains each way. On completion of the Pak-Arab fertiliser factory at Piran Ghaib, the traffic will increase further.

It has therefore become imperative to increase the line capacity to cope with anticipated traffic of 36 trains each way.

Track
Rail: 50 kg RE, 45 kg R BSS, 37.5 kg R BSS
Cross-ties (sleepers)

Type	Thickness	Spacing
PSC Monobloc	234 mm	1640/km
RCC twin-block	231.77 mm	1562/km
Wooden	125.152 mm	1562/km
Steel trough	106.36 mm	1562/km
CST 9 (cast iron plates joined with tie bar)	133.35 mm	1562/km

Fastenings
PSC/RCC sleepers: RM Type
Wooden sleepers: WI bearing plates with dog spikes; CI bearing plates with round spikes and keys
Steel trough sleepers: Mills spring loose jaws with keys
CST/9 CI plate sleepers: Keys
Minimum curvature radius: 10°
Max gradient: 4%
Max permissible axleload: 22.86 tonnes

Diesel locomotives

Class	Manufacturer's type reference	Wheel arrangement	Transmission	Rated power (kW)	Max speed km/h	Total weight tonnes	No in service 1988	Year first built	Builders — Mechanical parts	Builders — Engine & type	Builders — Transmission
HGMU-k30	TV6125A2	Co-Co	Elec	2462	120	120	30	1985	Thyssen Henschel	GM USA/16-645E3C	GM USA
GMU-30	GTCW-2	Co-Co	Elec	2238	122	114.95	36	1975	GM USA	GM USA/16-645E3	GM USA
GMU-15	GL-220	Co-Co	Elec	1119	122	85.44	32	1975	GM USA	GM USA/12-645E	GM USA
GMCU-15	G22CU	Co-Co	Elec	1119	122	86.90	30	1979	GM Canada	GM USA/12-645E	GM Canada
GEU-61	–	Bo-Bo	Elec	455	80	67.84	3	1954	GE USA	Cooper Bassmer/USA-FWL-67	GE USA
GEU-15	U-15-C	Co-Co	Elec	1492	122	83.00	23	1970	GE USA	GE USA/7FDL-B4	GE USA
GEU-20	U-20-C	Co-Co	Elec	1119	122	96.00	40	1971	GE USA	GE USA/7FDL-B11	GE USA
HAU-20	HFA-10A	Co-Co	Elec	746	72	120	4	1980	Hitachi Japan	Alco USA/6-251E	Hitachi Japan
HAU-20	HFA-22A	Co-Co	Elec	1492	120	102.6	28	1982	Hitachi Japan	Alco USA/12-251GE	Hitachi Japan
HBU 20	HFA-22B	Co-Co	Elec	1492	125	105	60	1986	Hitachi Japan	Bombardier/12-251C4	Hitachi Japan
HPU-k20	HFA-24P	Co-Co	Elec	1492	120	101.3	10	1982	Hitachi Japan	Pielstick/12PA4200VG	Hitachi Japan
ALU-95	DL-531	Co-Co	Elec	709	104	73.98	25	1958	Alco USA	Alco USA/6-251B	GE USA
ALU-12	DL-535	Co-Co	Elec	895	96	75.00	49	1962	Alco USA	Alco USA/6-251B	GE USA
ALU-18	DL-541	Co-Co	Elec	1343	120	96.00	27	1961	Alco USA	Alco USA/12-251B	GE USA
ALU-20	DL-543	Co-Co	Elec	1492	120	102	52	1962	Alco USA	Alco USA/12-251C	GE USA
ALU-24	DL-560	Co-Co	Elec	1790	120	112.44	21	1967	Alco USA	Alco USA/16-251B	GE USA
ALU-20R	DL-543	Co-Co	Elec	1492	120	102	3	1980	Alco USA	Bombardier/12-251G4	GE USA
ARP-20	DL-212	AIA-AIA	Elec	1492	120	109.06	29	1977	Alco USA	Bombardier/12-251C4	GE USA
ARU-20	E-1662	AIA-AIA	Elec	1492	120	111.9	26	1976	Alco USA	Bombardier/12-251C4	GE USA
ARPW-20	DL-500C	Co-Co	Elec	1492	120	102	42	1982	Alco USA	Bombardier/12-251C4	GE USA/Canada
FRAU-75	–	Bo-Bo	Elec	560	69	68	2	1979	Alsthom France	Pielstick/SEMT PA-4	Alsthom France

Diesel railcars

Class	Manufacturer's type reference	Cars per unit	Motored axles per motor car	Transmission	Rated power (kW)	Max speed km/h	Weight tonnes per car (M-motor T-trailer)	Total seating capacity per car (M-motor T-trailer)	Length per car (mm) (M-motor T-trailer)	No in service 1987-88	Year first built	Builders — Mechanical parts	Builders — Engine & type	Builders — Transmission
Diesel railcars	Hitachi Ltd	1	2	Hydraulic torque	313 kW per motor and 313 × 2 = 626 kW railcar	108	M 52.32 T 30.5	M 62 T 98	M 31 336 T 21 336	11	1966	Hitachi Japan	GM12V-71N (N65 injector) GM/USA	NIGATA/Japan

Electric locomotives

Class	Wheel arrangement	Line voltage	Rated output (kW) continuous	Max speed km/h	Weight tonnes	No in service 1988	Year first built	Builders — Mechanical parts	Builders — Electrical equipment
BCU-3DE	Bo-Bo	25 kV ac	2230	120	81.3	29	1966	AEI Traction Metropolitan Cammell	English Electric

Steam locomotives

Class	Wheel arrangement	Tractive effort (kg)	Max speed km/h	Weight tonnes	No in service 1988	Year first	Builders
1676 mm-gauge							
SG/S	0-6-0	11 760	72	90.15	19	1904 to 1923	NB Locomotive Co, Vulcan Foundry Ltd, England
SG/C	0-6-0	11 760	72	90.15	19	1908	NB Locomotive Co, Vulcan Foundry Ltd, England
CWD	2-8-2	15 909	80	146	53	1945 TO 1947	Montrial Locomotive Works, Canada
HG/S	2-8-0	15 490	72	122	25	1912 TO 1923	Kitson & Co, Vulcan Foundry Ltd, England
SP/S	4-4-0	–	72	94.20	21	1909 to 1913	NB Locomotive Co, Vulcan Foundry Ltd, England
1000 mm-gauge							
YD-3	2-8-2	10 050	56	94.5	8	1930	BB & CI Railway, Ajmer, India
YE	2-8-2	10 050	56	97.8	8	1952	Nippon Sharyo, Japan
M	4-6-0	6328	56	63.0	2	1913	Nasmyth Wilson & Co Ltd, England
MS	4-6-0	6414	64	64.0	3	Converted from 'M' Class in 1973	Nasmyth Wilson & Co Ltd, England
SP	4-6-0	7308	64	67.0	4	1921	Kerr Stuart & Co Ltd, California, USA
762 mm-gauge							
GS	2-8-2	–	40	60.963	7	1920	North British Locomotive Co Ltd
G	2-8-2	–	40	58.931	14	1909, 1914, 1917	NB Locomotive Co Ltd
ZE	2-8-2	–	40	65.027	4	1930	Nasmyth Wilson Ltd
ZB	2-6-2	–	450	65.027	10	1927, 1932	Hanomag, Germany

Panama

Chiriqui Land Company Railways

Chiriqui Land Company, Division de Armuelles, Apartado 6-2637, Estafeta El Dorado, Panama City

Telephone: +507 70 7243/5
Telex: 2292 clc arm pa
Telefax: +507 75 6810

General Manager: Freidrich Stargardter Bucka
Technical Services Manager: Alfonso Habeych De Andreis
Exportation & Transportation Superintendent: Francisco Rellán P
Trainmaster, Transportation Department: Miquel Angel Samudio
Agricultural Engineering Director: Diana K Alemán

Gauge: 914 mm
Length: 133 km

The railway, which is divided into the Armuelles and Bocas Divisions, is dedicated to banana transport and in 1987 recorded 387 497 tonnes of freight and 10.46 million tonne-km. It operates 17 diesel locomotives, eight diesel railcars, 10 passenger cars and 630 freight wagons. Most powerful traction units are five 700 hp Caterpillar-engined locomotives, one a Whitcomb unit of 1948, the remainder GE of 1959 and 1970. Standard coupler is knuckle-type and braking of vehicles mechanical. Track is formed of 30 kg/m rails spiked to wooden sleepers spaced 1600/km in plain track, 1700/km in curves, maximum permissible axleload is 20 tonnes.

Chiriqui National Railroad
Ferrocarril Nacional de Chiriqui

PO Box 12B, David City, Chiriqui

General Manager: C Augusto Sinclair
Superintendent: S L de Aguizola

Gauge: 914 mm
Length: 26 km

The railway, operated by the government of Panama, owns five diesel locomotives, four railcars, four passenger cars and 24 freight cars.

Panama Railroad
Ferrocarril de Panama

PO Box 2023, Estafeta de Balboa

Telephone: +507 32 6000 Telex: 3221 ferropan
Telefax: +507 32 5343

Director-General: Ing Robert Moreno
Assistant Director-General: Enrique Montenegro
Sub-Director: Adalberto Ferrer
Director, Engineering: Gustavo Paredes
  Administration: Abdiel Flynn ZJr
  Commercial: Javier Guardia
Public Relations: María Eugenia de Carles

Gauge: 1524 mm
Length: 76 km

Managed by the Ports Authority (Autoridad Portuaria Nacional), the railway owns three GM-EMD SW1200 diesel locomotives, six passenger cars and 107 freight wagons.

Construction of a new railway across the Panamanian isthmus is one of the three options considered by a US-Japanese-Panamanian consultancy team appointed to investigate the best course to protect the republic's role as an international trade corridor. The study has been part-financed by the Inter-American Development Bank. Landbridging via a modern rail line is advanced as an alternative to the upgrading of the existing Panama Canal or the digging of a new sea-level canal. At present the railway carries only 5 per cent of the containers transshipped at the ports of Cristobal and Balboa.

Track
Rail: 90 and 100 lb/yd
Sleepers: Wood spaced 2070/km
Fastenings: Track spike
Minimum curve radius: 250m
Max gradient: 1.3%
Max permissible axleload: 20 short tons

Paraguay

Ministry of Public Works and Communications

2° Piso-Gral, Diaz y Albridi, Asunción

Minister: P R Ruiz Diaz

Ferrocarril Presidente Carlos Antonio Lopez

PO Box 453, Calle Mexico 145, CC 453 Asunción

Telephone: +595 43273/46789
Cable: Carril, Asunción

President & Chairman of the Board of Directors: O S Gulino Alfieri
General Manager: Ramon Ayala A
Chief Accountant: Vicente Espindla
Director of Planning: Dr Wildo Netto
Departmental Managers; Statistics & Budget: Oscar Bolla A
Workshops: Francisco Knorr
Way & Works: J Jara S
Technical: G Leon S
Traction: N Encina
Chief Engineer: Hector Rojas
Purchases & Stores: Capt Carlos Royg Ferreira
Personnel: Jorge Gimmenez G
General Superintendent: A Vera Y

Gauge: 1435 mm
Route length: 441 km

Paraguay has four separate railways, only one being a passenger carrier, the FC Presidente Carlos Antonio Lopez, the others being industrial lines in western Paraguay and the Chaco.

The FC Presidente CA Lopez, government owned and operated, is the longest in the country, extending from Asunción south-east to Encarnación and Pacú-Cua (375 km) with a branch from San Salvador to Abai 65 km long. From Encarnación two wood-burning paddle-steamer train ferries, British-built in 1911–15, were until March 1990 providing a River Alto Parana crossing to connect at Posadas with the Argentine Railways (FC General Urquiza). But in March 1990 a fixed link was available for through freight trains. This, the 3km San Roque Gonzalez bridge, was formally inaugurated by the Presidents of Argentina and Paraguay in April 1990.

Traffic

Both passenger and freight traffic have been steadily rising since the mid-1970s. At last report annual passenger journeys totalled about 350 000, and annual freight 155 000 tonnes. The railway's market share of freight movement in Paraguay is 10 per cent.

Rehabilitation plan

The increased traffic expected to ensue from completion of the Parana river bridge between Encarnación and Posadas (see above) needs renewal of track throughout the 370 km Asunción-Encarnación line and replacement of its over-aged rolling stock, a good deal of which is reported unserviceable. Argentine consultants have recommended a US$66 million programme that includes replacement of steam by diesel power and installation of modern signalling and telecommunications. The Parana bridge may in time open up a link via Argentine Railways' Urquiza line with Brazil's putative Production Railway from Guaira to Asunción, which would afford the Paraguayan system access to the Brazilian port of Paranagua.

Motive power and rolling stock

The railway operates 26 mainly British-built wood-burning steam locomotives, nine passenger cars and 147 freight wagons.

Investment

With hydro-electric power coming on stream from the Itaipú dam scheme, 25 kV ac electrification, track reconstruction and resignalling of the 72 km route from Asunción to Pagaguari awaits government approval. Pending an electrification decision, the main priority is to relay the 140 km section from Villaria to General Artigas.

Peru

Ministry of Transport and Commications

Avenida 28 de Julio Lima

Telephone: +51 14 319206, 245088
Telex: 25511

Minister: G Parra Herrera

ENAFER-Peru
Empresa Nacional de Ferrocarriles del Peru

Apartado 1378, Ancash, 207, Lima

Telephone: +51 14 28 9440
Telex: 25068

Chairman: Dr Miguel Quiros Garcia
General Manager: Ing Erwin Ludman Paredes
Technical Manager: Americo Soto
Administration Manager: Jose Luis Luque
Finance Manager: Oscar Guillermo Greig Puyo
Development Manager: Jesus Castellares
Operations Manager: Juan Toche
Mechanical Adviser: John W M Wright
Permanent Way Adviser: Wilfredo Medina
Chief of Accounts: Felipe Cordova
Commercial Manager: Freddy Morales

Gauge: 1435 mm; 914 mm
Route length: 1372 km; 300 km

ENAFER was formed in 1972 with the nationalisation of The Peruvian Corporation railways, a private company which ran most of Peru's railways and the Lake Titicaca services. The system now comprises the Central and Southern Railways with headquarters in Lima and Arequipa respectively. As a whole, ENAFER achieves some 3.5 million passenger journeys (450 million passenger-km) and 2.5 million tonnes of freight (630 million tonne-km) a year.

In a six-year programme from 1984 to 1990 ENAFER hoped to build new workshops for the mechanical department of the Central Railway just north of Lima to replace the nineteenth century plant in Callao; to erect a floating rail bridge at Guaqui, Bolivia, on Lake Titicaca for the rail ferry service between Bolivia and Peru; and to investigate the possibility of building a new line from Tambo del Sol to Pucallpa, which would join the Atlantic with the Pacific via the river Amazon, on the Central Railway. ENAFER has hoped to invest in 24 more diesel-electric locomotives and an initial order for six GM-type JJ26CW-2B 3300 hp Co-Cos was delivered by Villares of Brazil in 1987. However, investment prospects were dimmed by the International Monetary Fund's 1987 declaration that Peru was ineligible for further credits, because of its defaults on loan repayments. World Bank loans were cut off in April 1987, but following some stringent corrective measures to stabilise the national economy the government was able to reopen negotiations with the World Bank in 1988.

Diesel locomotives

Class	Wheel arrangement	Transmission	Rated power (kW)	Max speed km/h	Total weight tonnes	Year first built	Builders Mechanical parts	Engine & type	Transmission
	0-6-0	Hyd	256	30	42	1964	Yorkshire Engine Co	Rolls-Royce C8TEL	Rolls-Royce
	0-6-0	Mech	140	20	32·6	1950	Hunslet	Gardner 863	Hunslet
DL-531	Co-Co	Elec	671	80	71·6	1958	Alco	Alco 6251B	GE
DL-532-B	Bo-Bo	Elec	708	80	69·4	1974	MLW	Alco 6251B	GE
DL-535-A	Co-Co	Elec	895	80	69·7	1967	Alco	Alco 6251C	GE
DL-535-B	Co-Co	Elec	895	80	81·4	1963	Alco	Alco 6251B	GE
DL-535B	Co-Co	Elec	895	80	80·7	1976	MLW	Alco 6251B	GE
DL-535D	Co-Co	Elec	895	80	80·7	1964	MLW	Alco 6251B	GE
DL-500-C	Co-Co	Elec	1342	110	104	1956	Alco	Alco 12251C	GE
DL-543	Co-Co	Elec	1491	110	110	1962/63	Alco	Alco 12551B	GE
DL-560-D	Co-Co	Elec	1789	105	110	1964/66	Alco	Alco 16251B	GE
DL-560-D	Co-Co	Elec	1789	105	110	1974	MLW	Alco 16251E	GE
GT-26CW-2	Co-Co	Elec	2237	105	116	1982	GM	GM 16-645E3B	GM
GT-26C2-2	Co-Co	Elec	2237	105	116	1983	GM	GM 16-645E3B	GM

Central Railway
ENAFER-Ferrocarril del Centro
Ferrocarril del Centro del Perú

Apartado 301, Lima

Telephone: +51 14 276620
Telex: 25068

Manager: David San Roman
Chief of Operations: Angel Bottino

Gauge: 1435 mm; 914 mm
Route length: 365 km; 128 km

The standard-gauge main line runs from Callao to Huancayo where it connects with the 914 mm-gauge line to Huancavelica. There are 66 tunnels with aggregate length of 8.9 km, 59 bridges and nine zig-zags (reversing stations) on the standard-gauge section and 38 tunnels on the narrow-gauge line.

The main line climbs from sea level to its highest point of 4782 metres in the Galera Tunnel in 171 km from Callao on an average gradient of 1 in 25 (4 per cent). The highest point on the system is 4829 metres at a siding at La Cima on the Ticlio-Morococha branch. This makes it the highest standard-gauge line in the world. The steepest gradients occur in the first 222 km from Callao, at sea level, to Oroya at 3726 metres above sea level.

Rolling stock

Three oil-burning steam, 31 diesel-electric, one diesel-mechanical locomotive, seven railcars, 1154 freight cars, 46 passenger cars.

Southern Railway
ENAFER-Ferrocarril del Sur
Ferrocarril del Sur

PO Box 194, Arequipa

Manager: Gino Olcese
Chief of Operations: Danilo Rodriquez

Gauge: 1435 mm; 914 mm
Route length: 924 km; 171 km

The standard-gauge main line runs from the ports of Matarani and Mollendo on the Pacific coast to Juliaca, 476 km, where the line divides, to Puno, 47 km, for connection with the Lake Titicaca steamer service to Bolivia; and to Cuzco, 338 km, where it connects with the 914 mm-gauge line to Quillabamba. A separate 62 km standard-gauge line connects Tacna and Arica Africa, in the far south.

The main line climbs from sea level to its highest point at Crucero Alto, 4477 metres, in 359 km from Matarani on an average gradient of 1 in 33 (3 per cent).

The steamer service on Lake Titicaca at 3818 metres is the highest in the world.

Rolling stock

50 diesel-electric, three diesel-hydraulic and five oil-burning steam locomotives, 982 freight cars, 160 passenger cars, 13 railcars.

Steamship service

Lake Titicaca 204 km from Puno, Peru to Guaqui, Bolivia.

Ships include one train ferry, three passenger-freight vessels, one dredger and two launches.

690 RAILWAY SYSTEMS / Peru—Philippines

Track
Standard rail
  80 lb/yd (39.7 kg/m) BS(R)
  75 lb/yd (37.2 kg/m) BSS
  75 lb/yd (37.2 kg/m) ASCE
  70 lb/yd (34.7 kg/m) ASCE
  70 lb/yd (34.7 kg/m) Livesey
Lengths: 24, 30, 33, 39 and 46 ft
Joints: 4-hole angle fishplates and bolts
Cross ties (sleepers): Peruvian hardwood, 8 in × 6 in × 8 ft (1435 mm track) 8 in × 6 in × 6 ft (914 mm track)
Made-up sleepers consisting of 2 blocks of reinforced concrete joined by a piece of used rail have been used in sidings and on straight stretches of main line

Spacing
  Main line: 1600-1720/km
  Branch line: 1365-1700/km

Rail fastenings
Soleplates and 7/8 in coachscrews
Soleplates and 5/8 in dogspikes
Pandrol fastenings are being fitted where new 80 lb/yd rail is being laid
Filling: 2–4 in broken stone ballast; 6 in under tie on main lines and 3 in on branch lines.
Max curvature: 17.5° = minimum radius 100 m
Max gradient: 4.7% (Central Railway), 4% (Southern Railway)
Worst combination of curve and grade: 156 m curve on 4.22% (1 in 23.7) grade for 235 m
Gauge widening on sharpest curve: ½ in (12.7 mm)
Super-elevation on sharpest curve: 4 in (101.6 mm) speed limited
Rate of slope of super-elevation: 1 in 360
Max altitude: 4839 m on Central Railways at La Cima sliding on Ticlio-Morococha branch, 173 km from Callao. On main line 4782 m inside Galera Tunnel, 172 km from Callao.
Max axleloading:
  Central Railway: 1435 mm, 18 tonnes; 914 mm, 14 tonnes
  Southern Railway: 1435 mm, 17 tonnes; 914 mm, 14 tonnes
  Tacna-Arica: 19.5 tonnes
Bridge loading: Cooper E-40
Max permitted speed
  Standard gauge:
    80 km/h on level and low gradient sections
    50 km/h on high gradient sections
  Narrow-gauge: 60 km/h

ML DI 560 at Desamparados station, Lima

Empresa Minera del Centro del Peru
(Division Ferrocarriles)

PO Box 2412, Edificio Salgas, Avenida Javier Prado Este s/n, San Borja, Lima 34

Telephone: 35 5467, 35 5924
Telex: 63839 pe centromi

Executive President: Dr J Cenzano
General Manager: Ing J Ortiz
Manager, General Services: Ing A Pérez
Superintendent of Railways: Ing J Chávez
Chief Operations Officer: V Zúñiga
Chief Mechanical Officer: Ing C A Hoyas
Chief Engineer, Way and Structures: Ing C Ortiz

Account of Railways: J Rodriguez

Gauge: 1435 mm
Route length: 212.2 km

The railway lies east of Lima and has two lines: La Oroya-Cerro de Pasco (132.2 km); and Pachacayo-Chaucha (80 km).

Motive power and rolling stock
The fleet in 1988 consisted of: one steam shunting locomotive; 12 line-haul diesel-electric locomotives; four petrol railcars; 13 passenger coaches; 607 freight wagons.

Traffic	1987	1988
Freight tonnage	99 962	697 066
Freight tonne-km (million)	113.097	80.978
Passenger-km (million)	17.74	15.66
Passenger journeys	253 487	212 700

Track
Rail: 9020 lb/yd (main line); 7040 lb/yd (Yauricocha line)
Cross ties (sleepers): Wood 8 ft × 8 in × 6 in; spacing 1850/km
Fastenings: Cut track spikes
Minimum curvature radius: 110° (main); 105° (Yauricocha)
Max gradient: 2.44% (main); 41.5% (Yauricocha)
Max permissible axleload: 13 tonnes

Type of braking in standard use: Air (valves K, AB, ABD Wabco Westinghouse)

Diesel locomotives

Class	Wheel arrangement	Transmission	Rated power (kW)	Max speed km/h	Total weight tonnes	No in service 1988	Year first built	Builders Mechanical parts	Engine & type	Transmission
GR-12	Co-Co	Elec	1310	105	174	7	1964	General Motors	GM 12/567C	GM
GA-8	Bo-Bo	Elec	800	72	173	3	1964	General Motors	GM 8/567C	GM
G22CW	Co-Co	Elec	1500	100	107	1	1976	General Motors	GM 12/645E	GM
G18W	Bo-Bo	Elec	1000	114	65·8	1	1976	General Motors	GM 8/645E	GM

Philippines

Ministry of Transport and Communications

Philcomcen Building, Oritgas Ave, Pasig, Metro-Manila

Telephone: +63 2 721 3781-92
Telex: 42219 motc pm

Minister: Rainerio O Reyes

Philippine National Railways (PNR)

Tutuban Station, 943 CM Recto Avenue, Manila

Telephone: +363 2 209375
Cable: Ferroco

Chairman: R de Vera
Vice-Chairman and General Manager: Pete Nicomedes Prado
Assistant General Manager, Finance and Administration: Jesus P Gotidoc
Department Managers
  Administration: Salvacion M Bundoc
  Railway Operations: Engr Cesar Casipit
  Material Management: E Laiz
  Budget and Planning: Engr Jose Nuguid
  Permanent Way Maintenance: Miguel Añonuevo
  Rolling Stock Maintenance: Prospero Yap
  Human Resources and Corporation Secretary: Mariano Abad
  Sales and Real Estate: Ramon Jimenez
Corporation Auditor: Jose de Vela
Controller: Francisco V Aure
Chief Construction Engineer: Justo Bonuel

Gauge: 1067 mm
Route length: 1058.8 km

The PNR rail system operates passenger and freight

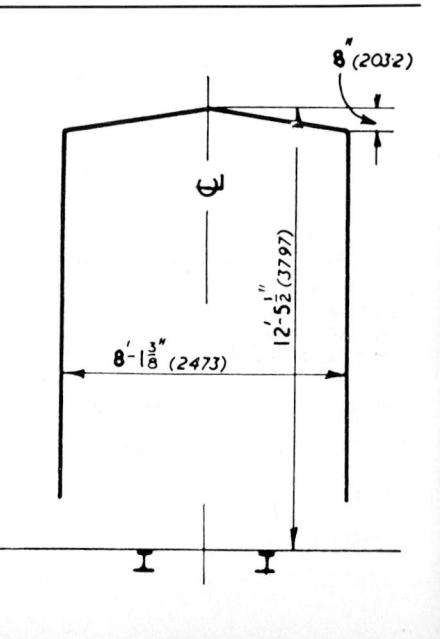

services in Luzon Island from Camilag, 14 km from the port of Legaspi in the south, to the northern railhead at San Fernando, via Manila.

Rehabilitation
A major project for the total rehabilitation of Philippine National Railways' 406 km Main Line South, from Manila to Camilag (the remaining 14 km to Legaspi has been closed since landslip damage in 1976), got under way in May 1979 following the granting of the US$24 million loan from the Asian Development Bank. In 1988 the country's National Economic Development Authority approved expenditure of a further 841 million pesos on the scheme. Completion of the project will be followed by a cut from 16 to 9 hours of passenger train timings over the 378 km between Manila and Naga. Purchase of 17 diesel locomotives was embodied in Phase I of the project, which now has 70 per cent funding from Japan. A new route is under construction from Camilag to Legaspi.

Following completion of work on its Main Line South, PNR hoped to refurbish similarly the 226 km Main Line North from Manila to San Fernando and to resuscitate its 92 km Cabanatuan branch at a cost of 547 million pesos.

Finance
PNR is heavily subsidised. Because inadequate investment has never fully recovered Second World War damage, deteriorating infrastructure and equipment have cost PNR a steady loss of main-line freight and passenger traffic; even the diesel multiple-unit commuter service established in the Manila area in the 1970s now logs only two-thirds of the passenger journeys recorded in 1977. However, usage has lately shown a sharp improvement. Between 1986 and 1989 total passenger-km rose 40 per cent to 244 million.

The mainspring was long-distance travel, for which cars have been refurbished; some trains now feature on-board video entertainment. Commuter travel remains seriously depressed, principally because of service cuts occasioned by defective diesel railcars. By 1992 PNR aims to have restored a fleet of up to 60 railcars and to have purchased 20 more.

PNR is inhibited from seeking new bulk freight flows because of the capital expense involved in restoring lifted tracks to the vicinity of several new heavy industrial plants. However, rehabilitation of the 60 km line from the port of Batanga to Calamba, to convey 880 000 tonnes of coal a year to eight cement works, has become a possibility with Canadian aid, though the project is in contention with a slurry pipeline scheme. Annual freight has lately totalled only some 65 000 tonnes and 16 million tonne-km.

Locomotives and rolling stock
PNR operates 62 diesel locomotives, 88 diesel railcars, 131 passenger cars and 619 freight cars.

Track
Standard rail
Main line: 65 lb/yd (32.2 kg/m) in 30 and 33 ft lengths
75 lb/yd (37.2 kg/m) in 33 ft lengths

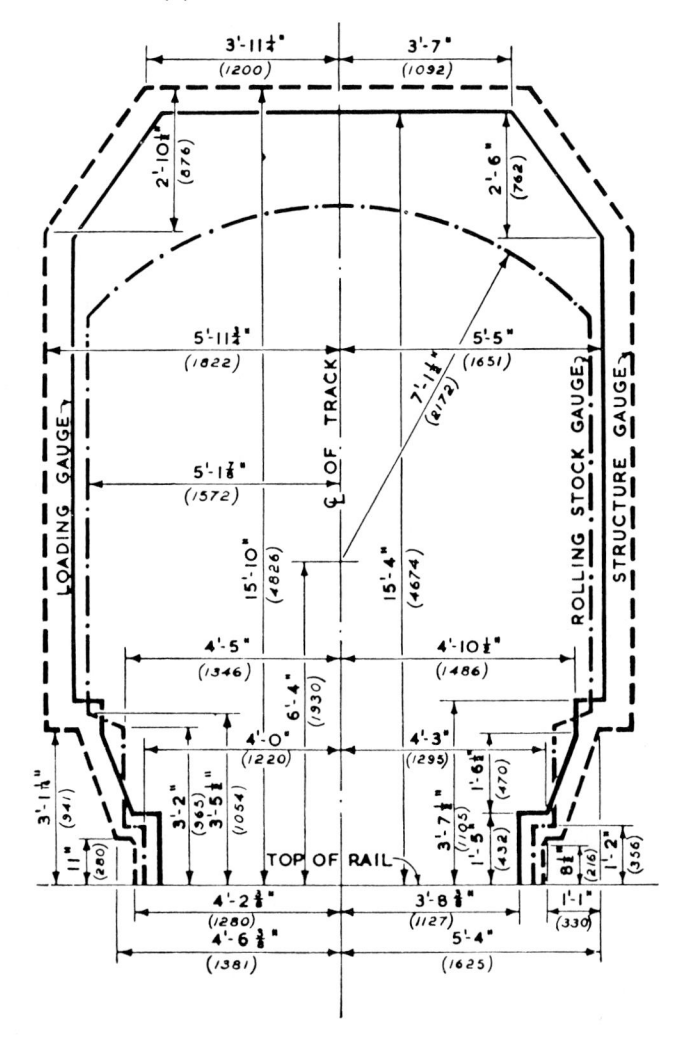

Branch lines: 65 lb/yd (32.2 kg/m) on 30 ft lengths
54 lb/yd (26.8 kg/m) in 30 ft lengths
45 lb/yd (22.3 kg/m) in 23 ft lengths
Rail joints: Angle bars with slots for spikes
Cross ties (sleepers)
Main line: 'Molave' wood, 5 in × 8 in × 7 ft (127 × 203 × 2133 mm), spaced at 22 in (558 mm)
Branch line: 'Molave' wood, 5 in × 8 in × 7 ft (127 × 203 × 2133 mm), spaced at 24 in (610 mm)
Bridge ties: 'Yacal' wood, 8 in × 8 in × 8 ft (203 × 203 × 2438 mm), spaced at 16 in (406 mm)
A limited number of steel ties are also used
Rail fastenings: Track spikes; bolts with square nuts; 'Hipower' nutlock washer, elastic rail spikes
Filing: Volcanic slag; river gravel with 15% sand; some crushed rock
Max curvature
Main line: 9.2° = minimum radius 190 m
Branch line: 11½° = minimum radius 150 m
Max gradient: Compensated 2.6% = 1 in 38½
Uncompensated, 1.2% = 1 in 83
Max axleload: 29.5 tonnes
Max permitted speed: 60 km/h
Signalling: In the Manila terminal area 13.6 km of double-track line with semaphore signals are controlled from interlocked cabins. On single-track lines elsewhere trains operated on English 'Staff' system or by telegraph or telephone communication from station to station.

Motive power

Type (road no)	900 type	1000 type	2000 type	1500 type	2500 type	3000 type	4000 type
Wheel (or axle) arrangement	C-C	C-C	C-C	B-B-B	B-B	B-B	B-B
Max speed	130 km/h	95 km/h	95 km/h	95 km/h	95 km/h	95 km/h	50 km/h
Dimensions (width)	2717 mm	2821 mm	2821 mm	2749 mm	2749 mm	2743 mm	2921 mm
(height)	3732 mm	3683 mm	3683 mm	3372 mm	3687 mm	3687 mm	3687 mm
Weight	81·6 tonnes	82·6 tonnes	87 tonnes	61·4 tonnes	54·4 tonnes	54·4 tonnes	47·1 tonnes
Builders	General Electric	General Electric	General Electric	Alsthom	General Electric	General Electric	General Electric
Tractive effort	24 495 kg	16 965 kg	16 965 kg	17 235 kg	11 975 kg	14 605 kg	74 840 kg

Poland
Ministry of Transport and Shipping

ul Chalubińskiego 4, 00-928 Warsaw

Telephone: +48 22 24 40 00
Telex: 813 898 pkp pl
Telefax: +48 22 21 2705

Minister: Dr Adam Wieladek

Polish State Railways (PKP)
Polskie Kokeje Państwowe

ul Chalubińskeigo 4, 00-928 Warsaw

Telephone: +48 22 24 44 00
Telex: 813898, 816651 pkp pl

Telefax: +48 22 212705

Director-General: Aleksander Janiszewski
Deputy Directors-General: J Franiewski
J Mäka
J Przewlocki
J Zalewski
Office of the Director-General: J Chmielewski

RAILWAY SYSTEMS / Poland

Directors
Transport: J Tymoszuk
Traction and Rolling Stock: E Kubik
Maintenance: W Ferenc
Signalling and Telecommunications: N Gruchala
International Co-operation: T Kaczmarek
Economics: T Slifirski
Investments and Development: B Kaczmarski
Press Service: J Wnukowski

Gauge: 1435 mm and 1524 mm; 1000, 785, 750 and 600 mm
Route length: 24 287 km; 2357 km
Electrification: 10 980 km at 3 kV dc; 35 km at 600 V dc

PKP entered the 1980s with the biggest traffic volume in Europe (excepting the Soviet Union) plus one of the most intensively-used railway systems anywhere in the world.

Freight traffic

In 1989 PKP again met all the freight transport demands laid upon the railway, but at 379.7 million, tonnage was 10 per cent down on the previous year. In the first quarter of 1990 tonnage was running no less than 28.4 per cent below the level in the same period of 1989. For the first time since the Second World War PKP had spare freight car capacity.

The main reason for the downturn was the drastic reduction of industrial output as the outcome of stringent measures to adjust the country to a free market economy. Political change has freed choice of transport and generated significant competition from road haulage for short-haul traffic.

PKP's traffic is dominated by annual movement of some 125 million tonnes of coal by unit train from Silesia to power stations, bigger industrial plants and ports employing rotary tippler or Talbot-system self-discharge hopper wagons. Thus it was not proportionately affected by the recession in industrial output, which was as much as 35 per cent in some sectors. Road haulage traffic was reported as halved in the first quarter of 1990. But delayed payments for coal movement were aggravating financial problems for PKP, which has relied on its bulk freight to cover losses elsewhere in its operation. The new regime is also pressing for attribution of real costs, which has further reduced the margin of income, including subsidies, over revenue and prejudiced the future rate of investment in the railway.

To counterattack in the merchandise market a PKP-Cargo system was launched in May 1990. This interconnects some 30 centres with direct trains that achieve siding-to-siding deliveries within 24 hours.

Negotiations have been undertaken to create a national piggyback company in partnership with haulage operator Pekaes, forwarding agents C Hartwig and several shipping firms including Polish Ocean Lines. The new organisation is expected to operate under the name PL-KOMBI.

Passenger traffic

Development of an intercity passenger network continues. It embraces 19 major centres and thereby 50 per cent of the country's urban population. Regular-interval service at varying frequency has been established on several routes. Several new connections with USSR centres were introduced in 1989, when seat capacity in PKP-USSR traffic was lifted by almost 50 per cent. In the 1990-91 timetable new services were launched between Poland and Western and Southern European countries. A computerised seat reservation system was expanded in 1989 to encompass 58 stations.

However, passenger traffic too was suffering from the economic pressures at the start of 1990, with passenger journeys down by 10.5 per cent in the year's first quarter, compared with the same period in 1989.

In 1995 PKP aims to celebrate the 150th anniversary of Polish railways by a lift of top passenger train speed on the Central Trunk Route to 200 km/h and achievement of 140 km/h or more commerical average speeds. Prerequisites will include deeper ballasting, replacement of a score of level crossings and equipment of the locomotives involved with cab signalling. Heavy freight using the line will have to be re-routed and trains of high-rated freight, including container trains, must be equipped for higher speed if they are to continue sharing the routes with high-speed passenger trains.

PKP has been testing prototype bogies designed for 160–200 km/h under cars of Warsaw-Szczecin train-

Class ET 22 electric Co-Co by Pafawag

Class SP 32 diesel locomotive by "23 August" Works, Romania

New Class WUA-22 railbus by Kolzam for lightly-used lines

Traffic	1985	1986	1987	1988	1989
Freight tonnage (million)	419.3	430.6	428.4	428.0	386.2
Freight tonne-km (million)	120 600	121 800	121 200	122 000	110 200
Passenger-km (million)	52 500	48 500	48 200	52 100	55 800
Passenger journeys (million)	1009.5	989.7	973.5	983.8	949.5

Class EN57 emu with thyristor control

Class EP08 electric locomotive by Pafawag

sets. In another preparation for 200 km/h operation on the Central Trunk Route a four-aspect signalling system, installed under Ericsson licence, is being applied to 214 km of the route between Warsaw and Katowice.

World Bank loan
In 1990 PKP was granted a World Bank loan of US$150 million for upgrading of rolling stock, track and signalling.

Motive power and rolling stock
The share of gross tonne-km performed by the three types of traction is developing as follows:

	Electric	Diesel	Steam
1980	61.1%	31.7%	7.2%
1982	67.3%	27%	5.7%
1985	74.3%	22.3%	3.4%
1986	76.4%	20.9%	2.7%
1987	78.2%	20.2%	1.6%
1988	80.8%	18.3%	0.9%
1989	82.9%	16.5%	0.6%

In 1989 PKP was operating 263 steam, 1941 electric, and 2591 diesel locomotives, 1041 emus, 35 diesel railcars, 6324 loco-hauled and diesel trailer passenger cars (including 235 sleeping, 246 couchette, 80 buffet and four restaurant cars) and 137 900 freight wagons.

Deliveries in 1989 comprised 44 Class ET 22 and 20 Class EU 07 electric locomotives, 7 Class SM 48 and 25 Class SP 32 diesel locomotives; 33 Class EN 57 emus; 372 passenger cars and 2817 freight wagons. Passenger car deliveries included the conclusion of an order for 160 bi-levels from VEB Waggonbau Görlitz of East Germany.

Orders placed in 1989 included one for 10 postal cars with 160 km/h capability, placed with Gosa of Yugoslavia.

Locomotive building concentrates on already proven types, notably the Type ET 22 Co-Co and the Type EU 07-3000 B-B. But in addition a series order is planned for the 160 km/h Pafawag Type E09 B-B. Pafawag has been completing a prototype six-car double-deck commuter emu.

The Minister of Transport has floated the possibility that after 1990, when it is hoped to have 75 per cent of the PKP system electrified, there might be resort to electro-diesel locomotives and battery-powered railcars for the remaining unelectrified areas of the system.

In 1989 three prototype three-car emus with thyristor control were under trial in Warsaw suburban service. For complete renewal of the Warsaw fleet PKP was expected to order for 1990-95 delivery a production series of 150, classified EN57.2.

Closure plan
Transfer of sparse rail traffic to road is possible for over 4000 km of 1435 mm-gauge and 1500 km of narrow-gauge.

A single-track electrified branch 35 km long is to be constructed by 1995 from Wieliczka, in the south-eastern Krakow suburbs, to Kasina, where it will make a triangular junction with the line parallelling the Czech border between Chsabowka and Novy Sacz. The objective is a direct route for passenger trains to the Tatra Mountains resorts in the far south. Along with the new construction the line from Chabowka to Novy Sacz will be electrified and a spur will be built at Novy Sacz to save the resort trains reversal there.

Class EP05 140-160km/h electric locomotive by Skoda

Minimum curvature radius

	Lowland	Foothills	Mountains
Newly constructed lines			
Trunk	2000 m	1500 m	800 m
Primary	1500 m	1000 m	600 m
Secondary	800 m	500 m	400 m
Local	500 m	300 m	300 m
Modernised lines			
Trunk	1500 m	1200 m	600 m
Primary	1200 m	600 m	400 m
Secondary	600 m	400 m	300 m
Local	400 m	250 m	200 m

Electrification
Route-distance electrified in 1989 totalled an impressive 507 km. By the end of the year 463 per cent of all PKP 1435 mm- gauge route-km was under wires, and 83 per cent of traffic electrically hauled.

The major achievement of 1989 was wiring of the 220 km from Bydgoszcz via Pila and Szczecinek to Bialogard. Other stretches concerted included: Wejherowo-Lebork-Slupsk (87km) and Grebów-Stalowa-Rudnik (40km). Electrification planned for

RAILWAY SYSTEMS / Poland

1990 totalled 366 km and included:

Poznań-Pila	93 km
Olsztyn-Korsze	67 km
Bialystok-Elk	99 km
Bielsko-Biala-Wadowice	41 km
Rudnik-Przeworsk Gorlicczyna	49 km
Slupsk-Ustka	17 km

Signalling and telecommunications

Installation of over 1000 electrically-powered sets of points, equipment of 200 km of lines with automatic interlockings, installation of automatic signalling and control at 106 level crossings, completion of radio-communication system over 700 km and automation of the Łódź Olechóe and Warsaw Glówna Towarowa marshalling yards were achieved in 1989. In 1990 the yard at Jaworzno Szczakowa was to be automated. Further yards to be rebuilt and automated are Krakow Prokocim, Lazy and Gliwice.

When these last three yards have been dealt with, PKP will have automated 16 of its most important yards which process some 55 per cent of its total freight traffic. In all, PKP has 102 marshalling yards, 28 of them dedicated exclusively to coal traffic.

Bi-directional four-aspect signalling of exclusively Polish manufacture is operative throughout the 224 km-long Central Trunk Route. PKP intends to install this type of equipment at the rate of 300 route-km per annum.

Permanent way

On main trunk routes UIC 60 rail is being laid and on other primary lines UIC 60 or S49 rail. With wooden sleepers up to 250 mm ballast depth is prescribed, with concrete sleepers up to 300 mm.

Rail welding is being carried out at the rate of some 2000 km a year. By the end of 1988 Cwr was installed over 20 600 route-km.

Track

Rail, type and weight: UIC 60 60.34 kg/m; S49 49.43 kg/m; S42 42.48 kg/m

Cross ties (sleepers)
Wooden: Types: IB, IIB, IIO thickness 150 mm; IIB, IIIO, IVO thickness 140 mm
Concrete: Types: BL-3 thickness 210 mm; INBK-3 thickness 202 mm; INBK-4 thickness 180 mm; INBK-7 thickness 190 mm; INBK-8 thickness 183 mm; PBS-1 thickness 180 mm

Spacing

Traditional track: 1566, 1600, 1720, 1733/km
Cwr: 1680 and 1700/km

Max gradient

Main trunk and primary: 0.6%
Secondary: 1%
Local: 2%

Minimum curve radius: 200 m
Max axleload: 20 tonnes, 22.5 tonnes on some sections

Diesel locomotives

Class	Wheel arrangement	Transmission	Rated power kW	Max speed km/h	Total weight tonnes	Year first built	Builders Mechanical parts	Builders Engine & type	Builders Transmission
SM 40/41	Bo-Bo	Elec	441	80	61.7	1958	Ganz-Mávag	Ganz XVI IV 170/240	Ganz
SM 03	B	Mech	111	45	24	1959	Fablok	Nowotko	"Zastal" Zielona-Góra
SM 30	Bo-Bo	Elec	257	58	36	1959	Fablok	Nowotko DVSa-350	Dolmel
SM 42	Bo-Bo	Elec	588	90	72	1963	Fablok	HCP 8 VCD22T	Dolmel
SP 42	Bo-Bo	Elec	588	90	70	1966	Fablok	HCP 8 VCD22T	Dolmel
ST 43	Co-Co	Elec	1544	100	116	1965	Ep Craiova	Sulzer 12 LDA 28	BBC
ST 44	Co-Co	Elec	1471	100	116	1966	WFBL-Voroshilovgrad	Kolomna 14D20	Charkow
SP 45	Co-Co	Elec	1287	100	96	1967	HCP	HCP Fiat 2112SFF	Dolmel
SU 46	Co-Co	Elec	1650	120	102	1974	HCP	HCP Fiat 2112SSF	Dolmel
SM 31	Co-Co	Elec	882	80	120	1976	Fablok	HCP	Dolmel
SM 48	Bo-Bo	Elec	882	100	116	1976	PZM-Lugansk	PDG-YM	Charkow
SP 32	Bo-Bo	Elec	1300	100	74	1985	23 August Bucaresti	23 August Bucaresti M820SR	Ep Craiova
SP 47	Co-Co	Elec	2200	140	114	1978	HCP	HCP Fiat 2116SSF	Dolmel

Electric multiple-units

Class	Cars per unit	Line voltage dc	Motor cars per unit	Motored axles per car	Rated output (kW) per motor	Max speed km/h	Weight tonnes per car (M-motor T-trailer)	Total seating capacity	Length per car mm (M-motor T-trailer)	Rate of acceleration m/s^2	Year first built	Builders Mechanical parts	Builders Electrical equipment
EW 55	3	3000	1	4	145	110	M 57 T 33	220	M 20 500 T 20 600	0.5	1959	Pafawag	Dolmel
EN 57	3	3000	1	4	145	110	M 57 T 34	212	M 21 570 T 20 700	0.5	1961	Pafawag	Dolmel
EN 71	4	3000	2	4	145	110	M 57 T 34	282	M 21 570 T 20 700	0.5	1974	Pafawag	Dolmel
EW 58	3	3000	2	4	206	120	total 146	212	M 21 300 T 20 940	0.75-1.0	1975	Pafawag	Dolmel
EN 94	2	600	2	2	56.5	80	total 40	80	total 26 800	0.3	1969	Pafawag	Dolmel

Electric locomotives

Class	Wheel arrangement	Line current	Rated output kW continuous/one-hour	Max speed km/h	Weight tonnes	Year first built	Builders Mechanical parts	Builders Electrical equipment
ET 21	Co-Co	3000 V dc	1860/2400	100	112	1957	Pafawag	Dolmel
EU 06/07	Bo-Bo	3000 V dc	2000/2080	125	80	1963	Pafawag	Dolmel
ET 22	Co-Co	3000 V dc	3000/3120	125	120	1971	Pafawag	Dolmel
EP 05	Bo-Bo	3000 V dc	2032/2344	140/160	80	1973	Skoda	Skoda
EP 08	Bo-Bo	3000 V dc	2080/3000	140	80	1973	Pafawag	Dolmel
ET 40	Bo-Bo + Bo-Bo	3000 V dc	4080/4680	100	164	1976	Skoda	Skoda
ET 41	Bo-Bo + Bo-Bo	3000 V dc	4000/4160	125	167	1978	Cegielski	Dolmel
ET 42	Bo-Bo + Bo-Bo	3000 V dc	4480/4840	100	164	1978	Novocherkassk	Novocherkassk
EP 09	Bo-Bo	3000 V dc	2920/3230	100	84	1986	Pafawag	Dolmel

Portugal
Ministry of Transport & Communications

Praca do Comércio, 1100 Lisbon Cedex

Telex: 13461 moptc p

Minister: Joao Oliveira Martins

Portuguese Railways (CP)
Caminhos de Ferro Portugueses

Calçada do Duque 20, 1294 Lisbon

Telephone: +351 1 36 31 81
Telex: 13334 ferros p

Board of Directors
Chairman: Eng Carvalho Carreira
Members: Eng José Fragoso
Eng Arménio Matias
Eng Antunes da Cunha
Eng Mário de Azevedo
Directors
 Planning: Eng Vilaça e Moura
 Commercial: Eng Apáricio dos Reis
 Economic & Financial: Dr Viegas de Barros
 Personnel: Dr Carlos Rodrigues
 Transport: Eng Ernesto Jorge Sanchez Martins de Brito
 Fixed Installations: João de Andrade Correia

 Rolling Stock: Eng Acúrcio dos Santos
Organisation and Data Processing Department: Eng Carlos Reis
Central Training Department: Dr Manuel Caetano
Supply Department: Eng A Oliveira Santos
Legal Office: Dr Almeida Coragem
Internal Audit Office: Eng Francisco Carapinha
Patrimony Valorisation Office: Dr Texeira da Mota
Innovation & Development: Eng Tiago Ferreira
Social Activities: Dr Lorga da Silva
Administration Secretariat: Dr Luis Beato
Public Relations: Dr Américo Ramalho
Director General, Production & Equipment: Vacant
Assistant Director General: Eng Soares Lopes
Safety & Quality Office: Eng Azevedo Batalha
Northern Region: Eng Fernando Avila
Central Region: Eng Alberto Grossinho
Southern Region: Eng João Lopes
Cascais Line; Eng João Cunha
Sintra and Circle Lines: Eng Conceição e Silva

Gauge: 1668 mm; 1000 mm
Route length: 2850 km; 758 km
Electrification: 1668 mm-gauge, 436 km at 25 kV 50 hZ ac; 26 m at 1.5 kV dc

Gauge conversion

Following Spain's decision to begin gauge conversion to 1435 mm, the Transport Minister asked CP at the end of 1988 to consider a similar move.

In 1990 the likeliest candidates for conversion or construction of completely new 1435 mm-gauge routes were Lisbon-Oporto (see below) and Lisbon-Madrid. The course of the latter is not certain. Spanish Railways (RENFE) have shown disinclination to upgrade their part of the present main rail route between Lisbon and Madrid, which in Portugal runs via Entroncamento and Marvao. They have preferred a more direct route, heading east straight from Lisbon and making for Badajoz in Spain; further east the prospective new route would join the new 250 km/h railway that is now taking shape from Madrid to Seville. This proposal would involve CP in costly creation of a new exit from Lisbon.

Other candidates for new 1435 mm-gauge infrastructure that have been mentioned are a route from Lisbon to the Algarve; and, should RENFE in time project its new Madrid-Seville high-speed line to Huelva, from the Algarve to Huelva.

Traffic (million)	1986	1987	1988
Freight tonnes	5.130	6.425	7.9
Freight tonne-km	1328	1614	1968
Passenger journeys	224.479	227.996	232
Passenger-km	5803	5909	6084

Dmu on the Douro Valley line

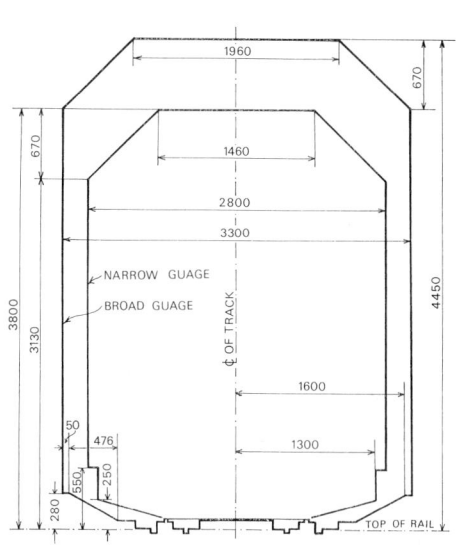

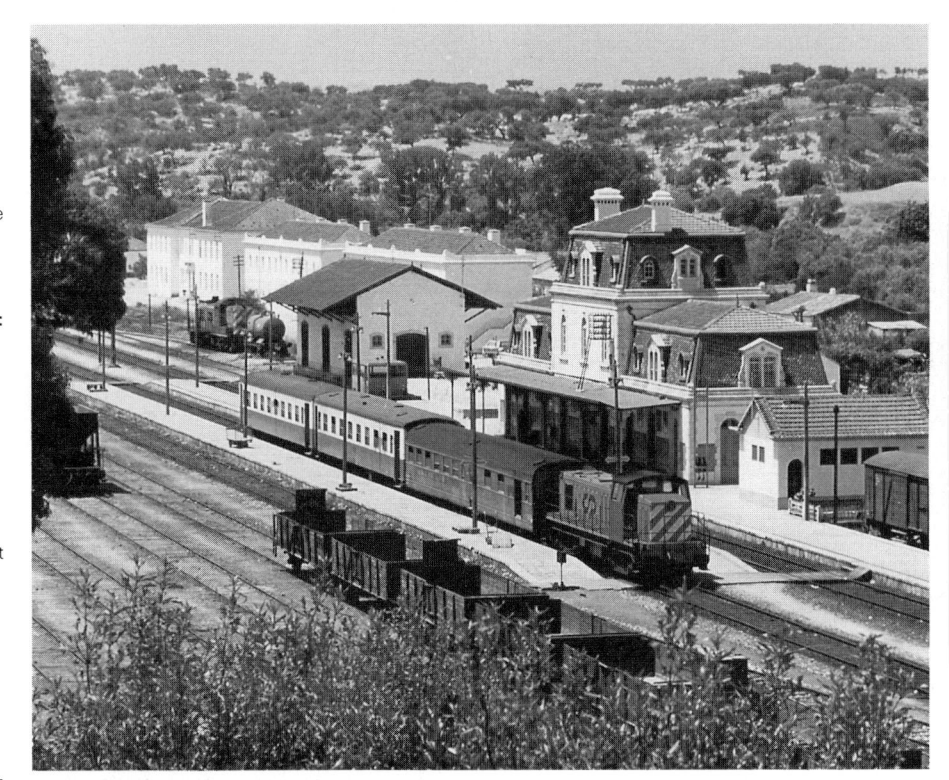

Funcheira station on the South line

Class 2601 electric locomotive crossing a new bridge on the North line near Cacia

RAILWAY SYSTEMS / Portugal

Finances (Contos* million)

Revenues	1985	1986	1988
Passengers and baggage	12.915	13.575	23.243
Freight and mail	3.8802	4.198	
Total	35.832	40.316	44.398†

Expenditure	1985	1986	1988
Staff/personnel	18.384	24.815	31.544
Materials and services	9.489	12.008	16.016
Depreciation	0.999	1.267	2.043
Financial charges	5.987	5.345	6.160
Total	38.628	46.087	55.823

* Conto = 1000 escudos
† Includes state support/compensation of contos 15.395

Investment and modernisation

The government has set CP's total investment money for the period from 1988 to 1994 at 225 200 million escudos. That is five times the rate of CP investment in the first half of the 1980s. Moreover, the character of the works agreed should build up a momentum that will make continuation of investment at this level in the later 1990s virtually unavoidable.

At the start of 1990 bold measures were announced to accelerate CP's adaptation to the transport demands of the post-1992 Single European Market. To concentrate resources and attention on important traffic axes, some 600 km of the narrow-gauge network in the sparsely-populated north would be progressively closed to passenger traffic, which would be switched to buses. The same would apply to some broad-gauge lines in the Alentejo, the area east and southeast of Lisbon.

A rationalisation of small-consignment freight would reduce from 126 to 18 the number of terminals handling such traffic by rail. A further 47 stations would stay in the business, but using road transport.

In October 1989 CP was granted a European Investment Bank (EIB) loan of 6000 million escudos towards its modernisation schemes. These latter included acquisition of 26 locomotives and seven diesel railcars, plus refurbishment of existing rolling stock, but the main use of the money would be for trunk route upgrading.

Improvement of lateral routes to Spain is as vital as regeneration of CP's north-south core. Consequently one priority is modernisation of CP's prime international freight route. This, the Beira Alta, runs from Pamphilhosa, south of Oporto on the Lisbon main line, to the Spanish border at Vilar Formoso; from here there is a direct Spanish route to the French border via Salamanca and Burgos. It is to be electrified and undergo substantial realignment to ease its most severe curves. This will entail complete reconstruction of two segments, in addition to which the 8km between Pampilhosa and Luso is to be double-tracked and level crossings will be eliminated. Completion may cut as much as 2 hours from contemporary Lisbon-Paris passenger train timings.

The electrified Lisbon-Oporto line generates half CP's income, and its redevelopment is the other priority. Its major handicap of the 1876-77 single-line Oporto bridge over the Douro, the frailty of which reduces train speeds to a crawl and prevents maximum loading of modern freight wagons, is at last heading for elimination. After some false starts, replacement of this antique Gustave Eiffel structure by a new double-track edifice, which will be one of the world's biggest prestressed concrete rail bridges, should be effected by 1992.

In 1989 the UK consultancy Transmark was commissioned to vet the case for a completely new 1435mm-gauge high-speed line between the two cities. Meanwhile, the existing route is undergoing track and bridge renewal, with a lift of maximum freight wagon axleloads to 25 tonnes one of the objectives. Part of the EIB loan mentioned above will be applied to resignalling and installation of the Ericsson ATP system; this, in conjunction with level crossing automation, will allow a rise of maximum passenger train speed to 160 km/h. Also planned is extension of the electrification north of Oporto to Braga.

North-south rail communication hits another snag at Lisbon. The first rail bridge over the Tagus river is some 55 km upstream from the city centre, and again only single-line. For passenger traffic CP has to maintain two Lisbon terminals, one on each side of the Tagus, with a ferry connection between them. The government has approved addition of two rail tracks to the 1966-built suspension road bridge over the Tagus within the city area. But finance will be confined to preparatory work in the 1987–94 period; completion is not expected until the second half of the decade. A major redevelopment of the Lisbon rail system is planned in conjunction with the new Tagus crossing, involving a new through station to the west of the city from which a new line would cross the bridge to Almada and run from there to a connection with the existing line to the south at Almada.

Meanwhile UK consultants Kennedy Henderson were in 1990 commissioned to consider a substantial relocation of Lisbon's Cascais suburban line. Lisbon's local passenger traffic has boomed and the final 8km of the Cascais line's entry to its Cais do Sodre terminus in the city is beset by level crossings. The study is to consider dropping the line into a cut-and-cover tunnel and extending it some 2km along the waterfront from Cais do Sodre to the Santa Apolonia main-line station.

Passenger

A powerful motivation to give CP a higher ranking in the country's investment priorities has been the extraordinary growth of rail passenger travel since the oil crisis. Measured in passenger journeys, volume has more than doubled since 1973 and ongoing growth at a rate of 2 per cent per annum is forecast.

The growth has been in commuter travel around Lisbon and Oporto, sparked by government-inspired fare schemes to encourage more use of the railway. Commuter traffic now accounts for 59 per cent of all

Bar car of Corall-type stock in Lisbon-Oporto 'Alfa' service

Alsthom 1000 mm-gauge diesel-electric railcar on Póvoa line

Alsthom-built Class 9000 diesel at Mirandela on narrow-gauge Tua line

Class 1961 diesel heads a pyrites train over the Marateca bridge on the new Poceirão branch line

CP passenger business. Further growth is now constrained by lack of operating capacity.

Freight
Until the 1960s national economic planning was obsessed with road transport. As a result rail connection was ignored when most post-war steel, cement, pulp and paper plants, and erected.

With the encouragement of CP's improving freight service quality, industries have lately been persuaded to lay in rail connections to their plants or to build a rail component into their overall transportation. The new contract with the state aims to increase the total of private sidings.

Concentration on quality service of major customers, including where necessary ancillary services of collection, delivery and warehousing, has lately lifted freight volume back to and beyond 1980 figures. As against 723 million tonne-km in 1973, CP registered 1327 million in 1986 and 1968 million in 1988. Growth continues at a rate of 7 per cent per annum. Advances have been significant in block train movement of cereals, timber, paper pulp and cereals. As much as 90 per cent of CP's freight now moves in unit trains.

CP's freight traffic is currently dominated by coal, cement, timber and cereals in roughly equal quantities, with petroleum products not far behind. CP has yet to develop a network of container terminals and dedicated container trains comparable with the TECO system of Spain's RENFE. But well-organised connections with TECO are in place to and from CP"s Alcantara Terra, Lisbon Beirolas, Leiria, Espinho and Oporto terminals. Twice-weekly 'TEC Iberico' trains dedicated to maritime container traffic interconnect Lisbon Beirolas and Leixoes with RENFE's Barcelona, Valencia, Algeciras, Cadiz and Bilbao terminals. Further terminal sites are under consideration at centres such as Mangualde, Setubal and Viana do Castelo. Metalsines has recently delivered 200 additional container flatcars.

Sines line
The long-discussed new line from Pinheiro, on the Lisbon-Algarve mainline, to Sines may be retrieved from the back-burner to which the idea was relegated when the port's industrial growth was faltering (and Portugal's economy was generally under pressure). Although in 1987 CP invited bids to prepare an alignment for the line, its construction has yet to be financed.

Need of the new line looms because, in the early 1990s, CP will be feeding new electricity generating plant at Pego annually with 3 million tonnes of imported coal offloaded at Sines. The railway will also lift the power station's fly ash to a cement works. In 1989 the national power generation company invited bids to build an 8.7 km branch to Pego, to install rapid discharge gear at the plant and to supply 160 65-tonne coal hopper wagons. CP is to electrify the branch from Entroncamento to Pego, and from Setil to Pinheiro, including connections to Barreiro. Numerous passing loops are being lengthend to accommodate the coal trains.

The port area of Sines is now a prime source of CP freight business, and this big addition of coal tonnage will raise access problems. Today's rail route to Sines takes in a considerable distance of the Faro main line, and that will be overburdened by the prospective flow of heavy coal trains. From Lisbon the Pego coal trains will take the electrified Oporto main line to Entoncamento.

Traction and rolling stock
In 1989 CP's broad-gauge stock comprised 176 diesel and 58 electric locomotives, 74 locotractors, 111 three-car emus, 39 two-car dmus, 35 diesel railcars, 524 passenger cars, 120 luggage vans and 5109 freight wagons. GEC-Alsthom has delivered a further nine Class 2600 electric locomotives, to supplement the series of 12 obtained in 1974.

The coaching stock includes four ex-SNCF 'Gril-Express' cafeteria cars.

The narrow-gauge stock in 1989 consisted of four steam and 17 diesel locomotives, 10 four-car and 22 two-car dmus, 10 diesel railcars, eight luggage vans and 395 freight wagons.

In 1989 six two-car diesel train-sets and 26 trailers were on order for the broad-gauge from Sorefame. At the end of the year bids were invited for the supply of 42 four-car emus for the Lisbon-Sintra commuter service, to be delivered fropm 1992 to 1996. The aim was for the units to be built by Sorefame in consort with a foreign traction equipment manufacturer. The specification called for asynchronous motors with a total rating per set of 3100kW, regenerative braking, 120 km/h top speed and a 1 m/s^2 acceleration rate. A subsequent call for supply of bi-level emus for the Cascais suburban line was anticipated.

Bids were also invited in late 1989 for the supply of 43 5600kW electric locomotives, 14 of them for the Beira Alta line electrification (see above) and the remainder to replace the elderly Classes 2500 and 2550. The GEC-Alsthom Sybic design for SNCF and Siemens' Class 120 of the DB were in contention for this order, as they had been in neighbouring Spain.

Forward plans include a 1988 order for 10 emus for the Lisbon-Sintra suburban service, and a number of dmus for the southern lines around Almeda and the Algarve coast.

Signalling
EB Corporation of Norway, part of the ABB Group, has, through its subsidiary, EB Signal, received a CP contract for the delivery of Ricsson-type ATP speed-control equipment for installation on the Lisbon-Oporto line. It will make possible an increase of train speed to 160 km/h. The contract, covers equipment for 300 locomotives. EB Signal's local partner in this project is EFACEC, who will be responsible for the installation work and will contribute, to a certain extent, in matters of design and production.

CP plans to concentrate signalling of its main-line network on five centres, to be located at Oporto, Coimbra, Entroncamento, Lisbon and Setubal.

Track
Standard rail
Broad-gauge: 30–55 kg/m in 8–18 m lengths
Narrow-gauge: 20–36 kg/m in 8 and 12 m lengths
Cross ties (sleepers)
Broad-gauge: 260 × 130 × 2600 mm, spacing 605 mm
Narrow-gauge: 230 × 120 × 1800 mm, spacing 820–850 mm
Rail fastening: Screw spikes or bolts. 'RN' flexible fastenings used with welded rail
Filling: Broken stone, gravel or earth

Max curvature
Broad-gauge: 5.9° = minimum radius 300 m
Narrow-gauge: 29° = minimum radius 60 m

Longest continuous gradient
Broad-gauge: 8.3 km of 1.4% grade with curves varying from 590 to 1501 m in radius
Narrow-gauge: 7.2 km of 2.5% grade with curves varying from 75 to 500 m in radius

Max gradient
Broad-gauge: 1.8% = 1 in 55½

Diesel locomotives

Class	Wheel arrangement	Transmission	Rated power hp	Tractive effort Max kg	Tractive effort Continuous at kg	Tractive effort Continuous at km/h	Max speed km/h	Wheel dia mm	Total weight tonnes	Length mm	No built	Year first built	Builders Mechanical parts	Builders Engine & type	Builders Transmission
9001/003	Bo-Bo	Elec	572	11 500	11 000	15	70	950	46	11 174	3	1959	Alsthom	SACM MGO	Alsthom
9004/006	Bo-Bo	Elec	590	11 500	9000	17·5	70	950	46	11 174	3	1959	Alsthom	SACM	Alsthom
9021/031	Bo-Bo	Elec	715	11 500	10 600	21·5	70	950	46·65	11 360	11	1976	Alsthom	SACM	Alsthom
1001/1006	C	Mech	160	7600	–	–	41·5	991	30·4	7815	6	1948	Drewry	Gardner	Sinclair
1021/1025	B	Elec	425	9720	9720	12	65	1050	36	9090	5	1968	Moyse	Deutz	Moyse
1051/1068	B	Elec	120	7000	7000	4	38	1050	28·3	7280	13	1955	Moyse	Moyse	Moyse
1101/1112	Bo-Bo	Elec	255	10 000	4258	10	56	965	41·2	10 210	11	1946	GE	Caterpillar	GE
1151/1186	C	Hyd	250	11 400	–	–	58	1090	42	8517	36	1966	Sorefame	Rolls-Royce	Rolls-Royce
1201/1225	Bo-Bo	Elec	600	16 000	12 200	13	80	1100	64·7	14 680	25	1961	Sorefame	SACM	Brissoneau & Lotz
1401/1467	Bo-Bo	Elec	1025	16 100	14 200	19	105	950	64·4	12 720	65	1967	Sorefame	EE	EE
1501/1521	A1A-A1A	Elec	1730		2100	21	120	1016	111	16 988	17	1948	Alco	Alco	GE
1551/1570	Co-Co	Elec	1700	24 300	19 300	22·5	120	1016	89·7	17 905	20	1973	MLW	MLW/Alco	Canadian-GE
1801/1810	Co-Co	Elec	2050	26 000	17 750	31	140	1100	110·3	18 680	10	1968	EE	EE	EE
1961/1973	Co-Co	Elec	2250	45 000	28 300	18·75	120	1016	121	19 895	13	1979	MLW	MLW	Canadian-GE
1901/13	Co-Co	Elec	3000	39 600	25 600	23·2	100	1100	120	19 100	13	1981	Sorefame	SACM	Alsthom
1931/47							120			18 800	17				

Electric locomotives

Class	Wheel arrangement	Line current	Continuous rating kW	One hour output	Tractive effort Max lb	Tractive effort Continuous at lb	Tractive effort Continuous at mph	Wheel diameter mm	Weight tonnes	Length mm	No built	Builders Mechanical parts	Builders Electrical equipment
2501-2515	Bo-Bo	25 kV ac 50 Hz	2116	2228	44 600	26 700	39	1300	72	15 380	15	50 c/s Group	50 c/s Group
2551-2570	Bo-Bo	25 kV ac 50 Hz	2116	2228	44 600	26 700	39	1300	70·5	15 380	20	Sorefame	50 c/s Group
2601-2629	B-B	25 kV ac 50 Hz	2940	3000	71 500* 46 800	42 000* 26 200	34 55	1140	78	17 480	21	Alsthom	50 c/s Group

* Low gear (monomotor bogie)

698 RAILWAY SYSTEMS / Portugal—Romania

Narrow-gauge: 2.5% = 1 in 40

Max altitude
Broad-gauge: 812.7 m
Narrow-gauge: 849.7 m

Max axleload
Broad-gauge: 19.5 tonnes
Narrow-gauge: 11 tonnes

Max permitted speed
Broad-gauge: 140 km/h
Narrow-gauge: 80 km/h

Welded rail: Thermit process is used. Rail used weighs 54, 50, 45, 40 kg/m in 18 and 24 m lengths. The length of continuous welded rail is usually 840 m but occasionally 950 m. Rails are secured to sleepers by RN flexible clips.

Diesel railcars

Series	Wheel arrangement	Trans-mission	Rated power hp	Tractive effort Max kg	Tractive effort Continuous at kg	Tractive effort Continuous at km/h	Max speed km/h	Wheel dia mm	Total weight tonnes	Length mm	No built	Year first built	Builders Mechanical parts	Builders Engine & type	Builders Transmission
9101/103 (NG)	B-B	Hyd	240	4100	—	—	70	700	22	15 500	3	1949	Nohab	Scania Vabis	Lisholm-Smith
9301/310 (NG)	Bo-Bo	Elec	320	9000	—	—	70	820	37	19 510	8	1954	Allan	AEC	Smith
9601/622 (NG)	BO 2' + 2' 2'	Elec	383	4500	2850	36	90	880	64·36	38 550	22	1976	Alsthom	SFAC	Alsthom
0101/115 (BG)	(1A) (A1)	Hyd	252	2500	—	—	100	700	33·3	22 490	12	1948	Nohab	Saab-Scania	Voith
0301/325 (BG)	Bo-Bo	Elec	360	—	—	—	100	920	5·5	23 630	24	1954	Allan	SSCM	Smith
0401/419 (BG)	(1A) (A1) + 2' 2'	Hyd	560	6200	—	—	110	850	94·1	51 960	19	1965	Sorefame	Rolls-Royce	Rolls-Royce
0601/0640 (BG)	2' B' + B' 2'	Hyd	775	11 400	7600	22	120	920	110	53 480	20	1979	Sorefame	SFAC	Voith
9701-40 (NG)	2B + B2 + 2B + B2 +	Mech	720	—	—	—	60	750	92	—	10	—	Fiat (acquired from Yugoslav Railways)		

Electric railcars

Class	Wheel arrangement	Line current	Rated output hp	Tractive effort Max kg	Tractive effort Continuous at kg	Tractive effort Continuous at km/h	Max speed km/h	Wheel dia mm	Weight tonnes	Length mm	No built	Year first built	Builders Mechanical parts	Builders Electrical equipment
2001/2025	Bo' Bo' + 2' 2' + 2' 2'	25 kV 50 Hz	1469	11 700	6000	40	90	1000-850*	117	71 060	24	1956	Sorefame	Siemens-AEG-Oerlikon
2051/2074-2082/2090	Bo' Bo' + 2' 2' + 2' 2'	25 kV 50 Hz	1469	11 700	6000	40	90	1000-850*	123·6	71 060	33	1956	Sorefame	Siemens-AEG-Oerlikon
2101/2124	2' 2' + Bo' Bo' + 2' 2'	25 kV 50 Hz	1716	11 700	6240	64	120	1000-850*	132·8	71 060	24	1970	Sorefame	Siemens-AEG-Oerlikon
2151/2168	2' 2' + Bo' Bo' + 2' 2'	25 kV 50 Hz	1716	11 700	6240	64	120	1000-850	132·8	71 060	18	1977	Sorefame	Siemens-AEG-Oerlikon
2201/2215	2' 2' + Bo' Bo' + 2' 2'	50 Hz	1716	11 700	6240	64	120	850	132·8	71 060	15	1984	Sorefame	Efalec

* Electric trailer cars

Romania

Romanian State Railways (CFR)
Caile Ferate Romane

Bd Dinicu Golescu 38, Bucharest 7

Telephone: +40 0 18 40 20/17 20 60/17 18 80
Telex: 10633 dci r

Minister of Transport and Communications: Pavel Aron
Heads of Railways Department: I Tudosie / A Dobre
Commercial and Operating Director: Ing M Munteanu
Motive Power and Rolling Stock Director: Ing I Bălănescu
Technical Director: M Negulesu
Way and Works Director: Ing C Ruianu
Personnel Director: F Vintilă
Financial Director: V Marghescu
Organisation and Audit Director: V Doborantu
Planning Director: A Mănescu
Director, Research Institute: Ing E Spirea
Director, Operation and Commercial: M Munteanu
Director, International Co-operation and External Traffic: C Alexandrescu
Director, Rail Projects: Ing I Antonescu
Director, Computer Centre: G Pătrascu
Director, Timetable Planning: Ing C Leu
Locomotive and Rolling Stock Engineer: Ing G H Tănase
Stores: Ing M Bălănescu

Gauge: 1435 mm; 610 and 762 mm

Route length: 10 565 km; 518km
Electrification: 2367 km at 25 kV 50 Hz ac

Electrification
Two electric main lines at present connect CFR with international traffic. Bucharest-Constanta and Bucharest-Craiova-Timisoara-Arad-Curtici. They allow electric operation from Curtici on the Hungarian western border to Constanta on the Black Sea coast. The other main electrified routes run north from Bucharest to Ploesti, Brasov, Dej, Buzau, Adjud and Bacau.

Two axle diesel railbus for CFR by "23 August" Works

Routes lately in course of electrification have included: Galati-Faurei and Bacau-Pascani (on the main Bucharest-Suceava line to the USSR border and Moscow) in the east of the country; the formidable Transylvania Alpine line of 229 km between Brasov and Teius, and the 27 km Ciulnita-Calarsi line. The area around Deva, in western Transylvania, is another focus of electrification work, covering the 55 km from Dej to Cluj in the north, a step towards creating a north-south route between the Ukraine and Bulgaria that avoids Bucharest, and continuation of the Transylvanian Alpine scheme beyond Sighisorara to Teius (170 km). Wiring from Simeria, near Deva, to the steel-manufacturing centre of Hunedoara (15 km) has been completed.

More new electrified branches have been or are being built. One of them is the 35 km Stoneasa link through the Zaranduli mountains connecting Brad with Deva, in the west, opening up a new route from Deva to Arad and relieving the 140 km main line along the Muresul valley, which is nevertheless being double-tracked. This project, completed in the summer of 1987, shortens the rail distance between the parallel Mures and Crisul Alb valleys by about 290 km. Another project is a 30 km branch connecting Tirgu Neamt with Pascani, on the main route from Bucharest to Suceava and Lvov. A new and much shorter route between Bucharest and Transylvania via Sibiu was being created by construction of a 50 km link between Ramnicu Vilcea and Vilceli; this scheme has been another complex engineering task, involving construction of nine viaducts, one of them 1.3 km long.

Civil engineering

New track construction will permit axleloading to be raised from 16–18 tonnes to 20.5 tonnes and enable a maximum running speed of 160 km/h. At present 60 and 65 kg/m rails is being installed on Type T16 and T17 concrete sleepers. Ballast depth is 300 mm and minimum curve radius 500 metres.

Welded rails have been laid on 70 per cent of trunk and main lines and about 700 km were to be welded annually during the 1980s.

A new 420 km, double-track bridge has been completed over the Danube between Fetesti and Cernavoda, some 150 km from Bucharest on the main line to Constanta, where a new 32-track marshalling yard was completed in 1981; the latter is to be automated. The previous river crossing here was single-track.

To enlarge operating capacity to and from the USSR, a 17 km branch has been completed from the Dornesti route into the USSR to Siret, where the new line will forge a link with a Soviet Railways branch.

Motive power and rolling stock

Both diesel-hydraulic locomotives (450, 750 and 1250 hp) and diesel-electric locomotives (2100, 3000 and 4000 hp versions with engines built under Sulzer, Alco and Maybach licences) are operated by the railway. Two types of electric locomotives are used on the single-phase 25 kV 50 Hz lines: a 5100 kW Co-Co built under an ASEA licence (240 are operating on CFR lines); and a 3400 kW Bo-Bo.

Signalling

Automatic block covers 3650 km. About 120 km per annum are being equipped with automatic block. CTC is not widespread. ATS covers the entire 1435 mm-gauge network.

Saudi Arabia

Saudi Government Railroad Organisation

PO Box 36, Dammam 31241

Telephone: +966 3 871 2222
Cable: Saudirail, Dammam
Telex: 801050 sarail sj
Telefax: +966 3 833 6337

President: Faysal M Al-Shehail
Vice President: Abdul Mohsin Bashawri
Vice-President, Operations: Fahad Zamil Al-Hazmi
Directors
  Administration and Finance: Abdulla Saleh Al-Wabil
  Maintenance: Salah Saleh Al-Ahmedi
  Operations: Mohammed Maraee (Acting)
  Motive Power & Equipment: Ali Abdulla Al-Qarnil
  Finance: Abdulla Ghanim Al-Oraini
  Accounts: Abdul Amir Al-Sunni
  Telecommunications: Abdul Aziz Al-Sayegh
  Planning and Budget: Khamis Mubarik Al-Dossary
  Personnel: Mohammed Ali Al-Jibreen
  Riyadh Region: Mohammed Dhaffar Qahtani
  Permanent Way: Turki Abdulla Al-Hajri
  Construction and Maintenance: Hassan Ali Al-Shaikh
  Purchasing: Abdul Aziz Ba Hussain
  Stores: Sa'ad Abdul Aziz Al-Abbad
  Electrical Equipment: Ahmed Ali Al-Tannaj
  Representative for UIC Affairs: Mohammed A Bubshait

Gauge: 1435 mm
Route length: 875 km

Dammam-Riyadh main line

Principal infrastructure project of the 1980s was the transformation of the Dammam-Riyadh main line. The 140 km of the existing route from Dammam to Hofuf were double-tracked and re-aligned for 150 km/h maximum speed, with continuously-welded UIC 60 rail on concrete sleepers, the latter manufactured in a plant established locally at Hofuf. Beyond Hofuf a new and direct double-track route of 308 km has been built and engineered for 150 km/h.

New stations have been built at Riyadh, Dammam and Hofuf. Traffic is controlled by route relay interlocking, tokenless block, with level crossing automatic barriers worked by soft-lead batteries recharged by solar power.

The next major project is to be construction of a 100 km line from Dammam to the Jubail steel manufacturing complex. This has been incorporated in the country's 1990–95 industrial development plan and a start of work scheduled for 1993. Completion is forecast in 1996.

Traction and rolling stock

In 1989 the railway was operating 59 diesel locomotives, 58 passenger cars (including nine restaurant cars) and 2340 freight wagons.

Type of coupler, passenger and freight: AAR Type E
Type of brake: Westinghouse air

Maintenance workshop at Dammam

A major maintenance workshop has been set up at Dammam. When complete the workshop will cater for a workload of 78 main-line locomotives and 33

Traffic	1985/86	1986/87	1987/88	1988/89
Freight tonne-km (000)	763 546	746 000	872 000	801 000
Freight tonnage (000)	1559·4	1626	1721	NA
Passenger-km (million)	66·514	70·719	88 006	121 000
Passengers carried	168 585	165 878	241 467	NA

Finances (Saudi Riyals 000)				
Revenue	1985/86	1986/87	1987/88	
Passengers and baggage	4389	5625	8202	
Freight and mail	37 129	36 234	50 787	
Other	23 614	9823	13 827	
Total	65 132	51 682	72 816	

Expenditure	1985/86	1986/87	1987/88
Staff/personnel	35 148	28 180	35 453
Materials and services	108 012	85 356	107 065
Depreciation	106 154	92 103	105 337
Financial charges	9822	5388	5936
Total	259 136	211 027	253 791

Diesel locomotives

Class	Wheel arrangement	Transmission	Rated power (kW)	Max speed km/h	Total weight tonnes	No in service 1988	Year first built	Builders Engine & type	Transmission
1100 (G18W)	Bo-Bo	Elec	746	110	62·2	16	1968, 1974 & 1976	EMD-GMC	EMD-GMC
1100 (SW1001)	Bo-Bo	Elec	746	110	104·3	5	1981	EMD-GMC	EMD-GMC
1500 (F7 & F9)	Bo-Bo	Elec	1119	110	118	6	1953, 1957	EMD-GMC	EMD-GMC
1200 (GP18)	Bo-Bo	Elec	1119	110	111·4	1	1961	EMD-GMC	EMD-GMC
2000 (GP38-2)	Bo-Bo	Elec	1492	110	113	1	1973	EMD-GMC	EMD-GMC
2000 (GT22CW)	Co-Co	Elec	1678·5	110	108	3	1976	EMD-GMC	EMD-GMC
2000 (SDL38-2)	Co-Co	Elec	1492	110	109·5	5	1978	EMD-GMC	EMD-GMC
3500 (SDL50)	Co-Co	Elec	2611	160	120·4	6	1981	EMD-GMC	EMD-GMC
						10*	1985*		
3600 (CSE 26-21)	Co-Co	Elec	2450	160	126	6	1981	Alco/Francorail	Jeumont Schneider

* With dynamic braking

RAILWAY SYSTEMS / Saudi Arabia—South Africa

shunting locomotives, with a maximum capacity of 20 locomotives at one time.

Track
All main-line track renewals are now being undertaken with continuously welded UIC 60 kg/m rail on prestressed concrete sleepers with elastic fastenings.

Rail types and weights: UIC 54, UIC 60
Cross ties (sleepers): Prestressed concrete, 200 mm thickness, 260 mm long
Spacing: 1667/km

Rail fastenings: Elastic, ballast cushion of 300 mm
Minimum curve radius: 565 m

Max gradient: 1%
Max permissible axleload: 29 tonnes

Senegal
Ministry of Equipment

Administrative Building, Dakar

Minister: R Sagna

Regie des Chemins de Fer du Sénégal (RCFS)

PO Box 175, Cité Ballabey, Thies

Telephone: +221 51 10 13
Telex: 7789 fersenegal

President: O S Thiaw
General Manager: M Diouf
Deputy General Manager: Louis Venault
Heads of Department
  Administration and Planning: Ndiaga Ndiaye
  Commercial: Momar Gueye
  Finance: Mor Kane
  Motive Power and Rolling Stock: Niokhar Sene
  Way and Works: Daouda Sene
  Stores: Babacar Gueye

Gauge: 1000 mm
Route length: 904 km

As one of West Africa's most industrialised countries, Senegal (which was united with Gambia in 1982) has a railway system comprising two basic main lines running from Dakar to St Louis and Linguère in the north-east and the border with Mali in the east. The system was originally part of the Federal West African Railway Authority (AOF) before transfer to the Mali Federation in 1960. The disintegration of the Mali Federation caused the division of the former Dakar-Niger system into two networks. The principal line extends 1286 km from Dakar in Senegal to Koulikoro, the terminus of the railway in Mali.

Status in dispute
RCFS is a public enterprise with, in theory, financial autonomy. In 1989 management was seeking new status that would relieve it of obligation to seek authorisation of its budget from the Transport Ministry, but the government was not in favour. Also in dispute, in this case with the railway labour unions, was a proposal that a separate company should be set up to expand Dakar's suburban rail service, at present confined to an unprofitable service to Tianoye, known as the 'Little Blue Train', that is in need of investment.

Ore line project
Subject to ability of the Eastern Senegal Iron Ore Mining Co to put together financing for its CFAfr 54 000 million cost, construction was to begin in 1992 of a 310 km railway from mines at Koudékourou to a junction with RCFS at Tambacounda. The new line, single track with three passing loops, will ferry an estimated 10 million tonnes of export ore to a port at Bargny, near Dakar. The operational plan is that 12 500-tonne trains of 90 ore wagons will be powered by four 2300 hp diesel locomotives. The track will be formed of 36 kg/m rail on twin-block concrete sleepers with a ruling gradient of 0/5 per cent against loaded trains and a minimum curve radius of 500m.

Traffic
In FY 1987-88 the railway recorded 984 000 passenger journeys, 178 million passenger-km, 3.21 million tonnes of freight and 530 million freight tonne-km.

Motive power and rolling stock
The stock of 29 diesel locomotives and eight railcars is mostly French-built. It was enlarged by three Bo-Bo and three Co-Co locomotives of 1600 hp in 1983/84, supplied by Spanish builders; four locomotives were delivered from General Motors of Canada, and three AD20C locomotives from GEC-Alsthom in 1987. French aid is financing GEC-Alsthom maintenance of the railway's Alsthom AD16B locomotives.

At the start of 1989 passenger cars totalled 100 (including 36 diesel railcar trailers) and freight wagons 825. In 1983 12 passenger cars, including three sleeping cars, were procured from Ateinsa of Spain. Complemented by a buffet car fashioned in RCF's own workshops, this equipment is applied to a daily Dakar-St Louis service.

RCFS train headed by first-class diesel railcar, Spanish built by La Maquinista Terrestre y Maritima (*Wilhelm Pflug*)

In October 1989 RCFS received from the SNCF the first of what was expected to be 14 of the French railway's Type B10t 'Bruhat' passenger cars. In its own workshops RCFS was refurbishing the cars and refitting them with ex-freight wagon metre-gauge bogies that had had their suspension refined. RCFS also placed an option on the 24 stainless steel SNCF 'Mistral' cars of the 1950s and their four generator cars, which the SNCF would be withdrawing from their own service in October 1990.

Track and signalling
With aid from France the first 270 km of the main line from Dakar to Kidra has been relaid. Italian aid was supporting renewal with 36 kg/m rail on concrete sleepers of the succeeding 193 km to Tambacounda. The concluding 180 km would lay 36 kg/m rail on reconditioned steel sleepers. Automatic block colour-light signalling is operative on the 70 km of double track between Dakar amd Thies.

South Africa
Ministry of Transport, Public Works & Land Affairs

Sanlam Centre, Pretoria (Ministry)

Forum Building, Struben Street, Pretoria (Departments)
Telephone: +27 12 322 1343

Room 215, Hendrik Verwoerd Building, Cape Town

Telephone: +27 21 45 1726/83

Minister: George Bartlett
Private Secretary to the Ministry of Transport Affairs: S J van Blommestein

Transnet
formerly **South African Transport Services (SATS)**

Paul Kruger Building, Wolmarans Street, Johannesburg 2001

Telephone: +27 11 773 2270
Telex: 4-24087; 4-24205
Telefax: +27 11 774 2665

Director General: Dr A T Moolman
Deputy General Managers
  Technical Services: Helmuth S F Hagen
  Financial Services: G M Holtz
  Airways: G D van der Veer
  Manpower Services: J G Benadé
  Railways: B J Lessing
Assistant General Managers
  Technical: H S F Hagen
  Services: A N Davidson
  Personnel: D M J Butler
  Rail Traffic: M F Myburgh
  Marketing: Dr G J S Coetzee
  Finance: T G Greef
  Financial Services: E Krüger
  Operating: A S Le Roux
  Airways: V C Lewis
Chief Directors
  Supporting Services, Railways: S G Wessels
  Rolling Stock: F J Nicholson
                    T N G Boshoff
  Infrastructure, Railways: V A Dixon
                                B J Van der Merwe
                                G Van der Merwe
Chief Engineers
  Supporting Services, Railways: C C Badenhorst
  Industrial Services: D J Erasmus
  Rolling Stock: W F Burger
  Infrastructure, Railways: D J van Zijl
  Workshops: F R Loygerenberg
  Harbours: N P Campbell
  Telecommunications: D C Coetzer
  Construction: W S Brass
  Technical Advisory Services: P C Lombard
Regional Managers
  Johannesburg: J C can der Merwe (Acting)
  Cape Town: B Heckroodt
  Durban: A E Fourie
  Pretoria: W P Burger
  Port Elizabeth: Dr F J Mülke
  East London: L D du Toit
  Windhoek: C J Brink
  Bloemfontein: J D J Uys
  Kimberley: J L Pretorius
  Saldanha: D J Barnado
  Richards Bay: W C Kuys

Gauge: 1065 mm; 610 mm
Route length: 23 244 km; 314 km
Electrification: 5831 km at 3 kV dc
  861 km at 50 kV ac
  1808 km at 25 kV ac
  15 km at dual 3 kV dc/25 kV ac

Restructure as Transnet Ltd
The bulk of South African Transport Services (SATS) activity was taken the first step down the road to privatisation in April 1990. From the start of that month all but SATS' loss-making suburban services were regrouped in a new public and profit-centred company, Transnet Ltd. This has five divisions: air services; roads; harbours; pipelines; and the railways, which are

now marketed under the name of Spoornet. Initially all Transnet equity is held by the government, but eventually shares will be put on the public market. A subsidised body, the South African Rail Commuter Corporation, is running SATS' heavily loss-making suburban passenger services under contract, at first to the government, though later it is intended that some of the subsidy will be taken over by local authorities. The rail division of the new public company has taken on SATS' lossmaking main-line passenger operations.

Finance
In FY 1987-88 the financial results of the railways before appropriation reflected a deficit of R788 million compared with a deficit of R429 million the previous year. But in FY 1988-89, with the help of an increased passenger service subsidy, this was turned into a R211 million profit, whereas a further deficit had been anticipated.

Freight traffic
Revenue-earning freight ton-km in FY 1987-88 totalled 85 629 million, 5.46 per cent less than the previous year. Coal and coke exported decreased by 4.39 per cent. Owing to the weak operating results SATS was obliged to increase tariffs twice during the 1987/88 financial year.

A major component of coal traffic is the export flow from the Transvaal fields to Richards Bay. The number of trains ferrying coal from the Transvaal and Natal coal fields to Richards Bay varies between 180 and 185 per week. Each train comprises either 88 or 176 air-braked CCR wagons (each with a payload of 58 tons) or 68 CCL-5 wagons (each with a payload of 84 tons) or 160 CCL-5 wagons; trains consisting of 160 CCL-5 wagons are presently loaded to a mass of 22 tons per axle (68 tons net) pending track improvements. The trains operate on a daily basis between Ermelo/Vryheid and Richards Bay.

The double-length trains, which are 2·3 km long, are headed by three Class 7E electric locomotives with a further five locomotives marshalled mid-train. Such trains convey a net load of approximately 10 208 tons (CCR wagons) or 10 880 tons (CCL-5 wagons).

In August 1989 several world records were claimed when a 71 600-tonne train was run the length of the 831 km Sishen-Saldanha ore line. The train, 7.2 km long, was formed of 660 wagons and powered by five Class 9E electric locomotives at the head end, four more cut in after the 470th wagon, and at the rear, to avoid overtaxing the traction current supply, seven Class 37 diesel locomotives plus a fuel tank car and brake coach. Locomotive crews had radio intercommunication. Maximum speed was 80 km/h and average speed for the whole run 37.9 km/h. The feat culminated a research programme directed to increase of the 14 500–21 800 tonne trainloads that are current practice on this line.

Up to four air-braked container trains, each consisting of 50 wagons, are operated daily in both directions between City Deep (Johannesburg) and Bayhead (Durban) terminals. Air-braked container trains consisting of 40 to 50 wagons are also run daily. Mondays to Fridays, in both directions between City Deep and Port Elizabeth, and between City Deep and Cape Town's Belcon terminal; the City Deep-Port Elizabeth trains additionally convey containers for Kroonstad, Welkom, Virginia, Bloemfontein and East London, with the containers for East London carried by ordinary goods trains between Bloemfontein and East London. Containers for Klerksdorp, De Aar and Namibia are conveyed on the City Deep-Cape Town trains; those for Namibia travel on from De Aar on ordinary goods trains. In 1989 SATS was completing delivery of 950 new container wagons.

Introduction of minicontainers has extended containerisation to smaller companies forwarding quantities of goods which do not justify the use of standard 3 m container. The minicontainer is of a size unique to Spoornet, with inside dimensions of 1·413 m (width) × 2·296 m (depth) × 2·461 m (height) and a capacity of 7·93 m³ (0·25 TEU); it can accommodate a payload of 3000 kg and fully loaded averages 3600 kg gross. It is constructed of reinforced glass fibre panels and a 3 CR12 stainless steel framework. The SATS cartage service has specially adapted vehicles fitted with frames to accommodate two or eight minicontainers.

Minicontainers are conveyed by the Fastfreight services, now extended country-wide, so that 51 Fastfreight trains operating daily over 18 routes interconnect all the major centres, in most cases overnight. Goods for small depots and stations are transshipped at these centres and forwarded by supplementary regional trains, while on branch lines goods are despatched with the first available train.

SATS now runs selected freight trains at 100 km/h maximum speed on its main lines from Johannesburg to Durban and Cape Town. Elsewhere the general limit remains 60 km/h. With the new Class 14E locomotives (see below) it is hoped to raise the maximum on key routes to 120 km/h in the 1990s but this may depend on the cost-effectiveness of curve easement in places, and also on the consequences for operating capacity of widening the freight train speed bend.

During 1990 Spoornet would be taking delivery of prototypes of locally-manufactured bi-modal and piggyback vehicles. Spoortrailer, the bi-modal, would follow the RoadRailer principle of a road trailer with retractable highway running gear that is mounted on a detachable bogie for use in the rail mode. Abba, the piggyback vehicle, would be a well-type wagon. Ten of the Abba were being built for trial use in Durban-Johannesburg container trains. Spoornet aimed to launch two daily dedicated Abba trains between Durban and Johannesburg, and another between Cape Town and Johannesburg, in 1992.

Passenger traffic
Main-line passenger services were further reduced by 58 per cent in November 1987, cutting the number of trains run weekly from 601 to 225. Since 1984 they have been cut in all by some 68 per cent, but regional passenger trains have been curtailed by 88 per cent. Rationalisation was forced on SATS by fierce competition from buses and combi-taxis as a direct result of the government's policy of deregulation and privatisation.

Except for a few weekend trains the main-line passenger service consists mainly of the following trains:
Blue Train: Pretoria-Cape Town-Pretoria;
Trans-Karoo: Johannesburg-Cape Town-Johannesburg;
Trans-Natal: Johannesburg-Durban-Johannesburg;
Trans-Orange: Cape Town-Durban-Cape Town;
Amatola: Johannesburg-East London-Johannesburg;
Algoa: Johannesburg-Port Elizabeth-Johannesburg;
Bosvelder: Johannesburg-Louis Trichardt-Johannesburg;
Komati: Johannesburg-Komatipoort-Johannesburg;
Suidwester: De Aar-Windhoek-De Aar.

The Blue Train is scheduled to do three round trips weekly from October to March, and one round trip weekly from April to September. An average occupancy of 90 per cent was achieved in FY 1987-88. This success was due to a striking revival of the domestic market as well as increase in foreign tourist patronage of the train.

A new line to Khayelitsha in the Cape Peninsula was completed and a commuter service implemented in March 1988. Eight new Class 8M emu sets, on order from Dorbyl Transport Products, were placed in service during 1988/89 on this line.

Electrification
The East London-Springfontein (475 route-km) ac electrification was inaugurated in October 1988 at an estimated cost of R153·362 million.

Richards Bay export coal train of 88 wagons, 7000 tons gross, leaving Bloomlager, Natal, behind four Class 7E1 locomotives (Hugh Ballantyne)

New Class 10E 3 kV dc heavy freight locomotive

Other major main line projects, notably Bloemfontein-Springfontein-Noupoort (378 route-km) and Beaconsfield-De Aar (231 route-km), have been shelved indefinitely because of SATS' financial problems.

Civil engineering
Construction projects and improvements generally have had to slacken pace because of the economic difficulties.

A R63 million scheme to eliminate the handicaps of sharp curvature and a 1 in 40 gradient confronting northbound traffic in the Hex River Pass, on the Johannesburg-Cape Town route, which necessitated load reduction over the affected section, was finished in 1988. The major item in the scheme was a new 13·3 km tunnel, the longest in South Africa; two other tunnels, one of 1·09 km, the other of 1·21 km length, were also necessary. The main tunnel has an 800 metre-long crossing loop at the midpoint of its bi-directionally-signalled single line, which is laid with concrete slab track. The new route eases the ruling gradient to 1 in 66 and sharpest curvature from 200 to 600 metres.

Although slab track has been used extensively inside tunnels in recent years, mainly because of the difficulty of maintaining conventional track in a confined space, concern nevertheless existed about the possible cracking of the concrete, long repair times required in case of derailments, and high initial costs. After intensive research, a slab-track system has been developed that largely eliminates the above drawbacks. The so-called PAN method was used in the Hex River tunnel.

Initial costs have been reduced to 40 per cent below those of previously available slab-track systems and now compare favourably with the costs of conventional-track systems of similar carrying capacity. Its use has also been considered in locations other than in tunnels and was, for the first time, used on a bridge, namely the viaduct on the Nasrec line.

The Ermelo-Richards Bay coal line is being progressively upgraded to permit an annual throughput of 80 million tonnes of coal and to sustain 26-tonne axleloads. Estimated to cost in all R200 million, the work includes realignments, deviations, multi-tracking installation of 60 kg/m chrome-manganese rails and movable-frog pointwork. At the same time the signalling and train radio system are being upgraded at a total cost of R208 million.

New coal line
In 1989 Iscor, the steel company, launched construction of a 123 km coal line from the neighbourhood of the Zimbabwe border at Tshikondeni to a junction with SATS' Groenbult-Beitbridge line at Huntleigh. The line will carry 3000-tonne, 50-wagon coal trains between Tshikondeni and Pietersburg, on the Groenbult-Pretoria line, hauled by four diesel locomotives, with each train making an out-and-back run within 22 hours.

Signalling and traffic control
Computers and microprocessors are being applied to a wide range of operations. Microprocessors have been incorporated in the mini-CTC system installed between De Aar and Touws River, in which eight centres each control 70 route-km. In these centres train descriptions are reproduced on vdus and operators can store routes.

All functions at the new Sentrarand marshalling yard are controlled by distributed microprocessor systems and at the new Durban signalling centre an automatic train routing based on microprocessors is employed.

RAILWAY SYSTEMS / South Africa

The Johannesburg-Durban main line (675 km) is now CTC-controlled from five central offices at Standerton, Vooruitsig, Newcastle, Ladysmith and Durban. Micro- and/or minicomputers are used to control time/distance graph plotters, automatic route calling, through routeing, route storage, train number stepping, etc. This is a double-track bi-directionally signalled route.

The upgrading of computer, signalling, telecommunication and radio systems on the Ermelo-Richards Bay coal line to allow a throughput of 80 million tonnes of coal per annum has been finished. The line is controlled from Ermelo, Vryheid and Richards Bay.

Large portions of the suburban network in and around Cape Town are being resignalled and the control is being centralised at the Windermere control centre. Automatic train routing will ultimately be provided for the whole of the Cape Town suburban network.

Spoornet has a computerised Operating Information and Control System which provides instant information on the last reported movement of all wagonloads of goods for the benefit of both clients and of all levels of transport management. Approximately 100 000 vehicles and 5500 locomotive movements on over 3000 trains are reported daily from some 100 locations country-wide to one of the largest computer complexes in the Southern Hemisphere. Automatic identification of vehicles has been introduced as a pilot scheme on certain sections.

Traction and rolling stock

At the start of 1989 the railway was operating 448 steam, 2350 electric and 1541 diesel locomotives, 4820 locomotive-hauled passenger cars, 1347 motor and 3314 trailer emu cars forming 337 emus, and 165 348 freight cars. Coaching stock included 102 lounge/catering cars, 2437 sleeping and 1112 couchette cars. Steam is to be eliminated by 1995-96.

In 1989 a further 50 Class 10E were ordered from GEC-Alsthom for local assembly by Union Carriage and Wagon. At the end of FY 1987-88 delivery of 91 Class 10E electric locomotives of the previous order was still awaited. A further 40 Class 7ED, 150 Class 10E, 41 Class 11E and 35 Class 14E locomotives were to be ordered.

Although SATS is now dedicated to Co-Cos for general main-line use, it took delivery in 1990 of three prototypes of a new Class 14E Bo-Bo design with dual-voltage 3 kV dc /25 kV ac capability. To have a 4000 kW output and 160 km/h top speed, the 14E features self-steering bogies, fully-suspended traction motors and three-phase asynchronous ac drive. SATS hopes to limit axleloads to 22 tonnes. The locomotives were built by SLM of Switzerland with electrical equipment from the 50 c/s Group. There is an option for a further 29 units of this type.

In 1990 a forecast order for 50 electro-diesel locomotives was placed with Siemens. These Class 38, to be assembled by Union Carriage & Wagon Co, will have a 1500kW rating as straight electrics and a 750kW engine to operate as diesel-electric. They will release diesel locomotives operating on electrified

Class 7M commuter emu

Steam locomotives

Class	Type	Stock at 29/2/88	Year into service
1065 mm-gauge			
Garratt articulated			
GMA/M	4-8-2 + 2-8-4	3	1953-58
Steam tender locomotives			
12-R	4-8-2	1	1912-22
12-AR	4-8-2	1	1912-22
15-AR	4-8-2	45	1914-25
15-CA	4-8-2	44	1926-30
1SE	4-8-2	1	NA
1SF	4-8-2	136	1938-49
16-E/DA	4-6-2	1	1930-35
19-C	4-8-2	1	1935
19-D	4-8-2	62	1937-49
23	4-8-2	1	1931-39
24	2-8-4	23	1949-50
25-C	4-8-4	1	1953-55
25-NC	4-8-4	127	1953-54
26*	4-8-4	1	NA
610 mm-gauge			
NG-15	2-8-2	8	1911-53
NGG-16	2-6-2 + 2-6-2	2	1929-59
Total		458	

* Converted from Class 25-C

Electric multiple-units

Class	Cars per unit	Line voltage	Motor cars per unit	Motored axles per train-set	Rated output (kW) per motor	Max speed km/h	Weight tonnes per car (M-motor T-trailer)	Total seating capacity (M-motor T-trailer)	Length per car mm	No of sets in service 29.2.88	Rate of acceleration m/s²	Year first built	Builders Mechanical parts	Builders Electrical equipment
5M2A	10	3 kV	4	16	220	100	M 61 T 31	M 56 T 67 } 1st M 43 T 50 } STD crush load 3850	18 600	335 (all series)	0·44 up to 42 km/h	1957	UCW	GEC
6M (2M1T)	4	3 kV	8	32	245	110	M 46·9 Mc 38 T 32·2	M 64 T 56 crush load 4424	22 940	1 (prototype)	0·8 up to 55 km/h	1983	Hitachi	Hitachi
7M (2M2T)	6	3 kV	6	24	290	110	M1 43·2 T1 35·6 M2 42·9 T2 34·6	M 62 T 56 crush load 4482	22 760	1 (prototype)	0·85 up to 60 km/h	1984	MAN	Siemens AEG BBC
8M (2M2T)	6	3 kV	6	24	245	110	M 47·4 T 32·4	M 64 T 56 crush load 4464	22 940	-	0·8 up to 50 km/h	1987	Dorbyl	Hitachi

South Africa / RAILWAY SYSTEMS

routes to accelerate the end of steam power.

Although the number of standard-gauge merchandise-carrying vehicles in service has decreased, the average carrying capacity per vehicle is rising. So as to utilise fully the intended upgrading of the most important main lines, all new wagons acquired for the bulk of the network are being designed with 80 tons glw but with 104 tons glw on the coal line. The programme to raise the carrying capacity of certain types of wagons in the existing fleet is continuing.

Type of braking: Vacuum and air
Type of coupler in standard use: Mainly E-type SASKOP (knuckle-type)

Electric suburban emu stock
Rated output of motors
Type 5M2/5M2A
One-hour: 1450 V, 230 A, 945 rpm; 302 kW full field
 1450 V, 255 A, 1075 rpm; 340 kW weak field
Continuous: 1450 V, 165 A, 1047 rpm; 220 kW full field
 1450 V, 180 A, 1212 rpm; 242 kW weak field

Type 4M1/4M2
One-hour: 1450 V, 170 A, 1040 rpm; 227·5 kW full field
 1450 V, 175 A, 1245 rpm; 235 kW weak field
Continuous: 1450 V, 150 A, 1070 rpm; 200 kW full field
 1450 V, 160 A, 1285 rpm; 208 kW weak field
Max speed: 97 m/h

	5M2/5M2A	4M1/4M2
Weight of motor coach	69 tons	67 tons
trailer	35 tons	33 tons
Average seating capacity		
motor coach	46	64
trailer	75	108
Length	18.38m	18.3m
Acceleration (normally loaded level tangent track)	0.44m/s^2	0.44m/s^2
Year first built	1958	1954
Builders:		
Mechanical	Union Carriage and Waggon Co	Metro Cammell
Electrical	General Electric Co	General Electric/Metro Vickers

Track
Rail: 60, 57, 48, 30 kg/m
Cross ties (sleepers)
Concrete: Fastenings: Fist, BTR, Pandrol
Steel: Thickness: 125/195 mm; fastenings; screws, chairs
Spacing: 1444/km plain tracks, 1429/km curves
Minimum curvature radius: 100 m
Max gradient: 2.5%
Max axleload: Rolling stock 26 tonnes, locomotives 28 tonnes

Coal, ore and minerals
Tonnages conveyed for export during the three most recent financial years:

Commodity	1984/85	1985/86	1986/87	1987/88	Increase or decrease (per cent)
Coal and Coke	37 802 139	39 427 632	42 366 483	40 506 594	−4·39
Iron ore	9 833 600	9 207 740	8 790 340	8 314 677	−5·41
Manganese ore	2 930 820	2 655 606	1 957 127	1 869 698	−4·47
Chrome ore	676 676	1 122 950	1 323 038	1 274 792	−3·65
Granite and marble	140 929	127 944	183 473	253 742	+38·3
Asbestos	28 832	49 875	23 125	24 590	+6·85
Clay and kaolin	10 790	1674	1612	8024	+398.7
Other minerals	376 315	452 457	631 161	703 354	+29·88

Traffic (million)	1984/85	1985/86	1986/87	1987/88
Revenue freight tonnage	164·765	170·649	169·589	161·085
Freight tonne-km	90 162·206	91 964·624	90 573·249	85 620·005
Passenger-km				
Main lines	5083·7	4468·1	2806·2	NA
Suburban	13 780·9	13 358	12 389·4	NA
Passenger journeys	686·168	658·7	612·4	578·4

Finances (railways only) (R million)				
Revenue	1984/85	1985/86	1986/87	1987/88
Transportation services				
Passengers	742·4	923·4	1105·1	954.35
Parcels	88·3	80·5	74·5	67.56
Mail	23·2	27·7	32·3	42.06
Goods	2621·8	2646·6	3098·1	3440.18
Coal	768·1	907·8	1033·5	1274.87
Livestock	13·4	12·5	12·3	NA
Rents and storage	34·4	26·2	27·8	32.03
Other transport services	68·0	67·4	81·9	108.69
Other revenue				
Interest received	174·3	176·6	245·5	299.57
Miscellaneous revenue	340·8	258·2	271·3	264.02
Subsidiary services				
Catering and bedding services	25·3	26·3	26·1	25.57
Publicity and advertising	—	—	—	—
Road Transport services	210·4	236·5	267·8	324.58
Tourist service	16·2	20·3	21·6	16.57
Loss carried to appropriation account	426·7	766·0	806·4	908.07
Total	5555·3	6176·0	7104·2	7759·1

Expenditure				
Transportation services				
Administrative and general charges	264·4	298·2	336·8	249.04
Maintenance of permanent way and works	826·4	935·9	983·3	1110.13
Maintenance of rolling stock	655·7	723·6	806·2	863.26
Motive power operating expenses	815·0	945·7	956·7	957.80
Traffic and vehicle running expenses	892·7	943·6	1026	1173
Cartage service	79·2	97·2	108·5	127.68
Depreciation	287·4	223·3	597·8	739.8
Higher replacement costs	441·1	324·1	—	—
Subsidiary services				
Catering and bedding services	34·0	36·5	37·6	38.54
Publicity and advertising	—	—	—	—
Road Transport service	213·0	245·9	270·5	353.1
Tourist service	15·7	20·1	21·3	11.48
Net revenue account				
Interest on funds	—	—	—	—
Financing costs	951·0	1301·1	1844·1	1739.16
Miscellaneous expenditure	77·7	80·8	1154·4	396·0
Total	555·3	6176·0	7104·2	7759·1

Diesel-electric locomotives

Class	Wheel arrangement	Rated power kW	Max axleload kg	Tractive effort continuous at kN	Tractive effort continuous at km/h	Max speed km/h	Wheel dia mm	Total mass tonnes	Length mm	No in service 29.2.88	Year first built	Builders Mechanical parts	Builders Engine & type	Builders Transmission
31-000	Bo-Bo	985/895	18 900	145	18	90	915	74	15 150	40	1958	GE	GE Cooper Bessemer 1 4-stroke V-8 turbocharged and aftercooled C-B type FVBL-8	General Electric 4 dc 4 pole axle-hung GE type BGE 761 A4
32-000	Co-Co	1475/1340	10 160/12 700	146	27	100	762/915	93	16 866	36*	1959	GE	GE Cooper Bessemer 1 4-stroke V12 turbocharged and aftercooled C-B type FVBL-12	General Electric 6 dc 4 pole axle-hung GE type 5GE 76 A3
32-200	Co-Co	1475/1340	10 160/12 700	146	27	100	767/915	93	16 866	10*	1966	GE	GE General Electric 1 4-stroke V-12 turbocharged and aftercooled GE type 7 FDL-12	6 dc 4 pole axle-hung GE type 5 GE 761 A9
33-000	Co-Co	1605/1490	15 749	178	24	100	915	91	16 866	61	1965	GE	GE General Electric 1 4-stroke V-12 turbocharged and aftercooled GE type 7 FDL-12	6 dc 4 pole axle-hung GE type 761 A6

Diesel-electric locomotives continued

Class	Wheel arrange-ment	Rated power kW	Max axle-load kg	Tractive effort continuous at kN	Tractive effort continuous at km/h	Max speed km/h	Wheel dia mm	Total mass tonnes	Length mm	No in service 29.2.88	Year first built	Builders Mechanical parts	Builders Engine & type	Builders Transmission
33-200	Co-Co	1640/ 1490	15 749	178	24	100	915	91	17 474	13	1966	EMD	EMD General Motors 1 2-stroke V-16 roots blown EMD type 16-645-E	6 dc 4 pole axle-hung EMD type D 29CC-7
33-400	Co-Co	1605/ 1490	15 749	178	24	100	915	91	16 866	112*	1968	GE	General Electric 1 4-stroke turbo-charged and aftercooled GE type 7 FDL-12	6 dc 4 pole axle-hung GE type 5 GE 761 A6
34-000	Co-Co	2050/ 1940	18 850	218	26	100	915	111	17 982	125	1971	GE	General Electric 1 4-stroke V-12 turbo-charged and aftercooled GE type 7 FDL-12	6 dc 4 pole axle-hung GE type 5 GE 761 A13
34-200	Co-Co	2145/ 1940	18 850	218	26	100	1016	111	19 242	50	1971	EMD	EMD General Motors 1 2-stroke V-16 turbo-charged and aftercooled EMD type 16-645-E3	6 dc 4 pole axle-hung EMD type 29B
34-400	Co-Co	2050/ 1940 1940	18 850	218	26	100	915	111	17 982	130	1973	GE	South African GE-DC Locomotive Group South Africa 1 4-stroke V-12 turbo-charged and aftercooled GE type 7 FDL-12	6 dc 4 pole axle-hung GE type 5 GE 761 A13
34-600	Co-Co	2245/ 1940	18 850	218	26	100	1016	111	19 202	98	1974	GM SA	General Motors South Africa (Pty) Ltd 1 2-stroke V-16 turbo-charged and aftercooled EMD type 16-645-E3	6 dc 4 pole axle-hung EMD type D 29B
34-800	Co-Co	2140/ 1940	18 850	218	26	100	1016	111	19 202	58	1978	GM SA	General Motors South African (Pty) Ltd 1 2-stroke V-16 turbo-charged and aftercooled EMD type 16-645-E3	6 dc 4 pole axle-hung EMD type 29B
34-900	Co-Co	2050/ 1940	18 850	218	26	100	915	111	17 982	30	1979	GE	South African GE-DL Locomotive Group 1 4-stroke V-12 turbo-charged and aftercooled GE type 7 FDL-12	6 dc 4 pole axle-hung GE type 5GE 761 A13
35-000	Co-Co	1230/ 1160	13 720	161	21	100	915	82	15 152	69	1972	GE	General Electric 1 4-stroke V-8 turbo-charged and aftercooled GE type 7 FDL-8	6 dc 4 pole axle-hung GE type 5GE 764-C
35-200	Co-Co	1195/ 1065	13 720	161	19	100	915	82	16 485	150	1974	EMD & GM SA	EMD General Motors-25 General Motors South African (Pty) Ltd-25 1 2-stroke V-8 turbo-charged and aftercooled EMD type 8-645-E3	6 dc 4 pole axle-hung EMD type D 29CCBT
35-400	Co-Co	1230/ 1160	13 720	161	21	100	915	82	15 152	100	1976	GE	South African GE-DL Locomotive Group South Africa 1 4-stroke V-8 turbo-charged and aftercooled GE type 7 FDL-8	6 dc 4 pole GE type 5GE 764-C1
35-600	Co-Co	1195/ 1065	13 720	161	19	100	915	82	16 485	100	1976	GM SA	General Motors South African (Pty) Ltd 1 2-stroke V-8 turbo-charged and aftercooled EMD type 8-645-E3	6 dc 4 pole axle-hung EMD type D29 CCBT
36-000	Bo-Bo	875/ 800	18 500	141	14	100	915	72	15 151	124	1975	GE	South African GE-DL Locomotive Group South Africa 1 4-stroke V-8 turbo-charged and aftercooled GE type 7 FDL-8	4 dc 4 pole axle-hung GE type 5GE 764-C1
36-200	Bo-Bo	875/ 800	18 500	141	14	90	1016	72	14 150	101	1980	GM SA	General Motors South African (Pty) Ltd 1 2-stroke V-8 roots blown EMD type 8-645-E	6 dc 4 pole axle-hung Type D29B
37-000	Co-Co	2340/ 2170	21 000	245	26	100	1016	125	19 202	99	1981	GM SA	General Motors South African (Pty) Ltd 1 2-stroke V-16 turbo-charged and aftercooled EMD type 16-645E-3B	6 dc 4 pole axle-hung EMD type D31
91-000	Bo-Bo	52/ 480	12 000	86	15	50	838	44	10 580	20	1973	GE GE	Caterpillar 1 4-stroke V-8 turbo-charged and aftercooled CAT type D 379	General Electric 4 dc 4 pole GE type 5GE 778 A1 gear case axle-mounted

* 36 Class 32-000, 10 Class 32-200 and 56 Class 33-400 are operated by SWA/Namibia Railways

Electric locomotives

Class	Wheel arrangement	Line current kV	Rated output (one-hour/ continuous) kW	Max load kg	Tractive effort (full field) Continuous at kN	Tractive effort (full field) km/h	Max speed km/h	Wheel dia mm	Total mass kg	Length mm	No in service 29.2.88	Year first built	Builders Mechanical parts	Builders Electrical equipment
5E	Bo-Bo	3	1508/1300	21 591	104	44	100	1219	86 364	15 494	106	1955	English Electric	4-EE 529 traction motors
5E1	Bo-Bo	3	1940/1456	21 591	122	43	100	1219	86 364	15 494	671	1959	Union Carriage and Wagon Co Ltd-555	Metro Vickers-135 4-MV 281 or 4-AEI 281 AZX or 4-AEI 281 AX or 4-AEI 281 X traction motors
6E	Bo-Bo	3	2492/2252	22 226	193	41	110	1219	88 904	15 494	80	1970	Union Carriage and Wagon Co Ltd	4-AEI 283 AZ traction motors
6E1	Bo-Bo	3	2492/2252	22 226	193	41	110	1219	88 904	15 494	957	1969	Union Carriage and Wagon Co Ltd	4-AEI 283 AZ traction motors
EXP/AC	Bo-Bo	25	2492/2252	22 226	190	41	110	1219	85 500	15 494	1	1975	Union Carriage and Wagon Co Ltd	50 c/s Group 4-AEI 283 AZ traction motors
7E	Co-Co	25	NA/3000	21 000	300	35	100	1220	123 115	18 430	99	1978	Union Carriage and Wagon Co Ltd	50 c/s Group
7EI	Co-Co	25	NA/3000	21 000	300	35	100	1220	123 115	18 430	50	1979	Dorman Long	Nissho Iwai 6-Hitachi HS-1054-GR traction motors
7E2 (Series 1)	Co-Co	25	3000	21 000	300	35	100	1220	125 500	18 465	25	1982	Union Carriage and Wagon Co Ltd	Siemens 6-MG 680 traction motors
7E2 (Series 2)	Co-Co	25	3000	21 000	300	35	100	1220	125 500	18 465	40	1983	Union Carriage and Wagon Co Ltd	Siemens 6-MG 680 traction motors
7E3 (Series 1)	Co-Co	25	3000	20 792	300	35	100	1220	124 750	18 430	60	1983	Dorbyl	Hitachi EFF20 HS-1054-HR traction motors
7E3 (Series 2)	Co-Co	25	3000	20 792	300	35	100	1220	124 750	18 430	25	1984	Dorbyl	Hitachi EFF20 HS-1054-HR traction motors
8E	Bo-Bo	3	800/704	21 171	145	17	75	1220	81 200	16 120	100	1983	Union Carriage and Wagon Co Ltd	BBC/Siemens 4-1 KB 2820-0TA 02 traction motors
9E 9E2	Co-Co	50	4068/3750	28 000	388	34·5	90	1220	166 300	21 132	25 6	1979 (ex-ISCOR 1978)	GEC Engineers (Pty) Ltd Union Carriage and Wagon Co Ltd	GEC Traction 6-GEC G415AZ traction motors
10E	Co-Co	3	3240/3090	21 210	310	35	90	1220	126 000	18 520	50	1985	Union Carriage and Wagon Co Ltd	Toshiba 6-SE-218 traction motors
11E	Co-Co	25	4000	28 000	400	34	90	1220	168 000	20 470	45	1985	General Motors (SA)	General Motors and ASEA 6X LJM 54D-1 traction motors
12E	Bo-Bo	3	2492/2252	24 470	–	–	165	1219	88 904	15 494	5	1983	Union Carriage and Wagon Co Ltd	4-AEI 283Z traction motors
10E1	Co-Co	3	3240/3090	–	–	–	90	–	126 000	18 520	6 (+50 on order)	1987	Union Carriage and Wagon Co Ltd	GEC Traction 6X G425 A2 traction motors
10E2	Co-Co	3	3240/3090	–	–	–	105	–	126 000	18 520	(25 on order)	1989	Union Carriage and Wagon Co Ltd	Toshiba 6X SE-218A traction motors
14E	Bo-Bo	3/25	4000	–	–	–	140	–	87 100	18 600	(3 on order)	1989	Swiss Locomotive Works	50 c/s Group

Spain

Ministry of Tourism, Transport & Communications

Plaza de San Juan de la Cruz, 1 Nuevos Ministerrios, 28003 Madrid

Telephone: +34 1 456 1144

Minister: José Barrionuevo Peña
General Director: Manuel Panadero Lopéz

Spanish National Railways (RENFE)
Rede Nacional de los Ferrocarriles Españoles

Las Caracolas, Final Av Pio XII s/n Charmartin, 28036 Madrid

Telephone: +34 1 733 6200
Telex: 27632
Telefax: +34 1 315 0384

President and Director General: Julián Garciá Valverde
Assistant Directors-General
 Operations, Personnel & Production: Damián Navascues Poyo
 Rolling Stock, Way and Works: Gonzalo Martin Baranda
 Planning, Urban Affairs & Control: José Rodes Biosca
 Purchases & Materials: Leopold Iglesia Lachica
Heads of Business Groups:
 Javier Pérez Sanz
 Antonio Barba Jiménez
 José Luis Villa de la Torre
 Directors
 Development & Corporate Management: Gonzalo Madrid
 Enterprise Group: José Rhodes
 Central Services: Eduardo Moreno
 Operations: Vincente Rallo Guinot
 Programming of Installations: Carlos Artegabeitia Velázquez
 Logistics & Transport: Pedro Antonio Martin Moreno
 Safety & Rules: Javier Moreno de Mesa
 High Speed Unit: Leopold Inglesial
 Traction: Manuel J Megiá
 Rolling Stock Maintenance: José Ignacio González Pisón
 Fixed Installations: Gonzalo Martin Baranda
 Commercial: José Maria Isla Sanchez
 Marketing: Emilio Arsuaga Navasqués
 Long-Distance Passenger Services: Abelardo Carillo
 Regional Passenger Services: Antonio Gómez Templado
 Suburban Services: Javier Bustunduy Fernándes
 International Relations: Miguel Corsini Freese

Public Affairs: Miguel Saráa Sanchez
Inspector General: José Escolano Paul
Secretary General: José L Virumbrales
Manager, Infrastructure: José Manuel Benegas
Zonal Directors
No 1, Madrid: Albertó Garćia Alvarez
No 2, Leon: Fernando Alfayate
No 3, Seville: Juan A Villaronte Martinéz
No 4, Valencia: Joaquín Romero Vera
No 5, Barcelona: Carlos Garciá Canibano
No 6, Bilbao: Angel Miguel Ruiz

Gauge: 168 mm; 1000 mm
Route length: 12 544 km; 19 km
Electrification: 1676 mm-gauge: 6258 km at 3 kV dc; 32 km at 1·5 kV dc
1000 mm-gauge: 19 km at 1·5 kV dc

New Rail Plan's big investment

Following changes in RENFE's administration, government approved a massive expenditure to fulfill a Rail Transport Plan (PTF) drafted by the Transport Ministry with RENFE's assistance. From 1987 to the century's end a total outlay of Pta 2 029 000 million was programmed. The state would provide a third of the total for the major infrastructure schemes proposed. RENFE was required to cover the remainder, towards which some loans from the European Investment Bank have been secured.

In early 1990, however, there was some fear that many PTF schemes would be deferred or even cancelled. That was because one of the PTF's high-speed bypass projects (see below) was subsequently expanded into a completely new, 1435mm-gauge high-speed route from Madrid to Seville, with a possible extension to the Portuguese border; and there was also the prospect of a similar line from Madrid to Barcelona and the French border. Together, these projects could absorb well over half the 1987 PTF budget. Furthermore, widespread gauge conversion of existing infrastructure was under consideration.

New high-speed bypasses

The main infrastructure projects embodied in the Rail Transport Plan were:

The Bilbao-Vitoria cut-off: about 50 km in length, to avoid a detour via Miranda de Ebro and obviate Bilbao's difficult approach via the sinuous Orduna incline through the eastern Cantabrian highlands. In collaboration with the Basque government this project was subsequently expanded to include a link with Irun. The scheme now forms a 'T' with a triangular junction at the head: the crossbar is a direct Bilbao-Irun line avoiding San Sebastian, the column the connection with Vitoria. Total new construction will be 160 route-km, of which half may have to be in tunnel and further 30km on viaducts because engineering for 250 km/h is envisaged. Preliminary design was begun in 1990.

The Guadarrama line: about 60 km long, to diverge from the Madrid-Avila main line about 40 km from Madrid near Escorial: thread the Guadarrama mountains in tunnel: cross the Madrid-Segovia-Medina del Campo line at Ortigosa del Monte and join the Medina-Valladolid main line 18 km south of Valladolid. To be engineered for 200 km/h. Completion should enable scheduling from Madrid to Valladolid at an average speed of 175 km/h.

The Brazatortas cut-off: to run for 105 km from Ciudad Real south to Alcolea, 8 km west of Cordoba on the present main line from Madrid to Andalucia. As already mentioned, this was subsequently expanded into a new high-speed route from Madrid to Seville (see below).

Lines to be upgraded for 200 km/h

The Rail Transport Plan provided for upgrading of the following routes: Madrid-Zaragoza-Barcelona. This includes construction of a 48·3 km cut-off between Yunguera de Henares and Baides, the first tenders for which were called in 1988.
Madrid-Valencia
Barcelona-Valencia

Lines to be double-tracked

Double-tracking was scheduled for the following routes: Castellon-Tarragona
Cordoba-Seville
La Encina-Jativa
Lastejon-Pamplona
Leon-Monteforte

Station renovation

The Plan tabled a station renovation programme covering 535 stations for a total cost of Pta 2907 million, almost all to come from RENFE's own resources. Works in progress range from improved access, provision of toilets, passenger information displays and platform lengthening or elevation to major rebuilding.

Prospective journey time on completion of the Plan

	After the Plan	*In 1988*	*Saving*	*Saving*
	h min	*h min*	*h min*	*%*
Madrid-Cordoba	2 00	4 20	2 20	54
Madrid-Seville	3 00	5 38	2 38	47
Madrid-Malaga	4 24	7 00	2 36	37
Madrid-Cádiz	4 44	7 31	2 47	37
Madrid-Huelva	4 41	7 23	2 42	37
Madrid-Valencia	3 45	4 15	30	12
Madrid-Alicante	3 15	3 49	34	15
Valencia-Barcelona	3 00	3 44	44	20
Madrid-Caceres	3 24	4 24	1 00	23
Madrid-Zaragoza	2 35	2 59	24	13
Zaragoza-Barcelona	2 34	3 28	54	26
Madrid-Valladolid*	1 08	2 20	1 12	51
Madrid-Burgos*	1 55	3 05	1 10	38
Madrid-Bilbao*	4 20	5 45	1 25	25
Madrid-Irun*	5 00	6 34	1 34	24
Madrid-Pamplona*	4 10	5 23	1 13	23
Madrid-Logroño*	3 55	6 05	2 10	36
Madrid-Santander*	4 20	5 40	1 20	24
Madrid-Leon*	2 45	4 10	1 25	34
Madrid-Gijon*	5 00	6 30	1 30	23
Madrid-Vigo*	5 59	7 55	1 56	24
Madrid-La Coruña*	6 44	8 35	1 51	22

* After completion of new access to Madrid from the north and northwest in 1993

Effects of the Plan

By 1991 RENFE aims to have 490 route-km fit for 250 km/h, 470 km passed for 200 km/h, and a further 1347 km passed for 160 km/h.

The Plan was reckoned to stimulate an annual traffic growth, year on year, of 3·8 per cent in passenger, 2·3 per cent in suburban and 3·2 per cent in freight business, where the emphasis would be on intermodal development and the hoped-for doubling of international traffic. In passenger-km terms, suburban passenger traffic in the Madrid metropolitan area was expected to double by the century's end, that of Barcelona to rise by 50 per cent.

In the passenger sector, the government would continue to subsidise and regulate the fares of all but intercity services. The latter RENFE is now required to make fully self-supporting.

Madrid-Seville high-speed line

The Brazatortas cut-off forms the core of a new high-speed 1435mm-gauge route under construction from Madrid to Seville. This, the first big Transport Plan project to be implemented, is expected to have its infrastructure ready for test running in late 1991. Commercial service inauguration is set for 1992, to coincide with Seville's celebration of the 500th anniversary of Columbus' discovery of America.

The new Madrid-Seville route is being engineered wherever possible for an initial top speed of 250 km/h, elsewhere for 200 km/h, and electrified at 25kV 50Hz ac. Ultimately it is hoped to run much of the route at 300 km/h. The line is also to be used by fast merchandise freight trains; as a result minimum curve radius will be 4000 m and the ruling gradient 1.25 per cent. Track will be 60 kg/m rail on monobloc concrete sleepers. A Spanish-German consortium of seven companies led by Siemens has the Pta 75 000 million to electrify and signal the new Madrid-Seville route. The DB's LZB system of cab signalling with continuous speed control has been adopted and is being installed by SEL. Siemens is supplying its Hicom ISDN communication system, which could become the basis of a system-wide network for transmission of speech, text, images and data.

For the first 15km out of Madrid Atocha to Getafe the route is traditional, but with the dedicated high-speed tracks rebuilt to 1435 mm gauge. The next 210 km to Brazatortas will be basically the earthworks of a single-track main line completely remodelled, realigned and laid with double track, and with a bypass around Ciudad Real. For 120km from Brazatortas to Cordoba a completely new infrastructure is being built through mountainous terrain. The final 130km from Cordoba to Seville will also be new, but in the general vicinity of the existing broad-gauge route.

The whole project is entailing major civil engineering works, including 16 tunnels with an aggregate length of 15.3 km, and 24 viaducts with a total length of 8.3 km. A fleet of 14 Class 319 diesel locomotives and some 500 wagons have been re-gauged to 1435 mm for construction trains. The line traverses several areas of great natural and wildlife value, and a considerable sum is being spent to palliate the project's effect on the environment.

The new route will cut out a tedious dog's-leg via Linares-Baeza, with its Dispenaperros Pass bottleneck, in the historic route from Madrid to the south. As a result the future 475 km Madrid-Seville high-speed route, now known as Nuevo Acceso Ferroviario a Andalucia (NAFA), will be 99 km shorter than the old. That and high speed will trim Madrid-Cordoba travel time from around 4½ to 2 hours, Madrid-Seville from over 5½ to less than 2 hours 50 minutes, Madrid-Malaga from over 7¼ to under 4¼ hours.

In 1989 it was forecast that NAFA would become the main route from Madrid to Lisbon. This would be achieved by construction of a line from Brazatortas to Badajoz, to link up with a remodelled Portuguese Railways' route from the border to Lisbon.

The journey time from Seville to Malaga is to be reduced from 1992 by 1½ hours from the present 3½ hours. This will ensue from the construction of two cut-offs, both aligned for high speed. One will extend for 40 km from Osuna to Bobadilla and avoid reversal at La Roda. The other will bypass Trinidad and run for 12·3 km from near Utrera to El Arahal.

By early 1990 cost overruns were reported, fuelling fears that the Madrid-Seville project would prejudice fulfilment of other elements of the PTF.

High-speed rolling stock

Fierce competition by French, German and Japanese industry for RENFE's high-speed rolling stock contracts was made the more intense by some high-level political interventions. The outcome was a shared European victory.

GEC-Alsthom won a Pta 51 400 million order for 24 train-sets to a design derived from the SNCF's TGV-Atlantique equipment. Each dual-voltage (3 kV dc/25kV ac) synchronous motor train-set would comprise two independent 4400kW power cars and eight articulated trailers, one of them a bar car. Accommodation elsewhere will include a business room with telephone, telefax and photocopier facilities. Seat spacing will be more generous than in a TGV-A unit and all saloons will have the video screens now becoming standard equipment in RENFE's intercity rolling stock.

German industry led by Siemens secured a Pta 33 900 million order for 75 5600kW 220 km/h Bo-Bo electric locomotives to a design based on the DB's Class 120. To become RENFE Class 252, the first 20 will be built to 1435mm gauge; the remainder will be built in tranches of 10 to standard or broad gauge as required.

Both orders were associated with a restructure of the Spanish rolling stock industry, with GEC-Alsthom taking a controlling interest in two companies. Consequently some components will be Spanish-built and 16 of the train-sets and 45 of the locomotives are being assembled in Spain. First deliveries were expected in 1991.

Meanwhile RENFE has modified four Class 269.200 chopper-controlled Bo-Bos and eight Class 354 diesel-hydraulic Talgo locomotives for a 200 km/h test programme. The electric locomotives have new bogies, transmission, axles and transformers, and a revised gearing. All 12 locomotives have been equipped with a new version of RENFE's ASFA automatic train control, which takes account of the flashing green signalling aspect adopted as a warning to reduce speed from 200 to 180 km/h.

Madrid-Barcelona-France high-speed line

In November 1988 the Transport Ministry proposed a second 1435mm-gauge high-speed line of some 700 km from Madrid to Barcelona and a connection with French Railways at Port-Bou. In the spring of 1990 the project still awaited government endorsement and the Treasury was known to be against it. In the hope of a favourable decision by midsummer, the Transport Ministry put up a proposal that RENFE, banks and contractors combine to raise a third of the cost under a deal by which this consortium would operate as well as build the line. The remainder of the capital would be derived from a government issue of variable interest bonds redeemable in 25–30 years. If the project were endorsed during 1990, the line could be operational by 1997. Its trains could cut Madrid-Barcelona journey time below three hours. RENFE suggests that the line could also be exploited by fast Madrid outer suburban trains.

Between Madrid and Barcelona northern and southern routeing options have been studied for each of the three sections of the line: Madrid-Zaragoza; Zaragoza-Lerida; and Lerida-Barcelona. Options were still open in the spring of 1990. The new route is likely to reach the Barcelona area from the northeast via Martorell. There would be a triangular layout to allow trains from both Madrid and Port Bou to terminate in Barcelona, but equally to permit Madrid-Port Bou trains to bypass the city centre.

Gauge conversion
With the 1988 decision to build the Brazatortas cutoff to 1435mm gauge, given Spain's new EEC bonding and the case for comparability with France's TGV system, the government asked for study of gauge conversion feasibility and costs in RENFE's existing system. RENFE put the likely cost of transforming the entire network, including rolling stock, at Pta 520 000 million. The purely infrastructure element of the change was costed in the Pta 200 000–300 000 million range. However, RENFE has also identified a limited programme related to the life-span of existing track. With the Treasury and Economic Ministry exercised by the cost, a government decision on general gauge conversion was in late 1989 deferred sine die, though by the spring of 1990 there was hope that a judgement might be reached in the following summer.

1988 contract
In April 1988, under a new contract programme concluded between the state and RENFE, the government approved total RENFE expenditure of Pta 1 040 000 million for the years 1988-91. Of this, Pta 56 100 million would be support for RENFE's deficit. Capital investment would total Pta 606 525 million. The state would fund capital investment totalling Pta 220 388 million, about three-quarters going on the three high-speed bypasses and the remainder on track doubling and other infrastructure improvements. Of the residue falling to RENFE's charge, Pta 119 500 million was allocated to new rolling stock, chiefly high-speed equipment for the new lines.

Apart from the high-speed bypasses, major works covered by the investment would be upgrading of the Madrid-Alicante line between Villarrobledo and La Encina, double-tracking between Castellon and Tarragona and between La Encina and Jativa. Completion of the Madrid suburban plan (see below) was covered.

The contract programme set out performance expectations for RENFE up to 1991. Influenced by a substantial rise in commuter travel, passenger-km were required to rise from 15 618 million in 1988 to 17 230 million; increased container traffic would be the main factor in a rise of freight tonne-km from 11 632 million to 12 510 million. By 1991 RENFE's annual loss was required by the contract to be no more than Pta 171 404 million, 25 per cent less than in 1987. RENFE was stimulated to raise its local passenger traffic by a new incentive proposal whereby its operating subsidy would be increased if its local service passenger-km and freight tonne-km targets were exceeded, but cut if either objective were not reached. A RENFE debt of Pta 16 340 million to the state was written off.

Under the new contract programme RENFE was to prepare a new and simplified pricing policy, which would inter alia seek a greater return from the new high-quality passenger services. It would also elaborate, with the aid of its new computer-based systems, a means of per-line and per-product analysis of results, and extend real-time monitoring of performance to traction and train crews.

Deficit still reducing
In 1989, for the fifth year in succession, RENFE reduced its annual deficit. The 1989 figure of some Pta 10 000 million compared with a loss of Pta 63 800 million five years earlier. During the same period accumulated debt was trimmed from Pta 232 800 million to Pta 188 000 million.

Management restructure
A further and major management reorganisation was begun in 1990. Based on principles of bottom-line financial responsibility and the primacy of the product over its means of production, the structure reforms management in three groups: commercial; infrastructure maintenance and train operation; traction and rolling stock maintenance. The production groups can sell their services to external parties as well as the commercial group; and the commercial group is at liberty to seek external bids for such services as coach maintenance. A separate corporate organisation deals with such central services as finance, administration and telecommunications.

Rapid spread of 160 km/h working
A major event since 1985 has been the spread of 160 km/h intercity operations. A further 846 route-km were passed for 160 km/h in time for the 1988 change of timetable. The 160 km/h trains are furnished by a variety of rolling stock and traction, for RENFE has a substantial number of vehicles arranged to run at this speed. Suitable motive power includes 220 electric locomotives of Classes 269, 250 and 251 (though riding problems compelled limitation of some Class 269 to 140 km/h in 1988) and 12 Class 354 Talgo diesel locomotives. The Class 444.500 emus, too, are designed for 160 km/h.

Talgo
The latest model of a Talgo coaching stock, the Talgo Pendular, has a passive body-tilting system designed to permit curve negotiation at a 20 per cent higher speed than the normal limit without discomfort to passengers. The range includes sleeping-car sets with wheel-sets adjustable to gauge-change for international services.

The Talgo body-tilting system employs no sensors, electronic detectors or hydraulic systems, but relies on a natural pendular action in reaction to centrifugal force. At 13·14 metres over couplers the 2·83 metre-wide Pendular cars are slightly longer than earlier Talgo models. They employ the patent Talgo automatic guidance system of their half-axles with independent wheels, and the Talgo air suspension, with disc brakes, and are designed for 180 km/h maximum speed. The bodies, monocoque structures of sound-proofed aluminium extrusions, are air-conditioned. The sleeper sets include a 30-seater restaurant, a 16-seater cafeteria-bar and a mix of cars with either six compartments for single- or double-berth accommodation, or five tourist-class compartments offering up to four berths each, also a baggage/generator car.

Talgo cars are owned by RENFE but maintained by the Talgo company under contract; Talgo also maintains the 12 Class 352, 353 and 354 diesel-hydraulic locomotives specially built for Talgo haulage.

The latest Talgo Pendular overnight train-sets include, in addition to restaurant, cafeteria, day, standard sleeping and luggage vehicles, a type of sleeping car classified Gran Class (GC). The GC cars not only have a new high standard of compartment furnishings, but also a private washroom-toilet with shower cubicle to each compartment (of which, consequently, there is room for only two within a Pendular trailer's 13·14 m length over neighbouring wheel centres).

A fresh order for 200 Talgo Pendular cars, the biggest Talgo built to date, was placed in April 1988. All have been built for 200 km/h top speed, and consequently have a new braking system; they also feature improved air-conditioning and soundproofing, and vacuum-retention toilets are standardised. The order comprised 119 variable-gauge cars for international service, including seven restaurant, seven kitchen-bar, 25 first-class, 43 tourist-class and 19 Gran Class sleeping cars; and 81 cars for domestic service, including eight restaurant and one kitchen-bar car.

Of the extra international cars, 76, including 55 sleepers (nine of them Gran Class), five restaurant and five bar cars, were required for a new overnight international service which was part-launched between Barcelona and Berne in May 1989. From 1990 this service, the 'Pablo Casals', became a Barcelona-Milan and Zurich train, dividing into Italian and Swiss sections at Chambéry, France. For this reason the baggage/generator cars in the new order are of revised internal design, with a central corridor to allow through passenger movement between sections prior to the train's division.

In 1990 the overnight Paris sleeper, the 'Barcelona Talgo' had its Talgo III train-sets replaced by new Pendular equipment with 200 km/h capability. (The Madrid-Paris overnight sleeper is already Pendular-equipped.) At the same time the day Barcelona-Geneva 'Catalan Talgo's' Talgo III sets were to be replaced by 200 km/h Pendular cars.

RENFE seeks to redeploy the displaced variable-gauge Talgo III sets (after their modernisation) on Barcelona-Toulouse (via Puigcerda) or Barcelona-Marseilles services. RENFE is investing Pta 500 million at Puigcerda, including installation of axle-changing apparatus, to develop this crossing into France (at La Tour de Carol, southeast of Toulouse) as an international passenger and freight thoroughfare.

Talgo Patentes expected in 1991 to roll out a prototype Talgo Pendular train-set with 250 km/h capability. Since 1988 the company has been engaged in development work on running gear, suspension, braking and body structure, the products of which have been embodied in a five-car test unit. The latter has been successfully run at up to 285 km/h in trials on a completed stretch of the DB's Hannover-Würzburg high-speed line. RENFE may order a production series of up to 20 train-sets.

Passenger traffic
Stimulated by faster transits and improved rolling stock, passenger traffic on medium- and long-haul services is now growing by 5 to 10 per cent a year.

On non-electrified routes RENFE has introduced an improved-quality diesel railcar service in its TER category. The tool is a version of the recent Class 592 emu modified with a first-class section, cafeteria and a top speed of 140 km/h. A total of 20, reclassified 592.200, has been modified to take over half the present TER services, such as Gandia-Madrid and Merida-Caceres-Madrid.

A total of 40 series 8000 sleeping cars have been retrofitted with shower rooms for incorporation in overnight 'Estrella' services.

At the end of May 1987 the Wagons-Lits company's historic contract for RENFE on-catering was terminated. Reasons cited were the size of the annual subsidy which the deal imposed on RENFE; and the need both to improve service quality and to adapt the character of the accelerating train service and changing

Passenger journeys (million)			1987	1988
Total			180·3	194.5
Passenger-km (million)	1985	1986	1987	1988*
Long-distance	9816	9340	9251	9439
Express trains	7270	6905	6799	6947
Talgo	1338	1381	1475	1576
TER	523	439	311	76
Emus	685	615	666	840
Local and regional	6163	6306	6143	6229
Total	15 976	15 646	15 394	15 716

* Provisional

Freight

Tonnage (000)	1985	1986	1987	1988
Total	31 682·3	31 027·2	36 242·5	36 587·7
Tonne-km (000)	1985	1986	1987	1988
Wagonload	8676·9	8232·9	8066	8074
Containers	2092·2	2163·6	2525	2609
Less-than-carload	209·7	199·3		
Parcels	57·2	54·9	884	1020
Internal service	335·2	307·5		
Mail	345·6	340·9		
Total	11 653·8	11 229·1	11 475	11 703

gastronomic habits. Under both these heads traditional meal service had become anachronistic. The new concession-holder is the Spanish company Cater, which operates widely in Morocco as well as Spain. Its RENFE activity is branded as 'Cater-Tren'.

Freight traffic

RENFE's container business, marketed under the brandname TECO, maintained its rapid growth in 1989, when traffic was 20 per cent up on the previous year and there was pressure on capacity. In 1989 the system embraced 18 TECO-operated terminals and 21 others. The flatcar fleet now includes 100 with interchangeable axle capability for international traffic, built by Ferrosud. Orders for 200 articulated three-axle flatcars were placed in 1990 with a partnership of Herederos de Ramon Mugica of Spain and Kolmex of Poland.

Dedicated container trains operate daily between Madrid and 14 centres, Barcelona and six centres, and Valencia and four centres. Operations include a refrigerated service for produce exports to the Far East between Algeciras and the Silla international shipment terminal near Valencia. The flatcars employed are fitted with petrol generator sets to supply the containers. RENFE has also launched its first 120 km/h container trains, between Silla and Madrid, which is likewise targeted at movement of fresh produce, and between Bilbao and Madrid, Bilbao and Barcelona, and Vigo and Barcelona.

A thrice-weekly overnight piggyback train service was inaugurated between Granollers and El Salobral in 1989.

RENFE has ordered from Ferrosud 20 units of the company's bi-modal road-rail transferable wagon (for details see Ferrosud entry in Freight vehicles section). These were to be evaluated alongside a RoadRailer-type bi-modal to be built by CAF.

All new freight wagons are being designed for 100 km/h running with 22·5-tonne axleloads or 120 km/h with 20-tonne axleloads. RENFE is also studying freight bogies for 200 km/h.

The freight business is supported by SACIM, a system-wide, real-time data transmission system for traffic monitoring and control. It derives its data from a total of 257 terminals throughout the rail transport.

New bypasses

A 7.6 km, 160 km/h bypass completed in 1989 completes a triangular junction at Venta de Baños. It has flying junctions at each end. The new double-track line connects the Madrid-Hendaye and Madrid-Santander lines north of their junction at Venta de Baños.

At La Encina a 13.2 km, 200 km/h double-track bypass is being built to eliminate the reversal there of trains between Alicante and Valencia. It would be finished in June 1990.

Barcelona remodelling

Work has begun on layout remodelling in the Barcelona area in preparation for the city's 1992 staging of the Olympic Games. The outstanding project will be elevation of the line from the city's suburban station as far as El Poble Nou. Other works will enable local trains from the Mataro line to reach Barcelona-Sants. The suburban Termino station, the city's original station, adjoins the site of the future Olympic village. It is to be substantially refurbished and, in conjunction with the layout remodelling, is to regain its historic role as a terminal for long-haul trains. It was closed for work to begin at the end of May 1988.

New stations for Seville and Cordoba

With Seville's 1992 celebration of the 500th anniversary of America's discovery in view, the Transport Ministry, the Andalusian and Seville authorities and RENFE are jointly financing a major reorganisation of Seville's rail facilities. The organisations mentioned will cover the whole of the Pta 18 000 million cost, except for an EEC contribution (see below).

At present the city is served by a terminus Plaza des Armas, branching from the Madrid-Huelva route, and a through station, San Bernardo, on the Madrid-Cadiz route. Both are to be abandoned. A new cross-city route, partly in tunnel, is being built to serve a new 12-platform station (plus two platforms for accompanied auto trains) at Santa Justa, about 1·5 km north of San Bernardo. A new north-to-west divergence for Huelva will be built north of Santa Justa at Majarabique, and the present Huelva line from there abandoned along with its Plaza des Armas terminal branch. The Huelva line will be reached from the new station by a triangular junction at Majarabique. The European Regional Development Fund has advanced Pta 1400 million towards this reorganisation. Some of the new terminal facilities and yards needed to replace those sacrificed in the abandonments will be transferred to Majarabique, others at La Negrilla, where the city's container terminal is now located.

The present Cordoba station is to be replaced by a new underground facility, for which the main Madrid-Seville line will be dropped into a covered cutting for 2·6 km. The Pta 12 000 million cost is being shared by the state, the province and the city, and also financed partly by commercial development. Completion is expected in 1993.

Madrid Suburban Plan

New and heavy investment in urban commuter rail services was announced by the government in the spring of 1990, much of it benefiting Madrid. A Pta 275 000 million plan by the Transport Ministry had as a priority provision of 200 more train-sets for intensification of the capital's suburban train services on a number of routes. At the same time the Prime Minister announced a Pta 197 500 million City Access programme for infrastructure and rolling stock development in the country's other major cities.

This followed earlier resuscitation of a Madrid Suburban Rail Plan formulated in 1979. That proposed a considerable expansion of services radiating from a reconstructed Madrid Atocha, where a new suburban station, Madrid Mediodia, was opened in May 1988. Seven of its tracks are through lines into the Atocha-Chamartin cross-city tunnel, which had previously carried far fewer trains than its designed capacity because of lack of progress in development of the suburban network. It now threads many more through trains between Madrid's northern and southern suburbs. The main-line Atocha station was closed in September 1988 for thorough reconstruction prior to the opening of the new high-speed route to the south.

Until 1983 development of the Suburban Plan had been limited to electrification and double-tracking of the branches from Villaverde Alto to Fuenlabrada and Parla, and a 2·6 km underground extension to Laguna, finished in January 1984, of the previously isolated line terminating at Aluche. A 3·9 km tunnel from Laguna to Embajadores was opened in 1989 and under a 1989–91 plan costing Pta 75 000 million extension from Embajadores was proceeding into Madrid Atocha to form on completion in September 1991 an important new suburban radial.

The 1989–91 plan provided for four-tracking between Villaverde Alto and Atocha via Ciudad de los Angeles, which was begun in October 1989, together with doubling of the present single line connecting Atocha with Madrid's Principe Pio station. Later in the 1990s it is hoped to move on to construction of new suburban branches. The 1990 investment plans mentioned

Finance (Pta million)	1985	1986	1987	1988
Revenue				
Passengers	55 307	58 201	59 453	63 524
Freight	47 211	46 250	54 431	56 019
Mail	6005	6050	NA	NA
Road transport	8380	9316	NA	NA
Other	12 375	13 636	37 733	32 485
Total commercial revenue	129 278	133 453	151 617	152 029
Compensation from state	92 115	97 209	107 111	109 447
Subvention of financial costs	64 965	62 444	62 348	59 980
Total all sources	286 358	293 106	NA	NA
Expenditure				
Personnel	142 655	143 056		
Energy and combustibles	21 209	21 524	253 645	244 853
Materials and services	80 410	83 111		
Amortisation	23 704	25 079	28 642	30 700
Financial costs	64 965	62 444	62 348	59 980
Total	322 943	335 214	344 635	335 533

Electric locomotives

Class	Wheel arrangement	Line current	Rated output kW	Max kg	Tractive effort (full field) Continuous at kg	km/h	Max speed km/h	Wheel dia mm	Weight tonnes	Length mm	No. in service 31.12.88	Year first built	Builders Mechanical parts	Electrical equipment
250	C-C	3000 V	4600	NA	20 090 / 32 220	80 / 50	160 / 100	1250	124	20 090	38	1982	Krauss-Maffei CAF-MTM	BBC
251	B-B-B	3000 V	4650	NA	NA	NA	160 / 100	NA	138	NA	30	1980	Mitsubishi-CAF	Westinghouse
269	B-B	3000 V	3100	34 200	16 620 / 26 820	66·3 / 40·3	140/80	1250	88	17 270	105	1973	Mitsubishi-CAF	Cenemesa (Westinghouse)
269-200/ 500/600	B-B	3000 V dc	3100	34 200	14 580 / 23 555	75·2 / 45·7	180/200*	1250	88	17 270	157	1973	CAF	Westinghouse
276	Co-Co	300 V dc	2208	33 600	16 500	49·5	110 / 110	1250	120	18 932	135		Alsthom-Macosa CAF-MTM Euskalduna Babcock & Wilcox	Alsthom-Sice, GEE-Oerlikon Exp Ind Westinghouse
277	Co-Co	3000 V dc	2000	31 300	13 850	58	110	1220	120	20 657	69	1952	Vulcan-Foundry	English Electric
278	Bo-Bo-Bo	3000 V dc	2200	31 710	16 800	48	130/ 100	1118	120	20 193	28	1954	Wesa-SE Construc Naval	Westinghouse
279	B-B	1500/ 3000 V	2700	31 200	14 000/ 22 500	69/ 43	80/ 65	1250 (1120)	80	17 270	16	1967	Mitsubishi-CAF	Mitsubishi-Cenemesa
281	Bo-Bo	3000 V dc	735	20 950			70 / 120	1400	74·8	11 912	3	1928	CAF	CAF
289	B-B	1500/ 3000 V	3100	22 400	12 100/ 20 700		70	1250	84	17 600	40	1967	Alsthom	Alsthom

* Four Class 269.600 only

above included provision for extra tracks on two of Madrid's suburban routes, the Pinar and Guadalajara.

A new connection has been built between Principe Pio and Chamartin stations. Previously movement between the two involved reversal at Pinar de la Rozas, junction of the exits from the two stations to the north. A new burrowing junction has created a double-track spur between the two routes that obviates the reversal. It came into service in December 1988.

All RENFE local passenger services in the metropolitan Madrid area are embodied in an integrated Consorcio de Transportes de Madrid, comprising also the city Metro, its municipal transport company (EMT) and its various concessionary bus transport operators.

Madrid airport link
RENFE, the Ministry of Works and the Madrid authorities have agreed construction of a 12.4km rail link with Madrid's Barajas airport. It will take the form of a loop off the main line from Chamartin to Barcelona and will serve the underground stations beneath both the domestic and the international terminals of the airport. The Madrid terminal of the interval airport service will be Nuevos Ministerios station on the Chamartin-Atocha cross-city underground connection. Construction bids were to be called in 1990.

Traction and rolling stock
At the start of 1989 RENFE operated 22 Talgo diesel locomotives, 348 other line-haul diesel locomotives, 366 diesel shunters, 621 electric locomotives, 664 Talgo trailers (including 74 baggage cars), 1709 locomotive-hauled passenger cars (including 86 restaurant/cafeteria, 356 sleeping and 331 couchette cars), 235 postal cars, 516 emu power, 921 emu trailer, 331 dmu motor and 203 dmu trailer vehicles (including railbuses) and 30 381 wagons (8549 privately-owned wagons were also in use).

In 1990 the emphasis of new deliveries was on commuter train-sets. In course of delivery were 150 three-car emus of a new Class 446 design. Each of its two power cars has a 960 kW motor with Mitsubishi chopper control and regenerative braking. Acceleration rate is 1 m/s^2 up to 60 km/h, 0.8 m/s^2 thereafter. Builders are CAF, Macosa, MTM, Cenemesa, Conelec and Melco (Mitsubishi). Orders for a further 100 Class 446 were anticipated, but during 1990 receipt was expected of the prototype of an improved version, the Class 447, with three-phase asynchronous motors, 15 per cent less weight and a 10 per cent lift of acceleration and deceleration rates. RENFE hoped to order a production series of 100 by the year's end.

New locomotive deliveries in 1990 were featuring 60 Class 310 diesel shunters to a new design with ac transmission based on the General Motors Type SW1001 Bo-Bo; and 60 Class 311, a European diesel shunter shunter design with an MTU engine.

Delivery of the third series of 20 Class 444·500 emus was completed in July 1989. By comparison with the previous series they feature modified primary suspension, a redesigned driving cab, a more elaborate bar-cafeteria, improved AEG video screens in the passenger saloons and a new external livery of blue and white.

RENFE was anticipating spring 1990 delivery of 60 bi-level cars for commuter service. Built by Ateinsa to GEC-Alsthom's SNCF design, they will be formed into five-car trains.

Signalling
Planned installation of AEG track-to-train radio is complete. In all AEG-Westinghouse has supplied equipment for 3850 route-km and 1065 traction units.

Other current signalling projects include major works in conjunction with suburban passenger development schemes in Barcelona and Madrid: these feature some bi-directional signalling and the equipment of control centres with timetable graph vdu displays and sophisticated train describer systems.

Early in 1989 General Railway Signal of the US announced that it had received from its Spanish licensee Abengoa SA of Seville, advice of a RENFE contract for the first large-scale deployment of its automatic vehicle identification equipment by a European railroad. GRS will supply equipment for over 2500 readers and several thousand transponders.

Track
Standard rail
Main lines: 54·5 kg/m for all relaying. 45 kg/m and UIC 54·1 kg/m in 12 and 18 m lengths.
Sleepers
Wooden: Mainly creosoted oak, pine, and sometimes beech, 2600 × 240 × 140 mm for ordinary track. For points, crossings etc, 3, 3·5, 4 and 4·5-m of same width and thickness (centre crossing sleeper being

Diesel locomotives (line-haul)

Class	Wheel arrangement	Transmission	Rated power kW	Max kg	Tractive effort Continuous at kg	km/h	Max speed km/h	Wheel dia mm	Total weight tonnes	Length mm	No in service 31.12.88	Year first built	Builders Mechanical parts	Engine & type	Transmission
313	Co-Co	Elec	743	18 480	19 300	14	120	1016	83·9	16 237	48	1965	Euskalduna Alco	Alco Products 251-D	General Electric GEE
314	Co-Co	Elec	824	18 450	18 625	16·4	120	1067	86	15 526	1	1967	Macosa	General Motors 567-V	General Motors
316	Co-Co	Elec	1105	24 090	18 200	21·7	120	1016	109·5	17 872	10	1955	Alco	Alco 251-C-3	General Electric
318	Co-Co	Elec	1105	24 090	18 200	21·7	120	1016	109·5	17 872	22	1958	Alco	Alco 251-B	General Electric
319-0	Co-Co	Elec	1154	23 100	18 450	21·6	120	1067	105/111	18 472	78	1965	EMD General Motors Macosa	EMD General Motors 567-C	EMD General Motors
319-200	Co-Co	Elec	1190	-	23 600	-	120	1067	110	19 700	20	1984	Macosa	General Motors 567C	WESA
321	Co-Co	Elec	1250	24 640	19 325	22·5	120	1016	111	18 567	76	1967 1970	Alco, CAF, Naval Euskalduna	Alco	General Electric GEE
333	Co-Co	Elec	1875	31 710	28 100	23·5	151	1067	120	20 700	93	1974	Macosa	General Motors 645 E 3	General Motors
352	B-B	Hyd	1470	22 100	16 400	20·5	140	950	76·3	17 450	10	1964	Krauss-Maffei Babcock & Wilcox	2 × Maybach-Mercedes MD 650/18	Maybach-Mercedes
353	B-B	Hyd	1668	25 500	19 100	20	180	1150	88	19 000	4	1969	Krauss-Maffei	2 × Maybach-Mercedes MD6652	Maybach-Mercedes
354	B-B	Hyd	2340	—	—	—	180	1150	80	19 000	8	1982	Krauss-Maffei	2 × Maybach-Mercedes MD 6652	Maybach-Mercedes

Note: Classes 352, 353 and 354 are 'Talgo' locomotives

Electric multiple-units

Class	Cars per unit	Line voltage	Motor cars per unit	Motored axles per motor car	Rated output kW per motor	Max speed km/h	Weight tonnes per car (M-motor T-trailer)	Total seating capacity	No in service 31.12.88	Year first built	Builders Mechanical parts	Electrical equipment
432	3	1500/3000 V	1	4	1160	140	M 60 T 40 T 50	212	18	1971	CAF-Macosa	Mitsubishi-Westinghouse
433	2	1500 V	1	4	600	100	M 60 T 46		7	1923	SECN	Westinghouse
434	2	1500 V	1	4	600	100	—	162	9	1961		
436-7-8	2/3	3000 V	1	4	880	110	M 58 T 33 T 31	252	150	1958	MTM-Macosa Schindler-Schlieren	BBC-Sécheron
439	2	1500/3000 V	1	4	1007	130	M 65 T 32	156	25	1967	Metropolitan C–CAF	ACEC-J Schneider Cenemesa
440	3	3000 V	1	4	1160	140	M 59 T 34 T 40	260	254	1974	CAF-Macosa	Melco-Westinghouse GEE
441	2	1500 V	1	4	600	90	M44 T 27	120	8	1977	CAF	Westinghouse
442	2	1500 V	1	4	524	60	M 35 T 19	88	6	1976	MTM	BBC
443	4	3000 V	1	4	1760	180	—	167	1	1980	CAF-Fiat CAF-Macosa	Melco-GEE
444	3	3000 V	1	4	1160	140	M 64 T 39 T 48	212	14			
444-500	3	3000 V	1	4	1160	160	NA	212	11	1988	CAF-Macosa	Melco-GEE
445	2	3000 V	2	2	1920	100	62·5	176	1	1985	CAF-Macosa-MTM	Cenemesa Conelec

RAILWAY SYSTEMS / Spain

4500 × 300 × 14 mm), and for expansion joints 2600 × 350 × 140 mm. Special sleepers of up to 6·2 m used for diagonals on double-track
Reinforced concrete: Type RS or monobloc, thickness 250 mm
Spacing: 1666 km

Rail fastenings: Screw spikes on wood sleepers and elastic clamps on reinforced concrete sleepers. Elastic fastenings for wood sleepers are also being tested.
Minimum curve radius: Generally 5·85° = 300 m
Max gradient: 4·25% on Ripoll-Puigcerdá line
Longest continuous gradient: 8·27 km of 2% (1 in 50) grade, with 5·85° curves (300 m radius) on 4·84 km
Max altitude: 1494 m on Ripoll-Puigcerdá line
Max axleload: 22·5 tonnes
Max permitted speed: Various, where permitted: 160 km/h

Diesel multiple-units

Class	Cars per unit	Motor cars per unit	Motored axles per motor car	Transmission	Rated power kW per motor	Max speed km/h	Weight tonnes per car (M-motor T-trailer)	Total seating capacity	Length per car m (M-motor T-trailer)	No in service 31.12.88	Year first built	Builders Mechanical parts	Engine & type	Transmission
591	2	1	2	Mech	277	90	M 21 T 11			20	1954	Macosa, CAF	Pegaso	Pegaso
597	2	1	2	Mech	381	120	M 52 T 44	128	M 12·7 T 12·7	49	1964	CAF, Fiat	Fiat	OM-(SDM)
592	3	2	2	Hyd	460	120	M 46 T 39	276	M 16·7 T 16·5	70	1981	Marcosa, Ateinsa	MAN	Voith
593	3	2	2	Mech	490	120	M 48 T 40	276	M 17·2 T 16·7	61	1982	CAF, BWE	Fiat	Fiat

Catalanes Railways (FGC)
Ferrocarriles de Generalitat de Catalunya

Plaza Cataluña 1, 08002 Barcelona

Telephone: +34 3 302 48 16
Telex: 97769 fcgd e
Telefax: +34 3 302 79 16

Chairman: Albert Vilalta i González
Director: Enric Roig i Solés
Deputy Director: Enric Taulés i Guinovart
Commercial Director: Tomàs Figueras i Riera
Administration Director: Antonî Herce
Managers
  Transport: Jésus Aragon Martin
  Workshops and Rolling Stock: Josep Lluís Arques Paton
  Electrical Installations and Communications: Enric Dominguez Saura
  Fixed Installations: Miguel Llevat Vallespinosa

Gauge: 1435 mm (Catalunya i Sarrià line); 1000 mm (Catalans and Ribes-Núria lines)
Length: 43·6 km; 138 km
Electrification: 1435 mm, 43·6 km at 1·2 kV dc
1000 mm, 61·95 km at 1·5 kV dc

FGC was created in 1979 to unite and modernise local railways in and around Barcelona. Besides the lines listed above FGC operates one cable car system and four funicular railways. FGC is basically an intensive passenger service operator, but from the Súria and Sallent freight-only branches at the extremity of the Catalans line there is significant freight movement of common and potassium salts from mines to Barcelona port.

Immediate aims for the 1435mm gauge system in 1990 were to complete double-tracking of the Sarrià line beyopnd Rubi, continue extension of train-sets from three to four cars and plan renewal of the Series 400 emus.

Plans for the Catalans line include resignalling and introduction of automatic train operation in the central Barcelona area to increase train frequency, and extension of ATP to the two sections beyond Sant Cugat that are presently without it. Also required is more double-tracking and a semi-underground relocation of Rubi station, to eliminate the line's last level crossing. Platform extension at stations is proposed to permit a new generation of four-car train-sets.

Three-car Type UT-211 emu for FGC 1435 mm-gauge

Renovated station at d'Olesa de Montserrat on Catalunya i Sarrià line

Metre-gauge version of Type 111 emu for Catalunya i Sarrià line

Finance (Pta million)
Revenues	1987	1988
Passengers and baggage	2042·456	2249·120
Freight, parcels and mail	584·045	616·365
Other income	209·373	290·259
Total	2835·874	3155·744

Expenditure	1987	1988
Staff/personnel	3724·355	3914·845
Materials and services	1549·340	1706·167
Depreciation	1008·659	1159·119
Financial charges	1428·519	1363·997
Total	7710·872	8144·128

Traffic	1987	1988	1989
Freight tonnes	1051 242	1061 163	1013 120
Freight tonne-km (million)	72·48	71·91	64·97
Passenger journeys (million)	41·73	42·27	44·4
Passenger-km (million)	476·62	486·24	507·2

In 1988 FGC was operating 10 Alsthom-built 690 kW diesel locomotives, 20 emus, five dmus and 405 wagons on the 1435 mm-gauge Catalans line, 37 emus on the metre-gauge Catalunya i Sarrià line.
In 1989 FGC ordered from Macosa three 1500hp diesel locomotives with three-phase motors for 1200-tonne mineral train haulage between Súria, Sallent and Barcelona port. The renovation and strengthening of Catalans line bridges to sustain 15-tone axleloads has been completed, and acquisition of 110 four-axle potassium wagons to replace existing two-axle wagons is contemplated.

Track
Rail: 100 mm-gauge: Vignole 45/kg/m
1435 mm-gauge: Vignole 54 kg/m
Minimum curvature radius: 150 m
Max gradient: 1%
Max axleload: 1000 mm-gauge: 10 tonnes
1435 mm-gauge: 12 tonnes

Spain / **RAILWAY SYSTEMS** 711

Electric multiple-units

Type	Cars per unit	Line voltage dc	Motor cars per unit	Motored axles per motor car	Rated output (kW) per motor	Max speed km/h	Weight tonnes per car (M-motor T-trailer)	Total seating capacity per car (M-motor T-trailer)	Length per car mm	No in service 1988	Year first built	Builders Mechanical parts	Builders Electrical equipment
Catalans line													
M 5000/T 6000	3	1500	2	4	477	75	M 35·8 T 21 M 35·8	M 36 T 46 M 42	15 200	3	1986	FGC	ABF
M 5000/T 6000	2	1500	1	4	477	75	M 35·8 T 22	M 36 T 40	15 200	3	1985	FGC	ABF
M 5000/T 2000/ T 6000	4	1500	1	4	477	80	M 37 T 16·6 T 20	M 56 T 52 M 48	15 200	4	1971	Naval	ABF
M 211/T 281/2	3	1500	1	4	276	90	M 36·4 T 26·2 T 29·7	M 34 T 37 T 34	17 200	5	1987	Macosa	Alsthom
M 211/T 282	2	1500	1	4	276	90	M 36·4 T 29·7	M 34 T 34	17 200	5	1987	Macosa	Alsthom
Catalunya i Sarrià line													
M 400/TM 700 T 800/M 500	3	1200	3	4	110	80	M 35·3 TM 35·3 T 23·5 M 35·3	M 52 TM 56 T 56 M 52	19 296	2	1943 (modernised 1985)	FGC	GEE
M 400/T 800 M 500	3	1200	2	4	110	80	M 35·3 T 23·5 M 23·5 M 35·3	M 52 T 56 T 56 M 52	19 296	12	1943 (modernised 1985)	FGC	GEE
M 600/T 600	3	1200	2	4	70	50	M 32·7	M 56	19 290	3	1953	FGC	GEE
M 111/T 181	3	1200	2	4	276	90	M 39·1 T 28·2 M 37·7	M 56 T 64 M 56	19 300	20	1983	La Maquinista Alsthom	

Diesel multiple-units

Type	Cars per unit	Motor cars per unit	Motored axles per motor car	Transmission	Rated power (kW) per motor	Max speed km/h	Total seating capacity per car (M-motor T-trailer)	Length per car mm	No in service 1988	Year first built	Builders
Catalans line											
M 3000/T 3000	3	2	2	Hyd (Voith)	156·6	90	M 51 T 37 M 51	17 260	5	1987	Macosa-Smaltbau

Spanish Narrow-Gauge Railways (FEVE)
Ferrocarriles Españoles de Via Estrecha

General Rodrigo 6, Parque de las Naciones, Madrid

Telephone: +34 2 53 70 00
Telex: 48690 feve
Telefax: +34 2 53 63 19/+34 2 54 63 19

Chairman: Joaquin Martinez-Vilanova
Deputy Director General: Jesús Maria Aristi Biurrun
Directors
  Administration and Finance: Francisco Laguna Palacios
  Commercial: Jesús María Fernández Acebes
  Equipment: Galo Antonio Heras de Santos
  Personnel: Paulino Gutiérrez Villa
  Information and Control: Javier Barreiro López
  Fixed Installation: José Antonio Laherrán Simon
  Press Relations: Adriana D'atri Remedi
  Operations, Northwest Lines: Juan de la Cruz Pacheco
  Operations, Northeast Lines: Juan-Carlos Albizuri Higuera
  Operations, Mallorca: Tomás Morell Marques
  Chief of Legal Services: José Benet Soler

Gauge: 1000 mm
Route length: 1374·7 km
Electrification: 123·7 km at 1·5 kV dc

FEVE is a public company under the Ministry of Transport, Tourism and Communications. It was set up in 1965 and operates the majority of public Spanish narrow-gauge railways, with the principal exception of those locally administered by the provincial administrations of Catalonia, Valencia and the Basque country.

The system comprises the following sections:
Northern Zone
Ferrol-Gijón; San Estaban de Pravia-Oviedo; Oviedo-Santander; Santander-Bilbao; León-Bilbao, and Gijón-Laviana
Cartegena Railways
Mallorca Railways

Merger with RENFE?
The government seeks to make FEVE a subsidiary of the national main-line railway, RENFE, by 1993.

Traffic
Passenger operations include a summer season land-cruise working covering a seven-day itinerary of 932 km between León, Bilbao, Santander, Oviedo and El Ferrol, with road coach side trips. The 10-car train-set employed on this 'Transcantabrico' service includes four six-compartment sleeping cars fashioned locally from diesel railcar bodies and, as saloons, two modified ex-FC Vascongados Pullman cars originally British-built in 1923. The train-set is available for private hire out of season.

Investment
In 1988 FEVE launched a new four-year investment programme costed in total at Pta 6500 million. Of this, Pta 5000 million was earmarked for infrastructure, the remainder for rolling stock. Aided by level crossing modernisation, passenger train speeds are being raised and frequency of suburban services intensified. A third of the total route-km has so far had its track renewed, and 80–90 per cent of the rolling stock has been replaced.

Class 2500 two-car demu

In 1990 FEVE secured a European Investment Bank loan of Ecu76 million for improvement of its lines in Bilbao and Santander. It was also to have a share of a Pta 200 000 million national government investment grant for new urban passenger rolling stock and urban rail infrastructure work.

Electrification
In 1990 FEVE announced that it was to electrify the Langreo line from Gijón to Laviana. Cost would be Pta 1300 million.

RAILWAY SYSTEMS / Spain

Traffic (million)	1988	1989
Total freight tonnage	4·731	4·672
Total freight tonne-km	209·921	219·512
Total passenger-km	239·025	228·143
Total passenger journeys	10·858	10·669

Finance (Pta 000)		
Revenue	1988	1989
Passengers and baggage	991·393	986·879
Freight, parcels and mail	1026·898	1080·94
Other incomes	588·983	658·589
Total	2607·274	2726·41
Expenditure		
Staff/personnel	5853·686	6431·519
Materials and services	1841·412	1759·15
Depreciation	2100·000	2100·00
Financial charges	1447·400	1931·818
Total	11 242·498	12 222·487

Traction and rolling stock

At the start of 1990 FEVE operated 87 diesel locomotives, 21 electric and 54 diesel train-sets, 19 diesel railcars with 22 trailer cars and 1146 freight cars. Recent deliveries have been headed by one more Class 1650 diesel-electric Bo-Bo from French industry and seven Class 2500 diesel-electric two-car train-sets.

In 1988 FEVE took delivery of a two-car dmu prototype, the FEMA, which was to be evaluated for six months as the prelude to an option for a 30-unit production series. The air-conditioned unit has electronic control of its 570 kW traction plant and is designed for 100 km/h speed.

Type of coupler in standard use: Passengers: automatic; freight cars: Alliance
Type of braking: Air and vacuum

Santander station

Electrification
The electrified sections within the FEVE network are: Gijón-Avilés-Pravia; Lierganes-Orejo-Santander-Puente San Miguel; and Cabezón de la Sal.

Track
Rail: 45 kg/m and 54 kg/m
Max axleload: 15 tonnes
Sleepers: Concrete and timber

Sleeper spacing: 1500 per km plain track, 1600 per km in curves
Minimum curvature radius: Main line 100 m
Average curvature radius: 250 m
Max gradient: 30% between Cartegena and Los Nietos
Max permissible axleload: 15 tonnes
Longest tunnel: 4 km, La Florida, between Gijón and Pola de Laviana

Diesel locomotives

FEVE Class	Wheel arrangement	Transmission	Rated power kW	Max speed km/h	Total weight tonnes	No in service 1989	Year first built	Builders Mechanical parts	Engine & type	Transmission
1000	Bo-Bo	Elec	625	70	48	10	1954	Alsthom	SACM-MGO.V12	Alsthom
1050	Bo-Bo	Elec	680	70	48	14	1954	Alsthom	SACM-MGO.V12	Alsthom
1600	Bo-Bo	Elec	1177	90	58	14	1982	MTM	SACM-MGO.V16	Alsthom
1650	Bo-Bo	Elec	1177	90	60	10	1985	MTM	SACM-MGO.V16	Alsthom
1400	B-B	Hyd	883	60	56	5	1964	Henschel	SACM-MGO.V12	Voith
1500	B-B	Elec	772	80	56	10	1965	GECO	Caterpillar	GECO
1200	B-B	Hyd	338	70	36	1	1954	Batignolles	Saurers GB	Voith
1300	B-B	Mech	207	28	33·5	7	1964	SECN	Rolls-Royce	Yorkshire
1300	B-B	Mech	161	28	33·5	16	1964	Westinghouse	Rolls-Royce	Yorkshire

Diesel railcars or multiple-units

Class	Cars per unit	Motor cars per unit	Motored axles per motor car	Transmission	Rated power kW per motor	Max speed km/h	Weight tonnes per car (M-motor T-trailer)	Total seating capacity	Length per car mm (M-motor T-trailer)	No in service 1989	Year first built	Builders Mechanical parts	Engine & type	Transmission
2500	2	2	2	Elec	250	80	M 34·2	M 42	17 100	1*	1987	MTM	Pegaso	ABB-MTM
2400	2	2	2	Elec	228	80	M 33·8 T 22·1	101	M 17 100 T 16 900	13	1983	MTM	MAN	BBC
2400	2	2	2	Elec	228	80	M 33·8	55	M 17 100	15	1985	MTM	MAN	BBC
2300	2	2	2	Hyd	154·5	80	M 23·2	89	M 17 000	25	Rebuilt 1984	CAF-Macosa-Babcock	Pegaso	Voith
2300	1	1	2	Hyd	154·5	80	M 23·2	46	M 17 100	7				
2200	1	1	4	Hyd	220	75	32	54	15 760	12	1959	Eslingen	Bussing	ZF

* Prototype

Electric railcars or multiple-units

Class	Cars per unit	Line voltage	Motor cars per unit	Motored axles per motor car	Rated output kW per motor	Max speed km/h	Weight tonnes per car (M-motor T-trailer)	Total seating capacity	Length per car mm	No in service 1989	Rate of acceleration m/s²	Year first built	Builders Mechanical parts	Electric equipment
3500	2	1500	1	4	4 × 121	80	M 29·7 Tc 24·5	32 30	16 000	2	0·8	1981	CAF	AEG-GEE
3500	3	1500	1	4	4 × 121	80	Ti 20·4 Tc 24·5	38		19	0·5-0·6	1981	CAF	AEG-GEE

Spain—Sri Lanka / **RAILWAY SYSTEMS** 713

Basque Railways (FV/ET)
Ferrocarriles Vascos SA

Atxuri 6, 48006 Bilbao

Telephone: +34 4 433 9500
Telex: 34076 etfv e
Telefax: +34 4 433 6009

Gauge: 100 mm
Route length: 202 km
Electrification: 202 km at 1.5 kV dc

Chairman: A Menoyo Camino
Director, Operations: J R Albizuri
Director, Administration & Finance: L F Escudero
Director, Data Processing: J L Isasi
Director, Way & Works: J C Lizundia
Director, Commercial: J E Urkijo

The Bilbao-San Sebastian line, the Bilbao suburban railways and branches formerly operated by FEVE were transferred in 1979 to a local railway administration controlled by the Basque government. The lines concerned were:
Bilbao-San Sebastian (108 km)
Amorebieta-Bermeo (29 km)
San Sebastian-Hendaye (21 km)
Bilbao suburban (44 km)

In 1990 the railway unveiled a three-year upgrading programme costed at Pta 8900 million. Of this total Pta 2700 million would be spent on new rolling stock. Schemes include double-tracking of the Hendaye-Donostia line and installation of CTC and train-to-ground radio communication.

The railway operates 17 electric locomotives, 80 electric railcars, 124 coaches and 54 wagons.

Sleeping compartment of 'Transcantabrico'

'Transcantabrico' 1000 mm-gauge land-cruise train

Valencia Railways (FGV)
Ferrocarriles de la Generalitat Valenciana

Cronista Rivelles 1, 46009 Valencia

Telephone: +34 96 347 3750
Telex: 64936
Telefax: +34 96 374 6783

Gauge: 1000 mm
Route length: 117 km
Electrification: 117km at 700V/1500V dc overhead

This organisation was created in 1986 to take over from FEVE the local railways in the Valencia area, which has been followed by integration of the city's five metre-gauge lines as a light S-Bahn through completion of a 6.8 km city-centre tunnel with eight underground stations. The Alboraya-Valencia line is now to be rebuilt as a second cross-city route. Re-electrification at 1.5 kV dc is in progress.

In 1989 a CTC centre with VDU control, supplied by Dimetronic, was inaugurated in Valencia.

CAF and Macosa supplied FGV's 30 chopper-controlled, air-conditioned LRVs with ABB electrical equipment which operate the Rafelbunol and Grao lines in the north. In 1989 FGV ordered 10 more, with an option for a further 20. Rolling stock is completed by 46 three-car emus.

FGV articulated LRV with ABB chopper-controlled motors and MICAS control, built by CAF and Macosa under Schindler Waggon licence

Sri Lanka
Ministry of Transport

PO Box 588, D R Wijewardana Mawatha, Colombo 10

Telephone: +94 1 31105/31308

Minister: Wijeyapala Mendis

Sri Lanka Government Railway (SLR)

PO Box No 355, Colombo 10

Telephone: +94 1 421281
Telex: 21674 rlyst ce
Telefax: +94 1 546490

General Manager: D C Lelwela
Additional General Manager (Administration):
  D M Dharmathilaka
Additional General Manager (Operations):
  T D de S W Jayasundera

Sales and Marketing Manager: P S P Samarasinghe
Commercial Superintendent: P Manatunga
Chief Engineer, Planning & Development:
  L P H Wijeratne
Chief Engineer, Mechanical Projects:
  D L D K Wijewardena
Chief Engineer, Civil Projects: T D W Peiris
Chief Engineer, Way and Works: W K B Weragama
Chief Signal and Telecommunications Engineer:
  U C N Fernando
Chief Mechanical Engineer: P W A K Silva
Chief Engineer, Motive Power: T Gunasekera
Stores Superintendent: P Samaranayaka
Chief Accountant: H K Pathirage

Gauge: 1676 mm; 762 mm
Route length: 1394 km; 59 km

SLR is based at Colombo, from where lines radiate north along the coast to Illarankulam, south to Matara and east to the Central Highlands. From the Central Highlands the main line runs to Talaimannar, where a ferry provides links with India's Southern Railway. Branch lines run to Trincomalee and Batticalo, ports on the Bay of Bengal. A narrow-gauge railway runs from Colombo inland to Ratnapura.

Brush-built Class M7 Bo-Bo at Kandy on Colombo express (Peter J Howard)

RAILWAY SYSTEMS / Sri Lanka

Traffic

Intercity services are now operated on three lines linking Colombo Fort with Kandy, Galle and Kankesanturai at distances of 121, 116 and 414 km respectively. An on-train radio communication system enables passengers to transmit urgent messages while on the move. Patronage of these services has of late been severely affected by the civil strife in the country.

Container traffic has continued to expand since it was begun in 1982 and is now managed by a dedicated company, Container Railway Freighters. In addition to the original container terminal at Colombo, there are now terminals in the tea plantations at Nuwara Eliya and Hatton. Another is likely to be established in the Katunayake free port and rail-served by an extension of the branch to Colombo airport. Further free trade zones to be established in the Colombo suburbs at Sapugaskande and at Koggala in the south offer fresh container traffic prospects. The aim is to develop unit container train services.

Early in 1989 delivery of 25 container wagons from Semaf of Egypt was completed and 75 more were to be ordered.

Electrification

The government has approved in principle a start to electrification of Colombo's suburban lines. Earlier design work for the lines from Colombo Fort to Polgahawela, Maradana to Kalutara South, and Ragama to Negombothe city to Negombo has been brought up to date and in 1990 funding for the projected Rs 69 million cost was being sought in the hope of starting work later in the year. The three lines together will entail wiring some 275 track-km. A need of 52 emu train-sets is forecast.

Signalling

Work continues on extension of a centralised traffic control system based on Colombo. The equipment is L M Ericsson's JZA 711 electronic system. Double-line tracks operated by CTC are signalled with automatic block signals with a minimum headway of three minutes at an average speed of 48 km/h. In 1989 a grant of R 16 million was secured from Sweden to finance colour-light resignalling in the Colombo area.

Infrastructure

India has assisted in a Rs 644 million rehabilitation of lines in the north-east of the country, under an agreement reached in 1988. The aid comprised both a US$15·4 million loan and on-the-spot oversight of the work. Indian credits are covering acquisition of 50 passenger cars.

More recently assistance from Japan's Overseas Economic Cooperation Fund has been obtained to begin a Rs 3000 million programme of infrastructure and locomotive rehabilitation. The lines affected are those from Colombo to Kalutara, Negombo and Veyangoda.

New line

The Transport Minister was seeking internal funds and Japanese aid to permit a 1989 start on construction of a 125 km, 1676 mm-gauge single-extension of the south coast line from Matara to the pilgrimage centre of Kataragama. A subsequent projection for a further 85 km to Badulla is a possibility. Radio signalling is proposed.

Communications

A new VHF/UHF telecommunications network supplied by ABB was completed at the end of 1989. It extends from Colombo to Anuradhapura and Nawalapitiya, and from Kandy to Badulla. The railway has begun a phased computerisation programme as part of its effort to establish and maintain a high degree of operational efficiency and management control. Preliminary work has already commenced.

Traffic	1985	1986	1987	1988	1989*
Freight tonnage (million)	1·681	1·574	1·497	1·5	1·3
Freight tonne-km (million)	247·07	203·62	194·99	197·5	127·5
Passenger-km (million)	2111	1972	1881·9	1859·1	1677
Passenger journeys (million)	59·902	59·737	59·7	54·9	50·2

Finances (Rs million)

Revenue	1985	1986	1987	1988	1989
Passengers and baggage	265·948	244·837	246·219	224·9	231·7
Freight, parcels and mail	186·871	202·342	209·714	205·6	182·3
Other income	20·686	34·823	31·22	33·4	44·8
Total	464·505	482·002	487·043	463·9	457·8

Expenditure	1985	1986	1987	1988	1989
Staff/personnel	360·99	388·227	393·765	450·3	507
Materials and services	151·77	363·965	419·052	393·3	355·2
Financial charges	17·139	19·017	22·058	19·4	20·2
Total	529·899	771·209	834·875	863·0	883·1

* Provisional

Motive power and rolling stock

At the start of 1990 SLR operated 8 steam and 153 diesel locomotives, 38 diesel railcars, 1149 passenger cars and 2781 freight wagons on 1676 mm-gauge. On 762 mm-gauge assets comprise 10 diesel locomotives, 68 passenger cars and 90 freight wagons.

In 1988 orders for 20 one power car four trailer dmus were placed with C Itoh, with Hitachi supplying the power cars and driving trailers, Hyundai of Korea the 60 intermediate trailers. Delivery was to begin in mid-1990, allowing withdrawal of the most elderly of the existing Colombo suburban dmus, unreliability of which has been a mounting concern.

In 1989-90 Mecanoexportimport of Romania was delivering 133 passenger cars. With the backing of Indian credits bids for the supply of 50 more were invited in 1988.

A new Paxman 1200 hp engine, the 12 SETCR, is being evaluated under an SLR Type S-6 dmu.

Type of braking: Vacuum
Track
Rail: Fb 39·9 and 36·26 kg/m
Cross ties (sleepers): Wood and concrete, spaced 1583/km
Fastenings: Dog and elastic spikes
Minimum curvature radius: 100·6 m
Max gradient: 1 in 44
Max axleload: 16·5 tonnes

Diesel railcars or multiple-units

Class	Cars per unit	Motor cars per unit	Motored axles per motor car	Transmission	Rated power kW per motor	Max speed km/h	Weight tonnes per car (M-motor T-trailer)	Total seating capacity	Length per car mm (M-motor T-trailer)	No in service 1989	Year first built	Builders Mechanical parts	Engine & type	Transmission
S3	4	1	4	Hyd	656	80	M 47-8-1	286	M 55 T 55	14	1959	MAN	MAN L 12V18/21	Maybach K 104 U
S4	4	1	4	Hyd	656	80	M 47-8-1	286	M 55 T 55	3	1959	MAN	MAN L 12V18/21	Maybach K 104 U
S5	4	2	4	Hyd	577	80	M 47-8-1	286	M 55 T 55	3	1970	Hitachi	Paxman 8Y JXL	MTU-Mekydro K 102 UB/55
S6	4	1	4	Hyd	869	80	M 51 T 28	286	M 55 T 55	8	1975	Hitachi	Paxman 12Y JXL	MTU-Mekydro K 102 UB
S7	4	1	4	Hyd	760	80	M 51 T 28	286	M 55 T 55	9	1977	Hitachi	Cummins KTA-2300L	Hitachi DW 2A

Diesel locomotives

Class	Wheel arrangement	Transmission	Rated power kW	Max speed km/h	Total weight tonnes	No in service 1989	Year first built	Builders Mechanical parts	Engine & type	Transmission
M2	A1A-A1A	Elec	1063	80	79		1954	General Motors	GM 12-567C	Generator D 12F
M2C	Bo-Bo	Elec	1063	80	79	13	1961	General Motors	GM 12-567C	Generator D 12F
M2D	A1A-A1A	Elec	977	80	79		1966	General Motors	GM 12-567E	Traction motor D 29
M4	Co-Co	Elec	1305	80	97·68	14	1975	MLW Industries	Alco 12-25 103	Generator GT 581PJ1
M5	Bo-Bo	Elec	1175	80	66	16	1979	Hitachi	MTC-Ikegai 12V652TD11	Alternator H1-503-Bb
M6	A1A-A1A	Elec	1230	80	85·5	15	1980	Henschel	GM 12-645E	Generator D 25L
M7	Bo-Bo	Elec	746	80	67	16	1981	Brush Electric	GM 08-645E	Main alternator/exciter BA 1004A/BAE/507A
W1	B-B	Hyd	857	80	60·55	33	1969	Henschel	Paxman 12YJXL	MTU-Mekydro K 102-1016 PS
W2	B-B	Hyd	1173	80	65·3	19	1969	VEB Lokomotivbau	Paxman 16YJXL	MTU-Mekydro K 182 BU
Y (shunting)	0-6-0	Hyd	410		45	28	1969	Hunslet Holding	Rolls-Royce DV 8T	Rolls-Royce torque convertor CF 13800
P1		Hyd	98	32	20·12	2	1950	Hunslet	Ruston Hornsby 6 VPH	Hunslet patent mechanical gear box & axle drive
N1	1-C-1	Hyd	367	32	41·17	4	1953	Fried Krupp	Deutz T8M233	Krupp LIB hydraulic transmission
N2	B-B	Hyd	447	32		3	1973	Kawasaki Heavy Industries	Detroit Diesel 16V71K Model 7163-X	Niigata hydraulic torque converter DBG-138

Sudan

Ministry of Transport & Communications

PO Box 300, Khartoum

Minister: Aldo Ago Deng

Sudan Railways (SRC)

PO Box 43, Atbara

Telephone: +249 21 2000, 2296
Telex: 40001 hadid sd

General Manager: Mohamed Ahmed el Tayeb
Deputy General Manager: Mohamed Khalifa Mohamed Ahmed
Chief Civil Engineer: Francis Murgos Mahrous
Chief Mechanical and Electrical Engineer: Abbas Sir El Khatim
Traffic Manager: Bela Abdel Rahman
Chief Accountant: Ahmed En Nour
Directors
Planning and Economic Research: Mohamed Gaili El Khalifa
Stores: Abdel Monem Shams Ed-Din
Personnel: Tag Elsir El Tayeb
Training: Mohamoud SMohd Mahmoud
Northern Region: El Fatih Nabag
Eastern Region: Mahmoud Shazali
Central Region: A/Azim El Tom
Southern Region: Mohamed Mahgoub
Western Region: M A Abu El-Khairat

Gauge: 1067 mm
Route length: 4954 km

The single-track railway used to be the main transport mode in Sudan, carrying nearly 75 per cent of the nation's passenger and freight traffic but its share has contracted sharply since the 1970s. Main reasons have been the halving of cotton production (with concommitant diversion of a high tonnage of ground nuts, previously railed for export, to conversion into domestic cooking oil), development of well-surfaced roads between Port Sudan and Khartoum, political interference and the railway's own serious shortcomings. There was a major change of SRC management in 1987.

SRC has been rigidly shackled by the government to uncommercial rates dating from its years of transport monopoly for its staple freight traffic. Acute shortage of foreign currency has prevented purchase of spares, fuel and particularly lubricating oil, as well as deferring badly needed capital expenditure.

The European Economic Community agreed in June 1985 to support an outlay of US$8 million, and the US government to furnish a further US$3 million, for track rehabilitation, installation of radio communication and repair of both steam and diesel locomotives so as to restore full rail grain movement capacity between Port Sudan and the west of the country, where drought has engendered severe famine.

EEC and UN representatives then joined a committee chaired by the Transport Minister which was charged with overseeing the emergency rail programme. Early decisions taken included the acquisition from General Electric do Brasil, funded with US aid, of 10 Type U20 diesel locomotives originally intended for Mozambique, and measures to return unserviceable locomotives to use. The latter included six Class 310 2-8-2 locomotives, the boilers of which were sent to Britain for overhaul; 10 GE diesel units which were dealt with by GE engineers in a project paid for with US aid; and 10 former English Electric diesel units, which were overhauled by GEC engineers from Britain. A total of 300 new air-braked wagons (since 1983 SRC had been converting from vacuum to air braking) that had been delivered knocked-down from Portugal but since then left untouched, were assembled at SRC's Atbara workshops.

Traffic	*1987*	*1988*
Total freight tonnes	735 505	676 277
Total freight tonne-km (million)	699	633
Total passenger-km (million)	357	667
Total passenger journeys (million)	1·021	0·334

Diesel locomotives owned

Series	*Transmission*	*Wheel arrangement*	*Rating*	*No purchased*	*Builder*	*Year first built*
100	Hyd	B	340 hp	6	RSH	1962
400	Elec	C	300 hp	3	English Electric/ Hawthorn Leslie	1936
403	Elec	C	350 hp	5	English Electric/ Dick Kerr	1951
450	Hyd	D	350 hp	4	Henschel	1958
460	Hyd	C	500 hp	2	Henschel	1962-64
600	Hyd	C	650 hp	30	Kawasaki	1968
700	Hyd	C	500 hp	20	Henschel	1976
1000	Elec	Co-Co	1850 hp	65	EE/Vulcan	1960-69
1500	Elec	A1A-A1A	1500 hp	20	Hitachi	1969
1601	Elec	Co-Co	1650 hp	10	Henschel	1981
1700	Elec	Co-Co	1650 hp	20	General Electric U15C	1975-81
1800	Elec	Co-Co	2300 hp	20	General Electric U22C	1975
1900	Elec	Co-Co	2500 hp	20	Henschel/ General Motors	1975
1950	Elec	Co-Co	2400 hp	10	General Motors JT22LC-2	1981

Finance (S£ million)	*1987*	*1988*
Revenue		
Passengers and baggage	20·3	30·049
Freight, parcels and mail	86·95	95·628
Other income	7·796	9·387
Total	115·046	135·784

Expenditure	*1987*	*1988*
Staff/personnel	123·631	118·938
Materials and services	51·763	16·136
Depreciation	10·37	11·759
Financial charges	22·472	6·5
Total	208·237	153·333

In 1988-89 loans were arranged from several sources to underwrite a US$100 million rehabilitation programme. It would be managed on the spot by experts from a consortium of Canadian Pacific Consulting Services, DE-Consult and Doshi Borgan. The programme will cover all aspects of infrastructure and rolling stock overhaul. Italy has given US$13 million to restore the Nyala-Babanusa line.

Signalling and telecommunication

Mechanical lower quadrant signalling is used throughout the system with absolute block working between stations. In some cases both points and signals are operated from signal cabins, but in others points are hand-operated individually or from ground frames at each end of the stations. The primary communication link is a lineside open pole route, over which SRC serves block instruments and block telephone, selective ringing telephones and a station-to-station telephone and telegraph system. In addition a manual morse telegraph operates. SRC has an HF radio link for voice communication between major centres throughout the rail network. Now it is considering introduction of radio signalling.

Investment

Sudan Railways is maintaining an emergency recovery programme which aims to resist further deterioration of operating performance, to improve utilisation of existing assets and capacity, and to strengthen and restructure SRC organisationally to enable it to re-establish itself as a financially sound and economically efficient participant in the economic development of the country. These objectives will be achieved through technical assistance, training, studies, spare parts and essential workshop equipment replacement, materials for top priority emergency track repairs, and signalling and telecommunication spares needed to maintain safe train operation.

Motive power and rolling stock

In 1988 Sudan Railways owned 89 steam locomotives and 200 diesel locomotives (137 main-line and 63 shunters), 440 passenger cars and 6246 freight cars. However, a large proportion of the stock was unserviceable. Over 2000 freight wagons were stopped for repairs. In 1989 the National Electricity Corporation took delivery from Japanese industry of three 2120 hp diesel locomotives with GE Canada 12-251C4 engines for use by SRC on power station coal trains between Port Sudan and Khartoum.

Egypt is to assist in creation of a coach building and repair plant at Port Sudan.

Track

Standard rail: Flat bottom, 50 lb/yd (24·7 kg/m) in lengths of 3 ft (9·14 m) and 75 lb/yd (37·2 kg/m) in lengths of 36 ft (10·97 m); joined by fishplates and bolts
Cross ties (sleepers): Steel; and wood impregnated under pressure in mixture of creosote and oil (½ and ½). Steel 6 ft 6 in by 10½ in by $\frac{13}{32}$ in. Timber 6 ft 9 in by 5 in. Concrete used in a few cases as an experiment
Spacing: 1274/km under 90 and 75 lb rail, 1320/km under 50 lb rail
Rail fastenings: 50 and 75 lb rails; screw spikes and elastic spikes
90 lb rail: cast iron baseplates and steel clips, or Pandrol fastenings and DE clips
Steel sleepers: steel keys being replaced by clips with bolts and nuts
Filling: Generally earth, but some stretches of quarry spoil and ballast
Max curvature: (Main line) 4·5°
Max gradient: 0·66% (1 in 150), except on section in Red Sea Hills between Summit and Port Sudan 1% (1 in 100). Gradient compensation for curves 0·04% per 1° curvature
Longest continuous gradient: Overall gradient from Port Sudan to Summit (129 km), 0·7% with continuous 3·75 km of 0·98%. Only short level sections, including 3 stations, in whole 129 km
Worst combination of gradient and curvature: 1% grade with 4½° curve-radius of 388 m
Gauge widening on curves: ¼ in (6·44mm) on curves of 4° and over
Super-elevation on sharpest curve: 3 in (76 mm) max
Rate of slope of super-elevation: ⅙ in (4·2 mm) per rail length for curves under 3° = radius of 1910 ft (582 m)
⅓ in (8·4 mm) per rail length for curves under 3° and over

Max axleload
76 lb track: 16½ tons
50 lb track: 12½ tons
Max speed
50 lb track: 50 km/h
75 lb track: 60 km/h
Max altitude: 918·5 m at Summit station on Port Sudan line

Swaziland

Ministry of Works, Power & Communications

PO Box 58, Mbabane

Telephone: +268 2321

Minister: W F Mklonza
Permanent Secretary: J S F Magogula

Swaziland Railway (SR)

Swaziland Railway Building, Johnston Street, PO Box 475, Mbabane

Telephone: +268 42486
Telex: 2053 wd
Telefax: +268 42775

Chairman: B Fitz-Patrick
Chief Executive Officer: J R Avery

Track	Ka Dake-Goba	Phuzumoya-Golela
Rail	40 kg/m	48 kg/m
	(sidings 30 kg/m)	
Sleepers	hardwood	concrete
Thickness	127 mm	200 mm
Spacing	814 mm	700 mm
Fastenings	soleplates and coachscrews	Fist BBR
Welded rail	126 km	92 km

Financial Director: L B Mabuza
Operating Director: M M Dlamini
Chief Civil Engineer: S Z Ngubane
Commercial Director: G J Mahlalela
Personnel Director: B N Fakudze

Swaziland's railway was completed in 1964. It is a corporate body established under the Swaziland Proclamation of 1962 and managed by a Railway Board appointed by the Minister of Works, Power and Communications. The main route is from Ka Dake to Goba (310 km), with lines from Phuzumoya to Lavumisa/Golela (92 km) and Mpaka to Komati Poort (55 km).

A 120 km link from Mpaka to Komati Poort in the eastern Transvaalwas opened in February 1986; 58 km is in Swaziland and 62 km in South Africa. The line provides a through north-south line to South Africa via the Mpaka-Phuzumoya section of the Ka Dake-Mlawula line and the 95 km Phuzumoya-Golela southern link. Traffic includes minerals and ores from eastern Transvaal, phosphoric acid, fruit, timber and containers are also carried.

Motive power and rolling stock
Eighteen Type 14R steam locomotives leased from South African Transport Services, three passenger cars and 786 freight wagons.

Sweden

Ministry of Transport & Communications

Vasagatan 8-10, 103 33 Stockholm

Telephone: +46 8 8763 1000
Telex: 17328
Telefax: +46 8 11 8943

Minister: Georg Andersson
Under-Secretary: Gunnel Färm
Secretary-General: Christine Striby

Swedish State Railways (SJ)
Statens Järnvägar

105 50 Stockholm C

Telephone: +46 8 762 2000
Cable: Statsbanan, Stockholm
Telex: 19410 sjtgmc s
Telefax: +46 8 111216

Chairman: Allan Larsson
Director General: Stig Larsson

HQ Functions
Financial Management: Gunnar Malm
Information: Gunnel Sundbom
Internal Auditing: Arne Kock
Legal Matters: Anders Iacobaeus
Personnel: Tage Persson
Corporate Planning: Anders Lundberg
Tele- and Radio Communications: Bo Larsson
Safety of Operations: Allan Bernhard

Passenger Traffic Division
Director: Karl-Erik Strand
Area Managers
  South Malmö: Lennart Serder
  West Goteborg: Lars Strömmer
  East Stockholm: Conny Adebåck
  North Gävle: Olle Dahlstedt
  Express Freight, Stockholm: Harry Rosengren
  Mass Transit, Stockholm: Karl-Axel Håkansson
  Terminal Operation, Stockholm: Ingemar Sjömalm

Freight Traffic Division
Director: Christer Beijbom
Area Managers
  West Göteborg: Lars Baeckström
  East Gävle: Harry Nordefors
  North Sundsvall: Bert Sarbäck
  Ferry Services, Malmö: Jochum Ressel
  Freight Wagons, Stockholm: Nils Stråhle
  Combined Transport, Stockholm: Gert Johansson
  Continental Transport, Stockholm: Göran Malmberg

Class Rc6 3600 kW electric locomotive

Class T44 diesel-electric locomotive built by Kalmar-Nohab

Ore Line, Kiruna: Thore Johansson
Mail Services, Norrköping: Jan Petersson

Mechanical Engineering Division
Director: Bernt Andersson
Traffic Workshops: Bernt Andersson
Maintenance Workshops: John Oscarsson
Technical: Per Leander

Real Estate Division
Director: Per Gunnar Andersson

Swedish National Rail Administration
Banverket (BV)

Klarabergsviadukten 78 S-105 50 Stockholm

Telephone: +46 8 762 2000
Telex: 19410 sjtgmc s
Telefax: +46 8 762 4274

Chairman: Lars-Erik Nicklasson
Director General: Jan Brandborn
Deputy Director-General: Karl Sicking
Chief Inspecting Officer of Railways: Yngve Gelotte
Directors
  Planning: Karl Sicking
  Engineering: Anders Sjöberg
  Economy: Tord Johansson
  Personnel: Lennart Zacke
  Service: Per-Olof Granbom

Heads of Regional Offices
  South (Malmö): Olof Sandberg
  West (Göteborg): Olle Pettersson
  East (Stockholm): Sven Bårström
  Middle (Gävle): Svante Murman
  North (Luleå): Olle Bylesjö

Division for Supply and Manufacture
Director (Nässjö): Claes Sandgren

Gauge: 1435 mm; 891 mm

Route length: 11 194 km; 97 km
Electrification: 6955 km at 15 kV 16⅔ Hz ac

In per capita terms, Sweden has the largest railway length in Europe (1·5 km of track per 1000 inhabitants) in spite of numerous branch lines closing during the 1970s.

Partition of SJ

In July 1988 Sweden followed the lead of Austria and Switzerland and assumed state responsibility for the upkeep of the railway's infrastructure. As a result SJ was partitioned. SJ became confined to operation of rail transport as a public but commercially-motivated enterprise. Its infrastructure, already state-owned, became the responsibility of Banverket (BV), (literally Track Authority in translation), which has been titled Swedish National Rail Administration in English. The move had two objectives: equalisation of the terms of competition between road and rail; and environmental protection. Like road transport, SJ's trains are now taxed for their use of state-funded infrastructure. At the same time road users had petrol prices lifted by 6 per cent and the tax on air fares was raised. Part of the extra money extracted from road users will be applied to rail infrastructure improvements.

Division of responsibilities

Under the government's new transport policy for the 1990s, the development of the railway sector is to be based on socio-economic costs and benefits and not only on commercial principles. Thus, decisions regarding new construction or reconstruction of railways will be based on socio-economic evaluation as is the case in the road sector. Principles and methods to be used will be developed and by Banverket, which is largely staffed by people from SJ. Banverket will also participate in developing the railways into a competitive transport system. In the next decade about SEK 10 000 million will be allocated to new projects.

Among other things, Banverket will decide upon the overall investment and maintenance plans for the state railway infrastructure. Within it there is an independent railway inspectorate, which will check on safety in the rail network and transportation. This body will also make inquiries about accidents.

Banverket is highly decentralised. Five regions with some 20 districts have responsibility for their own planning and economy. In addition, there is an Industrial Division with commercial responsibility for purchasing, production and storage of material for the entire administration.

The new policy makes provision for an injection of privatisation. As a government agency it is required to adopt a neutral attitude to transport companies, which may become competitors for future access to the tracks.

In brief, the responsibilities of Banverket cover:
Railway lines: sub-structure, superstructure and track, signals and other safety installations, electric traction equipment.
Terminals: all through tracks, certain storage tracks and sidings, passenger platforms, lighting and some major marshalling yards.
Fixed installations for traffic supervision and safety.
The responsibilities covered by SJ are:
Locomotives, wagons and coaches;
Terminal buildings and stations, including surrounding public services;
Goods terminals (except major marshalling yards) and combined road/rail transfer terminals;
Industry tracks;
Workshops for rolling stock.
Financing of Banverket will normally be effected through state budget grants. The transport companies will then have to pay fixed as well as variable fees for the use of the tracks.

New arrangements for social network

SJ has long been divided into a core that SJ has mandated to operate commercially; and a rural network that SJ has run under contract to the government, which has covered this system's inevitable losses. That segregation is now more emphatic.

The national railway system, where SJ has to run a fully self-supporting passenger and freight service, is established as 35 core routes totalling 6180 km. The strategic Lapland ore line from Kiruna to the ports of Lulea and Narvik (Norway), has been set apart as a special operation.

The residue consists of 23 lines aggregating 2220 route-km that currently offer both passenger and freight service; and 50 lines totalling 1370 route-km where SJ runs freight trains only. The new legislation has transferred responsibility for passenger service over these regional lines to country transport authorities. State financial support continues, but at reduced levels. These local authorities were given until July 1990 to decide whether they will persevere with trains, either under their own management or run for them by SJ under contract; or whether they will substitute bus service.

It also became possible for private enterprise to take on service in the social sector. From May 1990 a new company BK Tag AB, was to launch a coast-to-coast service of 450 km between Halmstad in the west and Oskarshama in the east.

SJ retains sole authority to run freight service over the regional lines. But under the new statute its former compensation for obligation to run unprofitable freight service is withdrawn and replaced by a subsidy for wagonload and intermodal system development.

Finance (SEK million)

Revenue	1987	1988
Passengers and baggage	4735	5296
Freight, parcels and mail	4242	4294
Other income	1028	1030
Total	10 005	10 620
Expenditure	*1987*	*1988*
Staff/personnel	6173	6384
Materials and services	3707	3922
Depreciation	482	554
Financial charges	110	187
Total	10 472	11 037

Freight organisation

The head of the new SJ Freight Traffic Division has separate staff functions responsible for economy, market and production. At ground level there are also business areas, four geographical and six delineated by function. Every business area has its own profit responsibility.

Ore for LKAB, steel for SSAB, wood products for SCA, Stora and Korsnas, engineering products for Volvo and Saab-Scania, foodstuffs for Felix, KF and ICA as well as transports for the Post Office Administration are some of the most important traffics. SJ Freight's 200 biggest customers are responsible for 90 per cent of receipts from full-load traffic. A key objective is to increase transport quality and efficiency mainly in co-operation with these 200 important customers.

A quality manager has been appointed at SJ Freight and his main task is to plan, develop and manage the quality by objectives.

Daily contacts between customers and SJ Freight have been made easier and improved through new customers' centres available at 22 places throughout the country. These effect wagon requests, reservations, loading guidance, quality follow-up, information on transits, etc. Extension of the SJ Freight data-based information system offers many advantages to the customer. A new electronic consignment note is fully based on data provided by the contract. The customer has only to indicate number of contract, destination station, wagon number and total weight of load. All other information is on the data base and all freight contracts are registered in the system. Customers of SJ Freight are invited to connnect their own data terminal to this information system.

The aim of SJ Freight, together with SJ's big customers, is to build rail transport into a manufacture and distribution process. For Felix SJ Freight delivers foodstuffs daily to some 30 places, and 40 per cent of these flows are completed to the final destination by road.

To achieve a maximum proportion of overnight transits between centres not covered by through trains, SJ has devised an operating plan focused on its Hallsberg yard, which is strategically placed at the junction west of Stockholm between the lines to Oslo, southwest to Gothenburg and south to Helingsborg and Malmö. Eight terminals that are major sources of intermodal business form each night complete trains of traffic for mixed destinations and forward them to Hallsberg. Here the wagons are swiftly sorted into fresh trains, each of which concentrates traffic for a single destination.

With a fixed Sweden-Denmark rail link still an uncertain project, further improvement of the train-ferry connections goes ahead. The year 1991 should see completion of the new ferry terminal at Helsingborg.

The Helsingborg city council has advanced SEK 700 million towards a whole series of local rail schemes arising out of the expansion of the train ferry service to and from Denmark. Construction will soon begin on a cross-city rail tunnel by which the Gothenburg-Malmö main line will be diverted through a new downtown station; at present Helsingborg is served by a branch from this route.

Helsingborg is the Swedish gateway to DanLink, the enhanced rail freight route to Northwest Europe developed jointly by SJ and the Danish State (DSB) and German Federal (DB) Railways in the earlier 1980s. From Helsingborg two capacious ferries, one DSB- and the other SJ-owned, ply to Copenhagen Freeport and the DSB; and the DSB is linked to the DB by the Rødby-Puttgarden ferry route.

The much increased size of the Helsingborg-Copenhagen ferries by comparison with those connecting the SJ with the DSB at Helsingör, and the better terminal facilities at Copenhagen, have eliminated a great deal of costly and time-wasting breakdowns of freight trains for the sea crossing. Volvo's daily train of containerised steel pressings from its factory at Olafstrom to its Ghent assembly plant in Belgium, for example, now crosses to Denmark intact in one shipment.

For the general market SJ has a network of overnight intermodal trains interlinking ports and key inland centres. Five nights a week there is also a dedicated Trans-Europ-Container-Express between Goteborg and Oslo.

SJ and DSB have been joined by Norway's NSB and Finland's VR in a Nordic European Rail Unit (NERU) to develop door-to-door intermodal service. So far as the rail element is concerned, the principle is that Helsingborg assembles traffic from each railway into one train for a non-stop long-haul via the DanLink route to a selected European rail centre.

The inaugural NERU venture was a North-Ruhr Express, run daily each way, Mondays to Fridays, to the Langendreer terminal at Bochum in the Ruhr. SJ's three gateways to the service are Gothenburg, Jonkoping and Stockholm's Arsta terminal. The service is open to piggybacked semi-trailers as well as containers and swapbodies, and the client can choose either to entrust the entire transit to NERU or organise his own cartage. The railways are also touting for term-based charters of whole trains to the same timings. NERU aimed in 1990 to launch a second service to Italy. Subsequent plans are for a combined Franco-Spanish and a Benelux service.

The potential of a rail-based intermodal system in freight transport between the Nordic countries and the rest of Europe has been highlighted in a study completed last autumn by COWIConsult for the Scandinavian Link Consortium and the four railways.

SJ, NSB and DSB are also co-operating in the development of a bi-modal system. Front-runner in 1989 was the TrailerTrain bi-modal of Britain's Tiger Europe company, which has sold a Scandinavian licence to build its model to NSB and Norwegian builders Strommens Verkstad. However, because the Scandinavian railways want to agree a standard bi-modal design with the DB and NS, they are committed to evaluating other bi-modal types.

SJ has other train ferry links with the rest of Europe besides Helsingborg-Helsingör and Helsingborg-Copenhagen. In 1988 a third ferry was added to the service between Ystad, east of Malmö, and Swinoujscie in Poland, which is operated by Polish Ocean Line, a joint venture of SJ and the Polish Railways (PKP). This is for through wagon traffic. PKP is also the intermediary in a recently-launched Vienna-Stockholm piggyback service for road trailers and swapbodies, which are transferred from rail to ro/ro ship at Gdynia.

DanLink now has three competitors for wagon traffic to and from Northwest Europe. Nordo-Link is running train ferries from Malmö to Lubeck Travemunde, TT Line from Trelleborg to the same West German port, and Stena Line from Göteborg to Frederikshaven in Denmark. From Frederikshaven wagons have an uninterrupted rail route into West Germany via Padborg.

Passenger traffic

In August 1986 SJ ordered 20 high-speed train-sets (see below) for the Stockholm-Gothenburg service. The order included an option on a further 30 train-sets for the Stockholm-Malmö, Malmö-Gothenburg and Stockholm-Sundsvall services. This order was, however, only one component of a new strategy that SJ is evolving in its passenger business.

A total of 800 passenger coaches dating from the

1960s are being rebuilt during a six-year period. One reason for this is that about 700 of them contain asbestos, on which a total ban has been imposed under legislation relating to hazardous substances, so that it must be removed as soon as possible from all these coaches.

In 1988 SJ introduced the first of a series of 10 prototype sleeping cars of revised interior concept prior to ordering a production series of 30 cars to a new design classified WL5. SJ's overnight travel is significant, but its sleeping cars date from the late 1950s and early 1960s. The prototypes, put into service as Type WL5 in autumn 1988, employ existing body-shells, which have been divided into five double-berth compartments each having their own toilet and shower, and six compartments with a washbasin. Based on the experience from this, SJ ordered 15 WL5R and 30 WL6 with an option for 45 more WL6. All sleeping cars have disc brakes. SJ expects to phase out three-berth sleeping compartments (except in 25 WL1R).

During 1988 22 Type B2R cars were delivered and 23 more would be delivered in 1989. Two new conference cars were ordered for delivery 1989-90. Another order is for five new cars of Type B7BR, specially designed for families and handicapped. These cars would come into service from December 1989 and during 1990 and will be delivered in two types, one with nursery room and playroom, the other designed for the handicapped with a wheelchair lift, a place for wheelchair and toilet for the handicapped.

Two new-designed office cars have been ordered for delivery in 1990; one car will consist of 10 single workrooms and a large conference compartment; the other will have 16 single workrooms. These cars will have PC, printing equipment, telephone, telefax and secretarial service. Each single workroom will have its own telephone. Passengers can also use their own PCs.

The top speed of Stockholm-Oslo trains was raised to 160 km/h in the 1989/90 timetable.

Development work on the 'total journey' concept, ie door-to-door and not simply between two railway stations is at present in progress. SJ is also actively engaged in the development of its railway stations as service points for rail passengers (see below). Better information facilities and improved station environments are envisaged.

An extensive reconstruction of Stockholm Central station is at present in progress. A modern departure hall with direct access to the platform via escalators and lifts has already been opened on the top floor of the station. Extensive reconstruction of and extensions to commuter railway stations in the Stockholm area were completed in 1986 (SJ's Stockholm suburban emus are now being repainted in the light-blue-with-white lining livery of the city's urban transport authority, Stockholm Lokaltrafik, or SL). Improvements were carried out in a number of other stations, where lifts and escalators were installed for the benefit of handicapped passengers.

PETRA, an important development project designed to boost SJ's competitiveness and cut down expenditure, was initiated in 1986. It is a computer-aided system which will come into operation in 1990 and supersede the present arrangements for booking and selling tickets. An important element in the future sales system will be the possibility of providing different kinds of service for different customer categories. It must be possible for customers who are used to computers to obtain information about travelling alternatives, and book whole travel packages, by means of a computer terminal at their office or by using computerised information and booking facilities at railway stations, post offices, etc.

Several other development projects using computerised systems are in progress. One is computer-aided traffic planning, on which the main work was carried out in 1987. The project embraces preparation of timetables, rostering of locomotives and rolling stock, work schedules for engine drivers and conductors and a daily updating of timetables including all extra trains and omitting all cancelled trains. The system will allow interactive handling of all these matters. One of its features is that it will provide for economic assessment of various timetable alternatives: this has been minimally possible with manual methods.

SJ and Sweden's international and domestic airlines, SAS and Linjeflyg, are combining their computer reservation systems to offer an integrated seat and hotel reservation service.

The first Type X2 tilt-body train-set

Saloon

First-class saloon of Stockholm-Gothenburg 'City Express'

Stations to become traffic centres
Station activity is to be restructured by SJ's new Real Estate Division. To make them convenient traffic centres with room for trains, buses, taxis and private cars as well as commercial services, increased co-operation with local authorities is being pursued. In certain cases the latter may take over the responsibility for smaller stations on the regional lines of the social network. Henceforth, if the Real Estate Division wants to sell property it will be enough to have the government's approval instead of that of Parliament as was earlier the case.

Land and property transactions
SJ is one of the largest land and property owners in Sweden. Until the transport policy decision of July 1988 these assets were surrounded by many restrictions on efficient development. In comparatively few cases has government approval been sufficient to sell land; generally Parliament has also had to give its approval. Although SJ now may sell land without government approval it has requested the government to agree a higher value limit for such transactions, freedom to choose sell-off methods and the right to make guarantee engagements. A comprehensive action programme has been worked out that will make a considerable contribution to SJ's commercial activities. It will be needed not least to plan and put through station environment projects at 50 major stations and at Stockholm Central.

Traction and rolling stock
In August 1986, after thorough examination of tenders from a number of European train manufacturers, SJ ordered from ASEA 20 high-speed tilt-body Series X2 train-sets, each consisting of a power car, four trailing cars and a driving trailer (for full specification, see ABB entry, Locomotives and Rolling Stock section). The order also included necessary workshop equipment, spare parts, training etc. Furthermore the contractor took the responsibility for fulfilment of contractual demands, for performance reliability and prescribed levels of operational and maintenance costs. The 20 train-sets will be put into service on the 456 km main line between Stockholm and Gothenburg, which they will run non-stop in less than 3 hours.

The first series of Type X2 train-sets would be delivered in November 1989 and the second one year later. The delivery rate will be six train-sets per year.

Deliveries in 1988 comprised three Class Rcb electric locomotives, seven Class X10 emus, three Class R4R dining cars, three Class A8R and 23 Class B4R passenger cars, three Class UA7 driving trailers (for electric pull-push train service) and 294 freight wagons.

At the close of 1988 items on order included 22 Class B4R passenger cars, 20 Class X2 high-speed train-sets and 50 freight wagons.

At the end of 1988 SJ operated 680 electric locomotives, 501 diesel locomotives, 186 emus, three dmus (includiing five powered railcars, eight intermediate trailers and two driving trailers), 105 other diesel railcars, 1348 passenger cars (including 86 buffet/dining cars and 266 sleeper/couchette cars), three driving trailers for push-pull service, 203 luggage/mail vans and 23 314 freight wagons.

Type of braking in standard use: Air
Type of coupler in standard use: Screw

ABB workshops takeover
ASEA Brown Boveri AB is to take over and run some of SJ's maintenance shops. It is planned to accomplish this through two companies jointly owned with SJ and others. One of these companies would include the maintenance shops in Malmö and Tillberga; it would be owned by ABB Traction AB, Västerås, and SJ. The maintenance shops in Gävle, Östersund, Fjällbo and Bollnäs would be transferred to a company owned by Ageve AB, Gävle with SJ. The new companies were scheduled to start up in January 1989. SJ's maintenance shops in Örebro, Notviken and Åmål are not affected by this agreement.

Banverket and the infrastructure
SJ's main lines allow speeds up to 130 km/h, but short stretches between Stockholm and Gothenburg are upgraded to 160 km/h. Double-track exists on the following lines:
Stockholm-Gothenburg.
Stockholm-Malmö.
Stockholm-Uppsala and some additional parts further to the north.

Traffic	1984	1985	1986	1987	1988	1989
Freight tonnage (million)	47.3	53.9	53.3	51.7	52.6	53.3
Tonne-km (million)	16 944	17 767	17 754	17 630	17 800	17 754
Passenger-km (million)	6483	6586	6152	6088	6050	NA
Passenger journeys (million)	77.7	76.9	73	70.8	72	71.0

About 25 km between Gothenburg and Malmö.
Frövi-Örebro-Hallsberg.

All major lines are electrified with catenary carrying. Axleload is normally 22.5 tonnes, but a design standard of 25 tonnes is now applied when upgrading track (eg by use of UIC-60 rail) and replacement of bridges on major lines.

Banverket's 1991–2000 Plan
In early 1990 Banverket issued a ten-year trunk line upgrading programme, to which it hoped for agreement by the year's end. The main items were:

Modification of the Stockholm-Malmö line for 200 km/h by 1995; cost SEK 1300 million;

Double-tracking of a further 25 per cent of the Göteborg-Malmö line, at its northern end, which involves boring a new 8km tunnel at Hallandsasen; cost SEK 2500 million;

Upgrading of the East Coast line, including provision for 200 km/h between Stockholm, Uppsala and Gävle;

Some double-tracking on the main line to the north to enlarge freight operating capacity;

Relaying of busy freight routes with UIC60 rail for 25-tonne maximum axleloads; Extension of CTC to most trunk routes.

To eliminate capacity problems on the existing Stockholm-Södertälje double track, an additional double-track line designed for 180 km/h has been decided for 30 km south of the capital. Estimated cost: SEK 3000 million, the works to be completed in 1994.

Other major projects
An additional third track is proposed through the central part of Stockholm. Existing historical monuments, new buildings and bridges for water passengers will incur high cost per unit length. About 3 km for a cost of some SEK 1000 million are planned and may be completed before the turn of the century.

To improve connections to Stockholm and between major cities in the Lake Mälar region vast improvements have been proposed and design work started. The plans include double track on a new alignment, alignment improvements, short cuts and terminal improvements. Estimated cost: SEK 4000 million, the works to be finished within the next 10-year period.

A second and more direct trunk route from Stockholm to Göteborg than the existing main line, which takes a near-westerly path through Hallsberg to Laxa before turning southwestward to Göteborg, has been promoted by the three regional authorities whose terrain it would thread. Known as the Gotlandsbanan, the new route would be formed by upgrading the existing line from Stockholm to Mjolby and Tranas, building 140 km of new line from Tranas through Jonkoping to Boras, and upgrading more existing track from Boras to Göteborg. The new route would be

Stockholm-Gothenburg 'City Express' restaurant car

Alpha-numerical operator's console and vdus in Hallsberg computer-based interlocking centre

prepared to the required standards for optimal use by the X2 tilting-body intercity trains.

The total cost of the scheme, which has the backing of both SJ and Banverket, is put at SEK 5·5 billion, the raising of which would be organised by the three regional governments. The project has been remitted to a steering group representing SJ and the regional authorities for preparation of a detailed proposal. Availability of the new route is unlikely until the next century.

In conjunction with SAS and the country's domestic airline, Linjeflyg, a scheme has been formed for a new 200 km/h railway between the Stockholm city centre and an underground station at Arlanda Airport, 40 km to the north. Means of financing the project are being discussed between the three promoters and the city and neighbouring local authorities. If funding were arranged in 1989, the city centre-airport link could be operational by 1995. There are plans for the line's subsequent projection to Stockholm's southern suburbs; if they mature, estimates are that by the next century about 40 per cent of Arlanda's users would arrive at and leave the airport by train. Estimated cost: SEK 3000 million.

Upgrading of electrification

In 1988 the first sections (about 150 km) of a single-phase 130 kV, 16⅔ Hz power transmission line were taken into operation. The transmission line will have a total length of about 800 km on the northern Boden-Hallsberg line. It will be completed by 1992 and make it possible to increase the electric traction load.

The upgrading of the power system involves insertion of transformer substations between existing converter substations, which at the same time gain power. This system also makes it possible to transmit power from one part of the network to another.

Signalling and traffic control

By the start of 1988 automatic train control (ATC) was operative over 4488 km of single- and 1550 km of double-track. Extension continues.

Hallsberg junction has been equipped with a fully electronic interlocking system. Hallsberg is the junction of the Stockholm-Gothenburg and Stockholm-Oslo main lines and also handles traffic from the north to the south of Sweden in its marshalling yard.

The interlocking system installed at Hallsberg is a further development of the system installed at Gothenburg in 1978 and at Malmö in 1981. The wayside apparatus control equipment has been redesigned from relay technology into microcomputer-based electronics. Communication between the central interlocking unit and the wayside apparatus control makes partial use of fibre-optic cabling.

Traffic flow at Hallsberg is extensive with about 1500 movements a day. This was formerly handled by three interlockings, one of which dates from 1932. The new electronic interlocking controls 200 signals, 190 points and some level crossings and platform equipment in an area within some 8 route-km.

In a SEK 170 million project the SJ/BV are applying track-to-train radio communication to over 600 vehicles from some 700 ground stations. Passenger cars are being equipped to allow direct broadcast to passengers. More than 80 long-haul cars are equipped with a public telephone facility.

Track

Standard rail: Type UIC 60 (60 kg/m) or SJ 50 (50 kg/m);
on secondary lines: SJ 43 (43 kg/m)
Cross ties (sleepers)
Concrete
Type B10: 320 × 222 × 2500 mm
Type S3: 320 × 250 × 2500 mm
Wooden
Type 1: 240 × 165 × 2600 mm
Rail fastenings:
Wooden sleepers
On main lines: Hey-Back
On secondary lines: spikes, normally with baseplate
Concrete sleeper: Pandrol
Sleeper spacing
On main lines: 1538 per km on plain track
1538 or 1667 per km in curves of less than 500 m radius
On secondary lines: 1333 per km
Number of sleepers is increased to 2000 per km on the Kiruna-Riksgränsen ore line
Minimum curve radius: 300 m
Max gradient: 2·5 per cent
Max permissible axleload: 22·5 tonnes (25 tonnes on the Kiruna-Riksgränsen ore line)

Ferries

The Swedish State Railways is linked to the continental railway network by four railway-operated ferry routes: Helsingborg-Helsingör (DSB), Helsingborg-Copenhagen (SJ-DSB), Trellerborg-Sassnitz (DR) and Ystad-Swinoujscie (PKP). Two of these are freight only, the Copenhagen and the Swinoujscie crossings.

Buses

SJ also operates some 1700 buses. Together with the SJ subsidiary GDB Biltrafik AB's 700 buses, this makes the SJ Group the biggest bus transport company in Sweden. About 90 per cent of the services are local and 6 per cent intercity. The remainder perform a hire-and-reward service.

Diesel railcars or multiple-units

Class	Cars per unit	Motor cars per unit	Motored axles per motor car	Transmission	Rated power kW per motor	Max speed km/h	Weight tonnes per car (M-motor T-trailer)	Total seating capacity	Length per car mm (M-motor T-trailer)	No in service end-1988 (M-motor T-trailer)	Year first built	Builders: Mechanical parts	Builders: Engine & type	Builders: Transmission
Y1	1	1	2	Hyd	147	130	46	68/76	24 400	88	1979	Fiat/Kalmar	Fiat 8217.12.150	Fiat SRM
YF1	1	1	2	Hyd	147	130	46	48	24 400	12	1981	Fiat	Fiat 8217.12.150	Fiat SRM
Y3 +	2-5	1-2	4	Hyd	460	140	M 64	34	M 19 620	M 5	1966	LHB	KHD BF 12 M 716	Voith, Gmeinder
U3 +							T 32	37-56	T 21 000	T 8	1966			
U3y							T 41·9	60	T 19 620	T 2	1966			
Y7	1	1	2	Mech/ Hyd	160	115	19	47	17 550	5	1957	ASJ, Eksjöv	Sc Vabis D 815	Vulcan, Sinclair, Wilson

Diesel locomotives

Class	Wheel arrangement	Transmission	Rated power hp (kW)	Max lb (kg)	Tractive effort: Continuous at lb (kg)	Tractive effort: Continuous at mph (km/h)	Max speed mph (km/h)	Wheel dia in (mm)	Axle load tonnes	Total weight tonnes	Length ft in (mm)	No in service end 1988	Year first built	Builders: Mechanical parts	Builders: Engine & type	Builders: Transmission
T21	D	Hyd	800 *(590)*	41 200 *(18 700)*	26 500 *(12 000)*	7·5 *(12)*	50 *(80)*	49⅜ *(1255)*	14·2	57	37′ 1″ *(11 300)*	29	1955 1956	MaK ASJ	MaK MA 301A	Voith and MaK
T43	Bo-Bo	Elec	1445 *(1065)*	47 600 *(21 600)*	28 200 *(12 800)*	14·3 *(23)*	59 *(95)*	40 *(1015)*	18	70	46′ 8¾″ *(14 240)*	50	1961	Nohab	GM 12-567D	ASEA (GM licence)
T44	Bo-Bo	Elec	1670 *(1230)*	48 600 *(22 100)*	36 000 *(16 500)*	11 *(17)*	56 *(90)*	40½ *(1030)*	19	76	50′ 6¼″ *(15 400)*	122	1968 1983	Nohab Kalmar	GM 12-645E	GM
Tb snow-plough	Bo-Bo	Elec	1670 *(1230)*	48 600 *(22 100)*	36 000 *(16 500)*	11 *(17)*	59 *(95)*	40½ *(1030)*	18	34	50′ 6½″ *(15 400)*	10	1969	Nohab	GM 12-645E	GM
V4	C	Hyd	625 *(460)*	34 800 *(15 800)*	30 400 *(13 800)*	3·1 *(5)*	43 *(70)*	38½ *(985)*	16	48	33′ 9½″ *(10 300)*	10	1972	Henschel	Deutz BF12M716	Voith and Gmeinder
V5	C	Hyd	625 *(460)*	34 800 *(15 800)*	30 400 *(13 800)*	3·1 *(5)*	43 *(70)*	38½ *(985)*	16	48	34′ 11″ *(10 640)*	40	1975	Henschel	Deutz BF12M716	Voith and Gmeinder Verkstads
Z43	B	Hyd	160 *(118)*	14 500 *(6600)*			34 *(55)*	38⅛ *(970)*	10	20	28′ 10⅛″ *(8800)*	45	1951 1958	Kockums Mek Kalmar Verkstads	Scania Vabis D812	Atlas Diesel and Kalmar Verkstads
Z64	B	Hyd	240/270 *(177/ 200)*	20 500 *(9300)*			31 *(53)*	33½ *(850)*	14	28	24′ 2¼″ *(7370)*	30	1953	Klöckner Humboldt Deutz	Deutz T4M 625 Scania Vabis DS140	Voith and KHD
Z65	B	Hyd	295 *(218)*	20 500 *(9300)*			37 *(60)*	38¾ *(985)*	14	28/30	30′ 3¾″ *(9240)*	102	1962	Kalmar Verkstads	Rolls-Royce C8TFL Mk IV KHD F12 M 716	Twin Disc and Deutsche Getriebe Gesellschaft
Z66	B	Hyd	295 *(218)*	21 160 *(9600)*			43 *(70)*	38¾ *(985)*	16	32/34	33′ 9½″ *(10 300)*	30	1971	Kalmar Verkstads	KHD F12 M 716	Voith and Gmeinder
Z67	B	Hyd	381 *(280)*	18 900 *(8600)*			43 *(70)*	38¾ *(985)*	15	32	30′ 6″ *(9300)*	31	1978 1981	Gmeinder Hägglunds	Cummins KT-1150-L	Voith and Gmeinder
Z68	Bo	Hydrostatic	438 *(322)*	15 385 *(7000)*			21 *(34)*	33¾ *(864)*	20	40	19′ 4½″ *(6960)*	2	1984	AGEVE Gavle	Scania Vabis DS1 14	Rexrath

Note: Class Z67 rebuilt from Z61, Z62 and Z63 locomotives

Sweden / **RAILWAY SYSTEMS**

Electric railcars or multiple-units

Class	Cars per unit	Line voltage	Motor cars per unit	Motored axles per motor car	Rated output kW per motor	Max speed km/h	Weight tonnes per car (M-motor T-trailer)	Total seating capacity	Length per car mm (M-motor T-trailer)	No in service end-1988 (M-motor T-trailer)	Rate of acceleration m/s^2	Year first built	Builders Mechanical parts	Builders Electrical equipment
X1	2	15 kV	1	4	280	120	M 50 T 31 M 53 T 32	98 + 98	M 24 500 T 24 500	93 2	0·9	1967	ASJ, KVAB	ASEA
X9	2-4	15 kV	2	2	170	115	M 26/21 T 16	24/26 30/54	M 17 500 T 17 400	M20	0·3	1960	H Carlsson	ASEA
X10	2	15 kV	1	4	280	140	M 60 T 41	92 + 92	24 659	T 38	0·8	1982	Hägglunds	ASEA

Electric locomotives

Class	Wheel arrangement	Line current	Rated output hp (kW)	Tractive effort (full field) Max lb (kg)	Tractive effort (full field) Continuous at lb (kg)	Tractive effort (full field) Continuous at mph (km/h)	Max speed mph (km/h)	Wheel dia in (mm)	Weight tonnes	Length ft in (mm)	No in service end-1988	Year first built	Builders Mechanical parts	Builders Electrical equipment
Da	1-C-1	15 kV 16⅔ Hz	2500 (1840)	45 200 (20 500)	21 200 (9600)	43·2 (69·5)	62 (100)	60⅜ (1530)	75	42' 8" (13 000)	90	1952	Nohab; ASJ; Motala	ASEA
Dm	1-D + D-1	15 kV 16⅔ Hz	5600 (4140) 6500 (4800)	137 000 (62 000) 137 000 (62 000)	63 500 (28 800) 63 500 (28 800)	32·4 (51·8) 37 (59)	47 (75) 47 (75)	60⅜ (1530) 60⅜ (1530)	180-186·4 190	82' 3¾" (25 100)	19 1	1953 1971	Nohab; ASJ Motala	ASEA
Dm3	1-D + D + D-1	15 kV 16⅔	8400 (6210)	205 000 (93 000)	96 000 (43 500)	32·4 (51·8)	47 (75)	60⅜ (1530)	258·4	15' 8" (32 250)	3	1960	Nohab; ASJ; Motala	ASEA
Dm3	1-D + D + D-1	15 kV 16⅔ Hz	9750 (7200)	205 000 (93 000)	96 000 (43 500)	37 (59)	47 (75)	60⅜ (1530)	273·2	115' 8" (32 250)	16*	1967	Nohab; ASJ; Motala	ASEA
Hg	Bo-Bo	15 kV 16⅔ Hz	1760 (1300)	40 200 (18 300)	18 500 (8400)	34·1 (54·9)	50 (80)	43⅜ (1100)	64·8	41' (12 500)	42	1942	Nohab; ASJ; Motala	ASEA
Ma	Co-Co	15 kV 16⅔ Hz	4500 (3300)	82 500 (37 400)	36 800 (16 700)	44·4 (71·5)	63 (100)	51¼ (1300)	105	55' 1½" (16 800)	29	1953	Nohab; ASJ; Motala	ASEA
Ra	Bo-Bo	15 kV 16⅔ Hz	3600 (2650)	43 200 (19 600)	20 000 (9100)	65·5 (104·5)	93 (150)	51¼ (1300)	64	49' 6½" (15 100)	6	1955	Nohab; ASJ; Motala	ASEA
Rc1	Bo-Bo	15 kV 16⅔ Hz	4900 (3600)	61 700 (28 000)	34 600 (15 700)	49 (78·8)	84 (135)	51¼ (1300)	80	50' 9" (15 470)	19	1967	Nohab; ASJ; Motala	ASEA
Rc2	Bo-Bo	15 kV 16⅔ Hz	4900 (3600)	61 700 (28 000)	34 600 (15 700)	49 (78·8)	84 (135)	51¼ (1300)	77	50' 11" (15 520)	97	1969	Nohab; ASJ; Motala	ASEA
Rc3	Bo-Bo	15 kV 16⅔ Hz	4900 (3600)	52 900 (24 000)	31 900 (14 500)	57 (91·8)	100 (160)	51¼ (1300)	77	50' 11" (15 520)	10	1970	Nohab; ASJ; Motala	ASEA
Rc4	Bo-Bo	15 kV 16⅔ Hz	4900 (3600)	61 700 (28 000)	34 600 (15 700)	48·5 (78)	84 (135)	51¼ (1300)	78	50' 9" (15 470)	128	1975-81	Nohab; KVAB	ASEA
Rc5	Bo-Bo	15 kV 16⅔ Hz	4900 (3600)	61 700 (28 000)	34 600 (15 700)	48·5 (78)	84 (135)	51¼ (1300)	78	50' 11" (15 520)	40	1982	Hägglunds	ASEA
Rc6	Bo-Bo	15 kV 16⅔ Hz	4900 (3600)	61 700 (28 000)	34 600 (15 700)	48·5 (78)	100 (160)	51¼ (1300)	78	50' 11" (15 520)	37	1985	Hägglunds	ASEA
Rm	Bo-Bo	15 kV 16⅔ Hz	4900 (3600)	65 000 (31 400)	50 600 (23 000)	34·2 (55)	63 (100)	49⅜ (1250)	92	50' 11" (15 570)	6	1977	Nohab	ASEA
Ub	C	15 kV 16⅔ Hz	690 (515) 830 (620) 940 (700)	29 800 (13 500)	16 700 (7600)	15·5 (25)	28 (45)	43⅜ (1100)	47·4	31' 6" (9600)	65	1930	Nohab; Motala	ASEA
Uc	C	15 kV 16⅔ Hz	940 (700)	29 800 (13 500)	16 700 (7600)	15·5 (25)	28 (45)	43⅜ (1100)	49·2	31' 6" (9600)	1	1933	Nohab	ASEA
Ud	C	15 kV 16⅔ Hz	830 (620) 940 (700)	28 600 (13 000)	15 200 (6900)	20 (32)	37 (60)	43⅜ (1100)	50·4	31' 6" (9600)	25	1955	Nohab; ASJ; Motala	ASEA
Ue†	C	15 kV 16⅔	940 (700)	28 600 (13 000)	16 700 (7600)	15·5 (25)	28 (45)	43⅜ (1100)	47·4	31' 6" (9600)	25	1987	Nohab; Motala; ASJ	ASEA

Notes: Class Rc and Rm, thyristor control   * Rebuilt from Class Dm to Dm3   † Rebuilt from Class Ub

TGOJ Railways
TGOJ AB

631 92 Eskilstuna

Telephone: +46 16 137585
Telefax: +46 16 122827

General Manager: R Johanson

Gauge: 1435 mm
Length: 300 km
Electrification: 300 km at 15 kV 16⅔ Hz ac

The railway, which operates in central Sweden, owns 19 electric locomotives, 12 emus, six diesel locomotives and 420 freight wagons. Its main route is entirely under CTC control.

TGOJ electric railcar at Linköping (*Marcel Vleugels*)

Nordmark Klarälvens Railways
Nordmark Klarälvens Järnvägar

Box 706, 683 01 Hagfors

Telephone: +46 563 17000

Chairman: H Bergström
Managing Director: R Khilberg

Motive Power Superintendent: L Carell

Gauge: 891 mm; 1435 mm
Length: 61 km; 8 km
Electrification: 69 km at 16 kV 16⅔ Hz ac

The railway, which operates in west central Sweden between Hagfors, Munkfors and Karlstad, operates six ASJ/ASEA 900 hp, 35·2-tonne electric and four 180 hp diesel-hydraulic shunters, all 891 mm-gauge, together with 400 freight wagons. Track employs 24·8 kg/m rail, minimum curve radius is 250 m, maximum gradient 1·45 per cent, and maximum axleloading 12 tonnes (20 tonnes on 1435 mm-gauge).

Freight traffic per annum total some 350 000 tonnes and 9 million freight tonne-km.

Switzerland

Ministry of Transport, Communications & Power

Bundeshaus Nord, 3003 Berne

Telephone: +41 31 61 57 11
Telex: 912791 bav ch
Telefax: +41 31 61 58 11

Minister: Adolf Ogi

Swiss Federal Railways
Schweizerische Bundesbahnen (SBB)
Chemins de Fer Fédéraux Suisses (CFF)
Ferrovie Federali Svizzere (FFS)

Hochschulstrasse 6, 3030 Berne

Telephone: +41 31 60 11 11
Telex: 99 11 21 gdsbb ch
Telefax: +41 31 60 43 58

Chairman: Carlos Grosjean
President and General Manager, Finance and Staff: : Hans Eisenring
Director, Marketing & Production: Dr Benedikt Weibel
Technical: Claude Roux
Heads of Division
  Secretariat: Dr Jean-Pierre Kälin
  Information Systems: Josef Egger
  Financial & Control: Michel Christe
  Personnel: Hans-Kaspar Dick
  Planning: Fritz Suter
  Medical: Dr Rudolf Gränicher
  Legal: Dr Eric Bertherin
  Freight Marketing: Dr Max Lehmann
  Passenger Marketing: Hans-Jörg Spillmann
  Marketing Services: Willi Werren
  Supplies & Purchases: Erwin Mauron
  Operating: Jakob Eberle
  Civil Engineering: Dr Peter Winter
  Traction and Maintenance: Dipl-Ing Theo Weiss
  Power Generation & Distribution: Jörg Stöcklin

Gauge: 1435 mm; 1000 mm
Route length: 2999 km; 74 km
Electrification: 1435 mm-gauge, 2983 km at 15 kV 16⅔ Hz ac
  1000 mm-gauge, 74 km at 15 kV 16⅔ Hz ac

Government finances infrastructure
The Federal government now assumes financial responsibility for SBB fixed installations except those deemed to have a direct connection with the SBB network's operation, notably principal workshops and traction current supply installations. The state's responsibility is purely financial, and in no way managerial. In its commercial sector, comprising intercity passenger, wagonload, container and less-than-wagonload traffic, SBB has managerial freedom and makes an annually predetermined contribution to infrastructure costs. If the budgeted figure is not fully utilised, the residue goes to SBB reserves. In 1989 SBB contributed SwFr 102 million, which was SwFr 76.8 million more than budgeted.

In the sector of SBB services designated as socially necessary, the government has assumed full financial responsibility for infrastructure and has the right to specify levels of service, in respect of which it refunds unrecovered costs. The SBB continues to exercise control of commercial action, operations and rolling stock, and refunds some of the infrastructure costs.

'Bahn 2000'
'Bahn 2000', the new nationwide rail passenger service development programme, surmounted its last legislative hurdle in late 1986 when the Federal Council, the Swiss parliament's upper chamber, gave it unanimous approval and approved a total expenditure of SwFr 5400 million on SBB projects over-shadowed in the plan. A matching credit of SwFr 930 million was later voted for complementary development on the country's private railways. Its final test was safely negotiated in December 1987, when 'Bahn 2000' was approved 57–43 per cent in a national referendum.

'Bahn 2000's' dominant theme is convenience. That is, optimisation of a Swiss rail station's easy accessibility (60 per cent of all Swiss households live within 1 km of a rail station and the average annual rail travel per inhabitant is about 1600 km) by a major increase and tightening of through and connecting services so that scarcely any internal journey is unappealing by rail; and intensification of intercity and other direct services on routes of maximum overall transportation demand. Higher speed is a secondary feature, sought only where needed (and at no higher level than needed) for competitiveness with improved highways, and also to satisfy a cardinal principle of the plan.

This principle centres on hourly cycling. The critical interchange points in the Swiss rail network as a whole are seen as the SBB stations at Basle, Berne, Biel, Lausanne, Lucerne, St Gallen, Sargans and Zurich. For symmetry direct trains need to run between each neighbouring pair of these centres on a timing that is slightly less than one hour, the residue of that hour being standing time for passenger interchange. Thus at each of these stations the full range of connections will be concentrated in a standard framework each hour of the day.

On key routes, however, 'Bahn 2000' doubles intercity or direct train service from hourly to half-hourly (which testifies to its precept that convenience counts for more than spectacular speed by selected trains, the latter at the cost of operating capacity). As a result some centres will have differing series of interconnections at alternative half-hours, a development that creates scope for introduction of additional through services connecting into and out of the direct trains, and reduces change of train on several routes off the main arteries. Thus at Berne connections will be grouped round east-west and north-south direct trains, and vice versa, on the hour; and around north-west and south-east direct trains and vice versa on the half-hour.

Some 40 to 50 stations over and above the eight hubs listed above will acquire new connectional significance through the intensification of direct train services. Major examples that will become gateways to wide areas are Montreux, Delémont and Wil SG. Others will be important interfaces with the private railways. Examples of trip acceleration:

	Journey time 1988 h min	2000 h min	Improvement (%)
Bern-Schaffhausen	2 14	1 44	22
Aarau-Biel/Bienne	57	40	30
Fribourg-Arth-Goldau	2 50	2 17	24
Biel/Bienne-Baden	1 41	1 12	29
Zug-Aarau	1 10	42	35
Stans-Meiringen	2 14	1 10	48
Basle SBB-Solothurn	1 10	42	31
Brugg-Biel/Bienne	1 30	58	36
Rotkreuz-Biel/Bienne	2 26	1 24	42
Chiasso-Geneva	6 24	5 34	15
Bellinzona-Martigny	4 20	3 16	25
Frauenfeld-Burgdorf	2 34	1 47	31
Locarno-Lausanne	4 45	3 42	22
Neuchâtel-St Gallen	3 10	2 32	20
Listal-Berne	1 14	41	45
Visp-Locarno (via Centovalli)	3 03	2 01	33
Weggi-Neuchâtel	2 38	2 06	20

Class Re 4/4 II and Geneva Airport-St Gallen InterCity service of Mk IV coaching stock *(John C Baker)*

New 200 km stretches
'Bahn 2000' calls for about 130 km of new 200 km/h-fit route, in part to secure competitive transit times, but no less importantly to bring feasible running time between all neighbouring hubs of the SBB network down to the one hour that the scheme predicates.

The longest stretches of new 200 km/h infrastructure will be on the Basle-Berne route: one of 34 km between Muttenz, on Basle's outskirts, and Olten (which entails tunnels of 4·7 and 12·8 km length, the Adler and Wisenberg respectively); and another of 54 km between the Olten area at Rothrist and Mattstetten, near Berne, this throwing off a branch to the Olten-Zofingen-Lucerne line. These schemes are a prerequisite for the 22-minute cut of Berne-Basle timings needed to secure the slightly-less-than-one-hour timing of direct trains between the two cities, and also to achieve the same objective between Berne and Lucerne or Zurich. But the effective four-tracking between Basle and Berne is equally essential to accommodate both the double direct passenger train frequency and also the anticipated extra volume of international freight traffic via the Berne area following completion of the BLS Lötschberg route's double-tracking.

The likely Olten-Mattstetten high-speed route takes a southerly course, parallel to the N1 motorway for a considerable distance and close to the existing railway as far as the region of Herzogenbuchsee, where it will throw off a branch to an existing secondary line to Solothurn; the latter will be upgraded to extend accelerated service to Biel. The project includes a 4·6 m tunnel, the Murgenthal near Rothrist.

A third stretch of 200 km/h track, 9 km in length, is to be between Zurich Airport and Winterthur. This is needed because the existing double-track between Effretikon and Winterthur, where the direct exit from Zurich and that from the Airport loop to St Gallen and Romanshorn in the far northeast merge, has inadequate capacity for the 'Bahn 2000' purposes. This stretch requires boring of the 8·4 km Brüttener Tunnel between Kloten and Winterthur. Finally 31 km of 200 km/h infrastructure are to be built between Vauderens and Villars-sur-Glâne, southwest of Fribourg on the main line from Lausanne to Berne; this is the only 200 km/h project with the sole aim of shortening transit time. The high-speed lines will be equipped with ATP speed-control and cab signalling.

Provision for 'Bahn 2000' requires various other works of double-tracking, curve realignment and infrastructure improvement. By the start of 1990 two such projects were under way, the laying of a third track from Basle to Muttenz (to be finished in 1993) and double-tracking of the Zoug-Lucerne line. But the four major new line schemes were still embroiled in planning processes. All have encountered strong local opposition.

Most forward were the Muttenz-Olten and Zurich Airport-Winterthur projects, which had reached the stage of ultimate Federal consideration of objections and determination of approved route. The SBB hoped to be free to start the Muttenz-Olten new line in 1993, immediately after completion of the Basle-Muttenz third track. Over the most controversial schemes, Vauderens-Villars and Mattstetten-Rothrist, the SBB was still locked in local negotiation, but it was determined to conclude that and proceed to the Federal approval stage by the end of 1990. It has faced powerful local pressure for some 16 km of the Rothrist-Mattstetten line to be in tunnel.

'Bahn 2000' train services

'Bahn 2000' aims to establish 13 new through services, among them Basle-Chur, Basle-Geneva, Geneva-Rorschach and Schaffhausen-Chiasso, to accelerate and eliminate changes from many cross-country services. This extra direct train service will be achieved without overtaxing track capacity by doubling up services as one train over portions of the route, each section with its traction unit in place. To avoid complex movements where such trains were separated or reassembled, each portion will be of push-pull format. A typical case for this concept is the Berne-Biel trains, which at Biel would divide for Basle and Chaux-de-Fonds.

'Bahn 2000' will exact a 60 per cent increase of SBB's annual intercity and direct train-km when fully implemented, but of only 30 per cent in total train-km, because most Regional train services already satisfy the 'Bahn 2000' prescription of at least hourly frequency in that category. It will be open to Cantonal or lower local authorities, if they wish, to negotiate (but in this event to subsidise) more intensive Regional train service in their territory.

The SBB sets great store by simplifying use of the train as well as revising the train service. It has therefore begun raising platform heights to 550 mm, which will cut out one of the four steps presently needed to climb aboard a train. It is also concerned to make ramp-approached inter-platform subways a standard station feature. On train, IC train public address systems are to employ pre-recorded information tapes. Installation of electronic ticket-issuing and reservation equipment at main stations has begun.

The first steps to implementation of 'Bahn 2000' were taken in the 1987-88 timetable, which expanded annual SBB passenger train-km by no less than 25 849, comprising a 18 per cent increase in IC, Eurocity and direct training working, 7 per cent in Regional train operation.

Two new Alpine base tunnels planned

The long-running debate over choice of new Alpine base tunnel route – the *Nouvelles Lignes Ferroviaires Alpines* policy or NLFA in French, NEAT in German – was in 1989 resolved by the country's Federal Council. It approved in principle both a Gotthard base tunnel and also, but in this case subject to EEC withdrawal of pressure for a 40-tonne road freight corridor through Switzerland, a Lötschberg base tunnel (for details of the latter proposal, see Bern Lötschberg-Simplon Railway entry). The Gotthard base tunnel cannot be finished until the year 2008 at the earliest. In the interim, to cater for the rise in transit traffic sure to follow the 1992 creation of the Single European Market, the government is to finance substantial enlargement of the existing Gotthard route's capacity for intermodal freight traffic in particular.

The Gotthard base tunnel plan envisages, in effect, four-tracking of the Gotthard route for about 49 km from the neighbourhood of Arth-Goldau to Limone, near Lugano, to create a transalpine operating capacity of some 400 trains a day. The base tunnel itself would extend from Amsteg to Bodio, but two tunnels would be needed north of it for the new double track, and to the south of it a tunnel under Monte Ceneri. One of the new northern tunnels, the Axen, might also absorb the existing Gotthard double track in a four-track bore, to reduce the environmental disturbance of Flüelen village. It would be possible to provide in the base tunnel for subsequent adoption of the 'Y' option that contemplated a mid-tunnel junction throwing off a branch to Chur in eastern Switzerland. The 'Y' project would add between SwFr 500 million and 1000 million to the NLFA bill.

Associated works contemplated include double-tracking between Brugg and Othmarsingen, to optimise the train operating capacity of the four routes feeding into the base tunnel, two from Basle and two from Zurich. There will also be clearance modification to match the approach to base tunnel's availability for piggybacking of road lorries 4·2 m high. There is concern to improve the international access from the Munich area, which will require upgrading of the Rhine Valley route in the St Gallen area and work on the Bodensee-Toggenburg/South Eastern Railways' (qv) route from St Gallen to Arth-Goldau or on the St Gallen-Zoug line.

South of the base tunnel the new tracks will first follow the alignment of the N2 motorway on the left bank of the Tessin valley, then join the alignment of the existing double track from Castione to Giubiasco before the new Monte Ceneri tunnel. The new line will feed into the Bellinzona-Luino single-track route as well as the main Chiasso route to Italy.

Interim transalpine capacity expansion

Meanwhile the government has allocated SwFr 1460 million, chiefly for the Gotthard route, to near-treble the transalpine railways' annual piggyback freight capacity to 360 000 tonnes by 1994. Infrastructure works will include: the NLFA double-tracking from Brugg to Othmarsingen; layout modifications and resignalling at some key stations, such as Dottikon where trains from the Basle and Schaffhousen directions may combine; an overtaking loop at Erstfeld; bi-directional resignalling on the Erstfeld-Flüelen and Bellinzona-Chiasso sections; reinforcement of the traction current supply; and new intermodal terminals at Basle, at a site yet to be determined on the Aarau-Arth Goldau line, and possibly at Chiasso too if the Italians cannot complete one in the Milan area.

The new terminals are required because the operating plan is to double piggyback train lengths to 30 or 36 cars, double-head the trains to Ertsfeld and there insert mid-train a third locomotive, radio controlled from the front end, for the climb to the Gotthard Tunnel. An extra 75 6100 kW locomotives were ordered, after invitation of international offers, in 1990 (see below). The intermodal company Hupac will itself finance procurement of 1200–1300 additional intermodal wagons.

In 1989 and early 1990 the record for a day's freight tonnage over the Gotthard route was re-set several times. On April 18 a new peak of 133 000 tonnes was recorded.

Performance in 1989

SBB freight traffic reached new record levels in 1989. Freight tonnes, rising 5.3 per cent, surpassed 50 million for the first time. rose 10·1 per cent and passenger-km 2·4 Star performer was again piggyback, up 22.8 per cent on 1988. Wagonload transit freight rose 7.8 per cent.

Passenger journeys in total improved by 0.2 per cent on the previous year, passenger-km by 2.1 per cent. International traffic revenue, climbing by 3.7 per cent, showed its best growth since 1985.

Total revenue was up 5.2 per cent on 1988, whereas total expenditure rose by 4.6 per cent. Staff costs accounted for 56 per cent of the latter total, and were responsible for 60 per cent of the cost increases. The end result was a surplus on the year's accounts of SwFr 70 million. That took account of Federal contributions of SwFr 523 million for provision of social passenger services and of SwFr 36 million for furtherance of piggyback freight.

Fixed installations investment in 1989 totalled SwFr 1205.5 million, and investment in traction and rolling stock SwFr 425.1 million.

In 1990 the SBB announced plans to remove staff from some 200 more passenger stations, which would leave roughly half the total unmanned: and also, in conjunction with intermodal development, to discontinue rail service at 160 of the 620 stations currently handling freight.

Passenger service developments

In May 1990, with the Zurich station works complete, the RENFE Talgo Pendular sleeper train from Barcelona, the 'Pablo Casals', could be extended beyond Berne to its originally planned Swiss terminal at Zurich.

The SBB is now likely to acquire tilt-body rolling stock of its own. One such move would relate to the overnight 'Hotel' trains which the SBB, OBB and DB are to launch with new rolling stock in 1994 (see below). In the interim the SBB and OBB are to follow the DB's load and adopt the latest type of Talgo Pendular overnight train-sets to serve as forerunners for the new concept. In the spring of 1990 the SBB Board approved the acquisition of two 14-car sets to run the Basel-Vienna 'Wiener Walzer' service. The DB's sets will run from Munich and Berlin to Zurich.

In the spring of 1990 the SBB was studying the case for acquisition of six to eight dual-voltage (15kV ac/ 3kV dc) Fiat Pendolino eight-car train-sets for service between Geneva/Berne and Milan, and possibly between Frankfurt/Mannheim and Milan (a service proposed for regular-interval frequency in the later 1990s). The possibility of combining Italy-bound units from Geneva and Berne at Brig has been under study. It was reported that the FS was averse to such SBB units continuing over the FS'own Pendolino intercity route from Milan to Rome, or to Venice.

Waggonfabrik Talbot, Simmering-Graz-Pauker and Schindler Waggon are between them to build 500 air-conditioned bi-level cars of new design for the 34 'Hotel' trains mentioned above. The SBB is to acquire six 10-car train-sets, which will each provide three levels of accommodation (for details see German Federal entry) and include a bar-lounge car. Destinations envisaged for 'Hotel' trains originating on the SBB include Hamburg, Vienna, Rome and Naples.

The Swiss Restaurant Car Co's' (SSG) monopoly of SBB on-train catering is being broken. In 1989 two former cafeteria cars were modernised and franchised to SA Minibuffet for exploitation between Basle and Brigue as 'Fronage-Express' on behalf of the Swiss cheesemaker's union (externally the two cars were vividly re-liveried in yellow overlaid with representations of Swiss cheeses). From May 1991 two cars on the Geneva-Biel-Basle IC service would be franchised to McDonald's.

In May 1989 some first-class cars on selected Geneva-Berne-St Gallen and Basle-Zurich-Chur Inter-City trains were designated 'Silence and Work Coaches'. They were identified by blue plaques with appropriate pictograms.

Work has begun on a new computer-based passenger sales and information system known as the PRISMA project. Its central bank of timetable and tariff data will be linked with travel agencies and a new generation of automatic machines at unmanned stations as well as station ticket offices.

Co-ordination with Swissair

Air travellers can now check in for Swissair flights at 13 main SBB stations. The number was to be increased in 1990. Berne station is now an IATA departure point, where passengers can buy inclusive tickets covering a rail leg to Zurich or Geneva Airport and the flights thereafter. Under the 'Fly-Rail-Baggage' scheme luggage for flights to any foreign destination can be checked in at 114 Swiss rail stations; the facility was used by 240 000 travellers in 1989. Conversely incoming passengers can have their luggage railed from the Swiss airport to a Swiss destination station without any intervention on their part.

Freight traffic

Cargo Rail, the SBB's brandname for orthodox wagon-load traffic, rose 2.5 per cent to a total of 41.1 million tonnes in 1989. Contributing 9.6 milion tonnes of this, transit traffic was up 7.8 per cent on 1988. Within the 23 per cent growth of Cargo Combi, the intermodal sector, container and swapbody traffic was up 27.7 per cent. Of 135 000 piggyback movements, 42 000 were accompanied road vehicles on *Rollende Landstrasse* ro/ro trains.

From May 1989 north-south international freight transits were shortened by a revision of marshalling arrangements at Basle and the formation of unit trains for Chiasso at internal Belgian, Dutch and German yards. North-south traffic marshalling still necessary at Basle is concentrated on the SBB's Muttenz yard and not processed successively at the DB's Badois yard as well as at Muttenz. Unit trains for Chiasso spend an average hour at Badois for all customs examinations and DB-SBB locomotive change: in the reverse direction this is done at Muttenz. Previously Chiasso traffic spent anything from 15 to 33 hours negotiating both Basle yards and their separate Swiss and German customs rituals.

At the end of 1988 the SBB and the private railways formed a new company, ACTS SA, to promote container traffic using a system developed by a Dutch company. This achieves road-rail transfer without need of cranage; the Type Rs-x rail wagons each have three 20 ft-long platforms that can be swung outwards to back up to the rear of a road vehicle chassis which is equipped with mechanism to slide a container from one vehicle to the other.

ACTS development figures in SBB plans to develop domestic intermodal service strongly in association with withdrawal of rail connections from least-profitable freight stations. Under a Cargo 2000 scheme the aim is to develop regular-interval container train shuttles between key terminals. A trial operation was

724 RAILWAY SYSTEMS / Switzerland

to be launched between Zurich, Berne and Lausanne Renens in June 1991.

In 1989 SBB was running 24 piggyback trains over the Gotthard route each weekday. The majority were conveying unaccompanied road trailers between Northwest Europe and Italy, or between Basle and Lugano only, but the Swiss piggyback company Hupac was operating ro/ro services for tractor-trailer rigs or lorries on low-floor wagons (*Rollende Landstrasse*) between Basle and Lugano, and between Freiburg-im-Breisgau (just inside Germany) and Lugano or Milan Greco Pirelli terminal. A further service, from Rielasingen to Milan Rogoredo, was launched in January 1990.

Corner height restrictions on road vehicles piggy-backed over the Gotthard route are 3·8 m for those in *Rollende Landstrasse* trains and 3·9 m for trailers conveyed on pocket wagons. If the pocket wagons are of the latest type, with pocket base lowered from 350 to 250 mm above rail, 4 m height is admissible provided that the road vehicles have air suspension that can be deflated during the rail transit. The new base tunnel will be built for a 4.2m clearance.

Investment 1990
In 1990 the SBB was budgeting for investment of SwFr 1653 million in fixed installations and of SwFr 408 million in traction and rolling stock. Major items on the fixed asset programme included: double-tracking between Bad Ragaz and Landquart, on the Sargans-Chur line; between Brugg and Birrfeld, and between Zurich Tiefenbrunnen and Zollikon. Also to be doubled by 1991 are the lines between Berne and Biel (see above) and the metre-gauge Brünig between Lucerne and Hergiswil. Double-tracking of 5 km of the Lucerne-Zoug line has begun (see above), and the Zoug junction layout is to be revised and resignalled at a cost of SwFr 37·4 million. The 1990 budget also provided for resignalling of the Simplon main line between Martigny and Sion, with remote control from Sion.

The rolling stock provision for 1990 covered 45 Class 450 Re4/4 locomotives for the Zurich S-Bahn/RER; 15 prototypes of the Bahn 2000 passenger car (see below); and 200 freight wagons.

Other infrastructure works in progress
Construction of a new Lucerne main station building, replacing the edifice destroyed by fire in 1971, would be completed for opening in February 1991. Reconstruction of Chur station, involving the dropping below ground of the Rhaetian Railway's Arosa approach and platforms, was to begin in 1990.

In October 1989 the SBB Board approved investment of SwFr 144 million in the double-tracking of the Lucerne-Zurich line between Rotkreuz and Ebikon. In the following month boring began on the 6.3 km tunnel that is the centrepiece of a new 9.5km bypass of Zollikofen by the Olten-Berne line. Zollikofen is a busy convergence of the present Olten-Berne and Biel-Berne lines, threading some 300 trains a day. With full implementation of 'Bahn 2000' the total will rise to 500, including eight pairs of IC trains in each hour. The bypass is to start 4km out of Berne at Berne-Löchligut and at its northern end will eventually join up end-on with the Olten-Mattstetten high-speed line. Due to be finished in 1995, the Grauholz bypass will allow inception of half-hourly Berne-Zurich IC service.

Simplon route upgrading
In late 1988 measures to sustain the Simplon line's international passenger route significance were approved. Complete renewal of track with heavier rail and higher-speed pointwork, realignments at Riddes and Ardon, renewal of the current wires, and resignalling accompanied by computer-based control, track-to-train radio and automatic speed control, will by 1995 equip the Martigny-Sion section for 200 km/h. At present the limit is 140 km/h, less through stations. There was provision for solid-state interlockings at Martigny and Sion in the SBB's 1989 investment plans. The sole remaining single-track section, the 5 km in difficult terrain between Salgesch and Leuk, will be replaced by a new double-track in tunnel. Here, and from Leuk to Visp and through the Simplon Tunnel the speed limit will be lifted to 160 km/h. Brig station, little changed since it was built in 1908 (before the arrival of the BLS and of the narrow-gauge railways in its forecourt), is being comprehensively rebuilt.

To achieve clearance for piggybacked trucks of 4.2m corner height, and to provide for the higher passenger train speed, the Simplon Tunnel's track is to be completely renewed and its bed lowered. At the same time a rigid traction current conductor will be installed in place of traditional catenary. The rigid conductor is closer to the tunnel crown so that another important benefit is 300–400 mm of extra clearance for inter-modal piggyback trains. To avoid unacceptable interference with traffic the works will be executed in January to April phases, at the least busy periods of the year, covering 3–5 km at a time, so that it will last from six to eight years.

Zurich RER
In a November 1981 referendum the Canton of Zurich public approved by a considerable majority creation of the so-called Zurich RER. The Canton itself voted credits of SwFr 523 million towards the infrastructure, leaving the SBB to bear SwFr 130 million in recognition of the scheme's side-benefit for other SBB traffics; rolling stock costs of SwFr 585 million have also been covered by the SBB.

The RER scheme provided for a new 11.5km cross-Zurich double-track line from a four-platform Museumstrasse underground station adjoining Zurich Hbf, passing beneath the Limmat and Sihl rivers, then veering north-east at Stadelhofen to junctions with existing lines at Dübendorf and Dietlikon. It unites existing Zurich suburban lines to create an integrated

Traffic (million)	1985	1986	1987	1988	1989
Freight tonnage	44·5	45·13	44·43	48·18	50·75
Freight tonne-km	7050	6966	6811	7502	8162
Passenger-km	9381	9325	10 680	10 804	11 034
Passengers carried	224·6	228·5	257·6	259·3	259·7

Finances (SwFr million)					
Expenditure	1985*	1986*	1987*	1988	1989
Personnel	2431	2502	2523·2	2644·9	2777
Materials and services	904	929	986·7	1058·3	1063
Depreciation	499	505	523·1	541·3	569
Financial charges	225	231	242·5	255·5	336
Major maintenance	85	82	66	96·1	113
On investment account	7	12	8·1	24·8	15
Contribution to state for use of infrastructure	—	—	218·5	135	102
Total	4151	4261	4568·1	4755·9	4975
Revenue					
Passengers	1191	1207	1262·3	1285·8	1370
Freight	1179	1179	1152·4	1179·3	1243
Federal compensation: regional passenger and piggyback freight	604	612	510	547·9	559
Support for infrastructure maintenance	—	—	794·5	883·2	950
Support for investment	NA	180·4	196·8	216·5	246
Other	808	840	675·4	685·4	677
Total	4151	3904	4591·4	4798·1	5045
Surplus (deficit)	281	357	23·3	42·2	70

* Costs and compensations reflect changed contract with state

Refurbished four-voltage ex-TEE train-set at Zurich Hbf on Milan-Winterthur 'Manzoni' EuroCity service *(John C Baker)*

Class Re 6/6 Bo-Bo-Bo and Geneva-Milan 'Cisalpin' EuroCity train on Rhône Valley main line near Aigle *(John C Baker)*

New first class car with 200 km/h operational capability for EuroCity service urban network. Several other infrastructure improvements have been executed in the RER area.

The RER service, embracing a network of some 380 km, was inaugurated in late May 1990. At the same time the Sihltal-Uetliberg Railway was extended to new platforms below the new Shopville commercial complex in the rebuilt Zurich main station.

Following a decision to raise platform heights rather than face the problem of vehicle design with mid-car entrances, the format of the Zurich RER train-sets was fixed on that of a 3200 kW Class 450 Type Re 4/4 V, three-phase motor locomotive forming a push-pull set with three bi-level cars of basically Netherlands Railways bi-level layout, with entrances above their air-sprung bogies. One of the cars is a driving trailer. The sets are arranged for multiple-unit operation in rakes of up to three offering a total seating of 1200.

ABB supplied all electrical equipment for the first 50 locomotives and 60 driving trailers and also the heating, ventilation and electrical services for all trailers. The latest three-phase ac motor technique, using induction motors and static converters with GTO thyristors, was chosen for the electric drives. Microprocessor technology is employed for the control systems. Maximum tractive effort is 240 kN. The mechanical parts of the 73-tonne Class Re 4/4 V locomotives have been supplied by the Swiss Locomotive and Machine Works (SLM), Winterthur. A feature of the mechanical part is that the bogies have drives using the SLM sliding bearing technique, which allows radial adjustment of the axles and hence optimum tracking.

Orders were placed with the Waggongruppe S-Bahn Zurich (Schindler Waggon, Pratteln, Flug- und Fahrzeugwerke, Altenrhein, Swiss Industrial Company, Neuhausen) for 90 S-Bahn bi-level coaches. A second series of 90 cars was ordered at the start of 1989.

In connection with the city's RER development the 20-year-old Zurich Hbf signalbox has been re-equipped and its area of control expanded. The new apparatus features automatic train describers and computerised storage of route-settings. A Deutsche Philips traffic monitoring system provides traffic controllers with computer aid in resolving problems of deviation from timetable.

The inaugural RER service comprised five routes taking in the underground cross-city line and seven more terminating in Zurich Hbf. Operation is complex because many of the routes share tracks with other traffic and convenient connections with IC services are deemed crucial.

In November 1989 Zurich Canton voters approved a contribution of SwFr 235 million to a further SwFr 444 million of infrastructure works to be completed by 1995. This will include three more double-tracking schemes, a flyover south of Effretikon, two new stations and signalling improvements. The outcome will be increased frequency on several routes.

Bi-levels for Basle and Geneva?

By the end of the century the SBB anticipates operation of a fleet of 140 bi-level train-sets of the Zurich type. By then negotiations for S-Bahn services taking in sections of the SNCF and DB at Basle, and of the SNCF at Geneva, should have borne fruit, and five prototype multi-voltage bi-level train-sets are likely to be running. Discussions continue with the SNCF on the project of Basle RER service that would take in Basle airport, which is just within French territory.

In 1989 Geneva published a public transport plan embracing an RER system, which the Geneva Canton would partly finance.

Traction and rolling stock

ASEA Brown Boveri and SLM were given an SwFr 80 million contract to develop and build the first 12 examples of a 6100 kW, 230 km/h, 20-tonne axleload locomotive capable of push-pull operation for the 'Bahn 2000' services. A further 12 were ordered in 1989.

To be classified Re 4/4 VI, or Class 460 in the new SBB scheme (see below), the locomotives will employ the three-phase ac propulsion technique developed by ABB with the locomotive body and bogie construction designed by SLM. Features of its electrical equipment include asynchronous traction motors, maintenance-free frequency converters with GTO thyristors, the MICAS programmable traction control system, interference-free fibre-optic transmission of control signals between the control electronics and the convertor unit, and also a diagnostics facility to enhance the locomotive's availability. Pinanfarina has been contracted for the exterior styling of the Re 4/4 VI.

Full-size mock-up of seating bay in new Panoramic car under construction in 1990

Class 450 pwer car propels RER bi-level train out of Zurich Hbf *(John C Baker)*

Model of Class Re 4/4 VI locomotive

Delivery of the first series would begin in June 1990 and be complete by mid-1991. The second series will have an ergonomically redesigned cab and microprocessor control of braking.

In 1990 the ABB/SLM consortium won the order for 75 6100kW locomotives for the prospective expansion of Gotthard route piggyback traffic (see above). The design will be derived from the Class 460 just described. The only other bidders were a Siemens-Krauss Maffei partnership offering a version of the DB Class 120.

The 19 new Mk IV restaurant cars now in service have a novel interior layout which raises seating capacity from the 48 of the four earliest prototypes to 56. On each side of the central gangway orthodox two-seat tables alternate with semi-circular five-seat tables. The cars operate with on-shore preparation (at a Geneva base) of vacuum-cooked dishes, re-heated on board the cars, to allow continuous meal availability during a journey. Unlike other Mk IV stock, these restaurant cars have air suspension bogies.

In 1989 the SBB decided to acquire a final batch of Mk IV cars; all first-class, the 30 vehicles would take the total Mk IV to 462 cars. At the close of the year delivery began from Schindler Wagon of 30 first- and 40 second-class EuroCity cars, a close relation of the Mk IV design but with modular component refinements and modifications essential for international service, including reinforced soundproofing, and electromagnetic brake and anti-wheel slide protection to permit 200 km/h operation. The SBB compartment cars of the 1960s and 1970s will be progressively rebuilt as saloons for other work. The SBB intends to form complete trains of the new EuroCity cars.

The last cars to be built on the basis of the Mk IV bodyshell will probably be 12 first-class 'Panorama' cars ordered in 1988. The design has a domed roof that peaks at a height of 4·28 m above rail. This allows the floor of the passenger saloon, approached by a slope from each end vestibule, to be raised to 1·7 m above rail level. Deep side windows follow the curve of the roof to within about 400 mm of its crown, for easy viewing of mountain scenery.

Class Ae 6/6 Co-Co and northbound freight at Momenthal *(John C Baker)*

From 1991 onwards SBB expects to take delivery of the first of a new generation of 'Bahn 2000' cars, designed for 230 km/h, probably aluminium-bodied to keep car weight to 42 tonnes tare and possibly fitted with a passive body-tilting system. Construction will be on a modular system. Internal layouts under consideration include family cars with playrooms and nursing mother compartments and saloon; and a business car with lounges, conference room, bar and a full range of office and conference equipment. The cars will be built by Schindler Waggon, but Design Triangle of the UK won the industrial design contract for the vehicles.

Orders for 15 'Bahn 2000' prototypes were placed in 1990. They would comprise three Type Apm first-class saloons, two Type Avm first-class saloon-compartment cars, eight Type Bpm second-class saloons, two Type Bm second-class cars incorporating space and WC for the handicapped, nursing mothers' compartment, children's playroom, telephone kiosk and minibar station, and two Type ADtm driving trailers. The control trailers were required to test a basic concept of

Electric locomotives

Class	New classifi-cation	Wheel arrange-ment	Line current	Rated output one-hour (kW)	Tractive effort (full field) Max (kN)	Continuous at (kN)	km/h	Max speed mph (km/h)	Wheel dia in (mm)	Weight tonnes	Length ft in (mm)	No in service 31.12.89	Year built	Builders: Mechanical parts	Electrical equipment
Ae 6/6 (11 401-02)	610	Co-Co	15 kV 16⅔ Hz	4300	324	209	74	78 *(125)*	49⅝ *(1260)*	124	60′ 4½″ *(18 400)*	120	1952-53	SLM	ABB; Oerlikon
(11 403-50)				4300	392	221	70	78 *(125)*	49⅝ *(1260)*	120	60′ 4½″ *(18 400)*		1955-60	SLM	ABB; Oerlikon
(11451-11520)				4300	392	221	70	78 *(125)*	49⅝ *(1260)*	120	60′ ½″ *(18 400)*		1962-66	SLM	ABB; Oerlikon
Re 4/4 I (10001-26)	410	Bo-Bo	15 kV 16⅔ Hz	1830	137	79	83	78 *(125)*	41 *(1040)*	57	48′ 2¾″ *(14 700)*	50	1946-48	SLM	ABB; Oerlikon
(10027-50)	411			1854	137	80	83	78 *(125)*	41 *(1040)*	57	48′ 10¾″ *(14 900)*		1950-51		Sécheron
Re 4/4 II (11101-106)	420	Bo-Bo	15 kV 16⅔ Hz	4700	255	170	100	87 *(140)*	48⅝ *(1260)*	80	48′ 6¾-50′11″ *(14 800-15 520)*	273	1964	SLM	ABB; Oerlikon; Sécheron
(11107-155)		Bo-Bo		4700	255	170	200	87 *(140)*	49⅝ *(1260)*	80			1967-68	SLM	ABB; Oerlikon; Sécheron
(11156-304)		Bo-Bo		4700	255	170	100	87 *(140)*	49⅝″ *(1260)*	80			1969-75	SLM	ABB; Oerlikon; Sécheron
(11305-49)		Bo-Bo											1981-83	SLM	ABB; Oerlikon
(11371-97)		Bo-Bo											1984-85	SLM	ABB; Oerlikon
Re 4/4 III (11354-11370)	430	Bo-Bo	15 kV 16⅔ Hz	4650	280	200	85	78 *(125)*	49⅝ *(1260)*	80	50′ 6¾″ *(15 410)*	17	1971	SLM	ABB; Oerlikon; Sécheron
Re 4/4 IV (10101-04)	440	Bo-Bo	15 kV 16⅔ Hz	4960	300	210	85	100 *(160)*	49⅝ *(1260)*	80	51′ 10″ *(15 800)*	4	1982	SLM	ABB
Re 4/4 IV	450	Bo-Bo	15 kV 16⅔ Hz	3000	240	NA	NA	80.8 *(130}*	NA	71	NA	13	1989	SLM	ABB
Re 6/6 (11601-689)	620	Bo-Bo-Bo	15 kV 16⅔ Hz	7850	394† 398	270 270	106* 104	87 *(140)*	49⅝ *(1260)*	120	63′4 ½″ *(19 310)*	89	1972/ 75-80	SLM	ABB Sécheron
Ae 3/6 I (10637-64-79-85)	396	2-Co-1	15 kV 16⅔ Hz	1560	147	86	65	68 *(110)*	63⅜ *(1610)*	93	48′ 5″ *(14 760)*	25	1925-27	SLM	ABB
(10690-11102)				1560	147	86	65	68 *(110)*	63⅜ *(1610)*	93	48′ 5″ *(14 760)*		1927-28	SLM	Oerlikon
Ae 4/7 (10901-72)	497	2-Do-1	15 kV 16⅔ Hz	2300	196	128	65	62 *(100)*	63⅜ *(1610)*	118	54′ 11¾″ *(16 760)*	107	1927-31		ABB (50);
(10974-002)				2300	196	128	65	62 *(100)*	63⅜ *(1610)*	123	56′ 1¼″ *(17 100)*		1931-34	SLM	Oerlikon (39); Sécheron (19)
(11003-27)				2300	196	128	65	2 *(100)*	63⅜ *(1610)*	118	54′ 11¾″ *(16 760)*		1931-34		
Ee 3/3 (16316-26)	930	C	15 kV 16⅔ Hz	428	88	56	27·5	2 *(40)*	41 *(1040)*	45	29′ 8¾″ *(9060)*	130	1928		
(16331-50)				428	88	56	27·5	25 *(40)*	41 *(1040)*	45	30′ 0¼″ *(9510)*		1930-31	SLM	ABB
(16351-76)				428	88	56	27·5	25 *(40)*	41 *(1040)*	45	31′ 11¾″ *(9150)*		1932-42		
16381-414)				502	98	61	29·6	31 *(50)*	41 *(1040)*	39	31′ 0¼″ *(9510)*		1944-47	SLM	ABB; Oerlikon; Sécheron
16421-30)				508	118	69	26·5	28 *(45)*	41 *(1040)*	45	31′ 0¼″ *(9510)*		1951 1956	SLM	ABB; Oerlikon;
(16431-36) (16440)				508	118	69	26·5	28 *(45)*	41 *(1040)*	45	31′ 0¼″ *(9510)*		1961 1962		Sécheron
(16441-60)				508	118	69	26·5	28 *(45)*	41 *(1040)*	44	31′ 0¼″ *(9510)*		1966	SLM	ABB; Oerlikon; Sécheron
Ee 3/3 II (16501-02)		C	2-current	506	132	69	26·5	28 *(45)*	41 *(1040)*	46	31′ 0¼″ *(9510)*	15	1957	SLM	ABB
(16503-04)				525	127	70	27	28 *(45)*	41 *(1040)*	46	31′ 0¼″ *(9510)*		1957	SLM	Oerlikon
(16505-06) (16511-19)				506	132	69	26·5	28 *(45)*	41 *(1040)*	52	30′ 8¾″ *(9420)*		1958 1962-63	SLM	Sécheron
Ee 3/3 IV (16551-60)		C	4-current	390	118	59	23·8	37 *(60)*	41 *(1040)*	48	32′ 8″ *(10 020)*	10	1962-63	SLM	Sécheron
Ee 6/6 (16801-02)		C + C	15 kV 16⅔ Hz	1008	235	137	26·5	28 *(45)*	41 *(1040)*	90	48′ 8¼″ *(14 840)*	2	1952	SLM	ABB; Sécheron
Ee 6/6 II (16811-20)	962	Co-Co	15 kV 16⅔ Hz	730	360	360	7·3	52 *(85)*	52 *(1260)*	107	58′ 6″ *(17 400)*	10	1980	SLM	ABB
Eem 6/6 (17001-04)		Co-Co	15 kV 16⅔ Hz	780/ 393‡	235	118	23·8/ 12†	40 *(65)*	41 *(1040)*	104	60′ 1″ *(17 875)*	4	1970-71	SLM	SAAS

Note-Series Ee 3/3 II operate on 15 kV 16⅔ Hz and 25 kV 50 Hz
Series 3e 3/3 IV operate on 15 kV 16⅔ Hz and 25 kV 50 Hz and on 1500 V and 3000 V dc
* New classifications have been reserved for forthcoming locomotives as follows:
450 Type Re 4/4 IV-Zurich S-Bahn locomotives
453 Possible three-voltage Re 4/4 V for Geneva and Basle S-Bahn projects
460 Type Re 4/4 VI-'Loco 2000'
462 Possible dual-voltage version of Re 4/4 VI
† Nos 11601-604 only
‡ On diesel motor

'Bahn 2000', the coupling of two independently-locomotive-powered push-pull train-sets in one formation over part of their itinerary.

In preparing its 'Bahn 2000' coaching stock, the SBB is to abandon its previous policy of 'cascading' superseded vehicles from IC through 'trains direct' to regional services. It is intended to equip all regional services with the latest type of 'Colibri' emu stock, and all city suburban services with bi-level train-sets of the Zurich S-Bahn type.

At the start of 1990 the SBB operated 701 electric locomotives, 232 electric power cars, 289 diesel locomotives and tractors, 934 tractors, 4496 passenger cars including 68 restaurant, 28 sleeping and 98 couchette cars. Freight wagons totalled 20 236, PTT-owned postal cars 609 and baggage cars 466; the last-mentioned included 10 ex-SNCF Corail baggage cars. Over 6700 privately-owned wagons were in use.

Delivery continued in 1989 of the so-called 'Colibri' RBDe 4/4 motor car-plus-driving trailer units. Each power car has thyristor-controlled motors with a total rating of 1680 kW and has regenerative braking. Maximum speed is 140 km/h. One bogie is equipped with electromagnetic brake and the unit's basic disc-and-shoe braking has a control device that regulates braking power according to vehicle load.

The SBB has bought seven refurbished DB Class 220 diesel-hydraulic locomotives for work train haulage where catenary is de-energised. These have been repainted in Swiss Federal livery and designed Class Am 4/4. In 1989 the SBB hired from the DB two Class 150 electric locomotives for work in the Basle harbour area, where they would release two Ae 6/6 for work elsewhere on the SBB.

New traction classification system

To suit today's computer-based data systems SBB traction, both locomotive and power car, has been given a new numerical classification. The new designations are indicated, along with the traditional, in the tables of this section.

Signalling and communications

The Siemens ZUB1100 ATP system has been selected and by 1996 it is to be applied to all main SBB routes, which involves equipment of 700 traction units and some 3500 signal locations. The latter plan will cover about 80 per cent of all block sections. First line to be equipped is the Zurich S-Bahn (see below).

With the aid of a Federal grant of SwFr 5 million, installation of track-to-train radio is being accelerated. The concept will be developed within the SBB's future traffic control framework of five higher-order operational centres and about 40 remote control centres at the major railway junctions. It will include means for communication with on-train staff in luggage vans as well as with traction unit cabs. In order that SBB locomotives may be reached abroad, or foreign locomotives within Switzerland, the new radio-communication system has to be compatible with that of UIC in a band between 457 and 468 MHz. It must also be able to handle encoded data, be extendable and possess tunnel antennae which will be able to serve the coming public railway telephone service, which will be independent of the train radio-communications facility. Technical execution has been entrusted to ABB. They are settting up the network, while Autophon AG, Solothurn, Switzerland, participates with supply of the mobile radio sets.

The main network will be sub-divided into area networks. From the central telephones in the operational control centres in Zurich, Lucerne, Lausanne, Biel and Bellinzona four-wire lines run to the telephones in the remote control centres and to the radio base stations spread along the main routes at intervals of 5 to 8 km. Completion of the whole network (secondary lines will be provided with simpler equipment) is planned for 1993.

In April 1989 the SBB commissioned its first fully-electronic interlocking at Chiasso in conjunction with layout revision covering the new Monte Olimpino Tunnel routing for Italian traffic. The contractor was Siemens. The scheme employs fibre-optic cabling as a protection against external electrical interference. At Arth-Goldau the SBB has been testing colour vdus as an operator aide; the train describer system also provides automatic route-setting.

Brünig line

The metre-gauge Brünig line, from Lucerne via Meiringen (reverse) to Interlaken, is a vital link between central Switzerland and the Bernese Oberland. Its route crosses the Brunig pass at a summit of 1002 m, which is approached from the Meiringen side by a gradient of 12 per cent and on the northern side, where the ascent is more gradual, on stretches of 10–11 per cent. This necessitates sections of Riggenbach rack totalling 9·28 km.

The Brünig traction fleet long comprised two Type HGe 4/4 I 1600 kW Bo-Bo locomotives built in 1954 and 16 Type Deh 4/6 930 kW six-axle motor luggage vans built in 1941-42. All were limited to 75 km/h, which is now a handicap on the easily-graded sections either side of the Brünig pass, as is a single motor luggage-van's limitation to a 60-tonne load on the rack sections. The line now has eight HGe 4/4 II Bo-Bos based on a general specification agreed with the BVZ, LSE and FO Railways (the FOB is taking three). These thyristor-controlled Type HGe 4/4 II have been built by SLM with Brown Boveri electrical equipment, have regenerative braking and, unlike the previous motor luggage-vans (in which the central two axles are exclusively for rack engagement), have their motored axles equipped with retractable rack engagement gear. Each axle is powered by a 483 kW motor (one-hour rating); maximum tractive effort with adhesion is 230 kN, with rack engaged 280 kN; and maximum speed with adhesion is 100 km/h, on rack 30 km/h uphill and 25 km/h downhill. An HGe 4/4 II can sustain 30 km/h with a 120-tonne trailing load on the rack.

Other Brünig rolling stock comprises 16 tractors of 70 to 260 kW, 119 passenger cars, 19 mail and baggage cars, and 173 freight wagons. Strikingly liveried with a reproduction of a popping champagne bottle top, a bar car created from an existing vehicle went into service in 1989.

With delivery of the new HGe 4/4 II locomotives a few of the Deh 4/6 power cars are being rebuilt without their central rack bogie as pure adhesion units to work solely regional trains on the level between Lucerne and Hergiswil, or Interlaken and Meiringen. The remainder will be withdrawn.

In the 1990s it is planned to order six or seven new power-car/trailer/control trailer sets for Lucerne-Giswil and Interlaken-Meiringen service

Intensification of Brünig service to hourly interval between Lucerne and Interlaken, and half-hourly between Lucerne and Giswil, Interlaken and Meiringen, is under consideration. The proposals will entail double-tracking from Meiringen to Brienz and from Lucerne to Hergiswil.

Articulated low-floor 'Jumbo' wagon of Swiss intermodal company Hupac carrying 9ft 6in ISO containers *(G Freeman Allen)*

New Brünig line Class HGe4/4 II locomotive at Meiringen on Interlaken-Lucerne train *(John C Baker)*

Diesel locomotives

Class	New classification	Wheel arrangement	Transmission	Rated power (hourly) kW	Tractive effort Max kN	Tractive effort Continuous at kN	Tractive effort Continuous at km/h	Max speed km/h	Wheel dia in (mm)	Total weight tons	Length ft in (mm)	No in service 31.12.89	Year first built	Builders Mechanical parts	Builders Engine & type	Builders Transmission
Am 4/4 (ex-DB) Cl 220	843	B-B	Hyd	1093	239	149	26·4	140	(950)	80	(18 470)	4	1956-59	Krupp	Krauss-Maffei	Maybach
Bm 4/4 II (18451-52)	842	Bo-Bo	Elec	611	112	59	37·5	75	41 (1040)	66	48'10¾" (14 900)	2	1939	SLM	Sulzer	ABB
Bm 4/4 18401-26	840	Bo-Bo	Elec	620	216	128	17·5	75	41 (1040)	72	41'6" (12 650)	26	1960-65	SLM	SLM	Sécheron
(18427-46)		Bo-Bo	Elec	620	216	128	17·5	75	41 (1040)	72	43'1¾" (13 150)	20	1968-70	SLM	SLM	Sécheron
Bm 6/6 (18501-14)		Co-Co	Elec	956	334	186	18·5	75	41 (1040)	106	55'9½" (17 000)	4 10	1954-55 1960-61	SLM	Sulzer	ABB; Sécheron
Em 3/3 (18801-06)	930	C	Elec	326	118	69	17	65	41 (1040)	49	32'10½" (10 020)	6	1959-60	SLM	SLM	ABB; Sécheron
(18807-41)			Elec	326	124	69	17	65	41 (1040)	49	32'10½" (10 020)	35	1962-63	SLM	SLM	ABB; Sécheron
Am 6/6 (18521-26)	863	Co-Co	Elec	1440	393	393	13·2	85	49 (1260)	111	57'1" (17 400)	6	1976	Thyssen-Industrie AG Henschel	Chantiers de l'Atlantique	ABB
Em 6/6 (ex-Eem 6/6)		C9-Co	Elec	393	235	118	12·0	65	41 (1040)	104	58'7" (17 870)	2	1971	SLM	SLM	SAAS SSB; ABB

728 **RAILWAY SYSTEMS** / Switzerland

Electric railcars or multiple-units

Class	New classification	Cars per unit	Line voltage	Motor cars per unit	Motored axles per motor car	Rated output (kW) per motor (hourly)	Max speed km/h	Total weight tonnes (M-motor T-trailer)	Total seating capacity	Total length mm	No in service 31.12.89	Year first built	Builders Mechanical parts	Builders Electrical equipment
RAe 2/4		1	15 kV	1	2	197	125	41	60	25 200	1	1935	SLM	ABB/MFO/SAAS/SBB
RAe/TEE	506	6	15 kV ac 25 kV ac 3 kV dc 1·5 kV dc	1	6	577·5	160	296	168	149 760	4 1	1961 1967	SIG	MFO
RABDe 12/12	511	3	15 kV	3	4	204	125	170	200	73 300	18	1965-67	SWP/FFA	SAAS/ABB
RABDe 8/16	512	4	15 kV	2	4	281	125	149	278	100 000	4	1976	SWS/SWP/SIG	SAAS
RBDe 4/4 + BT	532	2	15 kV	1	4	412	140	M 70 T 37	128	50 000	46	1984-88	FFA/SIG/SWP/SWA	ABB
RBe 4/4 (1401-06) (1407-82)	524	1	15 kV	1	4	497	125	64 68	64	23 700	6 75	1959-60 1963-66	SIG/SWS	ABB/MFO
Be 4/6	526	1	15 kV	1	4	157	90	72	56	20 000	9	1923-27	SIG/SWS	SAAS
Bde 4/4	536	1	15 kV	1	4	294	110	57	40	22 700	31	1952-55	SLM/SWP	ABB/MFO/SAAS
Bde 4/4 II + BT	533	2	1·5 kV dc	1	4	272	100	M 49 T 28	119	46 400	2	1956-57	SWS	SAAS
De 4/4	546	1	15 kV	1	4	201	75	58	–	15 180	10	1927-28	SIG/SWS	SAAS

Berne-Lötschberg-Simplon Railway (BLS)

Genfergasse 11, 3001 Berne

Telephone: +41 31 221182
Telex: 92238339
Telefax: +41 31 227027/910 5442

Manager: Martin Josi
Secretary: Heinrich Barben
Commercial Manager: Mathias Tromp
Traffic Manager: Fritz Krähenbüh
Traction and Workshops Manager: Kurt Müri
Production Manager: Franz Kilchenmann
Finance and Planning: Werner Dauwalder
Chief Engineer, Construction: Urs Graber

Route length: 115 km (BLS only); 130 km (other Group railways)
Electrification: 245 km at 15 kV 16⅔ Hz ac

Upon completion of the BLS main line from Frutigen through the Lötschberg Tunnel to Brig in 1913, a number of minor railways in the area, known as the 'Berne Decree Railways' and worked under special guarantees from the Canton of Berne, were incorporated in the Lötschberg system, though each retained separate financial and operating identity. As a result of this, subsequent amalgamations and other accessions to the Group, the BLS embraces the Spiez-Erlenbach-Zweisimmen Railway (SEZ), Gürbetal-Berne-Schwarzenburg Railway (GBS) and Berne-Neuchâtel Railway (BN). Rolling stock of these four companies and the BLS is pooled, but its use is recorded and each company correspondingly remunerated. The group also owns 18 Lake Thun and Lake Brienz ships and the Interlaken bus company, Auto AG.

The BLS system covers the main lines from Thun to Spiez and Interlaken, and from Spiez via the Lötschberg Tunnel to a junction with the Swiss Federal Railways at Brig. The Lötschberg route is one of Europe's most vital international rail links. BLS also owns the link through the Grenchenberg tunnel between Lengnau and Moutier (MLB), which forms part of the shortest route between Geneva and Basle.

Lötschberg base tunnel decision

The Federal Council's NLFA transalpine tunnel decision of 1989 (see SBB entry) has provided for construction of both Gotthard and Lötschberg base tunnels, but in the latter case subject to EEC withdrawal of pressure for a 40-tonne highway truck transit corridor through Switzerland to Italy. Earlier proposals for a Lötschberg base tunnel reaching all the way from the Spiez environs to Visp have been dropped in favour of a 28·4 km tunnel running from the neighbourhood of Kandergrund to a junction with the SBB's Rhone Valley main line at Raron.

Like the Gotthard base tunnel, the Lötschberg will have clearance for piggybacked 4·2 m-high lorries, which will also be able to thread the Simplon Tunnel following the latter's track lowering and equipment with a rigid traction current contact system (see SBB entry). Much of the cost of the Lötschberg scheme will be remunerated by road transport taxation. Plans for a Lötschberg road tunnel have been dropped.

In the meantime the existing Lötschberg Tunnel is to be adapted to clear piggybacked 4 m-high lorries and double the Swiss transalpine rail piggyback capacity by the mid-1990s. This is to be done by gauntleting a third track within one of the tunnel's present pair and nearer the bore's crown. To avoid modifying the catenary, this third track will be usable only by locomotives with an extra, off-centre pantograph to draw current from existing wires. Federal funds of SwFr 125 million have been made available to fit the BLS route for piggyback traffic, which it does not presently carry, but though it was hoped to complete this interim scheme by 1994, in early 1990 the government was not releasing the funds until it had EEC agreement to retention of the country's 28-tonne highway truck limit.

To minimise interference with other tracks, the tunnel's third track will be used only at night, when it is planned to run seven 30-car trains each way over the BLS between Basle and Italy. In 1989 the BLS began study of alternative four- and six-axle locomotive concepts for this and ultimate base tunnel service. Given pressure of rising freight traffic on traction resources at the start of 1990, it was possible that an order for six or eight locomotives might be placed later in the year.

After completion of the base tunnel and improvements of the Simplon route (see SBB entry) EuroCity journey time from Basle to Milan is forecast to come down from 5¼ hours to 3 hours 10 minutes. If and when the SBB and SNCF discussions on creation of a new TGV connection from Macon/Bourg-en-Bresse in France to Satigny, on the outskirts of Geneva, bear fruit and the present drastically speed-limited Paris-Geneva TGV route via Amberieu and Culoz is bypassed, multi-voltage TGVs could connect Paris and Milan in less than six hours.

SBB Class Re 4/4 IV heads away from Spiez with the Brig-Dortmund 'Lötschberg' EuroCity train (John C Baker)

A BLS Re 4/4 enters Kandersteg from the Lötschberg Tunnel with the Brig-Frankfurt 'Matterhorn' Euro-City (John C Baker)

BLS Type Ae 8/8 Bo-Bo+Bo-Bo heads a southbound freight through Kandersteg (John C Baker)

Lötschberg auto shuttle development

In 1989 the BLS started enlargement of its Goppenstein terminal and ordered from Waggonfabrik Talbot 20 new car-carriers to increase the hourly capacity of its Lötschberg Tunnel auto-carrier push-pull shuttle from 450 to 550 vehicles. Also ordered, from Schindler Waggon, were four driving trailers based on the latest BDt design, but with half their body laid out to accommodate motor-cycles. Total cost of the project will be SwFr 50 million.

The Waggonfabrik order, delivery of which was to be made in late 1990 and early 1991, comprises four drive on/drive off wagons, four ramp wagons and 20 intermediate low-floor wagons. For the last-mentioned Talbot evolved to BLS request a new two-axle 520 mm diameter-wheel bogie, which lowers the wagon floor to 650 mm above rail. Hence the need of intermediate

Switzerland / RAILWAY SYSTEMS

ramp wagons to lower the driveway from the 1275 mm height of the loading platforms to that of the train's central wagons.

In 1989 BLS operated four 16-carflat and two 10-carflat shuttle trains in a base service, with a reserve of two 14-carflat trains for peak demand. The ultimate potential is transport of 700 road vehicles an hour, subject to Federal investment of SwFr 110 million in terminal enlargement, resignalling and two additional shuttle trains with their locomotives and spare vehicles.

Carryings on this service have steadily risen since the provision of Federal subsidy that has halved the tolls charged to users of this and the other transalpine tunnel auto shuttles. In 1989 the Lötschberg service carried 1.1 milion vehicles, 12 per cent more than in 1988. From May 1990 the number of Kandersteg-Brig workings was being reduced to meet the demand for more Kandersteg-Iselle services taking in the Simplon as well as the Lötschberg tunnel.

Traffic (BLS only) (million)

	1986	1987	1988
Freight tonnes	4·291	4·194	4·568
Freight tonne-km	209·85	211·667	247·412
Passenger journeys	8·07	8·850	9·037
Passenger-km	197·53	221·694	228·025

International freight set new record levels in 1989, boosted particularly by intermodal and steel industry traffic. In concert with the SBB, some unit freight trains were taken over from the Gotthard route, including hauls of paper and cellulose from Scandinavia to Italy.

Mixed gauge to Interlaken

The BLS and SBB have agreed in principle the necessary measures to fulfil the metre-gauge MOB's ambition to operate its 'Panoramic Express' from Montreux through to Lucerne. It remained at the start of 1990 to obtain secure Federal funding for installation of mixed gauge from the MOB's terminal at Zweisimmen over the BLS branch from there to Spiez, and on to Interlaken Ost, where the train would pass to the SBB's metre-gauge Brünig line to accommodate the metre-gauge. The cost of laying the extra rail has been put at SwFr 45 million. Double that sum would be needed were it deemed essential to provide dual-voltage traction units to work the whole itinerary unchanged.

BLS Finances (SwFr 000)

Revenue	1986	1987	1988
Passengers	77 459	83 167	83 878
Freight, parcels and mail	42 182	41 127	43 553
Other	63 339	68 200	73 283
Total	188 98	192 494	200 714
Expenditure			
Staff expenses	122 832	123 559	127 142
Materials and services	46 604	48 604	50 703
Depreciation	19 526	18 832	31 104
Financial charges	316	1 419	656
Total	189 278	192 404	200 105

Traction and rolling stock

In 1989 BLS (including BN, SEZ and GBS) operated 52 electric locomotives, 10 electric shunters, nine diesel-electric shunters, 27 diesel shunters, 35 electric railcars, 36 control trailers, 203 passenger cars (including two restaurant cars), 29 baggage cars and 186 freight wagons (including 118 Lötschberg Tunnel car-carrying shuttle cars).

Delivery began from Schindler in late 1990 of a further 14 Mk IV cars, which would raise BLS stock of these vehicles to 26.

Double-tracking complete in 1990

At the start of 1990 the BLS was in the final stages of a 10-year programme to complete the double-tracking of the 84 km Lötschberg main line. In 1976 the Swiss Parliament voted credits of SwFr 620 million for the project, supplemented by SwFr 220 million in 1983, to cater for growing transalpine traffic and to equate the route's capacity with that of the Gotthard line (11 million tonnes).

Starting in June 1979, the work has been completed in stages. It has included driving an additional single-track tunnel at the approach to Spiez, the Hondrich (length 1·7 km), and another, the Mittalgraben (length 3 km) in the Lonza gorge. The existing tunnels were not built but completely finished off for a second track when built, and 20 tunnels with an aggregate length of 10·2 km had to be enlarged. A total of 19 new bridges and viaducts have been needed, including a second, 265 m Kander viaduct near Frutigen, and a new 85 m single-span bridge over the Rhône at Brig.

To step up the traction current supply for the line's doubled operating capacity, the BLS has been connected with the Swiss Federal Railway's 15 kV system at each end of the route.

In November 1990 the project would be fully completed with commissioning of its remaining two stages on the south side of the tunnel, Ausserberg-Lalden and Goppenstein-Hohtenn. Until the end of 1991, however, the double track would not be usable without restraint, as there was work to be done on the tunnel and avalanche shelter clearances surrounding the original track.

With both tracks in full use the route's daily operating capacity will be 68 passenger and 124 freight trains.

The route can now accept 22·5-tonne axleloads and piggybacked road trailers of 4 m height. Maximum permissible speed remains 80 km/h between Frutigen and Brig, but 125 km/h through the Lötschberg Tunnel. Ruling gradient on both approaches to the tunnel is 2·7 per cent.

The doubled Lötschberg route is signalled for reversible working throughout. When stations are closed it is remotely controlled from three centres, at Spiez, Kandersteg and Goppenstein. Track-to-train radio is now operational between Thun and Goppenstein.

Frutigen station has been rebuilt and that at Spiez is to be both reconstructed and enlarged. Spiez is also to have a new signalling centre.

Berne-Thun upgrading

The Berne-Thun section of the BLS is potentially one of the best-aligned high-speed stretches in Switzerland. In a SwFr 86·7 million programme its 20·8 km from Gümligen to Thun is being made fit for 160 km/h. The work involves complete renewal of the track, easing of four curves, strengthening of 52 bridges, station improvements, and resignalling for two-way working on each track. The work was sufficiently advanced for three pairs of Berne-Brig trains to be scheduled for 160 km/h between Gümligen and Wichtrach from the start of the 1989 summer timetable. This required their haulage by SBB Class Re 4/4 IV locomotives.

Track (BLS only)
Rail
SBB IV (UIC 54E), 54 kg/m
Cross ties (sleepers): Timber and concrete
Thickness: 150 mm timber, 235 mm concrete
Spacing: 1666/km

Brig-Kandersteg auto-carrier shuttle passes Hohtenn, on the southern climb to the Lötschberg Tunnel (John C Baker)

Two BLS Type Re 4/4 enter Spiez with a northbound intermodal train (John C Baker)

A BLS Type RBDe 4/4 railcar set leaves Spiez for Interlaken. (John C Baker)

RAILWAY SYSTEMS / Switzerland

Fastenings
Timber: Ke (bolted spring clips SKL 3)
Minimum curvature radius
Lötschberg line: 280 m

Other lines: 220 m
Max gradient
Lötschberg line: 2·7%
Other lines: 1·5%

Max axleload
Lötschberg line: 22·5 tonnes
Other lines: 20 tonnes

Electric locomotives

Class	Wheel arrangement	Line voltage	Rated output continuous	Max speed	Weight	No in service 1989	Year first built	Builders Mechanical parts	Electrical equipment
Re 4/4	Bo-Bo	15 kV ac	4990 kW	140 km/h	80 tonnes	35	1964	SLM	ABB
Ae 4/4	Bo-Bo	15 kV ac	2940 kW	125 km/h	80 tonnes	4	1944	SLM	ABB
Ae 6/8	1 Co-Co 1	15 kV ac	4400 kW	100 km/h	140 tonnes	4	1939	Breda, SLM	SAAS
Ae 8/8	Bo-Bo + Bo-Bo	15 kV ac	6470 kW	125 km/h	160 tonnes	5	1959	SLM	ABB
Ce 4/4	B-B	15 kV ac	735 kW	65 km/h	64 tonnes	3	1920	SLM	ABB
Ee 3/3	C (shunter)	15 kV ac	450 kW	40 km/h	38 tonnes	1	1943	SLM	SAAS

Electric railcars

Class	Cars per unit	Line voltage	Motor cars per unit	Motored axles per motor car	Rated output kW per motor	Max speed km/h	Weight tonnes per car	Total seating capacity	Length per car mm	No in service 1989	Rate of acceleration m/s²	Year first built	Builders Mechanical parts	Electrical equipment
Be 4/4	1*	15 kV ac	1	4	370	120	68	60	23 700	3	0·6	1953	SIG	SAAS
De 4/5	1	15 kV ac	1	4	290	90	70	†	20 900	1	NA	1929	SLM, SIG	SAAS
ABDe 4/8	2	15 kV ac	2	2	180	110	42·5	140	23 400	3	NA	1945	SIG	SAAS
ABDe 4/8	2*	15 kV ac	2	2	290	125	49·5	134	23 730	3	0·6	1954	SIG	ABB, SAAS
ABDe 4/8	2*	15 kV ac	2	2	290	125	49·5	132	23 650	2	0·6	1957	SIG	ABB, SAAS
ABDe 4/8	2*	15 kV ac	2	2	290	125	51	122	23 900	5	0·6	1964	SIG	ABB, SAAS
RBDe 4/4	1*	15 kV ac	1	4	400	125	69	55	25 000	18	0·8	1982	SIG, SWS, SWP	ABB

* Most of these railcars are operated with additional trailers (some driving) as three- or four-car emus
† Baggage car, 21 m² loading area

Appenzell Railway (AB)
Appenzeller Bahn

Bahnhofplatz 10, 9100 Herisau

Telephone: +41 71 51 1060
Telefax: +41 71 52 3040

Director: Martin Vogt

Gauge: 1000 mm
Route length: 59 km (5 km of rack rail)
Electrification: 59 km at 1·5 kV dc

The railway runs from Gossau, on the Swiss Federal St Gallen-Zurich main line, to Herisau, Appenzell and Wasserauen, in the Säntis mountain area, and attains a summit of 903 m above sea level at Gonten. It operates one steam, one electric and one diesel locomotive, three electric train-sets, 20 electric motor cars, 53 trailers (one including a buffet), one diesel-electric railcar and 112 freight wagons. In 1990 AB was contemplating purchase of four two-car train-sets, four rack-equipped trailers and a De 4/4 motor baggage van.

Recent developments include installation of Integra CTC over 25 km from Gossau to Appenzell.

In December 1988 it merged with the neighbouring St Gallen-Gais-Appenzell-Alstätten Railway. The resultant group became 10th for size in the league table of Swiss railways.

St Gallen-Gais-Appenzell-Alstätten Bahn train at Appenzell *(John C Baker)*

Rail type: 36 kg/m
Sleepers: Metal, spaced 1600/m
Max gradient: 3·7%

Minimum curve radius: 30 m
Max axleload: 13 tonnes

Electric railcars or multiple-units

Class	Cars per unit	Line voltage	Motor cars per unit	Motored axles per motor car	Rated output (kW) per motor	Max speed km/h	Weight tonnes per car (M-motor T-trailer)	Total seating capacity per car (M-motor T-trailer)	Length per car mm (M-motor T-trailer)	No in service 1989	Rate of acceleration m/s²	Year first built	Builders Mechanical parts	Electrical equipment
BDe 4/4' + ABt	2 (3)	1500 V	1	4	205	75	M 36 T 16	M 39 T 54	M 18 730 T 19 160	3	0·4	1986	FFA/SIG	ABB
ABe 4/4'	1	1500 V	1	4	113	65	34	52	16 700	2	0·3	1933	SIG	MFO
ABe 4/4"	1	1500 V	1	4	127	65	35	51	18 000	2	0·3	1949	SIG	MFO
BDe 4/4'	1	1500 V	1	4	130	75	37	32	18 900	2	0·4	1968	FFA	MFO
De 4/4	1	1500 V	1	4	130	65	32·5	—	13 000	1	0·4	1966	AB/FFA	MFO/AB
ABDeh 4/4'	1	1500 V	1	4	2 × 220	40	40	45	14 950	4	0·3	1931	SIG/SCM	ABB
ABDeh 4/4"	1	1500 V	1	4	4 × 118	55	36	38	15 800	3	0·3	1953	SLM	ABB
BDeh 4/4 + ABt	2 (3)	1500 V	1	4	4 × 205	65	M 44,5 T 14	M 40 T 43	M 17 410 T 17 100	5	0·4	1981	FFA/SCM	ABB

Bernese Oberland Railways (BOB)
Berner Oberland-Bahnen, Wengernalp-Bahn (WAB) and Jungfraubahn (JB)

3800 Interlaken

Telephone: +41 36 22 52 52
Telefax: +41 36 22 52 94

Director: Dr Roland Hirni
Chief of Operations: Christian Balmer
Chief of Traction & Workshops: Dr Hans Schlunegger
Chief Commercial Officer: Karl Schurter

The Group comprises the following railways:
Berner Oberland-Bahnen. Operates 24 route-km of metre-gauge from Interlaken Ost to Lauterbrunnen and Grindelwald, electrified at 1·5 kV dc. Sections of route employ Riggenbach rack to cope with maximum gradients of 1 in 11. A steam locomotive, privately owned, is operated on special excursions.

The railway also operates the 7·3 km, 800 mm-gauge, Riggenbach rack Schynige Platte mountain railway (SPB) starting from Wilderswil, which is electrified at 1·5 kV dc, and the Bergbahn Lauterbrunnen (BLM). The BLM comprises a cable funicular from Lauterbrunnen to Grütschalp and a metre-gauge line along the rim of the Lauterbrunnen valley's western wall from Grütschalp to Mürren.

The BOB's most modern rolling stock is three ABeh 4/4 II 43-tonne motor coaches and matching BDt control trailers. Each motor coach is powered by four newly-designed BBC Brown Boveri 314 kW series-wound dc motors. Another innovation is the braking system for direct-coupled dc motors, which is a combined regenerative and resistance brake with automatic changeover according to conditions in the supply system. The added control functions are performed by the BBC MICAS programmable system. Maximum speed is 70 km/h.

BOB records some 1.6 million passenger journeys a year.

A new signalling centre at Zweilütschinen, junction of the Lauterbrunnen and Grindelwald lines, now controls the whole line and its intermediate passing stations from Wilderswil, first station out of Interlaken, to the two termini.

In 1989 the BOB planned realignments between Wilderswil and Zweilütschinen and a longer loop in advance of the latter station. Completion would save 4 minutes of journey time and save two train-sets.

Wengernalp-Bahn (WAB). An 800 mm-gauge line, running from Grindelwald and Lauterbrunnen to Kleine Scheidegg, 2060 m above sea level and immediately below the Jungfrau mountain chain. It is electrified at 1·5 kV dc, and employs Riggenbach rack throughout.

WAB's latest rolling stock is four two-car Type BDhe 4/8 two-car sets and a matching control trailer by SLM/ABB. Each set has a continuous rating of 804 kW, a tare weight of 42·4 tonnes and seating for 64, with a total passenger capacity of 200. The units are designed for mu working up to a maximum formation of two twin-units and the control trailer. Features of the units include a transversal mounting of motors in relation to the bogie and microprocessor control of the regenerative braking.

The WAB records some 3.25 million passenger journeys a year.

Jungfraubahn (JB). This metre-gauge line, starting from Kleine Scheidegg, tunnels through the Jungfrau range to attain the highest altitude of any European railway at Jungfraujoch, 3454 metres above sea level on the ridge between the Jungfrau and Mönch mountains. It employs the Strub rack system and is electrified at 1100 V 50 Hz three-phase ac. A new station and 700-seater restaurant, replacing the hotel destroyed by fire in 1972, was opened at Jungfraujoch in 1988.

The Jungfraubahn records some 800 000 passenger journeys a year. In 1990 the BOB ordered for it four new two-car train-sets.

The Group also operates two other rope-worked funiculars, the Harderbahn at Interlaken and the Allmendhubel at Mürren.

BOB Railways

Railway	BOB	SPB	WAB	JB	BLM
Route-length	23·6 km	7·3 km	19·2 km	9·3 km	5·7 km
Max gradient	12%	25%	25%	25%	60%
Minimum curve radius	100 m	60 m	60 m	100 m	40 m
Steam locomotives	–	1	–	–	–
Electric locomotives	2	10	9	5	–
Electric railcars	73	–	28	10	4
Diesel tractors	2	–	–	–	–
Passenger cars	41	22	39	20	–
Baggage cars	10	–	–	–	–
Freight wagons	29	6	46*	15	4
Service vehicles	4	1	13	3	2

* Excluding ski-transporters

New WAB power cars and trailers en route from Grindelwald to Kleine Scheidegg; mountain in background is the Wetterhorn (John C Baker)

New BOB Type ABeh 4/4 II power car heads a Lauterbrunnen-Interlaken train towards Wilderswil (John C Baker)

BOB train at Lauterbrunnen; Jungfrau mountain on left background (John C Baker)

Bodensee-Toggenburg Railway (BT)
Bodensee-Toggenburg-Bahn

Bahnhofplatz 1a, 9001 St Gallen

Telephone: +41 71 23 19 12
Telefax: +41 71 23 19 52

General Manager: Walter Dietz

Gauge: 1435 mm
Route length: 65·9 km
Electrification: 65·9 km at 15 kV 16⅔ Hz ac

The BT is a concessionary undertaking, with just over 40 per cent of its capital owned by the Federation, 34·5 per cent by the Cantons of St Gallen, Thurgau and Appenzell, and 21·7 per cent by local communities in these Cantons.

Single-track throughout, the BT is an important cross-country operator. Starting from the Swiss Federal station at Romanshorn on Bodensee (Lake Constance), it rejoins Swiss Federal tracks for the passage of St Gallen; then, resuming on its own track, the BT line runs to Wattwil and there branches to its terminus at Nesslau-Neu St Johann. From Wattwil, however, BT operates over Swiss Federal lines to the junction with the South Eastern Railway (Südostbahn) at Rapperswil, whereby it runs a through Romanshorn-Gallen-Lucerne service jointly with the other two railways. Ruling gradient on the BT-owned route is 2·4 per cent.

Traffic	1986	1987	1988
Freight tonnage	594 143	539 668	595 758
Freight tonne-km (000)	7249	6607	7663
Passenger-km (000)	75 012	80 747	80 301
Passenger journeys (000)	5155	5522	5385·7

In 1989 BT registered a 10 per cent increase in freight traffic, largely because of new and regular traffic from recently-installed private sidings. Passenger traffic had a more modest increase.

Finances (SwFr 000)			
Revenue	1986	1987	1988
Passengers and baggage	12 716·6	13 016·7	13 034·4*
Freight, parcels and mail	4281·3	4066·1	4451·0
Other income	3228·7	6283·1*	5703·6*
Compensation	2332·2	NA	2469·1
Total	22 558·8	23 365·96	23 189·0

* Including compensations

Expenditure			
Staff/personnel expenses	16 297·4	16 557·1	17 379·4
Materials and services	7309·5	7777·2	7636·7
Depreciation	5738	5538·2	5548·2
Financial charges	8·2	5·4	1·3
Total	29 353·1	29 877·9	30 565·6

Bahn 2000
Under the 'Bahn 2000' programme BT aims to make the Lucerne-St Gallen service hourly (it is presently two-hourly) and from 1989 to extend some trains to

RAILWAY SYSTEMS / Switzerland

Konstanz. The hope is that Lucerne-St Gallen journey time can be cut from the present 2 hours 14 minutes to perhaps 2 hours.

Under BT's SwFr 44 million 1988-92 investment programme, a 1·2 km section between St Gallen Haggen and Herisau has been double-tracked. This allows trains to pass each other on the move and suffice to obtain the extra 'Bahn 2000' capacity on BT territory. However, on the Lucerne express route the SBB section may need creation of double-track sections each side of the single-track Ricken Tunnel to break up the 11 km of single line between Wattwil and Kaltbrunn block posts.

Traction and rolling stock
BT's most modern traction is six 3000 kW Bo-Bo locomotives. Builders were SLM, with electrical equipment by ABB. These multi-purpose locomotives have three-phase induction traction motors and a four-quadrant input converter for single-phase ac input at 15 kV 16⅔ Hz. GTO thyristors are used with pulse transmission by means of fibre-optics for the traction converters of traditional BBC oil-immersed design. Microprocessors provide control, protection and diagnoses at all control levers.

In 1989 the railway ordered six trailers for its RABDe 4/12 units, to increase set formats from three to four cars, starting in 1990. In early 1990, with Federal, Cantonal and local support, orders worth SwFr 25 million were placed for nine passenger cars of the SBB's Mk IV type, to enter Romanshorn-Lucerne service in 1991. The SBB has agreed to take over these cars should a design more suited to BT requirements become subsequently available.

At the start of 1990 BT operated nine line-haul electric, one shunting electric, eight diesel shunting and one steam locomotive (for special use only), 11 electric train-sets, one additional electric railcar and 24 other passenger cars (including two automat-buffet cars).

Type of coupler in standard use: Screw
Type of braking in standard use: Oerlikon

Signalling
The entire BT route-mileage is signalled by Integra Domino panels at stations.

Track
Rail: 46 kg/m
Cross ties (sleepers): Wood, thickness 150 mm
  Steel, thickness 11 mm
Spacing: 1166/km
Fastenings: K and Ae (screw)
Minimum curvature radius: 183 m
Max gradient: 2·4%
Max axleload: 20 tonnes

Type RABDe 4/12 emu on 99 metre-high Sitter Viaduct near St Gallen

Electric locomotives

Class	Wheel arrangement	Line voltage	Rated output continuous	Max speed	Weight	No in service 1990	Year first built	Builders Mechanical parts	Electrical equipment
Line-haul Re 4/4	Bo-Bo	15 kV 16⅔ Hz	3000 kW	130 km/h	68 tonnes	4	1987	SLM	ABB
Line-haul	Bo-Bo	15 kV 16⅔ Hz	1180 kW	80 km/h	66 tonnes	3	1931	SLM	SAAS
Shunting	B	15 kV 16⅔ Hz	238 kW	65 km/h	28 tonnes	1	1966	SLM	MFO

Electric railcars or multiple-units

Class	Cars per unit	Line voltage	Motor cars per unit	Motored axles per car	Rated output per motor kW	Max speed km/h	Weight per car tonnes (M-motor T-trailer)	Total seating capacity	Length per car m (M-motor T-trailer)	No in service 1990	Year first built	Builders Mechanical parts	Electrical equipment
Emu	3*	15 kV 16⅔ Hz	1	4	425 kW	125 km/h	M 71 tonnes T 36/35 tonnes	183	M 25 m T 25·3 m	6	1982	FZA/SIG	BBC
Emu (semi-permanent)	4	15 kV 16⅔ Hz	1	4	526 kW	110 km/h	M 73 tonnes T 32/30 tonnes	247	M 23·7 m T 24·03 m	4	1960	SIG	BBC
Emu	3	15 kV 16⅔ Hz	2	2	295 kW	90 km/h	M 58 tonnes T 31 tonnes	159	M 23·7/22.85 m T 23·7 m	1	1932 (modernised 1985)	SIG	SAAS
Railcar	1	15 kV 16⅔ Hz	1	3	295 kW	80 km/h	M 68 tonnes	34	M 22 m	1	1938 (modernised 1981)	SIG	SAAS

* To be increased to 4 cars, starting in 1990.

Brig-Visp-Zermatt Railway (BVZ)
Brig-Visp-Zermatt Bahn

Nordstrasse 20, 3900 Brig, Valais

Telephone: +41 28 23 13 33
Telex: 473 332 bvz ch

Manager: R Perren
Permanent Way: O Häberli
Electrical Engineer: K Hächler
Traction: H Tribolet
Finance: A Zurbriggen
Commercial: A Schmid
Chief Traffic Superintendent: H Favre

Gauge: 1000 m
Route length: 44 km
Electrification: 44 km at 11 kV 16⅔ Hz ac

The BVZ is part adhesion, part Abt rack (over four sections of its ascent from Visp to Zermatt, where the ruling gradient is 12·5 per cent). Between Visp and Zermatt the railway climbs a height of 955 m. It was the first Swiss railway to equip its whole route with CTC; this is controlled from a centre at Brig, with which all BVZ traction units are in radio communication through transmitter-receivers.

Zermatt station: reconstruction of station buildings now follows 1985 completion of platform roofing

Zermatt-Brig train descending the rack-assisted grade into Stalden-Saas (*G Freeman Allen*)

New Täsch shuttle Type BDk trailer in Zermatt station: note provision of trolleys and ease of loading for passengers conveying luggage to or from Täsch car park

BVZ also controls the metre-gauge, Abt track Gornergrat Railway from Zermatt to Gornergrat.

Single-line throughout, with passing loops, the busiest section of the BVZ is the final 5·6 km from Täsch to Zermatt; the former is the limit of other transport to Zermatt, which is kept inaccessible to most road vehicles. Over this section the basic service of 14 Brig-Zermatt trains each way daily is supplemented by a push-pull shuttle, the latest cars of which are arranged for easy loading and unloading of the 300 luggage trolleys which BVZ provides for passengers transferring luggage between Zermatt and the Täsch car parks. These cars also have automatic powered doors. The BVZ car park at Täsch is toll-free. To enable 2000 passengers an hour to be moved each way between Täsch and Zermatt in peak seasons, this section is provided with an automatically-controlled passing loop at Kalter Boden.

The BVZ has executed a comprehensive rebuilding of Zermatt station. To safeguard winter operation the station has been provided with overall cover and at the same time had its three-track layout rebuilt to provide four platforms, one of which is reserved for the Täsch shuttle and has raised platforms to simplify luggage trolley loading and unloading. A fifth track is reserved for vehicle servicing and standing.

In 1990 BVZ acquired two more of the trailers of novel design employed on the Zermatt-Täsch shuttle service. This enabled the formation of a third train-set. Designed in conjunction with the builders, Stadler Fahrzeuge AG, these Type BDk cars simplify passenger loading and unloading of the luggage trolleys that are provided for motorists parking their cars at Täsch. Between bogies the floor is lowered to 415 mm above rail level. This inter-bogie area of 9·3 × 2·54 m is for up to 23 luggage trolleys and passengers who wish to stand with them; its wide entrances from the platform have automatic power-operated doors and retracting loading ramps. The floor areas above the bogies each have 20 seats. Each Zermatt-Täsch shuttle train-set includes two such cars.

BVZ records some 2·7 million passenger journeys and 40 million passenger-km annually, and around 60 000 tonnes and 1·9 million tonne-km of freight.

Traction and rolling stock

BVZ operates six 736 kW electric, two diesel-electric and one steam locomotive, four diesel tractors, five 833/1178 kW electric motor coaches, eight driving trailers for the Zermatt-Täsch shuttle, four motor luggage vans, 51 hauled passenger cars, four baggage and mail cars, and 80 freight wagons.

In 1988 BVZ placed orders for five HGe 4/4 II 1750 kW electric locomotives of the same design as that supplied to the Furka-Oberalp Railway and the Brunig line of the SBB. Delivery was to begin in May 1990.

Emmental-Burgdorf-Thun Railway (EBT)

Emmental-Burgdorf-Thun-Bahn

Bucherstrasse 1, 3400 Burgdorf

Telephone: +41 34 22 3151
Telex: 99 12 32

Director: Dr Charles Kellerhals
Vice-Director: Dr D Gfeller
Technical Manager: P Dübi
Operations Manager: H Bleuler
Commercial Manager: I P Hubmann
Financial Manager: R Rohn

Gauge: 1435 mm
Route length: 71·2 km and 5 km of common route with SBB
Electrification: 76·2 m at 15 kV 16⅔ Hz ac

The EBT Group of railways connects the north and south of the Canton of Berne, and also reaches out to the hinterland of Lucerne. It comprises the following railways, which are under common management: Solothurn-Moutier (SMB); Solothurn-Burgdorf-Hasle-Rüegsau-Konolfingen-Thun, and Hasle-Rüegsau-Langnau (EBT); and Ramsei-Sumiswald-Langenthal-Huttwil-Wolhusen (VHB). There are eight interchange stations with the Swiss Federal Railways (SBB).

Emmental-Burgdorf-Thun-Bahn (EBT)

Gauge: 1435 mm
Length: 71·2 km and 5 km of common route with SBB
Electrification: 76·2 m at 15 kV 16⅔ Hz ac

Traffic (000)	1986	1987	1988
Freight tonnage	2049	2015	2187
Freight tonne-km	27 286	26 695	28 241
Passenger-km	46 717	49 941	50 576
Passenger journeys	4276	4913	4969

Southern-Münster-Bahn (SMB)

Gauge: 1435 mm
Length: 21·5 km and 1·5 km of common route with SSB
Electrification: 23 km at 15 kV 16⅔ Hz ac

Traffic (000)	1986	1987	1988
Freight tonnage	191	174	171
Freight tonne-km	4094	3721	3642
Passenger-km	5735	6049	6273
Passenger journeys	553	583	602

Vereinigte Huttwil-Bahnen (VHB)

Gauge: 1435 mm
Length: 63·1 km and 0·9 km of common route with SSB
Electrification: 64 km at 15 kV 16⅔ Hz ac

Traffic (000)	1986	1987	1988
Freight tonnage	834	754	820
Freight tonne-km	20 427	18 027	19 020
Passenger-km	18 371	20 172	20 194
Passenger journeys	1779	1979	1970

Traction and rolling stock

At the start of 1989 the ETB group was operating 10 Class Be 4/4 locomotives of 1932/53 build, five Class Re 4/4 III locomotives of 1969/83 build, four Class De 4/4 motor luggage vans, eight RBDe 4/41 (1974-74), three BDe 4/4 II (1966) and 13 Class RBDe 4/4 II (1984-85) electric railcars; 26 BT control trailers; 38 other passenger cars and 18 electric and 15 diesel shunting tractors.

Replacement of the elderly Class Be 4/4 freight locomotives is the next investment priority in rolling stock renewal.

RBDe 4/4 II + BT unit on Biglen-Thun service enters Obersiessbach (*John C Baker*)

RAILWAY SYSTEMS / Switzerland

Class Re 4/4 III locomotive brings freight into Grosshöchstetten, on the Burgdorf-Thun line *(John C Baker)*

Furka-Oberalp Railway (FO)
Furka-Oberalp Bahn

Postfach 256, 3900 Brig, Valais

Telephone: +41 28 23 66 66
Telex: 47 33 66 foba ch
Telefax: +41 28 24 23 23

Director: Alfred Gasser
Deputy Director: Peter Maurer
Manager, Operations & Marketing: Stephan Rechsteiner
Commercial Services: Hugo Summermatter
Construction: Emil Frey

Gauge: 1000 mm
Route length: 122·2 km, of which 22.87 km Abt rack-equipped
Electrification: 122·2 km at 11 kV 16⅔ Hz ac

The FO is the important central link in a metre-gauge route, formed by a trio of railways, from Zermatt on the Canton Valais to St Moritz and Chur in the Canton Grisons, the itinerary of the famous 'Glacier Express'. The FO section extends from Brig, junction with the Brig-Visp-Zermatt, to Disentis, junction with the Rhaetian. The FO employs the Abt rack system to negotiate maximum gradients of 11 per cent. Minimum curvature radius is 70 m.

Furka Base Tunnel
In June 1982 the new 15·44 km Furka Base Tunnel was formally opened. It bypasses the former exposed FO section from Oberwald to Realp, which was mostly between 2000 and 3000 m above sea level and always had to be closed to traffic annually between October and April. There are two crossing loops in the otherwise single-track bore. With the tunnel's completion adhesion working became possible throughout from Oberwald to Andermatt, cutting 30 minutes from journey times between these two points. Oberwald station is the terminus of an accompanied car-carrying shuttle service to and from Realp, on the other side of the tunnel. The 'Glacier Express' is now an all-year-round service.

In 1989 the FOB faced an unexpected need to renew rail in the tunnel. Serious corrosion had been discovered, caused primarily by melting, salt-impregnated snow dripping from the undersides of autos on the car-carrier trains in winter. As a first remedy the FOB was substituting audio-frequency for dc track circuits, which instigate galvanic action. Meanwhile the car-carrier shuttle traffic rises to the extent that in 1990 FOB was considering acquisition of two more train-sets and enlargement of the Oberwald and Realp car terminals.

The Federal Council has approved the plans of an organisation which seeks to reopen the original Oberwald-Realp line through the Furka pass as a steam-worked tourist operation. This body hoped to start service between Realp and Furka in 1990, to reach Gletsch by 1993 and Oberwald by 1996.

Traffic
The 'Glacier Express' is now so popular in the global

A Deh 4/4 motor car brings a stopping train from Andermatt into Disentis-Muster *(John C Baker)*

Push-pull local from Andermatt arrives at Realp *(John C Baker)*

Type HGe 4/4 II locomotive and train including Panoramic car tourist market that three trains each way daily between Zermatt and the Grisons via the FO are so titled in the timetable. But in the summer season some or all of these are frequently duplicated, one train being reserved for package tour parties and its duplicate catering for other travellers. In 1988 FO recorded increased passenger-km totalling 39.7 million; freight traffic totalled 209.46 million tonne-km.

Traction and rolling stock

In 1989 the FO was operating two diesel-electric, one diesel-hydraulic and 11 electric locomotives including three new HGe 4/4 II, five Type BDeh 2/4 and 11 Type Deh 4/4 electric power cars, 64 passenger cars (including 19 driving trailers), four baggage cars, 30 car-carriers and 67 freight wagons, plus service stock including nine powered vehicles and 11 powered snowploughs. All locomotives are equipped for radio communication with control centres at Brig and Andermatt.

As the SBB builds up its fleet of new HGe 4/4 II locomotives for its Brünig line, the first three of the type which it acquired as prototypes will be transferred to the FO by the 1990s at the latest, to join the latter's trio of the initial build, which were delivered in 1986 (for details of the HGe 4/4 II, see SBB Brünig entry).

Since 1986 the FOB has acquired four 'Panoramic' saloons with deep side windows and also window panels in the eaves, built by Ramseyer and Jenzer of Biel. A feature of these vehicles is the solar panels that cover their roof crowns and through which all their electrical power is obtainable, even in cloudy weather and when the roofs get covered with winter snow. Employed in 'Glacier Express' services, the cars were in 1990 to have their bus-layout seating rearranged in bays around tables.

The FOB was planning in 1989 to purchase three new locomotives and 10 passenger cars.

Lucerne-Stans-Engelberg Railway
Luzern-Stans-Engelberg Bahn

6362 Stansstad, Switzerland

Telephone: +41 41 61 25 25

Director: Dr R Braun

Gauge: 1000 mm
Length: 25 km, of which 1·4 km on Riggenbach rack
Electrification: 25 km at 15 kV 16⅔ Hz ac

The railway combines a commuter service for the outskirts of Lucerne with access to alpine resorts and facilities of the Engelberg valley and the Titlis mountains. In 1989 the railway decided on a realignment of its final rack section that lifts it from Obermatt into the Engelberg basin, so as to ease the gradient from 25 to 12 per cent. This would allow both use of longer train-sets and through working to Engelberg of SBB locomotive-hauled Brünig trains from Interlaken. The project will entail driving a 4km tunnel.

The railway operates eight 745 kW railcars and 23 trailers that form eight three-car train-sets and three diesel shunters.

LSE Engelberg-Lucerne train arrives at Stans (John C Baker)

Mittel-Thurgau Railway (MThB)
Mittel-Thurgau Bahn

Schützenstrasse 15, 8570 Weinfelden

Telephone: +41 72 22 3322
Telex: 99 3170 Telefax: +41 72 22 34 23

Director: Peter Joss

Gauge: 1435 mm
Route length: 43 km
Electrification: 43 km at 15 kV 16⅔ Hz ac

The railway runs from Wil, on the Swiss Federal Zurich-St Gallen main line, northwards to the Swiss Federal station at Weinfelden, and thence to Kreuzlingen; from here Swiss Federal tracks are used to Konstanz. The company also operates the metre-gauge, 1·2 kV dc Frauenfeld-Wil Railway of 18 km length. In 1989 MThB recorded 1.3 million passenger journeys, 21.576 million passenger-km, 656 000 tonnes and 13.445 million tonne-km of freight tonne-km.

The Mittel-Thurgau employs two electric (one an Re 4/4 II) and three diesel locomotives, six electric power cars, four trailers and five other passenger cars. Four ex-DB 'Rheingold' vista-dome observation cars are employed for land-cruise train operations organised by its associated travel agency company.

Track is formed of 46 kg/m rail on timber or steel sleepers. Minimum curve radius is 240 m, maximum gradient 20 per cent and maximum permissible axle-loading 20 tonnes.

The metre-gauge Frauenfeld-Wil Railway operates six Be 4/4 motor cars, four driving trailers and 32 carriers for transport of 1435 mm-gauge wagons.

Frauenfeld-Wil Railway power car and trailer recently supplied by FFA

Montreux-Oberland Bernois Railway (MOB)
Chemin de Fer Montreux-Oberland Bernois

Rue du Lac 36, 1820 Montreux

Telephone: +41 21 964 55 11
Telex: 453 129
Telefax: +41 21 964 64 48

Managing Director: E Styger
Assistant Director: M Sandoz
Marketing Director: H Richenbacher
Traffic Manager: A Bertholet
Way and Works Manager: G Brideraux
Traction and Workshops Manager: J M Forclaz

Zweisimmen-Montreux 'Panoramic Express' at Chernex (John C Baker)

RAILWAY SYSTEMS / Switzerland

The MOB Group comprises two railways and the Territet-Glion and Les Avants-Sonloup 1000 mm-gauge funiculars. The two railways are:

Montreux-Oberland Bernois

Gauge: 1000 mm
Route length: 75·3 m
Electrification: 75·3 km at 860 V dc

The main line runs from Montreux via Gstaad to Zweisimmen. Its climb away from the Lake of Geneva to Les Avants and the 2·4 km Col de Jaman tunnel, with stretches of 7·3 per cent gradient, is the steepest line in Switzerland worked by adhesion. The summit is 1269 metres above sea level. From Zweisimmen a branch runs to Lenk.

'Panoramic Express'

In 1979 MOB introduced Western Europe's first air-conditioned narrow-gauge rolling stock. New dome-roofed bodies were mounted on existing underframes to form a 'Panoramic Express', which runs twice daily from Montreux via Zweisimmen to Lenk and back (a bar-car is featured on two of the workings). The demand for the service prompted construction of a second four-car set, introduced on a Zweisimmen-Montreux return service in May 1982.

Two more 'Panoramic' cars were added to stock in 1989, raising the total to 15, and a further three were planned. The existing 13 cars were to be re-bogied by SIG in 1989.

The MOB's 'Panoramic Express' was such a commercial success that in 1985 the MOB created a two-car, first-class-only push-pull variant, the 'Super-Panoramic Express', operated to and from Lenk at weekends and public holidays only, and between Montreux and Bulle (GFM) once weekly, which includes a bar and the driving trailer of which has a cockpit cab so that its front is freed to become a passenger observation saloon.

Extension to Lucerne

The Swiss Federal Council has approved MOB's ambition to extend the 'Panoramic Express' to Lucerne, through a gauge-mixing of the BLS lines from Zweisimmen through Spiez to Interlaken Ost, where the train would pass on to the SBB's metre-gauge Brünig line to Lucerne. The MOB hopes to launch the through service in 1993, but up to early 1990 the Federal government had yet to advance the money for the BLS mixed-gauging. The BLS, though it is an agreeable party to the project, will not meet any of the cost; nor will it be involved in provision of traction and rolling stock, which will be exclusively an SBB-MOB concern. In 1989 the MOB was contemplating purchase of four more GDe 4/4 locomotives, which unlike their predecessors would be capable of modification to dual 900V dc/15 kV 16 2/3 Hz ac voltage for the through working from Montreux as far as Meiringen on the Brünig. They could not travel further, because the Brünig is rack-fitted through the pass of the same name and the MOB has no rack sections.

The MOB envisages four trains each way daily, half provided by its own 'Panoramic' trains, half by the SBB, under the brandname of 'Golden Pass'. Meanwhile, the MOB, BLS and SBB have co-operated to integrate train connections and launch a Montreux-Lucerne 'Golden Pass' package by existing means.

Bar car of first-class-only 'SuperPanoramic Express' push-pull unit

First-class only 'SuperPanoramic Express' push-pull unit with driving trailer leading at Chernex (*John C Baker*)

Glion railcars at Montreux (*John C Baker*)

Traffic	1986	1987	1988
Total freight tonnage	63 780	80 941	100 432
Total freight tonne-km (million)	1·442	1·820	2·266
Total passenger-km (million)	44·433	47·364	50·529
Total passenger journeys (million)	2·170	NA	NA

Finance (SwFr 000)

Revenue	1986	1987	1988
Passenger and baggage	12 218·3	13 145·2	15 891
Freight, parcels and mail	1249·3	1374·4	1539·2
Other income	3825	4100·3	4253
Total	17 292·6	18 619·8	21 683·2

Expenditure			
Staff/personnel	17 099·54	17 371·66	18 726·6
Materials and services	7335	8442·3	10 401·3
Depreciation	2907·48	2908	3050·5
Financial charges	629·41	530·6	403·8
Total	27 971·43	29 252·57	32 618·3

Electric locomotives

Class	Wheel arrangement	Line current	Rated output one hour kW	Max speed km/h	Weight tonnes	No in service 1.1.90	Year first built	Builders Mechanical parts	Electrical equipment
De 6/6	Bo-Bo-Bo	860 V dc	1230	55	63	2	1931	SIG Neuhausen	ABB
GDe 4/4	Bo-Bo	860 V dc	1432	100	50	4	1983	SLM Winterthur	ABB

Diesel locomotives

Class	Wheel arrangement	Transmission	Rated power continuous kW	Max speed km/h	Total weight tonnes	No in service 1.1.90	Year first built	Builders Mechanical parts	Engine & type	Transmission
Gm 4/4	Bo-Bo	Elec	575	80	44	2	1976	Moyse	Poyaud	Moyse-Leroy-Sommer
Tm 2/2	B-B	Hyd	115	33	15	2	1953 (rebuilt 1983/84)	Klöckner-Humboldt-Deutz	Deutz	Voith-Turbo

Investment

The MOB will be one of the recipients of the SwFr 930 million credits voted by the Federal Council for private railway development for 'Bahn 2000' needs. The MOB will apply its share to rolling stock acquisition and installation of automatic train stop.

In 1989 the three Cantons served by the railway agreed to loan half the cost of a three-year, SwFr 44 million modernisation plan. The rest of the money would be furnished by the Federal government. The plan includes enlargement of the 1.3 km Jaman tunnel crowning the climb out of Montreux, to allow passage through it of 1435 mm-gauge wagons on transporter bogies; reconstruction of the Kaltenbrunnen viaduct to ease curve radius; catenary renewal between Zweisimmen and Saanen; reconstruction of Zweisimmen's installations; and purchase of the four GDe 4/4 locomotives mentioned above, six passenger cars and 16 more standard-gauge wagon transporter bogies.

Track

The railway uses 30, 36 and 46 kg/m rail fixed to wood, steel or concrete sleepers, spaced 1660/km, by Swiss Federal Railways Type A fasteners. Minimum curve radius is 45 metres, maximum gradient 7·3 per cent and maximum axleloading 13 tonnes. The maximum gradient is the steepest in Switzerland operated by pure adhesion.

Traction and rolling stock

The MOB operates eight electric and two diesel locomotives, two diesel shunting tractors, 17 motored passenger units, 52 passenger cars and 112 freight wagons, plus numerous service vehicles.

Montreux-Glion-Rochers-de-Naye Railway

Gauge: 800 mm
Route length: 10·36 m

The railway employs the Abt rack system to cope with a ruling gradient of 13 per cent.

Electric railcars or multiple-units

Class	No in service 1.1.90	Year first built or rebuilt (*)	Rated output one-hour hp	Max speed km/h	Tare weight tonnes	Length mm	Total seating capacity First-class	Total seating capacity Second-class	Notes
Be 4/4 5001-2	2	1976	600	80	32·00	16 810	–	48	
5003-4	2	1979	600	80	32·00	16 810	–	48	
ABDe 8/8 4001-4	4	1968	1200	70	60·00	33 400	18	68	
BDe 4/4 3001	1	1981*	630	75	35·70	16 520	–	32	Built 1944
3002	1	1975*	630	75	35·70	16 520	–	32	Built 1944
3003-4	2	1944	630	75	35·70	16 520	–	32	
3005-6	2	1985*	630	75	36·00	16 620	–	24	Built 1946
Be 4/4 1001	1	1973*	420	45	30·00	17 500	–	64	Built 1955
1002	1	1975*	240	60	29·00	16 550	–	56	Built 1951
1003	1	1984*	300	55	31·00	16 270	–	56	Built 1958
BDe 4/4 18	1	1905	300	50	27·60	14 210	–	28	Service vehicle
20	1	1906	300	50	27·60	14 210	–	28	Service vehicle
De 4/4 25	1	1912	520	50	33·50	14 500	–	–	Service vehicle
26	1	1912	520	50	33·50	14 500	–	–	Service vehicle
BDe 4/4 27	1	1924	590	50	36·00	15 520	–	14	
28	1	1924	590	50	36·00	15 520	–	14	
ABt 5301-2	2	1976	–	80	17·50	16 810	17	31	
5303-4	2	1979	–	80	17·50	16 810	17	31	
ABt 3301	1	1979*	–	75	16·00	16 520	12	32	
3302	1	1974*	–	75	16·00	16 520	12	32	
Ast 116	1	1985	–	100	20·00	17 295	50	–	
117	1	1986	–	100	20·00	17 295	50	–	

Rhaetian Railway (RhB)
Rhätische Bahn

Bahnhofstrasse 25, 7002 Chur

Telephone: 081 21 91 21
Telex: 693 511

Director: Silvio Fasciati
Chief Engineer: W Altermatt
Chief Mechanical Engineer: F Skvor
Chief of Marketing and Operations: J Walter
Chief of Administration: N Michel

Gauge: 1000 mm
Route length: 375 km
Electrification: 276 km at 11 kV 16⅔ Hz ac
  26·5 km at 2·4 kV dc
  60·8 km at 1 kV dc
  13 km at 1·5 kV dc

The Rhaetian Railway is a vital means of communication in the mountainous east of Switzerland, where the Grisons have been termed the 'Canton of 150 Valleys'. Serving the Engadine, the valley of Poschiavo, the Davos area, Arosa and the Grisons Oberland, the railway connects the Canton with the Swiss Federal Railway system in Chur and Landquart, with the Furka-Oberalp Railway in Disentis/Muster, and with the Italian State Railways in Tirano. The territory is the most sparsely populated in Switzerland, with a population of some 170 000 averaging 23 per m².

The core of the Rhaetian network is electrified at 11 kV 16⅔ Hz, but the Bernina Railway from St Moritz to Tirano was electrified at its construction in 1908–10 at 1 kV dc and retains that system. The Bernina is the only Swiss transalpine line that avoids tunnelling, attaining a summit of 2253 m above sea level at Alp Grüm; for 27 km or 44 per cent of its total distance it is graded at 7 per cent but works entirely by adhesion. The Chur-Arosa Railway of 26·4 route-km, which the Rhaetian absorbed in 1943, is electrified at 2·4 kV dc; on this line the ruling gradient is 6 per cent.

The Rhaetian system as a whole has 118 tunnels and avalanche shelters aggregating 39 km in length and 498 bridges and viaducts totalling 12 km in length. Its longest tunnel is the 6 km Albula.

Income includes Cantonal subventions and compensations, and in accordance with the Federal law of 1957 concerning socially necessary private railways, 85 per cent of the final deficit is borne by the Federal government. Federal government and Canton also cover most of each year's normal investment needs.

Traffic	1988
Freight tonne-km	44 000
Passenger-km (000)	274 000

Total passenger-km in 1988 were the highest in the RhB's history. The tourist appeal of the Zermatt-St Moritz/Pontresina 'Glacier Express' and Chur/St Moritz-Tirano 'Bernina Express' services continues to grow. The former now records over 200 000 passengers a year over its RhB route segment, the latter over 185 000. The Bernina line's services as a whole log 570 000 passenger journeys a year.

Main constituents of RhB's considerable freight traffic are oil, cement, drinks, chemicals and timber. Wagon stock includes sliding-wall, insulated vans with electrical heating as well as cooling to provide for winter haulage of fresh produce; the vans' electrical power is taken by busline from a train's locomotive.

RhB Type Ge 4/4 II Bo-Bo at Scuol-Tarasp, on Lower Engadine line (*G Freeman Allen*)

RAILWAY SYSTEMS / Switzerland

RhB has a developing container traffic between Landquart and Thusis. It is developing a Bernina line terminal on the Italian frontier at Campocologno, believing that this route has all-weather advantages for traffic from northern Italy.

Investment 1988-92
The railway scheduled investment of around SwFr 200 million in the 1988-92 period. Major items are the relocation of the Arosa line's entry of Chur (see below) and its re-electrification at 11 kV 16⅔ Hz. Rolling stock purchases would comprise: six ABe 4/4 motor cars for the Bernina line (see below); six thyristor-controlled, three-phase motor Type Ge 4/4 III locomotives; five Type Tm 2/2 diesel tractors; 16 passenger cars; four baggage cars; and 42 freight wagons. Ground-to-train radio has been installed throughout the railway's network.

Traction and rolling stock
In 1989 the RhB operated 57 electric, three diesel and three electro-diesel locomotives, 38 electric railcars, 25 diesel and electric shunting tractors, three steam locomotives, 314 passenger cars (including six restaurant cars), 67 baggage and mail cars and 890 freight wagons, plus 144 service wagons.

The electric locomotive stock now comprises (ratings cited are one-hour): two Class Ge 2/2 of 250 kW; four Ge 2/4, two of 228 kW and two of 450 kW; two Class Ge 3/3 of 425 kW; one Class Ge 4/6 of 588 kW; 10 Class Ge 4/4 I of 1184 kW; 23 Class Ge 4/4 II of 1700 kW; five Class Ge 6/6 I of 940 kW ('Crocodiles'); and seven Class Ge 6/6 II of 1776 kW. The two Gem 4/4 electro-diesel locomotives take their electric current at I kV dc and thus are mainly used for freight haulage from the Bernina line to other parts of the system.

The most recent traction purchases have been six ABDe 4/4 motor cars for the Bernina line. These 1000kW units, employing ABB asynchronous motors, have raised the capability of a single motor car on the line's 1 in 14.2 ruling gradient from a 70 tonnes trailing load at 28 km/h to 95 tonnes at 40 km/h.

In 1990 RhB ordered six 11 kV ac 2400kW Type Ge 4/4 III Bo-Bos with ABB GTO thyristor inverter three-phase propulsion. These 61-tonne units will breach the RhB's existing axle-load limit of 12.5 tonnes and raise the system's maximum speed from 85 to 100 km/h. The locomotives will be delivered in 1992-93. For the Vereina tunnel service, and in connection with the reassignment of existing traction after re-electrification of the Chur-Arosa line to the RhB's standard 11 kV, the RhB expects to order 15 to 20 more Ge 4/4 III before the end of the decade.

Also ordered in 1990 were a further 16 passenger cars, 10 of them for the 'Bernina Express' service.

Automated Train Control
The RhB system is colour-light signalled under the oversight of seven control centres. The majority of passing loops can be switched for automatic operation by trains when their stations are unmanned. Main routes and their traction units are equipped with the Integra 79 Automatic Train Control system.

Klosters-Lavin cut-off
In March 1981 the RhB presented the Cantonal government with plans for a 22·3 km cut-off from Klosters to Lavin, on the line from Samedan to Scuol-Tarasp, which would halve the present journey times between Landquart and the Lower Engadine, at the extreme east of the RhB system, via the Albula line. Journey times to Scuol-Tarasp from Zurich and Chur would be cut by 135 and 100 minutes to 2 hours 40 minutes and 1½ hours respectively.

The project, refined in 1983, involves a 19·1 km tunnel under the Silvretta mountain range. This Vareina Tunnel will be single-track, intersected by a passing loop within the bore, on a ruling gradient of 1·5 per cent, and built to a loading gauge that will accommodate auto-transporter trains conveying road vehicles of up to 3·5 m height and also piggyback trains of all types of standard-gauge freight wagons. New road-rail transhipment terminals will be built at Klosters and Lavin. The track will be engineered for a maximum speed of 100 km/h, which will permit an initial operating capacity of five trains per hour each way, but the railway believes this capable of subsequent increase. A regular-interval operation at 12 minutes headway in each direction is envisaged at the daytime peaks, comprising one classic passenger and four auto-carrier trains each way. Klosters-Lavin transit time will be 17 minutes.

A Class Ge 6/6 II brings a Chur-St Moritz 'Glacier Express' into Samedan (G Freeman Allen)

The reinforced concrete Langwies Viaduct on the Chur-Arosa line

New ABe 4/4 power car with ABB three-phase ac motors climbs through the Bernina pass to the line's summit, the highest on Europe's transalpine routes

Cost in 1985 was estimated at a total of SwFr 538 million, of which SwFr 36 million would be for rolling stock. The Federal government has agreed to foot 85 per cent of the expenditure. The project was approved in a Cantonal referendum in the late summer of 1985 and a go-ahead for construction came with Federal Council approval in December 1986. Elektrowatt of Zurich have been appointed consultants for the project and Amberg AG of Chur have charge of planning and construction. Completion is set for 1999.

Tunnel to eliminate Chur street section
The RhB is to end the 2·3 km traversal of Chur's streets by the Arosa branch as it curves away from Chur's main station forecourt. The SwFr 100 million proposal will substitute a 3·3 km tunnel from the Sand depot on the town's outskirts to new underground platforms on the north side of a reconstructed Chur SBB station. The local authorities agreed credits for a start of the project in 1990.

Chur area shuttle train-set at Thusis *(John C Baker)*

Sihltal-Uetliberg Railway (SZU)
Sihltal-Zurich-Uetliberg Bahn

Manessestrasse 152, 8045 Zurich

Telephone: +41 1 202 8884

General Manager: H Tempelmann

Gauge: 1435 mm
Route length: 29 km
Electrification: 19 km (Sihltal line) at 15 kV 16⅔ Hz; 10 km (Uetliberg line) at 1·2 kV dc

The railway runs an intensive service from Zurich over the Sihltal line to Sihlbrugg and equally over the Uetliberg line. On the former it operates four electric and three diesel locomotives, seven electric motor cars and 15 trailers, and seven other passenger cars; on the latter, seven electric power cars, four trailers and four other passenger cars.

In conjunction with execution of the Swiss Federal's Zurich S-Bahn scheme, the SZU has moved from its Selnau station on the city's outskirts to the main SBB station, which it reaches by a new tunnel under the Sihl river that was completed in October 1988. Service commenced through the tunnel in May 1990.

In 1989 SZU ordered eight four-axle railcars of Class Be 4/4 for its Zurich-Uetliberg line. The order, valued at about SwFr 33 million, is being carried out jointly by SLM in Winterthur (mechanical part) and by Siemens Albis AG, Zurich (electrical equipment). Each railcar is to have an output of 800 kW, will be equipped with the latest three-phase converter technology and will provide seating accommodation for 64 and standing room for 74 passengers. The vehicles were due for delivery in 1991/92.

The SZU is considering acquisition of five bi-level train-sets. Its new tunnel approach to Zurich Hbf was designed to bi-level clearance parameter.

Model of new SZU Type Be 4/4 railcar

Solothurn-Zollikofen-Berne Railway (SZB)
Solothurn-Zollikofen-Bern Bahn

Berne-Worb Railways (VBW)
Vereinigte Bern-Worb Bahnen

Bahnhofhochhaus, Postfach 119, 3048 Worblaufen

Telephone: +41 31 58 58 11

Managr: P Scheidegger

Gauge: 1000 mm; mixed 1435 and 1000 mm
Route length: SZB: 34·5 km; 3·5 km
 VBW: 21 km; 4 km
Electrification: SZB 38 km at 1·25 kV dc
 VBW: 2·3 km at 600 V dc
 8·9 km at 800 V dc
 13·8 km at 1·25 kV dc

These two Berne suburban railways are jointly managed by Regionalverkehr Berne-Solothurn. Part of VBW is electrified at 800 V dc, the system of the Berne city tramway network with which both railways were connected before the 1960s. Then the SZB's original surface route into Berne was superseded by a new segregated double-track route from Worblaufen which finally tunnelled 1·2 km to a new four-platform terminus beneath the reconstructed Berne main station. The VBW was then mostly re-electrified at 1·25 kV and its route modified to funnel its trains into the new Berne subterranean terminus.

Traction and rolling stock
The SZB operates three electric and two diesel locomotives, eight electric power cars, 16 trailers, 12 two-car emus, and six passenger cars. The VBW operates three electric locomotives, eight electric power cars, seven trailers, nine two-car emus and seven passenger cars. All SZB train-sets are equipped with bars for the sale of both travel tickets to passengers boarding at unstaffed halts, and also of light refreshments. The two systems share 68 freight wagons, supplemented by 50 standard-gauge wagon transporters.

Track
Rail: VST 36 36 kg/m
Cross ties (sleepers): Wood (80%) 150 × 250 mm
Spacing: 1667/km
Fastenings: Type K with elastic spikes (SKL)
Minimum curvature radius: 100 m
Max gradient: 4·5%
Max axleload: 20 tonnes

South Eastern Railway
South Eastern Railway

Postfach 563, 8820 Wädenswil

Telephone: +41 1 780 31 57
Telefax: +41 1 780 37 56

Director: Ernest A Gross

Gauge: 1435 mm
Route length: 46·67 km
Electrification: 46·67 km at 15 kV 16⅔ Hz ac

The South Eastern Railway, together with the Swiss Federal and the Bodensee-Toggenburg, jointly operates an important cross-country intercity passenger service from Romanshorn and St Gallen to Lucerne, using the tracks of all three railways. The South Eastern segment of the route runs from Rapperswill to the Swiss Federal station at Pfäffikon, and from there to the Swiss Federal at Arth-Goldau. Branches serve Wädenswil and Einseideln.

Traffic	1988	1989
Freight tonnage	140 558	145 031
Freight tonne-km	1 654 000	1 701 000
Passenger-km	46 543 000	43 700 000
Passenger journeys	3 717 000	3 732 000

Finances (SwFr 000)

Revenue	1988	1989
Passengers and baggage	8 897	9 414
Freight, parcels and mail	3 133	3 488
Other income	2 575	3 025
Total	14 605	15 927

Expenditure	1988	1989
Staff/personnel expenses	13 547	14 936
Materials and services	8 148	8 786
Depreciation	2 624	2 632
Financial charges	2	1
Total	24 321	26 355

Traction and rolling stock
The railway operates four Re 4/4 III electric locomotives, six diesel tractors, 8 BDe 4/4 and 6 ABe 4/4 electric power cars, 11 driving trailers and 32 passenger cars (including two buffet cars). The railway recently

acquired two of the Re 4/4 III locomotives from the Swiss Federal Railway and adopted two of its passenger cars as driving trailers to form permanent push-pull train-sets with the Re 4/4 III as power cars.

To remedy shortage the railway purchased eight of the SBB's lightweight passenger cars in 1989. It also ordered four new cars of the SBB Mk IV type, to enter Lucerne-Romanshorn service in 1991; by the end of the decade, when a new design of car for Swiss private railways should be developed, these Mk IV cars may be sold to the SBB.

Track
Rail: SBB-profile type I, 46 kg/m
Cross ties (sleepers): Steel, concrete, wood, 150 × 260 mm
Spacing: 1667/km
Fastenings: K and W on wood and steel sleepers. A on steel sleepers, B on concrete sleepers
Minimum curvature radius: 143 m
Max gradient: 5%
Max axleload: 20 tonnes

South Eastern Railway Class Re 4/4 III and the push-pull format 'Konstanz-Rigi Express' near Samstagen en route to Arth-Goldau (*H H Isler*)

Electric railcars

Class	Cars per unit	Line voltage	Motor cars per unit	Motored axles per motor car	Rated output per motor/ one-hour kW	Max speed km/h	Weight per car tonnes	Length per car m	No in service 1989	Year first built	Builders Mechanical parts	Builders Electrical equipment
ABe 4/4	1	15 kV 16⅔ Hz	1	4	706	80	46·5	19·6	6	1939	SIG/SLM/SWS	ABB/MFO/SAAS
BDe 4/4	1	15 kV 16⅔ Hz	1	4	2060	110	72	23·7	8	1959	SIG	ABB

Electric locomotives

Class	Wheel arrangement	Line voltage	Rated output one-hour kW	Max speed km/h	Weight tonnes	No in service 1989	Year first built	Builders Mechanical parts	Builders Electrical equipment
Re 4/4 III	Bo-Bo	15 kV 16⅔ Hz	4700	125	80	4	1967	SLM	ABB/MFO

Syria
Ministry of Transport

Po Box 134, Damascus

Telephone: +963 213900-3
Telex: 331009 cfs sy

Minister: Youssef Ahmed

Chemins de Fer Syriens (CFS)

BP 182, Aleppo

Telephone: +963 11 213900; 213901
Telex: 331009 cfs sy

President and Director General: Ing Mohammed Ghassen El-Kaddour
Directors
Rolling Stock and Traction: Ing Abdel-Moneim El-Bourn
Movement and Traffic: Ing Mahmoud Hadj-Hassan
Fixed Installations: Dr-Ing Adnan Elias
Administration: Zouhay Moussali
Financial Affairs: M Mohamad Nadjar
Accounting: M Hussein El-Ahmed
Marketing: Ing Ghaleb Katerji
Signalling and Telecommunications: Ing Fahed Dassouki
International Relations: Zouheyr Moukayed
International Agreements: Berge Partdjian
Public Relations: Zouheyr Mimar
Railway Institute: Mme W Mimar

Chemin de Fer du Hedjaz

BP 134, Damascus

Telephone: +963 21 15 815

Director General: Ing Akil Ismail

Traffic	1984	1985	1986	1987	1988
Freight tonne-km (million)	966	1251	1417	1507	1570
Freight tonnage (000)	3897	4549	5000	5630	6000
Passenger-km (million)	746	933	893	1016	1122
Passenger journeys (000)	2853	3412	3300	3723	4000

Gauge: 1435 mm
Route length: 1525 km

All standard-gauge lines in Syria are operated by the Chemins de Fer Syriens, and comprise the lines from the Lebanese border via Homs and Aleppo to the Turkish border and in the north-east, the connecting line between the Turkish and Iraqi borders. A line runs from the oilfields of Kamechli to the port of Latakia (750 km). The final section of the Homs-Palmyra line was opened to phosphates traffic (destined for the port of Tartus) in 1980.

The extension of the railway from Homs southwards to Damascus (194 km) was opened to freight traffic in March 1983 and to passenger trains in November 1983. Laid with 50 kg/m rail, it has been engineered for a maximum speed of 120 km/h. The scheme heavily involved Soviet engineers, and earlier in 1981 a fresh Soviet loan was secured to enable a start on further lines from Deir Ezzor to Abou-Kemal on the Iraqi frontier (150 km) and from Tartus to Latakia (80 km). The first of these will link up with Iraq's new Baghdad-Husaiba line, and should be finished during the 1990s. The 80 km Tartus-Latakia line was heading for completion in 1990. A study has also been undertaken of a new 203 km line from Palmyra to Deir Ezzor, laid with 50 kg/m welded rail on sleepers spaced 1600 per km in 350 mm-deep ballast. The new lines are all being constructed with the aid of USSR engineers.

In November 1985 a further agreement was concluded for USSR engineering design of a 1435 mm-gauge line of 101 km from the outskirts of Damascus to Deraa, near the Jordanian frontier, to supersede the Syrian section of the 1050 mm-gauge Hedjaz Railway. The new line, which will have a branch from Sheikh Miskin to Suweida, will be engineered for 160 km/h operation. Completion is forecast during the 1990s. A new central station is to be built in Damascus.

CFS enjoys steadily rising freight traffic, particularly in bulk freight commodities such as phosphates and petroleum.

Traction and rolling stock
At the outset of 1989 the railway was operating 192 diesel locomotives, five diesel railcars, 459 passenger cars (including 19 restaurant and 45 sleeping cars), 33 baggage vans and 4166 freight wagons. It was taking delivery of 80 Type 114S 2800 hp diesel-electric locomotives from the USSR, 20 1500 hp shunters from Czechoslovak industry, 1400 freight wagons from firms in the German Democratic Republic and 49 passenger cars from Mecanoexportimport of Romania. For the opening of the Homs-Damascus line, VEB Bautzen and Görlitz supplied 358 new passenger cars including sleeping and restaurant cars and 100 air-conditioned first-class cars.

Directors, Traffic and Movements: Fouad Irabi
Traction and Rolling Stock: N El Mammami
Infrastructure: M El Sakbani
Manager, Accounts Department: Dib Habbouche

Gauge: 1050 mm
Route length: 246 km

In addition to its own route length, the CF du Hedjaz also operates the 67 km narrow-gauge Damascus-Zerghaya line on behalf of the Syrian government.

The Hedjaz Railway originally extended 1303 km from Damascus to Medine to carry pilgrims to the Holy Cities of Mecca and Medina. During the 1914–18 war the southern portion was severely damaged and the

844 km section from Maan in Jordan to Medina in Saudi Arabia was left derelict. In 1977, Syria, Jordan and Saudi Arabia formally agreed to commission from Dorsch Consult of West Germany a feasibility study for a replacement standard-gauge line using 60 kg/m rail, re-routed where necessary to improve alignment for high passenger speed, and designed to acceptable standards for operation of 25-tonne axleload freight wagons.

In 1981 Syria accepted the West German consultants' report and advised the Saudis and Jordanians that it was going ahead with the 114 km of the route from Damascus to Deraa, near the Jordanian border. With the Homs-Palmyra line finished in September 1980, the Damascus-Deraa extension was allocated the required funds in Syria's 1980–85 National Plan. Neither Jordan nor Saudi Arabia took complementary action. The Saudi government's reaction was that though it still regarded resurrection of the Hedjaz Railway throughout as a worthwhile long-term objective, it would not make a commitment to execute its part of the scheme without more exhaustive research.

In November 1982 an agreement was signed between the Syrian Ministry of Planning and the Soviet Administration of Economic Affairs with Foreign Countries to cover construction of the new Hedjaz Railway in Syria under the loan agreement signed in May 1981. A 1985 agreement took this project to the stage of engineering design (see above).

Traction and rolling stock
The railway owns 10 steam and seven diesel locomotives, six railcars, 51 passenger cars and 471 freight wagons.

Taiwan
Ministry of Communications

2 Cheng-Sha Street, Taipei

Telephone: +886 2 311 2661
Telex: 21733 gentel
Telefax: +886 2 311 9669

Minister: C P Chang

Taiwan Railway Administration (TRA)

2 Yen-Ping North Road, Section 1, Taipei

Telephone: +886 2 551 1131
Telex: 21837

Managing Director: S T Chang
Deputy Managing Directors
  T H Tu
  S F Chen
  K M Lee
Chief Engineer: K C Yen
Chief Secretary: H Chiang
Superintendents
  Transportation Department: T W Wang
  Civil Engineering Department: M C Chen
  Mechanical Engineering Department: H H Hsaio
  Electrical Engineering: H M Chen
  Purchase and Stores Department: T S Wu
  Planning Department: Y N Sheu
  Business: H C Lai
  Hualien Office: C K Chang
  General Affairs Department: H Chiang
  Accounting Department: Y Y Yeh
Chief, Personnel Office: C Y Hsieh
Chief, Electronic Data Processing Office: S Huang

Gauge: 1067 mm
Route length: 1071 km
Electrificatin: 498 km at 25 kV 60 Hz ac

The Taiwan Railway is the principal artery of transport on the island of Taiwan. It consists of three lines: the West Line with its branches; the East Line; and the new 79·2 km North Link Line from Suao-Idsin to Hualien. Completed in 1979 after six years' work at a cost of NT$7300 million, 39 per cent government-funded, this 1067 mm-gauge project ended the isolation of the 762 mm-gauge East Coast line. Conversion of the latter to 1067 mm has since been achieved.

The West Line, a double-tracked railway system, 1067 mm in gauge, stretches from north to south along the West Plain area of the island, linking the two big seaports of Keelung and Kaohsiung with the intermediate cities of Taipei, Hsinchu, Tai-chung, Changhua; Chia-i and Tai-nan. In the middle section of the system there are two routes from Chunan to Changhua; the Coast Line and the Mountain Line, 83.5 km in length, through the cities of Miao-Li, Feng-yuan, and Tai-chung.

Along a narrow valley area of the east coast the single-tracked 762 mm-gauge East Line from Hualien to Taitung (170 km) has now been converted to 1067 mm and through Taitung-Taipei service was inaugurated in July 1982. The scheme was also a further step in completion of an unbroken island ring route.

Traffic
TRA holds 29 per cent of national passenger travel market, but has only 19 per cent of the freight market. TRA runs some 350 freight trains daily but five times as many passenger trains. Bulk commodities account for 60 per cent of the freight tonnage, with cement, limestone and grain topping the list.

Through its Railway Freight Service (RFS), TRA offers a total transportation service, from door-to-door rail-and-truck transits between a dozen main centres to warehousing, responsibility for customs clearance and insurance. RFS has headquarters in Taipei, branch offices in eight other cities and service offices at 69 locations of the rail network.

TRA has two container terminals of its own at Kee Lung, one at Chi-Tu and the other at Wu-Tu. In addition the railway serves the United Container Terminal's installation at Pu-Hsui. TRA is also one of the financial backers of the China Container Terminal Corporation and its Wu-Tu Inland Terminal in the Kee-Lung suburbs. The railway has further port container terminals at Tai-Chung and Su-Ao, and a Taipei area terminal at Cheng-kung.

The Kee-Lung and Kao-Hsiung port terminals and the Taipei inland terminal are interconnected by eight dedicated container trains each way daily. TRA disposes of some 600 four-axle flatcars capable of carrying 40 ft ISO containers.

Traffic (million)	1986	1987	1988
Freight tonne-km	2265	2399	2178
Freight tonnage	17.3	19.1	18
Passenger-km	8305	8446	8223
Passengers carried	131.6	134.2	132

Civil engineering
Double-tracking of the Mountain Line between Chu-Nan and Chang-Hua began in 1984. The easiest part, the 26 km from Feng-Yuan to Cheng-kung, was finished in 1987. The rest, which is costing over three times as much per kilometre as the first stretch, cannot be achieved until 1992. Of the numerous tunnels that have had to be bored, one will be 6.7 km in length, and new bridge building has included a 1.1 km-long structure. Between San-I and Feng-Yuan the railway has been completely realigned for a distance that trims the route's length by 3 km.

The other key new line project currently in hand is construction of a 98 km-long South Coast Link line to connect the southern extremities of the West and East Trunk lines, respectively Fang-Liao and Pei-Nan (Tai-Tung). Here again TRA has had to negotiate a hostile mountain terrain, entailing construction of 34 tunnels aggregating 38 km, the longest of them extending for 8.07 km, and many bridges. Since 1983 this project has absorbed 40 per cent of TRA's capital investment.

Completion of this vital connection, mostly single-track but double in its mountain sector, was expected in 1990. With that the island would be orbited by a continuous trunk railway.

Double-tracking and upgrading with 50 kg/m rail of the West Trunk line's southernmost stub to the same infrastructure standards as the new South Coast Link, with which it connects at Fang-Liao, should be finished in 1991. Meantime, a computer-based Centralised Traffic Control system has been installed on the West Trunk south of Chang-Hua.

Electrification
Extension of the West Trunk electrification to the South Coast Link connection has been endorsed by the government, which of late has approved steadily and substantially rising capital investment in the railway. For 1989-91 TRA had authority to spend NT$206 billion.

High-speed line
In 1989 the Ministry of Communications announced ambitions to construct a new high-speed north-south line, engineered for 275–300 km/h line, from Kee-Lung

Electric multiple-unit for TRA by Socimi

to Kaohsiung. Three alternative routes are under study. The line would serve intermediate stations at Taipei, Hsin-chu and Tainan, possibly also at Taoyuan and Chia-i, and journey time from Taipei to Kaohsiung has been forecast as 1 hour 45 minutes, as compared with 4 hours by the existing route. In 1990 the scheme was endorsed by the country's Council for Economic Planning & Development, which has budgeted for investment of NT$ 600 million in it over a decade's span.

The high-speed project forms part of a 30-year transport infrastructure plan. Projected investment includes a metro for Kaohsiung, further development of the embryonic Taipei metro, and at a later stage metros for four other Taiwanese cities.

Taipei underground link
The trunk railway is being put underground in Taipei to eliminate the traffic congestion caused by level crossings on Chunghua Road and to establish a transport centre in the Taipei station area as a foundation for the emerging mass transit system in the Taipei Metropolitan Area. The project involves a new line starting from west of Sungchiang Road to the east of Wanhua station, including Taipei main station. Deutsche Eisenbahn Consulting GmbH was selected as general consultant for the project, and Saudi Arabia loaned US$83 million to finance the underground section's construction.

The first 4.8 km tunnel section between Wanhua and Huashan is complete and serves a new subterranean Taipei Main station. This phase cost NT$ 17.7 billion.The new Main station was formally inaugurated in September 1989 and has become a multi-level through station, instead of a terminal. Tunnelling continues over a further 5.5 km eastward, from Huashan to Sungshan, a work expected to take 4½ years at a cost of NT$18.5 billion.

Signalling
Computer-aided CTC has been installed between Chunghua, Tainan and Pintong.

Motive power and rolling stock
Electric locomotives	112
Diesel-electric locomotives	166
Diesel railcars	121
Diesel trailer cars	26
Emu cars	97

Passenger coaches	1341
Freight cars	5153

Recent deliveries have included eight three-car electric multiple-units and five three-car diesel multiple-units from Hitachi. Socimi of Italy has supplied eight three-car emus with electrical equipment by Bruch Electrical Machines for operation on the 25 kV 60 Hz West Coast main line from Taipei to Kaohsiung. Each three-car set has two power cars with total rating of 928 kW and a top speed of 120 km/h. The cars ride on air-suspension bogies.

In 1989 orders were placed with Union Carriage & Wagon of South Africa for 12 four-car emus. The traction equipment element would be supplied by GEC-Alsthom. Each unit's two power cars will have microprocessor-controlled braking and thyristor-controlled separately-excited dc motors.

Type of coupler
Passenger cars: Tight lock automatic AAR-H
Freight cars: AAR E Type automatic

Type of braking: AAR Westinghouse air

Track
Rail: 37 and 50 kg/m; 100 lb/yd

Cross ties (sleepers): Prestressed concrete 174 × 240 × 2000 mm
Timber: 140 × 200 × 215 mm

Spacing
In plain track: 1760/km (wood), 1640/km (concrete)
In curves: 1800/km for radii less than 437 m
Rail fastenings: Pandrol clip
Minimum curvature radius: 5.82°

Max gradient: 2.5%
Max axleload: 18 tonnes

Finances (NT$000)

Revenue	1986	1987
Passenger	8 050 863	8 267 736
Freight	2 056 466	2 184 170
Other	4 138 140	3 333 368
Total	14 245 469	13 785 274

Expenditure		
Staff	7 480 680	7 501 419
Materials and services	4 809 246	4 669 603
Depreciation	1 560 643	1 664 991
Financial charges	1 006 993	609 974
Other	—	—
Total	14 857 562	14 445 988

Diesel locomotives

Class	Wheel arrangement	Transmission	Related power hp	Max speed km/h	Total weight tonnes	Year first built	Builders Mechanical parts	Builders Engine & type	Builders Transmission
GM-EMD G-12	A1A-A1A	Elec	1425	100	78	1960	GM	GM 567C-12	GM
GM-EMD GA-18	B-B	Mech	1100	75	54	1970	GM	GM 645E-8	GM
GM-EMD G-22	A1A-A1A	Elec	1650	100	78	1970	GM	GM 645E-12	GM
GM-EMD G-22CU	Co-Co	Elec	1650	110	88	1973	GM	GM 645E-12	GM
GM-EMD GL-8	A1A-A1A	Elec	950	100	65	1960	GM	GM 567CR-8	GM
GM-EMD GA-8	B-B	Mech	950	75	54	1966	GM	GM 567-E-8	GM
Hitachi	Co-Co	Elec	1420	100	84	1960	Hitachi	Hitachi-MAN-V6V, 22/30 MAN L	Hitachi

Diesel railcars or multiple-units

Class	Cars per unit	Motor cars per unit	Motored axles per motor car	Transmission	Rated power hp per motor/rpm	Max speed km/h	Weight tonnes per car	Total seating capacity per car (M-motor T-trailer)	Length per car mm	Year first built	Builders Engine & type	Builders Transmission
DR 2100 DR 2200 DR 2300 DR 2400	1	1	1	Hydraulic	220/2100	95	35	66	19 916	1965	Cummins NHH-220	Niigata DBS-100
DR 2700	1		1	Hydraulic	335/2100	100	35	60	20 274	1966	Cummins NHHRTO-6-BI	Niigata DBSI-100
DR 2800	3	2	1	Hydraulic	335/2100	110	40	M 42 T 48	20 274	1983	Cummins NT855R4	Niigata DBSF-100
DR 2900	3	2	1	Hydraulic	335/2100	110	40	M 44 T 54	20 274	1986	Cummins NT85584	Niigata DBSF-100

Electric locomotives

Class	Wheel arrangement	Line current	Rated output kW	Tractive effort (full field) Continuous kg	Max speed km/h	Wheel dia mm	Weight tonnes	Length mm	Year built	Builders
E100	Bo-Bo	25 kV	2100	18 500	110	1220	72	14 050	1977	GEC, UK
E200	Co-Co	25 kV	2800	20 100	110	914	96	16 459	1977	GE, USA
E300	Co-Co	25 kV	3100	—	110	—	96	16 459	1977	GE, USA
E400	Co-Co	25 kV	3100	—	130	—	92	16 459	1980	GE, USA

Electric railcars

Class	Cars per unit	Power cars per unit	Motored axles per lower car	Line current	Rated output (kW) per motor	Tractive effort (full field) Continuous kg	Max speed km/h	Wheel dia mm	Weight tonnes (M-motor T-trailer)	Length mm	Year built	Builders Mechanical parts	Builders Electrical equipment
Emu 100	5	1	4	25 kV	310	6180	120	860	M 51·5 T 33·69	20 350	1979	BREL	GEC, UK
Emu 200	3	2	4	25 kV	125	NA	120	NA	M 49·5 T 39·8	20 000	1986	UCW (SA)	GEC, UK

Tanzania

Tanzanian Railways Corporation (TRC)

PO Box 468, Dar es Salaam

Telephone: +255 51 26241
Telex: 41308

Chairman: Prof A S Mawenya

General Manager: P C Bakilana
Assistant General Manager, Operations: E N Makoi
Assistant General Manager, Services: O R Kitenge
Assistant General Manager, Corporate Development: P R Kieran
Chief of Corporate Development and Research: G N Hizza
Chief Traffic Manager: K S Mtwangi
Chief Mechanical Engineer: H Sakwari
Chief Civil Engineer: P J Keysi
Chief of Manpower: A M Semaya
Chief Marketing Manager: L Mboma

Chief Supplies Manager: L Baseka
Chief of Finance: F B Matulile
Chief of Marine Operations: A S Kajiru
Chief of Road Services: A K Mwakalinga
Hotel and Catering Manager: M Chanda

Gauge: 1000 mm
Length: 2600 track-km

Following the formal break-up of the East African Railways Corporation in 1977, Tanzania set up the independent Tanzanian Railways Corporation to operate the former EAR lines wholly within Tanzania. In the succeeding years severance has posed TRC numerous problems.

In 1982 consultants completed a study sponsored by the Canadian International Development Agency (CIDA) and advocated both reorganisation measures and an investment equivalent to US$740 million over the next 20 years. Priorities were laid on staff training, improvement of communications and signalling, rolling stock purchases, and reballasting of track. Until these items had been covered, complete relaying of the main line to Kigoma should be suspended, since a higher level of traffic was needed to tax the strength of the existing rails, and plans for a new 540 km line from Arusha, present terminal of the TRC line north-westward from Tanga, to Musoma on Lake Victoria deferred. However, Pakistan Railways was in 1983 commissioned to undertake a feasibility study of the Arusha-Musoma project.

CIDA has followed earlier financial aid for rolling stock and infrastructure improvements with a sum of TSh 514 million chiefly for projects between Dar-es-Salaam and Morogoro, including a telecommunications system. Other aid for TRC's five-year rehabilitation scheme has been secured from Denmark and West Germany, for resignalling and telecommunications work respectively, and from the European Economic Community.

Investment

TRC is relaying the 115 km Manyoni-Singida line, which was uprooted in 1947. The objective is to stimulate social economic developments in the country. The work started in August 1985 but was still incomplete in 1989 for lack of funds. No more than 26 km had been laid because the government has provided only 10 per cent of the money needed. But 34 km of the Mruazi-Ruvu north-south Link line in the east of the country has been relaid and made serviceable.

TRC started relaying the central line with replacement of 60 lb/yd rail by heavy rail of 80 lb/yd. The Canadian International Development Agency (CIDA) has provided TRC with 320 km of rail, while Kuwait financed the purchase of 30 km of steel sleepers. Completion of this project will benefit both TRC and the economy as a whole by improved speed, safety and reliability of transport, and increased transit traffic, which is a foreign exchange earner.

To improve operations along the central line, installation of electric signals and power-operated points on a 465 km section from Dar es Salaam to Dodoma has been financed by the Italian government.

With the aid of the Federal Republic of Germany, TRC has constructed two diesel depots, at Moshi and Tabora. The existing workshops were antiquated and could not effectively meet the repair needs of locomotives due to inadequate facilities. In 1989 the German government granted aid worth DM 16 million to cover bridge rebuilding between Dar-es-Salaam and Kigoma.

Traffic

Freight traffic has receded since the 1970s in face of private road transport competition and limitation of imports, but has registered steady growth since the early 1980s.

Traffic (000)	1985	1986	1987
Freight tonnage	952	989	791
Freight tonne-km	770 000	NA	NA
Passenger-km	1 186 000	NA	NA
Passenger journeys	2912	3000	1700

Finance (TSh million)		
Revenue	1984	1985
Passengers and baggage	195	312
Freight, parcels and mail	436	589
Other	228	344
Total	859	1245
Expenditure		
Staff/personnel	209	228
Materials and services	785	828
Depreciation	88	102
Financial charges	265	236
Total	1347	1394

Traction and rolling stock

At last report 1987 TR owned 55 steam and 107 diesel locomotives, 225 passenger and baggage cars, including 81 sleeping and 21 restaurant/buffet cars, and 6060 freight wagons.

In 1986 TRC secured credits totalling US$25.6 million from various sources, including the World Bank, to carry out an emergency overhaul programme covering locomotives and freight wagons. By April 1989 it was reported that 87 line-haul and 20 shunting locomotives had been rehabiltated and around 600 of the 1000 or so freight wagons needing overhaul.

In 1990 the EEC agreed to put up a US$ 36.2 million grant for purchases of locomotives and wagons to move transit freight. The funds would be applied to purchase of nine line-haul and four shunting locomotives, and 80 freight wagons. Costmasnaga of Italy was supplying 30 container flatcars.

Signalling

Pursuant to an Italian government-financed study, WABCO Westinghouse was contracted to resignal the Dar-es-Salaam-Tabora section. The scheme is being executed in three phases: Dar es Salaam-Morogoro (201 km); Morogoro-Dodoma (456 km); and Dodoma-Tabora.

The colour-light, interlocked signalling scheme between Dar-es-Salaam and Tabora, a distance of 850 km, involves an entrance-exit electric interlocking system in four major stations, panel interlockings in all other stations, and tokenless block working throughout. Two wayside stations were already equipped with panel interlocking and operational, and at four other stations including Dar-es-Salaam signalling systems were under construction.

Type of coupler in standard use: MCA-DA

Type of brake in standard use: Automatic air, Type EST4d

Track

Rail: 55, 60 and 80 lb/yd
Cross ties (sleepers): Steel plain track, wood turnouts
Fastenings: Fish bolts and nuts, fishplates, screw spikes, coach screws, Pandrol
Spacing:
  55 lb/yd: 1430/km plain, 1540/km curved track
  60 lb/yd: 1405/km plain, 1485/km curved track
  80 lb/yd: 1402/km plain, 1482/km curved track
Minimum curve radius: 8°
Max gradient: 2.2%
Max axleload: 14.7 tonnes

Diesel locomotives

Class	Wheel arrangement	Transmission	Rated power kW	Max speed km/h	Total weight tonnes	No in service 1985	Year first built	Builders Mechanical parts	Engine & type	Transmission
35	C	Hyd	205	25	36·6	4	1973	Andrew Barclay	Paxman 8RPHL Mk 7	Voith L320V
36	C	Elec	244	25	36·2	20	1979	Brush	Ruston-Paxman	Brush
37	C	Hyd	295	25	36·2	5	1985	Thyssen-Henschel	MTU Type 6Y 396 TC12	Voith
64	B-B	Hyd	559	72	38·3	24	1979	Thyssen-Henschel	MTU Type EB 12V 396 TCII	Voith L520-UZ
72	1Bo-Bo1	Elec	925	72	68·86	2	1972	GEC Traction	Rushton-Paxman 8CVST	GEC
73	Co-Co	Elec	1003	96	72	15	1975	Varanasi	YDMA4	Varanasi
87	1Co-Co1	Elec	1370	72	101·4	8	1966/67	Eng Elec	Rushton-Paxman 12CVST	Eng Elec
88	1Co-Co1	Elec	1490	72	110·9	35	1972/80	MLW	Alco 251C	GE Canada

Tanzania-Zambia Railway Authority (TAZARA)

PO Box 2834, Dar-es-Salaam

Telephone: +255 51 64191
Telex: 41059

General Manager: Joseph Mayovu
Deputy General Manager: Ernest Abel Mulokozi
Corporation Secretary: J P Ngeleski
Chief Mechanical Engineer: L B J Chogo
Chief Civil Engineer: H S Mawona
Traffic Manager: J Mumba
Personnel Manager: S Chisamu
Supplies Manager: A S K Kilima
Finance Manager: M A Kashonda
Corporate Planning Manager: A S Mweemba
Regional Manager, Zambia: J Kasano
Regional Manager, Tanzania: R S Seme

Gauge: 1067 mm
Route length: 1860 km (891 km in Zambia, 969 km in Tanzania)

The Tanzania-Zambia Railway (TAZARA) was constructed following an agreement signed in September 1967 between the governments of Tanzania and Zambia, and of the People's Republic of China. Under the agreement, China provided finance and technical services for a rail link of approximately 1860 km from Dar es Salaam in Tanzania to Kapiri Mposhi in Zambia, together with equipment, two workshops and other auxiliary facilities, at an estimated cost of TSh 2 866 200 million. Operation began in 1975. The loan repayment was to commence in 1983 and to be spread over 30 years, with each country responsible for 50 per cent. Because of their economic problems, however, both countries agreed in 1983 to reschedule the repayment terms; the start of repayment of the main loan was put back 10 years.

The Tanzania-Zambia Railway is designed with a gauge that permits through goods traffic operations with contiguous railways in Central Africa, in particular Zambia Railways. Its performance, however, has been handicapped by serious problems of traction, rolling stock and track maintenance, of inadequate funds, and the international political strains of the continent. Whereas the railway's designed capacity was 5 million tonnes of freight a year, it has yet to register more than 1.5 million tonnes. In FY 1988-89 freight tonnage declined 4 per cent to 1.17 million, largely because of derailments and shortage of traction and rolling stock. Nevertheless, in FY 1988-89 the railway reported a profit for the third successive year and anticipated still better results in the two ensuing years.

With export/import traffic from Botswana, Malawi, Zaire, Zambia and Zimbabwe seeking to use Dar-es-Salaam instead of South African ports, pressure on TAZARA capacity has become intense. Co-ordinated by the Southern African Development Co-ordination Conference (SADCC), a 10-year, US$227 million rehabilitation of TAZARA was launched at the end of 1987. Almost a quarter of the sum was being put up by the World Bank; other aid was coming from Danish and Norwegian agencies, and from the African Development Bank. Swedish sources undertook to provide TAZARA with 200 of the 1000 freight wagons the railway needed to handle its rising traffic. Help was also promised by China in the rolling stock, signalling and communications fields.

In early 1990 Tazara's general manager forecast that by 1992 the railway would be carrying 2 million tonnes of freight. By then the railway would be well forward with its traction and rolling stock rehabilitation, and with repairs to the 1852 km line from Dar-es-Salaam to Kapiri Mposhi.

The Council of Ministers consisting of three

Ministers each from Zambia and Tanzania is the organ established by the two governments to exercise overall control on the railway. All the railway assets are vested in TAZARA, a corporate body whose principal organ is the Board of Directors consisting of five members each appointed by the two governments. For operational purposes, the whole railway is divided into two regions for Tanzania and Zambia, with respective regional headquarters at Dar-es-Salaam and Mpika.

Investment
In 1989 the US Agency for International Development (USAID) confirmed that it would put up US$ 17 million for eight new GE-built 3200 hp locomotives, plus provision for spares to overhaul the railway's GE-type locomotives that were German-built under licence, and also for local maintenance staff training. The new locomotives would be delivered in 1990-91. Re-engining of the Chinese DFH2 locomotives with MTU engines has continued. An agreement covering finance for 175 open and 25 tank wagons was signed with Sweden in March 1988; both orders were placed with Zimbabwean companies, for the open wagons with Zeco and for the tank wagons with More Wear of Zimbabwe.

A Danish supplier was appointed to begin provision of solar power panels, back-up radio links and teleprinters in April 1988. A financier has yet to be sought for a feasibility study of a future telecommunications system, CTC and ground-to-train radio. Switzerland provided a track recording car. Austria delivered two tampers and a ballast cleaner in 1988.

Motive power and rolling stock
At the start of 1989 TAZARA owned 95 diesel locomotives, 98 passenger coaches (including 10 restaurant cars) and 17960 freight wagons.

TAZARA has been modifying 150 DSO wagons into container-carriers to handle growing containerised traffic.

Type of coupler in standard use: Top action
Type of braking in standrd use
Passenger: Air
Freight cars: Air, vacuum

Track
Rail: 45 kg/m, 12.5 m length
Cross ties (sleepers): Prestressed concrete 195 × 208 × 272 mm
Spacing: 1520/km tangent, 1600/km curved track
Fastening: Electric (spring clip and bolt)
Minimum curvature: 200 m
Max gradient: 1 in 50
Max altitude: 1789.43 m, Uyole near Mbeya
Max axleload: 20 tonnes

Traffic	1986/87	1987/88
Freight tonnage	1 221 000	1 200 000
Freight tonne-km (million)	2960.9	NA
Passenger-km (million)	336 108	NA
Passenger journeys	1 335 000	1 500 000

Finance (TSh million)		
Revenue		1987/88
Passengers and baggage	78.89	117.89
Freight, parcels and mail	621.3	1662.5
Other	1.27	9.80
Total	701.46	1790.19

Expenditure		
Staff/personnel, materials and services	493.19	824.49
Depreciation	120	120
Total	613.19	944.49

Diesel locomotives

Class	Wheel arrangement	Transmission	Rated power hp	Max speed km/h	Total weight tonnes	No in service	Year first built	Builders – Mechanical parts	Builders – Engine & type	Builders – Transmission
1987										
1A (DFH1)	Bo-Bo	Hyd	1000	50	60	15	1971	Chintao Locomotive Works	Chintao Locomotive Works 12V 189ZL*	Chintao Locomotive Works SF 2010
1B (DFH-2)	Bo-Bo	Hyd	2000	100	80	66	1971	Chintao Locomotive Works	Chintao Locomotive Works 12V 180ZL (41 locos)* MTU 12V 396TC12 (25 locos)	Chintao Locomotive Works SE 2010 Chintao Locomotive Works SE2010
DE (U30C)	Co-Co	Elec	3200	100	120	12	1983	Krupp	General Electric 17 FDL 12HT	General Electric

* Class is being re-engined with MTU units

Thailand

Ministry of Communications

5 Rajdammern Avenue, Bangkok 10100

Telephone: +66 2 281 3422

Minister: J C Silapa-archa

State Railway of Thailand (SRT)

Rong Muang Road, Bangkok 10330

Telephone: +66 2 223 0341
Telex: 72242 srtbkk th
Telefax: +66 2 225 3801

Chairman: C Upong
General Manager: Somchai Chulacharitta
Railway Advisor: Sommai Tamthai
Deputy General Manager, Operations; Smaur Shavavai
Deputy General Manager, Development and Planning: Vatana Supornpaibul
Deputy General Manager, Administration: Amporn Larnlua
Assistant General Manager: Lieutenant Sutep Yuktasevi
Traffic Manager: Vichit Chansrakao
Deputy Traffic Manager, Operation: Suthep Bhichaibade
Service: Samnou Wacharasindhu
Chief Mechanical Engineer: Vacant
Deputy Chief Mechanical Engineer, Workshop: Paichit Tengtrirat
Motive Power: Twisvakorn Varavan
Chief Civil Engineer: Supoch Harindech
Deputy Chief Civil Engineer, Permanent Way: Aporn Phramalasoot
Modernisation: Vanich Pansuwan

Krupp-built diesel-hydraulic B-B locomotive

Kinki Sharyo stainless steel-bodied diesel-hydraulic dmu delivered in 1983

Personnel Manager: Thasanai Chantarangkul
Marketing Manager: Ithipol Sucaromn
Deputy Marketing Manager: Boonroeng Phonglumchiag
Director, Finance and Accounting Department: Pramte Chutima
Deputy Director, Finance and Accounting Department: Taweesak Maneepisith
Chief, Signalling and Telecommunication Bureau: Thavorn Ratanavaraha
Commander of Railway Police Division: Major General Pinit Soonsatham
Stores Superintendent: Kosol Chinda
Chief, Training and Development Bureau: Damrong Sooksmarn
Chief, Property Management & Development Bureau: Tanu Tammakul
Chief, Legal Bureau: Chookdi Sowamonmars
Chief, Medical Bureau: Dr Phadung Karnchanakul
Chief, Information System Bureau: Dr Chitsanti Danasobhon
Chief, Policy and Planning Bureau: Sriyoudh Sirivedhin
Chief, Internal Auditing Bureau: Navanit Palavichai
Chief, General Manager Bureau: Dr Nimitchai Snitbhan

Gauge: 1000 mm
Route length: 3924 km

SRT is playing a vital role in the nation's economic and industrial development following a decision by the government during the 1970s to invest heavily in railway projects.

Traffic (million)	*1986*	*1987*	*1988*
Freight tonnage	5.288	5.59	6.22
Freight tonne-km	2591.43	2736.46	2874.83
Passenger-km	9273.69	9582.74	10 381.4
Passenger journeys	76.702	77.931	82.71

Privatisation planned

The government is keen to privatise the metre-gauge State Railway of Thailand (SRT). Modest steps have already been taken in that direction; but World Bank and German consultants engaged in 1987 to work out a feasible scheme covering the whole system had a difficult remit.

So far private enterprise incursion is limited to operation of three intercity passenger services, between Bangkok and Phitsanulok, Surin and Khon Kaen. The companies concerned have leased from SRT their Japanese-built diesel train-sets, which include video entertainment and passenger telephones among their facilities.

No further progress was reported in 1989.

Traffic

In 1988 SRT carried 82.7 million passengers or 10 301.4 million passenger-km, representing increases of 6.2 and 7.5 per cent respectively over the previous year. The higher passenger traffic was due to addition of one express train on the Northern line and one rapid train in the Northeastern line.

In early 1990 bids for supply and installation of a computerised ticketing and reservation system were being evaluated. The project will be initiated at 11 stations in the Bangkok area and 26 stations further afield. Ultimately 35 more stations will be embraced by the scheme.

On the freight side, in 1988 SRT transported 6.2 million tonnes of carload freight and registered 2867.3 million tonne-km, representing increases of 10.7 and 5.1 per cent respectively from the previous year. This was the result of the increase of some commodities carried such as cement, rubber crude oil and petroleum products.

Road transport competition has sharpened considerably in this decade. Since 1980 the country's all-weather road system has been expanded by almost a third, and its highway truck resources likewise. Against that background, and in face of a national economic downturn, SRT has managed to contain its loss of freight volume at about 7 per cent.

SRT's own efforts to improve its finances have centred on a market-oriented management restructure, and concentration on services that optimise the railway's ability to turn a profit. Thus, in the freight sector the emphasis is on business that offers regular traffic in full siding-to-siding trainloads.

More than three-quarters of SRT's freight traffic is in commodities that lend themselves to unit train working – oil, refined as well as crude, rice, gypsum, maize, and rubber. To retain a viable stake in general merchandise SRT has abandoned construction of traditional box cars, cut down uneconomic wagonload working, and energetically expanded its container-carrying resources and train services. Container traffic has had a fillip from completion of the new 134 km line from Chachoengsao, east of Bangkok, to Sattahip port.

Finances (million Baht)			
Revenue	*1986*	*1987*	*1988*
Passenger and baggage	2064	2128	2309
Freight and mail	996	991	1006
Other	250	241	332
Total	3310	3360	3647
Expenditure			
Staff/personnel	2089	2070	2082
Materials and services	1338	1368	1355
Depreciation	442	487	378
Financial charges	435	375	378
Total	4304	4300	4193

Motive power and rolling stock

At the end of 1989 SRT was operating seven steam, 172 diesel-electric and 54 diesel-hydraulic locomotives, 53 shunters, 162 diesel railcars and 43 trailers, 1137 passenger cars (including 112 sleeping, 19 restaurant and 132 baggage cars) and 8633 freight wagons.

In November 1988 SRT made a contract with Waggonfabrik Talbot to purchase 24 freight cars financed by Kreditanstalt fur Wiederaufbau (KfW). The Overseas Economic Co-operation Fund (OECF) approved purchase of an additional 31 air-conditioned second-class sleeping cars from Daewoo in December 1988.

In 1989 SRT placed an order with BREL (1988) of the UK for 20 air-conditioned 120 km/h diesel railcars based on the design for British Rail's Class 158.

Conversion of vacuum to air brake of locomotives, passenger cars and freight continues. The equipment contractor is Knorr-Bremse. The changeover will cost the SRT approximately 210 million Baht.

Under the sixth five-year investment programme dating from 1987 SRT planned to acquire 22 diesel-electric locomotives, 36 diesel railcars, 18 passenger cars and 430 freight wagons.

Type of coupler in standard use: Passenger cars: Type E, AAR-10A automatic
Freight cars: Type E, AAR-10E automatic
Type of braking in standard use: Locomotive-hauled stock: vacuum and air

Electrification

A second study of the feasibility of the Northern line electrification from Bangkok to Chiang Mai by Deutsche Eisenbahn Consulting GmbH (DeConsult), financed by the government of the Federal Republic of Germany, has been completed with favourable recommendation for some sections. The Italian government offered a US$2.3 million grant for detailed engineering design of the Bangkok-Den Chai electrification; US$71 million (mixed credit) for construction of substations, contract lines, sectioning posts, signalling and telecommunications; and a US$500 000 grant for the study of feasible realignment between Den Chai and Chiang Mai. The Ministry of Communications was still studying these proposals in 1988.

Investment programme 1987–91

In general, an SRT investment programme includes only projects on lines already open. New line schemes are, in principle, government projects and are financed by the government accordingly (there are exceptions to the rule, however). The government gives no financial support to an SRT investment programme, but approval of the programme both in total and for each yearly slice of a project must first be obtained from the Council of Ministers before SRT can proceed with implementation.

The main features of the SRT's investment programme 1987–1991 were:
Rolling stock: 13 2400 hp diesel main-line locomotives, 36 diesel railcars, 18 passenger cars and 430 freight wagons. The 36 diesel-electric railcars would be air-conditioned and operated as intercity trains at a maximum speed of about 120 km/h.
Train electricity supply system: installation of diesel generating sets on 28 power cars and conversion of electrical equipment for 362 passenger cars.
Civil engineering: replacement of 2 350 000 sleepers; replacement of rails and switches; long-welding by thermit process; procurement of 1 million sets of fastenings for wooden sleepers; replacement of 107 timber bridges; and replacement/strengthening of 55 steel bridges.
Telecommunications: fibre-optic transmission system; centralised dispatcher telephone system; PABX; telex and facsimile system; passenger information services.

In 1989 the government released funds for a resignalling of the Bangkok suburban area by Westinghouse Brake & Signal, Australia. Another Australian company, Teknis International Rail Systems, was awarded a contract to resignal 31 km of the Maeklong line betwen Bangkok and Mahachai.

SRT was also pursuing a Railway Efficiency Equipment Project (IBRD), covering inter alia a tamping machine and two ballast regulators, 200 passenger car bogies, a driver training simulator, 200 computerised ticketing machines, vhf radio equipment for base stations and 40 locomotives, and an upgrading of SRT's central computer system.

In 1987 SRT negotiated a US$13 million World Bank loan. This would cover several items in the 1987–91 investment plan, such as the computerised management information system and the driver training simulator. It was hoped that a bigger loan would become available once SRT had completed some changes sought by the World Bank, such as detailed annual budgeting and revision of tariffs.

Civil engineering and new lines

A 134 km line from Sattahip to Chachoengsao, east of Bangkok, was finished in 1985. It has been engineered for 20-tonne axleloads and 100 km/h maximum speed, is operated by tokenless block between station interlockings associated with power-operated points, and runs passenger as well as freight trains. The freight includes unit mineral and container trains, the latter plying to and from new Bangkok terminals.

This new line was designed primarily as main trunk line to serve the government's plan of development and industrialisation of the eastern seaboard. In that context, construction of another three connecting lines was to be started. A 24 km extension beyond Sattahip to industrial development site at Map Ta Put was to be commenced by the end of 1990 and completed by 1992; an 11.2 km branch from the Chachoeng Sao-Sattahip line to Lam Cha Bang Deep Sea Port was to be completed by the end of 1990; and in early 1990 bids were invited for construction of the Klong Sip Kao-Kaeng Khoi line, an 82 km link between the existing Eastern and Northeastern lines.

In 1989 the government approved construction of a double-track rail landbridge of 180 km across the south of the country from Krabi on the Andaman Sea to Khanom on the Gulf of Thailand. The scheme envisages

RAILWAY SYSTEMS / Thailand

a road and pipelines alongside the railway, and construction of deep sea ports with industrial development potential at each end of the corridor.

A number of other new lines have been proposed, among them: Suphan Buri to Mae Sod via Tak, a segment of the Trans-Asian Railway concept conceived to link Asian and European rail systems, which could eventually connect SRT with the Union of Burma Railways; Suphan Buri to Lop Buri, to establish a link between Northern and Southern lines other than via Bangkok; a 186 km extension of the Southern lines' Khiri-Rattanikhom branch to the coast at Phuket, which has been submitted to feasibility study; and an 18.8 km connection from Thai territory to Vientienne in Laos, crossing the Mae Kong River.

Around and within the Bangkok area, proposals from the private investors have been canvassed for elevation of some 8.5 km of the approach lines from Bang Sue, and from Makkasan to Hua Lampong Terminus, which would obviate the present surface alignment's frequent intersection by road level crossings. For the benefit of urban transportation as well as relief of road traffic congestion in Bangkok, a plan to establish a new station in Bang Sue as terminus for southbound traffic has been developing, with an associated scheme to double the track between Bang Sue and Nakhon Pathom, a stretch of 57 km.

Substantial track and bridge renewal and strengthening started in 1985 has raised the maximum axleload to 15 tonnes. Further improvement plans have been set to cope with increased speed and traffic density and to minimise the cost of maintenance. One of them is a large-scale project to replace wooden sleepers by concrete sleepers. In the current four-year development plan laying of 900 000 concrete sleepers has been scheduled.

Colour-light signalling on the new Sattahip line

Diesel railcars

Class	Wheel arrangement	Transmission	Rated power hp	Max tractive effort at wheel rim kg @ % adhesion weight	Minimum continuous tractive effort kg @ km/h	Max speed km/h	Wheel dia mm	Service weight tons	Length mm	No in service 1.1.88	Year introduced	Builders Mechanical parts	Builders Engine & type	Builders Transmission
Niigata	2-4 wheel bogie driving trailer	Hyd-mech	320	4460	–	85	851	Power Type A 31 Type B 31 Trailer 33-75	20 800	1 power car 1 trailer	1962	Niigata, Japan	Cummins NHHRS-6-B	Niigata, Japan
Tokyu	2-4 wheel bogie driving trailer	Hyd-mech	220 × 2	4560	2260 @ 25	85	851	Power Type A 36·8 Type B 37 Trailer 26·9	20 800	1	1965	Tokyu, Japan	Cummins NHH-220-B-1	Niigata, Japan
Hitachi	2-4 wheel bogie driving trailer	Hyd-mech	220 × 2	4560	2310 @ 27	85	851	Power Type A 37·5 Type B 37·3 Trailer 27·5	20 800	9 (+ 1 trailer)	1967	Hitachi, Japan	Cummins NHH-220 B-1	Niigata, Japan
Hitachi	2-4 wheel bogie driving trailer	Hyd-mech	220 × 2	4380	2340 @ 25	90	851	Power Type A 38·5 Type B 38·3 Trailer 28·6	20 800	27 (+ 1 trailer)	1971	Nippon Sharyo & Hitachi, Japan	Cummins NHH-220-B-1	Niigata, Japan
Tokyo (stainless)	2-4 wheel bogie driving trailer	Hyd-mech	220	5400	2175 @ 30	70	851	Power Type A 33·6 Type B 32·2 Trailer 27·8	20 800	4	1971	Tokyu, Japan	Cummins NHH-220-B-1	Niigata, Japan
THN	2-4 wheel bogie driving trailer	Hyd torque converter	235	4090	–	100	851	35·38	20 800	20	1983	Tokyu Car, Hitachi Nippon Sharyo	Cummins N855-R2	Niigata, Japan
NKF	2-4 wheel bogie driving trailer	Hyd torque converter	235	4600	NA	100	851	35 534	20 800	32	1985	Nippon Sharyo, Kawasaki Fuji	Cummins N855-R2 Big Cam	Niigata, Japan
ATC	2-4 wheel bogie driving trailer	Hyd torque converter	235	4600	NA	100	851	38 132	20 800	6	1985	Tokyu Car	Cummins N855-R2 Big Cam	Niigata, Japan

Computerisation improvement

SRT plans to implement three fundamental on-line computerisation projects: Inventory and Material Management System (IMMS); Seat Ticketing And Reservation System (STARS); and Operation Control System (OCS). All three systems are considered top priority, to be implemented as early as possible.

For the Inventory and Material Management System (IMMS), SRT has received a grant for consultancy from the USA's Trade Development Programme (TDP). This includes a survey of SRT's present inventory and material management system, a study with SRT's personnel of software and practices in USA and Europe, evaluation of technical proposals as prepared by bidders, and assistance in the testing and system conversion. A local software manufacturer is to be hired by SRT to implement the project under supervision of SRT officials and the consultant.

The new IMMS will be on-line/real-time with information transferable from one store to another via a leased line from the Telephone Organisation of Thailand. SRT has selected as consultant SRT International.

The Seat Ticketing And Reservation System (STARS) project (see above) includes installation of 128 off-line ticket-issuing machines and 72 reservation work stations. In these installations only the reservation work stations, which are located in 32 stations will be connected by telephone lines to the host computer in Bangkok. STARS will be subcontracted on a turnkey basis. SRT has commissioned DeConsult to carry out the technical advisory consultation.

Under the third project, Operation Control System (OCS), SRT is to investigate the practices employed in some US and European railroads before finalising the technical requirement specification for the software package. The sytem would be on-line/real-time and the development on a turnkey basis. The consultant is Transurb of Belgium. The new system will enable SRT staff to identify instantly the status and location of wagons, which will help to reduce turnaround time and improve wagon utilisation. Wagon maintenance, currently ordered on a time basis, will be based on distance run as well as time.

Signalling and telecommunications

Four projects were in progress in 1989; the Sattahip port railway; installation of colour-light signals; installation of a train dispatcher telephone system project; and resignalling and CTC installation on the central main line.

For the Sattahip port railway, which is a government project supporting the development of the Eastern Seaboard, SRT signed a contract worth 175.8 million Baht in July 1985 with Westinghouse Signals Co Ltd of the UK for procurement and installation of signalling and telecommunications systems. This project is complete and work in 1989 was confined to rectification of minor problems.

The colour-light signals project has been supported by Japan's OECF's 12 800 million yen loan. The contract was awarded to GEC-General Signal (UK) in January 1989. The installation period would be 3½ years from commencement of works which envisages completion in September 1992. The works comprise:

Section	No of ARI stations	Covering distance (route-km)
Southern line		
Ratchaburi (exclusive) to Chumphon (inclusive) plus provisional three stations: Thonburi Khlong Kud and Khlong Prap	46	363.1

Section	No of ARI stations	Covering distance (route-km)
Northern line		
Lopburi (exclusive) to Phitsanulok (inclusive)	36	251.7
Northeastern line		
Banphachi junction (exclusive) to Thanonchira junction (inclusive)	30	171
Total	112	785.8

The contract for installation of a train dispatcher telephone system was awarded to GEC (UK) in November 1987. The new system comprises 13 dispatcher control centres and 518 wayside slave telephones. It covers the entire rail network and was scheduled to be complete in November 1989.

The resignalling and provision of Centralised Traffic Control project was awarded to Westinghouse Brake and Signals (Australia) in May 1989. The project area covers the following central main-line sections:

Section	No of CTC satellite stations	Covering distance (route-km)
Northern line		
Bangsue (exclusive) to Lopburi (inclusive)	21	115
Southern line		
Bangsue junction (exclusive) to Taling Chan junction (inclusive)	2	14.656
Total	23	129.656

The works include CTC, automatic block and train describer systems, optical fibre and digital transmission with automatic telephone system. Triple-aspect signals will be adopted with route indicators. The project's installation period will be three years eight months.

In the sixth and seventh National Economic Development Plan, SRT has proposed signalling and telecommunications system for four new lines: extension from Khao Shee Chan to Rayong; extension from Sri Racha to Laem Chabang; the bypass between Khlong Sib Kao and Kaeng Khoi; and the construction of elevated track between Bangkok and Bang Sue.

The turnkey contract for the installation of a train-dispatcher telephone system project was awarded to GEC Telecommunications of the UK in November 1987. The system comprises dispatching and slave telephones at 13 control centres and 518 wayside stations covering the entire rail network of 3750 route-km. Installation was completed in 1989.

Track

Rail Type	Weight (kg/m)
BS 50 R	24.8
BS 60 R & 60 ASCE	29.77
BS 70 R	34.76
BS 70 A & 70 ASCE	34.84
BS 80 A	39.8
Others	37, 37.5, 42.5

Minimum curvature radius: 180 m (turnouts 156 m)
Max gradient: 2.6%
Max altitude: 574.9 m
Max axleload: 15 tonnes

Sleepers				
Type	Untreated hardwood	Creosote-treated softwood	2-block concrete (RS-ype)	Monobloc prestressed concrete
Dimensions	150 × 200 × 1900-2000 mm	150 × 200 × 1900 mm	1710 mm long, block 209 × 274 × 600 mm	200 × 260 × 2000 mm
Spacing	1430-1540/km	1430-1540/km	1540/km	1666/km
Fastenings	Dog-spike, Dorken spike or Woodings clip	Dog-spike, Dorken spike or Woodings clip	RN clip	Hambo elastic

Type of coupler in standard use: Type E, AAR-10A automatic
Type of braking in standard use:
  locomotive-hauled stock: Vacuum

Diesel locomotives

Class	Wheel arrangement	Transmission	Rated power hp	Max tractive effort at wheel rim kg @ % adhesion weight	Minimum continuous tractive effort kg @ km/h	Max speed km/h	Wheel dia mm	Service weight tons	Length mm	No in service 1.1.88	Year introduced	Builders Mechanical parts	Builders Engine & type	Builders Transmission
Davenport	Bo-Bo	Elec	500	14 770 @ 30%	5700 @ 16	82	914	48.12	9893.2	24	1952	Davenport, USA	Caterpillar D 397	Westinghouse, USA
Davenport	Co-Co	Elec	1000	24 000 @ 30%	11 370 @ 16	92	914	80	16 954.4	10	1955	Davenport, USA	Caterpillar D 397	Westinghouse, USA
Hitachi	Co-Co	Elec	1040	21 600 @ 30%	13 140 @ 12.76	70	914	72	14 300	11	1958	Hitachi Japan	MAN W 8V 22/30 m AUL	Hitachi Japan
GE	Co-Co	Elec	1320	22 500 @ 30%	17 963 @ 13	103	914	75	16 288	50	1965	General Electric, USA	Cummins VT 12–825 B1, VTA-1710-L	General Electric, USA
Alsthom	Co-Co	Elec	2400	24 800 @ 30%	20 600 @ 21	95	914	82.5	16 258	52	1975	Alsthom, France, Krupp and Henschel, West Germany	SEMT Pielstick 16PA 4V.185	Alsthom, France
AHK	Co-Co	Elec	2400	24 800 @ 30%	20 600 @ 21	100	914	82.5	16 258	30	1980	Alsthom, Krupp, Henschel	SEMT Pielstick 16PA4 185VG	Alsthom, France
ALD	Co-Co	Elec	2400	25 700 @ 30%	20 600 @ 21.3	100	914	82.5	16 258	9	1983	Alsthom, France	SEMT Pielstick 16PA4 185VG	Alsthom, France
ADD	Co-Co	Elec	2400	25 700 @ 30%	20 600 @ 21.3	100	914	82.5	16 258	20	1985	Alsthom, France	SEMT Pielstick 16PA4 185VG	Alsthom, France
Krauss-Maffei	C	Hyd	440	12 000 @ 33.33%	7450 @ 7.55	27	1106	36	8350	5	1955	Kraus-Maffei, West Germany	MAN W 8V 17.5/22A	Voith, West Germany
Hunslet	C	Hyd	1240	19 100 @ 33%	2430 @ 12.1	19.5	1106	30	7658	4	1964	Hunslet, England	Gardner 8L 3B	Voith, West Germany
Henschel	B-B	Hyd	1200	17 160 @ 33%	14 900 @ 11	90	914	52	12 800	26	1964	Henschel, West Germany	Maybach MB, 12V 493 TY 10	Voith, West Germany
Krupp	B-B	Hyd	1500	18 150 @ 33%	15 250 @ 14.5	90	914	55	12 800	28	1969	Krupp, West Germany	Maybach MB, 12V 652 TB 10	Voith, West Germany
HAS	C	Hyd	704	12 240	11 730 @ 0.5	58	914	41.2	9600	10	1986	Henschel, Germany	MTU 6V 396 TC12	Voith, West Germany

748 RAILWAY SYSTEMS / Togo—Tunisia

Togo

Togo Railways

PO Box 340, Lomé

Telephone: +228 21 4301

President: P Y Tchalla
General Manager: T Kpekpassi
Superintendent, Administration & Finance:
  V K Dogbe-Tomi
  Rolling Stock & Motive Power: K Alfa
  Traffic: N Akoubia
  Infrastructure: Y Akakpo

Gauge: 1000 mm
Route length: 525 km

The railway extends three prongs inland from the port of Lomé, to Palime, Blitta and Anecho. It operates 10 line-haul and nine shunting diesel locomotives, three diesel railcars, 63 passenger cars and 450 freight wagons.

In late 1989 the railway was taking delivery of a tranche of new passenger cars from a local company, Socometo.

Alsthom-built diesel locomotive and local train at Lomé station (*Wilhelm Pflug*)

Tunisia

Tunisian National Railways (SNCFT)

Société Nationale des Chemins de Fer Tunisiens

67 avenue Farhat Hached, Tunis

Telephone: +216 1 249 999
Telex: 14109 tunis
Telefax: +216 1 245 044

President/Director General: N Chaouch
Deputy Director General, Technical: A Bazarbecha
Deputy Director General, Operations: K Ben Amor
Directors
  Administration: S Rached
  Finance: Hachmi Chabchoub
  Rolling Stock: Faika Daly
  Planning: Jameleddine Hamza
  Commercial: Abderrazak Nafti
  Purchases and Stores: R Toumi
  Infrastructure: A Jammali
  Signalling and Telecommunications: A Ghariani
  Workshops: M Chaouachi
  Computerisation: M Yangui
Chief, Systems and Control: S Khanfir
Chief, Administration and Finance: T Yalaoui
Chief, Concrete Factories: H Dahmouni

Gauge: 1435 mm; 1000 mm; mixed 1435/1000mm
Route length: 447 km; 1450 km; 10 km
Electrification: 24 km of 1000 m-gauge at 25 kV 50 Hz ac

Since the end of the 1970s SNCFT has undergone a major change in its affairs stemming largely from a 1979 agreement by the government to cover the cost of new infrastructure and to service the debts of loans for infrastructure payments.

Traffic (million)	1987	1988	1989
Freight tonne-km	1996	2156	2063
Freight tonnes	10.094	11.510.9	
Passenger-km	795	10 139	10 392
Passengers	25.13	28.19	28.96

Traffic
Both passenger and freight traffic registered sizeable gains in 1988. In terms of passenger-km, traffic in that sector was up 27.1 per cent. In the freight sector, bulk commodity tonne-km rose 13.2 per cent, fuelled by a sharp rise in phosphate exports from the south of the country and a 9.2 per cent growth in other traffics. Freight traffic fell back in 1989 but there was further growth in the passenger business. SNCFT operates an intensive commuter service over the double-track metre-gauge lines from Tunis to Hamman Lif and Bir Kassa. To these a Tunis-Djedei d-Tebourba operation can now be added, as the 24.7 km Tunis-Djedei da section became in July 1988 the first stretch of SNCFT standard gauge to be double-tracked.

Motive power and rolling stock
In 1989 SNCFT operated 6 electric, 136 line-haul and 53 shunting diesel locomotives, 39 diesel railcars, 83 trailers, six emus, 208 passenger cars and 5176 freight cars.

Delivery of 100 air-conditioned passenger cars (83 metre- and 171 435 mm-gauge; the order included buffet cars) was completed by Ganz-Mávag early in 1988. The passenger cars reproduce the accommodation standards of the three-car air-conditioned Ganz-Mávag diesel train-sets, which under the designation 'Autorail direct' have since the start of the 1980s sustained the bulk of the long-haul passenger service on both gauges. Even on the metre-gauge these units run in places at their maximum speed of 130 km/h. But in other areas their speed is severely restricted, particularly by the profusion of level crossings in built-up areas; and journey times are prolonged by the heavy occupation of single-track main lines beyond the metropolitan areas.

All railcars, locomotives and passenger cars are capable of bogie change and of operation on either gauge. Most of the passenger service has hitherto been provided by diesel railcars, but except for sets delivered by Alsthom in 1975 those used in secondary services are now elderly and inadequate to meet today's traffic levels.

In 1989 SNCFT invited bids for supply of 250 wagons of various types, chiefly hoppers and tankers. Of these 50 were to be delivered in 1990.

1992–2010 Development Plan
Considerable improvements have been executed and are planned at the approaches to Tunis. A new main station was inaugurated in 1980, segregating metre- and standard-gauge traffic, and completion of a chord on the outskirts has opened direct access to the freight yards and eliminated the reversal of standard-gauge freight trains in the passenger station.

Under a plan covering the 1992–2010 period SNCFT aims to double-track throughout the key metre-gauge main line from Tunis southward to Sousse, Sfax and Gabes. Extension of this trunk beyond Gabes to Medenine has begun, with ultimate projection to Tripoli in view. Reopening is scheduled of the line from Mateur to Tabarka, closed since 1984; of the Mateur-Jedeida connection; of the Mastouta-Merja link further south in the Second World War zone; and of the line southwest from Sousse to revive a through route from the coast to Kasserine.

Several new lines are on the agenda. It is planned to rebuild the former Cap Bon line from Fondouk Djedid to Henchir Lebna and extend it to Kelibia. Other schemes include two new north-south lines, one from Borj Mcherga to Kairouan and connections with the prospective Sousse-Kasserine route; and another further west from Gafour to Sidi Bouzid, whence there would be a fork southwest to Gafsa and southeast to Mazouna. Also projected is a new route around the coast from Monastir to Sfax via Mahdia.

In 1989 SNCFT gained a US$41 million European Investment Bank loan for trackwork, including renewal of some 180 km on the Tunis-Algiers and Tunis-Sfax-Gabes lines.

Electrification
Electrification at 25 kV 50 Hz of the 25 km between Sousse and Monastir, known as the Sahel metro, entrusted to Ansaldo Trasporti at a cost of 15 million dinars, was completed in March 1984. Six train-sets were supplied by Ganz-Mávag. The line is now being extended 45 km beyond Monastir to the fishing port of Mahdia and Ansaldo Trasporti has again won the electrification contract.

In 1990 SNCFT invited bids for a feasibility study of electrifying its Tunis-Borj Cedria and Tunis-Tebourba lines.

Signalling
Automatic block installation, operative throughout the Tunis-Sousse-Sfax-Gabès single line, with relay interlockings at crossing stations, is being extended to the sections from Tunis to Djedei da and Beja, Bir Kassa to Gafour, Sfax to Gabès and Gabès to Gafsa. The section from Sfax to Gafsa and Métlaoui has been experimentally equipped with track-to-train radio. All telephone lines are being progressively placed in ground-level ducts.

Track
Standard rail
Standard-gauge: Flat bottom, 36–46 kg/m in lengths of 12–18 m
Metre-gauge: Flat bottom, 25–36 kg/m in lengths of 7–8–12 m
Welded joints: Thermit welding of rail joints
Cross ties (sleepers): Oak impregnated with creosote; metal; concrete RS type
Standard-gauge: 120 × 220 × 2600 m
Metre-gauge: 120 × 220 × 2200 mm
Spacing: 1500/km
Rail fastenings: Wood sleepers; spikes
Metal sleepers: clips and bolts
Concrete sleepers: special resilient fittings
Filling: Broken stone
Max curvature
Standard-gauge: 7° = minimum radius 250 m
Metre-gauge: 11.6° = minimum radius 150 m
Max gradient: 2% = 1 in 50

Gradients	Standard gauge	Metre gauge
Level	29%	22%
Up to 0.5%	37%	26%
0.5 to 1%	20%	26%
1 to 2.5%	14%	26%

Max altitude: 952 m on line Haidra to Kasserine
Max speed, standard gauge
Railcars: 100 km/h
Diesel trains: 70 km/h
Max axleload
Standard-gauge: 21 tonnes
Metre-gauge: 18 tonnes

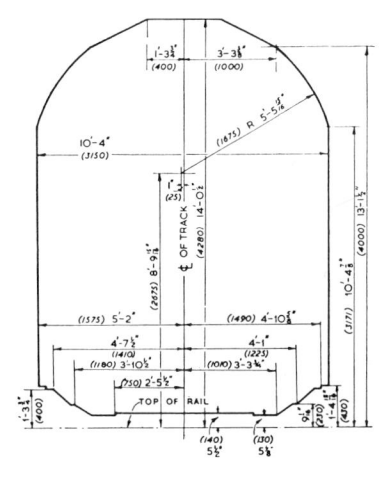

Standard gauge
All vehicles

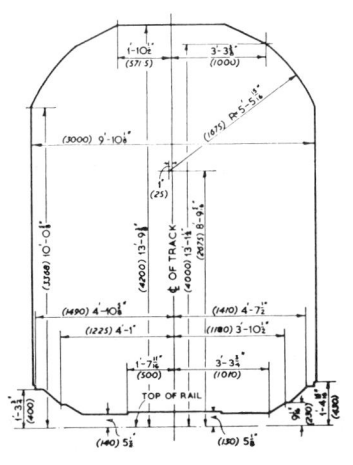

Metre gauge
Locomotives and passenger cars

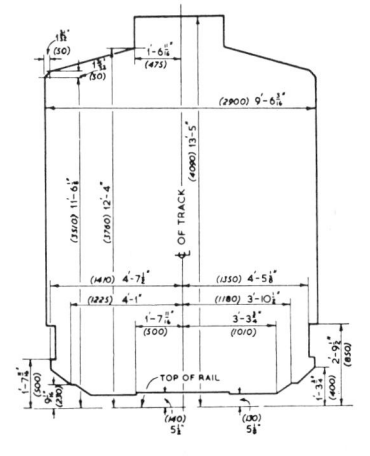

Metre gauge
Freight cars

Diesel locomotives

Class	Manufacturer	Wheel arrangement	Transmission	Rated power (kW)	Max speed km/h	Total weight tonnes	No in service 1989	Year first built
060GR12	General Motors	Co-Co	Elec	1047	100	92	5	1964/66
040 DF	General Motors	Bo-Bo	Elec	698	90	59	9	1965
040 DG	Traction	Bo-Bo	Elec	698	80	48	6	1967
060 DH	General Motors	Co-Co	Elec	1640	100	93	5	1973
060 DI	MLW	Co-Co	Elec	1604	114	90	22	1973
040 DK	MLW	Bo-Bo	Elec	895	116	64	20	1978
040 DL	Ganz Mávag	B-B	Hydr	1323	110	62	10	1981
060 DN	GE	Co-Co	Hydr	1862	114	89	19	1983
060 DP	Bombardier	Co-Co	Hydr	1764	130	91	20	1984
040 DO	Ganz Mávag	B-B	Hydr	1764	130	64	20	1985
040 DD	Alsthom	Bo-Bo	Elec	294	70	39	8	1958
040 GE	GE	Bo-Bo	Elec	446	96	49	4	1962
040 GE	GE	Bo-Bo	Elec	515	96	49	4	1965
060 DS	GE	Bo-Bo	Elec	466	103	64	9	1977
040 DM	GE	Bo-Bo	Elec	522	114	64	28	1983

Turkey
Ministry of Communications

Ankara

Telephone: +90 41 33 11 00
Telex: 42019

Minister: Cengiz Tuncer
Under-Secretary: Dr Ertan Yülek
Director-General of Land Transport: Atilla Tekelioğlu

Turkish State Railways (TCDD)
Türkiye Cumhuriyeti Devlet Demiryollari

Genel Müdürlüğu, Ankara

Telephone: +90 41 310 35 00
Telex: 42571 tcdd tr
Telefax: +90 41 312 32 15

President and Director General: Birkan Erdal
Members of the Board of Management
  Birkan Erdal
  Imdat Akmermer
  Tekin Çinar
  Nurhan Öç
  Cemal Akin
Deputy Directors General: Nurhan Öç
  Tekin Çinar
  Ismail Gültekin
  Talat Günsoy
  Dr Ercüment Türktan

Directors
  Board of Inspection: Rasih Civelekoğlu
  Secretariat of Security: Hikmet Güven
  Permanent Way: Arslan Aladağ
  Traction: Haluk Akova
  Commercial: Erol Özkut
  Financial: Murat Bostan
  Operations: Süleyman Yavuz
  Personnel: Bahattin Şahin
  Fixed Installations: Salim Selvi

Japanese-built Class 43 000 3180 kW electric locomotive at Haydarpasa (*Wolfram Veith*)

Krauss Maffei Class DE11000 diesel-electric locomotive

RAILWAY SYSTEMS / Turkey

Construction: Yavuz Denizer
Research and Planning: Fügen Findikoğlu
Training: Mehmet Onal
Foreign and Management Affairs: Necdet Kocabey
Law: Ahmet Gülleroğlu
Ports: Adnan Yardimci
Ankara Workshops: Boriş Beyhan
Purchasing: Mustafa Doğan
Real Estate: Sabiha Öncü
Data Processing: Ümran Özbozduman
Dining, Sleeping Cars & Tourism: Bedri Palamut
Affiliated companies
  TÜLOMSAS (Eskişehir Locomotive and Motor Industry Establishment): Hamdi Akfirat
  TÜVASAS (Adapazarı Wagon Industry Establishment): Metin Yerebakan
  TÜDEMAS (Sivas Railway Machine Industry Establishment): I Zeki Daloğlu

Gauge: 1435 mm
Route length: 8430 km
Electrification: 567 km at 25 kV 50 Hz ac

Master Transport Plan

In September 1982, as promised, the government endorsed a Master Transport Plan which greatly increased planned investment in TCDD up to 1990. The total budgeted for the period was 379 000 million Turkish lira. In addition, considerable funds have been separately allocated to the Ministry of Public Works for construction of a number of new lines.

Finance and traffic

TCDD still has to balance its books with the aid of a considerable state subsidy. But whereas, prior to 1982, TCDD still incurred a loss after accounting in the subsidy, it has since turned that loss into a modest surplus, and moreover achieved this margin on an amount of subsidy that from 1980 to 1986 was steadily reduced, though the amount of support has again been rising since 1987.

At the same time TCDD reversed the serious downward slide of its freight traffic. In the early 1970s TCDD had an annual gross of almost 16 million tonnes, but by 1980 the total had slumped to less than 11 million, largely because of the railway's inability to cope with the business offering. A gross of 14.4 million tonnes had been reached by 1988, but in 1989 there was a downturn to 13.1 million tonnes, largely because of strikes in the iron and steel industry. However, 1989 showed gains in international freight traffic, which reached 1.2 million tonnes. Local passenger traffic was up 9 per cent, long-haul by 4 per cent.

Financially, TCDD has also benefited from the rapid growth of traffic through the seven ports it manages (plus three piers elsewhere), following improvements achieved under Phase 1 of a World Bank US$75 million financing plan. At Haydarpasa, Mersin, Iskenderun and Samsun tonnage handled has virtually doubled since the start of the decade. The ports are now equipped to handle intermodal traffic.

Mainspring of the railways' turnround has been an attack on the inefficiencies which previously prevented TCDD from grasping all commercial opportunities. The unacceptably high ratio of unserviceable locomotives, for instance, has been halved by ordering workshops to give repairs priority over new building. TCDD has also been investing substantial sums to modernise and rationalise the activity of its vehicle workshops. Manufacture of new high-capacity bogie freight wagons is being concentrated on the Tüdemsaş plant at Sivas. A drive has also been mounted to improve wagon productivity, in part by imposing demurrage charges on customers who are lethargic in unloading their cargoes. This has already secured an improvement of about 10 per cent in turnround times.

However, TCDD's fundamental handicap persists, in that it cannot add competitive transit speeds to the considerable price advantage it offers over road transport, and to its availability when road movement is hobbled by winter conditions. Far too much of the rail system is still single-track, and furthermore beset by sharp curves and severe gradients.

Passenger business has expanded in recent years. A feature in its longhaul sector is the development of good quality, first-class-only services that are tagged as 'Blue Trains' which radiate from Ankara. Recent additions to the long-haul rolling stock include business cars with telephone, telex and data modem equipment, new day cars and sleeping cars.

Class DE 22 000 diesel locomotive and the newly-introduced Ankara-Istanbul 'Fatih Express', which includes new air-conditioned saloon cars.

One of 30 ex-German Federal diesel-hydraulic shunters, TCDD Class 6500, heads a Burdur-Gümüsgün passenger train (*Wolfram Veith*)

TCDD's latest type of open saloon car

Interior of new TCDD lounge car

Future passenger equipment plans

TCDD plans to introduce in the near future a new design of sleeping car with individual shower/WC facilities for each compartment. Also contemplated are self-powered tilt-body train-sets for several intercity connections.

Hopes are still cherished of constructing a new high-speed passenger line between Istanbul and Ankara. A build-operate-transfer approach is under consideration.

For short-haul service TCDD aims to begin local manufacture of diesel railbuses. It already operates 20 two-car railbus sets bought secondhand from the German Federal Railway.

Traffic (million)	1987	1988	1989
Freight tonne-km	7259	8006	7571
Freight tonnes	13.887	14.353	13.1
Passenger-km	6174	6708	6845
Passenger journeys	130	136	146

Finances (TL million)	1987	1988	1989
Revenue			
Passengers	28 407	53 435	90 705
Freight and mail	88 839	166 659	299 959
Other	206 455	102 703	192 142
Subsidies	56 262	84 195	205 231
Ports	78 506	124 989	209 743
Total	324 110	531 981	997 780
Expenditure	*1987*	*1988*	*1989*
Staff	129 890	207 845	487 947
Materials	108 634	96 172	208 110
Depreciation	52 710	92 869	159 015
Financial charges	52 743	131 341	152 147
Other		86 655	142 318
Total	343 979	614 882	1 149 537

Infrastructure improvements

The priority is to realign, double-track, resignal and electrify the 577 km iron ore route from the Divrigi mines in east central Turkey southwards to the ports of Adana and Iskenderun, also the site of a steelworks. A Saudi loan is financing this project and half its requirement of 80 4000 to 4500 kW locomotives. The high power is needed to attack the line's severe gradients. The objective is to double the line's present carrying capacity of 2 million tonnes a year. It was hoped to finish the three sections of double- tracking aggregating 439 km by 1993. The project includes resignalling (begun in late 1984) and installation of CTC throughout. In 1983 a West German-Yugoslav consortium led by Iskra Automatika and including SEL won a US$40 million signalling contract for the line.

Electrification is complicated by the route's 92 tunnels with an aggregate length of 22 km. The contract was awarded to a Franco-Turkish consortium led by Société de Construction des Lignes Electriques and GTM Entrepose Electricité. The project has been two-thirds funded by France, the Saudi Fund for Development and the Islamic Development Bank. Completion was forecast in 1990.

Other new lines included in the Master Plan are a 25 km branch from Menemen to the Alilaga oil refinery, in the west near Izmir; and 80 km cut-off between Toprakkala and Kömürler, north of Iskenderun, to bypass the steep gradients through Fevzipasa; another cut-off, of 65 km, between Bostankaya and Hanli in central Turkey, to avoid the detour through Sivas and Kalin, construction of which was authorised in 1986; and a new link of 140 km with Iraq to obviate transit traffic's present need to pass through Syria.

A feasibility study for an 8 km double-track tunnel under the Bosphorus between Yenikapi, in Istanbul, and Haydarpasa has been completed by Botek and the US consultancies, De Leuw, Cather and Sverdrup & Parcel. Responsibility for this project has been assumed by the Istanbul municipality, which has invited construction bids worldwide. Besides main-line traffic the tunnel would carry a suburban service connecting with the first line of the proposed Istanbul metro, between Topkapi and Levent on the European side of the Bosphorus. The government has allocated 806 000 million lira for fulfilment of this and other urban rail transport schemes.

World Bank loan

A 'Second Railway Project' goes ahead following the World Bank's advance of credits totalling US$ 187.75 million. Schemes that have gone ahead cover:
Track: Overhaul of 740 km and purchase of track construction and maintenance machinery would be completed in 1990. This has resulted in increase of permissible axleloading to 20 tonnes.
Signalling: In 1990 a consortium of ITT-SEL, Iskra and a local company, Alarko, gained a US$ 46 milion contract to resignal throughout a key freight sector from Cetinkaya east of Sivas, where the transversal main line makes a junction with the Divrigi ore line, to the Ankara suburbs at Kayas. A distance totalling some 700 km is involved.
Traction: Workshop modernisation, procurement of spares, rehabilitation of immobilised locomotives, study of diesel locomotive design to eradicate weak points, and improvement of telecommunications. Maintenance downtime has been reduced and locomotive availability advanced to 80-85 per cent.
Staff training: This has included despatch of 193 personnel for training on railways abroad.
MIS. The project is being advanced in three stages: computerisation of locomotive maintenance and operation, with cost accounting; computerisation of operational control systems; and establishment of integrated MIS.

Bids could be invited in 1987 for a thoroughgoing modernisation of that part of the historic Istanbul-Ankara route, from Haydarpasa to Sincan, which an aborted bypass scheme of the early 1980s would have avoided. The lowest tender, of around US$23 million, was submitted by a consortium of Japanese firms-Daido and C Itoh-and the Turkish companies Yuksel and Sasel.

Electrification

At present electrification is concentrated in the Istanbul and Ankara areas. In addition to the Divigi-Iskenderun/Adana route, routes between Kapikule and Çerzeköy (190 km), Kayaş and Çetinkaya (701 km) and Zonguldak and Sivas (953 km) have been the subject of recent electrification feasibility studies.

In 1988 Ircon was contracted to undertake the Sincan-Eskişehir wiring (238 km), which will complete

Interior of new saloon car

catenary throughout from Ankara to Haydarpasa. Other electrification was in progress in 1990 between Arifiye and Eskişehir (182 km) and (see above) Iskenderum and Divrigi (577 km).

Within the next five years TCDD hoped to undertake further electrification projects: Kayaş-Çetinkaya (701 km); Irmak-Karabük-Zonguldak (415 km), accompanied by resignalling; Menemen-Izmir-Cumaovasi (91km), accompanied by resignalling; and Çerkezköy-Hudut (189 km).

In 1989 Technoexport of the USSR was contracted to conduct a feasibility study of electrification from Halkali (Istanbul) to the Bulgarian border at Edirne (215 km).

Signalling

TCDD's 1990-94 plan scheduled resignalling over 1497 km. In 1990 schemes were in progress over these sectors: Iskerendum-Narli (192 km); Narli-Çetinkaya (320 km); and Çetinkaya-Divriği (65 km). Besides the projects already mentioned in association with new electrification schemes, it was hoped to resignal betwen Halkali and Hudut (290 km) in the first half of the 1990s.

CTC is operative over 1278 route-km of single-track main line. In 1990 it was in course of installation between Cetinkaya and Divrigi.

Traction and rolling stock

In 1989 29 SEMT-Pielstick 16-PA4V185-VG engines were ordered to re-equip the Class 24 000 locomotives. MTU of West Germany supplied 12 engines of each of its Series 183 and 396 type to repower the TCDD's ex-German Federal DN 11500 and DH 6500 locomotives, also some of the MAK diesel-hydraulics. With MTU engines also featuring in the TCDD's latest DE 11000 locomotives, the German company has set up a subsidiary in Turkey.

Diesel locomotives

Class (Railway's own designation)	Wheel arrangement	Transmission	Rated power hp	Max speed km/h	Total weight tonnes	No in service 1989	Year first built	Builders — Mechanical parts	Builders — Engine & type	Builders — Transmission
MAK 33100	C	Hyd	360-450	50	41·2	38	1953	MAK	Makms-304	Voith
MAK 44100	D	Hyd	-800	80	58·9	6	1955	MAK	Makma-301A	Voith
DH 6500	C	Hyd	-650	60	49·6	35	1960	Krupp-Esslingen	Maybach	Voith
DH 3600	C	Hyd	360-450	50	40·5	19	1968	ELEMS	ELEMS	Voith
DE 20000	Co-Co	Elec	1980	100	102	1	1957	GE	Cooper-Bessemer Fv12	Elec, GT, 581-C3
DE 21500	Co-Co	Elec	2150	114	111·6	35	1965	GE(USA)	GEFDL 12	GE
DE 24000	Co-Co	Elec	2400	120	112·8	328	1970	SMTE-ELMS	Pielstick 16 PA4-185	Alsthom
DE 24000	Co-Co	Elec	2000	120	112·8	41	1984	SMTE-ELMS	Hedemora	Alsthom
DE 18000	Bo-Bo	Elec	1800	80	80	3	1970	SMTE-ELMS	Pielstick 12 PA4-185	Alsthom
DE 18100	Bo-Bo	Elec	1800	80	105	18	1978	SMTE-ELMS	Pielstick 12 PA4-185	Alsthom
DE 22000	Co-Co	Elec	2200	120	122·5	86	1985	General Motors	GM 645 E	General Motors
DE 11000	Bo-Bo	Elec	1065	80	68	50	1985	Krauss-Maffei	MTU 8V396	GEC
DN 11500	B-B	Hyd	1100	100	62	10	1960	MAK	Mercedes MB 820 B6	Voith

Toshiba won a contract for 45 Bo-Bo-Bo 3180 kW, 120-tonne, 25 kV 50 Hz ac electric locomotives with thyristor converters and microprocessor control systems for the Divrigi-Iskenderun electrification. A technology transfer agreement confided part of the assembly work to TCDD's Eskisehir works.

In 1988 TCDD was prospecting for a high-speed bogie it could build under licence, with a view to developing 160–200 km/h coaching stock. It was also seeking bids for supply of railbuses capable of mainline service at speeds of 100 km/h.

TCDD'S 1990–94 plan provided for the following acquisitions: 425 main-line and 15 shunting diesel locomotives; 79 electric locomotives; 8 emus; 30 dmus; 425 passenger cars; and 10 500 freight wagons. It was hoped in 1990 to manufacture under licence 25 ABB-equipped locomotives and 15 Toshiba electric locomotives at Tülomsas, also 300 freight wagons; to build 600 freight cars at Tüdemsas; and 40 passenger cars and 15 emus at Tüvasas.

Locomotives in service (end-1989)

Steam	50
Electric	32
Diesel	572
Diesel shunters	103
Emus	86
Dmus	21

In addition the railway operated 1037 passenger coaches, among them 82 sleeping, 119 couchette and 11 restaurant cars and 20 719 freight wagons.

Type of coupling: Screw
Type of brake: Knorr and Westinghouse

Civil engineering

At present TCDD's maximum speed is 120 km/h, and that attainable only by the front-rank passenger train on parts of the Hydarpasa-Ankara route. TCDD has been aiming to ease main-line curves to a minimum 900 m radius with 160 km/h top speed as the target. Other objectives under TCDD's 1990-94 plan are renewal of 2424 km of track, double- or multi- tracking over 247 km and achievement of fully mechanised track maintenance.

Track

Rails: 49.5 kg/m
Cross ties (sleepers): Steel, wooden, concrete
Spacing: 600-750 km
Fastenings: DB, KHN
Minimum curvature radius: 200 m
Max gradient: 1.9%
Max axleload: 20 tonnes

Electric locomotives

Class	Wheel arrange-ment	Line current	Rated output kW Continuous	Tractive effort (full field) Max lb (kg)	Tractive effort (full field) Continuous at lb (kg)	Tractive effort (full field) Continuous at mph (km/h)	Max speed mph (km/h)	Wheel dia in (mm)	Weight tonnes	No in service 1989	Year built	Builders Mechanical parts	Builders Electrical equipment
4001-4003	Bo-Bo	25 kV 50 Hz	1620	41 900 (19 000)	23 150 (10 500)	39 (62·5)	56 (90)	51⅛ (1300)	77·5	3	1955	MTE	Alsthom-Jeumont-SW
40001	B-B	25 kV 50 Hz	2944	69 500 (31 500)	47 130 (21 350)	30·6 (49)	81 (130)	43¼ (1100)	77	13	1971	MTE	Groupement 50 Hz
43001	Bo-Bo-Bo	25 kV 50 Hz	3180	NA	NA	NA	56 (90)	NA	120	16	1987	Toshiba	Toshiba

Electric multiple-units

Class	Wheel arrange-ment	Line current	Rated output per set hp	Tractive effort (full field) Max lb (kg)	Tractive effort (full field) Continuous at lb (kg)	Tractive effort (full field) Continuous at mph (km/h)	Max speed mph (km/h)	Wheel dia in (mm)	Weight tonnes (M-motor T-trailer)	Length ft in (mm)	No in service 1989	Year built	Builders Mechanical parts	Builders Electrical equipment
8001-8030	BO² + 2′2′ + 2′2′ + BO²1²2	25 kV 50 Hz	1380	26 900 (12 200)	21 600 (9800)	30 (48)	56 (90)	43¼ (1100)	M 48 T 32	288′ 9″ (88 000)	28	1955	MTE	Alsthom
14001-14030	2B′0′ + 2′2′ +2′2′	25 kV 50 Hz	1400	41 300 (18 721)	13 600 (6171)	38 (61·3)	74 (119)	43¼ (1100)	M 51·5 T 22 DT 22	216′ 6″ (66 000)	58	1979-85	MTE	Groupement 50 Hz

Diesel multiple-units

Class	Cars per unit	Motor cars per unit	Motored axles per motor car	Trans-mission	Rated power (hp) per motor	Max speed km/h	Weight tonnes per car (M-motor T-trailer)	Total seating capacity	Length per car mm (M-motor T-trailer)	No in service 1989	Year first built	Builders Mechanical parts	Builders Engine & type	Builders Transmission
5400	1	1	2	Hyd	4 × 145	90	M 42·8 T 30.6	199	M 22 350 T 17700	9	1961	Fiat	2030/762	Fiat
5500	3	2	2	Hyd	2 × 170	90	42	52	17 000	12	1953	SCF	MAN W6V 14/18	AEG

Uganda

Uganda Railways Corporation (URC)

PO Box 7150, Nasser Road, Kampala

Telephone: +256 41 254961/ 250851
Telex: 61111 urail

Managing Director: C Karamanji
Senior Exeecutive Engineer: B Balumu
Chief Mechanical Engineer: E M Kwesiga
Chief Civil Engineer: M Kasimbazi
Chief Traffic Manager: E Mwemera
Chief Supplies Officer: A Wafakale-Mwambu
Planning and Development Officer: J Muhumuza
Chief Accountant: B M Marunganua

Gauge: 1000 mm
Route length: 1232 km

Uganda Railways Corporation (URC) was created after the 1977 dissolution of East African Railways. Since then it has suffered seriously from political dissention between its former partner countries in EAR, from the civil war in its own country and resultant damage, and from a decline in the performance of Uganda industry and agriculture.

URC started rehabilitation under a National Recovery Programme in 1980, commencing a signalling modernisation, financed by French aid, with station interlocking and tokenless block, the construction of a workshop at Nalukolong with the involvement of Henschel Export of the Federal Republic of Germany, new rolling stock orders, and construction of new Lake Victoria wagon ferries.

Alsthom-Atlantique supplied 14 2000 hp Co-Co diesel-electric locomotives of the manufacturer's Type AD20C, powered by a SEMT-Pielstick 12PA4185VG engine. To suit URC's present track, these units have a maximum axleload of only 12·5 tonnes. Also obtained were 20 1200 hp diesel-hydraulic locomotives from Thyssen Henschel, earlier suppliers of 10 other diesel-hydraulics and six diesel shunters. A fleet of 84 new passenger coaches was acquired from VEB Waggonbau Görlitz in the German Democratic Republic and 440 wagons from Indian builders.

In 1987 the government received an Italian consultants' study of a US$150 million ugrading of the 333 km Kampala-Kasese main line. By 1989 a US$153 million aid scheme had been formulated, largely underwritten by the World Bank and Italy, which would allow the work to go ahead. Completion would open up a valuable route from Mombasa to northeastern Zaire.

Train ferry service

As a member of the African Central Corridor transport system, Uganda benefited from the provision of European Economic Community funds for improvement of wagon ferry terminals and port facilities on Lake Victoria at Jinja, Port Bell, Mwanza, Musoma and Bukoba. Two train ferries ply between Jinja and Mwanza in Tanzania.

Traction and rolling stock

At latest report URC was operating 60 diesel locomotives, 82 passenger cars and 1113 freight wagons. The Spanish consortium Inirail was delivering 100 tank wagons in 1987-88; the order was 85 per cent supported by Spanish loans. Orders were placed for a further 600 wagons with More Wear of Zimbabwe in 1988. Alsthom was contracted to rehabilitate 11 diesel locomotives.

Delivery was to begin in 1989 of 13 more Type 73 diesel locomotives from Thyssen-Henschel.

Union of Soviet Socialist Republics

Soviet Union Railways (SZhD)

Ministry of Railway Transport, Novo Basmannaja 2, Moscow 107174

Telephone: +7 262 16 28

Administration
Minister of Railway Transport: Nikolai Konarev
First Deputy Ministers: G M Fadeev, V N Ginko
Department for International Communications:
  L V Malashko

Gauge: 1520 mm; 750-1435 mm
Route length: 145 000 km; 2608 km
Electrification: 25 534 km at 25 or 2 x 25 kV 50 Hz ac, 27 385 km at 3 kV dc.

The general management of main-line railways and underground (metro) rail transport throughout the whole of the Soviet Union is vested in the Ministry of Railway Transport, which has its headquarters in Moscow. The Ministry has several directories (departments) including the main directorate of transport, the main directorate of passenger traffic and other main directorates covering locomotive economy; rolling stock economy; track; electrification and electric power supply; signalling, communications and calculating technology; underground (metro) lines; container conveyancing and commercial work; industrial railway transport; safety of railway traffic; projects and capital construction; scientific-technical; economy; centralised bookkeeping and finance/accounts; material-technical supplies; repair of rolling stock and production of spare parts; cadre and training establishments; medical etc. There are also directorates of statistics, external (foreign) rail communications and others, as well as departments looking after improvement of the organisational structure, and legal matters. Perestroika has cut the staffing of the Ministry overall by 30 per cent.

Since the start of 1988 the railways have been put on a self-supporting footing and must finance their own development. All directorates have been given a bottom-line financial responsibility.

The whole railway network is divided into 32 railways each of which has an administrative structure similar to that of the Ministry.

The 32 railways are as follows:

Azerbaidzhanian	Alma Atinsk
Baikal-Amur	White Russian (Byelorussian)
East Siberian	Gorky
Far Eastern	Donetsk
Trans-Baikal	West Kazakhstan
West Siberian	Trans Caucasian
Krasnoyarsk	Kemerovsk
Kuibyshev	Lvovsk
Moldavian	Moscow
Odessa	Oktyabrsk
Baltic	Volga
Dniepr	Sverdlovsk
Northern	North Caucasian
Central Asian	Tselinn
South Eastern	South Western
Southern	South Ural

The system has some 11 000 passenger stations and 7000 freight depots.

Passenger traffic

In 1989 the Soviet railways recorded 3696.7 million passengers and 349 000 million passenger-km. During the period 1986–89 passenger traffic on Soviet railways rose by 230.2 million journeys, or 5.5 per cent.

The most effective method of coping with the increasing volume of passenger traffic has proved to be lengthening of trains. In such major rail centres with intensive suburban traffic as Leningrad, Kiev, Novosibirsk and in all areas of the Moscow railway system the standard electric trains now consist of 12 carriages. On numerous sections of the Gorky, October and other lines 20-car electric trains are now operated during peak periods. In 1989 there was discussion with France over possible adoption of SNCF bi-level car technology.

More drastic steps have been needed to cope with the continued growth of long-distance travel. After experiments in 1983, numerous trains on the Moscow-Kiev and Moscow-Smolensk routes had their formations increased from 18 to 24 cars and even more at peak periods. Outgoing formations of more than 30 cars have to be assembled from two halves at peripheral Moscow junctions, and conversely divided there on the return, as they cannot be accommodated intact in the Moscow terminal platforms.

In 1984 SZhD introduced to the Moscow-Leningrad route a high-speed train-set, the ER200, a 14-car formation with all 12 of its inner cars motored for a total rating of 11 500 kW. The ER200 has 200 km/h

Type VL86 10800kW twin-unit 25kV ac 50Hz electric locomotive

Type VL85 9400 kW twin-unit electric locomotive

Type 2TE121 8000 hp main-line diesel locomotive (Ralf Roman Rossberg)

Czech-built Type CS7 3 kV electric locomotive heads a Trans-Siberian train at Moscow (Günther Barths)

Type TE136 6000hp diesel-electric twin-unit locomotive

Type VL80R 25 kV electric locomotive

capability, which it can exploit over the 331 km of the route from Moscow to Bologoje. The remainder of the route to Leningrad allows only 160 to 180 km/h. The ER200 makes only one weekly return trip, to a schedule of 4 hours 30 minutes for the 650 km, partly because its route is normally so heavily used by freight that its passage requires up to 30 trains to be looped or re-routed. SZhD is anxious to standardise a 4-hour journey time between Moscow and Leningrad, and 10 more ER200 train-sets have been under construction at the Riga works for 1991–95 delivery.

Nine 'Ekspress-2' automatic ticket sales systems were operational in 1989. These are intended for complex ticket booking operations in large rail centres and can control the sale of tickets over whole sections of the network. 'Ekspress-2' terminals are installed in 2300 ticket offices on 13 routes of the European part of the USSR. It is intended that the 'Ekspress-2' system will serve all routes of the European part of the USSR, to be followed by the Ural, Siberian and Central Asian networks.

A unified computerised system of seat reservations has been introduced that embraces the majority of the larger rail centres with a passenger turnover of over 50 000 in a 24-hour period.

A complex automated reference-information system known as 'Ekasis' has been evolved based on the technology of 'Ekspress-2'. This provides real-time information for all enquiries relating to passenger traffic and the conveyance of luggage and cargo on trains at any given date. The 'Ekasis-I' system which automates the task of reference-information bureaux is now operational in the larger Soviet railway stations.

Automated machines dispensing suburban rail tickets, electronically-operated ticket- and change-giving machines, automated information machines and other technology are being introduced in Soviet railway stations to improve passenger service.

Freight traffic

In 1989 SZhD logged 3348 million tonnes of freight and 3221 000 million freight tonne-km. A gross of 4099 million tonnes was anticipated in 1990. The railway carries more than 68 per cent of all internal freight. Of this total 63 per cent is powered by electric traction and 37 per cent by diesel traction. On average, the SZhD conveys 11.2 million tonnes of national freight daily, of which almost 85 per cent consists of coal and coke, (mineral) oil, ores, timber, mineral construction materials, grain, and chemical and mineral fertilisers.

One of the most spectacular areas of growth is intermodal (reflected in considerable construction of suitable wagons). A gross of 75 million tonnes of container traffic by 1990 was forecast.

Policy is to increase the specific weight of heavy-weight containers to 20 tonnes gross and that of medium-weight containers to 5 tonnes gross weight. Further to increase the effectiveness of container traffic it is intended to develop production of containers of increased capacity with a gross weight of 24 tonnes, as well as that of the new universal containers of Types UUKP-3(5) and UUKP-5(6), with increased volume and carrying capacity. The railways also use special-purpose containers for the products of the chemical industry, ferrous, machine-building and fishing industries. To process this container traffic more than 1300 container-handling points are in operation, including approximately 170 for the heavy-weight containers. These terminals are laid out to process from 150 to 500 containers daily. A computer-based container traffic control system (ASUKP) has been introduced for international movements via the Trans-Siberian route and is to be extended to other routes.

SZhD currently operates some 7000 freight yards, already about 10 per cent fewer than in the early 1970s, and the number is to be further reduced. Revised sorting methods have cut by half to two-thirds the time needed to form trunk trains. The Krasnyj Liman marshalling yard was the first of SZhD's to be equipped with a fully automated hump processing system, employing computerised route-setting, radar computation of wagon speed for retarder braking control, and associated data transmission systems. SZhD's 50 principal yards are being similarly equipped.

Other moves to enhance productivity include civil engineering measures directed to raising maximum freight train speed from 90 to 120 km/h, and continued experiments in operation of heavier freight train loads. Loads commonly enter the 8000–10 000-tonne band. The biggest yet attempted, on the Tselinna Railway between Ekibastus and Tselinograd, where trains normally gross up to 18 000 tonnes, is 43 407 tonnes. This 6·5 km-long train was formed of three approximately 12 000-tonne and one 6000-tonne section, each with its own traction, and with the intermediate locomotives radio-controlled from the lead unit by a system known as SMET. SZhD is working to standardise 6000–8 000-tonne freight train loads on routes totalling 60 000 km. Timetables now provide special schedules for higher-load trains, and for double train formations grossing 12 000 tonnes.

The system-wide average weight of freight trains was planned to reach 3650 tonnes by 1995 and 4000 tonnes by the end of the decade. Maximum permitted axle loading on main lines is now 23·25 tonnes.

A computer-based system for real-time freight traffic operational planning and control, known as ASOUP, is under development. Its implementation on the Byelorussian Railway has been a factor in this system's recent drastic reduction of staff.

300 km/h line to the south

In 1987 the Railways Minister announced a decision to create a 300 km/h line from Moscow to the south. It would run through Tula, Orel Belgorod and Kharkov to Lozovaja. There it would fork, one branch heading southwest to Simferopol, in the heart of the Crimea, the other southeast to Rostov-on-Don. From Rostov-on-Don further branches would head to Tuapse, on the Black Sea 'Riveria', the other to Mineralnije Vody, a spa in the northern Caucasus on the line to Baku.

In all, the project involves some 3200 route-km. The first 60 km of the exit from Moscow would be on existing track. How much of the remainder would be new infrastructure, how much adaptation of existing route, has not been revealed. The 1987 announcement anticipated that the first 380 km from Moscow to Orel would be ready as early as 1990, the continuation to Simferopol by 1996 and that to Tuapse by 1999. However, there has been no report subsequently of a start on construction.

It was proposed that the line would carry six 160 km/h container or refrigerated produce trains as well as about 100 passenger trains each 24 hours. Because of the distance, much of the passenger movement would be overnight. Passenger trains were envisaged as 16-car formations of sleepers and day cars powered by a couple of 300 km/h locomotives to a design derived from the twin-unit CS200.

New lines

Centrepiece of new construction in recent years has the 3145 km Baikal-Amur Magistral (BAM). Tracklaying of the whole line was completed at the end of September 1984. Opening to traffic throughout, however, was not possible until the end of October 1989.

BAM was built in fearsome geological and climatic conditions, in territory where temperatures range from −60°C in winter to 40°C in summer. Almost half the route is in the permafrost area. In full operation, the BAM is expected to move some 35 million tonnes of bulk freight annually from east to west in unit trains of up to 9000 tonnes weight. Special importance is attached to the BAM's potential as a landbridge for Far East-European container movement, since its use on completion is predicted to reduce maritime transit times between the Far East and major western European centres by at least 20 per cent.

Inauguration of uninterrupted through working was delayed chiefly by inability to complete the majority of its tunnels through severe geological difficulties in the mountains northeast of Lake Baikal. In the case of the 15 km Severomuysk Tunnel, a deviation of 60 km to bypass it had to be put in hand.

A so-called 'Little BAM' extends 402 km from the BAM proper at Tynda through the permafrost and across the Aldan, Amga and Lena rivers to Berkatit. An 830 km northward extension via Tommok to the important town of Yakutsk at present rail-less, was given the go-ahead in 1984 and track-laying began in April 1985. This extension will tap important deposits of apatite at Seligdor, iron ore at Tayezhny and coal in South Yakutia and was scheduled for completion to Tommot (380 km) by 1990, throughout by 1995. Temperatures in the area of the Yakutsk extension can fall to −63°C. It will serve nine freight terminals. Staff settlements will be located at 150 km intervals.

A 120 km branch to the Usinsk oilfield is reaching out from the Moscow-Vorkuta route at Synya, north of Pechora. In the Georgian republic a line has been thrust through mountains (at a maximum height of

Traffic (million)	1980	1985	1986	1987	1988
Freight tonne-km	3 439 900	3 718 400	3 834 500	3 834 700	3 924 800
Freight tonnes	3728·2	3951	4076·3	4066·7	4115·6
Passenger-km	342 200	374 00	390 200	402 200	413 800
Passenger journeys	4072·2*	4165·8*	4345*	4360·3*	4394·9*

*Including metro traffic

2163 metres above sea level) between Marabda and Akhalkalaki, a distance of 160 km.

A new 180 km electrified line is being built over the Arkhot Pass from Tbilisi to Ordzhonikidza, the Aragvi valley and the Caucasus. Completion will reduce the rail journey from Tbilisi to Moscow by no less than 950 km. It will be double-track, electrified at 25 kV (with automatic changeover provision where it joins the 3 kV dc Trans-Caucasian line) and equipped with CTC from the start. More than half the route will be on the 1100 m contour and a third of it will involve tunnelling, bridging or gallery protection against avalanches. The total of 22 tunnels, aggregating 42·5 km in length, includes one of 23 km below the Arkhot Pass. Ruling gradient will generally be 1·9 per cent, but one section will be 3·5 per cent, necessitating triple-heading of trains. Construction of 70 major bridges is entailed. This is the most taxing new line project currently in hand; it will take at least a decade to complete. In neighbouring Tadzhikistan, construction has begun of a line from Kurgan to Tyube and Kulyab.

A 450 km line in central Asia from Makat north to Aleksandrov Gay will lop 1100 km from the present rail distance between Moscow and the other central Asian republics. It will equally ease pressure on the parallel line north from Tashkent to Kuibyshev.

A railway is being taken further north than any previously built in a project to extend a 540 km line from Labytnangi, just inside the Arctic Circle, up the Yamal Peninsula to a latitude of 73° north at Cape Kharasavel. The objective is conveyance of materials to natural gasified plants, the output of which will be carried south in a pipeline paralleling the new railway. A branch of the line will cater for Novvy Port on the Gulf of Ob. Construction, which began in mid-1986, is posing more problems of work in permafrost areas, in this case coupled with high salinity in certain sectors.

Electrification
Electrification of main-line routes continues rapidly, to increase the loads carried and economise on liquid fuel to the order of about 70–100 000 tonnes per annum on every 1000 km of electrified track. Some electrified routes are now amongst the world's longest, such as Brest-Moscow-Novosibirsk-Chita-Karymskaya (7600 km) and Leningrad-Moscow-Rostov-Tbilisi-Yerevan (3600 km).

Electrification of tracks is being carried out at both 3 kV dc and 25 kV single-phase ac. The introduction in service of a new automatic transformer system of 2 x 25 kV with feeder wires is continuing. This installation almost doubles the distance between substations, reduces the amount of work during electrification of lines thanks to a considerably reduced electro-magnetic influence on communications, lowers the expenditure incurred in maintaining electric power installations, provides power for heavier train loads and enables the headway between heavyweight trains to be curtailed.

To lessen the expenditure of copper in contact wires, use is made of low-alloy contact wires with tin and steel-aluminium alloy wires for suspension cables on ac sections. Increasing use is made of polymer insulators and frameless wire connections.

Early in 1989, the extent of electrified tracks totalled 52 900 km. During the 12th Five-Year Plan SZhD was required to develop further the technology of electric traction, by increasing the power and reliability of supply systems, introduction of computer-based information-control complexes, a change to remote control operations over 7500 km of electrified track, and the construction of electric power supply installations in 20 railway centres.

The 1986–90 Five-Year Plan targeted electrification throughout the Moscow-Kazan-Sverdlovsk Gorki Railway, Chita-Khabarovsk (Trans-Baikal) and Tselinograd-Mointy-Chu-Arys-Tashkent-Samarkand trunk routes.

Traction
At present the basic freight hauliers on ac electrified lines are the six-axle VL60 and the eight-axle twin-unit Type VL80, first introduced in 1971 and subsequently developed in different sub-types, such as the VL80R with thyristor control and regenerative braking. The versions chiefly in use are the 6520 kW VL80S and VL80T, both twin-units, but the VL80S also appears in a three-unit variant with a one-hour rating of 9780 kW to fit it for unit trains of up to 10 000 tonnes from the east.

For freight haulage on dc lines the standard VL10 Bo-Bo twin-unit has been developed into the 200-ton VL10U, with a one-hour rating of 5360 kW, which is also produced in a four-unit, 10 700 kW version for

Prototype Czech-built (ČKD) Type CME-5 eight-axle diesel locomotive; series production was anticipated in 1991 (Ralf Roman Rossberg)

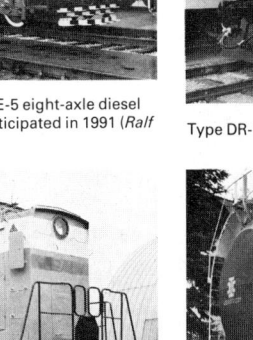

Type DR-1A diesel railcar (Ralf Roman Rossberg)

Eight-axle Type TEM-7 2000 hp diesel shunter (Ralf Roman Rossberg)

Eight-axle tank wagon (Ralf Roman Rossberg)

Type E29 25 kV electric train-set (Ralf Roman Rossberg)

10 000-tonne freight haulage, and the 12-axle VL11. The VL10U design has been further modified with additional transformer and rectifier as a dual-voltage unit, the VL82M, but SZhD does not yet have the justification to extend the limited number of this type to mass production.

Two new high-power models in production are each twin-units with 12 axles and weighing 300 tonnes. The ac unit is the VL85, with fully suspended traction motors, a one-hour tractive effort of 72 tonnes at 54 km/h, and a one-hour rating of 11 400 kW. Its mechanically similar dc counterpart is the VL15, with a one-hour rating of 10 560 kW and a tractive effort of 69 tonnes. The VL85 has regenerative rather than rheostatic braking because of the potentially damaging effect of the latter's heat dissipation on tunnelled structures in permafrost areas. A further prototype under development is the VL86F, a three-phase asynchronous 10 800 kW motor locomotive designed and built by the Novocherkassk works with the Finnish company, Kiumi Stromberg. SZhD aims to lift the power rating of this machine to 15 000 kW.

Passenger electric locomotives are supplied by Czechoslovak industry. For its dc lines SZhD has the CS200 8400 kW Bo-Bo twin-unit, which was designated with the proposed increase of maximum speed on the Moscow-Leningrad lines to 200 km/h in mind. At present the predominant ac type is the CS4T, introduced in 1973. For ability to deal with heavier trains under dc SZhD in 1982 unveiled the 8400 kW Bo-Bo twin-unit Type CS200, geared for a maximum speed of 160 km/h. Developments of this design are a 6160 kW, 160 km/h Bo-Bo + Bo-Bo classified CS7, with all traction motors series-connected for heavy haulage at medium speed, of which the first 10 were delivered by Škoda in 1984; and a mechanically- similar CS8 for the ac network. By mid-1987 Škoda had received orders for Type CS7 totalling 90 units.

Diesel-powered freight trains are hauled mainly by 12-axle twin-unit diesel locomotives of the TE3 and the 2TE10 series (in V and M modifications). A more powerful group comprises three- and four-unit diesel locomotives developing 9000 and 12 000 hp (the 3TE10M, 4TE10S and 4TE130S series), also the 3M62 developing 3 x 2000 hp, which is intended for work on the non-electrified sections of the BAM line in difficult winter conditions.

A new heavy freight haulier that went into series production in 1988 is the twin-unit 2TE121 diesel developing 2 x 4000 hp. The 2TE121 has dynamic braking. In addition, a prototype of the 6000 hp TE136 has been built, and project work is in hand on a twin-unit 2TE116, with five-axle bogies, developing 6000 hp per unit and powered by a new design of diesel

756 RAILWAY SYSTEMS / Union of Soviet Socialist Republics

Electric locomotives

Class	Wheel arrangement	Line voltage	Rated output (kW) continuous/one-hour	Max speed km/h	Weight tonnes	Year first built	Builders Mechanical parts	Electrical equipment
VL8	Bo + Bo + Bo + Bo	3000 V dc	3760/4200	100	184	1953	Novocherkassk	Novocherkassk
VL10	2 × Bo-Bo	3000 V dc	4500/5200	110	184	1961	Novocherkassk	Tbilisi
VL10U	2 × Bo-Bo	3000 V dc	4600/5360	110	184	1976	Novocherkassk	Tbilisi
VL11	2 × Bo-Bo	3000 V dc	4600/5360	110	184	1975	Novocherkassk	Tbilisi
ET42	2 × Bo-Bo	3000 V dc	4450/4840	100	164	1978	Novocherkassk	Novocherkassk
VL15	2 × Bo-Bo-Bo	3000 V dc	8400/10 560	100	300	1985	Novocherkassk	Tbilisi
VL60	Co-Co	25 kV 50 Hz	3330/4140	100	138	1957	Novocherkassk	Novocherkassk
VL60K	Co-Co	25 kV 50 Hz	4070/4590	100	138	1962	Novocherkassk	Novocherkassk
VL80K	2 × Bo-Bo	25 kV 50 Hz	6160/6520	110	184	1964	Novocherkassk	Novocherkassk
VL80T	2 × Bo-Bo	25 kV 50 Hz	6160/6520	110	184	1967	Novocherkassk	Novocherkassk
Sr1	Bo-Bo	25 kV 50 Hz	3100/3280	140/160	84	1973	Novocherkassk	Novocherkassk
VL80R	2 × Bo-Bo	25 kV 50 Hz	6160/6520	110	192	1974	Novocherkassk	Novocherkassk
VL80S	2 × Bo-Bo	25 kV 50 Hz	6160/6520	110	192	1980	Novocherkassk	Novocherkassk
VL85	2 × Bo-Bo-Bo	25 kV 50 Hz	9400/11 400	120	288	1983	Novocherkassk	Novocherkassk
VL86F	2 × Bo-Bo-Bo-Bo	25 kV 50 Hz	10 800	120	288	1985	Novocherkassk	Novocherkassk
VL82M dual-current	2 × Bo-Bo	25 kV 50 Hz 3000 V dc	5760/6040	110	200	1973	Novocherkassk	Novocherkassk
CS2T	Co-Co	3 kV dc	4080/4620	160	126	1974	Škoda	Škoda
CS4T	Co-Co	25 kV 50 Hz	4930/5200	180	126	1973	Škoda	Škoda
CS200	2 × Bo-Bo	3 kV dc	8000/8400	200	157	1975	Škoda	Škoda
CS7	2 × Bo-Bo	3 kV dc	6160/7200	180	172	1983	Škoda	Škoda
CS8	2 × Bo-Bo	25 kV 50 Hz	6160/7200	160	170	1983	Škoda	Škoda

engine. For diesel-powered passenger trains the SZhD uses the TEP60 series in both one-unit (3000 hp) and twin-unit (6000 hp) versions. For longer passenger trains (25–30 cars) the SZhD have begun series production of the TEP70 series of Co-Co powered by 4-stroke 16-cylinder diesel engines developing 4000 hp per unit. This locomotive weighs 129 tonnes and has a maximum speed of 160 km/h. A 6000 hp TEP80 is being designed.

The shunting park consists mainly of the TEM2 series locomotives with electric transmission, developing 1200 hp, the TEM7 (2000 hp) of Soviet as well as the ChME3 (1350 hp) of Czech manufacture.

Standard electric commuter trains produced by the Riga works since the mid-1960s have been of two series: the ER-2 for use on dc and ER-9 for ac. They have been improved as the ER-2ER and ER-9Ye series, with 21 m bodies. Each 10-car unit includes five power cars with all axles motored, for a total output of 4800 kW on dc and 3640 kW on ac lines. These trains have a max speed of 130 km/h. A more advanced series has recently appeared, the ER-24 for dc and ER-29 for ac, with 21·5 m long bodies and an acceleration rate of 0·72 m/s^2. They are all produced by the Riga works. A derivative of the ER-24, the dc ER-30, with a new type of traction control, was programmed for series production from 1989 onwards.

Rolling stock

The wagon fleet of the SZhD consists of four- and eight-axle universal open wagons, covered wagons, platforms and tanks, as well as special-purpose wagons intended for carrying cement, mineral fertilisers, grain, high-tonnage containers, flour, coke, peat and other cargoes. The passenger car fleet is based on all-metal carriages of 23·6 m body length.

All wagons are fitted with automatic coupling and automatic brakes; more than half of all freight wagons and all passenger carriages have roller bearings. A considerably higher payload is achieved by freight wagons of all-metal construction. Current construction of freight wagons is concerned with a further increase of load-carrying capacity, volume and area, to allow widespread use of mechanical means of loading and unloading. The most important new types in production are: a lengthened universal platform of 19·6 m length; a universal all-metal covered wagon of 140–150 m^3 capacity; and a platform with improved shock-absorber fittings for carrying high-tonnage containers.

An important feature of the development of special rolling stock is the increased production and variety of self-discharge covered hoppers. Under the 12th Five-Year Plan it was intended to increase the proportion of specialised wagons by 103–104 per cent.

All freight wagons in production have an axleload of 23 tonnes. Experimental models with axleloads of 25 tonnes were undergoing trials in 1989. The year 1990 was to see the completion of conversion of all freight wagons to roller bearings.

In 1988-89 2050 wagons were supplied by Rautarukki Oy of Finland. In 1990 this company was handed fresh orders for 1000 suto-carriers, 200 sulphur and 460 fertiliser wagons.

Track

The growth of traffic volume, higher-powered loco-

Heavy freight trains hauled by Class VL11 3 kV dc locomotives; the train above is fronted by one half of a VL11 twin-unit

Control centre of an automated yard

motives, heavier wagons and increased train speeds require strengthened tracks of improved construction, plus the availability and widespread use of high-productivity track repair machines which can accomplish heavy and difficult work at high speed and with minimal interruption of train traffic.

For track maintenance, use is made of more than 90 different types of specialised machine, mechanisms and devices. The level of mechanisation of capital repairs of track is now 88·7 per cent. Increase of mechanisation is a cardinal feature of the current Five-Year Plan.

Depending on traffic conditions, rail is of the following types:

Heavy, with thermically-treated R75 rails (75 kg/m) where load density is more than 80 million tonne-km annually per km;

Basic, with thermically-treated R65 rails (65 kg/m) where load density is from 25 to 80 million tonne-km annually per km. The R65 is also laid where load density is less than 25 million tonne-km annually if the line is used by passenger trains travelling at 120 km/h, and in suburban zones of especially intense traffic. R65 rails, not thermically-treated along their entire length, are used on lines with load density of 5–40 million tonne-km annually per km.

Light, employing R50 (approx 52 kg/m) rails, for line with a load density of 10–25 million tonne-km annually per km. R50 rail is not long-welded because of susceptibility to ambient temperature changes.

Sleepers
Wooden, saturated with oil antiseptics, length 2750 mm (for extra heavyweight traffic, 2850 mm), thickness 150–180 mm;
Ferro-concrete sleepers: S-56-2 and S-56-3, pre-stressed, length 2700 mm, height 193 mm at under-rail section, 135 mm at mean section. These are increasingly employed on heavy-duty routes.

Spacing
On straight sections: 1840/km;
On curves with radius of 1200 m and less; also with radius of 2000 m or less, where the speed of passenger trains is more than 120 km/h and that of freight trains more than 90 km/h; 2000/km.

Signalling
In 1986–1990 it was planned to install new automatic block signalling of USAB and TsAB types and CTC over about 9000 km of track.

For hump marshalling new types of retarders have been produced: the VZPG-VN11ZhT-3S with pneumo-hydraulic actuators and the VZP-BN11ZhT-5S with pneumatic actuators. Also being introduced is an automated train processing system (KGM) which is using microprocessor technology.

GEC-General Signal Ltd has won a contract to supply a comprehensive computer-based signalling and information system covering 167 route-km between Moscow and Kalinin. This stretch carries high-speed intercity, suburban and freight traffic. It includes 17 main-line stations, 25 halts and three major marshalling yards.

A new control centre will be created in Moscow containing a large over-view panel with 450 displayed berths. VDU fringe box units at six major junctions will provide input to the central computer and describe traffic entering the controlled area. Platform indicators will provide passenger information at stations and halts. Track-to-train data links will enable train description to be displayed in the driver's cab as determined by the control centre. Axle-counter equipment will record entry to and exits from the marshalling yards to provide information to centralised monitoring for maximum utilisation of yard capacity. At several curved station platforms closed-circuit television equipment will be installed to provide door monitoring. Computer-controlled route-setting and priority will be achieved by reference to the computer timetabling system. The central computer will also provide management reports and statistics and optimise maintenance, staffing and system capacity utilisation.

In 1989 the Ministry of Railways concluded an agreement for a Soviet-Italian joint venture involving Ansaldo Trasporti, Wabco Westinghouse and Fata for the modernisation of SZhD signalling.

Diesel locomotives

Class	Wheel arrangement	Transmission	Rated power hp	Max kg	Tractive effort Continuous at kg	Tractive effort Continuous at km/h	Max speed km/h	Wheel dia mm	Total weight tonnes	Length mm	Year first built	Builders Mechanical parts	Builders Engine & type	Builders Transmission
TE-3	2 × Co-Co	Elec	2 × 2000	58 200	40 400	20·5	100	1050	2 × 126	33 950	1953	Transmasch, Voroshilovgrad, Kharkov, Kolomna	2 × 2 D100	Elektrotyazh-masch
2TE-10M*	2 × Co-Co	Elec	2 × 3000	—	2 × 24 960	24·6	100	1050	2 × 138	2 × 16 969	1981	Voroshilovgrad	10 D100	Elektrotyazh-masch
TEP-10	Co-Co	Elec	3000	30 100 / 34 000	17 250 / 17 800	36 / 35	140	1050	129	18 160	1960	Transmach, Kharkov Voroshilovgrad	10 D100	Elektrotyazh-masch
2TE-10L	2 × Co-Co	Elec	2 × 3000	85 200	51 200 / 54 000	24 / 23	100	1050	2 × 129·3	33 938	1961	Voroshilovgrad	2 × 10 D100	Elektrtyazh-masch
2TE-10V	2 × Co-Co	Elec	2 × 3000	84 000	50 600	24·7	100	1050	2 × 138	33 938	1975	Voroshilovgrad	2 × 10 D100	Elektrotyazh-masch
TEP-60	Co-Co	Elec	3000	21 900 / 22 500	12 000 / 13 000	47 / 47·5	160	1050	126	19 250	1960	Kolomna	11 D45	Elektroyazh-masch
TEP-70	Co-Co	Elec (ac/dc)	4000	29 650	17 000	50	160	1220	129	21 700	1973	Kolomna	2A-5D49	Elektrotyazh-masch
M62†	Co-Co	Elec	2000	38 000	19 500	20	100	1050	116·5	17 400	1965	Voroshilovgrad	14 D40	Elektrotazh-masch
2TE-116	2 × Co-Co	Elec (ac/dc)	2 × 3000	92 000	2 × 26 000	24	100	1050	2 × 138	36 300	1972	Voroshilovgrad	2(a-5 D49)	Elektrotyazh-masch
2TE-121	2 × Co-Co	Elec (ac/dc)	2 × 4000	92 000	2 × 30 000	27	100	1250	2 × 150	42 000	1980	Voroshilovgrad	2(2V-5 D49) or 3 D70	Elektrotyazh-masch
4TE-130S	4 × Co-Co	Elec (ac/dc)	4 × 3000	—	4 × 26 000	24	100-120	1050	4 × 138	4 × 21 000	1982	Voroshilovgrad	4 × 2V-9DC (D49)	Elektrotyazh-masch
TE-136	Bo-Bo + Bo-Bo	Elec (ac/dc)	6000	—	48 000	25	100	1250	198	—	1984	Voroshilovgrad	1-20 DG (D49)	Electroyazh-masch
TEM-2	Co-Co	Elec	1200	36 000	21 000	11	100	1050	122·4	16 970	1960	Bryansk	PDIM	Elektrotyazh-masch
TEM-7	Bo-Bo + Bo-Bo	Elec (ac/dc)	2000	59 400/ 55 440	35 500/ 32 000	10·3/ 11·6	100	1050	180/ 168	21 500	1981	Lyudinovsk	2-26 DG (D49)	Elektrotyazh-masch
TEM-12	B-B	Elec	1200	—	24 000	10	40/80	1050	100	16 000	1978	Lyudinovsk	2-18 DG (D49)	Elektrotyazh-masch
CME-2	Bo-Bo	Elec	750	22 200	12 000/ 10 400	11·8	80	1050	74	13 260	1958	ČKD-Prague	6S 310DR	ČKD-Prague
CME-3‡	Co-Co	Elec	1350	36 900	23 000	11·4	95	1050	123	17 220	1963	ČKD-Prague	K6S 310DR	ČKD-Prague
TGM-6	B-B	Hyd	1200	26 100/ 29 700	14 000/ 25 190	14/8·5	80/40	1050	90	14 300	1970	Lyudinovsk	2A-6 D49	—
CEM-5	4 × Bo	Elec	4000	49 700	42 200	10·7	95	1050	168	20 220	1986	ČKD-Prague	K8S 310 DR	ČKD-Prague

* Also operated in triple-unit version (3TE-10M)   † Also operated in twin- and triple-unit versions (2M62, 2M63)   ‡ A variant is classified CME-3T

United Kingdom
Department of Transport

2 Marsham Street, London SW1P 3EB

Telephone: +44 71 276 3000
Telex: 22221 Telefax: +44 71 276 5179

Secretary of State, Transport: Cecil Parkinson
Minister of State Transport, with responsibility for railways: Roger Freeman
Deputy Secretary, Transport Industries:
Under-Secretary, Railway Directorate: J R Coates
Railway Inspectorate
Chief Inspecting Officer: R J Seymour

British Rail
British Railways Board

Euston House, 24 Eversholt Street, PO Box 100, London NW1 1DZ

Telephone +44 71 928 5151
Telex: 299431 brhqln
Telefax: +44 71 922 6994

Chairman: Sir Bob Reid
Deputy Chairman: Derek Fowler
Chief Executive, Railways: John K Welsby
Managing Director, Railways: D E Rayner
Managing Director, Group Services: John C P Edmonds
Members: Ms A Biss
Solicitor: S K Osborne

Business Sector Directors
  Freight: Colin J Driver
  Parcels: Adrian Shooter
  InterCity: Dr John Prideaux
  Provincial Services: Gordon C Pettitt
  Network SouthEast: C E W Green

British Rail Regional General Managers
  Anglia: D Burton
  Eastern Regions: J G Nelson
  London Midland Region: I W Warburton
  Scottish Region: C Bleasdale
  Southern: J R Ellis
  Western Region: B D Scott

Directors, Operations: Terry Worrall
  Civil Engineering: J S Cornell
  Mechanical and Electrical Engineering:
    David C Blake

Class 90 ac electric locomotive and London Euston-Blackpool InterCity at Wolverton *(John C Baker)*

758 RAILWAY SYSTEMS / United Kingdom

Signal and Telecommunications Engineering:
  K W Burrage
Research: Dr George Buckley
Procurement: P Keeling
Projects: Don Heath
Safety: Maurice Holmes
Quality: Brian Burdsall
Railfreight Distribution: Ian Brown
Trainload Freight: Leslie W Smith
Passenger Marketing Services: Alec McTavish
European Passenger Service: Richard Edgley
International Marketing: Ross Furby
Personnel: Trevor Toolan
Employee Relations: P Watkinson
Architecture & Design: Jane Priestman
Channel Tunnel: Malcolm Southgate
Finance: Robert Smith
Policy Unit: Charles Brown
Public Affairs: Jeremy Evans

Gauge: 1435 mm
Length: 16 584 km
Electrification: 2587·3 km at 25 kV 50 Hz ac 1958·2 km at 750 V dc third-rail

BR operates a system of business sector management for each of its five main activities: Railfreight; Parcels; InterCity passenger; Network SouthEast (formerly London and SouthEast); and Provincial Services. Sector directors have bottom-line financial responsibility for their prime-user assets and business results.

Financial objectives are set for each rail sector and subsidiary businesses covering a period of three to five years. Specific constraints, known as External Financing Limits (EFL) are imposed by the government on the funds which can be obtained by BR from government sources (including grants and loans) within a single financial year. For FY 1989-90 the EFL limit was set at £635 million.

Government objectives

In October 1986 the government revised its objectives, requiring that the InterCity, Railfreight and Parcels Businesses be self-supporting and in concert achieve a return of 2·7 per cent on their employed assets by March 1990. State support, through the annual Public Service Obligation (PSO) grant, would be limited to the Provincial Services and Network SouthEast passenger businesses. Within the non-supported sector, the BRB became free to adjust financial targets of each business as it saw fit so as to secure the overall objective.

Under the Railways Act 1974 BR receives an annual Public Service Obligation grant (PSO) with which it is required to sustain the same level and quality of service as existed in 1974, and at the same time cover total costs out of fare revenue and PSO grant combined. PSO grant supports only the Network SouthEast and Provincial businesses. Other business sectors are now required to be fully self-supporting and receive no government aid. Within the ceiling set for the PSO grant BR receives financial support from the provincial conurbation Passenger Transport Executives (PTEs) in Strathclyde (Greater Glasgow), Greater Manchester, Merseyside, West Midlands, Tyne & Wear, South Yorkshire and West Yorkshire where local train services are run to patterns and at fare levels specified by the PTEs as suits their overall, multi-modal public transport policy.

The government required a reduction of annual public money support to a total of £665 million by March 1990. In fact BR cut the level by that date to £574 million.

Fresh objectives set by the government have required BR by the end of FY 1992-93 to eliminate all need of public money support for Network Southeast, the essentially commuter system centred on London and embracing England's southeast quarter; to reduce to £345 million the annual support for the regional passenger services forming the Provincial business sector, which would then be the only one receiving subsidy; and to achieve profits for the other sectors of £95 million for InterCity passenger, £50 millions for Railfreight and £9 millions for Parcels.

Regions to go

In 1990 a fresh management restructure was beginning. The Regional tier of management would be gradually eliminated, leaving the previously subordinate Areas as the production units working to the specification and under the direct management of the Business sectors. The latter will develop further their present route or line management sub-divisions. Thus the General Managers of the Eastern, London Midland and Western Regions, for example, become respectively East Coast, West Coast and Great Western Main Line Route Directors reporting to the InterCity Business Sector Director.

During 1990 the Provincial Sector was to be renamed Regional Railways.

Class 86 ac electric locomotive and London-Norwich InterCity near Stowmarket *(John C Baker)*

Traffic	1987-88	1988-89	1989-90
Passenger journeys (million)	727·2	763·7	746·4
Passenger-km (million)	33 134	34 315	33 316
Freight net tonne-km (million)	17 462	18 099	16 738
Freight tonnes (million)	144·4	149·5	143·1

Finance

For the first time for five years the railway sustained in FY 1989-90 an overall loss, chiefly because of labour disputes that ignited a series of one-day strikes, but also because of tightness in the national economy that curtailed optional travel. At the same time the level of government financial support was again lowered, to a figure 58 per cent below that of 1983. The FY 1989-90 deficit of £26.4 million compared with an operating surplus of £107 million in the previous year. However, income from property sales boosted the overall group result for FY1989-90 to a surplus of £269.8 million, the third highest recorded since nationalisation. Investment totalling £715 milion for the year was the highest in real money values for 15 years.

In presenting these results the BR Board's new Chairman has admitted that the 1989-90 setback has made the objectives set for FY 1992-93 (see above) more difficult to achieve.

Investment

The biggest investment programme since nationalisation is in progress. The latest Corporate Plan, for the five years from FY 1989/90 to FY1993-94, planned expenditure totalling £4900 million. Major spending would be on renewing traction and rolling stock (£2576 million), infrastructure (£1494 million), and terminals (£836 million).

InterCity

In its second year as a fully commercial business without public money support, InterCity reported an operating surplus of £46.4 million and improved slightly on its profit objective, despite a loss of passenger-km through one-day labour strikes in 1989 and economic pressures that restrained leisure travel.

More Pullman services were introduced to serve the business travel market. Silver Standard, offering separate reserved accommodation and at-seat refreshments to business customers paying the full standard fare, was extended to trains between London and Tyneside after its successful launch on the London-Manchester and Liverpool routes.

InterCity planned to raise quality further by carrying out major improvements on the lines between Euston and Glasgow besides investing some £200 million completing electrification and resignalling of the lines between Kings Cross and Edinburgh. A full electric service will begin between London and Leeds from October 1989, when the next generation of InterCity trains is delivered.

InterCity's major investment, electrification of the East Coast main line (ECML) from London, progressed to the stage that a full London-Leeds electric service could start in October 1989. Energisation of the remainder of the route from London to Edinburgh remains due for inauguration by 1991. The project includes substantial resignalling schemes at Leeds, York and Newcastle, but the outlay involved in these has been considerably reduced by the advent of solid state interlocking technology with greater flexibility in its application than before.

ECML InterCity electric traction is provided by 31 Class 91 locomotives, an advanced 225 km/h design, though they are limited in public service to 200 km/h until the route is equipped with ATP (see below). However, a Class 91 has been run on test at 260 km/h between Grantham and Peterborough. Driving van trailers to allow push-pull working on both this and the West Coast main line were also emerging. On both ECML, West Coast main line (WCML) and the Anglian London-Norwich route, daytime electrically-powered InterCity service is now based on push-pull operation of fixed-formation train-sets, for which purpose a fleet of Driving Van Trailers (DVTs) has been built.

A contract for 283 Mk 4 passenger coaches and driving van trailers (DVT) of a new Mk 4 design for the electrified services on the East Coast main line was awarded to Metro-Cammell (now part of the GEC-

Propelled by a Class 91 ac electric locomotive and with Driving Van Trailer leading, a 200 km/h Leeds-London InterCity approaches Peterborough *(John C Baker)*

Rail Business Revenue (£ million)	1988-89	1989-90
InterCity	803·4	833·0
Network Southeast*	1 023·4	1 017·4
Provincial †	749·5	775·8
Trainload Freight	511·2	517·2
Parcels	125·5	119·8
Railfreight Distribution	170·0	176·7
Total	3 383·3	3 439·9

Rail Business Operating Expenditure (£ million)		
Total	3 209·2	3 315·3

* Includes grant support of £131·1 million in 1988-89, £87·4 million in 1989-90
† Includes grant support of £475·4 million in 1988-89, £499·4 million in 1989-90

Alsthom group). They sub-contracted to BREL (1988) for the manufacture of body shells, who in turn sub-contracted some of the work to Breda of Italy. Deliveries began in summer 1989. The Mk 4 cars run on SIG bogies, have power-operated external doors and provision for the future incorporation of on-train information systems. The 283 vehicles comprise 217 day coaches, 34 catering vehicles and 32 driving van trailers. The contract for 52 driving van trailers for West Coast main line push-pull services with an option for a further 10 vehicles, was awarded to BREL (1988).

Approval for an order of 31 more Mk 4 cars for the ECML was announced by the Transport Secretary in June 1989. They will enable InterCity to operate nine-coach push-pull trains instead of the eight-car, increasing the number of standard-class seats by 20 per cent on each train.

Inauguration of electric London-Leeds working enabled the fastest timing between the two cities to be cut to an unprecedented minute under 2 hours, by the southbound 'Yorkshire Pullman'. Some of the 200km/h diesel HST sets released by the ECML electrification to Leeds were dismantled to provide extra coaches for HSTs on the Great Western main line from London to Bristol, Wales and the West Country. Full train-sets were also transferred for intensified service on that line and between London and the East Midlands, enabling an hourly service to be operated between London and both Sheffield and Nottingham.

In June 1990 InterCity announced plans to invest £750 million in development of an InterCity 250 programme on the WCML. The immediate objective was to launch 250 km/h service between London and Manchester in May 1994, cutting present journey time for 304 km by at least 20 minutes to around 2 hours 15 minutes. The service will be provided by push-pull train-sets each comprising: a new-design Class 93 electric power car of around 5000 kW, not arranged like the Class 91 for independent operation as a locomotive on nocturnal sleeper or parcels trains; nine trailers of a new Mk 5 design, 26m long compared with the 23m of a Mk 4, probably fitted with a semi-active suspension, and in one car including a buffet; and a driving trailer which, unlike the DVTs currently in use will incorporate a kitchen for full meal service to its adjoining first-class trailers and be designated a DKT. Bids will be invited for supply of complete train-sets, whereas for the ECML's InterCity 225 locomotives and passenger cars were treated separately. The project includes further work to improve WCML alignments, which are historically less favourable to high speed than those of the ECML.

Work began in 1989 on an InterCity-sponsored £12 million electrification from Edinburgh to Carstairs, on the WCML to Glasgow. This will obtain faster service between Glasgow and northeast England, and between Edinburgh and northwest England and the Midlands.

Network SouthEast
Network SouthEast (NSE) had its original target of reducing PSO support to £149 million by March 1990 drastically revised to £94 million. Revenue loss of some £35 million from one-day strikes in 1989 and a recession of off-peak travel because of national economic pressures left the Sector needing £143 million of public support. But this compared in real money with £232 million of grant needed by the Sector in 1986.

Peak period traffic continued to rise. The average of 473 000 commuters conveyed into central London daily was a new record. It represented 42 per cent of all commuting into the city's centre.

NSE is in the course of investment totalling almost £2000 million in the five-year period up to FY1993-4. Roughly half is assigned to 1700 new multiple-unit cars (see below), to accelerate elimination of loco-motive-hauled train-sets and life-expired multiple-units of outdated design.

In May 1990 the cross-London Thameslink service was enhanced by demolition of London's Holborn Viaduct terminus and its replacement by a through St Paul's Thameslink station on the through route. At the same time south London coverage by the Thameslink service was extended to Guildford.

Third-rail dc electrification was completed between Southampton, Eastleigh and Portsmouth in 1990. Further third-rail dc electrification is planned from Wokingham to Reigate and Ashford to Hastings. In 1989 the government approved a 25 kV ac extension beyond Cambridge to Kings Lynn.

In August 1989 the government approved an order

Class 442 express emu on Weymouth-Waterloo 750 V dc third-rail service passes Basingstoke (*John C Baker*)

for the first 400 cars of a new generation of emu, the four-car Class 465 or 'Networker'. This first tranche will be for the third-rail dc lines in SE London and North Kent, where they will enter service in 1991/92. The order was divided between GEC-Alsthom (Metro-Cammell) and BREL 1988. The aluminium-bodied cars will feature GTO thyristor control of three-phase ac motors with regenerative braking, air suspension bogies, plug doors and dot matrix passenger information displays activated either by track-mounted transponders or track-to-train radio.

In 1990 work began on a four-year infrastructure programme to prepare for the Class 465 on routes out of London's Charing Cross, Cannon Street and Victoria termini. It included platform extension for 12-car train operation at 63 stations, upgrading of the traction current supply system, construction of a new maintenance depot at Slade Green and introduction of driver-only operation with train-to-ground radio back-up.

NSE has an option on a further 276 third-rail dc Class 465 emu cars to replace the existing inner suburban fleets serving Kent from London's Charing Cross, Cannon Street, Blackfriars and Victoria stations. A further 310 vehicles are needed for other inner suburban routes serving London Victoria and to meet future traffic growth. A tranche of 500 25 kV ac vehicles for the London Liverpool Street and London Fenchurch Street services is expected to follow from 1993.

Network SouthEast is also giving a £17 million facelift, with an increase of seating capacity, to its fleet of 768 Class 423 emu vehicles which operate the backbone of middle-distance commuter services south of the Thames.

Orders were placed in 1989 for 180 cars to form two- and three-car diesel-powered Class 165 'Networker Turbo' multiple-units for the non-electrified lines from London Marylebone to Aylesbury and Banbury, and from London Paddington to Reading, Newbury and Oxford. Built by BREL 1988, the first units were expected to appear in late 1991. The Class 165 will be powered by a new horizontal version of the Perkins Series 2000 engine, the Type 20006-TWH, which is turbocharged, intercooled and rated at 350 hp. The Class 165 will also be aluminium-bodied and feature dot-matrix passenger information displays and retention-tank toilets. On the London-Oxford/Newbury services Class 165 will run at up to 145 km/h.

In 1989 Network SouthEast placed an order for a further 780 self-service ticket machines for use at stations throughout the sector. These machines were in addition to previous orders, bringing the total number of machines to 1200. All the machines are manufactured by Ascom Autelca of Berne, Switzerland.

Two types of machines are being installed, one with a maximum of 40 destination buttons and the other with 92 destination buttons; each machine can issue up to 18 different ticket types. All machines will accept £5 and £10 notes as well as coins, can give change and issue magnetically-encoded tickets compatible with London Underground's ticketing systems.

Cross-London schemes
Early in 1989 a Central London Rail Study conducted jointly by Network SouthEast, London Underground and the Department of Transport to survey need in the light of traffic trends into the next century recommended construction of underground cross-town BR lines. One option, designated 'Full Cross', advocated two new BR routes: East-West Cross Rail, from Paddington/Marylebone to Liverpool Street via stations at Bond Street, Tottenham Court Road and Farringdon,

Interior of Class 442 emu standard-class saloon

Class 319 dual-voltage emu (25 kV ac/750 V dc third-rail) on Thameslink Bedford-Brighton cross-London service at Harpenden (*John C Baker*)

estimated cost £885 million; and North-South Cross Rail, from Euston/Kings Cross to Victoria, estimated cost £895 million. Alternatively, the study suggested combining the East-West Cross Rail with a new London Underground tube from Chelsea to Hackney. The government's immediate reaction was that means must be found to attract private capital to the schemes, though it would consider a measure of financial grant were benefits from reduced road congestion to be proven. Up to mid-1990 a decision to proceed with any of the schemes was still awaited.

Airport links
In association with the expansion of Stansted Airport, a rail connecting the airport with the Liverpool Street-Cambridge main line was under construction for

760 RAILWAY SYSTEMS / United Kingdom

opening in March 1991. Train service will be furnished by five Class 322 emus embodying special luggage areas, which will effect the 59km journey from airport to Liverpool Street in 41 minutes. The first emerged in July 1990.

In July 1988 the Transport Minister approved construction of a new rail link with London Heathrow Airport from London Paddington, promoted jointly by BR and the British Airports Authority. The project suffered delay in 1989 when the House of Lords rejected the route proposed in the Parliamentary Bill on environmental grounds. A surface approach to the airport was rejected.

The branch will leave the main line from Paddington west of Hayes station, where a flyover will carry Paddington-bound trains. It will then go immediately into tunnel to thread a first station under Heathrow Terminals 1,2 and 3, and terminate at a station under Terminal 4. The train service will be electric and all four main line tracks from Hayes to Paddington will be wired at 25 kV ac, though the 15 minute-interval Airport trains will normally use the fast lines. Journey times to Paddington will be 16 minutes from the Terminal 1-3 station, 20 minutes from Terminal 4. Given final Parliamantary approval for the revised scheme in 1990, the Heathrow Express service could be operational in 1994. The estimated £235 million capital cost of the project will be borne 80 per cent by BAA and 20 per cent by BR Network Southeast.

Provincial services

Provincial sector services, BR's regional passenger operations, increased their revenue in FY 1989-90, despite loss of income as a result of tbe one-day strikes in 1989. But the Sector was seriously affected by a major delay in delivery of new Class 158 Express dmus.

The first Class 158, with a top speed of 145 km/h, air-conditioning, trolley catering and facilities for the disabled traveller, were to have been introduced to Glasgow-Edinburgh service in 1989, when orders for a further 196 vehicles were placed to add to the 229 vehicles already being built. But because of difficulties in manufacture, a switch of this service to Class 158 was still impossible at the May 1990 change of timetable.

Other services scheduled to receive the Class 158 included the North Trans-Pennine from the Northwest to Middlesbrough, Newcastle, Scarborough and Hull; Cardiff to the Northwest, Southwest and Northwest, and from Norwich via Peterborough alternately to and from the Northwest and the North Midlands/North Wales. Non-arrival of Class 158 prevented redeployment of Class 150/1 Sprinter and Class 155/6 Super Sprinter dmus to replace 30-year-old, fallible and expensive-to-maintain vehicles on other services.

Private venture trolley catering is now a standard facility on all Express routes. In total this is a feature of 29 Provincial routes, which are covered by six catering companies.

Electric traction comes into Provincial's reckoning only when a service involves frequent stops or encounters stiff gradients (both of which put a premium on accelerative power); where there is a major growth potential; or where valuable maintenance savings are attainable. So TransPennine (discussed above) is the only Express route where electrification is a possibility.

Electrification prospects seem limited to one or two urban schemes, such as Birmingham cross-city (Lichfield-Redditch), in 1989 awaiting ministerial approval of the West Midlands PTA's £14·3 million-backed proposal; and the southward extension of Merseyrail to Ellesmere Port and Chester, which Merseytravel has agreed to support with £3·2 million.

These two investment undertakings typify the rising eagerness of local authorities to formulate cases for and to support new Provincial facilities. In 1989 about half the shire counties were actively pondering cases for support of new services. They included: Leicestershire, tor the parts of the Leicester-Burton line in its own territory; Nottinghamshire, in respect of Nottingham-Worksop; West Glamorgan, which was sponsoring a study of routes encircling Swansea; Mid-Glamorgan, which was looking at a westward projection over the main line from Cardiff; Cambridgeshire, in respect of Cambridge-St Ives; and West Yorkshire, working up to a five-year plan for development of routes and services.

Close partnership with local authorities has led to the opening or reopening of 103 Provincial stations since the sector was established in 1982. Plans were in hand in 1990 for more such inaugurations.

Class 321 25kV ac emu on London Euston-Birmingham semi-fast service near Wolverton *(John C Baker)*

Class 158 Express dmu for Provincial services on Birmingham-Norwich test run *((John C Baker)*

Electrification of a PTE-sponsored route, the Birmingham Cross-City line from Lichfield to Redditch, was approved in February 1990. For this scheme, and to replace life-expired emus in another PTE area, on lines radiating south of Manchester, a contract for 37 three-car Class 323 emus was awarded in June 1990 to Hunslet TPL. The aluminium-bodied cars will have three-phase ac drives supplied by Holec of the Netherlands.

The controversial closure of the Settle-Carlisle line, originally proposed in 1983, was finally rejected by the Transport Secretary. Abandonment had been sought because traffic volume could not cover the costs of repairing and maintaining the scenically-attractive line's structures, its Ribblehead Viaduct in particular. Extensive and repeated publicity for the great weight of objection raised to the closure proposal, and for the line's appeal, has substantially increased its passenger traffic. Effort is now directed to developing the line's business opportunities.

Railfreight

Railfreight, a business which has received no government support for 12 years, produced an operating surplus of £59·4 million in FY 1989/90, £10 million less than in the previous year. The Sector is now subdivided into Trainload Freight, covering the bulk commodities, metals and automotive; and Railfreight Distribution, dealing with intermodal, wagonload and international traffic.

In 1990 the Trainload business confronted uncertainties in its dominant traffic, the so-called Merry-Go-Round (MGR) conveyance of coal from pits to electricity generating stations by continuously circuiting trains of automatic-discharge hopper wagons. The newly-privatised electricity supply industry, though it has contracted to take from British Coal up to 1992 a tonnage little reduced from that bought by its nationalised predecessor, is expected to turn increasingly to imported coal for those plants using this fuel. This will involve Railfreight in creating competitive new MGR operations from ports to power stations. In one prospective case, a flow from Milford Haven port in South Wales, such a flow would entail mixing MGR trains with an intensive 200 km/h InterCity service on a double-track main line. But new power stations may well be gas-fired.

The Metals sub-sector took delivery in early 1990 of prototypes of a new range of versatile steel-carrying wagons. Fitted with retractable hood frames, the wagons have cradle-fitted wells below movable frame-level floors, so that they can be used either for coil transport or, with floor in place, for movement of metal slabs and sections.

Delivery to the Trainload businesses began in 1989 of 100 Class 60 3100 hp diesel-electric locomotives

Class 155 'Super Sprinter' dmu owned by West Yorkshire PTE (and in their livery) on Halifax-York service at East Garforth *(John C Baker)*

built by Brush Electrical Machines Ltd of Loughborough at a cost of around £120 million. All should be in service by the end of 1991. The latest adhesion aids and other technological advances will enable the Class 60 to haul much heavier loads than existing BR freight locomotives in Railfreight's core businesses: coal, construction materials, metals and petroleum.

A problem area in 1990 was the wagonload activity of Railfreight Distribution, known as the Speedlink system. It has proved impossible to reduce the high incidence of marshalling and local trip working in the overall cost of this operation, which was a main cause of Railfreight Distribution's FY1989-90 operating loss of £73·4 million on a turnover of £176.7 million. However, contraction of the business would be complicated on two counts: the fact that some of the private sidings contributing traffic were set up with the aid of government grants under Section 8 of the 1974 Railways Act; and the extent to which the traffic is carried in privately-capitalised wagons.

In May 1990 a £40 million order was placed with Arbel-Fauvet-Rail of France for 700 60ft container wagons to achieve a full renewal of the fleet employed in the Deepsea Freightliner services between ports and inland terminals. Whereas the existing Freightliner flatcars are in permanently-coupled five-car units, the new wagons will be arranged to form two- and three-car units.

For a proposed intermodal service from a new shipping terminal on the Isle of Grain, Kent, orders were placed in 1990 for 45 Lowliner wagons from Powell Duffryn Standard. These low-floor vehicles, employing the supplier's 520mm-wheel low track force bogies, can carry 9ft 6in-high swapbodies and containers within BR's W6 loading gauge.

Employing a leased stock of SNCF Multifret wagons, a 145 km/h Harwich Containerport-Warrington-Glasgow train service for import-export swapbodies was planned for launch in the spring of 1990. The train was to make a round trip within 24 hours. However, last-minute objections by the civil engineers compelled deferment. Pending modifications to the wagons, the service would be limited to 120 km/h and consequently be limited to operation between Harwich and Northwest England.

Investment of £175 million was approved in May 1990 for the first two projects preparing Railfreight Distribution for Continental service via the Channel Tunnel. One was the third-rail 750V dc electrification of the Tonbridge-Redhill line, the second of two routes west of Ashford, Kent, by which Continental freight trains will travel to and from London. The other, via Maidstone East, is already electrified. Also ordered, from Brush Electrical Machines, were the first 20 of a Class 92 dual-voltage (750V dc/25 kV ac) Co-Co locomotive type, for through freight train haulage between Fréthun yard, on the French side of the Channel Tunnel, and London's Continental traffic assembly yard at Willesden. A further 40 Class 92 may be ordered, to enable through train haulage between provincial centres and Fréthun, and also to haul overnight sleeping-car trains through the Tunnel.

Railfreight Distribution was seeking a further £135 million investment in Channel Tunnel-related schemes, which included enlargement of clearances between the Tunnel and London to BR's W6 loading gauge. Still awaited were full details of the 12 'freight villages' in prime British areas of consumption and production where concentration of international traffic origination and reception is planned.

The first of the new-technology intermodal systems to see revenue service with Railfreight will be the improved, four-axle version of Tiphook Rail's swing-deck well car for piggyback of the company's compatible semi-trailers. The Charterrail company leased 40, with an option for 60 more, and a matching fleet of semi-trailers for London area and Scottish distribution of Petfoods products from that company's Melton Mowbray factory.

Traction and rolling stock

In March 1990, BR was operating 1835 diesel locomotives, 260 electric locomotives, 197 HST power cars, 718 HST trailer cars, 2465 locomotive-hauled passenger cars, 1319 non-passenger cars, 2134 dmu and 7197 emu cars, 21 970 freight wagons (excluding service vehicles).

Ten Class 91 25 kV ac locomotives were delivered in 1989 for operation of the London-Leeds services from October 1989. A further 21 units would be completed by 1991 in time for the London-Edinburgh service. GEC-Alsthom is the main supplier. As recorded earlier, other locomotive developments included first deliveries of Class 60 freight locomotives and an order for Class 92 dual-voltage freight locomotives.

As mentioned above, from a 350 hp version of the Cummins engine, 425 Class 158 Express dmu vehicles have been ordered from BREL to conclude the replacement of locomotive-hauled services within the Provincial sector by multiple-units. To obtain maximum benefit, 10 intermediate vehicles are included in the Class 158 build to provide some three- and four-car formations. The first tranche has Cummins 350 hp engines, but BR has ordered the new Perkins Series d 2000 horizontal engine of 350 hp for a subsequent batch.

Emu builds under construction or in course of delivery in 1989 comprised 24 two-coach Class 456, to ease overcrowding on the London Waterloo suburban routes of Network SouthEast; 114 four-car Class 321 units for the Liverpool Street-Cambridge/Southend and other 25 kV ac outer suburban routes of Network SouthEast; 26 more Class 319 dual-voltage Thameslink units; 22 three-car Class 320, a variant of the Class 321 for Strathclyde PTE; and five four-car Class 322 emus for the Liverpool Street-Stansted Airport service. Ministerial approval for acquisition of seven more

Class 86 ac electric locomotive and Garston-Felixstowe Freightliner container train passes Milton Keynes (John C Baker)

Traffic	1985/86	1986/87	1987/88	1988/89
Passenger journeys (000)	685 900	689 400	727 200	763 700
Passenger-km (million)	30 374	30 812	33 134	34 315
Freight tonnes (million)	139·7	138·4	144·5	149·5
Net tonne miles (million)	9971	10 293	10 853	11 249
Operating Revenue	1985/86	1986/87	1987/88	1988/89
Passengers excluding government grant	1465·8	1591·3	1784·7	1969·8
Government grant	895·9	786·4	803·8	606·5
Freight	547·1	556·6	555·0	681·2
Parcels	127·1	118·9	120·3	125·5
Other				
Total	3035·9	3053·2	3263·8	3383
Operating Expenditure	1985/86	1986/87	1987/88	1988/89
Train operation, provision and maintenance	1150·0	1118·7	1103·2	1144·9
Operations control	170·0	172·1	179·0	187·9
Terminals	281·2	292·3	315·1	334·6
Commercial services and security	102·7	111·8	116·7	142·7
Track, signalling & telecommunications	594·9	575·0	650·0	621·7
General expenses	581·6	590·6	664·2	660·6
Total	2880·4	2860·5	3028·2	3091·5

Interior of Class 155 'Sprinter' dmu with folding tables on seat backs for use in conjunction with trolley refreshment service on cross-country routes

The first of Railfreight's new Class 60 diesel locomotives

Class 321 emus to serve the Cambridge-Kings Lynn electrification was obtained in 1989.

Specialist Rail Products, a subsidiary of RFS Industries, has been awarded a contract to develop a new lightweight Advanced Suburban Bogie for both emu and dmu units, in collaboration with BR Research and Mechanical & Electrical Engineering teams. This was to be followed in 1990 with invitations to tender for traction drive equipment to fit powered versions of the new bogie in emu applications.

Signalling

BR's signalling strategy envisages that the majority of InterCity, commuter and important freight routes will ultimately be controlled from about 75 signalling centres. To date about 50 centres have been established with the remainder of the system controlled from about 1800 manual or small power signalboxes.

Radio Electronic Token Block (RETB) schemes are now operational in the Dingwall-Wick/Thurso and East Suffolk lines, the West Highland line between Glasgow and Mallaig/Oban, and the Cambrian line between Shrewsbury and Aberystwyth/Pwllheli. This system replaces conventional signalboxes and block sections with a central dispatching system, whereby 'token' of authority to traverse a given section of line are transmitted by radio signals and are indicated electronically in the cab of suitably-fitted traction units.

RAILWAY SYSTEMS / United Kingdom

Electric locomotives

Class	Wheel arrangement	Supply voltage	Rated output kW	Max speed mph	Wheel dia mm	Total weight tonnes	Length m	No in service 1989	Year first built	Builders Mechanical parts	Builders Electrical equipment
73/0*	Bo	Third rail 660/750 V dc	Third rail dc 1190 Diesel 600 hp	80	1013	76·3	16·3	6	1962	BR/EE	EE
73/1*	Bo-Bo	Third rail 660/750 V dc	Third rail dc 1190 Diesel 600 hp	90	1013	76·8	16·3	45	1965	BR/EE	
81	Bo-Bo	25 kV dc	2390	80	1219	79·4	17·2	6	1959	BRCW	AEI
85/0 and 85/1	Bo-Bo	25 kV ac	2390	100	1219	82·5	17·2	29	1960	BR	AEI
86/1	Bo-Bo	25 kV ac	3730	110	1156	85	17·8	3	1965	BR/EE	AEI
86/2	Bo-Bo	25 kV ac	3010	100	1156	86·2	17·8	57	1965	BR/EE	AEI
86/4	Bo-Bo	25 kV ac	2680	100	1156	83	17·2	26	1965	BR/EE	AEI
86/6	Bo-Bo	25 kV ac	2680	75	1156	83	17·2		1965	BR/EE	AEI
87/0	Bo-Bo	25 kV ac	3730	110	1150	83·3	17·8	35	1973	BR/EE	AEI
87/1	Bo-Bo	25 kV ac	3620	110	1150	79·1	17·8	1	1975	BR/EE	AEI
89	Co-Co	25 kV ac	4350	125	1150	104	17·8	1	1987	Brush	Brush
90	Bo-Bo	25 kV ac	3730	110	1150	82·5	18·9	50	1987	BR	GEC-Alsthom
91	Bo-Bo	25 kV ac	4540	140	1000	82	19·4		1988	BR	GEC-Alsthom

* Electro-diesel

Diesel locomotives

Class	Wheel arrangement	Transmission	Rated output hp	Max speed mph	Wheel dia mm	Total weight tonnes	Length mm	Year first built	No in service 1989	Builders Mechanical parts	Builders Engine & type	Builders Transmission
03	0-6-0	Mech	204	28	1092	30·7	7920	1958	2	BR	Gardner 8L3	Fluidrive-SCG 23
08	0-6-0	Elec	400	15	1372	50·4	8920	1952	439	BR	EE 6KT	2 EE 506 motors
09	0-6-0	Elec	400	27	1372	50·4	8920	1959	25	BR	EE 6KT	2 EE 506 motors
20	Bo-Bo	Elec	1000	60	1092	73-74	14 250	1957	140	EE	EE 8SVT	4 EE traction motors
26/0	Bo-Bo	Elec	1160	60	1092	75	15 470	1958	12	BRCW	Sulzer 6LDA28	4 Crompton Parkinson
26/1	Bo-Bo	Elec	1160	60	1092	75	15 470	1958	18	BRCW	Sulzer 6LDA28	4 Crompton Parkinson T/Ms
31/1	A1A-A1A	Elec	1470	60	1003/1092	111	17 300	1958	124	Brush	EE 12SVLT	4 Brush traction motors
31/4	A1A/A1A	Elec	1470	90	1003/1092	112·6	17 300	1959	66	Brush	EE 12SVT	4 Brush traction motors
33/0	Bo-Bo	Elec	1550	85	1092	77·7	15 470	1960	32	BRCW	Sulzer 8LDA28	4 Crompton Parkinson T/Ms
33/1	Bo-Bo	Elec	1550	60	1092	78·5	15 470	1960	13	BRCW	Sulzer 8LDA28	4 Crompton Parkinson T/Ms
33/2	Bo-Bo	Elec	1550	60	1092	77·5	15 470	1962	9	BRCW	Sulzer 8LDA28	4 Crompton Parkinson T/Ms
37/0	Co-Co	Elec	1750	80	1092	102·2/107·7	18 750	1960	152	EE	EE 12CSVT	6 EE traction motors
37/3	Co-Co	Elec	1750	80	1092	102/108	18 750	1960	18	EE	EE 12CSVT	6 EE traction motors
37/4	Co-Co	Elec	1750	80	1092	102/108	18 750	1960	31	EE	EE 12CSVT	Altntr/6 EE traction motors
37/5	Co-Co	Elec	1750	80	1092	102/108	18 750	1960	54	EE	EE 12CSVT	Altntr/6 EE traction motors
37/7	Co-Co	Elec	1750	80	1092	120	18 750	1960	44	EE	EE 12CSVT	Altntr/6 EE traction motors
37/9	Co-Co	Elec	1800	80	1092	120	18 750	1960	6	EE	EE Mirrlees MB275T/ Ruston RK270T	Altntr/6 EE traction motors
47/0	Co-Co	Elec	2580	95	1143	112/125	19 380	1963	125	Brush/BR	Sulzer 12LDA28C	6 Brush traction motors
47/3	Co-Co	Elec	2580	75	1143	112/125	19 380	1963	80	Brush/BR	Sulzer 12LDA28C	6 Brush traction motors
47/4	Co-Co	Elec	2580	95	1143	125·1	19 380	1963	225	Brush/BR	Sulzer 12LDA28C	6 Brush traction motors
47/7	Co-Co	Elec	2580	100	1143	122·5	19 380	1979	16	BR	Sulzer 12LDA28C	6 Brush traction motors
47/9	Co-Co	Elec	3300	75	1143	113·7	19 380	1979	1	BR	Ruston RP12RK3CT	6 Brush traction motors
50	Co-Co	Elec	2700	100	1092	116·9	20 880	1967	39	EE	EE 16CVST	6 EE traction motors
56	Co-Co	Elec	3250	80	1143	125·2	19 355	1976	135	BR/Electroputere	GEC Diesels 16KT3CT	6 Brush traction motors
58	Co-Co	Elec	3300	80	1120	129	19 130	1982	50	BR	Ruston RK3ACT	6 Brush TM 73-62 motors
59	Co-Co	Elec	3300	60	1067	126	21 350	1985	5	GM-EMD	GM-EMD 645E3C	GM-EMD D77B
60	Co-Co	Elec	3100	60	1118	126	21 340	1989	5	Brush	Mirrlees MB27ST	Brush Sepex

Block posts are eliminated, and passing loops are fitted with self-restoring trailable points which are held locked for facing movements by hydropneumatic pressure. This system offers a very economical system of control for lightly-trafficked lines.

Solid State Interlocking (SSI) is intended to become the standard for the majority of British Rail's signalling centres. The system, conceived by BR, has been developed, manufactured, tested and installed under a collaboration agreement with the private sector.

The interlocking is performed centrally by microcomputers which communicate through serial data links with lineside terminals directly controlling signalling equipment. To achieve the required levels of safety and availability, cross-checking duplicate or triplicate systems are used (hardware redundancy). Built-in diagnostic facilities enable faults to be detected and rectified speedily.

Major resignalling schemes were completed or under way at Liverpool Street, York, Yoker (Glasgow North) and Newcastle in 1989. That at London Liverpool Street (which will be extended to cover the Great Eastern lines to Southend and Colchester) was the first to be based on the concept of the Integrated Electronic Control Centre (IECC).

In an IECC its area is controlled by a centralised solid state interlocking and, in place of a conventional panel, high-resolution colour VDUs are employed. Automatic route-setting is provided for the entire control area; manual route-setting is necessary only in exceptional cases, and is carried out by manipulation of a cursor on the VDU image using a tracker-ball, retaining the well-established entrance-exit principle. The signalling system provides data for comprehensive passenger and management information systems within an integrated communications network. This is intended to be a standard system for future large installations.

Other IECC-style control centres were being provided for York, Glasgow North and Newcastle. Several more were planned.

The last major resignalling scheme based on relay technology was likely to be the Waterloo Area resignalling on the southwest approaches to London. This scheme started in 1984 and, reaching completion in 1990, is based on free-wired route relay interlockings operated via electronic remote control systems from a conventional entrance-exit (NX) panel. The experience gained with the pilot Automatic Route Setting (ARS) at

Two Class 37 diesels return ore empties from the Scunthorpe steel complex to the Immingham import terminal (*John C Baker*)

Three Bridges has resulted in extensive use of ARS within the Waterloo scheme. This ARS experience has also been applied to the above IECC schemes.

Completion of the Waterloo scheme was delayed because of need to take account of the recommendations emerging from a government-commissioned enquiry by a leading lawyer, Anthony Hidden QC, into the causes and lessons of a collision of peak-hour trains near Clapham Junction in December 1988 which cost 35 lives.

One outcome was acceleration of work on an ATP system. In February 1990 contracts were placed for two pilot schemes. One, to be applied to the London Marylebone-Aylesbury/Banbury line, will adopt the SELCAB system of Standard Elektrik Lorenz. The other, to be installed on the London Paddington-Bristol main line, will employ the TBL track beacon system of ACEC. Availability for test commissioning was anticipated in 1991, followed by commitment to a national scheme in 1992.

Radio systems
The coverage of the 200 MHz National Radio Network (NRN) has progressed and in 1989 covered almost all the main-line network except in parts of Scotland. The first operational system was introduced covering the Kings Cross-Stoke Summit section of the East Coast main line coincident with the electrification from Royston to Huntingdon. Provision of NRN has avoided the need for provision of special electrification telephone facilities. Equipping of 1000 main-line locomotives with NRN overlay radio equipment was virtually complete by 1990. It was anticipated that all traction units would be equipped within five years.

Track
Rail: FB 113A, 56 kg/m
Cross ties (sleepers). Prestressed monobloc concrete, thickness 200 mm
Spacing: 1531/km in lines with speeds 160 km/h and over; 1422/km other lines except where curve radius is below 600 m, for which minimum spacing is 1531/km.
Fastenings: Pandrol clip
Minimum curvature radius: 400 m for cwr
Max gradient: 1:35
Max axleload: 25·4 tonnes

Trans-Manche Super-Trains (TMST)
In December 1989, at a ceremony in Brussels, contracts worth £500 million were signed for the first 30 Trans-Manche Super-Trains (TMST), the 300 km/h train-sets to operate the London-Paris/Brussels service. They will be built by the TMST Group, a tri-national consortium comprising two Belgian companies led by BN, three French companies and two from the UK, these both led by GEC-Alsthom. BR's share of the order represents 14 train-sets, the SNCF's 13 and the SNCB's 3 sets. Much of the technology will inevitably be derived from the SNCF's TGV design.

Each train will consist of 18 trailers, articulated in two easily separable rakes (as a safeguard against in-tunnel emergency) and flanked at each end by a 68-tonne power car. The latter has to be three-voltage (25 kV on SNCF, 3 kV on SNCB and 750 V on BR's Southern Region) but within a 17-tonne axleload maximum. Total continuous output under 25 kV wires will be some 14 000 kW, which will necessitate powering one outer bogie of each half of the trailer consist; on 3kV dc it will be 7200 kW and on 750V dc third-rail, 4300 kW. Asynchronous, inverter-controlled three-phase motors with microprocessor control and GTO thyristors will be employed.

Each train-set's air-conditioned cars will include two bar-buffet cars, two family compartments, special facilities for nursing mothers and accommodation for Customs and Immigration staff.

Further sets will be required for the proposed through services to centres north of London. As noted above, these sets will be divided on BR to cater for separate provincial areas. Consequently the trailers each side of the mid-train division point must be fitted with driving cabs designed so that passenger gangway access is uninterrupted when both halves of the set are coupled. Whether an acceptable design can be perfected in time will be a factor in the availability of these train-sets at the Tunnel's opening.

Delivery of two train-sets for evaluation is timed for early 1992. Series delivery is expected to follow from December 1992.

Until a new rail link is built from the British coast to London (see below), the standard timing for the London-Paris journey by these trains will be 3 hours,

Foster Yeoman-owned, GM-EMD-built Class 59 Co-Co heads an aggregates train from the Foster Yeoman quarry to a London railhead (John C Baker)

Class 58 Co-Co and Merry-Go-Round pit-to-power station coal train at Retford (John C Baker)

and for London-Brussels 2 hours 40 minutes. These times will perforce be extended by 10–14 minutes for trains leaving or arriving in London at the morning and evening peaks, because of conflict with BR's Network SouthEast commuter traffic. On the other side of the Tunnel the trains will use the SNCF/SNCB 300 km/h TGV-Nord and its branch to the tunnel (for details see SNCB and SNCF entries).

BR infrastructure plan
At the start of the tunnel operation, BR/SNCF-SNCB international passenger and freight trains will leave the BR Network SouthEast London-Folkestone main line at a junction between Dollands Moor, near Saltwood (16 km from Ashford) and Cheriton, the British Tunnel terminal. No new route will be built throughout from the Tunnel to London, but on the existing 750 V dc third-rail line signalling will be modified and the power supply improved to allow trains to accelerate to and maintain top line speed of 160 km/h between Tonbridge and the Tunnel.

Passenger trains will leave London (Waterloo) and join the traditional route to the Channel ports by a new flyover at Stewarts Lane, near Clapham Junction. Freight trains from the North and West will run via the West London line, then either use Clapham Junction, on the main Brighton line as far as Redhill then across to Tonbridge, joining the main route via Ashford to the tunnel; or via Swanley and Maidstone East. The Redhill-Tonbridge line will be upgraded, electrified, and have some clearances enlarged.

The West London line will be upgraded and resignalled. It will be electrified at 750 V dc from a reinstated connection at West London junction to the new TMST maintenance depot to be constructed alongside the Western Region main line at North Pole. Consideration is being given to electrification throughout from Clapham junction to Willesden Junction. The TSMT trains to and from the north will initially use this line until the new Kings Cross through station is available.

High-speed Tunnel-London Rail Link shelved
BR's initial dismissal of need to build a new line from the Tunnel incurred considerable criticism within its own country, as well as pressure from Eurotunnel for immediate moves to create a new London link. In 1987 BR set up a study team to review long-term need. At the Transport Secretary's request a preliminary report was completed and published by July 1988.

The report set out three options for a new high-speed link between London and the Tunnel, but observed that detailed design work and surveys to establish a preference could not be completed before 1990. Execution would take a further eight to ten years. The report concluded that there was no realistic alternative to building additional tracks either alongside existing routes or on new alignments, because of constraints that will ultimately extend over significant lengths of existing boat train routes. It emphasised that any proposals to build must show a proper commercial return to the BR and should also take account of its impact on the environment.

A new route, allowing for trains to run at up to 300 km/h through Kent, would reduce the journey time between London and Paris via the tunnel by some 25 minutes to just over 2 hours 30 minutes and that to Brussels to 2 hours 15 minutes.

The draft proposals aroused fierce environmental protests along much of the prospective lines of routes. Following extensive consultations with all interested parties, a definitive route was published in the summer of 1989. Earlier in the year BR had also decided to seek the necessary permissions to build a new international through station beneath London's Kings Cross terminus (see below).

The selected route, estimated to cost £1·7 billion to build, would run from Kings Cross in tunnel and from Waterloo on existing lines, the two approaches meeting at a sub-surface junction at Warwick Gardens, near Peckham Rye. From there twinbore tunnels would extend to beyond Swanley. From Swanley the high-speed line would run alongside existing tracks to South Darenth; then on new alignment to meet a new North Downs Tunnel before crossing the Medway at Halling on a new viaduct. From Detling new tracks would be laid alongside the M20 motorway and its Maidstone/Ashford extension, before the line entered a new tunnel under Ashford, emerging to run through a new Ashford station and alongside existing tracks to the Channel Tunnel. The line would be built to Berne gauge clearances.

764 RAILWAY SYSTEMS / United Kingdom

Of the 109·4 km between London and the Channel Tunnel, 37 km of this proposed Rail Link would be in tunnel, 25·3 km would run alongside existing railway and 22·5 km would follow the alignment of a motorway. Only 24 km (22 per cent) would be new surface transport corridor. To mollify environmental objectors the maximum speed on the route would be no higher than 220 km/h; that would be achievable over some 56 km of the route between North Downs Tunnel and Ashford Tunnel, between Willesborough, east of Ashford, and the Channel Tunnel.

The Thatcher government had incorporated in its Channel Tunnel legislation a provision that the project should not receive any state financial support. Given the high capital cost of the new Rail Link, and government wish that this too should be a privately-capitalised venture, BR therefore formed in November 1989 a Eurorail consortium with two private sector partners, Trafalgar House and BICC, to pursue the project. But it was quickly apparent, first, that because of the expense of the lengthy tunnelling proposed from Swanley to the centre of London, ways to make more use of surface alignments must be explored; and second, that even so the commercial return on the Rail Link investment would not meet the considerably higher criteria of the private sector companies. They sought at least a 12.5 per cent return, whereas BR needed 8 per cent to satisfy the Treasury.

Eurorail hoped that the government might be persuaded to inject money in the project without contravening its own legislation by basing its support on its powers to grant-aid urban transport improvements. BR proposed to use the Rail Link for a fast, limited-stop commuter service for Kent's long-distance London commuters as well as Continental trains. London travel time from Ashford could be halved, and savings of up to 40 minutes for commuters from Folkestone or Canterbury were forecast. Also contemplated was a mid-Kent Parkway station, north of Maidstone, with extensive car parking facilities, offering a journey time of less than 30 minutes to Kings Cross.

In June 1990 Transport Secretary Cecil Parkinson rejected Eurorail proposals for finance of the Rail Link, which he said amounted to requests for a total of £1900 million in government loans, grants and guarantees. The prospective benefits to London commuters were not commensurate, he objected.

BR's response was to move for a takeover of the Eurorail work and its partners' stakes therein, and to set out on its own to redevelop the Rail Link project. Its Chairman hoped to be able to submit a Parliamentary Bill in 1992 and have a Rail Link operational by the end of 1998.

New Kings Cross terminal

In 1988 BR selected Kings Cross as the site for a second international terminal in London. In November 1988 it deposited in Parliament a Bill for major improvements at Kings Cross and the neighbouring St Pancras terminus that would effectively merge the two stations.

The bill sought Parliamentary approval for the following major developments:

A new sub-surface (Low Level) station for international trains via the Channel Tunnel. It would have through platforms, enable international trains to continue journeys to destinations in the Midlands and North. The platforms would also be used by cross-London Thameslink suburban trains.

A major new passenger concourse building to be built between Kings Cross and St Pancras stations. The concourse would combine the separate stations into a single interchange with good access to London Underground. It would include the facilities, such as customs and immigration, required for access to the international platforms of the Low Level station.

Diversion of Network SouthEast trains which currently run into King's Cross to run instead into St Pancras station, over a new link across the northern part of the railway-owned lands in the area. The number of platforms in the St Pancras train shed would be increased from six to eight.

A new sub-surface ticket hall to give access to Thameslink suburban trains and the London Underground. This would replace the existing Thameslink station on the south side of Pentonville Road.

Reinstatement of railway tracks through to currently unused eastern bore of Gasworks Tunnel immediately north of Kings Cross station. This would permit the re-arrangement of the station throat to permit higher speeds and to provide for lengthened platforms.

It was envisaged that the railway improvements contained in the Bill would be constructed during the period 1990–95, although works in each area were expected to last considerably less than this period. However, this project has also excited controversy and in mid-1990 the Bill was still being deliberated in the Parliamentary processes. Nevertheless, BR hoped to have the new level platforms at Kings Cross operational by 1995. With the new Rail Link in abeyance, international trains would be directed into the low-level station via the Thameslink service's route.

In 1990 BR sought Parliamentary powers to construct a new connection, the West Hampstead chord, that will give access from Kings Cross to the WCML and Midland InterCity routes out of London.

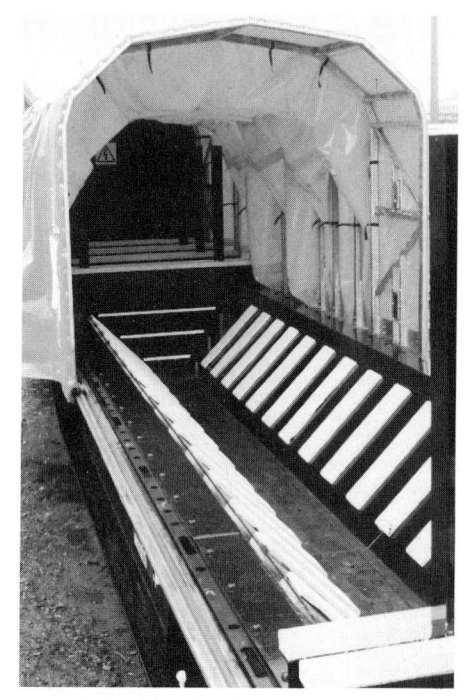

Rear end of Powell Duffryn Standard self-discharge hopper train operated on BR by Redland Aggregates, showing the rotatable discharge conveyor fed by a belt running the length of the train (John C Baker)

Interior of prototype Railfreight steel wagon, with well for coil conveyance uncovered and hood partially retracted (G Freeman Allen)

Northern Ireland Railways Co Ltd (NIR)

Central Station, East Bridge Street, Belfast BT1 3PB

Telephone: +44 232 235282
Telex: 747 623 nir
Telefax: +44 232 230630

Chairman: Sir Myles Humphreys
Chief Executive: Roy Beattie
Deputy Chief Executive: S G Shaw
General Managers, Freight: C S Myers
  Suburban: P R Thompson
  InterCity: D Grimshaw
  Mechanical Engineering: W Brown
  Civil Engineering: T McKinsty
  Signalling & Electrical: J Barnett
Company Secretary: R S Martin

Gauge: 1600 mm
Route length: 330 km

Class 110 diesel locomotive (Hugh Ballantyne)

United Kingdom—United States of America / **RAILWAY SYSTEMS** 765

Traffic	1986	1987	1988
Passengers journeys (million)	5·58	5·75	5·78

Finance (£000s)

Revenue	1985/86	1986/87	1987/88
Passengers and baggage	4901	5240	5574
Freight, parcels and mail	963	898	1914
Other income	5864	6631	6802
Total	11 728	12 769	14 291

Expenditure			
Staff/personnel	7866	8031	9117
Materials and services	3998	4209	5320
Depreciation	470	496	523
Financial charges	10	10	10
Total	12 353	12 746	14 960

Infrastructure
A Belfast cross-harbour rail link has been given the go-ahead by government and should be operational by 1994/95. The Department of the Environment will construct a new road linking the M2 and the Sydenham by-pass and a new rail link between the Larne line and Central station. The Department will construct the rail link up to track bed level and NIR will undertake the track work, signalling and commissioning of the railway. The road and rail links will cross the river Lagan about 200 m downstream of the Queen Elizabeth Bridge and will be elevated to provide vehicular headroom over existing roads.

Traction and rolling stock
The railway operates 12 diesel-electric and three diesel-hydraulic locomotives, 30 demus, one diesel railbus and 27 passenger cars (including two restaurant cars).

Track
Rail: 50 and 54 kg/m, 113 lb/yd
Cross ties (sleepers): Prestressed concrete, thickness 200 mm, spaced 1444/km in plain and 1536/km in curved track

Fastenings: Pandrol PR401
Minimum curvature radius: 200 m
Max gradient: 1·45%
Max axleload: 18 tonnes

Diesel locomotives

Class	Wheel arrangement	Transmission	Rated power kW	Max speed km/h	Total weight tonnes	No in service	Year first built	Builders — Mechanical parts	Builders — Engine & type	Builders — Transmission
110 (JT22CW)	Co-Co	Elec	1678	129	102	3	1980	General Motors	General Motors	General Motors
100	Bo-Bo	Elec	1007	129	69	3	1970	BREL/Hunslet	GEC Diesels/Paxman	GEC
—	C	Hyd	462	48	42	3	1969	GEC	Dorman 12QT	GEC
(Ex-CIE)	Bo-Bo	Elec	—	129	—	2	1956	Metro Vickers	GM-EMD 645E	AEI

Diesel railcars or multiple-units

Class	Transmission	Cars per unit	Motor car per unit	Motored axles per motor car	Rated output (kW) per motor	Max speed km/h	Weight tonnes per car (M-motor T-trailer)	Total seating capacity per car (M-motor T-trailer)	Length per car mm (M-motor T-trailer)	No in service 1987	Year first built	Builders
80	Elec	3	1	2	175	112	M 63 / T 28	M 45 / T 81	M 19812 / T 19812	21	1974	BREL
450	Elec	3	1	2	175	112	M 63	M 51	M 19812	9	1985	BREL
R3 Railbus	Mech	1	1	1	150	120	20	62	15240	1	1981	BREL

United States of America
Department of Transportation

400 7th Street SW, Washington DC 20590

Telephone: +1 202 366 4000

Secretary: Samuel Skinner
Deputy Secretary: Elaine L Chao
Asst Secretary, Budget & Programme: Kate Leader Moore
Public Affairs: David Prosperi
Policy & International Affairs: Jeffrey Shane
Executive Secretary: Ruth Drinkard Knouse

Federal Railroad Administration

Room 8206, 400 7th Street, SW, Washington DC 20590

Telephone: +1 202 366 0881
Telefax: +1 202 366 3055

Region 1: 55 Broadway, 10th Floor, Cambridge, Massachusetts 02142
Telephone: +1 617 494 2302
Region 2: 434 Walnut Street, Room 1020, Philadelphia, Pennsylvania 19106
Telephone: +1 215 597 0750
Region 3: 1720 Peachtree Road NW, Atlanta, Georgia 30309
Telephone: +1 404 881 2751
Region 4: 165 N Canal Street, Suite 1400-SA, Chicago, Illinois 60606
Telephone: +1 312 353 6203
Region 5: 819 Taylor Street, Room 7A35, Forth Worth, Texas 76102
Telephone: +1 817 334 3601
Region 6: 911 Walnut Street, Kansas City, Missouri 64106
Telephone: +1 816 374 2497
Region 7: 211 Main Street, Room 1085, San Francisco, California 94105
Telephone: +1 415 974 9845
Region 8: 1500 SW First Avenue, Room 250, Portland, Oregon 97201
Telephone: +1 503 221 3011

Administrator: Gilbert E Carmichael
Chief of Staff: Thomas M Fiorentino
Associate Administrator for Passenger and Freight Services: James T McQueen
Associate Administrator for Policy: William J Watt
Associate Administrator for Safety: Joseph W Walsh

Interstate Commerce Commission

12th & Constitution Ave NW, Washington DC 20423

Telephone: +1 202 275 7231
Telefax: +1 202 275 9237

Chairman: Edward J Philbin
Vice-Chairman: Karen Borlang Phillips
Commissioners: J J Simmons
Paul H Lamboley
Edward M Emmett
Secretary: Noreta R McGee
Chief of Staff: David M Konschnik

Urban Mass Transportation Administration (UMTA)

Department of Transportation, 400 7th Street SW, Washington DC 20590

Telephone: +1 202 366 4043
Telefax: +1 202 472 6944

Administrator: Brian W Clymer
Deputy Administrator: Roland J Ross
Associate Administrators
Budget and Policy: John A Cline
Administration: Thomas R Hunt
Technical Assistance: Lawrence L Schulman
Grants Management: Robert H McManus

UMTA is the Federal agency responsible for providing financial assistance to American cities to improve mass transportation. Hitherto, approximately 80 per cent of all transit capital improvements made in the United States have been financed with Federal funds from the agency, which also provides assistance in planning, research and development and operation of public transport systems.

766 RAILWAY SYSTEMS / United States of America

Class 1 railroads

The following main section lists class 1 railroads, which by the latest Interstate Commerce Commission definition are systems with a gross revenue of US$87·9 million or more. The second section lists the more important companies in the Class II (gross revenue US$17·7–87·8 million) and III category.

National Railroad Passenger Corporation (Amtrak)

Washington Union Station, 60 Massachusetts Avenue NE, Washington DC 20002

Telephone: +1 202 906 3000
Telefax: +1 202 906 3865

President and Chairman of the Board: W Graham Claytor Jnr
Executive Assistant: Beverly Balanda
Executive Vice President: William S Norman
Executive Vice President and Chief Operating Officer: Dennis F Sullivan
Vice President, Transportation: Robert C Vander Clute
Vice President, Law: Harold R Henderson
Vice President, Sales: Robert E Gall
Vice President, Passenger Marketing: Timothy P Gardner
Vice President, Engineering: Peter A Cannit
Vice President, Corporate Planning and Development: Elyse Wander
Vice President, Finance and Administration: Charles W Hayward
Assistant Vice President, Labour Relations: John P Lange
Vice President, Information Systems: Norris W Overton
Assistant Vice President, Personnel: Neil D Mann
Vice President, Passenger Services: Eugene N Eden
Assistant Vice President, Government and Public Affairs: Thomas J Gillespie
Assistant Vice President, Real Estate: Anthony De Angelo
Controller: Robert L Lewis
Treasurer: Richard T Klein

Gauge: 1435 mm
Route length owned: 557 km
Electrification: 554·6 km at 11 kV ac 25 Hz

Amtrak was created when the Rail Passenger Service Act was enacted in October 1970. Services began in May 1971, establishing the first nationwide rail passenger service under one management in the USA.

Except in the Boston-New York-Washington Northeast Corridor, Amtrak's rail passenger service is totally dependent upon the condition of track and related facilities that are owned, designed, maintained and operated by the private freight-hauling railroads. Amtrak has hitherto been supported by Federal capital and operating grants, the amount of which is annually budgeted by the Administration and approved by Congress.

The Amtrak legislation also provides for states or regional agencies to obtain service not included in the Basic System. Under this Clause 403(b) provision the local jurisdiction must at present assume 45 per cent of the short-term avoidable loss of operating the service for the first year and 65 per cent of the loss for each year thereafter, plus 50 per cent of the capital expenses for equipment, facilities or track repair in each year. New so-called '403(b)' services continue to be created.

Threat to Amtrak survival still averted

Since 1985 the Republican administrations have yearly proposed to eliminate all Federal funding for Amtrak. These proposals, however, have so far been rejected by Congress, which has appropriated grants sufficient to operate most existing trains, but not for Amtrak's requested capital requirements.

For FY 1990 President Bush left Congress to identify any cuts in funding. Amtrak was seeking US$656 million, to include US$100 million for capital improvements, plus US$56 million for work in the Northeast Corridor. The figure eventually set by Congress was US$615 million.

Amtrak has stressed its need not only for subsidies to meet its operating requirements, but for capital as well to improve its infrastructure and build new rolling stock. New cars and locomotives are desperately needed to cope with the rising demand for Amtrak services. Amtrak points to its significant financial and performance improvements despite reduced Federal support.

Bi-level Superliner (cars four to eight of the consist) in 'California Zephyr' service

Class AEM-7 electric locomotive and train of Amfleet II cars in the Northeast Corridor

Prototype 'Viewliner' sleeping car

However, President Bush's second Budget, for FY 1991, again sought to eliminate all funding of Amtrak (and also all operating subsidies for mass urban transit, another recurrent Republican move so far frustrated by Congress). Amtrak was requesting US$683 million. Of this US$495 million, US$35 million less than for the previous year, was sought for operations; the remainder, US$188 million, was requested for capital improvements, to enable Amtrak to leverage funds borrowed from the private sector for traction and rolling stock acquisitions, and for plant modernisation. Amtrak also sought US$58.5 million more for the Northeast Corridor Improvement Project (see below), towards extension of the Corridor's CETC system from Wilmington, Del, to Newark, NJ, under a scheme jointly funded by itself, UMTA, SEPTA and New Jersey Transit.

Financial achievements

In FY 1981 revenues covered only 48 per cent of total operating costs. In FY 1989 the ratio was 72 per cent, and a ratio of 78 per cent was anticipated in 1990. For the third year in succession short-term avoidable costs in FY 1989 were more than covered by revenue, by a ratio of 1·2 compared to 1·03 in 1987. Since FY 1981 Federal financial support for Amtrak as a percentage of the US Budget has been halved, and Federal operating subsidy cut by 40 per cent at 1981 money values. Over the same period Federal capital grants have been cut by 84 per cent at current money values.

Passenger revenue has been supplemented by diversification into activities such as a fibre-optics installation in Amtrak's Northeast Corridor right-of-way, transit car assembly (294 vehicles) for the Washington Metro on behalf of Breda at its Beech Grove maintenance shops in Indianapolis, and property development at its stations.

Finance (US$ million)

Revenues	1987	1988	1989
Passengers	655·2	765·5	870·2
Mail, baggage	32·6	34·9	37·0
Real estate	24·1	30·7	43·0
Contract	148·7	173·3	184·1
Interest	19·8	19·7	32·4
Other	93·0	82·6	102·4
Total	973·5	1106·7	1269·1
Expenditure			
Staff/personnel	910·1	993	1055·7
Materials and services	513·3	547·8	635·1
Depreciation	163·4	153·7	165·8
Financial charges	85·2	61·8	77·9
Total	1672·0	1757·1	1934·5

Traffic (million)

	1987	1988	1989
Passenger journeys	20·389	21·496	21·4
Passenger-miles	5221	5678	5859

Traffic

FY 1989 was another outstanding year in almost all respects. More passengers travelled greater distances, producing record revenues of US$1 270 million, a 14.7 per cent improvement on the previous year. Between 1985 and 1989 revenues rose 54 per cent, whereas expenses went up only 21 per cent, but in FY 1989 cost increases outstripped revenue growth, largely because of inflation in the cost of employee health and benefit schemes. Control of this factor was a crucial item of 1990 negotiations with the labour unions.

Amtrak carried 21·4 million intercity passengers in FY 1989, marginally less than in the year before, because of moves to boost revenue by giving preference on key trains to longer-haul passengers so as to boost revenue. Thus the total of intercity passenger miles rose from 5.7 billion in FY1988 to 5.86 billion, in contrast to the slight downturn in total of journeys. The 1989 total was considerably more than the 4.999 billion journeys logged in 1970, the last year of pre-Amtrak passenger service by the railroads over a significantly more extensive network and with more annual train-miles.

Amtrak is now the dominant carrier between New York and Washington, carrying more passengers than any one airline. Demand has been stimulated, amongst other things, by the newly-renovated Washington Union Station. This line's Metroliner trains recorded 8.5 per cent more passengers in FY 1989, lifting their annual total over 2 million. The service now includes four Express Metroliners that have reduced New York-Washington journey time to 2 hours 35 minutes.

'Viewliner' deluxe bedroom by night

'Viewliner' deluxe bedroom by day

'Horizon Fleet' car by Bombardier

Main Hall of restored Washington Union station

768 RAILWAY SYSTEMS / United States of America

Metroliner trains offer extra-fare first-class Club Service, providing complimentary meals served at seats and other service amenities, and run at up to 200 km/h. Amtrak also operates four Metroliner trains between New York and Boston on weekends, providing all-reserved seating in that growing segment of the Northeast Corridor.

Commuter ridership on trains Amtrak operates under contract for local transit agencies (see below) totalled 17.4 million journeys in FY1989.

System-wide, on-time reliability was improved from 71.4 to 75.1 per cent in FY 1989. Much of the control over the on-time performance of Amtrak trains lies with the freight railroads who own and control the tracks where the majority of them operate. In the Northeast Corridor, where Amtrak owns and controls most of the track, on-time performance improved over the previous year from 82·1 to 87 per cent, with the Metroliners showing 92.8 per cent. But outside the Corridor, on freight railroad-owned track, the average was only 67 per cent.

Amtrak is experimenting with automatic ticketing machines which may be used by customers during peak travel times when lines are long at the ticket windows. The self-service ticketing is available in New York, Washington, Philadelphia and in Los Angeles.

New services

A new high-frequency push-pull operation between Philadelphia and Atlantic City was inaugurated in May 1989. Considerable track work was required, and US$30 million was earmarked from Amtrak for that purpose. The remainder of the US$75 million costs for improvements have been paid by the state of New Jersey and local communities. Harmon Industries was awarded a US$3 million contract for design, manufacture and supply of an integrated signalling system for the mainly single-track route of 55 miles.

The route is served each weekday by four round-trips to Philadelphia and two to New York and Washington. From June 1990 three of the Philadelphia services were extended to Philadelphia International Airport, following an arrangement with Midway Airlines whereby airline passengers could book through tickets and air-rail baggage transfer to Atlantic City.

Initial patronage was disappointing because of the refusal of Atlantic City casino operators to offer railborne passengers the same inducements as they did to visitors coming by bus. But by early 1990 attitudes were changing. Approximately 11 New Jersey Transit commuter trains also use portions of the route. New Jersey Transit has built a new station within a convention centre complex at Atlantic City.

After two years of suspension because of track problems on the Boston & Maine Railroad, the 'Montrealer' was reinstated between Washington DC and Montreal via Vermont in July 1989, and ridership exceeded projections.

From November 1989 Amtrak was conveying on its Washington-Chicago 'Capitol Limited' the privately-owned cars of American European Express, a company offering premium-priced luxury overnight service of European 'Orient Express' character. In 1990 Transcisco Industries' new subsidiary, Trancisco Tours, contracted with Amtrak for operation of a similar train, the 'Transcisco 49er', twice weekly between San José, Oakland, Sacramento and Reno. The vehicles employed would be rebuilds of bi-level commuter gallery cars. A companion Los Angeles-Las Vegas service was planned.

With the January 1990 conversion of the Chicago-Houston/Los Angeles 'Texas Eagle' from thrice-weekly to daily operation, Amtrak was left with only two other services, the tri-weekly 'Cardinal' and 'Sunset Limited', to intensify for achievement of its goal of daily operation of all its trains. But for that acquisition of new cars was needed.

Meanwhile, deliveries of new short-haul coaches (see below) have permitted some modest expansions of shorter-distance services. A new '403b' service was launched between Chicago and Milwaukee in October 1989; and two months later an existing '403b' operation, the Bakersfield-Oakland 'San Joaquin', was expanded by a third service. A state-supported service between Birmingham and Mobile was inaugurated in October 1989. California's June 1990 vote for US$ 2 billion of bond sales and US$ 3 billion from higher petrol tax for rail passenger development was expected to result in further intensified 'San Joaquin' service and for extra trains in the Auburn-Sacramento-Oakland-San José corridor. Elsewhere, discussions and studies were in progress concerning new services between Seattle and Vancouver, Chicago and Florida, and through Oklahoma.

Interior of 'Horizon Fleet' car

Amtrak's 'Atlantic City Express' service detrains passengers within a few blocks of the resort's casinos

Northeast Corridor

Excluding sections owned by six Regional commuter authorities, Amtrak has owned the 585 km Boston-New York-Washington Northeast Corridor Route since 1976, including five of its stations: Baltimore, Wilmington, Philadelphia (30th Street), New York Penn station and Providence. An improvement project (NECIP) is nearing completion. This was originally budgeted at US$2500 million, but the Reagan administration's budget proposals limited funding authorisation up to end FY 1984 to US$2190 million. However, Congress subsequently authorised an extra US$98 million for FY 1985–89 to cover track, bridge-work, electrification and mechanical projects; and, as reported above, Amtrak was seeking a further sum for FY 1991. At present 440 km of the route has authority to be operated at 202 km/h.

In total 363 route-km and 1720·1 track-km of the Amtrak Northeast Corridor system are electrified at 12 kV ac 25 Hz. Conversion of 24·5 route-km between New York City and New Rochelle, New York, to 60 Hz was completed in 1987.

A project with long-term implications for Amtrak is New York's West Side Connection, the re-routing of trains now using Grand Central Terminal to take them down the west side of Pennsylvania station. This is a US$85 million project, with Amtrak funding 60 per cent of the cost; the remaining 40 per cent will be funded by New York state. When completed in 1991, it will save Amtrak the cost of using Grand Central Terminal.

Rail freight service on the Northeast Corridor, all operated by Conrail, Delaware & Hudson, Boston & Maine and Providence currently consists almost entirely of delivery and pick-up on industrial sidings and some through trains operating non-stop between major yards.

Commuter rail service is operated on the Northeast Corridor by the following agencies:
Maryland Department of Transportation (MARC):

Type	Wheel arrangement	Output hp	Max speed mph	Weight short tons	No in service 1989	Year built	Builders	Engine and type
Diesel locomotives								
F40PH	B-B	3000	103	130	29	1976/85	GM	16-645 E3B
F40PH	B-B	3000	103	131	179	1977/87	GM	16-645 E3B
F40AC	B-B	3000	103	133	1	1987	GM	16-645 E3B
F69AC	B-B	3000	103	NA	2	1989		12-710 G3
P30CH	C-C	3000	103	193	23	1975	GE	FOL16
FL9*	B-A1A	1750	89/103	145	6	1957	GM	16-657 C
GP40TC	B-B	3000	103	132	8	1966	GM	16-643E3
11 kV ac electric locomotives								
E60CP	C-C	5100	90	183	3	1975	GE	
E60MA	C-C	5100	90	183	9	1975	GE	
AEM-7	B-B	6200	125	91	52	1980	GM/ASEA	

*Dual-mode: diesel & electric dc

Turboliners

Class	Cars per unit	Motor cars per unit	Motored axles per motor car	Rated power (hp) per motor	Max speed mph	Weight short tons per set	Total seating capacity per car	Length per car ft in (M-motor T-trailer)	No in service 1988	Year first built	Builders Mechanical parts	Engine & type	Transmission
RTG	5	2	2	1 × 1100 1 × 1600	110	289	Food service 44, coach 72	M 86′ 8″ 83′ 7″	3	1973	ANF	Turmo III Turmo XII	Voith
RTL	5	2	2	1 × 1100 1 × 1600	110	309	Food service 44, coach 72	M 86′ 8″ T 83′ 7″	7	1976	ANF/Rohr	Turmo III Turmo XII	Voith

Baltimore-Washington;
Southeastern Pennsylvania Transportation Authority (SEPTA): Philadelphia-Trenton, Marcus Hook, Downington;
New Jersey Department of Transportation: Trenton and New York Penn station;
Metropolitan Transportation Authority: Penn station to the Borough of Queens;
Massachusetts Bay Transit Authority (MBTA): Attleboro to Boston.

The MARC and MBTA services are operated by Amtrak under contract.

Amtrak is concerned commuter and freight service users of the Corridor do not pay their fair share of the costs of maintaining and operating the route, and seeks to have UMTA meet the commuter train shortfall. This was estimated at US$ 33 million in 1990 and some US$47 million for 1991.

Talgo/LRC New York-Boston trials
In mid-1986 the Coalition of Northeast Governors (CONEG), representing seven states, formed a task force to study the 'feasibility, applicability and benefits' of high passenger rail speed to their region. The task force is concerned as a priority to see improvement between Boston and New York, where the Northeast Corridor Improvement Programme's financial cutbacks have prevented continuation of electrification from New Haven north to Boston and the originally proposed accelerations. The task force would like to have Boston-New York journey time trimmed from the present 4½–5 hours to 3 hours.

CONEG recommended evaluation of tilt-body equipment and in 1987 Amtrak reached an agreement with RENFE-Talgo, a joint venture of the Spanish National Railways and the Talgo car manufacturing concern, to import six Talgo Pendular cars for testing in the Boston-New York rail corridor. The cars were evaluated in the spring of 1988. RENFE-Talgo covered the shipping costs for the cars and provided technical advisors. Amtrak also tested Bombardier LRC equipment, of the type employed by VIA in Canada. A full report on the trials was submitted to CONEG and Congress early in 1989.

In early 1990 Amtrak, CONEG and the FRA were meeting to evolve an agreed plan for financing a New York-Boston development programme. Traction was apparently an issue, with CONEG pressing for resort to electro-diesel locomotives so as to accelerate introduction of a faster service, and Amtrak arguing for completion of electrification to Boston.

Signalling
The southern end of the NEC from Washington to Wilmington has been equipped with Chrysler's Centralized Electronic Traffic Control (CETC) system. Its functions include remote control of all substations. Amtrak was in 1990 seeking funds to extend this installation from Wilmington to Newark, NJ.

The northern end of the NEC was partially equipped with CETC in 1989. This initial installation, with a control centre in Boston South station, controls seven interlockings. It will be extended to reach Cranston, Rhode Island, taking in eight more interlockings.

Washington
The original Union station building, which opened in 1906, has been reconstructed and was reopened in September 1988.

More than 18 000 Amtrak passengers and Maryland commuters use the station every day, making it the third busiest in Amtrak's nationwide system of nearly 500 stations. Within the 80-year-old Beaux Arts building designed by Daniel Burnham, the barrel-vaulted Main Hall leads to the station concourse and a 20-position Amtrak ticket counter and baggage check-in facilities. Just behind the ticket counter is a large new waiting room with more than four times as many seats as Amtrak's previous temporary station. Escalators and elevators provide access to a new parking garage. There are new baggage carousels for retrieving checked baggage.

In further work continuing to 1990 Amtrak would achieve completion phase of its Union station facilities. First the old station would be demolished; then the tracks would be extended back toward the new station. In addition, Amtrak will build a new lounge for use by passengers who hold premium-fare tickets.

Union station already has an array of shops and restaurants in the concourse, and in the food court on the lower level. More shops, restaurants, and a nine-screen cinema were opened in 1989.

The restored Union station is the product of a public-private partnership that has invested more than US$150 million in the project.

Investment
Amtrak's objective of 100 per cent coverage of costs out of revenue by the end of the century is dependent on Federal, state and private sector funding support for renewal of its high ratio of life-expired traction and rolling stock, and for other investment in infrastructure and support services. The requirements are:
- Some 270 state-of-the-art locomotives, to cover expanded train formations and new services as well as renewals.
- About 175 Superliner and 307 Viewliner cars (see below). This would allow elimination of the 'Heritage' fleet of cars taken over from railroads at Amtrak's foundation.
- Updating of maintenance and overhaul facilities.
- Infrastructure work in the Northeast Corridor to obtain New York-Washington and New York-Boston journey times of at least 2 hours 30 minutes and 2 hours 59 minutes respectively.
- Means to improve Amtrak's capability of earning revenue from ancillary activity, such as its real estate, mail conveyance, commuter rail operation under contract, and car maintenance for other parties.

Amtrak points out that between 1985 and 1989 the amount of Federal capital grants it received, at US$156.4 million, contrasted sharply with its booked depreciation of US$815.9 million over the same period.

Congress did raise Amtrak's capital appropriation to US$83 million in FY 1990. To this Amtrak would add some US$50 million of income from its ancillary activities, but it would have to borrow from the private sector to complete the US$201 million it intended to invest in 1990. In ensuing years it would need to find at least US$300 million annually.

Traction and rolling stock
In 1984 Amtrak completed the design work for three new prototype cars, brandnamed Viewliner, with a view to replacement of the Heritage Fleet of former railroad-owned cars, including some vista-domes that have been converted by Amtrak to electrical powering of auxiliaries by head-end locomotive supply. The Budd Company was selected to detail design, and construct the shells. In 1985 the car shells were shipped to the Amtrak Beech Grove facility where the cars were completed as two sleeping and one dining car. In 1988 they were placed in revenue service on Amtrak's Auto Train and Capitol Limited. In 1989-90, however, all three prototypes were returned to Beech Grove Maintenance Facility for modifications.

Two prototype locomotives classified F69AC embodying Siemens' three-phase ac technology were to enter revenue service in August 1990. Built by GM-EMD, these 3000 hp diesel-electrics employ the builder's 12-710 G3 engine. Outshopped in the 1988 summer, they went first to the AAR test centre at Pueblo, Colorado, for commissioning.

In 1990 Amtrak purchased for US$2·3 million six FP40PH 3000 hp locomotives from Ontario, Canada's GO Transit. The locomotives have been in service there since their production by General Motors of Canada. The units were to be thoroughly overhauled and modified by Amtrak before taking up long-haul service.

In December 1988 Amtrak expanded from 50 to 104 the number of passenger cars it was purchasing from Bombardier. The increased car order was an option on Amtrak's original contract with Bombardier signed in June 1988, and the additional cars were ordered under the same terms as the first 50, at a cost of approximately US$50 million. The order was financed through the Export Development Corporation of Canada.

Delivery of the first 50 cars, designated the 'Horizon Fleet', was completed in August, 1989. The additional 54 cars were to be delivered between November 1989 and the spring of 1990.

The new order, consisting of 42 coach cars and 12 food service cars, were earmarked for several of Amtrak's short-distance routes, primarily in the Midwest and on the West Coast.

All the original Metroliner (MU) cars, now designated Capitoliners, have had their traction equipment removed and 23 have been rebuilt as push-pull control trailers, 10 for Los Angeles-San Diego, seven for Chicago-Detroit and six for the Philadelphia-Atlantic City service (see above). This work was performed at Amtrak's Wilmington, Delaware, Maintenance Facility. In 1990 a Metroliner cab car was being converted as a prototype club car with conference facilities.

In mid-1989 Amtrak ordered 70 second-generation Material Handling cars, delivered early in 1990, for its expanding mail express and baggage business. Like the original 60, they were built by Thrall Car, but the new vehicles have bogies designed for 200 km/h operation.

Because of the successful food service operations experienced on the Auto Train, Amtrak is modifying some of its Heritage diners. The modification permits the cars to provide either table-waited service or buffet service depending on passenger route densities. In addition, six former Santa Fe steam-heated dining cars were removed from storage for head-end electric auxiliary powering; these diners have also been modified to provide the more flexible food service.

At the start of 1990 Amtrak was operating 64 electric locomotives, 232 passenger train-hauling diesel-electric locomotives, 10 Turboliner cars, 1644 locomotive-hauled passenger cars, 230 baggage cars, and 59 bi- and tri-level auto carriers.

Track
Rail: 70 kg RE
Cross ties (sleepers)
Concrete: Thickness 241 mm, spacing 1584/km
Wood: Thickness 178 mm, spacing 1950/km
Fastenings: Concrete ties: Pandrol 601A
Wood ties: Cut spikes
Minimum curvature radius: 8° = 217 m
Max gradient: 1·34%
Max axleload: 29·58 tonnes

HIGH SPEED RAIL PROJECTS

In 1989-90 the following intercity corridors were the subject of high-speed passenger rail attention (excluding those affected by the Northeast Improvement Programme, for details of which see Amtrak entry):

Ohio High Speed Rail Authority

16 E Broad Street 1003, Columbus, OH 43215

Telephone: +1 614 466 2509

Chairman: Senator Robert J Boggs
Executive Director: Gregory Kostelac

Cleveland-Columbus-Cincinnati
Rebounding strongly following defeat of a proposal to fund development with a sales tax in an Ohio referendum of 1982, the state legislature in 1986 established an Ohio High Speed Rail Authority for study of a 270 km/h electrified railway interconnecting the three cities. This was advocated in the report of an Ohio High Speed Rail Task Force published in July 1986. The 170-mile line would be mostly over new infrastructure. Technology contenders were essentially French (TGV), German (ICE) and Japanese (Shinkansen).

In 1990 the Authority and the Ohio Railway Organization Inc were seeking private sector turnkey offers with a view to placing a build-and-operate plan before the state Governor and Assembly in 1991.

Michigan Department of Transportation

425 W Ottawa, Lansing, MI 48909

Telephone: +1 517 373 2953

Manager of Systems Planning: James Roach

Detroit-Chicago
Progress hinges on involvement of private capital, as the state is not prepared to offer financial aid for construction. In association with Bechtel and Budd in the Advanced Rail Consortium, British Rail has promoted its 200 km/h diesel traction technology for this project.

RAILWAY SYSTEMS / United States of America

Illinois, Minnesota and Wisconsin Departments of Transportation

Chicago-Milwaukee-Minneapolis and St Paul
In February 1990 the Transportation Departments of the three states agreed to combine to consider routeing and technology options and costs. Minnesota had obtained Federal funding for a Maglev study and was hopeful of private financing. Budd had previously completed a feasibility of a Transrapid Maglev system connecting Chicago, its O'Hare Airport and Milwaukee.

Florida High Speed Rail Passenger Commission

1440 Bricknell Avenue, Miami, FL 33131

Telephone: +1 305 358 4100

Chairman: David Blumberg
311 South Calhoun Street 202, Tallahassee, FL 32301
Telephone: +1 904 487 4261
Executive Director: Charles H Smith

Miami-Orlando-Tampa
This was in 1990 the US project closest to fulfilment. It was expected that in September 1991 a franchise would be granted to the Florida High Speed Rail Corporation, which will use a version of the ABB Type X-2 tilt-body train-set in production for Swedish State Railways. The Corporation was to produce a detailed financing and route plan in mid-1990; the route will start over the already Florida-owned ex-CSX Miami-West Palm Beach line and continue over a combination of railroad and highway rights-of-way. Completion of the 523-km Tampa-Miami route was forecast for 1995, operating initially at a top speed of 240 km/h, but later at 280 km/h as the infrastructure is improved.

Orlando Airport-Disney World
Maglev Transit Inc was expected in late 1990 to obtain a franchise to construct a 30 km Transrapid Maglev line from Orlando Airport to Orlando's Disney World.

California-Nevada SuperSpeed Ground Transportation Commission

211 Culver Boulevard, Suite G, Playa del Ray, CA 90293

Telephone: +1 213 578 9212
Telefax: +1 213 578 9227

Chairman: Arnie Adamson
Vice Chairman: Don R Roth
Executive Director: Paul Taylor

Las Vegas-Anaheim
In July 1990 three consortia were to submit proposals for a 100 per cent privately-financed 435km high-speed to run at least from Las Vegas to Anaheim, as the first step in creation of a network throughout the Pacific Southwest region. A spur to Palmdale would be included in the first phase if there were assurance of finance for an extension from there to Los Angeles. At least nine communities seek stations on the high-speed line.
The competing build-and-operate consortia were led by: Bechtel International, offering Transrapid Maglev; Morrison-Knudsen; and Bombardier with Rail Transportation Systems Inc, offering GEC-Alsthom TGV technology. Both states as well as the Commission must approve the chosen plan. Construction was expected to take from 1993 to 1997.

Empire Corridor

New York-Albany-Burlington-Montreal
Studies have shown likely revenues inadequate to amortise construction costs, but examination of up-grading feasibility on existing infrastructure continues, with particular attention to the New York-Albany segment.

Pennsylvania High Speed Rail Commission

Room 149, Main Capitol, Harrisburg, PA 17120

Telephone: +1 717 787 6419

Chairman: Representative Rick Geist
Executive Director: Robert J Casey

Pittsburgh-Harrisburg-Philadelphia
The Commission has favoured a Transrapid International proposal for a Maglev line from Pittsburgh to Harrisburg and upgrading of existing railroad between Harrisburg and Philadelphia. The Carnegie-Mellon University has conducted a feasibility study of a 30km Maglev line from central Pittsburgh to the city's airport as a pilot scheme for the bigger project.

Texas High Speed Rail Authority

8080 N Central Expressway, Suite 1100, Dallas, TX 75206-1806

Chairman: Charles J Wyly Jr

Dallas/Fort Worth-Houston-San Antonio-Austin
In 1990 the newly-constituted Authority was expecting to consider two proposals for an initial Dallas-Houston phase of a 300 km/h high-speed rail project. A consortium led by Morrison-Knudsen was offering the French TGV technology; another led by the Texas High Speed Rail Corporation was promoting the German ICE. A 1989 study performed for the Texas Turnpike Authority by a team including Morrison-Knudsen and Wilbur Smith Associates had confirmed the viability of a service using either TGV, ICE or Japanese Shinkansen technology on new infrastructure.

Georgia

Savannah-Macon-Atlanta
The state legislature has approved establishment of a high-speed rail commission, but by early 1990 the Governor had not appointed one. Atlanta delegates have visited France to study TGV technology.

Coalition of Northeastern Governors (CONEG) Task Force on High Speed Rail

400 N Capital Street, Washington, DC 20001

Chairman: Cheryl D Soon
Executive Director, CONEG: Anne D Stubbs

Boston and Maine Corporation
A subsidiary of Guilford Transportation Industries Inc Rail Division

Iron Horse Park, North Billerica, Massachusetts 01 862

Telephone: +1 617 663 9300
Telex: 951864
Telefax: +1 617 663 1199

Chairman and Chief Executive Officer: David A Fink
Executive Vice-President: F C Pease
Vice-President, Marketing and Sales: T F Steiniger
Vice-President, Human Resources: D J Kozak
Vice-President, Engineering: S F Nevero
Asst Vice-President, Engineering & Chief Engineer, Design & Construction: V V Mudholkar
General Attorney/Claims: J E O'Keefe
Vice-President, Finance: K C Austin
Vice-President, Law: J P Cronin
Vice-President, Transportation: S B Culliford
Vice-President, Mechanical: J P Coffin

Vice-President, Purchases & Stores: S P Park Jr
Director, Strategic Planning: R J Rooney
Engineer, Maintenance of Way: R F Dixon
Chief Engineer, Communications and Signals: J F West
Chief Engineer: J Parola

Gauge: 1435 mm
Length: 2532 km

Lines and territories
The principal lines of the Boston & Maine run north and west from Boston through the states of Maine, New Hampshire, Vermont, Massachusetts and in eastern New York State, where it makes connections at Albany and Schenectady with other lines.

Finance and ownership
In July 1983 Guilford Transportation Industries (GTI) formally took over B&M. GTI also owns the Maine Central. The two railroads preserve their separate identities, but are being operated as an integral system with common management. As a result of past disputes with the labour force over working practices, this management is exercised by another GTI subsidiary, the Springfield Terminal Railway Co. Early in March 1989 the long-running problems with employees were ended by signature of a deal with the employees' union accepting the Springfield Terminal arrangement and agreeing terms on key issues for the period up to 1994.

Traffic
About 85 per cent of B&M's freight tonnage is received from connecting lines and two-thirds of it terminates on the system. Forest products from northern New England or Canada predominate. Since bankruptcy the railroad has substantially contracted its network.

Locomotives and rolling stock
GTI rolling stock in total stands at 250 diesel-electric locomotives and 6933 freight cars.

Burlington Northern (BN)

777 Main, Fort Worth, Texas 76102

Telephone: +1 817 878 2000

President and Chief Executive Officer: Gerald Grinstein
Chief Operating Officer: William E Greenwood
Executive Vice-President, Operations: Joseph R Galassi
  Marketing and Sales: John Q Anderson
Executive Vice-President & Chief Financial Officer: P Jackson Bell
Executive Vice-President, Law & Government Affairs: Edmund W Burke

Senior Vice-President, Labour Relations: James B Dagnon
Vice-Presidents
  Transportation: Wayne A Hatton
  Information Systems: Brock Strom
  Communications & Public Affairs: John N Etchart
  Controller: Don S Snyder
  Coal Marketing: Nicholas P Moros
  Engineering and Technology: Donald W Henderson
  Equipment & Strategic Planning: Richard L Lewis
  Government Affairs: Alan M Fitzwater
  International Marketing and Sales: Ralph A Muellner
  Automotive: T Daniel Flood
  Human Resources: Donald W Scott

  Labour Relations: Joseph C Hilly
  Forest Products: Gary D Schlaeger
  Agricultural Commodities: Richard R Carter
  Industrial Products: Kenneth L Hagan
  Food & Consumer Products: Sharon S White
  Intermodal: Robert Ingram
  International Development: Michael H Karl
  Business Development: John T Hall
Regional Officers
Vice-Presidents
  Northern Region: William W Francis
  Southern Region: Robert S Howery

Gauge: 1435 mm
Length: 36 220 km plus 4767 km operated under trackage rights

United States of America / RAILWAY SYSTEMS

Lines and territories

Burlington Northern was formed in March 1970, by the merger of Chicago, Burlington & Quincy Railroad, Great Northern Railway, Northern Pacific Railway and Spokane, Portland and Seattle Railway. The territory it served covered 19 states and two Canadian provinces and reached from the Great Lakes and the Ohio river to California and the seaports of the Pacific Northwest. In addition, BN owned the Colorado and Southern Railway Co, and the Fort Worth and Denver Railway Co (now fully absorbed), which extended its territory via Denver to the Gulf of Mexico at Houston and Galveston, Texas.

The merger of the St Louis-San Francisco Railway Co (the Frisco) into Burlington Northern became effective in November 1980. The BN-Frisco merger created a rail system stretching from Washington and Oregon through the timber and mining regions of the Northern Tier States and the farming areas of the Midwest and as far south as Pensacola, Florida. The combined companies now operate in 25 states and two Canadian provinces. The Frisco has been integrated into BN's system and is not controlled separately, as has been the case in certain other recent railroad mergers.

BN has nine operating divisions, with headquarters in Seattle, Denver, Minneapolis, Fort Worth, Springfield, Mo, Fargo, ND, Lincoln, Neb, Galesburg, Ill, and Havre, Mont. In terms of track-km BN is the largest railroad in the US.

As a result of a decentralisation programme, BNRR now has three principal system offices, in St Paul, Minnesota; Overland Park, Kansas; and Fort Worth, Texas.

Finance and Traffic

In FY 1989 BN marked its first year as a pure railroad transportation company (it disposed of its trucking operation in 1988) with a net income of US$243 million, compared with US$156 million in FY1988. The Industrial Products unity's revenues rose sharply, due in part to good volume gains in petroleum products and industrial chemicals. The 1988 drought and a bad winter reduced grain traffic, but grain as well as coal traffic were strong in the final quarter of the year. Operating ratio in FY1989 deteriorated marginally to 85.4, compared with 85.2 in FY1988 and 84.8 in FY 1987.

Transportation of coal is BN's largest source of rail freight revenues, contributing almost a third of total income. About 91 per cent of the 1989 traffic originated in the Powder River Basin of Montana and Wyoming and was hauled to coal-burning electricity generating stations in the north central, south central, mountain and Pacific regions of the US. Nearly all the coal tonnage originated by BN is carried in unit trains and 99 per cent of the business is run under contract. The trains typically consist of 108 short tons of coal each and, depending on the difficulty of the grades encountered, from three to six locomotive units.

BN serves a significant area of the major grain-producing regions located in the Midwest and Great Plains and transports large quantities of whole grains to domestic feed lots, major milling centres, and to the Pacific Northwest, Gulf and western Great Lakes ports for export. Grain generated 15.59 per cent of revenues in FY1989.

Since 1988 BN has operated a Future Month Certificate Programme under which grain customers are guaranteed covered hopper availability subject to advance bidding and pre-payment. The railroad specifies the available number of 54-car unit trains at given times and sets a minimum rate for their use. Customers are then invited to bid with the minimum rate as a base. Upon acceptance of a bid and receipt of pre-payment, the client is guaranteed train availability on the specified date, or BN payment of per diem penalties until it does become available.

BN serves the timber producing regions of the Pacific Northwest and the Southeast, hauling significant volumes of lumber, plywood and structural panels, wood chips, wood pulp, paper and paper products. Fluctuations in the level of forest products traffic result from general economic conditions as reflected in new housing and levels of industrial production, from competition with other modes, and export demand.

Intermodal traffic

Increasing domestic containerisation benefited BN's intermodal traffic in 1989, when it generated 14.09 per cent of all revenue. Expanded use of double-stack equipment included its first use by BN America, the company's domestic COFC service, in selected traffic lanes. In 1990 BN was reported planning to start a RoadRailer bi-modal feeder system in conjunction with BN America. The FRA has approved the coupling via an adapter hitch of double-stack COFC cars and Road-Railers in the same train.

An important development has been conclusion of agreements with labour unions for operation of short, fast, single locomotive-powered intermodal trains named 'Expediter' with a two-man crew and no caboose. This has enabled BN to make a special marketing play for trucking company TOFC traffic. Since 1985 BN has been steadily expanding this service of trains limited to 30 flatcars in corridors such as St Louis-Dallas, Kansas City-Birmingham, Chicago and Memphis, Chicago and Minneapolis/St Paul, Seattle-Portland, Dallas-Houston, Chicago-Omaha, Kansas City-Omaha and Chicago-Dallas. The Chicago-Dallas operation was significant in that it breached the 850-mile limit previously set by the unions on two-man train-crewing.

Since 1982, 140 traditional rail ramps have been consolidated into 26 hub centres, with 25 satellites. The satellite hubs are managed by the parent hub centre and provide service to and from key markets within a 200-mile radius. These hubs and their satellites have used the highway networks to expand geographic markets to include customers and areas not previously served by BN. Eventually all hub centres will be able to handle a full dedicated intermodal train intact, without switching. In 1987 BN entered into an unprecedented joint agreement with Grand Trunk Western and now operates a hub centre on GTW property in Detroit, connecting the city to BN's entire intermodal network.

A significant proportion of the 25 hub centre satellites is without rail connection. That reflects the extent to which major railroads are now optimising deregulation licence to limit rail haulage to corridor flows justifying cost-effective haulage in dedicated full hub-to-hub trainloads; and to eliminate expensive handling of individual intermodal carloads by greatly extending the range of highway collection and delivery from each hub.

Another cost-cutting development is the commitment of intermodal terminal management to non-rail companies. Savings can include the management company's freedom from some of the railroad's more onerous labour union agreements; but much more is probably gained from the productivity incentive of contracts with these companies that are almost all of only a year's term, with a 30-day cancellation clause.

BN policy, in conjunction with its hub centre development, is to compress its entire intermodal traffic into dedicated train working. This now accounts for 90 per cent of BN's intermodal traffic. In 1990 BN was running 58 daily dedicated trains between the hubs at Houston, Dallas/Fort Worth, Amarillo, Denver, Billings, Spokane, Pasco, Portland, Kansas City, St Louis, Birmingham, Chicago, Memphis, Minneapolis-St Paul, Omaha, Mobile Tacoma, Tulsa, Springfield, Galesburg, Fargo, Seattle and Vancouver in Canada.

BN is one of the two major railroad owners of double-stack COFC equipment, with a fleet of 350 five-

Mile-long coal trains load on loop through overhead silo in Powder River region, Wyoming

GM-EMD GP-9 locomotive loads grain cars at an elevator in South Sioux City, Nebraska

platform units. A substantial proportion of these cars are assigned to the daily train service to and from Chicago and various terminals beyond which BN provides for the Port of Seattle. In association with Conrail, this double-stack COFC operation has been expanded to initiate the first coast-coast stack train not run to shipping line charter.

To improve its service capability further, BN has embarked on a clearance improvement programme to accommodate stack trains of the largest shipping containers now in use. This has involved modification of five through truss bridges and 26 tunnels, and undercutting the track under about 20 overhead structures. Tunnel clearance improvements are being made by track relocation or crown removal. Lowering the track through several tunnels to gain additional clearance was considered, but the typical large vertical correction needed made this procedure too disruptive to traffic and too costly. Clearance improvements between Seattle and Chicago via Vancouver, were completed in 1988. In 1989 work moved on to the Cascade route, which includes the 7·79-mile Cascade Tunnel, second longest in North America.

A January 1990 addition to the intermodal portfolio was a joint service with CSL Intermodal from the Pacific Northwest ports of Portland and Seattle/Tacoma to Atlanta and other southern centres. The agreement provided for additional through train service between BN's hub centres and Atlanta via Chicago and Memphis.

In 1990 BN concluded an agreement with three tank container operators to offer a BulkExpress domestic tank container service for bulk liquids.

Computer-satellite train monitoring

BN is testing a computer and satellite prototype system, called Advanced Railroad Electronics System (ARES) designed to show a train's location within 150 feet and its speed to within 1 mph. Two SD-19 locomotives used in transfer service in Minneapolis-St Paul between Northtown and Dayton's Bluff were equipped with on-board computers linked to video monitors and a network of satellites.

The initial tests proved that the ARES equipment works in stationary tests. BN is now evaluating ARES's use in controlling train operations in the Iron Range territory of north-eastern Minnesota.

The ARES system is being developed with the Collins Air Transport Division of Rockwell International Corp. The company is based in Cedar Rapids, Iowa, and manufactures avionics equipment, including components used by aircraft and ships to determine speed and position by satellite. The equipment picks up signals from Navstar satellites operated by the US Air Force. The signals are fed into on-board computers to show speed and position of BN trains.

In late 1989 BN ordered from Rockwell International 100 sets of locomotive condition monitoring equipment, including data and radio apparatus, for transmission of diagnostic data to three of BN's major locomotive maintenance shops.

Automatic Vehicle Identification (AVI)

Following 18 months' field-testing of two transponder-based systems, BN ordered 20 systems from Union Switch & Signal in 1989. Each system includes a controller, associated tags and programmers for locomotives, end-of-train devices, cabooses and fuel tenders. Further orders were expected in 1990.

Track

BN began in 1987 a six-year programme to install 3·5 million concrete sleepers in curves of 2 degrees or more over its routes bearing in excess of 20 million gross short tons of traffic a year. On completion, 4 per cent of BN route-mileage will support approximately 14 per cent total gross ton-miles on concrete sleepers. Because of curves and grades, this mileage traditionally has incurred some of the highest maintenance costs per mile. With concrete ties, not only will these maintenance costs be reduced, but there also will be a drastic reduction in train delays from maintenance operations. A further 700 000 concrete sleepers were to be installed under 1990's US$ 480 million capital investment programme.

Traction and rolling stock

Locomotive stock owned and leased at the end of 1989 totalled 1826 freight line-haul, 25 passenger, 260 multi-purpose and 198 switcher. Of this number, 1227 were leased and 1082 owned. BN also operated 141 leased commuter passenger cars and 61 778 owned and leased freight cars.

BN has been operating 200 locomotives under electrical-power purchase agreements by which BN commits to buy electrical power generated by locomotives acquired by a third-party energy supplier. The supplier of the locomotives retains responsibility for the investment in and acquisition, lease or sub-lease of locomotives to generate sufficient power to meet its obligations under the agreement. The supplier also contracts with the locomotive manufacturer to secure specific, long-term, maintenance- and performance-standard commitments.

BN's first agreements with third-party suppliers (Oakway Inc and LMX) covered respectively 100 GM-EMD SD60 and 100 GE Dash-8 locomotives. The manufacturers are responsible for the maintenance, repair and overhaul of the locomotives. However, this work is done by employees of BN and a BN subsidiary (Electro-Northern) directed by GE and EMD supervisors respectively. Overhauls, when due, are executed in the BN shop at West Burlington, Iowa.

In 1989 BN concluded an agreement with GM-EMD for acquisition of 100 more 3800 hp SD60 locomotives, to be maintained by BN shop employees under GM-EMD supervision. Deliveries began at the end of the year. BN had an option on a further 100 units. The SD60s are for coal haulage, superseding units of 1970s' vintage.

BN will also acquire GM-EMD's first freight units embodying Siemens three-phase ac traction, to be designated SD60MAC. These would be delivered in 1991, following testing of the first two at the AAR Centre, Pueblo.

In 1988 BN announced plans for the addition of 250 remanufactured low-horsepower locomotives from Morrison-Knudsen and the GM Electro-Motive Division to the railroad's fleet up to 1992. Once an initial order of 25 locomotives each from MK and EMD had been delivered in early 1989, orders for the remaining 200 remanufactured locomotives would be allocated among the two builders based on the quality and performance of their previously delivered remanufactured units. BN has also taken delivery from Generation II, Minneapolis, of 10 GP20 locomotives remanufactured with 2000 hp Caterpillar 3516 engines and designated GP20-C.

In June 1990 BN began to take delivery from Trinity Industries of 1000 high-capacity covered grain hopper cars with a 115 short-ton capacity and a gross loaded weight of 143 short tons. At the same time it was seeking bids for supply of 240 aluminium-bodies rotary coal gondolas of the same gross loaded weight. Other

Diesel-electric locomotives

Class	Wheel arrangement	Rated power hp	Tractive effort lb	Continuous at mph	Max speed mph	Wheel diameter in	Total weight tons	Length ft in	No operated end-1987	Year acquired	Builder
E9	B-B	2400	–	–	–	–	–	–	25	1944-56*	EMD
SW-10	B-B	1000	31 200	10	50	40	125	44' 8"	54	1966-72	EMD
SW-1	B-B	600	24 000	10	50	40	100	44' 5"	1	1940-50	EMD
SW-7	B-B	1200	35 600	10	50	40	125	44' 5"	1	1949-50	EMD
SW-9	B-B	1200	35 600	10	50	40	125	44' 5"	1	1950-53	EMD
SW-12	B-B	1200	35 600	10	50	40	125	44' 6"	69	1938-65	EMD
SW-15	B-B	1500	45 000	12	65	40	130	44' 8"	71	1967, 1973	EMD
NW-12	B-B	1200	31 200	10	50	40	125	44' 5"	2	1975-76	EMD
GP-5	B-B	1350	31 250	15	65	40	121	56' 2"	7	1958-59	EMD
MP-15	B-B	1500	45 000	9·3	65	40	131	47' 8"	5	1975	Alco
GP-15-1	B-B	1500	47 000	10	65	40	129	54' 11"	25	1977	Alco
GP-9 & GP-9B	B-B	1750	44 000	12	65	40	125	56' 2"	98	1954-59	EMD
GP-10	B-B	1800	44 000	14	65	40	128	55' 11"	21	1974-76	EMD
GP-18	B-B	1800	44 000	12	65	40	124	56' 2"	5	1960	EMD
GP-20	B-B	2000	45 000	14	65	40	128	56' 2"	19	1960-61	EMD
GP-38, GP-38X and GP-38B	B-B	2000	55 000	10·7	65	40	131	59' 2"	70	1970	EMD
GP-39-2	B-B	2300	58 200	8·5	65	40	131	59' 2"	40	1981	EMD
GP-38-2	B-B	2000	55 000	10·7	65	40	131	59' 2"	210	1972-74	EMD
GP-30	B-B	2250	51 000	12	65	40	130	56' 2"	30	1962-63	EMD
GP-35	B-B	2500	51 200	12	65	40	131	56' 2"	44	1963-65	EMD
GP-40	B-B	3000	48 000	13	77	40	150	59' 2"	36	1966-68	EMD
GP-40-2	B-B	3000	54 500	11·3	65	40	131	59' 2"	25	1979	EMD
GP-50	B-B	3500	62 000	9·7	70	40	138	59' 2"	63	1980/85	EMD
B-30-7A	B-B	3000	64 600	8·4	70	40	135	61' 2"	119	1982	GE
B-30-7	B-B	3000	52 000	15·2	70	40	138	62' 2"	8	1977	GE
B32-8	B-B	3200	–	–	–	–	–	–	3	1984	GE
U30B	B-B	3000	51 500	13	79	40	136	60' 2"	18	1966-68	GE
U30C	C-C	3000	90 500	8·4	70	40	206	67' 3"	149	1968-75	GE
			74 000	11·4	79	40	194				
C-30-7	C-C	3000	90 500	8·4	70	40	208	67' 3"	241	1976-80	GE
			82 000	8·4	70						
SD-9	C-C	1750	67 500	8	65	40	162	60' 8"	98	1954-58	EMD
SD-38-2	C-C	2000	81 000	6·8	65	40	196	68' 10"	4	1979	EMD
SD-40 & SDP-40	C-C	3000	74 500	9	77	40	191	65' 9½"	16	1966-71	EMD
SD-40-2	C-C	3000	71 000	13·2	65	40	193	68' 10"	820	1980	EMD
			90 474	8·5	65	40	208				
			74 500	9	77	40	193				
SD-42B	C-C	3000	–	9	–	–	–	–	2	1972-73	EMD
B39-8	B-B	3900	–	–	–	–	–	–	65	1987	GE
SD-60	C-C	3800	100 000	9·8	70	40	208	71' 2"	100	1986	EMD

* Rebuilt 1973-79

freight car purchases in 1990 were to be 460 autocarriers and 120 boxcars.

In conjunction with Bethlehem Steel's Freight Car Division, a freight car known as the Beth-Combo has been developed. This embodies a hydraulic, so-called 'walking floo' system of recessed blades which can sweep the vehicle clear after it has carried a powdered or granular load, so that it can be used for freight such as forest products or paper on the backhaul.

In partnership with the Mellon Institute and General Railway Signal, BN would to gain operational experience with the Smart Bolt. Replacing one standard bolt in a bearing cover plate, the Smart Bolt contains a heat sensor and a transmitter that radios to a locomotive cab display warning of any overheating in the bearing. BN has been concerned at the high cost of incidents ensuing from overheated freight car bearings.

Motive power utilisation has been improved by implementation of a computer system known as CAP-

Traffic	1985	1986	1987	1988	1989
Revenue ton-km (million)	296 204	301 242	331 906	359 704	374 135
Average net trainload (short tons)	3018	2939	2981	2997	3032
Average wagon load (short tons)	71·32	70·86	73	74	77
Finances (US$ million)	1985	1986	1987	1988	1989
Rail operating revenues	4098·5	3915·5	4065·2	4699·5	4606
Operating income	822·1	130.47	619.28	671.25	657
Operating ratio	80·7	86·7	84·8	85·2	85·4
Rail operating expenses		1986	1987	1988	1989
Total		3475·1	3661·7	4020·62	3949·8

MAC. Information derived from BN's COMPASS data system and supplemented by input from operators in the field presents operations department headquarters with advance data on train consists, tonnage, restrictive characteristics of routes to be followed by each train, and location and status of all traction, which is reproduced on a bank of colour vdus, each of which can display up to 36 consists with all relevant data.

Chicago and North Western Transportation Company

One North Western Center, Chicago, Illinois 60606

Telephone: +1 312 559 7000
Telefax: +1 312 559 6495

Chairman, President & Chief Executive Officer:
Robert Schmiege
Senior Vice Presidents
  Finance and Accounting: Thomas A Tingleff
  Administration: P C Conlon
  Law: James P Daley
  Operations: Robert A Jahnke
  Sales and Marketing: Arthur W Peters
Vice Presidents
  Equipment Management and Customer Services: R L Johnson
  Motive Power and Materials: D E Waller
  Safety, Rules and Casualty Prevention: J R Mann
  Engineering: R H McDonald
  Transportation: Jeffrey H Koch
  Corporate Communications and Taxes: J M Foote
  Labour Relations: R J Cuchna
  Human Resources: Robert F Ard
  Systems and Information Services: E A Lillig
  Revenue & Distribution Accounting: J L Liggett
  Comptroller: M S Morgan
  Acquisitions and Planning: J S Eberhardt
  Traffic Services: B W Bruce
  Business Development: D A Christensen
  Sales and Marketing, Autos and Steel: J W Leppert III
  Sales and Marketing, Bulk Consumer Goods: J P Toren
  Sales and Marketing, Energy: D G Weishaar
  Sales and Marketing, Grain: D C Berquist
  Corporate Quality Improvement/Assurance: J A McEleny

Gauge: 1435 mm
Length: 10 378 km

CNW was incorporated in Delaware in March 1970, under the name North Western Employees Transportation Corporation. Its present name was adopted in May 1972. The company has been engaged in business since 1972 when the employees purchased the transportation assets and assumed the transportation obligations of the former Chicago and North Western Railway Company and certain of its subsidiaries.

The company is engaged in hauling rail freight traffic in the Midwest. It operates in the nine states of Illinois, Wisconsin, Michigan, Iowa, Minnesota, Nebraska, South Dakota, Missouri and Wyoming. Besides its primary freight activity, in the Chicago metropolitan area the company also provides suburban passenger service.

CNW is the principal link in the central transcontinental freight corridor. Its 804 km-long heavy-density east-west main line between Chicago and the Missouri River gateway of Omaha-Fremont-Council Bluffs accounts for only 6 per cent of its mileage, but carries 47 per cent of its total traffic. In recent years, the CNW has also become an important north-south railroad, spending more than US$150 million to acquire and rehabilitate a new main line between the Twin Cities of Minneapolis-St Paul and Kansas City, Missouri. It is the only railroad in the US to operate trains on the left-hand track rather than on the right.

Management buy-out
In June 1989 CNW Corporation announced that CNW's Board of Directors had approved a definitive merger agreement with a corporation formed by Blackstone Capital Partners LP and investors including CNW senior management, Donaldson, Lufkin & Jenrette Securities Corporation and Union Pacific Corporation. The management group was led by CNW chairman and Chief Executive Officer Robert Schmiege. The total transaction size was approximately US$1·6 billion. Blackstone's acquisition of CNW Corporation's railroad subsidiaries was approved by the ICC in October 1989.

CNW had previously received an unsolicited offer by Japonica Partners to purchase CNW. As a result, a special committee conducted an auction of CNW, and the Blackstone-led group was selected as the winning bidder.

The financing structure of the acquisition provides for substantial capital expenditures to maintain high quality service on CNW's lines. A financing structure utilising new equity totalling in excess of US$300 million (including US$100 million of preferred stock to be held by Union Pacific) has been provided in order to ensure sufficient funds to enable CNW to make substantial capital improvements. In an agreement with Union Pacific, CNW would commit to spend a total of US$115 million up to end-1992, including US$40 million in the second half of 1989, to maintain and upgrade CNW's east-west main line in order to improve rail quality and shorten delivery times. Union Pacific relies on CNW's line from Chicago to Fremont, Nebraska, for east-west freight traffic.

Finance and Traffic
Freight revenues in FY 1989 were 4.3 per cent down on the previous year, despite a slight rise in carloads handled. One reason was the sale of 208 miles of railroad in Wisconsin to a subsidiary of the ITEL Corporation, completed in December 1988. Volume and revenues increased in two of CNW's five business groups, coal and intermodal. Coal loads were up 6.5 and intermodal 7.6 per cent, but automotive and steel fell by 8.8 and bulk and consumer products by 10.6 per cent.

Of the total coal traffic, 82.6 per cent was generated by the coal-hauling unit, Western Railroad Properties (see below), compared with 77.2 per cent in 1988. Intermodal revenue did not rise proportionately to the increase of traffic because of the shift from TOFC to double-stack COFC.

Wyoming coal project
A wholly-owned subsidiary, Western Railroad Properties, Inc (WRPI) was formed to construct the 56-mile (90 km) connector line from the company's existing line in east central Wyoming to a connection with the Union Pacific Railroad at Joyce, Nebraska, that taps Wyoming coal for CNW. Besides the 56 miles of new track, the project involved rehabilitation of 45 miles (72 km) of existing track to complete the link between Union Pacific at Joyce, Nebraska, and the 103-mile (166 km) Gillette line at the entrance to the Powder River Basin. The scheme was engineered for standard operation of 110-car trains, CNW coal haulage over the new lines began in mid-1984. Less than one year after gaining entry to the mines, coal had become the railroad's leading revenue-producing commodity. In 1989 CNW and WRPI coal traffic combined totalled 510 200 carloads.

Other traffic
CNW operates over 750 miles of 'grain gathering' lines in northern Iowa and southern Minnesota. These lines feed grain traffic into the North Western's main lines for shipment to processors, barge terminals or the gateways of Chicago, Omaha, Kansas City or St Louis for delivery to other railroads. CNW serves over 125

Finances (US$ million)	1985	1986	1987	1988	1989
Operating revenues					
Railroad freight	795	813.6	789.8	880.8	843
Suburban and other	102.7	104.2	109.4	114.6	111.6
Total	897.7	917.8	899.2	995.4	954.6
Operating expenditure					
Transportation	394.1	362.1	342.7	366.1	350.4
Way and structures	131.2	138	132.8	141.6	141.4
Equipment	187.4	189.1	182.5	186.5	176.1
Depreciation	48.8	50.1	52.5	53.8	60.7
General and administrative	72.8	80.5	76.9	89.4	76.3
Provision for employee reduction and relocation costs	24.5	11.7	–	26.3	24.0
Provision for litigation settlements	–	–	15	9	–
Corporate and other	1.3	9.8	11.5	13.4	4.5
Total	860.1	841.3	813.9	886.1	833.4
Operating income	37.6	76.5	85.3	109.3	121.1
Other income, net	17.7	40.1	18.4	62.1	(24.9)
Interest expense					
CNW railroad and other	64.2	57.9	58.7	53.7	113.3
Wyoming coal project	26.6	22.4	24.6	26.2	
Income (loss) from continuing operations before income taxes	(35.5)	36.3	20.4	91.5	(17.0)
Net income (loss)	(1.70)	2.31	1.29	4.34	(20.8)
Traffic					
Revenue short tons (000)	96 603	101 939	109 900	122 319	121 530
Revenue short ton-miles (millions)	27.5	30.8	33.7	37.4	35.7
Average haul (miles)	297	303	307	306	294

RAILWAY SYSTEMS / United States of America

multiple-car loading grain elevators, the majority in Iowa.

Grain volume fell 3 per cent from 268 800 carloads in 1988 to 260 700 in 1989.

The North Western delivers auto parts to and handles finished autos from assembly plants in Belvidere, Illinois (Chrysler) and Janesvile, Wisconsin (GM). The railroad also transports finished domestic and import vehicles to the North Western's regional distribution ramp facilities in West Chicago, Illinois, St Paul, Minnesota, and Milwaukee, Wisconsin.

CNW transports nearly one-third of its steel tonnage between Chicago and the Omaha gateway on its east-west main line for several of the largest steel companies in the USA. A substantial portion of steel's revenues are generated from iron ore, most of which is transferred to ships at the railroad's Escanaba, Michigan, ore port. The balance of the railroad's steel business consists of scrap steel shipped to electric-furnace customers and finished and semi-finished steel transported from basic-oxygen furnace customers.

Intermodal traffic

In view of the key intermediate role of CNW's Omaha/Fremont/Council Bluffs-Chicago route in the rapid development of double-stack COFC from West Coast ports to Chicago and the East, CNW invested US$51 million in two purpose-built Chicago yards, known as Global One and Two. Global One opened in 1986; Global Two was commissioned in November 1989.

A difference between One and Two is that the former was partly designed for rail-to-rail transfer of double-stacked containers that could not proceed further east in that mode because of clearance problems. Those limitations are now very largely eliminated. Global Two, on the west side of Chicago, is laid out with more concern for swift rail-to-highway trailer transfer; it also has longer tracks than One, with one able to take 17 articulated five-platform well cars, the other 13, whereas Global One's limit is 10.

The minimal handling of containers that characterises the two terminals enables double-stack train-sets to complete a West Coast-Chicago round trip within seven days. Global One can handle three double-stack trains, each bearing 200 containers, simultaneously, and turn each train-set round within 12 hours. Both terminals can execute 7000 lifts a week.

Besides the investment in Global One and Two, CNW has modified clearances along the 483 miles of its main line from Fremont to Chicago so that the route can accept trains stacking 9 ft 6 in-high containers atop each other (which demands room of 20 ft 4 in above track level).

Double-stack operations included 10 eastbound and 11 westbound double-stack trains for American President Intermodal (API), the shipping line's domestic arm. The average size of these trains is 25–28 cars or 250–280 containers per train. In 1988 CNW and API concluded a new agreement running to August 1995.

CNW has positioned itself as a wholesaler of intermodal transportation service. The railroad operates these trains for third parties based on their requirements for service. Under this system, shipper agents, shipper associations and vessel operators are responsible for arranging the transportation package between shipper and receiver.

The expansion of double-stack container traffic has surpassed initial expectations. In 1987, the intermodal business group handled 435 493 units. By the end of 1988, loads had increased 13·7 per cent to 495 199 units. Gross revenues for 1988 were approximately US$85·4 million, an improvement of 6·9 per cent compared with 1987.

To handle the expected growth in double-stack container traffic, a second facility was needed in 1989. Construction of Global Two, located near the railroad's existing Proviso classification yard, west of Chicago, began in spring 1989.

Despatching centralised

In a US$5 million project train despatching for the whole CNW system has been concentrated in a new Transportation Center in Chicago. The computerised installation is based on Harmon's Total Traffic Management (TTM) system.

Passenger service

North Western continues to operate a Chicago suburban commuter service under an agreement with the Commuter Rail Division of the Regional Transportation Authority (Metra). Under this agreement, expenses associated with the commuter operation which are not offset by commuter revenues are reimbursed by Metra. In addition, the railroad receives a small percentage of gross revenues as income. North Western continues to work toward its long-range goal of selling its commuter assets and transferring the operation to Metra.

The 10 000th unit coal train operated by CNW leaves the southern Powder River basin, Wyoming

Two GM-EMD GP-50 units head a double-stack train out of Global One

CNW locomotives at end 1988

Model	Horsepower	Builder	Locomotives
E-8	2250	EMD/CNW	7
F40PH	3200	EMD	41
F40PH-2	3200	EMD	29
F-7	1500	EMD	6
F-7B	1500	EMD	3
GP-7	1500	EMD	260
GP-15-1	1500	EMD	25
HE-15	1500	EMD/CNW	2
GP-9	1750	EMD	50
SD-18	1800	EMD	26
GP-38-2	2000	EMD	35
SD-38-2	2000	EMD	10
GP-30	2250	EMD	18
GP-35	2500	EMD	28
C-628	2750	Alco	25
GP-40	3000	EMD/CNW	38
SD-40	3000	EMD	44
SD-40-R	3000	EMD/CNW	1
SD-40-2	3000	EMD	132
GP-50	3500	EMD	50
SD-45	3600	EMD	91
SD-50	3600	EMD	35
SD-CAT	3800	EMD/CNW	1
SD-60	3800	EMD	55
Total			1016
Switcher			
MP-15	1500	EMD	15
SW 1200	1200	EMD	5
Total			20
Total locomotives			1036

Traction and rolling stock

C & NW operates 1129 diesel locomotives, 18 passenger cars and 31 020 freight cars.

In 1989 CNW acquired 30 new Dash 8-40C 4000 hp locomotives from General Electric at a cost of approximately US$40 million. The locomotives will be used to haul unit trains of coal from the southern Powder River Basin of Wyoming.

Conrail
Consolidated Rail Corporation

Six Penn Center Plaza, Philadelphia, Pennsylvania 19103-2959

Telephone: +1 215 977 4000
Telefax: +1 215 977 5567

Chairman, President, and Chief Executive Officer: James A Hagen
Senior Vice President, Finance: H William Brown
  Operations: Donald A Swanson
  Marketing and Sales: Gordon H Kuhn
Law: Bruce B Wilson
Vice President, Corporate Strategy: David M Levan
  Controller: Donald W Mattson
  Treasurer: John A McKelvey
  Washington Counsel: William B Newman Jr
  General Counsel: Timothy T O'Toole
  Engineering and Staff: Clifford W Owens
  Public Affairs: Saul Resnick
  Information Services and Administrative Services: Michael D Sims
  Resource Development: Richard C Sullivan
  Labour Relations: Robert E Swert
  Materials and Purchasing: Jeremy T Whatmough
  State & Local Affairs: G M Williams Jr
  Customer Service: Ralph von dem Hagen
Corporate Secretary and Assistant to the Chairman: Allan Schimmel

Gauge: 1435 mm
Length: 20 800 km

Conrail was created as a private, profit-making corporation by an Act of Congress and began operations in April 1976. It was comprised of most of the rail properties of the Central of New Jersey, Erie Lackawanna, Lehigh and Hudson River, Lehigh Valley, Penn-Central and Reading lines. Conrail is primarily a freight railroad providing the most extensive freight service in the north-east and Midwest quadrant of the USA.

Following an abortive attempt by the government to sell off Conrail to Norfolk Southern, the Federal 85 per cent stake in Conrail was floated on the open market in 1987. The flotation was successful and realised US$1650 million. Conrail thus remains a system intact.

In 1989 Conrail operated in 15 states (Connecticut, Delaware, Indiana, Illinois, Kentucky, Maryland, Massachusetts, Michigan, Missouri, New Jersey, New York, Ohio, Pennsylvania, Virginia, West Virginia), the District of Columbia and Canada.

Finance and Traffic 1989
In face of a soft national economy and competitive pricing pressures, freight volume measured in ton-miles declined 3.3 per cent in 1989 compared with 1988. Lower-revenue such as coal rose in volume, but higher-revenue freight such as autos and chemicals decreased. Earnings totalled US$ 148 million compared with US$ 306 million in the previous year, but this difference reflected a special 1989 charge concerned with voluntary retirement programmes and managerial restructuring that reduced net income by US$ 147 million.

Conrail's operating ratio (operating expenses as a percentage of revenues) declined to 94.2 per cent in 1989 from 86·2 per cent in 1988. Discounting the special charge (see above), the ratio would have been 87.3 per cent.

Monongahela purchase
In the spring of 1990 Conrail's newly-acquired control of the Monongahela Railway in Pennsylvania awaited ICC approval. In 1989 Conrail bought the Pittsburgh & Lake Erie Railroad's interest in the Monon; and in March 1990 Conrail reached agreement with CSX Transportation to purchase the latter's one-third interest in the Monon, which would complete Conrail's total share ownership.

Reorganisation
In 1988-89 Conrail consolidated three regional and 12 divisional offices into six divisions. The previous region and division structure was largely inherited from Conrail's six bankrupt predecessors, and did not adequately reflect the changes in routes, traffic flows and operations Conrail has made since it began operations. The six divisions are headquartered at Dearborn, Michigan, near Detroit; Harrisburg, Pennsylvania; Indianapolis; Philadelphia; Pittsburgh, Pennsylvania; and Selkirk, New York, near Albany.

In 1990 the Marketing & Sales department was restructured to dedicate a business group to each of seven major product areas. A new unit, Marketing Services, was created to provide pricing support services.

Service developments
Conrail has embarked on a broad programme of strategic partnerships to transform many of its terminals from end-of-the-line facilities to full-service, commodity-specific distribution hubs, offering a flexible array of transfer, storage, breakdown, and delivery capabilities all at a single price. Conrail's total distribution system offers strategically located distribution centres designed and operated to meet the specific handling and storage requirements of iron and steel, lumber and forest products, canned goods and dry groceries, automotive parts, and dry and liquid bulk commodities.

In 1989 Conrail expanded its SteelNET rail-truck distribution system by opening new facilities in Cleveland, Detroit, Ambridge and Sharon, Pennsylvania. The additions brought the number of SteelNET facilities to 15. Conrail transports iron and steel products in gondola and coiled steel railcars from most major mills in the Northeast and Midwest to the SteelNET facilities (or to warehouses on connecting railroads, giving shippers access to markets across the country). At the SteelNET centres, the shipments are stored and/or transferred to trucks for local delivery as needed. Each SteelNET center is operated by an independent warehouse company. Eleven of the SteelNET facilities are climate-controlled to meet special storage requirements for high-quality sheet steel used in the manufacture of motor vehicles and appliances.

In May 1989 SteelTrain, the first dedicated overnight train service for steel shipments on any major US railroad, was launched to link Chicago area steel mills with steel users in the Detroit and Jackson, Mich, areas, primarily auto manufacturers. At the end of its

Finances (US$ million)

Operating revenues	1985	1986	1987	1988	1989
Total	3208	3144	3247	3490	3411
Operating expenditure					
Way and structures	461	456	488	543	528
Equipment	733	735	732	752	748
Transportation	1317	1218	1271	1338	1341
General, administrative and other	300	332	339	375	362
Total	2811	2741	2830	3008	3218*
Income from operations	397	403	417	482	198

* Including special charge of US$234 million

Other income (expenditure)					
Interest	(89)	(87)	(80)	(85)	(82)
Unusual items	–	–	–	–	–
Other, net	134	115	108	94	117
Total	45	28	28	9	35
Net income	442	431	299	306	148

Traffic

	1985	1986	1987	1988	1989
Freight ton-miles (million)	NA	NA	NA	78 800	76 200

GE B36-7 and GM-EMD GP40-2 locomotives head double-stack COFC

The Chicago-Detroit and Jackson dedicated overnight SteelTrain

first year in May 1990, SteelTrain had posted a 98 per cent on-time record. Conrail refurbished 150 cars, including installation of hoods, for this operation in 1989 and was refurbishing

In 1989 Conrail launched a Paper Connection service, with six distribution centres in major paper-consuming markets. The principle was as for SteelNET, combining long-haul rail transportation, just-in-time local truck delivery, and storage, careful handling and computerised inventory management service by experienced, independent paper distribution center operators.

Conrail's Bulk Transfer Connection offers shippers door-to-door delivery of dry or liquid bulk commodities. The services include premium long-distance rail transportation and bulk transfer to tank or truck through a network of Conrail Flexi-Flo terminals and privately-owned facilities in 13 states and the District of Columbia.

Conrail is the first major railroad to adopt the self-discharge hopper train manufactured by Conveying and Mining Equipment Inc of Houston, Texas. The train, branded 'Conrail Conveyor', is used by a New Jersey company to deliver stone from a quarry to two asphalt plants, and also sand.

In service to the automobile industry, Conrail was the first railroad to offer so-called 'just-in-time' (JIT) service, in which shipments of parts are delivered to automobile assembly plants 'just-in-time' for that day's production. Conrail has lately built a new auto transloading terminal in Montgomery, Pennsylvania, and expanded its large facility near Albany, New York. In 1989 it completed improvements to a major auto terminal at Ridgefield Heights, New Jersey, in the metropolitan New York area.

Acquisition of fully enclosed multi-level railcars to transport new cars, vans and light trucks from assembly plants to distribution terminals is on a large

RAILWAY SYSTEMS / United States of America

scale. Conrail acquired 755 fully enclosed multi-levels in 1988, 850 more in 1989 and ordered a further 1000 for 1990 delivery.

In April 1989 Conrail and OHM Corporation agreed to form a joint venture to site, design, develop, and operate a network of state-of-the-art fixed base resource recovery, treatment and disposal facilities for solid and hazardous wastes.

Other initiatives launched in 1989 included: advances in simplified pricing and billing systems, and the electronic filing of rates which customers can access from their own computer terminals; and the start of computerised scheduling for each freight car movement, including local delivery performance and monitoring.

Intermodal development

Connecting railroads and Conrail provide dedicated double-stack mini-landbridge service for maritime containers from West Coast ports to metropolitan New York-New Jersey for American President Lines, Maersk Line, K-Line, Sea-Pac, Hanjin Container, Japan and NYK and Mitsui-OSK Lines.

By end-1990 Conrail would finish a five-year programme costing over US$90 million to achieve clearances for double-stack COFC service to all its key markets. In 1989 there remained work to do between Albany and Boston, and between Chicago and metropolitan New York.

In co-operation with Honda of America Mfg, a new exclusive double-stack terminal was opened in late 1989 at Marysville, Ohio; it complements the Columbus, Ohio, terminal, which caters for all types of intermodal traffic. In 1990 the Harrisburg intermodal terminal, hub of a fast-growing traffic, was undergoing an US$ 8 million expansion. Another US$ 6 million enlargement and development was under way at the Croxton double-stack terminal in New Jersey. Intermodal train service developments in 1989 included a joint venture with Norfolk Southern, the 'Atlanta Flyer', offering 36-hour transits between the Kearny, NJ, terminal and Atlanta, with connections there for Birmingham, Mobile, Ala and New Orleans.

From the start of 1989 Conrail became the first US railroad to give its customers truck-competitive loss and damage coverage and service throughout its dedicated intermodal network. Conrail hoped its example would persuade the railroad industry to offer the same loss and damage coverage for interline (a movement on two or more railroads) intermodal shipments, as Conrail and the Santa Fe have done since mid-1987 on their 76-hour run-through service between New York and California.

Persuaded that local shippers are the best versed in local markets and drayage, Conrail wholesales its intermodal train space, working through about 130 volume shippers (freight forwarders, shipper associations, motor carriers, etc) in nearly 400 locations. The third party organises the whole door-to-door transit for the individual consignment shipper, including highway collection and delivery, and bills the customer for the complete transit.

Two concerns, United Parcel Service (UPS) and the US Postal Service, account for a third of Conrail's intermodal business, and four of the railroad's 36 daily or near-daily intermodal trains (which Conrail brands 'TrailVan') are exclusive mail trains.

Expressly to win new traffic in traditional motor carrier corridors, not to compete with its existing intermodal retailers, Conrail formed a new wholly-owned subsidiary, Conrail Mercury, in October 1989. Working with appointed draying companies in key terminal areas, Conrail Mercury aims to offer a complete, totally reliable door-to-door intermodal service tailored to individual client need. Its small staff have the backing of a state-of-the-art computerised despatch centre.

Conrail operates 34 piggyback terminals and almost half its daily 'TrailVan' services link inland centres with the five major East Coast terminals at Baltimore, Maryland, Portside, South Kearny and North Bergen, all in New Jersey, and Morrisville, near Philadelphia.

Among the commodities hauled by Conrail's piggyback trains are fresh fruit and vegetables. Since perishables traffic was deregulated in 1979 (allowing railroads to compete with truckers for this business) Conrail's fresh fruit and vegetable volume has increased by 600 per cent. Most of these perishables originate on the West Coast and are brought to Chicago by BN and Santa Fe. From there Conrail hauls the produce to wholesale markets and supermarket distribution centres in Boston, New York-New Jersey and Philadelphia areas.

Traction and rolling stock

In mid-1989 Conrail owned 1988 line-haul and 379 switcher locomotives and 70 370 freight cars.

Diesel passenger units

Unit nos	Model	Make	Quantity
4020–4022	E8A	EMD	3
Total			3

Road freight diesel units

Unit nos	Model	Make	Quantity
2169–2249	GP30	EMD	63
2250–2394	GP35	EMD	59
3620–3691	GP35	EMD	29
3000–3274	GP40	EMD	69
3275–3403	GP40-2	EMD	127
6240–6357	SD40	EMD	108
6358–6524	SD40-2	EMD	165
6654–6666	SD45-2	EMD	13
6700–6834	SD50	EMD	135
6840–6867	SD60	EMD	28
Total EMD units			796
1900–2023	B23-7	GE	117
2800–2816	B23-7	GE	17
5000–5059	B36-7	GE	58
5060–5089	B40-8	GE	30
6600–6609	C30-7	GE	10
6550–6599	C30-7A	GE	50
6610–6619	C32-8	GE	10
6620–6644	C36-7	GE	25
6000–6021	C39-8	GE	22
6025–6045	C40-8	GE	25
2700–2798	U23B	GE	97
2971–2974	U36B	GE	4
Total GE units			465
Total road freight units			1261

Diesel road switcher units

Unit nos	Model	Make	Quantity
5400–5462	GP8	EMD	48
7001–7483	GP9	EMD	65
7513–7597	GP10	EMD	75
1600–1699	GP15-1	EMD	100
7635–7939	GP38	EMD	148
8040–8281	GP38-2	EMD	235
6925–6959	SD38	EMD	35
Total EMD units			706
6900–6918	U23C	GE	18
Total GE units			18
Total road switcher units			724

Diesel yard switcher units

Unit nos	Model	Make	Quantity
8600–8621	SW8	EMD	10
8690–8698	SW8	EMD	3
8666–8687	SW8M	EMD	13
8632–8646	SW900	EMD	7
8701–8721	SW900	EMD	15
9400–9424	SW1001	EMD	25
8838–9140	SW7, SW9	EMD	69
9315–9381	SW1200	EMD	58
9500–9620	SW1500	EMD	116
9621–9630	MP15	EMD	10
Total EMD units			326

Motor trailer units

Unit nos	Model	Make	Quantity
1000–1023	MT-4	ALT	24
1100–1118	MT-6	GE	19
1119–1128	MT-6	CD	10
Total motor trailer units (slugs)			53
Total diesel yard switcher units			379

In March 1989 Conrail ordered for 1990 delivery 100 more 4000 hp C40-8, valued at US$133 million, from General Electric. Including this order, Conrail has acquired or ordered a total of 485 high-horsepower locomotives since mid-1983.

A GM-EMD GP40 fronts a train of automotive parts in special high-roof boxcars deployed for this traffic

---

CSX Transportation Inc
A unit of CSX Corporation

500 Water Street, Jacksonville, Florida 32202

Telephone: +1 904 359 3100
Telefax: +1 904 359 1899

Rail Transportation Unit

President & Chief Executive Officer: A R Carpenter
Senior Vice-President, Corporate Services: J L Sweeney

Administration: G L Nichols
Executive Dept: A C Jones Jr
Transportation: Glenn P Michael
Vice-Presidents, Law: T L Samuel
Labour Relations: H G Anderson
Motive Power: W M Hart
Transportation Services: Franklin E Pursley
Operations Center: Sidney R Johnson
Operating Practices: R A Fliess
Comptroller & Accounts: C J O Wodehouse
Corporate Communications: Diane Liebman
Planning & Economic Analysis: B Schwinger
Risk Management: R A Bernard

Purchasing & Materials: J Basso
Human Resources: J W Warner
Property Services: J L Kiesler
Chief Engineer, Maintenance of Way: Jerry P Epting
Design & Construction: Paul E Van Cleeve
Communications and Signals: W J Scheerer
Chief Mechanical Officer, Locomotives: David G Orr

Gauge: 1435 mm
Length: 31 697 route-km

In November 1980 Chessie System Inc merged with Seaboard Coast Line Industries to form the CSX

Corporation. At first all maintaining their separate identities, managements and operations, the Corporation's constituents, Chessie System Railroads, Seaboard System Railroad (a revised title) and the 63 per cent-owned Richmond Fredericksburg & Potomac Railroad (RF&P), were co-ordinated into a single system serving 21 states, the District of Columbia, and a Canadian province. The Chicago South Shore & South Bend was sold to the Venango River Corp in 1984. A move by CSXT to fully merge the RF&P into its operations was called off in 1990 because of Virginian opposition.

In 1986 Chessie and Seaboard System railroads were merged into a unitary railroad, CSX Transportation. At the same time, a new multi-modal structure was developed to pursue the concept of 'One-Stop Shipping'. In other words, to maximise deregulation's opportunities and regard the train as a link in the total distribution chain; and to structure competitively credible door-to-door transportation. The railroads and the CSX trucking operation, Chessie Motor Express, were welded into a new total transportation system.

The new multi-modal CSX organisation has three strands. CSX Distribution Services has the 'One-Stop' marketing function, covering sales, pricing, billing and preparation of transportation specification. CSX Rail Transport is the rail operating group, charged with production of the required transportation, and thus with everything involved in efficient vehicle movement (including rail track maintenance). Finally, CSX Equipment Group is concerned with the supply, management and utilisation of vehicles.

In the spring of 1986 CSX bid successfully for control of Sea-Land, the major container shipping line, and the biggest intermodal client of the CSX railroads. This gave CSX control of Sea-Land terminals throughout the world, from Japan to the Middle East and Europe. To optimise the scope for synergies of its marine and land intermodal activity a new company CSX-Sea-Land Intermodal (CSLI), was formed to cover all CSXT intermodal operations. It became operational at the start of 1988.

Finance, rail only (US$ million)

	1987	1988	1989
Operating revenue	4634·2	5089	4988
Total operating expenditure	4075	5185*	4399
Operating income (loss)	533	(96)	589
Operating ratio	87·9	101·9	88·2

* Inclusive of a special charge

Lines and territories
The Chessie System principally comprised the former Chesapeake & Ohio and Baltimore & Ohio Railroads. The ex-Chesapeake & Ohio Railway's principle lines extend from the coal fields of southern West Virginia, eastern Kentucky and southern Ohio eastward to Newport News, Virginia, and Washington, DC, westward to Louisville, Cincinnati and Chicago, and northward through Colombus and Toledo to Detroit.

Another principal line extends from Chicago eastward through Grand Rapids and Detroit, to Buffalo. Owned mileage in Canada and trackage rights between St Thomas, Ontario, and Buffalo form a connecting line from the east through Detroit to Chicago and through Detroit to the eastern shore of Lake Michigan.

The former Baltimore & Ohio system operates in 11 states and the District Principal lines extend from Philadelphia, through Baltimore and Washington to Cumberland, Maryland, and from Cumberland by separate routes to Chicago and St Louis. A third important line extends from Cincinnati to Toledo. B & O lines also extend south-westward into the West Virginia coalfields and to Shippensburg, Pennsylvania.

Seaboard System was formed in January 1983 through the merger of Seaboard Coast Line Railroad and the Louisville and Nashville Railroad. The Seaboard System Railroad also encompassed the former Georgia and Clinchfield Railroads, as well as the Atlanta and West Point and the Western Railway of Alabama and other smaller lines.

Seaboard operated in the states of Alabama, Florida, Georgia, Illinois, Indiana, Kentucky, Louisiana, Mississippi, North Carolina, Ohio, South Carolina, Tennessee, and Virginia. Its main lines extend from Chicago to the Gulf of Mexico along the Atlantic coastal plain, forming a direct line from Richmond and Portsmouth to Atlanta, Birmingham, and Montgomery to the west, and to Jacksonville, Miami and Tampa to the south. It serves all major Atlantic ports from Virginia to Florida, including Norfolk, Virginia; Wilmington, North Carolina; Charleston, South Carolina; Savannah and Brunswick, Georgia; and Jacksonville and Miami, Florida. Seaboard also serves several ports on the Gulf of Mexico, including Mobile, Alabama; Pasagoula, Mississippi; New Orleans, Louisiana; and Tampa, Florida.

The ex-Seaboard System Railroad connects Richmond and Norfolk, Virginia, with major points throughout the Carolinas, Georgia, portions of Alabama and most of Florida. In the south and south-east the railroad serves the rich coal-producing fields of eastern Kentucky, and has main lines which connect Chicago, Cincinnati, St Louis and Louisville with Memphis, Nashville, Atlanta, Birmingham and New Orleans.

The ex-Seaboard System Railroad thus serves both as a major north-south railroad, and a major east-west artery, in the Midwest, south and south-east. With its ex-Chessie System partners in the total CSX rail network, it provides 'single-system' service between major markets from Canada, the Great Lakes, and the north-east all across the south and south-east.

Seaboard served more US ocean ports than any other US railroad, from Richmond and Norfolk on the Mid-Atlantic to New Orleans on the Gulf. In addition, it reached a large number of important ports on the Mississippi and Ohio Rivers.

Traffic and Finance 1989
A 2 per cent decline in revenue in 1989, compared with 1988, was attributed chiefly to decisions to shed marginal traffic in some merchandise sectors, and to restructure the intermodal network east of the Mississippi River with the closure of 13 unprofitable terminals; and also to the effect of an ICC adjustment of railroads' ability to up-price in relation to higher costs so as to take account of productivity gains. Discounting a special charge incurred in 1988, operating income in 1989 was 6 per cent lower than in the previous year.

The commodity moving in largest volume over the ex-Chessie System is bituminous coal. Coal originated on company lines comes principally from West Virginia and eastern Kentucky, and also from Pennsylvania, Ohio, Illinois, and Maryland. The railroad moves most of such coal north to the industrial Midwest and the Great Lakes region, east to the Chesapeake Bay region for shipment to domestic and foreign ports, and west to the Ohio River for loading on barges. Based on management estimates derived from reports of the US Geographical Survey, coal fields served by the railroad contain about 18 600 million tons of coal reserves. The company serves over 400 mine outlets and handles coal for export to foreign markets through coal-dumping facilities located at Newport News, Virginia, and Baltimore, Maryland.

In 1989 coal generated 1.9 million of CSXT's total 4.786 million freight carloads. The revenue derived was 2 per cent higher than in 1988, despite the impact of the ICC ruling mentioned above. In common with other railroads, CSXT's traffic in some higher-rated freight such as automotive, metals and chemicals business was weaker than in 1988, but exports stimulated significant growth in grain, phosphates and fertilisers. But in the last two-mentioned commodities hauls were mainly short, so that there was a decline in revenue.

All-line coverage from one CTC centre
Union Switch & Signal was in 1987 awarded a contract to consolidate all train dispatching operations for CSX in a new state-of-the-art CTC centre located in Jacksonville, Florida. This marks the first time a major US railroad has endeavoured to control all of its trackage from a single location.

Dubbed the 'Jacksonville Super Center', the new CTC office features a video-projected track diagram. The panoramic, colour-coded display of trackage, signals and trains pinpoints the locations and assigned routes of all trains operating on CSX trackage, including CTC and 'dark' territory, while a CRT located at each dispatcher's console offers detailed views of operations at any signal control point throughout the trackage. The new system provides for automatic meets and passes, train sheet compilation and other features.

CSX consolidated operations into the Jacksonville Super Centre in 1988. The total value of the contract was in excess of US$9 million.

Advanced Train Control (ACTS)
CSX is developing a pilot ATCS system on its Bone Valley line east of Tampa, Florida. Predominantly involved in phosphates haulage from mines to ports, this line is well suited to the trial because its traffic is

Ex-Chessie System diesel locomotives

Class	Wheel arrangement	Transmission	Rated power hp	Max speed mph	Total weight tons	Year first built	Builders Mechanical parts	Builders Engine & type
GP-7	Bo-Bo	Elec	1500	65	123·5	1950	EMD	16-567BC
GP-9	Bo-Bo	Elec	1750	65	127	1954	EMD	16-567C
GP 15-T	Bo-Bo	Elec	1500	65	122	1982	EMD	8-645BC
GP-30	Bo-Bo	Elec	2250	71	131	1962	EMD	16-567DB
GP-35	Bo-Bo	Elec	2500	71	131	1964	EMD	16-567DBA
GP-38	Bo-Bo	Elec	2000	71	138·5	1967	EMD	16-645-B
GP-39	Bo-Bo	Elec	2300	71	138·75	1969	EMD	12-645-B5
GP-40	Bo-Bo	Elec	3000	71	138·75	1966	EMD	16-645-E3
GP-40-2	Bo-Bo	Elec	3000	65	138·75	1972	EMD	16-645-E3
SD-7	Co-Co	Elec	1500	65	185	1953	EMD	16-567-BC
SD-9	Co-Co	Elec	1750	65	186	1954	EMD	16-567-C
SD-18	Co-Co	Elec	1800	65	181	1962	EMD	16-567-D1
SD-20-2	Co-Co	Elec	2000	65	193·25	1979	EMD	16-645-E
SE-35	Co-Co	Elec	2500	71	193·25	1964	EMD	16-567D3A
SD-40	Co-Co	Elec	3000	71	203	1969	EMD	16-645E3
SD-40-2	Co-Co	Elec	3000	65	198	1977	EMD	16-645E3
SD-50	Co-Co	Elec	3500	70	142	1984	EMD	16-645-F3B
SD-50	Co-Co	Elec	3600	70	142	1985	EMD	16-645-F3B
U23-B	Bo-Bo	Elec	2250	70	138·75	1969	GE	7F-DL12C4
U30-B	Bo-Bo	Elec	3000	70	138·75	1971	GE	7F-DL16E13
B-30-7	Bo-Bo	Elec	3000	70	138·75	1978	GE	7F-DL16
NW-2	Bo-Bo	Elec	1000	65	123	1949	EMD	12-567A
SW-7	Bo-Bo	Elec	1200	60	123	1950	EMD	12-567B
SW-9	Bo-Bo	Elec	1200	65	123·5	1951	EMD	12-567B
SW-12	Bo-Bo	Elec	1200	65	124	1957	EMD	12·567C
SW-900	Bo-Bo	Elec	900	65	115	1955	EMD	8-567C

778 RAILWAY SYSTEMS / United States of America

CSX intermodal terminal at Atlanta, Georgia

Unit train of export coal en route from West Virginia to Newport News, Va.

operated by a dedicated stud of locomotives. CSX is testing a work-order and train-location system with full data radio coverage.

Intermodal traffic
CSX operates 32 intermodal terminals in territory stretching from Chicago, Grand Rapids, Toledo, Baltimore and Philadelphia in the north down to New Orleans, Jacksonville, Tampa and Miami in the south, with other western gateways at East St Louis and Memphis. At Atlanta it recently opened a new terminal that is its largest, superseding two smaller facilities and handling 22 trains daily.

Over 40 per cent of CSX intermodal volume is now COFC. At present its dedicated intermodal train routes are predominantly north-south, from Chicago, Toledo and Philadelphia to the Sunbelt, but with important transferals from Chicago to Baltimore/ Philadelphia and between the Gulf and South Atlantic ports.

In conjunction with Grand Trunk Western, CSX-Sea-Land Intermodal in 1988 launched a through intermodal service, the DixieXpress, between Detroit and the southeast. The dedicated trains cut 36–48 hours from previous transits in this corridor. The company's first double-stack service into New England, from Chicago to Worcester, was launched in January 1989.

A new US$25 million bulk intermodal terminal (BIDS), the largest on CSX, was opened at Atlanta in 1988. The 23-acre site handles bulk distribution of such products as plastics, corn starch, oils and other dry and liquid products. There are now 45 such BIDS terminals in CSX territory. Annual throughput of all 45 BIDS terminals is 23 000 carloads.

In 1990 CSLI was expanding its Frequent Flyer transcontinental services for domestic container traffic. A daily service was introduced between Baltimore/ Philadelphia and southern California via Chicago, to be followed by connections with New York, Boston, Orlando, Tampa and Miami. CSLI and Burlington Northern Intermodal formed a partnership to provide through intermodal train service between Portland and Seattle/Tacoma, in the Pacific Northwest, and Atlanta.

Investment
In 1990 CSX Rail Transport planned to spend US$542 million on capital projects, compared with US$510 million in 1989. In addition equipment worth US$156 million would be acquired through leases.

Locomotives and rolling stock
In 1989 CSX Transportation owned or leased 3255 diesel locomotives. Freight car stock in use totalled 142 506.

In 1989 CSX expanded its freight car fleet, already the country's largest, with 1900 coal gondolas from Bethlehem Steel, 1400 covered hoppers from Trinity Industries and 1200 multi-level auto transporters from Thrall Car. In addition, US$244 million was invested in rebuilding of existing freight cars.

In 1988 CSXT ordered 40 GE Dash-840C 4000 hp locomotives and 10 GM-EMD 3800 hp SD60s. A further 54 Dash-840C were ordered in 1989, and 53 more in 1990. New locomotive deliveries in 1989 totalled 104, in addition to which 100 slugs were taken into service and also 45 rebuilt locomotives. A further 50 SD40-2 3000hp locomotives were being remanufactured by Morrison-Knudsen in 1990.

Delaware & Hudson Railway Company

PO Box 369, Fifth Street, Watervliet (Colonie), New York 12189

Telephone: +1 518 271 4400
Telefax: +1 518 271 4410

President & Chief Executive Officer: C P Belke
Trustee: F P Dicello
Executive Vice President: J J Parola
Secretary & Treasurer: S A Fisk

Gauge: 1435 mm
Length: 2734 km

The Delaware & Hudson, which operates 43 locomotives and 1328 freight cars, provides overhead and local service between Delson (Montreal), Quebec and Potomac Yard, Alexandria, Virginia and between its Mechanicville, New York connection to New England points and Buffalo, New York.

In 1988 a clearance improvement project was undertaken and double-stack service commenced in March 1989 from Buffalo to Albany and LaColle, Quebec (Montreal).

In 1989 the D&H let a contract for the overhaul of all its GP38-2 and GP39-2 locomotives. The locomotive stock comprises 12 GP39-2, 20 GP38- 2 by GM-EMD and six C424M and five RS11 units by Alco.

Chapter 11 bankruptcy
In June 1988 D&H obtained Chapter 11 bankruptcy protection, following 15 consecutive years of financial loss, after a filing by its then parent industry, Guilford Transportation. Until February 1990, when it took back operation, the D&H was operated by the New York, Susquehanna and Western Railroad under an ICC car service order, with financial support from CSX. The railroad's losses were in early 1990 being met temporarily by an alliance of state governments and interested shippers and railroads, the last-mentioned being CP Rail and CN rail of Canada, while efforts were resumed to find a buyer for D&H.

Numerous parties, including Conrail, showed interest in D&H, but the bid favoured by politicians, shippers and the labour force was from CP Rail. However, that collapsed early in 1990 because the Canadians failed to extract trackage rights from Conrail for access from the D&H to south-eastern railroads via Hagerstown.

The Denver and Rio Grande Western Railroad Company

(See Southern Pacific entry)

Florida East Coast Railway Company

1 Malaga Street, St Augustine, Florida 32084

Telephone: +1 904 829 3421
Telex: 56334

Chairman: W L Thornton
President: R W Wyckoff
Vice-President: W E Durham Jr
Vice-President, Transportation: M E Deputy
 Industrial Development: R J Barreto
 Marketing: D K Brideson
Secretary: C F Zellers Jr
Pricing: R W Herndon
General Manager, Transportation: R F Townsend
General Mechanical Superintendent: R Tardif
Chief Engineer: W S Stokely
Chief Engineer, Maintenance of Way: G E Clegg
Superintendent, Signalling and Communications:
 B L Burke

Gauge: 1435 mm
Length: 859 km

The core of the Florida East Coast system is its trunk route from Jacksonville to Miami. The railroad is notable for its determined acceptance of a confrontation over labour work-rules which struck it in 1963. As a result, uniquely among Class I US railroads, it is not bound by such constraints as the 100-mile working day for train crews, distinctions between road and yard crews, fixed numbers of train crew or separate seniority dates for different tasks. This has enabled FEC to surpass by a considerable margin the traction and rolling stock productivity norm of other railroads in its territory, even though it is a terminal system, with no bridge traffic between interchanges with other railroads. Its traffic development centres on intermodal business, particularly from the Miami and Jacksonville ports. Its main line is single track throughout, with

United States of America / **RAILWAY SYSTEMS** 779

3-mile passing loops at roughly 10-mile intervals.
In 1988 FEC recorded operating revenues of over US$150 million.

ATC installation
FEC has invested US$6 million on installation of automatic train control between Miami and Jacksonville.

The Ultra-Cab 40 system was supplied by Harmon Industries.

Finance (US$ million)

Revenue	1986	1987
Operating revenues	121·18	130·26
Operating expenses	91·002	86·469
Net operating income	25·44	29·61
Operating ratio	75·1	75·2

Traction and rolling stock
The company operates 71 line-haul, four switching diesel locomotives and 2544 freight cars.

Grand Trunk Corporation (GTC)

Grand Trunk Corporation is a holding company formed in 1971 to embrace the three Canadian railroads operating within the USA; Grand Trunk Western (GTW); Duluth, Winnipeg & Pacific (DWP); and Central Vermont (CV). DWP and CV are Class II railroads, and detailed on a following page. Since then, GTW has expanded considerably, first by acquisition of redundant Conrail trackage in the Saginaw Bay City-Midland, Michigan, region, then in 1980 by taking control of the 478-mile Detroit, Toledo & Ironton (DTI), which was merged into GTW at the end of 1983, and in 1981 of the 59-mile Detroit & Toledo Shore Line. The expanded GTW is now known as the Grand Trunk Rail System.

Pressed hard by competitive rate-making by deregulated neighbour railroads and trucking, Grand Trunk Corporation confronts rising losses on its railroads. It has been engaged in a 1987–91 plan to cut costs throughout its operation.

Grand Trunk Rail System
Grand Trunk Western Railroad Co

1333 Brewery Park Boulevard, Detroit, Michigan 48207

Finance (US$ million)

	1985	1986	1987
Operating revenues	342·947	323·03	307·72
Operating expenses			
Way and structures	42·874	41·14	39·28
Equipment	71·072	80·16	68·58
Depreciation	19·699	NA	NA
Total operating expenses	338·118	353·52	314·18
Operating ratio	98·59%	109·4	102·1
Net income (loss)	6·13	(16·45)	3·44

Telephone: +1 313 396 6000
Telex: 235463 Telefax: +1 313 396 6656

President: G L Maas
Senior Vice-President, Marketing: W H Cramer
  Finance and Administration: J F Corcoran
Vice-President, Operations: D L Wilson
  General Counsel: E C Opperthauser
  Planning: R A Walker
  Personnel & Labour Relations: J K Krikau
Chief Engineer: J M Letro
Chief Mechanical Officer: R G Lipmyer
Signal Engineer: L W Olson
Director, Purchases & Materials: M E Paisley
General Manager, Transportation: E E Shepard

Gauge: 1435 mm
Length: 1517 km

Intermodal
In 1990 GTW was investing US$7.2 million in expansion and modernisation of its MoTerm intermodal terminal at Detroit. This terminal is also used by BN, Santa Fe and CSLI. The daily Chicago-Detroit train service includes double-stack COFC traffic which GTW moves under contract for Mazda and American President Lines.

Traction and rolling stock
The railway operates 235 diesel locomotives and 8489 freight cars.

Illinois Central Railroad
(An IC Industries Company)

Two Illinois Center, 233 N Michigan Avenue, Chicago, Illinois 60601

Telephone: +1 312 819 7500
Telex: 25 3637

Chairman: W W McDowell Jr
President and Chief Executive Officer: E L Moyers
Senior Vice President, Marketing: Gerald F Mohan
  Law and Administration: Andrew F Reardon
  Chief Financial Officer: Richard P Bessette
Vice-Presidents, Chief Transportation Officer:
  E Hunter Harrison
  Chief Mechanical Officer: Henry M Chidgey
  Chief Engineer: David C Kelly
  Corporate Affairs: Frank J Aliston
  Market Development and Pricing: Robert J Neubauer
  Director, Materials Management: Daniel C Drier
  Amtrak Operations: R L Hoggard
Engineer, Maintenance of Way: David A Lowe

Signal Engineer: J T Sharkey

Gauge: 1435 mm
Length: 4637 km
Electrification: 64·5 km of 1·5 kV dc (Chicago commuter area)

Sale blocked
In 1988 Illinois Central Industries was proposing to spin-off the Illinois Central Gulf (ICG) railroad, now renamed Illinois Central (IC), to its shareholders for US$250 million. However, the ICG decided to investigate the proposal as a result of moves by a labour union and by Venango River Corporation; the latter was in dispute with IC over its purchase of the now financially troubled Chicago Missouri & Western system (qv).

Railroad activities include IC Industries' major transport subsidiary, the Illinois Central Railroad, its subsidiaries, and railroad real estate. The Illinois Central operates in eight states in the heartland of America and runs from the Great Lakes to the Gulf of Mexico, providing rail connection between some 2000 communities, including Chicago, St Louis, Memphis, New Orleans, Birmingham, Kansas City, and Mobile suburban area, over which it operates a fleet of 165 bi-level emu cars owned by the Chicago South Suburban Mass Transit District.

Since 1972 IC has reduced its network from 15 540 to 4637 route-km by sales of low-density trackage to newly-created regional or short-line railroads. With these sales, IC has naturally surrendered a lot of purely local traffic, but overall it has retained around 40 per cent of the lines' business through long-haul partnership with the new companies. The latter, of course, are not tied to the traditional work rules within which IC must operate, nor do they have to finance IC's accumulated debts, so that they have a much better chance to run the transferred lines profitably.

In May 1988 the IC approved sale to Norfolk Southern of some 200 route-miles from Haleyville, Alabama, to Fulton, Kentucky. That completed Illinois Central's downsizing programme.

Traffic
IC is the major railroad in Illinois. Through intensive marketing efforts and innovations, ICG has established itself as an integral part of the nation's grain distribution

Diesel-electric locomotives

Class	Wheel arrangement	Rated power hp	Tractive effort Continuous at lb / mph		Max speed mph	Wheel diameter in	Total weight tons	Length ft in	No in service 21.3.87	First built	Builders	Engine & type
BU-2	Bo-Bo	—	57 100	—	45	40	115	44′ 5″	10	1939	EMD	('Slug' remanufactured by UCG)
SW-9R	Bo-Bo	1200	31 000	12	45	40	124	44′ 5″	1	1951	EMD	12-567
SW-13/SW-13B	Bo-Bo	1300	28 000	11	45	40	125	44′ 5″	5	1939	EMD	12-567
SW-14	Bo-Bo	1300	31 000	12	45	40	125	44′ 5″	111	1950	EMD	12567
SD 28	Co-Co	1800	46 000	12	65	40	167	60′ 8″	2	1965	EMD	12-567D1
GP-9/18/28	Bo-Bo	1750/1800	40 000/44 600	11/12	65	40	124/123	56′ 2″	10	1950/1964	EMD	16-567/16-567C
GP-8/10/11	Bo-Bo	1600/1850	40 000/44 600	11/12	65	40	123/133	56′ 2″	309	1950/1954	EMD	16-567 (completely remanufactured by ICG) 16-645E
GP-38, 38A, 38-D	Bo-Bo	2000	46 715	12·8	76	40	131/133	59′ 2″	34	1970	EMD	16-567D3
GP-38-2	Bo-Bo	2000	46 000	10·9	65	40	129	56′ 2″	55	1962	EMD	16-567D3A
GP-30	Bo-Bo	2250	52 000	11·8	71	40	129	56′ 2″	8	1964	EMD	T/C 16-645E3
GP-35	Bo-Bo	2500	52 000	12	71	40	131	59′ 2″	7	1966	EMD	T/C 16-645E3
GP-40	Bo-Bo	3000	54 600	11	65	40	139	59′ 2″	38	1969	EMD	T/6 16 cyl Type FDL-16
GP-40A	Bo-Bo	3000	46 700	13	76	40	136	60′ 2″	13	1967	GE	T/C 16-645E3
SD 40/40A	Co-Co	3000	82 100	11·1	65	40	208	68′ 10″	40	1973	EMD	T/C 16-645E8
SD 40-2	Co-Co	3000	78 000	11·1	65	40	184/189	60′ 8″	15	1959	EMD	T/C 20-645E3
SD20	Co-Co	2000	48 000	12·8	65	40	198	65′ 9″	42	1966	EMD	16-567D3A
SD 45	Co-Co	3600	82 100	11·3	65	40	131	56′ 2″	1	1962	EMD	16-567D3A
GP-26	Bo-Bo	2250	52 000	11·8	71	40	124	44′ 5″	2	1951	EMD	

system by providing year-round service to the agricultural sector. IC maintains a strong advantage over other rail carriers as it provides a direct access to the Gulf of Mexico. Unit grain trains provide grain shippers with rates that are truck- and barge-competitive.

Approximately 95 per cent of IC coal traffic now moves in train load or unit train shipments. Of this total, 65 per cent is moved in non-IC equipment under reduced rates, thereby mimimising IC capital and equipment requirements. Coal is, and is expected to continue to be, a major contributor to IC's growth; it accounted for 16·1 per cent of revenues in 1986. IC is strategically positioned in the extensive Illinois Basin coal fields, encompassing Illinois, and western Kentucky, and containing an estimated 115 000 million tons of recoverable coal reserves.

A new prospect for IC is the development of foreign markets for coal from IC-served mines. IC has worked with overseas utilities and other coal users to bring to their attention the merits of using Illinois Basin coal and has co-operated with US coal companies to establish delivered BTU costs via the ports of New Orleans, Louisiana, and Mobile, Alabama, that are competitive with coal now moving through other ports.

At the southern end of the railroad, chemical complexes produce a significant contribution to ICs revenue mix. Louisiana, ranked first in chemical industry growth, represents a major portion of IC's loadings. IC is one of the largest US rail carriers of chemicals. The 145 km stretch between Baton Rouge and New Orleans is particularly rich in such natural resources as lime, salt, sulphur, crude oil and natural gas.

One of the nation's heaviest paper mill concentrations is the IC-served states of Alabama, Mississippi, Louisiana and Tennessee. Since IC is the major railroad in Mississippi, the growing wood and paper products industries of that state have benefited from IC innovations for moving both raw materials and finished products.

Intermodal traffic

In order to provide better road-to-rail TOFC operations, IC has implemented eight hub centres, truck/rail facilities which provide co-ordinated highway/rail access to customers within a 480 km radius within 21 states. This concept capitalises on main-line rail service, improves load balance, and increases equipment utilisation. Another intermodal development,

Plan V less-than-truckload (LTL), allows IC to compete with motor carriers in door-to-door service. It has recently obtained a 32-state trucking authority.

Daily dedicated trains connect Chicago with Memphis, Mobile and New Orleans. Undaunted by failure to make a remunerative activity of a 'Sprint'-type working between Chicago and St Louis, IC in 1986 launched a daily, two-man crew piggyback train service over the 316 miles from St Louis to Memphis. This operation makes connection at Memphis with trains to and from Jackson, Mobile and New Orleans.

IC is a double-stack COFC participant. It partners Southern Pacific (SP) in the operation of NYK Line's Los Angeles-St Louis and Mitsui OSK's Los Angeles-Chicago trains.

Results (US$ million)	1984	1985	1986
Sales and revenues	1013·4	909·8	715·5
Expenses	901·9	832·8	620·0
Operating income	111·5	77·0	95·5

Locomotives and rolling stock

At the end of 1989 IC was operating 630 locomotives. Freight car stock totalled 15 980.

Kansas City Southern Lines
(The Kansas City Southern and Louisiana & Arkansas Railway Companies)

114 West 11th Street, Kansas City, Missouri 64105

Telephone: +1 816 556 0303
Telefax: +1 816 556 0297

Chairman of the Board and Chief Executive Officer: Landon H Rowland
President and Chief Operating Officer: W N Deramus IV
Senior Vice President: L H Rowland
Senior Vice Presidents, Finance: D L Graf
  Marketing: L Larry R Parsons
  Law: R E Zimmerman
Vice Presidents
  Sales: D E Johnson
  Personnel: J L Deveney
  Governmental Affairs: P S Brown
  General Counsel: R P Bruening
  Operations: L D Fields
    James B Dehner
Comptroller: R L Brown II
Corporate Secretary: A P Mauro
Director, Purchases: S L Carpenter
Chief Mechanical Officer: E R Post
Superintendent of Locomotives: F Haywood
Chief Engineer: D W Brookings
Signal Engineer: S R Taylor

Gauge: 1435 mm
Length: 1419 km

Finance (US$ million)

	1985	1986	1987	1988
Operating revenues	316·7	306·2	315·1	316·6
Operating expenses				
Way and structures	48·662	67·5	53·89	64·35
Equipment	68·982	102·74	55·5	52·53
Depreciation	36·143	27·8	NA	NA
Total operating expenses	270·164	267·6	246·5	30·88
Operating ratio	85·3%	102·47%	80·6%	83·4%
Net income/(loss)	23·792	(2·86)*	31·28	(7·4)

*After capacity valuation adjustments

Locomotive fleet: all GM-EMD

Model	Rating	Year built	No in service end-1988
SD-40	3000	1966-71	30
SD-40-2	3000	1972-80	56
SD-40-X	3500	1979	4
SD-50	3500	1981	10
GP-40	3000	1966-68	45
GP-40-2	3000	1979-81	4
GP-38-2	2000	1974-78	12
GP-30	2250	1962	14
NW-2	1000	1938-48	5
GP-7	1500	1951-53	6
GP-9	1750	1954-59	2
SW-7	1200	1950-51	2
SW-1500	1500	1968-72	42
MP-15	1500	1975	4
Slug units			15

Kansas City Southern Lines is the largest unit of the Kansas City Southern Industries group of companies. KCSI owns fibre-optics and financial services companies. KCS itself runs south from Kansas City to Beaumont and Port Arthur, Texas; the L&A route extends from New Orleans to Farmville, Texas, with access to Dallas over Sante Fe tracks. The main freight yard, Deramus, is at Shreveport, where KCS and L&A lines intersect.

Traffic
Chief components of KCS traffic are the input and output of Gulf Coast refineries and chemical plants, forest products and most recently unit trains of coal. Intermodal business, chiefly between New Orleans and Dallas, is increasing.

Signalling
CTC is transmitted entirely by microwave, which also carries all other voice and data communications.

Traction and rolling stock
Traction and rolling stock (including Louisiana & Arkansas equipment) comprises 188 line-haul and 63 switcher diesel locomotives and 6858 freight cars.

In 1990 KCS was taking delivery of 10 GM-EMD 3800 hp SD60 locomotives, its first order of new traction units since 1981. A further 12 SD60s were ordered in 1990.

Norfolk Southern Corporation

PO Box 3609, One Commercial Place, Norfolk, Virginia 23510-2191

Telephone: +1 804 629 2600
Telefax: +1 804 629 2345

Chairman, President and Chief Executive: Arnold B McKinnon
Executive Vice President, Administration: Joseph R Nelkirk
Executive Vice President, Marketing: D Henry Watts
Executive Vice President, Law: John S Shannon
Executive Vice President, Finance: John R Turbyfill
Executive Vice President, Operations: Paul R Rudder
Vice President, Mechanical: Donald W Mayberry
Senior Vice President, Public Affairs: Edward T Breathitt
Vice President & Treasurer: Thomas H Kerwin
Vice President, Material Management: R Alan Brogan
Senior Vice President, Corporate Development & Real Estate: Robert E L deButts
Vice President, Management Information Services: Gerald C Durand
Vice President, Taxation: David R Goode
Vice President, Merchandise Marketing: William E Voltz
Vice President, Personnel & Labour Relations: Thomas C Sheller
Vice President, Engineering: Charles M Irvin
Vice President, Controller: Leslie I Prillaman, Jr
Vice President, Public Relations: Magda A Ratajski
Vice President, Coal & Ore Traffic: William B Bales
Vice President & General Counsel: Donald M Tolmie
Vice President, Law: James C Bishop
Vice President, Transportation: Stephen C Tobias
President and Chief Executive Officer, North American Van Lines, Inc, Fort Wayne, Ind: Joseph D Ruffolo
Corporate Secretary: Donald E Middleton

Gauge: 1435 mm
Route length: 25 734 km

Norfolk Southern Corporation (NS) is a holding company with headquarters at Norfolk, Virginia, established in 1982 to co-ordinate the merger of Norfolk & Western and Southern Railways, which was largely motivated by the 1980 creation of CSX (qv).

The merger was an end-to-end consolidation. The N&W stretches from Norfolk, Virginia, west to Kansas City, Missouri, and north into the key markets of Chicago, Detroit and Cleveland. The Southern blankets the southeast, from New Orleans, Louisiana, Mobile, Alabama, and Palatka, Florida, north to Cincinnati, Ohio, and Washington DC; and from East St Louis, Illinois, and Memphis, Tennessee, eastwards to the Atlantic ports of Norfolk, Virginia, Morehead City, North Carolina, Charleston, South Carolina, Savannah and Brunswick, Georgia, and Jacksonville, Florida. The railroads connect at 17 common points, with major connections at East St Louis; Cincinnati; Bristol, Altavista, Danville, Lynchburg, Norfolk and Norton, all in Virginia; and Winston-Salem and Durham, North Carolina.

A principal benefit was the establishment of five new major routes: the Altavista Gateway route, the Lynchburg-Knoxville Cutoff route, the Mid-South Corridor route, the Kansas City Gateway route and the Shenandoah Corridor route. Single-system service from Southern Railway points in the south-east is now offered by shorter, more efficient routes to the north via the Hagerstown, Maryland, gateway, to the Midwest via the Altavista, Bristol, Lynchburg and Cincinnati

United States of America / **RAILWAY SYSTEMS** 781

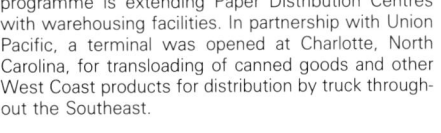

Finances (US$ million)	1985	1986	1987	1988	1989
Revenues					
Coal, coke and iron ore	1206·5	1137·2	1129·5	1219·6	1299·0
Merchandise	1868·7	1834·2	1848·4	2000·4	1929·9
Intermodal	244·9	247·1	251·1	248·7	351·1
Other	114·7	109·3	106·6	111·9	114·1
Total	3434·8	3327·8	3335·6	3616·6	3694·1
Expenditure					
Way and structures	490·7	510·9	533·2	565·7	575·3
Equipment	697·0	678·4	663·0	634·8	648·8
Transportation	1204·8	1085·2	1103·2	1137·1	1233·0
General and administrative	347·6	391·3	353·4	342·2	407·3
Total	2740·1	2665·8	2652·8	2679·8	2864·4
Net revenue from operations (including motor carrier)	719·0	702·0	105·0	945·2	825·2
Other income (expense)					
Interest income	171·7	215·8	232·93	108·4	158·2
Interest expense	(68·5)	(61·8)	(58·52)	(53·1)	(50·7)
Total	103·2	154·0	174·41	55·3	107·5
Income before taxes	822·2	856·0	279·45	1000·6	932·7
Provision for taxes	322·0	337·3	107·08	365·5	326·5
Net income	500·2	518·69	172·38	635·1	606·2

Unit coal train bound for Lamberts Point, Norfolk, Va near Williamson, West Virginia

gateways. N&W points in the Midwest such as Chicago, Detroit and Cleveland similarly obtain single-system service to Southern Railway points in the south such as Atlanta, Birmingham, New Orleans and Memphis.

Finance
Total transportation revenues rose 1.7 per cent in 1989, but expenses were up by 5.5 per cent. This, plus a sluggish national economy, meant that earnings of US$606.2 million did not match NS' record 1988 figure of US$635.1 million. Rail operations in isolation rose 2.1 per cent against expenses up by 6.9 per cent; coal, coke and iron ore revenues increased, but merchandise revenues declined slightly. The biggest downturns were in the construction and agriculture groups. NS has the lowest operating ratio of all Class 1 railroads; in 1989 it was 77.5, compared with 71.7 in 1988.

Thoroughbred Short Line Programme
In October 1987 Norfolk Southern announced a write-off of some 4350 km of railroad. Of this total around 2170 km were marked off for sale to regional operators under a Thoroughbred Shortline Program (NS' emblem is a prancing horse, hence its widespread promotional use of 'Thoroughbred'). By 1990 20 new short-line railroads had been created and the transfer of some 1770 route-km was either effected or approved. In all cases the objective was to encourage continued movement of carloads on to NS lines.

A major transaction near completion in the spring of 1990 was the transfer of 926.5 km of route that originally formed the Wheeling & Lake Erie, Akron Canton & Youngstown and Pittsburgh and West Virginia Railroads to the Wheeling Acquisition Corporation, which operate the resultant regional railroad under the Wheeling & Lake Erie name. The deal also covered lease to the new railroad by NS of 42 locomotives and 1297 freight cars.

Traffic
Coal, coke and iron ore are the dominant elements of NS freight. In 1989 NS railroads originated 122 million short tons of coal, 5.9 per cent more than in 1988, largely because of rising export demand. The gross shipped through the NS piers at Lamberts Point in Norfolk, Va, was 31.4 million short tons, of which a fifth was bound for Italy. The proportion of all NS coal tonnage moved under contract was 90 per cent. The principal sources were mines in Virginia, West Virginia, Kentucky and Tennessee.

Export coal cars generally stand loaded at Lamberts Point until their designated ship is available for loading. For better coal productivity NS was in 1989 preparing to build a ground storage facility with an 8 million-short tons' annual capacity some 48 km inland in Isle of Wight County.

Despite the downturn in domestic auto production, NS increased its automotive traffic in 1989. This was chiefly due to the establishment of new production facilities on NS territory by both US and Japanese manufacturers. NS itself opened a new auto distribution terminal at Petersburg, Va. Automative business now accounts for over 10 per cent of NS revenues.

NS continues to develop schemes that integrate rail and highway truck. Its Thoroughbred Bulk Transfer (TBT) system now embraces 30 terminals for trans-loading of liquid and dry bulk commodities. Another programme is extending Paper Distribution Centres with warehousing facilities. In partnership with Union Pacific, a terminal was opened at Charlotte, North Carolina, for transloading of canned goods and other West Coast products for distribution by truck throughout the Southeast.

Intermodal traffic
NS has in recent years been a frontrunner in intermodal business growth. That is partly because, healthily profitable from a huge coal traffic that once seemed set for indefinite expansion, it was a late-comer in earnest application to intermodal development. In 1989 its intermodal services, including the Triple Crown RoadRailer operation (see below), added 17.5 per cent in volume and 23.4 per cent in revenue.

NS joined the double-stack COFC trade by participation in American President Intermodal's New Orleans-Atlanta operation in 1985. In 1989 its double-stack traffic soared 83 per cent and by the end of the year NS was running 30 trains weekly for five shipping lines. Its traffic between Canada and the West Coast for Pacific Rim countries' trade, carried for Maersk and K-Line, grew fourfold during the year.

In 1990 NS was opening up one tunnel and enlarging another in Virginia so as to be able in 1991 to open up double-stack service to and from Norfolk, Va. New services were planned between that port and Chicago, St Louis and Kansas City. Also in 1990 NS was opening a new intermodal terminal at Columbus, O.

A boost for TOFC business in 1989 was a major new contract with United Parcels Service. Another new development was partnership with Conrail in the Atlanta Flyer, a through intermodal train connecting the New York-New Jersey area with Atlanta and other southern centres.

Daily NS piggyback services covering both COFC and TOFC operate between Kansas City, St Louis, New Orleans and Charlotte; Miami, Jacksonville, Charlotte, New Orleans, Atlanta, St Louis and Kansas City; Norfolk, Buffalo, Detroit, Chicago, St Louis and Kansas City; and Alexandria, Charlotte, Atlanta, Jacksonville, Miami and New Orleans.

RoadRailer service
NS' Triple Crown RoadRailer service, the first bi-modal network operation in the US, is run as an NS subsidiary, with its dedicated locomotives, road vehicles and staff. Triple Crown is based on a hub at Fort Wayne, Indiana, where trains exchange trailers, and where a new terminal was to be built in 1990. In 1990 a tenth Triple Crown terminal was opened at Kansas City and a new daily service begun to it from St Louis. Other RoadRailer routes were: Atlanta-Jacksonville; Chicago-St Louis; Chicago-Atlanta; Fort Wayne-Buffalo; and Alexandria-Atlanta. An Atlanta-Jacksonville service was launched in January 1989. Triple Crown runs well over 100 trains weekly, deploys over 2000 RoadRailer vehicles and in 1989 recorded 93 450 load vehicle movements.

In 1990 it was announced that Triple Crown was to acquire prototypes of a RoadRailer to carry 48ft containers and refrigerated units. Extension of the Triple Crown network to embrace Monteal and Toronto in Canada is a possibility.

Investment
For 1990 NS planned a capital budget for its railroads of US$683 million, 3 per cent more than the 1989 budget. This provided for 54 new locomotives and 1000 new open-top hoppers, also reconstruction of over 3000 existing freight cars. Infrastructure spending was projected at US$ 428 million, principally for intermodal terminals and auto handling facilities.

Motive power and rolling stock
At the close of 1989 NS operated 2 steam (for special trains only) and 2180 diesel locomotives and 127 669

Traffic	1986	1987	1988	1989
Total freight short tons (millions)	250·8	255·9	272·8	271·6
Total freight short ton-miles (millions)	91 418·1	94 265·9	100 800	99 600

RoadRailer in NS 'Triple Crown' service

Diesel locomotives

Type	Wheel arrangement	Transmission	Rated power kW	Max speed km/h	Total weight tonnes	Length mm	No in service 1989	Year first built	Builders Mechanical parts	Builders Engine & type	Builders Transmission
SW1	B-B	Elec	448	72	88.7	13,533	6	1950	EMD	EMD	EMD
SW12	B-B	Elec	895	105	111.6	13,612	3	1950	EMD	EMD	EMD
SW1500	B-B	Elec	1119	114	112.7	13,612	67	1970	EMD	EMD	EMD
TC10*	B-B	Elec	783	114	114.8	17,100	5	1983	EMD	Caterpillar	Kato
MP15	B-B	Elec	1119	105	116.6	14,832	87	1977	EMD	EMD	EMD
GP9	B-B	Elec	1306	105	111.2	17,121	5	1954	EMD	EMD	EMD
GP9R	B-B	Elec	1306	114	111.2	17,121	4	1978	EMD	EMD	EMD
SD9	C-C	Elec	1306	105	165.6	18,440	10	1957	EMD	EMD	EMD
GP18	B-B	Elec	1343	105	111.2	17,121	1	1959	EMD	EMD	EMD
GP20	B-B	Elec	1492	105	113.6	17,121	2	1980	EMD	EMD	EMD
GP30	B-B	Elec	1679	114	117.0	17,121	132	1962	EMD	EMD	EMD
GP35	B-B	Elec	1865	114	122.9	17,121	114	1963	EMD	EMD	EMD
GP38	B-B	Elec	1492	105	112.5	18,035	114	1969	EMD	EMD	EMD
GP38AC	B-B	Elec	1492	105	129.9	18,035	115	1971	EMD	EMD	EMD
GP38-2	B-B	Elec	1492	105	117.5	18,035	258	1972	EMD	EMD	EMD
GP40	B-B	Elec	2238	114	124.9	18,035	60	1966	EMD	EMD	EMD
GP40X	B-B	Elec	2611	114	121.5	18,318	3	1978	EMD	EMD	EMD
SD40	C-C	Elec	2238	114	175.5	20,113	73	1966	EMD	EMD	EMD
SD40-2	C-C	Elec	2238	113	175.5	20,979	289	1972	EMD	EMD	EMD
F40PH	B-B	Elec	2238	145	117.0	17,100	2	1977	EMD	EMD	EMD
GP49	B-B	Elec	2089	105	121.3	18,035	6	1980	EMD	EMD	EMD
GP50	B-B	Elec	2611	114	121.5	18,014	90	1980	EMD	EMD	EMD
SD50	C-C	Elec	2611	113	175.5	21,671	26	1980	EMD	EMD	EMD
GP59	B-B	Elec	2238	113	121.5	18,212	36	1986	EMD	EMD	EMD
SD60	C-C	Elec	2835	113	175.5	21,671	126	1984	EMD	EMD	EMD
U23B	B-B	Elec	1716	105	119.7	18,340	68	1972	GE	GE	GE
B23-7	B-B	Elec	1716	105	122.0	18,949	54	1978	GE	GE	GE
U30C	C-C	Elec	2238	113	175.5	20,498	3	1974	GE	GE	GE
B30-7A	B-B	Elec	2238	105	126.5	18,974	22	1982	GE	GE	GE
C30-7	C-C	Elec	2238	113	175.5	20,498	79	1978	GE	GE	GE
D8-32B	B-B	Elec	2387	113	121.5	19,385	45	1989	GE	GE	GE
B36-7	B-B	Elec	2686	105	125.1	18,645	6	1981	GE	GE	GE
C36-7	C-C	Elec	2686	113	175.5	20,498	43	1981	GE	GE	GE
C39-8	C-C	Elec	2909	113	175.5	21,537	138	1984	GE	GE	GE

* Retired GP9s rebuilt with Caterpillar engines and Kato transmission for local switching duty

freight cars. Locomotive deliveries in 1989 included the first of 33 GM-EMD 3000 hp Super Series GP59. These, the first Super Series models to use GM-EMD's 12-cylinder 710G engine, were to be used on Triple Crown RoadRailer trains as well as general freight traffic. Other acquisitions were 33 GE Dash 8-32B locomotives. The year's purchases also included 1450 coal hoppers from Trinity Industries (who were delivering a further 1000 open-top hoppers in 1990) and 100 wood chip gondolas, in addition to which 2500 coal hoppers were rebuilt.

In late 1990 NS would take delivery of 21 GE 8-40C locomotives, taking its stock of 'Dash-8' units beyond 200.

New communications systems

New developments foreseen include exploitation of the NAVSTAR Global Positioning System as a basis for control of all locomotive and train movement, without need of wayside signals. Also under development is the use of hand-held computers radio/microwave linked to mainframe computers at Roanoke and Atlanta, for handling of car billing data, workshop performance, bad order reporting and other items.

Meanwhile computer-aided despatching, currently covering about one-quarter of the Southern and one-fifth of the N&W network, is being expanded. The Fort Wayne installation by SafeTran controls an entire division embracing 660 route-miles of track between Chicago and Bellevue, Ohio, and Detroit and Cincinnati. This centre has three dispatcher consoles, but the whole territory can be controlled from any one of the three. The first NS solid state interlocking has been installed at Randolph Street, Roanoke.

Track

Rail type and weight: Chiefly 132 lb/yd, 65.6 kg/m; 115 lb/yd, 57 kg/m; 100 lb/yd, 49.6 kg/m; and 85 lb/yd, 42.2 kg/m.
Cross ties (sleepers): Wood, 7 in x 9 in x 8 ft 6 in; 6 in x 9 in x 8 ft 6 in
Spacing: 1970/km
Fastenings: 6 in cut spikes
Minimum curvature radius: 22°
Max gradient: 4.4%
Max permissible axleload (lb): 71 500±, 36 in dia wheels; 78 750±, 38 in dia wheels

Pittsburgh & Lake Erie Railroad Co

Commerce Court, 4 Station Square, Pittsburgh, Pennsylvania 15219

Telephone: +1 412 263 3813

Chairman, President and Chief Executive Officer: Gordon E Neuenschwander
Executive Vice-President and Chief Operating Officer: C Roy Holley
Vice-President, Finance: Donald F Heckathorne
Vice-President, Law: G Edward Yurcon
Chief Transportation Officer: Charles J Lukenas
Chief Mechanical Officers
  Locomotives: Robert J Costello
  Cars: Allan C Peters
  Motive Power Maintenance: John J Sullivan
Chief Engineer: Robert F Butter
Superintendant, Signals and Communications: Russell E Ross
Director, Purchase and Materials: Terry M Durko

Gauge: 1435 mm
Length: 650 km

The P&LE was part of the New York Central from 1889. NYC, originally a 50 per cent owner, acquired more stock after 1965, so that its successor, Penn Central, eventually owned over 90 per cent of the company. When Penn Central collapsed, P&LE fought for and secured an amendment to the Rail Reorganisation Act of 1973 that precluded the inclusion of solvent railroads in Conrail, which preserved P&LE's autonomy. In February 1979, with the aid of external finance, the sale of P&LE from Penn Central to a new Pittsburgh & Lake Erie Company based in Pittsburgh was achieved.

P&LE, with CSX and Conrail, has shared equally the ownership of the 146-mile (235 km) Monongahela Railway, but in 1990, with its own change of ownership (see below), P&LE was preparing to sell its share to Conrail. Other subsidiaries are the Montour, Youngstown & Southern and Pittsburgh, Chartiers & Youghiogheny Railroads.

Sell-off blocked

P&LE has been heavily dependent on the steel industry, the raw materials and products of which accounted for three-quarters of its annual loadings. By the early 1980s the railroad's steel business had collapsed, as unfulfilled pipeline prospects were aggravated by imported steel's savagery of local mills' outputs. From 1982 onwards P&LE accumulated losses of US$60 million and a mounting interest problem. In July 1987 the company arranged to sell the railroad to Chicago West Pullman Corporation, but was blocked by an Appeals Court ruling that such sale must involve agreement by the 14 labour unions involved because of its effects on their members.

Eventually, in early 1990, the ICC overruled labour union objections and in principle endorsed the sale of the railroad to the P&LE Acquisition Corp, a subsidiary of Railroad Development Corp. The prospective new owners planned to redevelop the railroad on a reduced traffic base.

Diesel locomotives

Class	Wheel arrangement	Transmission	Rated power hp	Max speed km/h	Total weight tonnes	No in service	Year first built	Builders Mechanical parts	Builders Engine & type	Builders Transmission
U28-B	B-B	Elec	2800	112	136.5	21	1966	GE	GE-7FDL16	GE
GP-38-2	B-B	Elec	2000	105	137.75	6	1977	EMD	EMD 645-E	EMD
GP-7	B-B	Elec	1500	88	123.4	2	1953	EMD	EMD 16 567-B	EMD
SW 1500	B-B	Elec	1500	105	128.7	37	1971	EMD	EMD 645-E	EMD
MP-15	B-B	Elec	1500	105	128.7	25	1975	EMD	EMD 645-E	EMD

Track
Rail: 65·48 kg/m
Cross ties (sleepers): Wooden, thickness 7 in
Spacing: 2019/km

Fastenings: Splice bars
Minimum curvature radius: 0°20'
Max gradient: 1·19%

Locomotives and rolling stock
In 1986 P&LE operated 38 line-haul and 54 switching diesel locomotives, three passenger cars and 13 636 freight cars.

Santa Fe Railway
Atchison, Topeka and Santa Fe Railway Company

80 East Jackson Boulevard, Chicago, Illinois 60604

Telephone: +1 312 347 3000
Telex: 253266
Telefax: +1 786 6219

President and Chief Executive Officer: R D Krebs
President & Chief Operating Officer: M R Haverty
Senior Vice President, Executive Dept: T J Fitzgerald
Assistant to President: B C Lancaster
Asst Vice President, Asset Mgt: L F Fox
Secretary and Treasurer: M W Prosser
Senior Vice-President, Finance: Glenn W Dodd
Asst Vice President, Accounting: J E Nolan
   Tax Counsel: S J Morrow
   Controller, Topeka: T N Hund
   Decision Support Systems, Topeka: C R Ice
Vice-President, Operations: A W Rees
Asst Vice President, Chief Transportation Officer: W C Lyman
   Chief Engineer: H G Webb
   Chief Mechanical Officer: D M Sizemore
   Staff Services, Topeka: C R Kaelin
Vice President, Purchases & Materials: W C Meares
   Law: J R Moreland
   Management Information Systems: C L Schultz
   Human Resources: R E Hagberg
   Intermodal: D G McInnes
Asst Vice President, Domestic Intermodal Mktg & Sales: S H Mitchell
   International Intermodal Mktg & Sales: R D Allen
   Intermodal Terminal Operations/Service: L C Jenkins
   Intermodal Operating Services: J L Fields
Vice President, Marketing & Sales: D H Skelton
   Marketing Services: P R O'Brien
Asst Vice-President, Chemicals: R W Brown
   Autos & Metals, Detroit: R W Gottschalk
   Grain, Kansas City: E Lyman
General Director, Equipment Management & Services: T A Murphy
   Intermodal Planning & Control Unit: S G Branscum

Gauge: 1435 mm
Length: 18 127 km

Lines and territories
The Santa Fe Railway is a subsidiary of Santa Fe Pacific Corporation. It extends from Chicago to the Gulf of Mexico and the Pacific coast.

In 1990 Santa Fe established a St Louis gateway for the first time in its history by obtaining trackage rights over the former Chicago Missouri & Western line from Kansas City, now the Gateway Western Railway; this followed the break-up and sale in two parts of the financially ailing Chicago Missouri & Western. Santa Fe was investigating the scope for similar arrangements with other railroads to extend its market range. Access to New Orleans was one objective.

Finance
In 1989 Santa Fe reported an operating loss, entirely due to extraordinary charges of US$389.6 million to estabish reserves covering restructure, which includes intention to sell or abandon some 4800 km of track, 9600 freight cars and 240 locomotives, and severance of some 2700 employees; and of US$52.2 million reflecting changes in assessment of personal injury liability. Discounting these charges, operating income on US$228.1 million was 4 per cent up on the previous year, whereas operating expenses rose only 3 per cent. Freight revenue per carload increased on average by 2 per cent.

A drastic 25 per cent decline in 1989 grain shipments because of drought was offset by a 9 per cent rise in carloadings of merchandise and improved shipments of coal, chemicals and non-metallic minerals. Intermodal traffic rose 8 per cent.

In the first quarter of 1990 Santa Fe was hit by a significant downturn in traffic, with auto and grain business off 47 and 40 per cent respectively. As a

GM-EMD FP45 units and double-stack COFC: Santa Fe has revived its historic 'war bonnet' red-and-silver livery for locomotives employed in prime intermodal service

New GE 4000hp 8-40B locomotives at Corwith yard, Chicago

Divisional Operations Centre, Kansas City

result some 850 staff were laid off, chiefly through suspension of heavy locomotive and freight car repairs, and reduction of staff in track gangs.

Line disposals
In 1989 five branch lines totalling 655 km were sold off. Sale of a further 1045 km was being pursued in 1990.

Management restructure
In 1989 the railway set up a separate intermodal business unit. The rest of its marketing and sales organisation was subdivided into seven business units each dealing with a specific commodity.

Intermodal traffic
The railroad's largest potential for growth is intermodal traffic, which now generates 40 per cent of its revenues. The proportion of COFC is rising, but TOFC still accounts for 65 per cent of the business.

Since the start of 1988 Santa Fe has acquired new articulated intermodal equipment representing more than 5000 platforms and half its intermodal equipment is now of this type. In 1989 additions to stock included 200 5-Pack articulated TOFC and 100 five-platform double-stack COFC well cars plus the first of 280 five-platform units adaptable to COFC or TOFC. In 1990 Santa Fe was to obtain 200 more of the last-mentioned type and a further 100 five-well double-stack units. At the end of 1989 the railway was operating 922 owned or leased 5-Pack and 10-Pack articulated units, including 270 double-stack.

In 1990 Santa Fe concluded an agreement with Rail-Bridge, a K-Line subsidiary, to set up a double-stack COFC operation branded the 'Azteca Service' from the K Line terminal at Long Beach, California, to the Mexican Railways' Pantaco terminal at Mexico City and to Monterrey, Mexico. Rail-Bridge was to provide the double-stack equipment.

Before the end of 1990 Santa Fe expected to be running double-stack trains carrying high-cube containers into and out of the San Francisco Bay area ports. This would follow clearance enlargement of three tunnels between Stockton and Richmond, California.

A two-year US$40 million intermodal capital improvement programme was launched in 1989. Its features included construction of new terminals at Amarillo, Texas, and San Diego and upgrading of eight existing terminals. Several arrangements have been made to extend the geographic scope of intermodal operations beyond Santa Fe lines. An example is Santa Fe's Intermodal Market Extension (IMX) concept, under which trucking firms provide a fast link between the IMX terminals and the railway. Customers drop off or pick up trailers or containers at IMX terminals and receive a single rate and service direct to destination. Santa Fe has four IMX terminals east of Chicago, with others located at Sacramento, California, Tucson, Nogales (Arizona) and most recently Laredo, Texas.

In late 1989 an alliance was forged with a major trucking company, J B Hunt Transport, to offer customised door-to-door transportation under a single rate, with a common communication system and billing, under the Quantum brand-name. Quantum was initially targeted at new business for both partners in the corridor between Los Angeles and eastern Michigan and central Ohio.

Santa Fe introduced another concept in 1988, called the 'Quality Distribution Center' (QDC) programme. This combines rail service with the expertise of independent warehouses to offer shippers a flexible, convenient distribution system. Santa Fe provides warehouses in 30 locations across the Midwest, Southwest and in California. This allows customers to maintain supplies near metropolitan areas and eliminate costly last-minute shipments by truck. In 1990 the QDC concept was extended to bulk commodities with the opening of the first of three bulk centres in Chicago and Los Angeles; a further nine centres were planned.

In October 1986 agreement was reached with operating unions for inauguration of a 'Quality Service Network' (QSN). QSN trains operate with three-man crews over longer crew districts than regular trains, and are designed to attract traffic in specified markets where trucks are dominant. The service, which is not restricted to intermodal traffic, operates daily between 15 city pairs: Denver-Oklahoma City; Denver-Dallas; Denver-Houston; Dallas-Houston; Kansas City-Denver; Chicago-Denver; Denver-Albuquerque; Denver-Phoenix; Kansas City-Albuquerque; Kansas City-Phoenix; Albuquerque-Phoenix; Denver-Los Angeles; and Albuquerque-Los Angeles. At QSN's inception, Santa Fe had only 0.5 per cent of the intercity tonnage moving within the network; by 1990 QSN was holding 9 per cent of it, ahead of original QSN forecasts.

In July 1988 Santa Fe, in conjunction with Conrail, launched a Quality Stack Service (QSS) for through double-stack COFC haulage of domestic freight between Los Angeles and Croxton, NJ. This service, equally successful, is now extended to take in northern California, Kansas City, Dallas and Houston.

Under a Voluntary Coordination Agreement (VCA) with Burlington Northern (BN), a dedicated intermodal train was initiated in December 1989 between Los Angeles and the Avard, Oklahoma, gateway. By May 1990 this had doubled Santa Fe traffic between California and the lower Midwest and Southeastern US. Launch of a double-stack COFC-based door-to-door service over this route was anticipated in July 1990.

Investment
For 1990 Santa Fe planned capital investment totalling US$305 million, compared with US$264 million in

Diesel locomotives

Class	Builders	Type	Horsepower	No in service end Jan 1989
1310	EMD	GP7	1500	20
1460	EMD	SWBLW	1500	1
1556	EMD	SD39	2500	20
2000	EMD	GP7	1500	21
2050	EMD	GP7	1500	169
2244	EMD	GP9	1750	53
2300	EMD	GP38	2000	58
2370	EMD	GP38-2	2000	11
2700	EMD	GP30	2500	79
2800	EMD	GP35	2500	152
3000	EMD	GP20	2000	71
3400	EMD	GP39-2	2300	50
3600	EMD	GP39-2	2300	17
3617	EMD	GP39-2	2300	1
3669	EMD	GP39-2	2300	13
3683	EMD	GP39-2	2300	11
3696	EMD	GP39-2	2300	10
3800	EMD	GP40X	3500	10
3810	EMD	GP50	3500	30
3840	EMD	GP50	3600	15
4000	EMD	GP60	3800	20
5000	EMD	SD40	3000	18
5020	EMD	SD40-2	3000	37
5058	EMD	SD40-2	3000	13
5071	EMD	SD40-2	3000	54
5125	EMD	SD40-2	3000	45
5170	EMD	SD40-2	3000	23
5200	EMD	SD40-2	3000	13
5250	EMD	SDF40-2	3000	18
5300	EMD	SD45	3600	4
5304	EMD	SD45	3600	104
5426	EMD	SD45	3500	4
5430	EMD	SD45	3500	8
5500	EMD	SD45	3600	2
5510	EMD	SD45-2	3600	8
5705	EMD	SD45-2	3600	9
5800	EMD	SD45-2	3600	69
5950	EMD	F45	3600	40
5990	EMD	FP45	3600	8
6350	GE	B23-7	2250	14
6364	GE	B23-7	2250	18
6390	GE	B23-7	2250	28
7200	GE	SF30B	3000	10
7400	GE	B39-8	3900	3
7410	GE	B40-8	4000	20
7484	GE	B36-7	3600	16
8010	GE	C30-7	3000	48
8058	GE	C30-7	3000	6
8064	GE	C30-7	3000	34
8099	GE	C30-7	3000	24
8123	GE	C30-7	3000	30
8153	GE	C30-7	3000	14
8736	GE	U36C	3600	27
9500	GE	SF30C	3000	70
Total				1671

Traffic	1984	1985	1986	1987	1988	1989
Revenue freight						
Carloads handled (000)	1514	1398	1350	1434	1550	1562
Revenue short ton-miles (million)	66 113	61 243	59 517	72 000	77 800	80 300
Operating ratio (%)	90·4	92·4	90·8	90·6	89·8	89·7*

* Before restructuring costs

Carloads by Principal Commodity*
(In thousands)

Commodity	1987	1988	1989
Grain	189	211	159
Food & Farm Products	157	159	156
Chemicals	101	109	111
Coal	250	265	273
Metal Products	28	31	33
Petroleum Products	41	46	49
Non Metallic Minerals	55	59	70
Paper Products	41	43	43
Lumber, Plywood & Logs	23	23	19
Vehicles & Parts	87	99	102
Merchandise	340	378	412
All Other	122	127	135
Total Carloads	1,434	1,550	1,562
TOFC/COFC Carloads Included in the Above	396	450	485

* Carloads per internal reporting based on the date car originated on line or was received from a connecting railroad.

1989. Of this US$119.8 million was earmarked for infrastructure. Acquisition of 123 locomotives was planned, 60 of them from GE on power-by-the-mile lease (see below), and rebuilding of 40 existing locomotives. More intermodal equipment would be procured on lease arrangements.

Productivity

During 1989 agreement was reached with the United Transportation Union providing for maximal three-man crewing of trains over approximately half the system. Up to 20 per cent of through trains could be run with a two-man crew. An agreement with the Brotherhood of Locomotive Engineers effective from the start of 1990 included provision for profit-sharing, a savings/retirement plan, increase of the basic working day from 108 to 120 miles, abolition of a premium for working with a reduced crew, work rule changes allowing more flexibility of employment, and a five-year moratorium on basic pay increases.

Motive power and rolling stock

At the end of 1989 Santa Fe was operating 1626 freight and 41 switcher diesel locomotives and 38 670 freight cars.

In 1989 Santa Fe took delivery of 40 GE 4000 hp 8-40B locomotives. A further 60 of this type were ordered for 1990 delivery, and would be supplied on a new power-by-the-mile lease arrangement.

In 1989 Santa Fe concluded its first power-by-the-mile agreement with General Electric. By end-1990 GE would assume responsibility for maintenance of the railway's entire fleet of 257 GE-built locomotives, for which Santa Fe would pay fees based on mileage operated. Santa Fe has undertaken to work its 100 new GE 8-40B units a minimum of almost 3 million miles over a 15-year period. Maintenance will be performed by Santa Fe staff under GE supervision.

A similar agreement covering 158 GM-EMD GP50 and GP60 locomotives was reached with that manufacturer early in 1990.

Soo Line Railroad Co

Soo Line Building, PO Box 530, Minneapolis, Minnesota 55440

Telephone: +1 612 347 8000
Telex: 290701
Telefax: +1 612 347 8059

Chairman: Donald F Swanson
President and Chief Executive Officer: Edwin V Dodge
Executive Vice President, Operations: P D Gilmore
Senior Vice-President and Chief Financial Officer: James A Lee
Senior Vice-President, Distribution Services: Peter M McNamee
Senior Vice-President and Chief Legal Officer: Wayne C Serkland
Vice-President, Engineering Services: Gerald A Nilsen
Mechanical Services: Larry D Bell
Sales: Edward A Delmoro
Agribusiness: Gregg F Haug
Natural Resources: Lee I Larson
Manufactured Goods: John D Winkler
Intermodal: William W Leedy
Information and Technology Services: J Michael Fox
Risk Management: Charles W Nelson
Labour Relations: Cathryn S Frankenberg
Resources Division: Larry W Harrington
Production: Warren B Peterson
Corporate Secretary: Fern B Albers
Treasurer: James A Mogen Sr

Route length: 9343·5 km

Soo Line Railroad Company is a wholly-owned subsidiary of Soo Line Corporation, a holding company involved in transportation and real estate. The railroad's routes extend from the Canadian borders through the Twin Cities and Chicago to Kansas City and Louisville. Soo handles a large volume of traffic flowing to and from Canada, serves industry in major midwestern population centres and has an extensive system of lines in grain areas.

Transportation revenues in 1988 came from farm products (21 per cent), chemicals (16 per cent), coal (11 per cent), automotive (9 per cent), food (9 per cent), lumber and wood (7 per cent), intermodal (6 per cent), pulp and paper (6 per cent) and all others (15 per cent).

Merger with Canadian Pacific

Soo's 56 per cent stockholder, Canadian Pacific Ltd, began a process in 1988 to identify a buyer for its interests in the Soo Line. During 1988, a joint labour-management group put forth a plan for employee ownership which was unsuccessful, whereupon CP decided in 1989 to retain its Soo holding.

At the end of 1989 an agreement was reached for Canadian Pacific Ltd to acquire all outstanding shares in Soo Line that it did not already hold. The plan provided for the Canadians' holding to rise to two-thirds of the total Soo Line shares. A wholly-owned CP subsidiary would be merged with Soo Line.

Kansas City-Chicago route sale

In 1989 Soo sold its Kansas City-Chicago route to Southern Pacific Lines, subject to ICC approval. Soo retains the right to run local trains over the line. Objections were raised by Burlington Northern, Chicago & North Western and Kansas City Southern Railroads, by the first two on the grounds that they shared ownership of sections of the route. However, these moves to block the proposal were voted down by the ICC, which looked set to issue a decision on the sale in mid-1990.

Traction and rolling stock

In 1988 the company operated 424 locomotives and a fleet of 12 295 freight cars.

Nearly half of Soo's locomotive fleet is made up of 3000 hp or higher units. Soo Line took delivery in 1989 of 42 new 3800 hp GM-EMD SD-60 locomotives valued at US$55 million; Soo had received 21 of these units in 1987.

Finance (US$ million)		
Operating revenues	*1987*	*1988*
Transportation	599·583	554·317
Real estate	13·541	16·179
Total	613·124	570·496
Operating expenses		
Transportation		
Operations	568·606	523·225
Special charges (credits)*	24·016	(6·960)
Total transportation	592·622	516·265
Real estate	1·024	269
Total	593·646	516·534
Operating income		
Transportation	6·961	38·052
Real estate	12·517	15·910
Total	19·478	53·962
Interest income	1·988	854
Other income – net	2·706	3·996
Interest expense	39·876	33·945
Income (loss) before		
income taxes	(15·704)	24·867
Provision (benefit) for		
income taxes	(7·200)	9·300
Net income (loss)	(8·504)	15·567

* Represents adjustments to employee reduction and equipment restructuring charges in 1988, loss on sale of Lake States Transportation Division in 1987, and restructuring charges in 1986

Southern Pacific Transportation Company

Southern Pacific Building, One Market Plaza, San Francisco, California 94105

Telephone: +1 415 541 1000
Telefax: +1 415 541 1929

Chairman: Philip Anschutz
Vice Chairmen: William J Holtman
                Robert F Starzel
President: D Michael Mohan
Executive Vice President, Distribution Services: George C Woodward
Senior Vice-President, Marketing & Sales: Roy Thiessen
Vice-President, Executive Department: Edward P Ahern
General Manager, Real Estate: Wallace Curtis
Management Services: Joseph M Graziani
General Counsel: Cannon Y Harvey
Purchases & Materials: William C Hoenig
Finance: Lawrence C Yarberry
Washington DC: Wiley N Jones
Operations: Kenneth A Moore
Transportation: Lloyd G Simpson
Real Estate Development: S David Steele
Public Affairs: Robert W Taggart
Treasurer: Edward F Grady
Secretary: Thomas F O'Donnell
Chief Special Agent: Glen D Barnett
Chief Mechanical Officer: Ron H Berry
Chief Engineer: Richard R Mahon

Gauge: 1435 mm
Length: 16 174 km

Merger with Rio Grande

The Interstate Commerce Commission in June 1987 conclusively rejected a Santa Fe-SP merger. It required the intended parent corporation of the two railroads to divest itself of either Southern Pacific or both. A little more than two months later, Santa Fe Southern Pacific Corp (SFSP) announced it would dispose of Southern Pacific. In late December 1987, SFSP agreed to sell Southern Pacific Transportation Company to Rio Grande Industries Incorporated, which is owned by the Anschutz Corporation. In 1988 this sale was approved by the Interstate Commerce Commission.

Lines and territory

The new Southern Pacific/Denver & Rio Grande Western railroad operates in the western, southwestern and midwestern sections of the United States. Western lines run from San Francisco north to Portland, Oregon, and east through Nevada, Utah, Colorado, to Kansas City, Kansas, and St Louis, and south to Los Angeles.

From Los Angeles, the line runs east, roughly parallel to the Mexican border, through Tucson and El Paso where it connects to a line northeast to Tucumcari, New Mexico, and on to Kansas City and St Louis with connections to Chicago (see also below). East from El Paso the line, known as the Sunset Route, continues to Houston, Dallas, New Orleans, Memphis and St Louis, all important interchange points for traffic.

The Northwestern Pacific Railroad Company and the St Louis Southwestern Railway Company (also known as the Cotton Belt) are subsidiaries of the new company. Southern Pacific Motor Trucking Company, a wholly-owned subsidiary, provides intermodal and other highway services nationwide.

Southern Pacific/Denver & Rio Grande Western own more than 300 000 acres of land in 15 states. Most of this consists of railroad rights-of-way, yard and other facilities. Long-range plans call for the sale of property not needed for railroad operations. The money will be used to reduce debt and pay for improvements to equipment and facilities.

After the merger

Immediately after consummation of the merger with D&RGW, plans were announced for property improvements and an upgrading of services on the Central and Southern transcontinental rail corridors. SP would be operated in combination with D&RGW to form the nation's fifth largest rail network. The combined services of the two lines are marketed under the Southern Pacific banner.

The combined rail system has single-line routes on both the Central and Southern corridors, with direct service to most major West Coast and Gulf Coast ports, and most Mexican and eastern gateways. This gives the new SP operating flexibility and a new edge in competition with trucks and other large rail lines in the United States.

SP's competitive stance would be strengthened by ICC approval of its 1989 purchase of Soo's 532-mile Kansas City-Chicago route. This would give it direct access to the heart of the Midwest from Los Angeles and northern California alongside Santa Fe and Union Pacific. However, three other railroads petitioned against the sale (see Soo Line entry). An ICC decision was expected by mid-1990. If SP gains possession, it plans a three-year investment of some US$50 million

786 **RAILWAY SYSTEMS** / United States of America

in the route to make it fit for 112.5 km/h and cut Kansas City-Chicago running time to about 2½ hours. Improvements would include installation of some 320 km of welded rail and of signalling over some 160 km of presently 'dark' territory.

New services
Four new daily intermodal and general freight trains between Oregon and northern California and St Louis and Memphis began service in October 1988. All operate via the Central Corridor through Nevada, Utah, Colorado, Kansas and Missouri. In connection with the new Oregon service, SP reopened its Modoc line through portions of Oregon, California and Nevada. The line was closed in January 1987 because of poor business. Using the Modoc line reduces routeings by 258 miles and improves transit time and delivery reliability for shipments to and from Oregon.

In January 1989 Southern Pacific inaugurated 13 additional new daily freight trains on faster schedules, designed to save customers transit times on several routes. These new transportation packages were the second round of significant services improvements resulting from the SP/Denver & Rio Grande Western combination. Included in the new schedule were three new 'Star Service' trains in each direction, joining the existing SP Lines' Track Star network. They were: the Lone Star (Houston/Dallas to El Paso and Phoenix/Tucson); the Kansas City Star (Kansas City to Denver); and the San Joaquin Star (a direct connection from Fresno for Central California shippers and receivers on Central and Pacific Northwest routes).

Intermodal traffic from the San Francisco Bay Area to the Southeast saves a day because of schedule improvements through Los Angeles. Shipments between southern California and Eastern markets also save a day through a revitalised system of direct, run-through trains connecting railroads at the Kansas City gateway. Other new 'run-through' services save time for customers between Eastern markets and the Denver and Salt Lake City areas, with trains at Kansas City being made up so that they can bypass intervening terminals.

SP has also instituted a new logistical approach to blocking trains called 'micro-blocking'. This is a system of identifying and consolidating blocks of time-sensitive shipments at origin to speed delivery to destinations with significant improvements in transit time consistency. As an example, the San Joaquin Star from Central California is micro-blocked for Midwestern, Eastern and Pacific Northwest markets before it leaves Fresno. This enables direct, high-priority connections without the need for further classification switching at California terminals.

In November 1989 SP began direct service to Chicago for the first time in its history. This became possible with parent Rio Grande Industries' purchase of the bankrupt Chicago, Missouri & Western's 282-mile St Louis-Chicago line.

Intermodal container transfer facility
The Intermodal Container Transfer Facility in Long Beach, California, celebrated its third anniversary in January 1990. In three years, the facility has handled more than 1 million containers. The reason for this growth is the rapidly increasing Pacific Rim imports and exports and emerging domestic containerisation. The ICTF has accommodated this growth by expanding to 237 acres from its original 150 acres. An average of 75 trains a week move containers in and out of the terminal, mostly for Pacific Rim shippers. The US$100 million facility, a joint venture of SP and the Ports of Los Angeles and Long Beach, is just 4 miles from the ports. It has 7 miles of track and can load and unload five double-stack trains simultaneously.

Double-stack COFC
In 1990 SP began twice-weekly double-stack COFC train service from the Long Beach ICTF to Mexico City, interchanging with the Mexican railway, FdeM, at El Paso/Juarez.

Intermodal network restructure
In 1990 SP was moving to concentrate its domestic intermodal service on major hubs and traffic corridors. Service would be withdrawn from corridors where volume was extremely low, two terminals would be closed and facilities reduced at some others.

New organisation
In January 1989 Southern Pacific created a new distribution services organisation to strengthen commercial efforts of the recently combined Southern Pacific and Denver & Rio Grande Western railroads. One of the major changes is that the marketing, sales and operation of intermodal traffic is now concentrated in a single Intermodal Department.

In the autumn of 1989 the operating department was reorganised. The number of divisions was increased from eight to 21, in conjunction with a reduction of management layers and devolution of considerable operating, maintenance and customer liaison authority and responsibilities to divisional superintendents. Train and crew dispatching were consolidated at two centres.

Customer service
By 1989 Southern Pacific was receiving 51·8 per cent of its bills of lading via Electronic Data Interchange, more than twice as many as any other railroad in the United States. SP has about 1800 customers using its various Liberator (EDI) packages. Liberator is a software program, provided to SP shippers, that links a customer's micro, mini or mainframe computer to SP's mainframe computer in San Francisco. Other Liberator programs allow customers to locate shipments, determine intermodal rates, request special customised reports, and specify car release data and time. The software program is available to any SP customer with an IBM compatible personal computer. The programs and the phone link are provided free by Southern Pacific.

The success of SP's Intermodal Container Transfer

ICTF intermodal terminal Long Beach

SP and DRGW locomotives symbolise the merger of the two railroads at Thistle, Utah

Finances (US$ million)	1985	1986	1987
Revenues			
Total	2464·5	2271·6	2305·6
Expenses			
Way and structures	332·5	341·4	NA
Equipment	675·2	599·6	NA
Transportation	1176·8	1014·3	NA
General and administrative	265·4	302·2	NA
Total	2449·9	2257·5	2214·5
Operating income	14·6	(587·2)*	91·1
Operating ratio	99·4%	99·4%†	96%

* Includes restructuring costs of US$601 million
† Before restructuring costs

Traffic	1985	1986
Revenue ton-miles (million)	77 700	75 000
Revenue carloads (million)	1·519	1·441
Average revenue per ton-mile (million)	3·05	2·92
Net ton-miles per freight train load (000s)	56·7	59·6

Facility in southern California is directly related to its broad application of advanced EDI to move international containers from the ports, on to railcars, and on their way across country, with substantial cost savings to shippers and the railroad. The EDI system is a combination of the terminal's own sophisticated data flow and the Liberator software program.

Investment
Proposed capital spending for 1990 totalled US$381 million, compared with US$408 million in 1989. Following delivery of 50 new locomotives in 1989, a further 50 would be acquired in 1990. A total of 970 new freight cars would include 160 double-stack COFC cars.

Fibre optics
Southern Pacific Telecommunications Company (SP Telecom), the company's fibre-optics subsidiary, completed a network between Houston and Los Angeles in 1989. In 1990 it was preparing to acquire Digital Signal Inc, which operates a nationwide 15 000-mile leased fibre-optic network serving more than 60 interexchange carriers.

Passenger traffic
Amtrak operates all intercity passenger services in Southern Pacific territory. Under contract with the state of California, SP operates a commuter service between San Francisco and San Jose. The state sets overall policy for this service. The railroad's contract with the state to operate this service expires in June 1990. Discussions began in late 1988 with local transit officials to sell the 50-mile right-of-way between the two cities.

SP has offered to sell three of its lines in the Los Angeles Basin to public agencies as components of a regional mass transit system.

Traction and rolling stock
Railroad equipment owned or leased at the start of 1989 consisted of 2034 diesel locomotives and 51 669 freight cars.

In 1988-89 SP took delivery of 35 4000 hp B40-8 locomotives from GE and 13 3800 hp GP60 locomotives from GM-EMD. A further 50 GP-60 and 15 B40-8 were ordered in 1989.

St Louis Southwestern Railway Co

Southern Pacific Bldg, One Market Plaza, San Francisco, Ca 94105

Telephone: +1 415 541 1000

Chairman and Chief Executive Officer: Philip F Anschutz
Executive Vice-President: D Michael Mohan
Senior Vice-President, Marketing and Sales: George C Woodward
Vice-President and General Manager: Rollin D Bredenberg
Vice-President, Finance: Eric L Johnson
Vice-President, Operations: K A Moore
Vice-President, Purchases: William C Hoenig
Vice-President, Automotive: Robert G Thruston
Chief Mechanical Officer: R H Berry
Signal Supervisor: K J Green
Engineer, Bridges & Roadway: M R Baker

Gauge: 1435 mm
Length: 3330 km

The railway operates in Illinois, Arkansas, Missouri, Tennessee, Louisiana, Texas, Kansas, Oklahoma and New Mexico. Familiarly known as the Cotton Belt system, since 1932 it has been under the control of the Southern Pacific and 98 per cent of its capital stock is now owned by the Southern Pacific Transportation Company. Under the corporate umbrella of this organisation the two Class I railroads together constitute one of the main rail links between the Middle West and the Pacific coast.

The St Louis Southwestern has a fleet of 225 line-haul and 41 switcher diesel locomotives and 14 426 freight cars.

Union Pacific Railroad Company

1416 Dodge Street, Omaha, Nevada, Nebraska 68179

Telephone: +1 402 271 5000
Telex: 484491; 484501

Chairman: Michael H Walsh
Executive Assistant: J J Adams
Special Assistant: J M Hildreth
Executive Vice-President, Marketing and Sales: Fred B Henderson
Executive Vice-President, Operations: Richard K Davidson
Vice-President, Sales: Ken Morrill
Finance: Jack Koraleski
Operations: Richard K Davidson
Law: James V Dolan
Labour Relations: Tom L Watts
Purchases and Materials: William A Bales
Engineering Services: Mike Kelly
Field Operations: Art Shoener
Customer Service: Bill Hillebrandt
Marketing: Jack Colvin
Strategic Planning: John H Rebensdorf
Chief Mechanical Officer: M L Wall
Chief Engineer, Maintenance: C D Barton
Chief Signal Engineer: P M Abaray

Gauge: 1435 mm
Length: 37 607 km

UP Railroad territory
Union Pacific Railroad (UP) is a subsidiary of Union Pacific Corporation. UP operates over 23 373 miles of railroad in 20 states, connecting leading Pacific Coast and Gulf ports with key midwestern gateways such as Chicago, Kansas City, St Louis and Memphis.

In 1982 the Interstate Commerce Commission approved a merger of Union Pacific and Missouri Pacific, and acquisition of Western Pacific by Union Pacific. Until 1985 Union Pacific and Missouri Pacific retained their separate identities, though Western Pacific had become a subsidiary of UP Railroad and was operated as the latter's fourth district. In 1985 the operating, mechanical and engineering functions of UP and MoPac were consolidated into unitary organisations. With that, the combined operations of all three railroads were brought within the umbrella title of Union Pacific Railroad.

In May 1985 agreement was reached with the Missouri-Kansas-Texas for purchase of that railroad from its parent corporation, Katy Industries. M-K-T was merged with Missouri Pacific within the UP System in August 1988.

In June 1990 Union Pacific Corporation purchased a 25 per cent stake in Chicago & North Western Railroad, to safeguard its access from Omaha to Chicago.

Diesel locomotives (Union Pacific and Western Pacific only) at end-1989

Series	Builders	Model	hp	No in service
Line-haul freight				
90-95	EMD	GP40X	3500	1
100-184, 257-259, 4600-4684	GE	B23-7	2250	84
200-254, 4800-4854	GE	B30-7A	3000	55
360-379	EMD	GP38-2	2200	13
541-561	GE	U23-B-L	2250	9
194-248, 581-683	EMD	GP40L	3000	66
170-181, 600-665	EMD	GP40	3000	23
782-799	EMD	GP35-L	2500	17
900-920	EMD	GP40-2	3000	15
951	EMD	E9	2400	1
954-9	EMD	GP-40X	3500	5
1555-1744	EMD	GP15-1	1500	190
1974-99	EMD	GP38L	2000	12
2000-2348	EMD	GP38-2	2000	365
4507-4527	GE	U23B	2500	4
2400-2539	GE	C30-7	3000	136
3000-3122, 4020-4069	EMD	SD40	3000	93
3123-4321, 6000-6073	EMD	SD40-2	3000	1019
50-79, 3500-3529	EMD	GP50	3500	30
5000-5059	EMD	SD50	3600	60
6000-84	EMD	SD60	3800	84
6085-6215	EMD	SD60M	3800	151
9000-9059	GE	C36-7	3750	60
9100-9405	GE	C40-8	4000	260
Yard switchers				
1000-1014, 1330-1392, 1530-1554	EMD	MP15	1500	80
1200-1274	EMD	SW10	1200	74
1501-1521	EMD	SW1500	1500	9
Total locomotives				2935

Traffic	1987	1988	1989
Revenue ton-miles (millions)	157 200	176 600	183 000
Finances (US$ million)			
Total revenue	3847·9	4390	4580
Expenditure			
Operating:			
Way and structures	513·56	648	583
Equipment	876·16	750	874
Total	3196·75	3530	3690

Sales to new short lines
Up to early 1988 UP had only sold off some 247 miles of its system, and created only one sizeable new short line, the Southeast Kansas Railroad of 104 miles. But in 1988 it identified over 1000 miles as disposable, principally between Baise, Idaho and eastern Oregon, and sale or leasing to short line carriers has since been negotiated.

Results in 1989
In 1989 Union Pacific achieved record profits for the fourth consecutive year. Net income reached US$547 million, a 6 per cent increase over 1988. Revenue was up 4 per cent to US$4580 million, through a 1 per cent rise in carloadings as a result of the M-K-T absorption coupled with selective price increases and favourable if slight shift in the traffic mix.

The largest percentage increases in carloadings were in aggregates (13 per cent), metals and ores (35 per cent) and merchandise, chiefly intermodal (7 per cent). There were falls principally in drought-hit grain (7 per cent), forest products (6 per cent), and food and

RAILWAY SYSTEMS / United States of America

food products (4 per cent).

Railroad operating expenses increased US$160 million, or 5 per cent. The operating ratio was 80.6, compared to 80.3 in 1988.

Management reorganisation

The Operating Department, which represents 85 per cent of the railroad's workforce, has been totally reorganised. Nine layers of management have been compressed to four, and a great deal of operating authority has been delegated to 30 regional superintendents.

The Marketing and Sales Department is reorganised into three areas of concentration. Forty-seven national account managers focus on UP's top 200 customers, or the largest segment of its business, while other account managers handle medium-to-large accounts.

Associated with this reorganisation is creation of a National Telemarketing Center in Omaha. The centre became operational in spring 1989, and was scheduled to be completed by phase in December 1994.

The Telemarketing Center will solicit freight traffic from selected customers. The staff of account representatives will develop transportation proposals for customers through the use of personal computers along with access to Union Pacific's extensive computer and communication systems.

Computerisation

Union Pacific's marketing strategy rests on one of the most advanced technical bases in the industry. The heart of UP's service operations, the National Customer Service Center, would be impossible without the Transportation Control System (TCS) and the Automatic Call Directing (ACD) system. TCS schedules and monitors rail operations and performs the accounting function on every item shipped on the railroad. It is being extended to the newly-acquired Missouri-Kansas-Texas Railroad. ACD distributes over 12 000 incoming calls a day, with a goal of handling over 90 per cent of them within 5 seconds.

A new work order reporting system connects TCS computers directly with UP locomotives, enabling customers to have their data communicated to trains en route. This new system is being developed in conjunction with ATCS (Advanced Train Control System) and will improve customer service and cut expenses by more than US$20 million a year.

Intermodal traffic

Serving all major West Coast and all Gulf Coast ports, UP focuses its intermodal operation on 21 hub centres, all fully mechanised and able to handle any type of intermodal shipment. Inland, each hub serves an area of up to 200 miles radius. In 1989 intermodal traffic constituted 15 per cent of UP's traffic volume and generated 9.7 per cent of its revenue.

UP has long been an advocate of intermodal traffic concentration into dedicated trains that are accorded the railroad's top operating policy (which is signified by a 'Z' in their letter designation codes, or 'train symbols'). Union Pacific is the nation's leader in double-stack COFC traffic. Most of the traffic runs between West Coast ports and midwestern cities or New York, but two double-stack trains also run each week between Houston and New Orleans. The fastest Chicago-Los Angeles double-stack train schedule is now 52 hours.

In addition to these double-stack COFC trains, UP runs numerous dedicated COFC/TOFC trains daily between its major city and port hubs. Besides through services, competitive intercity connections are augmented by scheduled interchange between a number of trains at North Platte, Nebraska.

American President Intermodal (API) owns a proportion of its extensive double-stack car fleet, the remainder being leased from Trailer Train. Maersk, US Lines and K-Line lease all of their equipment. Union Pacific does not own or lease any double-stack COFC cars. Double-stack trains are geared towards vessel arrivals and destination market service factors. They operate on a one-week cycle between a US West Coast port area and Chicago.

In 1990 UP and the Mexican national railway, FNdeM, were combining to set up double-stack COFC train service with a five-day transit time between Chicago and Mexico City/Monterrey via Laredo, the border town where trains previously terminated. Agreement was reached for UP locomotives to run through and for customs processing to be done at destination. Preparation involved considerable clearance enlargement on the Mexican side.

A new lightweight domestic refrigerated container system has been developed for UP by Fruehauf. The 48ft, 9ft 6in-high container, mostly of aluminium construction, has a lightweight, self-contained, nose-mounted all-electric refrigeration unit, of which the engine/generator is on a removable skid, easily detached for changeout or servicing. A lightweight highway chassis has been provided for the container. Four prototypes were in trial revenue service in 1990.

A US$14.5 million expansion of UP's Los Angeles intermodal terminal, UP's largest, was completed in 1989.

Automotive traffic

In 1988 UP signed a contract with Ford Motor Company under which the railroad will deliver all Ford automobiles being shipped into the Los Angeles

Double-stack COFC train on Williams Loop in Feather River Canyon, California

VDU touch-control of computerised CTC at North Platte, Nebraska

New GM-EMD Type SD60M locomotive with 'comfort cab'

Unit coal train in Wyoming, headed by GM-EMD SD40-2 locomotives

New GE 4000ho Type C40-8W units with 'comfort cabs' GM-EMD Type GP38-2 (*George R Cockle*)

market, commencing in 1990. In the first year alone, this involves the delivery of several hundred thousand vehicles a year into the Los Angeles area, which is the largest automobile market in the United States. A US$27 million auto loading facility was completed at Mira Loma, 64km east of Los Angeles, in December 1989. A similar facility was to open at nearby Montebello in April 1990. These two terminals together were expected to handle more than 200 000 autos a year for the southern California market.

In 1990 UP unveiled a stack container system for auto movement. Branded Secured Modular Automotive Rail Transport (SMART), the prototypes were built by Trinity Industries to UP specification. The modules are 53ft long, 8ft 6in wide and either 5ft 3in high for private autos, or 6 ft 3in for utility and sport vehicles. With doors at each end, the completely-enclosed modules are built of high-performance composite materials. To convey the materials an articulated, low-deck spine car with two 53ft-long platforms has been designed with newly-designed suspension and controlled-slack couplers. On this the modules can be stacked up to three high.

A US$2.2 million automobile distribution facility for Toyota was opened at West Memphis, Ark, in 1990.

Customer Service Center

The national Customer Service Center in St Louis interacts with Union Pacific's computerised transportation control system (TCS), which provides service representation with billing information and a profile of customer requirements, as well as on-line information on the status of shipments and the availability of cars. Shippers now have the ability to interact directly with Union Pacific's TCS system. By using personal computers they can order cars, trace shipments and enter billing information directly.

In 1990 UP introduced EDISTAR, a software package that enables customers to transmit shipping instructions, trace shipments and conduct billing and other electronic mail business on all major railroads with a single EDI system.

Advanced Train Control

For its ATCS development, UP has opted for interaction of track-mounted transponders and locomotive-mounted receivers and microprocessors. UP equipped its North Platte subdivision in Western Nebraska with a basic ATCS in 1987 at a cost of about US$2·5 million. By mid-1992 UP aimed to have 75 per cent of its locomotive fleet equipped to practise the work-order level of ATC throughout its system. In early 1990 the railroad had yet to set a target date for advance to full automatic train control.

New Omaha control centre

Union Switch & Signal has consolidated control of all UP trackage into the Harriman Dispatching Centre, located in Omaha, Nebraska, the railroad's headquarters. The most striking feature of the office is its panoramic, video-projected territory display. While this wall display provides summary information, a CRT at each dispatcher's console offers a detailed view of operations at any of the 1800 or so signal control points throughout the system.

The Harriman Centre employs computer-aided dispatching (CADS). Using auto-routeing, dispatchers assign an identity and priority to each train. The computer then takes over and routes trains according to priority, while also automatically determining meets and passes. CADS automatically updates and modifies its determinations based on actual train movements and changing track conditions. Although computers control the automatic mode, the system allows dispatchers to intervene and override the computer.

Another important feature of CADS is its operations reporting system, which integrates information gathering and reporting. The system performs functions such as train line-up status, track warrant control, and track and time permits; it gathers information on weather conditions through an interface to hotbox detectors across the railroad; and it exchanges data with the UP's crew-management and data-management computers.

The Omaha CADS includes important new capability that enables it to automatically predict and resolve traffic conflicts in CTC territory. New dark territory control functions facilitate displays indicating the locations of trains, reports of operation track bulletins, track warrant control, general orders and general line-up, as well as an enhanced double-track automatic block system.

The Harriman Centre's panoramic display employs a 150-projector rear-screen projection system, which tolerates a greater amount of ambient light in the viewing area; and, because the projectors are located behind the screen, allows for greater freedom of movement in the viewing area.

Each of the Harriman Centre's 30 dispatching stations is equipped with a colour CRT, two monochrome CRTs and a function keyboard. Each station can dispatch trains, and dispatchers initiate CTC control through their console keyboards. located at their consoles.

Capital investment

For 1990 UP projected capital investment of US$585 million, compared with US$708 million in 1989. Expenditure on freight cars would be roughly halved and investment in new locomotives cut from 152 to 50 units compared with 1989. Infrastructure expenditure would rise slightly, to US$261.8 million.

Track

Rail: 133 AREA, 66·2 kg/m
Cross ties (sleepers): Wooden, 7 in x 9 in x 9 ft
Spacing: 2019/km
Fastenings: ⅝ x 6¼ in cut track spikes; Portec curve blocs for radius in excess of 6°
Minimum curvature radius: 20°; exceptionally 12°
Max gradient: Main line 2·33%
Max axleload: 65 750 lb (unrestricted operation), 78 750 lb (with 40 mph speed restriction on main line and primary branch track)

Locomotives and rolling stock

At the end of 1989 Union Pacific owned or leased 3012 diesel-electric locomotives and 16 passenger cars, and had 76 162 revenue-earning freight cars owned and leased.

In 1989 UP invested US$196.5 million in 152 new locomotives. Delivery was taken of 106 GM-EMD Type SD60M with a new and roomier cab design that has become known as the 'comfort' cab (this is signified by the 'M' in the type designation). The 'comfort cab' features the first major revision of locomotive controls in 30 years. Controls are arranged in a console arrangement directly in front of the engineer. Even the horn control has been changed so the engineer can sound it with his foot, leaving his hands free to handle other controls. Numerous safety and health features have been designed into the new cabs, including improved collision protection, sound-proofing and central air ventilation. Outside air is filtered before it enters the central heating system. Thermal-pane windows are provided to help cope with the temperature extremes found along Union Pacific lines. The front windows are electrically heated to provide defrosting.

The cab interior includes a desk for the conductor, refrigerator, and four pedestal-mounted seats with arm rests. A fifth seat is available as a jump seat on the rear cab wall. Most existing locomotives have three seats. The nose area of the new locomotives includes a ventilated and heated toilet compartment and storage area for crew luggage.

In 1990 UP was taking delivery of a further 53 SD60M, and also of 50 4000hp 8-40CW locomotives from GE for coal haulage. The latter were also fitted with 'comfort cabs'. A further 53 8-40CW were on order. Further locomotive orders were anticipated in 1991, to complete UP's unprecedented three-year US$508 million programme for acquisition of 418 new locomotives.

In 1990 UP was leasing 550 aluminium rotary dump gondolas, built by Bethlehem Steel, to form five more unit trains for coal haulage out of the Powder River Basin, Wyoming.

Other selected US railroads

Note:* = Class II Railroad, with revenues in the US$10·50 million range

Aberdeen & Rockfish Railroad Co

PO Box 917, 101 East Main Street, Aberdeen, North Carolina 28315

Telephone: +1 919 944 2341

President: E A Lewis

47 route miles (75·6 km); four locomotives (GM-EMD GP7, F-7, GP18 and GP38); 172 freight cars. The company also owns the Pee Dee River and Dunn-Erwin railways in South and North Carolina.

RAILWAY SYSTEMS / United States of America

Diesel locomotives

Class	Wheel arrangement	Transmission	Rated power kW	Max speed km/h	Total weight tonnes	No in service 1989	Year first built (rebuilt)	Builders Mechanical parts	Builders Engine & type	Builders Transmission
1500 (F-7B)	B-B	dc Elec	1119	115	112	1	1952	EMD	EMD 16-567	EMD
1800 (GP-7)	B-B	dc Elec	1194	115	118	7	1951 (77)	EMD	EMD 16-567	EMD
2000 (GP-38-2)	B-B	ac/dc Elec	1492	113	116	8	1968	EMD	EMD 16-567	EMD
2500 (GP-35)	B-B	dc Elec	1865	115	118	3	1964	EMD	EMD 16-567	EMD
2800 (GP-49)	B-B	ac/dc Elec	2087	115	113	9	1983	EMD	EMd 12-645	EMD
3000 (GP-40-2)	B-B	ac/dc Elec	2238	115	121	21	1975	EMD	EMD 16-645	EMD

The Alaska Railroad
The Alaska Railroad Corporation

PO Box 107500, Anchorage, Alaska 99150-7500

Telephone: +1 907 265 2468
Telefax: +1 907 265 2443

President and Chief Executive Officer: Frank G Turpin
Vice-President, Operations: Arnold T Polanchek
Vice-President, Finance: Marvin J Yetter
Vice-President, Marketing and Sales: Richard J Knapp
Superintendent of Transportation: Terry R Blackwell
Chief Engineer: Francis C Weeks
Chief Mechanical Officer: John Kincaid
Director of Administration: James B Blasingame
Director, Human Resources: J D Wood
General Counsel: Larry Wood
Manager, Real Estate: Phillip L Cowart
Manager, Financial Services: Bruce E Carr
Manager, Security: Duane Bracken
Manager, Corporate Communications: Vivian Hamilton
Manager, Marketing Development: Marty Keale

Route length: 846 km

The Alaska Railroad runs a single-track main line of 756 km from the ports of Seward on the Gulf of Alaska, and Whittier, on Prince William Sound, northward through Anchorage and Denali (formerly McKinley) National Park to Fairbanks, and eastward to Eielson, with branches serving Eielson Air Force Base, Anchorage and Fairbanks International Airports and Palmer.

The Alaska Railroad was transferred from Federal to state ownership in January 1985. It is a quasi-public corporation with a seven-member board of directors appointed by the Governor of Alaska. Unique as the only full-service US railroad still offering both passenger and freight services, and also flag-stop service anywhere on the system, the railroad provides rail freight connections with the US rail system to the south via the Alaska Hydro-Train, CN Rail's AquaTrain, Sea-Land and TOTE.

Traffic	1986	1988	1989
Freight tonnage (000)	5005	4637	4979
Freight tonne-km (million)	1521·2	1483·9	1604·2
Passenger-km (000)	62 916	74 550	77 414
Passenger journeys	280 251	360 668	366 370

Finance (US$ million)
Revenues

Passengers and baggage		5·600	6·026
Freight, parcels and mail		44·872	48·342
Other income		8·579	7·506
Total		59·051	61·874

Expenditure

Staff/personnel	31·912	32·765
Materials and services	15·931	20·437
Depreciation	3·878	4·495
Financial charges	1·526	1·204
Total	53·247	58·901

Motive power and rolling stock
In service with the Alaska Railroad in 1989 were 49 diesel-electric locomotives, 4 RDC diesel railcars, 28 passenger cars (including 3 dome, 3 diner and 2 buffet cars) and 1222 freight cars.

In 1989 Daewoo of South Korea delivered six passenger cars, one diner and one buffet car to replace aged cars on the Anchorage-Fairbanks run.

Type of coupler in standard use: AAR Automatic Knuckle
Type of braking in standard use: AAR Standard Air

Track
Rail: 115 lb/yd RE–Standard Carbon (57·16 kg/m)
Cross ties (sleepers): Treated fir and hardwood 2045 x 203 x 178 mm
Spacing: 2019/km
Fastenings: 4- or 6-hole angle bars, steel spikes
Minimum curvature radius: 14·5%
Max gradient: 3%
Max axleload: 28·576 tonnes (67 750 lb)

Alabama & Florida Railroad

Po Box 150, Opp, Alabama 36467

Telephone: +1 205 493 3043

General Manager: R B Tomb

166 rote-km; the railway operates 8 diesel locomotives.

Aliquippa and Southern Railroad Co

PO Box 280, Aliquippa, Pennsylvania 15001

Telephone: +1 412 378 5801

General Superintendant: Stephen G Resek

46·5 route miles (74·75 km); 18 locomotives (including 12 GM-EMD SW1200); 160 freight cars

Allegheny Railroad Company

PO Box 628, 1111 Fourth Avenue, Warren, Pennsylvania 16365-0628

Telephone: +1 814 726 3550
Telefax: (814) 723 9661

President: H Leroy Weldner
General Manager: Gary E Landrio

149·2 route-miles (240 km); 4 locomotives (2 GM-EMD GP40, 2 GM-EMD CF7); 250 freight cars

Alton & Southern Railway Co

1000 S 22nd Street, E St Louis, Illinois 62207

Telephone: +1 618 482 3239
Telex: 44832

President: Davin M Mohan
Vice-President and General Manager: T G Todd

51 route-km; 20 diesel locomotives and 390 freight cars

The Apache Railway Company

PO Box E, Snowflake, Arizona 85937

Telephone: +1 602 536 4696

President: Alan Stone
Superintendant: Arthur E Rutledge

50·5 route miles (81·3 km); 7 locomotives (3 Alco 1800 hp RS-36; 4 Alco 2000 hp C-420); 215 freight cars

Apalachicola Northern Railroad Co*

A subsidiary of St Joe Industries

PO Box 250, 300 First Street, Port St Joe, Florida 32456

Telephone: +1 904 229 7411
Telefax: +1 904 227 1160

President: J C Belin
Vice-President: T E Johnston Jr
Director, Marketing & Sales: Gregg H Mahlkov
General Superintendent: R Wayne Parrish
Chief Mechanical Officer: B Keith Chiles

Apalachicola Northern unit coal train departs Port St Joe

United States of America / **RAILWAY SYSTEMS** 791

96.3 route miles (154.9 km); 14 locomotives (3 SW9, 8 SW 1500 and 3 GP15T, all GM-EMD); 1052 freight cars

All accounting, inventory, rating, billing and market analysis systems have been fully computerised and in mid-1989 the railroad went on-line with EDI to and from other North American railroads.

In 1989, a record year for traffic volume and revenue, the railroad purchased for development 20 acres of land and a dock with ocean-going ship berthing capability at Port St Joe.

Traffic	1987	1988	1989
Total freight tonnes (million)	3.815	3.24	3.91
Total freight tonne-km (million)	566.049	499.34	602.53
Finance (US$million)	1987	1988	1989
Revenues	10.376	10.589	11.710
Expenditure	7.30	7.926	7.398

Track
Rail: 66 and 45 kg/m
Cross ties (sleepers): Concrete, 305 × 203 × 2590 mm
Fastenings: Tru-Temper rail clips
Minimum curve radius: 6°
Max gradient: 1.2%
Max axleload: 30 short tons
Spacing: In plain track, 1415/km; in curves, 1650/km
Fastenings: Tru-Temper rail clips
Minimum curvature radius: 6°
Max gradient: 1.2%
Max permissible axleload: 30 tonnes

New Daewoo-built passenger cars skirt the Kenai Lake some 100 miles south of Anchorage

Arkansas & Louisiana Missouri Railway Company

PO Box 1653, 9th and Adams Streets, Monroe, Louisiana 71201

Telephone: +1 318 362 2250

Vice President, Operations: H B Wilson

54.4 route miles (87.5 km); 4 locomotives (2 SW9, 1 SW7 and 1 NW2, all GM-EMD); 197 freight cars

Arkansas & Missouri Railroad Co

107 N Commercial Street, Springdale, Arkansas 72764

Telephone: +1 501 751 5763
Telefax: +1 501 751 7603

President: J Anthony Hannold
Vice President & General Manager: G Brent McCready
Vice President, Sales & Marketing: J A Brooks
Chief Mechanical Officer: R P Hannold

138 route-miles (222 km). In 1989 the railroad moved 2.142 million tonnes of freight. It operates 15 Alco locomotives comprising 9 2000hp C420, 1 2000hp RS32, 3 1000hp T-6 and 2 1000hp RS-1.

Track is 90lb, 115cw and 132cw rail spiked to timber sleepers spaced 3000 per mile. Maximum gradient is 2.76 per cent, maximum permissible axleload 33.75 short tons.

Ashley, Drew and Northern Railway Company

PO Box 757, Crossett, Arkansas 71635

Telephone: +1 501 567 8631

President: S R Tedder
Vice-President, Operations: P H Schueth

41 route miles (66.1 km); 8 locomotives (3 GP-28, 2 GP-10, 2 CF7 and 1 SW1200, all GM-EMD Bo-Bos); 1757 freight wagons

Atlanta and St Andrews Bay Railway Company

PO Box 2775, 1 Everitt Avenue, Panama City, Florida 32402

Bangor and Aroostook Railroad Company

RR2, Northern Maine Junction Park, Bangor, Maine 04401

Telephone: +1 207 848 5711
Telex: 944459
Telefax: +1 207 848 5086

Chairman: Joseph B Ely II
Chief Executive Officer: James M Fitzgibbons
President: David J Hughes
Senior Vice President: R W Sprague
Vice-President, Operations: David M Krushwitz

Bay Colony Railroad Corporation

420 Bedford Street, Lexington, Massachusetts 02173

Telephone: +1 617 861 6480
Telefax: +1 617 862 8556

Vice-President Marketing: David C Kane
Director, Purchases: S C Hamlin
Chief Mechanical Officer: Marvin J BcBreairty
Chief Engineer: O D Anthony

Gauge: 1435 mm
Length: 436 route miles (701.5 km)

Track
Rail: 115 RE 57.05 kg/m; 112 RE 55.56 kg/m, 100 ARA 49.61 kg/m, 80 ARA 39.74 kg/m
Cross ties (sleepers): Treated hardwood, thickness 152.4 mm
Spacing: 1772 km
Fastenings: 178 × 304.8 mm Dbl sh 1:40 cant

Chairman and Chief Executive Officer: Gordon H Fay
General Manager, Transportation: Deane R Folsom
Superintendent, Operations and Maintenance: John F Pimentel Sr

Telephone: +1 904 769 6661

President: Alan Stone
Manager: Glenn Harvey
Director of Operations: D R Davis

89 route miles (143.2 km); 12 locomotives (3 GP7, 5 GP-38, 1 GP-39, 3 GP-38-2, all GM-EMD); 782 freight cars

In 1989 the company purchased the 27-mile Abbeville-Grimes Railway in southeast Alabama, which it is operating with Atlanta & Saint Andrews Bay Railway locomotives and equipment.

Austin & North Western Railroad

500 Canadian Street, Austin, Texas 78702

Telephone: +1 512 476 1791

General Manager: D R Kling

260 route-km: 8 diesel locomotives.

Minimum curvature radius: 10°
Max gradient: 1.25%
Max axleload: 62 750 lb unrestricted, 65 250 lb with restrictions

Traction and rolling stock
44 locomotives, comprised of GM-EMD F-3, BL-2, GP7, GP9 and GP38 types; 3213 freight cars

Baltimore & Pittsburgh Railroad

The company, a recently formed regional railroad, operates 369 route-miles of former CSX Transportation track.

123 route miles (198 km) formed of five unconnected lines in southeastern Massachusetts; 9 locomotives (chiefly EMD GP-7 and GP-9 type), 3 passenger cars and 127 freight cars

Belfast and Moosehead Lake Railroad

11 Water Street, Belfast, Maine 04915

Telephone: +1 207 338 2330

President: E M Christensen
General Manager: A L Socea

33 route miles (53.1 km); 5 locomotives; 5 freight cars

Belt Railway Company of Chicago

6900 South Central Avenue, Chicago, Illinois 60638

Telephone: +1 708 496 4000
Telefax: +1 708 496 4005

President: J E Martin
Vice-President, General Counsel: W M Cunningham
Superintendent, Transportation: J R Spano
  Motive Power: K H Smith
  Car Dept: J D Mowery
Chief Engineer: W G Taylor
Purchasing Agent: A L Payton
Secretary/Treasurer: R A Taylor

27 route miles (43.5 km); 48 diesel-electric locomotives

The Belt Line intersects and connects all Chicago trunk lines for interchange of traffic. Its focus is the automated Clearing Yard, one of the largest and most modern in the USA, which has a working capacity of 12 600 cars.

The principal functions of the Belt Railway are location and switching service for over 325 industries, and classification and interchange of freight cars for its nine owners and for other non-owner roads. In connection with this classification the Belt provides block train service for the benefit of many of its owners in connection with their run-through train operations.

Bessemer and Lake Erie Railroad Company

PO Box 68. Monroeville, Pennsylvania 15146

Telephone: +1 412 829 3465
Telex: 866222

President and Chief Executive Officer: Donald H Hoffman
Vice-President, Finance: R S Rosati
  Operations: M R Seipler
  Marketing: T J Siegel
General Manger, Operating: F J Habic
Superintendent, Mechanical: J L Neis
Chief Engineer: F H Morris
Signals and Communications Engineer: Dennis R Ojard

341·2km; 53 locomotives; 4542 freight cars

Birmingham Southern Railroad Co

PO Box 579, Fairfield, Alabama 35064

Telephone: +1 205 783 2821
Telex: 782589

President: Donald H Hoffman
Vice-President, Operations: M R Seipler
  Marketing: T J Siegel
  Finance: R S Rosati
General Manager: Frank J Habic III

84 route miles (135 km); 36 switcher locomotives; 215 freight cars

Black Mesa & Lake Powell Railroad

PO Box W, Page, Arizona 86040

Telephone: +1 602 645 8811

Superintendent: G Kester

78 route miles (126 km), electrified at 50 kV 60 Hz; operated by six 6000 hp, 220-tonne Co-Co electric and one 1600 hp diesel locomotive; 123 hopper wagons

The Black Mesa & Lake Powell Railroad carries coal from Peabody Coal Co's Kayenta mine on the Black Mesa to a generating station. The railroad was constructed by the Navajo Power Project at a cost of US$83 million. The electric locomotives were manufactured by General Electric, and the diesel locomotive, a back-up for the electric units, was supplied by Morrison-Knudsen. A total of 123 coal cars, 83 with a capacity of 122 tons, and 40 with a capacity of 100 tons, complete two trains.

California Western Railroad

PO Box 907, Foot of Laurel Street, Fort Bragg, California 95437

Telephone: +1 707 964 6371

President: W B Kyle
General Manager: G J Allen

40 route miles (64.4 km); 5 diesel (3 Alco RS11, 2 Alco RS12), 1 steam locomotive; 10 passenger train coaches

The so-called 'Skunk' line, the California Western, runs from Fort Bragg on the Mendocino coast, to Willits on US Highway 101. Originally a logging railroad, the California Western operates two passenger trains called 'Super Skunks', powered by diesel locomotives and featuring open observation cars on both. The trains make two round trips daily to Northspur, the halfway point on the line, during the summer months.

Camas Prairie Railroad Co

325 Mill Road, PO Box 1166, Lewiston, Idaho 83501

Telephone: +1 208 743 2115

President: Loren E Mueller

244.8 route miles (394 km)

The Camas Prairie Railroad is solely an operating company for the Union Pacific and Burlington Northern railroads.

Cambria & Indiana Railroad Co

1170 Eighth Avenue, Room 627, Martin Tower, Bethlehem, Pennsylvania 18018

Telephone: +1 215 694 5972

Chicago Central & Pacific Railroad Co*

PO Box 1800, Chicago Central Railroad Building, 501 Sycamore Street, Waterloo, Iowa 50704

Telephone: +1 319 236 9200

President: Carl W Eckenrode
Superintendent: Donald L Rauch
Chief Engineer: Patrick R Loughlin

27.9 route miles (44.9 km); 10 diesel locomotives; 614 freight wagons

Cedar Rapids and Iowa City Railway Co

PO Box 2951, Cedar Rapids, Iowa 52406

Telephone: +1 319 398 4597

President: Lee Liu
General Manager: O R Woods

53 route miles (85 km); 12 locomotives; 59 freight cars

Cedar Valley Railroad Co

PO Box 266, 223 Main Street, Osage, Iowa 50461

Telephone: +1 515 732 5817

President: John E Haley
General Manager: Willis L Hodge

113 miles (181.8 km); 6 locomotives (4 GP9 and 2 F7A, all GM-EMD); 29 freight cars

Central Montana Rail Inc

PO Box 928, Denton, Montana 59430

Telephone: +1 496 567 2223

General Manager: R Hitchcock

106 route-km; six diesel locomotives

President: Donald R Wood
Vice President, Operations: Lyle D Reed
  Finance: James B Lloyd
Chief Mechanical Officer: William K Brown
Chief Engineering Officer: John Adair

Gauge: 1435 mm

Central Vermont Railway

2 Federal Street, St Albans, Vermont 05478

Telephone: +1 802 524 9584
Telefax: +1 802 524 5423

Chairman: Ronald E Lawless
President: G L Maas
Vice-President: W H Cramer
General Manager: P C Larson
Mechanical Officer: R M Harmon
Chief Engineer: T J Faucett
Superintendent of Transportation: R A Viens
Director of Purchasing: M P Paisley
Corporate Secretary: W J McKnight

Gauge: 1435 mm
Length: 317 route miles (510)

Traffic (000)	1987	1988
Total freight tonnes	2764	2815

Finance (US$000)		
Revenue	*1987*	*1988*
Freight	20 060	22 497
Other income	1505	963
Total	21 565	23 460
Expenditure		
Staff/personnel	7972	8139
Materials and services	13 946	15 226
Depreciation	123	148
Total	22 041	23 513

The railway operates 26 road-switcher locomotives in Canadian National classification as follows: 7 EMD GR-20 2000 hp; and EMD GR-17 1750 hp. Freight stock totals 226 cars

Track
Rail: 85 to 115 lb/yd
Cross ties (sleepers): Wood, 6 in × 8 in ×8 ft 6 in
Spacing: 2900/mile
Fastenings: Cut spike
Minimum curvature radius: 12° (30 ft)
Max gradient: 1.289%
Max permissible axleload: 32.9 short tons

Route length: 797.7 miles (1283.5 km)

The company acquired and commenced operating the former Western Lines of the Illinois Central Gulf Railroad in December 1985. Its principal routes run 508 route-miles from Chicago to Council Bluffs, Iowa; and 128 miles from Tara to Sioux City, Iowa. The system connects with some 30 other railroads. Train-mileage has been doubled by comparison with operations under ICG and includes dedicated TOFC train service; the company has intermodal ramps at Chicago IMX, Rockford, Waterloo, Cedar Rapids, Fort Dodge, Council Bluffs and Sioux City. There is direct service of 96 grain elevators. The 374.3 miles from Chicago to Tara are equipped with a mix of automatic block, CTC and automatic train stop, permitting operation at up to 60 mph.

The company planned to purchase 220 new coal cars in 1990.

Traction and rolling stock
The railroad owns 93 GM-EMD diesel locomotives of Types SW-7R, SW13, SW14, GP8, GP9, GP10, GP18, GP28 and 20ER5, and operates 2066 freight wagons.

Track
Rail: 90-115 lb/yd
Cross ties (sleepers): Wood, treated, 7 in × 9 in × 8 ft 6 in
Spacing: 3150/mile
Fastenings: Spikes, plates and anchors
Minimum curvature radius: 11°
Max gradient: 1.1%
Max axleload: 35 short tons

Chicago and Illinois Midland Railway Co*

PO Box 139, Springfield, Illinois 62705

Telephone: +1 217 788 8602
Telefax: +1 217 788 8658

President: J F Compton
Executive Vice-President and General Manager: J F Hennecke
Senior Executive Vice-President, Operations and Chief Financial Officer: R Swan
Superintendent: M D Johnson
Director, Mechanical, Engineering, Purchasing and Stores: H L Bast
Chief Engineer: R E Pearson

Gauge: 1435 mm
Length: 194.7 km

The railroad is owned by a group of independent investors whose primary business is the haulage of coal for an electric utility.

Traffic	1986	1987	1988
Freight tonnage	7 287 000	4 040 118	5 607 119

Traction and rolling stock
18 locomotives, including 6 EMD SD38-2; 166 freight cars

Track
Rail: 132 lb/yd
Minimum curvature radius: 10°
Max gradient: 1.64%
Max axleload: 66 000 lb

Chicago Rail Link

2728 E 104th Street, Chicago, Illinois 60617-5766

Telephone: +1 312 721 4000

General Manager: M T Chilson

49 route-km; 5 locomotives; 121 freight cars

In 1990 the company's owner, Chicago West Pullman Transportation Corp, was seeking to purchase the Iowa Interstate Railroad, with which it shares a yard at Blue Island.

Chicago South Shore and South Bend Railroad (Electric)*

Carroll Avenue, Michigan City, Indiana 46360

Telephone: +1 219 874 4221

Chairman and Chief Executive Officer: J A Darling
President: T R Jorgenson

Vice-President, Operations and General Manager: Michael W Franke
Chief Mechanical Officer: Henry C Christie
Assistant Chief Engineer: R T Meyer

220 route miles (354 km) of which 91 route miles (146 km) electrified at 1.5 kV dc; 10 GM-EMD GP-38-2 diesel locomotives; 42 electric passenger cars supplied by Sumitomo; 251 freight cars

In 1984 the railroad was sold by Chessie System to Venango River Corp for US$31.7 million. The new owners aimed to develop freight service, which generates half of CSS&SB income and includes unit coal train flows to public utilities. However, in April 1989 the railroad filed for Chapter 11 bankruptcy.

In early 1990 South Shore Acquisition Co, a newly-formed subsidiary of investment bankers Anacostia & Pacific, which had been involved in several short-line schemes, had reached agreement to purchase most of the railroad's assets, subject to ICC approval. The new owners would operate freight. Northern Indiana Commuter Transportation District (NICTD) had agreed to takeover exclusive responsibility for the passenger service.

The line is entirely signalled by automatic block. Track is mostly 115 lb RE cwr on oak sleepers. Minimum curve radius is 8°, max gradient 2.5%.

Colorado & Wyoming Railway Co*

PO Box 316, Pueblo, Colorado 81002

Telephone: +1 303 561 6359

President: F J Villa

110.7 route miles (178 km); 18 GM-EMD locomotives (4 GP-7, 12 SW8 and 2 GP-38-2); 239 freight cars

Columbus and Greenville Railway Co

PO Box 6000, 201 19th Street North, Columbus, Mississippi 39701

Telephone: +1 601 328 6331

President and Chief Executive: Roger D Bell
Vice-President, Traffic and Treasurer: H L Gibson Jr
Chief Mechanical Officer: T Murrah

242 route miles (389 km); 14 locomotives (3 GP-9, 6 GP-7 and 5 CF-7); 949 freight cars

The Corinth and Counce Railroad Co

Highway 57, PO Box 128, Counce, Tennessee 38326

Telephone: +1 901 689 3145

President and General Manager: E W Rice Jr

26 route miles (41.8 km); 4 diesel-electric locomotives (3 SW-1001, 1 SW-900); 50 freight cars

Connects at Corinth, Mississippi with ICG, NS and Gulf & Mississippi Railroad; also connects with TVA line.

D & I Railroad Co

PO Box 829, 313 South Philips, Sioux Falls, South Dakota 57117

Telephone: +1 605 334 5000

President: Dennis A Sudbeck

222 route-km; 12 locomotives

Dakota Minnesota & Eastern Railroad Corporation*

PO Box 178, 337 22nd Avenue South, Brookings, South Dakota 57006

Telephone: +1 605 692 1666

Telefax: +1 605 692 5141

President: John C McIntyre
Vice-President, Traffic: L A Anderson
Engineering: Mike G Arter
Chief Financial Officer: Gregory W Watson
Transportation: Robert F Irwin

965 route miles (1553 km); 48 GM-EMD locomotives, comprising owned SD10, SD9 and GP9 units, and 9 leased SD40-2

The railroad, formed in 1986, was the first to be created by a major sale of Chicago & North Western trackage. It is the second longest US regional railroad, with Winona-Rapid City and Waseca-Mason City main lines as its core. Traffic in 1989 totalled 40 024 carloads and included unit grain trains to the Pacific Northwest.

Dakota Rail Inc

25 Adams Street N, Hutchinson, Minnesota 55350-2653

Telephone: +1 612 587 4018

President and General Manager: Jerry D Ross

44 route miles (70.8 km); 6 locomotives; 70 freight cars

Detroit & Mackinac Railway*

120 Oak Street, Tawas City, Michigan 48763

Telephone: +1 517 362 3461

President and General Manager: C A Pinkerton III
Executive Vice President: R C Moffatt
Vice President, Operations: R L Van Buskirk
Traffic & Equipment Manager: Richard B Moss

405 route miles (652 km); 12 locomotives (11 of them Alco types, including 4 C425M and 1 C420); 1320 freight cars

Duluth, Missabe and Iron Range Railway Company

599 Missabe Building, Duluth, Minnesota 55802

Telephone: +1 218 723 2115

President: Donald H Hoffman
Vice-President, Finance: R S Rosati
  Operations: Maurice R Seipler
  Marketing: Thomas J Siegel
General Manager: Clinton O Ferner
Locomotive Superintendent: Charles E Voss
Chief Engineer: William E Harrison
Signals and Communications Engineer: Wayne C Kelly

645 km; 66 locomotives; 3520 freight cars

This railway connects the Mesabi Range iron ore deposits with the ports of Duluth and Two Harbors on Lake Superior, from where the ore is shipped to the steel centres, throughout the Midwest. In 198 the railway carried 34.3 million tons and registered 3140 million revenue ton-miles.

Elgin, Joliet and Eastern Railway

PO Box 880, Maple Road, Joliet, Illinois 60434

Telephone: +1 815 740 6900

President: Donald H Hoffman
Vice-President, Operating: Maurice R Seipler
  Finance: R S Rosati
  Marketing: Thomas J Siegel
General Manager: George E Steins

320·2 km; 59 locomotives; 5352 freight cars

Eastern Shore Railroad

PO Box 312, Cape Charles, Virginia 23310-0312

Telephone: +1 804 331 1094
Telefax: +1 301 311 2772

Chief Executive Officer & General Manager: S M Gedney

113 route-km; 6 locomotives

Eureka Southern Railroad Co Inc

130 A Street, PO Box N, Eureka, California 95502

Telephone: +1 707 444 8055

General Manager: J H Kosack

168.6 miles (271.3 km), of which 3 miles operated under contract and not owned. The company owns four GP-38 diesel locomotives, one steam locomotive (stored serviceable) and 15 passenger cars. All rolling stock, which includes two parlour and three dining cars, was obtained secondhand in 1985. Trains are dispatched by microwave radio system. Annual traffic totals 480 000 net short tons and 8500 passenger journeys.

Fordyce & Princeton Railroad Co

PO Box 757, Crossett, Arkansas 71635

Telephone: +1 501 567 8631

President: S R Tedder
General Manager: R G McManus

57 route-miles (91.7 km); 3 locomotives (1 GP-28, 2 SW1500); 250 freight wagons

Fox River Valley Railroad

President: Stephen P Selby

Formed in early 1989, the railroad is a wholly-owned subsidiary of Itel Corp. It operates 208 route-miles of former Chicago & North Western track between Green Bay and Milwaukee, and Green Bay and Cleveland.

Gateway Western Railway

The railway was formed in 1989 to take over lines linking Kansas City, St Louis and Springfield, Ill, formerly owned by the bankrupt Chicago Missouri & Western. It has a long-term contract with Santa Fe for haulage of that railroad's freight between Kansas City and East St Louis.

Genesee & Wyoming Railroad Co

PO Box 101, 3546 Retsof Road, Retsof, New York 14539

Telephone: +1 716 243 3770

President: Gerald E Johnson
General Manager: David J Collins

47 route miles and 44 route miles trackage rights (total 146.4 km); 13 locomotives (3 Alco RS1, 2 Alco S4, 2 EMD MP15DC, 1 EMD SW1500, 2 EMD GP38, 3 Alco C424M); 558 freight cars

Gloster Southern Railroad Co

PO Box 757, Crossett, Arkansas 71635

Telephone: +1 501 547 8631

President: S R Tedder
Vice President, Operations: P H Schueth

65 route-miles (104.6 km); 3 locomotives (1 SW900, 2 CF-7); 101 freight wagons

Escanaba and Lake Superior Railroad

PO Box 158, One Larkin Plaza, Wells, Michigan 49894

Telephone: +1 906 786 0693
Telefax: +1 906 786 8012

Track
Rail: Mostly 54.5–65.5 kg/m (110–132 lb/yd)
Cross ties (sleepers): Creosoted fire, thickness 150 mm
Spacing: In plain track 1800–1900/km, in curves 1900–2000/km
Minimum curvature radius: 12°
Max gradient: 0.7%
Max axleload: 33 short tons (4-axle cars)

Farmrail lc

1750, 136 E Frisco Street, Clinton, Oklahoma 73601

Telephone: +1 405 323 1234

Grainbelt Corp

136 E Frisco Avenue, Clinton, Oklahoma 73601

Telephone: +1 405 323 1234

President: G C Betke Jr

300 route-km; 6 locomotives

Great Western Railway Co

Taylor Avenue Shops, PO Box 537, Loveland, Colorado 80539

Telephone: +1 303 667 2384
Telefax: +1 303 667 1444

President and Chief Executive Officer: W A Frederick Jr
General Manager: David L Lafferty

120 route miles (192 km); 13 diesel-electric locomotives, 3 freight cars. In 1989 the railroad carried 186 400 tons of freight. Revenues totalled US$ 906 470, expenses US$ 526 030.

Green Bay and Western Railroad Co*

PO Box 2507, Green Bay, Wisconsin 54306

Telephone: +1 414 497 0411
Telex: 263422

President: S P Selby
Executive Vice President: Jerry Bruley

254 route miles (409 km); 22 locomotives; 1687 freight cars. Six second-hand 2400 hp Alco RSD15 locomotives were acquired in 1989.

Green Mountain Railroad Corp

PO Box 498, Bellows Falls, Vermont 05101-0498

Telephone: +1 80) 463 9532

President, Chief Executive and General Manager: Glenn E Davis
Senior Vice-President and Chief Operating Officer: Robert W Adams
Vice-President and Chief Mechanical Officer: Jerome M Hebda

52.2 route miles (83.9 km); 4 locomotives (2 Alco RS1 and 2 EMD GP-9); 90 freight cars; 9 passenger coaches

Chairman: W W Larkin
President: J C Larkin
Secretary and Treasurer: A K Larkin

295.8 route miles (476 km); 21 locomotives; 182 freight cars

Chairman & Chief Executive Officer: G C Betke Jr

85 route-miles (143 route-km); 4 locomotives

Florida Central, Midland and Northern Railroads

PO Box 967, Plymouth, Florida 32768

Telephone: +1 407 880 8500
Telefax: +1 407 880 0203

General Manager: B J Biscan

171 route-km; 3 locomotives

Houston Belt & Terminal Railway Co

202 Union Station Building, Houston, Texas 77002

Telephone: +1 713 546 3101

President & General Manager: H W Ritter

53 route miles (85.3 km); 20 locomotives

Indiana & Ohio Rail Corp

8901 Blue Ash Road, Cincinnati, Ohio 45242

Telephone: +1 513 891 9191

President: T B McOwen

248 route-km; 12 locomotives, 4 passenger cars, 5 freight cars

Indiana Harbor Belt Railroad Co

PO Box 389, 2721 161st Street, Hammond, Indiana 46325

Telephone: +1 219 989 4703
Telex: 206581 ihb rr riva
Telefax: +1 219 989 4738

President: Richard C Sullivan
General Manager: Charles H Allen

120 route miles (193.2 km); 71 EMD locomotives (33 1000 hp NW2, 10 1200 hp SW7, 5 1200 hp SW9, 23 1500 hp SW15), three power boosters and three diesel hump trailers; 60 freight cars

In 1989 traffic totalled 535 836 carloads. Revenue grossed US$54 million against expenditures of US$46.2 million.
Track is 115 lb rail on wood sleepers with spike fastenings spaced 2031/mile. Minimum curve radius is 12½°, max gradient 1.5% and max permissible axleload 39 short tons.
Planned capital investment for 1990 included incorporation of four locations into the CTC system, installation of larger-capacity control computers and conversion of the system to entrance-exit route-setting.

Indiana Hi-Rail Corp

RR1, Connersville, Indiana 47331

Telephone: +1 317 825 0349

President: R Powell Felix
Vice President, General Manager: D L Smoot

Transportation: G E Bright
Equipment: C B Booker

425 route-miles (684 route-km); 26 diesel locomotives, 517 freight cars, 3 passenger cars

In 1990 a new Erie Division was formed of three lines aggregating 155 route-miles, leased from Norfolk Southern under the latter's Thoroughbred Shortline Program (qv).

Indiana Rail Road Co

PO Box 2464, 1500 South Senate Avenue, Indianapolis, Indiana 46206-2464

Telephone: +1 317 635 7028
Telefax: +1 317 636 8817

President & Chief Executive Officer:
 Thomas B Hoback
Vice President & General Manager:
 Thomas J Quigley
Manager, Equipment: R L Finlay

241 route-miles. In 1985 the company bought from Illinois Central 117 route-miles, serving southern Illinois coalfields, and has since extended; a further 91 route-miles were acquired in 1990.
 The railroad operates 10 GM-EMD F-7 1500 hp locomotives rebuilt as CF-7, 4 GM-EMD SD18 and 1 GM-EMD GP-9 and 40 freight cars. Max permissible axleload is 32.875 short tons.

Iowa Interstate Railroad Ltd*

111-115 Wright Street, Iowa City, Iowa 52240

Telephone: +1 319 338 1707

Chief Executive Officer: Paul H Banner

552 miles (888 km); 26 line-haul diesel locomotives and 416 freight cars

Overcoming opposition from the Chicago & North Western and Milwaukee, a shipper's group in 1984 bought the former Rock Island Iowa main line from Council Bluffs, Iowa, to Bureau, Illinois, and leased its operation to the Iowa Interstate Railroad. In April 1987 the company commenced double-stack COFC working for an independent operator: the traffic is Chicago-Los Angeles, exchanged with Union Pacific at Council Bluffs, Iowa.

Iowa Northern Railroad Co

PO Box 640, 113 North Second Street, Greene, Iowa 50636

Telephone: +1 515 823 5870
Telefax: +1 515 823 4816

Chairman: Harold Stark
President: C J Stoffer
Vice-President & General Manager: Carroll F Kaduce
 Sales & Marketing: Jerry L Swanson

127.2 route miles (204.7 km); 7 EMD GP-9 locomotives; 189 freight cars

Kiamichi Railroad Co Inc

PO Box 786, Hugo, Oklahoma 74743

Telephone: +1 405 326 8306
Telefax: +1 405 326 9353

President: Jack L Hadley
Vice-President, Operations: Charles L Harrison
Chief Engineer: Charles R Wallace

230 route-miles; no rolling stock. The company also operates the 60 route-mile Chaparral Railroad in Texas.

Kyle Railroad Company

PO Box 566, Third & Railroad Avenue, Philipsburg, Kansas 67661

Telephone: +1 913 543 6527

President: Willis B Kyle
Vice-President, General Manager: Rick D Cecil
Superintendent of Operations: Charles C Frankenfeld
Chief Mechanical Officer: John Gray
Accounts Manager: D O Tolle

410 route miles (660 km); 28 locomotives; 700 freight cars

Lake Erie, Franklin and Clarion Railroad

PO Box 689, East Wood Street, Clarion, Pennsylvania 16214

Telephone: +1 814 226 9684

Chairman: W Craig Smith

15 route miles (24.1 km); 4 EMD MP15DC locomotives; 568 freight cars

Lake Superior & Ishpeming Railroad Co*

105 East Washington Street, Marquette, Michigan 49855

Telephone: +1 906 228 7979

President and General Manager: Gerhart D Bantle
Chief Engineer: Theodor O Stokke

59 route miles (95 km); 19 diesel locomotives (6 Alco RSD12, 6 Alco RSD15, 5 GE U23C, 2 GE U25C); 2709 freight cars

Lamoille Valley Railroad Co

PO Box 790, Stafford Avenue, Morrisville, Vermont 05661

Telephone: +1 802 888 4255

President: Robert A Gensburg

99.4 route miles (160 km); 1 EMD 1500 hp GP-8, 5 Alco RS3 1600 hp Bo-Bo locomotives; 4 passenger cars; 59 freight cars. Annual traffic totals 2000 freight carloads and 10 000 passenger journeys

Laurinburg and Southern Railroad Co

PO Box 1929, Laurinburg, North Carolina 28352

Telephone: +1 919 276 0786

President: Murphy Evans

28 route miles (45.1 km); 37 locomotives (8 GM-EMD SW-1; 3 GM-EMD SW-2; 9 GM-EMD NW-2; 4 Alco S-2; 1 Alco S-4; 11 GE units; 1 Plymouth 35-ton unit); 364 freight cars

Long Island Rail Road Company*

93-02 Sutphin Boulevard, Jamaica Station, Jamaica, New York 11435

Telephone: +1 718 990 7400

President: Charles W Hoppe
Vice-President, Operations: J J Doherty
 Market and Public Affairs: Bonnie Stone
 Management & Financial Services: M Saggese
 Human Resources: Basil J Whiting
 Capital Program Mgt: T Marlow
General Counsel and Secretary: Thomas M Taranto
Chief Transportation Officer: Robert E Carbaugh

Chief Engineer: W B Dwinnell
Chief Mechanical Officer: Vacant
Director, Purchasing and Materials: B Kaplan
Assistant Chief Engineer, Signals and Communications, Power: E W Koch
 Maintenance of Way: D C George

Gauge: 1435 mm
Length: 1100 km (684 route miles)
Electrification: 237 km at 750 V dc third rail

LIRR is the third oldest railroad in the world still operating under its original name. It was demoted from the Class I category in 1983 at its own request, for savings in documentation and in view of its comparatively small freight traffic. The latter, however, may increase by up to 1500 carloads a year following LIRR's purchase of Conrail's Bay Ridge branch giving it access to the Brooklyn Waterfront and car floats thence to New Jersey.
 The railroad serves the Long Island suburban counties of Nassau and Suffolk as well as certain communities in eastern Queens. It has nine branches which feed into three western terminals in New York City: Penn station, Flatbush Avenue (Brooklyn) and Hunterspoint Avenue (open only in peak hours and served chiefly by diesel-powered trains). Penn station deals with 209 000 passengers daily. The focal point of the system is the eight-platform Jamaica station, which in the rush-hour averages a train movement every half minute and where eight of the nine branches and the three approaches to the New York City terminals converge. The nine branches provide extensive coverage of Long Island, and vary in length from 20 miles (the Port Washington branch) to 118 miles (the Montauk branch).
 LIRR runs over 700 passenger trains daily and records over 75 million passenger journeys a year.
 The LIRR is a wholly-owned subsidiary of the Metropolitan Transportation Authority, an agency of the State of New York, whose members constitute the railroad's Board of Directors.

Rolling stock
For passenger service the railroad operates 51 line-haul (28 GP-38-2 2000 hp and 23 MP-15 1500 hp) and three SW-1001 1000 hp switcher diesel locomotives. LIRR classifies them respectively E-20, E-15 and E-10. The fleet also includes five Alco-engined 2000 hp units designated Class L-2.
 The stock of 1167 passenger vehicles includes 761 Class M-1 multiple-unit passenger cars, covering service on its inner suburban electrified lines in New York City, Nassau and Suffolk counties, and 174 recently-delivered Type M-3 cars. Service to other points on the system is provided by diesel locomotive-hauled trains for which LIRR has a stock of 223 cars.
 The majority of diesel services are push-pull, with an EMD diesel locomotive at the east end and a power unit shell (traction motors removed) with engineer controls at the west end. The 150 coaches assigned to push-pull service were converted during 1971–80 from electric multiple-units.
 In 1987 LIRR was seeking suppliers of three prototype electro-diesel locomotives. Together with a dozen new cars the trio would be set to evaluate dual-mode working on the Port Jefferson branch. LIRR has also 10 prototype bi-level cars to work the Port Washington branch in push-pull mode with existing dual-mode FL-9 locomotives, of which NYMTA has recently ordered a further nine to eliminate locomotive changes at the approach to Manhattan.
 The bi-level order was placed with Mitsui (USA), but the cars are being outline-designed by Comeng to a derivative of that company's bi-level emu car series for New South Wales' Sydney services, Australia; detail design and manufacture was by Tokyu Car in Japan. The stainless, air-conditioned steel cars are profiled for operation through the East River tunnels into Penn station, New York. LIRR is likely to order 100 more bi-levels.

Investment programmes
Under a New York MTA 1987–91 US$1800 million capital improvement programme, LIRR was assigned US$1003 million. A major project is the comprehensive remodelling of the celebrated Jamaica junction, with a construction of flyovers at each end of the station and of a new fast route through the station. New York's Penn station will have track and structure modifications in association with Amtrak, and be equipped with a new control centre. Triplication of part of the main line track is proposed.

RAILWAY SYSTEMS / United States of America

Maine Central Railroad Company

Subsidiary of Guilford Transportation Industries Rail Division

PO Box 9701, Rigby Road West, Portland, Maine 04104

Telefax: +1 207 774 8240

Chairman, President and Chief Executive: David A Fink
Vice-President, Transportation: Sydney P Culliford
  Marketing and Sales: F C Pease
  Mechanical: James P Coffin
  Finance: C Austin

Gauge: 1435 mm
Length: 738 route miles (1187 km)

The Maine Central Railroad Company operates in Maine, New Hampshire, Vermont and New Brunswick. Maine Central serves all large population centres and with two exceptions the industrial centres of the State of Maine.

The Portland Terminal Company, a wholly-owned subsidiary, operates railroad facilities in Portland. It provides exclusive terminal services for Boston and Maine Corporation and Maine Central Railroad Company. It also provides for traffic to and from the Grand Trunk Railway (Canadian National) at Portland.

Three GE Type U-188 locomotives bring a freight from Portland into Bangor; two are in GTI livery, the centre unit in original Maine Central orange (*Peter J Howard*)

Traction and rolling stock
Number of locomotives in service: 73 line-haul units; 5 switchers. Freight train wagons: 3707.

Diesel locomotives

Class	Wheel arrangement	Transmission	Rated power kW	Max speed km/h	Total weight tonnes	Year first built	Builders		
							Mechanical parts	Engine & type	Transmission
U-25B	Bo-Bo	Elec	1864	112	132	1965	GE	GE	GE
U-18B	Bo-Bo	Elec	1342	112	125	1975	GE	GE	GE
GP-38	Bo-Bo	Elec	1491	104	128·5	1966	EMD	EMD	EMD
GP-9	Bo-Bo	Elec	1304	104	130	1963	EMD	EMD	EMD
GP-7R	Bo-Bo	Elec	1118	104	124	1950	EMD	EMD	EMD
SW-7	Bo-Bo	Elec	894	104	124	1950	EMD	EMD	EMD
SW-9	Bo-Bo	Elec	894	104	124	1951	EMD	EMD	EMD
RS-11	Bo-Bo	Elec	1342	104	123	1956	Alco	Alco	GE
S-3	Bo-Bo	Elec	492	96	98	1953	Alco	Alco	GE
S-1	Bo-Bo	Elec	492	96	98	1949	Alco	Alco	GE

Manufacturers Railway Co

2850 South Broadway, St Louis, Missouri 63118

Telephone: +1 314 577 1753
Telex: 44 7494

Chairman and Chief Executive Officer: August A Busch Jr
President: Roy W Chapman
Vice-President, Operations: Eldon D Harris
Mechanical Superintendent: Milbern Miller
Chief Engineer: Kem E Conrad

42.4 route miles (68.2 km); 11 locomotives (3 Alco S2, 1 Alco S4, 3 EMD MP15 and 3 EMD SW1500, 1 'slug'); 580 freight cars

Maryland & Delaware Railroad Co

106 Railroad Avenue, Federalsburg, Maryland 21632

Telephone: +1 301 754 5735
Telefax: +1 301 754 9528

President: J A Hannold
General Manager: Eric Callaway

117 route miles (188 km); 4 diesel locomotives

Maryland Midland Railway Inc

PO Box A, Union Bridge, Maryland 21791

Telephone: +1 301 775 7718
 +1 301 876 0392
Telefax: +1 301 775 2520

Chairman: Les F Dingman
President: Paul D Denton
Manager, Transportation: Alan M Novotny
Chief Mechanical Officer: Mike R Hambright
Manager, Track & Structures: Wayne E Weszka

67 route miles; 3 EMD GP-9, 2 EMD F7A diesel locomotives, 450 freight cars

In FY 1988-89 the railway recorded 4740 carloads of freight. Revenue totalled US$1.434 million against operating expenses of US$0.811 million.

Maryland and Pennsylvania Railroad Co

A subsidiary of Emons Industries Inc

1 West Market Street, York, Pennsylvania 17401

Telephone: +1 717 771 1700
Telefax: +1 717 854 6275

Chairman of the Board: R Grossman
President, Chief of Operations: A P Smith

25 route miles (40 km); 9 locomotives; 1739 freight cars

McCloud River Railroad Company

PO Box 1500, McCloud, California 96057

Telephone: +1 916 964 2141

President: Jeff Forbis

96 route miles (154 km); 3 EMD SD-38 and 1 EMD SD-38-2 locomotives; 900 freight cars

Michigan Interstate Railway
(formerly the Ann Arbor Railroad)

PO Box 380, 121 S Walnut Street, Howell, Michigan 48844

Telephone: +1 517 548 3930
Telex: 228555
Telefax: +1 517 548 3937

Chief Executive Officer: M J Barron
Vice-President Operations: E O Erickson
Chief Engineer: J M Chlipala

53.5 route miles (80 km); 3 EMD GP-38 locomotives; 119 freight cars

Michigan Northern Railway Co

PO Box U, Lake City, Michigan 49651

Telephone: +1 616 839 2039

President: E A Andrus

33 route miles (53 km); 8 diesel locomotives; 2 freight cars; 2 passenger cars

MidSouth Rail Corporation*

PO Box 1232, 111 E Capitol Street, Jackson, Mississippi 39215-1232

Telephone: +1 601 353 7508

Chairman: Mark M Levin
President and Chief Executive Officer: Frank K Turner
Vice-President, Chief Mechanical Officer: Robert A Gajewski
  Chief Engineer: John S Jacobsen
  Chief Transportation Officer: Hugh I Salmons

MidSouth Corporation owns and operates three subsidiary lines, MidSouth Rail Corporation, Mid-Louisiana Rail Corporation and SouthRail Corporation. MidSouth was created in 1986 by purchase from Illinois Central Gulf of a 474-mile east-west system from Meridian to Shreveport, and from Gulfport to Palmer in Mississippi. MidLouisiana Rail is the former North Louisiana & Gulf Railroad, and SouthRail the former Gulf & Mississippi; both were acquired in 1988. MidSouth now totals 1200 route-miles (1920 km) and operates 112 locomotives and 6010 freight cars.

MidSouth carloadings for 1989 rose to 241 200 from 214 500 in 1988. Revenues totalled US$87.096 million against total operating costs of US$62.513 million. MidSouth's operating ratio in 1989 was 72 per cent, still the lowest among publicly-held US railroads.

Mississippi Delta Railroad

PO Box 1446, 421 Fourth Street, Clarksdale, Mississippi 38614

Telephone: +1 615 624 4051

General Manager: B L Davis Jr

98 route-km; 6 diesel locomotives

Mississippi Export Railroad Co

PO Box 743, Moss Point, Mississippi 339563

Telephone: +1 601 475 3322

Vice President & General Manager: R A Paul

167 route-km; 4 locomotives, 325 freight cars

MNVA Railroad
Minnesota Valley Regional Rail Authority

262 First Street West, Morton, Minnesota 56270

Telephone: +1 507 697 6975

President: Larry C Wood
General Manager: Richard S Shaw

146 route miles (235 km); 6 EMD GP-9 locomotives and 388 freight cars

Monongahela Railway Company*

53 Market Street, Brownsville, Pennsylvania 15417

Telephone: +1 412 785 5300

President: Paul H Reistrup
Operations Superintendent: G L Staggers
Engineering Officer: D H Painter
Comptroller: D A Caldwell
Supervisor, Locomotives & Materials: D S Wargo

162 route miles (260.6 km); 13 locomotives. In 1988 the railway moved 17.3 million short tons of freight

In 1990 Conrail was moving to acquire the CSXT and P&LE one-third interests in the 'Monon' and increase its own stake to 100 per cent.

Montana Rail Link Inc

PO Box 8779, Missoula, Montana 59807

Telephone: +1 406 543 7245

President: W H Brodsky
Vice-President, Operations: G G Widle
Director, Purchases: H E Nash
Chief Engineer: R L Keller
Chief Mechanical Officer: M G Dinius

944 route-miles (1519 km); 69 GM-EMD locomotives; 977 freight cars

The company was formed in 1987 to run the Burlington Northern's ex-Northern Pacific main line through Montana as a regional railroad. The fiercely controversial sale provided, inter alia, for BN to continue use of the line, but at a lower cost because of new labour agreements; to control the new railroad's interchanges with other railroads; and to retain ownership of all TOFC terminals on the line.

Natchez Trace Railroad
A subsidiary of Kyle Railroads

PO Box 477, Holly Springs, Mississippi 38635

Telephone: +1 601 252 1263

General Manager: Steven W Leal

54.5 route miles (87.7 km); 3 EMD GP-87 locomotives; 135 freight cars

New England Southern Railroad

PO Box 958, Belchertown, Maryland 01007

Telephone: +1 413 256 8718

President & General Manager: P M Dearness

160 route-km; 5 diesel locomotives

New Orleans Public Belt Railroad

PO Box 51658, 1247 World Trade Center, New Orleans, Louisiana 70151

Telephone: +1 504 525 6282

President: Sidney J Barthelmy
General Manager: Moise Dumas Jr
Superintendent, Mechanical: Herbert C Lewis
Manager, Engineering and Maintenance: Donald D Childress

148.7 route miles (239 km); 7 locomotives; 352 freight cars

New York, Susquehanna and Western Railroad Corporation

1 Railroad Avenue, Cooperstown, New York 13326

Telephone: +1 607 547 2555

President and Chief Executive Officer: W G Rich
Vice President, NYS&W: Robert A Kurdock
Chief Financial Officer: William B Blatter
Engineering: Richard S Hensel
Operations: Joseph G Senchyshyn
Mechanical: David L Powell

Member of Delaware Otsego Corp, which also includes the: Cooperstown and Charlotte Valley Railway; Central New York; Rahway Valley; and Staten Island Railroads.

318.5 route miles; 51 locomotives (10 EMD SD45, 2 EMD F45, 24 GE B40-8, 3 Alco C430, 3 EMD GP-18, 1 Alco C420, 1 Alco RS3, 1 EMD SW9, 1 EMD NW2, 2 GE I6); 45 freight cars; 8 passenger cars

The NYS&W covers territory from Syracuse and Utica, NY, through Pennsylvania to the New Jersey coast. From its junction with Conrail at Bingamton, NY, it is now the regular route of Sea-Land double-stack COFC trains from the West Coast to the New York-New Jersey area. They are handled at the NYS&W-developed Little Ferry terminal, New Jersey. The railroad has also captured K-Line, Hanjin and NYK shipping lines' Pacific Rim-Northeast coast COFC, which is handled at a North Bergen terminal. The railroad also completes from Buffalo the haul of a K-Line double-stack service from Tacoma, Washington, to Montreal, using the bankrupt Delaware & Hudson, which the NYS&W was operating under government direction in 1989-90.

In 1989 20 new GE microprocessor-controlled B40-8 locomotives were leased from CSXT. A new subsidiary, Susquehanna Bulk Systems (SBS), was formed to prospect for sites and market bulk transfer facilities on the railroad's territory. Revenue in 1989 totalled US$108 million against expenses of US$106.4 million.

New NYS&W B40-8 locomotives and double-stack COFC near Endwell, NY (J J Young Jr)

Octoraro Railway Inc

PO Box 146, Kennett Square, Pennsylvania 19348

Telephone: +1 215 444 0238

President: S Babcock

72 route miles in service (116 km); 3 Alco diesel-electric locomotives

Oregon & Northwestern Railroad Co

PO Box 888, Hines, Oregon 97738

Telephone: +1 503 573 5281

President: T Turner
Manager: Paul L Taylor

51 route miles (82 km); 4 Baldwin locomotives; 175 freight cars

Oregon, California & Eastern Railway Co

PO Box 1088, Klamath Falls, Oregon 97601

Telephone: +1 503 882 5596

President: J P Tessier
Vice-President and General Manager: R S Coombes

66 route miles (105 km); 5 diesel locomotives; 140 freight wagons

Paducah & Louisville Railway*

1500 Kentucky Avenue, Paducah, Kentucky 42001

Telephone: +1 502 444 4300

President and Chief Operating Officer: Anthony V Reck
General Manager: Donald E Sill
Mechanical Superintendent: W O Albritton
Engineering Superintendent: W M D Sandefur
Director, Signals and Communications: D E Pflueger

309 route miles (497 km); 61 GM-EMD locomotives (1 SW-9, 8 SW-13, 1 SW-14, 7 GP-30, 13 GP-35, 6 GP-7 and 25 GP-9); 1639 freight cars. The company was formed in 1986 to take over Illinois Central Gulf trackage that is largely cwr and CTC-controlled, and also the ICG Paducah workshops.

Track is 56.98 cwr on 7 in × 9 in × 8 ft 6 in wood sleepers with cut spike fastenings. Minimum curve radius is 6°, max gradient 1.25% and max axleload 29.89 tonnes.

Patapsco & Back Rivers Railroad

1275 Daly Avenue, Bethlehem, Pennsylvania 18015

Telephone: +1 215 694 5972

President: C W Eckenrode
Superintendent: Michael J King
Chief Engineer: P R Loughlin

170 rote-km; 21 diesel locomotives; 278 freight cars

Peoria & Pekin Union Railway

101 Wesley Road, Creve Coeur, Illinois 61611

Telephone: +1 309 694 8600

President and General Manager: Charles E Hellums
Chief Engineer: Edward J Dean

150.87 route miles (243 km); 13 locomotives

Philadelphia, Bethlehem and New England Railroad Co

1170 Eighth Avenue, Martin Towrr, Bethlehem, Pennsylvania 18018

Telephone: +1 215 694 5972

President: Carl W Eckenrode
Superintendent: D H Boyer

56 route miles (94.6 km); 26 locomotives (8 EMD NW2, 3 EMD SW7, 4 EMD SW9, 5 EMD SW1200 and 5 'slugs'); 444 freight cars

Pittsburg and Shawmut Railroad

PO Box 45, One Glade Park, RD3, Kittaning, Pennsylvania 16201

Telephone: +1 412 543 2121

Executive Vice-President: G B Pettingell
Superintendent: M L Carrodus

96 route miles (154.5 km); 12 EMD locomotives (2 GP-7, 10 SW9); 939 freight cars.

Pocono Northeast Railway

1004 Exeter Avenue, Exeter, Pennsylvania 18643

Telephone: +1 717 655 8933

President: R McNichols
Superintendent: C F Kopetchny

150 route-km; 4 locomotives

Port Terminal Railroad

501, Crawford Street, Houston, Texas 77002

Telephone: +1 713 546 3304

General Manager: H E Handley

285 route-km; 21 locomotives

Providence and Worcester Railroad Co*

PO Box 1188, 382 Southbridge Street, Worcester, Maryland 01601

Telephone: +1 619 799 4472
Telex: 35 8217

President: O R Harrold
Vice-President: A E Kaulbach
Vice-President and General Manager: R P Chrzanowski
Chief Mechanical Officer: I M Filler
Chief Engineer, Track & Structures: P M Fetterman
Communications and Signalling: J B Cartier

360 route miles (576 km); 15 locomotives (5 MLW M420, 2 EMD GP-9, 6 EMD GP-38, 1 GE B23-7, 1 GE U18B); 395 freight cars.

Rarus Railway Company
(formerly the Butte, Anaconda & Pacific Railway)

300 West Commercial Avenue, Anaconda, Montana 59711

Telephone: +1 406 563 7121

President: W T McCarthy

Length: 88 route miles (141.5 km)

Traction and rolling stock
6 locomotives (2 1500 hp GP-7 and 4 1750 hp GP-9); 70 freight cars.

Track
Rail: 57.07 kg/m
Cross ties (sleepers): Fir, thickness 17.78 mm
Fastenings: Fishplate head-free joints
Minimum curvature radius: 10°
Max gradient: 4.01%
Max axleload: 34 tonnes

Red River Valley & Western Railroad Co

PO Box 608, 116 S 4th Street, Wahpeton, North Dakota 58075

Telephone: +1 701 642 8257

President: Thomas G Kotnour
Manager, Operations: C M Holwegner

667 route-miles (1073 km); 10 locomotives.

Richmond, Fredericksburg and Potomac Railroad Co*

2134 West Laburnum Avenue, Richmond, Virginia 23227. Mail address: PO Box 11281, Richmond, Virginia 23230

Telephone: +1 804 257 3200
Telex: 710 956 0164
Telefax: +1 804 257 3386

President: Frank A Crovo Jr
Vice President, Operations: James C Hobbs
Chief Traffic Officer, TOFC: J W Moore
Manager, Engineering: James R Smith Jr

113.8 route miles (183 km); 35 diesel locomotives; 1589 freight cars

The RF & P is an important 'bridge' from Washington DC in the north to Richmond, Virginia in the south, particularly for COFC/TOFC traffic. At Washington it connects with Conrail, CSX, NS and Delaware & Hudson; and at Richmond with CSX. Controlling interest is held by CSX Corporation (qv), which sought a full-scale merger in 1990, but abandoned the proposal in face of strong political opposition in Virginia.

Rochester & Southern Railroad Inc

1372 Brooks Avenue, Rochester, New York 14624

Telephone: +1 716 328 5190/5
Telefax: +1 716 328 6359

Chairman and Chief Executive: Mortimer B Fuller III
General Manager: Jack F Conser

106.9 route miles (172 km); 7 GM-EMD locomotives (6 GP-40, 1 SW-1200 purchased from Southern Pacific Railroad in 1987).

St Lawrence & Atlantic Railroad Co
Owned by Emons Holdings Inc

96 South George Street, Suite 520, York, Pennsylvania 17401

Telephone: +1 717 771 1700 Telefax: +1 717 854 6275

Chairman: R Grossman
President & Chief Operating officer: A P Smith

165 route-miles: 8 locomotives, 25 freight cars

The railroad was formed in 1989 by the purchase from Canadian National of a line from Portland, Maine through New Hampshire to Norton, Vermont.

Sacramento Northern Railway

1416 Dodge Street, Omaha, Nebraska 68179

Telephone: +1 402 271 5000

146.9 route miles (236.4 km); 3 diesel locomotives; 99 freight cars

San Diego & Imperial Valley Railroad Co

743 Imperial Avenue, San Diego, California 92101

Telephone: +1 619 239 7348

Vice-President and General Manager: Richard F Engle

171 route miles (275 km); 9 locomotives; 15 freight cars

San Francisco Belt Railroad

Suite 221, World Trade Center, San Francisco, California 94111

Telephone: +1 415 956 3874

President: W B Kyle
Vice-President: L T Cecil

20 route miles (32 km); 3 locomotives.
Operated by Port Railroads Inc.

Santa Maria Valley Railroad Company

PO Box 340, Santa Maria, California 93456

Telephone: +1 805 922 7941
Telefax: +1 805 928 9615

President: Marian M Hancock
Vice-President and Manager: Sue J Sword

14.8 route miles (23.8 km); 8 GE locomotives

Seminole Gulf Railway

2830 Winkler Avenue, Suite 201, Fort Myers, Florida 33916

Telephone: +1 813 275 6060
Telefax: +1 813 275 0581

118 route-miles (190 km); 8 GM-EMD GP-9 locomotives and 60 freight cars. In 1988 the railway carried 1.8 million short tons of freight.

Sierra Railroad Company

13645 Tuolumne Road, Sonora, California 95370

Telephone: +1 209 532 3685

President: J L Foster
Vice-President, Operations: R L Roy

49 route miles (78.8 km); 3 Baldwin diesel locomotives

South Buffalo Railway Co

2558 Hamburg Turnpike, Lackawanna, New York 14218

Telephone: +1 716 821 3631

President: C W Eckenrode
Superintendent: J M Ball
Chief Engineer: Patrick R Loughlin

108 route-km; 35 diesel locomotives; 200 freight cars.

South Central Tennessee Railroad Co
A subsidiary of Kyle Railways

PO Box 259, Centerville, Tennessee 37033

Telephone: +1 615 729 4227

General Manager: Wanda L Camp

51.5 route miles; 4 locomotives; 117 freight cars

United States of America / **RAILWAY SYSTEMS** 799

Spencerville & Elgin Railroad Co

PO Box 7, 109 E North Street, Spencerville, Ohio 45887

Telephone: +1 419 647 4373

General Manager and Chief Engineer: J W Kitson

30 route miles (48 km); 3 Alco diesel locomotives

Stockton Terminal & Eastern Railroad

1330 North Broadway Avenue, Stockton, California 95205

Telephone: +1 209 466 7001

President: B D Schneider
Superintendent: G N Carney

38 route miles (61 km); 5 Alco diesel locomotives; 147 refrigerator freight cars

Terminal Railroad Association of St Louis

2016 Madison Avenue, Granite City, Illinois 62040

Telephone: +1 618 451 8300
Telex: 724427

President: B C Davidson
General Manager: D C Weitzman

205 track-miles (329.8 km); 27 diesel locomotives (10 GM-EMD SW1200 and 17 GM-EMD SW1500) and five 'slugs'

In 1989 revenues grossed US$25.75 million against total expenses of US$26.29 million.

Texas Mexican Railway Co*

PO Box 419, Laredo, Texas 78042-0419

Telephone: +1 512 722 6411
Telex: 76 34 11
Telefax: +1 512 722 6431 Ext 166

Chairman of the Board and Chief Executive Officer:
 A R Ramos
President and Chief Operating Officer:
 C H Darnell Jr
Vice-President, Operations Manager: R J Spear
Finance and Comptroller: Z Solis III

Length: 157 route miles (253 km).

Track
Rail: 90 lb RA (43.74 kg/m); 100 lb RE (49.6 kg/m); 110 lb RE (54.56 kg/m); 115 lb RE (57.05 kg/m); 136 lb RE (67.46 kg/m)
Cross ties (sleepers): Wooden, thickness 7 in
Spacing: 1988/km
Fastenings: ⅝ × 6 in track spikes, 7 E 11 in tie plates, anchors etc
Max curvature radius: 6°
Max gradient: 0.75%

Traction and rolling stock
17 diesel locomotives; 1142 freight cars; 5 passenger cars

Texas & Northern Railway Co

PO Box 300, Lone Star, Texas 75668

Telephone: +1 214 656 3761

President: J K Pennington

7.6 route miles (12.2 km); 24 locomotives; 185 freight cars

Texas North Western Railway Co

Box 9, Route 1, Sunray, Texas 79086-9702

Telephone: +1 806 935 7474

President: J P Kleifgan
General Manager, Operations: W D Mathews

46 route miles (74 km); 1 GP-7, 1 GP-9 locomotives

Texas, Oklahoma & Eastern Railroad

412 E Lockesburg Street, Dequeen, Arkansas 71832

Telephone: +1 501 642 1309

Vice-President and General Manager: L E Gilliam

40 route miles (64 km); 10 EMD diesel locomotives (6 GP-40, 3 GP-40-2, 1 GP-35); 1332 freight cars

Toledo, Peoria & Western Railroad

281 route-miles

This line from Lomax, Illinois, to Logansport, Indiana, was sold by Santa Fe to a New Jersey group in February 1989. It is operated by 20 ex-Santa Fe GP20 locomotives. In February 1989 it combined with Santa Fe to operate double-track COFC service to an auto assembly plant in Illinois.

TransKentucky Transportation Railroad Inc

105 Winchester Street, Paris, Kentucky 40361

Telephone: +1 606 253 9200

President: C F Powell
Manager, Operations: R S Rogers

50 route miles (80 km); 24 locomotives; 50 freight cars

Tuscola & Saginaw Bay Railway

538 E Huron Street, Vassar, Michigan 48768

Telephone: +1 517 823 8331

President, Operations and General Manager:
 L R Judd
Chief Engineer: D A Schell
Engineer, Signalling and Communications:
 W R Wilder

531 route miles (854 km); 11 diesel locomotives (2 Alco, 1 EMD NW2, 8 EMD GP35); 93 freight cars

Union Railroad Co

PO Box 68, Monroeville, Pennsylvania 15146

Telephone: +1 412 829 3465

President and Chief Executive: D H Hoffman
Vice-President, Operations: M R Seipler
Superintendent Mechanical: J L Neis
Chief Engineer: F H Morris
Engineer, Signals and Communications: D R Ojard

206 route miles (331 km); 71 diesel locomotives; 1215 freight cars

Upper Merion and Plymouth Railroad Co

Member of Northbrook Corporation's Rail Division

PO Box 404, Conshohocken, Pennsylvania 19428

Telephone: +1 215 275 2066

President: E L Freeman

Vice-President and General Manager: James A Bogusky

15 route miles (24.1 km); 2 EMD locomotives; 959 freight cars

Utah Railway Co

136 E South Temple Street, Salt Lake City, Utah 84111

Telephone: +1 801 521 3447
President: D Gilson
Superintendent: D C Pilling

157 route-km; 14 locomotives

Vermont Railway Inc

One Railway Lane, Burlington, Vermont 05401

Telephone: +1 802 658 2550

President: J R Pennington
Vice-President, Operations: C H Bischoff
Chief Mechanical Officer: J A Martin IV

128.8 route miles (207.2 km); 4 EMD diesel locomotives; 231 freight cars

Washington Central Railroad Co Inc

6 West Arlington, Yakima, Washington 98902

Telephone: +1 509 453 9166

President: Nicholas B Temple

640 route-km); 6 diesel locomotives

Washington Terminal Co
Owned by Amtrak

Union Station, Washington DC 20002

Telephone: +1 202 289 2381

General Superintendent: E S Bagley Jr

33 track miles (53 km); 8 diesel locomotives

West Virginia Northern Railroad Inc

PO Box 458, Kingwood, West Virginia 26537

Telephone: +1 304 329 1050

Manager: Lloyd A Sturtevant

17 route miles (27.4 km); 2 EMD NW2 and 1 SW-1200 diesel locomotives

Services coal-mining companies and interchange with CSX Transportation at Tunnelton, West Virginia.

Winchester & Western Railroad Co

258 Elm Street, New Canaan, Connecticut 06840

Telephone: +1 703 662 2600

General Manager: Forrest Van Schwartz

120 route miles (193 km); 14 diesel locomotives (1 Alco RS-3, 2 Alco 900 hp S-6 and 3 Alco 1800 hp RS-11 Bo-Bo; 6 EMD 1750 hp GP-9 and 2 EMD 2000 hp GP-9M); 2 passenger cars, 299 freight cars

Track
Rail: 100-132 lb/yd
Cross ties (sleepers): Wood, 6 × 8, 7 × 9 in
Spacing: 1610/km
Fastenings: Cut spikes
Minimum curvature radius: 18°
Max gradient: 5% compensated

800 RAILWAY SYSTEMS / United States of America

Wisconsin & Southern Railroad Co

PO Box A, 511 Barstow Street, Horicon, Wisconsin 53032

Telephone: +1 414 485 4783

President: W E Gardner
Executive Vice President and Chief Operating Officer: James J Malloy Sr
Chief Mechanical Officer: James C Robertson

145 route-miles (233.3 km); 1 EMD NW2 and 4 EMD GP-9 locomotives; 438 freight cars

Wisconsin Central Ltd*

6250 N River Road, Suite 9000, Rosemont, Illinois 60018

Telephone: +1 708 318 4600
Telefax: +1 708 318 4615

President: Edward A Burkhardt
Executive Vice-President and Chief Financial Officer: Thomas F Power Jr
Vice-President and General Manager: John L Bradshaw
Vice President, Marketing: William R Schauer

Vice-President and Chief Engineer: Glenn J Kerbs
Vice-President and Chief Mechanical Officer: Robert F Nadrowski

Route length: 2047 miles (3296 km); 97 locomotives, 4657 freight cars

The longest regional railroad yet created, WCL began operating in October 1987 the former Lake States Division of Soo Line. Its system includes the former Soo main line between Chicago and Minneapolis, and reaches as far north as Sault Ste Marie in Ontario, Canada.

Commuter passenger systems and authorities

In certain conurbation areas regional authorities operate 'heavy rail' commuter services with their own equipment over 1435 mm-gauge trackage acquired from railroads, or have the services operated by railroads under contract. These operations are distinct from the metro and light rail activities covered in the Rapid Transit section.

California Department of Transportation (Caltrans)

1120 N Street, Sacramento, California
(Po Box 942874, Sacramento, CA 94274-0001)
Telephone: +1 916 322 5480

Director: R K Best
Chief of Office of Rail Services: C A Davis

In July 1980 Caltrans conducted a 10-year purchase-of-service contract with Southern Pacific for the latter's operation of the Peninsula Commuter Service (PCS) over the 75.6 km between San Francisco and San Jose. SP leases use of the trackage to Caltrans, but Caltrans has bought the stations. In 1989 the route was carrying 26 round train trips daily, reduced at weekends. Traffic totals over 5.6 million passenger journeys a year.

In 1989 a State law was enacted to provide for handover of the PCS to local control and management by July 1992. Extensions of service to the downtown San Francisco financial district and to Gilroy were under study by the relevant local agencies.

PCS service is furnished by 20 2400 hp F40PH locomotives from GM-EMD and 73 bi-level gallery cars from Nippon Sharyo Seizo Kaisha. The bi-levels include 21 push-pull cab control trailers. The F40PH units are arranged for a maximum speed of 134 km/h.

Caltrans also supports Amtrak 403(b) services on two routes: Los Angeles-San Diego, 206 km (of the eight daily round trips on this route, four are state-supported); Oakland-Bakersfield 513 km (three daily round trips, all state-supported); and Los Angeles-Santa Barbara (once daily each way). The services are supplemented by an extensive network of dedicated bus connections serving various off-line points such as San Francisco, Los Angeles, Sacramento, Long Beach, San Bernardino, Santa Barbara, San Jose, Santa Rosa and Chico.

In its 1989–94 Rail Passenger Development Plan, Caltrans recommended that services be expanded to 10 daily round trips between Los Angeles and San Diego, two between Los Angeles and Santa Barbara, and four between Oakland and Bakersfield during the plan's currency.

GM-EMD F40PH locomotive and Nippon Sharyo bi-levels

Connecticut Department of Transportation

Amtrak has been contracted to run a 33-mile service between Old Saybrook and New Haven, and develop five stations. The service, to start in the spring of 1990, was to be operated by two GE-EMD F7M locomotives and 10 passenger cars, including three control cab trailers, bought for US$1.7 million from the Port Authority of Allegheny County following the latter's discontinuance of commuter rail service.

Further start-ups were possible after the state's completion of a study of transportation needs.

Florida Department of Transportation (FDOT)

605 Suwannee Street, Burns Building, Tallahassee, Florida 32399-0450

Telephone: +1 904 488 5704
Telefax: +1 904 487 3403

Rail Program Administrator: J M Rankin
Rail Program Manager: A L Tompkins
Railroad Systems Engineer: G E Becdol

Tri-County Commuter Rail Organization: Tri-Rail

One River Plaza, 305 South Andrew's Avenue, 801 Fort Lauderdale, Florida 33301

Executive Director: Gilbert M Robert
Chief Mechanical Officer: George Kennedy

The Tri-Rail commuter service, funded by the Florida DoT, was launched over 67 route-miles of CSX tracks between Miami and West Palm Beach in January 1989. For this the Department obtained from UTDC of Canada 18 bi-level cars of GO Transport Toronto type and five GM-EMD F40PHL-2 locomotives re-manufactured by Morrison-Knudsen.

Florida purchased the 81-mile Miami-West Palm Beach line for US$264 million in 1988. The line continues to carry Amtrak and CSX trains. A Federal grant of US$10.5 million went toward a US$31 million upgrading of the CSX track and another of US$4 million towards creating an interchange with Amtrak and the Miami Metrorail in north Miami.

TRI-RAIL is operated by the Tri-County Commuter Rail Organization, so named because it represents three counties.

Maryland State Railroad Administration, Maryland Rail Commuter Service (MARC)

PO Box 8718, BWI Airport, Maryland 21240-8718

Telephone: +1 301 859 7422

Administrator: Richard J Keen
Director of Passenger Services: Joseph C Nessel III
Chief Engineer: Clyde A Raleigh
Assistant Director, Equipment: G F Payne
 Operations: F W Wengenroth

Maryland's Railroad Administration operates over 40 miles of Amtrak Northeast Corridor route (electrified at 11 kV ac 25 Hz) and 38 miles of CSX route with parallel Baltimore-Washington services, and a Brunswick (Maryland)-Washington service over 49 miles of CSX track.

Amtrak operates for MDOT a Washington-Baltimore service with four GM-EMD AEM-7 electric locomotives and MARC's new Japanese-built cars (see below). Two further services are run for MDOT by Chessie System. One is with Budd RDC railcars over Baltimore & Ohio tracks between Washington Union station and Baltimore Camden station. The other is between Washington, Brunswick, Maryland, and Martinsburg, West Virginia; this is worked by a mix of refurbished Budd RDC railcars and locomotive-hauled trains, the latter furnished by ex-B&O F7As, which Morrison-Knudsen rebuilt into F9PH units, and reconditioned ex-Pennsylvania cars, both updatings funded by MDOT. MARC also operates with a subsidy from Amtrak the latter's 'Blue Ridge' service between Washington and Martinsburg.

Equipment owned by MDOT includes five F9PH locomotives, 17 Budd RDC railcars (one of them leased), an auxiliary power/control unit fashioned from an F7A locomotive, and 35 ex-PRR head-end power passenger cars. Most modern equipment comprises

Japanese-built cars and AEM-7 locomotive head for Washington.

United States of America / **RAILWAY SYSTEMS** 801

28 stainless-steel push-pull cars from Sumitomo of Japan and four GM-EMD AEM-7 electric locomotives. In 1987-88 MARC received from Morrison-Knudsen five rebuilt EMD GP-39-2 2300 hp diesel locomotives with head-end auxiliary power.

A fresh order for 15 push-pull cars has been placed with Sumitomo with an option for a further 10 cars. Delivery was expected in 1991-92. Pending delivery, 13 cars were leased from NJ Transit; these were included in a 35-car refurbishing contract concluded with ABB Traction Inc in 1990.

Massachusetts Bay Transportation Authority (MBTA)

10 Park Plaza, Boston, Massachusetts 02116

Telephone: +1 617 722 5000
Telefax: +1 617 722 5841

General Manager, MBTA: Thomas Glynn
Director, Commuter Rail Operations: Ralph Duvall
Chief Transportation Officer: John F Flaherty
Manager, Administration, Marketing & Finances:
  Margaret Zirker
Chief Engineering Officer: William A MacDonald
Chief Mechanical Officer: Walter A Mark
Equipment Engineer: Paul W Frazier

MBTA operates 52 diesel locomotives and 243 passenger cars over eight routes covering 434 route-km of ex-Penn Central and Boston & Maine trackage bought in the 1970s. In 1988 the range of its services was extended to Providence, Rhode Island.

Delivery was completed in 1988, of 26 new F40PH-2C locomotives from GM- EMD and of 107 commuter cars, 67 from MBB of the Federal Republic of Germany and the remainder from Bombardier. The stock still included 49 elderly ex-B&M Budd RDC railcars, all of which have been modified by Morrison-Knudsen as non-powered trailers for locomotive haulage; though they retain their traction plant. The remainder of the EMD locomotive stock comprised 10 F40PH, 1 GP-9 and 15 FP10 locomotives; the FP10s are ex-Gulf Mobile & Ohio F3A and F7A units rebuilt in Illinois Central Gulf's Paducab workshops.

After a thorough analysis the MBTA has decided not to pursue another rebuild of the F10 locomotives. Instead it will purchase up to 25 new locomotives over the next four years. In mid-1989 it was not yet decided whether to employ three-phase traction motors.

Orders for a further 107 were placed with Bombardier in 1988, to permit operation of longer trains. Deliveries extended from June 1989 to June 1990. Another order was placed with Kawasaki for 75 bi-level cars, with an option for 75 more. These would be the first full double-deck commuter cars (as opposed to gallery cars) to operate in the US. Delivery would begin in June 1990.

Traffic

	1986	1987	1988
Total passenger-km (million)	344.383	413.944	503.265
Total passenger journeys (million)	12.048	14.649	17.81

Reconstruction of Boston South station was nearing completion in 1989. The rebuilt station will have new high-level platforms, foundations for air rights development above its platforms, a remodelled subway station on Boston's Red Line, and numerous new passenger amenities: it is expected to serve about 200 trains and 75 000 passengers daily. A rebuilding of Boston's North station was about to begin in 1989. This will provide high-level platforms, improved subway access and a major overhead commercial development.

A US$300 million rehabilitation of the Old Colony line, involving refurbishment of 93 miles of ex-Penn Central (former New Haven) track is in progress. Completion is scheduled for 1995.

Track
Rail: 65.5 kg/m

EMD FP10 locomotive enters Boston North station

Cross ties (sleepers): Wood and concrete, spaced 2011/km
Fastenings: Cut spikes with double shoulder tie plates or resilient fasteners with appropriate tie plates or adapters
Minimum curvature radius: 13°
Max gradient: 3%
Max permissible axleload: 31.75 tonnes

METRA
Chicago Commuter Rail Service Board
(Formerly Northeast Illinois Railroad Corporation)

547 W Jackson Blvd, Chicago, Illinois 60606

Telephone: +1 312 322 6900

Chairman: Jeffrey R Ladd
Executive Director: James E Cole
Department Heads
  Operations: G Richard Tidewell
  Finance: Frank M Racibozynski
  Transportation: Robert F Shive
  Mechanical: Dennis D Ramm
  Engineering: Vaughn L Stoner

Gauge: 1435 mm
Length: 693.2 km
Electrification: 98.95 km at 1.5kV dc

METRA is the commuter railroad operating arm of the Chicago Regional Transportation Authority (RTA).

Burlington Northern, Norfolk Southern, Chicago & North Western, Illinois Central Gulf and Amtrak run their own commuter services in the RTA area under METRA control. METRA itself owns and runs the former Illinois Central Gulf, Milwaukee Road and Rock Island services with its own train crews and equipment.

In 1990 METRA was analysing a network of ten new service corridors, designed to serve primarily the suburb-to-suburb travel market.

At the end of 1989 METRA owned 130 diesel locomotives, 173 electric railcars and 214 push-pull passenger cars. The most recently delivered equipment was 10 GM-EMD F40PH-2 locomotives

METRA plans to acquire 331 new bi-level cars, 173 of them control trailers, under a 10-year US$1900 million capital improvement programme. Enquiries for supply of the first 200 were initiated in 1990. Also planned is purchase of 20 new electric railcars.

In April 1990 METRA ordered from GM-EMD 30 new F40PH-2M locomotives, chiefly to replace the 25 E9 locomotives on former Burlington Northern routes. The new units will be similar to the F40PH-2, but will have a redesigned cab and nose. Their US$1.99 million-per-unit cost will be partly covered by METRA's share of Illinois' newly increased petrol tax; that is expected to be US$450–500 million over a five-year period.

Revenues (US$ million)	1988	1989
Passengers and baggage	140.671	144.446
Other income	16.482	21.039
Total	157.153	165.485
Total passenger-km (million)	2 363.9	2 417.1
Total passenger journey (million)	69.847	71.156

METRA locomotives

Class	Mfrs type	Wheel arrangement	Transmission	Rated power hp	Max speed km/h	Total weight tonnes	Length mm	No in service 1989	Year first built	Builders Mechanical	Builders Engine & type	Builders Transmission
B32A	F40PH	B-B	Elec	3200	142	118	17,117	50	1977	EMD	16-645E3B	EMD
B32B	F40PH-2	B-B	Elec	3200	142	118	17,117	24	1983	EMD	16-645E3C	EMD
B32C	F40PH-2	B-B	Elec	3200	142	120	17,117	11	1989	EMD	16-645E3B	EMD
C32A	F40C	C-C	Elec	3200	122	165	22,046	15	1973	EMD	16-645E	EMD
B12A	SW1200	B-B	Elec	1200	81	91	13,716	1	1954	EMD	12-567C	EMD
B15A	MP1500	B-B	Elec	1500	105	113	14,935	2	1970	EMD	12-645E2	EMD
B6A	SW1	B-B	Elec	600	81	82	11,582	2	1946	EMD	6-567A	EMD
A24D	E9	A-1-A	Elec	2400	158	150	21,336	25	1956	EMD	2/12-645E	EMD

METRA electric railcars or multiple-units

Class	No of cars per unit	Line voltage	No of motor cars per unit	No of Motored axles per motor car	Rated output (kW) per motor	Motor & control type	Max speed km/h	Weight tonnes per car (M-motor T-trailer)	Total seating capacity per car (M-motor T-trailer)	Length per car mm (M-motor T-trailer)	No in service 1989	Rate of acceleration m/s²	Year first built	Builders Mechanical parts	Builders Electrical equipment
S504A	1	1500 V dc	1	4	120	Cam	130	54	94	25,908	8	0.609	1982	Sumitomo	GE
MA3A	1	1500 V dc	1	4	120	Cam	121	62	150	25,908	130	0.457	1971	St Louis Car	GE
MA3B	1	1500 V dc	1	4	120	Cab	121	63	150	25,908	35	0.457	1978	Bombardier	GE

802   RAILWAY SYSTEMS / United States of America

Expenditure (US$ million)			Track	Fastenings: Rail anchors
Staff/personnel	168·549	180·096	Rail: 115, 119, 131, 132, 136 lb/yd	Minimum curvature radius: 7° 26'
Materials and services	92·753	97·806	Cross ties (sleepers): Wood	Max gradient: 1.75%
Depreciation	27·756	32·491	Thickness: 7 × 9 in	Max axleload: 65 000 lb
Total	289·058	310·393	Spacing: 1988/km	

Metro-North Commuter Railroad Co

347 Madison Avenue, New York, New York 10017

Telephone: +1 212 340 3000

President and General Manager: Peter E Stangl
Vice-President, Operations: D N Nelson
Vice-President, Planning and Capital Projects: W M Aston
Vice-President, Human Resources: M J Kurtz
Vice-President, Finance: G T Firnhaber
Vice-President, Marketing and Corporate Communications: J B Isenberg
Director, Engineering: R T Yutko
Chief Engineer: W G Lehn
Chief Mechanical Officer: R C Kirner

Length 454 km
Electrification: Hudson and Harlem lines (133 km), 600 V dc; New Haven line (111 km), 11 kV ac 60 Hz

Metro-North is an operating division of New York's Metropolitan Transportation Authority (MTA). It was created to take over Conrail commuter services at the start of 1983 and covers the Harlem and Hudson lines of the former New York Central and all ex-New Haven commuter lines. Metro-North is remunerated by the Connecticut Department of Transportation for extension of its activity into that state. These include some workings over lines owned by the Connecticut DOT (where freight service is undertaken by the Boston & Maine); Connecticut funded conversion of the New Haven line from 11 kV 25 Hz to 25 kV 60 Hz, a project completed in 1986.

Traffic
Annual ridership on Metro-North increased a further 2.6 per cent during 1989, motivated chiefly by rises in off-peak and within-suburb travel. Patronage, which has climbed 17 per cent since 1982 to an annual total of 55.9 million journeys, is now at its highest since World War II.

Five-year capital programme
Metro-North's US$749 million share of the New York MTA's 1987-91 capital improvement programme was used to buy 60 more M-4 cars for the New Haven line, new locomotives and more 'Shoreliner' cars for the Upper and West Hudson lines, renewal of the New Haven line catenary and substantial works at New York's Grand Central station.

Extensive improvements of the railroad's signal, electric, and data transmission systems were also part of the 1987–91 programme. Most main-line trackage is now equipped with cab signals and the remainder of the railroad will be so equipped over the next few years. Remote control of outlying interlockings from a centralised operations control centre is also progressing.

Construction of new substations on the Hudson and Harlem lines is continuing, along with replacement of third rail and feeder cables in Grand Central Terminal. The overhead catenary system on the New Haven line is also undergoing rehabilitation. Fibre-optic cables have been installed along main lines to replace leased telephone lines; and the 1990 capital investment programme provided for installation of automated public address at all stations.

Metro-North owns New York's Grand Central station. In 1990 a conceptual plan for restoration and redevelopment of the 77 year-old Beaux-Arts building was unveiled. Besides repair and essential renewal of utiltities, the plan envisaged modern additions, such as escalators, and major development of shopping, catering and entertainment, including provision of two cinemas and theatrical facilities.

Traction and rolling stock
The majority of Metro-North's 762 passenger cars are Type M-1 and M-2 emus serving the ex-NYC and New Haven electrified Hudson and Harlem lines employing 600 V dc third-rail. Non-electrified lines are worked by FL9 or ex-Conrail B23-7 locomotive-hauled push-pull trains, and Budd RDC and SPV-2000 diesel railcars. The FL9s are electro-diesel, equipped with third rail pick-up shoes to operate as straight electric locomotives for entry into New York. Almost 90 per cent of the Metro-North rolling stock is electric.

For the New Haven line 54 dual-voltage Type M-4 emu cars, an improved version of the M-2, were recently procured from Tokyu Car. They are arranged to form three-car units. For its locomotive-hauled services on the Upper Hudson and New Haven lines Metro-North has obtained 60 aluminium-bodied push-pull cars termed 'Shoreliners' from Bombardier; 40 were financed by New York, 20 by Connecticut. A further 20 cars were ordered from Bombardier in 1990.

Under the 1987-91 programme, a further 60 electric cars were to be ordered for the New Haven line and 13 push-pull cars for the Upper Hudson line.

In 1989 two emu cars were equipped with GTO inverter-fed asynchronous three-phase motors supplied by General Electric.

In April 1987 Metro-North signed an agreement with BBC Brown Boveri for the modernisation of 10 Type FL9 electro-diesel locomotives including their equipment with three-phase ac motors. However, Metro-North has joined New Jersey Transit and Long Island in the quest for a new dual-mode electro-diesel locomotive design, of which it intends to purchase seven units.

Budd-built Type M-1A 600 V dc emus alongside Hudson River near Tarrytown, New York

Class FL-9 electro-diesel and new Bombardier-built cars on Hudson line

New M-4 emu cars by Tokyu Car

Track
Rail: 119 RE predominantly, some 140, 132 and 127
Cross ties (sleepers): 7 in × 9 in × 8 ft 6 in

Spacing: 1968/km
Fastenings: Tie plates and cut spike
Minimum curvature radius: 16°

Max gradient: 3%
Max axleload: E72 loading for track design

Electric railcars or multiple-units

Class	Cars per unit	Line voltage	Motor cars per unit	Motored axles per motor car	Rated output (hp) per motor	Max speed mph	Weight short tons per car	Total seating capacity per unit	Length per car ft	No in service 1989	Rate of acceleration mph/s	Year first built	Builders Mechanical parts	Builders Electrical equipment
M-1A	2	600 dc	2	4	150	100	46	118 or 122	85	178	2·0	1971-73	Budd	General Electric
M-2*	2	600 dc and 11 000 ac	2	4	162	100	63 or 64·5	118 or 114	85	242	2·0	1973-76	General Electric	General Electric
M-3A	2	600 dc	2	4	140	100	55·3 or 53·8	120 or 114	85	142	2·0	1982-84	Budd	General Electric
M-4*	3	600 dc and 11 000 ac	3	4	162	100	64, 62·3 or 64·8	118, 113 or 120	85	54	2·0	1987	Tokyu Car	General Electric
ACMU	1	6000 dc	1	4	100	80	57·7	130	85	61	1·8	1962-65	Pullman-Standard	General Electric

* Dual-voltage

Electric locomotives

Class	Wheel arrangement	Line voltage	Rated output hp	Max speed mph	Weight tonnes	No in service 1989	Year first built	Builders Mechanical parts	Builders Electrical equipment
E10B	Bo-Bo	600 dc	750	35	96	3	1952	General Electric	General Electric

Diesel railcars or multiple-units

Class	Cars per unit	Motor cars per unit	Motored axles per motor car	Transmission	Rated power (hp) per motor	Max speed mph	Weight short tons per car	Total seating capacity	Length per car ft	No in service 1989	Year first built	Builders Mechanical parts	Builders Engine & type	Builders Transmission
RDC-1	1	1	4	Hyd	275 (2 engines)	80	58·8	89	85	5	1951-53	Budd	GMC 6-110	Allison
SPV-2000	1	1	4	Hyd	360 (2 engines)	80	63·5	109	85	13*	1981	Budd	Detroit Diesel 8.V-92	Twin Disc

* 10 SPV-2000 owned by Metro-North Commuter Railroad
3 SPV-2000 owned by Connecticut Dept of Transportation and dedicated to Metro-North service territory

Diesel locomotives

Class	Wheel arrangement	Transmission	Rated power hp	Max speed mph	Total weight short tons	No in service 1989	Year first built	Builders Mechanical parts	Builders Engine & type	Builders Transmission
FL-9	B + A1A	Elec	1800	89	141	30	1957-60	EMD	GM 567 C	EMD
B23-7	B + B	Elec	2300	71	134	7	1978	General Electric	GE 12-7 FDL	General Electric
GP-7u	B + B	Elec	1500	65	124·5	1	1953	EMD	GM 567 BC	EMD
GP-9	B + B	Elec	1750	65	125·5	1	1955	EMD	GE 567 C	EMD
RS-3M	B + B	Elec	1200	45	126	1	1952	Alco	GM 567 B	General Electric

New Jersey Transit Rail Operations Inc

1160 Raymond Blvd, Newark, New Jersey 07102

Telephone: +1 201 468 8000
Telefax: +1 201 468 8039

Executive Director: Thomas Gagliano
Chief Operating Officer: George Warrington
Vice President & General Manager: Joseph Crawford Jr
Deputy General Manager, Line Operations: William Knapp
System Operations: Ron Potkul
Technical Operations: Robert Randall
Support Operations: Michael Rienzi
Director, Safety: Carmen Bianco
Director, Passenger Communications: Pat Ballard

Route length, owned: 511.4 km
Trackage rights: 208.7 km
Electrification, owned: 107.6 km at 25 kV 60 Hz; 26.4 km at 11 kV 25 Hz; 25.4 km at 12 kV 60 Hz
Trackage rights: 93.5 km at 11 kV 25 Hv

From the start of 1983 former Conrail commuter passenger operations over ex-Erie, Lackawanna, Jersey Central, Pennsylvania and New York & Long Branch lines in New Jersey were added to those already managed and directly run for the New Jersey Department of Transportation.

NJT carries some 70 000 riders each weekday over nine routes into Newark, Hoboken and New York. It is the employer of the train crews, owns the rolling stock and also much of the track-mileage, except that of Conrail and Amtrak, together with 145 rail stations. This territory's previous 106.9 route-km of 3 kV dc has been converted to 25 kV 60 Hz ac.

On the former Pennsylvania/Central of New Jersey Coast Line from New York Penn station to Bay Head Junction NJT operates its 'Jersey Arrow' emus, and trains hauled by GP40P, FP40H and rebuilt E8 diesel locomotives. The Northeast Corridor service from Penn station to Trenton is performed by 'Jersey Arrow' emus; the ex-CNJ Raritan Valley line by FP40H-powered push-pulls; the ex-Lackawanna Morris and Essex lines by emus; and the ex-Lackawanna Boonton, ex-Erie Main Bergen and ex-Erie Pascack Valley lines by push-pulls with U34CH, FP40H and F7 locomotive power.

On these last-mentioned ex-Lackawanna and Erie lines the cars are 147 Pullman-Standard Comet 1 type built 1971-73 and refurbished in 1987. Other push-pull operations have been recently refreshed with Comet II cars built by Bombardier. A further 45 Comet IIB cars were delivered in 1986–89, and 50 Comet III cars were to be delivered by Bombardier in early 1991.

In 1987 NJ Transit applied to the Urban Mass Transportation Administration (UMTA) for funds to assist in the purchase of safety equipment such as ATC and the mid-life, US$207 million rehabilitation of 230 Arrow III cars, 130 of the latter to feature conversion from dc to an ac propulsion system. A contract covering 100 cars including ac motor conversion was placed with ABB Traction Inc in 1989.

At the same time NJT was promised UMTA grants totalling US$283 million for 1989-90. This made possible an order for 15 ALP-44 electric locomotives, of similar characteristics to the AEM-7 used by Amtrak and others, to be supplied by ABB. Delivery was to begin in March 1990. They would cover the withdrawal of Arrow III cars for modernisation (see above).

Capital projects
In 1987 NJ Transit unveiled a programme of investments to assist the state in meeting increased public transit travel demands through the 1990s. Rail recommendations included:

Increasing the capacity of New York's Penn station from 20 to 30 trains to operate from New Jersey to Manhattan in the peak hour;

Construction of the Secaucus Transfer and the restoration of passenger service on the West Shore line to create a major New Jersey public transit crossroad, with the potential for a unique private/public funding partnership. The Transfer station, in The Meadowlands, would provide access to mid-town Manhattan for commuters on three NJ Transit lines now providing service from Bergen County to Hoboken;

Construction of the Kearny Connection to link the Morris and Essex lines to the Northeast Corridor. The project would provide Morris and Essex commuters

with rail service to Manhattan, and link Newark's Broad Street station with New York's Penn station giving Newark a second major commuter link to support the city's flourishing downtown growth;
Construction of the Bay Street Connection to link the Boonton line to the Montclair Branch of the Morris and Essex lines in Montclair;
Construction of the Waterfront Connection between the Northeast Corridor and the Morris and Essex lines tracks in Harrison to permit direct service to Hoboken and the New Jersey Waterfront for lines now serving Newark Penn station, the Northeast Corridor, Raritan Valley and North Jersey Coast lines;
Expansion of service on the heavily-travelled Northeast Corridor and North Jersey Coast lines.

Atlantic City line revival
The abandoned line between Atlantic City and Philadelphia has been rehabilitated for intercity (by Amtrak) and commuter rail service. A new terminal station at Atlantic City has been constructed, and to this NJ Transit began train service from Lindenwold in September 1989. Lindenwold is a transfer point with the PATCo rapid transit line to Camden and Philadelphia.

Motive power and rolling stock
In 1989 NJT deployed eight electric and 56 diesel locomotives. 292 emu cars, 327 other passenger cars and 125 freight cars.

Track
Rail: New rail standard 132 lb/yd (65.5 kg/m)
Cross ties (sleepers): Hardwood
Thickness: Main lines 178 × 229 mm, yards 152 × 203 mm
Spacing: Running lines 1989/km; yards 1802/km
Fastenings: 152 mm cut spike, drive-on rail anchors
Minimum curvature radius: Running lines 194 m, yards 122 m
Max axleload: 20 tonnes at unrestricted speed; locomotives to 32.7 tonnes at restricted speed

Electric locomotives

Class	Wheel arrangement	Line voltage	Rated power kw	Max speed km/h	Weight tonnes	No in service 1989	Year first built	Builders Mechanical parts	Electrical equipment
E60CH	Co-Co	25 kV 60 Hz 12·5 kV 60 Hz 11 kV 25 Hz	4476	192	183	8	1973	General Electric NY Air Brake WABCO	General Electric

Electric 'Arrow III' multiple-units

Class	Cars per unit	Line voltage	Motor cars per unit	Motored axles per motor car	Rated output (kw) per motor	Max speed km/h	Weight tonnes per car	Total seating capacity	Length per car mm	No in service 1989	Rate of acceleration m/s²	Year first built	Builders Mechanical parts	Electrical equipment
MA-1G	2	25 kV 60 Hz 12·5 kV 60 Hz 11 kV 25 Hz	2	4	120	168	120/119	119/112	25 908	68	2·5	1973	GE	GE
MA-1H	2	–	2	4	120	168	123/120	115/119	25 908	224	2·5	1977	GE	GE
MA-1J	1	–	1	4	120	168	128	119	25 908	30	2·5	1977	GE	GE

Diesel locomotives

Class	Wheel arrangement	Transmission	Rated power kW	Max speed km/h	Total weight tonnes	No in service 1989	Year first built	Builders Mechanical parts	Engine & type
GP40PH	Bo-Bo	Elec	2238	104	144	13	1988	EMD	EMD 16-645 E3B
GP40FH-2	Bo-Bo	Elec	2238	160	144	15	1987	EMD/Morrison-Knudsen	EMD 16-645 E3
SW1500	Bo-Bo	Elec	1119	104	125	3	1972	EMD	EMD 12-645
U34CH	Co-Co	Elec	2562	120	190	3	1971	GE	GE 7FDL16
F40PH-2	Bo-Bo	Elec	2238	164	129.5	17	1982	EMD	EMD 16-645E3B
GP-7	Bo-Bo	Elec	1119	104	123.4	2	1952	EMD	EMD 12-567B
SW-9	Bo-Bo	Elec	895	104	123.9	2	1952	EMD	EMD 12-567B
GP-9	Bo-Bo	Elec	1305	104	123.6	1	1955	EMD	EMD 12-567B

Northern Indiana Commuter Transportation District

33 E US Highway 12, Chesterton, Indiana 46304

Telephone: +1 219 926 5744

Following the sale of the Chicago South Shore & South Bend Railroad (qv), the authority was to take over full responsibility for its passenger services.

Northern Virginia Transportation Commission (NVTC)

2009 14th Street N, Suite 300, Arlington, Virginia 22201

Telephone: +1 703 524 3322

Executive Director: Richard K Taube

NVTC planned to launch commuter operations in the 1991 autumn between Fredericksburg and Washington, DC, principally over the Richmond Fredericksburg & Potomac, but including a short stretch of Conrail metals at the approach to Washington and between Manassas and Washington over Norfolk Southern tracks. The service will be known as Virginia Railway Express.

Orders for 28 passenger cars with an option for 10 more have been placed with Mitsui USA, which is having them built by Mafersa of Brazil. Morrison-Knudsen is supplying eight remanufactured diesel locomotives.

Southeastern Pennsylvania Transportation Authority (SEPTA)

Sovereign Building, 714 Market Street, Philadelphia, Pennsylvania 19106

Telephone: +1 215 574 7300

Chairman: J C Undercofler III
General Manager: L J Gambaccini
Deputy General Manager: H H Roberts Jr
Assistant General Manager, Surface: J K MCormick
  Railroad: J W Palmer
  Suburban: T M Cain

Regional Rail Division
1515 Market Street (6th Floor), Philadelphia, Pennsylvania 19102

Telephone: +1 215 574 8451

General Manager: L J Gambaccini
Director, Planning & Development: E K Skoropowski
Assistant General Manager, Operations:
  C W Thomas

Route Length: 558km
Electrification: 558 km at 12 kV 25 Hz ac

SEPTA operates a multi-modal network of public transportation services throughout the five-county region of Southeastern Pennsylvania. The railway portion of the transit network consists of 13 11 kV ac-electrified lines radiating outward from Philadelphia. The Regional Rail service is operated chiefly by a fleet of 335 electric multiple-unit cars.

The present SEPTA Regional Rail system was formed in 1984 when the commuter railroad networks formerly operated by the Pennsylvania and Reading Railroads were linked by a four-track connection beneath Central Philadelphia. SEPTA operates seven Regional Rail routes between suburban points through Central Philadelphia over 330 route-km of tracks owned by SEPTA, Amtrak and Conrail. Complementing service connections are made with passenger railroad services provided by Amtrak and NJ Transit rail operations.

In January 1989, SEPTA extended Regional Rail service 15.5 route-km over the Amtrak Northeast Corridor to Wilmington, Delaware, under contract to the Delaware Transportation Authority. SEPTA also began to operate dedicated feeder bus routes that function as rubber-tyred extensions of Regional Rail service to suburban employment centres.

By April 1990 all rolling stock was to be fitted with

Automatic Train Stop (ATS). This would entail withdrawal of the 60 year-old RER 'Reading Blues' fleet, in which ATSD could not be installed.

Traffic (million)	1986	1987	1988
Total passenger journeys	22.6	22.92	23.8

Finance (US$ million)	1986	1987	1988
Revenue	45.849	49.837	50.932

Expenditure	1986	1987	1988
Staff/personnel	61.3	68.83	73.86
Materials and services	35.79	44.79	46.68
Traction power	14.99	14.48	11.26
Other	11.38	15.7	18.26
Total	123.46	143.8	150.06

Type of coupler in standard use: N2A (emus) Tightlock Knuckle (push/pull cars)

Type of braking in standard use: 26C, PS68 Brake air and blended rheostatic (Silverliner IV cars)

Track
Rail: 140 PS and RE, 132 RE, 131 RE, 130 REHF, 115 RE, 112 RE, 107 NH, 100 PS
Cross ties (sleepers): Wood, thickness 175 × 200 mm
Spacing: 530 mm
Fastenings: Pandol and spike
Minimum curvature radius: 125 m
Max gradient: 1 in 25

AEM-7 locomotive and Bombardier push-pull cars

Electric railcars or multiple-units

Class	Cars per unit	Line voltage ac	Motor cars per unit	Motored axles per motor car	Rated output (kw) per motor	Max speed km/h	Weight tonnes per car	Total seating capacity	Length per car mm	No in service 1989	Rate of acceleration m/s^2	Year first built	Builders Mechanical parts	Builders Electrical equipment
RER	1	11 500	1	2	105	120	59·4	84	15 000	26	0·45	1931	Bethlehem Steel	General Electric
Silverliner 1	1	11 500	1	4	75	120	40·5	123	25 650	5	0·45	1958	Budd Co	Westinghouse
Silverliner 2	1	11 500	1	4	110	135	45·9	123-125	25 650	36	0·9	1963	Budd Co	General Electric
Silverliner 2	1	11 500	1	4	110	135	45·9	123-125	25 650	17	0·9	1964	Budd Co	General Electric
Silverliner 3	1	11 500	1	4	110	135	45·9	90-122	25 650	20	0·9	1967	St Louis Car Co	General Electric
Silverliner 4	1	11 500	1	4	140	150	54·2	125	25 650	47	0·9	1974–75	General Electric	General Electric
Silverliner 4	2	11 500	2	4	140	150	53·1	125	25 650	184	0·9	1975–76	General Electric	General Electric

Uruguay

State Railways Administration (AFE)
Administración de Ferrocarriles del Estado

Casilla de Correro 419, Calle La Paz 1095, Montevideo

Telephone: +598 2 905866
Telex: 04 718 afecent
Telefax: +598 2 921530

President: Juan Berchesi
Vice-President: Victor Delgado
Directors: Jesus Fernandez
　　　　　　Luis Oscar Nunes
　　　　　　J Fernandez
Secretary General: Carlos Cipolina
General Manager: E Monchek
Assistant General Managers, Technical:
　Maximo Dellacasa
　Ing Francisco Puppo
Manager, Commercial: D Del Guercio
Manager, Services; Ing Horacio Chapuis
Manager, Operations: Ing Jorge Camaño

Manager, Traction: Humberto Preziosi
Manager, Way and Works: Dario Herrera
Chief Signalling and Communications: Daniel Gosweiller
Sales Manager: Fidel Russo

Gauge: 1435 mm
Route length: 3002 km

New rail links with Argentina have been the major features of recent planning. Objectives include development of the littoral line and continued extension of the central line northwards from 329 km. A new 2.8 km line over the Salto Grande Dam to a link with the General Urquiza Division of Argentine Railways was opened in August 1982, following which a through Salto-Concordia (Argentina) passenger service was inaugurated.

Traffic (million)	1986	1987	1988
Freight tonnage	0.867	0.943	0.98
Freight tonne-km	204	212.8	213

Drastic cuts end passenger service
At the start of 1988 AFE was ordered by the Transport Minister to close a third of its route system, withdraw all passenger services (then amounting to 2.24 million journeys and 140 million passenger-km a year), and to cut its labour force by 70 per cent over the next 15 years. This was partly to reduce the railway's state subsidy, partly to justify a government investment of US$100 million in a 15-year rehabilitation of AFE.

Signalling
In 1988 AFE invited bids to re-equip its network with a radio-based signalling and communications system.

Traction and rolling stock
The railway operates 39 GE 1500hp and 20 Alsthom 825 hp diesel locomotives, 7 steam locomotives and 2491 freight cars.

Track
Rail: 20 kg/m (529 km); 30–40 kg/m (1361 km); 40–50 kg/m (969 km); 50 kg/m or heavier (132 km)
Sleepers: Steel and timber
Minimum curve radius: Generally 500 m; less than 500 m over 97 km
Sleepers: Steel and timber
Minimum curve radius: Generally 500 m; less than 500 m over 97 km

Venezuela

Venezuelan State Railways (IAFE)
Instituto Autónomo Ferrocarriles del Estado

PO Box 146, Avenida Lecuna, Parque Central, Torre Este, Piso 45, Caracas

Telephone: +58 2 509 3500
Telex: 28522
Telefax: +58 2 574 7021

President and General Manager: Eduardo Santos Castillo

Vice-President: Ibsen Alvarez
Comptroller: Luisalva Morales de Torres
Legal Adviser: Débora Hecker
Manager, Construction: Ibsen Alvarez
　Operations: Carlos E Isturiz
　Administration and Finance: Carmen Carmona
　Lands: Ing Ricardo Gosselain
　Planning and Budget: Winston Briceno
　Personnel: María de Lourdes Berti

Gauge: 1435 mm
Route length: 362.6 km

National Network Plan
Progress with the plan to reverse the closures of the 1950s and create a 3700 km rail system by 1990 is considerably slower than anticipated and in 1984 ambitions were scaled down to a system of only 1300 km. So far the West Central Trunk from Puerto Cabello southwest to Barquisameto and Acarigua is the only main line operational.

Meanwhile design of the long-planned new east-west Central Trunk route has proceeded. This would extend 228 km from Caracas to Puerto Cabello via Charallave, Cú, Maracay and Valencia. It has now been designated a national government project. Electrification at 25 kV ac is envisaged. At Puerto Cabello the project would connect with the existing railway.

In early 1990 bids from three consortia for construction of the first section of the line, from Caracas to

Cúa, were being evaluated. The contestants were Contuy, Ferrofuv-Fiven and Europeo-Venezolano. This first stage traverses difficult terrain and will involve significant tunnelling and bridging.

Two other new main lines are proposed. One, the 862 km South Eastern Trunk, would start in the heart of the country's iron ore fields and steel industry at Ciudad de Puerto Ordaz and head for Maturin. From there a branch would lead to a deep-water port on the Gulf of Cariaco. The other fork would run from Maturin via Zaraza, Valle de La Pascua and San Juan de los Morros to a junction with the Central Trunk at Capua. Annual freight traffic of 15 million tonne-km is forecast for this Trunk.

Also planned is a South Western Trunk of 355 km connecting Ciudad de Maracaibo with La Fria. This would link the coal and phosphate mines in Táchira, Santo Domingo and Apure with the port of Santos Luzardo de Guasdualito on the Orinoco river.

Rapid transit scheme

A recent proposal regarded initially as a high priority concerns a 120 km/h rapid transit line of 32 km from Caracas to the Caribbean port of La Guaira, to be electrified at 1.5 kV dc and adhesion-worked despite the difference of 1000 m in altitude between Caracas and the coastline, also serving Simon Bolivar Airport. Construction was in 1982 entrusted to a West German group comprising MAN, Deutsche Eisenbahn Consulting, Siemens, Ferrostaal and AEG-Telefunken, which would supply 31 three-car emus (by MAN), signalling, track, traction current supply apparatus and a maintenance depot. The project lapsed, but was revived in 1986 with a commission for Sofrétu of France to study the scheme in detail.

Traffic	1988	1989
Freight tonnes	290 507	253 049
Freight tonne-km	40 247 144	38 627 405
Passenger-km	28 891 720	37 626 969
Passenger journeys	239 664	329 228

Finances (Bolivars 000)		
Revenue	1988	1989
Passengers and baggage	2774	3585
Freight, parcels and mail	22 124	29 433
Other income	37	66
Total	24 936	33 085
Expenditure		
Staff/personnel	48 202	88 343
Materials and services	8 195	23 377
Depreciation	12 706	8 400
Total	69 103	120 120

New coal line in suspense

In September 1982 the government authorised immediate construction of a 100 km line to ferry coal from a mine at Guasare, in the northwest of the country, to a power station and planned steelworks at Sur Maracaibo, on the western shore of Lake Maracaibo. Engineering design of the project was entrusted to MKI International-Cosa, an organisation including Morrison-Knudsen and a Venezuelan company. However, the contract was suspended and no construction work has been done.

Track

Rail employed is ASCE 49 kg/m and UIC 60kg/m on Dywidag concrete sleepers (2500 × 227 × 300 mm) spaced 1670 per km and 1336 per km in curves. Minimum curve radius is 800 metres, maximum gradient 1.4%, maximum permitted axle-load 31.75 tonnes, and maximum speed is 70 km/h.

Motive power and rolling stock

IAFE operates 11 diesel locomotives; types comprise Also M420 2000hp, GM-EMD GP9 and GP15-1 and GE 415 and 150 hp shunters. Other rolling stock comprises 14 passenger cars and 208 freight wagons. In 1988 100 mineral wagons were ordered from Cobrasma of Brazil.

Type of coupler in standard use: US Type E
Type of braking in standard use: Air

Viet-Nam

Viet-Nam Railways (DSVN)
Duong Sat Viet Nam

180 Nam Bo Street, Hanoi

Telephone: 54998; 58281

Director-General and Vice-Minister, Railways: Trau Lu
Vice Directors-General
  Administration: Trau Mau
  Rolling Stock: Dau Cao Hy
  Civil Engineering: Nguyen Tri
  Traffic: Nguyen Van Truy
  General Services: Pham Van Giap
  Development: Nguyen Van Tu

Gauge: 1435 mm; 1000 mm; mixed gauge
Route length: 170 km; 2500 km; 230 km

The railway is administered in three Divisions: Northern, based on Hanoi; Central, based on Donang; and Southern, based on Ho Chi Minh City.

The bulk of the network is formed by seven main lines: Hanoi-Ho Chi Minh City (1725.8km); Hanoi-Langson (148.5 km); Gialam-Haiphong (96.4km); Dong Anh-Quan Trieu (54.1 km); Kep-Halong (106 km); Kep-Thai Nguyen (55.6 km); and Yen Vien-Lao Kai (272.4 km). Hanoi has a western orbital route, built in the 1980s, which diverges from the main line to the north at Dong Anh, crosses the Red River on the Thang Long bridge, and joins the southern main line to Ho Chi Minh City at Thanh Tri. The orbital line is mixed gauge as far as Ha Dong, metre-gauge for the remaining distance to Thanh Tri.

Rehabilitation

A mammoth rehabilitation task remains. Trackwork is largely ancient and in poor condition, and a particularly critical problem is the state of the system's very numerous bridges and viaducts — 1658 of them, with a total length of some 39 km. Over many metal bridges a speed limit of 5 km/h is imposed because of corrosion or other weaknesses.

In 1989 the USSR undertook to fund new rolling stock and modernisation projects on the Hanoi-Ho Chi Minh City line.

Traffic

In 1989 the railway recorded 13 million passengers and 3.6 million tonnes of freight. The Hanoi-Ho Chi Minh City line logs 81 per cent of the passenger-km and 57 per cent of the freight tonne-km. By the end of the century traffic on this route is expected to have risen 60 per cent. Over the system as a whole forecast traffic by the end of the decade is 32 million passenger journeys and 5.2 million tonnes of freight.

Traction and rolling stock

In 1989 the railway owned 160 steam and 496 diesel locomotives, but of the latter only 365 were serviceable and only 180 or so in daily use. Only half a stock of about 1100 passenger cars and 5800 freight cars were serviceable. Delivery has lately been taken from India's Projects and Equipment Corporation of 15 1350 hp, 251 D-engined diesel-electric Co-Co locomotives, similar to Indian Railway's Type YDM4; and from Belgian industry of 16 1760 hp, 84-tonne diesel-electric Co-Cos with Cockerill engines. ČKD Praha of Czechoslovakia has delivered 10 1000 hp, 56-tonne Type DEV-736 diesel-electric locomotives for metre-gauge. Other diesel traction includes GE 00hp and Russian-built Type TY 400hp units.

Yugoslavia

Yugoslav Railways (JZ)
Zajednica Jugoslovenskih Zeleznica
(Community of Yugoslav Railways)

PO Box 563, Nemanjina 6/1, Belgrade 11000

Telephone: +38 11 685 722
Telex: 12495 yu zjz
Telfax: +38 11 683 548

General Manager: Nikola Zurković
Management Board
  Modernisation: Trajko Panev
  Technical: Mihallo Živadinović
  Organisation: Dr Petar Kovačević
  Commercial: Vene Gligorov
  Financial: Tima Ilin
  Development: Dr Streten Vuković
Regional Managers
  Belgrade: Petar Stošić
  Sarajevo: Alija Behmen
  Zagreb: Bartol Ivanuša
  Skoplje: Panče Kovačev
  Ljubljana: Jurij Pirš
  Titograd: Drago Vučinić
Directors
  Movements: Živojin Gotić
  Transport: Rotomir Vidaković
  Wagon Control: Djuradi Mastorović

Class 442 thryistor-controlled 25 kV 50 Hz ac Bo-Bo electric locomotive by Rade Koncar

Traction and Rolling Stock: Petar Gašić
Track: Gojko Vučković
Signalling and Telecommunications: Velibor Damjanović
Standardisation: Gregor Savinšek
Modernisation: Marko Tomanić
Commercial: Dr Savo Vasiljević
Finance: Dr Milka Damjanović
Law: Dr jur Tomislav Curic
Administration: Miloš Živić
International Relations: Vilibald Jurak

Gauge: 1435 mm
Route length: 9349 km
Electrification: 3004 km at 25 kV 50 Hz;
 756 km at 3 kV dc

Restructure under way

In conformity with the national move towards a market-driven economy, JZ embarked in 1989 on restructure as a market-oriented business. The government formed a special council to monitor and assist progress, and in June 1989 took a major step towards establishing conditions under which JZ could function as a business enterprise by adopting the Social Compact on Finance of Railway Infrastructure. This would equalise the previous imbalance whereby the share of infrastructure cost in the average JZ tariff was reckoned to be 29.47 per cent, compared with 7.74 per cent for air, and 3.44 per cent for both road and inland waterway transport.

The Federal government was next expected to announce measures to tackle the other problems hampering the transmutation of JZ into a public enterprise. As well as JZ's losses, these included the disposal of surplus staff. Since the mid-1980s the unhealthy state of the national economy has retarded capital projects. At the same time JZ freight traffic has been severely hit by road completion and its market share has slumped from 50 to 40 per cent.

Other projects besides the market-oriented restructure set by the Assembly of the Community of Yugoslav Railways in mid-1989 included: High Speed; Modernisation of the Jesenice/Sežana-Gevgelija/ Dimitrovgrad trunk route; Marketing; Transit Development; Intermodal Transport Development; and Development of Information Systems.

Traffic

In the passenger sector 1989 was marked by moves to segregate the timetabling of international and domestic trains, so as to improve the market orientation of the domestic service. In the latter more high-quality trains were introduced, including a new Zagreb-Belgrade train, the 'Matoš', for business travellers. Also improved was the seasonal train service to Adriatic coastal resorts. International developments included the 'Atika', a summer train conveying sleeping cars betwen Munich, Zagreb, Belgrade and Athens.

The number of international TEEM, TEE and intermodal services was increased. The percentage of unit train operation in domestic traffic has risen, and on 20 routes 'Cargo' trains have been introduced offering direct service between major centres of production and consumption. Provision for container transport has been slow to develop, but is now to be pressed ahead. A Belgrade terminal was opened in 1988 to complement those at Skopje and Ljubljana.

Finance (million dinars)
Revenues
Passengers and baggage	321.4
Freight, parcels and mail	1 752.9
Other income	1 425.1
Total	3 499.4

Expenditure
Staff/personnel	965.8
Materials and services	1 165.3
Depreciation	669.1
Financial charges	494.8
Other	461.9
Total	3 756.9

Investment

Financial difficulties are severely limiting JZ ability to meet its investment needs. In 1989 it could only complete 83.7 of 236 km of planned track renewal, and its locomotive, passenger car and freight wagon purchases were limited to 21.7, 19.6 and 3.8 per cent respectively of what had been planned. Particularly inadequate was investment in intermodal and information systems.

Type 713 diesel-hydraulic multiple-unit for 'Green Train' services

Class 412/16 emus manufactured by RVR Riga, USSR, at Titograd

Traffic control centre at Skopje

RAILWAY SYSTEMS / Yugoslavia

Traffic (million)	1985	1986	1987	1988	1989
Passenger journeys	126.385	131.7	119.8	115.7	117.5
Passenger-km	12 060	12 399	11 881	11 449	11 693
Freight tonnes	90.7	89.8	84.2	85.57	84.82
Freight tonne-km	28 700	27 573	26 070	25 414	25 921

The pressing need is to upgrade the Jesenice/Sežana-Gevgelija/Dimitrograd trunk, 1463 km long, which carries 80 per cent of JZ transit traffic and is a key link between Europe and the Near and Middle East. One aim is to complete the route's fitness for 160 km/h, which will cost US$2300 million spread over the rest of the 1990s. In 1989 the European Investment Bank loaned US$138 million towards this project, and JZ wil also apply US$200 million of a 7th World Bank loan to it.

A new line is being built from Tuzla to Zvornik (45.3 km). Its major civil engineering feature is the 4.8 km Krizevici tunnel. In early 1990 70 per cent of the civil engineering was complete. This will form part of a prospective new southern trunk route parallel to that from Jesenice to Gevgelija when another new line from Loznica to Valjevo (Serbia) (68 km) can be added.

High-speed line planned

In December 1989 design preparations were begun for a 200–250 km/h double-track line from Belgrade via Novi Sad to Subotica. It would be connected to a prospective high-speed line from Vienna to Budapest.

Electrification

Recent electrification has been at 25 kV 50 Hz, but in the far west of the country a few routes retain the 3 kV dc of early electrification. There was no extension in 1989. JZ had planned to convert the existing Zagreb-Rijeka route's 3 kV dc to 25 kV 50 Hz ac, and to double-track some of its length, but this was not economically possible. Conversion of voltage from Zagreb as far as Srpske Moravice was achieved in 1987.

After four years' work, electrification from Skopje to Gevgelija, on the Greek border, was finished in March 1987. Remote control of the electrification equipment was to be commissioned in 1990. The whole of the 1239 km axis from Jesenice to Gevgelija is now under wires.

The 129 km line from the Italian frontier at Sezana to Ljublijana is one of JZ's busiest, carrying some 10 million tonnes of freight a year, or 11 per cent of JZ's gross. It is still electrified at 3 kV dc and is on the agenda for conversion to 25 kV ac. Meanwhile, it is to be comprehensively realigned and relaid over a five-year period, equipped with new loops, and fitted with track-to-train radio (already operative over some 1500 km of JZ route and fitted to 400 traction units).

In the longer term, if and when finance allows, JZ aims to electrify the 386 km Macedonian transversal from Lapovo to Skopje and its 75 km Kralijevo-Pozega offshoot; the 134 km line between Subotica, near the Hungarian border, and Vinkovici, on the Belgrade-Zagreb route; also several Bosnian branches, including the 79 km between Tuzla and Brčko. To be electrified too is the 84 km line from Belgrade Dunav to Vrsac.

Data transmission systems

In 1989 JZ decided to begin integration with the HERMES and DOCIMEL computer systems of European railways. In November 1989 JZ's UNITS data transmission system, already operational in the Ljubljana, Zagreb and Sarajevo areas, was extended to Novi Sad. UNITS affords real-time monitoring and control of all traction, train crews, rolling stock and traffic, and programmes the operation of marshalling yards and distribution of freight wagons.

New Belgrade through route

Restraint of government expenditure has protracted the massive reformation of the Belgrade network, begun in 1976, which aims to supersede the dead-end central station and its inconvenient approach from Zagreb with a new 12-track one served by a through route tunnelled beneath the city.

The key elements of the scheme are a north-south line from Pont de Pancevo, near the Danube, to a junction with the existing south-eastern exit from Belgrade's terminus beyond Topcider; and, at National Library on this new line, a triangular junction with another new route threading the city via a route through central station, then bridging the Sava River to rejoin the present exit from Belgrade terminus to Zagreb at Novi Beograd. Thus, the finished scheme

Diesel locomotives

Class	Wheel arrangement	Trans-mission	Rated power kW	Max speed km/h	Wheel dia mm	Total weight tonnes	No in service 1989	Year first built	Builders Mechanical parts	Builders Engine	Builders Transmission
641	Bo-Bo	Elec	441	80	1040	59	110	1960	Mávag	Ganz	Ganz
642	Bo-Bo	Elec	606	80	1100	60·5	97	1960	Dj Djakovic	MGO	Br & Lotz
643	Bo-Bo	Elec	680	80	1100	67·2	51	1964	Br & Lotz/Dj Dj	MGO	Br & Lotz
644	A1A-A1A	Elec	1213	90	1016	79·5	25	1975	Macosa	GM	GM
645	A1A-A1A	Elec	1820	120		100	34	1981	GMF/Dj Dj	GM	GM
661	Co-Co	Elec	1933	124	1016	102	217	1961	GM	GM	GM
662	Co-Co	Elec	1212	120	1100	89	2	1965	Dj Djakovic	MGO/Dj Dj	R Končar/Sever
663	Co-Co	Elec	2426	124	1016	111	14	1972	GM	GM	GM
664	Co-Co	Elec	1617	124	1016	93	84	1972	GM	GM	GM
665	Co-Co	Elec	2022	127		111	10	1972	MLW	MLW/Alco	GE
731	C	Hyd	294	60	950	40	34	1958	Jenbach/Dj Dj	Jenbach	Voith L24
732	C	Hyd	441	80	950	42	109	1969	Dj Djakovic	Jenbach	Voith L26
733	C	Hyd	441	60	1250	46	32	1968	Dj Djakovic	MGO/Dj Dj	Voith L26
734	B-B	Hyd	478	60	1250	48	38	1960	MAK	Maybach GT06	Voith
743	B-B	Hyd	1176	120	950	60		1977	Dj Djakovic	MGO/V16	Voith

RK: Rade Koncar Zagreb. Br & L: Brissonneau & Lotz

Electric locomotives

Class	Wheel arrangement	kV	Line current type	Rated power kW	Max speed km/h	Wheel dia mm	Total weight tonnes	Length mm	No in service 1989	Year first built	Builders Mechanical parts	Builders Electrical equipment
342	Bo-Bo	3	dc	2000/2280	120	1250	79	15 800	40	1968	Ansaldo	Ansaldo
362	Bo-Bo-Bo	3	dc	2640/3150	120	1250	112	18 400	49	1961	Ansaldo	Ansaldo
363	Co-Co	3	dc	2750/2830	120	1100	115	20 100	38	1975	Alsthom	Alsthom
441	Bo-Bo	25	50 Hz ac	3400/4080	140	1250	78	15 500	284	1967	ASEA/R Končar	ASEA/R Končar
442	Bo-Bo	25	50 Hz ac	4400	160	1250	82	14 954	16	1983	Rade Koncar	Rade Koncar
461	Co-Co	25	50 Hz ac	5100/5400	120	1250	126	19 800	100	1972	Electroputere	Electroputere

Diesel railcars or multiple-units

Class	Cars per unit	Motor cars per unit	Motored axles per motor car	Trans-mission	Rated power (kW) per motor	Max speed km/h	Weight tonnes per car (M-motor T-trailer)	Total seating capacity	Length per car mm (M-motor T-trailer)	No of cars in service 1989	Year first built	Builders Mechanical parts	Builders Engine & type	Builders Transmission
610	5	2	4	Elec	277	120	M 59·3 T 43·4	204	M 25 600 T 24 700	6	1972	Br & Lotz	MG0	Br & Lotz
711	2	2	2	Hyd	235	120	46·7	116	47 160	10	1969	MBB	Mercedes	Voith
712	3	1	4	Hyd	120	120	M 34·1 T 26·8	145	M 17 730 T 17 700	69	1975	Macosa	MAN	Voith
811	4	2	2	Mech	370	118	M 61·0 T 37·5	151	94 760*	6	1959	Ganz-Mávag	Ganz-Mávag	Ganz-Mávag
812	2	1	1	Mech	90	90	M 21·2 T 16·2	123	M 13 330 T 13 330	151	1955	Goša Ganz-Mávag	MAN	MAN
813	2	1	1	Mech	150	100	M 44·5 T 34·6	150	M 22 110 T 22 110	47	1973	Fiat	Fiat	Fiat
713	2	1	2	Hyd	100	120	M 35·4 T 27·7	92	M 23 580 T 23 580	27	1983	MBB	Mercedes	Voith

* Four-car set in total

will create through running from both northeast and southeast to the Zagreb direction. The project involves in all 13 km of tunnelling, as well as an elevated approach to the new Sava River bridge, and these works were finished early in 1983. In late 1984 a suburban service was launched between the partially-finished main station and Novi Beograd. A connection linking together the lines from Nis, Bar and Mala Krsna was completed in 1988 to enable almost all Belgrade suburban and several main-line services to use the new station. That leaves the subterranean north-south line from Vrsac to Pancerb still to be built.

Signalling

In 1989 modernisation of equipment proceeded on the Jesenice-Gevgelija trunk. The work included installation of automatic block, automatic train stop, automation of level crossings and CTC. In preparation for higher speeds an ATP speed-control system is to be applied to the whole trunk route. Preparations were made for an electronic signalling installation at Zagreb.

Installation of track-to-train radio communication continued. It was completed between Niš and Preševo, and between Zidani and Most and Maribor, and proceeded between Sežana and Ljubljana.

Traction and rolling stock

At the start of 1990 JZ owned 26 steam, 522 electric and 849 diesel locomotives, 133 emu cars, 158 dmu power cars and 133 trailers, 2530 hauled passenger cars (including 188 sleeping, 162 couchette and 10 restaurant cars) and 52 925 freight wagons.

Acquisitions in 1988-89 included: 17 Class 442 electric locomotives from Rade Končar; 10 four-car emus from RVR Riga of the USSR; 18 UIC Type Z 200km/h, 5 Type Y sleeping and three postal cars from Goša, Yugoslavia; and 873 freight wagons from Yugoslav industry. Other recent additions to the diesel stock have been 38 surplus German Federal Railway Class 260/261 diesel-hydraulic shunters, designated JZ Class 734.

In May 1989 the Fiat ETR401 'Pendolino' prototype tilt-body train-set was demonstrated on JZ's 3 kV dc routes.

Tracks

Rail: S-49 (49.43 kg/m) and UIC 60 (60.34 kg/m)
Cross ties (sleepers): Wooden, 2600x260x160 mm; concrete, 2400x300x192mm.
Spacing: 1667/km
Fastenings: K, SKL-2 and Pandrol
Minimum curvature radius: 250 m
Max gradient: 2.5%
Max axleload: 22.5 tonnes

Electric railcars or multiple-units

Class	Cars per unit	Line voltage	Motor cars per unit	Motored axles per motor car	Rated output (kW) per motor	Max speed km/h	Weight tonnes per car (M-motor T-trailer)	Total seating capacity	Length per car mm (M-motor T-trailer)	Rate of acceleration m/s²	No of cars in service 1989	Year first built	Builders Mechanical parts	Builders Electrical equipment
311	3-4	3 kV dc	2	4	174	110	M 70 T 50.4	180-256	M 21 770 T 20 800	0.65	32	1964	Pafawag	Dolmel
411	3	25 kV ac	1	4	300	120	156	234	72 400*	0.6	48	1977	Ganz-Mávag	Ganz-Electric
412	4	25 kV ac	2	4	170	120	M 67.96 T 59.5	294	102 200	0.72	47	1981	RVR Riga	RVR Riga

* Three-car set in total

Zaïre

National Office of Transport & Communications (ONATRA)

BP 1 228, Kinshasa 1

Telephone: +243 12 22109/24 736

Minister: S K Milombe
President: U Kyamitala
Director, Land Transport: I Fingwafingwa

Gauge: 1067 mm
Route length: 366 km
ONATRA operates the Kinshasa-Matadi line under contract to SNCZ (see below)

Société Nationale des Chemins de Fer Zaïrois (SNCZ)

PO Box 297, Lubumbashi, Shaba Region

Telephone: +243 2 223430
Telex: 41056 sncz

President: B Mbatshi
Deputy Director-General: Pierre Meyreau
Director, Finance: Rubuz Difand
Director, Commercial: S Ngoy
Director, Operations: J F Strumane
Director, Administration: K Yandi
Director, Technical: Mbuyi Kapaya

Gauge: 1067 mm; 1000mm; 600mm
Route length: 3621 km; 125km; 1026 km

Electrification: 858 km of 1067 mm-gauge at 25 kV 50 Hz

SNCZ was created in 1974 by the merger of five former railways: La Compagnie des Chemins de Fer Kinshasa-Dilolo-Lubumbashi (KDL); Les Chemins de Fer des Grands Lacs (CFL); Matadi-Kinshasa (CFMK); Mayumbe (CFM); and Chemins de Fer Vicinaux Zaïrois (CVZ). SNCZ is state-owned.

The former KDL railway serves the important mining centres of the Shaba-Lubumbashi, Likasi, Kolwezi and Mososhi, and other important mining and industrial areas such as the manganese mine at Kisenge, cement works at Lubudi, collieries at Leuna, diamond mines at Mbuji-Mayi, etc. Expanding agricultural and forest product industries have developed along the line of its route. The electrified territory is the 606 km of ex-KDL line from Lubumbashi to Kamina, and part of the branch from the line's mid-point at Tenke to the Angolan border at Dilolo, 252 km.

The isolated Ubundu-Kisangani line is metre-gauge. The 600mm gauge, also isolated, is found on the Bumba-Mungbere line and its Bondo branch. Both these sections are in the east of the country. All SNCZ lines are single-track.

Internationally, SNCZ connects at Dilolo with the CF de Benguela (CFB) in Angola for access to the Atlantic port of Lobito; at Sakania with Zambia Railways and further on, Zimbabwe Railways and South Africa's Spoornet; and via Zambia with the Tazara railway for access to Dar-es-Salaam. However, the Lobito route, the most direct for Zaire's copper exports, has long been unusable because of the Angolan civil war. Half of the country's mineral exports have at present to take the 3500 km route via Zimbabwe to South African ports because of the limited capacity of the port of Dar es Salaam in Tanzania and other operational difficulties on the Tazara route, which is little used.

Voie Nationale handicaps

At present the principal export-import route is the so-called Voie Nationale. It consists of a rail segment Sakania to Ilebo, then river transport to Kinshasa, and finally use of the isolated rail segment from Kinshasa to the port of Matadi. The route's confinement to the territory of Zaire offsets the handicaps of its transhipments between river and road.

Plans to obviate the transhipments by building a new railway from Ilebo to Kinshasa are stalled by lack of finance. Likewise unfulfilled is a scheme to project the railway at Matadi via a new road-and-rail bridge over the Zaïre River, completed in 1984 by a Japanese consortium, to the future deep-water port of Banana, down river from Boma.

Finance

Since 1985 SNCZ expenditure has risen much faster than its revenue. As a result, from a slight surplus in 1985, the railway has fallen into rapidly rising loss, which in 1989 reached 46.7 billion Zaire.

Rehabilitation Project

A US$86 million credit from the African Development Association plus funds from other sources, including a US$75 million World Bank credit, was obtained in 1988/89 for renovation of the Lubumbashi Ilebo and Kinshasha-Matadi rail segments of the Voie Nationale. In 1989 the government looked set to obtain US$280 million for a major recovery programme, to include new electric locomotives, 300 km of track rehabilitation, and workshops and telecommunications equipment.

Electrification

At the end of 1980 Deutsche Eisenbahn Consulting completed a World Bank-financed study and advocated an extension of 25 kV 50 Hz ac electrification to the 365 km Matadi-Kinshasa 1067 mm-gauge railway. The scheme was forecast to cost over Z200 million. It would exploit hydro-electric power from plants on the Zaïre River at Inga and Zouga. The consultants proposed use of 2600 kW six-axle locomotives capable of working 1000-tonne trains. However, the World Bank has refused to finance execution of electrification.

Signalling

Colour-light signalling is being installed on the suburban section of the Kinshasa-Matadi line by Siemens, with the aid of a Federal German loan. Other improvements in the Kinshasa area are to include a new branch line south of the city, to be built with Japanese financial aid.

In 1988 Canac International Inc was awarded a C$4.3 million contract to rehabilitate and enhance telecommunications capabilities, supported by funding from the World Bank. Completion was scheduled for mid-1989.

When 23 existing microwave relay towers would have been rehabilitated and 52 new VHF ones installed between Kamina and Ilebo, SNCZ technicians would be trained to maintain both the microwave network, the VHF/FM system, and associated communications installations.

Traffic

	1986	1987	1988	1989
Freight tonne-km (million)	1834	1677	1698	1732
Passenger-km (million)	330	359.4	400	260

Traction and rolling stock

At the start of 1989 SNCZ owned, for 1067mm gauge operation, 86 line-haul and 59 shunter diesel locomotives, 51 electric locomotives, 282 passenger cars, 30 railcars and 4793 freight wagons. Metre-gauge stock comprised 3 diesel locomotives, 9 passenger cars and 78 freight wagons; and 600mm-gauge stock,

14 diesel locomotives, 5 diesel railcars, 16 passenger cars and 329 freight wagons.

In late 1987 Zaïre's National Transport Office signed a contract with Alsthom for supply of seven Type AD26C 2500 hp, single-cab diesel locomotives with Alco-Bombardier V12 engines, scheduled to be delivered around mid-1989. The contract also called for supply of a package of spare parts and was financed by the Caisse Centrale de Coopération Economique (CCCE). The locomotives will be used by ONATRA between Kinshasha and Matadi.

In 1989 ABB was contracted to supply 12 1000kW diesel locomotives to a design derived from Italian Railways' Type D145.2000, with asynchronous three-phase ac motors.

Track
Standard rail: 29.3 and 40 kg/m on KDL; 24.4 and 29.3 kg/m on CFL; 33.4 and 40 kg/m on ONATRA CFMK; 18 kg/m on ONATRA CFM; 9 to 33.4 kg/m elsewhere
Joints: Fishplates and bolts
Cross ties (sleepers): Chiefly steel, also wood and concrete
Spacing: 1250/km plain track, 1500 km in curves
Rail fastenings: By lugs of clips and bolts to steel sleepers. RN flexible fastenings to concrete sleepers
Max curvature: 100 m
Max gradient: 15%
Max altitude: 1614 at Dilongo-Yulu near Tenke on Bukama line
Max permitted speed
Electrified lines: 52 km/h
All other lines: 45 km/h
Max axleload: 15 tons nominal; 20 tons in special cases

Diesel locomotivies

Class	Wheel arrangement	Transmission	Rated power hp	Total weight tonnes	Year first built	Builders
Line-haul						
1200	A1A-A1A	Elec	1500	80	1968	Hitachi
1300	Co-Co	Elec	1650	87.3	1969	General Electric
1400	Co-Co	Elec	1650	87.3	1969	General Electric
1500	Bo-Bo	Elec	1310	56.5	1967	Krupp Krauss-Maffei
61/63	0-6-0	Hyd	250	13.5	1955	Atelier Metallurgique Tubize
81-85	B-B	Hyd	510	31	1969	Nippon Sharyo
86-92	B-B	Hyd	510	32	1974	Nippon Sharyo
Shunters						
71/73	0-4-0	Hyd	335	16	1958	Cockerill
1161-1173	0-2-0	Hyd	320	30	1965/68	Cockerill
1201-1241	B-B	Hyd	510	45	1968/69/72	Hitachi Kawasaki
501-510	B-B	Hyd	660	40	1973	Thyssen-Henschel
1011	2-8-0	–	1000	58	1959	ARB FUF/HSP
21/22/25	0-6-0	–	110	16	1958	SA Moteur Moes
506-508	Bo-Bo	–	60	40	1980	Waremme

Electric locomotives

Class	Wheel arrangement	Line voltage	Rated output kW	Max speed km/h	Weight tonnes	Year first built	Builders
2200	Bo-Bo	25 kV 50 Hz ac	1620	65	76	1956	ACEC
2300	Bo-Bo	25 kV 50 Hz ac	1505	65	73.7	1958	ACEC
2400	Bo-Bo	25 kV 50 Hz ac	1620	70	60	1960	ACEC
2450	Bo-Bo	25 kV 50 Hz ac	1620	75	60	1964 1970	ACEC
2500	Bo-Bo	25 kV 50 Hz ac	1600	70	62	1969 (5) 1972	Hitachi
2600	Bo-Bo	25 kV 50 Hz ac	2400	60	93	1976	Hitachi

Zambia

Ministry of Power, Transport & Communications

PO Box 50065, Block 33, Fairley Road, Ridgeway, Lusaka

Telephone: +260 1 215080/213211/213612
Telex: 41680 lusaka

Minister, Transport: Nephas Tembo
Permanent Secretary: N B Nyoni

Zambia Railways Ltd (ZR)

PO Box 80935, Corner of Buntungwa Street and Ghana Avenue, Kabwe

Telephone: +260 5 222201
Telex: 81000, 81230

Chairman: Oliver Chama
Managing Director: D B Mhango
Director, Technical Services: M S Shankaya
 Traffic & Marketing: N Makonde
 Finance: C Sengebwila
 Personnel and Administration: L Y Kalumba
 Corporate Planning: C C Ndyamba
 Public Relations : G C Sikazwe
Corporate Planning Manager: F Kangwa
Company Secretary and Legal Counsel: D H Lwiindi
Personnel Manager: Ms L Mufuzi
Marketing Manager: R Yikona
Chief Traffic Manager: D E Mwape
Purchasing and Stores Manager: C C Musonda
Data Processing Manager: H Kafwembe
Financial Manager: B Balasigamanay
Chief Internal Auditor: M R Musyani
General Manager, Workshops: B T Ching'andu
Corporate Planning Manager, Project Evaluation: B Hibajene
 Strategic Planning: I H Sichula
Chief of Safety: E M Ntalasha
Chief Civil Engineer: A R Udayansankar
Chief Mechanical & Electrical Engineer: B Lungu
Chief Signal and Telecommunications Engineer: H Nyimbili

Gauge: 1067 mm
Route length: 1273 km

Formerly part of Rhodesia Railways, Zambia Railways was segregated as an autonomous system in 1976. It comprises the old RR system north of the Victoria Falls Bridge, to which was added in 1970 the 164 km Zambesi Sawmills Railway from Livingstone to Mulobezi. Since its independence, ZR has been handicapped by the political crises in the region and the problems of some neighbouring railways, which have clouded definition of the landlocked country's rail routes to the sea ports with uncertainty. Rail outlets are of critical importance to Zambia's copper industry, which generates 90 per cent of its exports. The Tazara Railway's operating difficulties have restricted the potential of its route to Dar es Salaam, originally envisaged as Zambia's primary export rail route, and like the Benguela Railway to Lobito this route has been affected by the unrest to the west. Assignment of copper traffic to the Tazara or Victoria Falls routes is decided by the government.

Reorganisations as limited company

In 1979 the government moved to end unfettered competition between road and rail, influenced by concern to limit high-priced oil imports and highway wear and tear. ZR was brought within the orbit of ZIMCO, a holding company for all state-owned enterprises and which already embodies the country's two road haulage companies.

An investment plan for five years was developed during 1985 and identified projects valued at US$207 million as required to sustain the operations of the company. Its first stage, valued at US$80 million, was secured with the help of the International Development Association, the African Development Bank and others. The funds were applied to the rehabilitation of track, purchase of signalling and telecommunications equipment, replacement of rolling stock, purchase of various spare parts, training and technical assistance. (In 1990 the contract with RITES was extended for a further three years.) Also included was the purchase of various computer software to establish a management information system which will improve information flow in the company.

Traffic

Apart from the constraints of fallible equipment on performance, traffic growth has been hobbled by several factors: slow turn-round of wagons at customers' sidings and on neighbouring railways; inflation and the depreciation of the Kwacha, which has greatly increased the costs of imported inputs; and diversion of copper traffic to the Tazara route coupled with the loss of substantial amount of traffic to road transport.

However, an express freight service which has cut transit times between Kitwe and Livingstone, for example, to 40 hours as opposed to the previous timing of 100 hours, has achieved encouraging results. The copper mining industry has been a major beneficiary of the new service, which ZR hopes to sell to other companies for the transport of lead ore and manganese, sugar and chemical products. A key factor in the success has been the introduction of CTC.

Link with Malawi

In 1989 the government released funds to complete a 24 km line from Chipata to the Malawi border at Mchinji.

Traffic (million)	1985	1988
Total freight tonnage	4.9	4.6
Total freight tonne-km	1565.496	1335
Total passenger-km	558.176	422
Total passenger journeys	1.8	1.9

Electrification

In 1981 DEConsult was commissioned to undertake a feasibility study of electrification of the 421 km route between Kabwe and Nkana-Kitwe at 25 kV ac 50 Hz. Presented in 1982 and endorsed by ZR, the results of the study remain under consideration by the government. DEConsult studied a basic scheme covering the 565 km between Ndola and Choma, which bears about 65 per cent of ZR's freight, and for which the electrification cost was put at US$92.3 million; and addition of a further 274 km beyond Ndola to Nkana Kitwe, and from Choma to Livingstone on the

Zimbabwe border, which would have lifted the outlay to US$208.5 million. The scheme has been discussed with the World Bank.

Traction and rolling stock
In 1989 ZR was operating 57 General Electric U20C 1330 kW (US-built and delivered in batches from 1967 to 1976), 10 of the same type built by Krupp in 1980, and 12 General Electric U15C 1016 kW diesel-electric locomotives, 84 passenger cars and 7080 freight wagons. Delivery of a further 405 wagons, including 120 container flats, from Canadian builders, ordered with the aid of CIDA funding was completed in 1989; at the same time 100 wagons were received from Indian builders.

Type of coupler in standard use: AAR automatic, Contour 10A (Alliance I and II on some freight wagons)
Type of brake in standard use: Vacuum

Signalling and telecommunications
The 851 km in total from Livingstone to Ndola and the Copperbelt branch section between Ndola and Kitwe is controlled by CTC with multiple-aspect colour-light signals. Sections outside CTC territory are worked on the token block system or, in the Copper-belt, on the train staff system. The CTC system was installed during 1961–64 and utilised open wire carrier circuits along the line or rail. The CTC system has now been renewed with all-electronic apparatus, operating from a centre at Kabwe, by Siemens AG, at a cost of US$15.8 million. A total of 61 relay interlockings are remote-controlled from Kabwe, whilst a further six stations have locally-controlled relay interlockings. Mitsui has been contracted to install digital radio communication between Kabwe and Livingstone.

In 1988 Indian Railway Construction Co (IRCON) was awarded a US$6.9 million contract to install a signalling and radio communication system on the 851 km Kitwe-Livingstone main line.

Civil engineering
The main line between Livingstone and Kalomo consists of 80 lb rail on wooden sleepers laid in 1945 or earlier and badly in need of replacement. The stretch from Kalomo to Mookamunga has been relayed with 90 lb rail on concrete sleepers as part of the Third Railway Project of the World Bank and a further relay of 66 km using reclaimed 80 lb rail was in progress southward from Kaloma in 1989. On completion of these projects there would still remain some 100 km of sub-standard track in the section. In the section north of Mookamunga approximately 510 km is laid on wooden sleepers between 16 and 24 years old, most of which have outlived their useful lives. Plans to renew all these sleepers have had to be scaled down over the years and it is now planned to proceed on the basis of casual renewals only.

Thus, track condition is far from satisfactory and imposes speed restrictions ranging from 0 to 80 km/h. ZR now seeks funds to standardise an 80 km/h maximum by track upgrading.

Track
Rail: 45.13 kg/m
Cross ties (sleepers): Wood, 127 mm thickness; concrete, 200 mm thickness; spaced 1340/km in plain track, 1400/km in curves, for concrete, 1400/km in both cases for wood
Fastenings: Coach screw, clip and spring washer (triple coil) for wood, Pandrol for concrete sleepers
Minimum curve radius: 8.7°
Max gradient: 1.75%
Max axleload: 15.25 tonnes

Zimbabwe

Ministry of Transport

Causeway, Harare

Telephone: +263 0 700693

Minister: D Norman

National Railways of Zimbabwe (NRZ)

PO Box 596, Bulawayo

Telephone: +263 0 363111
Telex: 33173 nrz zw
Telefax: +263 0 263502

General Manager: Nau Nihal Singh
Assistant General Manager, Finance & Administration: A Nyalila (Acting)
  Corporate Services: S Zumbika
  Engineering and Supplies: M Dhliwayo (Acting)
  Traffic: A Mabena (A cting)
Chief Mechanical Engineer: Alvord Mabena
Chief Manpower Manager: G Chibanda
Chief Civil Engineer: T I Shepherd
Chief Accountant: H Westermann (Acting)
Chief Electrical Engineer: E S Marowa (Acting)
Chief Signal Engineer: Remigious Makumbe
Chief Planning Officer: A H S Madlela
Chief Traffic Manager: Welcome Phineas Lugube
Supplies & Stores Manager: B MacDowall (Acting)
Manager, Computer Services: R Wabatagore
Public Relations Officer: G N H Lupepe
Chief Internal Auditor: J M Doro (Acting)

Gauge: 1067 mm
Route length: 2759 mm
Electrification: 313 km at 25 kV 50 Hz ac

The NRZ system connects with those of Mozambique, South Africa, Botswana and Zambia. After 1978, when the border between Zambia and Zimbabwe was reopened at Victoria Falls, NRZ became responsible for operating services through Botswana. In April 1984, however, the Ramatlabama-Mahalapye section of the railway in Botswana was handed back to that country as the first step in a total switch to Botswana management, which was completed in January 1987.

Traffic
Freight traffic in 1989 was static at 13.6 million tonnes, but passenger traffic rebounded from 2.74 million journeys in 1988 to 3.126 milion.

Almost 80 per cent of the country's tobacco crop is exported in containers, along with tea, coffee, graphite, hides and skins, nickel and tin. Containerised imports for the Harare area's extensive industrial development include machinery, lubricants, bricks, iron and steel.

NRZ's 'liner trains' are a merry-go-round operation supplying ore from Ngezi (on the Somabhula-Rutenga section) and coal from Hwange to the state-owned ZISCO iron and steel manufacturing complex at Redcliff. The trains employ purpose-built rotary tippler wagons by ZECO of Zimbabwe, the coal wagons having aluminium bodysides; ore wagon payload capacity is 58.5 tonnes, that of a coal wagon 60.5 tonnes. Both iron ore and coal are loaded with trains on the move beneath overhead bunkers. Hauled by GM Class DE 10A 1678 kW locomotives, the liner trains are formed of 60 wagons grossing over 4500 tonnes, each powered by four DE 10A units. From loading to destination tippler takes 8 hours, while from Hwange source to Redcliff takes a coal train 16 hours.

In the autumn of 1989 NRZ was hit by a severe shortage of serviceable traction. At its worst, only two-thirds of daily power requirements could be met and 20 locomotives had to be hired from South Africa. The root of the problem was the diversity of NRZ's diesel locomotives and their power units, the obsolescence of several types, scarcity of spares because of shortage of foreign exchange, and inadequate skilled labour. Rationalisation of the locomotive fleet has begun (see below). Meanwhile, more withdrawals of steam power were suspended.

Class EL1 electric locomotive and container train head for the coast

Class DE 10A diesel leaves Bulawayo with the day train for Harare

Electrification
Feasibility studies of extending electrification to the Dabuka-Bulawayo and Harare-Mutare sections produced positive findings. For various reasons there was no firm follow-through until 1990 (see below).

Finance
In 1990 NRZ was negotiating a US$38.6 million World Bank loan. It was to support a 1991–97 development programme covering electrification extension, traction and rolling stock renewals, staff training and employment of consultancy services.

Signalling and telecommunications
NKF Kabel of the Netherlands completed a 269 km optical fibre communications system between Harare and Mutare in 1988. Installation of hot box detectors over CTC sections has been completed.

Traction and rolling stock
At the end of 1989 NRZ was operating 29 electric, 80 steam and 177 diesel locomotives, 362 passenger cars (including 28 buffet/dining, and 129 sleeping cars) and 13 274 freight cars.

RAILWAY SYSTEMS / Zimbabwe

Largely because of problems in procuring spares, NRZ plans to phase out some older diesel locomotive types and refurbish others with a standard range of engines.

Measures in hand in 1990 included rewiring and modifications of the Class DE4, which were re-engined with Ruston 8RK3CT units in 1981-82; and purchase of 10 Caterpillar Series 3512 813kW engines to repower the Class D9. GM of Canada has experimentally repowered an Alsthom Class DE8A with a GM-EMD 645E3B engine; if this rebuild, designated Class 10B, proves successful the change may be applied to the entirety of Classes DE8A and DE8B.

Tenders for the supply of 30 locomotives were invited in 1989 with government approval and placement of an order was anticipated in 1990. In 1988 European and Japanese builders were invited to tender for supply of 277 passenger cars over a period extending to 1997. A West German government loan of US$5.7 million was procured in 1989 for freight wagon purchases.

Type of coupler in standard use: Automatic centre buffer coupler, Alliance No 1 and 2 heads
  Passenger cars: 5 × 5 in, 5½ × 5 in shanks
  Freight cars: 8 × 6 in, 7 × 5 in shanks
Type of braking in standard use: Vacuum on passenger and freight stock except for liner train wagons, which are on direct release air-brakes.

Track
Rail: UICE standard 54 kg/m (307 km of main line only); remainder of main line BS45 kg/m; branch lines BS45, 40 and 30 kg/m. A new standard rail, BS90A, has been adopted for all future use.

Cross ties (sleepers)

Type	Thickness (under seat)
Concrete	226 mm
Hardwood	115 mm
Steel	10 mm; 13 mm

Spacing: 1429/km
Minimum curvature radius: Main line 550 m, branch lines 300 m

Max gradient: 1 in 50
Max axleload: 20 tonnes

Traffic

	1988	1989
Freight tonnes (000)	13 600	13 600
Freight tonne-km (million)	11 104	10 592
Passenger journeys (000)	2740	3126
Passenger-km (million)	708 828	870 403

Finance (Z$ million)

Revenue

	1988	1989
Passengers and baggage	20.76	23.987
Freight, parcels and mail	221.37	227.443
Other income	30.365	35.574
Total	272.495	286.994

Expenditure

	1988	1989
Staff/personnel	205.897	257.650
Materials and services	112.960	95.393
Depreciation	18.421	19.250
Financial charges	51.883	48.386
Total	391.161	420.679

Electric locomotivies

Class	Wheel arrangement	Line voltage	Rated output kW continuous	Max speed km/h	Weight tonnes	Length mm	No in service 1989	Year first built	Builders Mechanical parts	Builders Electrical equipment
EL1	Co-Co	25 kV 50 Hz	2400 at 34 km/h	100	114	19 040	30	1983	ZECO/SGP	50 c/s Group

Steam locomotives

Class	Wheel arrangement	Total weight tonnes	Max axleload tonnes	Tractive effort at 85% bwp tonnes	No in service 31.12.87	Year first built	Builders
14A	2-6-2 + 2-6-2	133·82	13·74	17·77	18	1953	Beyer Peacock
15/15A	4-6-4 + 4-6-4	189·79	15·43	21·54	36	1949	Beyer Peacock
16A	2-8-2 + 2-8-2	171·94	14·88	26·39	15	1953	Beyer Peacock
20	4-8-2 + 2-8-4	227·04	17·24	31·45	8	1954	Beyer Peacock
20A	4-8-2 + 2-8-4	229·18	17·42	31·45	11	1957	Beyer Peacock

* 87 locomotives refurbished during 1978 to 1981

Diesel locomotives

Class	Wheel arrangement	Transmission	Gross installed power (kW)	Max speed km/h	Total weight tonnes	No. owned 1988	Year first built	Builders Mechanical parts	Builders Engine & type	Builders Transmission
DE 2	1 Co-Co 1	Elec	1275	88	114·8	17	1955	English Electric	English Electric Type 16 SVT Mk II	English Electric
DE 3	1 Co-Co 1	Elec	1380	106	111·9	15	1962	English Electric	English Electric Type 12 CSVT	English Electric
DE 4	Co-Co	Elec	1327	96	93·48	14	1963	Brush Electric	GEC Type 8-RKCT	Brush Electric
DE 5	Co-Co	Elec	1690	96	103	34	1973	Siemens	MTU Type 12V956 TD	Siemens
DE 6	Co-Co	Elec	1559	116	90·84	9	1966	GE-USA	GE Type FDI	GE-USA
DE 7	Bo-Bo	Elec	785	67	52/56	32	1971	SGP-Austria	SGP Type T12b	SGP
DE 8	Co-Co	Elec	1730	80	120	14	1973	Alsthom (AD 28C)	Pielstick Type 16 PA4200	Alsthom
DE 8A	Co-Co	Elec	1730	80	120	17	1973	Alsthom (AD 28C)	Pielstick Type 16 PA4200	Alsthom
DE 8B	Co-Co	Elec	1730	80	102	19	1976	Alsthom (AD 28C)	Pielstick Type 16 PA4200	Alsthom
DE 9	Bo-Bo	Elec	686	103	56	20	1972	GE (U10B)	Caterpillar Type D398B	GE
DE 9A	Bo-Bo	Elec	895	103	61	44	1975	GE (U11B)	Pielstick Type 8 PA4200	GE
DE 10A	Co-Co	Elec	1678	107	94·35	61	1982	General Motors USA and Canada	EMD Type 645E3B	General Motors
DH 2A	0-6-0	Hyd	301	30	50·5	8	1975	SGP-Austria	SGP Type S108a	Voith

RELIABILITY

DAEWOO HEAVY INDUSTRIES: YOUR NAME FOR RELIABLE ROLLING STOCK OF THE FUTURE

We offer exciting innovation through experience, expertise and R&D

Daewoo Heavy Industries' rolling stock have rolled up reliability in more than 30 nations. We've produced over 12,000 units--locomotives, diesel multiple units, electric multiple units, deluxe passenger coaches, freight wagons, road trailers, etc. --as well as numerous components.

A variety of Daewoo's rolling stock and parts has been supplied not only to the domestic market but to many foreign countries such as America, Canada, Spain, Austria, New Zealand, Singapore, Thailand, Taiwan, Malaysia, Indonesia, the Philippines, Burma, Bangladesh, Jordan, Saudi-Arabia, Argentina, Mauritania, Nigeria, Ghana, Tunisia and Sudan, receiving our customer's wide acclaim.

As we head into the 21st century, we now concentrating on high-speed rolling stock and other futuristic models to meet the demands of a growing number of clients around the world. We combine experience, expertise, R&D and plenty of solid capability to bring you a better tomorrow through reliable rolling stock.

Rapid transit and underground

DAEWOO
DAEWOO HEAVY INDUSTRIES LTD

• SALES OFFICE: DAEWOO CENTER BLDG 20TH Fl 541, 5-GA, NAMDAEMOON-RO, JUNG-GU, SEOUL, KOREA C.P.O. BOX:7955 TLX:DHILTD K23301 TEL: 752-0211 • HEAD OFFICE & FACTORY: 6, MANSEOG-DONG, DONG-GU, INCHEON, KOREA TEL: INCHEON 762-1011, TELEX: DHILTD K28473 CABLE: DHILTD INCHEON • ROLLING STOCK FACTORY: 462-2, SAM-DONG, EUIWANG-CITY KYEONGGI-DO, KOREA TEL: ANYANG (043) 61-6170~80 TELEX: K25550

Rapid transit and underground railways

ALGERIA
Algiers 815

ARGENTINA
Buenos Aires 821

AUSTRALIA
Adelaide 815
Melbourne 835

AUSTRIA
Vienna 852

BELGIUM
Antwerp 815
Brussels 820
Charleroi 822
Liège 831

BRAZIL
Belo Horizonte 818
Goias 826
Porto Alegre 842
Recife 843
Rio de Janeiro 843
Sao Paulo 846

BULGARIA
Sofia 847

CANADA
Calgary 822
Edmonton 825
Montreal 836
Toronto 850
Vancouver 852

CHILE
Santiago 845

CHINA, PEOPLE'S REPUBLIC
Beijing 817
Guangzhou (Canton) 827
Shanghai 847
Tianjin 849

COLOMBIA
Bogota 819
Medellin 834

CUBA
Havana 827

CZECHOSLOVAKIA
Bratislava 820
Prague 842

EGYPT
Alexandria 815
Cairo 821

FINLAND
Helsinki 827

FRANCE
Bordeaux 819
Brest 820
Grenoble 826
Lille 831
Lyons 833
Marseilles 834
Nantes 837
Paris 840
Rennes 843
Rheims 843
Rouen 844
Toulouse 851

GERMANY, DEMOCRATIC REPUBLIC
Berlin (East) 818

GERMANY, FEDERAL REPUBLIC
Berlin (West) 818
Bochum 819
Cologne 823
Dortmund 824
Duisburg 824
Düsseldorf 824
Essen 825
Frankfurt am Main 825
Hamburg 827
Hannover 827
Karlsruhe 829
Mülheim 837
Munich 837
Nuremberg 839
Rhine-Ruhr 843
Stuttgart 848
Wuppertal 853

GREECE
Athens 816

HONG KONG
Hong Kong 828

HUNGARY
Budapest 820

INDIA
Calcutta 822
Delhi 824
Madras 833

IRAN
Tehran 849

IRAQ
Baghdad 816

ISRAEL
Haifa 827
Tel Aviv 849

ITALY
Bologna 819
Brescia 820
Florence 825
Genoa 826
Milan 835
Naples 837
Rome 844
Turin 851

IVORY COAST
Abidjan 815

JAPAN
Fukuoka 826
Hiroshima 828
Kobe 830
Kyoto 830
Nagoya 837
Osaka 840
Sapporo 846
Sendai 846
Tokyo 849
Yokohama 853

KOREA, DEMOCRATIC PEOPLE'S REPUBLIC
Pyongyang 843

KOREA, REPUBLIC
Pusan 843
Seoul 846

LIBYA
Tripoli 851

MEXICO
Guadalajara 826
Mexico City 835
Monterrey 836

MOROCCO
Casablanca 822

NETHERLANDS
Amsterdam 815
Rotterdam 844
Utrecht 851

NEW ZEALAND
Auckland 816

NORWAY
Oslo 840

PAKISTAN
Karachi 829

PERU
Lima 831

PHILIPPINES
Manila 834

POLAND
Lodz 832
Warsaw 852

PORTUGAL
Lisbon 831

ROMANIA
Bucharest 820

SINGAPORE
Singapore 847

SOUTH AFRICA
Johannesburg 829
Port Elizabeth 842

SPAIN
Barcelona 817
Bilbao 819
Madrid 833
Seville 847

SWEDEN
Gothenburg 826
Stockholm 848

SWITZERLAND
Lausanne 830
Neuchâtel 837

TAIWAN
Kaohsiung 829
Taipai 848

THAILAND
Bangkok 817

TUNISIA
Tunis 851

TURKEY
Ankara 815
Istanbul 829
Ismir 829

USSR
Alma-Ata 815
Baku 816
Chelyabinsk 823
Dnepropetrovsk 824
Erevan 825
Gorki 826
Kazan 829
Kharkov 829
Kiev 829
Krasnoyarsk 830
Krivoy Rog 830
Kulbyshev 830
Leningrad 831
Minsk 836
Moscow 836
Novosibirsk 839
Odessa 840
Omsk 840
Riga 843
Rostov-on-Don 844
Sverdlovsk 848
Tashkent 848
Tbilisi 848

UK
Birmingham 819
Bristol 820
Cambridge 822
Croydon 823
Edinburgh 824
Glasgow 826
Hull 829
Kingston-upon-Thames 830
Leeds-Bradford 831
London 832
Manchester 834
Middlesbrough 835
Newcastle-upon-Tyne 838
Nottingham 839
Sheffield 847

USA
Atlanta 816
Baltimore 817
Boston 819
Buffalo 821
Chicago 823
Cleveland 823
Dallas 823
Denver 824
Detroit 824
Honolulu 828
Houston 828
Jacksonville 829
Kansas City 829
Los Angeles 833
Miami 835
Minneapolis 836
New York 838
New York–New Jersey 839
New York (Staten Island) 839
Norfolk 839
Oklahoma City 840
Philadelphia 841
Pittsburgh 842
Portland 842
Sacramento 844
St Louis 845
San Antonio 845
San Diego 845
San Francisco 845
San Jose 845
Washington 852

VENEZUELA
Caracas 822
Valencia 852

Abidjan

Ministère des Travaux Publics et des Transports

Avenue Jean Paul II, Tour Administrative D, PO Box V6, Abidjan, Ivory Coast

Telephone: 29 13 67
Telex: 22108

Type of system: Planned metro

Further engineering studies of a north-south 17·3 km, metre-gauge metro were commissioned in 1984. Serving nine stations, it would run entirely at ground level, adopting in part the existing Abidjan-Niger Railway line, and operate six-car trains. No subsequent development, except for inclination to change to a light rail project on the same route.

Adelaide

For details see South Australia State Transport Authority entry, Railway Systems section

Alexandria

Alexandria Passenger Transport Authority

2 Aflatone Street, Chatby, PO Box 466, Alexandria, Egypt

Telephone: +20 3 596 1810, 597 5223
Telex: 54637 apta un

Chairman: Salah Eldin Abdel-Moneim
General Manager, Light Rail: Eng Abdel-Moneim Abdel Ghani
Chief Engineer: F Amin Abdel Malek

Type of system: Light rail and planned metro

Light rail (Ramleh lines)
Gauge: 1453 mm
Route length: 14.7 km
Number of lines: 6
Electrification: 600 V dc

Rolling stock: 36 three-car units by Kinki Nippon/Toshiba

Study by Italian consultants Transsystem SpA of a surface metro to connect the city centre with Bolkli and a projected new airport at Borg el Arab was completed and delivered to the city council in 1986. The authority also operates a city tram system of 28 route-km.

Algiers

Enterprise Metro d'Alger

13 Chemin de la Wilaya, 4 Kouba, Algiers, Algeria

Telephone: +213 2 585464/586768
Telex: 62567

Director: H Bellil

Type of system: Metro under construction

Construction began in 1989 of the first 11·5 km of Line 1 of a metro network planned eventually to have three lines totalling 64 km. The steel-wheel system (not rubber-tyre wheel, as was once envisaged) will take over SNTF surface tracks from Hamma to El Harrach, branching thereafter to Dar el Beida airport and Gué de Constantine in its first phase. This is set for completion in 1995. Second and third phases, scheduled to open in 1997 and 1999, will tunnel under the city centre via Algiers main station and terminate at Oued Koriche.

Alma-Ata

Alma-Ata, USSR

An 8·9 km line to link the main rail station with the city centre and its southwestern suburbs was committed to construction in 1984; opening expected in 1990. A second section will be of 3 km. In all, a three-line, 35·4 km system is planned.

Amsterdam

Gemeentevevoerbedrijf Amsterdam (GVBA)

Prins Hendrikkade 108-114, Postbox 2131, 1000 CC Amsterdam, Netherlands

Telephone: +31 20 5514911
Telex: 12708
Telefax: +31 20 5514250

Director: B J J Smit
Operating Manager: Ir G H Van Der Meer

Type of system: Full metro

Gauge: 1432 mm
Route length: 24 km
 (in tunnel): 3·5 km
 (elevated): 20·5 km
Number of stations: 20
 (in tunnel): 5
 (elevated): 15
Average distance between stations
 (in tunnel): 800–900 m
 (elevated): 1100–1300 m
Tunnel type: In order to keep out ground water sections of the underground portions were built by the pneumatic caisson method, which involved building pre-fabricated rectangular tunnel segments on the surface and sinking them into their final positions (with the tunnel roof 4·5 metres below surface level). Some 250 metres were achieved by cut-and-cover construction. The outer stretches of the initial line were all built on viaduct or embankment. The tunnels, 4·1 metres high above rail level and 8·3 metres wide, carry two tracks
Gradient (max): 3·2%
Curvature (max): 300 m
Speed (design max): 70 km/h
 (average commercial): 35 km/h
Rail type: 49 kg/m (S49) on wood sleeper, ballasted, both on surface and in tunnel
Signalling: Siemens ZUB100 cab signalling was adopted in 1989.
Electrification type: 750 V dc, third rail
Rolling stock
Two-car units, permanently coupled, built by Linke-Hofmann-Busch, each on four motored bogies, built by MAN, with electrical equipment by Siemens

Car type	Ml.1	Ml.2
Number of units: 44		
Car dimensions		
(length)	18·27 m	18·67 m
(width)	3·01 m	3·01 m
(height)	3·54 m	3·54 m
Passenger capacity: per twin-set:		
98 seated		
200 standing		
Power per unit: 4 × 195 kW at 33·5 km/h		
Rating	180 kWh	
Brakes	Rheostatic	
Weight (tare) (tonnes)	27	27

Trains are one-man operated with units multiplied up to a maximum of four; normal formation is two

Traffic
Train headways: Peak hour, on main line 3¾ minutes, on two extensions 7½ minutes and 10 minutes; off-peak, 5 minutes on main line
Passenger journeys: (1988) 124 000/working day, 66 000 Saturdays, 43 000 Sundays
Signalling: Automatic block system: signals, cables etc by ASI Utrecht; control panel, computers etc by AEG, West Berlin
Fare structure: Zonal fares, integrated with suburban trains and regional buses (local area only)

System development
Originally planned as a 78 km network, the Amsterdam metro's further extension has been blocked by vigorous opposition to further intrusion on the city's fabric. Curtailment of the original network plan has caused a serious revenue shortfall in relation to operating expenses. However, a hybrid metro-LRT line with additional 750 V dc overhead current wiring from Spaklerweg to Amstelveen was to be opened throughout in late 1990.

Ankara

Elektrik Gaz ve Otobüs Işletmesi Genel MÜdürlügü (EGO)
PO Box 294, Toros Sokak 20, 06042 Maltepe-Ankara, Turkey

Telephone: +90 41 231 7180
Telex: 42501 ego tr
Telefax: +90 41 230 8109

Director, Transport Planning & Rail Systems: M Aytekin
Project Manager: Yusuf Okçuoğlu
Director, Rail Construction: M Oral

Type of system: Light rail

After several false starts and vacillations between LRT and full metro, choice has now settled on a low-cost LRT system of 54·4 km with minimal tunnelling. The first 14·6 km line will run from the city centre along the Ataturk Boulevard to Batikent, west of the city. In 1988 UDTC won a build-operate-and-transfer contract to provide the first 14·5 km line running east-west from the city centre at Kizilay to Batikent. Opening is forecast for 1992.
Folowing a feasibility study, the city in 1990 invited turnkey design-and-build bids for an 8·6km light rail system from Sogutozu to Dikimevi.

Antwerp

Maatschappij voor het Intercommunaal Vervoer te Antwerpen (MIVA)

Grotehondstraat 58, 2018 Antwerp, Belgium

Telephone: +32 3 218 1411

Managing Director: A Blondé
Operating Manager: J du Mon
Rolling Stock Manager: G Vandenbril
Fixed Installation Manager: M Verdonck

Type of system: Pre-metro, light rail

Gauge: 1000 mm
Route length: tramway/light rail 101km; pre-metro 5.1km
Number of lines: 2 pre-metro, 8 conventional
Number of stations: Pre-metro 5 (all in tunnel)
Average distance between stations: 530 m
Rail weight and type: 61·7 kg/m grooved; 50 kg/m flat-bottomed (vignole) being systematically replaced
Track type: Normally sleepers on ballast; some sections rail directly on concrete with resilient pads
Tunnel-type: First two sections (in operation): bored double-track; all other sections (completed, in construction or planned): shield tunnelling (single-track), some sections by jacking of concrete pipes (single- or double-track)
Electrification type: 600 V dc, overhead

Rolling stock
Number of cars: 166 PCC cars all motored and one-man operated
Main supplier: NV Spoorwegmaterieel en Metaalconstructies, Bruges (formerly La Brugeoise et Nivelles); and ACEC, Charleroi
Car dimensions: Length 14.017 m, width 2·2 m, height 3·081 m
Capacity: 100 (crush) with 31 seated
Tare and loaded weights: 16·2/24·7 tonnes; tare weight of car with Scharfenberg couplers, 17 tonnes

The PCC cars' present traction equipment (starting resistances, 79 positions) is not well adapted to operation on long slopes or in long tunnels with a 4·5-6% gradient, as will occur on the future pre-metro section to the Left Bank district. Therefore preparatory studies have been started rebuilding the 105 vehicles for the opening of the Left Bank tunnel.
 The conversion would comprise:
Replacement of the starting resistances by chopper equipment;
Modification of all three doors and elimination of the central mullion; and
Replacement of all inflammable material in the interior (seats, panelling), and in electrical equipment and cables. The work is being carried out partly in MIVA shops and mostly by the constructor, BN of Bruges. This follows studies and experiments with converted

car 2050 equipped with chopper-controlled asynchronous motor drive.

Traffic
Total passenger journeys (1988) including those on 74 km of conventional tramways, 31·3 million

System development
The city decided in the late 1960s to start pre-metro conversion of the city-centre sections of the light rail system. The first 1·3 km double-track tunnel and 0·2 km single-track sections were opened in March 1975, and further 1·2 km double-track and 0·7 km single-track sections in April 1980; total, 5 stations. Ultimate length of the pre-metro network will be 15·6 km double-track and 1·6 km single-track, with 21 stations.

In 1989 a further 11·1 km of pre-metro route including a 1·53 km tunnel under the River Schelde was under construction. The first 3km including the Schelde tunnel were due to open in September 1990.

Athens

Athens-Piraeus Electric Railways Co Ltd (ISAP)

67 Athinas St, Athens 10552, Greece

Telephone: +30 1 324 9102
Telex: 21 9998
Telefax: +30 1 322 3935

Managing Director: Konstantinos Kostoulas

Type of system: Rapid transit

Gauge: 1435 mm
Route length: 25·84 km
 (in tunnel): 3 km
 (elevated): 0·76 km
Number of lines: 1
Number of stations: 23
 (in tunnel): 3
 (elevated): 1
Average distance between stations: 1·12 km
Track type: Flat-bottomed rail laid on timber sleepers and ballast
Tunnel type: Cut-and-cover
Electrification type: 720 V dc (to be raised to 750 V), third rail
Signalling: Electric automatic block (50 Hz)

Traffic
Train headways: 3 minutes (peak)
Passenger journeys: (1989) 100 million

Rolling stock
199 cars. Delivery was completed in 1985 of 15 five-car train-sets built by MAN/Siemen. Each set has three motor-cars with chopper control. Also in 1985 delivery was completed of 25 two-car train-sets built by LEW. All LEW cars are motored

Ministry of Environment and Public works
Ippokratous 196, Athens

Type of system: Full metro

Gauge: 1435 mm

Construction has begun of 8 km of a north-south Line 2 to link Peristeri and Iliopoulis. A three-line system is planned, with the Athens-Piraeus Railway (see above) forming Line 1 and a new east-west route Line 3.

Car type	M37/T37	M45/T30	M50
Number of cars	74	75	50
Car dimensions			
(length) (m)	17	17	14
(width) (m)	2·8	2·8	2·8
(height) (m)	3·6	3·6	3·6
Passenger capacity per car			
(total)	180	190	155
(seated)	56	33	35
Motors per 4-car train:	4	8	8
Brakes	rheostatic and air	regenerative and air	rheostatic and air
Body material	steel	stainless steel	aluminium
Motor rating	120/550 V	140/750 V	120/750 V
Maximum design speed (km/h)	80	80	70
Weight (empty, tonnes):			
Motor cars	37	31	22
Trailers	29	25	—

Atlanta

Metropolitan Atlanta Rapid Transit Authority (MARTA)

2424 Piedmont Avenue, Atlanta, Georgia 30324, USA

Telephone: +1 404 848 5000
Telex: 542948

Chairman: George Ivey Jr
General Manager: K M Gregor
General Manager, Transit Operations Rail: Theodore Williams
Assistant General Manager, Transit Systems Development: William Medley

Type of system: Full metro, integrated with bus feeder services

Gauge: 1435 mm
Number of lines: 2
Number of stations: 29
Total route length: 52·25 km
Rail weight and type: 119RE (52·12 kg/m)
Track type: Continuously-welded rail with Pandrol clips on concrete sleepers. Elastomer springing under track in residential areas to reduce vibration. Screens on surface and elevated sections to reduce noise
Axleload: 13.8 tonnes
Minimum curve radius: 230 m
Max gradient: 3%
Electrification type: 750 V dc, third rail
Signalling and control: General Railway Signal automatic train protection, automatic train operation and automatic line supervision

Rolling stock
Number of cars: 240
Supplier: Franco-Belge (now Soferval), 204; C Itoh/Hitachi, 36 with Garrett traction equipment
Car dimensions: Length 23 m, width 3·2 m, height 3·6 m
Capacity: 68 seats in cars with single driver's cab; 62 in cars with cab at each end; standing room for 140
Tare weight: 37 tonnes
Max speed: 114 km/h

Traffic
Passenger journeys: (1988) 66 million
Revenue control equipment: Cubic Western Data faregates

System development
The rail system is planned as a north-to-south, east- to-west cross of two lines aggregating (with branches) 98.12km in route-length, intersecting in downtown Atlanta's business district at Five Points. A third of the planned 100 km, 45-station system is to be elevated and 16 km underground, but completion in full is dependent on Federal funding.

Initial hopes of treating the network construction as one continuous project have been modified into a five-phase plan. In 1989 new construction centred on extension of the North line a further 9 km to Doraville, with opening set for 1992, and of the Northeast line by 15.93 km in five stages to Medical Center, which will be reached in 1995.

In 1989 the Atlanta Regional Commission published proposals costed at US$3900 million envisaging a further 119 km of orbital metro in the northern suburbs, and also 69 km of automated light metro.

Auckland

Auckland Regional Authority, New Zealand

131 Hobbson Street, Auckland 1, New Zealand

Telephone: +64 9 7945420

In conjunction with New Zealand Railways (NZR), plans have been finalised to convert NZR's suburban commuter service to a light rail by 1993-94. A two-line 45 km system is proposed, largely using existing NZR tracks but including 6km of new construction in the city-centre streets. New branches to the city airport and a developing suburb are possible. At the start of 1990 funding had still to be arranged.

Baghdad

Baghdad Rapid Transit Authority

Nisoor Square, Baghdad, Iraq

Telephone: +964 1 552 0013

General Manager, Metro Construction: J Al Saadi

Type of system: Metro under design

Gauge: 1435 mm
Number of lines: 2
Number of stations: 36
Route length: 32 km
Electrification type: 1·5 kV dc, overhead
Tunnel type: 60% bored, remainder cut-and-cover

Rolling stock: The metro will employ 83 three-car, air-conditioned train-sets, with a top speed of 80 km/h and acceleration of 1 m/s². They will seat 84 passengers in each car with room for 84 standees.

System development
The British Metro Consultants Group of 10 companies has been appointed to create the first stage of the Baghdad metro. Line 1 is to run from Aadhamiya to Al-Thawra, Line 2 from Masbah via Aqaba bin-Nasir Square to Mansour, with interchange in the central area at Khalani Street. Design of Line 1 began in 1986. The British Metro Consultants Group is advising.

Following Phase 1, extensions totalling 11 km with 10 stations are planned in Phase 2, and the addition of a third line to establish a regional system in Phase 3.

Baku

Baku Metropolitan

Ulitsa Inglaba 17, Baku 37063, USSR

Chief Executive: Igor Abasovich Khankishiev
Chief Engineer: Chingiz Mamedovich Rufullaev

Type of system: Full metro

Gauge: 1524 mm
Route length: 18·6 km
Number of lines: 2
Number of stations: 12
Average distance between stations: 1·8 km
Rail type: 50 kg/m
Minimum curve radius: 300 m
Max gradient: 4%
Electrification type: 825 V, third rail

Rolling stock
Car type (year introduced): 1960
Number of cars: 124 (all motored)
Car dimensions: (length) 18·8 m
 (width): 2·7 m
Passenger capacity: (per car)
 (total): 170
 (seated): 44
Weight: 32 tonnes
Motors per car: 4
Motor rating: 66 kW
Train composition (minimum): 5
 (maximum): 5
Brakes: Regenerative and electromagnetic
Body material: Steel

Signalling: Automatic train stop. Radio-telephone communication between trains and the central command post.

System development
In late 1967 the first 10·1 km section of line was opened, with seven stations, four of which lie at deep level and are served by high-speed escalators.

Under construction in 1980 were extensions of both lines, totalling 17·5 km. The ultimate scheme envisages three lines with a total of 52 km and 34 stations.

Baltimore

Maryland Department of Transportation, Mass Transit Administration (MTA)

300 West Lexington Street, Baltimore, Maryland 21201-3415, USA

Telephone: +1 301 333 3885
Telefax: +1 301 333 3279

Administrator and General Manager: Ronald Hartman
Assistant General Manager, Transit Operations: James Buckley
Assistant General Manager, Transit Development: Peter Schmidt

Type of system: Full metro

Gauge: 1435 mm
Route length: 22·4 km
  (in tunnel): 12·8 km
  (elevated): 7·2 km
Number of stations: 12 (6 in tunnel, 3 elevated)
Average distance between stations: 2 km
Gradient (max): 1 in 25
Curve radius (max): 186 m (main line)
Speed (design max): 112 km/h
  (average commercial): 43 km/h
Rail type: 57 kg/m RE continuous welded
Tunnel type: Horseshoe in rock (44%), shield-driven in soft earth (56%).

The Lexington Market tunnels were chosen for a demonstration project involving the use of precast concrete tunnel liners for the first time in a US rapid transit tunnel below the water table. Baltimore's other earth tunnels used steel liners. UMTA funded 100 per cent of the test programmes, and the cost differential, up to US$700 000, between the use of concrete tunnel liners and conventional steel liners.
Electrification type: 700 V dc, third rail
Signalling: Automatic train control (WABCO Union Switch and Signal AF-400 system), from operations control centre, directs trains from start to stop, regulates speeds at six levels from 19·2 to 112 km/h, spaces trains and routes them through switches and crossovers.

Rolling stock
Number of units: 100 cars, all motored, in twin units
Supplier: Transit America
Car dimensions
  length: 22·88 m
  width: 3·11 m
  height: 3·66 m
Number of doors per side: 3 sets bi-parting doors each side
Number of passengers per car (total): 166
  (seated): 76
Motors per car: 4
Motor rating: 130 kW
Acceleration (max): 3·0 mph/s
  (emergency): 3·2 mph/s
Max design speed: 113 km/h
Bogies: Transit America Pioneer
Brakes: Tread air brakes – WABCO
Weight: 38 tonnes

The Transit America-built cars were purchased in a joint venture with Miami. Bought under the Buy America provision of the Surface Transportation Act, the Baltimore-Miami vehicle was designed with general specifications in an effort to produce a car that would be standardised in the industry. Cars are of stainless steel, and designed to operate as married pairs. Microprocessor control for both propulsion and ATO is a feature of the Westinghouse regenerative chopper equipment. Trains are composed of a minimum of two cars and a maximum of six.

Traffic
Passenger journeys (daily): 52 000 Mondays-Fridays, 20 000 Saturdays
Max number of trains per hour (one way): 30

Train headways: 7 minutes (peak hours), 10 minutes (other)
Max train capacity (seated): 456
  (standing): 1200

System development
Ground was broken in spring 1989 for a further 2.3km extension, to the northeast to Johns Hopkins Hospital, a major employer in Baltimore. The 2·4 km extension, with two stations, is being built entirely in subway. The US$326 million price tag is being funded with 85% Federal money. No additional railcars will be purchased. The Johns Hopkins spur of the Metro will probably begin carrying passengers in mid-1994.

Type of system: Light rail under construction

A spring 1989 groundbreaking took place for a US$290 million, 44·2 km light rail line that will connect Hunt Valley in Baltimore County with Glen Burnie in Anne Arundel County by cutting through the centre of Baltimore City. A 2·4 km spur to Baltimore/Washington International Airport is also planned. The route mainly follows existing railroad rights-of-way. Thirty stops are proposed (half with parking), with patronage expected to be 33 000 daily trips after two or three years of operation. The central corridor light rail line should be open for service in late 1991. MTA feeder buses will serve selected light rail stops and the line will interface with the Baltimore Metro at the Lexington Market Metro and State Center stations. The state's share of the project is US$205 million.

In 1989 ABB Traction Inc was contracted to supply 35 articulated LRVs, with an option for up to 20 more. The LRVs will be a derivative of the Type M21 supplied by ABB to Göteborg, Sweden (qv).

Bangkok

Expressway and Rapid Transit Authority of Thailand

Phaholyothin Road, Bangkok 10900, Thailand

Telephone: +66 2 579 5380 9
Telex: 72346 etath
Telefax: +66 2 579 5205

General Manager: C Burapharat

Type of system: Planned metro

Gauge: 1435 mm
Route length: 36 km
  (elevated): 35 km
  (in tunnel): 1 km
Electrification: Linear motor
Number of lines: 2
Number of stations: 37

System development
The Expressway and Rapid Transit Authority of Thailand, formed in 1975, proposed a three-line mass transit rail system for Bangkok. The lines include: Pra-Khanong-Bangsue (23 km); Wongwien Yai-Lardphrao (20 km); Dao Khanong-Makasan (16 km).

By 1985 the project had been curtailed to an initial two-line, 36 km system, which the government undertook in May 1986 to finance to the extent of 25 per cent. The rest of the construction cost would have to be found by the private sector. The Minister of the Interior was mandated to find a suitable investor.

In 1989 Lavalin International was contracted to build and operate a Skytrain, linear motor-powered system of the type developed by UTDC for Vancouver (qv). The deal required Lavalin to raise US$1900 million for the project; the government would contribute only US$400 million. In 1989 negotiations with Lavalin hit problems and talks were reopened with an Asia-Euro consortium fronted by Leighton Industries. But in early 1990 a government created to review the situation came down in favour of Lavalin, which was required by the end of May to produce a new financial package.

Barcelona

FC Metropolitano de Barcelona SA (SPM)

PO Box 831, Calle 60 No 423, Sector A, Zona Franca, 08004 Barcelona, Spain

Telephone: +34 3 335 0812/1300/2770/3058

Telex: 93712
Telefax: +34 3 335 8630

Chairwoman: Mercè Sala Schnorkowski
Managing Director and General Manager: Jesús Zandueta Vera
Deputy General Manager: Guillermo Yenes Villa Fañes
Administration and Financial Manager: Francesco Bellver Creus
Labour Manager: Antonio Llardén Carratalá
Manager, Metro Operations: Augustin del Castillo Jiménez

Type of system: Full metro

The whole system is underground, except the Mercat Nou-Sta Eulalia section of Line 1 and a section in Boixeres station.

Gauge: 1674 mm (Line 1 only); 1435 mm
Route length: 70·8 km with 61·7 km in tunnel
Number of lines: 4 (Nos 1, 3, 4 and 5) all double-track
Number of stations: 98
  (in tunnel): 93
Average distance between stations: Line 1, 665 m; Line 3, 666 m; Line 4, 816 m; Line 5, 721 m
Rail weight and type: 54 kg/m UIC 54
Track type: New lines, sleepers on concrete; other lines, sleepers on ballast
Electrification type: Line 1, 1·5 kV dc; others, 1·2 kV dc
Current collection: Line 1, steel third-rail; Line 5, catenary; Lines 3 and 4 aluminium third-rail

Rolling stock
Number of cars: 481
Main suppliers (latest cars): Macosa, MTM, CAF, Cenemesa, Mitsubishi

The latest series 4000 cars are being concentrated on Line 1. Type 1000 cars are being rebuilt with air-conditioning.

Traffic
Train headways: Line 5, peak hours, 3 minutes 23 sec; Line 3, 3 minutes 40 sec; Line 1, 3 minutes 43 sec; Line 4, 4 minutes 22 sec.
Passenger journeys (1988): 264·8 million
Signalling: Automatic block, with ac track circuits, and colour-light signals. CTC on Lines 1, 3, 4 and 5. Automatic Train Protection (ATP) operational on Line 4, in preparation for other lines.

System development
Completion of a 1.8 km, two-station Line 1 extension to Ciudad Sanitaria in 1989 was being followed by a further extension from Sta Coloma to Cami de Fons, set to open in 1991. The same year will see completion of a 7.1 km Line 2 from Sagrada Familia to La Pau. An automated fare collection system is planned.

Planned light rail
Matra's VAL system has been selected for a 3km automated light metro to be built to connect the Metro with the 1992 Olympic Games site at Montjuic. Construction was expected to begin in the spring of 1990.

Ferrocarriles de Generalitat de Catalunya (FCG)

For details see Spain entry, Railway Systems section 1

Beijing

Beijing Metro Corporation

61 Suzhouhutong, Beijing, People's Republic of China

Telephone: +86 1 546252

General Manager: Feng Shuangsheng
Chief Engineer: Yas Jingdi

Type of system: Full metro

Gauge: 1435 mm
Route length: 40 km, all in tunnel
Number of lines: 2
Number of stations: 29
Average distance between stations: 1·4 km
Track type: Concrete slab
Tunnel type: Cut-and-cover, 4·1 m wide, 4·35 m high

Electrification type: 750 V dc, third rail
Minimum curve radius: 250 m
Max gradient: 3%
Signalling: Relay interlocking, automatic block, centralised traffic control, cab signalling, automatic train stop. Metro operated from one control room with electronic facilities for monitoring and controlling all turnouts and signals.

Rolling stock
Main suppliers: Changchun Rolling Stock Plant (Jilin province) and Xiangtan Electrical Machinery Plant (Hunan province); latest sets built under Japanese licence, based on one chopper-controlled prototype set delivered 1984 by Tokyu Car
Number of units: 200 cars, all motored, operated as four- and five-car sets
Types: 2000, 4000 and Tokyu
Max speed: 80 km/h
Capacity: 60 seats per car, 120 standing

Traffic
Train headways: Peak hours, 4 minutes; off-peak, 8–12 minutes
Passenger journeys daily: (1987) over 500 000

System development
A 53 km system is planned, to be built in three phases. To conclude the second phase, Line 1 is currently being extended 12 km from its present junction with the circular Line 2 at Fuxing Men, through a second interchange with the circle at Jianguo Men, to Bawangfen; construction began in mid-1989.

The third phase plans a fourth line. This would start as a 13 km cut-and-cover line from Xizhimen station on the circular Line 2 northwestward to the Summer Palace (Yike Yuan), with nine intermediate stations. It would eventually be projected eastward through the city, recrossing the circle at Dong Si-shi Tiao, then head northwestward to Shoudu Airport.

A French group comprising Sofrétu and Interinfra had been commissioned in 1987 to modernise Lines 1 and 2 for operation of six-car trains at 2-minute headways. But the Line modernisation contract was subsequently passed to a British group.

Belo Horizonte

Demetro-Consorcio Metropolitano del Belo Horizonte

Avenue Afonso Pena, 1500, 11° Andar, Belo Horizonte, Minas Gerias, CEP 30130, Brazil

Telephone: +55 31 201 4066
Telex: (031) 1289 tren

General Manager: C A Fonseca Salgado

Type of system: Regional metro

Gauge: 1600 mm
Route length: 16·7 km
Electrification type: 3 kV dc, overhead

System development
A French-Brazilian consortium, led by Francorail, was awarded a contract in 1981 to create a suburban railway network in Brazil's third largest city. The scheme involved construction of a new 1600 mm-gauge double track, partially adopting existing right-of-way, over the 38 km from Belo Horizonte south to Betim, and north of the city to Horto and São Paulo. The enterprise is managed by the CBTU (qv under Brazil, Railway Systems section).

A 6·5 km extension from Central to Sta Ines opened in 1989 and a further 3·4 km to Sao Paulo was to be commissioned in 1991. Also to be inaugurated in 1991 was a 10·3 km segment from Calafate to Barreiro. A subsequent 23·7 km extension to Betim is planned.

A fleet of 25 four-car emus, each with 1248 maximum passenger capacity, of similar character to that provided by the same builders for FEPASA, was being supplied by a Franco-Brazilian consortium involving Cobrasma and IEBB (Brazil); by 1989 only five had been delivered.

Type of System: Planned light rail
A 20.5 km light rail line is proposed for the north of the city. Only bid to build had been submitted by early 1990, from a Brazilian consortium offering Czech-designed LRVs.

Car type	A1	A2	E3*	G1
Car dimensions				
(length)	12·1 m	12·4 m	18·0 m	18·1 m
(width)	2·3 m	2·3 m	2·6 m	2·3 m
(height)	3·2 m	3·2 m	3·4 m	3·2 m
Passenger capacity per car				
(total)	129	122	163	129
(seated)	27	26 motor cars / 34 trailers	38	34
Motors per car	4	4	4	4
Rating	60 kW/h	60 kW/h	60 kW/h	60 kW/h

*Large profile, remainder small profile

Berlin (East)

VE Kombinat Berliner Verkehrs-Betriebe (VEB)

Rosa Luxemburgstrasse 2, Postfach 229, 1026 Berlin, German Democratic Republic

Telephone: +37 2 510311
Telex: 114774

Type of system: Full metro

Rolling stock: 464 cars, supplied by LEW Hennings-dorf. Additional stock for larger-profile Line E has been produced by rebuilding 51 former S-Bahn two-car units obtained from West Berlin.
Gauge: 1435 mm
Route length: 25·9 km
  (in tunnel): 12·4 km
Number of lines: 2
Number of stations: 31
Gradient (max): 4%
Curvature (max): 74 m
Electrification type: 750 V, third rail
Acceleration (max): 1015 m/s^2
Deceleration (emergency): 1·2/m/s^2
Brakes: Electro-pneumatic

Traffic
Train headways: 2½ minutes (peak)
Passenger journeys: (1988) 94.7 million

System development
A further extension of Line E to Hönow was completed in June 1989, bringing its length to 18·8 km.

Following the opening of the Berlin Wall, link-ups with the West Berlin system's two routes that cross East Berlin have been under discussion.

Berlin (West)

Berliner Verkehrs-Betriebe (BVG)

Postdamer Str 188, 1000 Berlin 30, Federal Republic of Germany

Telephone: +49 30 256-1
Telex: 183 329 vvr d
Telefax: +49 30 216 4186

Administration & Finance Manager: Hans Bernhard Ludwig
Engineering Manager: Dipl-Ing Helmut Döpfer
Personnel Manager: Harro Sachsse
Traffic Manager: Dipl-Kfm Konrad Lorenzen

Type of system: Full metro

Gauge: 1435 mm
Route length: 108·2 km (30·3 km small profile, 77·9 km large profile)
  (in tunnel): 93·7 km
  (elevated): 6·2 km
Number of lines: 8
Number of stations served: 119, including 16 interchange stations
  (in tunnel): 104
Average station spacing: 770 m
Rail weight and type: S 41, 41 kg/m
Track type: Conventional sleepers on ballast
Max gradient: 1 in 25 (4%)
Minimum curve radius: 74 m on running lines; 50 m on sidings
Tunnel type: There are two sizes of tunnel: 'large-profile' on the former North-South Company lines (now lines 6, 7, 8 and 9) and 'small-profile' on the former Elevated and Underground Company lines (now lines 1, 2, 3 and 4). All are double-track rectangular tunnels, with and without centre supports; the large-profile tunnels are 6·9 m wide and 3·6 m high for rail level, while the small-profile tunnels are 6·24 m wide and 3·4 m high. Construction was mostly by cut-and-cover method, the tunnels being generally just below surface level. Tunnel linings are of concrete.
Electrification type: 780 V dc, third rail
One-man operation: All trains
Signalling: Electromagnetic, Siemens
Automatic control: Seltrac ATO on Line 4. Trains start automatically and are operated at all stages over the line by the computer-based system. An inductive loop cable embedded in the track transmits instructions to the train. Two-way communication is independent of wheel/rail contact. Minicomputers at the control centre make it possible for despatchers to control operations over the line. Each train carries a microprocessor to intercept commands and transmit vehicle data back to control. Seltrac also transmits information to display units on trains, giving next station and destination.

Line 9 is equipped with the Siemens LZB500 system.

Rolling stock
Number of cars: 688 large profile, 360 small profile, all motored
Main suppliers: Waggon Union, O & K, electrical equipment AEG/Siemens. The 60 Type FS/FK 84 and 87 two-car units built by Waggon Union feature AEG/Siemens three-phase asynchronous motor traction. Types F79·3, F84 and F89 have ac drive.
Car dimensions: Small-profile lines, 12·53 m long (two-car set with Scharfenberg couplers, 25·66 m), 2·3 m wide; large profile lines, 15·5/16.05 m long, 2·65 m wide.
Number of seats: 38 (large-profile cars)
Capacity: Crush, 197 passengers
Tare weight: 1973–77 deliveries, FS/FK 18·68/19·62 tonnes; 1979 deliveries, FS/FK 19·1/19.05 tonnes; 1984 deliveries, FS/FK 21·8/21·3 tonnes
Permitted gross weight: 1973–77 deliveries, FS/FK 31·48/32·42 tonnes; 1979 deliveries, FS/FK 31·84/31·79 tonnes; 1984 deliveries, FS/FK 34·8/34·3 tonnes
Construction: Bodies frame-built light metal, bogies lightweight steel
Max speed: 70 km/h; Types F84/87, 80 km/h
Control: Automatic cam control mechanism
Braking system: Electric brake operated as separately excited resistance brake to standstill, thyristor-controlled.
Doors: Electropneumatic door closing installation. Doors remain closed until train stops.

Trains are equipped with a 24 V radio and 24 V radio-telephone, plus a 110 V PA system.

Traffic
Train headways: Peak hours, 3 minutes; off-peak, 5 minutes; evenings, 10 minutes
Passenger journeys: (1988) 359.15 million
Max number of cars per train: Large-profile lines 6; small-profile 8; minimum, 2 cars
Average scheduled speed (including stops)
Large-profile lines 32·7 km/h
Small-profile lines 30·0 km/h

System development
The BVG authority operates bus services in the western sector of Berlin in addition to its U-Bahn. There has been progressive building of new lines and extensions to existing lines in Berlin's western sector since the Second World War. On Line 8, a further 3·5 km extension from Paracelsus-Bad to Wittenau is scheduled for 1993-94 opening. Extension of Line U9 from Steglitz to Lankwitz is planned.

S-Bahn

Agreement was reached in 1984 for the transfer to BVG from German State Railway (DR) management of the city's S-Bahn. In its prime this was a network that carried 737 million passengers in 1943. Berlin's destruction enforced a total shutdown in April 1945, but by 1956 an electrified system of 345 km was back in use and carrying over 400 million passengers a year. The erection of the Berlin Wall in 1961 led to a West Berlin boycott of the system and a chain of after-effects which by 1980 had the DR restricting operation to 21 route-km.

By the end of 1986 the new BVG management resumed service over three lines to a total of 71·5 route-km and serving 37 stations.

It is now hoped to restore service to the southern orbital line in 1992; and to the northern orbital line, Spandau and Lichterfelde Sud in 1993-94. Up to the end of the 1990s rehabilitation of the system will require an outlay of about DM2500 million.

The 123 motor and 115 trailer cars of Series 275; all built in 1927–30 for the S-Bahn's 800 V dc third-rail routes, have been progressively refurbished by Waggon Union. Late in 1986, under a development contract, AEG, Siemens and Waggon Union delivered a prototype eight cars of Type BR480, featuring in each power car four 90 kW asynchronous motors under GTO thyristor and microprocessor control for evaluation prior to conclusion of a mass-production design for S-Bahn fleet renewal. Subsequently a series of 41 two-car sets was ordered for 1991 delivery.

M-Bahn

Type of system: Maglev people mover

System development
Funded by the Federal Ministry of Research and Technology and the West Berlin city authority, a 1·7 km system developed by Magnetbahn GmbH was completed from Gleisdrieck metro station to Philharmonie Hall in 1988. Public service was not immediately inaugurated, but non-revenue operation began in late 1989.

Bilbao

Bilbao Metropolitan

Transportes Urbanos Gran Bilbao

Cap C Haya 6, Bilbao, Spain

Telephone: +34 4 435 8200

Type of system: Metro under construction

Gauge: 1000 mm

In 1985 the Basque administration approved proposals to create a 31·2 km metre-gauge line from Erxebarri to the coast at Plentzia, of which 20 km would be adaptation of the existing local railway, ET (for details see Spain, Railway Systems section); and, in a second phase, a 10 km line from Sancurce to San Ignacio. The schemes involve 17·4 km of tunnelling and will serve 23 stations. Rolling stock will be the units already in use on ET's Plentzia line, lengthened from three to five cars per set.

Construction began in February 1990 of the first 3km, four-station city-centre section betwen Olaveaga and the Nervion river crossing at Ripa. Completion was expected in the late summer of 1992.

Birmingham

Centro
West Midlands Passenger Transport Executive

16 Summer Lane, Birmingham B19 3SD, England

Telephone: +44 21 200 2787
Telex: 333248
Telefax: +44 21 200 1224

Director-General: Robert J Tarr
Head of Metro Development: R L Hughes

Type of system: Planned light rail

West Midlands Passenger Transport Authority, which operates under the Centro name, plans an LRT network of some 200 km linking Birmingham with Wolverhampton and all the city's principal conurbation towns, and a separate network in the Coventry area.

A Parliamentary approval was obtained in November 1989 for construction of Midland Metro Line 1. Using a disused heavy rail line this will run 22km from Snow Hill in Birmingham City Centre via Sandwell to Wolverhampton. In mid-1990 Centro was seeking a Section 56 (1968 Transport Act) government grant towards the £73 million cost, in the hope of opening the route in 1993.

In mid-1990 application to build two more routes was before Parliament. One, chiefly using existing or disused rail alignments, will run from Wolverhampton to Dudley, interchanging with Line 1 at Sandwell. The other, involving city-centre tunnelling and new alignments elsewhere, will extend 26km from Birmingham Five Ways via the city's new Convention Centre and Chelmsley Wood to the National Exhibition Centre and Birmingham Airport.

In October submission to Parliament of a proposal for the first line in Coventry was planned. Further routes might be proposed in 1991.

Bochum-Gelsenkirchen

Bochum-Gelsenkirchener Strassenbahnen AG (Bogestra)

Universitätstrasse 58, Postfach 10349, 4630 Bochum 1, Federal Republic of Germany

Telephone: +49 234 3336-0
Telex: 82 58 51

Commercial Director: Dr Hans-Jürgen Sattler
Technical Director: Dipl-Ing Gerd Leidtke

Type of system: Pre-U-Bahn

Gauge: 1000 mm; 1435 mm (north-south line)
Route length: 7·2 km, all in tunnel
Number of lines: 2
Number of stations: 6
Average distance between stations: 550 m
Tunnel type: Built by New Austrian Tunnel Construction Method
Electrification type: 600 V dc, overhead

Rolling stock
Type M (articulated)
Car dimensions: Length 20·44 m, width 2·3 m, height 3·306 m
Average and crush capacity: 101/166 (36 seats)
Motors per car: 2
Motor rating: 150 kW
Floor height: 880 mm
Tare and loaded weight: 28·8/38·65 tonnes
Max speed: 80 km/h

Type B (north-south line)
Car dimensions: Length 28 m, width 2·65 m, height 3·365 m
Capacity: 72 seated, 112 standing
Motors per car: 2
Motor rating: 235 kW
Floor height: 1 m
Tare weight: 39 tonnes
Max speed: 80 km/h

System development
Converted from metre-gauge tramway, a 9·1 km stretch of a 1435 mm-gauge north-south line from Bochum Hbf to Herne, with 13 stations, was inaugurated in September 1989; this forms part of the embryonic Rhine-Ruhr Stadtbahn network (qv). A line to Gelsenkirchen is planned. The ultimate pre-U-Bahn system will total 63 km and be operated by 100 Type B LRVs.

Bogota

Secretaria de Obras Publicas Alcaldia de la Ciudad Distrito Especiale de Bogota

Bogota, Colombia

Type of system: Planned light rail

Feasibility studies were completed for a proposed 93 km, 1·5 kV dc metro, but the project is now transmuted into a three-line, 35 km light rail network. In 1987 the Ministry of Public Works and Transport received eight bids for a US$250 million turnkey constructions contract. In 1988 the contract was awarded to the Italian Intermetro consortium, but work was not expected to begin until late 1989.

Bologna

Bologna, Italy

Type of system: Planned light rail

Consultants engaged to draft a city development plan have recommended construction of a three-line light rail system, part underground and part elevated. East-west and north-south routes would be completed by a northern loop route. First to be built would be the 14 km east-west line.

Bordeaux

Réseau de Transports en Commun de la Communauté de Bordeaux

25 rue Commandant Marchard, 33082 Bordeaux, France

Telephone: +33 56 90 93 93
Telex: 550436 cfgte bx

Type of system: Planned light rail

Plans were finalised in March 1990 for the first two routes of an automated, rubber-tyre VAL system. Line 1 will initially run 6.7 km from Ravezies in the north to Saint-Jean in the south; Line 2 will run 6.4 km from Regional Hospital in the west to Thiers, east of the Gironde river, intersecting Line 1 at Quinconces. Completion is forecast in 1996. Extensions of both lines are planned, with Line 2 eventually serving the city's airport. Final system length will be 45km.

Boston

Massachusetts Bay Transportation Authority (MBTA)

110 Park Plaza, Boston, Massachusetts 02116, USA

Telephone: +1 617 722 5000
Telefax: +1 617 722 3340

Chairman: Frederick P Salvucci
General Manager: Thomas P Glynn
Director, Operations: Ronald J MacKay
Chief Mechanical Officer (Heavy Rail): Michael T Burns
Chief Engineer: James E Rooney

Type of system: Full metro (3 lines); light rail (1 line)

Gauge: 1435 mm
Route length: 126·5 km, including:
Orange Line (full metro) 17·5 km
Blue Line (full metro) 9·5 km
Red Line (full metro) 47·3 km
Green Line (light rail) 52.2 km
Length in tunnel: 24 km
Number of stations: 145
(in tunnel): 32

Rail weight and type: 38·556 kg/m (ASCE); 45·36 kg/m (ARA-B); 68·04 kg/m (RE)
Track type: Combination of conventional sleepers on ballast, wooden sleepers on steel and concrete sleepers with resilient pads. All rail renovations, line extensions and reconstruction will be with continuous welding and resilient pads.
Tunnel type
Orange Line, cut-and-cover and caisson
Blue Line, single bored and cut-and-cover
Green Line, cut-and-cover
Red Line, cut-and-cover and single bored (Red Line extension single bored)
Gradient (max): 5%
Curvature (max): 122 m
Speed (design speed): 80 km/h
Electrification type: All 600 V dc. Collection: Red Line, third rail; high speed section of Red Line, catenary; Orange Line, third rail; Blue Line, third rail and catenary; Green Line, catenary
Signalling: Blue Line, automatic block (GRS and Wabco); Orange and Red Line, automatic train opera-

tion (GRS) and automatic block (Wabco); Green Line, automatic block (Wabco)
Automatic control: Orange and Red Lines have automatic speed control. Station stops and starts under control of driver

Rolling stock: 408 rapid transit, 215 light rail and 12 PCC cars

Heavy Rail
Type of car: 'Redbird' and 'Silverbird'
No in service: 160
Main supplier: Pullman standard

Type of car: Orange Line and Blue Line
No in service: 190
Main supplier: Hawker Siddeley

Type of car: No 2 Red Line
No in service: 58
Main supplier: UTDC

Light Rail
Type of car: PCC (Picture Window)
No in service: 12
Main supplier: Pullman Standard

Type of car: LRV (Light Rail Vehicle)
Main suppliers (no in service): Boeing Vertol (116), Kinki Sharyo (99)

Traffic
Train headways: 4 minutes (peak); 8 minutes (off-peak)
Passenger journeys: (1989) 128 million

System development
With over US$2500 million invested in capital improvements during the 1980s and many major expansion projects completed, MBTA was in 1989-90 devoting capital resources to upgrading. Red and Orange Line stations have been lengthened to accommodate longer trains, and Green Line power supply was being improved for the same purpose. It was planned to lengthen Blue Line platforms for six-car trains. In 1989 light rail service was reinstated on the Green Line's Arborway branch.

Bratislava

Dopravné podniky hlavného mesta SSR Bratislava

ul Obrancov mieru č 1, 81452 Bratislava, Czechoslovakia

Telephone: +42 7 333226
Telex: 92269

General Manager: Ján Novotny

Type of system: Planned metro

The national 1981–85 Five-Year Plan included a 9·5 km rapid transit line from Bratislava to Petrzalka intended to form Line 1 of a three-route system. Finance for an initial 6km was approved by the government in mid-1989, but this may now be built as an LRT extension of existing tramway.

Brescia

Brescia, Italy

In mid-1989 the city authority disclosed plans for an LRT system. A 12km line, half on elevated structures, would include an underground section in the city centre.

Brest

Brest, France

The city council has approved in principle plans for a 12 km east-west light rail route, with a branch to the northwest.

Bristol

Advanced Transport for Avon (ATA) Ltd

76 Alma Vale Road, Clifton, Bristol, England

Telephone: +44 272 745270

Telefax: +44 272 743329

Chairman: Richard Cottrell
Managing Director: Brian T Tucker
Secretary: Peter Downey
Project Co-ordinator: Penelope Craven

ATA, a private sector enterprise, plans an extensive multi-route LRT network serving the county of Avon. A Bill for Parliamentary powers for the initial route was approved in May 1989. The initial 16 km represents a conversion of moribund British Rail track between Portishead and Wapping Wharf, in Bristol city centre, including some new construction, provision of a depot and supply of a fleet of 10 vehicles. Construction was expected to begin in late 1990 for a 1993 opening.

A second Bill was laid before Parliament to extend from Wapping Road, by means of street-running, across Bristol city centre to Temple Meads station, but in early 1990 this was snagged by Bristol City Council's unexpected objections to on-street tracks. From Temple Meads the line is to be projected, by adaptation of former or existing BR track, to serve extensive new residential and commercial development in the districts of Yate and Bradley Stoke.

Six further routes are planned, including extension to and within Bath, but in some cases fulfilment depends on agreement with British Rail for cession or share of operating rights on BR track currently in use.

Brussels

Société des Transports Intercommunaux de Bruxelles (STIB)
Maatschappij voor het Intercommunaal Vervoer te Brussel (MIVB)

Avenue de La Toison d'Or 15, 1060 Brussels, Belgium

Telephone: +32 2 515 2111/3111
Telex: 26520 ntbbru b

Chairman: August de Winter
Director General: Paul Appelmans
Director, Operating: Jacques Devroye
  Infrastructure: Roger Perlaux
  Rolling Stock: André Siraut

Type of system: Metro and pre-metro (light rail)

Gauge: 1435 mm
Route length: Metro, 39km; pre-metro, 11·9 km
Number of lines: Metro, 3; pre-metro, 2
Number of stations: Metro, 51; pre-metro, 17 (4 shared with Metro)
Tunnel type: Mainly rectangular 7·5 m wide, 4·5 m high, 96 m-long sections
Max gradient: 6·2%
Minimum curvature radius: 100 m
Electrification type: Metro, 900 V dc; pre-metro, 600–700 V dc

Tramway and pre-Metro rolling stock: 279 four-, six- and eight-axle cars
Metro rolling stock
Number of cars: (Metro) 80 two-car sets (32 cars on order to form three-car sets)
Suppliers: BN Constructions Ferroviaires et Metalliques with ACEC electrical equipment
Car dimensions: Length 18·2 m, width 2·7 m, height 3·42 m
Tare weight: 31 tonnes
Braking: Regenerative, rheostatic, pneumatic and electromagnetic emergency brakes
Control: Choppers
Motors per car: 2
Motor rating: 266·2 kW
Max acceleration: 1·16 m/s^2
Emergency deceleration: 1·7 m/s^2
Average commercial speed: 30 km/h
Max running speed: 72 km/h
Number of seated passengers: 40 per car
Total passenger capacity: 210 per car
Body material: Framework in light alloy

Traffic
Trains/track/hour: Main axis (peak hours) 20; (off-peak) 12
  Branches (peak hours) 10; (off-peak) 6
Passenger journeys: (1988) 186 million

System development
Completion of the transformation of tramways into a 60 km metro network has been hampered by lack of population growth and financial difficulties. Pre-metro segments are two cross-city centre tunnels.

Further extensions under way in 1989, with completion dates, were: Line 1B, Veeveyde to Bizet, 1990; Line 1A, Heysel to Amandiers, 1993; pre-metro Line 3, Midi to Place Albert, 1993; Line 2, Midi to Yorez, 1993.

Bucharest

Intreprinderea de Exploatare a Metroul București
(Bucharest Metro Operation Enterprise, operating under the Railway Division of the Ministry of Transport)

38 Bd Dinicu Golescu, Sector 1, 79917 Bucharest, Romania

Telephone: +40 41 00 90
Telex: 11665

Director: Dipl Eng Crasneanu Constantin

Type of system: Full metro

Gauge: 1432 mm
Route length: 60 km
Number of lines: 3
Number of stations: 38
Average distance between stations: 1·4 km
Rail weight and type: UIC 49 and UIC 60
Track type: Rail laid on timber sleepers and crushed stone ballast; reinforced concrete (duo-block) sleepers embedded in tunnel invert
Tunnel type: Rectangular box section including separate bores for each running track
Electrification type: 750 V dc
Signalling: Automatic block. Entry and exit signals transmitted automatically. Automatic train speed control with cab indications

Rolling stock
Number of cars: 200 two-car sets
Supplier: Arad works
Car dimensions: Length 18·6 m (38 m coupled unit); width 3·1 m; height 3·4 m
Capacity: 34 seats per car; 200 standing passengers at 5 passengers/m^2, 300 at 8/m^2
Motor rating: 185 kW
Tare weight: 36 tonnes
Minimum running curve radius: 150 m
Max speed: 80 km/h
Max acceleration: 1·35 m/s^2
Average deceleration: 1 m/s^2

The stock consists of permanently-coupled two-car sets in radio communication with the control centre, and with public address equipment. Improvements being considered include thyristor-controlled traction systems, regenerative braking, automatic train operation and use of new materials in construction.

Traffic
Train headways: Peak hours, 2 minutes, to be reduced to 1·5 minutes
Passenger journeys: (1989) 272 million

System development
The first segment of a third line was opened in 1989. This runs from Gara Nord eastwards, interchanging with Line 2 at Piata Victoriei, and has taken over part of Line 1 between Gara Nord and Eroilor.

Budapest

Budapesti Közlekedési Vallalat (BKV)

Akácfa utca 15, 1980 Budapest VII, Hungary

Telephone: +36 1 422 130
Telex: 226325 bkv h
Telefax: +36 1 225 200

General Manager: Dr József Zahumenszky

Type of system: Full metro

Gauge: 1435 mm
Route length: 27·1 km
Number of lines: 3 (including small-profile 'Millenium' Line 1)
Number of stations (total): 38
  (in tunnel): 24
Average distance between stations: 925 m

Rail weight: 48·5 kg/m
Gradient (max): 3·3%
Curvature (max): 250–450 m
Speed (design max): 80 km/h
   (average commercial): 33·8 km/h
Electrification type: 825 V dc, third rail; 'Millenium' Line 1, 600 V dc
Signalling: Centralised traffic control, Interelec of France has installed ATC on part of Line 3

Rolling stock
Number of cars: 373, all motored five-car sets, Line 2; six-car sets, Line 3; 'Millenium' Line 1, 23 three-car articulated sets
Main supplier: Mytischy, USSR; 'Millenium' Line 1, Ganz
Car dimensions: Length 20 m, width 2·7 m
Seating capacity: 42
Tare and loaded weight: 31·5/51·7 tonnes
Doors: Pneumatic operation, 1·218 m wide
Cars on order or under delivery: Prototypes, with chopper control of 230 kW, mono-motor bogies, by Ganz on trial

Traffic
Train capacity (passengers): 890 (five-car), 1093 (six-car)
Train headways: Metro: 2 minutes–2 minutes 20 seconds (peak); 4–6½ minutes (off-peak); Millenium line: 1 minute 40 seconds peak; 2¼–5½ minutes off-peak
Passenger journeys: (1989) 296.5 million

System development
The 4·4 km Line 1 was opened in 1896 and named 'Millenium' to mark the Hungarian state's 1000 years of existence. Its infrastructure and stations are now being modernised; completion in 1994-95 will be accompanied by provision of new train-sets.

A 4km, four-station northward extension of Line 3 was to be opened at the end of 1990. It will feature automated train control. A Line 4, running almost entirely in deep-level tubes from Bocskai út on the Danube's right bank to Ujpalota on the left bank, is planned, but route and length are still to be fixed. The next century may see a fifth line running from North Buda to Pest.

Local railways (HEV)
BKV also runs a 97·9 km, 1 kV dc-electrified Budapest surface suburban railway system, the HEV, with 124 two-car emus, 37 steam, 13 main-line, 18 shunting electric, four main-line and two shunting diesel locomotives and 187 wagons for freight. In 1989 the system registered 95.675 million passenger journeys and 6.026 million tonnes of freight.

BKV also manages the Budapest bus, trolleybus and tramway system. Almost all of the tramway is being converted to LRT standards and is undergoing rolling stock renewal.

Buenos Aires

Subterraneos de Buenos Aires (SUBTE)

Bartolomé Mitre 3342, Buenos Aires 1201 DF, Argentina

Telephone: +54 1 890631-38

President of Directorate: J A Barbero
Manager, Planning and Control: Ing Alejandro Nazard Anchorena
Technical Manager: Ing Eduardo Mariategui
Manager, Operations: R Lissarrague

Type of system: Full metro

Gauge: 1435 mm
Route length: 39 km
Number of lines: 5
Number of stations (all in tunnel): 63
Average distance between stations: 580 m
Rail weight: Line B, 44 kg/m; other lines, 45·5 kg/m
Track type: Timber sleepers on stone ballast; concrete sleepers on new sections
Tunnel type: Double-track, of cut-and-cover construction only in Line A and at some of the stations in Lines B, C and D. The other lines and stations were constructed by tunnelling. The Line A tunnel is 7·7 m wide, and 4·45 m high from rail level; it is of rectangular section without centre supports. Line B runs partly in tunnel of rectangular section, 8·45 m wide by 4·65 m high, with centre supports, and partly in tunnel with arches over each track.
Gradient (max): 4%
Curvature (max): 80 m
Electrification type: Line A, 1·1 kV dc, overhead collection; Line B, 600 V dc, third rail collection; Lines C, D and E, 1·5 kV dc, overhead collection. Electrification is to be standardised with existing lines converted and new lines equipped with 750 V dc supply.

Traffic
Passenger journeys: (1985) 223·7 million

System development
Lines A and D are in course of reconstruction, in the case of Line A involving also conversion to 1·5 kV dc. After years of inactivity, in 1989 an 8.5 km extension of Line A was begun to Liniers, with nine stations; this will take over suburban service from parallel FA tracks. Also under way in 1990 was a 3km, 4-station projection of Line D to Monroe.

Rolling stock
Number of cars: 435
Main suppliers: Fabricaciones Militares, Pullman Standard, General Electric (Spain), Materfer
Cars on order: 90 from Fiat/Siemens; delivery to start 1990

Type of system: Light rail

A 6 km Line E1 from Metro Line E at Plaza de los Virreyes to Gral Savio began public service in August 1987. At its outer end a terminal loop is under construction and extension to the Buenos Aires airport is considered.

Rolling stock: 25 six-axle LRVs from Fiat/Siemens/Materfer/AEG/Fab Militares consortium.

Buffalo

Niagara Frontier Transportation Authority

181 Elliot Street, PO Box 5008, Buffalo, New York 14205, USA

Telephone: +1 716 855 7300
Telefax: +1 716 855 7657

Chairman: Robert D Gioia
Executive Director: Alfred H Savage

Car type	Lines C, D, E		Lines A, C, D, E		Line B	
Number built	80	108	124	80	90	12
Car dimensions						
length (m)	17	17	15	17·8	17	17
width (m)	2·6	2·6	2·6	–	3·2	3·2
height (m)	2·52	2·34	3·41	–	2·6	2·6
Passenger capacity per car						
(total)	160	160	150	170	170	170
(seated)	42	40	42	41	42	42
Motors per car	4	–	2	4	2	2
Rating	116 kW	115 kW	115 kW	185 kW	109 hp	109 hp
Train composition (minimum) 2 (max) 6						
Body material	steel	steel	steel/wood	steel	steel	steel
Weight (tonnes)						
Motor car	30	32	28	32	32·5	32·5
Trailer	20	21	–	31·7	–	–

Type of system: Light rail

Gauge: 1435 mm
Route length: 10·3 km
   (in tunnel): 8·37 km; includes 5·63 km in rock tunnel, 2·74 km cut-and-cover
No of stations: 14
   (in tunnel): 8
Rail type: 115 RE cwr underground; 128 RE7 cwr on surface
Track type: Direct fixation to concrete roadbed or floating slabs
Electrification type: 650 V dc, overhead
Method of construction financing: 80% Federal (UMTA); 20% State of New York
Train headways: 5–6 minutes (peak hours)
Signalling: Centrally controlled cab signalling; 100 Hz track signals.

Carborne equipment operates under two modes of operation: cab signal control in the sub-surface area; and speed limit control on the surface or in small areas. For sub-surface operation, the carborne ATP consists of continuous inductive cab signalling equipment. This ATP equipment receives a coded 100 Hz phase selective signal from the running rails, and through proper decoding and relay logic, provides a signal for safe maximum speed indication. Surface speed is limited to 28 mph through relay logic.

Traffic
No of passengers: (1989) 8·071 million

Rolling stock
Tokyu Car Corp, Japan, supplied 27 four-axle cars each with capacity for 140 rush-hour passengers, including 51 seated. Each car is 20·37 m long and 2·67 m wide. Retractable steps provide for surface boarding in the surface transit mall, ramps are provided at surface stations to accommodate wheelchair and handicapped passengers. There is high-platform boarding at all underground stations.

System development
Most of the 1·93 km surface section is within a vehicular-free transit pedestrian mall, possibly the longest in the world, and the entire section, which traverses the central business district, is fare-free to stimulate retail development.

In 1990 NFTA was examining the feasibility of extending its line by 9.5 km in each of two corridors, one to the State University's North Campus, the other to the city of Tonawanda. The Authority has purchased 26.5 km of disused railroad rights-of-way for future extensions, which may be in other corridors also.

NFTA operates a unique combination of the HASTUS automated scheduling system and integrated graphics for formulation of interconnected rail and bus schedules and related vehicle and crew rosters.

Cairo

National Authority for Tunnels

56 El Ryad Street, El-Mohandiseen, Cairo, Egypt

Telephone: +20 2 346 7276/0458/7256
Telex: 93457 meteor un

Chairman: Eng M E Abdel Salam
Vice Chairman: Eng F Abdel Aziz
Chief Electrical and Mechanical: Dr Y Khattab
Chief Civil Engineer: Eng A Madkour
Transport Planning Authority
   Vice Chairman: Dr A K F Lashine

Type of system: Regional metro under construction

Route length: 42 km
Gauge: 1435 mm
Electrification: 1·5 kV dc, overhead
Rail weight: 54 kg/m

Rolling stock
The present fleet comprises 100 three-car M-T-M units, with each motor car powered by four 262 kW motors; total seating per set is 144, maximum speed 100 km/h and rate of acceleration 0·9 m/s^2.

System development
Egypt's Ministries of Economy and Planning approved plans in 1978 for a Greater Cairo rapid transit railway, which will run 42 km from El Marg via the city centre

to Helwan, with a complement of two urban metro lines aggregating 22 km. The first phase was completed in September 1987, when a 4·7 km cross-city tunnel was finished and Helwan trains were re-routed through it to a temporary terminus, Moubarak, under Rameses Square. A second phase, linking Moubarak with the El Marg line's terminus to join the two routes end-on, was completed in February 1989.

Current work is centred on upgrading, resignalling and electrifying the El Marg line. The final phase will be supplied by Alsthom of 48 more three-car emus.

Two urban metro lines totalling 24km are proposed: Line 1, running 16 km from Shubra-el-Kheima to El Giza, and Line 2 from Salah Salem to Imbaba. Both will interchange with the core route in the city centre. Bids to build Line 1 were called in 1989.

Calcutta

Metro Railway, Metro Rail Bhavan

33/1 Chowringhee Road, Calcutta 700071, India

Telephone: +91 22 29 4750
Telex: 021 7754 mrly in

Chief Engineer: Mir Liaquet Ali Aloke Sengupta
Chief Electrical Engineer: P Sahoo
Chief Signal and Telecommunications Engineer:
  M R Bhaskaran
Manager: B Chaudhuri

Type of system: Full metro, partly under construction

Gauge: 1676 mm
Route length: 16·43 km
  (in tunnel): 15·13 km (1·1 km in twin circular tunnel; 14·03 km in rectangular reinforced concrete box construction)
Number of stations (total): 17
  (in tunnel): 15
Max gradient: 2%
Minimum curve radius: 300 m
Rail weight: UIC 60 kg/m
Track type: Ballastless track with reinforced concrete bed
Tunnel type: Most of the line is being built by cut-and-cover, only a small section by shield tunnelling. Most stations have a mezzanine floor for passenger entrance and ticket sales. Tunnelling from Chitpur yard to the Shyambazar crossing has been carried out with Soviet-built tunnel shields, and of another tunnel near Chitpur yard with a Hungarian-built shield. Tunnels and stations have forced-air ventilation with the air scrubbed and cooled with chilled water. All entrances are constructed so their floor level is above the highest recorded level of flood water; any seepage of water will accumulate in sumps from where it will be regularly pumped out.
Electrification type: 750 V dc, third rail
Signalling: Cab signalling with automatic train protection. Central control

Rolling stock
Cars: 144 from Integral Coach Factory, Perambur, Madras, formed into eight-car sets, with traction equipment by the New Government Electric Factory, Bangalore. When in full operation the Metro will need 230 cars
Car dimensions: Length 20·3 m, width 2·74 m, height 3·7 m
Acceleration: 1 m/s^2
Capacity per car: 60 (trailer) or 54 (power car) seated; up to 240 standing
Max speed: 80 km/h (initially 50 km/h)

One-man operation: All cars suitable

Traffic (estimated)
Trains/track/hour: 24
Train capacity (passengers): 2300
Total passengers/track/hour (peak): 67 000
Train headway design: 2½ minutes initially, later 1½ minutes
Passenger journeys
  (daily): 1·73 million
  (annually): 442 million

System development
An 8 km section in the south and a 2·2 km section in the north of the 16·43 km north-south line are in revenue service. The central 6·5 km section is due to open in 1991. Eight-car trains are running between Esplanade and Tollyganj in the south, serving seven intermediate stations with a frequency of 12 minutes at peak hours. Daily traffic is about 60 000 passengers. When fully commissioned, the Dum Dum-Tollyganj line will carry about 1·73 million passengers per day.

Extension of the first line from Tollyganj southwards to New Garia, construction of an 18·3 km east-west line and of a second north-south line 27·6 km long have been surveyed in detail. These are yet to be approved by the government.

Calgary

City of Calgary Transportation Department

PO Box 2100, Calgary, Alberta T2P 2M5, Canada

Telephone: +1 403 277 9800
Telex: 03 822 652
Telefax: +1 403 230 1155

General Manager, Calgary Transit: G H Paton (Acting)
Manager, Light Rail Transit Construction Division:
  J Chaput

Type of system: Light rail

Gauge: 1435 mm
Route length: South Line 10·9 km
  Northeast Line: 9·8 km
  Downtown Transit Mall: 2 km
  Northwest Line: 5·6 km
  (in tunnel): 2·13 km
Rail weight and type: 60 kg/m (Ri 60) girder rail; 50 kg/m (ARA 100) 1 rail
Track type: 60 kg/m girder rail in-street; 50 kg/m rail on ballasted concrete sleepers and concrete slab (direct fixation). Continuously welded. Parallel track centre spacing: 4000 m
Electrification type: 600 V dc, overhead
Signalling: Block system, supplied by WABCO. Signalling can be adjusted to provide for 2½ minute headways

Rolling stock
Number of cars: 83 all motored
Main suppliers: Siemens Electric, Canada and Duewag, West Germany
Motor output: 2 × 150 kW per car
Car dimensions: Length 24·3 m, width 2·65 m, height 3·62 m
Capacity: 64 seated, 98 standing at 4/m^2
Tare weight: 32·5 tonnes
Service acceleration: 1·0 m/s^2
Service deceleration: 1·2 m/s^2
Max speed: 80 km/h

Traffic
Passenger journeys daily (1989)
South Line: 35 000
Northeast Line: 26 600
Downtown Free Fare Zone: 20 000
Northwest Line: 22 400
Total: 104 000

System development
Northwest leg forms a main-line system passing through the heart of the city along the exclusive, at-grade transit mall. The 5·6 km first stage of Northwest LRT extends from the city centre to the University of Calgary, site of the 1988 Winter Olympics. A 0·8 km extension of the Northwest line, to 31 Street NW was to open in September 1990. Further extensions are under review for 1991-95.

Cambridge

Cambridgeshire County Council, England

In 1990 consultants were conducting a feasibility study of a light rail system for an area that is one of the fastest-growing in England. The concept is based on parallel use of British Rail alignments, which approach the city from four directions, with city-centre on-street connection.

Caracas

CA Metro de Caracas

Multicentro Empresarial del Este Conjunto Miranda, Torre B pisos 1 al 7, Chacao, Caracao 1060, Venezuela

Telephone: +58 2 208 2111
Telex: 24936 metro vc

President: J González Lander
Manager, Design: R Alvarez
Equipment: S Marcano C

Type of system: Planned full metro

Gauge: 1435 m
Route length (open): 40 km
Number of lines: 2 open; 2 planned
Number of stations: 35
Gradient (max): 3·5%
Curvature (max): 225 m
Rail weight and type: 54 kg/m in 18 m lengths, continuously welded
Track type: Rails on Stedef twin-block sleepers laid on concrete in tunnels and on ballast on surface sections
Tunnel type: Cut-and-cover and bored
Electrification type: 750 V dc, third rail
Signalling: Automatic signalling and train control with on-board equipment similar to that on Paris Metro cars

Rolling stock
Number of cars: 378
Suppliers: Frameca consortium led by CIMT and including Alsthom-Atlantique, ANF-Industrie, Francorail and CEM-Oerlikon
Car dimensions: Length 21·35 m, width 3·05 m, height 2·498 m
Capacity: Cars with driver's cab, 54 sets; others 60; standing room for 120
Weight: 30 tonnes
Traction motors per car: 4 × 122 kW
Max speed: 80 km/h
Max acceleration: 1·35 m/s^2
Max deceleration: 1·1 m/s^2
Braking: Regenerative
Doors: 4 each side with 1·37 m openings
Car body construction: Aluminium extruded sections

Traffic
Passenger journeys: (1987) 240 million

System development
Line 1 was extended 4·7 km by 1988 and its remaining 4·4 km to Palo Verde was opened in November 1989. Construction of Line 3 extending 12·7 km from La Rinconada to the central area is under way. It is planned to finish this in 1993. A 9·5 km express line from Las Adjunkas to Los Teguesis planned.

Casablanca

Casablanca, Morocco

Japanese consultants have been studying a projected rapid transit system, most likely light rail. The first project would be an elevated cross-city line.

Charleroi

Société des Transports Intercommunaux de Charleroi (STIC)

Place des Tramways 9, Bte 1, 6000 Charleroi, Belgium

Telephone: +32 71 234111
Telefax: +32 71 234197

Director: G Delva

Type of system: Light rail

Gauge: 1000 m
Route length: 14·2 km (132 km planned)
Number of lines: 8 planned
Number of stations: 13; 75 planned
Track type: SNCB-type 50 kg/m rails laid on 'Angleur' tie-plates inclined 1.20; tie-plate laid on poplar plate, 5 mm thick for sound and vibration damping. Creosoted sleepers laid at 25/28 m on straight sections, 30/18 m on curves. Type U 69 safety guard rails laid in curves. 20/40 ballast layer, 20 cm thick, laid under sleepers.
  Rails welded to sections 600 m long. Switches activated by remote control from car by electromagnetic boxes supplied with 600 V current.
Electrification type: 600 V dc, overhead

Rolling stock
Number of cars: 50

Type: Six-axle articulated
Supplier: BN/ACEC
Car dimensions: Length 22·8 m, width 2·5 m, height 3·26 m
Capacity: 192, including 40 seated
Tare weight: 38 tonnes

The cars are of welded steel construction with four double doors on each side. They are equipped with regenerative and rheostatic braking for speeds above 4 km/h, with disk brakes mounted on all axles for speeds below 4 km/h, and thyristor chopper starting equipment.

System development
In 1976 Charleroi launched a scheme to convert its tramways into a light rail network consisting of a downtown 4·3 km ring line radiating eight branches. An east-west link, including the Beaux Arts-Nord section of the ring line, the radial lines to Chatelet and Gilly as far as Quatre-Bras, was nearing completion in 1989.

Completion of the planned system is now deferred and may not proceed as planned. Over-engineering of fixed installations has been alleged and traffic levels have been well below projections, leading to a revision of usage of forecasts.

Chelyabinsk

Chelyabinsk, USSR

Plans have been drafted for a 10 km line from the centre of this eastern USSR city to its northwestern suburbs, construction to begin possibly in 1990.

Chicago

Chicago Transit Authority (CTA)

Merchandise Mart Plaza, PO Box 3555, Chicago, Illinois 60654, USA

Telephone: +1 312 664 7200

Chairman: Clark Burns
Executive Director: Alfred Savage
Senior Deputy Executive Director: G Chevere

Type of system: Full metro

Gauge: 1435 mm
Route length: 157·5 km
 (in tunnel): 18 km
 (elevated): 59·1 km
Number of lines in operation: 6: North-South, West-Northwest, West-South, Ravenswood, Evanston, Skokie
Number of stations (total): 143
 (in tunnel): 21
 (elevated): 63
Gradient (max): 1 in 28·6 (3·5%)
Curvature (max): 27·4 m
Rail weight and type: 37·3 (50%), 41·4 (25%) and 47·6 (25%) kg/m flat-bottomed
Tunnel type: Single-track bored (14·2 km), cut-and-cover (3·6 km) and concrete caisson (0·2 km)
Electrification type: 600 V dc, third rail

Rolling stock
Number of cars: 1217
Main suppliers: St Louis Car, Pullman, Budd, Boeing Vertol
Main types: 6000 series (107); and 2000-2600 series (1110)

Car dimensions
6000 series: length 14·63 m, width 2·84 m, height 3·66 m
2000-2600 series: length 14·63 m, width 2·84 m, height 3·71 m
Capacity
6000 series: 46, 47, 50 or 51 seats depending on car type
2000-2600 series: 43, 45, 47, 49 or 51 seats
Motors per car: 4 (both series)
Automatic train control: All cars

Traffic
Train headways: Peak hours, 3–5 minutes depending on line; off-peak, 5–15 minutes
Capacity per train (seated): up to 400
 (standing): up to 800
Passenger journeys: (1989) 147·3 million

System development
Construction began in late 1984 on a project to reconfigure the system by connecting together the most heavily used branches of the West-South and North-South lines. The Dan Ryan branch of the present West-South line will be joined with the Howard branch of the present North-South line through the State Street Subway. When completed in 1991, the US$142 million Howard-Dan Ryan Thru-Route will shift the Dan Ryan from the Loop elevated structure in the city centre, where it shares tracks with two other routes, to unshared subway tracks nearby, enabling the presently overcrowded Dan Ryan rush-hour service to be increased up to 40 per cent. The project includes a 1·2 km subway-to-elevated connection; modernised and expanded car storage yards at 98th and Howard terminals, supported by new terminal trackwork and interlockings; a fully equipped 26-car maintenance workshop at Howard; and traction power and communications improvements.

The resultant re-configuration will connect together lines that have similar service requirements, allowing adequate service to be provided more economically on all the branches involved. Enlarging the yards at Howard and 98th will allow unproductive car mileage to be virtually eliminated, and improved terminal trackwork will increase terminal capacity and enable quicker turnbacks. The less heavily-used Englewood and Jackson Park branches of the present North-South line are expected to be through-routed with the Lake branch.

In 1986 construction started of a new 14·96 km line connecting the Loop elevated with Midway Airport on the city's southwest side. The project, budgeted at US$496 million, will include eight stations (seven with bus-rail interchange facilities), 72 new cars, a car storage yard and a car maintenance shop. Completion is expected in 1992/93.

Other planned capital projects include a US$156 million rehabilitation of the downtown Loop and Jackson Park branch portion of the elevated system, dating from 1990, and a US$26 million renovation of the central city subway system.

Specifications for a new generation of rolling stock, the Series 3200, have been drafted.

Cleveland

Greater Cleveland Regional Transit Authority

615 Superior NW St, Cleveland, Ohio 44113, USA

Telephone: +1 216 566 5100

General Manager: R J Tober

Type of system: Full metro (Red Line)

Gauge: 1435 m
Route length: 30·6 km
 (in tunnel): 0·8 km
 (at surface level): 29·8 km
Number of lines: 1
Number of stations: 18
 (in tunnel): 2
Rail weight and type: 45 kg/m ARA-A full-metro
Track type: Sleepers on ballast with continuous welded rail. Recently rebuilt sections use resilient fasteners in wood sleepers
Tunnel type: Cut-and-cover, or within structure
Electrification type: 600 V dc, overhead
Signalling: GRS three-aspect lights with automatic stop. All interlocks centrally controlled. Cab signal control will eventually be extended throughout the metro and light rail (see below) lines
Automatic control: Cab signalling between Tower City and Windermere, the eastern terminal on the GCRTA network. GCRTA may exercise an option for a fibre-optic transmission system together with a computerised alarm reporting system

Rolling stock
Number of cars: 60, all motored
Main supplier: Tokyu Car
Tare weight per car: 76 000 lb
Capacity

	Double cab car	Single cab car
Seating	80	84

Car dimensions: Length 75 ft (22·86 m), width 10 ft (3·15 m), height 12 ft 5½ in (3·66 m)
Max operating speed: 60 mph
Brakes: Electro-pneumatic with dynamic brakes
Acceleration: 2·75 m/s^2
Deceleration: Full service 3·0 mph/s, emergency 3·5 mph/s

Traffic
Train headways: Peak hours, 5–7 minutes; off-peak, 18 minutes
Passenger journeys: (1988) 4·6 million

System development
Cleveland's Red Line links the city's central area with the airport, where the station is in the terminal building.

Type of system: Light rail (Blue and Green lines)

Route length: 21·2 km
Number of lines: 2
Number of stops: 29
Average distance between stops: 0·8 km
Rail weight and type: 45 kg/m ARA-B light rail
Electrification type: 600 V dc, overhead

Rolling stock: 48, all motored
Main supplier: Breda (Italy)
Car dimensions: Length 23·504 m, width 2·821 m
Capacity: 84 seated, 270 crush
Tare and loaded weight: 38 102/56 472 kg
Doors: Folding, 1·249 m wide

Traffic
Train headways: Peak hours, 4–6 minutes; off-peak, 10 minutes
Passenger journeys: (1989) 3·35 million

Cologne

Kölner Verkehrsbetriebe AG

Scheidtweilerstrasse 38, Postfach 450 629, 5000 Cologne 41, Federal Republic of Germany

Telephone: +49 221 5471
Telex: 8881 701

Manager, Rail: Dr W Meyer

Type of system: Pre U-Bahn

Gauge: 1435 mm
Route length: 35·1 km (plus 14 tram routes totalling 105 km)
Number of stations: 28 (in tunnel)
Max gradient: 4%
Minimum curve radius: 60 m
Electrification type: 750 V dc, overhead

Rolling stock
Number of cars: 288 eight-axle trams of Duewag Types GT8 and B80
Car dimensions: Length 28/30 m, width 2·5/2·65 m, height 3·36 m
Passenger capacity: 282, 72 seated
Tare weight: 40 tonnes
Acceleration: 1·1 m/s^2
Deceleration: Normal, 1·6 m/s^2, emergency, 3 m/s^2
Cars on order: 9 Duewag B80

System development
Segregated rights of way are being progressively introduced for some 140 km of Cologne's tramway system, by the construction of cutting and embankment and by tunnelling. Completion of the total system is expected to take 70 to 80 years.

Croydon, England

Consultants have confirmed the feasibility and viability of a proposal formulated jointly by the local authority of this major south London suburb and business centre, London Regional Transport and British Rail for conversion to light rail of BR's West Croydon-Wimbledon and Addiscombe-Elmers End branches, their connection by a new cross-town line, and the addition of new Croydon-New Addington and Elmers End-Beckenham branches.

Dallas

Dallas Area Rapid Transit (DART)

601 Pacific Avenue, Dallas, Texas 75202, USA

Telephone: +1 214 748 3278

Chairman: Marvin M Lane
Executive Director: Charles S Anderson

Type of system: Planned light rail

After financial reconsideration and voter rejection of two earlier 1980s schemes, the electorate in 1989 endorsed a 'New Directions' transit plan embracing a light rail network totalling 106 km and a 29 km heavy rail commuter route. In that year DART bought 50 km of rail right-of-way from Union Pacific and secured operating rights over a further 65 km, to safeguard up to 80 per cent of the proposed light rail network and the heavy rail route.

Construction was to begin in 1990 of the first 32 km of the light rail system, from the northeast suburbs to the city centre. Opening was forecast for 1997. The heavy rail service was expected to start from South Irving Transit Center to Dallas Union Station in 1992.

Delhi
Metropolitan Transport Project (Railway)

35-36 Rani Jhansi Road, Motia Khan, Delhi 110 055, India

Type of system: Full metro and planned light rail

In 1989 RITES was contracted to undertake detailed design of the first east-west line of a full metro system. The city authorities envisage an eventual network of 220 km, partly underground, with about 150 stations.

A 300 km light rail system has also been under feasibility study. Besides serving the city centre, it would feed the electrified ring railway on which Indian Railways operates emu services. An east-west 36 km route from Vivek Vihar to Vikas Puri was approved by the Transport Minister in 1987.

Denver
Regional Transportation District

1600 Blake Street, Denver, Colorado 80202, USA

Telephone: +1 303 573 2330

General Manager: Richard Bauman

Type of system: Planned light rail

Plans for a 123 km light rail network were suspended by a new elected Board of Directors, following earlier rejection in a local referendum of the project's financing by a sales tax. In May 1987, however, the Colorado State Governor approved construction of a 27 km line on an existing rail alignment from the city centre southeastward. However, economic recession in the area delayed progress and in 1990 feasibility was back under discussion by the Colorado State legislature. The only adopted scheme under way was a 19 km bus/HOV lane on the North-I 25 highway.

Detroit
Suburban Mobility Authority for Regional Transportation (SMART)

660 Woodward Avenue, 13th Floor, First National Building, Detroit, Michigan 48226, USA

Telephone: +1 313 256 8600

Type of system: Planned light rail transit (LRT)

Gauge: 1435 mm
Route length: 42 km
 (in tunnel): to be decided
Number of stations: 20
Proposed electrification: 600 V dc, overhead
Signalling: Automatic block signals with train-stop protection

Rolling stock
Type of cars: Articulated light rail vehicles
Number required: 50 initially, 75 ultimately

System development
Detroit's planned light rail line would service both the Woodward Avenue and Gratiot Avenue corridors, with the former between Royal Oak and downtown Detroit to be initially constructed. With no source of funding in prospect SMART has no active plans to implement the light rail project and is concentrating on improvement and expansion of bus services.

Detroit Transportation Corporation

150 Michigan Avenue, Detroit, Michigan 48226, USA

Telephone: +1 313 224 2160

Type of system: People-mover

Operation began in August 1987 of a 4·8 km, 13-station single-track elevated downtown people-mover, creation of which has been 80 per cent Federally funded as a demonstration scheme. This is a steel rail loop of 1435 mm-gauge, and is the first US project to employ a driverless linear induction motor-powered system. Daily ridership has ranged from 5000 to 50 000 passengers, depending on special events, with a weekday average of 10 000 to 13 000 passengers.

Dnepropetrovsk
Upravlenie Metropolitena

Dnepropetrovsk, USSR

Type of system: Full metro

Gauge: 1524 mm
Route length: 11·2 km
Number of lines: 1
Electrification type: 825 V dc, third rail

Rolling stock: 52 cars
Supplier: Mytischy

System development
The first line was expected to open in 1990. Ultimate network plan covers 74 km.

Dortmund
Dortmunder Stadtwerke AG

Deggingstrasse 40, Postfach 105049, 4600 Dortmund 1, Federal Republic of Germany

Telephone: +49 231 555 0
Telex: 822183 dsw d
Telefax: +49 231 555 3300

Chairman: Prof Dr Hermann Flieger
Operating Manager: Dr-Ing Kurt Eckert

Type of system: Conventional tramway: 3 routes upgraded to pre-metro under the Rhine-Ruhr Stadtbahn project, with city-centre tunnels

Gauge: 1435 mm
Route length: 100·4 km (including tramway)
 reserved track: 58·8 km
Number of routes: 7
Number of stations: 190
Electrification type: 600 V dc, overhead

Rolling stock: 110 Duewag cars:
 N8C 8-axle 54
 GT8 8-axle 46
 B80C 6-axle 10
Cars on order: 34 Duewag Type B80C LRVs
Passenger journeys: (1987) approx 43·5 million

System development
The initial northern section of Line 2 (10·3 km), scheduled to open in 1990, will be followed by the two southern branches totalling 5·2 km. Line 3 and other extensions are still in the planning stage.

Under the Rhine-Ruhr Stadtbahn plan, which comprises four stages through to 2000, 10 branches of the tramway network are to be linked by three cross-city tunnels to create a light rail system of 41 km, with 59 stations, of which 20–25 km will be in tunnel. The remainder will be upgraded tramway, though much of the present system is already at or close to Stadtbahn standards (see under Rhine-Ruhr).

Duisburg
Duisberger Verkehrsgesellschaft AG

PO Box 10 04 52, Mülheimerstrasse 72-74, 4100 Duisburg 1, Federal Republic of Germany

Telephone: +49 203 3951

General Manager: Dipl-Kfm Dr Günter Erbe

Type of system: Pre U-Bahn and Stadtbahn

Gauge: 1435 mm
Route length: 63 km (including tramway)
Number of routes: 2
Electrification type: 600 V dc, overhead
Signalling: Long-loop, continuous inductive ATC to be installed

Rolling stock
Number of cars: 86 (Types B80, N8C, GT8)
Supplier: Duewag/Siemens

Traffic
Passenger journeys: (1988) 4·3 million

System development
A 40·5 km, two-line pre U-Bahn network is being created from parts of a tramway network, with the addition of 3·1 km of new construction (which should be finished in late 1991 or early 1992). The final system will form part of the Rhine-Ruhr Stadtbahn network eventually covering 400 km, and linking 11 cities with a total population of 16 million. The existing streetcar system to the south of the city was superseded by Stadtbahn operation in 1985 but its final form would not be achieved until 1991. That was to be followed by construction of inner-city tunnel to connect the southern system with Lines 2 and 3 in the north.

Düsseldorf
Rheinische Bahngesellschaft AG

Hansaallee 1, Postfach 6720, 4000 Düsseldorf 11, (Oberkassel) Federal Republic of Germany

Telephone: +49 211 58201
Telex: 858921
Telefax: +49 211 582 1966

General Manager: Dipl-Ing Georg Püttner

Type of system: Pre U-Bahn and Stadtbahn
Rolling stock: 87 Duewag B80 articulated LRVs and rebuilt trams

Traffic
Passenger journeys: (1988) 16.1 million

System development
Extensions, including a 2·2 km four-track tunnel under the central business area from Heinrich-Heine-Allee to Düsseldorf Hbf, were opened in May and August 1988. The tunnel is now used by five routes.

Two extensions totalling 2·6 km beyond the main station are set to open in 1992/93. Long-range plans envisage a four-line system of 68 km, with 15 km of it in tunnel.

The Düsseldorf system is also a component of the Rhine-Ruhr Stadtbahn, and connects with the Duisburg system.

Edinburgh
Edinburgh Metro Development Group, c/o Department of Planning, Lothian Regional Council

12 St Giles Street, Edinburgh EH1 1P7, Scotland

Telephone: +44 31 556 6933
Telefax: +44 557 0662

Leader, Metro Development Group:: David J S Scotney

Type of system: Planned light rail

The Council's public transport development strategy for the Edinburgh area includes development of a light rail system, electrified at 750V dc, known as the Edinburgh Metro. The programme envisages opening in 1998 of a 17.5 km north-south route from the Leith area to Cameron Toll West, and thence in branches to Burdiehouse and Gilmerton. The route would be formed from disused British Rail tunnel and surface route, new tunnels, roadside reservations and on-street track. An east-west route from the terminal area of the first line to Davidson's Main is proposed for opening in 2006. It was hoped during 1990 to finalise routes and then submit a Bill for Parliamentary approval.

Edmonton

Edmonton Transit

10th Floor, Century Place, 9803-102A Avenue, Edmonton, Alberta T5J 3A3, Canada

Telephone: +1 403 428 4145
Telex: 037 42725
Telefax: +1 403 478 3388

General Manager: John Schlumberger
Transit Manager: Gregory R Latham

Type of system: Light rail

Gauge: 1434 mm
Route length: 11·1 km
  (in tunnel): 2·8 km
Number of lines: 1
Number of stations (total): 9
  (in tunnel): 5
Rail weight and type: 100ARA (50 kg/m)
Tunnel type: Cut-and-cover and bored
Gradient (max): 4·5%
Curvature (max): main line 140 m, yard 30 m
Electrification type: 600 V dc, overhead

Rolling stock
Car types: 6-axle articulated motor cars, derived from Frankfurt U2 design
Number of units: 37
Car dimensions: Length 24·3 m, width 2·65 m, height 3·66 m
Number of doors per side: 4 double
Door width: 1·6 m
Number of passengers per car (total): 161
  (seated): 64
Motors per car: 2
Motor rating: 150 kWh
Power per train (minimum): single car, 300 kW
  (max): 5-car train, 1500 kW
Acceleration (max): 1·32 m/s^2
Deceleration (normal service): 1·3 m/s^2
  (emergency): 3·0 m/s^2
Max design speed: 80 km/h
Bogies (type and manufacturer): Duewag monomotor
Brakes: Dynamic/disc/magnetic
Weight (empty): 31 tonnes
Cars on track: 2 Duewag U2AC with three-phase ac motors

Traffic
Train headways (currrently): 5 minutes
Capacity per train (passengers seated): 192
  (passengers standing): 291. (Based on 3-car train crush load, 4 passengers/m^2)

System development
A 2·5 km, two-station extension was under construction in 1988 for completion throughout in September 1992; the first of its stations was opened in September 1989. This will extend the system southward across the river and to the University.

Erevan

Upravlenie Metropolitena

375010 Ploshchad Lenina, Dom Pravitelstva 2, Erevan, USSR

General Manager: R S Kaltakhchyan
Chief Engineer: Marlen Grigorievich Artiunov

Type of system: Full metro

Gauge: 1524 mm
Route length: 8·4 km
Number of lines: 1
Number of stations: 9
Average distance between stations: 1·44 km
Electrification type: 825 V, third rail

Rolling stock
Number of cars: 27 four-car sets

Traffic
Passenger journeys: (1986) 21 million

System development
The initial section, of which 5·7 km is underground, connects Erevan's main industrial area with its most heavily populated area via the main railway station. A 47 km network of two lines with a common, north-south central axis intersected by a third, east-west line, is envisaged.

Essen

Essener Verkehrs AG

Zweigerstrasse 34, Postfach 10 10 63, 4300 Essen 1, Federal Republic of Germany

Telephone: +49 201 826-0
Telex: 0857 688
Telefax: +49 201 826 1000

Directors: Wolfgang Teubner
  Hermann Derks Schärer
  Johannes K Schmidt
  Falkobert Obst
Managers, Rail: Hans Ahlbrecht
  Gerhard Boisserée
  Hans-Joachim Maab

Type of system: U-Stadtbahn (light rail) and tramway

Gauge: 1433 mm (tramway 1000 mm)
Route length: 1433mm-gauge: 16 km. 1000mm-gauge: 61 km
Length in tunnel: 13 km (tramway 6.5 km)
Number of lines: 3 (tramway:10)
Number of stations (total): 23
Rail type: S49, Ri59, NP4, Ri60
Track type: Conventional sleepers on ballast
Tunnel type: Cut-and-cover; bored single track; bored stations
Electrification type: 750V dc (some 600V dc on tramway)
One-man operation: All services
Signalling: Conventional block system by Siemens
Centralised control: Central control room with train identification system and process computer for point operation and vehicle identification. Radio control on all vehicles

Traffic
Passenger journeys: (1988) 1·38 million (Both systems)

Rolling stock
Number of cars: U-Stadtbahn: 24
Types: B80C: Cologne-type, six-axle, 2 × 235 kW motors by Duewag/ABB; 76 seats, standing room 161 passengers; 5 units. B100C: Cologne-type, six-axle 2 × 235 kW motors by Duewag/ABB/Siemens; 72 seats, standing room 187 passengers; 19 units.
The tramway system operates 19 Duewag Type M8S, 41 Duewag Type M8C (15 more were ordered for 1989/90 delivery), 1 Duewag Type M8D and 40 Duewag Type GT6/8 cars.

System development
The city's objective is a 58 km U-Bahn network, of which 12·5 km will be underground, to integrate with the overall Rhine-Ruhr Stadtbahn development. The surface sections are being created largely by conversion of metre-gauge tram tracks to 1433 mm in an eight-stage programme which has been absorbing a total investment of DM1697 million. The first five stages are over and two more were in progress in 1989. Some tunnel sections are in use with metre-gauge Type M8 tramcars in pre-metro service. Completion of the next stages was expected in the autumn of 1991, with a further stage to follow in 1995.

Florence

Florence, Italy

Feasibility studies of a two-line LRT system have been launched. North-south and east-west lines would aggregate 25 km.

Frankfurt am Main

Stadtwerke Frankfurt am Main

Börneplatz 3, Postfach 102 132, 6000 Frankfurt am Main 1, Federal Republic of Germany

Telephone: +49 69 213-1
Telex: 6997530
Telefax: +49 69 213 22740

Managing Director: Jürgen Wann
Traffic Manager: Dipl-Ing Dieter Oehm

Type of system: Metro

Gauge: 1435 mm
Route length: 51 km
Number of lines in operation: 7
Number of stations (total): 77
Rail type: S41, S49
Tunnel type: Box section, double-tracked 7·1 m wide internally and 4·8 m high, providing clearance for pantographs
Electrification type: 600 V dc, overhead
Signalling: A microcomputer-controlled interlocking installed on Line C by Siemens is claimed to be the largest for an underground to date. It controls a total of 141 points and signals on the 5·6 km section of Line C between Zoo and Industriehof stations. The extensions planned for Line C will come within its range of control.

Rolling stock
Number of cars: 99 articulated Type U2, 27 articulated Type U3, both six-axle; 100 articulated Type Pt8 (eight-axle)
Supplier: Duewag/Siemens/AEG
Car dimensions: Length 24·29 m (U2), 25·6 m (U3), 28·72 m (Pt8); width 2·65 m (U2/3), 2·35 m (Pt8); height 3·28 m (U2/3), 3·26 m (Pt8)
Average capacity: 64 seated, 97 standing (U2); 109 standing (U3); 62 seated, 108 standing (Pt8)
Motors per car: 4
  Motor rating: 150 kW (U2), 174 kW (U3), 120 kW (Pt8)
Max speed: 80 km/h
Tare weight: 31 tonnes (U2), 36 tonnes (U3), 34·5 tonnes (Pt8)
Doors: 4 double doors per side, 1·3 m openings, 1·9 m high, plus two single doors per side in Pt8 only. Electric drives and electromagnetic locks. Driver- or passenger-operated. Photoelectric cells for safety.
Bogies: Duewag monomotor with Duewag gearboxes
Suspension: Primary, rubber chevron axle box rings; secondary, coil springs
Articulation: Duewag with double ball-bearing ring and silentbloc bearings
Wheel diameter: 720 m
Acceleration: Average, 0–40 km/h, 1 m/s^2
Deceleration: Service brake, 1·3 m/s^2, emergency, 3 m/s^2

Traffic
Max number of trains per hour (one-way): 24
Train headways: 2·5 minutes
Passsenger journeys: (1988) 85·07 million
Peak track-hour capacity: 15 000

System development
After 14 years' work, the east-west Line C was completed from Industriehof to Zoo in October 1986. It serves eight underground and nine surface stations; in the city centre it threads through a four-track tunnel, common to both S-Bahn and U-Bahn trains between Hauptwache and Konstablerwache. Line C carries routes U6 and U7 from Ebelfield and Hausen in the city's northwest, connecting with north-south routes U1, U2 and U3 on Line A at Hauptwache, and with routes U4 and U5 on Line B at Konstablerwache. Line C is now being extended northeastwards from Zoo to Enkheim with nine stations, for 2·25 km underground with three stations, and 3 km above ground with six stations. Completion is expected in 1992. An extension of route U4 from Hauptbahnhof via the exhibition grounds (Messegelände) to Bockenheimer Warte should be finished in 1996.

Further plans include construction of a new 9 km line in tunnel from Bornheim to Ostbahnhof with eight stations, including a junction station with the existing north-south U-Bahn line at Theaterplatz and interchange with the S-Bahn at Hauptbahnhof. The ultimate U-Bahn network expanding north and south of the River Main will comprise 123 km of tunnel and segregated surface route.

Fukuoka

**Fukuoka-shi Kotsu Kyoku
(Municipal Transportation Bureau)**

2-5-31 Daimyo, Chuo-ku, Fukuoka 810, Japan

Telephone: +81 92 714 3211

Superintendent: H Oishi

Type of system: Full metro

Gauge: 1067 mm
Route length: 16·2 km (Line 1 trains also operate over 44.8km of JR Chikuhi line)
Number of lines: 2
Number of stations: 18
Electrification type: 1·5 kV dc, overhead

Rolling stock
Number of cars: 108, formed into six-car sets
Suppliers: Kinki Sharyo, Toshiba, Hitachi, Mitsubishi
Car dimensions: Length 19·5 m (motor), 20 m (driving trailer); width 2·86 m; height 4·135 m
Average capacity per train: 312 seated, 848 crush load
Motors per car: 2
Motor racing: 150 kW, chopper-controlled
Max speed: 90 km/h
Acceleration: 0·92 m/s^2
Deceleration: 0·97 m/s^2
Cars on order: 12 for 1993 delivery

Traffic
Passenger journeys: (1988) 84 million

System development
Line 1's 4 km extension to Fukuoka Airport should be finished in 1993. Trains provide through service to Karatsu City over 44·8 km of Japan Rail's Chikuhi line.

Genoa

Azienda Municipalizzata Trasporti

Via L Montaldo 2, PO Box 1756, 16137 Genoa, Italy

Telephone: +39 10 599 71
Telex: 271090
Telefax: +39 10 599 72100

Type of system: LRT under construction

General Manager: Dr Ing Domenico Mastropasqua

Gauge: 1435 mm
Route length: 8 km
No of stations: 11
Rail type: UNI 50
Electrification type: 750V dc
Rolling stock
Number of cars: 6 prototype six-axle cars, 15 kW motor each axle, maximum speed 75 km/h, built by OMS with Ansaldo Trasporti electrical equipment and ABB bogies and auxiliary systems

A former tramway tunnel, the Certosa, 1761 m long, which has proved unsuitable for substitute bus traffic, has been reactivated to carry an 8 km, 11-station LRT line from Brignole via Principe to Rivarolo, to be known as Metrogenova. Work began in 1981 and conversion of the Certosa tunnel for use as a test track was finished by the end of 1984, but subsequent progress has been limited. A 2·2 km segment was scheduled to open in 1990. Later the line may be projected to Staglieno, Foce, Begato, and Sampierdarena, for a total length of 22 km

Ansaldo Trasporti has a turnkey contract to build and equip the line. Six prototype cars have been delivered.

Metrogenova will be the first Italian light rail system with a fully automated driving system.

Glasgow

Strathclyde Passenger Transport Executive

Underground Railway: Broomloan Depot, Robert Street, Govan, Glasgow G51 2BY, Scotland

Telephone: +44 41 333 3159
Telex: 779746
Telefax: +44 41 425 1023

Underground Manager: R A Adams
Deputy Manager and Engineer: J K Wright

Type of system: Full metro

Gauge: 1220 mm
Route length: 10·4 km (all in tunnel)
Number of lines: 1
Number of stations: 15
Rail weight and type: 38 kg/m BS 80 A
Track type: Rails laid on concrete blocks with resilient rubber inserts, fixed to concrete bed
Max gradient: 1 in 16 (6·25%)
Minimum curve radius: 104 m on main line, 50 m in depot yard
Tunnel type: Double tubes, each of 3·35 m nominal diameter. Tunnelling was by means of shields. Depth of the tunnel top ranges from 2 to 35 m below surface; average depth is 8·84 m.
Electrification type: 600 V dc, third rail
Signalling: Two-aspect colour-light signalling operated by conventional track circuits and incorporating train-stops has been used. The track-to-train control signals are by passive transponders laid in the track. There is a radio communication link between all trains and the Central Control.

Rolling stock
Number of cars: 33, all motored
Main supplier: Metro-Cammell
Max number of cars per train: 3
Car dimensions: Length 12·75 m, width 2·34 m, height 2·65 m
Capacity: 90 crush, 36 seated
Tare weight: 19·4 tonnes
Doors: Air-worked sliding doors
Cars on order: 8 from Hunslet TPL for 1991 delivery

Traffic
Train headways: Peak hours, 4 minutes; off-peak, 5–8 minutes
Passenger journeys: (198) 13·37 million
Average schedule speed (including stops): 26 km/h

System development
New ticketing equipment ordered from Westinghouse Cubic for late 1990 delivery.

Goias

Goias, Brazil

Type of system: Planned light rail

In 1988 Matafer of Argentina gained a US$160 million turnkey contract to build a light rail system. Two lines, one of 6·7 km, the other of 13·5 km, will intersect in the city centre. Materfer will supply 50 articulated LRVs of its Buenos Aires Line E2 type.

Gorki

Upravlenia Metropolitena

Gorki, USSR

Type of system: Full metro

Gauge: 1524 mm
Route length: 9·8 km
Number of lines: 1
Number of stations: 8
Average distance between stations: 1·37 km
Electrification type: 825 V, third rail

Rolling stock
Number of cars: 36

System development
Under construction is a 15 km second line with nine stations. The metro will eventually have four lines extending a total of 75 km.

Gothenburg

Göteborgs Spårvägar

PO Box 424, Stampgatan 15, 401 26 Gothenburg, Sweden

Telephone: +46 31 80 05 00
Telefax: +46 31 80 20 33

General Manager: Harry Nordefors

Type of system: Light rail

Gauge: 1435 mm
Route length: 75·6 km
Number of lines: 8
Rail type and weight: Ri 60, 60 kg/m, on-street; SJ50, 50 kg/m elsewhere
Minimum curve radius: 17 m
Max gradient: 4% (streets)
2% (reserved tracks)
Electrification type: 600 V dc, with 9.3 km of Line 8 at 750 V dc, overhead

Rolling stock
Number of cars: 225 four-axle LRV, comprising 96 Type M25 by Hägglunds, 69 Type M28 by ASJ/ABB and 60 Type M29 by Hägglunds; 37 Type M21 six-axle LRVs by ABB
Rating per car: 4 × 50 kW (Types M25 and M29), 4 × 44 kW (Type M28), 4 × 75 kW (Type M21)
Capacity: 116 with 38 seats (Types M25, M28, M29); 182 with 57 seats (Type M21)
Doors: 1·57 m (double), 0·791 m (single), Types M25, M28, M29; 1·38 m (double), Type M21
Cars in course of delivery 1990–92: 43 further M21 from ABB. This type has four chopper-fed 75 kW traction motors, microprocessor control and fault diagnosis system. Maximum speed is 80 km/h. Seating capacity per car is 57, with standing room for 182. Braking systems combine regenerative, disc and emergency electro-pneumatic systems.

Traffic
Passenger journeys: (1988) 84.55 million, including bus and ferry services which account for about 40% of the total

System development
Reconstruction of city-centre Brunnsparken terminal under way for 1991 completion.

Grenoble

Société Mixte des Transports en Commun de L'Agglomération Grenobloise (SEMITAG)

15 avenue Salvador-Allende, 38130 Echirolles, PO Box 258X, 38044 Grenoble Cedex, France

Telephone: +33 76 33 04 04
Telex: 980 928

Chairman: M Descours
Operating Manager: H Guyot

Type of system: Light rail

Gauge: 1435 mm
Route length: Line A, 10 km; Line B (planned), 6 km
Number of lines: 1 operational; 1 in design
Number of stations: 21 (Line 1 only)
Track: Grooved rails secured on rubber pads to two-piece concrete sleepers linked by steel tie-bars
Electrification type: 750 V dc, overhead

Rolling stock
Number of cars: 35 six-axle low-floor LRVs
Main supplier: GEC-Alsthom
Overall length: 29·4 m
Width: 2·3 m
Floor height above motor bogies: 86 mm
Floor height in the main compartments: 34 mm
Length of low floor: 17·85 m
Seating capacity: 58
Standing capacity (4 passengers/m^2): 126
Tare weight: 44·6 tonnes
Rating: 2 × 275 kW
Max speed: 75 km/h

System development
A second line of 5 km under construction from French Railways' main station was to open in November 1990. At the start it shares tracks with Line A, then crosses the Isère River twice en route to the University in the northeast.

Guadalajara

Sistema de Transporte Colectivo de la Zona Metropolitana (Sistecozome)

Antiguo Central Camionera, Guadalajara Jal, Mexico

Telephone: +52 14 89 53/59

Director-General: Lic Eugenio Pelayo López
Operating Manager: Ing Carlos Branca

Type of system: Light rail under construction

Projected route length: 47 km, of which 15.5 km in service; 6.5 km in tunnel
Gauge: 1435mm
Number of lines: 1 in service; 2 more planned
Rail: 52 kg/m on concrete sleepers
Number of stations: 34
Electrification: 750V dc overhead
Rolling stock
Number of cars: 16 articulated LRVs built by Concarril with Duewag monomotor bogies, Japanese electrical equipment. Each traction motor has a 230kW continuous rating; maximum speed is 80 km/h.

System development
Originally planned as a full metro, but now revised as a light rail system, Guadalajara's first 10 km of a 16 km north-south line opened in the summer of 1989. The second, east-west line of 19 km is expected to open in 1994. The third line, of 18 km, will relieve congestion in the city's main street.

Guangzhou (Canton)

Guangzhou Underground Railway Preparatory Office, 204 Huan Shi Road, Guangzhou, People's Republic of China

Telephone: +86 20 665287
Telefax: +86 20 678232

Project Manager: Jin Feng

Feasibility studies of a two-line, 21.7 km metro system were finished in 1988. Hong Kong Mass Transit Railway Corporation assisted. Construction began in 1990.

Haifa

Municipal Corporation of Haifa

City Engineers Dept, 122 Hanassi Ave, Haifa, Israel

Telephone: +972 4 83765

Type of system: Funicular subway

Gauge: 1980 mm (rubber-tyred system)
Route length: 1.75 km (all in tunnel)
Number of lines: 1
Number of stations: 6 (all in tunnel)
Average distance between stations: 350 m
Track: Concrete strips with steel guide rails
Gradient (max): 15.5%
Speed (average commercial): 30 km/h
Electrification type: 1.2 kV

Rolling stock (rubber tyred)
Number of units: 4
Car dimensions: Length 15 m, width 2.4 m, height 3.8 m
Passenger capacity per car
(total): 160
(seated): 24
Train composition: 2
Brakes: Cable

System development
This railway, which was opened in 1959, has six stations and a train every six minutes. It commences about ¼ mile from the harbour at Paris station, in the town centre district, and runs in a straight line to its other terminus, Gen Haem, in the Carmel district, ascending nearly 274 m. In 1990 it was out of service until October 1991 for renovation,

Planned system: Full metro
A scheme for a 14 km full metro line has been approved and bids to build were sought in late 1988.

Hamburg

Hamburger Hochbahn Aktiengesellschaft

Steinstrasse 20, Postfach 10 27 20, 2000 Hamburg 1, Federal Republic of Germany

Telephone: +49 40 32 1041
Telex: 21 61 858 hha d

Traffic
Passenger journeys: (1988) 181.3 million

Rolling stock: 833 cars

Car type	DT 1	DT 2	DT 3	DT 4
Main supplier: Linke-Hofmann-Busch				
Number of cars per unit	2	2	3	4
Set dimensions				
(length)	27.91 m	27.98 m	39.06 m	60.28 m
(width)	2.55 m	2.51 m	2.48 m	2.58 m
(height)	3.37 m	3.36 m	3.35 m	3.32 m
Passenger capacity				
per set (total)	276	258	364	558
(seated)	80	82	92	183
Motors per set	8	4	8	8
Rating	8 × 74 kW	4 × 80 kW	8 × 80 kW	8 × 125 kW
Acceleration (max) (m/s^2)	1.14	0.8	1.2	1.2
Deceleration (emergency) (m/s^2)	1.19	1.25	1.2	1.2
Brakes: Regnerative				
Weight: (tonnes tare)				

Cars in delivery: 30 Type DT 4 with three-phase motors and microprocessor control; the first of these, with ASEA Brown Boveri electrical equipment, was delivered in May 1988 and deliveries were extending into 1991.

Telefax: +49 40 32 6406

Directors: DiplVolksw Josef Hoffstadt
Prof Dipl-Ing Hans Hermann Meyer
Heinz Wenzel
Operating Manager: Dipl-Ing Herbert Hussmann
Rolling Stock Manager: H Albert

Type of system: Full metro

Gauge: 1435 mm
Route length: 92.7 km
(in tunnel): 34.3 km
(elevated): 37 km
Number of lines: 3
Number of stations (total): 82
(in tunnel): 34
(elevated): 34
Rail weight and type: S49 (49 kg/m)
Track type: Conventional sleepers on ballast
Tunnel type: Bored single-track, concrete caisson, bored double-track

System development
A 2.4 km extension of Line U2 to Niendorf Nord and a 2.9 km extension of Line U3 to Mümmelmansberg were to open in 1990. A 2.7 km extension of Line U1 is planned.

Hannover

Hannoversche Verkehrsbetriebe AG (USTRA)

Am Hohen Ufer 6, Postfach 2540, 3000 Hannover 1, Federal Republic of Germany

Telephone: +49 511 16681
Telex: 0922425 fmd
Telefax: +49 511 1668 666

Director: Gerhard Knigge
Technical Director: Dipl Ing Bernd Kosiek
Operating Manager: K Platte

Type of system: Light rail

Gauge: 1435 mm
Route length: 69 km (plus 26 km tramway)
(in tunnel): 15.6km
Number of lines: 8 (plus 3 tramway)
Number of stations: 114 (including 6 interchanges)
(in tunnel): 16
Electrification type: 600 V dc, overhead
Control: Traffic is controlled by the computer-based BON system, in a project sponsored by the Federal Ministry of Research and Technology; it is designed for standardisation on all West German urban transit systems. All vehicles are in radio communication with the control centre and are equipped with on-board information displays

Passenger journeys: (1988) 97 million

Rolling stock
230 thyristor-controlled, eight-axle, double-articulated light rail vehicles by Duewag and Linke-Hofmann-Busch, with two monomotor bogies, thyristor-controlled, each with a 290 hp one-hour rating; tare weight is 38.8 tonnes, top speed 80 km/h and passenger capacity 150. Each vehicle has five double doors on each side. A further 25 cars were delivered by Linke-Hofmann-Busch in 1989; 20 more cars would be procured for 1993.

System development
Hannover's projected 90 km light rail transit system involves progressive tramway conversion and lowering of all city-centre routes below ground. Route C-Ost to Kirchrode and Roderbruch was ready for operation in autumn 1989. Extension of route C-Nord to Nordhafen has begun with completion set for 1993. An east-west route D is planned, and extensions of existing routes to densely-populated areas such as Auderten, Ahlem, Garbsen, Hemmlingen Langenhagen and Wettbergen. All surface track is segregated or on exclusive right-of-way; eventually the city-centre tracks will be entirely underground.

Havana

Havana, Cuba

With the support of the Transport Ministry and Soviet technical aid the city authorities have again planned a metro. The first line would run 25 km from northeast to southeast of the city. The government put up funds for the start of construction, but in 1989 the scheme was again in the melting-pot because of cooling USSR attitudes to further aid for Cuban projects.

Helsinki

Helsingin Kaupungin liikennelaitos (HKL)

PO Box 314, Toinen Linja 7, 00531 Helsinki, Finland

Telephone: +358 0 4721
Telex: 121872 cityh sf
Telefax: +358 0 715282

Managing Director: Martti Lund
Manager, Metro Operations: J Mannila

Type of system: Full metro

Gauge: 1524 mm
Route length: 15.9 km
(in tunnel): 4 km
Number of stations (total): 11
(in tunnel): 4
Gradient (max): 3.5 %
Curvature (minimum radius): main track 300 m, depot area 100 m
Rail type: UIC 54 kg/m
Electrification type: 750 V, third rail
Signalling: Fully automated control of traffic and train operation, from supervisory centres at Hakaniemi and Herttoniemi.

Rolling stock
Number of cars: 42 two-car sets
Main suppliers: Valmet Oy (mechanical), Oy Strömberg (electrical)
Car dimensions: Two-car set, length over couplers 44.2 m, width 3.2 m, height above rail 3.7 m
Total floor area: 66 m^2, standing area 30 m^2
Doors per side: 3
Door width: 1.4 m
Number of passengers per car (total): 200
(seated): 65

Motors per car: 4 (3-phase asynchronous motor fed by PWM-inverters)
Motor rating: 125 kW
Acceleration (max): 0–27 km/h, 1·2 m/s^2; 0–80 km/h, 0·9 m/s^2
Deceleration (normal service): 80–0 km/h, 1·2 m/s^2 (emergency): 80-0 km/h, 1·2 m/s^2
Max design speed: 90 km/h
Bogies: Air-sprung, two-motor bogies by Valmet
Brakes: Rheostatic/disc/electromagnetic track
Weight (empty): 30·2 tonnes

Traffic
Train headways (minutes): 5 during day, 10 late evenings and Sundays
Passenger journeys: (1988) 35·9 million

System development
An extension of 1·7 km from Kontula to Mellunmäki was opened in 1989. Another 1·1 km from Kamppi to Ruoholahti was under way for opening in 1992.

Hiroshima

Hiroshima Electric Railway Company (Hiroshima Dentetsu Hiroden)

2-9-29 Higash Senda-machi, Naka-ku, Hiroshima, Japan

Telephone: +81 82 241 1191

General Manager: Minoru Tonda

Type of system: Light rail

Gauge: 1435 mm
Route length: 16·1 km
Number of lines: 1
Number of stops: 20
Max gradient: 1·82%
Minimum curve radius: 161 m
Electrification type: 600 V dc, overhead

Rolling stock
Number of cars: 36
Main suppliers: Kawasaki Heavy Industries, Alna Koki and others
The latest addition to a very mixed fleet is Type 3800, introduced late in 1987. This is an articulated low-floor unit, designed for through running between light rail and street tramway. It consists of three air-conditioned car bodies with seats for 70 (70 standing), mounted on four bogies and with VVF inverter control. Tare weight is 38·4 tonnes. Supplier is Alna Koki.

Traffic
Train headways: Peak hours, 3–4 minutes; off-peak, 6 minutes

Hong Kong

Hong Kong Mass Transit Railway Corporation (MTRC)

33 Wai Yip Street, Kowloon Bay, Kowloon, Hong Kong

Telephone: +852 3 751 2111
Telex: 56257 tubes hx
Telefax: +852 3 798 8822

Chairman: H T Mathers
Operations Director: W R Donald

Type of system: Full metro

Gauge: 1432 mm
Route length: 43·2 km
 (in tunnel): 34·4 km
 (elevated): 7·6 km
Number of lines: 3
Number of stations: 38
 (in tunnel): 28
 (elevated): 9
Rail weight and type: UIC 60 60 kg/m, Island line; 90A 45 kg/m, Kwun Tong and Tsuen Wan lines
Track type: Continuously supported FB rail; discretely supported FB rail on overhead sections of Tsuen Wan extention
Tunnel type: Bored single-track, bored double-track and cut-and-cover
Max gradient: 3%
Minimum curve radius: 300 m
One-man operation: All trains

Signalling: Route relay interlocking by WBS. Installation has begun on the Island line of an automatic train regulation system that will be applied to all lines. A 10-year upgrading plan provides for adoption of solid state interlocking; first installation is at Eastern Harbour crossing
Automatic control: All tracks except within depots
Centralised control: All signalling, power supply and environment systems

Rolling stock
Number of cars: Total 671 (508 motored, 163 trailers)
Main supplier: Metro-Cammell (now GEC Alsthom)
Car dimensions: Length 22·85 m, width 3·116 m, height 3·7 m
Capacity: Seated 48, max standing (crush) 265
Tare and loaded weight: 39/60 tonnes (crush)
Doors: Electro-pneumatic belt-driven double sliding doors, 1·4 m wide, 1·8 m high
Motors: 4 per car, 90 kW GEC
Motor suspension: Nose-suspended, axle-hung
Motor voltage: 350 V dc
Gear ratio: 82 : 15
Gear drive: Parallel helical
Brake system (service): rheostatic/air
 (emergency): air

Traffic
Train headways: Peak hours, 2–2½ minutes; off-peak, 3–10 minutes
Max number of trains per hour: 30 (TWL line), 30 (KTL line), 21 (ISL line)
Capacity per train: 384 seated, 2116 standing
Passenger journeys: (1989) 687·6 million

System development
Hong Kong's Mass Transit Railway has been designed for the highest throughput of passengers per hour per track of any system in the world. The maximum carrying capacity provided is 75 000 passengers per hour per direction. In December 1985 the government announced the award of a franchise to the New Hong Kong Tunnel Co Ltd to build and operate a combined road and rail link from Cha Kwo Ling to Quarry Bay. This Eastern Harbour Crossing would provide the Corporation with an extension of its Kwun Tong line running from Kwun Tong, via a new station at Lam Tin and an immersed tube beneath the harbour, to its Quarry Bay station on the Island. Operated by MTRC as an integral part of its system under the terms of an 18½-year operating agreement, the Eastern Harbour Crossing came into operation in 1989.
A second Comprehensive Transport Study recommending further MTR extension was endorsed by the government in 1990. One extension would project the TWL line from Tseun Wan to an interchange with the Tuen Mun light rail system (see below) at Yuen Long. A second would extend the KTL line to a new town in the southeast at Junk Bay; and the third would involve a third harbour crossing to get the KTL line from Yau Ma Tei to Fortress Hill on Hong Kong Island. In the long term the study advocated construction of a fourth line from Sha Tin and Diamond Hill via Kowloon and Admiralty to Aberdeen.
A 33 km line to the new Chep Lak Kok airport on Lantau Island, which will be shared by conventional and 160 km/h express services, is to be opened by the end of 1996. The line will cross the water between Tsing Yi and Ma Wan islands on the world's longest single-span suspension bridge, which will carry a six-lane highway on its upper deck, two rail tracks and two typhoon-proof highway lanes on its lower.

Kowloon-Canton Railway Corporation
(for details of address, officers, etc see under Hong Kong in Railway systems section)

North West Rail

55-65 Lung Main Road, Tuen Mun, New Territories, Hong Kong

Telephone: +852 0 468 7660
Telex: 51618 lrt hx
Telefax: +852 0 455 0030

Director: Jonathan Yu
Operations Manager: M Brown

Type of system: Light rail

Gauge: 1435 mm
Route length: 23·3 km, 95% segregated, but having 56 junctions with road traffic
Number of lines: 6
Number of stations: 41
Track type: UIC 54 kg/m fb rail on concrete sleepers; some grooved rail; 3 km of paved track with UIC54/Ri60 rail
Max gradient: 8%
Minimum curve radius: 20 m
Electrification: 750 V dc, overhead

Rolling stock: 70 single-unit cars
Main supplier: Comeng
Max speed: 80 km/h

Traffic: (1989) 180 000 daily

System development
In November 1983 KCR was invited by Hong Kong's government to undertake, as a self-financing enterprise, construction of a light rail system in the new town of Tuen Mun, in the New Territories. The six-route Phase 1 system of 23 km of double track with 41 stops commenced public service in September 1988 after three years of construction.
The Corporation decided in January 1987 to construct six extensions aggregating 9·1 km by 1991. Five other possible future extensions totalling 7·2 km were also identified. Construction was to start in mid-1990 on the first three Phase 2 extensions with a total route length of some 5km and 10 additional stops. On completion of all the extensions, the Regional LRT system will comprise approximately 40 km of double track and around 70 stops. LRT patronage could increase to over half a million a day by 1996 on the full system.

Honolulu

Honolulu Rapid Transit Development

Department of Transportation Services, City and County of Honolulu, 650 South King Street, Honolulu, Hawaii 96813, USA

Director: Alfred J Thiede
Telephone: +1 808 523 4125
Project Manager: Amar Sappal
Telephone: +1 808 527 6975

Type of system: Planned automated advanced rapid transit

In March 1990 UMTA approved for circulation and review an Alternatives Analysis and Draft Environmental Impact Statement. Alternative alignments of some 29km in length from Waiawa to Moiliili, with branches to Waikiki and the University of Hawaii at Manoa, are being evaluated for a fully automated and electrified, grade-separated advanced rapid transit system. Turnkey bids were likely to be called in mid-1990.

Houston

Metropolitan Transit Authority (METRO), Harris County

PO Box 61429, 1202 Louisiana, Houston, Texas 77208-1429, USA

Telephone: +1 713 739 4000

Chairman: Anthony W Hall Jr
General Manager: Robert G MacLennan
Assistant General Manager Transportation: B G Fort

Type of system: To be determined

System development
METRO has now adopted a Regional Transit Plan, to be implemented in phases.
By the year 2000, buses will be unable to accommodate the commuter demand along the most densely-travelled corridors. Therefore, some type of rail component is being considered and a request for proposals from the private sector was being prepared in early 1990. This so-called System Connector will integrate the park-and-ride bus system (operating on the transitways) with the local bus system and the major employment centres (downtown, Texas Medical Center, Greenway Plaza, and Galleria-Post Oak).
The technology of the rail component (automated guideway transit, automated monorail, automated rail

transit, advanced rail transit or light rail) has yet to be determined by the Board of Directors. The Board has already committed to a grade-separated configuration for the initial segment.

Hull

Humberside County Council, Hull, England

Type of system: Proposed light rail

In 1989 consultants were engaged to undertake a feasibility study of a proposed light rail system.

Istanbul

Istanbul Metro (Istanbul Metrosu)

Istanbul Municipality, Istanbul, Turkey

Type of system: Light rail under construction

Gauge: 1435 m
Route length: 23 km
Number of lines: 1
Number of stations: 21
Electrification type: 750 V dc
Rolling stock: 105 articulated LRVs by ABB

In March 1986 ABB was awarded a contract valued at about US$340 million to build and equip a light rail system to serve the city of Istanbul. It will comprise a 23 km network with 21 stations and a service depot in the central parts of the city. The first phase of the scheme covers a line from Ferhatpasa to Yenikapi on the coast, to the south-east. Its initial 7 km section opened in March 1989. A second phase will project the line southwest from Ferhatpasa to Halkali, and a third from Halkali south to Cobancesme, beyond which the line will branch to Havaalani and to Ataköy.

Later extensions under consideration include a line encircling the western side of the city further out than the initial route, and running from Atisalani to Ataköy; a line heading northeastward from Atisalani to Abide; and a line from Yenikapi round the coastline to Sirkeci.

Type of system: Planned metro

In 1990 pre-qualification bids were invited for construction of a 16km, 13-station line from Topkapi to Yenikapi and, via a new bridge over the Golden Horn waterway, to Levent; and also for construction of a 13km railway involving a tunnel under the Bosphorus to project a line from Yenikapi via Sirkeci across the water to Uskūdar, then south to Sogütlücesme, near Haydapasa.

Type of system: Funicular

The Electricity, Tramway and Tunnel Administration (IETT) of the Istanbul Municipality operates a 0·573 km funicular railway linking Karaköy and Galatasary. Two vehicles are operated, carrying about 25 000 passengers a day.

Izmir

Izmir, Turkey

In 1990 the city authority was in discussion with several companies around tbe world concerning a proposal for a 4.5km light rail line from Bayramyeri to Konak.

Jacksonville

Jacksonville Transporation Authority

PO Drawer O, 100 North Myrtle Avenue, Jacksonville, Florida 32203, USA

Telephone: +1 904 630 3181

Director: John Meyer

Type of system: VAL

In 1985 Matra was awarded a contract to supply and install vehicles and sub-systems for a 1 km demonstration line based on the VAL technology (see Lille entry), which entered service in May 1989. It connects the city's central business district with the Jacksonville Convention Center and neighbouring car parks. This is an elevated line, which eases the constraint on vehicle width. Consequently Matra developed an enlarged car type, the VAL 256 (2·56 m wide), for the Jacksonville (and Chicago) schemes. With a carrying capacity some 20 per cent greater than that of the 206, the 256 enables a VAL system to move 25 000 passengers hourly each way. The 256 is a single, self-contained car capable of running in multiples of two, three or four cars. Each car is powered by two 150 kW motors.

Two extensions have been approved for construction up to 1998. In 1990 preliminary engineering was under way on a 2.5 km extension.

Johannesburg

Johannesburg, South Africa

Type of system: Full metro

The city's Mass Transport Committee has drafted proposals for a system comprising one east-west and two north-south routes which would interconnect in the city centre.

Kaohsiung

Kaohsiung, Taiwan

Type of system: Planned light rail

Construction was expected to begin in 1992 of the first stretch of a planned four-route, 71-station, 78km system, of which some 60 km will be below ground and 17 km elevated. Its first routes will be a 10.8km east-west Orange Line and a 30.9km north-south Red line intersecting mid-town. The 21.6km Blue Line will be orbital, starting from an interchange with the Red Line in the north and finishing in the harbour area. A 14.4km Brown Line will also be an east-west transversal.

Kansas City

Kansas City, USA

A proposal has been drafted by KCATA for a 4 km light rail line south from Crown Center along the Country Club Corridor.

Karachi

Karachi Development Agency, Karachi, Pakistan

Director, Mass Transit Programme: Dr Tahir Soomro

Type of system: Planned light rail

Construct-operate-transfer bids were likely to be called in 1990 for the first 16km route of a proposed 87km network. The World Bank has agreed to fund the provision of rolling stock, signalling and stations. The planned alignments will make part-use of an existing orbital rail line.

Karlsruhe

Stadtwerke Karlsruhe Verkehrsbetriebe

Postfach 6169, Tullastrasse 71, 7500 Karlsruhe 1, Federal Republic of Germany

Telephone: +49 721 599-1
Telex: (07) 825658
Telefax: +49 721 599 5899

Operating Director: Dipl-Ing Dieter Ludwig

Type of system: Light rail/tramway

Gauge: 1435 m
Route length: Over 100 km
Number of lines: 7
Rail type: Grooved NP 4/40; flat-bottomed S 41/10
Track type: Sleepers on ballast/concrete
Max gradient: 4%
Minimum curve radius: 21 m
Electrification type: 750 V dc, overhead

Rolling stock
Number of cars: 139
Main suppliers: Duewag, Waggon Union
Car dimensions: Length, Type T4, 14 m; Type T6 20 m; Type T8, 27 m; Type GT6-80C, 27·6 m; width, all 2·4 m except GT6-80C, 2·65 m
Tare weight: Type T4, 18 tonnes; Type T6, 22·8 tonnes; Type T8, 30·5 tonnes; Type GT6-80C, 42 tonnes

Traffic
Passenger journeys: (1988) 58.4 million

System development
A 4 km extension to Linkenheim-Hochstetten, a 1 km extension to the Siemens industrial complex and a projection of 6 km south to Rheinstetten were opened in 1989.

The system is now being connected to the German Federal Railway (DB) so that its LRVs can reach outer suburbs over DB tracks. The first connection will be at Karlsruhe-Durlach, from where the LRVs will use the DB main line for 2 km to the Grötzingen start of the 22km Bretten branch, which is to be electrified. The LRVs will largely supersede the branch's present DB diesel railcar service in 1991, serving 15 stops, nine of them new, but DB trains will still provide a semi-fast service to Heilbronn. The project is being 85 per cent funded by Federal and Land governments, 15 per cent by local administration. The extension will be operated by 10 eight-axle LRVs able to operate off the DB's 15 kV ac as well as the Stadtwerke's 750 V dc.

The Albtal-Verkehrs-GmbH electric interurban line from Karlsruhe to Bad Herrenalb and Ittersbach is now fully integrated in the Stadtwerke Karlsruhe system.

Kazan

Kazan, USSR

Construction is forecast to start in 1993 of the first 9.5km segment of a planned 20km metro system.

Kharkov

Kharkov Metropolitena

No 29 Ulitsa Engelsa, Kharkov 310012, USSR

Chief Executive: Nikolia Yakovlevich Bessonov
Chief Engineer: Lenoid Ivanovich Vstavskii

Type of system: Full metro

Gauge: 1524 mm
Route length: 22·9 km
Number of lines: 2
Number of stations: 20 (all in tunnel)
Max gradient: 4%
Minimum curve radius: 300 m
Electrification type: 825 V, third rail

Rolling stock
Number of cars: 171, all motored
Car dimensions: Length 18·77 m, width 2·7 m
Capacity: 170 (44 seated)
Motors per car: 4
Motor rating: 66 kW
Doors: 4 × 1·38 m
Braking: Rheostatic
Max speed: 90 km/h
Acceleration: 1·0 m/s^2
Deceleration: 1·2 m/s^2
Body material: Steel
Weight: Motor car, 30 tonnes

Traffic
Train headways: Peak hours, 2½ minutes; off-peak, 6 minutes
Passenger journeys: Approx 180 million a year
Signalling: Automatic train operation, but driver still carried. Cab signalling, with automatic speed control. Radio-telephone communication between the central control post and trains

System development
A third line will run from Alekseevka in the northwest to Kharkov airport in the southeast, intersecting the two earlier lines in the city centre; its first 6·1 km is to open in 1992. Trains are now operated as five-car sets.

Kiev

Kiev Metropolitena

Brest-Litovskii Prospekt 37a, Kiev 252055, USSR

Telephone: 29 90 00

Chief Executive: Stepan Pavlovich Kapitanyuk
Chief Engineer: Mikhail Ivanovich Mitrofanov

Type of system: Full metro

Gauge: 1524 mm
Route length: 32·5 km
Number of lines: 3
Number of stations: 29
Max gradient: 4%
Minimum curve radius: 400 m
Speed (design max): 75 km/h
  (average commercial): 38 km/h
Rail type: 50 kg/h
Electrification type: 825 V, third rail
Signalling: Automatic train stop. Radio-telephone communication between trains and central control post

Rolling stock
Number of cars: 385, all motored
Car dimensions: (All) length 18·77 m, width 2·7 m
Capacity: E-type, 170 (44 seated); D-type, 164 (44 seated)
Motor per car: 4
Motor rating: D-type cars supplied in 1960, 4 × 73 kW; E-type cars supplied 1965–79, 4 × 66 kW
Doors: E-type, 4 × 1·38 m; D-type, 4 × 1·05 m
Braking: Rheostatic (all)

Traffic
Trains/track/hour: 30
Train capacity (passengers): 750
Total passengers/track/hour (peak): 22 500
Train headways: 2 minutes
Passenger journeys: (1986) 368.6 million

System development
Three more lines are planned and 11 km of the third are under construction; its first section was opened in 1989. The ultimate five-line metro plan will aggregate 118 km. A monorail is to be built from the new suburb of Troeschchine to the Levoberezhnaya metro station on the River Dnieper's left bank.

Kingston-upon-Thames

Kingston-upon-Thames, Surrey, England

In 1990 the authority of this Royal Borough in the south-west London suburbs engaged consultants to consider the demand for and potential viability of a light rail system connecting Kingston-upon-Thames with neighbouring Epsom, Surbiton and Sunbury-on-Thames.

Kobe

Rapid Transit Department, Transportation Bureau (Kobe-shi Kotsu Kyoku)

5-1 6-chome, Kano-cho Chuo-ku, Kobe City, Japan

Telephone: +81 78 831 8181

General Manager: Kenji Tsubota

Type of system: Full metro

Gauge: 1435 mm
Route length: 22·6 km
Number of lines: 2
Number of stations: 16
Rail weight and type: 50 kg/m N long rail
Max gradient: 2·9%
Minimum curve radius: 300 m
Track type: Prestressed concrete and reinforced concrete sleepers with double elastic fastenings
Tunnel type: Bored single-track (shield tunnelling method), bored double-track (mountain tunnelling method) and cut-and-cover
Electrification type: 1·5 kV dc, overhead
Signalling: Cab signalling by Daido with ATC and CTC

Rolling stock
Number of cars: 110, all motored, in five-car sets, equipped with chopper control and regenerative braking
Main supplier: Kawasaki Heavy Industries
Car dimensions: Length 19 m, width 2·79 m
Capacity: 145, 56 seated
Tare and loaded weight: 35/55 tonnes
Doors: Sliding doors 1·3 m wide, 1·83 m high

Traffic
Train headways: Peak hours, 6 minutes; off-peak, 12 minutes
Passenger journeys: (1987) 25 million

System development
This important port has four surface railways, the Sanyo, Hankyu, Hanshin and Kobe Electric (besides the Japanese National Railways), whose terminal stations were until 1988 unconnected with each other by rail. With completion of its 7·75 km Yamate line in 1987 the Kobe Rapid Railway provided this connection.

Hokushin Express Electric Railway (Hokushin Kyuko Dentetsu)

Type of system: Full metro

A new private 1435 mm-gauge railway, electrified at 1·5 kV dc, overhead, connects the Hokushin Kyuko Dentetsu (Hokushin Express Electric Railway) at Tanigami with the Yamate line at Nunobiki. A joint venture with the Hankyu Railway, this 7·9 km line was opened in April 1988. Rolling stock is five Kawasaki-built five-car emus.

Kobe New Transit Co (Kobe Shin Kotsu Kyoku)

Minako-jima 6-chome, Chuo-ko, Kobe 650

Telephone: +81 78 802 2500

Type of system: Rubber-tyred automated light rail
Rolling stock: 12 six-car and 9 four-car trains
Main supplier: Kawasaki
Route length: 10·9 m
Number of lines: 2

Port Island is served from Sannomiya by the 6·4 km loop of the Kobe New Transit System, employing unmanned rubber-tyred vehicles on a guideway, using a technology devised by Kawasaki. A 3-minute headway service is provided and in 1986 moved 15 million passengers. In 1989 Kobe New Transit Co completed a second line of 4·5 km from Sumiyoshi station to Rokko Island in Osaka Bay.

Krasnoyarsk

Krasnoyarsk, USSR

Plans have been announced for the first 20 km line of a metro system.

Krivoy Rog

Krivoy Rog, USSR

Type of system: Light rail

The first 8.2km of a 12.2km Line 1 are in operation. Planned extensions total 24km.

Kuala Lumpur

Kuala Lumpur, Malaysia

Type of system: Light rail

Planned route length: 105 km
Number of lines: 3
Gauge: 1000 m
Electrification type: 750 V dc

After two years of consideration against a monorail alternative, the government in July 1984 authorised construction of the first 14·5 km Y-shaped line of a projected three-route system, to thread the city centre from Salak and Ampang to Puda Raya. The route will partly use KTM infrastructure, but about 8 km will be elevated. Rolling stock, comprising 14 cars initially, to be supplied by Comeng of Australia. In 1987 an Australian consortium gained the contract to design and build the first line, using existing KTM track in part. Extension of the first line to Port Klang, with branches to Subang airport and North Port, is envisaged; total route length would then be 62·5 km. Addition of two north-south routes would create a network totalling 105 km.

Kuibyshev

Kuibyshev, USSR

Type of system: Full metro

Gauge: 1524 mm
Route length: 12.5km
No of stations: 9
Electrification type: 825 V dc, third rail

System development
A further 3·5 km was completed in 1990. Line 1 will eventually extend 17km from Revolution Square in the western city to the Besymyanka industrial region. Line 2, the Station Line, will run from the main station northeastward and Line 3, the Samara Line, will diverge from Line 2 at Lenin Works to cater for a new residential area on the River Samara.

Of the 13 stations on Line 1, all but one are to be underground. This line will operate four-car trains at 2-minute headways in peak hours, and is expected to deal with 22 000 passengers an hour.

Kyoto

Kyoto Municipal Transportation Bureau (Kyoto-shi Kotsu Kyoku)

48 Bojocho, Mibu Nakagyo-ku, Kyoto City, Japan

Telephone: +81 75 841 9361

General Manager: Nisuharu Nakabo

Type of system: Full metro

Gauge: 1435 mm
Route length: 9.9 km
Number of lines: 1
Number of stations: 12
  in tunnel: 11
Rail weight: 60 kg/m
Track type: Sleepers on concrete with resilient pads, partly conventional sleepers on ballast
Tunnel type: Bored double-track plus some cut-and-cover
Electrification type: 1·5 V dc, overhead
Signalling: CTC and ATC

Rolling stock
Number of cars: 84, of which 56 motored: Hitachi/Kinki Sharyo Series 10
Car dimensions: Length 20 m, width 2·78 m
Capacity: 54 seated plus standees
Tare weight: 36 tonnes
Doors: 4 each side 1·3 m wide
Train capacity
  (seated): 214
  (standing): 426
Traction motors: 130 kW
Gear ratio: 16·99
Max speed: 105 km/h
Acceleration: 0·92 m/s^2
Service braking: 0·97 m/s^2
Emergency braking: 1·11 m/s^2

Traffic
Train headways: Peak hours, 4½ minutes; off-peak, 6½ minutes
Passenger journeys daily: (1988) 161 000

System development
A new 3·6 km section reached Takeda, in the southern part of the city, in 1988. It connected with the Kyoto line of the Kɪɴkɪ Nɪppon Railway, one of four private electric railways entering Kyoto (others include the Keihan and Hankyu), and allowed through running to Nara City. A northern extension from Kitaoji to Kitayama (1·5 km) was under way for 1990 inauguration.

The east-west Oike line of 30 km is now to be built by a separate concern, the Kyoto Rapid Railway, in which the Keihan Electric Railway has an interest. Construction of its first 12 km section began in 1988, for completion in 1995.

Lausanne

Tramway du Sud-Ouest Lausannois (TSOL)

Lausanne, Switzerland

Type of system: Light rail under construction

Gauge: 1435 mm
Route length: 7·9 km
  (in tunnel): 0·9 km
Number of lines: 1
Number of stations: 15

Electrification type: 750 V dc, overhead

Rolling stock: 12 articulated LRVs

A 7·9 km light rail line from the city centre to Dorigny and the Swiss Federal Railway station at Renens was to open in 1990.

Leeds

Metro (West Yorkshire Passenger Transport Executive)

40-50 Wellington Street, Leeds, West Yorkshire LS1 2DE, England

Telephone: +44 532 440988
Telefax: +44 532 340654

Director General: John Rhodes

Type of operation: Planned light rail

Proposals of 1988 for an 11.5km system in East Leeds were shelved at the request of Leeds City Council to allow consideration of alternative proposals, including those developed in 1989 for a fully automated Leeds Advanced Transport System (LATS) linking south and east Leeds on a largely elevated route. In view of major changes in road traffic levels, land use and economic activity in the city, the City Council and PTA launched a two-year study of future transport needs which aimed to produce options for public consultation late in 1990 and firm proposals for development by the autumn of 1991.

Leningrad

VI Leningradski Metropoliten

Moskovskii Prospekt 28, Leningrad 198013, USSR

Chief Executive: Victor Alexeivitch Elsukov
Chief Engineer: Konstantin Illarionovich Frolov

Type of system: Full metro

Gauge: 1524 mm
Route length: 83 km
  (in tunnel): 79·7 km
Number of lines: 4
Number of stations: 45
  (in tunnel): 40
Tunnel type: The line is of deep-level tube construction, and depending on the cambresian clay formation, is at places over 60 m below surface level. Each single-track tunnel is of metal and ferro-concrete tube construction and has an internal diameter of 5·1 m
Gradient (max): 4%
Speed (design max): 65 km/h
Electrification type: 825 V, third rail
Signalling: Automatic train stop; radio-telephone communications with trains. Central control room. Automatic train operation on three lines includes programmed traffic interlocking control and automatic train operation

Rolling stock
Number of cars: 1205, all motored

Traffic
Train headways: Peak hours, 1 minute 35 s; off-peak, 4 minutes
Train capacity (passengers): 1500
Passenger journeys: Approx 850 million annually

System development
The first section of east-west Line 4 was opened in 1989 and a further 9km to the southeast was due to open in 1990. A northward extension of Line 2 is under construction. A further cross-city route, Line 5, is planned, also an orbital Line 6, eventually raising the system's total distance to some 150 km.

Liège

Liège, Belgium

Plans for a light rail system to employ the fully automated, computer-controlled Transport Automatisé Urbain (TAU) system devised by BN and ACEC in collaboration with the Hainault Technological Research Centre have been abandoned.

Lille

Les Transports en Commun de la Communité (TCC)

PO Box 206, 908 avenue de la République, 59701 Marcq-en-Baroeul, France

Telephone: +33 20 98 04 04
Telex: 130898
Telefax: +33 20 40n41 35

Director General: Claude Rat
Director, Operations: D Fremaux
  Maintenance: C Beche

Type of system: Automated full metro (rubber-tyred), VAL system

Gauge: 2060 mm between H-type guide bars. Guide bars also used for power supply, one positive, the other negative, insulated with moulded polyester
Route length: 25.3km
  (in tunnel): 15·4 km
Number of stations: 34
Track type: Track consists of precast concrete longitudinal sleepers, with track heating provided by cables embedded in sleepers. Track equipment is similar to that used for other French rubber-tyred systems, but new VAL safety devices make additional steel security guide track unnecessary
Electrification type: 750 V dc, with collection by shoes from guide tracks
Signalling: Track equipment specific to system's fully automated train control includes 170 mm-wide strip carrying transmission lines; aluminium plate contacts used for command and control and regulation of traffic; ultrasonic transceiver at the entry and exit to every station. Sliding doors at the platform's edge open automatically when a train stops and the automated controls ensure that both trains and fixed doorways are in a precise correspondence. All station operation is automated.

Traffic
Train headways: Peak hours, 1 minute; off-peak, 3–5 minutes
Passenger journeys: (1988) 29.4 million; 120 000 daily

Rolling stock
The 83 train-sets supplied by CIMT/Alsthom each consist of two permanently-coupled cars, with a length per set of 26·14 m and a height of 3·25 m. Lateral surfaces are curved with the maximum width (2·06 m) at the seat level. Tare weight per set is 28·635 tonnes, 30 per cent less than for modern steel-wheeled underground stock with comparable load capacity. The light weight is achieved partly through the extensive use of light alloys, partly because the design uses pivoting axles with rubber-tyred wheels, instead of conventional bogies.

Switching is achieved via 320 mm diameter guide rollers making it possible to do without the steel guide wheels used on the Paris rubber-tyred stock. In the event of a loss of pressure in the tyres, rings mounted on the inner face of the tyres check slump and make it possible for the train to return to the maintenance depot without significant loss of speed.

Service braking is electrical, but emergency braking is provided via very large discs. The axle is linked to the body through flexible pneumatic suspension (frequency about 1·2 Hz) which filters vibrations and maintains a constant body floor level. Coupled with the use of wide doors and platforms, this arrangement permits ready access for the handicapped in wheel-chairs.

Each car is powered by two 120 kW traction motors, providing nearly 1·7 kW per tonne of unladen weight. Coupled with good tyre grip, this permits good acceleration (1·3 m/s^2 up to 35 km/h under normal loading). The set will also climb a 7 per cent grade even with one of the cars out of working order. The cars have chopper control and regenerative braking.

System development
VAL was the first metro in the world to plan operation of driverless trains from the start of public service. The design of its train-sets makes no provision for accompanying driver or conductor.

The 10km Line 1b from Gares to St Philibertin the west of Lille was opened in 1989 and by 1993 will be extended from Gares to the city's new TGV station, a year later to Mons-en-Baroeul. The first 10 km of Line 1b involved 6·86 km of tunnelling, 3·11 km of elevated route and 1·74 km of cut-and-cover trenching. For Line 1b 29 more vehicles were procured, along with a further 16 for Line 1, the two orders raising the fleet total to 83 cars.

The VAL network will be developed next in the northeast sector of the urban community, to create a network connecting Tourcoing and Roubaix as an extension of Line 1b. Completion is forecast for 1996.

Lima

Antoridad Autonoma del Tren Eléctrica de Lima

Lima, Peru

Type of system: Full metro

Gauge: 1435 mm
Route length: 20·8 km
Electrification: 1·5 kV dc

In 1989 a US$350 million contract to build the line was secured by an Italian consortium, Intermetro, with the backing of Italian government funding for the railway elements of the project, and also from Argentina. The Peruvian government will finance the civil works.

Ansaldo Trasporti and Ercole Marelli are the principals in the electrical, signalling and communications work. Breda and Fiat will supply an initial five M-T-T-M train-sets with chopper control, to a design derived from that for the Rome Metro's Line B.

The first section of 9·8 km is to be built by mid-1992.

Lisbon

Metropolitano de Lisboa SARL (ML)

28 Av Fontes Pereira de Melo, Lisbon 1098, Portugal

Telephone: +351 1 57 5457
Telex: 15681
Telefax: +351 1 57 4908

President: J M Consiglieri Pedro
Operating Manager: A Pinto Dantas

Type of system: Full metro

Gauge: 1435 mm
Route length: 16 km (all in tunnel)
Number of lines: 1 and 2 branches
Number of stations: 24
Rail weight and type: Vignole (FB), 50 kg/m, U50 profile
Track type: Timber sleepers, normally on ballast, with resilient pads; on concrete at stations; new lines, bi-bloc concrete sleepers, Stedep type
Tunnel type: Cut-and-cover except 1 km bored double-track
Gradient (max): 4%
Curvature (max): 150 m (100 m exceptionally)
Speed (design max): 60/72 km/h
Electrification type: 750 V dc, third rail
Signalling: Automatic block supplied by L M Ericsson, Sweden; latest line, Dimetronic
Centralised control: Computer-based system for signalling and points operation; train-to-control radio communication in course of installation

Rolling stock
Number of cars: 136 cars, all motored
Main suppliers: 1959/64 cars, Linke-Hofmann-Busch/Siemens; later cars, Sorefame/Siemens

Traffic
Train headways: Peak hours, 2⅓ minutes; off-peak 3–5 minutes
Passenger journeys: (1988) 136 million

System development
Under construction in 1990 for 1991 opening were a 1.8km elevated section from Cidade Universitária to Campo Grande, and one of 1.6 km from Alvalade to Campo Grande. By 1995 the present convergence of Lines 1 and 2 at Rotunda is to be disconnected and Line 1 projected to its own terminus at Rato. A southward extension of Line 2 will be completed from a Rossio/Restauradores triangular junction, where Line 2 presently merges into Line 3, to a terminus at the main-line station of Cais do Sodré. The metro will then comprise three independent lines. A northward extension of Line 2 to Lumiar and Odivelas is planned.

Car type (year introduced)	1959	1979	1988*
Car dimensions: (length)	16 m	16 m	16 m
(width)	2·7 m	2·7 m	2·79 m
(height)	3·45 m	3·45 m	3·53 m
Passenger capacity per car			
(total)	200	200	164
(seated)	36	36	40
Motors per car	4	4	4
Rating	90 kWh	100 kWh	217 kWh
Acceleration (max)	0·9 m/s^2	1·0 m/s^2	1·1 m/s^2
Deceleration (emergency)	1·2 m/s^2	1·0 m/s^2	1·4 m/s^2

Prototype on order

Lodz

Lodz, Poland

Plans for creation of a two-line pre-metro system of 23 km from the city's tramway network have been announced. Design has been entrusted to Metroproject of Warsaw. Opening is forecast for 1995.

London

London Underground Ltd
(a wholly-owned subsidiary of London Regional Transport)

55 Broadway, London SW1H 0BD, England

Telephone: +44 71 222 5600
Telefax: +44 71 222 6016

Chairman: C W Newton
Managing Director: D Tunnicliffe

Gauge: 1435 mm
Route length (managed): 392 km
  (run over): 408 km
  (in tunnel): 167 km
Number of lines: 11
Number of stations: 248 owned, 273 served
Rail weight and type: Running rail, 47 kg/m BH and 54 kg/m FB; conductor rail (open and sub-surface) 74 kg m FB and 53 kg m FB; conductor rail (tube tunnel) 64 kg/m rectangular
Track type: Conventional sleepers on ballast or in concrete: new track forms are under development
Tunnel type: Bored single-track and cut-and-cover; three lines (Metropolitan, District, Circle and East London) totalling 32 km cut-and-cover construction, remaining six lines bored tunnel. (A seventh bored tunnel, the Waterloo & City Line, is owned and operated by Southern Region of British Rail, with a design of rolling stock unique to that line; the Waterloo & City makes a passenger interchange with London Underground at Waterloo and Bank stations)
Electrification type: 630 V dc, third and fourth rail
Signalling: Colour-light signalling with automatic train stops all lines except the Victoria, which employs a 4-code ATO system with continuous track-circuit ATP and cab signalling; the driving system uses high-frequency codes. At present six lines are fully or partially controlled by centralised systems. Block jointless track circuits adopted for train detection in recent Bakerloo Line resignalling will be used in all future major schemes. All lines and trains are equipped with two-way radio, and on all lines except Central and Northern lines are one-person-operated.
  The Central Line will be resignalled in 1991 using a 9-code ATO system with platform transmission facilities to provide a two-way data link, including geographical data for the next two stations and train status, coupled with track-based safety codes to control train speed and provide ATP.
  Trials are being carried out to evaluate application of moving block signalling systems.
  The latest computer-based control centres for the Jubilee and Metropolitan lines provide automatic route-setting from an editable timetable and automatic regulation of trains to achieve even headways.

Rolling stock
Number of cars: 3950
Main supplier: Metro-Cammell (now GEC Alsthom)
Car types: London Transport operates two categories of rolling stock: surface and tube. Surface stock is constructed to a larger loading-gauge than tube stock. Tube stock is classed by the year of introduction. There are four basic car types: the driving motor car; the non-driving motor car; the un-coupling, non-driving motor car which forms the end of a unit, and has a shunting control position enabling the unit to be driven at reduced speed; and the non-motored trailer car

Tube stock
1956/1959: unpainted aluminium stock by Metro-Cammell used on the Northern Line. The three 1956 trains were prototypes and have minor differences.
1960: unpainted aluminium driving motor cars built by Cravens Ltd and now in use on the Woodford-Hainault branch of the Central Line, where trains are worked automatically.
1962: unpainted aluminium stock built by Metro-Cammell, except for 169 trailer cars built by British Railways at Derby. Used chiefly on the Central Line. Very similar to the 1956/1959 tube stock.
1967: unpainted aluminium trains built by Metro-Cammell for the Victoria Line. One-person operated and incorporate automatic train control.
1972: two types, both outwardly similar to the 1967 stock. The Mk II is used on the Bakerloo and the Mk I on the Northern Line.
1973: built by Metro-Cammell, used on the Piccadilly Line.
1983: built by Metro-Cammell, and used on the Jubilee Line. Passenger-operated doors.

Surface stock
Unpainted A60 and A62 aluminium stock built by Cravens and used on the Metropolitan main line and East London line.
Unpainted C69 aluminium stock built by Metro-Cammell originally for the Circle and Hammersmith & City lines. Entered service 1970.
Unpainted C77 aluminium stock built by Metro-Cammell for use on the Circle, Hammersmith & City and Edgware Road-Wimbledon lines. The trains are fully interchangeable with C69 stock and entered service 1978.
Unpainted D78 aluminium stock built by Metro-Cammell for the District Line. Entered service 1980. Passenger-operated doors.

Car dimensions: Tube stock
Type 1956, 1959 and 1962, width 2·59 m; length of driving motor car 15·93 m, other 15·62 m
Type 1960, length 15·85 m, width 2·59 m
Type 1967, width 2·64 m; length of driving motor car 16·08 m, trailer car 15·98 m
Type 1972, dimensions as Type 1967
Type 1973, width 2·63 m; length of driving motor car 17·47 m, others 17·68 m
Type 1983, width 2·63 m; length of driving motor car 17·22 m, trailer cars 17·67 m
Surface stock
Type A60 and A62, length 16·15 m, width 2·98 m
Type C69 and C77, width 2·92 m; length of driving motor car 16·03 m, trailer car 14·94 m
Type D78, length of driving motor car 18·36 m, other cars 18·11 m
Power per train (max): 847 kW; 7 cars, 1972 tube stock
Acceleration (max): 1·16 m/s^2, 1973 tube stock
Deceleration (normal service): 1·0 m/s^2
  (emergency): 1·34 m/s^2
Max design speed: 60 mph (96·6 km/h)
Brakes: Friction tread using two composite blocks per wheel controlled by electro-pneumatic valves with mercury switch retardation control. From 1967 onwards additional rheostatic braking on motor cars and brake blocks reduced to one per wheel on all cars. All with Westinghouse pneumatic emergency brake.
  1973 Tube stock and D78 have Westcode air brake and rheostatic braking with load weighting. Emergency brake is electrically controlled energised to release. All brake blocks are operated by individual brake units without rigging.
Cars on order: 680 tube cars of new design to form 85 eight-car trains for Central Line, built by BREL with Brush and ABB electrical equipment. Features will include chopper-controlled motors on all axles, driver's in-cab CCTV and dot-matrix interior as well as external destination displays.

Traffic
Train headways: 2–3 minutes at peak hours in central area
Passenger journeys: (1988/89) 815 million.

System development
In November 1989 the government approved a 15km extension of the Jubilee Line from Green Park to Stratford via Westminster, London Bridge and the Docklands Development Area. Completion is anticipated in 1995-96.
  It was hoped to submit in 1990 a Parliamentary Bill for an extension of the East London line south to East Dulwich and Peckham Rye, and north to Dalston via Bishopsgate.
  A Central London Rail Study set up by the government in 1988 proposed new cross-London routes. One, an East-West Crossrail, would be an RER/S-Bahn type connection between British Rail's main-line approach to Paddington terminus and Bethnal Green, at the approach to its Liverpool Street terminus; this would carry through trains from the western and north-western outer London suburbs to those east and northeast of the city.
  An alternative suggested to a similar North-South Crossrail was a Chelsea-Hackney London Underground line. This would take over the existing Wimbledon branch of the District Line and project it via Chelsea, Victoria, Piccadilly Circus, Kings Cross and Islington to Hackney, and thence to the suburbs at Hainault via the present Central Line tube branch.
  The government was evaluating these proposals in 1990 to arrive at the most cost-effective option. But curbs on public spending and a downturn in the property market, making public sector involvement less likely, discouraged hope of early approval for any of them.

Docklands Light Railway Ltd

PO Box 154, Prestons Road, London E14 9QA

Telephone: +44 71 538 0311
Telefax: +44 71 538 1508

Managing Director: John A Bygate
Railway Manager: Jim Gates

Type of system: Automated light metro

Gauge: 1435 mm
Route length: 12 km, mostly elevated
Number of lines: 2
Number of stations: 15
Track type: Running rail, 40 and 56 kg/m FB on ballasted concrete sleepers or concrete slab track
Electrification type: 750 V dc, third rail, underside contact
Rolling stock: 21 articulated cars from Linke-Hofmann-Busch and BREL; 44 on order from BN

The twin-unit articulated, driverless vehicles are of lightweight steel construction. There are 84 seats in each 28 m-long articulated vehicle, with standing room for a further 130 people. The bogies use rubber primary suspension and airbag secondary suspension. Each outer bogie is motored by a Type 1 KB 2021 traction motor manufactured by GEC Alsthom. The brake control scheme uses an advanced pulse width modulated electronic control from the ATO computer system to the individual brake control units. The GEC Alsthom-designed propulsion equipment uses GTO devices.
Automatic control system: Control is from a centre at Poplar with data processors linked to trainborne and trackside control and safety equipment through advanced data transmission links.
  Though trains carry a Train Captain in two-way radio communication with the Poplar centre, the latter's computer routes the train according to the timetable and determines appropriate performance profiles for each train's working from station to station. There are no lineside signals and the vehicles have no driving cabs. The Train Captain's only operating control functions are to close train doors at the conclusion of a station stop and initiate the train's departure.
Signalling: In 1990 the SEL Division of Alcatel Canada was contracted to re-equip the railway with its Seltrac transmission-based moving block system, to reduce headways below 22 minutes on the busiest sections. Completion was expected in late 1992.

Traffic: (1988–89) 6.6 million passenger journeys

System development
At the end of 1985 interests involved in creation of the £1500 million Canary Wharf financial complex on the Isle of Dogs, which the DLR will bisect, moved that the DLR must have its western terminus hard by the historic financial centre in the heart of the City of London, at the Bank of England, where LRT has a station, rather than at Tower Hill. This £170 million 1·5 km underground extension is in progress for 1991 completion, substantially financed by the Canary Wharf developers, Olympia York. Besides the Bank extension itself, the works include cover for its increased traffic throughout the system, which entails provision for peak-hour capacity of 6600 passengers as opposed to the initial 1760; lengthened platforms to accommodate longer trains; 44 more train-sets; signalling and electrification alterations; and installations of reversal facilities at Canary Wharf.

An eastwards extension of 7·5 km through the Royal Docks to Beckton, with 12 stations, is also under way for 1992 opening. Further extension from Island Gardens to Lewisham is planned but deferred.

Los Angeles

Southern California Rapid Transit District Metro Rail

425 South Main Street, Los Angeles, California 90013, USA

Telephone: +1 213 972 6000
Telefax: +1 212 972 6782

President: Gordana Swanson
General Manager: Alan F Pegg
Assistant General Manager, Transit Systems
  Development: Albert H Perdon
  Operations: Arthur T Leahy

Type of system: Full metro under construction

Gauge: 1435 mm
Length: 32·2 km
Electrification type: 750 V dc
Rolling stock: 30 cars on order from Breda

System development
Construction of the 7.1km city-centre section from Union Station to Alvarado, more than half complete in mid-1990, will be inaugurated in 1993. Construction cost of this section, known as Minimum Operable Segment-1 (MOS-1) is pegged at US$1354 million, of which UMTA is providing US$914 million; the remainder is shared by the state and local agencies.

The remainder of the route, to be known as the city's Red Line, will continue north through Hollywood and then under the Santa Monica Mountains to North Hollywood. The route will be primarily in tunnel with 17 stations.

Los Angeles County Transportation Commission (LACTC)

403 8th Street, Suite 500, Los Angeles, California 90014

Telephone: +1 213 626 0370

Executive Director, Rail Development: Neil Paterson

Type of system: Light rail under construction
Gauge: 1435mm
Route length: 68km
No of lines: 2
No of stations: 35
Electrification: 750 V dc
Rolling stock: Blue Line: 54 cars. Green Line: 36 cars
  The Blue Line's 54 six-axle articulated LRVs were ordered from Sumitomo, US agents of Nippon Sharyo, and the Japanese builders sub-contracted the 750 V dc overhead electric traction and other electrical equipment to ASEA Brown Boveri. ABB has supplied thyristor chopper-controlled 217kW motors with their MICAS programmable traction control system for the cars' monomotor bogies.
Car weight: 44.8 tonnes
Car passenger capacity: 237 (76 seated)
Maximum speed: 88 km/h
Acceleration rate: 4.8 km/h/s

System development
The 36km, 21-station Blue line, running from Los Angeles to Long Beach partly on street and partly on the alignment of the former Pacific Electric Railway, was mostly inaugurated in July 1990. In downtown Los Angeles the Blue Line goes underground to interchange at Wilshire Boulevard with the coming Metro Red Line (see above), and this northern tip of the route was not expected to be complete until July 1991. Though built by the Los Angeles County Transportation Commission, the line is operated by the Southern California Rapid Transit District and the full metro and light rail systems are being promoted as an integral Metro Rail network.

Construction of a 32 km, 14-station east-west route, the Green line, is under way for 1993 inauguration. Running from Norwalk to El Segundo, it will intersect the Blue line at Lynwood. Much of this second line will be located in the central reservation of a new Central Freeway. In 1988 it was decided that the Green line should be fully automated and operated by driverless single cars at short headways. This line will therefore have third-rail current collection.

Other routes under consideration include an extension from North Hollywood to Canoga Park, which could be either a projection of the metro Red line or light rail; Union Station-Pasadena; and Marina del Rey-Los Angeles International Airport.

Lyons

Operating authority: **Société Lyonnaise de Transports en Commun (TCL)**

PO Box 3167, 19 boulevard Vivier Merle, 69212 Lyons Cedex 3, France

Telephone: +33 78 60 25 53
Telex: 330102
Telefax: +33 72 33 84 62

Director: Jean Vallin

Construction authority:
Société d'Economie Mixte du Métropolitain de l'Agglomération Lyonnaise (SEMALY)

25 Cours Emile Zola, 69625 Villeurbanne Cedex, France

Telephone: +33 78 94 86 00
Telex: 380 801
Telefax: +33 78 89 68 57

General Manager: René Waldmann

Type of system: Rubber-tyred full metro (Lines A and B) plus rack railway (Line C)

Gauge: 1435 mm (for security rails)
Route length: Metro 14.3km; rack railway 2·4 km
  (in tunnel): 14 km
Number of lines: 3
Number of stations: 24
  (in tunnel): 22
Rail type and weight: Security rails, SNCF 36 kg/m Lines A, B; 50 kg/m Line C
Track type: Pneumatic rubber tyres run on 68 kg/m metal plates, with lateral guide bars from 100 × 100 × 25 mm angle iron. Security rails on RS-type concrete sleepers. Polyester insulating sleepers support guide rail, which carries power supply. Entire track system bedded in Stedef-type concrete slab, Lines A and B
Gradient (max): 6·5% Lines A and B; 20% Line C
Minimum curvature radius: 100 m Lines A and B; 80 m Line C
Speed (design max): 90 km/h
  (average commercial): 28 km/h
Tunnel type: Cut-and-cover 7·5 × 3·98 m
Electrification type: 750 V dc, collection from lateral bars on Lines A and B, overhead on Line C
Signalling: Centralised traffic control
Automatic control: Automatic train operation (ATO) and automatic train control (ATC)

Rolling stock
Lines A and B
Number of cars: Total 110, including 64 motored, 33 trailers; and 10 rack cars for Line C
Main suppliers: GEC Alsthom
Car dimensions: Length 18 m, width 2·89 m, height 3·4 m
Capacity: 52 seated, 74 standing; crush capacity, 200
Tare weight: 79 tonnes per 3-car set
Doors: 3 double sliding doors each car side

Line C (rack and adhesion)
Number of cars: 10, all motored
Main suppliers: SLM (1974/78); Alsthom-SLM (1982)
Car dimensions: Length 11·46 m, width 2·89 m, height 3·76 m
Capacity (per 2-car set): Crush load 252, seated 103
Tare weight: 65·3 tonnes per 2-car set
Motors (per car): 2 × 217 kW
Max speed (rack, level): 35 km/h
  (rack, 17·4%): 21 km/h
  (adhesion): 80 km/h

Traffic
Train headways: Peak hours, 2 minutes 48 s; off-peak, 5 minutes
Passenger journeys: (1988): 63 million

System development
Inauguration of the 12km, 13-station Line D from Gorge de Loup to Vénissieux, which makes an underwater crossing of the River Rhône between Wilson and University bridges and also of the River Saône, was set for May 1991. The transport authority has continued with the same rubber-tyred technology of Lines A and B for Line D, but construction of Line D has provided for possible future change to steel wheel. Operation of Line D will be fully automatic, using a system designated 'Maggaly' which has been developed by Matra from its VAL technology and from work on the now-aborted Aramis light rail scheme in Paris. Longer-term plans under study in 1990 included an extension to Satolas airport.

Madras

Metropolitan Transport Project (Railways)

Poonamallee High Road, Madras 600 008, India

Telephone: +91 44 39394
Telegrams: Bhoorail

Chief Project Manager: M G Mukundan
Chief Engineer: M S Mohan

Type of system: Planned rapid transit

Gauge: 1676 mm
Route length: 8·4 km
  (elevated): 5·8 km
Number of lines: 1
Number of stations: 8
  (elevated): 5
Electrification type: 25 kV ac, overhead

System development
Feasibility and other preliminary studies have been completed for a rapid transit line 21·7 km long from Kasturba Nagar to Tiruvottiyur, forming part of an inner circular rail system, and improvements to the existing metre-gauge and broad-gauge suburban railway systems. Construction has begun of the first, partly elevated section of 8·4 km from Madras Beach to Luz. Rolling stock will be of the Indian Railways standard broad-gauge emu type.

Madrid

Cia Metropolitano de Madrid

Cavanilles 56, Madrid 28007, Spain

Telephone: +34 1 552 49 00
Telex: 43361 mtro-e

Manager: Guillermo Vázquez Cabezas

Type of system: Full metro

Gauge: 1445 mm
Route length: 112·5 km
  (in tunnel): 107 km
Number of lines: 10
Number of stations: 155
  (in tunnel): 150
Rail weight and type: 45 kg/m and 54 kg/m flat-bottomed; laid in 18 m lengths on oak sleepers, with quartz ballast
Max gradient: 5%
Minimum gradient radius: 90 m
Tunnel type: Double-track tunnel 6·86 m wide. The height above rail level is 4·45 m on sections of cut-and-cover construction and 4·7 m on the majority distance tunnelled by the Belgian (gallery) method. Tunnel linings are of concrete, masonry or brick.

Electrification type: 600 V dc, overhead
Signalling: CTC with track circuits; ATO on Lines 6, 7, 8 and 9; ATP on Lines 1, 2, 3, 5 and 10

Rolling stock
Number of cars: 1014 including 774 motored
Car dimensions: Length 14·5 m, width 2·4 m (old lines); length 17·5 m, width 2·8 m (new lines 6, 7, 8, 9)
Average and crush capacities: 150/200
Tare and loaded weights: 32/50 tonnes
Doors: Automatic 2·2 m wide
Main supplier: CAF Zaragoza
Cars on order: 208 Series 2000 cars being delivered up to 1992

Traffic
Train headways: Peak, 2½–3 minutes; off-peak 3–5 minutes; night, 7½–15 minutes
Passenger journeys: (1989) 387 million

System development
Further extension of Line 1 from Portazgo to Sandi, and completion of the orbital Line 6 were to be started in 1990. Funds approved in 1989 cover the first, Laguna-Puerta del Angel segment of the missing Line 6 link, and this should be inaugurated in 1993.

Manchester

Greater Manchester Passenger Transport Executive (GMPTE)
Metrolink

PO Box 429, 9 Portland Street, Manchester M60 1HX, England

Telephone: +44 61 228 6400
Telefax: +44 61 228 3291

Managing Director: D Scott Hellewell

Type of system: Light rail under construction

Gauge: 1435mm
Route length: 31km
No of stations: 27
Electrification: 750V dc on-street; 1.5kV dc elsewhere

System development
In November 1985 the Greater Manchester Passenger Transport Authority endorsed plans formulated by the former County Council with British Rail and the Passenger Transport Executive for the creation of a 100 route-km system, known as Metrolink. The network would largely adapt five existing BR suburban lines into the city from Rochdale via Oldham, Bury, Glossop/Hadfield, Marple/Rose Hill and Altrincham. GMPTE subsequently put in further Bills to Parliament for extensions of the railway to Salford Quays and to Trafford Park. In the city centre new street-level tracks would be installed to connect Piccadilly, Victoria and Central (Deansgate) stations. A new route would be added to East Didsbury via Chorlton, resurrecting one closed in 1967.

Parliamentary powers for the first phase (Altrincham-Bury, and a city-centre link) were obtained in 1988. This first phase totals 31 route-km, of which 3·5 km including a spur to Piccadilly main-line station will be on-street. A design-build-maintain-operate contract was let to a GMA consortium comprising GEC Alsthom, Mowlem, AMEC and Greater Manchester Buses was let in 1989. Inauguration of the Altrincham-Bury line was anticipated in late 1991 and of the Piccadilly station spur in 1992.

The second phase of system development will convert the BR Rochdale-Oldham line and add the new routes to the Salford Quays development and the Trafford Park industrial estate.

Manila

Light Rail Transit Authority (Metrorail)

Administration Building, LRTA Compound, Aurora Boulevard, Pasay City, Metro Manila, Philippines

Telephone: +63 2 832 04 23/04 32/31 41
Telex: 64614 lrt pn

Administrator: A J Arevalo

Type of system: Light rail

Gauge: 1435 mm
Length: 15km, all elevated
Number of stations: 18
Max gradient: 0·4%
Minimum curve radius: 170 m
Rail weight: 50 kg/m EB50T
Track type: Conventional ballasted track on twin-block concrete bed
Electrification type: 750 V dc, overhead

Rolling stock
Number of cars: 64 double-articulated LRVs
Main suppliers: BN, ACEC
Car dimensions: Length 29·28 m, width 2·5 m, height 3·272 m
Capacity: Crush load 375 (81 seated)
Tare weight: 41·28 tonnes
Motors: 2 × 218 kW
Max speed: 60 km/h
Acceleration: 1 m/s^2
Braking (service): 1·3 m/s^2
(emergency): 2·1 m/s^2
Cars on order: 32, to increase set formats to 3 cars

Traffic
Train headways: Peak hours, 2½ minutes; off-peak, 3–5 minutes
Passenger journeys: (1987) 101.5 million

System development
Construction a 10km Line 2 from the west of the city centre to Cubao was approved in 1989. Further extensions totalling 120 km are under study in the framework of a 20-year plan that would project the system into the suburbs and neighbouring towns.

Marseilles

Construction authority:
Société du Métro de Marseille (SMM)

44 avenue Alexandre Dumas, 13008 Marseilles, France

Telephone: +33 91 23 25 25
Telefax: +33 91 71 05 87

Director General: Jean Clavier

Operating authority:
Régie des Transports de Marseille (RTM)

PO Box 334, 10-12 avenue Clot-Bley, 13008 Marseilles

Telephone: +33 91 95 55 55
Telex: 402880

Director General: Jacques de Plazaola

Type of system: Full metro

Gauge of guideway: 2000 mm
Gauge of auxiliary rail sections: 1435 mm
Route length: 19 km
(in tunnel): 15·5 km
Number of lines: 2
Number of stations: 22
(in tunnel): 17
Track type: 2 steel guideways for train's pneumatic tyres; 2 steel guidance rails fixed outside running guideways; 2 conventional rails for running in case of tyre punctures and guiding through sections without guidance rails
Gradient (max): 6%
Curvature (minimum): 150 m
Speed (design max): 80 km/h
(average commercial): 32 km/h
Tunnel (max): Bored or blasted. Double-track tunnel 7·63 m wide for plain track, 8·13 m wide through curves; twin single-track tunnels each 4·84 m wide. Concrete lined
Electrification type: 750 V dc, collected by side shoes from guidance rail
Signalling: Cab signalling. Continuous speed display instruction device in all trains. Automatic operations with monitored manual drive
Centralised control: Operation of line directed from control centre. Traffic control station or computer ensures regulation of traffic by modifying inter-station speeds and calculating stopping times at stations. Energy-control station ensures traction supply. Control centre also houses communications centre

Rolling stock
Main supplier: GEC Alsthom, ANF (bogies),

	Motor cars	Trailers
Number of units	108	36
Car dimensions		
(length)	16·2 m	15·4 m
(width)	2·6 m	2·6 m
(height)	3·55 m	3·55 m
Total floor area	29 m^2	30 m^2
Number of doors per side	3	3
Door width	1·3m	1·3m
Number of passengers per car		
(total)	116	120
(seated)	44	48

Motors per car: 4 × 130 kW, permanently coupled in series
Acceleration (max): 1·3 m/s^2
(emergency): 1·2–1·5 m/s^2
Max design speed: 80 km/h
Tare weight: 3-car set, about 70 tonnes
Braking: Regenerative and pneumatic. Electro-pneumatic parking brake
Bogies: Bimotor with steel rail wheels and pneumatic guideway wheels, pneumatic horizontal guidance wheels. Primary suspension, rubber/metal elements; secondary suspension, pneumatic pendular type with levelling valve

Traffic
Train headways: Peak hours, 2½ minutes; off-peak, 5 minutes; evenings, 15 minutes
Passenger journeys: (1987) 56·68 million
Max number of trains per hour (one way): 24
Capacity per train (passengers seated): 184
(passengers standing): 472

System development
A further extension of Line 1 eastward to La Timone is under way for opening in September 1992. A northward extension of Line 2 to Madrague-Ville is contemplated.

Medellin

Metro Medellin

Empresa de transporte Masivo del Valle de Aburrá ltda, Carrera 43A, 11A-80, 4° Piso, Apartado Aereo, 9128 Medellin, Colombia

Telephone: +57 4 266 0860
Telex: 65344
Telefax: +57 4 268 3635

General Manager: Jairo Hoyos Gómez

Type of system: Metro under construction

Gauge: 1435 mm
Route length: 29 km
(elevated): 11 km
Number of lines: 2
Number of stations: 25
Max gradient: 3·7%
Minimum curve radius: 150 m
Rail weight: 56 kg/m
Track type: Cut-and-cover
Electrification type: 1·5 kV dc, overhead

Rolling stock
42 three-car train-sets, each with two cars powered by 205 kW motors, maximum speed 80 km/h, built by MAN with Siemens electrical equipment

System development
The north-south Line 1, linking Bello and Itagui, will be 23 km long with 19 stations, and will be elevated for 7 km. The second, east-west Line 2 will be 6 km long and 5 km elevated, with six stations, including one interchange. No tunnelling will be involved on either route.

In December 1982 the government authorised the scheme. A consortium including Siemens, MAN and Aplicaciones Tecnicas Industriales and Entrecanales y Tavera of Spain had their US$650 million construction bid provisionally accepted in November 1983, but protests by unsuccessful tenderers at alleged irregularities delayed confirmation until mid-1984. Construction began in 1985.

The central section of Line 1 was due to open in June 1991, the remainder in the following February. Line 2 was also under construction in 1990.

Melbourne

Victoria Public Transport Corporation
The Met

Transport House, 589 Colins Street, Melbourne, Victoria 3000, Australia

Telephone: +61 3 619 1111
Telex: A 33801
Telefax: +61 3 619 2343

Chief General Manager: R Terrell
General Manager, Trains: D Watson
  Works & Services: G Brover

Type of system: Suburban rail

Gauge: 1600 mm
Route length: 219·5 km
Number of lines: 18
Number of stations: 209
Average distance between stations: 1·55 km
Track: 53 kg/m rail on timber/concrete sleepers
Electrification type: 1·5 kV dc, overhead (305 km only)

Rolling stock
Number of cars: 1212
Car types: 18 ex-VR Harris seven-car trains by Gloucester RC & W and Martin & King with GEC electrical equipment; 58 ex-VR six-car Hitachi trains in stainless steel by Martin & King with Hitachi electrical equipment; 95 six-car trains by Comeng (delivery completed in 1989).
Car dimensions: Length: Harris 15·99 m; Hitachi 23·01 m M, 22·86 m T; Comeng 23 m M, 22·5 m T
Capacity: 604 per six-car set
Motors per power car: Harris 4 × 107 kW; Hitachi 4 × 112 kW; Comeng 4 × 137 kW
Tare weight: Harris 36 tonnes M, 31 tonnes T; Hitachi 52 tonnes M, 36 tonnes T; Comeng 50 tonnes M, 34 tonnes T
Acceleration (max): Comeng 0·8 m/s²
Deceleration (max): 1·1 m/s²; 0·67 m/s² Hitachi
Max speed: 115 km/h
Doors: Power-operated
Cars to be ordered: Bi-level emus for Ringwood and Dandenong lines

Traffic
Passenger journeys: (1988/89) 94 million

System development
The City Loop scheme avoids terminal turnrounds at Flinders Street station. Four single-track tunnels connect with the four major groups of suburban lines: Eastern, passing through Burnley; Southeastern passing through Caulfield; Northeastern, passing through Clifton Hill; Northern and Western, passing through North Melbourne.

There are three city stations on the undergrond part of the system and all trains round the Loop also pass through Flinders and Spencer Street stations, so that passengers have the choice of five stations in the city area. In order to operate the Loop trains in the direction of the predominant traffic flow in each peak period, signalling is reversible. Each of the loops has an effective capacity of 24 trains an hour and, in addition to loop trains, at least another 60 trains an hour can, as a result of overall improvements to the suburban system, operate to and from Flinders Street station.

The Melbourne Metropolitan Train Control Centre (METROL) will eventually cover the whole suburban system. L M Ericsson, Sweden, is supplying the computer-based train describer which forms the heart of the system. The system provides a visual display to identify the position and status of all trains and signals, through links with wayside signals and signalboxes. Passenger information is displayed on colour VDUs on platforms.

(See also Victoria, Australia entry, Rail Systems section)

Mexico City

Sistema de Transporte Colectivo (STC)

Organismo Público Decentralizado, Postbox 06070, Delicias 67, Mexico 1, DF, Mexico

Telephone: +52 5 709 11 33
Telex: 01774667 stc me

Director-General: Ing Gerardo Ferrando Bravo
Deputy Director, Administrative: Lic Federico Valle Rodriguez
  Technical: Ing Juan Manuel Ramirez Caraza
  Planning: Oscar Barreiro Perera

Type of system: Full metro

Gauge: 1435 mm 9 auxiliary guide rails)
Route length: 141 m
  (in tunnel): 92·4 km
Number of lines: 8
Number of stations: (Total) 125
  (in tunnel): 79
Average distance between stations: 1029 m
Max gradient: 6·8%
Max curvature: 105 m
Speed: (design max) 80 km/h
Rail weight: 39·6 kg/m (80 ASCE)
Track type: Wood (concrete, Lines 6 and 7) sleepers on ballast
Tunnel type: Concrete caisson with double track
Electrification type: 750 V dc, collected with two lateral guide bars
One-man operation: All services
Signalling: Automatic block and interlocking, ATO

Rolling stock
Number of cars: Total 2269 including 1495 motored (head and intermediate) and 774 trailers forming six-car sets on Lines 4 and 6, nine-car sets elsewhere
Main suppliers: Alsthom, Bombardier, CNCF (Mexico)

	Control cars (M)	Intermediate motor cars and trailers (N)
Car dimensions		
(length)	17·2 m	16·2 m
(width)	2·5 m	2·5 m
(height)	3·6 m	3·6 m
Passenger capacity per car		
(total)	170	170
(seated)	38	39

Motors per car: 4
Rating: 110 to 128 kW
Train composition (minimum): 6
  (max): 9
Acceleration (max): 1·33 m/s²
Deceleration (emergency): 2·25 m/s²
Brakes: Electric or rheostatic air
Tare and loaded weight: 'M', 28·1/40 tonnes; 'N', motor 26·8/38·8 tonnes; trailer, 20·6/32·5 tonnes
Doors: Sliding type, 1·3 m wide
Cars on order: CNCF has rolling order to deliver 80 cars annually

Traffic
Train headways: Peak hours, Line 1, 1·9 minutes; Lines 2 and 3, 2·16 minutes; Line 4, 5·83 minutes; Line 5, 3·66 minutes; Line 6, 4·16 minutes; and Line 7, 4·08 minutes
Train capacity (passengers): 1530
Passenger journeys: (1988) 1476 million

System development
The Mexico City metro system is closely modelled on the Paris Metro, its architecture and pneumatic-tyred rolling stock particularly reflecting French influence. The latter country's interest extended to a 16-year loan to assist construction, besides consultancy as to its construction. The metro operates under a computerised electronic system of traffic control.

Construction of a further 60 route-km is planned up to 1994. The metro has long-range plans for enlargement of its system to 15 lines and 315 route-km by 2010, when daily usage is expected to exceed 12 million.

The upgrading of some tramways to light rail standards as metro feeders has been launched by STE, the Mexico City trolleybus operator. The first 11 km section was activated in early 1986 to cater for the World Cup soccer finals at Azteca stadium. A further 16 km were transformed in 1987, when PCC tramcars rebuilt as 52 articulated eight-axle LRVs became operational; in this conversion UTDC is aiding a local contractor. In 1990 a 13 km line was under construction from Pantitlan to Sta Marta.

Miami

Metro-Dade Country Transportation Administration

111 NW 1 Street, Suite 910, Miami, Florida 33128, USA

Telephone: +1 305 375 5675
Telefax: +1 305 375 4605

Executive Director: C E Colby
Deputy Director, Metrorail and Metromover
  Operation: F Martin

Type of system: Full metro

Gauge: 1435 mm
Route length: 34·5 km
  (at surface level): 1·6 km
  (elevated): 31·39 km
Number of lines: 1
Number of stations: 20
Track type: Wood sleepers on ballast over reinforced concrete structure. Direct fixation fasteners with resilient pads
Max gradient: 3%
Minimum curve radius: 305 m
Electrification type: 700 V dc, third rail
One-man operation: Total
Signalling: Union Switch & Signal Division, American Standard Company
Automatic control: Partial, with full operator override

Rolling stock
Number of cars: 136, all mounted
Main supplier: Transit America. Similar chopper-controlled Transit America cars have been ordered for Baltimore (qv for details)
Car dimensions: Length 22·86, width 3·175 m
Capacity: 74 seated, average crush load 166
Motors per car: 4 × 175 hp

Traffic
Passenger journeys: (1988) 12·6 million

System development
A 35·4 km Line 2 planned to connect the city centre with the airport, Little Havana and West Dade has been shelved in view of the initial line's unsatisfying traffic levels. Extension of Line 1 may go ahead.

Type of system: People-mover

Number of lines: 1
Number of stations: 9 (one connecting station with heavy rail)

The Metromover began operations in April 1986. Metromover consists of a double-loop, elevated people-mover system in downtown Miami providing service to nine stations on a 3·05 km radius. It is operated by 12 electrically-powered, automatically-controlled Westinghouse C-100 vehicles. Nominal capacity per vehicle is 96 passengers, with a maximum calculated crush load capacity of 155 passengers per vehicle. Maximum speed is 48 km/h; vehicle length, 39 ft (11·9 m) and weight 32 800/57 800 lb (14 909/26 273 kg).

Extensions north and south aggregating 4.1 km were approved in 1989. For these 15 more cars will be required. Inauguration is expected in 1994.

Middlesbrough

Cleveland County Council, Middlesbrough, England

Consultants were in 1989 engaged in feasibility, demand and financial studies to identify options for the first phase of a projected light rail system. A core line would connect Middlesbrough and Stockton-on-Tees.

Milan

Azienda Trasporti Municipali (ATM)

Foro Buonaparte 61, 20121 Milan, Italy

Telephone: +39 2 805 5841
Telex: 330564 atmi
Telefax: +39 2 805 0674

General Manager: Dr Elio Gambini
Director, Technical: L Calicchio

Planning & Development: P Silvestri
Manager, Metro & Tramway: E Kluzer

Metro Construction authority:
Metropolitana Milanese SpA

Via del Vecchio Politecnico 8, 20121 Milan

Telephone: +39 2 77 471
Telex: 334219 metrom i
Telefax: +39 2 780033

General Manager: Prof Ing Piero Ogna
Project Manager: A Colombo
Construction Manager: U Amagliani

Type of system: Full metro

Gauge: 1435 mm
Route length: 34·5 km (urban); plus 15 km Adda and 3·9 km (Cologno) suburban extensions of Green (No 2) Line; and 2·6 km suburban extension of Red (No 1) Line
Number of lines: 2
Number of stations: Red Line 1, 35, all in tunnel; Green Line 2, 31, of which 15 in tunnel
Rail weight and type: 50 kg/m (UNI)
Track type: Both ballasted and slab-track
Tunnel type: Large profile, double-track tunnels 7·5 m in width and 3·9 m in height (above rail level). Tunnelling was by the 'Milan' method of cut-and-cover which permitted the resumption of surface wheeled traffic, after a minimum period of interruption, over temporary surface while excavation proceeded below ground. Tunnel roofs are generally 3 m below street level, allowing space between tunnel extrados and street level for pedestrian subways and public utility services. The actual tunnel is of rectangular section in cast concrete. Part of Line 2 has been built in shield-driven tunnel to minimise surface traffic interference

Electrification type: Red Line 750 V dc, third rail collection and fourth the rail current return; Green Line 1·5 V dc, overhead
Signalling: Wayside light signals, cab signalling and automatic block with automatic train stop and CTC. Suppliers, Westinghouse and SASIB (GRS).
Line 3: ATO, ATP (employing audio-frequency track circuiting) and ATS (Automatic Train Supervision) under new computerised control centre. Remote control of stations using CCTV and voice/video data links via digital transmission and optic-fibre carrier-wave systems.

Rolling stock
Number of cars: 519 cars
Main suppliers: GAI (consortium of Italian suppliers)
Car dimensions: Length 17·5 m, width 2·85 m, height 3·55 m
Tare and loaded weight: Red Line, 32/50 tonnes; Green Line, motor cars, 29·5/44 tonnes; trailers 19·2/35·5 tonnes
Max speed: 90 km/h
Doors: All sliding; Red Line, 4 × 1·3 m; Green Line, 3 × 1·3 and 4 × 1·3 m

Cars in course of delivery 1989: For the new Yellow Line 3, six three-car trains by Socimi with Hitachi traction equipment; and 34 three-car trains with VVVF inverter-controlled 160kW asynchronous motors and microprocessor control from a Breda-Fiat-Firema consortium with electrical equipment by Ansaldo, Ercole Marelli, ABB and Parizzi. A further 20 train-sets will be needed for the Line 3 extension (see below)

Traffic
Train headways: Peak hours, Red Line 2¼ minutes; Green Line 3 minutes; off-peak, Red Line 3¾ minutes; Green Line 5 minutes
Passenger journeys: (1988) 270·2 million

System development
The new Yellow Line 3 runs 11·3 km with 15 stations under the old city centre at Piazzo Duomo to San Donato, among the highly populated industrial and residential suburb of the southwest. Entirely underground, it is electrified at 1·5 kV dc, overhead. The first 3.3km from Centrale to Duomo were inaugurated in May 1990; the remainder would be ready in early 1991. A 9·4 km northward extension of this line with 9 stations was likely to be started in 1991.

Other extensions under construction in 1989 were: Red Line 1 from Inganni to Bisceglie, 0·85 km, with one station; and Green Line 2 from Romolo to Missaglia (2·9 km, three stations).

A proposed Line 4, under feasibility study in 1990, is likely to run from the city centre to the northeastern suburbs. Other routes under study include city centre east-Linate Airport.

Minneapolis
Regional Transit Board

160 E Kellog Boulevard, St Paul, Minnesota 55410, USA

Chairman: Peter Stumpf

Type of system: Light rail proposed

Proposals outlining a three-line, 62 km system have been drafted. The state authority has endorsed detailed planning of one 22·5 km route from the city centre to Minnetonka, adapting an existing rail infrastructure, and has also approved property taxation as a contribution to construction costs. A preliminary engineering design contract was awarded in August 1988 and opening in 1991 is possible.

Minsk
Upravlenie Minsk Metropolitena

Novo Basmannaya 2, Moscow 107174, USSR

Type of system: Full metro

Gauge: 1524 mm
Number of lines: 1
Route length: 9·5 km
Number of stations: 9
Max gradient: 4%
Minimum curve radius: 400 m
Electrification type: 825 V, third rail

System development
The 6-station, 9km Line 2 is under construction. Two further lines are planned, to create eventually a 75 km network.

Monterrey
Metrorrey

Calz Madero, 990 pte, 64000, Monterrey, Mexico

Telephone: +52 83 728521

Type of system: Light rail under construction

Gauge: 1435mm
Route length: 17.5km
No of stations: 17
Electrification: 1.5kV dc overhead
Rolling stock: 25 articulated LRVs by CNCF

Construction began in 1988 of the first 17·5 km elevated section of a planned three-line 74 km system. The first route runs east-west and was inaugurated in March 1990. Siemens had the signalling, and Cubic Western Data the revenue collection contract.

Montreal
Société de Transport de la Communauté Urbaine de Montréal (STCUM)

159 St Antoine Street West, Montreal, Quebec H2Z 1HE, Canada

Telephone: +1 514 280 5656
Telex: 05-825570
Telefax: +1 514 280 5193

President and General Manager: Louis Roy
Executive Officer, Metro and Commuter Trains: Roger C Choquette
Construction, Maintenance, Security: Jacques Rompréd
Resource & Quality Development: Francis Therrien
Finance: Claire Monette

Type of system: Rubber-tyred full metro

Gauge: 1435 mm
Route length: 65 km
Number of lines: 4
Number of stations: 65
Track type: 35 kg/m security rails flanked by 254 mm-wide concrete running tracks and lateral guide bars.
Max gradient: 6·5%
Minimum curve radius: 140 m
Tunnel type: Double-track, 7·112 m wide; concrete-lined; vertical walls; arched roof 4·9 m high at centre. About 30% cut-and-cover using single rectangular concrete section. Depth varies from 6 m to 54·8 m
Electrification type: 750 V dc
Signalling: Cab signalling with ATC and ATO

Rolling stock
Number of cars: 759 (506 motored, 253 trailers)
Main supplier: Canadian-Vickers and Bombardier
Car dimensions: Motor cars: length 7·2 m, width 2·5 m; trailers: 16·5 m, width 2·5 m
Capacity: 160
Doors: 4 double doors on each side
Number of cars/train: 9
Average schedule speed: Line 1: 38·1 km/h; Line 2: 40 km/h; Line 4: 47·2 km/h, Line 5, 35·7 km/h. Cars are semi-permanently coupled in three-car sets consisting of two motor cars with a trailer in the centre. Maximum length of a nine-car train is 152·5 m. Each motor car has four 150 hp motors. Braking is dynamic (rheostatic on older rolling stock; regenerative on newer stock). Wooden shoes act on the steel security rails at slow speeds and for emergency stops. Top speed is 71·5 km/h

Traffic
Train headways: Line 1: 20 trains/h; Line 2: 26 trains/h; Line 4: 12 trains/h; Line 5, 15 trains/h.
Passenger journeys: (1988) 750 000 daily

System development
No extension active in 1989, but a newly-formed regional transport organisation embracing Montreal and the adjoining Laval and South Shore communities was seeking extension of Line 2 from Henri Bourassa to Laval. Other proposals advocated extensions of Lines 4 and 5 and construction of a new Line 8 to serve the east of the city.

Moscow
Moskovski Metropoliten Imeni VI Lenina

41 Mir Prospect, Moscow 129110, USSR

Telephone: +7 095 222 10 01

Chief Executive: Yevgeny Grigoryevich Dubchenko
Chief Engineer: Viktor Yakovlevich Gromov

Type of system: Full metro

Gauge: 1524 mm
Route length: 217 km
 (in tunnel): 179·7 km
Number of lines: 10
Number of stations: 135
 (in tunnel): 116
Max gradient: 4%
Minimum curve radius: 300 m
Rail type: 50 kg/m flat-bottomed, welded up to 325 m
Tunnel type: The earlier sections were partly of cut-and-cover construction, the tunnels being double-track and of rectangular section, 7·6 m wide by 3·9 m high from rail level. Subsequent lines have been largely of deep-level tube construction, each single-track tube tunnel having an internal diameter 5.46 m. Tube lines are as much as 40 m below surface level, eg at Dynamo station
Electrification type: 825 V dc, third rail
Signalling: Automatic train stop; central control; radio-telephone communication with all trains; complex automatic traffic control system with one-man train operation on Zhdanovsko-Krasnopresnienskaya and Kalininskaya lines; automatic speed control on Koltzeva and Sierpukhovskaya lines, also with one-man operations

Rolling stock
Number of cars: 3135, all motored
Ratings per car: 4 × 73 kW (type D); 4 × 66 kW (type E); 4 × 110 kW (Type 81-714/717)
Main supplier: Mytischy
Car dimensions: Length 18·77 m, width 2·7 m
Doors: Sliding 4 × 1·05 m wide per car (D); 4 × 1·38 m wide (E)
Braking: Rheostatic

Traffic
Train headways: Peak hours 1 minute 25 s on two lines recently equipped with ATC, 1 minute 20 s on other lines; off-peak, 2–4½ minutes
Passenger journeys: (1987) 2602 million
Trains per hour each way (max): 45
Cars per train (max): 8
Estimated capacity per car: 170 (including 40 seated)

System development
Additions in hand in 1989 concerned three existing lines and two new ones, aggregating 34·6 km, all for completion by 1990. The new routes are the first 14·6 km section of a cross-city line from Borovitskaya to Otradnoye, and the 7 km Lybulinski line. Existing routes involved in these extensions were: Kaluzhsko-Rizhskaya (6·7 km); Kirovsko-Frunzenski (3·9 km); and Filyevski (2·4 km).

Longer-term plans envisage at least one completely new route, an orbital Line 10, which would spread the metro system's length to some 370 km. In addition, three high-speed regional metro routes each of about 60 km length have been under discussion.

Mülheim

Betriebe der Stadt Mülheim and Ruhr, Federal Republic of Germany

Duisburger Strasse 78, 4330 Mülheim/Ruhr

Type of system: Tramway and light metro

One 7km route of the tramway system with 10 stations has been upgraded to light metro standards and further transmutation is in progress. Rolling stock includes 13 Duewag M6D six-axle LRVs with Siemens three-phase drive and Sibas 16 MC control units, which include comprehensive diagnostics.

Munich

Stadtwerke München Werkbereich Technik, Verkehrsbetriebe (SWM)

Einsteinstrasse 28, Postfach 20 22 22, Munich 2, Federal Republic of Germany

Telephone: +49 89 2191 1
Telex: 05 22 063
Telefax: +49 89 2191 2155

Manager: Dipl Ing Dieter Buhmann
Operations Manager: Dipl-Ing Reimar Wallisch
Chief Engineer: Dipl-Ing Heinz Halder

Type of system: Full metro (U-Bahn)

Gauge: 1435 mm
Route length: 56·5 km
Number of lines: 6
Number of stations: 63
Tunnel type: Shield driven 5·74 m diameter, conventional tunnelling and cut-and-cover
Electrification type: 750 kV dc, third rail
Signalling: Continuous automatic train control. SpDrL77 signalling and train control equipment with trackby Standard Elektrik Lorenz (SEL), 1980

Rolling stock
Number of cars: 466 (Types A1, A2, B1, B2)
35 Type B2 two-car units of a new generation from MAN GHH have Siemens three-phase ac motors, electrical equipment and microprocessor control
Main suppliers: MBB, MAN, O & K, Rathgeber
Car dimensions: Length 18 m (Type A2), 18·2 m (Type B2) width 2·9 m, height 3·55 m
Motors per car: 2 × 180 kW (A2), 2 × 188 kW three-phase (B2)
Average and crush capacity: 145/242 (49 seats per car)
Tare and loaded weight: 25·8/35·2 tonnes (4 passengers/m²)
Braking: Separately excited rheostatic brakes
Max speed: 80 km/h
Average speed: 35 km/h
Doors: Sliding with 1·3 m opening; 3 per side

Traffic
Train headways: 5 minutes
Passenger journeys: (1988) 219·8 million

System development
The U-Bahn development programme has been extended from 1985 to 1992 and the projected system expanded from a planned 52 km to 11 lines totalling around 80 km. In pursuance of the 1992 network plan of three main lines with 11 branches, work began in 1983 on a 7·7 km U3-South line with eight stations from Implerstrasse to Furstenried-West; the first 6·1 km and 6 stations were opened in late 1989 and the remainder was heading for inauguration in late 1991.

Also under construction in 1989 were: a 6·5 km U2-North line extension with seven stations to connect with the S-Bahn system at Feldmoching; a 3.3km, 3-station extension of Line U6-West from Holtzapfelkreuth to Klinikum Grosshadern; and a 3.5km projection of Line U1 south from Kolumbusplatz to Mangfallplatz, for completion in 1997.

Nagoya

Nagoya-shi Kotsu Kyoku (Nagoya Municipal Transportation Bureau)

City Hall Annex, 10th Floor, 1-1 Sannomaru 3-chome, Naka-ku, Nagoya 460, Japan

Telephone: +81 52 961 1111

General Manager: Kosuke Thomatsu

Type of system: Full metro

Gauge: 1435 mm; 1067 mm (Lines 3 and 6)
Route length: 41.2km; 25.3km
Number of lines: 5
Number of stations served: 66
Rail weight: 50 kg/m
Tunnel type: Mainly cut-and-cover
Electrification type: 600 V dc, third rail; 1·5 V dc, overhead (Lines 3 and 6)
Max gradient: 1 in 28 (3·5%)
Minimum curve radius: 125 m
Signalling: Automatic block with colour lights. Cab signalling and automatic train control introduced on three lines

Rolling stock
Number of cars: 605, of six types, four air-conditioned
Main suppliers: Hitachi, Nippon Sharyo
Car dimensions: Length 15·6 and 20 m, width 2·5, 2·6 and 2·8 m, height 3·43 and 3·5 m
Motors per car: 4
Doors: 3 or 4 per side

Traffic
Passenger journeys: (1986) 338·2 million
Max number of trains per hour each way: 30
Number of cars per train: 4-6
Average scheduled speed: 33 km/h

System development
Line 3 is being extended to the north by 1·4 km and completion set for 1992. Construction of a new 14.9 km Line 6 is under way; opening of the initial 6·3 km at its core was achieved in September 1989. An ultimate system of 130 km is planned, involving extensions of Lines 1, 4 and 6, and construction of three new lines.

Nantes

Société d'Economie Mixte des Transports en Commun de l'Agglomération Nantaise (SEMITAN)

3 rue Bellier, 44046 Nantes Cedex, France

Telephone: +33 40 29 99 00
Telex: 711 779 semitan f
Telefax: +33 40 74 64 09

President: Alain Chénard
Director General: Maudez Guillossou

Type of system: Light rail

Gauge: 1435 mm
Route length: 12·5 km
Number of routes: 1
Number of stations: 25
Track type: RI-60 grooved rail on highways, UIC50 rail conventionally ballasted elsewhere
Electrification type: 750 V dc

Rolling stock
Number of cars: 28 aluminium-bodied articulated LRVs; design in the French LRV standard
Main supplier: Consortium including MTE, CIMT, Creusot-Loire and TCO, headed by Alsthom
Car dimensions: Length 28·5 m, width 2·3 m
Capacity: 68 seated, 108 standing
Doors: 2 single, 4 double-leaf sliding

Traffic
Train headways: Peak hours 4 minutes, off-peak 6 minutes, late evenings and Sundays 10–20 minutes
Passenger journeys: (1988) 13.5 million

System development
An extension from Haluchère to La Beaujoirie was opened in April 1989. Work on a 5.1km, 13-station, second line south has begun. Its first section will open in September 1992 from a junction with the first line at Commerce to a Trocardière terminus in Rezé. Thereafter the line will be extended northward.

Naples

Assessorato ai Trasporti

Assessorato ai Trasporti and Regione Campania, Ferrovie dello Stato (FS), Naples, Italy

Director: Silvano Masciari

Construction authority:
Metropolitana Milanese (MM)

Via del Vecchio Politecnico 8, 20121 Milan

Telephone: +39 2 77 471
Telex: 334291

Type of system: Metro and light metro under construction

Gauge: 1435 mm
Planned route length: 40 km
Number of routes: 2
Number of stations: 11 (complete system 39)
Electrification type: 1·5 V dc, overhead
Max design speed: 80 km/h
Signalling: ATP, track-to-train data transmission system

Rolling stock
12 articulated LRVs by Firema with Ansaldo Trasporti chopper-controlled three-phase motors

System development
The geophysical character of Naples which shelves steeply away from the sea-front, poses severe metro design problems. Even with a spiral loop on 170 m-radius curves the full metro route approved by government and city in February 1982, to run from the Piazza Garibaldi and its main-line station to Colli Aminei, will have to be graded at 5·5 per cent of 8 km in its descent to the city centre. This section, from Vanvitelli to Piazza Garibaldi, being built by Metropolitana Milanese, may not be finished until 1997. The outer-city portion of the 16km Line 1, from Vanviteli to Secondigliano, may be inaugurated in 1992.

Meanwhile, the first in-tunnel 2.2 km and two stations, Augusto and Piedigrotto, of light metro Line 2 were opened in early summer 1990. This forms part of a 21 km Line 2 that will run mostly along the shoreline from Campi Flegrei to Ponticelli on the east. Ansaldo Trasporti is the main contractor for Line 2.

Naples is also served by the 140 km-long Circumvesuviana Railway (see under Italy).

Neuchâtel

Cis des Transports en Commun de Neuchâtel et Environs

5 Quai Ph-Godet, 2001 Neuchâtel, Switzerland

Telephone: +41 38 25 15 46
Telefax: +41 38 24 51 34

Director: H-P Gaze
Operating Director: D Blanchoud
Technical Director: P Moser

Type of system: Light rail

Gauge: 1000 mm
Route length: 9 km
(on own right-of-way): 9 km

Number of stations: 15
Average distance between stations: 650 m
Rail weight: 30/36 kg/m
Track type: Conventional sleepers on ballast
Electrification type: 630 V dc, overhead
Signalling: Simplified automatic block with cab radio on all trains; supplier Mauerhofer & Zuber (signalling) and Lier (radios)
Automatic control: Introduced 1981

Rolling stock
Number of cars: 10, including 6 motored
Main suppliers: SWS Schlieren/BBC Baden
Car dimensions: Length 18·38 m, width 2·4 m
Capacity: 88 seated, crush 220
Tare and loaded weight: Trailers 17·3/25·5 tonnes; motor cars 25·2/33 tonnes
Doors: 2 doors each side 1·3 m wide

Traffic
Train headways: Peak hours, 10 minutes; off-peak, 20 minutes
Passenger journeys: (1989) 2·7 million

Newark

Newark City Subway, NJ Transit Bus Operations Inc

180 Boyden Avenue, Maplewood, New Jersey 07040, USA

Telephone: +1 201 761 8300

Superintendent: J B Richardson

Type of system: Light rail

Gauge: 1435 mm
Route length: 6·9 km
  (in tunnel): 2 km
Number of stations: 11
  (in tunnel): 4
Rail weight: 110 lb (50 kg/m)
Track type: Conventional wood sleepers on ballast; in tunnel stations wood stub sleepers set in concrete
Tunnel type: Cut-and-cover, double track
Signalling: Single block, track circuit system

Rolling stock
Number of cars: 24, all motored
Main supplier: St Louis Car (built 1946 for Twin City Rapid Transit, Minneapolis)
Car dimensions: Length 14·14 m, width 2·74 m
Doors: Dual bi-fold 1·42 × 1·98 m

Traffic
Passenger journeys: (1988) 3.8 million

Harbourfront Rapid Transit
Hudson River Waterfront Unit

Director: Joseph A Martin

Type of system: Planned light rail

Plans were approved in October 1986 for a 24 km LRT project, partly over Conrail alignments, to connect the Hoboken-New Jersey City waterfront with Weekawken. Property acquisition has begun, supported by UMTA and Port Authority grants. New Jersey State has funded engineering studies with the aim of an opening in the late 1990s.

Newcastle upon Tyne

Tyne and Wear Passenger Transport Executive

Cuthbert House, All Saints, Newcastle upon Tyne NE1 2DA, England

Telephone: +44 91 261 0431
Telex: 537494
Telefax: +44 91 232 1192

Director General: D F Howard
Chief Finance Officer: T McCrady
Chief Planning Officer: I D Pauw
General Operations Manager: P J Neal
Chief Engineer: R Sproul

Type of system: Full metro

Gauge: 1435 mm
Route length: 55·6 km
  (in tunnel): 6·4 km
Number of lines: 3
Number of stations (total): 44
Gradient (max): 3·3%
Curvature (max): 50 m (service line)
  210 m (main line)
Speed (design max): 80 km/h
  (average commercial): 34·3 km/h
Rail type: BS 113A
Track type: Rail laid on tied concrete sleepers in tunnels; on concrete and timber sleepers with ballast on surface sections; on PACT slab track on Byker Viaduct.
Tunnel type: 4·75 m diameter to accommodate overhead electrification equipment. Mainly pre-cast segmental concrete linings; spheroidal graphite cast iron linings in unstable ground and 7 m diameter station tunnels
Electrification type: 1·5 kV dc, overhead
Signalling: Automatic Westinghouse two-aspect lineside signals with repeaters. Inductive train-stop equipment to halt trains overrunning signal
Automatic control: Philips Vetag vehicle indentification system combined with microprocessors for decentralised control from South Gosforth centre.

Traffic
Train headways: Mondays–Fridays: 3–4 minutes in South Gosforth to Heworth section; 5 minutes, St James to North Shields 0730–1830; 5 minutes in central area after 1830; 10 minutes elsewhere. Evenings and Sundays: 12 minutes.
Passenger journeys: (1989) 47·4 million
Max line capacity (one way): 10 000 passengers/h
Max number of trains per hour (one way): 18

Rolling stock
Car types: Articulated motor cars built by Metropolitan-Cammell, featuring monomotor bogies and articulation units built under licence; other equipment includes Duewag monomotor bogies and articulation, Westinghouse plug doors and Westcode braking system, BSI automatic couplers and Brecknell Willis pantograph
Number of units: 90
Car dimensions: Length 27·8 m, width 2·64 m, height (overall) 3·4 m
Number of doors per side: 4
Door width: 1·3 m
Number of passengers per car: 270 (crush load) (seated): 84
Motors per car: 2
Motor rating: 185 kW continuous/205 kWh
Power per train (minimum): 360 kW
  (max): 720 kW
Acceleration (max): 1 m/s^2
Deceleration (normal service): 1·3 m/s^2
  (emergency): 2·3 m/s^2
Max design speed: 80 km/h
Articulation: Two body halves connected to centre bogie through ball-race assembly
Suspension: Chevron rubber between bogie frame and axle box; air springing between bogie and body
Braking: Dynamic with Metcalfe/BSI ventilated discs on centre bogie; magnetic track brakes on all bogies for emergency use
Weight (empty): 38 tonnes

System development
Construction has begun of a branch from Bankfoot to Newcastle International Airport, set for opening in 1992. The feasibility of extension from Heworth into Sunderland town centre is under study.

New York

New York City Transit Authority (NYCTA)

370 Jay Street, Brooklyn, New York 11201, USA

Telephone: +1 718 330 3000

President: David L Gunn
Senior Vice-President: David F Feeley
Senior Vice-President, Operations: L G Reuter
Vice President, Rapid Transit: A R Goodlatte
Chief Electrical Officer: F Westfall
Chief Engineer, Track & Structures: C Stanford

Type of system: Full metro

Gauge: 1435 mm

Route length: 398 km
  (in tunnel): 246¾ km
  (elevated): 122 km
Number of lines: 7, A Division (IRT Lines), excluding 42nd Street shuttle
16, B Division (BMT-IND Lines), excluding Franklin shuttle
Number of routes: 25
Number of stations: 469
  (in tunnel): 277
  (elevated): 153
Rail weight: 49·6 kg/m
Track type: According to location (conventional sleepers on ballast, sleepers on concrete with resilient pads, etc)
Tunnel type: Cut-and-cover, under-river bored tunnel, cast-iron with concrete liners, some concrete horseshoe
Electrification type: 600 V dc, third rail with contact shoe current collector
Signalling: Wayside signals/train control; suppliers, Union Switch and Signal, General Railway Signal

Rolling stock
Number of cars: 6306
Main suppliers: St Louis Car, American Car & Foundry, Budd, Pullman-Standard, Kawasaki, Bombardier, Westinghouse-Amrail and Nissho-Iwai

In December 1981 the Metropoliitan Transportation Authority, the body created in 1967 to administer all public transport in New York and its seven surrounding suburban counties, authorised NYCTA to embark on the most massive car orders in the history of US rapid transit. The A Division has received a total of 1150 new R-62 cars for use on IRT Lines. The first order for 325 cars was secured by Nissho-Iwai and Kawasaki of Japan for US$274·5 million, with the backing of a US$126·143 million loan from the Export-Import Bank of Japan at very keen interest rates. The order for the remaining 825 R-62A cars, valued at US$836·8 million, went to Bombardier of Canada, with the help of US$563 million financing from the Canadian government at 9·7 per cent over 15 years.

Orders totalling 425 R-68 cars for the B Division, BMT-IND Lines, and valued at US$242·6 million, went to Westinghouse-Amrail, under a joint venture involving the then Francorail and Nippon Sharyo Seizo Kaisha. A further 200 R-68A cars were ordered from Nissho-Iwai and were delivered in 1989.

By end-1989 75 per cent of the entire fleet was either of 1980s build or newly overhauled and 90 per cent was air-conditioned. In January 1989 the Authority awarded a US$317 million contract for the heavy overhaul of its 752-car Class R-46 fleet. With this contract under way, only the 280-car Class R-44 remained to be committed to overhaul. By 1992 the Authority's entire fleet would be of 1980s construction or comprehensively overhauled.

Cars on order: A New Technology Test Programme has been launched to arrive at the design basis for the next generation of subway cars, of which 1500 are seen as required from 1992 to 2000. Under this project orders were placed in 1989 for two prototype tranches, one of 1051ft cars with NIAC/Kawasaki, the other of nine 67ft cars with Bombardier. The cars will feature ac motors with GTO thyristor control and solid-state door controls.

Traffic
Train headways: 2–4 minutes, peak; 5–15 minutes, off-peak; 24-hour service throughout the system
Passenger journeys: (1988) 1074 million
Max number of trains per hour each way: 34
Max number of cars per train: 10 local, 11 on IRT No 7 Line
Estimated capacity per car: A Division: 44 seated, 140 standing
B Division: 50–76 seated, 200–210 standing
Average scheduled speed (including stops): Express trains 35 km/h; local trains 32 km/h

System development
The five-year programme approved at the end of 1981 budgeted US$180 million for completion of the long-awaited East 63rd Street line's 5 km extension from 57th Street, Manhattan to 21st Street, Queens, via a two-level tunnel beneath the East River. This was inaugurated in October 1989.

In March 1990 the MTA and the Port Authority of New York & New Jersey, the city's airports operator, unveiled a plan for a rail link betwen John F Kennedy and La Guardia Airports. The proposed railway would cross Long Island alongside the Van Wyck Expressway and Grand Central Parkway, interchanging with the Long Island Railroad at Jamaica and with NYCTA's Line 7 at Shea Stadium, Flushing.

The 1981 programme was subsequently revised to accelerate the elements of it calculated to improve reliability and quality of service. Heavy overhauls of rolling stock, recovery of the backlog of track renewals and station improvements have had high priority. The New York State legislature approved a 1987–91 continuation of the capital programme and budgeted an additional US$8300 million for the purpose.

New York – New Jersey

Port Authority Trans-Hudson Corporation (PATH)
(a subsidiary of The Port Authority of New York and New Jersey)

1 World Trade Center-62W, New York, New York 10048, USA

Telephone: +1 212 466 7664
Telex: 424 747 panynj

Chairman: Philip D Kaltenbacher
President: Stephen Berger
Vice-President and General Manager: Richard R Kelly

Type of system: Full metro

Gauge: 1435 mm
Route length: 22·2 km
  (in tunnel): 11·9 km
Number of lines: 4
Number of stations: 13 (7 in New Jersey, 6 in New York)
  (in tunnel): 10
Average distance between stations: 1·9 km
Track type: Conventional sleepers on ballast, some sections on concrete trackbed with resilient pads, with 120 lb (60 kg/m) rail
Max gradient: 4·8%
Minimum curve radius: 27·4 m
Tunnel type: Single track, mainly cast iron or concrete type construction
Electrification type: 650 V dc, third rail
Signalling: Block signal system with automatic tripper. Main suppliers WABCO and GRS
Control centre: The John F Hoban operations control centre has overall control of all train operations: starting, switching, traction power, station monitoring and communications. The trainmaster can monitor the position of every train on the system by train describer; the status of traction power from PATH's seven power substations, displayed on a power board; and passenger flow through each of the 13 stations, shown on 71 closed-circuit television screens. He is in direct and immediate communication via radio, intercom and television with all PATH units, connecting carriers and essential services. The communications team can provide immediate information to PATH passngers via the all-points public address system. Additionally, turnstiles can be closed by remote control to prevent crowding on platforms

Rolling stock
Number of cars: 36 Type K (1958); 157 Type PA-1 (1965); 44 Type PA-2 (1967); 46 Type PA-3 (1972); 95 Type PA-4 (1986-87)
Main suppliers: St Louis Car, Hawker Siddeley, Canada; Nissho-Iwai American Corp
Car dimensions: K type, length 15·5 m, width 2·7 m, height 3·5 m; PA type, length 15·5 m, width 2·8 m, height 3·5 m
Capacity: K type, 44 seats, crush load 200; PA-1 type, 32 seats, crush load 200 or 31 seats, crush load 197, PA-3 type, 33 seats, crush load 222; PA-4 type, 31 seats, crush load 200
Doors: PA 1-3 cars have two sets of double folding doors, K cars have three sets of single-leaf doors on each side, and PA-4 cars three sets of double doors on each side. Manually-operated end doors permit emergency passage through the train
Motors per car: 4
Motor rating: 298 kW
Acceleration (max): 4·02 km/h/s
Max design speed: 115 km/h
Brakes: Westinghouse Air

Traffic
Max line capacity (one way): 400 cars/h
Max number of trains per hour (one way): 40

Train headways: 3 minutes (peak-hour)
Passenger journeys: (1987) 58·2 million

System development
PATH has been engaged on a US$830 million Capital Improvement Programme which has involved a comprehensive upgrading of its car fleet and car maintenance facilities, stations and utility systems.

An outmoded car shop in Jersey City, built in 1910, was to be superseded in the autumn of 1990 by a US$205 million car maintenance shop and yard in Harrison, New Jersey. In addition, PATH has completed major improvement programmes at six of its older stations in New York and New Jersey.

Other works include several electric power projects, track improvements and signal rehabilitation as well as a major rehabilitation of the Hackensack River Lift bridge on PATH's Newark Line between Jersey City and Harrison, New Jersey. PATH was also introducing from mid-1990 a magnetic-card AFC system.

New York

Staten Island Rapid Transit Operating Authority (SIRTOA)
(Agency of New York Metropolitan Transportation Authority)

358 St Marks Place, Staten Island, New York 10301, USA

Telephone: +1 718 816 8131
Telefax: +1 718 447 3643

Type of system: Full metro

General Manager: George J Governdale

Gauge: 1435 mm
Route length: 23 km
Number of stations (total): 22
Average distance between stations: 1040 m
Gradient (max): 1·9%
Speed (design max): 64 km/h (passenger); 48 km/h (freight), 48 km/h (average commercial)
Rail weight: 49·6 kg/m
Electrification type: 600 V, third rail

Rolling stock
Car types: R44 motor cars
Number of units: 52
Number of passengers per car (total): 300
  (seated): 74
Motors per car: 4
Motor rating: 86 kW
Bogies: General Steel Industries, St Louis Car Division
Brakes: WABCO RT-5-C

Traffic
Max number of trains per hour (one way): 7
Capacity per train (seated): 74
  (standing): 300
Passenger journeys: (1988) 6·2 million

Norfolk

Tidewater Transportation District

Norfolk, Virginia, USA

Type of system: Planned light rail

A 32 km route to connect Norfolk with Virginia Beach, adopting a disused main-line infrastructure, is under study.

Nottingham

Light Rapid Transit Project, Nottinghamshire County Council, County Hall, West Bridgford, Nottingham NG2 7QP, England

Telephone: +44 602 823823

Chairman, Joint Steering Group: County Councillor John Heppell

Type of system: Planned light rail

Nottingham Development Enterprise, a consortium of the County and City councils and private investors, proposed a 14·5 km railway which would run from Hucknall (north of Nottingham) alongside existing British Rail track, to Nottingham's Midland station.

From there it would descend to the level of the one-time Great Central Railway and proceed under the city centre to the shopping centre now occupying the site of the Great Central's former Victoria station.

In August 1989 consultants commissioned jointly by Nottingham Development Enterprise, Nottinghamshire County Council and Nottingham City Council confirmed the case for the system. In a further report of June 1990 they found that it would be feasible to route the LRT through the city centre on-street, instead of in tunnel, for considerable cost savings.

Novosibirsk

Upravlenie Novosibirski Metropolitena

Novo Basmannaya 2, Moscow 107174, USSR

Type of system: Full metro

Gauge: 1524 mm
Route length: 8·4 km
Number of lines: 1
Number of stations: 7
Average distance between stations: 1430 m
Electrification type: 825 V dc, third rail

System development
A three-line system totalling 52 km is planned.

Nuremberg

VAG Verkehrs-Aktiengesellschaft

Am Plärrer 27, Postfach 810220, 8500 Nuremberg 81, Federal Republic of Germany

Telephone: +49 911 283-0
Telex: 622249
Telefax: +49 911 271 3780

Chairman: Lothar Netter
Vice-Chairman: Dr-Ing Wolfgang Kung
Manager, Metro & Tram: Ernst Wentzel

Type of system: Full metro (U-Bahn)

Gauge: 1435 mm
Route length: 22·7 km
  (in tunnel): 17·2 km
Number of lines: 2
Number of stations: 31
  (in tunnel): 24
Track type: Track on concrete, without ballast
Max gradient: 4%
Minimum curve radius: 100 m
Tunnel type: Cut-and-cover with some bored single-track
Electrification type: 750 V dc, third rail
Centralised control: Central control room for all metro and surface operations
Speed (design max): 80 km/h

Rolling stock
Number of cars: 63 two-car sets, aluminium bodied, air-sprung, all motored, including 31 dc sets and 32 with three-phase ac drive
Main suppliers: MAN/Siemens
Car dimensions: Two-car set, length 37·15 m, width 2·9 m, height 3·55 m
Motors per car: 4
Motor rating: 180 kW (dc drive), 200 kW (three-phase ac drive cars)
Capacity: Average 290, crush 420
Tare and loaded weight: 52/71 tonnes (dc drive), 54/73 tonnes (three-phase ac drive)
Doors: Double doors (opening outside): 1·3 m wide, 1·95 m high

Traffic
Train headways: Peak hours, 3⅓ minutes; off-peak, 3⅓–10 minutes
Passenger journeys: (1989) 50 million

System development
Further progress to a planned 44 km network is in course of reappraisal. A northeasterly continuation of U2 from Hauptbahnhof to Rathenauplatz was to open in September 1990. Work was then in progress on a northeasterly extension of this line by 4.5km to Herrnhütte. A subsequent extension of 1.3km to Schoppenhof is likely. Extension to the airport is now unlikely until the later 1990s. A Line 3 of 12·4 km was in early 1990 suspended at the planning stage.

Odessa

Odessa, Ukraine, USSR

Type of system: Planned metro

A 55 km network is in design. The first 11 km line will connect the city centre with the new Black Sea port of Yuzhnyy and the southwestern suburbs. Start of construction not expected until 1994.

Oklahoma City

City Transit Department, 300 E California, Oklahoma City, Oklahoma 73104, USA

Telephone: +1 405 231 2601

Chairman: Harold Stansberry

Type of system: Planned light rail

In 1989 proposals for an LRT network to connect Oklahoma City and Tulsa were undergoing a feasibility study. Some portions of prospective right-of-way have been purchased.

Omsk

Omsk, USSR

Type of system: Planned metro

Design studies are under way for the first 7 km line of a proposed 17 km metro. The line will run from the city centre to industrial and residential development areas on the left bank of the River Irtish.

Osaka

Osaka Municipal Transportation Bureau

Kujo Minami-I, Nishi-ku, Osaka 550, Japan

Telephone: +81 6 582 1101

General Manager: Eiichi Sakaguchi

Type of system: Full metro

Gauge: 1435 mm
Route length: 99·1 km
  (in tunnel): 88·6 km
  (elevated): 10·5 km
Number of lines: 6
Number of stations: 79
  (in tunnel): 70
Rail type: 50 kg/m flat-bottomed
Max gradient: 3·5%
Minimum curve radius: 120 m
Tunnel type: Generally double-track, cut-and-cover tunnel, rectangular section, mostly in reinforced concrete with centre supports. At the city centre, parts of Lines 2 and 4 are at deep level in twin, single-track tube, internal diameter 5·7 m. The depth of rectangular tunnel below surface varies from 23 to 7·5 m
Electrification type: 750 V dc, third rail and (Line 6) 1·5 V dc, overhead
Signalling: All lines with CTC, and automatic block signalling by Nippon Signal and Kyosan Seisakusho. All lines with ATC

Rolling stock
Number of cars: 936, including 675 motored
Car dimensions: Length 17·7/18·9 m, height 2·84/2·89 m, width 3·74/3·75 m
Motors per power car: 4
Motor rating: 4 × 120 kW (Series 10 and 50 cars); 4 × 145 kW three-phase induction; VVVF inverter control (Series 20)
Capacity: 36 to 60 seats
Main suppliers: Hitachi, Kawasaki, Kinki, Tokyu, Nihon and Alna Koki
Doors: 3 or 4 sliding doors each side; 1·1 m and 1·3 m wide

Traffic
Train headways: 2–4 minutes at peak hours; 4–7 minutes off-peak
Passenger journeys: (1988/89) 947·7 million

System development
The metropolitan transport area of Osaka is served by a network of electrified lines, comprising the JR Osaka Loop Line and nine private railways, five of which have their terminals in the city centre. Between subway Lines 1, 4 and 6, and the Hankyu, Kintatu and Osaka North Express railways, there is reciprocal working of trains.

An extension from Dobutsuenmae to Tenga-chaya, 1·5 km, Line 6, was to be opened in April 1991.

A reduced-profile, 4·1 m diameter tube has been built with Transport Ministry funds as a test-bed for service with Series 70 linear-motored cars of outer suburban areas with lower traffic potential. Running 5·2 km from Kyobashi to Tsurumi-Ryukuchi and to be opened in March 1990, it would become Line 7.

Type of system: Intermediate Capacity Transit System (ICTS)

Under the same management as the Osaka subway, the elevated ICTS came into operation between the city and Nanko Port Town in March 1981. Operating on concrete guideways, the system's 64 rubber-tyred motor cars collect current from a third rail at 600 V ac.

Gauge: 1600 mm
Number of stations: 8
Route length: 6·6 km
Average distance between stations: 900 m
Electrification type: 600 V dc, third rail
Signalling: Fixed block (continuous transmission and receiving with check-in and check-out system), installed by Nihon Signal

Rolling stock
Cars: Supplied by Niigata Iron Works, the 64 motor cars are known as the 'Newtram'. Each has 24 seats with capacity for 51 standing passengers. Tare weight is 10·5 tonnes, loaded weight 15 tonnes. Length is 8 m, width 2·3 m, height 3·15 m. Each has a sliding door on either side

Traffic
Train headways: Peak hours, 2¾ minutes; off-peak, 7½ minutes
Passenger journeys: (1988/89) 20 million

System development
A 3 km extension in tunnel under the harbour to the Osakako terminus of the Chuo Line is under construction by the Osaka Port Authority.

Oslo

A/S Oslo Sporveier

Økernveien 9, Postbox 2857-Tøyen, 0608 Oslo 6, Norway

Telephone: +47 2 68 9580
Telefax: +47 2 57 1840

Managing Director: Knut Skuland
Director, Metro: Magne Glannes

Type of system: Full metro (Eastern lines) and suburban railway (Western lines)

Eastern lines
Gauge: 1435 mm
Route length: 49·4 km (double-track 37·2 km)
  (in tunnel): approx 13 km
Number of lines: 4
Number of stations: 44
  (in tunnel): 14
Electrification type: 750 V dc, third rail
Signalling: Cab signalling controlling speeds at 15, 30, 35, 50 and 70 km/h. Train services operate under central traffic control at Traffic Centre building at Tøyen. Trains' communication equipment includes radio and telephone

Rolling stock
Number of cars: 152, all motored
Main suppliers: Strømmens Verksted; traction motors from NEBB (Oslo) and electrical equipment from AEG (West Berlin)
Car dimensions: Length 17 m, width 3·2 m, height above rail 3·67 m
Capacity: Total 180 or 177 (63 or 60 seated)
Motors per car: 4
Motor rating: 98 kW
Max speed: 70 km/h
Acceleration: (0–40 km/h) 1·0 m/s^2
Tare weight: 29·7 tonnes

Cars on order: 20 from EB-Strømmens Verksted for 1992 delivery, equipped with both pantographs and third-rail shoes, for through running between eastern and western lines

Traffic
Passenger journeys: (1988) 36 million

System development
The metro in the east of the city has been connected with the western suburban lines by a 600 m tunnel extension between National Theatret and Storginget. A loop at Storginget provides for the turning of metro trains.

Western lines
Gauge: 1435 mm
Route length: 50·5 km
Number of lines: 4
Number of stations: 64
  (in tunnel): 3
Max gradient: 6%
Minimum curve radius: 70 m
Electrification type: 600 V dc, overhead

Traffic
Service interval: Peak hours, 15 minutes on each branch
Passenger journeys: (1988) 22.4 million

Rolling stock
Suburban railway: 78 cars, all motored

Main suppliers: Strømmens Verksted; traction motors from NEBB (Oslo), electrical equipment from AEG (Berlin)

System development
The Western suburban lines have been extended by 600 metres in tunnel to the new interchange station at Storginget. There is no through running between the two systems at this stage, but the possibility has been investigated.

Paris

Régie Autonome des Transports Parisiens (RATP)

53ter quai des Grands Augustins, 75271 Paris Cedex 06, France

Telephone: +33 1 40 46 41 41
Telex: 200 000 metrobu
Telefax: +33 1 40 46 42 59

President and Director General: Christian Blanc
Operating Manager, Metro: Pierre Faucheux
Electrical Equipment: Paul André Bolgert

Type of system: Full metro

Gauge: 1440 mm
Route length: 199 km double-track
Number of lines: 15 (13 radial, 2-circumference link lines), of which 4 worked by rubber-tyred trains
Number of stations: 367
Rail weight and type: 52 kg/m flat-bottomed in 18 m lengths
Minimum curve radius: 75 m and exceptionally 40 m
Max gradient: 4%
Tunnel type: Double-track tunnel of elliptical section, 7·1 m wide and 5·2 m high
Electrification type: 750 V dc, third rail
Signalling: All lines linked to central control and monitoring post (CCP) in Boulevard Bourdon. CCP receives all data on train movements and locations, issues appropriate instructions, and remotely controls all equipment installed along track, increasing carrying capacity on some lines by 10–15%. Automatic train operation (ATO) installed on all lines. Braking and acceleration instructions relayed from trackside cable. Full automation will probably be introduced first on Line 11.

Rolling stock
2193 cars. All are now of post-Second World War build.

Most numerous type of steel-wheel-on-steel-rail car in 1989 was the MF67 built in the mid-1970s. Close on 1000 were then in service of the MF77, built from 1978 to 1986. Aluminium-bodied, the MF77 cars are formed into five-car trains with driving motor car at each end, non-driving motor car in centre, and two intermediate trailers. Each car is 15·1 m long, with total length of five-car train, 77·5 m over couplers. Three large doors with 1·575 m openings supersede the four doors each side of previous Metro stock. Each of the three motor cars is equipped with two 270 kW chopper-controlled traction motors built by Alsthom and CEM-Oerlikon. Chopper control provides 30% energy saving and smoother acceleration. Top speed is 100 km/h.

Cars to be ordered: Replacement of cars built in early 1950 is now to begin. A new design designated MF88 has been evolved, with a rubber-tyred MP89 variant. Nine prototype MF88 sets were ordered in 1989, built by ANF-Industrie with GEC Alsthom GTO thyristors, asynchronous motors and microprocessor control, for commissioning on Line 7b in 1991-92.

The MF88 adopts a new RATP technology designated BOA. Bodies will be 10m long, mounted on two self-steering axles with independent wheels instead of orthodox bogies. Guidance is ensured by a mechanical device. A triangular shaft controls the axle's rotation about its point of attachment to the body; the extremity of this shaft is fixed to a half-tie rod that couples adjoining cars. A train-set's front and rearmost axles are steered by a guide axle fixed to the shaft. The concept secures full car-width passage between cars, the exteriors of which are connected by Faiveley flexible sheathing.

RATP was planning to take delivery from 1998 of 700 or 800 MF88 cars to supersede up to half the MF67 units.

The initial requirement for rubber-tyred MP89 cars would be 650 with cabs to replace the MP59 stock of the mid-1960s on Lines 1 and 11, this changeover to begin in 1992; and 120 cars without cabs for the new Meteor automated line (see below).

Traffic
Train headways: 1 minute 35 s–3 minutes 50 s depending on line
Passenger journeys: (1989) 1225 million

System development
Projection of Line 1 from Pont de Neuilly across the River Seine to La Défense (1·8 km) is to be ready by the end of 1992. A Ffr 70 million 1989–93 Paris public transport plan published by the government in February 1989 provides for extension of Line 13 to St Denis Université.

Also approved under the new plan is Meteor, a fully automated, driverless rubber-tyre train line from Maison Blanche to Tolbiax, Bercy, Châtelet, Madeleine and St Lazare to Brochant, where it will take over the present western branch of Line 13. At its southern end the line may later be extended to Porte d'Orléans. The train-sets will adopt BOA technology (see above). The first section of 8km from Tolbiac to St Lazare is to open by late 1995. Meteor will provide relief for overtaxed RER Line A.

Type of system: Regional express network (RER)

Gauge: 1435 mm
Route length: 103 km (RATP-operated; remainder, 249 km, SNCF)
Number of lines: 2, Lines A and B South; Lines B North and C (SNCF-operated)
Number of stations: 65 (remainder, 94, SNCF)
Rail weight and type: RER Line B: 46 and 55 kg/m in 16·5 or 18 m lengths; RER Line A: flat-bottomed, 60 kg/m, 144 m lengths welded in situ on underground sections; surface sections in 36 m lengths are fish-plated
Minimum curve radius: Line B 220 m, Line A 146 m
Max gradient: Line A, 3·6%; Line B, 4·08%
Electrification type: 1·5 kV dc
Signalling: To increase train frequency to 2-minute intervals, an ATO system known as SACEM has been installed on the central section of Line A.

The full SACEM concept combines in an integrated system Automatic Train Protection (ATP), Automatic Train Operation (ATO), train service regulation, cab signalling and maintenance diagnostics. In the initial RATP application, ATO capability has not been fully exploited; a measure of control remains with a train's driver.

SACEM transfers to on-train processors many ATP/ATO functions hitherto performed by trackside devices. As a result, operational parameters are not dictated by the performance characteristics of a line's least capable traction and rolling stock, or by its conventional block sectioning. Continuously pinpointing their location, determining their speed, and calculating a braking profile that will preserve safe headway in front of them, trains effectively create their own movable block sections. Track circuiting serves only for train detection, not train control. Thus, SACEM can be superimposed on existing track circuiting, as is the case on Line A.

Centralised control: As on Metro, each line linked to central control room for monitoring each train in service, communicating by telephone with each driver and taking appropriate measures in the event of disturbances on the network

Rolling stock
Number of cars: RATP, 492 motor and 355 trailer. Mainstay of the fleet is 324 M179 'Interconnexion' cars formed as four-car emus designed to operate on 1·5 kV dc or 25 kV ac supply and serve stations with varying platform heights. An improved version of the M179, classified M184, has been delivered to Line A in 80 four-car units. The early Type MS61 six-car emus have been comprehensively refurbished. Designs of a five-car emu to replace the MS61 in the later 1990s are under study

Traffic
Passenger journeys: (1989) 326.5 million (RATP sections only)

System development
The first phase of Interconnexion through service via the new underground Gare du Nord stations was inaugurated in May 1983 (see under French National Railways). In May 1988 the Cergy-Pontoise line was interconnected with Line A at Nanterre-Préfecture. Thereafter, and with the benefit of the M184 equipment, peak-hour headways of the busiest section of Line A, between Auber and Châtelet-les-Halles, were reduced with the aid of the new SACEM microprocessor-based continuous speed control system (see above) from 2·5 to 2 minutes to cope with an expected throughput of 55 000 passengers/hour. Line A trains were also extended to Poissy by May 1989. Trains arriving from Poissy now use the link with the Cergy-Pontoise line to run straight through Paris.

Through running between the SNCF's southeast suburban lines (involving Corbeil, Evry and Melun) and the Orry-la-Ville line of the northern suburbs via the Gare de Lyon-Châtelet-Gare du Nord tunnels has hitherto been deferred because of congestion on the RER core. This through service would become RER Line D serving a suburban population of 1 million. The government's 1989–93 Paris plan (see above) has now accorded top priority to construction of a second double-track tunnel between Châtelet and the present terminal underground platforms at Gare de Lyon. Costing Ffr 1550 million, this project is to be finished by 1995.

In addition, as mentioned in the metro section above, the government has approved further relief of Line A, by construction of the Meteor fully-automated rubber-tyred metro.

Extension of RER Line C via connection at Invalides to serve the Vallée de Montmorency, with branches to Argenteuil and Pontoise, was opened in October 1988. A new interchange between Lines B and C at St Michel Notre Dame was opened in February 1988. Line D services were extended 5 km north from Villiers-le-Bel to Goussainville on September 1988 and were projected a further 15 km to Orry-la-Ville in 1990.

Work has begun on an 11 km extension from Line A at Torcy to the Euro 'Disneyland' complex being built east of Paris. The government and the Ile de France Region will each cover 40 per cent of the Ffr 750 million infrastructure cost. The RER could eventually grow to a network of more than 450 km.

Type of system: Light rail under construction

As the first move in a plan to develop orbital Paris transport, a 9 km, 21-station, 750V dc electrified light rail line is being built in the northeast of the city between St Denis and Bobigny. Running on segregated tracks, mostly laid in central reservations, the line will interchange with metro Lines 5, 7 and 13. Set to open in 1992, it will be operated by 16 GEC Alsthom-built low-floor LRVs of the French standard design (see under Nantes). A second orbital route is under consideration for the southern suburbs.

Orlyval

Type of system: VAL light metro under construction
Route length: 7·2 km
(in tunnel): 1 km

Construction began in late 1988 of a VAL line to connect the Orly airport terminals with the RER Line C at Chemin d'Antony station. Completion is forecast for late 1991. Orlyval is a private enterprise in which Matra, the VAL system progenitors, have a 46·6 per cent interest, the domestic airline Air Inter 26·6 per cent, RATP 3·3 per cent and the remainder is with various banking institutions.

Philadelphia

Southeastern Pennsylvania Transportation Authority (SEPTA)

714 Market Street, Philadelphia, Pennsylvania 19106, USA

Telephone: +1 215 574 7300
Telefax: +1 215 580 7997

General Manager: Louis J Gambaccini
Assistant General Manager, Subway Elevated: H S Davidow
Surface: J H McCormick
Chief Engineer: R O Swindell

Type of system: Full metro

Gauge: Market Street-Frankford 1581 mm; Broad Street, Ridge-Eighth and Camden 1435 mm
Number of lines: 2: Market Street-Frankford subway-elevated; Broad Street subway-Broad-Ridge spur
Route length: Market Street-Frankford subway-elevated 20·6 km
  Broad Street subway 15·77 km
  Broad-Ridge spur 2·41 km
Number of stations: Market Street-Frankford subway-elevated: 28
  Broad Street subway and Broad-Ridge spur: 25
  (in tunnel): 33
Rail weight and type: 49·6 km/m flat bottomed
Max gradient: 5%
Minimum curve radius: Market Street-Frankford line, 32 m; Broad Street and Ridge-Eighth lines, 49 m
Tunnel type: Double or multiple-track tunnel, of rectangular section
Electrification type: 600 V dc, third rail (top contact, Broad Street and Ridge Avenue); bottom contact (Market Street-Frankford)
Signalling: Automatic block, with colour-light signals

Rolling stock
Number of cars: 383, all motored
Main suppliers: Budd (1956–60), 46 single and 221 coupled cars; Kawasaki (1982–83), 76 single- and 49 double-cabbed cars assembled by Boeing-Vertol for Broad Street line. These stainless steel vehicles have a maximum capacity of 230 passengers, and a maximum speed of 88 km/h.
Car dimensions: Budd, length 16·76 m, width 2·77 m, height 3·68 m; Kawasaki, length 20·57 m, width 3·068 m, height 3·71 m
Capacity: Budd, 54/56 seated; Kawasaki, 65/62 seated
Tare weight: Budd, 23·34 tonnes; Kawasaki, 31·7 tonnes

Traffic
Passenger journeys: (1988) 67·6 million
Train headways: Peak hours, 2–3½ minutes; off-peak 7½ minutes, 24-hour service

Type of system: Light rail/tramway

Suburban Transit Division-Norristown line

Gauge: 1435 mm
Route length: 21·9 km
Number of lines: 1
Number of stations: 22 (all high-level platform)
Electrification type: 600 V dc, top-contact third rail

Rolling stock
Number of cars: 17
Main supplier: J G Brill Co
Year introduced: 1924–31
Car dimensions: Length 16·89 m, width 2·79 m, height 3·2 m
Weight: 26·15 tonnes
Cars on order: ABB and Amtrak formed a consortium

to supply 26 cars, to enter service in early 1990. The cars, which have stainless steel bodies and can seat 64 passengers, can be run either individually or coupled together to form train-sets of up to four cars. They are the first LRVs in the US to use three-phase asynchronous propulsion. With a rating of 4 × 145 kW, they will have a maximum speed of 113 km/h. This was ABB's first mass transit contract in North America

Suburban Transit Division: Media and Sharon Hill lines

Gauge: 1581 mm
Route length: 19·15 km
Number of lines: 2
Number of stations: 51
Electrification type: 600 V dc, overhead

Rolling stock
Number of cars: 29 double-ended LRVs by Kawasaki

Traffic
Passenger journeys: (1988) 4·6 million

Port Authority Transit Corporation (PATCO)

Administrative and Maintenance Facility, Lindenwold, New Jersey 08021

Telephone: +1 609 772 6900
Telefax: +1 609 772 6915

President: J R Kelly
General Manager: R G Schwab

Type of system: Full metro

Gauge: 1435 mm
Route length: 23·3 km
  (in tunnel): 4·1 km
  (at surface level): 15·5 km
  (elevated): 3·7 km
Number of lines: 1
Number of stations: 13
  (in tunnel): 6
Rail weight and type: 66 kg/m continuous welded
Track type: In tunnel, sleepers encased three sides in concrete; at grade, wooden sleepers on ballast; on viaduct, no sleepers; track anchored directly to concrete deck with specially designed clips.
Tunnel type: Cut-and-cover
Max gradient: 5½%
Minimum curve radius: 61 m
Electrification type: 700 V dc, third rail
Signalling: Cab signals, with wayside signals at all interlockings, installed by WABCO
Automatic control: Full automation except for doors and PA announcements

Rolling stock
Number of cars: 121
Car type

(year introduced)	1968	1980
Builder	Budd	Vickers, Canada
Number of units	75	46
Car dimensions		
(length)	20·57 m	20·57 m
(width)	3·05 m	2·05 m
(height)	3·76 m	3·76 m
Passenger capacity per car		
(total)	120	120
(seated)	72*/80†	80
Motors per car	4	4
Rating	116 kW	116 kW
Train composition		
(minimum): 1		
(max): 8		
Acceleration		
(max)	1·34 m/s²	1·34 m/s²
Deceleration		
(emergency)	1·43 m/s²	1·43 m/s²

Brakes: Rheostatic and tread
Body material: Stainless steel
Weight (tonnes)
  motorcars   36·1*/33·9†   33·7
* single cars
† married pair cars

Traffic
Train headways: Morning peaks, down to 3½ minutes; evening peak, 2 minutes; off-peak, 10 minutes
Train capacity (passengers), six-car trains:
  seated 480
  standing 250
Passenger journeys: (1988) 11·1 million

System development
Three extensions have been studied and preliminary engineering completed: 9–6 km from Lindenwold (present terminal) to Berlin/Atco; 21 km east from Broadway station, Camden, to Mt Laurel; and 27 /km south from Broadway station to Glassboro, New Jersey. Implementation of all has been postponed indefinitely for lack of funding. Resources are currently concentrated on rehabilitation of existing assets.

Pittsburgh

Port Authority of Allegheny County (PAT)

Beaver and Island Avenue, Pittsburgh, Pennsylvania 15233, USA

Telephone: +1 412 237 7000
Telefax: +1 412 217 7101

Chairman: John P Robin
Executive Director: William W Millar

Type of system: Light rail

Gauge: 1580 mm
Route length: 16·89 km
  (in tunnel): 2·4 km
Rail type: 57·5 kg/m RE
Electrification type: 650 V dc, overhead

Rolling stock: 55 Type U3 articulated LRVs by Siemens-Duewag; 16 refurbished PCC cars

Traffic
Passenger journeys: (1988) 8·18 million

System development
PAT has completed Phase 1 of the conversion of its 36·2 km trolley system into a full LRT operation. Stage 1 covered complete rebuilding of the 42/38 Mt Lebanon via Beechview trolley line and a section of the Shannon Library and Shannon Drake Routes 35 and 36 south of Castle Shannon; an extension to the South Hills shopping centre in Upper St Clair; a new LRT tunnel under Washington Road in Mt Lebanon; an express entry into Pittsburgh town centre via the Panhandle railroad bridge; a town centre distribution system consisting of a subway alignment; and purchase of 55 new light rail vehicles to supplement 16 rehabilitated PCC cars.
By the end of 1990 PAT and the Allegheny County Board of Commissioners were to complete a study of a further series of major capital improvement projects. The latter could include development of a transit line connecting the North Side with downtown Pittsburgh, Oakland and Squirrel Hill (Spine Line).
In early 1989 PAT held a series of public meetings to discuss possible modernisation, abandonment or replacement of its Drake, Library and Overbrook trolley lines. By mid-1990 PAT expected to finish an analysis of the potential benefits and impacts of a Phase II Light Rail Modernisation Programme, which could include reconstruction of the lines between South Hills Village and downtown Pittsburgh via Castle Shannon, Mt Lebanon, Dormont and Beechview. The study was covering a comparison of light rail with busways and other transit alternatives with regard to preliminary ridership forecasts, operating and maintenance cost and capital expenditures.

Port Elizabeth

Port Elizabeth City Council, South Africa

Type of system: Planned light rail

Feasibility studies of a 21 km, 19-station light rail line from the city centre to Bethelsdorp, with a 9 km branch to Ibhayi, were accepted in 1988. No finance yet agreed.

Portland

Tri-County Transportation District of Oregon (Tri-Met)
Metropolitan Area Express (MAX)

4012 SE 17th Avenue, Portland, Oregon 97202, USA

Telephone: +1 503 238 5878

General Manager: James E Cowen
Director of Transportation: R Douglas

Type of system: Light rail

Gauge: 1435 mm
Route length: 24 km
Number of lines: 1
Number of stations: 27
Track type: Cwr on ballasted timber sleepers
Max gradient: 7%
Electrification type: 750 V dc, overhead

Rolling stock: 26 articulated six-axle LRVs
Main suppliers: Bombardier, under BN licence
Car dimensions: Length 26·82 m
Passenger capacity: 76 seated, 100 standing
Motors per car: 2 × 750 V
Tare weight: 45 tonnes
Max speed: 88 km/h

Traffic
Passenger journeys: (1988-89) 7·28 million

System development
The Metropolitan Area Express (MAX) system may be expanded to two lines with the addition of a western line to Beaverton. Preliminary engineering of this 19·3 km Westside line began in 1988, and there was a possibility construction would start in 1990. Planning continues in order to identify other potential light rail lines.

Porto Alegre

Empresa de Trens Urbanos de Porto Alegre SA

Rua Ernesto Neugebauer 1985, 90250 Porto Alegre, Rio Grande do Sul, Brazil

Telephone: +55 512 43 4111
Telex: 0512 5168 trsb

General Manager: Mansueto de Castro Serafini Filho
Operations Director: Wanderley José Brasil de Mello

Type of system: Full metro

Gauge: 1600 mm
Route length: 27·5 km
Number of lines: 1
Number of stations: 15
Track type: Conventional ballasted track, 57 kg/m rail, twin-block concrete sleepers
Max gradient: 2·5%
Minimum curve radius: 160 m
Electrification type: 3 kV dc, overhead
Signalling: Computer-aided CTC with automatic speed control

Rolling stock
Number of cars: 25 four-car sets
Main suppliers: Consortium of Hitachi, Nippon Sharyo and Mitsui
Car dimensions: Length 21·8 m, width 2·71 m
Passenger capacity: 228 seated, 850 standing per 2M + 2T set
Motor per motor car: 4 × 315 kW
Acceleration: 0·8 m/s²
Deceleration: 0·77 m/s²

Traffic
Passenger journeys: (1989) 37·99 million

System development
The line, to add a 15·4 km extension to Novo Hamburgo in 1990, has been fashioned largely from existing Brazilian Federal Railways (RFFSA) alignments. The project has been executed and is operated by Trensurb, a CBTU subsidiary (see Brazil entry, Railway Systems section).

Prague

Dopravní Podnik Hlavního Města Prahy Kombinat

Bubenska 1, 17026 Prague 7, Czechoslovakia

Telephone: +42 2 87 82 78
Telex: 122443 dopo c

Director: Ing Ladislav Slanička
Director, Metro: Ing Josef Němeček

Type of system: Full metro

Gauge: 1435 mm
Route length: 34·7 km
Number of lines: 3 (Lines A, B and C)
Number of stations: 36
Average distance between stations: Line A 822 m, Line B 800 m, Line C 1041 m
Tunnel type: Cut-and-cover and bored. Running tunnels, 5·1 m diameter. Deepest stations, three adjacent tunnels, each 7·8 m diameter. Over the Nusle Valley metro tunnel incorporated beneath highway on Nuselský bridge, 43 m above ground level
Electrification type: 750 V dc, third rail
Signalling: Automatic block colour light
Centralised control: Radio communications with trains individually or en masse. Ericsson graph system for safety working but fully automatic system planned.
Automatic control: Automatic train control equipment initiates brakes if signal overrun occurs.

Rolling stock
Number of cars: 355, all motored, Types Ecs and 81–717
Main supplier: Mytyshchinsky plant, USSR
Car dimensions: Length 18·81 m, width 2·71 m, height 3·662 m
Capacity: 262 with 42 seated
Motors per car: 4
Motor rating: 72 kW (Ecs) 110 kW (81-717)
Tare weight: 32·5 tonnes
Max speed: 90 km/h
Max acceleration: 1·2 m/s^2
Max deceleration: 1·2 m/s^2

Type 81-717 is an improved version of the Ecs retaining the same bogies and body structure, but with four 110 kW traction motors, battery-charging by thyristor converter, fluorescent lighting, automatic fuses and modernised electrical and pneumatic equipment.

Traffic
Train headways: Peak hours 2 minutes 10 s (Lines A and B), 1 minute 45 s (Line C)
Passenger journeys (daily): (1987) 1·182 million

System development
The network comprises three transverse lines, A, B and C meeting in a city-centre triangle.
  A further extension of Line B, from Sokolovská to Západockého, was to open in late 1990. Extension of Line C northward by 7 km, of Line B westwards by 5.1km and four stations, and a fourth line, north-south Line D, are planned.

Pusan

Pusan City Government

20 3-Ga Daegyo-Dong, Jung-Gu, Pusan, Republic of Korea

Telephone: +82 51 463 4206
Telex: 3345

Director: Lim Won Jae
Planning and Design: Lee Jae O

Type of system: Full metro

Gauge: 1435 mm
Route length: 25·3 km
Number of lines: 1
Number of stations: 22
Electrification type: 1·5 kV dc, overhead
Signalling: Automatic train control, but in 1989 operating under manual control

Rolling stock
Cars in use or on order: 186 formed into six-car sets to Marubeni Corp design, with Mitsubishi traction equipment, constructed by Hyundai in South Korea

System development
The objective is to complete a network of five lines aggregating 102 km by the end of the century.

Pyongyang

City Metro Dept, Transport & Communications Commission, Pyongyang, Democratic People's Republic of Korea

Type of system: Full metro

Gauge: 1435 mm
Route length: 22·5 km
Number of lines: 2
Number of stations: 17
Track type: Concrete trackbed
Tunnels: Bored and blasted to maximum depth of 150m; mostly single bore
Electrification type: 825 V dc, third rail
Signalling: Colour light, CTC

Rolling stock
Number of cars: 48, all motored, built locally

System development
Present system comprises two routes intersecting, but without connection, in city centre. A third cross-city line is proposed.

Recife

Metrorec

Rua José Natálio 478, Areias, 50000 Recife-Pe, Brazil

Telephone: +55 81 251 0933
Telex: 081 4390 trer br

President: Milton Torres Dantas
Engineering and Operations: Eng Eldenor Moraes

Type of system: Rapid transit railway

Gauge: 1600 mm
Route length: 20·5 km
Number of lines: 2
Number of stations: 17
Average distance between stations: 1·2 km
Electrification type: 3 kV dc
Signalling: Automatic train control
Track type: ARFA 57 kg/m rail, concrete sleepers

Rolling stock
Number of cars: 100 in four-car sets
Main suppliers: Santa Matilde, Villares, GEC Traction
Capacity (per set): 1040 normal, 1524 max
Max speed: 90 km/h

Traffic
Passenger journeys: (1989) 8.2 million

System development
A metre-gauge alignment of 16 km from Recife to Jaboatão and its 4 km Lacerde branch have been converted and electrified by GEC Transportation Projects. GEC Traction and its local licensee, Villares, provided traction equipment for 25 four-car emus built by Santa Matilde. Signalling and ATC were furnished by GEC-General Signal. The railway forms part of CBTU (see under RFFSA, Brazil, in Railway Systems section).
  In 1989 preparations were made for a 4.5k extension from Rodoviaria to Timbi.

Rennes

Syndicat Intercommunal des Transports en Commun de l'Agglomeration Rennaise (SITCAR), Rennes, France

Type of system: Planned VAL light metro

In 1990 SITCAR endorsed the vote of the municipal council to adopt the VAL system for a light metro line of 9.3 km (including 3.8 km in tunnel) and 17 stations. Provided state support for the construction costs were obtained, opening was foreseen in 1995.

Rheims

Rheims, France

Type of system: Planned light rail

Following a Sofrétu study, the city wants to start construction of a 7·4 km line, subject to promise of 50 per cent state funding.

Rhine-Ruhr

Verkehrsbund Rhein-Ruhr GmbH

Postfach 103052, 4650 Gelsenkirchen, Federal Republic of Germany

Telephone: +49 209 17006-0
Telefax: +49 209 17006 170

Type of system: Light rail (Stadtbahn)

Gauge: 1435 mm
Route length: 129·1 km
  (new Stadtbahn infrastructure): 72·8 km
  (upgraded tramway track): 56·3 km
Number of stations: 167
Electrification type: 750 V dc, overhead

System development
In addition to the German Federal Railway's S-Bahn a Stadtbahn network intended by 1995 to embrace 100 km of new reserved Stadtbahn infrastructure and 60 km of upgraded tramway track is being established in the area between Düsseldorf and Dortmund, which encloses Duisburg, Mülheim, Essen, Gelsenkirchen Bochum, Herne and Witten. By the end of 1989 investment in the scheme totalled DM6810 million. A further 9·5 km was created in September 1989 with the opening of a tunnel connecting Bochum and Herne.
  The system operates 137 articulated six-axle Stadtbahnwagen B LRVs, which are adaptable to either platform or street-level loading, so that it can operate routes integrating conventional tramway and new Stadtbahn via city-centre tunnels.
  The Rhine-Ruhr system is being assembled to common technical standards, which are of near-metro sophistication. One objective is right-of-way segregation from other road traffic to the maximum possible extent.

Riga

Riga, USSR

Type of system: Planned metro

The first 9·06 km line, electrified at 825 V dc, will link the city centre with an industrial area. The project was officially authorised in 1985 and construction began in 1986.

Rio de Janeiro

Companhia do Metropolitano do Rio de Janeiro Metro

Avenue NS de Copacabana 493, Rio de Janeiro, Brazil

Telephone: +55 21 255 9292
Telex: 021 021094

President: S M Sequeira de Barros
Director of Operations: Eng Luiz Carlos Téofilo
Engineering: S L C R Correia

Type of system: Full metro and light rail

Gauge: 1600 m
Route length: Metro (Line 1), 11·6 km (all in tunnel); (Line 2) 11 km
  Pre-metro: 8 km (service suspended)
Number of lines in operation: 3
Gradient (max): 4%
Minimum curve radius: 500 m
Speed (design max): 100 km/h (metro car), 80 km/h (pre-metro car)
Rail weight: 56·9 kg/m
Tunnel type: Mainly in cut-and-cover; Bernold system for 550 m; and New Austrian Tunnelling Method (NATM)
Electrification type: 750 V dc, third rail
Automatic control: Automatic train control computer-based

Rolling stock
Number of units: 124 Type A and B; 42 LRVs
Main suppliers: Mafersa (96 metro cars); Cobrasma (28 metro cars); BN (2 prototype and 6 pre-series pre-metro cars); Cobrasma (34 production pre-metro cars ordered)

Car type	A*	B†	Pre-metro
Car dimensions			
(length) (m)	21·885	21·75	25·476

(width) (m)	3·17	3·17	2·7
(height) (m)	3·65	3·65	5·75
Number of doors per side	3	3	4
Door width (m)	1·9	1·9	1·3
Number of passengers per car			
(total)	350	377	317
(seated)	40	48	58
Motors per car	4	4	2
Motor rating (kW)	143	143	200
Power per train (minimum)	3·432	3·432	8
Acceleration (max) (m/s^2)	1·12	1·12	1
Deceleration			
(normal service) (m/s^2)	1·2	1·2	1·2
(emergency) (m/s^2)	1·2	1·2	1·5
Max design speed (km/h)	100	100	80
Weight (empty in tons)	40	38	38

Braking: Regenerative/rheostatic/pneumatic; rheostatic/pneumatic/magnetic
* With cab
† Without cab

Traffic
Passenger journeys: (1988) 96 million

System development
Expansion of the system was halted in 1982, when local government funding was cut off with only a portion of the ordered metro and pre-metro rolling stock delivered. Pre-metro Line 2's continuation from Maria de Graça to Pavuna was suspended in 1986 to concentrate serviceable LRVs on its central section and thereafter vandalism and looting made the extension unusable.

In 1987 the state government changed tack and ordered Line 2's rehabilitation, an extension of Line 1 by 4 km from Botafogo through Copacabana to General Osório (due for completion in 1991) and purchase of 22 more metro and 22 pre-metro cars. A section of the disused Pavuna extension of Line 2 was likely to be rehabilitated in 1990. The line's central section is worked by pre-metro cars taking current from a third rail, as the overhead catenary is dismantled.

Rome

Azienda Consortile Trasporti Laziali (ACOTRAL)

Via Ostiense 131/1, 00154 Rome, Italy

Telephone: +39 6 57531

General Manager: Dr Ing Gastone Rossetti
Director, Rail: A Curci
Type of system: Full metro

Gauge: 1435 mm
Route length: 25·5 km
(in tunnel): 14·5 km
Number of lines: 2; double-track
Number of stations: 33
Average distance between stations: 670 m
Rail type: 50 kg/m Line A; 46·5 kg/m Line B
Max gradient: 4%
Minimum curve radius: 100 m
Electrification type: 1·5 kV dc, overhead
Signalling: Coded-current track circuits for continuous signal aspect repetition on-board
Automatic control: Programmer monitors train movements and amends scheduled timetable accordingly
Centralised controls: Remote traffic control from central point. All orders actuated automatically. System includes train number recognition

Rolling stock
Suppliers: Breda, electrical equipment by Ercole Marelli, TIBB, Ansaldo

ACOTRAL suburban rail systems

Route	Rome-Ostia Lido	Rome-Viterbo	Rome-Fiuggi
Gauge	1435 mm	1435 mm	950 mm
Route length	28·79 km	101·89 km	18·4 km
Electrification type	1·5 kV dc	3 kV dc	1·5 kV dc
Rails	46 kg/m	30, 36, 50 kg/m	36 kg/m
Minimum curvature radius	275 m	100 m	50 m
Max gradient	1·9%	3·2%	6%
Max axleload	15 tonnes	15 tonnes	9·25 tonnes

Total rolling stock: 16 electric locomotives, 43 emus, 83 other passenger cars

Car type	Line A	Line B
Number of cars	152	172
Car dimensions		
(length)	17·84 m	19·1 m
(width)	2·85 m	3·04 m
(height)	3·5 m	3·61 m
Doors per side	4	4
Door (width)	1·3 m	1·25 m
Passengers per car		
(total)	208	247
(seated)	32	52
Motors per car	4	4
Motor rating	110 kW	117 kW
Acceleration (max)	1·2 m/s^2	1·25 m/s^2
Deceleration (normal service)	1·2 m/s^2	0·84 m/s^2
Speed (max)	90 km/h	100 km/h

Cars on order: 53 aluminium-bodied, chopper-controlled two-car sets for the Line B extension from Breda, with electrical equipment by Ercole Marelli and Ansaldo Trasporti

Traffic
Passenger journeys: (1986) 152 million

System development
Extensions of both routes are in progress: of Line A by 3·7 km and three stations westward; and of Line B by 7·9 km and 10 stations northeast from Rome Termini to Rebibbia. Long-term proposals include a new cross-town line from Flamingo to Ostiense and a fourth line from southeast to northwest.

Intermetro, a consortium of engineering firms, is building the current extensions. It has lately published a scheme for 90 km of new lines up to the year 2006; the proposals range from new metro and light rail routes to conversion of some FS lines.

ACOTRAL also operates three Rome suburban rail lines: Rome-Viterbo; Rome-Lido; and Rome-Fiuggi, part of which is being adapted to form Line G of the Rome metro, and therefore extended to interchange with the latter's Lines A and B at Rome Termini.

Rostov-on-Don

Rostov-on-Don

A three-line metro system is proposed. The first stage would be construction of a 10·6 km, nine-station section.

Rotterdam

Rotterdamse Elektrische Tram (RET)

Kleiweg 244, 3051 SN Rotterdam, Netherlands

Telephone: +31 10 4546911
Telex: 25246
Telefax: +31 10 4546215

General Manager: J J Ph Kunst
Operating Manager: N Maas

Type of system: Full metro/light rail (Sneltram)

Gauge: 1435 mm
Route length: 42 km
(in tunnel): 11·5 km
(elevated): 14 km
Number of stations: 32
(in tunnel): 14
Distance between stations: 550–1600 m
Rail type and weight: NP46, 47 kg/m
Track type: Direct fastening of rail on concrete with resilient pads in tunnel and on viaduct; concrete sleepers, connected with galvanised steel tubes, on ballast on embankment
Minimum curve radius: 200 m
Max gradient: 4%
Electrification type: 750 V dc, third rail, with overhead collection at grade

One-man operations: All trains
Signalling: Cab signalling, installed by Siemens, with centralised control system

Rolling stock
Number of units: 142 articulated twin-unit
Main suppliers: Werkspoor, Duewag
Car dimensions: Length 28·6/29·8 m, width 2·68/2·73 m
Capacity: 80/72 seated, 155/294 standing passengers (4·5/m^2)
Tare and loaded weight: 41/64·4 tonnes
Doors: Pocket type, 1·3 m and 650 mm wide

Traffic
Train headways: Peak hours, 3 minutes
Passenger journeys: (1989) 66·5 million
Max number of trains per hour each way: 20
Max line capacity: 272 000 passengers per hour

System development
Of the two lines, the east-west becomes the Sneltram, with overhead current collection, when it reaches the suburban section at Capelsebrug. Half the rolling stock fleet is therefore fitted with pantographs for operation on the surface-level section north of Capelsebrug, as well as a normal third-rail current collector.

A new 3.3km branch of the Sneltram from Capelsebrug east to Capelle and IJssel is being built for completion by 1994.

Subsequent additions in view include: a northwards metro extension to the city's Zesitenhoven airport and an interchange at Kleiweg with the NS' The Hague-Hofplein line (which may be converted to metro operation); a metro branch from Zuidplein to an interchange with the NS at Lombardijen, with subsequent extension to Ridderkerk likely; and a Sneltram east-west Line 2 extension from Marconiplein via Schiedam to Vlaardingen.

Rouen

Rouen, France

Type of system: Planned light rail

In 1990 the city's mayor announced that construction would begin in 1991 of a 10.3km system, with 25 stations, running from Place du Boulingrin and the SNCF station in a 1·8 km tunnel down to the Seine, which will be crossed on the existing Jeanne d'Arc bridge. Beyond the river the line will branch to Sotteville-les-Rouen and to Le Grand Quevilly. The system will employ low-floor LRVs of the French standard pattern and be operated by TCAR, the city's public transport company.

Sacramento

Sacramento Regional Transit District

PO Box 2110, Sacramento, California 95812-2110, USA

Telephone: +1 916 321 2800
Telefax: +1 916 444 2156

General Manager: Thomas G Matoff

Type of system: Light rail

Gauge: 1435 mm
Route length: 29·3 km
Number of routes: 1
Number of stations: 27
Electrification type: 750 V dc, overhead

Rolling stock
Number of units: 26
Main supplier: Siemens-Allis/Duewag
Car type: Type U2A double-ended 6-axle articulated, air-conditioned with 189 kW motors, maximum speed 80 km/h, total sets 64
Car dimensions: Length 24·2 m, width 2·65 m, height 3·84 m
Cars on order: 10 U2A, ordered 1988
Capacity: 64 seated, 175 standing
Max speed: 80 km/h

System development
Four extensions are planned, but the next phase will be concerned with completion of double-tracking.

St Louis

Bi-State Development Agency
Metro Link

707 North First Street, St Louis, 63102, Missouri, USA

Telephone: +1 314 982 1400

Director, Metro Link Project: John R Muldoon

Type of system: Light rail under construction

Route length: 29 km
Gauge: 1435 mm
No of stations: 20
Electrification: 750 V dc overhead

An UMTA grant of US$10 million funded study of a Metro Link route running from the Lambert Field Airport to the city centre, Union station and across the Mississippi river to East St Louis mostly over derelict infrastructure, including an existing city-centre tunnel. The river would be crossed on an existing rail bridge. Only 7 km of new infrastructure would be required.

Funding agreement was reached with UMTA in 1988 and construction began in 1990 for 1993 inauguration. An initial fleet of 31 LRVs is foreseen.

San Antonio

San Antonio, Texas, USA

Type of system: Planned light rail

Adopting existing rail alignments, a 50 km network has been studied, to connect the airport, the University of Texas and the Sea World Amusement Park.

San Diego

San Diego Trolley Inc (SDTI)

12A South 13th Street, San Diego, California 92113, USA

Telephone: +1 619 239 6051

Managing Director: Langley C Powell

Type of system: Light rail

Gauge: 1435 mm
Route length: 53·4 km
Number of lines: 2
Number of stations: 30
Electrification type: 600 V dc, overhead

Rolling stock
Number of cars: 50 articulated, Type U2
Main supplier: Siemens/Duewag
Car dimensions: Length 24·28 m
Capacity: 64 seated, 86 standing

Traffic
Train headways: 15 minutes, 30 minutes at some periods
Passenger journeys: (1989) 11.3 million

System development
An 18·1 km extension to the East Line, the El Cajon project, to serve eastern suburbs was opened in June 1989. Funding for this extension came from UMTA (its first grant for SDTI), state and local funds. As with the South Line, the East Line adapts an existing rail freight line owned by the Metropolitan Transit Development Board (MTDB) of San Diego. Funding for a 3·2 km Bayside line was obtained and construction began in 1989 for inauguration in mid-1991.

Further routes are planned, including a 5·2 km East Line extension to Santee, and the first 5·3 km section of a projected 30·1 km North Line. Engineering design of both was under way in late 1989. Also proposed is a line to the airport.

The MTDB, of which San Diego Trolley is a subsidiary, plans and constructs the regional light rail projects; plans and provides the level of regional service through private and public bus and light rail transit operators; co-ordinates public transportation services under the umbrella identity of the Metropolitan Transit System; sets fares; and handles fund distribution for regional operators.

San Francisco

Bay Area Rapid Transit District (BART)

PO Box 12688, 800 Madison St, Oakland, California 94604-2688, USA

Telephone: +1 415 464 6000
Telefax: +1 415 464 7103

General Manager: Frank J Wilson

Type of system: Full metro

Gauge: 1676 mm
Route length: 115 km
(in tunnel): 37·4 km (including 6·44 km transbay tube)
(elevated): 37 km
Number of lines: 4
Number of stations: 34
(in tunnel): 14
(elevated): 13
Average distance between stations: 4 km
Gradient (max): 4%
Minimum curve radius: 120 m
Track type: Concrete sleepers on resilient pads
Tunnel type: Transbay tube: twin-section submerged caisson of steel and concrete, 7·32 m high, 14·64 m wide, designed for high resistance to seismic disturbances.
Electrification type: 1 kV dc, third rail
Signalling: Safety and signalling equipment supplied by Westinghouse Corporation for high level of automatic operation and control. Twin train control computers (one for backup) are installed at Lake Merritt station, Oakland. For operation, route is divided into blocks, 61–305 m in length, each with associated speed control equipment. Local station equipment can be used to lower speeds if block ahead has not been cleared. Automatic train control system safety functions are handled entirely by equipment at each station, along wayside and on each train. Central computer supervises functions to improve operational efficiency. Westinghouse equipment includes frequency modulation for track signalling, reliable speed-coding system, multiplexing of signals and solid-state transistorised circuitry. 52 mini-computers installed later in 26 stations to provide backup train protection system are known as SORS (Sequential Occupancy Release System).

October 1987 saw commissioning of a new computer-based Integrated Control System (ICS) to replace the existing computers. It would permit an increase in the number of trains in simultaneous operation from 49 to 75 (see below). ICS has been designed so that, by addition of fresh modules, the total of trains running simultaneously could be lifted to 150.

Rolling stock
Main supplier: Rohr Industries
Total number of cars: 599, all motored
Main supplies: Rohr, Types A and B; Alsthom, Type C

The A cars alone have a control cab, at one end only and with a slanted front, which makes them unsuitable for mid-train marshalling. BART later ordered from GEC Alsthom 150 cars of a new C type, with a flat-fronted cab at one end and chopper control, but otherwise similar to Type A. Final assembly was undertaken in the San Francisco area.

Traffic
Train headways: Peak hours, basic system 15 minutes (0600–0800, 1600–1800), central business district 3.5 minutes; off-peak, basic 15 minutes, central business district 5 minutes; evenings and weekends, 20 minutes
Passenger journeys: (1988/89) 60·5 million

System development
The fruits of a five-year US$491·3 million capacity expansion programme were starting to emerge in November 1989, when up to 98 of the new C cars had become available. That enabled an increase of trains simultaneously on line to 51 and a reduction of minimum scheduled headway to 3 min 10 sec. By October 1990 this was to come down to 2 min 30 sec, with a 52-train service. By October 1992, with a 58-train service, minimum headways throughout the peak periods would be 2 min 15 sec. This expansion of the operation had been delayed by late delivery of the C cars and subsequent problems with their availability.

The traction current supply system has been upgraded for better aptitude to the trains' characteristics and to cope with the more intensive operation.

An important factor in the increase of capacity, completed in 1989, is the three-track, 1·9 km Daly City Turnback and its yard, which enables BART to accelerate train turnrounds.

The regional plan of the Metropolitan Transportation Commission plots extensions totalling 105 km. Construction was expected to start in 1991 of the first three: one a 21 km branch from San Leandro to Dublin in Alameda County (set to open in 1995); one running 17 km from Concord to Pittsburg (expected to open in 1997); and the third an 8.6 km extension from Fremont to Warm Springs, also in Alameda County (to open in 1997). A 16.6 km branch from Daly City to San Francisco airport has planning approval and has been successfully negotiated with San Mateo County, which is not a member of BART; BART is not empowered to fund development or provide service outside its own territory. This line, unlikely to be finished before 2005, will terminate 1.6 km from the airport; the final link with the airport will be by Peoplemover.

Longer-term proposals include a Peoplemover connection with Oakland Airport, a further projection from Pittsburg to West and East Antioch, of the Dublin branch by 18km to Livermore, and on from Warm Springs to a meet with the San Jose LRT system (qv).

San Jose

County of Santa Clara Transportation Agency, Light Rail Division

101 W Younger Avenue, San Jose, California 95110, USA

Telephone: +1 408 299 8600

Director: James Reading
Assistant General Manager, Light Rail:
L A Washburn

Type of system: Light rail

Gauge: 1435 mm
Route length: 32 km planned
Number of lines: 1
Number of stations: 33 planned
Electrification type: 750 V dc, overhead

Rolling stock
Cars: 50
Main suppliers: UTDC
Type: 6-axle LRV, articulated
Motors per car: 2 or 4 dc
Car dimensions: Length 26·36 m, width 2·67 m, height 3·42 m
Capacity; 76 seats, 91 standing (4/m²)

System development
Known as the Guadalupe Corridor Light Rail System, the line has been built at a grade level, utilising both exclusive roadway (freeway) and city street median. The route connects southern residential to central San Jose and northern high technology employers (Silicon Valley). A north segment opened in December 1987, the central segment in June 1988, completing an initial route of 14 km with 17 stops. The final phase was to open in late 1991.

Santiago de Chile

Empresa de Transporte de Pasajeros Metro

Av Libertador B O'Higgins 1414, Santiago de Chile, Chile

Telephone: +56 2 562 698 8218
Telex: 240777 setop
Telefax: +56 2 562 699 2475

General Manager: Sergio Jimenez Moraga
Operating Manager: Patricio Rojo Trincado
Equipment Manager: Peter Himmel Konig

Type of system: Full rubber-tyred metro

Gauge: 1435 mm
Route length: 27·3 km
(in tunnel): 21·9 km
(at surface level): 5·4 km (in open cut)
(elevated): 1 km

Number of lines: 2
Number of stations: 37
(in tunnel): 29
Gradient (max): 4·8%
Minimum curve radius: 205 m
Speed (design max): 80 km/h
Track type: Concrete surface with 40 kg/m guide rail for rubber-tyred operation
Tunnel type: Cut-and-cover
Electrification type: 750 V dc, collected from 2 lateral guide rails
One-man operation: All trains
Signalling: Centralised control system. All signalling from Jeumont-Schneider, France
Automatic control of train operation: 100% except for start order

Rolling stock
Number of cars: 147 motor, 98 trailer
Main supplier: Alsthom
Train consist: Normally 3 motored plus 2 trailers
Motors per car: 2
Motor rating: 120 kW; 165 bhp
Car dimensions: Length 16 m, width 2·6 m
Capacity: 128 standing with 40 seated in motored cars; 177 standing, 24 seats in trailers
Tare weight: 28 tonnes (motored); 22 tonnes (trailers)
Doors: 4 automatic sliding doors each side

Traffic
Train headways: Peak hours, 2½ minutes; off-peak 4–8 minutes
Passenger journeys: (1988) 143 million

System development
Though the original metro design provided for a network of 60 km with four lines, progress has been retarded by the country's economic conditions and also the fact that the metro is the only state-owned public transport in an otherwise deregulated city market, which makes competition severe. However, it was expected that construction of 16 km of the proposed Line 3 would start in 1990, from Plaza Chacubuco to Plaza Ñuñoa. Although authorised in 1984, this was postponed due to the financial repercussions of the March 1985 earthquake. Also possible are short extensions of Line 1, to the east, and of Line 2 to the north and south.

São Paulo

Companhia do Metropolitano de São Paulo

Avenida Paulista 1842, 20° andar, Torre Norte, 01310 São Paulo, Brazil

Telephone: +55 11 283 4933
(011) 283 7483
Telex: 011 22013 mspo br
Telefax: +55 11 283 5228

President: Antonio Sergio Fernandez
Director, Engineering & Construction: D R Monaco Biani
Operations: C Giosa

Type of system: Full metro

Gauge: 1600 m
Route length: 40·3 km
(in tunnel): 18·4 km
(elevated): 6·3 km
Number of lines: 2
Number of stations: 38
(in tunnel): 20
(elevated): 7
Rail weight and type: AREA 57 (57 kg/m)
Track type: Continuous concrete beams in tunnels and on elevated sections; conventional concrete sleepers on surface sections
Gradient (max): 4%
Minimum curve radius: 300 m
Speed (design max): 100 km/h
Tunnel types: Double-track and cut-and-cover; single-track shield-driven bore
Electrification type: 750 V dc, third rail
Signalling and control: Automatic train supervision available, automatic train operation throughout. Both lines controlled from one centralised control centre. Automatic train operation and automatic train protection equipment by Westinghouse

Rolling stock
Number of cars: 588, all motored, formed into six-car trains
Main suppliers: Mafersa; Cobrasma/Francorail
Car dimensions: Length 21·2 m, width 3·17 m, height 3·55 m
Doors: Sliding leaf doors with 1·3 m openings
Capacity per car: 62 seated, total 333 crush load
Motors per car: All axles motored
Acceleration (max): 1·35 m/s²
Deceleration (normal service): 1·20 m/s²
Brakes: Rheostatic
Weight empty: Motors, 32·4 tonnes

Traffic
Train headways: Peak hours, 2 minutes 5 s (north-south), 2½ minutes (east-west); off-peak, 2 minutes 54 s (north-south), 4 minutes 10 s (east-west)
Passenger journeys: (1988) 565 million

System development
The ultimate metro plan envisages four lines and two branches totalling 95 km, with 80 stations, comprising: Line 1, cross-city, to link the northern suburb of Santana with Jabaquara in the south, with a branch to Moema, 21·5 km; Line 2, crossing the city east-westward from Corinthians Paulista for 22·9 km to Barra Funda; Line 3, crossing the city from the southwest to the southeast, from Três Poderos to Via Anchieta, with a branch to Vila Bertioga (total 25·5 km); and Line 4, running from Madalena in the northwest, southeast for 18·5 km to Oratório.

The lines at present in use are the north-south, which extends for 17·4 km, and the east-west which totals 22·9 km.

Construction has begun of the first 4.8km, 5-station segment of Line 3. This will interchange with the north-south Line 1 at Paraiso. Also under way is a 5.5km eastward extension of Line 2. Line 1 is to be extended by 3.5km from Santana to Tucuruvi.

Sapporo

Sapporo-shi Kotsu Kyoku
Sapporo City Transportation Bureau

Oyachi Higashi 2-4-1, Atubetu-ku, Sapporo 004, Japan

Telephone: +81 11 892 1133
Telefax: +81 11 892 2530

Managing Director: Konichi Osabe

Type of system: Full metro, rubber-tyred

Gauge and rail type
Line 1: pneumatic-tyred car 2180 mm wide. Centre-guide rail steel I-beam (310 × 446 mm). Running tracks paved with epoxy-resin plastics.
Line 2: pneumatic-tyred car 2150 mm wide. Centre-guide rail steel I-beam (311 × 399 mm). Running tracks paved with steel plates.
Route length: Line 1, 39·7 km; Line 2, 17.3km
(in tunnel): Line 1, 9·8 km; Line 2, 17·3 km
(elevated): Line 1, 4·5 km
Number of lines: 3
Number of stations: 42
Max gradient: Line 1: 4·3%
Lines 2 and 3: 3·5%
Minimum curve radius: Line 1: 200 m
Lines 2 and 3 : 201 m
Tunnel type: Generally double-track, cut-and-cover tunnel rectangular section, mostly reinforced concrete with centre supports. Under the Toyohira river the sections were constructed by caisson-method. Elevated section has circular aluminium shelter to protect against heavy snowfalls
Electrification type: Line 1: 750 V dc, third rail
Line 2: 1·5 kV dc, RS-AFB overhead conductor
Signalling and control: Automatic Train Control (ATC) and Automatic Train Operation (ATO) systems. In addition, an automatic vehicle control system has been introduced for the automated unmanned operation of empty trains over the 1·3 km to and from the depot.

A Total System has also been introduced to control and operate the following systems needed for subway operation through an integrated on-line optical transmission system: train traffic control system; electric power control system; disaster prevention system; closed-circuit television system; and automatic station operation system.

Rolling stock
Number of cars: Line 1, 176; Line 2, 144; Line 3, 60
Supplier: Marubeni Kawasaki
Manufacturer: Kawasaki Heavy Industries

Car type	Line 1	Lines 2 & 3
Units	176	204
Car dimensions		
(length)	13·8 m	18 m
(width)	3·08 m	3·08 m
(height)	3·7 m	3·9 m
Doors per side	2	3
Passengers per car	Type 2000	Type 3000
	90/96	82/96 116
Motors per car	2	2 8
Motors rating	90 kW	110 kW 70/75* kW
Max speed	70 km/h	70 km/h
Acceleration	1 m/s²	0·97 m/s²
Brakes	Electro-dynamic and hydraulic	Regenerative and hydraulic

*Line 3; each power car wheel is independently driven by a chopper-controlled 75 kW motor

Traffic
Passenger journeys: (1989) 224·8 million
Train headways: Peak hours, Line 1: 3½–4 minutes; Line 2: 4 minutes. Off-peak, Line 1: 6–7 minutes; Line 2: 6½–7 minutes

System development
The first 8·1 km, nine-station section of a new 18 km Line 3 from Sakaemachin in the north to Kitano was opened in December 1988. A 3 km extension of Line 2, from Kotoni to Teinehigashi, is set to open in 1995; and a 5·6 km extension of Line 3 from Housui to Fukuzumi in 1991, followed by a continuation of 3.2km to Kitano in 1995.

Sendai

Sendai-shi Kotsu Kyoku
(Sendai City Transportation Authority)

4-15 Kimachidori, 1-chome, Aoba-ku, Sendai City, Miyagi Pref 980, Japan

Telephone: +81 22 224 5111

Managing Director: Yoshio Tedo

Type of system: Full metro

Gauge: 1067 mm
Route length: 14·4 km
(in tunnel): 11·8 km
Number of lines: 1
Number of stations: 16
Rail weight: 60 kg/m
Max gradient: 3·5%
Minimum curve radius: 160 m
Electrification type: 1·5 kV dc, overhead

Traffic
Passenger journeys: (1989) 47 million

Rolling stock: 19 Series 1000 four-car train-sets by Kawasaki, each accommodating 144 persons per car. Designed for driver-only operation, Series 1000 has each motor car powered by four 160 kW motors under chopper control, and embodies on-board fault diagnosis and monitoring are optical fibres, with reports displayed on screen in driving cab

System development
A 1·2 km extension from Yaotome to the north was under construction in 1990, for opening in 1994.

Seoul

Seoul Metropolitan Subway Corporation (SMSC)

447-7 Bangbae-Dong, Kangnam-ku, Seoul, Republic of Korea

Telephone: +82 2 2 582 8892
Telex: 25172 smsco
Telefax: +82 2 582 9522

President: Jin-Hee Han
Director, Operations: Won Shin Kang

Type of system: Full metro

Gauge: 1435 mm
Route length: 116·5 km and additional 116·7 km planned
Number of lines: 4
Number of stations: 102
Rail weight: 50 kg/m
Gradient (max): 3·5%
Minimum curve radius: Main line: 180 m
  Platforms: 400 m
  Sidings: 76 m
Track type: Rail laid on timber sleepers and ballast. Track rubber-padded for protection of city's historic East and South gates
Tunnel type: Cut-and-cover, ASSM, NATM. Tunnels vibration-damped near East and South gates
Electrification type: 1·5 kV dc, overhead collection (Korean National Railroad suburban trains on Line 1 dual voltage, 25 kV 60 Hz and 1·5 kV dc)
Speed (design max): 100 km/h
  (average commercial): 35 km/h

Rolling stock
Number of cars: 862
Main suppliers: 476 cars for Lines 1 and 2 built in South Korea by Daewoo and Hyundai with mostly imported electrical and control equipment. Daewoo built 386 cars for Lines 3 and 4, with GEC Traction electrical equipment

Car type	Motor cars	Trailers
Car dimensions		
(length)	19·5 m	19·5 m
(width)	3·18 m	3·18 m
(height)	3·75–3·8 m	3·75–3·8 m
Doors per side	4	5
Doors (width)	1·3 m	1·3 m
Passengers per car		
(total)	160*	148*
(seated)	54	48
Motors per car	4	–
Motor rating	120–162 kW	–
Acceleration (max)	0·7–0·83 m/s²	–
Deceleration		
(normal service)	0·97 m/s²	–
(emergency)	1·25 m/s²	–
Speed (max)	100 km/h	–
Brakes: Electro-pneumatic, chopper regenerative		
Weight empty		
(tons)	43·5	34·5

* peak crush load 360 persons

Traffic
Train headways: Peak hours, 3–4·5 minutes; off-peak, 4–7 minutes
Passenger journeys: (1988) 927 million

System development
A new metropolitan plan drafted by Seoul city in 1988 tabled a nine-route network to counter growing road congestion, and segregation of Line 1 from its presently shared cross-city tracks with Korean National Railroad. Work would start immediately on three extensions, all suburban, and thus avoiding need of costly tunnelling. These comprise: a 20km projection of Line 3 northwest to a satellite town at Ilsan, and 8km southeast to Songnam; and a new 45km Line 5, an east-west route from Kimpo Airport to Kodok-Dong. Target date for completion of all three is the end of 1992.
  Lines 6, 7, 8 and 9 will all be cross-city. Lines 6 and 7 are to be started in the later 1990s.

Seville

Transportes Urbanos de Sevilla

Diego de Riano 2, Seville 41004, Spain

Telephone: +34 1 954 420011
Telefax: +34 1 954 418175

Director General: Miguel Bermejo Herrero

Type of system: Metro under construction

Opening of the first 5 km section of a proposed three-line metro was planned for 1982 but construction was halted and the Andalusian government and city authorities have since reappraised the original route plans for a 27 km system. Metro completion is now unlikely. An LRT solution is possible.

Shanghai

Shanghai Metro Corporation

10 Heng Shan Road, Shanghai, People's Republic of China

Telephone: +86 21 372809
Telex: 30235 smc cn

Director: Cai Jun Shi

Type of system: Planned metro

Gauge: 1435 mm
Route length: 176 km
Number of lines: 7
Electrification type: 1·5 kV dc, overhead

Construction began in March 1990 of the first 14·6 km of a north-south line, connecting the city's two main rail stations, to be built mostly by shield tunnelling with all but one of its 12 stations underground. Opening was forecast for 1994. A contract was signed with the German Shanghai Metro Group, which is fronted by AEG-Westinghouse and includes Siemens, Duewag and Waggon Union, for supply of the electrification and telecommunications equipment, and of 16 six-car train-sets.

Sheffield

South Yorkshire Passenger Transport Executive

Exchange Street, Sheffield S2 5SZ, England

Telephone: +44 742 768688
Telex: 547825 syptex g
Telefax: +44 742 759908

Director-General: J H M Russell

Type of system: Planned light rail ('Supertram')

In 1988 the PTE obtained Parliamentary powers for construction of an initial 22 km line, crossing the city from northwest to southeast between Hillsborough and Mosborough, mainly segregated in the southeast, but mostly on-street in the city centre and northwest. About half the route would be segregated from road traffic, utilising highway medians and laterals, two new viaducts and a new underpass, but no existing or former railway right-of-way. On-street, raised tram lanes would provide further partial segregation. Average stop spacing would be 500 m with a 5-minute headway across the city centre. Tenders to build were sought in 1989, with the aim of starting work in the autumn, but a start had to be deferred because of government refusal to include a financial grant in its immediate transport funding budget.
  A second 7 km line, largely segregated, to interchange with Line 1 and connect the city centre with the Lower Don Valley area, site of the 1991 World Student Games, was the subject of a Parliamentary Bill deposited in late 1988. The aim was to have this part of Line 2 operational by the spring of 1991, in time for the Games, but this has been frustrated by the refusal of immediate grant aid.

Singapore

Mass Rapid Transit Corporation

25K Paterson Road, Singapore 0923

Telephone: +65 732 4433
Telex: 20058
Telefax: +655 732 7758

Executive Director: Lim Leong Geok

Operator: Singapore MRT Ltd
OCC Bldg, 2 Victoria Road, Singapore 0718

Telephone: +65 339 0955
Telex: 24188
Telefax: +65 339 4892

Managing Director: L G Lim

Type of system: Full metro

Gauge: 1435 mm
Route length: 67 km
  (in tunnel): 18·93 km
Number of lines: 2, with spur off east-west line
Number of stations: 42
  (in tunnel): 9
  (elevated): 26
Track type: Timber sleepers on ballast on elevated and at grade sections, concrete set in slab in tunnels
Tunnel type: Single-track bored and cut-and-cover
Electrification type: 750 V dc, third rail
Signalling: Automatic train protection, automatic train operation and automatic line supervision, with central supervision. Suppliers: Westinghouse Brake & Signal
Innovations in design and construction: Platform screens in underground stations to reduce air-conditioning requirements. Screen doors operate automatically and are synchronised with the car doors

Traffic
Train headways: Peak hours, 3–6 minutes; off-peak, 5–8 minutes
Passenger journeys (1988-89): 460 000 daily

Rolling stock
Number of cars: 132 M-T-M three-car sets, cabbed at both ends, operated in six-car trains
Suppliers: Japanese consortium, led by Kawasaki, including Nippon Sharyo Seizo Kaisha, Tokyu Car, Kinki Sharyo; bogies by Duewag; inter-car gangways by SIG; air-conditioning by Stone International
Operating speed: 40–50 km/h
Car capacity: 62 seated, 238 standing

System development
The Singapore government concluded more than a decade of studies in 1981 with a decision to build the two-line, 67 km system. The Mass Rapid Transit Corporation, a statutory government board, assumed authority from the provisional planning agency in October 1983, and is responsible for building and operating the system. A private company, Singapore MRT Ltd, oversees operation.
  The initial segment of the system in use in 1989 began at Yishun on the north-south line and interchanged with the east-west line at City Hall. It is predominantly underground. The east-west line ran east from City Hall to Juron and west from City Hall to Lakeside. The final sections of the system, from Jurong to Pasir Ris, and from Lakeside to Boon Lay, were opened in July 1990 and completed Phase 2. A branch to Changi Airport had been proposed for the east-west line, but in mid-1990 it seemed probable that this would be deferred in favour of a northwest extension to Woodlands.
  In 1988 a Phase III programme involving a 15 km line to Punggol and Jalan Kayu in the island's northeast was approved.

Sofia

Construction authority:
Direction Metropolitene Aupres de Conseil Municipal de Sofia

34 Boulevarde Dondukov, Sofia, Bulgaria

Type of system: Full metro under construction

Gauge: 1435 mm
Proposed route length: 51·9 km (by 2000)
Proposed number of lines: 3
Number of stations: 48
Average distance between stations: 1·16 km
Tunnel type: Single and double-track, prefabricated concrete sections
Electrification type: 825 V dc, third rail
Automatic control: Automatic speed control
Signalling: CTC with cab signalling

Rolling stock
Number of cars: Plans for 250 cars, all motored, for operation in two-car sets; one driving control car with one motored car. Trains consist of up to four sets
Main suppliers: Probably Mytischy Machinery Plant, USSR
Car capacity: Crush, 270 in driving car and 300 in rear car

System development
Sofia's Metro is planned to have three lines crossing the city centre, but construction made slow progress until a speed-up was ordered in late 1989. Line 1, now under construction, will start at the Lyulin housing estate in the northwest. The first section will terminate in the city centre, and this was expected to be ready by late 1991. Work will then take the line under the Boulevarde Dondukov to Iskr station in the southeast, centre of a big industrial complex. The line will have 16 stations.

848 RAPID TRANSIT / Sofia—Tbilisi

The north-south line will run 18 km from another industrial zone, Ilyantsi, beneath the main Bulgarian State Railways station and under the Boulevarde Dimitrov to reach the Mladoct housing area. It will have 17 stations. Construction of this line has also begun.

The third line will run 15·7 km beneath the Boulevarde Botevgradsko Chaussee, under the Poduyane railway station, to terminate at Knayshevo. The line will have 15 stations.

Stockholm

AB Storstockholms Lokaltrafik (Rail Division)

Tegnérgatan 2A, Box 6301, 113 81 Stockholm
Sweden

Telephone: +46 8 786 10 00
Telex: 19159 sl transis
Telefax: +46 8 786 15 80

General Manager: Leif Axén
Manager, Rail Division: Gunnar Rehnström

Type of system: Full metro (T-Bana)

Gauge: 1435 mm
Route length: 110 km
  (in tunnel): 62 km
Number of lines: 3 with branches
Number of stations: (total): 99
  (in tunnel): 53
Average distance between stations: 1000 m
Speed (design max): 80–90 km/h
  (average commercial): 30–40 km/h
Rail type: Flat-bottomed 50 kg/m
Tunnel type: Concrete, rock and steel
Gradient (max): 4%, (exceptional): 4·8%
Minimum curve radius: 200 m, (exceptional): 120 m
Electrification type: 650–750 V, third rail
One-man operation: All trains one-man operated with cab signalling
Signalling: Cab signalling with two speed ranges; up to 15 and 50 km/h, with a third for higher speeds. Signalling provides for 90 s train intervals and 30 s stops at station. Fixed lineside signals are installed only at junctions. Central Control Office is linked to all trains through radio communication

Rolling stock
Car types: C2-C9; C12-C15
Number of cars: 962
Main suppliers: ABB in co-operation with Svenska Järnvägsverkstäderna and Hägglund. Latest 15 two-car sets supplied in 1988 have chopper control, air-suspension and are single-cabbed
Car dimensions: Length 17 m, width 2·7–2·8 m, height 3·7 m
Number of doors per side: 3 × 2
Door width: 1·2 m
Number of passengers per car (total): 158
  (seated): 48
Motors per car: 4
Motor rating: 4 × 87 kW-4 × 100 kW
Power per 8-car train (minimum): 175 kN
  (max): 415 kN
Acceleration (max): 1·0–1·3 m/s^2
Deceleration (normal service): 1·1 m/s^2
  (emergency): 1·0 m/s^2
Max design speed: 80–90 k/h
Bogies: 2 motor air-rubber-suspended ABB
Brakes: Electrodynamic and compressed air
Weight (empty): 23·6–30 tonnes (motor cars)
Each car has six double-leaf automatic sliding doors and each is equipped with centre buffer couplers. All recently delivered cars have air suspension and driver's cab at one end only

Traffic
Train headways: Peak hours: tube 1, 2 minutes; tube 2, 2½ minutes; tube 3, 5 minutes. Off-peak hours: tube 1, 2⅖–2⅔ minutes; tube 2, 4–6⅔ minutes; tube 3, 6–10 minutes
Passenger journeys: (1988) 229 million

System development
A 2 km, two-station extension from Bagarmossen to Skarpnäck is being built for opening in 1994.

Stuttgart

Stuttgarter Strassenbahnen AG (SSB)

Postbox 801006, Schockenriedstrasse 50, 7000 Stuttgart 80, Federal Republic of Germany

Telephone: +49 711 78850
Telex: 725771 ssb d
Telefax: +49 711 7885 2891

Chief Officers: Roland Batzill
  Manfred Bonz
  Dr Peter Höflinger

Type of system: Stadtbahn light rail created from tramway

Gauge: Stadtbahn 1435 mm; tramway 1000 mm
Route length: Stadtbahn and mixed gauge in operation, 45 km; tramway, 66 km
  (in tunnel): 12 km
Number of lines: Stadtbahn 4; tramway 6; also a rack-assisted railway and funicular
Number of stations: Stadtbahn and mixed operation, 75; tramway, 126
Max gradient: 7%; tramway 8·5%
Minimum curve radius: 50 m; tramway 18 m
Electrified type: 660 V dc, overhead, to be modified to 750 V dc
Rolling stock
Number of cars: 225 Type GT4 (1000 mm gauge): 65 Type DT8 (1435 mm gauge)
Main suppliers: Maschinenfabrik Esslingen (Type GT4); Duewag (Type DT8)
Car dimensions: GT4, length 18 m, width 2·2 m; DT8, length complete two-car set 38·05 m, width 2·65 m, height 3·715 m
Capacity: GT4, 96 seated, 114 standing; DT8, 110 seated, 124 standing. Four passengers/m^2
Traffic
Train headways: Peak hours, 6/7–8/10 minutes; off-peak, 12 minutes
Passenger journeys: (1989) 93.3 million

System development
The tramway system, already lowered below ground in the city centre and elsewhere substantially placed on segregated tracks, is in course of a two-stage conversion to a light rail Stadtbahn, which by 1995 is planned to embrace 95 route-km; 20 km will be in tunnel. The gauge is being changed from 1000 to 1435 mm at the same time, but to simplify transition some routes are being dual-gauged to allow flexible use of existing cars. Lines 1, 3, 9 and 14 have had their conversion completed. The air-conditioned, high-density seating of the DT8 units is to be standardised in the 1435 mm-gauge fleet and 40 GT4 were being modified to these characteristics in 1990–92.

Lines 5 and 6 would be converted to 1435 mm by the end of 1990, raising the light rail distance to some 70 km. Metre-gauge tramway operation will be eliminated by the end of the 1990s.

Sverdlovsk

Sverdlovsk, USSR

Type of system: Full metro under construction

Gauge: 1524 mm
Electrification type: 825 V dc

System development
Construction of the Sverdlovsk metro has begun. The first 8·2 km section with six stations is heading for completion in 1990. A three-line system is planned.

Taipei

Department of Rapid Transit Systems (DORTS) Taipei Municipal Government (TMG)

10th Floor, 746 Minsheng E Road, Taipei, Taiwan 10580

Telephone: +886 2 712 1104/ 713 7710
Telex: 29795 dorts
Telefax: +886 2 712 1085

Director General: Benjamin P C Chi

Type of system: Métro under construction

Gauge: 1435 mm
Planned route length: 70 km
Number of lines: 5
Number of stations: 110
Electrification: Third-rail dc

Rolling stock
Cars on order: 132 cars, being built in the USA by United Rail Car Partnership, an alliance of Nissho Iwai American Corp and Kawasaki Rolling Stock (USA), with AEG-Westinghouse ac traction equipment

The first phase of the project, started in 1988, is a 22·9 km Red Line 1 from the main station that will take over Taiwan Railways' Tamshui line for its final 7·9 km. Of the remaining distance, 3km will be in cut-and-cover tunnel and 12km elevated. Opening is anticipated in 1993.

In design are a 10 km Green Line, a 19 km Blue Line and a 6 km Orange Line. In June 1988 contracts for a 14 km Brown Line to employ automated rubber-tyred trains were signed with Matra; this is to open in late 1991.

Long term, the 'initial planning network' will be extended to a full network of 107km covering the entire Taipei metropolitan area.

Tashkent

Tashkent Metropolitane

Ulitsa Tarasa Shevchenko 62, Tashkent 600015, USSR

Chief Executive: Shainoyat Rakhimovich Shaabdurakhimov
Chief Engineer: Khakim Gafurovich Gafurov

Type of system: Full metro

Gauge: 1524 mm
Route length: 24 km
No of lines: 2
Number of stations: 19
Gradient (max): 4%
Electrification type: 825 V dc, third rail

Rolling stock
Number of cars: 137, all motored, operated in four-car sets
Car type: Mytischy EJ-T
Car dimensions:
  (length): 19·2 m
  (width): 2·7 m
Doors per side: 4
Passengers per car:
  (total): 170
  (seated): 44
Motors per car: 4
Motor rating: 66 kW
Brakes: Rheostatic

Traffic
Train frequencies: 20 pairs/h
Passenger journeys: (1988) 132 million

System development
The first underground railway to be built in an earthquake zone, the Tashkent metro's construction entailed special protective techniques and precautions, which satisfactorily survived the region's two severe earthquakes in late 1980. The metro is characterised by a higher degree of automated control than other USSR metros.

A 50 km system with three lines is planned. A further 2.5km of Line 2 was to open in 1989 and another 2km extension was under construction.

Tbilisi

Tbilisi Metropolitane

Ploshchad Vokzalnaya 2, Tbilisi 38012, USSR

Chief Executive: Igor Grigoroviech Melkadze
Chief Engineer: Jondo Gerontevich Jinjikhadze

Type of system: Full metro

Gauge: 1524 mm
Route length: 23 km
  (in tunnel): 16·4 km
Number of lines: 2
Number of stations: 20
  (in tunnel): 13
Max gradient: 4%
Minimum curve radius: 400 m

Speed (average commercial): 45·8 km/h
Electrification type: 825 V dc, third rail
Signalling: Automatic train stop. Radio-telephone communication between trains and central command post

Rolling stock
Car type: Mytischy E-60
Number: 161, all motored
Car dimensions
(length): 18·8 m
(width): 2·7 m
(height): 3·7 m
Doors per side: 4
Door (width): 1·38 m
Passengers per car
(total): 170
(seated): 44
Motors per car: 4
Motor rating: 68 kW (94 hp)
Brakes: Rheostatic

Traffic
Train headways: 2½ minutes (peak hours), 4 minutes (off-peak)
Passenger journeys: (1985) 145 million

System development
The first 8km of Line 3 was to open in 1990, and a further 11km in 1995. Line 1 is to be extended at each end.

Tehran

Tehran Urban and Suburban Railway Co

PO Box 4661, 37 Miremad Street, 15875 Tehran, Iran

Telephone: +98 21 838051 Telex: 215676 tusr ir

Managing Director: A Ebrahimi

Type of system: Full metro under construction

Gauge: 1435 mm
Route length: 48 km
(in tunnel): 32 km
Number of lines: 2
Number of stations: 43
Rail weight: 54 kg/m
Track bed: Reinforced concrete
Electrification: 750 V dc, third rail
Estimated passenger volume for the first period of operation: 40 000 passengers/h one way
Train headways during first period of operation: Approx 3 minutes

Rolling stock
Number of cars required: 720 in four-car sets. Bids to supply were invited in 1990
Type of operation: Automatic and manual

System development
Work began in 1977 in the Abas Abad area, following detailed planning by Sofretu, but was suspended in 1979. In 1986 the Iranian Minister of the Interior required some changes in the proposed design, after which construction of Lines 1 and 2 was resumed in 1987 by local industry. The first section is set to open in 1992.
The ultimate network will comprise four lines aggregating 72km.
Also under construction is a 42km regional metro line, to be electrified at 25kV ac, from the Line 2 terminus of Ayatolah Kashani to the satellite city of Karadj.

Tel Aviv

Tel Aviv Metropolitan Area Rapid Transit

Ministry of Transport, 97 Jaffa Road, Jerusalem, Israel

Telephone: +972 2 229211
Telex: 3507

Plans are being formulated for a four-route, 60km, 1435mm-gauge system with 35 stations and 8km in tunnel. Not yet decided is whether the system would be metro or light rail.

Tianjin

Tianjin Metro

Xin Hei Li No 7, Qi-Xiang-Tai Road, He-Ping, Tianjin, People's Republic of China

Telephone: +86 21 319567/311434

Deputy Director: Li Zhong-Xin
Manager: Liu Yu Xi
Chief Engineer: Liu Yu Xi

Type of system: Metro

Gauge: 1435 mm
Route length: 8 km
Number of lines: 1
Number of stations: 8
Rail weight: 50 kg/m
Track type: Conventional, rail laid on concrete sleepers
Tunnel type: Cut-and-cover 2 m beneath surface
Max gradient: 3%
Minimum curve radius: 300 m
Electrification type: Third rail
Signalling: Automatic block with three-aspect signals
Service hours: Initial operations restricted to peak periods 0600–0900, 1630–1900

Rolling stock
Number of cars: 12
Type: BJ-III three-car sets
Supplier: Changchun Rolling Stock Plant
Max speed: 70 km/h
The cars are similar to those operating on the Beijing metro. Further cars are on order

Lines planned: 24 km circling inner city area, with present line extended to Liutan; opening of the latter was anticipated in 1989.

Tokyo

The present subway network in Tokyo consists of ten lines with a total length of 211·7 km of which seven lines, 150·2 km, are operated by the Teito Rapid Transit Authority.
The outer part of the city proper and its suburbs are served by seven major private railway companies.

Teito Kosokudu Kotsu Eidan (Teito Rapid Transit Authority)

19-6, Higashi Ueno 3-chome, Taito-ku, Tokyo, Japan

Telephone: +81 3 832 2111
Telefax: +81 3 337 7048

President: S Nakamura
Operations Manager: J Ono

Type of system: Full metro

Gauge: 1435 mm (Ginza and Marunouchi lines); 1067 mm
Route length: 154·6 km
(in tunnel): 128·1 km
(elevated): 26·5 km
Number of lines: 7
Number of stations: 142
Rail type and weight: Main-line, 50 and 60 kg/m; sidings 30–50 kg/m
Track type: In tunnel, solid bed; at surface level, sleepers on ballast
Tunnel type: Shield driven and cut-and-cover
Max gradient: 4%
Minimum curve radius: 90 m
Electrification type: 600 V dc, third rail (Ginza and Marunouchi lines); 1·5 kV dc, overhead
Signalling: Wayside signals on four lines, cab signalling on three lines. Suppliers and installers; Kyosan Electric, Nippon Signal and Daido Signal
Automatic train control: Hibiya, Tozai, Chiyoda, Yuraku-cho and Hanzoman lnes; automatic train-stop, Ginza and Marunouchi lines

Rolling stock
Number of cars: 1677 motor, 536 trailers
Suppliers: Mechanical, Kawasaki Heavy Industries, Tokyu Car, Kinki Sharyo, Nippon Sharyo. Electrical equipment, Mitsubishi Electric, Toshiba and Hitachi
Cars on order: 18 chopper cars for Marunouchi line, 20 for Yurakucho line, 24 for Hibiya line and 30 for Tozai line

Traffic
Train headways: Peak hours, 1 minute 50 s; off-peak, 2–8 minutes
Passenger journeys: (1988) 2045 million

System development
Teito is the capital's principal metro operator. Its network includes the original Ginza line of 1927, electrified at 600 V dc. A 0·9 km continuation of the Hanzomon line to Kakigaracho was to open in 1990.
Construction was in hand, for 1991 inauguration, of the first 6·8 km of Line 7, which will run 21·2 km to the west of central Tokyo from Iwabuchi-cho to Nakameguni on the south side of the city and afford through running to Tokyu Railway's Mekama line. The remainder will open in 1995. At the eastern end of the Tozai line a 16·2 km extension, known as the Toyo Rapid Railway, is being built by the Japan Railway Construction Corporation. This was to open in two stages.
The Council for Transport Policy's proposals include a 8·3 km branch of the Yurakucho line from Toyosu northwards. The Hanzomon line would be projected east to Sumiyoshi then north, diverging to reach Matsudo, a total of 16.7km. A 25.5km Line 13 is planned to run on new track from Shibuya to Kotake-Mukaihara, then take over the existing section of Yurakucho line to Wakoshi and run through to the Tobu Railway's Tojo line.
In 1989 the Transport Ministry moved for construction of two deep-level metro routes, one of which would be built jointly by Teito Rapid Transit and JR-East. This would extend 6km from Marunouchi to Shinjuku.

Tokyo-to Kotsu Kyoku TOEI (Transportation Bureau of Tokyo Metropolitan Government)

10-1, 2-chome Yurakucho, Chiyoda-ku, Tokyo, Japan

Telephone: +81 3 216 1411
Telefax: +81 3 216 2924

General Manager: Tsuneharu Ochi
Assistant General Manager: F Tozawa
Chief Engineer: Takao Okamoto

Type of system: Full metro

Gauge: 1067 mm; 1372 mm; 1435 mm
Route length: 64·3 mm
(in tunnel): 56·7 km
Number of lines: 3
Number of stations: 65
(in tunnel): 57
Rail weight and type: 50 kg/m T-rail
Max gradient: 3·5%
Minimum curve radius: 164 m
Track type: Conventional sleepers on ballast, sleepers on concrete and slab track
Tunnel type: Cut-and-cover, shield driven and concrete caisson
Electrification type: 1·5 kV dc, overhead
Signalling: Automatic block with three-aspect colour-light signalling and ATS, cab signalling and ATC

Traffic
Train headways: Peak hours, 2½–4 minutes; off-peak 5–8 minutes
Passenger journeys: (1988/89) 496 million

System development
A 2·8 km extension of Line 10, the Shinjuku line, from Shinozaki to Motoyawata was inaugurated in 1989.
Construction has begun of a small-profile metro route, Line 12, which will encircle central Tokyo in a 26 km loop and also run 22·9 km north from Shinjuku to Niiza-shi. The first 4·8 km segment was to open in 1991. Tunnels will be 4·2 m in diameter instead of 6·2 m. Gauge will be 1435 mm and current supply 1·5 kV dc. A prototype eight-car train-set has been built in which cars are 16.25 m long, 2·5 m wide and 3·05 m in height.
The Council for Transport Policy proposes further extension of the Shinjuku line beyond Mokoyawata, reached by a 2·8 km extension in 1989, and a 3·9 km extension of the Mita line to a connection with Teito's new Line 7 at Seishoko, for through running to Meguro.

850 RAPID TRANSIT / Tokyo—Toronto

Line	Ginza and Marunouchi	Ginza	Marunouchi	Marunouchi	Hibiya	Hibiya	Tozai	Tozai and Chiyoda	Chiyoda	Yuraku-cho	Hanzoman
Car type	2000	01	02	500 and others	03	3000	05	5000	6000	7000	8000
Gauge (mm)	1435	1435	1435	1435	1067	1067	1067	1067	1067	1067	1067
Electrification type	600 V dc third rail	600 V dc third rail	600 V dc third rail	600 V dc third rail	1500 V dc overhead	1500 V dc overhead	1500 V dc overhead	1500 V dc overhead	1500 V dc overhead	1500 V dc overhead	1500 V dc overhead
Number of cars	Ginza: 34 Marunouchi: 18	138	24	296	40	280	60	Tozai: 420 Chiyoda: 6	343	320	166
Car dimensions											
(length) (m)	16	16	18	18	18	18	20	20	20	20	20
(width) (m)	2·55	2·55	2·83	2·79	2·83	2·79	2·85	2·8	2·8	2·8	2·78
(height) (m)	3·495	3·465	3·495	3·495	3·598	3·6	3·67	3·625	3·625	3·67	3·67
Number of doors per side	3	3	3	3	3	3	4	4	4	4	4
Door width (m)	1·3	1·3	1·4	1·3	1·4	1·3	1·3	1·3	1·3	1·3	1·3
Number of passengers per car											
(total)	100-102	100-102	124-136	120-132	124-136	120-128	142-154	136-144	136-144	136-144	136-144
(seated)	36-44	36-44	42-52	44-58	44-52	48-56	48-54	50-58	48-54	48-54	48-54
Body materials	steel	aluminium	aluminium	steel	aluminium	semi-stainless steel	aluminium	semi-stainless steel	aluminium	aluminium	aluminium
Control system	rheostatic	chopper	chopper	rheostatic	chopper	rheostatic	chopper	rheostatic	chopper	chopper	chopper
Motors per car	4	4	4	4	4	4	4	4	4	4	4
Motor rating (kW) (1 h rating)	55	120	120	75	160	75	160	100	145	150	160
Acceleration (m/s^2)	0·78	0·83	0·83	0·89	0·92	1·11	0·92	0·97	0·92	0·92	0·92
Deceleration (normal service) (m/s^2)	1·11	0·97	1·11	1·11	1·11	1·11	0·97	1·11	1·03	0·97	0·97
(emergency) (m/s^2)	1·39	1·25	1·39	1·39	1·39	1·39	1·39	1·30	1·31	1·25	1·25
Electric brakes	–	regenerative	regenerative	rheostatic	regenerative	rheostatic	regenerative	rheostatic	regenerative	regenerative	regenerative
Weight (empty) (tonnes) approx	28-35	22-29·5	22·8-30·5	34-40	22·7-32·7	31-33	23·1-33·7	26·5-36	22·5-35·3	23·7-36·3	26·3-35·8

Rolling stock
Main suppliers: Tokyu Car, Nippon Sharyo

Car type	5000/5200 (Line 1), Asakusa	6000 (Line 6), Mita	10 000 (Line 10), Shinjuku
Units	164	168	192
Car dimensions			
(length)	18 m	20 m	20 m
(width)	2·8 m	2·8 m	2·8 m
(height)	4·05 m	4·05 m	4·1 m
Doors per side	3	4	4
Passengers per car			
(total)	140 (MC), 150 (M)	150 (MC), 170 (M)	150 (TC), 170 (M)
(seated)	48 (MC), 52 (M)	50 (MC), 58 (M)	50 (TC), 58 (M)
Motors per car	4	4	4
Motor rating	85 kW	100 kW	165 kW
	117 hp	137 hp	226 hp
Acceleration (max)	0·97 m/s^2	0·97 m/s^2	0·92 m/s^2
Deceleration			
(normal service)	1·1 m/s^2	1·1 m/s^2	1·1 m/s^2
(emergency)	1·3 m/s^2	1·3 m/s^2	1·3 m/s^2
Brakes	Rheostatic/air	Rheostatic/air	Regenerative/air
Weight empty (tons)			
M	33	36	40
T	–	–	30

Toronto

Toronto Transit Commission

1900 Yonge Street, Toronto, Ontario M4S 1Z2, Canada

Telephone: +1 416 393 4000
Telex: 0652 4670
Telefax: +1 416 393 4899

Chairman: Lois Griffin
Chief General Manager: Allan Leach

Type of system: Full metro

Gauge: 1495 mm
Route length: 54·4 km
Number of lines: 2
Number of stations: 60 (50 in tunnel, 5 elevated, 5 at surface)
Rail weight and type: 100 lb/yd (49·6 kg/m) and 115 lb/yd (57·5 kg/m) T-rail
Track type: Open cut, conventional sleepers on ballast and concrete sleepers (on new sections) on ballast. Bored tunnel, rail laid on concrete bed; and rail laid on oversize concrete sleepers on resilient rubber pads
Tunnel type: Cut-and-cover sections, steel-reinforced poured concrete box structures; 4·1 m high, 8·6 m wide in tunnel, 14·5 m wide in stations. Bored tunnels, shield driven precast concrete or cast iron linings; 4·8 m wide in tunnel, 7·2 m wide in stations
Max gradient: 3·45%
Electrification type: 600 V dc, third rail
Signalling: Automatic block and interlocking signals and wayside signals; suppliers, Siemens and General Electric Railway Signal Company, GRS, WABCO, Wismer and Becker, Transcontrol and Imperial Electric Company Division of Burwall Electric (Bloor-Danforth extensions 1980)
Centralised control: Centralised train despatch and control system

Rolling stock
Number of cars: 623 motor cars
Number of units per train: 4, 6 or 8
Main suppliers: Gloucester RCW, MLW, Hawker Siddeley Canada, UTDC/Can-Car Rail

Traffic
Train headways: Yonge-University-Spadina line, peak hours, 2 minutes 10 s; off-peak, 3 minutes 42 s (day), 5 minutes 50 s (Sundays), Bloor-Danforth line, peak hours, 2 minutes 17 s; off-peak, 4¾ minutes (day), 5 minutes 52 s (Sundays)
Passenger journeys: (1988) 178·6 million

System development
In April 1990 Ontario's Transport Minister announced a network development plan that would extend the system to 140km. The priority will be the Downtown line, a connection of the Spadina and Yonge lines to complete a circular route. Next on the list are a new line, the Sheppard, to run east-west in the northern suburbs; an extension westward of the Spadina line to Sherway Gardens; and another new line, the Eglinton West, to run from Spadina to Etobicoke. A study group was to report in late 1990 on means of financing and progressing the plan.

Type of system: Intermediate Capacity Transit System (ICTS)

Gauge: 1435 mm
Route length: 6·52 km
  (in tunnel): 0·3 km
  (elevated): 2·3 km
Number of routes: 1
Number of stations: 6
  (elevated): 4
Track type: 115 lb/yd continuously welded T-rail fixed to concrete base with rubber insulation pads
Max gradient: 5·25%
Electrification type: 600 V dc, collection two live and one reaction rail
Signalling: Full automatic control of trains, save for door operation, under moving block signalling based on Seltrac system and installed by SEL Canada.

Rolling stock
Number of cars: 28
Main supplier: UTDC/Venture Trans
Car dimensions: Length 12·7 m, width 2·5 m, height 3·1 m
Capacity: 30 seated, 70 standing, 109 crush
Tare weight: 15·5 tonnes
Cars to be ordered: 16

Traffic
Passenger journeys: (1987) 3·36 million, 36 000 daily

Rolling stock						
Car type (all motored)	G1, 3, 4*	M1	H1, H2	H4	H5	H6
Number of cars	58	36	236	88	136	126
Number of units per train	6-8	4-6	4-6	4-6	4-6	4-6
Car dimensions						
(length)	17·4 m	22·8 m	22·8 m	22·8 m	22·8 m	22·8 m
(width)	3·1 m	3·1 m	3·1 m	3·1 m	3·1 m	3·1 m
(height)	3·65 m	3·65 m	3·65 m	3·65 m	3·65 m	3·65 m
Number of doors per side	3	4	4	4	4	4
Door width	1·14 m	1·14 m	1·14 m	1·14 m	1·14 m	1·14 m
Number of passengers per car (crush load)	232	301	307	307	307	307
(seated)	62	83	83	77	76	76
Motors per car	4	4	4	4	4	4
Motor rating (kW) (1 h rating)	51	90	86½	86½	94	92
Acceleration (max)	0·85 m/s^2	1·12 m/s^2	1·12 m/s^2	1·12 m/s^2	1·12 m/s^2	1·12 m/s^2
Deceleration (normal service)	1·25 m/s^2	1·25 m/s^2	1·25 m/s^2	1·25 m/s^2	1·25 m/s^2	1·25 m/s^2
(emergency)	1·35 m/s^2	1·35 m/s^2	1·35 m/s^2	1·35 m/s^2	1·35 m/s^2	1·35 m/s^2
Bogies	GRCW	Dofasco	Dofasco	Dofasco	Dofasco	MAN
Brakes: rheostatic, electro-pneumatic, pneumatic service, pneumatic emergency brake	No rheostatic	All	All	All	No rheostatic but regenerative	No rheostatic but regenerative
Weight (empty in tonnes) per car	33-38	27	26	26	30·5 (air-conditioning fitted)	32·5 (air-conditioning fitted)

* All stored in 1989; replaced by new H6 cars

Train headways: Peak hours, 3 minutes 20 seconds; off-peak, 5 minutes

System development
The Scarborough line, opened in March 1985, employs the Intermediate Capacity Transit (ICTS) system of Canada's UTDC. The main features of ICTS are: lightweight vehicles operating single or in trains; steel wheel/steel rail suspension; standard-gauge continuously welded track; radial car bogies; linear induction motor propulsion with regenerative braking; concrete elevated guideways; moving block automatic train control; and 600 V dc wayside power distribution.

The 1990 city transport plan (see above) proposed a 2.9km northeastern extension of the line.

Toulouse

Société d'Economie Mixte des Transports Publics de Voyageurs de l'Agglomération Toulousaine (SEMVAT)

49 rue de Gironis, 31081 Toulouse Cedex, France

Telephone: +33 61 41 11 41
Telex: 521723 semvat f
Telefax: +33 61 41 70 39

Director General: Michael Montazel

Type of operation: Rubber-tyred VAL metro under construction

In July 1985 the city transport authority voted by a narrow majority to adopt the rubber-tyred VAL system. An initial 10 km north-south line, Line 1 from Jolimont to Centre Regional du Mirail with 8 km in tunnel and 15 stations, is under construction for completion in 1993. Service will commence with 29 train-sets, each with 154-passenger capacity, at a frequency of 1¾ minutes. Three lines with a total length of 28 km are planned. The second line will intersect with the first in the city centre; a third will run west from the city centre to Colomiers.

Tripoli

Tripoli, Libya

A contract to design an urban railway system was granted to Uvaterv of Hungary in 1984. A 70 km network is planned, with 20 km underground, but no progress reported.

Tunis

Société du Métro Léger de Tunis (SLMT)

6 Rue Khartoum, Tunis 1002, Tunisia

Telephone: +216 1 780 100
Telex: 14072

Director General: L Riahi

Type of system: Light rail

Gauge: 1440 mm
Route length: 19 km
Number of lines: 2
Number of stations: 26
Electrification type: 750 V dc, overhead

Rolling stock
Number of cars: 78 twin-unit articulated
Main suppliers: Siemens/Duewag/MAN
Car dimensions: Length 30 m, width 2·47 m, height 3·91 m
Motors: 2 × 240 kW, chopper-controlled, per bogie
Acceleration: 0·9 m/s^2
Max speed: 70 km/h
Passenger capacity: 52 seated; 234 standing
Tare weight: 40·3 tonnes
Cars on order: 26, for delivery in 1991

Traffic
Train headways: Peak hours, 6 minutes; off-peak, 8 minutes
Number of passengers: 70 000 daily

System development
The 7.1km North line from Place Barcelone in Tunis to Ariana was inaugurated in 1989. The 7km Northwest line to Ettahrir was to open in July 1990, and its 5.5km branch to Den Den late in 1991. An extension of the Northwest line to Ettadhamen was to go ahead for inauguration in 1992.

An existing 19·5 km, 18-station railway between Tunis and La Marsa, the TGM, operating emus at 750 V dc, third-rail has been converted to overhead current supply for integration with the light rail system. It is operated by 36 cars supplied by Duewag/MAN/Siemens.

Turin

Consorzio Trasporti Torinesi – Azienda Tranvie Municipali (TT-ATM)

Corso Turati 19/6, Turin 10128, Italy

Telephone: +39 11 57641
Telex: 224345
Telefax: +39 11 5764 291

Chairman: Dr Girogio Perinetti
Director General: Dr Ing Giovanni Fava
Operating Manager: Dr Ing Antonio Ardissone

Type of system: Light rail

Gauge: 1445 mm
Route length: 21.5km
Number of lines: 2
Rail type: 50 or 51 kg/m
Track type: Ballasted concrete sleepers
Minimum curve radius: 25m
Maximum gradient: 4 per cent
Electrification type: 600 V dc, overhead

Rolling stock
Number of cars Lines 4 and 10: 51 Fiat Type ML 7000 six-axle single articulated vehicles equipped with two monomotòr bogies and one unpowered bogie; the rating per motor is 210 kW at 1165 rpm. Three-phase inverter ac traction equipment is by Ansaldo (30 vehicles) and AEG (20 vehicles)
Car dimensions: Length 29.7 m, width 2·5 m, height rail to floor 850 mm
Tare weight: 62·8 tonnes
Wheel diameter: 680 mm
Service brakes: Regenerative and rheostatic
Emergency brakes: Electro-dynamic disc brakes and magnetic rail brake
Max speed: 75 km/h
Service acceleration: 1 m/s^2
Service deceleration: 1·4 m/s^2
Emergency deceleration: 2·6 m/s^2
Crush capacity: Seats 56, standing 234

Lines 3 and 9: In 1989 delivery was taken of the first two of 50 Fiat Type TPR 5000 six-axle articulated low-floor tramcars with Ansaldo Trasporti chopper-controlled dc motors. Each car has two 150 kW monomotor bogies. Tare weight is 42 tonnes, passenger capacity 51 seated and 129 standing, and maximum speed 60km/h. Braking equipment is as for LRVs (see above)

System development
In 1990 the system's first route, east-west Line 3, was supplemented by a 1.2km connection to the city's football stadium in time for the World Cup, and the 10.5 km Line 9 was finished from Torino Esposizioni in the southeast via Porta Nuova FS station to Piazza Stampalia.

Upgrading of further tram routes to LRT standards is planned.

Utrecht

NV Verenigd Streekvervoer Westnederland

PO Box 3 Hoogeveenseweg 7, 2770 AA Boskop, Netherlands

Telephone: +31 1 727 2105
Telefax: +31 1 727 16071

Director: P Van Fliet
Manager, Sneltram: A O Pot

Type of system: Light rail

Gauge: 1435 mm
Route length: 17·9 km
Number of lines: 1, with branch to Nieuwegein Zuid
Number of stations: 23
Track type: 46 kg/m rails on concrete sleepers. About 90% on exclusive right-of-way, with about 40 road crossings
Electrification type: 750 V dc, overhead
Signalling: Ordinary street traffic lights or automatic half-barriers, except for 1·5 km of conventional signalling at level crossing

Rolling stock
Number of cars: 27, all motored
Main suppliers: SIG, Switzerland; Holec (electrical

equipment); BBC (traction motors)
Car output: 2 × 228 kW
Axle arrangement: Bo-Bo-Bo
Car dimensions: Length 29·8 m, width 2·65 m
Capacity: 98 seated, 160 standing

Traffic
Train headways: 7½ minutes day, 10 minutes evening on main section; alternate trains will run to IJsselstein and Nieuwegein Zuid
Passenger journeys: (1987) 7·4 million

System development
An extension from the Central station to the university at De Uithof is planned, for opening in 1996. As it will thread narrow city streets, a new type of shorter, low-floor vehicle will be required.

Valencia

Valencia, Venezuela

Type of system: Planned metro under construction

Venezuela's second city has plans for a 60 km metro system with three lines intersecting in the city centre. The first 10 km line, with 11 stations, is under construction, but pace is slow because of economic difficulties.

Vancouver

British Columbia Rapid Transit

6800 14th Avenue, Burnaby, British Columbia V3N 4S7, Canada

Telephone: +1 604 520 3641
Telefax: +1 604 521 5818

Type of system: Automated light metro ('Skytrain')

Route length: 22·2 km
  (in tunnel): 1·6 km
  (elevated): 13 km
Number of stations: 16
  (in tunnel): 2
Track type: Mainly lightweight, pre-stressed elevated concrete guideways
Max gradient: 4%
Electrification type: 600 V dc, collected by brushes from side rails (2 in vertical series) and fed to linear induction motors
Signalling: Full automation, using SELTRAC system with central computer control. Trains are unmanned

Traffic
Passenger journeys: (1988/89) 23.3 million
Headways: 3–5 minutes

Rolling stock
Number of cars: 114
Main supplier: Metro Canada (construction division of Urban Transportation Development Corporation of Ontario)

The lightweight cars feature linear induction motors, steerable bogies to reduce noise and vibration and wheel track wear; an automated train control system permits headways of 1 minute

System development
A 0·8 km extension to Colombia was opened in February 1989.
Phase 2, scheduled for completion by the winter of 1990, will carry the line over the Fraser River on a dedicated cable-stayed bridge and into Surrey, adding 4 km and three more stations. Further extensions are planned at each end of the system.

Vienna

Wiener Stadtwerke Verkehrsbetriebe

Favoritenstrasse 9-11, 1040 Vienna, Austria

Telephone: +43 1 501 30
Telex: 3221278 wstwvb
Telefax: +43 1 501 30 2550

Director: Dipl-Ing Josef Sailler
Operating Manager: Dipl-Ing Günther Grois

Type of system: Full metro (U-Bahn)

Gauge: 1435 mm
Route length: 30·1 km
  (in tunnel): 18·6 km
Number of lines: 3
Number of stations: 40
  (in tunnel): 21
Rail weight and type: Flat-bottomed S48-U, 48·33 kg/m; S49, 49 kg/m
Track type: Timber sleeper on ballast bed and soundproofed superstructure with synthetic sleeper
Max gradient: 4%
Minimum curve radius: 100 m
Tunnel type: Partly single-track ring segment (steel) tunnel, covered construction; partly double-track, reinforced concrete, rectangular section in cut-and-cover construction.
Electrification type: 750 V dc, third rail
Signalling: Continuous automatic train running control, supplied by Siemens, with centralised control

Rolling stock
Number of cars: 136 Type U with 4 × 200 kW motors; 9 Type U11 of 1986 with 8 × 120 kW motors; 5 Type U1 of 1986 with 8 × 125kW motors.
Main supplier: Simmering-Graz-Pauker
Car dimensions: Two-car sets, length 36·8 m, width 2·8 m, height 3·5 m
Tare weight: Type U, 52·6 tonnes; Type U11, 56 tonnes; Type U1, 58 tonnes

Traffic
Train headways: Peak hours, 3 minutes; off-peak, 7.5 minutes
Passenger journeys: (1989) 199·6 million

System development
Vienna's tramway system is the most extensive and the largest of Vienna's carriers, with 196 km of route. As part of the declared policy to separate public transport from other traffic, some central tram routes are being diverted underground and converted into a U-Bahn.
Line U1, extended in 1982, now begins at the elevated Zentrum Kagran station, in the heart of a commercial complex on the Danube's east bank, and runs approximately 10 km via Praterstern southward, under the city centre and via Favoritenstrasse to Reumannplatz, just beyond the Gürtel (outer ring road). Tunnel construction was partly cut-and-cover, partly shield-driven. Line U4 runs from Heiligenstadt to Hütteldorf in the west. Line U2 is an inner city ring route. Line U3, a cross-city line, interchanging with the existing three routes, will run from Erdberg in the east to Ottakring in the west.
Line U3's extension from Erdberg to Volkstheater (4·9 km) was expected to open in 1991. Its next 3·5 km will open in 1993/94, and the final section to Ottakring in 1996. Construction works for Line U6 started in 1983 over 14·8 km from Siebenhirten to Heiligenstadt and should be complete in 1995. The 9·3 km of U6 from Philadelphiabrücke to Heiligenstadt with 14 stations was inaugurated October 1989, as this was an upgrading of an existing tram route. Further extension to Neue Donau should be completed in 1995, and further projection to Florisdorf in 1996-97.
Vienna is also served by a surface rapid transit railway, the Austrian Federal Railway's Schnellbahn. A common fare tariff applies to the Vienna region's public transport systems.

Type of system: Light rail (Stadtbahn)

Gauge: 1435 mm
Route length: 10·6 km
  (in tunnel): 3·6km
  (elevated): 7·4 km
Number of lines: 1
Number of stations: 14
  (in tunnel): 2
  (elevated): 12
Electrification type: 750 V dc, overhead
Signalling: Magnetic train control

Rolling stock
Number of cars: 45 Type E6 motored cars and 39 trailers. The E6, built by Bombardier in 1976, has two 190 kW motors
Main supplier: Bombardier/Rotax
Motor output: 2 × 190 kW
Tare weight: Train (3-car set), 75·4 tonnes; motor car, 28 tonnes

Traffic
Train headways: Peak hours, 5 minutes; off-peak, 10 minutes
Passenger journeys: (1989) 28·7 million

System development
The line is now designated part of U6 in the metro scheme, though still operated by LRVs. In 1989 it was extended 2.1km to Philadelphiabrücke. A six-axle articulated low-floor LRV is to be developed for this line by Bombardier-Rotax; four prototypes will be produced by 1994 as a preface to a production order for 64 vehicles.

Warsaw

Generalria Dyrekcja Metra w Warszawie

ul Marszalkowska 77/79, 00-683 Warsaw, Poland

Telephone: +48 22 21 49 84
Telex: 816109 gdpm pl

Director: J Brzostek

Type of system: Full metro under construction

Gauge: 1435 mm
Route length: 90 km
Number of lines: 4
Number of stations: 90
Average distance between stations: Central area, 600–700 m; suburbs, 1300 m
Max gradient: 3·1%
Minimum curve radius: 300 m
Electrification type: 825 V dc, third rail

Traffic
Train headways: 1½ minutes (2½ minutes initially)
Capacity: 40 000 passengers/h

System development
Work commenced in August 1983 on construction of a planned 4-line, 105 km metro system. Considerable Soviet aid was then made available for the project.
The first section of the new system will be 12 km of Line 1 with 11 stations, and should be finished in 1992, but financial constraints may defer inauguration to 1993. Line 1 will eventually extend for 23·1 km, with a total of 23 stations, entirely in tunnel, running from north to south through the city centre and should be fully open by 1996. All tunnels will be about 4 m below ground level. The system will be operated with six-car train-sets built in the USSR, the first 10 of which were being delivered in 1990.

Washington

Washington Metropolitan Area Transit Authority

600 Fifth Street NW, Washington DC 20001, USA

Telephone: +1 202 962 1234
Telefax: +1 202 962 1133

General Manager: Carmen E Turner

Type of system: Full metro

Gauge: 1435 mm
Route length: 112 km
  (in tunnel): 52·8 km
  (at surface level): 49·2 km
  (elevated): 10·4 km
Number of lines: 4 (Red, Orange, Blue, Yellow)
Number of stations: 64
  (in tunnel): 38
  (elevated): 4
Average distance between stations: 1·0 km
Rail type: 51·16 kg/m solid steel
Max gradient: 4%
Minimum curve radius: 213 m
Electrification type: 750 V dc, third rail
One-man operation: All trains
Signalling: Wayside and cab signals, installed by GRS
Automatic control: Although each train carries an operator, the train is actually operated by an automatic train control (ATC) system. The operator makes station announcements, closes doors and monitors passenger activity. The ATC system is made up of three subsystems: automatic train supervision (ATS), automatic train operation (ATO), and automatic train protection (ATP). The ATS system takes information from one of two digital computers and, under orders to

operate an on-time high-performance rail network, can 'advise' Metro trains of speeds, spacing intervals, dwell times in stations and other performance requirements. The ATO converts signals from the ATS into operating instructions to trains. Before these directions are relayed, the ATP system comes into play as a safeguard. It can stop trains or set safe speed limits and other restrictions on train operations, no matter what the ATS demands, to assure on-time performance, functioning as a watchful eye over activities of ATO to protect passengers and equipment. A variety of fail-safe features has been designed into the ATC system to ensure that operating instructions are not misinterpreted, false signals are not transmitted, actual signals do not go astray, and any malfunctioning of components results in a safer, rather than more dangerous, situation. The fail-safe principle will cause a train to slow down and stop rather than run away in the event of a part failure.

Trains are monitored from a central control room in the operations headquarters building in Washington. Six consoles with colour cathode-ray tubes show the train system in colour code, the position and identity of each train, and other aspects of the operating system. The communication system enables Central Control to speak to train operators and stations individually or collectively. Communications with trains underground is by 'leaky line' antenna. Operators in the control room can call up and magnify on the CRTS special sections of the system at will.

Rolling stock
Number of cars: 664 (operated in married pairs), all motored
Average and crush capacities: Seated 80; average standing 95; crush standing 140
Tare weight: 80 000lb
Car dimensions: Length 22·8 m, width 3·09 m, height 3·3 m
Doors: Three automatic double doors per side 1930 × 1282 mm
Main supplier: Rohr Industries, Breda (Italy). The Breda batch of 366 cars, delivered from 1983 onwards, have per-car seating reduced by 12, improved air-conditioning and braking, and other detail changes.
Cars on order: 68 cars from Breda for 1991-92 delivery with an option for 32 more

Traffic
Train headways: Peak hours: Red Line 3 minutes; Blue 6 minutes; Orange 6 minutes; Yellow 6 minutes. Off-peak: Red 7 minutes; Orange/Blue/Yellow 12 minutes
Passenger journeys: (1989) 144 million

System development
Federal funding limitations now restrict eventual network size to 144 km, which should be attained by 1994. WMATA remains committed to the originally planned aggregate of 165 km with 87 stations.

Five more extensions are planned for the 1990–93 period. On the Green Line, a section from Gallery Place to U Street-Howard University station in the central district of Columbia was to open in 1990, and a section southeast under the Anacostia River to Anacostia was to open in 1991. Construction from Fort Totten to Greenbelt is under way in north Prince George's County and this segment is to open in 1993. On the Red Line, a segment from Silver Spring to Wheaton was to open in September 1990, and a Yellow Line segment from King Street to Van Dorn Street in 1991.

Wuppertal

Wuppertal Stadtwerke AG

Bromberger Str 39-41, 5600 Wuppertal 2, Federal Republic of Germany

Telephone: +49 202 5691
Telex: 8591 788 wsw d
Telefax: +49 202 511693

General Manager: Dr-Ing Kurt Sunkel
Operating Manager: Dieter Sack

Type of system: Suspended monorail

Route length: 13·3 km
Number of lines: 1
Number of stations: 19
Average distance between stations: 739 m
Gradient (max): 4%
Minimum curve radius: 75 m
Speed (design max): 60 km/h
(average commercial): 26·6 km/h
Electrification type: 600 V dc

Rolling stock
Number of units: 28 articulated units
Car dimensions: Length 24·05 m, width 2·2 m, height 2·5 m
Doors per side: 4
Door width: 1·3 m
Number of passengers per car (total): 204
(seated): 48
Motors per car: 4
Acceleration (max): 1·1 m/s^2
Deceleration (normal service): 0·8 m/s^2
(emergency): 1·2 m/s^2
Bogies: Aluminium, MAN
Brakes: E1 Disc
Weight (empty): 22·175 tonnes

Traffic
Max number of trains per hour (one way): 21
Train headways: 3 minutes
Passenger journeys: (1989) 15·99 million

Yokohama

Yokohama Municipal Transportation Bureau (Yokohama-shi Kotsu Kyoku)

1-1 Minatocho, Naka-ku, 231 Yokohama, Japan

Telephone: +81 45 671 3201
Telex: 045 641 6700

Type of system: Full metro

Gauge: 1435 mm
Route length: 22·1 km (all in tunnel)
Number of lines: 2
Number of stations: 20
Speed (design max): 90 km/h
Electrification type: 750 V dc, third rail
Signalling: ATC with cab signalling and central traffic control

Rolling stock
Units: 138 in six-car sets
Car dimensions: Length 18 m, width 2·78 m, height 3·54 m
Doors per side: 3
Door width: 1·3 m
Passengers per car
(total): 145
(seated): 52
Motors per car: 4
Motor rating: 140 kW, 165 bhp

Traffic
Train headways: Peak hours, 5 minutes; off-peak, 8 minutes
Passenger journeys: (1988) 87 million

System development
The rapid transit project calls for the construction of four lines with a total length of 67·8 km. Priority was given to the important rapid transit routes 1 and 3 passing through the city's central area. A 10·9 km extension of Line 3 from Shin-Yokohama to the new town of Kohuku and to Azamino is in progress.

The network will consist of sub-surface lines in box-type tunnel under urban Yokohama, rising to elevated tracks in the suburbs.

In 1990 the Transport Ministry proposed construction of an 8km deep-level metro line, the Sagami Railway, from central Yokohama west to Futamatagawa.

INDEX

A

Aabacas Engineering Co Ltd	402
AB	730
ABB	4, 78, 152, 176, 216, 282, 339, 388
ABB Ageve	8, 232
ABB British Wheelset	293
ABB Scandia A/S	59, 79, 134
ABB Traction AB	79
ABC	152, 266, 282, 348
Aberdeen & Rockfish Railroad Co	789
Abetong-Sabema	348
ABEX Corporation	266, 388
Abidjan	815
ABRF-Atalier Bréton de Réparation Ferroviarie	232
Abtus Co	348
Accent Marketing and Research	462
ACEC	8, 79, 152, 176, 216, 330, 338, 388
ACER Consultants Ltd	430
ACET Ltd	430
ACF Industries, Inc	232
Adams & Westlake Co	216
Adelaide	815
Aebi	8
AEG Westinghouse	8, 80, 177, 216, 330, 338, 388, 402
Afghanistan	464
AFE	805
AFNE	9, 232
AFR Arbel-Fauvet-Rail Co	9, 232
Air Industrie-Faiveley	216
A & K Railroad Materials Inc	348
ACPF	423
AFEDEF	423
AKZO	348
AL	80
Alabama & Florida Railroad	790
Alaska Railroad, The	789
Albania	464
Albanian Railways (HRPSSL)	464
Albtal Railway (AVG)	586
Alcan Canada Products	192, 233
Alco Power Inc	152
Aldon Co	348, 388
Alexander & Co Ltd, Walter	80
Alexandria	815
Algeco SA	410
Algeria	464
Algerian National Railways (SNTF)	464
Algiers	815
Algoma Central Railway	520
Algoma Steel Corporation	348
Alice Springs-Darwin Railway	472
Aliquippa & Southern Railroad Co	790
ALK Associates Inc	430
Allegheny Rail Products	350
Allegheny Railroad Co	790
Allen Cranes (Northampton) Ltd	388
Allied Insulators	338
Allis Chalmers	388
Alma Ata	815
Almex Control Systems	330
Alna Koki Co	80, 192, 217, 233
Altai Wagon Works	233
Alton & Southern Railway Co	790
Altona-Kaltenkirchen-Neumünster Railway	586
Aluminothermique, L'	350
Alusuisse – Lonza Services Ltd	80, 192
Alzmetall	402
Amatek	351
American Association of Railroad Superintendents	426
American Koyo Corporation	296
American Public Transit Association (APTA)	426
American Railroad Curvelining Corporation	351
American Railroad Truck Lines Association	426
American Railway Car Institute	426
American Railway Development Association	426
American Railway Engineering Association	426
American Refrigerator Transit Co	414
American Short Line Railroad Association	426
American Society of Mechanical Engineers Rail Transportation Division	426
American Transit Corporation	430
Ametek	302
Amherst Industries	233
Amman & Whitney	430
Ammendorf, VEB Waggonbau	192
Ampcontrol	338
Amsted	266
Amsterdam	815
Amtech Corporation	302
Amtrack	767
Anbel, The Anbel Group	9, 233, 414
ANF-Industrie	82, 193
Angola	467
Ankara	815
Ansaldo Trasporti	83, 180, 302, 338, 389, 430
ANT	324
Antenna Specialists Co	302
Antofagasta (Chile) & Bolivia Railway plc (FCAB)	539
Antwerp	815
Apache Railway Co	790
Apalachicola Northern Railroad Co	790
Appenzell Railway	730
Aqaba Railway Corporation (ARC)	657
Arab Union of Railways (UACF)	422
Arad Car & Passenger Coach Bogies	193, 233, 283
ARC	658
Arezzo Railways	628
Argentina	468
Argentine Railways (FA)	468
Argentinian Chamber of Railway Industries	424
Arinc Research Corporation	431
Arkansas & Louisiana Missouri Railway Co	791
Arkansas & Missouri Railway Co	791
Armita	410
Arneke	351
Artimsa SAIC	351
AS & I	324
Ascom Radiocom	302
ASEA Brown Boveri (see ABB)	
ASEA Brown Boveri-Sécheron	339
ASF	266, 283
Ashley, Drew & Northern Railway Co	791
Association of American Railroad	426
Association of Consulting Engineers	425
Association of European Railway Component Manufacturers (AFEDEF)	423
Association of Independent Railways	425
Association of Private Railway Wagon Owners	425
Association of Railroad Advertising and Marketing	426
Association of Railway Communicators	426
Association of Wagon Builders and Repairers	425
Astarsa	9
Aston Martin Tickford Ltd	431
ATEINSA	9, 84, 193
Athens	816
Atkins, W S & Partners	431
Atlanta	816
Atlanta & St Andrews Bay Railway Co	791
Atlantic Track & Turnout Co	351
Atlas Copco (Great Britain) Ltd	266, 351
Atlas Hydraulic Loaders Ltd	351
Atlos Weyhausen GmbH	352
Auckland	816
'August 23' Works	10, 84, 153
Ausilaire	410
Austin & North Western Railroad	791
Australia	469
Australia, Railways of, Committee	424
Australia National Committee on Railway Engineering	424
Australian National Railways	469
Australia, Railtrack Association of	424
Austria	490
Austrian Federal Railways (ÖBB)	490
Austrian Federation of Cable Railways	424
Austrian Federation of Private Railways	424
Automatic Systems Ltd	330
Avon Industrial Polymers Ltd	266, 283
AWS	296
Aydin	303

B

Babcock & Wilcox Española	10, 84, 194, 233, 389
Badische Waggonfabrik	233
Badoni, Antonio	10
Baghdad	816
Baker, Michael Jr Inc	431
Baku	816
Balfour Beatty Power Construction Ltd	340, 352
Baltimore	817
Baltimore & Pittsburgh Railroad	791
Bance R & Co	352
Bandegua Railways	593
Bangkok	817
Bangladesh	498
Bangladesh Railway	498
Bangor & Aroostook Railroad Co	791
Banks & Associates Inc, R L	431
Barcelona	817
Barclay, Andrew	11
Barclay Brothers	340
Bari-Nord Railway	628
Barton-Aschman Associates Inc	431
Basque Railways (FV/ET)	713
Batiruhr	11
Bautista Buriasco Ltd	233
Bautzen, VEB Waggonbau	194
Bay Colony Railroad Corporation	791
Bayham Ltd	217
BBC Sécheron	181, 266, 283
BBN Laboratories Inc	431
BBR	352
BBW	266
BDZ	517
BC Rail (Canada)	520
Beall Manufacturing Co	283
Bechtel Civil Inc	432
Beclawat/Bode	217
Beijing	11, 153, 817
Beilhack GmbH, Martin	353
Belfast and Moosehead Lake Railroad	792
Belgium	499
Belo Horizonte	818
Belt Railway Company of Chicago	792
Belz, August Apparatebau GmbH	217
BEML	195
Benevento-Naples Railway	628
Benin	505
Bentheim Railway	586
Berema	353
Berlin (East)	818
Berlin (West)	818
Berne-Lötschberg-Simplon Railway (BLS)	728
Bernese Oberland Railways (BOB)	731
Berne-Worb Railways (VBW)	739
Bessemer & Lake Erie Railroad Co	792
Bethlehem Steel Corporation	233, 353
Betran Hnos	233
BG Checo International Ltd	303, 324
Bharat Brakes & Valves Ltd	266
Bharat Heavy Electricals (BHEL)	12, 181
Bharat Wagon & Engineering	233
BHP Rail Products	353
BHP Long Products Division	353
BIC	422
BICC Ltd	340
Bilbao	819
Birmingham	819
Birmingham Southern Railroad Co	792
BJLJ Engineers	432
Black Mesa and Lake Powell Railroad	792
Blatchford & Co, Ralph	233
Blauvelt Engineering Co	432
BLS	728
BN Constructions Ferroviaires et Métalliques	12, 85, 195, 234
BOB	731
Bochum	819
Bodensee-Toggenburg Railway (BT)	731
Bogota	819
Bolivia	506
Bolivian National Railways	506
Bologna	819
Bomag GmbH	354
Bombardier Inc	86, 195
Bombardier-Rotax-Wien	89
Bong Mining Co	663
Booz, Allen & Hamilton Inc	432
Bordeaux	819
Boston	819
Boston & Maine Corporation	770
Botswana	507
Botswana Railways (BR)	507
Boulonnerie de Thiant	354
BP-Battioni & Pagani	234, 389
BP Solar International	303
Bradken Consolidated Ltd	266, 283
Braine-le-Compte SA	283
Braithwaite & Co	235
Bratislava	820

INDEX / B–D

Bratstvo 235
Brazil 508
BR 507
BRB 498
BREC 235
Brecknell, Willis & Co 183, 340
Breda Costruzioni Ferroviarie SpA 13, 87, 196
BREL, British Rail Engineering Ltd 13, 88, 196, 284
Bremer Waggonbau GmbH 196, 236
Brenco Inc 296
Brescia 820
Brescia North Railway 628
Brest 820
Brig-Visp-Zermatt Railway (BVZ) 732
Briggs & Turivas Inc 236
Bristol 820
Bristol Pneumatic Ltd 183
British Rail 758
British Steel Track Products 354
Broken Hill 341
Brookville 14
Brose, Carl 324
Brown & Root Vickers 402
Bruckner & Thomas GBR 355
Bruff 355
Brush Electrical Machines Ltd 14, 153, 183
Brussels 820
BSI 153, 182, 267
BT 731
BTR Ltd 355
BTR Permali RP Ltd 356
BTS 324
Bucharest 820
Buckeye Steel Castings 267, 284
Budapest 820
Budavox 303
Buenos Aires 821
Buffalo 821
Buffalo Brake Beam Co 267
Buhlmann SA 267, 356
Bulgaria 517
Bulgarian State Railways (BDZ) 517
Bumar-Fablok 14
Burkina Faso 518
Burkino Faso Railway 518
Burle Industries 303
Burlington Northern (BN) 770
Burma (Myanmar) 518
Burma Railways Corporation (BRC) 518
Burn Standard Co 236
Burro Crane Inc 356
Butzbacher 356
BVC-Berliner Verkehrs-Consulting GmbH 431
BVZ 732
BWR 236
Bylin 356

C

Cadoux, International 236
CAF 15, 90, 196, 237
CAIB 410
Caillard Levage 389
Cairo 820
Calabria-Lucana Railways 629
Calcutta 822
Calgary 822
California Department of Transportation (Caltrans) 800
California-Nevada Superspeed Ground Transportation Commission 770
California Western Railroad 792
Callegari, José 237
CAM Industries Inc 403
CAM International Inc 433
Camas Prairie Railroad Co 792
Cambodia Railways 658
Cambria & Indiana Railroad Co 792
Cambridge 822
Cameroon 520
Caminho de Ferro do Amboim 467
Caminho de Ferro de Benguela 467
Caminhose de Ferro de Angola 467
Camp-Alcatel 330
CANAC International Inc 433
Canada 520
Canada - National Transportation Agency of 424
Canada, Railway Association of 424
Canadian Institute of Guided Transport 424
Canadian Pacific Consulting Services Ltd 433
Canadian Railway & Transit Manufacturers Association 424
Canadian Urban Transit Association 424
Canton Motive Power Machinery Works 15
Caracas 822
Cardwell Westinghouse Co 268
Carr Smith Associates 433
Carrier Khéops Bac 217
Cartier Railway 531
Cartner Display Systems 324
Casablanca 822
Casaire 408
Casaralta SpA 15, 92, 197, 237
CAT 237
Catalanes Railways (FGC) 710
Caterpillar Co 153
Cattaneo SA 237
CBTU 512
CCC 197, 237
Cedar Rapids & Iowa City Railway Co 792
Cedar Valley Railroad Co 792
CEFF 237
Cegielski Locomotive and Wagon Works 16, 92, 197
Cemafer Gleisbaumaschinen und Gerate GmbH 356
CENEMESA 183
Central Engineering 217
Central Japan Railway Co (JR-Tokai) 641
Central Manufacturing 389
Central Montana Rail Inc 792
Central Railway (ENAFER) 659
Central Railway (IR) 602
Central Vermont Railway 792
Centro-Maskin 356
Centurion Industries 237
Century Engineering Inc 433
CERCI 324
CFC 197, 237
CFD 16, 92
CFF 356
CF&I Steel 356
CFL 664
CFM 674
CFR 698
CFS 740
CGE 183, 341
CGTX Inc 414
Changchow Diesel Locomotive Factory 16
Changchun Railway Passenger Car Works 92, 197
Charleroi 822
Chartered Institute of Transport 425
Chelyabinsk 823
Chemetron Railway Products Inc 356
Chemico 390
Chemin de Fer de la Guinée (ONCFG) 593
Chemins de Fer de l'Etat Libanais (CEL) 662
Chemins de Fer du Hedjaz 740
Chemins de Fer du Mali (RCFM) 669
Chemins de Fer Syriens (CFS) 740
Chiang An Rolling Stock Plant 237
Chicago 823
Chicago Central & Pacific Railroad Co 792
Chicago Freight Car Leasing Co 414
Chicago & Illinois Midland Railway Co 793
Chicago & North Western Transportation Co 773
Chicago Rail Link 793
Chicago, South Shore & South Bend Railroad (Electric) 793
Chichibu Railway 649
Chile 536
Chilean State Railways (EFE) 536
China National Railway Locomotive & Rolling Stock Industry Corporation 16, 93, 197, 237
China Railway Signal & Communication Co 303
Chiriqui Land Company Railways 688
Chiriqui National Railroad 688
Chrysler Electronics 303
Cimmco International 217, 237, 268, 284, 356, 403
Circumvesuviana Railway 629
CIT 422
CIWLT 418
ČKD Praha 17
Cleveland 823
Clough Harbour & Associates 433
Clouth Gummiwerke AG 356
CLW 17
Clyde Engineering Co 18, 183, 390
CMI 19, 154
CNCFSA 237
CN Rail 523
Coborail-Extrapo 356
Coalition of Northeastern Governors (CONEG) Task Force on High Speed Rail 770
Coast Engineering and Manufacturing Co 389
Cobra Railroad Friction Products Corporation 268, 356
Cobrasma SA 93, 197, 237, 268, 357
Cobreq 268
Cockerill Forges & Ringmill 284
COGIFER 357
Colebrand Ltd 357
Cole, Sherman & Associates Ltd 433
Collins Associates Inc, Terence J 434
Cologne 823
Cologne-Bonn Railways 587
Cologne-Frechen-Benzelraeth Railway 587
Colorado & Wyoming Railway Co 793
Colston, Budd, Wardrop & Hunt 434
Columbus & Greenville Railway Co 793
Comeng 19, 93, 197, 238, 268
Comet Industries Inc 296
Cometal-Mometal SARL 238
Cometarsa SAIC 20, 238
Community of European Railways 423
Compagnie Générale d'Automatisme 330
Companhia Brasileira de Trans Urbanos (CBTU) 512
Companhia Vale de Rio Doce (CVRD) 516
Comsal LTDA 238
Comsteel 268, 284
Comsul Ltd 434
Conbrako (Pty) Ltd 217, 268, 357
Concarril 95, 238
CONEG 770
Congo 626
Connecticut Department of Transportation 799
Conrail 774
Contransimex 341
Convoy-Contigas BV 410
Cooper & Turner 357
Coopers & Lybrand Associates 434
Corinth & Counce Railroad Co 793
Costain Concrete Co 357
Costamasnaga SpA 197, 238
Couplomatic 268
CP Rail 528
Cowans Boyd NEI Ltd 358, 390
CP 695
Cragg Railcharger 303
Craswell Scientific 303
Crocker, Trevor & Partners 461
Crouzet SA 331
Crown Agents for Oversea Governments and Administrations (UK) 425
Croydon 823
CSEE 303
CSX Transportation Inc 776
Cuba 545
Cuban National Railways (FdeC) 545
Cubic Western Data 331
Cummins Engine Co 155
CVRD 516
CXT 358
Czechoslovakia 547
Czechoslovak State Railways (ČSD) 547
Czechoslovak Wagon Works 95, 198, 239

D

Daewoo Heavy Industries Ltd 20, 96, 198, 239
Daido Steel Co Ltd 358
Dakota Minnesota & Eastern Railroad Corporation 793
Dakota Rail Inc 793
Dalian Locomotive and Rolling Stock Works 21, 155, 239
Dallas 823
D&I Railroad Co 793
Daniel, Mann, Johnson & Mendenhall 434
Danish State Railways (DSB) 549
DanRail Consult 434
Datarail 435
Datong Locomotive Works 21
David Brown Corp 156
Davies & Metcalfe Ltd 268
Davis Ltd, W H 240
Dawson-Aquamatic 390
Deans Powered Doors 217
Dearmedelec SAIC 183
DEConsult 435
De Dietrich & Cie 97, 198, 285, 391
Dehé et Cie 358
Delachaux SA, C 358
Delaware Car Co 217
Delaware & Hudson Railway Co 778
Delcan Corporation 435

D–G / INDEX 857

De Leuw, Cather & Company (DCCO) ... 435
Delhi ... 824
Dellner-Malmco ... 269
Delon Hampton & Associates ... 442
Delta Crompton Cables Ltd ... 341
Denmark ... 549
Denmark Institution of Railway Signal Engineers ... 424
Denver ... 824
Denver & Rio Grande Western Railroad Co ... 778
Design Triangle ... 436
Desquenne et Giral ... 358
Dessau, VEB Waggonbau ... 240
Detroit ... 824
Detroit Diesel Corp ... 156
Detroit & Mackinac Railway ... 793
Deuta-Werke GmbH ... 304
Deutz, MWM ... 156
D'Huart & Cie ... 359
Dickertmann Hebezeugfabrik AG ... 391, 403
Diema GmbH ... 21
Difco Inc ... 240
Dimetal SA ... 199, 269
Dimetronic SA ... 304
Diversey Wyandotte ... 391
Dixie Precast ... 304
DKS Associates ... 437
DLW ... 22
Dnepropetrovsk ... 824
Dobbie and Partners, C H ... 437
Domange-Jarrett ... 269, 391
Dominican Government Railway ... 554
Dominican Republic ... 554
Donelli SpA ... 359
Dorsey Trailers ... 241
Dortmund ... 824
Dortmund Railway ... 587
Dow Mac Concrete ... 359
Dowty RFL Industries ... 304
Dowty Electronics ... 324
Drallim Telecommunications Ltd ... 304
DSG ... 418
DSI ... 305
DSL ... 305
DSVN ... 805
Dubin, Dubin, and Moutoussamy ... 437
Duewag Aktiengesellschaft ... 98
Duisburg ... 824
Duluth, Missabe & Iron Range Railway Co ... 793
Durbin-Durco Inc ... 391
Duro Daković Industries ... 23, 100, 199
Düsseldorf ... 824
Dyer Inc, Thomas K ... 437
Dynatrend Inc ... 437

E

East Hanover Railway ... 587
East Japan Railway Co (JR-East) ... 633
Eastern Railway (IR) ... 604
Eastern Shore Railroad ... 794
EB Signal ... 305, 392
EBT ... 733
Ecuador ... 554
Edgar Allen Engineering Ltd ... 359
Edinburgh ... 824
Edmonton ... 825
Edwards and Kelcey ... 437
EFE (Chile) ... 536
EFE North America ... 269
EFE North America Inc ... 184, 341
EFF ... 217
EVFM ... 516
Egypt ... 555
Egyptian Railways (ER) ... 555
EKA ... 392
EKE Group ... 218
Elbe-Weser Railway ... 587
Electric Rails Ltd ... 341
Electrologic ... 360
Electronique Serge Dassault ... 331
Electroputere ... 23
Elektrim ... 306, 341
Elektro-Mechanik GmbH (EMG) ... 157
Electrowatt Engineering Services Ltd ... 438
Elektro-Thermit GmbH ... 360
Elgeba Gerätebau GmbH ... 331
Elgin, Joliet & Eastern Railway ... 793
Elin Energieanwendung ... 24
Ellcon-National Inc ... 218, 269
Elrail Consultants Pty Ltd ... 438
El Salvador ... 556
El Salvador National Railways (FENADESAL) ... 556
Emaq ... 24
EMJ Engineers Inc ... 438
Emmental-Burgdorf-Thun Railway (EBT) ... 733
Empire Corridor ... 770
Empresa Minera del Centro del Peru ... 690
Empresa Nacional de Ferrocarriles (ENFE, Bolivia) ... 555
Emu Bay Railway Co Ltd, The ... 482
EMX International Ltd ... 306
ENAFER-Peru ... 689
Energomachexport, VO 24, 100, 172, k241, 270, 285, 360
Engesa-FNV ... 100, 199, 241
Envirodyne Engineers, Inc ... 439
Equip Rail ... 218
Ercole Marelli Trazrone (EMT) ... 341
Erevan ... 825
Erico Products Inc ... 306
ESAB AB ... 360
Escanaba & Lake Superior Railroad ... 794
Essen ... 825
Ethiopia ... 557
ETRA ... 410
Eureka Southern Railroad Co Inc ... 794
European Company for the Financing of Railroad Rolling Stock (EUROFIMA) ... 423
European Conference of Ministers of Transport (ECMT) ... 423
European Diesel and Electric Locomotive Manufacturers' Association (CELTE) ... 423
European Freight Timetable Conference ... 423
European Passenger Timetable and Conference ... 423
European Wagon Pool (Europ Agreement) ... 423
Eurosystems Datacol ... 328
Euro-Trac Ltd ... 360
Eurotunnel ... 423
EVA ... 410
EVAC AB ... 218
Evershed & Vignoles ... 324
Ewbank Preece Consulting Group ... 439
EWEM BV ... 360
EXIM ... 360

F

Fabrika Vagona Kraljevo ... 270
FAGA ... 218
FAG Bearings Corporation ... 296
FAG Kugelfischer Georg Schäfer & Co ... 296
Fairfield-Mabey Ltd ... 360
Fairhurst & Partners, W A ... 439
Faiveley SA ... 184, 218
Famatex SRL ... 361
FAO ... 361
Farmrail ... 794
FCAB ... 539
Federal Railroad Administration ... 765
Federation of Civil Engineering Contractors ... 425
FEGUA ... 593
Fenadesal ... 555
FEPASA ... 514
Fergusson Co, Alex C ... 392
Ferotrack Engineering ... 361
Ferranti International ... 307
Ferraz SA ... 184, 219, 285, 341
Ferrocarril de Panama ... 688
Ferrocarril Nacional de Chiriqui ... 689
Ferrocarril Presidente Carlos Antonio Lopez ... 688
Ferrocarriles Nacionales de Mexico (FN de M) ... 670
Ferrostaal AG ... 25, 100, 199, 242, 285, 361
Ferrosud SpA ... 25, 100, 199, 242
Ferrovia Paulista SA (FEPASA) ... 514
Ferrovias y Siderurgia SA ... 361
Fert & Cie ... 410
FEVE ... 711
FGC ... 710
FGE, Fruit Growers Express Co ... 414
FGV ... 714
Fiat-Concord SAIC ... 157
Fiat Ferroviaria SpA 25, 100, 157, 199, 242, 285
Field & Grant Ltd ... 307
Findlay, Irvine Ltd ... 361
Finland ... 557
Finnish State Railways (VR) ... 557
Finsam A/S ... 242
Firema Consortium ... 25, 102, 200, 243
Fischer Industries ... 307
FKI Godwin Warren ... 392
Fleming Corp ... 439
Florence ... 825
Florida Department of Transportation (FDOT) ... 800
Florida East Coast Railway Co ... 778
Florida High Speed, Rail Passenger Commission ... 770
Fluor Daniel Australia Limited ... 439
FM Industries ... 270
FNdeM ... 670
FNH ... 594
FNME ... 629
FO ... 734
Fordyce & Princeton Railroad Co ... 794
Forges de Fresnes ... 270
Forja Argentina SA ... 285
Foss Manufacturing Co Inc ... 362
Foster Co, L B ... 362
Foster Engineering Inc ... 439
Fox River Valley Railroad ... 794
FRAMAFER ... 362
France ... 561
Frankfurt am Main ... 825
French National Railways (SNCF) ... 560
French Railway Industries Association ... 424
Freños Calefaccion y Señales ... 270
Fresinbra Industrial SA ... 219, 270, 307
Frichs A/S ... 26, 103
FS ... 619
Fuji Car Manufacturing Co ... 103, 200, 243
Fuji Electric ... 157, 184, 341
Fuji Heavy Industries Ltd ... 104, 200
Fukuoka ... 826
Furka-Oberalp Railway (FO) ... 734
Furrer & Frey ... 341
Futurit Werk AG ... 307
FV/ET ... 713
FWZ, VEB Federwerk Zittau ... 286

G

Gabon ... 574
Gabon State Railways (OCTRA) ... 574
Gallinari SpA ... 200
Gannett Fleming ... 439
Ganz Electric Works ... 26, 104, 185, 307, 341
Ganz Hunslet ... 26, 200
Ganz Machinery Works ... 157
Ganz Máveg Locomotive & Railway Carriage Works ... 27, 105, 286
Gardner & Sons Ltd ... 158
Gateway Western Railway ... 794
GATX ... 414
GCE Gas Control Equipment AB ... 362
GC-Hydraulik A/S ... 403
GEC Alsthom 30, 106, 159, 179, 201, 286, 308, 324, 341, 392
GEC Alsthom Australia Ltd ... 33, 308
GEC Diesels ... 159
GEC General Signal ... 308
GEC Plessey Telecommunications Ltd ... 309
GEC Transmission and Distribution Projects Ltd ... 185, 220
GEC Alsthom Transportation Projects Ltd ... 440
Geismar, SA ... 342, 362
Gellman Research Associates Inc ... 440
Gemco Ltd ... 363
General Electric Co (GE) ... 27, 158, 342
General Electric do Brasil SA ... 33
General Electric Canada ... 33
General Electric Railcar Services Corp ... 415
General Motors, Argentina ... 36
General Motors Electromotive Division ... 34, 160
General Motors of Canada ... 36
General Railway Signal Co ... 309, 392
General Standard ... 296
Genesee & Wyoming Railroad Co ... 794
GenFare International ... 332
Genoa ... 826
German Federal Railway (DB) ... 577
German Rail Service Co (DSG) ... 418
German State Railway (DR) ... 575
Germany, Democratic Republic ... 575
Germany, Federal Republic ... 577
Germany, Federal Republic
Locomotive Industry Ass ... 424
Private Railways Ass of ... 424
Railway Rolling Stock Industry Ass ... 424
Rolled Steel Ass Permanent Way Group ... 424
Switch & Crossing Manufacturers Ass ... 424
Getzner Chemie GmbH ... 363
GEZ ... 220
Ghana ... 590
Ghana Railway Corporation (GRC) ... 590
GIA Industrie AB ... 364

INDEX / G–K

Gibb, Sir Alexander, & Partners ... 440
Gibbs & Hill Inc ... 440
Girling, Lucas Ltd ... 270
Glasgow ... 826
Gleismac Italiana SpA ... 37, 109
Gloster Southern Railroad Co ... 794
GMD ... 160
GMT ... 161
GNB Inc ... 309
GO Transit ... 531
Godwin Warren Engineering Inc ... 392
Goias ... 826
Goldsworthy Railway ... 488
Goninan & Co ... 37, 201, 243
Gorki ... 826
Görlitz, VEB Waggonbau ... 201, 286, 342
GOŠA, SOUR Industria ... 202, 243
Gotha, Getriebewerk ... 161
Gothenburg ... 826
Gottwald GmbH ... 364
Graaff Kommanditgesellschaft ... 243
Graham-White Manufacturing ... 270
Grainbelt Corp ... 794
Grand Trunk Corporation (GTC) ... 779
Grant Lyon Eagre Ltd ... 364
Graviner Ltd ... 220
Graz-Köflacher Railway ... 497
Great Western Railway Co ... 794
Greece ... 591
Green Bay & Western Railroad Co ... 794
Green Mountain Railroad Corp ... 794
Greenville Steel Car Co ... 243
Gregg Company Ltd ... 243
Greiner Engineering Inc ... 441
Grenoble ... 826
Gresham & Craven Ltd ... 270
Greysham & Co ... 270, 343
Griffin Wheel Co ... 270, 286
Grinaker Precast (Pty) Ltd ... 364
Groupe Design MBD ... 441
Groupement 50 Hz ... 38, 185, 343
Grove Coles ... 364
GRS ... 309, 392
GSI ... 286
GTG ... 365
Guadalajara ... 826
Guangzhou (Canton) ... 827
Guatamala ... 593
Guatemala Railways (FEGUA) ... 593
Guinea ... 593
Gunderson Inc ... 243
Gutteridge Haskins & Davey Pty Ltd ... 441
Györ-Sopron-Ebenfurt Railway GySEV ... 599

H

Haacon Hebetechnik ... 392
Haifa ... 827
Halais, Georges ... 220
Halcrow, Sir William & Partners Ltd ... 441
Hamburg ... 827
Hamburg-Consult ... 442
Hamersley Iron Ore Railways ... 488
Hankyu Corporation ... 649
Hanning & Kahl ... 309
Hannover ... 827
Harbridge House Inc ... 442
Harris Corporation ... 310
Harris Miller Miller & Hanson Inc ... 442
Harza Engineering Company ... 442
Hasler AG ... 310
Haswell, Charles & Partners (Far East) ... 443
Hauhinco Maschinenfabrik GmbH ... 392
Havana ... 827
Hawker Siddeley Canada Ltd ... 244
Hawker Siddeley Rail Projects Ltd ... 343, 443
HDA Forgings ... 286
HDC ... 365
HDR Engineering Inc ... 443
Hedjaz Jordan Railway (HJR) ... 657
Hegenscheidt, W ... 403
Hellenic Railways Organisation (OSE) ... 591
Helsinki ... 827
Henry Williams Electrical ... 310, 343
Henshall Ltd ... 220
Heredos de Ramon Mugica ... 244
Hersfeld Railway ... 588
Hidromecanica ... 161
High Speed Rail Association ... 426
Hill International Inc ... 444
Hiroshima ... 828
Hitachi Cable Ltd ... 343

Hitachi Ltd ... 39, 161, 185, 221
HJR ... 657
Hoesch Rothe Erde-Schmiedag ... 365
Hoesch Maschinenfabrik ... 393, 404
Hohenzoller Provincial Railway ... 588
Hokkaido Railway Co (JR-Hokkaido) ... 638
Hokuriku Railway ... 649
Holec Machines & Apparaten BV ... 185
Holland Co ... 365
Holmes International ... 393
Honduras ... 594
Honduras National Railway (FNH) ... 594
Hong Kong ... 594, 828
Honolulu ... 828
Houston ... 828
Houston Belt & Terminal Railway Co ... 794
Howden, James & Co ... 245
Howden Sirocco ... 221
Hudson (South Africa) Pty Ltd, Robert ... 39, 245
Hull ... 829
Humes ... 365
Hungary ... 596
Hungarian Railway Carriage ... 39, 202
Hungarian Shipyards & Crane Factory ... 393
Hungarian State Railways (MÁV) ... 596
Hunslet Engine Co ... 39, 365
Hunslet Precision Engineering Ltd ... 161
Hunslet Taylor Consolidated Pty Ltd ... 40
Hunslet TPL ... 202
Hurth, Maschinen-und Zahnrad Fabrik ... 161
HWD ... 365
Hyland Joy & Associates Pty Ltd ... 444
Hyster Europe Ltd ... 393
Hyundai Precision & Ind Co Ltd (HDPIC) ... 40, 202, 245
Hywema Lifting Systems ... 404

I

IAFE ... 805
Iarnród Eireann ... 616
IBR ... 311
ICF ... 203
IFE ... 221
Iffland Kavanagh Waterbury PC ... 444
IGG Systems ... 324
IIRR ... 613
Ilium Associates, Inc ... 444
IIT Research Institute ... 444
Illinois Central Railroad ... 770, 779
ILVA ... 365
Imesi SpA ... 41, 202, 245
Impco Products Inc ... 393
India ... 599
Indian Government Railways (IR) ... 599
Indiana Harbor Belt Railroad Co ... 794
Indiana Hi-Rail Corp ... 794
Indiana & Ohio Railroad Corp ... 794
Indiana Railroad Co ... 795
Indonesia ... 610
Indonesian State Railways (PJKA) ... 610
Inirail ... 41
Institution of Civil Engineers ... 425
Institution of Diesel & Gas Turbine Engineers ... 425
Institution of Electrical Engineers ... 425
Institution of Mechanical Engineers,
 Railway Division ... 426
Institution of Railway Signal Engineers ... 426
Insulation Equipments ... 221
Inta-Eimar ... 245
Integra Signum ... 311, 394
Intercontainer ... 418
Interelec ... 311
Interfrigo ... 418
Intergovernmental Organisation for
 International Carriage by Rail (OTIF) ... 422
Interinfra ... 444
International Association of Rolling Stock
 Builders ... 422
International Container Bureau (BIC) ... 422
International Metal Service ... 286
International Organisation for
 Standardisation (ISO) ... 422
International Rail Consultants ... 444
International Rail Transport Committee (CIT) ... 422
International Railway Congress Association
 (IRCA) ... 422
International Sleeping Car Company (CIWLT) ... 418
International Track Systems Inc ... 366
International Union of Private Railway Wagon
 Owners' Associations (UIP) ... 422
International Union of Public Transport

(UITP) ... 422
International Union of Railway Medical
 Services (UIMC) ... 422
International Union of Railways (UIC) ... 422
Intraflug AG ... 418
Intramatic SA ... 366
Invar Manufacturing Ltd ... 287
Invatra ... 410
IOS ... 422
Iowa Interstate Railroad Ltd ... 795
Iowa Northern Railroad Co ... 795
IPA ... 366
IR ... 599
Iran ... 613
Iraq ... 614
Iraqi Railways (IRR) ... 614
IRCA ... 422
Ireland (CIE) ... 615
Iskra ... 348
Islamic Iranian Republic Railways (ISR) ... 613
Isotta Fraschini SpA ... 162
Israel ... 618
Israel State Railways (ISR) ... 618
Istanbul ... 829
Italian Association of Electrotechnical
 and Electronics Industries ... 425
Italian (College of) Railway Engineers ... 425
Italian Railways (FS) ... 620
Italsider SpA ... 366
Italtrafo ... 41
Italy ... 620
Itel Rail ... 415
ITI/CLM ... 366
Ivory Coast ... 632
Iyo Railway ... 649
Izmir ... 829
Izu Express ... 650
Izu Hakone Railway ... 650

J

Jackson Jordan Inc ... 366
Jacksonville ... 829
Jakem Timbers ... 366
Jamaica ... 632
Jamaica Railway Corporation (JRC) ... 632
Jambes-Namur SA ... 41, 366, 394
Janakpur Railway (JR) ... 675
Japan ... 633
Japan Freight Railway Co ... 643
Japan Private Railways Ass ... 425
Japan Railway Construction Corp ... 425
Japan Railway Electrification Ass Inc ... 425
Japan Railway Engineers Ass ... 425
Japan Railways Group (JR) ... 633
Japan Rolling Stock Exporters Ass ... 425
Japan Society of Mechanical Engineers ... 425
Japan Transportation Consultants Inc ... 445
Jaragua ... 366
JARTS ... 444
Jenbacher Werke AG ... 41, 162, 203
Jessop & Co ... 203
Johannesburg ... 829
Johnson Inc, Bernard ... 445
Jones GCM 599 Ltd ... 394
Jordan ... 657
Joshin Electric Railway ... 650
JR ... 633, 675
JRC ... 632
JR Shikoku ... 642
JR Tokai ... 641
Jung Locomotivfabrik GmbH ... 41
Jurid Werke GmbH ... 270
JW James Walker & Co ... 366
JZ ... 806

K

Kaelble u Gmeinder, Carl, GmbH & Co ... 42, 162
KAGO-A Kaufman AG ... 367
Kaiser Engineers Inc ... 445
Kalmar Lagab ... 394
Kalmar Verkstads AB ... 42, 203, 245
Kampsax International A/S ... 445
Kampuchea ... 658
Kango Ltd ... 367
Kansas City ... 829
Kansas City Southern Lines ... 780
Kaohsiung ... 829
Karachi ... 829

Karlsruhe	829
Kawasaki Heavy Industries Ltd	43, 204, 245
Kazan	829
KCR	594
Kearney Inc, A T	445
Keifuku Electric Railway	650
Keihan Electric Railway Co Ltd	650
Keihin Electric Express Railway	651
Keio Teito Electric Railway	652
Keisei Electric Railway	652
Keller SpA	246
Kenelec	311
Kennedy Henderson Ltd	445
Kenya	658
Kenya Railways (KR)	658
Kershaw Manufacturing Co Ltd	367, 394
Kharkov	829
KHD Deutz	162
Kiamichi Railroad Co Inc	795
Kiepe Elektrik	186
Kiev	829
KIHN	367
Kilo-Wate Inc	246
Kim Hotstart	162
Kingston upon Thames	830
Kinki Nippon Railway	653
Kinki Sharyo Co	204, 246
Kismotor Es-Gepgyar	221
Klein, Etablissements Georges	221, 332
Klöckner-Werke AG	367
Kloos Kinderdijk BV	368
Knight & Associates Inc, Lester B	446
Knorr-Bremse GmbH	270
KNR	660
Kobe	830
Kobe Electric Railway	653
Koehring GmbH	368
Kolmex	43, 204, 246, 271
Kolomna	163
Konan Railway	653
Kone Corp Crane Division	394
Koni BV	287
Konstal Steel Construction Works	246
Koppers Company Inc	368
Korea, Republic	660
Korea, Democratic People's Republic	660
Korea Shipbuilding & Engineering	204, 246
Korean National Railroad (KNR) (Republic of Korea)	660
Kowloon-Canton Railway	594
Koyo Seiko Co	296
KR	658
Krasnoyarsk	830
Krauss-Maffei AG	43, 311
Krautkrämer GmbH	368
Krivoy Rog	830
Krone (UK) Technique Ltd	324
Krupp Brüninghaus GmbH	287
Krupp Maschinentechnik	44, 247
KSFB	247
K T Steel Industries Pvt	247
Kuala Lumpur	830
Kuckuck Bau Stromungstechnischer Apparate	221
Kuibyshev	830
Kuibyshev Diesel Locomotive Works	46
Kuttner, Collins Group	446
Kyle Railroad Co	795
Kyosan Electric Manufacturing Co	311, 394
Kyosan Kogyo	46
Kyoto	830
Kyushu Railway Co (JR-Kyushi)	640

L

Lagab	247
Lake Erie, Franklin & Clarion Railroad	795
Lake Superior & Ishpeming Railroad Co	795
Lamco Railroad	663
Lamoille Valley Railroad Co	795
Lamp Manufacturing & Railway Supplies Ltd	368
L & M Radiator Inc	163
Laramore, Douglass and Popham	446
Latin American Railway Association	422
Laurinburg & Southern Railroad Co	795
Lausanne	830
Lauwaert & Cie SA	368
LDA	272
Leas & Associates Inc, J W	447
Lebanon	662
Leeds-Bradford	831
Leningrad	831

MANNESMANN DEMAG

Gottwald Railway Cranes

Gottwald Railway Breakdown Cranes operate on all track gauges worldwide:
- up to 300 tons lifting capacity
- tailor-made according to customer specifications

Photo shows:
150 t Gottwald Railway Breakdown Crane working with railways in Middle East.

Mannesmann Demag
Gottwald GmbH
Reisholzer Werftstrasse
Postfach 130329
D-4000 Düsseldorf 13
Phone (211) 79 56-0
Telefax (211) 79 56-252
Telex 8 582 638

GOTTWALD

860 INDEX / L–O

Letourneau Co, Marathon . . . 247, 394
LEW . . . 46, 287
Liberia . . . 663
Libya . . . 664
Liebherr Container Cranes Ltd . . . 247, 394
Liège . . . 831
Liga de Propietaries de Vagones de España . . . 410
Light Rail Transit Consultants GmbH . . . 447
Lille . . . 831
Lima . . . 831
Lindapter . . . 368
Linsinger . . . 368
Lisbon . . . 831
Litton Interconnection Products . . . 272
Lloyd (ABC Couplers) Ltd . . . 272
Locomotive Maintenance Officers' Association . . . 426
Lodz . . . 831
London . . . 831
London Transport International Services Ltd . . . 447
Long Island Rail Road Company . . . 795
Loram Maintenance of Way Inc . . . 368
Lord Corporation . . . 287, 368
Los Angeles . . . 833
LTK Engineering Services . . . 447
Lucas Automotive . . . 343
Lucas Girling Ltd . . . 272
Lucerne-Stans-Engelberg Railway . . . 735
Luwa GmbH . . . 221
Luxembourg . . . 664
Luxembourg Railways (CFL) . . . 664
Lyons . . . 833

M

McGregor Paving Ltd . . . 370
McKay Rail Products . . . 370
Macosa . . . 47, 204, 221, 247, 272, 287
Madagascar . . . 665
Madras . . . 833
Madrid . . . 833
MAEL Computer . . . 332
Mafersa . . . 248, 287
Magnordata . . . 332
Magnus/Farley Industries Co. Inc . . . 297
Maguire Group Inc . . . 447
Maine Central Railroad Company . . . 796
MaK Maschinenbau GmbH . . . 47, 163
Makomat . . . 332
Malawi . . . 667
Malawi Railways Ltd (MR) . . . 667
Malayan Railway Administration (KTM) . . . 667
Malaysia . . . 667
Mali . . . 669
MAN GHH . . . 205, 248, 288
Manchester . . . 834
Manila . . . 834
Manta, NV . . . 222
Manufacturers Railway Co . . . 796
Maquinista, La Terrestre y Maritima SA . . . 48, 204, 248
Marconi Electronic Devices . . . 187
Marseilles . . . 834
Maryland & Delaware Railroad Co . . . 796
Maryland & Pennsylvania Railroad Co . . . 796
Maryland Midland Railway Inc . . . 796
Maryland Rail Commuter Service (MARC) . . . 800
Massachusetts Bay Transportation Authority . . . 801
Matema Materiali Meccanici SpA . . . 368
Materfer . . . 49, 205
Matérial de Voie SA . . . 369
Matisa . . . 369
Matisa SpA . . . 369
Matix-Industries . . . 369
Matra Transport SA . . . 311
Matrix . . . 272
Maunsell Consultants Pty Ltd . . . 448
Mauritania . . . 670
Mauritanian National Railways (TFM-SNIM) . . . 670
MÁV . . . 596
Maxon Electronics . . . 311
MBB . . . 206
McCloud River Railroad Co . . . 796
ME Mischiatti Elettronica . . . 325
Mealstream (UK) Ltd . . . 222
Mecanoexportimport . . . 49, 206, 248, 272
Medellin . . . 834
Melbourne . . . 835
Merz and McLellan . . . 449
Metalsines . . . 248
Metalastik . . . 288
METRA . . . 801
Metransa . . . 410
Metro-North Commuter Railroad Co . . . 802
Metropolitan Transit Authority (Melbourne) . . . 485
Mexico . . . 670
Mexico City . . . 835
Miami . . . 835
Miba Gleitlager AG . . . 297
Michigan Dept of Transportation . . . 769
Michigan Interstate Railway . . . 796
Michigan Northern Railway Co . . . 796
Microphor . . . 222
Mid South Rail Corporation . . . 796
Middleton Sheet Metal Co . . . 222
Middlesbrough . . . 835
Midwest Electronics Industries . . . 325
Midwest Steel . . . 370
Milan . . . 835
Minden Local Railways (MKB) . . . 588
Mineral Haul Ltd . . . 410
Miner Enterprises Inc . . . 272
Miner Railcar Services Inc . . . 206, 249
Miner y Mendez de Mexico SA . . . 273
Minneapolis . . . 836
Minsk . . . 836
MIO . . . 371
Mirrlees Blackstone Ltd . . . 163
Mississippi Delta Railroad . . . 797
Mississippi Export Railroad . . . 797
Mitchell Equipment Corp . . . 371
Mitsubishi Electric Corporation . . . 50, 273
Mitsubishi Heavy Industries Ltd . . . 273, 394
Mitsukawa Metal Works . . . 371
Mittel-Thurgau Railway (MThB) . . . 735
ML . . . 187
MNVA Railroad . . . 797
MOB . . . 735
Modern Industries Inc . . . 394
Modern Track Machinery Canada Ltd . . . 371
Modjeski & Masters . . . 449
Modulex Systems . . . 332
Moës SA, Moteurs . . . 51, 164
Mongolia . . . 672
Monogram Sanitation . . . 222
Monongahela Railway Co . . . 797
Montana Rail Link Inc . . . 797
Monterrey . . . 836
Monterrey IFSA . . . 371
Montreal . . . 836
Montreal Urban Community Transport Commission (MUCTC) . . . 532
Montreux-Oberland Bernois Railway (MOB) . . . 735
Moore & Steele Corp . . . 371
More Wear Industries (Pvt) Ltd . . . 249
Moroccan Railways (ONCFM) . . . 672
Morocco . . . 672
Morrison-Knudsen Company Inc . . . 51, 449
Morrison-Knudsen Engineers Inc . . . 450
Mors Techniphone . . . 311
Moscow . . . 836
Moss, George Pty Ltd . . . 51, 249, 371
Motorola Canada . . . 312
Motorola Communications & Electronics Inc . . . 312
Mott MacDonald Group . . . 450
Mount Newman Railroad . . . 489
Mozambique . . . 674
Mozambique Ports & Railways (CFM) . . . 674
MPM . . . 164
MR . . . 667
MTLB . . . 735
MTU . . . 164
Mülheim . . . 837
Muller-Munk Associates, Peter . . . 452
Multi-Service Supply Inc . . . 273, 297
Munich . . . 837
MVA Consultancy, The . . . 452
Myanmar (Burma) . . . 518
MZ Tito-Skopje . . . 273

N

NABCO . . . 273
Nachi-Fujikoshi Corporation . . . 297
Nagoya . . . 837
Nagoya Railroad . . . 653
Namibe Railway . . . 467
Namibia . . . 674
Nankai Electric Railway . . . 654
Nantes . . . 837
Naples . . . 837
Narita Seisakusho . . . 222
Natchez Trace Railroad . . . 797
National Castings Inc . . . 288
National City Management Co . . . 452
National Electrical Carbon . . . 187
Nationale Maatschappij der Belgische Spoorwegen (NMBS) . . . 499
National Mediation Board . . . 426
National Railroad Construction & Maintenance Association Inc . . . 426
National Railroad Intermodal Association . . . 426
National Railroad Passenger Corporation (Amtrak) . . . 766
National Railway Labor Conference . . . 427
National Railways of Colombia (FNdeC) . . . 543
National Railways of Zimbabwe (NRZ) . . . 811
National Steel Car Ltd . . . 249
National Transportation Safety Board . . . 427
National Transport Corporation of Namibia (NVK) . . . 674
Nelcon BV . . . 250
Nepal . . . 675
Nepal Government Railway (NR) . . . 675
Nesite Industri Finland Oy . . . 222
Netherlands . . . 675
Netherlands Railways (NS) . . . 675
Neuchâtel . . . 837
Neumann Elektronik GmbH & Co KG . . . 325
New England Southern Railroad . . . 797
New Jersey Transit Rail Operations Inc . . . 803
New Orleans Public Belt Railroad . . . 797
New York . . . 838
New York Air Brake Co, NYAB . . . 274
New York-New Jersey (PATH) . . . 839
New York-Staten Island Rapid Transit Operating Authority (SIRTOA) . . . 839
New York, Susquehanna & Western Railroad Corp . . . 797
New Zealand . . . 679
New Zealand Railways Corporation (NZR) . . . 679
Newag GmbH & Co. KG . . . 52, 273, 371
Newark . . . 838
Newcastle upon Tyne . . . 838
Nicaragua . . . 681
Nicaragua Railway . . . 681
Niederrhein Railway . . . 588
Niesky, VEB Waggonbau . . . 250
Nigeria . . . 681
Nigerian Railway Corporation (NRC) . . . 681
Niigata Converter Co (NICO) . . . 165
Niigata Engineering Co . . . 52, 165
Nikex Hungarian Trading Co . . . 288
Nippon Air Brake Co (NABCO) . . . 223
Nippon Kido Kogyo Co . . . 371
Nippon KK . . . 371
Nippon Seiko KK (NSK) . . . 297
Nippon Sharyo Ltd . . . 52, 206, 250
Nippon Signal Co . . . 223, 273, 312, 332, 395
NIR . . . 764
Nishi Nippon Railroad . . . 654
NKF Kabel . . . 312
NMBS . . . 499
Nogradi Szenbanyak . . . 408
Noord-Nederlandsche Machinenfabriek BV . . . 371, 395
Nordco . . . 371
Nordmark Klarälvens Railways . . . 722
Norfolk Southern Corporation . . . 780
Northbrook Corporation . . . 415
North Eastern Railway (IR) . . . 605
North Korea Railway . . . 660
North Milan Railway (FNME) . . . 629
Northeast Frontier Railway (IR) . . . 605
Northern Indiana Commuter Transportation District . . . 804
Northern Ireland Railways Co Ltd (NIR) . . . 764
Northern Railway (IR) . . . 605
Northern Virginia Transportation Commission (NVTC) . . . 804
Nortrak . . . 372
Norway . . . 682
Norwegian State Railways (NSB) . . . 682
Nottingham . . . 839
Novocherkassk . . . 52
Novosibirsk . . . 839
NR . . . 675
NRC . . . 681
NRZ . . . 811
NSB . . . 682
NTN Toyo Bearing Co . . . 297
Nuremberg . . . 839
NZR . . . 679

O

ÖBB . . . 490

O-S / INDEX

OB Transit Products (EFE) ... 269
Oberrhein Railway ... 588
OCBN ... 505
Octoraro Railway Inc ... 797
OCTRA ... 574
Odakyu Electric Railway ... 654
Odessa ... 840
Oerlikon Brakes ... 274
OEVA ... 411
OFV ... 206, 250
Ohio High Speed Rail Authority ... 769
O & K (Orenstein & Koppel) AG ... 250
Oklahoma City ... 840
Oleo Pneumatics Ltd ... 250, 274, 372, 395
Omeca ... 206
Omega Electronics ... 325
Omi Railway ... 655
Omron ... 333
OMS ... 52, 206, 250
Omsk ... 840
ONATRA ... 809
ONCFG ... 593
ONCFM ... 672
Ontario Northland Railway ... 533
Oregon California & Eastern Railway Co ... 797
Oregon & Northwestern Railroad Co ... 797
Organisation for the Collaboration of Railways (OSShD) ... 422
Organisation Commune Benin-Niger des Chemins de Fer et des Transports (OCBN) ... 505
Organisme Repartiteur Central du Pool-TEN ... 418
Orlians & Co ... 313
Ortner Freight Car Co ... 251
Orton McCullough Crane Co ... 372
Orval, Ateliers de Matériel Ferroviaire d' ... 251
Osaka ... 840
OSE ... 591
Oslo ... 840
Osmose Railroad Div ... 372
OTIF ... 422
OTP Rail and Transit ... 313

P

Padane Railways ... 630
Paducah & Louisville Railway ... 797
Pafawag, PFW ... 52, 187, 207, 288
Pakistan ... 685
Pakistan Railway (PR) ... 685
Pakistan Railways Carriage Factory ... 207, 251
Pan American Railway Congress Association (ACPF) ... 423
Panama ... 688
Panama Railroad ... 688
Pandrol Ltd ... 373
Paraguay ... 688
Paris ... 840
Parisini ... 313
Parizzi ... 187
Parma-Suzzara Railway ... 630
Parsons Co, Ralph M ... 453
Parsons Brinckerhoff Centec International Inc ... 452
Patapsco & Back Rivers Railroad ... 797
Paulstra Hutchinson ... 166, 274
PEC Projects & Equipment Corporation of India ... 53, 207, 251
Peine-Salzgitter Transport ... 588
Peiner ... 251, 395
Penetone Corporation ... 395
Penn Machine Co ... 289
Pennsylvania High Speed Rail Commission ... 770
Peoria & Pekin Union Railway ... 797
Peregrine & Partners ... 453
Perkins Engines Group ... 166
Permali Gloucester Ltd ... 223, 373
Permanent Way Institution ... 426
Permaquip ... 373
Perry Engineering Division ... 251
Peru ... 689
Pettibone Corp ... 373
Philadelphia ... 841
Philadelphia, Bethlehem & New England Railroad Co ... 798
Philippine National Railways (PNR) ... 690
Philippines ... 690
Philips Telecommunicatie Industrie BV ... 313
Phoenix AG ... 223, 289, 373
Pintsch Bamag Antriebs-und Verkehrstechnik GmbH ... 224, 313, 373
Pirelli Construction Co ... 343
Pirelli General Cable Works ... 313

Pittsburgh ... 842
Pittsburgh & Lake Erie Railroad Co ... 782
Pittsburg & Shawmut Railroad ... 798
PJKA ... 610
PKP ... 691
Planning Research & Systems plc ... 453
Plasser Australia ... 343
Plasser American Corp ... 374
Plasser & Theurer ... 374
Plastica Kunststoffwerk GmbH ... 375
Plessey Controls Ltd ... 313
Plymouth Locomotive Works ... 53
PNR ... 690
Pocono Northeast Railway ... 798
Poland ... 691
Polish State Railways (PKP) ... 691
Port Elizabeth ... 842
Port Terminal Railroad ... 798
Portec Inc ... 251, 375, 404
Portec (UK) Ltd ... 376
Portland ... 842
Porto Alegre ... 842
Porto e Caminhos de Ferro de Luanda ... 467
Portugal ... 695
Portuguese Railways (CP) ... 695
Pouget, Etablissements SA ... 376
Powell Duffryn Standard ... 251, 289
Powernetics ... 343
PR ... 685
Pragoinvest ... 54
Prague ... 842
Prati-Vazquez Iglesias SA ... 252
Precision National Corporation ... 54
Premesa SA ... 376
Price Ltd, A & G ... 55, 253
Probat-Werke ... 405
Proceco Inc ... 405
Procor Ltd, Rail Car Division ... 415
Procor Engineering ... 253
Prodata ... 333
Providence & Worcester Railroad Co ... 798
PS Concrete Co Ltd ... 376
PSI ... 55
Pullman Leasing Co ... 415
Pullman Standard ... 253
Pullman Technology Inc ... 453
Pulse Electronics Inc ... 313
Purdy Co ... 275
Pusan ... 843
Pu Zhen Rolling Stock Works ... 207
PW Consulting ... 453
Pyongyang ... 843

Q

Qiqihar Rolling Stock Works ... 253
Qishuyen Rolling Stock ... 55
Quebec North Shore & Labrador Railway ... 533
Queensland Government Railways ... 477
Queensland Railways Consulting Services ... 453

R

Racal Acoustics Ltd ... 325
Racine Railroad Products Inc ... 376
Rafil ... 290
Railbox Co ... 415
Railfone Inc ... 313
Railgon Co ... 415
Rail India Technical & Economic Services Ltd (RITES) ... 453
Railko Ltd ... 297
Railquip Inc ... 405
Railroad Personnel Association ... 427
Railroad Public Relations Association ... 427
Railroad Retirement Board ... 427
Rails Co ... 377
Railway Engineering-Maintenance Suppliers Association Inc (REMSA) ... 427
Railway Industry Association of Great Britain ... 426
Railway Progress Institute ... 427
Railway Supply Association ... 427
Railway Systems Design Inc ... 454
Railway Systems Suppliers, Inc ... 427
Rail-Wel Inc ... 377
Ranzi-Legnano SRL ... 405
Rarus Railway Company ... 798
Rauma-Repola Oy ... 378
Rautaruukki Oy ... 254
Rawie ... 378

Raychem Corp (USA) ... 378
Ray Smith Demountables ... 254
RCFM ... 669
RCL ... 326
Real Estate Research Corporation ... 454
Recife ... 843
Red River Valley & Western Railroad Co ... 798
Rede Ferroviaria Federal SA (RFFSA) ... 508
Regental Railway ... 588
Reggiane ... 55, 207, 255
Regie Nationale des Chemins de Fer du Cameroun (Regifercam) ... 519
Regional Railroads of America ... 427
Reid Crowther ... 454
REMAFER ... 255
Rendel, Palmer & Tritton Ltd ... 454
RENFE ... 705
Rennes ... 842
Republic ... 56
Research Products/Blankenship Corporation ... 224
Reservoir, Le ... 275
RFS Engineering Ltd ... 56, 207, 255, 275, 290
RFS Projects Ltd ... 454
RhB ... 737
RHP ... 298
Rhaetian Railway (RhB) ... 737
Rheims ... 843
Rhine-Ruhr ... 843
Richardson & Cruddas (1972) Ltd ... 378
Richmond, Fredericksburg and Potomac Railroad Co ... 798
Ries Maschinenbau GmbH ... 57
Riga ... 843
Ringfeder GmbH ... 275
Ringrollers ... 290
Rio de Janeiro ... 843
Ripper Systems ... 326
RNCFM ... 665
Roadmasters and Maintenance Way Association of America ... 427
RoadRailer ... 255
Robel GmbH ... 378
Robe River Railroad ... 490
Rochester & Southern Railroad Inc ... 798
Rockwell International ... 313
Rolba Co ... 379
Romania ... 698
Romanian State Railways (CFR) ... 698
Rome ... 844
Ross & White Co ... 395
Rostov-on-Don ... 844
Rotterdam ... 844
Rouen ... 844
Roundel Design Group ... 454
RPS Rail Passenger Services Inc ... 207
RSD ... 57, 256, 290
Ruhfus GmbH, A ... 290
Ruhrthaler Maschinenfabrik ... 57
R W Mac Co ... 290

S

Saalasti Oy ... 57, 275, 395
SAB Brake Regulator Co Ltd ... 276
SAB WABCO ... 275, 290
Sable Sièges Industrielles ... 224
Sacramento ... 844
Sacramento Northern Railway ... 798
SAE Sadelmi ... 344
SAE (India) ... 344
Safetran Systems Corporation ... 314, 395
SAFT ... 225, 344
Sagami Railway ... 655
Sait Electronics ... 315, 326
Salient Systems Inc ... 379
St Lawrence & Atlantic Railroad Co ... 798
St Louis ... 845
St Louis Southwestern Railway Co ... 787
Sambre et Meuse, Usines et Acieries de ... 277, 290
San Antonio ... 845
San Diego ... 845
San Diego & Imperial Valley Railroad Co ... 798
SAN Engineering & Locomotive Co ... 58
San Francisco ... 845
San Francisco Belt Railroad ... 798
Sangritana Railway ... 631
San Jose ... 845
San Severo-Peschici Railway ... 631
Santa Fe Railway ... 783
Santa Maria Valley Railroad Co ... 798
Santa Matilde ... 256
Santiago de Chile ... 845

Sanyo Electric Railway	655	
São Paulo	846	
Sapporo	846	
Sardinian Minor Railways	631	
Sardinian Railways	631	
SASIB	315	
Sassuolo-Modena Railway	631	
Sateba	380	
SATO	380	
SATI	411	
Saudi Government Railroad Organisation	699	
Savesa SA	411	
ScanAcoustic	326	
Scandia Randers *See* ABB Scandia A/S		
Scania	166, 380	
Scanpoint	333	
SCC Signalcom Canada Corp	315	
SCG	167	
Schaltbau	225	
Scharfenberg GmbH	277	
Scheidt & Bachmann GmbH	315, 333	
Schienenfahrzeuge Export-Import	59, 207, 256	
Schimpeler Corradino Associates	454	
Schindler Carriage & Wagon Co	208, 256	
Schindler Waggon Altenrhein	208	
Schlatter AG HA	380	
Schlumberger Industrie	333	
Schöma GmbH	59	
Schramm Inc	380	
SCI Speciality Concepts Inc	316	
SCIF	209, 256	
SECEMM	380	
Sécheron	189	
SEE Société Européenne d'Engrenages	277	
SEFAC	405	
Seibu Railway	655	
Seitu	326	
SEL	316, 395	
SEL Canada	316	
SEMA	316	
SEMAF	209, 257	
Semco	225	
Seminole Gulf Railway	798	
Semperit	380	
SEMT-Pielstick	168	
Sendai	846	
Senegal	700	
Seoul	846	
Servo Corporation of America	316	
SET Schadt	344	
Seville	847	
SEWAR	411	
SFC-Daval	257	
SFL	60	
SGI	209, 257	
S-G-P AG	60, 210, 257	
SGTE	455	
SGTL	411	
SGW	411	
Shanghai	847	
Sheffield	847	
Shikoku Railway Co. (JR-Shikoku)	642	
Shimbara Railway	656	
Shinkansen Property Corp	646	
Shin Keisei Electric Railway	646	
Shinko Engineering Co	169	
SIAM SA	225, 277	
SICF	632	
SICFA SpA	381	
Siemens AG	60, 170, 188, 210, 225, 316, 326, 344, 395	
Siemens Electric	344	
Siemens Energy & Automation Inc	188, 345	
Siemens Plessey	188	
Sierra Railroad Company	798	
Siette	345	
Siferdec	316	
SIG	225, 290	
SIGLA	186, 345	
Sigmaform Corporation	381	
Signarail Canada	326	
Sihltal-Uetliberg Railway (SZU)	739	
Sika Ltd	381, 395	
SILEC	318, 326	
Silentbloc	291	
SILF Srl	381	
Simmons Machine Tool Corp	405	
Simotra	411	
Simpson & Curtin	455	
Singapore	847	
SJ	716	
Skelton H J	381	
SKF, Aktiebolaget	298	
SKF Argentina SA	277, 298	
Škoda, Plzeň	62	
SLM	63	
SLR	713	
SMC Pneumatic (Australia) Pty Ltd	188, 225, 277, 345	
Smith & Egan Associates Inc	455	
Smith Bros & Webb Ltd	395	
SNCB	499	
SNCFT	748	
SNCZ	808	
Société d'Etat Réseau National des Chemins de Fer Malagasy (RNCFM)	665	
Société de Transports de Vehicules Automobiles (TVA)	411	
Société Nationale des Chemins de Fer Belges (SNCB)	499	
Société Nationale des Chemins de Fer Zaïrois (SNCZ)	809	
Socimi	66, 188, 210, 226, 277, 291	
Sodeteg-Tai	455	
Sofanor	226	
SOFER, Officine Ferroviere SpA	66, 210	
Sofia	847	
Sofrerail	455	
Sofretu	456	
Sola	381	
Solari Udine SpA	326	
Solothurn-Zollikofen-Berne Railway (SZB)	739	
Soma Equipamentos Industrias SA	66, 273	
Sonatest plc	381	
Sonit	382	
Soo Line Railroad Co	785	
Sorefame	66, 149, 210	
Soulé SA	141, 210, 273	
South Africa	700	
South African Transport Services (SATS)	700	
South Australia State Transport Authority	481	
South Buffalo Railway Co	798	
South Central Railway (IR)	606	
South Central Tennessee Railroad Co	798	
South Eastern Railway (IR)	607	
South Eastern Railway (Italy)	631	
South Eastern Railway (Switzerland)	739	
Southeastern Pennsylvania Transportation Authority (SEPTA)	804	
Southern Pacific Transportation Company	785	
Southern Railway ENAFER	689	
Southern Railway (IR)	606	
South-West German Railways	589	
Soviet Union Railways (SZhD)	753	
Spain	705	
Spanish Narrow-Gauge Railways (FEVE)	711	
Spanish National Railways (RENFE)	705	
Specialist Rail Products	292	
Spencerville and Elgin Railroad Co	799	
Speno International SA	382	
Sperry Rail Service	383	
SPIE Batignolles	345, 383	
Sri Lanka	713	
Sri Lanka Railways (SLR)	713	
SR	716	
SRC	715	
SRM Hydromekanik AB	170	
SRS	383	
SRT	744	
SSG	418	
Stabeg Apparatengesellschaft GmbH	277	
Standard Car Truck Co	292	
Standard Radio & Telefon	318	
State Railway Authority/SRA (New South Wales)	472	
State Railway of Thailand (SRT)	744	
STC	318	
STCUM	532	
Stedef	384	
Steele & Co, E G	396, 411	
Steer, Davies & Gleave	456	
Stemmann	189	
Stockholm	848	
Stockton Terminal & Eastern Railroad	799	
Stone Ibérica	226	
Stone India Ltd	226, 278	
Stone International Ltd	226	
Stone McColl	226, 327	
Stone Nycal	226	
Stone Safety Corp	226	
Stone Transportation	226	
Stothert & Pitt Ltd	396	
Strachan & Henshaw	396	
Stratos Ventilation Products Ltd	406	
Strojexport	142, 210, 345	
Strömberg	188	
Strømens Vaerksted A/S (NEBB)	142, 210	
Strömungsmaschinen, VEB	170	
Strukton Spoorwegboun	384	
Stuart Turner Ltd	226	
Stucki Co, A	292, 298	
Stuttgart	848	
STV Engineers	455	
Sudan	715	
Sudan Railways (SRC)	715	
Suecobras Industria e Comercio Ltda	278	
Sumitomo Metal Industries Ltd	278, 292, 406	
Sundberg-Ferar Inc	457	
Suzzara-Ferrara Railway	631	
Sverdlovsk	848	
Sverdrup Corporation	437	
Swaziland	716	
Swaziland Railway (SR)	716	
Sweden	716	
Swederail Consulting AB	457	
Swedish National Rail Administration	716	
Swedish State Railways (SJ)	716	
Swingmaster Corporation	384	
Swiss Federal Railways	722	
Switzerland	722	
SYCAFER	384	
Sydney-Canberra-Melbourne VFT	472	
Sydney Steel Corp	384	
Syria	740	
Syscon Corporation	457	
Szarka Enterprises Inc	384	
SZB	739	
SZhD	753	
SZU	739	

T

TAFESA	211
Taipei	848
Taiwan	741
Taiwan Railway Administration (TRA)	741
Takraf VVB	397
Talbot, Waggonfabrik	143, 211
Talgo	221
Talleres de Amurio	292, 384
Tamper Corp	384
Tamper-Holland Welding Services	384
TAMS Consultants Inc	457
Tanzania	742
Tanzania Railway Corporation (TRC)	742
Tanzania-Zambia Railway Authority (TAZARA)	743
Tashkent	848
TAU	143
TAZARA	743
Tbilisi	848
TBL Limited	278

SPECIALIST RAIL PRODUCTS

- High Performance Bogies for passenger and freight vehicles
- Complete Cab Systems and Electrical Equipment
- Suspension Systems

Specialist Rail Products Limited
PO Box 76
Hexthorpe Trading Park
Doncaster DN4 0EH
Telephone: (0302) 328080
Fax: (0302) 329911
Telex: 548208

RFS
A Member of the
RFS Industries Group

Transport design consortium

The Transport design consortium is a project based consultancy comprising the combined creative talents of some of the rail industry's foremost design companies; Industrial designers Jones Garrard, corporate and graphic designers Roundel Design Group, interior designers and architects Tilney Lumsden Shane and engineering designers RFS Projects. Each is an acknowledged leader in its own discipline, frequently setting new standards in its specialist field. Every project is undertaken by a dedicated and cohesive team, co-ordinated to achieve a precise balance of appropriate technical and professional skills. If you would like to know more, please contact Marvin Shane or Barbara Baker at the address below.

Transport design consortium, 5 Heathmans Road, Parsons Green, London SW6 4TJ. Telephone: 071-731 8190, Fax: 071-736 3356.

TEDD	749
Tebel Pneumatik	226
Technopol	345
Tehran	848
Teklite Lighting	397
Teknis	318, 327
Tela Railroad Company	594
Tel Aviv	849
Telemotive UK Ltd	318, 406
Telephone Cables Ltd	319
Telkor (Pty) Ltd	319
Temperature Ltd	226
Tempered Spring Co	385
Temple Barker & Sloane Inc	457
Templeton, Kenly & Co	385
Terminal Railroad Assoc of St Louis	799
Terni SpA	293
Tetsudo Kiki Kaisha Ltd	385
Teutoburger Wald Railway	589
Texas High Speed Rail Authority	770
Texas Mexican Railway Co	799
Texas & Northern Railway Co	799
Texas North Western Railway Co	799
Texas, Oklahoma & Eastern Railroad	799
Textar GmbH Brems-und Kupplungsbeläge	278
TFM-SNIM	670
TGOJ Railways	721
Thailand	744
Thebra do Brazil	385
Thermit Welding (GB) Ltd	385
Thomas Robinson & Son	385
Thorn EMI	227, 319, 327, 334, 345
Thos W Ward Ltd	385
Thyssen AG	397
Thyssen Engineering GmbH	385
Thyssen Henschel	67, 170
Tianjin	849
TIBB	68, 189, 293, 345
Tiger Rail Ltd	411
Timken Co	298
Tipco	385
Tiphook Rail Ltd	411
Tobu Railway	656
Togo Railways	748
Tokyo	849
Tokyo Express Electric Railway	656
Tokyo Keiki Co Ltd	385
Tokyu Car Corporation	143, 212, 278
Toledo, Peoria & Western Railroad	799
Toronto	850
Toshiba Corporation	69, 144, 189, 227, 319, 334, 345, 398, 407
Toulouse	851
Toyama Chicho Railway	657
Toyo Denki Seizo KK	71, 189, 227, 334
Toyo Kizai Co Ltd	386
TRA	741
Trackmaster (Pty) Ltd	386
Trackmobile Inc	398
Trailer Train	279, 412, 415
Tramesa	412
Transcisco	415
Transcontrol Corporation	319
Transfesa	412, 418
Transit Control Systems	319
Transit & Tunnel Consultants Inc	457
TransKentucky Transportation Railroad Inc	799
Transmark	458
Transmitton	345
Transnet	700
Transportation and Distribution Associates	458
Transportation Planning Associates	458
Transport Canada	520
Transport Design Consortium	458
Transrapid International	145
Transurb Consult SC	459
Transystem SpA	460
Travers Morgan International Ltd	460
TRC	742
Trento-Male Railway	632
Triax-Davis	279
Tri-County Commuter Rail Organization	800
Triplex Safety Glass Co	227
Tripoli	851
True Temper	386
TSO	386
Tudor Engineering Co	461
Tunis	851
Tunisia	748
Tunisian National Railways (SNCFT)	748
Turbomeca	170
Turin	851
Turin-Ceres Railway	632
Turk & Hillinger	387
Turkey	749
Turkish State Railways (TCDD)	749
Turnu-Severin Wagon Works	212
Tuscola & Saginaw Bay Railway	799
TVA	411
Twiflex Ltd	171
Twin Disc Co	171
Tysol Products Inc	398

U

UACF	422
UAR	423
UCMR Resita	171
Uganda Railways Corporation (URC)	752
UIC	422
UIMC	422
UIP	422
UIRR	418
UITP	422
Ultra Hydraulics Ltd	398
Umbria Railway	632
UNI Diesel Sales and Marketing Co	171
Unilokomotive Ltd	71, 398
Union Carriage & Wagon Co	72, 147, 212
Union of European Railway Industries (UNIFE)	423
Union Pacific Railroad Co	787
Union Rail Co	799
Union of Soviet Socialist Republics	753
Union Switch & Signal Division	319
Union Tank Car Co	416
Unit Rail Anchor Co	387
United Kingdom	757
United Nations Economic Commission for Europe	423
United States of America	765
Unity Railway Supply Co	299
Upper Merion & Plymouth Railroad Co	799
Urban Mass Transportation Administration (UMTA)	765
Urbitran Associates	461
URC	752
URS Company	461
URS Consultants Inc	461
Uruguay State Railways Administration (AFE)	805
Utah Railway Co	799
UTDC Urban Transport Development Corporation	147, 212
Utrecht	851
Uzinexportimport	279

V

Vagones Frigorificos SA	412
VAI	387
Valencia	852
Valencia Railways (FGV)	713
Va Leo	279
Valmet Corporation	72, 148, 213, 398
Vancouver	852
Vapor Corporation	228, 320
Vaughan	320, 327
VBW	739

Layrub

Flexible couplings & high speed shafts

EFFICIENT, RELIABLE and VERSATILE

Combinations of couplings and shafts to suit most applications solving problems of shock, vibration, misalignment, noise, restricted space, servicing costs and high speeds.

TWIFLEX Twiflex Ltd, The Green, Twickenham TW2 5AQ
Phone: 081-894 1161 Telex: 261704 Fax: 081-894 6056 **TWIFLEX**

Venezuelan State Railways (IAFE) 805
Ventra Locomotives Ltd 73
Vermont Railway Inc 799
VeVy Engineering Works 148, 282
VIA Rail Canada 534
Vienna 852
Viet-Nam Railways (DSVN) 806
Villares 73, 148
Vitoria a Minas Railway (EVFM) 515
Voest-Alpine AG 387
Voith J M GmbH 173
Vollert 399
Von Roll Habegger Ltd 148, 387
Voroshilovgrad Diesel Locomotive Works 73
Vossloh-Werke GmbH 387
VR 557
VSOE-Venice-Simplon-Orient-Express Ltd 418
VTG 413
VTG (UK) Ltd 413
Vultron International Ltd 327

W

WABCO Locomotive & Rubber Products
  Division 279
WABCO Passenger Transit Division 279
WABCO Westinghouse Air Brake Division 279
WABCO Westinghouse Compagnia Freni SpA . 279
WABCO Westinghouse Equipements
  Ferroviaires 280
WABCO Westinghouse Compagnia Segnali
  SpA 321
WABCO Westinghouse Steuerungstechnic 280
Waggon Union GmbH 148, 213, 282
Wagner Maschinenfabrik, Gustav 407
Walkers Ltd 149
Wallace, Roberts and Todd 461
Walton Products Inc 280
Wanne-Bochum-Herner Railway 589
Warrington Tractors 399
Warsaw 852
Washington 852
Washington Central Railroad Co Inc 799
Washington Terminal Co 799
Weese & Associates, Harry 461
Wegmann & Co 293
Wells-Krautkamer 387
Western Australian Government Railway
  (Westrail) 485
Western-Cullen-Hayes Inc 387
Western Railway (IR) 607
Westinghouse Brakes 280, 327
Westinghouse Cubic 334
Westinghouse Door System 228
Westinghouse Electric 321, 346
Westinghouse Saxby Farmer 321
Westinghouse Signals 321, 399
West Japan Railway Co (JR-West) 636
Westphalian Provincial Railway 589
West Virginia Northern Railroad Inc 799
Wheel & Axle Plant, Indian Railways 293
Whipp & Bourne 346
Whiting Corporation 407
Wickham & Co 149, 293, 346, 387
Wilbur Smith & Associates 461
William Nicholas Bodouva & Associates PC ... 462
Wilson, Inrig & Associates 462
Winchester & Western Railroad Co 799
Windhoff, Rheiner Maschinenfabrik AG-
                                    74, 399, 407
Wisconsin & Southern Railroad Co 800
Wisconsin Central Ltd 800
Wispeco Widney 229
Wuppertal 853
Württemberg Railway 589

X

Xamax AG 334
Xiangtan 74

Y

Yokohama 853
Young Commercial Windows Ltd 229
Yugoslav Railways (JZ) 806
Yusoki Kogyo KK 229, 325

Z

Zagro Bahn-und Baumaschinen GmbH 399
Zaire 809
Zambia Railways Ltd (ZR) 810
Zeco Zimbabwe Engineering 75
Zephir SpA 75
Zhuzou Rolling Stock Works 75
Zimbabwe (NRZ) 811
ZT 462
Zweiweg-Fahrzeug 386
Zwicky Engineering 386